Less managing. More teaching. Greater learning.

INSTRUCTORS...

Would you like your **students** to show up for class **more prepared**? *(Let's face it, class is much more fun if everyone is engaged and prepared...)*

Want an **easy way to assign** homework online and track student **progress**? *(Less time grading means more time teaching...)*

Want an **instant view** of student or class performance relative to learning objectives? *(No more wondering if students understand...)*

Need to **collect data and generate reports** required for administration or accreditation? *(Say goodbye to manually tracking student learning outcomes...)*

Want to **record and post your lectures** for students to view online?

With **McGraw-Hill's** *Connect*™ *Plus Accounting*,

INSTRUCTORS GET:

- Simple **assignment management**, allowing you to spend more time teaching.
- **Auto-graded** assignments, quizzes, and tests.
- **Detailed Visual Reporting** where student and section results can be viewed and analyzed.
- Sophisticated **online testing** capability.
- A **filtering and reporting** function that allows you to easily assign and report on materials that are correlated to accreditation standards, learning outcomes, and Bloom's taxonomy.
- An easy-to-use **lecture capture** tool.
- The option to **upload course documents** for student access.

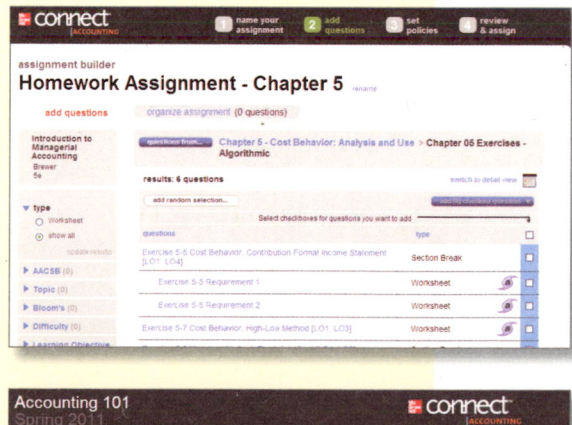

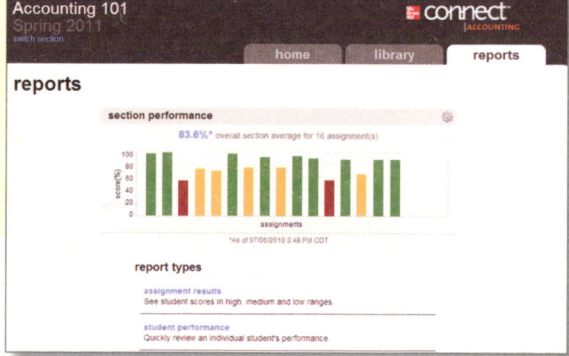

Want an online, searchable version of your textbook?

Wish your textbook could be available online while you're doing your assignments?

 ### Connect™ Plus Accounting eBook

If you choose to use *Connect™ Plus Accounting*, you have an affordable and searchable online version of your book integrated with your other online tools.

Connect™ Plus Accounting eBook offers features like:

- Topic search
- Direct links from assignments
- Adjustable text size
- Jump to page number
- Print by section

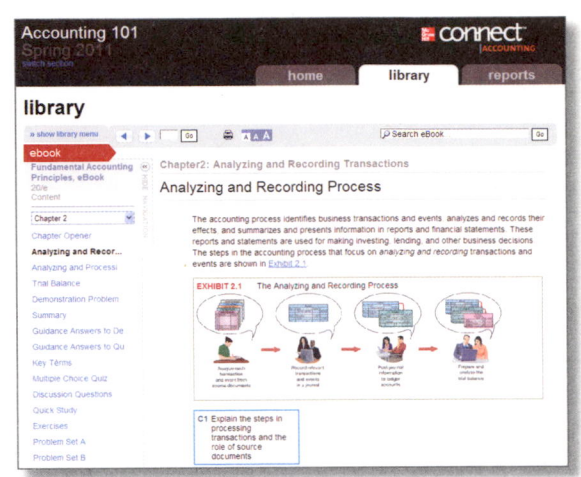

 Want to get more value from your textbook purchase?

Think learning accounting should be a bit more interesting?

 ### Check out the STUDENT RESOURCES section under the *Connect™* Library tab.

Here you'll find a wealth of resources designed to help you achieve your goals in the course. You'll find things like **quizzes, PowerPoints, and Internet activities** to help you study. Every student has different needs, so explore the STUDENT RESOURCES to find the materials best suited to you.

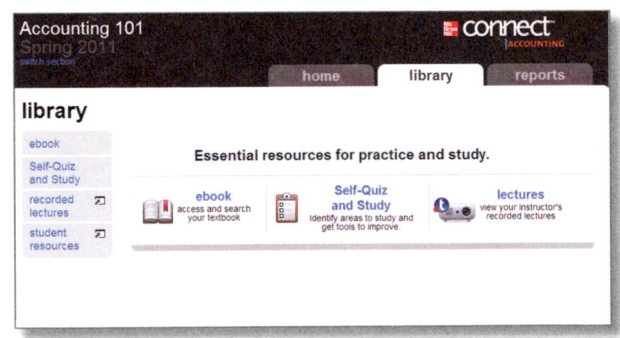

Financial & Managerial Accounting

4th edition

INFORMATION FOR DECISIONS

John J. Wild

University of Wisconsin at Madison

Ken W. Shaw

University of Missouri at Columbia

Barbara Chiappetta

Nassau Community College

McGraw-Hill Irwin

The McGraw·Hill Companies

McGraw-Hill Irwin

To my students and family, especially **Kimberly, Jonathan, Stephanie,** and **Trevor.**
To my wife **Linda** and children, **Erin, Emily,** and **Jacob.**
To my mother, husband **Bob,** and sons **Michael** and **David.**

FINANCIAL AND MANAGERIAL ACCOUNTING: INFORMATION FOR DECISIONS
Published by McGraw-Hill/Irwin, a business unit of The McGraw-Hill Companies, Inc., 1221 Avenue of the Americas, New York, NY, 10020. Copyright © 2011, 2009, 2007, 2005 by The McGraw-Hill Companies, Inc. All rights reserved. No part of this publication may be reproduced or distributed in any form or by any means, or stored in a database or retrieval system, without the prior written consent of The McGraw-Hill Companies, Inc., including, but not limited to, in any network or other electronic storage or transmission, or broadcast for distance learning.

Some ancillaries, including electronic and print components, may not be available to customers outside the United States.

This book is printed on acid-free paper.

1 2 3 4 5 6 7 8 9 0 DOW/DOW 1 0 9 8 7 6 5 4 3 2 1 0

ISBN 978-0-07-811088-7 (combined edition)
MHID 0-07-811088-2 (combined edition)
ISBN 978-0-07-731835-2 (with working papers volume 1, chapters 1-13)
MHID 0-07-731835-8 (with working papers volume 1, chapters 1-13)
ISBN 978-0-07-731839-0 (with working papers volume 2, chapters 12-24)
MHID 0-07-731839-0 (with working papers volume 2, chapters 12-24)

Vice president and editor-in-chief: *Brent Gordon*
Editorial director: *Stewart Mattson*
Publisher: *Tim Vertovec*
Executive editor: *Steve Schuetz*
Executive director of development: *Ann Torbert*
Senior development editor: *Christina A. Sanders*
Vice president and director of marketing: *Robin J. Zwettler*
Marketing director: *Brad Parkins*
Marketing manager: *Michelle Heaster*
Vice president of editing, design, and production: *Sesha Bolisetty*
Managing editor: *Lori Koetters*

Senior buyer: *Carol A. Bielski*
Lead designer: *Matthew Baldwin*
Senior photo research coordinator: *Jeremy Cheshareck*
Photo researcher: *Sarah Evertson*
Lead media project manager: *Brian Nacik*
Media project manager: *Ron Nelms*
Interior and cover design: *Laurie Entringer*
Cover image: *© Getty Images*
Typeface: *10.5/12 Times Roman*
Compositor: *Aptara®, Inc.*
Printer: *R. R. Donnelley*

Library of Congress Cataloging-in-Publication Data

Wild, John J.
    Financial and managerial accounting: information for decisions / John J. Wild, Ken
W. Shaw, Barbara Chiappetta.—4th ed.
        p. cm.
    Includes index.
    ISBN-13: 978-0-07-811088-7 (combined edition : alk. paper)
    ISBN-10: 0-07-811088-2 (combined edition : alk. paper)
    ISBN-13: 978-0-07-731835-2 (volume 1, chapters 1-13 : alk. paper)
    ISBN-10: 0-07-731835-8 (volume 1, chapters 1-13 : alk. paper)
    [etc.]
    1. Accounting. 2. Managerial accounting. I. Shaw, Ken W. II. Chiappetta, Barbara.
III. Title.
HF5636.W674 2011
658.15′11—dc22
                                                                                2010038609

www.mhhe.com

Dear Colleagues/Friends,

As we roll out the new edition of *Financial and Managerial Accounting*, we thank each of you who provided suggestions to improve our textbook. As teachers, we know how important it is to select the right book for our course. This new edition reflects the advice and wisdom of many dedicated reviewers, students, instructors, and symposium and workshop participants. Our book consistently rates number one in customer loyalty because of you. Together, we have created the most readable, concise, current, accurate, and innovative accounting book available today.

Throughout the writing process, we steered this book in the manner you directed. Reviewers, instructors, and students say this book's enhanced presentation, graphics, and technology cater to different learning styles and helps students better understand accounting. *Connect Accounting Plus* offers new features to improve student learning and to assist instructor teaching and grading. Our iPod content lets students study on the go, while our Algorithmic Test Bank provides an infinite variety of exam problems. You and your students will find all these tools easy to apply.

We owe the success of this book to our colleagues who graciously took time to help us focus on the changing needs of today's instructors and students. We feel fortunate to have witnessed our profession's extraordinary devotion to teaching. Your feedback and suggestions are reflected in everything we write. Please accept our heartfelt thanks for your dedication in helping today's students learn, understand, and appreciate accounting.

With kindest regards,

John J. Wild   Ken W. Shaw   Barbara Chiappetta

About the Authors

JOHN J. WILD is a distinguished professor of accounting at the University of Wisconsin at Madison. He previously held appointments at Michigan State University and the University of Manchester in England. He received his BBA, MS, and PhD from the University of Wisconsin.

Professor Wild teaches accounting courses at both the undergraduate and graduate levels. He has received numerous teaching honors, including the Mabel W. Chipman Excellence-in-Teaching Award, the departmental Excellence-in-Teaching Award, and the Teaching Excellence Award from the 2003 and 2005 business graduates at the University of Wisconsin. He also received the Beta Alpha Psi and Roland F. Salmonson Excellence-in-Teaching Award from Michigan State University. Professor Wild has received several research honors and is a past KPMG Peat Marwick National Fellow and is a recipient of fellowships from the American Accounting Association and the Ernst and Young Foundation.

Professor Wild is an active member of the American Accounting Association and its sections. He has served on several committees of these organizations, including the Outstanding Accounting Educator Award, Wildman Award, National Program Advisory, Publications, and Research Committees. Professor Wild is author of *Fundamental Accounting Principles*, *Financial Accounting*, *Managerial Accounting*, and *College Accounting*, each published by McGraw-Hill/Irwin. His research articles on accounting and analysis appear in *The Accounting Review*; *Journal of Accounting Research*; *Journal of Accounting and Economics*; *Contemporary Accounting Research*; *Journal of Accounting, Auditing, and Finance*; *Journal of Accounting and Public Policy*; and other journals. He is past associate editor of *Contemporary Accounting Research* and has served on several editorial boards including *The Accounting Review*.

In his leisure time, Professor Wild enjoys hiking, sports, travel, people, and spending time with family and friends.

KEN W. SHAW is an associate professor of accounting and the Deloitte Professor at the University of Missouri. He previously was on the faculty at the University of Maryland at College Park. He received an accounting degree from Bradley University and an MBA and PhD from the University of Wisconsin. He is a Certified Public Accountant with work experience in public accounting.

Professor Shaw teaches financial accounting at the undergraduate and graduate levels. He received the Williams-Keepers LLC Teaching Excellence award in 2007, was voted the "Most Influential Professor" by the 2005, 2006, and 2010 School of Accountancy graduating classes, and is a two-time recipient of the O'Brien Excellence in Teaching Award. He is the advisor to his school's chapter of the Association of Certified Fraud Examiners.

Professor Shaw is an active member of the American Accounting Association and its sections. He has served on many committees of these organizations and presented his research papers at national and regional meetings. Professor Shaw's research appears in *The Accounting Review*; *Journal of Accounting Research*; *Contemporary Accounting Research*; *Journal of Financial and Quantitative Analysis*; *Journal of the American Taxation Association*; *Journal of Accounting, Auditing, and Finance*; *Journal of Financial Research*; *Research in Accounting Regulation*; and other journals. He has served on the editorial boards of *Issues in Accounting Education*, the *Journal of Business Research*, and *Research in Accounting Regulation*. Professor Shaw is co-author of *Fundamental Accounting Principles*, *Managerial Accounting*, and *College Accounting*, all published by McGraw-Hill/Irwin.

In his leisure time, Professor Shaw enjoys tennis, cycling, music, and coaching his children's sports teams.

BARBARA CHIAPPETTA received her BBA in Accountancy and MS in Education from Hofstra University and is a tenured full professor at Nassau Community College. For the past two decades, she has been an active executive board member of the Teachers of Accounting at Two-Year Colleges (TACTYC), serving 10 years as vice president and as president from 1993 through 1999. As an active member of the American Accounting Association, she has served on the Northeast Regional Steering Committee, chaired the Curriculum Revision Committee of the Two-Year Section, and participated in numerous national committees. Professor Chiappetta has been inducted into the American Accounting Association Hall of Fame for the Northeast Region.

She had also received the Nassau Community College dean of instruction's Faculty Distinguished Achievement Award. Professor Chiappetta was honored with the State University of New York Chancellor's Award for Teaching Excellence in 1997. As a confirmed believer in the benefits of the active learning pedagogy, Professor Chiappetta has authored *Student Learning Tools*, an active learning workbook for a first-year accounting course, published by McGraw-Hill/Irwin.

In her leisure time, Professor Chiappetta enjoys tennis and participates on a U.S.T.A. team. She also enjoys the challenge of bridge. Her husband, Robert, is an entrepreneur in the leisure sport industry. She has two sons—Michael, a lawyer, specializing in intellectual property law in New York, and David, a composer, pursuing a career in music for film in Los Angeles.

Helping Students Achieve Peak Performance

Financial and Managerial Accounting 4e

Great performances result from pushing the limits through quality practices and reinforcing feedback. Assist your students in achieving their peak performance by giving them what they need to succeed in today's introductory accounting course.

Whether the goal is to become an accountant or a businessperson, or simply to be an informed consumer of accounting information, *Financial and Managerial Accounting (FinMan)* has helped generations of students succeed. FinMan provides leading-edge accounting content that engages students, which is then paired with state-of-the-art technology that elevates a student's understanding of key accounting principles.

With *FinMan* on your side, you'll be provided with **engaging content** in a **motivating style** to help students see the relevance of accounting. Students are motivated when reading materials that are clear and pertinent. *FinMan* excels at engaging students. Its chapter-opening vignettes showcase dynamic, successful entrepreneurial individuals and companies guaranteed to **interest and excite students**. This edition's featured companies—**Research In Motion** (maker of BlackBerry), **Apple**, **Nokia**, and **Palm**—captivate students with their products and annual reports, which are a pathway for learning financial statements. Further, this book's coverage of the accounting cycle fundamentals is widely praised for its clarity and effectiveness.

FinMan also delivers innovative technology to help student performance. **Connect Accounting** provides students with instant grading and feedback for assignments that are completed online. **Connect Accounting Plus** integrates an online version of the textbook with *Connect Accounting*. Our algorithmic test bank offers infinite variations of numerical test bank questions. The Self-Quiz and Study, Interactive Presentations, and LearnSmart all provide additional support to help reinforce concepts and keep students motivated.

We're confident you'll agree that *FinMan* **will help your students achieve peak performance**.

© Getty Images

 **ACCOUNTING** Your Students' Connection to

McGraw-Hill *Connect Accounting* is an online assignment and assessment solution that connects your students with the tools and resources needed to achieve success through faster learning, more efficient studying, and higher retention of knowledge.

Online Assignments: *Connect Accounting* helps students learn more efficiently by providing feedback and practice material when they need it, where they need it. *Connect* grades homework automatically and gives immediate feedback on any questions students may have missed.

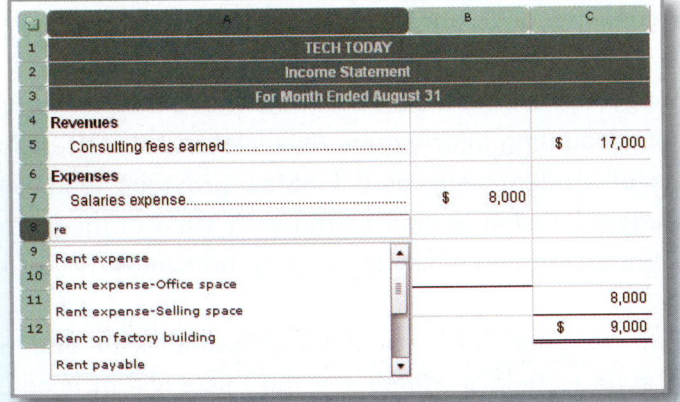

Interactive Presentations: The interactive presentations provide engaging narratives of all chapter learning objectives in an interactive online format. The presentations are tied specifically to *Financial and Managerial Accounting 4e*. They follow the structure of the text and are organized to match the learning objectives within each chapter. While the interactive presentations are not meant to replace the textbook in this course, they provide additional explanation and enhancement of material from the text chapter, allowing students to learn, study, and practice with instant feedback at their own pace.

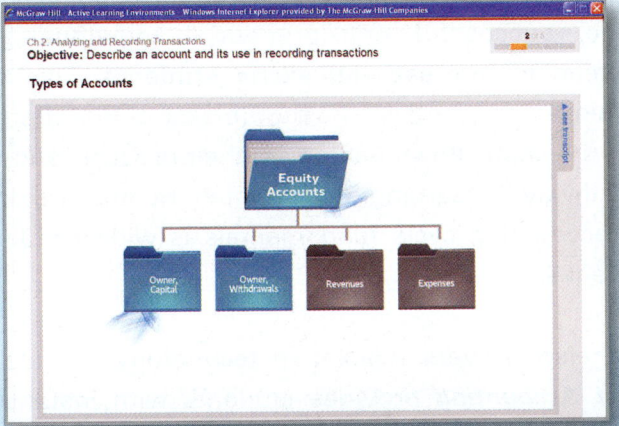

Student Resource Library: The *Connect Accounting* Student Study Center gives access to additional resources such as recorded lectures, online practice materials, an eBook, and more.

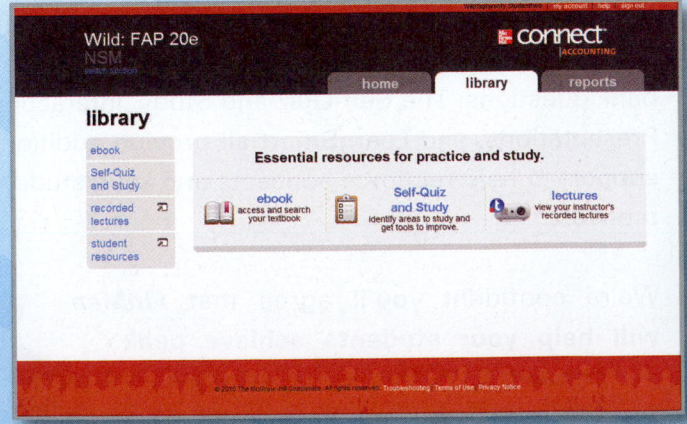

Reach Peak Performance!

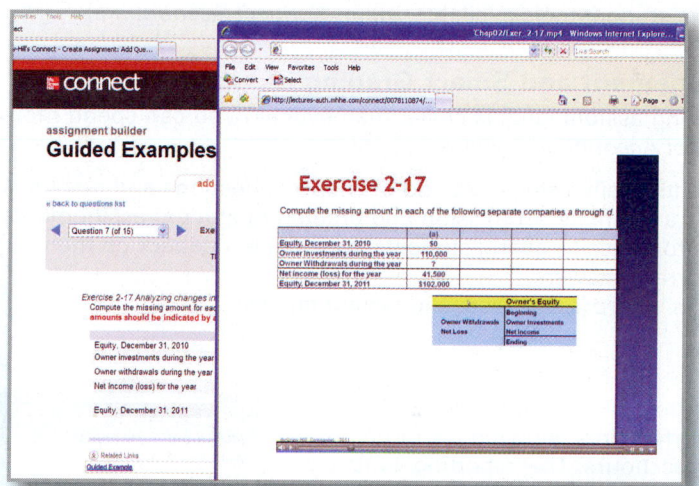

Guided Examples: The Guided Examples in *Connect Accounting* provide a narrated, animated, step-by-step walk-through of select exercises similar to those assigned. These short presentations provide reinforcement when students need it most.

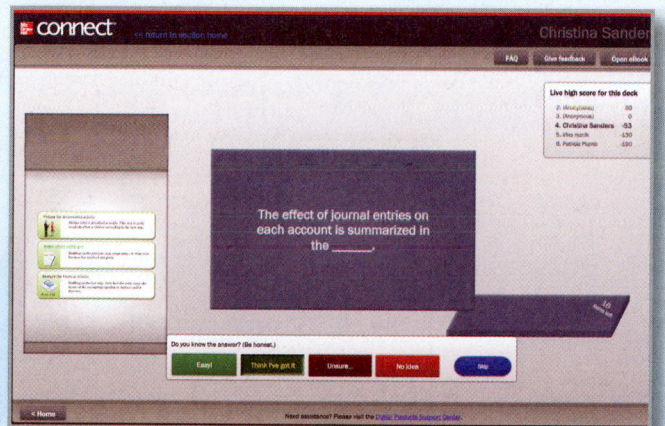

LearnSmart: LearnSmart adaptive self-study technology within *Connect Accounting* helps students make the best use of their study time. LearnSmart provides a seamless combination of practice, assessment, and remediation for every concept in the textbook. LearnSmart's intelligent software adapts to students by supplying questions on a new concept when they are ready to learn it. With LearnSmart, students will spend less time on topics they understand and practice more on those they have yet to master.

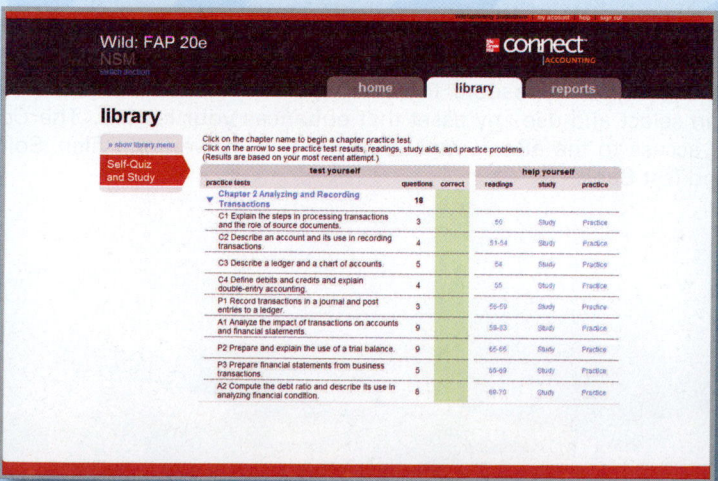

Self-Quiz and Study: The Self-Quiz and Study (SQS) connects students to the learning resources students need to succeed in the course. For each chapter, students can take a practice quiz and immediately see how well they performed. A study plan then recommends specific readings from the text, supplemental study material, and practice exercises that will improve students' understanding and mastery of each learning objective.

Connect Accounting

Connect Accounting offers a number of powerful tools and features to make managing assignments easier, so faculty can spend more time teaching. With *Connect Accounting*, students can engage with their coursework anytime and anywhere, making the learning process more accessible and efficient. (Please see previous page for a description of the student tools available within *Connect Accounting*.)

Simple Assignment Management and Smart Grading

With *Connect Accounting*, creating assignments is easier than ever, so you can spend more time teaching and less time managing. *Connect Accounting* enables you to:

- Create and deliver assignments easily with select end-of-chapter questions and test bank items.
- Go paperless with the eBook and online submission and grading of student assignments.
- Have assignments scored automatically, giving students immediate feedback on their work and side-by-side comparisons with correct answers.
- Reinforce classroom concepts with practice tests and instant quizzes.

Student Reporting

Connect Accounting keeps instructors informed about how each student, section, and class is performing, allowing for more productive use of lecture and office hours. The reporting function enables you to:

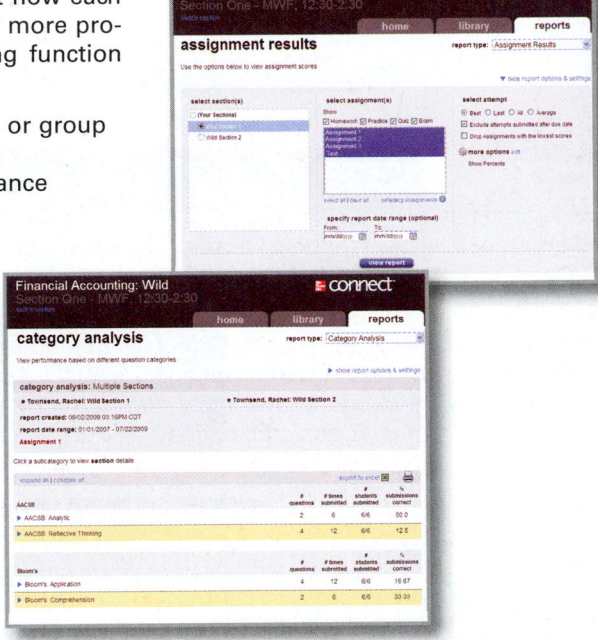

- View scored work immediately and track individual or group performance with assignment and grade reports.
- Access an instant view of student or class performance relative to learning objectives.
- Collect data and generate reports required by many accreditation organizations, such as AACSB and AICPA.

Instructor Library

The *Connect Accounting* Instructor Library is your repository for additional resources to improve student engagement in and out of class. You can select and use any asset that enhances your lecture. The *Connect Accounting* Instructor Library includes: access to the eBook version of the text, PowerPoint files, Solutions Manual, Instructor Resource Manual, and Test Bank.

Tools for Instructors

McGraw-Hill *Connect Plus Accounting*

McGraw-Hill reinvents the textbook learning experience for the modern student with *Connect Plus Accounting*. A seamless integration of an eBook and *Connect Accounting, Connect Plus Accounting* provides all of the *Connect Accounting* features plus:

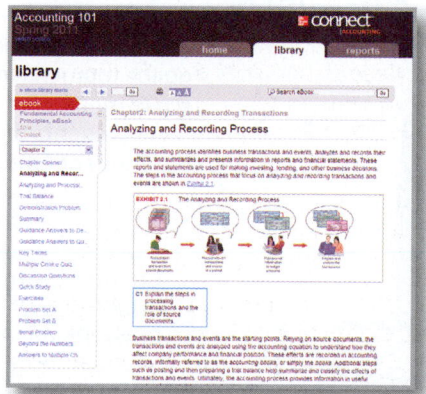

- An integrated eBook, allowing for anytime, anywhere access to the textbook.
- Dynamic links between the problems or questions you assign to your students and the location in the eBook where that problem or question is covered.
- A powerful search function to pinpoint and connect key concepts in a snap.

For more information about *Connect*, go to **www.mcgrawhillconnect.com**, or contact your local McGraw-Hill sales representative.

Tegrity Campus: Lectures 24/7

Tegrity Campus is a service that makes class time available 24/7 by automatically capturing every lecture. With a simple one-click start-and-stop process, you capture all computer screens and corresponding audio in a format that is easily searchable, frame by frame. Students can replay any part of any class with easy-to-use browser-based viewing on a PC or Mac, an iPod, or other mobile device.

Educators know that the more students can see, hear, and experience class resources, the better they learn. In fact, studies prove it. Tegrity Campus's unique search feature helps students efficiently find what they need, when they need it, across an entire semester of class recordings. Help turn your students' study time into learning moments immediately supported by your lecture. With Tegrity Campus, you also increase intent listening and class participation by easing students' concerns about note-taking. Lecture Capture will make it more likely you will see students' faces, not the tops of their heads.

To learn more about Tegrity watch a two-minute Flash demo at **http://tegritycampus.mhhe.com**.

McGraw-Hill Customer Care Contact Information

At McGraw-Hill, we understand that getting the most from new technology can be challenging. That's why our services don't stop after you purchase our products. You can e-mail our Product Specialists 24 hours a day to get product training online. Or you can search our knowledge bank of Frequently Asked Questions on our support Website. For Customer Support, call 800-331-5094 or visit **www.mhhe.com/support**. One of our Technical Support Analysts will be able to assist you in a timely fashion.

© Getty Images

How Can Text-Related Web Resources Enrich My Course?

Online Learning Center (OLC)

© Okea; iStockphoto

We offer an Online Learning Center (OLC) that follows *Financial and Managerial Accounting* chapter by chapter. It doesn't require any building or maintenance on your part. It's ready to go the moment you and your students type in the URL: *www.mhhe.com/wildFINMAN4e*

As students study and learn from *Financial and Managerial Accounting*, they can visit the Student Edition of the OLC Website to work with a multitude of helpful tools:

- Generic Template Working Papers
- Chapter Learning Objectives
- Interactive Chapter Quizzes
- PowerPoint® Presentations
- Narrated PowerPoint® Presentations*
- Excel Template Assignments
- iPod Content*

* indicates Premium Content

A secured Instructor Edition stores essential course materials to save you prep time before class. Everything you need to run a lively classroom and an efficient course is included. All resources available to students, plus . . .

- Instructor's Resource Manual
- Solutions Manual
- Solutions to Excel Template Assignments
- Test Bank
- Solutions to CYGL, Peachtree, and QuickBooks templates

The OLC Website also serves as a doorway to other technology solutions, like course management systems.

> "This is a well-written, clearly illustrated, easy to understand accounting textbook. The supplemental material provided to faculty, as well as students, is awesome."
>
> **—Jerri Tittle, Rose State College**

www.blackboard.com

Online Course Management

No matter what online course management system you use (WebCT, BlackBoard, or eCollege), we have a course content ePack available for *Financial and Managerial Accounting* 4e. Our new ePacks are specifically designed to make it easy for students to navigate and access content online. They are easier than ever to install on the latest version of the course management system available today.

Don't forget that you can count on the highest level of service from McGraw-Hill. Our online course management specialists are ready to assist you with your online course needs. They provide training and will answer any questions you have throughout the life of your adoption. So try our new ePack for *Financial and Managerial Accounting* 4e and make online course content delivery easy and fun.

CourseSmart

CourseSmart is a new way to find and buy eTextbooks. CourseSmart has the largest selection of eTextbooks available anywhere, offering thousands of the most commonly adopted textbooks from a wide variety of higher education publishers. CourseSmart eTextbooks are available in one standard online reader with full text search, notes, and highlighting, and email tools for sharing between classmates. Visit **www.CourseSmart.com** for more information on ordering.

How Students Can Study On the Go Using Their iPods

iPod Content

Harness the power of one of the most popular technology tools students use today—the Apple iPod. Our innovative approach allows students to download audio and video presentations right into their iPods and take learning materials with them wherever they go. Students just need to visit the Online Learning Center at **www.mhhe.com/wildFINMAN4e** to download our iPod content. For each chapter of the book they will be able to download audio narrated lecture presentations for use on various versions of iPods. iPod Touch users can even access self-quizzes.

It makes review and study time as easy as putting on headphones.

How Can McGraw-Hill Help Teach My Course Online?

Improve Student Learning Outcomes and Save Instructor Time with ALEKS®

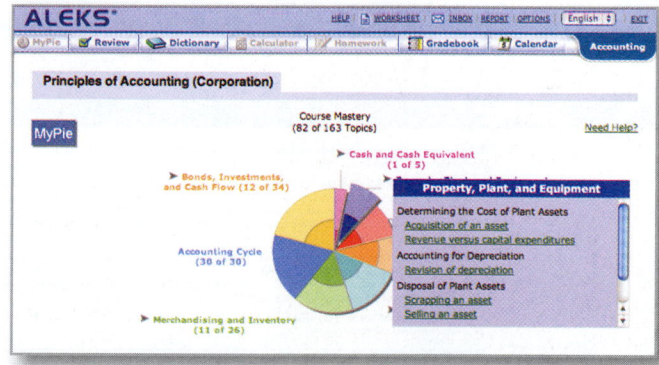

ALEKS is an assessment and learning program that provides individualized instruction in accounting. Available online in partnership with McGraw-Hill/Irwin, ALEKS interacts with students much like a skilled human tutor, with the ability to assess precisely a student's knowledge and provide instruction on the exact topics the student is most ready to learn. By providing topics to meet individual students' needs, allowing students to move between explanation and practice, correcting and analyzing errors, and defining terms, ALEKS helps students to master course content quickly and easily.

ALEKS also includes an Instructor Module with powerful, assignment-driven features and extensive content flexibility. The complimentary Instructor Module provides a course calendar, a customizable gradebook with automatically graded homework, textbook integration, and dynamic reports to monitor student and class progress. ALEKS simplifies course management and allows instructors to spend less time with administrative tasks and more time directing student learning.

To learn more about ALEKS, visit **www.aleks.com/highered/business**.

ALEKS is a registered trademark of ALEKS Corporation.

Innovative Textbook Features

Using Accounting for Decisions

Whether we prepare, analyze, or apply accounting information, one skill remains essential: decision-making. To help develop good decision-making habits and to illustrate the relevance of accounting, our book uses a unique pedagogical framework we call the Decision Center. This framework is comprised of a variety of approaches and subject areas, giving students insight into every aspect of business decision-making; see three examples to the right and one below. Answers to Decision Maker and Ethics boxes are at the end of each chapter.

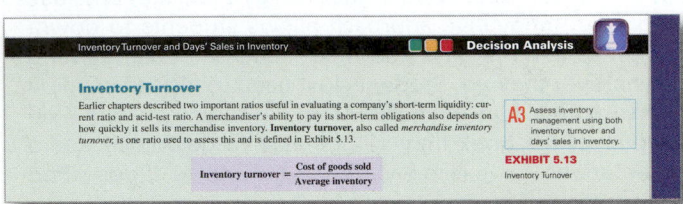

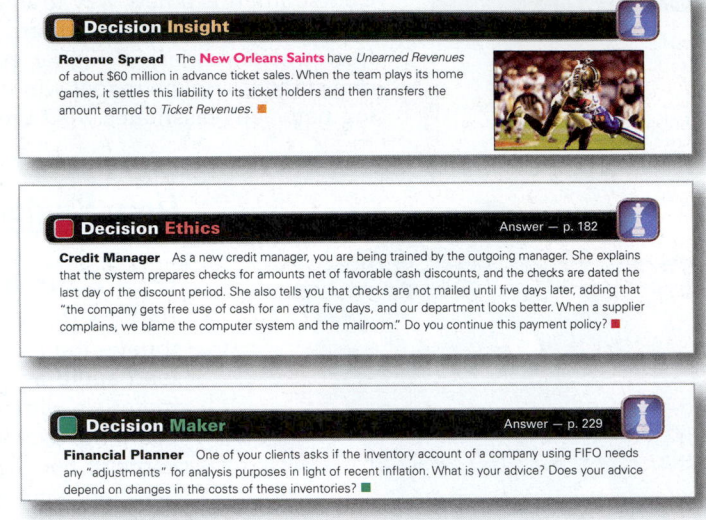

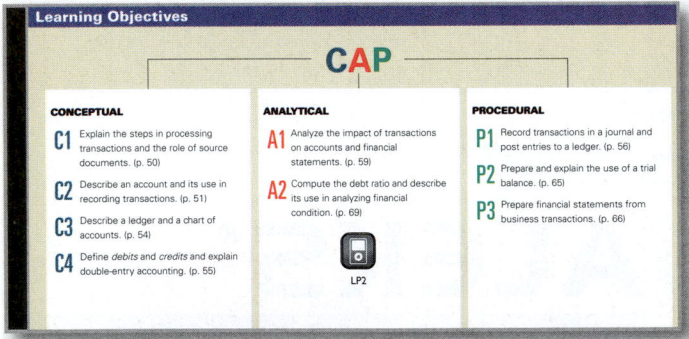

CAP Model

The Conceptual/Analytical/Procedural (CAP) Model allows courses to be specially designed to meet your teaching needs or those of a diverse faculty. This model identifies learning objectives, textual materials, assignments, and test items by C, A, or P, allowing different instructors to teach from the same materials, yet easily customize their courses toward a conceptual, analytical, or procedural approach (or a combination thereof) based on personal preferences.

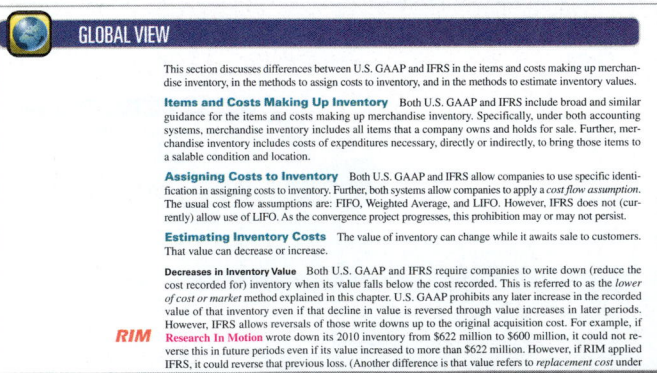

New Global View

This section explains international accounting practices relating to the material covered in that chapter. This section is purposefully located at the end of each chapter so that each instructor can decide what emphasis, if at all, is to be assigned to it. The aim of this Global View section is to describe accounting practices and to identify the similarities and differences in international accounting practices versus that in the U.S. As we move toward global convergence in accounting practices, and as we witness the likely conversion of U.S. GAAP to IFRS, the importance of student familiarity with international accounting grows. This innovative section helps us begin down that path of learning and teaching global accounting practices.

> "...the 'real world' examples that are at the beginning of each chapter are great for the students to understand that accounting is a very practical skill that every business needs."
>
> —**Mark Fronke, Cerritos College**

Bring Accounting To Life

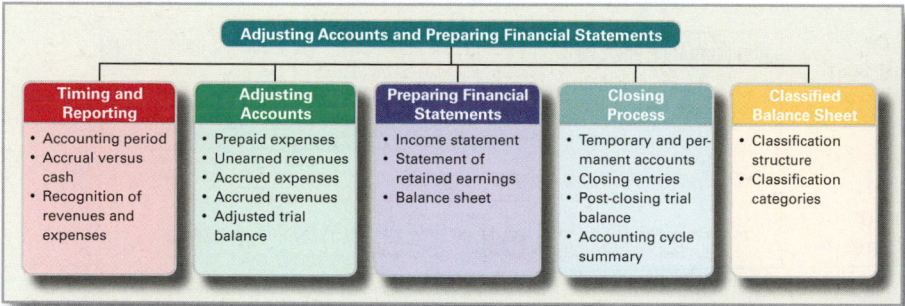

Chapter Preview With Flowchart

This feature provides a handy textual/visual guide at the start of every chapter. Students can now begin their reading with a clear understanding of what they will learn and when, allowing them to stay more focused and organized along the way.

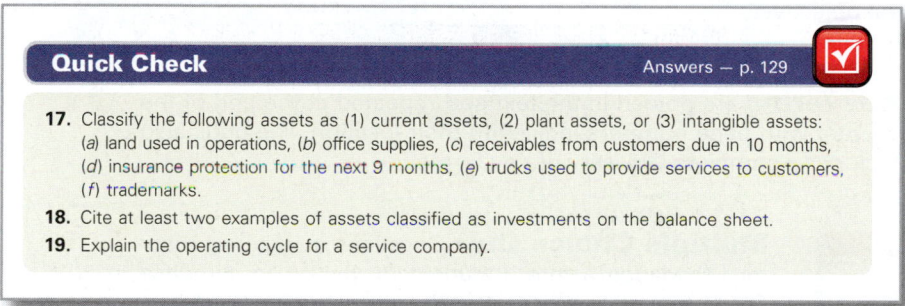

Quick Check

These short question/answer features reinforce the material immediately preceding them. They allow the reader to pause and reflect on the topics described, then receive immediate feedback before going on to new topics. Answers are provided at the end of each chapter.

"I think the Wild text is a superior introduction to financial and managerial accounting. I believe the content is well selected and explained. The exercises and problems are among the best I have used and the inclusion of ethics scenarios is very useful. The presentation is contemporary and attractive. I have had better success with the Wild text than with previous texts."

—David Diehl, Aurora University

Marginal Student Annotations

mployees handling large amounts of cash and oyee is *bonded* when a company purchases an n theft by that employee. Bonding reduces the nded employees know an independent bonding ered and is unlikely to be sympathetic with an

Point: The Association of Certified Fraud Examiners (**cfenet.com**) estimates that employee fraud costs small companies more than $100,000 per incident.

These annotations provide students with additional hints, tips, and examples to help them more fully understand the concepts and retain what they have learned. The annotations also include notes on global implications of accounting and further examples.

Outstanding Assignment Material

Once a student has finished reading the chapter, how well he or she retains the material can depend greatly on the questions, exercises, and problems that reinforce it. This book leads the way in comprehensive, accurate assignments.

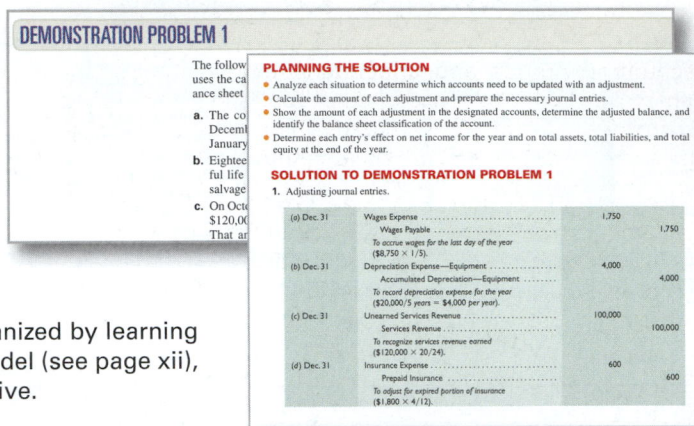

Demonstration Problems present both a problem and a complete solution, allowing students to review the entire problem-solving process and achieve success.

Chapter Summaries provide students with a review organized by learning objectives. Chapter Summaries are a component of the CAP model (see page xii), which recaps each conceptual, analytical, and procedural objective.

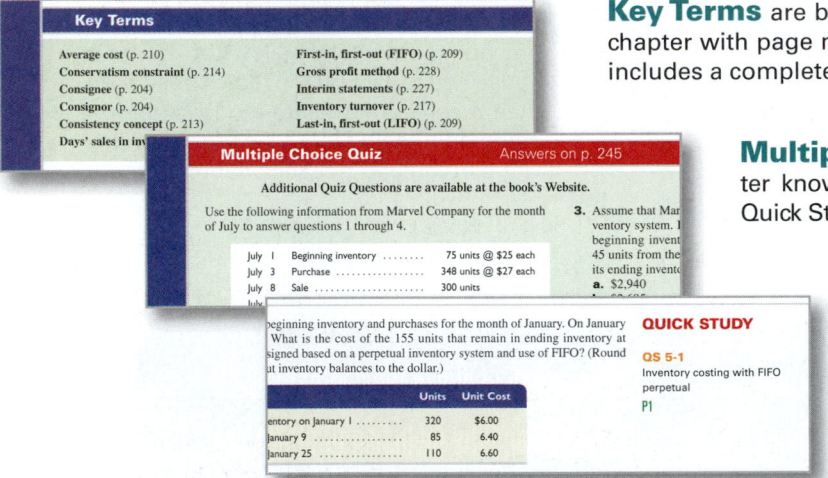

Key Terms are bolded in the text and repeated at the end of the chapter with page numbers indicating their location. The book also includes a complete Glossary of Key Terms.

Multiple Choice Quiz Questions quickly test chapter knowledge before a student moves on to complete Quick Studies, Exercises, and Problems.

Quick Study assignments are short exercises that often focus on one learning objective. Most are included in *Connect Accounting*. There are usually 8-10 Quick Study assignments per chapter.

Exercises are one of this book's many strengths and a competitive advantage. There are about 10-15 per chapter and most are included in *Connect Accounting*.

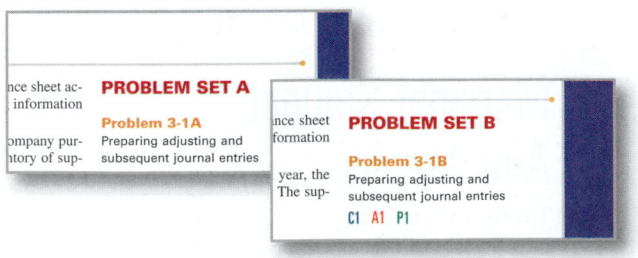

Problem Sets A & B are proven problems that can be assigned as homework or for in-class projects. All problems are coded according to the CAP model (see page xii), and Set A is included in *Connect Accounting*.

PUT AWAY YOUR RED PEN!

We pride ourselves on the accuracy of this book's assignment materials. Independent research reports that instructors and reviewers point to the accuracy of this book's assignment materials as one of its key competitive advantages.

Helps Students Master Key Concepts

Beyond the Numbers exercises ask students to use accounting figures and understand their meaning. Students also learn how accounting applies to a variety of business situations. These creative and fun exercises are all new or updated, and are divided into sections:

- Reporting in Action
- Comparative Analysis
- Ethics Challenge
- Communicating in Practice
- Taking It To The Net
- Teamwork in Action
- Hitting the Road
- Entrepreneurial Decision
- Global Decision

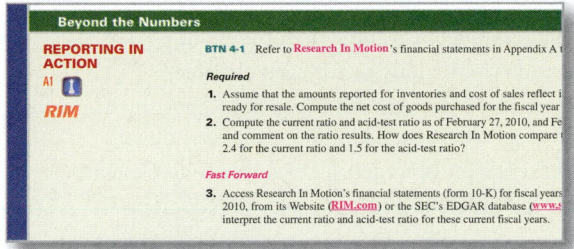

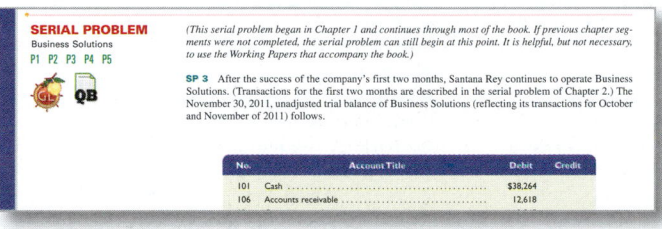

Serial Problem uses a continuous running case study to illustrate chapter concepts in a familiar context. The Serial Problem can be followed continuously from the first chapter or picked up at any later point in the book; enough information is provided to ensure students can get right to work.

The End of the Chapter Is Only the Beginning Our valuable and proven assignments aren't just confined to the book. From problems that require technological solutions to materials found exclusively online, this book's end-of-chapter material is fully integrated with its technology package.

 • Quick Studies, Exercises, and Problems available in *Connect* are marked with an icon.

 • Problems supported by the General Ledger Application Software, Peachtree, or Quickbooks are marked with an icon.

 • Online Learning Center (OLC) includes Interactive Quizzes, Excel template assignments, and more.

 • Problems supported with Microsoft Excel template assignments are marked with an icon.

 • Material that receives additional coverage (slide shows, videos, audio, etc.) available in iPod ready format are marked with an icon.

 • Assignments that focus on global accounting practices and companies are often identified with an icon.

The authors extend a special thanks to accuracy checkers Barbara Schnathorst, The Write Solution, Inc.; Helen Roybark, Radford University; Donna Grace, Sheridan College; Yvonne Phang, Borough of Manhattan Community College; Mitchell Franklin, Syracuse University; and David Krug, Johnson County Community College.

Enhancements in This Edition

This edition's revisions are driven by instructors and students. General revisions to the entire book are in the bulleted list that follows (including chapter-by-chapter revisions listed below):

- Revised and updated assignments throughout
- Updated ratio (tool) analyses for each chapter
- New material on International Financial Reporting Standards (IFRS) in most chapters, including global examples
- New and revised entrepreneurial examples and elements
- Revised serial problem through nearly all chapters
- New art program, visual info-graphics and text layout

- New Research In Motion (maker of BlackBerry) annual report with comparisons to Apple, Palm, and Nokia (IFRS) with new assignments for each
- Updated graphics added to each chapter's analysis section
- New technology content integrated and referenced in the book
- New Global View section in each chapter referencing international accounting including examples using global companies
- New assignments covering international accounting

Chapter 1

Facebook NEW opener with new entrepreneurial assignment
Streamlined and consolidated learning objectives
New section on International Standards and convergence
Revised section on accounting principles, assumptions, and constraints
New visual layouts for conceptual framework and the building blocks of GAAP
New discussion of conceptual framework linked to IFRS
New graphic discussing fraud control in accounting
Updated compensation data in exhibit

Chapter 2

CitySlips NEW opener with new entrepreneurial assignment
Reorganized and streamlined learning objectives
Revised introduction of double-entry accounting
New 4-step process for analyzing, recording, and posting transactions
Revised layout for transaction analysis
New discussion on accounting quality

Chapter 3

Cheezburger Network NEW opener with new entrepreneurial assignment
Updated 3-step process for adjusting accounts
Enhanced and streamlined presentation of accounting adjustments
Revised info-graphics for adjusting entries
Enhanced exhibit on steps in preparing financial statements
Expanded discussion of global accounting
Slightly revised steps 1 and 2 of work sheet
Enhanced graphics for closing process
Enhanced details for general ledger after the closing process
Updated color-coded work sheet

Chapter 4

Heritage Link Brands NEW opener with new entrepreneurial assignment
Streamlined learning objectives
New 2-step presentation for recording merchandise sales and its costs
Revised presentation on purchase returns
New discussion on fraud and invoices
Revised discussion of gross margin

Chapter 5

Fitness Anywhere NEW opener with new entrepreneurial assignment
Streamlined presentation for lower of cost or market (LCM)
Color-coded graphic for introducing cost flow assumptions
Enhanced graphics for learning inventory errors
Expanded discussion on inventory controls
Expanded explanation of inventory accounting under IFRS

Chapter 6

Dylan's Candy Bar REVISED opener with new entrepreneurial assignment
Enhanced SOX discussion of controls, including the role of COSO
Streamlined learning objectives
New material on drivers of human fraud
New graphic introducing a bank reconciliation with links to bank and book balances
Updated graphic on frequent cyber frauds
New graphic on drivers of financial misconduct

Chapter 7

LaserMonks NEW opener with new entrepreneurial assignment
Streamlined learning objectives
Reorganized recording of credit sales
Further clarification of interest formula
Enhanced graphics for bad debts estimation

Chapter 8

Games2U NEW opener with new entrepreneurial assignment
Reorganized learning objectives
Added entry to record impairment
Enhanced discussion of asset sales
Expanded explanation of asset valuation under IFRS
Updated all real world examples and graphics

Chapter 9

SnorgTees NEW opener with new entrepreneurial assignment
Updated tax illustrations and assignments using most recent government rates
New data on frauds involving employee payroll
New entry to reclassify long- to short-term debt
Updated all real world examples and graphics

Chapter 10

CakeLove NEW opener with new entrepreneurial assignment
Enhanced graphics for bonds and notes
Revised discussion of debt-to-equity
Enhanced explanation of how U.S. GAAP and IFRS determine fair value
New arrow lines linking effective interest amortization tables to journal entries

Chapter 11

Clean Air Lawn Care NEW opener with new entrepreneurial assignment
Streamlined learning objectives
Inserted numerous key margin computations for entries involving equity
Updated statement of stockholders' equity
Updated all real world examples and graphics
Explained accounting for equity under IFRS

For Better Learning

Chapter 12

Animoto NEW opener with new entrepreneurial assignment
Streamlined learning objectives
Enhanced graphics on cash inflows and outflows involving operating, investing, and financing
Highlighted 5-step process to prepare the statement of cash flows
New discussion of different classifications for certain cash flows under IFRS
Increased number and range of assignments

Chapter 13

Motley Fool REVISED opener with new entrepreneurial assignment
Streamlined learning objectives
New companies—Research In Motion, Apple, Palm, and Nokia—data throughout the chapter, exhibits, and illustrations
Enhanced horizontal and vertical analysis using new company and industry data
Enhanced discussion of common-size graphics
Enhanced ratio analysis using new company and industry data

Chapter 14

Hot Box Cookies NEW opener with new entrepreneurial assignment
Revised learning objectives
Enhanced discussion of trends in managerial accounting, including e-commerce and role of services
New exhibit and discussion of the value chain
Discussion of fraud and ethics in managerial accounting moved to earlier in chapter
New discussion of global trends in managerial accounting

Chapter 15

Liberty Tax Service NEW opener with new entrepreneurial assignment
Enhanced explanation of events in job order costing, including new 3-step process
Added new arrow lines to exhibits as learning aids
Enhanced discussion of adjusting factory overhead
New factory overhead T-account exhibit
New exhibit on entries to adjust factory overhead account
Added several new assignments

Chapter 16

IdeaPaint NEW opener with new entrepreneurial assignment
Streamlined learning objectives
Updated list of companies applying process operations
Enhanced several exhibits for better learning
New section on trends in process operations, including discussion of just-in-time, automation, role of services, and customer focus
Increased number and range of assignments

Chapter 17

Three Twins Ice Cream NEW opener with new entrepreneurial assignment
New exhibit summarizing overhead cost allocation methods
New section on assessing the plantwide and departmental overhead rate methods
New discussion of global use of lean accounting
Revised discussion of activity-based costing for added clarity
Increased number and range of assignments

Chapter 18

Johnny Cupcakes NEW opener with new entrepreneurial assignment
Streamlined learning objectives
Revised cost exhibits for added clarity and learning
New discussion on global use of contribution margin

Chapter 19

Samanta Shoes NEW opener with new entrepreneurial assignment
Streamlined learning objectives
Revised section on absorption costing
New section on variable costing for service firms

Chapter 20

Smathers and Branson NEW opener with new entrepreneurial assignment
Reorganized learning objectives
New discussion on potential outcomes of participatory budgeting
Enhanced discussion and exhibits for cash budgets

New exhibit on general formula for preparing the cash budget
Added Decision Insight box on Apple's cash cushion
Enhanced discussion of computing cash disbursements for purchases, including new exhibit
Increased number and range of assignments

Chapter 21

SewWhat? NEW opener with new entrepreneurial assignment
Streamlined learning objectives
Simplified presentation of overhead variances to focus on controllable and volume variances
Moved detailed overhead variances and standard cost system journal entries to (new) Appendix 21
Increased number and range of assignments

Chapter 22

Skullcandy NEW opener with new entrepreneurial assignment
Streamlined learning objectives
Revised section on departmental reporting and analysis
Added Serial Problem to end of chapter assignments

Chapter 23

Dogswell NEW opener with new entrepreneurial assignment
Streamlined learning objectives
Added section and assignments on decision to keep or replace equipment
Increased number and range of assignments

Chapter 24

Gamer Grub NEW opener with new entrepreneurial assignment
Updated graphic on industry cost of capital estimates

Instructor Supplements

Instructor's Resource CD-ROM
Chapters 1-24
ISBN13: 9780077318307
ISBN10: 0077318307

This is your all-in-one resource. It allows you to create custom presentations from your own materials or from the following text-specific materials provided in the CD's asset library:

- **Instructor's Resource Manual**

  Written by April Mohr, Jefferson Community and Technical College SW.

  This manual contains (for each chapter) a Lecture Outline, a chart linking all assignment materials to Learning Objectives, a list of relevant active learning activities, and additional visuals with transparency masters.

- **Solutions Manual**
- **Test Bank, Computerized Test Bank**

  Prepared by Stacie Mayes, Rose State College, and Margaret Tanner, University of Arkansas–Fort Smith.

- **PowerPoint® Presentations**

  Prepared by Debra Schmidt, Cerritos College.

  Presentations allow for revision of lecture slides, and includes a viewer, allowing screens to be shown with or without the software.

- **Link to PageOut**

Solutions Manual
Vol. 1, Chapters 1-13
ISBN13: 9780077318376
ISBN10: 0077318374

Vol. 2, Chapters 14-24
ISBN13: 9780077318413
ISBN10: 0077318412

Written by John J. Wild, Ken W. Shaw, and Anita Kroll, University of Wisconsin–Madison.

Student Supplements

Excel Working Papers CD
Vol. 1, Chapters 1-13
ISBN13: 9780077318369
ISBN10: 0077318366

Vol. 2, Chapters 13-24
ISBN13: 9780077318406
ISBN10: 0077318404

Written by John J. Wild.

Working Papers delivered in Excel spreadsheets. These Excel Working Papers are available on CD-ROM and can be bundled with the printed Working Papers; see your representative for information.

Working Papers
Vol. 1, Chapters 1-13
ISBN13: 9780077318383
ISBN10: 0077318382

Vol. 2, Chapters 13-24
ISBN13: 9780077318420
ISBN10: 0077318420

Study Guide
ISBN13: 9780077318345
ISBN10: 007731834X

Written by April Mohr, Jefferson Community and Technical College SW.

Covers each chapter and appendix with reviews of the learning objectives, outlines of the chapters, summaries of chapter materials, and additional problems with solutions.

Carol Yacht's General Ledger and Peachtree Complete CD-ROM
ISBN13: 9780077318239
ISBN10: 0077318234

The CD-ROM includes fully functioning versions of McGraw-Hill's own General Ledger Application software and Peachtree Complete. Problem templates prepared by Carol Yacht and student user guides are included that allow you to assign text problems for working in Yacht's General Ledger or Peachtree.

QuickBooks Pro 2011 Student Guide and Templates
ISBN13: 9780077455316
ISBN10: 0077455312

Prepared by Carol Yacht.

To better prepare students for accounting in the real world, select end-of-chapter material in the text is tied to QuickBooks software. The accompanying student guide provides a step-by-step walkthrough for students on how to complete the problem in the software.

Assurance of Learning Ready

Many educational institutions today are focused on the notion of assurance of learning, an important element of some accreditation standards. *Financial and Managerial Accounting* is designed specifically to support your assurance of learning initiatives with a simple, yet powerful solution. Each test bank question for *Financial and Managerial Accounting* maps to a specific chapter learning objective listed in the text. You can use our test bank software, EZ Test and EZ Test Online, or *Connect Accounting* to easily query for learning objectives that directly relate to the learning objectives for your course. You can then use the reporting features of EZ Test to aggregate student results in similar fashion, making the collection and presentation of assurance of learning data simple and easy.

> "This textbook is a very well-structured comprehensive accounting textbook that presents material that is easy to follow and understand."
>
> — Scott Williams, County College of Morris

AACSB Statement

The McGraw-Hill Companies is a proud corporate member of AACSB International. Understanding the importance and value of AACSB accreditation, *Financial and Managerial Accounting* recognizes the curricula guidelines detailed in the AACSB standards for business accreditation by connecting selected questions in the test bank to the six general knowledge and skill guidelines in the AACSB standards. The statements contained in *Financial and Managerial Accounting* are provided only as a guide for the users of this textbook. The AACSB leaves content coverage and assessment within the purview of individual schools, the mission of the school, and the faculty. While *Financial and Managerial Accounting* and the teaching package make no claim of any specific AACSB qualification or evaluation, we have within *Financial and Managerial Accounting* labeled select questions according to the six general knowledge and skills areas.

The authors extend a special thanks to our contributing and technology supplement authors:

Contributing Author: Anita Kroll, University of Wisconsin–Madison
LearnSmart Authors: Anna Boulware, St. Charles Community College; Brenda Mattison, Tri County Technical College; and Dominique Svarc, William Rainey Harper College
Online Quizzes: Constance Hylton, George Mason University
Connect Self-Quiz and Study: Jeannine Metzler, Northampton Community College, and Karen Wisniewski, County College of Morris
Interactive Presentations: Kathleen O'Donnell, Onondaga Community College, and Jeannie Folk, College of DuPage

Acknowledgments

John J. Wild, Ken W. Shaw, Barbara Chiappetta, and McGraw-Hill/Irwin would like to recognize the following instructors for their valuable feedback and involvement in the development of *Financial and Managerial Accounting* 4e. We are thankful for their suggestions, counsel, and encouragement.

Nelson Alino, Quinnipiac University

David Alldredge, Salt Lake Community College

Sheila Ammons, Austin Community College

Victoria Badura, Chadron State College

Susan Baker, University of Michigan-Dearborn

Charles Scott Barhight, Northampton Community College

Rick Barnhart, Grand Rapids Community College

Robert Beebe, Morrisville State University

Teri Bernstein, Santa Monica College

Swati Bhandarkar, University of Georgia

Jaswinder Bhangal, Chabot College

Anna Boulware, St. Charles Community College

Nina Brown, Tarrant County Community College

Philip Brown, Harding University

Jay Buchanon, Burlington County College-Pemberton

Mary Burnell, Fairmont State University

Nathaniel Calloway, University of Maryland

Sal Cardiel, Chaffey College

Hong Chen, Northeastern Illinois University

Stanley Chu, Borough of Manhattan Community College

Kwang-Hyun Chung, Pace University

Shifei Chung, Rowan University

Robert Churchman, Harding University

Marilyn Ciolino, Delgado Community College

Lisa Cole, Johnson County Community College

Howard A. Collins, SUNY at Stony Brook

William Cooper, North Carolina A &T University

Suzie Cordes, Johnson County Community College

James Cosby, John Tyler Community College

Richard Culp, Ball State University

Alan Czyzewski, Indiana State University-Terre Haute

Walter DeAguero, Saddleback College

Mike Deschamps, Mira Costa College

Rosemond Desir, Colorado State University

Vincent Dicalogero, Suffolk County Community College

Carol Dickerson, Chaffey College

David Diehl, Aurora University

Jap Efendi, University of Texas-Arlington

Terry Elliott Morehead State University

James M. Emig, Villanova University

Steven Englert, Ivy Tech Community College

Caroline Falconetti, Nassau Community College

Stephanie Farewell, University of Arkansas-Little Rock

Laura Farrell, Wagner College

Charles Fazzi, Saint Vincent College

Ronald A. Feinberg, Suffolk Community College

Kathleen Fitzpatrick, University of Toledo-Scott Park

Jeannie Folk, College of DuPage

Mary Foster, Illinois Central College

Mitchell Franklin, Syracuse University

Paul Franklin, Kaplan University Online

Mark Fronke, Cerritos College

Kim Gatzke, Delgado Community College

Rich Geglein, Ivy Tech Community College

Barbara Gershowitz, Nashville State Technical Community College

Richard Gordon, Columbia Southern

Richard P. Green II, Texas A& M University

Tony Greig, Purdue University

Lillian Grose, Delgado Community College

Betty Habiger, New Mexico State University

Francis Haggerty, Lee College

Betty Harper, Middle Tennessee State University

Jeannie Harrington, Middle Tennessee State University

John L. Haverty, St. Joseph's University

Laurie Hays, Western Michigan University

Shelley Henke, Fox Valley Technical College

Lyle Hicks, Danville Area Community College

Cecil Hill, Jackson State University

Patricia Holmes, Des Moines Area Community College

Margaret Houston, Wright State University

Calvin M. Hoy, County College of Morris

Constance Hylton, George Mason University

Gary Allen Hypes, Mount Aloysius College

Peggy Jenkins, SUNY Canton

Catherine Jeppson, Caifornia State University–Northridge

Gina M. Jones, Aims Community College

Rita Jones, Columbus State University

Christine Jonick, Gainesville State College

Thomas Kam, Hawaii Pacific University

Jack Karbens, Hawaii Pacific University

Connie Kelt, San Juan College

Karen Kettelson, Western Technical College

Randy Kidd, Longview Community College

Irene Kim, George Washington University

James Kinard, Ohio State University-Columbus

Rita Kingery-Cook, University of Delaware

Frank Klaus, Cleveland State University

Shirly A. Kleiner, Johnson County Community College

Morris Knapp, Miami-Dade College

Jill Kolody, Anne Arundel Community College

Phillip Korb, University of Baltimore

Emil Koren, St. Leo University

David Krug, Johnson County Community College

Charles Lacey, Henry Ford Community College

Tara Laken, Joliet Junior College

Beth Lasky, Delgado Community College

Phillip Lee, Nashville State Technical Community College

Jerry Lehman, Madison Area Technical College

Frederic Lerner, New York University

Roger Lewis, West Virginia University-Parkersburg

Eric Lindquist, Lansing Community College

Danny Litt, University of California-Los Angeles

Jeannie Liu, Chaffey College

Don Lucy, Indian River State College

Sylvester A. Marino, SUNY Westchester Community College

Brenda Mattison, Tri-County Technical College

Stacie Mayes, Rose State College

Jeanine Metzler, Northampton Community College

Pam Meyer, University of Louisiana-Lafayette

Kathleen Michele, Sun Prairie College

Tim Miller, El Camino College

April Mohr, Jefferson Community and Technical College, SW

Robbie Morse, Ivy Tech Community College

Linda Muren, Cuyahoga Community College—West Campus

Ramesh Narasimhan, Montclair State University

Mary Beth Nelson, North Shore Community College

Deborah Niemer, Oakland Community College

Kathleen O'Donnell, Onondaga Community College

Ahmed Omar, Burlington County College

Ginger Parker, Miami-Dade College

Joel Peralto, Hawaii Community College

Yvonne Phang, Borough of Manhattan Community College

Susan Pope, University of Akron

Jean Price, Marshall University

Debbie Rankin, Lincoln University

Susan Reeves, University of South Carolina

Jenny Resnick, Santa Monica College

Ruthie Reynolds, Howard University

Carla Rich, Pensacola Junior College

Jill Roberts, Campbellsville University

Karen Robinson, Morgan State University

Richard Roding, Red Rocks Community College

Joel Rosenfeld, New York University

Pamela Rouse, Butler University

Helen Roybark, Radford University

Alphonse Ruggiero, Suffolk County Community College

Martin Sabo, Community College of Denver

Judith Sage, Texas A&M International University

Nathaniel Samba, Ivy Tech Community College

Linda Schain, Hoefstra University

Christine Schalow, University of Wisconsin-Stevens Point

Geeta Shankar, University of Dayton

Regina Shea, Community College of Baltimore County—Essex

Gerald Smith, University of Northern Iowa

Robert Smolin, Citrus College

Charles Spector, State University of New York College

Jane Stam, Onondaga Community College

Douglas P. Stives, Monmouth University

Jacqueline Stoute, Baruch University

Beverly Strachan, Troy University

Dominique Svarc, William Rainey Harper College

Paul Swanson, Illinois Central College

Margaret Tanner, University of Arkansas–Fort Smith

Anthony Teng, Saddleback College

Sue Terizan, Wright State University

Leslie Thysell, John Tyler Community College

Jerri Tittle, Rose State College

Michael Ulinski, Pace University-Pleasantville

Bob Urell, Irvine Valley College

Alonda Vaughn, Strayer University-Tampa East

Ari Vega, Fashion Institute of Technology

Adam Vitalis, University of Wisconsin

Li Wang, University of Akron

Doris Warmflash, SUNY Westchester Community College

Janis Weber, University of Louisiana-Monroe

David Welch, Franklin University

Jean Wells, Howard University

Robert A. Widman, Brooklyn College CUNY

Christopher Widmer, Tidewater Community College

Jane Wiese, Valencia Community College

Kenneth L. Wild, University of London

Scott Williams, County College of Morris

Karen Wisniewski, County College of Morris

Wanda Wong, Chabot College

Darryl Woolley, University of Idaho

Lorenzo Ybarra, West Los Angeles College

Laura Young, University of Central Arkansas

Judith Zander, Grossmont College

In addition to the helpful and generous colleagues listed above, we thank the entire McGraw-Hill/Irwin *Financial and Managerial Accounting* 4e team, including Stewart Mattson, Tim Vertovec, Steve Schuetz, Christina Sanders, Aaron Downey of Matrix Productions, Lori Koetters, Matthew Baldwin, Carol Bielski, Patricia Plumb, and Brian Nacik. We also thank the great marketing and sales support staff, including Michelle Heaster, Kathleen Klehr, and Simi Dutt. Many talented educators and professionals worked hard to create the supplements for this book, and for their efforts we're grateful. Finally, many more people we either did not meet or whose efforts we did not personally witness nevertheless helped to make this book everything that it is, and we thank them all.

John J. Wild   Ken W. Shaw   Barbara Chiappetta

Brief Contents

* Appendixes D & E are available on the book's Website, mhhe.com/wildFINMAN4e, and as print copy from a McGraw-Hill representative.

Contents

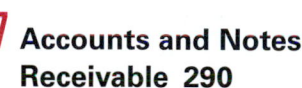

9 Current Liabilities 366

10 Long-Term Liabilities 410

11 Corporate Reporting and Analysis 454

* Appendixes D & E are available on the book's Website, <u>mhhe.com/wildFINMAN4e</u>, and as print copy
from a McGraw-Hill representative.

Financial & Managerial Accounting

INFORMATION FOR DECISIONS

1

Introducing Accounting in Business

A Look at This Chapter

Accounting is crucial in our information age. In this chapter, we discuss the importance of accounting to different types of organizations and describe its many users and uses. We explain that ethics are essential to accounting. We also explain business transactions and how they are reflected in financial statements.

A Look Ahead

Chapter 2 describes and analyzes business transactions. We explain the analysis and recording of transactions, the ledger and trial balance, and the double-entry system. More generally, Chapters 2 and 3 show (via the accounting cycle) how financial statements reflect business activities.

Learning Objectives

Learning Objectives are classified as conceptual, analytical, or procedural.

CAP

CONCEPTUAL

C1 Explain the purpose and importance of accounting. (p. 4)

C2 Identify users and uses of, and opportunities in, accounting. (p. 5)

C3 Explain why ethics are crucial to accounting. (p. 8)

C4 Explain generally accepted accounting principles and define and apply several accounting principles. (p. 9)

C5 *Appendix 1B*—Identify and describe the three major activities of organizations. (p. 26)

ANALYTICAL

A1 Define and interpret the accounting equation and each of its components. (p. 14)

A2 Compute and interpret return on assets. (p. 22)

A3 *Appendix 1A*—Explain the relation between return and risk. (p. 26)

LP I

PROCEDURAL

P1 Analyze business transactions using the accounting equation. (p. 15)

P2 Identify and prepare basic financial statements and explain how they interrelate. (p. 19)

Accounting for Facebook

A ***Decision Feature*** *launches each chapter showing the relevance of accounting for a real entrepreneur. An* ***Entrepreneurial Decision*** *problem at the end of the assignments returns to this feature with a mini-case.*

"We are focused on . . . helping people share information"

—MARK ZUCKERBERG

PALO ALTO, CA—"Open Society" conjures up philosophical thoughts and political ideologies. However, for Mark Zuckerberg, his vision of an open society "is to give people the power to share and make the world more open and connected." That vision led Mark to create **Facebook** (**Facebook.com**) from his college dorm. Today, Facebook is the highest-profile social networking site. Along the way, Mark had to learn accounting and the details of preparing and interpreting financial statements.

"It's all been very interesting," says Mark. Important questions involving business formation, transaction analysis, and financial reporting arose. Mark answered them and in the process has set his company apart. "I'm here to build something for the long term," declares Mark. "Anything else is a distraction."

Information is the focus—both within Facebook and within its accounting records. Mark recalls that when he launched his business, there were "all these reasons why they could not aggregate this [personal] information." He took a similar tactic in addressing accounting information. "There's an intense focus on . . . information, as both an ideal and a practical strategy to get things done," insists Mark. This includes using accounting information to make key business decisions.

While Facebook is the language of social networking, accounting is the language of business networking. "As a company we are very focused on what we are building," says Mark. "We are adding a certain amount of value to people's lives if we build a very good product." That value is reflected in its financial statements, which are based on transaction analysis and accounting concepts.

Facebook's success is reflected in its revenues, which continue to grow and exhibit what people call the monetizing of social networking. "Social Ads are doing pretty well," asserts Mark. "We are happy with how we are doing in terms of numbers of advertisers and revenue." Facebook also tracks its expenses and asset purchases. "We expect to achieve . . . profitability next year," states Mark. "It means we will be able to fund all of our operations and server purchases from the cash we generate." This is saying a lot as Facebook's operating expenditures must support nearly 1 billion photo uploads and 8 million video uploads per day.

Mark emphasizes that his financial house must be in order for Facebook to realize its full potential—and that potential is in his sights. "We believe really deeply that if people are sharing more, then the world will be a more open place where people can understand what is going on with the people around them."

[Sources: *Facebook Website,* January 2011; *CNN,* October 2008; *Mercury News,* April 2009; *VentureBeat,* March 2008; *FastCompany.com,* May 2007; *Wired,* June 2009]

Today's world is one of information—its preparation, communication, analysis, and use. Accounting is at the core of this information age. Knowledge of accounting gives us career opportunities and the insight to take advantage of them. This book introduces concepts, procedures, and analyses that help us make better decisions, including career choices. In this chapter we describe accounting, the users and uses of accounting information, the forms and activities of organizations, and several accounting principles. We also introduce transaction analysis and financial statements.

Introducing Accounting in Business

Importance of Accounting	Fundamentals of Accounting	Transaction Analysis	Financial Statements
• Accounting information users • Opportunities in accounting	• Ethics—key concept • Generally accepted accounting principles • International standards	• Accounting equation • Transaction analysis—illustrated	• Income statement • Statement of retained earnings • Balance sheet • Statement of cash flows

IMPORTANCE OF ACCOUNTING

C1 Explain the purpose and importance of accounting.

Why is accounting so popular on campuses? Why are there so many accounting jobs for graduates? Why is accounting so important to companies? Why do politicians and business leaders focus on accounting regulations? The answer is that we live in an information age, where that information, and its reliability, impacts the financial well-being of us all.

Accounting is an information and measurement system that identifies, records, and communicates relevant, reliable, and comparable information about an organization's business activities. *Identifying* business activities requires selecting transactions and events relevant to an organization. Examples are the sale of iPhones by **Apple** and the receipt of ticket money by **TicketMaster**. *Recording* business activities requires keeping a chronological log of transactions and events measured in dollars and classified and summarized in a useful format. *Communicating* business activities requires preparing accounting reports such as financial statements. It also requires analyzing and interpreting such reports. (The financial statements and notes of **Research In Motion**, the maker of *BlackBerry*, are shown in Appendix A near the end of this book. This appendix also shows the financial statements of **Apple**, **Palm**, and **Nokia**.) Exhibit 1.1 summarizes accounting activities.

Real company names are printed in bold magenta.

We must guard against a narrow view of accounting. Our most common contact with accounting is through credit approvals, checking accounts, tax forms, and payroll. These experiences are limited and tend to focus on the recordkeeping parts of accounting. **Recordkeeping,** or **bookkeeping,** is the recording of transactions and events, either manually or electronically. This is just one part of accounting. Accounting also identifies and communicates information on transactions and events, and it includes the crucial processes of analysis and interpretation.

EXHIBIT 1.1

Accounting Activities

Identifying	Recording	Communicating
Select transactions and events	Input, measure, and classify	Prepare, analyze, and interpret

Technology is a key part of modern business and plays a major role in accounting. Technology reduces the time, effort, and cost of recordkeeping while improving clerical accuracy. Some small organizations continue to perform various accounting tasks manually, but even they are impacted by technology. As technology has changed the way we store, process, and summarize masses of data, accounting has been freed to expand. Consulting, planning, and other financial services are now closely linked to accounting. These services require sorting through data, interpreting their meaning, identifying key factors, and analyzing their implications.

Point: Technology is only as useful as the accounting data available, and users' decisions are only as good as their understanding of accounting. The best software and recordkeeping cannot make up for lack of accounting knowledge.

Margin notes further enhance the textual material.

Users of Accounting Information

Accounting is often called the *language of business* because all organizations set up an accounting information system to communicate data to help people make better decisions. Exhibit 1.2 shows that the accounting information system serves many kinds of users (this is a partial listing) who can be divided into two groups: external users and internal users.

External users

- Lenders
- Shareholders
- Governments
- Consumer groups
- External auditors
- Customers

Internal users

- Officers
- Managers
- Internal auditors
- Sales staff
- Budget officers
- Controllers

EXHIBIT 1.2

Users of Accounting Information

Infographics reinforce key concepts through visual learning.

External Information Users   **External users** of accounting information are *not* directly involved in running the organization. They include shareholders (investors), lenders, directors, customers, suppliers, regulators, lawyers, brokers, and the press. External users have limited access to an organization's information. Yet their business decisions depend on information that is reliable, relevant, and comparable.

C2   Identify users and uses of, and opportunities in, accounting.

   Financial accounting is the area of accounting aimed at serving external users by providing them with *general-purpose financial statements*. The term *general-purpose* refers to the broad range of purposes for which external users rely on these statements.

   Each external user has special information needs depending on the types of decisions to be made. *Lenders* (creditors) loan money or other resources to an organization. Banks, savings and loans, co-ops, and mortgage and finance companies are lenders. Lenders look for information to help them assess whether an organization is likely to repay its loans with interest. *Shareholders* (investors) are the owners of a corporation. They use accounting reports in deciding whether to buy, hold, or sell stock. Shareholders typically elect a *board of directors* to oversee their interests in an organization. Since directors are responsible to shareholders, their information needs are similar. *External* (independent) *auditors* examine financial statements to verify that they are prepared according to generally accepted accounting principles. *Nonexecutive employees* and *labor unions* use financial statements to judge the fairness of wages, assess job prospects, and bargain for better wages. *Regulators* often have legal authority over certain activities of organizations. For example, the Internal Revenue Service (IRS) and other tax authorities require organizations to file accounting reports in computing taxes. Other regulators include utility boards that use accounting information to set utility rates and securities regulators that require reports for companies that sell their stock to the public.

   Accounting serves the needs of many other external users. *Voters, legislators,* and *government officials* use accounting information to monitor and evaluate government receipts and expenses. *Contributors* to nonprofit organizations use accounting information to evaluate the use and impact of their donations. *Suppliers* use accounting information to judge the soundness of a customer before making sales on credit, and *customers* use financial reports to assess the staying power of potential suppliers.

Internal Information Users   **Internal users** of accounting information are those directly involved in managing and operating an organization. They use the information to help improve the efficiency and effectiveness of an organization. **Managerial accounting** is the area of accounting that serves the decision-making needs of internal users. Internal reports are not subject to the same rules as external reports and instead are designed with the special needs of internal users in mind.

There are several types of internal users, and many are managers of key operating activities. *Research and development managers* need information about projected costs and revenues of any proposed changes in products and services. *Purchasing managers* need to know what, when, and how much to purchase. *Human resource managers* need information about employees' payroll, benefits, performance, and compensation. *Production managers* depend on information to monitor costs and ensure quality. *Distribution managers* need reports for timely, accurate, and efficient delivery of products and services. *Marketing managers* use reports about sales and costs to target consumers, set prices, and monitor consumer needs, tastes, and price concerns. *Service managers* require information on the costs and benefits of looking after products and services. Decisions of these and other internal users depend on accounting reports.

Both internal and external users rely on internal controls to monitor and control company activities. *Internal controls* are procedures set up to protect company property and equipment, ensure reliable accounting reports, promote efficiency, and encourage adherence to company policies. Examples are good records, physical controls (locks, passwords, guards), and independent reviews.

Decision Insight boxes highlight relevant items from practice.

Decision **Insight**

Virtuous Returns   Virtue is not always its own reward. Compare the S&P 500 with the Domini Social Index (DSI), which covers 400 companies that have especially good records of social responsibility. We see that returns for companies with socially responsible behavior are at least as high as those of the S&P 500. ■

Copyright © 2009 by KLD Research & Analytics, Inc. The "Domini 400 Social Index" is a service mark of KLD Research & Analytics.

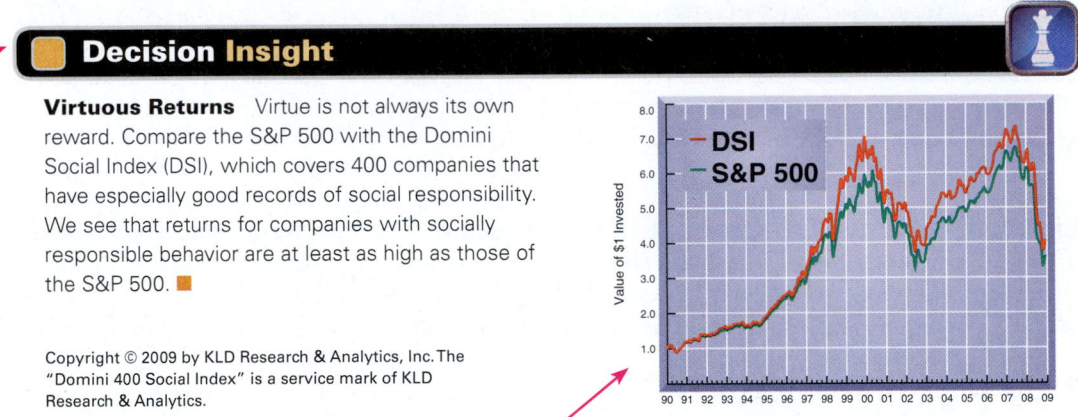

Graphical displays are often used to illustrate key points.

Opportunities in Accounting

Accounting information affects many aspects of our lives. When we earn money, pay taxes, invest savings, budget earnings, and plan for the future, we are influenced by accounting. Accounting has four broad areas of opportunities: financial, managerial, taxation, and accounting-related. Exhibit 1.3 lists selected opportunities in each area.

EXHIBIT 1.3

Accounting Opportunities

The majority of accounting opportunities are in *private accounting,* which are employees working for businesses, as shown in Exhibit 1.4. *Public accounting* offers the next largest number of opportunities, which involve services such as auditing and tax advice to a vast range of businesses. Still other opportunities exist in government and not-for-profit agencies, including business regulation and investigation of law violations.

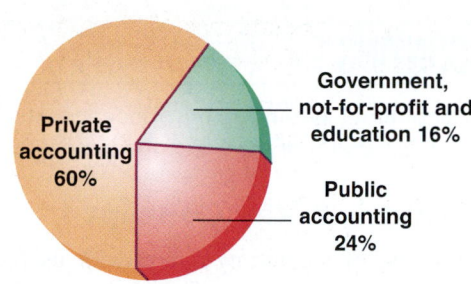

EXHIBIT 1.4

Accounting Jobs by Area

Accounting specialists are highly regarded and their professional standing is often denoted by a certificate. Certified public accountants (CPAs) must meet education and experience requirements, pass an examination, and exhibit ethical character. Many accounting specialists hold certificates in addition to or instead of the CPA. Two of the most common are the certificate in management accounting (CMA) and the certified internal auditor (CIA). Employers also look for specialists with designations such as certified bookkeeper (CB), certified payroll professional (CPP), personal financial specialist (PFS), certified fraud examiner (CFE), and certified forensic accountant (CrFA).

Individuals with accounting knowledge are always in demand as they can help with financial analysis, strategic planning, e-commerce, product feasibility analysis, information technology, and financial management. Benefit packages can include flexible work schedules, telecommuting options, career path alternatives, casual work environments, extended vacation time, and child and elder care.

Demand for accounting specialists is strong. Exhibit 1.5 reports average annual salaries for several accounting positions. Salary variation depends on location, company size, professional designation, experience, and other factors. For example, salaries for chief financial officers (CFO) range from under $75,000 to more than $1 million per year. Likewise, salaries for bookkeepers range from under $30,000 to more than $80,000.

Point: The largest accounting firms are Deloitte, Ernst & Young, KPMG, and PricewaterhouseCoopers.

Point: Census Bureau (2009) reports that for workers 18 and over, higher education yields higher average pay:
Advanced degree $80,977
Bachelor's degree   57,181
High school degree   31,286
No high school degree   21,484

Field	Title (experience)	2009 Salary	2014 Estimate*
Public Accounting	Partner	$191,000	$211,000
	Manager (6–8 years)	94,500	104,000
	Senior (3–5 years)	72,000	79,500
	Junior (0–2 years)	51,500	57,000
Private Accounting	CFO	232,000	256,000
	Controller/Treasurer	147,500	163,000
	Manager (6–8 years)	87,500	96,500
	Senior (3–5 years)	72,500	80,000
	Junior (0–2 years)	49,000	54,000
Recordkeeping	Full-charge bookkeeper	57,500	63,500
	Accounts manager	51,000	56,500
	Payroll manager	54,500	60,000
	Accounting clerk (0–2 years)	37,500	41,500

EXHIBIT 1.5

Accounting Salaries for Selected Fields

Point: For updated salary information: **Abbott-Langer.com** **www.AICPA.org** **Kforce.com**

* Estimates assume a 2% compounded annual increase over current levels (rounded to nearest $500).

Quick Check

Answers — p. 28

Quick Check is a chance to stop and reflect on key points.

1. What is the purpose of accounting?
2. What is the relation between accounting and recordkeeping?
3. Identify some advantages of technology for accounting.
4. Who are the internal and external users of accounting information?
5. Identify at least five types of managers who are internal users of accounting information.
6. What are internal controls and why are they important?

FUNDAMENTALS OF ACCOUNTING

Accounting is guided by principles, standards, concepts, and assumptions. This section describes several of these key fundamentals of accounting.

Ethics—A Key Concept

 C3 Explain why ethics are crucial to accounting.

The goal of accounting is to provide useful information for decisions. For information to be useful, it must be trusted. This demands ethics in accounting. **Ethics** are beliefs that distinguish right from wrong. They are accepted standards of good and bad behavior.

Identifying the ethical path is sometimes difficult. The preferred path is a course of action that avoids casting doubt on one's decisions. For example, accounting users are less likely to trust an auditor's report if the auditor's pay depends on the success of the client's business. To avoid such concerns, ethics rules are often set. For example, auditors are banned from direct investment in their client and cannot accept pay that depends on figures in the client's reports. Exhibit 1.6 gives guidelines for making ethical decisions.

Point: **Sarbanes-Oxley Act** requires each issuer of securities to disclose whether it has adopted a code of ethics for its senior financial officers and the contents of that code.

EXHIBIT 1.6

Guidelines for Ethical Decision Making

Identify ethical concerns	Analyze options	Make ethical decision

Use personal ethics to recognize an ethical concern.	Consider all good and bad consequences.	Choose best option after weighing all consequences.

Providers of accounting information often face ethical choices as they prepare financial reports. These choices can affect the price a buyer pays and the wages paid to workers. They can even affect the success of products and services. Misleading information can lead to a wrongful closing of a division that harms workers, customers, and suppliers. There is an old saying: *Good ethics are good business.*

Some people extend ethics to *social responsibility,* which refers to a concern for the impact of actions on society. An organization's social responsibility can include donations to hospitals, colleges, community programs, and law enforcement. It also can include programs to reduce pollution, increase product safety, improve worker conditions, and support continuing education. These programs are not limited to large companies. For example, many small businesses offer discounts to students and senior citizens. Still others help sponsor events such as the Special Olympics and summer reading programs.

Point: The American Institute of Certified Public Accountants' *Code of Professional Conduct* is available at **www.AICPA.org**.

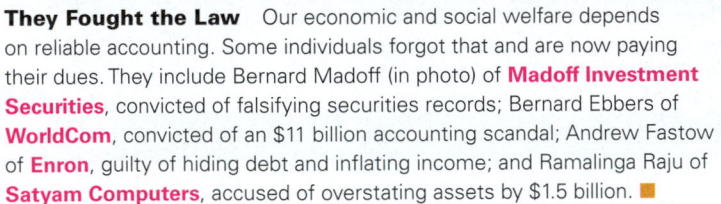

> **◆ Decision Insight**
>
> **They Fought the Law**   Our economic and social welfare depends on reliable accounting. Some individuals forgot that and are now paying their dues. They include Bernard Madoff (in photo) of **Madoff Investment Securities**, convicted of falsifying securities records; Bernard Ebbers of **WorldCom**, convicted of an $11 billion accounting scandal; Andrew Fastow of **Enron**, guilty of hiding debt and inflating income; and Ramalinga Raju of **Satyam Computers**, accused of overstating assets by $1.5 billion. ◼

Generally Accepted Accounting Principles

Financial accounting practice is governed by concepts and rules known as **generally accepted accounting principles (GAAP).** To use and interpret financial statements effectively, we need to understand these principles, which can change over time in response to the demands of users.

GAAP aims to make information in financial statements *relevant, reliable,* and *comparable.* Relevant information affects the decisions of its users. Reliable information is trusted by users. Comparable information is helpful in contrasting organizations.

In the United States, the **Securities and Exchange Commission (SEC),** a government agency, has the legal authority to set GAAP. The SEC also oversees proper use of GAAP by companies that raise money from the public through issuances of their stock and debt. Those companies that issue their stock on U.S. exchanges include both *U.S. SEC registrants* (companies incorporated in the United States) and *non-U.S. SEC registrants* (companies incorporated under non-U.S. laws). The SEC has largely delegated the task of setting U.S. GAAP to the **Financial Accounting Standards Board (FASB),** which is a private-sector group that sets both broad and specific principles.

> **C4** Explain generally accepted accounting principles and define and apply several accounting principles.

> **Point:** State ethics codes require CPAs who audit financial statements to disclose areas where those statements fail to comply with GAAP. If CPAs fail to report noncompliance, they can lose their licenses and be subject to criminal and civil actions and fines.

International Standards

In today's global economy, there is increased demand by external users for comparability in accounting reports. This demand often arises when companies wish to raise money from lenders and investors in different countries. To that end, the **International Accounting Standards Board (IASB),** an independent group (consisting of individuals from many countries), issues **International Financial Reporting Standards (IFRS)** that identify preferred accounting practices.

If standards are harmonized, one company can potentially use a single set of financial statements in all financial markets. Differences between U.S. GAAP and IFRS are slowly fading as the FASB and IASB pursue a *convergence* process aimed to achieve a single set of accounting standards for global use. More than 115 countries now require or permit companies to prepare financial reports following IFRS. Further, non-U.S. SEC registrants can use IFRS in financial reports filed with the SEC (with no reconciliation to U.S. GAAP). This means there are *two* sets of accepted accounting principles in the United States: (1) U.S. GAAP for U.S. SEC registrants and (2) either IFRS or U.S. GAAP for non-U.S. SEC registrants.

The convergence process continues and, in late 2008, the SEC set a roadmap for use of IFRS by publicly traded U.S. companies. This roadmap proposes that large U.S. companies adopt IFRS by 2014, with midsize and small companies following in 2015 and 2016, respectively. Early adoption is permitted for large multinationals that meet certain criteria. For updates on this roadmap, we can check with the AICPA (**IFRS.com**), FASB (**FASB.org**), and IASB (**IASB.org.uk**).

 **IFRS**

Like the FASB, the IASB uses a conceptual framework to aid in revising or drafting new standards. However, unlike the FASB, the IASB's conceptual framework is used as a reference when specific guidance is lacking. The IASB also requires that transactions be accounted for according to their substance (not only their legal form), and that financial statements give a fair presentation, whereas the FASB narrows that scope to fair presentation *in accordance with U.S. GAAP.* ∎

Conceptual Framework and Convergence

The FASB and IASB are attempting to converge and enhance the **conceptual framework** that guides standard setting. The framework consists broadly of the following:

- **Objectives**—to provide information useful to investors, creditors, and others.
- **Qualitative Characteristics**—to require information that is relevant, reliable, and comparable.
- **Elements**—to define items that financial statements can contain.
- **Recognition and Measurement**—to set criteria that an item must meet for it to be recognized as an element; and how to measure that element.

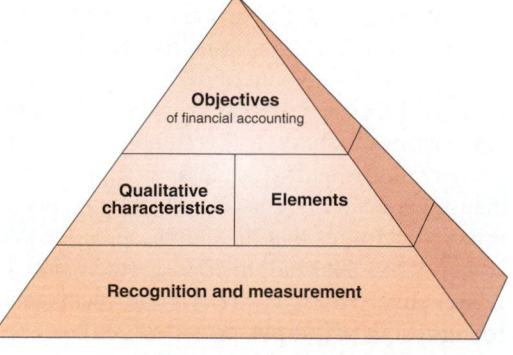

For updates on this joint FASB and IASB conceptual framework convergence we can check with **FASB.org** or **IASB.org.uk** Websites. We must remember that U.S. GAAP and IFRS are two similar, but not identical, systems. However, their similarities greatly outweigh any differences. The remainder of this section describes key principles and assumptions of accounting.

Decision Insight

Principles and Scruples Auditors, directors, and lawyers are using principles to improve accounting reports. Examples include accounting restatements at **Navistar**, financial restatements at **Nortel**, accounting reviews at **Echostar**, and expense adjustments at **Electronic Data Systems**. Principles-based accounting has led accounting firms to drop clients deemed too risky. Examples include **Grant Thornton**'s resignation as auditor of **Fremont General** due to alleged failures in providing information when promised, and **Ernst and Young**'s resignation as auditor of **Catalina Marketing** due to alleged accounting errors. ■

Principles and Assumptions of Accounting Accounting principles (and assumptions) are of two types. *General principles* are the basic assumptions, concepts, and guidelines for preparing financial statements. *Specific principles* are detailed rules used in reporting business transactions and events. General principles stem from long-used accounting practices. Specific principles arise more often from the rulings of authoritative groups.

EXHIBIT 1.7

Building Blocks for GAAP

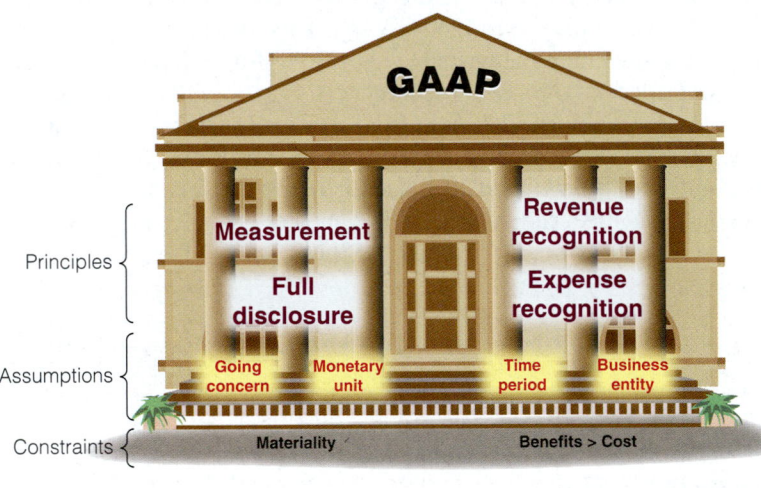

We need to understand both general and specific principles to effectively use accounting information. Several general principles are described in this section that are relied on in later chapters. General principles (in purple font with white shading) and assumptions (in red font with yellow shading) are portrayed as building blocks of GAAP in Exhibit 1.7. The specific principles are described as we encounter them in the book.

Accounting Principles General principles consist of at least four basic principles, four assumptions, and two constraints.

Point: The cost principle is also called the *historical cost principle.*

The **measurement principle,** also called the **cost principle,** usually means that accounting information is based on actual cost (with a potential for subsequent adjustments to market). Cost is measured on a cash or equal-to-cash basis. This means if cash is given for a service, its cost is measured as the amount of cash paid. If something besides cash is exchanged (such as a car traded for a truck), cost is measured as the cash value of what is given up or received. The cost principle emphasizes reliability and verifiability, and information based on cost is considered objective. *Objectivity* means that information is supported by independent, unbiased evidence; it demands more than a person's opinion. To illustrate, suppose a company pays $5,000 for equipment. The cost principle requires that this purchase be recorded at a cost of $5,000. It makes no difference if the owner thinks this equipment is worth $7,000. Later in the book we introduce *fair value* measures.

Revenue (sales) is the amount received from selling products and services. The **revenue recognition principle** provides guidance on when a company must recognize revenue. To *recognize* means to record it. If revenue is recognized too early, a company would look more profitable than it is. If revenue is recognized too late, a company would look less profitable than it is.

Three concepts are important to revenue recognition. (1) *Revenue is recognized when earned.* The earnings process is normally complete when services are performed or a seller transfers ownership of products to the buyer. (2) *Proceeds from selling products and services need not be in cash.* A common noncash proceed received by a seller is a customer's promise to pay at a future date, called *credit sales.* (3) *Revenue is measured by the cash received plus the cash value of any other items received.*

The **expense recognition principle,** also called the **matching principle,** prescribes that a company record the expenses it incurred to generate the revenue reported. The principles of matching and revenue recognition are key to modern accounting.

The **full disclosure principle** prescribes that a company report the details behind financial statements that would impact users' decisions. Those disclosures are often in footnotes to the statements.

Decision Insight

Revenues for the **Green Bay Packers** and **Dallas Cowboys** football teams include ticket sales, television and cable broadcasts, radio rights, concessions, and advertising. Revenues from ticket sales are earned when the NFL team plays each game. Advance ticket sales are not revenues; instead, they represent a liability until the NFL team plays the game for which the ticket was sold. At that point, the liability is removed and revenues are reported.

Accounting Assumptions   There are four accounting assumptions: the going concern assumption, the monetary unit assumption, the time period assumption, and the business entity assumption.

The **going-concern assumption** means that accounting information reflects a presumption that the business will continue operating instead of being closed or sold. This implies, for example, that property is reported at cost instead of, say, liquidation values that assume closure.

The **monetary unit assumption** means that we can express transactions and events in monetary, or money, units. Money is the common denominator in business. Examples of monetary units are the dollar in the United States, Canada, Australia, and Singapore; and the peso in Mexico, the Philippines, and Chile. The monetary unit a company uses in its accounting reports usually depends on the country where it operates, but many companies today are expressing reports in more than one monetary unit.

The **time period assumption** presumes that the life of a company can be divided into time periods, such as months and years, and that useful reports can be prepared for those periods.

The **business entity assumption** means that a business is accounted for separately from other business entities, including its owner. The reason for this assumption is that separate information about each business is necessary for good decisions. A business entity can take one of three legal forms: *proprietorship, partnership,* or *corporation.*

1. A **sole proprietorship,** or simply **proprietorship,** is a business owned by one person in which that person and the company are viewed as one entity for tax and liability purposes. No special legal requirements must be met to start a proprietorship. It is a separate entity for accounting purposes, but it is *not* a separate legal entity from its owner. This means, for example, that a court can order an owner to sell personal belongings to pay a proprietorship's debt. This *unlimited liability* of a proprietorship is a disadvantage. However, an advantage is that a proprietorship's income is not subject to a business income tax but is instead reported and taxed on the owner's personal income tax return. Proprietorship attributes are summarized in Exhibit 1.8, including those for partnerships and corporations.

2. A **partnership** is a business owned by two or more people, called *partners,* which are jointly liable for tax and other obligations. Like a proprietorship, no special legal requirements must be met in starting a partnership. The only requirement is an agreement between

EXHIBIT 1.8

Attributes of Businesses

Attribute Present	Proprietorship	Partnership	Corporation
One owner allowed	yes	no	yes
Business taxed	no	no	yes
Limited liability	no*	no*	yes
Business entity	yes	yes	yes
Legal entity	no	no	yes
Unlimited life	no	no	yes

* Proprietorships and partnerships that are set up as LLCs provide limited liability.

partners to run a business together. The agreement can be either oral or written and usually indicates how income and losses are to be shared. A partnership, like a proprietorship, is *not* legally separate from its owners. This means that each partner's share of profits is reported and taxed on that partner's tax return. It also means *unlimited liability* for its partners. However, at least three types of partnerships limit liability. A *limited partnership* (*LP*) includes a general partner(s) with unlimited liability and a limited partner(s) with liability restricted to the amount invested. A *limited liability partnership* (*LLP*) restricts partners' liabilities to their own acts and the acts of individuals under their control. This protects an innocent partner from the negligence of another partner, yet all partners remain responsible for partnership debts. A *limited liability company* (*LLC*) offers the limited liability of a corporation and the tax treatment of a partnership (and proprietorship). Most proprietorships and partnerships are now organized as LLCs.

Point: Proprietorships and partnerships are usually managed by their owners. In a corporation, the owners (shareholders) elect a board of directors who appoint managers to run the business.

3. A **corporation,** also called *C corporation,* is a business legally separate from its owner or owners, meaning it is responsible for its own acts and its own debts. Separate legal status means that a corporation can conduct business with the rights, duties, and responsibilities of a person. A corporation acts through its managers, who are its legal agents. Separate legal status also means that its owners, who are called **shareholders** (or **stockholders**), are not personally liable for corporate acts and debts. This limited liability is its main advantage. A main disadvantage is what's called *double taxation*—meaning that (1) the corporation income is taxed and (2) any distribution of income to its owners through dividends is taxed as part of the owners' personal income, usually at the 15% rate. (For lower income taxpayers, the dividend tax is less than 15%, and in some cases zero.) An *S corporation,* a corporation with special attributes, does not owe corporate income tax. Owners of S corporations report their share of corporate income with their personal income. Ownership of all corporations is divided into units called **shares** or **stock.** When a corporation issues only one class of stock, we call it **common stock** (or *capital stock*).

Decision Ethics boxes are role-playing exercises that stress ethics in accounting and business.

Decision Ethics

Answer — p. 27

Entrepreneur   You and a friend develop a new design for in-line skates that improves speed by 25% to 30%. You plan to form a business to manufacture and market those skates. You and your friend want to minimize taxes, but your prime concern is potential lawsuits from individuals who might be injured on these skates. What form of organization do you set up? ■

Accounting Constraints   There are two basic constraints on financial reporting. The **materiality constraint** prescribes that only information that would influence the decisions of a reasonable person need be disclosed. This constraint looks at both the importance and relative size of an amount. The **cost-benefit constraint** prescribes that only information with benefits of disclosure greater than the costs of providing it need be disclosed.

Sarbanes–Oxley (SOX)

Point: An **audit** examines whether financial statements are prepared using GAAP. It does *not* attest to absolute accuracy of the statements.

Congress passed the **Sarbanes–Oxley Act,** also called *SOX,* to help curb financial abuses at companies that issue their stock to the public. SOX requires that these public companies apply both accounting oversight and stringent internal controls. The desired results include more transparency, accountability, and truthfulness in reporting transactions.

Compliance with SOX requires documentation and verification of internal controls and increased emphasis on internal control effectiveness. Failure to comply can yield financial penalties, stock market delisting, and criminal prosecution of executives. Management must issue a report stating that internal controls are effective. CEOs and CFOs who knowingly sign off on bogus accounting reports risk millions of dollars in fines and years in prison. **Auditors** also must verify the effectiveness of internal controls.

Point: *BusinessWeek* reports that external audit costs run about $35,000 for start-ups, up from $15,000 pre-SOX.

A listing of some of the more publicized accounting scandals in recent years follows.

Company	Alleged Accounting Abuses
Enron	Inflated income, hid debt, and bribed officials
WorldCom	Understated expenses to inflate income and hid debt
Fannie Mae	Inflated income
Adelphia Communications	Understated expenses to inflate income and hid debt
AOL Time Warner	Inflated revenues and income
Xerox	Inflated income
Bristol-Myers Squibb	Inflated revenues and income
Nortel Networks	Understated expenses to inflate income
Global Crossing	Inflated revenues and income
Tyco	Hid debt, and CEO evaded taxes
Halliburton	Inflated revenues and income
Qwest Communications	Inflated revenues and income

To reduce the risk of accounting fraud, companies set up *governance systems.* A company's governance system includes its owners, managers, employees, board of directors, and other important stakeholders, who work together to reduce the risk of accounting fraud and increase confidence in accounting reports.

The impact of SOX regulations for accounting and business is discussed throughout this book. Ethics and investor confidence are key to company success. Lack of confidence in accounting numbers impacts company value as evidenced by huge stock price declines for **Enron**, **WorldCom**, **Tyco**, and **ImClone** after accounting misconduct was uncovered.

Decision Insight

Economic Downturn, Fraud Upturn? Executives polled show that 80% believe that the economic downturn has or will have a significant impact on fraud control in their companies (Deloitte 2009). The top three responses to the question "What activity would best counter this increased fraud risk?" are tallied in the graphic to the right. ∎

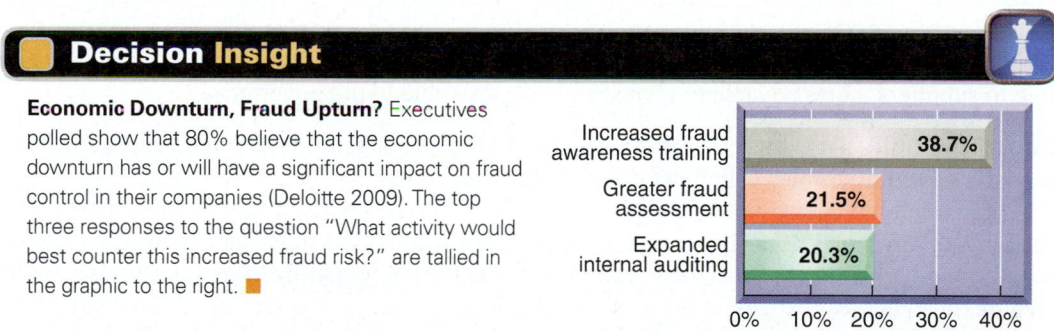

Increased fraud awareness training	38.7%
Greater fraud assessment	21.5%
Expanded internal auditing	20.3%

0% 10% 20% 30% 40%

Quick Check

Answers — p. 28

7. What three-step guidelines can help people make ethical decisions?
8. Why are ethics and social responsibility valuable to organizations?
9. Why are ethics crucial in accounting?
10. Who sets U.S. accounting rules?
11. How are U.S. companies affected by international accounting standards?
12. How are the objectivity concept and cost principle related?
13. Why is the business entity assumption important?
14. Why is the revenue recognition principle important?
15. What are the three basic forms of business organization?
16. Identify the owners of corporations and the terminology for ownership units.

TRANSACTION ANALYSIS AND THE ACCOUNTING EQUATION

To understand accounting information, we need to know how an accounting system captures relevant data about transactions, and then classifies, records, and reports data.

Accounting Equation

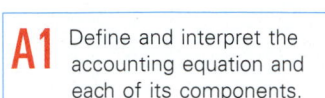

A1 Define and interpret the accounting equation and each of its components.

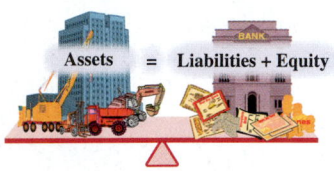

Assets = Liabilities + Equity

The accounting system reflects two basic aspects of a company: what it owns and what it owes. *Assets* are resources a company owns or controls. Examples are cash, supplies, equipment, and land, where each carries expected benefits. The claims on a company's assets—what it owes—are separated into owner and nonowner claims. *Liabilities* are what a company owes its nonowners (creditors) in future payments, products, or services. *Equity* (also called owner's equity or capital) refers to the claims of its owner(s). Together, liabilities and equity are the source of funds to acquire assets. The relation of assets, liabilities, and equity is reflected in the following **accounting equation:**

$$\text{Assets} = \text{Liabilities} + \text{Equity}$$

Liabilities are usually shown before equity in this equation because creditors' claims must be paid before the claims of owners. (The terms in this equation can be rearranged; for example, Assets − Liabilities = Equity.) The accounting equation applies to all transactions and events, to all companies and forms of organization, and to all points in time. For example, **Research In Motion**'s assets equal $10,204,409, its liabilities equal $2,601,746, and its equity equals $7,602,663 ($ in thousands). Let's now look at the accounting equation in more detail.

Assets   Assets are resources a company owns or controls. These resources are expected to yield future benefits. Examples are Web servers for an online services company, musical instruments for a rock band, and land for a vegetable grower. The term *receivable* is used to refer to an asset that promises a future inflow of resources. A company that provides a service or product on credit is said to have an account receivable from that customer.

Point: The phrases "on credit" and "on account" imply that cash payment will occur at a future date.

Liabilities   Liabilities are creditors' claims on assets. These claims reflect company obligations to provide assets, products or services to others. The term *payable* refers to a liability that promises a future outflow of resources. Examples are wages payable to workers, accounts payable to suppliers, notes payable to banks, and taxes payable to the government.

Equity   Equity is the owner's claim on assets. Equity is equal to assets minus liabilities. This is the reason equity is also called *net assets* or *residual equity*.

Key **terms** are printed in bold and defined again in the end-of-book **glossary**.

A corporation's equity—often called stockholders' or shareholders' equity—has two parts: contributed capital and retained earnings. **Contributed capital** refers to the amount that stockholders invest in the company—included under the title **common stock. Retained earnings** refer to **income** (revenues less expenses) that has *not* been distributed to its stockholders. The distribution of assets to stockholders is called **dividends,** which reduce retained earnings. **Revenues** increase retained earnings (via net income) and are resources generated from a company's earnings activities. Examples are consulting services provided, sales of products, facilities rented to others, and commissions from services. **Expenses** decrease retained earnings and are the cost of assets or services used to earn revenues. Examples are costs of employee time, use of supplies, and advertising, utilities, and insurance services from others. In sum, retained earnings is the accumulated revenues less the accumulated expenses and dividends since the company began. This breakdown of equity yields the following **expanded accounting equation:**

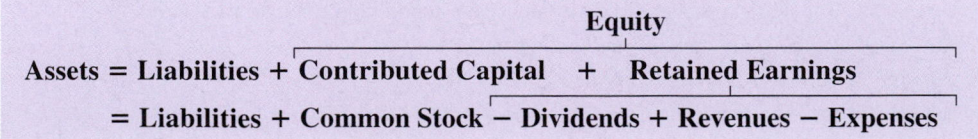

Equity

Assets = Liabilities + Contributed Capital + Retained Earnings

= Liabilities + Common Stock − Dividends + Revenues − Expenses

Net income occurs when revenues exceed expenses. Net income increases equity. A **net loss** occurs when expenses exceed revenues, which decreases equity.

Decision Insight

Web Info   Most organizations maintain Websites that include accounting data— see **Research In Motion** (**RIM.com**) as an example. The SEC keeps an online database called **EDGAR** (**www.SEC.gov/edgar.shtml**), which has accounting information for thousands of companies that issue stock to the public (EDGAR is being upgraded and renamed **IDEA**). Information services such as **Finance.Google.com** and **Finance.Yahoo.com** offer additional online data and analysis. ■

Transaction Analysis

Business activities can be described in terms of transactions and events. **External transactions** are exchanges of value between two entities, which yield changes in the accounting equation. An example is the sale of ad space by **Facebook**. **Internal transactions** are exchanges within an entity, which may or may not affect the accounting equation. An example is Facebook's use of its supplies, which are reported as expenses when used. **Events** refer to happenings that affect the accounting equation *and* are reliably measured. They include business events such as changes in the market value of certain assets and liabilities and natural events such as floods and fires that destroy assets and create losses. They do not include, for example, the signing of service or product contracts, which by themselves do not impact the accounting equation.

   This section uses the accounting equation to analyze 11 selected transactions and events of FastForward, a start-up consulting (service) business, in its first month of operations. Remember that each transaction and event leaves the equation in balance and that assets *always* equal the sum of liabilities and equity.

P1   Analyze business transactions using the accounting equation.

Transaction 1: Investment by Owner   On December 1, Chas Taylor forms a consulting business, named FastForward and set up as a corporation, that focuses on assessing the performance of footwear and accessories. Taylor owns and manages the business. The marketing plan for the business is to focus primarily on publishing online reviews and consulting with clubs, athletes, and others who place orders for footwear and accessories with manufacturers. Taylor personally invests $30,000 cash in the new company and deposits the cash in a bank account opened under the name of FastForward. After this transaction, the cash (an asset) and the stockholders' equity each equal $30,000. The source of increase in equity is the owner's investment (stock issuance), which is included in the column titled Common Stock. The effect of this transaction on FastForward is reflected in the accounting equation as follows:

Point: There are 3 basic types of company operations: (1) **Services**— providing customer services for profit, (2) **Merchandisers**—buying products and re-selling them for profit, and (3) **Manufacturers**—creating products and selling them for profit.

	Assets	=	Liabilities	+	Equity
	Cash	=			**Common Stock**
(1)	+$30,000	=			+$30,000

Transaction 2: Purchase Supplies for Cash   FastForward uses $2,500 of its cash to buy supplies of brand name footwear for performance testing over the next few months. This transaction is an exchange of cash, an asset, for another kind of asset, supplies. It merely changes the form of assets from cash to supplies. The decrease in cash is exactly equal to the increase in supplies. The supplies of footwear are assets because of the expected future benefits from the test results of their performance. This transaction is reflected in the accounting equation as follows:

	Assets			=	Liabilities	+	Equity
	Cash	+	**Supplies**	=			**Common Stock**
Old Bal.	$30,000			=			$30,000
(2)	−2,500	+	$2,500				
New Bal.	$27,500	+	$ 2,500	=			$30,000
		$30,000				$30,000	

Transaction 3: Purchase Equipment for Cash   FastForward spends $26,000 to acquire equipment for testing footwear. Like transaction 2, transaction 3 is an exchange of one asset, cash, for another asset, equipment. The equipment is an asset because of its expected future benefits from testing footwear. This purchase changes the makeup of assets but does not change the asset total. The accounting equation remains in balance.

	Assets					=	Liabilities	+	Equity
	Cash	+	**Supplies**	+	**Equipment**	=			**Common Stock**
Old Bal.	$27,500	+	$2,500			=			$30,000
(3)	−26,000			+	$26,000				
New Bal.	$ 1,500	+	$2,500	+	$ 26,000	=			$30,000
			$30,000					$30,000	

Example: If FastForward pays $500 cash in transaction 4, how does this partial payment affect the liability to CalTech? What would be FastForward's cash balance? *Answers:* The liability to CalTech would be reduced to $6,600 and the cash balance would be reduced to $1,000.

Transaction 4: Purchase Supplies on Credit   Taylor decides more supplies of footwear and accessories are needed. These additional supplies total $7,100, but as we see from the accounting equation in transaction 3, FastForward has only $1,500 in cash. Taylor arranges to purchase them on credit from CalTech Supply Company. Thus, FastForward acquires supplies in exchange for a promise to pay for them later. This purchase increases assets by $7,100 in supplies, and liabilities (called *accounts payable* to CalTech Supply) increase by the same amount. The effects of this purchase follow:

	Assets					=	Liabilities	+	Equity
	Cash	+	**Supplies**	+	**Equipment**	=	**Accounts Payable**	+	**Common Stock**
Old Bal.	$1,500	+	$2,500	+	$26,000	=			$30,000
(4)		+	7,100				+$7,100		
New Bal.	$1,500	+	$9,600	+	$26,000	=	$ 7,100	+	$30,000
			$37,100					$37,100	

Transaction 5: Provide Services for Cash   FastForward earns revenues by selling online ad space to manufacturers and by consulting with clients about test results on footwear and accessories. It earns net income only if its revenues are greater than its expenses incurred in earning them. In one of its first jobs, FastForward provides consulting services to a power-walking club and immediately collects $4,200 cash. The accounting equation reflects this increase in cash of $4,200 and in equity of $4,200. This increase in equity is identified in the far right column under Revenues because the cash received is earned by providing consulting services.

	Assets					=	Liabilities	+	Equity		
	Cash	+	**Supplies**	+	**Equipment**	=	**Accounts Payable**	+	**Common Stock**	+	**Revenues**
Old Bal.	$1,500	+	$9,600	+	$26,000	=	$7,100	+	$30,000		
(5)	+4,200									+	$4,200
New Bal.	$5,700	+	$9,600	+	$26,000	=	$7,100	+	$30,000	+	$ 4,200
			$41,300					$41,300			

Transactions 6 and 7: Payment of Expenses in Cash   FastForward pays $1,000 rent to the landlord of the building where its facilities are located. Paying this amount allows FastForward to occupy the space for the month of December. The rental payment is reflected in the following accounting equation as transaction 6. FastForward also pays the biweekly $700 salary of the company's only employee. This is reflected in the accounting equation as transaction 7. Both transactions 6 and 7 are December expenses for FastForward. The costs of both rent and salary are expenses, as opposed to assets, because their benefits are used in December (they have no future benefits after December). These transactions also use up an asset (cash) in carrying out FastForward's operations. The accounting equation shows that both transactions reduce cash and equity. The far right column identifies these decreases as Expenses.

By definition, increases in expenses yield decreases in equity.

	Assets					=	Liabilities	+			Equity			
	Cash	+	Supplies	+	Equipment	=	Accounts Payable	+	Common Stock	+	Revenues	−	Expenses
Old Bal.	$5,700	+	$9,600	+	$26,000	=	$7,100	+	$30,000	+	$4,200		
(6)	−1,000											−	$1,000
Bal.	4,700	+	9,600	+	26,000	=	7,100	+	30,000	+	4,200	−	1,000
(7)	− 700											−	700
New Bal.	$4,000	+	$9,600	+	$26,000	=	$7,100	+	$30,000	+	$4,200	−	$ 1,700
			$39,600							$39,600			

Transaction 8: Provide Services and Facilities for Credit

FastForward provides consulting services of $1,600 and rents its test facilities for $300 to a podiatric services center. The rental involves allowing members to try recommended footwear and accessories at FastForward's testing area. The center is billed for the $1,900 total. This transaction results in a new asset, called *accounts receivable,* from this client. It also yields an increase in equity from the two revenue components reflected in the Revenues column of the accounting equation:

	Assets								=	Liabilities	+			Equity			
	Cash	+	Accounts Receivable	+	Supplies	+	Equipment	=	Accounts Payable	+	Common Stock	+	Revenues	−	Expenses
Old Bal.	$4,000	+		+	$9,600	+	$26,000	=	$7,100	+	$30,000	+	$4,200	−	$1,700
(8)		+	$1,900									+	1,600		
												+	300		
New Bal.	$4,000	+	$ 1,900	+	$9,600	+	$26,000	=	$7,100	+	$30,000	+	$6,100	−	$1,700
			$41,500									$41,500			

Transaction 9: Receipt of Cash from Accounts Receivable

The client in transaction 8 (the podiatric center) pays $1,900 to FastForward 10 days after it is billed for consulting services. This transaction 9 does not change the total amount of assets and does not affect liabilities or equity. It converts the receivable (an asset) to cash (another asset). It does not create new revenue. Revenue was recognized when FastForward rendered the services in transaction 8, not when the cash is now collected. This emphasis on the earnings process instead of cash flows is a goal of the revenue recognition principle and yields useful information to users. The new balances follow:

Point: Receipt of cash is not always a revenue.

	Assets								=	Liabilities	+			Equity			
	Cash	+	Accounts Receivable	+	Supplies	+	Equipment	=	Accounts Payable	+	Common Stock	+	Revenues	−	Expenses
Old Bal.	$4,000	+	$1,900	+	$9,600	+	$26,000	=	$7,100	+	$30,000	+	$6,100	−	$1,700
(9)	+1,900	−	1,900												
New Bal.	$5,900	+	$ 0	+	$9,600	+	$26,000	=	$7,100	+	$30,000	+	$6,100	−	$1,700
			$41,500									$41,500			

Transaction 10: Payment of Accounts Payable

FastForward pays CalTech Supply $900 cash as partial payment for its earlier $7,100 purchase of supplies (transaction 4), leaving $6,200 unpaid. The accounting equation shows that this transaction decreases FastForward's cash by $900 and decreases its liability to CalTech Supply by $900. Equity does not change. This event does not create an expense even though cash flows out of FastForward (instead the expense is recorded when FastForward derives the benefits from these supplies).

	Assets				=	Liabilities	+		Equity		
	Cash	+ Accounts Receivable	+ Supplies	+ Equipment	=	Accounts Payable	+	Common Stock	+ Revenues	− Expenses	
Old Bal.	$5,900	+ $ 0	+ $9,600	+ $26,000	=	$7,100	+	$30,000	+ $6,100	− $1,700	
(10)	− 900					− 900					
New Bal.	$5,000	+ $ 0	+ $9,600	+ $26,000	=	$6,200	+	$30,000	+ $6,100	− $1,700	

$40,600 $40,600

Transaction 11: Payment of Cash Dividend   FastForward declares and pays a $200 cash dividend to its owner. Dividends (decreases in equity) are not reported as expenses because they are not part of the company's earnings process. Since dividends are not company expenses, they are not used in computing net income.

By definition, increases in dividends yield decreases in equity.

	Assets				=	Liabilities	+		Equity			
	Cash	+ Accounts Receivable	+ Supplies	+ Equipment	=	Accounts Payable	+	Common Stock	− Dividends	+ Revenues	− Expenses	
Old Bal.	$5,000	+ $ 0	+ $9,600	+ $26,000	=	$6,200	+	$30,000		+ $6,100	− $1,700	
(11)	− 200								− $200			
New Bal.	$4,800	+ $ 0	+ $9,600	+ $26,000	=	$6,200	+	$30,000	− $200	+ $6,100	− $1,700	

$40,400 $40,400

Summary of Transactions

We summarize in Exhibit 1.9 the effects of these 11 transactions of FastForward using the accounting equation. First, we see that the accounting equation remains in balance after each transaction. Second, transactions can be analyzed by their effects on components of the

EXHIBIT 1.9

Summary of Transactions Using the Accounting Equation

	Assets				=	Liabilities +		Equity			
	Cash	+ Accounts Receivable	+ Supplies	+ Equipment	=	Accounts Payable	+ Common Stock	− Dividends	+ Revenues	− Expenses
(1)	$30,000				=		$30,000			
(2)	− 2,500		+ $2,500							
Bal.	27,500		+ 2,500		=		30,000			
(3)	−26,000			+ $26,000						
Bal.	1,500		+ 2,500	+ 26,000	=		30,000			
(4)			+ 7,100			+$7,100				
Bal.	1,500		+ 9,600	+ 26,000	=	7,100	+ 30,000			
(5)	+ 4,200								+ $4,200	
Bal.	5,700		+ 9,600	+ 26,000	=	7,100	+ 30,000		+ 4,200	
(6)	− 1,000									− $1,000
Bal.	4,700		+ 9,600	+ 26,000	=	7,100	+ 30,000		+ 4,200	− 1,000
(7)	− 700									− 700
Bal.	4,000		+ 9,600	+ 26,000	=	7,100	+ 30,000		+ 4,200	− 1,700
(8)		+ $1,900							+ 1,600	
									+ 300	
Bal.	4,000	+ 1,900	+ 9,600	+ 26,000	=	7,100	+ 30,000		+ 6,100	− 1,700
(9)	+ 1,900	− 1,900								
Bal.	5,900	+ 0	+ 9,600	+ 26,000	=	7,100	+ 30,000		+ 6,100	− 1,700
(10)	− 900					− 900				
Bal.	5,000	+ 0	+ 9,600	+ 26,000	=	6,200	+ 30,000		+ 6,100	− 1,700
(11)	− 200							− $200		
Bal.	$ 4,800	+ $ 0	+ $ 9,600	+ $ 26,000	=	$ 6,200	+ $ 30,000	− $ 200	+ $6,100	− $1,700

accounting equation. For example, in transactions 2, 3, and 9, one asset increased while another asset decreased by equal amounts.

Point: Knowing how financial statements are prepared improves our analysis of them. We develop the skills for analysis of financial statements throughout the book. Chapter 13 focuses on financial statement analysis.

Quick Check   Answers — p. 28

17. When is the accounting equation in balance, and what does that mean?
18. How can a transaction not affect any liability and equity accounts?
19. Describe a transaction increasing equity and one decreasing it.
20. Identify a transaction that decreases both assets and liabilities.

FINANCIAL STATEMENTS

This section introduces us to how financial statements are prepared from the analysis of business transactions. The four financial statements and their purposes are:

P2 Identify and prepare basic financial statements and explain how they interrelate.

1. **Income statement**—describes a company's revenues and expenses along with the resulting net income or loss over a period of time due to earnings activities.
2. **Statement of retained earnings**—explains changes in retained earnings from net income (or loss) and from any dividends over a period of time.
3. **Balance sheet**—describes a company's financial position (types and amounts of assets, liabilities, and equity) at a point in time.
4. **Statement of cash flows**—identifies cash inflows (receipts) and cash outflows (payments) over a period of time.

We prepare these financial statements, in this order, using the 11 selected transactions of FastForward. (These statements are technically called *unadjusted*—we explain this in Chapters 2 and 3.)

Income Statement

FastForward's income statement for December is shown at the top of Exhibit 1.10. Information about revenues and expenses is conveniently taken from the Equity columns of Exhibit 1.9. Revenues are reported first on the income statement. They include consulting revenues of $5,800 from transactions 5 and 8 and rental revenue of $300 from transaction 8. Expenses are reported after revenues. (For convenience in this chapter, we list larger amounts first, but we can sort expenses in different ways.) Rent and salary expenses are from transactions 6 and 7. Expenses reflect the costs to generate the revenues reported. Net income (or loss) is reported at the bottom of the statement and is the amount earned in December. Stockholders' investments and dividends are *not* part of income.

Point: Net income is sometimes called *earnings* or *profit.*

Statement of Retained Earnings

The statement of retained earnings reports information about how retained earnings changes over the reporting period. This statement shows beginning retained earnings, events that increase it (net income), and events that decrease it (dividends and net loss). Ending retained earnings is computed in this statement and is carried over and reported on the balance sheet. FastForward's statement of retained earnings is the second report in Exhibit 1.10. The beginning balance is measured as of the start of business on December 1. It is zero because FastForward did not exist before then. An existing business reports the beginning balance equal to that as of the end of the prior reporting period (such as from November 30). FastForward's statement shows the $4,400 of net income earned during the period. This links the income statement to the statement of retained earnings (see line ①). The statement also reports the $200 cash dividend and FastForward's end-of-period retained earnings balance.

Point: The statement of retained earnings is also called the *statement of changes in retained earnings.* Note: Beg. Retained Earnings + Net Income − Dividends = End. Retained Earnings

EXHIBIT 1.10

Financial Statements and Their Links

Point: A statement's heading identifies the company, the statement title, and the date or time period.

Point: Arrow lines show how the statements are linked. (1) Net income is used to compute equity. (2) Retained earnings is used to prepare the balance sheet. (3) Cash from the balance sheet is used to reconcile the statement of cash flows.

Point: The income statement, the statement of retained earnings, and the statement of cash flows are prepared for a *period* of time. The balance sheet is prepared as of a *point* in time.

Point: A single ruled line denotes an addition or subtraction. Final totals are double underlined. Negative amounts are often in parentheses.

FASTFORWARD
Income Statement
For Month Ended December 31, 2011

Revenues		
Consulting revenue ($4,200 + $1,600)	$ 5,800	
Rental revenue	300	
Total revenues		$ 6,100
Expenses		
Rent expense	1,000	
Salaries expense	700	
Total expenses		1,700
Net income		**$ 4,400** (1)

FASTFORWARD
Statement of Retained Earnings
For Month Ended December 31, 2011

Retained earnings, December 1, 2011	$ 0
Plus: Net income	**4,400** (1)
	4,400
Less: Dividends	200
Retained earnings, December 31, 2011	**$ 4,200** (2)

FASTFORWARD
Balance Sheet
December 31, 2011

Assets		**Liabilities**	
Cash (3)	**$ 4,800**	Accounts payable	$ 6,200
Supplies	9,600	Total liabilities	6,200
Equipment	26,000	**Equity**	
		Common stock	30,000
		Retained earnings	**4,200** (2)
		Total equity	34,200
Total assets	$ 40,400	Total liabilities and equity	$ 40,400

FASTFORWARD
Statement of Cash Flows
For Month Ended December 31, 2011

Cash flows from operating activities		
Cash received from clients ($4,200 + $1,900)	$ 6,100	
Cash paid for supplies ($2,500 + $900)	(3,400)	
Cash paid for rent	(1,000)	
Cash paid to employee	(700)	
Net cash provided by operating activities		$ 1,000
Cash flows from investing activities		
Purchase of equipment	(26,000)	
Net cash used by investing activities		(26,000)
Cash flows from financing activities		
Investments by stockholder	30,000	
Dividends to stockholder	(200)	
Net cash provided by financing activities		29,800
Net increase in cash		$ 4,800
Cash balance, December 1, 2011		0
Cash balance, December 31, 2011 (3)		**$ 4,800**

Balance Sheet

FastForward's balance sheet is the third report in Exhibit 1.10. This statement refers to Fast-Forward's financial condition at the close of business on December 31. The left side of the balance sheet lists FastForward's assets: cash, supplies, and equipment. The upper right side of the balance sheet shows that FastForward owes $6,200 to creditors. Any other liabilities (such as a bank loan) would be listed here. The equity balance is $34,200. Line ② shows the link between the ending balance of the statement of retained earnings and the retained earnings balance on the balance sheet. (This presentation of the balance sheet is called the *account form:* assets on the left and liabilities and equity on the right. Another presentation is the *report form:* assets on top, followed by liabilities and then equity at the bottom. Either presentation is acceptable.) As always, we see the accounting equation applies: Assets of $40,400 = Liabilities of $6,200 + Equity of $34,200.

Decision Maker boxes are role-playing exercises that stress the relevance of accounting.

Decision Maker   Answer — p. 28

Retailer   You open a wholesale business selling entertainment equipment to retail outlets. You find that most of your customers demand to buy on credit. How can you use the balance sheets of these customers to help you decide which ones to extend credit to? ■

Statement of Cash Flows

FastForward's statement of cash flows is the final report in Exhibit 1.10. The first section reports cash flows from *operating activities*. It shows the $6,100 cash received from clients and the $5,100 cash paid for supplies, rent, and employee salaries. Outflows are in parentheses to denote subtraction. Net cash provided by operating activities for December is $1,000. If cash paid exceeded the $5,100 cash received, we would call it "cash used by operating activities." The second section reports *investing activities,* which involve buying and selling assets such as land and equipment that are held for *long-term use* (typically more than one year). The only investing activity is the $26,000 purchase of equipment. The third section shows cash flows from *financing activities,* which include the *long-term* borrowing and repaying of cash from lenders and the cash investments from, and dividends to, stockholders. FastForward reports $30,000 from the owner's initial investment and the $200 cash dividend. The net cash effect of all financing transactions is a $29,800 cash inflow. The final part of the statement shows FastForward increased its cash balance by $4,800 in December. Since it started with no cash, the ending balance is also $4,800—see line ③. We see that cash flow numbers are different from income statement (*accrual*) numbers, which is common.

Point: Statement of cash flows has three main sections: operating, investing, and financing.

Point: Payment for supplies is an operating activity because supplies are expected to be used up in short-term operations (typically less than one year).

Point: Investing activities refer to long-term asset investments by the company, *not* to owner investments.

Quick Check   Answers — p. 28

21. Explain the link between the income statement and the statement of retained earnings.
22. Describe the link between the balance sheet and the statement of retained earnings.
23. Discuss the three major sections of the statement of cash flows.

GLOBAL VIEW

Accounting according to U.S. GAAP is similar, but not identical, to IFRS. Throughout the book we use this last section to identify major similarities and differences between IFRS and U.S. GAAP for the materials in each chapter.

Basic Principles   Both U.S. GAAP and IFRS include broad and similar guidance for accounting. However, neither system specifies particular account names nor the detail required. (A typical *chart of accounts* is shown near the end of this book.) IFRS does require certain minimum line items be reported in the balance sheet along with other minimum disclosures that U.S. GAAP does not. On the other hand, U.S. GAAP requires disclosures for the current and prior two years for the income statement, statement of cash flows, and statement of retained earnings (equity), while IFRS requires disclosures for the current and prior year. Still, the basic principles behind these two systems are similar.

Transaction Analysis   Both U.S. GAAP and IFRS apply transaction analysis identically as shown in this chapter. Although some variations exist in revenue and expense recognition and other principles, all of the transactions in this chapter are accounted for identically under these two systems. It is often said that U.S. GAAP is more *rules-based* whereas IFRS is more *principles-based*. The main difference on the rules versus principles focus is with the approach in deciding how to account for certain transactions. Under U.S. GAAP, the approach is more focused on strictly following the accounting rules; under IFRS, the approach is more focused on a review of the situation and how accounting can best reflect it. This difference typically impacts advanced topics beyond the introductory course.

NOKIA

Financial Statements   Both U.S. GAAP and IFRS prepare the same four basic financial statements. To illustrate, a condensed version of **Nokia**'s income statement follows (numbers are in euros millions). Nokia is a leader in mobile technology, from smartphones to mobile computers. Similar condensed versions can be prepared for the other three statements.

NOKIA Income Statement (in € millions) For Year Ended December 31, 2009	
Net sales	40,984
Cost of sales	27,720
Research, selling, administrative, and other expenses	12,302
Taxes	702
Net income (profit)	260

Decision Analysis (a section at the end of each chapter) introduces and explains ratios helpful in decision making using real company data. Instructors can skip this section and cover all ratios in Chapter 13.

Decision Analysis    Return on Assets

---

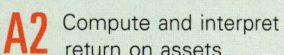
A2 Compute and interpret return on assets.

A *Decision Analysis* section at the end of each chapter is devoted to financial statement analysis. We organize financial statement analysis into four areas: (1) liquidity and efficiency, (2) solvency, (3) profitability, and (4) market prospects—Chapter 13 has a ratio listing with definitions and groupings by area. When analyzing ratios, we need benchmarks to identify good, bad, or average levels. Common benchmarks include the company's prior levels and those of its competitors.

This chapter presents a profitability measure: return on assets. Return on assets is useful in evaluating management, analyzing and forecasting profits, and planning activities. **Dell** has its marketing department compute return on assets for *every* order. **Return on assets (ROA),** also called *return on investment (ROI)*, is defined in Exhibit 1.11.

EXHIBIT 1.11

Return on Assets

$$\text{Return on assets} = \frac{\text{Net income}}{\text{Average total assets}}$$

Net income is from the annual income statement, and average total assets is computed by adding the beginning and ending amounts for that same period and dividing by 2. To illustrate, **Best Buy** reports net income of $1,317 million for fiscal year 2010. At the beginning of fiscal 2010, its total assets are $15,826 million and at the end of fiscal 2010, they total $18,302 million. Best Buy's return on assets for fiscal 2010 is:

$$\text{Return on assets} = \frac{\$1,317 \text{ million}}{(\$15,826 \text{ million} + \$18,302 \text{ million})/2} = 7.7\%$$

Is a 7.7% return on assets good or bad for Best Buy? To help answer this question, we compare (benchmark) Best Buy's return with its prior performance, the returns of competitors (such as **RadioShack**, **Conn's**, and **Rex Stores**), and the returns from alternative investments. Best Buy's return for each of the prior five years is in the second column of Exhibit 1.12, which ranges from 7.0% to 10.8%.

Fiscal Year	Return on Assets	
	Best Buy	Industry
2010	7.7%	2.9%
2009	7.0	2.5
2008	10.7	3.4
2007	10.8	3.5
2006	10.3	3.3

EXHIBIT 1.12

Best Buy and Industry Returns

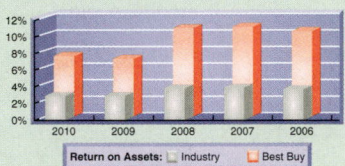

Best Buy shows a fairly stable pattern of good returns that reflect its productive use of assets. There is a decline in its 2009 return reflecting the recessionary period. We compare Best Buy's return to the normal return for similar merchandisers of electronic products (third column). Industry averages are available from services such as **Dun & Bradstreet**'s *Industry Norms and Key Ratios* and **The Risk Management Association**'s *Annual Statement Studies*. When compared to the industry, Best Buy performs well.

*Each **Decision Analysis** section ends with a role-playing scenario to show the usefulness of ratios.*

Decision Maker   Answer — p. 28

Business Owner   You own a small winter ski resort that earns a 21% return on its assets. An opportunity to purchase a winter ski equipment manufacturer is offered to you. This manufacturer earns a 19% return on its assets. The industry return for this manufacturer is 14%. Do you purchase this manufacturer? ■

*The **Demonstration Problem** is a review of key chapter content. The Planning the Solution offers strategies in solving the problem.*

DEMONSTRATION PROBLEM

After several months of planning, Jasmine Worthy started a haircutting business called Expressions. The following events occurred during its first month of business.

a. On August 1, Worthy invested $3,000 cash and $15,000 of equipment in Expressions in exchange for its common stock.

b. On August 2, Expressions paid $600 cash for furniture for the shop.

c. On August 3, Expressions paid $500 cash to rent space in a strip mall for August.

d. On August 4, it purchased $1,200 of equipment on credit for the shop (using a long-term note payable).

e. On August 5, Expressions opened for business. Cash received from haircutting services in the first week and a half of business (ended August 15) was $825.

f. On August 15, it provided $100 of haircutting services on account.

g. On August 17, it received a $100 check for services previously rendered on account.

h. On August 17, it paid $125 cash to an assistant for hours worked during the grand opening.

i. Cash received from services provided during the second half of August was $930.

j. On August 31, it paid a $400 installment toward principal on the note payable entered into on August 4.

k. On August 31, it paid $900 in cash dividends to Worthy.

Required

1. Arrange the following asset, liability, and equity titles in a table similar to the one in Exhibit 1.9: Cash; Accounts Receivable; Furniture; Store Equipment; Note Payable; Common Stock; Dividends; Revenues; and Expenses. Show the effects of each transaction using the accounting equation.

2. Prepare an income statement for August.

3. Prepare a statement of retained earnings for August.

4. Prepare a balance sheet as of August 31.

5. Prepare a statement of cash flows for August.

6. Determine the return on assets ratio for August.

PLANNING THE SOLUTION

- Set up a table like Exhibit 1.9 with the appropriate columns for accounts.
- Analyze each transaction and show its effects as increases or decreases in the appropriate columns. Be sure the accounting equation remains in balance after each transaction.
- Prepare the income statement, and identify revenues and expenses. List those items on the statement, compute the difference, and label the result as *net income* or *net loss*.
- Use information in the Equity columns to prepare the statement of retained earnings.
- Use information in the last row of the transactions table to prepare the balance sheet.
- Prepare the statement of cash flows; include all events listed in the Cash column of the transactions table. Classify each cash flow as operating, investing, or financing.
- Calculate return on assets by dividing net income by average assets.

SOLUTION TO DEMONSTRATION PROBLEM

1.

	Cash	+	Accounts Receivable	+	Furniture	+	Store Equipment	=	Note Payable	+	Common Stock	−	Dividends	+	Revenues	−	Expenses
a.	$3,000						$15,000				$18,000						
b.	− 600			+	$600												
Bal.	2,400	+		+	600	+	15,000	=			18,000						
c.	− 500															−	$500
Bal.	1,900	+		+	600	+	15,000	=			18,000					−	500
d.						+	1,200		+$1,200								
Bal.	1,900	+		+	600	+	16,200	=	1,200	+	18,000					−	500
e.	+ 825													+	$ 825		
Bal.	2,725	+		+	600	+	16,200	=	1,200	+	18,000			+	825	−	500
f.			+	$100											+	100		
Bal.	2,725	+	100	+	600	+	16,200	=	1,200	+	18,000			+	925	−	500
g.	+ 100	−	100														
Bal.	2,825	+	0	+	600	+	16,200	=	1,200	+	18,000			+	925	−	500
h.	− 125															−	125
Bal.	2,700	+	0	+	600	+	16,200	=	1,200	+	18,000			+	925	−	625
i.	+ 930													+	930		
Bal.	3,630	+	0	+	600	+	16,200	=	1,200	+	18,000			+	1,855	−	625
j.	− 400								− 400								
Bal.	3,230	+	0	+	600	+	16,200	=	800	+	18,000			+	1,855	−	625
k.	− 900											−	$900				
Bal.	$ 2,330	+	0	+	$600	+	$ 16,200	=	$ 800	+	$ 18,000	−	$900	+	$1,855	−	$625

2.

EXPRESSIONS
Income Statement
For Month Ended August 31

Revenues		
Haircutting services revenue		$1,855
Expenses		
Rent expense	$500	
Wages expense	125	
Total expenses		625
Net Income		$1,230

3.

EXPRESSIONS Statement of Retained Earnings For Month Ended August 31	
Retained earnings, August 1*	$ 0
Plus: Net income	1,230
	1,230
Less: Dividend to owner	900
Retained earnings, August 31	$ 330

* If Expressions had been an existing business from a prior period, the beginning retained earnings balance would equal the retained earnings balance from the end of the prior period.

4.

EXPRESSIONS Balance Sheet August 31			
Assets		**Liabilities**	
Cash	$ 2,330	Note payable	$ 800
Furniture	600	**Equity**	
Store equipment	16,200	Common stock	18,000
		Retained earnings.	330
		Total equity	18,330
Total assets	$19,130	Total liabilities and equity.	$19,130

5.

EXPRESSIONS Statement of Cash Flows For Month Ended August 31		
Cash flows from operating activities		
Cash received from customers	$1,855	
Cash paid for rent	(500)	
Cash paid for wages	(125)	
Net cash provided by operating activities		$1,230
Cash flows from investing activities		
Cash paid for furniture		(600)
Cash flows from financing activities		
Investments from stockholders	3,000	
Cash dividends to stockholders	(900)	
Partial repayment of (long-term) note payable	(400)	
Net cash provided by financing activities		1,700
Net increase in cash.		$2,330
Cash balance, August 1		0
Cash balance, August 31.		$2,330

6. Return on assets $= \dfrac{\text{Net income}}{\text{Average assets}} = \dfrac{\$1,230}{(\$18,000^* + \$19,130)/2} = \dfrac{\$1,230}{\$18,565} = \mathbf{6.63\%}$

 * Uses the initial $18,000 investment as the beginning balance for the *start-up period only*.

1A

Return and Risk Analysis

A3 Explain the relation between return and risk.

This appendix explains return and risk analysis and its role in business and accounting.

Net income is often linked to **return.** Return on assets (ROA) is stated in ratio form as income divided by assets invested. For example, banks report return from a savings account in the form of an interest return such as 4%. If we invest in a savings account or in U.S. Treasury bills, we expect a return of around 2% to 7%. We could also invest in a company's stock, or even start our own business. How do we decide among these investment options? The answer depends on our trade-off between return and risk.

Risk is the uncertainty about the return we will earn. All business investments involve risk, but some investments involve more risk than others. The lower the risk of an investment, the lower is our expected return. The reason that savings accounts pay such a low return is the low risk of not being repaid with interest (the government guarantees most savings accounts from default). If we buy a share of eBay or any other company, we might obtain a large return. However, we have no guarantee of any return; there is even the risk of loss.

EXHIBIT 1A.1

Average Returns for Bonds with Different Risks

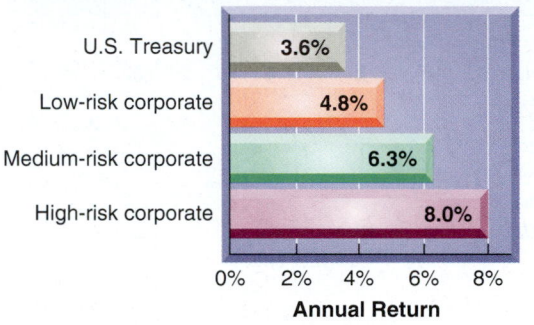

The bar graph in Exhibit 1A.1 shows recent returns for 10-year bonds with different risks. *Bonds* are written promises by organizations to repay amounts loaned with interest. U.S. Treasury bonds provide a low expected return, but they also offer low risk since they are backed by the U.S. government. High-risk corporate bonds offer a much larger potential return but with much higher risk.

The trade-off between return and risk is a normal part of business. Higher risk implies higher, but riskier, expected returns. To help us make better decisions, we use accounting information to assess both return and risk.

1B

Business Activities and the Accounting Equation

C5 Identify and describe the three major activities of organizations.

This appendix explains how the accounting equation is derived from business activities.

There are three major types of business activities: financing, investing, and operating. Each of these requires planning. *Planning* involves defining an organization's ideas, goals, and actions. Most public corporations use the *Management Discussion and Analysis* section in their annual reports to communicate plans. However, planning is not cast in stone. This adds *risk* to both setting plans and analyzing them.

Financing *Financing activities* provide the means organizations use to pay for resources such as land, buildings, and equipment to carry out plans. Organizations are careful in acquiring and managing financing activities because they can determine success or failure. The two sources of financing are owner and nonowner. *Owner financing* refers to resources contributed by the owner along with any income the owner leaves in the organization. *Nonowner* (or *creditor*) *financing* refers to resources contributed by creditors (lenders). *Financial management* is the task of planning how to obtain these resources and to set the right mix between owner and creditor financing.

Point: Management must understand accounting data to set financial goals, make financing and investing decisions, and evaluate operating performance.

Investing *Investing activities* are the acquiring and disposing of resources (assets) that an organization uses to acquire and sell its products or services. Assets are funded by an organization's financing. Organizations differ on the amount and makeup of assets. Some require land and factories to operate. Others need only an office. Determining the amount and type of assets for operations is called *asset management*. Invested amounts are referred to as *assets*. Financing is made up of creditor and owner financing, which hold claims on assets. Creditors' claims are called *liabilities,* and the owner's claim is called *equity.* This basic equality is called the *accounting equation* and can be written as: Assets = Liabilities + Equity.

Point: Investing (assets) and financing (liabilities plus equity) totals are *always* equal.

Operating   *Operating activities* involve using resources to research, develop, purchase, produce, distribute, and market products and services. Sales and revenues are the inflow of assets from selling products and services. Costs and expenses are the outflow of assets to support operating activities. *Strategic management* is the process of determining the right mix of operating activities for the type of organization, its plans, and its market.

Exhibit 1B.1 summarizes business activities. Planning is part of each activity and gives them meaning and focus. Investing (assets) and financing (liabilities and equity) are set opposite each other to stress their balance. Operating activities are below investing and financing activities to show that operating activities are the result of investing and financing.

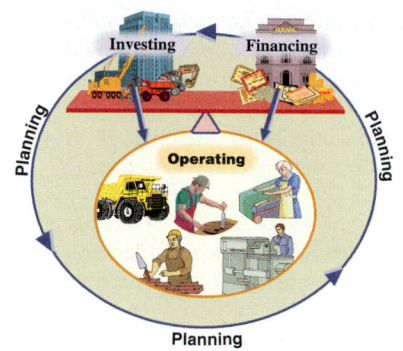

EXHIBIT 1B.1

Activities of Organizations

Summary ← *A **Summary** organized by learning objectives concludes each chapter.*

C1 **Explain the purpose and importance of accounting.** Accounting is an information and measurement system that aims to identify, record, and communicate relevant, reliable, and comparable information about business activities. It helps assess opportunities, products, investments, and social and community responsibilities.

C2 **Identify users and uses of, and opportunities in, accounting.** Users of accounting are both internal and external. Some users and uses of accounting include (a) managers in controlling, monitoring, and planning; (b) lenders for measuring the risk and return of loans; (c) shareholders for assessing the return and risk of stock; (d) directors for overseeing management; and (e) employees for judging employment opportunities. Opportunities in accounting include financial, managerial, and tax accounting. They also include accounting-related fields such as lending, consulting, managing, and planning.

C3 **Explain why ethics are crucial to accounting.** The goal of accounting is to provide useful information for decision making. For information to be useful, it must be trusted. This demands ethical behavior in accounting.

C4 **Explain generally accepted accounting principles and define and apply several accounting principles.** Generally accepted accounting principles are a common set of standards applied by accountants. Accounting principles aid in producing relevant, reliable, and comparable information. Four principles underlying financial statements were introduced: cost, revenue recognition, matching, and full disclosure. Financial statements also reflect four assumptions: going-concern, monetary unit, time period, and business entity.

C5^B **Identify and describe the three major activities of organizations.** Organizations carry out three major activities: financing, investing, and operating. Financing is the means used to

pay for resources such as land, buildings, and machines. Investing refers to the buying and selling of resources used in acquiring and selling products and services. Operating activities are those necessary for carrying out the organization's plans.

A1 **Define and interpret the accounting equation and each of its components.** The accounting equation is: Assets = Liabilities + Equity. Assets are resources owned by a company. Liabilities are creditors' claims on assets. Equity is the owner's claim on assets (*the residual*). The expanded accounting equation is: Assets = Liabilities + [Common Stock − Dividends + Revenues − Expenses].

A2 **Compute and interpret return on assets.** Return on assets is computed as net income divided by average assets. For example, if we have an average balance of $100 in a savings account and it earns $5 interest for the year, the return on assets is $5/$100, or 5%.

A3^A **Explain the relation between return and risk.** *Return* refers to income, and *risk* is the uncertainty about the return we hope to make. All investments involve risk. The lower the risk of an investment, the lower is its expected return. Higher risk implies higher, but riskier, expected return.

P1 **Analyze business transactions using the accounting equation.** A *transaction* is an exchange of economic consideration between two parties. Examples include exchanges of products, services, money, and rights to collect money. Transactions always have at least two effects on one or more components of the accounting equation. This equation is always in balance.

P2 **Identify and prepare basic financial statements and explain how they interrelate.** Four financial statements report on an organization's activities: balance sheet, income statement, statement of retained earnings, and statement of cash flows.

Guidance Answers to Decision Maker and Decision Ethics

Entrepreneur   You should probably form the business as a corporation if potential lawsuits are of prime concern. The corporate form of organization protects your personal property from lawsuits directed at the business and places only the corporation's resources at risk. A downside of the corporate form is double taxation: The corporation must pay taxes on its income, and you normally must pay taxes

on any money distributed to you from the business (even though the corporation already paid taxes on this money). You should also examine the ethical and socially responsible aspects of starting a business in which you anticipate injuries to others. Formation as an LLC or S corp. should also be explored.

Retailer   You can use the accounting equation (Assets = Liabilities + Equity) to help identify risky customers to whom you would likely not want to extend credit. A balance sheet provides amounts for each of these key components. The lower a customer's equity is relative to liabilities, the less likely you would be to extend credit. A low equity means the business has little value that does not already have creditor claims to it.

Business Owner   The 19% return on assets for the manufacturer exceeds the 14% industry return (and many others). This is a positive

factor for a potential purchase. Also, the purchase of this manufacturer is an opportunity to spread your risk over two businesses as opposed to one. Still, you should hesitate to purchase a business whose return of 19% is lower than your current resort's return of 21%. You are probably better off directing efforts to increase investment in your resort, assuming you can continue to earn a 21% return.

Guidance Answers to Quick Checks

1. Accounting is an information and measurement system that identifies, records, and communicates relevant information to help people make better decisions.

2. Recordkeeping, also called *bookkeeping,* is the recording of financial transactions and events, either manually or electronically. Recordkeeping is essential to data reliability; but accounting is this and much more. Accounting includes identifying, measuring, recording, reporting, and analyzing business events and transactions.

3. Technology offers increased accuracy, speed, efficiency, and convenience in accounting.

4. External users of accounting include lenders, shareholders, directors, customers, suppliers, regulators, lawyers, brokers, and the press. Internal users of accounting include managers, officers, and other internal decision makers involved with strategic and operating decisions.

5. Internal users (managers) include those from research and development, purchasing, human resources, production, distribution, marketing, and servicing.

6. Internal controls are procedures set up to protect assets, ensure reliable accounting reports, promote efficiency, and encourage adherence to company policies. Internal controls are crucial for relevant and reliable information.

7. Ethical guidelines are threefold: (1) identify ethical concerns using personal ethics, (2) analyze options considering all good and bad consequences, and (3) make ethical decisions after weighing all consequences.

8. Ethics and social responsibility yield good behavior, and they often result in higher income and a better working environment.

9. For accounting to provide useful information for decisions, it must be trusted. Trust requires ethics in accounting.

10. Two major participants in setting rules include the SEC and the FASB. (*Note:* Accounting rules reflect society's needs, not those of accountants or any other single constituency.)

11. Most U.S. companies are not directly affected by international accounting standards. International standards are put forth as preferred accounting practices. However, stock exchanges and other parties are increasing the pressure to narrow differences in worldwide accounting practices. International accounting standards are playing an important role in that process.

12. The objectivity concept and cost principle are related in that most users consider information based on cost as objective. Information prepared using both is considered highly reliable and often relevant.

13. Users desire information about the performance of a specific entity. If information is mixed between two or more entities, its usefulness decreases.

14. The revenue recognition principle gives preparers guidelines on when to recognize (record) revenue. This is important; for example, if revenue is recognized too early, the statements report revenue sooner than it should and the business looks more profitable than it is. The reverse is also true.

15. The three basic forms of business organization are sole proprietorships, partnerships, and corporations.

16. Owners of corporations are called *shareholders* (or *stockholders*). Corporate ownership is divided into units called *shares* (or *stock*). The most basic of corporate shares is common stock (or capital stock).

17. The accounting equation is: Assets = Liabilities + Equity. This equation is always in balance, both before and after each transaction.

18. A transaction that changes the makeup of assets would not affect liability and equity accounts. FastForward's transactions 2 and 3 are examples. Each exchanges one asset for another.

19. Earning revenue by performing services, as in FastForward's transaction 5, increases equity (and assets). Incurring expenses while servicing clients, such as in transactions 6 and 7, decreases equity (and assets). Other examples include owner investments (stock issuances) that increase equity and dividends that decrease equity.

20. Paying a liability with an asset reduces both asset and liability totals. One example is FastForward's transaction 10 that reduces a payable by paying cash.

21. An income statement reports a company's revenues and expenses along with the resulting net income or loss. A statement of retained earnings shows changes in retained earnings, including that from net income or loss. Both statements report transactions occurring over a period of time.

22. The balance sheet describes a company's financial position (assets, liabilities, and equity) at a point in time. The retained earnings amount in the balance sheet is obtained from the statement of retained earnings.

23. Cash flows from operating activities report cash receipts and payments from the primary business the company engages in. Cash flows from investing activities involve cash transactions from buying and selling long-term assets. Cash flows from financing activities include long-term cash borrowings and repayments to lenders and the cash investments from, and dividends to, the stockholders.

A list of key terms with page references concludes each chapter (a complete glossary is at the end of the book and also on the book's Website).

Key Terms   mhhe.com/wildFINMAN4e

Accounting (p. 4)
Accounting equation (p. 14)
Assets (p. 14)
Audit (p. 12)
Auditors (p. 13)
Balance sheet (p. 19)
Bookkeeping (p. 4)
Business entity assumption (p. 11)
Common stock (p. 12)
Conceptual framework (p. 9)
Contributed capital (p. 14)
Corporation (p. 12)
Cost-benefit constraint (p. 12)
Cost principle (p. 10)
Dividends (p. 14)
Equity (p. 14)
Ethics (p. 8)
Events (p. 15)
Expanded accounting equation (p. 14)
Expense recognition principle (p. 11)
Expenses (p. 14)
External transactions (p. 15)

External users (p. 5)
Financial accounting (p. 5)
Financial Accounting Standards Board (FASB) (p. 9)
Full disclosure principle (p. 11)
Generally accepted accounting principles (GAAP) (p. 8)
Going-concern assumption (p. 11)
Income statement (p. 19)
Internal transactions (p. 15)
Internal users (p. 6)
International Accounting Standards Board (IASB) (p. 9)
International Financial Reporting Standards (IFRS) (p. 9)
Liabilities (p. 14)
Managerial accounting (p. 6)
Matching principle (p. 11)
Materiality constraint (p. 12)
Measurement principle (p. 10)
Monetary unit assumption (p. 11)
Net income (p. 14)
Net loss (p. 14)

Partnership (p. 11)
Proprietorship (p. 11)
Recordkeeping (p. 4)
Retained earnings (p. 14)
Return (p. 26)
Return on assets (p. 22)
Revenue recognition principle (p. 10)
Revenues (p. 14)
Risk (p. 26)
Sarbanes–Oxley Act (p. 12)
Securities and Exchange Commission (SEC) (p. 9)
Shareholders (p. 12)
Shares (p. 12)
Sole proprietorship (p. 11)
Statement of cash flows (p. 19)
Statement of retained earnings (p. 19)
Stock (p. 12)
Stockholders (p. 12)
Time period assumption (p. 11)

Multiple Choice Quiz   Answers on p. 47   mhhe.com/wildFINMAN4e

Additional Quiz Questions are available at the book's Website.

1. A building is offered for sale at $500,000 but is currently assessed at $400,000. The purchaser of the building believes the building is worth $475,000, but ultimately purchases the building for $450,000. The purchaser records the building at:
   a. $50,000
   b. $400,000
   c. $450,000
   d. $475,000
   e. $500,000

2. On December 30, 2010, **KPMG** signs a $150,000 contract to provide accounting services to one of its clients in 2011. KPMG has a December 31 year-end. Which accounting principle or assumption requires KPMG to record the accounting services revenue from this client in 2011 and not 2010?
   a. Business entity assumption
   b. Revenue recognition principle
   c. Monetary unit assumption
   d. Cost principle
   e. Going-concern assumption

3. If the assets of a company increase by $100,000 during the year and its liabilities increase by $35,000 during the same

year, then the change in equity of the company during the year must have been:
   a. An increase of $135,000.
   b. A decrease of $135,000.
   c. A decrease of $65,000.
   d. An increase of $65,000.
   e. An increase of $100,000.

4. **Brunswick** borrows $50,000 cash from Third National Bank. How does this transaction affect the accounting equation for Brunswick?
   a. Assets increase by $50,000; liabilities increase by $50,000; no effect on equity.
   b. Assets increase by $50,000; no effect on liabilities; equity increases by $50,000.
   c. Assets increase by $50,000; liabilities decrease by $50,000; no effect on equity.
   d. No effect on assets; liabilities increase by $50,000; equity increases by $50,000.
   e. No effect on assets; liabilities increase by $50,000; equity decreases by $50,000.

5. Geek Squad performs services for a customer and bills the customer for $500. How would Geek Squad record this transaction?

   a. Accounts receivable increase by $500; revenues increase by $500.

   b. Cash increases by $500; revenues increase by $500.

   c. Accounts receivable increase by $500; revenues decrease by $500.

   d. Accounts receivable increase by $500; accounts payable increase by $500.

   e. Accounts payable increase by $500; revenues increase by $500.

$^{A(B)}$ *Superscript letter A (B) denotes assignments based on Appendix 1A (1B).*

🛈 Icon denotes assignments that involve decision making.

Discussion Questions

1. What is the purpose of accounting in society?
2. Technology is increasingly used to process accounting data. Why then must we study and understand accounting?
3. 🛈 Identify four kinds of external users and describe how they use accounting information.
4. 🛈 What are at least three questions business owners and managers might be able to answer by looking at accounting information?
5. Identify three actual businesses that offer services and three actual businesses that offer products.
6. 🛈 Describe the internal role of accounting for organizations.
7. Identify three types of services typically offered by accounting professionals.
8. 🛈 What type of accounting information might be useful to the marketing managers of a business?
9. Why is accounting described as a service activity?
10. What are some accounting-related professions?
11. How do ethics rules affect auditors' choice of clients?
12. What work do tax accounting professionals perform in addition to preparing tax returns?
13. What does the concept of *objectivity* imply for information reported in financial statements? Why?
14. A business reports its own office stationery on the balance sheet at its $400 cost, although it cannot be sold for more than $10 as scrap paper. Which accounting principle and/or assumption justifies this treatment?
15. Why is the revenue recognition principle needed? What does it demand?
16. Describe the three basic forms of business organization and their key attributes.
17. Define (a) *assets*, (b) *liabilities*, (c) *equity*, and (d) *net assets*.

18. What events or transactions change equity?
19. Identify the two main categories of accounting principles.
20. What do accountants mean by the term *revenue?*
21. Define *net income* and explain its computation.
22. Identify the four basic financial statements of a business.
23. 🛈 What information is reported in an income statement?
24. Give two examples of expenses a business might incur.
25. What is the purpose of the statement of retained earnings?
26. 🛈 What information is reported in a balance sheet?
27. The statement of cash flows reports on what major activities?
28. 🛈 Define and explain return on assets.
29.^{A}🛈 Define return and risk. Discuss the trade-off between them.
30.^{B} Describe the three major business activities in organizations.
31.^{B} Explain why investing (assets) and financing (liabilities and equity) totals are always equal.
32. Refer to the financial statements of **Research In Motion** in Appendix A near the end of the book. To what level of significance are dollar amounts rounded? What time period does its income statement cover?   **RIM**
33. Identify the dollar amounts of **Apple**'s 2009 assets, liabilities, and equity as reported in its statements in Appendix A near the end of the book.   Apple
34. Refer to **Nokia**'s balance sheet in Appendix A near the end of the book. Confirm that its total assets equal its total liabilities plus total equity.   **NOKIA**
35. 🛈 Access the SEC EDGAR database (<u>www.sec.gov</u>) and retrieve **Palm**'s 2009 10-K (filed July 24, 2009; ticker PALM). Identify its auditor. What responsibility does its independent auditor claim regarding Palm's financial statements?   **Palm**

Connect reproduces assignments online, in static or algorithmic mode, which allows instructors to monitor, promote, and assess student learning. It can be used for practice, homework, or exams.

Quick Study exercises give readers a brief test of key elements.

QUICK STUDY

QS 1-1
Identifying accounting terms   **C1**

Reading and interpreting accounting reports requires some knowledge of accounting terminology. (*a*) Identify the meaning of these accounting-related acronyms: GAAP, SEC, FASB, IASB and IFRS. (*b*) Briefly explain the importance of the knowledge base or organization that is referred to for each of the accounting-related acronyms.

An important responsibility of many accounting professionals is to design and implement internal control procedures for organizations. Explain the purpose of internal control procedures. Provide two examples of internal controls applied by companies.

QS 1-2
Explaining internal control
C1

Identify the following users as either external users (E) or internal users (I).

a. Lenders   **d.** Sales staff   **g.** Brokers   **j.** Managers
b. Controllers   **e.** FBI and IRS   **h.** Suppliers   **k.** Business press
c. Shareholders   **f.** Consumer group   **i.** Customers   **l.** District attorney

QS 1-3
Identifying accounting users
C2

There are many job opportunities for those with accounting knowledge. Identify at least three main areas of opportunities for accounting professionals. For each area, identify at least three job possibilities linked to accounting.

QS 1-4
Accounting opportunities   **C2**

Accounting professionals must sometimes choose between two or more acceptable methods of accounting for business transactions and events. Explain why these situations can involve difficult matters of ethical concern.

QS 1-5
Identifying ethical concerns   **C3**

This icon highlights assignments that enhance decision-making skills.

Identify which accounting principle or assumption best describes each of the following practices:

a. If $51,000 cash is paid to buy land, the land is reported on the buyer's balance sheet at $51,000.
b. Alissa Kees owns both Sailing Passions and Dockside Supplies. In preparing financial statements for Dockside Supplies, Kees makes sure that the expense transactions of Sailing Passions are kept separate from Dockside's transactions and financial statements.
c. In December 2010, Ace Landscaping received a customer's order and cash prepayment to install sod at a new house that would not be ready for installation until March 2011. Ace should record the revenue from the customer order in March 2011, not in December 2010.

QS 1-6
Identifying accounting principles
C4

---

a. Total assets of Caldwell Company equal $40,000 and its equity is $10,000. What is the amount of its liabilities?
b. Total assets of Waterworld equal $55,000 and its liabilities and equity amounts are equal to each other. What is the amount of its liabilities? What is the amount of its equity?

QS 1-7
Applying the accounting equation
A1

Use the accounting equation to compute the missing financial statement amounts (a), (b), and (c).

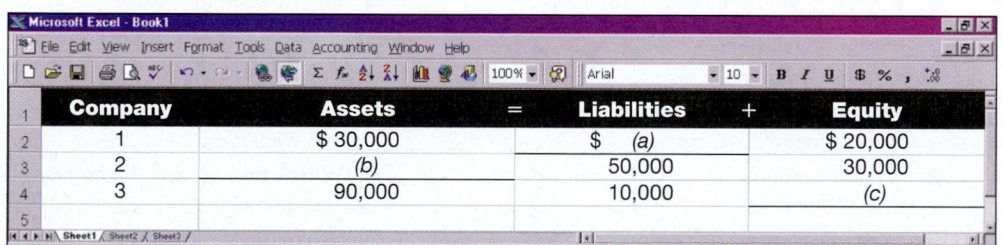

Company	Assets	=	Liabilities	+	Equity
1	$ 30,000		$ (a)		$ 20,000
2	(b)		50,000		30,000
3	90,000		10,000		(c)

QS 1-8
Applying the accounting equation
A1

Accounting provides information about an organization's business transactions and events that both affect the accounting equation and can be reliably measured. Identify at least two examples of both (a) business transactions and (b) business events that meet these requirements.

QS 1-9
Identifying transactions and events   **P1**

Use **Apple**'s September 26, 2009, financial statements, in Appendix A near the end of the book, to answer the following:

a. Identify the dollar amounts of Apple's 2009 (1) assets, (2) liabilities, and (3) equity.
b. Using Apple's amounts from part a, verify that Assets = Liabilities + Equity.

QS 1-10
Identifying and computing assets, liabilities, and equity
P1

QS 1-11
Computing and interpreting
return on assets

A2

In a recent year's financial statements, **Home Depot** reported the following results. Compute and interpret Home Depot's return on assets (assume competitors average a 5% return on assets).

Sales	$71,288 million
Net income	2,260 million
Average total assets	42,744 million

QS 1-12
Identifying items with financial
statements

P2

Indicate in which financial statement each item would most likely appear: income statement (I), balance sheet (B), statement of retained earnings (RE), or statement of cash flows (CF).

a. Assets   **d.** Equipment   **g.** Total liabilities and equity

b. Revenues   **e.** Dividends   **h.** Cash from operating activities

c. Liabilities   **f.** Expenses   **i.** Net decrease (or increase) in cash

---

QS 1-13
International accounting
standards   C4

 This icon highlights assignments that focus on IFRS-related content.

Answer each of the following questions related to international accounting standards.

a. The International Accounting Standards Board (IASB) issues preferred accounting practices that are referred to as what?

b. The FASB and IASB are working on a convergence process for what purpose?

c. The SEC has proposed a roadmap for use of IFRS by U.S. companies. What is the proposed adoption date for large U.S. companies to adopt IFRS?

EXERCISES

Exercise 1-1
Classifying activities reflected in
the accounting system

C1

Accounting is an information and measurement system that identifies, records, and communicates relevant, reliable, and comparable information about an organization's business activities. Classify the following activities as part of the identifying (I), recording (R), or communicating (C) aspects of accounting.

_____ **1.** Determining employee tasks behind a service.

_____ **2.** Establishing revenues generated from a product.

_____ **3.** Maintaining a log of service costs.

_____ **4.** Measuring the costs of a product.

_____ **5.** Preparing financial statements.

_____ **6.** Analyzing and interpreting reports.

_____ **7.** Presenting financial information.

Exercise 1-2
Identifying accounting
users and uses

C2

Part A. Identify the following users of accounting information as either an internal (I) or an external (E) user.

_____ **1.** Shareholders

_____ **2.** Creditors

_____ **3.** Nonexecutive employee

_____ **4.** Research and development director

_____ **5.** Purchasing manager

_____ **6.** Human resources director

_____ **7.** Production supervisors

_____ **8.** Distribution managers

Part B. Identify the following questions as most likely to be asked by an internal (I) or an external (E) user of accounting information.

_____ **1.** What are the costs of our service to customers?

_____ **2.** Should we make a five-year loan to that business?

_____ **3.** Should we spend further research on our product?

_____ **4.** Do income levels justify the current stock price?

_____ **5.** What are reasonable payroll benefits and wages?

_____ **6.** Which firm reports the highest sales and income?

_____ **7.** What are the costs of our product's ingredients?

Exercise 1-3
Describing accounting
responsibilities

C2

Many accounting professionals work in one of the following three areas:

A. Managerial accounting   **B.** Financial accounting   **C.** Tax accounting

Identify the area of accounting that is most involved in each of the following responsibilities:

_____ **1.** Reviewing reports for SEC compliance.

_____ **2.** Planning transactions to minimize taxes.

_____ **3.** Investigating violations of tax laws.

_____ **4.** Preparing external financial statements.

_____ **5.** Budgeting.

_____ **6.** Cost accounting.

_____ **7.** External auditing.

_____ **8.** Internal auditing.

Assume the following role and describe a situation in which ethical considerations play an important part in guiding your decisions and actions:

a. You are a student in an introductory accounting course.

b. You are an accounting professional with audit clients that are competitors in business.

c. You are an accounting professional preparing tax returns for clients.

d. You are a manager with responsibility for several employees.

Exercise 1-4
Identifying ethical concerns
C3

Match each of the numbered descriptions with the term or phrase it best reflects. Indicate your answer by writing the letter for the term or phrase in the blank provided.

A. Audit   **C.** Ethics   **E.** SEC   **G.** Net income

B. GAAP   **D.** Tax accounting **F.** Public accountants **H.** IASB

_____ **1.** Amount a business earns after paying all expenses and costs associated with its sales and revenues.

_____ **2.** An examination of an organization's accounting system and records that adds credibility to financial statements.

_____ **3.** Principles that determine whether an action is right or wrong.

_____ **4.** Accounting professionals who provide services to many clients.

_____ **5.** An accounting area that includes planning future transactions to minimize taxes paid.

Exercise 1-5
Learning the language of business
C1–C3

Match each of the numbered descriptions with the principle or assumption it best reflects. Enter the letter for the appropriate principle or assumption in the blank space next to each description.

A. Cost principle   **E.** General accounting principle

B. Matching principle   **F.** Business entity assumption

C. Specific accounting principle **G.** Revenue recognition principle

D. Full disclosure principle   **H.** Going-concern assumption

_____ **1.** Revenue is recorded only when the earnings process is complete.

_____ **2.** Information is based on actual costs incurred in transactions.

_____ **3.** Usually created by a pronouncement from an authoritative body.

_____ **4.** Financial statements reflect the assumption that the business continues operating.

_____ **5.** A company reports details behind financial statements that would impact users' decisions.

_____ **6.** A company records the expenses incurred to generate the revenues reported.

_____ **7.** Derived from long-used and generally accepted accounting practices.

_____ **8.** Every business is accounted for separately from its owner or owners.

Exercise 1-6
Identifying accounting principles and assumptions
C4

The following describe several different business organizations. Determine whether the description refers to a sole proprietorship, partnership, or corporation.

a. A-1 pays its own income taxes and has two owners.

b. Ownership of Zeller Company is divided into 1,000 shares of stock.

c. Waldron is owned by Mary Malone, who is personally liable for the company's debts.

d. Micah Douglas and Nathan Logan own Financial Services, a financial services provider. Neither Douglas nor Logan has personal responsibility for the debts of Financial Services.

e. Bailey and Kay own Squeaky Clean, a cleaning service. Both are personally liable for the debts of the business.

f. Plasto Products does not pay income taxes and has one owner.

g. Ian LLC does not have separate legal existence apart from the one person who owns it.

Exercise 1-7
Distinguishing business organizations
C4

Answer the following questions. (*Hint:* Use the accounting equation.)

a. Office Mart has assets equal to $123,000 and liabilities equal to $53,000 at year-end. What is the total equity for Office Mart at year-end?

b. At the beginning of the year, Logan Company's assets are $200,000 and its equity is $150,000. During the year, assets increase $70,000 and liabilities increase $30,000. What is the equity at the end of the year?

c. At the beginning of the year, Keller Company's liabilities equal $60,000. During the year, assets increase by $80,000, and at year-end assets equal $180,000. Liabilities decrease $10,000 during the year. What are the beginning and ending amounts of equity?

Exercise 1-8
Using the accounting equation
A1 P1

Check (c) Beg. equity, $40,000

Exercise 1-9
Using the accounting equation
A1

Determine the missing amount from each of the separate situations *a*, *b*, and *c* below.

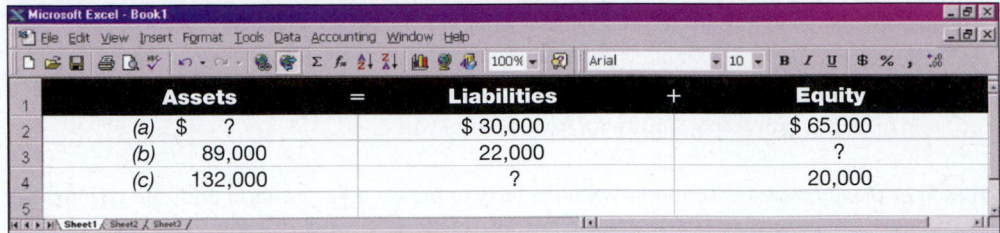

	Assets	=	Liabilities	+	Equity
(a)	$?		$ 30,000		$ 65,000
(b)	89,000		22,000		?
(c)	132,000		?		20,000

Exercise 1-10
Identifying effects of transactions on the accounting equation
P1

Provide an example of a transaction that creates the described effects for the separate cases *a* through *g*.

a. Increases an asset and decreases an asset.
b. Decreases an asset and decreases a liability.
c. Decreases a liability and increases a liability.
d. Increases an asset and increases a liability.

e. Decreases an asset and decreases equity.
f. Increases a liability and decreases equity.
g. Increases an asset and increases equity.

Exercise 1-11
Identifying effects of transactions using the accounting equation
P1

Lena Gold began a professional practice on June 1 and plans to prepare financial statements at the end of each month. During June, Gold (the owner) completed these transactions:

a. Owner invested $50,000 cash in the company along with equipment that had a $10,000 market value in exchange for common stock.
b. The company paid $1,600 cash for rent of office space for the month.
c. The company purchased $12,000 of additional equipment on credit (payment due within 30 days).
d. The company completed work for a client and immediately collected the $2,000 cash earned.
e. The company completed work for a client and sent a bill for $7,000 to be received within 30 days.
f. The company purchased additional equipment for $8,000 cash.
g. The company paid an assistant $2,400 cash as wages for the month.
h. The company collected $5,000 cash as a partial payment for the amount owed by the client in transaction *e*.
i. The company paid $12,000 cash to settle the liability created in transaction *c*.
j. The company paid $500 cash for dividends.

Required

Check Net income, $5,000

Create a table like the one in Exhibit 1.9, using the following headings for columns: Cash; Accounts Receivable; Equipment; Accounts Payable; Common Stock; Dividends; Revenues; and Expenses. Then use additions and subtractions to show the effects of the transactions on individual items of the accounting equation. Show new balances after each transaction.

Exercise 1-12
Analysis using the accounting equation
P1

Zelda began a new consulting firm on January 5. The accounting equation showed the following balances after each of the company's first five transactions. Analyze the accounting equation for each transaction and describe each of the five transactions with their amounts.

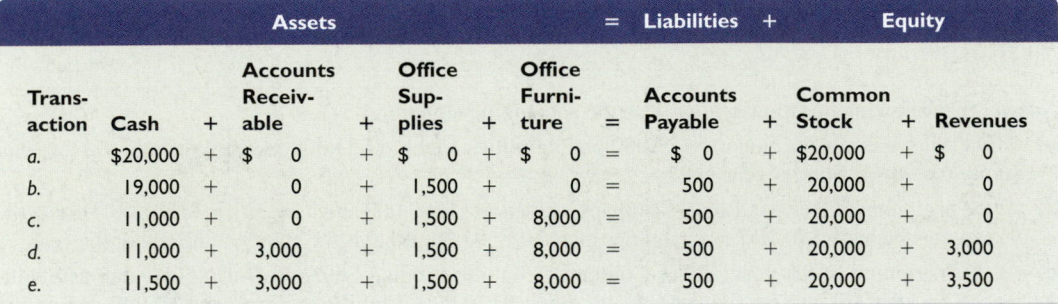

			Assets						=	Liabilities	+		Equity		
Trans- action	Cash	+	Accounts Receiv- able	+	Office Sup- plies	+	Office Furni- ture	=	Accounts Payable	+	Common Stock	+	Revenues
a.	$20,000	+	$ 0	+	$ 0	+	$ 0	=	$ 0	+	$20,000	+	$ 0
b.	19,000	+	0	+	1,500	+	0	=	500	+	20,000	+	0
c.	11,000	+	0	+	1,500	+	8,000	=	500	+	20,000	+	0
d.	11,000	+	3,000	+	1,500	+	8,000	=	500	+	20,000	+	3,000
e.	11,500	+	3,000	+	1,500	+	8,000	=	500	+	20,000	+	3,500

The following table shows the effects of five transactions (*a* through *e*) on the assets, liabilities, and equity of Vera's Boutique. Write short descriptions of the probable nature of each transaction.

Exercise 1-13
Identifying effects of transactions on accounting equation
P1

	Cash	+	Accounts Receivable	+	Office Supplies	+	Land	=	Accounts Payable	+	Common Stock	+	Revenues
	$ 10,500	+	$ 0	+	$1,500	+	$ 9,500	=	$ 0	+	$21,500	+	$ 0
a.	− 2,000					+	2,000						
b.				+	500				+500				
c.		+	950									+	950
d.	− 500								−500				
e.	+ 950	−	950										
	$ 8,950	+	$ 0	+	$2,000	+	$11,500	=	$ 0	+	$21,500	+	$950

On October 1, Natalie King organized Real Solutions, a new consulting firm. On October 31, the company's records show the following items and amounts. Use this information to prepare an October income statement for the business.

Exercise 1-14
Preparing an income statement
P2

Cash	$ 2,000	Cash dividends	$ 3,360
Accounts receivable	13,000	Consulting fees earned	15,000
Office supplies	4,250	Rent expense	2,550
Land	36,000	Salaries expense	6,000
Office equipment	28,000	Telephone expense	660
Accounts payable	7,500	Miscellaneous expenses	680
Common stock	74,000		

Check   Net income, $5,110

Use the information in Exercise 1-14 to prepare an October statement of retained earnings for Real Solutions.

Exercise 1-15
Preparing a statement of retained earnings   P2

Use the information in Exercise 1-14 (if completed, you can also use your solution to Exercise 1-15) to prepare an October 31 balance sheet for Real Solutions.

Exercise 1-16
Preparing a balance sheet   P2

Use the information in Exercise 1-14 to prepare an October 31 statement of cash flows for Real Solutions. Also assume the following:

Exercise 1-17
Preparing a statement of cash flows
P2

a. The owner's initial investment consists of $38,000 cash and $36,000 in land in exchange for common stock.
b. The company's $28,000 equipment purchase is paid in cash.
c. The accounts payable balance of $7,500 consists of the $4,250 office supplies purchase and $3,250 in employee salaries yet to be paid.
d. The company's rent, telephone, and miscellaneous expenses are paid in cash.
e. $2,000 has been collected on the $15,000 consulting fees earned.

Check   Net increase in cash, $2,000

Geneva Group reports net income of $20,000 for 2011. At the beginning of 2011, Geneva Group had $100,000 in assets. By the end of 2011, assets had grown to $150,000. What is Geneva Group's 2011 return on assets? How would you assess its performance if competitors average a 10% return on assets?

Exercise 1-18
Analysis of return on assets
A2

Indicate the section where each of the following would appear on the statement of cash flows.
A. Cash flows from operating activity
B. Cash flows from investing activity
C. Cash flows from financing activity

Exercise 1-19
Identifying sections of the statement of cash flows
P2

_____ **1.** Cash paid for wages
_____ **2.** Cash paid for dividends
_____ **3.** Cash purchase of equipment
_____ **4.** Cash paid for advertising
_____ **5.** Cash paid on an account payable
_____ **6.** Cash recieved from stock issued
_____ **7.** Cash received from clients
_____ **8.** Cash paid for rent

Exercise 1-20ᴮ

Identifying business activities

C5

Match each transaction or event to one of the following activities of an organization: financing activities (F), investing activities (I), or operating activities (O).

1. _____ An owner contributes resources to the business in exchange for stock.
2. _____ An organization purchases equipment.
3. _____ An organization advertises a new product.
4. _____ The organization borrows money from a bank.
5. _____ An organization sells some of its land.

Exercise 1-21

Preparing an income statement for a global company

P2

Nintendo Company reports the following income statement accounts for the year ended March 31, 2009. (Japanese yen in millions.)

Net sales	¥1,838,622
Cost of sales	1,044,981
Selling, general and administrative expenses	238,378
Other expenses	276,174

Use this information to prepare Nintendo's income statement for the year ended March 31, 2009.

Problem Set B located at the end of Problem Set A is provided for each problem to reinforce the learning process.

PROBLEM SET A

Problem 1-1A

Identifying effects of transactions on financial statements

A1 P1

Identify how each of the following separate transactions affects financial statements. For the balance sheet, identify how each transaction affects total assets, total liabilities, and total equity. For the income statement, identify how each transaction affects net income. For the statement of cash flows, identify how each transaction affects cash flows from operating activities, cash flows from financing activities, and cash flows from investing activities. For increases, place a "+" in the column or columns. For decreases, place a "−" in the column or columns. If both an increase and a decrease occur, place a "+/−" in the column or columns. The first transaction is completed as an example.

		Balance Sheet			Income Statement	Statement of Cash Flows		
	Transaction	Total Assets	Total Liab.	Total Equity	Net Income	Operating Activities	Financing Activities	Investing Activities
1	Owner invests cash for stock	+		+			+	
2	Incurs legal costs on credit							
3	Pays cash for employee wages							
4	Borrows cash by signing long-term note payable							
5	Receives cash for services provided							
6	Buys land by signing note payable							
7	Buys office equipment for cash							
8	Provides services on credit							
9	Collects cash on receivable from (8)							
10	Pays cash dividend							

The following financial statement information is from five separate companies:

Problem 1-2A

Computing missing information using accounting knowledge

A1   P1

	Company A	Company B	Company C	Company D	Company E
December 31, 2010					
Assets.........................	$45,000	$35,000	$29,000	$80,000	$123,000
Liabilities	23,500	22,500	14,000	38,000	?
December 31, 2011					
Assets.........................	48,000	41,000	?	125,000	112,500
Liabilities	?	27,500	19,000	64,000	75,000
During year 2011					
Stock issuances	5,000	1,500	7,750	?	4,500
Net income (loss)	7,500	?	9,000	12,000	18,000
Cash dividends	2,500	3,000	3,875	0	9,000

Required

1. Answer the following questions about Company A:
   a. What is the amount of equity on December 31, 2010?
   b. What is the amount of equity on December 31, 2011?
   c. What is the amount of liabilities on December 31, 2011?
2. Answer the following questions about Company B:
   a. What is the amount of equity on December 31, 2010?
   b. What is the amount of equity on December 31, 2011?
   c. What is net income for year 2011?
3. Calculate the amount of assets for Company C on December 31, 2011.
4. Calculate the amount of stock issuances for Company D during year 2011.
5. Calculate the amount of liabilities for Company E on December 31, 2010.

Check   (1*b*) $31,500

(2*c*) $2,500

(3) $46,875

The following is selected financial information for Affiliated Company as of December 31, 2011: liabilities, $34,000; equity, $56,000; assets, $90,000.

Required

Prepare the balance sheet for Affiliated Company as of December 31, 2011.

Problem 1-3A

Preparing a balance sheet

P2

The following is selected financial information for Sun Energy Company for the year ended December 31, 2011: revenues, $65,000; expenses, $50,000; net income, $15,000.

Required

Prepare the 2011 calendar-year income statement for Sun Energy Company.

Problem 1-4A

Preparing an income statement

P2

Following is selected financial information for Boardwalk for the year ended December 31, 2011.

Retained earnings, Dec. 31, 2011.........	$15,000	Cash dividends	$2,000
Net income	9,000	Retained earnings, Dec. 31, 2010	8,000

Required

Prepare the 2011 statement of retained earnings for Boardwalk.

Problem 1-5A

Preparing a statement of retained earnings

P2

Problem 1-6A
Preparing a statement of
cash flows

P2

Following is selected financial information of Trimark for the year ended December 31, 2011.

Cash used by investing activities	$(3,000)
Net increase in cash	200
Cash used by financing activities	(3,800)
Cash from operating activities	7,000
Cash, December 31, 2010	3,300

Check Cash balance, Dec. 31,
2011, $3,500

Required

Prepare the 2011 statement of cash flows for Trimark Company.

Problem 1-7A
Analyzing effects of transactions

C4 P1 P2 A1

Miranda Right started Right Consulting, a new business, and completed the following transactions during its first year of operations.

a. M. Right invests $60,000 cash and office equipment valued at $30,000 in the company in exchange for common stock.

b. The company purchased a $300,000 building to use as an office. Right paid $50,000 in cash and signed a note payable promising to pay the $250,000 balance over the next ten years.

c. The company purchased office equipment for $6,000 cash.

d. The company purchased $4,000 of office supplies and $1,000 of office equipment on credit.

e. The company paid a local newspaper $1,000 cash for printing an announcement of the office's opening.

f. The company completed a financial plan for a client and billed that client $4,000 for the service.

g. The company designed a financial plan for another client and immediately collected an $8,000 cash fee.

h. The company paid $1,800 cash for dividends.

i. The company received $3,000 cash as partial payment from the client described in transaction *f*.

j. The company made a partial payment of $500 cash on the equipment purchased in transaction *d*.

k. The company paid $2,500 cash for the office secretary's wages for this period.

Required

1. Create a table like the one in Exhibit 1.9, using the following headings for the columns: Cash; Accounts Receivable; Office Supplies; Office Equipment; Building; Accounts Payable; Notes Payable; Common Stock; Dividends; Revenues; and Expenses.

Check (2) Ending balances: Cash,
$9,200; Expenses, $3,500; Notes
Payable, $250,000

(3) Net income, $8,500

2. Use additions and subtractions within the table created in part *1* to show the dollar effects of each transaction on individual items of the accounting equation. Show new balances after each transaction.

3. Once you have completed the table, determine the company's net income.

Problem 1-8A
Analyzing transactions and
preparing financial statements

C4 P1 P2

mhhe.com/wildFINMAN4e

J. D. Simpson started The Simpson Co., a new business that began operations on May 1. The Simpson Co. completed the following transactions during its first month of operations.

May 1   J. D. Simpson invested $60,000 cash in the company in exchange for common stock.
     1   The company rented a furnished office and paid $3,200 cash for May's rent.
     3   The company purchased $1,680 of office equipment on credit.
     5   The company paid $800 cash for this month's cleaning services.
     8   The company provided consulting services for a client and immediately collected $4,600 cash.
    12   The company provided $3,000 of consulting services for a client on credit.
    15   The company paid $850 cash for an assistant's salary for the first half of this month.
    20   The company received $3,000 cash payment for the services provided on May 12.
    22   The company provided $2,800 of consulting services on credit.
    25   The company received $2,800 cash payment for the services provided on May 22.
    26   The company paid $1,680 cash for the office equipment purchased on May 3.
    27   The company purchased $60 of advertising in this month's (May) local paper on credit; cash payment is due June 1.
    28   The company paid $850 cash for an assistant's salary for the second half of this month.
    30   The company paid $200 cash for this month's telephone bill.
    30   The company paid $480 cash for this month's utilities.
    31   The company paid $1,200 cash for dividends.

Required

1. Arrange the following asset, liability, and equity titles in a table like Exhibit 1.9: Cash; Accounts Receivable; Office Equipment; Accounts Payable; Common Stock; Dividends; Revenues; and Expenses.

2. Show effects of the transactions on the accounts of the accounting equation by recording increases and decreases in the appropriate columns. Do not determine new account balances after each transaction. Determine the final total for each account and verify that the equation is in balance.

Check   (2) Ending balances: Cash, $61,140; Expenses, $6,440

3. Prepare an income statement for May, a statement of retained earnings for May, a May 31 balance sheet, and a statement of cash flows for May.

(3) Net income, $3,960; Total assets, $62,820

Curtis Hamilton started a new business and completed these transactions during December.

Problem 1-9A

Analyzing transactions and preparing financial statements

C4 P1 P2

mhhe.com/wildFINMAN4e

Dec.	1	Curtis Hamilton transferred $56,000 cash from a personal savings account to a checking account in the name of Hamilton Electric in exchange for common stock.
	2	The company rented office space and paid $800 cash for the December rent.
	3	The company purchased $14,000 of electrical equipment by paying $3,200 cash and agreeing to pay the $10,800 balance in 30 days.
	5	The company purchased office supplies by paying $900 cash.
	6	The company completed electrical work and immediately collected $1,000 cash for these services.
	8	The company purchased $3,800 of office equipment on credit.
	15	The company completed electrical work on credit in the amount of $4,000.
	18	The company purchased $500 of office supplies on credit.
	20	The company paid $3,800 cash for the office equipment purchased on December 8.
	24	The company billed a client $600 for electrical work completed; the balance is due in 30 days.
	28	The company received $4,000 cash for the work completed on December 15.
	29	The company paid the assistant's salary of $1,200 cash for this month.
	30	The company paid $440 cash for this month's utility bill.
	31	The company paid $700 cash for dividends.

Required

1. Arrange the following asset, liability, and equity titles in a table like Exhibit 1.9: Cash; Accounts Receivable; Office Supplies; Office Equipment; Electrical Equipment; Accounts Payable; Common Stock; Dividends; Revenues; and Expenses.

2. Use additions and subtractions to show the effects of each transaction on the accounts in the accounting equation. Show new balances after each transaction.

Check   (2) Ending balances: Cash, $49,960, Accounts Payable, $11,300

3. Use the increases and decreases in the columns of the table from part 2 to prepare an income statement, a statement of retained earnings, and a statement of cash flows—each of these for the current month. Also prepare a balance sheet as of the end of the month.

(3) Net income, $3,160; Total assets, $69,760

Analysis Component

4. Assume that the owner investment transaction on December 1 was $40,000 cash instead of $56,000 and that Hamilton Electric obtained another $16,000 in cash by borrowing it from a bank. Explain the effect of this change on total assets, total liabilities, and total equity.

Nolan manufactures, markets, and sells cellular telephones. The average total assets for Nolan is $250,000. In its most recent year, Nolan reported net income of $55,000 on revenues of $455,000.

Problem 1-10A

Determining expenses, liabilities, equity, and return on assets

A1 A2

Required

1. What is Nolan's return on assets?

2. Does return on assets seem satisfactory for Nolan given that its competitors average a 12% return on assets?

3. What are total expenses for Nolan in its most recent year?

4. What is the average total amount of liabilities plus equity for Nolan?

Check   (3) $400,000
(4) $250,000

Coca-Cola and **PepsiCo** both produce and market beverages that are direct competitors. Key financial figures (in $ millions) for these businesses over the past year follow.

Problem 1-11A

Computing and interpreting return on assets

A2

Key Figures ($ millions)	Coca-Cola	PepsiCo
Sales	$30,990	$43,232
Net income	6,906	5,979
Average assets	44,595	37,921

Required

1. Compute return on assets for (*a*) Coca-Cola and (*b*) PepsiCo.
2. Which company is more successful in its total amount of sales to consumers?
3. Which company is more successful in returning net income from its assets invested?

Analysis Component

4. Write a one-paragraph memorandum explaining which company you would invest your money in and why. (Limit your explanation to the information provided.)

Problem 1-12A[A]

Identifying risk and return

A3

All business decisions involve aspects of risk and return.

Required

Identify both the risk and the return in each of the following activities:

1. Investing $1,000 in a 4% savings account.
2. Placing a $1,000 bet on your favorite sports team.
3. Investing $10,000 in Yahoo! stock.
4. Taking out a $10,000 college loan to earn an accounting degree.

Problem 1-13A[B]

Describing organizational activities   C5

An organization undertakes various activities in pursuit of business success. Identify an organization's three major business activities, and describe each activity.

Problem 1-14A[B]

Describing organizational activities

C5

A start-up company often engages in the following transactions in its first year of operations. Classify those transactions in one of the three major categories of an organization's business activities.

F. Financing   **I.** Investing   **O.** Operating

_____ **1.** Owner investing land in business.
_____ **2.** Purchasing a building.
_____ **3.** Purchasing land.
_____ **4.** Borrowing cash from a bank.

_____ **5.** Purchasing equipment.
_____ **6.** Selling and distributing products.
_____ **7.** Paying for advertising.
_____ **8.** Paying employee wages.

PROBLEM SET B

Problem 1-1B

Identifying effects of transactions on financial statements   A1   P1

Identify how each of the following separate transactions affects financial statements. For the balance sheet, identify how each transaction affects total assets, total liabilities, and total equity. For the income statement, identify how each transaction affects net income. For the statement of cash flows, identify how each transaction affects cash flows from operating activities, cash flows from financing activities, and cash flows from investing activities. For increases, place a "+" in the column or columns. For decreases, place a "−" in the column or columns. If both an increase and a decrease occur, place "+/−" in the column or columns. The first transaction is completed as an example.

		Balance Sheet			Income Statement	Statement of Cash Flows		
	Transaction	Total Assets	Total Liab.	Total Equity	Net Income	Operating Activities	Financing Activities	Investing Activities
1	Owner invests cash for stock	+		+			+	
2	Buys building by signing note payable							
3	Pays cash for salaries incurred							
4	Provides services for cash							
5	Pays cash for rent incurred							
6	Incurs utilities costs on credit							
7	Buys store equipment for cash							
8	Pays cash dividend							
9	Provides services on credit							
10	Collects cash on receivable from (9)							

The following financial statement information is from five separate companies.

Problem 1-2B
Computing missing information using accounting knowledge

A1 P1

	Company V	Company W	Company X	Company Y	Company Z
December 31, 2010					
Assets.............................	$45,000	$70,000	$121,500	$82,500	$124,000
Liabilities	30,000	50,000	58,500	61,500	?
December 31, 2011					
Assets.............................	49,000	90,000	136,500	?	160,000
Liabilities	26,000	?	55,500	72,000	52,000
During year 2011					
Stock issuances	6,000	10,000	?	38,100	40,000
Net income or (loss)............	?	30,000	16,500	24,000	32,000
Cash dividends	4,500	2,000	0	18,000	6,000

Required

1. Answer the following questions about Company V:
   a. What is the amount of equity on December 31, 2010?
   b. What is the amount of equity on December 31, 2011?
   c. What is the net income or loss for the year 2011?
2. Answer the following questions about Company W:
   a. What is the amount of equity on December 31, 2010?
   b. What is the amount of equity on December 31, 2011?
   c. What is the amount of liabilities on December 31, 2011?
3. Calculate the amount of stock issuances for Company X during 2011.
4. Calculate the amount of assets for Company Y on December 31, 2011.
5. Calculate the amount of liabilities for Company Z on December 31, 2010.

Check (1*b*) $23,000

(2*c*) $32,000

(4) $137,100

The following is selected financial information for RWB Company as of December 31, 2011.

Problem 1-3B
Preparing a balance sheet

P2

Liabilities	$74,000	Equity	$40,000	Assets	$114,000

Required

Prepare the balance sheet for RWB Company as of December 31, 2011.

Selected financial information for Online Company for the year ended December 31, 2011, follows.

Problem 1-4B
Preparing an income statement

P2

Revenues	$58,000	Expenses	$30,000	Net income	$28,000

Required

Prepare the 2011 income statement for Online Company.

Following is selected financial information of ComEx for the year ended December 31, 2011.

Problem 1-5B
Preparing a statement of retained earnings

P2

Retained earnings, Dec. 31, 2011	$47,000	Cash dividends	$ 8,000
Net income	6,000	Retained earnings, Dec. 31, 2010	49,000

Required

Prepare the 2011 statement of retained earnings for ComEx.

Problem 1-6B
Preparing a statement of
cash flows

P2

Selected financial information of BuyRight Company for the year ended December 31, 2011, follows.

Cash from investing activities	$2,600
Net increase in cash	1,400
Cash from financing activities	2,800
Cash used by operating activities	(4,000)
Cash, December 31, 2010	1,300

Required

Prepare the 2011 statement of cash flows for BuyRight Company.

Problem 1-7B
Analyzing effects of transactions

C4 P1 P2 A1

Tiana Moore started a new business, Tiana's Solutions, and completed the following transactions during its first year of operations.

a. T. Moore invests $95,000 cash and office equipment valued at $20,000 in the company in exchange for common stock.

b. The company purchased a $120,000 building to use as an office. It paid $20,000 in cash and signed a note payable promising to pay the $100,000 balance over the next ten years.

c. The company purchased office equipment for $20,000 cash.

d. The company purchased $1,400 of office supplies and $3,000 of office equipment on credit.

e. The company paid a local newspaper $400 cash for printing an announcement of the office's opening.

f. The company completed a financial plan for a client and billed that client $1,800 for the service.

g. The company designed a financial plan for another client and immediately collected a $2,000 cash fee.

h. The company paid $5,000 cash for dividends.

i. The company received $1,800 cash from the client described in transaction f.

j. The company made a payment of $2,000 cash on the equipment purchased in transaction d.

k. The company paid $2,000 cash for the office secretary's wages.

Required

1. Create a table like the one in Exhibit 1.9, using the following headings for the columns: Cash; Accounts Receivable; Office Supplies; Office Equipment; Building; Accounts Payable; Notes Payable; Common Stock; Dividends; Revenues; and Expenses.

2. Use additions and subtractions within the table created in part 1 to show the dollar effects of each transaction on individual items of the accounting equation. Show new balances after each transaction.

3. Once you have completed the table, determine the company's net income.

Check (2) Ending balances: Cash, $49,400; Expenses, $2,400; Notes Payable, $100,000

(3) Net income, $1,400

Problem 1-8B
Analyzing transactions and
preparing financial statements

C4 P1 P2

Ken Stone launched a new business, Ken's Maintenance Co., that began operations on June 1. The following transactions were completed by the company during that first month.

June	1	K. Stone invested $120,000 cash in the company in exchange for common stock.
	2	The company rented a furnished office and paid $4,500 cash for June's rent.
	4	The company purchased $2,400 of equipment on credit.
	6	The company paid $1,125 cash for this month's advertising of the opening of the business.
	8	The company completed maintenance services for a customer and immediately collected $750 cash.
	14	The company completed $6,300 of maintenance services for City Center on credit.
	16	The company paid $900 cash for an assistant's salary for the first half of the month.
	20	The company received $6,300 cash payment for services completed for City Center on June 14.
	21	The company completed $3,500 of maintenance services for Skyway Co. on credit.
	24	The company completed $825 of maintenance services for Comfort Motel on credit.
	25	The company received $3,500 cash payment from Skyway Co. for the work completed on June 21.
	26	The company made payment of $2,400 cash for equipment purchased on June 4.
	28	The company paid $900 cash for an assistant's salary for the second half of this month.
	29	The company paid $2,000 cash for dividends.
	30	The company paid $120 cash for this month's telephone bill.
	30	The company paid $525 cash for this month's utilities.

Required

1. Arrange the following asset, liability, and equity titles in a table like Exhibit 1.9: Cash; Accounts Receivable; Equipment; Accounts Payable; Common Stock; Dividends; Revenues; and Expenses.

2. Show the effects of the transactions on the accounts of the accounting equation by recording increases and decreases in the appropriate columns. Do not determine new account balances after each transaction. Determine the final total for each account and verify that the equation is in balance.

3. Prepare a June income statement, a June statement of retained earnings, a June 30 balance sheet, and a June statement of cash flows.

Check   (2) Ending balances: Cash, $118,080; Expenses, $8,070

(3) Net income, $3,305; Total assets, $121,305

Swender Excavating Co., owned by Patrick Swender, began operations in July and completed these transactions during that first month of operations.

Problem 1-9B
Analyzing transactions and preparing financial statements

C4 P1 P2

July 1   P. Swender invested $60,000 cash in the company in exchange for common stock.
2   The company rented office space and paid $500 cash for the July rent.
3   The company purchased excavating equipment for $4,000 by paying $800 cash and agreeing to pay the $3,200 balance in 30 days.
6   The company purchased office supplies for $500 cash.
8   The company completed work for a customer and immediately collected $2,200 cash for the work.
10   The company purchased $3,800 of office equipment on credit.
15   The company completed work for a customer on credit in the amount of $2,400.
17   The company purchased $1,920 of office supplies on credit.
23   The company paid $3,800 cash for the office equipment purchased on July 10.
25   The company billed a customer $5,000 for work completed; the balance is due in 30 days.
28   The company received $2,400 cash for the work completed on July 15.
30   The company paid an assistant's salary of $1,260 cash for this month.
31   The company paid $260 cash for this month's utility bill.
31   The company paid $1,200 cash for dividends.

Required

1. Arrange the following asset, liability, and equity titles in a table like Exhibit 1.9: Cash; Accounts Receivable; Office Supplies; Office Equipment; Excavating Equipment; Accounts Payable; Common Stock; Dividends; Revenues; and Expenses.

2. Use additions and subtractions to show the effects of each transaction on the accounts in the accounting equation. Show new balances after each transaction.

3. Use the increases and decreases in the columns of the table from part 2 to prepare an income statement, a statement of retained earnings, and a statement of cash flows—each of these for the current month. Also prepare a balance sheet as of the end of the month.

Check   (2) Ending balances: Cash, $56,280; Accounts Payable, $5,120

(3) Net income, $7,580; Total assets, $71,500

Analysis Component

4. Assume that the $4,000 purchase of excavating equipment on July 3 was financed from an owner investment of another $4,000 cash in the business in exchange for more common stock (instead of the purchase conditions described in the transaction). Explain the effect of this change on total assets, total liabilities, and total equity.

Aspen Company manufactures, markets, and sells ATV and snowmobile equipment and accessories. The average total assets for Aspen is $2,000,000. In its most recent year, Aspen reported net income of $100,000 on revenues of $1,200,000.

Problem 1-10B
Determining expenses, liabilities, equity, and return on assets

A1 A2

Required

1. What is Aspen Company's return on assets?

2. Does return on assets seem satisfactory for Aspen given that its competitors average a 9.5% return on assets?

3. What are the total expenses for Aspen Company in its most recent year?

4. What is the average total amount of liabilities plus equity for Aspen Company?

Check   (3) $1,100,000

(4) $2,000,000

AT&T and **Verizon** produce and market telecommunications products and are competitors. Key financial figures (in $ millions) for these businesses over the past year follow.

Problem 1-11B
Computing and interpreting return on assets

A2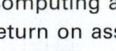

Key Figures ($ millions)	AT&T	Verizon
Sales	$123,018	$107,808
Net income	12,535	10,358
Average assets	266,999	214,937

Required

1. Compute return on assets for (*a*) AT&T and (*b*) Verizon.
2. Which company is more successful in the total amount of sales to consumers?
3. Which company is more successful in returning net income from its assets invested?

Analysis Component

4. Write a one-paragraph memorandum explaining which company you would invest your money in and why. (Limit your explanation to the information provided.)

Problem 1-12B[A]
Identifying risk and return

A3

All business decisions involve aspects of risk and return.

Required

Identify both the risk and the return in each of the following activities:

1. Stashing $1,000 cash under your mattress.
2. Placing a $500 bet on a horse running in the Kentucky Derby.
3. Investing $10,000 in Nike stock.
4. Investing $10,000 in U.S. Savings Bonds.

Problem 1-13B[B]
Describing organizational activities C5

Identify in outline format the three major business activities of an organization. For each of these activities, identify at least two specific transactions or events normally undertaken by the business's owners or its managers.

Problem 1-14B[B]
Describing organizational activities

C5

A start-up company often engages in the following activities during its first year of operations. Classify each of the following activities into one of the three major activities of an organization.

A. Financing   **B.** Investing   **C.** Operating

_____ **1.** Providing client services.   _____ **5.** Supervising workers.
_____ **2.** Obtaining a bank loan.   _____ **6.** Owner investing money in business.
_____ **3.** Purchasing machinery.   _____ **7.** Renting office space.
_____ **4.** Research for its products.   _____ **8.** Paying utilities expenses.

This serial problem starts in this chapter and continues throughout most chapters of the book. It is most readily solved if you use the Working Papers that accompany this book (but working papers are not required).

SERIAL PROBLEM
Business Solutions

C4   P1

SP 1   On October 1, 2011, Santana Rey launched a computer services company, **Business Solutions,** that is organized as a corporation and provides consulting services, computer system installations, and custom program development. Rey adopts the calendar year for reporting purposes and expects to prepare the company's first set of financial statements on December 31, 2011.

Required

Create a table like the one in Exhibit 1.9 using the following headings for columns: Cash; Accounts Receivable; Computer Supplies; Computer System; Office Equipment; Accounts Payable; Common Stock; Dividends; Revenues; and Expenses. Then use additions and subtractions within the table created to show the dollar effects for each of the following October transactions for Business Solutions on the individual items of the accounting equation. Show new balances after each transaction.

Oct.   1   S. Rey invested $45,000 cash, a $20,000 computer system, and $8,000 of office equipment in the company in exchange for common stock.
       3   The company purchased $1,420 of computer supplies on credit from Harris Office Products.
       6   The company billed Easy Leasing $4,800 for services performed in installing a new Web server.
       8   The company paid $1,420 cash for the computer supplies purchased from Harris Office Products on October 3.
      10   The company hired Lyn Addie as a part-time assistant for $125 per day, as needed.
      12   The company billed Easy Leasing another $1,400 for services performed.
      15   The company received $4,800 cash from Easy Leasing as partial payment toward its account.
      17   The company paid $805 cash to repair computer equipment damaged when moving it.
      20   The company paid $1,728 cash for advertisements published in the local newspaper.
      22   The company received $1,400 cash from Easy Leasing toward its account.
      28   The company billed IFM Company $5,208 for services performed.
      31   The company paid $875 cash for Lyn Addie's wages for seven days of work this month.
      31   The company paid $3,600 cash for dividends.

> *Beyond the Numbers (BTN)* is a special problem section aimed to refine communication, conceptual, analysis, and research skills. It includes many activities helpful in developing an active learning environment.

Beyond the Numbers

BTN 1-1 Key financial figures for **Research In Motion**'s fiscal year ended February 27, 2010, follow.

Key Figure	In Millions
Liabilities + Equity.........	$10,204
Net income	2,457
Revenues	14,953

REPORTING IN ACTION

A1 A2 A3

RIM

Required

1. What is the total amount of assets invested in Research In Motion?
2. What is Research In Motion's return on assets? Its assets at February 28, 2009, equal $8,101 (in millions).
3. How much are total expenses for Research In Motion for the year ended February 27, 2010?
4. Does Research In Motion's return on assets seem satisfactory if competitors average an 18% return?

Check (2) 26.8%

Fast Forward

5. Access Research In Motion's financial statements (Form 10-K) for fiscal years ending after February 27, 2010, from its Website (**RIM.com**) or from the SEC Website (**www.SEC.gov**) and compute its return on assets for those fiscal years. Compare the February 27, 2010, fiscal year-end return on assets to any subsequent years' returns you are able to compute, and interpret the results.

BTN 1-2 Key comparative figures ($ millions) for both **Research In Motion** and **Apple** follow.

Key Figure	Research In Motion	Apple
Liabilities + Equity.........	$10,204	$47,501
Net income	2,457	8,235
Revenues and sales	14,953	42,905

COMPARATIVE ANALYSIS

A1 A2 A3

RIM

Apple

Required

1. What is the total amount of assets invested in (*a*) Research In Motion and (*b*) Apple?
2. What is the return on assets for (*a*) Research In Motion and (*b*) Apple? Research In Motion's beginning-year assets equal $8,101 (in millions) and Apple's beginning-year assets equal $36,171 (in millions).
3. How much are expenses for (*a*) Research In Motion and (*b*) Apple?
4. Is return on assets satisfactory for (*a*) Research In Motion and (*b*) Apple? (Assume competitors average an 18% return.)
5. What can you conclude about Research In Motion and Apple from these computations?

Check (2b) 19.7%

BTN 1-3 Madison Thorne works in a public accounting firm and hopes to eventually be a partner. The management of Allnet Company invites Thorne to prepare a bid to audit Allnet's financial statements. In discussing the audit fee, Allnet's management suggests a fee range in which the amount depends on the reported profit of Allnet. The higher its profit, the higher will be the audit fee paid to Thorne's firm.

ETHICS CHALLENGE

C3 C4

Required

1. Identify the parties potentially affected by this audit and the fee plan proposed.
2. What are the ethical factors in this situation? Explain.
3. Would you recommend that Thorne accept this audit fee arrangement? Why or why not?
4. Describe some ethical considerations guiding your recommendation.

COMMUNICATING IN PRACTICE

A1 C2

BTN 1-4 Refer to this chapter's opening feature about **Facebook**.® Assume that Mark Zuckerberg desires to expand his online services to meet people's demands. He decides to meet with his banker to discuss a loan to allow Facebook to expand.

Required

1. Prepare a half-page report outlining the information you would request from Mark Zuckerberg if you were the loan officer.
2. Indicate whether the information you request and your loan decision are affected by the form of business organization for Facebook.

TAKING IT TO THE NET

A2

BTN 1-5 Visit the EDGAR database at (**www.sec.gov**). Access the Form 10-K report of **Rocky Mountain Chocolate Factory** (ticker RMCF) filed on May 26, 2009, covering its 2009 fiscal year.

Required

1. Item 6 of the 10-K report provides comparative financial highlights of RMCF for the years 2005–2009. How would you describe the revenue trend for RMCF over this five-year period?
2. Has RMCF been profitable (see net income) over this five-year period? Support your answer.

TEAMWORK IN ACTION

C1

BTN 1-6 Teamwork is important in today's business world. Successful teams schedule convenient meetings, maintain regular communications, and cooperate with and support their members. This assignment aims to establish support/learning teams, initiate discussions, and set meeting times.

Required

1. Form teams and open a team discussion to determine a regular time and place for your team to meet between each scheduled class meeting. Notify your instructor via a memorandum or e-mail message as to when and where your team will hold regularly scheduled meetings.
2. Develop a list of telephone numbers and/or e-mail addresses of your teammates.

ENTREPRENEURIAL DECISION

A1 P1

BTN 1-7 Refer to this chapter's opening feature about **Facebook**. Assume that Mark Zuckerberg decides to open a new Website devoted to social networking for accountants and those studying accounting. This new company will be called AccountBook.

Required

1. AccountBook obtains a $500,000 loan and Mark Zuckerberg contributes $250,000 of his own assets in exchange for common stock in the new company.
   a. What is the new company's total amount of liabilities plus equity?
   b. What is the new company's total amount of assets?
2. If the new company earns $80,000 in net income in the first year of operation, compute its return on asset (assume average assets equal $750,000). Assess its performance if competitors average a 10% return.

Check   (2) 10.7%

HITTING THE ROAD

C2

BTN 1-8 You are to interview a local business owner. (This can be a friend or relative.) Opening lines of communication with members of the business community can provide personal benefits of business networking. If you do not know the owner, you should call ahead to introduce yourself and explain your position as a student and your assignment requirements. You should request a thirty minute appointment for a face-to-face or phone interview to discuss the form of organization and operations of the business. Be prepared to make a good impression.

Required

1. Identify and describe the main operating activities and the form of organization for this business.
2. Determine and explain why the owner(s) chose this particular form of organization.
3. Identify any special advantages and/or disadvantages the owner(s) experiences in operating with this form of business organization.

BTN 1-9   Nokia (www.Nokia.com) is a leading manufacturer of mobile devices and services, and it competes to some extent with both **Research In Motion** and **Apple**. Key financial figures for Nokia follow.

GLOBAL DECISION

A1 A2 A3

NOKIA
RIM
Apple

Key Figure*	Euro (EUR) in Millions
Average assets.................	37,660
Net income	260
Revenue	40,984
Return on assets	0.7%

* Figures prepared in accordance with International Financial Reporting Standards.

Required

1. Identify any concerns you have in comparing Nokia's income and revenue figures to those of Research In Motion and Apple (in BTN 1-2) for purposes of making business decisions.

2. Identify any concerns you have in comparing Nokia's return on assets ratio to those of Research In Motion and Apple (computed for BTN 1-2) for purposes of making business decisions.

ANSWERS TO MULTIPLE CHOICE QUIZ

1. c; $450,000 is the actual cost incurred.
2. b; revenue is recorded when earned.
3. d;

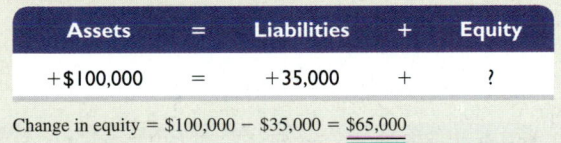

Assets	=	Liabilities	+	Equity
+$100,000	=	+35,000	+	?

Change in equity = $100,000 − $35,000 = $65,000

4. a
5. a

2

Analyzing and Recording Transactions

A Look Back

Chapter 1 defined accounting and introduced financial statements. We described forms of organizations and identified users and uses of accounting. We defined the accounting equation and applied it to transaction analysis.

A Look at This Chapter

This chapter focuses on the accounting process. We describe transactions and source documents, and we explain the analysis and recording of transactions. The accounting equation, T-account, general ledger, trial balance, and debits and credits are key tools in the accounting process.

A Look Ahead

Chapter 3 extends our focus on processing information. We explain the importance of adjusting accounts and the procedures in preparing financial statements.

Learning Objectives

CONCEPTUAL

C1 Explain the steps in processing transactions and the role of source documents. (p. 50)

C2 Describe an account and its use in recording transactions. (p. 51)

C3 Describe a ledger and a chart of accounts. (p. 54)

C4 Define *debits* and *credits* and explain double-entry accounting. (p. 55)

ANALYTICAL

A1 Analyze the impact of transactions on accounts and financial statements. (p. 59)

A2 Compute the debt ratio and describe its use in analyzing financial condition. (p. 69)

LP2

PROCEDURAL

P1 Record transactions in a journal and post entries to a ledger. (p. 56)

P2 Prepare and explain the use of a trial balance. (p. 65)

P3 Prepare financial statements from business transactions. (p. 66)

Sole Sisters

"Every way we can cut costs, we do!"

—SUSIE LEVITT (on right)

NEW YORK—"High heels were killing our feet, but we didn't want to give them up because we aren't the tallest people out there," insists Susie Levitt, who stands no taller than 5'2". "So we came up with the idea of emergency footwear." Susie, along with Katie Shea, designed a stylish, foldable slip-on ballet flat with a pouch that is readily tucked into a handbag and pulled out when their feet cry for mercy. The empty pouch then expands into a tote bag to hold their "killer" heels for carrying home. Launched from their college apartment, Susie and Katie invested "less than $10,000" for the cost of their first order of 1,000 pairs, including Website design, to launch **CitySlips** (**www.cityslips.com**).

To pursue their business ambitions, Susie and Katie took business courses, including accounting. They learned and applied recordkeeping processes, transaction analysis, inventory accounting, and financial statement reporting. We were careful to get a handle on our financial situation, says Katie. Today, the two are running a profitable business and have a reliable accounting system to help them make good business decisions.

We had to account for product costs, design expenses, supplier payments, patent fees, and other expenses, says Susie. At the same time, the two have grown sales and expanded their product line. "It was all done online," says Susie. "We became nocturnal!"

The two insist that it is crucial to track and account for all revenues and expenses, and what is invested in the business. They maintain that success requires proper accounting for and analysis of the financial side. Susie also suggests that young entrepreneurs "network with your professors and other staff members. They have years of experience and can often help you, or introduce you to people who can help you, with your business."

The bigger message of our company, says Susie, is promoting comfort and confidence for women. Adds Katie, "Regardless of what your business is, the story of starting while in college, differentiates you from the beginning!"

[Sources: *CitySlips Website,* January 2011; *Entrepreneur,* December 2009; *Examiner.com,* December 2009; *CNN.com,* August 2009; *Daily News,* May 2009]

Financial statements report on the financial performance and condition of an organization. Knowledge of their preparation, organization, and analysis is important. A main goal of this chapter is to illustrate how transactions are recorded, how they are reflected in financial statements, and how they impact analysis of financial statements. Debits and credits are introduced and identified as a tool in helping analyze and process transactions.

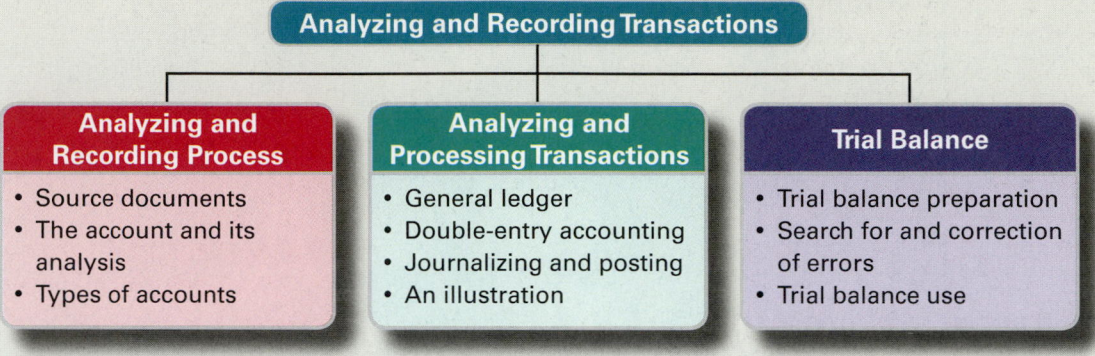

Analyzing and Recording Transactions

Analyzing and Recording Process	**Analyzing and Processing Transactions**	**Trial Balance**
• Source documents • The account and its analysis • Types of accounts	• General ledger • Double-entry accounting • Journalizing and posting • An illustration	• Trial balance preparation • Search for and correction of errors • Trial balance use

ANALYZING AND RECORDING PROCESS

EXHIBIT 2.1

The Analyzing and Recording Process

The accounting process identifies business transactions and events, analyzes and records their effects, and summarizes and presents information in reports and financial statements. These reports and statements are used for making investing, lending, and other business decisions. The steps in the accounting process that focus on *analyzing and recording* transactions and events are shown in Exhibit 2.1.

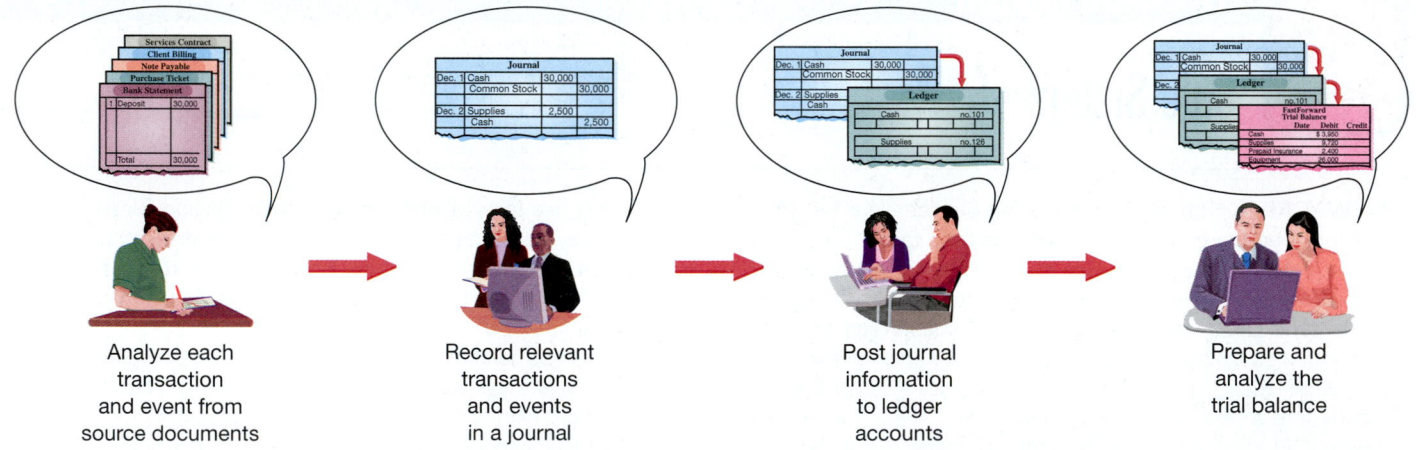

| Analyze each transaction and event from source documents | Record relevant transactions and events in a journal | Post journal information to ledger accounts | Prepare and analyze the trial balance |

C1 Explain the steps in processing transactions and the role of source documents.

Business transactions and events are the starting points. Relying on source documents, the transactions and events are analyzed using the accounting equation to understand how they affect company performance and financial position. These effects are recorded in accounting records, informally referred to as the *accounting books,* or simply the *books*. Additional steps such as posting and then preparing a trial balance help summarize and classify the effects of transactions and events. Ultimately, the accounting process provides information in useful reports or financial statements to decision makers.

Source Documents

Source documents identify and describe transactions and events entering the accounting process. They are the sources of accounting information and can be in either hard copy or electronic form. Examples are sales tickets, checks, purchase orders, bills from suppliers, employee earnings records, and bank statements. To illustrate, when an item is purchased on credit, the seller usually prepares at least two copies of a sales invoice. One copy is given to the buyer. Another copy, often sent electronically, results in an entry in the seller's information system to record the sale. Sellers use invoices for recording sales and for control; buyers use them for recording purchases and for monitoring purchasing activity. Many cash registers record information for each sale on a tape or electronic file locked inside the register. This record can be used as a source document for recording sales in the accounting records. Source documents, especially if obtained from outside the organization, provide objective and reliable evidence about transactions and events and their amounts.

Point: To ensure that all sales are rung up on the register, most sellers require customers to have their receipts to exchange or return purchased items.

■ **Decision Ethics**   Answer — p. 74

Cashier   Your manager requires that you, as cashier, immediately enter each sale. Recently, lunch hour traffic has increased and the assistant manager asks you to avoid delays by taking customers' cash and making change without entering sales. The assistant manager says she will add up cash and enter sales after lunch. She says that, in this way, the register will always match the cash amount when the manager arrives at three o'clock. What do you do? ■

The Account and Its Analysis

An **account** is a record of increases and decreases in a specific asset, liability, equity, revenue, or expense item. Information from an account is analyzed, summarized, and presented in reports and financial statements. The **general ledger,** or simply **ledger,** is a record containing all accounts used by a company. The ledger is often in electronic form. While most companies' ledgers contain similar accounts, a company often uses one or more unique accounts because of its type of operations. As shown in Exhibit 2.2, accounts are classified into three general categories based on the accounting equation: asset, liability, or equity.

C2 Describe an account and its use in recording transactions.

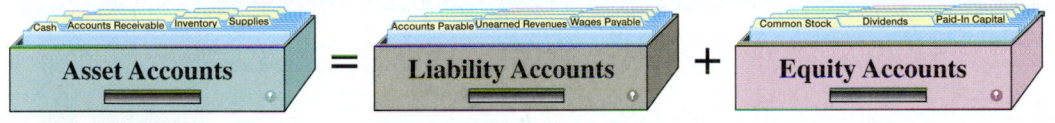

EXHIBIT 2.2

Accounts Organized by the Accounting Equation

Asset Accounts   Assets are resources owned or controlled by a company, and those resources have expected future benefits. Most accounting systems include (at a minimum) separate accounts for the assets described here.

A *Cash* account reflects a company's cash balance. All increases and decreases in cash are recorded in the Cash account. It includes money and any medium of exchange that a bank accepts for deposit (coins, checks, money orders, and checking account balances).

Accounts receivable are held by a seller and refer to promises of payment from customers to sellers. These transactions are often called *credit sales* or *sales on account* (or *on credit*). Accounts receivable are increased by credit sales and are decreased by customer payments. A company needs a separate record for each customer, but for now, we use the simpler practice of recording all increases and decreases in receivables in a single account called Accounts Receivable.

Point: Customers and others who owe a company are called its **debtors.**

A *note receivable,* or promissory note, is a written promise of another entity to pay a definite sum of money on a specified future date to the holder of the note. A company holding a promissory note signed by another entity has an asset that is recorded in a Note (or Notes) Receivable account.

Prepaid accounts (also called *prepaid expenses*) are assets that represent prepayments of future expenses (*not* current expenses). When the expenses are later incurred, the amounts in prepaid accounts are transferred to expense accounts. Common examples of prepaid accounts include prepaid insurance, prepaid rent, and prepaid services (such as club memberships). Prepaid accounts expire with the passage of time (such as with rent) or through use (such as with prepaid meal tickets). When financial statements are prepared, prepaid accounts are adjusted so that (1) all expired and used prepaid accounts are recorded as regular expenses and (2) all unexpired and unused prepaid accounts are recorded as assets (reflecting future use in

Point: A college parking fee is a prepaid account from the student's standpoint. At the beginning of the term, it represents an asset that entitles a student to park on or near campus. The benefits of the parking fee expire as the term progresses. At term-end, prepaid parking (asset) equals zero as it has been entirely recorded as parking expense.

Point: Prepaid accounts that apply to current and future periods are assets. These assets are adjusted at the end of each period to reflect only those amounts that have not yet expired, and to record as expenses those amounts that have expired.

future periods). To illustrate, when an insurance fee, called a *premium,* is paid in advance, the cost is typically recorded in the asset account Prepaid Insurance. Over time, the expiring portion of the insurance cost is removed from this asset account and reported in expenses on the income statement. Any unexpired portion remains in Prepaid Insurance and is reported on the balance sheet as an asset. (An exception exists for prepaid accounts that will expire or be used before the end of the current accounting period when financial statements are prepared. In this case, the prepayments *can* be recorded immediately as expenses.)

Supplies are assets until they are used. When they are used up, their costs are reported as expenses. The costs of unused supplies are recorded in a Supplies asset account. Supplies are often grouped by purpose—for example, office supplies and store supplies. *Office supplies* include stationery, paper, toner, and pens. *Store supplies* include packaging materials, plastic and paper bags, gift boxes and cartons, and cleaning materials. The costs of these unused supplies can be recorded in an Office Supplies or a Store Supplies asset account. When supplies are used, their costs are transferred from the asset accounts to expense accounts.

Equipment is an asset. When equipment is used and gets worn down, its cost is gradually reported as an expense (called depreciation). Equipment is often grouped by its purpose—for example, office equipment and store equipment. *Office equipment* includes computers, printers, desks, chairs, and shelves. Costs incurred for these items are recorded in an Office Equipment asset account. The Store Equipment account includes the costs of assets used in a store, such as counters, showcases, ladders, hoists, and cash registers.

Point: Some assets are described as *intangible* because they do not have physical existence or their benefits are highly uncertain. A recent balance sheet for **Coca-Cola Company** shows nearly $1 billion in intangible assets.

Buildings such as stores, offices, warehouses, and factories are assets because they provide expected future benefits to those who control or own them. Their costs are recorded in a Buildings asset account. When several buildings are owned, separate accounts are sometimes kept for each of them.

The cost of *land* owned by a business is recorded in a Land account. The cost of buildings located on the land is separately recorded in one or more building accounts.

Decision Insight

Women Entrepreneurs   The Center for Women's Business Research reports that women-owned businesses, such as **CitySlips**, are growing and that they:

- Total approximately 11 million and employ nearly 20 million workers.
- Generate $2.5 trillion in annual sales and tend to embrace technology.
- Are philanthropic—70% of owners volunteer at least once per month.
- Are more likely funded by individual investors (73%) than venture firms (15%). ■

Liability Accounts   Liabilities are claims (by creditors) against assets, which means they are obligations to transfer assets or provide products or services to others. **Creditors** are individuals and organizations that have rights to receive payments from a company. If a company fails to pay its obligations, the law gives creditors a right to force the sale of that company's assets to obtain the money to meet creditors' claims. When assets are sold under these conditions, creditors are paid first, but only up to the amount of their claims. Any remaining money, the residual, goes to the owners of the company. Creditors often use a balance sheet to help decide whether to loan money to a company. A loan is less risky if the borrower's liabilities are small in comparison to assets because this means there are more resources than claims on resources. Common liability accounts are described here.

Point: Accounts payable are also called *trade payables.*

Accounts payable refer to oral or implied promises to pay later, which usually arise from purchases of merchandise. Payables can also arise from purchases of supplies, equipment, and services. Accounting systems keep separate records about each creditor. We describe these individual records in Chapter 4.

A *note payable* refers to a formal promise, usually denoted by the signing of a promissory note, to pay a future amount. It is recorded in either a short-term Note Payable account or a long-term Note Payable account, depending on when it must be repaid. We explain details of short- and long-term classification in Chapter 3.

Unearned revenue refers to a liability that is settled in the future when a company delivers its products or services. When customers pay in advance for products or services (before revenue is earned), the revenue recognition principle requires that the seller consider this payment as unearned revenue. Examples of unearned revenue include magazine subscriptions collected in advance by a publisher, sales of gift certificates by stores, and season ticket sales by sports teams. The seller would record these in liability accounts such as Unearned Subscriptions, Unearned Store Sales, and Unearned Ticket Revenue. When products and services are later delivered, the earned portion of the unearned revenue is transferred to revenue accounts such as Subscription Fees, Store Sales, and Ticket Sales.[1]

Accrued liabilities are amounts owed that are not yet paid. Examples are wages payable, taxes payable, and interest payable. These are often recorded in separate liability accounts by the same title. If they are not large in amount, one or more ledger accounts can be added and reported as a single amount on the balance sheet. (Financial statements often have amounts reported that are a summation of several ledger accounts.)

Point: If a subscription is canceled, the publisher is expected to refund the unused portion to the subscriber.

Decision **Insight**

Revenue Spread   The **New Orleans Saints** have *Unearned Revenues* of about $60 million in advance ticket sales. When the team plays its home games, it settles this liability to its ticket holders and then transfers the amount earned to *Ticket Revenues*. ∎

Equity Accounts   The owner's claim on a company's assets is called *equity*, or *stockholders' equity*, or *shareholders' equity*. Equity is the owners' *residual interest* in the assets of a business after deducting liabilities. Equity is impacted by four types of accounts: common stock, dividends, revenues, and expenses. We show this visually in Exhibit 2.3 by expanding the accounting equation. (As Chapter 1 explains, the accounts for dividends, revenues, and expenses are reflected in the retained earnings account, and that account is reported in the balance sheet.)

Point: Equity is also called *net assets*.

EXHIBIT 2.3

Expanded Accounting Equation

When an owner invests in a company in exchange for common stock, the invested amount is recorded in an account titled **Common Stock.** Any further owner investments are recorded in this account. When the company pays any cash dividends, it decreases both the company's assets and its total equity. Dividends are not expenses of the business. They are simply the opposite of owner investments. A **Dividends** account is used in recording asset distributions to stockholders (owners).

Point: The Dividends account is sometimes referred to as a *contra equity* account because it reduces the normal balance of equity.

Revenues and expenses also impact equity. Examples of revenue accounts are Sales, Commissions Earned, Professional Fees Earned, Rent Revenue, and Interest Revenue. *Revenues increase equity* and result from products and services provided to customers. Examples of expense accounts are Advertising Expense, Store Supplies Expense, Office Salaries Expense, Office Supplies Expense, Rent Expense, Utilities Expense, and Insurance Expense. *Expenses decrease equity* and result from assets and services used in a company's operations. The variety of revenues and expenses can be seen by looking at the *chart of accounts* that follows the index at the

Point: The withdrawal of assets by the owners of a corporation is called a *dividend*.

---

[1] In practice, account titles vary. As one example, Subscription Fees is sometimes called Subscription Fees Revenue, Subscription Fees Earned, or Earned Subscription Fees. As another example, Rent Earned is sometimes called Rent Revenue, Rental Revenue, or Earned Rent Revenue. We must use good judgment when reading financial statements because titles can differ even within the same industry. For example, product sales are called *revenue* at **Research In Motion**, but *net sales* at **Apple**. Generally, the term *revenues* or *fees* is more commonly used with service businesses, and *net sales* or *sales* with product businesses.

back of this book. (Different companies sometimes use different account titles than those in this book's chart of accounts. For example, some might use Interest Revenue instead of Interest Earned, or Rental Expense instead of Rent Expense. It is important only that an account title describe the item it represents.)

Decision Insight

Sporting Accounts   The **Los Angeles Lakers** and the other NBA teams have the following major revenue and expense accounts:

Revenues	Expenses
Basketball ticket sales	Team salaries
TV & radio broadcast fees	Game costs
Advertising revenues	NBA franchise costs
Basketball playoff receipts	Promotional costs ■

ANALYZING AND PROCESSING TRANSACTIONS

This section explains several tools and processes that comprise an accounting system. These include a ledger, T-account, debits and credits, double-entry accounting, journalizing, and posting.

Ledger and Chart of Accounts

 C3 Describe a ledger and a chart of accounts.

The collection of all accounts and their balances for an information system is called a *ledger* (or *general ledger*). If accounts are in files on a hard drive, the sum of those files is the ledger. If the accounts are pages in a file, that file is the ledger. A company's size and diversity of operations affect the number of accounts needed. A small company can get by with as few as 20 or 30 accounts; a large company can require several thousand. The **chart of accounts** is a list of all ledger accounts and includes an identification number assigned to each account. A small business might use the following numbering system for its accounts:

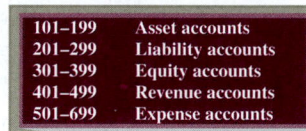

101–199	Asset accounts
201–299	Liability accounts
301–399	Equity accounts
401–499	Revenue accounts
501–699	Expense accounts

These numbers provide a three-digit code that is useful in recordkeeping. In this case, the first digit assigned to asset accounts is a 1, the first digit assigned to liability accounts is a 2, and so on. The second and third digits relate to the accounts' subcategories. Exhibit 2.4 shows a partial chart of accounts for FastForward, the focus company of Chapter 1. (Please review the more complete chart of accounts that follows the index at the back of this book.)

EXHIBIT 2.4

Partial Chart of Accounts for FastForward

Acct. No.	Account Name	Acct. No.	Account Name	Acct. No.	Account Name
101	Cash	236	Unearned consulting revenue	406	Rental revenue
106	Accounts receivable			622	Salaries expense
126	Supplies	307	Common stock	637	Insurance expense
128	Prepaid insurance	318	Retained earnings	640	Rent expense
167	Equipment	319	Dividends	652	Supplies expense
201	Accounts payable	403	Consulting revenue	690	Utilities expense

Debits and Credits

A **T-account** represents a ledger account and is a tool used to understand the effects of one or more transactions. Its name comes from its shape like the letter **T**. The layout of a T-account, shown in Exhibit 2.5, is (1) the account title on top, (2) a left, or debit side, and (3) a right, or credit, side.

The left side of an account is called the **debit** side, often abbreviated *Dr.* The right side is called the **credit** side, abbreviated *Cr.*[2] To enter amounts on the left side of an account is to *debit* the account. To enter amounts on the

Account Title	
(Left side)	(Right side)
Debit	**Credit**

right side is to *credit* the account. Do not make the error of thinking that the terms *debit* and *credit* mean increase or decrease. Whether a debit or a credit is an increase or decrease depends on the account. For an account where a debit is an increase, the credit is a decrease; for an account where a debit is a decrease, the credit is an increase. The difference between total debits and total credits for an account, including any beginning balance, is the **account balance.** When the sum of debits exceeds the sum of credits, the account has a *debit balance*. It has a *credit balance* when the sum of credits exceeds the sum of debits. When the sum of debits equals the sum of credits, the account has a *zero balance*.

Double-Entry Accounting

Double-entry accounting requires that for each transaction:

- At least two accounts are involved, with at least one debit and one credit.
- The total amount debited must equal the total amount credited.
- The accounting equation must not be violated.

This means the sum of the debits for all entries must equal the sum of the credits for all entries, and the sum of debit account balances in the ledger must equal the sum of credit account balances.

The system for recording debits and credits follows from the usual accounting equation—see Exhibit 2.6. Two points are important here. First, like any simple mathematical relation, net increases or decreases on one side have equal net effects on the other side. For example, a net increase in assets must be accompanied by an identical net increase on the liabilities and equity

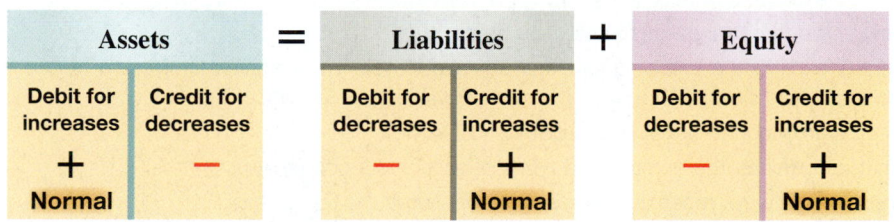

side. Recall that some transactions affect only one side of the equation, meaning that two or more accounts on one side are affected, but their net effect on this one side is zero. Second, the left side is the *normal balance* side for assets, and the right side is the *normal balance* side for liabilities and equity. This matches their layout in the accounting equation where assets are on the left side of this equation, and liabilities and equity are on the right.

Recall that equity increases from revenues and stock issuances, and it decreases from expenses and dividends. These important equity relations are conveyed by expanding the accounting equation to include debits and credits in double-entry form as shown in Exhibit 2.7.

Increases (credits) to common stock and revenues *increase* equity; increases (debits) to dividends and expenses *decrease* equity. The normal balance of each account (asset, liability, common stock, dividends, revenue, or expense) refers to the left or right (debit or credit) side where

---

[2] These abbreviations are remnants of 18th-century English recordkeeping practices where the terms *debitor* and *creditor* were used instead of *debit* and *credit*. The abbreviations use the first and last letters of these terms, just as we still do for Saint (St.) and Doctor (Dr.).

C4   Define *debits* and *credits* and explain double-entry accounting.

EXHIBIT 2.5

The T-Account

Point: Think of *debit* and *credit* as accounting directions for left and right.

"Total debits equal total credits for each entry."

EXHIBIT 2.6

Debits and Credits in the Accounting Equation

Point: Debits and credits do not mean favorable or unfavorable. A debit to an asset increases it, as does a debit to an expense. A credit to a liability increases it, as does a credit to a revenue.

EXHIBIT 2.7

Debit and Credit Effects for
Component Accounts

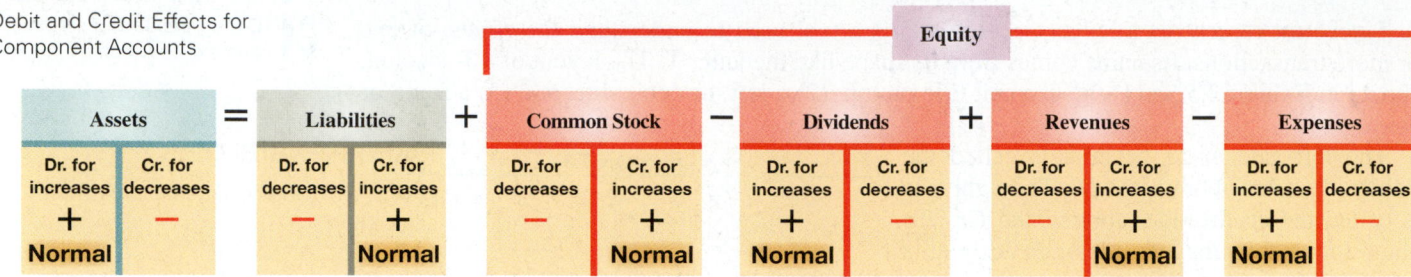

increases are recorded. Understanding these diagrams and rules is required to prepare, analyze, and interpret financial statements.

The T-account for FastForward's Cash account, reflecting its first 11 transactions (from Exhibit 1.9), is shown in Exhibit 2.8. The total increases in its Cash account are $36,100, the total decreases are $31,300, and the account's debit balance is $4,800. (We illustrate use of T-accounts later in this chapter.)

EXHIBIT 2.8

Computing the Balance for
a T-Account

Point: The ending balance is on the side with the larger dollar amount. Also, a plus (+) and minus (−) are not used in a T-account.

Cash			
Receive investment by owner for stock	30,000	Purchase of supplies	2,500
Consulting services revenue earned	4,200	Purchase of equipment	26,000
Collection of account receivable	1,900	Payment of rent	1,000
		Payment of salary	700
		Payment of account payable	900
		Payment of cash dividend	200
Balance	4,800		

Quick Check

Answers — p. 75

1. Identify examples of accounting source documents.
2. Explain the importance of source documents.
3. Identify each of the following as either an asset, a liability, or equity: (*a*) Prepaid Rent, (*b*) Unearned Fees, (*c*) Building, (*d*) Wages Payable, and (*e*) Office Supplies.
4. What is an account? What is a ledger?
5. What determines the number and types of accounts a company uses?
6. Does *debit* always mean increase and *credit* always mean decrease?
7. Describe a chart of accounts.

Journalizing and Posting Transactions

 P1 Record transactions in a journal and post entries to a ledger.

Processing transactions is a crucial part of accounting. The four usual steps of this process are depicted in Exhibit 2.9. Steps 1 and 2—involving transaction analysis and the accounting equation—were introduced in prior sections. This section extends that discussion and focuses on steps 3 and 4 of the accounting process. Step 3 is to record each transaction chronologically in a journal. A **journal** gives a complete record of each transaction in one place. It also shows debits and credits for each transaction. The process of recording transactions in a journal is called **journalizing.** Step 4 is to transfer (or *post*) entries from the journal to the ledger. The process of transferring journal entry information to the ledger is called **posting.**

Journalizing Transactions   The process of journalizing transactions requires an understanding of a journal. While companies can use various journals, every company uses a **general journal.** It can be used to record any transaction and includes the following information about each transaction: ⓐ date of transaction, ⓑ titles of affected accounts, ⓒ dollar amount of each

Step 1: Identify transactions and source documents.

Step 2: Analyze transactions using the accounting equation.

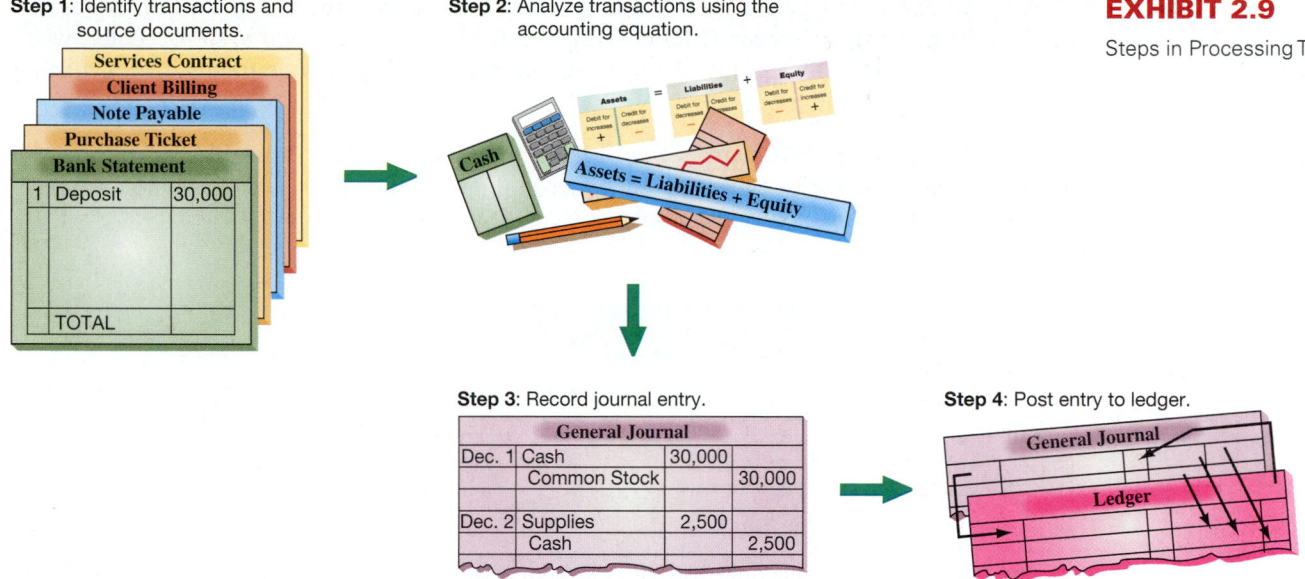

EXHIBIT 2.9

Steps in Processing Transactions

Step 3: Record journal entry.

Step 4: Post entry to ledger.

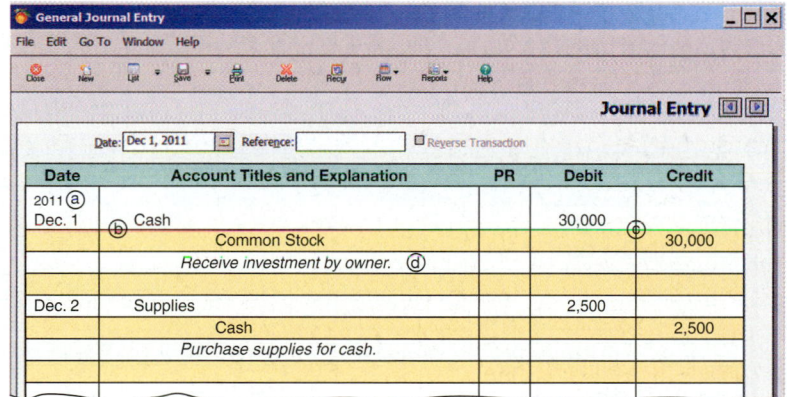

debit and credit, and ⓓ explanation of the transaction. Exhibit 2.10 shows how the first two transactions of FastForward are recorded in a general journal. This process is similar for manual and computerized systems. Computerized journals are often designed to look like a manual journal page, and also include error-checking routines that ensure debits equal credits for each entry. Shortcuts allow recordkeepers to select account names and numbers from pull-down menus.

EXHIBIT 2.10

Partial General Journal for FastForward

To record entries in a general journal, apply these steps; refer to the entries in Exhibit 2.10 when reviewing these steps. (1) Date the transaction: Enter the year at the top of the first column and the month and day on the first line of each journal entry. (2) Enter titles of accounts debited and then enter amounts in the Debit column on the same line. Account titles are taken from the chart of accounts and are aligned with the left margin of the Account Titles and Explanation column. (3) Enter titles of accounts credited and then enter amounts in the Credit column on the same line. Account titles are from the chart of accounts and are indented from the left margin of the Account Titles and Explanation column to distinguish them from debited accounts. (4) Enter a brief explanation of the transaction on the line below the entry (it often references a source document). This explanation is indented about half as far as the credited account titles to avoid confusing it with accounts, and it is italicized.

Point: There are no exact rules for writing journal entry explanations. An explanation should be short yet describe why an entry is made.

 **IFRS** _____

IFRS requires that companies report the following four basic financial statements with explanatory notes:

- Balance sheet
- Income statement
- Statement of changes in equity (or statement of recognized revenue and expense)
- Statement of cash flows

IFRS does not prescribe specific formats; and comparative information is required for the preceding period only. ∎

A blank line is left between each journal entry for clarity. When a transaction is first recorded, the **posting reference (PR) column** is left blank (in a manual system). Later, when posting entries to the ledger, the identification numbers of the individual ledger accounts are entered in the PR column.

Balance Column Account   T-accounts are simple and direct means to show how the accounting process works. However, actual accounting systems need more structure and therefore use **balance column accounts,** such as that in Exhibit 2.11.

EXHIBIT 2.11

Cash Account in Balance Column Format

	Cash				Account No. 101
Date	Explanation	PR	Debit	Credit	Balance
2011					
Dec. 1		G1	30,000		30,000
Dec. 2		G1		2,500	27,500
Dec. 3		G1		26,000	1,500
Dec. 10		G1	4,200		5,700

The balance column account format is similar to a T-account in having columns for debits and credits. It is different in including transaction date and explanation columns. It also has a column with the balance of the account after each entry is recorded. To illustrate, FastForward's Cash account in Exhibit 2.11 is debited on December 1 for the $30,000 owner investment, yielding a $30,000 debit balance. The account is credited on December 2 for $2,500, yielding a $27,500 debit balance. On December 3, it is credited again, this time for $26,000, and its debit balance is reduced to $1,500. The Cash account is debited for $4,200 on December 10, and its debit balance increases to $5,700; and so on.

The heading of the Balance column does not show whether it is a debit or credit balance. Instead, an account is assumed to have a *normal balance*. Unusual events can sometimes temporarily

Point: Explanations are typically included in ledger accounts only for unusual transactions or events.

EXHIBIT 2.12

Posting an Entry to the Ledger

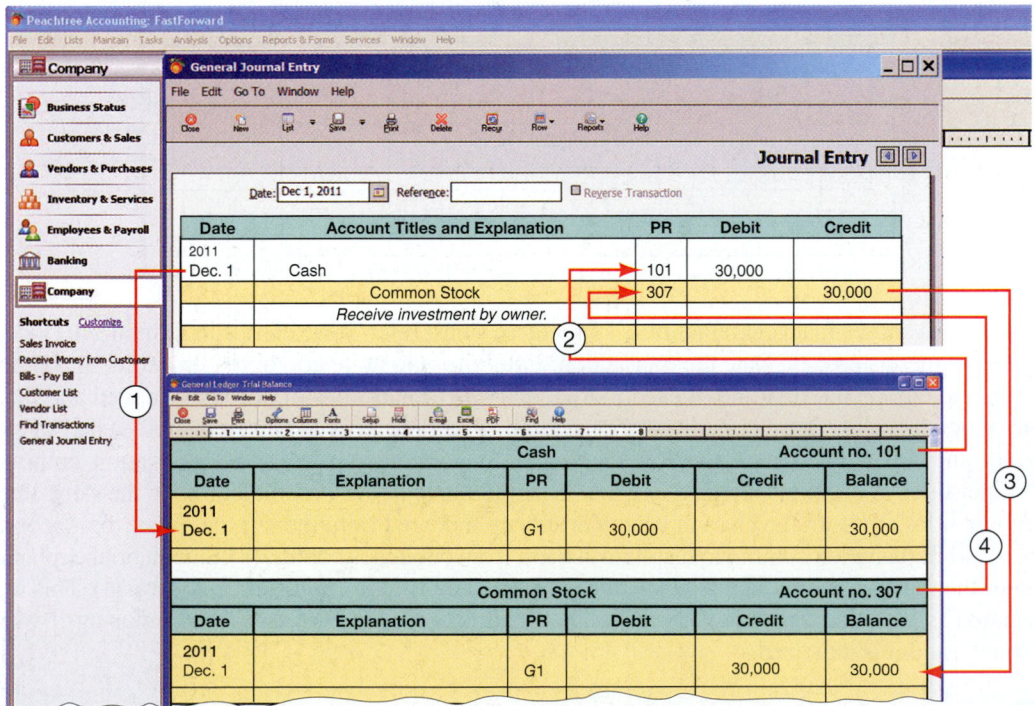

Point: The fundamental concepts of a manual (pencil-and-paper) system are identical to those of a computerized information system.

Key: (1) Identify debit account in Ledger: enter date, journal page, amount, and balance.
      (2) Enter the debit account number from the Ledger in the PR column of the journal.
      (3) Identify credit account in Ledger: enter date, journal page, amount, and balance.
      (4) Enter the credit account number from the Ledger in the PR column of the journal.

give an account an abnormal balance. An *abnormal balance* refers to a balance on the side where decreases are recorded. For example, a customer might mistakenly overpay a bill. This gives that customer's account receivable an abnormal (credit) balance. An abnormal balance is often identified by circling it or by entering it in red or some other unusual color. A zero balance for an account is usually shown by writing zeros or a dash in the Balance column to avoid confusion between a zero balance and one omitted in error.

Posting Journal Entries   Step 4 of processing transactions is to post journal entries to ledger accounts (see Exhibit 2.9). To ensure that the ledger is up-to-date, entries are posted as soon as possible. This might be daily, weekly, or when time permits. All entries must be posted to the ledger before financial statements are prepared to ensure that account balances are up-to-date. When entries are posted to the ledger, the debits in journal entries are transferred into ledger accounts as debits, and credits are transferred into ledger accounts as credits. Exhibit 2.12 shows the *four steps to post a journal entry*. First, identify the ledger account that is debited in the entry; then, in the ledger, enter the entry date, the journal and page in its PR column, the debit amount, and the new balance of the ledger account. (The letter *G* shows it came from the General Journal.) Second, enter the ledger account number in the PR column of the journal. Steps 3 and 4 repeat the first two steps for credit entries and amounts. The posting process creates a link between the ledger and the journal entry. This link is a useful cross-reference for tracing an amount from one record to another.

> **Point:** Computerized systems often provide a code beside a balance such as *dr.* or *cr.* to identify its balance. Posting is automatic and immediate with accounting software.

> **Point:** A journal is often referred to as the *book of original entry*. The ledger is referred to as the *book of final entry* because financial statements are prepared from it.

Analyzing Transactions — An Illustration

We return to the activities of FastForward to show how double-entry accounting is useful in analyzing and processing transactions. Analysis of each transaction follows the four steps of Exhibit 2.9.

> **A1** Analyze the impact of transactions on accounts and financial statements.

Step 1 Identify the transaction and any source documents.

Step 2 Analyze the transaction using the accounting equation.

Step 3 Record the transaction in journal entry form applying double-entry accounting.

Step 4 Post the entry (for simplicity, we use T-accounts to represent ledger accounts).

Study each transaction thoroughly before proceeding to the next. The first 11 transactions are from Chapter 1, and we analyze five additional December transactions of FastForward (numbered 12 through 16) that were omitted earlier.

1. Receive Investment by Owner

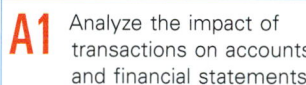

1 IDENTIFY FastForward receives $30,000 cash from Chas Taylor in exchange for common stock.

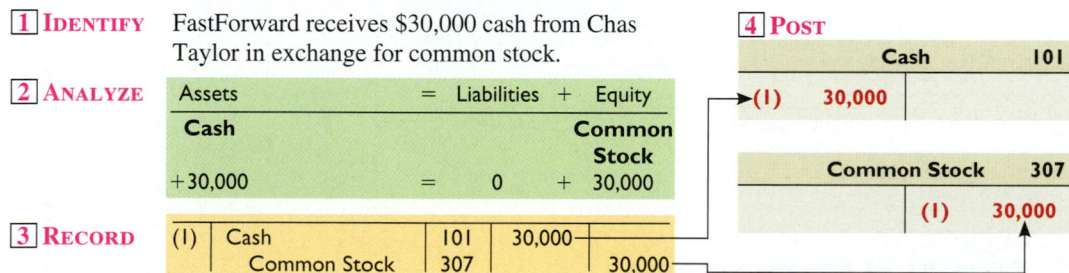

2. Purchase Supplies for Cash

1 IDENTIFY FastForward pays $2,500 cash for supplies.

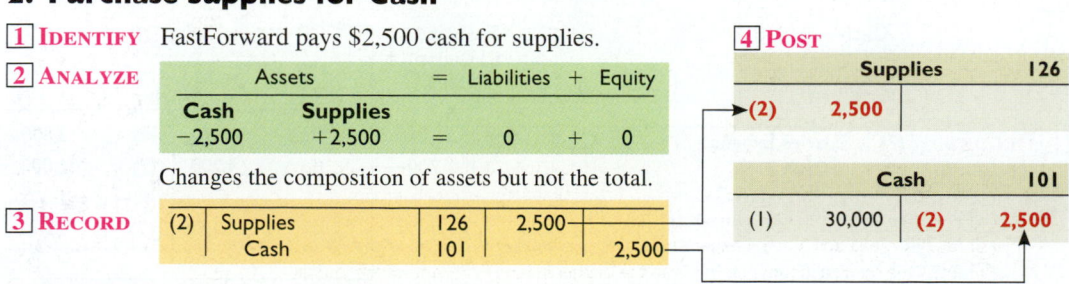

3. Purchase Equipment for Cash

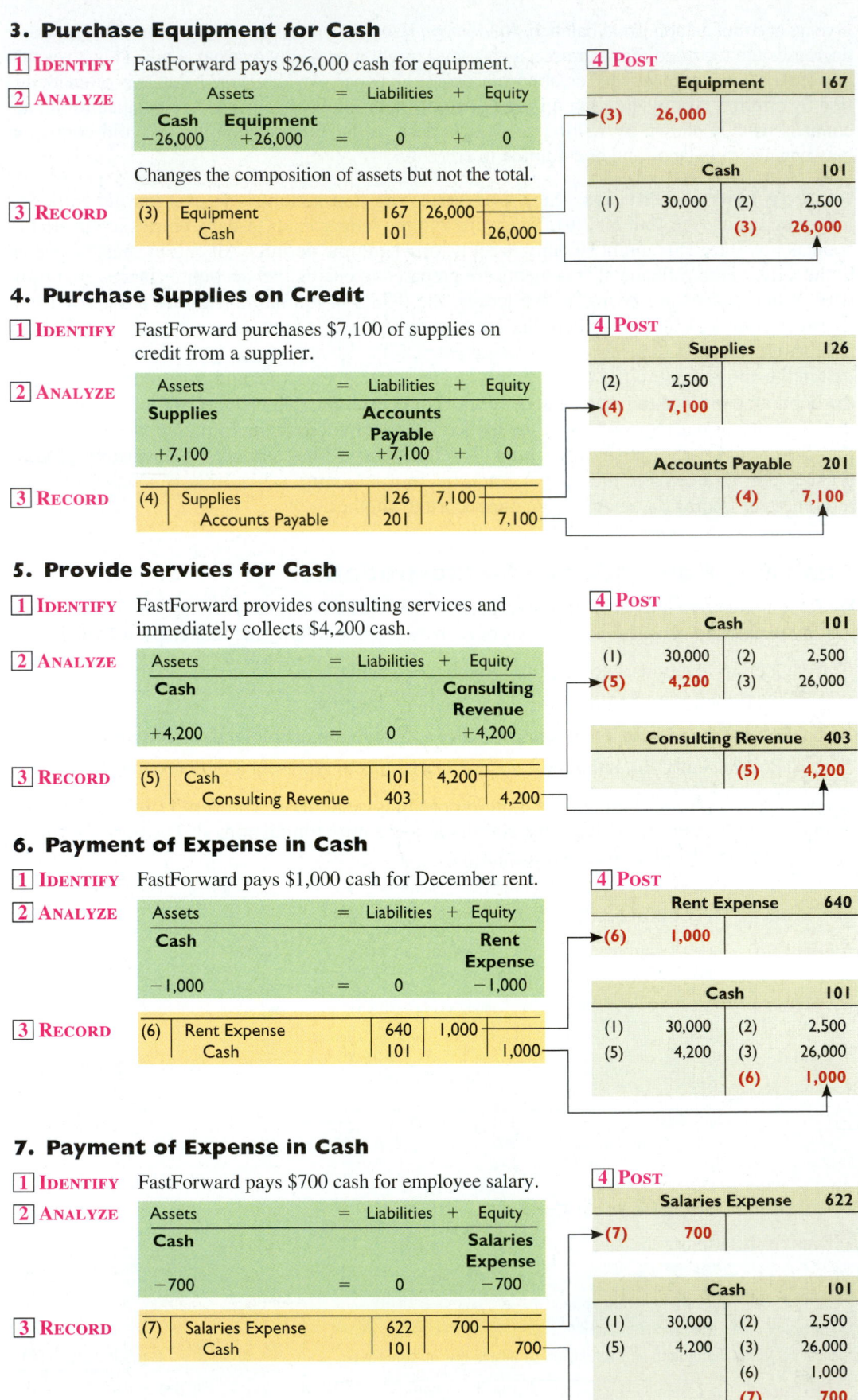

1 IDENTIFY   FastForward pays $26,000 cash for equipment.

2 ANALYZE

	Assets		=	Liabilities	+	Equity
	Cash	**Equipment**				
	−26,000	+26,000	=	0	+	0

Changes the composition of assets but not the total.

3 RECORD

(3)	Equipment	167	26,000	
	Cash	101		26,000

4 POST

Equipment			167
(3)	26,000		

Cash			101
(1)	30,000	(2)	2,500
		(3)	26,000

4. Purchase Supplies on Credit

1 IDENTIFY   FastForward purchases $7,100 of supplies on credit from a supplier.

2 ANALYZE

	Assets	=	Liabilities	+	Equity
	Supplies		**Accounts Payable**		
	+7,100	=	+7,100	+	0

3 RECORD

(4)	Supplies	126	7,100	
	Accounts Payable	201		7,100

4 POST

Supplies			126
(2)	2,500		
(4)	7,100		

Accounts Payable			201
		(4)	7,100

5. Provide Services for Cash

1 IDENTIFY   FastForward provides consulting services and immediately collects $4,200 cash.

2 ANALYZE

	Assets	=	Liabilities	+	Equity
	Cash				**Consulting Revenue**
	+4,200	=	0		+4,200

3 RECORD

(5)	Cash	101	4,200	
	Consulting Revenue	403		4,200

4 POST

Cash			101
(1)	30,000	(2)	2,500
(5)	4,200	(3)	26,000

Consulting Revenue			403
		(5)	4,200

6. Payment of Expense in Cash

1 IDENTIFY   FastForward pays $1,000 cash for December rent.

2 ANALYZE

	Assets	=	Liabilities	+	Equity
	Cash				**Rent Expense**
	−1,000	=	0		−1,000

3 RECORD

(6)	Rent Expense	640	1,000	
	Cash	101		1,000

4 POST

Rent Expense			640
(6)	1,000		

Cash			101
(1)	30,000	(2)	2,500
(5)	4,200	(3)	26,000
		(6)	1,000

7. Payment of Expense in Cash

Point: *Salary* usually refers to compensation for an employee who receives a fixed amount for a given time period, whereas *wages* usually refers to compensation based on time worked.

1 IDENTIFY   FastForward pays $700 cash for employee salary.

2 ANALYZE

	Assets	=	Liabilities	+	Equity
	Cash				**Salaries Expense**
	−700	=	0		−700

3 RECORD

(7)	Salaries Expense	622	700	
	Cash	101		700

4 POST

Salaries Expense			622
(7)	700		

Cash			101
(1)	30,000	(2)	2,500
(5)	4,200	(3)	26,000
		(6)	1,000
		(7)	700

8. Provide Consulting and Rental Services on Credit

1 IDENTIFY FastForward provides consulting services of $1,600 and rents its test facilities for $300. The customer is billed $1,900 for these services.

2 ANALYZE

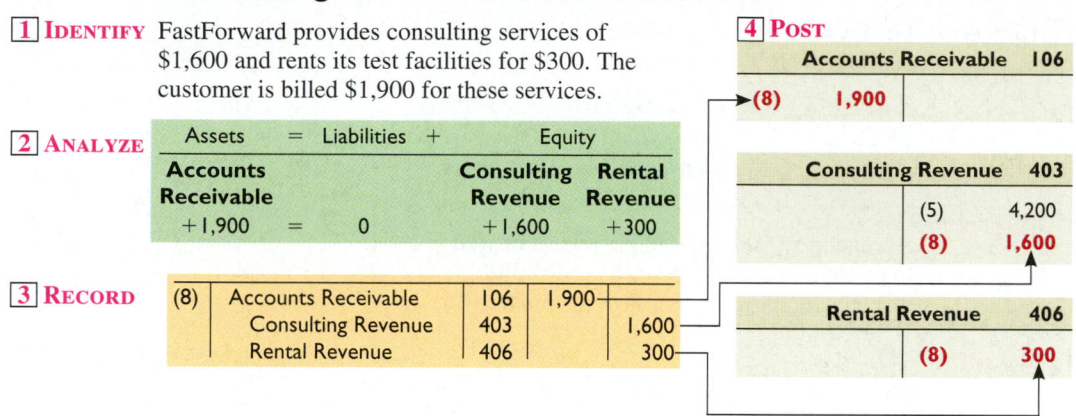

Assets	=	Liabilities	+	Equity	
Accounts Receivable				**Consulting Revenue**	**Rental Revenue**
+1,900	=	0		+1,600	+300

3 RECORD

(8)	Accounts Receivable	106	1,900	
	Consulting Revenue	403		1,600
	Rental Revenue	406		300

4 POST

Accounts Receivable		106	
(8)	1,900		

Consulting Revenue		403	
		(5)	4,200
		(8)	1,600

Rental Revenue		406	
		(8)	300

Point: Transaction 8 is a **compound journal entry,** which affects three or more accounts.

9. Receipt of Cash on Account

1 IDENTIFY FastForward receives $1,900 cash from the client billed in transaction 8.

2 ANALYZE

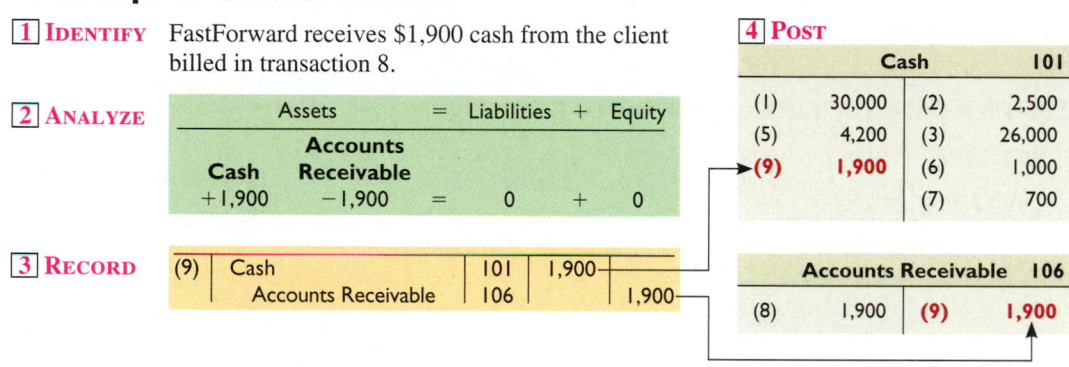

Assets		=	Liabilities	+	Equity
Cash	**Accounts Receivable**				
+1,900	−1,900	=	0	+	0

3 RECORD

(9)	Cash	101	1,900	
	Accounts Receivable	106		1,900

4 POST

		Cash		101	
(1)	30,000		(2)	2,500
(5)	4,200		(3)	26,000
(9)	1,900		(6)	1,000
			(7)	700

Accounts Receivable		106	
(8)	1,900	(9)	1,900

Point: The *revenue recognition principle* requires revenue to be recognized when earned, which is when the company provides products and services to a customer. This is not necessarily the same time that the customer pays. A customer can pay before or after products or services are provided.

10. Partial Payment of Accounts Payable

1 IDENTIFY FastForward pays CalTech Supply $900 cash toward the payable of transaction 4.

2 ANALYZE

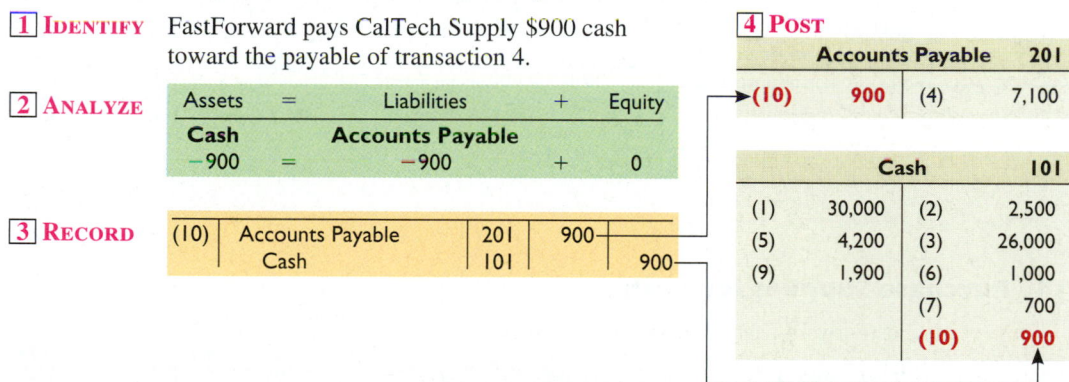

Assets	=	Liabilities	+	Equity
Cash		**Accounts Payable**		
−900	=	−900	+	0

3 RECORD

(10)	Accounts Payable	201	900	
	Cash	101		900

4 POST

Accounts Payable		201	
(10)	900	(4)	7,100

		Cash		101	
(1)	30,000		(2)	2,500
(5)	4,200		(3)	26,000
(9)	1,900		(6)	1,000
			(7)	700
			(10)	900

11. Payment of Cash Dividend

1 IDENTIFY FastForward pays $200 cash for dividends

2 ANALYZE

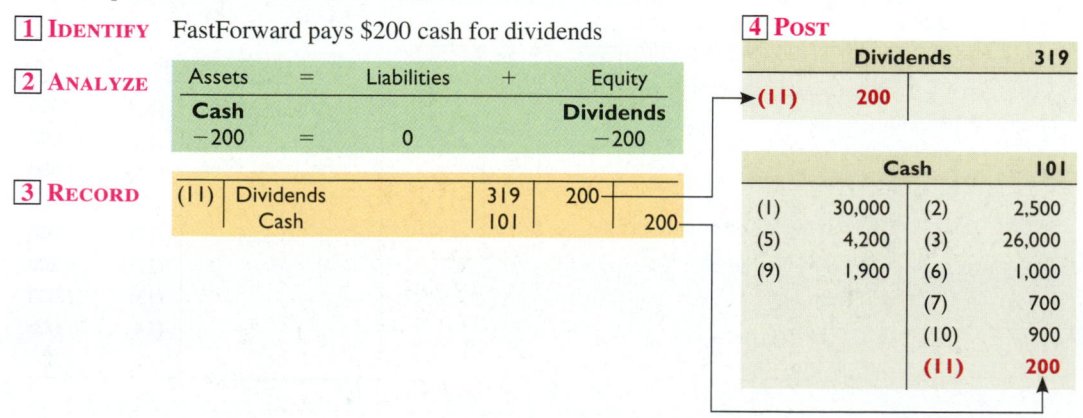

Assets	=	Liabilities	+	Equity
Cash				**Dividends**
−200	=	0		−200

3 RECORD

(11)	Dividends	319	200	
	Cash	101		200

4 POST

Dividends		319	
(11)	200		

		Cash		101	
(1)	30,000		(2)	2,500
(5)	4,200		(3)	26,000
(9)	1,900		(6)	1,000
			(7)	700
			(10)	900
			(11)	200

12. Receipt of Cash for Future Services

1 IDENTIFY   FastForward receives $3,000 cash in advance of providing consulting services to a customer.

2 ANALYZE

Accepting $3,000 cash obligates FastForward to perform future services and is a liability. No revenue is earned until services are provided.

3 RECORD

4 POST

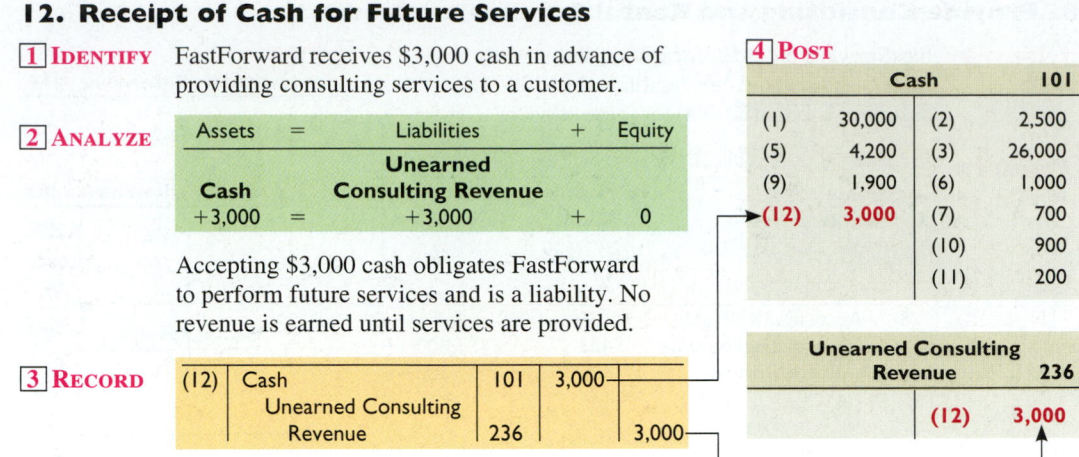

13. Pay Cash for Future Insurance Coverage

1 IDENTIFY   FastForward pays $2,400 cash (insurance premium) for a 24-month insurance policy. Coverage begins on December 1.

2 ANALYZE

Changes the composition of assets from cash to prepaid insurance. Expense is incurred as insurance coverage expires.

3 RECORD

4 POST

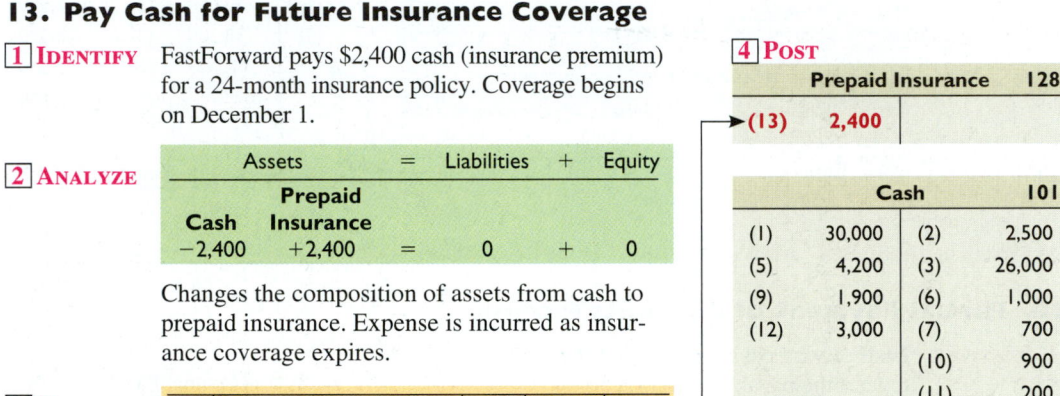

14. Purchase Supplies for Cash

1 IDENTIFY   FastForward pays $120 cash for supplies.

2 ANALYZE

3 RECORD

4 POST

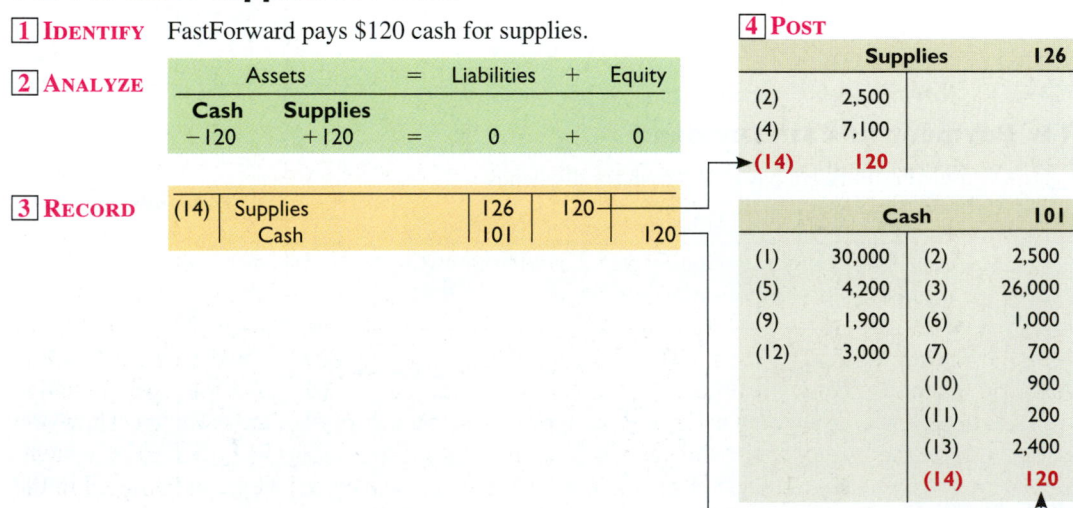

15. Payment of Expense in Cash

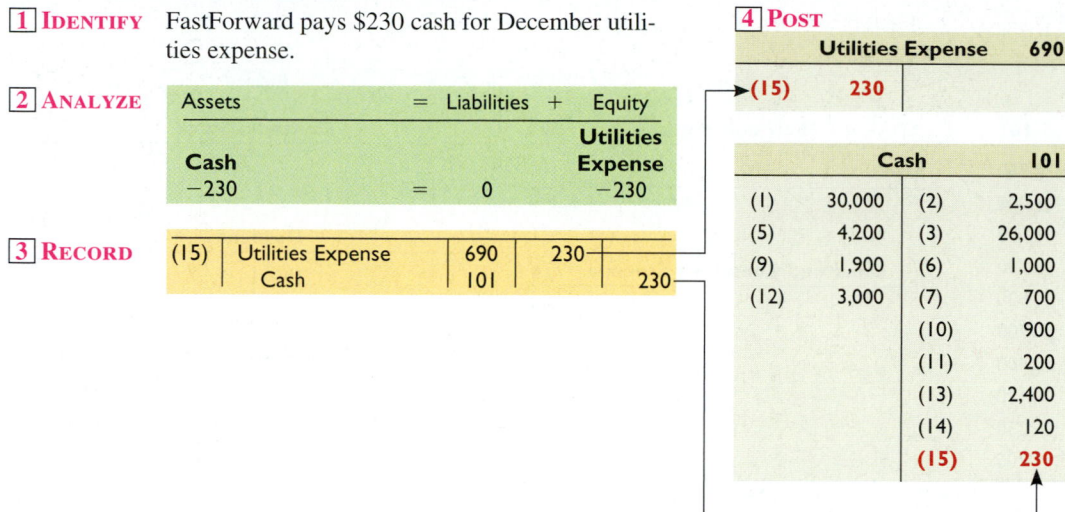

1 IDENTIFY FastForward pays $230 cash for December utilities expense.

2 ANALYZE

Assets	=	Liabilities	+	Equity
Cash				Utilities Expense
−230	=	0		−230

3 RECORD

| (15) | Utilities Expense | 690 | 230 | |
| | Cash | 101 | | 230 |

4 POST

Utilities Expense 690
(15) 230

Cash			101
(1)	30,000	(2)	2,500
(5)	4,200	(3)	26,000
(9)	1,900	(6)	1,000
(12)	3,000	(7)	700
		(10)	900
		(11)	200
		(13)	2,400
		(14)	120
		(15)	230

16. Payment of Expense in Cash

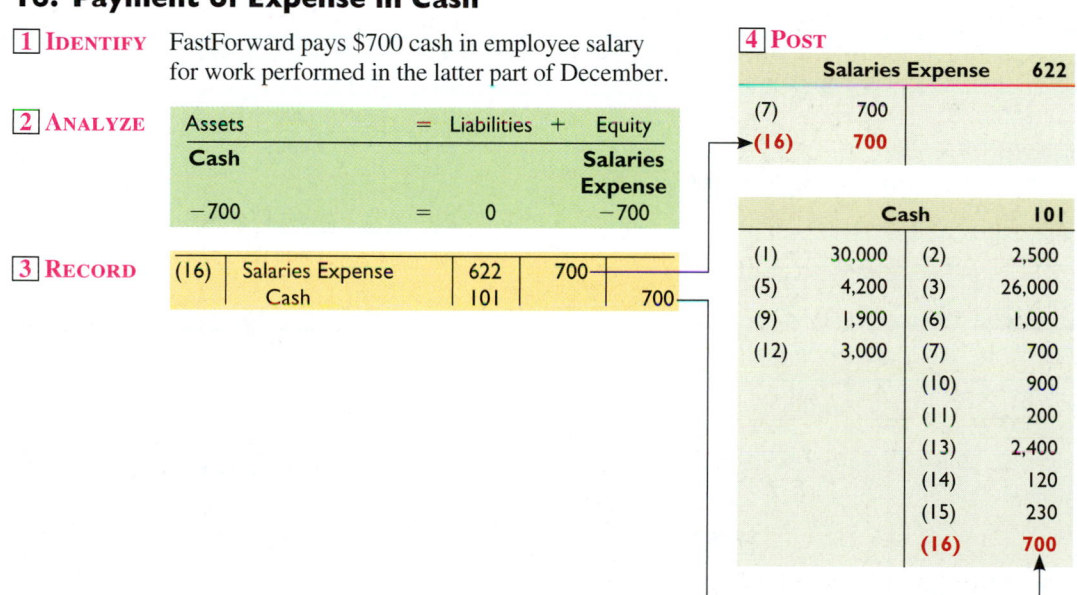

1 IDENTIFY FastForward pays $700 cash in employee salary for work performed in the latter part of December.

2 ANALYZE

Assets	=	Liabilities	+	Equity
Cash				Salaries Expense
−700	=	0		−700

3 RECORD

| (16) | Salaries Expense | 622 | 700 | |
| | Cash | 101 | | 700 |

4 POST

Salaries Expense 622
(7) 700
(16) 700

Cash			101
(1)	30,000	(2)	2,500
(5)	4,200	(3)	26,000
(9)	1,900	(6)	1,000
(12)	3,000	(7)	700
		(10)	900
		(11)	200
		(13)	2,400
		(14)	120
		(15)	230
		(16)	700

Point: We could merge transactions 15 and 16 into one *compound entry.*

Accounting Equation Analysis

Exhibit 2.13 shows the ledger accounts (in T-account form) of FastForward after all 16 transactions are recorded and posted and the balances computed. The accounts are grouped into three major columns corresponding to the accounting equation: assets, liabilities, and equity. Note several important points. First, as with each transaction, the totals for the three columns must obey the accounting equation. Specifically, assets equal $42,470 ($4,350 + $0 + $9,720 + $2,400 + $26,000); liabilities equal $9,200 ($6,200 + $3,000); and equity equals $33,270 ($30,000 − $200 + $5,800 + $300 − $1,400 − $1,000 − $230). These numbers prove the accounting equation: Assets of $42,470 = Liabilities of $9,200 + Equity of $33,270. Second, the common stock, dividends, revenue, and expense accounts reflect the transactions that change equity. The latter three account categories underlie the statement of retained earnings. Third, the revenue and expense account balances will be summarized and reported in the income statement. Fourth, increases and decreases in the cash account make up the elements reported in the statement of cash flows.

Debit and Credit Rules

Accounts	Increase (normal bal.)	Decrease
Asset	Debit	Credit
Liability	Credit	Debit
Common stock	Credit	Debit
Dividends	Debit	Credit
Revenue	Credit	Debit
Expense	Debit	Credit

Point: Technology does not provide the judgment required to analyze most business transactions. Analysis requires the expertise of skilled and ethical professionals.

EXHIBIT 2.13

Ledger for FastForward (in T-Account Form)

Assets			=	Liabilities			+	Equity		

Assets

Cash   101

(1)	30,000	(2)	2,500
(5)	4,200	(3)	26,000
(9)	1,900	(6)	1,000
(12)	3,000	(7)	700
		(10)	900
		(11)	200
		(13)	2,400
		(14)	120
		(15)	230
		(16)	700
Balance	4,350		

Accounts Receivable   106

(8)	1,900	(9)	1,900
Balance	0		

Supplies   126

(2)	2,500	
(4)	7,100	
(14)	120	
Balance	9,720	

Prepaid Insurance   128

(13)	2,400	

Equipment   167

(3)	26,000	

$42,470

Liabilities

Accounts Payable   201

(10)	900	(4)	7,100
		Balance	6,200

Unearned Consulting Revenue   236

		(12)	3,000

$9,200

Equity

Common Stock   307

		(1)	30,000

Dividends   319

(11)	200	

Consulting Revenue   403

		(5)	4,200
		(8)	1,600
		Balance	5,800

Rental Revenue   406

		(8)	300

Salaries Expense   622

(7)	700	
(16)	700	
Balance	1,400	

Rent Expense   640

(6)	1,000	

Utilities Expense   690

(15)	230	

Accounts in this white area reflect those reported on the income statement.

$33,270

Quick Check

Answers — p. 75

8. What types of transactions increase equity? What types decrease equity?

9. Why are accounting systems called *double-entry?*

10. For each transaction, double-entry accounting requires which of the following? (*a*) Debits to asset accounts must create credits to liability or equity accounts, (*b*) a debit to a liability account must create a credit to an asset account, or (*c*) total debits must equal total credits.

11. An owner invests $15,000 cash along with equipment having a market value of $23,000 in a company in exchange for common stock. Prepare the necessary journal entry.

12. Explain what a compound journal entry is.

13. Why are posting reference numbers entered in the journal when entries are posted to ledger accounts?

TRIAL BALANCE

Double-entry accounting requires the sum of debit account balances to equal the sum of credit account balances. A trial balance is used to confirm this. A **trial balance** is a list of accounts and their balances at a point in time. Account balances are reported in their appropriate debit or credit columns of a trial balance. A trial balance can be used to confirm this and to follow up on any abnormal or unusual balances. Exhibit 2.14 shows the trial balance for FastForward after its 16 entries have been posted to the ledger. (This is an *unadjusted* trial balance—Chapter 3 explains the necessary adjustments.)

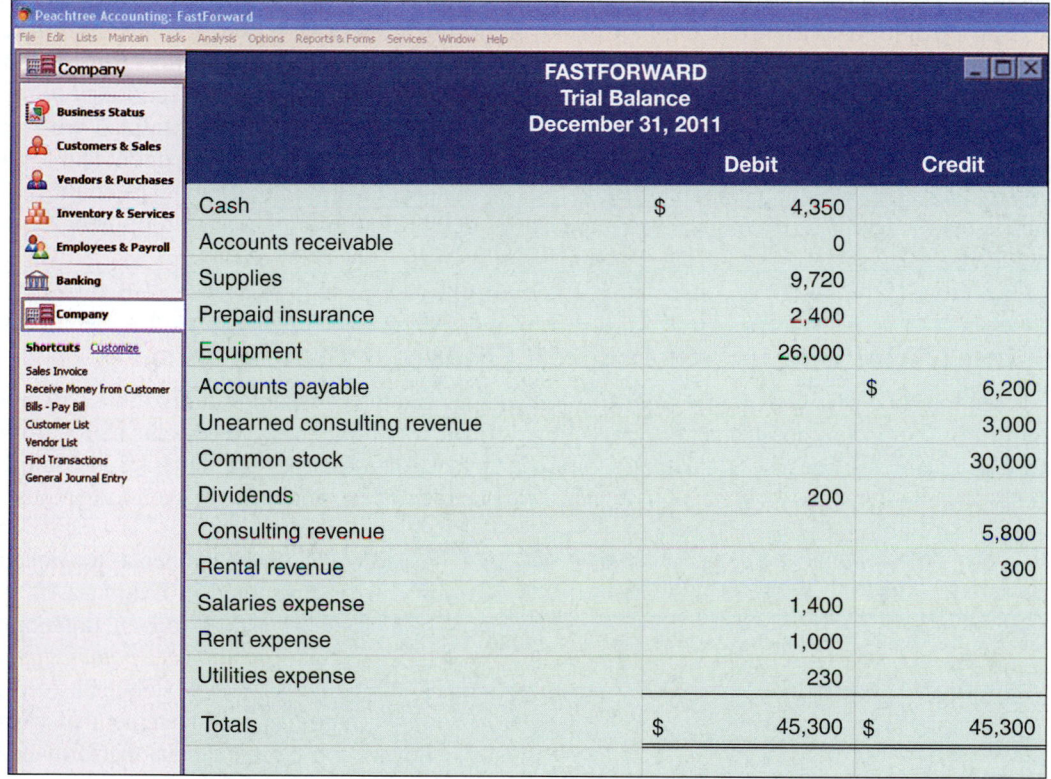

EXHIBIT 2.14

Trial Balance (Unadjusted)

	Debit	Credit
Cash	$ 4,350	
Accounts receivable	0	
Supplies	9,720	
Prepaid insurance	2,400	
Equipment	26,000	
Accounts payable		$ 6,200
Unearned consulting revenue		3,000
Common stock		30,000
Dividends	200	
Consulting revenue		5,800
Rental revenue		300
Salaries expense	1,400	
Rent expense	1,000	
Utilities expense	230	
Totals	$ 45,300	$ 45,300

Point: The ordering of accounts in a trial balance typically follows their identification number from the chart of accounts.

Preparing a Trial Balance

Preparing a trial balance involves three steps:

1. List each account title and its amount (from ledger) in the trial balance. If an account has a zero balance, list it with a zero in its normal balance column (or omit it entirely).
2. Compute the total of debit balances and the total of credit balances.
3. Verify (*prove*) total debit balances equal total credit balances.

P2 Prepare and explain the use of a trial balance.

The total of debit balances equals the total of credit balances for the trial balance in Exhibit 2.14. Equality of these two totals does not guarantee that no errors were made. For example, the column totals still will be equal when a debit or credit of a correct amount is made to a wrong account. Another error that does not cause unequal column totals occurs when equal debits and credits of an incorrect amount are entered.

Searching for and Correcting Errors   If the trial balance does not balance (when its columns are not equal), the error (or errors) must be found and corrected. An efficient

Point: A trial balance is *not* a financial statement but a mechanism for checking equality of debits and credits in the ledger. Financial statements do not have debit and credit columns.

Example: If a credit to Unearned Revenue was incorrectly posted from the journal as a credit to the Revenue ledger account, would the ledger still balance? Would the financial statements be correct? *Answers:* The ledger would balance, but liabilities would be understated, equity would be overstated, and income would be overstated (all because of overstated revenues).

Point: The IRS requires companies to keep records that can be audited.

way to search for an error is to check the journalizing, posting, and trial balance preparation in *reverse order*. Step 1 is to verify that the trial balance columns are correctly added. If step 1 fails to find the error, step 2 is to verify that account balances are accurately entered from the ledger. Step 3 is to see whether a debit (or credit) balance is mistakenly listed in the trial balance as a credit (or debit). A clue to this error is when the difference between total debits and total credits equals twice the amount of the incorrect account balance. If the error is still undiscovered, Step 4 is to recompute each account balance in the ledger. Step 5 is to verify that each journal entry is properly posted. Step 6 is to verify that the original journal entry has equal debits and credits. At this point, the errors should be uncovered.[3]

If an error in a journal entry is discovered before the error is posted, it can be corrected in a manual system by drawing a line through the incorrect information. The correct information is written above it to create a record of change for the auditor. Many computerized systems allow the operator to replace the incorrect information directly.

If an error in a journal entry is not discovered until after it is posted, we do not strike through both erroneous entries in the journal and ledger. Instead, we correct this error by creating a *correcting entry* that removes the amount from the wrong account and records it to the correct account. As an example, suppose a $100 purchase of supplies is journalized with an incorrect debit to Equipment, and then this incorrect entry is posted to the ledger. The Supplies ledger account balance is understated by $100, and the Equipment ledger account balance is overstated by $100. The correcting entry is: debit Supplies and credit Equipment (both for $100).

Using a Trial Balance to Prepare Financial Statements

P3   Prepare financial statements from business transactions.

This section shows how to prepare *financial statements* from the trial balance in Exhibit 2.14 and from information on the December transactions of FastForward. These statements differ from those in Chapter 1 because of several additional transactions. These statements are also more precisely called *unadjusted statements* because we need to make some further accounting adjustments (described in Chapter 3).

EXHIBIT 2.15

Links between Financial Statements across Time

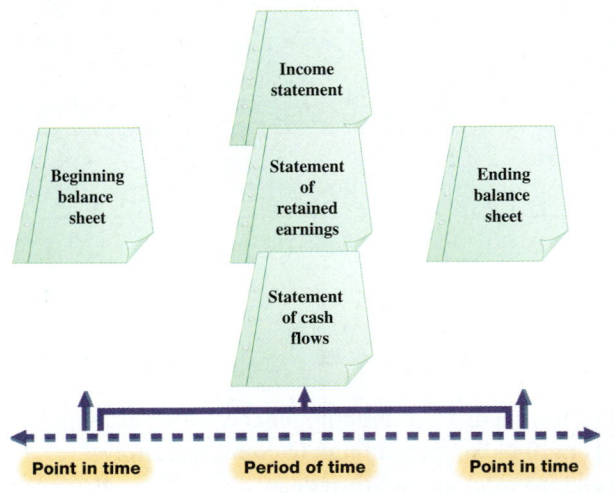

How financial statements are linked in time is illustrated in Exhibit 2.15. A balance sheet reports on an organization's financial position at a *point in time*. The income statement, statement of retained earnings, and statement of cash flows report on financial performance over a *period of time*. The three statements in the middle column of Exhibit 2.15 link balance sheets from the beginning to the end of a reporting period. They explain how financial position changes from one point to another.

Preparers and users (including regulatory agencies) determine the length of the reporting period. A one-year, or

---

[3] *Transposition* occurs when two digits are switched, or transposed, within a number. If transposition is the only error, it yields a difference between the two trial balance totals that is evenly divisible by 9. For example, assume that a $691 debit in an entry is incorrectly posted to the ledger as $619. Total credits in the trial balance are then larger than total debits by $72 ($691 − $619). The $72 error is *evenly* divisible by 9 (72/9 = 8). The first digit of the quotient (in our example it is 8) equals the difference between the digits of the two transposed numbers (the 9 and the 1). The number of digits in the quotient also tells the location of the transposition, starting from the right. The quotient in our example had only one digit (8), so it tells us the transposition is in the first digit. Consider another example where a transposition error involves posting $961 instead of the correct $691. The difference in these numbers is $270, and its quotient is 30 (270/9). The quotient has two digits, so it tells us to check the second digit from the right for a transposition of two numbers that have a difference of 3.

annual, reporting period is common, as are semiannual, quarterly, and monthly periods. The one-year reporting period is known as the *accounting,* or *fiscal, year.* Businesses whose accounting year begins on January 1 and ends on December 31 are known as *calendar-year* companies. Many companies choose a fiscal year ending on a date other than December 31. **Research In Motion** is a *noncalendar-year* company as reflected in the headings of its February 27 year-end financial statements in Appendix A near the end of the book.

Income Statement   An income statement reports the revenues earned less the expenses incurred by a business over a period of time. FastForward's income statement for December is shown at the top of Exhibit 2.16. Information about revenues and expenses is conveniently taken from the trial balance in Exhibit 2.14. Net income of $3,470 is reported at the bottom of the statement. Owner investments and dividends are *not* part of income.

Statement of Retained Earnings   The statement of retained earnings reports information about how retained earnings changes over the reporting period. FastForward's statement of retained earnings is the second report in Exhibit 2.16. It shows the $3,470 of net income, the $200 dividend, and the $3,270 end-of-period balance. (The beginning balance in the statement of

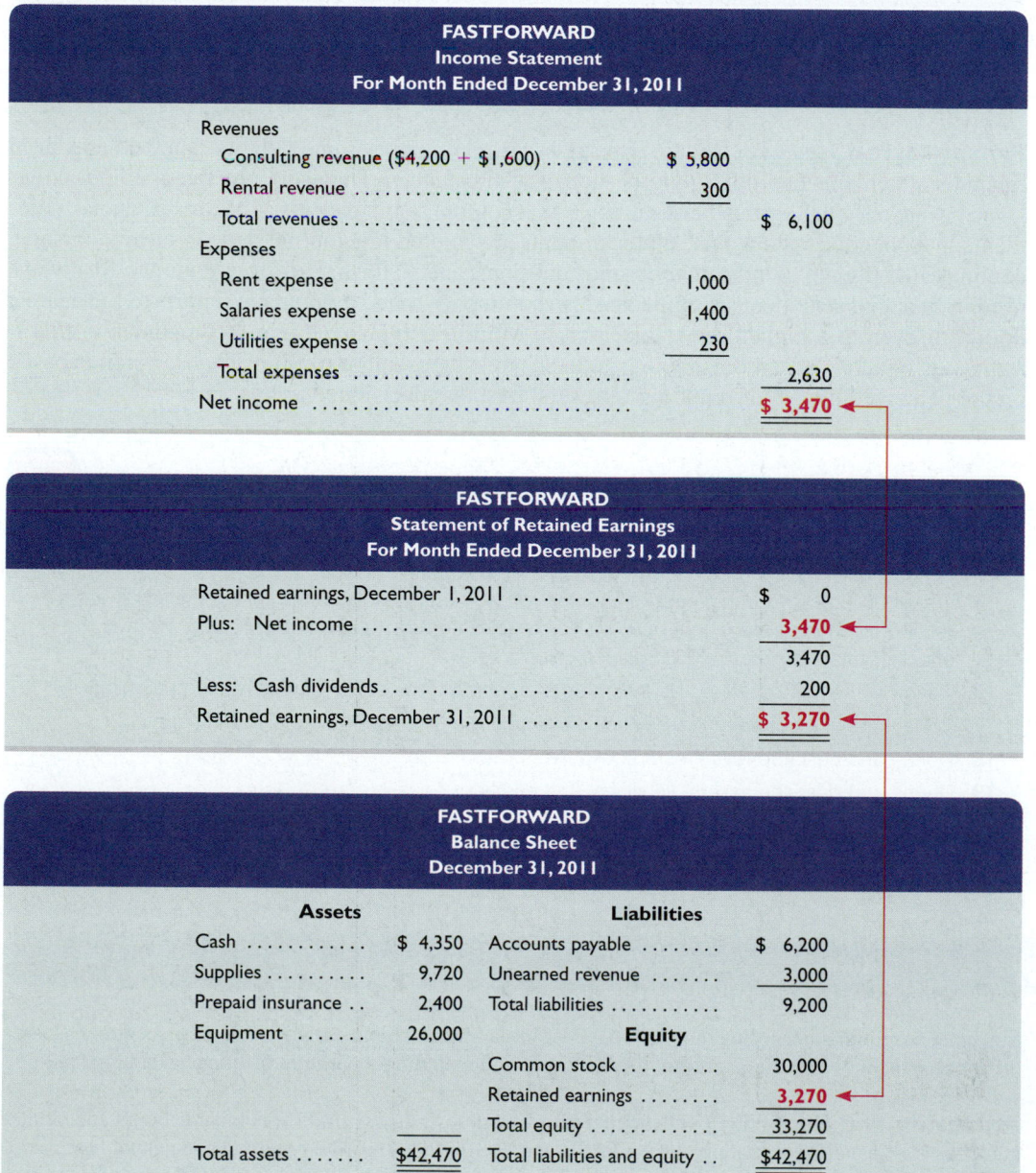

EXHIBIT 2.16

Financial Statements and Their Links

retained earnings is rarely zero; an exception is for the first period of operations. The beginning retained earnings balance in January 2012 is $3,270, which is December's ending balance.)

Balance Sheet   The balance sheet reports the financial position of a company at a point in time, usually at the end of a month, quarter, or year. FastForward's balance sheet is the third report in Exhibit 2.16. This statement refers to financial condition at the close of business on December 31. The left side of the balance sheet lists its assets: cash, supplies, prepaid insurance, and equipment. The upper right side of the balance sheet shows that it owes $6,200 to creditors and $3,000 in services to customers who paid in advance. The equity section shows an ending balance of $33,270. Note the link between the ending balance of the statement of retained earnings and the retained earnings balance. (Recall that this presentation of the balance sheet is called the *account form:* assets on the left and liabilities and equity on the right. Another presentation is the *report form:* assets on top, followed by liabilities and then equity. Either presentation is acceptable.)

Decision Maker   Answer — p. 74

Entrepreneur   You open a wholesale business selling entertainment equipment to retail outlets. You find that most of your customers demand to buy on credit. How can you use the balance sheets of these customers to decide which ones to extend credit to? ◼

Presentation Issues   Dollar signs are not used in journals and ledgers. They do appear in financial statements and other reports such as trial balances. The usual practice is to put dollar signs beside only the first and last numbers in a column. **Research In Motion**'s financial statements in Appendix A show this. When amounts are entered in a journal, ledger, or trial balance, commas are optional to indicate thousands, millions, and so forth. However, commas are always used in financial statements. Companies also commonly round amounts in reports to the nearest dollar, or even to a higher level. Research In Motion is typical of many companies in that it rounds its financial statement amounts to the nearest thousand or million. This decision is based on the perceived impact of rounding for users' business decisions.

off the mark.com   by Mark Parisi

COULD YOU PLEASE STOP TOUCHING THINGS FOR ONE MOMENT?! I CAN'T KEEP UP!

offthemark.com

KING MIDAS' ACCOUNTANT

Quick Check   Answers — p. 75

14. Where are dollar signs typically entered in financial statements?
15. If a $4,000 debit to Equipment in a journal entry is incorrectly posted to the ledger as a $4,000 credit, and the ledger account has a resulting debit balance of $20,000, what is the effect of this error on the Trial Balance column totals?
16. Describe the link between the income statement and the statement of retained earnings.
17. Explain the link between the balance sheet and the statement of retained earnings.
18. Define and describe revenues and expenses.
19. Define and describe assets, liabilities, and equity.

GLOBAL VIEW

Financial accounting according to U.S. GAAP is similar, but not identical, to IFRS. This section discusses differences in analyzing and recording transactions, and with the preparation of financial statements.

Analyzing and Recording Transactions   Both U.S. GAAP and IFRS include broad and similar guidance for financial accounting. As the FASB and IASB work toward a common conceptual framework over the next few years, even those differences will fade. Further, both U.S. GAAP and IFRS apply transaction

Point: An income statement is also called an *earnings statement, a statement of operations,* or a *P&L* (profit and loss) statement. A balance sheet is also called a *statement of financial position.*

Point: While revenues increase equity, and expenses decrease equity, the amounts are not reported in detail in the statement of retained earnings. Instead, their effects are reflected through net income.

Point: Knowing how financial statements are prepared improves our analysis of them.

analysis and recording as shown in this chapter—using the same debit and credit system and accrual account-ing. Although some variations exist in revenue and expense recognition and other accounting principles, all of the transactions in this chapter are accounted for identically under these two systems.

Financial Statements   Both U.S. GAAP and IFRS prepare the same four basic financial state-ments. A few differences within each statement do exist and we will discuss those throughout the book. For example, both U.S. GAAP and IFRS require balance sheets to separate current items from noncurrent items. However, while U.S. GAAP balance sheets report current items first, IFRS balance sheets normally (but are not required to) present noncurrent items first, and equity before liabilities. To illustrate, a con-densed version of **Nokia**'s balance sheet follows (numbers using euros in millions).

NOKIA

NOKIA Balance Sheet (in EUR millions) December 31, 2009			
Assets		**Equity and Liabilities**	
Noncurrent assets	12,125	Total equity	14,749
Current assets	23,613	Noncurrent liabilities	5,801
		Current liabilities	15,188
Total assets	35,738	Total equity and liabilities	35,738

Accounting Controls and Assurance   Accounting systems depend on control procedures that assure the proper principles were applied in processing accounting information. The passage of SOX leg-islation strengthened U.S. control procedures in recent years. However, global standards for control are diverse and so are enforcement activities. Consequently, while global accounting standards are converg-ing, their application in different countries can yield different outcomes depending on the quality of their auditing standards and enforcement.

Decision **Insight**

Accounting Control   Recording valid transactions, and not recording fraudulent transactions, enhances the quality of financial statements. The graph here shows the percentage of employees in information technology that report observing specific types of misconduct within the past year. ■

[Source: KPMG 2009]

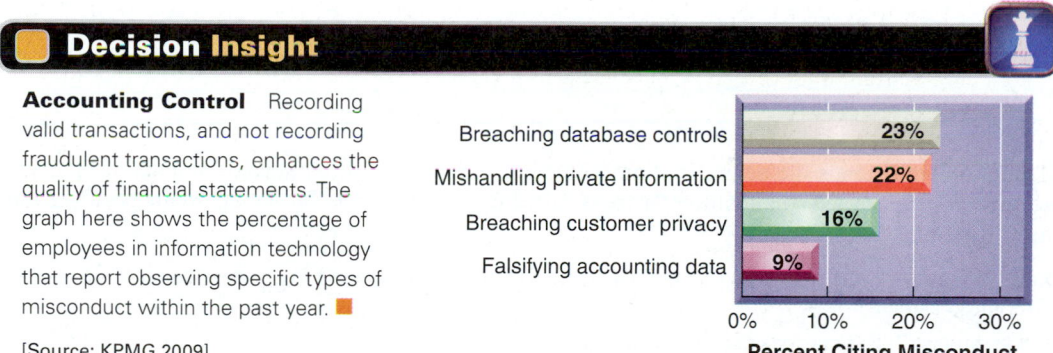

Breaching database controls — 23%
Mishandling private information — 22%
Breaching customer privacy — 16%
Falsifying accounting data — 9%

Percent Citing Misconduct

Debt Ratio    **Decision Analysis**

An important business objective is gathering information to help assess a company's risk of failing to pay its debts. Companies finance their assets with either liabilities or equity. A company that finances a rela-tively large portion of its assets with liabilities is said to have a high degree of *financial leverage*. Higher financial leverage involves greater risk because liabilities must be repaid and often require regular interest payments (equity financing does not). The risk that a company might not be able to meet such required payments is higher if it has more liabilities (is more highly leveraged). One way to assess the risk associ-ated with a company's use of liabilities is to compute the **debt ratio** as in Exhibit 2.17.

A2 Compute the debt ratio and describe its use in analyzing financial condition.

$$\text{Debt ratio} = \frac{\text{Total liabilities}}{\text{Total assets}}$$

EXHIBIT 2.17

Debt Ratio

Point: Compare the equity amount to the liability amount to assess the extent of owner versus nonowner financing.

To see how to apply the debt ratio, let's look at **Skechers**'s liabilities and assets. The company designs, markets, and sells footwear for men, women, and children under the Skechers brand. Exhibit 2.18 computes and reports its debt ratio at the end of each year from 2005 to 2009.

EXHIBIT 2.18

Computation and Analysis of Debt Ratio

$ in millions	2009	2008	2007	2006	2005
Total liabilities	$246	$204	$201	$288	$238
Total assets	$996	$876	$828	$737	$582
Debt ratio	0.25	0.23	0.24	0.39	0.41
Industry debt ratio	0.51	0.50	0.46	0.48	0.47

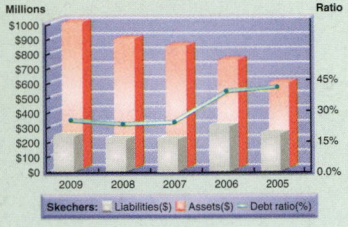

Skechers's debt ratio ranges from a low of 0.23 to a high of 0.41—also, see graph in margin. Its ratio is lower, and has been generally declining, compared with the industry ratio. This analysis implies a low risk from its financial leverage. Is financial leverage good or bad for Skechers? To answer that question we need to compare the company's return on the borrowed money to the rate it is paying creditors. If the company's return is higher, it is successfully borrowing money to make more money. A company's success with making money from borrowed money can quickly turn unprofitable if its own return drops below the rate it is paying creditors.

■ Decision Maker　　　　　　　　　Answer — p. 74

Investor　You consider buying stock in **Converse**. As part of your analysis, you compute its debt ratio for 2009, 2010, and 2011 as: 0.35, 0.74, and 0.94, respectively. Based on the debt ratio, is Converse a low-risk investment? Has the risk of buying Converse stock changed over this period? (The industry debt ratio averages 0.40.) ■

DEMONSTRATION PROBLEM

(This problem extends the demonstration problem of Chapter 1.) After several months of planning, Jasmine Worthy started a haircutting business called Expressions. The following events occurred during its first month.

a. On August 1, Worthy invested $3,000 cash and $15,000 of equipment in Expressions in exchange for common stock.

b. On August 2, Expressions paid $600 cash for furniture for the shop.

c. On August 3, Expressions paid $500 cash to rent space in a strip mall for August.

d. On August 4, it purchased $1,200 of equipment on credit for the shop (using a long-term note payable).

e. On August 5, Expressions opened for business. Cash received from haircutting services in the first week and a half of business (ended August 15) was $825.

f. On August 15, it provided $100 of haircutting services on account.

g. On August 17, it received a $100 check for services previously rendered on account.

h. On August 17, it paid $125 to an assistant for hours worked during the grand opening.

i. Cash received from services provided during the second half of August was $930.

j. On August 31, it paid a $400 installment toward principal on the note payable entered into on August 4.

k. On August 31, it paid $900 cash for dividends.

Required

1. Open the following ledger accounts in balance column format (account numbers are in parentheses): Cash (101); Accounts Receivable (102); Furniture (161); Store Equipment (165); Note Payable (240); Common Stock (307); Dividends (319); Haircutting Services Revenue (403); Wages Expense (623); and Rent Expense (640). Prepare general journal entries for the transactions.

2. Post the journal entries from (1) to the ledger accounts.

3. Prepare a trial balance as of August 31.

4. Prepare an income statement for August.

5. Prepare a statement of retained earnings for August.

6. Prepare a balance sheet as of August 31.

7. Determine the debt ratio as of August 31.

Extended Analysis

8. In the coming months, Expressions will experience a greater variety of business transactions. Identify which accounts are debited and which are credited for the following transactions. (*Hint:* We must use some accounts not opened in part 1.)

a. Purchase supplies with cash.

b. Pay cash for future insurance coverage.

c. Receive cash for services to be provided in the future.

d. Purchase supplies on account.

PLANNING THE SOLUTION

- Analyze each transaction and use the debit and credit rules to prepare a journal entry for each.
- Post each debit and each credit from journal entries to their ledger accounts and cross-reference each amount in the posting reference (PR) columns of the journal and ledger.
- Calculate each account balance and list the accounts with their balances on a trial balance.
- Verify that total debits in the trial balance equal total credits.
- To prepare the income statement, identify revenues and expenses. List those items on the statement, compute the difference, and label the result as *net income* or *net loss*.
- Use information in the ledger to prepare the statement of retained earnings.
- Use information in the ledger to prepare the balance sheet.
- Calculate the debt ratio by dividing total liabilities by total assets.
- Analyze the future transactions to identify the accounts affected and apply debit and credit rules.

SOLUTION TO DEMONSTRATION PROBLEM

1. General journal entries:

General Journal Entry

Page 1

Date	Account Titles and Explanation	PR	Debit	Credit
Aug. 1	Cash	101	3,000	
	Store Equipment	165	15,000	
	Common Stock	307		18,000
	Owner's investment for stock.			
2	Furniture	161	600	
	Cash	101		600
	Purchased furniture for cash.			
3	Rent Expense	640	500	
	Cash	101		500
	Paid rent for August.			
4	Store Equipment	165	1,200	
	Note Payable	240		1,200
	Purchased additional equipment on credit.			
15	Cash	101	825	
	Haircutting Services Revenue	403		825
	Cash receipts from first half of August.			

[continued on next page]

[continued from previous page]

15	Accounts Receivable	102	100	
	Haircutting Services Revenue	403		100
	To record revenue for services provided on account.			
17	Cash	101	100	
	Accounts Receivable	102		100
	To record cash received as payment on account.			
17	Wages Expense....................................	623	125	
	Cash	101		125
	Paid wages to assistant.			
31	Cash	101	930	
	Haircutting Services Revenue	403		930
	Cash receipts from second half of August.			
31	Note Payable	240	400	
	Cash	101		400
	Paid an installment on the note payable.			
31	Dividends	319	900	
	Cash	101		900
	Paid cash dividend.			

2. Post journal entries from part 1 to the ledger accounts:

General Ledger

Cash — Account No. 101

Date	PR	Debit	Credit	Balance
Aug. 1	G1	3,000		3,000
2	G1		600	2,400
3	G1		500	1,900
15	G1	825		2,725
17	G1	100		2,825
17	G1		125	2,700
31	G1	930		3,630
31	G1		400	3,230
31	G1		900	2,330

Accounts Receivable — Account No. 102

Date	PR	Debit	Credit	Balance
Aug. 15	G1	100		100
17	G1		100	0

Furniture — Account No. 161

Date	PR	Debit	Credit	Balance
Aug. 2	G1	600		600

Store Equipment — Account No. 165

Date	PR	Debit	Credit	Balance
Aug. 1	G1	15,000		15,000
4	G1	1,200		16,200

Note Payable — Account No. 240

Date	PR	Debit	Credit	Balance
Aug. 4	G1		1,200	1,200
31	G1	400		800

Common Stock — Account No. 307

Date	PR	Debit	Credit	Balance
Aug. 1	G1		18,000	18,000

Dividends — Account No. 319

Date	PR	Debit	Credit	Balance
Aug. 31	G1	900		900

Haircutting Services Revenue — Account No. 403

Date	PR	Debit	Credit	Balance
Aug. 15	G1		825	825
15	G1		100	925
31	G1		930	1,855

Wages Expense — Account No. 623

Date	PR	Debit	Credit	Balance
Aug. 17	G1	125		125

Rent Expense — Account No. 640

Date	PR	Debit	Credit	Balance
Aug. 3	G1	500		500

3. Prepare a trial balance from the ledger:

EXPRESSIONS Trial Balance August 31		
	Debit	Credit
Cash	$ 2,330	
Accounts receivable	0	
Furniture	600	
Store equipment	16,200	
Note payable		$ 800
Common stock		18,000
Dividends	900	
Haircutting services revenue		1,855
Wages expense	125	
Rent expense	500	
Totals	$20,655	$20,655

4.

EXPRESSIONS Income Statement For Month Ended August 31		
Revenues		
Haircutting services revenue		$1,855
Operating expenses		
Rent expense	$500	
Wages expense	125	
Total operating expenses		625
Net income		$1,230

5.

EXPRESSIONS Statement of Retained Earnings For Month Ended August 31	
Retained earnings, August 1	$ 0
Plus: Net income	1,230
	1,230
Less: Cash dividends	900
Retained earnings, August 31	$ 330

6.

EXPRESSIONS Balance Sheet August 31			
Assets		**Liabilities**	
Cash	$ 2,330	Note payable	$ 800
Furniture	600	**Equity**	
Store equipment	16,200	Common stock.................	18,000
		Retained earnings	330
		Total equity...................	18,330
Total assets	$19,130	Total liabilities and equity	$19,130

7. Debt ratio $= \dfrac{\text{Total liabilities}}{\text{Total assets}} = \dfrac{\$800}{\$19,130} = \underline{\underline{4.18\%}}$

8a. Supplies *debited*
       Cash *credited*

8b. Prepaid Insurance *debited*
       Cash *credited*

8c. Cash *debited*
       Unearned Services Revenue *credited*

8d. Supplies *debited*
       Accounts Payable *credited*

Summary

C1 **Explain the steps in processing transactions and the role of source documents.** The accounting process identifies business transactions and events, analyzes and records their effects, and summarizes and prepares information useful in making decisions. Transactions and events are the starting points in the accounting process. Source documents identify and describe transactions and events. Examples are sales tickets, checks, purchase orders, bills, and bank statements. Source documents provide objective and reliable evidence, making information more useful. The effects of transactions and events are recorded in journals. Posting along with a trial balance helps summarize and classify these effects.

C2 **Describe an account and its use in recording transactions.** An account is a detailed record of increases and decreases in a specific asset, liability, equity, revenue, or expense. Information from accounts is analyzed, summarized, and presented in reports and financial statements for decision makers.

C3 **Describe a ledger and a chart of accounts.** The ledger (or general ledger) is a record containing all accounts used by a company and their balances. It is referred to as the *books*. The chart of accounts is a list of all accounts and usually includes an identification number assigned to each account.

C4 **Define *debits* and *credits* and explain double-entry accounting.** *Debit* refers to left, and *credit* refers to right. Debits increase assets, expenses, and dividends while credits decrease them. Credits increase liabilities, common stock, and revenues; debits decrease them. Double-entry accounting means each transaction affects at least two accounts and has at least one debit and one credit. The system for recording debits and credits follows from the accounting equation. The left side of an account is the normal balance for assets, dividends, and expenses, and the right side is the normal balance for liabilities, common stock, and revenues.

A1 **Analyze the impact of transactions on accounts and financial statements.** We analyze transactions using concepts of double-entry accounting. This analysis is performed by determining a transaction's effects on accounts. These effects are recorded in journals and posted to ledgers.

A2 **Compute the debt ratio and describe its use in analyzing financial condition.** A company's debt ratio is computed as total liabilities divided by total assets. It reveals how much of the assets are financed by creditor (nonowner) financing. The higher this ratio, the more risk a company faces because liabilities must be repaid at specific dates.

P1 **Record transactions in a journal and post entries to a ledger.** Transactions are recorded in a journal. Each entry in a journal is posted to the accounts in the ledger. This provides information that is used to produce financial statements. Balance column accounts are widely used and include columns for debits, credits, and the account balance.

P2 **Prepare and explain the use of a trial balance.** A trial balance is a list of accounts from the ledger showing their debit or credit balances in separate columns. The trial balance is a summary of the ledger's contents and is useful in preparing financial statements and in revealing recordkeeping errors.

P3 **Prepare financial statements from business transactions.** The balance sheet, the statement of retained earnings, the income statement, and the statement of cash flows use data from the trial balance (and other financial statements) for their preparation.

Guidance Answers to Decision Maker and Decision Ethics

Cashier The advantages to the process proposed by the assistant manager include improved customer service, fewer delays, and less work for you. However, you should have serious concerns about internal control and the potential for fraud. In particular, the assistant manager could steal cash and simply enter fewer sales to match the remaining cash. You should reject her suggestion without the manager's approval. Moreover, you should have an ethical concern about the assistant manager's suggestion to ignore store policy.

Entrepreneur We can use the accounting equation (Assets = Liabilities + Equity) to help us identify risky customers to whom we would likely not want to extend credit. A balance sheet provides amounts for each of these key components. The lower a customer's equity is relative to liabilities, the less likely you would extend credit. A low equity means the business has little value that does not already have creditor claims to it.

Investor The debt ratio suggests the stock of Converse is of higher risk than normal and that this risk is rising. The average industry ratio of 0.40 further supports this conclusion. The 2011 debt ratio for Converse is twice the industry norm. Also, a debt ratio approaching 1.0 indicates little to no equity.

Guidance Answers to Quick Checks

1. Examples of source documents are sales tickets, checks, purchase orders, charges to customers, bills from suppliers, employee earnings records, and bank statements.

2. Source documents serve many purposes, including record-keeping and internal control. Source documents, especially if obtained from outside the organization, provide objective and reliable evidence about transactions and their amounts.

3.

Assets	Liabilities	Equity
a,c,e	b,d	—

4. An account is a record in an accounting system that records and stores the increases and decreases in a specific asset, liability, equity, revenue, or expense. The ledger is a collection of all the accounts of a company.

5. A company's size and diversity affect the number of accounts in its accounting system. The types of accounts depend on information the company needs to both effectively operate and report its activities in financial statements.

6. No. Debit and credit both can mean increase or decrease. The particular meaning in a circumstance depends on the *type of account*. For example, a debit increases the balance of asset, dividends, and expense accounts, but it decreases the balance of liability, common stock, and revenue accounts.

7. A chart of accounts is a list of all of a company's accounts and their identification numbers.

8. Equity is increased by revenues and by owner investments. Equity is decreased by expenses and dividends.

9. The name *double-entry* is used because all transactions affect at least two accounts. There must be at least one debit in one account and at least one credit in another account.

10. The answer is (c).

11.

Cash	15,000	
Equipment	23,000	
Common Stock		38,000
Investment by owner of cash and equipment.		

12. A compound journal entry affects three or more accounts.

13. Posting reference numbers are entered in the journal when posting to the ledger as a cross-reference that allows the record-keeper or auditor to trace debits and credits from one record to another.

14. At a minimum, dollar signs are placed beside the first and last numbers in a column. It is also common to place dollar signs beside any amount that appears after a ruled line to indicate that an addition or subtraction has occurred.

15. The Equipment account balance is incorrectly reported at $20,000—it should be $28,000. The effect of this error understates the trial balance's Debit column total by $8,000. This results in an $8,000 difference between the column totals.

16. An income statement reports a company's revenues and expenses along with the resulting net income or loss. A statement of retained earnings reports changes in retained earnings, including that from net income or loss. Both statements report transactions occurring over a period of time.

17. The balance sheet describes a company's financial position (assets, liabilities, and equity) at a point in time. The retained earnings amount in the balance sheet is obtained from the statement of retained earnings.

18. Revenues are inflows of assets in exchange for products or services provided to customers as part of the main operations of a business. Expenses are outflows or the using up of assets that result from providing products or services to customers.

19. Assets are the resources a business owns or controls that carry expected future benefits. Liabilities are the obligations of a business, representing the claims of others against the assets of a business. Equity reflects the owner's claims on the assets of the business after deducting liabilities.

Key Terms

mhhe.com/wildFINMAN4e

Account (p. 51)
Account balance (p. 55)
Balance column account (p. 58)
Chart of accounts (p. 54)
Common stock (p. 53)
Compound journal entry (p. 61)
Credit (p. 55)
Creditors (p. 52)
Debit (p. 55)

Debtors (p. 51)
Debt ratio (p. 69)
Dividends (p. 53)
Double-entry accounting (p. 55)
General journal (p. 56)
General ledger (p. 51)
Journal (p. 56)
Journalizing (p. 56)
Ledger (p. 51)

Posting (p. 56)
Posting reference (PR) column (p. 58)
Source documents (p. 50)
T-account (p. 55)
Trial balance (p. 65)
Unearned revenue (p. 52)

Additional Quiz Questions are available at the book's Website.

1. Amalia Company received its utility bill for the current period of $700 and immediately paid it. Its journal entry to record this transaction includes a
   a. Credit to Utility Expense for $700.
   b. Debit to Utility Expense for $700.
   c. Debit to Accounts Payable for $700.
   d. Debit to Cash for $700.
   e. Credit to Common Stock for $700.

2. On May 1, Mattingly Lawn Service collected $2,500 cash from a customer in advance of five months of lawn service. Mattingly's journal entry to record this transaction includes a
   a. Credit to Unearned Lawn Service Fees for $2,500.
   b. Debit to Lawn Service Fees Earned for $2,500.
   c. Credit to Cash for $2,500.
   d. Debit to Unearned Lawn Service Fees for $2,500.
   e. Credit to Common Stock for $2,500.

3. Liang Shue contributed $250,000 cash and land worth $500,000 to open his new business, Shue Consulting Corporation. Which of the following journal entries does Shue Consulting make to record this transaction?
   a. Cash Assets 750,000
      Common Stock   750,000
   b. Common Stock 750,000
      Assets   750,000
   c. Cash 250,000
      Land 500,000
      Common Stock   750,000

   d. Common Stock 750,000
      Cash   250,000
      Land   500,000

4. A trial balance prepared at year-end shows total credits exceed total debits by $765. This discrepancy could have been caused by
   a. An error in the general journal where a $765 increase in Accounts Payable was recorded as a $765 decrease in Accounts Payable.
   b. The ledger balance for Accounts Payable of $7,650 being entered in the trial balance as $765.
   c. A general journal error where a $765 increase in Accounts Receivable was recorded as a $765 increase in Cash.
   d. The ledger balance of $850 in Accounts Receivable was entered in the trial balance as $85.
   e. An error in recording a $765 increase in Cash as a credit.

5. Bonaventure Company has total assets of $1,000,000, liabilities of $400,000, and equity of $600,000. What is its debt ratio (rounded to a whole percent)?
   a. 250%
   b. 167%
   c. 67%
   d. 150%
   e. 40%

[i] Icon denotes assignments that involve decision making.

Discussion Questions

1. Provide the names of two (a) asset accounts, (b) liability accounts, and (c) equity accounts.
2. What is the difference between a note payable and an account payable?
3. [i] Discuss the steps in processing business transactions.
4. What kinds of transactions can be recorded in a general journal?
5. Are debits or credits typically listed first in general journal entries? Are the debits or the credits indented?
6. If assets are valuable resources and asset accounts have debit balances, why do expense accounts also have debit balances?
7. Should a transaction be recorded first in a journal or the ledger? Why?
8. [i] Why does the recordkeeper prepare a trial balance?
9. If an incorrect amount is journalized and posted to the accounts, how should the error be corrected?
10. Identify the four financial statements of a business.
11. [i] What information is reported in an income statement?

12. [i] Why does the user of an income statement need to know the time period that it covers?
13. [i] What information is reported in a balance sheet?
14. Define (a) assets, (b) liabilities, (c) equity, and (d) net assets.
15. Which financial statement is sometimes called the statement of financial position?
16. [i] Review the **Research In Motion** balance sheet in Appendix A. Identify three accounts on its balance sheet that carry debit balances and three accounts on its balance sheet that carry credit balances. **RIM**
17. Review the **Apple** balance sheet in Appendix A. Identify an asset with the word receivable in its account title and a liability with the word payable in its account title. **Apple**
18. Locate **Palm**'s income statement in Appendix A. What is the title of its revenue account? **Palm**
19. Refer to **Nokia**'s balance sheet in Appendix A. What does Nokia title its current asset referring to merchandise available for sale? **NOKIA**

connect

Identify the financial statement(s) where each of the following items appears. Use I for income statement, E for statement of retained earnings, and B for balance sheet.

a. Accounts payable	**d.** Office supplies	**g.** Office equipment
b. Cash	**e.** Prepaid insurance	**h.** Cash dividends
c. Rent expense	**f.** Revenue	**i.** Unearned rent revenue

QUICK STUDY

QS 2-1
Identifying financial statement items
C2 P3

Identify the items from the following list that are likely to serve as source documents.

a. Bank statement	**d.** Trial balance	**g.** Company revenue account
b. Sales ticket	**e.** Telephone bill	**h.** Balance sheet
c. Income statement	**f.** Invoice from supplier	**i.** Prepaid rent

QS 2-2
Identifying source documents
C1

Identify whether a debit or credit yields the indicated change for each of the following accounts.

a. To increase Store Equipment	**f.** To decrease Unearned Revenue
b. To increase Land	**g.** To decrease Prepaid Insurance
c. To decrease Cash	**h.** To increase Notes Payable
d. To increase Utilities Expense	**i.** To decrease Accounts Receivable
e. To increase Fees Earned	**j.** To increase Common Stock

QS 2-3
Analyzing debit or credit by account
A1

Identify the normal balance (debit or credit) for each of the following accounts.

a. Equipment	**d.** Office Supplies	**g.** Prepaid Insurance
b. Wages Expense	**e.** Dividends	**h.** Wages Payable
c. Repair Services Revenue	**f.** Accounts Receivable	**i.** Common Stock

QS 2-4
Identifying normal balance
C4

Indicate whether a debit or credit *decreases* the normal balance of each of the following accounts.

a. Land	**e.** Salaries Expense	**i.** Interest Revenue
b. Service Revenue	**f.** Common Stock	**j.** Dividends
c. Interest Payable	**g.** Prepaid Insurance	**k.** Unearned Revenue
d. Accounts Receivable	**h.** Buildings	**l.** Accounts Payable

QS 2-5
Linking debit or credit with normal balance
C4

Prepare journal entries for each of the following selected transactions.

a. On January 15, Kolby Anderson opens a remodeling company called Fancy Kitchens by investing $75,000 cash along with equipment having a $30,000 value in exchange for common stock.

b. On January 21, Fancy Kitchens purchases office supplies on credit for $650.

c. On January 25, Fancy Kitchens receives $8,700 cash for performing remodeling services.

d. On January 30, Fancy Kitchens receives $4,000 cash in advance of providing remodeling services to a customer.

QS 2-6
Preparing journal entries
P1

A trial balance has total debits of $20,000 and total credits of $24,500. Which one of the following errors would create this imbalance? Explain.

a. A $2,250 debit posting to Accounts Receivable was posted mistakenly to Cash.

b. A $4,500 debit posting to Equipment was posted mistakenly to Supplies.

c. An entry debiting Cash and crediting Accounts Payable for $4,500 was mistakenly not posted.

d. A $2,250 credit to Revenue in a journal entry is incorrectly posted to the ledger as a $2,250 debit, leaving the Revenue account with a $6,300 credit balance.

e. A $4,500 debit to Rent Expense in a journal entry is incorrectly posted to the ledger as a $4,500 credit, leaving the Rent Expense account with a $750 debit balance.

f. A $2,250 debit to Utilities Expense in a journal entry is incorrectly posted to the ledger as a $2,250 credit, leaving the Utilities Expense account with a $3,000 debit balance.

QS 2-7
Identifying a posting error
P2

QS 2-8
Classifying accounts in
financial statements
P3

Indicate the financial statement on which each of the following items appears. Use I for income statement, E for statement of retained earnings, and B for balance sheet.

a. Buildings	**e.** Rental Revenue	**i.** Accounts Receivable
b. Interest Expense	**f.** Insurance Expense	**j.** Salaries Expense
c. Dividends	**g.** Services Revenue	**k.** Equipment
d. Office Supplies	**h.** Interest Payable	**l.** Prepaid Insurance

QS 2-9
International accounting
standards
C4

Answer each of the following questions related to international accounting standards.

a. What type of entry system is applied when accounting follows IFRS?

b. Identify the number and usual titles of the financial statements prepared under IFRS.

c. How do differences in accounting controls and enforcement impact accounting reports prepared across different countries?

McGraw Hill **connect**

EXERCISES

Exercise 2-1
Steps in analyzing and recording
transactions   C1

Order the following steps in the accounting process that focus on analyzing and recording transactions.

_____ **a.** Record relevant transactions in a journal.

_____ **b.** Prepare and analyze the trial balance.

_____ **c.** Analyze each transaction from source documents.

_____ **d.** Post journal information to ledger accounts.

Exercise 2-2
Identifying and classifying
accounts
C2

Enter the number for the item that best completes each of the descriptions below.

1. Account	**3.** Asset	**5.** Equity
2. Three	**4.** Liability	

a. Common stock and dividends are examples of _____ accounts.

b. Accounts payable, unearned revenue, and note payable are examples of _____ accounts.

c. Accounts receivable, prepaid accounts, supplies, and land are examples of _____ accounts.

d. Accounts are arranged into _____ general categories

e. An _____ is a record of increases and decreases in a specific asset, liability, equity, revenue, or expense item.

Exercise 2-3
Identifying a ledger and chart
of accounts
C3

Enter the number for the item that best completes each of the descriptions below.

1. General ledger   **2.** Chart

a. The _____ is a record containing all accounts used by a company.

b. A _____ of accounts is a list of all accounts a company uses.

Exercise 2-4
Identifying type and normal
balances of accounts
C4

For each of the following (1) identify the type of account as an asset, liability, equity, revenue, or expense, (2) identify the normal balance of the account, and (3) enter *debit* (*Dr.*) or *credit* (*Cr.*) to identify the kind of entry that would increase the account balance.

a. Fees Earned	**e.** Cash	**i.** Accounts Receivable
b. Equipment	**f.** Legal Expense	**j.** Dividends
c. Notes Payable	**g.** Prepaid Insurance	**k.** License Fee Revenue
d. Common Stock	**h.** Land	**l.** Unearned Revenue

Exercise 2-5
Analyzing effects of
transactions on accounts
A1

Taylor Co. bills a client $48,000 for services provided and agrees to accept the following three items in full payment: (1) $7,500 cash, (2) computer equipment worth $75,000, and (3) to assume responsibility for a $34,500 note payable related to the computer equipment. The entry Taylor makes to record this transaction includes which one or more of the following?

a. $34,500 increase in a liability account	**d.** $48,000 increase in an asset account
b. $7,500 increase in the Cash account	**e.** $48,000 increase in a revenue account
c. $7,500 increase in a revenue account	**f.** $34,500 increase in an equity account

Use the information in each of the following separate cases to calculate the unknown amount.

a. During October, Shandra Company had $97,500 of cash receipts and $101,250 of cash disbursements. The October 31 Cash balance was $16,800. Determine how much cash the company had at the close of business on September 30.

b. On September 30, Mordish Co. had a $97,500 balance in Accounts Receivable. During October, the company collected $88,950 from its credit customers. The October 31 balance in Accounts Receivable was $100,500. Determine the amount of sales on account that occurred in October.

c. Nasser Co. had $147,000 of accounts payable on September 30 and $136,500 on October 31. Total purchases on account during October were $270,000. Determine how much cash was paid on accounts payable during October.

Exercise 2-6
Analyzing account entries and balances

A1

Prepare general journal entries for the following transactions of a new company called Pose for Pics.

Aug. 1   Kasey Madison, the owner, invested $7,500 cash and $32,500 of photography equipment in the company in exchange for common stock.
       2   The company paid $3,000 cash for an insurance policy covering the next 24 months.
       5   The company purchased office supplies for $1,400 cash.
      20   The company received $2,650 cash in photography fees earned.
      31   The company paid $875 cash for August utilities.

Exercise 2-7
Preparing general journal entries

P1

Use the information in Exercise 2-7 to prepare an August 31 trial balance for Pose for Pics. Begin by opening these T-accounts: Cash; Office Supplies; Prepaid Insurance; Photography Equipment; Common Stock; Photography Fees Earned; and Utilities Expense. Then, post the general journal entries to these T-accounts (which will serve as the ledger), and prepare the trial balance.

Exercise 2-8
Preparing T-accounts (ledger) and a trial balance   P2

Prepare general journal entries to record the transactions below for Dexter Company by using the following accounts: Cash; Accounts Receivable; Office Supplies; Office Equipment; Accounts Payable; Common Stock; Dividends; Fees Earned; and Rent Expense. Use the letters beside each transaction to identify entries. After recording the transactions, post them to T-accounts, which serves as the general ledger for this assignment. Determine the ending balance of each T-account.

a. Macy Dexter, owner, invested $12,750 cash in the company in exchange for common stock.
b. The company purchased office supplies for $375 cash.
c. The company purchased $7,050 of office equipment on credit.
d. The company received $1,500 cash as fees for services provided to a customer.
e. The company paid $7,050 cash to settle the payable for the office equipment purchased in transaction *c*.
f. The company billed a customer $2,700 as fees for services provided.
g. The company paid $525 cash for the monthly rent.
h. The company collected $1,125 cash as partial payment for the account receivable created in transaction *f*.
i. The company paid $1,000 cash for dividends.

Exercise 2-9
Recording effects of transactions in T-accounts

A1

Check   Cash ending balance, $6,425

After recording the transactions of Exercise 2-9 in T-accounts and calculating the balance of each account, prepare a trial balance. Use May 31, 2011, as its report date.

Exercise 2-10
Preparing a trial balance   P2

Examine the following transactions and identify those that create revenues for Jade Services, a company owned by Mia Jade. Prepare general journal entries to record those revenue transactions and explain why the other transactions did not create revenues.

a. Mia Jade invests $38,250 cash in the company in exchange for common stock.
b. The company provided $1,350 of services on credit.
c. The company provided services to a client and immediately received $1,575 cash.
d. The company received $9,150 cash from a client in payment for services to be provided next year.
e. The company received $4,500 cash from a client in partial payment of an account receivable.
f. The company borrowed $150,000 cash from the bank by signing a promissory note.

Exercise 2-11
Analyzing and journalizing revenue transactions

A1 P1

Exercise 2-12
Analyzing and journalizing expense transactions

A1 P1

Examine the following transactions and identify those that create expenses for Jade Services. Prepare general journal entries to record those expense transactions and explain why the other transactions did not create expenses.

a. The company paid $14,100 cash for payment on a 14-month old liability for office supplies.

b. The company paid $1,125 cash for the just completed two-week salary of the receptionist.

c. The company paid $45,000 cash for equipment purchased.

d. The company paid $930 cash for this month's utilities.

e. The company paid $5,000 cash for dividends.

Exercise 2-13
Preparing an income statement

C3 P3

Dominick Lopez operates a consulting firm called Tech Today, which began operations on August 1. On August 31, the company's records show the following accounts and amounts for the month of August. Use this information to prepare an August income statement for the business.

Cash.....................	$ 8,360	Dividends	$ 3,000
Accounts receivable	17,000	Consulting fees earned...............	17,000
Office supplies	3,250	Rent expense	4,550
Land	46,000	Salaries expense	8,000
Office equipment	18,000	Telephone expense...................	560
Accounts payable	8,000	Miscellaneous expenses	280
Common Stock	84,000		

Check   Net income, $3,610

Exercise 2-14
Preparing a statement of retained earnings   P3

Check   End. Ret. Earn., $610

Use the information in Exercise 2-13 to prepare an August statement of retained earnings for Tech Today. (The owner invested $84,000 cash in the company in exchange for common stock on August 1.)

Exercise 2-15
Preparing a balance sheet   P3

Use the information in Exercise 2-13 (if completed, you can also use your solution to Exercise 2-14) to prepare an August 31 balance sheet for Tech Today.

Exercise 2-16
Computing net income

A1

A corporation had the following assets and liabilities at the beginning and end of this year.

	Assets	Liabilities
Beginning of the year	$ 70,000	$30,000
End of the year	115,000	46,000

Determine the net income earned or net loss incurred by the business during the year for each of the following *separate* cases:

a. Owner made no investments in the business and no dividends were paid during the year.

b. Owner made no investments in the business, but dividends were $1,250 cash per month.

c. No dividends were paid during the year, but the owner did invest an additional $45,000 cash in exchange for common stock.

d. Dividends were $1,250 cash per month and the owner invested an additional $25,000 cash in exchange for common stock.

Exercise 2-17
Analyzing changes in a company's equity

P3

Compute the missing amount for each of the following separate companies *a* through *d*.

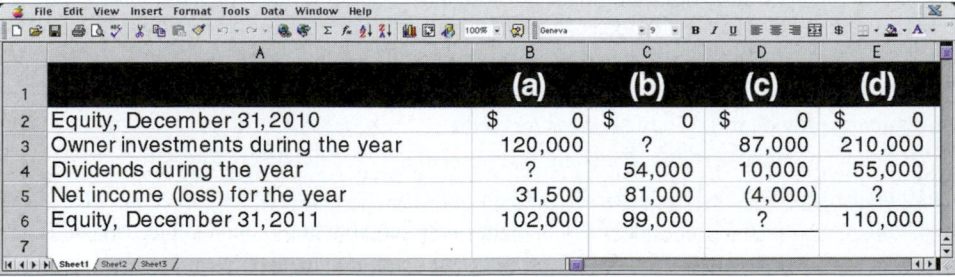

	(a)	(b)	(c)	(d)
Equity, December 31, 2010	$ 0	$ 0	$ 0	$ 0
Owner investments during the year	120,000	?	87,000	210,000
Dividends during the year	?	54,000	10,000	55,000
Net income (loss) for the year	31,500	81,000	(4,000)	?
Equity, December 31, 2011	102,000	99,000	?	110,000

Assume the following T-accounts reflect Joy Co.'s general ledger and that seven transactions *a* through *g* are posted to them. Provide a short description of each transaction. Include the amounts in your descriptions.

Exercise 2-18
Interpreting and describing transactions from T-accounts

A1

Cash			
(a)	7,000	(b)	3,600
(e)	2,500	(c)	600
		(f)	2,400
		(g)	700

Office Supplies	
(c)	600
(d)	200

Prepaid Insurance	
(b)	3,600

Equipment	
(a)	5,600
(d)	9,400

Automobiles	
(a)	11,000

Accounts Payable			
(f)	2,400	(d)	9,600

Common Stock			
		(a)	23,600

Delivery Services Revenue			
		(e)	2,500

Gas and Oil Expense	
(g)	700

Use information from the T-accounts in Exercise 2-18 to prepare general journal entries for each of the seven transactions *a* through *g*.

Exercise 2-19
Preparing general journal entries

P1

Posting errors are identified in the following table. In column (1), enter the amount of the difference between the two trial balance columns (debit and credit) due to the error. In column (2), identify the trial balance column (debit or credit) with the larger amount if they are not equal. In column (3), identify the account(s) affected by the error. In column (4), indicate the amount by which the account(s) in column (3) is under- or overstated. Item (a) is completed as an example.

Exercise 2-20
Identifying effects of posting errors on the trial balance

A1 P2

	Description of Posting Error	(1) Difference between Debit and Credit Columns	(2) Column with the Larger Total	(3) Identify Account(s) Incorrectly Stated	(4) Amount that Account(s) Is Over- or Understated
a.	$2,400 debit to Rent Expense is posted as a $1,590 debit.	$810	Credit	Rent Expense	Rent Expense understated $810
b.	$4,050 credit to Cash is posted twice as two credits to Cash.				
c.	$9,900 debit to the Dividends account is debited to Common Stock.				
d.	$2,250 debit to Prepaid Insurance is posted as a debit to Insurance Expense.				
e.	$42,000 debit to Machinery is posted as a debit to Accounts Payable.				
f.	$4,950 credit to Services Revenue is posted as a $495 credit.				
g.	$1,440 debit to Store Supplies is not posted.				

You are told the column totals in a trial balance are not equal. After careful analysis, you discover only one error. Specifically, a correctly journalized credit purchase of a computer for $16,950 is posted from the journal to the ledger with a $16,950 debit to Office Equipment and another $16,950 debit to Accounts Payable. The Office Equipment account has a debit balance of $40,100 on the trial balance. Answer each of the following questions and compute the dollar amount of any misstatement.

Exercise 2-21
Analyzing a trial balance error

A1 P2

a. Is the debit column total of the trial balance overstated, understated, or correctly stated?

b. Is the credit column total of the trial balance overstated, understated, or correctly stated?

c. Is the Office Equipment account balance overstated, understated, or correctly stated in the trial balance?

d. Is the Accounts Payable account balance overstated, understated, or correctly stated in the trial balance?

e. If the debit column total of the trial balance is $360,000 before correcting the error, what is the total of the credit column before correction?

Exercise 2-22
Interpreting the debt ratio and return on assets
A2

a. Calculate the debt ratio and the return on assets using the year-end information for each of the following six separate companies ($ thousands).

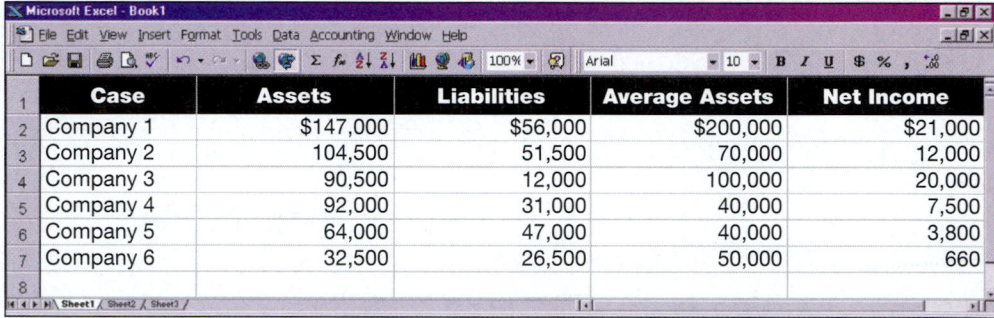

Case	Assets	Liabilities	Average Assets	Net Income
Company 1	$147,000	$56,000	$200,000	$21,000
Company 2	104,500	51,500	70,000	12,000
Company 3	90,500	12,000	100,000	20,000
Company 4	92,000	31,000	40,000	7,500
Company 5	64,000	47,000	40,000	3,800
Company 6	32,500	26,500	50,000	660

b. Of the six companies, which business relies most heavily on creditor financing?

c. Of the six companies, which business relies most heavily on equity financing?

d. Which two companies indicate the greatest risk?

e. Which two companies earn the highest return on assets?

f. Which one company would investors likely prefer based on the risk–return relation?

Exercise 2-23
Preparing a balance sheet following IFRS
P3

BMW reports the following balance sheet accounts for the year ended December 31, 2009 (euro in millions). Prepare the balance sheet for this company as of December 31, 2009, following the usual IFRS formats.

Current liabilities	€ 8,350	Noncurrent liabilities	€10,943
Current assets	17,663	Noncurrent assets	6,984
Total equity	5,354		

connect

PROBLEM SET A

Problem 2-1A
Preparing and posting journal entries; preparing a trial balance
C3 C4 A1 P1 P2

mhhe.com/wildFINMAN4e

Gary Bauer opens a computer consulting business called Technology Consultants and completes the following transactions in April.

April 1 Bauer invested $100,000 cash along with $24,000 in office equipment in the company in exchange for common stock.
       2 The company prepaid $7,200 cash for twelve months' rent for an office. (*Hint:* Debit Prepaid Rent for $7,200.)
       3 The company made credit purchases of office equipment for $12,000 and office supplies for $2,400. Payment is due within 10 days.
       6 The company completed services for a client and immediately received $2,000 cash.
       9 The company completed an $8,000 project for a client, who must pay within 30 days.
      13 The company paid $14,400 cash to settle the account payable created on April 3.
      19 The company paid $6,000 cash for the premium on a 12-month insurance policy. (*Hint:* Debit Prepaid Insurance for $6,000.)
      22 The company received $6,400 cash as partial payment for the work completed on April 9.
      25 The company completed work for another client for $2,640 on credit.
      28 The company paid $6,200 cash for dividends.
      29 The company purchased $800 of additional office supplies on credit.
      30 The company paid $700 cash for this month's utility bill.

Required

1. Prepare general journal entries to record these transactions (use the account titles listed in part 2).

2. Open the following ledger accounts—their account numbers are in parentheses (use the balance column format): Cash (101); Accounts Receivable (106); Office Supplies (124); Prepaid Insurance (128);

Prepaid Rent (131); Office Equipment (163); Accounts Payable (201); Common Stock (307); Dividends (319); Services Revenue (403); and Utilities Expense (690). Post the journal entries from part 1 to the ledger accounts and enter the balance after each posting.

3. Prepare a trial balance as of the end of April.

Check   (2) Ending balances: Cash, $73,900; Accounts Receivable, $4,240; Accounts Payable, $800

(3) Total debits, $137,440

Shelton Engineering completed the following transactions in the month of June.

a. Shana Shelton, the owner, invested $105,000 cash, office equipment with a value of $6,000, and $45,000 of drafting equipment to launch the company in exchange for common stock.

b. The company purchased land worth $54,000 for an office by paying $5,400 cash and signing a long-term note payable for $48,600.

c. The company purchased a portable building with $75,000 cash and moved it onto the land acquired in *b*.

d. The company paid $6,000 cash for the premium on an 18-month insurance policy.

e. The company completed and delivered a set of plans for a client and collected $5,700 cash.

f. The company purchased $22,500 of additional drafting equipment by paying $10,500 cash and signing a long-term note payable for $12,000.

g. The company completed $12,000 of engineering services for a client. This amount is to be received in 30 days.

h. The company purchased $2,250 of additional office equipment on credit.

i. The company completed engineering services for $18,000 on credit.

j. The company received a bill for rent of equipment that was used on a recently completed job. The $1,200 rent cost must be paid within 30 days.

k. The company collected $7,200 cash in partial payment from the client described in transaction *g*.

l. The company paid $1,500 cash for wages to a drafting assistant.

m. The company paid $2,250 cash to settle the account payable created in transaction *h*.

n. The company paid $675 cash for minor maintenance of its drafting equipment.

o. The company paid $9,360 cash for dividends.

p. The company paid $1,500 cash for wages to a drafting assistant.

q. The company paid $3,000 cash for advertisements in the local newspaper during June.

Required

1. Prepare general journal entries to record these transactions (use the account titles listed in part 2).

2. Open the following ledger accounts—their account numbers are in parentheses (use the balance column format): Cash (101); Accounts Receivable (106); Prepaid Insurance (108); Office Equipment (163); Drafting Equipment (164); Building (170); Land (172); Accounts Payable (201); Notes Payable (250); Common Stock (307); Dividends (319); Engineering Fees Earned (402); Wages Expense (601); Equipment Rental Expense (602); Advertising Expense (603); and Repairs Expense (604). Post the journal entries from part 1 to the accounts and enter the balance after each posting.

3. Prepare a trial balance as of the end of June.

Problem 2-2A
Preparing and posting journal entries; preparing a trial balance

C3 C4 A1 P1 P2

Check   (2) Ending balances: Cash, $2,715; Accounts Receivable, $22,800; Accounts Payable, $1,200

(3) Trial balance totals, $253,500

The accounting records of Fabiano Distribution show the following assets and liabilities as of December 31, 2010 and 2011.

December 31	2010	2011
Cash	$ 52,500	$ 18,750
Accounts receivable	28,500	22,350
Office supplies	4,500	3,300
Office equipment	138,000	147,000
Trucks	54,000	54,000
Building	0	180,000
Land	0	45,000
Accounts payable	7,500	37,500
Note payable	0	105,000

Problem 2-3A
Computing net income from equity analysis, preparing a balance sheet, and computing the debt ratio

C2 A1 A2 P3

mhhe.com/wildFINMAN4e

Late in December 2011, the business purchased a small office building and land for $225,000. It paid $120,000 cash toward the purchase and a $105,000 note payable was signed for the balance. Mr. Fabiano had to invest $35,000 cash in the business (in exchange for stock) to enable it to pay the $120,000 cash. The business also pays $3,000 cash per month for dividends.

Required

1. Prepare balance sheets for the business as of December 31, 2010 and 2011. (*Hint:* Report only total equity on the balance sheet and remember that total equity equals the difference between assets and liabilities.)

Check   (2) Net income, $58,900

2. By comparing equity amounts from the balance sheets and using the additional information presented in this problem, prepare a calculation to show how much net income was earned by the business during 2011.

(3) Debt ratio, 30.29%

3. Compute the 2011 year-end debt ratio for the business.

Problem 2-4A

Preparing and posting journal entries; preparing a trial balance

C3 C4 A1 P1 P2

Santo Birch opens a Web consulting business called Show-Me-the-Money and completes the following transactions in its first month of operations.

March	1	Birch invests $150,000 cash along with office equipment valued at $22,000 in the company in exchange for common stock.
	2	The company prepaid $6,000 cash for twelve months' rent for office space. (*Hint:* Debit Prepaid Rent for $6,000.)
	3	The company made credit purchases for $3,000 in office equipment and $1,200 in office supplies. Payment is due within 10 days.
	6	The company completed services for a client and immediately received $4,000 cash.
	9	The company completed a $7,500 project for a client, who must pay within 30 days.
	13	The company paid $4,200 cash to settle the account payable created on March 3.
	19	The company paid $5,000 cash for the premium on a 12-month insurance policy. (*Hint:* Debit Prepaid Insurance for $5,000.)
	22	The company received $3,500 cash as partial payment for the work completed on March 9.
	25	The company completed work for another client for $3,820 on credit.
	29	The company paid $5,100 cash for dividends.
	30	The company purchased $600 of additional office supplies on credit.
	31	The company paid $200 cash for this month's utility bill.

Required

1. Prepare general journal entries to record these transactions (use account titles listed in part 2).

Check   (2) Ending balances:
Cash, $137,000; Accounts
Receivable, $7,820; Accounts
Payable, $600

2. Open the following ledger accounts—their account numbers are in parentheses (use the balance column format): Cash (101); Accounts Receivable (106); Office Supplies (124); Prepaid Insurance (128); Prepaid Rent (131); Office Equipment (163); Accounts Payable (201); Common Stock (307); Dividends (319); Services Revenue (403); and Utilities Expense (690). Post journal entries from part 1 to the ledger accounts and enter the balance after each posting.

(3) Total debits, $187,920

3. Prepare a trial balance as of March 31.

Problem 2-5A

Recording transactions; posting to ledger; preparing a trial balance

C3 A1 P1 P2

Business transactions completed by Eric Pense during the month of September are as follows.

- **a.** Pense invested $23,000 cash along with office equipment valued at $12,000 in exchange for common stock of a new company named EP Consulting.
- **b.** The company purchased land valued at $8,000 and a building valued at $33,000. The purchase is paid with $15,000 cash and a long-term note payable for $26,000.
- **c.** The company purchased $600 of office supplies on credit.
- **d.** Pense invested his personal automobile in the company in exchange for more common stock. The automobile has a value of $7,000 and is to be used exclusively in the business.
- **e.** The company purchased $1,100 of additional office equipment on credit.
- **f.** The company paid $800 cash salary to an assistant.
- **g.** The company provided services to a client and collected $2,700 cash.
- **h.** The company paid $430 cash for this month's utilities.
- **i.** The company paid $600 cash to settle the account payable created in transaction *c*.
- **j.** The company purchased $4,000 of new office equipment by paying $4,000 cash.
- **k.** The company completed $2,400 of services for a client, who must pay within 30 days.
- **l.** The company paid $800 cash salary to an assistant.
- **m.** The company received $1,000 cash in partial payment on the receivable created in transaction *k*.
- **n.** The company paid $1,050 cash for dividends.

Required

1. Prepare general journal entries to record these transactions (use account titles listed in part 2).
2. Open the following ledger accounts—their account numbers are in parentheses (use the balance column format): Cash (101); Accounts Receivable (106); Office Supplies (108); Office Equipment (163); Automobiles (164); Building (170); Land (172); Accounts Payable (201); Notes Payable (250); Common Stock (307); Dividends (319); Fees Earned (402); Salaries Expense (601); and Utilities Expense (602). Post the journal entries from part 1 to the ledger accounts and enter the balance after each posting.
3. Prepare a trial balance as of the end of September.

Check   (2) Ending balances: Cash, $4,020; Office Equipment, $17,100

(3) Trial balance totals, $74,200

Carlos Beltran started an engineering firm called Beltran Engineering. He began operations and completed seven transactions in May, which included his initial investment of $17,000 cash. After those seven transactions, the ledger included the following accounts with normal balances.

Problem 2-6A
Analyzing account balances and reconstructing transactions
C1 C3 A1 P2

Cash	$26,660
Office supplies	660
Prepaid insurance	3,200
Office equipment	16,500
Accounts payable	16,500
Common Stock	17,000
Dividends	3,740
Engineering fees earned	24,000
Rent expense	6,740

Required

1. Prepare a trial balance for this business as of the end of May.

Check   (1) Trial balance totals, $57,500

Analysis Components

2. Analyze the accounts and their balances and prepare a list that describes each of the seven most likely transactions and their amounts.
3. Prepare a report of cash received and cash paid showing how the seven transactions in part 2 yield the $26,660 ending Cash balance.

(3) Cash paid, $14,340

Shaw Management Services opens for business and completes these transactions in November.

PROBLEM SET B

Problem 2-1B
Preparing and posting journal entries; preparing a trial balance
C3 C4 A1 P1 P2

Nov. 1   Kita Shaw, the owner, invested $30,000 cash along with $15,000 of office equipment in the company in exchange for common stock.
  2   The company prepaid $4,500 cash for six months' rent for an office. (*Hint:* Debit Prepaid Rent for $4,500.)
  4   The company made credit purchases of office equipment for $2,500 and of office supplies for $600. Payment is due within 10 days.
  8   The company completed work for a client and immediately received $3,400 cash.
  12   The company completed a $10,200 project for a client, who must pay within 30 days.
  13   The company paid $3,100 cash to settle the payable created on November 4.
  19   The company paid $1,800 cash for the premium on a 24-month insurance policy.
  22   The company received $5,200 cash as partial payment for the work completed on November 12.
  24   The company completed work for another client for $1,750 on credit.
  28   The company paid $5,300 cash for dividends.
  29   The company purchased $249 of additional office supplies on credit.
  30   The company paid $531 cash for this month's utility bill.

Required

1. Prepare general journal entries to record these transactions (use account titles listed in part 2).
2. Open the following ledger accounts—their account numbers are in parentheses (use the balance column format): Cash (101); Accounts Receivable (106); Office Supplies (124); Prepaid Insurance (128); Prepaid Rent (131); Office Equipment (163); Accounts Payable (201); Common Stock (307); Dividends (319); Services Revenue (403); and Utilities Expense (690). Post the journal entries from part 1 to the ledger accounts and enter the balance after each posting.
3. Prepare a trial balance as of the end of November.

Check   (2) Ending balances: Cash, $23,369; Accounts Receivable, $6,750; Accounts Payable, $249

(3) Total debits, $60,599

Problem 2-2B

Preparing and posting journal entries; preparing a trial balance

C3 C4 A1 P1 P2

At the beginning of April, Brooke Gable launched a custom computer solutions company called Softways. The company had the following transactions during April.

a. Brooke Gable invested $45,000 cash, office equipment with a value of $4,500, and $28,000 of computer equipment in the company in exchange for common stock.

b. The company purchased land worth $24,000 for an office by paying $4,800 cash and signing a long-term note payable for $19,200.

c. The company purchased a portable building with $21,000 cash and moved it onto the land acquired in *b*.

d. The company paid $6,600 cash for the premium on a two-year insurance policy.

e. The company provided services to a client and immediately collected $3,200 cash.

f. The company purchased $3,500 of additional computer equipment by paying $700 cash and signing a long-term note payable for $2,800.

g. The company completed $3,750 of services for a client. This amount is to be received within 30 days.

h. The company purchased $750 of additional office equipment on credit.

i. The company completed client services for $9,200 on credit.

j. The company received a bill for rent of a computer testing device that was used on a recently completed job. The $320 rent cost must be paid within 30 days.

k. The company collected $4,600 cash in partial payment from the client described in transaction *i*.

l. The company paid $1,600 cash for wages to an assistant.

m. The company paid $750 cash to settle the payable created in transaction *h*.

n. The company paid $425 cash for minor maintenance of the company's computer equipment.

o. The company paid $3,875 cash for dividends.

p. The company paid $1,600 cash for wages to an assistant.

q. The company paid $800 cash for advertisements in the local newspaper during April.

Required

1. Prepare general journal entries to record these transactions (use account titles listed in part 2).

Check   (2) Ending balances: Cash, $10,650; Accounts Receivable, $8,350; Accounts Payable, $320

2. Open the following ledger accounts—their account numbers are in parentheses (use the balance column format): Cash (101); Accounts Receivable (106); Prepaid Insurance (108); Office Equipment (163); Computer Equipment (164); Building (170); Land (172); Accounts Payable (201); Notes Payable (250); Common Stock (307); Dividends (319); Fees Earned (402); Wages Expense (601); Computer Rental Expense (602); Advertising Expense (603); and Repairs Expense (604). Post the journal entries from part 1 to the accounts and enter the balance after each posting.

(3) Trial balance totals, $115,970

3. Prepare a trial balance as of the end of April.

Problem 2-3B

Computing net income from equity analysis, preparing a balance sheet, and computing the debt ratio

C2 A1 A2 P3

The accounting records of Schmit Co. show the following assets and liabilities as of December 31, 2010 and 2011.

December 31	2010	2011
Cash	$14,000	$ 10,000
Accounts receivable	25,000	30,000
Office supplies	10,000	12,500
Office equipment	60,000	60,000
Machinery	30,500	30,500
Building	0	260,000
Land	0	65,000
Accounts payable	5,000	15,000
Note payable	0	260,000

Late in December 2011, the business purchased a small office building and land for $325,000. It paid $65,000 cash toward the purchase and a $260,000 note payable was signed for the balance. Janet Schmit, the owner, had to invest an additional $25,000 cash (in exchange for common stock) to enable it to pay the $65,000 cash toward the purchase. The company also pays $1,000 cash per month for dividends.

Required

1. Prepare balance sheets for the business as of December 31, 2010 and 2011. (*Hint:* Report only total equity on the balance sheet and remember that total equity equals the difference between assets and liabilities.)

2. By comparing equity amounts from the balance sheets and using the additional information presented in the problem, prepare a calculation to show how much net income was earned by the business during 2011.

3. Calculate the December 31, 2011, debt ratio for the business.

Check (2) Net income, $45,500

(3) Debt ratio, 58.76%

Lummus Management Services opens for business and completes these transactions in September.

Sept. 1 Rhonda Lummus, the owner, invests $28,000 cash along with office equipment valued at $25,000 in the company in exchange for common stock.

2 The company prepaid $10,500 cash for 12 months' rent for office space. (*Hint:* Debit Prepaid Rent for $10,500.)

4 The company made credit purchases for $9,000 in office equipment and $1,200 in office supplies. Payment is due within 10 days.

8 The company completed work for a client and immediately received $2,600 cash.

12 The company completed a $13,400 project for a client, who must pay within 30 days.

13 The company paid $10,200 cash to settle the payable created on September 4.

19 The company paid $5,200 cash for the premium on an 18-month insurance policy. (*Hint:* Debit Prepaid Insurance for $5,200.)

22 The company received $7,800 cash as partial payment for the work completed on September 12.

24 The company completed work for another client for $1,900 on credit.

28 The company paid $5,300 cash for dividends.

29 The company purchased $1,700 of additional office supplies on credit.

30 The company paid $460 cash for this month's utility bill.

Problem 2-4B
Preparing and posting journal entries; preparing a trial balance
C3 C4 A1 P1 P2

Required

1. Prepare general journal entries to record these transactions (use account titles listed in part 2).

2. Open the following ledger accounts—their account numbers are in parentheses (use the balance column format): Cash (101); Accounts Receivable (106); Office Supplies (124); Prepaid Insurance (128); Prepaid Rent (131); Office Equipment (163); Accounts Payable (201); Common Stock (307); Dividends (319); Service Fees Earned (401); and Utilities Expense (690). Post journal entries from part 1 to the ledger accounts and enter the balance after each posting.

3. Prepare a trial balance as of the end of September.

Check (2) Ending balances: Cash, $6,740; Accounts Receivable, $7,500; Accounts Payable, $1,700

(3) Total debits, $72,600

Cooke Consulting completed the following transactions during June.

a. Chris Cooke, the owner, invested $80,000 cash along with office equipment valued at $30,000 in the new company in exchange for common stock.

b. The company purchased land valued at $30,000 and a building valued at $170,000. The purchase is paid with $40,000 cash and a long-term note payable for $160,000.

c. The company purchased $2,400 of office supplies on credit.

d. C. Cooke invested his personal automobile in the company in exchange for more common stock. The automobile has a value of $18,000 and is to be used exclusively in the business.

e. The company purchased $6,000 of additional office equipment on credit.

f. The company paid $1,500 cash salary to an assistant.

g. The company provided services to a client and collected $6,000 cash.

h. The company paid $800 cash for this month's utilities.

i. The company paid $2,400 cash to settle the payable created in transaction c.

j. The company purchased $20,000 of new office equipment by paying $20,000 cash.

k. The company completed $5,200 of services for a client, who must pay within 30 days.

l. The company paid $1,500 cash salary to an assistant.

m. The company received $3,800 cash in partial payment on the receivable created in transaction k.

n. The company paid $6,400 cash for dividends.

Problem 2-5B
Recording transactions; posting to ledger; preparing a trial balance
C3 A1 P1 P2

Required

1. Prepare general journal entries to record these transactions (use account titles listed in part 2).

2. Open the following ledger accounts—their account numbers are in parentheses (use the balance column format): Cash (101); Accounts Receivable (106); Office Supplies (108); Office Equipment (163); Automobiles (164); Building (170); Land (172); Accounts Payable (201); Notes Payable (250); Common Stock (307); Dividends (319); Fees Earned (402); Salaries Expense (601); and Utilities Expense (602). Post the journal entries from part 1 to the ledger accounts and enter the balance after each posting.

3. Prepare a trial balance as of the end of June.

Check (2) Ending balances: Cash, $17,200; Office Equipment, $56,000

(3) Trial balance totals, $305,200

Problem 2-6B
Analyzing account balances
and reconstructing
transactions

C1 C3 A1 P2

Michael Gould started a Web consulting firm called Gould Solutions. He began operations and completed seven transactions in April that resulted in the following accounts, which all have normal balances.

Cash	$12,485
Office supplies	560
Prepaid rent	1,500
Office equipment	11,450
Accounts payable	11,450
Common Stock	10,000
Dividends	6,200
Consulting fees earned	16,400
Operating expenses	5,655

Required

Check   (1) Trial balance total, $37,850

1. Prepare a trial balance for this business as of the end of April.

Analysis Component

2. Analyze the accounts and their balances and prepare a list that describes each of the seven most likely transactions and their amounts.

(3) Cash paid, $13,915

3. Prepare a report of cash received and cash paid showing how the seven transactions in part 2 yield the $12,485 ending Cash balance.

SERIAL PROBLEM
Business Solutions

A1 P1 P2

(This serial problem started in Chapter 1 and continues through most of the chapters. If the Chapter 1 segment was not completed, the problem can begin at this point. It is helpful, but not necessary, to use the Working Papers that accompany this book.)

SP 2   On October 1, 2011, Santana Rey launched a computer services company called **Business Solutions,** which provides consulting services, computer system installations, and custom program development. Rey adopts the calendar year for reporting purposes and expects to prepare the company's first set of financial statements on December 31, 2011. The company's initial chart of accounts follows.

Account	No.	Account	No.
Cash	101	Common Stock....................	307
Accounts Receivable	106	Dividends	319
Computer Supplies	126	Computer Services Revenue	403
Prepaid Insurance	128	Wages Expense....................	623
Prepaid Rent	131	Advertising Expense	655
Office Equipment	163	Mileage Expense	676
Computer Equipment	167	Miscellaneous Expenses	677
Accounts Payable	201	Repairs Expense—Computer.........	684

Required

1. Prepare journal entries to record each of the following transactions for Business Solutions.

Oct. 1 S. Rey invested $45,000 cash, a $20,000 computer system, and $8,000 of office equipment in the company in exchange for its common stock.

2 The company paid $3,300 cash for four months' rent. (*Hint:* Debit Prepaid Rent for $3,300.)

3 The company purchased $1,420 of computer supplies on credit from Harris Office Products.

5 The company paid $2,220 cash for one year's premium on a property and liability insurance policy. (*Hint:* Debit Prepaid Insurance for $2,220.)

6 The company billed Easy Leasing $4,800 for services performed in installing a new Web server.

8 The company paid $1,420 cash for the computer supplies purchased from Harris Office Products on October 3.

10 The company hired Lyn Addie as a part-time assistant for $125 per day, as needed.

12 The company billed Easy Leasing another $1,400 for services performed.

15   The company received $4,800 cash from Easy Leasing as partial payment on its account.

17   The company paid $805 cash to repair computer equipment that was damaged when moving it.

20   The company paid $1,728 cash for advertisements published in the local newspaper.

22   The company received $1,400 cash from Easy Leasing on its account.

28   The company billed IFM Company $5,208 for services performed.

31   The company paid $875 cash for Lyn Addie's wages for seven days' work.

31   The company paid $3,600 cash for dividends.

Nov. 1   The company reimbursed S. Rey in cash for business automobile mileage allowance (Rey logged 1,000 miles at $0.32 per mile).

2   The company received $4,633 cash from Liu Corporation for computer services performed.

5   The company purchased computer supplies for $1,125 cash from Harris Office Products.

8   The company billed Gomez Co. $5,668 for services performed.

13   The company received notification from Alex's Engineering Co. that Business Solutions' bid of $3,950 for an upcoming project is accepted.

18   The company received $2,208 cash from IFM Company as partial payment of the October 28 bill.

22   The company donated $250 cash to the United Way in the company's name.

24   The company completed work for Alex's Engineering Co. and sent it a bill for $3,950.

25   The company sent another bill to IFM Company for the past-due amount of $3,000.

28   The company reimbursed S. Rey in cash for business automobile mileage (1,200 miles at $0.32 per mile).

30   The company paid $1,750 cash for Lyn Addie's wages for 14 days' work.

30   The company paid $2,000 cash for dividends.

2. Open ledger accounts (in balance column format) and post the journal entries from part 1 to them.

3. Prepare a trial balance as of the end of November.

Check   (2) Cash, Nov. 30 bal., $38,264

(3) Trial bal. totals, $98,659

Beyond the Numbers

BTN 2-1   Refer to **Research In Motion**'s financial statements in Appendix A for the following questions.

REPORTING IN ACTION

A1 A2

RIM

Required

1. What amount of total liabilities does it report for each of the fiscal years ended February 28, 2009, and February 27, 2010?

2. What amount of total assets does it report for each of the fiscal years ended February 28, 2009, and February 27, 2010?

3. Compute its debt ratio for each of the fiscal years ended February 28, 2009, and February 27, 2010.

4. In which fiscal year did it employ more financial leverage (February 28, 2009, or February 27, 2010)? Explain.

Fast Forward

5. Access its financial statements (10-K report) for a fiscal year ending after February 27, 2010, from its Website (**RIM.com**) or the SEC's EDGAR database (**www.SEC.gov**). Recompute its debt ratio for any subsequent year's data and compare it with the debt ratio for 2009 and 2010.

BTN 2-2   Key comparative figures for **Research In Motion** and **Apple** follow.

COMPARATIVE ANALYSIS

A1 A2

RIM

Apple

($ millions)	Research In Motion		Apple	
	Current Year	Prior Year	Current Year	Prior Year
Total liabilities	$ 2,602	$ 2,227	$15,861	$13,874
Total assets	10,204	8,101	47,501	36,171

1. What is the debt ratio for Research In Motion in the current year and for the prior year?

2. What is the debt ratio for Apple in the current year and for the prior year?

3. Which of the two companies has the higher degree of financial leverage? What does this imply?

ETHICS CHALLENGE
C1

BTN 2-3   Review the *Decision Ethics* case from the first part of this chapter involving the cashier. The guidance answer suggests that you should not comply with the assistant manager's request.

Required

Propose and evaluate two other courses of action you might consider, and explain why.

COMMUNICATING IN PRACTICE
C1 C2 A1 P3

BTN 2-4   Mora Stanley is an aspiring entrepreneur and your friend. She is having difficulty understanding the purposes of financial statements and how they fit together across time.

Required

Write a one-page memorandum to Stanley explaining the purposes of the four financial statements and how they are linked across time.

TAKING IT TO THE NET
A1

BTN 2-5   Access EDGAR online (www.sec.gov) and locate the 2009 year 10-K report of **Amazon.com** (ticker AMZN) filed on January 29, 2010. Review its financial statements reported for years ended 2009, 2008, and 2007 to answer the following questions.

Required

1. What are the amounts of its net income or net loss reported for each of these three years?
2. Does Amazon's operating activities provide cash or use cash for each of these three years?
3. If Amazon has a 2009 net income of more than $900 million and 2009 operating cash flows of more than $3,000 million, how is it possible that its cash balance at December 31, 2009, increases by less than $700 million relative to its balance at December 31, 2008?

TEAMWORK IN ACTION
C1 C2 C4 A1

BTN 2-6   The expanded accounting equation consists of assets, liabilities, common stock, dividends, revenues, and expenses. It can be used to reveal insights into changes in a company's financial position.

Required

1. Form *learning teams* of six (or more) members. Each team member must select one of the six components and each team must have at least one expert on each component: (*a*) assets, (*b*) liabilities, (*c*) common stock, (*d*) dividends, (*e*) revenues, and (*f*) expenses.
2. Form *expert teams* of individuals who selected the same component in part 1. Expert teams are to draft a report that each expert will present to his or her learning team addressing the following:
   a. Identify for its component the (i) increase and decrease side of the account and (ii) normal balance side of the account.
   b. Describe a transaction, with amounts, that increases its component.
   c. Using the transaction and amounts in (*b*), verify the equality of the accounting equation and then explain any effects on the income statement and statement of cash flows.
   d. Describe a transaction, with amounts, that decreases its component.
   e. Using the transaction and amounts in (*d*), verify the equality of the accounting equation and then explain any effects on the income statement and statement of cash flows.
3. Each expert should return to his/her learning team. In rotation, each member presents his/her expert team's report to the learning team. Team discussion is encouraged.

ENTREPRENEURIAL DECISION
A1 A2 P3

BTN 2-7   Assume Susie Levitt and Katie Shea of **CitySlips** plan on expanding their business to accommodate more product lines. They are considering financing their expansion in one of two ways: (1) contributing more of their own funds to the business or (2) borrowing the funds from a bank.

Required

Identify at least two issues that Susie and Katie should consider when trying to decide on the method for financing their expansion.

BTN 2-8   Lisa Langely is a young entrepreneur who operates Langely Music Services, offering singing lessons and instruction on musical instruments. Langely wishes to expand but needs a $15,000 loan. The bank requests Langely to prepare a balance sheet and key financial ratios. Langely has not kept formal records but is able to provide the following accounts and their amounts as of December 31, 2011.

Cash	$ 1,800	Accounts Receivable	$4,800	Prepaid Insurance	$	750
Prepaid Rent	4,700	Store Supplies	3,300	Equipment		25,000
Accounts Payable	1,100	Unearned Lesson Fees . . .	7,800	Total Equity*		31,450
Annual net income . . .	20,000					

* The total equity amount reflects all owner investments, dividends, revenues, and expenses as of December 31, 2011.

Required

1. Prepare a balance sheet as of December 31, 2011, for Langely Music Services. (Report only the total equity amount on the balance sheet.)
2. Compute Langely's debt ratio and its return on assets (the latter ratio is defined in Chapter 1). Assume average assets equal its ending balance.
3. Do you believe the prospects of a $15,000 bank loan are good? Why or why not?

BTN 2-9   Obtain a recent copy of the most prominent newspaper distributed in your area. Research the classified section and prepare a report answering the following questions (attach relevant classified clippings to your report). Alternatively, you may want to search the Web for the required information. One suitable Website is **CareerOneStop** (**www.CareerOneStop.org**). For documentation, you should print copies of Websites accessed.

1. Identify the number of listings for accounting positions and the various accounting job titles.
2. Identify the number of listings for other job titles, with examples, that require or prefer accounting knowledge/experience but are not specifically accounting positions.
3. Specify the salary range for the accounting and accounting-related positions if provided.
4. Indicate the job that appeals to you, the reason for its appeal, and its requirements.

BTN 2-10   **Nokia** (**www.Nokia.com**) is a leading global manufacturer of mobile devices and services, and it competes to some extent with both **Research In Motion** and **Apple**. Key financial ratios for the current fiscal year follow.

Key Figure	Nokia	Research In Motion	Apple
Return on assets	0.7%	26.8%	19.7%
Debt ratio	58.7%	25.5%	33.4%

Required

1. Which company is most profitable according to its return on assets?
2. Which company is most risky according to the debt ratio?
3. Which company deserves increased investment based on a joint analysis of return on assets and the debt ratio? Explain.

ANSWERS TO MULTIPLE CHOICE QUIZ

1. b; debit Utility Expense for $700, and credit Cash for $700.
2. a; debit Cash for $2,500, and credit Unearned Lawn Service Fees for $2,500.
3. c; debit Cash for $250,000, debit Land for $500,000, and credit Common Stock for $750,000.
4. d
5. e; Debt ratio = $400,000/$1,000,000 = 40%

3

Adjusting Accounts and Preparing Financial Statements

A Look Back

Chapter 2 explained the analysis and recording of transactions. We showed how to apply and interpret company accounts, T-accounts, double-entry accounting, ledgers, postings, and trial balances.

A Look at This Chapter

This chapter explains the timing of reports and the need to adjust accounts. Adjusting accounts is important for recognizing revenues and expenses in the proper period. We describe how to prepare financial statements from an adjusted trial balance, and how the closing process works.

A Look Ahead

Chapter 4 looks at accounting for merchandising activities. We describe the sale and purchase of merchandise and their implications for preparing and analyzing financial statements.

Learning Objectives

CAP

CONCEPTUAL

C1 Explain the importance of periodic reporting and the time period assumption. (p. 94)

C2 Explain accrual accounting and how it improves financial statements. (p. 95)

C3 Identify steps in the accounting cycle. (p. 112)

C4 Explain and prepare a classified balance sheet. (p. 113)

ANALYTICAL

A1 Explain how accounting adjustments link to financial statements. (p. 105)

A2 Compute profit margin and describe its use in analyzing company performance. (p. 117)

A3 Compute the current ratio and describe what it reveals about a company's financial condition. (p. 117)

LP3

PROCEDURAL

P1 Prepare and explain adjusting entries. (p. 96)

P2 Explain and prepare an adjusted trial balance. (p. 106)

P3 Prepare financial statements from an adjusted trial balance. (p. 106)

P4 Describe and prepare closing entries. (p. 108)

P5 Explain and prepare a post-closing trial balance. (p. 110)

P6 *Appendix 3A*—Explain the alternatives in accounting for prepaids. (p. 121)

P7 *Appendix 3B*—Prepare a work sheet and explain its usefulness. (p. 123)

P8 *Appendix 3C*—Prepare reversing entries and explain their purpose. (p. 126)

Decision Insight

Huh? Yes!

"Make sure that whatever commitment you make . . . you keep"
—BEN HUH

SEATTLE—"When we were starting this thing, people asked who was going to run it, and I said, 'I will, and my wife.' And they said, 'You're crazy.' And I said, 'Yes!' " Meet Ben Huh. His thing? **Cheezburger Network (Cheezburger.com/sites),** which controls over 30 Websites devoted to Internet memes. (Memes are running gags, usually in JPEG or video format, which spawn and spread on the Web.) His sites include ICanHasCheezburger?, FailBlog, IHasAHotdog!, ROFLrazzi, and TotallyLooksLike. Since launching his company just a few years ago, his network has nearly 200 million page views per month and annual revenue in the millions. Revenue comes from display ads, along with some merchandise sales.

Ben explains that he set up an accounting system early on to account for all business activities, including cash, revenues, receivables, and payables. He also had to learn about the deferral and accrual of revenues and expenses. Setting up a good accounting system is an important part of success, explains Ben. "I learned how to keep costs low."

In spite of his quirky business, Ben insists "it is very serious business." He also seriously monitors the adjusting of accounts so that revenues and expenses are properly reported so that good decisions are made. Adds Ben, "No matter how strange or ridiculous a business looks, those fundamentals still need to be there."

Financial statement preparation and analysis is a process that Ben emphasizes. Although he insists on timely and accurate accounting reports, Ben says "we're just having fun . . . we've always been very much counterculture." To achieve the fun part, Ben first took time to understand accounting adjustments and their effects. It is part of the larger picture. We "make people happy for five minutes every day." But, for Ben to do that, he insists that a reliable accounting system is necessary . . . otherwise his business would fail.

"We'd like to continue to do what we do . . . build bigger communities and just kind of evangelize the idea that the user is great at creating excellent content," says Ben. "The market is far more efficient than any one company . . . but we haven't applied that theory to [Web] content."

[Sources: *Cheezburger Website* and *BenHuh Website,* January 2011; *Entrepreneur,* August 2009; *Wired,* February 2010; *The New York Times,* April 2009; *Time,* August 2009]

Chapters 1 and 2 described how transactions and events are analyzed, journalized, and posted. This chapter describes important adjustments that are often necessary to properly reflect revenues when earned and expenses when incurred. This chapter also describes financial statement preparation. It explains the closing process that readies revenue, expense, and dividend accounts for the next reporting period and updates retained earnings. It also explains how accounts are classified on a balance sheet to increase their usefulness to decision makers.

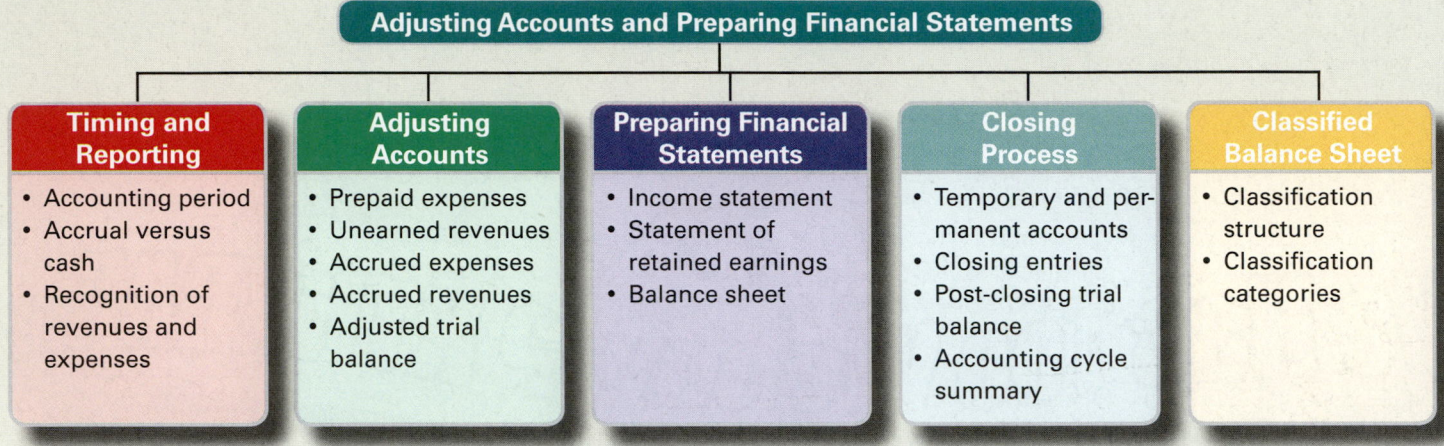

Adjusting Accounts and Preparing Financial Statements

Timing and Reporting	Adjusting Accounts	Preparing Financial Statements	Closing Process	Classified Balance Sheet
• Accounting period • Accrual versus cash • Recognition of revenues and expenses	• Prepaid expenses • Unearned revenues • Accrued expenses • Accrued revenues • Adjusted trial balance	• Income statement • Statement of retained earnings • Balance sheet	• Temporary and permanent accounts • Closing entries • Post-closing trial balance • Accounting cycle summary	• Classification structure • Classification categories

TIMING AND REPORTING

This section describes the importance of reporting accounting information at regular intervals and its impact for recording revenues and expenses.

The Accounting Period

C1 Explain the importance of periodic reporting and the time period assumption.

The value of information is often linked to its timeliness. Useful information must reach decision makers frequently and promptly. To provide timely information, accounting systems prepare reports at regular intervals. This results in an accounting process impacted by the time period (or periodicity) assumption. The **time period assumption** presumes that an organization's activities can be divided into specific time periods such as a month, a three-month quarter, a six-month interval, or a year. Exhibit 3.1 shows various **accounting,** or *reporting,* **periods.** Most organizations use a year as their primary accounting period. Reports covering a one-year period are known as **annual financial statements.** Many organizations also prepare **interim financial statements** covering one, three, or six months of activity.

"RIM announces annual income of . . ."

EXHIBIT 3.1

Accounting Periods

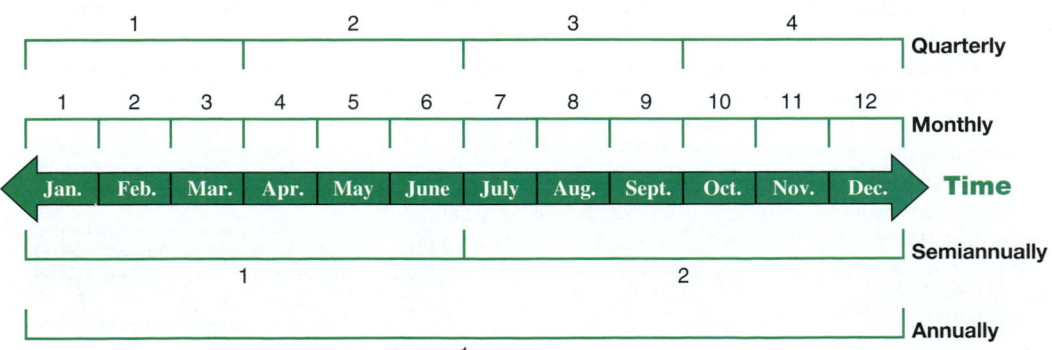

The annual reporting period is not always a calendar year ending on December 31. An organization can adopt a **fiscal year** consisting of any 12 consecutive months. It is also acceptable to adopt an annual reporting period of 52 weeks. For example, **Gap**'s fiscal year consistently ends the final week of January or the first week of February each year.

Companies with little seasonal variation in sales often choose the calendar year as their fiscal year. The financial statements of **The Kellogg Company** (the company that controls characters such as Tony the Tiger, Snap! Crackle! Pop!, and Keebler Elf) reflect a fiscal year that ends on the Saturday nearest December 31. Companies experiencing seasonal variations in sales often choose a **natural business year** end, which is when sales activities are at their lowest level for the year. The natural business year for retailers such as **Walmart**, **Target**, and **Macy's** usually ends around January 31, after the holiday season.

Accrual Basis versus Cash Basis

After external transactions and events are recorded, several accounts still need adjustments before their balances appear in financial statements. This need arises because internal transactions and events remain unrecorded. **Accrual basis accounting** uses the adjusting process to recognize revenues when earned and expenses when incurred (matched with revenues).

C2 Explain accrual accounting and how it improves financial statements.

Cash basis accounting recognizes revenues when cash is received and records expenses when cash is paid. This means that cash basis net income for a period is the difference between cash receipts and cash payments. Cash basis accounting is not consistent with generally accepted accounting principles (neither U.S. GAAP nor IFRS).

It is commonly held that accrual accounting better reflects business performance than information about cash receipts and payments. Accrual accounting also increases the *comparability* of financial statements from one period to another. Yet cash basis accounting is useful for several business decisions—which is the reason companies must report a statement of cash flows.

To see the difference between these two accounting systems, let's consider FastForward's Prepaid Insurance account. FastForward paid $2,400 for 24 months of insurance coverage that began on December 1, 2011. Accrual accounting requires that $100 of insurance expense be reported on December 2011's income statement. Another $1,200 of expense is reported in year 2012, and the remaining $1,100 is reported as expense in the first 11 months of 2013. Exhibit 3.2 illustrates this allocation of insurance cost across these three years. Any unexpired premium is reported as a Prepaid Insurance asset on the accrual basis balance sheet.

EXHIBIT 3.2

Accrual Accounting for Allocating Prepaid Insurance to Expense

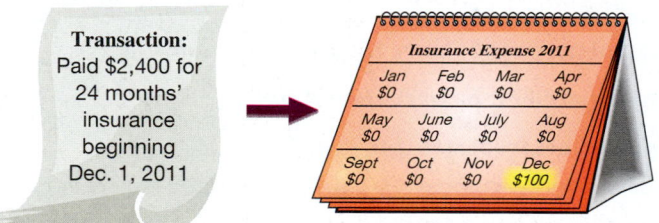

Alternatively, a cash basis income statement for December 2011 reports insurance expense of $2,400, as shown in Exhibit 3.3. The cash basis income statements for years 2012 and 2013 report no insurance expense. The cash basis balance sheet never reports an insurance asset because it is immediately expensed. This shows that cash basis income for 2011–2013 fails to match the cost of insurance with the insurance benefits received for those years and months.

EXHIBIT 3.3

Cash Accounting for Allocating Prepaid Insurance to Expense

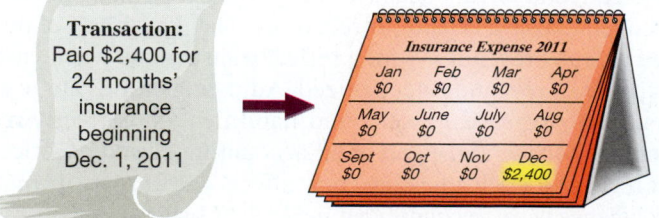

Recognizing Revenues and Expenses

We use the time period assumption to divide a company's activities into specific time periods, but not all activities are complete when financial statements are prepared. Thus, adjustments often are required to get correct account balances.

We rely on two principles in the adjusting process: revenue recognition and expense recognition (the latter is often referred to as matching). Chapter 1 explained that the *revenue recognition principle* requires that revenue be recorded when earned, not before and not after. Most companies earn revenue when they provide services and products to customers. A major goal of the adjusting process is to have revenue recognized (reported) in the time period when it is earned. The **expense recognition** (or **matching**) **principle** aims to record expenses in the same accounting period as the revenues that are earned as a result of those expenses. This matching of expenses with the revenue benefits is a major part of the adjusting process.

Matching expenses with revenues often requires us to predict certain events. When we use financial statements, we must understand that they require estimates and therefore include measures that are not precise. **Walt Disney**'s annual report explains that its production costs from movies, such as *Alice in Wonderland,* are matched to revenues based on a ratio of current revenues from the movie divided by its predicted total revenues.

Quick Check   Answers — p. 128

1. Describe a company's annual reporting period.
2. Why do companies prepare interim financial statements?
3. What two accounting principles most directly drive the adjusting process?
4. Is cash basis accounting consistent with the matching principle? Why or why not?
5. If your company pays a $4,800 premium on April 1, 2011, for two years' insurance coverage, how much insurance expense is reported in 2012 using cash basis accounting?

ADJUSTING ACCOUNTS

Adjusting accounts is a 3-step process:

> **Step 1:**   **Determine what the current account balance *equals*.**
>
> **Step 2:**   **Determine what the current account balance *should equal*.**
>
> **Step 3:**   **Record an adjusting entry to get from step *1* to step *2*.**

Framework for Adjustments

P1 Prepare and explain adjusting entries.

Adjustments are necessary for transactions and events that extend over more than one period. It is helpful to group adjustments by the timing of cash receipt or cash payment in relation to the recognition of the related revenues or expenses. Exhibit 3.4 identifies four types of adjustments.

The upper half of this exhibit shows prepaid expenses (including depreciation) and unearned revenues, which reflect transactions when cash is paid or received *before* a related expense or revenue is recognized. They are also called *deferrals* because the recognition of an expense (or revenue) is *deferred* until after the related cash is paid (or received). The lower half of this exhibit shows accrued expenses and accrued revenues, which reflect transactions when cash is paid or received *after* a related expense or revenue is recognized. Adjusting entries are necessary for each of these so that revenues, expenses, assets, and liabilities are correctly reported. Specifically, an **adjusting entry** is made at the end of an accounting period to reflect a transaction or event that is not yet recorded. Each adjusting entry affects one or more income statement accounts *and* one or more balance sheet accounts (but never the Cash account).

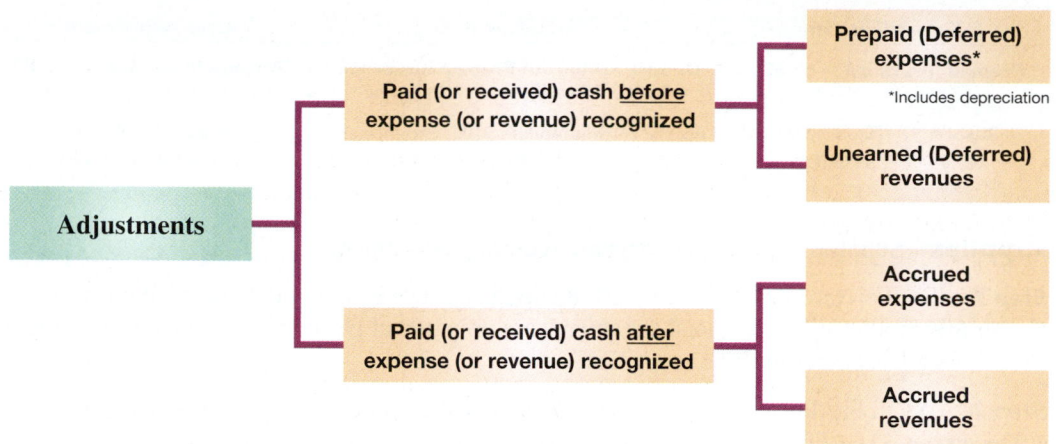

EXHIBIT 3.4

Types of Adjustments

Prepaid (Deferred) Expenses

Prepaid expenses refer to items *paid for* in advance of receiving their benefits. Prepaid expenses are assets. When these assets are used, their costs become expenses. Adjusting entries for prepaids increase expenses and decrease assets as shown in the T-accounts of Exhibit 3.5. Such adjustments reflect transactions and events that use up prepaid expenses (including passage of time). To illustrate the accounting for prepaid expenses, we look at prepaid insurance, supplies, and depreciation.

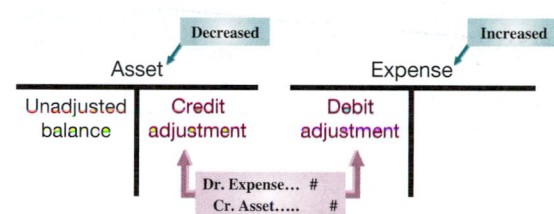

EXHIBIT 3.5

Adjusting for Prepaid Expenses

Prepaid Insurance   We use our 3-step process for this and all accounting adjustments.

Step 1:   We determine that the current balance of FastForward's prepaid insurance is equal to its $2,400 payment for 24 months of insurance benefits that began on December 1, 2011.

Step 2:   With the passage of time, the benefits of the insurance gradually expire and a portion of the Prepaid Insurance asset becomes expense. For instance, one month's insurance coverage expires by December 31, 2011. This expense is $100, or 1/24 of $2,400, which leaves $2,300.

Step 3:   The adjusting entry to record this expense and reduce the asset, along with T-account postings, follows:

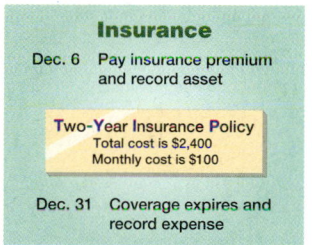

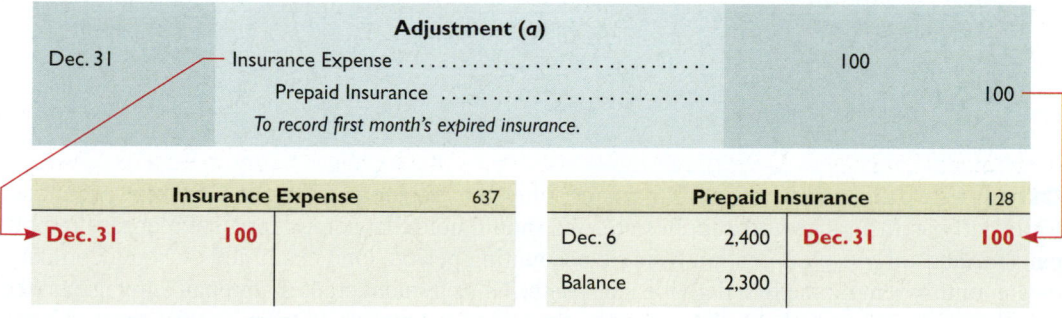

Assets = Liabilities + Equity
−100   −100

Explanation   After adjusting and posting, the $100 balance in Insurance Expense and the $2,300 balance in Prepaid Insurance are ready for reporting in financial statements. *Not* making the adjustment on or before December 31 would (1) understate expenses by $100 and overstate net income by $100 for the December income statement and (2) overstate both prepaid insurance (assets) and equity (because of net income) by $100 in the December 31 balance sheet. (Exhibit 3.2 showed that 2012's adjustments must transfer a total of $1,200 from Prepaid Insurance to Insurance Expense, and 2013's adjustments must transfer the remaining $1,100 to Insurance Expense.) The following table highlights the December 31, 2011, adjustment for prepaid insurance.

Point: Many companies record adjusting entries only at the end of each year because of the time and cost necessary.

Before Adjustment	Adjustment	After Adjustment
Prepaid Insurance = $2,400	**Deduct $100 from Prepaid Insurance Add $100 to Insurance Expense**	**Prepaid Insurance = $2,300**
Reports $2,400 policy for 24-months' coverage.	Record current month's $100 insurance expense and $100 reduction in prepaid amount.	Reports $2,300 in coverage for remaining 23 months.

Supplies   Supplies are a prepaid expense requiring adjustment.

Supplies

Dec. 2,6,26   Purchase supplies and record asset

Dec. 31   Supplies used and record expense

Step 1:   FastForward purchased $9,720 of supplies in December and some of them were used during this month. When financial statements are prepared at December 31, the cost of supplies used during December must be recognized.

Step 2:   When FastForward computes (takes physical count of) its remaining unused supplies at December 31, it finds $8,670 of supplies remaining of the $9,720 total supplies. The $1,050 difference between these two amounts is December's supplies expense.

Step 3:   The adjusting entry to record this expense and reduce the Supplies asset account, along with T-account postings, follows:

Assets = Liabilities + Equity
−1,050   −1,050

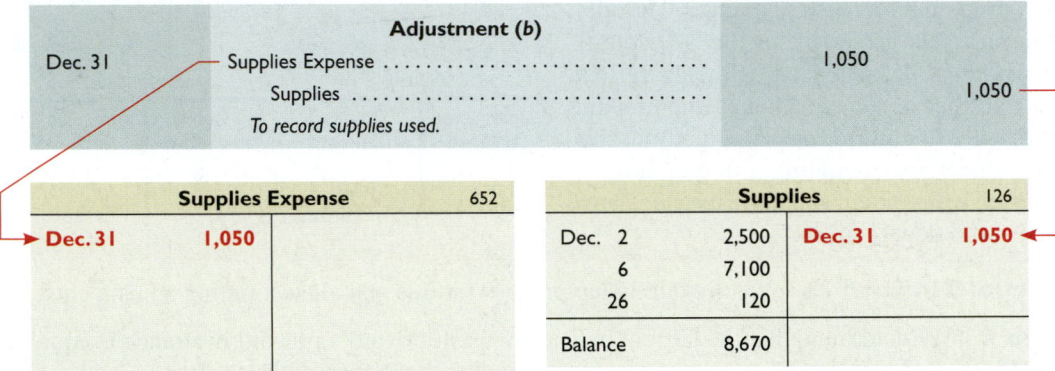

	Adjustment (b)		
Dec. 31	Supplies Expense	1,050	
	Supplies		1,050
	To record supplies used.		

Supplies Expense		652
Dec. 31	**1,050**	

Supplies			126
Dec. 2	2,500	**Dec. 31**	**1,050**
6	7,100		
26	120		
Balance	8,670		

Explanation   The balance of the Supplies account is $8,670 after posting—equaling the cost of the remaining supplies. *Not* making the adjustment on or before December 31 would (1) understate expenses by $1,050 and overstate net income by $1,050 for the December income statement and (2) overstate both supplies and equity (because of net income) by $1,050 in the December 31 balance sheet. The following table highlights the adjustment for supplies.

Before Adjustment	Adjustment	After Adjustment
Supplies = $9,720	**Deduct $1,050 from Supplies Add $1,050 to Supplies Expense**	**Supplies = $8,670**
Reports $9,720 in supplies.	Record $1,050 in supplies used and $1,050 as supplies expense.	Reports $8,670 in supplies.

Other Prepaid Expenses   Other prepaid expenses, such as Prepaid Rent, are accounted for exactly as Insurance and Supplies are. We should note that some prepaid expenses are both paid for and fully used up within a single accounting period. One example is when a company pays monthly rent on the first day of each month. This payment creates a prepaid expense on the first day of each month that fully expires by the end of the month. In these special cases, we can record the cash paid with a debit to an expense account instead of an asset account. This practice is described more completely later in the chapter.

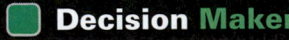 **Decision Maker**   Answer — p. 128

Investor   A small publishing company signs a well-known athlete to write a book. The company pays the athlete $500,000 to sign plus future book royalties. A note to the company's financial statements says that "prepaid expenses include $500,000 in author signing fees to be matched against future expected sales." Is this accounting for the signing bonus acceptable? How does it affect your analysis? ■

Depreciation A special category of prepaid expenses is **plant assets,** which refers to long-term tangible assets used to produce and sell products and services. Plant assets are expected to provide benefits for more than one period. Examples of plant assets are buildings, machines, vehicles, and fixtures. All plant assets, with a general exception for land, eventually wear out or decline in usefulness. The costs of these assets are deferred but are gradually reported as expenses in the income statement over the assets' useful lives (benefit periods). **Depreciation** is the process of allocating the costs of these assets over their expected useful lives. Depreciation expense is recorded with an adjusting entry similar to that for other prepaid expenses.

Point: Plant assets are also called *Plant & Equipment,* or *Property, Plant & Equipment.*

Point: Depreciation does not necessarily measure decline in market value.

Point: An asset's expected value at the end of its useful life is called *salvage value.*

Step 1: Recall that FastForward purchased equipment for $26,000 in early December to use in earning revenue. This equipment's cost must be depreciated.

Step 2: The equipment is expected to have a useful life (benefit period) of four years and to be worth about $8,000 at the end of four years. This means the *net* cost of this equipment over its useful life is $18,000 ($26,000 − $8,000). We can use any of several methods to allocate this $18,000 net cost to expense. FastForward uses a method called **straight-line depreciation,** which allocates equal amounts of the asset's net cost to depreciation during its useful life. Dividing the $18,000 net cost by the 48 months in the asset's useful life gives a monthly cost of $375 ($18,000/48).

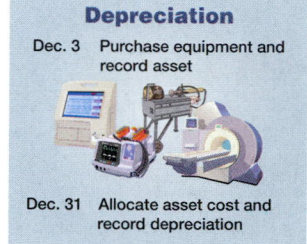

Depreciation

Dec. 3 Purchase equipment and record asset

Dec. 31 Allocate asset cost and record depreciation

Step 3: The adjusting entry to record monthly depreciation expense, along with T-account postings, follows:

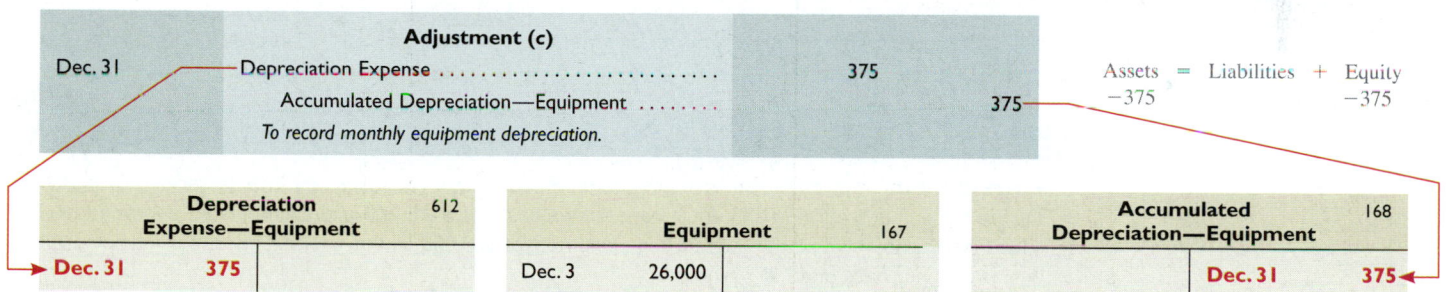

Dec. 31	**Adjustment (c)**		
	Depreciation Expense	375	
	Accumulated Depreciation—Equipment		375
	To record monthly equipment depreciation.		

Assets = Liabilities + Equity
−375   −375

Depreciation Expense—Equipment	612		**Equipment**	167		**Accumulated Depreciation—Equipment**	168
Dec. 31	**375**		Dec. 3	26,000		**Dec. 31**	**375**

Explanation After posting the adjustment, the Equipment account ($26,000) less its Accumulated Depreciation ($375) account equals the $25,625 net cost (made up of $17,625 for the 47 remaining months in the benefit period plus the $8,000 value at the end of that time). The $375 balance in the Depreciation Expense account is reported in the December income statement. *Not* making the adjustment at December 31 would (1) understate expenses by $375 and overstate net income by $375 for the December income statement and (2) overstate both assets and equity (because of income) by $375 in the December 31 balance sheet. The following table highlights the adjustment for depreciation.

Before Adjustment	Adjustment	After Adjustment
Equipment, net = $26,000	**Deduct $375 from Equipment, net** **Add $375 to Depreciation Expense**	Equipment, net = $25,625
Reports $26,000 in equipment.	Record $375 in depreciation and $375 as accumulated depreciation, which is deducted from equipment.	Reports $25,625 in equipment, net of accumulated depreciation.

Accumulated depreciation is kept in a separate contra account. A **contra account** is an account linked with another account, it has an opposite normal balance, and it is reported as a subtraction from that other account's balance. For instance, FastForward's contra account of Accumulated Depreciation—Equipment is subtracted from the Equipment account in the balance sheet (see Exhibit 3.7). This contra account allows balance sheet readers to know both the full costs of assets and the total depreciation.

The title of the contra account, *Accumulated Depreciation,* reveals that this account includes total depreciation expense for all prior periods for which the asset was used. To illustrate, the Equipment and the Accumulated Depreciation accounts appear as in Exhibit 3.6 on February 28, 2012, after three months of adjusting entries. The $1,125 balance in the accumulated depreciation account can be subtracted from its related $26,000 asset cost. The difference ($24,875) between these two balances is the cost of the asset that has not yet been depreciated. This difference is

Point: The cost principle requires an asset to be initially recorded at acquisition cost. Depreciation causes the asset's book value (cost less accumulated depreciation) to decline over time.

EXHIBIT 3.6

Accounts after Three Months of
Depreciation Adjustments

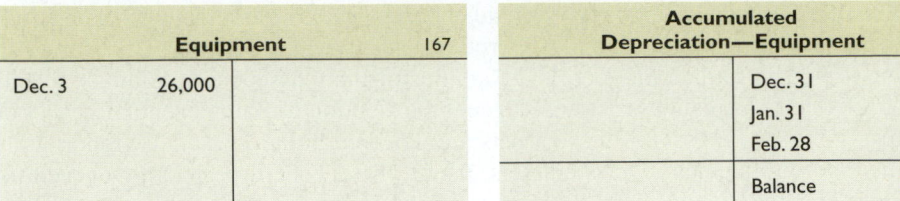

Equipment		167
Dec. 3	26,000	

Accumulated Depreciation—Equipment		168
Dec. 31		375
Jan. 31		375
Feb. 28		375
Balance		**1,125**

Point: The net cost of equipment is
also called the *depreciable basis.*

called the **book value,** or the *net amount,* which equals the asset's costs less its accumulated
depreciation.

These account balances are reported in the assets section of the February 28 balance sheet in
Exhibit 3.7.

EXHIBIT 3.7

Equipment and Accumulated
Depreciation on February 28
Balance Sheet

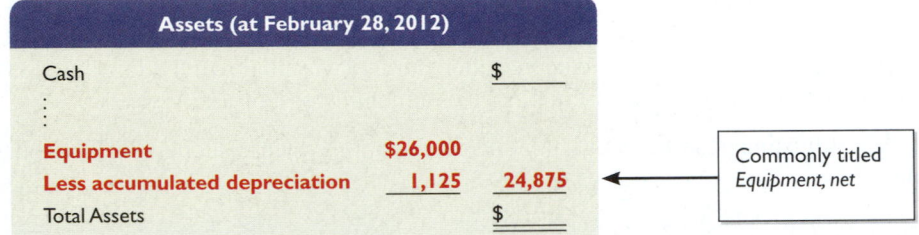

Assets (at February 28, 2012)		
Cash		$ _____
⋮		
Equipment	**$26,000**	
Less accumulated depreciation	**1,125**	**24,875**
Total Assets		$ _____

Commonly titled
Equipment, net

Decision Maker   Answer — p. 128

Entrepreneur   You are preparing an offer to purchase a family-run restaurant. The depreciation schedule
for the restaurant's building and equipment shows costs of $175,000 and accumulated depreciation of
$155,000. This leaves a net for building and equipment of $20,000. Is this information useful in helping you
decide on a purchase offer? ■

Unearned (Deferred) Revenues

The term **unearned revenues** refers to cash received in advance of providing products and
services. Unearned revenues, also called *deferred revenues,* are liabilities. When cash is accepted, an obligation to provide products
or services is accepted. As products or services are provided, the unearned revenues
become *earned* revenues. Adjusting entries
for unearned revenues involve increasing
revenues and decreasing unearned revenues, as shown in Exhibit 3.8.

EXHIBIT 3.8

Adjusting for Unearned Revenues

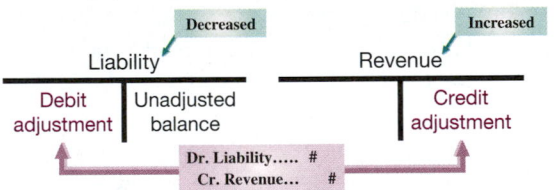

Point: To *defer* is to postpone. We
postpone reporting amounts received
as revenues until they are earned.

An example of unearned revenues is from **The New York Times Company**, which reports
unexpired (unearned) subscriptions of $81 million: "Proceeds from … subscriptions are de-
ferred at the time of sale and are recognized in earnings on a pro rata basis over the terms of
the subscriptions." Unearned revenues are nearly 10% of the current liabilities for the Times.
Another example comes from the **Boston Celtics**. When the Celtics receive cash from advance
ticket sales and broadcast fees, they record it in an unearned revenue account called *Deferred
Game Revenues.* The Celtics recognize this unearned revenue with adjusting entries on a game-
by-game basis. Since the NBA regular season begins in October and ends in April, revenue
recognition is mainly limited to this period. For a recent season, the Celtics' quarterly revenues were $0 million for July–September; $34 million for October–December; $48 million
for January–March; and $17 million for April–June.

Returning to FastForward, it also has unearned revenues. It agreed on December 26 to provide consulting services to a client for a fixed fee of $3,000 for 60 days.

Unearned Revenues

Dec. 26   Cash received in advance
and record liability

*Thanks for cash in
advance. I'll work now
through Feb. 24*

Dec. 31   Provided services and
record revenue

Step 1:   On December 26, the client paid the 60-day fee in advance, covering the period
December 27 to February 24. The entry to record the cash received in advance is

Dec. 26	Cash	3,000	
	Unearned Consulting Revenue		3,000
	Received advance payment for services over the next 60 days.		

Assets = Liabilities + Equity
+3,000   +3,000

This advance payment increases cash and creates an obligation to do consulting work over the next 60 days.

Step 2:   As time passes, FastForward earns this payment through consulting. By December 31, it has provided five days' service and earned 5/60 of the $3,000 unearned revenue. This amounts to $250 ($3,000 × 5/60). The *revenue recognition principle* implies that $250 of unearned revenue must be reported as revenue on the December income statement.

Step 3:   The adjusting entry to reduce the liability account and recognize earned revenue, along with T-account postings, follows:

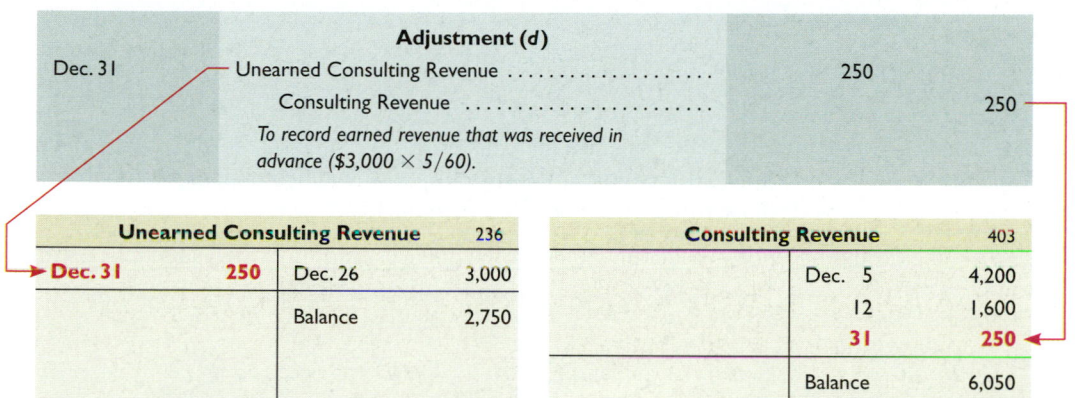

	Adjustment (*d*)		
Dec. 31	Unearned Consulting Revenue	250	
	Consulting Revenue		250
	To record earned revenue that was received in advance ($3,000 × 5/60).		

Assets = Liabilities + Equity
            −250   +250

Unearned Consulting Revenue		236
Dec. 31	250	Dec. 26	3,000
		Balance	2,750

Consulting Revenue		403
	Dec. 5	4,200
	12	1,600
	31	250
	Balance	6,050

Explanation   The adjusting entry transfers $250 from unearned revenue (a liability account) to a revenue account. *Not* making the adjustment (1) understates revenue and net income by $250 in the December income statement and (2) overstates unearned revenue and understates equity by $250 on the December 31 balance sheet. The following highlights the adjustment for unearned revenue.

Before Adjustment	**Adjustment**	**After Adjustment**
Unearned Consulting Revenue = $3,000	**Deduct $250 from Unearned Consulting Revenue Add $250 to Consulting Revenue**	**Unearned Consulting Revenue = $2,750**
Reports $3,000 in unearned revenue for consulting services promised for 60 days.	Record 5 days of earned consulting revenue, which is 5/60 of unearned amount.	Reports $2,750 in unearned revenue for consulting services owed over next 55 days.

Accounting for unearned revenues is crucial to many companies. For example, the **National Retail Federation** reports that gift card sales, which are unearned revenues for sellers, exceed $20 billion annually. Gift cards are now the top selling holiday gift.

Accrued Expenses

Accrued expenses refer to costs that are incurred in a period but are both unpaid and unrecorded. Accrued expenses must be reported on the income statement of the period when incurred. Adjusting entries for recording accrued expenses involve increasing expenses and increasing liabilities as shown in Exhibit 3.9. This adjustment recognizes expenses incurred in a period but not yet paid. Common examples of accrued expenses are salaries, interest, rent, and taxes. We use salaries and interest to show how to adjust accounts for accrued expenses.

Point: Accrued expenses are also called accrued liabilities.

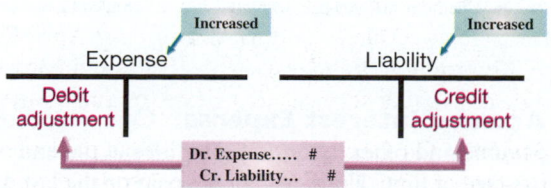

EXHIBIT 3.9

Adjusting for Accrued Expenses

Accrued Salaries Expense   FastForward's employee earns $70 per day, or $350 for a five-day workweek beginning on Monday and ending on Friday.

Step 1:   Its employee is paid every two weeks on Friday. On December 12 and 26, the wages are paid, recorded in the journal, and posted to the ledger.

Step 2:   The calendar in Exhibit 3.10 shows three working days after the December 26 payday (29, 30, and 31). This means the employee has earned three days' salary by the close of business

EXHIBIT 3.10

Salary Accrual and Paydays

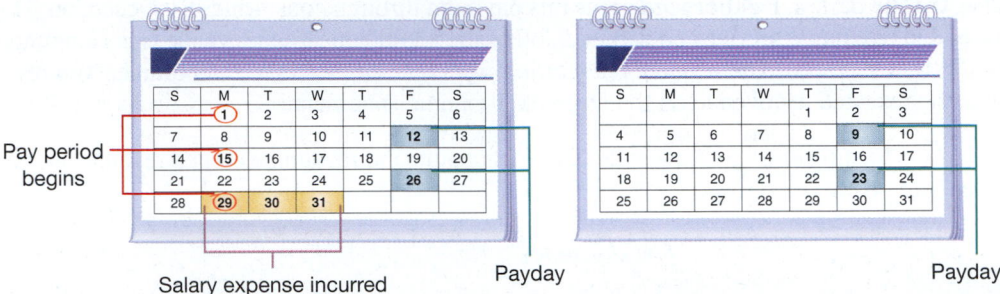

Pay period begins

Salary expense incurred   Payday   Payday

Point: An employer records salaries expense and a vacation pay liability when employees earn vacation pay.

on Wednesday, December 31, yet this salary cost has not been paid or recorded. The financial statements would be incomplete if FastForward fails to report the added expense and liability to the employee for unpaid salary from December 29, 30, and 31.

Step 3:   The adjusting entry to account for accrued salaries, along with T-account postings, follows:

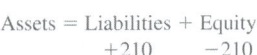

Assets = Liabilities + Equity
         +210   −210

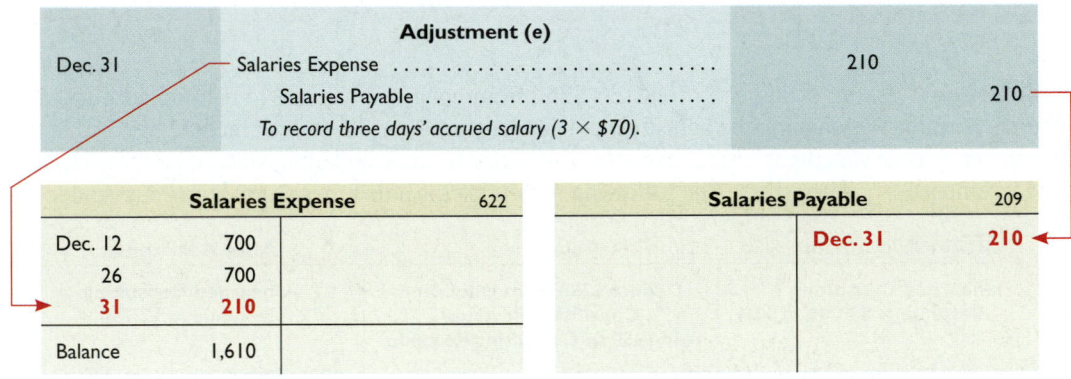

Adjustment (e)

Dec. 31	Salaries Expense	210	
	Salaries Payable		210
	To record three days' accrued salary (3 × $70).		

Salaries Expense		622
Dec. 12	700	
26	700	
31	210	
Balance	1,610	

| **Salaries Payable** | | 209 |
| | Dec. 31 | 210 |

Explanation   Salaries expense of $1,610 is reported on the December income statement and $210 of salaries payable (liability) is reported in the balance sheet. *Not* making the adjustment (1) understates salaries expense and overstates net income by $210 in the December income statement and (2) understates salaries payable (liabilities) and overstates equity by $210 on the December 31 balance sheet. The following highlights the adjustment for salaries incurred.

Before Adjustment	Adjustment	After Adjustment
Salaries Payable = $0	Add $210 to Salaries Payable Add $210 to Salaries Expense	Salaries Payable = $210
Reports $0 from employee salaries incurred but not yet paid in cash.	Record 3 days' salaries owed to employee, but not yet paid, at $70 per day.	Reports $210 salaries payable to employee but not yet paid.

Accrued Interest Expense   Companies commonly have accrued interest expense on notes payable and other long-term liabilities at the end of a period. Interest expense is incurred with the passage of time. Unless interest is paid on the last day of an accounting period, we need to adjust for interest expense incurred but not yet paid. This means we must accrue interest cost from the most recent payment date up to the end of the period. The formula for computing accrued interest is:

Principal amount owed × Annual interest rate × Fraction of year since last payment date.

To illustrate, if a company has a $6,000 loan from a bank at 6% annual interest, then 30 days' accrued interest expense is $30—computed as $6,000 × 0.06 × 30/360. The adjusting entry would be to debit Interest Expense for $30 and credit Interest Payable for $30.

Point: Interest computations assume a 360-day year; known as the *bankers' rule*.

Future Payment of Accrued Expenses   Adjusting entries for accrued expenses foretell cash transactions in future periods. Specifically, accrued expenses at the end of one accounting period result in *cash payment* in a *future period*(s). To illustrate, recall that FastForward recorded accrued salaries of $210. On January 9, the first payday of the next period, the following entry settles the accrued liability (salaries payable) and records salaries expense for seven days of work in January:

Jan. 9	Salaries Payable (3 days at $70 per day)	210	
	Salaries Expense (7 days at $70 per day)	490	
	Cash		700
	Paid two weeks' salary including three days accrued in December.		

Assets = Liabilities + Equity
−700   −210   −490

The $210 debit reflects the payment of the liability for the three days' salary accrued on December 31. The $490 debit records the salary for January's first seven working days (including the New Year's Day holiday) as an expense of the new accounting period. The $700 credit records the total amount of cash paid to the employee.

Accrued Revenues

The term **accrued revenues** refers to revenues earned in a period that are both unrecorded and not yet received in cash (or other assets). An example is a technician who bills customers only when the job is done. If one-third of a job is complete by the end of a period, then the technician must record one-third of the expected billing as revenue in that period—even though there is no billing or collection. The adjusting entries for accrued revenues increase assets and increase revenues as shown in Exhibit 3.11. Accrued revenues commonly arise from services, products, interest, and rent. We use service fees and interest to show how to adjust for accrued revenues.

Point: Accrued revenues are also called *accrued assets.*

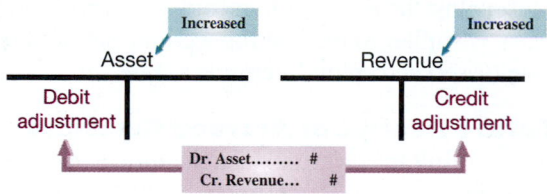

EXHIBIT 3.11

Adjusting for Accrued Revenues

Accrued Services Revenue   Accrued revenues are not recorded until adjusting entries are made at the end of the accounting period. These accrued revenues are earned but unrecorded because either the buyer has not yet paid for them or the seller has not yet billed the buyer. FastForward provides an example.

Step 1:   In the second week of December, it agreed to provide 30 days of consulting services to a local fitness club for a fixed fee of $2,700. The terms of the initial agreement call for FastForward to provide services from December 12, 2011, through January 10, 2012, or 30 days of service. The club agrees to pay FastForward $2,700 on January 10, 2012, when the service period is complete.

Step 2:   At December 31, 2011, 20 days of services have already been provided. Since the contracted services have not yet been entirely provided, FastForward has neither billed the club nor recorded the services already provided. Still, FastForward has earned two-thirds of the 30-day fee, or $1,800 ($2,700 × 20/30). The *revenue recognition principle* implies that it must report the $1,800 on the December income statement. The balance sheet also must report that the club owes FastForward $1,800.

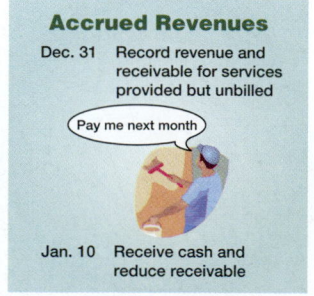

Accrued Revenues

Dec. 31   Record revenue and receivable for services provided but unbilled

Pay me next month

Jan. 10   Receive cash and reduce receivable

Step 3: The year-end adjusting entry to account for accrued services revenue is

Assets = Liabilities + Equity
+1,800   +1,800

	Adjustment (f)		
Dec. 31	Accounts Receivable	1,800	
	Consulting Revenue		1,800
	To record 20 days' accrued revenue.		

Accounts Receivable			106
Dec. 12	1,900	Dec. 22	1,900
31	**1,800**		
Balance	1,800		

Consulting Revenue		403
	Dec. 5	4,200
	12	1,600
	31	250
	31	**1,800**
	Balance	7,850

Example: What is the adjusting entry if the 30-day consulting period began on December 22? *Answer:* One-third of the fee is earned:
Accounts Receivable 900
   Consulting Revenue.... 900

Explanation   Accounts receivable are reported on the balance sheet at $1,800, and the $7,850 total of consulting revenue is reported on the income statement. *Not* making the adjustment would understate (1) both consulting revenue and net income by $1,800 in the December income statement and (2) both accounts receivable (assets) and equity by $1,800 on the December 31 balance sheet. The following table highlights the adjustment for accrued revenue.

Before Adjustment	Adjustment	After Adjustment
Accounts Receivable = $0	Add $1,800 to Accounts Receivable Add $1,800 to Consulting Revenue	Accounts Receivable = $1,800
Reports $0 from revenue earned but not yet received in cash.	Record 20 days of earned consulting revenue, which is 20/30 of total contract amount.	Reports $1,800 in accounts receivable from consulting services provided.

Accrued Interest Revenue   In addition to the accrued interest expense we described earlier, interest can yield an accrued revenue when a debtor owes money (or other assets) to a company. If a company is holding notes or accounts receivable that produce interest revenue, we must adjust the accounts to record any earned and yet uncollected interest revenue. The adjusting entry is similar to the one for accruing services revenue. Specifically, we debit Interest Receivable (asset) and credit Interest Revenue.

Future Receipt of Accrued Revenues   Accrued revenues at the end of one accounting period result in *cash receipts* in a *future period*(s). To illustrate, recall that FastForward made an adjusting entry for $1,800 to record 20 days' accrued revenue earned from its consulting contract. When FastForward receives $2,700 cash on January 10 for the entire contract amount, it makes the following entry to remove the accrued asset (accounts receivable) and recognize the revenue earned in January. The $2,700 debit reflects the cash received. The $1,800 credit reflects the removal of the receivable, and the $900 credit records the revenue earned in January.

Assets = Liabilities + Equity
+2,700   +900
−1,800

Jan. 10	Cash	2,700	
	Accounts Receivable (20 days at $90 per day)		1,800
	Consulting Revenue (10 days at $90 per day)		900
	Received cash for the accrued asset and recorded earned consulting revenue for January.		

● **Decision Maker**   Answer — p. 128

Loan Officer   The owner of an electronics store applies for a business loan. The store's financial statements reveal large increases in current-year revenues and income. Analysis shows that these increases are due to a promotion that let consumers buy now and pay nothing until January 1 of next year. The store recorded these sales as accrued revenue. Does your analysis raise any concerns? ■

Links to Financial Statements

The process of adjusting accounts is intended to bring an asset or liability account balance to its correct amount. It also updates a related expense or revenue account. These adjustments are necessary for transactions and events that extend over more than one period. (Adjusting entries are posted like any other entry.)

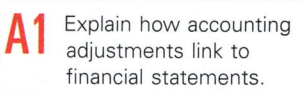

A1   Explain how accounting adjustments link to financial statements.

   Exhibit 3.12 summarizes the four types of transactions requiring adjustment. Understanding this exhibit is important to understanding the adjusting process and its importance to financial statements. Remember that each adjusting entry affects one or more income statement accounts *and* one or more balance sheet accounts (but never cash).

EXHIBIT 3.12

Summary of Adjustments and Financial Statement Links

| Category | BEFORE Adjusting | | Adjusting Entry |
	Balance Sheet	Income Statement	
Prepaid expenses†	Asset overstated	Expense understated	**Dr. Expense**
	Equity overstated		**Cr. Asset***
Unearned revenues†	Liability overstated	Revenue understated	**Dr. Liability**
	Equity understated		**Cr. Revenue**
Accrued expenses	Liability understated	Expense understated	**Dr. Expense**
	Equity overstated		**Cr. Liability**
Accrued revenues	Asset understated	Revenue understated	**Dr. Asset**
	Equity understated		**Cr. Revenue**

* For depreciation, the credit is to Accumulated Depreciation (contra asset).

† Exhibit assumes that prepaid expenses are initially recorded as assets and that unearned revenues are initially recorded as liabilities.

   Information about some adjustments is not always available until several days or even weeks after the period-end. This means that some adjusting and closing entries are recorded later than, but dated as of, the last day of the period. One example is a company that receives a utility bill on January 10 for costs incurred for the month of December. When it receives the bill, the company records the expense and the payable as of December 31. Other examples include long-distance phone usage and costs of many Web billings. The December income statement reflects these additional expenses incurred, and the December 31 balance sheet includes these payables, although the amounts were not actually known on December 31.

Decision Ethics   Answer — p. 128

Financial Officer   At year-end, the president instructs you, the financial officer, not to record accrued expenses until next year because they will not be paid until then. The president also directs you to record in current-year sales a recent purchase order from a customer that requires merchandise to be delivered two weeks after the year-end. Your company would report a net income instead of a net loss if you carry out these instructions. What do you do? ■

Quick Check   Answers — p. 128

6. If an adjusting entry for accrued revenues of $200 at year-end is omitted, what is this error's effect on the year-end income statement and balance sheet?

7. What is a contra account? Explain its purpose.

8. What is an accrued expense? Give an example.

9. Describe how an unearned revenue arises. Give an example.

Adjusted Trial Balance

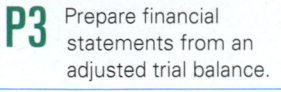

P2   Explain and prepare an adjusted trial balance.

An **unadjusted trial balance** is a list of accounts and balances prepared *before* adjustments are recorded. An **adjusted trial balance** is a list of accounts and balances prepared *after* adjusting entries have been recorded and posted to the ledger.

Exhibit 3.13 shows both the unadjusted and the adjusted trial balances for FastForward at December 31, 2011. The order of accounts in the trial balance is usually set up to match the order in the chart of accounts. Several new accounts arise from the adjusting entries.

EXHIBIT 3.13

Unadjusted and Adjusted Trial Balances

FASTFORWARD
Trial Balances
December 31, 2011

Acct. No.	Account Title	Unadjusted Trial Balance Dr.	Unadjusted Trial Balance Cr.	Adjustments Dr.	Adjustments Cr.	Adjusted Trial Balance Dr.	Adjusted Trial Balance Cr.
101	Cash	$ 4,350				$ 4,350	
106	Accounts receivable	0		(f) $1,800		1,800	
126	Supplies	9,720			(b) $1,050	8,670	
128	Prepaid insurance	2,400			(a) 100	2,300	
167	Equipment	26,000				26,000	
168	Accumulated depreciation—Equip.		$ 0		(c) 375		$ 375
201	Accounts payable		6,200				6,200
209	Salaries payable		0		(e) 210		210
236	Unearned consulting revenue		3,000	(d) 250			2,750
307	Common stock		30,000				30,000
318	Retained earnings		0				0
319	Dividends	200				200	
403	Consulting revenue		5,800		(d) 250		7,850
					(f) 1,800		
406	Rental revenue		300				300
612	Depreciation expense—Equip.	0		(c) 375		375	
622	Salaries expense	1,400		(e) 210		1,610	
637	Insurance expense	0		(a) 100		100	
640	Rent expense	1,000				1,000	
652	Supplies expense	0		(b) 1,050		1,050	
690	Utilities expense	230				230	
	Totals	$45,300	$45,300	$3,785	$3,785	$47,685	$47,685

Each adjustment (see middle columns) is identified by a letter in parentheses that links it to an adjusting entry explained earlier. Each amount in the Adjusted Trial Balance columns is computed by taking that account's amount from the Unadjusted Trial Balance columns and adding or subtracting any adjustment(s). To illustrate, Supplies has a $9,720 Dr. balance in the unadjusted columns. Subtracting the $1,050 Cr. amount shown in the adjustments columns yields an adjusted $8,670 Dr. balance for Supplies. An account can have more than one adjustment, such as for Consulting Revenue. Also, some accounts might not require adjustment for this period, such as for Accounts Payable.

PREPARING FINANCIAL STATEMENTS

P3   Prepare financial statements from an adjusted trial balance.

We can prepare financial statements directly from information in the *adjusted* trial balance. An adjusted trial balance (see the right-most columns in Exhibit 3.13) includes all accounts and balances appearing in financial statements, and is easier to work from than the entire ledger when preparing financial statements.

EXHIBIT 3.14

Preparing Financial Statements (Adjusted Trial Balance from Exhibit 3.13)

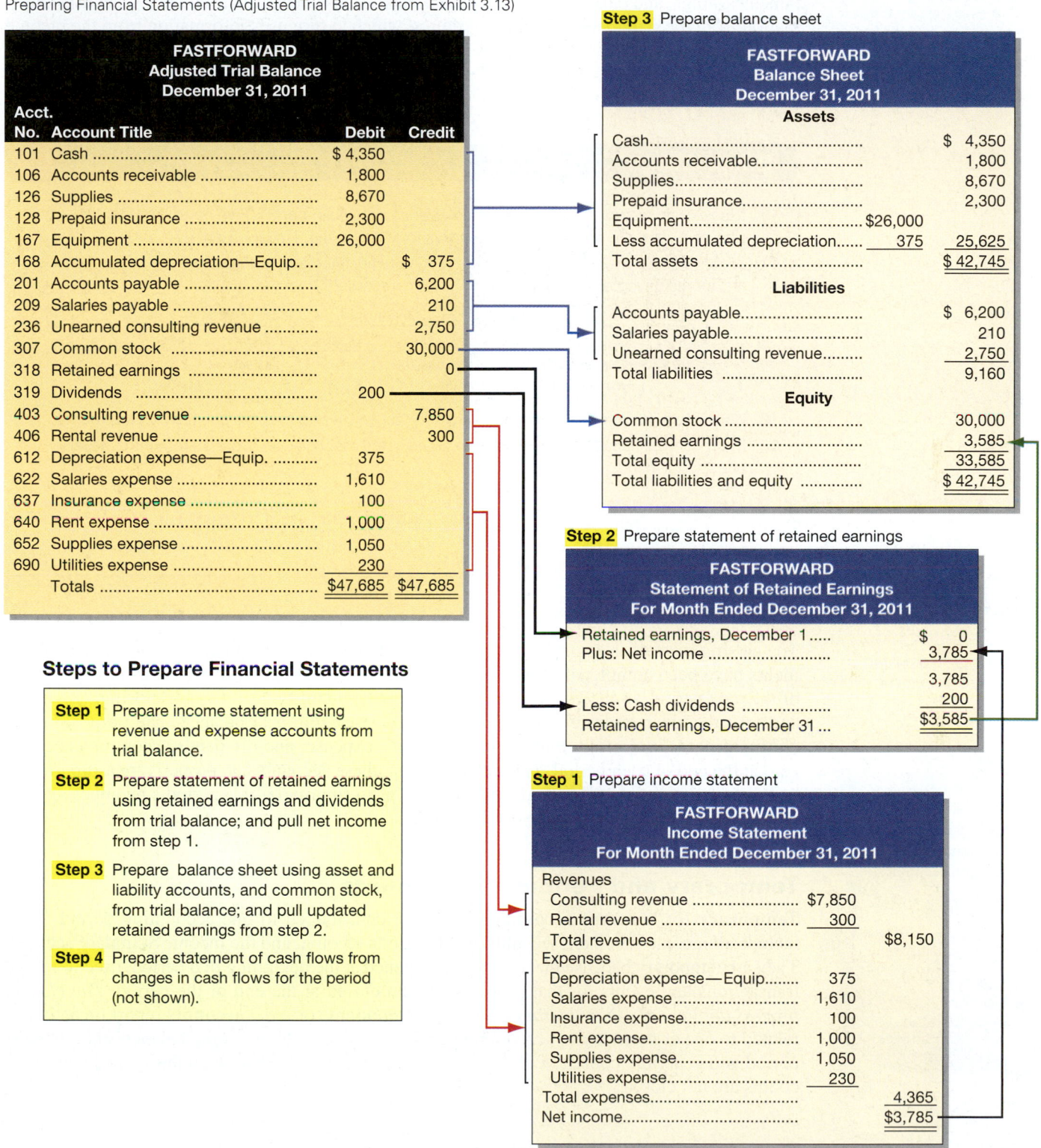

Exhibit 3.14 shows how revenue and expense balances are transferred from the adjusted trial balance to the income statement (red lines). The net income and the dividends amount are then used to prepare the statement of retained earnings (black lines). Asset and liability balances on the adjusted trial balance are then transferred to the balance sheet (blue lines). The ending retained earnings is determined on the statement of retained earnings and transferred to the balance sheet (green lines).

Point: Sarbanes-Oxley Act requires that financial statements filed with the SEC be certified by the CEO and CFO, including a declaration that the statements fairly present the issuer's operations and financial condition. Violators can receive fines and/or prison terms.

Point: Each trial balance amount is used in only *one* financial statement and, when financial statements are completed, each account will have been used once.

We prepare financial statements in the following order: income statement, statement of retained earnings, and balance sheet. This order makes sense because the balance sheet uses information from the statement of retained earnings, which in turn uses information from the income statement. The statement of cash flows is usually the final statement prepared.

Quick Check   Answers — p. 128

10. Music-Mart records $1,000 of accrued salaries on December 31. Five days later, on January 5 (the next payday), salaries of $7,000 are paid. What is the January 5 entry?

11. Jordan Air has the following information in its unadjusted and adjusted trial balances. What are the adjusting entries that Jordan Air likely recorded?

	Unadjusted		Adjusted	
	Debit	Credit	Debit	Credit
Prepaid insurance	$6,200		$5,900	
Salaries payable		$ 0		$1,400

12. What accounts are taken from the adjusted trial balance to prepare an income statement?

13. In preparing financial statements from an adjusted trial balance, what statement is usually prepared second?

CLOSING PROCESS

P4 Describe and prepare closing entries.

The **closing process** is an important step at the end of an accounting period *after* financial statements have been completed. It prepares accounts for recording the transactions and the events of the *next* period. In the closing process we must (1) identify accounts for closing, (2) record and post the closing entries, and (3) prepare a post-closing trial balance. The purpose of the closing process is twofold. First, it resets revenue, expense, and dividends account balances to zero at the end of each period. This is done so that these accounts can properly measure income and dividends for the next period. Second, it helps in summarizing a period's revenues and expenses. This section explains the closing process.

Temporary Accounts
(closed at period-end)
Revenues
Expenses
Dividends
Income Summary

Temporary and Permanent Accounts

Temporary (or *nominal*) **accounts** accumulate data related to one accounting period. They include all income statement accounts, the dividends account, and the Income Summary account. They are temporary because the accounts are opened at the beginning of a period, used to record transactions and events for that period, and then closed at the end of the period. *The closing process applies only to temporary accounts.* **Permanent** (or *real*) **accounts** report on activities related to one or more future accounting periods. They carry their ending balances into the next period and generally consist of all balance sheet accounts. These asset, liability, and equity accounts are not closed.

Permanent Accounts
(not closed at period-end)
Assets
Liabilities
Common Stock
Retained Earnings

Recording Closing Entries

To record and post **closing entries** is to transfer the end-of-period balances in revenue, expense, and dividends accounts to the permanent retained earnings account. Closing entries are necessary at the end of each period after financial statements are prepared because

- Revenue, expense, and dividends accounts must begin each period with zero balances.
- Retained earnings must reflect prior periods' revenues, expenses, and dividends.

An income statement aims to report revenues and expenses for a *specific accounting period*. The statement of retained earnings reports similar information, including dividends. Since revenue, expense, and dividends accounts must accumulate information separately for each period, they must start each period with zero balances. To close these accounts, we transfer their balances first to an account called *Income Summary*. **Income Summary** is a temporary account (only used for the closing process) that contains a credit for the sum of all revenues (and gains) and a debit for the sum of all expenses (and losses). Its balance equals net income or net loss and it is transferred to retained earnings. Next the dividends account balance is transferred to retained earnings. After these closing entries are posted, the revenue, expense, dividends, and Income Summary accounts have zero balances. These accounts are then said to be *closed* or *cleared*.

Exhibit 3.15 uses the adjusted account balances of FastForward (from the left side of Exhibit 3.14) to show the four steps necessary to close its temporary accounts. We explain each step.

Point: To understand the closing process, focus on its *outcomes*—*updating* the retained earnings account balance to its proper ending balance, and getting *temporary accounts* to show *zero balances* for purposes of accumulating data for the next period.

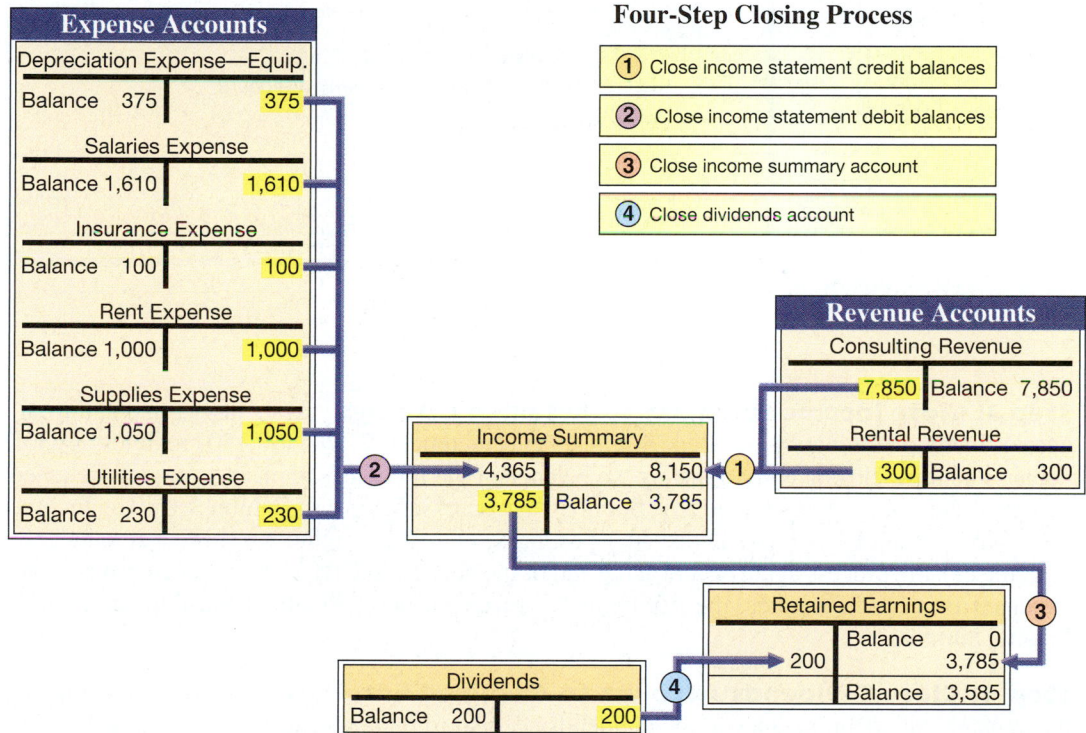

Four-Step Closing Process

① Close income statement credit balances
② Close income statement debit balances
③ Close income summary account
④ Close dividends account

EXHIBIT 3.15

Four-Step Closing Process

Point: Retained Earnings is the only *permanent account* in Exhibit 3.15.

Step 1: Close Credit Balances in Revenue Accounts to Income Summary

The first closing entry transfers credit balances in revenue (and gain) accounts to the Income Summary account. We bring accounts with credit balances to zero by debiting them. For FastForward, this journal entry is step 1 in Exhibit 3.16. This entry closes revenue accounts and leaves them with zero balances. The accounts are now ready to record revenues when they occur in the next period. The $8,150 credit entry to Income Summary equals total revenues for the period.

Step 2: Close Debit Balances in Expense Accounts to Income Summary

The second closing entry transfers debit balances in expense (and loss) accounts to the Income Summary account. We bring expense accounts' debit balances to zero by crediting them. With a balance of zero, these accounts are ready to accumulate a record of expenses for the next period. This second closing entry for FastForward is step 2 in Exhibit 3.16. Exhibit 3.15 shows that posting this entry gives each expense account a zero balance.

Point: It is possible to close revenue and expense accounts directly to retained earnings. Computerized accounting systems do this.

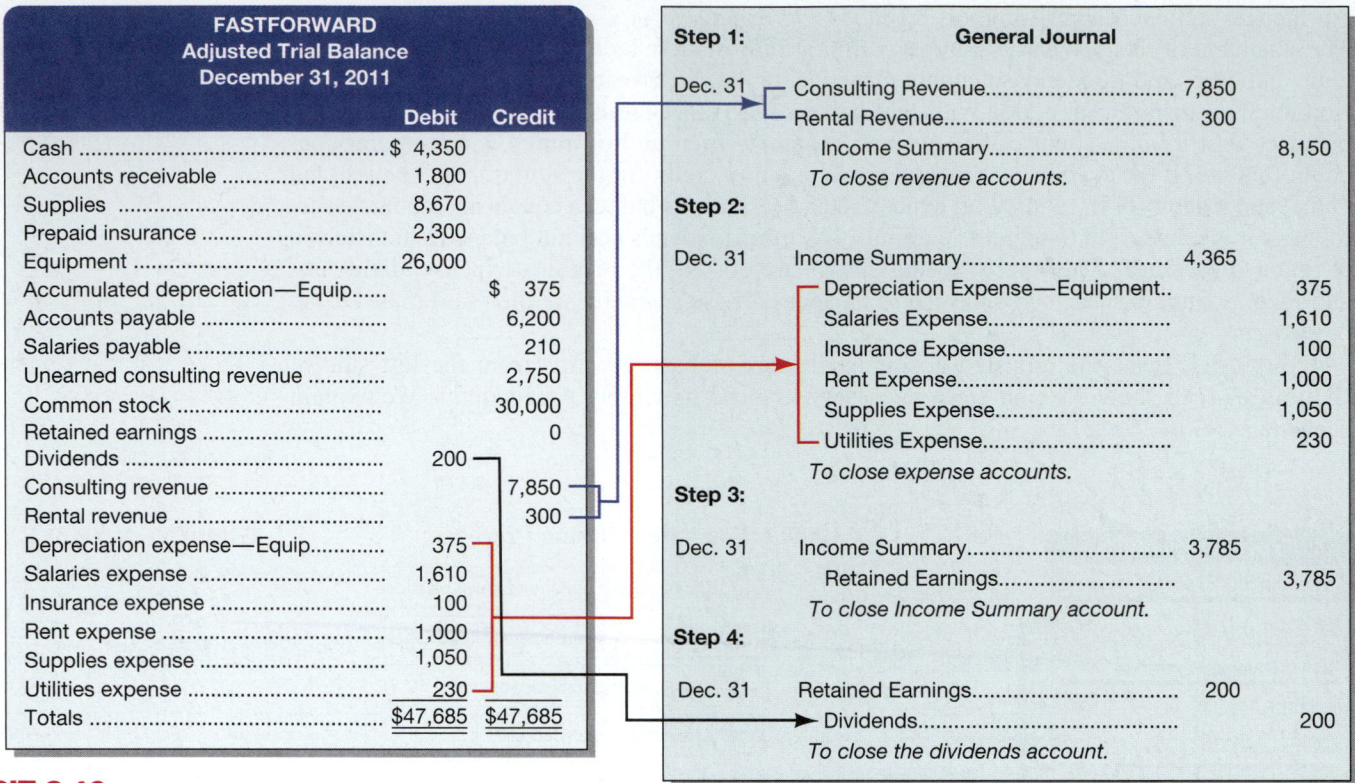

EXHIBIT 3.16

Preparing Closing Entries

Step 3: Close Income Summary to Retained Earnings

After steps 1 and 2, the balance of Income Summary is equal to December's net income of $3,785 ($8,150 credit less $4,365 debit). The third closing entry transfers the balance of the Income Summary account to retained earnings. This entry closes the Income Summary account–see step 3 in Exhibit 3.16. The Income Summary account has a zero balance after posting this entry. It continues to have a zero balance until the closing process again occurs at the end of the next period. (If a net loss occurred because expenses exceeded revenues, the third entry is reversed: debit Retained Earnings and credit Income Summary.)

Step 4: Close Dividends Account to Retained Earnings

The fourth closing entry transfers any debit balance in the dividends account to retained earnings—see step 4 in Exhibit 3.16. This entry gives the dividends account a zero balance, and the account is now ready to accumulate next period's dividends. This entry also reduces the retained earnings balance to the $3,585 amount reported on the balance sheet.

   We could also have selected the accounts and amounts needing to be closed by identifying individual revenue, expense, and dividends accounts in the ledger. This is illustrated in Exhibit 3.16 where we prepare closing entries using the adjusted trial balance. (Information for closing entries is also in the financial statement columns of a work sheet—see Appendix 3B.)

Post-Closing Trial Balance

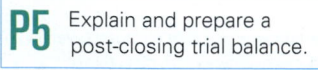

Exhibit 3.17 shows the entire ledger of FastForward as of December 31 after adjusting and closing entries are posted. (The transaction entries are in Chapter 2.) The temporary accounts (revenues, expenses, and dividends) have ending balances equal to zero.

   A **post-closing trial balance** is a list of permanent accounts and their balances from the ledger after all closing entries have been journalized and posted. It lists the balances for all accounts not closed. These accounts comprise a company's assets, liabilities, and equity, which are identical to those in the balance sheet. The aim of a post-closing trial balance is to verify that

EXHIBIT 3.17

General Ledger after the Closing Process for FastForward

Asset Accounts

Cash — Acct. No. 101

Date	Explan.	PR	Debit	Credit	Balance
2011					
Dec. 1	(1)	G1	30,000		30,000
2	(2)	G1		2,500	27,500
3	(3)	G1		26,000	1,500
5	(5)	G1	4,200		5,700
6	(13)	G1		2,400	3,300
12	(6)	G1		1,000	2,300
12	(7)	G1		700	1,600
22	(9)	G1	1,900		3,500
24	(10)	G1		900	2,600
24	(11)	G1		200	2,400
26	(12)	G1	3,000		5,400
26	(14)	G1		120	5,280
26	(15)	G1		230	5,050
26	(16)	G1		700	**4,350**

Accounts Receivable — Acct. No. 106

Date	Explan.	PR	Debit	Credit	Balance
2011					
Dec. 12	(8)	G1	1,900		1,900
22	(9)	G1		1,900	0
31	Adj.(f)	G1	1,800		**1,800**

Supplies — Acct. No. 126

Date	Explan.	PR	Debit	Credit	Balance
2011					
Dec. 2	(2)	G1	2,500		2,500
6	(4)	G1	7,100		9,600
26	(14)	G1	120		9,720
31	Adj.(b)	G1		1,050	**8,670**

Prepaid Insurance — Acct. No. 128

Date	Explan.	PR	Debit	Credit	Balance
2011					
Dec. 6	(13)	G1	2,400		2,400
31	Adj.(a)	G1		100	**2,300**

Equipment — Acct. No. 167

Date	Explan.	PR	Debit	Credit	Balance
2011					
Dec. 3	(3)	G1	26,000		**26,000**

Accumulated Depreciation— Equipment — Acct. No. 168

Date	Explan.	PR	Debit	Credit	Balance
2011					
Dec. 31	Adj.(c)	G1		375	**375**

Liability and Equity Accounts

Accounts Payable — Acct. No. 201

Date	Explan.	PR	Debit	Credit	Balance
2011					
Dec. 6	(4)	G1		7,100	7,100
24	(10)	G1	900		**6,200**

Salaries Payable — Acct. No. 209

Date	Explan.	PR	Debit	Credit	Balance
2011					
Dec. 31	Adj.(e)	G1		210	**210**

Unearned Consulting Revenue — Acct. No. 236

Date	Explan.	PR	Debit	Credit	Balance
2011					
Dec. 26	(12)	G1		3,000	3,000
31	Adj.(d)	G1	250		**2,750**

Common Stock — Acct. No. 307

Date	Explan.	PR	Debit	Credit	Balance
2011					
Dec. 1	(1)	G1		30,000	30,000

Retained Earnings — Acct. No. 318

Date	Explan.	PR	Debit	Credit	Balance
2011					
Dec. 31	Clos.(3)	G1		3,785	3,785
31	Clos.(4)	G1	200		3,585

Dividends — Acct. No. 319

Date	Explan.	PR	Debit	Credit	Balance
2011					
Dec. 24	(11)	G1	200		200
31	Clos.(4)	G1		200	0

Revenue and Expense Accounts (Including Income Summary)

Consulting Revenue — Acct. No. 403

Date	Explan.	PR	Debit	Credit	Balance
2011					
Dec. 5	(5)	G1		4,200	4,200
12	(8)	G1		1,600	5,800
31	Adj.(d)	G1		250	6,050
31	Adj.(f)	G1		1,800	**7,850**
31	Clos.(1)	G1	7,850		0

Rental Revenue — Acct. No. 406

Date	Explan.	PR	Debit	Credit	Balance
2011					
Dec. 12	(8)	G1		300	**300**
31	Clos.(1)	G1	300		0

Depreciation Expense— Equipment — Acct. No. 612

Date	Explan.	PR	Debit	Credit	Balance
2011					
Dec. 31	Adj.(c)	G1	375		**375**
31	Clos.(2)	G1		375	0

Salaries Expense — Acct. No. 622

Date	Explan.	PR	Debit	Credit	Balance
2011					
Dec. 12	(7)	G1	700		700
26	(16)	G1	700		1,400
31	Adj.(e)	G1	210		**1,610**
31	Clos.(2)	G1		1,610	0

Insurance Expense — Acct. No. 637

Date	Explan.	PR	Debit	Credit	Balance
2011					
Dec. 31	Adj.(a)	G1	100		**100**
31	Clos.(2)	G1		100	0

Rent Expense — Acct. No. 640

Date	Explan.	PR	Debit	Credit	Balance
2011					
Dec. 12	(6)	G1	1,000		**1,000**
31	Clos.(2)	G1		1,000	0

Supplies Expense — Acct. No. 652

Date	Explan.	PR	Debit	Credit	Balance
2011					
Dec. 31	Adj.(b)	G1	1,050		**1,050**
31	Clos.(2)	G1		1,050	0

Utilities Expense — Acct. No. 690

Date	Explan.	PR	Debit	Credit	Balance
2011					
Dec. 26	(15)	G1	230		**230**
31	Clos.(2)	G1		230	0

Income Summary — Acct. No. 901

Date	Explan.	PR	Debit	Credit	Balance
2011					
Dec. 31	Clos.(1)	G1		8,150	8,150
31	Clos.(2)	G1	4,365		3,785
31	Clos.(3)	G1	3,785		0

(1) total debits equal total credits for permanent accounts and (2) all temporary accounts have zero balances. FastForward's post-closing trial balance is shown in Exhibit 3.18. The post-closing trial balance usually is the last step in the accounting process.

EXHIBIT 3.18

Post-Closing Trial Balance

FASTFORWARD Post-Closing Trial Balance December 31, 2011		
	Debit	Credit
Cash	$ 4,350	
Accounts receivable	1,800	
Supplies	8,670	
Prepaid insurance	2,300	
Equipment	26,000	
Accumulated depreciation—Equipment		$ 375
Accounts payable		6,200
Salaries payable		210
Unearned consulting revenue		2,750
Common stock		30,000
Retained earnings		3,585
Totals	$43,120	$43,120

Accounting Cycle

 C3 Identify steps in the accounting cycle.

The term **accounting cycle** refers to the steps in preparing financial statements. It is called a *cycle* because the steps are repeated each reporting period. Exhibit 3.19 shows the 10 steps in the cycle, beginning with analyzing transactions and ending with a post-closing trial balance or

EXHIBIT 3.19

Steps in the Accounting Cycle*

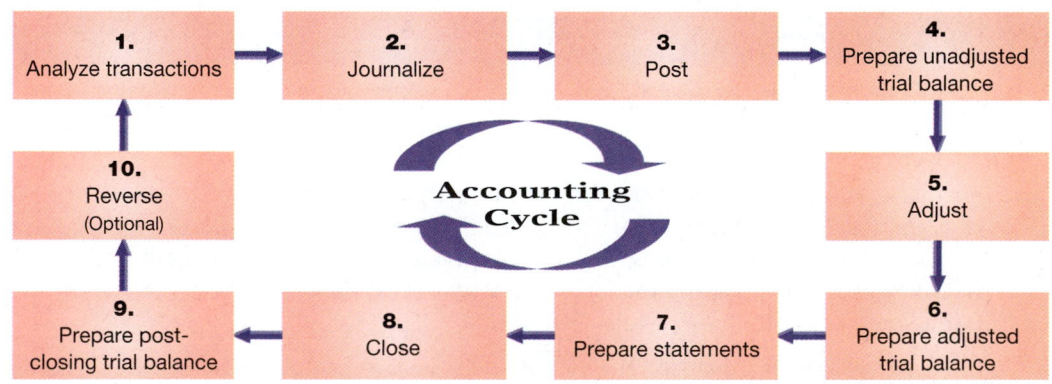

Explanations

1. Analyze transactions	Analyze transactions to prepare for journalizing.
2. Journalize	Record accounts, including debits and credits, in a journal.
3. Post	Transfer debits and credits from the journal to the ledger.
4. Prepare unadjusted trial balance	Summarize unadjusted ledger accounts and amounts.
5. Adjust	Record adjustments to bring account balances up to date; journalize and post adjustments.
6. Prepare adjusted trial balance	Summarize adjusted ledger accounts and amounts.
7. Prepare statements	Use adjusted trial balance to prepare financial statements.
8. Close	Journalize and post entries to close temporary accounts.
9. Prepare post-closing trial balance	Test clerical accuracy of the closing procedures.
10. Reverse (optional)	Reverse certain adjustments in the next period—optional step; see Appendix 3C.

* Steps 4, 6, and 9 can be done on a work sheet. A work sheet is useful in planning adjustments, but adjustments (step 5) must always be journalized and posted. Steps 3, 4, 6, and 9 are automatic with a computerized system.

reversing entries. Steps 1 through 3 usually occur regularly as a company enters into transactions. Steps 4 through 9 are done at the end of a period. *Reversing entries* in step 10 are optional and are explained in Appendix 3C.

Quick Check
Answers — p. 128

14. What are the major steps in preparing closing entries?
15. Why are revenue and expense accounts called *temporary?* Identify and list the types of temporary accounts.
16. What accounts are listed on the post-closing trial balance?

CLASSIFIED BALANCE SHEET

Our discussion to this point has been limited to unclassified financial statements. This section describes a classified balance sheet. The next chapter describes a classified income statement. An **unclassified balance sheet** is one whose items are broadly grouped into assets, liabilities, and equity. One example is FastForward's balance sheet in Exhibit 3.14. A **classified balance sheet** organizes assets and liabilities into important subgroups that provide more information to decision makers.

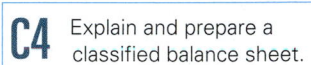

C4   Explain and prepare a classified balance sheet.

Classification Structure

A classified balance sheet has no required layout, but it usually contains the categories in Exhibit 3.20. One of the more important classifications is the separation between current and noncurrent items for both assets and liabilities. Current items are those expected to come due (either collected or owed) within one year or the company's operating cycle, whichever is longer. The **operating cycle** is the time span from when *cash is used* to acquire goods and services until *cash is received* from the sale of goods and services. "Operating" refers to company operations and "cycle" refers to the circular flow of cash used for company inputs and then cash received from its outputs. The length of a company's operating cycle depends on its activities. For a service company, the operating cycle is the time span between (1) paying employees who perform the services and (2) receiving cash from customers. For a merchandiser selling products, the operating cycle is the time span between (1) paying suppliers for merchandise and (2) receiving cash from customers.

Assets	Liabilities and Equity
Current assets	Current liabilities
Noncurrent assets	Noncurrent liabilities
Long-term investments	Equity
Plant assets	
Intangible assets	

EXHIBIT 3.20

Typical Categories in a Classified Balance Sheet

Most operating cycles are less than one year. This means most companies use a one-year period in deciding which assets and liabilities are current. A few companies have an operating cycle longer than one year. For instance, producers of certain beverages (wine) and products (ginseng) that require aging for several years have operating cycles longer than one year. A balance sheet lists current assets before noncurrent assets and current liabilities before noncurrent liabilities. This consistency in presentation allows users to quickly identify current assets that are most easily converted to cash and current liabilities that are shortly coming due. Items in current assets and current liabilities are listed in the order of how quickly they will be converted to, or paid in, cash.

EXHIBIT 3.21

Example of a Classified
Balance Sheet

SNOWBOARDING COMPONENTS
Balance Sheet
January 31, 2011

Assets

Current assets

Cash	$ 6,500	
Short-term investments	2,100	
Accounts receivable, net	4,400	
Merchandise inventory	27,500	
Prepaid expenses	2,400	
Total current assets		$ 42,900
Long-term investments		
Notes receivable	1,500	
Investments in stocks and bonds	18,000	
Land held for future expansion	48,000	
Total long-term investments		67,500
Plant assets		
Equipment and buildings	203,200	
Less accumulated depreciation	53,000	
Equipment and buildings, net		150,200
Land		73,200
Total plant assets		223,400
Intangible assets		10,000
Total assets		$343,800

Liabilities

Current liabilities

Accounts payable	$ 15,300	
Wages payable	3,200	
Notes payable	3,000	
Current portion of long-term liabilities	7,500	
Total current liabilities		$ 29,000
Long-term liabilities (net of current portion)		150,000
Total liabilities		179,000

Equity

Common stock		50,000
Retained earnings		114,800
Total equity		164,800
Total liabilities and equity		$343,800

Classification Categories

This section describes the most common categories in a classified balance sheet. The balance sheet for Snowboarding Components in Exhibit 3.21 shows the typical categories. Its assets are classified as either current or noncurrent. Its noncurrent assets include three main categories: long-term investments, plant assets, and intangible assets. Its liabilities are classified as either current or long-term. Not all companies use the same categories of assets and liabilities for their balance sheets. **K2 Inc.,** a manufacturer of snowboards, reported a balance sheet with only three asset classes: current assets; property, plant and equipment; and other assets.

Current Assets   **Current assets** are cash and other resources that are expected to be sold, collected, or used within one year or the company's operating cycle, whichever is longer. Examples are cash, short-term investments, accounts receivable, short-term notes receivable, goods for sale (called *merchandise* or *inventory*), and prepaid expenses. The individual prepaid expenses of a company are usually small in amount compared to many other assets and are often combined and shown as a single item. The prepaid expenses likely include items such as prepaid insurance, prepaid rent, office supplies, and store supplies. Prepaid expenses are usually listed last because they will not be converted to cash (instead, they are used).

Point: Current is also called *short-term*, and noncurrent is also called *long-term.*

Long-Term Investments   A second major balance sheet classification is **long-term** (or *noncurrent*) **investments.** Notes receivable and investments in stocks and bonds are long-term assets when they are expected to be held for more than the longer of one year or the operating cycle. Land held for future expansion is a long-term investment because it is *not* used in operations.

Plant Assets   Plant assets are tangible assets that are both *long-lived* and *used to produce* or *sell products and services.* Examples are equipment, machinery, buildings, and land that are used to produce or sell products and services. The order listing for plant assets is usually from most liquid to least liquid such as equipment and machinery to buildings and land.

Point: Plant assets are also called *fixed assets; property, plant and equipment;* or *long-lived assets.*

Intangible Assets   **Intangible assets** are long-term resources that benefit business operations, usually lack physical form, and have uncertain benefits. Examples are patents, trademarks, copyrights, franchises, and goodwill. Their value comes from the privileges or rights granted to or held by the owner. **K2, Inc.,** reported intangible assets of $228 million, which is nearly 20 percent of its total assets. Its intangibles included trademarks, patents, and licensing agreements.

Current Liabilities   **Current liabilities** are obligations due to be paid or settled within one year or the operating cycle, whichever is longer. They are usually settled by paying out current assets such as cash. Current liabilities often include accounts payable, notes payable, wages payable, taxes payable, interest payable, and unearned revenues. Also, any portion of a long-term liability due to be paid within one year or the operating cycle, whichever is longer, is a current liability. Unearned revenues are current liabilities when they will be settled by delivering products or services within one year or the operating cycle, whichever is longer. Current liabilities are reported in the order of those to be settled first.

Point: Many financial ratios are distorted if accounts are not classified correctly.

Long-Term Liabilities   **Long-term liabilities** are obligations *not* due within one year or the operating cycle, whichever is longer. Notes payable, mortgages payable, bonds payable, and lease obligations are common long-term liabilities. If a company has both short- and long-term items in each of these categories, they are commonly separated into two accounts in the ledger.

Point: Only assets and liabilities are classified as current or noncurrent.

Equity   Equity is the owner's claim on assets. The equity section for a corporation is divided into two main subsections, common stock and retained earnings.

Quick Check   Answers — p. 129

17. Classify the following assets as (1) current assets, (2) plant assets, or (3) intangible assets: (*a*) land used in operations, (*b*) office supplies, (*c*) receivables from customers due in 10 months, (*d*) insurance protection for the next 9 months, (*e*) trucks used to provide services to customers, (*f*) trademarks.
18. Cite at least two examples of assets classified as investments on the balance sheet.
19. Explain the operating cycle for a service company.

GLOBAL VIEW

We explained that accounting under U.S. GAAP is similar, but not identical, to that under IFRS. This section discusses differences in adjusting accounts, preparing financial statements, and reporting assets and liabilities on a balance sheet.

Adjusting Accounts   Both U.S. GAAP and IFRS include broad and similar guidance for adjusting accounts. Although some variations exist in revenue and expense recognition and other principles, all of the adjustments in this chapter are accounted for identically under the two systems. In later chapters we describe how certain assets and liabilities can result in different adjusted amounts using fair value measurements.

Preparing Financial Statements   Both U.S. GAAP and IFRS prepare the same four basic financial statements following the same process discussed in this chapter. Chapter 2 explained how both U.S. GAAP and IFRS require current items to be separated from noncurrent items on the balance sheet (yielding a classified balance sheet). U.S. GAAP balance sheets report current items first. Assets are listed from most liquid to least liquid, where liquid refers to the ease of converting an asset to cash. Liabilities are listed from nearest to maturity to furthest from maturity, maturity refers to the nearness of paying off the liability. IFRS balance sheets normally present noncurrent items first (and equity before liabilities), but this is not a requirement. Other differences with financial statements exist, which we identify in later chapters. Nokia provides the following example of IFRS reporting for its assets, liabilities, and equity within the balance sheet:

NOKIA

NOKIA Balance Sheet (in EUR millions) December 31, 2009			
Assets		**Equity and Liabilities**	
Noncurrent assets		Total equity	14,749
Goodwill and other intangibles	8,076	Noncurrent liabilities	
Property, plant and equipment	1,867	Long-term interest-bearing liabilities	4,432
Other noncurrent assets	2,182	Other long-term liabilities	1,369
Total noncurrent assets	12,125	Total noncurrent liabilities	5,801
Current assets		Current liabilities	
Inventories............................	1,865	Current portion of long-term loans	44
Accounts receivable, net	7,981	Short-term borrowings and other liabilities ...	972
Prepaid expenses and accrued income	4,551	Accounts payable	4,950
Other current assets	8,074	Accrued expenses	6,504
Cash	1,142	Provisions	2,718
Total current assets	23,613	Total current liabilities	15,188
Total assets	35,738	Total equity and liabilities	35,738

Closing Process   The closing process is identical under U.S. GAAP and IFRS. Although unique accounts can arise under either system, the closing process remains the same.

 **IFRS** _____

Revenue and expense recognition are key to recording accounting adjustments. IFRS tends to be more *principles-based* relative to U.S. GAAP, which is viewed as more *rules-based.* A principles-based system depends heavily on control procedures to reduce the potential for fraud or misconduct. Failure in judgment led to improper accounting adjustments at **Fannie Mae**, **Xerox**, **WorldCom**, and others. A KPMG 2009 survey of accounting and finance employees found that 13% of them had witnessed falsification or manipulation of accounting data within the past year. Internal controls and governance processes are directed at curtailing such behavior. ■

Profit Margin and Current Ratio **Decision Analysis**

A useful measure of a company's operating results is the ratio of its net income to net sales. This ratio is called **profit margin,** or *return on sales,* and is computed as in Exhibit 3.22.

A2 Compute profit margin and describe its use in analyzing company performance.

$$\text{Profit margin} = \frac{\text{Net income}}{\text{Net sales}}$$

EXHIBIT 3.22

Profit Margin

This ratio is interpreted as reflecting the percent of profit in each dollar of sales. To illustrate how we compute and use profit margin, let's look at the results of **Limited Brands, Inc.,** in Exhibit 3.23 for its fiscal years 2006 through 2010.

EXHIBIT 3.23

Limited Brands' Profit Margin

$ in millions	2010	2009	2008	2007	2006
Net income	$ 448	$ 220	$ 718	$ 676	$ 683
Net sales	$8,632	$9,043	$10,134	$10,671	$9,699
Profit margin	**5.2%**	**2.4%**	**7.1%**	**6.3%**	**7.0%**
Industry profit margin	0.9%	0.3%	1.1%	1.6%	1.5%

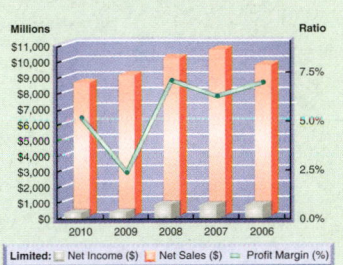

The Limited's average profit margin is 5.6% during this 5-year period. This favorably compares to the average industry profit margin of 1.1%. However, Limited's profit margin has declined in the most recent two years—from 7.1% in 2008 to 2.4% and 5.2% for the recent recessionary periods (see margin graph). Future success depends on Limited maintaining its market share and increasing its profit margin.

Current Ratio

An important use of financial statements is to help assess a company's ability to pay its debts in the near future. Such analysis affects decisions by suppliers when allowing a company to buy on credit. It also affects decisions by creditors when lending money to a company, including loan terms such as interest rate, due date, and collateral requirements. It can also affect a manager's decisions about using cash to pay debts when they come due. The **current ratio** is one measure of a company's ability to pay its short-term obligations. It is defined in Exhibit 3.24 as current assets divided by current liabilities.

A3 Compute the current ratio and describe what it reveals about a company's financial condition.

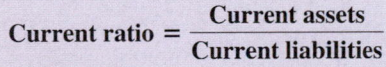

EXHIBIT 3.24

Current Ratio

Using financial information from **Limited Brands, Inc.,** we compute its current ratio for the recent four-year period. The results are in Exhibit 3.25.

EXHIBIT 3.25

Limited Brands' Current Ratio

$ in millions	2010	2009	2008	2007	2006
Current assets	$3,250	$2,867	$2,919	$2,771	$2,784
Current liabilities	$1,322	$1,255	$1,374	$1,709	$1,575
Current ratio	**2.5**	**2.3**	**2.1**	**1.6**	**1.8**
Industry current ratio	1.9	2.0	2.1	2.3	2.4

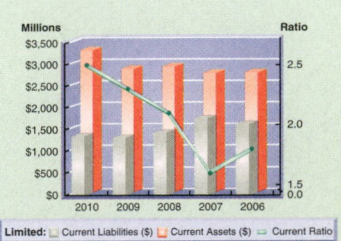

Limited Brands' current ratio averaged 2.1 for its fiscal years 2006 through 2010. The current ratio for each of these years suggests that the company's short-term obligations can be covered with its short-term assets. However, if its ratio would approach 1.0, Limited would expect to face challenges in covering liabilities. If the ratio were *less* than 1.0, current liabilities would exceed current assets, and the company's ability to pay short-term obligations could be in doubt.

 **Decision** Maker   Answer — p. 128

Analyst You are analyzing the financial condition of a company to assess its ability to meet upcoming loan payments. You compute its current ratio as 1.2. You also find that a major portion of accounts receivable is due from one client who has not made any payments in the past 12 months. Removing this receivable from current assets lowers the current ratio to 0.7. What do you conclude? ■

DEMONSTRATION PROBLEM 1

The following information relates to Fanning's Electronics on December 31, 2011. The company, which uses the calendar year as its annual reporting period, initially records prepaid and unearned items in balance sheet accounts (assets and liabilities, respectively).

a. The company's weekly payroll is $8,750, paid each Friday for a five-day workweek. Assume December 31, 2011, falls on a Monday, but the employees will not be paid their wages until Friday, January 4, 2012.

b. Eighteen months earlier, on July 1, 2010, the company purchased equipment that cost $20,000. Its useful life is predicted to be five years, at which time the equipment is expected to be worthless (zero salvage value).

c. On October 1, 2011, the company agreed to work on a new housing development. The company is paid $120,000 on October 1 in advance of future installation of similar alarm systems in 24 new homes. That amount was credited to the Unearned Services Revenue account. Between October 1 and December 31, work on 20 homes was completed.

d. On September 1, 2011, the company purchased a 12-month insurance policy for $1,800. The transaction was recorded with an $1,800 debit to Prepaid Insurance.

e. On December 29, 2011, the company completed a $7,000 service that has not been billed and not recorded as of December 31, 2011.

Required

1. Prepare any necessary adjusting entries on December 31, 2011, in relation to transactions and events *a* through *e*.

2. Prepare T-accounts for the accounts affected by adjusting entries, and post the adjusting entries. Determine the adjusted balances for the Unearned Revenue and the Prepaid Insurance accounts.

3. Complete the following table and determine the amounts and effects of your adjusting entries on the year 2011 income statement and the December 31, 2011, balance sheet. Use up (down) arrows to indicate an increase (decrease) in the Effect columns.

Entry	Amount in the Entry	Effect on Net Income	Effect on Total Assets	Effect on Total Liabilities	Effect on Total Equity

PLANNING THE SOLUTION

● Analyze each situation to determine which accounts need to be updated with an adjustment.
● Calculate the amount of each adjustment and prepare the necessary journal entries.
● Show the amount of each adjustment in the designated accounts, determine the adjusted balance, and identify the balance sheet classification of the account.
● Determine each entry's effect on net income for the year and on total assets, total liabilities, and total equity at the end of the year.

SOLUTION TO DEMONSTRATION PROBLEM 1

1. Adjusting journal entries.

(a) Dec. 31	Wages Expense	1,750	
	Wages Payable		1,750
	To accrue wages for the last day of the year ($8,750 × 1/5).		
(b) Dec. 31	Depreciation Expense—Equipment	4,000	
	Accumulated Depreciation—Equipment		4,000
	To record depreciation expense for the year ($20,000/5 years = $4,000 per year).		
(c) Dec. 31	Unearned Services Revenue	100,000	
	Services Revenue		100,000
	To recognize services revenue earned ($120,000 × 20/24).		
(d) Dec. 31	Insurance Expense	600	
	Prepaid Insurance		600
	To adjust for expired portion of insurance ($1,800 × 4/12).		
(e) Dec. 31	Accounts Receivable	7,000	
	Services Revenue		7,000
	To record services revenue earned.		

2. T-accounts for adjusting journal entries *a* through *e*.

Wages Expense					Wages Payable		
(a)	1,750					(a)	1,750

Depreciation Expense—Equipment					Accumulated Depreciation—Equipment		
(b)	4,000					(b)	4,000

Unearned Revenue				Services Revenue		
		Unadj. Bal.	120,000		(c)	100,000
(c)	100,000				(e)	7,000
		Adj. Bal.	20,000		Adj. Bal.	107,000

Insurance Expense				Prepaid Insurance		
(d)	600		Unadj. Bal.	1,800		
					(d)	600

Accounts Receivable				Prepaid Insurance (cont.)		
(e)	7,000		Adj. Bal.	1,200		

3. Financial statement effects of adjusting journal entries.

Entry	Amount in the Entry	Effect on Net Income	Effect on Total Assets	Effect on Total Liabilities	Effect on Total Equity
a	$ 1,750	$ 1,750 ↓	No effect	$ 1,750 ↑	$ 1,750 ↓
b	4,000	4,000 ↓	$4,000 ↓	No effect	4,000 ↓
c	100,000	100,000 ↑	No effect	$100,000 ↓	100,000 ↑
d	600	600 ↓	$ 600 ↓	No effect	600 ↓
e	7,000	7,000 ↑	$7,000 ↑	No effect	7,000 ↑

DEMONSTRATION PROBLEM 2

Use the following adjusted trial balance to answer questions 1–3.

CHOI COMPANY Adjusted Trial Balance December 31		
	Debit	**Credit**
Cash	$ 3,050	
Accounts receivable	400	
Prepaid insurance	830	
Supplies	80	
Equipment	217,200	
Accumulated depreciation—Equipment		$ 29,100
Wages payable		880
Interest payable		3,600
Unearned rent		460
Long-term notes payable		150,000
Common stock...............................		10,000
Retained earnings		30,340
Dividends	21,000	
Rent earned		57,500
Wages expense	25,000	
Utilities expense	1,900	
Insurance expense	3,200	
Supplies expense	250	
Depreciation expense—Equipment	5,970	
Interest expense	3,000	
Totals	$281,880	$281,880

1. Prepare the annual income statement from the adjusted trial balance of Choi Company.

Answer:

CHOI COMPANY Income Statement For Year Ended December 31		
Revenues		
Rent earned		$57,500
Expenses		
Wages expense	$25,000	
Utilities expense	1,900	
Insurance expense	3,200	
Supplies expense	250	
Depreciation expense—Equipment	5,970	
Interest expense	3,000	
Total expenses		39,320
Net income		$18,180

2. Prepare a statement of retained earnings from the adjusted trial balance of Choi Company.

Answer:

CHOI COMPANY Statement of Retained Earnings For Year Ended December 31	
Retained earnings, December 31 prior year-end	$30,340
Plus: Net income	18,180
	48,520
Less: Dividends....................................	21,000
Retained earnings, December 31 current year-end	$27,520

3. Prepare a balance sheet from the adjusted trial balance of Choi Company.

Answer:

CHOI COMPANY
Balance Sheet
December 31

Assets

Cash		$ 3,050
Accounts receivable		400
Prepaid insurance		830
Supplies		80
Equipment	$217,200	
Less accumulated depreciation	29,100	188,100
Total assets		$192,460

Liabilities

Wages payable		$ 880
Interest payable		3,600
Unearned rent		460
Long-term notes payable		150,000
Total liabilities		154,940

Equity

Common stock		10,000
Retained earnings		27,520
Total equity		37,520
Total liabilities and equity		$192,460

Alternative Accounting for Prepayments

This appendix explains an alternative in accounting for prepaid expenses and unearned revenues.

Recording Prepayment of Expenses in Expense Accounts An alternative method is to record *all* prepaid expenses with debits to expense accounts. If any prepaids remain unused or unexpired at the end of an accounting period, then adjusting entries must transfer the cost of the unused portions from expense accounts to prepaid expense (asset) accounts. This alternative method is acceptable. The financial statements are identical under either method, but the adjusting entries are different. To illustrate the differences between these two methods, let's look at FastForward's cash payment of December 6 for 24 months of insurance coverage beginning on December 1. FastForward recorded that payment with a debit to an asset account, but it could have recorded a debit to an expense account. These alternatives are shown in Exhibit 3A.1.

P6 Explain the alternatives in accounting for prepaids.

EXHIBIT 3A.1

Alternative Initial Entries for Prepaid Expenses

		Payment Recorded as Asset		Payment Recorded as Expense	
Dec. 6	Prepaid Insurance	2,400			
	Cash		2,400		
Dec. 6	Insurance Expense			2,400	
	Cash				2,400

At the end of its accounting period on December 31, insurance protection for one month has expired. This means $100 ($2,400/24) of insurance coverage expired and is an expense for December. The adjusting entry depends on how the original payment was recorded. This is shown in Exhibit 3A.2.

EXHIBIT 3A.2

Adjusting Entry for Prepaid Expenses for the Two Alternatives

			Payment Recorded as Asset	Payment Recorded as Expense
Dec. 31	Insurance Expense		100	
	Prepaid Insurance		100	
Dec. 31	Prepaid Insurance			2,300
	Insurance Expense			2,300

When these entries are posted to the accounts in the ledger, we can see that these two methods give identical results. The December 31 adjusted account balances in Exhibit 3A.3 show Prepaid Insurance of $2,300 and Insurance Expense of $100 for both methods.

EXHIBIT 3A.3

Account Balances under Two Alternatives for Recording Prepaid Expenses

Payment Recorded as Asset				Payment Recorded as Expense			

Prepaid Insurance			128
Dec. 6	2,400	Dec. 31	100
Balance	2,300		

Prepaid Insurance			128
Dec. 31	2,300		

Insurance Expense			637
Dec. 31	100		

Insurance Expense			637
Dec. 6	2,400	Dec. 31	2,300
Balance	100		

Recording Prepayment of Revenues in Revenue Accounts   As with prepaid expenses, an alternative method is to record *all* unearned revenues with credits to revenue accounts. If any revenues are unearned at the end of an accounting period, then adjusting entries must transfer the unearned portions from revenue accounts to unearned revenue (liability) accounts. This alternative method is acceptable. The adjusting entries are different for these two alternatives, but the financial statements are identical. To illustrate the accounting differences between these two methods, let's look at FastForward's December 26 receipt of $3,000 for consulting services covering the period December 27 to February 24. FastForward recorded this transaction with a credit to a liability account. The alternative is to record it with a credit to a revenue account, as shown in Exhibit 3A.4.

EXHIBIT 3A.4

Alternative Initial Entries for Unearned Revenues

			Receipt Recorded as Liability	Receipt Recorded as Revenue
Dec. 26	Cash		3,000	
	Unearned Consulting Revenue		3,000	
Dec. 26	Cash			3,000
	Consulting Revenue			3,000

By the end of its accounting period on December 31, FastForward has earned $250 of this revenue. This means $250 of the liability has been satisfied. Depending on how the initial receipt is recorded, the adjusting entry is as shown in Exhibit 3A.5.

	Receipt Recorded as Liability	Receipt Recorded as Revenue
Dec. 31	Unearned Consulting Revenue	250	
	Consulting Revenue		250
Dec. 31	Consulting Revenue	2,750	
	Unearned Consulting Revenue		2,750

EXHIBIT 3A.5

Adjusting Entry for Unearned Revenues for the Two Alternatives

After adjusting entries are posted, the two alternatives give identical results. The December 31 adjusted account balances in Exhibit 3A.6 show unearned consulting revenue of $2,750 and consulting revenue of $250 for both methods.

EXHIBIT 3A.6

Account Balances under Two Alternatives for Recording Unearned Revenues

Receipt Recorded as Liability

Unearned Consulting Revenue			236
Dec. 31	250	Dec. 26	3,000
		Balance	**2,750**

Consulting Revenue		403
	Dec. 31	**250**

Receipt Recorded as Revenue

Unearned Consulting Revenue			236
		Dec. 31	**2,750**

Consulting Revenue			403
Dec. 31	2,750	Dec. 26	3,000
		Balance	**250**

Work Sheet as a Tool

3B

Information preparers use various analyses and internal documents when organizing information for internal and external decision makers. Internal documents are often called **working papers.** One widely used working paper is the **work sheet,** which is a useful tool for preparers in working with accounting information. It is usually not available to external decision makers.

Benefits of a Work Sheet (Spreadsheet)   A work sheet is *not* a required report, yet using a manual or electronic work sheet has several potential benefits. Specifically, a work sheet:

P7 Prepare a work sheet and explain its usefulness.

- Aids the preparation of financial statements.
- Reduces the possibility of errors when working with many accounts and adjustments.
- Links accounts and adjustments to their impacts in financial statements.
- Assists in planning and organizing an audit of financial statements—as it can be used to reflect any adjustments necessary.
- Helps in preparing interim (monthly and quarterly) financial statements when the journalizing and posting of adjusting entries are postponed until the year-end.
- Shows the effects of proposed or "what if" transactions.

Use of a Work Sheet (Spreadsheet)   When a work sheet is used to prepare financial statements, it is constructed at the end of a period before the adjusting process. The complete work sheet includes a list of the accounts, their balances and adjustments, and their sorting into financial statement columns. It provides two columns each for the unadjusted trial balance, the adjustments, the adjusted trial balance, the income statement, and the balance sheet. To describe and interpret the work sheet, we

Point: Since a work sheet is *not* a required report or an accounting record, its format is flexible and can be modified by its user to fit his/her preferences.

use the information from FastForward. Preparing the work sheet has five important steps. Each step, 1 through 5, is color-coded and explained with reference to Exhibit 3B.1.

① Step 1. Enter Unadjusted Trial Balance

The first step in preparing a work sheet is to list the title of every account and its account number that is expected to appear on its financial statements. This includes all accounts in the ledger plus any new ones from adjusting entries. Most adjusting entries—including expenses from salaries, supplies, depreciation, and insurance—are predictable and recurring. The unadjusted balance for each account is then entered in the appropriate Debit or Credit column of the unadjusted trial balance columns. The totals of these two columns must be equal. Exhibit 3B.1 shows FastForward's work sheet after completing this first step. Sometimes blank lines are left on the work sheet based on past experience to indicate where lines will be needed for adjustments to certain accounts. Exhibit 3B.1 shows Consulting Revenue as one example. An alternative is to squeeze adjustments on one line or to combine the effects of two or more adjustments in one amount. In the unusual case when an account is not predicted, we can add a new line for such an account following the *Totals* line.

② Step 2. Enter Adjustments

The second step in preparing a work sheet is to enter adjustments in the Adjustments columns. The adjustments shown are the same ones shown in Exhibit 3.13. An identifying letter links the debit and credit of each adjusting entry. This is called *keying* the adjustments. After preparing a work sheet, adjusting entries must still be entered in the journal and posted to the ledger. The Adjustments columns provide the information for those entries.

③ Step 3. Prepare Adjusted Trial Balance

Point: To avoid omitting the transfer of an account balance, start with the first line (cash) and continue in account order.

The adjusted trial balance is prepared by combining the adjustments with the unadjusted balances for each account. As an example, the Prepaid Insurance account has a $2,400 debit balance in the Unadjusted Trial Balance columns. This $2,400 debit is combined with the $100 credit in the Adjustments columns to give Prepaid Insurance a $2,300 debit in the Adjusted Trial Balance columns. The totals of the Adjusted Trial Balance columns confirm the equality of debits and credits.

④ Step 4. Sort Adjusted Trial Balance Amounts to Financial Statements

This step involves sorting account balances from the adjusted trial balance to their proper financial statement columns. Expenses go to the Income Statement Debit column and revenues to the Income Statement Credit column. Assets and Dividends go to the Balance Sheet Debit column. Liabilities, Retained Earnings, and Common Stock go to the Balance Sheet Credit column.

⑤ Step 5. Total Statement Columns, Compute Income or Loss, and Balance Columns

Each financial statement column (from Step 4) is totaled. The difference between the totals of the Income Statement columns is net income or net loss. This occurs because revenues are entered in the Credit column and expenses in the Debit column. If the Credit total exceeds the Debit total, there is net income. If the Debit total exceeds the Credit total, there is a net loss. For FastForward, the Credit total exceeds the Debit total, giving a $3,785 net income.

The net income from the Income Statement columns is then entered in the Balance Sheet Credit column. Adding net income to the last Credit column implies that it is to be added to retained earnings. If a loss occurs, it is added to the Debit column. This implies that it is to be subtracted from retained earnings. The ending balance of retained earnings does not appear in the last two columns as a single amount, but it is computed in the statement of retained earnings using these account balances. When net income or net loss is added to the proper Balance Sheet column, the totals of the last two columns must balance. If they do not, one or more errors have been made. The error can either be mathematical or involve sorting one or more amounts to incorrect columns.

Work Sheet Applications and Analysis   A work sheet does not substitute for financial statements. It is a tool we can use at the end of an accounting period to help organize data and prepare financial statements. FastForward's financial statements are shown in Exhibit 3.14. Its income statement amounts are taken from the Income Statement columns of the work sheet. Similarly, amounts for its balance sheet and its statement of retained earnings are taken from the Balance Sheet columns of the work sheet.

Work sheets are also useful in analyzing the effects of proposed, or what-if, transactions. This is done by entering financial statement amounts in the Unadjusted (what-if) columns. Proposed transactions are then entered in the Adjustments columns. We then compute "adjusted" amounts from these proposed transactions. The extended amounts in the financial statement columns show the effects of these proposed transactions. These financial statement columns yield **pro forma financial statements** because they show the statements *as if* the proposed transactions occurred.

Work Sheet

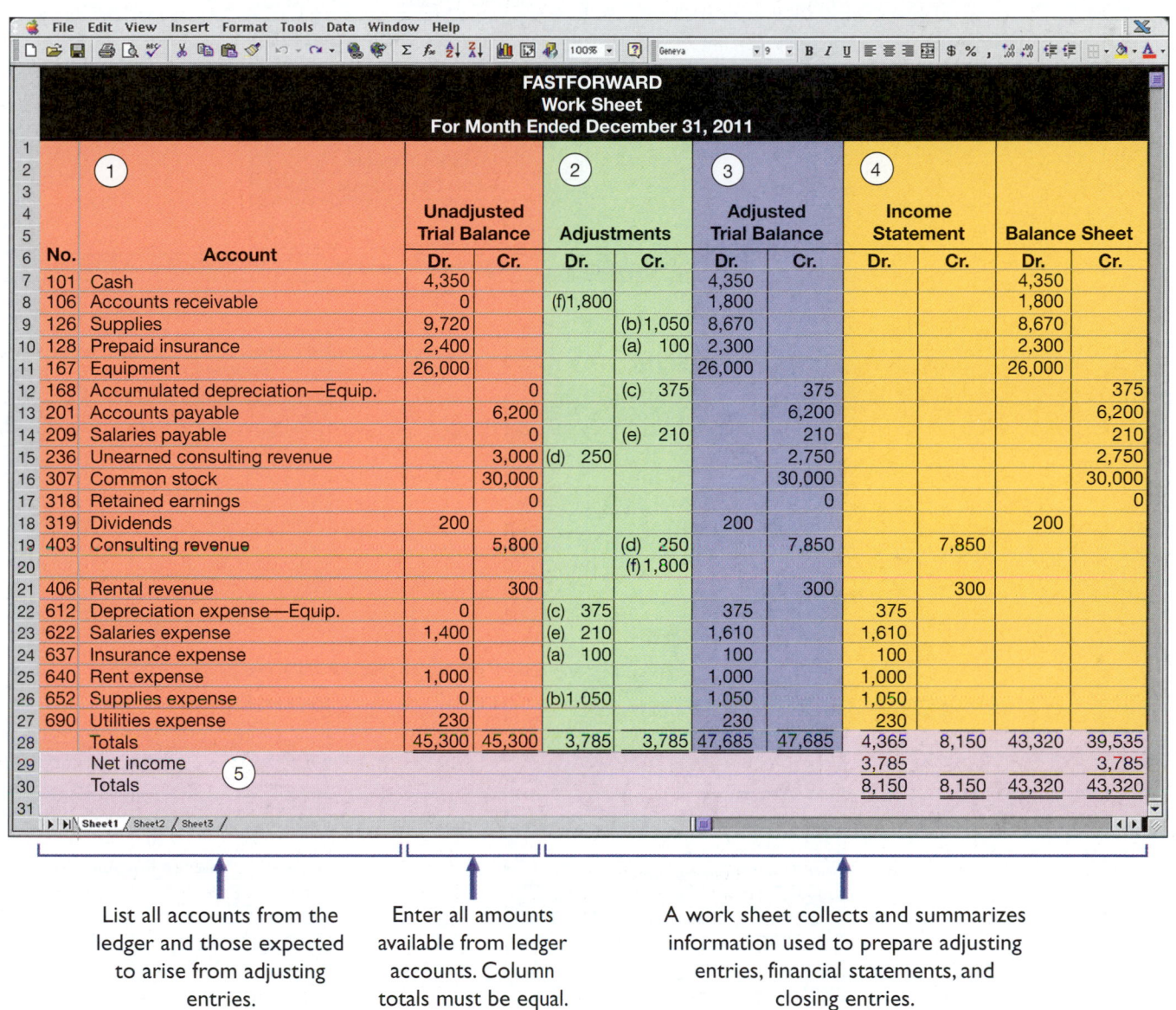

List all accounts from the ledger and those expected to arise from adjusting entries.

Enter all amounts available from ledger accounts. Column totals must be equal.

A work sheet collects and summarizes information used to prepare adjusting entries, financial statements, and closing entries.

APPENDIX

Reversing Entries

3C

Reversing entries are optional. They are recorded in response to accrued assets and accrued liabilities that were created by adjusting entries at the end of a reporting period. The purpose of reversing entries is to simplify a company's recordkeeping. Exhibit 3C.1 shows an example of FastForward's reversing entries. The top of the exhibit shows the adjusting entry FastForward recorded on December 31 for its employee's earned but unpaid salary. The entry recorded three days' salary of $210, which increased December's total salary expense to $1,610. The entry also recognized a liability of $210. The expense is reported on December's income statement. The expense account is then closed. The ledger on January 1, 2012, shows a $210 liability and a zero balance in the Salaries Expense account. At this point, the choice is made between using or not using reversing entries.

Point: As a general rule, adjusting entries that create new asset or liability accounts are likely candidates for reversing.

EXHIBIT 3C.1

Reversing Entries for an
Accrued Expense

Accrue salaries expense on December 31, 2011

| Salaries Expense | 210 | |
| Salaries Payable | | 210 |

Salaries Expense

Date	Expl.	Debit	Credit	Balance
2011				
Dec. 12	(7)	700		700
26	(16)	700		1,400
31	(e)	210		1,610

Salaries Payable

Date	Expl.	Debit	Credit	Balance
2011				
Dec. 31	(e)		210	210

WITHOUT Reversing Entries ◄─── — OR — ───► **WITH Reversing Entries**

No reversing entry recorded on January 1, 2012

NO ENTRY

Salaries Expense

Date	Expl.	Debit	Credit	Balance
2012				

Salaries Payable

Date	Expl.	Debit	Credit	Balance
2011				
Dec. 31	(e)		210	210
2012				

Reversing entry recorded on January 1, 2012

| Salaries Payable | 210 | |
| Salaries Expense | | 210 |

Salaries Expense*

Date	Expl.	Debit	Credit	Balance
2012				
Jan. 1			210	(210)

Salaries Payable

Date	Expl.	Debit	Credit	Balance
2011				
Dec. 31	(e)		210	210
2012				
Jan. 1		210		0

Pay the accrued and current salaries on January 9, the first payday in 2012

Salaries Expense	490	
Salaries Payable	210	
Cash		700

Salaries Expense

Date	Expl.	Debit	Credit	Balance
2012				
Jan. 9		490		**490**

Salaries Payable

Date	Expl.	Debit	Credit	Balance
2011				
Dec. 31	(e)		210	210
2012				
Jan. 9		210		**0**

| Salaries Expense | 700 | |
| Cash | | 700 |

Salaries Expense*

Date	Expl.	Debit	Credit	Balance
2012				
Jan. 1			210	(210)
Jan. 9		700		**490**

Salaries Payable

Date	Expl.	Debit	Credit	Balance
2011				
Dec. 31	(e)		210	210
2012				
Jan. 1		210		**0**

Under both approaches, the expense and liability accounts have
identical balances after the cash payment on January 9.

| Salaries Expense | $490 |
| Salaries Payable | $ 0 |

*Circled numbers in the *Balance* column indicate abnormal balances.*

Accounting *without* Reversing Entries   The path down the left side of Exhibit 3C.1 is described in the chapter. To summarize here, when the next payday occurs on January 9, we record payment with a compound entry that debits both the expense and liability accounts and credits Cash. Posting that entry creates a $490 balance in the expense account and reduces the liability account balance to zero because the debt has been settled. The disadvantage of this approach is the slightly more complex entry required on January 9. Paying the accrued liability means that this entry differs from the routine entries made on all other paydays. To construct the proper entry on January 9, we must recall the effect of the December 31 adjusting entry. Reversing entries overcome this disadvantage.

P8 Prepare reversing entries and explain their purpose.

Accounting *with* Reversing Entries   The right side of Exhibit 3C.1 shows how a reversing entry on January 1 overcomes the disadvantage of the January 9 entry when not using reversing entries.

A reversing entry is the exact opposite of an adjusting entry. For FastForward, the Salaries Payable liability account is debited for $210, meaning that this account now has a zero balance after the entry is posted. The Salaries Payable account temporarily understates the liability, but this is not a problem since financial statements are not prepared before the liability is settled on January 9. The credit to the Salaries Expense account is unusual because it gives the account an *abnormal credit balance*. We highlight an abnormal balance by circling it. Because of the reversing entry, the January 9 entry to record payment is straightforward. This entry debits the Salaries Expense account and credits Cash for the full $700 paid. It is the same as all other entries made to record 10 days' salary for the employee. Notice that after the payment entry is posted, the Salaries Expense account has a $490 balance that reflects seven days' salary of $70 per day (see the lower right side of Exhibit 3C.1). The zero balance in the Salaries Payable account is now correct. The lower section of Exhibit 3C.1 shows that the expense and liability accounts have exactly the same balances whether reversing entries are used or not. This means that both approaches yield identical results.

Summary

C1 Explain the importance of periodic reporting and the time period assumption. The value of information is often linked to its timeliness. To provide timely information, accounting systems prepare periodic reports at regular intervals. The time period assumption presumes that an organization's activities can be divided into specific time periods for periodic reporting.

C2 Explain accrual accounting and how it improves financial statements. Accrual accounting recognizes revenue when earned and expenses when incurred—not necessarily when cash inflows and outflows occur. This information is valuable in assessing a company's financial position and performance.

C3 Identify steps in the accounting cycle. The accounting cycle consists of 10 steps: (1) analyze transactions, (2) journalize, (3) post, (4) prepare an unadjusted trial balance, (5) adjust accounts, (6) prepare an adjusted trial balance, (7) prepare statements, (8) close, (9) prepare a post-closing trial balance, and (10) prepare (optional) reversing entries.

C4 Explain and prepare a classified balance sheet. Classified balance sheets report assets and liabilities in two categories: current and noncurrent. Noncurrent assets often include long-term investments, plant assets, and intangible assets. A corporation separates equity into common stock and retained earnings.

A1 Explain how accounting adjustments link to financial statements. Accounting adjustments bring an asset or liability account balance to its correct amount. They also update related expense or revenue accounts. Every adjusting entry affects one or more income statement accounts *and* one or more balance sheet accounts. An adjusting entry never affects cash.

A2 Compute profit margin and describe its use in analyzing company performance. *Profit margin* is defined as the reporting period's net income divided by its net sales. Profit margin reflects on a company's earnings activities by showing how much income is in each dollar of sales.

A3 Compute the current ratio and describe what it reveals about a company's financial condition. A company's current ratio is defined as current assets divided by current liabilities. We use it to evaluate a company's ability to pay its current liabilities out of current assets.

P1 Prepare and explain adjusting entries. *Prepaid expenses* refer to items paid for in advance of receiving their benefits. Prepaid expenses are assets. Adjusting entries for prepaids involve increasing (debiting) expenses and decreasing (crediting) assets. *Unearned (or prepaid) revenues* refer to cash received in advance of providing products and services. Unearned revenues are liabilities. Adjusting entries for unearned revenues involve increasing (crediting) revenues and decreasing (debiting) unearned revenues. *Accrued expenses* refer to costs incurred in a period that are both unpaid and unrecorded. Adjusting entries for recording accrued expenses involve increasing (debiting) expenses and increasing (crediting) liabilities. *Accrued revenues* refer to revenues earned in a period that are both unrecorded and not yet received in cash. Adjusting entries for recording accrued revenues involve increasing (debiting) assets and increasing (crediting) revenues.

P2 Explain and prepare an adjusted trial balance. An adjusted trial balance is a list of accounts and balances prepared after recording and posting adjusting entries. Financial statements are often prepared from the adjusted trial balance.

P3 Prepare financial statements from an adjusted trial balance. Revenue and expense balances are reported on the income statement. Asset, liability, and equity balances are reported on the balance sheet. We usually prepare statements in the following order: income statement, statement of retained earnings, balance sheet, and statement of cash flows.

P4 Describe and prepare closing entries. Closing entries involve four steps: (1) close credit balances in revenue (and gain) accounts to Income Summary, (2) close debit balances in expense (and loss) accounts to Income Summary, (3) close Income Summary to retained earnings, and (4) close dividends account to retained earnings.

P5 Explain and prepare a post-closing trial balance. A post-closing trial balance is a list of permanent accounts and their balances after all closing entries have been journalized and posted. Its purpose is to verify that (1) total debits equal total credits for permanent accounts and (2) all temporary accounts have zero balances.

P6ᴬ Explain the alternatives in accounting for prepaids. Charging all prepaid expenses to expense accounts when they are purchased is acceptable. When this is done, adjusting entries must transfer any unexpired amounts from expense accounts to asset accounts. Crediting all unearned revenues to revenue accounts when cash is received is also acceptable. In this case, the adjusting entries must transfer any unearned amounts from revenue accounts to unearned revenue accounts.

P7ᴮ **Prepare a work sheet and explain its usefulness.** A work sheet can be a useful tool in preparing and analyzing financial statements. It is helpful at the end of a period in preparing adjusting entries, an adjusted trial balance, and financial statements. A work sheet usually contains five pairs of columns: Unadjusted Trial Balance, Adjustments, Adjusted Trial Balance, Income Statement, and Balance Sheet & Statement of Equity.

P8ᶜ **Prepare reversing entries and explain their purpose.** Reversing entries are an optional step. They are applied to accrued expenses and revenues. The purpose of reversing entries is to simplify subsequent journal entries. Financial statements are unaffected by the choice to use or not use reversing entries.

Guidance Answers to Decision Maker and Decision Ethics

Investor   Prepaid expenses are items paid for in advance of receiving their benefits. They are assets and are expensed as they are used up. The publishing company's treatment of the signing bonus is acceptable provided future book sales can at least match the $500,000 expense. As an investor, you are concerned about the risk of future book sales. The riskier the likelihood of future book sales is, the more likely your analysis is to treat the $500,000, or a portion of it, as an expense, not a prepaid expense (asset).

Entrepreneur   Depreciation is a process of cost allocation, not asset valuation. Knowing the depreciation schedule is not especially useful in your estimation of what the building and equipment are currently worth. Your own assessment of the age, quality, and usefulness of the building and equipment is more important.

Loan Officer   Your concern in lending to this store arises from analysis of current-year sales. While increased revenues and income are fine, your concern is with collectibility of these promotional sales. If the owner sold products to customers with poor records of

paying bills, then collectibility of these sales is low. Your analysis must assess this possibility and recognize any expected losses.

Financial Officer   Omitting accrued expenses and recognizing revenue early can mislead financial statement users. One action is to request a second meeting with the president so you can explain that accruing expenses when incurred and recognizing revenue when earned are required practices. If the president persists, you might discuss the situation with legal counsel and any auditors involved. Your ethical action might cost you this job, but the potential pitfalls for falsification of statements, reputation and personal integrity loss, and other costs are too great.

Analyst   A current ratio of 1.2 suggests that current assets are sufficient to cover current liabilities, but it implies a minimal buffer in case of errors in measuring current assets or current liabilities. Removing the past due receivable reduces the current ratio to 0.7. Your assessment is that the company will have some difficulty meeting its loan payments.

Guidance Answers to Quick Checks

1. An annual reporting (or accounting) period covers one year and refers to the preparation of annual financial statements. The annual reporting period is not always a calendar year that ends on December 31. An organization can adopt a fiscal year consisting of any consecutive 12 months or 52 weeks.

2. Interim financial statements (covering less than one year) are prepared to provide timely information to decision makers.

3. The revenue recognition principle and the expense recognition (matching) principle lead most directly to the adjusting process.

4. No. Cash basis accounting is not consistent with the matching principle because it reports revenue when received, not necessarily when earned, and expenses when paid, not necessarily in the period when the expenses were incurred as a result of the revenues earned.

5. No expense is reported in 2012. Under cash basis accounting, the entire $4,800 is reported as an expense in April 2011 when the premium is paid.

6. If the accrued revenues adjustment of $200 is not made, then both revenues and net income are understated by $200 on the current year's income statement, and both assets and equity are understated by $200 on the balance sheet.

7. A contra account is an account that is subtracted from the balance of a related account. Use of a contra account provides more information than simply reporting a net amount.

8. An accrued expense is a cost incurred in a period that is both unpaid and unrecorded prior to adjusting entries. One example is salaries earned but not yet paid at period-end.

9. An unearned revenue arises when a firm receives cash (or other assets) from a customer before providing the services or products to the customer. A magazine subscription paid in advance is one example; season ticket sales is another.

10.
Salaries Payable	1,000	
Salaries Expense	6,000	
Cash		7,000
Paid salary including accrual from December.		

11. The probable adjusting entries of Jordan Air are:

Insurance Expense	300	
Prepaid Insurance		300
To record insurance expired.		
Salaries Expense	1,400	
Salaries Payable		1,400
To record accrued salaries.		

12. Revenue accounts and expense accounts.

13. Statement of retained earnings.

14. The major steps in preparing closing entries are to close (1) credit balances in revenue accounts to Income Summary, (2) debit balances in expense accounts to Income Summary,

(3) Income Summary to retained earnings, and (4) any dividends account to retained earnings.

15. Revenue (and gain) and expense (and loss) accounts are called *temporary* because they are opened and closed each period. The Income Summary and Dividends accounts are also temporary.

16. Permanent accounts make up the post-closing trial balance, which consist of asset, liability, and equity accounts.

17. Current assets: (*b*), (*c*), (*d*). Plant assets: (*a*), (*e*). Item (*f*) is an intangible asset.

18. Investment in common stock, investment in bonds, and land held for future expansion.

19. For a service company, the operating cycle is the usual time between (1) paying employees who do the services and (2) receiving cash from customers for services provided.

Key Terms
mhhe.com/wildFINMAN4e

Accounting cycle (p. 112)
Accounting period (p. 94)
Accrual basis accounting (p. 95)
Accrued expenses (p. 101)
Accrued revenues (p. 103)
Adjusted trial balance (p. 106)
Adjusting entry (p. 96)
Annual financial statements (p. 94)
Book value (p. 100)
Cash basis accounting (p. 95)
Classified balance sheet (p. 113)
Closing entries (p. 108)
Closing process (p. 108)
Contra account (p. 99)
Current assets (p. 114)

Current liabilities (p. 115)
Current ratio (p. 117)
Depreciation (p. 99)
Expense recognition (or **matching**) **principle** (p. 96)
Fiscal year (p. 95)
Income Summary (p. 109)
Intangible assets (p. 115)
Interim financial statements (p. 94)
Long-term investments (p. 115)
Long-term liabilities (p. 115)
Natural business year (p. 95)
Operating cycle (p. 113)
Permanent accounts (p. 108)
Plant assets (p. 99)

Post-closing trial balance (p. 110)
Prepaid expenses (p. 97)
Pro forma financial statements (p. 124)
Profit margin (p. 117)
Reversing entries (p. 125)
Straight-line depreciation method (p. 99)
Temporary accounts (p. 108)
Time period assumption (p. 94)
Unadjusted trial balance (p. 106)
Unclassified balance sheet (p. 113)
Unearned revenues (p. 100)
Working papers (p. 123)
Work sheet (p. 123)

Multiple Choice Quiz
Answers on p. 153   mhhe.com/wildFINMAN4e

Additional Quiz Questions are available at the book's Website.

1. A company forgot to record accrued and unpaid employee wages of $350,000 at period-end. This oversight would
   a. Understate net income by $350,000.
   b. Overstate net income by $350,000.
   c. Have no effect on net income.
   d. Overstate assets by $350,000.
   e. Understate assets by $350,000.

2. Prior to recording adjusting entries, the Supplies account has a $450 debit balance. A physical count of supplies shows $125 of unused supplies still available. The required adjusting entry is:
   a. Debit Supplies $125; Credit Supplies Expense $125.
   b. Debit Supplies $325; Credit Supplies Expense $325.
   c. Debit Supplies Expense $325; Credit Supplies $325.
   d. Debit Supplies Expense $325; Credit Supplies $125.
   e. Debit Supplies Expense $125; Credit Supplies $125.

3. On May 1, 2011, a two-year insurance policy was purchased for $24,000 with coverage to begin immediately. What is the amount of insurance expense that appears on the company's income statement for the year ended December 31, 2011?
   a. $4,000
   b. $8,000

   c. $12,000
   d. $20,000
   e. $24,000

4. On November 1, 2011, Stockton Co. receives $3,600 cash from Hans Co. for consulting services to be provided evenly over the period November 1, 2011, to April 30, 2012—at which time Stockton credited $3,600 to Unearned Consulting Fees. The adjusting entry on December 31, 2011 (Stockton's year-end) would include a
   a. Debit to Unearned Consulting Fees for $1,200.
   b. Debit to Unearned Consulting Fees for $2,400.
   c. Credit to Consulting Fees Earned for $2,400.
   d. Debit to Consulting Fees Earned for $1,200.
   e. Credit to Cash for $3,600.

5. If a company had $15,000 in net income for the year, and its sales were $300,000 for the same year, what is its profit margin?
   a. 20%
   b. 2,000%
   c. $285,000
   d. $315,000
   e. 5%

6. Based on the following information from Repicor Company's balance sheet, what is Repicor Company's current ratio?

Current assets	$ 75,000	Current liabilities	$ 50,000	**a.** 2.10	**d.** 0.95
Investments	30,000	Long-term liabilities . . .	60,000	**b.** 1.50	**e.** 0.67
Plant assets	300,000	Common stock	295,000	**c.** 1.00	

A(B,C)   *Superscript letter A(B,C) denotes assignments based on Appendix 3A(3B,3C).*

🔲 Icon denotes assignments that involve decision making.

Discussion Questions

1. What is the difference between the cash basis and the accrual basis of accounting?

2. 🔲 Why is the accrual basis of accounting generally preferred over the cash basis?

3. What type of business is most likely to select a fiscal year that corresponds to its natural business year instead of the calendar year?

4. What is a prepaid expense and where is it reported in the financial statements?

5. 🔲 What type of assets require adjusting entries to record depreciation?

6. 🔲 What contra account is used when recording and reporting the effects of depreciation? Why is it used?

7. **Apple** has unearned revenue. What is unearned revenue and where is it reported in financial statements? **Apple**

8. What is an accrued revenue? Give an example.

9.^AIf a company initially records prepaid expenses with debits to expense accounts, what type of account is debited in the adjusting entries for those prepaid expenses?

10. 🔲 Review the balance sheet of **Research In Motion** in Appendix A. Identify one asset account that requires adjustment before annual financial statements can be prepared. What would be the effect on the income statement if this asset account were not adjusted? **RIM**

11. 🔲 Review the balance sheet of **Nokia** in Appendix A. Identify the amount for property, plant, and equipment. What adjusting entry is necessary (no numbers required) for this account when preparing financial statements? **NOKIA**

12. 🔲 Refer to **Palm**'s balance sheet in Appendix A. If it made an adjustment for unpaid wages at year-end, where would the accrued wages be reported on its balance sheet? **Palm**

13. What accounts are affected by closing entries? What accounts are not affected?

14. 🔲 What two purposes are accomplished by recording closing entries?

15. What are the steps in recording closing entries?

16. What is the purpose of the Income Summary account?

17. 🔲 Explain whether an error has occurred if a post-closing trial balance includes a Depreciation Expense account.

18.^B What tasks are aided by a work sheet?

19.^B Why are the debit and credit entries in the Adjustments columns of the work sheet identified with letters?

20. What is a company's operating cycle?

21. What classes of assets and liabilities are shown on a typical classified balance sheet?

22. How is unearned revenue classified on the balance sheet?

23. What are the characteristics of plant assets?

24.^C How do reversing entries simplify recordkeeping?

25.^C If a company recorded accrued salaries expense of $500 at the end of its fiscal year, what reversing entry could be made? When would it be made?

26. 🔲 Refer to the balance sheet for **Research In Motion** in Appendix A. What five main noncurrent asset categories are used on its classified balance sheet? **RIM**

27. Refer to **Nokia**'s balance sheet in Appendix A. Identify and list its 9 current assets. **NOKIA**

28. 🔲 Refer to **Apple**'s balance sheet in Appendix A. Identify the three accounts listed as current liabilities. **Apple**

29. 🔲 Refer to **Palm**'s financial statements in Appendix A. What journal entry was likely recorded as of May 31, 2009, to close its Income Summary account? **Palm**

QUICK STUDY

QS 3-1

Identifying accounting adjustments

P1

Classify the following adjusting entries as involving prepaid expenses (PE), unearned revenues (UR), accrued expenses (AE), or accrued revenues (AR).

a. _____ To record revenue earned that was previously received as cash in advance.

b. _____ To record annual depreciation expense.

c. _____ To record wages expense incurred but not yet paid (nor recorded).

d. _____ To record revenue earned but not yet billed (nor recorded).

e. _____ To record expiration of prepaid insurance.

a. On July 1, 2011, Baxter Company paid $1,800 for six months of insurance coverage. No adjustments have been made to the Prepaid Insurance account, and it is now December 31, 2011. Prepare the journal entry to reflect expiration of the insurance as of December 31, 2011.

b. Tyrell Company has a Supplies account balance of $1,000 on January 1, 2011. During 2011, it purchased $3,000 of supplies. As of December 31, 2011, a supplies inventory shows $1,300 of supplies available. Prepare the adjusting journal entry to correctly report the balance of the Supplies account and the Supplies Expense account as of December 31, 2011.

QS 3-2
Adjusting prepaid expenses
P1

---

a. Carlos Company purchases $30,000 of equipment on January 1, 2011. The equipment is expected to last five years and be worth $5,000 at the end of that time. Prepare the entry to record one year's depreciation expense of $5,000 for the equipment as of December 31, 2011.

b. Chaves Company purchases $40,000 of land on January 1, 2011. The land is expected to last indefinitely. What depreciation adjustment, if any, should be made with respect to the Land account as of December 31, 2011?

QS 3-3
Adjusting for depreciation
P1

---

a. Eager Co. receives $20,000 cash in advance for 4 months of legal services on October 1, 2011, and records it by debiting Cash and crediting Unearned Revenue both for $20,000. It is now December 31, 2011, and Eager has provided legal services as planned. What adjusting entry should Eager make to account for the work performed from October 1 through December 31, 2011?

b. Rutherford Co. started a new publication called *Contest News*. Its subscribers pay $48 to receive 12 issues. With every new subscriber, Rutherford debits Cash and credits Unearned Subscription Revenue for the amounts received. The company has 100 new subscribers as of July 1, 2011. It sends *Contest News* to each of these subscribers every month from July through December. Assuming no changes in subscribers, prepare the journal entry that Rutherford must make as of December 31, 2011, to adjust the Subscription Revenue account and the Unearned Subscription Revenue account.

QS 3-4
Adjusting for unearned revenues

A1 P1

Marsha Moder employs one college student every summer in her coffee shop. The student works the five weekdays and is paid on the following Monday. (For example, a student who works Monday through Friday, June 1 through June 5, is paid for that work on Monday, June 8.) Moder adjusts her books monthly, if needed, to show salaries earned but unpaid at month-end. The student works the last week of July—Friday is August 1. If the student earns $100 per day, what adjusting entry must Moder make on July 31 to correctly record accrued salaries expense for July?

QS 3-5
Accruing salaries
A1 P1

Adjusting entries affect at least one balance sheet account and at least one income statement account. For the following entries, identify the account to be debited and the account to be credited. Indicate which of the accounts is the income statement account and which is the balance sheet account.

a. Entry to record revenue earned that was previously received as cash in advance.

b. Entry to record annual depreciation expense.

c. Entry to record wage expenses incurred but not yet paid (nor recorded).

d. Entry to record revenue earned but not yet billed (nor recorded).

e. Entry to record expiration of prepaid insurance.

QS 3-6
Recording and analyzing adjusting entries
A1

In its first year of operations, Harden Co. earned $39,000 in revenues and received $33,000 cash from these customers. The company incurred expenses of $22,500 but had not paid $2,250 of them at year-end. The company also prepaid $3,750 cash for expenses that would be incurred the next year. Calculate the first year's net income under both the cash basis and the accrual basis of accounting.

QS 3-7
Computing accrual and cash income

C2 A1

The following information is taken from Cruz Company's unadjusted and adjusted trial balances.

QS 3-8
Interpreting adjusting entries
C2 P2

	Unadjusted		Adjusted	
	Debit	Credit	Debit	Credit
Prepaid insurance.........	$4,100		$3,700	
Interest payable		$ 0		$800

Given this information, which of the following is likely included among its adjusting entries?

a. A $400 credit to Prepaid Insurance and an $800 debit to Interest Payable.

b. A $400 debit to Insurance Expense and an $800 debit to Interest Payable.

c. A $400 debit to Insurance Expense and an $800 debit to Interest Expense.

QS 3-9
Determining effects of adjusting entries
A1

In making adjusting entries at the end of its accounting period, Gomez Consulting failed to record $1,600 of insurance coverage that had expired. This $1,600 cost had been initially debited to the Prepaid Insurance account. The company also failed to record accrued salaries expense of $1,000. As a result of these two oversights, the financial statements for the reporting period will [choose one] (1) understate assets by $1,600; (2) understate expenses by $2,600; (3) understate net income by $1,000; or (4) overstate liabilities by $1,000.

QS 3-10
Preparing adjusting entries
P1

During the year, Lyle Co. recorded prepayments of expenses in asset accounts, and cash receipts of unearned revenues in liability accounts. At the end of its annual accounting period, the company must make three adjusting entries: (1) accrue salaries expense, (2) adjust the Unearned Services Revenue account to recognize earned revenue, and (3) record services revenue earned for which cash will be received the following period. For each of these adjusting entries (1), (2), and (3), indicate the account from *a* through *i* to be debited and the account to be credited.

a. Prepaid Salaries	**d.** Salaries Payable	**g.** Unearned Services Revenue
b. Salaries Expense	**e.** Equipment	**h.** Accounts Receivable
c. Services Revenue	**f.** Cash	**i.** Accounts Payable

QS 3-11
Analyzing profit margin A2

Yang Company reported net income of $37,925 and net sales of $390,000 for the current year. Calculate the company's profit margin and interpret the result. Assume that its competitors earn an average profit margin of 15%.

QS 3-12^A
Preparing adjusting entries
P6

Diego Consulting initially records prepaid and unearned items in income statement accounts. Given this company's accounting practices, which of the following applies to the preparation of adjusting entries at the end of its first accounting period?

a. Earned but unbilled (and unrecorded) consulting fees are recorded with a debit to Unearned Consulting Fees and a credit to Consulting Fees Earned.

b. Unpaid salaries are recorded with a debit to Prepaid Salaries and a credit to Salaries Expense.

c. The cost of unused office supplies is recorded with a debit to Supplies Expense and a credit to Office Supplies.

d. Unearned fees (on which cash was received in advance earlier in the period) are recorded with a debit to Consulting Fees Earned and a credit to Unearned Consulting Fees.

QS 3-13
International accounting standards P3

Answer each of the following questions related to international accounting standards.

a. Do financial statements prepared under IFRS normally present assets from least liquid to most liquid or vice-versa?

b. Do financial statements prepared under IFRS normally present liabilities from furthest from maturity to nearest to maturity or vice-versa?

QS 3-14
Identifying the accounting cycle
C3

List the following steps of the accounting cycle in their proper order.

a. Preparing the post-closing trial balance.	**f.** Analyzing transactions and events.
b. Posting the journal entries.	**g.** Preparing the financial statements.
c. Journalizing and posting adjusting entries.	**h.** Preparing the unadjusted trial balance.
d. Preparing the adjusted trial balance.	**i.** Journalizing transactions and events.
e. Journalizing and posting closing entries.	

QS 3-15
Identifying current accounts and computing the current ratio
A3

Compute Jamar Company's current ratio using the following information.

Accounts receivable	$15,000	Long-term notes payable	$20,000
Accounts payable	10,000	Office supplies	1,800
Buildings	42,000	Prepaid insurance	2,500
Cash	6,000	Unearned services revenue	4,000

The following are common categories on a classified balance sheet.

A. Current assets	**D.** Intangible assets
B. Long-term investments	**E.** Current liabilities
C. Plant assets	**F.** Long-term liabilities

QS 3-16
Classifying balance sheet items
C4

For each of the following items, select the letter that identifies the balance sheet category where the item typically would appear.

_____ **1.** Trademarks   _____ **5.** Cash

_____ **2.** Accounts receivable   _____ **6.** Wages payable

_____ **3.** Land not currently used in operations   _____ **7.** Store equipment

_____ **4.** Notes payable (due in three years)   _____ **8.** Accounts payable

---

The ledger of Avril Company includes the following accounts with normal balances: Common Stock $6,000; Dividends $400; Services Revenue $10,000; Wages Expense $5,200; and Rent Expense $800. Prepare the necessary closing entries from the available information at December 31.

QS 3-17
Prepare closing entries from the ledger **P4**

Identify the accounts listed in QS 3-17 that would be included in a post-closing trial balance.

QS 3-18
Identify post-closing accounts **P5**

The ledger of Terrel Company includes the following unadjusted normal balances: Prepaid Rent $800, Services Revenue $11,600, and Wages Expense $5,000. Adjusting entries are required for (a) accrued rent expense $240; (b) accrued services revenue $180; and (c) accrued wages expense $160. Enter these unadjusted balances and the necessary adjustments on a work sheet and complete the work sheet for these accounts. *Note:* Also include the following accounts: Accounts Receivable, Wages Payable, and Rent Expense.

QS 3-19ᴮ
Preparing a partial work sheet
P7

On December 31, 2010, Lester Co. prepared an adjusting entry for $6,700 of earned but unrecorded management fees. On January 16, 2011, Lester received $15,500 cash in management fees, which included the accrued fees earned in 2010. Assuming the company uses reversing entries, prepare the January 1, 2011, reversing entry and the January 16, 2011, cash receipt entry.

QS 3-20ᶜ
Reversing entries
P8

---

connect
_____

For each of the following separate cases, prepare adjusting entries required of financial statements for the year ended (date of) December 31, 2011. (Assume that prepaid expenses are initially recorded in asset accounts and that fees collected in advance of work are initially recorded as liabilities.)

EXERCISES

Exercise 3-1
Preparing adjusting entries
P1

a. One-third of the work related to $30,000 cash received in advance is performed this period.

b. Wages of $9,000 are earned by workers but not paid as of December 31, 2011.

c. Depreciation on the company's equipment for 2011 is $19,127.

d. The Office Supplies account had a $480 debit balance on December 31, 2010. During 2011, $5,349 of office supplies are purchased. A physical count of supplies at December 31, 2011, shows $587 of supplies available.

e. The Prepaid Insurance account had a $5,000 balance on December 31, 2010. An analysis of insurance policies shows that $2,200 of unexpired insurance benefits remain at December 31, 2011.

Check (*e*) Dr. Insurance Expense, $2,800; (*f*) Cr. Interest Revenue, $750

f. The company has earned (but not recorded) $750 of interest from investments in CDs for the year ended December 31, 2011. The interest revenue will be received on January 10, 2012.

g. The company has a bank loan and has incurred (but not recorded) interest expense of $3,500 for the year ended December 31, 2011. The company must pay the interest on January 2, 2012.

Prepare adjusting journal entries for the year ended (date of) December 31, 2011, for each of these separate situations. Assume that prepaid expenses are initially recorded in asset accounts. Also assume that fees collected in advance of work are initially recorded as liabilities.

Exercise 3-2
Preparing adjusting entries
P1

a. Depreciation on the company's equipment for 2011 is computed to be $16,000.

b. The Prepaid Insurance account had a $7,000 debit balance at December 31, 2011, before adjusting for the costs of any expired coverage. An analysis of the company's insurance policies showed that $1,040 of unexpired insurance coverage remains.

c. The Office Supplies account had a $300 debit balance on December 31, 2010; and $2,680 of office supplies were purchased during the year. The December 31, 2011, physical count showed $354 of supplies available.

Check (*c*) Dr. Office Supplies Expense, $2,626; (*e*) Dr. Insurance Expense, $4,600

d. One-half of the work related to $10,000 of cash received in advance was performed this period.

e. The Prepaid Insurance account had a $5,600 debit balance at December 31, 2011, before adjusting for the costs of any expired coverage. An analysis of insurance policies showed that $4,600 of coverage had expired.

f. Wage expenses of $4,000 have been incurred but are not paid as of December 31, 2011.

Exercise 3-3

Adjusting and paying accrued expenses

A1

Check (b) May 20 Dr. Interest Expense, $4,160

The following three separate situations require adjusting journal entries to prepare financial statements as of April 30. For each situation, present both the April 30 adjusting entry and the subsequent entry during May to record the payment of the accrued expenses.

a. On April 1, the company retained an attorney for a flat monthly fee of $2,500. This amount is paid to the attorney on the 12th day of the following month in which it was earned.

b. A $780,000 note payable requires 9.6% annual interest, or $6,240 to be paid at the 20th day of each month. The interest was last paid on April 20 and the next payment is due on May 20. As of April 30, $2,080 of interest expense has accrued.

c. Total weekly salaries expense for all employees is $9,000. This amount is paid at the end of the day on Friday of each five-day workweek. April 30 falls on Tuesday of this year, which means that the employees had worked two days since the last payday. The next payday is May 3.

Exercise 3-4

Determining cost flows through accounts

C1   A1

Determine the missing amounts in each of these four separate situations *a* through *d*.

	a	b	c	d
Supplies available—prior year-end	$ 300	$1,600	$1,360	?
Supplies purchased during the current year	2,100	5,400	?	$6,000
Supplies available—current year-end	750	?	1,840	800
Supplies expense for the current year	?	1,300	9,600	6,575

Exercise 3-5

Adjusting and paying accrued wages

C1   P1

Pablo Management has five part-time employees, each of whom earns $100 per day. They are normally paid on Fridays for work completed Monday through Friday of the same week. They were paid in full on Friday, December 28, 2011. The next week, the five employees worked only four days because New Year's Day was an unpaid holiday. Show (*a*) the adjusting entry that would be recorded on Monday, December 31, 2011, and (*b*) the journal entry that would be made to record payment of the employees' wages on Friday, January 4, 2012.

Exercise 3-6

Analyzing and preparing adjusting entries

A1   P3

Following are two income statements for Kendall Co. for the year ended December 31. The left column is prepared before any adjusting entries are recorded, and the right column includes the effects of adjusting entries. The company records cash receipts and payments related to unearned and prepaid items in balance sheet accounts. Analyze the statements and prepare the eight adjusting entries that likely were recorded. (*Note:* 30% of the $6,000 adjustment for Fees Earned has been earned but not billed, and the other 70% has been earned by performing services that were paid for in advance.)

KENDALL CO. Income Statements For Year Ended December 31		
	Unadjusted	**Adjusted**
Revenues		
Fees earned	$24,000	$30,000
Commissions earned	42,500	42,500
Total revenues	66,500	72,500
Expenses		
Depreciation expense—Computers	0	1,500
Depreciation expense—Office furniture	0	1,750
Salaries expense	12,500	14,950
Insurance expense	0	1,300
Rent expense	4,500	4,500
Office supplies expense	0	480
Advertising expense	3,000	3,000
Utilities expense	1,250	1,320
Total expenses	21,250	28,800
Net income	$45,250	$43,700

Use the following information to compute profit margin for each separate company *a* through *e*.

	Net Income	Net Sales		Net Income	Net Sales
a.	$ 5,390	$ 44,830	**d.**	$55,234	$1,458,999
b.	87,644	398,954	**e.**	70,158	435,925
c.	93,385	257,082			

Which of the five companies is the most profitable according to the profit margin ratio? Interpret that company's profit margin ratio.

Exercise 3-7
Computing and interpreting profit margin

A2

Corbel Company experienced the following events and transactions during July.

July 1 Received $2,000 cash in advance of performing work for Beth Oker.
     6 Received $8,400 cash in advance of performing work for Lisa Poe.
    12 Completed the job for Oker.
    18 Received $7,500 cash in advance of performing work for Henry Coe.
    27 Completed the job for Poe.
    31 None of the work for Coe has been performed.

a. Prepare journal entries (including any adjusting entries as of the end of the month) to record these events using the procedure of initially crediting the Unearned Fees account when payment is received from a customer in advance of performing services.

b. Prepare journal entries (including any adjusting entries as of the end of the month) to record these events using the procedure of initially crediting the Fees Earned account when payment is received from a customer in advance of performing services.

c. Under each method, determine the amount of earned fees reported on the income statement for July and the amount of unearned fees reported on the balance sheet as of July 31.

Exercise 3-8ᴬ
Recording and reporting revenues received in advance
P6

Check (c) Fees Earned—using entries from part b, $10,400

On-The-Mark Construction began operations on December 1. In setting up its accounting procedures, the company decided to debit expense accounts when it prepays its expenses and to credit revenue accounts when customers pay for services in advance. Prepare journal entries for items *a* through *d* and the adjusting entries as of its December 31 period-end for items *e* through *g*.

a. Supplies are purchased on December 1 for $3,000 cash.

b. The company prepaid its insurance premiums for $1,440 cash on December 2.

c. On December 15, the company receives an advance payment of $12,000 cash from a customer for remodeling work.

d. On December 28, the company receives $3,600 cash from another customer for remodeling work to be performed in January.

e. A physical count on December 31 indicates that On-The-Mark has $1,920 of supplies available.

f. An analysis of the insurance policies in effect on December 31 shows that $240 of insurance coverage had expired.

g. As of December 31, only one remodeling project has been worked on and completed. The $6,300 fee for this project had been received in advance and recorded as unearned remodeling fees.

Exercise 3-9ᴬ
Adjusting for prepaids recorded as expenses and unearned revenues recorded as revenues
P6

Check (f) Cr. Insurance Expense, $1,200; (g) Dr. Remodeling Fees Earned, $9,300

adidas AG reports the following balance sheet accounts for the year ended December 31, 2009 (euros in millions). Prepare the balance sheet for this company as of December 31, 2009, following usual IFRS practices.

Tangible and other assets	€1,410	Intangible assets	€2,980
Total equity	3,776	Total current liabilities	2,836
Receivables and financial assets	1,753	Inventories	1,471
Total noncurrent liabilities	2,263	Total liabilities	5,099
Cash and cash equivalents	775	Other current assets	486
Total current assets	4,485	Total noncurrent assets	4,390

Exercise 3-10
Preparing a balance sheet following IFRS
P3

Use the following adjusted trial balance of Webb Trucking Company to prepare the (1) income statement and (2) statement of retained earnings, for the year ended December 31, 2011. The retained earnings account balance is $151,000 at December 31, 2010.

Exercise 3-11
Preparing financial statements
C3 P3

Account Title	Debit	Credit
Cash	$ 7,000	
Accounts receivable	16,500	
Office supplies	2,000	
Trucks	170,000	
Accumulated depreciation—Trucks		$ 35,000
Land	75,000	
Accounts payable		11,000
Interest payable		3,000
Long-term notes payable		52,000
Common stock		10,000
Retained earnings		151,000
Dividends	19,000	
Trucking fees earned		128,000
Depreciation expense—Trucks	22,500	
Salaries expense	60,000	
Office supplies expense	7,000	
Repairs expense—Trucks	11,000	
Totals	$390,000	$390,000

Exercise 3-12

Preparing a classified balance sheet **C4**

Check Total assets, $235,500;

Use the information in the adjusted trial balance reported in Exercise 3-11 to prepare Webb Trucking Company's classified balance sheet as of December 31, 2011.

Exercise 3-13

Computing the current ratio

A3

Use the information in the adjusted trial balance reported in Exercise 3-11 to compute the current ratio as of the balance sheet date (round the ratio to two decimals). Interpret the current ratio for the Webb Trucking Company. (Assume that the industry average for the current ratio is 1.5.)

Exercise 3-14

Computing and analyzing the current ratio

A3

Calculate the current ratio in each of the following separate cases (round the ratio to two decimals). Identify the company case with the strongest liquidity position. (These cases represent competing companies in the same industry.)

	Current Assets	Current Liabilities
Case 1	$ 78,000	$31,000
Case 2	104,000	75,000
Case 3	44,000	48,000
Case 4	84,500	80,600
Case 5	60,000	99,000

Exercise 3-15ᴬ

Preparing reversing entries

P8

The following two events occurred for Tanger Co. on October 31, 2011, the end of its fiscal year.

a. Tanger rents a building from its owner for $3,200 per month. By a prearrangement, the company delayed paying October's rent until November 5. On this date, the company paid the rent for both October and November.

b. Tanger rents space in a building it owns to a tenant for $750 per month. By prearrangement, the tenant delayed paying the October rent until November 8. On this date, the tenant paid the rent for both October and November.

Required

1. Prepare adjusting entries that the company must record for these events as of October 31.

2. Assuming Tanger does *not* use reversing entries, prepare journal entries to record Tanger's payment of rent on November 5 and the collection of rent on November 8 from Tanger's tenant.

3. Assuming that the company uses reversing entries, prepare reversing entries on November 1 and the journal entries to record Tanger's payment of rent on November 5 and the collection of rent on November 8 from Tanger's tenant.

Following are **Nintendo**'s revenue and expense accounts for a recent calendar year (yen in millions). Prepare the company's closing entries for its revenues and its expenses.

Net sales	¥1,838,622
Cost of sales	1,044,981
Advertising expense	117,308
Other expense, net	397,244

Exercise 3-16
Preparing closing entries

P4

The following data are taken from the unadjusted trial balance of the Madison Company at December 31, 2011. Each account carries a normal balance and the accounts are shown here in alphabetical order.

Accounts Payable.................	$ 2	Prepaid Insurance ..	$ 6	Retained earnings	$11
Accounts Receivable	4	Revenue	25	Dividends	2
Accumulated Depreciation—Equip. ..	5	Salaries Expense....	6	Unearned Revenue	4
Cash..........................	7	Supplies	8	Utilities Expense	4
Equipment	13	Common stock.....	3		

Exercise 3-17
Completing a worksheet

P7

1. Use the data above to prepare a worksheet. Enter the accounts in proper order and enter their balances in the correct debit or credit column.

2. Use the following adjustment information to complete the worksheet.

   a. Depreciation on equipment, $1   **d.** Supplies available at December 31, 2011, $5

   b. Accrued salaries, $2   **e.** Expired insurance, $5

   c. The $4 of unearned revenue has been earned

connect

Meyer Co. follows the practice of recording prepaid expenses and unearned revenues in balance sheet accounts. The company's annual accounting period ends on December 31, 2011. The following information concerns the adjusting entries to be recorded as of that date.

a. The Office Supplies account started the year with a $3,000 balance. During 2011, the company purchased supplies for $12,400, which was added to the Office Supplies account. The inventory of supplies available at December 31, 2011, totaled $2,640.

b. An analysis of the company's insurance policies provided the following facts.

Policy	Date of Purchase	Months of Coverage	Cost
A	April 1, 2010	24	$15,840
B	April 1, 2011	36	13,068
C	August 1, 2011	12	2,700

PROBLEM SET A

Problem 3-1A
Preparing adjusting and subsequent journal entries

C1 A1 P1

The total premium for each policy was paid in full (for all months) at the purchase date, and the Prepaid Insurance account was debited for the full cost. (Year-end adjusting entries for Prepaid Insurance were properly recorded in all prior years.)

c. The company has 15 employees, who earn a total of $2,100 in salaries each working day. They are paid each Monday for their work in the five-day workweek ending on the previous Friday. Assume that December 31, 2011, is a Tuesday, and all 15 employees worked the first two days of that week. Because New Year's Day is a paid holiday, they will be paid salaries for five full days on Monday, January 6, 2012.

d. The company purchased a building on January 1, 2011. It cost $855,000 and is expected to have a $45,000 salvage value at the end of its predicted 30-year life. Annual depreciation is $27,000.

e. Since the company is not large enough to occupy the entire building it owns, it rented space to a tenant at $2,400 per month, starting on November 1, 2011. The rent was paid on time on November 1, and the amount received was credited to the Rent Earned account. However, the tenant has not paid the December rent. The company has worked out an agreement with the tenant, who has promised to pay both December and January rent in full on January 15. The tenant has agreed not to fall behind again.

f. On November 1, the company rented space to another tenant for $2,175 per month. The tenant paid five months' rent in advance on that date. The payment was recorded with a credit to the Unearned Rent account.

Required

1. Use the information to prepare adjusting entries as of December 31, 2011.
2. Prepare journal entries to record the first subsequent cash transaction in 2012 for parts *c* and *e*.

Problem 3-2A

Identifying adjusting entries with explanations

P1

For each of the following entries, enter the letter of the explanation that most closely describes it in the space beside each entry. (You can use letters more than once.)

A. To record receipt of unearned revenue.   **E.** To record an accrued expense.
B. To record this period's earning of prior   **F.** To record an accrued revenue.
     unearned revenue.   **G.** To record this period's use of a prepaid expense.
C. To record payment of an accrued expense.   **H.** To record payment of a prepaid expense.
D. To record receipt of an accrued revenue.   **I.** To record this period's depreciation expense.

_____	1.	Rent Expense	2,000	
		Prepaid Rent		2,000
_____	2.	Interest Expense	1,000	
		Interest Payable		1,000
_____	3.	Depreciation Expense	4,000	
		Accumulated Depreciation		4,000
_____	4.	Unearned Professional Fees	3,000	
		Professional Fees Earned		3,000
_____	5.	Insurance Expense	4,200	
		Prepaid Insurance		4,200
_____	6.	Salaries Payable	1,400	
		Cash		1,400
_____	7.	Prepaid Rent	4,500	
		Cash		4,500
_____	8.	Salaries Expense	6,000	
		Salaries Payable		6,000
_____	9.	Interest Receivable	5,000	
		Interest Revenue		5,000
_____	10.	Cash	9,000	
		Accounts Receivable (from consulting)		9,000
_____	11.	Cash	7,500	
		Unearned Professional Fees		7,500
_____	12.	Cash	2,000	
		Interest Receivable		2,000

Problem 3-3A

Preparing adjusting entries, adjusted trial balance, and financial statements

A1 P1 P2 P3

mhhe.com/wildFINMAN4e

Watson Technical Institute (WTI), a school owned by Tom Watson, provides training to individuals who pay tuition directly to the school. WTI also offers training to groups in off-site locations. Its unadjusted trial balance as of December 31, 2011, follows. WTI initially records prepaid expenses and unearned revenues in balance sheet accounts. Descriptions of items *a* through *h* that require adjusting entries on December 31, 2011, follow.

Additional Information Items

a. An analysis of WTI's insurance policies shows that $3,000 of coverage has expired.
b. An inventory count shows that teaching supplies costing $2,600 are available at year-end 2011.
c. Annual depreciation on the equipment is $12,000.
d. Annual depreciation on the professional library is $6,000.
e. On November 1, WTI agreed to do a special six-month course (starting immediately) for a client. The contract calls for a monthly fee of $2,200, and the client paid the first five months' fees in advance. When the cash was received, the Unearned Training Fees account was credited. The fee for the sixth month will be recorded when it is collected in 2012.

f. On October 15, WTI agreed to teach a four-month class (beginning immediately) for an individual for $3,000 tuition per month payable at the end of the class. The class started on October 15, but no payment has yet been received. (WTI's accruals are applied to the nearest half-month; for example, October recognizes one-half month accrual.)

g. WTI's two employees are paid weekly. As of the end of the year, two days' salaries have accrued at the rate of $100 per day for each employee.

h. The balance in the Prepaid Rent account represents rent for December.

	Debit	Credit
WATSON TECHNICAL INSTITUTE Unadjusted Trial Balance December 31, 2011		
Cash	$ 26,000	
Accounts receivable	0	
Teaching supplies	10,000	
Prepaid insurance	15,000	
Prepaid rent	2,000	
Professional library	30,000	
Accumulated depreciation — Professional library		$ 9,000
Equipment	70,000	
Accumulated depreciation — Equipment		16,000
Accounts payable		36,000
Salaries payable		0
Unearned training fees		11,000
Common stock		10,000
Retained earnings		53,600
Dividends	40,000	
Tuition fees earned		102,000
Training fees earned		38,000
Depreciation expense — Professional library	0	
Depreciation expense — Equipment	0	
Salaries expense	48,000	
Insurance expense	0	
Rent expense	22,000	
Teaching supplies expense	0	
Advertising expense	7,000	
Utilities expense	5,600	
Totals	$ 275,600	$ 275,600

Required

1. Prepare T-accounts (representing the ledger) with balances from the unadjusted trial balance.
2. Prepare the necessary adjusting journal entries for items *a* through *h* and post them to the T-accounts. Assume that adjusting entries are made only at year-end.
3. Update balances in the T-accounts for the adjusting entries and prepare an adjusted trial balance.
4. Prepare Watson Technical Institute's income statement and statement of retained earnings for the year 2011 and prepare its balance sheet as of December 31, 2011.

Check (2*e*) Cr. Training Fees Earned, $4,400; (2*f*) Cr. Tuition Fees Earned, $7,500; (3) Adj. Trial balance totals, $301,500; (4) Net income, $38,500;

A six-column table for JJW Company follows. The first two columns contain the unadjusted trial balance for the company as of July 31, 2011. The last two columns contain the adjusted trial balance as of the same date.

Required

Analysis Component

1. Analyze the differences between the unadjusted and adjusted trial balances to determine the eight adjustments that likely were made. Show the results of your analysis by inserting these adjustment amounts in the table's two middle columns. Label each adjustment with a letter *a* through *h* and provide a short description of it at the bottom of the table.

Problem 3-4A

Interpreting unadjusted and adjusted trial balances, and preparing financial statements

A1 P1 P2 P3

mhhe.com/wildFINMAN4e

Preparation Component

2. Use the information in the adjusted trial balance to prepare the company's (*a*) income statement and its statement of retained earnings for the year ended July 31, 2011 (*note:* retained earnings at July 31, 2010, was $23,420, and the current-year dividends were $10,000), and (*b*) the balance sheet as of July 31, 2011.

	Unadjusted Trial Balance		Adjustments		Adjusted Trial Balance	
Cash	$ 27,000				$ 27,000	
Accounts receivable	12,000				22,460	
Office supplies	18,000				3,000	
Prepaid insurance	7,320				4,880	
Office equipment	92,000				92,000	
Accum. depreciation— Office equip.		$ 12,000				$ 18,000
Accounts payable		9,300				10,200
Interest payable		0				800
Salaries payable		0				6,600
Unearned consulting fees		16,000				14,300
Long-term notes payable		44,000				44,000
Common stock		5,000				5,000
Retained earnings		23,420				23,420
Dividends	10,000				10,000	
Consulting fees earned		156,000				168,160
Depreciation expense— Office equip.	0				6,000	
Salaries expense	71,000				77,600	
Interest expense	1,400				2,200	
Insurance expense	0				2,440	
Rent expense	13,200				13,200	
Office supplies expense	0				15,000	
Advertising expense	13,800				14,700	
Totals	$265,720	$265,720			$290,480	$290,480

Problem 3-5A

Preparing financial statements from the adjusted trial balance and calculating profit margin

P3   A1   A2

The adjusted trial balance for Callahay Company as of December 31, 2011, follows.

	Debit	Credit
Cash	$ 22,000	
Accounts receivable	44,000	
Interest receivable	10,000	
Notes receivable (due in 90 days)	160,000	
Office supplies	8,000	
Automobiles	160,000	
Accumulated depreciation—Automobiles		$ 42,000
Equipment	130,000	
Accumulated depreciation—Equipment		10,000
Land	70,000	
Accounts payable		88,000
Interest payable		12,000
Salaries payable		11,000
Unearned fees		22,000
Long-term notes payable		130,000
Common stock		20,000

[continued on next page]

[continued from previous page]

Retained earnings..........................		227,800
Dividends	38,000	
Fees earned		420,000
Interest earned		16,000
Depreciation expense—Automobiles	18,000	
Depreciation expense—Equipment	10,000	
Salaries expense	180,000	
Wages expense	32,000	
Interest expense	24,000	
Office supplies expense	26,000	
Advertising expense	50,000	
Repairs expense—Automobiles	16,800	
Totals	$998,800	$998,800

Required

1. Use the information in the adjusted trial balance to prepare (*a*) the income statement for the year ended December 31, 2011; (*b*) the statement of retained earnings for the year ended December 31, 2011; and (*c*) the balance sheet as of December 31, 2011.

2. Calculate the profit margin for year 2011.

Check (1) Total assets, $552,000

In the blank space beside each numbered balance sheet item, enter the letter of its balance sheet classification. If the item should not appear on the balance sheet, enter a *Z* in the blank.

A. Current assets **D.** Intangible assets **F.** Long-term liabilities

B. Long-term investments **E.** Current liabilities **G.** Equity

C. Plant assets

Problem 3-6A
Determining balance sheet classifications

C4

_____	**1.** Office equipment	_____ **11.** Depreciation expense—Building
_____	**2.** Office supplies	_____ **12.** Prepaid rent
_____	**3.** Buildings	_____ **13.** Interest receivable
_____	**4.** Store supplies	_____ **14.** Taxes payable
_____	**5.** Accumulated depreciation—Trucks	_____ **15.** Automobiles
_____	**6.** Land (used in operations)	_____ **16.** Notes payable (due in 3 years)
_____	**7.** Repairs expense	_____ **17.** Accounts payable
_____	**8.** Cash	_____ **18.** Prepaid insurance
_____	**9.** Current portion of long-term note payable	_____ **19.** Common stock
_____	**10.** Long-term investment in stock	_____ **20.** Unearned services revenue

---

On April 1, 2011, Jennifer Stafford created a new travel agency, See-It-Now Travel. The following transactions occurred during the company's first month.

April 1 Stafford invested $20,000 cash and computer equipment worth $40,000 in the company in exchange for common stock.

2 The company rented furnished office space by paying $1,700 cash for the first month's (April) rent.

3 The company purchased $1,100 of office supplies for cash.

10 The company paid $3,600 cash for the premium on a 12-month insurance policy. Coverage begins on April 11.

14 The company paid $1,800 cash for two weeks' salaries earned by employees.

24 The company collected $7,900 cash on commissions from airlines on tickets obtained for customers.

28 The company paid $1,800 cash for two weeks' salaries earned by employees.

29 The company paid $250 cash for minor repairs to the company's computer.

30 The company paid $650 cash for this month's telephone bill.

30 The company paid $1,500 cash for dividends.

Problem 3-7A
Applying the accounting cycle

 P1 P2 P3 P4 P5

mhhe.com/wildFINMAN4e

The company's chart of accounts follows:

No.	Account	No.	Account
101	Cash	405	Commissions Earned
106	Accounts Receivable	612	Depreciation Expense—Computer Equip.
124	Office Supplies	622	Salaries Expense
128	Prepaid Insurance	637	Insurance Expense
167	Computer Equipment	640	Rent Expense
168	Accumulated Depreciation—Computer Equip.	650	Office Supplies Expense
209	Salaries Payable	684	Repairs Expense
307	Common Stock	688	Telephone Expense
318	Retained Earnings	901	Income Summary
319	Dividends		

Required

Check (3) Unadj. trial balance totals, $67,900

     (4a) Dr. Insurance Expense, $200

1. Use the balance column format to set up each ledger account listed in its chart of accounts.
2. Prepare journal entries to record the transactions for April and post them to the ledger accounts. The company records prepaid and unearned items in balance sheet accounts.
3. Prepare an unadjusted trial balance as of April 30.
4. Use the following information to journalize and post adjusting entries for the month:
   a. Two-thirds of one month's insurance coverage has expired.
   b. At the end of the month, $700 of office supplies are still available.
   c. This month's depreciation on the computer equipment is $600.
   d. Employees earned $320 of unpaid and unrecorded salaries as of month-end.
   e. The company earned $1,650 of commissions that are not yet billed at month-end.

     (5) Net income, $1,830; Total assets, $60,650

5. Prepare the income statement and the statement of retained earnings for the month of April and the balance sheet at April 30, 2011.
6. Prepare journal entries to close the temporary accounts and post these entries to the ledger.

     (7) P-C trial balance totals, $61,250

7. Prepare a post-closing trial balance.

Problem 3-8A
Preparing closing entries,
financial statements, and ratios

C4 A2 A3 P3 P4

The adjusted trial balance for Sharp Construction as of December 31, 2011, follows.

	SHARP CONSTRUCTION Adjusted Trial Balance December 31, 2011		
No.	**Account Title**	**Debit**	**Credit**
101	Cash	$ 4,000	
104	Short-term investments	22,000	
126	Supplies	7,100	
128	Prepaid insurance	6,000	
167	Equipment	39,000	
168	Accumulated depreciation—Equipment		$ 20,000
173	Building	130,000	
174	Accumulated depreciation—Building		55,000
183	Land	45,000	
201	Accounts payable		15,500
203	Interest payable		1,500
208	Rent payable		2,500
210	Wages payable		1,500
213	Property taxes payable		800
233	Unearned professional fees		6,500

[continued on next page]

[continued from previous page]

251	Long-term notes payable		66,000
307	Common stock		20,000
318	Retained earnings		62,700
319	Dividends	12,000	
401	Professional fees earned		96,000
406	Rent earned		13,000
407	Dividends earned		1,900
409	Interest earned		1,000
606	Depreciation expense—Building	10,000	
612	Depreciation expense—Equipment	5,000	
623	Wages expense	31,000	
633	Interest expense	4,100	
637	Insurance expense	9,000	
640	Rent expense	12,400	
652	Supplies expense	6,400	
682	Postage expense	3,200	
683	Property taxes expense	4,000	
684	Repairs expense	7,900	
688	Telephone expense	2,200	
690	Utilities expense	3,600	
	Totals	$363,900	$363,900

J. Sharp invested $50,000 cash in the business in exchange for more common stock during year 2011 (the December 31, 2010, credit balance of retained earnings was $62,700). Sharp Construction is required to make a $6,600 payment on its long-term notes payable during 2012.

Required

1. Prepare the income statement and the statement of retained earnings for the calendar year 2011 and the classified balance sheet at December 31, 2011.

Check (1) Total assets (12/31/2011), $178,100; Net income, $13,100

2. Prepare the necessary closing entries at December 31, 2011.

3. Use the information in the financial statements to compute these ratios: (*a*) return on assets (total assets at December 31, 2010, was $200,000), (*b*) debt ratio, (*c*) profit margin ratio (use total revenues as the denominator), and (*d*) current ratio.

Nomo Co. follows the practice of recording prepaid expenses and unearned revenues in balance sheet accounts. The company's annual accounting period ends on October 31, 2011. The following information concerns the adjusting entries that need to be recorded as of that date.

PROBLEM SET B

Problem 3-1B
Preparing adjusting and subsequent journal entries

C1 A1 P1

a. The Office Supplies account started the fiscal year with a $500 balance. During the fiscal year, the company purchased supplies for $3,650, which was added to the Office Supplies account. The supplies available at October 31, 2011, totaled $700.

b. An analysis of the company's insurance policies provided the following facts.

Policy	Date of Purchase	Months of Coverage	Cost
A	April 1, 2010	24	$3,000
B	April 1, 2011	36	3,600
C	August 1, 2011	12	660

The total premium for each policy was paid in full (for all months) at the purchase date, and the Prepaid Insurance account was debited for the full cost. (Year-end adjusting entries for Prepaid Insurance were properly recorded in all prior fiscal years.)

c. The company has four employees, who earn a total of $800 for each workday. They are paid each Monday for their work in the five-day workweek ending on the previous Friday. Assume that October 31, 2011, is a Monday, and all four employees worked the first day of that week. They will be paid salaries for five full days on Monday, November 7, 2011.

d. The company purchased a building on November 1, 2010, that cost $155,000 and is expected to have a $20,000 salvage value at the end of its predicted 25-year life. Annual depreciation is $5,400.

e. Since the company does not occupy the entire building it owns, it rented space to a tenant at $600 per month, starting on September 1, 2011. The rent was paid on time on September 1, and the amount received was credited to the Rent Earned account. However, the October rent has not been paid. The company has worked out an agreement with the tenant, who has promised to pay both October and November rent in full on November 15. The tenant has agreed not to fall behind again.

f. On September 1, the company rented space to another tenant for $525 per month. The tenant paid five months' rent in advance on that date. The payment was recorded with a credit to the Unearned Rent account.

Required

Check (1*b*) Dr. Insurance Expense, $2,675; (1*d*) Dr. Depreciation Expense, $5,400.

1. Use the information to prepare adjusting entries as of October 31, 2011.

2. Prepare journal entries to record the first subsequent cash transaction in November 2011 for parts *c* and *e*.

Problem 3-2B
Identifying adjusting entries with explanations

P1

For each of the following entries, enter the letter of the explanation that most closely describes it in the space beside each entry. (You can use letters more than once.)

A. To record payment of a prepaid expense.
B. To record this period's use of a prepaid expense.
C. To record this period's depreciation expense.
D. To record receipt of unearned revenue.
E. To record this period's earning of prior unearned revenue.
F. To record an accrued expense.
G. To record payment of an accrued expense.
H. To record an accrued revenue.
I. To record receipt of accrued revenue.

___	1.	Unearned Professional Fees	6,000
		Professional Fees Earned	6,000
___	2.	Interest Receivable	3,500
		Interest Revenue	3,500
___	3.	Salaries Payable	9,000
		Cash	9,000
___	4.	Depreciation Expense	8,000
		Accumulated Depreciation	8,000
___	5.	Cash	9,000
		Unearned Professional Fees	9,000
___	6.	Insurance Expense	4,000
		Prepaid Insurance	4,000
___	7.	Interest Expense	5,000
		Interest Payable	5,000
___	8.	Cash	1,500
		Accounts Receivable (from services)	1,500
___	9.	Salaries Expense	7,000
		Salaries Payable	7,000
___	10.	Cash	1,000
		Interest Receivable	1,000
___	11.	Prepaid Rent	3,000
		Cash	3,000
___	12.	Rent Expense	7,500
		Prepaid Rent	7,500

Following is the unadjusted trial balance for Alcorn Institute as of December 31, 2011, which initially records prepaid expenses and unearned revenues in balance sheet accounts. The Institute provides one-on-one training to individuals who pay tuition directly to the business and offers extension training to groups in off-site locations. Shown after the trial balance are items *a* through *h* that require adjusting entries as of December 31, 2011.

Problem 3-3B
Preparing adjusting entries, adjusted trial balance, and financial statements

A1 P1 P2 P3

	ALCORN INSTITUTE Unadjusted Trial Balance December 31, 2011	
	Debit	**Credit**
Cash	$ 50,000	
Accounts receivable	0	
Teaching supplies	60,000	
Prepaid insurance	18,000	
Prepaid rent	2,600	
Professional library	10,000	
Accumulated depreciation—Professional library		$ 1,500
Equipment	30,000	
Accumulated depreciation—Equipment		16,000
Accounts payable		12,200
Salaries payable		0
Unearned training fees		27,600
Common stock		12,000
Retained earnings		56,500
Dividends	20,000	
Tuition fees earned		105,000
Training fees earned		62,000
Depreciation expense—Professional library	0	
Depreciation expense—Equipment	0	
Salaries expense	43,200	
Insurance expense	0	
Rent expense	28,600	
Teaching supplies expense	0	
Advertising expense	18,000	
Utilities expense	12,400	
Totals	$ 292,800	$292,800

Additional Information Items

a. An analysis of the Institute's insurance policies shows that $6,400 of coverage has expired.

b. An inventory count shows that teaching supplies costing $2,500 are available at year-end 2011.

c. Annual depreciation on the equipment is $4,000.

d. Annual depreciation on the professional library is $2,000.

e. On November 1, the Institute agreed to do a special four-month course (starting immediately) for a client. The contract calls for a $4,600 monthly fee, and the client paid the first two months' fees in advance. When the cash was received, the Unearned Training Fees account was credited. The last two months' fees will be recorded when collected in 2012.

f. On October 15, the Institute agreed to teach a four-month class (beginning immediately) to an individual for $2,200 tuition per month payable at the end of the class. The class started on October 15, but no payment has yet been received. (Alcorn's accruals are applied to the nearest half-month; for example, October recognizes one-half month accrual.)

g. The Institute's only employee is paid weekly. As of the end of the year, three days' salaries have accrued at the rate of $180 per day.

h. The balance in the Prepaid Rent account represents rent for December.

Required

1. Prepare T-accounts (representing the ledger) with balances from the unadjusted trial balance.
2. Prepare the necessary adjusting journal entries for items *a* through *h*, and post them to the T-accounts. Assume that adjusting entries are made only at year-end.
3. Update balances in the T-accounts for the adjusting entries and prepare an adjusted trial balance.
4. Prepare the company's income statement and statement of retained earnings for the year 2011, and prepare its balance sheet as of December 31, 2011.

Problem 3-4B

Interpreting unadjusted and adjusted trial balances, and preparing financial statements

A1 P1 P2 P3

A six-column table for Daxu Consulting Company follows. The first two columns contain the unadjusted trial balance for the company as of December 31, 2011, and the last two columns contain the adjusted trial balance as of the same date.

	Unadjusted Trial Balance		Adjustments		Adjusted Trial Balance	
Cash	$ 48,000				$ 48,000	
Accounts receivable	70,000				76,660	
Office supplies	30,000				7,000	
Prepaid insurance	13,200				8,600	
Office equipment	150,000				150,000	
Accumulated depreciation— Office equip.		$ 30,000				$ 40,000
Accounts payable		36,000				42,000
Interest payable		0				1,600
Salaries payable		0				11,200
Unearned consulting fees		30,000				17,800
Long-term notes payable		80,000				80,000
Common stock		4,000				4,000
Retained earnings		66,200				66,200
Dividends	10,000				10,000	
Consulting fees earned		264,000				282,860
Depreciation expense— Office equip.	0				10,000	
Salaries expense	115,600				126,800	
Interest expense	6,400				8,000	
Insurance expense	0				4,600	
Rent expense	24,000				24,000	
Office supplies expense	0				23,000	
Advertising expense	43,000				49,000	
Totals	$510,200	$510,200			$545,660	$545,660

Required

Analysis Component

1. Analyze the differences between the unadjusted and adjusted trial balances to determine the eight adjustments that likely were made. Show the results of your analysis by inserting these adjustment amounts in the table's two middle columns. Label each adjustment with a letter *a* through *h* and provide a short description of it at the bottom of the table.

Preparation Component

2. Use the information in the adjusted trial balance to prepare this company's (*a*) income statement and its statement of retained earnings for the year ended December 31, 2011 (*note:* retained earnings at December 31, 2010, was $66,200, and the current-year dividends were $10,000), and (*b*) the balance sheet as of December 31, 2011.

The adjusted trial balance for Lightning Courier as of December 31, 2011, follows.

Problem 3-5B
Preparing financial statements from the adjusted trial balance and calculating profit margin

P3 A1 A2

	Debit	Credit
Cash	$ 48,000	
Accounts receivable	110,000	
Interest receivable	6,000	
Notes receivable (due in 90 days)	200,000	
Office supplies	12,000	
Trucks	124,000	
Accumulated depreciation—Trucks		$ 48,000
Equipment	260,000	
Accumulated depreciation—Equipment		190,000
Land	90,000	
Accounts payable		124,000
Interest payable		22,000
Salaries payable		30,000
Unearned delivery fees		110,000
Long-term notes payable		190,000
Common stock		15,000
Retained earnings		100,000
Dividends	40,000	
Delivery fees earned		580,000
Interest earned		24,000
Depreciation expense—Trucks	24,000	
Depreciation expense—Equipment	46,000	
Salaries expense	64,000	
Wages expense	290,000	
Interest expense	25,000	
Office supplies expense	33,000	
Advertising expense	26,400	
Repairs expense—Trucks	34,600	
Totals	$1,433,000	$1,433,000

Required

1. Use the information in the adjusted trial balance to prepare (*a*) the income statement for the year ended December 31, 2011, (*b*) the statement of retained earnings for the year ended December 31, 2011, and (*c*) the balance sheet as of December 31, 2011.

2. Calculate the profit margin for year 2011.

Check (1) Total assets, $612,000

In the blank space beside each numbered balance sheet item, enter the letter of its balance sheet classification. If the item should not appear on the balance sheet, enter a *Z* in the blank.

Problem 3-6B
Determining balance sheet classifications

C4

A. Current assets

B. Long-term investments

C. Plant assets

D. Intangible assets

E. Current liabilities

F. Long-term liabilities

G. Equity

_____ **1.** Machinery

_____ **2.** Prepaid insurance

_____ **3.** Current portion of long-term note payable

_____ **4.** Interest receivable

_____ **5.** Rent receivable

_____ **6.** Land (used in operations)

_____ **7.** Copyrights

_____ **8.** Rent revenue

_____ **9.** Depreciation expense—Trucks

_____ **10.** Long-term investment in stock
_____ **11.** Office supplies
_____ **12.** Interest payable
_____ **13.** Common stock
_____ **14.** Notes receivable (due in 120 days)
_____ **15.** Accumulated depreciation—Trucks
_____ **16.** Salaries payable
_____ **17.** Commissions earned
_____ **18.** Income taxes payable
_____ **19.** Office equipment
_____ **20.** Notes payable (due in 15 years)

Problem 3-7B

Applying the accounting cycle

P1 P2 P3 P4 P5

On July 1, 2011, Lucinda Fogle created a new self-storage business, KeepSafe Co. The following transactions occurred during the company's first month.

July   1   Fogle invested $20,000 cash and buildings worth $120,000 in the company in exchange for common stock.
      2   The company rented equipment by paying $1,800 cash for the first month's (July) rent.
      5   The company purchased $2,300 of office supplies for cash.
    10   The company paid $5,400 cash for the premium on a 12-month insurance policy. Coverage begins on July 11.
    14   The company paid an employee $900 cash for two weeks' salary earned.
    24   The company collected $8,800 cash for storage fees from customers.
    28   The company paid $900 cash for two weeks' salary earned by an employee.
    29   The company paid $850 cash for minor repairs to a leaking roof.
    30   The company paid $300 cash for this month's telephone bill.
    31   The company paid $1,600 cash for dividends.

The company's chart of accounts follows:

101	Cash		401	Storage Fees Earned
106	Accounts Receivable		606	Depreciation Expense—Buildings
124	Office Supplies		622	Salaries Expense
128	Prepaid Insurance		637	Insurance Expense
173	Buildings		640	Rent Expense
174	Accumulated Depreciation—Buildings		650	Office Supplies Expense
209	Salaries Payable		684	Repairs Expense
307	Common Stock		688	Telephone Expense
318	Retained Earnings		901	Income Summary
319	Dividends			

Required

1. Use the balance column format to set up each ledger account listed in its chart of accounts.
2. Prepare journal entries to record the transactions for July and post them to the ledger accounts. Record prepaid and unearned items in balance sheet accounts.
3. Prepare an unadjusted trial balance as of July 31.
4. Use the following information to journalize and post adjusting entries for the month:
   a. Two-thirds of one month's insurance coverage has expired.
   b. At the end of the month, $1,550 of office supplies are still available.
   c. This month's depreciation on the buildings is $1,200.
   d. An employee earned $180 of unpaid and unrecorded salary as of month-end.
   e. The company earned $950 of storage fees that are not yet billed at month-end.
5. Prepare the income statement and the statement of retained earnings for the month of July and the balance sheet at July 31, 2011.
6. Prepare journal entries to close the temporary accounts and post these entries to the ledger.
7. Prepare a post-closing trial balance.

Check   (3) Unadj. trial balance totals, $148,800

(4a) Dr. Insurance Expense, $300

(5) Net income, $2,570; Total assets, $141,150

(7) P-C trial balance totals, $142,350

The adjusted trial balance for Giovanni Co. as of December 31, 2011, follows.

Problem 3-8B
Preparing closing entries,
financial statements, and ratios
C4 A2 A3 P3 P4

GIOVANNI COMPANY Adjusted Trial Balance December 31, 2011			
No.	Account Title	Debit	Credit
101	Cash	$ 6,400	
104	Short-term investments	10,200	
126	Supplies	3,600	
128	Prepaid insurance	800	
167	Equipment	18,000	
168	Accumulated depreciation—Equipment		$ 3,000
173	Building	90,000	
174	Accumulated depreciation—Building		9,000
183	Land	28,500	
201	Accounts payable		2,500
203	Interest payable		1,400
208	Rent payable		200
210	Wages payable		1,180
213	Property taxes payable		2,330
233	Unearned professional fees		650
251	Long-term notes payable		32,000
307	Common stock		30,000
318	Retained earnings		61,800
319	Dividends	6,000	
401	Professional fees earned		47,000
406	Rent earned		3,600
407	Dividends earned		500
409	Interest earned		1,120
606	Depreciation expense—Building	2,000	
612	Depreciation expense—Equipment	1,000	
623	Wages expense	17,500	
633	Interest expense	1,200	
637	Insurance expense	1,425	
640	Rent expense	1,800	
652	Supplies expense	900	
682	Postage expense	310	
683	Property taxes expense	3,825	
684	Repairs expense	579	
688	Telephone expense	421	
690	Utilities expense	1,820	
	Totals	$196,280	$196,280

J. Giovanni invested $30,000 cash in the business in exchange for more common stock during year 2011 (the December 31, 2010, credit balance of retained earnings was $61,800). Giovanni Company is required to make a $6,400 payment on its long-term notes payable during 2012.

Required

1. Prepare the income statement and the statement of retained earnings for the calendar year 2011 and the classified balance sheet at December 31, 2011.

2. Prepare the necessary closing entries at December 31, 2011.

3. Use the information in the financial statements to calculate these ratios: (*a*) return on assets (total assets at December 31, 2010, were $150,000), (*b*) debt ratio, (*c*) profit margin ratio (use total revenues as the denominator), and (*d*) current ratio.

Check   (1) Total assets (12/31/2011),
$145,500; Net income, $19,440

SERIAL PROBLEM
Business Solutions
P1 P2 P3 P4 P5

(This serial problem began in Chapter 1 and continues through most of the book. If previous chapter segments were not completed, the serial problem can still begin at this point. It is helpful, but not necessary, to use the Working Papers that accompany the book.)

SP 3   After the success of the company's first two months, Santana Rey continues to operate Business Solutions. (Transactions for the first two months are described in the serial problem of Chapter 2.) The November 30, 2011, unadjusted trial balance of Business Solutions (reflecting its transactions for October and November of 2011) follows.

No.	Account Title	Debit	Credit
101	Cash	$38,264	
106	Accounts receivable	12,618	
126	Computer supplies	2,545	
128	Prepaid insurance	2,220	
131	Prepaid rent	3,300	
163	Office equipment	8,000	
164	Accumulated depreciation—Office equipment		$ 0
167	Computer equipment	20,000	
168	Accumulated depreciation—Computer equipment		0
201	Accounts payable		0
210	Wages payable		0
236	Unearned computer services revenue		0
307	Common stock		73,000
318	Retained earnings		0
319	Dividends	5,600	
403	Computer services revenue		25,659
612	Depreciation expense—Office equipment	0	
613	Depreciation expense—Computer equipment	0	
623	Wages expense	2,625	
637	Insurance expense	0	
640	Rent expense	0	
652	Computer supplies expense	0	
655	Advertising expense	1,728	
676	Mileage expense	704	
677	Miscellaneous expenses	250	
684	Repairs expense—Computer	805	
	Totals	$98,659	$98,659

Business Solutions had the following transactions and events in December 2011.

Dec.   2   Paid $1,025 cash to Hillside Mall for Business Solutions' share of mall advertising costs.
      3   Paid $500 cash for minor repairs to the company's computer.
      4   Received $3,950 cash from Alex's Engineering Co. for the receivable from November.
    10   Paid cash to Lyn Addie for six days of work at the rate of $125 per day.
    14   Notified by Alex's Engineering Co. that Business Solutions' bid of $7,000 on a proposed project has been accepted. Alex's paid a $1,500 cash advance to Business Solutions.
    15   Purchased $1,100 of computer supplies on credit from Harris Office Products.
    16   Sent a reminder to Gomez Co. to pay the fee for services recorded on November 8.
    20   Completed a project for Liu Corporation and received $5,625 cash.
22–26   Took the week off for the holidays.
    28   Received $3,000 cash from Gomez Co. on its receivable.
    29   Reimbursed S. Rey for business automobile mileage (600 miles at $0.32 per mile).
    31   The business paid $1,500 cash for dividends.

The following additional facts are collected for use in making adjusting entries prior to preparing financial statements for the company's first three months:

a. The December 31 inventory count of computer supplies shows $580 still available.

b. Three months have expired since the 12-month insurance premium was paid in advance.

c. As of December 31, Lyn Addie has not been paid for four days of work at $125 per day.

d. The computer system, acquired on October 1, is expected to have a four-year life with no salvage value.

e. The office equipment, acquired on October 1, is expected to have a five-year life with no salvage value.

f. Three of the four months' prepaid rent has expired.

Required

1. Prepare journal entries to record each of the December transactions and events for Business Solutions. Post those entries to the accounts in the ledger.

2. Prepare adjusting entries to reflect *a* through *f*. Post those entries to the accounts in the ledger.

3. Prepare an adjusted trial balance as of December 31, 2011.

4. Prepare an income statement for the three months ended December 31, 2011.

5. Prepare a statement of retained earnings for the three months ended December 31, 2011.

6. Prepare a balance sheet as of December 31, 2011.

7. Record and post the necessary closing entries for Business Solutions.

8. Prepare a post-closing trial balance as of December 31, 2011.

Check   (3) Adjusted trial balance totals, $109,034

(6) Total assets, $83,460

Check   Post-closing trial balance totals, $85,110

Beyond the Numbers

BTN 3-1   Refer to **Research In Motion**'s financial statements in Appendix A to answer the following.

1. Identify and write down the revenue recognition principle as explained in the chapter.

2. Review Research In Motion's footnotes to discover how it applies the revenue recognition principle and when it recognizes revenue. Report what you discover.

3. What is Research In Motion's profit margin for fiscal years ended February 28, 2009, and February 27, 2010.

4. For the fiscal year ended February 27, 2010, what amount is credited to Income Summary to summarize its revenues earned?

5. For the fiscal year ended February 27, 2010, what amount is debited to Income Summary to summarize its expenses incurred?

6. For the fiscal year ended February 27, 2010, what is the balance of its Income Summary account before it is closed?

REPORTING IN ACTION

C1 C2 A1 A2 P4

RIM

Fast Forward

7. Access RIM's annual report (10-K) for fiscal years ending after February 27, 2010, at its Website (**RIM.com**) or the SEC's EDGAR database (**www.sec.gov**). Assess and compare the February 27, 2010, fiscal year profit margin to any subsequent year's profit margin that you compute.

BTN 3-2   Key figures for the recent two years of both **Research In Motion** and **Apple** follow.

($ millions)	Research In Motion		Apple	
	Current Year	**Prior Year**	**Current Year**	**Prior Year**
Net income	$ 2,457	$ 1,893	$ 8,235	$ 6,119
Net sales	14,953	11,065	42,905	37,491
Current assets	5,813	4,842	31,555	30,006
Current liabilities	2,432	2,115	11,506	11,361

COMPARATIVE ANALYSIS

A2 A3

RIM

Apple

Required

1. Compute profit margins for (*a*) Research In Motion and (*b*) Apple for the two years of data shown.
2. Which company is more successful on the basis of profit margin? Explain.
3. Compute the current ratio for both years for both companies.
4. Which company has the better ability to pay short-term obligations according to the current ratio?
5. Analyze and comment on each company's current ratios for the past two years.
6. How do RIM's and Apple's current ratios compare to their industry (assumed) average ratio of 2.4?

ETHICS CHALLENGE
C1 C2 A1

BTN 3-3 Jackie Bergez works for Sea Biscuit Co. She and Bob Welch, her manager, are preparing adjusting entries for annual financial statements. Bergez computes depreciation and records it as

Depreciation Expense—Equipment	123,000	
Accumulated Depreciation—Equipment		123,000

Welch agrees with her computation but says the credit entry should be directly to the Equipment account. Welch argues that while accumulated depreciation is technically correct, "it is less hassle not to use a contra account and just credit the Equipment account directly. And besides, the balance sheet shows the same amount for total assets under either method."

Required

1. How should depreciation be recorded? Do you support Bergez or Welch?
2. Evaluate the strengths and weaknesses of Welch's reasons for preferring his method.
3. Indicate whether the situation Bergez faces is an ethical problem. Explain.

COMMUNICATING IN PRACTICE
P4

BTN 3-4 Assume that one of your classmates states that a company's books should be ongoing and therefore not closed until that business is terminated. Write a half-page memo to this classmate explaining the concept of the closing process by drawing analogies between (1) a scoreboard for an athletic event and the revenue and expense accounts of a business or (2) a sports team's record book and retained earnings. (*Hint:* Think about what would happen if the scoreboard is not cleared before the start of a new game.)

TAKING IT TO THE NET
C1 A2

BTN 3-5 Access EDGAR online (<u>www.sec.gov</u>) and locate the 10-K report of **The Gap, Inc.,** (ticker GPS) filed on March 26, 2010. Review its financial statements reported for the year ended January 30, 2010, to answer the following questions.

Required

1. What are Gap's main brands?
2. What is Gap's fiscal year-end?
3. What is Gap's net sales for the period ended January 30, 2010?
4. What is Gap's net income for the period ended January 30, 2010?
5. Compute Gap's profit margin for the year ended January 30, 2010.
6. Do you believe Gap's decision to use a year-end of late January or early February relates to its natural business year? Explain.

TEAMWORK IN ACTION
A1 P1

BTN 3-6 Four types of adjustments are described in the chapter: (1) prepaid expenses, (2) unearned revenues, (3) accrued expenses, and (4) accrued revenues.

Required

1. Form *learning teams* of four (or more) members. Each team member must select one of the four adjustments as an area of expertise (each team must have at least one expert in each area).

2. Form *expert teams* from the individuals who have selected the same area of expertise. Expert teams are to discuss and write a report that each expert will present to his or her learning team addressing the following:

   a. Description of the adjustment and why it's necessary.

   b. Example of a transaction or event, with dates and amounts, that requires adjustment.

   c. Adjusting entry(ies) for the example in requirement *b*.

   d. Status of the affected account(s) before and after the adjustment in requirement *c*.

   e. Effects on financial statements of not making the adjustment.

3. Each expert should return to his or her learning team. In rotation, each member should present his or her expert team's report to the learning team. Team discussion is encouraged.

BTN 3-7   Review the opening feature of this chapter dealing with **Cheezburger Network**.

Required

1. Assume that Cheezburger Network sells a $300 gift certificate to a customer, collecting the $300 cash in advance. Prepare the journal entry for the (*a*) collection of the cash for delivery of the gift certificate to the customer and (*b*) revenue from the subsequent delivery of merchandise when the gift certificate is used.

2. How can keeping less inventory help to improve Cheezburger Network's profit margin?

3. Ben Huh understands that many companies carry considerable inventory, and Ben is thinking of carrying additional inventory of merchandise for sale. Ben desires your advice on the pros and cons of carrying such inventory. Provide at least one reason for and one reason against carrying additional inventory.

ENTREPRENEURIAL DECISION

A2

BTN 3-8   Select a company that you can visit in person or interview on the telephone. Call ahead to the company to arrange a time when you can interview an employee (preferably an accountant) who helps prepare the annual financial statements. Inquire about the following aspects of its *accounting cycle:*

1. Does the company prepare interim financial statements? What time period(s) is used for interim statements?

2. Does the company use the cash or accrual basis of accounting?

3. Does the company use a work sheet in preparing financial statements? Why or why not?

4. Does the company use a spreadsheet program? If so, which software program is used?

5. How long does it take after the end of its reporting period to complete annual statements?

HITTING THE ROAD

C1

BTN 3-9   Nokia (**www.Nokia.com**) is a leading global manufacturer of mobile devices and services.

Required

1. Locate the notes to its December 31, 2009, financial statements at the company's Website, and read note *1 Accounting Principles—Revenue Recognition,* first paragraph only. When is revenue recognized by Nokia?

2. Refer to Nokia's financials in Appendix A. What is Nokia's profit margin for the year ended December 31, 2009?

3. Compute Nokia's current ratio for both the current year and the prior year.

4. Comment on any change from the prior year to the current year for the current ratio.

GLOBAL DECISION

A2 A3 C1 C2

NOKIA

ANSWERS TO MULTIPLE CHOICE QUIZ

1. b; the forgotten adjusting entry is: *dr.* Wages Expense, *cr.* Wages Payable.
2. c; Supplies used = $450 − $125 = $325
3. b; Insurance expense = $24,000 × (8/24) = $8,000; adjusting entry is: *dr.* Insurance Expense for $8,000, *cr.* Prepaid Insurance for $8,000.

4. a; Consulting fees earned = $3,600 × (2/6) = $1,200; adjusting entry is: *dr.* Unearned Consulting Fee for $1,200, *cr.* Consulting Fees Earned for $1,200.
5. e; Profit margin = $15,000/$300,000 = 5%
6. b

4

Accounting for Merchandising Operations

A Look Back

Chapter 3 focused on the final steps of the accounting process. We explained the importance of proper revenue and expense recognition and described the adjusting and closing processes. We also prepared financial statements.

A Look at This Chapter

This chapter emphasizes merchandising activities. We explain how reporting merchandising activities differs from reporting service activities. We also analyze and record merchandise purchases and sales transactions, and explain the adjustments and closing process for merchandisers.

A Look Ahead

Chapter 5 extends our analysis of merchandising activities and focuses on the valuation of inventory. Topics include the items in inventory, costs assigned, costing methods used, and inventory estimation techniques.

Learning Objectives

CAP

CONCEPTUAL

C1 Describe merchandising activities and identify income components for a merchandising company. (p. 156)

C2 Identify and explain the inventory asset and cost flows of a merchandising company. (p. 157)

ANALYTICAL

A1 Compute the acid-test ratio and explain its use to assess liquidity. (p. 172)

A2 Compute the gross margin ratio and explain its use to assess profitability. (p. 172)

LP4

PROCEDURAL

P1 Analyze and record transactions for merchandise purchases using a perpetual system. (p. 158)

P2 Analyze and record transactions for merchandise sales using a perpetual system. (p. 163)

P3 Prepare adjustments and close accounts for a merchandising company. (p. 166)

P4 Define and prepare multiple-step and single-step income statements. (p. 168)

P5 *Appendix 4A*—Record and compare merchandising transactions using both periodic and perpetual inventory systems. (p. 177)

Decision Insight

Out of Africa

"We are changing history and . . . we are all going to make a whole lot of money"

—SELENA CUFFE

LOS ANGELES—Selena Cuffe was in Johannesburg as part of a student exchange program when she discovered wine at the Soweto Wine Festival. "They have wine here?" asked a puzzled Selena. That festival unleashed Selena's passion to pursue the merchandising of wine. But not just any wine—she would import and distribute wine produced by indigenous African vintners. She and her husband, Khary, launched **Heritage Link Brands (HeritageLinkBrands.com).** Our mission, says Selena, is "to showcase the very best wines from Africa and the African Diaspora."

But the start-up was a struggle. "Our business is a family business so whatever decisions we make have to be made with the best interest of my family and those we work with," explains Selena. She describes how the business required a merchandising accounting system to account for purchases and sales transactions and to effectively track the levels of the various wines. Inventory was especially important to account for and monitor. Khary explains, "It is very easy to underestimate expenses."

To succeed, Selena and Khary needed to make smart business decisions. They set up an accounting system to capture and communicate costs and sales information. Tracking merchandising activities was necessary to set prices and to manage discounts, allowances, and returns of both sales and purchases. A perpetual inventory system enabled them to stock the right kind and amount of merchandise and to avoid the costs of out-of-stock and excess inventory. Khary stressed that they monitored current assets and current liabilities (working capital). "Understand working capital," insists Khary. "If you don't understand working capital, stop right here and open an accounting book."

Mastering accounting for merchandising is a means to an end for Selena and Khary. "My training is really about how to run a successful business," says Selena. "How to get the most profit you can out of something." Still, Selena recognizes that her merchandising business is more than profits and losses. "What we're able to do and how we're able to make an impact with this business only matters in as much as the people here and on the continent are able to be successful and thrive."

[Sources: *Heritage Link Brands Website,* January 2011; *TIME,* September 2007; *Black Enterprise,* May 2009; *Inc,* March 2009]

Buyers of merchandise expect many products, discount prices, inventory on demand, and high quality. This chapter introduces the accounting practices used by companies engaged in merchandising. We show how financial statements reflect merchandising activities and explain the new financial statement items created by merchandising activities. We also analyze and record merchandise purchases and sales, and explain the adjustments and the closing process for these companies.

Accounting for Merchandising Operations

Merchandising Activities	Merchandising Purchases	Merchandising Sales	Accounting Cycle	Financial Statement Formats
• Reporting income • Reporting inventory • Operating cycles • Inventory systems	• Purchase discounts • Purchase returns and allowances • Transportation costs	• Sales of merchandise • Sales discounts • Sales returns and allowances	• Adjusting entries • Preparing financial statements • Closing entries	• Multiple-step income statement • Single-step income statement • Classified balance sheet

MERCHANDISING ACTIVITIES

C1 Describe merchandising activities and identify income components for a merchandising company.

Previous chapters emphasized the accounting and reporting activities of service companies. A merchandising company's activities differ from those of a service company. **Merchandise** consists of products, also called *goods,* that a company acquires to resell to customers. A **merchandiser** earns net income by buying and selling merchandise. Merchandisers are often identified as either wholesalers or retailers. A **wholesaler** is an *intermediary* that buys products from manufacturers or other wholesalers and sells them to retailers or other wholesalers. A **retailer** is an intermediary that buys products from manufacturers or wholesalers and sells them to consumers. Many retailers sell both products and services.

Reporting Income for a Merchandiser

Net income for a merchandiser equals revenues from selling merchandise minus both the cost of merchandise sold to customers and the cost of other expenses for the period, see Exhibit 4.1. The

EXHIBIT 4.1

Computing Income for a Merchandising Company versus a Service Company

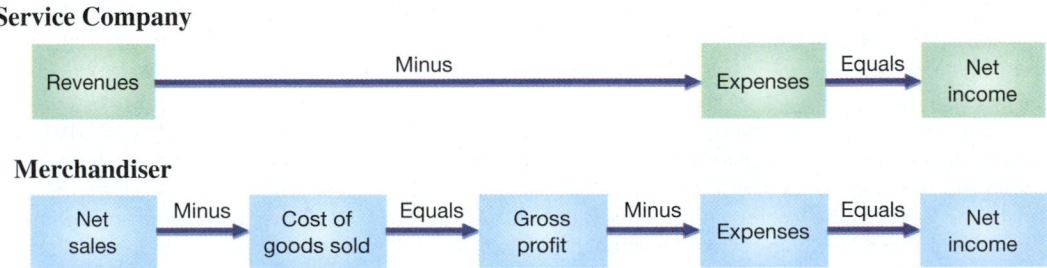

usual accounting term for revenues from selling merchandise is *sales,* and the term used for the expense of buying and preparing the merchandise is **cost of goods sold.** (Some service companies use the term *sales* instead of revenues; and cost of goods sold is also called *cost of sales.*)

The income statement for Z-Mart in Exhibit 4.2 illustrates these key components of a merchandiser's net income. The first two lines show that products are acquired at a cost of $230,400 and sold for $314,700. The third line shows an $84,300 **gross profit,** also called

Point: Fleming, SuperValu, and **SYSCO** are wholesalers. **Gap, Oakley, Target,** and **Walmart** are retailers.

Z-MART
Income Statement
For Year Ended December 31, 2011

Net sales	$314,700
Cost of goods sold	**230,400**
Gross profit	**84,300**
Expenses	71,400
Net income	$ 12,900

EXHIBIT 4.2

Merchandiser's Income Statement

gross margin, which equals net sales less cost of goods sold. Additional expenses of $71,400 are reported, which leaves $12,900 in net income.

Point: Analysis of gross profit is important to effective business decisions, and is described later in the chapter.

Reporting Inventory for a Merchandiser

A merchandiser's balance sheet includes a current asset called *merchandise inventory,* an item not on a service company's balance sheet. **Merchandise inventory,** or simply *inventory,* refers to products that a company owns and intends to sell. The cost of this asset includes the cost incurred to buy the goods, ship them to the store, and make them ready for sale.

C2 Identify and explain the inventory asset and cost flows of a merchandising company.

Operating Cycle for a Merchandiser

A merchandising company's operating cycle begins by purchasing merchandise and ends by collecting cash from selling the merchandise. The length of an operating cycle differs across the types of businesses. Department stores often have operating cycles of two to five months. Operating cycles for grocery merchants usually range from two to eight weeks.

Exhibit 4.3 illustrates an operating cycle for a merchandiser with credit sales. The cycle moves from (*a*) cash purchases of merchandise to (*b*) inventory for sale to (*c*) credit sales to (*d*) accounts receivable to (*e*) cash. Companies try to keep their operating cycles short because assets tied up in inventory and receivables are not productive. Cash sales shorten operating cycles.

(e) Cash collection — Cash — (a) Purchases
(d) Accounts receivable
(b) Merchandise inventory
(c) Credit sales

EXHIBIT 4.3

Merchandiser's Operating Cycle

Inventory Systems

Cost of goods sold is the cost of merchandise sold to customers during a period. It is often the largest single expense on a merchandiser's income statement. **Inventory** refers to products a company owns and expects to sell in its normal operations. Exhibit 4.4 shows that a company's merchandise available for sale consists of what it begins with (beginning inventory) and what it

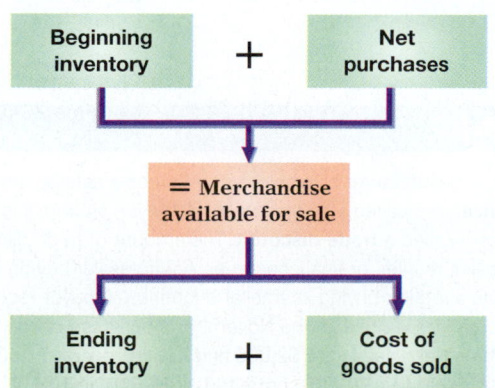

Beginning inventory + Net purchases
= Merchandise available for sale
Ending inventory + Cost of goods sold

EXHIBIT 4.4

Merchandiser's Cost Flow for a Single Time Period

Point: Mathematically, Exhibit 4.4 says

$$BI + NP = MAS,$$

where BI is beginning inventory, NP is net purchases, and MAS is merchandise available for sale. Exhibit 4.4 also says

$$MAS = EI + COGS,$$

which can be rewritten as MAS − EI = COGS or MAS − COGS = EI, where EI is ending inventory and COGS is cost of goods sold.

purchases (net purchases). The merchandise available is either sold (cost of goods sold) or kept for future sales (ending inventory).

Two alternative inventory accounting systems can be used to collect information about cost of goods sold and cost of inventory: *perpetual system* or *periodic system*. The **perpetual inventory system** continually updates accounting records for merchandising transactions—specifically, for those records of inventory available for sale and inventory sold. The **periodic inventory system** updates the accounting records for merchandise transactions only at the *end of a period*. Technological advances and competitive pressures have dramatically increased the use of the perpetual system. It gives managers immediate access to detailed information on sales and inventory levels, where they can strategically react to sales trends, cost changes, consumer tastes, and so forth, to increase gross profit. (Some companies use a *hybrid* system where the perpetual system is used for tracking units available and the periodic system is used to compute cost of sales.)

Point: Growth of superstores such as **Costco** and **Sam's** is fueled by efficient use of perpetual inventory.

Quick Check

Answers — p. 183

1. Describe a merchandiser's cost of goods sold.
2. What is gross profit for a merchandising company?
3. Explain why use of the perpetual inventory system has dramatically increased.

The following sections, consisting of the next 10 pages on purchasing, selling, and adjusting merchandise, use the perpetual system. Appendix 4A uses the periodic system (with the perpetual results on the side). An instructor can choose to cover either one or both inventory systems.

ACCOUNTING FOR MERCHANDISE PURCHASES

P1 Analyze and record transactions for merchandise purchases using a perpetual system.

Assets = Liabilities + Equity
+1,200
−1,200

The cost of merchandise purchased for resale is recorded in the Merchandise Inventory asset account. To illustrate, Z-Mart records a $1,200 cash purchase of merchandise on November 2 as follows:

Nov. 2	Merchandise Inventory	1,200	
	Cash		1,200
	Purchased merchandise for cash.		

The invoice for this merchandise is shown in Exhibit 4.5. The buyer usually receives the original invoice, and the seller keeps a copy. This *source document* serves as the purchase invoice of Z-Mart (buyer) and the sales invoice for Trex (seller). The amount recorded for merchandise inventory includes its purchase cost, shipping fees, taxes, and any other costs necessary to make it ready for sale. This section explains how we compute the recorded cost of merchandise purchases.

Point: The Merchandise Inventory account reflects the cost of goods available for resale.

Decision Insight

Trade Discounts   When a manufacturer or wholesaler prepares a catalog of items it has for sale, it usually gives each item a **list price,** also called a *catalog price*. However, an item's intended *selling price* equals list price minus a given percent called a **trade discount.** The amount of trade discount usually depends on whether a buyer is a wholesaler, retailer, or final consumer. A wholesaler buying in large quantities is often granted a larger discount than a retailer buying in smaller quantities. A buyer records the net amount of list price minus trade discount. For example, in the November 2 purchase of merchandise by Z-Mart, the merchandise was listed in the seller's catalog at $2,000 and Z-Mart received a 40% trade discount. This meant that Z-Mart's purchase price was $1,200, computed as $2,000 − (40% × $2,000). ∎

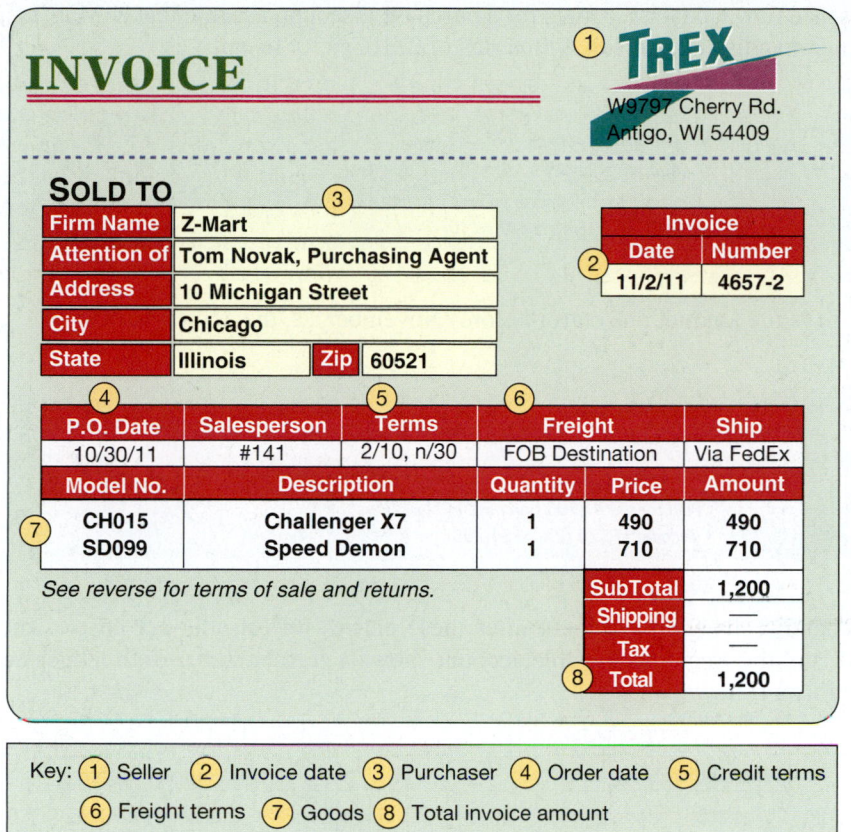

EXHIBIT 4.5

Invoice

Purchase Discounts

The purchase of goods on credit requires a clear statement of expected future payments and dates to avoid misunderstandings. **Credit terms** for a purchase include the amounts and timing of payments from a buyer to a seller. Credit terms usually reflect an industry's practices. To illustrate, when sellers require payment within 10 days after the end of the month of the invoice date, the invoice will show credit terms as "n/10 EOM," which stands for net 10 days after end of month (**EOM**). When sellers require payment within 30 days after the invoice date, the invoice shows credit terms of "n/30," which stands for *net 30 days*.

Exhibit 4.6 portrays credit terms. The amount of time allowed before full payment is due is called the **credit period.** Sellers can grant a **cash discount** to encourage buyers to pay earlier. A buyer views a cash discount as a **purchase discount.** A seller views a cash discount as a **sales discount.** Any cash discounts are described in the credit terms on the invoice. For example, credit terms of "2/10, n/60" mean that full payment is due within a 60-day credit period, but the buyer can deduct 2% of the invoice amount if payment is made within 10 days of the invoice date. This reduced payment applies only for the **discount period.**

Point: Since both the buyer and seller know the invoice date, this date is used in setting the discount and credit periods.

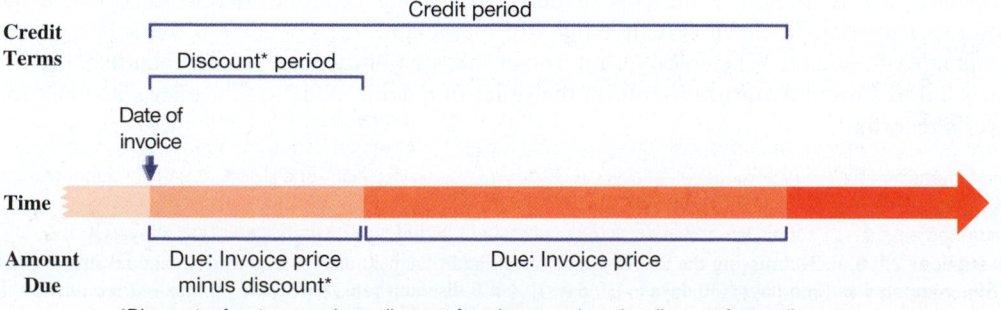

EXHIBIT 4.6

Credit Terms

To illustrate how a buyer accounts for a purchase discount, assume that Z-Mart's $1,200 purchase of merchandise is on credit with terms of 2/10, n/30. Its entry is

Assets = Liabilities + Equity
+1,200   +1,200

(a) Nov. 2	Merchandise Inventory	1,200	
	Accounts Payable		1,200
	Purchased merchandise on credit, invoice		
	dated Nov. 2, terms 2/10, n/30.		

If Z-Mart pays the amount due on (or before) November 12, the entry is

Assets = Liabilities + Equity
−24   −1,200
−1,176

(b) Nov. 12	Accounts Payable	1,200	
	Merchandise Inventory		24
	Cash		1,176
	Paid for the $1,200 purchase of Nov. 2 less the		
	discount of $24 (2% × $1,200).		

The Merchandise Inventory account after these entries reflects the net cost of merchandise purchased, and the Accounts Payable account shows a zero balance. Both ledger accounts, in T-account form, follow:

Merchandise Inventory			
Nov. 2	1,200	Nov. 12	24
Balance	1,176		

Accounts Payable			
Nov. 12	1,200	Nov. 2	1,200
		Balance	0

A buyer's failure to pay within a discount period can be expensive. To illustrate, if Z-Mart does not pay within the 10-day 2% discount period, it can delay payment by 20 more days. This delay costs Z-Mart $24, computed as 2% × $1,200. Most buyers take advantage of a purchase discount because of the usually high interest rate implied from not taking it.[1] Also, good cash management means that no invoice is paid until the last day of the discount or credit period.

Decision Maker   Answer — p. 182

Entrepreneur   You purchase a batch of products on terms of 3/10, n/90, but your company has limited cash and you must borrow funds at an 11% annual rate if you are to pay within the discount period. Do you take advantage of the purchase discount? ■

Purchase Returns and Allowances

Purchase returns refer to merchandise a buyer acquires but then returns to the seller. A *purchase allowance* is a reduction in the cost of defective or unacceptable merchandise that a buyer acquires. Buyers often keep defective but still marketable merchandise if the seller grants an acceptable allowance. When a buyer returns or takes an allowance on merchandise, the buyer issues a **debit memorandum** to inform the seller of a debit made to the seller's account in the buyer's records.

---

[1] The *implied annual interest rate* formula is:

(365 days ÷ [Credit period − Discount period]) × Cash discount rate.

For terms of 2/10, n/30, missing the 2% discount for an additional 20 days is equal to an annual interest rate of 36.5%, computed as [365 days/(30 days − 10 days)] × 2% discount rate. *Favorable purchase discounts* are those with implied annual interest rates that exceed the purchaser's annual rate for borrowing money.

Purchase Allowances   To illustrate purchase allowances, assume that on November 15, Z-Mart (buyer) issues a $300 debit memorandum for an allowance from Trex for defective merchandise. Z-Mart's November 15 entry to update its Merchandise Inventory account to reflect the purchase allowance is

(c) Nov. 15	Accounts Payable..................................	300	
	Merchandise Inventory		300
	Allowance for defective merchandise.		

Assets = Liabilities + Equity
−300   −300

The buyer's allowance for defective merchandise is usually offset against the buyer's current account payable balance to the seller. When cash is refunded, the Cash account is debited instead of Accounts Payable.

Purchase Returns   Returns are recorded at the net costs charged to buyers. To illustrate the accounting for returns, suppose Z-Mart purchases $1,000 of merchandise on June 1 with terms 2/10, n/60. Two days later, Z-Mart returns $100 of goods before paying the invoice. When Z-Mart later pays on June 11, it takes the 2% discount only on the $900 remaining balance. When goods are returned, a buyer can take a purchase discount on only the remaining balance of the invoice. The resulting discount is $18 (2% × $900) and the cash payment is $882 ($900 − $18). The following entries reflect this illustration.

June 1	Merchandise Inventory	1,000	
	Accounts Payable		1,000
	Purchased merchandise, invoice dated June 1,		
	terms 2/10, n/60.		
June 3	Accounts Payable...............................	100	
	Merchandise Inventory		100
	Returned merchandise to seller.		
June 11	Accounts Payable...............................	900	
	Merchandise Inventory		18
	Cash		882
	Paid for $900 merchandise ($1,000 − $100)		
	less $18 discount (2% × $900).		

Example: Assume Z-Mart pays $980 cash for $1,000 of merchandise purchased within its 2% discount period. Later, it returns $100 of the original $1,000 merchandise. The return entry is
Cash 98
    Merchandise Inventory 98

■ Decision Ethics   Answer — p. 182

Credit Manager   As a new credit manager, you are being trained by the outgoing manager. She explains that the system prepares checks for amounts net of favorable cash discounts, and the checks are dated the last day of the discount period. She also tells you that checks are not mailed until five days later, adding that "the company gets free use of cash for an extra five days, and our department looks better. When a supplier complains, we blame the computer system and the mailroom." Do you continue this payment policy? ■

Transportation Costs and Ownership Transfer

The buyer and seller must agree on who is responsible for paying any freight costs and who bears the risk of loss during transit for merchandising transactions. This is essentially the same as asking at what point ownership transfers from the seller to the buyer. The point of transfer is called the **FOB** (*free on board*) point, which determines who pays transportation costs (and often other incidental costs of transit such as insurance).

Exhibit 4.7 identifies two alternative points of transfer. (1) *FOB shipping point,* also called *FOB factory,* means the buyer accepts ownership when the goods depart the seller's place of business. The buyer is then responsible for paying shipping costs and bearing the risk of damage or loss when goods are in transit. The goods are part of the buyer's inventory when they are in transit since ownership has transferred to the buyer. **1-800-FLOWERS.COM**, a floral and gift

EXHIBIT 4.7

Ownership Transfer and
Transportation Costs

	Ownership Transfers When Goods Passed to	Transportation Costs Paid by
FOB shipping point	Carrier	Buyer
FOB destination	Buyer	Seller

Point: The party not responsible for shipping costs sometimes pays the carrier. In these cases, the party paying these costs either bills the party responsible or, more commonly, adjusts its account payable or account receivable with the other party. For example, a buyer paying a carrier when terms are FOB destination can decrease its account payable to the seller by the amount of shipping cost.

merchandiser, and **Bare Escentuals**, a cosmetic manufacturer, both use FOB shipping point. (2) *FOB destination* means ownership of goods transfers to the buyer when the goods arrive at the buyer's place of business. The seller is responsible for paying shipping charges and bears the risk of damage or loss in transit. The seller does not record revenue from this sale until the goods arrive at the destination because this transaction is not complete before that point. **Kyocera**, a manufacturer, uses FOB destination.

Z-Mart's $1,200 purchase on November 2 is on terms of FOB destination. This means Z-Mart is not responsible for paying transportation costs. When a buyer is responsible for paying transportation costs, the payment is made to a carrier or directly to the seller depending on the agreement. The cost principle requires that any necessary transportation costs of a buyer (often called *transportation-in* or *freight-in*) be included as part of the cost of purchased merchandise. To illustrate, Z-Mart's entry to record a $75 freight charge from an independent carrier for merchandise purchased FOB shipping point is

Assets = Liabilities + Equity
+75
−75

(d) Nov. 24	Merchandise Inventory	75	
	Cash		75
	Paid freight costs on purchased merchandise.		

A seller records the costs of shipping goods to customers in a Delivery Expense account when the seller is responsible for these costs. Delivery Expense, also called *transportation-out* or *freight-out,* is reported as a selling expense in the seller's income statement.

In summary, purchases are recorded as debits to Merchandise Inventory. Any later purchase discounts, returns, and allowances are credited (decreases) to Merchandise Inventory. Transportation-in is debited (added) to Merchandise Inventory. Z-Mart's itemized costs of merchandise purchases for year 2011 are in Exhibit 4.8.

EXHIBIT 4.8

Itemized Costs of
Merchandise Purchases

Z-MART	
Itemized Costs of Merchandise Purchases	
For Year Ended December 31, 2011	
Invoice cost of merchandise purchases	$ 235,800
Less: Purchase discounts received	(4,200)
Purchase returns and allowances	(1,500)
Add: Costs of transportation-in	2,300
Total cost of merchandise purchases	**$232,400**

Point: Some companies have separate accounts for purchase discounts, returns and allowances, and transportation-in. These accounts are then transferred to Merchandise Inventory at period-end. This is a *hybrid system* of perpetual and periodic. That is, Merchandise Inventory is updated on a perpetual basis but only for purchases and cost of goods sold.

The accounting system described here does not provide separate records (accounts) for total purchases, total purchase discounts, total purchase returns and allowances, and total transportation-in. Yet nearly all companies collect this information in supplementary records because managers need this information to evaluate and control each of these cost elements. **Supplementary records,** also called *supplemental records,* refer to information outside the usual general ledger accounts.

Quick Check

Answers — p. 183

4. How long are the credit and discount periods when credit terms are 2/10, n/60?

5. Identify which items are subtracted from the *list* amount and not recorded when computing purchase price: (*a*) freight-in; (*b*) trade discount; (*c*) purchase discount; (*d*) purchase return.

6. What does *FOB* mean? What does *FOB destination* mean?

ACCOUNTING FOR MERCHANDISE SALES

Merchandising companies also must account for sales, sales discounts, sales returns and allowances, and cost of goods sold. A merchandising company such as Z-Mart reflects these items in its gross profit computation, as shown in Exhibit 4.9. This section explains how this information is derived from transactions.

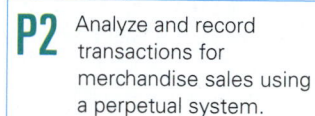

P2 Analyze and record transactions for merchandise sales using a perpetual system.

EXHIBIT 4.9

Gross Profit Computation

Z-MART Computation of Gross Profit For Year Ended December 31, 2011		
Sales.		$321,000
Less: Sales discounts	$4,300	
Sales returns and allowances	2,000	6,300
Net sales		314,700
Cost of goods sold		230,400
Gross profit		**$ 84,300**

Sales of Merchandise

Each sales transaction for a seller of merchandise involves two parts.

1. **Revenue received in the form of an asset from the customer.**
2. **Recognition of the cost of merchandise sold to the customer.**

Accounting for a sales transaction under the perpetual system requires recording information about both parts. This means that each sales transaction for merchandisers, whether for cash or on credit, requires *two entries:* one for revenue and one for cost. To illustrate, Z-Mart sold $2,400 of merchandise on credit on November 3. The revenue part of this transaction is recorded as

(e) Nov. 3	Accounts Receivable	2,400	
	Sales		2,400
	Sold merchandise on credit.		

Assets = Liabilities + Equity
+2,400   +2,400

This entry reflects an increase in Z-Mart's assets in the form of accounts receivable. It also shows the increase in revenue (Sales). If the sale is for cash, the debit is to Cash instead of Accounts Receivable.

The cost part of each sales transaction ensures that the Merchandise Inventory account under a perpetual inventory system reflects the updated cost of the merchandise available for sale. For example, the cost of the merchandise Z-Mart sold on November 3 is $1,600, and the entry to record the cost part of this sales transaction is

(e) Nov. 3	Cost of Goods Sold	1,600	
	Merchandise Inventory		1,600
	To record the cost of Nov. 3 sale.		

Assets = Liabilities + Equity
−1,600   −1,600

Decision Insight

Suppliers and Demands Large merchandising companies often bombard suppliers with demands. These include discounts for bar coding and technology support systems, and fines for shipping errors. Merchandisers' goals are to reduce inventories, shorten lead times, and eliminate errors. ■

Sales Discounts

Sales discounts on credit sales can benefit a seller by decreasing the delay in receiving cash and reducing future collection efforts. At the time of a credit sale, a seller does not know whether a customer will pay within the discount period and take advantage of a discount. This means the seller usually does not record a sales discount until a customer actually pays within the discount period. To illustrate, Z-Mart completes a credit sale for $1,000 on November 12 with terms of 2/10, n/60. The entry to record the revenue part of this sale is

Assets = Liabilities + Equity
+1,000   +1,000

Nov. 12	Accounts Receivable	1,000	
	Sales		1,000
	Sold merchandise under terms of 2/10, n/60.		

This entry records the receivable and the revenue as if the customer will pay the full amount. The customer has two options, however. One option is to wait 60 days until January 11 and pay the full $1,000. In this case, Z-Mart records that payment as

Assets = Liabilities + Equity
+1,000
−1,000

Jan. 11	Cash	1,000	
	Accounts Receivable		1,000
	Received payment for Nov. 12 sale.		

The customer's second option is to pay $980 within a 10-day period ending November 22. If the customer pays on (or before) November 22, Z-Mart records the payment as

Assets = Liabilities + Equity
+980   −20
−1,000

Nov. 22	Cash	980	
	Sales Discounts	20	
	Accounts Receivable		1,000
	Received payment for Nov. 12 sale less discount.		

Sales Discounts is a contra revenue account, meaning the Sales Discounts account is deducted from the Sales account when computing a company's net sales (see Exhibit 4.9). Management monitors Sales Discounts to assess the effectiveness and cost of its discount policy.

Sales Returns and Allowances

Point: Published income statements rarely disclose sales discounts, returns and allowances.

Sales returns refer to merchandise that customers return to the seller after a sale. Many companies allow customers to return merchandise for a full refund. *Sales allowances* refer to reductions in the selling price of merchandise sold to customers. This can occur with damaged or defective merchandise that a customer is willing to purchase with a decrease in selling price. Sales returns and allowances usually involve dissatisfied customers and the possibility of lost future sales, and managers monitor information about returns and allowances.

Sales Returns To illustrate, recall Z-Mart's sale of merchandise on November 3 for $2,400 that had cost $1,600. Assume that the customer returns part of the merchandise on

November 6, and the returned items sell for $800 and cost $600. The revenue part of this transaction must reflect the decrease in sales from the customer's return of merchandise as follows:

(f) Nov. 6	Sales Returns and Allowances	800	
	Accounts Receivable		800
	Customer returns merchandise of Nov. 3 sale.		

Assets = Liabilities + Equity
−800   −800

If the merchandise returned to Z-Mart is not defective and can be resold to another customer, Z-Mart returns these goods to its inventory. The entry to restore the cost of such goods to the Merchandise Inventory account is

Nov. 6	Merchandise Inventory	600	
	Cost of Goods Sold		600
	Returned goods added to inventory.		

Assets = Liabilities + Equity
+600   +600

This entry changes if the goods returned are defective. In this case the returned inventory is recorded at its estimated value, not its cost. To illustrate, if the goods (costing $600) returned to Z-Mart are defective and estimated to be worth $150, the following entry is made: Dr. Merchandise Inventory for $150, Dr. Loss from Defective Merchandise for $450, and Cr. Cost of Goods Sold for $600.

Decision Insight

Return to Sender Book merchandisers such as **Barnes & Noble**, **Borders Books**, **Books-A-Million**, and **Waldenbooks** can return unsold books to publishers at purchase price. Publishers say returns of new hardcover books run between 35% and 50%. ■

Sales Allowances   To illustrate sales allowances, assume that $800 of the merchandise Z-Mart sold on November 3 is defective but the buyer decides to keep it because Z-Mart offers a $100 price reduction. Z-Mart records this allowance as follows:

Nov. 6	Sales Returns and Allowances	100	
	Accounts Receivable		100
	To record sales allowance on Nov. 3 sale.		

Assets = Liabilities + Equity
−100   −100

The seller usually prepares a credit memorandum to confirm a buyer's return or allowance. A seller's **credit memorandum** informs a buyer of the seller's credit to the buyer's Account Receivable (on the seller's books).

Point: The sender (maker) of a credit memorandum will *credit* the account of the receiver. The receiver of a credit memorandum will *debit* the sender's account.

Quick Check

Answers — p. 183

7. Why are sales discounts and sales returns and allowances recorded in contra revenue accounts instead of directly in the Sales account?

8. Under what conditions are two entries necessary to record a sales return?

9. When merchandise is sold on credit and the seller notifies the buyer of a price allowance, does the seller create and send a credit memorandum or a debit memorandum?

COMPLETING THE ACCOUNTING CYCLE

Exhibit 4.10 shows the flow of merchandising costs during a period and where these costs are reported at period-end. Specifically, beginning inventory plus the net cost of purchases is the merchandise available for sale. As inventory is sold, its cost is recorded in cost of goods sold on the income statement; what remains is ending inventory on the balance sheet. A period's ending inventory is the next period's beginning inventory.

EXHIBIT 4.10

Merchandising Cost Flow in the Accounting Cycle

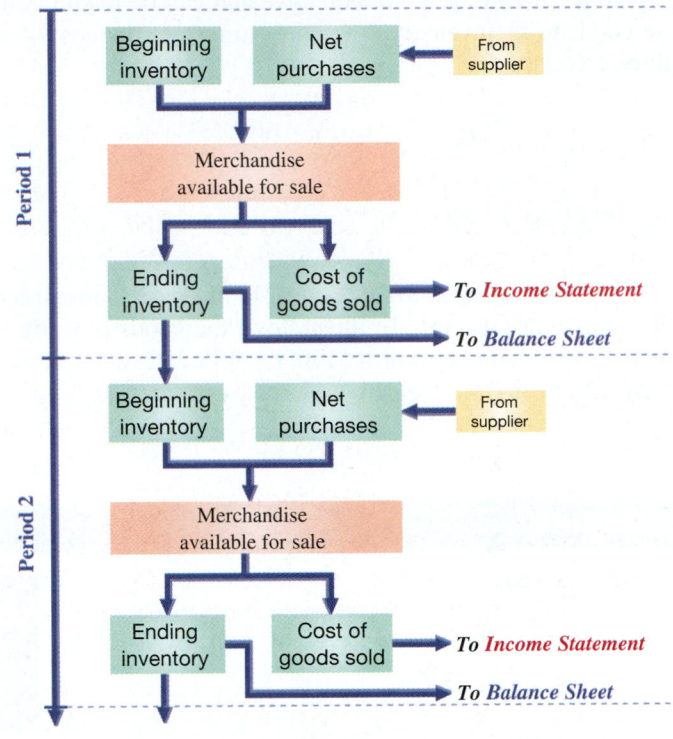

Adjusting Entries for Merchandisers

P3 Prepare adjustments and close accounts for a merchandising company.

Each of the steps in the accounting cycle described in the prior chapter for a service company applies to a merchandiser. This section and the next two further explain three steps of the accounting cycle for a merchandiser—adjustments, statement preparation, and closing.

Adjusting entries are generally the same for merchandising companies and service companies, including those for prepaid expenses (including depreciation), accrued expenses, unearned revenues, and accrued revenues. However, a merchandiser using a perpetual inventory system is usually required to make another adjustment to update the Merchandise Inventory account to reflect any loss of merchandise, including theft and deterioration. **Shrinkage** is the term used to refer to the loss of inventory and it is computed by comparing a physical count of inventory with recorded amounts. A physical count is usually performed at least once annually.

To illustrate, Z-Mart's Merchandise Inventory account at the end of year 2011 has a balance of $21,250, but a physical count reveals that only $21,000 of inventory exists. The adjusting entry to record this $250 shrinkage is

Point: About two-thirds of shoplifting losses are thefts by employees.

Assets = Liabilities + Equity
−250   −250

Dec. 31	Cost of Goods Sold	250	
	Merchandise Inventory		250
	To adjust for $250 shrinkage revealed by a physical count of inventory.		

Preparing Financial Statements

The financial statements of a merchandiser, and their preparation, are similar to those for a service company described in Chapters 2 and 3. The income statement mainly differs by the inclusion of *cost of goods sold* and *gross profit*. Also, net sales is affected by discounts, returns, and allowances, and some additional expenses are possible such as delivery expense and loss from defective merchandise. The balance sheet mainly differs by the inclusion of *merchandise inventory* as part of current assets. The statement of retained earnings is unchanged. A work sheet can be used to help prepare these statements, and one is illustrated in Appendix 4B for Z-Mart.

Point: Staples's costs of shipping merchandise to its stores is included in its costs of inventories as required by the cost principle.

Closing Entries for Merchandisers

Closing entries are similar for service companies and merchandising companies using a perpetual system. The difference is that we must close some new temporary accounts that arise from merchandising activities. Z-Mart has several temporary accounts unique to merchandisers: Sales (of goods), Sales Discounts, Sales Returns and Allowances, and Cost of Goods Sold. Their existence in the ledger means that the first two closing entries for a merchandiser are slightly different from the ones described in the prior chapter for a service company. These differences are set in **red boldface** in the closing entries of Exhibit 4.11.

Point: The Inventory account is not affected by the closing process under a perpetual system.

Step 1: Close Credit Balances in Temporary Accounts to Income Summary.

Dec. 31	**Sales**	**321,000**	
	Income Summary		321,000
	To close credit balances in temporary accounts.		

Step 2: Close Debit Balances in Temporary Accounts to Income Summary.

Dec. 31	Income Summary	308,100	
	Sales Discounts		**4,300**
	Sales Returns and Allowances		**2,000**
	Cost of Goods Sold		**230,400**
	Depreciation Expense		3,700
	Salaries Expense		43,800
	Insurance Expense		600
	Rent Expense		9,000
	Supplies Expense		3,000
	Advertising Expense		11,300
	To close debit balances in temporary accounts.		

Step 3: Close Income Summary to Retained Earnings.

The third closing entry is identical for a merchandising company and a service company. The $12,900 amount is net income reported on the income statement.

Dec. 31	Income Summary	12,900	
	Retained Earnings		12,900
	To close the Income Summary account.		

Step 4: Close Dividends Account to Retained Earnings.

The fourth closing entry is identical for a merchandising company and a service company. It closes the Dividends account and adjusts the Retained Earnings account to the amount shown on the balance sheet.

Dec. 31	Retained Earnings	4,000	
	Dividends		4,000
	To close the Dividends account.		

EXHIBIT 4.11

Closing Entries for a Merchandiser

Summary of Merchandising Entries

Exhibit 4.12 summarizes the key adjusting and closing entries of a merchandiser (using a perpetual inventory system) that are different from those of a service company described in prior chapters (the Demonstration Problem 2 illustrates these merchandising entries).

EXHIBIT 4.12

Summary of Merchandising Entries

Merchandising Transactions	Merchandising Entries	Dr.	Cr.
Purchases Purchasing merchandise for resale.	Merchandise Inventory	#	
	Cash or Accounts Payable		#
Paying freight costs on purchases; FOB shipping point.	Merchandise Inventory	#	
	Cash		#
Paying within discount period.	Accounts Payable	#	
	Merchandise Inventory		#
	Cash		#
Recording purchase returns or allowances.	Cash or Accounts Payable	#	
	Merchandise Inventory		#
Sales Selling merchandise.	Cash or Accounts Receivable	#	
	Sales		#
	Cost of Goods Sold	#	
	Merchandise Inventory		#
Receiving payment within discount period.	Cash	#	
	Sales Discounts	#	
	Accounts Receivable		#
Granting sales returns or allowances.	Sales Returns and Allowances	#	
	Cash or Accounts Receivable		#
	Merchandise Inventory	#	
	Cost of Goods Sold		#
Paying freight costs on sales; FOB destination.	Delivery Expense	#	
	Cash		#

Merchandising Events	Adjusting and Closing Entries		
Adjusting Adjusting due to shrinkage (occurs when recorded amount larger than physical inventory).	Cost of Goods Sold	#	
	Merchandise Inventory		#
Closing Closing temporary accounts with credit balances.	Sales	#	
	Income Summary		#
Closing temporary accounts with debit balances.	Income Summary	#	
	Sales Returns and Allowances		#
	Sales Discounts		#
	Cost of Goods Sold		#
	Delivery Expense		#
	"Other Expenses"		#

Quick Check   Answers — p. 183

10. When a merchandiser uses a perpetual inventory system, why is it sometimes necessary to adjust the Merchandise Inventory balance with an adjusting entry?

11. What temporary accounts do you expect to find in a merchandising business but not in a service business?

12. Describe the closing entries normally made by a merchandising company.

FINANCIAL STATEMENT FORMATS

P4 Define and prepare multiple-step and single-step income statements.

Generally accepted accounting principles do not require companies to use any one presentation format for financial statements so we see many different formats in practice. This section describes two common income statement formats: multiple-step and single-step. The classified balance sheet of a merchandiser is also explained.

Multiple-Step Income Statement

A **multiple-step income statement** format shows detailed computations of net sales and other costs and expenses, and reports subtotals for various classes of items. Exhibit 4.13 shows a multiple-step income statement for Z-Mart. The statement has three main parts: (1) *gross profit,* determined by net sales less cost of goods sold, (2) *income from operations,* determined by gross profit less operating expenses, and (3) *net income,* determined by income from operations adjusted for nonoperating items.

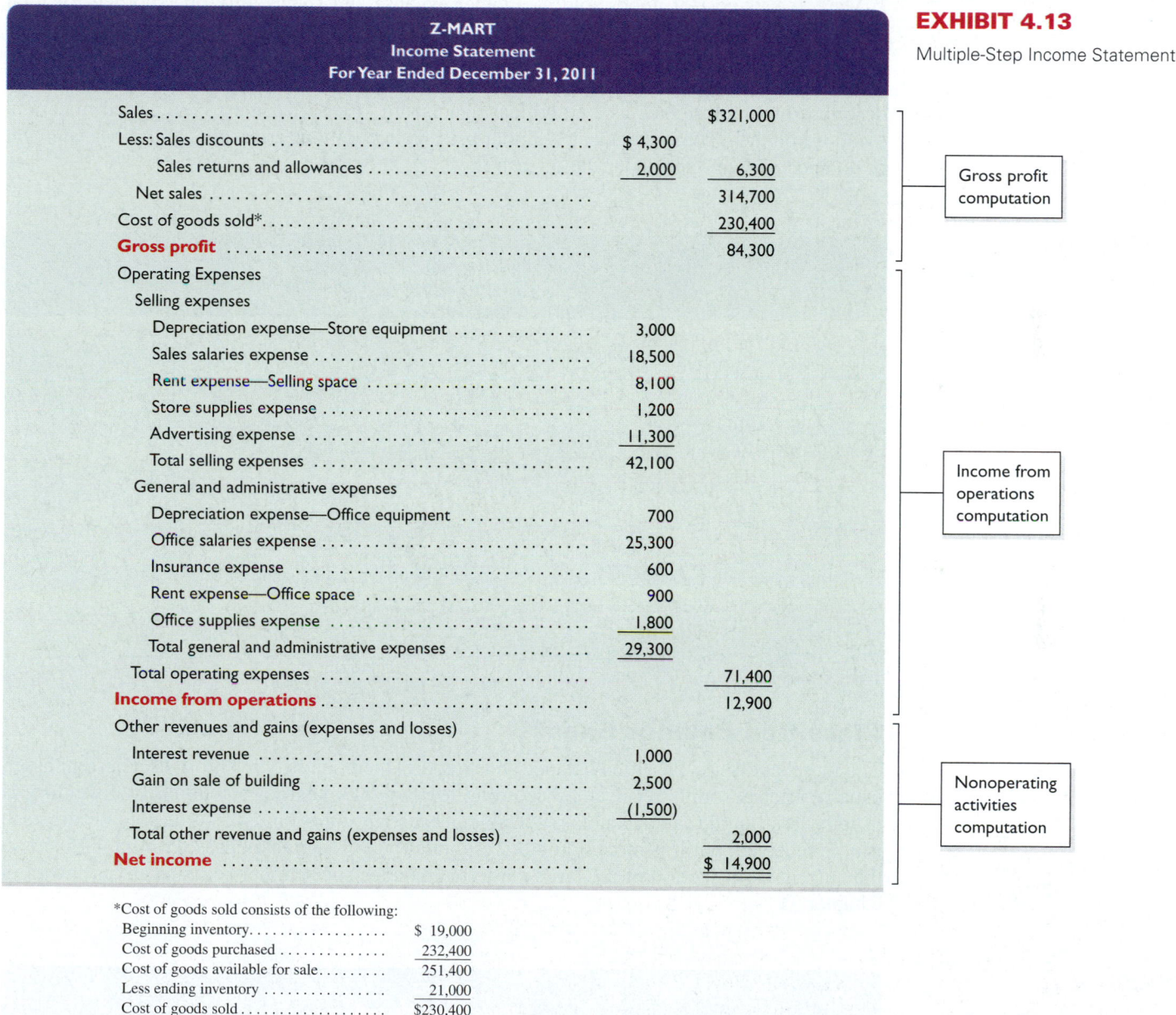

EXHIBIT 4.13

Multiple-Step Income Statement

Z-MART
Income Statement
For Year Ended December 31, 2011

Sales...		$321,000
Less: Sales discounts	$ 4,300	
Sales returns and allowances	2,000	6,300
Net sales		314,700
Cost of goods sold*................................		230,400
Gross profit		84,300
Operating Expenses		
Selling expenses		
Depreciation expense—Store equipment	3,000	
Sales salaries expense	18,500	
Rent expense—Selling space	8,100	
Store supplies expense	1,200	
Advertising expense	11,300	
Total selling expenses	42,100	
General and administrative expenses		
Depreciation expense—Office equipment	700	
Office salaries expense	25,300	
Insurance expense	600	
Rent expense—Office space	900	
Office supplies expense	1,800	
Total general and administrative expenses	29,300	
Total operating expenses		71,400
Income from operations		12,900
Other revenues and gains (expenses and losses)		
Interest revenue	1,000	
Gain on sale of building	2,500	
Interest expense	(1,500)	
Total other revenue and gains (expenses and losses)		2,000
Net income		$ 14,900

*Cost of goods sold consists of the following:

Beginning inventory...................	$ 19,000
Cost of goods purchased	232,400
Cost of goods available for sale.........	251,400
Less ending inventory	21,000
Cost of goods sold...................	$230,400

Gross profit computation

Income from operations computation

Nonoperating activities computation

Operating expenses are classified into two sections. **Selling expenses** include the expenses of promoting sales by displaying and advertising merchandise, making sales, and delivering goods to customers. **General and administrative expenses** support a company's overall operations and include expenses related to accounting, human resource management, and financial management. Expenses are allocated between sections when they contribute to more than one. Z-Mart allocates rent expense of $9,000 from its store building between two sections: $8,100 to selling expense and $900 to general and administrative expense.

Nonoperating activities consist of other expenses, revenues, losses, and gains that are unrelated to a company's operations. *Other revenues and gains* commonly include interest revenue,

Point: Z-Mart did not have any nonoperating activities; however, Exhibit 4.13 includes some for illustrative purposes.

dividend revenue, rent revenue, and gains from asset disposals. *Other expenses and losses* commonly include interest expense, losses from asset disposals, and casualty losses. When a company has no reportable nonoperating activities, its income from operations is simply labeled net income.

Single-Step Income Statement

Point: Many companies report interest expense and interest revenue in separate categories after operating income and before subtracting income tax expense. As one example, see **Palm**'s income statement in Appendix A.

A **single-step income statement** is another widely used format and is shown in Exhibit 4.14 for Z-Mart. It lists cost of goods sold as another expense and shows only one subtotal for total expenses. Expenses are grouped into very few, if any, categories. Many companies use formats that combine features of both the single- and multiple-step statements. Provided that income statement items are shown sensibly, management can choose the format. (In later chapters, we describe some items, such as extraordinary gains and losses, that must be reported in certain locations on the income statement.) Similar presentation options are available for the statement of retained earnings and statement of cash flows.

EXHIBIT 4.14

Single-Step Income Statement

Z-MART		
Income Statement		
For Year Ended December 31, 2011		
Revenues		
Net sales		$314,700
Interest revenue		1,000
Gain on sale of building		2,500
Total revenues		318,200
Expenses		
Cost of goods sold	$230,400	
Selling expenses	42,100	
General and administrative expenses	29,300	
Interest expense	1,500	
Total expenses.		303,300
Net income		$ 14,900

Classified Balance Sheet

The merchandiser's classified balance sheet reports merchandise inventory as a current asset, usually after accounts receivable according to an asset's nearness to liquidity. Inventory is usually less liquid than accounts receivable because inventory must first be sold before cash can be received; but it is more liquid than supplies and prepaid expenses. Exhibit 4.15 shows the current asset section of Z-Mart's classified balance sheet (other sections are as shown in Chapter 3).

EXHIBIT 4.15

Classified Balance Sheet (partial) of a Merchandiser

Z-MART	
Balance Sheet (partial)	
December 31, 2011	
Current assets	
Cash	$ 8,200
Accounts receivable	11,200
Merchandise inventory	**21,000**
Office supplies	550
Store supplies	250
Prepaid insurance	300
Total current assets	$ 41,500

Decision Insight

Merchandising Shenanigans Accurate invoices are important to both sellers and buyers. Merchandisers rely on invoices to make certain they receive all monies for products provided—no more, no less. To achieve this, controls are set up. Still, failures arise. A survey reports that 9% of employees in sales and marketing witnessed false or misleading invoices sent to customers. Another 14% observed employees violating contract terms with customers (KPMG 2009). ∎

GLOBAL VIEW

This section discusses similarities and differences between U.S. GAAP and IFRS in accounting and reporting for merchandise purchases and sales, and for the income statement.

Accounting for Merchandise Purchases and Sales Both U.S. GAAP and IFRS include broad and similar guidance for the accounting of merchandise purchases and sales. Specifically, all of the transactions presented and illustrated in this chapter are accounted for identically under the two systems. The closing process for merchandisers also is identical for U.S. GAAP and IFRS. In the next chapter we describe how inventory valuation can, in some cases, be different for the two systems.

Income Statement Presentation We explained that net income, profit, and earnings refer to the same (*bottom line*) item. However, IFRS tends to use the term *profit* more than any other term, whereas U.S. statements tend to use *net income* more than any other term. Both U.S. GAAP and IFRS income statements begin with the net sales or net revenues (*top line*) item. For merchandisers and manufacturers, this is followed by cost of goods sold. The presentation is similar for the remaining items with the following differences.

- U.S. GAAP offers little guidance about the presentation or order of expenses. IFRS requires separate disclosures for financing costs (interest expense), income tax expense, and some other special items.
- Both systems require separate disclosure of items when their size, nature, or frequency are important for proper interpretation.
- IFRS permits expenses to be presented by their function or their nature. U.S. GAAP provides no direction but the SEC requires presentation by function.
- Neither U.S. GAAP nor IFRS define *operating* income; this means classification of expenses into operating or nonoperating reflects considerable management discretion.
- IFRS permits alternative measures of income on the income statement; U.S. GAAP prohibits disclosure of alternative income measures in financial statements.

Nokia provides the following example of income statement reporting.   **NOKIA**

NOKIA	
Income Statement (in Euros million)	
For Year Ended December 31, 2009	
Net sales	40,984
Cost of sales	27,720
Gross profit	13,264
Research and development expenses	5,909
Selling and marketing expenses	3,933
Administrative and general expenses	1,145
Other income and expenses	1,080
Operating profit	1,197
Financial income and expenses (and other)	235
Profit before tax	962
Tax	702
Profit	260

Balance Sheet Presentation Chapters 2 and 3 explained how both U.S. GAAP and IFRS require current items to be separated from noncurrent items on the balance sheet (yielding a *classified balance sheet*). As discussed, U.S. GAAP balance sheets report current items first. Assets are listed from most liquid to least liquid, whereas liabilities are listed from nearest to maturity to furthest from maturity. IFRS balance sheets normally present noncurrent items first (and equity before liabilities), but this is *not* a requirement. Nokia provides an example of IFRS reporting for the balance sheet in Appendix A.

Decision Analysis    Acid-Test and Gross Margin Ratios

Acid-Test Ratio

A1 Compute the acid-test ratio and explain its use to assess liquidity.

For many merchandisers, inventory makes up a large portion of current assets. Inventory must be sold and any resulting accounts receivable must be collected before cash is available. Chapter 3 explained that the current ratio, defined as current assets divided by current liabilities, is useful in assessing a company's ability to pay current liabilities. Because it is sometimes unreasonable to assume that inventories are a source of payment for current liabilities, we look to other measures.

   One measure of a merchandiser's ability to pay its current liabilities (referred to as its *liquidity*) is the acid-test ratio. It differs from the current ratio by excluding less liquid current assets such as inventory and prepaid expenses that take longer to be converted to cash. The **acid-test ratio,** also called *quick ratio,* is defined as *quick assets* (cash, short-term investments, and current receivables) divided by current liabilities—see Exhibit 4.16.

EXHIBIT 4.16

Acid-Test (Quick) Ratio

$$\text{Acid-test ratio} = \frac{\text{Cash and cash equivalents} + \text{Short-term investments} + \text{Current receivables}}{\text{Current liabilities}}$$

   Exhibit 4.17 shows both the acid-test and current ratios of retailer **JCPenney** for fiscal years 2007 through 2010—also see margin graph. JCPenney's acid-test ratio reveals a general increase from 2007 through 2010 that exceeds the industry average. Further, JCPenney's current ratio (never less than 1.90) suggests that its short-term obligations can be confidently covered with short-term assets.

EXHIBIT 4.17

JCPenney's Acid-Test and Current Ratios

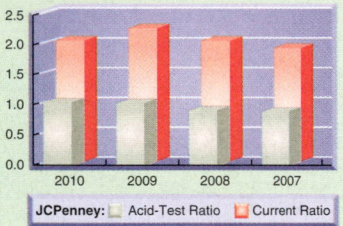

JCPenney: ☐ Acid-Test Ratio ☐ Current Ratio

($ millions)	2010	2009	2008	2007
Total quick assets	$3,406	$2,704	$2,845	$2,901
Total current assets	$6,652	$6,220	$6,751	$6,648
Total current liabilities	$3,249	$2,794	$3,338	$3,492
Acid-test ratio	**1.05**	**0.97**	**0.85**	**0.83**
Current ratio	**2.05**	**2.23**	**2.02**	**1.90**
Industry acid-test ratio	0.59	0.63	0.62	0.58
Industry current ratio	2.15	2.31	2.39	2.43

   An acid-test ratio less than 1.0 means that current liabilities exceed quick assets. A rule of thumb is that the acid-test ratio should have a value near, or higher than, 1.0 to conclude that a company is unlikely to face near-term liquidity problems. A value much less than 1.0 raises liquidity concerns unless a company can generate enough cash from inventory sales or if much of its liabilities are not due until late in the next period. Similarly, a value slightly larger than 1.0 can hide a liquidity problem if payables are due shortly and receivables are not collected until late in the next period. Analysis of JCPenney shows no need for concern regarding its liquidity even though its acid-test ratio is less than one. This is because retailers such as JCPenney pay many current liabilities from inventory sales. Further, in all years, JCPenney's acid-test ratios exceed the industry norm (and its inventory is fairly liquid).

Point: Successful use of a just-in-time inventory system can narrow the gap between the acid-test ratio and the current ratio.

☐ Decision Maker   Answer — p. 182

Supplier   A retailer requests to purchase supplies on credit from your company. You have no prior experience with this retailer. The retailer's current ratio is 2.1, its acid-test ratio is 0.5, and inventory makes up most of its current assets. Do you extend credit? ■

Gross Margin Ratio

A2 Compute the gross margin ratio and explain its use to assess profitability.

The cost of goods sold makes up much of a merchandiser's expenses. Without sufficient gross profit, a merchandiser will likely fail. Users often compute the gross margin ratio to help understand this relation. It differs from the profit margin ratio in that it excludes all costs except cost of goods sold. The **gross margin ratio** (also called *gross profit ratio*) is defined as *gross margin* (net sales minus cost of goods sold) divided by net sales—see Exhibit 4.18.

EXHIBIT 4.18

Gross Margin Ratio

$$\text{Gross margin ratio} = \frac{\text{Net sales} - \text{Cost of goods sold}}{\text{Net sales}}$$

Exhibit 4.19 shows the gross margin ratio of **JCPenney** for fiscal years 2007 through 2010. For JCPenney, each $1 of sales in 2010 yielded about 39.4¢ in gross margin to cover all other expenses and still produce a net income. This 39.4¢ margin is up from 39.3¢ in 2007. This slight increase is a favorable development. Success for merchandisers such as JCPenney depends on adequate gross margin. For example, the 0.1¢ increase in the gross margin ratio, computed as 39.4¢ − 39.3¢, means that JCPenney has $17.6 million more in gross margin! (This is computed as net sales of $17,556 million multiplied by the 0.1% increase in gross margin.) Management's discussion in its annual report attributes this improvement to its "strategy to sell a greater portion of merchandise at regular promotional prices and less at clearance prices."

Point: The power of a ratio is often its ability to identify areas for more detailed analysis.

($ millions)	2010	2009	2008	2007
Gross margin	$ 6,910	$ 6,915	$ 7,671	$ 7,825
Net sales	$17,556	$18,486	$19,860	$19,903
Gross margin ratio	39.4%	37.4%	38.6%	39.3%

EXHIBIT 4.19
JCPenney's Gross Margin Ratio

Decision Maker   Answer — p. 183

Financial Officer   Your company has a 36% gross margin ratio and a 17% net profit margin ratio. Industry averages are 44% for gross margin and 16% for net profit margin. Do these comparative results concern you? ■

DEMONSTRATION PROBLEM 1

Use the following adjusted trial balance and additional information to complete the requirements.

KC ANTIQUES Adjusted Trial Balance December 31, 2011	Debit	Credit
Cash	$ 7,000	
Accounts receivable	13,000	
Merchandise inventory	60,000	
Store supplies	1,500	
Equipment	45,600	
Accumulated depreciation—Equipment		$ 16,600
Accounts payable		9,000
Salaries payable		2,000
Common stock		20,000
Retained earnings		59,000
Dividends	10,000	
Sales		343,250
Sales discounts	5,000	
Sales returns and allowances	6,000	
Cost of goods sold	159,900	
Depreciation expense—Store equipment	4,100	
Depreciation expense—Office equipment	1,600	
Sales salaries expense	30,000	
Office salaries expense	34,000	
Insurance expense	11,000	
Rent expense (70% is store, 30% is office)	24,000	
Store supplies expense	5,750	
Advertising expense	31,400	
Totals	$449,850	$449,850

KC Antiques' *supplementary records* for 2011 reveal the following itemized costs for merchandising activities:

Invoice cost of merchandise purchases	$150,000
Purchase discounts received	2,500
Purchase returns and allowances	2,700
Cost of transportation-in	5,000

Required

1. Use the supplementary records to compute the total cost of merchandise purchases for 2011.
2. Prepare a 2011 multiple-step income statement. (Inventory at December 31, 2010, is $70,100.)
3. Prepare a single-step income statement for 2011.
4. Prepare closing entries for KC Antiques at December 31, 2011.
5. Compute the acid-test ratio and the gross margin ratio. Explain the meaning of each ratio and interpret them for KC Antiques.

PLANNING THE SOLUTION

- Compute the total cost of merchandise purchases for 2011.
- To prepare the multiple-step statement, first compute net sales. Then, to compute cost of goods sold, add the net cost of merchandise purchases for the year to beginning inventory and subtract the cost of ending inventory. Subtract cost of goods sold from net sales to get gross profit. Then classify expenses as selling expenses or general and administrative expenses.
- To prepare the single-step income statement, begin with net sales. Then list and subtract the expenses.
- The first closing entry debits all temporary accounts with credit balances and opens the Income Summary account. The second closing entry credits all temporary accounts with debit balances. The third entry closes the Income Summary account to the retained earnings account, and the fourth entry closes the dividends account to the retained earnings account.
- Identify the quick assets on the adjusted trial balance. Compute the acid-test ratio by dividing quick assets by current liabilities. Compute the gross margin ratio by dividing gross profit by net sales.

SOLUTION TO DEMONSTRATION PROBLEM 1

1.

Invoice cost of merchandise purchases	$150,000
Less: Purchases discounts received	2,500
Purchase returns and allowances	2,700
Add: Cost of transportation-in	5,000
Total cost of merchandise purchases	$149,800

2. Multiple-step income statement

KC ANTIQUES		
Income Statement		
For Year Ended December 31, 2011		
Sales		$343,250
Less: Sales discounts	$ 5,000	
Sales returns and allowances	6,000	11,000
Net sales		332,250
Cost of goods sold*		159,900
Gross profit		172,350
Expenses		
Selling expenses		
Depreciation expense—Store equipment	4,100	
Sales salaries expense	30,000	
Rent expense—Selling space	16,800	
Store supplies expense	5,750	
Advertising expense	31,400	
Total selling expenses	88,050	

[continued on next page]

[continued from previous page]

General and administrative expenses

Depreciation expense—Office equipment	1,600	
Office salaries expense	34,000	
Insurance expense	11,000	
Rent expense—Office space	7,200	
Total general and administrative expenses	53,800	
Total operating expenses		141,850
Net income		$ 30,500

* Cost of goods sold can also be directly computed (applying concepts from Exhibit 4.4):

Merchandise inventory, December 31, 2010	$ 70,100
Total cost of merchandise purchases (from part 1)	149,800
Goods available for sale	219,900
Merchandise inventory, December 31, 2011	60,000
Cost of goods sold	$159,900

3. Single-step income statement

KC ANTIQUES
Income Statement
For Year Ended December 31, 2011

Net sales		$332,250
Expenses		
Cost of goods sold	$159,900	
Selling expenses	88,050	
General and administrative expenses	53,800	
Total expenses		301,750
Net income		$ 30,500

4.

Dec. 31	Sales	343,250	
	Income Summary		343,250
	To close credit balances in temporary accounts.		
Dec. 31	Income Summary	312,750	
	Sales Discounts		5,000
	Sales Returns and Allowances		6,000
	Cost of Goods Sold		159,900
	Depreciation Expense—Store Equipment		4,100
	Depreciation Expense—Office Equipment		1,600
	Sales Salaries Expense		30,000
	Office Salaries Expense		34,000
	Insurance Expense		11,000
	Rent Expense		24,000
	Store Supplies Expense		5,750
	Advertising Expense		31,400
	To close debit balances in temporary accounts.		
Dec. 31	Income Summary	30,500	
	Retained Earnings		30,500
	To close the Income Summary account.		
Dec. 31	Retained Earnings	10,000	
	Dividends		10,000
	To close the Dividends account.		

5. Acid-test ratio = (Cash and equivalents + Short-term investments + Current receivables)/ Current liabilities

= (Cash + Accounts receivable/(Accounts payable + Salaries payable)

= ($7,000 + $13,000)/($9,000 + $2,000) = $20,000/$11,000 = 1.82

Gross margin ratio = Gross profit/Net sales = $172,350/$332,250 = 0.52 (or 52%)

KC Antiques has a healthy acid-test ratio of 1.82. This means it has more than $1.80 in liquid assets to satisfy each $1.00 in current liabilities. The gross margin of 0.52 shows that KC Antiques spends 48¢ ($1.00 − $0.52) of every dollar of net sales on the costs of acquiring the merchandise it sells. This leaves 52¢ of every dollar of net sales to cover other expenses incurred in the business and to provide a net profit.

DEMONSTRATION PROBLEM 2

Prepare journal entries to record the following merchandising transactions for both the seller (BMX) and buyer (Sanuk).

May 4   BMX sold $1,500 of merchandise on account to Sanuk, terms FOB shipping point, n/45, invoice dated May 4. The cost of the merchandise was $900.

May 6   Sanuk paid transportation charges of $30 on the May 4 purchase from BMX.

May 8   BMX sold $1,000 of merchandise on account to Sanuk, terms FOB destination, n/30, invoice dated May 8. The cost of the merchandise was $700.

May 10   BMX paid transportation costs of $50 for delivery of merchandise sold to Sanuk on May 8.

May 16   BMX issued Sanuk a $200 credit memorandum for merchandise returned. The merchandise was purchased by Sanuk on account on May 8. The cost of the merchandise returned was $140.

May 18   BMX received payment from Sanuk for purchase of May 8.

May 21   BMX sold $2,400 of merchandise on account to Sanuk, terms FOB shipping point, 2/10, n/EOM. BMX prepaid transportation costs of $100, which were added to the invoice. The cost of the merchandise was $1,440.

May 31   BMX received payment from Sanuk for purchase of May 21, less discount (2% × $2,400).

SOLUTION TO DEMONSTRATION PROBLEM 2

	BMX (Seller)				Sanuk (Buyer)		
May 4	Accounts Receivable—Sanuk	1,500			Merchandise Inventory	1,500	
	Sales		1,500		Accounts Payable—BMX		1,500
	Cost of Goods Sold	900					
	Merchandise Inventory		900				
6	No entry.				Merchandise Inventory	30	
					Cash		30
8	Accounts Receivable—Sanuk	1,000			Merchandise Inventory	1,000	
	Sales		1,000		Accounts Payable—BMX		1,000
	Cost of Goods Sold	700					
	Merchandise Inventory		700				
10	Delivery Expense	50			No entry.		
	Cash		50				
16	Sales Returns & Allowances	200			Accounts Payable—BMX	200	
	Accounts Receivable—Sanuk		200		Merchandise Inventory		200
	Merchandise Inventory	140					
	Cost of Goods Sold		140				
18	Cash	800			Accounts Payable—BMX	800	
	Accounts Receivable—Sanuk		800		Cash		800
21	Accounts Receivable—Sanuk	2,400			Merchandise Inventory	2,500	
	Sales		2,400		Accounts Payable—BMX		2,500
	Accounts Receivable—Sanuk	100					
	Cash		100				
	Cost of Goods Sold	1,440					
	Merchandise Inventory		1,440				
31	Cash	2,452			Accounts Payable—BMX	2,500	
	Sales Discounts	48			Merchandise Inventory		48
	Accounts Receivable—Sanuk		2,500		Cash		2,452

Periodic Inventory System

A periodic inventory system requires updating the inventory account only at the *end of a period* to reflect the quantity and cost of both the goods available and the goods sold. Thus, during the period, the Merchandise Inventory balance remains unchanged. It reflects the beginning inventory balance until it is updated at the end of the period. During the period the cost of merchandise is recorded in a temporary *Purchases* account. When a company sells merchandise, it records revenue **but not the cost of the goods sold.** At the end of the period when a company prepares financial statements, it takes a *physical count of inventory* by counting the quantities and costs of merchandise available. The cost of goods sold is then computed by subtracting the ending inventory amount from the cost of merchandise available for sale.

Recording Merchandise Transactions   Under a periodic system, purchases, purchase returns and allowances, purchase discounts, and transportation-in transactions are recorded in separate temporary accounts. At period-end, each of these temporary accounts is closed and the Merchandise Inventory account is updated. To illustrate, journal entries under the periodic inventory system are shown for the most common transactions (codes *a* through *f* link these transactions to those in the chapter, and we drop explanations for simplicity). For comparison, perpetual system journal entries are shown to the right of each periodic entry, where differences are in green font.

> **P5** Record and compare merchandising transactions using both periodic and perpetual inventory systems.

Purchases   The periodic system uses a temporary *Purchases* account that accumulates the cost of all purchase transactions during each period. Z-Mart's November 2 entry to record the purchase of merchandise for $1,200 on credit with terms of 2/10, n/30 is

(a)

Periodic		
Purchases	1,200	
Accounts Payable		1,200

Perpetual		
Merchandise Inventory	1,200	
Accounts Payable		1,200

Purchase Discounts   The periodic system uses a temporary *Purchase Discounts* account that accumulates discounts taken on purchase transactions during the period. If payment in (*a*) is delayed until after the discount period expires, the entry is to debit Accounts Payable and credit Cash for $1,200 each. However, if Z-Mart pays the supplier for the previous purchase in (*a*) within the discount period, the required payment is $1,176 ($1,200 × 98%) and is recorded as

(b)

Periodic		
Accounts Payable	1,200	
Purchase Discounts		24
Cash		1,176

Perpetual		
Accounts Payable	1,200	
Merchandise Inventory		24
Cash		1,176

Purchase Returns and Allowances   Z-Mart returned merchandise purchased on November 2 because of defects. In the periodic system, the temporary *Purchase Returns and Allowances* account accumulates the cost of all returns and allowances during a period. The recorded cost (including discounts) of the defective merchandise is $300, and Z-Mart records the November 15 return with this entry:

(c)

Periodic		
Accounts Payable	300	
Purchase Returns		
and Allowances		300

Perpetual		
Accounts Payable	300	
Merchandise Inventory		300

Transportation-In   Z-Mart paid a $75 freight charge to transport merchandise to its store. In the periodic system, this cost is charged to a temporary *Transportation-In* account.

(d)

Periodic			Perpetual		
Transportation-In	75		Merchandise Inventory	75	
Cash		75	Cash		75

Sales   Under the periodic system, the cost of goods sold is *not* recorded at the time of each sale. (We later show how to compute total cost of goods sold at the end of a period.) Z-Mart's November 3 entry to record sales of $2,400 in merchandise on credit (when its cost is $1,600) is:

(e)

Periodic			Perpetual		
Accounts Receivable	2,400		Accounts Receivable	2,400	
Sales		2,400	Sales		2,400
			Cost of Goods Sold	1,600	
			Merchandise Inventory		1,600

Sales Returns   A customer returned part of the merchandise from the transaction in (*e*), where the returned items sell for $800 and cost $600. (*Recall:* The periodic system records only the revenue effect, not the cost effect, for sales transactions.) Z-Mart restores the merchandise to inventory and records the November 6 return as

(f)

Periodic			Perpetual		
Sales Returns and			Sales Returns and		
Allowances	800		Allowances	800	
Accounts Receivable . . .		800	Accounts Receivable		800
			Merchandise Inventory	600	
			Cost of Goods Sold		600

Sales Discounts   To illustrate sales discounts, assume that the remaining $1,600 of receivables (computed as $2,400 from *e* less $800 for *f*) has credit terms of 3/10, n/90 and that customers all pay within the discount period. Z-Mart records this payment as

Periodic			Perpetual		
Cash	1,552		Cash	1,552	
Sales Discounts ($1,600 × .03)	48		Sales Discounts ($1,600 × .03) . . .	48	
Accounts Receivable . . .		1,600	Accounts Receivable		1,600

Adjusting and Closing Entries   The periodic and perpetual inventory systems have slight differences in adjusting and closing entries. The period-end Merchandise Inventory balance (unadjusted) is $19,000 under the periodic system and $21,250 under the perpetual system. Since the periodic system does not update the Merchandise Inventory balance during the period, the $19,000 amount is the beginning inventory. However, the $21,250 balance under the perpetual system is the recorded ending inventory before adjusting for any inventory shrinkage.

A physical count of inventory taken at the end of the period reveals $21,000 of merchandise available. The adjusting and closing entries for the two systems are shown in Exhibit 4A.1. The periodic system records the ending inventory of $21,000 in the Merchandise Inventory account (which includes

EXHIBIT 4A.1

Comparison of Adjusting and Closing Entries—Periodic and Perpetual

PERIODIC			PERPETUAL		
Adjusting Entry—Shrinkage			**Adjusting Entry—Shrinkage**		
None			Cost of Goods Sold	250	
			Merchandise Inventory		250

[continued on next page]

[continued from previous page]

PERIODIC		
Closing Entries		
(1) Sales	321,000	
Merchandise Inventory	**21,000**	
Purchase Discounts	**4,200**	
Purchase Returns and Allowances	**1,500**	
Income Summary		347,700
(2) Income Summary	334,800	
Sales Discounts		4,300
Sales Returns and Allowances		2,000
Merchandise Inventory		**19,000**
Purchases		**235,800**
Transportation-In		**2,300**
Depreciation Expense		3,700
Salaries Expense		43,800
Insurance Expense		600
Rent Expense		9,000
Supplies Expense		3,000
Advertising Expense		11,300
(3) Income Summary	12,900	
Retained Earnings		12,900
(4) Retained Earnings	4,000	
Dividends		4,000

PERPETUAL		
Closing Entries		
(1) Sales	321,000	
Income Summary		321,000
(2) Income Summary	308,100	
Sales Discounts		4,300
Sales Returns and Allowances		2,000
Cost of Goods Sold		**230,400**
Depreciation Expense		3,700
Salaries Expense		43,800
Insurance Expense		600
Rent Expense		9,000
Supplies Expense		3,000
Advertising Expense		11,300
(3) Income Summary	12,900	
Retained Earnings		12,900
(4) Retained Earnings	4,000	
Dividends		4,000

shrinkage) in the first closing entry and removes the $19,000 beginning inventory balance from the account in the second closing entry.[2]

By updating Merchandise Inventory and closing Purchases, Purchase Discounts, Purchase Returns and Allowances, and Transportation-In, the periodic system transfers the cost of goods sold amount to Income Summary. Review the periodic side of Exhibit 4A.1 and notice that the **boldface** items affect Income Summary as follows.

Credit to Income Summary in the first closing entry includes amounts from:	
Merchandise inventory (ending)	$ 21,000
Purchase discounts	4,200
Purchase returns and allowances	1,500
Debit to Income Summary in the second closing entry includes amounts from:	
Merchandise inventory (beginning)	(19,000)
Purchases	(235,800)
Transportation-in	(2,300)
Net effect on Income Summary	**$(230,400)**

This $230,400 effect on Income Summary is the cost of goods sold amount. The periodic system transfers cost of goods sold to the Income Summary account but without using a Cost of Goods Sold account. Also, the periodic system does not separately measure shrinkage. Instead, it computes cost of goods available

---

[2] This approach is called the *closing entry method.* An alternative approach, referred to as the *adjusting entry method,* would not make any entries to Merchandise Inventory in the closing entries of Exhibit 4A.1, but instead would make two adjusting entries. Using Z-Mart data, the two adjusting entries would be: (1) Dr. Income Summary and Cr. Merchandise Inventory for $19,000 each, and (2) Dr. Merchandise Inventory and Cr. Income Summary for $21,000 each. The first entry removes the beginning balance of Merchandise Inventory, and the second entry records the actual ending balance.

for sale, subtracts the cost of ending inventory, and defines the difference as cost of goods sold, which includes shrinkage.

Preparing Financial Statements   The financial statements of a merchandiser using the periodic system are similar to those for a service company described in prior chapters. The income statement mainly differs by the inclusion of *cost of goods sold* and *gross profit*—of course, net sales is affected by discounts, returns, and allowances. The cost of goods sold section under the periodic system follows

Calculation of Cost of Goods Sold For Year Ended December 31, 2011	
Beginning inventory	$ 19,000
Cost of goods purchased	232,400
Cost of goods available for sale	251,400
Less ending inventory	21,000
Cost of goods sold	$230,400

The balance sheet mainly differs by the inclusion of *merchandise inventory* in current assets—see Exhibit 4.15. The statement of retained earnings is unchanged. A work sheet can be used to help prepare these statements. The only differences under the periodic system from the work sheet illustrated in Appendix 4B using the perpetual system are highlighted as follows in **blue boldface** font.

File Edit View Insert Format Tools Data Accounting Window Help

	No.	Account	Unadjusted Trial Balance Dr.	Cr.	Adjustments Dr.	Cr.	Adjusted Trial Balance Dr.	Cr.	Income Statement Dr.	Cr.	Balance Sheet Dr.	Cr.
3	101	Cash	8,200				8,200				8,200	
4	106	Accounts receivable	11,200				11,200				11,200	
5	119	**Merchandise Inventory**	19,000				19,000		19,000	21,000	21,000	
6	126	Supplies	3,800			(b) 3,000	800				800	
7	128	Prepaid insurance	900			(a) 600	300				300	
8	167	Equipment	34,200				34,200				34,200	
9	168	Accumulated depr.—Equip.		3,700		(c) 3,700		7,400				7,400
10	201	Accounts payable		16,000				16,000				16,000
11	209	Salaries payable				(d) 800		800				800
12	307	Common stock		10,000				10,000				10,000
13	318	Retained earnings		32,600				32,600				32,600
14	319	Dividends	4,000				4,000				4,000	
15	413	Sales		321,000				321,000		321,000		
16a	414	Sales returns and allowances	2,000				2,000		2,000			
16b	415	Sales discounts	4,300				4,300		4,300			
16c	505	**Purchases**	**235,800**				**235,800**		**235,800**			
16d	506	**Purchases returns & allowance**		**1,500**				**1,500**		**1,500**		
17	507	**Purchases discounts**		**4,200**				**4,200**		**4,200**		
18	508	**Transportation-in**	**2,300**				**2,300**		**2,300**			
19	612	Depreciation expense—Equip.			(c) 3,700		3,700		3,700			
20	622	Salaries expense	43,000		(d) 800		43,800		43,800			
21	637	Insurance expense			(a) 600		600		600			
22	640	Rent expense	9,000				9,000		9,000			
23	652	Supplies expense			(b) 3,000		3,000		3,000			
24	655	Advertising expense	11,300				11,300		11,300			
25		Totals	389,000	389,000	8,100	8,100	393,500	393,500	334,800	347,700	79,700	66,800
26		Net income							12,900			12,900
27		Totals							347,700	347,700	79,700	79,700

Sheet1   Sheet2   Sheet3

Quick Check

Answers — p. 183

13. What account is used (for journalizing entries) in a perpetual inventory system but not in a periodic system?

14. Which of the following accounts are temporary accounts under a periodic system? (*a*) Merchandise Inventory; (*b*) Purchases; (*c*) Transportation-In.

15. How is cost of goods sold computed under a periodic inventory system?

16. Do reported amounts of ending inventory and net income differ if the adjusting entry method of recording the change in inventory is used instead of the closing entry method?

APPENDIX

Work Sheet—Perpetual System

4B

Exhibit 4B.1 shows the work sheet for preparing financial statements of a merchandiser. It differs slightly from the work sheet layout in Chapter 3—the differences are in **red boldface**. Also, the adjustments in the work sheet reflect the following: (*a*) Expiration of $600 of prepaid insurance. (*b*) Use of $3,000 of supplies. (*c*) Depreciation of $3,700 for equipment. (*d*) Accrual of $800 of unpaid salaries. (*e*) Inventory shrinkage of $250. Once the adjusted amounts are extended into the financial statement columns, the information is used to develop financial statements.

EXHIBIT 4B.1

Work Sheet for Merchandiser (using a perpetual system)

No.	Account	Unadjusted Trial Balance Dr.	Cr.	Adjustments Dr.	Cr.	Adjusted Trial Balance Dr.	Cr.	Income Statement Dr.	Cr.	Balance Sheet Dr.	Cr.
101	Cash	8,200				8,200				8,200	
106	Accounts receivable	11,200				11,200				11,200	
119	**Merchandise Inventory**	**21,250**			(e) 250	21,000				**21,000**	
126	Supplies	3,800			(b) 3,000	800				800	
128	Prepaid insurance	900			(a) 600	300				300	
167	Equipment	34,200				34,200				34,200	
168	Accumulated depr.—Equip.		3,700		(c) 3,700		7,400				7,400
201	Accounts payable		16,000				16,000				16,000
209	Salaries payable				(d) 800		800				800
307	Common stock		10,000				10,000				10,000
318	Retained earnings		32,600				32,600				32,600
319	Dividends	4,000				4,000				4,000	
413	**Sales**		**321,000**				321,000		321,000		
414	**Sales returns and allowances**	**2,000**				2,000		2,000			
415	**Sales discounts**	**4,300**				4,300		4,300			
502	**Cost of goods sold**	**230,150**		(e) 250		230,400		230,400			
612	Depreciation expense—Equip.			(c) 3,700		3,700		3,700			
622	Salaries expense	43,000		(d) 800		43,800		43,800			
637	Insurance expense			(a) 600		600		600			
640	Rent expense	9,000				9,000		9,000			
652	Supplies expense			(b) 3,000		3,000		3,000			
655	Advertising expense	11,300				11,300		11,300			
	Totals	383,300	383,300	8,350	8,350	387,800	387,800	308,100	321,000	79,700	66,800
	Net income							12,900			12,900
	Totals							321,000	321,000	79,700	79,700

Summary

C1 **Describe merchandising activities and identify income components for a merchandising company.** Merchandisers buy products and resell them. Examples of merchandisers include Walmart, Home Depot, The Limited, and Barnes & Noble. A merchandiser's costs on the income statement include an amount for cost of goods sold. Gross profit, or gross margin, equals sales minus cost of goods sold.

C2 **Identify and explain the inventory asset and cost flows of a merchandising company.** The current asset section of a merchandising company's balance sheet includes *merchandise inventory,* which refers to the products a merchandiser sells and are available for sale at the balance sheet date. Cost of merchandise purchases flows into Merchandise Inventory and from there to Cost of Goods Sold on the income statement. Any remaining inventory is reported as a current asset on the balance sheet.

A1 **Compute the acid-test ratio and explain its use to assess liquidity.** The acid-test ratio is computed as quick assets (cash, short-term investments, and current receivables) divided by current liabilities. It indicates a company's ability to pay its current liabilities with its existing quick assets. An acid-test ratio equal to or greater than 1.0 is often adequate.

A2 **Compute the gross margin ratio and explain its use to assess profitability.** The gross margin ratio is computed as gross margin (net sales minus cost of goods sold) divided by net sales. It indicates a company's profitability before considering other expenses.

P1 **Analyze and record transactions for merchandise purchases using a perpetual system.** For a perpetual inventory system, purchases of inventory (net of trade discounts) are added to the Merchandise Inventory account. Purchase discounts and purchase returns and allowances are subtracted from Merchandise Inventory, and transportation-in costs are added to Merchandise Inventory.

P2 **Analyze and record transactions for merchandise sales using a perpetual system.** A merchandiser records sales at list price less any trade discounts. The cost of items sold is transferred from Merchandise Inventory to Cost of Goods Sold. Refunds or credits given to customers for unsatisfactory merchandise are recorded in Sales Returns and Allowances, a contra account to Sales. If merchandise is returned and restored to inventory, the cost of this merchandise is removed from Cost of Goods Sold and transferred back to Merchandise Inventory. When cash discounts from the sales price are offered and customers pay within the discount period, the seller records Sales Discounts, a contra account to Sales.

P3 **Prepare adjustments and close accounts for a merchandising company.** With a perpetual system, it is often necessary to make an adjustment for inventory shrinkage. This is computed by comparing a physical count of inventory with the Merchandise Inventory balance. Shrinkage is normally charged to Cost of Goods Sold. Temporary accounts closed to Income Summary for a merchandiser include Sales, Sales Discounts, Sales Returns and Allowances, and Cost of Goods Sold.

P4 **Define and prepare multiple-step and single-step income statements.** Multiple-step income statements include greater detail for sales and expenses than do single-step income statements. They also show details of net sales and report expenses in categories reflecting different activities.

P5^A **Record and compare merchandising transactions using both periodic and perpetual inventory systems.** A perpetual inventory system continuously tracks the cost of goods available for sale and the cost of goods sold. A periodic system accumulates the cost of goods purchased during the period and does not compute the amount of inventory or the cost of goods sold until the end of a period. Transactions involving the sale and purchase of merchandise are recorded and analyzed under both the periodic and perpetual inventory systems. Adjusting and closing entries for both inventory systems are illustrated and explained.

Guidance Answers to Decision Maker and Decision Ethics

Entrepreneur For terms of 3/10, n/90, missing the 3% discount for an additional 80 days equals an implied annual interest rate of 13.69%, computed as (365 days ÷ 80 days) × 3%. Since you can borrow funds at 11% (assuming no other processing costs), it is better to borrow and pay within the discount period. You save 2.69% (13.69% − 11%) in interest costs by paying early.

Credit Manager Your decision is whether to comply with prior policy or to create a new policy and not abuse discounts offered by suppliers. Your first step should be to meet with your superior to find out if the late payment policy is the actual policy and, if so, its rationale. If it is the policy to pay late, you must apply your own sense of ethics. One point of view is that the late payment policy is unethical. A deliberate plan to make late payments means the company lies when it pretends to make payment within the discount period. Another view is that the late payment policy is acceptable. In some markets, attempts to take discounts through late payments are accepted as a continued phase of "price negotiation." Also, your company's suppliers can respond by billing your company for the discounts not accepted because of late payments. However, this is a dubious viewpoint, especially since the prior manager proposes that you dishonestly explain late payments as computer or mail problems and since some suppliers have complained.

Supplier A current ratio of 2.1 suggests sufficient current assets to cover current liabilities. An acid-test ratio of 0.5 suggests, however, that quick assets can cover only about one-half of current liabilities. This implies that the retailer depends on money from sales of inventory to pay current liabilities. If sales of inventory decline or profit margins decrease, the likelihood that this retailer will default on its payments increases. Your decision is probably not to extend credit. If you do extend credit, you are likely to closely monitor the retailer's financial condition. (It is better to hold unsold inventory than uncollectible receivables.)

Financial Officer   Your company's net profit margin is about equal to the industry average and suggests typical industry performance. However, gross margin reveals that your company is paying far more in cost of goods sold or receiving far less in sales price than competitors. Your attention must be directed to finding the problem with cost of goods sold, sales, or both. One positive note is that your company's expenses make up 19% of sales (36% − 17%). This favorably compares with competitors' expenses that make up 28% of sales (44% − 16%).

Guidance Answers to Quick Checks

1. Cost of goods sold is the cost of merchandise purchased from a supplier that is sold to customers during a specific period.

2. Gross profit (or gross margin) is the difference between net sales and cost of goods sold.

3. Widespread use of computing and related technology has dramatically increased the use of the perpetual inventory system.

4. Under credit terms of 2/10, n/60, the credit period is 60 days and the discount period is 10 days.

5. (*b*) trade discount.

6. *FOB* means "free on board." It is used in identifying the point when ownership transfers from seller to buyer. *FOB destination* means that the seller transfers ownership of goods to the buyer when they arrive at the buyer's place of business. It also means that the seller is responsible for paying shipping charges and bears the risk of damage or loss during shipment.

7. Recording sales discounts and sales returns and allowances separately from sales gives useful information to managers for internal monitoring and decision making.

8. When a customer returns merchandise *and* the seller restores the merchandise to inventory, two entries are necessary. One entry records the decrease in revenue and credits the customer's account. The second entry debits inventory and reduces cost of goods sold.

9. Credit memorandum—seller credits accounts receivable from buyer.

10. Merchandise Inventory may need adjusting to reflect shrinkage.

11. Sales (of goods), Sales Discounts, Sales Returns and Allowances, and Cost of Goods Sold (and maybe Delivery Expense).

12. Four closing entries: (1) close credit balances in temporary accounts to Income Summary, (2) close debit balances in temporary accounts to Income Summary, (3) close Income Summary to retained earnings, and (4) close dividends account to retained earnings.

13. Cost of Goods Sold.

14. (*b*) Purchases and (*c*) Transportation-In.

15. Under a periodic inventory system, the cost of goods sold is determined at the end of an accounting period by adding the net cost of goods purchased to the beginning inventory and subtracting the ending inventory.

16. Both methods report the same ending inventory and income.

Key Terms   mhhe.com/wildFINMAN4e

Acid-test ratio (p. 172)
Cash discount (p. 159)
Cost of goods sold (p. 156)
Credit memorandum (p. 165)
Credit period (p. 159)
Credit terms (p. 159)
Debit memorandum (p. 160)
Discount period (p. 159)
EOM (p. 159)
FOB (p. 161)
General and administrative expenses (p. 169)

Gross margin (p. 157)
Gross margin ratio (p. 172)
Gross profit (p. 156)
Inventory (p. 157)
List price (p. 158)
Merchandise (p. 156)
Merchandise inventory (p. 157)
Merchandiser (p. 156)
Multiple-step income statement (p. 169)
Periodic inventory system (p. 158)
Perpetual inventory system (p. 158)

Purchase discount (p. 159)
Retailer (p. 156)
Sales discount (p. 159)
Selling expenses (p. 169)
Shrinkage (p. 166)
Single-step income statement (p. 170)
Supplementary records (p. 162)
Trade discount (p. 158)
Wholesaler (p. 156)

Multiple Choice Quiz   Answers on p. 201   mhhe.com/wildFINMAN4e

Additional Quiz Questions are available at the book's Website.

1. A company has $550,000 in net sales and $193,000 in gross profit. This means its cost of goods sold equals
    a. $743,000
    b. $550,000
    c. $357,000
    d. $193,000
    e. $(193,000)

2. A company purchased $4,500 of merchandise on May 1 with terms of 2/10, n/30. On May 6, it returned $250 of that merchandise. On May 8, it paid the balance owed for merchandise, taking any discount it is entitled to. The cash paid on May 8 is
   a. $4,500
   b. $4,250
   c. $4,160
   d. $4,165
   e. $4,410

3. A company has cash sales of $75,000, credit sales of $320,000, sales returns and allowances of $13,700, and sales discounts of $6,000. Its net sales equal
   a. $395,000
   b. $375,300
   c. $300,300
   d. $339,700
   e. $414,700

4. A company's quick assets are $37,500, its current assets are $80,000, and its current liabilities are $50,000. Its acid-test ratio equals
   a. 1.600
   b. 0.750
   c. 0.625
   d. 1.333
   e. 0.469

5. A company's net sales are $675,000, its costs of goods sold are $459,000, and its net income is $74,250. Its gross margin ratio equals
   a. 32%
   b. 68%
   c. 47%
   d. 11%
   e. 34%

A(B) *Superscript letter A (B) denotes assignments based on Appendix 4A (4B).*
🛈 Icon denotes assignments that involve decision making.

Discussion Questions

1. In comparing the accounts of a merchandising company with those of a service company, what additional accounts would the merchandising company likely use, assuming it employs a perpetual inventory system?

2. What items appear in financial statements of merchandising companies but not in the statements of service companies?

3. 🛈 Explain how a business can earn a positive gross profit on its sales and still have a net loss.

4. 🛈 Why do companies offer a cash discount?

5. How does a company that uses a perpetual inventory system determine the amount of inventory shrinkage?

6. Distinguish between cash discounts and trade discounts. Is the amount of a trade discount on purchased merchandise recorded in the accounts?

7. What is the difference between a sales discount and a purchase discount?

8. 🛈 Why would a company's manager be concerned about the quantity of its purchase returns if its suppliers allow unlimited returns?

9. Does the sender (maker) of a debit memorandum record a debit or a credit in the recipient's account? What entry (debit or credit) does the recipient record?

10. What is the difference between the single-step and multiple-step income statement formats?

11. 🛈 Refer to the balance sheet and income statement for **Research In Motion** in Appendix A. What **RIM** does the company title its inventory account? Does the company present a detailed calculation of its cost of sales?

12. Refer to **Nokia**'s income statement in Appendix A. What title does it use for cost of goods sold? **NOKIA**

13. Refer to the income statement for **Apple** in Appendix A. What does Apple title its cost of goods sold account? **Apple**

14. Refer to the income statement of **Palm** in Appendix A. Does its income statement report a gross profit figure? If yes, what is the amount? **Palm**

15. 🛈 Buyers negotiate purchase contracts with suppliers. What type of shipping terms should a buyer attempt to negotiate to minimize freight-in costs?

connect

QUICK STUDY

QS 4-1

Applying merchandising terms

C1

Enter the letter for each term in the blank space beside the definition that it most closely matches.

A. Cash discount
B. Credit period
C. Discount period
D. FOB destination

E. FOB shipping point
F. Gross profit
G. Merchandise inventory

H. Purchase discount
I. Sales discount
J. Trade discount

——— **1.** Ownership of goods is transferred when delivered to the buyer's place of business.
——— **2.** Time period in which a cash discount is available.
——— **3.** Difference between net sales and the cost of goods sold.
——— **4.** Reduction in a receivable or payable if it is paid within the discount period.
——— **5.** Purchaser's description of a cash discount received from a supplier of goods.
——— **6.** Ownership of goods is transferred when the seller delivers goods to the carrier.
——— **7.** Reduction below list or catalog price that is negotiated in setting the price of goods.
——— **8.** Seller's description of a cash discount granted to buyers in return for early payment.
——— **9.** Time period that can pass before a customer's payment is due.
——— **10.** Goods a company owns and expects to sell to its customers.

The cost of merchandise inventory includes which of the following:

a. Costs incurred to buy the goods.
b. Costs incurred to ship the goods to the store(s).
c. Costs incurred to make the goods ready for sale.
d. Both a and b.
e. a, b, and c.

QS 4-2
Identifying inventory costs
C2

Prepare journal entries to record each of the following purchases transactions of a merchandising company. Show supporting calculations and assume a perpetual inventory system.

Mar. 5   Purchased 500 units of product at a cost of $5 per unit. Terms of the sale are 2/10, n/60; the invoice is dated March 5.
Mar. 7   Returned 50 defective units from the March 5 purchase and received full credit.
Mar. 15   Paid the amount due from the March 5 purchase, less the return on March 7.

QS 4-3
Recording purchases— perpetual system
P1

Prepare journal entries to record each of the following sales transactions of a merchandising company. Show supporting calculations and assume a perpetual inventory system.

Apr. 1   Sold merchandise for $2,000, granting the customer terms of 2/10, EOM; invoice dated April 1. The cost of the merchandise is $1,400.
Apr. 4   The customer in the April 1 sale returned merchandise and received credit for $500. The merchandise, which had cost $350, is returned to inventory.
Apr. 11   Received payment for the amount due from the April 1 sale less the return on April 4.

QS 4-4
Recording sales— perpetual system
P2

Compute net sales, gross profit, and the gross margin ratio for each separate case *a* through *d*. Interpret the gross margin ratio for case *a*.

QS 4-5
Computing and analyzing gross margin
A2

	a	b	c	d
Sales	$130,000	$512,000	$35,700	$245,700
Sales discounts	4,200	16,500	400	3,500
Sales returns and allowances	17,000	5,000	5,000	700
Cost of goods sold	76,600	326,700	21,300	125,900

Nix'It Company's ledger on July 31, its fiscal year-end, includes the following selected accounts that have normal balances (Nix'It uses the perpetual inventory system).

QS 4-6
Accounting for shrinkage— perpetual system
P3

Merchandise inventory	$ 34,800	Sales returns and allowances	$ 3,500
Retained earnings	115,300	Cost of goods sold	102,000
Dividends	7,000	Depreciation expense	7,300
Sales	157,200	Salaries expense	29,500
Sales discounts	1,700	Miscellaneous expenses	2,000

A physical count of its July 31 year-end inventory discloses that the cost of the merchandise inventory still available is $32,900. Prepare the entry to record any inventory shrinkage.

QS 4-7
Closing entries   **P3**

Refer to QS 4-6 and prepare journal entries to close the balances in temporary revenue and expense accounts. Remember to consider the entry for shrinkage that is made to solve QS 4-6.

QS 4-8
Computing and interpreting acid-test ratio

A1

Use the following information on current assets and current liabilities to compute and interpret the acid-test ratio. Explain what the acid-test ratio of a company measures.

Cash	$1,200	Prepaid expenses	$ 600
Accounts receivable	2,700	Accounts payable	4,750
Inventory	5,000	Other current liabilities	950

QS 4-9
Contrasting liquidity ratios   **A1**

Identify similarities and differences between the acid-test ratio and the current ratio. Compare and describe how the two ratios reflect a company's ability to meet its current obligations.

QS 4-10
Multiple-step income statement

P4

The multiple-step income statement normally includes which of the following:
a. Detailed computations of net sales.
b. Detailed computations of expenses, including subtotals for various expense categories.
c. Operating expenses are usually classified into (1) selling expenses and (2) general and administrative expenses.
d. Both a and c.
e. a, b, and c.

QS 4-11[A]
Contrasting periodic and perpetual systems

P5

Identify whether each description best applies to a periodic or a perpetual inventory system.
a. Provides more timely information to managers.
b. Requires an adjusting entry to record inventory shrinkage.
c. Markedly increased in frequency and popularity in business within the past decade.
d. Records cost of goods sold each time a sales transaction occurs.
e. Updates the inventory account only at period-end.

QS 4-12[A]
Recording purchases—periodic system   **P5**

Refer to QS 4-3 and prepare journal entries to record each of the merchandising transactions assuming that the periodic inventory system is used.

QS 4-13[A]
Recording purchases—periodic system   **P5**

Refer to QS 4-4 and prepare journal entries to record each of the merchandising transactions assuming that the periodic inventory system is used.

QS 4-14
IFRS income statement presentation

P4

Income statement information for **adidas**, a German footwear, apparel, and accessories manufacturer, for the year ended December 31, 2009, follows. The company applies IFRS, as adopted by the European Union, and reports its results in millions of euros. Prepare its calendar year 2009 (1) multiple-step income statement and (2) single-step income statement.

Net income	€ 245
Financial income	19
Financial expenses	169
Operating profit	508
Cost of sales	5,669
Income taxes	113
Income before taxes	358
Gross profit........................	4,712
Royalty and commission income	86
Other operating income	100
Other operating expenses	4,390
Net sales	10,381

Answer each of the following questions related to international accounting standards.

a. Explain how the accounting for merchandise purchases and sales is different between accounting under IFRS versus U.S. GAAP.

b. Income statements prepared under IFRS usually report an item titled *finance costs*. What do finance costs refer to?

c. U.S. GAAP prohibits alternative measures of income reported on the income statement. Does IFRS permit such alternative measures on the income statement?

QS 4-15
International accounting standards

C1

 connect

EXERCISES

Prepare journal entries to record the following transactions for a retail store. Assume a perpetual inventory system.

Apr. 2 Purchased merchandise from Blue Company under the following terms: $3,600 price, invoice dated April 2, credit terms of 2/15, n/60, and FOB shipping point.

3 Paid $200 for shipping charges on the April 2 purchase.

4 Returned to Blue Company unacceptable merchandise that had an invoice price of $600.

17 Sent a check to Blue Company for the April 2 purchase, net of the discount and the returned merchandise.

18 Purchased merchandise from Fox Corp. under the following terms: $7,500 price, invoice dated April 18, credit terms of 2/10, n/30, and FOB destination.

21 After negotiations, received from Fox a $2,100 allowance on the April 18 purchase.

28 Sent check to Fox paying for the April 18 purchase, net of the discount and allowance.

Exercise 4-1
Recording entries for merchandise purchases
P1

Check   April 28, Cr. Cash $5,292

Taos Company purchased merchandise for resale from Tuscon Company with an invoice price of $22,000 and credit terms of 3/10, n/60. The merchandise had cost Tuscon $15,000. Taos paid within the discount period. Assume that both buyer and seller use a perpetual inventory system.

1. Prepare entries that the buyer should record for (*a*) the purchase and (*b*) the cash payment.

2. Prepare entries that the seller should record for (*a*) the sale and (*b*) the cash collection.

3. Assume that the buyer borrowed enough cash to pay the balance on the last day of the discount period at an annual interest rate of 11% and paid it back on the last day of the credit period. Compute how much the buyer saved by following this strategy. (Assume a 365-day year and round dollar amounts to the nearest cent, including computation of interest per day.)

Exercise 4-2
Analyzing and recording merchandise transactions— both buyer and seller

P1   P2

Check   (3) $338.50 savings (rounded)

The operating cycle of a merchandiser with credit sales includes the following five activities. Starting with merchandise acquisition, identify the chronological order of these five activities.

a. _____ purchases of merchandise.

b. _____ credit sales to customers.

c. _____ inventory made available for sale.

d. _____ cash collections from customers.

e. _____ accounts receivable accounted for.

Exercise 4-3
Operating cycle for merchandiser

C2

Spare Parts was organized on May 1, 2011, and made its first purchase of merchandise on May 3. The purchase was for 1,000 units at a price of $10 per unit. On May 5, Spare Parts sold 600 of the units for $14 per unit to DeSoto Co. Terms of the sale were 2/10, n/60. Prepare entries for Spare Parts to record the May 5 sale and each of the following separate transactions *a* through *c* using a perpetual inventory system.

a. On May 7, DeSoto returns 200 units because they did not fit the customer's needs. Spare Parts restores the units to its inventory.

b. On May 8, DeSoto discovers that 50 units are damaged but are still of some use and, therefore, keeps the units. Spare Parts sends DeSoto a credit memorandum for $300 to compensate for the damage.

c. On May 15, DeSoto discovers that 72 units are the wrong color. DeSoto keeps 43 of these units because Spare Parts sends a $92 credit memorandum to compensate. DeSoto returns the remaining 29 units to Spare Parts. Spare Parts restores the 29 returned units to its inventory.

Exercise 4-4
Recording sales returns and allowances   **P2**

Check   (c) Dr. Merchandise Inventory $290

Refer to Exercise 4-4 and prepare the appropriate journal entries for DeSoto Co. to record the May 5 purchase and each of the three separate transactions *a* through *c*. DeSoto is a retailer that uses a perpetual inventory system and purchases these units for resale.

Exercise 4-5
Recording purchase returns and allowances   **P1**

Exercise 4-6

Analyzing and recording merchandise transactions— both buyer and seller

P1 P2

Check (1) May 20, Cr. Cash $27,936

On May 11, Smythe Co. accepts delivery of $30,000 of merchandise it purchases for resale from Hope Corporation. With the merchandise is an invoice dated May 11, with terms of 3/10, n/90, FOB shipping point. The goods cost Hope $20,000. When the goods are delivered, Smythe pays $335 to Express Shipping for delivery charges on the merchandise. On May 12, Smythe returns $1,200 of goods to Hope, who receives them one day later and restores them to inventory. The returned goods had cost Hope $800. On May 20, Smythe mails a check to Hope Corporation for the amount owed. Hope receives it the following day. (Both Smythe and Hope use a perpetual inventory system.)

1. Prepare journal entries that Smythe Co. records for these transactions.

2. Prepare journal entries that Hope Corporation records for these transactions.

Exercise 4-7

Sales returns and allowances

C1

Business decision makers desire information on sales returns and allowances. (1) Explain why a company's manager wants the accounting system to record customers' returns of unsatisfactory goods in the Sales Returns and Allowances account instead of the Sales account. (2) Explain whether this information would be useful for external decision makers.

Exercise 4-8

Recording effects of merchandising activities

P1 P2

The following supplementary records summarize Titus Company's merchandising activities for year 2011. Set up T-accounts for Merchandise Inventory and Cost of Goods Sold. Then record the summarized activities in those T-accounts and compute account balances.

Cost of merchandise sold to customers in sales transactions	$186,000
Merchandise inventory, December 31, 2010	27,000
Invoice cost of merchandise purchases	190,500
Shrinkage determined on December 31, 2011	700
Cost of transportation-in	1,900
Cost of merchandise returned by customers and restored to inventory	2,200
Purchase discounts received	1,600
Purchase returns and allowances	4,100

Check Year-End Merchandise Inventory Dec. 31, $29,200

Exercise 4-9

Computing revenues, expenses, and income

C1 C2

Using your accounting knowledge, fill in the blanks in the following separate income statements *a* through *e*. Identify any negative amount by putting it in parentheses.

	a	b	c	d	e
Sales	$60,000	$42,500	$36,000	$?	$23,600
Cost of goods sold					
Merchandise inventory (beginning)	6,000	17,050	7,500	7,000	2,560
Total cost of merchandise purchases	36,000	?	?	32,000	5,600
Merchandise inventory (ending)	?	(2,700)	(9,000)	(6,600)	?
Cost of goods sold	34,050	15,900	?	?	5,600
Gross profit	?	?	3,750	45,600	?
Expenses	9,000	10,650	12,150	2,600	6,000
Net income (loss)	$?	$15,950	$ (8,400)	$43,000	$?

Exercise 4-10

Preparing adjusting and closing entries for a merchandiser

P3

The following list includes selected permanent accounts and all of the temporary accounts from the December 31, 2011, unadjusted trial balance of Deacon Co., a business owned by Julie Deacon. Use these account balances along with the additional information to journalize (*a*) adjusting entries and (*b*) closing entries. Deacon Co. uses a perpetual inventory system.

	Debit	Credit
Merchandise inventory	$ 28,000	
Prepaid selling expenses	5,000	
Dividends	2,200	
Sales		$429,000
Sales returns and allowances	16,500	
Sales discounts	4,000	
Cost of goods sold	211,000	
Sales salaries expense	47,000	
Utilities expense	14,000	
Selling expenses	35,000	
Administrative expenses	95,000	

[continued on next page]

Additional Information

Accrued sales salaries amount to $1,600. Prepaid selling expenses of $2,000 have expired. A physical count of year-end merchandise inventory shows $27,450 of goods still available.

Check Entry to close Income Summary: Cr. Retained Earnings $2,350

A retail company recently completed a physical count of ending merchandise inventory to use in preparing adjusting entries. In determining the cost of the counted inventory, company employees failed to consider that $2,000 of incoming goods had been shipped by a supplier on December 31 under an FOB shipping point agreement. These goods had been recorded in Merchandise Inventory as a purchase, but they were not included in the physical count because they were in transit. Explain how this overlooked fact affects the company's financial statements and the following ratios: return on assets, debt ratio, current ratio, and acid-test ratio.

Exercise 4-11
Interpreting a physical count error as inventory shrinkage
A1

Refer to the information in Exercise 4-11 and explain how the error in the physical count affects the company's gross margin ratio and its profit margin ratio.

Exercise 4-12
Physical count error and profits
A2

Compute the current ratio and acid-test ratio for each of the following separate cases. (Round ratios to two decimals.) Which company case is in the best position to meet short-term obligations? Explain.

	Case A	Case B	Case C
Cash.......................	$ 800	$ 510	$3,200
Short-term investments	0	0	1,100
Current receivables............	0	790	800
Inventory	2,000	1,600	1,900
Prepaid expenses..............	1,200	600	300
Total current assets	$4,000	$3,500	$7,300
Current liabilities..............	$2,200	$1,100	$3,650

Exercise 4-13
Computing and analyzing acid-test and current ratios
A1

Journalize the following merchandising transactions for CSI Systems assuming it uses a perpetual inventory system.

1. On November 1, CSI Systems purchases merchandise for $1,400 on credit with terms of 2/5, n/30, FOB shipping point; invoice dated November 1.
2. On November 5, CSI Systems pays cash for the November 1 purchase.
3. On November 7, CSI Systems discovers and returns $100 of defective merchandise purchased on November 1 for a cash refund.
4. On November 10, CSI Systems pays $80 cash for transportation costs with the November 1 purchase.
5. On November 13, CSI Systems sells merchandise for $1,500 on credit. The cost of the merchandise is $750.
6. On November 16, the customer returns merchandise from the November 13 transaction. The returned items would sell for $200 and cost $100; the items were not damaged and were returned to inventory.

Exercise 4-14
Preparing journal entries—perpetual system
P1 P2

A company reports the following sales related information: Sales (gross) of $100,000; Sales discounts of $2,000; Sales returns and allowances of $8,000; Sales salaries expense of $5,000. Prepare the net sales portion only of this company's multiple-step income statement.

Exercise 4-15
Multiple-step income statement
P4

Refer to Exercise 4-1 and prepare journal entries to record each of the merchandising transactions assuming that the periodic inventory system is used.

Exercise 4-16^A
Recording purchases—periodic system P5

Refer to Exercise 4-2 and prepare journal entries to record each of the merchandising transactions assuming that the periodic inventory system is used by both the buyer and the seller. (Skip the part 3 requirement.)

Exercise 4-17^A
Recording purchases and sales—periodic system P5

Exercise 4-18^A
Buyer and seller transactions—
periodic system   P5

Refer to Exercise 4-6 and prepare journal entries to record each of the merchandising transactions assuming that the periodic inventory system is used by both the buyer and the seller.

Exercise 4-19^A
Recording purchases—
periodic system   P5

Refer to Exercise 4-14 and prepare journal entries to record each of the merchandising transactions assuming that the periodic inventory system is used.

Exercise 4-20
Preparing an income statement
following IFRS

P4

L'Oréal reports the following income statement accounts for the year ended December 31, 2009 (euros in millions). Prepare the income statement for this company for the year ended December 31, 2009, following usual IFRS practices.

Net profit	€ 1,794.9	Income tax expense	€ 676.1
Finance costs	76.0	Profit before tax expense	2,471.0
Net sales	17,472.6	Research and development expense	609.2
Gross profit	12,311.0	Selling, general and administrative expense	3,735.5
Other expense	30.6	Advertising and promotion expense	5,388.7
Cost of sales	5,161.6		

PROBLEM SET A

Problem 4-1A
Preparing journal entries for
merchandising activities—
perpetual system

P1 P2

Check Aug. 9, Dr. Delivery
Expense, $120

Aug. 18, Cr. Cash $4,695

Aug. 29, Dr. Cash $2,970

Prepare journal entries to record the following merchandising transactions of Stone Company, which applies the perpetual inventory system. (*Hint:* It will help to identify each receivable and payable; for example, record the purchase on August 1 in Accounts Payable—Abilene.)

Aug. 1   Purchased merchandise from Abilene Company for $6,000 under credit terms of 1/10, n/30, FOB destination, invoice dated August 1.

4   At Abilene's request, Stone paid $100 cash for freight charges on the August 1 purchase, reducing the amount owed to Abilene.

5   Sold merchandise to Lux Corp. for $4,200 under credit terms of 2/10, n/60, FOB destination, invoice dated August 5. The merchandise had cost $3,000.

8   Purchased merchandise from Welch Corporation for $5,300 under credit terms of 1/10, n/45, FOB shipping point, invoice dated August 8. The invoice showed that at Stone's request, Welch paid the $240 shipping charges and added that amount to the bill. (*Hint:* Discounts are not applied to freight and shipping charges.)

9   Paid $120 cash for shipping charges related to the August 5 sale to Lux Corp.

10   Lux returned merchandise from the August 5 sale that had cost Stone $500 and been sold for $700. The merchandise was restored to inventory.

12   After negotiations with Welch Corporation concerning problems with the merchandise purchased on August 8, Stone received a credit memorandum from Welch granting a price reduction of $800.

15   Received balance due from Lux Corp. for the August 5 sale less the return on August 10.

18   Paid the amount due Welch Corporation for the August 8 purchase less the price reduction granted.

19   Sold merchandise to Trax Co. for $3,600 under credit terms of 1/10, n/30, FOB shipping point, invoice dated August 19. The merchandise had cost $2,500.

22   Trax requested a price reduction on the August 19 sale because the merchandise did not meet specifications. Stone sent Trax a $600 credit memorandum to resolve the issue.

29   Received Trax's cash payment for the amount due from the August 19 sale.

30   Paid Abilene Company the amount due from the August 1 purchase.

Problem 4-2A
Preparing journal entries for
merchandising activities—
perpetual system

P1 P2

Prepare journal entries to record the following merchandising transactions of Bask Company, which applies the perpetual inventory system. (*Hint:* It will help to identify each receivable and payable; for example, record the purchase on July 1 in Accounts Payable—Black.)

July 1   Purchased merchandise from Black Company for $6,000 under credit terms of 1/15, n/30, FOB shipping point, invoice dated July 1.

2   Sold merchandise to Coke Co. for $800 under credit terms of 2/10, n/60, FOB shipping point, invoice dated July 2. The merchandise had cost $500.

3   Paid $100 cash for freight charges on the purchase of July 1.

8   Sold merchandise that had cost $1,200 for $1,600 cash.

9   Purchased merchandise from Lane Co. for $2,300 under credit terms of 2/15, n/60, FOB desti-
    nation, invoice dated July 9.

11 Received a $200 credit memorandum from Lane Co. for the return of part of the merchandise
    purchased on July 9.

12 Received the balance due from Coke Co. for the invoice dated July 2, net of the discount.

16 Paid the balance due to Black Company within the discount period.

19 Sold merchandise that cost $900 to AKP Co. for $1,250 under credit terms of 2/15, n/60, FOB
    shipping point, invoice dated July 19.

21 Issued a $150 credit memorandum to AKP Co. for an allowance on goods sold on July 19.

24 Paid Lane Co. the balance due after deducting the discount.

30 Received the balance due from AKP Co. for the invoice dated July 19, net of discount.

31 Sold merchandise that cost $3,200 to Coke Co. for $5,000 under credit terms of 2/10, n/60,
    FOB shipping point, invoice dated July 31.

Check July 12, Dr. Cash $784
July 16, Cr. Cash $5,940

July 24, Cr. Cash $2,058
July 30, Dr. Cash $1,078

The following unadjusted trial balance is prepared at fiscal year-end for Rex Company.

Problem 4-3A
Preparing adjusting entries
and income statements; and
computing gross margin, acid-
test, and current ratios

A1 A2 P3 P4

mhhe.com/wildFINMAN4e

File Edit View Insert Format Tools Data Accounting Window Help		
REX COMPANY		
Unadjusted Trial Balance		
January 31, 2011		
	Debit	**Credit**
1		
2 Cash	$ 2,200	
3 Merchandise inventory	11,500	
4 Store supplies	4,800	
5 Prepaid insurance	2,300	
6 Store equipment	41,900	
7 Accumulated depreciation—Store equipment		$ 15,000
8 Accounts payable		9,000
9 Common stock		5,000
10 Retained earnings		27,000
11 Dividends	2,000	
12 Sales		104,000
13 Sales discounts	1,000	
14 Sales returns and allowances	2,000	
15 Cost of goods sold	37,400	
16 Depreciation expense—Store equipment	0	
17 Salaries expense	31,000	
18 Insurance expense	0	
19 Rent expense	14,000	
20 Store supplies expense	0	
21 Advertising expense	9,900	
22 Totals	$160,000	$160,000
23		

Rent expense and salaries expense are equally divided between selling activities and the general and administrative activities. Rex Company uses a perpetual inventory system.

Required

1. Prepare adjusting journal entries to reflect each of the following:

a. Store supplies still available at fiscal year-end amount to $1,650.

b. Expired insurance, an administrative expense, for the fiscal year is $1,500.

c. Depreciation expense on store equipment, a selling expense, is $1,400 for the fiscal year.

d. To estimate shrinkage, a physical count of ending merchandise inventory is taken. It shows $11,100
    of inventory is still available at fiscal year-end.

2. Prepare a multiple-step income statement for fiscal year 2011.

3. Prepare a single-step income statement for fiscal year 2011.

4. Compute the current ratio, acid-test ratio, and gross margin ratio as of January 31, 2011.

Problem 4-4A
Computing merchandising amounts and formatting income statements

C2   P4

BizKid Company's adjusted trial balance on August 31, 2011, its fiscal year-end, follows.

	Debit	Credit
Merchandise inventory	$ 31,000	
Other (noninventory) assets	120,400	
Total liabilities		$ 35,000
Common stock		10,000
Retained earnings		91,650
Dividends	8,000	
Sales		212,000
Sales discounts	3,250	
Sales returns and allowances	14,000	
Cost of goods sold	82,600	
Sales salaries expense	29,000	
Rent expense—Selling space	10,000	
Store supplies expense	2,500	
Advertising expense	18,000	
Office salaries expense	26,500	
Rent expense—Office space	2,600	
Office supplies expense	800	
Totals	$348,650	$348,650

On August 31, 2010, merchandise inventory was $25,000. Supplementary records of merchandising activities for the year ended August 31, 2011, reveal the following itemized costs.

Invoice cost of merchandise purchases	$91,000
Purchase discounts received	1,900
Purchase returns and allowances	4,400
Costs of transportation-in	3,900

Required

1. Compute the company's net sales for the year.

2. Compute the company's total cost of merchandise purchased for the year.

3. Prepare a multiple-step income statement that includes separate categories for selling expenses and for general and administrative expenses.

4. Prepare a single-step income statement that includes these expense categories: cost of goods sold, selling expenses, and general and administrative expenses.

Problem 4-5A
Preparing closing entries and interpreting information about discounts and returns

C2   P3

Use the data for BizKid Company in Problem 4-4A to complete the following requirements.

Required

1. Prepare closing entries as of August 31, 2011 (the perpetual inventory system is used).

Analysis Component

2. The company makes all purchases on credit, and its suppliers uniformly offer a 3% sales discount. Does it appear that the company's cash management system is accomplishing the goal of taking all available discounts? Explain.

3. In prior years, the company experienced a 5% returns and allowance rate on its sales, which means approximately 5% of its gross sales were eventually returned outright or caused the company to grant allowances to customers. How do this year's results compare to prior years' results?

Refer to the data and information in Problem 4-3A.

Required

Prepare and complete the entire 10-column work sheet for Rex Company. Follow the structure of Exhibit 4B.1 in Appendix 4B.

Problem 4-6A[B]
Preparing a work sheet for a merchandiser
P3

Prepare journal entries to record the following merchandising transactions of Wave Company, which applies the perpetual inventory system. (*Hint:* It will help to identify each receivable and payable; for example, record the purchase on July 3 in Accounts Payable—CAP.)

PROBLEM SET B

Problem 4-1B
Preparing journal entries for merchandising activities—perpetual system
P1 P2

July 3 Purchased merchandise from CAP Corp. for $15,000 under credit terms of 1/10, n/30, FOB destination, invoice dated July 3.
  4 At CAP's request, Wave paid $250 cash for freight charges on the July 3 purchase, reducing the amount owed to CAP.
  7 Sold merchandise to Morris Co. for $10,500 under credit terms of 2/10, n/60, FOB destination, invoice dated July 7. The merchandise had cost $7,500.
  10 Purchased merchandise from Murdock Corporation for $14,200 under credit terms of 1/10, n/45, FOB shipping point, invoice dated July 10. The invoice showed that at Wave's request, Murdock paid the $600 shipping charges and added that amount to the bill. (*Hint:* Discounts are not applied to freight and shipping charges.)
  11 Paid $300 cash for shipping charges related to the July 7 sale to Morris Co.
  12 Morris returned merchandise from the July 7 sale that had cost Wave $1,250 and been sold for $1,750. The merchandise was restored to inventory.
  14 After negotiations with Murdock Corporation concerning problems with the merchandise purchased on July 10, Wave received a credit memorandum from Murdock granting a price reduction of $2,000.
  17 Received balance due from Morris Co. for the July 7 sale less the return on July 12.
  20 Paid the amount due Murdock Corporation for the July 10 purchase less the price reduction granted.
  21 Sold merchandise to Ulsh for $9,000 under credit terms of 1/10, n/30, FOB shipping point, invoice dated July 21. The merchandise had cost $6,250.
  24 Ulsh requested a price reduction on the July 21 sale because the merchandise did not meet specifications. Wave sent Ulsh a credit memorandum for $1,500 to resolve the issue.
  30 Received Ulsh's cash payment for the amount due from the July 21 sale.
  31 Paid CAP Corp. the amount due from the July 3 purchase.

Check July 17, Dr. Cash $8,575
July 20, Cr. Cash $12,678

July 30, Dr. Cash $7,425

Prepare journal entries to record the following merchandising transactions of Yang Company, which applies the perpetual inventory system. (*Hint:* It will help to identify each receivable and payable; for example, record the purchase on May 2 in Accounts Payable—Bots.)

Problem 4-2B
Preparing journal entries for merchandising activities—perpetual system
P1 P2

May 2 Purchased merchandise from Bots Co. for $9,000 under credit terms of 1/15, n/30, FOB shipping point, invoice dated May 2.
  4 Sold merchandise to Chase Co. for $1,200 under credit terms of 2/10, n/60, FOB shipping point, invoice dated May 4. The merchandise had cost $750.
  5 Paid $150 cash for freight charges on the purchase of May 2.
  9 Sold merchandise that had cost $1,800 for $2,400 cash.
  10 Purchased merchandise from Snyder Co. for $3,450 under credit terms of 2/15, n/60, FOB destination, invoice dated May 10.
  12 Received a $300 credit memorandum from Snyder Co. for the return of part of the merchandise purchased on May 10.
  14 Received the balance due from Chase Co. for the invoice dated May 4, net of the discount.
  17 Paid the balance due to Bots Co. within the discount period.
  20 Sold merchandise that cost $1,450 to Tex Co. for $2,800 under credit terms of 2/15, n/60, FOB shipping point, invoice dated May 20.
  22 Issued a $400 credit memorandum to Tex Co. for an allowance on goods sold from May 20.
  25 Paid Snyder Co. the balance due after deducting the discount.
  30 Received the balance due from Tex Co. for the invoice dated May 20, net of discount and allowance.
  31 Sold merchandise that cost $4,800 to Chase Co. for $7,500 under credit terms of 2/10, n/60, FOB shipping point, invoice dated May 31.

Check May 14, Dr. Cash $1,176
May 17, Cr. Cash $8,910

May 30, Dr. Cash $2,352

Problem 4-3B

Preparing adjusting entries and income statements; and computing gross margin, acid-test, and current ratios

A1 A2 P3 P4

The following unadjusted trial balance is prepared at fiscal year-end for FAB Products Company.

		Debit	Credit
	File Edit View Insert Format Tools Data Accounting Window Help		
	FAB PRODUCTS COMPANY		
	Unadjusted Trial Balance		
	October 31, 2011		
1		**Debit**	**Credit**
2	Cash	$ 4,400	
3	Merchandise inventory	23,000	
4	Store supplies	9,600	
5	Prepaid insurance	4,600	
6	Store equipment	83,800	
7	Accumulated depreciation—Store equipment		$ 30,000
8	Accounts payable		16,000
9	Common stock		4,000
10	Retained earnings		60,000
11	Dividends	2,000	
12	Sales		208,000
13	Sales discounts	2,000	
14	Sales returns and allowances	4,000	
15	Cost of goods sold	74,800	
16	Depreciation expense—Store equipment	0	
17	Salaries expense	62,000	
18	Insurance expense	0	
19	Rent expense	28,000	
20	Store supplies expense	0	
21	Advertising expense	19,800	
22	Totals	$318,000	$318,000
23			

Rent expense and salaries expense are equally divided between selling activities and the general and administrative activities. FAB Products Company uses a perpetual inventory system.

Required

1. Prepare adjusting journal entries to reflect each of the following.
    a. Store supplies still available at fiscal year-end amount to $3,300.
    b. Expired insurance, an administrative expense, for the fiscal year is $3,000.
    c. Depreciation expense on store equipment, a selling expense, is $2,800 for the fiscal year.
    d. To estimate shrinkage, a physical count of ending merchandise inventory is taken. It shows $22,200 of inventory is still available at fiscal year-end.

Check   (2) Gross profit, $126,400; (3) Total expenses, $197,500; Net income, $4,500

2. Prepare a multiple-step income statement for fiscal year 2011.
3. Prepare a single-step income statement for fiscal year 2011.
4. Compute the current ratio, acid-test ratio, and gross margin ratio as of October 31, 2011.

Problem 4-4B

Computing merchandising amounts and formatting income statements

C1 C2 P4

Albin Company's adjusted trial balance on March 31, 2011, its fiscal year-end, follows.

	Debit	Credit
Merchandise inventory	$ 46,500	
Other (noninventory) assets	190,600	
Total liabilities		$ 52,500
Common stock		12,000
Retained earnings		140,475
Dividends	2,000	

[continued on next page]

[continued from previous page]

Sales		318,000
Sales discounts	4,875	
Sales returns and allowances	21,000	
Cost of goods sold	123,900	
Sales salaries expense	43,500	
Rent expense—Selling space	15,000	
Store supplies expense	3,750	
Advertising expense	27,000	
Office salaries expense	39,750	
Rent expense—Office space	3,900	
Office supplies expense	1,200	
Totals	$522,975	$522,975

On March 31, 2010, merchandise inventory was $37,500. Supplementary records of merchandising activities for the year ended March 31, 2011, reveal the following itemized costs.

Invoice cost of merchandise purchases	$136,500
Purchase discounts received	2,850
Purchase returns and allowances	6,600
Costs of transportation-in	5,850

Required

1. Calculate the company's net sales for the year.
2. Calculate the company's total cost of merchandise purchased for the year.
3. Prepare a multiple-step income statement that includes separate categories for selling expenses and for general and administrative expenses.
4. Prepare a single-step income statement that includes these expense categories: cost of goods sold, selling expenses, and general and administrative expenses.

Check (2) $132,900;

(3) Gross profit, $168,225;
Net income, $34,125;

(4) Total expenses, $258,000

Use the data for Albin Company in Problem 4-4B to complete the following requirements.

Required

1. Prepare closing entries as of March 31, 2011 (the perpetual inventory system is used).

Analysis Component

2. The company makes all purchases on credit, and its suppliers uniformly offer a 3% sales discount. Does it appear that the company's cash management system is accomplishing the goal of taking all available discounts? Explain.
3. In prior years, the company experienced a 5% returns and allowance rate on its sales, which means approximately 5% of its gross sales were eventually returned outright or caused the company to grant allowances to customers. How do this year's results compare to prior years' results?

Problem 4-5B
Preparing closing entries and interpreting information about discounts and returns

C2 P3

Check (1) $34,125 Dr. to close Income Summary

(3) Current-year rate, 6.6%

Refer to the data and information in Problem 4-3B.

Required

Prepare and complete the entire 10-column work sheet for FAB Products Company. Follow the structure of Exhibit 4B.1 in Appendix 4B.

Problem 4-6B[B]
Preparing a work sheet for a merchandiser

P3

SERIAL PROBLEM
Business Solutions

P1   P2   P3   P4

(This serial problem began in Chapter 1 and continues through most of the book. If previous chapter segments were not completed, the serial problem can begin at this point. It is helpful, but not necessary, to use the Working Papers that accompany the book.)

SP 4   Santana Rey created Business Solutions on October 1, 2011. The company has been successful, and its list of customers has grown. To accommodate the growth, the accounting system is modified to set up separate accounts for each customer. The following chart of accounts includes the account number used for each account and any balance as of December 31, 2011. Santana Rey decided to add a fourth digit with a decimal point to the 106 account number that had been used for the single Accounts Receivable account. This change allows the company to continue using the existing chart of accounts.

No.	Account Title	Dr.	Cr.
101	Cash	$48,372	
106.1	Alex's Engineering Co.	0	
106.2	Wildcat Services	0	
106.3	Easy Leasing	0	
106.4	IFM Co.........................	3,000	
106.5	Liu Corp.	0	
106.6	Gomez Co......................	2,668	
106.7	Delta Co.	0	
106.8	KC, Inc........................	0	
106.9	Dream, Inc.	0	
119	Merchandise inventory	0	
126	Computer supplies	580	
128	Prepaid insurance	1,665	
131	Prepaid rent	825	
163	Office equipment	8,000	
164	Accumulated depreciation—Office equipment		$ 400
167	Computer equipment	20,000	
168	Accumulated depreciation—Computer equipment		1,250
201	Accounts payable		1,100

No.	Account Title	Dr.	Cr.
210	Wages payable		$ 500
236	Unearned computer services revenue		1,500
307	Common stock		73,000
318	Retained earnings............................		7,360
319	Dividends	$0	
403	Computer services revenue		0
413	Sales		0
414	Sales returns and allowances	0	
415	Sales discounts	0	
502	Cost of goods sold	0	
612	Depreciation expense—Office equipment	0	
613	Depreciation expense—Computer equipment	0	
623	Wages expense	0	
637	Insurance expense	0	
640	Rent expense...............................	0	
652	Computer supplies expense	0	
655	Advertising expense	0	
676	Mileage expense	0	
677	Miscellaneous expenses	0	
684	Repairs expense—Computer	0	

In response to requests from customers, S. Rey will begin selling computer software. The company will extend credit terms of 1/10, n/30, FOB shipping point, to all customers who purchase this merchandise. However, no cash discount is available on consulting fees. Additional accounts (Nos. 119, 413, 414, 415, and 502) are added to its general ledger to accommodate the company's new merchandising activities. Also, Business Solutions does not use reversing entries and, therefore, all revenue and expense accounts have zero beginning balances as of January 1, 2012. Its transactions for January through March follow:

Jan.   4   The company paid cash to Lyn Addie for five days' work at the rate of $125 per day. Four of the five days relate to wages payable that were accrued in the prior year.

      5   Santana Rey invested an additional $25,000 cash in the company in exchange for more common stock.

      7   The company purchased $5,800 of merchandise from Kansas Corp. with terms of 1/10, n/30, FOB shipping point, invoice dated January 7.

      9   The company received $2,668 cash from Gomez Co. as full payment on its account.

11 The company completed a five-day project for Alex's Engineering Co. and billed it $5,500, which is the total price of $7,000 less the advance payment of $1,500.

Check   Jan. 11, Dr. Unearned Computer Services Revenue $1,500

13 The company sold merchandise with a retail value of $5,200 and a cost of $3,560 to Liu Corp., invoice dated January 13.

15 The company paid $600 cash for freight charges on the merchandise purchased on January 7.

16 The company received $4,000 cash from Delta Co. for computer services provided.

17 The company paid Kansas Corp. for the invoice dated January 7, net of the discount.

20 Liu Corp. returned $500 of defective merchandise from its invoice dated January 13. The returned merchandise, which had a $320 cost, is discarded. (The policy of Business Solutions is to leave the cost of defective products in cost of goods sold.)

Check   Jan. 20, No entry to Cost of Goods Sold

22 The company received the balance due from Liu Corp., net of both the discount and the credit for the returned merchandise.

24 The company returned defective merchandise to Kansas Corp. and accepted a credit against future purchases. The defective merchandise invoice cost, net of the discount, was $496.

26 The company purchased $9,000 of merchandise from Kansas Corp. with terms of 1/10, n/30, FOB destination, invoice dated January 26.

26 The company sold merchandise with a $4,640 cost for $5,800 on credit to KC, Inc., invoice dated January 26.

31 The company paid cash to Lyn Addie for 10 days' work at $125 per day.

Feb. 1 The company paid $2,475 cash to Hillside Mall for another three months' rent in advance.

3 The company paid Kansas Corp. for the balance due, net of the cash discount, less the $496 amount in the credit memorandum.

5 The company paid $600 cash to the local newspaper for an advertising insert in today's paper.

11 The company received the balance due from Alex's Engineering Co. for fees billed on January 11.

15 The company paid $4,800 cash for dividends.

23 The company sold merchandise with a $2,660 cost for $3,220 on credit to Delta Co., invoice dated February 23.

26 The company paid cash to Lyn Addie for eight days' work at $125 per day.

27 The company reimbursed Santana Rey for business automobile mileage (600 miles at $0.32 per mile).

Mar. 8 The company purchased $2,730 of computer supplies from Harris Office Products on credit, invoice dated March 8.

9 The company received the balance due from Delta Co. for merchandise sold on February 23.

11 The company paid $960 cash for minor repairs to the company's computer.

16 The company received $5,260 cash from Dream, Inc., for computing services provided.

19 The company paid the full amount due to Harris Office Products, consisting of amounts created on December 15 (of $1,100) and March 8.

24 The company billed Easy Leasing for $9,047 of computing services provided.

25 The company sold merchandise with a $2,002 cost for $2,800 on credit to Wildcat Services, invoice dated March 25.

30 The company sold merchandise with a $1,048 cost for $2,220 on credit to IFM Company, invoice dated March 30.

31 The company reimbursed Santana Rey for business automobile mileage (400 miles at $0.32 per mile).

The following additional facts are available for preparing adjustments on March 31 prior to financial statement preparation:

a. The March 31 amount of computer supplies still available totals $2,005.

b. Three more months have expired since the company purchased its annual insurance policy at a $2,220 cost for 12 months of coverage.

c. Lyn Addie has not been paid for seven days of work at the rate of $125 per day.

d. Three months have passed since any prepaid rent has been transferred to expense. The monthly rent expense is $825.

e. Depreciation on the computer equipment for January 1 through March 31 is $1,250.

f. Depreciation on the office equipment for January 1 through March 31 is $400.

g. The March 31 amount of merchandise inventory still available totals $704.

Required

1. Prepare journal entries to record each of the January through March transactions.

2. Post the journal entries in part 1 to the accounts in the company's general ledger. (*Note:* Begin with the ledger's post-closing adjusted balances as of December 31, 2011.)

3. Prepare a partial work sheet consisting of the first six columns (similar to the one shown in Exhibit 4B.1) that includes the unadjusted trial balance, the March 31 adjustments (*a*) through (*g*), and the adjusted trial balance. Do not prepare closing entries and do not journalize the adjustments or post them to the ledger.

4. Prepare an income statement (from the adjusted trial balance in part 3) for the three months ended March 31, 2012. Use a single-step format. List all expenses without differentiating between selling expenses and general and administrative expenses.

5. Prepare a statement of retained earnings (from the adjusted trial balance in part 3) for the three months ended March 31, 2012.

6. Prepare a classified balance sheet (from the adjusted trial balance) as of March 31, 2012.

Beyond the Numbers

REPORTING IN ACTION

A1

RIM

BTN 4-1   Refer to **Research In Motion**'s financial statements in Appendix A to answer the following.

Required

1. Assume that the amounts reported for inventories and cost of sales reflect items purchased in a form ready for resale. Compute the net cost of goods purchased for the fiscal year ended February 27, 2010.

2. Compute the current ratio and acid-test ratio as of February 27, 2010, and February 28, 2009. Interpret and comment on the ratio results. How does Research In Motion compare to the industry average of 2.4 for the current ratio and 1.5 for the acid-test ratio?

Fast Forward

3. Access Research In Motion's financial statements (form 10-K) for fiscal years ending after February 27, 2010, from its Website (**RIM.com**) or the SEC's EDGAR database (**www.sec.gov**). Recompute and interpret the current ratio and acid-test ratio for these current fiscal years.

COMPARATIVE ANALYSIS

A2

RIM

Apple

BTN 4-2   Key comparative figures for both **Research In Motion** and **Apple** follow.

($ millions)	Research In Motion		Apple	
	Current Year	Prior Year	Current Year	Prior Year
Revenues (net sales)	$14,953	$11,065	$42,905	$37,491
Cost of sales	8,369	5,968	25,683	24,294

Required

1. Compute the dollar amount of gross margin and the gross margin ratio for the two years shown for each of these companies.

2. Which company earns more in gross margin for each dollar of net sales? How do they compare to the industry average of 40.0%?

3. Did the gross margin ratio improve or decline for these companies?

BTN 4-3   Ashton Martin is a student who plans to attend approximately four professional events a year at her college. Each event necessitates a financial outlay of $100 to $200 for a new suit and accessories. After incurring a major hit to her savings for the first event, Ashton developed a different approach. She buys the suit on credit the week before the event, wears it to the event, and returns it the next week to the store for a full refund on her charge card.

ETHICS CHALLENGE

C1   P2

Required

1. Comment on the ethics exhibited by Ashton and possible consequences of her actions.

2. How does the merchandising company account for the suits that Ashton returns?

BTN 4-4   You are the financial officer for Music Plus, a retailer that sells goods for home entertainment needs. The business owner, Jamie Madsen, recently reviewed the annual financial statements you prepared and sent you an e-mail stating that he thinks you overstated net income. He explains that although he has invested a great deal in security, he is sure shoplifting and other forms of inventory shrinkage have occurred, but he does not see any deduction for shrinkage on the income statement. The store uses a perpetual inventory system.

COMMUNICATING IN PRACTICE

C2   P3   P5

Required

Prepare a brief memorandum that responds to the owner's concerns.

BTN 4-5   Access the SEC's EDGAR database (www.SEC.gov) and obtain the March 19, 2010, filing of its fiscal 2010 10-K report (for year ended January 30, 2010) for **J. Crew Group, Inc** (ticker: JCG).

TAKING IT TO THE NET

A2   C1

Required

Prepare a table that reports the gross margin ratios for J. Crew using the revenues and cost of goods sold data from J. Crew's income statement for each of its most recent three years. Analyze and comment on the trend in its gross margin ratio.

BTN 4-6   Best Brands' general ledger and supplementary records at the end of its current period reveal the following.

TEAMWORK IN ACTION

C1   C2

Sales	$430,000	Merchandise inventory (beginning of period)	$ 49,000
Sales returns and allowances	18,000	Invoice cost of merchandise purchases	180,000
Sales discounts	6,600	Purchase discounts received	4,500
Cost of transportation-in	11,000	Purchase returns and allowances	5,500
Operating expenses	20,000	Merchandise inventory (end of period)	42,000

Required

1. *Each* member of the team is to assume responsibility for computing *one* of the following items. You are not to duplicate your teammates' work. Get any necessary amounts to compute your item from the appropriate teammate. Each member is to explain his or her computation to the team in preparation for reporting to the class.

    a. Net sales   **d.** Gross profit

    b. Total cost of merchandise purchases   **e.** Net income

    c. Cost of goods sold

2. Check your net income with the instructor. If correct, proceed to step 3.

3. Assume that a physical inventory count finds that actual ending inventory is $38,000. Discuss how this affects previously computed amounts in step 1.

Point: In teams of four, assign the same student *a* and *e*. Rotate teams for reporting on a different computation and the analysis in step 3.

ENTREPRENEURIAL DECISION

C1 C2 P4

BTN 4-7   Refer to the opening feature about **Heritage Link Brands**. Assume that Selena and Khary Cuffe report current annual sales at approximately $10 million and disclose the following income statement.

Heritage Link Brands Income Statement For Year Ended January 31, 2010	
Net sales	$10,000,000
Cost of sales	6,100,000
Expenses (other than cost of sales)	2,000,000
Net income	$ 1,900,000

Selena and Khary Cuffe sell to various individuals and retailers, ranging from small shops to large chains. Assume that they currently offer credit terms of 1/15, n/60, and ship FOB destination. To improve their cash flow, they are considering changing credit terms to 3/10, n/30. In addition, they propose to change shipping terms to FOB shipping point. They expect that the increase in discount rate will increase net sales by 9%, but the gross margin ratio (and ratio of cost of sales divided by net sales) is expected to remain unchanged. They also expect that delivery expenses will be zero under this proposal; thus, expenses other than cost of sales are expected to increase only 6%.

Required

1. Prepare a forecasted income statement for the year ended January 31, 2011, based on the proposal.
2. Based on the forecasted income statement alone (from your part 1 solution), do you recommend that Selena and Khary implement the new sales policies? Explain.
3. What else should Selena and Khary consider before deciding whether or not to implement the new policies? Explain.

HITTING THE ROAD

C1

Point: This activity complements the Ethics Challenge assignment.

BTN 4-8   Arrange an interview (in person or by phone) with the manager of a retail shop in a mall or in the downtown area of your community. Explain to the manager that you are a student studying merchandising activities and the accounting for sales returns and sales allowances. Ask the manager what the store policy is regarding returns. Also find out if sales allowances are ever negotiated with customers. Inquire whether management perceives that customers are abusing return policies and what actions management takes to counter potential abuses. Be prepared to discuss your findings in class.

GLOBAL DECISION

A2 P4

BTN 4-9   **Nokia** (**www.Nokia.com**), **Research In Motion**, and **Apple** are competitors in the global marketplace. Key comparative figures for each company follow.

	Net Sales	Cost of Sales
Nokia*	40,984	27,720
Research In Motion[†]	$14,953	$ 8,369
Apple[†]	$42,905	$25,683

* EUR millions for Nokia.

[†] $ millions for Research In Motion and Apple.

Required

1. Rank the three companies (highest to lowest) based on the gross margin ratio.
2. Which of the companies uses a multiple-step income statement format? (These companies' income statements are in Appendix A.)

ANSWERS TO MULTIPLE CHOICE QUIZ

1. c; Gross profit = $550,000 − $193,000 = $357,000

2. d; ($4,500 − $250) × (100% − 2%) = $4,165

3. b; Net sales = $75,000 + $320,000 − $13,700 − $6,000 = $375,300

4. b; Acid-test ratio = $37,500/$50,000 = 0.750

5. a; Gross margin ratio = ($675,000 − $459,000)/$675,000 = 32%

5

Inventories and Cost of Sales

A Look Back

Chapter 4 focused on merchandising activities and how they are reported. We analyzed and recorded purchases and sales and explained accounting adjustments and closing for merchandisers.

A Look at This Chapter

This chapter emphasizes accounting for inventory. We describe methods for assigning costs to inventory and we explain the items and costs making up merchandise inventory. We also discuss methods of estimating and measuring inventory.

A Look Ahead

Chapter 6 focuses on internal controls and accounting for cash and cash equivalents. We explain good internal control procedures and their importance to accounting.

Learning Objectives

CAP

CONCEPTUAL

C1 Identify the items making up merchandise inventory. (p. 204)

C2 Identify the costs of merchandise inventory. (p. 205)

ANALYTICAL

A1 Analyze the effects of inventory methods for both financial and tax reporting. (p. 212)

A2 Analyze the effects of inventory errors on current and future financial statements. (p. 214)

A3 Assess inventory management using both inventory turnover and days' sales in inventory. (p. 217)

LP5

PROCEDURAL

P1 Compute inventory in a perpetual system using the methods of specific identification, FIFO, LIFO, and weighted average. (p. 206)

P2 Compute the lower of cost or market amount of inventory. (p. 213)

P3 *Appendix 5A*—Compute inventory in a periodic system using the methods of specific identification, FIFO, LIFO, and weighted average. (p. 222)

P4 *Appendix 5B*—Apply both the retail inventory and gross profit methods to estimate inventory. (p. 227)

Decision Insight

The Gizmo!

"I wanted to re-create the SEAL team environment"
—**RANDY HETRICK**

SAN FRANCISCO—The Navy SEALs call it "the gizmo." This gizmo, created by former Navy SEAL Randy Hetrick, CEO of Fitness Anywhere, Inc and the inventor of Suspension Training®, is a resistance exercise device officially named the TRX Suspension Trainer. It is the hallmark product of Randy's start-up exercise equipment business, **Fitness Anywhere Inc. (FitnessAnywhere.com)**.

Randy explains that to keep himself in shape for clandestine missions, he stitched parachute webbing into straps that he could fasten to almost anything and then use as a pulley system where his own body weight served as resistance. After leaving the Navy, Randy headed to business school and devoted himself to producing and marketing his new invention.

However, the entrepreneurial road was rough. Randy struggled with inventory production and sales planning, and had to deal with discounts, returns, and allowances. A major challenge was maintaining appropriate inventories while controlling costs. Randy admits that mistakes are part of entrepreneurial endeavors, but that he just had to throw himself into it and learn.

And, learn he did. Applying inventory management, and old-fashion trial-and-error, Randy learned to fill orders, collect money, and maintain the right inventory. "I wanted to re-create the SEAL team environment," explains Randy. To help, he set up a

perpetual inventory system to account for inventory sales and purchases in real time. Randy insists that it is really important to serve customers' needs, which demands sound inventory accounting.

But business success requires more than good products and perpetual inventory management, explains Randy. It requires commitment, patience, energy, faith, and maybe some luck. "I thought this was a commando tool, pure and simple," laughs Randy. "Man, was I wrong!"

While Randy continues to measure, monitor, and manage inventories and costs, his success and growth are pushing him into new products and opportunities. He explains that he now has a line of portable, resistance exercise devices. Still, Randy demands that his business stay true to "the small, flat, high-performance . . . kind of [SEALs] culture." His inventory procedures and office setting contribute to that lean and mean culture. "Working out [in the office] is not only sanctioned," says Randy, "it almost is required."

[Sources: *FitnessAnywhere Website,* January 2011; *Entrepreneur,* February 2010; *Triathlete Magazine,* December 2009; *Wall Street Journal,* September 2009]

Merchandisers' activities include the purchasing and reselling of merchandise. We explained accounting for merchandisers in Chapter 4, including that for purchases and sales. In this chapter, we extend the study and analysis of inventory by explaining the methods used to assign costs to merchandise inventory *and* to cost of goods sold. Retailers, wholesalers, and other merchandising companies that purchase products for resale use the principles and methods described here. Understanding inventory accounting helps in the analysis and interpretation of financial statements and helps people run their businesses.

Inventories and Cost of Sales

Inventory Basics
- Determining inventory items
- Determining inventory costs
- Internal control of inventory
- Taking a physical count

Inventory Costing under a Perpetual System
- Cost flow assumptions
- Specific identification
- First-in, first-out
- Last-in, first-out
- Weighted average
- Financial statement effects

Inventory Valuation and Errors
- Inventory valuation at lower of cost or market
- Financial statement effects of inventory errors

INVENTORY BASICS

This section identifies the items and costs making up merchandise inventory. It also describes the importance of internal controls in taking a physical count of inventory.

Determining Inventory Items

C1 Identify the items making up merchandise inventory.

Merchandise inventory includes all goods that a company owns and holds for sale. This rule holds regardless of where the goods are located when inventory is counted. Certain inventory items require special attention, including goods in transit, goods on consignment, and goods that are damaged or obsolete.

Goods in Transit   Does a purchaser's inventory include goods in transit from a supplier? The answer is that if ownership has passed to the purchaser, the goods are included in the purchaser's inventory. We determine this by reviewing the shipping terms: *FOB destination* or *FOB shipping point.* If the purchaser is responsible for paying freight, ownership passes when goods are loaded on the transport vehicle. If the seller is responsible for paying freight, ownership passes when goods arrive at their destination.

Goods on Consignment   Goods on consignment are goods shipped by the owner, called the **consignor,** to another party, the **consignee.** A consignee sells goods for the owner. The consignor continues to own the consigned goods and reports them in its inventory. **Upper Deck**, for instance, pays sports celebrities such as Tony Romo of the Dallas Cowboys to sign memorabilia, which are offered to shopping networks on consignment. Upper Deck, the consignor, must report these items in its inventory until sold.

Goods Damaged or Obsolete   Damaged and obsolete (and deteriorated) goods are not counted in inventory if they cannot be sold. If these goods can be sold at a reduced price, they are included in inventory at a conservative estimate of their **net realizable value.** Net realizable value is sales price minus the cost of making the sale. The period when damage or obsolescence (or deterioration) occurs is the period when the loss in value is reported.

A wireless portable device with a two-way radio allows clerks to quickly record inventory by scanning bar codes and to instantly send and receive inventory data. It gives managers access to up-to-date information on inventory and its location. ■

Determining Inventory Costs

Merchandise inventory includes costs of expenditures necessary, directly or indirectly, to bring an item to a salable condition and location. This means that the cost of an inventory item includes its invoice cost minus any discount, and plus any incidental costs necessary to put it in a place and condition for sale. Incidental costs can include import duties, freight, storage, insurance, and costs incurred in an aging process (for example, aging wine or cheese).

> **C2** Identify the costs of merchandise inventory.

Accounting principles prescribe that incidental costs be added to inventory. Also, the *matching (expense recognition) principle* states that inventory costs should be recorded against revenue in the period when inventory is sold. However, some companies use the *materiality constraint (cost-to-benefit constraint)* to avoid assigning some incidental costs of acquiring merchandise to inventory. Instead, they expense them when incurred. These companies argue either that those incidental costs are immaterial or that the effort in assigning them outweighs the benefit.

Internal Controls and Taking a Physical Count

The Inventory account under a perpetual system is updated for each purchase and sale, but events can cause the Inventory account balance to differ from the actual inventory available. Such events include theft, loss, damage, and errors. Thus, nearly all companies take a *physical count of inventory* at least once each year—informally called *taking an inventory*. This often occurs at the end of a fiscal year or when inventory amounts are low. This physical count is used to adjust the Inventory account balance to the actual inventory available.

A company applies internal controls when taking a physical count of inventory that usually include the following:

- *Prenumbered inventory tickets* are prepared and distributed to the *counters*—each ticket must be accounted for.
- Counters of inventory are assigned and do not include those responsible for inventory.
- Counters confirm the validity of inventory, including its existence, amount, and quality.
- A second count is taken by a different counter.
- A manager confirms that all inventories are ticketed once, and only once.

> **Point:** The Inventory account is a controlling account for the inventory subsidiary ledger. This *subsidiary ledger* contains a separate record (units and costs) for each separate product, and it can be in electronic or paper form. Subsidiary records assist managers in planning and monitoring inventory.

Quick Check   Answers — p. 229 ☑

1. What accounting principle most guides the allocation of cost of goods available for sale between ending inventory and cost of goods sold?
2. If **Skechers** sells goods to **Target** with terms FOB shipping point, which company reports these goods in its inventory while they are in transit?
3. An art gallery purchases a painting for $11,400 on terms FOB shipping point. Additional costs in obtaining and offering the artwork for sale include $130 for transportation-in, $150 for import duties, $100 for insurance during shipment, $180 for advertising, $400 for framing, and $800 for office salaries. For computing inventory, what cost is assigned to the painting?

INVENTORY COSTING UNDER A PERPETUAL SYSTEM

Accounting for inventory affects both the balance sheet and the income statement. A major goal in accounting for inventory is to properly match costs with sales. We use the *matching principle* to decide how much of the cost of the goods available for sale is deducted from sales and how much is carried forward as inventory and matched against future sales.

Management decisions in accounting for inventory involve the following:

- Items included in inventory and their costs.
- Costing method (specific identification, FIFO, LIFO, or weighted average).
- Inventory system (perpetual or periodic).
- Use of market values or other estimates.

The first point was explained on the prior two pages. The second and third points will be addressed now. The fourth point is the focus at the end of this chapter. Decisions on these points affect the reported amounts for inventory, cost of goods sold, gross profit, income, current assets, and other accounts.

One of the most important issues in accounting for inventory is determining the per unit costs assigned to inventory items. When all units are purchased at the same unit cost, this process is simple. When identical items are purchased at different costs, however, a question arises as to which amounts to record in cost of goods sold and which amounts remain in inventory.

Four methods are commonly used to assign costs to inventory and to cost of goods sold: (1) specific identification; (2) first-in, first-out; (3) last-in, first-out; and (4) weighted average.

EXHIBIT 5.1

Frequency in Use of Inventory Methods

Exhibit 5.1 shows the frequency in the use of these methods.

Other* 3%

FIFO 50%

Weighted Average 20%

LIFO 27%

*Includes specific identification.

Each method assumes a particular pattern for how costs flow through inventory. Each of these four methods is acceptable whether or not the actual physical flow of goods follows the cost flow assumption. Physical flow of goods depends on the type of product and the way it is stored. (Perishable goods such as fresh fruit demand that a business attempt to sell them in a first-in, first-out physical flow. Other products such as crude oil and minerals such as coal, gold, and decorative stone can be sold in a last-in, first-out physical flow.) **Physical flow and cost flow need not be the same.**

Inventory Cost Flow Assumptions

P1 Compute inventory in a perpetual system using the methods of specific identification, FIFO, LIFO, and weighted average.

Point: It is helpful to recall the cost flow of inventory from Exhibit 4.4.

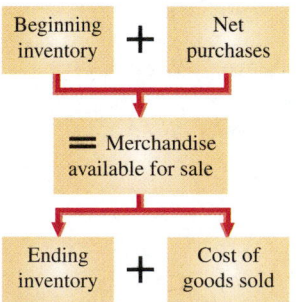

Beginning inventory + Net purchases

= Merchandise available for sale

Ending inventory + Cost of goods sold

This section introduces inventory cost flow assumptions. For this purpose, assume that three identical units are purchased separately at the following three dates and costs: May 1 at $45, May 3 at $65, and May 6 at $70. One unit is then sold on May 7 for $100. Exhibit 5.2 gives a visual layout of the flow of costs to either the gross profit section of the income statement or the inventory reported on the balance sheet for FIFO, LIFO, and weighted average.

(1) *FIFO assumes costs flow in the order incurred.* The unit purchased on May 1 for $45 is the earliest cost incurred—it is sent to cost of goods sold on the income statement first. The remaining two units ($65 and $70) are reported in inventory on the balance sheet.

(2) *LIFO assumes costs flow in the reverse order incurred.* The unit purchased on May 6 for $70 is the most recent cost incurred—it is sent to cost of goods sold on the income statement. The remaining two units ($45 and $65) are reported in inventory on the balance sheet.

(3) *Weighted average assumes costs flow at an average of the costs available.* The units available at the May 7 sale average $60 in cost, computed as ($45 + $65 + $70)/3. One unit's $60 average cost is sent to cost of goods sold on the income statement. The remaining two units' average costs are reported in inventory at $120 on the balance sheet.

Cost flow assumptions can markedly impact gross profit and inventory numbers. Exhibit 5.2 shows that gross profit as a percent of net sales ranges from 30% to 55% due to nothing else but the cost flow assumption.

The following sections on inventory costing use the perpetual system. Appendix 5A uses the periodic system. An instructor can choose to cover either one or both systems. If the perpetual system is skipped, then read Appendix 5A and return to the section (seven pages ahead) titled "Valuing Inventory at LCM and . . ."

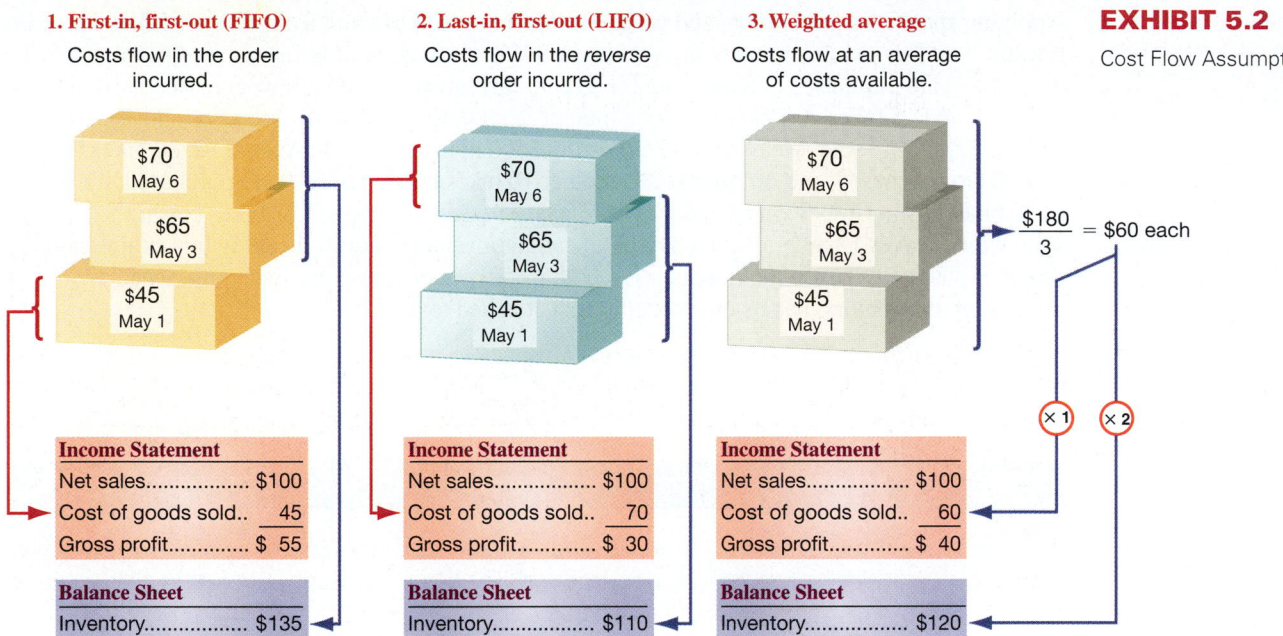

EXHIBIT 5.2

Cost Flow Assumptions

Inventory Costing Illustration

This section provides a comprehensive illustration of inventory costing methods. We use information from Trekking, a sporting goods store. Among its many products, Trekking carries one type of mountain bike whose sales are directed at resorts that provide inexpensive mountain bikes for complimentary guest use. Its customers usually purchase in amounts of 10 or more bikes. We use Trekking's data from August. Its mountain bike (unit) inventory at the beginning of August and its purchases and sales during August are shown in Exhibit 5.3. It ends August with 12 bikes remaining in inventory.

Date	Activity	Units Acquired at Cost	Units Sold at Retail	Unit Inventory
Aug. 1	Beginning inventory	10 units @ $ 91 = $ 910		10 units
Aug. 3	Purchases	15 units @ $106 = $ 1,590		25 units
Aug. 14	Sales		20 units @ $130	5 units
Aug. 17	Purchases	20 units @ $115 = $ 2,300		25 units
Aug. 28	Purchases	10 units @ $119 = $ 1,190		35 units
Aug. 31	Sales		23 units @ $150	**12 units**
	Totals	**55 units** **$5,990**	**43 units**	

EXHIBIT 5.3

Purchases and Sales of Goods

Trekking uses the perpetual inventory system, which means that its merchandise inventory account is continually updated to reflect purchases and sales. **(Appendix 5A describes the assignment of costs to inventory using a periodic system.)** Regardless of what inventory method or system is used, cost of goods available for sale must be allocated between cost of goods sold and ending inventory.

Point: The perpetual inventory system is now the most dominant system for U.S. businesses.

Point: Cost of goods sold plus ending inventory equals cost of goods available for sale.

Specific Identification

When each item in inventory can be identified with a specific purchase and invoice, we can use **specific identification** (also called *specific invoice inventory pricing*) to assign costs. We also need sales records that identify exactly which items were sold and when. Trekking's internal documents reveal the following specific unit sales:

August 14   Sold 8 bikes costing $91 each and 12 bikes costing $106 each

August 31   Sold 2 bikes costing $91 each, 3 bikes costing $106 each, 15 bikes costing $115 each, and 3 bikes costing $119 each

Applying specific identification, and using the information above and from Exhibit 5.3, we prepare Exhibit 5.4. This exhibit starts with 10 bikes at $91 each in beginning inventory. On August 3, 15 more bikes are purchased at $106 each for $1,590. Inventory available now consists of 10 bikes at $91 each and 15 bikes at $106 each, for a total of $2,500. On August 14 (see sales above), 20 bikes costing $2,000 are sold—leaving 5 bikes costing $500 in inventory. On August 17, 20 bikes costing $2,300 are purchased, and on August 28, another 10 bikes costing $1,190 are purchased, for a total of 35 bikes costing $3,990 in inventory. On August 31 (see sales above), 23 bikes costing $2,582 are sold, which leaves 12 bikes costing $1,408 in ending inventory. Carefully study this exhibit and the boxed explanations to see the flow of costs both in and out of inventory. Each unit, whether sold or remaining in inventory, has its own specific cost attached to it.

EXHIBIT 5.4

Specific Identification Computations

For the 20 units sold on Aug. 14, the company specifically identified that 8 of those had cost $91 and 12 had cost $106.

For the 23 units sold on Aug. 31, the company specifically identified each bike sold and its acquisition cost from prior purchases.

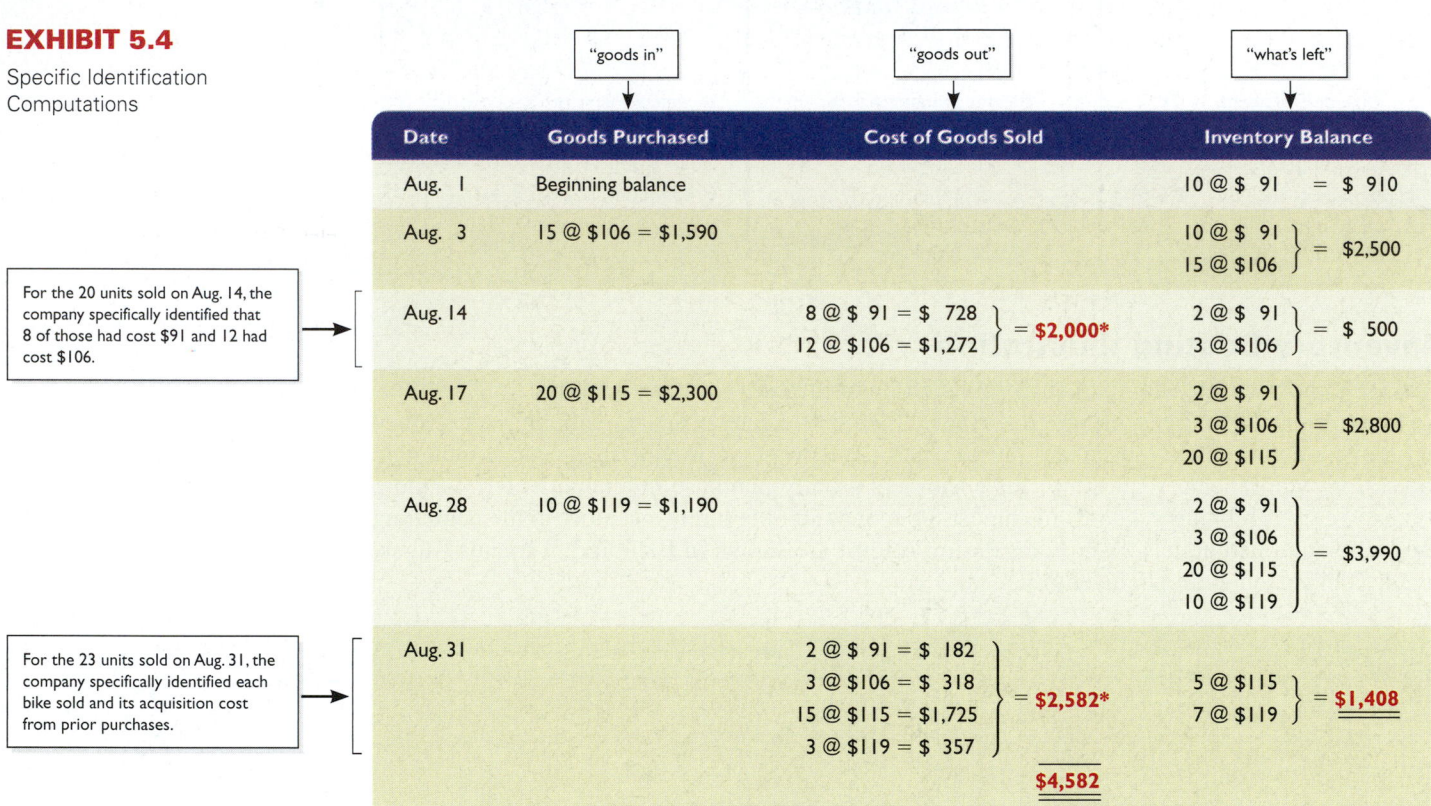

Date	Goods Purchased	Cost of Goods Sold	Inventory Balance
Aug. 1	Beginning balance		10 @ $ 91 = $ 910
Aug. 3	15 @ $106 = $1,590		10 @ $ 91 ⎫ = $2,500 15 @ $106 ⎭
Aug. 14		8 @ $ 91 = $ 728 ⎫ = **$2,000*** 12 @ $106 = $1,272 ⎭	2 @ $ 91 ⎫ = $ 500 3 @ $106 ⎭
Aug. 17	20 @ $115 = $2,300		2 @ $ 91 ⎫ 3 @ $106 ⎬ = $2,800 20 @ $115 ⎭
Aug. 28	10 @ $119 = $1,190		2 @ $ 91 ⎫ 3 @ $106 ⎪ 20 @ $115 ⎬ = $3,990 10 @ $119 ⎭
Aug. 31		2 @ $ 91 = $ 182 ⎫ 3 @ $106 = $ 318 ⎪ = **$2,582*** 15 @ $115 = $1,725 ⎬ 3 @ $119 = $ 357 ⎭ **$4,582**	5 @ $115 ⎫ = **$1,408** 7 @ $119 ⎭

* Identification of items sold (and their costs) is obtained from internal documents that track each unit from its purchase to its sale.

When using specific identification, Trekking's cost of goods sold reported on the income statement totals **$4,582**, the sum of $2,000 and $2,582 from the third column of Exhibit 5.4. Trekking's ending inventory reported on the balance sheet is **$1,408**, which is the final inventory balance from the fourth column of Exhibit 5.4.

The purchases and sales entries for Exhibit 5.4 follow (the colored boldface numbers are those impacted by the cost flow assumption).

Purchases				**Sales**			
Aug. 3	Merchandise Inventory	1,590		Aug. 14	Accounts Receivable	2,600	
	Accounts Payable		1,590		Sales		2,600
17	Merchandise Inventory	2,300		14	Cost of Goods Sold	**2,000**	
	Accounts Payable		2,300		Merchandise Inventory		**2,000**
28	Merchandise Inventory	1,190		31	Accounts Receivable	3,450	
	Accounts Payable		1,190		Sales		3,450
				31	Cost of Goods Sold	**2,582**	
					Merchandise Inventory		**2,582**

First-In, First-Out

The **first-in, first-out (FIFO)** method of assigning costs to both inventory and cost of goods sold assumes that inventory items are sold in the order acquired. When sales occur, the costs of the earliest units acquired are charged to cost of goods sold. This leaves the costs from the most recent purchases in ending inventory. Use of FIFO for computing the cost of inventory and cost of goods sold is shown in Exhibit 5.5.

This exhibit starts with beginning inventory of 10 bikes at $91 each. On August 3, 15 more bikes costing $106 each are bought for $1,590. Inventory now consists of 10 bikes at $91 each and 15 bikes at $106 each, for a total of $2,500. On August 14, 20 bikes are sold—applying FIFO, the first 10 sold cost $91 each and the next 10 sold cost $106 each, for a total cost of $1,970. This leaves 5 bikes costing $106 each, or $530, in inventory. On August 17, 20 bikes costing $2,300 are purchased, and on August 28, another 10 bikes costing $1,190 are purchased, for a total of 35 bikes costing $4,020 in inventory. On August 31, 23 bikes are sold—applying FIFO, the first 5 bikes sold cost $530 and the next 18 sold cost $2,070, which leaves 12 bikes costing $1,420 in ending inventory.

Point: The "Goods Purchased" column is identical for all methods. Data are taken from Exhibit 5.3.

Date	Goods Purchased	Cost of Goods Sold	Inventory Balance
Aug. 1	Beginning balance		10 @ $ 91 = $ 910
Aug. 3	15 @ $106 = $1,590		10 @ $ 91 ⎫ 15 @ $106 ⎭ = $2,500
Aug. 14		10 @ $ 91 = $ 910 ⎫ 10 @ $106 = $1,060 ⎭ = **$1,970**	5 @ $106 = $ 530
Aug. 17	20 @ $115 = $2,300		5 @ $106 ⎫ 20 @ $115 ⎭ = $2,830
Aug. 28	10 @ $119 = $1,190		5 @ $106 ⎫ 20 @ $115 ⎬ = $4,020 10 @ $119 ⎭
Aug. 31		5 @ $106 = $ 530 ⎫ 18 @ $115 = $2,070 ⎭ = **$2,600** **$4,570**	2 @ $115 ⎫ 10 @ $119 ⎭ = **$1,420**

EXHIBIT 5.5

FIFO Computations— Perpetual System

For the 20 units sold on Aug. 14, the first 10 sold are assigned the earliest cost of $91 (from beg. bal.). The next 10 sold are assigned the next earliest cost of $106.

For the 23 units sold on Aug. 31, the first 5 sold are assigned the earliest available cost of $106 (from Aug. 3 purchase). The next 18 sold are assigned the next earliest cost of $115 (from Aug. 17 purchase).

Trekking's FIFO cost of goods sold reported on its income statement (reflecting the 43 units sold) is **$4,570** ($1,970 + $2,600), and its ending inventory reported on the balance sheet (reflecting the 12 units unsold) is **$1,420**.

The purchases and sales entries for Exhibit 5.5 follow (the colored boldface numbers are those affected by the cost flow assumption).

Point: Under FIFO, a unit sold is assigned the earliest (oldest) cost from inventory. This leaves the most recent costs in ending inventory.

Purchases			
Aug. 3	Merchandise Inventory	1,590	
	Accounts Payable		1,590
17	Merchandise Inventory	2,300	
	Accounts Payable		2,300
28	Merchandise Inventory	1,190	
	Accounts Payable		1,190

Sales			
Aug. 14	Accounts Receivable	2,600	
	Sales		2,600
14	Cost of Goods Sold	**1,970**	
	Merchandise Inventory		**1,970**
31	Accounts Receivable	3,450	
	Sales		3,450
31	Cost of Goods Sold	**2,600**	
	Merchandise Inventory		**2,600**

Last-In, First-Out

The **last-in, first-out (LIFO)** method of assigning costs assumes that the most recent purchases are sold first. These more recent costs are charged to the goods sold, and the costs of the earliest purchases are assigned to inventory. As with other methods, LIFO is acceptable even when the physical flow of goods does not follow a last-in, first-out pattern. One appeal of LIFO is that by assigning costs from the most recent purchases to cost of goods sold, LIFO comes closest to matching current costs of goods sold with revenues (compared to FIFO or weighted average).

Exhibit 5.6 shows the LIFO computations. It starts with beginning inventory of 10 bikes at $91 each. On August 3, 15 more bikes costing $106 each are bought for $1,590. Inventory now consists of 10 bikes at $91 each and 15 bikes at $106 each, for a total of $2,500. On August 14, 20 bikes are sold—applying LIFO, the first 15 sold are from the most recent purchase costing $106 each, and the next 5 sold are from the next most recent purchase costing $91 each, for a total cost of $2,045. This leaves 5 bikes costing $91 each, or $455, in inventory. On August 17, 20 bikes costing $2,300 are purchased, and on August 28, another 10 bikes costing $1,190 are purchased, for a total of 35 bikes costing $3,945 in inventory. On August 31, 23 bikes are sold—applying LIFO, the first 10 bikes sold are from the most recent purchase costing $1,190, and the next 13 sold are from the next most recent purchase costing $1,495, which leaves 12 bikes costing $1,260 in ending inventory.

EXHIBIT 5.6

LIFO Computations—
Perpetual System

For the 20 units sold on Aug. 14, the first 15 sold are assigned the most recent cost of $106. The next 5 sold are assigned the next most recent cost of $91.

For the 23 units sold on Aug. 31, the first 10 sold are assigned the most recent cost of $119. The next 13 sold are assigned the next most recent cost of $115.

Date	Goods Purchased	Cost of Goods Sold	Inventory Balance
Aug. 1	Beginning balance		10 @ $ 91 = $ 910
Aug. 3	15 @ $106 = $1,590		10 @ $ 91 } 15 @ $106 } = $ 2,500
Aug. 14		15 @ $106 = $1,590 } 5 @ $ 91 = $ 455 } = **$2,045**	5 @ $ 91 = $ 455
Aug. 17	20 @ $115 = $2,300		5 @ $ 91 } 20 @ $115 } = $ 2,755
Aug. 28	10 @ $119 = $1,190		5 @ $ 91 } 20 @ $115 } 10 @ $119 } = $ 3,945
Aug. 31		10 @ $119 = $1,190 } 13 @ $115 = $1,495 } = **$2,685**	5 @ $ 91 } 7 @ $115 } = **$1,260**
		$4,730	

Trekking's LIFO cost of goods sold reported on the income statement is **$4,730** ($2,045 + $2,685), and its ending inventory reported on the balance sheet is **$1,260**.

The purchases and sales entries for Exhibit 5.6 follow (the colored boldface numbers are those affected by the cost flow assumption).

	Purchases		
Aug. 3	Merchandise Inventory	1,590	
	Accounts Payable		1,590
17	Merchandise Inventory	2,300	
	Accounts Payable		2,300
28	Merchandise Inventory	1,190	
	Accounts Payable		1,190

	Sales		
Aug. 14	Accounts Receivable	2,600	
	Sales		2,600
14	Cost of Goods Sold	**2,045**	
	Merchandise Inventory		**2,045**
31	Accounts Receivable	3,450	
	Sales		3,450
31	Cost of Goods Sold	**2,685**	
	Merchandise Inventory		**2,685**

Weighted Average

The **weighted average** (also called **average cost**) method of assigning cost requires that we use the weighted average cost per unit of inventory at the time of each sale. Weighted average cost per unit at the time of each sale equals the cost of goods available for sale divided by the units available. The results using weighted average (WA) for Trekking are shown in Exhibit 5.7.

This exhibit starts with beginning inventory of 10 bikes at $91 each. On August 3, 15 more bikes costing $106 each are bought for $1,590. Inventory now consists of 10 bikes at $91 each and 15 bikes at $106 each, for a total of $2,500. The average cost per bike for that inventory is $100, computed as $2,500/(10 bikes + 15 bikes). On August 14, 20 bikes are sold—applying

EXHIBIT 5.7

Weighted Average
Computations—Perpetual System

Date	Goods Purchased	Cost of Goods Sold	Inventory Balance
Aug. 1	Beginning balance		10 @ $ 91 = $ 910
Aug. 3	15 @ $106 = $1,590		10 @ $ 91 ⎫ = $2,500 (or $100 per unit)[a] 15 @ $106 ⎭
Aug. 14		20 @ $100 = **$2,000**	5 @ $100 = $ 500 (or $100 per unit)[b]
Aug. 17	20 @ $115 = $2,300		5 @ $100 ⎫ = $2,800 (or $112 per unit)[c] 20 @ $115 ⎭
Aug. 28	10 @ $119 = $1,190		5 @ $100 ⎫ 20 @ $115 ⎬ = $3,990 (or $114 per unit)[d] 10 @ $119 ⎭
Aug. 31		23 @ $114 = **$2,622**	12 @ $114 = **$1,368** (or $114 per unit)[e]
		$4,622	

For the 20 units sold on Aug. 14, the cost assigned is the $100 *average cost* per unit from the inventory balance column at the time of sale.

For the 23 units sold on Aug. 31, the cost assigned is the $114 *average cost* per unit from the inventory balance column at the time of sale.

[a] $100 per unit = ($2,500 inventory balance ÷ 25 units in inventory).
[b] $100 per unit = ($500 inventory balance ÷ 5 units in inventory).
[c] $112 per unit = ($2,800 inventory balance ÷ 25 units in inventory).
[d] $114 per unit = ($3,990 inventory balance ÷ 35 units in inventory).
[e] $114 per unit = ($1,368 inventory balance ÷ 12 units in inventory).

WA, the 20 sold are assigned the $100 average cost, for a total cost of $2,000. This leaves 5 bikes with an average cost of $100 each, or $500, in inventory. On August 17, 20 bikes costing $2,300 are purchased, and on August 28, another 10 bikes costing $1,190 are purchased, for a total of 35 bikes costing $3,990 in inventory at August 28. The average cost per bike for the August 28 inventory is $114, computed as $3,990/(5 bikes + 20 bikes + 10 bikes). On August 31, 23 bikes are sold—applying WA, the 23 sold are assigned the $114 average cost, for a total cost of $2,622. This leaves 12 bikes costing $1,368 in ending inventory.

Trekking's cost of goods sold reported on the income statement (reflecting the 43 units sold) is **$4,622** ($2,000 + $2,622), and its ending inventory reported on the balance sheet (reflecting the 12 units unsold) is **$1,368**.

The purchases and sales entries for Exhibit 5.7 follow (the colored boldface numbers are those affected by the cost flow assumption).

Point: Under weighted average, a unit sold is assigned the average cost of all items currently available for sale at the date of each sale.

Purchases

Aug. 3	Merchandise Inventory	1,590	
	Accounts Payable		1,590
17	Merchandise Inventory	2,300	
	Accounts Payable		2,300
28	Merchandise Inventory	1,190	
	Accounts Payable		1,190

Sales

Aug. 14	Accounts Receivable	2,600	
	Sales		2,600
14	Cost of Goods Sold	**2,000**	
	Merchandise Inventory		**2,000**
31	Accounts Receivable	3,450	
	Sales		3,450
31	Cost of Goods Sold	**2,622**	
	Merchandise Inventory		**2,622**

This completes computations under the four most common perpetual inventory costing methods. Advances in technology have greatly reduced the cost of a perpetual inventory system. Many companies now ask whether they can afford *not* to have a perpetual inventory system because timely access to inventory information is a competitive advantage and it can help reduce the amount of inventory, which reduces costs.

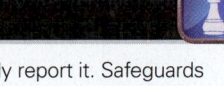

Decision Insight

Inventory Control   SOX demands that companies safeguard inventory and properly report it. Safeguards include restricted access, use of authorized requisitions, security measures, and controlled environments to prevent damage. Proper accounting includes matching inventory received with purchase order terms and quality requirements, preventing misstatements, and controlling access to inventory records. A study reports that 23% of employees in purchasing and procurement observed inappropriate kickbacks or gifts from suppliers (KPMG 2009). Another 23% of employees in production witnessed fabrication of product quality results. ■

A1   Analyze the effects of
      inventory methods for
      both financial and tax
      reporting.

Financial Statement Effects of Costing Methods

When purchase prices do not change, each inventory costing method assigns the same cost amounts to inventory and to cost of goods sold. When purchase prices are different, however, the methods nearly always assign different cost amounts. We show these differences in Exhibit 5.8 using Trekking's data.

EXHIBIT 5.8

Financial Statement Effects of Inventory Costing Methods

| | **TREKKING COMPANY** For Month Ended August 31 | | | |
	Specific Identification	FIFO	LIFO	Weighted Average
Income Statement				
Sales	$ 6,050	$ 6,050	$ 6,050	$ 6,050
Cost of goods sold	4,582	4,570	4,730	4,622
Gross profit	1,468	1,480	1,320	1,428
Expenses	450	450	450	450
Income before taxes	1,018	1,030	870	978
Income tax expense (30%)	305	309	261	293
Net income	$ 713	$ 721	$ 609	$ 685
Balance Sheet				
Inventory	$1,408	$1,420	$1,260	$1,368

This exhibit reveals two important results. First, when purchase costs *regularly rise,* as in Trekking's case, the following occurs:

Point: Managers prefer FIFO when costs are rising *and* incentives exist to report higher income for reasons such as bonus plans, job security, and reputation.

- FIFO assigns the lowest amount to cost of goods sold—yielding the highest gross profit and net income.
- LIFO assigns the highest amount to cost of goods sold—yielding the lowest gross profit and net income, which also yields a temporary tax advantage by postponing payment of some income tax.
- Weighted average yields results between FIFO and LIFO.
- Specific identification always yields results that depend on which units are sold.

Point: LIFO inventory is often less than the inventory's replacement cost because LIFO inventory is valued using the oldest inventory purchase costs.

Second, when costs *regularly decline,* the reverse occurs for FIFO and LIFO. Namely, FIFO gives the highest cost of goods sold—yielding the lowest gross profit and income. However, LIFO then gives the lowest cost of goods sold—yielding the highest gross profit and income.

All four inventory costing methods are acceptable. However, a company must disclose the inventory method it uses in its financial statements or notes. Each method offers certain advantages as follows:

- FIFO assigns an amount to inventory on the balance sheet that approximates its current cost; it also mimics the actual flow of goods for most businesses.
- LIFO assigns an amount to cost of goods sold on the income statement that approximates its current cost; it also better matches current costs with revenues in computing gross profit.
- Weighted average tends to smooth out erratic changes in costs.
- Specific identification exactly matches the costs of items with the revenues they generate.

Decision Maker   Answer — p. 229

Financial Planner   One of your clients asks if the inventory account of a company using FIFO needs any "adjustments" for analysis purposes in light of recent inflation. What is your advice? Does your advice depend on changes in the costs of these inventories? ■

Tax Effects of Costing Methods   Trekking's segment income statement in Exhibit 5.8 includes income tax expense (at a rate of 30%) because it was formed as a corporation. Since inventory costs affect net income, they have potential tax effects. Trekking gains a temporary tax advantage by using LIFO. Many companies use LIFO for this reason.

Companies can and often do use different costing methods for financial reporting and tax reporting. *The only exception is when LIFO is used for tax reporting; in this case, the IRS requires that it also be used in financial statements*—called the LIFO conformity rule.

Consistency in Using Costing Methods

The **consistency concept** prescribes that a company use the same accounting methods period after period so that financial statements are comparable across periods—the only exception is when a change from one method to another will improve its financial reporting. The *full-disclosure principle* prescribes that the notes to the statements report this type of change, its justification, and its effect on income.

The consistency concept does *not* require a company to use one method exclusively. For example, it can use different methods to value different categories of inventory.

Decision Ethics   Answer — p. 229

Inventory Manager   Your compensation as inventory manager includes a bonus plan based on gross profit. Your superior asks your opinion on changing the inventory costing method from FIFO to LIFO. Since costs are expected to continue to rise, your superior predicts that LIFO would match higher current costs against sales, thereby lowering taxable income (and gross profit). What do you recommend? ■

Quick Check   Answers — p. 229

4. Describe one advantage for each of the inventory costing methods: specific identification, FIFO, LIFO, and weighted average.
5. When costs are rising, which method reports higher net income—LIFO or FIFO?
6. When costs are rising, what effect does LIFO have on a balance sheet compared to FIFO?
7. A company takes a physical count of inventory at the end of 2010 and finds that ending inventory is understated by $10,000. Would this error cause cost of goods sold to be overstated or understated in 2010? In year 2011? If so, by how much?

VALUING INVENTORY AT LCM AND THE EFFECTS OF INVENTORY ERRORS

This section examines the role of market costs in determining inventory on the balance sheet and also the financial statement effects of inventory errors.

Lower of Cost or Market

We explained how to assign costs to ending inventory and cost of goods sold using one of four costing methods (FIFO, LIFO, weighted average, or specific identification). However, *accounting principles require that inventory be reported at the market value (cost) of replacing inventory when market value is lower than cost.* Merchandise inventory is then said to be reported on the balance sheet at the **lower of cost or market (LCM).**

> **P2** Compute the lower of cost or market amount of inventory.

Computing the Lower of Cost or Market   *Market* in the term *LCM* is defined as the current replacement cost of purchasing the same inventory items in the usual manner. A decline in replacement cost reflects a loss of value in inventory. When the recorded cost of inventory is higher than the replacement cost, a loss is recognized. When the recorded cost is lower, no adjustment is made.

LCM is applied in one of three ways: (1) to each individual item separately, (2) to major categories of items, or (3) to the whole of inventory. The less similar the items that make up inventory, the more likely companies are to apply LCM to individual items or categories. With the increasing application of technology and inventory tracking, companies increasingly apply

EXHIBIT 5.9

Lower of Cost or Market
Computations

$140,000 is the lower of $160,000
or $140,000

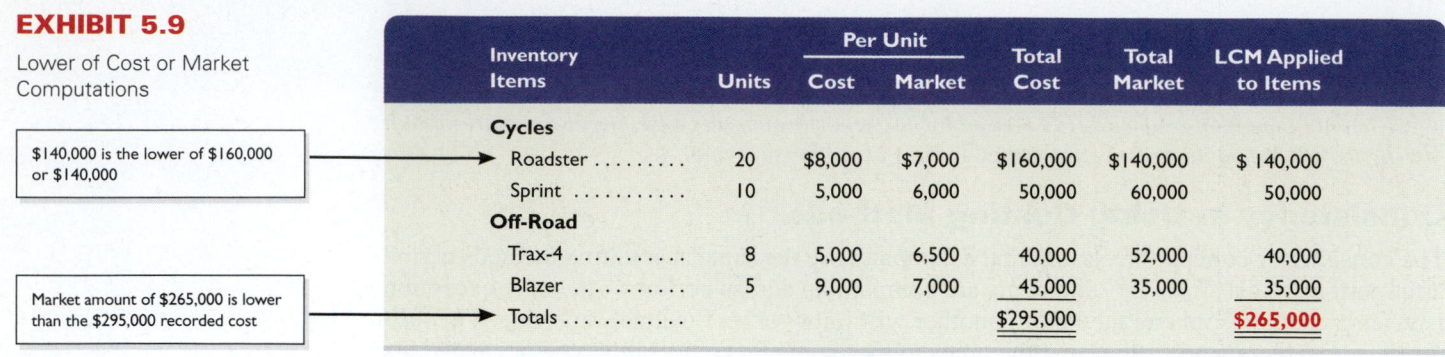

Inventory Items	Units	Per Unit Cost	Per Unit Market	Total Cost	Total Market	LCM Applied to Items
Cycles						
Roadster	20	$8,000	$7,000	$160,000	$140,000	$ 140,000
Sprint	10	5,000	6,000	50,000	60,000	50,000
Off-Road						
Trax-4	8	5,000	6,500	40,000	52,000	40,000
Blazer	5	9,000	7,000	45,000	35,000	35,000
Totals				$295,000		$265,000

Market amount of $265,000 is lower
than the $295,000 recorded cost

LCM to each individual item separately. Accordingly, we show that method only; however, advanced courses cover the other two methods. To illustrate LCM, we apply it to the ending inventory of a motorsports retailer in Exhibit 5.9.

LCM Applied to Individual Items When LCM is applied to individual *items* of inventory, the number of comparisons equals the number of items. For Roadster, $140,000 is the lower of the $160,000 cost and the $140,000 market. For Sprint, $50,000 is the lower of the $50,000 cost and the $60,000 market. For Trax-4, $40,000 is the lower of the $40,000 cost and the $52,000 market. For Blazer, $35,000 is the lower of the $45,000 cost and the $35,000 market. This yields a $265,000 reported inventory, computed from $140,000 for Roadster plus $50,000 for Sprint plus $40,000 for Trax-4 plus $35,000 for Blazer.

Point: Advances in technology encourage the individual-item approach for LCM.

RIM   The manufacturer **Research In Motion** applies LCM and reports that its "inventories are stated at the lower of cost and net realizable value [or replacement cost]."

Recording the Lower of Cost or Market Inventory must be adjusted downward when market is less than cost. To illustrate, if LCM is applied to the individual items of inventory in Exhibit 5.9, the Merchandise Inventory account must be adjusted from the $295,000 recorded cost down to the $265,000 market amount as follows.

Cost of Goods Sold	30,000	
Merchandise Inventory		30,000
To adjust inventory cost to market.		

Accounting rules require that inventory be adjusted to market when market is less than cost, but inventory normally cannot be written up to market when market exceeds cost. If recording inventory down to market is acceptable, why are companies not allowed to record inventory up to market? One view is that a gain from a market increase should not be realized until a sales transaction verifies the gain. However, this problem also applies when market is less than cost. A second and primary reason is the **conservatism constraint,** which prescribes the use of the less optimistic amount when more than one estimate of the amount to be received or paid exists and these estimates are about equally likely.

Financial Statement Effects of Inventory Errors

A2 Analyze the effects of inventory errors on current and future financial statements.

Companies must take care in both taking a physical count of inventory and in assigning a cost to it. An inventory error causes misstatements in cost of goods sold, gross profit, net income, current assets, and equity. It also causes misstatements in the next period's statements because ending inventory of one period is the beginning inventory of the next. As we consider the financial statement effects in this section, it is helpful if we recall the following *inventory relation.*

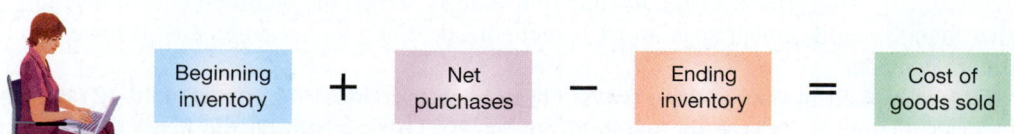

Income Statement Effects Exhibit 5.10 shows the effects of inventory errors on key amounts in the current and next periods' income statements. Let's look at row 1 and year 1. We see that understating ending inventory overstates cost of goods sold. This can be seen from the above inventory relation where we subtract a smaller ending inventory amount in computing cost of goods sold. Then a higher cost of goods sold yields a lower income.

To understand year 2 of row 1, remember that an understated ending inventory for year 1 becomes an understated beginning inventory for year 2. Using the above inventory relation, we see that if beginning inventory is understated, then cost of goods sold is understated (because we are starting with a smaller amount). A lower cost of goods sold yields a higher income.

Turning to overstatements, let's look at row 2 and year 1. If ending inventory is overstated, we use the inventory relation to see that cost of goods sold is understated. A lower cost of goods sold yields a higher income.

For year 2 of row 2, we again recall that an overstated ending inventory for year 1 becomes an overstated beginning inventory for year 2. If beginning inventory is overstated, we use the inventory relation to see that cost of goods sold is overstated. A higher cost of goods sold yields a lower income.

EXHIBIT 5.10

Effects of Inventory Errors on the Income Statement

	Year 1		Year 2	
Ending Inventory	**Cost of Goods Sold**	**Net Income**	**Cost of Goods Sold**	**Net Income**
Understated↓	Overstated↑	Understated↓	Understated↓	Overstated↑
Overstated*↑	Understated↓	Overstated↑	Overstated↑	Understated↓

* This error is less likely under a perpetual system because it implies more inventory than is recorded (or less shrinkage than expected). Management will normally follow up and discover and correct this error before it impacts any accounts.

To illustrate, consider an inventory error for a company with $100,000 in sales for each of the years 2010, 2011, and 2012. If this company maintains a steady $20,000 inventory level during this period and makes $60,000 in purchases in each of these years, its cost of goods sold is $60,000 and its gross profit is $40,000 each year.

Ending Inventory Understated—Year 1   Assume that this company errs in computing its 2010 ending inventory and reports $16,000 instead of the correct amount of $20,000. The effects of this error are shown in Exhibit 5.11. The $4,000 understatement of 2010 ending inventory causes a $4,000 overstatement in 2010 cost of goods sold and a $4,000 understatement in both gross profit and net income for 2010. We see that these effects match the effects predicted in Exhibit 5.10.

EXHIBIT 5.11

Effects of Inventory Errors on Three Periods' Income Statements

	Income Statements		
	2010	**2011**	**2012**
Sales	$100,000	$100,000	$100,000
Cost of goods sold			
Beginning inventory	$20,000	→$16,000*	→$20,000
Cost of goods purchased	60,000	60,000	60,000
Goods available for sale	80,000	76,000	80,000
Ending inventory	16,000*	20,000	20,000
Cost of goods sold	64,000†	56,000†	60,000
Gross profit	36,000	44,000	40,000
Expenses	10,000	10,000	10,000
Net income	$ 26,000	$ 34,000	$ 30,000

Correct income is $30,000 for each year

* Correct amount is $20,000.   † Correct amount is $60,000.

Ending Inventory Understated—Year 2   The 2010 understated ending inventory becomes the 2011 understated *beginning* inventory. We see in Exhibit 5.11 that this error causes an understatement in 2011 cost of goods sold and a $4,000 overstatement in both gross profit and net income for 2011.

Ending Inventory Understated—Year 3   Exhibit 5.11 shows that the 2010 ending inventory error affects only that period and the next. It does not affect 2012 results or any period thereafter. An inventory error is said to be *self-correcting* because it always yields an offsetting error in the next period. This does not reduce the severity of inventory errors. Managers, lenders, owners, and others make important decisions from analysis of income and costs.

Example: If 2010 ending inventory in Exhibit 5.11 is overstated by $3,000 (not understated by $4,000), what is the effect on cost of goods sold, gross profit, assets, and equity? *Answer:* Cost of goods sold is understated by $3,000 in 2010 and overstated by $3,000 in 2011. Gross profit and net income are overstated in 2010 and understated in 2011. Assets and equity are overstated in 2010.

Point: A former internal auditor at **Coca-Cola** alleges that just before midnight at a prior calendar year-end, fully loaded Coke trucks were ordered to drive about 2 feet away from the loading dock so that Coke could record millions of dollars in extra sales.

We can also do an analysis of beginning inventory errors. The income statement effects are the opposite of those for ending inventory.

Balance Sheet Effects   Balance sheet effects of an inventory error can be seen by considering the accounting equation: Assets = Liabilities + Equity. For example, understating ending inventory understates both current and total assets. An understatement in ending inventory also yields an understatement in equity because of the understatement in net income. Exhibit 5.12 shows the effects of inventory errors on the current period's balance sheet amounts. Errors in *beginning* inventory do not yield misstatements in the end-of-period balance sheet, but they do affect that current period's income statement.

EXHIBIT 5.12

Effects of Inventory Errors on Current Period's Balance Sheet

Ending Inventory	Assets	Equity
Understated ↓	Understated ↓	Understated ↓
Overstated ↑	Overstated ↑	Overstated ↑

Quick Check   Answers — p. 230

8. Use LCM applied separately to the following individual items to compute ending inventory.

Product	Units	Unit Recorded Cost	Unit Market Cost
A	20	$ 6	$ 5
B	40	9	8
C	10	12	15

GLOBAL VIEW

This section discusses differences between U.S. GAAP and IFRS in the items and costs making up merchandise inventory, in the methods to assign costs to inventory, and in the methods to estimate inventory values.

Items and Costs Making Up Inventory   Both U.S. GAAP and IFRS include broad and similar guidance for the items and costs making up merchandise inventory. Specifically, under both accounting systems, merchandise inventory includes all items that a company owns and holds for sale. Further, merchandise inventory includes costs of expenditures necessary, directly or indirectly, to bring those items to a salable condition and location.

Assigning Costs to Inventory   Both U.S. GAAP and IFRS allow companies to use specific identification in assigning costs to inventory. Further, both systems allow companies to apply a *cost flow assumption*. The usual cost flow assumptions are: FIFO, Weighted Average, and LIFO. However, IFRS does not (currently) allow use of LIFO. As the convergence project progresses, this prohibition may or may not persist.

Estimating Inventory Costs   The value of inventory can change while it awaits sale to customers. That value can decrease or increase.

Decreases in Inventory Value   Both U.S. GAAP and IFRS require companies to write down (reduce the cost recorded for) inventory when its value falls below the cost recorded. This is referred to as the *lower of cost or market* method explained in this chapter. U.S. GAAP prohibits any later increase in the recorded value of that inventory even if that decline in value is reversed through value increases in later periods. However, IFRS allows reversals of those write downs up to the original acquisition cost. For example, if *RIM* **Research In Motion** wrote down its 2010 inventory from $622 million to $600 million, it could not reverse this in future periods even if its value increased to more than $622 million. However, if RIM applied IFRS, it could reverse that previous loss. (Another difference is that value refers to *replacement cost* under U.S. GAAP, but *net realizable value* under IFRS.)

Increases in Inventory Value   Neither U.S. GAAP nor IFRS allow inventory to be adjusted upward beyond the original cost. (One exception is that IFRS requires agricultural assets such as animals, forests, and plants to be measured at fair value less point-of-sale costs.)

Nokia provides the following description of its inventory valuation procedures:

> Inventories are stated at the lower of cost or net realizable value. Cost ... approximates actual cost on a FIFO (First-in First-out) basis. Net realizable value is the amount that can be realized from the sale of the inventory in the normal course of business after allowing for the costs of realization.

Inventory Turnover and Days' Sales in Inventory   **Decision Analysis**

Inventory Turnover

Earlier chapters described two important ratios useful in evaluating a company's short-term liquidity: current ratio and acid-test ratio. A merchandiser's ability to pay its short-term obligations also depends on how quickly it sells its merchandise inventory. **Inventory turnover,** also called *merchandise inventory turnover,* is one ratio used to assess this and is defined in Exhibit 5.13.

$$\text{Inventory turnover} = \frac{\text{Cost of goods sold}}{\text{Average inventory}}$$

This ratio reveals how many *times* a company turns over (sells) its inventory during a period. If a company's inventory greatly varies within a year, average inventory amounts can be computed from interim periods such as quarters or months.

Users apply inventory turnover to help analyze short-term liquidity and to assess whether management is doing a good job controlling the amount of inventory available. A low ratio compared to that of competitors suggests inefficient use of assets. The company may be holding more inventory than it needs to support its sales volume. Similarly, a very high ratio compared to that of competitors suggests inventory might be too low. This can cause lost sales if customers must back-order merchandise. Inventory turnover has no simple rule except to say *a high ratio is preferable provided inventory is adequate to meet demand.*

Days' Sales in Inventory

To better interpret inventory turnover, many users measure the adequacy of inventory to meet sales demand. **Days' sales in inventory,** also called *days' stock on hand,* is a ratio that reveals how much inventory is available in terms of the number of days' sales. It can be interpreted as the number of days one can sell from inventory if no new items are purchased. This ratio is often viewed as a measure of the buffer against out-of-stock inventory and is useful in evaluating liquidity of inventory. It is defined in Exhibit 5.14.

$$\text{Days' sales in inventory} = \frac{\text{Ending inventory}}{\text{Cost of goods sold}} \times 365$$

Days' sales in inventory focuses on ending inventory and it estimates how many days it will take to convert inventory at the end of a period into accounts receivable or cash. Days' sales in inventory focuses on *ending* inventory whereas inventory turnover focuses on *average* inventory.

Decision Insight

Dell-ocity From its roots in a college dorm room, **Dell** now sells over 50 million dollars' worth of computers each day from its Website. The speed of Web technology has allowed Dell to slash inventories. Dell's inventory turnover is 88 and its days' sales in inventory is 5 days. Michael Dell asserts, "Speed is everything in this business." ■

Analysis of Inventory Management

Inventory management is a major emphasis for merchandisers. They must both plan and control inventory purchases and sales. **Toys "R" Us** is one of those merchandisers. Its inventory in fiscal year 2009 was $1,781 million. This inventory constituted 59% of its current assets and 21% of its total assets. We apply the analysis tools in this section to Toys "R" Us, as shown in Exhibit 5.15—also see margin graph.

A3 Assess inventory management using both inventory turnover and days' sales in inventory.

EXHIBIT 5.13
Inventory Turnover

Point: We must take care when comparing turnover ratios across companies that use different costing methods (such as FIFO and LIFO).

Point: Inventory turnover is higher and days' sales in inventory is lower for industries such as foods and other perishable products. The reverse holds for nonperishable product industries.

EXHIBIT 5.14
Days' Sales in Inventory

Point: Days' sales in inventory for many Ford models has risen: Freestyle, 122 days; Montego, 109 days; Five Hundred, 118 days. The industry average is 73 days. (*BusinessWeek*)

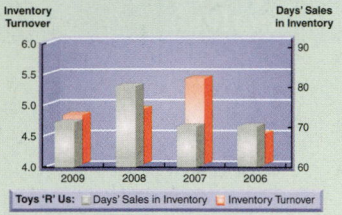

($ millions)	2009	2008	2007	2006
Cost of goods sold	$8,976	$8,987	$8,638	$7,652
Ending inventory	$1,781	$1,998	$1,690	$1,488
Inventory turnover	**4.8** times	**4.9** times	**5.4** times	**4.5** times
Industry inventory turnover	3.2 times	3.4 times	3.0 times	2.8 times
Days' sales in inventory	**72** days	**81** days	**71** days	**71** days
Industry days' sales in inventory	124 days	135 days	129 days	135 days

Its 2009 inventory turnover of 4.8 times means that Toys "R" Us turns over its inventory 4.8 times per year, or once every 76 days (365 days ÷ 4.8). We prefer inventory turnover to be high provided inventory is not out of stock and the company is not losing customers. The second metric, the 2009 days' sales in inventory of 72 days, reveals that it is carrying 72 days of sales in inventory. This inventory buffer seems more than adequate. Toys "R" Us would benefit from further management efforts to increase inventory turnover and reduce inventory levels.

Decision Maker   Answer — p. 229

Entrepreneur   Analysis of your retail store yields an inventory turnover of 5.0 and a days' sales in inventory of 73 days. The industry norm for inventory turnover is 4.4 and for days' sales in inventory is 74 days. What is your assessment of inventory management? ■

DEMONSTRATION PROBLEM

Craig Company uses a perpetual inventory system for its one product. Its beginning inventory, purchases, and sales during calendar year 2011 follow.

Date	Activity	Units Acquired at Cost	Units Sold at Retail	Unit Inventory
Jan. 1	Beg. Inventory	400 units @ $14 = $ 5,600		400 units
Jan. 15	Sale		200 units @ $30	200 units
March 10	Purchase	200 units @ $15 = $ 3,000		400 units
April 1	Sale		200 units @ $30	200 units
May 9	Purchase	300 units @ $16 = $ 4,800		500 units
Sept. 22	Purchase	250 units @ $20 = $ 5,000		750 units
Nov. 1	Sale		300 units @ $35	450 units
Nov. 28	Purchase	100 units @ $21 = $ 2,100		550 units
	Totals	1,250 units $20,500	700 units	

Additional tracking data for specific identification: (1) January 15 sale—200 units @ $14, (2) April 1 sale—200 units @ $15, and (3) November 1 sale—200 units @ $14 and 100 units @ $20.

Required

1. Calculate the cost of goods available for sale.

2. Apply the four different methods of inventory costing (FIFO, LIFO, weighted average, and specific identification) to calculate ending inventory and cost of goods sold under each method.

3. Compute gross profit earned by the company for each of the four costing methods in part 2. Also, report the inventory amount reported on the balance sheet for each of the four methods.

4. In preparing financial statements for year 2011, the financial officer was instructed to use FIFO but failed to do so and instead computed cost of goods sold according to LIFO. Determine the impact on year 2011's income from the error. Also determine the effect of this error on year 2012's income. Assume no income taxes.

5. Management wants a report that shows how changing from FIFO to another method would change net income. Prepare a table showing (1) the cost of goods sold amount under each of the four methods, (2) the amount by which each cost of goods sold total is different from the FIFO cost of goods sold, and (3) the effect on net income if another method is used instead of FIFO.

PLANNING THE SOLUTION

- Compute cost of goods available for sale by multiplying the units of beginning inventory and each purchase by their unit costs to determine the total cost of goods available for sale.
- Prepare a perpetual FIFO table starting with beginning inventory and showing how inventory changes after each purchase and after each sale (see Exhibit 5.5).
- Prepare a perpetual LIFO table starting with beginning inventory and showing how inventory changes after each purchase and after each sale (see Exhibit 5.6).
- Make a table of purchases and sales recalculating the average cost of inventory prior to each sale to arrive at the weighted average cost of ending inventory. Total the average costs associated with each sale to determine cost of goods sold (see Exhibit 5.7).
- Prepare a table showing the computation of cost of goods sold and ending inventory using the specific identification method (see Exhibit 5.4).
- Compare the year-end 2011 inventory amounts under FIFO and LIFO to determine the misstatement of year 2011 income that results from using LIFO. The errors for year 2011 and 2012 are equal in amount but opposite in effect.
- Create a table showing cost of goods sold under each method and how net income would differ from FIFO net income if an alternate method is adopted.

SOLUTION TO DEMONSTRATION PROBLEM

1. Cost of goods available for sale (this amount is the same for all methods).

Date		Units	Unit Cost	Cost
Jan. 1	Beg. Inventory	400	$14	$ 5,600
March 10	Purchase..............	200	15	3,000
May 9	Purchase..............	300	16	4,800
Sept. 22	Purchase..............	250	20	5,000
Nov. 28	Purchase..............	100	21	2,100
	Total goods available for sale.........	1,250		$20,500

2a. FIFO perpetual method.

Date	Goods Purchased	Cost of Goods Sold	Inventory Balance	
Jan. 1	Beginning balance		400 @ $14	= $ 5,600
Jan. 15		200 @ $14 = $2,800	200 @ $14	= $ 2,800
Mar. 10	200 @ $15 = $3,000		200 @ $14 200 @ $15	= $ 5,800
April 1		200 @ $14 = $2,800	200 @ $15	= $ 3,000
May 9	300 @ $16 = $4,800		200 @ $15 300 @ $16	= $ 7,800
Sept. 22	250 @ $20 = $5,000		200 @ $15 300 @ $16 250 @ $20	= $12,800
Nov. 1		200 @ $15 = $3,000 100 @ $16 = $1,600	200 @ $16 250 @ $20	= $ 8,200
Nov. 28	100 @ $21 = $2,100		200 @ $16 250 @ $20 100 @ $21	= $10,300
Total cost of goods sold		**$10,200**		

Note to students: **In a classroom situation,** once we compute cost of goods available for sale, we can compute the amount for either cost of goods sold or ending inventory—it is a matter of preference. **In practice,** the costs of items sold are identified as sales are made and immediately transferred from the inventory account to the cost of goods sold account. The previous solution showing the line-by-line approach illustrates actual application in practice. The following alternate solutions illustrate that, once the concepts are understood, other solution approaches are available. Although this is only shown for FIFO, it could be shown for all methods.

Alternate Methods to Compute FIFO Perpetual Numbers

[FIFO Alternate No. 1: Computing cost of goods sold first]

Cost of goods available for sale (from part 1)		$ 20,500
Cost of goods sold		
Jan. 15 Sold (200 @ $14)	$2,800	
April 1 Sold (200 @ $14)	2,800	
Nov. 1 Sold (200 @ $15 and 100 @ $16)	4,600	**10,200**
Ending inventory		**$10,300**

[FIFO Alternate No. 2: Computing ending inventory first]

Cost of goods available for sale (from part 1)		$ 20,500
Ending inventory*		
Nov. 28 Purchase (100 @ $21)	$2,100	
Sept. 22 Purchase (250 @ $20)	5,000	
May 9 Purchase (200 @ $16)	3,200	
Ending inventory		**10,300**
Cost of goods sold		**$10,200**

* Since FIFO assumes that the earlier costs are the first to flow out, we determine ending inventory by assigning the most recent costs to the remaining items.

2b.   LIFO perpetual method.

Date	Goods Purchased	Cost of Goods Sold	Inventory Balance
Jan. 1	Beginning balance		400 @ $14 = $ 5,600
Jan. 15		200 @ $14 = $2,800	200 @ $14 = $ 2,800
Mar. 10	200 @ $15 = $3,000		200 @ $14 200 @ $15 } = $ 5,800
April 1		200 @ $15 = $3,000	200 @ $14 = $ 2,800
May 9	300 @ $16 = $4,800		200 @ $14 300 @ $16 } = $ 7,600
Sept. 22	250 @ $20 = $5,000		200 @ $14 300 @ $16 250 @ $20 } = $12,600
Nov. 1		250 @ $20 = $5,000 50 @ $16 = $ 800	200 @ $14 250 @ $16 } = $ 6,800
Nov. 28	100 @ $21 = $2,100		200 @ $14 250 @ $16 100 @ $21 } = **$ 8,900**
Total cost of goods sold		**$11,600**	

2c. Weighted average perpetual method.

Date	Goods Purchased	Cost of Goods Sold	Inventory Balance	
Jan. 1	Beginning balance		400 @ $14	= $ 5,600
Jan. 15		200 @ $14 = $2,800	200 @ $14	= $ 2,800
Mar. 10	200 @ $15 = $3,000		200 @ $14 200 @ $15 (avg. cost is $14.5)	= $ 5,800
April 1		200 @ $14.5 = $2,900	200 @ $14.5	= $ 2,900
May 9	300 @ $16 = $4,800		200 @ $14.5 300 @ $16 (avg. cost is $15.4)	= $ 7,700
Sept. 22	250 @ $20 = $5,000		200 @ $14.5 300 @ $16 250 @ $20 (avg. cost is $16.93)	= $ 12,700
Nov. 1		300 @ $16.93 = $5,079	450 @ $16.93	= $ 7,618.5
Nov. 28	100 @ $21 = $2,100		450 @ $16.93 100 @ $21	= **$9,718.5**
Total cost of goods sold*		**$10,779**		

* The cost of goods sold ($10,779) plus ending inventory ($9,718.5) is $2.5 less than the cost of goods available for sale ($20,500) due to rounding.

2d. Specific identification method.

Date	Goods Purchased	Cost of Goods Sold	Inventory Balance	
Jan. 1	Beginning balance		400 @ $14	= $ 5,600
Jan. 15		200 @ $14 = $2,800	200 @ $14	= $ 2,800
Mar. 10	200 @ $15 = $3,000		200 @ $14 200 @ $15	= $ 5,800
April 1		200 @ $15 = $3,000	200 @ $14	= $ 2,800
May 9	300 @ $16 = $4,800		200 @ $14 300 @ $16	= $ 7,600
Sept. 22	250 @ $20 = $5,000		200 @ $14 300 @ $16 250 @ $20	= $ 12,600
Nov. 1		200 @ $14 = $2,800 100 @ $20 = $2,000	300 @ $16 150 @ $20	= $ 7,800
Nov. 28	100 @ $21 = $2,100		300 @ $16 150 @ $20 100 @ $21	= **$ 9,900**
Total cost of goods sold		**$10,600**		

3.

	FIFO	LIFO	Weighted Average	Specific Identification
Income Statement				
Sales*	$ 22,500	$22,500	$ 22,500	$22,500
Cost of goods sold	10,200	11,600	10,779	10,600
Gross profit	$ 12,300	$10,900	$ 11,721	$11,900
Balance Sheet				
Inventory	$10,300	$ 8,900	$9,718.5	$ 9,900

* Sales = (200 units × $30) + (200 units × $30) + (300 units × $35) = $22,500

4. Mistakenly using LIFO when FIFO should have been used overstates cost of goods sold in year 2011 by $1,400, which is the difference between the FIFO and LIFO amounts of ending inventory. It understates income in 2011 by $1,400. In year 2012, income is overstated by $1,400 because of the understatement in beginning inventory.

5. Analysis of the effects of alternative inventory methods.

	Cost of Goods Sold	Difference from FIFO Cost of Goods Sold	Effect on Net Income If Adopted Instead of FIFO
FIFO	$10,200	—	—
LIFO	11,600	+$1,400	$1,400 lower
Weighted average	10,779	+ 579	579 lower
Specific identification	10,600	+ 400	400 lower

APPENDIX

5A   Inventory Costing under a Periodic System

P3 Compute inventory in a periodic system using the methods of specific identification, FIFO, LIFO, and weighted average.

The basic aim of the periodic system and the perpetual system is the same: to assign costs to inventory and cost of goods sold. The same four methods are used to assign costs under both systems: specific identification; first-in, first-out; last-in, first-out; and weighted average. We use information from Trekking to show how to assign costs using these four methods with a periodic system. Data for sales and purchases are in Exhibit 5A.1. Also, recall that we explained the accounting entries under a periodic system in Appendix 4A.

EXHIBIT 5A.1

Purchases and Sales of Goods

Date	Activity	Units Acquired at Cost	Units Sold at Retail	Unit Inventory
Aug. 1	Beginning inventory	10 units @ $ 91 = $ 910		10 units
Aug. 3	Purchases	15 units @ $106 = $ 1,590		25 units
Aug. 14	Sales		20 units @ $130	5 units
Aug. 17	Purchases	20 units @ $115 = $ 2,300		25 units
Aug. 28	Purchases.............	10 units @ $119 = $ 1,190		35 units
Aug. 31	Sales................		23 units @ $150	12 units
	Totals	55 units $5,990	43 units	

Specific Identification   We use the above sales and purchases information and the specific identification method to assign costs to ending inventory and units sold. Trekking's internal data reveal the following specific unit sales:

August 14   Sold 8 bikes costing $91 each and 12 bikes costing $106 each

August 31   Sold 2 bikes costing $91 each, 3 bikes costing $106 each, 15 bikes costing $115 each, and 3 bikes costing $119 each

Applying specific identification and using the information above, we prepare Exhibit 5A.2. This exhibit starts with 10 bikes at $91 each in beginning inventory. On August 3, 15 more bikes are purchased at $106 each for $1,590. Inventory available now consists of 10 bikes at $91 each and 15 bikes at $106 each, for a total of $2,500. On August 14 (see specific sales data above), 20 bikes costing $2,000 are sold—leaving 5 bikes costing $500 in inventory. On August 17, 20 bikes costing $2,300 are purchased, and on August 28, another 10 bikes costing $1,190 are purchased, for a total of 35 bikes costing $3,990 in inventory. On August 31 (see specific sales above), 23 bikes costing $2,582 are sold, which leaves 12 bikes costing $1,408 in ending inventory. Carefully study Exhibit 5A.2 to see the flow of costs both in and out of inventory. Each unit, whether sold or remaining in inventory, has its own specific cost attached to it.

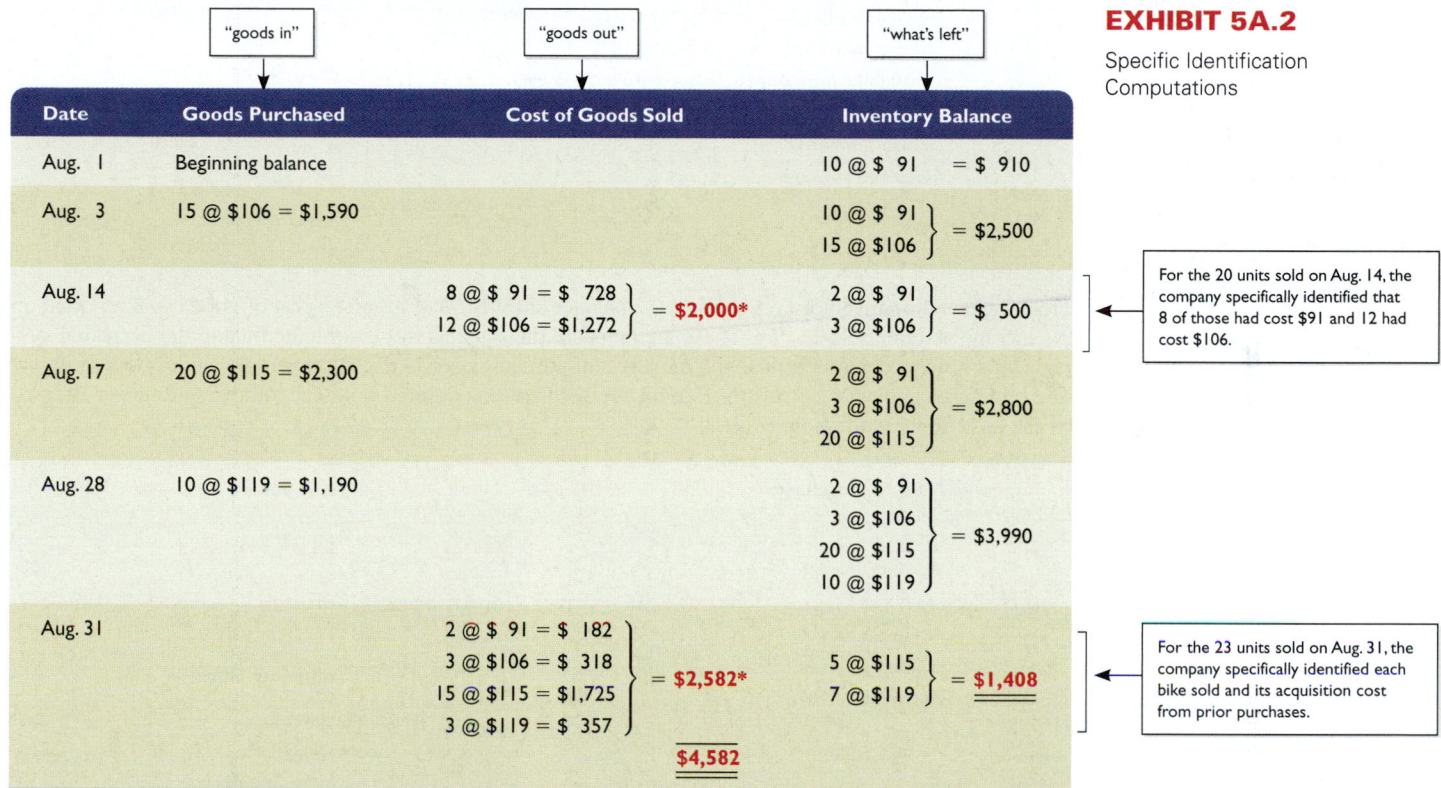

EXHIBIT 5A.2

Specific Identification Computations

Date	Goods Purchased	Cost of Goods Sold	Inventory Balance
Aug. 1	Beginning balance		10 @ $ 91 = $ 910
Aug. 3	15 @ $106 = $1,590		10 @ $ 91 ⎱ = $2,500 15 @ $106 ⎰
Aug. 14		8 @ $ 91 = $ 728 ⎱ = $2,000* 12 @ $106 = $1,272 ⎰	2 @ $ 91 ⎱ = $ 500 3 @ $106 ⎰
Aug. 17	20 @ $115 = $2,300		2 @ $ 91 ⎫ 3 @ $106 ⎬ = $2,800 20 @ $115 ⎭
Aug. 28	10 @ $119 = $1,190		2 @ $ 91 ⎫ 3 @ $106 ⎪ = $3,990 20 @ $115 ⎬ 10 @ $119 ⎭
Aug. 31		2 @ $ 91 = $ 182 ⎫ 3 @ $106 = $ 318 ⎪ = $2,582* 15 @ $115 = $1,725 ⎬ 3 @ $119 = $ 357 ⎭ **$4,582**	5 @ $115 ⎱ = **$1,408** 7 @ $119 ⎰

"goods in" → Goods Purchased

"goods out" → Cost of Goods Sold

"what's left" → Inventory Balance

For the 20 units sold on Aug. 14, the company specifically identified that 8 of those had cost $91 and 12 had cost $106.

For the 23 units sold on Aug. 31, the company specifically identified each bike sold and its acquisition cost from prior purchases.

* Identification of items sold (and their costs) is obtained from internal documents that track each unit from its purchase to its sale.

When using specific identification, Trekking's cost of goods sold reported on the income statement totals **$4,582**, the sum of $2,000 and $2,582 from the third column of Exhibit 5A.2. Trekking's ending inventory reported on the balance sheet is **$1,408**, which is the final inventory balance from the fourth column. The purchases and sales entries for Exhibit 5A.2 follow (the colored boldface numbers are those affected by the cost flow assumption).

Point: The assignment of costs to the goods sold and to inventory using specific identification is the same for both the perpetual and periodic systems.

Purchases		
Aug. 3 Purchases	1,590	
Accounts Payable		1,590
17 Purchases	2,300	
Accounts Payable		2,300
28 Purchases	1,190	
Accounts Payable		1,190

Sales		
Aug. 14 Accounts Receivable	2,600	
Sales...................		2,600
31 Accounts Receivable	3,450	
Sales...................		3,450
Adjusting Entry		
31 Merchandise Inventory	**1,408**	
Income Summary.........		498
Merchandise Inventory		**910**

First-In, First-Out

The first-in, first-out (FIFO) method of assigning costs to inventory assumes that inventory items are sold in the order acquired. When sales occur, the costs of the earliest units acquired are charged to cost of goods sold. This leaves the costs from the most recent purchases in ending inventory. Use of FIFO for computing the cost of inventory and cost of goods sold is shown in Exhibit 5A.3.

This exhibit starts with computing $5,990 in total units available for sale—this is given to us at the start of this appendix. Applying FIFO, we know that the 12 units in ending inventory will be reported at the cost of the most recent 12 purchases. Reviewing purchases in reverse order, we assign costs to the 12 bikes in ending inventory as follows: $119 cost to 10 bikes and $115 cost to 2 bikes. This yields 12 bikes costing $1,420 in ending inventory. We then subtract this $1,420 in ending inventory from $5,990 in cost of goods available to get $4,570 in cost of goods sold.

EXHIBIT 5A.3

FIFO Computations—
Periodic System

> Exhibit 5A.1 shows that the 12 units in ending inventory consist of 10 units from the latest purchase on Aug. 28 and 2 units from the next latest purchase on Aug. 17.

Total cost of 55 units available for sale (from Exhibit 5A.1)	$5,990
Less ending inventory priced using FIFO	
10 units from August 28 purchase at $119 each $1,190	
2 units from August 17 purchase at $115 each 230	
Ending inventory	**1,420**
Cost of goods sold	**$4,570**

Trekking's ending inventory reported on the balance sheet is **$1,420**, and its cost of goods sold reported on the income statement is **$4,570**. These amounts are the same as those computed using the perpetual system. This always occurs because the most recent purchases are in ending inventory under both systems. The purchases and sales entries for Exhibit 5A.3 follow (the colored boldface numbers are those affected by the cost flow assumption).

Point: The assignment of costs to the goods sold and to inventory using FIFO is the same for both the perpetual and periodic systems.

Purchases				**Sales**		
Aug. 3	Purchases.....................	1,590		Aug. 14	Accounts Receivable 2,600	
	Accounts Payable..........		1,590		Sales	2,600
17	Purchases.....................	2,300		31	Accounts Receivable 3,450	
	Accounts Payable..........		2,300		Sales	3,450
28	Purchases.....................	1,190			**Adjusting Entry**	
	Accounts Payable..........		1,190	31	Merchandise Inventory **1,420**	
					Income Summary	510
					Merchandise Inventory	**910**

Last-In, First-Out   The last-in, first-out (LIFO) method of assigning costs assumes that the most recent purchases are sold first. These more recent costs are charged to the goods sold, and the costs of the earliest purchases are assigned to inventory. LIFO results in costs of the most recent purchases being assigned to cost of goods sold, which means that LIFO comes close to matching current costs of goods sold with revenues. Use of LIFO for computing cost of inventory and cost of goods sold is shown in Exhibit 5A.4.

This exhibit starts with computing $5,990 in total units available for sale—this is given to us at the start of this appendix. Applying LIFO, we know that the 12 units in ending inventory will be reported at the cost of the earliest 12 purchases. Reviewing the earliest purchases in order, we assign costs to the 12 bikes in ending inventory as follows: $91 cost to 10 bikes and $106 cost to 2 bikes. This yields 12 bikes costing $1,122 in ending inventory. We then subtract this $1,122 in ending inventory from $5,990 in cost of goods available to get $4,868 in cost of goods sold.

EXHIBIT 5A.4

LIFO Computations—
Periodic System

> Exhibit 5A.1 shows that the 12 units in ending inventory consist of 10 units from the earliest purchase (beg. inv.) and 2 units from the next earliest purchase on Aug. 3.

Total cost of 55 units available for sale (from Exhibit 5A.1)	$5,990
Less ending inventory priced using LIFO	
10 units in beginning inventory at $91 each $910	
2 units from August 3 purchase at $106 each.................. 212	
Ending inventory	**1,122**
Cost of goods sold......................................	**$4,868**

Trekking's ending inventory reported on the balance sheet is **$1,122**, and its cost of goods sold reported on the income statement is **$4,868**. When LIFO is used with the periodic system, cost of goods sold is assigned costs from the most recent purchases for the period. With a perpetual system, cost of goods sold is assigned costs from the most recent purchases at the point of *each sale*. The purchases and sales entries for Exhibit 5A.4 follow (the colored boldface numbers are those affected by the cost flow assumption).

Purchases		
Aug. 3 Purchases	1,590	
Accounts Payable		1,590
17 Purchases	2,300	
Accounts Payable		2,300
28 Purchases	1,190	
Accounts Payable		1,190

Sales		
Aug. 14 Accounts Receivable	2,600	
Sales		2,600
31 Accounts Receivable	3,450	
Sales		3,450
Adjusting Entry		
31 Merchandise Inventory	**1,122**	
Income Summary		212
Merchandise Inventory		**910**

Weighted Average The **weighted average** or **WA** (also called **average cost**) method of assigning cost requires that we use the average cost per unit of inventory at the end of the period. Weighted average cost per unit equals the cost of goods available for sale divided by the units available. The weighted average method of assigning cost involves three important steps. The first two steps are shown in Exhibit 5A.5. First, multiply the per unit cost for beginning inventory and each particular purchase by the corresponding number of units (from Exhibit 5A.1). Second, add these amounts and divide by the total number of units available for sale to find the weighted average cost per unit.

Step 1:	10 units @ $ 91 = $ 910
	15 units @ $106 = 1,590
	20 units @ $115 = 2,300
	10 units @ $119 = 1,190
	55 **$5,990**
Step 2:	$5,990/55 units = **$108.91** weighted average cost per unit

EXHIBIT 5A.5

Weighted Average Cost per Unit

The third step is to use the weighted average cost per unit to assign costs to inventory and to the units sold as shown in Exhibit 5A.6.

Step 3:	Total cost of 55 units available for sale (from Exhibit 5A.1)..........	$ 5,990
	Less **ending inventory** priced on a weighted average cost basis: 12 units at $108.91 each (from Exhibit 5A.5)...........	**1,307**
	Cost of goods sold	**$4,683**

Example: In Exhibit 5A.5, if 5 more units had been purchased at $120 each, what would be the weighted average cost per unit?
Answer: $109.83 ($6,590/60)

EXHIBIT 5A.6

Weighted Average Computations—Periodic

Trekking's ending inventory reported on the balance sheet is **$1,307**, and its cost of goods sold reported on the income statement is **$4,683** when using the weighted average (periodic) method. The purchases and sales entries for Exhibit 5A.6 follow (the colored boldface numbers are those affected by the cost flow assumption).

Purchases		
Aug. 3 Purchases.....................	1,590	
Accounts Payable..........		1,590
17 Purchases....................	2,300	
Accounts Payable..........		2,300
28 Purchases....................	1,190	
Accounts Payable..........		1,190

Sales		
Aug. 14 Accounts Receivable	2,600	
Sales....................		2,600
31 Accounts Receivable	3,450	
Sales....................		3,450
Adjusting Entry		
31 Merchandise Inventory	**1,307**	
Income Summary		397
Merchandise Inventory		**910**

Point: Weighted average usually yields different results for the perpetual and the periodic systems because under a perpetual system it recomputes the per unit cost prior to each sale, whereas under a periodic system, the per unit cost is computed only at the end of a period.

Point: LIFO inventory is often less than the inventory's replacement cost because LIFO inventory is valued using the oldest inventory purchase costs.

Financial Statement Effects   When purchase prices do not change, each inventory costing method assigns the same cost amounts to inventory and to cost of goods sold. When purchase prices are different, however, the methods nearly always assign different cost amounts. We show these differences in Exhibit 5A.7 using Trekking's data.

EXHIBIT 5A.7

Financial Statement Effects of Inventory Costing Methods

TREKKING COMPANY For Month Ended August 31				
	Specific Identification	FIFO	LIFO	Weighted Average
Income Statement				
Sales	$ 6,050	$ 6,050	$ 6,050	$ 6,050
Cost of goods sold	4,582	4,570	4,868	4,683
Gross profit	1,468	1,480	1,182	1,367
Expenses......................	450	450	450	450
Income before taxes..............	1,018	1,030	732	917
Income tax expense (30%).........	305	309	220	275
Net income	$ 713	$ 721	$ 512	$ 642
Balance Sheet				
Inventory	$1,408	$1,420	$1,122	$1,307

This exhibit reveals two important results. First, when purchase costs *regularly rise,* as in Trekking's case, observe the following:

● FIFO assigns the lowest amount to cost of goods sold—yielding the highest gross profit and net income.
● LIFO assigns the highest amount to cost of goods sold—yielding the lowest gross profit and net income, which also yields a temporary tax advantage by postponing payment of some income tax.
● Weighted average yields results between FIFO and LIFO.
● Specific identification always yields results that depend on which units are sold.

Second, when costs *regularly decline,* the reverse occurs for FIFO and LIFO. FIFO gives the highest cost of goods sold—yielding the lowest gross profit and income. And LIFO gives the lowest cost of goods sold—yielding the highest gross profit and income.

All four inventory costing methods are acceptable in practice. A company must disclose the inventory method it uses. Each method offers certain advantages as follows:

● FIFO assigns an amount to inventory on the balance sheet that approximates its current cost; it also mimics the actual flow of goods for most businesses.
● LIFO assigns an amount to cost of goods sold on the income statement that approximates its current cost; it also better matches current costs with revenues in computing gross profit.
● Weighted average tends to smooth out erratic changes in costs.
● Specific identification exactly matches the costs of items with the revenues they generate.

Quick Check

Answers — p. 230

9. A company reports the following beginning inventory and purchases, and it ends the period with 30 units in inventory.

       Beginning inventory .... 100 units at $10 cost per unit
       Purchase 1 .... 40 units at $12 cost per unit
       Purchase 2 .... 20 units at $14 cost per unit

  a. Compute ending inventory using the FIFO periodic system.
  b. Compute cost of goods sold using the LIFO periodic system.

Inventory Estimation Methods

5B

Inventory sometimes requires estimation for two reasons. First, companies often require **interim statements** (financial statements prepared for periods of less than one year), but they only annually take a physical count of inventory. Second, companies may require an inventory estimate if some casualty such as fire or flood makes taking a physical count impossible. Estimates are usually only required for companies that use the periodic system. Companies using a perpetual system would presumably have updated inventory data.

This appendix describes two methods to estimate inventory.

> **P4** Apply both the retail inventory and gross profit methods to estimate inventory.

Retail Inventory Method   To avoid the time-consuming and expensive process of taking a physical inventory each month or quarter, some companies use the **retail inventory method** to estimate cost of goods sold and ending inventory. Some companies even use the retail inventory method to prepare the annual statements. **Home Depot**, for instance, says in its annual report: "Inventories are stated at the lower of cost (first-in, first-out) or market, as determined by the retail inventory method." A company may also estimate inventory for audit purposes or when inventory is damaged or destroyed.

The retail inventory method uses a three-step process to estimate ending inventory. We need to know the amount of inventory a company had at the beginning of the period in both *cost* and *retail* amounts. We already explained how to compute the cost of inventory. The *retail amount of inventory* refers to its dollar amount measured using selling prices of inventory items. We also need to know the net amount of goods purchased (minus returns, allowances, and discounts) in the period, both at cost and at retail. The amount of net sales at retail is also needed. The process is shown in Exhibit 5B.1.

The reasoning behind the retail inventory method is that if we can get a good estimate of the cost-to-retail ratio, we can multiply ending inventory at retail by this ratio to estimate ending inventory at cost. We show in Exhibit 5B.2 how these steps are applied to estimate ending inventory for a typical company. First, we find that $100,000 of goods (at retail selling prices) were available for sale. We see that $70,000 of these goods were sold, leaving $30,000 (retail value) of merchandise in ending inventory. Second, the cost of these goods is 60% of the $100,000 retail value. Third, since cost for these goods is 60% of retail, the estimated cost of ending inventory is $18,000.

> **Point:** When a retailer takes a physical inventory, it can restate the retail value of inventory to a cost basis by applying the cost-to-retail ratio. It can also estimate the amount of shrinkage by comparing the inventory computed with the amount from a physical inventory.

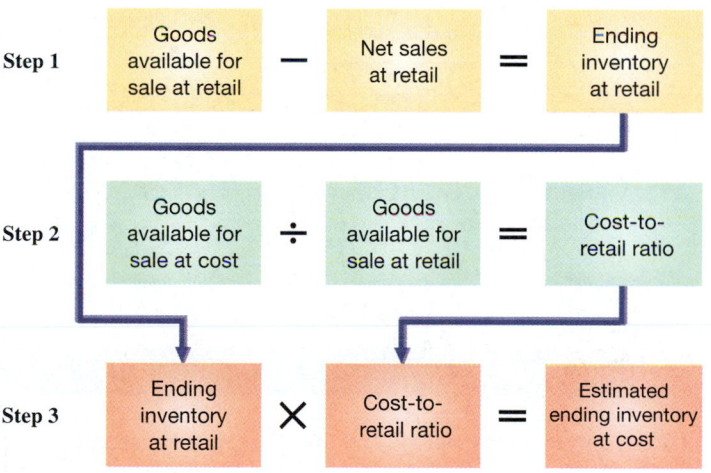

EXHIBIT 5B.1

Retail Inventory Method of Inventory Estimation

> **Example:** What is the cost of ending inventory in Exhibit 5B.2 if the cost of beginning inventory is $22,500 and its retail value is $34,500? *Answer:* $30,000 × 62% = $18,600

EXHIBIT 5B.2

Estimated Inventory Using the Retail Inventory Method

	At Cost	At Retail
Goods available for sale		
Beginning inventory	$ 20,500	$ 34,500
Cost of goods purchased.	39,500	65,500
Goods available for sale	60,000	100,000
Step 1: Deduct net sales at retail		70,000
Ending inventory at retail		$ 30,000
Step 2: Cost-to-retail ratio: ($60,000 ÷ $100,000) = 60%		
Step 3: Estimated ending inventory at cost ($30,000 × 60%)	$18,000	

Gross Profit Method   The **gross profit method** estimates the cost of ending inventory by applying the gross profit ratio to net sales (at retail). This type of estimate often is needed when inventory is destroyed, lost, or stolen. These cases require an inventory estimate so that a company can file a claim with its insurer. Users also apply this method to see whether inventory amounts from a physical count are rea-

EXHIBIT 5B.3

Gross Profit Method of Inventory Estimation

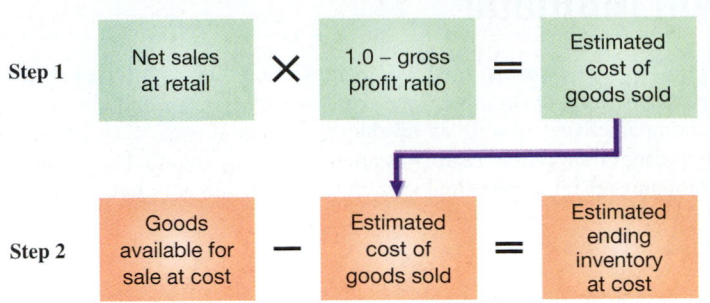

sonable. This method uses the historical relation between cost of goods sold and net sales to estimate the proportion of cost of goods sold making up current sales. This cost of goods sold estimate is then subtracted from cost of goods available for sale to estimate the ending inventory at cost. These two steps are shown in Exhibit 5B.3.

To illustrate, assume that a company's inventory is destroyed by fire in March 2011. When the fire occurs, the company's accounts show the following balances for January through March: sales, $31,500; sales returns, $1,500; inventory (January 1, 2011), $12,000; and cost of goods purchased, $20,500. If this company's gross profit ratio is 30%, then 30% of each net sales dollar is gross profit and 70% is cost of goods sold. We show in Exhibit 5B.4 how this 70% is used to estimate lost inventory of $11,500. To understand this exhibit, think of subtracting the cost of goods sold from the goods available for sale to get the ending inventory.

Point: A fire or other catastrophe can result in an insurance claim for lost inventory or income. Backup and off-site storage of data help ensure coverage for such losses.

Point: Reliability of the gross profit method depends on a good estimate of the gross profit ratio.

EXHIBIT 5B.4

Estimated Inventory Using the Gross Profit Method

Goods available for sale		
Inventory, January 1, 2011		$12,000
Cost of goods purchased		20,500
Goods available for sale (at cost)		32,500
Net sales at retail ($31,500 − $1,500)		$30,000
Step 1: **Estimated cost of goods sold ($30,000 × 70%)**		**(21,000)** ← × 0.70
Step 2: **Estimated March inventory at cost**		**$11,500**

Quick Check

Answer — p. 230

10. Using the retail method and the following data, estimate the cost of ending inventory.

	Cost	Retail
Beginning inventory	$324,000	$530,000
Cost of goods purchased	195,000	335,000
Net sales		320,000

Summary

C1   **Identify the items making up merchandise inventory.**
Merchandise inventory refers to goods owned by a company and held for resale. Three special cases merit our attention. Goods in transit are reported in inventory of the company that holds ownership rights. Goods on consignment are reported in the consignor's inventory. Goods damaged or obsolete are reported in inventory at their net realizable value.

C2   **Identify the costs of merchandise inventory.** Costs of merchandise inventory include expenditures necessary to bring an

item to a salable condition and location. This includes its invoice cost minus any discount plus any added or incidental costs necessary to put it in a place and condition for sale.

A1   **Analyze the effects of inventory methods for both financial and tax reporting.** When purchase costs are rising or falling, the inventory costing methods are likely to assign different costs to inventory. Specific identification exactly matches costs and revenues. Weighted average smooths out cost changes. FIFO assigns an amount to inventory closely approximating current replacement cost. LIFO assigns the most recent costs incurred to cost of goods sold and likely better matches current costs with revenues.

A2   Analyze the effects of inventory errors on current and future financial statements. An error in the amount of ending inventory affects assets (inventory), net income (cost of goods sold), and equity for that period. Since ending inventory is next period's beginning inventory, an error in ending inventory affects next period's cost of goods sold and net income. Inventory errors in one period are offset in the next period.

A3   Assess inventory management using both inventory turnover and days' sales in inventory. We prefer a high inventory turnover, provided that goods are not out of stock and customers are not turned away. We use days' sales in inventory to assess the likelihood of goods being out of stock. We prefer a small number of days' sales in inventory if we can serve customer needs and provide a buffer for uncertainties.

P1   Compute inventory in a perpetual system using the methods of specific identification, FIFO, LIFO, and weighted average. Costs are assigned to the cost of goods sold account *each time* a sale occurs in a perpetual system. Specific identification assigns a cost to each item sold by referring to its actual cost (for example, its net invoice cost). Weighted average assigns a cost to items sold by dividing the current balance in the inventory account by the total items available for sale to determine cost per unit. We then multiply the number of units sold by this cost per unit to get the cost of each sale. FIFO assigns cost to items sold assuming that the earliest units purchased are the first units sold. LIFO assigns cost to items sold assuming that the most recent units purchased are the first units sold.

P2   Compute the lower of cost or market amount of inventory. Inventory is reported at market cost when market is *lower* than recorded cost, called the *lower of cost or market (LCM) inventory*. Market is typically measured as replacement cost. Lower of cost or market can be applied separately to each item, to major categories of items, or to the entire inventory.

P3^A   Compute inventory in a periodic system using the methods of specific identification, FIFO, LIFO, and weighted average. Periodic inventory systems allocate the cost of goods available for sale between cost of goods sold and ending inventory *at the end of a period*. Specific identification and FIFO give identical results whether the periodic or perpetual system is used. LIFO assigns costs to cost of goods sold assuming the last units purchased for the period are the first units sold. The weighted average cost per unit is computed by dividing the total cost of beginning inventory and net purchases for the period by the total number of units available. Then, it multiplies cost per unit by the number of units sold to give cost of goods sold.

P4^B   Apply both the retail inventory and gross profit methods to estimate inventory. The retail inventory method involves three steps: (1) goods available at retail minus net sales at retail equals ending inventory at retail, (2) goods available at cost divided by goods available at retail equals the cost-to-retail ratio, and (3) ending inventory at retail multiplied by the cost-to-retail ratio equals estimated ending inventory at cost. The gross profit method involves two steps: (1) net sales at retail multiplied by 1 minus the gross profit ratio equals estimated cost of goods sold, and (2) goods available at cost minus estimated cost of goods sold equals estimated ending inventory at cost.

Guidance Answers to Decision Maker and Decision Ethics

Financial Planner   The FIFO method implies that the oldest costs are the first ones assigned to cost of goods sold. This leaves the most recent costs in ending inventory. You report this to your client and note that in most cases, the ending inventory of a company using FIFO is reported at or near its replacement cost. This means that your client need not in most cases adjust the reported value of inventory. Your answer changes only if there are major increases in replacement cost compared to the cost of recent purchases reported in inventory. When major increases in costs occur, your client might wish to adjust inventory (for internal reports) for the difference between the reported cost of inventory and its replacement cost. (*Note:* Decreases in costs of purchases are recognized under the lower of cost or market adjustment.)

Inventory Manager   It seems your company can save (or at least postpone) taxes by switching to LIFO, but the switch is likely to reduce bonus money that you think you have earned and deserve. Since

the U.S. tax code requires companies that use LIFO for tax reporting also to use it for financial reporting, your options are further constrained. Your best decision is to tell your superior about the tax savings with LIFO. You also should discuss your bonus plan and how this is likely to hurt you unfairly. You might propose to compute inventory under the LIFO method for reporting purposes but use the FIFO method for your bonus calculations. Another solution is to revise the bonus plan to reflect the company's use of the LIFO method.

Entrepreneur   Your inventory turnover is markedly higher than the norm, whereas days' sales in inventory approximates the norm. Since your turnover is already 14% better than average, you are probably best served by directing attention to days' sales in inventory. You should see whether you can reduce the level of inventory while maintaining service to customers. Given your higher turnover, you should be able to hold less inventory.

Guidance Answers to Quick Checks

1. The matching principle.
2. Target reports these goods in its inventory.
3. Total cost assigned to the painting is $12,180, computed as $11,400 + $130 + $150 + $100 + $400.
4. Specific identification exactly matches costs and revenues. Weighted average tends to smooth out cost changes. FIFO

assigns an amount to inventory that closely approximates current replacement cost. LIFO assigns the most recent costs incurred to cost of goods sold and likely better matches current costs with revenues.

5. FIFO—it gives a lower cost of goods sold, a higher gross profit, and a higher net income when costs are rising.

6. When costs are rising, LIFO gives a lower inventory figure on the balance sheet as compared to FIFO. FIFO's inventory amount approximates current replacement costs.

7. Cost of goods sold would be overstated by $10,000 in 2010 and understated by $10,000 in year 2011.

8. The reported LCM inventory amount (using items) is $540, computed as [(20 × $5) + (40 × $8) + (10 × $12)].

9.[A] **a.** FIFO periodic inventory = (20 × $14) + (10 × $12)
$$= \$400$$

b. LIFO periodic cost of goods sold
$$= (20 \times \$14) + (40 \times \$12) + (70 \times \$10)$$
$$= \$1,460$$

10.[B] Estimated ending inventory (at cost) is $327,000. It is computed as follows:

Step 1:   ($530,000 + $335,000) − $320,000 = $545,000

Step 2: $\dfrac{\$324,000 + \$195,000}{\$530,000 + \$335,000} = 60\%$

Step 3: $545,000 \times 60\% = \underline{\$327,000}$

Key Terms

Average cost (p. 210)

Conservatism constraint (p. 214)

Consignee (p. 204)

Consignor (p. 204)

Consistency concept (p. 213)

Days' sales in inventory (p. 217)

First-in, first-out (FIFO) (p. 209)

Gross profit method (p. 228)

Interim statements (p. 227)

Inventory turnover (p. 217)

Last-in, first-out (LIFO) (p. 209)

Lower of cost or market (LCM) (p. 213)

Net realizable value (p. 204)

Retail inventory method (p. 227)

Specific identification (p. 207)

Weighted average (p. 210)

Multiple Choice Quiz   Answers on p. 245   mhhe.com/wildFINMAN4e

Additional Quiz Questions are available at the book's Website.

Use the following information from Marvel Company for the month of July to answer questions 1 through 4.

July 1	Beginning inventory	75 units @ $25 each
July 3	Purchase	348 units @ $27 each
July 8	Sale	300 units
July 15	Purchase	257 units @ $28 each
July 23	Sale	275 units

1. Assume that Marvel uses a perpetual FIFO inventory system. What is the dollar value of its ending inventory?
 a. $2,940   **d.** $2,852
 b. $2,685   **e.** $2,705
 c. $2,625

2. Assume that Marvel uses a perpetual LIFO inventory system. What is the dollar value of its ending inventory?
 a. $2,940   **d.** $2,852
 b. $2,685   **e.** $2,705
 c. $2,625

3. Assume that Marvel uses a perpetual specific identification inventory system. Its ending inventory consists of 20 units from beginning inventory, 40 units from the July 3 purchase, and 45 units from the July 15 purchase. What is the dollar value of its ending inventory?
 a. $2,940   **d.** $2,852
 b. $2,685   **e.** $2,840
 c. $2,625

4.[A] Assume that Marvel uses a *periodic* FIFO inventory system. What is the dollar value of its ending inventory?
 a. $2,940   **d.** $2,852
 b. $2,685   **e.** $2,705
 c. $2,625

5. A company has cost of goods sold of $85,000 and ending inventory of $18,000. Its days' sales in inventory equals:
 a. 49.32 days   **d.** 77.29 days
 b. 0.21 days   **e.** 1,723.61 days
 c. 4.72 days

[A(B)]   *Superscript letter A (B) denotes assignments based on Appendix 5A (5B).*
 🅘 Icon denotes assignments that involve decision making.

Discussion Questions

1. Describe how costs flow from inventory to cost of goods sold for the following methods: (*a*) FIFO and (*b*) LIFO.

2. Where is the amount of merchandise inventory disclosed in the financial statements?

3. Why are incidental costs sometimes ignored in inventory costing? Under what accounting constraint is this permitted?

4. 🅘 If costs are declining, will the LIFO or FIFO method of inventory valuation yield the lower cost of goods sold? Why?

5. What does the full-disclosure principle prescribe if a company changes from one acceptable accounting method to another?

6. Can a company change its inventory method each accounting period? Explain.

7. 🚹 Does the accounting concept of consistency preclude any changes from one accounting method to another?

8. 🚹 If inventory errors are said to correct themselves, why are accounting users concerned when such errors are made?

9. Explain the following statement: "Inventory errors correct themselves."

10. What is the meaning of *market* as it is used in determining the lower of cost or market for inventory?

11. 🚹 What guidance does the accounting constraint of conservatism offer?

12. What factors contribute to (or cause) inventory shrinkage?

13.ᴬ What accounts are used in a periodic inventory system but not in a perpetual inventory system?

14. Refer to **Research In Motion**'s financial statements in Appendix A. On February 27, 2010, what percent of current assets are represented by inventory? *RIM*

15. Refer to **Apple**'s financial statements in Appendix A and compute its cost of goods available for sale for the year ended September 26, 2009. *Apple*

16. Refer to **Nokia**'s financial statements in Appendix A. Compute its cost of goods available for sale for the year ended December 31, 2009. *NOKIA*

17. Refer to **Palm**'s financial statements in Appendix A. What percent of its current assets are inventory as of May 31, 2008 and 2009? *Palm*

18.ᴮ When preparing interim financial statements, what two methods can companies utilize to estimate cost of goods sold and ending inventory?

connect

A company reports the following beginning inventory and purchases for the month of January. On January 26, the company sells 360 units. What is the cost of the 155 units that remain in ending inventory at January 31, assuming costs are assigned based on a perpetual inventory system and use of FIFO? (Round per unit costs to three decimals, but inventory balances to the dollar.)

	Units	Unit Cost
Beginning inventory on January 1	320	$6.00
Purchase on January 9	85	6.40
Purchase on January 25	110	6.60

QUICK STUDY

QS 5-1
Inventory costing with FIFO perpetual
P1

Refer to the information in QS 5-1 and assume the perpetual inventory system is used. Determine the costs assigned to ending inventory when costs are assigned based on LIFO. (Round per unit costs to three decimals, but inventory balances to the dollar.)

QS 5-2
Inventory costing with LIFO perpetual P1

Refer to the information in QS 5-1 and assume the perpetual inventory system is used. Determine the costs assigned to ending inventory when costs are assigned based on weighted average. (Round per unit costs to three decimals, but inventory balances to the dollar.)

QS 5-3
Inventory costing with weighted average perpetual P1
Check $960

Segoe Company reports beginning inventory of 10 units at $50 each. Every week for four weeks it purchases an additional 10 units at respective costs of $51, $52, $55 and $60 per unit for weeks 1 through 4. Calculate the cost of goods available for sale and the units available for sale for this four-week period. Assume that no sales occur during those four weeks.

QS 5-4
Computing goods available for sale P1

Mercedes Brown starts a merchandising business on December 1 and enters into three inventory purchases:

December 7	10 units @ $ 9 cost
December 14	20 units @ $10 cost
December 21	15 units @ $12 cost

Brown sells 18 units for $35 each on December 15. Seven of the sold units are from the December 7 purchase and eleven are from the December 14 purchase. Brown uses a perpetual inventory system. Determine the costs assigned to the December 31 ending inventory based on FIFO. (Round per unit costs to three decimals, but inventory balances to the dollar.)

QS 5-5
Assigning costs with FIFO perpetual
P1

QS 5-6

Inventory costing with LIFO
perpetual   **P1**

Refer to the information in QS 5-5 and assume the perpetual inventory system is used. Determine the costs assigned to ending inventory when costs are assigned based on LIFO. (Round per unit costs to three decimals, but inventory balances to the dollar.)

QS 5-7

Inventory costing with weighted
average perpetual   **P1**

Check   End. Inv. = $296

Refer to the information in QS 5-5 and assume the perpetual inventory system is used. Determine the costs assigned to ending inventory when costs are assigned based on weighted average. (Round per unit costs to three decimals, but inventory balances to the dollar.)

QS 5-8

Inventory costing with specific
identification perpetual   **P1**

Refer to the information in QS 5-5 and assume the perpetual inventory system is used. Determine the costs assigned to ending inventory when costs are assigned based on specific identification. (Round per unit costs to three decimals, but inventory balances to the dollar.)

QS 5-9

Contrasting inventory
costing methods

A1

Identify the inventory costing method best described by each of the following separate statements. Assume a period of increasing costs.

1. The preferred method when each unit of product has unique features that markedly affect cost.

2. Matches recent costs against net sales.

3. Provides a tax advantage (deferral) to a corporation when costs are rising.

4. Yields a balance sheet inventory amount often markedly less than its replacement cost.

5. Results in a balance sheet inventory amount approximating replacement cost.

QS 5-10

Inventory ownership

C1

Crafts Galore, a distributor of handmade gifts, operates out of owner Jenny Finn's house. At the end of the current period, Jenny reports she has 1,500 units (products) in her basement, 30 of which were damaged by water and cannot be sold. She also has another 250 units in her van, ready to deliver per a customer order, terms FOB destination, and another 70 units out on consignment to a friend who owns a retail store. How many units should Jenny include in her company's period-end inventory?

QS 5-11

Inventory costs

C2

A car dealer acquires a used car for $3,000, terms FOB shipping point. Additional costs in obtaining and offering the car for sale include $150 for transportation-in, $200 for import duties, $50 for insurance during shipment, $25 for advertising, and $250 for sales staff salaries. For computing inventory, what cost is assigned to the used car?

QS 5-12

Applying LCM to inventories

P2

Tailspin Trading Co. has the following products in its ending inventory. Compute lower of cost or market for inventory applied separately to each product.

Product	Quantity	Cost per Unit	Market per Unit
Mountain bikes	9	$360	$330
Skateboards	12	210	270
Gliders	25	480	420

QS 5-13

Inventory errors

A2

In taking a physical inventory at the end of year 2011, Nadir Company forgot to count certain units. Explain how this error affects the following: (*a*) 2011 cost of goods sold, (*b*) 2011 gross profit, (*c*) 2011 net income, (*d*) 2012 net income, (*e*) the combined two-year income, and (*f*) income for years after 2012.

QS 5-14

Analyzing inventory   **A3**

Market Company begins the year with $200,000 of goods in inventory. At year-end, the amount in inventory has increased to $230,000. Cost of goods sold for the year is $1,600,000. Compute Market's inventory turnover and days' sales in inventory. Assume that there are 365 days in the year.

QS 5-15ᴬ

Assigning costs with FIFO
periodic   **P3**

Refer to the information in QS 5-1 and assume the periodic inventory system is used. Determine the costs assigned to the ending inventory when costs are assigned based on FIFO. (Round per unit costs to three decimals, but inventory balances to the dollar.)

Refer to the information in QS 5-1 and assume the periodic inventory system is used. Determine the costs assigned to ending inventory when costs are assigned based on LIFO. (Round per unit costs to three decimals, but inventory balances to the dollar.)

QS 5-16ᴬ
Inventory costing with LIFO periodic P3

Refer to the information in QS 5-1 and assume the periodic inventory system is used. Determine the costs assigned to ending inventory when costs are assigned based on weighted average. (Round per unit costs to three decimals, but inventory balances to the dollar.)

QS 5-17ᴬ
Inventory costing with weighted average periodic P3

Refer to the information in QS 5-5 and assume the periodic inventory system is used. Determine the costs assigned to the December 31 ending inventory when costs are assigned based on FIFO. (Round per unit costs to three decimals, but inventory balances to the dollar.)

QS 5-18ᴬ
Inventory costing with FIFO periodic P3

Refer to the information in QS 5-5 and assume the periodic inventory system is used. Determine the costs assigned to ending inventory when costs are assigned based on LIFO. (Round per unit costs to three decimals, but inventory balances to the dollar.)

QS 5-19ᴬ
Inventory costing with LIFO periodic P3

Refer to the information in QS 5-5 and assume the periodic inventory system is used. Determine the costs assigned to ending inventory when costs are assigned based on weighted average. (Round per unit costs to three decimals, but inventory balances to the dollar.)

QS 5-20ᴬ
Inventory costing with weighted average periodic P3

Refer to the information in QS 5-5 and assume the periodic inventory system is used. Determine the costs assigned to ending inventory when costs are assigned based on specific identification. (Round per unit costs to three decimals, but inventory balances to the dollar.)

QS 5-21ᴬ
Inventory costing with specific identification periodic P3

Dooling Store's inventory is destroyed by a fire on September 5, 2011. The following data for year 2011 are available from the accounting records. Estimate the cost of the inventory destroyed.

QS 5-22ᴮ
Estimating inventories—gross profit method

P4

Jan. 1 inventory	$180,000
Jan. 1 through Sept. 5 purchases (net)	$342,000
Jan. 1 through Sept. 5 sales (net)	$675,000
Year 2011 estimated gross profit rate	42%

Answer each of the following questions related to international accounting standards.

a. Explain how the accounting for items and costs making up merchandise inventory is different between IFRS and U.S. GAAP.

b. Can companies reporting under IFRS apply a cost flow assumption in assigning costs to inventory? If yes, identify at least two acceptable cost flow assumptions.

c. Both IFRS and U.S. GAAP apply the lower of cost or market method for reporting inventory values. If inventory is written down from applying the lower of cost or market method, explain in general terms how IFRS and U.S. GAAP differ in accounting for any subsequent period reversal of that reported decline in inventory value.

QS 5-23
International accounting standards

C1 C2 P2

![McGraw Hill] **connect**™

1. Jolie Company has shipped $500 of goods to China Co., and China Co. has arranged to sell the goods for Jolie. Identify the consignor and the consignee. Which company should include any unsold goods as part of its inventory?

2. At year-end, Jolie Co. had shipped $850 of merchandise FOB destination to China Co. Which company should include the $850 of merchandise in transit as part of its year-end inventory?

EXERCISES

Exercise 5-1
Inventory ownership C1

Duke Associates, antique dealers, purchased the contents of an estate for $37,500. Terms of the purchase were FOB shipping point, and the cost of transporting the goods to Duke Associates' warehouse was $1,200. Duke Associates insured the shipment at a cost of $150. Prior to putting the goods up for sale, they cleaned and refurbished them at a cost of $490. Determine the cost of the inventory acquired from the estate.

Exercise 5-2
Inventory costs

C2

Exercise 5-3
Inventory costing
methods—perpetual

P1

Park Company reported the following March purchases and sales data for its only product.

Date	Activities	Units Acquired at Cost	Units Sold at Retail
Mar. 1	Beginning inventory	150 units @ $7.00 = $1,050	
Mar. 10	Sales		90 units @ $15
Mar. 20	Purchase	220 units @ $6.00 = 1,320	
Mar. 25	Sales		145 units @ $15
Mar. 30	Purchase	90 units @ $5.00 = 450	
	Totals	460 units $2,820	235 units

Park uses a perpetual inventory system. Determine the cost assigned to ending inventory and to cost of goods sold using (*a*) specific identification, (*b*) weighted average, (*c*) FIFO, and (*d*) LIFO. (Round per unit costs to three decimals, but inventory balances to the dollar.) For specific identification, ending inventory consists of 225 units, where 90 are from the March 30 purchase, 80 are from the March 20 purchase, and 55 are from beginning inventory.

Check   Ending inventory: LIFO, $1,320; WA, $1,289

Exercise 5-4
Income effects of
inventory methods

A1

Use the data in Exercise 5-3 to prepare comparative income statements for the month of January for Park Company similar to those shown in Exhibit 5.8 for the four inventory methods. Assume expenses are $1,600, and that the applicable income tax rate is 30%.

1. Which method yields the highest net income?

2. Does net income using weighted average fall between that using FIFO and LIFO?

3. If costs were rising instead of falling, which method would yield the highest net income?

Exercise 5-5
Inventory costing methods
(perpetual)—FIFO and LIFO

P1

Harold Co. reported the following current-year purchases and sales data for its only product.

Date	Activities	Units Acquired at Cost	Units Sold at Retail
Jan. 1	Beginning inventory	100 units @ $10 = $ 1,000	
Jan. 10	Sales		90 units @ $40
Mar. 14	Purchase	250 units @ $15 = 3,750	
Mar. 15	Sales		140 units @ $40
July 30	Purchase	400 units @ $20 = 8,000	
Oct. 5	Sales		300 units @ $40
Oct. 26	Purchase	600 units @ $25 = 15,000	
	Totals	1,350 units $27,750	530 units

Check   Ending inventory: LIFO, $18,750

Harold uses a perpetual inventory system. Determine the costs assigned to ending inventory and to cost of goods sold using (*a*) FIFO and (*b*) LIFO. Compute the gross margin for each method.

Exercise 5-6
Specific identification   P1

Refer to the data in Exercise 5-5. Assume that ending inventory is made up of 100 units from the March 14 purchase, 120 units from the July 30 purchase, and all 600 units from the October 26 purchase. Using the specific identification method, calculate (*a*) the cost of goods sold and (*b*) the gross profit.

Exercise 5-7
Lower of cost or market

P2

Ripken Company's ending inventory includes the following items. Compute the lower of cost or market for ending inventory applied separately to each product.

		Per Unit	
Product	Units	Cost	Market
Helmets	22	$50	$54
Bats	15	78	72
Shoes	36	95	91
Uniforms	40	36	36

Check   LCM = $6,896

Ringo Company had $900,000 of sales in each of three consecutive years 2010–2012, and it purchased merchandise costing $500,000 in each of those years. It also maintained a $200,000 physical inventory from the beginning to the end of that three-year period. In accounting for inventory, it made an error at the end of year 2010 that caused its year-end 2010 inventory to appear on its statements as $180,000 rather than the correct $200,000.

1. Determine the correct amount of the company's gross profit in each of the years 2010–2012.
2. Prepare comparative income statements as in Exhibit 5.11 to show the effect of this error on the company's cost of goods sold and gross profit for each of the years 2010–2012.

Exercise 5-8
Analysis of inventory errors

A2

Check   2010 reported gross profit, $380,000

Chess Company uses LIFO for inventory costing and reports the following financial data. It also recomputed inventory and cost of goods sold using FIFO for comparison purposes.

	2011	2010
LIFO inventory	$150	$100
LIFO cost of goods sold	730	670
FIFO inventory	220	125
FIFO cost of goods sold	685	—
Current assets (using LIFO)	210	180
Current liabilities	190	170

1. Compute its current ratio, inventory turnover, and days' sales in inventory for 2011 using (*a*) LIFO numbers and (*b*) FIFO numbers. (Round answers to one decimal.)
2. Comment on and interpret the results of part 1.

Exercise 5-9
Comparing LIFO numbers to FIFO numbers; ratio analysis

A1 A3

Check   (1) FIFO: Current ratio, 1.5; Inventory turnover, 4.0 times

---

Use the following information for Ryder Co. to compute inventory turnover for 2011 and 2010, and its days' sales in inventory at December 31, 2011 and 2010. (Round answers to one decimal.) Comment on Ryder's efficiency in using its assets to increase sales from 2010 to 2011.

	2011	2010	2009
Cost of goods sold	$643,825	$426,650	$391,300
Ending inventory	96,400	86,750	91,500

Exercise 5-10
Inventory turnover and days' sales in inventory

A3

Refer to Exercise 5-3 and assume the periodic inventory system is used. Determine the costs assigned to ending inventory and to cost of goods sold using (*a*) specific identification, (*b*) weighted average, (*c*) FIFO, and (*d*) LIFO. (Round per unit costs to three decimals, but inventory balances to the dollar.)

Exercise 5-11[A]
Inventory costing—periodic system **P3**

Refer to Exercise 5-5 and assume the periodic inventory system is used. Determine the costs assigned to ending inventory and to cost of goods sold using (*a*) FIFO and (*b*) LIFO. Then (*c*) compute the gross margin for each method.

Exercise 5-12[A]
Inventory costing—periodic system **P3**

Lopez Co. reported the following current-year data for its only product. The company uses a periodic inventory system, and its ending inventory consists of 300 units—100 from each of the last three purchases. Determine the cost assigned to ending inventory and to cost of goods sold using (*a*) specific identification, (*b*) weighted average, (*c*) FIFO, and (*d*) LIFO. (Round per unit costs to three decimals, but inventory balances to the dollar.) Which method yields the highest net income?

Exercise 5-13[A]
Alternative cost flow assumptions—periodic

P3

Jan.	1	Beginning inventory	200 units @ $2.00 = $	400
Mar.	7	Purchase	440 units @ $2.25 =	990
July	28	Purchase	1080 units @ $2.50 =	2,700
Oct.	3	Purchase	960 units @ $2.80 =	2,688
Dec.	19	Purchase	320 units @ $2.90 =	928
		Totals	3,000 units	$7,706

Check   Inventory; LIFO, $625; FIFO, $870

Exercise 5-14^A

Alternative cost flow
assumptions—periodic

P3

Candis Gifts reported the following current-year data for its only product. The company uses a periodic inventory system, and its ending inventory consists of 300 units—100 from each of the last three purchases. Determine the cost assigned to ending inventory and to cost of goods sold using (a) specific identification, (b) weighted average, (c) FIFO, and (d) LIFO. (Round per unit costs to three decimals, but inventory balances to the dollar.) Which method yields the lowest net income?

Jan.	1	Beginning inventory	280 units @ $3.00 = $ 840
Mar.	7	Purchase	600 units @ $2.80 = 1,680
July	28	Purchase	800 units @ $2.50 = 2,000
Oct.	3	Purchase	1,100 units @ $2.30 = 2,530
Dec.	19	Purchase	250 units @ $2.00 = 500
		Totals	3,030 units $7,550

Check   Inventory: LIFO, $896;
          FIFO, $615

Exercise 5-15^B

Estimating ending inventory—
retail method

P4

In 2011, Wichita Company had net sales (at retail) of $130,000. The following additional information is available from its records at the end of 2011. Use the retail inventory method to estimate Wichita's 2011 ending inventory at cost.

	At Cost	At Retail
Beginning inventory	$ 31,900	$64,200
Cost of goods purchased	57,810	98,400

Check   End. Inventory, $17,930

Exercise 5-16^B

Estimating ending inventory—
gross profit method

P4

On March 1, KB Shop had $450,000 of inventory at cost. In the first quarter of the year, it purchased $1,590,000 of merchandise, returned $23,100, and paid freight charges of $37,600 on purchased merchandise, terms FOB shipping point. The company's gross profit averages 30%, and the store had $2,000,000 of net sales (at retail) in the first quarter of the year. Use the gross profit method to estimate its cost of inventory at the end of the first quarter.

Exercise 5-17

Accounting for inventory
following IFRS

P2

Samsung Electronics reports the following regarding its accounting for inventories.

> Inventories are stated at the lower of cost or net realizable value. Cost is determined using the average cost method, except for materials-in-transit which are stated at actual cost as determined using the specific identification method. Losses on valuation of inventories and losses on inventory obsolescence are recorded as part of cost of sales. As of December 31, 2008, losses on valuation of inventories amounted to ₩651,296 million (₩ is Korean won).

1. What cost flow assumption(s) does Samsung apply in assigning costs to its inventories?

2. What has Samsung recorded for 2008 as a write-down on valuation of its inventories?

3. If at year-end 2009 there was an increase in the value of its inventories such that there was a reversal of ₩900 million for the 2008 write-down, how would Samsung account for this under IFRS? Would Samsung's accounting be different for this reversal if it reported under U.S. GAAP? Explain.

PROBLEM SET A

Problem 5-1A

Alternative cost
flows—perpetual

P1

Anthony Company uses a perpetual inventory system. It entered into the following purchases and sales transactions for March.

Date	Activities	Units Acquired at Cost	Units Sold at Retail
Mar. 1	Beginning inventory	50 units @ $50/unit	
Mar. 5	Purchase...................	200 units @ $55/unit	
Mar. 9	Sales		210 units @ $85/unit
Mar. 18	Purchase...................	60 units @ $60/unit	
Mar. 25	Purchase...................	100 units @ $62/unit	
Mar. 29	Sales	_____	80 units @ $95/unit
	Totals	410 units	290 units

Required

1. Compute cost of goods available for sale and the number of units available for sale.
2. Compute the number of units in ending inventory.
3. Compute the cost assigned to ending inventory using (*a*) FIFO, (*b*) LIFO, (*c*) weighted average, and (*d*) specific identification. (Round per unit costs to three decimals, but inventory balances to the dollar.) For specific identification, the March 9 sale consisted of 40 units from beginning inventory and 170 units from the March 5 purchase; the March 29 sale consisted of 20 units from the March 18 purchase and 60 units from the March 25 purchase.
4. Compute gross profit earned by the company for each of the four costing methods in part 3.

Check (3) Ending Inventory: FIFO, $7,400; LIFO, $6,840, WA, $7,176

(4) LIFO gross profit, $8,990

Marlow Company uses a perpetual inventory system. It entered into the following calendar-year 2011 purchases and sales transactions.

Problem 5-2A
Alternative cost flows—perpetual
P1

Date	Activities	Units Acquired at Cost	Units Sold at Retail
Jan. 1	Beginning inventory	600 units @ $44/unit	
Feb. 10	Purchase	200 units @ $40/unit	
Mar. 13	Purchase	100 units @ $20/unit	
Mar. 15	Sales		400 units @ $75/unit
Aug. 21	Purchase	160 units @ $60/unit	
Sept. 5	Purchase	280 units @ $48/unit	
Sept. 10	Sales		200 units @ $75/unit
	Totals	1,340 units	600 units

Required

1. Compute cost of goods available for sale and the number of units available for sale.
2. Compute the number of units in ending inventory.
3. Compute the cost assigned to ending inventory using (*a*) FIFO, (*b*) LIFO, (*c*) specific identification—units sold consist of 500 units from beginning inventory and 100 units from the March 13 purchase, and (*d*) weighted average. (Round per unit costs to three decimals, but inventory balances to the dollar.)
4. Compute gross profit earned by the company for each of the four costing methods in part 3.

Check (3) Ending inventory: FIFO, $33,040; LIFO, $35,440; WA, $34,055;

(4) LIFO gross profit, $21,000

Analysis Component

5. If the company's manager earns a bonus based on a percent of gross profit, which method of inventory costing will the manager likely prefer?

A physical inventory of Helmke Company taken at December 31 reveals the following.

Problem 5-3A
Lower of cost or market
P2

		Per Unit	
Item	**Units**	**Cost**	**Market**
Audio equipment			
Receivers	335	$ 90	$ 98
CD players	250	111	100
MP3 players	316	86	95
Speakers	194	52	41
Video equipment			
Handheld LCDs	470	150	125
VCRs	281	93	84
Camcorders	202	310	322
Car audio equipment			
Satellite radios	175	70	84
CD/MP3 radios	160	97	105

Required

1. Calculate the lower of cost or market for the inventory applied separately to each item.
2. If the market amount is less than the recorded cost of the inventory, then record the LCM adjustment to the Merchandise Inventory account.

Check $263,024

Problem 5-4A

Analysis of inventory errors

A2

mhhe.com/wildFINMAN4e

Doubletree Company's financial statements show the following. The company recently discovered that in making physical counts of inventory, it had made the following errors: Inventory on December 31, 2010, is understated by $50,000, and inventory on December 31, 2011, is overstated by $20,000.

For Year Ended December 31		2010	2011	2012
(a)	Cost of goods sold	$ 725,000	$ 955,000	$ 790,000
(b)	Net income......................	268,000	275,000	250,000
(c)	Total current assets	1,247,000	1,360,000	1,230,000
(d)	Total equity	1,387,000	1,580,000	1,245,000

Required

1. For each key financial statement figure—(a), (b), (c), and (d) above—prepare a table similar to the following to show the adjustments necessary to correct the reported amounts.

Figure: _____	2010	2011	2012
Reported amount	_____	_____	_____
Adjustments for: 12/31/2010 error	_____	_____	_____
12/31/2011 error	_____	_____	_____
Corrected amount	======	======	======

Check (1) Corrected net income:
2010, $318,000; 2011, $205,000;
2012, $270,000

Analysis Component

2. What is the error in total net income for the combined three-year period resulting from the inventory errors? Explain.

3. Explain why the understatement of inventory by $50,000 at the end of 2010 results in an understatement of equity by the same amount in that year.

Problem 5-5A[A]

Alternative cost flows—periodic

P3

mhhe.com/wildFINMAN4e

Viper Company began year 2011 with 20,000 units of product in its January 1 inventory costing $15 each. It made successive purchases of its product in year 2011 as follows. The company uses a periodic inventory system. On December 31, 2011, a physical count reveals that 35,000 units of its product remain in inventory.

Mar. 7	28,000 units @ $18 each
May 25	30,000 units @ $22 each
Aug. 1	20,000 units @ $24 each
Nov. 10	33,000 units @ $27 each

Required

1. Compute the number and total cost of the units available for sale in year 2011.

Check (2) Cost of goods sold:
FIFO, $1,896,000; LIFO, $2,265,000;
WA, $2,077,557

2. Compute the amounts assigned to the 2011 ending inventory and the cost of goods sold using (a) FIFO, (b) LIFO, and (c) weighted average. (Round per unit costs to three decimals, but inventory balances to the dollar.)

Problem 5-6A[A]

Income comparisons and cost flows—periodic

A1 P3

Botch Corp. sold 5,500 units of its product at $45 per unit in year 2011 and incurred operating expenses of $6 per unit in selling the units. It began the year with 600 units in inventory and made successive purchases of its product as follows.

Jan. 1	Beginning inventory	600 units @ $18 per unit
Feb. 20	Purchase	1,500 units @ $19 per unit
May 16	Purchase	700 units @ $20 per unit
Oct. 3	Purchase	400 units @ $21 per unit
Dec. 11	Purchase	3,300 units @ $22 per unit
	Total	6,500 units

Required

Check (1) Net income: FIFO,
$71,540; LIFO, $69,020; WA, $70,603

1. Prepare comparative income statements similar to Exhibit 5.8 for the three inventory costing methods of FIFO, LIFO, and weighted average. (Round per unit costs to three decimals, but inventory balances to the dollar.) Include a detailed cost of goods sold section as part of each statement. The company uses a periodic inventory system, and its income tax rate is 30%.

2. How would the financial results from using the three alternative inventory costing methods change if Botch had been experiencing declining costs in its purchases of inventory?

3. What advantages and disadvantages are offered by using (*a*) LIFO and (*b*) FIFO? Assume the continuing trend of increasing costs.

The records of Nilson Company provide the following information for the year ended December 31.

	At Cost	At Retail
January 1 beginning inventory	$ 471,350	$ 927,150
Cost of goods purchased	3,276,030	6,279,350
Sales		5,495,700
Sales returns		44,600

Problem 5-7A[B]
Retail inventory method

P4

Required

1. Use the retail inventory method to estimate the company's year-end inventory at cost.

2. A year-end physical inventory at retail prices yields a total inventory of $1,675,800. Prepare a calculation showing the company's loss from shrinkage at cost and at retail.

Check (1) Inventory, $912,808 cost;
(2) Inventory shortage at cost, $41,392

Wayman Company wants to prepare interim financial statements for the first quarter. The company wishes to avoid making a physical count of inventory. Wayman's gross profit rate averages 35%. The following information for the first quarter is available from its records.

January 1 beginning inventory	$ 300,260
Cost of goods purchased	939,050
Sales	1,191,150
Sales returns	9,450

Problem 5-8A[B]
Gross profit method

P4

Required

Use the gross profit method to estimate the company's first quarter ending inventory.

Check Estimated ending inventory, $471,205

CCO Company uses a perpetual inventory system. It entered into the following purchases and sales transactions for April.

Date	Activities	Units Acquired at Cost	Units Sold at Retail
Apr. 1	Beginning inventory	15 units @ $3,000/unit	
Apr. 6	Purchase	35 units @ $3,500/unit	
Apr. 9	Sales		18 units @ $12,000/unit
Apr. 17	Purchase	8 units @ $4,500/unit	
Apr. 25	Purchase	10 units @ $4,580/unit	
Apr. 30	Sales		30 units @ $14,000/unit
	Total	68 units	48 units

PROBLEM SET B

Problem 5-1B
Alternative cost flows—perpetual

P1

Required

1. Compute cost of goods available for sale and the number of units available for sale.

2. Compute the number of units in ending inventory.

3. Compute the cost assigned to ending inventory using (*a*) FIFO, (*b*) LIFO, (*c*) weighted average, and (*d*) specific identification. (Round per unit costs to three decimals, but inventory balances to the dollar.) For specific identification, the April 9 sale consisted of 8 units from beginning inventory and 10 units from the April 6 purchase; the April 30 sale consisted of 20 units from the April 6 purchase and 10 units from the April 25 purchase.

4. Compute gross profit earned by the company for each of the four costing methods in part 3.

Check (3) Ending inventory: FIFO, $88,800; LIFO, $62,500; WA, $75,600;

(4) LIFO gross profit, $449,200

Problem 5-2B
Alternative cost
flows—perpetual

P1

Venus Company uses a perpetual inventory system. It entered into the following calendar-year 2011 purchases and sales transactions.

Date	Activities	Units Acquired at Cost	Units Sold at Retail
Jan. 1	Beginning inventory	600 units @ $55/unit	
Jan. 10	Purchase	450 units @ $56/unit	
Feb. 13	Purchase	200 units @ $57/unit	
Feb. 15	Sales		430 units @ $90/unit
July 21	Purchase	230 units @ $58/unit	
Aug. 5	Purchase	345 units @ $59/unit	
Aug. 10	Sales		335 units @ $90/unit
	Total	1,825 units	765 units

Required

1. Compute cost of goods available for sale and the number of units available for sale.
2. Compute the number of units in ending inventory.

Check (3) Ending inventory: FIFO, $61,055; LIFO, $59,250; WA, $60,293;

3. Compute the cost assigned to ending inventory using (*a*) FIFO, (*b*) LIFO, (*c*) specific identification—units sold consist of 600 units from beginning inventory and 165 units from the February 13 purchase, and (*d*) weighted average. (Round per unit costs to three decimals, but inventory balances to the dollar.)

(4) LIFO gross profit, $24,805

4. Compute gross profit earned by the company for each of the four costing methods in part 3.

Analysis Component

5. If the company's manager earns a bonus based on a percent of gross profit, which method of inventory costing will the manager likely prefer?

Problem 5-3B
Lower of cost or market

P2

A physical inventory of Office Deals taken at December 31 reveals the following.

Item	Units	Per Unit Cost	Per Unit Market
Office furniture			
Desks	436	$261	$305
Credenzas	295	227	256
Chairs	587	49	43
Bookshelves	321	93	82
Filing cabinets			
Two-drawer	214	81	70
Four-drawer	398	135	122
Lateral	175	104	118
Office equipment			
Fax machines	430	168	200
Copiers	545	317	288
Telephones	352	125	117

Required

Check $584,444

1. Compute the lower of cost or market for the inventory applied separately to each item.
2. If the market amount is less than the recorded cost of the inventory, then record the LCM adjustment to the Merchandise Inventory account.

Problem 5-4B
Analysis of inventory errors

A2

Watson Company's financial statements show the following. The company recently discovered that in making physical counts of inventory, it had made the following errors: Inventory on December 31, 2010, is overstated by $70,000, and inventory on December 31, 2011, is understated by $55,000.

For Year Ended December 31	2010	2011	2012
(a) Cost of goods sold	$ 655,000	$ 957,000	$ 799,000
(b) Net income	225,000	277,000	244,000
(c) Total current assets	1,251,000	1,360,000	1,200,000
(d) Total equity	1,387,000	1,520,000	1,250,000

Required

1. For each key financial statement figure—(a), (b), (c), and (d) above—prepare a table similar to the following to show the adjustments necessary to correct the reported amounts.

Figure: _____	2010	2011	2012
Reported amount			
Adjustments for: 12/31/2010 error			
12/31/2011 error			
Corrected amount			

Check (1) Corrected net income: 2010, $155,000; 2011, $402,000; 2012, $189,000

Analysis Component

2. What is the error in total net income for the combined three-year period resulting from the inventory errors? Explain.

3. Explain why the overstatement of inventory by $70,000 at the end of 2010 results in an overstatement of equity by the same amount in that year.

Solaris Co. began year 2011 with 6,300 units of product in its January 1 inventory costing $35 each. It made successive purchases of its product in year 2011 as follows. The company uses a periodic inventory system. On December 31, 2011, a physical count reveals that 16,500 units of its product remain in inventory.

Problem 5-5B[A]
Alternative cost flows—periodic

P3

Jan. 4	10,500 units @ $33 each
May 18	13,000 units @ $32 each
July 9	12,000 units @ $29 each
Nov. 21	15,500 units @ $26 each

Required

1. Compute the number and total cost of the units available for sale in year 2011.

2. Compute the amounts assigned to the 2011 ending inventory and the cost of goods sold using (a) FIFO, (b) LIFO, and (c) weighted average. (Round per unit costs to three decimals, but inventory balances to the dollar.)

Check (2) Cost of goods sold: FIFO, $1,302,000; LIFO, $1,176,900; WA, $1,234,681

Rikkers Company sold 2,500 units of its product at $98 per unit in year 2011 and incurred operating expenses of $14 per unit in selling the units. It began the year with 740 units in inventory and made successive purchases of its product as follows.

Problem 5-6B[A]
Income comparisons and cost flows—periodic

A1 P3

Jan. 1	Beginning inventory	740 units @ $58 per unit
April 2	Purchase	700 units @ $59 per unit
June 14	Purchase	600 units @ $61 per unit
Aug. 29	Purchase	500 units @ $64 per unit
Nov. 18	Purchase	800 units @ $65 per unit
	Total	3,340 units

Required

1. Prepare comparative income statements similar to Exhibit 5.8 for the three inventory costing methods of FIFO, LIFO, and weighted average. (Round per unit costs to three decimals, but inventory balances to the dollar.) Include a detailed cost of goods sold section as part of each statement. The company uses a periodic inventory system, and its income tax rate is 25%.

2. How would the financial results from using the three alternative inventory costing methods change if the company had been experiencing decreasing prices in its purchases of inventory?

3. What advantages and disadvantages are offered by using (a) LIFO and (b) FIFO? Assume the continuing trend of increasing costs.

Check (1) Net income: LIFO, $40,500; FIFO, $44,805; WA, $42,519

The records of Saturn Co. provide the following information for the year ended December 31.

Problem 5-7B[B]
Retail inventory method

P4

	At Cost	At Retail
January 1 beginning inventory	$ 81,670	$114,610
Cost of goods purchased	492,250	751,730
Sales		786,120
Sales returns		4,480

Required

1. Use the retail inventory method to estimate the company's year-end inventory.

2. A year-end physical inventory at retail prices yields a total inventory of $78,550. Prepare a calculation showing the company's loss from shrinkage at cost and at retail.

Problem 5-8B[B]
Gross profit method
P4

Ernst Equipment Co. wants to prepare interim financial statements for the first quarter. The company wishes to avoid making a physical count of inventory. Ernst's gross profit rate averages 30%. The following information for the first quarter is available from its records.

January 1 beginning inventory	$ 752,880
Cost of goods purchased	2,159,630
Sales	3,710,250
Sales returns	74,200

Required

Use the gross profit method to estimate the company's first quarter ending inventory.

SERIAL PROBLEM
Business Solutions

P2 A3

(This serial problem began in Chapter 1 and continues through most of the book. If previous chapter segments were not completed, the serial problem can begin at this point.)

SP 5

Part A

Santana Rey of Business Solutions is evaluating her inventory to determine whether it must be adjusted based on lower of cost or market rules. Business Solutions has three different types of software in its inventory and the following information is available for each.

		Per Unit	
Inventory Items	Units	Cost	Market
Office productivity	3	$ 76	$ 74
Desktop publishing	2	103	100
Accounting	3	90	96

Required

1. Compute the lower of cost or market for ending inventory assuming Rey applies the lower of cost or market rule to inventory as a whole. Must Rey adjust the reported inventory value? Explain.

2. Assume that Rey had instead applied the lower of cost or market rule to each product in inventory. Under this assumption, must Rey adjust the reported inventory value? Explain.

Part B

Selected accounts and balances for the three months ended March 31, 2012, for Business Solutions follow.

January 1 beginning inventory	$ 0
Cost of goods sold	14,052
March 31 ending inventory	704

Required

1. Compute inventory turnover and days' sales in inventory for the three months ended March 31, 2012.

2. Assess the company's performance if competitors average 15 times for inventory turnover and 25 days for days' sales in inventory.

Beyond the Numbers

REPORTING IN ACTION

C2 A3

RIM

BTN 5-1   Refer to **Research In Motion**'s financial statements in Appendix A to answer the following.

Required

1. What amount of inventories did Research In Motion report as a current asset on February 27, 2010? On February 28, 2009?

2. Inventories represent what percent of total assets on February 27, 2010? On February 28, 2009?

3. Comment on the relative size of Research In Motion's inventories compared to its other types of assets.

4. What accounting method did Research In Motion use to compute inventory amounts on its balance sheet?

5. Compute inventory turnover for fiscal year ended February 27, 2010, and days' sales in inventory as of February 27, 2010.

Fast Forward

6. Access Research In Motion's financial statements for fiscal years ended after February 27, 2010, from its Website (**RIM.com**) or the SEC's EDGAR database (**www.sec.gov**). Answer questions 1 through 5 using the current RIM information and compare results to those prior years.

BTN 5-2 Comparative figures for **Research In Motion** and **Apple** follow.

($ millions)	Research In Motion			Apple		
	Current Year	One Year Prior	Two Years Prior	Current Year	One Year Prior	Two Years Prior
Inventory	$ 622	$ 682	$ 396	$ 455	$ 509	$ 346
Cost of sales	8,369	5,968	2,929	25,683	24,294	16,426

COMPARATIVE ANALYSIS

A3

RIM

Apple

Required

1. Compute inventory turnover for each company for the most recent two years shown.

2. Compute days' sales in inventory for each company for the three years shown.

3. Comment on and interpret your findings from parts 1 and 2. Assume an industry average for inventory turnover of 10.

BTN 5-3 Golf Mart is a retail sports store carrying golf apparel and equipment. The store is at the end of its second year of operation and is struggling. A major problem is that its cost of inventory has continually increased in the past two years. In the first year of operations, the store assigned inventory costs using LIFO. A loan agreement the store has with its bank, its prime source of financing, requires the store to maintain a certain profit margin and current ratio. The store's owner is currently looking over Golf Mart's preliminary financial statements for its second year. The numbers are not favorable. The only way the store can meet the required financial ratios agreed on with the bank is to change from LIFO to FIFO. The store originally decided on LIFO because of its tax advantages. The owner recalculates ending inventory using FIFO and submits those numbers and statements to the loan officer at the bank for the required bank review. The owner thankfully reflects on the available latitude in choosing the inventory costing method.

ETHICS CHALLENGE

A1

Required

1. How does Golf Mart's use of FIFO improve its net profit margin and current ratio?

2. Is the action by Golf Mart's owner ethical? Explain.

BTN 5-4 You are a financial adviser with a client in the wholesale produce business that just completed its first year of operations. Due to weather conditions, the cost of acquiring produce to resell has escalated during the later part of this period. Your client, Raphaela Gonzalez, mentions that because her business sells perishable goods, she has striven to maintain a FIFO flow of goods. Although sales are good, the increasing cost of inventory has put the business in a tight cash position. Gonzalez has expressed concern regarding the ability of the business to meet income tax obligations.

COMMUNICATING IN PRACTICE

A1

Required

Prepare a memorandum that identifies, explains, and justifies the inventory method you recommend your client, Ms. Gonzalez, adopt.

BTN 5-5 Access the 2009 annual 10-K report for **Polaris Industries** (Ticker PII), filed on March 1, 2010, from the EDGAR filings at **www.sec.gov**.

TAKING IT TO THE NET

A3

Required

1. What products are manufactured by Polaris?

2. What inventory method does Polaris use? (*Hint:* See the Note 1 to its financial statements.)

3. Compute its gross margin and gross margin ratio for the 2009 calendar year. Comment on your computations—assume an industry average of 27% for the gross margin ratio.

4. Compute its inventory turnover and days' sales in inventory for the year ended December 31, 2009. Comment on your computations—assume an industry average of 5.9 for inventory turnover and 55 for days' sales in inventory.

TEAMWORK IN ACTION

A1   P1

Point: Step 1 allows four choices or areas for expertise. Larger teams will have some duplication of choice, but the specific identification method should not be duplicated.

BTN 5-6   Each team member has the responsibility to become an expert on an inventory method. This expertise will be used to facilitate teammates' understanding of the concepts relevant to that method.

1. Each learning team member should select an area for expertise by choosing one of the following inventory methods: specific identification, LIFO, FIFO, or weighted average.

2. Form expert teams made up of students who have selected the same area of expertise. The instructor will identify where each expert team will meet.

3. Using the following data, each expert team must collaborate to develop a presentation that illustrates the relevant concepts and procedures for its inventory method. Each team member must write the presentation in a format that can be shown to the learning team.

Data

The company uses a perpetual inventory system. It had the following beginning inventory and current year purchases of its product.

Jan. 1	Beginning inventory.........	50 units @ $10 = $ 500
Jan. 14	Purchase	150 units @ $12 = 1,800
Apr. 30	Purchase	200 units @ $15 = 3,000
Sept. 26	Purchase	300 units @ $20 = 6,000

The company transacted sales on the following dates at a $35 per unit sales price.

Jan. 10	30 units	(specific cost: 30 @ $10)
Feb. 15	100 units	(specific cost: 100 @ $12)
Oct. 5	350 units	(specific cost: 100 @ $15 and 250 @ $20)

Concepts and Procedures to Illustrate in Expert Presentation

a. Identify and compute the costs to assign to the units sold. (Round per unit costs to three decimals.)

b. Identify and compute the costs to assign to the units in ending inventory. (Round inventory balances to the dollar.)

c. How likely is it that this inventory costing method will reflect the actual physical flow of goods? How relevant is that factor in determining whether this is an acceptable method to use?

d. What is the impact of this method versus others in determining net income and income taxes?

e. How closely does the ending inventory amount reflect replacement cost?

4. Re-form learning teams. In rotation, each expert is to present to the team the presentation developed in part 3. Experts are to encourage and respond to questions.

ENTREPRENEURIAL DECISION

A3

BTN 5-7   Review the chapter's opening feature highlighting Randy Hetrick and his company, **Fitness Anywhere**. Assume that Fitness Anywhere consistently maintains an inventory level of $300,000, meaning that its average and ending inventory levels are the same. Also assume its annual cost of sales is $1,200,000. To cut costs, Randy proposes to slash inventory to a constant level of $150,000 with no impact on cost of sales. He plans to work with suppliers to get quicker deliveries and to order smaller quantities more often.

Required

1. Compute the company's inventory turnover and its days' sales in inventory under (*a*) current conditions and (*b*) proposed conditions.

2. Evaluate and comment on the merits of his proposal given your analysis for part 1. Identify any concerns you might have about the proposal.

HITTING THE ROAD

C1   C2

BTN 5-8   Visit four retail stores with another classmate. In each store, identify whether the store uses a bar-coding system to help manage its inventory. Try to find at least one store that does not use bar-coding. If a store does not use bar-coding, ask the store's manager or clerk whether he or she knows which type of inventory method the store employs. Create a table that shows columns for the name of store visited, type of merchandise sold, use or nonuse of bar-coding, and the inventory method used if bar-coding is not employed. You might also inquire as to what the store's inventory turnover is and how often physical inventory is taken.

BTN 5-9   Key figures (EUR millions) for **Nokia** (**www.Nokia.com**), which is a leading global manufacturer of mobile devices and services, follow.

EUR millions	Current Year	One Year Prior	Two Years Prior
Inventory	1,865	2,533	2,876
Cost of sales	27,720	33,337	33,781

GLOBAL DECISION

A3

NOKIA

RIM

Apple

Required

1. Use these data and those from BTN 5-2 to compute (*a*) inventory turnover and (*b*) days' sales in inventory for the most recent two years shown for **Nokia**, **Research In Motion**, and **Apple**.

2. Comment on and interpret your findings from part 1.

ANSWERS TO MULTIPLE CHOICE QUIZ

1. a; FIFO perpetual

Date	Goods Purchased	Cost of Goods Sold	Inventory Balance
July 1			75 units @ $25 = $ 1,875
July 3	348 units @ $27 = $9,396		75 units @ $25 } = $ 11,271 348 units @ $27 }
July 8		75 units @ $25 } = $ 7,950 225 units @ $27 }	123 units @ $27 = $ 3,321
July 15	257 units @ $28 = $7,196		123 units @ $27 } = $ 10,517 257 units @ $28 }
July 23		123 units @ $27 } = $ 7,577 152 units @ $28 }	105 units @ $28 = **$ 2,940**
		$15,527	

2. b; LIFO perpetual

Date	Goods Purchased	Cost of Goods Sold	Inventory Balance
July 1			75 units @ $25 = $ 1,875
July 3	348 units @ $27 = $9,396		75 units @ $25 } = $ 11,271 348 units @ $27 }
July 8		300 units @ $27 = $ 8,100	75 units @ $25 } = $ 3,171 48 units @ $27 }
July 15	257 units @ $28 = $7,196		75 units @ $25 } 48 units @ $27 } = $ 10,367 257 units @ $28 }
July 23		257 units @ $28 } = $ 7,682 18 units @ $27 }	75 units @ $25 } = **$ 2,685** 30 units @ $27 }
		$15,782	

3. e; Specific identification perpetual—Ending inventory computation.

20 units @ $25	$ 500
40 units @ $27	1,080
45 units @ $28	1,260
105 units	$2,840

4. a; FIFO periodic—Ending inventory computation.
105 units @ $28 each = $2,940; The FIFO periodic inventory computation is identical to the FIFO perpetual inventory computation (see question 1).

5. d; Days' sales in inventory = (Ending inventory/Cost of goods sold × 365)
= ($18,000/$85,000) × 365 = 77.29 days

6

Cash and Internal Controls

A Look Back

Chapters 4 and 5 focused on merchandising activities and accounting for inventory. We explained inventory systems, accounting for inventory transactions, and assigning costs to inventory.

A Look at This Chapter

This chapter extends our study of accounting to internal control and the analysis of cash. We describe procedures that are good for internal control. We also explain the control of and the accounting for cash, including control features of banking activities.

A Look Ahead

Chapter 7 focuses on receivables. We explain how to account and report on receivables and their related accounts. This includes estimating uncollectible receivables and computing interest earned.

Learning Objectives

CAP

CONCEPTUAL

C1 Define internal control and identify its purpose and principles. (p. 248)

C2 Define cash and cash equivalents and explain how to report them. (p. 253)

ANALYTICAL

A1 Compute the days' sales uncollected ratio and use it to assess liquidity. (p. 267)

LP6

PROCEDURAL

P1 Apply internal control to cash receipts and disbursements. (p. 254)

P2 Explain and record petty cash fund transactions. (p. 258)

P3 Prepare a bank reconciliation. (p. 263)

P4 *Appendix 6A*—Describe the use of documentation and verification to control cash disbursements. (p. 270)

P5 *Appendix 6B*—Apply the net method to control purchase discounts. (p. 273)

Decision Insight

Candyland Biz

"It's a creative outlet for me . . . it doesn't feel like work"
—DYLAN LAUREN

NEW YORK—A 10-foot chocolate bunny greets you as you enter the store—that should be warning enough! This elite designer candy store, christened **Dylan's Candy Bar (DylansCandyBar.com),** is the brainchild of co-founder Dylan Lauren. Explains Dylan, "I got a business plan together and set out to make candy my livelihood."

This sweet-lovers' heaven offers more than 5,000 different choices of sweets from all over the world. It has become a hip hangout for locals and tourists—and it has made candy cool. Says Dylan, "Park Avenue women come in, and the first thing they ask for is Gummi bears. They love that it's very childhood, nostalgic."

Although marketing is an important part of its success, Dylan's management of internal controls and cash is equally impressive. Several control procedures monitor its business activities and safeguard its assets. An example is the biometric time and attendance control system using fingerprint characteristics. Says Dylan, "There's no fooling the system! It is going to help us remotely manage our employees while eliminating human error and

dishonesty. [It] is a cost-effective and important business management tool." Similar controls are applied throughout the store. Dylan explains that such controls raise productivity and cut expenses.

The store's cash management practices are equally impressive, including controls over cash receipts, disbursements, and petty cash. The use of bank reconciliations further helps with the store's control and management of cash. Dylan explains that she takes advantage of available banking services to enhance controls over cash.

Internal controls are crucial when on a busy day its stores bring in thousands of customers, and their cash. They have already expanded to three stores in New York, and one each in Houston and Orlando. Through it all, Dylan says it is "totally fun."

[Sources: *Dylan's Candy Bar Website,* January 2011; *Entrepreneur,* June 2005; *NYC Official City Guide,* July 2009; *The New York Times,* June & March 2009; *Dolce Vita Magazine,* June 2009; *Luxury Insider,* March 2009.]

We all are aware of theft and fraud. They affect us in several ways: We lock doors, chain bikes, review sales receipts, and acquire alarm systems. A company also takes actions to safeguard, control, and manage what it owns. Experience tells us that small companies are most vulnerable, usually due to weak internal controls. It is management's responsibility to set up policies and procedures to safeguard a company's assets, especially cash. To do so, management *and* employees must understand and apply principles of internal control. This chapter describes these principles and how to apply them. It focuses special attention on cash because it is easily transferable and is often at high risk of loss.

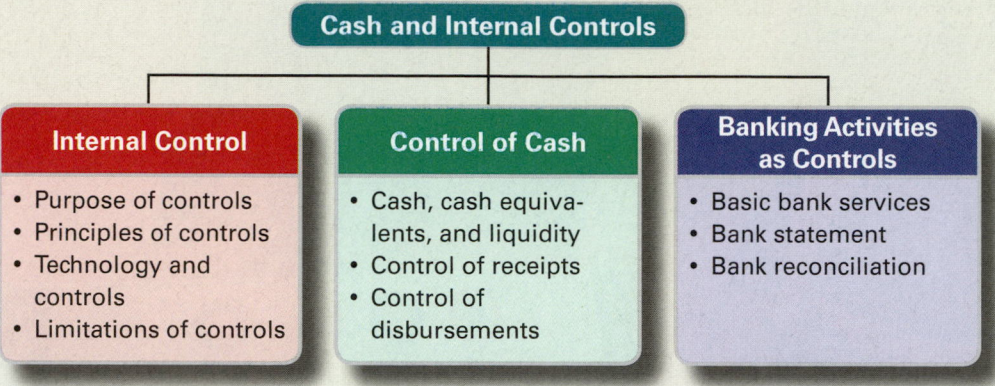

INTERNAL CONTROL

This section describes internal control and its fundamental principles. We also discuss the impact of technology on internal control and the limitations of control procedures.

Purpose of Internal Control

C1 Define internal control and identify its purpose and principles.

Managers (or owners) of small businesses often control the entire operation. These managers usually purchase all assets, hire and manage employees, negotiate all contracts, and sign all checks. They know from personal contact and observation whether the business is actually receiving the assets and services paid for. Most companies, however, cannot maintain this close personal supervision. They must delegate responsibilities and rely on formal procedures rather than personal contact in controlling business activities.

Internal Control System   Managers use an internal control system to monitor and control business activities. An **internal control system** consists of the policies and procedures managers use to

- Protect assets.
- Ensure reliable accounting.
- Promote efficient operations.
- Urge adherence to company policies.

A properly designed internal control system is a key part of systems design, analysis, and performance. Managers place a high priority on internal control systems because they can prevent avoidable losses, help managers plan operations, and monitor company and employee performance. Internal controls do not provide guarantees, but they lower the company's risk of loss.

Sarbanes-Oxley Act (SOX)   The **Sarbanes-Oxley Act (SOX)** requires the managers and auditors of companies whose stock is traded on an exchange (called *public companies*) to document and certify the system of internal controls. Following are some of the specific requirements:

- Auditors must evaluate internal controls and issue an internal control report.
- Auditors of a client are restricted as to what consulting services they can provide that client.
- The person leading an audit can serve no more than seven years without a two-year break.
- Auditors' work is overseen by the *Public Company Accounting Oversight Board* (PCAOB).
- Harsh penalties exist for violators—sentences up to 25 years in prison with severe fines.

SOX has markedly impacted companies, and the costs of its implementation are high. Importantly, **Section 404** of SOX requires that managers document and assess the effectiveness of all internal control processes that can impact financial reporting. The benefits include greater confidence in accounting systems and their related reports. However, the public continues to debate the costs versus the benefits of SOX as nearly all business activities of these companies are impacted by SOX. Section 404 of SOX requires that managers document and assess their internal controls *and* that auditors provide an opinion on managers' documentation and assessment. Costs of complying with Section 404 for companies is reported to average $4 million (source: Financial Executives Institute).

Principles of Internal Control

Internal control policies and procedures vary from company to company according to such factors as the nature of the business and its size. Certain fundamental internal control principles apply to all companies. The **principles of internal control** are to

1. Establish responsibilities.
2. Maintain adequate records.
3. Insure assets and bond key employees.
4. Separate recordkeeping from custody of assets.
5. Divide responsibility for related transactions.
6. Apply technological controls.
7. Perform regular and independent reviews.

This section explains these seven principles and describes how internal control procedures minimize the risk of fraud and theft. These procedures also increase the reliability and accuracy of accounting records. A framework for how these seven principles improve the quality of financial reporting is provided by the **Committee of Sponsoring Organizations (COSO)** (**www.COSO.org**). Specifically, these principles link to five aspects of internal control: control activities, control environment, risk assessment, monitoring, and communication.

Point: Sarbanes-Oxley Act (SOX) requires that each annual report contain an *internal control report,* which must: (1) state managers' responsibility for establishing and maintaining adequate internal controls for financial reporting; and (2) assess the effectiveness of those controls.

Establish Responsibilities   Proper internal control means that responsibility for a task is clearly established and assigned to one person. When a problem occurs in a company where responsibility is not identified, determining who is at fault is difficult. For instance, if two salesclerks share the same cash register and there is a cash shortage, neither clerk can be held accountable. To prevent this problem, one clerk might be given responsibility for handling all cash sales. Alternately, a company can use a register with separate cash drawers for each clerk. Most of us have waited at a retail counter during a shift change while employees swap cash drawers.

Point: Many companies have a mandatory vacation policy for employees who handle cash. When another employee must cover for the one on vacation, it is more difficult to hide cash frauds.

Maintain Adequate Records   Good recordkeeping is part of an internal control system. It helps protect assets and ensures that employees use prescribed procedures. Reliable records are also a source of information that managers use to monitor company activities. When detailed records of equipment are kept, for instance, items are unlikely to be lost or stolen without detection. Similarly, transactions are less likely to be entered in wrong accounts if a chart of accounts is set up and carefully used. Many preprinted forms and internal documents are also designed for use in a good internal control system. When sales slips are properly designed, for instance, sales personnel can record needed information efficiently with less chance of errors or delays to customers. When sales slips are prenumbered and controlled, each one issued is the responsibility of one salesperson, preventing the salesperson from pocketing cash by making a sale and destroying the sales slip. Computerized point-of-sale systems achieve the same control results.

Insure Assets and Bond Key Employees   Good internal control means that assets are adequately insured against casualty and that employees handling large amounts of cash and easily transferable assets are bonded. An employee is *bonded* when a company purchases an insurance policy, or a bond, against losses from theft by that employee. Bonding reduces the risk of loss. It also discourages theft because bonded employees know an independent bonding company will be involved when theft is uncovered and is unlikely to be sympathetic with an employee involved in theft.

Point: The Association of Certified Fraud Examiners (**cfenet.com**) estimates that employee fraud costs small companies more than $100,000 per incident.

Separate Recordkeeping from Custody of Assets A person who controls or has access to an asset must not keep that asset's accounting records. This principle reduces the risk of theft or waste of an asset because the person with control over it knows that another person keeps its records. Also, a recordkeeper who does not have access to the asset has no reason to falsify records. This means that to steal an asset and hide the theft from the records, two or more people must *collude*—or agree in secret to commit the fraud.

Divide Responsibility for Related Transactions Good internal control divides responsibility for a transaction or a series of related transactions between two or more individuals or departments. This is to ensure that the work of one individual acts as a check on the other. This principle, often called *separation of duties,* is not a call for duplication of work. Each employee or department should perform unduplicated effort. Examples of transactions with divided responsibility are placing purchase orders, receiving merchandise, and paying vendors. These tasks should not be given to one individual or department. Assigning responsibility for two or more of these tasks to one party increases mistakes and perhaps fraud. Having an independent person, for example, check incoming goods for quality and quantity encourages more care and attention to detail than having the person who placed the order do the checking. Added protection can result from identifying a third person to approve payment of the invoice. A company can even designate a fourth person with authority to write checks as another protective measure.

Point: There's a new security device—a person's ECG (electrocardiogram) reading—that is as unique as a fingerprint and a lot harder to lose or steal than a PIN. ECGs can be read through fingertip touches. An ECG also shows that a living person is actually there, whereas fingerprint and facial recognition software can be fooled.

Apply Technological Controls Cash registers, check protectors, time clocks, and personal identification scanners are examples of devices that can improve internal control. Technology often improves the effectiveness of controls. A cash register with a locked-in tape or electronic file makes a record of each cash sale. A check protector perforates the amount of a check into its face and makes it difficult to alter the amount. A time clock registers the exact time an employee both arrives at and departs from the job. Mechanical change and currency counters quickly and accurately count amounts, and personal scanners limit access to only authorized individuals. Each of these and other technological controls are an effective part of many internal control systems.

Perform Regular and Independent Reviews Changes in personnel, stress of time pressures, and technological advances present opportunities for shortcuts and lapses. To counter these factors, regular reviews of internal control systems are needed to ensure that procedures are followed. These reviews are preferably done by internal auditors not directly involved in the activities. Their impartial perspective encourages an evaluation of the efficiency as well as the effectiveness of the internal control system. Many companies also pay for audits by independent, external auditors. These external auditors test the company's financial records to give an opinion as to whether its financial statements are presented fairly. Before external auditors decide on how much testing is needed, they evaluate the effectiveness of the internal control system. This evaluation is often helpful to a client.

Decision Maker   Answer — p. 275

Entrepreneur   As owner of a start-up information services company, you hire a systems analyst. One of her first recommendations is to require all employees to take at least one week of vacation per year. Why would she recommend a "forced vacation" policy? ■

Technology and Internal Control

The fundamental principles of internal control are relevant no matter what the technological state of the accounting system, from purely manual to fully automated systems. Technology impacts an internal control system in several important ways. Perhaps the most obvious is that technology allows us quicker access to databases and information. Used effectively, technology greatly improves managers' abilities to monitor and control business activities. This section describes some technological impacts we must be alert to.

Reduced Processing Errors   Technologically advanced systems reduce the number of errors in processing information. Provided the software and data entry are correct, the risk of mechanical and mathematical errors is nearly eliminated. However, we must remember that erroneous software or data entry does exist. Also, less human involvement in data processing can cause data entry errors to go undiscovered. Moreover, errors in software can produce consistent but erroneous processing of transactions. Continually checking and monitoring all types of systems are important.

More Extensive Testing of Records   A company's review and audit of electronic records can include more extensive testing when information is easily and rapidly accessed. When accounting records are kept manually, auditors and others likely select only small samples of data to test. When data are accessible with computer technology, however, auditors can quickly analyze large samples or even the entire database.

Limited Evidence of Processing   Many data processing steps are increasingly done by computer. Accordingly, fewer hard-copy items of documentary evidence are available for review. Yet technologically advanced systems can provide new evidence. They can, for instance, record who made the entries, the date and time, the source of the entry, and so on. Technology can also be designed to require the use of passwords or other identification before access to the system is granted. This means that internal control depends more on the design and operation of the information system and less on the analysis of its resulting documents.

Crucial Separation of Duties   Technological advances in accounting information systems often yield some job eliminations or consolidations. While those who remain have the special skills necessary to operate advanced programs and equipment, a company with a reduced workforce risks losing its crucial separation of duties. The company must establish ways to control and monitor employees to minimize risk of error and fraud. For instance, the person who designs and programs the information system must not be the one who operates it. The company must also separate control over programs and files from the activities related to cash receipts and disbursements. For instance, a computer operator should not control check-writing activities. Achieving acceptable separation of duties can be especially difficult and costly in small companies with few employees.

Increased E-Commerce   Technology has encouraged the growth of e-commerce. **Amazon.com** and **eBay** are examples of companies that have successfully exploited e-commerce. Most companies have some e-commerce transactions. All such transactions involve at least three risks. (1) *Credit card number theft* is a risk of using, transmitting, and storing such data online. This increases the cost of e-commerce. (2) *Computer viruses* are malicious programs that attach themselves to innocent files for purposes of infecting and harming other files and programs. (3) *Impersonation* online can result in charges of sales to bogus accounts, purchases of inappropriate materials, and the unknowing giving up of confidential information to hackers. Companies use both firewalls and encryption to

Point: Information on Internet fraud can be found at these Websites: sec.gov/investor/pubs/cyberfraud.htm ftc.gov/bcp/consumer.shtm www.fraud.org

Point: Evidence of any internal control failure for a company reduces user confidence in its financial statements.

Point: We look to several sources when assessing a company's internal controls. Sources include the auditor's report, management report on controls (if available), management discussion and analysis, and financial press.

Point: COSO organizes control components into five types:
• Control environment
• Control activities
• Risk assessment
• Monitoring
• Information and communication

"Worst case of identity theft I've ever seen!"

Copyright 2004 by Randy Glasbergen. www.glasbergen.com

combat some of these risks—firewalls are points of entry to a system that require passwords to continue, and encryption is a mathematical process to rearrange contents that cannot be read without the process code. Nearly 5% of Americans already report being victims of identity theft, and roughly 10 million say their privacy has been compromised.

Decision Insight

Cheery Fraud Victim   Certified Fraud Examiners Website reports the following: Andrew Cameron stole Jacqueline Boanson's credit card. Cameron headed to the racetrack and promptly charged two bets for $150 on the credit card—winning $400. Unfortunately for Cameron the racetrack refused to pay him cash as its internal control policy is to credit winnings from bets made on a credit card to that same card. Cameron was later nabbed; and the racetrack let Ms. Boanson keep the winnings. ■

Limitations of Internal Control

All internal control policies and procedures have limitations that usually arise from either (1) the human element or (2) the cost–benefit principle.

Internal control policies and procedures are applied by people. This human element creates several potential limitations that we can categorize as either (1) human error or (2) human fraud. *Human error* can occur from negligence, fatigue, misjudgment, or confusion. *Human fraud* involves intent by people to defeat internal controls, such as *management override,* for personal gain. Fraud also includes collusion to thwart the separation of duties. The human element highlights the importance of establishing an *internal control environment* to convey management's commitment to internal control policies and procedures. Human fraud is driven by the *triple-threat* of fraud:

- **Opportunity**—refers to internal control deficiencies in the workplace.
- **Pressure**—refers to financial, family, society, and other stresses to succeed.
- **Rationalization**—refers to employees justifying fraudulent behavior.

The second major limitation on internal control is the *cost–benefit principle,* which dictates that the costs of internal controls must not exceed their benefits. Analysis of costs and benefits must consider all factors, including the impact on morale. Most companies, for instance, have a legal right to read employees' e-mails, yet companies seldom exercise that right unless they are confronted with evidence of potential harm to the company. The same holds for drug testing, phone tapping, and hidden cameras. The bottom line is that managers must establish internal control policies and procedures with a net benefit to the company.

Point: Cybercrime.gov pursues computer and intellectual property crimes, including that of e-commerce.

Address   www.hacker'sguidetocyberspace.com   GO

Hacker's Guide to Cyberspace

Pharming   Viruses attached to e-mails and Websites load software onto your PC that monitors keystrokes; when you sign on to financial Websites, it steals your passwords.

Phishing   Hackers send e-mails to you posing as banks; you are asked for information using fake Websites where they reel in your passwords and personal data.

Wl-Phishing   Cybercrooks set up wireless networks hoping you use them to connect to the Web; your passwords and data are stolen as you use their network.

Bot-Networking   Hackers send remote-control programs to your PC that take control to send out spam and viruses; they even rent your bot to other cybercrooks.

Typo-Squatting   Hackers set up Websites with addresses similar to legit outfits; when you make a typo and hit their sites, they infect your PC with viruses or take them over as bots.

Quick Check   Answers — p. 275

1. Principles of internal control suggest that (choose one): (*a*) Responsibility for a series of related transactions (such as placing orders, receiving and paying for merchandise) should be assigned to one employee; (*b*) Responsibility for individual tasks should be shared by more than one employee so that one serves as a check on the other; or (*c*) Employees who handle considerable cash and easily transferable assets should be bonded.

2. What are some impacts of computing technology on internal control?

CONTROL OF CASH

Cash is a necessary asset of every company. Most companies also own *cash equivalents* (defined below), which are assets similar to cash. Cash and cash equivalents are the most liquid of all assets and are easily hidden and moved. An effective system of internal controls protects these assets and it should meet three basic guidelines:

1. Handling cash is separate from recordkeeping of cash.
2. Cash receipts are promptly deposited in a bank.
3. Cash disbursements are made by check.

The first guideline applies separation of duties to minimize errors and fraud. When duties are separated, two or more people must collude to steal cash and conceal this action in the accounting records. The second guideline uses immediate (say, daily) deposits of all cash receipts to produce a timely independent record of the cash received. It also reduces the likelihood of cash theft (or loss) and the risk that an employee could personally use the money before depositing it. The third guideline uses payments by check to develop an independent bank record of cash disbursements. This guideline also reduces the risk of cash theft (or loss).

This section begins with definitions of cash and cash equivalents. Discussion then focuses on controls and accounting for both cash receipts and disbursements. The exact procedures used to achieve control over cash vary across companies. They depend on factors such as company size, number of employees, volume of cash transactions, and sources of cash.

Cash, Cash Equivalents, and Liquidity

Good accounting systems help in managing the amount of cash and controlling who has access to it. Cash is the usual means of payment when paying for assets, services, or liabilities. **Liquidity** refers to a company's ability to pay for its near-term obligations. Cash and similar assets are called **liquid assets** because they can be readily used to settle such obligations. A company needs liquid assets to effectively operate.

C2 Define cash and cash equivalents and explain how to report them.

Cash includes currency and coins along with the amounts on deposit in bank accounts, checking accounts (called *demand deposits*), and many savings accounts (called *time deposits*). Cash also includes items that are acceptable for deposit in these accounts such as customer checks, cashier's checks, certified checks, and money orders. **Cash equivalents** are short-term, highly liquid investment assets meeting two criteria: (1) readily convertible to a known cash amount and (2) sufficiently close to their due date so that their market value is not sensitive to interest rate changes. Only investments purchased within three months of their due date usually satisfy these criteria. Examples of cash equivalents are short-term investments in assets such as U.S. Treasury bills and money market funds. To increase their return, many companies invest idle cash in cash equivalents. Most companies combine cash equivalents with cash as a single item on the balance sheet.

Point: The most liquid assets are usually reported first on a balance sheet; the least liquid assets are reported last.

Point: Google reports cash and cash equivalents of $10,198 million in its balance sheet. This amount makes up nearly 25% of its total assets.

Cash Management

When companies fail, one of the most common causes is their inability to manage cash. Companies must plan both cash receipts and cash payments. The goals of cash management are twofold:

1. Plan cash receipts to meet cash payments when due.
2. Keep a minimum level of cash necessary to operate.

The *treasurer* of the company is responsible for cash management. Effective cash management involves applying the following cash management principles.

- **Encourage collection of receivables.** The more quickly customers and others pay the company, the more quickly that company can use the money. Some companies have cash-only sales policies. Others might offer discounts for payments received early.
- **Delay payment of liabilities.** The more delayed a company is in paying others, the more time it has to use the money. Some companies regularly wait to pay their bills until the last possible day allowed—although, a company must take care not to hurt its credit standing.
- **Keep only necessary levels of assets.** The less money tied up in idle assets, the more money to invest in productive assets. Some companies maintain *just-in-time* inventory; meaning they plan inventory to be available at the same time orders are filled. Others might lease out excess warehouse space or rent equipment instead of buying it.
- **Plan expenditures.** Money should be spent only when it is available. Companies must look at seasonal and business cycles to plan expenditures.
- **Invest excess cash.** Excess cash earns no return and should be invested. Excess cash from seasonal cycles can be placed in a bank account or other short-term investment for income. Excess cash beyond what's needed for regular business should be invested in productive assets like factories and inventories.

Decision **Insight**

Days' Cash Expense Coverage   The ratio of *cash (and cash equivalents) to average daily cash expenses* indicates the number of days a company can operate without additional cash inflows. It reflects on company liquidity and on the potential of excess cash. ■

Control of Cash Receipts

P1 Apply internal control to cash receipts and disbursements.

Internal control of cash receipts ensures that cash received is properly recorded and deposited. Cash receipts can arise from transactions such as cash sales, collections of customer accounts, receipts of interest earned, bank loans, sales of assets, and owner investments. This section explains internal control over two important types of cash receipts: over-the-counter and by mail.

Over-the-Counter Cash Receipts   For purposes of internal control, over-the-counter cash receipts from sales should be recorded on a cash register at the time of each sale. To help ensure that correct amounts are entered, each register should be located so customers can read the amounts entered. Clerks also should be required to enter each sale before wrapping merchandise and to give the customer a receipt for each sale. The design of each cash register should provide a permanent, locked-in record of each transaction. In many systems, the register is directly linked with computing and accounting services. Less advanced registers simply print a record of each transaction on a paper tape or electronic file locked inside the register.

Proper internal control prescribes that custody over cash should be separate from its record-keeping. For over-the-counter cash receipts, this separation begins with the cash sale. The clerk who has access to cash in the register should not have access to its locked-in record. At the end of the clerk's work period, the clerk should count the cash in the register, record the amount, and turn over the cash and a record of its amount to the company cashier. The cashier, like the clerk, has access to the cash but should not have access to accounting records (or the register tape or file). A third employee, often a supervisor, compares the record of total register transactions (or the register tape or file) with the cash receipts reported by the cashier. This record is the basis for a journal entry recording over-the-counter cash receipts. The third employee has access to the records for cash but not to the actual cash. The clerk and the cashier have access to cash but not to the accounting records. None of them can make a mistake or divert cash without the difference being revealed—see the following diagram.

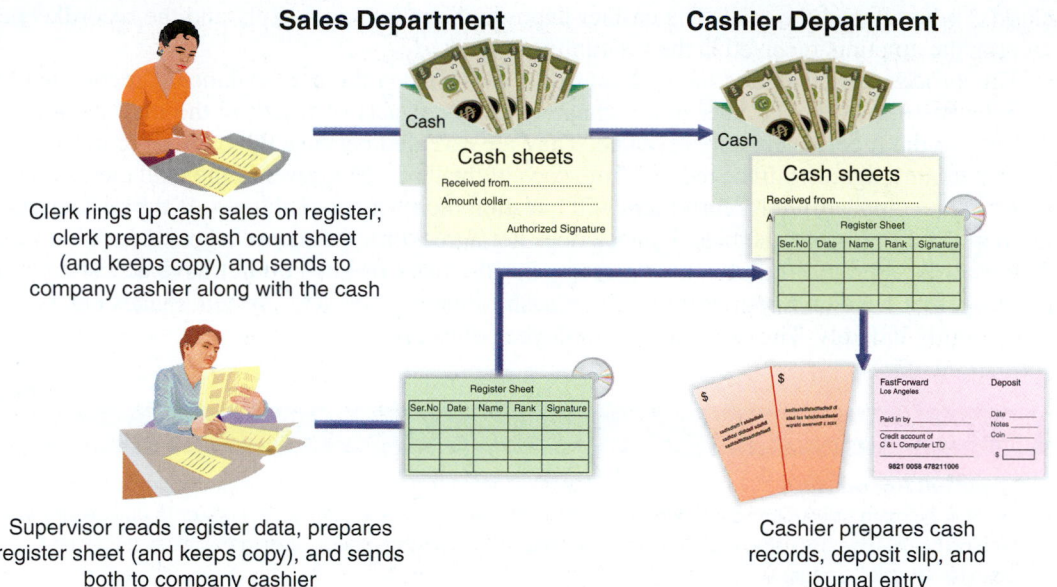

Sales Department

Clerk rings up cash sales on register; clerk prepares cash count sheet (and keeps copy) and sends to company cashier along with the cash

Supervisor reads register data, prepares register sheet (and keeps copy), and sends both to company cashier

Cashier Department

Cashier prepares cash records, deposit slip, and journal entry

Cash over and short.   Sometimes errors in making change are discovered from differences between the cash in a cash register and the record of the amount of cash receipts. Although a clerk is careful, one or more customers can be given too much or too little change. This means that at the end of a work period, the cash in a cash register might not equal the record of cash receipts. This difference is reported in the **Cash Over and Short** account, also called *Cash Short and Over,* which is an income statement account recording the income effects of cash overages and cash shortages. To illustrate, if a cash register's record shows $550 but the count of cash in the register is $555, the entry to record cash sales and its overage is

Point: Retailers often require cashiers to restrictively endorse checks immediately on receipt by stamping them "For deposit only."

Cash	555	
Cash Over and Short		5
Sales		550
To record cash sales and a cash overage.		

Assets = Liabilities + Equity
+555   +   5
                                   +550

On the other hand, if a cash register's record shows $625 but the count of cash in the register is $621, the entry to record cash sales and its shortage is

Cash	621	
Cash Over and Short	4	
Sales		625
To record cash sales and a cash shortage.		

Assets = Liabilities + Equity
+621   −   4
                                   +625

Since customers are more likely to dispute being shortchanged than being given too much change, the Cash Over and Short account usually has a debit balance at the end of an accounting period. A debit balance reflects an expense. It is reported on the income statement as part of general and administrative expenses. (Since the amount is usually small, it is often combined with other small expenses and reported as part of *miscellaneous expenses—*or as part of *miscellaneous revenues* if it has a credit balance.)

Point: Merchants begin a business day with a *change fund* in their cash register. The accounting for a change fund is similar to that for petty cash, including that for cash shortages or overages.

Cash Receipts by Mail   Control of cash receipts that arrive through the mail starts with the person who opens the mail. Preferably, two people are assigned the task of, and are present for, opening the mail. In this case, theft of cash receipts by mail requires collusion between these two employees. Specifically, the person(s) opening the mail enters a list (in triplicate) of money received. This list should contain a record of each sender's name, the amount, and an explanation of why the money is sent. The first copy is sent with the money to the cashier. A second copy is sent to the recordkeeper in the accounting area. A third copy is kept by the

Point: Collusion implies that two or more individuals are knowledgeable or involved with the activities of the other(s).

clerk(s) who opened the mail. The cashier deposits the money in a bank, and the recordkeeper records the amounts received in the accounting records.

This process reflects good internal control. That is, when the bank balance is reconciled by another person (explained later in the chapter), errors or acts of fraud by the mail clerks, the cashier, or the recordkeeper are revealed. They are revealed because the bank's record of cash deposited must agree with the records from each of the three. Moreover, if the mail clerks do not report all receipts correctly, customers will question their account balances. If the cashier does not deposit all receipts, the bank balance does not agree with the recordkeeper's cash balance. The recordkeeper and the person who reconciles the bank balance do not have access to cash and therefore have no opportunity to divert cash to themselves. This system makes errors and fraud highly unlikely. The exception is employee collusion.

Decision Insight

Perpetual Accounting   **Walmart** uses a network of information links with its point-of-sale cash registers to coordinate sales, purchases, and distribution. Its supercenters, for instance, ring up 15,000 separate sales on heavy days. By using cash register information, the company can fix pricing mistakes quickly and capitalize on sales trends. ■

Control of Cash Disbursements

Control of cash disbursements is especially important as most large thefts occur from payment of fictitious invoices. One key to controlling cash disbursements is to require all expenditures to be made by check. The only exception is small payments made from petty cash. Another key is to deny access to the accounting records to anyone other than the owner who has the authority to sign checks. A small business owner often signs checks and knows from personal contact that the items being paid for are actually received. This arrangement is impossible in large businesses. Instead, internal control procedures must be substituted for personal contact. Such procedures are designed to assure the check signer that the obligations recorded are properly incurred and should be paid. This section describes these and other internal control procedures, including the voucher system and petty cash system. A method for management of cash disbursements for purchases is described in Appendix 6B.

Decision Insight

Cash Budget   Projected cash receipts and cash disbursements are often summarized in a *cash budget*. Provided that sufficient cash exists for effective operations, companies wish to minimize the cash they hold because of its risk of theft and its low return versus other investment opportunities. ■

Voucher System of Control   A **voucher system** is a set of procedures and approvals designed to control cash disbursements and the acceptance of obligations. The voucher system of control establishes procedures for

- Verifying, approving, and recording obligations for eventual cash disbursement.
- Issuing checks for payment of verified, approved, and recorded obligations.

A reliable voucher system follows standard procedures for every transaction. This applies even when multiple purchases are made from the same supplier.

A voucher system's control over cash disbursements begins when a company incurs an obligation that will result in payment of cash. A key factor in this system is that only approved departments and individuals are authorized to incur such obligations. The system often limits the type of obligations that a department or individual can incur. In a large retail store, for instance, only a purchasing department should be authorized to incur obligations for merchandise inventory. Another key factor is that procedures for purchasing, receiving, and paying for merchandise are divided among several departments (or individuals). These departments include the one requesting the purchase, the purchasing department, the receiving department, and the accounting department. To coordinate and control responsibilities of these departments, a company uses

Point: MCI, formerly **WorldCom,** paid a whopping $500 million in SEC fines for accounting fraud. Among the charges were that it inflated earnings by as much as $10 billion. Its CEO, Bernard Ebbers, was sentenced to 25 years.

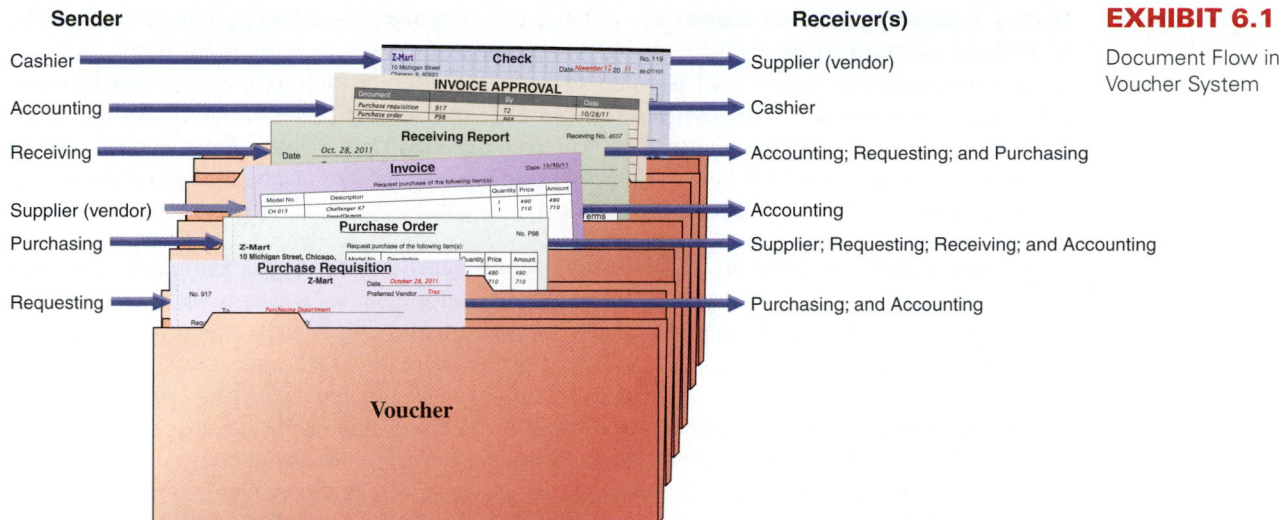

EXHIBIT 6.1

Document Flow in a
Voucher System

several different business documents. Exhibit 6.1 shows how documents are accumulated in a
voucher, which is an internal document (or file) used to accumulate information to control cash
disbursements and to ensure that a transaction is properly recorded. This specific example begins
with a *purchase requisition* and concludes with a *check* drawn against cash. Appendix 6A
describes the documentation and verification necessary for a voucher system of control. It also
describes the internal control objective served by each document.

A voucher system should be applied not only to purchases of inventory but to all expenditures.
To illustrate, when a company receives a monthly telephone bill, it should review and verify the
charges, prepare a voucher (file), and insert the bill. This transaction is then recorded with a journal
entry. If the amount is currently due, a check is issued. If not, the voucher is filed for payment on
its due date. If no voucher is prepared, verifying the invoice and its amount after several days or
weeks can be difficult. Also, without records, a dishonest employee could collude with a dishonest
supplier to get more than one payment for an obligation, payment for excessive amounts, or payment for goods and services not received. An effective voucher system helps prevent such frauds.

Point: A *voucher* is an internal
document (or file).

Point: The basic purposes of paper
and electronic documents are similar.
However, the internal control system
must change to reflect different risks,
including confidential and competitive-
sensitive information that is at greater
risk in electronic systems.

Decision Insight

Cyber Setup The FTC is on the cutting edge of cyber-
sleuthing. Opportunists in search of easy money are lured to
WeMarket4U.net/SundaeStation and **WeMarket4U.net/**
FatFoe. Take the bait and you get warned. The top 5 fraud
complaints as compiled by the Bureau of Consumer Protection
are shown to the right. ■

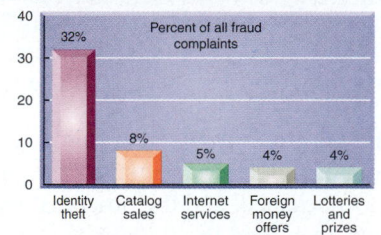

Quick Check   Answers — p. 275

3. Why must a company hold liquid assets?

4. Why does a company hold cash equivalent assets in addition to cash?

5. Identify at least two assets that are classified as cash equivalents.

6. Good internal control procedures for cash include which of the following? (*a*) All cash
   disbursements, other than those for very small amounts, are made by check; (*b*) One employee
   counts cash received from sales and promptly deposits cash receipts; or (*c*) Cash receipts by
   mail are opened by one employee who is then responsible for recording and depositing them.

7. Should all companies require a voucher system? At what point in a company's growth would
   you recommend a voucher system?

Petty Cash System of Control   A basic principle for controlling cash disbursements is that all payments must be made by check. An exception to this rule is made for *petty cash disbursements,* which are the small payments required for items such as postage, courier fees, minor repairs, and low-cost supplies. To avoid the time and cost of writing checks for small amounts, a company sets up a petty cash fund to make small payments. (**Petty cash** activities are part of an *imprest system,* which designates advance money to establish the fund, to withdraw from the fund, and to reimburse the fund.)

Operating a petty cash fund.   Establishing a petty cash fund requires estimating the total amount of small payments likely to be made during a short period such as a week or month. A check is then drawn by the company cashier for an amount slightly in excess of this estimate. This check is recorded with a debit to the Petty Cash account (an asset) and a credit to Cash. The check is cashed, and the currency is given to an employee designated as the *petty cashier* or *petty cash custodian.* The petty cashier is responsible for keeping this cash safe, making payments from the fund, and keeping records of it in a secure place referred to as the *petty cashbox.*

> **Point:** A petty cash fund is used only for business expenses.

When each cash disbursement is made, the person receiving payment should sign a prenumbered *petty cash receipt,* also called *petty cash ticket*—see Exhibit 6.2. The petty cash receipt is then placed in the petty cashbox with the remaining money. Under this system, the sum of all receipts plus the remaining cash equals the total fund amount. A $100 petty cash fund, for instance, contains any combination of cash and petty cash receipts that totals $100 (examples are $80 cash plus $20 in receipts, or $10 cash plus $90 in receipts). Each disbursement reduces cash and increases the amount of receipts in the petty cashbox.

EXHIBIT 6.2

Petty Cash Receipt

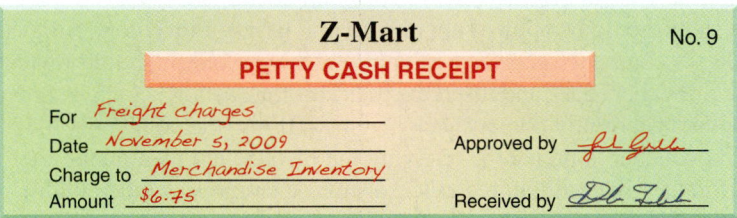

> **Point:** Petty cash receipts with either no signature or a forged signature usually indicate misuse of petty cash. Companies respond with surprise petty cash counts for verification.

The petty cash fund should be reimbursed when it is nearing zero and at the end of an accounting period when financial statements are prepared. For this purpose, the petty cashier sorts the paid receipts by the type of expense or account and then totals the receipts. The petty cashier presents all paid receipts to the company cashier, who stamps all receipts *paid* so they cannot be reused, files them for recordkeeping, and gives the petty cashier a check for their sum. When this check is cashed and the money placed in the cashbox, the total money in the cashbox is restored to its original amount. The fund is now ready for a new cycle of petty cash payments.

Illustrating a petty cash fund.   To illustrate, assume Z-Mart establishes a petty cash fund on November 1 and designates one of its office employees as the petty cashier. A $75 check is drawn, cashed, and the proceeds given to the petty cashier. The entry to record the setup of this petty cash fund is

Assets = Liabilities + Equity
+75
−75

Nov. 1	Petty Cash	75	
	Cash		75
	To establish a petty cash fund.		

> **Point:** Reducing or eliminating a petty cash fund requires a credit to Petty Cash.

> **Point:** Although *individual* petty cash disbursements are not evidenced by a check, the initial petty cash fund is evidenced by a check, and later petty cash expenditures are evidenced by a check to replenish them *in total.*

After the petty cash fund is established, the Petty Cash account is not debited or credited again unless the amount of the fund is changed. (A fund should be increased if it requires reimbursement too frequently. On the other hand, if the fund is too large, some of its money should be redeposited in the Cash account.)

Next, assume that Z-Mart's petty cashier makes several November payments from petty cash. Each person who received payment is required to sign a receipt. On November 27, after making a $26.50 cash payment for tile cleaning, only $3.70 cash remains in the fund. The petty cashier then summarizes and totals the petty cash receipts as shown in Exhibit 6.3.

EXHIBIT 6.3

Petty Cash Payments Report

| Z-MART |
| Petty Cash Payments Report |

Miscellaneous Expenses

Nov. 2	Cleaning of LCD panels	$20.00	
Nov. 27	Tile cleaning	26.50	$ 46.50

Merchandise Inventory (transportation-in)

| Nov. 5 | Transport of merchandise purchased | 6.75 | |
| Nov. 20 | Transport of merchandise purchased | 8.30 | 15.05 |

Delivery Expense

| Nov. 18 | Customer's package delivered | | 5.00 |

Office Supplies Expense

| Nov. 15 | Purchase of office supplies immediately used | | 4.75 |
| **Total** | | | **$71.30** |

Point: This report can also include receipt number and names of those who approved and received cash payment (see Demo Problem 2).

The petty cash payments report and all receipts are given to the company cashier in exchange for a $71.30 check to reimburse the fund. The petty cashier cashes the check and puts the $71.30 cash in the petty cashbox. The company records this reimbursement as follows.

Nov. 27	Miscellaneous Expenses	46.50	
	Merchandise Inventory	15.05	
	Delivery Expense	5.00	
	Office Supplies Expense	4.75	
	Cash		71.30
	To reimburse petty cash.		

Assets = Liabilities + Equity
−71.30   −46.50
                        −15.05
                        − 5.00
                        − 4.75

A petty cash fund is usually reimbursed at the end of an accounting period so that expenses are recorded in the proper period, even if the fund is not low on money. If the fund is not reimbursed at the end of a period, the financial statements would show both an overstated cash asset and understated expenses (or assets) that were paid out of petty cash. Some companies do not reimburse the petty cash fund at the end of each period under the notion that this amount is immaterial to users of financial statements.

Point: To avoid errors in recording petty cash reimbursement, follow these steps: (1) prepare payments report, (2) compute cash needed by subtracting cash remaining from total fund amount, (3) record entry, and (4) check "Dr. = Cr." in entry. Any difference is Cash Over and Short.

Increasing or decreasing a petty cash fund. A decision to increase or decrease a petty cash fund is often made when reimbursing it. To illustrate, assume Z-Mart decides to *increase* its petty cash fund from $75 to $100 on November 27 when it reimburses the fund. The entries required are to (1) reimburse the fund as usual (see the preceding November 27 entry) and (2) increase the fund amount as follows.

Nov. 27	Petty Cash	25	
	Cash		25
	To increase the petty cash fund amount.		

Alternatively, if Z-Mart *decreases* the petty cash fund from $75 to $55 on November 27, the entry is to (1) credit Petty Cash for $20 (decreasing the fund from $75 to $55) and (2) debit Cash for $20 (reflecting the $20 transfer from Petty Cash to Cash).

Cash over and short. Sometimes a petty cashier fails to get a receipt for payment or overpays for the amount due. When this occurs and the fund is later reimbursed, the petty cash payments report plus the cash remaining will not total to the fund balance. This mistake causes the fund to be *short*. This shortage is recorded as an expense in the reimbursing entry with a debit to the Cash Over and Short account. (An overage in the petty cash fund is recorded with a credit to Cash Over and Short in the reimbursing entry.) To illustrate, prepare the June 1 entry

Summary of Petty Cash Accounting			
Event	**Petty Cash**	**Cash**	**Expenses**
Set up fund	Dr.	Cr.	—
Reimburse fund	—	Cr.	Dr.
Increase fund	Dr.	Cr.	—
Decrease fund	Cr.	Dr.	—

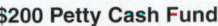

$200 Petty Cash Fund

to reimburse a $200 petty cash fund when its payments report shows $178 in miscellaneous expenses and $15 cash remains.

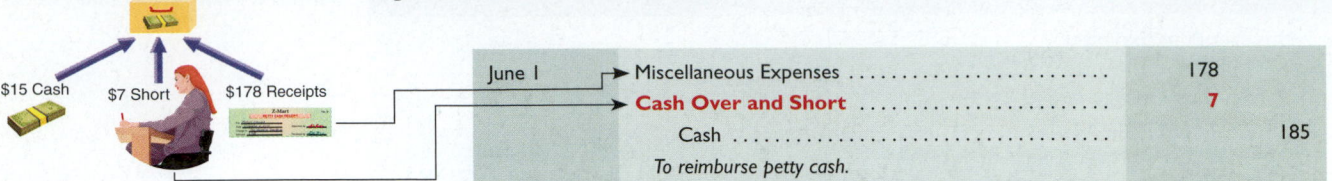

$15 Cash $7 Short $178 Receipts

June 1	Miscellaneous Expenses	178	
	Cash Over and Short	7	
	Cash		185
	To reimburse petty cash.		

Decision Insight

Warning Signs   There are clues to internal control violations. Warning signs from accounting include (1) an increase in customer refunds—could be fake, (2) missing documents—could be used for fraud, (3) differences between bank deposits and cash receipts—could be cash embezzled, and (4) delayed recording—could reflect fraudulent records. Warning signs from employees include (1) lifestyle change—could be embezzlement, (2) too close with suppliers—could signal fraudulent transactions, and (3) failure to leave job, even for vacations—could conceal fraudulent activities. ∎

Quick Check   Answers — p. 275

8. Why are some cash payments made from a petty cash fund and not by check?
9. Why should a petty cash fund be reimbursed at the end of an accounting period?
10. Identify at least two results of reimbursing a petty cash fund.

BANKING ACTIVITIES AS CONTROLS

Banks (and other financial institutions) provide many services, including helping companies control cash. Banks safeguard cash, provide detailed and independent records of cash transactions, and are a source of cash financing. This section describes these services and the documents provided by banking activities that increase managers' control over cash.

Basic Bank Services

This section explains basic bank services—such as the bank account, the bank deposit, and checking—that contribute to the control of cash.

Bank Account, Deposit, and Check   A *bank account* is a record set up by a bank for a customer. It permits a customer to deposit money for safekeeping and helps control withdrawals. To limit access to a bank account, all persons authorized to write checks on the account must sign a **signature card,** which bank employees use to verify signatures on checks. Many companies have more than one bank account to serve different needs and to handle special transactions such as payroll.

Point: Online banking services include the ability to stop payment on a check, move money between accounts, get up-to-date balances, and identify cleared checks and deposits.

Each bank deposit is supported by a **deposit ticket,** which lists items such as currency, coins, and checks deposited along with their corresponding dollar amounts. The bank gives the customer a copy of the deposit ticket or a deposit receipt as proof of the deposit. Exhibit 6.4 shows one type of deposit ticket.

To withdraw money from an account, the depositor can use a **check,** which is a document signed by the depositor instructing the bank to pay a specified amount of money to a designated recipient. A check involves three parties: a *maker* who signs the check, a *payee* who is the recipient, and a *bank* (or *payer*) on which the check is drawn. The bank provides a depositor the checks that are serially numbered and imprinted with the name and address of both the depositor and bank. Both checks and deposit tickets are imprinted with identification codes in magnetic ink

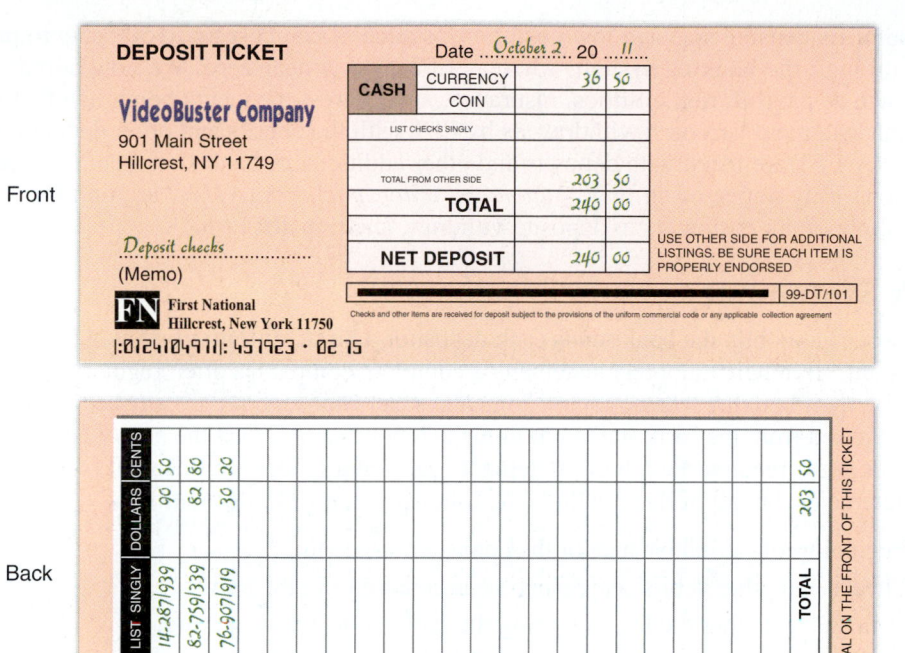

EXHIBIT 6.4

Deposit Ticket

for computer processing. Exhibit 6.5 shows one type of check. It is accompanied with an optional *remittance advice* explaining the payment. When a remittance advice is unavailable, the *memo* line is often used for a brief explanation.

Electronic Funds Transfer   **Electronic funds transfer (EFT)** is the electronic transfer of cash from one party to another. No paper documents are necessary. Banks simply transfer cash from one account to another with a journal entry. Companies are increasingly using EFT

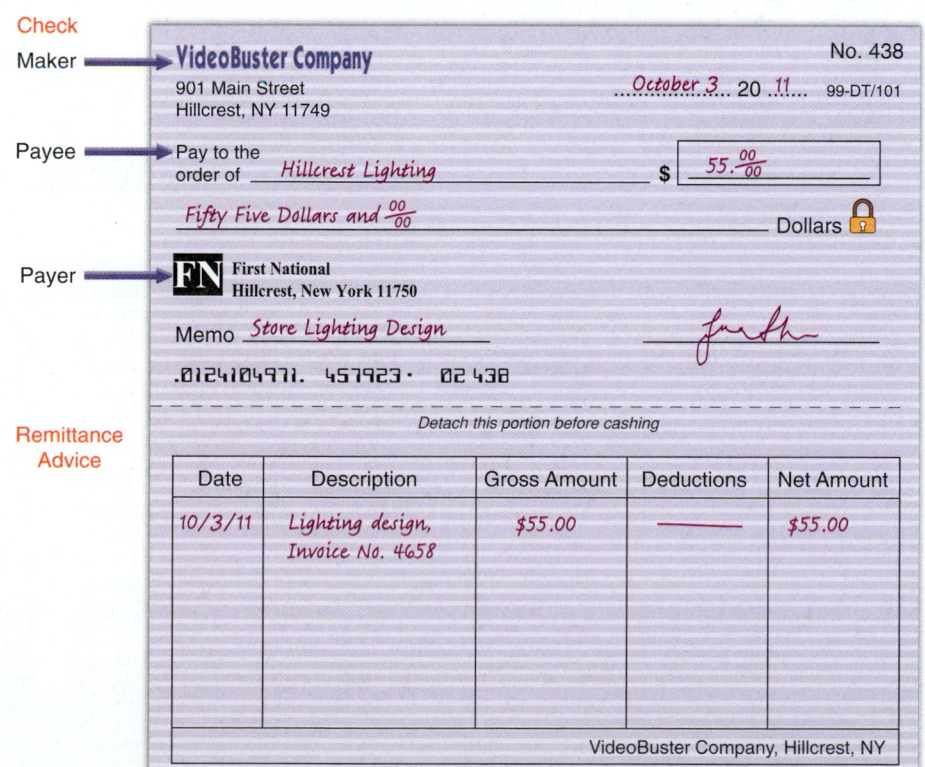

EXHIBIT 6.5

Check with Remittance Advice

because of its convenience and low cost. For instance, it can cost up to 50 cents to process a check through the banking system, whereas EFT cost is near zero. We now commonly see items such as payroll, rent, utilities, insurance, and interest payments being handled by EFT. The bank statement lists cash withdrawals by EFT with the checks and other deductions. Cash receipts by EFT are listed with deposits and other additions. A bank statement is sometimes a depositor's only notice of an EFT. *Automated teller machines (ATMs)* are one form of EFT, which allows bank customers to deposit, withdraw, and transfer cash.

Bank Statement

Point: Good internal control is to deposit all cash receipts daily and make all payments for goods and services by check. This controls access to cash and creates an independent record of all cash activities.

Usually once a month, the bank sends each depositor a **bank statement** showing the activity in the account. Although a monthly statement is common, companies often regularly access information on their banking transactions. (Companies can choose to record any accounting adjustments required from the bank statement immediately or later, say, at the end of each day, week, month, or when reconciling a bank statement.) Different banks use different formats for their bank statements, but all of them include the following items of information:

1. Beginning-of-period balance of the depositor's account.
2. Checks and other debits decreasing the account during the period.
3. Deposits and other credits increasing the account during the period.
4. End-of-period balance of the depositor's account.

This information reflects the bank's records. Exhibit 6.6 shows one type of bank statement. Identify each of these four items in that statement. Part Ⓐ of Exhibit 6.6 summarizes changes in the account. Part Ⓑ lists paid checks along with other debits. Part Ⓒ lists deposits and credits to the account, and part Ⓓ shows the daily account balances.

In reading a bank statement note that a depositor's account is a liability on the bank's records. This is so because the money belongs to the depositor, not the bank. When a depositor increases

EXHIBIT 6.6

Bank Statement

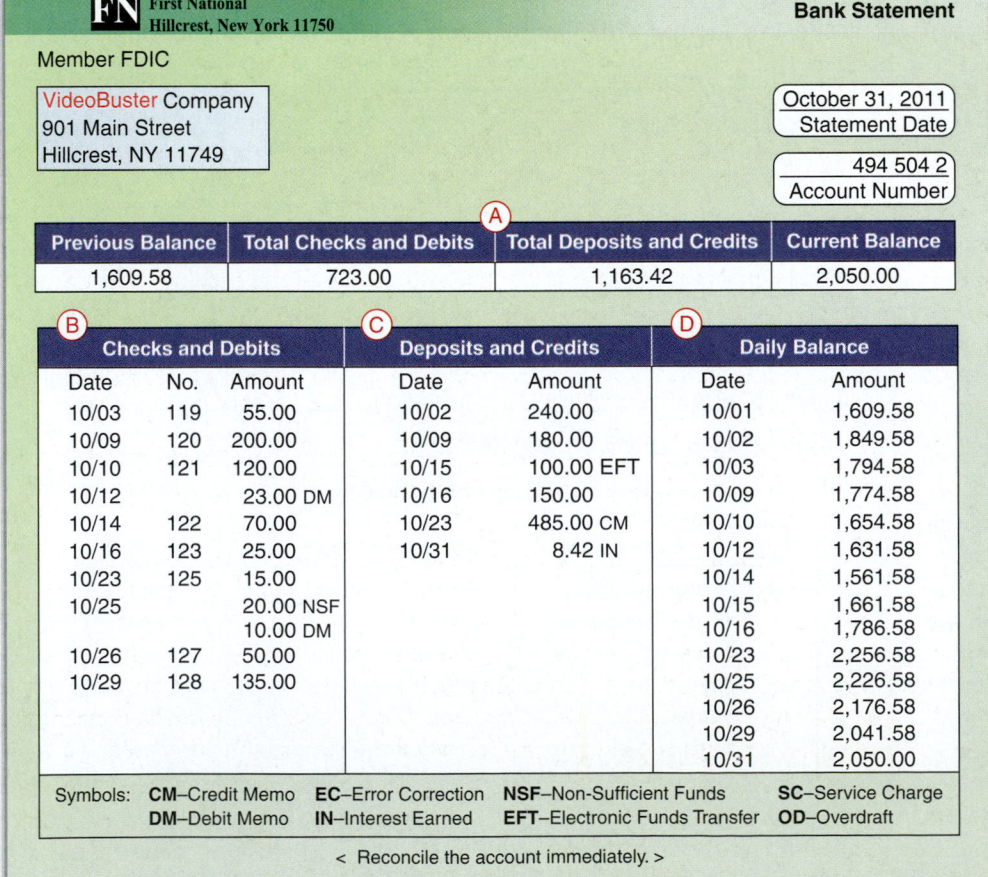

Point: Many banks separately report other debits and credits apart from checks and deposits.

the account balance, the bank records it with a *credit* to that liability account. This means that debit memos from the bank produce *credits* on the depositor's books, and credit memos from the bank produce *debits* on the depositor's books.

Enclosed with a bank statement is a list of the depositor's canceled checks (or the actual canceled checks) along with any debit or credit memoranda affecting the account. Increasingly, banks are showing canceled checks electronically via online access to accounts. **Canceled checks** are checks the bank has paid and deducted from the customer's account during the period. Other deductions that can appear on a bank statement include (1) service charges and fees assessed by the bank, (2) checks deposited that are uncollectible, (3) corrections of previous errors, (4) withdrawals through automated teller machines (ATMs), and (5) periodic payments arranged in advance by a depositor. (Most company checking accounts do not allow ATM withdrawals because of the company's desire to make all disbursements by check.) Except for service charges, the bank notifies the depositor of each deduction with a debit memorandum when the bank reduces the balance. A copy of each debit memorandum is usually sent with the statement (again, this information is often available earlier via online access and notifications).

Transactions that increase the depositor's account include amounts the bank collects on behalf of the depositor and the corrections of previous errors. Credit memoranda notify the depositor of all increases when they are recorded. A copy of each credit memorandum is often sent with the bank statement. Banks that pay interest on checking accounts often compute the amount of interest earned on the average cash balance and credit it to the depositor's account each period. In Exhibit 6.6, the bank credits $8.42 of interest to the account.

Global: If cash is in more than one currency, a company usually translates these amounts into U.S. dollars using the exchange rate as of the balance sheet date. Also, a company must disclose any restrictions on cash accounts located outside the U.S.

Bank Reconciliation

When a company deposits all cash receipts and makes all cash payments (except petty cash) by check, it can use the bank statement for proving the accuracy of its cash records. This is done using a **bank reconciliation,** which is a report explaining any differences between the checking account balance according to the depositor's records and the balance reported on the bank statement. The figure below reflects this process, which we describe in the following sections.

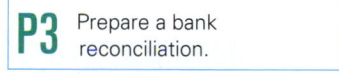

P3   Prepare a bank reconciliation.

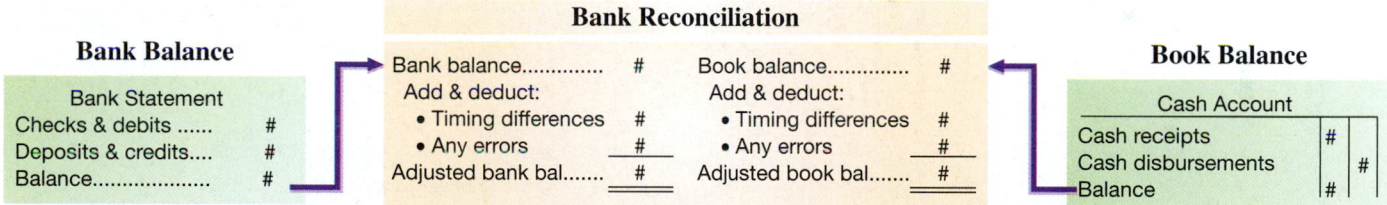

Purpose of Bank Reconciliation   The balance of a checking account reported on the bank statement rarely equals the balance in the depositor's accounting records. This is usually due to information that one party has that the other does not. We must therefore prove the accuracy of both the depositor's records and those of the bank. This means we must *reconcile* the two balances and explain or account for any differences in them. Among the factors causing the bank statement balance to differ from the depositor's book balance are these:

- **Outstanding checks. Outstanding checks** are checks written (or drawn) by the depositor, deducted on the depositor's records, and sent to the payees but not yet received by the bank for payment at the bank statement date.

- **Deposits in transit** (also called **outstanding deposits**). **Deposits in transit** are deposits made and recorded by the depositor but not yet recorded on the bank statement. For example, companies can make deposits (in the night depository) at the end of a business day after the bank is closed. If such a deposit occurred on a bank statement date, it would not appear on this period's statement. The bank would record such a deposit on the next business day, and it would appear on the next period's bank statement. Deposits mailed to the bank near the end of a period also can be in transit and unrecorded when the statement is prepared.

- **Deductions for uncollectible items and for services.** A company sometimes deposits another party's check that is uncollectible (usually meaning the balance in that party's account is not large enough to cover the check). This check is called a *non-sufficient funds (NSF)* check. The bank would have initially credited the depositor's account for the amount of the

Forms of Check Fraud (CkFraud.org)
- Forged signatures—legitimate blank checks with fake payer signature
- Forged endorsements—stolen check that is endorsed and cashed by someone other than the payee
- Counterfeit checks—fraudulent checks with fake payer signature
- Altered checks—legitimate check altered (such as changed payee or amount) to benefit perpetrator
- Check kiting—deposit check from one bank account (without sufficient funds) into a second bank account

check. When the bank learns the check is uncollectible, it debits (reduces) the depositor's account for the amount of that check. The bank may also charge the depositor a fee for processing an uncollectible check and notify the depositor of the deduction by sending a debit memorandum. The depositor should record each deduction when a debit memorandum is received, but an entry is sometimes not made until the bank reconciliation is prepared. Other possible bank charges to a depositor's account that are first reported on a bank statement include printing new checks and service fees.

- **Additions for collections and for interest.** Banks sometimes act as collection agents for their depositors by collecting notes and other items. Banks can also receive electronic funds transfers to the depositor's account. When a bank collects an item, it is added to the depositor's account, less any service fee. The bank also sends a credit memorandum to notify the depositor of the transaction. When the memorandum is received, the depositor should record it; yet it sometimes remains unrecorded until the bank reconciliation is prepared. The bank statement also includes a credit for any interest earned.

- **Errors.** Both banks and depositors can make errors. Bank errors might not be discovered until the depositor prepares the bank reconciliation. Also, depositor errors are sometimes discovered when the bank balance is reconciled. Error testing includes: (a) comparing deposits on the bank statement with deposits in the accounting records and (b) comparing canceled checks on the bank statement with checks recorded in the accounting records.

Illustration of a Bank Reconciliation   We follow nine steps in preparing the bank reconciliation. It is helpful to refer to the bank reconciliation in Exhibit 6.7 when studying steps ① through ⑨.

EXHIBIT 6.7

Bank Reconciliation

VIDEOBUSTER Bank Reconciliation October 31, 2011						
① Bank statement balance		$ 2,050.00	⑤ Book balance			$ 1,404.58
② Add			⑥ Add			
Deposit of Oct. 31 in transit		145.00	Collect $500 note less $15 fee	$485.00		
		2,195.00	Interest earned	8.42		493.42
③ Deduct						1,898.00
Outstanding checks			⑦ Deduct			
No. 124	$150.00		Check printing charge	23.00		
No. 126	200.00	350.00	NSF check plus service fee	30.00		53.00
④ **Adjusted bank balance**		**$1,845.00**	⑧ **Adjusted book balance**			**$1,845.00**

⑨ Balances are equal (reconciled)

① Identify the bank statement balance of the cash account (*balance per bank*). VideoBuster's bank balance is $2,050.

② Identify and list any unrecorded deposits and any bank errors understating the bank balance. Add them to the bank balance. VideoBuster's $145 deposit placed in the bank's night depository on October 31 is not recorded on its bank statement.

③ Identify and list any outstanding checks and any bank errors overstating the bank balance. Deduct them from the bank balance. VideoBuster's comparison of canceled checks with its books shows two checks outstanding: No. 124 for $150 and No. 126 for $200.

④ Compute the *adjusted bank balance,* also called the *corrected* or *reconciled balance.*

⑤ Identify the company's book balance of the cash account (*balance per book*). VideoBuster's book balance is $1,404.58.

⑥ Identify and list any unrecorded credit memoranda from the bank, any interest earned, and errors understating the book balance. Add them to the book balance. VideoBuster's bank statement includes a credit memorandum showing the bank collected a note receivable for the company on October 23. The note's proceeds of $500 (minus a $15 collection fee) are credited to the company's account. VideoBuster's bank statement also shows a credit of $8.42 for interest earned on the average cash balance. There was no prior notification of this item, and it is not yet recorded.

7 Identify and list any unrecorded debit memoranda from the bank, any service charges, and errors overstating the book balance. Deduct them from the book balance. Debits on Video-Buster's bank statement that are not yet recorded include (a) a $23 charge for check printing and (b) an NSF check for $20 plus a related $10 processing fee. (The NSF check is dated October 16 and was included in the book balance.)

8 Compute the *adjusted book balance,* also called *corrected* or *reconciled balance.*

9 Verify that the two adjusted balances from steps 4 and 8 are equal. If so, they are reconciled. If not, check for accuracy and missing data to achieve reconciliation.

Point: Adjusting entries can be combined into one compound entry.

Adjusting Entries from a Bank Reconciliation   A bank reconciliation often identifies unrecorded items that need recording by the company. In VideoBuster's reconciliation, the adjusted balance of $1,845 is the correct balance as of October 31. But the company's accounting records show a $1,404.58 balance. We must prepare journal entries to adjust the book balance to the correct balance. It is important to remember that only the items reconciling the book balance require adjustment. A review of Exhibit 6.7 indicates that four entries are required for VideoBuster.

Collection of note.   The first entry is to record the proceeds of its note receivable collected by the bank less the expense of having the bank perform that service.

Oct. 31	Cash	485	
	Collection Expense	15	
	Notes Receivable...........................		500
	To record the collection fee and proceeds		
	for a note collected by the bank.		

Assets = Liabilities + Equity
+485   −15
−500

Interest earned.   The second entry records interest credited to its account by the bank.

Oct. 31	Cash	8.42	
	Interest Revenue		8.42
	To record interest earned on the cash		
	balance in the checking account.		

Assets = Liabilities + Equity
+8.42   +8.42

Check printing.   The third entry records expenses for the check printing charge.

Oct. 31	Miscellaneous Expenses........................	23	
	Cash		23
	Check printing charge.		

Assets = Liabilities + Equity
−23   −23

NSF check.   The fourth entry records the NSF check that is returned as uncollectible. The $20 check was originally received from T. Woods in payment of his account and then deposited. The bank charged $10 for handling the NSF check and deducted $30 total from VideoBuster's account. This means the entry must reverse the effects of the original entry made when the check was received and must record (add) the $10 bank fee.

Point: The company will try to collect the entire NSF amount of $30 from customer.

Oct. 31	Accounts Receivable—T. Woods	30	
	Cash		30
	To charge Woods' account for $20 NSF check		
	and $10 bank fee.		

Assets = Liabilities + Equity
+30
−30

Point: The Demo Problem I shows an adjusting entry for an error correction.

Cash			
Unadj. bal.	1,404.58		
⑥	485.00	⑦	23.00
⑥	8.42	⑦	30.00
Adj. bal.	1,845.00		

After these four entries are recorded, the book balance of cash is adjusted to the correct amount of $1,845 (computed as $1,404.58 + $485 + $8.42 − $23 − $30). The Cash T-account to the side shows the same computation, where entries are keyed to the numerical codes in Exhibit 6.7.

Decision Insight

Fraud A survey reports that 74% of employees had 'personally seen' or had 'firsthand knowledge of' fraud or misconduct in their company within the past year. These employees also identified factors that would drive employees and managers to engage in misconduct. They cited pressures to meet targets, lack of standards, and other root causes—see graphic (KPMG 2009). ■

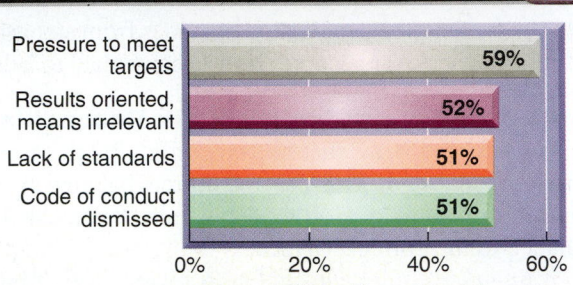

Percent Citing These Root Causes

Quick Check

Answers — p. 275

11. What is a bank statement?
12. What is the meaning of the phrase *to reconcile a bank balance?*
13. Why do we reconcile the bank statement balance of cash and the depositor's book balance of cash?
14. List at least two items affecting the *bank balance* side of a bank reconciliation and indicate whether the items are added or subtracted.
15. List at least three items affecting the *book balance* side of a bank reconciliation and indicate whether the items are added or subtracted.

GLOBAL VIEW

This section discusses similarities and differences between U.S. GAAP and IFRS regarding internal controls and in the accounting and reporting of cash.

Internal Control Purposes, Principles, and Procedures   Both U.S. GAAP and IFRS aim for high-quality financial reporting. That aim translates into enhanced internal controls worldwide. Specifically, the purposes and principles of internal control systems are fundamentally the same across the globe. However, culture and other realities suggest different emphases on the mix of control procedures, and some sensitivity to different customs and environments when establishing that mix. Nevertheless, the discussion in this chapter applies internationally. **Nokia** provides the following description of its control activities.

NOKIA

> Nokia has an internal audit function that acts as an independent appraisal function by examining and evaluating the adequacy and effectiveness of the company's system of internal control.

Control of Cash   Accounting definitions for cash are similar for U.S. GAAP and IFRS. The need for control of cash is universal and applies globally. This means that companies worldwide desire to apply cash management procedures as explained in this chapter and aim to control both cash receipts and disbursements. Accordingly, systems that employ tools such as cash monitoring mechanisms, verification of documents, and petty cash processes are applied worldwide. The basic techniques explained in this chapter are part of those control procedures.

Banking Activities as Controls   There is a global demand for banking services, bank statements, and bank reconciliations. To the extent feasible, companies utilize banking services as part of their effective control procedures. Further, bank statements are similarly used along with bank reconciliations to control and monitor cash.

 IFRS _____

Internal controls are crucial to companies that convert from U.S. GAAP to IFRS. Major risks include misstatement of financial information and fraud. Other risks are ineffective communication of the impact of this change for investors, creditors and others, and management's inability to certify the effectiveness of controls over financial reporting. ■

Days' Sales Uncollected    **Decision Analysis**

An important part of cash management is monitoring the receipt of cash from receivables. If customers and others who owe money to a company are delayed in payment, then that company can find it difficult to pay its obligations when they are due. A company's customers are crucial partners in its cash management. Many companies attract customers by selling to them on credit. This means that cash receipts from customers are delayed until accounts receivable are collected.

One measure of how quickly a company can convert its accounts receivable into cash is the **days' sales uncollected,** also called _days' sales in receivables_. This measure is computed by dividing the current balance of receivables by net credit sales over the year just completed and then multiplying by 365 (number of days in a year). Since net credit sales usually are not reported to external users, the net sales (or revenues) figure is commonly used in the computation as in Exhibit 6.8.

A1 Compute the days' sales uncollected ratio and use it to assess liquidity.

$$\text{Days' sales uncollected} = \frac{\text{Accounts receivable}}{\text{Net sales}} \times 365$$

EXHIBIT 6.8

Days' Sales Uncollected

We use days' sales uncollected to estimate how much time is likely to pass before the current amount of accounts receivable is received in cash. For evaluation purposes, we need to compare this estimate to that for other companies in the same industry. We also make comparisons between current and prior periods.

To illustrate, we select data from the annual reports of two toy manufacturers, **Hasbro** and **Mattel**. Their days' sales uncollected figures are shown in Exhibit 6.9.

EXHIBIT 6.9

Analysis Using Days' Sales Uncollected

Company	Figure ($ millions)	2009	2008	2007	2006	2005
Hasbro	Accounts receivable	$1,039	$612	$655	$556	$523
	Net sales	$4,068	$4,022	$3,838	$3,151	$3,088
	Days' sales uncollected	93 days	56 days	62 days	64 days	62 days
Mattel	Accounts receivable	$749	$874	$991	$944	$761
	Net sales	$5,431	$5,918	$5,970	$5,650	$5,179
	Days' sales uncollected	50 days	54 days	61 days	61 days	54 days

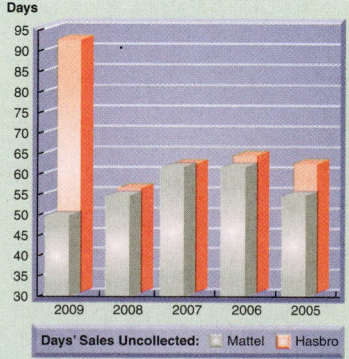

Days' Sales Uncollected: ☐ Mattel ☐ Hasbro

Days' sales uncollected for Hasbro in 2009 is computed as ($1,039/$4,068) × 365 days = 93 days. This means that it will take about 93 days to collect cash from ending accounts receivable. This number reflects one or more of the following factors: a company's ability to collect receivables, customer financial health, customer payment strategies, and discount terms. To further assess days' sales uncollected for Hasbro, we compare it to four prior years and to those of Mattel. We see that Hasbro's days' sales uncollected has worsened in 2009 as it takes much longer to collect its receivables relative to the prior four years. In comparison, Mattel fluctuated on days' sales uncollected for each of those years—from 54 days, to 61 days for two years, then back down to 54 days, and then down to the current 50 days. For all years, Mattel is superior to Hasbro on this measure of cash management. The less time that money is tied up in receivables often translates into increased profitability.

 Decision Maker   Answer — p. 275

Sales Representative   The sales staff is told to take action to help reduce days' sales uncollected for cash management purposes. What can you, a salesperson, do to reduce days' sales uncollected? ■

DEMONSTRATION PROBLEM 1

Prepare a bank reconciliation for Jamboree Enterprises for the month ended November 30, 2011. The following information is available to reconcile Jamboree Enterprises' book balance of cash with its bank statement balance as of November 30, 2011:

a. After all posting is complete on November 30, the company's book balance of Cash has a $16,380 debit balance, but its bank statement shows a $38,520 balance.

b. Checks No. 2024 for $4,810 and No. 2026 for $5,000 are outstanding.

c. In comparing the canceled checks on the bank statement with the entries in the accounting records, it is found that Check No. 2025 in payment of rent is correctly drawn for $1,000 but is erroneously entered in the accounting records as $880.

d. The November 30 deposit of $17,150 was placed in the night depository after banking hours on that date, and this amount does not appear on the bank statement.

e. In reviewing the bank statement, a check written by Jumbo Enterprises in the amount of $160 was erroneously drawn against Jamboree's account.

f. A credit memorandum enclosed with the bank statement indicates that the bank collected a $30,000 note and $900 of related interest on Jamboree's behalf. This transaction was not recorded by Jamboree prior to receiving the statement.

g. A debit memorandum for $1,100 lists a $1,100 NSF check received from a customer, Marilyn Welch. Jamboree had not recorded the return of this check before receiving the statement.

h. Bank service charges for November total $40. These charges were not recorded by Jamboree before receiving the statement.

PLANNING THE SOLUTION

- Set up a bank reconciliation with a bank side and a book side (as in Exhibit 6.7). Leave room to both add and deduct items. Each column will result in a reconciled, equal balance.
- Examine each item *a* through *h* to determine whether it affects the book or the bank balance and whether it should be added or deducted from the bank or book balance.
- After all items are analyzed, complete the reconciliation and arrive at a reconciled balance between the bank side and the book side.
- For each reconciling item on the book side, prepare an adjusting entry. Additions to the book side require an adjusting entry that debits Cash. Deductions on the book side require an adjusting entry that credits Cash.

SOLUTION TO DEMONSTRATION PROBLEM 1

JAMBOREE ENTERPRISES
Bank Reconciliation
November 30, 2011

Bank statement balance		$ 38,520	Book balance			$ 16,380
Add			Add			
Deposit of Nov. 30	$17,150		Collection of note	$30,000		
Bank error (Jumbo)	160	17,310	Interest earned	900	30,900	
		55,830			47,280	
Deduct			Deduct			
Outstanding checks			NSF check (M. Welch)	1,100		
No. 2024	4,810		Recording error (# 2025)...	120		
No. 2026	5,000	9,810	Service charge	40	1,260	
Adjusted bank balance ...		**$46,020**	**Adjusted book balance**		**$46,020**	

Required Adjusting Entries for Jamboree

Nov. 30	Cash	30,900	
	Notes Receivable		30,000
	Interest Earned		900
	To record collection of note with interest.		
Nov. 30	Accounts Receivable—M. Welch	1,100	
	Cash		1,100
	To reinstate account due from an NSF check.		
Nov. 30	Rent Expense	120	
	Cash		120
	To correct recording error on check no. 2025.		
Nov. 30	Bank Service Charges	40	
	Cash		40
	To record bank service charges.		

Point: Error correction can alternatively involve (1) reversing the error entry, and (2) recording the correct entry.

DEMONSTRATION PROBLEM 2

Bacardi Company established a $150 petty cash fund with Dean Martin as the petty cashier. When the fund balance reached $19 cash, Martin prepared a petty cash payment report, which follows.

Petty Cash Payments Report				
Receipt No.	**Account Charged**		**Approved by**	**Received by**
12	Delivery Expense	$ 29	Martin	A. Smirnoff
13	Merchandise Inventory	18	Martin	J. Daniels
15	(Omitted)	32	Martin	C. Carlsberg
16	Miscellaneous Expense	41	(Omitted)	J. Walker
	Total	$120		

Required

1. Identify four internal control weaknesses from the payment report.

2. Prepare general journal entries to record:

   a. Establishment of the petty cash fund.

   b. Reimbursement of the fund. (Assume for this part only that petty cash receipt no. 15 was issued for miscellaneous expenses.)

3. What is the Petty Cash account balance immediately before reimbursement? Immediately after reimbursement?

SOLUTION TO DEMONSTRATION PROBLEM 2

1. Four internal control weaknesses are

   a. Petty cash ticket no. 14 is missing. Its omission raises questions about the petty cashier's management of the fund.

   b. The $19 cash balance means that $131 has been withdrawn ($150 − $19 = $131). However, the total amount of the petty cash receipts is only $120 ($29 + $18 + $32 + $41). The fund is $11 short of cash ($131 − $120 = $11). Was petty cash receipt no. 14 issued for $11? Management should investigate.

   c. The petty cashier (Martin) did not sign petty cash receipt no. 16. This omission could have been an oversight on his part or he might not have authorized the payment. Management should investigate.

   d. Petty cash receipt no. 15 does not indicate which account to charge. This omission could have been an oversight on the petty cashier's part. Management could check with C. Carlsberg and the petty cashier (Martin) about the transaction. Without further information, debit Miscellaneous Expense.

2. Petty cash general journal entries.

a. Entry to establish the petty cash fund.   **b.** Entry to reimburse the fund.

Petty Cash	150	
Cash		150

Delivery Expense	29	
Merchandise Inventory	18	
Miscellaneous Expense ($41 + $32)	73	
Cash Over and Short	11	
Cash		131

3. The Petty Cash account balance *always* equals its fund balance, in this case $150. This account balance does not change unless the fund is increased or decreased.

APPENDIX

6A   Documentation and Verification

This appendix describes the important business documents of a voucher system of control.

P4 Describe the use of documentation and verification to control cash disbursements.

Purchase Requisition   Department managers are usually not allowed to place orders directly with suppliers for control purposes. Instead, a department manager must inform the purchasing department of its needs by preparing and signing a **purchase requisition,** which lists the merchandise needed and requests that it be purchased—see Exhibit 6A.1. Two copies of the purchase requisition are sent to the purchasing department, which then sends one copy to the accounting department. When the accounting department receives a purchase requisition, it creates and maintains a voucher for this transaction. The requesting department keeps the third copy.

EXHIBIT 6A.1

Purchase Requisition

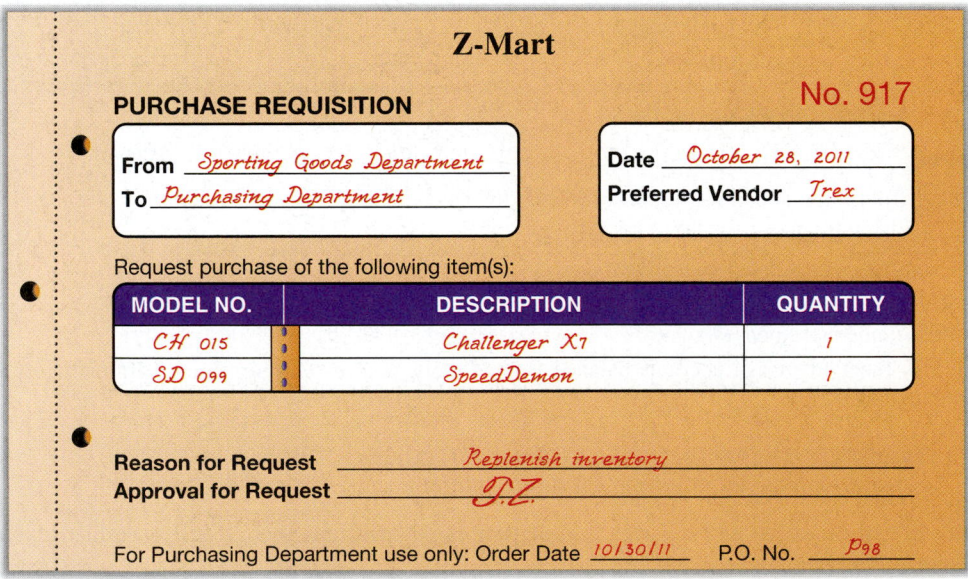

Point: A voucher system is designed to uniquely meet the needs of a specific business. Thus, we should read this appendix as one example of a common voucher system design, but *not* the only design.

Purchase Order   A **purchase order** is a document the purchasing department uses to place an order with a **vendor** (seller or supplier). A purchase order authorizes a vendor to ship ordered merchandise at the stated price and terms—see Exhibit 6A.2. When the purchasing department receives a purchase requisition, it prepares at least five copies of a purchase order. The copies are distributed as follows: *copy 1* to the vendor as a purchase request and as authority to ship merchandise; *copy 2,* along with a copy of the purchase requisition, to the accounting department, where it is entered in the voucher and used in approving payment of the invoice; *copy 3* to the requesting department to inform its manager that action is being taken; *copy 4* to the receiving department without order quantity so it can compare with goods received and provide independent count of goods received; and *copy 5* retained on file by the purchasing department.

EXHIBIT 6A.2

Purchase Order

Z-Mart
10 Michigan Street
Chicago, Illinois 60521

PURCHASE ORDER

No. P98

Date	10/30/11
FOB	Destination
Ship by	As soon as possible
Terms	2/15, n/30

To: Trex
W9797 Cherry Road
Antigo, Wisconsin 54409

Request shipment of the following item(s):

Model No.	Description	Quantity	Price	Amount
CH 015	Challenger X7	1	490	490
SD 099	SpeedDemon	1	710	710

All shipments and invoices must include purchase order number

J.W.

ORDERED BY

Invoice   An **invoice** is an itemized statement of goods prepared by the vendor listing the customer's name, items sold, sales prices, and terms of sale. An invoice is also a bill sent to the buyer from the supplier. From the vendor's point of view, it is a *sales invoice*. The buyer, or **vendee,** treats it as a *purchase invoice.* When receiving a purchase order, the vendor ships the ordered merchandise to the buyer and includes or mails a copy of the invoice covering the shipment to the buyer. The invoice is sent to the buyer's accounting department where it is placed in the voucher. (Refer back to Exhibit 4.5, which shows Z-Mart's purchase invoice.)

Receiving Report   Many companies maintain a separate department to receive all merchandise and purchased assets. When each shipment arrives, this receiving department counts the goods and checks them for damage and agreement with the purchase order. It then prepares four or more copies of a **receiving report,** which is used within the company to notify the appropriate persons that ordered goods have been received and to describe the quantities and condition of the goods. One copy is sent to accounting and placed in the voucher. Copies are also sent to the requesting department and the purchasing department to notify them that the goods have arrived. The receiving department retains a copy in its files.

Invoice Approval   When a receiving report arrives, the accounting department should have copies of the following documents in the voucher: purchase requisition, purchase order, and invoice. With the information in these documents, the accounting department can record the purchase and approve its payment. In approving an invoice for payment, it checks and compares information across all documents. To facilitate this checking and to ensure that no step is omitted, it often uses an **invoice approval,** also called *check authorization*—see Exhibit 6A.3. An invoice approval is a checklist of steps necessary for approving an invoice for recording and payment. It is a separate document either filed in the voucher or preprinted (or stamped) on the voucher.

EXHIBIT 6A.3

Invoice Approval

INVOICE APPROVAL

DOCUMENT			BY	DATE
Purchase requisition		917	TZ	10/28/11
Purchase order		P98	JW	10/30/11
Receiving report		R85	SK	11/03/11
Invoice:		4657		11/12/11
Price			JK	11/12/11
Calculations			JK	11/12/11
Terms			JK	11/12/11
Approved for payment			BC	

Point: Recording a purchase is initiated by an invoice approval, not an invoice. An invoice approval verifies that the amount is consistent with that requested, ordered, and received. This controls and verifies purchases and related liabilities.

As each step in the checklist is approved, the person initials the invoice approval and records the current date. Final approval implies the following steps have occurred:

1. **Requisition check:** Items on invoice are requested per purchase requisition.
2. **Purchase order check:** Items on invoice are ordered per purchase order.
3. **Receiving report check:** Items on invoice are received per receiving report.
4. **Invoice check: Price:** Invoice prices are as agreed with the vendor.
           Calculations: Invoice has no mathematical errors.
           Terms: Terms are as agreed with the vendor.

Voucher   Once an invoice has been checked and approved, the voucher is complete. A complete voucher is a record summarizing a transaction. Once the voucher certifies a transaction, it authorizes recording an obligation. A voucher also contains approval for paying the obligation on an appropriate date. The physical form of a voucher varies across companies. Many are designed so that the invoice and other related source documents are placed inside the voucher, which can be a folder.

Completion of a voucher usually requires a person to enter certain information on both the inside and outside of the voucher. Typical information required on the inside of a voucher is shown in Exhibit 6A.4, and that for the outside is shown in Exhibit 6A.5. This information is taken from the invoice and the supporting documents filed in the voucher. A complete voucher is sent to an authorized individual (often called an *auditor*). This person performs a final review, approves the accounts and amounts for debiting (called the *accounting distribution*), and authorizes recording of the voucher.

EXHIBIT 6A.4

Inside of a Voucher

After a voucher is approved and recorded (in a journal called a **voucher register**), it is filed by its due date. A check is then sent on the payment date from the cashier, the voucher is marked "paid," and the voucher is sent to the accounting department and recorded (in a journal called the **check register**). The person issuing checks relies on the approved voucher and its signed supporting documents as proof that an obligation has been incurred and must be paid. The purchase requisition and purchase order confirm the purchase was authorized. The receiving report shows that items have been received, and the invoice approval form verifies that the invoice has been checked for errors. There is little chance for error and even less chance for fraud without collusion unless all the documents and signatures are forged.

EXHIBIT 6A.5

Outside of a Voucher

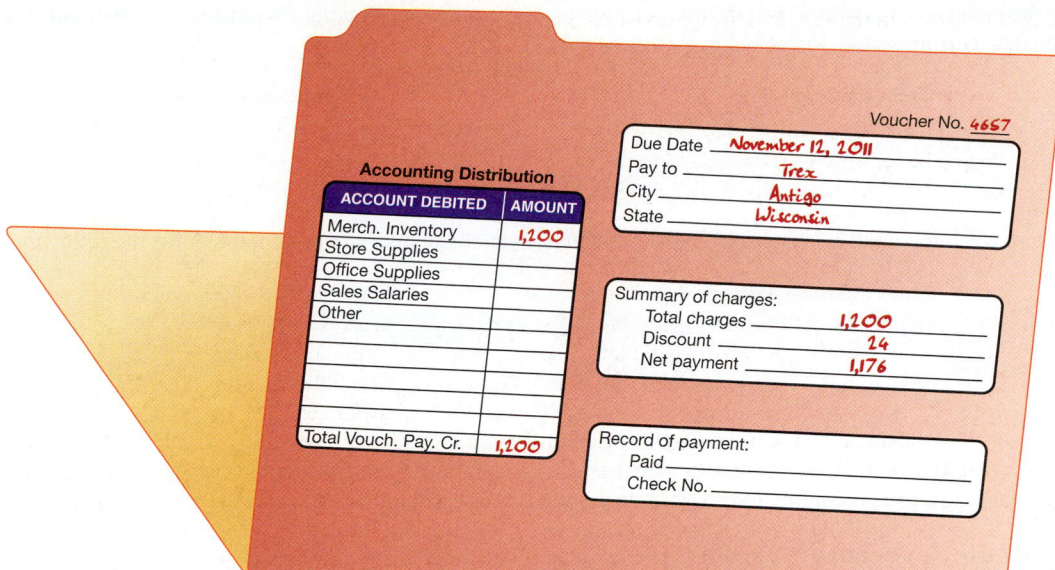

APPENDIX

Control of Purchase Discounts

6B

This appendix explains how a company can better control its cash *disbursements* to take advantage of favorable purchases discounts. Chapter 4 described the entries to record the receipt and payment of an invoice for a merchandise purchase with and without discount terms. Those entries were prepared under what is called the **gross method** of recording purchases, which initially records the invoice at its *gross* amount ignoring any cash discount.

> **P5** Apply the net method to control purchase discounts.

The **net method** is another means of recording purchases, which initially records the invoice at its *net* amount of any cash discount. The net method gives management an advantage in controlling and monitoring cash payments involving purchase discounts.

To explain, when invoices are recorded at *gross* amounts, the amount of any discounts taken is deducted from the balance of the Merchandise Inventory account when cash payment is made. This means that the amount of any discounts lost is not reported in any account or on the income statement. Lost discounts recorded in this way are unlikely to come to the attention of management. When purchases are recorded at *net* amounts, a **Discounts Lost** expense account is recorded and brought to management's attention. Management can then seek to identify the reason for discounts lost such as oversight, carelessness, or unfavorable terms. (Chapter 4 explains how managers assess whether a discount is favorable or not.)

Perpetual Inventory System   To illustrate, assume that a company purchases merchandise on November 2 at a $1,200 invoice price with terms of 2/10, n/30. Its November 2 entries under the gross and net methods are

Gross Method—Perpetual			Net Method—Perpetual		
Merchandise Inventory	1,200		Merchandise Inventory	1,176	
Accounts Payable		1,200	Accounts Payable		1,176

If the invoice is paid on November 12 within the discount period, it records the following:

Gross Method—Perpetual			Net Method—Perpetual		
Accounts Payable	1,200		Accounts Payable	1,176	
Merchandise Inventory		24	Cash		1,176
Cash		1,176			

If the invoice is *not* paid within the discount period, it records the following November 12 entry (which is the date corresponding to the end of the discount period):

Gross Method—Perpetual			**Net Method—Perpetual**		
No entry			Discounts Lost	24	
			Accounts Payable		24

Then, when the invoice is later paid on December 2, outside the discount period, it records the following:

Gross Method—Perpetual			**Net Method—Perpetual**		
Accounts Payable	1,200		Accounts Payable	1,200	
Cash		1,200	Cash		1,200

(The discount lost can be recorded when the cash payment is made with a single entry. However, in this case, when financial statements are prepared after a discount is lost and before the cash payment is made, an adjusting entry is required to recognize any unrecorded discount lost in the period when incurred.)

Periodic Inventory System   The preceding entries assume a perpetual inventory system. If a company is using a periodic system, its November 2 entries under the gross and net methods are

Gross Method—Periodic			**Net Method—Periodic**		
Purchases	1,200		Purchases	1,176	
Accounts Payable		1,200	Accounts Payable		1,176

If the invoice is paid on November 12 within the discount period, it records the following:

Gross Method—Periodic			**Net Method—Periodic**		
Accounts Payable	1,200		Accounts Payable	1,176	
Purchases Discounts		24	Cash		1,176
Cash		1,176			

If the invoice is *not* paid within the discount period, it records the following November 12 entry:

Gross Method—Periodic			**Net Method—Periodic**		
No entry			Discounts Lost	24	
			Accounts Payable		24

Then, when the invoice is later paid on December 2, outside the discount period, it records the following:

Gross Method—Periodic			**Net Method—Periodic**		
Accounts Payable	1,200		Accounts Payable	1,200	
Cash		1,200	Cash		1,200

Summary

C1   **Define internal control and identify its purpose and principles.** An internal control system consists of the policies and procedures managers use to protect assets, ensure reliable accounting, promote efficient operations, and urge adherence to company policies. It can prevent avoidable losses and help managers both plan operations and monitor company and human performance. Principles of good internal control include establishing responsibilities, maintaining adequate records, insuring assets and bonding employees, separating recordkeeping from custody of assets, dividing responsibilities for related transactions, applying technological controls, and performing regular independent reviews.

C2   **Define cash and cash equivalents and explain how to report them.** Cash includes currency, coins, and amounts on (or acceptable for) deposit in checking and savings accounts. Cash equivalents are short-term, highly liquid investment assets readily convertible to a known cash amount and sufficiently close to their maturity date so that market value is not sensitive to interest rate changes. Cash and cash equivalents are liquid assets because they are readily converted into other assets or can be used to pay for goods, services, or liabilities.

A1 **Compute the days' sales uncollected ratio and use it to assess liquidity.** Many companies attract customers by selling to them on credit. This means that cash receipts from customers are delayed until accounts receivable are collected. Users want to know how quickly a company can convert its accounts receivable into cash. The days' sales uncollected ratio, one measure reflecting company liquidity, is computed by dividing the ending balance of receivables by annual net sales, and then multiplying by 365.

P1 **Apply internal control to cash receipts and disbursements.** Internal control of cash receipts ensures that all cash received is properly recorded and deposited. Attention focuses on two important types of cash receipts: over-the-counter and by mail. Good internal control for over-the-counter cash receipts includes use of a cash register, customer review, use of receipts, a permanent transaction record, and separation of the custody of cash from its record-keeping. Good internal control for cash receipts by mail includes at least two people assigned to open mail and a listing of each sender's name, amount, and explanation. (Banks offer several services that promote the control and safeguarding of cash.)

P2 **Explain and record petty cash fund transactions.** Petty cash disbursements are payments of small amounts for items such as postage, courier fees, minor repairs, and supplies. A company usually sets up one or more petty cash funds. A petty cash fund cashier is responsible for safekeeping the cash, making payments from this fund, and keeping receipts and records. A Petty Cash account

is debited only when the fund is established or increased in amount. When the fund is replenished, petty cash disbursements are recorded with debits to expense (or asset) accounts and a credit to cash.

P3 **Prepare a bank reconciliation.** A bank reconciliation proves the accuracy of the depositor's and the bank's records. The bank statement balance is adjusted for items such as outstanding checks and unrecorded deposits made on or before the bank statement date but not reflected on the statement. The book balance is adjusted for items such as service charges, bank collections for the depositor, and interest earned on the account.

P4^A **Describe the use of documentation and verification to control cash disbursements.** A voucher system is a set of procedures and approvals designed to control cash disbursements and acceptance of obligations. The voucher system of control relies on several important documents, including the voucher and its supporting files. A key factor in this system is that only approved departments and individuals are authorized to incur certain obligations.

P5^B **Apply the net method to control purchase discounts.** The net method aids management in monitoring and controlling purchase discounts. When invoices are recorded at gross amounts, the amount of discounts taken is deducted from the balance of the Inventory account. This means that the amount of any discounts lost is not reported in any account and is unlikely to come to the attention of management. When purchases are recorded at net amounts, a Discounts Lost account is brought to management's attention as an operating expense. Management can then seek to identify the reason for discounts lost, such as oversight, carelessness, or unfavorable terms.

Guidance Answers to Decision Maker and Decision Ethics

Entrepreneur   A forced vacation policy is part of a good system of internal controls. When employees are forced to take vacations, their ability to hide any fraudulent behavior decreases because others must perform the vacationers' duties. A replacement employee potentially can uncover fraudulent behavior or falsified records. A forced vacation policy is especially important for employees in sensitive positions of handling money or in control of easily transferable assets.

Sales Representative   A salesperson can take several steps to reduce days' sales uncollected. These include (1) decreasing the ratio of sales on account to total sales by encouraging more cash sales, (2) identifying customers most delayed in their payments and encouraging earlier payments or cash sales, and (3) applying stricter credit policies to eliminate credit sales to customers that never pay.

Guidance Answers to Quick Checks

1. (*c*)
2. Technology reduces processing errors. It also allows more extensive testing of records, limits the amount of hard evidence, and highlights the importance of separation of duties.
3. A company holds liquid assets so that it can purchase other assets, buy services, and pay obligations.
4. It owns cash equivalents because they yield a return greater than what cash earns (and are readily exchanged for cash).
5. Examples of cash equivalents are 90-day (or less) U.S. Treasury bills, money market funds, and commercial paper (notes).
6. (*a*)
7. A voucher system is used when an owner/manager can no longer control purchasing procedures through personal supervision and direct participation.

8. If all cash payments are made by check, numerous checks for small amounts must be written. Since this practice is expensive and time-consuming, a petty cash fund is often established for making small (immaterial) cash payments.
9. If the petty cash fund is not reimbursed at the end of an accounting period, the transactions involving petty cash are not yet recorded and the petty cash asset is overstated.
10. First, petty cash transactions are recorded when the petty cash fund is reimbursed. Second, reimbursement provides cash to allow the fund to continue being used. Third, reimbursement identifies any cash shortage or overage in the fund.
11. A bank statement is a report prepared by the bank describing the activities in a depositor's account.

12. To reconcile a bank balance means to explain the difference between the cash balance in the depositor's accounting records and the cash balance on the bank statement.

13. The purpose of the bank reconciliation is to determine whether the bank or the depositor has made any errors and whether the bank has entered any transactions affecting the account that the depositor has not recorded.

14. Unrecorded deposits—added
Outstanding checks—subtracted

15. Interest earned—added   Debit memos—subtracted
Credit memos—added   NSF checks—subtracted
                            Bank service charges—subtracted

Key Terms   mhhe.com/wildFINMAN4e

Bank reconciliation (p. 263)

Bank statement (p. 262)

Canceled checks (p. 263)

Cash (p. 253)

Cash equivalents (p. 253)

Cash Over and Short (p. 255)

Check (p. 260)

Check register (p. 272)

Committee of Sponsoring Organizations (COSO) (p. 249)

Days' sales uncollected (p. 267)

Deposit ticket (p. 260)

Deposits in transit (p. 263)

Discounts lost (p. 273)

Electronic funds transfer (EFT) (p. 261)

Gross method (p. 273)

Internal control system (p. 248)

Invoice (p. 271)

Invoice approval (p. 271)

Liquid assets (p. 253)

Liquidity (p. 253)

Net method (p. 273)

Outstanding checks (p. 263)

Petty cash (p. 258)

Principles of internal control (p. 249)

Purchase order (p. 270)

Purchase requisition (p. 270)

Receiving report (p. 271)

Sarbanes-Oxley Act (p. 248)

Section 404 (of SOX) (p. 249)

Signature card (p. 260)

Vendee (p. 271)

Vendor (p. 270)

Voucher (p. 257)

Voucher register (p. 272)

Voucher system (p. 256)

Multiple Choice Quiz   Answers on p. 289   mhhe.com/wildFINMAN4e

Additional Quiz Questions are available at the book's Website.

1. A company needs to replenish its $500 petty cash fund. Its petty cash box has $75 cash and petty cash receipts of $420. The journal entry to replenish the fund includes
   a. A debit to Cash for $75.
   b. A credit to Cash for $75.
   c. A credit to Petty Cash for $420.
   d. A credit to Cash Over and Short for $5.
   e. A debit to Cash Over and Short for $5.

2. The following information is available for Hapley Company:
   • The November 30 bank statement shows a $1,895 balance.
   • The general ledger shows a $1,742 balance at November 30.
   • A $795 deposit placed in the bank's night depository on November 30 does not appear on the November 30 bank statement.
   • Outstanding checks amount to $638 at November 30.
   • A customer's $335 note was collected by the bank in November. A collection fee of $15 was deducted by the bank and the difference deposited in Hapley's account.
   • A bank service charge of $10 is deducted by the bank and appears on the November 30 bank statement.

   How will the customer's note appear on Hapley's November 30 bank reconciliation?
   a. $320 appears as an addition to the book balance of cash.
   b. $320 appears as a deduction from the book balance of cash.
   c. $320 appears as an addition to the bank balance of cash.

   d. $320 appears as a deduction from the bank balance of cash.
   e. $335 appears as an addition to the bank balance of cash.

3. Using the information from question 2, what is the reconciled balance on Hapley's November 30 bank reconciliation?
   a. $2,052
   b. $1,895
   c. $1,742
   d. $2,201
   e. $1,184

4. A company had net sales of $84,000 and accounts receivable of $6,720. Its days' sales uncollected is
   a. 3.2 days
   b. 18.4 days
   c. 230.0 days
   d. 29.2 days
   e. 12.5 days

5.[B] A company records its purchases using the net method. On August 1, it purchases merchandise on account for $6,000 with terms of 2/10, n/30. The August 1 journal entry to record this transaction includes a
   a. Debit to Merchandise Inventory for $6,000.
   b. Debit to Merchandise Inventory for $5,880.
   c. Debit to Merchandise Inventory for $120.
   d. Debit to Accounts Payable for $5,880.
   e. Credit to Accounts Payable for $6,000.

A(B) *Superscript letter A(B) denotes assignments based on Appendix 6A (6B).*

  Icon denotes assignments that involve decision making.

Discussion Questions

1. List the seven broad principles of internal control.

2. Internal control procedures are important in every business, but at what stage in the development of a business do they become especially critical?

3. Why should responsibility for related transactions be divided among different departments or individuals?

4. Why should the person who keeps the records of an asset not be the person responsible for its custody?

5. When a store purchases merchandise, why are individual departments not allowed to directly deal with suppliers?

6. What are the limitations of internal controls?

7. Which of the following assets is most liquid? Which is least liquid? Inventory, building, accounts receivable, or cash.

8. What is a petty cash receipt? Who should sign it?

9. Why should cash receipts be deposited on the day of receipt?

10. **Research In Motion**'s statement of cash flows in Appendix A describes changes in cash and cash   *RIM*   equivalents for the year ended February 27, 2010. What total amount is provided (used) by investing activities? What amount is provided (used) by financing activities?

11. Refer to **Apple**'s financial statements in Appendix A. Identify Apple's net income for the year ended December 31, 2009. Is its net income equal to the increase in cash and cash equivalents for the year? Explain the difference between net income and the increase in cash and cash equivalents.   *Apple*

12. Refer to **Nokia**'s balance sheet in Appendix A. How does its cash (titled "bank and cash") compare with its other current assets (both in amount and percent) as of December 31, 2009? Compare and assess its cash at December 31, 2009, with its cash at December 31, 2008.   **NOKIA**

13. **Palm**'s balance sheet in Appendix A reports that cash and equivalents decreased during the fiscal year ended May, 31, 2009. Identify the cash generated (or used) by operating activities, by investing activities, and by financing activities.   **Palm**

connect

An internal control system consists of all policies and procedures used to protect assets, ensure reliable accounting, promote efficient operations, and urge adherence to company policies.

1. What is the main objective of internal control procedures? How is that objective achieved?

2. Why should recordkeeping for assets be separated from custody over those assets?

3. Why should the responsibility for a transaction be divided between two or more individuals or departments?

QUICK STUDY

QS 6-1
Internal control objectives
C1

A good system of internal control for cash provides adequate procedures for protecting both cash receipts and cash disbursements.

1. What are three basic guidelines that help achieve this protection?

2. Identify two control systems or procedures for cash disbursements.

QS 6-2
Internal control for cash
P1

Good accounting systems help in managing cash and controlling who has access to it.

1. What items are included in the category of cash?

2. What items are included in the category of cash equivalents?

3. What does the term *liquidity* refer to?

QS 6-3
Cash and equivalents
C2

---

1. The petty cash fund of the Rio Agency is established at $75. At the end of the current period, the fund contained $14 and had the following receipts: film rentals, $19, refreshments for meetings, $23 (both expenditures to be classified as Entertainment Expense); postage, $6; and printing, $13. Prepare journal entries to record (*a*) establishment of the fund and (*b*) reimbursement of the fund at the end of the current period.

2. Identify the two events that cause a Petty Cash account to be credited in a journal entry.

QS 6-4
Petty cash accounting
P2

---

1. For each of the following items, indicate whether its amount (i) affects the bank or book side of a bank reconciliation and (ii) represents an addition or a subtraction in a bank reconciliation.

   a. Outstanding checks   **d.** Unrecorded deposits   **g.** Bank service charges
   b. Debit memos   **e.** Interest on cash balance
   c. NSF checks   **f.** Credit memos

2. Which of the items in part 1 require an adjusting journal entry?

QS 6-5
Bank reconciliation
P3

QS 6-6
Bank reconciliation
P3

Cruz Company deposits all cash receipts on the day when they are received and it makes all cash payments by check. At the close of business on June 30, 2011, its Cash account shows an $11,352 debit balance. Cruz's June 30 bank statement shows $10,332 on deposit in the bank. Prepare a bank reconciliation for Cruz Company using the following information.

a. Outstanding checks as of June 30 total $1,713.

b. The June 30 bank statement included a $23 debit memorandum for bank services; Cruz has not yet recorded the cost of these services.

c. In reviewing the bank statement, a $90 check written by Cruz Company was mistakenly recorded in Cruz Company's books at $99.

d. June 30 cash receipts of $2,724 were placed in the bank's night depository after banking hours and were not recorded on the June 30 bank statement.

e. The bank statement included a $5 credit for interest earned on the cash in the bank.

QS 6-7
Days' sales uncollected
A1

The following annual account balances are taken from ProTeam Sports at December 31.

	2011	2010
Accounts receivable	$ 75,692	$ 70,484
Net sales	2,591,933	2,296,673

What is the change in the number of days' sales uncollected between years 2010 and 2011? According to this analysis, is the company's collection of receivables improving? Explain.

QS 6-8^A
Documents in a voucher system
P4

Management uses a voucher system to help control and monitor cash disbursements. Identify and describe at least four key documents that are part of a voucher system of control.

QS 6-9^B
Purchase discounts   P5

An important part of cash management is knowing when, and if, to take purchase discounts.

a. Which accounting method uses a Discounts Lost account?

b. What is the advantage of this method for management?

QS 6-10
International accounting and internal controls
C1 P1

Answer each of the following related to international accounting standards.

a. Explain how the purposes and principles of internal controls are different between accounting systems reporting under IFRS versus U.S. GAAP.

b. Cash presents special internal control challenges. How do internal controls for cash differ for accounting systems reporting under IFRS versus U.S. GAAP? How do the procedures applied differ across those two accounting systems?

QS 6-11
Reviewing bank statements
P3

An entrepreneur commented that a bank reconciliation may not be necessary as she regularly reviews her online bank statement for any unusual items and errors.

a. Describe how a bank reconciliation and an online review (or reading) of the bank statement are not equivalent.

b. Identify and explain at least two frauds or errors that would be uncovered through a bank reconciliation and that would *not* be uncovered through an online review of the bank statement.

EXERCISES

Exercise 6-1
Internal control recommendations
C1

What internal control procedures would you recommend in each of the following situations?

1. A concession company has one employee who sells towels, coolers, and sunglasses at the beach. Each day, the employee is given enough towels, coolers, and sunglasses to last through the day and enough cash to make change. The money is kept in a box at the stand.

2. An antique store has one employee who is given cash and sent to garage sales each weekend. The employee pays cash for any merchandise acquired that the antique store resells.

Cantu Company is a rapidly growing start-up business. Its recordkeeper, who was hired nine months ago, left town after the company's manager discovered that a large sum of money had disappeared over the past three months. An audit disclosed that the recordkeeper had written and signed several checks made payable to her fiancé and then recorded the checks as salaries expense. The fiancé, who cashed the checks but never worked for the company, left town with the recordkeeper. As a result, the company incurred an uninsured loss of $84,000. Evaluate Cantu's internal control system and indicate which principles of internal control appear to have been ignored.

Exercise 6-2

Analyzing internal control

C1

Some of Chester Company's cash receipts from customers are received by the company with the regular mail. Chester's recordkeeper opens these letters and deposits the cash received each day. (*a*) Identify any internal control problem(s) in this arrangement. (*b*) What changes to its internal control system do you recommend?

Exercise 6-3

Control of cash receipts by mail

P1

Good accounting systems help with the management and control of cash and cash equivalents.
1. Define and contrast the terms *liquid asset* and *cash equivalent*.
2. Why would companies invest their idle cash in cash equivalents?
3. Identify five principles of effective cash management.

Exercise 6-4

Cash, liquidity, and return

C2

Hawk Company establishes a $400 petty cash fund on September 9. On September 30, the fund shows $166 in cash along with receipts for the following expenditures: transportation-in, $32; postage expenses, $113; and miscellaneous expenses, $87. The petty cashier could not account for a $2 shortage in the fund. Hawk uses the perpetual system in accounting for merchandise inventory. Prepare (1) the September 9 entry to establish the fund, (2) the September 30 entry to reimburse the fund, and (3) an October 1 entry to decrease the fund to $300.

Exercise 6-5

Petty cash fund with a shortage

P2

Check   (2) Cr. Cash $234 and (3) Dr. Cash $100

NetPerks Co. establishes a $200 petty cash fund on January 1. On January 8, the fund shows $28 in cash along with receipts for the following expenditures: postage, $64; transportation-in, $19; delivery expenses, $36; and miscellaneous expenses, $53. NetPerks uses the perpetual system in accounting for merchandise inventory. Prepare journal entries to (1) establish the fund on January 1, (2) reimburse it on January 8, and (3) both reimburse the fund and increase it to $500 on January 8, assuming no entry in part 2. (*Hint*: Make two separate entries for part 3.)

Exercise 6-6

Petty cash fund accounting

P2

Check   (3) Cr. Cash $472 (total)

Prepare a table with the following headings for a monthly bank reconciliation dated September 30.

Exercise 6-7

Bank reconciliation and adjusting entries

P3

Bank Balance		Book Balance			Not Shown on the Reconciliation
Add	Deduct	Add	Deduct	Adjust	

For each item 1 through 12, place an *x* in the appropriate column to indicate whether the item should be added to or deducted from the book or bank balance, or whether it should not appear on the reconciliation. If the book balance is to be adjusted, place a *Dr.* or *Cr.* in the Adjust column to indicate whether the Cash balance should be debited or credited. At the left side of your table, number the items to correspond to the following list.
1. Bank service charge for September.
2. Checks written and mailed to payees on October 2.
3. Checks written by another depositor but charged against this company's account.
4. Principal and interest on a note receivable to this company is collected by the bank but not yet recorded by the company.
5. Special bank charge for collection of note in part 4 on this company's behalf.
6. Check written against the company's account and cleared by the bank; erroneously not recorded by the company's recordkeeper.
7. Interest earned on the September cash balance in the bank.
8. Night deposit made on September 30 after the bank closed.
9. Checks outstanding on August 31 that cleared the bank in September.
10. NSF check from customer is returned on September 25 but not yet recorded by this company.
11. Checks written by the company and mailed to payees on September 30.
12. Deposit made on September 5 and processed by the bank on September 6.

Exercise 6-8
Voucher system
P1

The voucher system of control is designed to control cash disbursements and the acceptance of obligations.
1. The voucher system of control establishes procedures for what two processes?
2. What types of expenditures should be overseen by a voucher system of control?
3. When is the voucher initially prepared? Explain.

Exercise 6-9
Bank reconciliation
P3

Frederick Clinic deposits all cash receipts on the day when they are received and it makes all cash payments by check. At the close of business on June 30, 2011, its Cash account shows a $15,141 debit balance. Frederick Clinic's June 30 bank statement shows $14,275 on deposit in the bank. Prepare a bank reconciliation for Frederick Clinic using the following information:
a. Outstanding checks as of June 30 total $2,500.
b. The June 30 bank statement included a $125 debit memorandum for bank services.
c. Check No. 919, listed with the canceled checks, was correctly drawn for $645 in payment of a utility bill on June 15. Frederick Clinic mistakenly recorded it with a debit to Utilities Expense and a credit to Cash in the amount of $654.

Check   Reconciled bal., $15,025

d. The June 30 cash receipts of $3,250 were placed in the bank's night depository after banking hours and were not recorded on the June 30 bank statement.

Exercise 6-10
Adjusting entries from bank
reconciliation   **P3**

Prepare the adjusting journal entries that Frederick Clinic must record as a result of preparing the bank reconciliation in Exercise 6-9.

Exercise 6-11
Bank reconciliation
P3

Chung Company deposits all cash receipts on the day when they are received and it makes all cash payments by check. At the close of business on May 31, 2011, its Cash account shows a $15,500 debit balance. Chung's May 31 bank statement shows $13,800 on deposit in the bank. Prepare a bank reconciliation for Chung Company using the following information.
a. May 31 cash receipts of $2,200 were placed in the bank's night depository after banking hours and were not recorded on the May 31 bank statement.
b. Outstanding checks as of May 31 total $1,600.
c. The May 31 bank statement included a $100 debit memorandum for bank services; Chung has not yet recorded the cost of these services.
d. In reviewing the bank statement, a $400 check written by Wald Company was mistakenly drawn against Chung's account.

Check   Reconciled bal., $14,800

e. A debit memorandum for $600 refers to a $600 NSF check from a customer; Chung has not yet recorded this NSF check.

Exercise 6-12
Liquid assets and
accounts receivable

A1

Deacon Co. reported annual net sales for 2010 and 2011 of $565,000 and $647,000, respectively. Its year-end balances of accounts receivable follow: December 31, 2010, $51,000; and December 31, 2011, $83,000. (a) Calculate its days' sales uncollected at the end of each year. (b) Evaluate and comment on any changes in the amount of liquid assets tied up in receivables.

Exercise 6-13^A
Documents in a voucher system
P4

Match each document in a voucher system in column one with its description in column two.

Document	Description
1. Voucher	A. A document used to notify the appropriate persons that ordered goods have arrived, including a description of the quantities and condition of goods.
2. Invoice approval	B. An internal file used to store documents and information to control cash disbursements and to ensure that a transaction is properly authorized and recorded.
3. Receiving report	
4. Invoice	C. A document used to place an order with a vendor that authorizes the vendor to ship ordered merchandise at the stated price and terms.
5. Purchase order	
6. Purchase requisition	D. A checklist of steps necessary for the approval of an invoice for recording and payment; also known as a check authorization.
	E. A document used by department managers to inform the purchasing department to place an order with a vendor.
	F. An itemized statement of goods prepared by the vendor listing the customer's name, items sold, sales prices, and terms of sale.

USA Imports uses the perpetual system in accounting for merchandise inventory and had the following transactions during the month of October. Prepare entries to record these transactions assuming that USA Imports records invoices (*a*) at gross amounts and (*b*) at net amounts.

Oct. 2   Purchased merchandise at a $4,000 price, invoice dated October 2, terms 2/10, n/30.
    10   Received a $400 credit memorandum (at full invoice price) for the return of merchandise that it purchased on October 2.
    17   Purchased merchandise at a $4,400 price, invoice dated October 16, terms 2/10, n/30.
    26   Paid for the merchandise purchased on October 17, less the discount.
    31   Paid for the merchandise purchased on October 2. Payment was delayed because the invoice was mistakenly filed for payment today. This error caused the discount to be lost.

Exercise 6-14^B

Record invoices at gross or net amounts

P5

---

connect

For each of these five separate cases, identify the principle(s) of internal control that is violated. Recommend what the business should do to ensure adherence to principles of internal control.

1. Heather Flat records all incoming customer cash receipts for her employer and posts the customer payments to their respective accounts.

2. At Netco Company, Jeff and Jose alternate lunch hours. Jeff is the petty cash custodian, but if someone needs petty cash when he is at lunch, Jose fills in as custodian.

3. Nadine Cox posts all patient charges and payments at the Dole Medical Clinic. Each night Nadine backs up the computerized accounting system to a tape and stores the tape in a locked file at her desk.

4. Barto Sayles prides himself on hiring quality workers who require little supervision. As office manager, Barto gives his employees full discretion over their tasks and for years has seen no reason to perform independent reviews of their work.

5. Desi West's manager has told her to reduce costs. Desi decides to raise the deductible on the plant's property insurance from $5,000 to $10,000. This cuts the property insurance premium in half. In a related move, she decides that bonding the plant's employees is a waste of money since the company has not experienced any losses due to employee theft. Desi saves the entire amount of the bonding insurance premium by dropping the bonding insurance.

PROBLEM SET A

Problem 6-1A
Analyzing internal control

C1

Shawnee Co. set up a petty cash fund for payments of small amounts. The following transactions involving the petty cash fund occurred in May (the last month of the company's fiscal year).

May 1   Prepared a company check for $250 to establish the petty cash fund.
    15   Prepared a company check to replenish the fund for the following expenditures made since May 1.
        a.   Paid $78 for janitorial services.
        b.   Paid $63.68 for miscellaneous expenses.
        c.   Paid postage expenses of $43.50.
        d.   Paid $57.15 to *The County Gazette* (the local newspaper) for an advertisement.
        e.   Counted $11.15 remaining in the petty cash box.
    16   Prepared a company check for $200 to increase the fund to $450.
    31   The petty cashier reports that $293.39 cash remains in the fund. A company check is drawn to replenish the fund for the following expenditures made since May 15.
        f.   Paid postage expenses of $48.36.
        g.   Reimbursed the office manager for business mileage, $38.50.
        h.   Paid $39.75 to deliver merchandise to a customer, terms FOB destination.
    31   The company decides that the May 16 increase in the fund was too large. It reduces the fund by $50, leaving a total of $400.

Problem 6-2A
Establish, reimburse, and adjust petty cash

P2

Required

1. Prepare journal entries to establish the fund on May 1, to replenish it on May 15 and on May 31, and to reflect any increase or decrease in the fund balance on May 16 and May 31.

Check   (1) Cr. to Cash: May 15; $238.85; May 16, $200.00

Analysis Component

2. Explain how the company's financial statements are affected if the petty cash fund is not replenished and no entry is made on May 31.

Problem 6-3A

Establish, reimburse, and increase petty cash

P2

Shelton Gallery had the following petty cash transactions in February of the current year.

Feb. 2 Wrote a $300 check, cashed it, and gave the proceeds and the petty cashbox to Bo Brown, the petty cashier.

  5 Purchased bond paper for the copier for $10.13 that is immediately used.

  9 Paid $22.50 COD shipping charges on merchandise purchased for resale, terms FOB shipping point. Shelton uses the perpetual system to account for merchandise inventory.

  12 Paid $9.95 postage to express mail a contract to a client.

  14 Reimbursed Alli Buck, the manager, $58 for business mileage on her car.

  20 Purchased stationery for $77.76 that is immediately used.

  23 Paid a courier $18 to deliver merchandise sold to a customer, terms FOB destination.

  25 Paid $15.10 COD shipping charges on merchandise purchased for resale, terms FOB shipping point.

  27 Paid $64 for postage expenses.

  28 The fund had $21.23 remaining in the petty cash box. Sorted the petty cash receipts by accounts affected and exchanged them for a check to reimburse the fund for expenditures.

  28 The petty cash fund amount is increased by $100 to a total of $400.

Required

1. Prepare the journal entry to establish the petty cash fund.

2. Prepare a petty cash payments report for February with these categories: delivery expense, mileage expense, postage expense, merchandise inventory (for transportation-in), and office supplies expense. Sort the payments into the appropriate categories and total the expenditures in each category.

Check (3a & 3b) Total Cr. to Cash $378.77

3. Prepare the journal entries for part 2 to both (*a*) reimburse and (*b*) increase the fund amount.

Problem 6-4A

Prepare a bank reconciliation and record adjustments

P3

mhhe.com/wildFINMAN4e

The following information is available to reconcile Clark Company's book balance of cash with its bank statement cash balance as of July 31, 2011.

a. On July 31, the company's Cash account has a $26,193 debit balance, but its July bank statement shows a $28,020 cash balance.

b. Check No. 3031 for $1,380 and Check No. 3040 for $552 were outstanding on the June 30 bank reconciliation. Check No. 3040 is listed with the July canceled checks, but Check No. 3031 is not. Also, Check No. 3065 for $336 and Check No. 3069 for $2,148, both written in July, are not among the canceled checks on the July 31 statement.

c. In comparing the canceled checks on the bank statement with the entries in the accounting records, it is found that Check No. 3056 for July rent was correctly written and drawn for $1,250 but was erroneously entered in the accounting records as $1,230.

d. A credit memorandum enclosed with the July bank statement indicates the bank collected $9,000 cash on a non-interest-bearing note for Clark, deducted a $45 collection fee, and credited the remainder to its account. Clark had not recorded this event before receiving the statement.

e. A debit memorandum for $805 lists a $795 NSF check plus a $10 NSF charge. The check had been received from a customer, Jim Shaw. Clark has not yet recorded this check as NSF.

f. Enclosed with the July statement is a $15 debit memorandum for bank services. It has not yet been recorded because no previous notification had been received.

g. Clark's July 31 daily cash receipts of $10,152 were placed in the bank's night depository on that date, but do not appear on the July 31 bank statement.

Required

1. Prepare the bank reconciliation for this company as of July 31, 2011.

Check (1) Reconciled balance, $34,308; (2) Cr. Note Receivable $9,000

2. Prepare the journal entries necessary to bring the company's book balance of cash into conformity with the reconciled cash balance as of July 31, 2011.

Analysis Component

3. Assume that the July 31, 2011, bank reconciliation for this company is prepared and some items are treated incorrectly. For each of the following errors, explain the effect of the error on (i) the adjusted bank statement cash balance and (ii) the adjusted cash account book balance.

  a. The company's unadjusted cash account balance of $26,193 is listed on the reconciliation as $26,139.

  b. The bank's collection of the $9,000 note less the $45 collection fee is added to the bank statement cash balance on the reconciliation.

Els Company most recently reconciled its bank statement and book balances of cash on August 31 and it reported two checks outstanding, No. 5888 for $1,038.05 and No. 5893 for $484.25. The following information is available for its September 30, 2011, reconciliation.

Problem 6-5A
Prepare a bank reconciliation and record adjustments

P3

mhhe.com/wildFINMAN4e

From the September 30 Bank Statement

PREVIOUS BALANCE	TOTAL CHECKS AND DEBITS	TOTAL DEPOSITS AND CREDITS	CURRENT BALANCE
16,800.45	9,620.05	11,182.85	18,363.25

CHECKS AND DEBITS			DEPOSITS AND CREDITS		DAILY BALANCE	
Date	No.	Amount	Date	Amount	Date	Amount
09/03	5888	1,038.05	09/05	1,103.75	08/31	16,800.45
09/04	5902	731.90	09/12	2,226.90	09/03	15,762.40
09/07	5901	1,824.25	09/21	4,093.00	09/04	15,030.50
09/17		588.25 NSF	09/25	2,351.70	09/05	16,134.25
09/20	5905	937.00	09/30	22.50 IN	09/07	14,310.00
09/22	5903	399.10	09/30	1,385.00 CM	09/12	16,536.90
09/22	5904	2,080.00			09/17	15,948.65
09/28	5907	213.85			09/20	15,011.65
09/29	5909	1,807.65			09/21	19,104.65
					09/22	16,625.55
					09/25	18,977.25
					09/28	18,763.40
					09/29	16,955.75
					09/30	18,363.25

From Els Company's Accounting Records

Cash Receipts Deposited				Cash Disbursements		
Date		Cash Debit		Check No.		Cash Credit
Sept.	5	1,103.75		5901		1,824.25
	12	2,226.90		5902		731.90
	21	4,093.00		5903		399.10
	25	2,351.70		5904		2,050.00
	30	1,582.75		5905		937.00
		11,358.10		5906		859.30
				5907		213.85
				5908		276.00
				5909		1,807.65
						9,099.05

Cash					Acct. No. 101	
Date		Explanation	PR	Debit	Credit	Balance
Aug.	31	Balance				15,278.15
Sept.	30	Total receipts	R12	11,358.10		26,636.25
	30	Total disbursements	D23		9,099.05	17,537.20

Additional Information

Check No. 5904 is correctly drawn for $2,080 to pay for computer equipment; however, the recordkeeper misread the amount and entered it in the accounting records with a debit to Computer Equipment and a credit to Cash of $2,050. The NSF check shown in the statement was originally received from a customer, S. Nilson, in payment of her account. Its return has not yet been recorded by the company. The credit memorandum is from the collection of a $1,400 note for Els Company by the bank. The bank deducted a $15 collection fee. The collection and fee are not yet recorded.

Required

Check (1) Reconciled balance, $18,326.45 (2) Cr. Note Receivable $1,400

1. Prepare the September 30, 2011, bank reconciliation for this company.

2. Prepare the journal entries to adjust the book balance of cash to the reconciled balance.

Analysis Component

3. The bank statement reveals that some of the prenumbered checks in the sequence are missing. Describe three situations that could explain this.

PROBLEM SET B

Problem 6-1B

Analyzing internal control

C1

For each of these five separate cases, identify the principle(s) of internal control that is violated. Recommend what the business should do to ensure adherence to principles of internal control.

1. Latoya Tally is the company's computer specialist and oversees its computerized payroll system. Her boss recently asked her to put password protection on all office computers. Latoya has put a password in place that allows only the boss access to the file where pay rates are changed and personnel are added or deleted from the payroll.

2. Lake Theater has a computerized order-taking system for its tickets. The system is active all week and backed up every Friday night.

3. X2U Company has two employees handling acquisitions of inventory. One employee places purchase orders and pays vendors. The second employee receives the merchandise.

4. The owner of Super-Aid Pharmacy uses a check protector to perforate checks, making it difficult for anyone to alter the amount of the check. The check protector is on the owner's desk in an office that contains company checks and is normally unlocked.

5. LeAnn Company is a small business that has separated the duties of cash receipts and cash disbursements. The employee responsible for cash disbursements reconciles the bank account monthly.

Problem 6-2B

Establishing, reimbursing, and adjusting petty cash

P2

Pepco Co. establishes a petty cash fund for payments of small amounts. The following transactions involving the petty cash fund occurred in January (the last month of the company's fiscal year).

Jan. 3   A company check for $150 is written and made payable to the petty cashier to establish the petty cash fund.

    14   A company check is written to replenish the fund for the following expenditures made since January 3.
  a. Purchased office supplies for $16.29 that are immediately used up.
  b. Paid $17.60 COD shipping charges on merchandise purchased for resale, terms FOB shipping point. Pepco uses the perpetual system to account for inventory.
  c. Paid $36.57 to All-Tech for minor repairs to a computer.
  d. Paid $14.82 for items classified as miscellaneous expenses.
  e. Counted $62.28 remaining in the petty cash box.

    15   Prepared a company check for $25 to increase the fund to $175.

    31   The petty cashier reports that $17.35 remains in the fund. A company check is written to replenish the fund for the following expenditures made since January 14.
  f. Paid $40 to *The Smart Shopper* for an advertisement in January's newsletter.
  g. Paid $38.19 for postage expenses.
  h. Paid $58 to Take-You-There for delivery of merchandise, terms FOB destination.

    31   The company decides that the January 15 increase in the fund was too little. It increases the fund by another $75, leaving a total of $250.

Required

Check (1) Cr. to Cash: Jan. 14, $87.72; Jan. 31 (total), $232.65

1. Prepare journal entries to establish the fund on January 3, to replenish it on January 14 and January 31, and to reflect any increase or decrease in the fund balance on January 15 and 31.

Analysis Component

2. Explain how the company's financial statements are affected if the petty cash fund is not replenished and no entry is made on January 31.

RPM Music Center had the following petty cash transactions in March of the current year.

March 5   Wrote a $200 check, cashed it, and gave the proceeds and the petty cashbox to Liz Buck, the petty cashier.

6   Paid $14.50 COD shipping charges on merchandise purchased for resale, terms FOB shipping point. RPM uses the perpetual system to account for merchandise inventory.

11   Paid $8.75 delivery charges on merchandise sold to a customer, terms FOB destination.

12   Purchased file folders for $12.13 that are immediately used.

14   Reimbursed Will Nelson, the manager, $9.65 for office supplies purchased and used.

18   Purchased printer paper for $22.54 that is immediately used.

27   Paid $47.10 COD shipping charges on merchandise purchased for resale, terms FOB shipping point.

28   Paid postage expenses of $16.

30   Reimbursed Nelson $58.80 for business car mileage.

31   Cash of $11.53 remained in the fund. Sorted the petty cash receipts by accounts affected and exchanged them for a check to reimburse the fund for expenditures.

31   The petty cash fund amount is increased by $50 to a total of $250.

Required

1. Prepare the journal entry to establish the petty cash fund.

2. Prepare a petty cash payments report for March with these categories: delivery expense, mileage expense, postage expense, merchandise inventory (for transportation-in), and office supplies expense. Sort the payments into the appropriate categories and total the expenses in each category.

3. Prepare the journal entries for part 2 to both (*a*) reimburse and (*b*) increase the fund amount.

Problem 6-3B
Establish, reimburse, and increase petty cash
P2

Check   (2) Total expenses $189.47

(3a & 3b) Total Cr. to Cash $238.47

The following information is available to reconcile Style Co.'s book balance of cash with its bank statement cash balance as of December 31, 2011.

a. The December 31 cash balance according to the accounting records is $31,743.70, and the bank statement cash balance for that date is $45,091.80.

b. Check No. 1273 for $1,084.20 and Check No. 1282 for $390, both written and entered in the accounting records in December, are not among the canceled checks. Two checks, No. 1231 for $2,289 and No. 1242 for $370.50, were outstanding on the most recent November 30 reconciliation. Check No. 1231 is listed with the December canceled checks, but Check No. 1242 is not.

c. When the December checks are compared with entries in the accounting records, it is found that Check No. 1267 had been correctly drawn for $2,435 to pay for office supplies but was erroneously entered in the accounting records as $2,453.

d. Two debit memoranda are enclosed with the statement and are unrecorded at the time of the reconciliation. One debit memorandum is for $749.50 and dealt with an NSF check for $732 received from a customer, Titus Industries, in payment of its account. The bank assessed a $17.50 fee for processing it. The second debit memorandum is a $79 charge for check printing. Style did not record these transactions before receiving the statement.

e. A credit memorandum indicates that the bank collected $20,000 cash on a note receivable for the company, deducted a $20 collection fee, and credited the balance to the company's Cash account. Style did not record this transaction before receiving the statement.

f. Style's December 31 daily cash receipts of $7,666.10 were placed in the bank's night depository on that date, but do not appear on the December 31 bank statement.

Required

1. Prepare the bank reconciliation for this company as of December 31, 2011.

2. Prepare the journal entries necessary to bring the company's book balance of cash into conformity with the reconciled cash balance as of December 31, 2011.

Analysis Component

3. Explain the nature of the communications conveyed by a bank when the bank sends the depositor (*a*) a debit memorandum and (*b*) a credit memorandum.

Problem 6-4B
Prepare a bank reconciliation and record adjustments
P3

Check   (1) Reconciled balance, $50,913.20; (2) Cr. Note Receivable $20,000

Problem 6-5B

Prepare a bank reconciliation and record adjustments

P3

Safe Systems most recently reconciled its bank balance on April 30 and reported two checks outstanding at that time, No. 1771 for $781 and No. 1780 for $1,325.90. The following information is available for its May 31, 2011, reconciliation.

From the May 31 Bank Statement

PREVIOUS BALANCE	TOTAL CHECKS AND DEBITS	TOTAL DEPOSITS AND CREDITS	CURRENT BALANCE
18,290.70	12,898.90	16,416.80	21,808.60

CHECKS AND DEBITS			DEPOSITS AND CREDITS		DAILY BALANCE	
Date	No.	Amount	Date	Amount	Date	Amount
05/01	1771	781.00	05/04	2,438.00	04/30	18,290.70
05/02	1783	195.30	05/14	2,898.00	05/01	17,509.70
05/04	1782	1,285.50	05/22	1,801.80	05/02	17,314.40
05/11	1784	1,449.60	05/25	7,200.00 CM	05/04	18,466.90
05/18		431.80 NSF	05/26	2,079.00	05/11	17,017.30
05/25	1787	8,032.50			05/14	19,915.30
05/26	1785	157.20			05/18	19,483.50
05/29	1788	554.00			05/22	21,285.30
05/31		12.00 SC			05/25	20,452.80
					05/26	22,374.60
					05/29	21,820.60
					05/31	21,808.60

From Safe Systems' Accounting Records

Cash Receipts Deposited			
Date			Cash Debit
May	4		2,438.00
	14		2,898.00
	22		1,801.80
	26		2,079.00
	31		2,526.30
			11,743.10

Cash Disbursements		
Check No.		Cash Credit
1782		1,285.50
1783		195.30
1784		1,449.60
1785		157.20
1786		353.10
1787		8,032.50
1788		544.00
1789		639.50
		12,656.70

Cash						Acct. No. 101
Date		Explanation	PR	Debit	Credit	Balance
Apr.	30	Balance				16,183.80
May	31	Total receipts	R7	11,743.10		27,926.90
	31	Total disbursements	D8		12,656.70	15,270.20

Additional Information

Check No. 1788 is correctly drawn for $554 to pay for May utilities; however, the recordkeeper misread the amount and entered it in the accounting records with a debit to Utilities Expense and a credit to Cash for $544. The bank paid and deducted the correct amount. The NSF check shown in the statement was originally received from a customer, S. Bax, in payment of her account. The company has not yet recorded its return. The credit memorandum is from a $7,300 note that the bank collected for the company. The bank deducted a $100 collection fee and deposited the remainder in the company's account. The collection and fee have not yet been recorded.

Required

1. Prepare the May 31, 2011, bank reconciliation for Safe Systems.

2. Prepare the journal entries to adjust the book balance of cash to the reconciled balance.

Check   (1) Reconciled balance, $22,016.40; (2) Cr. Note Receivable $7,300

Analysis Component

3. The bank statement reveals that some of the prenumbered checks in the sequence are missing. Describe three possible situations to explain this.

(This serial problem began in Chapter 1 and continues through most of the book. If previous chapter segments were not completed, the serial problem can begin at this point. It is helpful, but not necessary, to use the Working Papers that accompany the book.)

SERIAL PROBLEM
Business Solutions
P3

SP 6   Santana Rey receives the March bank statement for Business Solutions on April 11, 2012. The March 31 bank statement shows an ending cash balance of $67,566. A comparison of the bank statement with the general ledger Cash account, No. 101, reveals the following.

a. S. Rey notices that the bank erroneously cleared a $500 check against her account in March that she did not issue. The check documentation included with the bank statement shows that this check was actually issued by a company named Business Systems.

b. On March 25, the bank issued a $50 debit memorandum for the safety deposit box that Business Solutions agreed to rent from the bank beginning March 25.

c. On March 26, the bank issued a $102 debit memorandum for printed checks that Business Solutions ordered from the bank.

d. On March 31, the bank issued a credit memorandum for $33 interest earned on Business Solutions' checking account for the month of March.

e. S. Rey notices that the check she issued for $128 on March 31, 2012, has not yet cleared the bank.

f. S. Rey verifies that all deposits made in March do appear on the March bank statement.

g. The general ledger Cash account, No. 101, shows an ending cash balance per books of $68,057 as of March 31 (prior to any reconciliation).

Required

1. Prepare a bank reconciliation for Business Solutions for the month ended March 31, 2012.

Check   (1) Adj. bank bal. $67,938

2. Prepare any necessary adjusting entries. Use Miscellaneous Expenses, No. 677, for any bank charges. Use Interest Revenue, No. 404, for any interest earned on the checking account for the month of March.

Beyond the Numbers

BTN 6-1   Refer to **Research In Motion**'s financial statements in Appendix A to answer the following.

REPORTING IN ACTION

C2 A1

RIM

1. For both fiscal year-ends February 27, 2010, and February 28, 2009, identify the total amount of cash and cash equivalents. Determine the percent this amount represents of total current assets, total current liabilities, total shareholders' equity, and total assets for both years. Comment on any trends.

2. For fiscal years ended February 27, 2010, and February 28, 2009, use the information in the statement of cash flows to determine the percent change between the beginning and ending year amounts of cash and cash equivalents.

3. Compute the days' sales uncollected as of February 27, 2010, and February 28, 2009. Has the collection of receivables improved? Are accounts receivable an important asset for Research In Motion? Explain.

Fast Forward

4. Access Research In Motion's financial statements for fiscal years ending after February 27, 2010, from its Website (**RIM.com**) or the SEC's EDGAR database (**www.sec.gov**). Recompute its days' sales uncollected for fiscal years ending after February 27, 2010. Compare this to the days' sales uncollected for 2010 and 2009.

COMPARATIVE ANALYSIS

A1

RIM

Apple

BTN 6-2   Key comparative figures for **Research In Motion** and **Apple** follow.

| ($ millions) | Research In Motion | | Apple | |
	Current Year	Prior Year	Current Year	Prior Year
Accounts receivable	$ 2,594	$ 2,112	$ 3,361	$ 2,422
Net sales	14,953	11,065	42,905	37,491

Required

Compute days' sales uncollected for these companies for each of the two years shown. Comment on any trends for the companies. Which company has the largest percent change in days' sales uncollected?

ETHICS CHALLENGE

C1

BTN 6-3   Carol Benton, Sue Knox, and Marcia Diamond work for a family physician, Dr. Gwen Conrad, who is in private practice. Dr. Conrad is knowledgeable about office management practices and has segregated the cash receipt duties as follows. Benton opens the mail and prepares a triplicate list of money received. She sends one copy of the list to Knox, the cashier, who deposits the receipts daily in the bank. Diamond, the recordkeeper, receives a copy of the list and posts payments to patients' accounts. About once a month the office clerks have an expensive lunch they pay for as follows. First, Knox endorses a patient's check in Dr. Conrad's name and cashes it at the bank. Benton then destroys the remittance advice accompanying the check. Finally, Diamond posts payment to the customer's account as a miscellaneous credit. The three justify their actions by their relatively low pay and knowledge that Dr. Conrad will likely never miss the money.

Required

1. Who is the best person in Dr. Conrad's office to reconcile the bank statement?
2. Would a bank reconciliation uncover this office fraud?
3. What are some procedures to detect this type of fraud?
4. Suggest additional internal controls that Dr. Conrad could implement.

COMMUNICATING IN PRACTICE

P5

BTN 6-4^B   Assume you are a business consultant. The owner of a company sends you an e-mail expressing concern that the company is not taking advantage of its discounts offered by vendors. The company currently uses the gross method of recording purchases. The owner is considering a review of all invoices and payments from the previous period. Due to the volume of purchases, however, the owner recognizes that this is time-consuming and costly. The owner seeks your advice about monitoring purchase discounts in the future. Provide a response in memorandum form.

TAKING IT TO THE NET

C1 P1

BTN 6-5   Visit the Association of Certified Fraud Examiners Website at **cfenet.com**. Find and open the file "2008 Report to the Nation." Read the two-page Executive Summary and fill in the following blanks. (The report is under its *Fraud Resources* tab or under its *About the ACFE* tab [under Press Room]; we can also use the *Search* tab.)

1. The median loss caused by occupational frauds was $_____.
2. More than _____ of fraud cases caused at least $1 million in losses.
3. Companies lose ___% of their annual revenues to fraud; this figure translates to $_____ billion in fraud losses.
4. The typical length of fraud schemes was _____ years from the time the fraud began until it was detected.
5. Companies that conducted surprise audits suffered a median loss of $_____, whereas those without surprise audits had a median loss of $_____.
6. The median loss suffered by companies with fewer than 100 employees was $_____ per scheme.
7. _____ and _____ were the most common small business fraud schemes.
8. ___% of respondents cited inadequate internal controls as the primary contributing factor in the frauds investigated.
9. Only ___% of the perpetrators had convictions prior to committing their frauds.

BTN 6-6 Organize the class into teams. Each team must prepare a list of 10 internal controls a consumer could observe in a typical retail department store. When called upon, the team's spokesperson must be prepared to share controls identified by the team that have not been shared by another team's spokesperson.

TEAMWORK IN ACTION

C1

BTN 6-7 Review the opening feature of this chapter that highlights Dylan Lauren and her company **Dylan's Candy Bar**.

Required

1. List the seven principles of internal control and explain how Dylan could implement each of them in her retail stores.
2. Do you believe that Dylan will need to add controls as her business expands? Explain.

ENTREPRENEURIAL DECISION

C1 P1

BTN 6-8 Visit an area of your college that serves the student community with either products or services. Some examples are food services, libraries, and bookstores. Identify and describe between four and eight internal controls being implemented.

HITTING THE ROAD

C1

BTN 6-9 The following information is from Nokia (www.Nokia.com), which is a leading global manufacturer of mobile devices and services.

GLOBAL DECISION

C2 A1

EUR millions	Current Year	Prior Year
Cash	1,142	1,706
Accounts receivable	7,981	9,444
Current assets	23,613	24,470
Total assets	35,738	39,582
Current liabilities	15,188	20,355
Shareholders' equity	14,749	16,510
Net sales	40,984	50,710

Required

1. For each year, compute the percentage that cash represents of current assets, total assets, current liabilities, and shareholders' equity. Comment on any trends in these percentages.
2. Determine the percentage change between the current and prior year cash balances.
3. Compute the days' sales uncollected at the end of both the current year and the prior year. Has the collection of receivables improved? Explain.

ANSWERS TO MULTIPLE CHOICE QUIZ

1. e; The entry follows.

Debits to expenses (or assets)	420
Cash Over and Short	5
Cash	425

2. a; recognizes cash collection of note by bank.
3. a; the bank reconciliation follows.

4. d; ($6,720/$84,000) × 365 = <u>29.2 days</u>
5. b; The entry follows.

Merchandise Inventory*	5,880	
Accounts Payable		5,880

*$6,000 × 98%

Bank Reconciliation November 30			
Balance per bank statement	$1,895	Balance per books	$1,742
Add: Deposit in transit	795	Add: Note collected less fee	320
Deduct: Outstanding checks	(638)	Deduct: Service charge	(10)
Reconciled balance	$2,052	Reconciled balance	$2,052

7

Accounts and Notes Receivable

A Look Back

Chapter 6 focused on internal control and reporting for cash. We described internal control procedures and the accounting for and management of cash.

A Look at This Chapter

This chapter emphasizes receivables. We explain that they are liquid assets and describe how companies account for and report them. We also discuss the importance of estimating uncollectibles.

A Look Ahead

Chapter 8 focuses on plant assets, natural resources, and intangible assets. We explain how to account for, report, and analyze these long-term assets.

Learning Objectives

CONCEPTUAL

C1 Describe accounts receivable and how they occur and are recorded. (p. 292)

C2 Describe a note receivable, the computation of its maturity date, and the recording of its existence. (p. 302)

C3 Explain how receivables can be converted to cash before maturity. (p. 305)

ANALYTICAL

A1 Compute accounts receivable turnover and use it to help assess financial condition. (p. 307)

LP7

PROCEDURAL

P1 Apply the direct write-off method to account for accounts receivable. (p. 295)

P2 Apply the allowance method and estimate uncollectibles based on sales and accounts receivable. (p. 298)

P3 Record the honoring and dishonoring of a note and adjustments for interest. (p. 304)

Monk E-Business

"We are not wearing bling . . . I mean, we are still monks"
—BROTHER BERNARD McCOY

SPARTA, WI—"My printer ran out of toner," recalls Brother Bernard McCoy. "I was just appalled at the cost of the black dust . . . the markup on toner is sinfully high!" So, Bernard, who is part of a handful of monks living at and trying to keep a remote monastery in rural Wisconsin going, started thinking. "Nine hundred years ago, my brothers were copying manuscripts and making their own paper and ink," explains Bernard. His response was to launch **LaserMonks** (**LaserMonks.com**), a supplier of toner and ink products (and other goods).

Sales quickly soared, and Bernard, along with what he calls his monk-helper angels, had to contend with accounting activities, receivables management, and other day-to-day record-keeping needs. Special attention was focused on monitoring receivables. Decisions on credit sales and policies for extending credit can make or break a start-up, and Bernard was determined to succeed in spite of the demands of a monk's life. "We spend about five hours a day in Gregorian chant, and another couple of hours in prayers," explains Bernard. "We're monks . . . we do monk things!"

Nevertheless, Bernard and his angels ensured that credit sales were extended to customers in good credit standing. Further, his team knows their customers, including who pays and when. Explains Bernard, we understand our customers—inside and out—including cash payment patterns that allow them to estimate uncollectibles and minimize bad debts. Bernard points out, however, that "we use the money for good works and to support monks who dedicate their lives to serving God and neighbor."

A commitment to quality customers and products is propelling LaserMonks' sales and shattering Bernard's most optimistic goals. "The results have been beyond anything we could imagine," affirms Bernard. Both accounts and notes receivables receive his attention. Bernard and his team's financial focus includes reviewing the allowance for doubtful accounts monthly. "We're scrambling to keep up with growth," adds Bernard. "[We're] continuing to negotiate with suppliers . . . processing orders between our times of prayer."

Bernard's focus on serving people is unwavering. "Our customer service is following our order's tradition of hospitality," explains Bernard. "We try to transfer monastic hospitality into commerce hospitality . . . we try to treat every single customer with kid gloves." Bernard says he wishes that all customers "be abundantly blessed with prosperity of soul."

[Sources: *LaserMonks Website,* January 2011; *Entrepreneur,* September 2009; *CBS Broadcasting,* August 2006; *Religion & Ethics Newsweekly,* September 2009; *Consumer Reports,* February 2010]

This chapter focuses on accounts receivable and short-term notes receivable. We describe each of these assets, their uses, and how they are accounted for and reported in financial statements. This knowledge helps us use accounting information to make better business decisions. It can also help in predicting future company performance and financial condition as well as in managing one's own business.

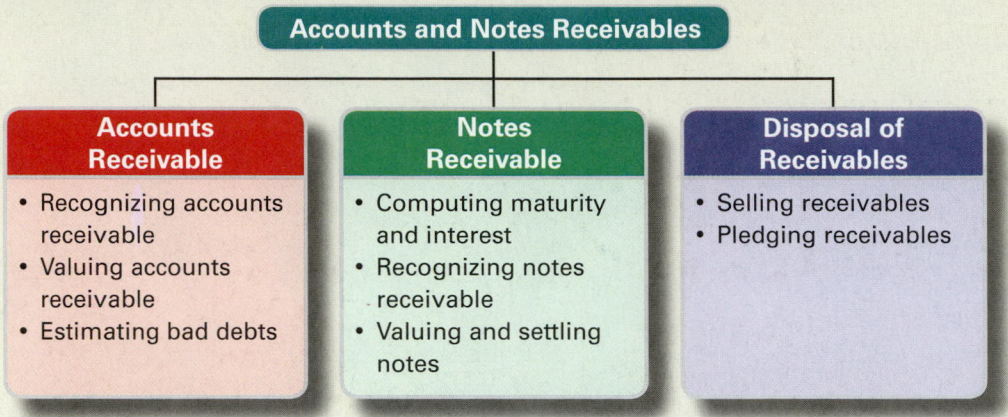

Accounts and Notes Receivables

Accounts Receivable	Notes Receivable	Disposal of Receivables
• Recognizing accounts receivable • Valuing accounts receivable • Estimating bad debts	• Computing maturity and interest • Recognizing notes receivable • Valuing and settling notes	• Selling receivables • Pledging receivables

ACCOUNTS RECEIVABLE

A *receivable* is an amount due from another party. The two most common receivables are accounts receivable and notes receivable. Other receivables include interest receivable, rent receivable, tax refund receivable, and receivables from employees. **Accounts receivable** are amounts due from customers for credit sales. This section begins by describing how accounts receivable occur. It includes receivables that occur when customers use credit cards issued by third parties and when a company gives credit directly to customers. When a company does extend credit directly to customers, it (1) maintains a separate account receivable for each customer and (2) accounts for bad debts from credit sales.

Recognizing Accounts Receivable

C1 Describe accounts receivable and how they occur and are recorded.

Accounts receivable occur from credit sales to customers. The amount of credit sales has increased in recent years, reflecting several factors including an efficient financial system. Retailers such as **Costco** and **Best Buy** hold millions of dollars in accounts receivable. Similar amounts are held by wholesalers such as **SUPERVALU** and **SYSCO**. Exhibit 7.1 shows recent dollar amounts of receivables and their percent of total assets for four well-known companies.

EXHIBIT 7.1

Accounts Receivable for Selected Companies

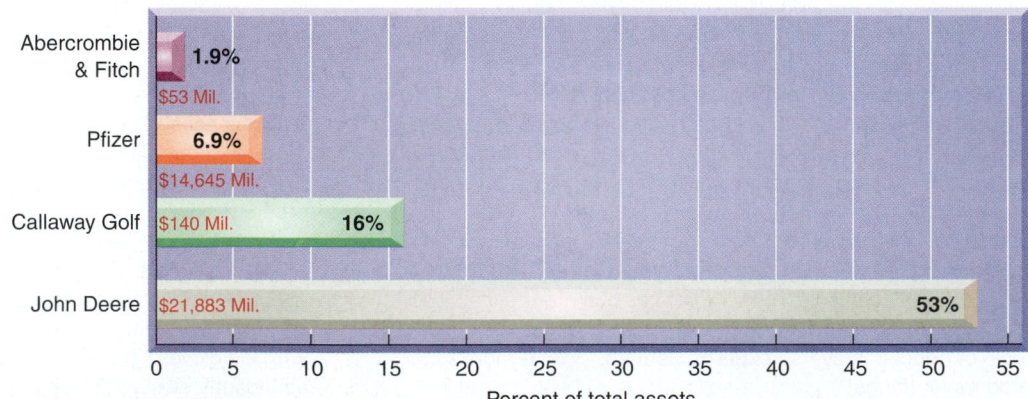

Abercrombie & Fitch — 1.9% — $53 Mil.
Pfizer — 6.9% — $14,645 Mil.
Callaway Golf — $140 Mil. — 16%
John Deere — $21,883 Mil. — 53%

Percent of total assets

Sales on Credit Credit sales are recorded by increasing (debiting) Accounts Receivable. A company must also maintain a separate account for each customer that tracks how much that customer purchases, has already paid, and still owes. This information provides the basis for sending bills to customers and for other business analyses. To maintain this information, companies that extend credit directly to their customers keep a separate account receivable for each one of them. The general ledger continues to have a single Accounts Receivable account along with the other financial statement accounts, but a supplementary record is created to maintain a separate account for each customer. This supplementary record is called the *accounts receivable ledger*.

Exhibit 7.2 shows the relation between the Accounts Receivable account in the general ledger and its individual customer accounts in the accounts receivable ledger for TechCom, a small electronics wholesaler. This exhibit reports a $3,000 ending balance of TechCom's accounts receivable for June 30. TechCom's transactions are mainly in cash, but it has two major credit customers: CompStore and RDA Electronics. Its *schedule of accounts receivable* shows that the $3,000 balance of the Accounts Receivable account in the general ledger equals the total of its two customers' balances in the accounts receivable ledger.

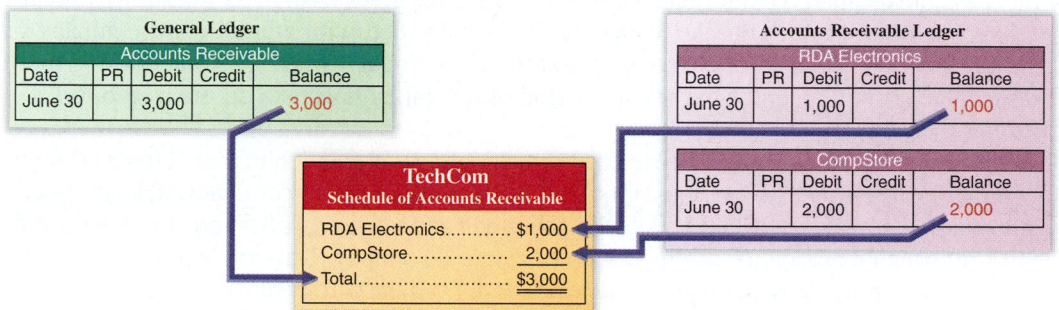

EXHIBIT 7.2

General Ledger and the Accounts Receivable Ledger (before July 1 transactions)

To see how accounts receivable from credit sales are recognized in the accounting records, we look at two transactions on July 1 between TechCom and its credit customers—see Exhibit 7.3. The first is a credit sale of $950 to CompStore. A credit sale is posted with both a debit to the Accounts Receivable account in the general ledger and a debit to the customer account in the accounts receivable ledger. The second transaction is a collection of $720 from RDA Electronics from a prior credit sale. Cash receipts from a credit customer are posted with a credit to the Accounts Receivable account in the general ledger and flow through to credit the customer account in the accounts receivable ledger. (Posting debits or credits to Accounts Receivable in two separate ledgers does not violate the requirement that debits equal credits. The equality of debits and credits is maintained in the general ledger. The accounts receivable ledger is a *supplementary* record providing information on each customer.)

EXHIBIT 7.3

Accounts Receivable Transactions

July 1	Accounts Receivable—CompStore	950	
	Sales		950
	*To record credit sales**		
July 1	Cash	720	
	Accounts Receivable—RDA Electronics		720
	To record collection of credit sales.		

Assets = Liabilities + Equity
\+ 950   +950

Assets = Liabilities + Equity
+720
−720

* We omit the entry to Dr. Cost of Sales and Cr. Merchandise Inventory to focus on sales and receivables.

Exhibit 7.4 shows the general ledger and the accounts receivable ledger after recording the two July 1 transactions. The general ledger shows the effects of the sale, the collection, and the resulting balance of $3,230. These events are also reflected in the individual customer accounts: RDA Electronics has an ending balance of $280, and CompStore's ending balance is $2,950.

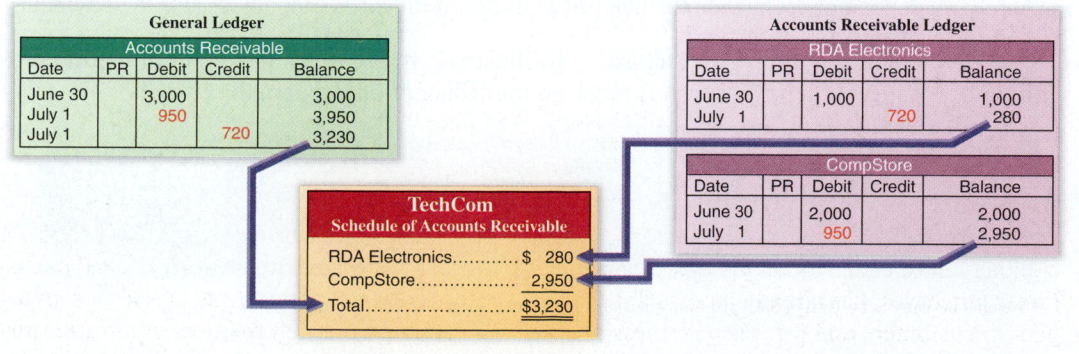

EXHIBIT 7.4

General Ledger and the Accounts Receivable Ledger (after July 1 transactions)

The $3,230 sum of the individual accounts equals the debit balance of the Accounts Receivable account in the general ledger.

Like TechCom, many large retailers such as **Sears** and **JCPenney** sell on credit. Many also maintain their own credit cards to grant credit to approved customers and to earn interest on any balance not paid within a specified period of time. This allows them to avoid the fee charged by credit card companies. The entries in this case are the same as those for TechCom except for the possibility of added interest revenue. If a customer owes interest on a bill, we debit Interest Receivable and credit Interest Revenue for that amount.

Credit Card Sales   Many companies allow their customers to pay for products and services using third-party credit cards such as **Visa**, **MasterCard**, or **American Express**, and debit cards (also called ATM or bank cards). This practice gives customers the ability to make purchases without cash or checks. Once credit is established with a credit card company or bank, the customer does not have to open an account with each store. Customers using these cards can make single monthly payments instead of several payments to different creditors and can defer their payments.

Many sellers allow customers to use third-party credit cards and debit cards instead of granting credit directly for several reasons. First, the seller does not have to evaluate each customer's credit standing or make decisions about who gets credit and how much. Second, the seller avoids the risk of extending credit to customers who cannot or do not pay. This risk is transferred to the card company. Third, the seller typically receives cash from the card company sooner than had it granted credit directly to customers. Fourth, a variety of credit options for customers offers a potential increase in sales volume. **Sears** historically offered credit only to customers using a Sears card but later changed its policy to permit customers to charge purchases to third-party credit card companies in a desire to increase sales. It reported: "SearsCharge increased its share of Sears retail sales even as the company expanded the payment options available to its customers with the acceptance ... of Visa, MasterCard, and American Express in addition to the [Sears] Card."

There are guidelines in how companies account for credit card and debit card sales. Some credit cards, but nearly all debit cards, credit a seller's Cash account immediately upon deposit. In this case the seller deposits a copy of each card sales receipt in its bank account just as it deposits a customer's check. The majority of credit cards, however, require the seller to remit a copy (often electronically) of each receipt to the card company. Until payment is received, the seller has an account receivable from the card company. In both cases, the seller pays a fee for services provided by the card company, often ranging from 1% to 5% of card sales. This charge is deducted from the credit to the seller's account or the cash payment to the seller.

Point: Visa USA now transacts more than $1 trillion from its credit, debit, and prepaid cards.

Point: Web merchants pay twice as much in credit card association fees as other retailers because they suffer 10 times as much fraud.

Decision Insight

Debit Card vs. Credit Card   A buyer's debit card purchase reduces the buyer's cash account balance at the card company, which is often a bank. Since the buyer's cash account balance is a liability (with a credit balance) for the card company to the buyer, the card company would debit that account for a buyer's purchase—hence, the term *debit card*. A credit card reflects authorization by the card company of a line of credit for the buyer with preset interest rates and payment terms—hence, the term *credit card*. Most card companies waive interest charges if the buyer pays its balance each month. ■

The procedures used in accounting for credit card sales depend on whether cash is received immediately on deposit or cash receipt is delayed until the credit card company makes the payment.

Cash Received Immediately on Deposit   To illustrate, if TechCom has $100 of credit card sales with a 4% fee, and its $96 cash is received immediately on deposit, the entry is

Assets = Liabilities + Equity
+96   +100
                        −4

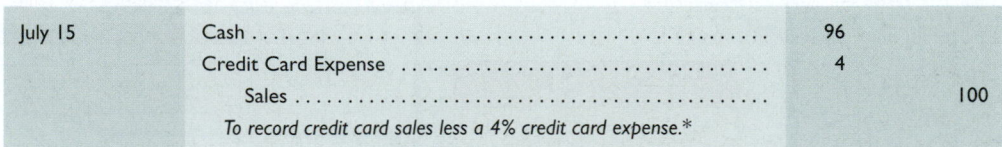

July 15	Cash	96	
	Credit Card Expense	4	
	Sales		100
	*To record credit card sales less a 4% credit card expense.**		

* We omit the entry to Dr. Cost of Sales and Cr. Merchandise Inventory to focus on credit card expense.

Cash Received Some Time after Deposit   However, if instead TechCom must remit electronically the credit card sales receipts to the credit card company and wait for the $96 cash payment, the entry on the date of sale is

July 15	Accounts Receivable—Credit Card Co.	96	
	Credit Card Expense	4	
	Sales		100
	*To record credit card sales less 4% credit card expense.**		

Assets = Liabilities + Equity
+96   +100
                            −4

* We omit the entry to Dr. Cost of Sales and Cr. Merchandise Inventory to focus on credit card expense.

When cash is later received from the credit card company, usually through electronic funds transfer, the entry is

July 20	Cash	96	
	Accounts Receivable—Credit Card Co.		96
	To record cash receipt.		

Assets = Liabilities + Equity
+96
−96

Some firms report credit card expense in the income statement as a type of discount deducted from sales to get net sales. Other companies classify it as a selling expense or even as an administrative expense. Arguments can be made for each approach.

Point: Third-party credit card costs can be large. JCPenney reported third-party credit card costs exceeding $10 million.

Installment Sales and Receivables   Many companies allow their credit customers to make periodic payments over several months. For example, **Ford Motor Company** reports more than $75 billion in installment receivables. The seller refers to such assets as *installment accounts* (or *finance*) *receivable,* which are amounts owed by customers from credit sales for which payment is required in periodic amounts over an extended time period. Source documents for installment accounts receivable include sales slips or invoices describing the sales transactions. The customer is usually charged interest. Although installment accounts receivable can have credit periods of more than one year, they are classified as current assets if the seller regularly offers customers such terms.

Decision Maker   Answer — p. 310

Entrepreneur   As a small retailer, you are considering allowing customers to buy merchandise using credit cards. Until now, your store accepted only cash and checks. What analysis do you use to make this decision? ■

Quick Check   Answers — p. 311

1. In recording credit card sales, when do you debit Accounts Receivable and when do you debit Cash?
2. A company accumulates sales receipts and remits them to the credit card company for payment. When are the credit card expenses recorded? When are these expenses incurred?

Valuing Accounts Receivable—Direct Write-Off Method

When a company directly grants credit to its customers, it expects that some customers will not pay what they promised. The accounts of these customers are *uncollectible accounts,* commonly called **bad debts.** The total amount of uncollectible accounts is an expense of selling on credit. Why do companies sell on credit if they expect some accounts to be uncollectible? The answer is that companies believe that granting credit will increase total sales and net income enough to offset bad debts. Companies use two methods to account for uncollectible accounts: (1) direct write-off method and (2) allowance method. We describe both.

P1 Apply the direct write-off method to account for accounts receivable.

Recording and Writing Off Bad Debts   The **direct write-off method** of accounting for bad debts records the loss from an uncollectible account receivable when it is determined to

Point: Managers realize that some portion of credit sales will be uncollectible, but which credit sales are uncollectible is unknown.

be uncollectible. No attempt is made to predict bad debts expense. To illustrate, if TechCom determines on January 23 that it cannot collect $520 owed to it by its customer J. Kent, it recognizes the loss using the direct write-off method as follows:

Assets = Liabilities + Equity
−520   −520

Jan. 23	Bad Debts Expense	520	
	Accounts Receivable—J. Kent		520
	To write off an uncollectible account.		

The debit in this entry charges the uncollectible amount directly to the current period's Bad Debts Expense account. The credit removes its balance from the Accounts Receivable account in the general ledger (and its subsidiary ledger).

Recovering a Bad Debt   Although uncommon, sometimes an account written off is later collected. This can be due to factors such as continual collection efforts or a customer's good fortune. If the account of J. Kent that was written off directly to Bad Debts Expense is later collected in full, the following two entries record this recovery.

Assets = Liabilities + Equity
+520   +520

Assets = Liabilities + Equity
+520   +520
−520

Mar. 11	Accounts Receivable—J. Kent	520	
	Bad Debts Expense		520
	To reinstate account previously written off.		
Mar. 11	Cash	520	
	Accounts Receivable—J. Kent		520
	To record full payment of account.		

Assessing the Direct Write-Off Method   Examples of companies that use the direct write-off method include **Rand Medical Billing**, **Gateway Distributors**, **Microwave Satellite Technologies**, **First Industrial Realty**, **New Frontier Energy**, and **Sub Surface Waste Management**. The following disclosure by **Pharma-Bio Serv** is typical of the justification for this method: Bad debts are accounted for using the direct write-off method whereby an expense is recognized only when a specific account is determined to be uncollectible. The effect of using this method approximates that of the allowance method. Companies must weigh at least two accounting concepts when considering the use of the direct write-off method: the (1) matching principle and (2) materiality constraint.

Matching principle applied to bad debts.   The **matching (expense recognition) principle** requires expenses to be reported in the same accounting period as the sales they helped produce. This means that if extending credit to customers helped produce sales, the bad debts expense linked to those sales is matched and reported in the same period. The direct write-off method usually does *not* best match sales and expenses because bad debts expense is not recorded until an account becomes uncollectible, which often occurs in a period after that of the credit sale. To match bad debts expense with the sales it produces therefore requires a company to estimate future uncollectibles.

Materiality constraint applied to bad debts.   The **materiality constraint** states that an amount can be ignored if its effect on the financial statements is unimportant to users' business decisions. The materiality constraint permits the use of the direct write-off method when bad debts expenses are very small in relation to a company's other financial statement items such as sales and net income.

Valuing Accounts Receivable—Allowance Method

The **allowance method** of accounting for bad debts matches the *estimated* loss from uncollectible accounts receivable against the sales they helped produce. We must use estimated losses because when sales occur, management does not know which customers will not pay their bills. This means that at the end of each period, the allowance method requires an estimate of the total bad debts expected to result from that period's sales. This method has two advantages over the direct write-off method: (1) it records estimated bad debts expense in the period when the related sales are recorded and (2) it reports accounts receivable on the balance sheet at the estimated amount of cash to be collected.

Point: If a customer fails to pay within the credit period, most companies send out repeated billings and make other efforts to collect.

Point: Harley-Davidson reports $169 million of credit losses matched against $4,782 million of total revenues.

Point: Under direct write-off, expense is recorded each time an account is written off. Under the allowance method, expense is recorded with an adjusting entry equal to the total estimated uncollectibles for that period's sales.

Recording Bad Debts Expense   The allowance method estimates bad debts expense at the end of each accounting period and records it with an adjusting entry. TechCom, for instance, had credit sales of $300,000 during its first year of operations. At the end of the first year, $20,000 of credit sales remained uncollected. Based on the experience of similar businesses, TechCom estimated that $1,500 of its accounts receivable would be uncollectible. This estimated expense is recorded with the following adjusting entry.

Dec. 31	Bad Debts Expense	1,500	
	Allowance for Doubtful Accounts		1,500
	To record estimated bad debts.		

Assets = Liabilities + Equity
−1,500   −1,500

The estimated Bad Debts Expense of $1,500 is reported on the income statement (as either a selling expense or an administrative expense) and offsets the $300,000 credit sales it helped produce. The **Allowance for Doubtful Accounts** is a contra asset account. A contra account is used instead of reducing accounts receivable directly because at the time of the adjusting entry, the company does not know which customers will not pay. After the bad debts adjusting entry is posted, TechCom's account balances (in T-account form) for Accounts Receivable and its Allowance for Doubtful Accounts are as shown in Exhibit 7.5.

Point: Credit approval is usually not assigned to the selling dept. because its goal is to increase sales, and it may approve customers at the cost of increased bad debts. Instead, approval is assigned to a separate credit-granting or administrative dept.

Accounts Receivable			Allowance for Doubtful Accounts		
Dec. 31	20,000			Dec. 31	1,500

EXHIBIT 7.5
General Ledger Entries after Bad Debts Adjusting Entry

The Allowance for Doubtful Accounts credit balance of $1,500 has the effect of reducing accounts receivable to its estimated realizable value. **Realizable value** refers to the expected proceeds from converting an asset into cash. Although credit customers owe $20,000 to TechCom, only $18,500 is expected to be realized in cash collections from these customers. In the balance sheet, the Allowance for Doubtful Accounts is subtracted from Accounts Receivable and is often reported as shown in Exhibit 7.6.

Point: Bad Debts Expense is also called *Uncollectible Accounts Expense.* The Allowance for Doubtful Accounts is also called *Allowance for Uncollectible Accounts.*

Current assets		
Accounts receivable...............................	$20,000	
Less allowance for doubtful accounts	1,500	$18,500

EXHIBIT 7.6
Balance Sheet Presentation of the Allowance for Doubtful Accounts

Sometimes the Allowance for Doubtful Accounts is not reported separately. This alternative presentation is shown in Exhibit 7.7 (also see Appendix A).

Current assets	
Accounts receivable (net of $1,500 doubtful accounts)	$18,500

EXHIBIT 7.7
Alternative Presentation of the Allowance for Doubtful Accounts

Writing Off a Bad Debt   When specific accounts are identified as uncollectible, they are written off against the Allowance for Doubtful Accounts. To illustrate, TechCom decides that J. Kent's $520 account is uncollectible and makes the following entry to write it off.

Jan. 23	Allowance for Doubtful Accounts	520	
	Accounts Receivable—J. Kent		520
	To write off an uncollectible account.		

Assets = Liabilities + Equity
+520
−520

Posting this write-off entry to the Accounts Receivable account removes the amount of the bad debt from the general ledger (it is also posted to the accounts receivable subsidiary ledger). The general ledger accounts now appear as in Exhibit 7.8 (assuming no other transactions affecting these accounts).

Point: The Bad Debts Expense account is not debited in the write-off entry because it was recorded in the period when sales occurred.

Accounts Receivable			Allowance for Doubtful Accounts		
Dec. 31	20,000			Dec. 31	1,500
		Jan. 23 520	Jan. 23 520		

EXHIBIT 7.8
General Ledger Entries after Write-Off

The write-off does *not* affect the realizable value of accounts receivable as shown in Exhibit 7.9. Neither total assets nor net income is affected by the write-off of a specific account. Instead, both assets and net income are affected in the period when bad debts expense is predicted and recorded with an adjusting entry.

EXHIBIT 7.9

Realizable Value before and after Write-Off of a Bad Debt

	Before Write-Off	After Write-Off
Accounts receivable	$ 20,000	$ 19,480
Less allowance for doubtful accounts	1,500	980
Estimated realizable accounts receivable	$18,500	$18,500

Recovering a Bad Debt   When a customer fails to pay and the account is written off as uncollectible, his or her credit standing is jeopardized. To help restore credit standing, a customer sometimes volunteers to pay all or part of the amount owed. A company makes two entries when collecting an account previously written off by the allowance method. The first is to reverse the write-off and reinstate the customer's account. The second entry records the collection of the reinstated account. To illustrate, if on March 11 Kent pays in full his account previously written off, the entries are

Assets = Liabilities + Equity
+520
−520

Assets = Liabilities + Equity
+520
−520

Mar. 11	Accounts Receivable—J. Kent.	520	
	Allowance for Doubtful Accounts		520
	To reinstate account previously written off.		
Mar. 11	Cash	520	
	Accounts Receivable—J. Kent		520
	To record full payment of account.		

In this illustration, Kent paid the entire amount previously written off, but sometimes a customer pays only a portion of the amount owed. A question then arises as to whether the entire balance of the account or just the amount paid is returned to accounts receivable. This is a matter of judgment. If we believe this customer will later pay in full, we return the entire amount owed to accounts receivable, but if we expect no further collection, we return only the amount paid.

Decision **Insight**

PayPal   PayPal is legally just a money transfer agent, but it is increasingly challenging big credit card brands—see chart. PayPal is successful because: (1) online credit card processing fees often exceed $0.15 per dollar, but PayPal's fees are under $0.10 per dollar. (2) PayPal's merchant fraud losses are under 0.2% of revenues, which compares to nearly 2% for online merchants using credit cards. ■

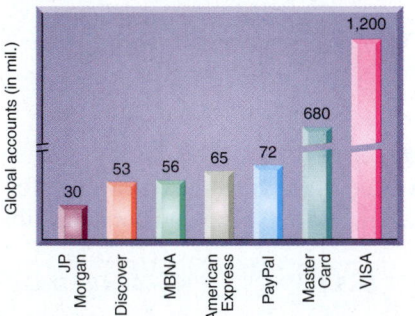

Estimating Bad Debts—Percent of Sales Method

The allowance method requires an estimate of bad debts expense to prepare an adjusting entry at the end of each accounting period. There are two common methods. One is based on the income statement relation between bad debts expense and sales. The second is based on the balance sheet relation between accounts receivable and the allowance for doubtful accounts.

The *percent of sales method,* also referred to as the *income statement method,* is based on the idea that a given percent of a company's credit sales for the period is uncollectible. To illustrate, assume that Musicland has credit sales of $400,000 in year 2011. Based on past experience,

Musicland estimates 0.6% of credit sales to be uncollectible. This implies that Musicland expects $2,400 of bad debts expense from its sales (computed as $400,000 × 0.006). The adjusting entry to record this estimated expense is

Dec. 31	Bad Debts Expense	2,400	
	Allowance for Doubtful Accounts		2,400
	To record estimated bad debts.		

Assets = Liabilities + Equity
−2,400   −2,400

The allowance account ending balance on the balance sheet for this method would rarely equal the bad debts expense on the income statement. This is so because unless a company is in its first period of operations, its allowance account has a zero balance only if the prior amounts written off as uncollectible *exactly* equal the prior estimated bad debts expenses. (When computing bad debts expense as a percent of sales, managers monitor and adjust the percent so it is not too high or too low.)

Point: When using the *percent of sales method* for estimating uncollectibles, the estimate of bad debts is the number used in the adjusting entry.

Estimating Bad Debts—Percent of Receivables Method

The *accounts receivable methods,* also referred to as *balance sheet methods,* use balance sheet relations to estimate bad debts—mainly the relation between accounts receivable and the allowance amount. The goal of the bad debts adjusting entry for these methods is to make the Allowance for Doubtful Accounts balance equal to the portion of accounts receivable that is estimated to be uncollectible. The estimated balance for the allowance account is obtained in one of two ways: (1) computing the percent uncollectible from the total accounts receivable or (2) aging accounts receivable.

The *percent of accounts receivable method* assumes that a given percent of a company's receivables is uncollectible. This percent is based on past experience and is impacted by current conditions such as economic trends and customer difficulties. The total dollar amount of all receivables is multiplied by this percent to get the estimated dollar amount of uncollectible accounts—reported in the balance sheet as the Allowance for Doubtful Accounts.

To illustrate, assume that Musicland has $50,000 of accounts receivable on December 31, 2011. Experience suggests 5% of its receivables is uncollectible. This means that *after* the adjusting entry is posted, we want the Allowance for Doubtful Accounts to show a $2,500 credit balance (5% of $50,000). We are also told that its beginning balance is $2,200, which is 5% of the $44,000 accounts receivable on December 31, 2010—see Exhibit 7.10.

Point: When using an accounts receivable method for estimating uncollectibles, the allowance account balance is adjusted to equal the estimate of uncollectibles.

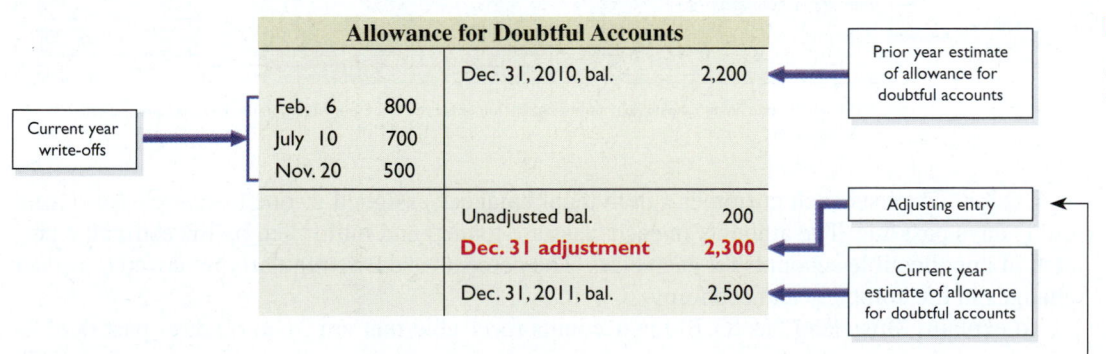

EXHIBIT 7.10

Allowance for Doubtful Accounts after Bad Debts Adjusting Entry

During 2011, accounts of customers are written off on February 6, July 10, and November 20. Thus, the account has a $200 credit balance *before* the December 31, 2011, adjustment. The adjusting entry to give the allowance account the estimated $2,500 balance is

Dec. 31	Bad Debts Expense	2,300	
	Allowance for Doubtful Accounts		2,300
	To record estimated bad debts.		

Assets = Liabilities + Equity
−2,300   −2,300

Decision Insight

Aging Pains Experience shows that the longer a receivable is past due, the lower is the likelihood of its collection. An *aging schedule* uses this knowledge to estimate bad debts. The chart here is from a survey that reported estimates of bad debts for receivables grouped by how long they were past their due dates. Each company sets its own estimates based on its customers and its experiences with those customers' payment patterns. ■

Bad debts percentage

Months past due	
1	6%
2	15%
3–5	27%
6–8	43%
9–11	58%
12–23	76%
>24	89%

0% — 100%

Estimating Bad Debts—Aging of Receivables Method

The **aging of accounts receivable** method uses both past and current receivables information to estimate the allowance amount. Specifically, each receivable is classified by how long it is past its due date. Then estimates of uncollectible amounts are made assuming that the longer an amount is past due, the more likely it is to be uncollectible. Classifications are often based on 30-day periods. After the amounts are classified (or aged), experience is used to estimate the percent of each uncollectible class. These percents are applied to the amounts in each class and then totaled to get the estimated balance of the Allowance for Doubtful Accounts. This computation is performed by setting up a schedule such as Exhibit 7.11.

EXHIBIT 7.11

Aging of Accounts Receivable

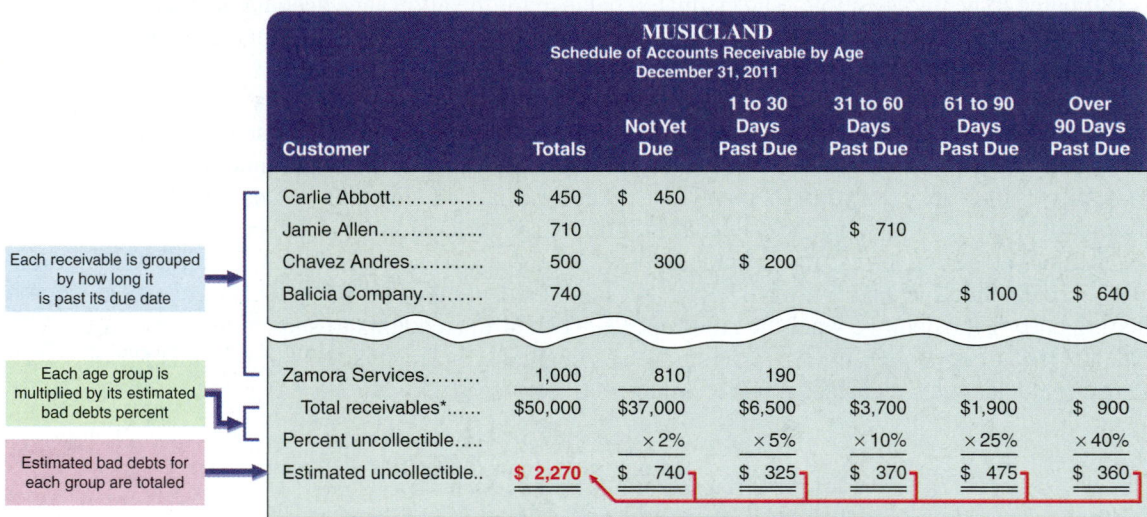

MUSICLAND — Schedule of Accounts Receivable by Age — December 31, 2011						
Customer	Totals	Not Yet Due	1 to 30 Days Past Due	31 to 60 Days Past Due	61 to 90 Days Past Due	Over 90 Days Past Due
Carlie Abbott..............	$ 450	$ 450				
Jamie Allen.................	710			$ 710		
Chavez Andres............	500	300	$ 200			
Balicia Company..........	740				$ 100	$ 640
Zamora Services.........	1,000	810	190			
Total receivables*......	$50,000	$37,000	$6,500	$3,700	$1,900	$ 900
Percent uncollectible.....		×2%	×5%	×10%	×25%	×40%
Estimated uncollectible..	$ 2,270	$ 740	$ 325	$ 370	$ 475	$ 360

- Each receivable is grouped by how long it is past its due date
- Each age group is multiplied by its estimated bad debts percent
- Estimated bad debts for each group are totaled

*The "white line break" means that additional customer accounts are not shown in the table but are included in each column's total.

Exhibit 7.11 lists each customer's individual balances assigned to one of five classes based on its days past due. The amounts in each class are totaled and multiplied by the estimated percent of uncollectible accounts for each class. The percents used are regularly reviewed to reflect changes in the company and economy.

To explain, Musicland has $3,700 in accounts receivable that are 31 to 60 days past due. Its management estimates 10% of the amounts in this age class are uncollectible, or a total of $370 (computed as $3,700 × 10%). Similar analysis is done for each of the other four classes. The final total of $2,270 ($740 + $325 + 370 + $475 + $360) shown in the first column is the estimated balance for the Allowance for Doubtful Accounts. Exhibit 7.12 shows that since the allowance

EXHIBIT 7.12

Computation of the Required Adjustment for the Accounts Receivable Method

Unadjusted balance	$ 200 credit
Estimated balance	2,270 credit
Required adjustment	**$2,070 credit**

account has an unadjusted credit balance of $200, the required adjustment to the Allowance for Doubtful Accounts is $2,070. (We could also use a T-account for this analysis as shown in the margin.) This yields the following end-of-period adjusting entry.

Allowance for Doubtful Accounts	
	Unadj. bal. 200
	Req. adj. 2,070
	Estim. bal. 2,270

Dec. 31	Bad Debts Expense	2,070	
	Allowance for Doubtful Accounts		2,070
	To record estimated bad debts.		

Assets = Liabilities + Equity
−2,070   −2,070

Alternatively, if the allowance account had an unadjusted *debit* balance of $500 (instead of the $200 credit balance), its required adjustment would be computed as follows. (Again, a T-account can be used for this analysis as shown in the margin.)

Point: A debit balance implies that write-offs for that period exceed the total allowance.

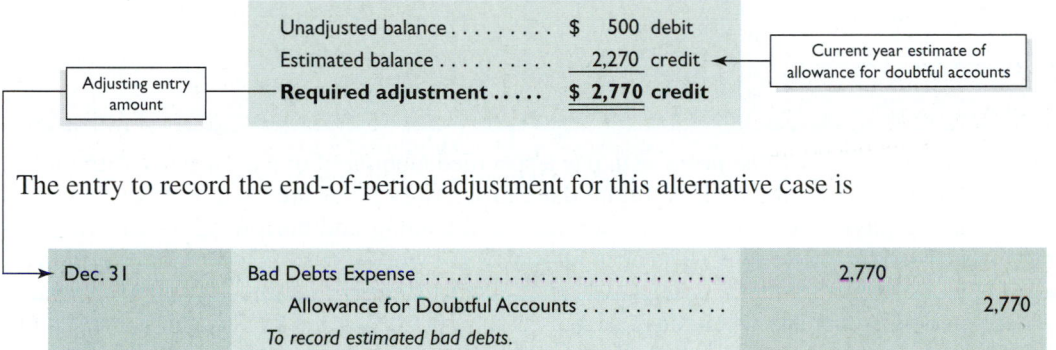

Allowance for Doubtful Accounts	
Unadj. bal. 500	
	Req. adj. 2,770
	Estim. bal. 2,270

The entry to record the end-of-period adjustment for this alternative case is

Dec. 31	Bad Debts Expense	2,770	
	Allowance for Doubtful Accounts		2,770
	To record estimated bad debts.		

Assets = Liabilities + Equity
−2,770   −2,770

The aging of accounts receivable method is an examination of specific accounts and is usually the most reliable of the estimation methods.

Estimating Bad Debts—Summary of Methods   Exhibit 7.13 summarizes the principles guiding all three estimation methods and their focus of analysis. Percent of sales, with its income statement focus, does a good job at matching bad debts expense with sales. The accounts receivable methods, with their balance sheet focus, do a better job at reporting accounts receivable at realizable value.

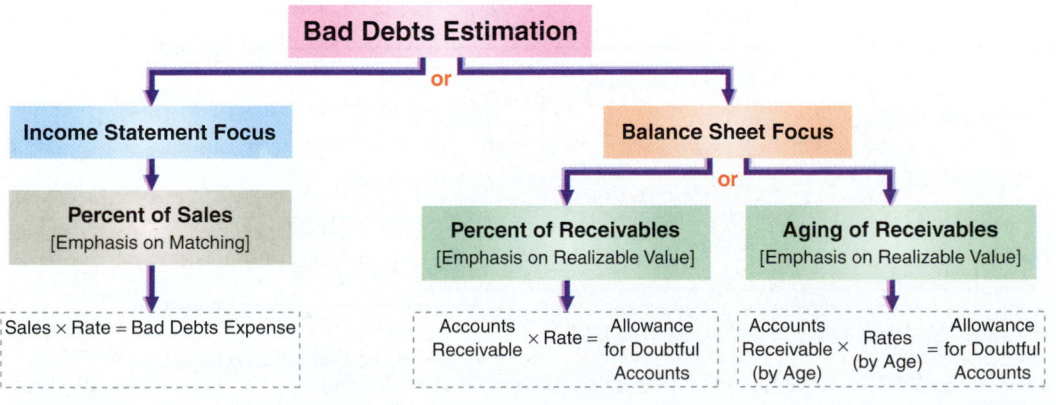

EXHIBIT 7.13

Methods to Estimate Bad Debts

Decision Maker   Answer — p. 311

Labor Union Chief   One week prior to labor contract negotiations, financial statements are released showing no income growth. A 10% growth was predicted. Your analysis finds that the company increased its allowance for uncollectibles from 1.5% to 4.5% of receivables. Without this change, income would show a 9% growth. Does this analysis impact negotiations? ■

Quick Check   Answers — p. 311

3. Why must bad debts expense be estimated if such an estimate is possible?

4. What term describes the balance sheet valuation of Accounts Receivable less the Allowance for Doubtful Accounts?

5. Why is estimated bad debts expense credited to a contra account (Allowance for Doubtful Accounts) rather than to the Accounts Receivable account?

6. SnoBoard Company's year-end balance in its Allowance for Doubtful Accounts is a credit of $440. By aging accounts receivable, it estimates that $6,142 is uncollectible. Prepare SnoBoard's year-end adjusting entry for bad debts.

7. Record entries for these transactions assuming the allowance method is used:

   Jan. 10   The $300 account of customer Cool Jam is determined uncollectible.

   April 12   Cool Jam unexpectedly pays in full the account deemed uncollectible on Jan. 10.

NOTES RECEIVABLE

C2 Describe a note receivable, the computation of its maturity date, and the recording of its existence.

A **promissory note** is a written promise to pay a specified amount of money, usually with interest, either on demand or at a definite future date. Promissory notes are used in many transactions, including paying for products and services, and lending and borrowing money. Sellers sometimes ask for a note to replace an account receivable when a customer requests additional time to pay a past-due account. For legal reasons, sellers generally prefer to receive notes when the credit period is long and when the receivable is for a large amount. If a lawsuit is needed to collect from a customer, a note is the buyer's written acknowledgment of the debt, its amount, and its terms.

Exhibit 7.14 shows a simple promissory note dated July 10, 2011. For this note, Julia Browne promises to pay TechCom or to its order (according to TechCom's instructions) a specified amount of money ($1,000), called the **principal of a note,** at a definite future date (October 8, 2011). As the one who signed the note and promised to pay it at maturity, Browne is the **maker of the note.** As the person to whom the note is payable, TechCom is the **payee of the note.** To Browne, the note is a liability called a *note payable*. To TechCom, the same note is an asset called a *note receivable*. This note bears interest at 12%, as written on the note. **Interest** is the charge for using the money until its due date. To a borrower, interest is an expense. To a lender, it is revenue.

EXHIBIT 7.14

Promissory Note

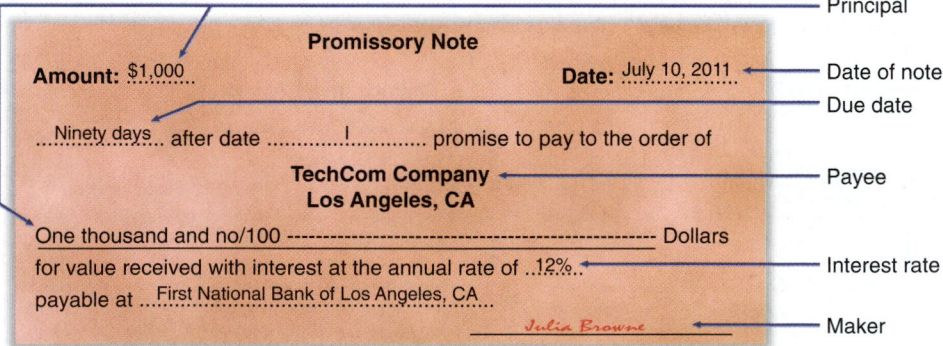

Computing Maturity and Interest

This section describes key computations for notes including the determination of maturity date, period covered, and interest computation.

Maturity Date and Period   The **maturity date of a note** is the day the note (principal and interest) must be repaid. The *period* of a note is the time from the note's (contract) date to its maturity date. Many notes mature in less than a full year, and the period they cover is often expressed in days. When the time of a note is expressed in days, its maturity date is the specified number of days after the note's date. As an example, a five-day note dated June 15 matures and is due on June 20. A 90-day note dated July 10 matures on October 8. This October 8 due date is computed as shown in Exhibit 7.15. The period of a note is sometimes expressed in months or years. When months are used, the note matures and is payable in the month of its maturity on the *same day of the month* as its original date. A nine-month note dated July 10, for instance, is payable on April 10. The same analysis applies when years are used.

Days in July	31
Minus the date of the note	<u>10</u>
Days remaining in July	21 ← July 11–31
Add days in August	31 ← Aug. 1–31
Add days in September	30 ← Sept. 1–30
Days to equal 90 days, or **maturity date of October 8**	<u>8</u> ← Oct. 1–8
Period of the note in days	90

EXHIBIT 7.15

Maturity Date Computation

Interest Computation   *Interest* is the cost of borrowing money for the borrower or, alternatively, the profit from lending money for the lender. Unless otherwise stated, the rate of interest on a note is the rate charged for the use of the principal for one year. The formula for computing interest on a note is shown in Exhibit 7.16.

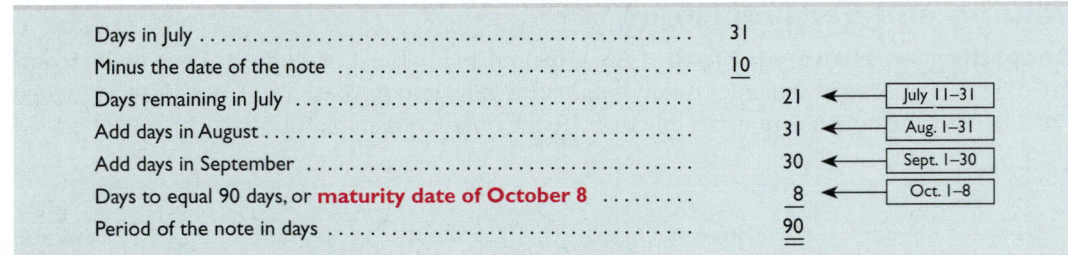

$$\text{Principal of the note} \times \text{Annual interest rate} \times \text{Time expressed in fraction of year} = \text{Interest}$$

EXHIBIT 7.16

Computation of Interest Formula

To simplify interest computations, a year is commonly treated as having 360 days (called the *banker's rule* in the business world and widely used in commercial transactions). **We treat a year as having 360 days for interest computations in the examples and assignments**. Using the promissory note in Exhibit 7.14 where we have a 90-day, 12%, $1,000 note, the total interest is computed as follows.

$$\$1,000 \times 12\% \times \frac{90}{360} = \$1,000 \times 0.12 \times 0.25 = \$30$$

Recognizing Notes Receivable

Notes receivable are usually recorded in a single Notes Receivable account to simplify record-keeping. The original notes are kept on file, including information on the maker, rate of interest, and due date. (When a company holds a large number of notes, it sometimes sets up a controlling account and a subsidiary ledger for notes. This is similar to the handling of accounts receivable.) To illustrate the recording for the receipt of a note, we use the $1,000, 90-day, 12% promissory note in Exhibit 7.14. TechCom received this note at the time of a product sale to Julia Browne. This transaction is recorded as follows.

July 10*	Notes Receivable	1,000	
	Sales		1,000
	Sold goods in exchange for a 90-day, 12% note.		

Assets = Liabilities + Equity
+1,000   +1,000

* We omit the entry to Dr. Cost of Sales and Cr. Merchandise Inventory to focus on sales and receivables.

When a seller accepts a note from an overdue customer as a way to grant a time extension on a past-due account receivable, it will often collect part of the past-due balance in cash. This partial payment forces a concession from the customer, reduces the customer's debt (and the seller's risk), and produces a note for a smaller amount. To illustrate, assume that Tech-Com agreed to accept $232 in cash along with a $600, 60-day, 15% note from Jo Cook to

Point: Notes receivable often are a major part of a company's assets. Likewise, notes payable often are a large part of a company's liabilities.

settle her $832 past-due account. TechCom made the following entry to record receipt of this cash and note.

Assets = Liabilities + Equity
+232
+600
−832

Oct. 5	Cash	232	
	Notes Receivable	600	
	Accounts Receivable—J. Cook		832
	Received cash and note to settle account.		

Valuing and Settling Notes

Recording an Honored Note The principal and interest of a note are due on its maturity date. The maker of the note usually *honors* the note and pays it in full. To illustrate, when J. Cook pays the note above on its due date, TechCom records it as follows.

P3 Record the honoring and dishonoring of a note and adjustments for interest.

Assets = Liabilities + Equity
+615   +15
−600

Dec. 4	Cash	615	
	Notes Receivable		600
	Interest Revenue		15
	Collect note with interest of $600 × 15% × 60/360.		

Interest Revenue, also called *Interest Earned,* is reported on the income statement.

Recording a Dishonored Note When a note's maker is unable or refuses to pay at maturity, the note is *dishonored.* The act of dishonoring a note does not relieve the maker of the obligation to pay. The payee should use every legitimate means to collect. How do companies report this event? The balance of the Notes Receivable account should include only those notes that have not matured. Thus, when a note is dishonored, we remove the amount of this note from the Notes Receivable account and charge it back to an account receivable from its maker. To illustrate, TechCom holds an $800, 12%, 60-day note of Greg Hart. At maturity, Hart dishonors the note. TechCom records this dishonoring of the note as follows.

Point: When posting a dishonored note to a customer's account, an explanation is included so as not to misinterpret the debit as a sale on account.

Assets = Liabilities + Equity
+816   +16
−800

Oct. 14	Accounts Receivable—G. Hart	816	
	Interest Revenue		16
	Notes Receivable		800
	To charge account of G. Hart for a dishonored note		
	and interest of $800 × 12% × 60/360.		

Point: Reporting the details of notes is consistent with the **full disclosure principle,** which requires financial statements (including footnotes) to report all relevant information.

Charging a dishonored note back to the account of its maker serves two purposes. First, it removes the amount of the note from the Notes Receivable account and records the dishonored note in the maker's account. Second, and more important, if the maker of the dishonored note applies for credit in the future, his or her account will reveal all past dealings, including the dishonored note. Restoring the account also reminds the company to continue collection efforts from Hart for both principal and interest. The entry records the full amount, including interest, to ensure that it is included in collection efforts.

Recording End-of-Period Interest Adjustment When notes receivable are outstanding at the end of a period, any accrued interest earned is computed and recorded. To illustrate, on December 16, TechCom accepts a $3,000, 60-day, 12% note from a customer in granting an extension on a past-due account. When TechCom's accounting period ends on December 31, $15 of interest has accrued on this note ($3,000 × 12% × 15/360). The following adjusting entry records this revenue.

Assets = Liabilities + Equity
+15   +15

Dec. 31	Interest Receivable	15	
	Interest Revenue		15
	To record accrued interest earned.		

Interest Revenue appears on the income statement, and Interest Receivable appears on the balance sheet as a current asset. When the December 16 note is collected on February 14, TechCom's entry to record the cash receipt is

Feb. 14	Cash	3,060	
	Interest Revenue		45
	Interest Receivable		15
	Notes Receivable		3,000
	Received payment of note and its interest.		

Assets = Liabilities + Equity
+3,060   +45
−15
−3,000

Total interest earned on the 60-day note is $60. The $15 credit to Interest Receivable on February 14 reflects the collection of the interest accrued from the December 31 adjusting entry. The $45 interest earned reflects TechCom's revenue from holding the note from January 1 to February 14 of the current period.

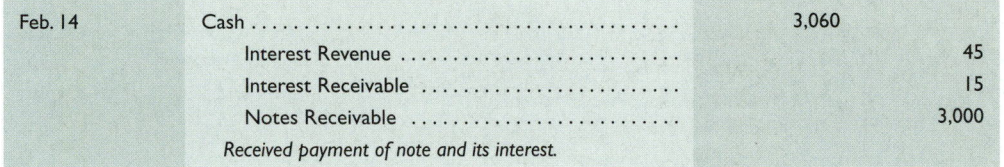

Quick Check

Answers — p. 311

8. Irwin purchases $7,000 of merchandise from Stamford on December 16, 2011. Stamford accepts Irwin's $7,000, 90-day, 12% note as payment. Stamford's accounting period ends on December 31, and it does not make reversing entries. Prepare entries for Stamford on December 16, 2011, and December 31, 2011.

9. Using the information in Quick Check 8, prepare Stamford's March 16, 2012, entry if Irwin dishonors the note.

DISPOSAL OF RECEIVABLES

Companies can convert receivables to cash before they are due. Reasons for this include the need for cash or the desire not to be involved in collection activities. Converting receivables is usually done either by (1) selling them or (2) using them as security for a loan. A recent survey shows that about 20% of companies obtain cash from either selling receivables or pledging them as security. In some industries such as textiles, apparel and furniture, this is common practice.

C3 Explain how receivables can be converted to cash before maturity.

Selling Receivables

A company can sell all or a portion of its receivables to a finance company or bank. The buyer, called a *factor,* charges the seller a *factoring fee* and then the buyer takes ownership of the receivables and receives cash when they come due. By incurring a factoring fee, the seller receives cash earlier and can pass the risk of bad debts to the factor. The seller can also choose to avoid costs of billing and accounting for the receivables. To illustrate, if TechCom sells $20,000 of its accounts receivable and is charged a 4% factoring fee, it records this sale as follows.

Global: Firms in export sales increasingly sell their receivables to factors.

Aug. 15	Cash	19,200	
	Factoring Fee Expense	800	
	Accounts Receivable		20,000
	Sold accounts receivable for cash, less 4% fee.		

Assets = Liabilities + Equity
+19,200   −800
−20,000

The accounting for sales of notes receivable is similar to that for accounts receivable. The detailed entries are covered in advanced courses.

Pledging Receivables

A company can raise cash by borrowing money and *pledging* its receivables as security for the loan. Pledging receivables does not transfer the risk of bad debts to the lender because the borrower retains ownership of the receivables. If the borrower defaults on the loan, the lender has a right to be paid from the cash receipts of the receivable when collected. To illustrate, when TechCom borrows $35,000 and pledges its receivables as security, it records this transaction as follows.

Assets = Liabilities + Equity
+35,000   +35,000

Aug. 20	Cash	35,000	
	Notes Payable		35,000
	Borrowed money with a note secured by pledging receivables.		

Since pledged receivables are committed as security for a specific loan, the borrower's financial statements disclose the pledging of them. TechCom, for instance, includes the following note with its statements: Accounts receivable of $40,000 are pledged as security for a $35,000 note payable.

Decision Insight

What's the Proper Allowance?   How can we assess whether a company has properly estimated its allowance for uncollectibles? One way is to compute the ratio of the allowance account to the gross accounts receivable. When this ratio is analyzed over several consecutive periods, trends often emerge that reflect on the adequacy of the allowance amount. ∎

GLOBAL VIEW

This section discusses similarities and differences between U.S. GAAP and IFRS regarding the recognition, measurement, and disposition of receivables.

Recognition of Receivables   Both U.S. GAAP and IFRS have similar asset criteria that apply to recognition of receivables. Further, receivables that arise from revenue-generating activities are subject to broadly similar criteria for U.S. GAAP and IFRS. Specifically, both refer to the realization principle and an earnings process. The realization principle under U.S. GAAP implies an *arm's-length transaction* occurs, whereas under IFRS this notion is applied in terms of reliable measurement and likelihood of economic benefits. Regarding U.S. GAAP's reference to an earnings process, IFRS instead refers to risk transfer and ownership reward. While these criteria are broadly similar, differences do exist, and they arise mainly from industry-specific guidance under U.S. GAAP, which is very limited under IFRS.

Valuation of Receivables   Both U.S. GAAP and IFRS require that receivables be reported net of estimated uncollectibles. Further, both systems require that the expense for estimated uncollectibles be recorded in the same period when any revenues from those receivables are recorded. This means that for accounts receivable, both U.S. GAAP and IFRS require the allowance method for uncollectibles (unless uncollectibles are immaterial). The allowance method using percent of sales, percent of receivables, and aging was explained in this chapter. **Nokia** reports the following for its allowance for uncollectibles:

NOKIA

> Management specifically analyzes accounts receivables and historical bad debt, customer concentrations, customer creditworthiness, current economic trends and changes in our customer payment terms when evaluating the adequacy of the allowance.

Disposition of Receivables   Both U.S. GAAP and IFRS apply broadly similar rules in recording dispositions of receivables. Those rules are discussed in this chapter. We should be aware of an important difference in terminology. Companies reporting under U.S. GAAP disclose Bad Debts Expense, which is also referred to as Provision for Bad Debts or the Provision for Uncollectible Accounts. For U.S. GAAP, *provision* here refers to expense. Under IFRS, the term *provision* usually refers to a liability whose amount or timing (or both) is uncertain.

Accounts Receivable Turnover 🟩🟨🟥 **Decision Analysis**

For a company selling on credit, we want to assess both the quality and liquidity of its accounts receivable. *Quality* of receivables refers to the likelihood of collection without loss. Experience shows that the longer receivables are outstanding beyond their due date, the lower the likelihood of collection. *Liquidity* of receivables refers to the speed of collection. **Accounts receivable turnover** is a measure of both the quality and liquidity of accounts receivable. It indicates how often, on average, receivables are received and collected during the period. The formula for this ratio is shown in Exhibit 7.17.

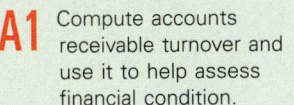

A1 Compute accounts receivable turnover and use it to help assess financial condition.

$$\text{Accounts receivable turnover} = \frac{\text{Net sales}}{\text{Average accounts receivable, net}}$$

EXHIBIT 7.17

Accounts Receivable Turnover

We prefer to use net *credit* sales in the numerator because cash sales do not create receivables. However, since financial statements rarely report net credit sales, our analysis uses net sales. The denominator is the *average* accounts receivable balance, computed as (Beginning balance + Ending balance) ÷ 2. TechCom has an accounts receivable turnover of 5.1. This indicates its average accounts receivable balance is converted into cash 5.1 times during the period. Exhibit 7.18 shows graphically this turnover activity for TechCom.

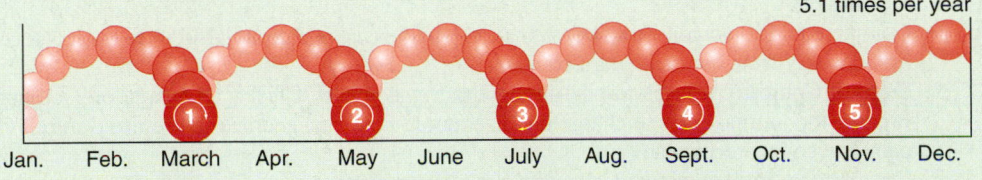

5.1 times per year

Jan. Feb. March Apr. May June July Aug. Sept. Oct. Nov. Dec.

EXHIBIT 7.18

Rate of Accounts Receivable Turnover for TechCom

Accounts receivable turnover also reflects how well management is doing in granting credit to customers in a desire to increase sales. A high turnover in comparison with competitors suggests that management should consider using more liberal credit terms to increase sales. A low turnover suggests management should consider stricter credit terms and more aggressive collection efforts to avoid having its resources tied up in accounts receivable.

Point: Credit risk ratio is computed by dividing the Allowance for Doubtful Accounts by Accounts Receivable. The higher this ratio, the higher is credit risk.

To illustrate, we take fiscal year data from two competitors: **Dell** and **Apple**. Exhibit 7.19 shows accounts receivable turnover for both companies.

EXHIBIT 7.19

Analysis Using Accounts Receivable Turnover

Company	Figure ($ millions)	2008	2007	2006	2005
Dell	Net sales	$61,101	$61,133	$57,420	$55,788
	Average accounts receivable, net	$ 5,346	$ 5,292	$ 4,352	$ 3,826
	Accounts receivable turnover	**11.4**	**11.6**	**13.2**	**14.6**
Apple	Net sales	$32,479	$24,006	$19,315	$13,931
	Average accounts receivable, net	$ 2,030	$ 1,445	$ 1,074	$ 835
	Accounts receivable turnover	**16.0**	**16.6**	**18.0**	**16.7**

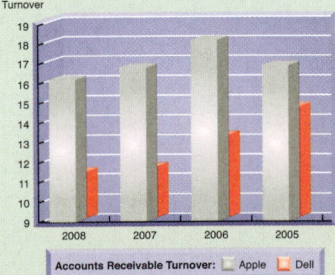

Dell's 2008 turnover is 11.4, computed as $61,101/$5,346 ($ millions). This means that Dell's average accounts receivable balance was converted into cash 11.4 times in 2008. Its turnover declined in 2008, as it has for each of the past 3 years. Apple's turnover exceeds that for Dell in each of the past 4 years. Is either company's turnover too high? Since sales are stable or markedly growing over this time period, each company's turnover rate does not appear to be too high. Instead, both Dell and Apple seem to be doing well in managing receivables. This is especially true given the recession-ary period of 2008 and 2009. Turnover for competitors is generally in the range of 7 to 12 for this same period.[1]

 **Decision** Maker   Answer — p. 311

Family Physician   Your medical practice is barely profitable, so you hire a health care analyst. The ana-lyst highlights several points including the following: *"Accounts receivable turnover is too low. Tighter credit policies are recommended along with discontinuing service to those most delayed in payments."* How do you interpret these recommendations? What actions do you take? ∎

DEMONSTRATION PROBLEM

Clayco Company completes the following selected transactions during year 2011.

July 14   Writes off a $750 account receivable arising from a sale to Briggs Company that dates to 10 months ago. (Clayco Company uses the allowance method.)

        30   Clayco Company receives a $1,000, 90-day, 10% note in exchange for merchandise sold to Sumrell Company (the merchandise cost $600).

Aug. 15   Receives $2,000 cash plus a $10,000 note from JT Co. in exchange for merchandise that sells for $12,000 (its cost is $8,000). The note is dated August 15, bears 12% interest, and matures in 120 days.

Nov. 1   Completed a $200 credit card sale with a 4% fee (the cost of sales is $150). The cash is received immediately from the credit card company.

        3   Sumrell Company refuses to pay the note that was due to Clayco Company on October 28. Prepare the journal entry to charge the dishonored note plus accrued interest to Sumrell Com-pany's accounts receivable.

        5   Completed a $500 credit card sale with a 5% fee (the cost of sales is $300). The payment from the credit card company is received on Nov. 9.

        15   Received the full amount of $750 from Briggs Company that was previously written off on July 14. Record the bad debts recovery.

Dec. 13   Received payment of principal plus interest from JT for the August 15 note.

Required

1. Prepare journal entries to record these transactions on Clayco Company's books.

2. Prepare an adjusting journal entry as of December 31, 2011, assuming the following:

   a. Bad debts are estimated to be $20,400 by aging accounts receivable. The unadjusted balance of the Allowance for Doubtful Accounts is $1,000 debit.

   b. Alternatively, assume that bad debts are estimated using the percent of sales method. The Allowance for Doubtful Accounts had a $1,000 debit balance before adjustment, and the company estimates bad debts to be 1% of its credit sales of $2,000,000.

PLANNING THE SOLUTION

● Examine each transaction to determine the accounts affected, and then record the entries.

● For the year-end adjustment, record the bad debts expense for the two approaches.

---

[1] As an estimate of *average days' sales uncollected,* we compute how many days (*on average*) it takes to collect receivables as follows: 365 days ÷ accounts receivable turnover. An increase in this *average collection period* can signal a decline in customers' financial condition.

SOLUTION TO DEMONSTRATION PROBLEM

1.

July 14	Allowance for Doubtful Accounts	750	
	Accounts Receivable—Briggs Co.		750
	Wrote off an uncollectible account.		
July 30	Notes Receivable—Sumrell Co.	1,000	
	Sales		1,000
	Sold merchandise for a 90-day, 10% note.		
July 30	Cost of Goods Sold	600	
	Merchandise Inventory		600
	To record the cost of July 30 sale.		
Aug. 15	Cash	2,000	
	Notes Receivable—JT Co.	10,000	
	Sales		12,000
	Sold merchandise to customer for $2,000 cash and $10,000 note.		
Aug. 15	Cost of Goods Sold	8,000	
	Merchandise Inventory		8,000
	To record the cost of Aug. 15 sale.		
Nov. 1	Cash	192	
	Credit Card Expense	8	
	Sales		200
	To record credit card sale less a 4% credit card expense.		
Nov. 1	Cost of Goods Sold	150	
	Merchandise Inventory		150
	To record the cost of Nov. 1 sale.		
Nov. 3	Accounts Receivable—Sumrell Co.	1,025	
	Interest Revenue		25
	Notes Receivable—Sumrell Co.		1,000
	To charge account of Sumrell Company for a $1,000 dishonored note and interest of $1,000 × 10% × 90/360.		
Nov. 5	Accounts Receivable—Credit Card Co.	475	
	Credit Card Expense	25	
	Sales		500
	To record credit card sale less a 5% credit card expense.		
Nov. 5	Cost of Goods Sold	300	
	Merchandise Inventory		300
	To record the cost of Nov. 5 sale.		
Nov. 9	Cash	475	
	Accounts Receivable—Credit Card Co.		475
	To record cash receipt from Nov. 5 sale.		
Nov. 15	Accounts Receivable—Briggs Co.	750	
	Allowance for Doubtful Accounts		750
	To reinstate the account of Briggs Company previously written off.		
Nov. 15	Cash	750	
	Accounts Receivable—Briggs Co.		750
	Cash received in full payment of account.		
Dec. 13	Cash	10,400	
	Interest Revenue		400
	Note Receivable—JT Co.		10,000
	Collect note with interest of $10,000 × 12% × 120/360.		

2a. Aging of accounts receivable method.

Dec. 31	Bad Debts Expense	21,400	
	Allowance for Doubtful Accounts		21,400
	To adjust allowance account from a $1,000 debit balance to a $20,400 credit balance.		

2b. Percent of sales method.*

Dec. 31	Bad Debts Expense	20,000	
	Allowance for Doubtful Accounts		20,000
	To provide for bad debts as 1% × $2,000,000 in credit sales.		

* For the income statement approach, which requires estimating bad debts as a percent of sales or credit sales, the Allowance account balance is *not* considered when making the adjusting entry.

Summary

C1 **Describe accounts receivable and how they occur and are recorded.** Accounts receivable are amounts due from customers for credit sales. A subsidiary ledger lists amounts owed by each customer. Credit sales arise from at least two sources: (1) sales on credit and (2) credit card sales. *Sales on credit* refers to a company's granting credit directly to customers. Credit card sales involve customers' use of third-party credit cards.

C2 **Describe a note receivable, the computation of its maturity date, and the recording of its existence.** A note receivable is a written promise to pay a specified amount of money at a definite future date. The maturity date is the day the note (principal and interest) must be repaid. Interest rates are normally stated in annual terms. The amount of interest on the note is computed by expressing time as a fraction of one year and multiplying the note's principal by this fraction and the annual interest rate. A note received is recorded at its principal amount by debiting the Notes Receivable account. The credit amount is to the asset, product, or service provided in return for the note.

C3 **Explain how receivables can be converted to cash before maturity.** Receivables can be converted to cash before maturity in three ways. First, a company can sell accounts receivable to a factor, who charges a factoring fee. Second, a company can borrow money by signing a note payable that is secured by pledging the accounts receivable. Third, notes receivable can be discounted at (sold to) a financial institution.

A1 **Compute accounts receivable turnover and use it to help assess financial condition.** Accounts receivable turnover is a measure of both the quality and liquidity of accounts receivable.

The accounts receivable turnover measure indicates how often, on average, receivables are received and collected during the period. Accounts receivable turnover is computed as net sales divided by average accounts receivable.

P1 **Apply the direct write-off method to account for accounts receivable.** The direct write-off method charges Bad Debts Expense when accounts are written off as uncollectible. This method is acceptable only when the amount of bad debts expense is immaterial.

P2 **Apply the allowance method and estimate uncollectibles based on sales and accounts receivable.** Under the allowance method, bad debts expense is recorded with an adjustment at the end of each accounting period that debits the Bad Debts Expense account and credits the Allowance for Doubtful Accounts. The uncollectible accounts are later written off with a debit to the Allowance for Doubtful Accounts. Uncollectibles are estimated by focusing on either (1) the income statement relation between bad debts expense and credit sales or (2) the balance sheet relation between accounts receivable and the allowance for doubtful accounts. The first approach emphasizes the matching principle using the income statement. The second approach emphasizes realizable value of accounts receivable using the balance sheet.

P3 **Record the honoring and dishonoring of a note and adjustments for interest.** When a note is honored, the payee debits the money received and credits both Notes Receivable and Interest Revenue. Dishonored notes are credited to Notes Receivable and debited to Accounts Receivable (to the account of the maker in an attempt to collect), and Interest Revenue is recorded for interest earned for the time the note is held.

Guidance Answers to Decision Maker and Decision Ethics

Entrepreneur Analysis of credit card sales should weigh the benefits against the costs. The primary benefit is the potential to increase sales by attracting customers who prefer the convenience of credit cards. The primary cost is the fee charged by the credit card company for providing this service. Analysis should therefore estimate the expected increase in dollar sales from allowing credit card sales and then subtract (1) the normal costs and expenses and (2) the credit card fees associated with this expected increase in dollar sales. If your analysis shows an increase in profit from allowing credit card sales, your store should probably accept them.

Labor Union Chief Yes, this information is likely to impact your negotiations. The obvious question is why the company markedly increased this allowance. The large increase in this allowance means a substantial increase in bad debts expense *and* a decrease in earnings. This change (coming immediately prior to labor contract discussions) also raises concerns since it reduces the union's bargaining power for increased compensation. You want to ask management for supporting documentation justifying this increase. You also want data for two or three prior years and similar data from competitors.

These data should give you some sense of whether the change in the allowance for uncollectibles is justified.

Family Physician The recommendations are twofold. First, the analyst suggests more stringent screening of patients' credit standing. Second, the analyst suggests dropping patients who are most overdue in payments. You are likely bothered by both suggestions. They are probably financially wise recommendations, but you are troubled by eliminating services to those less able to pay. One alternative is to follow the recommendations while implementing a care program directed at patients less able to pay for services. This allows you to continue services to patients less able to pay and lets you discontinue services to patients able but unwilling to pay.

Guidance Answers to Quick Checks

1. If cash is immediately received when credit card sales receipts are deposited, the company debits Cash at the time of sale. If the company does not receive payment until after it submits receipts to the credit card company, it debits Accounts Receivable at the time of sale. (Cash is later debited when payment is received from the credit card company.)

2. Credit card expenses are usually *recorded* and *incurred* at the time of their related sales, not when cash is received from the credit card company.

3. If possible, bad debts expense must be matched with the sales that gave rise to the accounts receivable. This requires that companies estimate future bad debts at the end of each period before they learn which accounts are uncollectible.

4. Realizable value (also called *net realizable value*).

5. The estimated amount of bad debts expense cannot be credited to the Accounts Receivable account because the specific customer accounts that will prove uncollectible cannot yet be identified and removed from the accounts receivable subsidiary ledger. Moreover, if only the Accounts Receivable account is credited, its balance would not equal the sum of its subsidiary account balances.

6.

| Dec. 31 | Bad Debts Expense | 5,702 | |
| | Allowance for Doubtful Accounts | | 5,702 |

7.

Jan. 10	Allowance for Doubtful Accounts	300	
	Accounts Receivable—Cool Jam		300
Apr. 12	Accounts Receivable—Cool Jam	300	
	Allowance for Doubtful Accounts		300
Apr. 12	Cash	300	
	Accounts Receivable—Cool Jam		300

8.

Dec. 16	Note Receivable—Irwin	7,000	
	Sales		7,000
Dec. 31	Interest Receivable	35	
	Interest Revenue		35
	($7,000 × 12% × 15/360)		

9.

Mar. 16	Accounts Receivable—Irwin	7,210	
	Interest Revenue		175
	Interest Receivable		35
	Notes Receivable—Irwin		7,000

Key Terms
mhhe.com/wildFINMAN4e

Multiple Choice Quiz   Answers on p. 323   mhhe.com/wildFINMAN4e

Additional Quiz Questions are available at the book's Website.

1. A company's Accounts Receivable balance at its December 31 year-end is $125,650, and its Allowance for Doubtful Accounts has a credit balance of $328 before year-end adjustment. Its net sales are $572,300. It estimates that 4% of outstanding accounts receivable are uncollectible. What amount of Bad Debts Expense is recorded at December 31?
   a. $5,354
   b. $328
   c. $5,026
   d. $4,698
   e. $34,338

2. A company's Accounts Receivable balance at its December 31 year-end is $489,300, and its Allowance for Doubtful Accounts has a debit balance of $554 before year-end adjustment. Its net sales are $1,300,000. It estimates that 6% of outstanding accounts receivable are uncollectible. What amount of Bad Debts Expense is recorded at December 31?
   a. $29,912
   b. $28,804
   c. $78,000
   d. $29,358
   e. $554

3. Total interest to be earned on a $7,500, 5%, 90-day note is
   a. $93.75
   b. $375.00
   c. $1,125.00
   d. $31.25
   e. $125.00

4. A company receives a $9,000, 8%, 60-day note. The maturity value of the note is
   a. $120
   b. $9,000
   c. $9,120
   d. $720
   e. $9,720

5. A company has net sales of $489,600 and average accounts receivable of $40,800. What is its accounts receivable turnover?
   a. 0.08
   b. 30.41
   c. 1,341.00
   d. 12.00
   e. 111.78

🔢 Icon denotes assignments that involve decision making.

Discussion Questions

1. 🔢 How do sellers benefit from allowing their customers to use credit cards?

2. 🔢 Why does the direct write-off method of accounting for bad debts usually fail to match revenues and expenses?

3. Explain the accounting constraint of materiality.

4. Explain why writing off a bad debt against the Allowance for Doubtful Accounts does not reduce the estimated realizable value of a company's accounts receivable.

5. 🔢 Why does the Bad Debts Expense account usually not have the same adjusted balance as the Allowance for Doubtful Accounts?

6. Why might a business prefer a note receivable to an account receivable?

7. 🔢 Refer to the financial statements and notes of **Research In Motion** in Appendix A. In its presenta- *RIM* tion of accounts receivable on the balance sheet, how does it

title accounts receivable? What does it report for its allowance as of February 27, 2010?

8. 🔢 Refer to the balance sheet of **Apple** in Appendix A. Does it use the direct write-off method or allowance *Apple* method in accounting for its Accounts Receivable? What is the realizable value of its receivable's balance as of September 26, 2009?

9. Refer to the financial statements of **Palm** in Appendix A. What are Palm's gross accounts receivable at *Palm* May 31, 2009? What percentage of its accounts receivable does it believe to be uncollectible at this date?

10. Refer to the December 31, 2009, financial statements of **Nokia** in Appendix A. What does it title *NOKIA* its accounts receivable on its statement of financial position? What percent of its accounts receivable does it believe to be uncollectible?

📊 connect

QUICK STUDY

QS 7-1
Credit card sales
C1

Prepare journal entries for the following credit card sales transactions (the company uses the perpetual inventory system).

1. Sold $10,000 of merchandise, that cost $7,500, on MasterCard credit cards. The net cash receipts from sales are immediately deposited in the seller's bank account. MasterCard charges a 5% fee.

2. Sold $3,000 of merchandise, that cost $1,500, on an assortment of credit cards. Net cash receipts are received 7 days later, and a 4% fee is charged.

Milner Corp. uses the allowance method to account for uncollectibles. On October 31, it wrote off a $1,000 account of a customer, C. Schaub. On December 9, it receives a $200 payment from Schaub.

1. Prepare the journal entry or entries for October 31.

2. Prepare the journal entry or entries for December 9; assume no additional money is expected from Schaub.

QS 7-2
Allowance method for bad debts
P2

Wecker Company's year-end unadjusted trial balance shows accounts receivable of $89,000, allowance for doubtful accounts of $500 (credit), and sales of $270,000. Uncollectibles are estimated to be 1.5% of accounts receivable.

1. Prepare the December 31 year-end adjusting entry for uncollectibles.

2. What amount would have been used in the year-end adjusting entry if the allowance account had a year-end unadjusted debit balance of $200?

QS 7-3
Percent of accounts receivable method
P2

Assume the same facts as in QS 7-3, except that Wecker estimates uncollectibles as 1.0% of sales. Prepare the December 31 year-end adjusting entry for uncollectibles.

QS 7-4
Percent of sales method   **P2**

On August 2, 2011, JLK Co. receives a $5,500, 90-day, 12% note from customer Tom Menke as payment on his $9,000 account. (1) Compute the maturity date for this note. (2) Prepare JLK's journal entry for August 2.

QS 7-5
Note receivable   **C2**

Refer to the information in QS 7-5 and prepare the journal entry assuming the note is honored by the customer on October 31, 2011.

QS 7-6
Note receivable   **P3**

Dekon Company's December 31 year-end unadjusted trial balance shows a $8,000 balance in Notes Receivable. This balance is from one 6% note dated December 1, with a period of 45 days. Prepare any necessary journal entries for December 31 and for the note's maturity date assuming it is honored.

QS 7-7
Note receivable   **P3**

Record the sale by Kroll Company of $1,000 in accounts receivable on May 1. Kroll is charged a 3% factoring fee.

QS 7-8
Disposing receivables   **C3**

Krugg Company determines on May 1 that it cannot collect $1,000 of its accounts receivable from its customer P. Carroll. Apply the direct write-off method to record this loss as of May 1.

QS 7-9
Direct write-off method   **P1**

Refer to the information in QS 7-9. On May 30, P. Carroll unexpectedly paid his account in full to Krugg Company. Record Krugg's entry(ies) to reflect this recovery of this bad debt.

QS 7-10
Recovering a bad debt   **P1**

The following data are taken from the comparative balance sheets of Fulton Company. Compute and interpret its accounts receivable turnover for year 2011 (competitors average a turnover of 7.5).

QS 7-11
Accounts receivable turnover

A1

	2011	2010
Accounts receivable, net	$152,900	$133,700
Net sales	754,200	810,600

Answer each of the following related to international accounting standards.

a. Explain (in general terms) how the accounting for recognition of receivables is different between IFRS and U.S. GAAP.

b. Explain (in general terms) how the accounting for valuation of receivables is different between IFRS and U.S. GAAP.

QS 7-12
International accounting standards

C1

EXERCISES

Exercise 7-1
Accounting for credit card sales
C1

Petri Company uses the perpetual inventory system and allows customers to use two credit cards in charging purchases. With the Omni Bank Card, Petri receives an immediate credit to its account when it deposits sales receipts. Omni assesses a 4% service charge for credit card sales. The second credit card that Petri accepts is the Continental Card. Petri sends its accumulated receipts to Continental on a weekly basis and is paid by Continental about a week later. Continental assesses a 2.5% charge on sales for using its card. Prepare journal entries to record the following selected credit card transactions of Petri Company.

Apr. 8   Sold merchandise for $9,200 (that had cost $6,800) and accepted the customer's Omni Bank Card. The Omni receipts are immediately deposited in Petri's bank account.
      12   Sold merchandise for $5,400 (that had cost $3,500) and accepted the customer's Continental Card. Transferred $5,400 of credit card receipts to Continental, requesting payment.
      20   Received Continental's check for the April 12 billing, less the service charge.

Exercise 7-2
Accounts receivable subsidiary ledger; schedule of accounts receivable
C1

Sami Company recorded the following selected transactions during November 2011.

Nov. 5	Accounts Receivable—Surf Shop	4,417	
	Sales		4,417
10	Accounts Receivable—Yum Enterprises	1,250	
	Sales		1,250
13	Accounts Receivable—Matt Albin	733	
	Sales		733
21	Sales Returns and Allowances	189	
	Accounts Receivable—Matt Albin		189
30	Accounts Receivable—Surf Shop	2,606	
	Sales		2,606

1. Open a general ledger having T-accounts for Accounts Receivable, Sales, and Sales Returns and Allowances. Also open an accounts receivable subsidiary ledger having a T-account for each customer. Post these entries to both the general ledger and the accounts receivable ledger.

Check Accounts Receivable ending balance, $8,817

2. Prepare a schedule of accounts receivable (see Exhibit 7.4) and compare its total with the balance of the Accounts Receivable controlling account as of November 30.

Exercise 7-3
Direct write-off method
P1

Diablo Company applies the direct write-off method in accounting for uncollectible accounts. Prepare journal entries to record the following selected transactions of Diablo.

June 11   Diablo determines that it cannot collect $9,000 of its accounts receivable from its customer Chaffey Company.
      29   Chaffey Company unexpectedly pays its account in full to Diablo Company. Diablo records its recovery of this bad debt.

Exercise 7-4
Percent of sales method; write-off
P2

At year-end (December 31), Alvare Company estimates its bad debts as 0.5% of its annual credit sales of $875,000. Alvare records its Bad Debts Expense for that estimate. On the following February 1, Alvare decides that the $420 account of P. Coble is uncollectible and writes it off as a bad debt. On June 5, Coble unexpectedly pays the amount previously written off. Prepare the journal entries of Alvare to record these transactions and events of December 31, February 1, and June 5.

Exercise 7-5
Percent of accounts receivable method
P2

At each calendar year-end, Cabool Supply Co. uses the percent of accounts receivable method to estimate bad debts. On December 31, 2011, it has outstanding accounts receivable of $53,000, and it estimates that 4% will be uncollectible. Prepare the adjusting entry to record bad debts expense for year 2011 under the assumption that the Allowance for Doubtful Accounts has (a) a $915 credit balance before the adjustment and (b) a $1,332 debit balance before the adjustment.

Exercise 7-6
Aging of receivables method
P2

Hecter Company estimates uncollectible accounts using the allowance method at December 31. It prepared the following aging of receivables analysis.

			Days Past Due			
	Total	0	1 to 30	31 to 60	61 to 90	Over 90
Accounts receivable	$190,000	$132,000	$30,000	$12,000	$6,000	$10,000
Percent uncollectible		1%	2%	4%	7%	12%

a. Estimate the balance of the Allowance for Doubtful Accounts using the aging of accounts receivable method.

b. Prepare the adjusting entry to record Bad Debts Expense using the estimate from part *a*. Assume the unadjusted balance in the Allowance for Doubtful Accounts is a $600 credit.

c. Prepare the adjusting entry to record Bad Debts Expense using the estimate from part *a*. Assume the unadjusted balance in the Allowance for Doubtful Accounts is a $400 debit.

Refer to the information in Exercise 7-6 to complete the following requirements.

a. Estimate the balance of the Allowance for Doubtful Accounts assuming the company uses 3.5% of total accounts receivable to estimate uncollectibles, instead of the aging of receivables method.

b. Prepare the adjusting entry to record Bad Debts Expense using the estimate from part *a*. Assume the unadjusted balance in the Allowance for Doubtful Accounts is a $300 credit.

c. Prepare the adjusting entry to record Bad Debts Expense using the estimate from part *a*. Assume the unadjusted balance in the Allowance for Doubtful Accounts is a $200 debit.

Exercise 7-7
Percent of receivables method

P2

Refer to the information in Exercise 7-6 to complete the following requirements.

a. On February 1 of the next period, the company determined that $1,900 in customer accounts is uncollectible; specifically, $400 for Oxford Co. and $1,500 for Brookes Co. Prepare the journal entry to write off those accounts.

b. On June 5 of that next period, the company unexpectedly received a $400 payment on a customer account, Oxford Company, that had previously been written off in part *a*. Prepare the entries necessary to reinstate the account and to record the cash received.

Exercise 7-8
Writing off receivables

P2

At December 31, GreenTea Company reports the following results for its calendar-year.

Cash sales	$1,200,000
Credit sales	900,000

Its year-end unadjusted trial balance includes the following items.

Accounts receivable	$195,000 debit
Allowance for doubtful accounts	3,000 debit

a. Prepare the adjusting entry to record Bad Debts Expense assuming uncollectibles are estimated to be 1.5% of credit sales.

b. Prepare the adjusting entry to record Bad Debts Expense assuming uncollectibles are estimated to be 0.5% of total sales.

c. Prepare the adjusting entry to record Bad Debts Expense assuming uncollectibles are estimated to be 6% of year-end accounts receivable.

Exercise 7-9
Estimating bad debts

P2

Check Dr. Bad Debts Expense:
(*a*) $13,500

(*c*) $14,700

On June 30, Roman Co. has $125,900 of accounts receivable. Prepare journal entries to record the following selected July transactions. Also prepare any footnotes to the July 31 financial statements that result from these transactions. (The company uses the perpetual inventory system.)

July   4   Sold $6,295 of merchandise (that had cost $4,000) to customers on credit.
       9   Sold $18,000 of accounts receivable to Center Bank. Center charges a 4% factoring fee.
      17   Received $3,436 cash from customers in payment on their accounts.
      27   Borrowed $10,000 cash from Center Bank, pledging $13,000 of accounts receivable as security for the loan.

Exercise 7-10
Selling and pledging accounts receivable

C3

Prepare journal entries to record these selected transactions for Eduardo Company.

Nov. 1   Accepted a $5,000, 180-day, 6% note dated November 1 from Melosa Allen in granting a time extension on her past-due account receivable.
Dec. 31   Adjusted the year-end accounts for the accrued interest earned on the Allen note.
Apr. 30   Allen honors her note when presented for payment; February has 28 days for the current year.

Exercise 7-11
Honoring a note

P3

Exercise 7-12

Dishonoring a note

P3

Prepare journal entries to record the following selected transactions of Paloma Company.

Mar. 21   Accepted a $3,100, 180-day, 10% note dated March 21 from Salma Hernandez in granting a time extension on her past-due account receivable.

Sept. 17   Hernandez dishonors her note when it is presented for payment.

Dec. 31   After exhausting all legal means of collection, Paloma Company writes off Hernandez's account against the Allowance for Doubtful Accounts.

Exercise 7-13

Notes receivable transactions

C2

Check Dec. 31, Cr. Interest Revenue $40

Prepare journal entries for the following selected transactions of Deshawn Company for 2010.

2010

Dec. 13   Accepted a $10,000, 45-day, 8% note dated December 13 in granting Latisha Clark a time extension on her past-due account receivable.

31   Prepared an adjusting entry to record the accrued interest on the Clark note.

Exercise 7-14

Notes receivable transactions

P3

Check Jan. 27, Dr. Cash $10,100

June 1, Dr. Cash $4,100

Refer to the information in Exercise 7-13 and prepare the journal entries for the following selected transactions of Deshawn Company for 2011.

2011

Jan. 27   Received Clark's payment for principal and interest on the note dated December 13.

Mar. 3   Accepted a $4,000, 10%, 90-day note dated March 3 in granting a time extension on the past-due account receivable of Shandi Company.

17   Accepted a $2,000, 30-day, 9% note dated March 17 in granting Juan Torres a time extension on his past-due account receivable.

Apr. 16   Torres dishonors his note when presented for payment.

May 1   Wrote off the Torres account against the Allowance for Doubtful Accounts.

June 1   Received the Shandi payment for principal and interest on the note dated March 3.

Exercise 7-15

Accounts receivable turnover

A1

The following information is from the annual financial statements of Waseem Company. Compute its accounts receivable turnover for 2010 and 2011. Compare the two years results and give a possible explanation for any change (competitors average a turnover of 11).

	2011	2010	2009
Net sales	$305,000	$236,000	$288,000
Accounts receivable, net (year-end)	22,900	20,700	17,400

Exercise 7-16

Accounting for bad debts following IFRS

P2

Hitachi, Ltd., reports total revenues of ¥10,000,369 million for its fiscal year ending March 31, 2009, and its March 31, 2009, unadjusted trial balance reports a debit balance for trade receivables (gross) of ¥2,179,764 million.

a. Prepare the adjusting entry to record its Bad Debts Expense assuming uncollectibles are estimated to be 0.4% of total revenues and its unadjusted trial balance reports a credit balance of ¥10,000 million.

b. Prepare the adjusting entry to record Bad Debts Expense assuming uncollectibles are estimated to be 2.1% of year-end trade receivables (gross) and its unadjusted trial balance reports a credit balance of ¥10,000 million.

---

 connect

PROBLEM SET A

Problem 7-1A

Sales on account and credit card sales

C1

Atlas Co. allows select customers to make purchases on credit. Its other customers can use either of two credit cards: Zisa or Access. Zisa deducts a 3% service charge for sales on its credit card and credits the bank account of Atlas immediately when credit card receipts are deposited. Atlas deposits the Zisa credit card receipts each business day. When customers use Access credit cards, Atlas accumulates the receipts for several days before submitting them to Access for payment. Access deducts a 2% service charge and usually pays within one week of being billed. Atlas completes the following transactions in June. (The terms of all credit sales are 2/15, n/30, and all sales are recorded at the gross price.)

June 4   Sold $750 of merchandise (that had cost $500) on credit to Anne Cianci.

5   Sold $5,900 of merchandise (that had cost $3,200) to customers who used their Zisa cards.

   6   Sold $4,800 of merchandise (that had cost $2,800) to customers who used their Access cards.

   8   Sold $3,200 of merchandise (that had cost $1,900) to customers who used their Access cards.

  10   Submitted Access card receipts accumulated since June 6 to the credit card company for payment.

  13   Wrote off the account of Nakia Wells against the Allowance for Doubtful Accounts. The $329 balance in Wells's account stemmed from a credit sale in October of last year.

  17   Received the amount due from Access.

  18   Received Cianci's check in full payment for the purchase of June 4.

Check June 17, Dr. Cash $7,840

Required

Prepare journal entries to record the preceding transactions and events. (The company uses the perpetual inventory system. Round amounts to the nearest dollar.)

Lopez Company began operations on January 1, 2010. During its first two years, the company completed a number of transactions involving sales on credit, accounts receivable collections, and bad debts. These transactions are summarized as follows.

Problem 7-2A
Accounts receivable transactions and bad debts adjustments

C1 P2

2010

a. Sold $1,803,750 of merchandise (that had cost $1,475,000) on credit, terms n/30.

b. Wrote off $20,300 of uncollectible accounts receivable.

c. Received $789,200 cash in payment of accounts receivable.

d. In adjusting the accounts on December 31, the company estimated that 1.5% of accounts receivable will be uncollectible.

Check (*d*) Dr. Bad Debts Expense $35,214

2011

e. Sold $1,825,700 of merchandise (that had cost $1,450,000) on credit, terms n/30.

f. Wrote off $28,800 of uncollectible accounts receivable.

g. Received $1,304,800 cash in payment of accounts receivable.

h. In adjusting the accounts on December 31, the company estimated that 1.5% of accounts receivable will be uncollectible.

(*h*) Dr. Bad Debts Expense $36,181

Required

Prepare journal entries to record Lopez's 2010 and 2011 summarized transactions and its year-end adjustments to record bad debts expense. (The company uses the perpetual inventory system. Round amounts to the nearest dollar.)

At December 31, 2011, Ethan Company reports the following results for its calendar-year.

Problem 7-3A
Estimating and reporting bad debts

P2

Cash sales	$1,803,750
Credit sales	3,534,000

In addition, its unadjusted trial balance includes the following items.

Accounts receivable	$1,070,100 debit
Allowance for doubtful accounts	15,750 debit

Required

1. Prepare the adjusting entry for this company to recognize bad debts under each of the following independent assumptions.

  a. Bad debts are estimated to be 2% of credit sales.

  b. Bad debts are estimated to be 1% of total sales.

  c. An aging analysis estimates that 5% of year-end accounts receivable are uncollectible.

Check Bad Debts Expense: (1*a*) $70,680, (1*c*) $69,255

2. Show how Accounts Receivable and the Allowance for Doubtful Accounts appear on its December 31, 2011, balance sheet given the facts in part 1*a*.

3. Show how Accounts Receivable and the Allowance for Doubtful Accounts appear on its December 31, 2011, balance sheet given the facts in part 1*c*.

Problem 7-4A
Aging accounts receivable and
accounting for bad debts

P2

Carmack Company has credit sales of $2.6 million for year 2011. On December 31, 2011, the company's Allowance for Doubtful Accounts has an unadjusted credit balance of $13,400. Carmack prepares a schedule of its December 31, 2011, accounts receivable by age. On the basis of past experience, it estimates the percent of receivables in each age category that will become uncollectible. This information is summarized here.

File Edit View Insert Format Tools Data Accounting Window Help

December 31, 2011 Accounts Receivable	Age of Accounts Receivable	Expected Percent Uncollectible
$730,000	Not yet due	1.25%
354,000	1 to 30 days past due	2.00
76,000	31 to 60 days past due	6.50
48,000	61 to 90 days past due	32.75
12,000	Over 90 days past due	68.00

Sheet1 / Sheet2 / Sheet3 /

Required

1. Estimate the required balance of the Allowance for Doubtful Accounts at December 31, 2011, using the aging of accounts receivable method.

Check (2) Dr. Bad Debts Expense
$31,625

2. Prepare the adjusting entry to record bad debts expense at December 31, 2011.

Analysis Component

3. On June 30, 2012, Carmack Company concludes that a customer's $3,750 receivable (created in 2011) is uncollectible and that the account should be written off. What effect will this action have on Carmack's 2012 net income? Explain.

Problem 7-5A
Analyzing and journalizing notes
receivable transactions

C2 C3 P3

The following selected transactions are from Ohlde Company.

2010

Dec. 16   Accepted a $9,600, 60-day, 9% note dated this day in granting Todd Duke a time extension on his past-due account receivable.
      31   Made an adjusting entry to record the accrued interest on the Duke note.

2011

Check Feb. 14, Cr. Interest
Revenue $108

Feb. 14   Received Duke's payment of principal and interest on the note dated December 16.
Mar. 2   Accepted an $4,120, 8%, 90-day note dated this day in granting a time extension on the past-due account receivable from Mare Co.
      17   Accepted a $2,400, 30-day, 7% note dated this day in granting Jolene Halaam a time extension on her past-due account receivable.
Apr. 16   Halaam dishonored her note when presented for payment.

June 2, Cr. Interest
Revenue $82

June 2   Mare Co. refuses to pay the note that was due to Ohlde Co. on May 31. Prepare the journal entry to charge the dishonored note plus accrued interest to Mare Co.'s accounts receivable.
July 17   Received payment from Mare Co. for the maturity value of its dishonored note plus interest for 46 days beyond maturity at 8%.
Aug. 7   Accepted an $5,440, 90-day, 10% note dated this day in granting a time extension on the past-due account receivable of Birch and Byer Co.
Sept. 3   Accepted a $2,080, 60-day, 10% note dated this day in granting Kevin York a time extension on his past-due account receivable.

Nov. 2, Cr. Interest
Revenue $35

Nov. 2   Received payment of principal plus interest from York for the September 3 note.
Nov. 5   Received payment of principal plus interest from Birch and Byer for the August 7 note.
Dec. 1   Wrote off the Jolene Halaam account against Allowance for Doubtful Accounts.

Required

1. Prepare journal entries to record these transactions and events. (Round amounts to the nearest dollar.)

Analysis Component

2. What reporting is necessary when a business pledges receivables as security for a loan and the loan is still outstanding at the end of the period? Explain the reason for this requirement and the accounting principle being satisfied.

Able Co. allows select customers to make purchases on credit. Its other customers can use either of two credit cards: Commerce Bank or Aztec. Commerce Bank deducts a 3% service charge for sales on its credit card and immediately credits the bank account of Able when credit card receipts are deposited. Able deposits the Commerce Bank credit card receipts each business day. When customers use the Aztec card, Able accumulates the receipts for several days and then submits them to Aztec for payment. Aztec deducts a 2% service charge and usually pays within one week of being billed. Able completed the following transactions in August (terms of all credit sales are 2/10, n/30; and all sales are recorded at the gross price).

PROBLEM SET B

Problem 7-1B
Sales on account and credit card sales
C1

Aug. 4   Sold $2,780 of merchandise (that had cost $1,750) on credit to Stacy Dalton.
      10   Sold $3,248 of merchandise (that had cost $2,456) to customers who used their Commerce Bank credit cards.
      11   Sold $1,575 of merchandise (that had cost $1,150) to customers who used their Aztec cards.
      14   Received Dalton's check in full payment for the purchase of August 4.
      15   Sold $2,960 of merchandise (that had cost $1,758) to customers who used their Aztec cards.
      18   Submitted Aztec card receipts accumulated since August 11 to the credit card company for payment.
      22   Wrote off the account of Ness City against the Allowance for Doubtful Accounts. The $398 balance in Ness City's account stemmed from a credit sale in November of last year.
      25   Received the amount due from Aztec.

Check Aug. 25, Dr. Cash $4,444

Required

Prepare journal entries to record the preceding transactions and events. (The company uses the perpetual inventory system. Round amounts to the nearest dollar.)

Crist Co. began operations on January 1, 2010, and completed several transactions during 2010 and 2011 that involved sales on credit, accounts receivable collections, and bad debts. These transactions are summarized as follows.

Problem 7-2B
Accounts receivable transactions and bad debts adjustments

C1   P2

2010

a. Sold $673,490 of merchandise (that had cost $500,000) on credit, terms n/30.
b. Received $437,250 cash in payment of accounts receivable.
c. Wrote off $8,330 of uncollectible accounts receivable.
d. In adjusting the accounts on December 31, the company estimated that 1% of accounts receivable will be uncollectible.

Check (d) Dr. Bad Debts Expense $10,609

2011

e. Sold $930,100 of merchandise (that had cost $650,000) on credit, terms n/30.
f. Received $890,220 cash in payment of accounts receivable.
g. Wrote off $10,090 of uncollectible accounts receivable.
h. In adjusting the accounts on December 31, the company estimated that 1% of accounts receivable will be uncollectible.

(h) Dr. Bad Debts Expense $10,388

Required

Prepare journal entries to record Crist's 2010 and 2011 summarized transactions and its year-end adjusting entry to record bad debts expense. (The company uses the perpetual inventory system. Round amounts to the nearest dollar.)

At December 31, 2011, Klimek Company reports the following results for the year.

Problem 7-3B
Estimating and reporting bad debts

P2

Cash sales	$1,015,000
Credit sales	1,241,000

In addition, its unadjusted trial balance includes the following items.

Accounts receivable	$475,000 debit
Allowance for doubtful accounts	5,200 credit

Required

1. Prepare the adjusting entry for Klimek Co. to recognize bad debts under each of the following independent assumptions.

   a. Bad debts are estimated to be 2.5% of credit sales.

   b. Bad debts are estimated to be 1.5% of total sales.

   c. An aging analysis estimates that 6% of year-end accounts receivable are uncollectible.

2. Show how Accounts Receivable and the Allowance for Doubtful Accounts appear on its December 31, 2011, balance sheet given the facts in part 1*a*.

3. Show how Accounts Receivable and the Allowance for Doubtful Accounts appear on its December 31, 2011, balance sheet given the facts in part 1*c*.

Check   Bad debts expense:
(1*b*) $33,840, (1*c*) $23,300

Problem 7-4B

Aging accounts receivable and accounting for bad debts

P2

Quisp Company has credit sales of $3.5 million for year 2011. At December 31, 2011, the company's Allowance for Doubtful Accounts has an unadjusted debit balance of $4,100. Quisp prepares a schedule of its December 31, 2011, accounts receivable by age. On the basis of past experience, it estimates the percent of receivables in each age category that will become uncollectible. This information is summarized here.

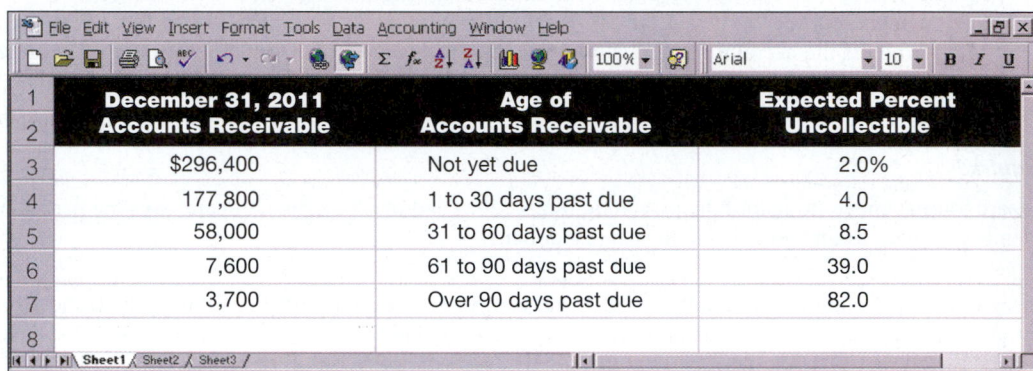

December 31, 2011 Accounts Receivable	Age of Accounts Receivable	Expected Percent Uncollectible
$296,400	Not yet due	2.0%
177,800	1 to 30 days past due	4.0
58,000	31 to 60 days past due	8.5
7,600	61 to 90 days past due	39.0
3,700	Over 90 days past due	82.0

Required

1. Compute the required balance of the Allowance for Doubtful Accounts at December 31, 2011, using the aging of accounts receivable method.

2. Prepare the adjusting entry to record bad debts expense at December 31, 2011.

Check   (2) Dr. Bad Debts Expense
$28,068

Analysis Component

3. On July 31, 2012, Quisp concludes that a customer's $2,345 receivable (created in 2011) is uncollectible and that the account should be written off. What effect will this action have on Quisp's 2012 net income? Explain.

Problem 7-5B

Analyzing and journalizing notes receivable transactions

C2 C3 P3

The following selected transactions are from Seeker Company.

2010

Nov.   1   Accepted a $4,800, 90-day, 8% note dated this day in granting Julie Stephens a time extension on her past-due account receivable.

Dec. 31   Made an adjusting entry to record the accrued interest on the Stephens note.

2011

Jan. 30   Received Stephens's payment for principal and interest on the note dated November 1.

Feb. 28   Accepted a $12,600, 6%, 30-day note dated this day in granting a time extension on the past-due account receivable from Kramer Co.

Mar.   1   Accepted a $6,200, 60-day, 8% note dated this day in granting Shelly Myers a time extension on her past-due account receivable.

      30   The Kramer Co. dishonored its note when presented for payment.

April 30   Received payment of principal plus interest from Myers for the March 1 note.

June 15   Accepted a $2,000, 60-day, 10% note dated this day in granting a time extension on the past-due account receivable of Rhonda Rye.

      21   Accepted a $9,500, 90-day, 12% note dated this day in granting J. Striker a time extension on his past-due account receivable.

Aug. 14   Received payment of principal plus interest from R. Rye for the note of June 15.

Sep. 19   Received payment of principal plus interest from J. Striker for the June 21 note.

Nov. 30   Wrote off Kramer's account against Allowance for Doubtful Accounts.

Check   Jan. 30, Cr. Interest
Revenue $32

April 30, Cr. Interest
Revenue $83

Sep. 19, Cr. Interest
Revenue $285

Required

1. Prepare journal entries to record these transactions and events. (Round amounts to the nearest dollar.)

Analysis Component

2. What reporting is necessary when a business pledges receivables as security for a loan and the loan is still outstanding at the end of the period? Explain the reason for this requirement and the accounting principle being satisfied.

SERIAL PROBLEM
Business Solutions
P1 P2

(This serial problem began in Chapter 1 and continues through most of the book. If previous chapter segments were not completed, the serial problem can begin at this point. It is helpful, but not necessary, to use the Working Papers that accompany the book.)

SP 7   Santana Rey, owner of Business Solutions, realizes that she needs to begin accounting for bad debts expense. Assume that Business Solutions has total revenues of $44,000 during the first three months of 2012, and that the Accounts Receivable balance on March 31, 2012, is $22,867.

Required

1. Prepare the adjusting entry needed for Business Solutions to recognize bad debts expense on March 31, 2012, under each of the following independent assumptions (assume a zero unadjusted balance in the Allowance for Doubtful Accounts at March 31).

  a. Bad debts are estimated to be 1% of total revenues. (Round amounts to the dollar.)

  b. Bad debts are estimated to be 2% of accounts receivable. (Round amounts to the dollar.)

2. Assume that Business Solutions' Accounts Receivable balance at June 30, 2012, is $20,250 and that one account of $100 has been written off against the Allowance for Doubtful Accounts since March 31, 2012. If S. Rey uses the method prescribed in Part 1b, what adjusting journal entry must be made to recognize bad debts expense on June 30, 2012?

3. Should S. Rey consider adopting the direct write-off method of accounting for bad debts expense rather than one of the allowance methods considered in part 1? Explain.

Check (2) Bad Debts Expense, $48

Beyond the Numbers

BTN 7-1 Refer to **Research In Motion**'s financial statements in Appendix A to answer the following.
1. What is the amount of Research In Motion's accounts receivable as of February 27, 2010?
2. Compute Research In Motion's accounts receivable turnover as of February 27, 2010.
3. How long does it take, *on average*, for the company to collect receivables? Do you believe that customers actually pay the amounts due within this short period? Explain.
4. Research In Motion's most liquid assets include (*a*) cash and cash equivalents, (*b*) short-term investments, and (*c*) receivables. Compute the percentage that these liquid assets make up of current liabilities as of February 27, 2010. Do the same computations for February 28, 2009. Comment on the company's ability to satisfy its current liabilities as of its 2010 fiscal year-end compared to its 2009 fiscal year-end.
5. What criteria did Research In Motion use to classify items as cash equivalents?

Fast Forward

6. Access Research In Motion's financial statements for fiscal years after February 27, 2010, at its Website (**www.RIM.com**) or the SEC's EDGAR database (**www.SEC.gov**). Recompute parts 2 and 4 and comment on any changes since February 27, 2010.

REPORTING IN ACTION
A1
RIM

BTN 7-2 Comparative figures for **Research In Motion** and **Apple** follow.

COMPARATIVE ANALYSIS
A1 P2
RIM
Apple

	Research In Motion			Apple		
($ millions)	Current Year	One Year Prior	Two Years Prior	Current Year	One Year Prior	Two Years Prior
Accounts receivable, net	$ 2,594	$ 2,112	$1,175	$ 3,361	$ 2,422	$ 1,637
Net sales	14,953	11,065	6,009	42,905	37,491	24,578

Required

1. Compute the accounts receivable turnover for Research In Motion and Apple for each of the two most recent years using the data shown.

2. Using results from part 1, compute how many days it takes each company, *on average,* to collect receivables. Compare the collection periods for RIM and Apple, and suggest at least one explanation for the difference.

3. Which company is more efficient in collecting its accounts receivable? Explain.

Hint: Average collection period equals 365 divided by the accounts receivable turnover.

ETHICS CHALLENGE

P2

BTN 7-3   Kelly Steinman is the manager of a medium-size company. A few years ago, Steinman persuaded the owner to base a part of her compensation on the net income the company earns each year. Each December she estimates year-end financial figures in anticipation of the bonus she will receive. If the bonus is not as high as she would like, she offers several recommendations to the accountant for year-end adjustments. One of her favorite recommendations is for the controller to reduce the estimate of doubtful accounts.

Required

1. What effect does lowering the estimate for doubtful accounts have on the income statement and balance sheet?

2. Do you believe Steinman's recommendation to adjust the allowance for doubtful accounts is within her right as manager, or do you believe this action is an ethics violation? Justify your response.

3. What type of internal control(s) might be useful for this company in overseeing the manager's recommendations for accounting changes?

COMMUNICATING IN PRACTICE

P2

BTN 7-4   As the accountant for Pure-Air Distributing, you attend a sales managers' meeting devoted to a discussion of credit policies. At the meeting, you report that bad debts expense is estimated to be $59,000 and accounts receivable at year-end amount to $1,750,000 less a $43,000 allowance for doubtful accounts. Sid Omar, a sales manager, expresses confusion over why bad debts expense and the allowance for doubtful accounts are different amounts. Write a one-page memorandum to him explaining why a difference in bad debts expense and the allowance for doubtful accounts is not unusual. The company estimates bad debts expense as 2% of sales.

TAKING IT TO THE NET

C1

BTN 7-5   Access **eBay**'s, February 17, 2010, filing of its 10-K report for the year ended December 31, 2009, at **www.sec.gov**.

Required

1. What is the amount of eBay's net accounts receivable at December 31, 2009, and at December 31, 2008?

2. "Financial Statement Schedule II" to its financial statements lists eBay's allowance for doubtful accounts (including authorized credits). For the two years ended December 31, 2009 and 2008, compute its allowance for doubtful accounts (including authorized credits) as a percent of gross accounts receivable.

3. Do you believe that these percentages are reasonable based on what you know about eBay? Explain.

TEAMWORK IN ACTION

P2

BTN 7-6   Each member of a team is to participate in estimating uncollectibles using the aging schedule and percents shown in Problem 7-4A. The division of labor is up to the team. Your goal is to accurately complete this task as soon as possible. After estimating uncollectibles, check your estimate with the instructor. If the estimate is correct, the team then should prepare the adjusting entry and the presentation of accounts receivable (net) for the December 31, 2011, balance sheet.

ENTREPRENEURIAL DECISION

C1

BTN 7-7   Bernard McCoy of **LaserMonks** is introduced in the chapter's opening feature. Bernard currently sells his products through multiple outlets. Assume that he is considering two new selling options.

Plan A. LaserMonks would begin selling additional products online directly to customers, which are only currently sold directly to outlet stores. These new online customers would use their credit cards. It currently has the capability of selling through its Website with no additional investment in hardware or software. Credit sales are expected to increase by $250,000 per year. Costs associated with this plan are: cost of these sales will be $135,500, credit card fees will be 4.75% of sales, and additional recordkeeping and shipping costs will be 6% of sales. These online sales will reduce the sales to stores by $35,000 because some customers will now purchase items online. Sales to stores have a 25% gross margin percentage.

Plan B. LaserMonks would expand its market to more outlet stores. It would make additional credit sales of $500,000 to those stores. Costs associated with those sales are: cost of sales will be $375,000, additional recordkeeping and shipping will be 4% of sales, and uncollectible accounts will be 6.2% of sales.

Required

1. Compute the additional annual net income or loss expected under (a) Plan A and (b) Plan B.
2. Should LaserMonks pursue either plan? Discuss both the financial and nonfinancial factors relevant to this decision.

Check (1*b*) Net income, $74,000

BTN 7-8 Many commercials include comments similar to the following: "We accept **VISA**" or "We do not accept **American Express**." Conduct your own research by contacting at least five companies via interviews, phone calls, or the Internet to determine the reason(s) companies discriminate in their use of credit cards. Collect information on the fees charged by the different cards for the companies contacted. (The instructor can assign this as a team activity.)

HITTING THE ROAD

C1

BTN 7-9 Key information from Nokia (www.Nokia.com), which is a leading global manufacturer of mobile devices and services, follows.

GLOBAL DECISION

C1 P2

NOKIA

RIM

Apple

EUR millions	Current Year	Prior Year
Accounts receivable, net*	7,981	9,444
Sales	40,984	50,710

*Nokia refers to it as "Accounts receivable, net of allowance for doubtful accounts."

1. Compute the accounts receivable turnover for the current year.
2. How long does it take on average for Nokia to collect receivables?
3. Refer to BTN 7-2. How does Nokia compare to Research In Motion and Apple in terms of its accounts receivable turnover and its collection period?
4. Nokia reports an aging analysis of its receivables, based on due dates, as follows (in EUR millions) as of December 31, 2009. Compute the percent of receivables in each category.

EUR millions	Total Receivables
Current	7,302
Past due 1–30 days	393
Past due 31–180 days	170
More than 180 days	116

ANSWERS TO MULTIPLE CHOICE QUIZ

1. d; Desired balance in Allowance for Doubtful Accounts = $ 5,026 cr.
   ($125,650 × 0.04)
   Current balance in Allowance for Doubtful Accounts = (328) cr.
   Bad Debts Expense to be recorded = $ 4,698
2. a; Desired balance in Allowance for Doubtful Accounts = $29,358 cr.
   ($489,300 × 0.06)
   Current balance in Allowance for Doubtful Accounts = 554 dr.
   Bad Debts Expense to be recorded = $29,912
3. a; $7,500 × 0.05 × 90/360 = $93.75

4. c; Principal amount $9,000
   Interest accrued . . . . 120 ($9,000 × 0.08 × 60/360)
   Maturity value $9,120
5. d; $489,600/$40,800 = 12

8

Long-Term Assets

A Look Back

Chapters 6 and 7 focused on short-term assets: cash, cash equivalents, and receivables. We explained why they are known as liquid assets and described how companies account and report for them.

A Look at This Chapter

This chapter introduces us to long-term assets. We explain how to account for a long-term asset's cost, the allocation of an asset's cost to periods benefiting from it, the recording of additional costs after an asset is purchased, and the disposal of an asset.

A Look Ahead

Chapter 9 focuses on current liabilities. We explain how they are computed, recorded, and reported in financial statements. We also explain the accounting for company payroll and contingencies.

Learning Objectives

CAP

CONCEPTUAL

C1 Explain the cost principle for computing the cost of plant assets. (p. 327)

C2 Explain depreciation for partial years and changes in estimates. (p. 334)

C3 Distinguish between revenue and capital expenditures, and account for them. (p. 336)

ANALYTICAL

A1 Compute total asset turnover and apply it to analyze a company's use of assets. (p. 345)

LP8

PROCEDURAL

P1 Compute and record depreciation using the straight-line, units-of-production, and declining-balance methods. (p. 330)

P2 Account for asset disposal through discarding or selling an asset. (p. 338)

P3 Account for natural resource assets and their depletion. (p. 340)

P4 Account for intangible assets. (p. 341)

P5 *Appendix 8A*—Account for asset exchanges. (p. 348)

Gaming Assets

"We want the average kid to have a party like a rock star"
—**DAVID PIKOFF**

AUSTIN, TX—Fun and games are the common bond for brothers Stuart and David Pikoff. That bond was also the driving force for an excursion into business. "We're both fun guys, we love kids, and we love games," explains David. "So we thought, 'Why not create our own game franchise?'" What they did was create **Games2U (Games2U.com),** a business focused on bringing fun and games to children and adults, using vans and trailers outfitted with state-of-the-art games and activities.

The brothers started operations by scraping up just enough money. However, long-term assets such as mobile vehicles outfitted with video games, large flat-screen displays, high-quality sound systems, and laser-light and fog machines for effects, are very expensive. David explains that financing such equipment, machinery, and similar assets is a struggle. "We would be much bigger, much quicker, if we didn't have that challenge." The owners had to work out depreciation schedules and estimate payback for different games and accessories.

Games2U is now rocking—employing nearly 20 workers, offering franchise agreements to others interested in mimicking their fun and games business, and generating several million in annual sales. Still, a constant challenge for the brothers is maintaining the right kind and amount of assets to meet people's demands and be profitable. "That made us hone in on product development," explains David. "How do we provide unique entertainment at your doorstep?" Games2U's success depends on monitoring and controlling those asset costs, which range from a mobile 4-D movie theater to decked-out trailers to a patented seven-foot tall kid-controlled robot.

Each of these tangible and intangible assets commands Stuart and David's attention. The brothers account for, manage, and focus on recovering all costs of these long-term assets. "We're never done," says David. "We're always challenging ourselves." Their success in asset management permits them to pursue further expansion and new ideas for gaming experiences. They have expanded into outdoor laser tag, human gyros, air cannons, and a version of capture-the-flag called "Booger Wars." "We have a unique concept, a solid infrastructure," explains David. "We provide unique entertainment."

[Sources: *Games2U Website,* January 2011; *Entrepreneur,* June 2009; *The Wall Street Journal,* March 2010; *Inc.com* October 2009; *The Monitor,* September 2009; *Franchise Update,* August 2009]

This chapter focuses on long-term assets, which can be grouped into plant assets, natural resource assets, and intangible assets. Plant assets make up a large part of assets on most balance sheets, and they yield depreciation, often one of the largest expenses on income statements. The acquisition or building of a plant asset is often referred to as a *capital expenditure*. Capital expenditures are important events because they impact both the short- and long-term success of a company. Natural resource assets and intangible assets have similar impacts. This chapter describes the purchase and use of these assets. We also explain what distinguishes these assets from other types of assets, how to determine their cost, how to allocate their costs to periods benefiting from their use, and how to dispose of them.

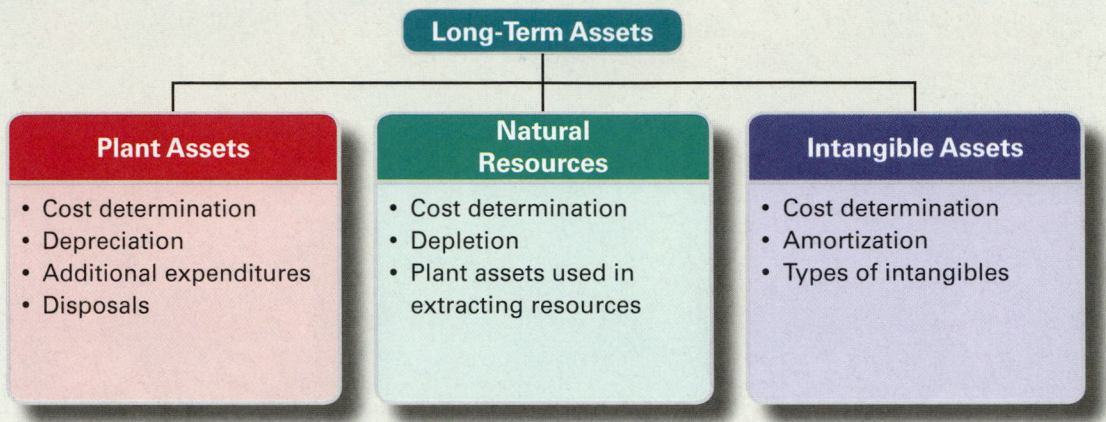

Long-Term Assets

Plant Assets
- Cost determination
- Depreciation
- Additional expenditures
- Disposals

Natural Resources
- Cost determination
- Depletion
- Plant assets used in extracting resources

Intangible Assets
- Cost determination
- Amortization
- Types of intangibles

Section 1—Plant Assets

Plant assets are tangible assets used in a company's operations that have a useful life of more than one accounting period. Plant assets are also called *plant and equipment; property, plant, and equipment;* or *fixed assets.* For many companies, plant assets make up the single largest class of assets they own. Exhibit 8.1 shows plant assets as a per-cent of total assets for several companies. Not only do they make up a large percent of many companies' assets, but their dollar values are large. **McDonald's** plant assets, for instance, are reported at more than $20 billion, and **Walmart** reports plant assets of more than $92 billion.

EXHIBIT 8.1

Plant Assets of Selected Companies

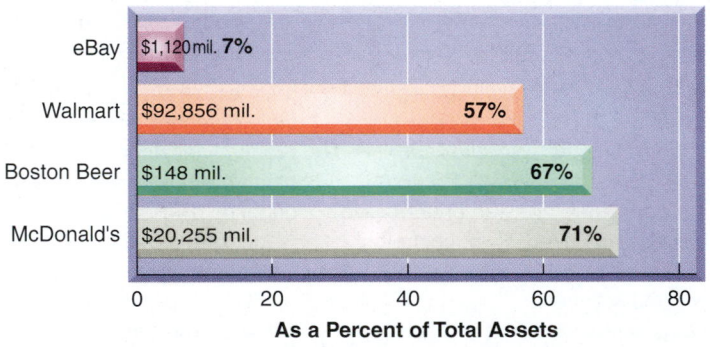

eBay $1,120 mil. **7%**

Walmart $92,856 mil. **57%**

Boston Beer $148 mil. **67%**

McDonald's $20,255 mil. **71%**

0   20   40   60   80

As a Percent of Total Assets

Plant assets are set apart from other assets by two important features. First, *plant assets are used in operations.* This makes them different from, for instance, inventory that is held for sale and not used in operations. The distinctive feature here is use, not type of asset. A company that purchases a computer to resell it reports it on the balance sheet as inventory. If the same company purchases this computer to use in operations, however, it is a plant asset. Another example is land held for future expansion, which is reported as a long-term investment. However, if this land holds a factory used in operations, the land is part of plant assets. Another example is equipment held for use in the event of a breakdown or for peak periods of production, which is reported in plant assets. If this same equipment is removed from use and held for sale, how-ever, it is not reported in plant assets.

The second important feature is that *plant assets have useful lives extending over more than one accounting period.* This makes plant assets different from current assets such as supplies that are normally consumed in a short time period after they are placed in use.

The accounting for plant assets reflects these two features. Since plant assets are used in operations, we try to match their costs against the revenues they generate. Also, since their useful lives extend over more than one period, our matching of costs and revenues must extend over several periods. Specifically, we value plant assets (balance sheet effect) and then, for many of them, we allocate their costs to periods benefiting from their use (income statement effect). An important exception is land; land cost is not allocated to expense when we expect it to have an indefinite life.

Exhibit 8.2 shows four main issues in accounting for plant assets: (1) computing the costs of plant assets, (2) allocating the costs of most plant assets (less any salvage amounts) against revenues for the periods they benefit, (3) accounting for expenditures such as repairs and improvements to plant assets, and (4) recording the disposal of plant assets. The following sections discuss these issues.

Point: It can help to view plant assets as prepaid expenses that benefit several future accounting periods.

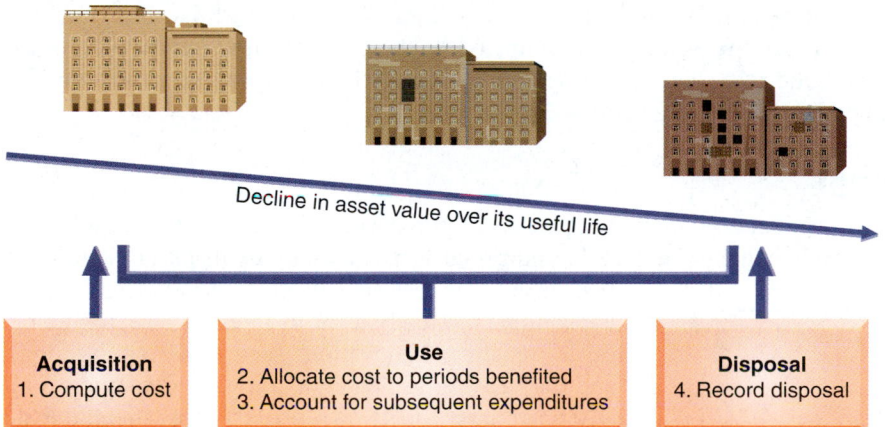

EXHIBIT 8.2

Issues in Accounting for Plant Assets

COST DETERMINATION

Plant assets are recorded at cost when acquired. This is consistent with the *cost principle.* **Cost** includes all normal and reasonable expenditures necessary to get the asset in place and ready for its intended use. The cost of a factory machine, for instance, includes its invoice cost less any cash discount for early payment, plus any necessary freight, unpacking, assembling, installing, and testing costs. Examples are the costs of building a base or foundation for a machine, providing electrical hookups, and testing the asset before using it in operations.

C1 Explain the cost principle for computing the cost of plant assets.

To be recorded as part of the cost of a plant asset, an expenditure must be normal, reasonable, and necessary in preparing it for its intended use. If an asset is damaged during unpacking, the repairs are not added to its cost. Instead, they are charged to an expense account. Nor is a paid traffic fine for moving heavy machinery on city streets without a proper permit part of the machinery's cost; but payment for a proper permit is included in the cost of machinery. Charges are sometimes incurred to modify or customize a new plant asset. These charges are added to the asset's cost. We explain in this section how to determine the cost of plant assets for each of its four major classes.

Land

When land is purchased for a building site, its cost includes the total amount paid for the land, including any real estate commissions, title insurance fees, legal fees, and any accrued property taxes paid by the purchaser. Payments for surveying, clearing, grading, and draining also are included in the cost of land. Other costs include government assessments, whether incurred at the time of purchase or later, for items such as public roadways, sewers, and sidewalks. These assessments are included because they permanently add to the land's value. Land purchased as a building site sometimes includes structures that must be removed. In such cases, the total purchase price is charged to the Land account as is the cost of removing the structures, less any amounts recovered through sale of salvaged materials. To illustrate, assume that **Starbucks** paid $167,000 cash to acquire land for a retail store. This land had an old service garage that was removed at a net cost of

EXHIBIT 8.3

Computing Cost of Land

Cash price of land	$ 167,000
Net cost of garage removal	13,000
Closing costs	10,000
Cost of land	**$190,000**

$13,000 ($15,000 in costs less $2,000 proceeds from salvaged materials). Additional closing costs total $10,000, consisting of brokerage fees ($8,000), legal fees ($1,500), and title costs ($500). The cost of this land to Starbucks is $190,000 and is computed as shown in Exhibit 8.3.

Land Improvements

Land has an indefinite (unlimited) life and is not usually used up over time. **Land improvements** such as parking lot surfaces, driveways, fences, shrubs, and lighting systems, however, have limited useful lives and are used up. While the costs of these improvements increase the usefulness of the land, they are charged to a separate Land Improvement account so that their costs can be allocated to the periods they benefit.

Buildings

A Building account is charged for the costs of purchasing or constructing a building that is used in operations. When purchased, a building's costs usually include its purchase price, brokerage

fees, taxes, title fees, and attorney fees. Its costs also include all expenditures to ready it for its intended use, including any necessary repairs or renovations such as wiring, lighting, flooring, and wall coverings. When a company constructs a building or any plant asset for its own use, its costs include materials and labor plus a reasonable amount of indirect overhead cost. Overhead includes the costs of items such as heat, lighting, power, and depreciation on machinery used to construct the asset. Costs of construction also include design fees, building permits, and insurance during construction. However, costs such as insurance to cover the asset *after* it is placed in use are operating expenses.

Machinery and Equipment

The costs of machinery and equipment consist of all costs normal and necessary to purchase them and prepare them for their intended use. These include the purchase price, taxes, transportation charges, insurance while in transit, and the installing, assembling, and testing of the machinery and equipment.

Lump-Sum Purchase

Example: If appraised values in Exhibit 8.4 are land, $24,000; land improvements, $12,000; and building, $84,000, what cost is assigned to the building? *Answer:*
(1) $24,000 + $12,000 + $84,000 = $120,000 (total appraisal)
(2) $84,000/$120,000 = 70% (building's percent of total)
(3) 70% × $90,000 = $63,000 (building's apportioned cost)

Plant assets sometimes are purchased as a group in a single transaction for a lump-sum price. This transaction is called a *lump-sum purchase,* or *group, bulk,* or *basket purchase.* When this occurs, we allocate the cost of the purchase among the different types of assets acquired based on their *relative market values,* which can be estimated by appraisal or by using the tax-assessed valuations of the assets. To illustrate, assume **CarMax** paid $90,000 cash to acquire a group of items consisting of land appraised at $30,000, land improvements appraised at $10,000, and a building appraised at $60,000. The $90,000 cost is allocated on the basis of these appraised values as shown in Exhibit 8.4.

EXHIBIT 8.4

Computing Costs in a Lump-Sum Purchase

	Appraised Value	Percent of Total	Apportioned Cost
Land	$ 30,000	30% ($30,000/$100,000)	**$27,000** ($90,000 × 30%)
Land improvements	10,000	10 ($10,000/$100,000)	**9,000** ($90,000 × 10%)
Building	60,000	60 ($60,000/$100,000)	**54,000** ($90,000 × 60%)
Totals	$100,000	100%	$ 90,000

Quick Check

Answers — p. 351

1. Identify the asset class for each of the following: (*a*) supplies, (*b*) office equipment, (*c*) inventory, (*d*) land for future expansion, and (*e*) trucks used in operations.
2. Identify the account charged for each of the following: (*a*) the purchase price of a vacant lot to be used in operations and (*b*) the cost of paving that same vacant lot.
3. Compute the amount recorded as the cost of a new machine given the following payments related to its purchase: gross purchase price, $700,000; sales tax, $49,000; purchase discount taken, $21,000; freight cost—terms FOB shipping point, $3,500; normal assembly costs, $3,000; cost of necessary machine platform, $2,500; cost of parts used in maintaining machine, $4,200.

DEPRECIATION

Depreciation is the process of allocating the cost of a plant asset to expense in the accounting periods benefiting from its use. Depreciation does not measure the decline in the asset's market value each period, nor does it measure the asset's physical deterioration. Since depreciation reflects the cost of using a plant asset, depreciation charges are only recorded when the asset is actually in service. This section describes the factors we must consider in computing depreciation, the depreciation methods used, revisions in depreciation, and depreciation for partial periods.

Factors in Computing Depreciation

Factors that determine depreciation are (1) cost, (2) salvage value, and (3) useful life.

Cost   The **cost** of a plant asset consists of all necessary and reasonable expenditures to acquire it and to prepare it for its intended use.

Salvage Value   The total amount of depreciation to be charged off over an asset's benefit period equals the asset's cost minus its salvage value. **Salvage value,** also called *residual value* or *scrap value,* is an estimate of the asset's value at the end of its benefit period. This is the amount the owner expects to receive from disposing of the asset at the end of its benefit period. If the asset is expected to be traded in on a new asset, its salvage value is the expected trade-in value.

Point: If we expect additional costs in preparing a plant asset for disposal, the salvage value equals the expected amount from disposal less any disposal costs.

Useful Life   The **useful life** of a plant asset is the length of time it is productively used in a company's operations. Useful life, also called *service life,* might not be as long as the asset's total productive life. For example, the productive life of a computer can be eight years or more. Some companies, however, trade in old computers for new ones every two years. In this case, these computers have a two-year useful life, meaning the cost of these computers (less their expected trade-in values) is charged to depreciation expense over a two-year period.

Point: Useful life and salvage value are estimates. Estimates require judgment based on all available information.

Several variables often make the useful life of a plant asset difficult to predict. A major variable is the wear and tear from use in operations. Two other variables, inadequacy and obsolescence, also require consideration. **Inadequacy** refers to the insufficient capacity of a company's plant assets to meet its growing productive demands. **Obsolescence** refers to the condition of a plant asset that is no longer useful in producing goods or services with a competitive advantage because of new inventions and improvements. Both inadequacy and obsolescence are difficult to predict because of demand changes, new inventions, and improvements. A company usually disposes of an inadequate or obsolete asset before it wears out.

A company is often able to better predict a new asset's useful life when it has past experience with a similar asset. When it has no such experience, a company relies on the experience of others or on engineering studies and judgment. In note 1 of its annual report, **Tootsie Roll**, a snack food manufacturer, reports the following useful lives:

Buildings	20–35 years
Machinery and Equipment	5–20 years

Decision Insight

Life Line   Life expectancy of plant assets is often in the eye of the beholder. For instance, **Hershey Foods** and **Tootsie Roll** are competitors and apply similar manufacturing processes, yet their equipment's life expectancies are different. Hershey depreciates equipment over 3 to 15 years, but Tootsie Roll depreciates them over 5 to 20 years. Such differences markedly impact financial statements. ■

Depreciation Methods

P1 Compute and record depreciation using the straight-line, units-of-production, and declining-balance methods.

Depreciation methods are used to allocate a plant asset's cost over the accounting periods in its useful life. The most frequently used method of depreciation is the straight-line method. Another common depreciation method is the units-of-production method. We explain both of these methods in this section. This section also describes accelerated depreciation methods, with a focus on the declining-balance method.

The computations in this section use information about a machine that inspects athletic shoes before packaging. Manufacturers such as **Converse**, **Reebok**, **adidas**, and **Fila** use this machine. Data for this machine are in Exhibit 8.5.

EXHIBIT 8.5

Data for Athletic Shoe-Inspecting Machine

Cost	$10,000
Salvage value	1,000
Depreciable cost	$ 9,000
Useful life	
Accounting periods	5 years
Units inspected	36,000 shoes

Straight-Line Method   **Straight-line depreciation** charges the same amount of expense to each period of the asset's useful life. A two-step process is used. We first compute the *depreciable cost* of the asset, also called the *cost to be depreciated*. It is computed by subtracting the asset's salvage value from its total cost. Second, depreciable cost is divided by the number of accounting periods in the asset's useful life. The formula for straight-line depreciation, along with its computation for the inspection machine just described, is shown in Exhibit 8.6.

EXHIBIT 8.6

Straight-Line Depreciation Formula and Example

$$\frac{\text{Cost} - \text{Salvage value}}{\text{Useful life in periods}} = \frac{\$10,000 - \$1,000}{5 \text{ years}} = \$1,800 \text{ per year}$$

If this machine is purchased on December 31, 2010, and used throughout its predicted useful life of five years, the straight-line method allocates an equal amount of depreciation to each of the years 2011 through 2015. We make the following adjusting entry at the end of each of the five years to record straight-line depreciation of this machine.

Assets	=	Liabilities	+	Equity
−1,800				−1,800

Dec. 31	Depreciation Expense	1,800	
	Accumulated Depreciation—Machinery		1,800
	To record annual depreciation.		

Example: If the salvage value of the machine is $2,500, what is the annual depreciation? *Answer:* ($10,000 − $2,500)/5 years = $1,500

The $1,800 Depreciation Expense is reported on the income statement among operating expenses. The $1,800 Accumulated Depreciation is a contra asset account to the Machinery account in the balance sheet. The graph on the left in Exhibit 8.7 shows the $1,800 per year expenses reported in each of the five years. The graph on the right shows the amounts reported on each of the six December 31 balance sheets.

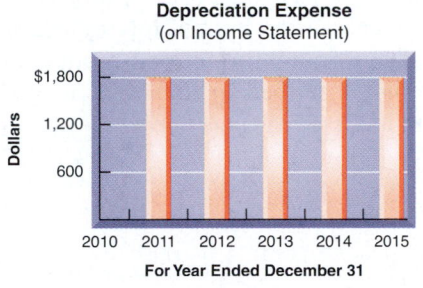

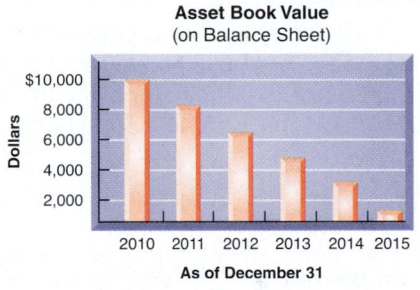

EXHIBIT 8.7

Financial Statement Effects of Straight-Line Depreciation

The net balance sheet amount is the **asset book value,** or simply *book value,* and is computed as the asset's total cost less its accumulated depreciation. For example, at the end of year 2 (December 31, 2012), its book value is $6,400 and is reported in the balance sheet as follows:

Machinery	$10,000	
Less accumulated depreciation	3,600	$6,400

The book value of this machine declines by $1,800 each year due to depreciation. From the graphs in Exhibit 8.7 we can see why this method is called straight-line.

We also can compute the *straight-line depreciation rate,* defined as 100% divided by the number of periods in the asset's useful life. For the inspection machine, this rate is 20% (100% ÷ 5 years, or 1/5 per period). We use this rate, along with other information, to compute the machine's *straight-line depreciation schedule* shown in Exhibit 8.8. Note three points in this exhibit. First, depreciation expense is the same each period. Second, accumulated depreciation is the sum of current and prior periods' depreciation expense. Third, book value declines each period until it equals salvage value at the end of the machine's useful life.

Point: Depreciation requires estimates for salvage value and useful life. Ethics are relevant when managers might be tempted to choose estimates to achieve desired results on financial statements.

	Depreciation for the Period			End of Period	
Annual Period	**Depreciable Cost***	**Depreciation Rate**	**Depreciation Expense**	**Accumulated Depreciation**	**Book Value†**
2010	—	—	—	—	$10,000
2011	$9,000	20%	**$1,800**	$1,800	8,200
2012	9,000	20	**1,800**	3,600	6,400
2013	9,000	20	**1,800**	5,400	4,600
2014	9,000	20	**1,800**	7,200	2,800
2015	9,000	20	**1,800**	9,000	**1,000**

EXHIBIT 8.8

Straight-Line Depreciation Schedule

* $10,000 − $1,000.   † Book value is total cost minus accumulated depreciation.

Units-of-Production Method   The straight-line method charges an equal share of an asset's cost to each period. If plant assets are used up in about equal amounts each accounting period, this method produces a reasonable matching of expenses with revenues. However, the use of some plant assets varies greatly from one period to the next. A builder, for instance, might use a piece of construction equipment for a month and then not use it again for several months. When equipment use varies from period to period, the units-of-production depreciation method can better match expenses with revenues. **Units-of-production depreciation** charges a varying amount to expense for each period of an asset's useful life depending on its usage.

A two-step process is used to compute units-of-production depreciation. We first compute *depreciation per unit* by subtracting the asset's salvage value from its total cost and then dividing by the total number of units expected to be produced during its useful life. Units of production can be expressed in product or other units such as hours used or miles driven. The second step is to compute depreciation expense for the period by multiplying the units produced in the period by the depreciation per unit. The formula for units-of-production depreciation, along with its computation for the machine described in Exhibit 8.5, is shown in Exhibit 8.9. (7,000 shoes are inspected and sold in its first year.)

EXHIBIT 8.9

Units-of-Production Depreciation Formula and Example

Step 1

$$\text{Depreciation per unit} = \frac{\text{Cost} - \text{Salvage value}}{\text{Total units of production}} = \frac{\$10,000 - \$1,000}{36,000 \text{ shoes}} = \$0.25 \text{ per shoe}$$

Step 2

$$\text{Depreciation expense} = \text{Depreciation per unit} \times \text{Units produced in period}$$
$$\$0.25 \text{ per shoe} \times 7,000 \text{ shoes} = \$1,750$$

Using data on the number of shoes inspected by the machine, we can compute the *units-of-production depreciation schedule* shown in Exhibit 8.10. For example, depreciation for the first year is $1,750 (7,000 shoes at $0.25 per shoe). Depreciation for the second year is $2,000 (8,000 shoes at $0.25 per shoe). Other years are similarly computed. Exhibit 8.10 shows that (1) depreciation expense depends on unit output, (2) accumulated depreciation is the sum of current and prior periods' depreciation expense, and (3) book value declines each period until it equals salvage value at the end of the asset's useful life. **Deltic Timber** is one of many companies using the units-of-production depreciation method. It reports that depreciation "is calculated over the estimated useful lives of the assets by using the units of production method for machinery and equipment."

Example: Refer to Exhibit 8.10. If the number of shoes inspected in 2015 is 5,500, what is depreciation for 2015? *Answer:* $1,250 (never depreciate below salvage value)

EXHIBIT 8.10

Units-of-Production Depreciation Schedule

Annual Period	Number of Units	Depreciation per Unit	Depreciation Expense	Accumulated Depreciation	Book Value
2010	—	—	—	—	$10,000
2011	7,000	$0.25	$1,750	$1,750	8,250
2012	8,000	0.25	2,000	3,750	6,250
2013	9,000	0.25	2,250	6,000	4,000
2014	7,000	0.25	1,750	7,750	2,250
2015	5,000	0.25	1,250	9,000	1,000

Declining-Balance Method   An **accelerated depreciation method** yields larger depreciation expenses in the early years of an asset's life and less depreciation in later years. The most common accelerated method is the **declining-balance method** of depreciation, which uses a depreciation rate that is a multiple of the straight-line rate and applies it to the asset's beginning-of-period book value. The amount of depreciation declines each period because book value declines each period.

A common depreciation rate for the declining-balance method is double the straight-line rate. This is called the *double-declining-balance (DDB)* method. This method is applied in three steps: (1) compute the asset's straight-line depreciation rate, (2) double the straight-line rate, and (3) compute depreciation expense by multiplying this rate by the asset's beginning-of-period book value. To illustrate, let's return to the machine in Exhibit 8.5 and apply the double-declining-balance method to compute depreciation expense. Exhibit 8.11 shows the first-year depreciation computation for the machine. The three-step process is to (1) divide 100% by five years to determine the straight-line rate of 20%, or 1/5, per year, (2) double this 20% rate to get the

Point: In the DDB method, *double* refers to the rate and *declining balance* refers to book value. The rate is applied to beginning book value each period.

declining-balance rate of 40%, or 2/5, per year, and (3) compute depreciation expense as 40%, or 2/5, multiplied by the beginning-of-period book value.

EXHIBIT 8.11

Double-Declining-Balance
Depreciation Formula*

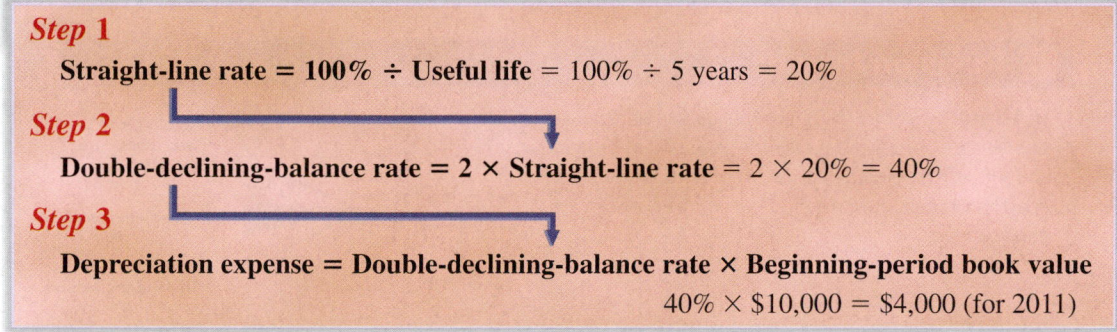

Step 1

   Straight-line rate = 100% ÷ Useful life = 100% ÷ 5 years = 20%

Step 2

   Double-declining-balance rate = 2 × Straight-line rate = 2 × 20% = 40%

Step 3

   Depreciation expense = Double-declining-balance rate × Beginning-period book value
   40% × $10,000 = $4,000 (for 2011)

* To simplify: DDB depreciation = (2 × Beginning-period book value)/Useful life.

The *double-declining-balance depreciation schedule* is shown in Exhibit 8.12. The schedule follows the formula except for year 2015, when depreciation expense is $296. This $296 is not equal to 40% × $1,296, or $518.40. If we had used the $518.40 for depreciation expense in 2015, the ending book value would equal $777.60, which is less than the $1,000 salvage value. Instead, the $296 is computed by subtracting the $1,000 salvage value from the $1,296 book value at the beginning of the fifth year (the year when DDB depreciation cuts into salvage value).

Example: What is the DDB depreciation expense in year 2014 if the salvage value is $2,000?
Answer: $2,160 − $2,000 = $160

EXHIBIT 8.12

Double-Declining-Balance
Depreciation Schedule

	Depreciation for the Period			End of Period	
Annual Period	**Beginning of Period Book Value**	**Depreciation Rate**	**Depreciation Expense**	**Accumulated Depreciation**	**Book Value**
2010	—	—	—	—	$10,000
2011	$10,000	40%	**$4,000**	$4,000	6,000
2012	6,000	40	**2,400**	6,400	3,600
2013	3,600	40	**1,440**	7,840	2,160
2014	2,160	40	**864**	8,704	1,296
2015	1,296	40	**296***	9,000	**1,000**

* Year 2015 depreciation is $1,296 − $1,000 = $296 (never depreciate book value below salvage value).

Comparing Depreciation Methods   Exhibit 8.13 shows depreciation expense for each year of the machine's useful life under each of the three depreciation methods. While depreciation expense per period differs for different methods, total depreciation expense of $9,000 is the same over the machine's useful life.

EXHIBIT 8.13

Depreciation Expense for the
Different Methods

	Period	Straight-Line	Units-of-Production	Double-Declining-Balance
1	**Period**	**Straight-Line**	**Units-of-Production**	**Double-Declining-Balance**
2	2011	$1,800	$1,750	$4,000
3	2012	1,800	2,000	2,400
4	2013	1,800	2,250	1,440
5	2014	1,800	1,750	864
6	2015	1,800	1,250	296
7	Totals	**$9,000**	**$9,000**	**$9,000**
8				

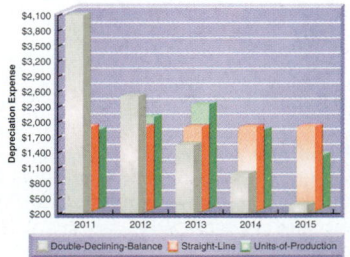

Each method starts with a total cost of $10,000 and ends with a salvage value of $1,000. The difference is the pattern in depreciation expense over the useful life. The book value of the asset when using straight-line is always greater than the book value from using double-declining-balance, except at the beginning and end of the asset's useful life, when it is the same. Also, the straight-line method yields a steady pattern of depreciation expense while the units-of-production depreciation depends on the number of units produced. Each of these methods is acceptable because it allocates cost in a systematic and rational manner.

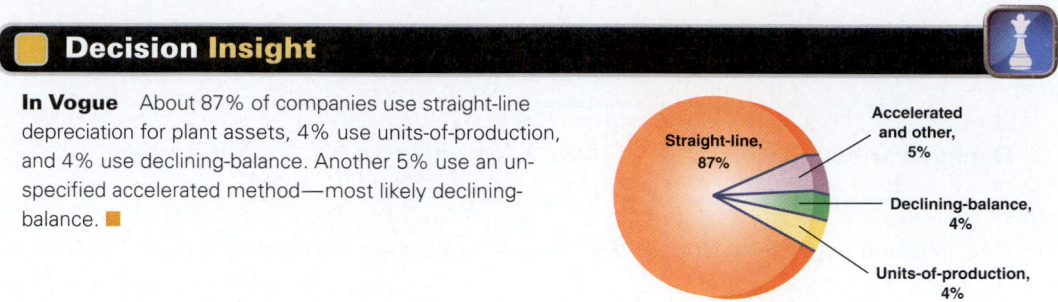

Decision Insight

In Vogue About 87% of companies use straight-line depreciation for plant assets, 4% use units-of-production, and 4% use declining-balance. Another 5% use an unspecified accelerated method—most likely declining-balance. ■

Straight-line, 87%

Accelerated and other, 5%

Declining-balance, 4%

Units-of-production, 4%

Depreciation for Tax Reporting The records a company keeps for financial accounting purposes are usually separate from the records it keeps for tax accounting purposes. This is so because financial accounting aims to report useful information on financial performance and position, whereas tax accounting reflects government objectives in raising revenues. Differences between these two accounting systems are normal and expected. Depreciation is a common example of how the records differ. For example, many companies use accelerated depreciation in computing taxable income. Reporting higher depreciation expense in the early years of an asset's life reduces the company's taxable income in those years and increases it in later years, when the depreciation expense is lower. The company's goal here is to *postpone* its tax payments.

The U.S. federal income tax law has rules for depreciating assets. These rules include the **Modified Accelerated Cost Recovery System (MACRS),** which allows straight-line depreciation for some assets but requires accelerated depreciation for most kinds of assets. MACRS separates depreciable assets into different classes and defines the depreciable life and rate for each class. MACRS is *not* acceptable for financial reporting because it often allocates costs over an arbitrary period that is less than the asset's useful life and it fails to estimate salvage value. Details of MACRS are covered in tax accounting courses.

Partial-Year Depreciation

Plant assets are purchased and disposed of at various times. When an asset is purchased (or disposed of) at a time other than the beginning or end of an accounting period, depreciation is recorded for part of a year. This is done so that the year of purchase or the year of disposal is charged with its share of the asset's depreciation.

To illustrate, assume that the machine in Exhibit 8.5 is purchased and placed in service on October 8, 2010, and the annual accounting period ends on December 31. Since this machine is purchased and used for nearly three months in 2010, the calendar-year income statement should report depreciation expense on the machine for that part of the year. Normally, depreciation assumes that the asset is purchased on the first day of the month nearest the actual date of purchase. In this case, since the purchase occurred on October 8, we assume an October 1 purchase date. This means that three months' depreciation is recorded in 2010. Using straight-line depreciation, we compute three months' depreciation of $450 as follows.

$$\frac{\$10,000 - \$1,000}{5 \text{ years}} \times \frac{3}{12} = \$450$$

A similar computation is necessary when an asset disposal occurs during a period. To illustrate, assume that the machine is sold on June 24, 2015. Depreciation is recorded for the period January 1 through June 24 when it is disposed of. This partial year's depreciation, computed to the nearest whole month, is

$$\frac{\$10,000 - \$1,000}{5 \text{ years}} \times \frac{6}{12} = \$900$$

Change in Estimates for Depreciation

Depreciation is based on estimates of salvage value and useful life. During the useful life of an asset, new information may indicate that these estimates are inaccurate. If our estimate of an asset's useful life and/or salvage value changes, what should we do? The answer is to use the new estimate to compute depreciation for current and future periods. This means that we revise the depreciation expense computation by spreading the cost yet to be depreciated over the remaining useful life. This approach is used for all depreciation methods.

Let's return to the machine described in Exhibit 8.8 using straight-line depreciation. At the beginning of this asset's third year, its book value is $6,400, computed as $10,000 minus $3,600. Assume that at the beginning of its third year, the estimated number of years remaining in its useful life changes from three to four years *and* its estimate of salvage value changes from $1,000 to $400. Straight-line depreciation for each of the four remaining years is computed as shown in Exhibit 8.14.

$$\frac{\text{Book value} - \text{Revised salvage value}}{\text{Revised remaining useful life}} = \frac{\$6,400 - \$400}{4 \text{ years}} = \$1,500 \text{ per year}$$

Thus, $1,500 of depreciation expense is recorded for the machine at the end of the third through sixth years—each year of its remaining useful life. Since this asset was depreciated at $1,800 per year for the first two years, it is tempting to conclude that depreciation expense was overstated in the first two years. However, these expenses reflected the best information available at that time. We do not go back and restate prior years' financial statements for this type of new information. Instead, we adjust the current and future periods' statements to reflect this new information. Revising an estimate of the useful life or salvage value of a plant asset is referred to as a **change in an accounting estimate** and is reflected in current and future financial statements, not in prior statements.

Reporting Depreciation

Both the cost and accumulated depreciation of plant assets are reported on the balance sheet or in its notes. **Dale Jarrett Racing Adventure**, for instance, reports the following.

Office furniture and equipment	$ 54,593
Shop and track equipment	202,973
Race vehicles and other	975,084
Property and equipment, gross	1,232,650
Less accumulated depreciation	628,355
Property and equipment, net	$ 604,295

Many companies also show plant assets on one line with the net amount of cost less accumulated depreciation. When this is done, the amount of accumulated depreciation is disclosed in a note. **Apple** reports only the net amount of its property, plant and equipment in its balance sheet in Appendix A. To satisfy the full-disclosure principle, Apple describes its depreciation methods in its Note 1 and the amounts comprising plant assets in its Note 5—see its 10-K at **www.SEC.gov**.

Reporting both the cost and accumulated depreciation of plant assets helps users compare the assets of different companies. For example, a company holding assets costing $50,000 and accumulated depreciation of $40,000 is likely in a situation different from a company with new assets costing $10,000. While the net undepreciated cost of $10,000 is the same in both cases, the first company may have more productive capacity available but likely is facing the need to replace older assets. These insights are not provided if the two balance sheets report only the $10,000 book values.

Users must remember that plant assets are reported on a balance sheet at their undepreciated costs (book value), not at fair (market) values. This emphasis on costs rather than fair values is based on the *going-concern assumption* described in Chapter 1. This assumption states that, unless there is evidence to the contrary, we assume that a company continues in business. This implies

Point: Remaining depreciable cost equals book value less revised salvage value at the point of revision.

Point: Income is overstated (and depreciation understated) when useful life is too high; when useful life is too low, the opposite results.

EXHIBIT 8.14

Computing Revised Straight-Line Depreciation

Example: If at the beginning of its second year the machine's remaining useful life changes from four to three years and salvage value from $1,000 to $400, how much straight-line depreciation is recorded in remaining years?
Answer: Revised depreciation = ($8,200 − $400)/3 = $2,600.

Point: A company usually keeps records for each asset showing its cost and depreciation to date. The combined records for individual assets are a type of *plant asset subsidiary ledger.*

that plant assets are held and used long enough to recover their cost through the sale of products and services. Because plant assets are not for sale, their fair values are not reported. An exception is when there is a *permanent decline* in the fair value of an asset relative to its book value, called an asset **impairment.** In this case the company writes the asset down to this fair value (details for the two-step process for assessing and computing the impairment loss are in advanced courses).

Accumulated Depreciation is a contra asset account with a normal credit balance. It does *not* reflect funds accumulated to buy new assets when the assets currently owned are replaced. If a company has funds available to buy assets, the funds are shown on the balance sheet among liquid assets such as Cash or Investments.

Decision Ethics

Answer — p. 350

Controller You are the controller for a struggling company. Its operations require regular investments in equipment, and depreciation is its largest expense. Its competitors frequently replace equipment—often depreciated over three years. The company president instructs you to revise useful lives of equipment from three to six years and to use a six-year life on all new equipment. What actions do you take? ◼

Quick Check

Answers — p. 351

4. On January 1, 2011, a company pays $77,000 to purchase office furniture with a zero salvage value. The furniture's useful life is somewhere between 7 and 10 years. What is the year 2011 straight-line depreciation on the furniture using (*a*) a 7-year useful life and (*b*) a 10-year useful life?

5. What does the term *depreciation* mean in accounting?

6. A company purchases a machine for $96,000 on January 1, 2011. Its useful life is five years or 100,000 units of product, and its salvage value is $8,000. During 2011, 10,000 units of product are produced. Compute the book value of this machine on December 31, 2011, assuming (*a*) straight-line depreciation and (*b*) units-of-production depreciation.

7. In early January 2011, a company acquires equipment for $3,800. The company estimates this equipment to have a useful life of three years and a salvage value of $200. Early in 2013, the company changes its estimates to a total four-year useful life and zero salvage value. Using the straight-line method, what is depreciation for the year ended 2013?

ADDITIONAL EXPENDITURES

 C3 Distinguish between revenue and capital expenditures, and account for them.

After a company acquires a plant asset and puts it into service, it often makes additional expenditures for that asset's operation, maintenance, repair, and improvement. In recording these expenditures, it must decide whether to capitalize or expense them (to capitalize an expenditure is to debit the asset account). The issue is whether these expenditures are reported as current period expenses or added to the plant asset's cost and depreciated over its remaining useful life.

Revenue expenditures, also called *income statement expenditures,* are additional costs of plant assets that do not materially increase the asset's life or productive capabilities. They are recorded as expenses and deducted from revenues in the current period's income statement. Examples of revenue expenditures are cleaning, repainting, adjustments, and lubricants. **Capital expenditures,** also called *balance sheet expenditures,* are additional costs of plant assets that provide benefits extending beyond the current period. They are debited to asset accounts and reported on the balance sheet. Capital expenditures increase or improve the type or amount of service an asset provides. Examples are roofing replacement, plant expansion, and major overhauls of machinery and equipment.

Financial statements are affected for several years by the accounting choice of recording costs as either revenue expenditures or capital expenditures. This decision is based on whether the expenditures are identified as ordinary repairs or as betterments and extraordinary repairs.

	Financial Statement Effect	
	Accounting	**Expense Timing**
Revenue expenditure	Income stmt. account debited	Expensed currently
Capital expenditure	Balance sheet account debited	Expensed in future

Ordinary Repairs

Ordinary repairs are expenditures to keep an asset in normal, good operating condition. They are necessary if an asset is to perform to expectations over its useful life. Ordinary repairs do not extend an asset's useful life beyond its original estimate or increase its productivity beyond original expectations. Examples are normal costs of cleaning, lubricating, adjusting, and replacing small parts of a machine. Ordinary repairs are treated as *revenue expenditures.* This means their costs are reported as expenses on the current period income statement. Following this rule, **Brunswick** reports that "maintenance and repair costs are expensed as incurred." If Brunswick's current year repair costs are $9,500, it makes the following entry.

Point: Many companies apply the *materiality constraint* to treat *low-cost plant assets* (say, less than $500) as revenue expenditures. This practice is referred to as a "capitalization policy."

Dec. 31	Repairs Expense	9,500	
	Cash		9,500
	To record ordinary repairs of equipment.		

Assets = Liabilities + Equity
−9,500   −9,500

Betterments and Extraordinary Repairs

Accounting for betterments and extraordinary repairs is similar—both are treated as *capital expenditures.*

Betterments (Improvements)   **Betterments,** also called *improvements,* are expenditures that make a plant asset more efficient or productive. A betterment often involves adding a component to an asset or replacing one of its old components with a better one, and does not always increase an asset's useful life. An example is replacing manual controls on a machine with automatic controls. One special type of betterment is an *addition,* such as adding a new wing or dock to a warehouse. Since a betterment benefits future periods, it is debited to the asset account as a capital expenditure. The new book value (less salvage value) is then depreciated over the asset's remaining useful life. To illustrate, suppose a company pays $8,000 for a machine with an eight-year useful life and no salvage value. After three years and $3,000 of depreciation, it adds an automated control system to the machine at a cost of $1,800. This results in reduced labor costs in future periods. The cost of the betterment is added to the Machinery account with this entry.

Example: Assume a firm owns a Web server. Identify each cost as a revenue or capital expenditure: (1) purchase price, (2) necessary wiring, (3) platform for operation, (4) circuits to increase capacity, (5) cleaning after each month of use, (6) repair of a faulty switch, and (7) replaced a worn fan. *Answer:* Capital expenditures: 1, 2, 3, 4; revenue expenditures: 5, 6, 7.

Jan. 2	Machinery	1,800	
	Cash		1,800
	To record installation of automated system.		

Assets = Liabilities + Equity
+1,800
−1,800

After the betterment is recorded, the remaining cost to be depreciated is $6,800, computed as $8,000 − $3,000 + $1,800. Depreciation expense for the remaining five years is $1,360 per year, computed as $6,800/5 years.

Point: Both extraordinary repairs and betterments require revising future depreciation.

Extraordinary Repairs (Replacements)   **Extraordinary repairs** are expenditures extending the asset's useful life beyond its original estimate. Extraordinary repairs are *capital expenditures* because they benefit future periods. Their costs are debited to the asset account (or to accumulated depreciation). For example, **Delta Air Lines** reports, "modifications that ... extend the useful lives of airframes or engines are capitalized and amortized [depreciated] over the remaining estimated useful life of the asset."

 **Decision Maker**   Answer — p. 351

Entrepreneur   Your start-up Internet services company needs cash, and you are preparing financial statements to apply for a short-term loan. A friend suggests that you treat as many expenses as possible as capital expenditures. What are the impacts on financial statements of this suggestion? What do you think is the aim of this suggestion? ■

DISPOSALS OF PLANT ASSETS

Plant assets are disposed of for several reasons. Some are discarded because they wear out or become obsolete. Others are sold because of changing business plans. Regardless of the reason, disposals of plant assets occur in one of three basic ways: discarding, sale, or exchange. The general steps in accounting for a disposal of plant assets are described in Exhibit 8.15.

EXHIBIT 8.15

Accounting for Disposals of Plant Assets

1. Record depreciation up to the date of disposal—this also updates Accumulated Depreciation.
2. Record the removal of the disposed asset's account balances—including its Accumulated Depreciation.
3. Record any cash (and/or other assets) received or paid in the disposal.
4. Record any gain or loss—computed by comparing the disposed asset's book value with the market value of any assets received.*

* An exception to step 4 is the case of an exchange that lacks *commercial substance*—see Appendix 8A.

Discarding Plant Assets

P2 Account for asset disposal through discarding or selling an asset.

A plant asset is *discarded* when it is no longer useful to the company and it has no market value. To illustrate, assume that a machine costing $9,000 with accumulated depreciation of $9,000 is discarded. When accumulated depreciation equals the asset's cost, it is said to be *fully depreciated* (zero book value). The entry to record the discarding of this asset is

Assets = Liabilities + Equity
+9,000
−9,000

June 5	Accumulated Depreciation—Machinery	9,000	
	Machinery		9,000
	To discard fully depreciated machinery.		

This entry reflects all four steps of Exhibit 8.15. Step 1 is unnecessary since the machine is fully depreciated. Step 2 is reflected in the debit to Accumulated Depreciation and credit to Machinery. Since no other asset is involved, step 3 is irrelevant. Finally, since book value is zero and no other asset is involved, no gain or loss is recorded in step 4.

How do we account for discarding an asset that is not fully depreciated or one whose depreciation is not up-to-date? To answer this, consider equipment costing $8,000 with accumulated depreciation of $6,000 on December 31 of the prior fiscal year-end. This equipment is being depreciated using the straight-line method over eight years with zero salvage. On July 1 of the current year it is discarded. Step 1 is to bring depreciation up-to-date.

Point: Recording depreciation expense up-to-date gives an up-to-date book value for determining gain or loss.

Assets = Liabilities + Equity
−500   −500

July 1	Depreciation Expense	500	
	Accumulated Depreciation—Equipment		500
	To record 6 months' depreciation ($1,000 × 6/12).		

Steps 2 through 4 of Exhibit 8.15 are reflected in the second (and final) entry.

Assets = Liabilities + Equity
+6,500   −1,500
−8,000

July 1	Accumulated Depreciation—Equipment	6,500	
	Loss on Disposal of Equipment	1,500	
	Equipment		8,000
	To discard equipment with a $1,500 book value.		

Point: Gain or loss is determined by comparing "value given" (book value) to "value received."

This loss is computed by comparing the equipment's $1,500 book value ($8,000 − $6,000 − $500) with the zero net cash proceeds. The loss is reported in the Other Expenses and Losses section of the income statement. Discarding an asset can sometimes require a cash payment that would increase the loss.

Selling Plant Assets

Companies often sell plant assets when they restructure or downsize operations. To illustrate the accounting for selling plant assets, we consider BTO's March 31 sale of equipment that cost $16,000 and has accumulated depreciation of $12,000 at December 31 of the prior calendar year-end. Annual depreciation on this equipment is $4,000 computed using straight-line depreciation. Step 1 of this sale is to record depreciation expense and update accumulated depreciation to March 31 of the current year.

March 31	Depreciation Expense	1,000	
	Accumulated Depreciation—Equipment		1,000
	To record 3 months' depreciation ($4,000 × 3/12).		

Assets	= Liabilities +	Equity
−1,000		−1,000

Steps 2 through 4 of Exhibit 8.15 can be reflected in one final entry that depends on the amount received from the asset's sale. We consider three different possibilities.

Sale at Book Value If BTO receives $3,000 cash, an amount equal to the equipment's book value as of March 31 (book value = $16,000 − $12,000 − $1,000), no gain or loss occurs on disposal. The entry is

 Sale price = Book value → No gain or loss

March 31	Cash	3,000	
	Accumulated Depreciation—Equipment	13,000	
	Equipment		16,000
	To record sale of equipment for no gain or loss.		

Assets	= Liabilities +	Equity
+3,000		
+13,000		
−16,000		

Sale above Book Value If BTO receives $7,000, an amount that is $4,000 above the equipment's $3,000 book value as of March 31, a gain on disposal occurs. The entry is

 Sale price > Book value → Gain

March 31	Cash	7,000	
	Accumulated Depreciation—Equipment	13,000	
	Gain on Disposal of Equipment		4,000
	Equipment		16,000
	To record sale of equipment for a $4,000 gain.		

Assets	= Liabilities +	Equity
+7,000		+4,000
+13,000		
−16,000		

Sale below Book Value If BTO receives $2,500, an amount that is $500 below the equipment's $3,000 book value as of March 31, a loss on disposal occurs. The entry is

Sale price < Book value → Loss

March 31	Cash	2,500	
	Loss on Disposal of Equipment	500	
	Accumulated Depreciation—Equipment	13,000	
	Equipment		16,000
	To record sale of equipment for a $500 loss.		

Assets	= Liabilities +	Equity
+2,500		−500
+13,000		
−16,000		

 **IFRS**

Unlike U.S. GAAP, IFRS requires an annual review of useful life and salvage value estimates. IFRS also permits revaluation of plant assets to market value if market value is reliably determined. ∎

Quick Check
Answers — p. 351

8. Early in the fifth year of a machine's six-year useful life, it is overhauled, and its useful life is extended to nine years. This machine originally cost $108,000 and the overhaul cost is $12,000. Prepare the entry to record the overhaul cost.

9. Explain the difference between revenue expenditures and capital expenditures and how both are recorded.

10. What is a betterment? How is a betterment recorded?

11. A company acquires equipment on January 10, 2011, at a cost of $42,000. Straight-line depreciation is used with a five-year life and $7,000 salvage value. On June 27, 2012, the company sells this equipment for $32,000. Prepare the entry(ies) for June 27, 2012.

Section 2—Natural Resources

P3	Account for natural resource assets and their depletion.

Natural resources are assets that are physically consumed when used. Examples are standing timber, mineral deposits, and oil and gas fields. Since they are consumed when used, they are often called *wasting assets*. These assets represent soon-to-be inventories of raw materials that will be converted into one or more products by cutting, mining, or pumping. Until that conversion takes place, they are noncurrent assets and are shown in a balance sheet using titles such as timberlands, mineral deposits, or oil reserves. Natural resources are reported under either plant assets or their own separate category. **Alcoa**, for instance, reports its natural resources under the balance sheet title *Properties, plants and equipment*. In a note to its financial statements, Alcoa reports a separate amount for *Land and land rights, including mines.* **Weyerhaeuser**, on the other hand, reports its timber holdings in a separate balance sheet category titled *Timber and timberlands*.

Cost Determination and Depletion

Natural resources are recorded at cost, which includes all expenditures necessary to acquire the resource and prepare it for its intended use. **Depletion** is the process of allocating the cost of a natural resource to the period when it is consumed. Natural resources are reported on the balance sheet at cost less *accumulated depletion*. The depletion expense per period is usually based on units extracted from cutting, mining, or pumping. This is similar to units-of-production depreciation. **Exxon Mobil** uses this approach to amortize the costs of discovering and operating its oil wells.

To illustrate depletion of natural resources, let's consider a mineral deposit with an estimated 250,000 tons of available ore. It is purchased for $500,000, and we expect zero salvage value. The depletion charge per ton of ore mined is $2, computed as $500,000 ÷ 250,000 tons. If 85,000 tons are mined and sold in the first year, the depletion charge for that year is $170,000. These computations are detailed in Exhibit 8.16.

EXHIBIT 8.16

Depletion Formula and Example

Step 1

$$\text{Depletion per unit} = \frac{\text{Cost} - \text{Salvage value}}{\text{Total units of capacity}} = \frac{\$500,000 - \$0}{250,000 \text{ tons}} = \$2 \text{ per ton}$$

Step 2

$$\text{Depletion expense} = \text{Depletion per unit} \times \text{Units extracted and sold in period}$$
$$= \$2 \times 85,000 = \$170,000$$

Depletion expense for the first year is recorded as follows.

Assets	=	Liabilities	+	Equity
−170,000				−170,000

Dec. 31	Depletion Expense—Mineral Deposit	170,000	
	Accumulated Depletion—Mineral Deposit		170,000
	To record depletion of the mineral deposit.		

The period-end balance sheet reports the mineral deposit as shown in Exhibit 8.17.

EXHIBIT 8.17

Balance Sheet Presentation of Natural Resources

Mineral deposit	$500,000	
Less accumulated depletion	**170,000**	$330,000

Since all 85,000 tons of the mined ore are sold during the year, the entire $170,000 of depletion is reported on the income statement. If some of the ore remains unsold at year-end, however, the depletion related to the unsold ore is carried forward on the balance sheet and reported as

Ore Inventory, a current asset. To illustrate, and continuing with our example, assume that 40,000 tons are mined in the second year, but only 34,000 tons are sold. We record depletion of $68,000 (34,000 tons × $2 depletion per unit) and the remaining Ore Inventory of $12,000 (6,000 tons × $2 depletion per unit) as follows.

Dec. 31	Depletion Expense—Mineral Deposit	68,000	
	Ore Inventory	12,000	
	Accumulated Depletion—Mineral Deposit		80,000
	To record depletion and inventory of mineral deposit.		

Assets = Liabilities + Equity
−80,000   −68,000
+12,000

Plant Assets Used in Extracting

The conversion of natural resources by mining, cutting, or pumping usually requires machinery, equipment, and buildings. When the usefulness of these plant assets is directly related to the depletion of a natural resource, their costs are depreciated using the units-of-production method in proportion to the depletion of the natural resource. For example, if a machine is permanently installed in a mine and 10% of the ore is mined and sold in the period, then 10% of the machine's cost (less any salvage value) is allocated to depreciation expense. The same procedure is used when a machine is abandoned once resources have been extracted. If, however, a machine will be moved to and used at another site when extraction is complete, the machine is depreciated over its own useful life.

Decision Insight

Asset Control   Long-term assets must be safeguarded against theft, misuse, and other damages. Controls take many forms depending on the asset, including use of security tags, the legal monitoring of rights infringements, and approvals of all asset disposals. A study reports that 44% of employees in operations and service areas witnessed the wasting, mismanaging, or abusing of assets in the past year (KPMG 2009). Another 21% in general management and administration observed stealing or misappropriation of assets. ■

Section 3—Intangible Assets

Intangible assets are nonphysical assets (used in operations) that confer on their owners long-term rights, privileges, or competitive advantages. Examples are patents, copyrights, licenses, leaseholds, franchises, goodwill, and trademarks. Lack of physical substance does not necessarily imply an intangible asset. Notes and accounts receivable, for instance, lack physical substance, but they are not intangibles. This section identifies the more common types of intangible assets and explains the accounting for them.

P4 Account for intangible assets.

Cost Determination and Amortization

An intangible asset is recorded at cost when purchased. Intangibles are then separated into those with limited lives or indefinite lives. If an intangible has a **limited life,** its cost is systematically allocated to expense over its estimated useful life through the process of **amortization.** If an intangible asset has an **indefinite life**—meaning that no legal, regulatory, contractual, competitive, economic, or other factors limit its useful life—it should not be amortized. (If an intangible with an indefinite life is later judged to have a limited life, it is amortized over that limited life.) Amortization of intangible assets is similar to depreciation of plant assets and the depletion of natural resources in that it is a process of cost allocation. However, only the straight-line method is used for amortizing intangibles *unless* the company can show that another method is preferred. The effects of amortization are recorded in a contra account (Accumulated Amortization). The gross acquisition cost of intangible assets is disclosed in the balance sheet along with their accumulated amortization (these disclosures are new). The eventual disposal of an intangible asset involves removing its book value, recording any other asset(s) received or given up, and recognizing any gain or loss for the difference.

Many intangibles have limited lives due to laws, contracts, or other asset characteristics. Examples are patents, copyrights, and leaseholds. Other intangibles such as goodwill, trademarks, and trade names have lives that cannot be easily determined. The cost of intangible assets is amortized over the periods expected to benefit by their use, but in no case can this period be longer than the asset's legal existence. The values of some intangible assets such as goodwill continue indefinitely into the future and are not amortized. (An intangible asset that is not amortized is tested annually for **impairment**—if necessary, an impairment loss is recorded. Details for this test are in advanced courses.)

Intangible assets are often shown in a separate section of the balance sheet immediately after plant assets. **Callaway Golf**, for instance, follows this approach in reporting nearly $150 million of intangible assets in its balance sheet. Companies usually disclose their amortization periods for intangibles. The remainder of our discussion focuses on accounting for specific types of intangible assets.

Types of Intangibles

Patents   The federal government grants patents to encourage the invention of new technology, mechanical devices, and production processes. A **patent** is an exclusive right granted to its owner to manufacture and sell a patented item or to use a process for 20 years. When patent rights are purchased, the cost to acquire the rights is debited to an account called Patents. If the owner engages in lawsuits to successfully defend a patent, the cost of lawsuits is debited to the Patents account. However, the costs of research and development leading to a new patent are expensed when incurred.

A patent's cost is amortized over its estimated useful life (not to exceed 20 years). If we purchase a patent costing $25,000 with a useful life of 10 years, we make the following adjusting entry at the end of each of the 10 years to amortize one-tenth of its cost.

Assets = Liabilities + Equity
−2,500   −2,500

Dec. 31	Amortization Expense—Patents	2,500	
	Accumulated Amortization—Patents		2,500
	To amortize patent costs over its useful life.		

The $2,500 debit to Amortization Expense appears on the income statement as a cost of the product or service provided under protection of the patent. The Accumulated Amortization—Patents account is a contra asset account to Patents.

Decision Insight

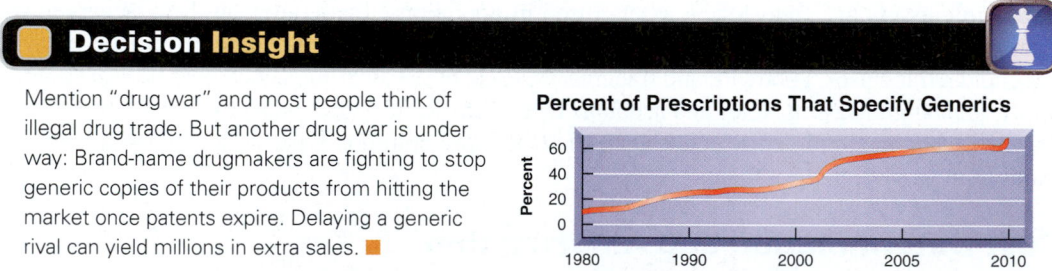

Mention "drug war" and most people think of illegal drug trade. But another drug war is under way: Brand-name drugmakers are fighting to stop generic copies of their products from hitting the market once patents expire. Delaying a generic rival can yield millions in extra sales. ■

Percent of Prescriptions That Specify Generics

Copyrights   A **copyright** gives its owner the exclusive right to publish and sell a musical, literary, or artistic work during the life of the creator plus 70 years, although the useful life of most copyrights is much shorter. The costs of a copyright are amortized over its useful life. The only identifiable cost of many copyrights is the fee paid to the Copyright Office of the federal government or international agency granting the copyright. If this fee is immaterial, it is charged directly to an expense account; but if the identifiable costs of a copyright are material, they are capitalized (recorded in an asset account) and periodically amortized by debiting an account called Amortization Expense—Copyrights.

Franchises and Licenses   **Franchises** and **licenses** are rights that a company or government grants an entity to deliver a product or service under specified conditions. Many organizations grant franchise and license rights—**McDonald's**, **Pizza Hut**, and **Major**

League Baseball are just a few examples. The costs of franchises and licenses are debited to a Franchises and Licenses asset account and are amortized over the lives of the agreements. If an agreement is for an indefinite or perpetual period, those costs are not amortized.

Trademarks and Trade Names   Companies often adopt unique symbols or select unique names and brands in marketing their products. A **trademark** or **trade (brand) name** is a symbol, name, phrase, or jingle identified with a company, product, or service. Examples are Nike swoosh, Marlboro Man, Big Mac, Coca-Cola, and Corvette. Ownership and exclusive right to use a trademark or trade name are often established by showing that one company used it before another. Ownership is best established by registering a trademark or trade name with the government's Patent Office. The cost of developing, maintaining, or enhancing the value of a trademark or trade name (such as advertising) is charged to expense when incurred. If a trademark or trade name is purchased, however, its cost is debited to an asset account and then amortized over its expected life. If the company plans to renew indefinitely its right to the trademark or trade name, the cost is not amortized.

Point: McDonald's "golden arches" are one of the world's most valuable trademarks, yet this asset is not shown on McDonald's balance sheet.

Goodwill   **Goodwill** has a specific meaning in accounting. Goodwill is the amount by which a company's value exceeds the value of its individual assets and liabilities. This usually implies that the company as a whole has certain valuable attributes not measured among its individual assets and liabilities. These can include superior management, skilled workforce, good supplier or customer relations, quality products or services, good location, or other competitive advantages.

To keep accounting information from being too subjective, goodwill is not recorded unless an entire company or business segment is purchased. Purchased goodwill is measured by taking the purchase price of the company and subtracting the market value of its individual net assets (excluding goodwill). For instance, **Yahoo!** paid nearly $3.0 billion to acquire **GeoCities**; about $2.8 of the $3.0 billion was for goodwill and other intangibles.

Goodwill is measured as the excess of the cost of an acquired entity over the value of the acquired net assets. Goodwill is recorded as an asset, and it is *not* amortized. Instead, goodwill is annually tested for impairment. If the book value of goodwill does not exceed its fair (market) value, goodwill is not impaired. However, if the book value of goodwill does exceed its fair value, an impairment loss is recorded equal to that excess. (Details of this test are in advanced courses.)

Point: Amortization of goodwill is different for financial accounting and tax accounting. The IRS requires the amortization of goodwill over 15 years.

Example: Assume goodwill carries a book value of $500 and has an implied fair value of $475, *and* this $25 decline in value meets the 2-step impairment test. The entry to record this impairment is:
Impairment Loss $25
  Goodwill $25

Leaseholds   Property is rented under a contract called a **lease**. The property's owner, called the **lessor,** grants the lease. The one who secures the right to possess and use the property is called the **lessee**. A **leasehold** refers to the rights the lessor grants to the lessee under the terms of the lease. A leasehold is an intangible asset for the lessee.

Certain leases require no advance payment from the lessee but require monthly rent payments. In this case, we do not set up a Leasehold account. Instead, the monthly payments are debited to a Rent Expense account. If a long-term lease requires the lessee to pay the final period's rent in advance when the lease is signed, the lessee records this advance payment with a debit to the Leasehold account. Since the advance payment is not used until the final period, the Leasehold account balance remains intact until that final period when its balance is transferred to Rent Expense. (Some long-term leases give the lessee essentially the same rights as a purchaser. This results in a tangible asset and a liability reported by the lessee. Chapter 10 describes these so-called *capital leases*.)

A long-term lease can increase in value when current rental rates for similar property rise while the required payments under the lease remain constant. This increase in value of a lease is not reported on the lessee's balance sheet. However, if the property is subleased and the new tenant makes a cash payment to the original lessee for the rights under the old lease, the new tenant debits this payment to a Leasehold account, which is amortized to Rent Expense over the remaining life of the lease.

Point: A leasehold account implies existence of future benefits that the lessee controls because of a prepayment. It also meets the definition of an asset.

Leasehold Improvements   A lessee sometimes pays for alterations or improvements to the leased property such as partitions, painting, and storefronts. These alterations and improvements are called **leasehold improvements,** and the lessee debits these costs to a Leasehold Improvements account. Since leasehold improvements become part of the property and revert to the lessor at the end of the lease, the lessee amortizes these costs over the life of the lease or the life of the improvements, whichever is shorter. The amortization entry debits

Amortization Expense—Leasehold Improvements and credits Accumulated Amortization—Leasehold Improvements.

Other Intangibles   There are other types of intangible assets such as *software, noncompete covenants, customer lists,* and so forth. Our accounting for them is the same. First, we record the intangible asset's costs. Second, we determine whether the asset has a limited or indefinite life. If limited, we allocate its costs over that period. If indefinite, its costs are not amortized.

Quick Check   Answers — p. 351

12. Give an example of a natural resource and of an intangible asset.
13. A company pays $650,000 for an ore deposit. The deposit is estimated to have 325,000 tons of ore that will be mined over the next 10 years. During the first year, it mined, processed, and sold 91,000 tons. What is that year's depletion expense?
14. On January 6, 2011, a company pays $120,000 for a patent with a remaining 17-year legal life to produce a toy expected to be marketable for three years. Prepare entries to record its acquisition and the December 31, 2011, amortization entry.

GLOBAL VIEW

This section discusses similarities and differences between U.S. GAAP and IFRS in accounting and reporting for plant assets and intangible assets.

Accounting for Plant Assets   Issues involving cost determination, depreciation, additional expenditures, and disposals of plant assets are subject to broadly similar guidance for both U.S. GAAP and IFRS. Although differences exist, the similarities vastly outweigh the differences. **Nokia** describes its accounting for plant assets as follows:

NOKIA

> Property, plant and equipment are stated at cost less accumulated depreciation. Depreciation is recorded on a straight-line basis over the expected useful lives of the assets. Maintenance, repairs and renewals are generally charged to expense during the financial period in which they are incurred. However, major renovations are capitalized and included in the carrying amount of the asset . . . Major renovations are depreciated over the remaining useful life of the related asset.

One area where notable differences exist is in accounting for changes in the value of plant assets (between the time they are acquired and when disposed of). Namely, how do IFRS and U.S. GAAP treat decreases and increases in the value of plant assets subsequent to acquisition?

Decreases in the Value of Plant Assets   When the value of plant assets declines after acquisition, but before disposition, both U.S. GAAP and IFRS require companies to record those decreases as *impairment losses*. While the *test for impairment* uses a different base between U.S. GAAP and IFRS, a more fundamental difference is that U.S. GAAP revalues impaired plant assets to *fair value* whereas IFRS revalues them to a *recoverable amount* (defined as fair value less costs to sell).

Increases in the Value of Plant Assets   U.S. GAAP prohibits companies from recording increases in the value of plant assets. However, IFRS permits upward *asset revaluations*. Namely, under IFRS, if an impairment was previously recorded, a company would reverse that impairment to the extent necessary and record that increase in income. If the increase is beyond the original cost, that increase is recorded in comprehensive income.

Accounting for Intangible Assets   For intangible assets, the accounting for cost determination, amortization, additional expenditures, and disposals is subject to broadly similar guidance for U.S. GAAP and IFRS. Although differences exist, the similarities vastly outweigh differences. Again, and consistent with the accounting for plant assets, U.S. GAAP and IFRS handle decreases and increases in the value of intangible assets differently. However, IFRS requirements for recording increases in the value of intangible assets are so restrictive that such increases are rare. **Nokia** describes its accounting for intangible assets as follows:

[Intangible assets] are capitalized and amortized using the straight-line method over their useful lives. Where an indication of impairment exists, the carrying amount of any intangible asset is assessed and written down to its recoverable amount.

NOKIA

Total Asset Turnover   **Decision Analysis**

A company's assets are important in determining its ability to generate sales and earn income. Managers devote much attention to deciding what assets a company acquires, how much it invests in assets, and how to use assets most efficiently and effectively. One important measure of a company's ability to use its assets is **total asset turnover,** defined in Exhibit 8.18.

A1 Compute total asset turnover and apply it to analyze a company's use of assets.

EXHIBIT 8.18

Total Asset Turnover

$$\text{Total asset turnover} = \frac{\text{Net sales}}{\text{Average total assets}}$$

The numerator reflects the net amounts earned from the sale of products and services. The denominator reflects the average total resources devoted to operating the company and generating sales.

To illustrate, let's look at total asset turnover in Exhibit 8.19 for two competing companies: **Molson Coors** and **Boston Beer**.

EXHIBIT 8.19

Analysis Using Total Asset Turnover

Company	Figure ($ millions)	2009	2008	2007	2006	2005
Molson Coors	Net sales	$ 3,032.4	$ 4,774.3	$ 6,190.6	$ 5,845.0	$ 5,506.9
	Average total assets	$11,203.9	$11,934.1	$12,527.5	$11,701.4	$ 8,228.4
	Total asset turnover	**0.27**	**0.40**	**0.49**	**0.50**	**0.67**
Boston Beer	Net sales	$ 415.053	$ 398.400	$ 341.647	$ 285.431	$238.304
	Average total assets	$ 241.347	$ 208.856	$ 176.215	$ 136.765	$113.258
	Total asset turnover	**1.72**	**1.91**	**1.94**	**2.09**	**2.10**

To show how we use total asset turnover, let's look at Molson Coors. We express Molson Coors's use of assets in generating net sales by saying "it turned its assets over 0.27 times during 2009." This means that each $1.00 of assets produced $0.27 of net sales. Is a total asset turnover of 0.27 good or bad? It is safe to say that all companies desire a high total asset turnover. Like many ratio analyses, however, a company's total asset turnover must be interpreted in comparison with those of prior years and of its competitors. Interpreting the total asset turnover also requires an understanding of the company's operations. Some operations are capital intensive, meaning that a relatively large amount is invested in assets to generate sales. This suggests a relatively lower total asset turnover. Other companies' operations are labor intensive, meaning that they generate sales more by the efforts of people than the use of assets. In that case, we expect a higher total asset turnover. Companies with low total asset turnover require higher profit margins (examples are hotels and real estate); companies with high total asset turnover can succeed with lower profit margins (examples are food stores and toy merchandisers). Molson Coors's turnover recently declined and is now much lower than that for Boston Beer and many other competitors. Total asset turnover for Molson Coors's competitors, available in industry publications such as Dun & Bradstreet, is generally in the range of 0.5 to 1.0 over this same period. Overall, Molson Coors must improve relative to its competitors on total asset turnover.

Total Asset Turnover: ☐ Molson Coors ☐ Boston Beer

Point: An estimate of **plant asset useful life** equals the plant asset cost divided by depreciation expense.

Point: The **plant asset age** is estimated by dividing accumulated depreciation by depreciation expense. Older plant assets can signal needed asset replacements; they may also signal less efficient assets.

■ **Decision Maker**   Answer — p. 351

Environmentalist   A paper manufacturer claims it cannot afford more environmental controls. It points to its low total asset turnover of 1.9 and argues that it cannot compete with companies whose total asset turnover is much higher. Examples cited are food stores (5.5) and auto dealers (3.8). How do you respond? ■

DEMONSTRATION PROBLEM

On July 14, 2011, Tulsa Company pays $600,000 to acquire a fully equipped factory. The purchase involves the following assets and information.

Asset	Appraised Value	Salvage Value	Useful Life	Depreciation Method
Land	$160,000			Not depreciated
Land improvements	80,000	$ 0	10 years	Straight-line
Building	320,000	100,000	10 years	Double-declining-balance
Machinery	240,000	20,000	10,000 units	Units-of-production*
Total	$800,000			

* The machinery is used to produce 700 units in 2011 and 1,800 units in 2012.

Required

1. Allocate the total $600,000 purchase cost among the separate assets.
2. Compute the 2011 (six months) and 2012 depreciation expense for each asset, and compute the company's total depreciation expense for both years.
3. On the last day of calendar year 2013, Tulsa discarded machinery that had been on its books for five years. The machinery's original cost was $12,000 (estimated life of five years) and its salvage value was $2,000. No depreciation had been recorded for the fifth year when the disposal occurred. Journalize the fifth year of depreciation (straight-line method) and the asset's disposal.
4. At the beginning of year 2013, Tulsa purchased a patent for $100,000 cash. The company estimated the patent's useful life to be 10 years. Journalize the patent acquisition and its amortization for the year 2013.
5. Late in the year 2013, Tulsa acquired an ore deposit for $600,000 cash. It added roads and built mine shafts for an additional cost of $80,000. Salvage value of the mine is estimated to be $20,000. The company estimated 330,000 tons of available ore. In year 2013, Tulsa mined and sold 10,000 tons of ore. Journalize the mine's acquisition and its first year's depletion.
6.^{A} On the first day of 2013, Tulsa exchanged the machinery that was acquired on July 14, 2011, along with $5,000 cash for machinery with a $210,000 market value. Journalize the exchange of these assets assuming the exchange lacked commercial substance. (Refer to background information in parts 1 and 2.)

PLANNING THE SOLUTION

- Complete a three-column table showing the following amounts for each asset: appraised value, percent of total value, and apportioned cost.
- Using allocated costs, compute depreciation for 2011 (only one-half year) and 2012 (full year) for each asset. Summarize those computations in a table showing total depreciation for each year.
- Remember that depreciation must be recorded up-to-date before discarding an asset. Calculate and record depreciation expense for the fifth year using the straight-line method. Since salvage value is not received at the end of a discarded asset's life, the amount of any salvage value becomes a loss on disposal. Record the loss on the disposal as well as the removal of the discarded asset and its related accumulated depreciation.
- Record the patent (an intangible asset) at its purchase price. Use straight-line amortization over its useful life to calculate amortization expense.
- Record the ore deposit (a natural resource asset) at its cost, including any added costs to ready the mine for use. Calculate depletion per ton using the depletion formula. Multiply the depletion per ton by the amount of tons mined and sold to calculate depletion expense for the year.
- Remember that gains and losses on asset exchanges that lack commercial substance are not recognized. Make a journal entry to add the acquired machinery to the books and to remove the old machinery, along with its accumulated depreciation, and to record the cash given in the exchange.

SOLUTION TO DEMONSTRATION PROBLEM

1. Allocation of the total cost of $600,000 among the separate assets.

Asset	Appraised Value	Percent of Total Value	Apportioned Cost
Land	$160,000	20%	**$120,000** ($600,000 × 20%)
Land improvements	80,000	10	**60,000** ($600,000 × 10%)
Building	320,000	40	**240,000** ($600,000 × 40%)
Machinery	240,000	30	**180,000** ($600,000 × 30%)
Total	$800,000	100%	$ 600,000

2. Depreciation for each asset. (Land is not depreciated.)

Land Improvements

Cost	$ 60,000
Salvage value	0
Depreciable cost	$ 60,000
Useful life	10 years
Annual depreciation expense ($60,000/10 years)	$ 6,000
2011 depreciation ($6,000 × 6/12)	**$ 3,000**
2012 depreciation	**$ 6,000**

Building

Straight-line rate = 100%/10 years = 10%	
Double-declining-balance rate = 10% × 2 = 20%	
2011 depreciation ($240,000 × 20% × 6/12)	**$ 24,000**
2012 depreciation [($240,000 − $24,000) × 20%]	**$ 43,200**

Machinery

Cost	$180,000
Salvage value	20,000
Depreciable cost	$160,000
Total expected units of production	10,000 units
Depreciation per unit ($160,000/10,000 units)	$ 16
2011 depreciation ($16 × 700 units)	**$ 11,200**
2012 depreciation ($16 × 1,800 units)	**$ 28,800**

Total depreciation expense for each year:

	2011	2012
Land improvements	$ 3,000	$ 6,000
Building	24,000	43,200
Machinery	11,200	28,800
Total	$38,200	$78,000

3. Record the depreciation up-to-date on the discarded asset.

Depreciation Expense—Machinery	2,000	
Accumulated Depreciation—Machinery		2,000
To record depreciation on date of disposal: ($12,000 − $2,000)/5		

Record the removal of the discarded asset and its loss on disposal.

Accumulated Depreciation—Machinery	10,000	
Loss on Disposal of Machinery	2,000	
Machinery		12,000
To record the discarding of machinery with a $2,000 book value.		

4.

Patent	100,000	
Cash		100,000
To record patent acquisition.		

Amortization Expense—Patent	10,000	
Accumulated Amortization—Patent		10,000
To record amortization expense: $100,000/10 years = $10,000.		

5.

Ore Deposit	680,000	
Cash		680,000
To record ore deposit acquisition and its related costs.		

Depletion Expense—Ore Deposit	20,000	
Accumulated Depletion—Ore Deposit		20,000
To record depletion expense: ($680,000 − $20,000)/330,000 tons =		
$2 per ton. 10,000 tons mined and sold × $2 = $20,000 depletion.		

6. Record the asset exchange: The book value on the exchange date is $180,000 (cost) − $40,000 (accumulated depreciation). The book value of the machinery given up in the exchange ($140,000) plus the $5,000 cash paid is less than the $210,000 value of the machine acquired. The entry to record this exchange of assets that lacks commercial substance does not recognize the $65,000 "gain."

Machinery (new)	145,000*	
Accumulated Depreciation—Machinery (old)	40,000	
Machinery (old)		180,000
Cash		5,000
To record asset exchange that lacks commercial substance.		

    * Market value of the acquired asset of $210,000 minus $65,000 "gain."

8A

Exchanging Plant Assets

P5A Account for asset exchanges.

Many plant assets such as machinery, automobiles, and office equipment are disposed of by exchanging them for newer assets. In a typical exchange of plant assets, a *trade-in allowance* is received on the old asset and the balance is paid in cash. Accounting for the exchange of assets depends on whether the transaction has *commercial substance* (per *SFAS 153,* commercial substance implies that it alters the company's future cash flows). If an asset exchange has commercial substance, a gain or loss is recorded based on the difference between the book value of the asset(s) given up and the market value of the asset(s) received. If an asset exchange lacks commercial substance, no gain or loss is recorded, and the asset(s) received is recorded based on the book value of the asset(s) given up. An exchange has commercial substance if the company's future cash flows change as a result of the transaction. This section describes the accounting for the exchange of assets.

Exchange with Commercial Substance: A Loss A company acquires $42,000 in new equipment. In exchange, the company pays $33,000 cash and trades in old equipment. The old equipment originally cost $36,000 and has accumulated depreciation of $20,000, which implies a $16,000 book value at the time of exchange. We are told this exchange has commercial substance and that the old equipment has a trade-in allowance of $9,000. This exchange yields a loss as computed in the middle (Loss) columns of Exhibit 8A.1; the loss is computed as Asset received − Assets given = $42,000 − $49,000 = $(7,000). We can also compute the loss as Trade-in allowance − Book value of asset given = $9,000 − $16,000 = $(7,000).

Asset Exchange Has Commercial Substance	Loss		Gain	
Market value of asset received		$42,000		$52,000
Book value of assets given:				
Equipment ($36,000 − $20,000)	$16,000		$16,000	
Cash	33,000	49,000	33,000	49,000
Gain (loss) on exchange		$(7,000)		$ 3,000

EXHIBIT 8A.1

Computing Gain or Loss on Asset Exchange with Commercial Substance

The entry to record this asset exchange is

Jan. 3	Equipment (**new**)...............................	42,000	
	Loss on Exchange of Assets	7,000	
	Accumulated Depreciation—Equipment (**old**)........	20,000	
	Equipment (**old**)		36,000
	Cash		33,000
	To record exchange (with commercial substance) of old equipment and cash for new equipment.		

Assets   =   Liabilities +   Equity
+42,000   −7,000
+20,000
−36,000
−33,000

Point: Parenthetical notes to "new" and "old" equipment are for illustration only. Both the debit and credit are to the same Equipment account.

Exchange with Commercial Substance: A Gain   Let's assume the same facts as in the preceding asset exchange *except* that the new equipment received has a market value of $52,000 instead of $42,000. We are told that this exchange has commercial substance and that the old equipment has a trade-in allowance of $19,000. This exchange yields a gain as computed in the right-most (Gain) columns of Exhibit 8A.1; the gain is computed as Asset received − Assets given = $52,000 − $49,000 = $3,000. We can also compute the gain as Trade-in allowance − Book value of asset given = $19,000 − $16,000 = $3,000. The entry to record this asset exchange is

Jan. 3	Equipment (**new**)	52,000	
	Accumulated Depreciation—Equipment (**old**)	20,000	
	Equipment (**old**)		36,000
	Cash		33,000
	Gain on Exchange of Assets		3,000
	To record exchange (with commercial substance) of old equipment and cash for new equipment.		

Assets   =   Liabilities +   Equity
+52,000   +3,000
+20,000
−36,000
−33,000

Exchanges without Commercial Substance   Let's assume the same facts as in the preceding asset exchange involving new equipment received with a market value of $52,000, but let's instead assume the transaction *lacks commercial substance*. The entry to record this asset exchange is

Jan. 3	Equipment (**new**)	49,000	
	Accumulated Depreciation—Equipment (**old**)	20,000	
	Equipment (**old**)		36,000
	Cash		33,000
	To record exchange (without commercial substance) of old equipment and cash for new equipment.		

Assets   =   Liabilities +   Equity
+49,000
+20,000
−36,000
−33,000

The $3,000 gain recorded when the transaction has commercial substance is *not* recognized in this entry because of the rule prohibiting recording a gain or loss on asset exchanges without commercial substance. The $49,000 recorded for the new equipment equals its cash price ($52,000) less the unrecognized gain ($3,000) on the exchange. The $49,000 cost recorded is called the *cost basis* of the new machine. This cost basis is the amount we use to compute depreciation and its book value. The cost basis of the new asset also can be computed by summing the book values of the assets given up as shown in Exhibit 8A.2. The same analysis and approach are taken for a loss on an asset exchange without commercial substance.

Point: No gain or loss is recorded for exchanges *without* commercial substance.

EXHIBIT 8A.2

Cost Basis of New Asset When Gain Not Recorded on Asset Exchange without Commercial Substance

Cost of old equipment	$ 36,000
Less accumulated depreciation	20,000
Book value of old equipment	16,000
Cash paid in the exchange	33,000
Cost recorded for new equipment	**$49,000**

Quick Check
Answer — p. 351

15. A company trades an old Web server for a new one. The cost of the old server is $30,000, and its accumulated depreciation at the time of the trade is $23,400. The new server has a cash price of $45,000. Prepare entries to record the trade under two different assumptions where the company receives a trade-in allowance of (a) $3,000 and the exchange has commercial substance, and (b) $7,000 and the exchange lacks commercial substance.

Summary

C1 Explain the cost principle for computing the cost of plant assets. Plant assets are set apart from other tangible assets by two important features: use in operations and useful lives longer than one period. Plant assets are recorded at cost when purchased. Cost includes all normal and reasonable expenditures necessary to get the asset in place and ready for its intended use. The cost of a lump-sum purchase is allocated among its individual assets.

C2 Explain depreciation for partial years and changes in estimates. Partial-year depreciation is often required because assets are bought and sold throughout the year. Depreciation is revised when changes in estimates such as salvage value and useful life occur. If the useful life of a plant asset changes, for instance, the remaining cost to be depreciated is spread over the remaining (revised) useful life of the asset.

C3 Distinguish between revenue and capital expenditures, and account for them. Revenue expenditures expire in the current period and are debited to expense accounts and matched with current revenues. Ordinary repairs are an example of revenue expenditures. Capital expenditures benefit future periods and are debited to asset accounts. Examples of capital expenditures are extraordinary repairs and betterments.

A1 Compute total asset turnover and apply it to analyze a company's use of assets. Total asset turnover measures a company's ability to use its assets to generate sales. It is defined as net sales divided by average total assets. While all companies desire a high total asset turnover, it must be interpreted in comparison with those for prior years and its competitors.

P1 Compute and record depreciation using the straight-line, units-of-production, and declining-balance methods. *Depreciation* is the process of allocating to expense the cost of a plant asset over the accounting periods that benefit from its use. Depreciation does not measure the decline in a plant asset's market value or its physical deterioration. Three factors determine depreciation:

cost, salvage value, and useful life. Salvage value is an estimate of the asset's value at the end of its benefit period. Useful (service) life is the length of time an asset is productively used. The straight-line method divides cost less salvage value by the asset's useful life to determine depreciation expense per period. The units-of-production method divides cost less salvage value by the estimated number of units the asset will produce over its life to determine depreciation per unit. The declining-balance method multiplies the asset's beginning-of-period book value by a factor that is often double the straight-line rate.

P2 Account for asset disposal through discarding or selling an asset. When a plant asset is discarded or sold, its cost and accumulated depreciation are removed from the accounts. Any cash proceeds from discarding or selling an asset are recorded and compared to the asset's book value to determine gain or loss.

P3 Account for natural resource assets and their depletion. The cost of a natural resource is recorded in a noncurrent asset account. Depletion of a natural resource is recorded by allocating its cost to depletion expense using the units-of-production method. Depletion is credited to an Accumulated Depletion account.

P4 Account for intangible assets. An intangible asset is recorded at the cost incurred to purchase it. The cost of an intangible asset with a definite useful life is allocated to expense using the straight-line method, and is called *amortization*. Goodwill and intangible assets with an indefinite useful life are not amortized—they are annually tested for impairment. Intangible assets include patents, copyrights, leaseholds, goodwill, and trademarks.

P5ᴬ Account for asset exchanges. For an asset exchange with commercial substance, a gain or loss is recorded based on the difference between the book value of the asset given up and the market value of the asset received. For an asset exchange without commercial substance, no gain or loss is recorded, and the asset received is recorded based on the book value of the asset given up.

Guidance Answers to Decision Maker and Decision Ethics

Controller   The president's instructions may reflect an honest and reasonable prediction of the future. Since the company is struggling financially, the president may have concluded that the normal pattern of replacing assets every three years cannot continue. Perhaps the strategy is to avoid costs of frequent replacements and stretch use of equipment a few years longer until financial conditions improve.

However, if you believe the president's decision is unprincipled, you might confront the president with your opinion that it is unethical to change the estimate to increase income. Another possibility is to wait and see whether the auditor will prohibit this change in estimate. In either case, you should insist that the statements be based on reasonable estimates.

Entrepreneur   Treating an expense as a capital expenditure means that reported expenses will be lower and income higher in the short run. This is so because a capital expenditure is not expensed immediately but is spread over the asset's useful life. Treating an expense as a capital expenditure also means that asset and equity totals are reported at larger amounts in the short run. This continues until the asset is fully depreciated. Your friend is probably trying to help, but the suggestion is misguided. Only an expenditure benefiting future periods is a capital expenditure.

Environmentalist   The paper manufacturer's comparison of its total asset turnover with food stores and auto dealers is misdirected. These other industries' turnovers are higher because their profit margins are lower (about 2%). Profit margins for the paper industry are usually 3% to 3.5%. You need to collect data from competitors in the paper industry to show that a 1.9 total asset turnover is about the norm for this industry. You might also want to collect data on this company's revenues and expenses, along with compensation data for its high-ranking officers and employees.

Guidance Answers to Quick Checks

1. **a.** Supplies—current assets
    b. Office equipment—plant assets
    c. Inventory—current assets
    d. Land for future expansion—long-term investments
    e. Trucks used in operations—plant assets
2. **a.** Land   **b.** Land Improvements
3. $700,000 + $49,000 − $21,000 + $3,500 + $3,000 + $2,500 = $737,000
4. **a.** Straight-line with 7-year life: ($77,000/7) = $11,000
    b. Straight-line with 10-year life: ($77,000/10) = $7,700
5. Depreciation is a process of allocating the cost of plant assets to the accounting periods that benefit from the assets' use.
6. **a.** Book value using straight-line depreciation:
    $96,000 − [($96,000 − $8,000)/5] = $78,400
    b. Book value using units of production:
    $96,000 − [($96,000 − $8,000) × (10,000/100,000)]
    = $87,200
7. ($3,800 − $200)/3 = $1,200 (original depreciation per year)
    $1,200 × 2 = $2,400 (accumulated depreciation)
    ($3,800 − $2,400)/2 = $700 (revised depreciation)

8.

Machinery	12,000	
Cash		12,000

9. A revenue expenditure benefits only the current period and should be charged to expense in the current period. A capital expenditure yields benefits that extend beyond the end of the current period and should be charged to an asset.
10. A betterment involves modifying an existing plant asset to make it more efficient, usually by replacing part of the asset with an improved or superior part. The cost of a betterment is debited to the asset account.

11.

Depreciation Expense	3,500	
Accumulated Depreciation		3,500

Cash	32,000	
Accumulated Depreciation	10,500	
Gain on Sale of Equipment		500
Equipment		42,000

12. Examples of natural resources are timberlands, mineral deposits, and oil reserves. Examples of intangible assets are patents, copyrights, leaseholds, leasehold improvements, goodwill, trademarks, and licenses.
13. ($650,000/325,000 tons) × 91,000 tons = $182,000

14.

Jan. 6	Patents		120,000	
	Cash			120,000
Dec. 31	Amortization Expense		40,000*	
	Accumulated			
	Amortization—Patents			40,000

* $120,000/3 years = $40,000.

15.

(a) Equipment (new)		45,000	
Loss on Exchange of Assets		3,600	
Accumulated Depreciation—Equipment (old)		23,400	
Equipment (old)			30,000
Cash ($45,000 − $3,000)			42,000

(b) Equipment (new)*		44,600	
Accumulated Depreciation—Equipment (old)		23,400	
Equipment (old)			30,000
Cash ($45,000 − $7,000)			38,000

* Includes $400 unrecognized gain.

Land improvements (p. 328)

Lease (p. 343)

Leasehold (p. 343)

Leasehold improvements (p. 343)

Lessee (p. 343)

Lessor (p. 343)

Licenses (p. 342)

Limited life (p. 341)

Modified Accelerated Cost Recovery System (MACRS) (p. 334)

Natural resources (p. 340)

Obsolescence (p. 329)

Ordinary repairs (p. 336)

Patent (p. 342)

Plant asset age (p. 345)

Plant assets (p. 326)

Revenue expenditures (p. 336)

Salvage value (p. 329)

Straight-line depreciation (p. 330)

Total asset turnover (p. 345)

Trademark or trade (brand) name (p. 343)

Units-of-production depreciation (p. 331)

Useful life (p. 329)

Multiple Choice Quiz   Answers on p. 365   mhhe.com/wildFINMAN4e

Additional Quiz Questions are available at the book's Website.

1. A company paid $326,000 for property that included land, land improvements, and a building. The land was appraised at $175,000, the land improvements were appraised at $70,000, and the building was appraised at $105,000. What is the allocation of property costs to the three assets purchased?
   a. Land, $150,000; Land Improvements, $60,000; Building, $90,000
   b. Land, $163,000; Land Improvements, $65,200; Building, $97,800
   c. Land, $150,000; Land Improvements, $61,600; Building, $92,400
   d. Land, $159,000; Land Improvements, $65,200; Building, $95,400
   e. Land, $175,000; Land Improvements, $70,000; Building, $105,000

2. A company purchased a truck for $35,000 on January 1, 2011. The truck is estimated to have a useful life of four years and an estimated salvage value of $1,000. Assuming that the company uses straight-line depreciation, what is the depreciation expense on the truck for the year ended December 31, 2012?
   a. $8,750
   b. $17,500
   c. $8,500
   d. $17,000
   e. $25,500

3. A company purchased machinery for $10,800,000 on January 1, 2011. The machinery has a useful life of 10 years and an estimated salvage value of $800,000. What is the depreciation expense on the machinery for the year ended December 31, 2012, assuming that the double-declining-balance method is used?
   a. $2,160,000
   b. $3,888,000
   c. $1,728,000
   d. $2,000,000
   e. $1,600,000

4. A company sold a machine that originally cost $250,000 for $120,000 when accumulated depreciation on the machine was $100,000. The gain or loss recorded on the sale of this machine is
   a. $0 gain or loss.
   b. $120,000 gain.
   c. $30,000 loss.
   d. $30,000 gain.
   e. $150,000 loss.

5. A company had average total assets of $500,000, gross sales of $575,000, and net sales of $550,000. The company's total asset turnover is
   a. 1.15
   b. 1.10
   c. 0.91
   d. 0.87
   e. 1.05

A   *Superscript letter A denotes assignments based on Appendix 8A.*

🔲 Icon denotes assignments that involve decision making.

Discussion Questions

1. 🔲 What characteristics of a plant asset make it different from other assets?
2. What is the general rule for cost inclusion for plant assets?
3. What is different between land and land improvements?
4. Why is the cost of a lump-sum purchase allocated to the individual assets acquired?

5. 🔲 Does the balance in the Accumulated Depreciation—Machinery account represent funds to replace the machinery when it wears out? If not, what does it represent?
6. Why is the Modified Accelerated Cost Recovery System not generally accepted for financial accounting purposes?

7. What accounting concept justifies charging low-cost plant asset purchases immediately to an expense account?

8. What is the difference between ordinary repairs and extraordinary repairs? How should each be recorded?

9. Identify events that might lead to disposal of a plant asset.

10. What is the process of allocating the cost of natural resources to expense as they are used?

11. Is the declining-balance method an acceptable way to compute depletion of natural resources? Explain.

12. What are the characteristics of an intangible asset?

13. What general procedures are applied in accounting for the acquisition and potential cost allocation of intangible assets?

14. When do we know that a company has goodwill? When can goodwill appear in a company's balance sheet?

15. Assume that a company buys another business and pays for its goodwill. If the company plans to incur costs each year to maintain the value of the goodwill, must it also amortize this goodwill?

16. How is total asset turnover computed? Why would a financial statement user be interested in total asset turnover?

17. Refer to **Research In Motion**'s balance sheet in Appendix A. What property, plant and equipment assets does RIM list on its balance sheet? What is the book value of its total net property, plant and equipment assets at February 27, 2010?   *RIM*

18. **Apple** lists its plant assets as "Property, plant and equipment, net." What does "net" mean in this title?   *Apple*

19. Refer to **Nokia**'s balance sheet in Appendix A. What does it title its plant assets? What is the book value of its plant assets at December 31, 2009?   **NOKIA**

20. Refer to the May 31, 2009, balance sheet of **Palm** in Appendix A. What long-term assets discussed in this chapter are reported by the company?   **Palm**

Mc Graw Hill connect

Strike Bowling installs automatic scorekeeping equipment with an invoice cost of $180,000. The electrical work required for the installation costs $8,000. Additional costs are $3,000 for delivery and $12,600 for sales tax. During the installation, a component of the equipment is carelessly left on a lane and hit by the automatic lane-cleaning machine. The cost of repairing the component is $2,250. What is the total recorded cost of the automatic scorekeeping equipment?

QUICK STUDY

QS 8-1
Cost of plant assets C1

Identify the main difference between (1) plant assets and inventory, (2) plant assets and current assets, and (3) plant assets and long-term investments.

QS 8-2
Defining assets C1

On January 2, 2011, the Crossover Band acquires sound equipment for concert performances at a cost of $55,900. The band estimates it will use this equipment for four years, during which time it anticipates performing about 120 concerts. It estimates that after four years it can sell the equipment for $1,900. During year 2011, the band performs 40 concerts. Compute the year 2011 depreciation using the straight-line method.

QS 8-3
Straight-line depreciation
P1

Refer to the information in QS 8-3. Compute the year 2011 depreciation using the units-of-production method.

QS 8-4
Units-of-production depreciation
P1

Refer to the facts in QS 8-3. Assume that the Crossover Band uses straight-line depreciation but realizes at the start of the second year that due to concert bookings beyond expectations, this equipment will last only a total of three years. The salvage value remains unchanged. Compute the revised depreciation for both the second and third years.

QS 8-5
Computing revised depreciation
C2

A fleet of refrigerated delivery trucks is acquired on January 5, 2011, at a cost of $930,000 with an estimated useful life of eight years and an estimated salvage value of $150,000. Compute the depreciation expense for the first three years using the double-declining-balance method.

QS 8-6
Double-declining-balance method P1

Assume a company's equipment carries a book value of $4,000 ($4,500 cost less $500 accumulated depreciation) and a fair value of $3,750, *and* that the $250 decline in fair value in comparison to the book value meets the 2-step impairment test. Prepare the entry to record this $250 impairment.

QS 8-7
Recording plant asset impairment C2

QS 8-8
Revenue and capital
expenditures

C3

1. Classify the following as either revenue or capital expenditures.
   a. Completed an addition to an office building for $250,000 cash.
   b. Paid $160 for the monthly cost of replacement filters on an air-conditioning system.
   c. Paid $300 cash per truck for the cost of their annual tune-ups.
   d. Paid $50,000 cash to replace a compressor on a refrigeration system that extends its useful life by four years.
2. Prepare the journal entries to record transactions *a* and *d* of part 1.

QS 8-9
Disposal of assets   P2

Horizon Co. owns equipment that cost $138,750, with accumulated depreciation of $81,000. Horizon sells the equipment for cash. Record the sale of the equipment assuming Horizon sells the equipment for (1) $63,000 cash, (2) $57,750 cash, and (3) $46,500 cash.

QS 8-10
Natural resources and depletion
P3

Diamond Company acquires an ore mine at a cost of $1,300,000. It incurs additional costs of $200,000 to access the mine, which is estimated to hold 500,000 tons of ore. The estimated value of the land after the ore is removed is $150,000.
1. Prepare the entry(ies) to record the cost of the ore mine.
2. Prepare the year-end adjusting entry if 90,000 tons of ore are mined and sold the first year.

QS 8-11
Classify assets

P3 P4

Which of the following assets are reported on the balance sheet as intangible assets? Which are reported as natural resources? (*a*) timberland, (*b*) patent, (*c*) leasehold, (*d*) Oil well, (*e*) equipment, (*f*) copyright, (*g*) franchise, (*h*) gold mine.

QS 8-12
Intangible assets and amortization   P4

On January 4 of this year, Larsen Boutique incurs a $95,000 cost to modernize its store. Improvements include new floors, ceilings, wiring, and wall coverings. These improvements are estimated to yield benefits for 10 years. Larsen leases its store and has eight years remaining on the lease. Prepare the entry to record (1) the cost of modernization and (2) amortization at the end of this current year.

QS 8-13
Computing total asset turnover
A1

Eastman Company reports the following ($ 000s): net sales of $13,557 for 2011 and $12,670 for 2010; end-of-year total assets of $14,968 for 2011 and $18,810 for 2010. Compute its total asset turnover for 2011, and assess its level if competitors average a total asset turnover of 2.0 times.

QS 8-14[A]
Asset exchange
P5

Esteban Co. owns a machine that costs $38,400 with accumulated depreciation of $20,400. Esteban exchanges the machine for a newer model that has a market value of $48,000. (1) Record the exchange assuming Esteban paid $32,000 cash and the exchange has commercial substance. (2) Record the exchange assuming Esteban pays $24,000 cash and the exchange lacks commercial substance.

QS 8-15
International accounting standards

C1 C3

Answer each of the following related to international accounting standards.
a. Accounting for plant assets involves cost determination, depreciation, additional expenditures, and disposals. Is plant asset accounting broadly similar or dissimilar between IFRS and U.S. GAAP? Identify one notable difference between IFRS and U.S. GAAP in accounting for plant assets.
b. Describe how IFRS and U.S. GAAP treat increases in the value of plant assets subsequent to their acquisition (but before their disposition).

EXERCISES

Exercise 8-1
Cost of plant assets

C1

Farha Co. purchases a machine for $11,500, terms 2/10, n/60, FOB shipping point. The seller prepaid the $260 freight charges, adding the amount to the invoice and bringing its total to $11,760. The machine requires special steel mounting and power connections costing $795. Another $375 is paid to assemble the machine and get it into operation. In moving the machine to its steel mounting, $190 in damages occurred. Materials costing $30 are used in adjusting the machine to produce a satisfactory product. The adjustments are normal for this machine and are not the result of the damages. Compute the cost recorded for this machine. (Farha pays for this machine within the cash discount period.)

Cerner Manufacturing purchases a large lot on which an old building is located as part of its plans to build a new plant. The negotiated purchase price is $225,000 for the lot plus $120,000 for the old building. The company pays $34,500 to tear down the old building and $51,000 to fill and level the lot. It also pays a total of $1,440,000 in construction costs—this amount consists of $1,354,500 for the new building and $85,500 for lighting and paving a parking area next to the building. Prepare a single journal entry to record these costs incurred by Cerner, all of which are paid in cash.

Exercise 8-2
Recording costs of assets
C1

Ming Yue Company pays $368,250 for real estate plus $19,600 in closing costs. The real estate consists of land appraised at $166,320; land improvements appraised at $55,440; and a building appraised at $174,240. Allocate the total cost among the three purchased assets and prepare the journal entry to record the purchase.

Exercise 8-3
Lump-sum purchase of plant assets **C1**

In early January 2011, LabTech purchases computer equipment for $147,000 to use in operating activities for the next four years. It estimates the equipment's salvage value at $30,000. Prepare a table showing depreciation and book value for each of the four years assuming straight-line depreciation.

Exercise 8-4
Straight-line depreciation **P1**

Refer to the information in Exercise 8-4. Prepare a table showing depreciation and book value for each of the four years assuming double-declining-balance depreciation.

Exercise 8-5
Double-declining-balance depreciation **P1**

Feng Company installs a computerized manufacturing machine in its factory at the beginning of the year at a cost of $42,300. The machine's useful life is estimated at 10 years, or 363,000 units of product, with a $6,000 salvage value. During its second year, the machine produces 35,000 units of product. Determine the machine's second-year depreciation under the straight-line method.

Exercise 8-6
Straight-line depreciation
P1

Refer to the information in Exercise 8-6. Determine the machine's second-year depreciation using the units-of-production method.

Exercise 8-7
Units-of-production depreciation
P1

Refer to the information in Exercise 8-6. Determine the machine's second-year depreciation using the double-declining-balance method.

Exercise 8-8
Double-declining-balance depreciation **P1**

On April 1, 2010, Stone's Backhoe Co. purchases a trencher for $250,000. The machine is expected to last five years and have a salvage value of $25,000. Compute depreciation expense for both 2010 and 2011 assuming the company uses the straight-line method.

Exercise 8-9
Straight-line, partial-year depreciation **C2**

Refer to the information in Exercise 8-9. Compute depreciation expense for both 2010 and 2011 assuming the company uses the double-declining-balance method.

Exercise 8-10
Double-declining-balance, partial-year depreciation **C2**

Supreme Fitness Club uses straight-line depreciation for a machine costing $21,750, with an estimated four-year life and a $2,250 salvage value. At the beginning of the third year, Supreme determines that the machine has three more years of remaining useful life, after which it will have an estimated $1,800 salvage value. Compute (1) the machine's book value at the end of its second year and (2) the amount of depreciation for each of the final three years given the revised estimates.

Exercise 8-11
Revising depreciation
C2

Check (2) $3,400

Mulan Enterprises pays $235,200 for equipment that will last five years and have a $52,500 salvage value. By using the equipment in its operations for five years, the company expects to earn $85,500 annually, after deducting all expenses except depreciation. Prepare a table showing income before depreciation, depreciation expense, and net (pretax) income for each year and for the total five-year period, assuming straight-line depreciation.

Exercise 8-12
Straight-line depreciation and income effects **P1**

Refer to the information in Exercise 8-12. Prepare a table showing income before depreciation, depreciation expense, and net (pretax) income for each year and for the total five-year period, assuming double-declining-balance depreciation is used.

Exercise 8-13
Double-declining-balance depreciation **P1**

Check Year 3 NI, $53,328

Exercise 8-14
Extraordinary repairs;
plant asset age

C3

Check (3) $207,450

Passat Company owns a building that appears on its prior year-end balance sheet at its original $561,000 cost less $420,750 accumulated depreciation. The building is depreciated on a straight-line basis assuming a 20-year life and no salvage value. During the first week in January of the current calendar year, major structural repairs are completed on the building at a $67,200 cost. The repairs extend its useful life for 7 years beyond the 20 years originally estimated.

1. Determine the building's age (plant asset age) as of the prior year-end balance sheet date.
2. Prepare the entry to record the cost of the structural repairs that are paid in cash.
3. Determine the book value of the building immediately after the repairs are recorded.
4. Prepare the entry to record the current calendar year's depreciation.

Exercise 8-15
Ordinary repairs, extraordinary
repairs and betterments

C3

Patterson Company pays $262,500 for equipment expected to last four years and have a $30,000 salvage value. Prepare journal entries to record the following costs related to the equipment.

1. During the second year of the equipment's life, $21,000 cash is paid for a new component expected to increase the equipment's productivity by 10% a year.
2. During the third year, $5,250 cash is paid for normal repairs necessary to keep the equipment in good working order.
3. During the fourth year, $13,950 is paid for repairs expected to increase the useful life of the equipment from four to five years.

Exercise 8-16
Disposal of assets

P2

Millworks Company owns a milling machine that cost $125,000 and has accumulated depreciation of $91,000. Prepare the entry to record the disposal of the milling machine on January 5 under each of the following independent situations.

1. The machine needed extensive repairs, and it was not worth repairing. Millworks disposed of the machine, receiving nothing in return.
2. Millworks sold the machine for $17,500 cash.
3. Millworks sold the machine for $34,000 cash.
4. Millworks sold the machine for $40,000 cash.

Exercise 8-17
Partial-year depreciation;
disposal of plant asset

P2

Finesse Co. purchases and installs a machine on January 1, 2011, at a total cost of $92,750. Straight-line depreciation is taken each year for four years assuming a seven-year life and no salvage value. The machine is disposed of on July 1, 2015, during its fifth year of service. Prepare entries to record the partial year's depreciation on July 1, 2015, and to record the disposal under the following separate assumptions: (1) the machine is sold for $35,000 cash and (2) Finesse receives an insurance settlement of $30,000 resulting from the total destruction of the machine in a fire.

Exercise 8-18
Depletion of natural resources

P1 P3

On April 2, 2011, Idaho Mining Co. pays $3,633,750 for an ore deposit containing 1,425,000 tons. The company installs machinery in the mine costing $171,000, with an estimated seven-year life and no salvage value. The machinery will be abandoned when the ore is completely mined. Idaho begins mining on May 1, 2011, and mines and sells 156,200 tons of ore during the remaining eight months of 2011. Prepare the December 31, 2011, entries to record both the ore deposit depletion and the mining machinery depreciation. Mining machinery depreciation should be in proportion to the mine's depletion.

Exercise 8-19
Amortization of intangible assets

P4

Busch Gallery purchases the copyright on an oil painting for $236,700 on January 1, 2011. The copyright legally protects its owner for 12 more years. The company plans to market and sell prints of the original for 15 years. Prepare entries to record the purchase of the copyright on January 1, 2011, and its annual amortization on December 31, 2011.

Exercise 8-20
Goodwill

P4

On January 1, 2011, Timothy Company purchased Macys Company at a price of $3,750,000. The fair market value of the net assets purchased equals $2,700,000.

1. What is the amount of goodwill that Timothy records at the purchase date?
2. Explain how Timothy would determine the amount of goodwill amortization for the year ended December 31, 2011.
3. Timothy Company believes that its employees provide superior customer service, and through their efforts, Timothy Company believes it has created $1,350,000 of goodwill. How would Timothy Company record this goodwill?

Refer to the statement of cash flows for **Apple** in Appendix A for the fiscal year ended September 26, 2009, to answer the following.

1. What amount of cash is used to purchase property, plant, and equipment?

2. How much depreciation, amortization, and accretion are recorded?

3. What total amount of net cash is used in investing activities?

Exercise 8-21
Cash flows related to assets

C1

Apple

Joy Co. reports net sales of $4,862,000 for 2010 and $7,542,000 for 2011. End-of-year balances for total assets are 2009, $1,586,000; 2010, $1,700,000; and 2011, $1,882,000. (*a*) Compute Joy's total asset turnover for 2010 and 2011. (*b*) Comment on Joy's efficiency in using its assets if its competitors average a total asset turnover of 3.0.

Exercise 8-22
Evaluating efficient use of assets

A1

Ramond Construction trades in an old tractor for a new tractor, receiving a $31,850 trade-in allowance and paying the remaining $93,275 in cash. The old tractor had cost $107,900, and straight-line accumulated depreciation of $58,500 had been recorded to date under the assumption that it would last eight years and have a $14,300 salvage value. Answer the following questions assuming the exchange has commercial substance.

1. What is the book value of the old tractor at the time of exchange?

2. What is the loss on this asset exchange?

3. What amount should be recorded (debited) in the asset account for the new tractor?

Exercise 8-23^A
Exchanging assets

P5

Check (2) $17,550

On January 5, 2011, Holstrom Co. disposes of a machine costing $65,500 with accumulated depreciation of $35,284. Prepare the entries to record the disposal under each of the following separate assumptions.

1. The machine is sold for $25,343 cash.

2. The machine is traded in for a newer machine having an $86,125 cash price. A $31,912 trade-in allowance is received, and the balance is paid in cash. Assume the asset exchange lacks commercial substance.

3. The machine is traded in for a newer machine having an $86,125 cash price. A $23,393 trade-in allowance is received, and the balance is paid in cash. Assume the asset exchange has commercial substance.

Exercise 8-24^A
Recording plant asset disposals

P2 P5

Check (2) Dr. Machinery (new), $84,429

Volkswagen Group reports the following information for property, plant and equipment as of December 31, 2008, along with additions, disposals, depreciation, and impairments for the year ended December 31, 2008 (euros in millions):

Exercise 8-25
Accounting for plant assets under IFRS

C2 P1 P2

Property, plant and equipment, net	€23,121
Additions to property, plant and equipment	6,651
Disposals of property, plant and equipment	2,322
Depreciation on property, plant and equipment	4,625
Impairments to property, plant and equipment	184

1. Prepare Volkswagen's journal entry to record its depreciation for 2008.

2. Prepare Volkswagen's journal entry to record its additions for 2008 assuming they are paid in cash and are treated as "betterments (improvements)" to the assets.

3. Prepare Volkswagen's journal entry to record its €2,322 in disposals for 2008 assuming it receives €700 cash in return and the accumulated depreciation on the disposed assets totals €1,322.

4. Volkswagen reports €184 of impairments. Do these impairments increase or decrease the property, plant and equipment account? And, by what amount?

---

connect

Xavier Construction negotiates a lump-sum purchase of several assets from a company that is going out of business. The purchase is completed on January 1, 2011, at a total cash price of $787,500 for a building, land, land improvements, and four vehicles. The estimated market values of the assets are building, $408,000; land, $289,000; land improvements, $42,500; and four vehicles, $110,500. The company's fiscal year ends on December 31.

PROBLEM SET A

Problem 8-1A
Plant asset costs; depreciation methods **C1 P1**

Required

1. Prepare a table to allocate the lump-sum purchase price to the separate assets purchased (round percents to the nearest 1%). Prepare the journal entry to record the purchase.

Check   (2) $23,490

     (3) $15,750

2. Compute the depreciation expense for year 2011 on the building using the straight-line method, assuming a 15-year life and a $25,650 salvage value.

3. Compute the depreciation expense for year 2011 on the land improvements assuming a five-year life and double-declining-balance depreciation.

Analysis Component

4. Defend or refute this statement: Accelerated depreciation results in payment of less taxes over the asset's life.

Problem 8-2A
Asset cost allocation;
straight-line depreciation

C1   P1

mhhe.com/wildFINMAN4e

In January 2011, Keona Co. pays $2,800,000 for a tract of land with two buildings on it. It plans to demolish Building 1 and build a new store in its place. Building 2 will be a company office; it is appraised at $641,300, with a useful life of 20 years and an $80,000 salvage value. A lighted parking lot near Building 1 has improvements (Land Improvements 1) valued at $408,100 that are expected to last another 14 years with no salvage value. Without the buildings and improvements, the tract of land is valued at $1,865,600. The company also incurs the following additional costs:

Cost to demolish Building 1	$ 422,600
Cost of additional land grading	167,200
Cost to construct new building (Building 3), having a useful life of 25 years and a $390,100 salvage value	2,019,000
Cost of new land improvements (Land Improvements 2) near Building 2 having a 20-year useful life and no salvage value	158,000

Required

Check   (1) Land costs, $2,381,800; Building 2 costs, $616,000

1. Prepare a table with the following column headings: Land, Building 2, Building 3, Land Improvements 1, and Land Improvements 2. Allocate the costs incurred by Keona to the appropriate columns and total each column (round percents to the nearest 1%).

2. Prepare a single journal entry to record all the incurred costs assuming they are paid in cash on January 1, 2011.

(3) Depr.—Land Improv. 1 and 2, $28,000 and $7,900

3. Using the straight-line method, prepare the December 31 adjusting entries to record depreciation for the 12 months of 2011 when these assets were in use.

Problem 8-3A
Computing and revising
depreciation; revenue and
capital expenditures

C1   C2   C3

Clarion Contractors completed the following transactions and events involving the purchase and operation of equipment in its business.

2010

Jan.   1   Paid $255,440 cash plus $15,200 in sales tax and $2,500 in transportation (FOB shipping point) for a new loader. The loader is estimated to have a four-year life and a $34,740 salvage value. Loader costs are recorded in the Equipment account.

Jan.   3   Paid $3,660 to enclose the cab and install air conditioning in the loader to enable operations under harsher conditions. This increased the estimated salvage value of the loader by another $1,110.

Check   Dec. 31, 2010, Dr. Depr. Expense—Equip., $60,238

Dec. 31   Recorded annual straight-line depreciation on the loader.

2011

Jan.   1   Paid $4,500 to overhaul the loader's engine, which increased the loader's estimated useful life by two years.

Feb. 17   Paid $920 to repair the loader after the operator backed it into a tree.

Check   Dec. 31, 2011, Dr. Depr. Expense—Equip., $37,042

Dec. 31   Recorded annual straight-line depreciation on the loader.

Required

Prepare journal entries to record these transactions and events.

Problem 8-4A
Computing and revising
depreciation; selling plant assets

C2   P1   P2

Chen Company completed the following transactions and events involving its delivery trucks.

2010

Jan.   1   Paid $19,415 cash plus $1,165 in sales tax for a new delivery truck estimated to have a five-year life and a $3,000 salvage value. Delivery truck costs are recorded in the Trucks account.

Dec. 31   Recorded annual straight-line depreciation on the truck.

2011

Dec. 31 Due to new information obtained earlier in the year, the truck's estimated useful life was changed from five to four years, and the estimated salvage value was increased to $3,500. Recorded annual straight-line depreciation on the truck.

Check Dec. 31, 2011, Dr. Depr. Expense—Trucks, $4,521

2012

Dec. 31 Recorded annual straight-line depreciation on the truck.
Dec. 31 Sold the truck for $6,200 cash.

Dec. 31, 2012, Dr. Loss on Disposal of Trucks, $1,822

Required

Prepare journal entries to record these transactions and events.

A machine costing $210,000 with a four-year life and an estimated $20,000 salvage value is installed in Calhoon Company's factory on January 1. The factory manager estimates the machine will produce 475,000 units of product during its life. It actually produces the following units: year 1, 121,400; year 2, 122,400; year 3, 119,600; and year 4, 118,200. The total number of units produced by the end of year 4 exceeds the original estimate—this difference was not predicted. (The machine must not be depreciated below its estimated salvage value.)

Problem 8-5A
Depreciation methods
P1

Required

Prepare a table with the following column headings and compute depreciation for each year (and total depreciation of all years combined) for the machine under each depreciation method.

Year	Straight-Line	Units-of-Production	Double-Declining-Balance

Check Year 4: units-of-production depreciation, $44,640; DDB depreciation, $6,250

Saturn Co. purchases a used machine for $167,000 cash on January 2 and readies it for use the next day at an $3,420 cost. On January 3, it is installed on a required operating platform costing $1,080, and it is further readied for operations. The company predicts the machine will be used for six years and have a $14,600 salvage value. Depreciation is to be charged on a straight-line basis. On December 31, at the end of its fifth year in operations, it is disposed of.

Problem 8-6A
Disposal of plant assets
C1 P1 P2

Required

1. Prepare journal entries to record the machine's purchase and the costs to ready and install it. Cash is paid for all costs incurred.

2. Prepare journal entries to record depreciation of the machine at December 31 of (*a*) its first year in operations and (*b*) the year of its disposal.

3. Prepare journal entries to record the machine's disposal under each of the following separate assumptions: (*a*) it is sold for $13,500 cash; (*b*) it is sold for $45,000 cash; and (*c*) it is destroyed in a fire and the insurance company pays $24,000 cash to settle the loss claim.

Check (2*b*) Depr. Exp., $26,150

(3*c*) Dr. Loss from Fire, $16,750

On July 23 of the current year, Dakota Mining Co. pays $4,836,000 for land estimated to contain 7,800,000 tons of recoverable ore. It installs machinery costing $390,000 that has a 10-year life and no salvage value and is capable of mining the ore deposit in eight years. The machinery is paid for on July 25, seven days before mining operations begin. The company removes and sells 400,000 tons of ore during its first five months of operations ending on December 31. Depreciation of the machinery is in proportion to the mine's depletion as the machinery will be abandoned after the ore is mined.

Problem 8-7A
Natural resources
P3

Required

Prepare entries to record (*a*) the purchase of the land, (*b*) the cost and installation of machinery, (*c*) the first five months' depletion assuming the land has a net salvage value of zero after the ore is mined, and (*d*) the first five months' depreciation on the machinery.

Check (*c*) Depletion, $248,000
(*d*) Depreciation, $20,000

Analysis Component

Describe both the similarities and differences in amortization, depletion, and depreciation.

Problem 8-8A
Intangible assets

P4

On July 1, 2006, Sweetman Company signed a contract to lease space in a building for 15 years. The lease contract calls for annual (prepaid) rental payments of $70,000 on each July 1 throughout the life of the lease and for the lessee to pay for all additions and improvements to the leased property. On June 25, 2011, Sweetman decides to sublease the space to Kirk & Associates for the remaining 10 years of the lease—Kirk pays $185,000 to Sweetman for the right to sublease and it agrees to assume the obligation to pay the $70,000 annual rent to the building owner beginning July 1, 2011. After taking possession of the leased space, Kirk pays for improving the office portion of the leased space at a $129,840 cost. The improvements are paid for by Kirk on July 5, 2011, and are estimated to have a useful life equal to the 16 years remaining in the life of the building.

Required

1. Prepare entries for Kirk to record (*a*) its payment to Sweetman for the right to sublease the building space, (*b*) its payment of the 2011 annual rent to the building owner, and (*c*) its payment for the office improvements.

Check   Dr. Rent Expense for (2*a*) $9,250, (2*c*) $35,000

2. Prepare Kirk's year-end adjusting entries required at December 31, 2011, to (*a*) amortize the $185,000 cost of the sublease, (*b*) amortize the office improvements, and (*c*) record rent expense.

PROBLEM SET B

Problem 8-1B
Plant asset costs; depreciation methods

C1 P1

Racerback Company negotiates a lump-sum purchase of several assets from a contractor who is relocating. The purchase is completed on January 1, 2011, at a total cash price of $1,610,000 for a building, land, land improvements, and six trucks. The estimated market values of the assets are building, $784,800; land, $540,640; land improvements, $226,720; and six trucks, $191,840. The company's fiscal year ends on December 31.

Required

1. Prepare a table to allocate the lump-sum purchase price to the separate assets purchased (round percents to the nearest 1%). Prepare the journal entry to record the purchase.

Check   (2) $52,000

2. Compute the depreciation expense for year 2011 on the building using the straight-line method, assuming a 12-year life and a $100,500 salvage value.

(3) $41,860

3. Compute the depreciation expense for year 2011 on the land improvements assuming a 10-year life and double-declining-balance depreciation.

Analysis Component

4. Defend or refute this statement: Accelerated depreciation results in payment of more taxes over the asset's life.

Problem 8-2B
Asset cost allocation; straight-line depreciation

C1 P1

In January 2011, InTech Co. pays $1,350,000 for a tract of land with two buildings. It plans to demolish Building A and build a new shop in its place. Building B will be a company office; it is appraised at $472,770, with a useful life of 15 years and a $90,000 salvage value. A lighted parking lot near Building B has improvements (Land Improvements B) valued at $125,145 that are expected to last another six years with no salvage value. Without the buildings and improvements, the tract of land is valued at $792,585. The company also incurs the following additional costs.

Cost to demolish Building A	$ 117,000
Cost of additional land grading	172,500
Cost to construct new building (Building C), having a useful life of 20 years and a $295,500 salvage value	1,356,000
Cost of new land improvements (Land Improvements C) near Building C, having a 10-year useful life and no salvage value	101,250

Required

Check   (1) Land costs, $1,059,000; Building B costs, $459,000

1. Prepare a table with the following column headings: Land, Building B, Building C, Land Improvements B, and Land Improvements C. Allocate the costs incurred by InTech to the appropriate columns and total each column (round percents to the nearest 1%).

2. Prepare a single journal entry to record all incurred costs assuming they are paid in cash on January 1, 2011.

(3) Depr.—Land Improv. B and C, $20,250 and $10,125

3. Using the straight-line method, prepare the December 31 adjusting entries to record depreciation for the 12 months of 2011 when these assets were in use.

Xpress Delivery Service completed the following transactions and events involving the purchase and operation of equipment for its business.

2010

Jan. 1 Paid $24,950 cash plus $1,950 in sales tax for a new delivery van that was estimated to have a five-year life and a $3,400 salvage value. Van costs are recorded in the Equipment account.

Jan. 3 Paid $1,550 to install sorting racks in the van for more accurate and quicker delivery of packages. This increases the estimated salvage value of the van by another $200.

Dec. 31 Recorded annual straight-line depreciation on the van.

2011

Jan. 1 Paid $1,970 to overhaul the van's engine, which increased the van's estimated useful life by two years.

May 10 Paid $600 to repair the van after the driver backed it into a loading dock.

Dec. 31 Record annual straight-line depreciation on the van. (Round to the nearest dollar.)

Required

Prepare journal entries to record these transactions and events.

Problem 8-3B
Computing and revising depreciation; revenue and capital expenditures
C1 C2 C3

Check Dec. 31, 2010, Dr. Depr. Expense—Equip., $4,970

Check Dec. 31, 2011, Dr. Depr. Expense—Equip., $3,642

Field Instruments completed the following transactions and events involving its machinery.

2010

Jan. 1 Paid $106,600 cash plus $6,400 in sales tax for a new machine. The machine is estimated to have a six-year life and a $9,800 salvage value.

Dec. 31 Recorded annual straight-line depreciation on the machinery.

2011

Dec. 31 Due to new information obtained earlier in the year, the machine's estimated useful life was changed from six to four years, and the estimated salvage value was increased to $13,050. Recorded annual straight-line depreciation on the machinery.

2012

Dec. 31 Recorded annual straight-line depreciation on the machinery.

Dec. 31 Sold the machine for $25,240 cash.

Required

Prepare journal entries to record these transactions and events.

Problem 8-4B
Computing and revising depreciation; selling plant assets
C2 P1 P2

Check Dec. 31, 2011, Dr. Depr. Expense—Machinery, $27,583

Dec. 31, 2012, Dr. Loss on Disposal of Machinery, $15,394

On January 2, Gannon Co. purchases and installs a new machine costing $312,000 with a five-year life and an estimated $28,000 salvage value. Management estimates the machine will produce 1,136,000 units of product during its life. Actual production of units is as follows: year 1, 245,600; year 2, 230,400; year 3, 227,000; year 4, 232,600; and year 5, 211,200. The total number of units produced by the end of year 5 exceeds the original estimate—this difference was not predicted. (The machine must not be depreciated below its estimated salvage value.)

Required

Prepare a table with the following column headings and compute depreciation for each year (and total depreciation of all years combined) for the machine under each depreciation method.

Year	Straight-Line	Units-of-Production	Double-Declining-Balance

Problem 8-5B
Depreciation methods
P1

Check DDB Depreciation, Year 3, $44,928; U-of-P Depreciation, Year 4, $58,150

On January 1, Jefferson purchases a used machine for $130,000 and readies it for use the next day at a cost of $3,390. On January 4, it is mounted on a required operating platform costing $4,800, and it is further readied for operations. Management estimates the machine will be used for seven years and have an $18,000 salvage value. Depreciation is to be charged on a straight-line basis. On December 31, at the end of its sixth year of use, the machine is disposed of.

Problem 8-6B
Disposal of plant assets
C1 P1 P2

Required

1. Prepare journal entries to record the machine's purchase and the costs to ready and install it. Cash is paid for all costs incurred.

2. Prepare journal entries to record depreciation of the machine at December 31 of (*a*) its first year in operations and (*b*) the year of its disposal.

3. Prepare journal entries to record the machine's disposal under each of the following separate assumptions: (*a*) it is sold for $30,000 cash; (*b*) it is sold for $50,000 cash; and (*c*) it is destroyed in a fire and the insurance company pays $20,000 cash to settle the loss claim.

Problem 8-7B
Natural resources
P3

On February 19 of the current year, Rock Chalk Co. pays $4,450,000 for land estimated to contain 5 million tons of recoverable ore. It installs machinery costing $200,000 that has a 16-year life and no salvage value and is capable of mining the ore deposit in 12 years. The machinery is paid for on March 21, eleven days before mining operations begin. The company removes and sells 352,000 tons of ore during its first nine months of operations ending on December 31. Depreciation of the machinery is in proportion to the mine's depletion as the machinery will be abandoned after the ore is mined.

Required

Prepare entries to record (*a*) the purchase of the land, (*b*) the cost and installation of the machinery, (*c*) the first nine months' depletion assuming the land has a net salvage value of zero after the ore is mined, and (*d*) the first nine months' depreciation on the machinery.

Analysis Component

Describe both the similarities and differences in amortization, depletion, and depreciation.

Problem 8-8B
Intangible assets
P4

On January 1, 2004, Liberty Co. entered into a 12-year lease on a building. The lease contract requires (1) annual (prepaid) rental payments of $26,400 each January 1 throughout the life of the lease and (2) for the lessee to pay for all additions and improvements to the leased property. On January 1, 2011, Liberty decides to sublease the space to Moberly Co. for the remaining five years of the lease—Moberly pays $30,000 to Liberty for the right to sublease and agrees to assume the obligation to pay the $26,400 annual rent to the building owner beginning January 1, 2011. After taking possession of the leased space, Moberly pays for improving the office portion of the leased space at an $18,000 cost. The improvements are paid for by Moberly on January 3, 2011, and are estimated to have a useful life equal to the 13 years remaining in the life of the building.

Required

1. Prepare entries for Moberly to record (*a*) its payment to Liberty for the right to sublease the building space, (*b*) its payment of the 2011 annual rent to the building owner, and (*c*) its payment for the office improvements.

2. Prepare Moberly's year-end adjusting entries required on December 31, 2011, to (*a*) amortize the $30,000 cost of the sublease, (*b*) amortize the office improvements, and (*c*) record rent expense.

SERIAL PROBLEM
Business Solutions
P1 A1

(This serial problem began in Chapter 1 and continues through most of the book. If previous chapter segments were not completed, the serial problem can begin at this point. It is helpful, but not necessary, to use the Working Papers that accompany the book.)

SP 8   Selected ledger account balances for Business Solutions follow.

	For Three Months Ended December 31, 2011	For Three Months Ended March 31, 2012
Office equipment	$ 8,000	$ 8,000
Accumulated depreciation— Office equipment	400	800
Computer equipment	20,000	20,000
Accumulated depreciation— Computer equipment	1,250	2,500
Total revenue	31,284	44,000
Total assets	83,460	120,268

Required

1. Assume that Business Solutions does not acquire additional office equipment or computer equipment in 2012. Compute amounts for *the year ended* December 31, 2012, for Depreciation Expense—Office Equipment and for Depreciation Expense—Computer Equipment (assume use of the straight-line method).

2. Given the assumptions in part 1, what is the book value of both the office equipment and the computer equipment as of December 31, 2012?

3. Compute the three-month total asset turnover for Business Solutions as of March 31, 2012. Use total revenue for the numerator and average the December 31, 2011, total assets and the March 31, 2012, total assets for the denominator. Interpret its total asset turnover if competitors average 2.5 for annual periods. (Round turnover to two decimals.)

Check (3) Three-month (annual) turnover = 0.43 (1.73 annual)

Beyond the Numbers

BTN 8-1 Refer to the financial statements of **Research In Motion** in Appendix A to answer the following.

1. What percent of the original cost of RIM's property, plant and equipment remains to be depreciated as of February 27, 2010, and at February 28, 2009? Assume these assets have no salvage value.

2. Over what length(s) of time is RIM depreciating its major categories of property, plant and equipment?

3. What is the change in total property, plant and equipment (before accumulated depreciation) for the year ended February 27, 2010? What is the amount of cash provided (used) by investing activities for property, plant and equipment for the year ended February 27, 2010? What is one possible explanation for the difference between these two amounts?

4. Compute its total asset turnover for the year ended February 27, 2010, and the year ended February 28, 2009. Assume total assets at March 1, 2008, are $5,511 ($ millions).

Fast Forward

5. Access RIM's financial statements for fiscal years ending after February 27, 2010, at its Website (**RIM.com**) or the SEC's EDGAR database (**www.sec.gov**). Recompute RIM's total asset turnover for the additional years' data you collect. Comment on any differences relative to the turnover computed in part 4.

REPORTING IN ACTION

A1

RIM

BTN 8-2 Comparative figures for **Research In Motion** and **Apple** follow.

($ millions)	Research In Motion			Apple		
	Current Year	One Year Prior	Two Years Prior	Current Year	One Year Prior	Two Years Prior
Total assets	$10,204	$ 8,101	$5,511	$47,501	$36,171	$25,347
Net sales	14,953	11,065	6,009	42,905	37,491	24,578

COMPARATIVE ANALYSIS

A1

RIM

Apple

Required

1. Compute total asset turnover for the most recent two years for Research In Motion and Apple using the data shown.

2. Which company is more efficient in generating net sales given the total assets it employs? Assume an industry average of 1.0 for asset turnover.

BTN 8-3 Flo Choi owns a small business and manages its accounting. Her company just finished a year in which a large amount of borrowed funds was invested in a new building addition as well as in equipment and fixture additions. Choi's banker requires her to submit semiannual financial statements so he can monitor the financial health of her business. He has warned her that if profit margins erode, he might raise the interest rate on the borrowed funds to reflect the increased loan risk from the bank's point of view. Choi knows profit margin is likely to decline this year. As she prepares year-end adjusting entries, she decides to apply the following depreciation rule: All asset additions are considered to be in use on the first day of the following month. (The previous rule assumed assets are in use on the first day of the month nearest to the purchase date.)

ETHICS CHALLENGE

C1

Required

1. Identify decisions that managers like Choi must make in applying depreciation methods.
2. Is Choi's rule an ethical violation, or is it a legitimate decision in computing depreciation?
3. How will Choi's new depreciation rule affect the profit margin of her business?

COMMUNICATING IN PRACTICE

A1

BTN 8-4 Teams are to select an industry, and each team member is to select a different company in that industry. Each team member is to acquire the financial statements (Form 10-K) of the company selected—see the company's Website or the SEC's EDGAR database (**www.SEC.gov**). Use the financial statements to compute total asset turnover. Communicate with teammates via a meeting, e-mail, or telephone to discuss the meaning of this ratio, how different companies compare to each other, and the industry norm. The team must prepare a one-page report that describes the ratios for each company and identifies the conclusions reached during the team's discussion.

TAKING IT TO THE NET

P4

BTN 8-5 Access the **Yahoo!** (ticker: YHOO) 10-K report for the year ended December 31, 2009, filed on February 26, 2010, at **www.SEC.gov**.

Required

1. What amount of goodwill is reported on Yahoo!'s balance sheet? What percentage of total assets does its goodwill represent? Is goodwill a major asset for Yahoo!? Explain.
2. Locate Note 5 to its financial statements. Identify the change in goodwill from December 31, 2008, to December 31, 2009. Comment on the change in goodwill over this period.
3. Locate Note 6 to its financial statements. What are the three categories of intangible assets that Yahoo! reports at December 31, 2009? What proportion of total assets do the intangibles represent?
4. What does Yahoo! indicate is the life of "Trade names, trademarks, and domain names" according to its Note 6? Comment on the difference between the estimated useful life and the legal life of Yahoo!'s trademark.

TEAMWORK IN ACTION

P1

BTN 8-6 Each team member is to become an expert on one depreciation method to facilitate teammates' understanding of that method. Follow these procedures:

a. Each team member is to select an area for expertise from one of the following depreciation methods: straight-line, units-of-production, or double-declining-balance.

b. Expert teams are to be formed from those who have selected the same area of expertise. The instructor will identify the location where each expert team meets.

c. Using the following data, expert teams are to collaborate and develop a presentation answering the requirements. Expert team members must write the presentation in a format they can show to their learning teams.

Point: This activity can follow an overview of each method. Step 1 allows for three areas of expertise. Larger teams will have some duplication of areas, but the straight-line choice should not be duplicated. Expert teams can use the book and consult with the instructor.

Data and Requirements On January 8, 2009, Waverly Riders purchases a van to transport rafters back to the point of departure at the conclusion of the rafting adventures they operate. The cost of the van is $44,000. It has an estimated salvage value of $2,000 and is expected to be used for four years and driven 60,000 miles. The van is driven 12,000 miles in 2009, 18,000 miles in 2010, 21,000 in 2011, and 10,000 in 2012.

1. Compute the annual depreciation expense for each year of the van's estimated useful life.
2. Explain when and how annual depreciation is recorded.
3. Explain the impact on income of this depreciation method versus others over the van's life.
4. Identify the van's book value for each year of its life and illustrate the reporting of this amount for any one year.

d. Re-form original learning teams. In rotation, experts are to present to their teams the results from part *c*. Experts are to encourage and respond to questions.

ENTREPRENEURIAL DECISION

A1

BTN 8-7 Review the chapter's opening feature involving **Games2U**. Assume that the company currently has net sales of $8,000,000, and that it is planning an expansion that will increase net sales by $4,000,000. To accomplish this expansion, Games2U must increase its average total assets from $2,500,000 to $3,000,000.

Required

1. Compute the company's total asset turnover under (*a*) current conditions and (*b*) proposed conditions.
2. Evaluate and comment on the merits of the proposal given your analysis in part 1. Identify any concerns you would express about the proposal.

BTN 8-8   Team up with one or more classmates for this activity. Identify companies in your community or area that must account for at least one of the following assets: natural resource; patent; lease; leasehold improvement; copyright; trademark; or goodwill. You might find a company having more than one type of asset. Once you identify a company with a specific asset, describe the accounting this company uses to allocate the cost of that asset to the periods benefited from its use.

HITTING THE ROAD

P3 P4

BTN 8-9   **Nokia** (**www.Nokia.com**), **Research In Motion**, and **Apple** are all competitors in the global marketplace. Comparative figures for these companies' recent annual accounting periods follow.

GLOBAL DECISION

A1

NOKIA

RIM

Apple

(in millions, except turnover)	Nokia (EUR millions)			Research In Motion		Apple	
	Current Year	Prior Year	Two Years Prior	Current Year	Prior Year	Current Year	Prior Year
Total assets	35,738	39,582	37,599	$10,204	$ 8,101	$47,501	$36,171
Net sales	40,984	50,710	51,058	14,953	11,065	42,905	37,491
Total asset turnover	?	?	—	1.63	1.63	1.03	1.22

Required

1. Compute total asset turnover for the most recent two years for Nokia using the data shown.
2. Which company is most efficient in generating net sales given the total assets it employs?

ANSWERS TO MULTIPLE CHOICE QUIZ

1. b;

	Appraisal Value	%	Total Cost	Allocated
Land	$175,000	50%	$326,000	$163,000
Land improvements	70,000	20	326,000	65,200
Building	105,000	30	326,000	97,800
Totals	$350,000			$326,000

2. c; ($35,000 − $1,000)/4 years = $8,500 per year.
3. c; 2011: $10,800,000 × (2 × 10%) = $2,160,000
    2012: ($10,800,000 − $2,160,000) × (2 × 10%) = $1,728,000
4. c;

Cost of machine	$250,000
Accumulated depreciation	100,000
Book value	150,000
Cash received	120,000
Loss on sale	$ 30,000

5. b; $550,000/$500,000 = 1.10

9

Current Liabilities

A Look Back

Chapter 8 focused on long-term assets including plant assets, natural resources, and intangibles. We showed how to account for and analyze those assets.

A Look at This Chapter

This chapter explains how to identify, compute, record, and report current liabilities in financial statements. We also analyze and interpret these liabilities, including those related to employee costs.

A Look Ahead

Chapter 10 focuses on long-term liabilities. We explain how to value, record, amortize, and report these liabilities in financial statements.

Learning Objectives

CONCEPTUAL

C1 Describe current and long-term liabilities and their characteristics. (p. 368)

C2 Identify and describe known current liabilities. (p. 370)

C3 Explain how to account for contingent liabilities. (p. 380)

ANALYTICAL

A1 Compute the times interest earned ratio and use it to analyze liabilities. (p. 382)

LP9

PROCEDURAL

P1 Prepare entries to account for short-term notes payable. (p. 371)

P2 Compute and record *employee* payroll deductions and liabilities. (p. 374)

P3 Compute and record *employer* payroll expenses and liabilities. (p. 375)

P4 Account for estimated liabilities, including warranties and bonuses. (p. 377)

P5 *Appendix 9A*—Identify and describe the details of payroll reports, records, and procedures. (p. 385)

No Stuffed Shirts

"Part of the fun is the journey . . . working til 2 am every day"
—MATT WALLS

ATLANTA, GA—Brothers Matt and Bryan Walls never planned to be entrepreneurs in the T-shirt business. "[It was] an idea we had while hanging out in our parents' basement," explains Matt. "We were naive and, like many first-time entrepreneurs, just dove right in." Matt and Bryan's plans involved making T-shirts with visual humor and pop culture themes. Their company, **SnorgTees (SnorgTees.com)**, had a shaky start but soon found its groove with best-selling T-shirts such as "With a shirt like this, who needs pants?" "Don't act like you're not impressed," and "I'm kind of a big deal."

"We dreamed it would be successful overnight," recalls Matt. "But when things first started we had a huge reality check, and at that point I don't know if I believed." Today their business is thriving. Their commitment to success carries over to the financial side. They especially focus on the important task of managing liabilities for payroll, supplies, employee wages, training, and taxes. Both insist that effective management of liabilities, especially payroll and employee benefits, is crucial. They stress that monitoring and controlling liabilities are a must.

To help control liabilities, Matt and Bryan describe how they began by working out of their parents' home to reduce liabilities. "Most people think all we do is sit around and think up funny ideas," explains Matt. "In reality most of the time is spent on executing projects and managing the business . . . [including] order fulfillment, supply chain management, marketing, and accounting." In short, creative reduction of liabilities can mean success or failure.

The two continue to monitor liabilities and their payment patterns. "I'm pretty conservative about spending money," admits Matt. "If you want to run a successful company, you can't forget all the details." The two insist that accounting for and monitoring liabilities are one key to a successful start-up. Their company now generates sufficient income to pay for liabilities and produces revenue growth for expansion. "We plan to keep having fun," insists Matt. "We do business with people all over the world."

[Sources: *SnorgTees Website,* January 2011; *Entrepreneur,* September 2009; *RetireAt21.com,* October 2008; *Business to Business,* January 2008; *WannaBeMogul.com,* November 2007.]

Previous chapters introduced liabilities such as accounts payable, notes payable, wages payable, and unearned revenues. This chapter further explains these liabilities and additional ones such as warranties, taxes, payroll, vacation pay, and bonuses. It also describes contingent liabilities and introduces long-term liabilities. The focus is on how to define, classify, measure, report, and analyze these liabilities so that this information is useful to business decision makers.

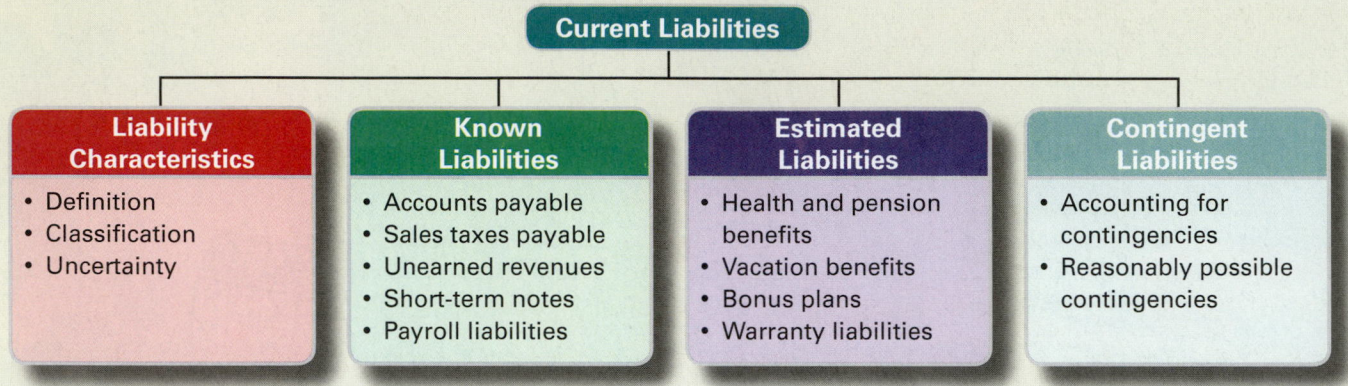

Current Liabilities

Liability Characteristics	Known Liabilities	Estimated Liabilities	Contingent Liabilities
• Definition • Classification • Uncertainty	• Accounts payable • Sales taxes payable • Unearned revenues • Short-term notes • Payroll liabilities	• Health and pension benefits • Vacation benefits • Bonus plans • Warranty liabilities	• Accounting for contingencies • Reasonably possible contingencies

CHARACTERISTICS OF LIABILITIES

This section discusses important characteristics of liabilities and how liabilities are classified and reported.

Defining Liabilities

C1 Describe current and long-term liabilities and their characteristics.

A *liability* is a probable future payment of assets or services that a company is presently obligated to make as a result of past transactions or events. This definition includes three crucial factors:

1. A past transaction or event.
2. A present obligation.
3. A future payment of assets or services.

These three important elements are portrayed visually in Exhibit 9.1. Liabilities reported in financial statements exhibit those characteristics. No liability is reported when one or more of those characteristics is absent. For example, most companies expect to pay wages to their employees in upcoming months and years, but these future payments are *not* liabilities because no past event such as employee work resulted in a present obligation. Instead, such liabilities arise when employees perform their work and earn the wages.

EXHIBIT 9.1

Characteristics of a Liability

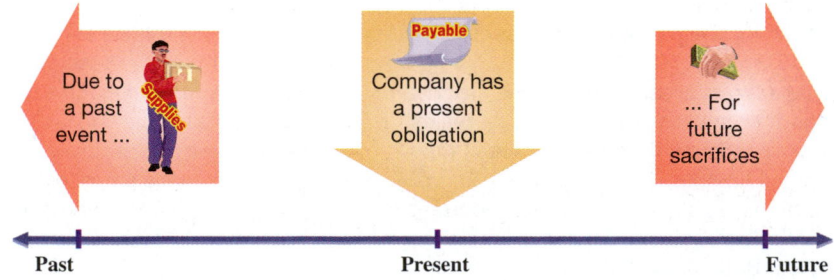

Due to a past event ...   Company has a present obligation   ... For future sacrifices

Past   Present   Future

Classifying Liabilities

Information about liabilities is more useful when the balance sheet identifies them as either current or long term. Decision makers need to know when obligations are due so they can plan for them and take appropriate action.

Current Liabilities   **Current liabilities,** also called *short-term liabilities,* are obligations due within one year or the company's operating cycle, whichever is longer. They are expected to be paid using current assets or by creating other current liabilities. Common examples of current liabilities are accounts payable, short-term notes payable, wages payable, warranty liabilities, lease liabilities, taxes payable, and unearned revenues.

Current liabilities differ across companies because they depend on the type of company operations. **MGM Mirage**, for instance, included the following current liabilities related to its gaming, hospitality and entertainment operations ($000s):

Advance deposits and ticket sales	$104,911
Casino outstanding chip liability	83,957
Casino front money deposits	80,944

Harley-Davidson reports a much different set of current liabilities. It discloses current liabilities made up of items such as warranty, recall, and dealer incentive liabilities.

Long-Term Liabilities   A company's obligations not expected to be paid within the longer of one year or the company's operating cycle are reported as **long-term liabilities.** They can include long-term notes payable, warranty liabilities, lease liabilities, and bonds payable. They are sometimes reported on the balance sheet in a single long-term liabilities total or in multiple categories. **Domino's Pizza**, for instance, reports long-term liabilities of $1,555 million. They are reported after current liabilities. A single liability also can be divided between the current and noncurrent sections if a company expects to make payments toward it in both the short and long term. Domino's reports ($ millions) long-term debt, $1,522; and current portion of long-term debt, $50. The second item is reported in current liabilities. We sometimes see liabilities that do not have a fixed due date but instead are payable on the creditor's demand. These are reported as current liabilities because of the possibility of payment in the near term. Exhibit 9.2 shows amounts of current liabilities and as a percent of total liabilities for selected companies.

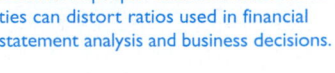
Point: Improper classification of liabilities can distort ratios used in financial statement analysis and business decisions.

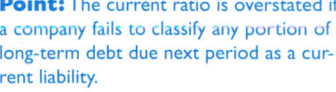
Point: The current ratio is overstated if a company fails to classify any portion of long-term debt due next period as a current liability.

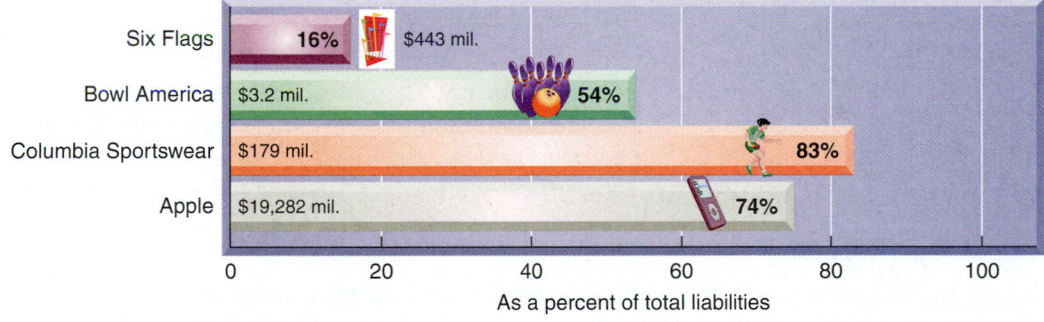

EXHIBIT 9.2

Current Liabilities of Selected Companies

Chart: As a percent of total liabilities (0 to 100)
- Six Flags: $443 mil., 16%
- Bowl America: $3.2 mil., 54%
- Columbia Sportswear: $179 mil., 83%
- Apple: $19,282 mil., 74%

Uncertainty in Liabilities

Accounting for liabilities involves addressing three important questions: Whom to pay? When to pay? How much to pay? Answers to these questions are often decided when a liability is incurred. For example, if a company has a $100 account payable to a specific individual, payable on March 15, the answers are clear. The company knows whom to pay, when to pay, and how much to pay. However, the answers to one or more of these questions are uncertain for some liabilities.

Uncertainty in Whom to Pay   Liabilities can involve uncertainty in whom to pay. For instance, a company can create a liability with a known amount when issuing a note that is payable to its holder. In this case, a specific amount is payable to the note's holder at a specified date, but the company does not know who the holder is until that date. Despite this uncertainty, the company reports this liability on its balance sheet.

Point: An *accrued expense* is an unpaid expense, and is also called an *accrued liability.*

Uncertainty in When to Pay A company can have an obligation of a known amount to a known creditor but not know when it must be paid. For example, a legal services firm can accept fees in advance from a client who plans to use the firm's services in the future. This means that the firm has a liability that it settles by providing services at an unknown future date. Although this uncertainty exists, the legal firm's balance sheet must report this liability. These types of obligations are reported as current liabilities because they are likely to be settled in the short term.

Uncertainty in How Much to Pay A company can be aware of an obligation but not know how much will be required to settle it. For example, a company using electrical power is billed only after the meter has been read. This cost is incurred and the liability created before a bill is received. A liability to the power company is reported as an estimated amount if the balance sheet is prepared before a bill arrives.

 IFRS

IFRS records a contingent liability when an obligation exists from a past event if there is a 'probable' outflow of resources and the amount can be estimated reliably. However, IFRS defines probable as 'more likely than not' while U.S. GAAP defines it as 'likely to occur.' ■

Quick Check   Answers — p. 393

1. What is a liability? Identify its crucial characteristics.
2. Is every expected future payment a liability?
3. If a liability is payable in 15 months, is it classified as current or long term?

KNOWN LIABILITIES

C2 Identify and describe known current liabilities.

Most liabilities arise from situations with little uncertainty. They are set by agreements, contracts, or laws and are measurable. These liabilities are **known liabilities,** also called *definitely determinable liabilities.* Known liabilities include accounts payable, notes payable, payroll, sales taxes, unearned revenues, and leases. We describe how to account for these known liabilities in this section.

Accounts Payable

Accounts payable, or trade accounts payable, are amounts owed to suppliers for products or services purchased on credit. Accounting for accounts payable is primarily explained and illustrated in our discussion of merchandising activities in Chapters 4 and 5.

Sales Taxes Payable

Nearly all states and many cities levy taxes on retail sales. Sales taxes are stated as a percent of selling prices. The seller collects sales taxes from customers when sales occur and remits these collections (often monthly) to the proper government agency. Since sellers currently owe these collections to the government, this amount is a current liability. **Home Depot**, for instance, reports sales taxes payable of $362 million in its recent annual report. To illustrate, if Home Depot sells materials on August 31 for $6,000 cash that are subject to a 5% sales tax, the revenue portion of this transaction is recorded as follows:

Assets = Liabilities + Equity
+6,300   +300   +6,000

Aug. 31	Cash..	6,300	
	Sales.......................................		6,000
	Sales Taxes Payable ($6,000 × 0.05)............		300
	To record cash sales and 5% sales tax.		

Sales Taxes Payable is debited and Cash credited when it remits these collections to the government. Sales Taxes Payable is not an expense. It arises because laws require sellers to collect this cash from customers for the government.[1]

Unearned Revenues

Unearned revenues (also called *deferred revenues, collections in advance,* and *prepayments*) are amounts received in advance from customers for future products or services. Advance ticket sales for sporting events or music concerts are examples. **Beyonce**, for instance, has "deferred revenues" from advance ticket sales. To illustrate, assume that Beyonce sells $5 million in tickets for eight concerts; the entry is

June 30	Cash	5,000,000	
	Unearned Ticket Revenue		5,000,000
	To record sale of concert tickets.		

Point: To *defer* a revenue means to postpone recognition of a revenue collected in advance until it is earned. Sport teams must defer recognition of ticket sales until games are played.

Assets	=	Liabilities	+ Equity
+5,000,000		+5,000,000	

When a concert is played, Beyonce would record revenue for the portion earned.

Oct. 31	Unearned Ticket Revenue	625,000	
	Ticket Revenue		625,000
	To record concert ticket revenues earned.		

Assets	=	Liabilities	+	Equity
		−625,000		+625,000

Unearned Ticket Revenue is an unearned revenue account and is reported as a current liability. Unearned revenues also arise with airline ticket sales, magazine subscriptions, construction projects, hotel reservations, and custom orders.

🟨 Decision Insight

Reward Programs Gift card sales now exceed $100 billion annually, and reward (also called loyalty) programs are growing. There are no exact rules for how retailers account for rewards. When **Best Buy** launched its "Reward Zone," shoppers earned $5 on each $125 spent and had 90 days to spend it. Retailers make assumptions about how many reward program dollars will be spent and how to report it. Best Buy sets up a liability and reduces revenue by the same amount. **Talbots** does not reduce revenue but instead increases selling expense. **Men's Wearhouse** records rewards in cost of goods sold, whereas **Neiman Marcus** subtracts them from revenue. The FASB continues to review reward programs. ■

Short-Term Notes Payable

A **short-term note payable** is a written promise to pay a specified amount on a definite future date within one year or the company's operating cycle, whichever is longer. These promissory notes are negotiable (as are checks), meaning they can be transferred from party to party by endorsement. The written documentation provided by notes is helpful in resolving disputes and for pursuing legal actions involving these liabilities. Most notes payable bear interest to compensate for use of the money until payment is made. Short-term notes payable can arise from many transactions. A company that purchases merchandise on credit can sometimes extend the credit period by signing a note to replace an account payable. Such notes also can arise when money is borrowed from a bank. We describe both of these cases.

P1 Prepare entries to account for short-term notes payable.

Point: Required characteristics for negotiability of a note: (1) unconditional promise, (2) in writing, (3) specific amount, and (4) definite due date.

---

[1] Sales taxes can be computed from total sales receipts when sales taxes are not separately identified on the register. To illustrate, assume a 5% sales tax and $420 in total sales receipts (which includes sales taxes). Sales are computed as follows:

$$\text{Sales} = \text{Total sales receipts}/(1 + \text{Sales tax percentage}) = \$420/1.05 = \$400$$

Thus, the sales tax amount equals total sales receipts minus sales, or $420 − $400 = $20.

Note Given to Extend Credit Period   A company can replace an account payable with a note payable. A common example is a creditor that requires the substitution of an interest-bearing note for an overdue account payable that does not bear interest. A less common situation occurs when a debtor's weak financial condition motivates the creditor to accept a note, sometimes for a lesser amount, and to close the account to ensure that this customer makes no additional credit purchases.

To illustrate, let's assume that on August 23, Brady Company asks to extend its past-due $600 account payable to McGraw. After some negotiations, McGraw agrees to accept $100 cash and a 60-day, 12%, $500 note payable to replace the account payable. Brady records the transaction with this entry:

Assets = Liabilities + Equity
−100   −600
            +500

Aug. 23	Accounts Payable—McGraw	600	
	Cash		100
	Notes Payable—McGraw		500
	Gave $100 cash and a 60-day, 12% note for payment on account.		

Point: Accounts payable are detailed in a subsidiary ledger, but notes payable are sometimes not. A file with copies of notes can serve as a subsidiary ledger.

Signing the note does not resolve Brady's debt. Instead, the form of debt is changed from an account payable to a note payable. McGraw prefers the note payable over the account payable because it earns interest and it is written documentation of the debt's existence, term, and amount. When the note comes due, Brady pays the note and interest by giving McGraw a check for $510. Brady records that payment with this entry:

Assets = Liabilities + Equity
−510   −500   −10

Oct. 22	Notes Payable—McGraw	500	
	Interest Expense	10	
	Cash		510
	Paid note with interest ($500 × 12% × 60/360).		

Point: Commercial companies commonly compute interest using a 360-day year. This is known as the *banker's rule.*

Interest expense is computed by multiplying the principal of the note ($500) by the annual interest rate (12%) for the fraction of the year the note is outstanding (60 days/360 days).

Note Given to Borrow from Bank   A bank nearly always requires a borrower to sign a promissory note when making a loan. When the note matures, the borrower repays the note with an amount larger than the amount borrowed. The difference between the amount borrowed and the amount repaid is *interest*. This section considers a type of note whose signer promises to pay *principal* (the amount borrowed) plus interest. In this case, the *face value* of the note equals principal. Face value is the value shown on the face (front) of the note. To illustrate, assume that a company needs $2,000 for a project and borrows this money from a bank at 12% annual interest. The loan is made on September 30, 2011, and is due in 60 days. Specifically, the borrowing company signs a note with a face value equal to the amount borrowed. The note includes a statement similar to this: *"I promise to pay $2,000 plus interest at 12% within 60 days after September 30."* This simple note is shown in Exhibit 9.3.

Point: When money is borrowed from a bank, the loan is reported as an asset (receivable) on the bank's balance sheet.

EXHIBIT 9.3

Note with Face Value Equal to
Amount Borrowed

Promissory Note

$2,000   Sept. 30, 2011
Face Value   **Date**

Sixty days   after date, ___I___ promise to pay to the order of
                    National Bank
                    Boston, MA
Two thousand and no/100 -------------------------- **Dollars**

plus interest at the annual rate of __12%__ .

                            Janet Lee

The borrower records its receipt of cash and the new liability with this entry:

Sept. 30	Cash	2,000	
	Notes Payable		2,000
	Borrowed $2,000 cash with a 60-day, 12%, $2,000 note.		

Assets = Liabilities + Equity
+2,000   +2,000

When principal and interest are paid, the borrower records payment with this entry:

Nov. 29	Notes Payable	2,000	
	Interest Expense	40	
	Cash		2,040
	Paid note with interest ($2,000 × 12% × 60/360).		

Assets = Liabilities + Equity
−2,040   −2,000   −40

End-of-period interest adjustment.   When the end of an accounting period occurs between the signing of a note payable and its maturity date, the *matching principle* requires us to record the accrued but unpaid interest on the note. To illustrate, let's return to the note in Exhibit 9.3, but assume that the company borrows $2,000 cash on December 16, 2011, instead of September 30. This 60-day note matures on February 14, 2012, and the company's fiscal year ends on December 31. Thus, we need to record interest expense for the final 15 days in December. This means that one-fourth (15 days/60 days) of the $40 total interest is an expense of year 2011. The borrower records this expense with the following adjusting entry:

2011			
Dec. 31	Interest Expense	10	
	Interest Payable		10
	To record accrued interest on note ($2,000 × 12% × 15/360).		

Assets = Liabilities + Equity
               +10   −10

When this note matures on February 14, the borrower must recognize 45 days of interest expense for year 2012 and remove the balances of the two liability accounts:

Example: If this note is dated Dec. 1 instead of Dec. 16, how much expense is recorded on Dec. 31? *Answer:* $2,000 × 12% × 30/360 = $20

2012			
Feb. 14	Interest Expense*	30	
	Interest Payable	10	
	Notes Payable	2,000	
	Cash		2,040
	*Paid note with interest. *($2,000 × 12% × 45/360)*		

Assets = Liabilities + Equity
−2,040   −10   −30
                    −2,000

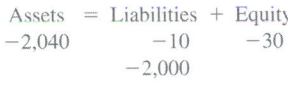 **Decision Insight**

Many franchisors such as **Baskin-Robbins**, **Dunkin' Donuts**, and **Cold Stone Creamery**, use notes to help entrepreneurs acquire their own franchises, including using notes to pay for the franchise fee and any equipment. Payments on these notes are usually collected monthly and often are secured by the franchisees' assets. ■

Payroll Liabilities

An employer incurs several expenses and liabilities from having employees. These expenses and liabilities are often large and arise from salaries and wages earned, from employee benefits, and from payroll taxes levied on the employer. **Boston Beer**, for instance, reports payroll-related current liabilities of more than $6.6 million from accrued "employee wages, benefits and reimbursements." We discuss payroll liabilities and related accounts in this section. Appendix 9A describes details about payroll reports, records, and procedures.

P2 Compute and record *employee* payroll deductions and liabilities.

Point: Deductions at some companies, such as those for insurance coverage, are "required" under its own labor contracts.

EXHIBIT 9.4

Payroll Deductions

Employee Payroll Deductions **Gross pay** is the total compensation an employee earns including wages, salaries, commissions, bonuses, and any compensation earned before deductions such as taxes. (*Wages* usually refer to payments to employees at an hourly rate. *Salaries* usually refer to payments to employees at a monthly or yearly rate.) **Net pay,** also called *take-home pay,* is gross pay less all deductions. **Payroll deductions,** commonly called *withholdings,* are amounts withheld from an employee's gross pay, either required or voluntary. Required deductions result from laws and include income taxes and Social Security taxes. Voluntary deductions, at an employee's option, include pension and health contributions, health and life insurance premiums, union dues, and charitable giving. Exhibit 9.4 shows the typical payroll deductions of an employee. The employer withholds payroll deductions from employees' pay and is obligated to transmit this money to the designated organization. The employer records payroll deductions as current liabilities until these amounts are transmitted. This section discusses the major payroll deductions.

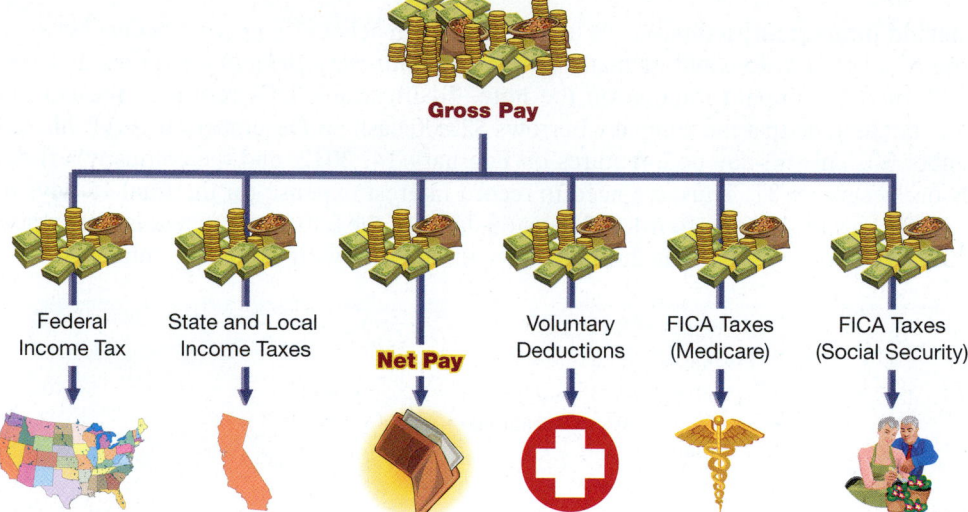

Employee FICA taxes. The federal Social Security system provides retirement, disability, survivorship, and medical benefits to qualified workers. Laws *require* employers to withhold **Federal Insurance Contributions Act (FICA) taxes** from employees' pay to cover costs of the system. Employers usually separate FICA taxes into two groups: (1) retirement, disability, and survivorship and (2) medical. For the first group, the Social Security system provides monthly cash payments to qualified retired workers for the rest of their lives. These payments are often called *Social Security benefits.* Taxes related to this group are often called *Social Security taxes.* For the second group, the system provides monthly payments to deceased workers' surviving families and to disabled workers who qualify for assistance. These payments are commonly called *Medicare benefits;* like those in the first group, they are paid with *Medicare taxes* (part of FICA taxes).

Law requires employers to withhold FICA taxes from each employee's salary or wages on each payday. The taxes for Social Security and Medicare are computed separately. For example, for the year 2010, the amount withheld from each employee's pay for Social Security tax was 6.2% of the first $106,800 the employee earns in the calendar year, or a maximum of $6,621.60. The Medicare tax was 1.45% of *all* amounts the employee earns; there is no maximum limit to Medicare tax.

Employers must pay withheld taxes to the Internal Revenue Service (IRS) on specific filing dates during the year. Employers who fail to send the withheld taxes to the IRS on time can be assessed substantial penalties. Until all the taxes are sent to the IRS, they are included in employers' current liabilities. For any changes in rates or with the maximum earnings level, check the IRS Website at **www.IRS.gov** or the SSA Website at **www.SSA.gov**.

Employee income tax. Most employers are required to withhold federal income tax from each employee's paycheck. The amount withheld is computed using tables published by the IRS. The amount depends on the employee's annual earnings rate and the number of *withholding allowances* the employee claims. Allowances reduce the amount of taxes one owes the government. The more allowances one claims, the less tax the employer will withhold. Employees

Point: The sources of U.S. tax receipts are roughly as follows:
50%　Personal income tax
35　FICA and FUTA taxes
10　Corporate income tax
5　Other taxes

Point: Part-time employees may claim "exempt from withholding" if they did not have any income tax liability in the prior year and do not expect any in the current year.

can claim allowances for themselves and their dependents. They also can claim additional allowances if they expect major declines in their taxable income for medical expenses. (An employee who claims more allowances than appropriate is subject to a fine.) Most states and many local governments require employers to withhold income taxes from employees' pay and to remit them promptly to the proper government agency. Until they are paid, withholdings are reported as a current liability on the employer's balance sheet.

Point: IRS withholding tables are based on projecting weekly (or other period) pay into an annual figure.

Employee voluntary deductions. Beyond Social Security, Medicare, and income taxes, employers often withhold other amounts from employees' earnings. These withholdings arise from employee requests, contracts, unions, or other agreements. They can include amounts for charitable giving, medical and life insurance premiums, pension contributions, and union dues. Until they are paid, such withholdings are reported as part of employers' current liabilities.

Recording employee payroll deductions. Employers must accrue payroll expenses and liabilities at the end of each pay period. To illustrate, assume that an employee earns a salary of $2,000 per month. At the end of January, the employer's entry to accrue payroll expenses and liabilities for this employee is

Jan. 31	Salaries Expense	2,000	
	FICA—Social Security Taxes Payable (6.2%)		124
	FICA—Medicare Taxes Payable (1.45%)		29
	Employee Federal Income Taxes Payable*		213
	Employee Medical Insurance Payable*		85
	Employee Union Dues Payable*		25
	Salaries Payable		1,524
	To record accrued payroll for January.		

Assets	=	Liabilities	+	Equity
		+124		−2,000
		+29		
		+213		
		+85		
		+25		
		+1,524		

* Amounts taken from employer's accounting records.

Salaries Expense (debit) shows that the employee earns a gross salary of $2,000. The first five payables (credits) show the liabilities the employer owes on behalf of this employee to cover FICA taxes, income taxes, medical insurance, and union dues. The Salaries Payable account (credit) records the $1,524 net pay the employee receives from the $2,000 gross pay earned. When the employee is paid, another entry (or a series of entries) is required to record the check written and distributed (or funds transferred). The entry to record cash payment to this employee is to debit Salaries Payable and credit Cash for $1,524.

Salaries Payable	1,524	
Cash		1,524

Decision **Insight**

A company's delay or failure to pay withholding taxes to the government has severe consequences. For example, a 100% penalty can be levied, with interest, on the unpaid balance. The government can even close a company, take its assets, and pursue legal actions against those involved. ■

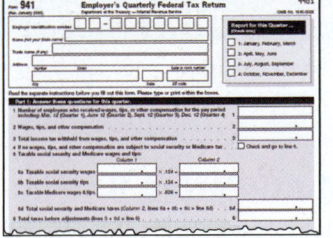

Employer Payroll Taxes Employers must pay payroll taxes in addition to those required of employees. Employer taxes include FICA and unemployment taxes.

Employer FICA tax. Employers must pay FICA taxes *equal in amount to* the FICA taxes withheld from their employees. An employer's tax is credited to the same FICA Taxes Payable accounts used to record the Social Security and Medicare taxes withheld from employees. (A self-employed person must pay both the employee and employer FICA taxes.)

P3 Compute and record *employer* payroll expenses and liabilities.

Federal and state unemployment taxes. The federal government participates with states in a joint federal and state unemployment insurance program. Each state administers its program. These programs provide unemployment benefits to qualified workers. The federal government approves state programs and pays a portion of their administrative expenses.

Federal Unemployment Taxes (FUTA). Employers are subject to a federal unemployment tax on wages and salaries paid to their employees. For the year 2010, employers were required to pay FUTA taxes of as much as 6.2% of the first $7,000 earned by each employee. This federal tax can be reduced by a credit of up to 5.4% for taxes paid to a state program. As a result, the net federal unemployment tax is often only 0.8%.

State Unemployment Taxes (SUTA). All states support their unemployment insurance programs by placing a payroll tax on employers. (A few states require employees to make a contribution. In the book's assignments, we assume that this tax is only on the employer.) In most states, the base rate for SUTA taxes is 5.4% of the first $7,000 paid each employee. This base rate is adjusted according to an employer's merit rating. The state assigns a **merit rating** that reflects a company's stability or instability in employing workers. A good rating reflects stability in employment and means an employer can pay less than the 5.4% base rate. A low rating reflects high turnover or seasonal hirings and layoffs. To illustrate, an employer with 50 employees each of whom earns $7,000 or more per year saves $15,400 annually if it has a merit rating of 1.0% versus 5.4%. This is computed by comparing taxes of $18,900 at the 5.4% rate to only $3,500 at the 1.0% rate.

Recording employer payroll taxes. Employer payroll taxes are an added expense beyond the wages and salaries earned by employees. These taxes are often recorded in an entry separate from the one recording payroll expenses and deductions. To illustrate, assume that the $2,000 recorded salaries expense from the previous example is earned by an employee whose earnings have not yet reached $5,000 for the year. This means the entire salaries expense for this period is subject to tax because year-to-date pay is under $7,000. Also assume that the federal unemployment tax rate is 0.8% and the state unemployment tax rate is 5.4%. Consequently, the FICA portion of the employer's tax is $153, computed by multiplying both the 6.2% and 1.45% by the $2,000 gross pay. Moreover, state unemployment (SUTA) taxes are $108 (5.4% of the $2,000 gross pay), and federal unemployment (FUTA) taxes are $16 (0.8% of $2,000). The entry to record the employer's payroll tax expense and related liabilities is

Example: If the employer's merit rating in this example reduces its SUTA rate to 2.9%, what is its SUTA liability? *Answer:* SUTA payable = $2,000 × 2.9% = $58

Assets = Liabilities + Equity
　　　　+124　　　−277
　　　　+29
　　　　+108
　　　　+16

Jan. 31			
	Payroll Taxes Expense	277	
	FICA—Social Security Taxes Payable (6.2%)		124
	FICA—Medicare Taxes Payable (1.45%)		29
	State Unemployment Taxes Payable		108
	Federal Unemployment Taxes Payable		16
	To record employer payroll taxes.		

Point: Internal control is important for payroll accounting. Managers must monitor (1) employee hiring, (2) timekeeping, (3) payroll listings, and (4) payroll payments. Poor controls led the U.S. Army to pay nearly $10 million to deserters, fictitious soldiers, and other unauthorized entities.

■ **Decision Ethics**　　　　　Answer — p. 392

Web Designer　You take a summer job working for a family friend who runs a small IT service. On your first payday, the owner slaps you on the back, gives you full payment in cash, winks, and adds: "No need to pay those high taxes, eh." What action, if any, do you take? ■

Multi-Period Known Liabilities

Many known liabilities extend over multiple periods. These often include unearned revenues and notes payable. For example, if **Sports Illustrated** sells a four-year magazine subscription, it records amounts received for this subscription in an Unearned Subscription Revenues account. Amounts in this account are liabilities, but are they current or long term? They are *both.* The portion of the Unearned Subscription Revenues account that will be fulfilled in the next year is reported as a current liability. The remaining portion is reported as a long-term liability.

The same analysis applies to notes payable. For example, a borrower reports a three-year note payable as a long-term liability in the first two years it is outstanding. In the third year, the borrower reclassifies this note as a current liability since it is due within one year or the operating cycle, whichever is longer. The **current portion of long-term debt** refers to that part of long-term debt due within one year or the operating cycle, whichever is longer. Long-term debt is reported under long-term liabilities, but the *current portion due* is reported under current liabilities. To illustrate, assume that a $7,500 debt is paid in installments of $1,500 per year for five years. The $1,500 due within the year is reported as a current liability. No journal entry is necessary for this reclassification. Instead, we simply classify the amounts for debt as either current or long term when the balance sheet is prepared.

Some known liabilities are rarely reported in long-term liabilities. These include accounts payable, sales taxes, and wages and salaries.

Point: Some accounting systems do make an entry to transfer the current amount due out of Long-Term Debt and into the Current Portion of Long-Term Debt as follows:

Long-Term Debt 1,500
   Current Portion of L-T Debt . . . 1,500

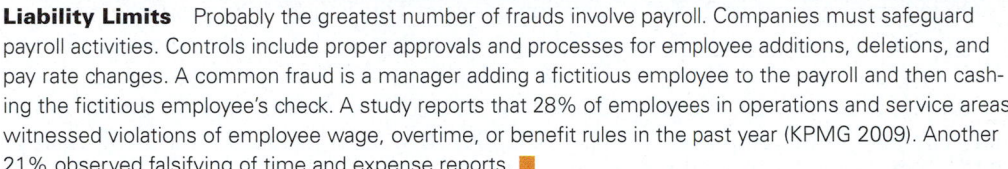

Decision Insight

Liability Limits Probably the greatest number of frauds involve payroll. Companies must safeguard payroll activities. Controls include proper approvals and processes for employee additions, deletions, and pay rate changes. A common fraud is a manager adding a fictitious employee to the payroll and then cashing the fictitious employee's check. A study reports that 28% of employees in operations and service areas witnessed violations of employee wage, overtime, or benefit rules in the past year (KPMG 2009). Another 21% observed falsifying of time and expense reports. ■

Quick Check

Answers — p. 393

4. Why does a creditor prefer a note payable to a past-due account payable?

5. A company pays its one employee $3,000 per month. This company's FUTA rate is 0.8% on the first $7,000 earned; its SUTA rate is 4.0% on the first $7,000; its Social Security tax rate is 6.2% of the first $106,800; and its Medicare tax rate is 1.45% of all amounts earned. The entry to record this company's March payroll includes what amount for total payroll taxes expense?

6. Identify whether the employer or employee or both incurs each of the following: (*a*) FICA taxes, (*b*) FUTA taxes, (*c*) SUTA taxes, and (*d*) withheld income taxes.

ESTIMATED LIABILITIES

An **estimated liability** is a known obligation that is of an uncertain amount but that can be reasonably estimated. Common examples are employee benefits such as pensions, health care and vacation pay, and warranties offered by a seller. We discuss each of these in this section. Other examples of estimated liabilities include property taxes and certain contracts to provide future services.

P4 Account for estimated liabilities, including warranties and bonuses.

Health and Pension Benefits

Many companies provide **employee benefits** beyond salaries and wages. An employer often pays all or part of medical, dental, life, and disability insurance. Many employers also contribute to *pension plans,* which are agreements by employers to provide benefits (payments) to employees after retirement. Many companies also provide medical care and insurance benefits to their retirees. When payroll taxes and charges for employee benefits are totaled, payroll cost often exceeds employees' gross earnings by 25% or more.

To illustrate, assume that an employer agrees to (1) pay an amount for medical insurance equal to $8,000 and (2) contribute an additional 10% of the employees' $120,000 gross salary to a retirement program. The entry to record these accrued benefits is

Dec. 31	Employee Benefits Expense	20,000	
	Employee Medical Insurance Payable		8,000
	Employee Retirement Program Payable		12,000
	To record costs of employee benefits.		

Assets = Liabilities + Equity
         +8,000 −20,000
         +12,000

Vacation Benefits

Many employers offer paid vacation benefits, also called *paid absences*. To illustrate, assume that salaried employees earn 2 weeks' vacation per year. This benefit increases employers' payroll expenses because employees are paid for 52 weeks but work for only 50 weeks. Total annual salary is the same, but the cost per week worked is greater than the amount paid per week. For example, if an employee is paid $20,800 for 52 weeks but works only 50 weeks, the total weekly expense to the employer is $416 ($20,800/50 weeks) instead of the $400 cash paid weekly to the employee ($20,800/52 weeks). The $16 difference between these two amounts is recorded weekly as follows:

Assets = Liabilities + Equity
         +16   −16

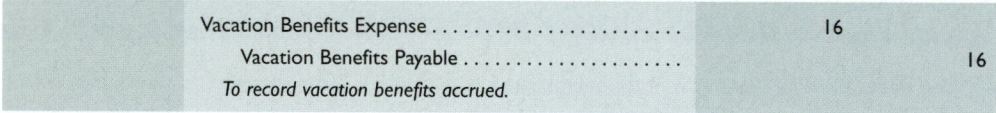

Vacation Benefits Expense	16	
Vacation Benefits Payable		16
To record vacation benefits accrued.		

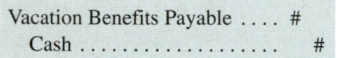

Vacation Benefits Payable .... #		
Cash		#

Vacation Benefits Expense is an operating expense, and Vacation Benefits Payable is a current liability. When the employee takes a vacation, the employer reduces (debits) the Vacation Benefits Payable and credits Cash (no additional expense is recorded).

Bonus Plans

Many companies offer bonuses to employees, and many of the bonuses depend on net income. To illustrate, assume that an employer offers a bonus to its employees equal to 5% of the company's annual net income (to be equally shared by all). The company's expected annual net income is $210,000. The year-end adjusting entry to record this benefit is

Assets = Liabilities + Equity
         +10,000   −10,000

Dec. 31	Employee Bonus Expense*	10,000	
	Bonus Payable		10,000
	To record expected bonus costs.		

* Bonus Expense (B) equals 5% of net income, which equals $210,000 minus the bonus; this is computed as:

$$B = 0.05 (\$210,000 - B)$$
$$B = \$10,500 - 0.05B$$
$$1.05B = \$10,500$$
$$\mathbf{B = \$10,500/1.05 = \$10,000}$$

When the bonus is paid, Bonus Payable is debited and Cash is credited for $10,000.

Warranty Liabilities

Point: Kodak recently reported $60 million in warranty obligations.

A **warranty** is a seller's obligation to replace or correct a product (or service) that fails to perform as expected within a specified period. Most new cars, for instance, are sold with a warranty covering parts for a specified period of time. **Ford Motor Company** reported more than $15 billion in "dealer and customer allowances and claims" in its annual report. To comply with the *full disclosure* and *matching principles,* the seller reports the expected warranty expense in the period when revenue from the sale of the product or service is reported. The seller reports this warranty obligation as a liability, although the existence, amount, payee, and date of future sacrifices are uncertain. This is because such warranty costs are probable and the amount can be estimated using, for instance, past experience with warranties.

To illustrate, a dealer sells a used car for $16,000 on December 1, 2011, with a maximum one-year or 12,000-mile warranty covering parts. This dealer's experience shows that warranty expense averages about 4% of a car's selling price, or $640 in this case ($16,000 × 4%). The dealer records the estimated expense and liability related to this sale with this entry:

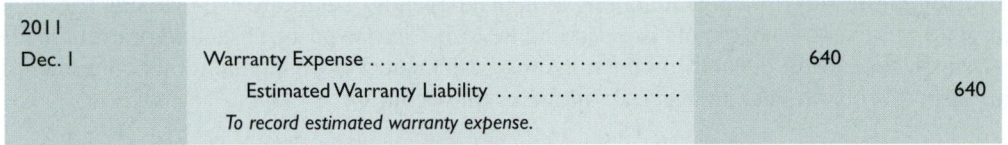

2011			
Dec. 1	Warranty Expense	640	
	Estimated Warranty Liability		640
	To record estimated warranty expense.		

Assets = Liabilities + Equity
　　　　　+640　　　 −640

This entry alternatively could be made as part of end-of-period adjustments. Either way, the estimated warranty expense is reported on the 2011 income statement and the warranty liability on the 2011 balance sheet. To further extend this example, suppose the customer returns the car for warranty repairs on January 9, 2012. The dealer performs this work by replacing parts costing $200. The entry to record partial settlement of the estimated warranty liability is

Point: Recognition of warranty liabilities is necessary to comply with the matching and full disclosure principles.

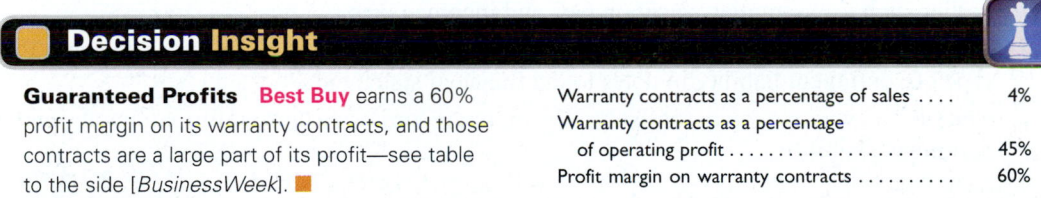

2012			
Jan. 9	Estimated Warranty Liability	200	
	Auto Parts Inventory		200
	To record costs of warranty repairs.		

Assets = Liabilities + Equity
−200　　　 −200

This entry reduces the balance of the estimated warranty liability. Warranty expense was previously recorded in 2011, the year the car was sold with the warranty. Finally, what happens if total warranty expenses are more or less than the estimated 4%, or $640? The answer is that management should monitor actual warranty expenses to see whether the 4% rate is accurate. If experience reveals a large difference from the estimate, the rate for current and future sales should be changed. Differences are expected, but they should be small.

Point: Both U.S. GAAP and IFRS account for restructuring costs in a manner similar to accounting for warranties.

Decision Insight

Guaranteed Profits   **Best Buy** earns a 60% profit margin on its warranty contracts, and those contracts are a large part of its profit—see table to the side [*BusinessWeek*]. ■

Warranty contracts as a percentage of sales	4%
Warranty contracts as a percentage of operating profit	45%
Profit margin on warranty contracts	60%

Multi-Period Estimated Liabilities

Estimated liabilities can be both current and long term. For example, pension liabilities to employees are long term to workers who will not retire within the next period. For employees who are retired or will retire within the next period, a portion of pension liabilities is current. Other examples include employee health benefits and warranties. Specifically, many warranties are for 30 or 60 days in length. Estimated costs under these warranties are properly reported in current liabilities. Many other automobile warranties are for three years or 36,000 miles. A portion of these warranties is reported as long term.

Quick Check   Answers — p. 393

7. Estimated liabilities involve an obligation to pay which of these? (*a*) An uncertain but reasonably estimated amount owed on a known obligation or (*b*) A known amount to a specific entity on an uncertain due date.

8. A car is sold for $15,000 on June 1, 2011, with a one-year warranty on parts. Warranty expense is estimated at 1.5% of selling price at each calendar year-end. On March 1, 2012, the car is returned for warranty repairs costing $135. The amount recorded as warranty expense on March 1 is (*a*) $0; (*b*) $60; (*c*) $75; (*d*) $135; (*e*) $225.

CONTINGENT LIABILITIES

C3 Explain how to account for contingent liabilities.

A **contingent liability** is a potential obligation that depends on a future event arising from a past transaction or event. An example is a pending lawsuit. Here, a past transaction or event leads to a lawsuit whose result depends on the outcome of the suit. Future payment of a contingent liability depends on whether an uncertain future event occurs.

Accounting for Contingent Liabilities

Accounting for contingent liabilities depends on the likelihood that a future event will occur and the ability to estimate the future amount owed if this event occurs. Three different possibilities are identified in the following chart: record liability, disclose in notes, or no disclosure.

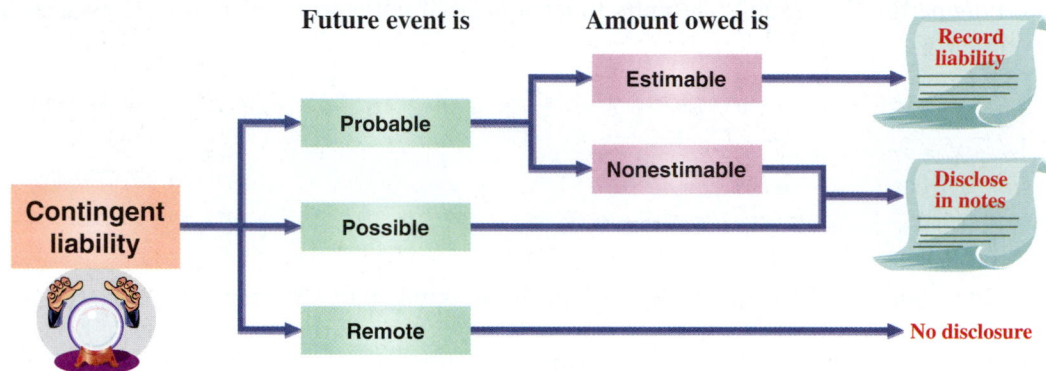

The conditions that determine each of these three possibilities follow:

1. The future event is *probable* (likely) and the amount owed can be *reasonably estimated.* We then record this amount as a liability. Examples are the estimated liabilities described earlier such as warranties, vacation pay, and income taxes.
2. The future event is *reasonably possible* (could occur). We disclose information about this type of contingent liability in notes to the financial statements.
3. The future event is *remote* (unlikely). We do not record or disclose information on remote contingent liabilities.

Point: A contingency is an *if.* Namely, if a future event occurs, then financial consequences are likely for the entity.

Reasonably Possible Contingent Liabilities

This section identifies and discusses contingent liabilities that commonly fall in the second category—when the future event is reasonably possible. Disclosing information about contingencies in this category is motivated by the *full-disclosure principle,* which requires information relevant to decision makers be reported and not ignored.

Point: A sale of a note receivable is often a contingent liability. It becomes a liability if the original signer of the note fails to pay it at maturity.

Potential Legal Claims   Many companies are sued or at risk of being sued. The accounting issue is whether the defendant should recognize a liability on its balance sheet or disclose a contingent liability in its notes while a lawsuit is outstanding and not yet settled. The answer is that a potential claim is recorded in the accounts *only* if payment for damages is probable and the amount can be reasonably estimated. If the potential claim cannot be reasonably estimated or is less than probable but reasonably possible, it is disclosed. **Ford Motor Company**, for example, includes the following note in its annual report: "Various legal actions, governmental investigations and proceedings and claims are pending . . . arising out of alleged defects in our products."

Debt Guarantees   Sometimes a company guarantees the payment of debt owed by a supplier, customer, or another company. The guarantor usually discloses the guarantee in its financial statement notes as a contingent liability. If it is probable that the debtor will default, the guarantor needs to record and report the guarantee in its financial statements as a liability. The **Boston Celtics** report a unique guarantee when it comes to coaches and players: "Certain of the contracts provide for guaranteed payments which must be paid even if the employee [player] is injured or terminated."

Other Contingencies   Other examples of contingencies include environmental damages, possible tax assessments, insurance losses, and government investigations. **Sunoco**, for instance, reports that "federal, state and local laws . . . result in liabilities and loss contingencies. Sunoco accrues . . . cleanup costs [that] are probable and reasonably estimable. Management believes it is reasonably possible (i.e., less than probable but greater than remote) that additional . . . losses will be incurred." Many of Sunoco's contingencies are revealed only in notes.

Point: Auditors and managers often have different views about whether a contingency is recorded, disclosed, or omitted.

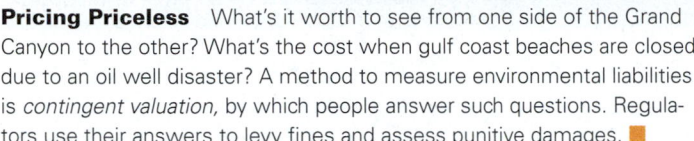

Decision Insight

Pricing Priceless   What's it worth to see from one side of the Grand Canyon to the other? What's the cost when gulf coast beaches are closed due to an oil well disaster? A method to measure environmental liabilities is *contingent valuation,* by which people answer such questions. Regulators use their answers to levy fines and assess punitive damages. ■

Uncertainties that Are Not Contingencies

All organizations face uncertainties from future events such as natural disasters and the development of new competing products or services. These uncertainties are not contingent liabilities because they are future events *not* arising from past transactions. Accordingly, they are not disclosed.

Quick Check   Answers — p. 393

9. A future payment is reported as a liability on the balance sheet if payment is contingent on a future event that (*a*) is reasonably possible but the payment cannot be reasonably estimated; (*b*) is probable and the payment can be reasonably estimated; or (*c*) is not probable but the payment is known.

10. Under what circumstances is a future payment reported in the notes to the financial statements as a contingent liability?

GLOBAL VIEW

This section discusses similarities and differences between U.S. GAAP and IFRS in accounting and reporting for current liabilities.

Characteristics of Liabilities   The definitions and characteristics of current liabilities are broadly similar for both U.S. GAAP and IFRS. Although differences exist, the similarities vastly outweigh any differences. Remembering that "provision" is typically used under IFRS to refer to what is titled "liability" under U.S. GAAP, **Nokia** describes its recognition of liabilities as follows:

NOKIA

> Provisions are recognized when the Group has a present legal or constructive obligation as a result of past events, it is probable that an outflow of resources will be required to settle the obligation and a reliable estimate of the amount can be made.

Known (Determinable) Liabilities   When there is little uncertainty surrounding current liabilities, both U.S. GAAP and IFRS require companies to record them in a similar manner. This correspondence in accounting applies to accounts payable, sales taxes payable, unearned revenues, short-term notes, and payroll liabilities. Of course, tax regulatory systems of countries are different, which implies use of different rates and levels. Still, the basic approach is the same.

Estimated Liabilities   When there is a known current obligation that involves an uncertain amount, but one that can be reasonably estimated, both U.S. GAAP and IFRS require similar treatment. This treatment extends to many obligations such as those arising from vacations, warranties, restructurings, pensions, and health care. Both accounting systems require that companies record estimated expenses related to these obligations when they can reasonably estimate the amounts. Nokia reports wages, salaries and bonuses of €5,658 million. It also reports pension expenses of €427 million.

 **Decide Analysis**    Times Interest Earned Ratio

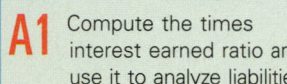
A1 Compute the times interest earned ratio and use it to analyze liabilities.

A company incurs interest expense on many of its current and long-term liabilities. Examples extend from its short-term notes and the current portion of long-term liabilities to its long-term notes and bonds. Interest expense is often viewed as a *fixed expense* because the amount of these liabilities is likely to remain in one form or another for a substantial period of time. This means that the amount of interest is unlikely to vary due to changes in sales or other operating activities. While fixed expenses can be advantageous when a company is growing, they create risk. This risk stems from the possibility that a company might be unable to pay fixed expenses if sales decline. To illustrate, consider Diego Co.'s results for 2011 and two possible outcomes for year 2012 in Exhibit 9.5.

EXHIBIT 9.5

Actual and Projected Results

		2012 Projections	
($ thousands)	2011	Sales Increase	Sales Decrease
Sales	$600	$900	$300
Expenses (75% of sales)	450	675	225
Income before interest	150	225	75
Interest expense (fixed)	60	60	60
Net income	$ 90	$165	$ 15

Expenses excluding interest are at, and expected to remain at, 75% of sales. Expenses such as these that change with sales volume are called *variable expenses*. However, interest expense is at, and expected to remain at, $60,000 per year due to its fixed nature.

The middle numerical column of Exhibit 9.5 shows that Diego's income increases by 83% to $165,000 if sales increase by 50% to $900,000. In contrast, the far right column shows that income decreases by 83% if sales decline by 50%. These results reveal that the amount of fixed interest expense affects a company's risk of its ability to pay interest, which is numerically reflected in the **times interest earned** ratio in Exhibit 9.6.

EXHIBIT 9.6

Times Interest Earned

$$\text{Times interest earned} = \frac{\text{Income before interest expense and income taxes}}{\text{Interest expense}}$$

For 2011, Diego's times interest earned is computed as $150,000/$60,000, or 2.5 times. This ratio suggests that Diego faces low to moderate risk because its sales must decline sharply before it would be unable to cover its interest expenses. (Diego is an LLC and does not pay income taxes.)

Experience shows that when times interest earned falls below 1.5 to 2.0 and remains at that level or lower for several periods, the default rate on liabilities increases sharply. This reflects increased risk for companies and their creditors. We also must interpret the times interest earned ratio in light of information about the variability of a company's income before interest. If income is stable from year to year or if it is growing, the company can afford to take on added risk by borrowing. If its income greatly varies from year to year, fixed interest expense can increase the risk that it will not earn enough income to pay interest.

 **Decision Maker**   Answer — p. 392

Entrepreneur   You wish to invest in a franchise for either one of two national chains. Each franchise has an expected annual net income *after* interest and taxes of $100,000. Net income for the first franchise includes a regular fixed interest charge of $200,000. The fixed interest charge for the second franchise is $40,000. Which franchise is riskier to you if sales forecasts are not met? Does your decision change if the first franchise has more variability in its income stream? ■

DEMONSTRATION PROBLEM

The following transactions and events took place at Kern Company during its recent calendar-year reporting period (Kern does not use reversing entries).

a. In September 2011, Kern sold $140,000 of merchandise covered by a 180-day warranty. Prior experience shows that costs of the warranty equal 5% of sales. Compute September's warranty expense and prepare the adjusting journal entry for the warranty liability as recorded at September 30. Also prepare the journal entry on October 8 to record a $300 cash expenditure to provide warranty service on an item sold in September.

b. On October 12, 2011, Kern arranged with a supplier to replace Kern's overdue $10,000 account payable by paying $2,500 cash and signing a note for the remainder. The note matures in 90 days and has a 12% interest rate. Prepare the entries recorded on October 12, December 31, and January 10, 2012, related to this transaction.

c. In late December, Kern learns it is facing a product liability suit filed by an unhappy customer. Kern's lawyer advises that although it will probably suffer a loss from the lawsuit, it is not possible to estimate the amount of damages at this time.

d. Sally Bline works for Kern. For the pay period ended November 30, her gross earnings are $3,000. Bline has $800 deducted for federal income taxes and $200 for state income taxes from each paycheck. Additionally, a $35 premium for her health care insurance and a $10 donation for the United Way are deducted. Bline pays FICA Social Security taxes at a rate of 6.2% and FICA Medicare taxes at a rate of 1.45%. She has not earned enough this year to be exempt from any FICA taxes. Journalize the accrual of salaries expense of Bline's wages by Kern.

e. On November 1, Kern borrows $5,000 cash from a bank in return for a 60-day, 12%, $5,000 note. Record the note's issuance on November 1 and its repayment with interest on December 31.

f. [B] Kern has estimated and recorded its quarterly income tax payments. In reviewing its year-end tax adjustments, it identifies an additional $5,000 of income tax expense that should be recorded. A portion of this additional expense, $1,000, is deferrable to future years. Record this year-end income taxes expense adjusting entry.

g. For this calendar-year, Kern's net income is $1,000,000, its interest expense is $275,000, and its income taxes expense is $225,000. Calculate Kern's times interest earned ratio.

PLANNING THE SOLUTION

● For *a,* compute the warranty expense for September and record it with an estimated liability. Record the October expenditure as a decrease in the liability.

● For *b,* eliminate the liability for the account payable and create the liability for the note payable. Compute interest expense for the 80 days that the note is outstanding in 2011 and record it as an additional liability. Record the payment of the note, being sure to include the interest for the 10 days in 2012.

● For *c,* decide whether the company's contingent liability needs to be disclosed or accrued (recorded) according to the two necessary criteria: probable loss and reasonably estimable.

● For *d,* set up payable accounts for all items in Bline's paycheck that require deductions. After deducting all necessary items, credit the remaining amount to Salaries Payable.

● For *e,* record the issuance of the note. Calculate 60 days' interest due using the 360-day convention in the interest formula.

● For *f,* determine how much of the income taxes expense is payable in the current year and how much needs to be deferred.

● For *g,* apply and compute times interest earned.

SOLUTION TO DEMONSTRATION PROBLEM

a. Warranty expense = 5% × $140,000 = $7,000

Sept. 30	Warranty Expense	7,000	
	Estimated Warranty Liability		7,000
	To record warranty expense for the month.		
Oct. 8	Estimated Warranty Liability	300	
	Cash		300
	To record the cost of the warranty service.		

b. Interest expense for 2011 = 12% × $7,500 × 80/360 = $200
Interest expense for 2012 = 12% × $7,500 × 10/360 = $25

Oct. 12	Accounts Payable	10,000	
	Notes Payable		7,500
	Cash		2,500
	Paid $2,500 cash and gave a 90-day, 12% note		
	to extend the due date on the account.		
Dec. 31	Interest Expense	200	
	Interest Payable		200
	To accrue interest on note payable.		
Jan. 10	Interest Expense	25	
	Interest Payable	200	
	Notes Payable	7,500	
	Cash		7,725
	Paid note with interest, including the accrued		
	interest payable.		

c. Disclose the pending lawsuit in the financial statement notes. Although the loss is probable, no liability can be accrued since the loss cannot be reasonably estimated.

d.

Nov. 30	Salaries Expense	3,000.00	
	FICA—Social Security Taxes Payable (6.2%)		186.00
	FICA—Medicare Taxes Payable (1.45%)		43.50
	Employee Federal Income Taxes Payable		800.00
	Employee State Income Taxes Payable		200.00
	Employee Medical Insurance Payable		35.00
	Employee United Way Payable		10.00
	Salaries Payable		1,725.50
	To record Bline's accrued payroll.		

e.

Nov. 1	Cash	5,000	
	Notes Payable		5,000
	Borrowed cash with a 60-day, 12% note.		

When the note and interest are paid 60 days later, Kern Company records this entry:

Dec. 31	Notes Payable	5,000	
	Interest Expense	100	
	Cash		5,100
	Paid note with interest ($5,000 × 12% × 60/360).		

f.

Dec. 31	Income Taxes Expense	5,000	
	Income Taxes Payable		4,000
	Deferred Income Tax Liability		1,000
	To record added income taxes expense and the deferred tax liability.		

g. Times interest earned $= \dfrac{\$1{,}000{,}000 + \$275{,}000 + \$225{,}000}{\$275{,}000} = \underline{\underline{5.45 \text{ times}}}$

Payroll Reports, Records, and Procedures

Understanding payroll procedures and keeping adequate payroll reports and records are essential to a company's success. This appendix focuses on payroll accounting and its reports, records, and procedures.

Payroll Reports   Most employees and employers are required to pay local, state, and federal payroll taxes. Payroll expenses involve liabilities to individual employees, to federal and state governments, and to other organizations such as insurance companies. Beyond paying these liabilities, employers are required to prepare and submit reports explaining how they computed these payments.

> **P5** Identify and describe the details of payroll reports, records, and procedures.

Reporting FICA Taxes and Income Taxes   The Federal Insurance Contributions Act (FICA) requires each employer to file an Internal Revenue Service (IRS) **Form 941,** the *Employer's Quarterly Federal Tax Return,* within one month after the end of each calendar quarter. A sample Form 941 is shown in Exhibit 9A.1 for Phoenix Sales & Service, a landscape design company. Accounting information and software are helpful in tracking payroll transactions and reporting the accumulated information on Form 941. Specifically, the employer reports total wages subject to income tax withholding on line 2 of Form 941. (For simplicity, this appendix uses *wages* to refer to both wages and salaries.) The income tax withheld is reported on line 3. The combined amount of employee and employer FICA (Social Security) taxes for Phoenix Sales & Service is reported on line 5a (taxable Social Security wages, $36,599 × 12.4% = $4,538.28). The 12.4% is the sum of the Social Security tax withheld, computed as 6.2% tax withheld from the employee wages for the quarter plus the 6.2% tax levied on the employer. The combined amount of employee Medicare wages is reported on line 5c. The 2.9% is the sum of 1.45% withheld from employee wages for the quarter plus 1.45% tax levied on the employer. Total FICA taxes are reported on line 5d and are added to the total income taxes withheld of $3,056.47 to yield a total of $8,656.12. For this year, assume that income up to $106,800 is subject to Social Security tax. There is no income limit on amounts subject to Medicare tax. Congress sets annual limits on the amount owed for Social Security tax.

   Federal depository banks are authorized to accept deposits of amounts payable to the federal government. Deposit requirements depend on the amount of tax owed. For example, when the sum of FICA taxes plus the employee income taxes is less than $2,500 for a quarter, the taxes can be paid when Form 941 is filed. Companies with large payrolls are often required to pay monthly or even semiweekly.

Reporting FUTA Taxes and SUTA Taxes   An employer's federal unemployment taxes (FUTA) are reported on an annual basis by filing an *Annual Federal Unemployment Tax Return,* IRS **Form 940.** It must be mailed on or before January 31 following the end of each tax year. Ten more days are allowed if all required tax deposits are filed on a timely basis and the full amount of tax is paid on or before January 31. FUTA payments are made quarterly to a federal depository bank if the total amount due exceeds $500. If $500 or less is due, the taxes are remitted annually. Requirements for paying and reporting state unemployment taxes (SUTA) vary depending on the laws of each state. Most states require quarterly payments and reports.

Form **941**	Employer's QUARTERLY Federal Tax Return

Department of the Treasury — Internal Revenue Service

(EIN)
Employer identification number: 8 6 – 3 2 1 4 5 8 7

Name *(not your trade name)*: Phoenix Sales & Service

Trade name *(if any)*:

Address: 1214   Mill Road
Number   Street   Suite or room number

Phoenix   AZ   85621
City   State   ZIP code

Report for this Quarter ...
(Check one.)

☐ 1: January, February, March
☐ 2: April, May, June
☐ 3: July, August, September
☒ 4: October, November, December

Part 1: Answer these questions for this quarter.

1 Number of employees who received wages, tips, or other compensation for the pay period including: *Mar. 12 (Quarter 1)*, *June 12 (Quarter 2)*, *Sept. 12 (Quarter 3)*, *Dec. 12 (Quarter 4)*   **1**   1

2 Wages, tips, and other compensation   **2**   36,599.00

3 Total income tax withheld from wages, tips, and other compensation   **3**   3,056.47

4 If no wages, tips, and other compensation are subject to social security or Medicare tax   ☐ Check and go to line 6.

5 Taxable social security and Medicare wages and tips:

	Column 1		Column 2
5a Taxable social security wages	36,599.00	× .124 =	4,538.28
5b Taxable social security tips	.	× .124 =	.
5c Taxable Medicare wages & tips	36,599.00	× .029 =	1,061.37

5d Total social security and Medicare taxes (*Column 2, lines 5a + 5b + 5c = line 5d*)   **5d**   5,599.65

6 Total taxes before adjustments (lines 3 + 5d = line 6)   **6**   8,656.12

7 **TAX ADJUSTMENTS** (Read the instructions for line 7 before completing lines 7a through 7h.):

7a Current quarter's fractions of cents   .

7b Current quarter's sick pay   .

7c Current quarter's adjustments for tips and group-term life insurance   .

7d Current year's income tax withholding (attach Form 941c)   .

7e Prior quarters' social security and Medicare taxes (attach Form 941c)   .

7f Special additions to federal income tax (attach Form 941c)   .

7g Special additions to social security and Medicare (attach Form 941c)   .

7h **TOTAL ADJUSTMENTS** (Combine all amounts: lines 7a through 7g.)   **7h**   0.00

8 Total taxes after adjustments (Combine lines 6 and 7h.)   **8**   8,656.12

9 Advance earned income credit (EIC) payments made to employees   **9**   .

10 Total taxes after adjustment for advance EIC (lines 8 – line 9 = line 10)   **10**   8,656.12

11 Total deposits for this quarter, including overpayment applied from a prior quarter   **11**   8,656.12

12 Balance due (If line 10 is more than line 11, write the difference here.)   **12**   0.00
Make checks payable to *United States Treasury*.

13 Overpayment (If line 11 is more than line 10, write the difference here.)   0.00   Check one ☐ Apply to next return. ☐ Send a refund.

Part 2: Tell us about your deposit schedule and tax liability for this quarter.

If you are unsure about whether you are a monthly schedule depositor or a semiweekly schedule depositor, see *Pub. 15 (Circular E), section 11.*

14 A Z   Write the state abbreviation for the state where you made your deposits OR write "MU" if you made your deposits in *multiple* states.

15 Check one: ☐ Line 10 is less than $2,500. Go to Part 3.

☒ You were a monthly schedule depositor for the entire quarter. Fill out your tax liability for each month. Then go to Part 3.

Tax liability: Month 1   3,079.11

   Month 2   2,049.77

   Month 3   3,527.24

   Total liability for quarter   8,656.12   Total must equal line 10.

☐ You were a semiweekly schedule depositor for any part of this quarter. Fill out *Schedule B (Form 941): Report of Tax Liability for Semiweekly Schedule Depositors*, and attach it to this form.

Part 3: Tell us about your business. If a question does NOT apply to your business, leave it blank.

16 If your business has closed or you stopped paying wages   ☐ Check here, and
enter the final date you paid wages   /   /

17 If you are a seasonal employer and you do not have to file a return for every quarter of the year   ☐ Check here.

Part 4: May we speak with your third-party designee?

Do you want to allow an employee, a paid tax preparer, or another person to discuss this return with the IRS? See the instructions for details.

☐ Yes. Designee's name

Phone ( ) –   Personal Identification Number (PIN) ☐ ☐ ☐ ☐ ☐

☒ No.

Part 5: Sign here. You MUST fill out both sides of this form and SIGN it.

Under penalties of perjury, I declare that I have examined this return, including accompanying schedules and statements, and to the best of my knowledge and belief, it is true, correct, and complete.

✗ Sign your name here

Print name and title

Date   /   /   Phone ( ) –

Reporting Wages and Salaries Employers are required to give each employee an annual report of his or her wages subject to FICA and federal income taxes along with the amounts of these taxes withheld. This report is called a *Wage and Tax Statement,* or **Form W-2.** It must be given to employees before January 31 following the year covered by the report. Exhibit 9A.2 shows Form W-2 for one of the employees at Phoenix Sales & Service. Copies of the W-2 Form must be sent to the Social Security Administration, where the amount of the employee's wages subject to FICA taxes and FICA taxes withheld are posted to each employee's Social Security account. These posted amounts become the basis for determining an employee's retirement and survivors' benefits. The Social Security Administration also transmits to the IRS the amount of each employee's wages subject to federal income taxes and the amount of taxes withheld.

EXHIBIT 9A.2

Form W-2

Payroll Records Employers must keep payroll records in addition to reporting and paying taxes. These records usually include a payroll register and an individual earnings report for each employee.

Payroll Register A **payroll register** usually shows the pay period dates, hours worked, gross pay, deductions, and net pay of each employee for each pay period. Exhibit 9A.3 shows a payroll register for Phoenix Sales & Service. It is organized into nine columns:

Col. 1 Employee identification (ID); Employee name; Social Security number (SS No.); Reference (check number); and Date (date check issued)
Col. 2 Pay Type (regular and overtime)
Col. 3 Pay Hours (number of hours worked as regular and overtime)
Col. 4 Gross Pay (amount of gross pay)[2]
Col. 5 FIT (federal income taxes withheld); FUTA (federal unemployment taxes)
Col. 6 SIT (state income taxes withheld); SUTA (state unemployment taxes)
Col. 7 FICA-SS_EE (social security taxes withheld, employee); FICA-SS_ER (social security taxes, employer)
Col. 8 FICA-Med_EE (medicare tax withheld, employee); FICA-Med_ER (medicare tax, employer)
Col. 9 Net pay (Gross pay less amounts withheld from employees)

---

[2] The Gross Pay column shows regular hours worked on the first line multiplied by the regular pay rate—this equals regular pay. Overtime hours multiplied by the overtime premium rate equals overtime premium pay reported on the second line. If employers are engaged in interstate commerce, federal law sets a minimum overtime rate of pay to employees. For this company, workers earn 150% of their regular rate for hours in excess of 40 per week.

EXHIBIT 9A.3

Payroll Register

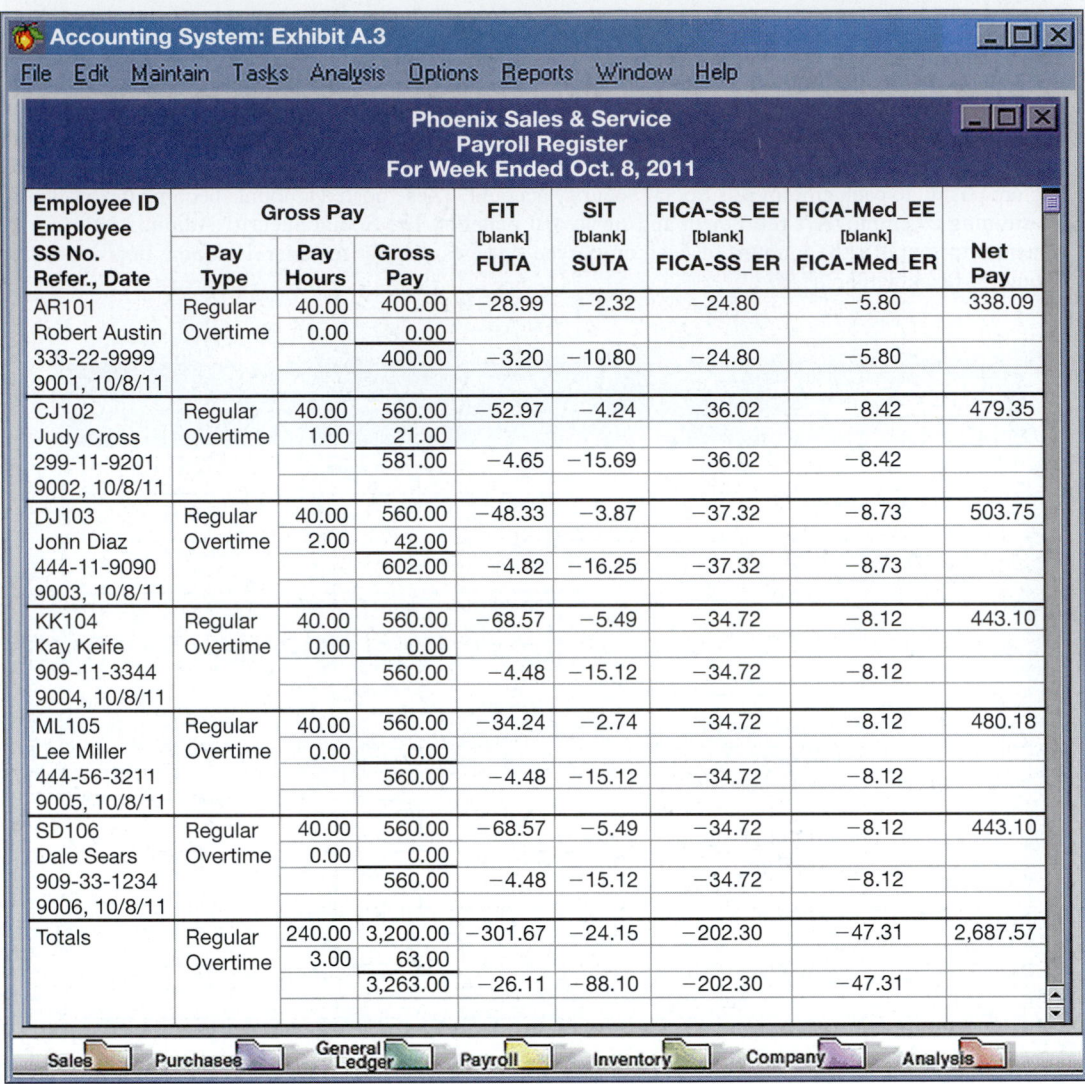

Net pay for each employee is computed as gross pay minus the items on the first line of columns 5–8. The employer's payroll tax for each employee is computed as the sum of items on the third line of columns 5–8. A payroll register includes all data necessary to record payroll. In some software programs the entries to record payroll are made in a special *payroll journal*.

Payroll Check   Payment of payroll is usually done by check or electronic funds transfer. Exhibit 9A.4 shows a *payroll check* for a Phoenix employee. This check is accompanied with a detachable *statement of earnings* (at top) showing gross pay, deductions, and net pay.

Employee Earnings Report   An **employee earnings report** is a cumulative record of an employee's hours worked, gross earnings, deductions, and net pay. Payroll information on this report is taken from the payroll register. The employee earnings report for R. Austin at Phoenix Sales & Service is shown in Exhibit 9A.5. An employee earnings report accumulates information that can show when an employee's earnings reach the tax-exempt points for FICA, FUTA, and SUTA taxes. It also gives data an employer needs to prepare Form W-2.

Payroll Procedures   Employers must be able to compute federal income tax for payroll purposes. This section explains how we compute this tax and how to use a payroll bank account.

Computing Federal Income Taxes   To compute the amount of taxes withheld from each employee's wages, we need to determine both the employee's wages earned and the employee's number of *withholding*

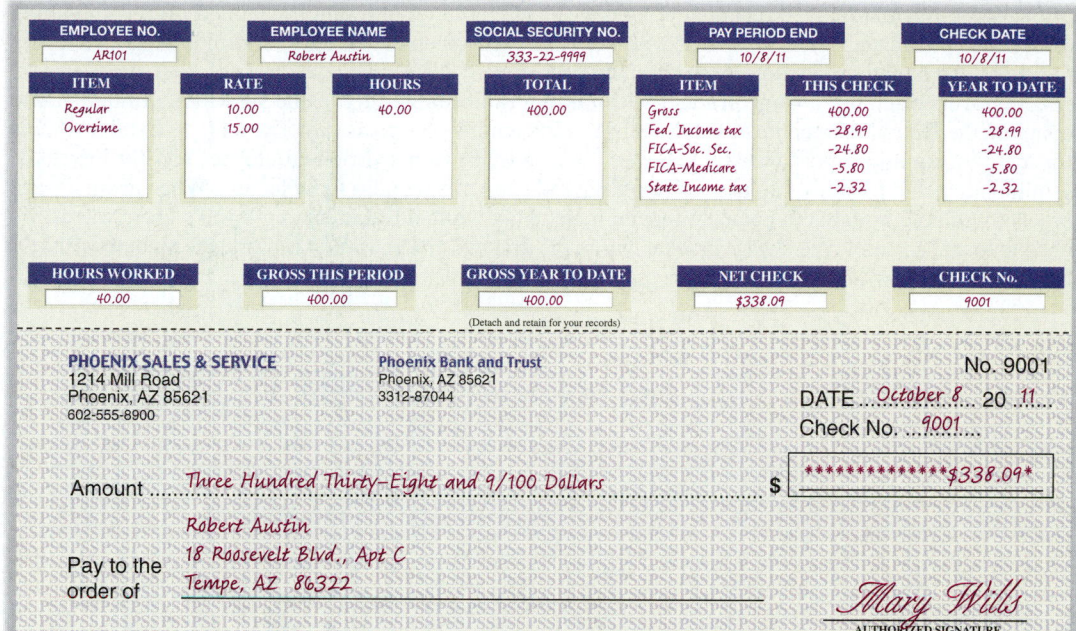

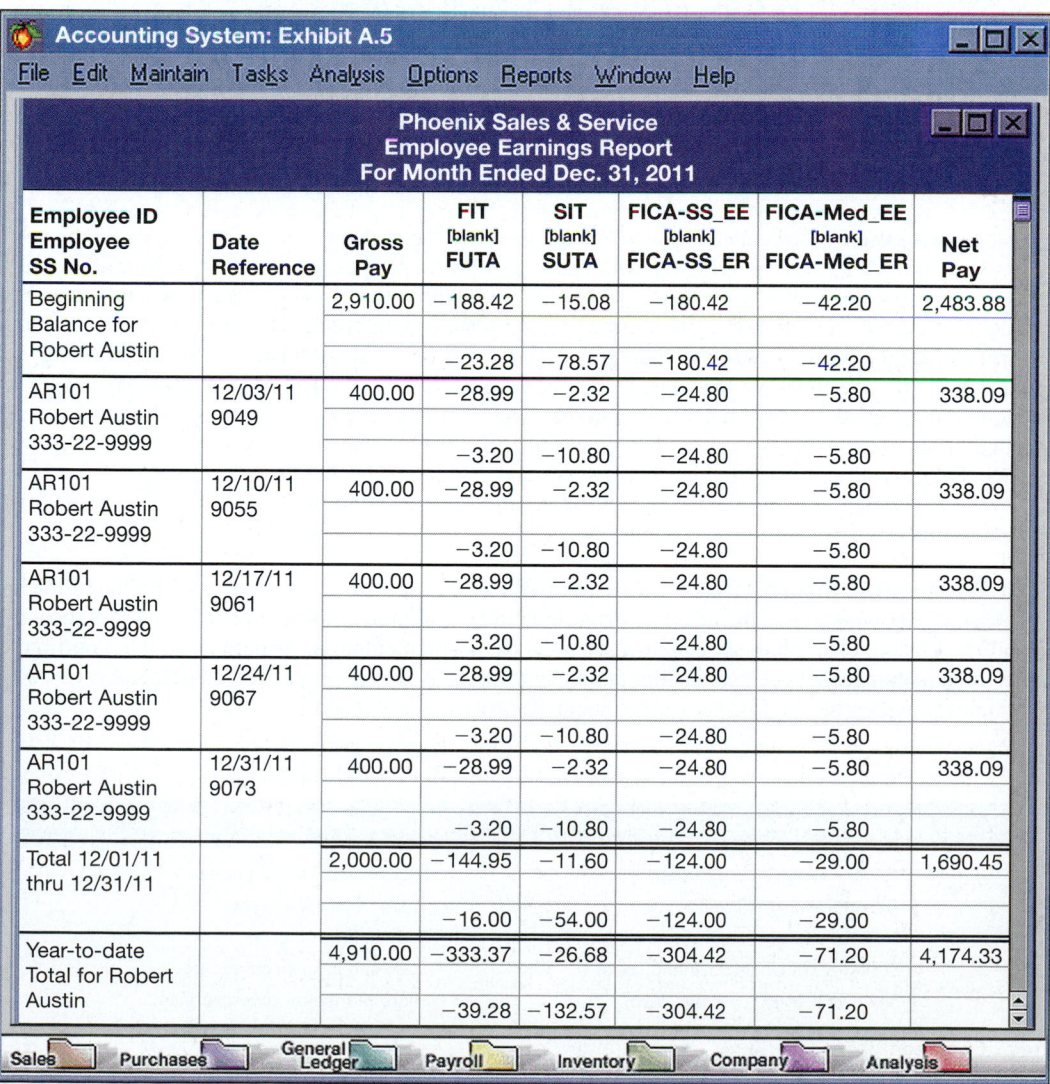

allowances. Each employee records the number of withholding allowances claimed on a withholding allowance certificate, **Form W-4,** filed with the employer. When the number of withholding allowances increases, the amount of income taxes withheld decreases.

Employers often use a **wage bracket withholding table** similar to the one shown in Exhibit 9A.6 to compute the federal income taxes withheld from each employee's gross pay. The table in Exhibit 9A.6 is for a single employee paid weekly. Tables are also provided for married employees and for biweekly, semimonthly, and monthly pay periods (most payroll software includes these tables). When using a wage bracket withholding table to compute federal income tax withheld from an employee's gross wages, we need to locate an employee's wage bracket within the first two columns. We then find the amount withheld by looking in the withholding allowance column for that employee.

EXHIBIT 9A.6

Wage Bracket Withholding Table

SINGLE Persons—WEEKLY Payroll Period

If the wages are—		And the number of withholding allowances claimed is—										
At least	But less than	0	1	2	3	4	5	6	7	8	9	10
		The amount of income tax to be withheld is—										
$600	$610	$76	$67	$58	$49	$39	$30	$21	$12	$6	$0	$0
610	620	79	69	59	50	41	32	22	13	7	1	0
620	630	81	70	61	52	42	33	24	15	8	2	0
630	640	84	72	62	53	44	35	25	16	9	3	0
640	650	86	73	64	55	45	36	27	18	10	4	0
650	660	89	75	65	56	47	38	28	19	11	5	0
660	670	91	76	67	58	48	39	30	21	12	6	0
670	680	94	78	68	59	50	41	31	22	13	7	1
680	690	96	81	70	61	51	42	33	24	14	8	2
690	700	99	83	71	62	53	44	34	25	16	9	3
700	710	101	86	73	64	54	45	35	27	17	10	4
710	720	104	88	74	65	56	47	37	28	19	11	5
720	730	106	91	76	67	57	48	39	30	20	12	6
730	740	109	93	78	68	59	50	40	31	22	13	7
740	750	111	96	80	70	60	51	42	33	23	14	8

Payroll Bank Account Companies with few employees often pay them with checks drawn on the company's regular bank account. Companies with many employees often use a special **payroll bank account** to pay employees. When this account is used, a company either (1) draws one check for total payroll on the regular bank account and deposits it in the payroll bank account or (2) executes an *electronic funds transfer* to the payroll bank account. Individual payroll checks are then drawn on this payroll bank account. Since only one check for the total payroll is drawn on the regular bank account each payday, use of a special payroll bank account helps with internal control. It also helps in reconciling the regular bank account. When companies use a payroll bank account, they usually include check numbers in the payroll register. The payroll register in Exhibit 9A.3 shows check numbers in column 1. For instance, Check No. 9001 is issued to Robert Austin. With this information, the payroll register serves as a supplementary record of wages earned by and paid to employees.

Who Pays What Payroll Taxes and Benefits We conclude this appendix with the following table identifying who pays which payroll taxes and which common employee benefits such as medical, disability, pension, charitable, and union costs. Who pays which employee benefits, and what portion, is subject to agreements between companies and their workers. Also, self-employed workers must pay both the employer and employee FICA taxes for Social Security and Medicare.

Employer Payroll Taxes and Costs	Employee Payroll Deductions
• FICA—Social Security Taxes	• FICA—Social Security taxes
• FICA—Medicare Taxes	• FICA—Medicare taxes
• FUTA (Federal Unemployment Taxes)	• Federal Income taxes
• SUTA (State Unemployment Taxes)	• State and local income taxes
• Share of medical coverage, if any	• Share of medical coverage, if any
• Share of pension coverage, if any	• Share of pension coverage, if any
• Share of other benefits, if any	• Share of other benefits, if any

Quick Check

Answers — p. 393

11. What three items determine the amount deducted from an employee's wages for federal income taxes?

12. What amount of income tax is withheld from the salary of an employee who is single with three withholding allowances and earnings of $675 in a week? (*Hint:* Use the wage bracket withholding table in Exhibit 9A.6.)

13. Which of the following steps are executed when a company draws one check for total payroll and deposits it in a special payroll bank account? (*a*) Write a check to the payroll bank account for the total payroll and record it with a debit to Salaries Payable and a credit to Cash. (*b*) Deposit a check (or transfer funds) for the total payroll in the payroll bank account. (*c*) Issue individual payroll checks drawn on the payroll bank account. (*d*) All of the above.

APPENDIX

Corporate Income Taxes

9B

This appendix explains current liabilities involving income taxes for corporations.

Income Tax Liabilities   Corporations are subject to income taxes and must estimate their income tax liability when preparing financial statements. Since income tax expense is created by earning income, a liability is incurred when income is earned. This tax must be paid quarterly under federal regulations. To illustrate, consider a corporation that prepares monthly financial statements. Based on its income in January 2011, this corporation estimates that it owes income taxes of $12,100. The following adjusting entry records this estimate:

Jan. 31	Income Taxes Expense	12,100	
	Income Taxes Payable		12,100
	To accrue January income taxes.		

Assets	=	Liabilities	+	Equity
		+12,100		−12,100

The tax liability is recorded each month until the first quarterly payment is made. If the company's estimated taxes for this first quarter total $30,000, the entry to record its payment is

Apr. 10	Income Taxes Payable	30,000	
	Cash		30,000
	Paid estimated quarterly income taxes based on first quarter income.		

Assets	=	Liabilities	+	Equity
−30,000		−30,000		

This process of accruing and then paying estimated income taxes continues through the year. When annual financial statements are prepared at year-end, the corporation knows its actual total income and the actual amount of income taxes it must pay. This information allows it to properly record income taxes expense for the fourth quarter so that the total of the four quarters' expense amounts equals the actual taxes paid to the government.

Deferred Income Tax Liabilities   An income tax liability for corporations can arise when the amount of income before taxes that the corporation reports on its income statement is not the same as the amount of income reported on its income tax return. This difference occurs because income tax laws and GAAP measure income differently. (Differences between tax laws and GAAP arise because Congress uses tax laws to generate receipts, stimulate the economy, and influence behavior, whereas GAAP are intended to provide financial information useful for business decisions. Also, tax accounting often follows the cash basis, whereas GAAP follows the accrual basis.)

Some differences between tax laws and GAAP are temporary. *Temporary differences* arise when the tax return and the income statement report a revenue or expense in different years. As an example, companies are often able to deduct higher amounts of depreciation in the early years of an asset's life and smaller amounts in later years for tax reporting in comparison to GAAP. This means that in the early years, depreciation for tax reporting is often more than depreciation on the income statement. In later years, depreciation for tax reporting is often less than depreciation on the income statement. When temporary differences exist between taxable income on the tax return and the income before taxes on the income statement, corporations compute income taxes expense based on the income reported on the income statement. The result is that income taxes expense reported in the income statement is often different from the amount of income taxes payable to the government. This difference is the **deferred income tax liability.**

To illustrate, assume that in recording its usual quarterly income tax payments, a corporation computes $25,000 of income taxes expense. It also determines that only $21,000 is currently due and $4,000 is deferred to future years (a timing difference). The entry to record this end-of-period adjustment is

Assets = Liabilities + Equity
+21,000   −25,000
+4,000

Dec. 31	Income Taxes Expense	25,000	
	Income Taxes Payable		21,000
	Deferred Income Tax Liability		4,000
	To record tax expense and deferred tax liability.		

The credit to Income Taxes Payable reflects the amount currently due to be paid. The credit to Deferred Income Tax Liability reflects tax payments deferred until future years when the temporary difference reverses.

Temporary differences also can cause a company to pay income taxes *before* they are reported on the income statement as expense. If so, the company reports a *Deferred Income Tax Asset* on its balance sheet.

Summary

C1   **Describe current and long-term liabilities and their characteristics.** Liabilities are probable future payments of assets or services that past transactions or events obligate an entity to make. Current liabilities are due within one year or the operating cycle, whichever is longer. All other liabilities are long term.

C2   **Identify and describe known current liabilities.** Known (determinable) current liabilities are set by agreements or laws and are measurable with little uncertainty. They include accounts payable, sales taxes payable, unearned revenues, notes payable, payroll liabilities, and the current portion of long-term debt.

C3   **Explain how to account for contingent liabilities.** If an uncertain future payment depends on a probable future event and the amount can be reasonably estimated, the payment is recorded as a liability. The uncertain future payment is reported as a contingent liability (in the notes) if (*a*) the future event is reasonably possible but not probable or (*b*) the event is probable but the payment amount cannot be reasonably estimated.

A1   **Compute the times interest earned ratio and use it to analyze liabilities.** Times interest earned is computed by dividing a company's net income before interest expense and income taxes by the amount of interest expense. The times interest earned ratio reflects a company's ability to pay interest obligations.

P1   **Prepare entries to account for short-term notes payable.** Short-term notes payable are current liabilities; most bear

interest. When a short-term note's face value equals the amount borrowed, it identifies a rate of interest to be paid at maturity.

P2   **Compute and record *employee* payroll deductions and liabilities.** Employee payroll deductions include FICA taxes, income taxes, and voluntary deductions such as for pensions and charities. They make up the difference between gross and net pay.

P3   **Compute and record *employer* payroll expenses and liabilities.** An employer's payroll expenses include employees' gross earnings, any employee benefits, and the payroll taxes levied on the employer. Payroll liabilities include employees' net pay amounts, withholdings from employee wages, any employer-promised benefits, and the employer's payroll taxes.

P4   **Account for estimated liabilities, including warranties and bonuses.** Liabilities for health and pension benefits, warranties, and bonuses are recorded with estimated amounts. These items are recognized as expenses when incurred and matched with revenues generated.

P5^A   **Identify and describe the details of payroll reports, records, and procedures.** Employers report FICA taxes and federal income tax withholdings using Form 941. FUTA taxes are reported on Form 940. Earnings and deductions are reported to each employee and the federal government on Form W-2. An employer's payroll records often include a payroll register for each pay period, payroll checks and statements of earnings, and individual employee earnings reports.

Guidance Answers to Decision Maker and Decision Ethics

Web Designer   You need to be concerned about being an accomplice to unlawful payroll activities. Not paying federal and state taxes on wages earned is illegal and unethical. Such payments also will not provide the employee with Social Security and some Medicare credits. The best course of action is to request payment by check. If this fails to change the owner's payment practices, you must consider quitting this job.

Entrepreneur   Risk is partly reflected by the times interest earned ratio. This ratio for the first franchise is 1.5 [($100,000 +

$200,000)/$200,000], whereas the ratio for the second franchise is 3.5 [($100,000 + $40,000)/$40,000]. This analysis shows that the first franchise is more at risk of incurring a loss if its sales decline. The second question asks about variability of income. If income greatly varies, this increases the risk an owner will not earn sufficient income to cover interest. Since the first franchise has the greater variability, it is a riskier investment.

Guidance Answers to Quick Checks

1. A liability involves a probable future payment of assets or services that an entity is presently obligated to make as a result of past transactions or events.

2. No, an expected future payment is not a liability unless an existing obligation was created by a past event or transaction.

3. In most cases, a liability due in 15 months is classified as long term. It is classified as a current liability if the company's operating cycle is 15 months or longer.

4. A creditor prefers a note payable instead of a past-due account payable so as to (*a*) charge interest and/or (*b*) have evidence of the debt and its terms for potential litigation or disputes.

5. $1,000* × (.008) + $1,000* × (.04) + $3,000 × (.062) + $3,000 × (.0145) = <u>$277.50</u>

—————

* $1,000 of the $3,000 March pay is subject to FUTA and SUTA—the entire $6,000 pay from January and February was subject to them.

6. (*a*) FICA taxes are incurred by both employee and employer.
(*b*) FUTA taxes are incurred by the employer.
(*c*) SUTA taxes are incurred by the employer.
(*d*) Withheld income taxes are incurred by the employee.

7. (*a*)

8. (*a*) Warranty expense was previously estimated and recorded.

9. (*b*)

10. A future payment is reported in the notes as a contingent liability if (*a*) the uncertain future event is probable but the amount of payment cannot be reasonably estimated or (*b*) the uncertain future event is not probable but has a reasonable possibility of occurring.

11. An employee's marital status, gross earnings and number of withholding allowances determine the deduction for federal income taxes.

12. $59

13. (*d*)

Key Terms

mhhe.com/wildFINMAN4e

Contingent liability (p. 380)
Current liabilities (p. 369)
Current portion of long-term debt (p. 377)
Deferred income tax liability (p. 392)
Employee benefits (p. 377)
Employee earnings report (p. 388)
Estimated liability (p. 377)
Federal depository bank (p. 385)
Federal Insurance Contributions Act (FICA) taxes (p. 374)

Federal Unemployment Taxes (FUTA) (p. 376)
Form 940 (p. 385)
Form 941 (p. 385)
Form W-2 (p. 387)
Form W-4 (p. 390)
Gross pay (p. 374)
Known liabilities (p. 370)
Long-term liabilities (p. 369)
Merit rating (p. 376)

Net pay (p. 374)
Payroll bank account (p. 390)
Payroll deductions (p. 374)
Payroll register (p. 387)
Short-term note payable (p. 371)
State Unemployment Taxes (SUTA) (p. 376)
Times interest earned (p. 382)
Wage bracket withholding table (p. 390)
Warranty (p. 378)

Multiple Choice Quiz

Answers on p. 409   mhhe.com/wildFINMAN4e

Additional Quiz Questions are available at the book's Website.

1. On December 1, a company signed a $6,000, 90-day, 5% note payable, with principal plus interest due on March 1 of the following year. What amount of interest expense should be accrued at December 31 on the note?
   a. $300
   b. $25
   c. $100
   d. $75
   e. $0

2. An employee earned $50,000 during the year. FICA tax for social security is 6.2% and FICA tax for Medicare is 1.45%. The employer's share of FICA taxes is
   a. Zero, since the employee's pay exceeds the FICA limit.
   b. Zero, since FICA is not an employer tax.
   c. $3,100
   d. $725
   e. $3,825

3. Assume the FUTA tax rate is 0.8% and the SUTA tax rate is 5.4%. Both taxes are applied to the first $7,000 of an employee's pay. What is the total unemployment tax an employer must pay on an employee's annual wages of $40,000?
   a. $2,480
   b. $434
   c. $56
   d. $378
   e. Zero; the employee's wages exceed the $7,000 maximum.

4. A company sells big screen televisions for $3,000 each. Each television has a two-year warranty that covers the replacement of defective parts. It is estimated that 1% of all televisions sold will be returned under warranty at an average cost of $250 each. During July, the company sold 10,000 big screen televisions, and 80 were serviced under the warranty during July at a total cost of $18,000. The credit balance in the Estimated

Warranty Liability account at July 1 was $26,000. What is the company's warranty expense for the month of July?

a. $51,000
b. $1,000
c. $25,000
d. $33,000
e. $18,000

5. Employees earn vacation pay at the rate of 1 day per month. During October, 150 employees qualify for one vacation day

each. Their average daily wage is $175 per day. What is the amount of vacation benefit expense for October?

a. $26,250
b. $175
c. $2,100
d. $63,875
e. $150

A(B) *Superscript letter A (B) denotes assignments based on Appendix 9A (9B).*

 Icon denotes assignments that involve decision making.

Discussion Questions

1. What are the three important questions concerning the uncertainty of liabilities?

2. What is the difference between a current and a long-term liability?

3. What is an estimated liability?

4. If $988 is the total of a sale that includes its sales tax of 4%, what is the selling price of the item only?

5. What is the combined amount (in percent) of the employee and employer Social Security tax rate?

6. What is the current Medicare tax rate? This rate is applied to what maximum level of salary and wages?

7. What determines the amount deducted from an employee's wages for federal income taxes?

8. Which payroll taxes are the employee's responsibility and which are the employer's responsibility?

9. What is an employer's unemployment merit rating? How are these ratings assigned to employers?

10. Why are warranty liabilities usually recognized on the balance sheet as liabilities even when they are uncertain?

11. Suppose that a company has a facility located where disastrous weather conditions often occur. Should it report a probable loss from a future disaster as a liability on its balance sheet? Explain.

12.A What is a wage bracket withholding table?

13.A What amount of income tax is withheld from the salary of an employee who is single with two withholding allowances and earning $725 per week? What if the employee earned $625 and has no withholding allowances? (Use Exhibit 9A.6.)

14. Refer to **Research In Motion**'s balance sheet in Appendix A. What revenue-related liability does Research In Motion report at February 27, 2010? **RIM**

15. Refer to **Apple**'s balance sheet in Appendix A. What is the amount of Apple's accounts payable as of September 26, 2009? **Apple**

16. Refer to **Nokia**'s balance sheet in Appendix A. List Nokia's current liabilities as of December 31, 2009. **NOKIA**

17. Refer to **Palm**'s balance sheet in Appendix A. What current liabilities related to income taxes are on its balance sheet? Explain the meaning of each income tax account identified. **Palm**

connect

QUICK STUDY

QS 9-1
Classifying liabilities C1

Which of the following items are normally classified as a current liability for a company that has a 15-month operating cycle?

1. Salaries payable.
2. Note payable due in 19 months.
3. FICA taxes payable.
4. Note payable maturing in 3 years.
5. Note payable due in 10 months.
6. Portion of long-term note due in 15 months.

QS 9-2
Accounting for sales taxes
C2

Wrecker Computing sells merchandise for $5,000 cash on September 30 (cost of merchandise is $2,900). The sales tax law requires Wrecker to collect 4% sales tax on every dollar of merchandise sold. Record the entry for the $5,000 sale and its applicable sales tax. Also record the entry that shows the remittance of the 4% tax on this sale to the state government on October 15.

QS 9-3
Unearned revenue C2

Tickets, Inc., receives $5,500,000 cash in advance ticket sales for a four-date tour of Bruce Springsteen. Record the advance ticket sales on October 31. Record the revenue earned for the first concert date of November 8, assuming it represents one-fourth of the advance ticket sales.

The following legal claims exist for Kalamazoo Co. Identify the accounting treatment for each claim as either (*a*) a liability that is recorded or (*b*) an item described in notes to its financial statements.

1. Kalamazoo (defendant) estimates that a pending lawsuit could result in damages of $1,000,000; it is reasonably possible that the plaintiff will win the case.
2. Kalamazoo faces a probable loss on a pending lawsuit; the amount is not reasonably estimable.
3. Kalamazoo estimates damages in a case at $2,500,000 with a high probability of losing the case.

QS 9-4
Accounting for contingent liabilities
C3

On November 7, 2011, Ortez Company borrows $150,000 cash by signing a 90-day, 8% note payable with a face value of $150,000. (1) Compute the accrued interest payable on December 31, 2011, (2) prepare the journal entry to record the accrued interest expense at December 31, 2011, and (3) prepare the journal entry to record payment of the note at maturity.

QS 9-5
Interest-bearing note transactions   **P1**

On January 14, the end of the first bi-weekly pay period of the year, Rockin Company's payroll register showed that its employees earned $14,000 of sales salaries. Withholdings from the employees' salaries include FICA Social Security taxes at the rate of 6.2%, FICA Medicare taxes at the rate of 1.45%, $2,600 of federal income taxes, $309 of medical insurance deductions, and $120 of union dues. No employee earned more than $7,000 in this first period. Prepare the journal entry to record Rockin Company's January 14 (employee) payroll expenses and liabilities.

QS 9-6
Record employee payroll taxes
P2

Merger Co. has ten employees, each of whom earns $2,000 per month and has been employed since January 1. FICA Social Security taxes are 6.2% of the first $106,800 paid to each employee, and FICA Medicare taxes are 1.45% of gross pay. FUTA taxes are 0.8% and SUTA taxes are 5.4% of the first $7,000 paid to each employee. Prepare the March 31 journal entry to record the March payroll taxes expense.

QS 9-7
Record employer payroll taxes
P3

On September 11, 2010, Home Store sells a mower for $400 with a one-year warranty that covers parts. Warranty expense is estimated at 5% of sales. On July 24, 2011, the mower is brought in for repairs covered under the warranty requiring $35 in materials taken from the Repair Parts Inventory. Prepare the July 24, 2011, entry to record the warranty repairs.

QS 9-8
Recording warranty repairs
P4

Paris Company offers an annual bonus to employees if the company meets certain net income goals. Prepare the journal entry to record a $10,000 bonus owed to its workers (to be shared equally) at calendar year-end.

QS 9-9
Accounting for bonuses   **P4**

Chester Co.'s salaried employees earn four weeks vacation per year. It pays $192,000.12 in total employee salaries for 52 weeks but its employees work only 48 weeks. This means Chester's total weekly expense is $4,000 ($192,000/48 weeks) instead of the $3,692.31 cash paid weekly to the employees ($192,000/52 weeks). Record Chester's weekly vacation benefits expense.

QS 9-10
Accounting for vacations
P4

Compute the times interest earned for Weltin Company, which reports income before interest expense and income taxes of $2,044,000, and interest expense of $350,000. Interpret its times interest earned (assume that its competitors average a times interest earned of 4.0).

QS 9-11
Times interest earned   **A1**

The payroll records of Clix Software show the following information about Trish Farqua, an employee, for the weekly pay period ending September 30, 2011. Farqua is single and claims one allowance. Compute her Social Security tax (6.2%), Medicare tax (1.45%), federal income tax withholding, state income tax (1.0%), and net pay for the current pay period. (Use the withholding table in Exhibit 9A.6 and round tax amounts to the nearest cent.)

QS 9-12ᴬ
Net pay and tax computations
P5

Total (gross) earnings for current pay period	$ 735
Cumulative earnings of previous pay periods	9,700

Check   Net pay, $578.42

Cather Corporation has made and recorded its quarterly income tax payments. After a final review of taxes for the year, the company identifies an additional $30,000 of income tax expense that should be recorded. A portion of this additional expense, $8,000, is deferred for payment in future years. Record Cather's year-end adjusting entry for income tax expense.

QS 9-13ᴮ
Record deferred income tax liability   **P4**

Answer each of the following related to international accounting standards.

a. In general, how similar or different are the definitions and characteristics of current liabilities between IFRS and U.S. GAAP?
b. Companies reporting under IFRS often reference a set of current liabilities with the title *financial liabilities*. Identify two current liabilities that would be classified under financial liabilities per IFRS. (*Hint:* **Nokia** provides examples in this chapter and in Appendix A.)

QS 9-14
International accounting standards

C1 C2

EXERCISES

Exercise 9-1

Classifying liabilities

C1

The following items appear on the balance sheet of a company with a two-month operating cycle. Identify the proper classification of each item as follows: *C* if it is a current liability, *L* if it is a long-term liability, or *N* if it is not a liability.

_____ **1.** Sales taxes payable.	_____ **6.** Notes payable (due in 6 to 12 months).
_____ **2.** FUTA taxes payable.	_____ **7.** Notes payable (due in 120 days).
_____ **3.** Accounts receivable.	_____ **8.** Current portion of long-term debt.
_____ **4.** Wages payable.	_____ **9.** Notes payable (mature in five years).
_____ **5.** Salaries payable.	_____**10.** Notes payable (due in 13 to 24 months).

Exercise 9-2

Recording known current liabilities

C2

Prepare any necessary adjusting entries at December 31, 2011, for Yacht Company's year-end financial statements for each of the following separate transactions and events.

1. Yacht Company records an adjusting entry for $2,000,000 of previously unrecorded cash sales (costing $1,000,000) and its sales taxes at a rate of 5%.

2. The company earned $40,000 of $100,000 previously received in advance for services.

Exercise 9-3

Accounting for contingent liabilities

C3

Prepare any necessary adjusting entries at December 31, 2011, for Moor Company's year-end financial statements for each of the following separate transactions and events.

1. A disgruntled employee is suing Moor Company. Legal advisers believe that the company will probably need to pay damages, but the amount cannot be reasonably estimated.

2. Moor Company guarantees the $5,000 debt of a supplier. The supplier will probably not default on the debt.

Exercise 9-4

Accounting for note payable

P1

Check (2b) Interest expense, $1,880

Perfect Systems borrows $94,000 cash on May 15, 2011, by signing a 60-day, 12% note.

1. On what date does this note mature?

2. Suppose the face value of the note equals $94,000, the principal of the loan. Prepare the journal entries to record (*a*) issuance of the note and (*b*) payment of the note at maturity.

Exercise 9-5

Interest-bearing notes payable with year-end adjustments

P1

Check (2) $2,250
       (3) $1,125

Kwon Co. borrows $150,000 cash on November 1, 2011, by signing a 90-day, 9% note with a face value of $150,000.

1. On what date does this note mature? (Assume that February of 2011 has 28 days.)

2. How much interest expense results from this note in 2011? (Assume a 360-day year.)

3. How much interest expense results from this note in 2012? (Assume a 360-day year.)

4. Prepare journal entries to record (*a*) issuance of the note, (*b*) accrual of interest at the end of 2011, and (*c*) payment of the note at maturity.

Exercise 9-6

Computing payroll taxes

P2 P3

Check (*a*) FUTA, $4.80; SUTA, $17.40

MRI Company has one employee. FICA Social Security taxes are 6.2% of the first $106,800 paid to its employee, and FICA Medicare taxes are 1.45% of gross pay. For MRI, its FUTA taxes are 0.8% and SUTA taxes are 2.9% of the first $7,000 paid to its employee. Compute MRI's amounts for each of these four taxes as applied to the employee's gross earnings for September under each of three separate situations (*a*), (*b*), and (*c*).

	Gross Pay through August	Gross Pay for September
a.	$ 6,400	$ 800
b.	18,200	2,100
c.	100,500	8,000

Exercise 9-7

Payroll-related journal entries   P2

Using the data in situation *a* of Exercise 9-6, prepare the employer's September 30 journal entries to record salary expense and its related payroll liabilities for this employee. The employee's federal income taxes withheld by the employer are $135 for this pay period.

Exercise 9-8

Payroll-related journal entries   P3

Using the data in situation *a* of Exercise 9-6, prepare the employer's September 30 journal entries to record the *employer's* payroll taxes expense and its related liabilities.

For the year ended December 31, 2011, Winter Company has implemented an employee bonus program equal to 3% of Winter's net income, which employees will share equally. Winter's net income (prebonus) is expected to be $1,000,000, and bonus expense is deducted in computing net income.

1. Compute the amount of the bonus payable to the employees at year-end (use the method described in the chapter and round to the nearest dollar).
2. Prepare the journal entry at December 31, 2011, to record the bonus due the employees.
3. Prepare the journal entry at January 19, 2012, to record payment of the bonus to employees.

Exercise 9-9
Computing and recording bonuses **P4**

Check (1) $29,126

Prepare any necessary adjusting entries at December 31, 2011, for Jester Company's year-end financial statements for each of the following separate transactions and events.

1. During December, Jester Company sold 3,000 units of a product that carries a 60-day warranty. December sales for this product total $120,000. The company expects 8% of the units to need warranty repairs, and it estimates the average repair cost per unit will be $15.
2. Employees earn vacation pay at a rate of one day per month. During December, 20 employees qualify for one vacation day each. Their average daily wage is $120 per employee.

Exercise 9-10
Accounting for estimated liabilities
P4

Chang Co. sold a copier costing $3,800 with a two-year parts warranty to a customer on August 16, 2011, for $5,500 cash. Chang uses the perpetual inventory system. On November 22, 2012, the copier requires on-site repairs that are completed the same day. The repairs cost $199 for materials taken from the Repair Parts Inventory. These are the only repairs required in 2012 for this copier. Based on experience, Chang expects to incur warranty costs equal to 4% of dollar sales. It records warranty expense with an adjusting entry at the end of each year.

1. How much warranty expense does the company report in 2011 for this copier?
2. How much is the estimated warranty liability for this copier as of December 31, 2011?
3. How much warranty expense does the company report in 2012 for this copier?
4. How much is the estimated warranty liability for this copier as of December 31, 2012?
5. Prepare journal entries to record (*a*) the copier's sale; (*b*) the adjustment on December 31, 2011, to recognize the warranty expense; and (*c*) the repairs that occur in November 2012.

Exercise 9-11
Warranty expense and liability computations and entries
P4

Check (1) $220

(4) $21

Use the following information from separate companies *a* through *f* to compute times interest earned. Which company indicates the strongest ability to pay interest expense as it comes due?

	Net Income (Loss)	Interest Expense	Income Taxes
a.	$140,000	$48,000	$ 35,000
b.	140,000	15,000	50,000
c.	140,000	8,000	70,000
d.	265,000	12,000	130,000
e.	79,000	12,000	30,000
f.	(4,000)	12,000	0

Exercise 9-12
Computing and interpreting times interest earned

A1

Check (b) 13.67

Tony Newbern, an unmarried employee, works 48 hours in the week ended January 12. His pay rate is $12 per hour, and his wages are subject to no deductions other than FICA—Social Security, FICA—Medicare, and federal income taxes. He claims two withholding allowances. Compute his regular pay, overtime pay (for this company, workers earn 150% of their regular rate for hours in excess of 40 per week), and gross pay. Then compute his FICA tax deduction (use 6.2% for the Social Security portion and 1.45% for the Medicare portion), income tax deduction (use the wage bracket withholding table of Exhibit 9A.6), total deductions, and net pay. (Round tax amounts to the nearest cent.)

Exercise 9-13ᴬ
Gross and net pay computation
P5

Check Net pay, $515.26

Ming Corporation prepares financial statements for each month-end. As part of its accounting process, estimated income taxes are accrued each month for 30% of the current month's net income. The income taxes are paid in the first month of each quarter for the amount accrued for the prior quarter. The following information is available for the fourth quarter of year 2011. When tax computations are completed on January 20, 2012, Ming determines that the quarter's Income Taxes Payable account balance should be $29,100 on December 31, 2011 (its unadjusted balance is $23,640).

Exercise 9-14ᴮ
Accounting for income taxes
P4

October 2011 net income	$27,900	
November 2011 net income	18,200	
December 2011 net income	32,700	

1. Determine the amount of the accounting adjustment (dated as of December 31, 2011) to produce the proper ending balance in the Income Taxes Payable account.

2. Prepare journal entries to record (*a*) the December 31, 2011, adjustment to the Income Taxes Payable account and (*b*) the January 20, 2012, payment of the fourth-quarter taxes.

Exercise 9-15
Accounting for current liabilities under IFRS

P4

Volvo Group reports the following information for its product warranty costs as of December 31, 2008, along with provisions and utilizations of warranty liabilities for the year ended December 31, 2008 (SEK in millions).

Product warranty costs

Estimated costs for product warranties are charged to cost of sales when the products are sold. Estimated warranty costs include contractual warranty and goodwill warranty. Warranty provisions are estimated with consideration of historical claims statistics, the warranty period, the average time-lag between faults occurring and claims to the company, and anticipated changes in quality indexes. Differences between actual warranty claims and the estimated claims generally affect the recognized expense and provisions in future periods. At December 31, 2008, warranty cost provisions amounted to 10,354.

Product warranty liabilities, December 31, 2007	SEK 9,373
Additional provisions to product warranty liabilities	6,201
Utilizations and reductions of product warranty liabilities	(5,220)
Product warranty liabilities, December 31, 2008	10,354

1. Prepare Volvo's journal entry to record its estimated warranty liabilities (provisions) for 2008.

2. Prepare Volvo's journal entry to record its costs (utilizations) related to its warranty program for 2008. Assume those costs involve replacements taken out of Inventory, with no cash involved.

3. How much warranty expense does Volvo report for 2008?

Exercise 9-16
Recording payroll

P2 P3

The following monthly data are taken from Nunez Company at July 31: Sales salaries, $120,000; Office salaries, $60,000; Federal income taxes withheld, $45,000; State income taxes withheld, $10,000; Social security taxes withheld, $11,160; Medicare taxes withheld, $2,610; Medical insurance premiums, $7,000; Life insurance premiums, $4,000; Union dues deducted, $1,000; and Salaries subject to unemployment taxes, $50,000. The employee pays forty percent of medical and life insurance premiums.

Prepare journal entries to record: (1) accrued payroll, including employee deductions, for July; (2) cash payment of the net payroll (salaries payable) for July; (3) accrued employer payroll taxes, and other related employment expenses, for July—assume that FICA taxes are identical to those on employees and that SUTA taxes are 5.4% and FUTA taxes are 0.8%; and (4) cash payment of all liabilities related to the July payroll.

Exercise 9-17
Computing payroll taxes

P2 P3

Madison Company has nine employees. FICA Social Security taxes are 6.2% of the first $106,800 paid to each employee, and FICA Medicare taxes are 1.45% of gross pay. FUTA taxes are 0.8% and SUTA taxes are 5.4% of the first $7,000 paid to each employee. Cumulative pay for the current year for each of its employees follows.

Employee	Cumulative Pay	Employee	Cumulative Pay	Employee	Cumulative Pay
Steve S.	$ 6,000	Christina S.	$156,800	Dana W.	$116,800
Tim V.	60,000	Michelle H.	106,800	Stewart M.	36,800
Brent G.	87,000	Kathleen K.	110,000	Sankha B.	4,000

a. Prepare a table with the following column headings: Employee; Cumulative Pay; Pay Subject to FICA Social Security Taxes; Pay Subject to FICA Medicare Taxes; Pay Subject to FUTA Taxes; Pay Subject to SUTA Taxes. Compute the amounts in this table for each employee and total the columns.

b. For the company, compute each total for: FICA Social Security taxes, FICA Medicare taxes, FUTA taxes, and SUTA taxes. (*Hint:* Remember to include in those totals any employee share of taxes that the company must collect.)

Exercise 9-18
Preparing payroll register and related entries   P5

SP Company has five employees. Employees paid by the hour receive a $10 per hour pay rate for the regular 40-hour work week plus one and one-half times the hourly rate for each overtime hour beyond the 40-hours per week. Hourly employees are paid every two weeks, but salaried employees are paid monthly on the last biweekly payday of each month. FICA Social Security taxes are 6.2% of the first $106,800 paid to each employee, and FICA Medicare taxes are 1.45% of gross pay. FUTA taxes are 0.8% and SUTA taxes are 5.4% of the first $7,000 paid to each employee. The company has a benefits plan that includes medical insurance, life insurance, and retirement funding for employees. Under this plan, employees must contribute 5 percent of their gross income as a payroll withholding, which the company matches with double the amount. Following is the partially completed payroll register for the biweekly period ending August 31, which is the last payday of August.

Employee	Cumulative Pay (Excludes Current Period)	Pay Type	Pay Hours	Gross Pay	FIT / SIT	FUTA / SUTA	FICA-SS_EE / FICA-SS_ER	FICA-Med_EE / FICA-Med_ER	EE-Ben_Plan Withholding / ER-Ben_Plan Withholding	Employee Net Pay
Kathleen	$105,000.00	Salary	---	$7,000.00	$2,000.00 / 300.00					
Nichole	6,800.00	Salary	---	500.00	80.00 / 20.00					
Anthony	15,000.00	Regular / Overtime	80 / 8		110.00 / 25.00					
Zoey	6,500.00	Regular / Overtime	80 / 4		100.00 / 22.00					
Gracie	5,000.00	Regular / Overtime	74 / 0	740.00 / 0.00	90.00 / 21.00					
Totals	138,300.00				2,380.00 / 388.00					

* Table abbreviations follow those in Exhibit 9A.3 (see pages 387–388); and, "Ben_Plan" refers to employee (EE) or employer (ER) withholding for the benefits plan.

a. Complete this payroll register by filling in all cells for the pay period ended August 31. *Hint:* See Exhibit 9A.3 for guidance. (Round amounts to cents.)

b. Prepare the August 31 journal entry to record the accrued biweekly payroll and related liabilities for deductions.

c. Prepare the August 31 journal entry to record the employer's cash payment of the net payroll of part *b.*

d. Prepare the August 31 journal entry to record the employer's payroll taxes including the contribution to the benefits plan.

e. Prepare the August 31 journal entry to pay all liabilities (expect net payroll in part *c*) for this biweekly period.

Tytus Co. entered into the following transactions involving short-term liabilities in 2010 and 2011.

2010

Apr. 20 Purchased $38,500 of merchandise on credit from Frier, terms are 1/10, n/30. Tytus uses the perpetual inventory system.

May 19 Replaced the April 20 account payable to Frier with a 90-day, $30,000 note bearing 9% annual interest along with paying $8,500 in cash.

July 8 Borrowed $60,000 cash from Community Bank by signing a 120-day, 10% interest-bearing note with a face value of $60,000.

? Paid the amount due on the note to Frier at the maturity date.

? Paid the amount due on the note to Community Bank at the maturity date.

Nov. 28 Borrowed $21,000 cash from UMB Bank by signing a 60-day, 8% interest-bearing note with a face value of $21,000.

Dec. 31 Recorded an adjusting entry for accrued interest on the note to UMB Bank.

2011

? Paid the amount due on the note to UMB Bank at the maturity date.

Required

1. Determine the maturity date for each of the three notes described.

2. Determine the interest due at maturity for each of the three notes. (Assume a 360-day year.)

3. Determine the interest expense to be recorded in the adjusting entry at the end of 2010.

4. Determine the interest expense to be recorded in 2011.

5. Prepare journal entries for all the preceding transactions and events for years 2010 and 2011.

PROBLEM SET A

Problem 9-1A
Short-term notes payable transactions and entries

P1

mhhe.com/wildFINMAN4e

Check (2) Frier, $675
(3) $154
(4) $126

Problem 9-2A
Warranty expense and
liability estimation
P4

On October 29, 2010, Lue Co. began operations by purchasing razors for resale. Lue uses the perpetual inventory method. The razors have a 90-day warranty that requires the company to replace any nonworking razor. When a razor is returned, the company discards it and mails a new one from Merchandise Inventory to the customer. The company's cost per new razor is $18 and its retail selling price is $80 in both 2010 and 2011. The manufacturer has advised the company to expect warranty costs to equal 7% of dollar sales. The following transactions and events occurred.

2010

Nov. 11   Sold 75 razors for $6,000 cash.
     30   Recognized warranty expense related to November sales with an adjusting entry.
Dec. 9   Replaced 15 razors that were returned under the warranty.
     16   Sold 210 razors for $16,800 cash.
     29   Replaced 30 razors that were returned under the warranty.
     31   Recognized warranty expense related to December sales with an adjusting entry.

2011

Jan. 5   Sold 130 razors for $10,400 cash.
     17   Replaced 50 razors that were returned under the warranty.
     31   Recognized warranty expense related to January sales with an adjusting entry.

Required

1. Prepare journal entries to record these transactions and adjustments for 2010 and 2011.
2. How much warranty expense is reported for November 2010 and for December 2010?
3. How much warranty expense is reported for January 2011?
4. What is the balance of the Estimated Warranty Liability account as of December 31, 2010?
5. What is the balance of the Estimated Warranty Liability account as of January 31, 2011?

Check   (3) $728
            (4) $786 Cr.
            (5) $614 Cr.

Problem 9-3A
Computing and analyzing times interest earned
A1

Shown here are condensed income statements for two different companies (both are organized as LLCs and pay no income taxes).

Ace Company	
Sales	$500,000
Variable expenses (80%)	400,000
Income before interest	100,000
Interest expense (fixed)	30,000
Net income	$ 70,000

Deuce Company	
Sales	$500,000
Variable expenses (60%)	300,000
Income before interest	200,000
Interest expense (fixed)	130,000
Net income	$ 70,000

Required

1. Compute times interest earned for Ace Company.
2. Compute times interest earned for Deuce Company.
3. What happens to each company's net income if sales increase by 30%?
4. What happens to each company's net income if sales increase by 50%?
5. What happens to each company's net income if sales increase by 80%?
6. What happens to each company's net income if sales decrease by 10%?
7. What happens to each company's net income if sales decrease by 20%?
8. What happens to each company's net income if sales decrease by 40%?

Check   (3) Ace net income,
$100,000 (43% increase)

(6) Deuce net income,
$50,000 (29% decrease)

Analysis Component

9. Comment on the results from parts 3 through 8 in relation to the fixed-cost strategies of the two companies and the ratio values you computed in parts 1 and 2.

Problem 9-4A
Payroll expenses, withholdings, and taxes
P2   P3

Legal Stars has four employees. FICA Social Security taxes are 6.2% of the first $106,800 paid to each employee, and FICA Medicare taxes are 1.45% of gross pay. Also, for the first $7,000 paid to each employee, the company's FUTA taxes are 0.8% and SUTA taxes are 2.15%. The company is preparing its payroll calculations for the week ended August 25. Payroll records show the following information for the company's four employees.

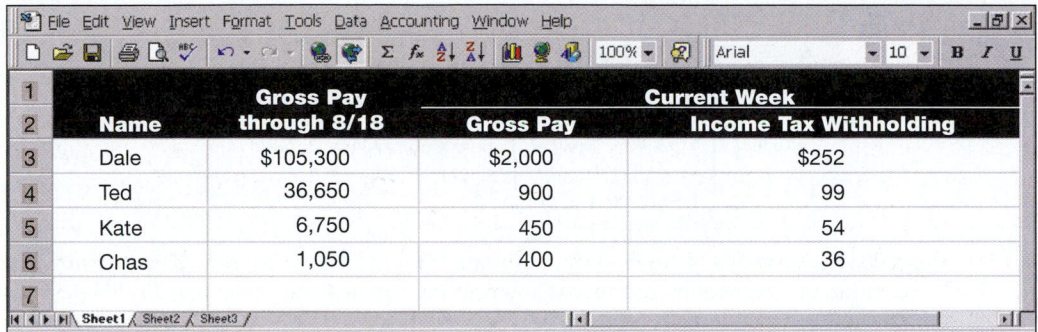

In addition to gross pay, the company must pay one-half of the $32 per employee weekly health insurance; each employee pays the remaining one-half. The company also contributes an extra 8% of each employee's gross pay (at no cost to employees) to a pension fund.

Required

Compute the following for the week ended August 25 (round amounts to the nearest cent):

1. Each employee's FICA withholdings for Social Security.

2. Each employee's FICA withholdings for Medicare.

3. Employer's FICA taxes for Social Security.

4. Employer's FICA taxes for Medicare.

5. Employer's FUTA taxes.

6. Employer's SUTA taxes.

7. Each employee's net (take-home) pay.

8. Employer's total payroll-related expense for each employee.

Check (3) $201.50

(4) $54.38

(5) $5.20

(7) Total net pay, $2,989.12

On January 8, the end of the first weekly pay period of the year, Royal Company's payroll register showed that its employees earned $11,380 of office salaries and $32,920 of sales salaries. Withholdings from the employees' salaries include FICA Social Security taxes at the rate of 6.2%, FICA Medicare taxes at the rate of 1.45%, $6,340 of federal income taxes, $670 of medical insurance deductions, and $420 of union dues. No employee earned more than $7,000 in this first period.

Problem 9-5A
Entries for payroll transactions
P2 P3

Required

1. Calculate FICA Social Security taxes payable and FICA Medicare taxes payable. Prepare the journal entry to record Royal Company's January 8 (employee) payroll expenses and liabilities.

2. Prepare the journal entry to record Royal's (employer) payroll taxes resulting from the January 8 payroll. Royal's merit rating reduces its state unemployment tax rate to 4% of the first $7,000 paid each employee. The federal unemployment tax rate is 0.8%.

Check (1) Cr. Salaries Payable, $33,481.05

(2) Dr. Payroll Taxes Expense, $5,515.35

Polo Company has 10 employees, each of whom earns $2,600 per month and is paid on the last day of each month. All 10 have been employed continuously at this amount since January 1. Polo uses a payroll bank account and special payroll checks to pay its employees. On March 1, the following accounts and balances exist in its general ledger:

Problem 9-6A[A]
Entries for payroll transactions
P2 P3 P5

a. FICA—Social Security Taxes Payable, $3,224; FICA—Medicare Taxes Payable, $754. (The balances of these accounts represent total liabilities for *both* the employer's and employees' FICA taxes for the February payroll only.)

b. Employees' Federal Income Taxes Payable, $3,900 (liability for February only).

c. Federal Unemployment Taxes Payable, $416 (liability for January and February together).

d. State Unemployment Taxes Payable, $2,080 (liability for January and February together).

During March and April, the company had the following payroll transactions.

Mar. 15   Issued check payable to Fleet Bank, a federal depository bank authorized to accept employers' payments of FICA taxes and employee income tax withholdings. The $7,878 check is in payment of the February FICA and employee income taxes.

31   Recorded the March payroll and transferred funds from the regular bank account to the payroll bank account. Issued checks payable to each employee in payment of the March payroll. The payroll register shows the following summary totals for the March pay period.

Check March 31: Cr. Salaries Payable, $20,111

Salaries and Wages					
Office Salaries	Shop Wages	Gross Pay	FICA Taxes*	Federal Income Taxes	Net Pay
$10,400	$15,600	$26,000	$1,612	$3,900	$20,111
			$ 377		

* FICA taxes are Social Security and Medicare, respectively.

March 31: Dr. Payroll Taxes Expenses, $2,853

April 15: Cr. Cash, $7,878 (Fleet Bank)

31   Recorded the employer's payroll taxes resulting from the March payroll. The company has a merit rating that reduces its state unemployment tax rate to 4.0% of the first $7,000 paid each employee. The federal rate is 0.8%.

Apr. 15   Issued check to Fleet Bank in payment of the March FICA and employee income taxes.

15   Issued check to the State Tax Commission for the January, February, and March state unemployment taxes. Mailed the check and the first quarter tax return to the Commission.

30   Issued check payable to Fleet Bank in payment of the employer's FUTA taxes for the first quarter of the year.

30   Mailed Form 941 to the IRS, reporting the FICA taxes and the employees' federal income tax withholdings for the first quarter.

Required

Prepare journal entries to record the transactions and events for both March and April.

PROBLEM SET B

Problem 9-1B
Short-term notes payable transactions and entries
P1

Bargen Co. entered into the following transactions involving short-term liabilities in 2010 and 2011.

2010

Apr. 22   Purchased $4,000 of merchandise on credit from Quinn Products, terms are 1/10, n/30. Bargen uses the perpetual inventory system.

May 23   Replaced the April 22 account payable to Quinn Products with a 60-day, $3,600 note bearing 15% annual interest along with paying $400 in cash.

July 15   Borrowed $9,000 cash from Blackhawk Bank by signing a 120-day, 10% interest-bearing note with a face value of $9,000.

___?___   Paid the amount due on the note to Quinn Products at maturity.

___?___   Paid the amount due on the note to Blackhawk Bank at maturity.

Dec. 6   Borrowed $16,000 cash from City Bank by signing a 45-day, 9% interest-bearing note with a face value of $16,000.

31   Recorded an adjusting entry for accrued interest on the note to City Bank.

2011

___?___   Paid the amount due on the note to City Bank at maturity.

Required

Check (2) Quinn, $90
(3) $100
(4) $80

1. Determine the maturity date for each of the three notes described.

2. Determine the interest due at maturity for each of the three notes. (Assume a 360-day year.)

3. Determine the interest expense to be recorded in the adjusting entry at the end of 2010.

4. Determine the interest expense to be recorded in 2011.

5. Prepare journal entries for all the preceding transactions and events for years 2010 and 2011.

Problem 9-2B
Warranty expense and liability estimation
P4

On November 10, 2011, Byung Co. began operations by purchasing coffee grinders for resale. Byung uses the perpetual inventory method. The grinders have a 60-day warranty that requires the company to replace any nonworking grinder. When a grinder is returned, the company discards it and mails a new one from Merchandise Inventory to the customer. The company's cost per new grinder is $14 and its retail selling price is $35 in both 2011 and 2012. The manufacturer has advised the company to expect warranty costs to equal 10% of dollar sales. The following transactions and events occurred.

2011

Nov. 16   Sold 50 grinders for $1,750 cash.

30   Recognized warranty expense related to November sales with an adjusting entry.

Dec. 12   Replaced six grinders that were returned under the warranty.

18   Sold 150 grinders for $5,250 cash.

28   Replaced 17 grinders that were returned under the warranty.

31   Recognized warranty expense related to December sales with an adjusting entry.

2012

Jan. 7 Sold 60 grinders for $2,100 cash.
   21 Replaced 38 grinders that were returned under the warranty.
   31 Recognized warranty expense related to January sales with an adjusting entry.

Required

1. Prepare journal entries to record these transactions and adjustments for 2011 and 2012.
2. How much warranty expense is reported for November 2011 and for December 2011?
3. How much warranty expense is reported for January 2012?
4. What is the balance of the Estimated Warranty Liability account as of December 31, 2011?
5. What is the balance of the Estimated Warranty Liability account as of January 31, 2012?

Check (3) $210
(4) $378 Cr.
(5) $56 Cr.

Shown here are condensed income statements for two different companies (both are organized as LLCs and pay no income taxes).

Problem 9-3B
Computing and analyzing times interest earned

A1

Virgo Company	
Sales	$120,000
Variable expenses (50%)	60,000
Income before interest	60,000
Interest expense (fixed)	45,000
Net income	$ 15,000

Zodiac Company	
Sales	$120,000
Variable expenses (75%)	90,000
Income before interest	30,000
Interest expense (fixed)	15,000
Net income	$ 15,000

Required

1. Compute times interest earned for Virgo Company.
2. Compute times interest earned for Zodiac Company.
3. What happens to each company's net income if sales increase by 10%?
4. What happens to each company's net income if sales increase by 40%?
5. What happens to each company's net income if sales increase by 90%?
6. What happens to each company's net income if sales decrease by 20%?
7. What happens to each company's net income if sales decrease by 50%?
8. What happens to each company's net income if sales decrease by 80%?

Check (4) Virgo net income,
$39,000 (160% increase)

(6) Zodiac net income,
$9,000 (40% decrease)

Analysis Component

9. Comment on the results from parts 3 through 8 in relation to the fixed-cost strategies of the two companies and the ratio values you computed in parts 1 and 2.

Sea Biz Co. has four employees. FICA Social Security taxes are 6.2% of the first $106,800 paid to each employee, and FICA Medicare taxes are 1.45% of gross pay. Also, for the first $7,000 paid to each employee, the company's FUTA taxes are 0.8% and SUTA taxes are 1.75%. The company is preparing its payroll calculations for the week ended September 30. Payroll records show the following information for the company's four employees.

Problem 9-4B
Payroll expenses, withholdings, and taxes

P2 P3

File Edit View Insert Format Tools Data Accounting Window Help

	Name	Gross Pay through 9/23	Current Week	
			Gross Pay	Income Tax Withholding
3	Alli	$104,300	$2,500	$198
4	Eve	36,650	1,515	182
5	Hong	6,650	475	52
6	Juan	22,200	600	48

Sheet1 Sheet2 Sheet3

In addition to gross pay, the company must pay one-half of the $44 per employee weekly health insurance; each employee pays the remaining one-half. The company also contributes an extra 5% of each employee's gross pay (at no cost to employees) to a pension fund.

Required

Compute the following for the week ended September 30 (round amounts to the nearest cent):

1. Each employee's FICA withholdings for Social Security.
2. Each employee's FICA withholdings for Medicare.
3. Employer's FICA taxes for Social Security.
4. Employer's FICA taxes for Medicare.
5. Employer's FUTA taxes.
6. Employer's SUTA taxes.
7. Each employee's net (take-home) pay.
8. Employer's total payroll-related expense for each employee.

Check (3) $315.58
(4) $73.81
(5) $2.80
(7) Total net pay, $4,132.61

Problem 9-5B
Entries for payroll transactions
P2 P3

Palmer Company's first weekly pay period of the year ends on January 8. On that date, the column totals in Palmer's payroll register indicate its sales employees earned $69,490, its office employees earned $42,450, and its delivery employees earned $2,060. The employees are to have withheld from their wages FICA Social Security taxes at the rate of 6.2%, FICA Medicare taxes at the rate of 1.45%, $17,250 of federal income taxes, $2,320 of medical insurance deductions, and $275 of union dues. No employee earned more than $7,000 in the first pay period.

Required

Check (1) Cr. Salaries Payable, $85,434

(2) Dr. Payroll Taxes Expense, $13,509

1. Calculate FICA Social Security taxes payable and FICA Medicare taxes payable. Prepare the journal entry to record Palmer Company's January 8 (employee) payroll expenses and liabilities.
2. Prepare the journal entry to record Palmer's (employer) payroll taxes resulting from the January 8 payroll. Palmer's merit rating reduces its state unemployment tax rate to 3.4% of the first $7,000 paid each employee. The federal unemployment tax rate is 0.8%.

Problem 9-6B^A
Entries for payroll transactions
P2 P3 P5

JLK Company has five employees, each of whom earns $1,200 per month and is paid on the last day of each month. All five have been employed continuously at this amount since January 1. JLK uses a payroll bank account and special payroll checks to pay its employees. On June 1, the following accounts and balances exist in its general ledger:

a. FICA—Social Security Taxes Payable, $744; FICA—Medicare Taxes Payable, $174. (The balances of these accounts represent total liabilities for *both* the employer's and employees' FICA taxes for the May payroll only.)
b. Employees' Federal Income Taxes Payable, $900 (liability for May only).
c. Federal Unemployment Taxes Payable, $96 (liability for April and May together).
d. State Unemployment Taxes Payable, $480 (liability for April and May together).

During June and July, the company had the following payroll transactions.

June 15 Issued check payable to Security Bank, a federal depository bank authorized to accept employers' payments of FICA taxes and employee income tax withholdings. The $1,818 check is in payment of the May FICA and employee income taxes.
30 Recorded the June payroll and transferred funds from the regular bank account to the payroll bank account. Issued checks payable to each employee in payment of the June payroll. The payroll register shows the following summary totals for the June pay period.

Check June 30: Cr. Salaries Payable, $4,641

Salaries and Wages					
Office Salaries	Shop Wages	Gross Pay	FICA Taxes*	Federal Income Taxes	Net Pay
$2,000	$4,000	$6,000	$372	$900	$4,641
			$ 87		

* FICA taxes are Social Security and Medicare, respectively.

Check June 30: Dr. Payroll Taxes Expenses, $699

July 15: Cr. Cash $1,818 (Security Bank)

30 Recorded the employer's payroll taxes resulting from the June payroll. The company has a merit rating that reduces its state unemployment tax rate to 4.0% of the first $7,000 paid each employee. The federal rate is 0.8%.
July 15 Issued check payable to Security Bank in payment of the June FICA and employee income taxes.
15 Issued check to the State Tax Commission for the April, May and June state unemployment taxes. Mailed the check and the second quarter tax return to the State Tax Commission.
31 Issued check payable to Security Bank in payment of the employer's FUTA taxes for the first quarter of the year.
31 Mailed Form 941 to the IRS, reporting the FICA taxes and the employees' federal income tax withholdings for the second quarter.

Required

Prepare journal entries to record the transactions and events for both June and July.

SERIAL PROBLEM
Business Solutions
P2 P3 C2

(This serial problem began in Chapter 1 and continues through most of the book. If previous chapter segments were not completed, the serial problem can begin at this point. It is helpful, but not necessary, to use the Working Papers that accompany the book.)

SP 9 Review the February 26 and March 25 transactions for Business Solutions (SP 4) from Chapter 4.

Required

1. Assume that Lyn Addie is an unmarried employee. Her $1,000 of wages are subject to no deductions other than FICA Social Security taxes, FICA Medicare taxes, and federal income taxes. Her federal income taxes for this pay period total $159. Compute her net pay for the eight days' work paid on February 26. (Round amounts to the nearest cent.)

2. Record the journal entry to reflect the payroll payment to Lyn Addie as computed in part 1.

3. Record the journal entry to reflect the (employer) payroll tax expenses for the February 26 payroll payment. Assume Lyn Addie has not met earnings limits for FUTA and SUTA—the FUTA rate is 0.8% and the SUTA rate is 4% for Business Solutions. (Round amounts to the nearest cent.)

4. Record the entry(ies) for the merchandise sold on March 25 if a 4% sales tax rate applies.

CP 9 Bug-Off Exterminators provides pest control services and sells extermination products manufactured by other companies. The following six-column table contains the company's unadjusted trial balance as of December 31, 2011.

COMPREHENSIVE PROBLEM
Bug-Off Exterminators
(Review of Chapters 1–9)

BUG-OFF EXTERMINATORS December 31, 2011	Unadjusted Trial Balance		Adjustments	Adjusted Trial Balance
Cash	$ 17,000			
Accounts receivable	4,000			
Allowance for doubtful accounts		$ 828		
Merchandise inventory	11,700			
Trucks	32,000			
Accum. depreciation—Trucks		0		
Equipment	45,000			
Accum. depreciation—Equipment		12,200		
Accounts payable		5,000		
Estimated warranty liability		1,400		
Unearned services revenue		0		
Interest payable		0		
Long-term notes payable		15,000		
Common stock		10,000		
Retained earnings		49,700		
Dividends	10,000			
Extermination services revenue		60,000		
Interest revenue		872		
Sales (of merchandise)		71,026		
Cost of goods sold	46,300			
Depreciation expense—Trucks	0			
Depreciation expense—Equipment	0			
Wages expense	35,000			
Interest expense	0			
Rent expense	9,000			
Bad debts expense	0			
Miscellaneous expense	1,226			
Repairs expense	8,000			
Utilities expense	6,800			
Warranty expense	0			
Totals	$226,026	$226,026		

The following information in *a* through *h* applies to the company at the end of the current year.

a. The bank reconciliation as of December 31, 2011, includes the following facts.

Cash balance per bank	$15,100
Cash balance per books	17,000
Outstanding checks	1,800
Deposit in transit	2,450
Interest earned (on bank account)	52
Bank service charges (miscellaneous expense)	15

Reported on the bank statement is a canceled check that the company failed to record. (Information from the bank reconciliation allows you to determine the amount of this check, which is a payment on an account payable.)

b. An examination of customers' accounts shows that accounts totaling $679 should be written off as uncollectible. Using an aging of receivables, the company determines that the ending balance of the Allowance for Doubtful Accounts should be $700.

c. A truck is purchased and placed in service on January 1, 2011. Its cost is being depreciated with the straight-line method using the following facts and estimates.

Original cost	$32,000
Expected salvage value	8,000
Useful life (years)	4

d. Two items of equipment (a sprayer and an injector) were purchased and put into service in early January 2009. They are being depreciated with the straight-line method using these facts and estimates.

	Sprayer	Injector
Original cost	$27,000	$18,000
Expected salvage value	3,000	2,500
Useful life (years)	8	5

e. On August 1, 2011, the company is paid $3,840 cash in advance to provide monthly service for an apartment complex for one year. The company began providing the services in August. When the cash was received, the full amount was credited to the Extermination Services Revenue account.

f. The company offers a warranty for the services it sells. The expected cost of providing warranty service is 2.5% of the extermination services revenue of $57,760 for 2011. No warranty expense has been recorded for 2011. All costs of servicing warranties in 2011 were properly debited to the Estimated Warranty Liability account.

g. The $15,000 long-term note is an 8%, five-year, interest-bearing note with interest payable annually on December 31. The note was signed with First National Bank on December 31, 2011.

h. The ending inventory of merchandise is counted and determined to have a cost of $11,700. Bug-Off uses a perpetual inventory system.

Required

1. Use the preceding information to determine amounts for the following items.

Check (1*a*) Cash bal. $15,750
(1*b*) $551 credit

a. Correct (reconciled) ending balance of Cash, and the amount of the omitted check.

b. Adjustment needed to obtain the correct ending balance of the Allowance for Doubtful Accounts.

c. Depreciation expense for the truck used during year 2011.

d. Depreciation expense for the two items of equipment used during year 2011.

e. The adjusted 2011 ending balances of the Extermination Services Revenue and Unearned Services Revenue accounts.

(1*f*) Estim. warranty liability, $2,844 Cr.

f. The adjusted 2011 ending balances of the accounts for Warranty Expense and Estimated Warranty Liability.

g. The adjusted 2011 ending balances of the accounts for Interest Expense and Interest Payable. (Round amounts to nearest whole dollar.)

2. Use the results of part 1 to complete the six-column table by first entering the appropriate adjustments for items *a* through *g* and then completing the adjusted trial balance columns. (*Hint:* Item *b* requires two adjustments.)

(2) Adjusted trial balance totals, $238,207

3. Prepare journal entries to record the adjustments entered on the six-column table. Assume Bug-Off's adjusted balance for Merchandise Inventory matches the year-end physical count.

4. Prepare a single-step income statement, a statement of retained earnings (cash dividends declared during 2011 were $10,000), and a classified balance sheet.

(4) Net income, $9,274; Total assets, $82,771

Beyond the Numbers

BTN 9-1 Refer to the financial statements of **Research In Motion** in Appendix A to answer the following.

1. Compute times interest earned for the fiscal years ended 2010, 2009, and 2008. Comment on RIM's ability to cover its interest expense for this period. Assume interest expense of $1, $502, and $31 for fiscal years ended 2010, 2009, and 2008 ($ thousands); and, assume an industry average of 18.1 for times interest earned.

2. RIM's current liabilities include "deferred revenue"; assume that this account reflects "Unredeemed gift card liabilities." Explain how this liability is created and how RIM satisfies this liability.

3. Does RIM have any commitments or contingencies? Briefly explain them.

REPORTING IN ACTION

A1 P4

RIM

Fast Forward

4. Access RIM's financial statements for fiscal years ending after February 27, 2010, at its Website (**RIM.com**) or the SEC's EDGAR database (**www.sec.gov**). Compute its times interest earned for years ending after February 27, 2010, and compare your results to those in part 1.

BTN 9-2 Key figures for **Research In Motion** and **Apple** follow. (Interest expense figures for Apple are assumed as it has no interest expense for these years.)

COMPARATIVE ANALYSIS

A1

RIM

Apple

($ millions)	Research In Motion			Apple		
	Current Year	One Year Prior	Two Years Prior	Current Year	One Year Prior	Two Years Prior
Net income	$2,457.144	$1,892.616	$1,293.867	$8,235	$6,119	$3,495
Income taxes	809.366	907.747	516.653	3,831	2,828	1,511
Interest expense	.001	.502	.031	3	2	1

Required

1. Compute times interest earned for the three years' data shown for each company.

2. Comment on which company appears stronger in its ability to pay interest obligations if income should decline. Assume an industry average of 18.1.

BTN 9-3 Connor Bly is a sales manager for an automobile dealership. He earns a bonus each year based on revenue from the number of autos sold in the year less related warranty expenses. Actual warranty expenses have varied over the prior 10 years from a low of 3% of an automobile's selling price to a high of 10%. In the past, Bly has tended to estimate warranty expenses on the high end to be conservative. He must work with the dealership's accountant at year-end to arrive at the warranty expense accrual for cars sold each year.

1. Does the warranty accrual decision create any ethical dilemma for Bly?

2. Since warranty expenses vary, what percent do you think Bly should choose for the current year? Justify your response.

ETHICS CHALLENGE

P4

BTN 9-4 Dustin Clemens is the accounting and finance manager for a manufacturer. At year-end, he must determine how to account for the company's contingencies. His manager, Madeline Pretti, objects to Clemens's proposal to recognize an expense and a liability for warranty service on units of a new product introduced in the fourth quarter. Pretti comments, "There's no way we can estimate this warranty cost. We don't owe anyone anything until a product fails and it is returned. Let's report an expense if and when we do any warranty work."

COMMUNICATING IN PRACTICE

C3

Required

Prepare a one-page memorandum for Clemens to send to Pretti defending his proposal.

**TAKING IT TO
THE NET**

C1   A1

BTN 9-5   Access the February 26, 2010, filing of the December 31, 2009, annual 10-K report of **McDonald's Corporation** (Ticker: MCD), which is available from **www.sec.gov**.

Required

1. Identify the current liabilities on McDonald's balance sheet as of December 31, 2009.
2. What portion (in percent) of McDonald's long-term debt matures within the next 12 months?
3. Use the consolidated statement of income for the year ended December 31, 2009, to compute McDonald's times interest earned ratio. Comment on the result. Assume an industry average of 12.0.

**TEAMWORK IN
ACTION**

C2   P1

BTN 9-6   Assume that your team is in business and you must borrow $6,000 cash for short-term needs. You have been shopping banks for a loan, and you have the following two options.

A. Sign a $6,000, 90-day, 10% interest-bearing note dated June 1.
B. Sign a $6,000, 120-day, 8% interest-bearing note dated June 1.

Required

1. Discuss these two options and determine the best choice. Ensure that all teammates concur with the decision and understand the rationale.
2. Each member of the team is to prepare *one* of the following journal entries.
    a. Option A—at date of issuance.
    b. Option B—at date of issuance.
    c. Option A—at maturity date.
    d. Option B—at maturity date.
3. In rotation, each member is to explain the entry he or she prepared in part 2 to the team. Ensure that all team members concur with and understand the entries.
4. Assume that the funds are borrowed on December 1 (instead of June 1) and your business operates on a calendar-year reporting period. Each member of the team is to prepare *one* of the following entries.
    a. Option A—the year-end adjustment.
    b. Option B—the year-end adjustment.
    c. Option A—at maturity date.
    d. Option B—at maturity date.
5. In rotation, each member is to explain the entry he or she prepared in part 4 to the team. Ensure that all team members concur with and understand the entries.

**ENTREPRENEURIAL
DECISION**

A1

BTN 9-7   Review the chapter's opening feature about Matt and Bryan Walls, and their start-up company, **SnorgTees**. Assume that these young entrepreneurs are considering expanding their business to open an outlet in Europe. Assume their current income statement is as follows.

SNORGTEES Income Statement For Year Ended December 31, 2011	
Sales	$1,000,000
Cost of goods sold (30%)	300,000
Gross profit	700,000
Operating expenses (25%)	250,000
Net income	$ 450,000

SnorgTees currently has no interest-bearing debt. If it expands to open a European location, it will require a $300,000 loan. SnorgTees has found a bank that will loan it the money on a 7% note payable. The company believes that, at least for the first few years, sales at its European location will be $250,000, and that all expenses (including cost of goods sold) will follow the same patterns as its current locations.

Required

1. Prepare an income statement (showing three separate columns for current operations, European, and total) for SnorgTees assuming that it borrows the funds and expands to Europe. Annual revenues for current operations are expected to remain at $1,000,000.

2. Compute SnorgTees' times interest earned under the expansion assumptions in part 1.

3. Assume sales at its European location are $400,000. Prepare an income statement (with columns for current operations, European, and total) for the company and compute times interest earned.

4. Assume sales at its European location are $100,000. Prepare an income statement (with columns for current operations, European, and total) for the company and compute times interest earned.

5. Comment on your results from parts 1 through 4.

BTN 9-8   Check your phone book or the Social Security Administration Website (www.ssa.gov) to locate the Social Security office near you. Visit the office to request a personal earnings and estimate form. Fill out the form and mail according to the instructions. You will receive a statement from the Social Security Administration regarding your earnings history and future Social Security benefits you can receive. (Formerly the request could be made online. The online service has been discontinued and is now under review by the Social Security Administration due to security concerns.) It is good to request an earnings and benefit statement every 5 to 10 years to make sure you have received credit for all wages earned and for which you and your employer have paid taxes into the system.

HITTING THE ROAD

P2

BTN 9-9   **Nokia**, **Research In Motion**, and **Apple** are all competitors in the global marketplace. Comparative figures for Nokia (www.Nokia.com), along with selected figures from Research In Motion and Apple, follow.

GLOBAL DECISION

A1

NOKIA

RIM

Apple

Key Figures	Nokia (EUR millions)		Research In Motion		Apple	
	Current Year	Prior Year	Current Year	Prior Year	Current Year	Prior Year
Net income	260	3,889	—	—	—	—
Income taxes	702	1,081	—	—	—	—
Interest expense	243	185	—	—	—	—
Times interest earned	?	?	3,267	5,579	4,023	4,475

Required

1. Compute the times interest earned ratio for the most recent two years for Nokia using the data shown.

2. Which company of the three presented provides the best coverage of interest expense? Explain.

ANSWERS TO MULTIPLE CHOICE QUIZ

1. b; $6,000 × 0.05 × 30/360 = $25
2. e; $50,000 × (.062 + .0145) = $3,825
3. b; $7,000 × (.008 + .054) = $434

4. c; 10,000 television sets × .01 × $250 = $25,000
5. a; 150 employees × $175 per day × 1 vacation day earned = $26,250

10

Long-Term Liabilities

A Look Back

Chapter 9 focused on how current liabilities are identified, computed, recorded, and reported. Attention was directed at notes, payroll, sales taxes, warranties, employee benefits, and contingencies.

A Look at This Chapter

This chapter describes the accounting for and analysis of bonds and notes. We explain their characteristics, payment patterns, interest computations, retirement, and reporting requirements. An appendix to this chapter introduces leases and pensions.

A Look Ahead

Chapter 11 focuses on corporate equity transactions, including stock issuances and dividends. We also explain how to report and analyze income, earnings per share, and retained earnings.

Learning Objectives

CAP

CONCEPTUAL

C1 Explain the types and payment patterns of notes. (p. 422)

C2 *Appendix 10A*—Explain and compute the present value of an amount(s) to be paid at a future date(s). (p. 430)

C3 *Appendix 10C*—Describe interest accrual when bond payment periods differ from accounting periods. (p. 434)

C4 *Appendix 10D*—Describe accounting for leases and pensions. (p. 436)

ANALYTICAL

A1 Compare bond financing with stock financing. (p. 412)

A2 Assess debt features and their implications. (p. 426)

A3 Compute the debt-to-equity ratio and explain its use. (p. 426)

LP10

PROCEDURAL

P1 Prepare entries to record bond issuance and interest expense. (p. 414)

P2 Compute and record amortization of bond discount. (p. 415)

P3 Compute and record amortization of bond premium. (p. 418)

P4 Record the retirement of bonds. (p. 421)

P5 Prepare entries to account for notes. (p. 424)

Love At First Bite

"Each individual problem you face is totally surmountable"
—**WARREN BROWN**

WASHINGTON, DC—Warren Brown started baking cakes in his apartment after work each evening. He sold his sweet concoctions mostly to coworkers and friends, and even held a cake open house at the local art gallery. But Warren was determined to grow his business. He took a course in entrepreneurship at his local community college, and there he discovered the importance of financial reporting and accounting.

Launching his fledgling cake business presented Warren with many challenges. He needed to especially focus on the important task of managing liabilities for payroll, baking supplies, employee benefits, training, and taxes. Warren insists that effective management of liabilities, especially long-term financing from sources such as bonds and notes, is crucial to business success. "Everything feels like a disaster when it's right in your face," says Warren. "You just have to be calm, look at what you're doing, and fix the problem."

Warren fixed the problems and unveiled his business called **Cake Love (CakeLove.com),** funded with short- and long-term notes. "I opened up this tiny retail, walk-up bakery . . . [to sell] goodies that are baked from scratch," Warren explains. Today Cake Love entices the neighborhood with a gentle scent of fresh bakery and a sidewalk view into the kitchen. Warmly painted

walls, comfy window seats, and free wireless Internet encourage customers to lounge for hours. "I want it to be relaxed and comfortable," says Warren. "People can bring their work, their kids, their friends, and just relax."

Warren continues to monitor liabilities and their payment patterns, and he is not shy about striving to better learn the accounting side. "I'm always getting better, improving my skills," he explains. Warren insists that accounting for and monitoring liabilities of long-term financing are important ingredients to a successful start-up. His company now generates sufficient income to pay for liabilities of interest and principal on long-term debt and still produces revenue growth for expansion. He shows a keen appetite for using accounting information to make good business decisions. "But," says Warren, "I love eating what I make more."

"The bigger message of Cake Love is finding your passion and working to reach your goals," explains Warren. That's a slice of advice worth more than any amount of dough.

[Sources: *Cake Love Website,* January 2011; *Black Enterprise,* September 2004; *Georgetown Voice,* March 2005; *National Public Radio (NPR) Website,* May 2005; *Inc.com,* April 2005]

Individuals, companies, and governments issue bonds to finance their activities. In return for financing, bonds promise to repay the lender with interest. This chapter explains the basics of bonds and the accounting for their issuance and retirement. The chapter also describes long-term notes as another financing source. We explain how present value concepts impact both the accounting for and reporting of bonds and notes. Appendixes to this chapter discuss present value concepts applicable to liabilities, effective interest amortization, and the accounting for leases and pensions.

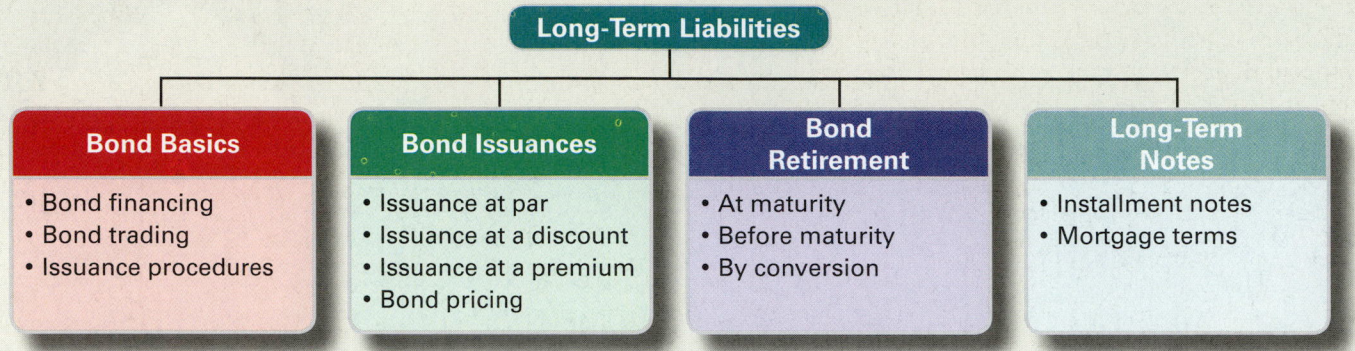

Long-Term Liabilities

Bond Basics	Bond Issuances	Bond Retirement	Long-Term Notes
• Bond financing • Bond trading • Issuance procedures	• Issuance at par • Issuance at a discount • Issuance at a premium • Bond pricing	• At maturity • Before maturity • By conversion	• Installment notes • Mortgage terms

BASICS OF BONDS

This section explains the basics of bonds and a company's motivation for issuing them.

Bond Financing

A1 Compare bond financing with stock financing.

Projects that demand large amounts of money often are funded from bond issuances. (Both for-profit and nonprofit companies, as well as governmental units, such as nations, states, cities, and school districts, issue bonds.) A **bond** is its issuer's written promise to pay an amount identified as the par value of the bond with interest. The **par value of a bond,** also called the *face amount* or *face value,* is paid at a specified future date known as the bond's *maturity date.* Most bonds also require the issuer to make semiannual interest payments. The amount of interest paid each period is determined by multiplying the par value of the bond by the bond's contract rate of interest for that same period. This section explains both advantages and disadvantages of bond financing.

Advantages of Bonds   There are three main advantages of bond financing:

1. *Bonds do not affect owner control.* Equity financing reflects ownership in a company, whereas bond financing does not. A person who contributes $1,000 of a company's $10,000 equity financing typically controls one-tenth of all owner decisions. A person who owns a $1,000, 11%, 20-year bond has no ownership right. This person, or bondholder, is to receive from the bond issuer 11% interest, or $110, each year the bond is outstanding and $1,000 when it matures in 20 years.

2. *Interest on bonds is tax deductible.* Bond interest payments are tax deductible for the issuer, but equity payments (distributions) to owners are not. To illustrate, assume that a corporation with no bond financing earns $15,000 in income *before* paying taxes at a 40% tax rate, which amounts to $6,000 ($15,000 × 40%) in taxes. If a portion of its financing is in bonds, however, the resulting bond interest is deducted in computing taxable income. That is, if bond interest expense is $10,000, the taxes owed would be $2,000 ([$15,000 − $10,000] × 40%), which is less than the $6,000 owed with no bond financing.

3. *Bonds can increase return on equity.* A company that earns a higher return with borrowed funds than it pays in interest on those funds increases its return on equity. This process is called *financial leverage* or *trading on the equity.*

Point: Financial leverage reflects issuance of bonds, notes, or preferred stock.

To illustrate the third point, consider Magnum Co., which has $1 million in equity and is planning a $500,000 expansion to meet increasing demand for its product. Magnum predicts the

$500,000 expansion will yield $125,000 in additional income before paying any interest. It currently earns $100,000 per year and has no interest expense. Magnum is considering three plans. Plan A is to not expand. Plan B is to expand and raise $500,000 from equity financing. Plan C is to expand and issue $500,000 of bonds that pay 10% annual interest ($50,000). Exhibit 10.1 shows how these three plans affect Magnum's net income, equity, and return on equity (net income/equity). The owner(s) will earn a higher return on equity if expansion occurs. Moreover, the preferred expansion plan is to issue bonds. Projected net income under Plan C ($175,000) is smaller than under Plan B ($225,000), but the return on equity is larger because of less equity investment. Plan C has another advantage if income is taxable. This illustration reflects a general rule: *Return on equity increases when the expected rate of return from the new assets is higher than the rate of interest expense on the debt financing.*

Example: Compute return on equity for all three plans if Magnum currently earns $150,000 instead of $100,000.
Answer ($ 000s):
Plan A = 15%   ($150/$1,000)
Plan B = 18.3%   ($275/$1,500)
Plan C = 22.5%   ($225/$1,000)

EXHIBIT 10.1

Financing with Bonds versus Equity

	Plan A: Do Not Expand	Plan B: Equity Financing	Plan C: Bond Financing
Income before interest expense	$ 100,000	$ 225,000	$ 225,000
Interest expense	—	—	(50,000)
Net income	**$ 100,000**	**$ 225,000**	**$ 175,000**
Equity	$1,000,000	$1,500,000	$1,000,000
Return on equity	**10.0%**	**15.0%**	**17.5%**

Disadvantages of Bonds   The two main disadvantages of bond financing are these:

1. *Bonds can decrease return on equity.* When a company earns a lower return with the borrowed funds than it pays in interest, it decreases its return on equity. This downside risk of financial leverage is more likely to arise when a company has periods of low income or net losses.

2. *Bonds require payment of both periodic interest and the par value at maturity.* Bond payments can be especially burdensome when income and cash flow are low. Equity financing, in contrast, does not require any payments because cash withdrawals (dividends) are paid at the discretion of the owner (or board).

Point: Debt financing is desirable when interest is tax deductible, when owner control is preferred, and when return on equity exceeds the debt's interest rate.

A company must weigh the risks and returns of the disadvantages and advantages of bond financing when deciding whether to issue bonds to finance operations.

Bond Trading

Bonds are securities that can be readily bought and sold. A large number of bonds trade on both the New York Exchange and the American Exchange. A bond *issue* consists of a number of bonds, usually in denominations of $1,000 or $5,000, and is sold to many different lenders. After bonds are issued, they often are bought and sold by investors, meaning that any particular bond probably has a number of owners before it matures. Since bonds are exchanged (bought and sold) in the market, they have a market value (price). For convenience, bond market values are expressed as a percent of their par (face) value. For example, a company's bonds might be trading at 103½, meaning they can be bought or sold for 103.5% of their par value. Bonds can also trade below par value. For instance, if a company's bonds are trading at 95, they can be bought or sold at 95% of their par value.

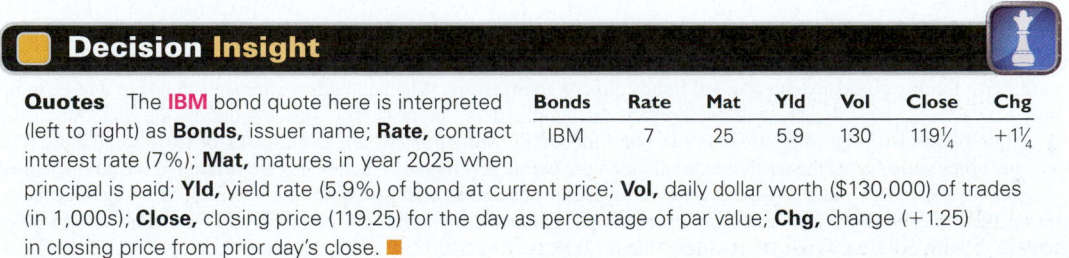

Decision Insight

Quotes   The **IBM** bond quote here is interpreted (left to right) as **Bonds,** issuer name; **Rate,** contract interest rate (7%); **Mat,** matures in year 2025 when principal is paid; **Yld,** yield rate (5.9%) of bond at current price; **Vol,** daily dollar worth ($130,000) of trades (in 1,000s); **Close,** closing price (119.25) for the day as percentage of par value; **Chg,** change (+1.25) in closing price from prior day's close. ∎

Bonds	Rate	Mat	Yld	Vol	Close	Chg
IBM	7	25	5.9	130	119¼	+1¼

Bond-Issuing Procedures

State and federal laws govern bond issuances. Bond issuers also want to ensure that they do not violate any of their existing contractual agreements when issuing bonds. Authorization of bond issuances includes the number of bonds authorized, their par value, and the contract interest rate. The legal document identifying the rights and obligations of both the bondholders and the issuer is called the **bond indenture,** which is the legal contract between the issuer and the bondholders. A bondholder may also receive a bond certificate as evidence of the company's debt. A **bond certificate,** such as that shown in Exhibit 10.2, includes specifics such as the issuer's name, the par value, the contract interest rate, and the maturity date. Many companies reduce costs by not issuing paper certificates to bondholders.[1]

EXHIBIT 10.2

Bond Certificate

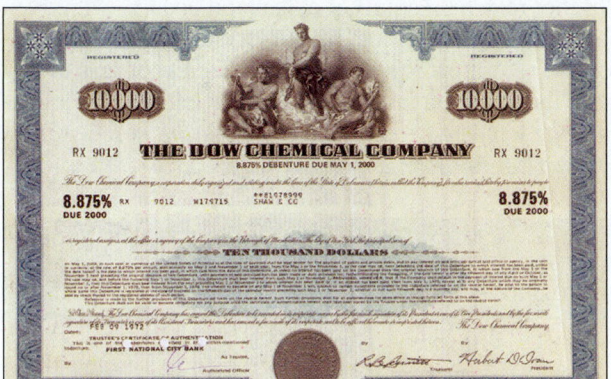

Point: *Indenture* refers to a bond's legal contract; *debenture* refers to an unsecured bond.

BOND ISSUANCES

This section explains accounting for bond issuances at par, below par (discount), and above par (premium). It also describes how to amortize a discount or premium and record bonds issued between interest payment dates.

Issuing Bonds at Par

P1 Prepare entries to record bond issuance and interest expense.

To illustrate an issuance of bonds at par value, suppose a company receives authorization to issue $800,000 of 9%, 20-year bonds dated January 1, 2011, that mature on December 31, 2030, and pay interest semiannually on each June 30 and December 31. After accepting the bond indenture on behalf of the bondholders, the trustee can sell all or a portion of the bonds to an underwriter. If all bonds are sold at par value, the issuer records the sale as follows.

Assets = Liabilities + Equity
+800,000   +800,000

2011			
Jan. 1	Cash	800,000	
	Bonds Payable		800,000
	Sold bonds at par.		

This entry reflects increases in the issuer's cash *and* long-term liabilities.

The issuer records the first semiannual interest payment as follows.

Assets = Liabilities + Equity
−36,000   −36,000

2011			
June 30	Bond Interest Expense	36,000	
	Cash		36,000
	Paid semiannual interest (9% × $800,000 × ½ year).		

Point: The *spread* between the dealer's cost and what buyers pay can be huge. Dealers earn more than $25 billion in annual spread revenue.

Global: In the United Kingdom, government bonds are called *gilts*— short for gilt-edged investments.

[1] The issuing company normally sells its bonds to an investment firm called an *underwriter,* which resells them to the public. An issuing company can also sell bonds directly to investors. When an underwriter sells bonds to a large number of investors, a *trustee* represents and protects the bondholders' interests. The trustee monitors the issuer to ensure that it complies with the obligations in the bond indenture. Most trustees are large banks or trust companies. The trustee writes and accepts the terms of a bond indenture before it is issued. When bonds are offered to the public, called *floating an issue,* they must be registered with the Securities and Exchange Commission (SEC). SEC registration requires the issuer to file certain financial information. Most company bonds are issued in par value units of $1,000 or $5,000. A *baby bond* has a par value of less than $1,000, such as $100.

The issuer pays and records its semiannual interest obligation every six months until the bonds mature. When they mature, the issuer records its payment of principal as follows.

2030			
Dec. 31	Bonds Payable	800,000	
	Cash		800,000
	Paid bond principal at maturity.		

Assets = Liabilities + Equity
−800,000 −800,000

Bond Discount or Premium

The bond issuer pays the interest rate specified in the indenture, the **contract rate,** also referred to as the *coupon rate, stated rate,* or *nominal rate*. The annual interest paid is determined by multiplying the bond par value by the contract rate. The contract rate is usually stated on an annual basis, even if interest is paid semiannually. For example, if a company issues a $1,000, 8% bond paying interest semiannually, it pays annual interest of $80 (8% × $1,000) in two semiannual payments of $40 each.

The contract rate sets the amount of interest the issuer pays in *cash,* which is not necessarily the *bond interest expense* actually incurred by the issuer. Bond interest expense depends on the bond's market value at issuance, which is determined by market expectations of the risk of lending to the issuer. The bond's **market rate** of interest is the rate that borrowers are willing to pay and lenders are willing to accept for a particular bond and its risk level. As the risk level increases, the rate increases to compensate purchasers for the bonds' increased risk. Also, the market rate is generally higher when the time period until the bond matures is longer due to the risk of adverse events occurring over a longer time period.

Many bond issuers try to set a contract rate of interest equal to the market rate they expect as of the bond issuance date. When the contract rate and market rate are equal, a bond sells at par value, but when they are not equal, a bond does not sell at par value. Instead, it is sold at a *premium* above par value or at a *discount* below par value. Exhibit 10.3 shows the relation between the contract rate, market rate, and a bond's issue price.

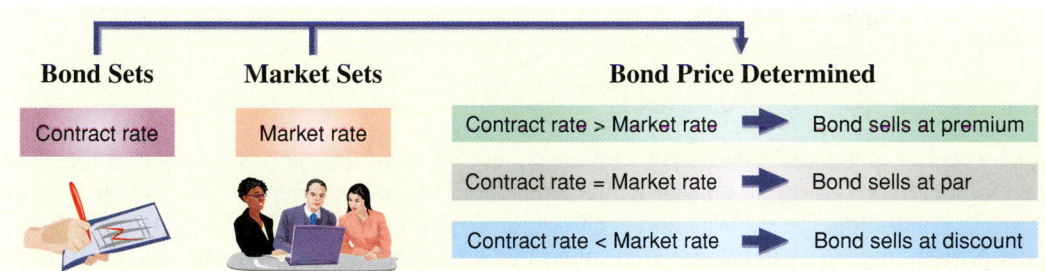

Bond Sets	Market Sets	Bond Price Determined	
Contract rate	Market rate	Contract rate > Market rate	Bond sells at premium
		Contract rate = Market rate	Bond sells at par
		Contract rate < Market rate	Bond sells at discount

EXHIBIT 10.3

Relation between Bond Issue Price, Contract Rate, and Market Rate

Quick Check

Answers — p. 439

1. A company issues $10,000 of 9%, 5-year bonds dated January 1, 2011, that mature on December 31, 2015, and pay interest semiannually on each June 30 and December 31. Prepare the entry to record this bond issuance and the first semiannual interest payment.
2. How do you compute the amount of interest a bond issuer pays in cash each year?
3. When the contract rate is above the market rate, do bonds sell at a premium or a discount? Do purchasers pay more or less than the par value of the bonds?

Issuing Bonds at a Discount

A **discount on bonds payable** occurs when a company issues bonds with a contract rate less than the market rate. This means that the issue price is less than par value. To illustrate, assume that **Fila** announces an offer to issue bonds with a $100,000 par value, an 8% annual contract rate (paid semiannually), and a two-year life. Also assume that the market rate for Fila bonds is

P2 Compute and record amortization of bond discount.

Point: The difference between the contract rate and the market rate of interest on a new bond issue is usually a fraction of a percent. We use a difference of 2% to emphasize the effects.

10%. These bonds then will sell at a discount since the contract rate is less than the market rate. The exact issue price for these bonds is stated as 96.454 (implying 96.454% of par value, or $96,454); we show how to compute this issue price later in the chapter. These bonds obligate the issuer to pay two separate types of future cash flows:

1. Par value of $100,000 cash at the end of the bonds' two-year life.
2. Cash interest payments of $4,000 (4% × $100,000) at the end of each semiannual period during the bonds' two-year life.

The exact pattern of cash flows for the Fila bonds is shown in Exhibit 10.4.

EXHIBIT 10.4

Cash Flows for Fila Bonds

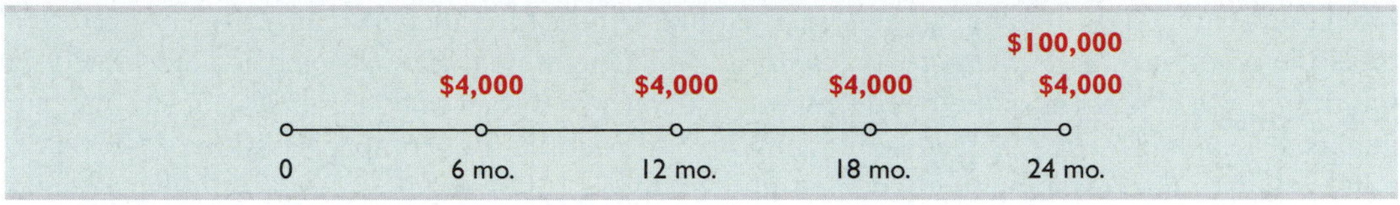

When Fila accepts $96,454 cash for its bonds on the issue date of December 31, 2011, it records the sale as follows.

Assets	=	Liabilities	+	Equity
+96,454		+100,000		
		−3,546		

Dec. 31	Cash	96,454	
	Discount on Bonds Payable	3,546	
	Bonds Payable		100,000
	Sold bonds at a discount on their issue date.		

Point: Book value at issuance always equals the issuer's cash borrowed.

These bonds are reported in the long-term liability section of the issuer's December 31, 2011, balance sheet as shown in Exhibit 10.5. A discount is deducted from the par value of bonds to yield the **carrying (book) value of bonds.** Discount on Bonds Payable is a contra liability account.

EXHIBIT 10.5

Balance Sheet Presentation of Bond Discount

Long-term liabilities		
Bonds payable, 8%, due December 31, 2013	$100,000	
Less discount on bonds payable	3,546	$96,454

Amortizing a Bond Discount Fila receives $96,454 for its bonds; in return it must pay bondholders $100,000 after two years (plus semiannual interest payments). The $3,546 discount is paid to bondholders at maturity and is part of the cost of using the $96,454 for two years. The upper portion of panel A in Exhibit 10.6 shows that total bond interest expense of $19,546 is the difference between the total amount repaid to bondholders ($116,000) and the amount borrowed from bondholders ($96,454). Alternatively, we can compute total bond interest expense as the sum of the four interest payments and the bond discount. This alternative computation is shown in the lower portion of panel A.

Point: *Zero-coupon bonds* do not pay periodic interest (contract rate is zero). These bonds always sell at a discount because their 0% contract rate is always below the market rate.

The total $19,546 bond interest expense must be allocated across the four semiannual periods in the bonds' life, and the bonds' carrying value must be updated at each balance sheet date. This is accomplished using the straight-line method (or the effective interest method in Appendix 10B). Both methods systematically reduce the bond discount to zero over the two-year life. This process is called *amortizing a bond discount.*

Straight-Line Method The **straight-line bond amortization** method allocates an equal portion of the total bond interest expense to each interest period. To apply the straight-line method to Fila's bonds, we divide the total bond interest expense of $19,546 by 4 (the number of semiannual periods in the bonds' life). This gives a bond interest expense of $4,887 per period, which is $4,886.5 rounded to the nearest dollar per period (all computations, including those for assignments, are rounded to the nearest whole dollar). Alternatively, we can find this number by first dividing the $3,546 discount by 4, which yields the $887 amount of discount to be amortized each interest period. When the $887 is added to the $4,000 cash payment, the bond

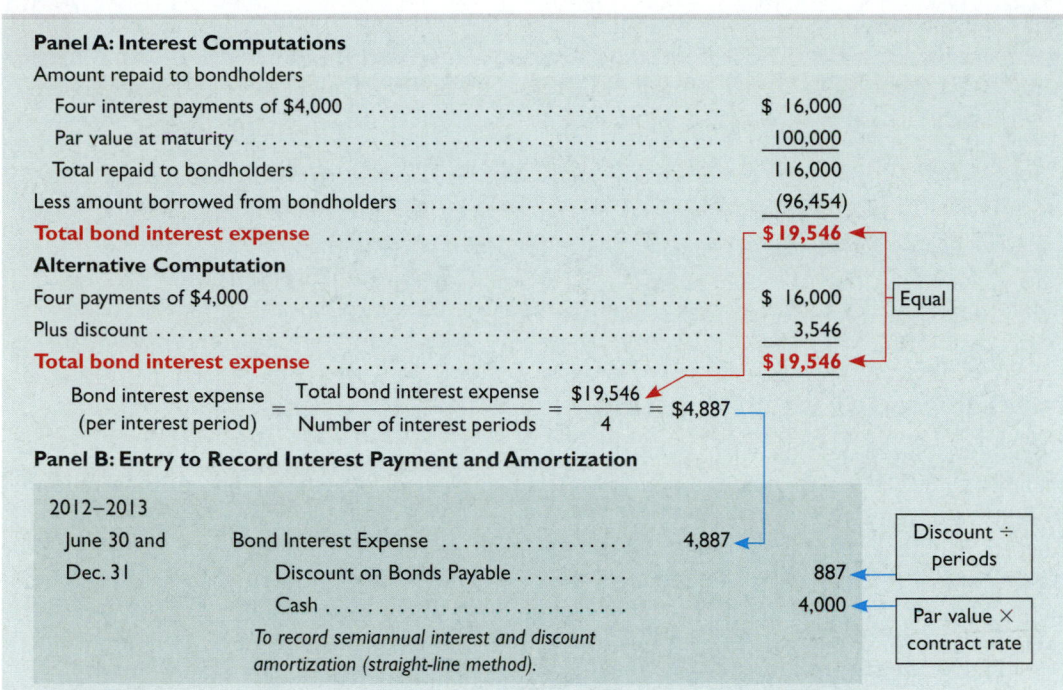

EXHIBIT 10.6

Interest Computation and Entry for Bonds Issued at a Discount

interest expense for each period is $4,887. Panel B of Exhibit 10.6 shows how the issuer records bond interest expense and updates the balance of the bond liability account at the end of *each* of the four semiannual interest periods (June 30, 2012, through December 31, 2013).

Exhibit 10.7 shows the pattern of decreases in the Discount on Bonds Payable account and the pattern of increases in the bonds' carrying value. The following points summarize the discount bonds' straight-line amortization:

1. At issuance, the $100,000 par value consists of the $96,454 cash received by the issuer plus the $3,546 discount.

2. During the bonds' life, the (unamortized) discount decreases each period by the $887 amortization ($3,546/4), and the carrying value (par value less unamortized discount) increases each period by $887.

Semiannual Period-End		Unamortized Discount*	Carrying Value†
(0)	12/31/2011	$3,546	$ 96,454
(1)	6/30/2012	2,659	97,341
(2)	12/31/2012	1,772	98,228
(3)	6/30/2013	885	99,115
(4)	12/31/2013	0‡	100,000

* Total bond discount (of $3,546) less accumulated periodic amortization ($887 per semiannual interest period).

† Bond par value (of $100,000) less unamortized discount.

‡ Adjusted for rounding.

EXHIBIT 10.7

Straight-Line Amortization of Bond Discount

The two columns always sum to par value for a discount bond.

3. At maturity, the unamortized discount equals zero, and the carrying value equals the $100,000 par value that the issuer pays the holder.

We see that the issuer incurs a $4,887 bond interest expense each period but pays only $4,000 cash. The $887 unpaid portion of this expense is added to the bonds' carrying value. (The total $3,546 unamortized discount is "paid" when the bonds mature; $100,000 is paid at maturity but only $96,454 was received at issuance.)

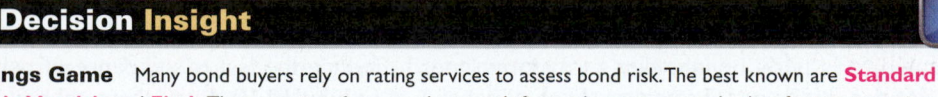

Decision **Insight**

Ratings Game Many bond buyers rely on rating services to assess bond risk. The best known are **Standard & Poor's**, **Moody's**, and **Fitch**. These services focus on the issuer's financial statements and other factors in setting ratings. Standard & Poor's ratings, from best quality to default, are AAA, AA, A, BBB, BB, B, CCC, CC, C, and D. Ratings can include a plus (+) or minus (−) to show relative standing within a category. ∎

Five-year, 6% bonds with a $100,000 par value are issued at a price of $91,893. Interest is paid semiannually, and the bonds' market rate is 8% on the issue date. Use this information to answer the following questions:

4. Are these bonds issued at a discount or a premium? Explain your answer.
5. What is the issuer's journal entry to record the issuance of these bonds?
6. What is the amount of bond interest expense recorded at the first semiannual period using the straight-line method?

Issuing Bonds at a Premium

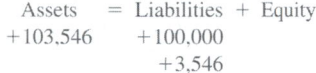

P3   Compute and record amortization of bond premium.

When the contract rate of bonds is higher than the market rate, the bonds sell at a price higher than par value. The amount by which the bond price exceeds par value is the **premium on bonds.** To illustrate, assume that **Adidas** issues bonds with a $100,000 par value, a 12% annual contract rate, semiannual interest payments, and a two-year life. Also assume that the market rate for Adidas bonds is 10% on the issue date. The Adidas bonds will sell at a premium because the contract rate is higher than the market rate. The issue price for these bonds is stated as 103.546 (implying 103.546% of par value, or $103,546); we show how to compute this issue price later in the chapter. These bonds obligate the issuer to pay out two separate future cash flows:

1. Par value of $100,000 cash at the end of the bonds' two-year life.
2. Cash interest payments of $6,000 (6% × $100,000) at the end of each semiannual period during the bonds' two-year life.

The exact pattern of cash flows for the Adidas bonds is shown in Exhibit 10.8.

EXHIBIT 10.8

Cash Flows for Adidas Bonds

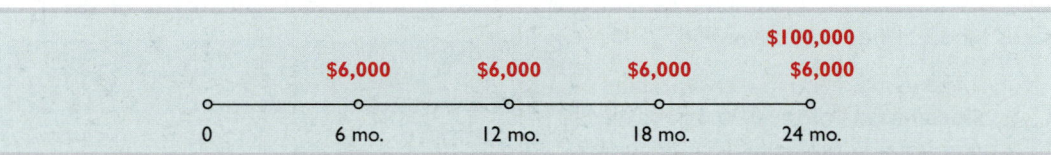

When Adidas accepts $103,546 cash for its bonds on the issue date of December 31, 2011, it records this transaction as follows.

Assets	= Liabilities + Equity
+103,546	+100,000
	+3,546

Dec. 31	Cash	103,546	
	Premium on Bonds Payable		3,546
	Bonds Payable		100,000
	Sold bonds at a premium on their issue date.		

These bonds are reported in the long-term liability section of the issuer's December 31, 2011, balance sheet as shown in Exhibit 10.9. A premium is added to par value to yield the carrying (book) value of bonds. Premium on Bonds Payable is an adjunct (also called *accretion*) liability account.

EXHIBIT 10.9

Balance Sheet Presentation of Bond Premium

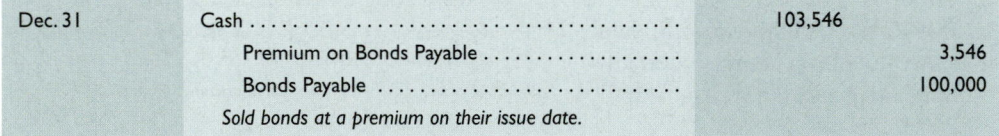

Amortizing a Bond Premium   Adidas receives $103,546 for its bonds; in return, it pays bondholders $100,000 after two years (plus semiannual interest payments). The $3,546 premium not repaid to issuer's bondholders at maturity goes to reduce the issuer's expense of using the $103,546 for two years. The upper portion of panel A of Exhibit 10.10 shows that total bond interest expense of $20,454 is the difference between the total amount repaid to bondholders ($124,000) and the amount borrowed from bondholders ($103,546). Alternatively, we can compute total bond interest expense as the sum of the four interest payments less the bond premium. The premium is

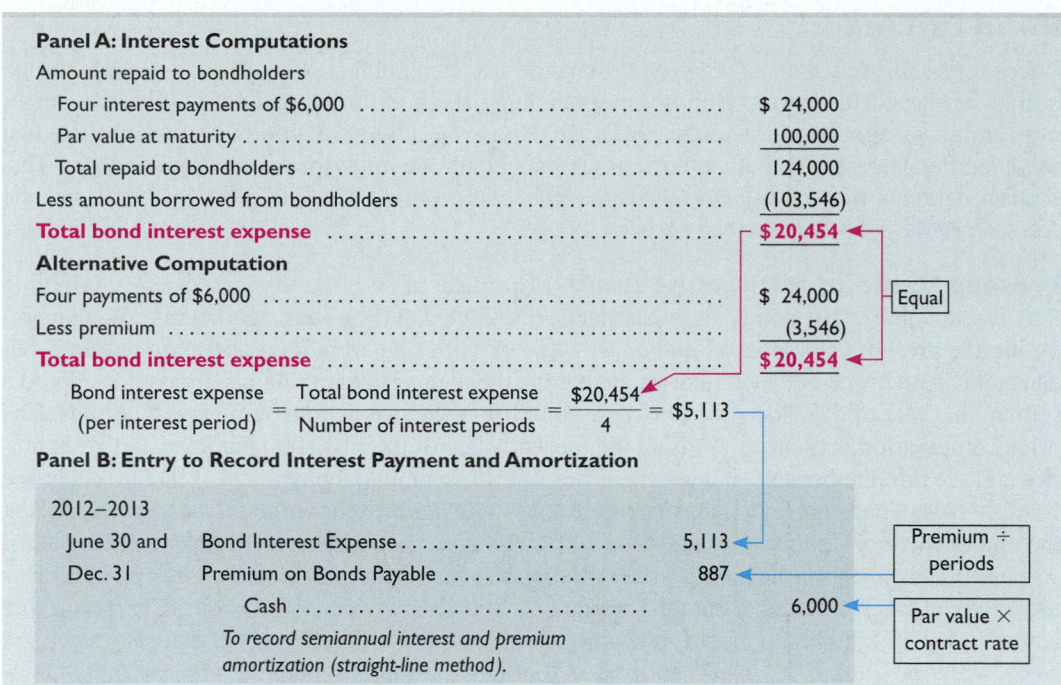

EXHIBIT 10.10

Interest Computation and Entry for Bonds Issued at a Premium

subtracted because it will not be paid to bondholders when the bonds mature; see the lower portion of panel A. Total bond interest expense must be allocated over the four semiannual periods using the straight-line method (or the effective interest method in Appendix 10B).

Straight-Line Method The straight-line method allocates an equal portion of total bond interest expense to each of the bonds' semiannual interest periods. To apply this method to Adidas bonds, we divide the two years' total bond interest expense of $20,454 by 4 (the number of semiannual periods in the bonds' life). This gives a total bond interest expense of $5,113 per period, which is $5,113.5 rounded down so that the journal entry balances and for simplicity in presentation (alternatively, one could carry cents). Panel B of Exhibit 10.10 shows how the issuer records bond interest expense and updates the balance of the bond liability account for *each* semiannual period (June 30, 2012, through December 31, 2013).

Exhibit 10.11 shows the pattern of decreases in the unamortized Premium on Bonds Payable account and in the bonds' carrying value. The following points summarize straight-line amortization of the premium bonds:

Point: A premium decreases Bond Interest Expense; a discount increases it.

EXHIBIT 10.11

Straight-Line Amortization of Bond Premium

Semiannual Period-End	Unamortized Premium*	Carrying Value†
(0) 12/31/2011	$3,546	$103,546
(1) 6/30/2012	2,659	102,659
(2) 12/31/2012	1,772	101,772
(3) 6/30/2013	885	100,885
(4) 12/31/2013	0‡	100,000

* Total bond premium (of $3,546) less accumulated periodic amortization ($887 per semiannual interest period).

† Bond par value (of $100,000) plus unamortized premium.

‡ Adjusted for rounding.

During the bond life, carrying value is adjusted to par and the amortized premium to zero.

1. At issuance, the $100,000 par value plus the $3,546 premium equals the $103,546 cash received by the issuer.
2. During the bonds' life, the (unamortized) premium decreases each period by the $887 amortization ($3,546/4), and the carrying value decreases each period by the same $887.
3. At maturity, the unamortized premium equals zero, and the carrying value equals the $100,000 par value that the issuer pays the holder.

The next section describes bond pricing. An instructor can choose to cover bond pricing or not. Assignments requiring the next section are Quick Study 10-5, and Exercises 10-9 & 10-10.

Bond Pricing

Prices for bonds traded on an organized exchange are often published in newspapers and through online services. This information normally includes the bond price (called *quote*), its contract rate, and its current market (called *yield*) rate. However, only a fraction of bonds are traded on organized exchanges. To compute the price of a bond, we apply present value concepts. This section explains how to use *present value concepts* to price the Fila discount bond and the Adidas premium bond described earlier.

Present Value of a Discount Bond   The issue price of bonds is found by computing the present value of the bonds' cash payments, discounted at the bonds' market rate. When computing the present value of the Fila bonds, we work with *semiannual* compounding periods because this is the time between interest payments; the annual market rate of 10% is considered a semiannual rate of 5%. Also, the two-year bond life is viewed as four semiannual periods. The price computation is twofold: (1) Find the present value of the $100,000 par value paid at maturity and (2) find the present value of the series of four semiannual payments of $4,000 each; see Exhibit 10.4. These present values can be found by using *present value tables*. Appendix B at the end of this book shows present value tables and describes their use. Table B.1 at the end of Appendix B is used for the single $100,000 maturity payment, and Table B.3 in Appendix B is used for the $4,000 series of interest payments. Specifically, we go to Table B.1, row 4, and across to the 5% column to identify the present value factor of 0.8227 for the maturity payment. Next, we go to Table B.3, row 4, and across to the 5% column, where the present value factor is 3.5460 for the series of interest payments. We compute bond price by multiplying the cash flow payments by their corresponding present value factors and adding them together; see Exhibit 10.12.

Point: InvestingInBonds.com is a bond research and learning source.

Point: A bond's market value (price) at issuance equals the present value of its future cash payments, where the interest (discount) rate used is the bond's market rate.

Point: Many calculators have present value functions for computing bond prices.

EXHIBIT 10.12

Computing Issue Price for the Fila Discount Bonds

Cash Flow	Table	Present Value Factor	Amount	Present Value
$100,000 par (maturity) value	B.1	0.8227	× $100,000 =	$82,270
$4,000 interest payments	B.3	3.5460	× 4,000 =	14,184
Price of bond				**$96,454**

Present Value of a Premium Bond   We find the issue price of the Adidas bonds by using the market rate to compute the present value of the bonds' future cash flows. When computing the present value of these bonds, we again work with *semiannual* compounding periods because this is the time between interest payments. The annual 10% market rate is applied as a semiannual rate of 5%, and the two-year bond life is viewed as four semiannual periods. The computation is twofold: (1) Find the present value of the $100,000 par value paid at maturity and (2) find the present value of the series of four payments of $6,000 each; see Exhibit 10.8. These present values can be found by using present value tables. First, go to Table B.1, row 4, and across to the 5% column where the present value factor is 0.8227 for the maturity payment. Second, go to Table B.3, row 4, and across to the 5% column, where the present value factor is 3.5460 for the series of interest payments. The bonds' price is computed by multiplying the cash flow payments by their corresponding present value factors and adding them together; see Exhibit 10.13.

Point: There are nearly 5 million individual U.S. bond issues, ranging from huge treasuries to tiny municipalities. This compares to about 12,000 individual U.S. stocks that are traded.

EXHIBIT 10.13

Computing Issue Price for the Adidas Premium Bonds

Cash Flow	Table	Present Value Factor	Amount	Present Value
$100,000 par (maturity) value	B.1	0.8227	× $100,000 =	$ 82,270
$6,000 interest payments	B.3	3.5460	× 6,000 =	21,276
Price of bond				**$103,546**

Quick Check

Answers — p. 439

On December 31, 2010, a company issues 16%, 10-year bonds with a par value of $100,000. Interest is paid on June 30 and December 31. The bonds are sold to yield a 14% annual market rate at an issue price of $110,592. Use this information to answer questions 7 through 9:

7. Are these bonds issued at a discount or a premium? Explain your answer.

8. Using the straight-line method to allocate bond interest expense, the issuer records the second interest payment (on December 31, 2011) with a debit to Premium on Bonds Payable in the amount of (*a*) $7,470, (*b*) $530, (*c*) $8,000, or (*d*) $400.

9. How are these bonds reported in the long-term liability section of the issuer's balance sheet as of December 31, 2011?

BOND RETIREMENT

This section describes the retirement of bonds (1) at maturity, (2) before maturity, and (3) by conversion to stock.

P4 Record the retirement of bonds.

Bond Retirement at Maturity

The carrying value of bonds at maturity always equals par value. For example, both Exhibits 10.7 (a discount) and 10.11 (a premium) show that the carrying value of bonds at the end of their lives equals par value ($100,000). The retirement of these bonds at maturity, assuming interest is already paid and entered, is recorded as follows:

2013			
Dec. 31	Bonds Payable	100,000	
	Cash		100,000
	To record retirement of bonds at maturity.		

Assets	=	Liabilities	+	Equity
−100,000		−100,000		

Bond Retirement before Maturity

Issuers sometimes wish to retire some or all of their bonds prior to maturity. For instance, if interest rates decline greatly, an issuer may wish to replace high-interest-paying bonds with new low-interest bonds. Two common ways to retire bonds before maturity are to (1) exercise a call option or (2) purchase them on the open market. In the first instance, an issuer can reserve the right to retire bonds early by issuing callable bonds. The bond indenture can give the issuer an option to *call* the bonds before they mature by paying the par value plus a *call premium* to bondholders. In the second case, the issuer retires bonds by repurchasing them on the open market at their current price. Whether bonds are called or repurchased, the issuer is unlikely to pay a price that exactly equals their carrying value. When a difference exists between the bonds' carrying value and the amount paid, the issuer records a gain or loss equal to the difference.

Point: Bond retirement is also referred to as *bond redemption.*

Point: Gains and losses from retiring bonds were *previously* reported as extraordinary items. New standards require that they now be judged by the "unusual and infrequent" criteria for reporting purposes.

To illustrate the accounting for retiring callable bonds, assume that a company issued callable bonds with a par value of $100,000. The call option requires the issuer to pay a call premium of $3,000 to bondholders in addition to the par value. Next, assume that after the June 30, 2011, interest payment, the bonds have a carrying value of $104,500. Then on July 1, 2011, the issuer calls these bonds and pays $103,000 to bondholders. The issuer recognizes a $1,500 gain from the difference between the bonds' carrying value of $104,500 and the retirement price of $103,000. The issuer records this bond retirement as follows.

July 1	Bonds Payable	100,000	
	Premium on Bonds Payable	4,500	
	Gain on Bond Retirement		1,500
	Cash		103,000
	To record retirement of bonds before maturity.		

Assets	=	Liabilities	+	Equity
−103,000		−100,000		+1,500
		−4,500		

An issuer usually must call all bonds when it exercises a call option. However, to retire as many or as few bonds as it desires, an issuer can purchase them on the open market. If it retires less than the entire class of bonds, it recognizes a gain or loss for the difference between the carrying value of those bonds retired and the amount paid to acquire them.

Bond Retirement by Conversion

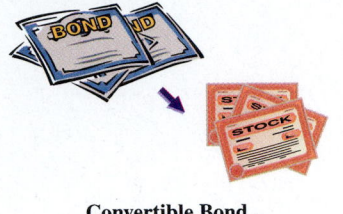

Convertible Bond

Holders of convertible bonds have the right to convert their bonds to stock. When conversion occurs, the bonds' carrying value is transferred to equity accounts and no gain or loss is recorded. (We further describe convertible bonds in the Decision Analysis section of this chapter.)

To illustrate, assume that on January 1 the $100,000 par value bonds of **Converse**, with a carrying value of $100,000, are converted to 15,000 shares of $2 par value common stock. The entry to record this conversion follows (the market prices of the bonds and stock are *not* relevant to this entry; the material in Chapter 11 is helpful in understanding this transaction):

Assets	=	Liabilities	+	Equity
		−100,000		+30,000
				+70,000

Jan. 1	Bonds Payable	100,000	
	Common Stock		30,000
	Paid-In Capital in Excess of Par Value		70,000
	To record retirement of bonds by conversion.		

Decision Insight

Junk Bonds Junk bonds are company bonds with low credit ratings due to a higher than average likelihood of default. On the upside, the high risk of junk bonds can yield high returns if the issuer survives and repays its debt. ■

Quick Check   Answer — p. 439

10. Six years ago, a company issued $500,000 of 6%, eight-year bonds at a price of 95. The current carrying value is $493,750. The company decides to retire 50% of these bonds by buying them on the open market at a price of 102½. What is the amount of gain or loss on the retirement of these bonds?

LONG-TERM NOTES PAYABLE

 C1 Explain the types and payment patterns of notes.

Like bonds, notes are issued to obtain assets such as cash. Unlike bonds, notes are typically transacted with a *single* lender such as a bank. An issuer initially records a note at its selling price—that is, the note's face value minus any discount or plus any premium. Over the note's life, the amount of interest expense allocated to each period is computed by multiplying the market rate (at issuance of the note) by the beginning-of-period note balance. The note's carrying (book) value at any time equals its face value minus any unamortized discount or plus any unamortized premium; carrying value is also computed as the present value of all remaining payments, discounted using the market rate at issuance.

Installment Notes

An **installment note** is an obligation requiring a series of payments to the lender. Installment notes are common for franchises and other businesses when lenders and borrowers agree to spread payments over several periods. To illustrate, assume that Foghog borrows $60,000 from a bank to purchase equipment. It signs an 8% installment note requiring six annual payments of principal plus interest and it records the note's issuance at January 1, 2011, as follows.

Jan. 1	Cash	60,000	
	Notes Payable		60,000
	Borrowed $60,000 by signing an 8%, six-year installment note.		

Assets = Liabilities + Equity
+60,000   +60,000

Payments on an installment note normally include the accrued interest expense plus a portion of the amount borrowed (the *principal*). This section describes an installment note with equal payments.

The equal total payments pattern consists of changing amounts of both interest and principal. To illustrate, assume that Foghog borrows $60,000 by signing a $60,000 note that requires six *equal payments* of $12,979 at the end of each year. (The present value of an annuity of six annual payments of $12,979, discounted at 8%, equals $60,000; we show this computation in footnote 2 on the next page.) The $12,979 includes both interest and principal, the amounts of which change with each payment. Exhibit 10.14 shows the pattern of equal total payments and its two parts, interest and principal. Column A shows the note's beginning balance. Column B shows accrued interest for each year at 8% of the beginning note balance. Column C shows the impact on the note's principal, which equals the difference between the total payment in column D and the interest expense in column B. Column E shows the note's year-end balance.

Years

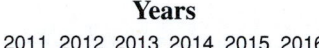
2011 2012 2013 2014 2015 2016

$12,979 $12,979 $12,979 $12,979 $12,979 $12,979

Point: Most consumer notes are installment notes that require equal total payments.

EXHIBIT 10.14

Installment Note: Equal Total Payments

		Payments			
Period Ending Date	**(A) Beginning Balance**	**(B) Debit Interest Expense 8% × (A)**	**(C) Debit Notes Payable (D) − (B)**	**(D) Credit Cash (computed)**	**(E) Ending Balance (A) − (C)**
(1) 12/31/2011	$60,000	$ 4,800	$ 8,179	$12,979	$51,821
(2) 12/31/2012	51,821	4,146	8,833	12,979	42,988
(3) 12/31/2013	42,988	3,439	9,540	12,979	33,448
(4) 12/31/2014	33,448	2,676	10,303	12,979	23,145
(5) 12/31/2015	23,145	1,852	11,127	12,979	12,018
(6) 12/31/2016	12,018	961	12,018	12,979	0
		$17,874	$60,000	$77,874	

Decreasing Accrued Interest ↓ — Increasing Principal Component ↓ — Equal Total Payments ↓

☐ Interest ☐ Principal

End of Year		
2011	$4,800	$8,179
2012	$4,146	$8,833
2013	$3,439	$9,540
2014	$2,676	$10,303
2015	$1,852	$11,127
2016	$961	$12,018

0 $2,500 $5,000 $7,500 $10,000 $12,500 $15,000
Cash Payment Pattern

Decision Insight

Hidden Debt   A study reports that 13% of employees in finance and accounting witnessed the falsifying or manipulating of accounting information in the past year (KPMG 2009). This is of special concern with long-term liabilities. For example, Enron violated GAAP to keep debt off its balance sheet. This concern extends to hidden environment liabilities. That same study reports 27% of employees in quality, safety, and environmental areas observed violations of environmental standards, which can yield massive liabilities. ■

P5 Prepare entries to account for notes.

Although the six cash payments are equal, accrued interest decreases each year because the principal balance of the note declines. As the amount of interest decreases each year, the portion of each payment applied to principal increases. This pattern is graphed in the lower part of Exhibit 10.14. Foghog uses the amounts in Exhibit 10.14 to record its first two payments (for years 2011 and 2012) as follows:

Assets = Liabilities + Equity
−12,979   −8,179   −4,800

2011			
Dec. 31	Interest Expense	4,800	
	Notes Payable	8,179	
	Cash		12,979
	To record first installment payment.		

Assets = Liabilities + Equity
−12,979   −8,833   −4,146

2012			
Dec. 31	Interest Expense	4,146	
	Notes Payable	8,833	
	Cash		12,979
	To record second installment payment.		

Foghog records similar entries but with different amounts for each of the remaining four payments. After six years, the Notes Payable account balance is zero.[2]

Mortgage Notes and Bonds

Point: The Truth-in-Lending Act requires lenders to provide information about loan costs including finance charges and interest rate.

A **mortgage** is a legal agreement that helps protect a lender if a borrower fails to make required payments on notes or bonds. A mortgage gives the lender a right to be paid from the cash proceeds of the sale of a borrower's assets identified in the mortgage. A legal document, called a *mortgage contract,* describes the mortgage terms.

Mortgage notes carry a mortgage contract pledging title to specific assets as security for the note. Mortgage notes are especially popular in the purchase of homes and the acquisition of plant assets. Less common *mortgage bonds* are backed by the issuer's assets. Accounting for mortgage notes and bonds is similar to that for unsecured notes and bonds, except that the mortgage agreement must be disclosed. For example, **TIBCO Software** reports that its "mortgage note payable . . . is collateralized by the commercial real property acquired [corporate headquarters]."

Global: Countries vary in the preference given to debtholders vs. stockholders when a company is in financial distress. Some countries such as Germany, France, and Japan give preference to stockholders over debtholders.

Example: Suppose the $60,000 installment loan has an 8% interest rate with eight equal annual payments. What is the annual payment? *Answer* (using Table B.3): $60,000/5.7466 = $10,441

[2] Table B.3 in Appendix B is used to compute the dollar amount of the six payments that equal the initial note balance of $60,000 at 8% interest. We go to Table B.3, row 6, and across to the 8% column, where the present value factor is 4.6229. The dollar amount is then computed by solving this relation:

Table	Present Value Factor		Dollar Amount		Present Value
B.3	4.6229	×	?	=	$60,000

The dollar amount is computed by dividing $60,000 by 4.6229, yielding $12,979.

Decision Maker   Answer — p. 439

Entrepreneur   You are an electronics retailer planning a holiday sale on a custom stereo system that requires no payments for two years. At the end of two years, buyers must pay the full amount. The system's suggested retail price is $4,100, but you are willing to sell it today for $3,000 cash. What is your holiday sale price if payment will not occur for two years and the market interest rate is 10%? ■

Quick Check   Answers — p. 439

11. Which of the following is true for an installment note requiring a series of equal total cash payments? (*a*) Payments consist of increasing interest and decreasing principal; (*b*) payments consist of changing amounts of principal but constant interest; or (*c*) payments consist of decreasing interest and increasing principal.

12. How is the interest portion of an installment note payment computed?

13. When a borrower records an interest payment on an installment note, how are the balance sheet and income statement affected?

GLOBAL VIEW

This section discusses similarities and differences between U.S. GAAP and IFRS in accounting and reporting for long-term liabilities such as bonds and notes.

Accounting for Bonds and Notes   The definitions and characteristics of bonds and notes are broadly similar for both U.S. GAAP and IFRS. Although slight differences exist, accounting for bonds and notes under U.S. GAAP and IFRS is similar. Specifically, the accounting for issuances (including recording discounts and premiums), market pricing, and retirement of both bonds and notes follows the procedures in this chapter. **Nokia** describes its accounting for bonds, which follows the amortized cost approach explained in this chapter (and in Appendix 10B), as follows: Loans payable [bonds] are recognized initially at fair value, net of transaction costs incurred. In the subsequent periods, they are stated at amortized cost.

NOKIA

   Both U.S. GAAP and IFRS allow companies to account for bonds and notes using fair value (different from the amortized value described in this chapter). This method is referred to as the **fair value option.** This method is similar to that applied in measuring and accounting for debt and equity securities. *Fair value* is the amount a company would receive if it settled a liability (or sold an asset) in an orderly transaction as of the balance sheet date. Companies can use several sources of inputs to determine fair value, and those inputs fall into three classes (ranked in order of preference):

Level 1: Observable quoted market prices in active markets for identical items.
Level 2: Observable inputs other than those in Level 1 such as prices from inactive markets or from similar, but not identical, items.
Level 3: Unobservable inputs reflecting a company's assumptions about value.

The exact procedures for marking liabilities to fair value at each balance sheet date are in advanced courses.

Accounting for Leases and Pensions   Both U.S. GAAP and IFRS require companies to distinguish between operating leases and capital leases; the latter is referred to as *finance leases* under IFRS. The accounting and reporting for leases are broadly similar for both U.S. GAAP and IFRS. The main difference is the criteria for identifying a lease as a capital lease are more general under IFRS. However, the basic approach applies. **Nokia** describes its accounting for operating leases as follows: the payments . . . are treated as rentals and recognized in the profit and loss account.

   For pensions, both U.S. GAAP and IFRS require companies to record costs of retirement benefits as employees work and earn them. The basic methods are similar in accounting and reporting for pensions.

Decision Analysis    Debt Features and the Debt-to-Equity Ratio

Collateral agreements can reduce the risk of loss for both bonds and notes. Unsecured bonds and notes are riskier because the issuer's obligation to pay interest and principal has the same priority as all other unsecured liabilities in the event of bankruptcy. If a company is unable to pay its debts in full, the unsecured creditors (including the holders of debentures) lose all or a portion of their balances. These types of legal agreements and other characteristics of long-term liabilities are crucial for effective business decisions. The first part of this section describes the different types of features sometimes included with bonds and notes. The second part explains and applies the debt-to-equity ratio.

 A2 Assess debt features and their implications.

Features of Bonds and Notes

This section describes common features of debt securities.

Secured Debt

Unsecured Debt

Secured or Unsecured   **Secured bonds** (and notes) have specific assets of the issuer pledged (or *mortgaged*) as collateral. This arrangement gives holders added protection against the issuer's default. If the issuer fails to pay interest or par value, the secured holders can demand that the collateral be sold and the proceeds used to pay the obligation. **Unsecured bonds** (and notes), also called *debentures,* are backed by the issuer's general credit standing. Unsecured debt is riskier than secured debt. *Subordinated debentures* are liabilities that are not repaid until the claims of the more senior, unsecured (and secured) liabilities are settled.

Term or Serial   **Term bonds** (and notes) are scheduled for maturity on one specified date. **Serial bonds** (and notes) mature at more than one date (often in series) and thus are usually repaid over a number of periods. For instance, $100,000 of serial bonds might mature at the rate of $10,000 each year from 6 to 15 years after they are issued. Many bonds are **sinking fund bonds,** which to reduce the holder's risk require the issuer to create a *sinking fund* of assets set aside at specified amounts and dates to repay the bonds.

Registered or Bearer   Bonds issued in the names and addresses of their holders are **registered bonds.** The issuer makes bond payments by sending checks (or cash transfers) to registered holders. A registered holder must notify the issuer of any ownership change. Registered bonds offer the issuer the practical advantage of not having to actually issue bond certificates. Bonds payable to whoever holds them (the *bearer*) are called **bearer bonds** or *unregistered bonds*. Sales or exchanges might not be recorded, so the holder of a bearer bond is presumed to be its rightful owner. As a result, lost bearer bonds are difficult to replace. Many bearer bonds are also **coupon bonds.** This term reflects interest coupons that are attached to the bonds. When each coupon matures, the holder presents it to a bank or broker for collection. At maturity, the holder follows the same process and presents the bond certificate for collection. Issuers of coupon bonds cannot deduct the related interest expense for taxable income. This is to prevent abuse by taxpayers who own coupon bonds but fail to report interest income on their tax returns.

Convertible Debt

Callable Debt

Convertible and/or Callable   **Convertible bonds** (and notes) can be exchanged for a fixed number of shares of the issuing corporation's common stock. Convertible debt offers holders the potential to participate in future increases in stock price. Holders still receive periodic interest while the debt is held and the par value if they hold the debt to maturity. In most cases, the holders decide whether and when to convert debt to stock. **Callable bonds** (and notes) have an option exercisable by the issuer to retire them at a stated dollar amount before maturity.

 Decision Insight

Munis   More than a million municipal bonds, or "munis," exist, and many are tax exempt. Munis are issued by state, city, town, and county governments to pay for public projects including schools, libraries, roads, bridges, and stadiums. ■

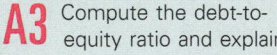 **A3** Compute the debt-to-equity ratio and explain its use.

Debt-to-Equity Ratio

Beyond assessing different characteristics of debt as just described, we want to know the level of debt, especially in relation to total equity. Such knowledge helps us assess the risk of a company's financing structure. A company financed mainly with debt is more risky because liabilities must be repaid—usually with periodic interest—whereas equity financing does not. A measure to assess the risk of a company's financing structure is the **debt-to-equity ratio** (see Exhibit 10.15).

$$\text{Debt-to-equity} = \frac{\text{Total liabilities}}{\text{Total equity}}$$

EXHIBIT 10.15

Debt-to-Equity Ratio

The debt-to-equity ratio varies across companies and industries. Industries that are more variable tend to have lower ratios, while more stable industries are less risky and tend to have higher ratios. To apply the debt-to-equity ratio, let's look at this measure for **Cedar Fair** in Exhibit 10.16.

($ millions)	2009	2008	2007	2006	2005
Total liabilities	$2,017.577	$2,079.297	$2,133.576	$2,100.306	$590.560
Total equity	$ 127.862	$ 106.786	$ 285.092	$ 410.615	$434.234
Debt-to-equity	**15.8**	**19.5**	**7.5**	**5.1**	**1.4**
Industry debt-to-equity	11.4	10.3	5.7	3.2	1.2

EXHIBIT 10.16

Cedar Fair's Debt-to-Equity Ratio

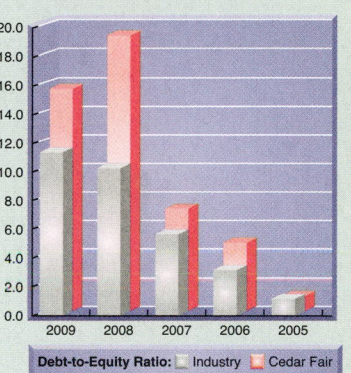

Cedar Fair's 2009 debt-to-equity ratio is 15.8, meaning that debtholders contributed $15.8 for each $1 contributed by equityholders. This implies a fairly risky financing structure for Cedar Fair. A similar concern is drawn from a comparison of Cedar Fair with its competitors, where the 2009 industry ratio is 11.4. Analysis across the years shows that Cedar Fair's financing structure has grown increasingly risky in recent years. Given its sluggish revenues and increasing operating expenses in recent years (see its annual report), Cedar Fair is increasingly at risk of financial distress.

 **Decision Maker**   Answer — p. 439

Bond Investor   You plan to purchase debenture bonds from one of two companies in the same industry that are similar in size and performance. The first company has $350,000 in total liabilities, and $1,750,000 in equity. The second company has $1,200,000 in total liabilities, and $1,000,000 in equity. Which company's debenture bonds are less risky based on the debt-to-equity ratio? ■

DEMONSTRATION PROBLEM

Water Sports Company (WSC) patented and successfully test-marketed a new product. To expand its ability to produce and market the new product, WSC needs to raise $800,000 of financing. On January 1, 2011, the company obtained the money in two ways:

a. WSC signed a $400,000, 10% installment note to be repaid with five equal annual installments to be made on December 31 of 2011 through 2015.

b. WSC issued five-year bonds with a par value of $400,000. The bonds have a 12% annual contract rate and pay interest on June 30 and December 31. The bonds' annual market rate is 10% as of January 1, 2011.

Required

1. For the installment note, (*a*) compute the size of each annual payment, (*b*) prepare an amortization table such as Exhibit 10.14, and (*c*) prepare the journal entry for the first payment.

2. For the bonds, (*a*) compute their issue price; (*b*) prepare the January 1, 2011, journal entry to record their issuance; (*c*) prepare an amortization table using the straight-line method; (*d*) prepare the June 30, 2011, journal entry to record the first interest payment; and (*e*) prepare a journal entry to record retiring the bonds at a $416,000 call price on January 1, 2013.

3.ᴮRedo parts 2(*c*), 2(*d*), and 2(*e*) assuming the bonds are amortized using the effective interest method.

PLANNING THE SOLUTION

- For the installment note, divide the borrowed amount by the annuity factor (from Table B.3) using the 10% rate and five payments to compute the amount of each payment. Prepare a table similar to Exhibit 10.14 and use the numbers in the table's first line for the journal entry.
- Compute the bonds' issue price by using the market rate to find the present value of their cash flows (use tables found in Appendix B). Then use this result to record the bonds' issuance. Next, prepare an amortization table like Exhibit 10.11 (and Exhibit 10B.2) and use it to get the numbers needed for the journal entry. Also use the table to find the carrying value as of the date of the bonds' retirement that you need for the journal entry.

SOLUTION TO DEMONSTRATION PROBLEM

Part 1: Installment Note

a. Annual payment = Note balance/Annuity factor = $400,000/3.7908 = $105,519 (The annuity factor is for five payments and a rate of 10%.)

b. An amortization table follows.

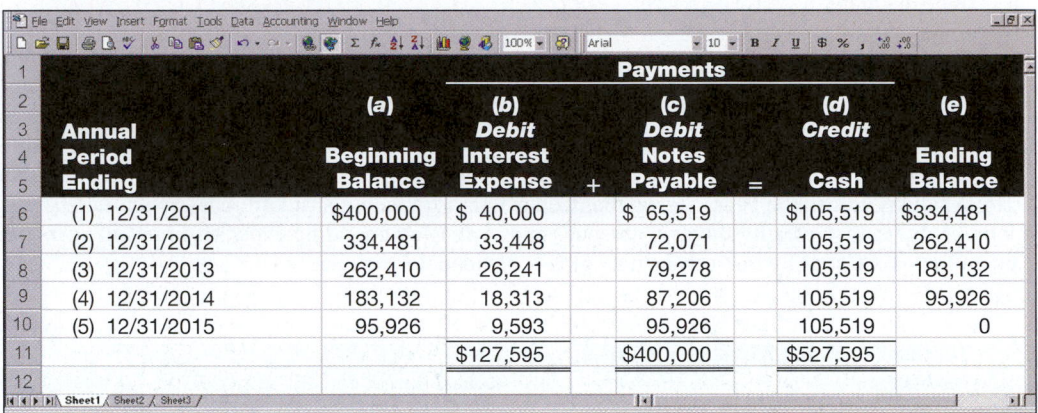

Annual Period Ending	(a) Beginning Balance	(b) Debit Interest Expense	+	(c) Debit Notes Payable	=	(d) Credit Cash	(e) Ending Balance
(1) 12/31/2011	$400,000	$ 40,000		$ 65,519		$105,519	$334,481
(2) 12/31/2012	334,481	33,448		72,071		105,519	262,410
(3) 12/31/2013	262,410	26,241		79,278		105,519	183,132
(4) 12/31/2014	183,132	18,313		87,206		105,519	95,926
(5) 12/31/2015	95,926	9,593		95,926		105,519	0
		$127,595		$400,000		$527,595	

c. Journal entry for December 31, 2011, payment.

Dec. 31	Interest Expense	40,000	
	Notes Payable	65,519	
	Cash		105,519
	To record first installment payment.		

Part 2: Bonds (Straight-Line Amortization)

a. Compute the bonds' issue price.

Cash Flow	Table	Present Value Factor*	Amount	Present Value
Par (maturity) value	B.1 in App. B (PV of 1)	0.6139	× 400,000	= $245,560
Interest payments	B.3 in App. B (PV of annuity)	7.7217	× 24,000	= 185,321
Price of bond				$430,881

* Present value factors are for 10 payments using a semiannual market rate of 5%.

b. Journal entry for January 1, 2011, issuance.

Jan. 1	Cash	430,881	
	Premium on Bonds Payable		30,881
	Bonds Payable		400,000
	Sold bonds at a premium.		

c. Straight-line amortization table for premium bonds.

Semiannual Period-End	Unamortized Premium	Carrying Value
(0) 1/1/2011	$30,881	$430,881
(1) 6/30/2011	27,793	427,793
(2) 12/31/2011	24,705	424,705
(3) 6/30/2012	21,617	421,617
(4) 12/31/2012	18,529	418,529
(5) 6/30/2013	15,441	415,441
(6) 12/31/2013	12,353	412,353
(7) 6/30/2014	9,265	409,265
(8) 12/31/2014	6,177	406,177
(9) 6/30/2015	3,089	403,089
(10) 12/31/2015	0*	400,000

* Adjusted for rounding.

d. Journal entry for June 30, 2011, bond payment.

June 30	Bond Interest Expense	20,912	
	Premium on Bonds Payable	3,088	
	Cash		24,000
	Paid semiannual interest on bonds.		

e. Journal entry for January 1, 2013, bond retirement.

Jan. 1	Bonds Payable	400,000	
	Premium on Bonds Payable	18,529	
	Cash		416,000
	Gain on Retirement of Bonds		2,529
	To record bond retirement (carrying value as of Dec. 31, 2012).		

Part 3: Bonds (Effective Interest Amortization)[B]

c. The effective interest amortization table for premium bonds.

	Semiannual Interest Period	(A) Cash Interest Paid 6% × $400,000	(B) Interest Expense 5% × Prior (E)	(C) Premium Amortization (A) − (B)	(D) Unamortized Premium Prior (D) − (C)	(E) Carrying Value $400,000 + (D)
(0)	1/1/2011				$30,881	$430,881
(1)	6/30/2011	$ 24,000	$ 21,544	$ 2,456	28,425	428,425
(2)	12/31/2011	24,000	21,421	2,579	25,846	425,846
(3)	6/30/2012	24,000	21,292	2,708	23,138	423,138
(4)	12/31/2012	24,000	21,157	2,843	20,295	420,295
(5)	6/30/2013	24,000	21,015	2,985	17,310	417,310
(6)	12/31/2013	24,000	20,866	3,134	14,176	414,176
(7)	6/30/2014	24,000	20,709	3,291	10,885	410,885
(8)	12/31/2014	24,000	20,544	3,456	7,429	407,429
(9)	6/30/2015	24,000	20,371	3,629	3,800	403,800
(10)	12/31/2015	24,000	20,200*	3,800	0	400,000
		$240,000	$209,119	$30,881		

* Adjusted for rounding

d. Journal entry for June 30, 2011, bond payment.

June 30	Bond Interest Expense	21,544	
	Premium on Bonds Payable	2,456	
	Cash		24,000
	Paid semiannual interest on bonds.		

e. Journal entry for January 1, 2013, bond retirement.

Jan. 1	Bonds Payable	400,000	
	Premium on Bonds Payable	20,295	
	Cash		416,000
	Gain on Retirement of Bonds		4,295
	To record bond retirement (carrying value as of December 31, 2012).		

APPENDIX

10A — Present Values of Bonds and Notes

This appendix explains how to apply present value techniques to measure a long-term liability when it is created and to assign interest expense to the periods until it is settled. Appendix B at the end of the book provides additional discussion of present value concepts.

C2 Explain and compute the present value of an amount(s) to be paid at a future date(s).

Present Value Concepts   The basic present value concept is that cash paid (or received) in the future has less value now than the same amount of cash paid (or received) today. To illustrate, if we must pay $1 one year from now, its present value is less than $1. To see this, assume that we borrow $0.9259 today that must be paid back in one year with 8% interest. Our interest expense for this loan is computed as $0.9259 × 8%, or $0.0741. When the $0.0741 interest is added to the $0.9259 borrowed, we get the $1 payment necessary to repay our loan with interest. This is formally computed in Exhibit 10A.1. The $0.9259 borrowed is the present value of the $1 future payment. More generally, an amount borrowed equals the present value of the future payment. (This same interpretation applies to an investment. If $0.9259 is invested at 8%, it yields $0.0741 in revenue after one year. This amounts to $1, made up of principal and interest.)

EXHIBIT 10A.1

Components of a One-Year Loan

Amount borrowed	$0.9259
Interest for one year at 8%	0.0741
Amount owed after 1 year	$ 1.0000

To extend this example, assume that we owe $1 two years from now instead of one year, and the 8% interest is compounded annually. *Compounded* means that interest during the second period is based on the total of the amount borrowed plus the interest accrued from the first period. The second period's interest is then computed as 8% multiplied by the sum of the amount borrowed plus interest earned in the first period. Exhibit 10A.2 shows how we compute the present value of $1 to be paid in two years. This amount is $0.8573. The first year's interest of $0.0686 is added to the principal so that the second year's interest is based on $0.9259. Total interest for this two-year period is $0.1427, computed as $0.0686 plus $0.0741.

Point: Benjamin Franklin is said to have described compounding as "the money, money makes, makes more money."

EXHIBIT 10A.2

Components of a Two-Year Loan

Amount borrowed	$0.8573
Interest for first year ($0.8573 × 8%)	0.0686
Amount owed after 1 year	0.9259
Interest for second year ($0.9259 × 8%)	0.0741
Amount owed after 2 years	$ 1.0000

Present Value Tables   The present value of $1 that we must repay at some future date can be computed by using this formula: $1/(1 + i)^n$. The symbol i is the interest rate per period and n is the number of periods until the future payment must be made. Applying this formula to our two-year loan, we get $1/(1.08)^2$, or $0.8573. This is the same value shown in Exhibit 10A.2. We can use this formula to find any present value. However, a simpler method is to use a *present value table,* which lists present values computed with this formula for various interest rates and time periods. Many people find it helpful in learning present value concepts to first work with the table and then move to using a calculator.

Exhibit 10A.3 shows a present value table for a future payment of 1 for up to 10 periods at three different interest rates. Present values in this table are rounded to four decimal places. This table is drawn from the larger and more complete Table B.1 in Appendix B at the end of the book. Notice that the first value in the 8% column is 0.9259, the value we computed earlier for the present value of a $1 loan for one year at 8% (see Exhibit 10A.1). Go to the second row in the same 8% column and find the present value of 1 discounted at 8% for two years, or 0.8573. This $0.8573 is the present value of our obligation to repay $1 after two periods at 8% interest (see Exhibit 10A.2).

EXHIBIT 10A.3

Present Value of 1

Periods	Rate 6%	8%	10%
1	0.9434	**0.9259**	0.9091
2	0.8900	**0.8573**	0.8264
3	0.8396	0.7938	0.7513
4	0.7921	0.7350	0.6830
5	0.7473	0.6806	0.6209
6	0.7050	0.6302	0.5645
7	0.6651	0.5835	0.5132
8	0.6274	0.5403	0.4665
9	0.5919	0.5002	0.4241
10	0.5584	0.4632	0.3855

Example: Use Exhibit 10A.3 to find the present value of $1 discounted for 2 years at 6%. *Answer:* $0.8900

Applying a Present Value Table   To illustrate how to measure a liability using a present value table, assume that a company plans to borrow cash and repay it as follows: $2,000 after one year, $3,000 after two years, and $5,000 after three years. How much does this company receive today if the interest rate on this loan is 10%? To answer, we need to compute the present value of the three future payments, discounted at 10%. This computation is shown in Exhibit 10A.4 using present values from Exhibit 10A.3. The company can borrow $8,054 today at 10% interest in exchange for its promise to make these three payments at the scheduled dates.

EXHIBIT 10A.4

Present Value of a Series of Unequal Payments

Periods	Payments	Present Value of 1 at 10%	Present Value of Payments
1	$2,000	0.9091	$ 1,818
2	3,000	0.8264	2,479
3	5,000	0.7513	3,757
Present value of all payments			$8,054

Present Value of an Annuity   The $8,054 present value for the loan in Exhibit 10A.4 equals the sum of the present values of the three payments. When payments are not equal, their combined present value is best computed by adding the individual present values as shown in Exhibit 10A.4. Sometimes payments follow an **annuity,** which is a series of *equal* payments at equal time intervals. The present value of an annuity is readily computed.

To illustrate, assume that a company must repay a 6% loan with a $5,000 payment at each year-end for the next four years. This loan amount equals the present value of the four payments discounted at 6%. Exhibit 10A.5 shows how to compute this loan's present value of $17,326 by multiplying each payment by its matching present value factor taken from Exhibit 10A.3.

However, the series of $5,000 payments is an annuity, so we can compute its present value with either of two shortcuts. First, the third column of Exhibit 10A.5 shows that the sum of the present values of 1 at 6% for periods 1 through 4 equals 3.4651. One shortcut is to multiply this total of 3.4651 by the $5,000 annual payment to get the combined present value of $17,326. It requires one multiplication instead of four.

EXHIBIT 10A.5

Present Value of a Series of Equal Payments (Annuity) by Discounting Each Payment

Periods	Payments	Present Value of 1 at 6%	Present Value of Payments
1	$5,000	0.9434	$ 4,717
2	5,000	0.8900	4,450
3	5,000	0.8396	4,198
4	5,000	0.7921	3,961
Present value of all payments		3.4651	$17,326

EXHIBIT 10A.6

Present Value of an Annuity of 1

Periods	Rate		
	6%	8%	10%
1	0.9434	0.9259	0.9091
2	1.8334	1.7833	1.7355
3	2.6730	2.5771	2.4869
4	**3.4651**	3.3121	3.1699
5	4.2124	3.9927	3.7908
6	4.9173	4.6229	4.3553
7	5.5824	5.2064	4.8684
8	6.2098	5.7466	5.3349
9	6.8017	6.2469	5.7590
10	7.3601	6.7101	6.1446

Example: Use Exhibit 10A.6 to find the present value of an annuity of eight $15,000 payments with an 8% interest rate. *Answer:* $15,000 × 5.7466 = $86,199

Example: If this borrower makes five semiannual payments of $8,000, what is the present value of this annuity at a 12% rate? *Answer:* 4.2124 × $8,000 = $33,699

The second shortcut uses an *annuity table* such as the one shown in Exhibit 10A.6, which is drawn from the more complete Table B.3 in Appendix B. We go directly to the annuity table to get the present value factor for a specific number of payments and interest rate. We then multiply this factor by the amount of the payment to find the present value of the annuity. Specifically, find the row for four periods and go across to the 6% column, where the factor is 3.4651. This factor equals the present value of an annuity with four payments of 1, discounted at 6%. We then multiply 3.4651 by $5,000 to get the $17,326 present value of the annuity.

Compounding Periods Shorter Than a Year The present value examples all involved periods of one year. In many situations, however, interest is compounded over shorter periods. For example, the interest rate on bonds is usually stated as an annual rate but interest is often paid every six months (semiannually). This means that the present value of interest payments from such bonds must be computed using interest periods of six months.

Assume that a borrower wants to know the present value of a series of 10 *semiannual payments* of $4,000 made over five years at an *annual interest rate* of 12%. The interest rate is stated as an annual rate of 12%, but it is actually a rate of 6% per semiannual interest period. To compute the present value of this series of $4,000 payments, go to row 10 of Exhibit 10A.6 and across to the 6% column to find the factor 7.3601. The present value of this annuity is $29,440 (7.3601 × $4,000).

Appendix B further describes present value concepts and includes more complete present value tables and assignments.

Quick Check

Answers — p. 439

14. A company enters into an agreement to make four annual year-end payments of $1,000 each, starting one year from now. The annual interest rate is 8%. The present value of these four payments is (*a*) $2,923, (*b*) $2,940, or (*c*) $3,312.

15. Suppose a company has an option to pay either (*a*) $10,000 after one year or (*b*) $5,000 after six months and another $5,000 after one year. Which choice has the lower present value?

APPENDIX

10B

Effective Interest Amortization

Effective Interest Amortization of a Discount Bond The straight-line method yields changes in the bonds' carrying value while the amount for bond interest expense remains constant. This gives the impression of a changing interest rate when users divide a constant bond interest expense over a changing carrying value. As a result, accounting standards allow use of the straight-line method only when its results do not differ materially from those obtained using the effective interest method. The **effective interest method,** or simply *interest method,* allocates total bond interest expense over the bonds' life in a way that yields a constant rate of interest. This constant rate of interest is the market rate at the issue date. Thus, bond interest expense for a period equals the carrying value of the bond at the beginning of that period multiplied by the market rate when issued.

Point: The effective interest method computes bond interest expense using the market rate at issuance. This rate is applied to a changing carrying value.

Exhibit 10B.1 shows an effective interest amortization table for the Fila bonds (as described in Exhibit 10.4). The key difference between the effective interest and straight-line methods lies in computing bond interest expense. Instead of assigning an equal amount of bond interest expense to each period, the effective interest method assigns a bond interest expense amount that increases over the life of a discount bond. **Both methods allocate the *same* $19,546 of total bond interest expense to the bonds' life, but in different patterns.** Specifically, the amortization table in Exhibit 10B.1 shows that the balance of the discount (column D) is amortized until it reaches zero. Also, the bonds' carrying value (column E) changes each period until it equals par value at maturity. Compare columns D and E to the corresponding columns in Exhibit 10.7 to see the amortization patterns. Total bond interest expense is $19,546, consisting of $16,000 of semiannual cash payments and $3,546 of the original bond discount, the same for both methods.

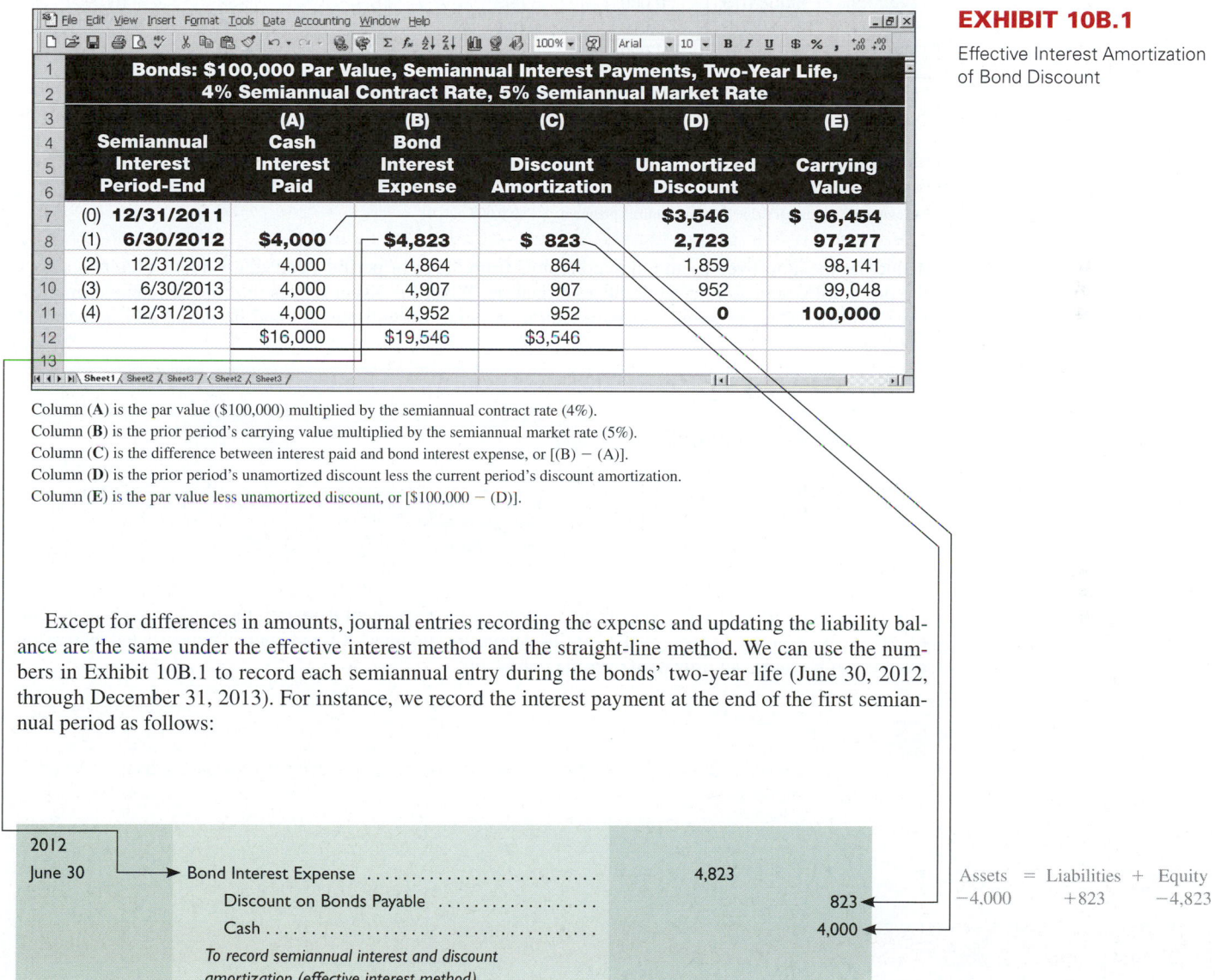

EXHIBIT 10B.1

Effective Interest Amortization of Bond Discount

Bonds: $100,000 Par Value, Semiannual Interest Payments, Two-Year Life, 4% Semiannual Contract Rate, 5% Semiannual Market Rate

Semiannual Interest Period-End	(A) Cash Interest Paid	(B) Bond Interest Expense	(C) Discount Amortization	(D) Unamortized Discount	(E) Carrying Value
(0) 12/31/2011				$3,546	$ 96,454
(1) 6/30/2012	$4,000	$4,823	$ 823	2,723	97,277
(2) 12/31/2012	4,000	4,864	864	1,859	98,141
(3) 6/30/2013	4,000	4,907	907	952	99,048
(4) 12/31/2013	4,000	4,952	952	0	100,000
	$16,000	$19,546	$3,546		

Column (**A**) is the par value ($100,000) multiplied by the semiannual contract rate (4%).
Column (**B**) is the prior period's carrying value multiplied by the semiannual market rate (5%).
Column (**C**) is the difference between interest paid and bond interest expense, or [(B) − (A)].
Column (**D**) is the prior period's unamortized discount less the current period's discount amortization.
Column (**E**) is the par value less unamortized discount, or [$100,000 − (D)].

Except for differences in amounts, journal entries recording the expense and updating the liability balance are the same under the effective interest method and the straight-line method. We can use the numbers in Exhibit 10B.1 to record each semiannual entry during the bonds' two-year life (June 30, 2012, through December 31, 2013). For instance, we record the interest payment at the end of the first semiannual period as follows:

2012			
June 30	Bond Interest Expense	4,823	
	Discount on Bonds Payable		823
	Cash		4,000
	To record semiannual interest and discount amortization (effective interest method).		

Assets	=	Liabilities	+	Equity
−4,000		+823		−4,823

Effective Interest Amortization of a Premium Bond Exhibit 10B.2 shows the amortization table using the effective interest method for the Adidas bonds (as described in Exhibit 10.8). Column A lists the semiannual cash payments. Column B shows the amount of bond interest expense, computed as the 5% semiannual market rate at issuance multiplied by the beginning-of-period carrying value. The amount of cash paid in column A is larger than the bond interest expense because the cash payment is based on the higher 6% semiannual contract rate. The excess cash payment over the interest expense reduces the principal. These amounts are shown in column C. Column E shows the carrying value after

EXHIBIT 10B.2

Effective Interest Amortization of Bond Premium

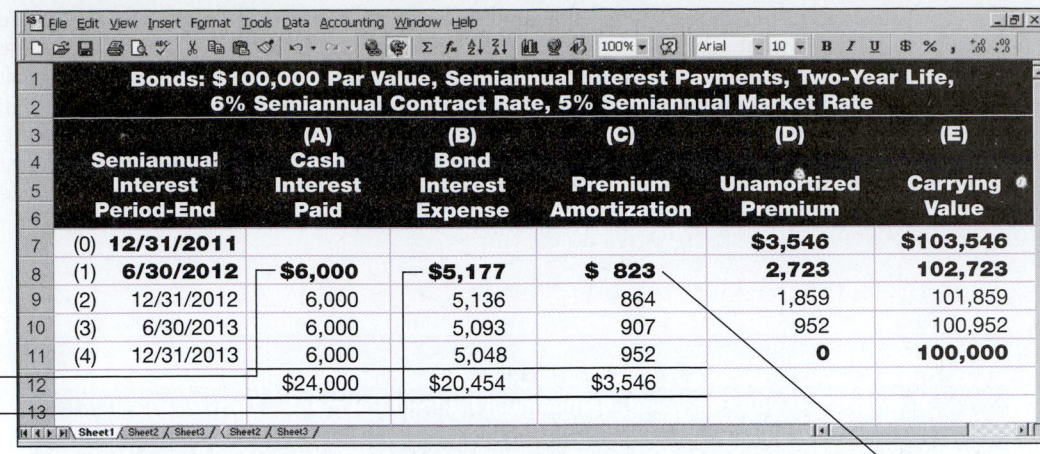

Bonds: $100,000 Par Value, Semiannual Interest Payments, Two-Year Life, 6% Semiannual Contract Rate, 5% Semiannual Market Rate					
Semiannual Interest Period-End	(A) Cash Interest Paid	(B) Bond Interest Expense	(C) Premium Amortization	(D) Unamortized Premium	(E) Carrying Value
(0) 12/31/2011				$3,546	$103,546
(1) 6/30/2012	$6,000	$5,177	$ 823	2,723	102,723
(2) 12/31/2012	6,000	5,136	864	1,859	101,859
(3) 6/30/2013	6,000	5,093	907	952	100,952
(4) 12/31/2013	6,000	5,048	952	0	100,000
	$24,000	$20,454	$3,546		

Column (**A**) is the par value ($100,000) multiplied by the semiannual contract rate (6%).
Column (**B**) is the prior period's carrying value multiplied by the semiannual market rate (5%).
Column (**C**) is the difference between interest paid and bond interest expense, or [(A) − (B)].
Column (**D**) is the prior period's unamortized premium less the current period's premium amortization.
Column (**E**) is the par value plus unamortized premium, or [$100,000 + (D)].

deducting the amortized premium in column C from the prior period's carrying value. Column D shows the premium's reduction by periodic amortization. When the issuer makes the first semiannual interest payment, the effect of premium amortization on bond interest expense and bond liability is recorded as follows:

Assets = Liabilities + Equity
−6,000   −823   −5,177

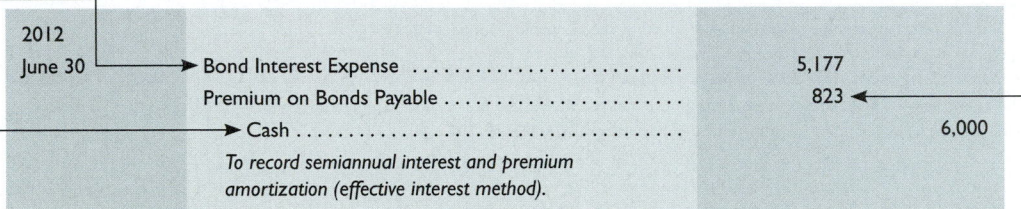

2012
June 30
    Bond Interest Expense   5,177
    Premium on Bonds Payable   823
        Cash   6,000
    To record semiannual interest and premium
    amortization (effective interest method).

Similar entries with different amounts are recorded at each payment date until the bond matures at the end of 2013. The effective interest method yields decreasing amounts of bond interest expense and increasing amounts of premium amortization over the bonds' life.

IFRS

Unlike U.S. GAAP, IFRS requires that interest expense be computed using the effective interest method with *no exemptions.* ■

APPENDIX

10C

Issuing Bonds between Interest Dates

C3 Describe interest accrual when bond payment periods differ from accounting periods.

An issuer can sell bonds at a date other than an interest payment date. When this occurs, the buyers normally pay the issuer the purchase price plus any interest accrued since the prior interest payment date. This accrued interest is then repaid to these buyers on the next interest payment date. To illustrate, suppose **Avia** sells $100,000 of its 9% bonds at par on March 1, 2011, 60 days after the stated issue date. The interest on Avia bonds is payable semiannually on each June 30 and December 31. Since 60 days have passed, the issuer collects accrued interest from the buyers at the time of issuance. This amount is $1,500 ($100,000 × 9% × $^{60}/_{360}$ year). This case is reflected in Exhibit 10C.1.

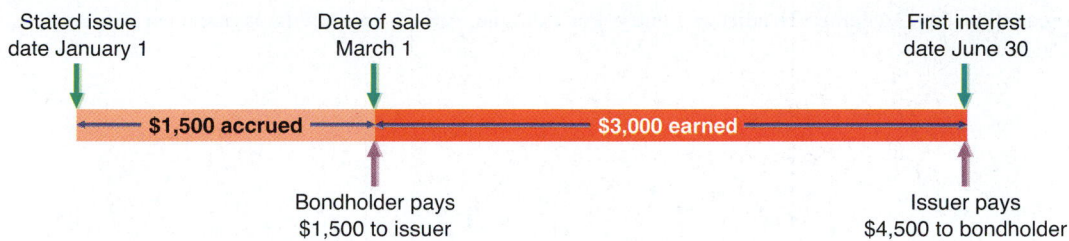

Avia records the issuance of these bonds on March 1, 2011, as follows:

Mar. I	Cash	101,500	
	Interest Payable		1,500
	Bonds Payable.		100,000
	Sold bonds at par with accrued interest.		

Assets   = Liabilities + Equity
+101,500   +100,000
+1,500

Liabilities for interest payable and bonds payable are recorded in separate accounts. When the June 30, 2011, semiannual interest date arrives, Avia pays the full semiannual interest of $4,500 ($100,000 × 9% × ½ year) to the bondholders. This payment includes the four months' interest of $3,000 earned by the bondholders from March 1 to June 30 *plus* the repayment of the 60 days' accrued interest collected by Avia when the bonds were sold. Avia records this first semiannual interest payment as follows:

Example: How much interest is collected from a buyer of $50,000 of Avia bonds sold at par 150 days after the contract issue date? *Answer:* $1,875 (computed as $50,000 × 9% × $^{150}/_{360}$ year)

June 30	Interest Payable	1,500	
	Bond Interest Expense.	3,000	
	Cash		4,500
	Paid semiannual interest on the bonds.		

Assets   = Liabilities + Equity
−4,500   −1,500   −3,000

The practice of collecting and then repaying accrued interest with the next interest payment is to simplify the issuer's administrative efforts. To explain, suppose an issuer sells bonds on 15 or 20 different dates between the stated issue date and the first interest payment date. If the issuer does not collect accrued interest from buyers, it needs to pay different amounts of cash to each of them according to the time that passed after purchasing the bonds. The issuer needs to keep detailed records of buyers and the dates they bought bonds. Issuers avoid this recordkeeping by having each buyer pay accrued interest at purchase. Issuers then pay the full semiannual interest to all buyers, regardless of when they bought bonds.

Accruing Bond Interest Expense   If a bond's interest period does not coincide with the issuer's accounting period, an adjusting entry is needed to recognize bond interest expense accrued since the most recent interest payment. To illustrate, assume that the stated issue date for Adidas bonds described in Exhibit 10.10 is September 1, 2011, instead of December 31, 2011, and that the bonds are sold on September 1, 2011. As a result, four months' interest (and premium amortization) accrue before the end of the 2011 calendar year. Interest for this period equals $3,409, or ⅔ of the first six months' interest of $5,113. Also, the premium amortization is $591, or ⅔ of the first six months' amortization of $887. The sum of the bond interest expense and the amortization is $4,000 ($3,409 + $591), which equals ⅔ of the $6,000 cash payment due on February 28, 2012. Adidas records these effects with an adjusting entry at December 31, 2011.

Point: Computation of accrued bond interest may use months instead of days for simplicity purposes. For example, the accrued interest computation for the Adidas bonds is based on months.

Dec. 31	Bond Interest Expense	3,409	
	Premium on Bonds Payable	591	
	Interest Payable		4,000
	To record four months' accrued interest and		
	premium amortization.		

Assets   = Liabilities + Equity
                −591   −3,409
                +4,000

Similar entries are made on each December 31 throughout the bonds' two-year life. When the $6,000 cash payment occurs on each February 28 interest payment date, Adidas must recognize bond interest expense and amortization for January and February. It must also eliminate the interest payable liability created by the December 31 adjusting entry. For example, Adidas records its payment on February 28, 2012, as follows:

Assets = Liabilities + Equity
−6,000　　−4,000　　−1,704
　　　　　−296

Feb. 28	Interest Payable	4,000	
	Bond Interest Expense ($5,113 × ⅔)	1,704	
	Premium on Bonds Payable ($887 × ⅔)	296	
	Cash		6,000
	To record 2 months' interest and amortization, and eliminate accrued interest liability.		

The interest payments made each August 31 are recorded as usual because the entire six-month interest period is included within this company's calendar-year reporting period.

Decision Maker

Answer — p. 439

Bond Rater　You must assign a rating to a bond that reflects its risk to bondholders. Identify factors you consider in assessing bond risk. Indicate the likely levels (relative to the norm) for the factors you identify for a bond that sells at a discount. ∎

Quick Check

Answer — p. 439

16. On May 1, a company sells 9% bonds with a $500,000 par value that pay semiannual interest on each January 1 and July 1. The bonds are sold at par plus interest accrued since January 1. The issuer records the first semiannual interest payment on July 1 with (*a*) a debit to Interest Payable for $15,000, (*b*) a debit to Bond Interest Expense for $22,500, or (*c*) a credit to Interest Payable for $7,500.

APPENDIX

10D

Leases and Pensions

This appendix briefly explains the accounting and analysis for both leases and pensions.

C4　Describe accounting for leases and pensions.

Lease Liabilities　A **lease** is a contractual agreement between a *lessor* (asset owner) and a *lessee* (asset renter or tenant) that grants the lessee the right to use the asset for a period of time in return for cash (rent) payments. Nearly one-fourth of all equipment purchases are financed with leases. The advantages of lease financing include the lack of an immediate large cash payment and the potential to deduct rental payments in computing taxable income. From an accounting perspective, leases can be classified as either operating or capital leases.

Point: Home Depot reports that its rental expenses from operating leases total more than $900 million.

Operating Leases　**Operating leases** are short-term (or cancelable) leases in which the lessor retains the risks and rewards of ownership. Examples include most car and apartment rental agreements. The lessee records such lease payments as expenses; the lessor records them as revenue. The lessee does not report the leased item as an asset or a liability (it is the lessor's asset). To illustrate, if an employee of Amazon leases a car for $300 at an airport while on company business, Amazon (lessee) records this cost as follows:

Assets = Liabilities + Equity
−300　　　　　　　−300

July 4	Rental Expense	300	
	Cash		300
	To record lease rental payment.		

Capital Leases   **Capital leases** are long-term (or noncancelable) leases by which the lessor transfers substantially all risks and rewards of ownership to the lessee.[3] Examples include most leases of airplanes and department store buildings. The lessee records the leased item as its own asset along with a lease liability at the start of the lease term; the amount recorded equals the present value of all lease payments. To illustrate, assume that K2 Co. enters into a six-year lease of a building in which it will sell sporting equipment. The lease transfers all building ownership risks and rewards to K2 (the present value of its $12,979 annual lease payments is $60,000). K2 records this transaction as follows:

2011			
Jan. 1	Leased Asset—Building	60,000	
	Lease Liability		60,000
	To record leased asset and lease liability.		

Assets = Liabilities + Equity
+60,000   +60,000

K2 reports the leased asset as a plant asset and the lease liability as a long-term liability. The portion of the lease liability expected to be paid in the next year is reported as a current liability.[4] At each year-end, K2 records depreciation on the leased asset (assume straight-line depreciation, six-year lease term, and no salvage value) as follows:

Point: Home Depot reports *"certain locations ... are leased under capital leases."* The net present value of this Lease Liability is about $400 million.

Dec. 31	Depreciation Expense—Building	10,000	
	Accumulated Depreciation—Building		10,000
	To record depreciation on leased asset.		

Assets = Liabilities + Equity
−10,000   −10,000

K2 also accrues interest on the lease liability at each year-end. Interest expense is computed by multiplying the remaining lease liability by the interest rate on the lease. Specifically, K2 records its annual interest expense as part of its annual lease payment ($12,979) as follows (for its first year):

2011			
Dec. 31	Interest Expense	4,800	
	Lease Liability	8,179	
	Cash		12,979
	*To record first annual lease payment.**		

Assets = Liabilities + Equity
−12,979   −8,179   −4,800

* These numbers are computed from a *lease payment schedule*. For simplicity, we use the same numbers from Exhibit 10.14 for this lease payment schedule—with different headings as follows:

Period Ending Date	(A) Beginning Balance of Lease Liability	(B) Debit Interest on Lease Liability 8% × (A)	+	(C) Debit Lease Liability (D) − (B)	=	(D) Credit Cash Lease Payment	(E) Ending Balance of Lease Liability (A) − (C)
12/31/2011	$60,000	$ 4,800		$ 8,179		$12,979	$51,821
12/31/2012	51,821	4,146		8,833		12,979	42,988
12/31/2013	42,988	3,439		9,540		12,979	33,448
12/31/2014	33,448	2,676		10,303		12,979	23,145
12/31/2015	23,145	1,852		11,127		12,979	12,018
12/31/2016	12,018	961		12,018		12,979	0
		$17,874		$60,000		$77,874	

[3] A *capital lease* meets any one or more of four criteria: (1) transfers title of leased asset to lessee, (2) contains a bargain purchase option, (3) has a lease term that is 75% or more of the leased asset's useful life, or (4) has a present value of lease payments that is 90% or more of the leased asset's market value.

[4] Most lessees try to keep leased assets and lease liabilities off their balance sheets by failing to meet any one of the four criteria of a capital lease. This is because a lease liability increases a company's total liabilities, making it more difficult to obtain additional financing. The acquisition of assets without reporting any related liabilities (or other asset outflows) on the balance sheet is called **off-balance-sheet financing.**

Point: Fringe benefits are often 40% or more of salaries and wages, and pension benefits make up nearly 15% of fringe benefits.

Pension Liabilities   A **pension plan** is a contractual agreement between an employer and its employees for the employer to provide benefits (payments) to employees after they retire. Most employers pay the full cost of the pension, but sometimes employees pay part of the cost. An employer records its payment into a pension plan with a debit to Pension Expense and a credit to Cash. A *plan administrator* receives payments from the employer, invests them in pension assets, and makes benefit payments to *pension recipients* (retired employees). Insurance and trust companies often serve as pension plan administrators.

Point: Two types of pension plans are (1) *defined benefit plan*—the retirement benefit is defined and the employer estimates the contribution necessary to pay these benefits—and (2) *defined contribution plan*—the pension contribution is defined and the employer and/or employee contributes amounts specified in the pension agreement.

Many pensions are known as *defined benefit plans* that define future benefits; the employer's contributions vary, depending on assumptions about future pension assets and liabilities. Several disclosures are necessary in this case. Specifically, a pension liability is reported when the accumulated benefit obligation is *more than* the plan assets, a so-called *underfunded plan*. The accumulated benefit obligation is the present value of promised future pension payments to retirees. *Plan assets* refer to the market value of assets the plan administrator holds. A pension asset is reported when the accumulated benefit obligation is *less than* the plan assets, a so-called *overfunded plan*. An employer reports pension expense when it receives the benefits from the employees' services, which is sometimes decades before it pays pension benefits to employees. (*Other Postretirement Benefits* refer to nonpension benefits such as health care and life insurance benefits. Similar to a pension, costs of these benefits are estimated and liabilities accrued when the employees earn them.)

Summary

C1   **Explain the types and payment patterns of notes.** Notes repaid over a period of time are called *installment notes* and usually follow one of two payment patterns: (1) decreasing payments of interest plus equal amounts of principal or (2) equal total payments. Mortgage notes also are common.

C2ᴬ   **Explain and compute the present value of an amount(s) to be paid at a future date(s).** The basic concept of present value is that an amount of cash to be paid or received in the future is worth less than the same amount of cash to be paid or received today. Another important present value concept is that interest is compounded, meaning interest is added to the balance and used to determine interest for succeeding periods. An annuity is a series of equal payments occurring at equal time intervals. An annuity's present value can be computed using the present value table for an annuity (or a calculator).

C3ᶜ   **Describe interest accrual when bond payment periods differ from accounting periods.** Issuers and buyers of debt record the interest accrued when issue dates or accounting periods do not coincide with debt payment dates.

C4ᴰ   **Describe accounting for leases and pensions.** A lease is a rental agreement between the lessor and the lessee. When the lessor retains the risks and rewards of asset ownership (an *operating lease*), the lessee debits Rent Expense and credits Cash for its lease payments. When the lessor substantially transfers the risks and rewards of asset ownership to the lessee (a *capital lease*), the lessee capitalizes the leased asset and records a lease liability. Pension agreements can result in either pension assets or pension liabilities.

A1   **Compare bond financing with stock financing.** Bond financing is used to fund business activities. Advantages of bond financing versus stock include (1) no effect on owner control, (2) tax savings, and (3) increased earnings due to financial leverage. Disadvantages include (1) interest and principal payments and (2) amplification of poor performance.

A2   **Assess debt features and their implications.** Certain bonds are secured by the issuer's assets; other bonds, called *debentures,* are unsecured. Serial bonds mature at different points in time;

term bonds mature at one time. Registered bonds have each bondholder's name recorded by the issuer; bearer bonds are payable to the holder. Convertible bonds are exchangeable for shares of the issuer's stock. Callable bonds can be retired by the issuer at a set price. Debt features alter the risk of loss for creditors.

A3   **Compute the debt-to-equity ratio and explain its use.** Both creditors and equity holders are concerned about the relation between the amount of liabilities and the amount of equity. A company's financing structure is at less risk when the debt-to-equity ratio is lower, as liabilities must be paid and usually with periodic interest.

P1   **Prepare entries to record bond issuance and interest expense.** When bonds are issued at par, Cash is debited and Bonds Payable is credited for the bonds' par value. At bond interest payment dates (usually semiannual), Bond Interest Expense is debited and Cash credited—the latter for an amount equal to the bond par value multiplied by the bond contract rate.

P2   **Compute and record amortization of bond discount.** Bonds are issued at a discount when the contract rate is less than the market rate, making the issue (selling) price less than par. When this occurs, the issuer records a credit to Bonds Payable (at par) and debits both Discount on Bonds Payable and Cash. The amount of bond interest expense assigned to each period is computed using either the straight-line or effective interest method.

P3   **Compute and record amortization of bond premium.** Bonds are issued at a premium when the contract rate is higher than the market rate, making the issue (selling) price greater than par. When this occurs, the issuer records a debit to Cash and credits both Premium on Bonds Payable and Bonds Payable (at par). The amount of bond interest expense assigned to each period is computed using either the straight-line or effective interest method. The Premium on Bonds Payable is allocated to reduce bond interest expense over the life of the bonds.

P4   **Record the retirement of bonds.** Bonds are retired at maturity with a debit to Bonds Payable and a credit to Cash at par value. The issuer can retire the bonds early by exercising a call option or purchasing them in the market. Bondholders can also retire bonds early by exercising a conversion feature on convertible bonds. The issuer recognizes a gain or loss for the difference between the amount paid and the bond carrying value.

P5 Prepare entries to account for notes. Interest is allocated to each period in a note's life by multiplying its beginning-

period carrying value by its market rate at issuance. If a note is repaid with equal payments, the payment amount is computed by dividing the borrowed amount by the present value of an annuity factor (taken from a present value table) using the market rate and the number of payments.

Guidance Answers to Decision Maker

Entrepreneur This is a "present value" question. The market interest rate (10%) and present value ($3,000) are known, but the payment required two years later is unknown. This amount ($3,630) can be computed as $3,000 \times 1.10 \times 1.10$. Thus, the sale price is $3,630 when no payments are received for two years. The $3,630 received two years from today is equivalent to $3,000 cash today.

Bond Investor The debt-to-equity ratio for the first company is 0.2 ($350,000/$1,750,000) and for the second company is 1.2 ($1,200,000/$1,000,000), suggesting that the financing structure of

the second company is more risky than that of the first company. Consequently, as a buyer of unsecured debenture bonds, you prefer the first company (all else equal).

Bond Rater Bonds with longer repayment periods (life) have higher risk. Also, bonds issued by companies in financial difficulties or facing higher than normal uncertainties have higher risk. Moreover, companies with higher than normal debt and large fluctuations in earnings are considered of higher risk. Discount bonds are more risky on one or more of these factors.

Guidance Answers to Quick Checks

1.

2011			
Jan. 1	Cash	10,000	
	Bonds Payable		10,000
June 30	Bond Interest Expense	450	
	Cash		450

2. Multiply the bond's par value by its contract rate of interest.

3. Bonds sell at a premium when the contract rate exceeds the market rate and the purchasers pay more than their par value.

4. The bonds are issued at a discount, meaning that issue price is less than par value. A discount occurs because the bond contract rate (6%) is less than the market rate (8%).

5.

Cash	91,893	
Discount on Bonds Payable	8,107	
Bonds Payable		100,000

6. $3,811 (total bond interest expense of $38,107 divided by 10 periods; or the $3,000 semiannual cash payment plus the $8,107 discount divided by 10 periods).

7. The bonds are issued at a premium, meaning issue price is higher than par value. A premium occurs because the bonds' contract rate (16%) is higher than the market rate (14%).

8. (*b*) For each semiannual period: $10,592/20 periods = $530 premium amortization.

9.

Bonds payable, 16%, due 12/31/2020	$100,000
Plus premium on bonds payable	9,532* $109,532

* Original premium balance of $10,592 less $530 and $530 amortized on 6/30/2011 and 12/31/2011, respectively.

10. $9,375 loss, computed as the difference between the repurchase price of $256,250 [50% of ($500,000 × 102.5%)] and the carrying value of $246,875 (50% of $493,750).

11. (*c*)

12. The interest portion of an installment payment equals the period's beginning loan balance multiplied by the market interest rate at the time of the note's issuance.

13. On the balance sheet, the account balances of the related liability (note payable) and asset (cash) accounts are decreased. On the income statement, interest expense is recorded.

14. (*c*), computed as 3.3121 × $1,000 = $3,312.

15. The option of paying $10,000 after one year has a lower present value. It postpones paying the first $5,000 by six months. More generally, the present value of a further delayed payment is always lower than a less delayed payment.

16. (*a*) Reflects payment of accrued interest recorded back on May 1; $500,000 × 9% × ¹⁄₁₂ = $15,000.

Key Terms

mhhe.com/wildFINMAN4e

Annuity (p. 431)	Bond certificate (p. 414)	Capital leases (p. 437)
Bearer bonds (p. 426)	Bond indenture (p. 414)	Carrying (book) value of bonds (p. 416)
Bond (p. 412)	Callable bonds (p. 426)	Contract rate (p. 415)

Convertible bonds (p. 426)
Coupon bonds (p. 426)
Debt-to-equity ratio (p. 427)
Discount on bonds payable (p. 415)
Effective interest method (p. 432)
Fair value option (p. 425)
Installment note (p. 422)
Lease (p. 436)

Market rate (p. 415)
Mortgage (p. 424)
Off-balance-sheet financing (p. 437)
Operating leases (p. 436)
Par value of a bond (p. 412)
Pension plan (p. 438)
Premium on bonds (p. 418)
Registered bonds (p. 426)

Secured bonds (p. 426)
Serial bonds (p. 426)
Sinking fund bonds (p. 426)
Straight-line bond amortization (p. 416)
Term bonds (p. 426)
Unsecured bonds (p. 426)

Multiple Choice Quiz   Answers on p. 453   mhhe.com/wildFINMAN4e

Additional Quiz Questions are available at the book's Website.

1. A bond traded at 97½ means that
   a. The bond pays 97½% interest.
   b. The bond trades at $975 per $1,000 bond.
   c. The market rate of interest is below the contract rate of interest for the bond.
   d. The bonds can be retired at $975 each.
   e. The bond's interest rate is 2½%.

2. A bondholder that owns a $1,000, 6%, 15-year bond has
   a. The right to receive $1,000 at maturity.
   b. Ownership rights in the bond issuing entity.
   c. The right to receive $60 per month until maturity.
   d. The right to receive $1,900 at maturity.
   e. The right to receive $600 per year until maturity.

3. A company issues 8%, 20-year bonds with a par value of $500,000. The current market rate for the bonds is 8%. The amount of interest owed to the bondholders for each semiannual interest payment is
   a. $40,000.
   b. $0.
   c. $20,000.

   d. $800,000.
   e. $400,000.

4. A company issued 5-year, 5% bonds with a par value of $100,000. The company received $95,735 for the bonds. Using the straight-line method, the company's interest expense for the first semiannual interest period is
   a. $2,926.50.
   b. $5,853.00.
   c. $2,500.00.
   d. $5,000.00.
   e. $9,573.50.

5. A company issued 8-year, 5% bonds with a par value of $350,000. The company received proceeds of $373,745. Interest is payable semiannually. The amount of premium amortized for the first semiannual interest period, assuming straight-line bond amortization, is
   a. $2,698.
   b. $23,745.
   c. $8,750.
   d. $9,344.
   e. $1,484.

B(C,D) *Superscript letter B(C, D) denotes assignments based on Appendix 10B (10C, 10D).*
🔲 Icon denotes assignments that involve decision making.

Discussion Questions

1. What is the main difference between a bond and a share of stock?
2. What is the main difference between notes payable and bonds payable?
3. 🔲 What is the advantage of issuing bonds instead of obtaining financing from the company's owners?
4. What are the duties of a trustee for bondholders?
5. What is a bond indenture? What provisions are usually included in it?
6. What are the *contract* rate and the *market* rate for bonds?
7. 🔲 What factors affect the market rates for bonds?

8.B 🔲 Does the straight-line or effective interest method produce an interest expense allocation that yields a constant rate of interest over a bond's life? Explain.
9.C Why does a company that issues bonds between interest dates collect accrued interest from the bonds' purchasers?
10. 🔲 If you know the par value of bonds, the contract rate, and the market rate, how do you compute the bonds' price?
11. What is the issue price of a $2,000 bond sold at 98¼? What is the issue price of a $6,000 bond sold at 101½?
12. Describe the debt-to-equity ratio and explain how creditors and owners would use this ratio to evaluate a company's risk.

13. What obligation does an entrepreneur (owner) have to investors that purchase bonds to finance the business?

14. Refer to **Research In Motion**'s annual report in Appendix A. Is there any indication that RIM has issued **RIM** bonds?

15. By what amount did **Palm**'s long-term debt increase or decrease in 2009? **Palm**

16. Refer to the statement of cash flows for **Nokia** in Appendix A. For the year ended December 31, 2009, what was the amount for repayment of bank loans? **NOKIA**

17. Refer to the annual report for **Apple** in Appendix A. For the year ended September 26, 2009, what is its debt-to-equity ratio? What does this ratio tell us? **Apple**

18.^D When can a lease create both an asset and a liability for the lessee?

19.^D Compare and contrast an operating lease with a capital lease.

20.^D Describe the two basic types of pension plans.

---

connect

Round dollar amounts to the nearest whole dollar.

Enter the letter of the description *A* through *H* that best fits each term or phrase 1 through 8.

A. Records and tracks the bondholders' names.

B. Is unsecured; backed only by the issuer's credit standing.

C. Has varying maturity dates for amounts owed.

D. Identifies rights and responsibilities of the issuer and the bondholders.

E. Can be exchanged for shares of the issuer's stock.

F. Is unregistered; interest is paid to whoever possesses them.

G. Maintains a separate asset account from which bondholders are paid at maturity.

H. Pledges specific assets of the issuer as collateral.

1. _____ Debenture
2. _____ Bond indenture
3. _____ Bearer bond
4. _____ Registered bond
5. _____ Sinking fund bond
6. _____ Convertible bond
7. _____ Secured bond
8. _____ Serial bond

QUICK STUDY

QS 10-1
Bond features and terminology
A2

Alberto Company issues 8%, 10-year bonds with a par value of $350,000 and semiannual interest payments. On the issue date, the annual market rate for these bonds is 10%, which implies a selling price of 87½. The straight-line method is used to allocate interest expense.

1. What are the issuer's cash proceeds from issuance of these bonds?

2. What total amount of bond interest expense will be recognized over the life of these bonds?

3. What is the amount of bond interest expense recorded on the first interest payment date?

QS 10-2
Bond computations—
straight-line
P1 P2

Sanchez Company issues 10%, 15-year bonds with a par value of $120,000 and semiannual interest payments. On the issue date, the annual market rate for these bonds is 8%, which implies a selling price of 117¼. The effective interest method is used to allocate interest expense.

1. What are the issuer's cash proceeds from issuance of these bonds?

2. What total amount of bond interest expense will be recognized over the life of these bonds?

3. What amount of bond interest expense is recorded on the first interest payment date?

QS 10-3^B
Bond computations—
effective interest
P1 P3

Prepare the journal entries for the issuance of the bonds in both QS 10-2 and QS 10-3. Assume that both bonds are issued for cash on January 1, 2011.

QS 10-4
Journalize bond issuance P1

Using the bond details in both QS 10-2 and QS 10-3, confirm that the bonds' selling prices given in each problem are approximately correct. Use the present value tables B.1 and B.3 in Appendix B.

QS 10-5
Computing bond price P2 P3

QS 10-6

Recording bond issuance and discount amortization   P1   P2

Bellvue Company issues 10%, five-year bonds, on December 31, 2010, with a par value of $100,000 and semiannual interest payments. Use the following straight-line bond amortization table and prepare journal entries to record (*a*) the issuance of bonds on December 31, 2010; (*b*) the first interest payment on June 30, 2011; and (*c*) the second interest payment on December 31, 2011.

Semiannual Period-End		Unamortized Discount	Carrying Value
(0)	12/31/2010	$7,360	$92,640
(1)	6/30/2011	6,624	93,376
(2)	12/31/2011	5,888	94,112

QS 10-7

Bond retirement by call option

P4

On July 1, 2011, Jackson Company exercises a $5,000 call option (plus par value) on its outstanding bonds that have a carrying value of $208,000 and par value of $200,000. The company exercises the call option after the semiannual interest is paid on June 30, 2011. Record the entry to retire the bonds.

QS 10-8

Bond retirement by stock conversion   P4

On January 1, 2011, the $1,000,000 par value bonds of Gruden Company with a carrying value of $1,000,000 are converted to 500,000 shares of $0.50 par value common stock. Record the entry for the conversion of the bonds.

QS 10-9

Computing payments for an installment note   C1

Valdez Company borrows $170,000 cash from a bank and in return signs an installment note for five annual payments of equal amount, with the first payment due one year after the note is signed. Use Table B.3 in Appendix B to compute the amount of the annual payment for each of the following annual market rates: (*a*) 4%, (*b*) 8%, and (*c*) 12%.

QS 10-10

Debt-to-equity ratio

A2

Compute the debt-to-equity ratio for each of the following companies. Which company appears to have a riskier financing structure? Explain.

	Canal Company	Sears Company
Total liabilities	$492,000	$ 384,000
Total equity	656,000	1,200,000

QS 10-11^C

Issuing bonds between interest dates   P1

Kemper Company plans to issue 6% bonds on January 1, 2011, with a par value of $1,000,000. The company sells $900,000 of the bonds on January 1, 2011. The remaining $100,000 sells at par on March 1, 2011. The bonds pay interest semiannually as of June 30 and December 31. Record the entry for the March 1 cash sale of bonds.

QS 10-12^D

Recording operating leases   C4

Lauren Wright, an employee of ETrain.com, leases a car at O'Hare airport for a three-day business trip. The rental cost is $350. Prepare the entry by ETrain.com to record Lauren's short-term car lease cost.

QS 10-13^D

Recording capital leases   C4

Juicyfruit, Inc., signs a five-year lease for office equipment with Office Solutions. The present value of the lease payments is $20,859. Prepare the journal entry that Juicyfruit records at the inception of this capital lease.

QS 10-14

International liabilities disclosures

P1   P2

Vodafone Group Plc reports the following information among its bonds payable as of March 31, 2009 (pounds in millions).

Financial Long-Term Liabilities Measured at Amortised Cost			
(£ millions)	Nominal (par) Value	Carrying Value	Fair Value
4.625% (US dollar 500 million) bond due July 2018	£350	£392	£315

a. What is the par value of the 4.625% bond issuance? What is its book (carrying) value?

b. Was the 4.625% bond sold at a discount or a premium? Explain.

Refer to the information in QS 10-14 for **Vodafone Group Plc**. The following price quotes (from Yahoo! Finance Bond Center) relate to its bonds payable as of late 2009. For example, the price quote indicates that the 4.625% bonds have a market price of 98.0 (98.0% of par value), resulting in a yield to maturity of 4.899%.

QS 10-15
International liabilities disclosures and interpretations

P1   P2

Price	Contract Rate (coupon)	Maturity Date	Market Rate (YTM)
98.0	4.625%	15-Jul-2018	4.899%

a. Assuming that the 4.625% bonds were originally issued at par value, what does the market price reveal about interest rate changes since bond issuance? (Assume that Vodafone's credit rating has remained the same.)

b. Does the change in market rates since the issuance of these bonds affect the amount of interest expense reported on Vodafone's income statement? Explain.

c. How much cash would Vodafone need to pay to repurchase the 4.625% bonds at the quoted market price of 98.0? (Assume no interest is owed when the bonds are repurchased.)

d. Assuming that the 4.625% bonds remain outstanding until maturity, at what market price will the bonds sell on the due date in 2018?

☒ connect™

Round dollar amounts to the nearest whole dollar. Assume no reversing entries are used.

EXERCISES

On January 1, 2011, Kidman Enterprises issues bonds that have a $1,700,000 par value, mature in 20 years, and pay 9% interest semiannually on June 30 and December 31. The bonds are sold at par.

1. How much interest will Kidman pay (in cash) to the bondholders every six months?

2. Prepare journal entries to record (*a*) the issuance of bonds on January 1, 2011; (*b*) the first interest payment on June 30, 2011; and (*c*) the second interest payment on December 31, 2011.

3. Prepare the journal entry for issuance assuming the bonds are issued at (*a*) 98 and (*b*) 102.

Exercise 10-1
Recording bond issuance and interest

P1

Moss issues bonds with a par value of $90,000 on January 1, 2011. The bonds' annual contract rate is 8%, and interest is paid semiannually on June 30 and December 31. The bonds mature in three years. The annual market rate at the date of issuance is 10%, and the bonds are sold for $85,431.

1. What is the amount of the discount on these bonds at issuance?

2. How much total bond interest expense will be recognized over the life of these bonds?

3. Prepare an amortization table like the one in Exhibit 10.7 for these bonds; use the straight-line method to amortize the discount.

Exercise 10-2
Straight-line amortization of bond discount

P2

Welch issues bonds dated January 1, 2011, with a par value of $250,000. The bonds' annual contract rate is 9%, and interest is paid semiannually on June 30 and December 31. The bonds mature in three years. The annual market rate at the date of issuance is 12%, and the bonds are sold for $231,570.

1. What is the amount of the discount on these bonds at issuance?

2. How much total bond interest expense will be recognized over the life of these bonds?

3. Prepare an amortization table like the one in Exhibit 10B.1 for these bonds; use the effective interest method to amortize the discount.

Exercise 10-3[B]
Effective interest amortization of bond discount

P2

Prairie Dunes Co. issues bonds dated January 1, 2011, with a par value of $800,000. The bonds' annual contract rate is 13%, and interest is paid semiannually on June 30 and December 31. The bonds mature in three years. The annual market rate at the date of issuance is 12%, and the bonds are sold for $819,700.

1. What is the amount of the premium on these bonds at issuance?

2. How much total bond interest expense will be recognized over the life of these bonds?

3. Prepare an amortization table like the one in Exhibit 10.11 for these bonds; use the straight-line method to amortize the premium.

Exercise 10-4
Straight-line amortization of bond premium

P3

Exercise 10-5ᴮ
Effective interest amortization of bond premium   **P3**

Refer to the bond details in Exercise 10-4 and prepare an amortization table like the one in Exhibit 10B.2 for these bonds using the effective interest method to amortize the premium.

Exercise 10-6
Recording bond issuance and premium amortization
P1 P3

Jobbs Company issues 10%, five-year bonds, on December 31, 2010, with a par value of $100,000 and semiannual interest payments. Use the following straight-line bond amortization table and prepare journal entries to record (*a*) the issuance of bonds on December 31, 2010; (*b*) the first interest payment on June 30, 2011; and (*c*) the second interest payment on December 31, 2011.

Semiannual Period-End	Unamortized Premium	Carrying Value
(0) 12/31/2010	$8,111	$108,111
(1) 6/30/2011	7,300	107,300
(2) 12/31/2011	6,489	106,489

Exercise 10-7
Recording bond issuance and discount amortization
P1 P2

Matchbox Company issues 6%, four-year bonds, on December 31, 2011, with a par value of $100,000 and semiannual interest payments. Use the following straight-line bond amortization table and prepare journal entries to record (*a*) the issuance of bonds on December 31, 2011; (*b*) the first interest payment on June 30, 2012; and (*c*) the second interest payment on December 31, 2012.

Semiannual Period-End	Unamortized Discount	Carrying Value
(0) 12/31/2011	$6,733	$93,267
(1) 6/30/2012	5,891	94,109
(2) 12/31/2012	5,049	94,951

Exercise 10-8
Recording bond issuance and discount amortization
P1 P2

Oneil Company issues 5%, two-year bonds, on December 31, 2011, with a par value of $100,000 and semiannual interest payments. Use the following straight-line bond amortization table and prepare journal entries to record (*a*) the issuance of bonds on December 31, 2011; (*b*) the first through fourth interest payments on each June 30 and December 31; and (*c*) the maturity of the bond on December 31, 2013.

Semiannual Period-End	Unamortized Discount	Carrying Value
(0) 12/31/2011	$6,000	$ 94,000
(1) 6/30/2012	4,500	95,500
(2) 12/31/2012	3,000	97,000
(3) 6/30/2013	1,500	98,500
(4) 12/31/2013	0	100,000

Exercise 10-9
Computing bond interest and price; recording bond issuance
P2

Jester Company issues bonds with a par value of $600,000 on their stated issue date. The bonds mature in 10 years and pay 6% annual interest in semiannual payments. On the issue date, the annual market rate for the bonds is 8%.

1. What is the amount of each semiannual interest payment for these bonds?
2. How many semiannual interest payments will be made on these bonds over their life?
3. Use the interest rates given to determine whether the bonds are issued at par, at a discount, or at a premium.
4. Compute the price of the bonds as of their issue date.
5. Prepare the journal entry to record the bonds' issuance.

Check   (4) $518,465

Exercise 10-10
Computing bond interest and price; recording bond issuance
P3

Metro Company issues bonds with a par value of $75,000 on their stated issue date. The bonds mature in five years and pay 10% annual interest in semiannual payments. On the issue date, the annual market rate for the bonds is 8%.

1. What is the amount of each semiannual interest payment for these bonds?
2. How many semiannual interest payments will be made on these bonds over their life?
3. Use the interest rates given to determine whether the bonds are issued at par, at a discount, or at a premium.

4. Compute the price of the bonds as of their issue date.

5. Prepare the journal entry to record the bonds' issuance.

Check   (4) $81,086

On January 1, 2011, Steadman issues $350,000 of 10%, 15-year bonds at a price of 97¾. Six years later, on January 1, 2017, Steadman retires 20% of these bonds by buying them on the open market at 104½. All interest is accounted for and paid through December 31, 2016, the day before the purchase. The straight-line method is used to amortize any bond discount.

1. How much does the company receive when it issues the bonds on January 1, 2011?

2. What is the amount of the discount on the bonds at January 1, 2011?

3. How much amortization of the discount is recorded on the bonds for the entire period from January 1, 2011, through December 31, 2016?

4. What is the carrying (book) value of the bonds as of the close of business on December 31, 2016? What is the carrying value of the 20% soon-to-be-retired bonds on this same date?

5. How much did the company pay on January 1, 2017, to purchase the bonds that it retired?

6. What is the amount of the recorded gain or loss from retiring the bonds?

7. Prepare the journal entry to record the bond retirement at January 1, 2017.

Exercise 10-11
Bond computations, straight-line amortization, and bond retirement
P2 P4

Check   (6) $4,095 loss

On May 1, 2011, Fellenger Enterprises issues bonds dated January 1, 2011, that have a $1,700,000 par value, mature in 20 years, and pay 9% interest semiannually on June 30 and December 31. The bonds are sold at par plus four months' accrued interest.

1. How much accrued interest do the bond purchasers pay Fellenger on May 1, 2011?

2. Prepare Fellenger's journal entries to record (*a*) the issuance of bonds on May 1, 2011; (*b*) the first interest payment on June 30, 2011; and (*c*) the second interest payment on December 31, 2011.

Exercise 10-12^C
Recording bond issuance with accrued interest
C4   P1

Check   (1) $51,000

Simon issues four-year bonds with a $50,000 par value on June 1, 2011, at a price of $47,974. The annual contract rate is 7%, and interest is paid semiannually on November 30 and May 31.

1. Prepare an amortization table like the one in Exhibit 10.7 for these bonds. Use the straight-line method of interest amortization.

2. Prepare journal entries to record the first two interest payments and to accrue interest as of December 31, 2011.

Exercise 10-13
Straight-line amortization and accrued bond interest expense
P1 P2

On January 1, 2011, Randa borrows $25,000 cash by signing a four-year, 7% installment note. The note requires four equal total payments of accrued interest and principal on December 31 of each year from 2011 through 2014.

1. Compute the amount of each of the four equal total payments.

2. Prepare an amortization table for this installment note like the one in Exhibit 10.14.

Exercise 10-14
Installment note with equal total payments   **C1 P5**

Check   (1) $7,381

Use the information in Exercise 10-14 to prepare the journal entries for Randa to record the loan on January 1, 2011, and the four payments from December 31, 2011, through December 31, 2014.

Exercise 10-15
Installment note entries   **P5**

Ramirez Company is considering a project that will require a $500,000 loan. It presently has total liabilities of $220,000, and total assets of $620,000.

1. Compute Ramirez's (*a*) present debt-to-equity ratio and (*b*) the debt-to-equity ratio assuming it borrows $500,000 to fund the project.

2. Evaluate and discuss the level of risk involved if Ramirez borrows the funds to pursue the project.

Exercise 10-16
Applying debt-to-equity ratio
A3

Indicate whether the company in each separate case 1 through 3 has entered into an operating lease or a capital lease.

1. The present value of the lease payments is 95% of the leased asset's market value, and the lease term is 70% of the leased asset's useful life.

2. The title is transferred to the lessee, the lessee can purchase the asset for $1 at the end of the lease, and the lease term is five years. The leased asset has an expected useful life of six years.

3. The lessor retains title to the asset, and the lease term is three years on an asset that has a five-year useful life.

Exercise 10-17^D
Identifying capital and operating leases
C4

Exercise 10-18^D

Accounting for capital lease

C4

Flyer (lessee) signs a five-year capital lease for office equipment with a $20,000 annual lease payment. The present value of the five annual lease payments is $82,000, based on a 7% interest rate.

1. Prepare the journal entry Flyer will record at inception of the lease.
2. If the leased asset has a five-year useful life with no salvage value, prepare the journal entry Flyer will record each year to recognize depreciation expense related to the leased asset.

Exercise 10-19^D

Analyzing lease options

C2 C3 C4

General Motors advertised three alternatives for a 25-month lease on a new Blazer: (1) zero dollars down and a lease payment of $1,750 per month for 25 months, (2) $5,000 down and $1,500 per month for 25 months, or (3) $38,500 down and no payments for 25 months. Use the present value Table B.3 in Appendix B to determine which is the best alternative (assume you have enough cash to accept any alternative and the annual interest rate is 12% compounded monthly).

Exercise 10-20

Accounting for long-term liabilities under IFRS

P1 P2 P3

Heineken N.V. reports the following information for its Loans and Borrowings as of December 31, 2008, including proceeds and repayments for the year ended December 31, 2008 (euros in millions).

Loans and borrowings (noncurrent liabilities)	
Loans and borrowings, December 31, 2008	€ 9,084
Proceeds (cash) from issuances of loans and borrowings	6,361
Repayments (in cash) of loans and borrowings	(2,532)

1. Prepare Heineken's journal entry to record its cash proceeds from issuances of its loans and borrowings for 2008. Assume that the par value of these issuances is €6,000.
2. Prepare Heineken's journal entry to record its cash repayments of its loans and borrowings for 2008. Assume that the par value of these issuances is €2,400, and the premium on them is €32.
3. Compute the discount or premium on its loans and borrowings as of December 31, 2008, assuming that the par value of these liabilities is €9,000.
4. Given the facts in part 3 and viewing the entirety of loans and borrowings as one issuance, was the contract rate on these loans and borrowings higher or lower than the market rate at the time of issuance? Explain. (Assume that Heineken's credit rating has remained the same.)

---

connect

PROBLEM SET A

> Round dollar amounts to the nearest whole dollar. Assume no reversing entries are used.

Problem 10-1A

Computing bond price and recording issuance

P1 P2 P3

Check (1) Premium, $2,718

(3) Discount, $2,294

Stowers Research issues bonds dated January 1, 2011, that pay interest semiannually on June 30 and December 31. The bonds have a $20,000 par value and an annual contract rate of 10%, and they mature in 10 years.

Required

For each of the following three separate situations, (*a*) determine the bonds' issue price on January 1, 2011, and (*b*) prepare the journal entry to record their issuance.

1. The market rate at the date of issuance is 8%.
2. The market rate at the date of issuance is 10%.
3. The market rate at the date of issuance is 12%.

Problem 10-2A

Straight-line amortization of bond discount

P1 P2

mhhe.com/wildFINMAN4e

Check (3) $2,071,776

(4) 12/31/2012 carrying value, $1,764,460

Heathrow issues $2,000,000 of 6%, 15-year bonds dated January 1, 2011, that pay interest semiannually on June 30 and December 31. The bonds are issued at a price of $1,728,224.

Required

1. Prepare the January 1, 2011, journal entry to record the bonds' issuance.
2. For each semiannual period, compute (*a*) the cash payment, (*b*) the straight-line discount amortization, and (*c*) the bond interest expense.
3. Determine the total bond interest expense to be recognized over the bonds' life.
4. Prepare the first two years of an amortization table like Exhibit 10.7 using the straight-line method.
5. Prepare the journal entries to record the first two interest payments.

Refer to the bond details in Problem 10-2A, *except* assume that the bonds are issued at a price of $2,447,990.

Required

1. Prepare the January 1, 2011, journal entry to record the bonds' issuance.
2. For each semiannual period, compute (*a*) the cash payment, (*b*) the straight-line premium amortization, and (*c*) the bond interest expense.
3. Determine the total bond interest expense to be recognized over the bonds' life.
4. Prepare the first two years of an amortization table like Exhibit 10.7 using the straight-line method.
5. Prepare the journal entries to record the first two interest payments.

Problem 10-3A
Straight-line amortization of bond premium

P1 P3

Check (3) $1,352,010
(4) 12/31/2012 carrying value, $2,388,258

Saturn issues 6.5%, five-year bonds dated January 1, 2011, with a $500,000 par value. The bonds pay interest on June 30 and December 31 and are issued at a price of $510,666. The annual market rate is 6% on the issue date.

Required

1. Calculate the total bond interest expense over the bonds' life.
2. Prepare a straight-line amortization table like Exhibit 10.11 for the bonds' life.
3. Prepare the journal entries to record the first two interest payments.

Problem 10-4A
Straight-line amortization of bond premium

P1 P3

mhhe.com/wildFINMAN4e

Check (2) 6/30/2013 carrying value, $505,331

Refer to the bond details in Problem 10-4A.

Required

1. Compute the total bond interest expense over the bonds' life.
2. Prepare an effective interest amortization table like the one in Exhibit 10B.2 for the bonds' life.
3. Prepare the journal entries to record the first two interest payments.
4. Use the market rate at issuance to compute the present value of the remaining cash flows for these bonds as of December 31, 2013. Compare your answer with the amount shown on the amortization table as the balance for that date (from part 2) and explain your findings.

Problem 10-5A[B]
Effective interest amortization of bond premium; computing bond price **P1 P3**

Check (2) 6/30/2013 carrying value, $505,728

(4) $504,653

Patton issues $650,000 of 5%, four-year bonds dated January 1, 2011, that pay interest semiannually on June 30 and December 31. They are issued at $584,361 and their market rate is 8% at the issue date.

Required

1. Prepare the January 1, 2011, journal entry to record the bonds' issuance.
2. Determine the total bond interest expense to be recognized over the bonds' life.
3. Prepare a straight-line amortization table like the one in Exhibit 10.7 for the bonds' first two years.
4. Prepare the journal entries to record the first two interest payments.

Analysis Component

5. Assume the market rate on January 1, 2011, is 4% instead of 8%. Without providing numbers, describe how this change affects the amounts reported on Patton's financial statements.

Problem 10-6A
Straight-line amortization of bond discount

P1 P2

Check (2) $195,639
(3) 12/31/2012 carrying value, $617,181

Refer to the bond details in Problem 10-6A.

Required

1. Prepare the January 1, 2011, journal entry to record the bonds' issuance.
2. Determine the total bond interest expense to be recognized over the bonds' life.
3. Prepare an effective interest amortization table like the one in Exhibit 10B.1 for the bonds' first two years.
4. Prepare the journal entries to record the first two interest payments.

Problem 10-7A[B]
Effective interest amortization of bond discount **P1 P2**

Check (2) $195,639
(3) 12/31/2012 carrying value, $614,614

mhhe.com/wildFINMAN4e

Problem 10-8A^B

Effective interest amortization of bond premium; retiring bonds

P1 P3 P4

Check (3) 6/30/2012 carrying value, $91,224

(5) $2,635 gain

mhhe.com/wildFINMAN4e

McFad issues $90,000 of 11%, three-year bonds dated January 1, 2011, that pay interest semiannually on June 30 and December 31. They are issued at $92,283. Their market rate is 10% at the issue date.

Required

1. Prepare the January 1, 2011, journal entry to record the bonds' issuance.
2. Determine the total bond interest expense to be recognized over the bonds' life.
3. Prepare an effective interest amortization table like Exhibit 10B.2 for the bonds' first two years.
4. Prepare the journal entries to record the first two interest payments.
5. Prepare the journal entry to record the bonds' retirement on January 1, 2013, at 98.

Analysis Component

6. Assume that the market rate on January 1, 2011, is 12% instead of 10%. Without presenting numbers, describe how this change affects the amounts reported on McFad's financial statements.

Problem 10-9A

Installment notes

C1 P5

Check (2) 10/31/2015 ending balance, $92,759

On November 1, 2011, Leetch Ltd. borrows $400,000 cash from a bank by signing a five-year installment note bearing 8% interest. The note requires equal total payments each year on October 31.

Required

1. Compute the total amount of each installment payment.
2. Complete an amortization table for this installment note similar to the one in Exhibit 10.14.
3. Prepare the journal entries in which Leetch records (a) accrued interest as of December 31, 2011 (the end of its annual reporting period), and (b) the first annual payment on the note.

Problem 10-10A

Applying the debt-to-equity ratio

A3

At the end of the current year, the following information is available for both Kumar Company and Asher Company.

	Kumar Company	Asher Company
Total assets	$2,254,500	$1,123,500
Total liabilities	904,500	598,500
Total equity	1,350,000	525,000

Required

1. Compute the debt-to-equity ratios for both companies.
2. Comment on your results and discuss the riskiness of each company's financing structure.

Problem 10-11A^D

Capital lease accounting

C4

Check (1) $79,854

(3) Year 3 ending balance, $35,664

Montana Company signs a five-year capital lease with Elway Company for office equipment. The annual lease payment is $20,000, and the interest rate is 8%.

Required

1. Compute the present value of Montana's five-year lease payments.
2. Prepare the journal entry to record Montana's capital lease at its inception.
3. Complete a lease payment schedule for the five years of the lease with the following headings. Assume that the beginning balance of the lease liability (present value of lease payments) is $79,854. (*Hint:* To find the amount allocated to interest in year 1, multiply the interest rate by the beginning-of-year lease liability. The amount of the annual lease payment not allocated to interest is allocated to principal. Reduce the lease liability by the amount allocated to principal to update the lease liability at each year-end.)

Period Ending Date	Beginning Balance of Lease Liability	Interest on Lease Liability	Reduction of Lease Liability	Cash Lease Payment	Ending Balance of Lease Liability

4. Use straight-line depreciation and prepare the journal entry to depreciate the leased asset at the end of year 1. Assume zero salvage value and a five-year life for the office equipment.

PROBLEM SET B

Sedona Systems issues bonds dated January 1, 2011, that pay interest semiannually on June 30 and December 31. The bonds have a $45,000 par value and an annual contract rate of 12%, and they mature in five years.

Problem 10-1B
Computing bond price and recording issuance

P1 P2 P3

Required

For each of the following three separate situations, (*a*) determine the bonds' issue price on January 1, 2011, and (*b*) prepare the journal entry to record their issuance.

1. The market rate at the date of issuance is 10%.
2. The market rate at the date of issuance is 12%.
3. The market rate at the date of issuance is 14%.

Check   (1) Premium, $3,475

(3) Discount, $3,162

ParFour issues $1,700,000 of 10%, 10-year bonds dated January 1, 2011, that pay interest semiannually on June 30 and December 31. The bonds are issued at a price of $1,505,001.

Problem 10-2B
Straight-line amortization of bond discount

P1 P2

Required

1. Prepare the January 1, 2011, journal entry to record the bonds' issuance.
2. For each semiannual period, compute (*a*) the cash payment, (*b*) the straight-line discount amortization, and (*c*) the bond interest expense.
3. Determine the total bond interest expense to be recognized over the bonds' life.
4. Prepare the first two years of an amortization table like Exhibit 10.7 using the straight-line method.
5. Prepare the journal entries to record the first two interest payments.

Check   (3) $1,894,999

(4) 6/30/2012 carrying value, $1,534,251

Refer to the bond details in Problem 10-2B, *except* assume that the bonds are issued at a price of $2,096,466.

Problem 10-3B
Straight-line amortization of bond premium

P1 P3

Required

1. Prepare the January 1, 2011, journal entry to record the bonds' issuance.
2. For each semiannual period, compute (*a*) the cash payment, (*b*) the straight-line premium amortization, and (*c*) the bond interest expense.
3. Determine the total bond interest expense to be recognized over the bonds' life.
4. Prepare the first two years of an amortization table like Exhibit 10.7 using the straight-line method.
5. Prepare the journal entries to record the first two interest payments.

Check   (3) $1,303,534

(4) 6/30/2012 carrying value, $2,036,997

Zooba Company issues 9%, five-year bonds dated January 1, 2011, with a $160,000 par value. The bonds pay interest on June 30 and December 31 and are issued at a price of $166,494. Their annual market rate is 8% on the issue date.

Problem 10-4B
Straight-line amortization of bond premium

P1 P3

Required

1. Calculate the total bond interest expense over the bonds' life.
2. Prepare a straight-line amortization table like Exhibit 10.11 for the bonds' life.
3. Prepare the journal entries to record the first two interest payments.

Check   (2) 6/30/2013 carrying value, $163,249

Refer to the bond details in Problem 10-4B.

Problem 10-5B[B]
Effective interest amortization of bond premium; computing bond price **P1 P3**

Required

1. Compute the total bond interest expense over the bonds' life.
2. Prepare an effective interest amortization table like the one in Exhibit 10B.2 for the bonds' life.
3. Prepare the journal entries to record the first two interest payments.
4. Use the market rate at issuance to compute the present value of the remaining cash flows for these bonds as of December 31, 2013. Compare your answer with the amount shown on the amortization table as the balance for that date (from part 2) and explain your findings.

Check   (2) 6/30/2013 carrying value, $163,568

(4) $162,903

Problem 10-6B
Straight-line amortization of
bond discount

P1 P2

Check (2) $128,753

(3) 6/30/2012 carrying
value, $101,323

Roney issues $120,000 of 6%, 15-year bonds dated January 1, 2011, that pay interest semiannually on June 30 and December 31. They are issued at $99,247, and their market rate is 8% at the issue date.

Required

1. Prepare the January 1, 2011, journal entry to record the bonds' issuance.
2. Determine the total bond interest expense to be recognized over the life of the bonds.
3. Prepare a straight-line amortization table like the one in Exhibit 10.7 for the bonds' first two years.
4. Prepare the journal entries to record the first two interest payments.

Problem 10-7B^B

Problem 10-7B[B]
Effective interest amortization of
bond discount

P1 P2

Check (2) $128,753;

(3) 6/30/2012 carrying
value, $100,402

Refer to the bond details in Problem 10-6B.

Required

1. Prepare the January 1, 2011, journal entry to record the bonds' issuance.
2. Determine the total bond interest expense to be recognized over the bonds' life.
3. Prepare an effective interest amortization table like the one in Exhibit 10B.1 for the bonds' first two years.
4. Prepare the journal entries to record the first two interest payments.

Problem 10-8B[B]
Effective interest amortization of
bond premium; retiring bonds

P1 P3 P4

Check (3) 6/30/2012 carrying value,
$958,406

(5) $6,174 loss

Hutton issues $900,000 of 13%, four-year bonds dated January 1, 2011, that pay interest semiannually on June 30 and December 31. They are issued at $987,217, and their market rate is 10% at the issue date.

Required

1. Prepare the January 1, 2011, journal entry to record the bonds' issuance.
2. Determine the total bond interest expense to be recognized over the bonds' life.
3. Prepare an effective interest amortization table like the one in Exhibit 10B.2 for the bonds' first two years.
4. Prepare the journal entries to record the first two interest payments.
5. Prepare the journal entry to record the bonds' retirement on January 1, 2013, at 106.

Analysis Component

6. Assume that the market rate on January 1, 2011, is 14% instead of 10%. Without presenting numbers, describe how this change affects the amounts reported on Hutton's financial statements.

Problem 10-9B
Installment notes

C1 P5

Check (2) 9/30/2013 ending
balance, $109,673

On October 1, 2011, Milan Enterprises borrows $300,000 cash from a bank by signing a three-year install-ment note bearing 10% interest. The note requires equal total payments each year on September 30.

Required

1. Compute the total amount of each installment payment.
2. Complete an amortization table for this installment note similar to the one in Exhibit 10.14.
3. Prepare the journal entries to record (*a*) accrued interest as of December 31, 2011 (the end of its annual reporting period) and (*b*) the first annual payment on the note.

Problem 10-10B
Applying the debt-to-equity ratio

A3

At the end of the current year, the following information is available for both West Elm Company and East Park Company.

	West Elm Company	East Park Company
Total assets	$396,396	$1,650,000
Total liabilities	178,596	1,237,500
Total equity	217,800	412,500

Required

1. Compute the debt-to-equity ratios for both companies.
2. Comment on your results and discuss what they imply about the relative riskiness of these companies.

Preston Company signs a five-year capital lease with Starbuck Company for office equipment. The annual lease payment is $10,000, and the interest rate is 10%.

Required

1. Compute the present value of Preston's lease payments.
2. Prepare the journal entry to record Preston's capital lease at its inception.
3. Complete a lease payment schedule for the five years of the lease with the following headings. Assume that the beginning balance of the lease liability (present value of lease payments) is $37,908. (*Hint:* To find the amount allocated to interest in year 1, multiply the interest rate by the beginning-of-year lease liability. The amount of the annual lease payment not allocated to interest is allocated to principal. Reduce the lease liability by the amount allocated to principal to update the lease liability at each year-end.)

Period Ending Date	Beginning Balance of Lease Liability	Interest on Lease Liability	Reduction of Lease Liability	Cash Lease Payment	Ending Balance of Lease Liability

4. Use straight-line depreciation and prepare the journal entry to depreciate the leased asset at the end of year 1. Assume zero salvage value and a five-year life for the office equipment.

(This serial problem began in Chapter 1 and continues through most of the book. If previous chapter segments were not completed, the serial problem can begin at this point. It is helpful, but not necessary, to use the Working Papers that accompany the book.)

SP 10   Santana Rey has consulted with her local banker and is considering financing an expansion of her business by obtaining a long-term bank loan. Selected account balances at March 31, 2012, for Business Solutions follow.

Total assets	$120,268	Total liabilities	$875	Total equity	$119,393

Required

1. The bank has offered a long-term secured note to Business Solutions. The bank's loan procedures require that a client's debt-to-equity ratio not exceed 0.8. As of March 31, 2012, what is the maximum amount that Business Solutions could borrow from this bank (rounded to nearest dollar)?
2. If Business Solutions borrows the maximum amount allowed from the bank, what percentage of assets would be financed (*a*) by debt and (*b*) by equity?
3. What are some factors Santana Rey should consider before borrowing the funds?

Beyond the Numbers

BTN 10-1   Refer to **Research In Motion**'s financial statements in Appendix A to answer the following.

1. Identify the items, if any, that make up RIM's long-term debt as reported on its balance sheet at February 27, 2010.
2. Assume that RIM has $402,000 thousand in convertible debentures that carry a 2.25% contract rate of interest. How much annual cash interest must be paid on those convertible debentures?
3. How much cash did it generate from issuance of debt for the year-ended February 27, 2010? How much cash did it use for repayments of debt for that same year?

Fast Forward

4. Access Research In Motion's financial statements for the years ending after February 27, 2010, from its Website (**RIM.com**) or the SEC's EDGAR database (**www.sec.gov**). Has it issued additional long-term debt since the year-end February 27, 2010? If yes, identify the amount(s).

Problem 10-11B^D — rendered as [D]

Problem 10-11B[D]
Capital lease accounting
C4

Check   (1) $37,908

(3) Year 3 ending balance, $17,356

SERIAL PROBLEM
Business Solutions
A1   A3

Check   (1) $94,639

REPORTING IN ACTION
A1   A2

RIM

COMPARATIVE ANALYSIS

A3

RIM

Apple

BTN 10-2   Key figures for **Research In Motion** and **Apple** follow.

($ millions)	Research In Motion		Apple	
	Current Year	Prior Year	Current Year	Prior Year
Total assets	$10,204	$8,101	$47,501	$36,171
Total liabilities	2,602	2,227	15,861	13,874
Total equity	7,603	5,874	31,640	22,297

Required

1. Compute the debt-to-equity ratios for Research In Motion and Apple for both the current year and the prior year.
2. Use the ratios you computed in part 1 to determine which company's financing structure is least risky. Assume an industry average of 0.64 for debt-to-equity.

ETHICS CHALLENGE

C4   A1

BTN 10-3   Holly County needs a new county government building that would cost $24 million. The politicians feel that voters will not approve a municipal bond issue to fund the building since it would increase taxes. They opt to have a state bank issue $24 million of tax-exempt securities to pay for the building construction. The county then will make yearly lease payments (of principal and interest) to repay the obligation. Unlike conventional municipal bonds, the lease payments are not binding obligations on the county and, therefore, require no voter approval.

Required

1. Do you think the actions of the politicians and the bankers in this situation are ethical?
2. How do the tax-exempt securities used to pay for the building compare in risk to a conventional municipal bond issued by Holly County?

COMMUNICATING IN PRACTICE

P3

BTN 10-4   Your business associate mentions that she is considering investing in corporate bonds currently selling at a premium. She says that since the bonds are selling at a premium, they are highly valued and her investment will yield more than the going rate of return for the risk involved. Reply with a memorandum to confirm or correct your associate's interpretation of premium bonds.

TAKING IT TO THE NET

A2

BTN 10-5   Access the March 25, 2010, filing of the 10-K report of **Home Depot** for the year ended January 31, 2010, from **www.sec.gov** (Ticker: HD). Refer to Home Depot's balance sheet, including its note 4 (on debt).

Required

1. Identify Home Depot's long-term liabilities and the amounts for those liabilities from Home Depot's balance sheet at January 31, 2010.
2. Review Home Depot's note 5. The note reports that as of January 31, 2010, it had $2.96 billion of "5.875% Senior Notes; due December 16, 2036; interest payable semiannually on June 16 and December 16." These notes have a face value of $3.0 billion and were originally issued at $2.958 billion.
   a. Why would Home Depot issue $3.0 billion of its notes for only $2.958 billion?
   b. How much cash interest must Home Depot pay each June 16 and December 16 on these notes?

TEAMWORK IN ACTION

P2   P3

BTN 10-6ᴮ   Break into teams and complete the following requirements related to effective interest amortization for a premium bond.

1. Each team member is to independently prepare a blank table with proper headings for amortization of a bond premium. When all have finished, compare tables and ensure that all are in agreement.

Parts 2 and 3 require use of these facts: On January 1, 2010, Caleb issues $100,000, 9%, five-year bonds at 104.1. The market rate at issuance is 8%. Caleb pays interest semiannually on June 30 and December 31.

2. In rotation, *each* team member must explain how to complete *one* line of the bond amortization table, including all computations for his or her line. (Round amounts to the nearest dollar.) All members are to fill in their tables during this process. You need not finish the table; stop after all members have explained a line.

3. In rotation, *each* team member is to identify a separate column of the table and indicate what the final number in that column will be and explain the reasoning.

4. Reach a team consensus as to what the total bond interest expense on this bond issue will be if the bond is not retired before maturity.

5. As a team, prepare a list of similarities and differences between the amortization table just prepared and the amortization table if the bond had been issued at a discount.

Hint: Rotate teams to report on parts 4 and 5. Consider requiring entries for issuance and interest payments.

BTN 10-7   Warren Brown is the founder of **Cake Love**. Assume that his company currently has $250,000 in equity, and he is considering a $100,000 expansion to meet increased demand. The $100,000 expansion would yield $16,000 in additional annual income before interest expense. Assume that the business currently earns $40,000 annual income before interest expense of $10,000, yielding a return on equity of 12% ($30,000/$250,000). To fund the expansion, he is considering the issuance of a 10-year, $100,000 note with annual interest payments (the principal due at the end of 10 years).

ENTREPRENEURIAL DECISION

A1

Required

1. Using return on equity as the decision criterion, show computations to support or reject the expansion if interest on the $100,000 note is (*a*) 10%, (*b*) 15%, (*c*) 16%, (*d*) 17%, and (*e*) 20%.

2. What general rule do the results in part 1 illustrate?

BTN 10-8   Visit your city or county library. Ask the librarian to help you locate the recent financial records of your city or county government. Examine those records.

HITTING THE ROAD

A1

Required

1. Determine the amount of long-term bonds and notes currently outstanding.

2. Read the supporting information to your municipality's financial statements and record

   a. The market interest rate(s) when the bonds and/or notes were issued.

   b. The date(s) when the bonds and/or notes will mature.

   c. Any rating(s) on the bonds and/or notes received from **Moody's**, **Standard & Poor's**, or another rating agency.

BTN 10-9   **Nokia (www.Nokia.com)**, **Research In Motion**, and **Apple** are competitors in the global marketplace. Selected results from these companies follow.

GLOBAL DECISION

A3

NOKIA

RIM

Apple

Key Figures	Nokia (EURm) Current Year	Nokia (EURm) Prior Year	Research In Motion ($ millions) Current Year	Research In Motion ($ millions) Prior Year	Apple ($ millions) Current Year	Apple ($ millions) Prior Year
Total assets	€35,738	€39,582	$10,204	$8,101	$47,501	$36,171
Total liabilities	20,989	23,072	2,602	2,227	15,861	13,874
Total equity	14,749	16,510	7,603	5,874	31,640	22,297
Debt-to-equity ratio	?	?	0.34	0.38	0.50	0.62

Required

1. Compute Nokia's debt-to-equity ratios for the current year and the prior year.

2. Use the data provided and the ratios computed in part 1 to determine which company's financing structure is least risky.

ANSWERS TO MULTIPLE CHOICE QUIZ

1. b

2. a

3. c; $500,000 × 0.08 × ½ year = $20,000

4. a; Cash interest paid = $100,000 × 5% × ½ year = $2,500
Discount amortization = ($100,000 − $95,735)/10 periods = $426.50
Interest expense = $2,500.00 + $426.50 = $2,926.50

5. e; ($373,745 − $350,000)/16 periods = $1,484

11

Corporate Reporting and Analysis

A Look Back

Chapter 10 focused on long-term liabilities, which are a main part of most companies' financing. We explained how to value, record, amortize, and report these liabilities in financial statements.

A Look at This Chapter

This chapter emphasizes details of the corporate form of organization. The accounting concepts and procedures for equity transactions are explained. We also describe how to report and analyze income, earnings per share, and retained earnings.

A Look Ahead

Chapter 12 focuses on reporting and analyzing a company's cash flows. Special emphasis is directed at the statement of cash flows and the methods for reporting that statement.

Learning Objectives

CONCEPTUAL

C1 Identify characteristics of corporations and their organization. (p. 456)

C2 Explain characteristics of, and distribute dividends between, common and preferred stock. (p. 466)

C3 Explain the items reported in retained earnings. (p. 472)

ANALYTICAL

A1 Compute earnings per share and describe its use. (p. 475)

A2 Compute price-earnings ratio and describe its use in analysis. (p. 475)

A3 Compute dividend yield and explain its use in analysis. (p. 476)

A4 Compute book value and explain its use in analysis. (p. 476)

LP11

PROCEDURAL

P1 Record the issuance of corporate stock. (p. 460)

P2 Record transactions involving cash dividends, stock dividends, and stock splits. (p. 463)

P3 Record purchases and sales of treasury stock and the retirement of stock. (p. 470)

Greener Lawns

"Every part of our business is . . . profitable"

—**KELLY GIARD**

FORT COLLINS, CO—According to the U.S. Environmental Protection Agency, a gas-powered lawn mower produces as much air pollution as 43 new cars each driven 12,000 miles. "At least 5 percent of pollution is caused by gas-powered maintenance equipment," explains Kelly Giard, owner of **Clean Air Lawn Care** (**CleanAirLawnCare.com**). "This is one of the last dirty frontiers in America that can be easily solved."

Kelly launched his business four years ago, which is a full-service sustainable lawn care company dedicated to using clean electrical and biodiesel powered equipment. His equipment is charged by solar panels during the day and by wind power overnight. "I started [it] out of my garage mostly for fun," says Kelly. "And business took off."

Kelly explains that his success would not have been possible without equity financing and knowledge of business operations. To make it happen, says Kelly, he studied corporate formation, equity issuance, stock types, retaining earnings, and dividend policies. After that analysis, Kelly set up Clean Air Lawn Care as a corporation, which had several benefits given his business goals and strategies. With his corporate structure in place, Kelly was ready to attack the market. "Only about 1% of the country uses an electrical mower," says Kelly. "That's awful, and that's something we're committed to changing."

The success of Kelly's corporate structure and his equity financing brings both opportunities and challenges. The positive is being part of the green movement, yielding "a ripple effect where there's profit, happy customers and an environmental benefit." The challenge is effectively using accounting for equity as a tool to achieve those objectives. That includes his knowledge of corporate formation, stock types, and equity transactions. "This is critical to us doing well in the long term," explains Kelly. Still, the focus remains on the environment. "We want [consumers] to have a choice when they hire a service: sustainable vs. dirty."

[Sources: *Clean Air Lawn Care Website,* January 2011; *Entrepreneur,* January 2010; *Lawn & Landscape,* April 2010; *Charles & Hudson Website,* 2010]

Chapter Preview

This chapter focuses on equity transactions. The first part of the chapter describes the basics of the corporate form of organization and explains the accounting for common and preferred stock. We then focus on several special financing transactions, including cash and stock dividends, stock splits, and treasury stock. The final section considers accounting for retained earnings, including prior period adjustments, retained earnings restrictions, and reporting guidelines.

Corporate Reporting and Analysis

Corporations	Common Stock	Dividends	Preferred Stock	Treasury Stock	Reporting on Equity
• Characteristics • Organization and management • Stockholders • Stock basics	• Par value • No-par value • Stated value • Stock for non-cash assets	• Cash dividends • Stock dividends • Stock splits	• Issuance • Dividend preferences • Convertible preferred • Callable preferred	• Purchasing treasury stock • Reissuing treasury stock • Retiring stock	• Statement of retained earnings • Statement of stockholders' equity • Stock options

CORPORATE FORM OF ORGANIZATION

C1 Identify characteristics of corporations and their organization.

A **corporation** is an entity created by law that is separate from its owners. It has most of the rights and privileges granted to individuals. Owners of corporations are called *stockholders* or *shareholders*. Corporations can be separated into two types. A *privately held* (or *closely held*) corporation does not offer its stock for public sale and usually has few stockholders. A *publicly held* corporation offers its stock for public sale and can have thousands of stockholders. *Public sale* usually refers to issuance and trading on an organized stock market.

Characteristics of Corporations

Corporations represent an important type of organization. Their unique characteristics offer advantages and disadvantages.

Advantages of Corporate Characteristics

- **Separate legal entity:** A corporation conducts its affairs with the same rights, duties, and responsibilities of a person. It takes actions through its agents, who are its officers and managers.

- **Limited liability of stockholders:** Stockholders are liable for neither corporate acts nor corporate debt.

- **Transferable ownership rights:** The transfer of shares from one stockholder to another usually has no effect on the corporation or its operations except when this causes a change in the directors who control or manage the corporation.

- **Continuous life:** A corporation's life continues indefinitely because it is not tied to the physical lives of its owners.

- **Lack of mutual agency for stockholders:** A corporation acts through its agents, who are its officers and managers. Stockholders, who are not its officers and managers, do not have the power to bind the corporation to contracts—referred to as *lack of mutual agency*.

- **Ease of capital accumulation:** Buying stock is attractive to investors because (1) stockholders are not liable for the corporation's acts and debts, (2) stocks usually are transferred easily, (3) the life of the corporation is unlimited, and (4) stockholders are not corporate agents. These advantages enable corporations to accumulate large amounts of capital from the combined investments of many stockholders.

Point: The *business entity assumption* requires a corporation to be accounted for separately from its owners (shareholders).

Global: U.S., U.K., and Canadian corporations finance much of their operations with stock issuances, but companies in countries such as France, Germany, and Japan finance mainly with note and bond issuances.

Disadvantages of Corporate Characteristics

- **Government regulation:** A corporation must meet requirements of a state's incorporation laws, which subject the corporation to state regulation and control. Proprietorships and partnerships avoid many of these regulations and governmental reports.
- **Corporate taxation:** Corporations are subject to the same property and payroll taxes as proprietorships and partnerships plus *additional* taxes. The most burdensome of these are federal and state income taxes that together can take 40% or more of corporate pretax income. Moreover, corporate income is usually taxed a second time as part of stockholders' personal income when they receive cash distributed as dividends. This is called *double taxation.* (The usual dividend tax is 15%; however, it is less than 15% for lower income taxpayers, and in some cases zero.)

 Point: Proprietorships and partnerships are not subject to income taxes. Their income is taxed as the personal income of their owners.

Point: Double taxation is less severe when a corporation's owner-manager collects a salary that is taxed only once as part of his or her personal income.

 **Decision Insight**

Stock Financing Marc Andreessen cofounded **Netscape** at age 22, only four months after earning his degree. One year later, he and friends issued Netscape shares to the public. The stock soared, making Andreessen a multimillionaire. ■

Corporate Organization and Management

This section describes the incorporation, costs, and management of corporate organizations.

Incorporation A corporation is created by obtaining a charter from a state government. A charter application usually must be signed by the prospective stockholders called *incorporators* or *promoters* and then filed with the proper state official. When the application process is complete and fees paid, the charter is issued and the corporation is formed. Investors then purchase the corporation's stock, meet as stockholders, and elect a board of directors. Directors oversee a corporation's affairs.

Point: A corporation is not required to have an office in its state of incorporation.

Organization Expenses Organization expenses (also called *organization costs*) are the costs to organize a corporation; they include legal fees, promoters' fees, and amounts paid to obtain a charter. The corporation records (debits) these costs to an expense account called *Organization Expenses*. Organization costs are expensed as incurred because it is difficult to determine the amount and timing of their future benefits.

Management of a Corporation The ultimate control of a corporation rests with stockholders who control a corporation by electing its *board of directors,* or simply, *directors.* Each stockholder usually has one vote for each share of stock owned. This control relation is shown in Exhibit 11.1. Directors are responsible for and have final authority for managing corporate activities. A board can act only as a collective body and usually limits its actions to setting general policy.

A corporation usually holds a stockholder meeting at least once a year to elect directors and transact business as its bylaws require. A group of stockholders owning or controlling votes of more than a 50% share of a corporation's stock can elect the board and control the corporation. Stockholders who do not attend stockholders' meetings must have an opportunity to delegate their voting rights to an agent by signing a **proxy,** a document that gives a designated agent the right to vote the stock.

EXHIBIT 11.1

Corporate Structure

Stockholders → Board of Directors → President, Vice President, and Other Officers → Employees of the Corporation

Day-to-day direction of corporate business is delegated to executive officers appointed by the board. A corporation's chief executive officer (CEO) is often its president. Several vice presidents, who report to the president, are commonly assigned specific areas of management responsibility such as finance, production, and marketing. One person often has the dual role

Point: *Bylaws* are guidelines that govern the behavior of individuals employed by and managing the corporation.

of chairperson of the board of directors and CEO. In this case, the president is usually designated the chief operating officer (COO).

Decision Insight

Seed Money   Sources for start-up money include (1) "angel" investors such as family, friends, or anyone who believes in a company, (2) employees, investors, and even suppliers who can be paid with stock, and (3) venture capitalists (investors) who have a record of entrepreneurial success. See the National Venture Capital Association (**NVCA.org**) for information. ■

Stockholders of Corporations

This section explains stockholder rights, stock purchases and sales, and the role of registrar and transfer agents.

Rights of Stockholders   When investors buy stock, they acquire all *specific* rights the corporation's charter grants to stockholders. They also acquire *general* rights granted stockholders by the laws of the state in which the company is incorporated. When a corporation has only one class of stock, it is identified as **common stock.** State laws vary, but common stockholders usually have the general right to

1. Vote at stockholders' meetings.
2. Sell or otherwise dispose of their stock.
3. Purchase their proportional share of any common stock later issued by the corporation. This **preemptive right** protects stockholders' proportionate interest in the corporation. For example, a stockholder who owns 25% of a corporation's common stock has the first opportunity to buy 25% of any new common stock issued.
4. Receive the same dividend, if any, on each common share of the corporation.
5. Share in any assets remaining after creditors and preferred stockholders are paid when, and if, the corporation is liquidated. Each common share receives the same amount.

Stockholders also have the right to receive timely financial reports.

Stock Certificates and Transfer   Investors who buy a corporation's stock, sometimes receive a *stock certificate* as proof of share ownership. Many corporations issue only one certificate for each block of stock purchased. A certificate can be for any number of shares. Exhibit 11.2 shows a stock certificate of the **Green Bay Packers**. A certificate shows the company name, stockholder name, number of shares, and other crucial information. Issuance of certificates is becoming less common. Instead, many stockholders maintain accounts with the corporation or their stockbrokers and never receive actual certificates.

EXHIBIT 11.2

Stock Certificate

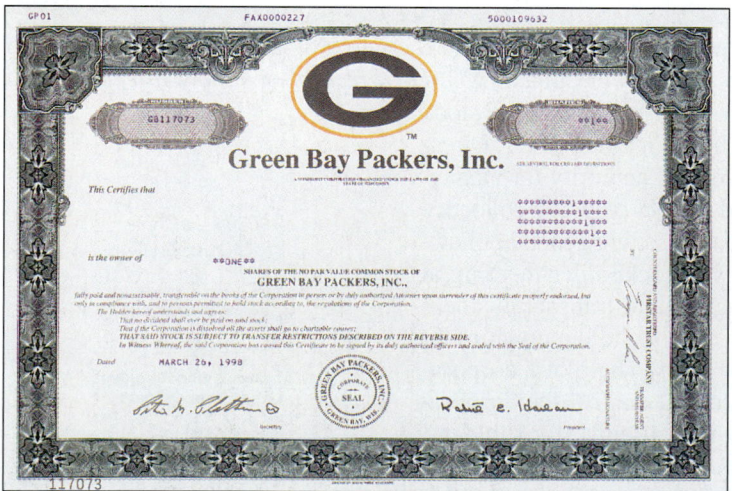

Registrar and Transfer Agents   If a corporation's stock is traded on a major stock exchange, the corporation must have a registrar and a transfer agent. A *registrar* keeps stockholder records and prepares official lists of stockholders for stockholder meetings and dividend payments. A *transfer agent* assists with purchases and sales of shares by receiving and issuing certificates as necessary. Registrars and transfer agents are usually large banks or trust companies with computer facilities and staff to do this work.

> **Decision Insight**
>
> **Pricing Stock** A prospectus accompanies a stock's initial public offering (IPO), giving financial information about the company issuing the stock. A prospectus should help answer these questions to price an IPO: (1) Is the underwriter reliable? (2) Is there growth in revenues, profits, and cash flows? (3) What is management's view of operations? (4) Are current owners selling? (5) What are the risks? ■

Basics of Capital Stock

Capital stock is a general term that refers to any shares issued to obtain capital (owner financing). This section introduces terminology and accounting for capital stock.

Authorized Stock **Authorized stock** is the number of shares that a corporation's charter allows it to sell. The number of authorized shares usually exceeds the number of shares issued (and outstanding), often by a large amount. (*Outstanding stock* refers to issued stock held by stockholders.) No formal journal entry is required for stock authorization. A corporation must apply to the state for a change in its charter if it wishes to issue more shares than previously authorized. A corporation discloses the number of shares authorized in the equity section of its balance sheet or notes. **Apple**'s balance sheet in Appendix A reports 1.8 billion common shares authorized as of the start of its 2010 fiscal year.

Subcategories of Authorized Stock

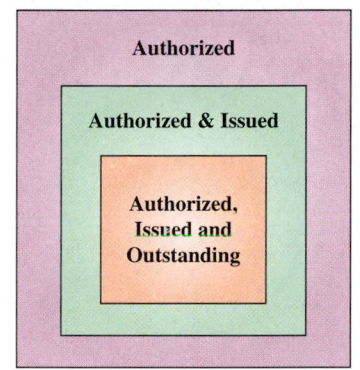

Selling (Issuing) Stock A corporation can sell stock directly or indirectly. To *sell directly,* it advertises its stock issuance to potential buyers. This type of issuance is most common with privately held corporations. To *sell indirectly,* a corporation pays a brokerage house (investment banker) to issue its stock. Some brokerage houses *underwrite* an indirect issuance of stock; that is, they buy the stock from the corporation and take all gains or losses from its resale.

Market Value of Stock **Market value per share** is the price at which a stock is bought and sold. Expected future earnings, dividends, growth, and other company and economic factors influence market value. Traded stocks' market values are available daily in newspapers such as *The Wall Street Journal* and online. The current market value of previously issued shares (for example, the price of stock in trades between investors) does not impact the issuing corporation's stockholders' equity.

Classes of Stock When all authorized shares have the same rights and characteristics, the stock is called *common stock.* A corporation is sometimes authorized to issue more than one class of stock, including preferred stock and different classes of common stock. **American Greetings**, for instance, has two types of common stock: Class A stock has 1 vote per share and Class B stock has 10 votes per share.

Par Value Stock **Par value stock** is stock that is assigned a **par value,** which is an amount assigned per share by the corporation in its charter. For example, **Palm**'s common stock has a par value of $0.001. Other commonly assigned par values are $10, $5, $1 and $0.01. There is no restriction on the assigned par value. In many states, the par value of a stock establishes **minimum legal capital,** which refers to the least amount that the buyers of stock must contribute to the corporation or be subject to paying at a future date. For example, if a corporation issues 1,000 shares of $10 par value stock, the corporation's minimum legal capital in these states would be $10,000. Minimum legal capital is intended to protect a corporation's creditors. Since creditors cannot demand payment from stockholders' personal assets, their claims are limited to the corporation's assets and any minimum legal capital. At liquidation, creditor claims are paid before any amounts are distributed to stockholders.

Point: Managers are motivated to set a low par value when minimum legal capital or state issuance taxes are based on par value.

Point: Minimum legal capital was intended to protect creditors by requiring a minimum level of net assets.

No-Par Value Stock **No-par value stock,** or simply *no-par stock,* is stock *not* assigned a value per share by the corporate charter. Its advantage is that it can be issued at any price without the possibility of a minimum legal capital deficiency.

Point: Par, no-par, and stated value do *not* set the stock's market value.

EXHIBIT 11.3

Equity Composition

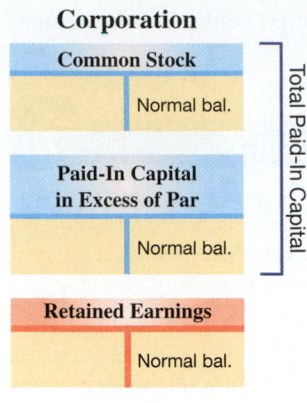

Point: Paid-in capital comes from stock-related transactions, whereas retained earnings comes from operations.

Stated Value Stock Stated value stock is no-par stock to which the directors assign a "stated" value per share. Stated value per share becomes the minimum legal capital per share in this case.

Stockholders' Equity A corporation's equity is known as **stockholders' equity,** also called *shareholders' equity* or *corporate capital.* Stockholders' equity consists of (1) paid-in (or contributed) capital and (2) retained earnings; see Exhibit 11.3. **Paid-in capital** is the total amount of cash and other assets the corporation receives from its stockholders in exchange for its stock. **Retained earnings** is the cumulative net income (and loss) not distributed as dividends to its stockholders.

Decision Insight

Stock Quote The **Best Buy** stock quote is interpreted as (left to right): **Hi,** highest price in past 52 weeks; **Lo,** lowest price in past 52 weeks;

52 Weeks				Yld		Vol				Net
Hi	Lo	Sym	Div	%	PE	mil.	Hi	Lo	Close	Chg
54.15	41.85	BBY	0.13	0.98	19	7.2	53.14	52.36	52.91	+0.20

Sym, company exchange symbol; **Div,** dividends paid per share in past year; **Yld %,** dividend divided by closing price; **PE,** stock price per share divided by earnings per share; **Vol mil.,** number (in millions) of shares traded; **Hi,** highest price for the day; **Lo,** lowest price for the day; **Close,** closing price for the day; **Net Chg,** change in closing price from prior day. ■

Quick Check   Answers — p. 481

1. Which of the following is *not* a characteristic of the corporate form of business? (*a*) Ease of capital accumulation, (*b*) Stockholder responsibility for corporate debts, (*c*) Ease in transferability of ownership rights, or (*d*) Double taxation.
2. Why is a corporation's income said to be taxed twice?
3. What is a proxy?

COMMON STOCK

P1 Record the issuance of corporate stock.

Accounting for the issuance of common stock affects only paid-in (contributed) capital accounts; no retained earnings accounts are affected.

Issuing Par Value Stock

Par value stock can be issued at par, at a premium (above par), or at a discount (below par). In each case, stock can be exchanged for either cash or noncash assets.

Issuing Par Value Stock at Par When common stock is issued at par value, we record amounts for both the asset(s) received and the par value stock issued. To illustrate, the entry to record Dillon Snowboards' issuance of 30,000 shares of $10 par value stock for $300,000 cash on June 5, 2011, follows.

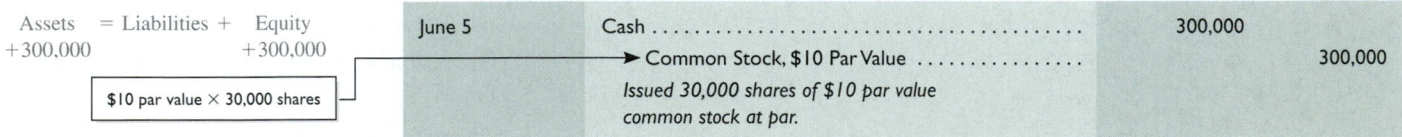

Exhibit 11.4 shows the stockholders' equity of Dillon Snowboards at year-end 2011 (its first year of operations) after income of $65,000 and no dividend payments.

Stockholders' Equity	
Common Stock—$10 par value; 50,000 shares authorized;	
30,000 shares issued and outstanding	$300,000
Retained earnings	65,000
Total stockholders' equity	$365,000

EXHIBIT 11.4

Stockholders' Equity for Stock Issued at Par

Issuing Par Value Stock at a Premium   A **premium on stock** occurs when a corporation sells its stock for more than par (or stated) value. To illustrate, if Dillon Snowboards issues its $10 par value common stock at $12 per share, its stock is sold at a $2 per share premium. The premium, known as **paid-in capital in excess of par value,** is reported as part of equity; it is not revenue and is not listed on the income statement. The entry to record Dillon Snowboards' issuance of 30,000 shares of $10 par value stock for $12 per share on June 5, 2011, follows

Point: A *premium* is the amount by which issue price exceeds par (or stated) value. It is recorded in the "Paid-In Capital in Excess of Par Value, Common Stock" account; also called "Additional Paid-In Capital, Common Stock."

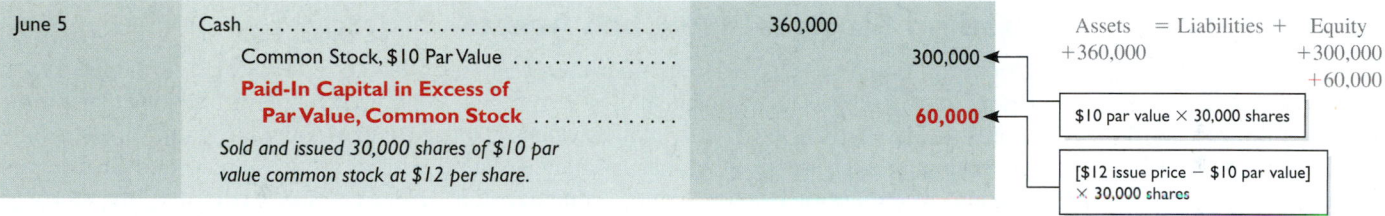

The Paid-In Capital in Excess of Par Value account is added to the par value of the stock in the equity section of the balance sheet as shown in Exhibit 11.5.

Point: The *Paid-In Capital* terminology is interchangeable with *Contributed Capital.*

EXHIBIT 11.5

Stockholders' Equity for Stock Issued at a Premium

Stockholders' Equity	
Common Stock—$10 par value; 50,000 shares authorized;	
30,000 shares issued and outstanding	$300,000
Paid-in capital in excess of par value, common stock	**60,000**
Retained earnings	65,000
Total stockholders' equity	$425,000

Issuing Par Value Stock at a Discount   A **discount on stock** occurs when a corporation sells its stock for less than par (or stated) value. Most states prohibit the issuance of stock at a discount. In states that allow stock to be issued at a discount, its buyers usually become contingently liable to creditors for the discount. If stock is issued at a discount, the amount by which issue price is less than par is debited to a *Discount on Common Stock* account, a contra to the common stock account, and its balance is subtracted from the par value of stock in the equity section of the balance sheet. This discount is not an expense and does not appear on the income statement.

Point: Retained earnings can be negative, reflecting accumulated losses. Amazon.com had an accumulated deficit of $730 million at the start of 2009.

Issuing No-Par Value Stock

When no-par stock is issued and is not assigned a stated value, the amount the corporation receives becomes legal capital and is recorded as Common Stock. This means that the entire proceeds are credited to a no-par stock account. To illustrate, a corporation records its October 20 issuance of 1,000 shares of no-par stock for $40 cash per share as follows.

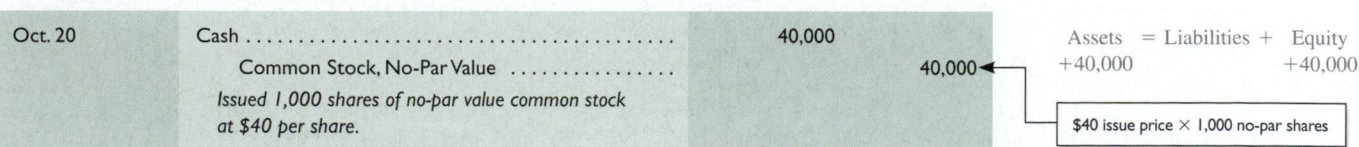

Frequency of Stock Types

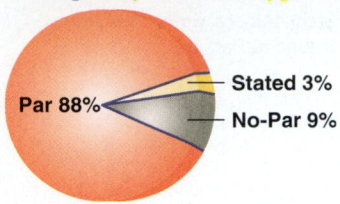

Par 88%
Stated 3%
No-Par 9%

Issuing Stated Value Stock

When no-par stock is issued and assigned a stated value, its stated value becomes legal capital and is credited to a stated value stock account. Assuming that stated value stock is issued at an amount in excess of stated value (the usual case), the excess is credited to Paid-In Capital in Excess of Stated Value, Common Stock, which is reported in the stockholders' equity section. To illustrate, a corporation that issues 1,000 shares of no-par common stock having a stated value of $40 per share in return for $50 cash per share records this as follows.

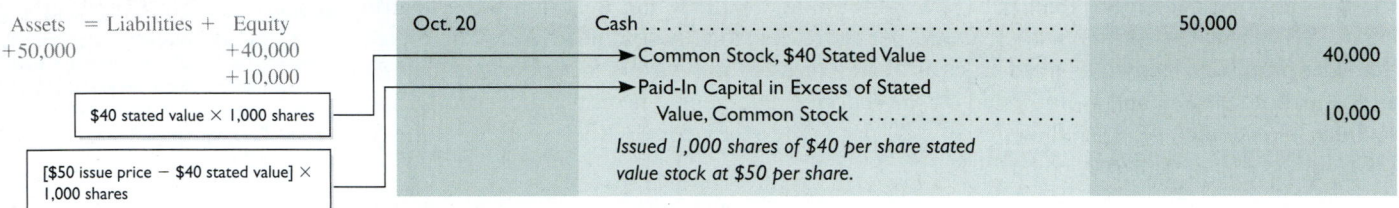

Assets	= Liabilities +	Equity
+50,000		+40,000
		+10,000

$40 stated value × 1,000 shares

[$50 issue price − $40 stated value] × 1,000 shares

Oct. 20	Cash	50,000	
	Common Stock, $40 Stated Value		40,000
	Paid-In Capital in Excess of Stated		
	Value, Common Stock		10,000
	Issued 1,000 shares of $40 per share stated value stock at $50 per share.		

Issuing Stock for Noncash Assets

Point: Stock issued for noncash assets should be recorded at the market value of either the stock or the noncash asset, whichever is more clearly determinable.

A corporation can receive assets other than cash in exchange for its stock. (It can also assume liabilities on the assets received such as a mortgage on property received.) The corporation records the assets received at their market values as of the date of the transaction. The stock given in exchange is recorded at its par (or stated) value with any excess recorded in the Paid-In Capital in Excess of Par (or Stated) Value account. (If no-par stock is issued, the stock is recorded at the assets' market value.) To illustrate, the entry to record receipt of land valued at $105,000 in return for issuance of 4,000 shares of $20 par value common stock on June 10 is

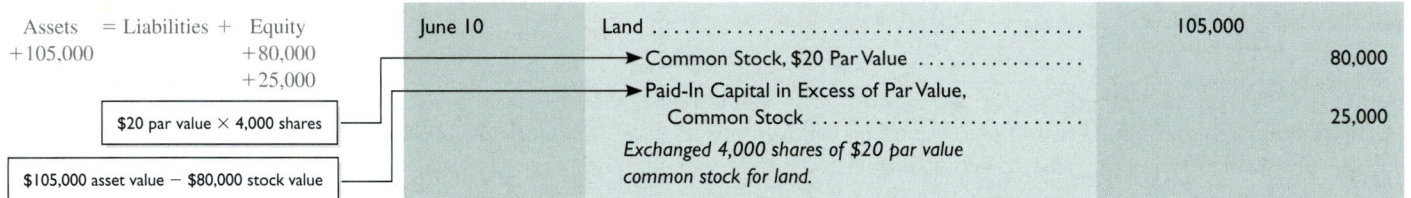

Assets	= Liabilities +	Equity
+105,000		+80,000
		+25,000

$20 par value × 4,000 shares

$105,000 asset value − $80,000 stock value

June 10	Land	105,000	
	Common Stock, $20 Par Value		80,000
	Paid-In Capital in Excess of Par Value,		
	Common Stock		25,000
	Exchanged 4,000 shares of $20 par value common stock for land.		

Point: Any type of stock can be issued for noncash assets.

A corporation sometimes gives shares of its stock to promoters in exchange for their services in organizing the corporation, which the corporation records as **Organization Expenses.** The entry to record receipt of services valued at $12,000 in organizing the corporation in return for 600 shares of $15 par value common stock on June 5 is

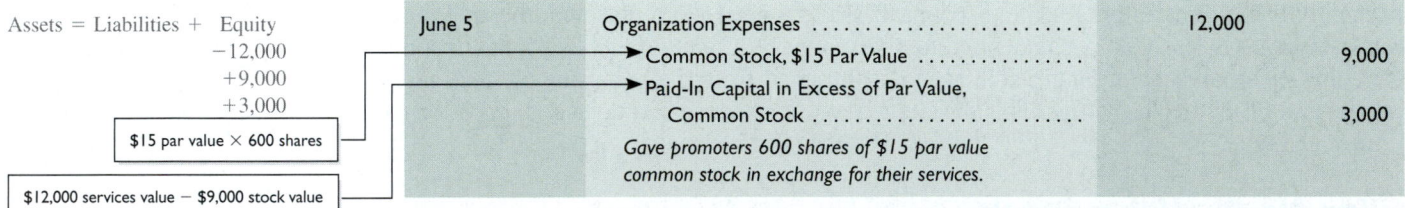

Assets = Liabilities +	Equity
	−12,000
	+9,000
	+3,000

$15 par value × 600 shares

$12,000 services value − $9,000 stock value

June 5	Organization Expenses	12,000	
	Common Stock, $15 Par Value		9,000
	Paid-In Capital in Excess of Par Value,		
	Common Stock		3,000
	Gave promoters 600 shares of $15 par value common stock in exchange for their services.		

Quick Check

Answers — p. 481

4. A company issues 7,000 shares of its $10 par value common stock in exchange for equipment valued at $105,000. The entry to record this transaction includes a credit to (*a*) Paid-In Capital in Excess of Par Value, Common Stock, for $35,000. (*b*) Retained Earnings for $35,000. (*c*) Common Stock, $10 Par Value, for $105,000.

5. What is a premium on stock issuance?

6. Who is intended to be protected by minimum legal capital?

DIVIDENDS

This section describes both cash and stock dividend transactions.

Cash Dividends

The decision to pay cash dividends rests with the board of directors and involves more than evaluating the amounts of retained earnings and cash. The directors, for instance, may decide to keep the cash to invest in the corporation's growth, to meet emergencies, to take advantage of unexpected opportunities, or to pay off debt. Alternatively, many corporations pay cash dividends to their stockholders at regular dates. These cash flows provide a return to investors and almost always affect the stock's market value.

P2	Record transactions involving cash dividends, stock dividends, and stock splits.

Accounting for Cash Dividends   Dividend payment involves three important dates: declaration, record, and payment. **Date of declaration** is the date the directors vote to declare and pay a dividend. This creates a legal liability of the corporation to its stockholders. **Date of record** is the future date specified by the directors for identifying those stockholders listed in the corporation's records to receive dividends. The date of record usually follows the date of declaration by at least two weeks. Persons who own stock on the date of record receive dividends. **Date of payment** is the date when the corporation makes payment; it follows the date of record by enough time to allow the corporation to arrange checks, money transfers, or other means to pay dividends.

Percent of Corporations Paying Dividends

Cash Dividend to Common — 75%

Cash Dividend to Preferred — 22%

0%   20%   40%   60%   80%   100%

To illustrate, the entry to record a January 9 declaration of a $1 per share cash dividend by the directors of Z-Tech, Inc., with 5,000 outstanding shares is

Date of Declaration

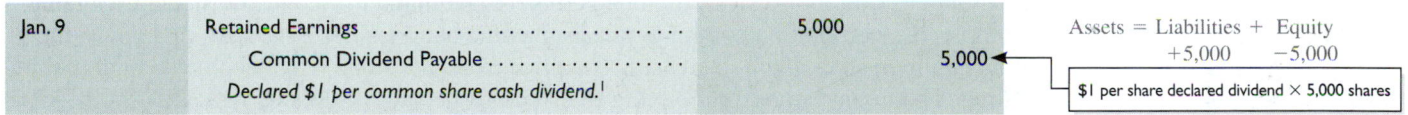

Jan. 9	Retained Earnings	5,000	
	Common Dividend Payable		5,000
	Declared $1 per common share cash dividend.[1]		

Assets = Liabilities + Equity
        +5,000   −5,000

$1 per share declared dividend × 5,000 shares

Common Dividend Payable is a current liability. The date of record for the Z-Tech dividend is January 22. *No formal journal entry is needed on the date of record.* The February 1 date of payment requires an entry to record both the settlement of the liability and the reduction of the cash balance, as follows:

Date of Payment

Feb. 1	Common Dividend Payable	5,000	
	Cash		5,000
	Paid $1 per common share cash dividend.		

Assets = Liabilities + Equity
−5,000   −5,000

Deficits and Cash Dividends   A corporation with a debit (abnormal) balance for retained earnings is said to have a **retained earnings deficit,** which arises when a company incurs cumulative losses and/or pays more dividends than total earnings from current and prior years. A deficit is reported as a deduction on the balance sheet, as shown in Exhibit 11.6. Most states prohibit a corporation with a deficit from paying a cash dividend to its stockholders. This legal restriction is designed to protect creditors by preventing distribution of assets to stockholders when the company may be in financial difficulty.

Point: It is often said a dividend is a distribution of retained earnings, but it is more precise to describe a dividend as a distribution of assets to satisfy stockholder claims.

Point: The Retained Earnings Deficit account is also called *Accumulated Deficit.*

---

[1] An alternative entry is to debit Dividends instead of Retained Earnings. The balance in Dividends is then closed to Retained Earnings at the end of the reporting period. The effect is the same: Retained Earnings is decreased and a Dividend Payable is increased. For simplicity, all assignments in this chapter use the Retained Earnings account to record dividend declarations.

EXHIBIT 11.6

Stockholders' Equity
with a Deficit

Common stock—$10 par value, 5,000 shares authorized, issued, and outstanding	$50,000
Retained earnings deficit	**(6,000)**
Total stockholders' equity	$44,000

Some state laws allow cash dividends to be paid by returning a portion of the capital contributed by stockholders. This type of dividend is called a **liquidating cash dividend,** or simply *liquidating dividend,* because it returns a part of the original investment back to the stockholders. This requires a debit entry to one of the contributed capital accounts instead of Retained Earnings at the declaration date.

Point: Amazon.com has never declared a cash dividend.

Quick Check   Answers — p. 482

7. What type of an account is the Common Dividend Payable account?
8. What three crucial dates are involved in the process of paying a cash dividend?
9. When does a dividend become a company's legal obligation?

Stock Dividends

A **stock dividend,** declared by a corporation's directors, is a distribution of additional shares of the corporation's own stock to its stockholders without the receipt of any payment in return. Stock dividends and cash dividends are different. A stock dividend does not reduce assets and equity but instead transfers a portion of equity from retained earnings to contributed capital.

Reasons for Stock Dividends   Stock dividends exist for at least two reasons. First, directors are said to use stock dividends to keep the market price of the stock affordable. For example, if a corporation continues to earn income but does not issue cash dividends, the price of its common stock likely increases. The price of such a stock may become so high that it discourages some investors from buying the stock (especially in lots of 100 and 1,000). When a corporation has a stock dividend, it increases the number of outstanding shares and lowers the per share stock price. Another reason for a stock dividend is to provide evidence of management's confidence that the company is doing well and will continue to do well.

Accounting for Stock Dividends   A stock dividend affects the components of equity by transferring part of retained earnings to contributed capital accounts, sometimes described as *capitalizing* retained earnings. Accounting for a stock dividend depends on whether it is a small or large stock dividend. A **small stock dividend** is a distribution of 25% or less of previously outstanding shares. It is recorded by capitalizing retained earnings for an amount equal to the market value of the shares to be distributed. A **large stock dividend** is a distribution of more than 25% of previously outstanding shares. A large stock dividend is recorded by capitalizing retained earnings for the minimum amount required by state law governing the corporation. Most states require capitalizing retained earnings equal to the par or stated value of the stock.

To illustrate stock dividends, we use the equity section of Quest's balance sheet shown in Exhibit 11.7 just *before* its declaration of a stock dividend on December 31.

EXHIBIT 11.7

Stockholders' Equity *before* Declaring a Stock Dividend

Stockholders' Equity (before dividend)	
Common stock—$10 par value, 15,000 shares authorized,	
10,000 shares issued and outstanding	$100,000
Paid-in capital in excess of par value, common stock	8,000
Retained earnings	35,000
Total stockholders' equity	$143,000

Recording a small stock dividend.   Assume that Quest's directors declare a 10% stock dividend on December 31. This stock dividend of 1,000 shares, computed as 10% of its 10,000 issued and outstanding shares, is to be distributed on January 20 to the stockholders of record on January 15. Since the market price of Quest's stock on December 31 is $15 per share, this small stock dividend declaration is recorded as follows:

Point: Small stock dividends are recorded at market value.

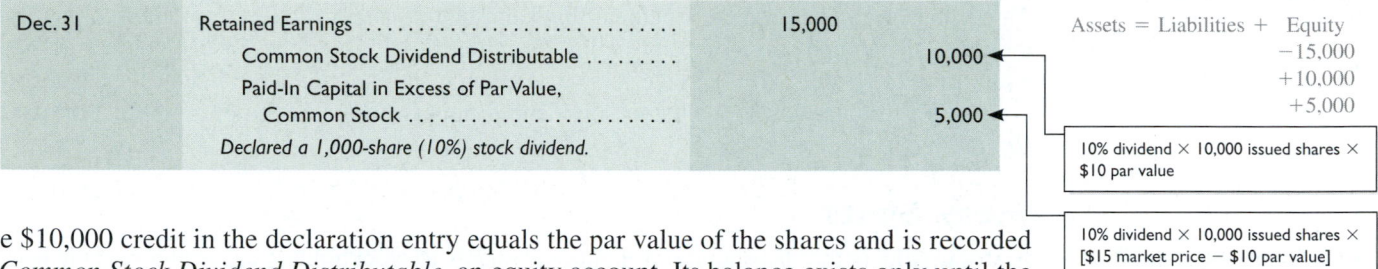

Date of Declaration—Small Stock Dividend

Dec. 31	Retained Earnings	15,000	
	Common Stock Dividend Distributable		10,000
	Paid-In Capital in Excess of Par Value,		
	Common Stock		5,000
	Declared a 1,000-share (10%) stock dividend.		

Assets = Liabilities + Equity
                          −15,000
                          +10,000
                          +5,000

10% dividend × 10,000 issued shares × $10 par value

10% dividend × 10,000 issued shares × [$15 market price − $10 par value]

The $10,000 credit in the declaration entry equals the par value of the shares and is recorded in *Common Stock Dividend Distributable,* an equity account. Its balance exists only until the shares are issued. The $5,000 credit equals the amount by which market value exceeds par value. This amount increases the Paid-In Capital in Excess of Par Value account in anticipation of the issuance of shares. In general, the balance sheet changes in three ways when a stock dividend is declared. First, the amount of equity attributed to common stock increases; for Quest, from $100,000 to $110,000 for 1,000 additional declared shares. Second, paid-in capital in excess of par increases by the excess of market value over par value for the declared shares. Third, retained earnings decreases, reflecting the transfer of amounts to both common stock and paid-in capital in excess of par. The stockholders' equity of Quest is shown in Exhibit 11.8 *after* its 10% stock dividend is declared on December 31—the items impacted are in bold.

Point: The term *Distributable* (not *Payable*) is used for stock dividends. A stock dividend is never a liability because it never reduces assets.

Point: The credit to Paid-In Capital in Excess of Par Value is recorded when the stock dividend is declared. This account is not affected when stock is later distributed.

EXHIBIT 11.8

Stockholders' Equity *after* Declaring a Stock Dividend

Stockholders' Equity (after dividend)	
Common stock—$10 par value, 15,000 shares authorized,	
10,000 shares issued and outstanding	$100,000
Common stock dividend distributable—1,000 shares	**10,000**
Paid-in capital in excess of par value, common stock	**13,000**
Retained earnings	**20,000**
Total stockholders' equity	$143,000

No entry is made on the date of record for a stock dividend. On January 20, the date of payment, Quest distributes the new shares to stockholders and records this entry:

Date of Payment—Small Stock Dividend

Jan. 20	Common Stock Dividend Distributable	10,000	
	Common Stock, $10 Par Value		10,000
	To record issuance of common stock dividend.		

Assets = Liabilities + Equity
                          −10,000
                          +10,000

The combined effect of these stock dividend entries is to transfer (or capitalize) $15,000 of retained earnings to paid-in capital accounts. The amount of capitalized retained earnings equals the market value of the 1,000 issued shares ($15 × 1,000 shares). A stock dividend has no effect on the ownership percent of individual stockholders.

Point: A stock dividend does not affect assets.

Recording a large stock dividend.   A corporation capitalizes retained earnings equal to the minimum amount required by state law for a large stock dividend. For most states, this amount is the par or stated value of the newly issued shares. To illustrate, suppose Quest's board declares a stock dividend of 30% instead of 10% on December 31. Since this dividend is more

Point: Large stock dividends are recorded at par or stated value.

than 25%, it is treated as a large stock dividend. Thus, the par value of the 3,000 dividend shares is capitalized at the date of declaration with this entry:

Date of Declaration—Large Stock Dividend

Dec. 31	Retained Earnings	30,000	
	Common Stock Dividend Distributable		30,000
	Declared a 3,000-share (30%) stock dividend.		

Assets = Liabilities + Equity
−30,000
+30,000

30% dividend × 10,000 issued shares × $10 par value

This transaction decreases retained earnings and increases contributed capital by $30,000. On the date of payment the company debits Common Stock Dividend Distributable and credits Common Stock for $30,000. The effects from a large stock dividend on balance sheet accounts are similar to those for a small stock dividend except for the absence of any effect on paid-in capital in excess of par.

Stock Splits

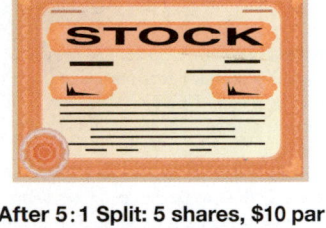

Before 5:1 Split: 1 share, $50 par

After 5:1 Split: 5 shares, $10 par

A **stock split** is the distribution of additional shares to stockholders according to their percent ownership. When a stock split occurs, the corporation "calls in" its outstanding shares and issues more than one new share in exchange for each old share. Splits can be done in any ratio, including 2-for-1, 3-for-1, or higher. Stock splits reduce the par or stated value per share. The reasons for stock splits are similar to those for stock dividends.

To illustrate, CompTec has 100,000 outstanding shares of $20 par value common stock with a current market value of $88 per share. A 2-for-1 stock split cuts par value in half as it replaces 100,000 shares of $20 par value stock with 200,000 shares of $10 par value stock. Market value is reduced from $88 per share to about $44 per share. The split does not affect any equity amounts reported on the balance sheet or any individual stockholder's percent ownership. Both the Paid-In Capital and Retained Earnings accounts are unchanged by a split, and *no journal entry is made.* The only effect on the accounts is a change in the stock account description. CompTec's 2-for-1 split on its $20 par value stock means that after the split, it changes its stock account title to Common Stock, $10 Par Value. This stock's description on the balance sheet also changes to reflect the additional authorized, issued, and outstanding shares and the new par value.

Point: Berkshire Hathaway has resisted a stock split. Its recent stock price was $150,000 per share.

Point: A *reverse stock split* is the opposite of a stock split. It increases both the market value per share and the par or stated value per share with a split ratio less than 1-for-1, such as 1-for-2. A reverse split results in fewer shares.

The difference between stock splits and large stock dividends is often blurred. Many companies report stock splits in their financial statements without calling in the original shares by simply changing their par value. This type of "split" is really a large stock dividend and results in additional shares issued to stockholders by capitalizing retained earnings or transferring other paid-in capital to Common Stock. This approach avoids administrative costs of splitting the stock. **Harley-Davidson** recently declared a 2-for-1 stock split executed in the form of a 100% stock dividend.

Decision Maker   Answer – p. 481

Entrepreneur A company you cofounded and own stock in announces a 50% stock dividend. Has the value of your stock investment increased, decreased, or remained the same? Would it make a difference if it was a 3-for-2 stock split executed in the form of a dividend? ■

Quick Check   Answers – p. 482

10. How does a stock dividend impact assets and retained earnings?
11. What distinguishes a large stock dividend from a small stock dividend?
12. What amount of retained earnings is capitalized for a small stock dividend?

PREFERRED STOCK

C2 Explain characteristics of, and distribute dividends between, common and preferred stock.

A corporation can issue two basic kinds of stock, common and preferred. **Preferred stock** has special rights that give it priority (or senior status) over common stock in one or more areas. Special rights typically include a preference for receiving dividends and for the distribution of assets if the corporation is liquidated. Preferred stock carries all rights of common stock unless the corporate charter nullifies them. Most preferred stock, for instance, does not confer the right to vote. Exhibit 11.9 shows that preferred stock is issued by about one-fourth of corporations. All corporations issue common stock.

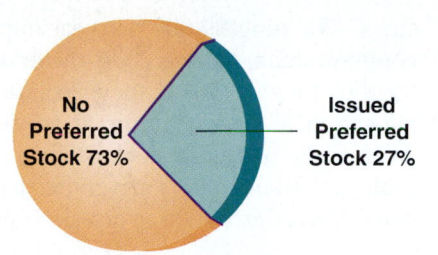

EXHIBIT 11.9

Corporations and Preferred Stock

Issuance of Preferred Stock

Preferred stock usually has a par value. Like common stock, it can be sold at a price different from par. Preferred stock is recorded in its own separate capital accounts. To illustrate, if Dillon Snowboards issues 50 shares of $100 par value preferred stock for $6,000 cash on July 1, 2011, the entry is

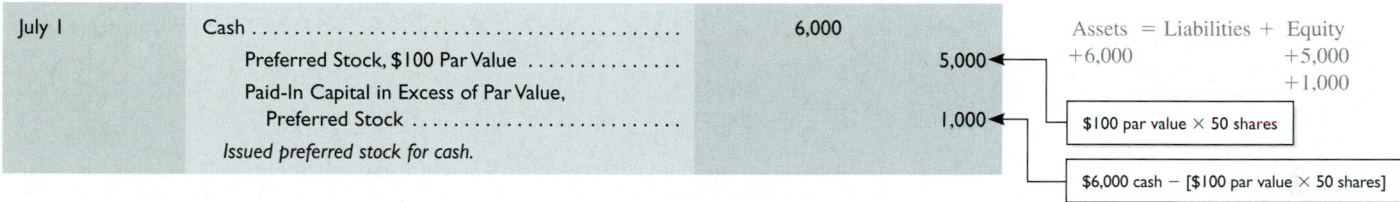

The equity section of the year-end balance sheet for Dillon Snowboards, including preferred stock, is shown in Exhibit 11.10. (This exhibit assumes that common stock was issued at par.) Issuing no-par preferred stock is similar to issuing no-par common stock. Also, the entries for issuing preferred stock for noncash assets are similar to those for common stock.

Stockholders' Equity	
Common stock—$10 par value; 50,000 shares authorized; 30,000 shares issued and outstanding	$300,000
Preferred stock—$100 par value; 1,000 shares authorized; 50 shares issued and outstanding	5,000
Paid-in capital in excess of par value, preferred stock	1,000
Retained earnings	65,000
Total stockholders' equity	$371,000

EXHIBIT 11.10

Stockholders' Equity with Common and Preferred Stock

Dividend Preference of Preferred Stock

Preferred stock usually carries a preference for dividends, meaning that preferred stockholders are allocated their dividends before any dividends are allocated to common stockholders. The dividends allocated to preferred stockholders are usually expressed as a dollar amount per share or a percent applied to par value. A preference for dividends does *not* ensure dividends. If the directors do not declare a dividend, neither the preferred nor the common stockholders receive one.

Cumulative or Noncumulative Dividend   Most preferred stocks carry a cumulative dividend right. **Cumulative preferred stock** has a right to be paid both the current and all prior periods' unpaid dividends before any dividend is paid to common stockholders. When preferred stock is cumulative and the directors either do not declare a dividend to preferred stockholders or declare one that does not cover the total amount of cumulative dividend, the unpaid dividend amount is called **dividend in arrears.** Accumulation of dividends in arrears on cumulative preferred stock does not guarantee they will be paid. **Noncumulative preferred stock** confers no right to prior periods' unpaid dividends if they were not declared in those prior periods.

To illustrate the difference between cumulative and noncumulative preferred stock, assume that a corporation's outstanding stock includes (1) 1,000 shares of $100 par, 9% preferred

Point: Dividend preference does not imply that preferred stockholders receive more dividends than common stockholders, nor does it guarantee a dividend.

stock—yielding $9,000 per year in potential dividends, and (2) 4,000 shares of $50 par value common stock. During 2010, the first year of operations, the directors declare cash dividends of $5,000. In year 2011, they declare cash dividends of $42,000. See Exhibit 11.11 for the allocation of dividends for these two years. Allocation of year 2011 dividends depends on whether the preferred stock is noncumulative or cumulative. With noncumulative preferred, the preferred stockholders never receive the $4,000 skipped in 2010. If the preferred stock is cumulative, the $4,000 in arrears is paid in 2011 before any other dividends are paid.

EXHIBIT 11.11

Allocation of Dividends (noncumulative vs. cumulative preferred stock)

Example: What dividends do cumulative preferred stockholders receive in 2011 if the corporation paid only $2,000 of dividends in 2010? How does this affect dividends to common stockholders in 2011? *Answers:* $16,000 ($7,000 dividends in arrears, plus $9,000 current preferred dividends). Dividends to common stockholders decrease to $26,000.

	Preferred	Common
Preferred Stock Is Noncumulative		
Year 2010	$ 5,000	$ 0
Year 2011		
Step 1: Current year's preferred dividend	$ 9,000	
Step 2: Remainder to common		$33,000
Preferred Stock Is Cumulative		
Year 2010	$ 5,000	$ 0
Year 2011		
Step 1: Dividend in arrears	$ 4,000	
Step 2: Current year's preferred dividend	9,000	
Step 3: Remainder to common		$29,000
Totals for year 2011	$13,000	$29,000

A liability for a dividend does not exist until the directors declare a dividend. If a preferred dividend date passes and the corporation's board fails to declare the dividend on its cumulative preferred stock, the dividend in arrears is not a liability. The *full-disclosure principle* requires a corporation to report (usually in a note) the amount of preferred dividends in arrears as of the balance sheet date.

Participating or Nonparticipating Dividend   **Nonparticipating preferred stock** has a feature that limits dividends to a maximum amount each year. This maximum is often stated as a percent of the stock's par value or as a specific dollar amount per share. Once preferred stockholders receive this amount, the common stockholders receive any and all additional dividends. **Participating preferred stock** has a feature allowing preferred stockholders to share with common stockholders in any dividends paid in excess of the percent or dollar amount stated on the preferred stock. This participation feature does not apply until common stockholders receive dividends equal to the preferred stock's dividend percent. Many corporations are authorized to issue participating preferred stock but rarely do, and most managers never expect to issue it.[2]

Convertible Preferred Stock

Preferred stock is more attractive to investors if it carries a right to exchange preferred shares for a fixed number of common shares. **Convertible preferred stock** gives holders the option to

---

[2] Participating preferred stock is usually authorized as a defense against a possible corporate *takeover* by an "unfriendly" investor (or a group of investors) who intends to buy enough voting common stock to gain control. Taking a term from spy novels, the financial world refers to this type of plan as a *poison pill* that a company swallows if enemy investors threaten its capture. A poison pill usually works as follows: A corporation's common stockholders on a given date are granted the right to purchase a large amount of participating preferred stock at a very low price. This right to purchase preferred shares is *not* transferable. If an unfriendly investor buys a large block of common shares (whose right to purchase participating preferred shares does *not* transfer to this buyer), the board can issue preferred shares at a low price to the remaining common shareholders who retained the right to purchase. Future dividends are then divided between the newly issued participating preferred shares and the common shares. This usually transfers value from common shares to preferred shares, causing the unfriendly investor's common stock to lose much of its value and reduces the potential benefit of a hostile takeover.

exchange their preferred shares for common shares at a specified rate. When a company prospers and its common stock increases in value, convertible preferred stockholders can share in this success by converting their preferred stock into more valuable common stock.

Callable Preferred Stock

Callable preferred stock gives the issuing corporation the right to purchase (retire) this stock from its holders at specified future prices and dates. The amount paid to call and retire a preferred share is its **call price,** or *redemption value,* and is set when the stock is issued. The call price normally includes the stock's par value plus a premium giving holders additional return on their investment. When the issuing corporation calls and retires a preferred stock, the terms of the agreement often require it to pay the call price *and* any dividends in arrears.

Point: The issuing corporation has the right, or option, to retire its callable preferred stock.

 **IFRS**

Like U.S. GAAP, IFRS requires that preferred stocks be classified as debt or equity based on analysis of the stock's contractual terms. However, IFRS uses different criteria for such classification. ■

Reasons for Issuing Preferred Stock

Corporations issue preferred stock for several reasons. One is to raise capital without sacrificing control. For example, suppose a company's organizers have $100,000 cash to invest and organize a corporation that needs $200,000 of capital to start. If they sell $200,000 worth of common stock (with $100,000 to the organizers), they would have only 50% control and would need to negotiate extensively with other stockholders in making policy. However, if they issue $100,000 worth of common stock to themselves and sell outsiders $100,000 of 8%, cumulative preferred stock with no voting rights, they retain control.

A second reason to issue preferred stock is to boost the return earned by common stockholders. To illustrate, suppose a corporation's organizers expect to earn an annual after-tax income of $24,000 on an investment of $200,000. If they sell and issue $200,000 worth of common stock, the $24,000 income produces a 12% return on the $200,000 of common stockholders' equity. However, if they issue $100,000 of 8% preferred stock to outsiders and $100,000 of common stock to themselves, their own return increases to 16% per year, as shown in Exhibit 11.12.

Net (after-tax) income	$24,000
Less preferred dividends at 8%	(8,000)
Balance to common stockholders	$16,000
Return to common stockholders ($16,000/$100,000)	16%

EXHIBIT 11.12

Return to Common Stockholders When Preferred Stock Is Issued

Common stockholders earn 16% instead of 12% because assets contributed by preferred stockholders are invested to earn $12,000 while the preferred dividend is only $8,000. Use of preferred stock to increase return to common stockholders is an example of **financial leverage** (also called *trading on the equity*). As a general rule, when the dividend rate on preferred stock is less than the rate the corporation earns on its assets, the effect of issuing preferred stock is to increase (or *lever)* the rate earned by common stockholders.

Other reasons for issuing preferred stock include its appeal to some investors who believe that the corporation's common stock is too risky or that the expected return on common stock is too low.

Point: Financial leverage also occurs when debt is issued and the interest rate paid on it is less than the rate earned from using the assets the creditors lend the company.

 **Decision Maker**   Answer — p. 481

Concert Organizer   Assume that you alter your business strategy from organizing concerts targeted at under 1,000 people to those targeted at between 5,000 to 20,000 people. You also incorporate because of increased risk of lawsuits and a desire to issue stock for financing. It is important that you control the company for decisions on whom to schedule. What types of stock do you offer? ■

Quick Check

Answers — p. 482

13. In what ways does preferred stock often have priority over common stock?

14. Increasing the return to common stockholders by issuing preferred stock is an example of (*a*) Financial leverage. (*b*) Cumulative earnings. (*c*) Dividend in arrears.

15. A corporation has issued and outstanding (i) 9,000 shares of $50 par value, 10% cumulative, nonparticipating preferred stock and (ii) 27,000 shares of $10 par value common stock. No dividends have been declared for the two prior years. During the current year, the corporation declares $288,000 in dividends. The amount paid to common shareholders is (*a*) $243,000. (*b*) $153,000. (*c*) $135,000.

TREASURY STOCK

P3 Record purchases and sales of treasury stock and the retirement of stock.

Corporations and Treasury Stock

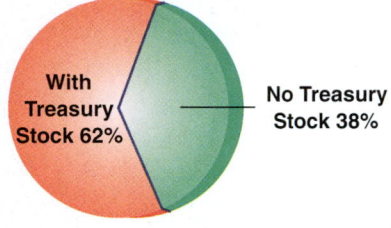

Corporations acquire shares of their own stock for several reasons: (1) to use their shares to acquire another corporation, (2) to purchase shares to avoid a hostile takeover of the company, (3) to reissue them to employees as compensation, and (4) to maintain a strong market for their stock or to show management confidence in the current price.

A corporation's reacquired shares are called **treasury stock,** which is similar to unissued stock in several ways: (1) neither treasury stock nor unissued stock is an asset, (2) neither receives cash dividends or stock dividends, and (3) neither allows the exercise of voting rights. However, treasury stock does differ from unissued stock in one major way: The corporation can resell treasury stock at less than par without having the buyers incur a liability, provided it was originally issued at par value or higher. Treasury stock purchases also require management to exercise ethical sensitivity because funds are being paid to specific stockholders instead of all stockholders. Managers must be sure the purchase is in the best interest of all stockholders. These concerns cause companies to fully disclose treasury stock transactions.

Purchasing Treasury Stock

Purchasing treasury stock reduces the corporation's assets and equity by equal amounts. (We describe the *cost method* of accounting for treasury stock, which is the most widely used method. The *par value* method is another method explained in advanced courses.) To illustrate, Exhibit 11.13 shows Cyber Corporation's account balances *before* any treasury stock purchase (Cyber has no liabilities).

EXHIBIT 11.13

Account Balances *before* Purchasing Treasury Stock

Assets		Stockholders' Equity	
Cash	$ 30,000	Common stock—$10 par; 10,000 shares	
Other assets	95,000	authorized, issued, and outstanding	$100,000
		Retained earnings	25,000
Total assets	$125,000	Total stockholders' equity	$125,000

Cyber then purchases 1,000 of its own shares for $11,500 on May 1, which is recorded as follows.

Assets = Liabilities + Equity
−11,500   −11,500

$11.50 cost per share × 1,000 shares

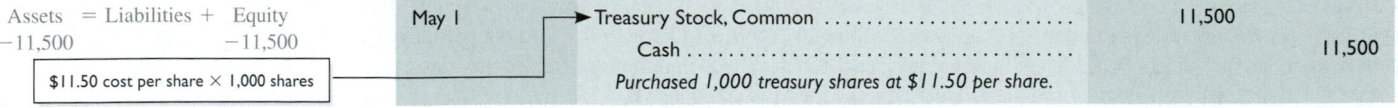

May 1	Treasury Stock, Common	11,500	
	Cash		11,500
	Purchased 1,000 treasury shares at $11.50 per share.		

This entry reduces equity through the debit to the Treasury Stock account, which is a contra equity account. Exhibit 11.14 shows account balances *after* this transaction.

Assets		Stockholders' Equity	
Cash	$ 18,500	Common stock—$10 par; 10,000 shares	
Other assets	95,000	authorized and issued; 1,000 shares in treasury	$100,000
		Retained earnings, $11,500 restricted by	
		treasury stock purchase	25,000
		Less cost of treasury stock	**(11,500)**
Total assets	$113,500	Total stockholders' equity	$113,500

EXHIBIT 11.14

Account Balances *after* Purchasing Treasury Stock

The treasury stock purchase reduces Cyber's cash, total assets, and total equity by $11,500 but does not reduce the balance of either the Common Stock or the Retained Earnings account. The equity reduction is reported by deducting the cost of treasury stock in the equity section. Also, two disclosures are evident. First, the stock description reveals that 1,000 issued shares are in treasury, leaving only 9,000 shares still outstanding. Second, the description for retained earnings reveals that it is partly restricted.

Point: The Treasury Stock account is *not* an asset. Treasury stock does not carry voting or dividend rights.

Point: A treasury stock purchase is also called a *stock buyback*.

Reissuing Treasury Stock

Treasury stock can be reissued by selling it at cost, above cost, or below cost.

Selling Treasury Stock at Cost If treasury stock is reissued at cost, the entry is the reverse of the one made to record the purchase. For instance, if on May 21 Cyber reissues 100 of the treasury shares purchased on May 1 at the same $11.50 per share cost, the entry is

May 21	Cash	1,150	
	Treasury Stock, Common		1,150
	Received $11.50 per share for 100 treasury shares costing $11.50 per share.		

Assets = Liabilities + Equity
+1,150   +1,150

$11.50 cost per share × 100 shares

Selling Treasury Stock *above* Cost If treasury stock is sold for more than cost, the amount received in excess of cost is credited to the Paid-In Capital, Treasury Stock account. This account is reported as a separate item in the stockholders' equity section. No gain is ever reported from the sale of treasury stock. To illustrate, if Cyber receives $12 cash per share for 400 treasury shares costing $11.50 per share on June 3, the entry is

Point: Treasury stock does not represent ownership. A company cannot own a part of itself.

June 3	Cash	4,800	
	Treasury Stock, Common		4,600
	Paid-In Capital, Treasury Stock		200
	Received $12 per share for 400 treasury shares costing $11.50 per share.		

Assets = Liabilities + Equity
+4,800   +4,600
                                +200

$11.50 cost per share × 400 shares

[$12 issue price − $11.50 cost per share] × 400 shares

Selling Treasury Stock *below* Cost When treasury stock is sold below cost, the entry to record the sale depends on whether the Paid-In Capital, Treasury Stock account has a credit balance. If it has a zero balance, the excess of cost over the sales price is debited to Retained Earnings. If the Paid-In Capital, Treasury Stock account has a credit balance, it is debited for the excess of the cost over the selling price but not to exceed the balance in this account. When the credit balance in this paid-in capital account is eliminated, any remaining difference between the cost and selling price is debited to Retained Earnings. To illustrate, if Cyber sells its remaining 500 shares of treasury stock at $10 per share on July 10, equity is

Point: The phrase *treasury stock* is believed to arise from the fact that reacquired stock is held in a corporation's treasury.

Point: The Paid-In Capital, Treasury Stock account can have a zero or credit balance but never a debit balance.

reduced by $750 (500 shares × $1.50 per share excess of cost over selling price), as shown in this entry:

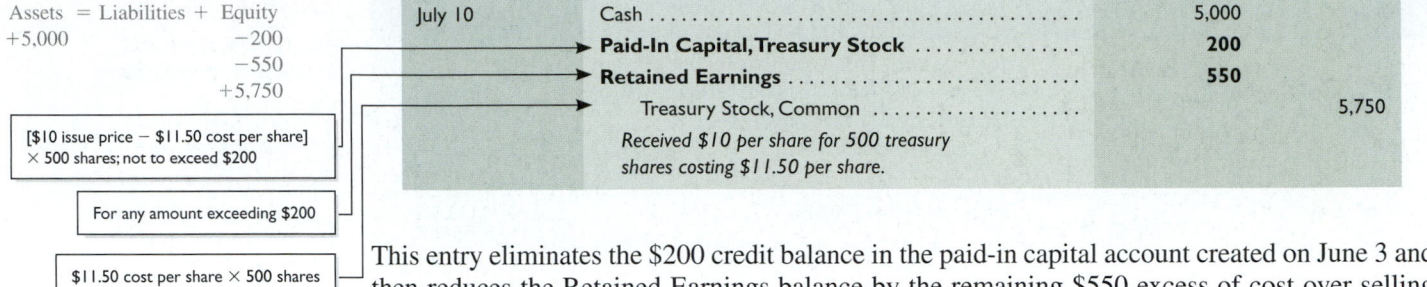

Assets = Liabilities + Equity
+5,000   −200
                          −550
                        +5,750

[$10 issue price − $11.50 cost per share] × 500 shares; not to exceed $200

For any amount exceeding $200

$11.50 cost per share × 500 shares

July 10	Cash	5,000	
	Paid-In Capital, Treasury Stock	200	
	Retained Earnings	550	
	Treasury Stock, Common		5,750
	Received $10 per share for 500 treasury shares costing $11.50 per share.		

This entry eliminates the $200 credit balance in the paid-in capital account created on June 3 and then reduces the Retained Earnings balance by the remaining $550 excess of cost over selling price. A company never reports a loss (or gain) from the sale of treasury stock.

Retiring Stock

Point: Recording stock retirement results in canceling the equity from the original issuance of the shares.

A corporation can purchase its own stock and retire it. Retiring stock reduces the number of issued shares. Retired stock is the same as authorized and unissued shares. Purchases and retirements of stock are permissible under state law only if they do not jeopardize the interests of creditors and stockholders. When stock is purchased for retirement, we remove all capital amounts related to the retired shares. If the purchase price exceeds the net amount removed, this excess is debited to Retained Earnings. If the net amount removed from all capital accounts exceeds the purchase price, this excess is credited to the Paid-In Capital from Retirement of Stock account. A company's assets and equity are always reduced by the amount paid for the retiring stock.

Quick Check   Answers — p. 482

16. Purchase of treasury stock (*a*) has no effect on assets; (*b*) reduces total assets and total equity by equal amounts; or (*c*) is recorded with a debit to Retained Earnings.

17. Southern Co. purchases shares of Northern Corp. Should either company classify these shares as treasury stock?

18. How does treasury stock affect the authorized, issued, and outstanding shares?

19. When a company purchases treasury stock, (*a*) retained earnings are restricted by the amount paid; (*b*) Retained Earnings is credited; or (*c*) it is retired.

REPORTING OF EQUITY

 C3 Explain the items reported in retained earnings.

Statement of Retained Earnings

Retained earnings generally consist of a company's cumulative net income less any net losses and dividends declared since its inception. Retained earnings are part of stockholders' claims on the company's net assets, but this does *not* imply that a certain amount of cash or other assets is available to pay stockholders. For example, **Research In Motion** has $5,274,365 thousand in retained earnings, but only $1,550,861 thousand in cash. This section describes events and transactions affecting retained earnings and how retained earnings are reported.

Restrictions and Appropriations   The term **restricted retained earnings** refers to both statutory and contractual restrictions. A common *statutory* (or *legal*) *restriction* is to limit treasury stock purchases to the amount of retained earnings. The balance sheet in Exhibit 11.14 provides an example. A common *contractual restriction* involves loan agreements that restrict paying dividends beyond a specified amount or percent of retained earnings. Restrictions are usually described in the notes. The term **appropriated retained earnings** refers to a voluntary transfer of amounts from the Retained Earnings account to the Appropriated Retained Earnings account to inform users of special activities that require funds.

Prior Period Adjustments   **Prior period adjustments** are corrections of material errors in prior period financial statements. These errors include arithmetic mistakes, unacceptable accounting, and missed facts. Prior period adjustments are reported in the *statement of retained earnings* (or the statement of stockholders' equity), net of any income tax effects. Prior period adjustments result in changing the beginning balance of retained earnings for events occurring prior to the earliest period reported in the current set of financial statements. To illustrate, assume that ComUS makes an error in a 2009 journal entry for the purchase of land by incorrectly debiting an expense account. When this is discovered in 2011, the statement of retained earnings includes a prior period adjustment, as shown in Exhibit 11.15. This exhibit also shows the usual format of the statement of retained earnings.

Point: If a year 2009 error is discovered in 2010, the company records the adjustment in 2010. But if the financial statements include 2009 and 2010 figures, the statements report the correct amounts for 2009, and a note describes the correction.

EXHIBIT 11.15

Statement of Retained Earnings with a Prior Period Adjustment

ComUS Statement of Retained Earnings For Year Ended December 31, 2011	
Retained earnings, Dec. 31, 2010, as previously reported	$4,745,000
Prior period adjustment	
Cost of land incorrectly expensed (net of $63,000 income taxes)	147,000
Retained earnings, Dec. 31, 2010, as adjusted	4,892,000
Plus net income	1,224,300
Less cash dividends declared	(301,800)
Retained earnings, Dec. 31, 2011	$5,814,500

Many items reported in financial statements are based on estimates. Future events are certain to reveal that some of these estimates were inaccurate even when based on the best data available at the time. These inaccuracies are *not* considered errors and are *not* reported as prior period adjustments. Instead, they are identified as **changes in accounting estimates** and are accounted for in current and future periods. To illustrate, we know that depreciation is based on estimated useful lives and salvage values. As time passes and new information becomes available, managers may need to change these estimates and the resulting depreciation expense for current and future periods.

Point: Accounting for changes in estimates is sometimes criticized as two wrongs to make a right. Consider a change in an asset's life. Depreciation neither before nor after the change is the amount computed if the revised estimate were originally selected. Regulators chose this approach to avoid restating prior period numbers.

Closing Process   The closing process was explained earlier in the book as: (1) Close credit balances in revenue accounts to Income Summary, (2) Close debit balances in expense accounts to Income Summary, and (3) Close Income Summary to Retained Earnings. If dividends are recorded in a Dividends account, and not as an immediate reduction to Retained Earnings (as shown in this chapter), a fourth step is necessary to close the Dividends account to Retained Earnings.

Statement of Stockholders' Equity

Instead of a separate statement of retained earnings, companies commonly report a statement of stockholders' equity that includes changes in retained earnings. A **statement of stockholders' equity** lists the beginning and ending balances of key equity accounts and describes the changes that occur during the period. The companies in Appendix A report such a statement. The usual format is to provide a column for each component of equity and use the rows to describe events occurring in the period. Exhibit 11.16 shows a condensed statement for **Apple**.

Reporting Stock Options

The majority of corporations whose shares are publicly traded issue **stock options,** which are rights to purchase common stock at a fixed price over a specified period. As the stock's price rises, the option's value increases. **Starbucks** and **Home Depot** offer stock options to both full- and part-time employees. Stock options are said to motivate managers and employees to

EXHIBIT 11.16

Statement of Stockholders' Equity

Apple

APPLE Statement of Stockholders' Equity					
($ millions, shares in thousands)	Common Stock Shares	Common Stock Amount	Retained Earnings	Other	Total Equity
Balance, Sept. 27, 2008	888,326	$7,177	$15,129	$(9)	$22,297
Net income	—	—	8,235	—	8,235
Issuance of Common Stock	11,480	404	(11)	—	393
Other	—	629	—	86	715
Cash Dividends ($0.00 per share)	—	—	—	—	—
Balance, Sept. 26, 2009	899,806	$8,210	$23,353	$77	$31,640

(1) focus on company performance, (2) take a long-run perspective, and (3) remain with the company. A stock option is like having an investment with no risk ("a carrot with no stick").

To illustrate, Quantum grants each of its employees the option to purchase 100 shares of its $1 par value common stock at its current market price of $50 per share anytime within the next 10 years. If the stock price rises to $70 per share, an employee can exercise the option at a gain of $20 per share (acquire a $70 stock at the $50 option price). With 100 shares, a single employee would have a total gain of $2,000, computed as $20 × 100 shares. Companies report the cost of stock options in the income statement. Measurement of this cost is explained in advanced courses.

GLOBAL VIEW

This section discusses similarities and differences between U.S. GAAP and IFRS in accounting and reporting for equity.

Accounting for Common Stock   The accounting for and reporting of common stock under U.S. GAAP and IFRS are similar. Specifically, procedures for issuing common stock at par, at a premium, at a discount, and for noncash assets are similar across the two systems. However, we must be aware of legal and cultural differences across the world that can impact the rights and responsibilities of common share-

NOKIA

holders. Nokia's terminology is a bit different as it uses the phrase "share capital" in reference to what U.S. GAAP would title "common shares" (see Appendix A). It also discloses that it has issued (and outstanding) shares of 3,744,956,052.

Accounting for Dividends   Accounting for and reporting of dividends under U.S. GAAP and IFRS are consistent. This applies to cash dividends, stock dividends, and stock splits. For Nokia, a "dividend of EUR 0.40 per share is to be paid out on the shares of the Company." Nokia, like many other companies, follows a dividend policy set by management and its board.

Accounting for Preferred Stock   Accounting and reporting for preferred stock are similar for U.S. GAAP and IFRS, but there are some important differences. First, preferred stock that is redeemable at the option of the preferred stockholders is reported *between* liabilities and equity in U.S. GAAP balance sheets. However, that same stock is reported as a liability in IFRS balance sheets. Second, the issue price of convertible preferred stock (and bonds) is recorded entirely under preferred stock (or bonds) *and none is assigned to the conversion feature* under U.S. GAAP. However, IFRS requires that a portion of the issue price be allocated to the conversion feature when it exists. Nokia has no preferred stock.

Accounting for Treasury Stock   Both U.S. GAAP and IFRS apply the principle that companies do not record gains or losses on transactions involving their own stock. This applies to purchases, reissuances, and retirements of treasury stock. Consequently, the accounting for treasury stock explained in this chapter is consistent with that under IFRS. However, IFRS in this area is less detailed than that of U.S. GAAP. Nokia's policy regarding treasury stock follows: "[It] recognizes acquired treasury shares as a deduction from equity at their acquisition cost."

Earnings per Share, Price-Earnings Ratio, Dividend Yield, and
Book Value per Share

 **Decision Analysis**

Earnings per Share

The income statement reports **earnings per share,** also called *EPS* or *net income per share,* which is
the amount of income earned per each share of a company's outstanding common stock. The **basic
earnings per share** formula is shown in Exhibit 11.17. When a company has no preferred stock, then
preferred dividends are zero. The weighted-average common shares outstanding is measured over the
income reporting period; its computation is explained in advanced courses.

 A1 Compute earnings per share and describe its use.

$$\text{Basic earnings per share} = \frac{\text{Net income} - \text{Preferred dividends}}{\text{Weighted-average common shares outstanding}}$$

EXHIBIT 11.17

Basic Earnings per Share

To illustrate, assume that Quantum Co. earns $40,000 net income in 2011 and declares dividends of
$7,500 on its noncumulative preferred stock. (If preferred stock is *non*cumulative, the income available
[numerator] is the current period net income less any preferred dividends *declared* in that same period.
If preferred stock is cumulative, the income available [numerator] is the current period net income less
the preferred dividends whether declared or not.) Quantum has 5,000 weighted-average common shares
outstanding during 2011. Its basic EPS[3] is

$$\text{Basic earnings per share} = \frac{\$40,000 - \$7,500}{5,000 \text{ shares}} = \$6.50$$

Price-Earnings Ratio

A stock's market value is determined by its *expected* future cash flows. A comparison of a company's
EPS and its market value per share reveals information about market expectations. This comparison is
traditionally made using a **price-earnings (or PE) ratio,** expressed also as *price earnings, price to earnings,* or *PE.* Some analysts interpret this ratio as what price the market is willing to pay for a company's
current earnings stream. Price-earnings ratios can differ across companies that have similar earnings
because of either higher or lower expectations of future earnings. The price-earnings ratio is defined in
Exhibit 11.18.

 A2 Compute price-earnings ratio and describe its use in analysis.

Point: The average PE ratio of stocks in the 1950–2010 period is about 14.

$$\text{Price-earnings ratio} = \frac{\text{Market value (price) per share}}{\text{Earnings per share}}$$

EXHIBIT 11.18

Price-Earnings Ratio

This ratio is often computed using EPS from the most recent period (for Amazon, its PE is 52; for Altria,
its PE is 13). However, many users compute this ratio using *expected* EPS for the next period.

Some analysts view stocks with high PE ratios (higher than 20 to 25) as more likely to be overpriced
and stocks with low PE ratios (less than 5 to 8) as more likely to be underpriced. These investors prefer to
sell or avoid buying stocks with high PE ratios and to buy or hold stocks with low PE ratios. However,
investment decision making is rarely so simple as to rely on a single ratio. For instance, a stock with a
high PE ratio can prove to be a good investment if its earnings continue to increase beyond current
expectations. Similarly, a stock with a low PE ratio can prove to be a poor investment if its earnings
decline below expectations.

Point: Average PE ratios for U.S. stocks increased over the past two decades. Some analysts interpret this as a signal the market is overpriced. But higher ratios can at least partly reflect accounting changes that have reduced reported earnings.

---

[3] A corporation can be classified as having either a simple or complex capital structure. The term **simple capital structure** refers to a company with only common stock and nonconvertible preferred stock outstanding. The term **complex
capital structure** refers to companies with dilutive securities. **Dilutive securities** include options, rights to purchase
common stock, and any bonds or preferred stock that are convertible into common stock. A company with a complex
capital structure must often report two EPS figures: basic and diluted. **Diluted earnings per share** is computed by
adding all dilutive securities to the denominator of the basic EPS computation. It reflects the decrease in basic EPS
assuming that all dilutive securities are converted into common shares.

Decision Maker   Answer — p. 481

Money Manager   You plan to invest in one of two companies identified as having identical future prospects. One has a PE of 19 and the other a PE of 25. Which do you invest in? Does it matter if your *estimate* of PE for these two companies is 29 as opposed to 22? ■

Dividend Yield

 A3 Compute dividend yield and explain its use in analysis.

Investors buy shares of a company's stock in anticipation of receiving a return from either or both cash dividends and stock price increases. Stocks that pay large dividends on a regular basis, called *income stocks,* are attractive to investors who want recurring cash flows from their investments. In contrast, some stocks pay little or no dividends but are still attractive to investors because of their expected stock price increases. The stocks of companies that distribute little or no cash but use their cash to finance expansion are called *growth stocks*. One way to help identify whether a stock is an income stock or a growth stock is to analyze its dividend yield. **Dividend yield,** defined in Exhibit 11.19, shows the annual amount of cash dividends distributed to common shares relative to their market value.

EXHIBIT 11.19

Dividend Yield

$$\text{Dividend yield} = \frac{\text{Annual cash dividends per share}}{\text{Market value per share}}$$

Dividend yield can be computed for current and prior periods using actual dividends and stock prices and for future periods using expected values. Exhibit 11.20 shows recent dividend and stock price data for **Amazon** and **Altria Group** to compute dividend yield.

EXHIBIT 11.20

Dividend and Stock Price Information

Company	Cash Dividends per Share	Market Value per Share	Dividend Yield
Amazon	$0.00	$80	0.0%
Altria Group.	1.68	20	8.4

Point: The *payout ratio* equals cash dividends declared on common stock divided by net income. A low payout ratio suggests that a company is retaining earnings for future growth.

Dividend yield is zero for Amazon, implying it is a growth stock. An investor in Amazon would look for increases in stock prices (and eventual cash from the sale of stock). Altria has a dividend yield of 8.4%, implying it is an income stock for which dividends are important in assessing its value.

Book Value per Share

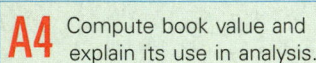 **A4** Compute book value and explain its use in analysis.

Case 1: Common Stock (Only) Outstanding. **Book value per common share,** defined in Exhibit 11.21, reflects the amount of equity applicable to *common* shares on a per share basis. To illustrate, we use Dillon Snowboards' data from Exhibit 11.4. Dillon has 30,000 outstanding common shares, and the stockholders' equity applicable to common shares is $365,000. Dillon's book value per common share is $12.17, computed as $365,000 divided by 30,000 shares.

EXHIBIT 11.21

Book Value per Common Share

$$\text{Book value per common share} = \frac{\text{Stockholders' equity applicable to common shares}}{\text{Number of common shares outstanding}}$$

Point: Book value per share is also referred to as *stockholders' claim to assets on a per share basis.*

Case 2: Common and Preferred Stock Outstanding. To compute book value when both common and preferred shares are outstanding, we allocate total equity between the two types of shares. The **book value per preferred share** is computed first; its computation is shown in Exhibit 11.22.

EXHIBIT 11.22

Book Value per Preferred Share

$$\text{Book value per preferred share} = \frac{\text{Stockholders' equity applicable to preferred shares}}{\text{Number of preferred shares outstanding}}$$

The equity applicable to preferred shares equals the preferred share's call price (or par value if the preferred is not callable) plus any cumulative dividends in arrears. The remaining equity is the portion applicable to common shares. To illustrate, consider LTD's equity in Exhibit 11.23. Its preferred stock is callable at $108 per share, and two years of cumulative preferred dividends are in arrears.

EXHIBIT 11.23

Stockholders' Equity with Preferred and Common Stock

Stockholders' Equity	
Preferred stock—$100 par value, 7% cumulative, 2,000 shares authorized, 1,000 shares issued and outstanding	$100,000
Common stock—$25 par value, 12,000 shares authorized, 10,000 shares issued and outstanding	250,000
Paid-in capital in excess of par value, common stock	15,000
Retained earnings	82,000
Total stockholders' equity	$447,000

The book value computations are in Exhibit 11.24. Equity is first allocated to preferred shares before the book value of common shares is computed.

EXHIBIT 11.24

Computing Book Value per Preferred and Common Share

Total stockholders' equity		$447,000
Less equity applicable to preferred shares		
Call price (1,000 shares × $108)	$108,000	
Dividends in arrears ($100,000 × 7% × 2 years)	14,000	(122,000)
Equity applicable to common shares		$325,000
Book value per preferred share ($122,000/1,000 shares)		**$122.00**
Book value per common share ($325,000/10,000 shares)		**$ 32.50**

Book value per share reflects the value per share if a company is liquidated at balance sheet amounts. Book value is also the starting point in many stock valuation models, merger negotiations, price setting for public utilities, and loan contracts. The main limitation in using book value is the potential difference between recorded value and market value for assets and liabilities. Investors often adjust their analysis for estimates of these differences.

 **Decision Maker**   Answer — p. 481

Investor   You are considering investing in **BMX**, whose book value per common share is $4 and price per common share on the stock exchange is $7. From this information, are BMX's net assets priced higher or lower than its recorded values? ■

DEMONSTRATION PROBLEM 1

Barton Corporation began operations on January 1, 2010. The following transactions relating to stockholders' equity occurred in the first two years of the company's operations.

2010

Jan. 1   Authorized the issuance of 2 million shares of $5 par value common stock and 100,000 shares of $100 par value, 10% cumulative, preferred stock.

Jan. 2   Issued 200,000 shares of common stock for $12 cash per share.

Jan. 3   Issued 100,000 shares of common stock in exchange for a building valued at $820,000 and merchandise inventory valued at $380,000.

Jan. 4   Paid $10,000 cash to the company's founders for organization activities.

Jan. 5   Issued 12,000 shares of preferred stock for $110 cash per share.

2011

June 4   Issued 100,000 shares of common stock for $15 cash per share.

Required

1. Prepare journal entries to record these transactions.

2. Prepare the stockholders' equity section of the balance sheet as of December 31, 2010, and December 31, 2011, based on these transactions.

3. Prepare a table showing dividend allocations and dividends per share for 2010 and 2011 assuming Barton declares the following cash dividends: 2010, $50,000, and 2011, $300,000.

4. Prepare the January 2, 2010, journal entry for Barton's issuance of 200,000 shares of common stock for $12 cash per share assuming

   a. Common stock is no-par stock without a stated value.

   b. Common stock is no-par stock with a stated value of $10 per share.

PLANNING THE SOLUTION

- Record journal entries for the transactions for 2010 and 2011.
- Determine the balances for the 2010 and 2011 equity accounts for the balance sheet.
- Prepare the contributed capital portion of the 2010 and 2011 balance sheets.
- Prepare a table similar to Exhibit 11.11 showing dividend allocations for 2010 and 2011.
- Record the issuance of common stock under both specifications of no-par stock.

SOLUTION TO DEMONSTRATION PROBLEM 1

1. Journal entries.

2010			
Jan. 2	Cash	2,400,000	
	Common Stock, $5 Par Value		1,000,000
	Paid-In Capital in Excess of Par Value, Common Stock		1,400,000
	Issued 200,000 shares of common stock.		
Jan. 3	Building	820,000	
	Merchandise Inventory	380,000	
	Common Stock, $5 Par Value		500,000
	Paid-In Capital in Excess of Par Value, Common Stock		700,000
	Issued 100,000 shares of common stock.		
Jan. 4	Organization Expenses	10,000	
	Cash		10,000
	Paid founders for organization costs.		
Jan. 5	Cash	1,320,000	
	Preferred Stock, $100 Par Value		1,200,000
	Paid-In Capital in Excess of Par Value, Preferred Stock		120,000
	Issued 12,000 shares of preferred stock.		
2011			
June 4	Cash	1,500,000	
	Common Stock, $5 Par Value		500,000
	Paid-In Capital in Excess of Par Value, Common Stock		1,000,000
	Issued 100,000 shares of common stock.		

2. Balance sheet presentations (at December 31 year-end).

	2011	2010
Stockholders' Equity		
Preferred stock—$100 par value, 10% cumulative, 100,000 shares authorized, 12,000 shares issued and outstanding	$1,200,000	$1,200,000
Paid-in capital in excess of par value, preferred stock	120,000	120,000
Total paid-in capital by preferred stockholders	1,320,000	1,320,000
Common stock—$5 par value, 2,000,000 shares authorized, 300,000 shares issued and outstanding in 2010, and 400,000 shares issued and outstanding in 2011	2,000,000	1,500,000
Paid-in capital in excess of par value, common stock	3,100,000	2,100,000
Total paid-in capital by common stockholders	5,100,000	3,600,000
Total paid-in capital	$6,420,000	$4,920,000

3. Dividend allocation table.

	Common	Preferred
2010 ($50,000)		
Preferred—current year (12,000 shares × $10 = $120,000)	$ 0	$ 50,000
Common—remainder (300,000 shares outstanding)	0	0
Total for the year	$ 0	$ 50,000
2011 ($300,000)		
Preferred—dividend in arrears from 2010 ($120,000 − $50,000)	$ 0	$ 70,000
Preferred—current year	0	120,000
Common—remainder (400,000 shares outstanding)	110,000	0
Total for the year	$110,000	$190,000
Dividends per share		
2010	$ 0.00	$ 4.17
2011	$ 0.28	$ 15.83

4. Journal entries.
   a. For 2010 (no-par stock without a stated value):

Jan. 2	Cash	2,400,000	
	Common Stock, No-Par Value		2,400,000
	Issued 200,000 shares of no-par common stock at $12 per share.		

   b. For 2010 (no-par stock with a stated value):

Jan. 2	Cash	2,400,000	
	Common Stock, $10 Stated Value		2,000,000
	Paid-In Capital in Excess of		
	Stated Value, Common Stock		400,000
	Issued 200,000 shares of $10 stated value common stock at $12 per share.		

DEMONSTRATION PROBLEM 2

Precision Company began year 2011 with the following balances in its stockholders' equity accounts.

Common stock—$10 par, 500,000 shares authorized, 200,000 shares issued and outstanding	$2,000,000
Paid-in capital in excess of par, common stock	1,000,000
Retained earnings	5,000,000
Total	$8,000,000

All outstanding common stock was issued for $15 per share when the company was created. Prepare journal entries to account for the following transactions during year 2011.

Jan. 10 The board declared a $0.10 cash dividend per share to shareholders of record Jan. 28.
Feb. 15 Paid the cash dividend declared on January 10.
Mar. 31 Declared a 20% stock dividend. The market value of the stock is $18 per share.
May 1   Distributed the stock dividend declared on March 31.
July 1   Purchased 30,000 shares of treasury stock at $20 per share.
Sept. 1   Sold 20,000 treasury shares at $26 cash per share.
Dec. 1   Sold the remaining 10,000 shares of treasury stock at $7 cash per share.

PLANNING THE SOLUTION

- Calculate the total cash dividend to record by multiplying the cash dividend declared by the number of shares as of the date of record.
- Decide whether the stock dividend is a small or large dividend. Then analyze each event to determine the accounts affected and the appropriate amounts to be recorded.

SOLUTION TO DEMONSTRATION PROBLEM 2

Jan. 10	Retained Earnings	20,000	
	Common Dividend Payable		20,000
	Declared a $0.10 per share cash dividend.		
Feb. 15	Common Dividend Payable	20,000	
	Cash		20,000
	Paid $0.10 per share cash dividend.		
Mar. 31	Retained Earnings	720,000	
	Common Stock Dividend Distributable		400,000
	Paid-In Capital in Excess of Par Value, Common Stock		320,000
	Declared a small stock dividend of 20% or 40,000 shares; market value is $18 per share.		
May 1	Common Stock Dividend Distributable	400,000	
	Common Stock		400,000
	Distributed 40,000 shares of common stock.		
July 1	Treasury Stock, Common	600,000	
	Cash		600,000
	Purchased 30,000 common shares at $20 per share.		
Sept. 1	Cash	520,000	
	Treasury Stock, Common		400,000
	Paid-In Capital, Treasury Stock		120,000
	Sold 20,000 treasury shares at $26 per share.		
Dec. 1	Cash	70,000	
	Paid-In Capital, Treasury Stock	120,000	
	Retained Earnings	10,000	
	Treasury Stock, Common		200,000
	Sold 10,000 treasury shares at $7 per share.		

Summary

C1 **Identify characteristics of corporations and their organization.** Corporations are legal entities whose stockholders are not liable for its debts. Stock is easily transferred, and the life of a corporation does not end with the incapacity of a stockholder. A corporation acts through its agents, who are its officers and managers. Corporations are regulated and subject to income taxes. Authorized stock is the stock that a corporation's charter authorizes it to sell. Issued stock is the portion of authorized shares sold. Par value stock is a value per share assigned by the charter. No-par value stock is stock *not* assigned a value per share by the charter. Stated value stock is no-par stock to which the directors assign a value per share.

C2 **Explain characteristics of, and distribute dividends between, common and preferred stock.** Preferred stock has a priority (or senior status) relative to common stock in one or more areas, usually (1) dividends and (2) assets in case of liquidation. Preferred stock usually does not carry voting rights and can be

convertible or callable. Convertibility permits the holder to convert preferred to common. Callability permits the issuer to buy back preferred stock under specified conditions. Preferred stockholders usually hold the right to dividend distributions before common stockholders. When preferred stock is cumulative and in arrears, the amount in arrears must be distributed to preferred before any dividends are distributed to common.

C3 **Explain the items reported in retained earnings.** Stockholders' equity is made up of (1) paid-in capital and (2) retained earnings. Paid-in capital consists of funds raised by stock issuances. Retained earnings consists of cumulative net income (losses) not distributed. Many companies face statutory and contractual restrictions on retained earnings. Corporations can voluntarily appropriate retained earnings to inform others about their disposition. Prior period adjustments are corrections of errors in prior financial statements.

A1 **Compute earnings per share and describe its use.** A company with a simple capital structure computes basic EPS by dividing net income less any preferred dividends by the weighted-average number of outstanding common shares. A company with a complex capital structure must usually report both basic and diluted EPS.

A2 **Compute price-earnings ratio and describe its use in analysis.** A common stock's price-earnings (PE) ratio is computed by dividing the stock's market value (price) per share by its EPS. A stock's PE is based on expectations that can prove to be better or worse than eventual performance.

A3 **Compute dividend yield and explain its use in analysis.** Dividend yield is the ratio of a stock's annual cash dividends per share to its market value (price) per share. Dividend yield can be compared with the yield of other companies to determine whether the stock is expected to be an income or growth stock.

A4 **Compute book value and explain its use in analysis.** Book value per common share is equity applicable to common shares divided by the number of outstanding common shares. Book value per preferred share is equity applicable to preferred shares divided by the number of outstanding preferred shares.

P1 **Record the issuance of corporate stock.** When stock is issued, its par or stated value is credited to the stock account and any excess is credited to a separate contributed capital account. If a stock has neither par nor stated value, the entire proceeds are credited to the stock account. Stockholders must contribute assets equal to minimum legal capital or be potentially liable for the deficiency.

P2 **Record transactions involving cash dividends, stock dividends, and stock splits.** Cash dividends involve three events. On the date of declaration, the directors bind the company to pay the dividend. A dividend declaration reduces retained earnings and creates a current liability. On the date of record, recipients of the dividend are identified. On the date of payment, cash is paid to stockholders and the current liability is removed. Neither a stock dividend nor a stock split alters the value of the company. However, the value of each share is less due to the distribution of additional shares. The distribution of additional shares is according to individual stockholders' ownership percent. Small stock dividends (≤25%) are recorded by capitalizing retained earnings equal to the market value of distributed shares. Large stock dividends (>25%) are recorded by capitalizing retained earnings equal to the par or stated value of distributed shares. Stock splits do not necessitate journal entries but do necessitate changes in the description of stock.

P3 **Record purchases and sales of treasury stock and the retirement of stock.** When a corporation purchases its own previously issued stock, it debits the cost of these shares to Treasury Stock. Treasury stock is subtracted from equity in the balance sheet. If treasury stock is reissued, any proceeds in excess of cost are credited to Paid-In Capital, Treasury Stock. If the proceeds are less than cost, they are debited to Paid-In Capital, Treasury Stock to the extent a credit balance exists. Any remaining amount is debited to Retained Earnings. When stock is retired, all accounts related to the stock are removed.

Guidance Answers to Decision Maker and Decision Ethics

Entrepreneur The 50% stock dividend provides you no direct income. A stock dividend often reveals management's optimistic expectations about the future and can improve a stock's marketability by making it affordable to more investors. Accordingly, a stock dividend usually reveals "good news" and because of this, it likely increases (slightly) the market value for your stock. The same conclusions apply to the 3-for-2 stock split.

Concert Organizer You have two basic options: (1) different classes of common stock or (2) common and preferred stock. Your objective is to issue to yourself stock that has all or a majority of the voting power. The other class of stock would carry limited or no voting rights. In this way, you maintain control and are able to raise the necessary funds.

Money Manager Since one company requires a payment of $19 for each $1 of earnings, and the other requires $25, you would prefer the stock with the PE of 19; it is a better deal given identical prospects. You should make sure these companies' earnings computations are roughly the same, for example, no extraordinary items, unusual events, and so forth. Also, your PE estimates for these companies do matter. If you are willing to pay $29 for each $1 of earnings for these companies, you obviously expect both to exceed current market expectations.

Investor Book value reflects recorded values. BMX's book value is $4 per common share. Stock price reflects the market's expectation of net asset value (both tangible and intangible items). BMX's market value is $7 per common share. Comparing these figures suggests BMX's market value of net assets is higher than its recorded values (by an amount of $7 versus $4 per share).

Guidance Answers to Quick Checks

1. (b)

2. A corporation pays taxes on its income, and its stockholders normally pay personal income taxes (at the 15% rate or lower) on any cash dividends received from the corporation.

3. A proxy is a legal document used to transfer a stockholder's right to vote to another person.

4. (a)

5. A stock premium is an amount in excess of par (or stated) value paid by purchasers of newly issued stock.

6. Minimum legal capital intends to protect creditors of a corporation by obligating stockholders to some minimum level of equity financing and by constraining a corporation from excessive payments to stockholders.

7. Common Dividend Payable is a current liability account.

8. The date of declaration, date of record, and date of payment.

9. A dividend is a legal liability at the date of declaration, on which date it is recorded as a liability.

10. A stock dividend does not transfer assets to stockholders, but it does require an amount of retained earnings to be transferred to a contributed capital account(s).

11. A small stock dividend is 25% or less of the previous outstanding shares. A large stock dividend is more than 25%.

12. Retained earnings equal to the distributable shares' market value should be capitalized for a small stock dividend.

13. Typically, preferred stock has a preference in receipt of dividends and in distribution of assets.

14. (a)

15. (b)

Total cash dividend	$288,000
To preferred shareholders	135,000*
Remainder to common shareholders	$153,000

* 9,000 × $50 × 10% × 3 years = $135,000.

16. (b)

17. No. The shares are an investment for Southern Co. and are issued and outstanding shares for Northern Corp.

18. Treasury stock does not affect the number of authorized or issued shares, but it reduces the outstanding shares.

19. (a)

Key Terms

mhhe.com/wildFINMAN4e

Appropriated retained earnings (p. 473)
Authorized stock (p. 459)
Basic earnings per share (p. 475)
Book value per common share (p. 476)
Book value per preferred share (p. 476)
Call price (p. 469)
Callable preferred stock (p. 469)
Capital stock (p. 459)
Changes in accounting estimates (p. 473)
Common stock (p. 458)
Complex capital structure (p. 475)
Convertible preferred stock (p. 468)
Corporation (p. 456)
Cumulative preferred stock (p. 467)
Date of declaration (p. 463)
Date of payment (p. 463)
Date of record (p. 463)
Diluted earnings per share (p. 475)
Dilutive securities (p. 475)

Discount on stock (p. 461)
Dividend in arrears (p. 467)
Dividend yield (p. 476)
Earnings per share (EPS) (p. 475)
Financial leverage (p. 469)
Large stock dividend (p. 464)
Liquidating cash dividend (p. 464)
Market value per share (p. 459)
Minimum legal capital (p. 459)
Noncumulative preferred stock (p. 467)
Nonparticipating preferred stock (p. 468)
No-par value stock (p. 459)
Organization expenses (p. 457)
Paid-in capital (p. 460)
Paid-in capital in excess of par value (p. 461)
Participating preferred stock (p. 468)
Par value (p. 459)
Par value stock (p. 459)

Preemptive right (p. 458)
Preferred stock (p. 466)
Premium on stock (p. 461)
Price-earnings (PE) ratio (p. 475)
Prior period adjustments (p. 473)
Proxy (p. 457)
Restricted retained earnings (p. 472)
Retained earnings (p. 460)
Retained earnings deficit (p. 463)
Reverse stock split (p. 466)
Simple capital structure (p. 475)
Small stock dividend (p. 464)
Stated value stock (p. 460)
Statement of stockholders' equity (p. 473)
Stock dividend (p. 464)
Stock options (p. 473)
Stock split (p. 466)
Stockholders' equity (p. 460)
Treasury stock (p. 470)

Multiple Choice Quiz   Answers on p. 497   mhhe.com/wildFINMAN4e

Additional Quiz Questions are available at the book's Website.

1. A corporation issues 6,000 shares of $5 par value common stock for $8 cash per share. The entry to record this transaction includes:
   a. A debit to Paid-In Capital in Excess of Par Value for $18,000.
   b. A credit to Common Stock for $48,000.
   c. A credit to Paid-In Capital in Excess of Par Value for $30,000.
   d. A credit to Cash for $48,000.
   e. A credit to Common Stock for $30,000.

2. A company reports net income of $75,000. Its weighted-average common shares outstanding is 19,000. It has no other stock outstanding. Its earnings per share is:
   a. $4.69
   b. $3.95
   c. $3.75
   d. $2.08
   e. $4.41

3. A company has 5,000 shares of $100 par preferred stock and 50,000 shares of $10 par common stock outstanding. Its total stockholders' equity is $2,000,000. Its book value per common share is:
  a. $100.00
  b. $ 10.00
  c. $ 40.00
  d. $ 30.00
  e. $ 36.36

4. A company paid cash dividends of $0.81 per share. Its earnings per share is $6.95 and its market price per share is $45.00. Its dividend yield is:
  a. 1.8%
  b. 11.7%

  c. 15.4%
  d. 55.6%
  e. 8.6%

5. A company's shares have a market value of $85 per share. Its net income is $3,500,000, and its weighted-average common shares outstanding is 700,000. Its price-earnings ratio is:
  a.   5.9
  b. 425.0
  c. 17.0
  d. 10.4
  e. 41.2

Icon denotes assignments that involve decision making.

Discussion Questions

1. What are organization expenses? Provide examples.

2. How are organization expenses reported?

3. Who is responsible for directing a corporation's affairs?

4. What is the preemptive right of common stockholders?

5. List the general rights of common stockholders.

6. What is the difference between authorized shares and outstanding shares?

7. Why would an investor find convertible preferred stock attractive?

8. What is the difference between the market value per share and the par value per share?

9. What is the difference between the par value and the call price of a share of preferred stock?

10. Identify and explain the importance of the three dates relevant to corporate dividends.

11. Why is the term *liquidating dividend* used to describe cash dividends debited against paid-in capital accounts?

12. How does declaring a stock dividend affect the corporation's assets, liabilities, and total equity? What are the effects of the eventual distribution of that stock?

13. What is the difference between a stock dividend and a stock split?

14. Courts have ruled that a stock dividend is not taxable income to stockholders. What justifies this decision?

15. How does the purchase of treasury stock affect the purchaser's assets and total equity?

16. Why do laws place limits on treasury stock purchases?

17. How are EPS results computed for a corporation with a simple capital structure?

18. What is a stock option?

19. How is book value per share computed for a corporation with no preferred stock? What is the main limitation of using book value per share to value a corporation?

20. Review the 2009 balance sheet for **Nokia** in Appendix A and list the amounts for treasury shares and retained earnings.   **NOKIA**

21. Refer to **Research In Motion**'s 2010 balance sheet in Appendix A. How many shares of common stock are authorized? How many shares of voting common stock are issued?   *RIM*

22. Refer to the 2009 balance sheet for **Palm** in Appendix A. What is the par value per share of its common stock? Suggest a rationale for the amount of par value it assigned.   **Palm**

23. Refer to the financial statements for **Apple** in Appendix A. What are its cash proceeds from issuance of common stock *and* its cash repurchases of common stock for the year ended September 26, 2009? Explain.   Apple

---

connect

Of the following statements, which are true for the corporate form of organization?

1. Owners are not agents of the corporation.

2. It is a separate legal entity.

3. It has a limited life.

4. Capital is more easily accumulated than with most other forms of organization.

5. Corporate income that is distributed to shareholders is usually taxed twice.

6. Owners have unlimited liability for corporate debts.

7. Ownership rights cannot be easily transferred.

QUICK STUDY

QS 11-1
Characteristics of corporations
C1

QS 11-2
Issuance of common stock
P1

Prepare the journal entry to record Channel One Company's issuance of 100,000 shares of $0.50 par value common stock assuming the shares sell for:

a. $0.50 cash per share.

b. $2 cash per share.

QS 11-3
Issuance of no-par common stock
P1

Prepare the journal entry to record Selectist Company's issuance of 104,000 shares of no-par value common stock assuming the shares:

a. Sell for $15 cash per share.

b. Are exchanged for land valued at $1,560,000.

QS 11-4
Issuance of par and stated value common stock
P1

Prepare the journal entry to record Typist Company's issuance of 250,000 shares of its common stock assuming the shares have a:

a. $1 par value and sell for $10 cash per share.

b. $1 stated value and sell for $10 cash per share.

QS 11-5
Issuance of common stock
P1

Prepare the issuer's journal entry for each separate transaction. (*a*) On March 1, Edgar Co. issues 44,500 shares of $4 par value common stock for $255,000 cash. (*b*) On April 1, GT Co. issues no-par value common stock for $50,000 cash. (*c*) On April 6, MTV issues 2,000 shares of $20 par value common stock for $35,000 of inventory, $135,000 of machinery, and acceptance of an $84,000 note payable.

QS 11-6
Issuance of preferred stock
P1 P2

a. Prepare the journal entry to record Stefan Company's issuance of 12,000 shares of $50 par value 6% cumulative preferred stock for $75 cash per share.

b. Assuming the facts in part 1, if Stefan declares a year-end cash dividend, what is the amount of dividend paid to preferred shareholders? (Assume no dividends in arrears.)

QS 11-7
Accounting for cash dividends
P2

Prepare journal entries to record the following transactions for Emerson Corporation.

April 15   Declared a cash dividend payable to common stockholders of $40,000.
May 15   Date of record is May 15 for the cash dividend declared on April 15.
May 31   Paid the dividend declared on April 15.

QS 11-8
Dividend allocation between classes of shareholders
C2

Stockholders' equity of STIX Company consists of 75,000 shares of $5 par value, 8% cumulative preferred stock and 200,000 shares of $1 par value common stock. Both classes of stock have been outstanding since the company's inception. STIX did not declare any dividends in the prior year, but it now declares and pays a $108,000 cash dividend at the current year-end. Determine the amount distributed to each class of stockholders for this two-year-old company.

QS 11-9
Accounting for small stock dividend
P2

The stockholders' equity section of Zacman Company's balance sheet as of April 1 follows. On April 2, Zacman declares and distributes a 10% stock dividend. The stock's per share market value on April 2 is $25 (prior to the dividend). Prepare the stockholders' equity section immediately after the stock dividend.

Common stock—$5 par value, 375,000 shares authorized, 150,000 shares issued and outstanding	$ 750,000
Paid-in capital in excess of par value, common stock	352,500
Retained earnings	633,000
Total stockholders' equity	$1,735,500

QS 11-10
Accounting for changes in estimates; error adjustments
C3

Answer the following questions related to a company's activities for the current year:

1. After using an expected useful life of 20 years and no salvage value to depreciate its office equipment over the preceding 15 years, the company decided early this year that the equipment will last only two more years. How should the effects of this decision be reported in the current year financial statements?

2. A review of the notes payable files discovers that two years ago the company reported the entire amount of a payment (principal and interest) on an installment note payable as interest expense. This mistake had a material effect on the amount of income in that year. How should the correction be reported in the current year financial statements?

On May 3, Lassman Corporation purchased 3,000 shares of its own stock for $27,000 cash. On November 4, Lassman reissued 750 shares of this treasury stock for $7,080. Prepare the May 3 and November 4 journal entries to record Lassman's purchase and reissuance of treasury stock.

QS 11-11
Purchase and sale of treasury stock P3

Barnes Company earned net income of $450,000 this year. The number of common shares outstanding during the entire year was 200,000, and preferred shareholders received a $10,000 cash dividend. Compute Barnes Company's basic earnings per share.

QS 11-12
Basic earnings per share A1

Campbell Company reports net income of $1,200,000 for the year. It has no preferred stock, and its weighted-average common shares outstanding is 300,000 shares. Compute its basic earnings per share.

QS 11-13
Basic earnings per share A1

Compute Fox Company's price-earnings ratio if its common stock has a market value of $30.75 per share and its EPS is $4.10. Would an analyst likely consider this stock potentially over- or underpriced? Explain.

QS 11-14
Price-earnings ratio A2

Fiona Company expects to pay a $2.10 per share cash dividend this year on its common stock. The current market value of Fiona stock is $28.50 per share. Compute the expected dividend yield on the Fiona stock. Would you classify the Fiona stock as a growth or an income stock? Explain.

QS 11-15
Dividend yield A3

The stockholders' equity section of Axel Company's balance sheet follows. The preferred stock's call price is $30. Determine the book value per share of the common stock.

QS 11-16
Book value per common share
A4

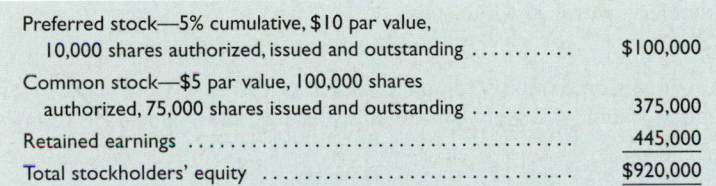

Preferred stock—5% cumulative, $10 par value, 10,000 shares authorized, issued and outstanding	$100,000
Common stock—$5 par value, 100,000 shares authorized, 75,000 shares issued and outstanding	375,000
Retained earnings	445,000
Total stockholders' equity	$920,000

Air France-KLM reports the following equity information for its fiscal year ended March 31, 2009 (euros in millions). Prepare its journal entry, using its account titles, to record the issuance of capital stock assuming that its entire par value stock was issued on March 31, 2009, for cash.

QS 11-17
International equity disclosures

P1

March 31	2009
Issued capital	€2,552
Additional paid-in capital	765

Describe how each of the following characteristics of organizations applies to corporations.

EXERCISES

1. Duration of life	5. Owner authority and control
2. Owner liability	6. Ease of formation
3. Legal status	7. Transferability of ownership
4. Tax status of income	8. Ability to raise large capital amounts

Exercise 11-1
Characteristics of corporations
C1

Aloha Corporation issues 6,000 shares of its common stock for $144,000 cash on February 20. Prepare journal entries to record this event under each of the following separate situations.
1. The stock has neither par nor stated value.
2. The stock has a $20 par value.
3. The stock has an $8 stated value.

Exercise 11-2
Accounting for par, stated, and no-par stock issuances

P1

Exercise 11-3

Recording stock issuances

P1

Prepare journal entries to record the following four separate issuances of stock.

1. A corporation issued 2,000 shares of no-par common stock to its promoters in exchange for their efforts, estimated to be worth $30,000. The stock has no stated value.

2. A corporation issued 2,000 shares of no-par common stock to its promoters in exchange for their efforts, estimated to be worth $30,000. The stock has a $1 per share stated value.

3. A corporation issued 4,000 shares of $10 par value common stock for $70,000 cash.

4. A corporation issued 1,000 shares of $100 par value preferred stock for $120,000 cash.

Exercise 11-4

Stock issuance for noncash assets

P1

Soku Company issues 36,000 shares of $9 par value common stock in exchange for land and a building. The land is valued at $225,000 and the building at $360,000. Prepare the journal entry to record issuance of the stock in exchange for the land and building.

Exercise 11-5

Identifying characteristics of preferred stock

C2

Match each description 1 through 6 with the characteristic of preferred stock that it best describes by writing the letter of that characteristic in the blank next to each description.

A. Cumulative   **B.** Noncumulative   **C.** Convertible

D. Callable   **E.** Nonparticipating   **F.** Participating

_____ **1.** Holders of the stock lose any dividends that are not declared in the current year.

_____ **2.** The issuing corporation can retire the stock by paying a prespecified price.

_____ **3.** Holders of the stock can receive dividends exceeding the stated rate under certain conditions.

_____ **4.** Holders of the stock are not entitled to receive dividends in excess of the stated rate.

_____ **5.** Holders of this stock can exchange it for shares of common stock.

_____ **6.** Holders of the stock are entitled to receive current and all past dividends before common stockholders receive any dividends.

Exercise 11-6

Stock dividends and splits

P2

On June 30, 2011, Quinn Corporation's common stock is priced at $31 per share before any stock dividend or split, and the stockholders' equity section of its balance sheet appears as follows.

Common stock—$10 par value, 60,000 shares	
authorized, 25,000 shares issued and outstanding	$250,000
Paid-in capital in excess of par value, common stock	100,000
Retained earnings	330,000
Total stockholders' equity	$680,000

1. Assume that the company declares and immediately distributes a 100% stock dividend. This event is recorded by capitalizing retained earnings equal to the stock's par value. Answer these questions about stockholders' equity as it exists *after* issuing the new shares.

   a. What is the retained earnings balance?

Check   (1*b*) $680,000

   b. What is the amount of total stockholders' equity?

   c. How many shares are outstanding?

2. Assume that the company implements a 2-for-1 stock split instead of the stock dividend in part 1. Answer these questions about stockholders' equity as it exists *after* issuing the new shares.

(2*a*) $330,000

   a. What is the retained earnings balance?

   b. What is the amount of total stockholders' equity?

   c. How many shares are outstanding?

3. Explain the difference, if any, to a stockholder from receiving new shares distributed under a large stock dividend versus a stock split.

Exercise 11-7

Stock dividends and per share book values

P2

The stockholders' equity of Whiz.com Company at the beginning of the day on February 5 follows.

Common stock—$25 par value, 150,000 shares	
authorized, 60,000 shares issued and outstanding	$1,500,000
Paid-in capital in excess of par value, common stock	525,000
Retained earnings	675,000
Total stockholders' equity	$2,700,000

On February 5, the directors declare a 20% stock dividend distributable on February 28 to the February 15 stockholders of record. The stock's market value is $40 per share on February 5 before the stock dividend. The stock's market value is $34 per share on February 28.

1. Prepare entries to record both the dividend declaration and its distribution.
2. One stockholder owned 750 shares on February 5 before the dividend. Compute the book value per share and total book value of this stockholder's shares immediately before *and* after the stock dividend of February 5.
3. Compute the total market value of the investor's shares in part 2 as of February 5 and February 28.

Check   (2) Book value per share: before, $45; after, $37.50

Wade's outstanding stock consists of 40,000 shares of *noncumulative* 7.5% preferred stock with a $10 par value and also 100,000 shares of common stock with a $1 par value. During its first four years of operation, the corporation declared and paid the following total cash dividends.

Exercise 11-8
Dividends on common and noncumulative preferred stock
C2

2011	$ 10,000
2012	24,000
2013	100,000
2014	196,000

Determine the amount of dividends paid each year to each of the two classes of stockholders: preferred and common. Also compute the total dividends paid to each class for the four years combined.

Check   4-year total paid to preferred, $94,000

Use the data in Exercise 11-8 to determine the amount of dividends paid each year to each of the two classes of stockholders assuming that the preferred stock is *cumulative*. Also determine the total dividends paid to each class for the four years combined.

Exercise 11-9
Dividends on common and cumulative preferred stock   C2

On October 10, the stockholders' equity of Noble Systems appears as follows.

Exercise 11-10
Recording and reporting treasury stock transactions
P3

Common stock—$10 par value, 36,000 shares authorized, issued, and outstanding	$360,000
Paid-in capital in excess of par value, common stock	108,000
Retained earnings	432,000
Total stockholders' equity	$900,000

1. Prepare journal entries to record the following transactions for Noble Systems.
   a. Purchased 4,500 shares of its own common stock at $30 per share on October 11.
   b. Sold 1,200 treasury shares on November 1 for $36 cash per share.
   c. Sold all remaining treasury shares on November 25 for $25 cash per share.
2. Explain how the company's equity section changes after the October 11 treasury stock purchase, and prepare the revised equity section of its balance sheet at that date.

Check   (1c) Dr. Retained Earnings, $9,300

The following information is available for Ballard Company for the year ended December 31, 2011.
a. Balance of retained earnings, December 31, 2010, prior to discovery of error, $850,000.
b. Cash dividends declared and paid during 2011, $15,000.
c. It neglected to record 2009 depreciation expense of $55,600, which is net of $5,500 in income taxes.
d. The company earned $205,000 in 2011 net income.
Prepare a 2011 statement of retained earnings for Ballard Company.

Exercise 11-11
Preparing a statement of retained earnings
C3

Guess Company reports $648,500 of net income for 2011 and declares $102,500 of cash dividends on its preferred stock for 2011. At the end of 2011, the company had 260,000 weighted-average shares of common stock.

1. What amount of net income is available to common stockholders for 2011?
2. What is the company's basic EPS for 2011?

Exercise 11-12
Earnings per share
A1

Check   (2) $2.10

Exercise 11-13
Earnings per share
A1

Check   (2) $3.56

Franklin Company reports $698,000 of net income for 2011 and declares $75,500 of cash dividends on its preferred stock for 2011. At the end of 2011, the company had 175,000 weighted-average shares of common stock.

1. What amount of net income is available to common stockholders for 2011?
2. What is the company's basic EPS for 2011? Round your answer to the nearest whole cent.

Exercise 11-14
Dividend yield computation and interpretation
A3

Compute the dividend yield for each of these four separate companies. Which company's stock would probably *not* be classified as an income stock? Explain.

Company	Annual Cash Dividend per Share	Market Value per Share
1	$15.00	$216.00
2	12.00	128.00
3	6.00	61.00
4	1.20	86.00

Exercise 11-15
Price-earnings ratio computation and interpretation
A2

Compute the price-earnings ratio for each of these four separate companies. Which stock might an analyst likely investigate as being potentially undervalued by the market? Explain.

Company	Earnings per Share	Market Value per Share
1	$10.00	$166.00
2	9.00	90.00
3	6.50	84.50
4	40.00	240.00

Exercise 11-16
Book value per share
A4

The equity section of Webster Corporation's balance sheet shows the following.

Preferred stock—5% cumulative, $10 par value, $15 call price, 10,000 shares issued and outstanding	$100,000
Common stock—$10 par value, 55,000 shares issued and outstanding	550,000
Retained earnings	267,500
Total stockholders' equity	$917,500

Determine the book value per share of the preferred and common stock under two separate situations.

Check   (1) Book value of common, $13.95

1. No preferred dividends are in arrears.
2. Three years of preferred dividends are in arrears.

Exercise 11-17
Accounting for equity under IFRS
C3   P1

Unilever Group reports the following equity information for the years ended December 31, 2007 and 2008 (euros in millions).

December 31	2008	2007
Share capital	€ 484	€ 484
Share premium	121	153
Other reserves	(6,469)	(3,412)
Retained profit	15,812	15,162
Shareholders' equity	€ 9,948	€12,387

1. For each of the three account titles *share capital*, *share premium*, and *retained profit*, match it with the usual account title applied under U.S. GAAP from the following options:

   a. Paid-in capital in excess of par value, common stock

   b. Retained earnings

   c. Common stock, par value

2. Prepare Unilever's journal entry, using its account titles, to record the issuance of capital stock assuming that its entire par value stock was issued on December 31, 2007, for cash.

3. What were Unilever's 2008 dividends assuming that only dividends and income impacted retained profit for 2008 and that its 2008 income totaled €2,692?

Kroll Corporation reports the following components of stockholders' equity on December 31, 2011.

Exercise 11-18
Cash dividends, treasury stock, and statement of retained earnings

C3 P2 P3

Common stock—$25 par value, 40,000 shares authorized, 30,000 shares issued and outstanding	$ 750,000
Paid-in capital in excess of par value, common stock	50,000
Retained earnings	260,000
Total stockholders' equity	$1,060,000

In year 2012, the following transactions affected its stockholders' equity accounts.

Jan.	2	Purchased 2,000 shares of its own stock at $25 cash per share.
Jan.	7	Directors declared a $2 per share cash dividend payable on Feb. 28 to the Feb. 9 stockholders of record.
Feb. 28		Paid the dividend declared on January 7.
July	9	Sold 500 of its treasury shares at $30 cash per share.
Aug. 27		Sold 1,500 of its treasury shares at $23 cash per share.
Sept.	9	Directors declared a $2 per share cash dividend payable on October 22 to the September 23 stockholders of record.
Oct. 22		Paid the dividend declared on September 9.
Dec. 31		Closed the $8,000 credit balance (from net income) in the Income Summary account to Retained Earnings.

Required

1. Prepare journal entries to record each of these transactions for 2012.
2. Prepare a statement of retained earnings for the year ended December 31, 2012.
3. Prepare the stockholders' equity section of the company's balance sheet as of December 31, 2012.

connect

Oxygen Co. is incorporated at the beginning of this year and engages in a number of transactions. The following journal entries impacted its stockholders' equity during its first year of operations.

PROBLEM SET A

Problem 11-1A
Stockholders' equity transactions and analysis

C2 P1

a.	Cash	150,000	
	Common Stock, $25 Par Value		125,000
	Paid-In Capital in Excess of Par Value, Common Stock		25,000
b.	Organization Expenses	75,000	
	Common Stock, $25 Par Value		62,500
	Paid-In Capital in Excess of Par Value, Common Stock		12,500
c.	Cash	21,500	
	Accounts Receivable	7,500	
	Building	30,000	
	Notes Payable		19,000
	Common Stock, $25 Par Value		25,000
	Paid-In Capital in Excess of Par Value, Common Stock		15,000

[continued on next page]

[continued from previous page]

d.	Cash	60,000	
	Common Stock, $25 Par Value		37,500
	Paid-In Capital in Excess of Par Value, Common Stock		22,500

Required

1. Explain the transaction(s) underlying each journal entry (*a*) through (*d*).

Check (2) 10,000 shares

(3) $250,000

(4) $325,000

2. How many shares of common stock are outstanding at year-end?

3. What is the amount of minimum legal capital (based on par value) at year-end?

4. What is the total paid-in capital at year-end?

5. What is the book value per share of the common stock at year-end if total paid-in capital plus retained earnings equals $347,500?

Problem 11-2A
Cash dividends, treasury stock, and statement of retained earnings

C3 P2 P3

Context Corporation reports the following components of stockholders' equity on December 31, 2011.

Common stock—$10 par value, 50,000 shares authorized, 20,000 shares issued and outstanding	$200,000
Paid-in capital in excess of par value, common stock	30,000
Retained earnings	135,000
Total stockholders' equity	$365,000

In year 2012, the following transactions affected its stockholders' equity accounts.

Jan.	1	Purchased 2,000 shares of its own stock at $20 cash per share.
Jan.	5	Directors declared a $2 per share cash dividend payable on Feb. 28 to the Feb. 5 stockholders of record.
Feb.	28	Paid the dividend declared on January 5.
July	6	Sold 750 of its treasury shares at $24 cash per share.
Aug.	22	Sold 1,250 of its treasury shares at $17 cash per share.
Sept.	5	Directors declared a $2 per share cash dividend payable on October 28 to the September 25 stockholders of record.
Oct.	28	Paid the dividend declared on September 5.
Dec.	31	Closed the $194,000 credit balance (from net income) in the Income Summary account to Retained Earnings.

Required

1. Prepare journal entries to record each of these transactions for 2012.

Check (2) Retained earnings, Dec. 31, 2012, $252,250.

2. Prepare a statement of retained earnings for the year ended December 31, 2012.

3. Prepare the stockholders' equity section of the company's balance sheet as of December 31, 2012.

Problem 11-3A
Equity analysis—journal entries and account balances

P2

At September 30, the end of Excel Company's third quarter, the following stockholders' equity accounts are reported.

Common stock, $12 par value	$720,000
Paid-in capital in excess of par value, common stock	180,000
Retained earnings	640,000

In the fourth quarter, the following entries related to its equity are recorded.

Oct. 2	Retained Earnings	120,000	
	Common Dividend Payable		120,000
Oct. 25	Common Dividend Payable	120,000	
	Cash		120,000
Oct. 31	Retained Earnings	150,000	
	Common Stock Dividend Distributable		72,000
	Paid-In Capital in Excess of Par Value, Common Stock		78,000

[continued on next page]

[continued from previous page]

Nov. 5	Common Stock Dividend Distributable	72,000	
	Common Stock, $12 Par Value		72,000
Dec. 1	Memo—Change the title of the common stock account to reflect the new par value of $4.		
Dec. 31	Income Summary	420,000	
	Retained Earnings		420,000

Required

1. Explain the transaction(s) underlying each journal entry.

2. Complete the following table showing the equity account balances at each indicated date (include the balances from September 30).

	Oct. 2	Oct. 25	Oct. 31	Nov. 5	Dec. 1	Dec. 31
Common stock	$_____	$_____	$_____	$_____	$_____	$_____
Common stock dividend distributable	_____	_____	_____	_____	_____	_____
Paid-in capital in excess of par, common stock	_____	_____	_____	_____	_____	_____
Retained earnings	_____	_____	_____	_____	_____	_____
Total equity	$_____	$_____	$_____	$_____	$_____	$_____

Check Total equity: Oct. 2, $1,420,000; Dec. 31, $1,840,000

The equity sections from Salazar Group's 2011 and 2012 year-end balance sheets follow.

Problem 11-4A
Analysis of changes in stockholders' equity accounts

C3 P2 P3

Stockholders' Equity (December 31, 2011)	
Common stock—$4 par value, 50,000 shares authorized, 20,000 shares issued and outstanding	$ 80,000
Paid-in capital in excess of par value, common stock	60,000
Retained earnings	160,000
Total stockholders' equity	$300,000

Stockholders' Equity (December 31, 2012)	
Common stock—$4 par value, 50,000 shares authorized, 23,700 shares issued, 1,500 shares in treasury	$ 94,800
Paid-in capital in excess of par value, common stock	89,600
Retained earnings ($15,000 restricted by treasury stock)	200,000
	384,400
Less cost of treasury stock	(15,000)
Total stockholders' equity	$369,400

The following transactions and events affected its equity during year 2012.

Jan.	5	Declared a $0.50 per share cash dividend, date of record January 10.
Mar.	20	Purchased treasury stock for cash.
Apr.	5	Declared a $0.50 per share cash dividend, date of record April 10.
July	5	Declared a $0.50 per share cash dividend, date of record July 10.
July	31	Declared a 20% stock dividend when the stock's market value is $12 per share.
Aug.	14	Issued the stock dividend that was declared on July 31.
Oct.	5	Declared a $0.50 per share cash dividend, date of record October 10.

Required

1. How many common shares are outstanding on each cash dividend date?

2. What is the total dollar amount for each of the four cash dividends?

3. What is the amount of the capitalization of retained earnings for the stock dividend?

4. What is the per share cost of the treasury stock purchased?

5. How much net income did the company earn during year 2012?

Check (3) $44,400

(4) $10

(5) $124,000

Problem 11-5A
Computation of book values and
dividend allocations

C2   A4

Razz Corporation's common stock is currently selling on a stock exchange at $170 per share, and its current balance sheet shows the following stockholders' equity section.

Preferred stock—5% cumulative, $___ par value, 1,000 shares authorized, issued, and outstanding	$100,000
Common stock—$___ par value, 4,000 shares authorized, issued, and outstanding	160,000
Retained earnings	300,000
Total stockholders' equity	$560,000

Required (Round per share amounts to cents.)

1. What is the current market value (price) of this corporation's common stock?

2. What are the par values of the corporation's preferred stock and its common stock?

3. If no dividends are in arrears, what are the book values per share of the preferred stock and the common stock?

Check (4) Book value of common, $112.50

(5) Book value of common, $110

(6) Dividends per common share, $1.25

4. If two years' preferred dividends are in arrears, what are the book values per share of the preferred stock and the common stock?

5. If two years' preferred dividends are in arrears and the preferred stock is callable at $110 per share, what are the book values per share of the preferred stock and the common stock?

6. If two years' preferred dividends are in arrears and the board of directors declares cash dividends of $20,000, what total amount will be paid to the preferred and to the common shareholders? What is the amount of dividends per share for the common stock?

Analysis Component

7. What are some factors that can contribute to a difference between the book value of common stock and its market value (price)?

PROBLEM SET B

Problem 11-1B
Stockholders' equity
transactions and analysis

C2   P1

Nilson Company is incorporated at the beginning of this year and engages in a number of transactions. The following journal entries impacted its stockholders' equity during its first year of operations.

a.	Cash	60,000	
	Common Stock, $1 Par Value		1,500
	Paid-In Capital in Excess of Par Value, Common Stock		58,500
b.	Organization Expenses	20,000	
	Common Stock, $1 Par Value		500
	Paid-In Capital in Excess of Par Value, Common Stock		19,500
c.	Cash	6,650	
	Accounts Receivable	4,000	
	Building	12,500	
	Notes Payable		3,150
	Common Stock, $1 Par Value		400
	Paid-In Capital in Excess of Par Value, Common Stock		19,600
d.	Cash	30,000	
	Common Stock, $1 Par Value		600
	Paid-In Capital in Excess of Par Value, Common Stock		29,400

Required

1. Explain the transaction(s) underlying each journal entry (a) through (d).

Check (2) 3,000 shares

(3) $3,000

2. How many shares of common stock are outstanding at year-end?

3. What is the amount of minimum legal capital (based on par value) at year-end?

4. What is the total paid-in capital at year-end?

(4) $130,000

5. What is the book value per share of the common stock at year-end if total paid-in capital plus retained earnings equals $141,500?

Baycore Corp. reports the following components of stockholders' equity on December 31, 2011.

Problem 11-2B
Cash dividends, treasury stock, and statement of retained earnings

C3 P2 P3

Common stock—$1 par value, 160,000 shares authorized, 100,000 shares issued and outstanding	$ 100,000
Paid-in capital in excess of par value, common stock	700,000
Retained earnings	1,080,000
Total stockholders' equity	$1,880,000

It completed the following transactions related to stockholders' equity in year 2012.

Jan. 10   Purchased 20,000 shares of its own stock at $12 cash per share.
Mar. 2   Directors declared a $1.50 per share cash dividend payable on March 31 to the March 15 stockholders of record.
Mar. 31   Paid the dividend declared on March 2.
Nov. 11   Sold 12,000 of its treasury shares at $13 cash per share.
Nov. 25   Sold 8,000 of its treasury shares at $9.50 cash per share.
Dec. 1   Directors declared a $2.50 per share cash dividend payable on January 2 to the December 10 stockholders of record.
Dec. 31   Closed the $536,000 credit balance (from net income) in the Income Summary account to Retained Earnings.

Required

1. Prepare journal entries to record each of these transactions for 2012.
2. Prepare a statement of retained earnings for the year ended December 31, 2012.
3. Prepare the stockholders' equity section of the company's balance sheet as of December 31, 2012.

Check   (2) Retained earnings, Dec. 31, 2012, $1,238,000

At December 31, the end of Intertec Communication's third quarter, the following stockholders' equity accounts are reported.

Problem 11-3B
Equity analysis—journal entries and account balances

P2

Common stock, $10 par value	$480,000
Paid-in capital in excess of par value, common stock	192,000
Retained earnings	800,000

In the fourth quarter, the following entries related to its equity are recorded.

Jan. 17	Retained Earnings	48,000	
	Common Dividend Payable		48,000
Feb. 5	Common Dividend Payable	48,000	
	Cash		48,000
Feb. 28	Retained Earnings	126,000	
	Common Stock Dividend Distributable		60,000
	Paid-In Capital in Excess of Par Value, Common Stock		66,000
Mar. 14	Common Stock Dividend Distributable	60,000	
	Common Stock, $10 Par Value		60,000
Mar. 25	Memo—Change the title of the common stock account to reflect the new par value of $5.		
Mar. 31	Income Summary	360,000	
	Retained Earnings		360,000

Required

1. Explain the transaction(s) underlying each journal entry.
2. Complete the following table showing the equity account balances at each indicated date (include the balances from December 31).

	Jan. 17	Feb. 5	Feb. 28	Mar. 14	Mar. 25	Mar. 31
Common stock	$_____	$_____	$_____	$_____	$_____	$_____
Common stock dividend distributable	_____	_____	_____	_____	_____	_____
Paid-in capital in excess of par, common stock	_____	_____	_____	_____	_____	_____
Retained earnings	_____	_____	_____	_____	_____	_____
Total equity	$_____	$_____	$_____	$_____	$_____	$_____

Check   Total equity: Jan. 17, $1,424,000; Mar. 31, $1,784,000

Problem 11-4B

Analysis of changes in stockholders' equity accounts

C3   P2   P3

The equity sections from Jetta Corporation's 2011 and 2012 balance sheets follow.

Stockholders' Equity (December 31, 2011)

Common stock—$20 par value, 15,000 shares authorized, 8,500 shares issued and outstanding	$170,000
Paid-in capital in excess of par value, common stock	30,000
Retained earnings	135,000
Total stockholders' equity	$335,000

Stockholders' Equity (December 31, 2012)

Common stock—$20 par value, 15,000 shares authorized, 9,500 shares issued, 500 shares in treasury	$190,000
Paid-in capital in excess of par value, common stock	52,000
Retained earnings ($20,000 restricted by treasury stock)	147,600
	389,600
Less cost of treasury stock	(20,000)
Total stockholders' equity	$369,600

The following transactions and events affected its equity during year 2012.

Feb. 15   Declared a $0.40 per share cash dividend, date of record five days later.
Mar. 2   Purchased treasury stock for cash.
May 15   Declared a $0.40 per share cash dividend, date of record five days later.
Aug. 15   Declared a $0.40 per share cash dividend, date of record five days later.
Oct. 4   Declared a 12.5% stock dividend when the stock's market value is $42 per share.
Oct. 20   Issued the stock dividend that was declared on October 4.
Nov. 15   Declared a $0.40 per share cash dividend, date of record five days later.

Required

1. How many common shares are outstanding on each cash dividend date?
2. What is the total dollar amount for each of the four cash dividends?
3. What is the amount of the capitalization of retained earnings for the stock dividend?
4. What is the per share cost of the treasury stock purchased?
5. How much net income did the company earn during year 2012?

Check   (3) $42,000
       (4) $40
       (5) $68,000

Problem 11-5B

Computation of book values and dividend allocations

C2   A4

Scotch Company's common stock is currently selling on a stock exchange at $45 per share, and its current balance sheet shows the following stockholders' equity section.

Preferred stock—8% cumulative, $___ par value, 1,500 shares authorized, issued, and outstanding	$ 187,500
Common stock—$___ par value, 18,000 shares authorized, issued, and outstanding	450,000
Retained earnings	562,500
Total stockholders' equity	$1,200,000

Required (Round per share amounts to cents.)

1. What is the current market value (price) of this corporation's common stock?
2. What are the par values of the corporation's preferred stock and its common stock?
3. If no dividends are in arrears, what are the book values per share of the preferred stock and the common stock? (Round per share values to the nearest cent.)
4. If two years' preferred dividends are in arrears, what are the book values per share of the preferred stock and the common stock? (Round per share values to the nearest cent.)
5. If two years' preferred dividends are in arrears and the preferred stock is callable at $140 per share, what are the book values per share of the preferred stock and the common stock? (Round per share values to the nearest cent.)
6. If two years' preferred dividends are in arrears and the board of directors declares cash dividends of $50,000, what total amount will be paid to the preferred and to the common shareholders? What is the amount of dividends per share for the common stock? (Round per share values to the nearest cent.)

Check (4) Book value of common, $54.58

(5) Book value of common, $53.33

(6) Dividends per common share, $0.28

Analysis Component

7. Discuss why the book value of common stock is not always a good estimate of its market value.

(This serial problem began in Chapter 1 and continues through most of the book. If previous chapter segments were not completed, the serial problem can begin at this point. It is helpful, but not necessary, to use the Working Papers that accompany the book.)

SERIAL PROBLEM
Business Solutions

P1 C1 C2

SP 11 Santana Rey created Business Solutions on October 1, 2011. The company has been successful, and Santana plans to expand her business. She believes that an additional $86,000 is needed and is investigating three funding sources.

a. Santana's sister Cicely is willing to invest $86,000 in the business as a common shareholder. Since Santana currently has about $129,000 invested in the business, Cicely's investment will mean that Santana will maintain about 60% ownership, and Cicely will have 40% ownership of Business Solutions.

b. Santana's uncle Marcello is willing to invest $86,000 in the business as a preferred shareholder. Marcello would purchase 860 shares of $100 par value, 7% preferred stock.

c. Santana's banker is willing to lend her $86,000 on a 7%, 10-year note payable. She would make monthly payments of $1,000 per month for 10 years.

Required

1. Prepare the journal entry to reflect the initial $86,000 investment under each of the options (a), (b), and (c).
2. Evaluate the three proposals for expansion, providing the pros and cons of each option.
3. Which option do you recommend Santana adopt? Explain.

Beyond the Numbers

BTN 11-1 Refer to **Research In Motion**'s financial statements in Appendix A to answer the following.

1. How many shares of common stock are issued and outstanding at February 27, 2010, and February 28, 2009? How do these numbers compare with the basic weighted-average common shares outstanding at February 27, 2010, and February 28, 2009?
2. What is the book value of its entire common stock at February 27, 2010?
3. What is the total amount of cash dividends paid to common stockholders for the years ended February 27, 2010, and February 28, 2009?
4. Identify and compare basic EPS amounts across fiscal years 2010, 2009, and 2008. Identify and comment on any notable changes.
5. How many shares does Research In Motion hold in treasury stock, if any, as of February 27, 2010? As of February 28, 2009?

REPORTING IN ACTION

C2 A1 A4

RIM

Fast Forward

6. Access Research In Motion's financial statements for fiscal years ending after February 27, 2010, from its Website (**RIM.com**) or the SEC's EDGAR database (**www.sec.gov**). Has the number of common shares outstanding increased since that date? Has the company increased the total amount of cash dividends paid compared to the total amount for fiscal year 2010?

COMPARATIVE ANALYSIS

A1 A2 A3 A4

RIM
Palm
Apple

BTN 11-2 Key comparative figures for **Research In Motion**, **Palm**, and **Apple** follow.

Key Figures	Research In Motion	Palm	Apple
Net income (in millions)	$2,457	$ (753)	$8,235
Cash dividends declared per common share	$ —	$ —	$ —
Common shares outstanding (in millions)	557	140	900
Weighted-average common shares outstanding (in mil.)	564	116	893
Market value (price) per share	$69.76	$12.19	$184.40
Equity applicable to common shares (in millions)	$7,603	$ (414)	$31,640

Required

1. Compute the book value per common share for each company using these data.
2. Compute the basic EPS for each company using these data.
3. Compute the dividend yield for each company using these data. Does the dividend yield of any of the companies characterize it as an income or growth stock? Explain.
4. Compute, compare, and interpret the price-earnings ratio for each company using these data.

ETHICS CHALLENGE

C3

BTN 11-3 Gianna Tuck is an accountant for Post Pharmaceuticals. Her duties include tracking research and development spending in the new product development division. Over the course of the past six months, Gianna notices that a great deal of funds have been spent on a particular project for a new drug. She hears "through the grapevine" that the company is about to patent the drug and expects it to be a major advance in antibiotics. Gianna believes that this new drug will greatly improve company performance and will cause the company's stock to increase in value. Gianna decides to purchase shares of Post in order to benefit from this expected increase.

Required

What are Gianna's ethical responsibilities, if any, with respect to the information she has learned through her duties as an accountant for Post Pharmaceuticals? What are the implications to her planned purchase of Post shares?

COMMUNICATING IN PRACTICE

A1 A2

Hint: Make a transparency of each team's memo for a class discussion.

BTN 11-4 Teams are to select an industry, and each team member is to select a different company in that industry. Each team member then is to acquire the selected company's financial statements (or Form 10-K) from the SEC site (**www.sec.gov**). Use these data to identify basic EPS. Use the financial press (or **finance.yahoo.com**) to determine the market price of this stock, and then compute the price-earnings ratio. Communicate with teammates via a meeting, e-mail, or telephone to discuss the meaning of this ratio, how companies compare, and the industry norm. The team must prepare a single memorandum reporting the ratio for each company and identifying the team conclusions or consensus of opinion. The memorandum is to be duplicated and distributed to the instructor and teammates.

TAKING IT TO THE NET

C1 C3

BTN 11-5 Access the February 26, 2010, filing of the 2009 calendar-year 10-K report of **McDonald's**, (ticker MCD) from **www.sec.gov**.

Required

1. Review McDonald's balance sheet and identify how many classes of stock it has issued.
2. What are the par values, number of authorized shares, and issued shares of the classes of stock you identified in part 1?
3. Review its statement of cash flows and identify what total amount of cash it paid in 2009 to purchase treasury stock.
4. What amount did McDonald's pay out in common stock cash dividends for 2009?

TEAMWORK IN ACTION

P3

Hint: Instructor should be sure each team accurately completes part 1 before proceeding.

BTN 11-6 This activity requires teamwork to reinforce understanding of accounting for treasury stock.

1. Write a brief team statement (*a*) generalizing what happens to a corporation's financial position when it engages in a stock "buyback" and (*b*) identifying reasons why a corporation would engage in this activity.
2. Assume that an entity acquires 100 shares of its $100 par value common stock at a cost of $134 cash per share. Discuss the entry to record this acquisition. Next, assign *each* team member to prepare *one* of the following entries (assume each entry applies to all shares):
   a. Reissue treasury shares at cost.
   b. Reissue treasury shares at $150 per share.

    c. Reissue treasury shares at $120 per share; assume the paid-in capital account from treasury shares has a $1,500 balance.

    d. Reissue treasury shares at $120 per share; assume the paid-in capital account from treasury shares has a $1,000 balance.

    e. Reissue treasury shares at $120 per share; assume the paid-in capital account from treasury shares has a zero balance.

3. In sequence, each member is to present his/her entry to the team and explain the *similarities* and *differences* between that entry and the previous entry.

BTN 11-7   Assume that Kelly Giard of Clean Air Lawn Care decides to launch a new retail chain to market electrical mowers. This chain, named Mow Green, requires $500,000 of start-up capital. Kelly contributes $375,000 of personal assets in return for 15,000 shares of common stock, but he must raise another $125,000 in cash. There are two alternative plans for raising the additional cash. *Plan A* is to sell 3,750 shares of common stock to one or more investors for $125,000 cash. *Plan B* is to sell 1,250 shares of cumulative preferred stock to one or more investors for $125,000 cash (this preferred stock would have a $100 par value, an annual 8% dividend rate, and be issued at par).

ENTREPRENEURIAL DECISION

C2 P2

1. If the new business is expected to earn $72,000 of after-tax net income in the first year, what rate of return on beginning equity will Kelly earn under each alternative plan? Which plan will provide the higher expected return?

2. If the new business is expected to earn $16,800 of after-tax net income in the first year, what rate of return on beginning equity will Kelly earn under each alternative plan? Which plan will provide the higher expected return?

3. Analyze and interpret the differences between the results for parts 1 and 2.

BTN 11-8   Review 30 to 60 minutes of financial news programming on television. Take notes on companies that are catching analysts' attention. You might hear reference to over- and undervaluation of firms and to reports about PE ratios, dividend yields, and earnings per share. Be prepared to give a brief description to the class of your observations.

HITTING THE ROAD

A1 A2 A3

BTN 11-9   Financial information for Nokia Corporation (<u>www.nokia.com</u>) follows.

Net income (in millions)	€ 260
Cash dividends declared (in millions)	€ 1,481
Cash dividends declared per share	€ 0.40
Number of shares outstanding (in millions)*	3,708
Equity applicable to shares (in millions)	€14,749

    * Assume that for Nokia the year-end number of shares outstanding approximates the weighted-average shares outstanding.

GLOBAL DECISION

A1 C3

NOKIA

Required

1. Compute book value per share for Nokia.

2. Compute earnings per share (EPS) for Nokia.

3. Compare Nokia's dividends per share with its EPS. Is Nokia paying out a large or small amount of its income as dividends? Explain.

ANSWERS TO MULTIPLE CHOICE QUIZ

1. e; Entry to record this stock issuance is:

Cash (6,000 × $8)	48,000	
Common Stock (6,000 × $5)		30,000
Paid-In Capital in Excess of Par Value,		
Common Stock		18,000

2. b; $75,000/19,000 shares = $3.95 per share

3. d; Preferred stock = 5,000 × $100 = $500,000
    Book value per share = ($2,000,000 − $500,000)/50,000 shares = $30 per common share

4. a; $0.81/$45.00 = 1.8%

5. c; Earnings per share = $3,500,000/700,000 shares = $5 per share
    PE ratio = $85/$5 = 17.0

12

Reporting Cash Flows

A Look Back

Chapter 11 focused on corporate equity transactions, including stock issuances and dividends. We also explained how to report and analyze income, earnings per share, and retained earnings.

A Look at This Chapter

This chapter focuses on reporting and analyzing cash inflows and cash outflows. We emphasize how to prepare and interpret the statement of cash flows.

A Look Ahead

Chapter 13 focuses on tools to help us analyze financial statements. We also describe comparative analysis and the application of ratios for financial analysis.

Learning Objectives

CONCEPTUAL

C1 Distinguish between operating, investing, and financing activities, and describe how noncash investing and financing activities are disclosed. (p. 501)

ANALYTICAL

A1 Analyze the statement of cash flows and apply the cash flow on total assets ratio. (p. 518)

LP12

PROCEDURAL

P1 Prepare a statement of cash flows. (p. 504)

P2 Compute cash flows from operating activities using the indirect method. (p. 507)

P3 Determine cash flows from both investing and financing activities. (p. 513)

P4 *Appendix 12A*—Illustrate use of a spreadsheet to prepare a statement of cash flows. (p. 522)

P5 *Appendix 12B*—Compute cash flows from operating activities using the direct method. (p. 525)

Shape Up Your Images

"We feel like we have a great competitive advantage"
—**BRAD JEFFERSON**

NEW YORK—"I don't know about you, but I get shown so many boring slideshows of my friends' trips," admits Jason Hsiao. "It's like 20 minutes, and you're like, 'Kill me now.'" However, unlike the rest of us, Jason decided to do something about it. He, along with childhood buddies Brad Jefferson, Stevie Clifton, and Tom Clifton, launched **Animoto (Animoto.com).** Its Website describes their service as "a web application that automatically . . . analyzes and combines user-selected images, video clips, and music."

"We want to help users create professional-quality content," explains Jason. "So it doesn't matter what you give us, we'll take that and put it in our magic black box, and in a couple minutes, we'll deliver something that . . . you never could have dreamed of doing on your own." The owners point out that they can create a 30-second video for free. This has cash flow implications. "We decided that we would make a *freemium* model, which allows people to get a taste of the Animoto service for free," says Brad. However, longer videos and videos with more user-options require cash payments, which generate positive cash inflows.

User traffic at Animoto has grown to over 1 million per month. That type of growth has obvious cash implications for technology support, accounting, and other operating and investing cash outflows. The owners emphasize the importance of monitoring and tracking cash inflows and cash outflows. Jason admits, "There's no possible way we could handle [growth] . . . without quickly digging ourselves into a multimillion dollar hole!"

Accordingly, the young owners learned to monitor and control cash flows for each of their operating, investing, and financing activities. Their focus on controlling cash flows led them to apply *cloud computing,* which is a pay-as-you-go model. "[We] could not have existed . . . without cloud computing," admits Jason. A review of Animoto's statement of cash flows, and its individual cash inflows and outflows, led them to this cash flow model. Explains Brad, "We use Amazon . . . for all IT infrastructure . . . PayPal and Google . . . for billing/payment . . . SaaS for email and sales." This model highlights those activities that generate the most cash and those that are cash drains. Adds Jason, "The only real asset we have in our office [is] . . . a fancy espresso machine!"

Yet cash management has not curtailed the team's fun-loving approach. Their Website describes themselves as "a bunch of techies . . . who decided to lock themselves in a room together and nerd out!" Adds Brad, "We're going through the process of figuring out where we want the future to take us."

[Sources: *Animoto Website,* January 2011; *Entrepreneur,* January 2009; *Fast Company,* September 2008; *Bellevue Reporter,* May 2008]

A company cannot achieve or maintain profits without carefully managing cash. Managers and other users of information pay attention to a company's cash position and the events and transactions affecting cash. This chapter explains how we prepare, analyze, and interpret a statement of cash flows. It also discusses the importance of cash flow information for predicting future performance and making managerial decisions. More generally, effectively using the statement of cash flows is crucial for managing and analyzing the operating, investing, and financing activities of businesses.

Reporting Cash Flows

Basics of Cash Flow Reporting	Cash Flows from Operating	Cash Flows from Investing	Cash Flows from Financing
• Purpose • Importance • Measurement • Classification • Noncash activities • Format and preparation	• Indirect and direct methods of reporting • Application of indirect method of reporting • Summary of indirect method adjustments	• Three-stage process of analysis • Analysis of noncurrent assets • Analysis of other assets	• Three-stage process of analysis • Analysis of non-current liabilities • Analysis of equity

BASICS OF CASH FLOW REPORTING

This section describes the basics of cash flow reporting, including its purpose, measurement, classification, format, and preparation.

Purpose of the Statement of Cash Flows

The purpose of the **statement of cash flows** is to report cash receipts (inflows) and cash payments (outflows) during a period. This includes separately identifying the cash flows related to operating, investing, and financing activities. The statement of cash flows does more than simply report changes in cash. It is the detailed disclosure of individual cash flows that makes this statement useful to users. Information in this statement helps users answer questions such as these:

- How does a company obtain its cash?
- Where does a company spend its cash?
- What explains the change in the cash balance?

Point: Internal users rely on the statement of cash flows to make investing and financing decisions. External users rely on this statement to assess the amount and timing of a company's cash flows.

The statement of cash flows addresses important questions such as these by summarizing, classifying, and reporting a company's cash inflows and cash outflows for each period.

Importance of Cash Flows

Information about cash flows can influence decision makers in important ways. For instance, we look more favorably at a company that is financing its expenditures with cash from operations than one that does it by selling its assets. Information about cash flows helps users decide whether a company has enough cash to pay its existing debts as they mature. It is also relied upon to evaluate a company's ability to meet unexpected obligations and pursue unexpected opportunities. External information users especially want to assess a company's ability to take advantage of new business opportunities. Internal users such as managers use cash flow information to plan day-to-day operating activities and make long-term investment decisions.

Macy's striking turnaround is an example of how analysis and management of cash flows can lead to improved financial stability. Several years ago Macy's obtained temporary protection from bankruptcy, at which time it desperately needed to improve its cash flows. It did so by engaging in aggressive cost-cutting measures. As a result, Macy's annual cash flow rose to $210 million, up from a negative cash flow of $38.9 million in the prior year. Macy's eventually met its financial obligations and then successfully merged with Federated Department Stores.

The case of **W. T. Grant Co.** is a classic example of the importance of cash flow information in predicting a company's future performance and financial strength. Grant reported net income of more than $40 million per year for three consecutive years. At that same time, it was experiencing an alarming decrease in cash provided by operations. For instance, net cash outflow was more than $90 million by the end of that three-year period. Grant soon went bankrupt. Users who relied solely on Grant's income numbers were unpleasantly surprised. This reminds us that cash flows as well as income statement and balance sheet information are crucial in making business decisions.

Decision Insight

Cash Savvy "A lender must have a complete understanding of a borrower's cash flows to assess both the borrowing needs and repayment sources. This requires information about the major types of cash inflows and outflows. I have seen many companies, whose financial statements indicate good profitability, experience severe financial problems because the owners or managers lacked a good understanding of cash flows."—Mary E. Garza, **Bank of America** ■

Measurement of Cash Flows

Cash flows are defined to include both *cash* and *cash equivalents*. The statement of cash flows explains the difference between the beginning and ending balances of cash and cash equivalents. We continue to use the phrases *cash flows* and the *statement of cash flows,* but we must remember that both phrases refer to cash and cash equivalents. Recall that a cash equivalent must satisfy two criteria: (1) be readily convertible to a known amount of cash and (2) be sufficiently close to its maturity so its market value is unaffected by interest rate changes. In most cases, a debt security must be within three months of its maturity to satisfy these criteria. Companies must disclose and follow a clear policy for determining cash and cash equivalents and apply it consistently from period to period. **American Express**, for example, defines its cash equivalents as "time deposits and other highly liquid investments with original maturities of 90 days or less."

Classification of Cash Flows

Since cash and cash equivalents are combined, the statement of cash flows does not report transactions between cash and cash equivalents such as cash paid to purchase cash equivalents and cash received from selling cash equivalents. However, all other cash receipts and cash payments are classified and reported on the statement as operating, investing, or financing activities. Individual cash receipts and payments for each of these three categories are labeled to identify their originating transactions or events. A net cash inflow (source) occurs when the receipts in a category exceed the payments. A net cash outflow (use) occurs when the payments in a category exceed the receipts.

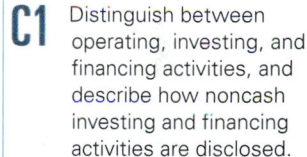

C1 Distinguish between operating, investing, and financing activities, and describe how noncash investing and financing activities are disclosed.

Operating Activities   **Operating activities** include those transactions and events that determine net income. Examples are the production and purchase of merchandise, the sale of goods and services to customers, and the expenditures to administer the business. Not all items in income, such as unusual gains and losses, are operating activities (we discuss these exceptions later in the chapter). Exhibit 12.1 lists the more common cash inflows and outflows from operating activities. (Although cash receipts and cash payments from buying and selling trading

EXHIBIT 12.1

Cash Flows from Operating Activities

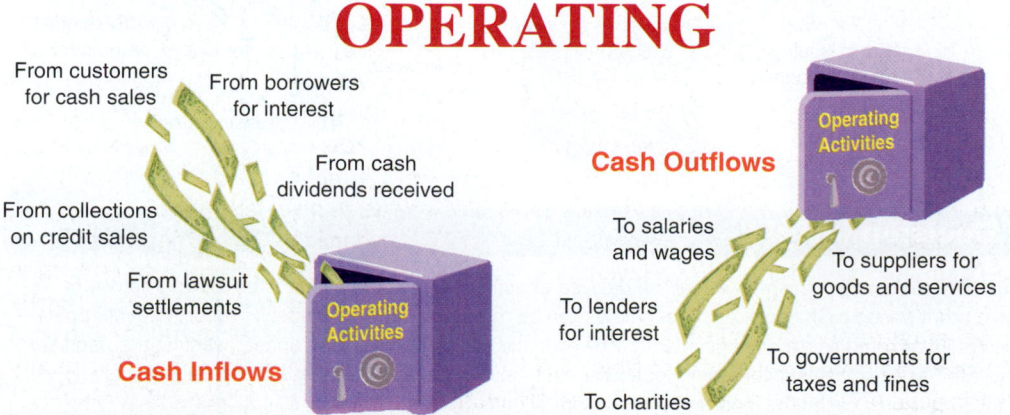

securities are often reported under operating activities, new standards require that these receipts and payments be classified based on the nature and purpose of those securities.)

Investing Activities   **Investing activities** generally include those transactions and events that affect long-term assets—namely, the purchase and sale of long-term assets. They also include (1) the purchase and sale of short-term investments in the securities of other entities, other than cash equivalents and trading securities and (2) lending and collecting money for notes receivable. Exhibit 12.2 lists examples of cash flows from investing activities. Proceeds from collecting the principal amounts of notes deserve special mention. If the note results from sales to customers, its cash receipts are classed as operating activities whether short-term or long-term. If the note results from a loan to another party apart from sales, however, the cash receipts from collecting the note principal are classed as an investing activity. The FASB requires that the collection of interest on loans be reported as an operating activity.

Point: The FASB requires that *cash dividends received* and *cash interest received* be reported as operating activities.

EXHIBIT 12.2

Cash Flows from Investing Activities

INVESTING

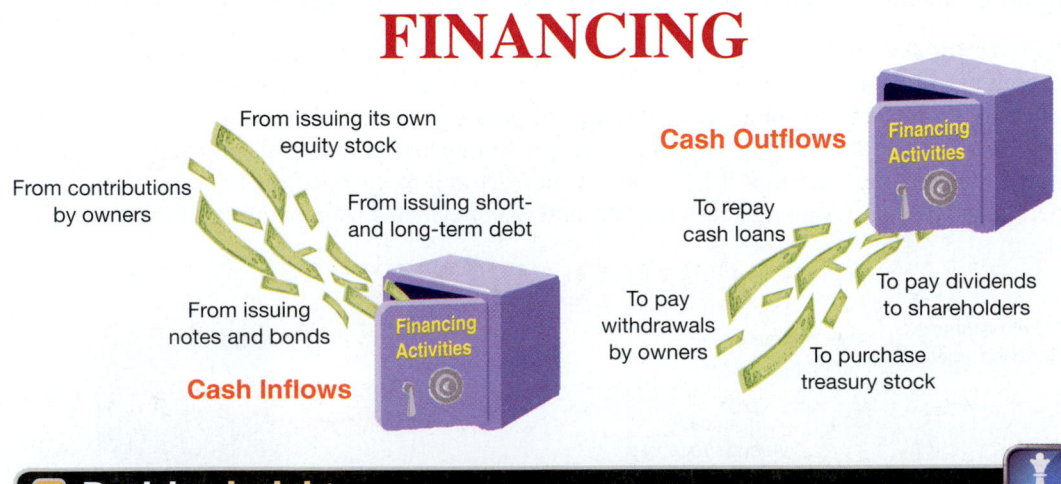

Financing Activities   **Financing activities** include those transactions and events that affect long-term liabilities and equity. Examples are (1) obtaining cash from issuing debt and repaying the amounts borrowed and (2) receiving cash from or distributing cash to owners. These activities involve transactions with a company's owners and creditors. They also often involve borrowing and repaying principal amounts relating to both short- and long-term debt. GAAP requires that payments of interest expense be classified as operating activities. Also, cash payments to settle credit purchases of merchandise, whether on account or by note, are operating activities. Exhibit 12.3 lists examples of cash flows from financing activities.

EXHIBIT 12.3

Cash Flows from Financing Activities

FINANCING

From issuing its own equity stock

From contributions by owners

From issuing short- and long-term debt

Cash Outflows   Financing Activities

From issuing notes and bonds   Financing Activities

Cash Inflows

To repay cash loans

To pay withdrawals by owners

To pay dividends to shareholders

To purchase treasury stock

Point: Interest payments on a loan are classified as operating activities, but payments of loan principal are financing activities.

Decision Insight

Cash Monitoring   Cash flows can be delayed or accelerated at the end of a period to improve or reduce current period cash flows. Also, cash flows can be misclassified. Cash outflows reported under operations are interpreted as expense payments. However, cash outflows reported under investing activities are interpreted as a positive sign of growth potential. Thus, managers face incentives to misclassify cash flows. For these reasons, cash flow reporting warrants our scrutiny. ■

Noncash Investing and Financing

When important investing and financing activities do not affect cash receipts or payments, they are still disclosed at the bottom of the statement of cash flows or in a note to the statement because of their importance and the *full-disclosure principle*. One example of such a transaction is the purchase of long-term assets using a long-term note payable (loan). This transaction involves both investing and financing activities but does not affect any cash inflow or outflow and is not reported in any of the three sections of the statement of cash flows. This disclosure rule also extends to transactions with partial cash receipts or payments.

To illustrate, assume that Goorin purchases land for $12,000 by paying $5,000 cash and trading in used equipment worth $7,000. The investing section of the statement of cash flows reports only the $5,000 cash outflow for the land purchase. The $12,000 investing transaction is only partially described in the body of the statement of cash flows, yet this information is potentially important to users because it changes the makeup of assets. Goorin could either describe the transaction in a footnote or include information at the bottom of its statement that lists the $12,000 land purchase along with the cash financing of $5,000 and a $7,000 trade-in of equipment. As another example, Borg Co. acquired $900,000 of assets in exchange for $200,000 cash and a $700,000 long-term note, which should be reported as follows:

Point: A stock dividend transaction involving a transfer from retained earnings to common stock or a credit to contributed capital is *not* considered a noncash investing and financing activity because the company receives no consideration for shares issued.

Fair value of assets acquired	$900,000
Less cash paid	200,000
Liabilities incurred or assumed	$700,000

Exhibit 12.4 lists transactions commonly disclosed as noncash investing and financing activities.

- Retirement of debt by issuing equity stock.
- Conversion of preferred stock to common stock.
- Lease of assets in a capital lease transaction.
- Purchase of long-term assets by issuing a note or bond.
- Exchange of noncash assets for other noncash assets.
- Purchase of noncash assets by issuing equity or debt.

EXHIBIT 12.4

Examples of Noncash Investing and Financing Activities

Format of the Statement of Cash Flows

Accounting standards require companies to include a statement of cash flows in a complete set of financial statements. This statement must report information about a company's cash receipts and cash payments during the period. Exhibit 12.5 shows the usual format. A company must report cash flows from three activities: operating, investing, and financing. The statement

EXHIBIT 12.5

Format of the Statement of Cash Flows

COMPANY NAME	
Statement of Cash Flows	
For *period* Ended *date*	
Cash flows from operating activities	
[List of individual inflows and outflows]	
Net cash provided (used) by operating activities	$ #
Cash flows from investing activities	
[List of individual inflows and outflows]	
Net cash provided (used) by investing activities	#
Cash flows from financing activities	
[List of individual inflows and outflows]	
Net cash provided (used) by financing activities	#
Net increase (decrease) in cash	$ #
Cash (and equivalents) balance at prior period-end	#
Cash (and equivalents) balance at current period-end	$ #

Separate schedule or note disclosure of any "noncash investing and financing transactions" is required.

explains how transactions and events impact the prior period-end cash (and cash equivalents) balance to produce its current period-end balance.

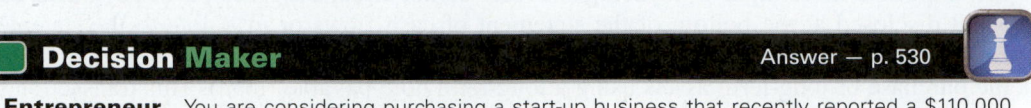

Decision Maker   Answer — p. 530

Entrepreneur   You are considering purchasing a start-up business that recently reported a $110,000 annual net loss and a $225,000 annual net cash inflow. How are these results possible? ■

Quick Check   Answers — p. 530

1. Does a statement of cash flows report the cash payments to purchase cash equivalents? Does it report the cash receipts from selling cash equivalents?
2. Identify the three categories of cash flows reported separately on the statement of cash flows.
3. Identify the cash activity category for each transaction: (*a*) purchase equipment for cash, (*b*) cash payment of wages, (*c*) sale of common stock for cash, (*d*) receipt of cash dividends from stock investment, (*e*) cash collection from customers, (*f*) notes issued for cash.

Preparing the Statement of Cash Flows

P1 Prepare a statement of cash flows.

Preparing a statement of cash flows involves five steps: 1 compute the net increase or decrease in cash; 2 compute and report the net cash provided or used by operating activities (using either the direct or indirect method; both are explained); 3 compute and report the net cash provided or used by investing activities; 4 compute and report the net cash provided or used by financing activities; and 5 compute the net cash flow by combining net cash provided or used by operating, investing, and financing activities and then *prove it* by adding it to the beginning cash balance to show that it equals the ending cash balance.

Step 1 Compute net increase or decrease in cash

Step 2 Compute net cash from operating activities

Step 3 Compute net cash from investing activities

Step 4 Compute net cash from financing activities

Step 5 Prove and report beginning and ending cash balances

Computing the net increase or net decrease in cash is a simple but crucial computation. It equals the current period's cash balance minus the prior period's cash balance. This is the *bottom-line* figure for the statement of cash flows and is a check on accuracy. The information we need to prepare a statement of cash flows comes from various sources including comparative balance sheets at the beginning and end of the period, and an income statement for the period. There are two alternative approaches to preparing the statement: (1) analyzing the Cash account and (2) analyzing noncash accounts.

Point: View the change in cash as a *target* number that we will fully explain and prove in the statement of cash flows.

Analyzing the Cash Account   A company's cash receipts and cash payments are recorded in the Cash account in its general ledger. The Cash account is therefore a natural place to look for information about cash flows from operating, investing, and financing activities. To illustrate, review the summarized Cash T-account of Genesis, Inc., in Exhibit 12.6. Individual cash transactions are summarized in this Cash account according to the major types of cash receipts and cash payments. For instance, only the total of cash receipts from all customers is listed. Individual cash transactions underlying these totals can number in the thousands. Accounting software is available to provide summarized cash accounts.

Preparing a statement of cash flows from Exhibit 12.6 requires determining whether an individual cash inflow or outflow is an operating, investing, or financing activity, and then listing each by

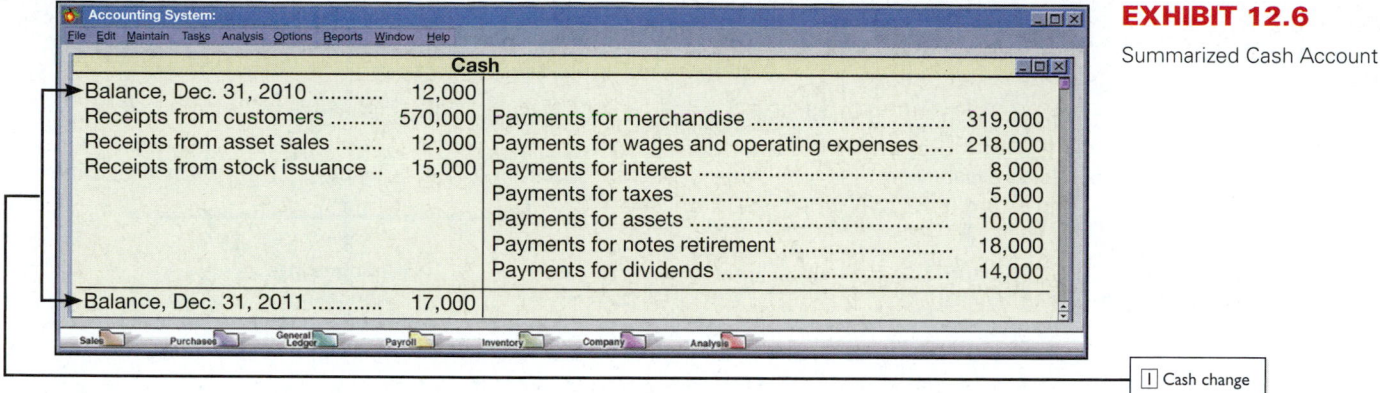

EXHIBIT 12.6

Summarized Cash Account

activity. This yields the statement shown in Exhibit 12.7. However, preparing the statement of cash flows from an analysis of the summarized Cash account has two limitations. First, most companies have many individual cash receipts and payments, making it difficult to review them all. Accounting software minimizes this burden, but it is still a task requiring professional judgment for many transactions. Second, the Cash account does not usually carry an adequate description of each cash transaction, making assignment of all cash transactions according to activity difficult.

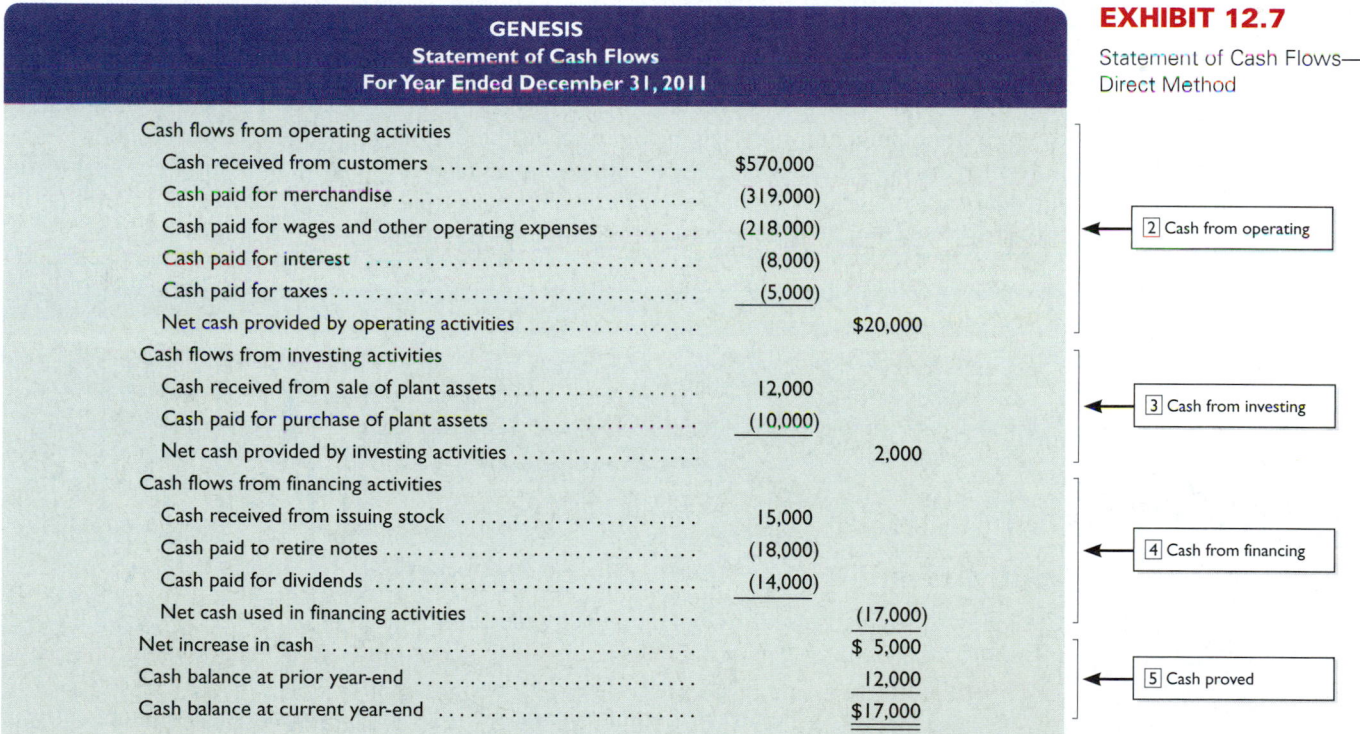

EXHIBIT 12.7

Statement of Cash Flows—Direct Method

Analyzing Noncash Accounts   A second approach to preparing the statement of cash flows is analyzing noncash accounts. This approach uses the fact that when a company records cash inflows and outflows with debits and credits to the Cash account (see Exhibit 12.6), it also records credits and debits in noncash accounts (reflecting double-entry accounting). Many of these noncash accounts are balance sheet accounts—for instance, from the sale of land for cash. Others are revenue and expense accounts that are closed to equity. For instance, the sale of services for cash yields a credit to Services Revenue that is closed to Retained Earnings for a corporation. In sum, *all cash transactions eventually affect noncash balance sheet accounts*. Thus, we can determine cash inflows and outflows by analyzing changes in noncash balance sheet accounts.

Exhibit 12.8 uses the accounting equation to show the relation between the Cash account and the noncash balance sheet accounts. This exhibit starts with the accounting equation at the

EXHIBIT 12.8

Relation between Cash and
Noncash Accounts

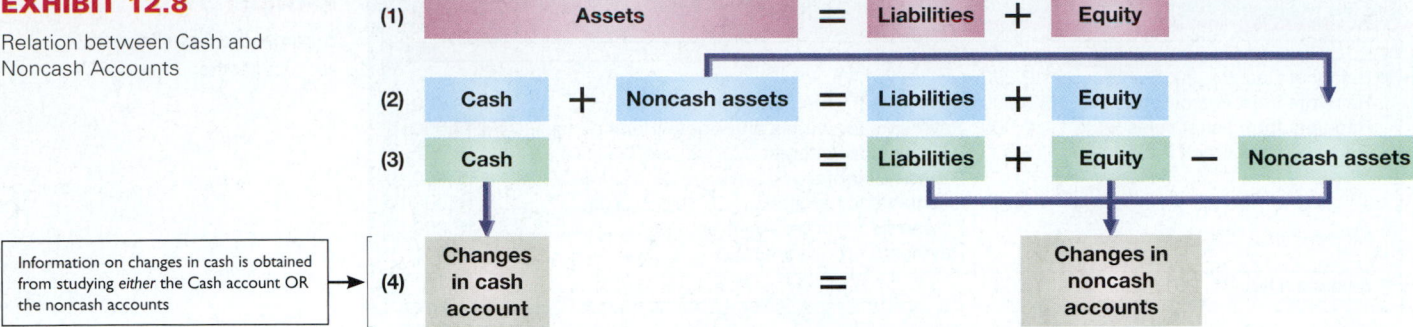

Information on changes in cash is obtained from studying *either* the Cash account OR the noncash accounts

top. It is then expanded in line (2) to separate cash from noncash asset accounts. Line (3) moves noncash asset accounts to the right-hand side of the equality where they are subtracted. This shows that cash equals the sum of the liability and equity accounts *minus* the noncash asset accounts. Line (4) points out that *changes* on one side of the accounting equation equal *changes* on the other side. It shows that we can explain changes in cash by analyzing changes in the noncash accounts consisting of liability accounts, equity accounts, and noncash asset accounts. By analyzing noncash balance sheet accounts and any related income statement accounts, we can prepare a statement of cash flows.

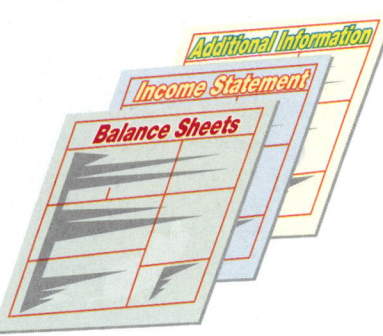

Information to Prepare the Statement   Information to prepare the statement of cash flows usually comes from three sources: (1) comparative balance sheets, (2) the current income statement, and (3) additional information. Comparative balance sheets are used to compute changes in noncash accounts from the beginning to the end of the period. The current income statement is used to help compute cash flows from operating activities. Additional information often includes details on transactions and events that help explain both the cash flows and noncash investing and financing activities.

Decision Insight

e-Cash   Every credit transaction on the Net leaves a trail that a hacker or a marketer can pick up. Enter e-cash—or digital money. The encryption of e-cash protects your money from snoops and thieves and cannot be traced, even by the issuing bank. ■

CASH FLOWS FROM OPERATING

Indirect and Direct Methods of Reporting

Cash flows provided (used) by operating activities are reported in one of two ways: the *direct method* or the *indirect method.* **These two different methods apply only to the operating activities section.**

The **direct method** separately lists each major item of operating cash receipts (such as cash received from customers) and each major item of operating cash payments (such as cash paid for merchandise). The cash payments are subtracted from cash receipts to determine the net cash provided (used) by operating activities. The operating activities section of Exhibit 12.7 reflects the direct method of reporting operating cash flows.

The **indirect method** reports net income and then adjusts it for items necessary to obtain net cash provided or used by operating activities. It does *not* report individual items of cash inflows and cash outflows from operating activities. Instead, the indirect method reports the necessary adjustments to reconcile net income to net cash provided or used by operating activities. The operating activities section for Genesis prepared under the indirect method is shown in Exhibit 12.9. **The net cash amount provided by operating activities is *identical* under both the direct and indirect methods.**

EXHIBIT 12.9

Operating Activities Section—
Indirect Method

Cash flows from operating activities		
Net income	$ 38,000	
Adjustments to reconcile net income to net cash provided by operating activities		
Increase in accounts receivable......................	(20,000)	
Increase in merchandise inventory	(14,000)	
Increase in prepaid expenses........................	(2,000)	
Decrease in accounts payable	(5,000)	
Decrease in interest payable	(1,000)	
Increase in income taxes payable	10,000	
Depreciation expense	24,000	
Loss on sale of plant assets	6,000	
Gain on retirement of notes	(16,000)	
Net cash provided by operating activities..........		**$20,000**

This equality always exists. The difference in these methods is with the computation and presentation of this amount. The FASB recommends the direct method, but because it is not required and the indirect method is arguably easier to compute, nearly all companies report operating cash flows using the indirect method.

To illustrate, we prepare the operating activities section of the statement of cash flows for Genesis. Exhibit 12.10 shows the December 31, 2010 and 2011, balance sheets of Genesis along with its 2011 income statement. We use this information to prepare a statement of cash flows that explains the $5,000 increase in cash for 2011 as reflected in its balance sheets. This $5,000 is computed as Cash of $17,000 at the end of 2011 minus Cash of $12,000 at the end of 2010. Genesis discloses additional information on its 2011 transactions:

a. The accounts payable balances result from merchandise inventory purchases.

b. Purchased $70,000 in plant assets by paying $10,000 cash and issuing $60,000 of notes payable.

c. Sold plant assets with an original cost of $30,000 and accumulated depreciation of $12,000 for $12,000 cash, yielding a $6,000 loss.

d. Received $15,000 cash from issuing 3,000 shares of common stock.

e. Paid $18,000 cash to retire notes with a $34,000 book value, yielding a $16,000 gain.

f. Declared and paid cash dividends of $14,000.

The next section describes the indirect method. Appendix 12B describes the direct method. An instructor can choose to cover either one or both methods. Neither section depends on the other.

Application of the Indirect Method of Reporting

Net income is computed using accrual accounting, which recognizes revenues when earned and expenses when incurred. Revenues and expenses do not necessarily reflect the receipt and payment of cash. The indirect method of computing and reporting net cash flows from operating activities involves adjusting the net income figure to obtain the net cash provided or used by operating activities. This includes subtracting noncash increases (credits) from net income and adding noncash charges (debits) back to net income.

To illustrate, the indirect method begins with Genesis's net income of $38,000 and adjusts it to obtain net cash provided by operating activities of $20,000. Exhibit 12.11 shows the results of the indirect method of reporting operating cash flows, which adjusts net income for three types of adjustments. There are adjustments ① to reflect changes in noncash current assets and current liabilities related to operating activities, ② to income statement items involving operating activities that do not affect cash inflows or outflows, and ③ to eliminate gains and losses resulting from investing and financing activities (not part of operating activities). This section describes each of these adjustments.

Point: To better understand the direct and indirect methods of reporting operating cash flows, identify similarities and differences between Exhibits 12.7 and 12.11.

P2 Compute cash flows from operating activities using the indirect method.

Point: *Noncash credits* refer to *revenue* amounts reported on the income statement that are *not collected in cash* this period. *Noncash charges* refer to *expense* amounts reported on the income statement that are *not paid* this period.

EXHIBIT 12.10

Financial Statements

GENESIS Income Statement For Year Ended December 31, 2011		
Sales		$590,000
Cost of goods sold	$300,000	
Wages and other operating expenses	216,000	
Interest expense	7,000	
Depreciation expense	24,000	(547,000)
		43,000
Other gains (losses)		
Gain on retirement of notes	16,000	
Loss on sale of plant assets	(6,000)	10,000
Income before taxes		53,000
Income taxes expense		(15,000)
Net income		$ 38,000

GENESIS Balance Sheets December 31, 2011 and 2010		
	2011	**2010**
Assets		
Current assets		
Cash	$ 17,000	$ 12,000
Accounts receivable	60,000	40,000
Merchandise inventory	84,000	70,000
Prepaid expenses	6,000	4,000
Total current assets	167,000	126,000
Long-term assets		
Plant assets	250,000	210,000
Accumulated depreciation	(60,000)	(48,000)
Total assets	$357,000	$288,000
Liabilities		
Current liabilities		
Accounts payable	$ 35,000	$ 40,000
Interest payable	3,000	4,000
Income taxes payable	22,000	12,000
Total current liabilities	60,000	56,000
Long-term notes payable	90,000	64,000
Total liabilities	150,000	120,000
Equity		
Common stock, $5 par	95,000	80,000
Retained earnings	112,000	88,000
Total equity	207,000	168,000
Total liabilities and equity	$357,000	$288,000

① **Adjustments for Changes in Current Assets and Current Liabilities**   This section describes adjustments for changes in noncash current assets and current liabilities.

Point: Operating activities are typically those that determine income, which are often reflected in changes in current assets and current liabilities.

Adjustments for changes in noncash current assets.   Changes in noncash current assets normally result from operating activities. Examples are sales affecting accounts receivable and building usage affecting prepaid rent. Decreases in noncash current assets yield the following adjustment:

Decreases in noncash current assets are added to net income.

To see the logic for this adjustment, consider that a decrease in a noncash current asset such as accounts receivable suggests more available cash at the end of the period compared to the beginning. This is so because a decrease in accounts receivable implies higher cash receipts than reflected in sales. We add these higher cash receipts (from decreases in noncash current assets) to net income when computing cash flow from operations.

In contrast, an increase in noncash current assets such as accounts receivable implies less cash receipts than reflected in sales. As another example, an increase in prepaid rent indicates that more cash is paid for rent than is deducted as rent expense. Increases in noncash current assets yield the following adjustment:

Increases in noncash current assets are subtracted from net income.

To illustrate, these adjustments are applied to the noncash current assets in Exhibit 12.10.

Accounts receivable. Accounts receivable *increase* $20,000, from a beginning balance of $40,000 to an ending balance of $60,000. This increase implies that Genesis collects less cash than is reported in sales. That is, some of these sales were in the form of accounts receivable and that amount increased during the period. To see this it is helpful to use *account analysis*. This usually involves setting up a T-account and reconstructing its major entries to compute cash receipts or payments. The following reconstructed Accounts Receivable T-account reveals that cash receipts are less than sales:

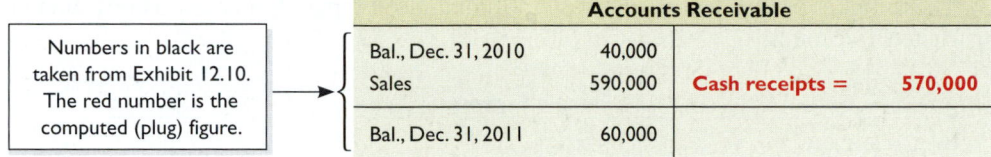

Numbers in black are taken from Exhibit 12.10. The red number is the computed (plug) figure.		**Accounts Receivable**		
	Bal., Dec. 31, 2010	40,000		
	Sales	590,000	**Cash receipts =**	**570,000**
	Bal., Dec. 31, 2011	60,000		

We see that sales are $20,000 greater than cash receipts. This $20,000—as reflected in the $20,000 increase in Accounts Receivable—is subtracted from net income when computing cash provided by operating activities (see Exhibit 12.11).

Merchandise inventory. Merchandise inventory *increases* by $14,000, from a $70,000 beginning balance to an $84,000 ending balance. This increase implies that Genesis had greater cash purchases than cost of goods sold. This larger amount of cash purchases is in the form of inventory, as reflected in the following account analysis:

Merchandise Inventory			
Bal., Dec. 31, 2010	70,000		
Purchases =	**314,000**	Cost of goods sold	300,000
Bal., Dec. 31, 2011	84,000		

GENESIS
Statement of Cash Flows
For Year Ended December 31, 2011

Cash flows from operating activities		
Net income	$ 38,000	
Adjustments to reconcile net income to net cash provided by operating activities		
① Increase in accounts receivable.	(20,000)	
Increase in merchandise inventory	(14,000)	
Increase in prepaid expenses	(2,000)	
Decrease in accounts payable.	(5,000)	
Decrease in interest payable.	(1,000)	
Increase in income taxes payable	10,000	
② Depreciation expense.	24,000	
③ Loss on sale of plant assets.	6,000	
Gain on retirement of notes.	(16,000)	
Net cash provided by operating activities		$20,000
Cash flows from investing activities		
Cash received from sale of plant assets	12,000	
Cash paid for purchase of plant assets	(10,000)	
Net cash provided by investing activities		2,000
Cash flows from financing activities		
Cash received from issuing stock	15,000	
Cash paid to retire notes	(18,000)	
Cash paid for dividends.	(14,000)	
Net cash used in financing activities		(17,000)
Net increase in cash		$ 5,000
Cash balance at prior year-end.		12,000
Cash balance at current year-end		$17,000

EXHIBIT 12.11

Statement of Cash Flows—Indirect Method

Point: Refer to Exhibit 12.10 and identify the $5,000 change in cash. This change is what the statement of cash flows explains; it serves as a check.

The amount by which purchases exceed cost of goods sold—as reflected in the $14,000 increase in inventory—is subtracted from net income when computing cash provided by operating activities (see Exhibit 12.11).

Prepaid expenses. Prepaid Expenses *increase* $2,000, from a $4,000 beginning balance to a $6,000 ending balance, implying that Genesis's cash payments exceed its recorded prepaid expenses. These higher cash payments increase the amount of Prepaid Expenses, as reflected in its reconstructed T-account:

Prepaid Expenses			
Bal., Dec. 31, 2010	4,000		
Cash payments =	**218,000**	Wages and other operating exp.	216,000
Bal., Dec. 31, 2011	6,000		

The amount by which cash payments exceed the recorded operating expenses—as reflected in the $2,000 increase in Prepaid Expenses—is subtracted from net income when computing cash provided by operating activities (see Exhibit 12.11).

Adjustments for changes in current liabilities.   Changes in current liabilities normally result from operating activities. An example is a purchase that affects accounts payable. Increases in current liabilities yield the following adjustment to net income when computing operating cash flows:

Increases in current liabilities are added to net income.

To see the logic for this adjustment, consider that an increase in the Accounts Payable account suggests that cash payments are less than the related (cost of goods sold) expense. As another example, an increase in wages payable implies that cash paid for wages is less than the recorded wages expense. Since the recorded expense is greater than the cash paid, we add the increase in wages payable to net income to compute net cash flow from operations.

Conversely, when current liabilities decrease, the following adjustment is required:

Decreases in current liabilities are subtracted from net income.

To illustrate, these adjustments are applied to the current liabilities in Exhibit 12.10.

Accounts payable. Accounts payable *decrease* $5,000, from a beginning balance of $40,000 to an ending balance of $35,000. This decrease implies that cash payments to suppliers exceed purchases by $5,000 for the period, which is reflected in the reconstructed Accounts Payable T-account:

Accounts Payable			
		Bal., Dec. 31, 2010	40,000
Cash payments =	**319,000**	Purchases	314,000
		Bal., Dec. 31, 2011	35,000

The amount by which cash payments exceed purchases—as reflected in the $5,000 decrease in Accounts Payable—is subtracted from net income when computing cash provided by operating activities (see Exhibit 12.11).

Interest payable. Interest payable *decreases* $1,000, from a $4,000 beginning balance to a $3,000 ending balance. This decrease indicates that cash paid for interest exceeds interest expense by $1,000, which is reflected in the Interest Payable T-account:

Interest Payable			
		Bal., Dec. 31, 2010	4,000
Cash paid for interest =	**8,000**	Interest expense	7,000
		Bal., Dec. 31, 2011	3,000

The amount by which cash paid exceeds recorded expense—as reflected in the $1,000 decrease in Interest Payable—is subtracted from net income (see Exhibit 12.11).

Income taxes payable. Income taxes payable *increase* $10,000, from a $12,000 beginning balance to a $22,000 ending balance. This increase implies that reported income taxes exceed the cash paid for taxes, which is reflected in the Income Taxes Payable T-account:

Income Taxes Payable			
	Bal., Dec. 31, 2010	12,000
Cash paid for taxes = 5,000	Income taxes expense	15,000
	Bal., Dec. 31, 2011	22,000

Summary Adjustments for Changes in Current Assets and Current Liabilities		
Account	Increases	Decreases
Noncash current assets	Deduct from NI	Add to NI
Current liabilities......	Add to NI	Deduct from NI

The amount by which cash paid falls short of the reported taxes expense—as reflected in the $10,000 increase in Income Taxes Payable—is added to net income when computing cash provided by operating activities (see Exhibit 12.11).

② **Adjustments for Operating Items Not Providing or Using Cash** The income statement usually includes some expenses that do not reflect cash outflows in the period. Examples are depreciation, amortization, depletion, and bad debts expense. The indirect method for reporting operating cash flows requires that

Expenses with no cash outflows are added back to net income.

To see the logic of this adjustment, recall that items such as depreciation, amortization, depletion, and bad debts originate from debits to expense accounts and credits to noncash accounts. These entries have *no* cash effect, and we add them back to net income when computing net cash flows from operations. Adding them back cancels their deductions.

Similarly, when net income includes revenues that do not reflect cash inflows in the period, the indirect method for reporting operating cash flows requires that

Revenues with no cash inflows are subtracted from net income.

We apply these adjustments to the Genesis operating items that do not provide or use cash.

Depreciation. Depreciation expense is the only Genesis operating item that has no effect on cash flows in the period. We must add back the $24,000 depreciation expense to net income when computing cash provided by operating activities. (We later explain that any cash outflow to acquire a plant asset is reported as an investing activity.)

③ **Adjustments for Nonoperating Items** Net income often includes losses that are not part of operating activities but are part of either investing or financing activities. Examples are a loss from the sale of a plant asset and a loss from retirement of notes payable. The indirect method for reporting operating cash flows requires that

Nonoperating losses are added back to net income.

To see the logic, consider that items such as a plant asset sale and a notes retirement are normally recorded by recognizing the cash, removing all plant asset or notes accounts, and recognizing any loss or gain. The cash received or paid is not part of operating activities but is part of either investing or financing activities. *No* operating cash flow effect occurs. However, because the nonoperating loss is a deduction in computing net income, we need to add it back to net income when computing cash flow from operations. Adding it back cancels the deduction.

Similarly, when net income includes gains not part of operating activities, the indirect method for reporting operating cash flows requires that

Nonoperating gains are subtracted from net income.

To illustrate these adjustments, we consider the nonoperating items of Genesis.

Point: An income statement reports revenues, gains, expenses, and losses on an accrual basis. The statement of cash flows reports cash received and cash paid for operating, financing, and investing activities.

Loss on sale of plant assets.   Genesis reports a $6,000 loss on sale of plant assets as part of net income. This loss is a proper deduction in computing income, but it is *not part of operating activities*. Instead, a sale of plant assets is part of investing activities. Thus, the $6,000 nonoperating loss is added back to net income (see Exhibit 12.11). Adding it back cancels the loss. We later explain how to report the cash inflow from the asset sale in investing activities.

Gain on retirement of debt.   A $16,000 gain on retirement of debt is properly included in net income, but it is *not part of operating activities*. This means the $16,000 nonoperating gain must be subtracted from net income to obtain net cash provided by operating activities (see Exhibit 12.11). Subtracting it cancels the recorded gain. We later describe how to report the cash outflow to retire debt.

Summary of Adjustments for Indirect Method

Exhibit 12.12 summarizes the most common adjustments to net income when computing net cash provided or used by operating activities under the indirect method.

EXHIBIT 12.12

Summary of Selected Adjustments for Indirect Method

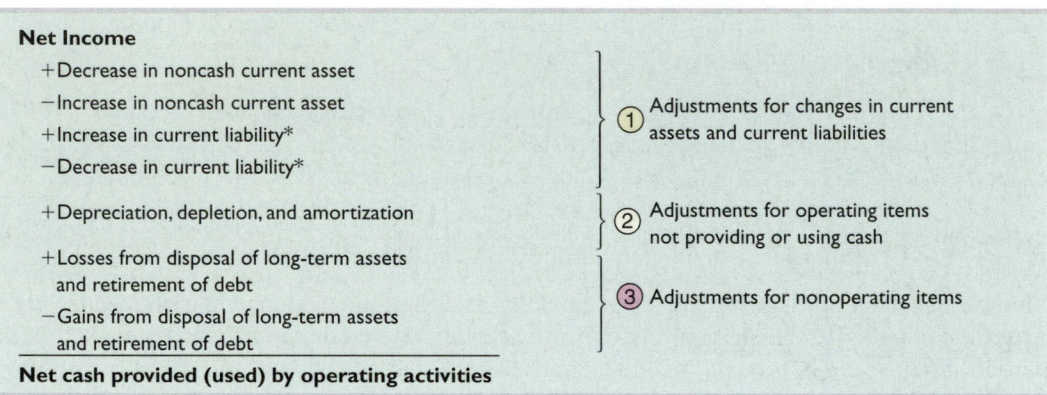

* Excludes current portion of long-term debt and any (nonsales-related) short-term notes payable—both are financing activities.

The computations in determining cash provided or used by operating activities are different for the indirect and direct methods, but the result is identical. Both methods yield the same $20,000 figure for cash from operating activities for Genesis; see Exhibits 12.7 and 12.11.

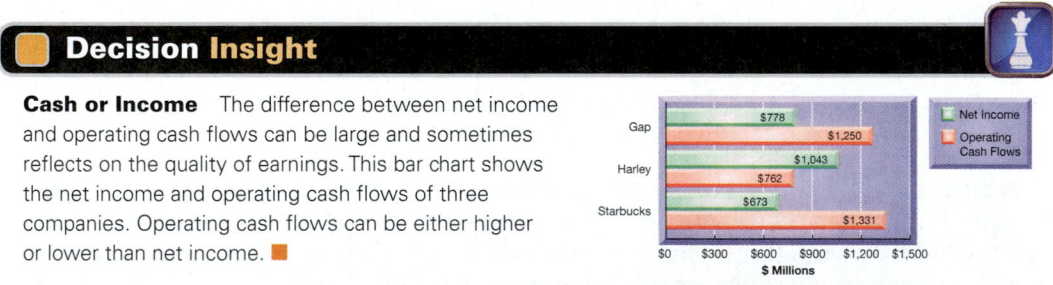

Decision Insight

Cash or Income   The difference between net income and operating cash flows can be large and sometimes reflects on the quality of earnings. This bar chart shows the net income and operating cash flows of three companies. Operating cash flows can be either higher or lower than net income. ■

Quick Check   Answers — p. 530

4. Determine the net cash provided or used by operating activities using the following data: net income, $74,900; decrease in accounts receivable, $4,600; increase in inventory, $11,700; decrease in accounts payable, $1,000; loss on sale of equipment, $3,400; payment of cash dividends, $21,500.

5. Why are expenses such as depreciation and amortization added to net income when cash flow from operating activities is computed by the indirect method?

6. A company reports net income of $15,000 that includes a $3,000 gain on the sale of plant assets. Why is this gain subtracted from net income in computing cash flow from operating activities using the indirect method?

CASH FLOWS FROM INVESTING

The third major step in preparing the statement of cash flows is to compute and report cash flows from investing activities. We normally do this by identifying changes in (1) all noncurrent asset accounts and (2) the current accounts for both notes receivable and investments in securities (excluding trading securities). We then analyze changes in these accounts to determine their effect, if any, on cash and report the cash flow effects in the investing activities section of the statement of cash flows. **Reporting of investing activities is identical under the direct method and indirect method.**

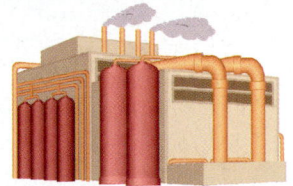

Three-Stage Process of Analysis

Information to compute cash flows from investing activities is usually taken from beginning and ending balance sheets and the income statement. We use a three-stage process to determine cash provided or used by investing activities: (1) identify changes in investing-related accounts, (2) explain these changes using reconstruction analysis, and (3) report their cash flow effects.

P3 Determine cash flows from both investing and financing activities.

Analysis of Noncurrent Assets

Information about the Genesis transactions provided earlier reveals that the company both purchased and sold plant assets during the period. Both transactions are investing activities and are analyzed for their cash flow effects in this section.

Plant Asset Transactions   The first stage in analyzing the Plant Assets account and its related Accumulated Depreciation is to identify any changes in these accounts from comparative balance sheets in Exhibit 12.10. This analysis reveals a $40,000 increase in plant assets from $210,000 to $250,000 and a $12,000 increase in accumulated depreciation from $48,000 to $60,000.

The second stage is to explain these changes. Items *b* and *c* of the additional information for Genesis (page 507) are relevant in this case. Recall that the Plant Assets account is affected by both asset purchases and sales, while its Accumulated Depreciation account is normally increased from depreciation and decreased from the removal of accumulated depreciation in asset sales. To explain changes in these accounts and to identify their cash flow effects, we prepare *reconstructed entries* from prior transactions; *they are not the actual entries by the preparer*.

To illustrate, item *b* reports that Genesis purchased plant assets of $70,000 by issuing $60,000 in notes payable to the seller and paying $10,000 in cash. The reconstructed entry for analysis of item *b* follows:

Point: Investing activities include (1) purchasing and selling long-term assets, (2) lending and collecting on notes receivable, and (3) purchasing and selling short-term investments other than cash equivalents and trading securities.

Point: Financing and investing info is available in ledger accounts to help explain changes in comparative balance sheets. Post references lead to relevant entries and explanations.

Reconstruction	Plant Assets	70,000	
	Notes Payable		60,000
	Cash		**10,000**

This entry reveals a $10,000 cash outflow for plant assets and a $60,000 noncash investing and financing transaction involving notes exchanged for plant assets.

Next, item *c* reports that Genesis sold plant assets costing $30,000 (with $12,000 of accumulated depreciation) for $12,000 cash, resulting in a $6,000 loss. The reconstructed entry for analysis of item *c* follows:

Reconstruction	**Cash**	**12,000**	
	Accumulated Depreciation	12,000	
	Loss on Sale of Plant Assets	6,000	
	Plant Assets		30,000

This entry reveals a $12,000 cash inflow from assets sold. The $6,000 loss is computed by comparing the asset book value to the cash received and does not reflect any cash inflow or outflow. We also reconstruct the entry for Depreciation Expense using information from the income statement.

| Reconstruction | Depreciation Expense .... | 24,000 | |
| | Accumulated Depreciation .... | | 24,000 |

This entry shows that Depreciation Expense results in no cash flow effect. These three reconstructed entries are reflected in the following plant asset and related T-accounts.

Plant Assets					Accumulated Depreciation—Plant Assets			
Bal., Dec. 31, 2010	210,000						Bal., Dec. 31, 2010	48,000
Purchase	70,000	Sale	30,000		Sale	12,000	Depr. expense	24,000
Bal., Dec. 31, 2011	250,000						Bal., Dec. 31, 2011	60,000

This reconstruction analysis is complete in that the change in plant assets from $210,000 to $250,000 is fully explained by the $70,000 purchase and the $30,000 sale. Also, the change in accumulated depreciation from $48,000 to $60,000 is fully explained by depreciation expense of $24,000 and the removal of $12,000 in accumulated depreciation from an asset sale. (Preparers of the statement of cash flows have the entire ledger and additional information at their disposal, but for brevity reasons only the information needed for reconstructing accounts is given.)

The third stage looks at the reconstructed entries for identification of cash flows. The two identified cash flow effects are reported in the investing section of the statement as follows (also see Exhibit 12.7 or 12.11):

Cash flows from investing activities	
Cash received from sale of plant assets	$12,000
Cash paid for purchase of plant assets	(10,000)

Example: If a plant asset costing $40,000 with $37,000 of accumulated depreciation is sold at a $1,000 loss, what is the cash flow? What is the cash flow if this asset is sold at a gain of $3,000? *Answers:* +$2,000; +$6,000.

The $60,000 portion of the purchase described in item *b* and financed by issuing notes is a non-cash investing and financing activity. It is reported in a note or in a separate schedule to the statement as follows:

Noncash investing and financing activity	
Purchased plant assets with issuance of notes	$60,000

Analysis of Other Assets

Many other asset transactions (including those involving current notes receivable and investments in certain securities) are considered investing activities and can affect a company's cash flows. Since Genesis did not enter into other investing activities impacting assets, we do not need to extend our analysis to these other assets. If such transactions did exist, we would analyze them using the same three-stage process illustrated for plant assets.

Quick Check

Answer — p. 530

7. Equipment costing $80,000 with accumulated depreciation of $30,000 is sold at a loss of $10,000. What is the cash receipt from this sale? In what section of the statement of cash flows is this transaction reported?

CASH FLOWS FROM FINANCING

The fourth major step in preparing the statement of cash flows is to compute and report cash flows from financing activities. We normally do this by identifying changes in all noncurrent liability accounts (including the current portion of any notes and bonds) and the equity accounts. These accounts include long-term debt, notes payable, bonds payable, common stock, and retained earnings. Changes in these accounts are then analyzed using available information to determine their effect, if any, on cash. Results are reported in the financing activities section of the statement. **Reporting of financing activities is identical under the direct method and indirect method.**

Three-Stage Process of Analysis

We again use a three-stage process to determine cash provided or used by financing activities: (1) identify changes in financing-related accounts, (2) explain these changes using reconstruction analysis, and (3) report their cash flow effects.

Analysis of Noncurrent Liabilities

Information about Genesis provided earlier reveals two transactions involving noncurrent liabilities. We analyzed one of those, the $60,000 issuance of notes payable to purchase plant assets. This transaction is reported as a significant noncash investing and financing activity in a footnote or a separate schedule to the statement of cash flows. The other remaining transaction involving noncurrent liabilities is the cash retirement of notes payable.

Point: Financing activities generally refer to changes in the noncurrent liability and the equity accounts. Examples are (1) receiving cash from issuing debt or repaying amounts borrowed and (2) receiving cash from or distributing cash to owners.

Notes Payable Transactions   The first stage in analysis of notes is to review the comparative balance sheets from Exhibit 12.10. This analysis reveals an increase in notes payable from $64,000 to $90,000.

The second stage explains this change. Item *e* of the additional information for Genesis (page 507) reports that notes with a carrying value of $34,000 are retired for $18,000 cash, resulting in a $16,000 gain. The reconstructed entry for analysis of item *e* follows:

Reconstruction	Notes Payable	34,000	
	Gain on retirement of debt		16,000
	Cash		**18,000**

This entry reveals an $18,000 cash outflow for retirement of notes and a $16,000 gain from comparing the notes payable carrying value to the cash received. This gain does not reflect any cash inflow or outflow. Also, item *b* of the additional information reports that Genesis purchased plant assets costing $70,000 by issuing $60,000 in notes payable to the seller and paying $10,000 in cash. We reconstructed this entry when analyzing investing activities: It showed a $60,000 increase to notes payable that is reported as a noncash investing and financing transaction. The Notes Payable account reflects (and is fully explained by) these reconstructed entries as follows:

Notes Payable			
		Bal., Dec. 31, 2010	64,000
Retired notes	34,000	**Issued notes**	**60,000**
		Bal., Dec. 31, 2011	90,000

The third stage is to report the cash flow effect of the notes retirement in the financing section of the statement as follows (also see Exhibit 12.7 or 12.11):

Cash flows from financing activities	
Cash paid to retire notes	$(18,000)

Analysis of Equity

The Genesis information reveals two transactions involving equity accounts. The first is the issuance of common stock for cash. The second is the declaration and payment of cash dividends. We analyze both.

Common Stock Transactions   The first stage in analyzing common stock is to review the comparative balance sheets from Exhibit 12.10, which reveal an increase in common stock from $80,000 to $95,000.

The second stage explains this change. Item *d* of the additional information (page 507) reports that 3,000 shares of common stock are issued at par for $5 per share. The reconstructed entry for analysis of item *d* follows:

| Reconstruction | **Cash** .... | **15,000** | |
| | Common Stock .... | | 15,000 |

This entry reveals a $15,000 cash inflow from stock issuance and is reflected in (and explains) the Common Stock account as follows:

Common Stock		
	Bal., Dec. 31, 2010	80,000
	Issued stock	**15,000**
	Bal., Dec. 31, 2011	95,000

The third stage discloses the cash flow effect from stock issuance in the financing section of the statement as follows (also see Exhibit 12.7 or 12.11):

Cash flows from financing activities
Cash received from issuing stock $15,000

Retained Earnings Transactions   The first stage in analyzing the Retained Earnings account is to review the comparative balance sheets from Exhibit 12.10. This reveals an increase in retained earnings from $88,000 to $112,000.

The second stage explains this change. Item *f* of the additional information (page 507) reports that cash dividends of $14,000 are paid. The reconstructed entry follows:

| Reconstruction | Retained Earnings .... | 14,000 | |
| | Cash .... | | 14,000 |

This entry reveals a $14,000 cash outflow for cash dividends. Also see that the Retained Earnings account is impacted by net income of $38,000. (Net income was analyzed under the operating section of the statement of cash flows.) The reconstructed Retained Earnings account follows:

Retained Earnings			
		Bal., Dec. 31, 2010	88,000
Cash dividend	**14,000**	**Net income**	**38,000**
		Bal., Dec. 31, 2011	112,000

Point: Financing activities not affecting cash flow include *declaration* of a cash dividend, *declaration* of a stock dividend, payment of a stock dividend, and a stock split.

The third stage reports the cash flow effect from the cash dividend in the financing section of the statement as follows (also see Exhibit 12.7 or 12.11):

Cash flows from financing activities
Cash paid for dividends..................... $(14,000)

Global: There are no requirements to separate domestic and international cash flows, leading some users to ask, "Where in the world is cash flow?"

We now have identified and explained all of the Genesis cash inflows and cash outflows and one noncash investing and financing transaction. Specifically, our analysis has reconciled changes in all noncash balance sheet accounts.

Proving Cash Balances

The fifth and final step in preparing the statement is to report the beginning and ending cash balances and prove that the *net change in cash* is explained by operating, investing, and financing cash flows. This step is shown here for Genesis.

Net cash provided by operating activities	$20,000
Net cash provided by investing activities	2,000
Net cash used in financing activities	(17,000)
Net increase in cash	**$ 5,000**
Cash balance at 2010 year-end	12,000
Cash balance at 2011 year-end	$17,000

The preceding table shows that the $5,000 net increase in cash, from $12,000 at the beginning of the period to $17,000 at the end, is reconciled by net cash flows from operating ($20,000 inflow), investing ($2,000 inflow), and financing ($17,000 outflow) activities. This is formally reported at the bottom of the statement of cash flows as shown in both Exhibits 12.7 and 12.11.

Decision Maker Answer — p. 530

Reporter Management is in labor contract negotiations and grants you an interview. It highlights a recent $600,000 net loss that involves a $930,000 extraordinary loss and a total net cash outflow of $550,000 (which includes net cash outflows of $850,000 for investing activities and $350,000 for financing activities). What is your assessment of this company? ■

GLOBAL VIEW

The statement of cash flows, which explains changes in cash (including cash equivalents) from period to period, is required under both U.S. GAAP and IFRS. This section discusses similarities and differences between U.S. GAAP and IFRS in reporting that statement.

Reporting Cash Flows from Operating Both U.S. GAAP and IFRS permit the reporting of cash flows from operating activities using either the direct or indirect method. Further, the basic requirements underlying the application of both methods are fairly consistent across these two accounting systems. Appendix A shows that **Nokia** reports its cash flows from operating activities using the indirect method, and in a manner similar to that explained in this chapter. Further, the definition of cash and cash equivalents is roughly similar for U.S. GAAP and IFRS.

NOKIA

There are, however, some differences between U.S. GAAP and IFRS in reporting operating cash flows. We mention two of the more notable. First, U.S. GAAP requires cash inflows from interest revenue and dividend revenue be classified as operating, whereas IFRS permits classification under operating or investing provided that this classification is consistently applied across periods. Nokia reports its cash from interest received under operating, consistent with U.S. GAAP (no mention is made of any dividends received). Second, U.S. GAAP requires cash outflows for interest expense be classified as operating, whereas IFRS again permits classification under operating or financing provided that it is consistently applied across periods. (Some believe that interest payments, like dividends payments, are better classified as financing because they represent payments to financiers.) Nokia reports cash outflows for interest under operating, which is consistent with U.S. GAAP and acceptable under IFRS.

Reporting Cash Flows from Investing and Financing U.S. GAAP and IFRS are broadly similar in computing and classifying cash flows from investing and financing activities. A quick review of these two sections for **Nokia**'s statement of cash flows shows a structure similar to that explained in this chapter. One notable exception is that U.S. GAAP requires cash outflows for income tax be classified as operating, whereas IFRS permits the splitting of those cash flows among operating, investing, and financing depending on the sources of that tax. Nokia reports its cash outflows for income tax under operating, which is similar to U.S. GAAP.

Decision Analysis

Cash Flow Analysis

Analyzing Cash Sources and Uses

A1 Analyze the statement of cash flows and apply the cash flow on total assets ratio.

Most managers stress the importance of understanding and predicting cash flows for business decisions. Creditors evaluate a company's ability to generate cash before deciding whether to lend money. Investors also assess cash inflows and outflows before buying and selling stock. Information in the statement of cash flows helps address these and other questions such as (1) How much cash is generated from or used in operations? (2) What expenditures are made with cash from operations? (3) What is the source of cash for debt payments? (4) What is the source of cash for distributions to owners? (5) How is the increase in investing activities financed? (6) What is the source of cash for new plant assets? (7) Why is cash flow from operations different from income? (8) How is cash from financing used?

To effectively answer these questions, it is important to separately analyze investing, financing, and operating activities. To illustrate, consider data from three different companies in Exhibit 12.13. These companies operate in the same industry and have been in business for several years.

EXHIBIT 12.13

Cash Flows of Competing Companies

($ thousands)	BMX	ATV	Trex
Cash provided (used) by operating activities	$90,000	$40,000	$(24,000)
Cash provided (used) by investing activities			
Proceeds from sale of plant assets			26,000
Purchase of plant assets	(48,000)	(25,000)	
Cash provided (used) by financing activities			
Proceeds from issuance of debt			13,000
Repayment of debt	(27,000)		
Net increase (decrease) in cash	$15,000	$15,000	$ 15,000

Each company generates an identical $15,000 net increase in cash, but its sources and uses of cash flows are very different. BMX's operating activities provide net cash flows of $90,000, allowing it to purchase plant assets of $48,000 and repay $27,000 of its debt. ATV's operating activities provide $40,000 of cash flows, limiting its purchase of plant assets to $25,000. Trex's $15,000 net cash increase is due to selling plant assets and incurring additional debt. Its operating activities yield a net cash outflow of $24,000. Overall, analysis of these cash flows reveals that BMX is more capable of generating future cash flows than is ATV or Trex.

☐ Decision **Insight**

Free Cash Flows Many investors use cash flows to value company stock. However, cash-based valuation models often yield different stock values due to differences in measurement of cash flows. Most models require cash flows that are "free" for distribution to shareholders. These *free cash flows* are defined as cash flows available to shareholders after operating asset reinvestments and debt payments. Knowledge of the statement of cash flows is key to proper computation of free cash flows. A company's growth and financial flexibility depend on adequate free cash flows. ■

Cash Flow on Total Assets

Cash flow information has limitations, but it can help measure a company's ability to meet its obligations, pay dividends, expand operations, and obtain financing. Users often compute and analyze a cash-based ratio similar to return on total assets except that its numerator is net cash flows from operating activities. The **cash flow on total assets** ratio is in Exhibit 12.14.

EXHIBIT 12.14

Cash Flow on Total Assets

$$\text{Cash flow on total assets} = \frac{\text{Cash flow from operations}}{\text{Average total assets}}$$

This ratio reflects actual cash flows and is not affected by accounting income recognition and measurement. It can help business decision makers estimate the amount and timing of cash flows when planning and analyzing operating activities.

To illustrate, the 2009 cash flow on total assets ratio for **Nike** is 13.5%—see Exhibit 12.15. Is a 13.5% ratio good or bad? To answer this question, we compare this ratio with the ratios of prior years (we could also compare its ratio with those of its competitors and the market). Nike's cash flow on total assets ratio for several prior years is in the second column of Exhibit 12.15. Results show that its 13.5% return is the lowest return over the past several years. This is probably reflective of the recent recessionary period.

EXHIBIT 12.15

Nike's Cash Flow on Total Assets

Year	Cash Flow on Total Assets	Return on Total Assets
2009.........	13.5%	11.6%
2008.........	16.7	16.3
2007.........	18.3	14.5
2006.........	17.9	14.9
2005.........	18.8	14.5

As an indicator of *earnings quality*, some analysts compare the cash flow on total assets ratio to the return on total assets ratio. Nike's return on total assets is provided in the third column of Exhibit 12.15. Nike's cash flow on total assets ratio exceeds its return on total assets in each of the five years, leading some analysts to infer that Nike's earnings quality is high for that period because more earnings are realized in the form of cash.

Decision Insight

Cash Flow Ratios   Analysts use various other cash-based ratios, including the following two:

$$(1) \qquad \text{Cash coverage of growth} = \frac{\text{Operating cash flow}}{\text{Cash outflow for plant assets}}$$

where a low ratio (less than 1) implies cash inadequacy to meet asset growth, whereas a high ratio implies cash adequacy for asset growth.

$$(2) \qquad \text{Operating cash flow to sales} = \frac{\text{Operating cash flow}}{\text{Net sales}}$$

When this ratio substantially and consistently differs from the operating income to net sales ratio, the risk of accounting improprieties increases. ■

Point: The following ratio helps assess whether operating cash flow is adequate to meet long-term obligations:
Cash coverage of debt = Cash flow from operations ÷ Noncurrent liabilities. A low ratio suggests a higher risk of insolvency; a high ratio suggests a greater ability to meet long-term obligations.

DEMONSTRATION PROBLEM

Umlauf's comparative balance sheets, income statement, and additional information follow.

UMLAUF COMPANY
Balance Sheets
December 31, 2011 and 2010

	2011	2010
Assets		
Cash	$ 43,050	$ 23,925
Accounts receivable	34,125	39,825
Merchandise inventory	156,000	146,475
Prepaid expenses	3,600	1,650
Equipment	135,825	146,700
Accum. depreciation—Equipment	(61,950)	(47,550)
Total assets	$310,650	$311,025
Liabilities and Equity		
Accounts payable	$ 28,800	$ 33,750
Income taxes payable	5,100	4,425
Dividends payable	0	4,500
Bonds payable	0	37,500
Common stock, $10 par	168,750	168,750
Retained earnings	108,000	62,100
Total liabilities and equity	$310,650	$311,025

UMLAUF COMPANY
Income Statement
For Year Ended December 31, 2011

Sales		$446,100
Cost of goods sold	$222,300	
Other operating expenses	120,300	
Depreciation expense	25,500	(368,100)
		78,000
Other gains (losses)		
Loss on sale of equipment	3,300	
Loss on retirement of bonds ..	825	(4,125)
Income before taxes		73,875
Income taxes expense		(13,725)
Net income		$ 60,150

Additional Information

a. Equipment costing $21,375 with accumulated depreciation of $11,100 is sold for cash.

b. Equipment purchases are for cash.

c. Accumulated Depreciation is affected by depreciation expense and the sale of equipment.

d. The balance of Retained Earnings is affected by dividend declarations and net income.

e. All sales are made on credit.

f. All merchandise inventory purchases are on credit.

g. Accounts Payable balances result from merchandise inventory purchases.

h. Prepaid expenses relate to "other operating expenses."

Required

1. Prepare a statement of cash flows using the indirect method for year 2011.

2.B Prepare a statement of cash flows using the direct method for year 2011.

PLANNING THE SOLUTION

- Prepare two blank statements of cash flows with sections for operating, investing, and financing activities using the (1) indirect method format and (2) direct method format.
- Compute the cash paid for equipment and the cash received from the sale of equipment using the additional information provided along with the amount for depreciation expense and the change in the balances of equipment and accumulated depreciation. Use T-accounts to help chart the effects of the sale and purchase of equipment on the balances of the Equipment account and the Accumulated Depreciation account.
- Compute the effect of net income on the change in the Retained Earnings account balance. Assign the difference between the change in retained earnings and the amount of net income to dividends declared. Adjust the dividends declared amount for the change in the Dividends Payable balance.
- Compute cash received from customers, cash paid for merchandise, cash paid for other operating expenses, and cash paid for taxes as illustrated in the chapter.
- Enter the cash effects of reconstruction entries to the appropriate section(s) of the statement.
- Total each section of the statement, determine the total net change in cash, and add it to the beginning balance to get the ending balance of cash.

SOLUTION TO DEMONSTRATION PROBLEM

Supporting computations for cash receipts and cash payments.

(1)	*Cost of equipment sold	$ 21,375
	Accumulated depreciation of equipment sold	(11,100)
	Book value of equipment sold	10,275
	Loss on sale of equipment	(3,300)
	Cash received from sale of equipment	**$ 6,975**
	Cost of equipment sold	$ 21,375
	Less decrease in the equipment account balance	(10,875)
	Cash paid for new equipment	**$ 10,500**
(2)	Loss on retirement of bonds	$ 825
	Carrying value of bonds retired	37,500
	Cash paid to retire bonds	**$ 38,325**
(3)	Net income	$ 60,150
	Less increase in retained earnings	45,900
	Dividends declared	14,250
	Plus decrease in dividends payable	4,500
	Cash paid for dividends	**$ 18,750**
(4)B	Sales	$ 446,100
	Add decrease in accounts receivable	5,700
	Cash received from customers	**$451,800**

[continued on next page]

[continued from previous page]

(5)B Cost of goods sold	$ 222,300
Plus increase in merchandise inventory	9,525
Purchases	231,825
Plus decrease in accounts payable	4,950
Cash paid for merchandise	**$236,775**
(6)B Other operating expenses	$ 120,300
Plus increase in prepaid expenses	1,950
Cash paid for other operating expenses	**$122,250**
(7)B Income taxes expense	$ 13,725
Less increase in income taxes payable	(675)
Cash paid for income taxes	**$ 13,050**

* Supporting T-account analysis for part 1 follows:

Equipment			
Bal., Dec. 31, 2010	146,700		
Cash purchase	10,500	Sale	21,375
Bal., Dec. 31, 2011	135,825		

Accumulated Depreciation—Equipment			
		Bal., Dec. 31, 2010	47,550
Sale	11,100	Depr. expense	25,500
		Bal., Dec. 31, 2011	61,950

UMLAUF COMPANY
Statement of Cash Flows (Indirect Method)
For Year Ended December 31, 2011

Cash flows from operating activities		
Net income	$60,150	
Adjustments to reconcile net income to net cash provided by operating activities		
Decrease in accounts receivable	5,700	
Increase in merchandise inventory	(9,525)	
Increase in prepaid expenses	(1,950)	
Decrease in accounts payable	(4,950)	
Increase in income taxes payable	675	
Depreciation expense	25,500	
Loss on sale of plant assets	3,300	
Loss on retirement of bonds	825	
Net cash provided by operating activities		$79,725
Cash flows from investing activities		
Cash received from sale of equipment	6,975	
Cash paid for equipment	(10,500)	
Net cash used in investing activities		(3,525)
Cash flows from financing activities		
Cash paid to retire bonds payable	(38,325)	
Cash paid for dividends	(18,750)	
Net cash used in financing activities		(57,075)
Net increase in cash		$19,125
Cash balance at prior year-end		23,925
Cash balance at current year-end		$43,050

UMLAUF COMPANY
Statement of Cash Flows (Direct Method)
For Year Ended December 31, 2011

Cash flows from operating activities		
Cash received from customers	$451,800	
Cash paid for merchandise	(236,775)	
Cash paid for other operating expenses	(122,250)	
Cash paid for income taxes	(13,050)	
Net cash provided by operating activities		$79,725
Cash flows from investing activities		
Cash received from sale of equipment	6,975	
Cash paid for equipment	(10,500)	
Net cash used in investing activities		(3,525)
Cash flows from financing activities		
Cash paid to retire bonds payable	(38,325)	
Cash paid for dividends	(18,750)	
Net cash used in financing activities		(57,075)
Net increase in cash		$19,125
Cash balance at prior year-end		23,925
Cash balance at current year-end		$43,050

APPENDIX

12A

Spreadsheet Preparation of the Statement of Cash Flows

This appendix explains how to use a spreadsheet to prepare the statement of cash flows under the indirect method.

P4 Illustrate use of a spreadsheet to prepare a statement of cash flows.

Preparing the Indirect Method Spreadsheet   Analyzing noncash accounts can be challenging when a company has a large number of accounts and many operating, investing, and financing transactions. A *spreadsheet,* also called *work sheet* or *working paper,* can help us organize the information needed to prepare a statement of cash flows. A spreadsheet also makes it easier to check the accuracy of our work. To illustrate, we return to the comparative balance sheets and income statement shown in Exhibit 12.10. We use the following identifying letters *a* through *g* to code changes in accounts, and letters *h* through *m* for additional information, to prepare the statement of cash flows:

a. Net income is $38,000.
b. Accounts receivable increase by $20,000.
c. Merchandise inventory increases by $14,000.
d. Prepaid expenses increase by $2,000.
e. Accounts payable decrease by $5,000.
f. Interest payable decreases by $1,000.
g. Income taxes payable increase by $10,000.
h. Depreciation expense is $24,000.
i. Plant assets costing $30,000 with accumulated depreciation of $12,000 are sold for $12,000 cash. This yields a loss on sale of assets of $6,000.
j. Notes with a book value of $34,000 are retired with a cash payment of $18,000, yielding a $16,000 gain on retirement.

k. Plant assets costing $70,000 are purchased with a cash payment of $10,000 and an issuance of notes payable for $60,000.

l. Issued 3,000 shares of common stock for $15,000 cash.

m. Paid cash dividends of $14,000.

Exhibit 12A.1 shows the indirect method spreadsheet for Genesis. We enter both beginning and ending balance sheet amounts on the spreadsheet. We also enter information in the Analysis of Changes columns (keyed to the additional information items *a* through *m*) to explain changes in the accounts and determine the cash flows for operating, investing, and financing activities. Information about noncash investing and financing activities is reported near the bottom.

EXHIBIT 12A.1

Spreadsheet for Preparing Statement of Cash Flows— Indirect Method

	File Edit View Insert Format Tools Data Accounting Window Help						
	GENESIS						
	Spreadsheet for Statement of Cash Flows—Indirect Method						
	For Year Ended December 31, 2011						
		Dec. 31, 2010	**Analysis of Changes**			**Dec. 31, 2011**	
			Debit		**Credit**		
8	**Balance Sheet—Debit Bal. Accounts**						
9	Cash	$ 12,000					$ 17,000
10	Accounts receivable	40,000	*(b)*	$ 20,000			60,000
11	Merchandise inventory	70,000	*(c)*	14,000			84,000
12	Prepaid expenses	4,000	*(d)*	2,000			6,000
13	Plant assets	210,000	*(k1)*	70,000	*(i)*	$ 30,000	250,000
14		$336,000					$417,000
16	**Balance Sheet—Credit Bal. Accounts**						
17	Accumulated depreciation	$ 48,000	*(i)*	12,000	*(h)*	24,000	$ 60,000
18	Accounts payable	40,000	*(e)*	5,000			35,000
19	Interest payable	4,000	*(f)*	1,000			3,000
20	Income taxes payable	12,000			*(g)*	10,000	22,000
21	Notes payable	64,000	*(j)*	34,000	*(k2)*	60,000	90,000
22	Common stock, $5 par value	80,000			*(l)*	15,000	95,000
23	Retained earnings	88,000	*(m)*	14,000	*(a)*	38,000	112,000
24		$336,000					$417,000
26	**Statement of Cash Flows**						
27	Operating activities						
28	Net income		*(a)*	38,000			
29	Increase in accounts receivable				*(b)*	20,000	
30	Increase in merchandise inventory				*(c)*	14,000	
31	Increase in prepaid expenses				*(d)*	2,000	
32	Decrease in accounts payable				*(e)*	5,000	
33	Decrease in interest payable				*(f)*	1,000	
34	Increase in income taxes payable		*(g)*	10,000			
35	Depreciation expense		*(h)*	24,000			
36	Loss on sale of plant assets		*(i)*	6,000			
37	Gain on retirement of notes				*(j)*	16,000	
38	Investing activities						
39	Receipts from sale of plant assets		*(i)*	12,000			
40	Payment for purchase of plant assets				*(k1)*	10,000	
41	Financing activities						
42	Payment to retire notes				*(j)*	18,000	
43	Receipts from issuing stock		*(l)*	15,000			
44	Payment of cash dividends				*(m)*	14,000	
46	**Noncash Investing and Financing Activities**						
47	Purchase of plant assets with notes		*(k2)*	60,000	*(k1)*	60,000	
48				$337,000		$337,000	

Sheet1 / Sheet2 / Sheet3 /

Entering the Analysis of Changes on the Spreadsheet   The following sequence of procedures is used to complete the spreadsheet after the beginning and ending balances of the balance sheet accounts are entered:

① Enter net income as the first item in the Statement of Cash Flows section for computing operating cash inflow (debit) and as a credit to Retained Earnings.

② In the Statement of Cash Flows section, adjustments to net income are entered as debits if they increase cash flows and as credits if they decrease cash flows. Applying this same rule, adjust net income for the change in each noncash current asset and current liability account related to operating activities. For each adjustment to net income, the offsetting debit or credit must help reconcile the beginning and ending balances of a current asset or current liability account.

③ Enter adjustments to net income for income statement items not providing or using cash in the period. For each adjustment, the offsetting debit or credit must help reconcile a noncash balance sheet account.

④ Adjust net income to eliminate any gains or losses from investing and financing activities. Because the cash from a gain must be excluded from operating activities, the gain is entered as a credit in the operating activities section. Losses are entered as debits. For each adjustment, the related debit and/or credit must help reconcile balance sheet accounts and involve reconstructed entries to show the cash flow from investing or financing activities.

⑤ After reviewing any unreconciled balance sheet accounts and related information, enter the remaining reconciling entries for investing and financing activities. Examples are purchases of plant assets, issuances of long-term debt, stock issuances, and dividend payments. Some of these may require entries in the noncash investing and financing section of the spreadsheet (reconciled).

⑥ Check accuracy by totaling the Analysis of Changes columns and by determining that the change in each balance sheet account has been explained (reconciled).

Point: Analysis of the changes on the spreadsheet are summarized here:
1. Cash flows from operating activities generally affect net income, current assets, and current liabilities.
2. Cash flows from investing activities generally affect noncurrent asset accounts.
3. Cash flows from financing activities generally affect noncurrent liability and equity accounts.

We illustrate these steps in Exhibit 12A.1 for Genesis:

Step	Entries
①·········	(a)
②·········	(b) through (g)
③·········	(h)
④·········	(i) through (j)
⑤·········	(k) through (m)

Since adjustments *i*, *j*, and *k* are more challenging, we show them in the following debit and credit format. These entries are for purposes of our understanding; they are *not* the entries actually made in the journals. Changes in the Cash account are identified as sources or uses of cash.

		Debit	Credit
i.	Loss from sale of plant assets	6,000	
	Accumulated depreciation	12,000	
	Receipt from sale of plant assets **(source of cash)**	12,000	
	Plant assets		30,000
	To describe sale of plant assets.		
j.	Notes payable	34,000	
	Payments to retire notes **(use of cash)**		18,000
	Gain on retirement of notes		16,000
	To describe retirement of notes.		
k1.	Plant assets	70,000	
	Payment to purchase plant assets **(use of cash)**		10,000
	Purchase of plant assets financed by notes		60,000
	To describe purchase of plant assets.		
k2.	Purchase of plant assets financed by notes	60,000	
	Notes payable		60,000
	To issue notes for purchase of assets.		

APPENDIX

Direct Method of Reporting Operating Cash Flows

12B

We compute cash flows from operating activities under the direct method by adjusting accrual-based income statement items to the cash basis. The usual approach is to adjust income statement accounts related to operating activities for changes in their related balance sheet accounts as follows:

P5 Compute cash flows from operating activities using the direct method.

| Revenue or expense | **+** or **−** | Adjustments for changes in related balance sheet accounts | **=** | Cash receipts or cash payments |

The framework for reporting cash receipts and cash payments for the operating section of the cash flow statement under the direct method is shown in Exhibit 12B.1. We consider cash receipts first and then cash payments.

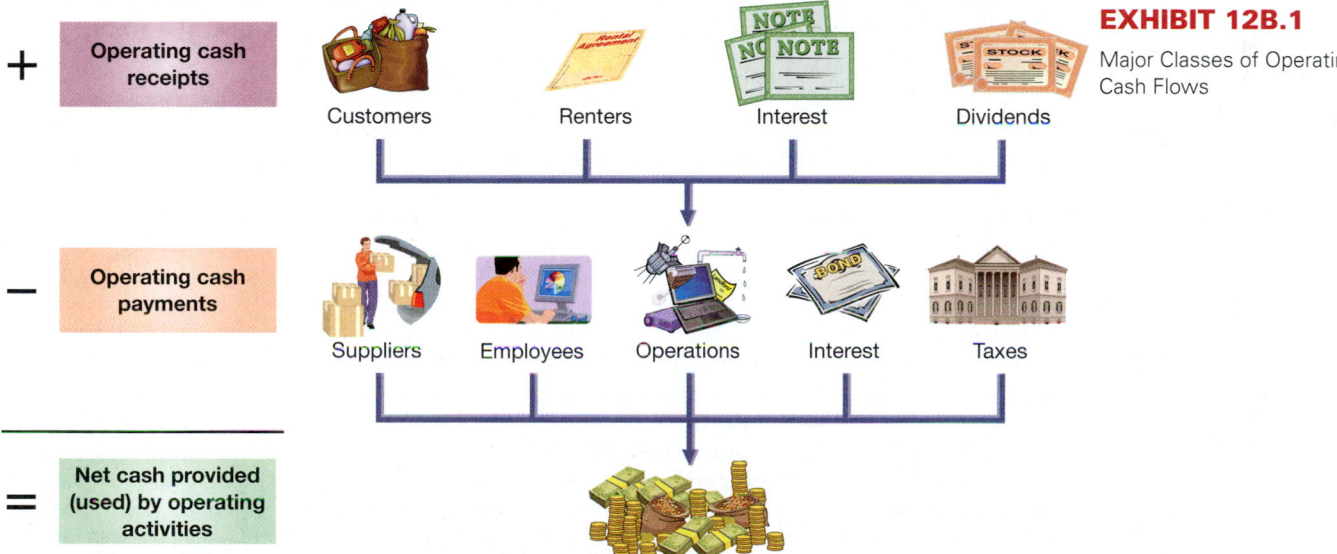

+ Operating cash receipts

Customers   Renters   Interest   Dividends

− Operating cash payments

Suppliers   Employees   Operations   Interest   Taxes

= Net cash provided (used) by operating activities

EXHIBIT 12B.1

Major Classes of Operating Cash Flows

Operating Cash Receipts   A review of Exhibit 12.10 and the additional information reported by Genesis suggests only one potential cash receipt: sales to customers. This section, therefore, starts with sales to customers as reported on the income statement and then adjusts it as necessary to obtain cash received from customers to report on the statement of cash flows.

Cash Received from Customers   If all sales are for cash, the amount received from customers equals the sales reported on the income statement. When some or all sales are on account, however, we must adjust the amount of sales for the change in Accounts Receivable. It is often helpful to use *account analysis* to do this. This usually involves setting up a T-account and reconstructing its major entries, with emphasis on cash receipts and payments. To illustrate, we use a T-account that includes accounts receivable balances for Genesis on December 31, 2010 and 2011. The beginning balance is $40,000 and the ending balance is $60,000. Next, the income statement shows sales of $590,000, which we enter on the debit side of this account. We now can reconstruct the Accounts Receivable account to determine the amount of cash received from customers as follows:

Point: An accounts receivable increase implies that cash received from customers is less than sales (the converse is also true).

Accounts Receivable			
Bal., Dec. 31, 2010	40,000		
Sales	590,000	**Cash receipts =**	**570,000**
Bal., Dec. 31, 2011	60,000		

EXHIBIT 12B.2

Formula to Compute Cash Received from Customers— Direct Method

This T-account shows that the Accounts Receivable balance begins at $40,000 and increases to $630,000 from sales of $590,000, yet its ending balance is only $60,000. This implies that cash receipts from customers are $570,000, computed as $40,000 + $590,000 − [?] = $60,000. This computation can be rearranged to express cash received as equal to sales of $590,000 minus a $20,000 increase in accounts receivable. This computation is summarized as a general rule in Exhibit 12B.2. The statement of cash flows in Exhibit 12.7 reports the $570,000 cash received from customers as a cash inflow from operating activities.

$$\text{Cash received from customers} = \text{Sales} \begin{cases} + \text{ Decrease in accounts receivable} \\ \quad\quad\quad\quad\quad\quad \text{or} \\ - \text{ Increase in accounts receivable} \end{cases}$$

Other Cash Receipts   While Genesis's cash receipts are limited to collections from customers, we often see other types of cash receipts, most commonly cash receipts involving rent, interest, and dividends. We compute cash received from these items by subtracting an increase in their respective receivable or adding a decrease. For instance, if rent receivable increases in the period, cash received from renters is less than rent revenue reported on the income statement. If rent receivable decreases, cash received is more than reported rent revenue. The same logic applies to interest and dividends. The formulas for these computations are summarized later in this appendix.

Operating Cash Payments   A review of Exhibit 12.10 and the additional Genesis information shows four operating expenses: cost of goods sold; wages and other operating expenses; interest expense; and taxes expense. We analyze each expense to compute its cash amounts for the statement of cash flows. (We then examine depreciation and the other losses and gains.)

Cash Paid for Merchandise   We compute cash paid for merchandise by analyzing both cost of goods sold and merchandise inventory. If all merchandise purchases are for cash and the ending balance of Merchandise Inventory is unchanged from the beginning balance, the amount of cash paid for merchandise equals cost of goods sold—an uncommon situation. Instead, there normally is some change in the Merchandise Inventory balance. Also, some or all merchandise purchases are often made on credit, and this yields changes in the Accounts Payable balance. When the balances of both Merchandise Inventory and Accounts Payable change, we must adjust the cost of goods sold for changes in both accounts to compute cash paid for merchandise. This is a two-step adjustment.

First, we use the change in the account balance of Merchandise Inventory, along with the cost of goods sold amount, to compute cost of purchases for the period. An increase in merchandise inventory implies that we bought more than we sold, and we add this inventory increase to cost of goods sold to compute cost of purchases. A decrease in merchandise inventory implies that we bought less than we sold, and we subtract the inventory decrease from cost of goods sold to compute purchases. We illustrate the *first step* by reconstructing the Merchandise Inventory account of Genesis:

Merchandise Inventory			
Bal., Dec. 31, 2010	70,000		
Purchases =	**314,000**	Cost of goods sold	300,000
Bal., Dec. 31, 2011	84,000		

The beginning balance is $70,000, and the ending balance is $84,000. The income statement shows that cost of goods sold is $300,000, which we enter on the credit side of this account. With this information, we determine the amount for cost of purchases to be $314,000. This computation can be rearranged to express cost of purchases as equal to cost of goods sold of $300,000 plus the $14,000 increase in inventory.

The second step uses the change in the balance of Accounts Payable, and the amount of cost of purchases, to compute cash paid for merchandise. A decrease in accounts payable implies that we paid for more goods than we acquired this period, and we would then add the accounts payable decrease to cost of purchases to compute cash paid for merchandise. An increase in accounts payable implies that we paid for less than the amount of goods acquired, and we would subtract the accounts payable increase from purchases to compute cash paid for merchandise. The *second step* is applied to Genesis by reconstructing its Accounts Payable account:

Accounts Payable			
		Bal., Dec. 31, 2010	40,000
Cash payments =	**319,000**	Purchases	314,000
		Bal., Dec. 31, 2011	35,000

Its beginning balance of $40,000 plus purchases of $314,000 minus an ending balance of $35,000 yields cash paid of $319,000 (or $40,000 + $314,000 − [?] = $35,000). Alternatively, we can express cash paid for merchandise as equal to purchases of $314,000 plus the $5,000 decrease in accounts payable. The $319,000 cash paid for merchandise is reported on the statement of cash flows in Exhibit 12.7 as a cash outflow under operating activities.

We summarize this two-step adjustment to cost of goods sold to compute cash paid for merchandise inventory in Exhibit 12B.3.

Example: If the ending balances of Inventory and Accounts Payable are $60,000 and $50,000, respectively (instead of $84,000 and $35,000), what is cash paid for merchandise? *Answer:* $280,000

EXHIBIT 12B.3

Two Steps to Compute Cash Paid for Merchandise—Direct Method

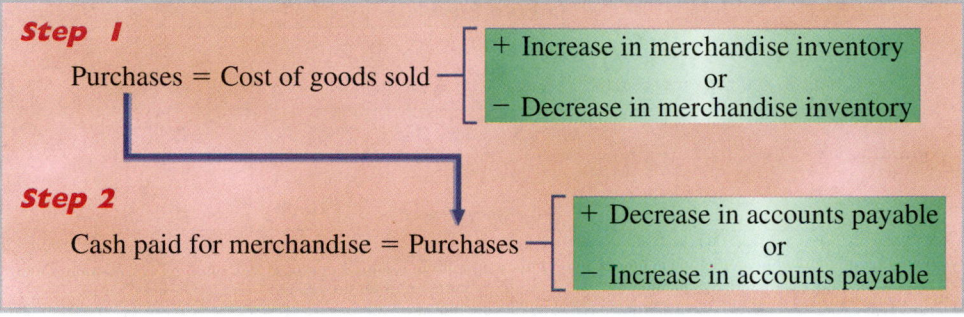

Step 1

Purchases = Cost of goods sold
+ Increase in merchandise inventory
or
− Decrease in merchandise inventory

Step 2

Cash paid for merchandise = Purchases
+ Decrease in accounts payable
or
− Increase in accounts payable

Cash Paid for Wages and Operating Expenses (Excluding Depreciation)   The income statement of Genesis shows wages and other operating expenses of $216,000 (see Exhibit 12.10). To compute cash paid for wages and other operating expenses, we adjust this amount for any changes in their related balance sheet accounts. We begin by looking for any prepaid expenses and accrued liabilities related to wages and other operating expenses in the balance sheets of Genesis in Exhibit 12.10. The balance sheets show prepaid expenses but no accrued liabilities. Thus, the adjustment is limited to the change in prepaid expenses. The amount of adjustment is computed by assuming that all cash paid for wages and other operating expenses is initially debited to Prepaid Expenses. This assumption allows us to reconstruct the Prepaid Expenses account:

Prepaid Expenses			
Bal., Dec. 31, 2010	4,000		
Cash payments =	**218,000**	Wages and other operating exp.	216,000
Bal., Dec. 31, 2011	6,000		

Prepaid Expenses increase by $2,000 in the period, meaning that cash paid for wages and other operating expenses exceeds the reported expense by $2,000. Alternatively, we can express cash paid for wages and other operating expenses as equal to its reported expenses of $216,000 plus the $2,000 increase in prepaid expenses.[1]

Exhibit 12B.4 summarizes the adjustments to wages (including salaries) and other operating expenses. The Genesis balance sheet did not report accrued liabilities, but we include them in the formula to explain the adjustment to cash when they do exist. A decrease in accrued liabilities implies that we paid cash for more goods or services than received this period, so we add the decrease in accrued liabilities to the expense amount to obtain cash paid for these goods or services. An increase in accrued liabilities implies that we paid cash for less than what was acquired, so we subtract this increase in accrued liabilities from the expense amount to get cash paid.

Point: A decrease in prepaid expenses implies that reported expenses include an amount(s) that did not require a cash outflow in the period.

---

[1] The assumption that all cash payments for wages and operating expenses are initially debited to Prepaid Expenses is not necessary for our analysis to hold. If cash payments are debited directly to the expense account, the total amount of cash paid for wages and other operating expenses still equals the $216,000 expense plus the $2,000 increase in Prepaid Expenses (which arise from end-of-period adjusting entries).

EXHIBIT 12B.4

Formula to Compute Cash Paid for Wages and Operating Expenses—Direct Method

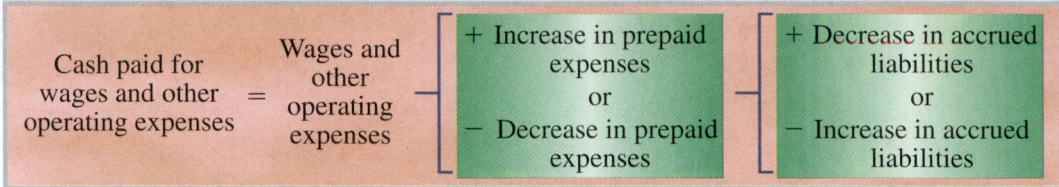

Cash paid for interest and income taxes   Computing operating cash flows for interest and taxes is similar to that for operating expenses. Both require adjustments to their amounts reported on the income statement for changes in their related balance sheet accounts. We begin with the Genesis income statement showing interest expense of $7,000 and income taxes expense of $15,000. To compute the cash paid, we adjust interest expense for the change in interest payable and then the income taxes expense for the change in income taxes payable. These computations involve reconstructing both liability accounts:

Interest Payable		
	Bal., Dec. 31, 2010	4,000
Cash paid for interest = **8,000**	Interest expense	7,000
	Bal., Dec. 31, 2011	3,000

Income Taxes Payable		
	Bal., Dec. 31, 2010	12,000
Cash paid for taxes = **5,000**	Income taxes expense	15,000
	Bal., Dec. 31, 2011	22,000

These accounts reveal cash paid for interest of $8,000 and cash paid for income taxes of $5,000. The formulas to compute these amounts are in Exhibit 12B.5. Both of these cash payments are reported as operating cash outflows on the statement of cash flows in Exhibit 12.7.

EXHIBIT 12B.5

Formulas to Compute Cash Paid for Both Interest and Taxes—Direct Method

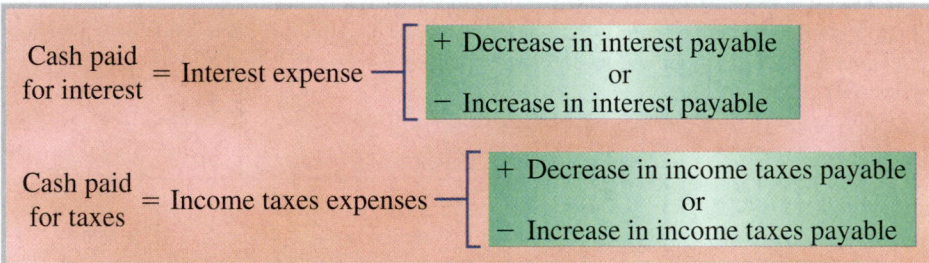

Analysis of Additional Expenses, Gains, and Losses   Genesis has three additional items reported on its income statement: depreciation, loss on sale of assets, and gain on retirement of debt. We must consider each for its potential cash effects.

Depreciation Expense   Depreciation expense is $24,000. It is often called a *noncash expense* because depreciation has no cash flows. Depreciation expense is an allocation of an asset's depreciable cost. The cash outflow with a plant asset is reported as part of investing activities when it is paid for. Thus, depreciation expense is *never* reported on a statement of cash flows using the direct method; nor is depletion or amortization expense.

Loss on Sale of Assets   Sales of assets frequently result in gains and losses reported as part of net income, but the amount of recorded gain or loss does *not* reflect any cash flows in these transactions. Asset sales result in cash inflow equal to the cash amount received, regardless of whether the asset was sold at a gain or a loss. This cash inflow is reported under investing activities. Thus, the loss or gain on a sale of assets is *never* reported on a statement of cash flows using the direct method.

Gain on Retirement of Debt   Retirement of debt usually yields a gain or loss reported as part of net income, but that gain or loss does *not* reflect cash flow in this transaction. Debt retirement results in cash outflow equal to the cash paid to settle the debt, regardless of whether the debt is retired at a gain or loss.

This cash outflow is reported under financing activities; the loss or gain from retirement of debt is *never* reported on a statement of cash flows using the direct method.

Summary of Adjustments for Direct Method   Exhibit 12B.6 summarizes common adjustments for net income to yield net cash provided (used) by operating activities under the direct method.

Item	From Income Statement	Adjustments to Obtain Cash Flow Numbers	
Receipts			
From sales	Sales Revenue	+ Decrease in Accounts Receivable − Increase in Accounts Receivable	
From rent	Rent Revenue	+ Decrease in Rent Receivable − Increase in Rent Receivable	
From interest	Interest Revenue	+ Decrease in Interest Receivable − Increase in Interest Receivable	
From dividends	Dividend Revenue	+ Decrease in Dividends Receivable − Increase in Dividends Receivable	
Payments			
To suppliers	Cost of Goods Sold	+ Increase in Inventory − Decrease in Inventory	+ Decrease in Accounts Payable − Increase in Accounts Payable
For operations	Operating Expense	+ Increase in Prepaids − Decrease in Prepaids	+ Decrease in Accrued Liabilities − Increase in Accrued Liabilities
To employees	Wages (Salaries) Expense	+ Decrease in Wages (Salaries) Payable − Increase in Wages (Salaries) Payable	
For interest	Interest Expense	+ Decrease in Interest Payable − Increase in Interest Payable	
For taxes	Income Tax Expense	+ Decrease in Income Tax Payable − Increase in Income Tax Payable	

EXHIBIT 12B.6

Summary of Selected Adjustments for Direct Method

Direct Method Format of Operating Activities Section   Exhibit 12.7 shows the Genesis statement of cash flows using the direct method. Major items of cash inflows and cash outflows are listed separately in the operating activities section. The format requires that operating cash outflows be subtracted from operating cash inflows to get net cash provided (used) by operating activities. The FASB recommends that the operating activities section of the statement of cash flows be reported using the direct method, which is considered more useful to financial statement users. *However, the FASB requires a reconciliation of net income to net cash provided (used) by operating activities when the direct method is used* (which can be reported in the notes). This reconciliation is similar to preparation of the operating activities section of the statement of cash flows using the indirect method.

Point: Some preparers argue that it is easier to prepare a statement of cash flows using the indirect method. This likely explains its greater frequency in financial statements.

 **IFRS** _____

Like U.S. GAAP, IFRS allows cash flows from operating activities to be reported using either the indirect method or the direct method. ∎

Quick Check   Answers — p. 530

8. Net sales in a period are $590,000, beginning accounts receivable are $120,000, and ending accounts receivable are $90,000. What cash amount is collected from customers in the period?

9. The Merchandise Inventory account balance decreases in the period from a beginning balance of $32,000 to an ending balance of $28,000. Cost of goods sold for the period is $168,000. If the Accounts Payable balance increases $2,400 in the period, what is the cash amount paid for merchandise inventory?

10. This period's wages and other operating expenses total $112,000. Beginning-of-period prepaid expenses totaled $1,200, and its ending balance is $4,200. There were no beginning-of-period accrued liabilities, but end-of-period wages payable equal $5,600. How much cash is paid for wages and other operating expenses?

Summary

C1   **Distinguish between operating, investing, and financing activities, and describe how noncash investing and financing activities are disclosed.** The purpose of the statement of cash flows is to report major cash receipts and cash payments relating to operating, investing, or financing activities. Operating activities include transactions and events that determine net income. Investing activities include transactions and events that mainly affect long-term assets. Financing activities include transactions and events that mainly affect long-term liabilities and equity. Noncash investing and financing activities must be disclosed in either a note or a separate schedule to the statement of cash flows. Examples are the retirement of debt by issuing equity and the exchange of a note payable for plant assets.

A1   **Analyze the statement of cash flows and apply the cash flow on total assets ratio.** To understand and predict cash flows, users stress identification of the sources and uses of cash flows by operating, investing, and financing activities. Emphasis is on operating cash flows since they derive from continuing operations. The cash flow on total assets ratio is defined as operating cash flows divided by average total assets. Analysis of current and past values for this ratio can reflect a company's ability to yield regular and positive cash flows. It is also viewed as a measure of earnings quality.

P1   **Prepare a statement of cash flows.** Preparation of a statement of cash flows involves five steps: (1) Compute the net increase or decrease in cash; (2) compute net cash provided or used by operating activities (*using either the direct or indirect method*); (3) compute net cash provided or used by investing activities; (4) compute net cash

provided or used by financing activities; and (5) report the beginning and ending cash balance and prove that it is explained by net cash flows. Noncash investing and financing activities are also disclosed.

P2   **Compute cash flows from operating activities using the indirect method.** The indirect method for reporting net cash provided or used by operating activities starts with net income and then adjusts it for three items: (1) changes in noncash current assets and current liabilities related to operating activities, (2) revenues and expenses not providing or using cash, and (3) gains and losses from investing and financing activities.

P3   **Determine cash flows from both investing and financing activities.** Cash flows from both investing and financing activities are determined by identifying the cash flow effects of transactions and events affecting each balance sheet account related to these activities. All cash flows from these activities are identified when we can explain changes in these accounts from the beginning to the end of the period.

P4ᴬ   **Illustrate use of a spreadsheet to prepare a statement of cash flows.** A spreadsheet is a useful tool in preparing a statement of cash flows. Six key steps (see Appendix 12A) are applied when using the spreadsheet to prepare the statement.

P5ᴮ   **Compute cash flows from operating activities using the direct method.** The direct method for reporting net cash provided or used by operating activities lists major operating cash inflows less cash outflows to yield net cash inflow or outflow from operations.

Guidance Answers to Decision Maker

Entrepreneur   Several factors might explain an increase in net cash flows when a net loss is reported, including (1) early recognition of expenses relative to revenues generated (such as research and development), (2) cash advances on long-term sales contracts not yet recognized in income, (3) issuances of debt or equity for cash to finance expansion, (4) cash sale of assets, (5) delay of cash payments, and (6) cash prepayment on sales. Analysis needs to focus on the components of both the net loss and the net cash flows and their implications for future performance.

Reporter   Your initial reaction based on the company's $600,000 loss with a $550,000 decrease in net cash flows is not positive. However, closer scrutiny reveals a more positive picture of this company's performance. Cash flow from operating activities is $650,000, computed as [?] − $850,000 − $350,000 = $(550,000). You also note that net income *before* the extraordinary loss is $330,000, computed as [?] − $930,000 = $(600,000).

Guidance Answers to Quick Checks

1. No to both. The statement of cash flows reports changes in the sum of cash plus cash equivalents. It does not report transfers between cash and cash equivalents.

2. The three categories of cash inflows and outflows are operating activities, investing activities, and financing activities.

3. **a.** Investing   **c.** Financing   **e.** Operating
       b. Operating   **d.** Operating   **f.** Financing

4. $74,900 + $4,600 − $11,700 − $1,000 + $3,400 = $70,200

5. Expenses such as depreciation and amortization do not require current cash outflows. Therefore, adding these expenses back to

net income eliminates these noncash items from the net income number, converting it to a cash basis.

6. A gain on the sale of plant assets is subtracted from net income because a sale of plant assets is not an operating activity; it is an investing activity for the amount of cash received from its sale. Also, such a gain yields no cash effects.

7. $80,000 − $30,000 − $10,000 = $40,000 cash receipt. The $40,000 cash receipt is reported as an investing activity.

8. $590,000 + ($120,000 − $90,000) = $620,000

9. $168,000 − ($32,000 − $28,000) − $2,400 = $161,600

10. $112,000 + ($4,200 − $1,200) − $5,600 = $109,400

Key Terms

mhhe.com/wildFINMAN4e

Cash flow on total assets (p. 518)
Direct method (p. 506)
Financing activities (p. 502)

Indirect method (p. 506)
Investing activities (p. 502)

Operating activities (p. 501)
Statement of cash flows (p. 500)

Multiple Choice Quiz   Answers on p. 551   mhhe.com/wildFINMAN4e

Additional Quiz Questions are available at the book's Website.

1. A company uses the indirect method to determine its cash flows from operating activities. Use the following information to determine its net cash provided or used by operating activities.

Net income	$15,200
Depreciation expense	10,000
Cash payment on note payable	8,000
Gain on sale of land	3,000
Increase in inventory	1,500
Increase in accounts payable	2,850

a. $23,550 used by operating activities
b. $23,550 provided by operating activities
c. $15,550 provided by operating activities
d. $42,400 provided by operating activities
e. $20,850 provided by operating activities

2. A machine with a cost of $175,000 and accumulated depreciation of $94,000 is sold for $87,000 cash. The amount reported as a source of cash under cash flows from investing activities is
a. $81,000.
b. $6,000.
c. $87,000.
d. Zero; this is a financing activity.
e. Zero; this is an operating activity.

3. A company settles a long-term note payable plus interest by paying $68,000 cash toward the principal amount and $5,440 cash for interest. The amount reported as a use of cash under cash flows from financing activities is
a. Zero; this is an investing activity.
b. Zero; this is an operating activity.

c. $73,440.
d. $68,000.
e. $5,440.

4. The following information is available regarding a company's annual salaries and wages. What amount of cash is paid for salaries and wages?

Salaries and wages expense	$255,000
Salaries and wages payable, prior year-end	8,200
Salaries and wages payable, current year-end	10,900

a. $252,300
b. $257,700
c. $255,000
d. $274,100
e. $235,900

5. The following information is available for a company. What amount of cash is paid for merchandise for the current year?

Cost of goods sold	$545,000
Merchandise inventory, prior year-end	105,000
Merchandise inventory, current year-end	112,000
Accounts payable, prior year-end	98,500
Accounts payable, current year-end	101,300

a. $545,000
b. $554,800
c. $540,800
d. $535,200
e. $549,200

A(B) *Superscript letter A (B) denotes assignments based on Appendix 12A (12B).*
Icon denotes assignments that involve decision making.

Discussion Questions

1. What is the reporting purpose of the statement of cash flows? Identify at least two questions that this statement can answer.
2. Describe the direct method of reporting cash flows from operating activities.
3. When a statement of cash flows is prepared using the direct method, what are some of the operating cash flows?

4. Describe the indirect method of reporting cash flows from operating activities.
5. What are some investing activities reported on the statement of cash flows?
6. What are some financing activities reported on the statement of cash flows?

7. Where on the statement of cash flows is the payment of cash dividends reported?

8.  Assume that a company purchases land for $100,000, paying $20,000 cash and borrowing the remainder with a long-term note payable. How should this transaction be reported on a statement of cash flows?

9.  On June 3, a company borrows $50,000 cash by giving its bank a 160-day, interest-bearing note. On the statement of cash flows, where should this be reported?

10.  If a company reports positive net income for the year, can it also show a net cash outflow from operating activities? Explain.

11.  Is depreciation a source of cash flow?

12.  Refer to **Research In Motion**'s statement of cash flows in Appendix A. (*a*) Which method is used to compute its net cash provided by operating activities? **RIM**

(*b*) While its balance sheet shows an increase in working capital (current assets less current liabilities) from fiscal years 2009 to 2010, why is this increase in working capital subtracted when computing net cash provided by operating activities for the year ended February 27, 2010?

13.  Refer to **Palm**'s statement of cash flows in Appendix A. What are its cash flows from financing activities for the year ended May 31, 2009? List items and amounts. **Palm**

14.  Refer to **Nokia**'s statement of cash flows in Appendix A. List its cash flows from operating activities, investing activities, and financing activities. **NOKIA**

15.  Refer to **Apple**'s statement of cash flows in Appendix A. What investing activities result in cash outflows for the year ended September 26, 2009? List items and amounts. **Apple**

 **connect**

QUICK STUDY

QS 12-1
Transaction classification by activity
C1

Classify the following cash flows as operating, investing, or financing activities.

1. Paid cash for property taxes on building.
2. Paid cash dividends.
3. Paid cash for wages and salaries.
4. Purchased inventories for cash.
5. Received cash payments from customers.

6. Received cash from sale of land at a loss.
7. Received cash interest on a note.
8. Paid cash interest on outstanding notes.
9. Issued common stock for cash.
10. Sold long-term investments for cash.

QS 12-2
Statement of cash flows
C1

The statement of cash flows is one of the four primary financial statements.

1. Describe the content and layout of a statement of cash flows, including its three sections.
2. List at least three transactions classified as significant noncash financing and investing activities in the statement of cash flows.
3. List at least three transactions classified as financing activities in a statement of cash flows.
4. List at least three transactions classified as investing activities in a statement of cash flows.

QS 12-3
Computing cash from operations (indirect)
P2

Use the following information to determine this company's cash flows from operating activities using the indirect method.

LING COMPANY Selected Balance Sheet Information December 31, 2011 and 2010		
	2011	**2010**
Current assets		
Cash	$338,600	$107,200
Accounts receivable	100,000	128,000
Inventory	240,000	216,400
Current liabilities		
Accounts payable	121,600	102,800
Income taxes payable	8,200	8,800

LING COMPANY Income Statement For Year Ended December 31, 2011		
Sales		$2,060,000
Cost of goods sold		1,326,400
Gross profit		733,600
Operating expenses		
Depreciation expense	$144,000	
Other expenses	486,000	630,000
Income before taxes		103,600
Income taxes expense		30,800
Net income		$ 72,800

The following selected information is from Mooney Company's comparative balance sheets.

At December 31	2011	2010
Furniture	$155,000	$ 260,000
Accumulated depreciation—Furniture	(74,400)	(121,400)

The income statement reports depreciation expense for the year of $36,000. Also, furniture costing $105,000 was sold for its book value. Compute the cash received from the sale of furniture.

QS 12-4
Computing cash from asset sales
P3

The following selected information is from the Teeter Company's comparative balance sheets.

At December 31	2011	2010
Common stock, $10 par value	$ 310,000	$300,000
Paid-in capital in excess of par	1,134,000	684,000
Retained earnings	627,000	575,000

The company's net income for the year ended December 31, 2011, was $196,000.
1. Compute the cash received from the sale of its common stock during 2011.
2. Compute the cash paid for dividends during 2011.

QS 12-5
Computing financing cash flows
P3

For each of the following separate cases, compute cash flows from operations. The list includes all balance sheet accounts related to operating activities.

	Case A	Case B	Case C
Net income	$ 20,000	$125,000	$105,000
Depreciation expense	60,000	16,000	48,000
Accounts receivable increase (decrease)	80,000	40,000	(8,000)
Inventory increase (decrease)	(40,000)	(20,000)	21,000
Accounts payable increase (decrease)	28,000	(44,000)	16,000
Accrued liabilities increase (decrease)	(88,000)	10,000	(16,000)

QS 12-6
Computing cash flows from operations (indirect)
P2

Compute cash flows from investing activities using the following company information.

Sale of short-term investments	$16,000
Cash collections from customers	44,000
Purchase of used equipment	10,000
Depreciation expense	6,000

QS 12-7
Computing cash flows from investing
P3

Compute cash flows from financing activities using the following company information.

Additional short-term borrowings	$88,000
Purchase of short-term investments	25,000
Cash dividends paid	32,000
Interest paid	17,000

QS 12-8
Computing cash flows from financing
P3

QS 12-9

Computing cash from operations (indirect) **P2**

Use the following balance sheets and income statement to answer QS 12-9 through QS 12-14.

Use the indirect method to prepare the cash provided or used from operating activities section only of the statement of cash flows for this company.

ORWELL, INC.
Income Statement
For Year Ended December 31, 2011

Sales		$468,000
Cost of goods sold		312,000
Gross profit		156,000
Operating expenses		
Depreciation expense	$38,600	
Other expenses	57,000	95,600
Income before taxes		60,400
Income taxes expense		24,600
Net income		$ 35,800

ORWELL, INC.
Comparative Balance Sheets
December 31, 2011

	2011	2010
Assets		
Cash	$ 95,800	$ 25,000
Accounts receivable, net	42,000	52,000
Inventory	86,800	96,800
Prepaid expenses	6,400	5,200
Furniture	110,000	120,000
Accum. depreciation—Furniture	(18,000)	(10,000)
Total assets	$323,000	$289,000
Liabilities and Equity		
Accounts payable	$ 16,000	$ 22,000
Wages payable	10,000	6,000
Income taxes payable	2,400	3,600
Notes payable (long-term)	30,000	70,000
Common stock, $5 par value	230,000	180,000
Retained earnings	34,600	7,400
Total liabilities and equity	$323,000	$289,000

QS 12-10

Computing cash from asset sales **P3**

Refer to the data in QS 12-9.
Furniture costing $54,000 is sold at its book value in 2011. Acquisitions of furniture total $44,000 cash, on which no depreciation is necessary because it is acquired at year-end. What is the cash inflow related to the sale of furniture?

QS 12-11

Computing financing cash outflows **P3**

Refer to the data in QS 12-9.
1. Assume that all common stock is issued for cash. What amount of cash dividends is paid during 2011?
2. Assume that no additional notes payable are issued in 2011. What cash amount is paid to reduce the notes payable balance in 2011?

QS 12-12ᴮ

Computing cash received from customers **P5**

Refer to the data in QS 12-9.
1. How much cash is received from sales to customers for year 2011?
2. What is the net increase or decrease in cash for year 2011?

QS 12-13ᴮ

Computing operating cash outflows **P5**

Refer to the data in QS 12-9.
1. How much cash is paid to acquire merchandise inventory during year 2011?
2. How much cash is paid for operating expenses during year 2011?

QS 12-14ᴮ

Computing cash from operations (direct) **P5**

Refer to the data in QS 12-9.
Use the direct method to prepare the cash provided or used from operating activities section only of the statement of cash flows for this company.

QS 12-15

Analyses of sources and uses of cash **A1**

Financial data from three competitors in the same industry follow.
1. Which of the three competitors is in the strongest position as shown by its statement of cash flows?
2. Analyze and compare the strength of Z-Best's cash flow on total assets ratio to that of Lopez.

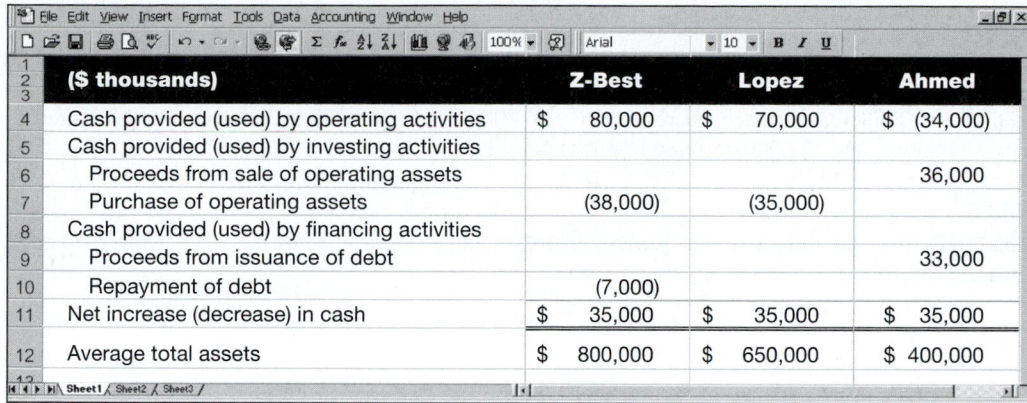

($ thousands)	Z-Best	Lopez	Ahmed
Cash provided (used) by operating activities	$ 80,000	$ 70,000	$ (34,000)
Cash provided (used) by investing activities			
Proceeds from sale of operating assets			36,000
Purchase of operating assets	(38,000)	(35,000)	
Cash provided (used) by financing activities			
Proceeds from issuance of debt			33,000
Repayment of debt	(7,000)		
Net increase (decrease) in cash	$ 35,000	$ 35,000	$ 35,000
Average total assets	$ 800,000	$ 650,000	$ 400,000

When a spreadsheet for a statement of cash flows is prepared, all changes in noncash balance sheet accounts are fully explained on the spreadsheet. Explain how these noncash balance sheet accounts are used to fully account for cash flows on a spreadsheet.

QS 12-16^A
Noncash accounts
on a spreadsheet **P4**

Use the following financial statements and additional information to (1) prepare a statement of cash flows for the year ended December 31, 2012, using the *indirect method,* and (2) analyze and briefly discuss the statement prepared in part 1 with special attention to operating activities and to the company's cash level.

QS 12-17
Preparation of statement
of cash flows (indirect)

P1

KRUG INC.
Comparative Balance Sheets
December 31, 2012 and 2011

	2012	2011
Assets		
Cash	$ 26,400	$ 30,550
Accounts receivable, net	14,050	12,150
Inventory	90,100	70,150
Equipment	49,900	44,500
Accum. depreciation—Equipment	(22,500)	(18,300)
Total assets	$157,950	$139,050
Liabilities and Equity		
Accounts payable	$ 23,350	$ 25,400
Salaries payable	1,050	600
Common stock, no par value	107,000	100,000
Retained earnings	26,550	13,050
Total liabilities and equity	$157,950	$139,050

KRUG INC.
Income Statement
For Year Ended December 31, 2012

Sales		$47,575
Cost of goods sold		(17,950)
Gross profit		29,625
Operating expenses		
Depreciation expense	$4,200	
Other expenses	8,550	
Total operating expense		12,750
Income before taxes		16,875
Income tax expense		3,375
Net income		$13,500

Additional Information

a. No dividends are declared or paid in 2012.

b. Issued additional stock for $7,000 cash in 2012.

c. Purchased equipment for cash in 2012; no equipment was sold in 2012.

Answer each of the following related to international accounting standards.

1. Which method, indirect or direct, is acceptable for reporting operating cash flows under IFRS?

2. For each of the following four cash flows, identify whether it is reported under the operating, investing, or financing section (or some combination) within the indirect format of the statement of cash flows reported under IFRS and under U.S. GAAP.

QS 12-18
International cash flow
disclosures

C1

Cash Flow Source	US GAAP Reporting	IFRS Reporting
a. Interest paid		
b. Dividends paid		
c. Interest received		
d. Dividends received		

EXERCISES

Exercise 12-1

Cash flow from operations (indirect)

P2

Rasheed Company reports net income of $390,000 for the year ended December 31, 2011. It also reports $70,000 depreciation expense and a $10,000 gain on the sale of machinery. Its comparative balance sheets reveal a $30,000 increase in accounts receivable, $16,000 increase in accounts payable, $8,000 decrease in prepaid expenses, and $12,000 decrease in wages payable.

Required

Prepare only the operating activities section of the statement of cash flows for 2011 using the *indirect method*.

Exercise 12-2

Cash flow classification (indirect)

C1

The following transactions and events occurred during the year. Assuming that this company uses the *indirect method* to report cash provided by operating activities, indicate where each item would appear on its statement of cash flows by placing an *x* in the appropriate column.

	Statement of Cash Flows			Noncash Investing and Financing Activities	Not Reported on Statement or in Notes
	Operating Activities	Investing Activities	Financing Activities		
a. Accounts receivable decreased in the year	——	——	——	——	——
b. Purchased land by issuing common stock	——	——	——	——	——
c. Paid cash to purchase inventory	——	——	——	——	——
d. Sold equipment for cash, yielding a loss	——	——	——	——	——
e. Accounts payable decreased in the year	——	——	——	——	——
f. Income taxes payable increased in the year	——	——	——	——	——
g. Declared and paid a cash dividend	——	——	——	——	——
h. Recorded depreciation expense	——	——	——	——	——
i. Paid cash to settle long-term note payable	——	——	——	——	——
j. Prepaid expenses increased in the year	——	——	——	——	——

Exercise 12-3[B]

Cash flow classification (direct)

C1 P5

The following transactions and events occurred during the year. Assuming that this company uses the *direct method* to report cash provided by operating activities, indicate where each item would appear on the statement of cash flows by placing an *x* in the appropriate column.

	Statement of Cash Flows			Noncash Investing and Financing Activities	Not Reported on Statement or in Notes
	Operating Activities	Investing Activities	Financing Activities		
a. Accepted six-month note receivable in exchange for plant assets	——	——	——	——	——
b. Recorded depreciation expense	——	——	——	——	——
c. Paid cash to acquire treasury stock	——	——	——	——	——
d. Collected cash from sales	——	——	——	——	——
e. Borrowed cash from bank by signing a nine-month note payable	——	——	——	——	——
f. Paid cash to purchase a patent	——	——	——	——	——
g. Retired long-term notes payable by issuing common stock	——	——	——	——	——
h. Paid cash toward accounts payable	——	——	——	——	——
i. Sold inventory for cash	——	——	——	——	——
j. Paid cash dividend that was declared in a prior period	——	——	——	——	——

Roney Company's calendar-year 2011 income statement shows the following: Net Income, $364,000; Depreciation Expense, $45,000; Amortization Expense, $8,200; Gain on Sale of Plant Assets, $7,000. An examination of the company's current assets and current liabilities reveals the following changes (all from operating activities): Accounts Receivable decrease, $18,100; Merchandise Inventory decrease, $52,000; Prepaid Expenses increase, $3,700; Accounts Payable decrease, $9,200; Other Payables increase, $1,400. Use the *indirect method* to compute cash flow from operating activities.

Exercise 12-4
Cash flows from operating activities (indirect)
P2

For each of the following three separate cases, use the information provided about the calendar-year 2012 operations of Sahim Company to compute the required cash flow information.

Exercise 12-5[B]
Computation of cash flows (direct)
P5

Case A: Compute cash received from customers:

Sales	$510,000
Accounts receivable, December 31, 2011	25,200
Accounts receivable, December 31, 2012	34,800

Case B: Compute cash paid for rent:

Rent expense	$140,800
Rent payable, December 31, 2011	8,800
Rent payable, December 31, 2012	7,200

Case C: Compute cash paid for merchandise:

Cost of goods sold	$528,000
Merchandise inventory, December 31, 2011	159,600
Accounts payable, December 31, 2011	67,800
Merchandise inventory, December 31, 2012	131,400
Accounts payable, December 31, 2012	84,000

Use the following income statement and information about changes in noncash current assets and current liabilities to prepare only the cash flows from operating activities section of the statement of cash flows using the *indirect* method.

Exercise 12-6
Cash flows from operating activities (indirect)
P2

BEKHAM COMPANY		
Income Statement		
For Year Ended December 31, 2011		
Sales		$1,818,000
Cost of goods sold		891,000
Gross profit		927,000
Operating expenses		
Salaries expense	$248,535	
Depreciation expense	43,200	
Rent expense	48,600	
Amortization expenses—Patents	5,400	
Utilities expense	19,125	364,860
		562,140
Gain on sale of equipment		7,200
Net income		$ 569,340

Changes in current asset and current liability accounts for the year that relate to operations follow.

Accounts receivable	$40,500 increase	Accounts payable	$13,500 decrease
Merchandise inventory	27,000 increase	Salaries payable	4,500 decrease

---

Refer to the information about Bekham Company in Exercise 12-6.
Use the *direct method* to prepare only the cash provided or used by operating activities section of the statement of cash flows for this company.

Exercise 12-7[B]
Cash flows from operating activities (direct) **P5**

Exercise 12-8

Cash flows from investing activities

P3

Use the following information to determine this company's cash flows from investing activities.

a. Sold land costing $315,000 for $400,000 cash, yielding a gain of $15,000.
b. Paid $106,000 cash for a new truck.
c. Equipment with a book value of $80,500 and an original cost of $165,000 was sold at a loss of $34,000.
d. Long-term investments in stock were sold for $94,700 cash, yielding a gain of $15,750.

Exercise 12-9

Cash flows from financing activities

P3

Use the following information to determine this company's cash flows from financing activities.

a. Net income was $472,000.
b. Issued common stock for $75,000 cash.
c. Paid cash dividend of $13,000.
d. Paid $120,000 cash to settle a note payable at its $120,000 maturity value.
e. Paid $118,000 cash to acquire its treasury stock.
f. Purchased equipment for $92,000 cash.

Exercise 12-10

Preparation of statement of cash flows (indirect) P1

Use the following financial statements and additional information to (1) prepare a statement of cash flows for the year ended June 30, 2011, using the *indirect method,* and (2) compute the company's cash flow on total assets ratio for its fiscal year 2011.

GECKO INC.
Income Statement
For Year Ended June 30, 2011

Sales		$668,000
Cost of goods sold		412,000
Gross profit		256,000
Operating expenses		
Depreciation expense	$58,600	
Other expenses	67,000	
Total operating expenses		125,600
		130,400
Other gains (losses)		
Gain on sale of equipment		2,000
Income before taxes		132,400
Income taxes expense		45,640
Net income		$ 86,760

GECKO INC.
Comparative Balance Sheets
June 30, 2011 and 2010

	2011	2010
Assets		
Cash	$ 85,800	$ 45,000
Accounts receivable, net	70,000	52,000
Inventory	66,800	96,800
Prepaid expenses	5,400	5,200
Equipment	130,000	120,000
Accum. depreciation—Equipment	(28,000)	(10,000)
Total assets	$330,000	$309,000
Liabilities and Equity		
Accounts payable	$ 26,000	$ 32,000
Wages payable	7,000	16,000
Income taxes payable	2,400	3,600
Notes payable (long term)	40,000	70,000
Common stock, $5 par value	230,000	180,000
Retained earnings	24,600	7,400
Total liabilities and equity	$330,000	$309,000

Additional Information

a. A $30,000 note payable is retired at its $30,000 carrying (book) value in exchange for cash.
b. The only changes affecting retained earnings are net income and cash dividends paid.
c. New equipment is acquired for $58,600 cash.
d. Received cash for the sale of equipment that had cost $48,600, yielding a $2,000 gain.
e. Prepaid Expenses and Wages Payable relate to Other Expenses on the income statement.
f. All purchases and sales of merchandise inventory are on credit.

Check (b) Cash dividends, $69,560

(d) Cash from equip. sale, $10,000

Refer to the data in Exercise 12-10.
Using the *direct method,* prepare the statement of cash flows for the year ended June 30, 2011.

Use the following information about the cash flows of Kansas Company to prepare a complete statement of cash flows (*direct method*) for the year ended December 31, 2011. Use a note disclosure for any noncash investing and financing activities.

Cash and cash equivalents balance, December 31, 2010	$ 25,000
Cash and cash equivalents balance, December 31, 2011	70,000
Cash received as interest	2,500
Cash paid for salaries	72,500
Bonds payable retired by issuing common stock (no gain or loss on retirement)	187,500
Cash paid to retire long-term notes payable	125,000
Cash received from sale of equipment	61,250
Cash received in exchange for six-month note payable	25,000
Land purchased by issuing long-term note payable	106,250
Cash paid for store equipment	23,750
Cash dividends paid	15,000
Cash paid for other expenses	40,000
Cash received from customers	485,000
Cash paid for merchandise	252,500

The following summarized Cash T-account reflects the total debits and total credits to the Cash account of Texas Corporation for calendar year 2011.

(1) Use this information to prepare a complete statement of cash flows for year 2011. The cash provided or used by operating activities should be reported using the *direct method.*

(2) Refer to the statement of cash flows prepared for part 1 to answer the following questions *a* through *d*: (*a*) Which section—operating, investing, or financing—shows the largest cash (i) inflow and (ii) outflow? (*b*) What is the largest individual item among the investing cash outflows? (*c*) Are the cash proceeds larger from issuing notes or issuing stock? (*d*) Does the company have a net cash inflow or outflow from borrowing activities?

Accounting System:

File Edit Maintain Tasks Analysis Options Reports Window Help

Cash

Balance, Dec. 31, 2010	135,200			
Receipts from customers	6,000,000	Payments for merchandise	1,590,000	
Receipts from dividends	208,400	Payments for wages	550,000	
Receipts from land sale	220,000	Payments for rent	320,000	
Receipts from machinery sale	710,000	Payments for interest	218,000	
Receipts from issuing stock	1,540,000	Payments for taxes	450,000	
Receipts from borrowing	2,600,000	Payments for machinery	2,236,000	
		Payments for long-term investments	2,260,000	
		Payments for note payable	386,000	
		Payments for dividends	500,000	
		Payments for treasury stock	218,000	
Balance, Dec. 31, 2011	$?			

Sales   Purchases   General Ledger   Payroll   Inventory   Company   Analysis

Exercise 12-14
Reporting cash flows from
operations (indirect)

P2

Harold Company reports the following information for its recent calendar year.

Sales	$70,000
Expenses	
Cost of goods sold	40,000
Salaries expense	12,000
Depreciation expense	6,000
Net income	$12,000
Accounts receivable increase	$ 9,000
Inventory decrease	3,000
Salaries payable increase	800

Required

Prepare the operating activities section of the statement of cash flows for Harold Company using the indirect method.

Exercise 12-15
Reporting and interpreting cash
flows from operations (indirect)

P2

Oregon Company disclosed the following information for its recent calendar year.

Revenues	$100,000
Expenses	
Salaries expense	68,000
Utilities expense	28,000
Depreciation expense	29,200
Other expenses	6,800
Net loss	$ (32,000)
Accounts receivable decrease	$ 28,000
Purchased a machine	20,000
Salaries payable increase	26,000
Other accrued liabilities decrease	16,000

Required

1. Prepare the operating activities section of the statement of cash flows using the indirect method.
2. What were the major reasons that this company was able to report a net loss but positive cash flow from operations?
3. Of the potential causes of differences between cash flow from operations and net income, which are the most important to investors?

Exercise 12-16
Analyses of cash flow on
total assets   A1

A company reported average total assets of $248,000 in 2010 and $302,000 in 2011. Its net operating cash flow in 2010 was $20,575 and $27,750 in 2011. Calculate its cash flow on total assets ratio for both years. Comment on the results and any change in performance.

Exercise 12-17
Cash flows spreadsheet
(indirect method)

P4

Complete the following spreadsheet in preparation of the statement of cash flows. (The statement of cash flows is not required.) Prepare the spreadsheet as in Exhibit 12A.1; report operating activities under the indirect method. Identify the debits and credits in the Analysis of Changes columns with letters that correspond to the following transactions and events *a* through *h*.

  a. Net income for the year was $30,000.
  b. Dividends of $10,000 cash were declared and paid.
  c. Stylish's only noncash expense was $50,000 of depreciation.
  d. The company purchased plant assets for $70,000 cash.
  e. Notes payable of $40,000 were issued for $40,000 cash.
  f. Change in accounts receivable.
  g. Change in merchandise inventory.
  h. Change in accounts payable.

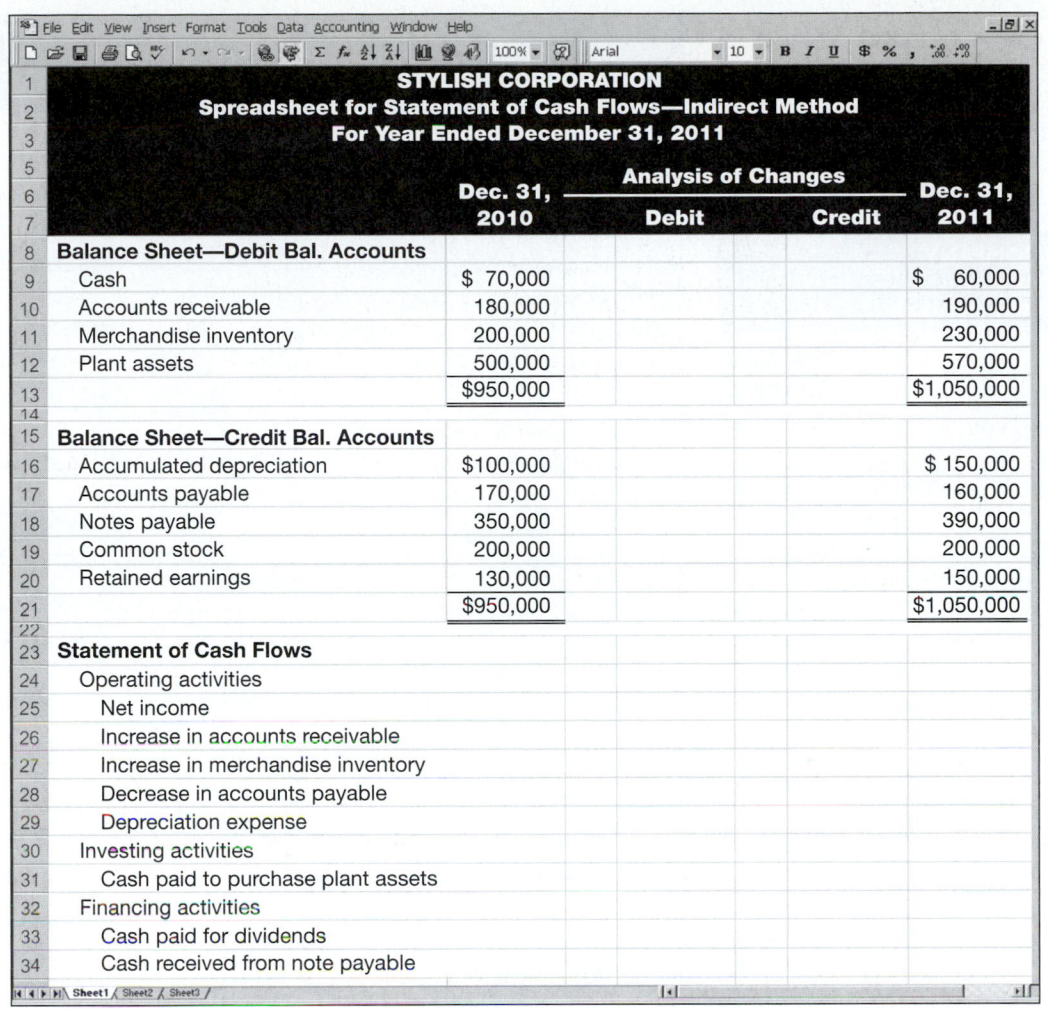

Spreadsheet — STYLISH CORPORATION, Statement of Cash Flows—Indirect Method, For Year Ended December 31, 2011:

	Dec. 31, 2010	Analysis of Changes Debit	Analysis of Changes Credit	Dec. 31, 2011
Balance Sheet—Debit Bal. Accounts				
Cash	$ 70,000			$ 60,000
Accounts receivable	180,000			190,000
Merchandise inventory	200,000			230,000
Plant assets	500,000			570,000
	$950,000			$1,050,000
Balance Sheet—Credit Bal. Accounts				
Accumulated depreciation	$100,000			$ 150,000
Accounts payable	170,000			160,000
Notes payable	350,000			390,000
Common stock	200,000			200,000
Retained earnings	130,000			150,000
	$950,000			$1,050,000
Statement of Cash Flows				
Operating activities				
Net income				
Increase in accounts receivable				
Increase in merchandise inventory				
Decrease in accounts payable				
Depreciation expense				
Investing activities				
Cash paid to purchase plant assets				
Financing activities				
Cash paid for dividends				
Cash received from note payable				

Peugeot S.A. reports the following financial information for the year ended December 31, 2008 (euros in millions). Prepare its statement of cash flows under the indirect method.

Exercise 12-18
Statement of cash flows under IFRS (indirect)

P1

Net loss	€ 500	Cash from sales of treasury stock and other	€ 812
Depreciation and amortization	3,679	Cash paid for dividends	361
Gains on disposals and other	(362)	Cash from disposal of plant assets and intangibles	88
Net increase in current assets	(417)	Cash paid for plant assets and intangibles	(3,331)
Net decrease in current liabilities ...	(2,338)	Cash and cash equivalents, December 31, 2007	5,937

connect

Kazaam Company, a merchandiser, recently completed its calendar-year 2011 operations. For the year, (1) all sales are credit sales, (2) all credits to Accounts Receivable reflect cash receipts from customers, (3) all purchases of inventory are on credit, (4) all debits to Accounts Payable reflect cash payments for inventory, and (5) Other Expenses are paid in advance and are initially debited to Prepaid Expenses. The company's balance sheets and income statement follow.

PROBLEM SET A

Problem 12-1A
Statement of cash flows (indirect method)

A1 P1 P2 P3

KAZAAM COMPANY
Comparative Balance Sheets
December 31, 2011 and 2010

	2011	2010
Assets		
Cash	$ 53,875	$ 76,625
Accounts receivable	65,000	49,625
Merchandise inventory	273,750	252,500
Prepaid expenses	5,375	6,250
Equipment	159,500	110,000
Accum. depreciation—Equipment	(34,625)	(44,000)
Total assets	$522,875	$451,000
Liabilities and Equity		
Accounts payable	$ 88,125	$116,625
Short-term notes payable	10,000	6,250
Long-term notes payable	93,750	53,750
Common stock, $5 par value	168,750	156,250
Paid-in capital in excess of par, common stock	32,500	0
Retained earnings	129,750	118,125
Total liabilities and equity	$522,875	$451,000

KAZAAM COMPANY
Income Statement
For Year Ended December 31, 2011

Sales		$496,250
Cost of goods sold		250,000
Gross profit		246,250
Operating expenses		
Depreciation expense	$ 18,750	
Other expenses.................	136,500	155,250
Other gains (losses)		
Loss on sale of equipment		5,125
Income before taxes		85,875
Income taxes expense		12,125
Net income		$ 73,750

Additional Information on Year 2011 Transactions

a. The loss on the cash sale of equipment was $5,125 (details in *b*).

b. Sold equipment costing $46,875, with accumulated depreciation of $28,125, for $13,625 cash.

c. Purchased equipment costing $96,375 by paying $25,000 cash and signing a long-term note payable for the balance.

d. Borrowed $3,750 cash by signing a short-term note payable.

e. Paid $31,375 cash to reduce the long-term notes payable.

f. Issued 2,500 shares of common stock for $18 cash per share.

g. Declared and paid cash dividends of $62,125.

Required

Check Cash from operating activities, $33,375

1. Prepare a complete statement of cash flows; report its operating activities using the *indirect method*. Disclose any noncash investing and financing activities in a note.

Analysis Component

2. Analyze and discuss the statement of cash flows prepared in part 1, giving special attention to the wisdom of the cash dividend payment.

Problem 12-2A^B
Statement of cash flows (direct method) P1 P3 P5

Check Cash used in financing activities, $(44,750)

Refer to Kazaam Company's financial statements and related information in Problem 12-1A.

Required

Prepare a complete statement of cash flows; report its operating activities according to the *direct method*. Disclose any noncash investing and financing activities in a note.

Problem 12-3A^A
Cash flows spreadsheet (indirect method)

P1 P2 P3 P4

Refer to the information reported about Kazaam Company in Problem 12-1A.

Required

Prepare a complete statement of cash flows using a spreadsheet as in Exhibit 12A.1; report its operating activities using the indirect method. Identify the debits and credits in the Analysis of Changes columns with letters that correspond to the following list of transactions and events.

a. Net income was $73,750.

b. Accounts receivable increased.

c. Merchandise inventory increased.

d. Prepaid expenses decreased.

e. Accounts payable decreased.

f. Depreciation expense was $18,750.

g. Sold equipment costing $46,875, with accumulated depreciation of $28,125, for $13,625 cash. This yielded a loss of $5,125.

h. Purchased equipment costing $96,375 by paying $25,000 cash and **(i.)** by signing a long-term note payable for the balance.

j. Borrowed $3,750 cash by signing a short-term note payable.

k. Paid $31,375 cash to reduce the long-term notes payable.

l. Issued 2,500 shares of common stock for $18 cash per share.

m. Declared and paid cash dividends of $62,125.

Check Analysis of Changes column totals, $515,375

Galley Corp., a merchandiser, recently completed its 2011 operations. For the year, (1) all sales are credit sales, (2) all credits to Accounts Receivable reflect cash receipts from customers, (3) all purchases of inventory are on credit, (4) all debits to Accounts Payable reflect cash payments for inventory, (5) Other Expenses are all cash expenses, and (6) any change in Income Taxes Payable reflects the accrual and cash payment of taxes. The company's balance sheets and income statement follow.

Problem 12-4A
Statement of cash flows
(indirect method)
P1 P2 P3

mhhe.com/wildFINMAN4e

GALLEY CORPORATION Comparative Balance Sheets December 31, 2011 and 2010		
	2011	**2010**
Assets		
Cash	$ 174,000	$117,000
Accounts receivable	93,000	81,000
Merchandise inventory	609,000	534,000
Equipment..............................	333,000	297,000
Accum. depreciation—Equipment	(156,000)	(102,000)
Total assets	$1,053,000	$927,000
Liabilities and Equity		
Accounts payable	$ 69,000	$ 96,000
Income taxes payable	27,000	24,000
Common stock, $2 par value.............	582,000	558,000
Paid-in capital in excess of par value, common stock.............	198,000	162,000
Retained earnings	177,000	87,000
Total liabilities and equity	$1,053,000	$927,000

GALLEY CORPORATION Income Statement For Year Ended December 31, 2011		
Sales		$1,992,000
Cost of goods sold		1,194,000
Gross profit		798,000
Operating expenses		
Depreciation expense	$ 54,000	
Other expenses..............	501,000	555,000
Income before taxes		243,000
Income taxes expense		42,000
Net income		$ 201,000

Additional Information on Year 2011 Transactions

a. Purchased equipment for $36,000 cash.

b. Issued 12,000 shares of common stock for $5 cash per share.

c. Declared and paid $111,000 in cash dividends.

Required

Prepare a complete statement of cash flows; report its cash inflows and cash outflows from operating activities according to the *indirect method*.

Check Cash from operating activities, $144,000

Refer to Galley Corporation's financial statements and related information in Problem 12-4A.

Required

Prepare a complete statement of cash flows; report its cash flows from operating activities according to the *direct method*.

Problem 12-5A[B]
Statement of cash flows (direct method) P1 P3 P5

mhhe.com/wildFINMAN4e

Check Cash used in financing activities, $(51,000)

Problem 12-6A^A

Cash flows spreadsheet
(indirect method)

P1 P2 P3 P4

mhhe.com/wildFINMAN4e

Check Analysis of Changes column totals, $579,000

Refer to the information reported about Galley Corporation in Problem 12-4A.

Required

Prepare a complete statement of cash flows using a spreadsheet as in Exhibit 12A.1; report operating activities under the indirect method. Identify the debits and credits in the Analysis of Changes columns with letters that correspond to the following list of transactions and events.

a. Net income was $201,000.

b. Accounts receivable increased.

c. Merchandise inventory increased.

d. Accounts payable decreased.

e. Income taxes payable increased.

f. Depreciation expense was $54,000.

g. Purchased equipment for $36,000 cash.

h. Issued 12,000 shares at $5 cash per share.

i. Declared and paid $111,000 of cash dividends.

Problem 12-7A

Computing cash flows from operations (indirect)

P2

Rapture Company's 2011 income statement and selected balance sheet data at December 31, 2010 and 2011, follow ($ thousands).

RAPTURE COMPANY
Selected Balance Sheet Accounts

At December 31	2011	2010
Accounts receivable	$380	$390
Inventory	99	77
Accounts payable	120	130
Salaries payable	44	35
Utilities payable	11	8
Prepaid insurance	13	14
Prepaid rent	11	9

RAPTURE COMPANY
Income Statement
For Year Ended December 31, 2011

Sales revenue	$58,600
Expenses	
Cost of goods sold	21,000
Depreciation expense	6,000
Salaries expense	11,000
Rent expense	2,500
Insurance expense	1,900
Interest expense	1,800
Utilities expense	1,400
Net income	$13,000

Required

Check Cash from operating activities, $18,989

Prepare the cash flows from operating activities section only of the company's 2011 statement of cash flows using the indirect method.

Problem 12-8A^B

Computing cash flows from operations (direct)

P5

Refer to the information in Problem 12-7A.

Required

Prepare the cash flows from operating activities section only of the company's 2011 statement of cash flows using the direct method.

PROBLEM SET B

Problem 12-1B

Statement of cash flows
(indirect method)

A1 P1 P2 P3

Kite Corporation, a merchandiser, recently completed its calendar-year 2011 operations. For the year, (1) all sales are credit sales, (2) all credits to Accounts Receivable reflect cash receipts from customers, (3) all purchases of inventory are on credit, (4) all debits to Accounts Payable reflect cash payments for inventory, and (5) Other Expenses are paid in advance and are initially debited to Prepaid Expenses. The company's balance sheets and income statement follow.

KITE CORPORATION Comparative Balance Sheets December 31, 2011 and 2010		
	2011	**2010**
Assets		
Cash	$136,500	$ 71,550
Accounts receivable	74,100	90,750
Merchandise inventory	454,500	490,200
Prepaid expenses	17,100	19,200
Equipment	278,250	216,000
Accum. depreciation—Equipment	(108,750)	(93,000)
Total assets	$851,700	$794,700
Liabilities and Equity		
Accounts payable	$117,450	$123,450
Short-term notes payable	17,250	11,250
Long-term notes payable	112,500	82,500
Common stock, $5 par	465,000	450,000
Paid-in capital in excess of par, common stock	18,000	0
Retained earnings	121,500	127,500
Total liabilities and equity	$851,700	$794,700

KITE CORPORATION Income Statement For Year Ended December 31, 2011		
Sales		$1,083,000
Cost of goods sold		585,000
Gross profit		498,000
Operating expenses		
Depreciation expense	$ 36,600	
Other expenses	392,850	
Total operating expenses		429,450
		68,550
Other gains (losses)		
Loss on sale of equipment		2,100
Income before taxes		66,450
Income taxes expense		9,450
Net income		$ 57,000

Additional Information on Year 2011 Transactions

a. The loss on the cash sale of equipment was $2,100 (details in *b*).

b. Sold equipment costing $51,000, with accumulated depreciation of $20,850, for $28,050 cash.

c. Purchased equipment costing $113,250 by paying $38,250 cash and signing a long-term note payable for the balance.

d. Borrowed $6,000 cash by signing a short-term note payable.

e. Paid $45,000 cash to reduce the long-term notes payable.

f. Issued 3,000 shares of common stock for $11 cash per share.

g. Declared and paid cash dividends of $63,000.

Required

1. Prepare a complete statement of cash flows; report its operating activities using the *indirect method*. Disclose any noncash investing and financing activities in a note.

Check Cash from operating activities, $144,150

Analysis Component

2. Analyze and discuss the statement of cash flows prepared in part 1, giving special attention to the wisdom of the cash dividend payment.

Refer to Kite Corporation's financial statements and related information in Problem 12-1B.

Required

Prepare a complete statement of cash flows; report its operating activities according to the *direct method*. Disclose any noncash investing and financing activities in a note.

Problem 12-2B[B]
Statement of cash flows (direct method) P1 P3 P5

Check Cash used in financing activities, $(69,000)

Refer to the information reported about Kite Corporation in Problem 12-1B.

Required

Prepare a complete statement of cash flows using a spreadsheet as in Exhibit 12A.1; report its operating activities using the *indirect method*. Identify the debits and credits in the Analysis of Changes columns with letters that correspond to the following list of transactions and events.

Problem 12-3B[A]
Cash flows spreadsheet (indirect method)

P1 P2 P3 P4

a. Net income was $57,000.

b. Accounts receivable decreased.

c. Merchandise inventory decreased.

d. Prepaid expenses decreased.

e. Accounts payable decreased.

f. Depreciation expense was $36,600.

g. Sold equipment costing $51,000, with accumulated depreciation of $20,850, for $28,050 cash. This yielded a loss of $2,100.

h. Purchased equipment costing $113,250 by paying $38,250 cash and (i.) by signing a long-term note payable for the balance.

j. Borrowed $6,000 cash by signing a short-term note payable.

k. Paid $45,000 cash to reduce the long-term notes payable.

l. Issued 3,000 shares of common stock for $11 cash per share.

m. Declared and paid cash dividends of $63,000.

Check Analysis of Changes column totals, $540,300

Problem 12-4B

Statement of cash flows (indirect method)

P1 P2 P3

Taurasi Company, a merchandiser, recently completed its 2011 operations. For the year, (1) all sales are credit sales, (2) all credits to Accounts Receivable reflect cash receipts from customers, (3) all purchases of inventory are on credit, (4) all debits to Accounts Payable reflect cash payments for inventory, (5) Other Expenses are cash expenses, and (6) any change in Income Taxes Payable reflects the accrual and cash payment of taxes. The company's balance sheets and income statement follow.

TAURASI COMPANY
Comparative Balance Sheets
December 31, 2011 and 2010

	2011	2010
Assets		
Cash	$ 53,925	$ 31,800
Accounts receivable	19,425	23,250
Merchandise inventory	175,350	139,875
Equipment	105,450	76,500
Accum. depreciation—Equipment	(48,300)	(30,600)
Total assets	$305,850	$240,825
Liabilities and Equity		
Accounts payable	$ 38,475	$ 35,625
Income taxes payable	4,500	6,750
Common stock, $2 par value	165,000	150,000
Paid-in capital in excess of par, common stock	42,000	15,000
Retained earnings	55,875	33,450
Total liabilities and equity	$305,850	$240,825

TAURASI COMPANY
Income Statement
For Year Ended December 31, 2011

Sales		$609,750
Cost of goods sold		279,000
Gross profit		330,750
Operating expenses		
Depreciation expense	$ 17,700	
Other expenses	179,775	197,475
Income before taxes		133,275
Income taxes expense		44,850
Net income		$ 88,425

Additional Information on Year 2011 Transactions

a. Purchased equipment for $28,950 cash.

b. Issued 3,000 shares of common stock for $14 cash per share.

c. Declared and paid $66,000 of cash dividends.

Required

Check Cash from operating activities, $75,075

Prepare a complete statement of cash flows; report its cash inflows and cash outflows from operating activities according to the *indirect method*.

Problem 12-5B[B]

Statement of cash flows (direct method) P1 P3 P5

Check Cash used by financing activities, $(24,000)

Refer to Taurasi Company's financial statements and related information in Problem 12-4B.

Required

Prepare a complete statement of cash flows; report its cash flows from operating activities according to the *direct method*.

Refer to the information reported about Taurasi Company in Problem 12-4B.

Required

Prepare a complete statement of cash flows using a spreadsheet as in Exhibit 12A.1; report operating activities under the *indirect method.* Identify the debits and credits in the Analysis of Changes columns with letters that correspond to the following list of transactions and events.

a. Net income was $88,425.

b. Accounts receivable decreased.

c. Merchandise inventory increased.

d. Accounts payable increased.

e. Income taxes payable decreased.

f. Depreciation expense was $17,700.

g. Purchased equipment for $28,950 cash.

h. Issued 3,000 shares at $14 cash per share.

i. Declared and paid $66,000 of cash dividends.

Problem 12-6B[A]
Cash flows spreadsheet
(indirect method)
P1 P2 P3 P4

Check Analysis of Changes column totals, $287,475

Tyra Company's 2011 income statement and selected balance sheet data at December 31, 2010 and 2011, follow ($ thousands).

Problem 12-7B
Computing cash flows from
operations (indirect)
P2

TYRA COMPANY Income Statement For Year Ended December 31, 2011	
Sales revenue	$412,000
Expenses	
Cost of goods sold	244,000
Depreciation expense	64,000
Salaries expense	30,000
Rent expense	20,000
Insurance expense	5,200
Interest expense	4,800
Utilities expense	4,000
Net income	$ 40,000

TYRA COMPANY Selected Balance Sheet Accounts		
At December 31	2011	2010
Accounts receivable	$820	$700
Inventory	272	296
Accounts payable	480	520
Salaries payable	280	220
Utilities payable	40	0
Prepaid insurance	28	36
Prepaid rent	40	60

Required

Prepare the cash flows from operating activities section only of the company's 2011 statement of cash flows using the indirect method.

Check Cash from operating activities, $103,992

Refer to the information in Problem 12-7B.

Required

Prepare the cash flows from operating activities section only of the company's 2011 statement of cash flows using the direct method.

Problem 12-8B[B]
Computing cash flows from
operations (direct)
P5

(This serial problem began in Chapter 1 and continues through most of the book. If previous chapter segments were not completed, the serial problem can begin at this point. It is helpful, but not necessary, to use the Working Papers that accompany the book.)

SERIAL PROBLEM
Business Solutions
P1 P2 P3

SP 12   Santana Rey, owner of Business Solutions, decides to prepare a statement of cash flows for her business. (Although the serial problem allowed for various ownership changes in earlier chapters, we will prepare the statement of cash flows using the following financial data.)

BUSINESS SOLUTIONS
Income Statement
For Three Months Ended March 31, 2012

Computer services revenue		$25,307
Net sales		18,693
Total revenue		44,000
Cost of goods sold	$14,052	
Depreciation expense— Office equipment	400	
Depreciation expense— Computer equipment	1,250	
Wages expense	3,250	
Insurance expense	555	
Rent expense	2,475	
Computer supplies expense	1,305	
Advertising expense	600	
Mileage expense	320	
Repairs expense—Computer	960	
Total expenses		25,167
Net income		$18,833

BUSINESS SOLUTIONS
Comparative Balance Sheets
December 31, 2011, and March 31, 2012

	2012	2011
Assets		
Cash	$ 68,057	$48,372
Accounts receivable	22,867	5,668
Merchandise inventory	704	0
Computer supplies	2,005	580
Prepaid insurance	1,110	1,665
Prepaid rent	825	825
Office equipment	8,000	8,000
Accumulated depreciation—Office equipment	(800)	(400)
Computer equipment	20,000	20,000
Accumulated depreciation— Computer equipment	(2,500)	(1,250)
Total assets	$120,268	$83,460
Liabilities and Equity		
Accounts payable	$ 0	$ 1,100
Wages payable	875	500
Unearned computer service revenue	0	1,500
Common stock	98,000	73,000
Retained earnings	21,393	7,360
Total liabilities and equity	$120,268	$83,460

Required

Check   Cash flows used by operations: $(515)

Prepare a statement of cash flows for Business Solutions using the *indirect method* for the three months ended March 31, 2012. Recall that the owner Santana Rey contributed $25,000 to the business in exchange for additional stock in the first quarter of 2012 and has received $4,800 in cash dividends.

Beyond the Numbers

REPORTING IN ACTION

A1

RIM

BTN 12-1   Refer to **Research In Motion**'s financial statements in Appendix A to answer the following.

1. Is Research In Motion's statement of cash flows prepared under the direct method or the indirect method? How do you know?
2. For each fiscal year 2010, 2009, and 2008, is the amount of cash provided by operating activities more or less than the cash paid for dividends?
3. What is the largest amount in reconciling the difference between net income and cash flow from operating activities in 2010? In 2009? In 2008?
4. Identify the largest cash inflow and outflow for investing *and* for financing activities in 2010 and in 2009.

Fast Forward

5. Obtain Research In Motion's financial statements for a fiscal year ending after February 27, 2010, from either its Website (**RIM.com**) or the SEC's database (**www.SEC.gov**). Since February 27, 2010, what are Research In Motion's largest cash outflows and cash inflows in the investing and in the financing sections of its statement of cash flows?

BTN 12-2 Key figures for **Research In Motion** and **Apple** follow.

($ millions)	Research In Motion			Apple		
	Current Year	1 Year Prior	2 Years Prior	Current Year	1 Year Prior	2 Years Prior
Operating cash flows	$ 3,035	$1,452	$1,577	$10,159	$ 9,596	$ 5,470
Total assets	10,204	8,101	5,511	47,501	36,171	25,347

COMPARATIVE ANALYSIS

A1

RIM

Apple

Required

1. Compute the recent two years' cash flow on total assets ratios for Research In Motion and Apple.
2. What does the cash flow on total assets ratio measure?
3. Which company has the highest cash flow on total assets ratio for the periods shown?
4. Does the cash flow on total assets ratio reflect on the quality of earnings? Explain.

BTN 12-3 Lisa Gish is preparing for a meeting with her banker. Her business is finishing its fourth year of operations. In the first year, it had negative cash flows from operations. In the second and third years, cash flows from operations were positive. However, inventory costs rose significantly in year 4, and cash flows from operations will probably be down 25%. Gish wants to secure a line of credit from her banker as a financing buffer. From experience, she knows the banker will scrutinize operating cash flows for years 1 through 4 and will want a projected number for year 5. Gish knows that a steady progression upward in operating cash flows for years 1 through 4 will help her case. She decides to use her discretion as owner and considers several business actions that will turn her operating cash flow in year 4 from a decrease to an increase.

ETHICS CHALLENGE

C1 A1

Required

1. Identify two business actions Gish might take to improve cash flows from operations.
2. Comment on the ethics and possible consequences of Gish's decision to pursue these actions.

BTN 12-4 Your friend, Jessica Willard, recently completed the second year of her business and just received annual financial statements from her accountant. Willard finds the income statement and balance sheet informative but does not understand the statement of cash flows. She says the first section is especially confusing because it contains a lot of additions and subtractions that do not make sense to her. Willard adds, "The income statement tells me the business is more profitable than last year and that's most important. If I want to know how cash changes, I can look at comparative balance sheets."

COMMUNICATING IN PRACTICE

C1

Required

Write a half-page memorandum to your friend explaining the purpose of the statement of cash flows. Speculate as to why the first section is so confusing and how it might be rectified.

BTN 12-5 Access the March 19, 2010, filing of the 10-K report (for fiscal year ending January 30, 2010) of **J. Crew Group, Inc.** (ticker JCG), at **www.sec.gov**.

TAKING IT TO THE NET

A1

Required

1. Does J. Crew use the direct or indirect method to construct its consolidated statement of cash flows?
2. For the fiscal year ended January 30, 2010, what is the largest item in reconciling the net income to net cash provided by operating activities?
3. In the recent three years, has the company been more successful in generating operating cash flows or in generating net income? Identify the figures to support the answer.
4. In the year ended January 30, 2010, what was the largest cash outflow for investing activities *and* for financing activities?
5. What item(s) does J. Crew report as supplementary cash flow information?
6. Does J. Crew report any noncash financing activities for fiscal year 2010? Identify them, if any.

TEAMWORK IN ACTION
C1 A1 P2 P5

BTN 12-6 Team members are to coordinate and independently answer one question within each of the following three sections. Team members should then report to the team and confirm or correct teammates' answers.

1. Answer *one* of the following questions about the statement of cash flows.
   a. What are this statement's reporting objectives?
   b. What two methods are used to prepare it? Identify similarities and differences between them.
   c. What steps are followed to prepare the statement?
   d. What types of analyses are often made from this statement's information?

2. Identify and explain the adjustment from net income to obtain cash flows from operating activities using the indirect method for *one* of the following items.
   a. Noncash operating revenues and expenses.
   b. Nonoperating gains and losses.
   c. Increases and decreases in noncash current assets.
   d. Increases and decreases in current liabilities.

3.ᴮIdentify and explain the formula for computing cash flows from operating activities using the direct method for *one* of the following items.
   a. Cash receipts from sales to customers.
   b. Cash paid for merchandise inventory.
   c. Cash paid for wages and operating expenses.
   d. Cash paid for interest and taxes.

Note: For teams of more than four, some pairing within teams is necessary. Use as an in-class activity or as an assignment. If used in class, specify a time limit on each part. Conclude with reports to the entire class, using team rotation. Each team can prepare responses on a transparency.

ENTREPRENEURIAL DECISION
C1 A1

BTN 12-7 Review the chapter's opener involving **Animoto** and its four young entrepreneurial owners.

Required

1. In a business such as Animoto, monitoring cash flow is always a priority. Even though Animoto now has thousands in annual sales and earns a positive net income, explain how cash flow can lag behind earnings.

2. Animoto is a closely held corporation. What are potential sources of financing for its future expansion?

C1 A1

BTN 12-8 Jenna and Matt Wilder are completing their second year operating Mountain High, a downhill ski area and resort. Mountain High reports a net loss of $(10,000) for its second year, which includes an $85,000 extraordinary loss from fire. This past year also involved major purchases of plant assets for renovation and expansion, yielding a year-end total asset amount of $800,000. Mountain High's net cash outflow for its second year is $(5,000); a summarized version of its statement of cash flows follows:

Net cash flow provided by operating activities	$295,000
Net cash flow used by investing activities	(310,000)
Net cash flow provided by financing activities	10,000

Required

Write a one-page memorandum to the Wilders evaluating Mountain High's current performance and assessing its future. Give special emphasis to cash flow data and their interpretation.

HITTING THE ROAD
C1

BTN 12-9 Visit **The Motley Fool**'s Website (**Fool.com**). Enter the *Fool's School* (at *Fool.com/School*). Identify and select the link *How to Value Stocks*.

Required

1. Click on *Introduction to Valuation Methods,* and then *Cash-Flow-Based Valuations.* How does the Fool's school define cash flow? What is the school's reasoning for this definition?

2. Per the school's instruction, why do analysts focus on earnings before interest and taxes (EBIT)?

3. Visit other links at this Website that interest you such as "How to Read a Balance Sheet," or find out what the "Fool's Ratio" is. Write a half-page report on what you find.

BTN 12-10   Key comparative information for **Nokia** (**www.Nokia.com**), which is a leading global manufacturer of mobile devices and services, follows (in EUR).

(Euro millions)	Current Year	1 Year Prior	2 Years Prior
Operating cash flows	3,247	3,197	7,882
Total assets	35,738	39,582	37,599

Required

1. Compute the recent two years' cash flow on total assets ratio for Nokia.
2. How does Nokia's ratio compare to Research In Motion's and Apple's ratios from BTN 12-2?

ANSWERS TO MULTIPLE CHOICE QUIZ

1. b;

Net income	$15,200
Depreciation expense	10,000
Gain on sale of land	(3,000)
Increase in inventory	(1,500)
Increase in accounts payable	2,850
Net cash provided by operations	$23,550

2. c; cash received from sale of machine is reported as an investing activity.

3. d; FASB requires cash interest paid to be reported under operating.
4. a; Cash paid for salaries and wages = $255,000 + $8,200 − $10,900 = $252,300
5. e; Increase in inventory = $112,000 − $105,000 = $7,000
   Increase in accounts payable = $101,300 − $98,500 = $2,800
   Cash paid for merchandise = $545,000 + $7,000 − $2,800 = $549,200

13

Analysis of Financial Statements

A Look Back

Chapter 12 focused on reporting and analyzing cash inflows and cash outflows. We explained how to prepare, analyze, and interpret the statement of cash flows.

A Look at This Chapter

This chapter emphasizes the analysis and interpretation of financial statement information. We learn to apply horizontal, vertical, and ratio analyses to better understand company performance and financial condition.

A Look Ahead

Chapter 14 introduces us to managerial accounting. We discuss its purposes, concepts, and roles in helping managers gather and organize information for decisions. We also explain basic management principles.

Learning Objectives

CONCEPTUAL

C1 Explain the purpose and identify the building blocks of analysis. (p. 554)

C2 Describe standards for comparisons in analysis. (p. 556)

ANALYTICAL

A1 Summarize and report results of analysis. (p. 574)

A2 *Appendix 13A*—Explain the form and assess the content of a complete income statement. (p. 578)

LP13

PROCEDURAL

P1 Explain and apply methods of horizontal analysis. (p. 556)

P2 Describe and apply methods of vertical analysis. (p. 561)

P3 Define and apply ratio analysis. (p. 564)

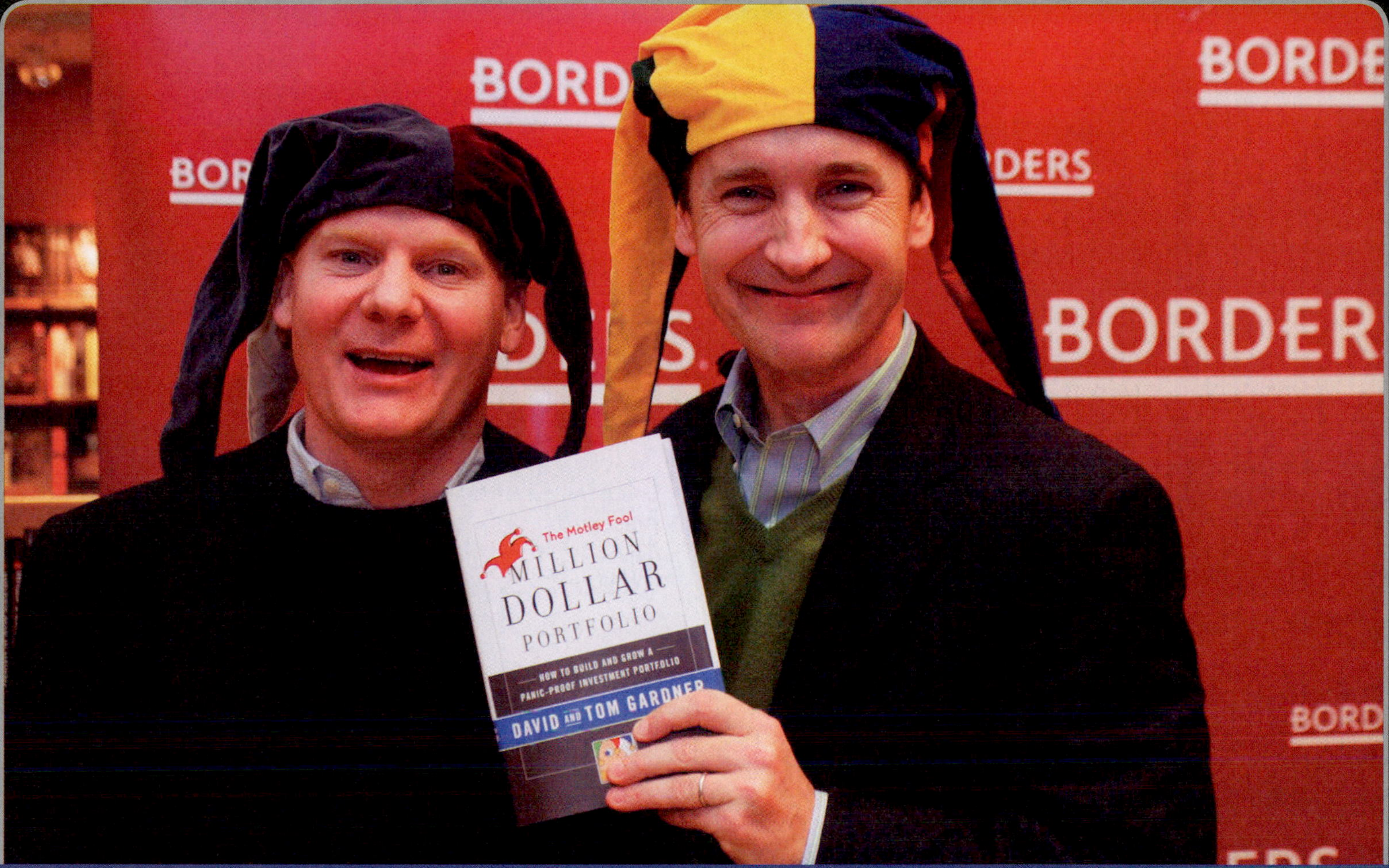

Decision Insight

Motley Fool

ALEXANDRIA, VA—In Shakespeare's Elizabethan comedy *As You Like It,* only the fool could speak truthfully to the King without getting his head lopped off. Inspired by Shakespeare's stage character, Tom and David Gardner vowed to become modern-day fools who tell it like it is. With under $10,000 in start-up money, the brothers launched **The Motley Fool** (**Fool.com**). And befitting of a Shakespearean play, the two say they are "dedicated to educating, amusing, and enriching individuals in search of the truth."

The Gardners do not fear the wrath of any King, real or fictional. They are intent on exposing the truth, as they see it, "that the financial world preys on ignorance and fear." As Tom explains, "There is such a great need in the general populace for financial information." Who can argue, given their brilliant success through practically every medium, including their Website, radio shows, newspaper columns, online store, investment newsletters, and global expansion.

Despite the brothers' best efforts, however, ordinary people still do not fully use information contained in financial state-

ments. For instance, discussions keep appearing on The Motley Fool's online bulletin board that can be easily resolved using reliable and available accounting data. So, it would seem that the Fools must continue their work of "educating and enriching" individuals and showing them the advantages of financial statement analysis.

Following The Motley Fool's objectives, this chapter introduces horizontal and vertical analyses—tools used to reveal crucial trends and insights from financial information. It also expands on ratio analysis, which gives insight into a company's financial condition and performance. By arming ourselves with the information contained in this chapter and the investment advice of The Motley Fool, *we* can be sure to not play the fool in today's financial world.

[Sources: *Motley Fool Website,* January 2011; *Entrepreneur,* July 1997; *What to Do with Your Money Now,* June 2002; *USA Weekend,* July 2004; *Washington Post,* November 2007; *Money after 40,* April 2007]

This chapter shows how we use financial statements to evaluate a company's financial performance and condition. We explain financial statement analysis, its basic building blocks, the information available, standards for comparisons, and tools of analysis. Three major analysis tools are presented: horizontal analysis, vertical analysis, and ratio analysis. We apply each of these tools using **Research In Motion**'s financial statements, and we introduce comparative analysis using **Apple** and **Nokia** (and sometimes **Palm**). This chapter expands and organizes the ratio analyses introduced at the end of each chapter.

Analysis of Financial Statements

Basics of Analysis	Horizontal Analysis	Vertical Analysis	Ratio Analysis
• Purpose • Building blocks • Information • Standards for comparisons • Tools	• Comparative balance sheets • Comparative income statements • Trend analysis	• Common-size balance sheet • Common-size income statement • Common-size graphics	• Liquidity and efficiency • Solvency • Profitability • Market prospects • Ratio summary

BASICS OF ANALYSIS

C1 Explain the purpose and identify the building blocks of analysis.

Financial statement analysis applies analytical tools to general-purpose financial statements and related data for making business decisions. It involves transforming accounting data into more useful information. Financial statement analysis reduces our reliance on hunches, guesses, and intuition as well as our uncertainty in decision making. It does not lessen the need for expert judgment; instead, it provides us an effective and systematic basis for making business decisions. This section describes the purpose of financial statement analysis, its information sources, the use of comparisons, and some issues in computations.

Purpose of Analysis

Internal users of accounting information are those involved in strategically managing and operating the company. They include managers, officers, internal auditors, consultants, budget directors, and market researchers. The purpose of financial statement analysis for these users is to provide strategic information to improve company efficiency and effectiveness in providing products and services.

External users of accounting information are *not* directly involved in running the company. They include shareholders, lenders, directors, customers, suppliers, regulators, lawyers, brokers, and the press. External users rely on financial statement analysis to make better and more informed decisions in pursuing their own goals.

Point: Financial statement analysis tools are also used for personal financial investment decisions.

Point: Financial statement analysis is a topic on the CPA, CMA, CIA, and CFA exams.

We can identify other uses of financial statement analysis. Shareholders and creditors assess company prospects to make investing and lending decisions. A board of directors analyzes financial statements in monitoring management's decisions. Employees and unions use financial statements in labor negotiations. Suppliers use financial statement information in establishing credit terms. Customers analyze financial statements in deciding whether to establish supply relationships. Public utilities set customer rates by analyzing financial statements. Auditors use financial statements in assessing the "fair presentation" of their clients' financial results. Analyst services such as **Dun & Bradstreet**, **Moody's**, and **Standard & Poor's** use financial statements in making buy-sell recommendations and in setting credit ratings. The common goal of these users is to evaluate company performance and financial condition. This includes evaluating (1) past and current performance, (2) current financial position, and (3) future performance and risk.

Building Blocks of Analysis

Financial statement analysis focuses on one or more elements of a company's financial condition or performance. Our analysis emphasizes four areas of inquiry—with varying degrees of importance. These four areas are described and illustrated in this chapter and are considered the *building blocks* of financial statement analysis:

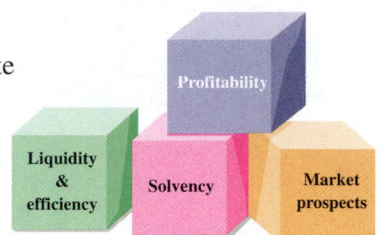

- **Liquidity** and **efficiency**—ability to meet short-term obligations and to efficiently generate revenues.
- **Solvency**—ability to generate future revenues and meet long-term obligations.
- **Profitability**—ability to provide financial rewards sufficient to attract and retain financing.
- **Market prospects**—ability to generate positive market expectations.

Applying the building blocks of financial statement analysis involves determining (1) the objectives of analysis and (2) the relative emphasis among the building blocks. We distinguish among these four building blocks to emphasize the different aspects of a company's financial condition or performance, yet we must remember that these areas of analysis are interrelated. For instance, a company's operating performance is affected by the availability of financing and short-term liquidity conditions. Similarly, a company's credit standing is not limited to satisfactory short-term liquidity but depends also on its profitability and efficiency in using assets. Early in our analysis, we need to determine the relative emphasis of each building block. Emphasis and analysis can later change as a result of evidence collected.

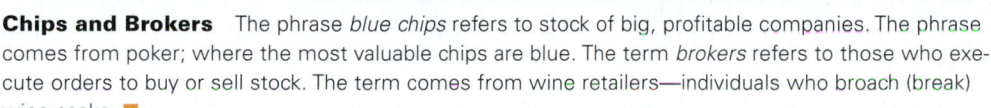

Decision Insight

Chips and Brokers   The phrase *blue chips* refers to stock of big, profitable companies. The phrase comes from poker; where the most valuable chips are blue. The term *brokers* refers to those who execute orders to buy or sell stock. The term comes from wine retailers—individuals who broach (break) wine casks. ■

Information for Analysis

Some users, such as managers and regulatory authorities, are able to receive special financial reports prepared to meet their analysis needs. However, most users must rely on **general-purpose financial statements** that include the (1) income statement, (2) balance sheet, (3) statement of stockholders' equity (or statement of retained earnings), (4) statement of cash flows, and (5) notes to these statements.

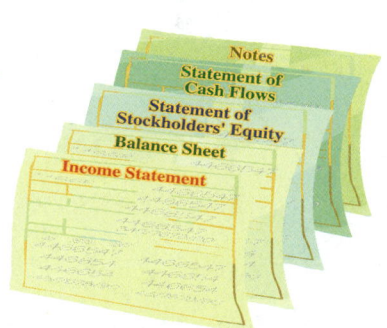

Financial reporting refers to the communication of financial information useful for making investment, credit, and other business decisions. Financial reporting includes not only general-purpose financial statements but also information from SEC 10-K or other filings, press releases, shareholders' meetings, forecasts, management letters, auditors' reports, and Webcasts.

Management's Discussion and Analysis (MD&A) is one example of useful information outside traditional financial statements. **Research In Motion**'s MD&A (available at **RIM.com**), for example, begins with an overview, followed by critical accounting policies and restatements of previous statements. It then discusses operating results followed by financial condition (liquidity, capital resources, and cash flows). The final few parts discuss legal proceedings, market risk of financial instruments, disclosure controls, and internal controls. The MD&A is an excellent starting point in understanding a company's business activities.

Decision Insight

Analysis Online   Many Websites offer free access and screening of companies by key numbers such as earnings, sales, and book value. For instance, **Standard & Poor's** has information for more than 10,000 stocks (**www.standardandpoors.com**). ■

C2   Describe standards for comparisons in analysis.

Standards for Comparisons

When interpreting measures from financial statement analysis, we need to decide whether the measures indicate good, bad, or average performance. To make such judgments, we need standards (benchmarks) for comparisons that include the following:

- *Intracompany*—The company under analysis can provide standards for comparisons based on its own prior performance and relations between its financial items. **Research In Motion**'s current net income, for instance, can be compared with its prior years' net income and in relation to its revenues or total assets.
- *Competitor*—One or more direct competitors of the company being analyzed can provide standards for comparisons. **Coca-Cola**'s profit margin, for instance, can be compared with **PepsiCo**'s profit margin.
- *Industry*—Industry statistics can provide standards of comparisons. Such statistics are available from services such as **Dun & Bradstreet**, **Standard & Poor's**, and **Moody's**.
- *Guidelines (rules of thumb)*—General standards of comparisons can develop from experience. Examples are the 2:1 level for the current ratio or 1:1 level for the acid-test ratio. Guidelines, or rules of thumb, must be carefully applied because context is crucial.

Point: Each chapter's *Reporting in Action* problems engage students in *intracompany* analysis, whereas *Comparative Analysis* problems require competitor analysis (RIM vs. Apple and often vs. Palm).

All of these comparison standards are useful when properly applied, yet measures taken from a selected competitor or group of competitors are often best. Intracompany and industry measures are also important. Guidelines or rules of thumb should be applied with care, and then only if they seem reasonable given past experience and industry norms.

Tools of Analysis

Three of the most common tools of financial statement analysis are

1. **Horizontal analysis**—Comparison of a company's financial condition and performance across time.
2. **Vertical analysis**—Comparison of a company's financial condition and performance to a base amount.
3. **Ratio analysis**—Measurement of key relations between financial statement items.

The remainder of this chapter describes these analysis tools and how to apply them.

Quick Check   Answers — p. 581

1. Who are the intended users of general-purpose financial statements?
2. General-purpose financial statements consist of what information?
3. Which of the following is *least* useful as a basis for comparison when analyzing ratios? (*a*) Company results from a different economic setting. (*b*) Standards from past experience. (*c*) Rule-of-thumb standards. (*d*) Industry averages.
4. What is the preferred basis of comparison for ratio analysis?

HORIZONTAL ANALYSIS

Analysis of any single financial number is of limited value. Instead, much of financial statement analysis involves identifying and describing relations between numbers, groups of numbers, and changes in those numbers. Horizontal analysis refers to examination of financial statement data *across time*. [The term *horizontal analysis* arises from the left-to-right (or right-to-left) movement of our eyes as we review comparative financial statements across time.]

Comparative Statements

P1   Explain and apply methods of horizontal analysis.

Comparing amounts for two or more successive periods often helps in analyzing financial statements. **Comparative financial statements** facilitate this comparison by showing financial amounts in side-by-side columns on a single statement, called a *comparative format*. Using figures from **Research In Motion**'s financial statements, this section explains how to compute dollar changes and percent changes for comparative statements.

Computation of Dollar Changes and Percent Changes   Comparing financial statements over relatively short time periods—two to three years—is often done by analyzing changes in line items. A change analysis usually includes analyzing absolute dollar amount changes and percent changes. Both analyses are relevant because dollar changes can yield large percent changes inconsistent with their importance. For instance, a 50% change from a base figure of $100 is less important than the same percent change from a base amount of $100,000 in the same statement. Reference to dollar amounts is necessary to retain a proper perspective and to assess the importance of changes. We compute the *dollar change* for a financial statement item as follows:

Example: What is a more significant change, a 70% increase on a $1,000 expense or a 30% increase on a $400,000 expense? *Answer:* The 30% increase.

$$\text{Dollar change} = \text{Analysis period amount} - \text{Base period amount}$$

Analysis period is the point or period of time for the financial statements under analysis, and *base period* is the point or period of time for the financial statements used for comparison purposes. The prior year is commonly used as a base period. We compute the *percent change* by dividing the dollar change by the base period amount and then multiplying this quantity by 100 as follows:

$$\text{Percent change (\%)} = \frac{\text{Analysis period amount} - \text{Base period amount}}{\text{Base period amount}} \times 100$$

We can always compute a dollar change, but we must be aware of a few rules in working with percent changes. To illustrate, look at four separate cases in this chart:

Case	Analysis Period	Base Period	Change Analysis Dollar	Change Analysis Percent
A	$ 1,500	$(4,500)	$ 6,000	—
B	(1,000)	2,000	(3,000)	—
C	8,000	—	8,000	—
D	0	10,000	(10,000)	(100%)

When a negative amount appears in the base period and a positive amount in the analysis period (or vice versa), we cannot compute a meaningful percent change; see cases A and B. Also, when no value is in the base period, no percent change is computable; see case C. Finally, when an item has a value in the base period and zero in the analysis period, the decrease is 100 percent; see case D.

Example: When there is a value in the base period and zero in the analysis period, the decrease is 100%. Why isn't the reverse situation an increase of 100%? *Answer:* A 100% increase of zero is still zero.

It is common when using horizontal analysis to compare amounts to either average or median values from prior periods (average and median values smooth out erratic or unusual fluctuations).[1] We also commonly round percents and ratios to one or two decimal places, but practice on this matter is not uniform. Computations are as detailed as necessary, which is judged by whether rounding potentially affects users' decisions. Computations should not be excessively detailed so that important relations are lost among a mountain of decimal points and digits.

Comparative Balance Sheets   Comparative balance sheets consist of balance sheet amounts from two or more balance sheet dates arranged side by side. Its usefulness is often improved by showing each item's dollar change and percent change to highlight large changes.

Analysis of comparative financial statements begins by focusing on items that show large dollar or percent changes. We then try to identify the reasons for these changes and, if possible, determine whether they are favorable or unfavorable. We also follow up on items with small changes when we expected the changes to be large.

Point: Spreadsheet programs can help with horizontal, vertical, and ratio analyses, including graphical depictions of financial relations.

---

[1] *Median* is the middle value in a group of numbers. For instance, if five prior years' incomes are (in 000s) $15, $19, $18, $20, and $22, the median value is $19. When there are two middle numbers, we can take their average. For instance, if four prior years' sales are (in 000s) $84, $91, $96, and $93, the median is $92 (computed as the average of $91 and $93).

EXHIBIT 13.1

Comparative Balance Sheets

RIM

RESEARCH IN MOTION Comparative Balance Sheets February 27, 2010 and February 28, 2009				
($ thousands)	2010	2009	Dollar Change	Percent Change
Assets				
Cash and cash equivalents	$ 1,550,861	$ 835,546	$ 715,315	85.6%
Short-term investments	360,614	682,666	(322,052)	(47.2)
Accounts receivable, net	2,593,742	2,112,117	481,625	22.8
Other receivables	206,373	157,728	48,645	30.8
Inventories	621,611	682,400	(60,789)	(8.9)
Other current assets	285,539	187,257	98,282	52.5
Deferred income tax asset	193,916	183,872	10,044	5.5
Total current assets	5,812,656	4,841,586	971,070	20.1
Long-term investments	958,248	720,635	237,613	33.0
Property, plant and equipment, net	1,956,581	1,334,648	621,933	46.6
Intangible assets, net	1,326,363	1,066,527	259,836	24.4
Goodwill	150,561	137,572	12,989	9.4
Deferred income tax asset	0	404	(404)	(100.0)
Total assets	$10,204,409	$8,101,372	$2,103,037	26.0
Liabilities				
Accounts payable	$ 615,620	$ 448,339	$ 167,281	37.3%
Accrued liabilities	1,638,260	1,238,602	399,658	32.3
Income taxes payable	95,650	361,460	(265,810)	(73.5)
Deferred revenue	67,573	53,834	13,739	25.5
Deferred income tax liability	14,674	13,116	1,558	11.9
Total current liabilities	2,431,777	2,115,351	316,426	15.0
Deferred income tax liability	141,382	87,917	53,465	60.8
Income taxes payable	28,587	23,976	4,611	19.2
Total liabilities	2,601,746	2,227,244	374,502	16.8
Shareholders' Equity				
Capital stock	2,207,609	2,208,235	(626)	0.0
Treasury stock	(94,463)	0	(94,463)	—
Retained earnings	5,274,365	3,545,710	1,728,655	48.8
Additional paid-in capital	164,060	119,726	44,334	37.0
Accumulated other comprehensive income	51,092	457	50,635	11,079
Total stockholders' equity	7,602,663	5,874,128	1,728,535	29.4
Total liabilities and stockholders' equity	$10,204,409	$8,101,372	$2,103,037	26.0

Exhibit 13.1 shows comparative balance sheets for **Research In Motion** (RIM). A few items stand out. Many asset categories substantially increase, which is probably not surprising because RIM is a growth company. Much of the increase in current assets is from the 85.6% increase in cash and equivalents and the 22.8% increase in accounts receivable; although the 47.2% decline in short-term investments dampened this growth. The long-term assets of property, plant and equipment, intangible assets, and long-term investments also markedly increased. Of course, its sizeable total asset growth of 26.0% must be accompanied by future income to validate RIM's growth strategy.

We likewise see substantial increases on the financing side, the most notable ones (in amount) being accounts payable and accrued liabilities totaling $566,939 thousand. The increase in these items is probably related to the recessionary period covering this report. RIM also reinvested much of its income as reflected in the $1,728,655 thousand increase in retained earnings. Again, we must monitor these increases in investing and financing activities to be sure they are reflected in increased operating performance.

Comparative Income Statements   Comparative income statements are prepared similarly to comparative balance sheets. Amounts for two or more periods are placed side by side, with additional columns for dollar and percent changes. Exhibit 13.2 shows Research In Motion's comparative income statements.

RESEARCH IN MOTION Comparative Income Statements For Years Ended February 27, 2010 and February 28, 2009				
($ thousands, except per share data)	2010	2009	Dollar Change	Percent Change
Revenue	$14,953,224	$11,065,186	$3,888,038	35.1%
Cost of sales	8,368,958	5,967,888	2,401,070	40.2
Gross profit	6,584,266	5,097,298	1,486,968	29.2
Research and development	964,841	684,702	280,139	40.9
Selling, marketing, and administration	1,907,398	1,495,697	411,701	27.5
Amortization	310,357	194,803	115,554	59.3
Litigation	163,800	—	163,800	—
Income from operations	3,237,870	2,722,096	515,774	18.9
Investment income	28,640	78,267	(49,627)	(63.4)
Income before income taxes	3,266,510	2,800,363	466,147	16.6
Provision for income taxes	809,366	907,747	(98,381)	(10.8)
Net income	$ 2,457,144	$ 1,892,616	564,528	29.8
Basic earnings per share	$ 4.35	$ 3.35	$ 1.00	29.9
Diluted earnings per share	$ 4.31	$ 3.30	$ 1.01	30.6

EXHIBIT 13.2

Comparative Income Statements

RIM

RIM has substantial revenue growth of 35.1% in 2010. This finding helps support management's growth strategy as reflected in the comparative balance sheets. RIM evidences some ability to control costs of selling, marketing, and administration, which increased 27.5% (versus the 35.1% revenue increase). However, cost of sales increased 40.2% and other expenses also increased at a rate more than that for sales. RIM's net income growth of 29.8% on revenue growth of 35.1% is still good.

Point: Percent change can also be computed by dividing the current period by the prior period and subtracting 1.0. For example, the 35.1% revenue increase of Exhibit 13.2 is computed as: ($14,953,224/$11,065,186) − 1.

Trend Analysis

Trend analysis, also called *trend percent analysis* or *index number trend analysis,* is a form of horizontal analysis that can reveal patterns in data across successive periods. It involves computing trend percents for a series of financial numbers and is a variation on the use of percent changes. The difference is that trend analysis does not subtract the base period amount in the numerator. To compute trend percents, we do the following:

1. Select a *base period* and assign each item in the base period a weight of 100%.
2. Express financial numbers as a percent of their base period number.

Specifically, a *trend percent,* also called an *index number,* is computed as follows:

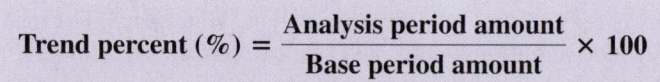

$$\text{Trend percent (\%)} = \frac{\text{Analysis period amount}}{\text{Base period amount}} \times 100$$

Point: *Index* refers to the comparison of the analysis period to the base period. Percents determined for each period are called *index numbers.*

To illustrate trend analysis, we use the **Research In Motion** data shown in Exhibit 13.3.

EXHIBIT 13.3

Revenue and Expenses

(in thousands)	2010	2009	2008	2007	2006
Revenue	$14,953,224	$11,065,186	$6,009,395	$3,037,103	$2,065,845
Cost of sales	8,368,958	5,967,888	2,928,814	1,379,301	925,598
Operating expenses	3,346,396	2,375,202	1,349,422	850,974	523,155

These data are from RIM's current and prior financial statements. The base period is 2006 and the trend percent is computed in each subsequent year by dividing that year's amount by its 2006 amount. For instance, the revenue trend percent for 2010 is 723.8%, computed as $14,953,224/$2,065,845. The trend percents—using the data from Exhibit 13.3—are shown in Exhibit 13.4.

EXHIBIT 13.4

Trend Percents for Revenue and Expenses

	2010	2009	2008	2007	2006
Revenue	723.8%	535.6%	290.9%	147.0%	100.0%
Cost of sales	904.2	644.8	316.4	149.0	100.0
Operating expenses	639.7	454.0	257.9	162.7	100.0

Point: Trend analysis expresses a percent of base, not a percent of change.

Graphical depictions often aid analysis of trend percents. Exhibit 13.5 shows the trend percents from Exhibit 13.4 in a *line graph,* which can help us identify trends and detect changes in direction or magnitude. It reveals that the trend line for revenue consistently falls short of that for cost of sales. Moreover, the magnitude of that difference has slightly grown. This result does not bode well for RIM because its cost of sales are by far its largest cost, and the company fails to show an ability to control these expenses as it expands. The line graph also reveals a consistent increase in each of these accounts, which is typical of growth companies. The trend line for operating expenses is more encouraging because it falls short of the revenue trend line in 2008, 2009 and 2010. Still, the bad news is that much of the shift in cost of sales occurred in the most recent two years. Management must try to better control those costs in future years.

EXHIBIT 13.5

Trend Percent Lines for Revenue and Expenses of Research In Motion

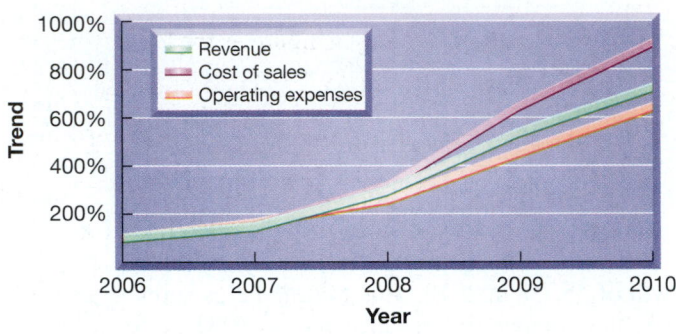

Exhibit 13.6 compares **RIM**'s revenue trend line to that of **Apple** and **Palm** for this same period. RIM's revenues sharply increased over this time period while those of Apple exhibited less growth, and those for Palm were declining. These data indicate that RIM's products and services have met with considerable consumer acceptance.

Trend analysis of financial statement items can include comparisons of relations between items on different financial statements. For instance, Exhibit 13.7 compares RIM's revenue and total assets. The rate of increase in total assets (440.9%) is less than the increase in revenues (723.8%) since 2006. Is this result favorable or not? The answer is that RIM was *more* efficient in using its assets in 2010. Management has generated revenues sufficient to compensate for this asset growth.

EXHIBIT 13.6

Trend Percent Lines—Research In Motion, Apple and Palm

RIM

Apple

Palm

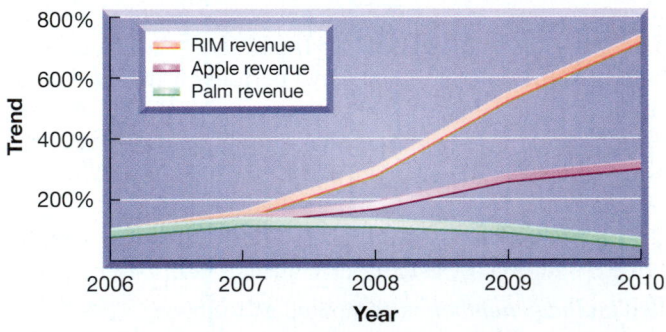

EXHIBIT 13.7

Revenue and Asset Data for Research In Motion

($ thousands)	2010	2006	Trend Percent (2010 vs. 2006)
Revenue	$14,953,224	$2,065,845	723.8%
Total assets	10,204,409	2,314,349	440.9

Overall we must remember that an important role of financial statement analysis is identifying questions and areas of interest, which often direct us to important factors bearing on a company's future. Accordingly, financial statement analysis should be seen as a continuous process of refining our understanding and expectations of company performance and financial condition.

□ Decision Maker   Answer – p. 580

Auditor   Your tests reveal a 3% increase in sales from $200,000 to $206,000 and a 4% decrease in expenses from $190,000 to $182,400. Both changes are within your "reasonableness" criterion of ±5%, and thus you don't pursue additional tests. The audit partner in charge questions your lack of follow-up and mentions the *joint relation* between sales and expenses. To what is the partner referring? ■

VERTICAL ANALYSIS

Vertical analysis is a tool to evaluate individual financial statement items or a group of items in terms of a specific base amount. We usually define a key aggregate figure as the base, which for an income statement is usually revenue and for a balance sheet is usually total assets. This section explains vertical analysis and applies it to **Research In Motion**. [The term *vertical analysis* arises from the up-down (or down-up) movement of our eyes as we review common-size financial statements. Vertical analysis is also called *common-size analysis*.]

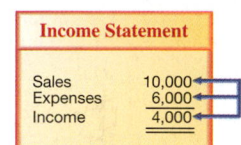

Common-Size Statements

The comparative statements in Exhibits 13.1 and 13.2 show the change in each item over time, but they do not emphasize the relative importance of each item. We use **common-size financial statements** to reveal changes in the relative importance of each financial statement item. All individual amounts in common-size statements are redefined in terms of common-size percents. A *common-size percent* is measured by dividing each individual financial statement amount under analysis by its base amount:

P2 Describe and apply methods of vertical analysis.

$$\text{Common-size percent (\%)} = \frac{\text{Analysis amount}}{\text{Base amount}} \times 100$$

Common-Size Balance Sheets   Common-size statements express each item as a percent of a *base amount,* which for a common-size balance sheet is usually total assets. The base amount is assigned a value of 100%. (This implies that the total amount of liabilities plus equity equals 100% since this amount equals total assets.) We then compute a common-size percent for each asset, liability, and equity item using total assets as the base amount. When we present a company's successive balance sheets in this way, changes in the mixture of assets, liabilities, and equity are apparent.

Exhibit 13.8 shows common-size comparative balance sheets for RIM. Some relations that stand out on both a magnitude and percentage basis include (1) a 4.9% point increase in cash and equivalents, which is likely balanced with a 4.9% point decline in short-term investments, (2) a 2.3% point decline in inventories, (3) a 2.7% point increase in net property, plant and equipment, (4) a 3.6% point decline in taxes payable, and (5) a marked increase in retained earnings. Many of these changes are characteristic of a growth/stable company. The concern, if any, is whether RIM can continue to generate sufficient revenue and income to support its asset buildup within a very competitive industry.

Common-Size Income Statements   Analysis also benefits from use of a common-size income statement. Revenue is usually the base amount, which is assigned a value of 100%. Each common-size income statement item appears as a percent of revenue. If we think of the 100%

Point: The *base* amount in common-size analysis is an *aggregate* amount from that period's financial statement.

Point: Common-size statements often are used to compare two or more companies in the same industry.

Point: Common-size statements are also useful in comparing firms that report in different currencies.

EXHIBIT 13.8

Common-Size Comparative
Balance Sheets

RIM

			Common-Size Percents*	
RESEARCH IN MOTION **Common-Size Comparative Balance Sheets** **February 27, 2010 and February 28, 2009**				
(in thousands)	2010	2009	2010	2009
Assets				
Cash and cash equivalents	$ 1,550,861	$ 835,546	15.2%	10.3%
Short-term investments	360,614	682,666	3.5	8.4
Accounts receivable, net	2,593,742	2,112,117	25.4	26.1
Other receivables	206,373	157,728	2.0	1.9
Inventories	621,611	682,400	6.1	8.4
Other current assets	285,539	187,257	2.8	2.3
Deferred income tax asset	193,916	183,872	1.9	2.3
Total current assets	5,812,656	4,841,586	57.0	59.8
Long-term investments	958,248	720,635	9.4	8.9
Property, plant and equipment, net	1,956,581	1,334,648	19.2	16.5
Intangible assets, net	1,326,363	1,066,527	13.0	13.2
Goodwill	150,561	137,572	1.5	1.7
Deferred income tax asset	0	404	0.0	0.0
Total assets	$10,204,409	$8,101,372	100.0%	100.0%
Liabilities				
Accounts payable	$ 615,620	$ 448,339	6.0%	5.5%
Accrued liabilities	1,638,260	1,238,602	16.1	15.3
Income taxes payable	95,650	361,460	0.9	4.5
Deferred revenue	67,573	53,834	0.7	0.7
Deferred income tax liability	14,674	13,116	0.1	0.2
Total current liabilities	2,431,777	2,115,351	23.8	26.1
Deferred income tax liability	141,382	87,917	1.4	1.1
Income taxes payable	28,587	23,976	0.3	0.3
Total liabilities	2,601,746	2,227,244	25.5	27.5
Shareholders' Equity				
Capital stock	2,207,609	2,208,235	21.6	27.3
Treasury stock	(94,463)	0	(0.9)	0.0
Retained earnings	5,274,365	3,545,710	51.7	43.8
Additional paid-in capital	164,060	119,726	1.6	1.5
Accumulated other comprehensive income	51,092	457	0.5	0.0
Total stockholders' equity	7,602,663	5,874,128	74.5	72.5
Total liabilities and stockholders' equity	$10,204,409	$8,101,372	100.0%	100.0%

* Percents are rounded to tenths and thus may not exactly sum to totals and subtotals.

revenue amount as representing one sales dollar, the remaining items show how each revenue dollar is distributed among costs, expenses, and income.

Exhibit 13.9 shows common-size comparative income statements for each dollar of RIM's revenue. The past two years' common-size numbers are similar with a few exceptions. The bad news is that RIM has given up 0.7 cent in earnings per revenue dollar—evidenced by the 17.1% to 16.4% decline in earnings as a percentage of revenue. This implies that management is not effectively controlling costs. Much of this is attributed to the rise in cost of sales from 53.9% to 56.0% as a percentage of revenue. This is a concern given the price-competitive smartphone market. Some good news is apparent with the decline in selling, marketing, and administration expenses as a percentage of revenue. Analysis here shows that common-size percents for successive income statements can uncover potentially important changes in a company's expenses. Evidence of no changes, especially when changes are expected, is also informative.

Global: International companies sometimes disclose "convenience" financial statements, which are statements translated in other languages and currencies. However, these statements rarely adjust for differences in accounting principles across countries.

RESEARCH IN MOTION Common-Size Comparative Income Statements For Years Ended February 27, 2010 and February 28, 2009			Common-Size Percents*	
($ thousands)	2010	2009	2010	2009
Revenue	$14,953,224	$11,065,186	100.0%	100.0%
Cost of sales	8,368,958	5,967,888	56.0	53.9
Gross margin	6,584,266	5,097,298	44.0	46.1
Research and development	964,841	684,702	6.5	6.2
Selling, marketing, and administration	1,907,398	1,495,697	12.8	13.5
Amortization	310,357	194,803	2.1	1.8
Litigation	163,800	—	1.1	0.0
Income from operations	3,237,870	2,722,096	21.7	24.6
Investment income	28,640	78,267	0.2	0.7
Income before income taxes	3,266,510	2,800,363	21.8	25.3
Provision for income taxes	809,366	907,747	5.4	8.2
Net income	$ 2,457,144	$ 1,892,616	16.4%	17.1%

EXHIBIT 13.9

Common-Size Comparative Income Statements

RIM

* Percents are rounded to tenths and thus may not exactly sum to totals and subtotals.

Common-Size Graphics

Two of the most common tools of common-size analysis are trend analysis of common-size statements and graphical analysis. The trend analysis of common-size statements is similar to that of comparative statements discussed under vertical analysis. It is not illustrated here because the only difference is the substitution of common-size percents for trend percents. Instead, this section discusses graphical analysis of common-size statements.

An income statement readily lends itself to common-size graphical analysis. This is so because revenues affect nearly every item in an income statement. Exhibit 13.10 shows **RIM**'s 2010 common-size income statement in graphical form. This pie chart highlights the contribution of each cost component of revenue for net income, excluding investment income.

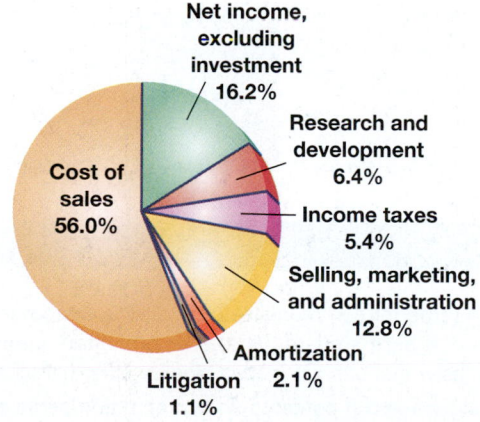

EXHIBIT 13.10

Common-Size Graphic of Income Statement

Exhibit 13.11 previews more complex graphical analyses available and the insights they provide. The data for this exhibit are taken from **RIM**'s *Segments* footnote. RIM has at least two reportable segments: (1) United States, and (2) outside the United States (titled Non-U.S.).

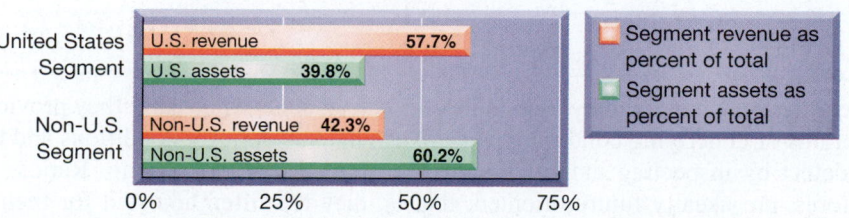

EXHIBIT 13.11

Revenue and Total Asset Breakdown by Segment

EXHIBIT 13.12

Common-Size Graphic of
Asset Components

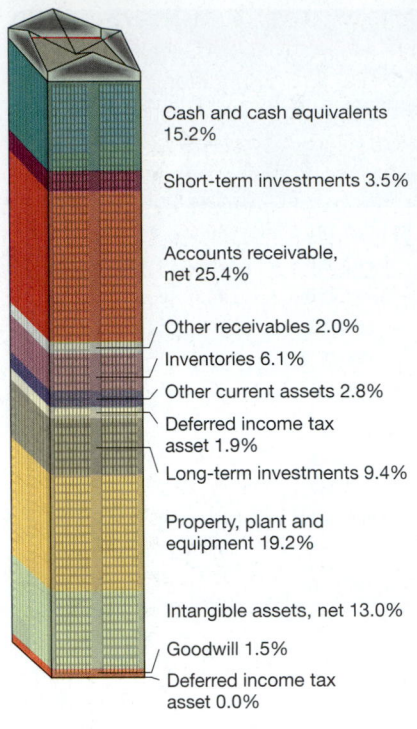

Cash and cash equivalents
15.2%

Short-term investments 3.5%

Accounts receivable,
net 25.4%

Other receivables 2.0%

Inventories 6.1%

Other current assets 2.8%

Deferred income tax
asset 1.9%

Long-term investments 9.4%

Property, plant and
equipment 19.2%

Intangible assets, net 13.0%

Goodwill 1.5%

Deferred income tax
asset 0.0%

The upper set of bars in Exhibit 13.11 shows the percent of revenues from, and the assets invested in, its U.S. segment. Its U.S. segment generates 57.7% of its revenue, while only 39.8% of its assets are in the United States. The lower set of bars shows that 42.3% of its revenue is generated outside the United States, while 60.2% of its assets are outside the United States. This can lead to questions about the revenue generated per assets invested across different countries. This type of information can help users in determining strategic analyses and actions.

Graphical analysis is also useful in identifying (1) sources of financing including the distribution among current liabilities, noncurrent liabilities, and equity capital and (2) focuses of investing activities, including the distribution among current and noncurrent assets. To illustrate, Exhibit 13.12 shows a common-size graphical display of RIM's assets. Common-size balance sheet analysis can be extended to examine the composition of these subgroups. For instance, in assessing liquidity of current assets, knowing what proportion of *current* assets consists of inventories is usually important, and not simply what proportion inventories are of *total* assets.

Common-size financial statements are also useful in comparing different companies. Exhibit 13.13 shows common-size graphics of **RIM**, **Apple** and **Nokia** on financing sources. This graphic highlights the larger percent of equity financing for RIM and Apple than for Nokia. It also highlights the much larger noncurrent (debt) financing of Nokia and Apple versus RIM. Comparison of a company's common-size statements with competitors' or industry common-size statistics alerts us to differences in the structure or distribution of its financial statements but not to their dollar magnitude.

EXHIBIT 13.13

Common-Size Graphic of Financing
Sources—Competitor Analysis

RIM

Apple

NOKIA

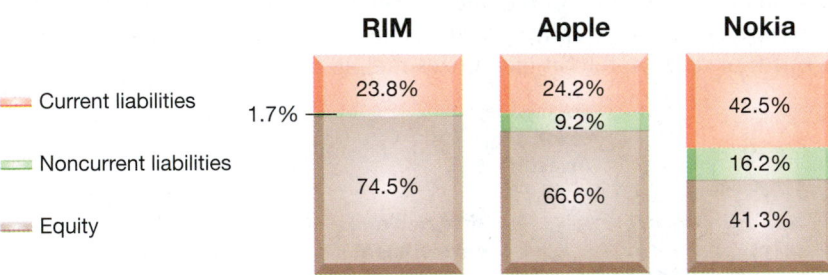

	RIM	Apple	Nokia
Current liabilities	23.8%	24.2%	42.5%
Noncurrent liabilities	1.7%	9.2%	16.2%
Equity	74.5%	66.6%	41.3%

Quick Check   Answers — p. 581

5. Which of the following is true for common-size comparative statements? (*a*) Each item is expressed as a percent of a base amount. (*b*) Total assets often are assigned a value of 100%. (*c*) Amounts from successive periods are placed side by side. (*d*) All are true. (*e*) None is true.

6. What is the difference between the percents shown on a comparative income statement and those shown on a common-size comparative income statement?

7. Trend percents are (*a*) shown on comparative income statements and balance sheets, (*b*) shown on common-size comparative statements, or (*c*) also called *index numbers*.

RATIO ANALYSIS

 P3 Define and apply ratio analysis.

Ratios are among the more widely used tools of financial analysis because they provide clues to and symptoms of underlying conditions. A ratio can help us uncover conditions and trends difficult to detect by inspecting individual components making up the ratio. Ratios, like other analysis tools, are usually future oriented; that is, they are often adjusted for their probable future trend and magnitude, and their usefulness depends on skillful interpretation.

A ratio expresses a mathematical relation between two quantities. It can be expressed as a percent, rate, or proportion. For instance, a change in an account balance from $100 to $250 can be expressed as (1) 150% increase, (2) 2.5 times, or (3) 2.5 to 1 (or 2.5:1). Computation of a ratio is a simple arithmetic operation, but its interpretation is not. To be meaningful, a ratio must refer to an economically important relation. For example, a direct and crucial relation exists between an item's sales price and its cost. Accordingly, the ratio of cost of goods sold to sales is meaningful. In contrast, no obvious relation exists between freight costs and the balance of long-term investments.

This section describes an important set of financial ratios and its application. The selected ratios are organized into the four building blocks of financial statement analysis: (1) liquidity and efficiency, (2) solvency, (3) profitability, and (4) market prospects. All of these ratios were explained at relevant points in prior chapters. The purpose here is to organize and apply them under a summary framework. We use four common standards, in varying degrees, for comparisons: intracompany, competitor, industry, and guidelines.

Point: Some sources for industry norms are *Annual Statement Studies* by Robert Morris Associates, *Industry Norms & Key Business Ratios* by Dun & Bradstreet, *Standard & Poor's Industry Surveys*, and Reuters.com/finance.

Liquidity and Efficiency

Liquidity refers to the availability of resources to meet short-term cash requirements. It is affected by the timing of cash inflows and outflows along with prospects for future performance. Analysis of liquidity is aimed at a company's funding requirements. *Efficiency* refers to how productive a company is in using its assets. Efficiency is usually measured relative to how much revenue is generated from a certain level of assets.

Both liquidity and efficiency are important and complementary. If a company fails to meet its current obligations, its continued existence is doubtful. Viewed in this light, all other measures of analysis are of secondary importance. Although accounting measurements assume the company's continued existence, our analysis must always assess the validity of this assumption using liquidity measures. Moreover, inefficient use of assets can cause liquidity problems. A lack of liquidity often precedes lower profitability and fewer opportunities. It can foretell a loss of owner control. To a company's creditors, lack of liquidity can yield delays in collecting interest and principal payments or the loss of amounts due them. A company's customers and suppliers of goods and services also are affected by short-term liquidity problems. Implications include a company's inability to execute contracts and potential damage to important customer and supplier relationships. This section describes and illustrates key ratios relevant to assessing liquidity and efficiency.

Working Capital and Current Ratio The amount of current assets less current liabilities is called **working capital,** or *net working capital.* A company needs adequate working capital to meet current debts, to carry sufficient inventories, and to take advantage of cash discounts. A company that runs low on working capital is less likely to meet current obligations or to continue operating. When evaluating a company's working capital, we must not only look at the dollar amount of current assets less current liabilities, but also at their ratio. The *current ratio* is defined as follows (see Chapter 3 for additional explanation):

$$\text{Current ratio} = \frac{\text{Current assets}}{\text{Current liabilities}}$$

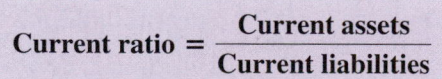

Drawing on information in Exhibit 13.1, **RIM**'s working capital and current ratio for both 2010 and 2009 are shown in Exhibit 13.14. Also, **Apple** (2.74), **Palm** (1.03), and the Industry's current ratio (2.4) are shown in the margin. RIM's 2010 ratio (2.39) is between the competitors' ratios, and it does not appear in danger of defaulting on loan payments. A high current ratio suggests a strong liquidity position and an ability to meet current obligations. A company can, however, have a current ratio that is too high. An excessively high current ratio means that the company has invested too much in current assets compared to its current obligations.

($ thousands)	2010	2009
Current assets	$ 5,812,656	$ 4,841,586
Current liabilities	2,431,777	2,115,351
Working capital	**$3,380,879**	**$2,726,235**
Current ratio		
$5,812,656/$2,431,777 =	**2.39 to 1**	
$4,841,586/$2,115,351 =		**2.29 to 1**

EXHIBIT 13.14

RIM's Working Capital and Current Ratio

Current ratio
Apple = 2.74
Palm = 1.03
Industry = 2.4

An excessive investment in current assets is not an efficient use of funds because current assets normally generate a low return on investment (compared with long-term assets).

Many users apply a guideline of 2:1 (or 1.5:1) for the current ratio in helping evaluate a company's debt-paying ability. A company with a 2:1 or higher current ratio is generally thought to be a good credit risk in the short run. Such a guideline or any analysis of the current ratio must recognize at least three additional factors: (1) type of business, (2) composition of current assets, and (3) turnover rate of current asset components.

Type of business.   A service company that grants little or no credit and carries few inventories can probably operate on a current ratio of less than 1:1 if its revenues generate enough cash to pay its current liabilities. On the other hand, a company selling high-priced clothing or furniture requires a higher ratio because of difficulties in judging customer demand and cash receipts. For instance, if demand falls, inventory may not generate as much cash as expected. Accordingly, analysis of the current ratio should include a comparison with ratios from successful companies in the same industry and from prior periods. We must also recognize that a company's accounting methods, especially choice of inventory method, affect the current ratio. For instance, when costs are rising, a company using LIFO tends to report a smaller amount of current assets than when using FIFO.

Point: When a firm uses LIFO in a period of rising costs, the standard for an adequate current ratio usually is lower than if it used FIFO.

Composition of current assets.   The composition of a company's current assets is important to an evaluation of short-term liquidity. For instance, cash, cash equivalents, and short-term investments are more liquid than accounts and notes receivable. Also, short-term receivables normally are more liquid than inventory. Cash, of course, can be used to immediately pay current debts. Items such as accounts receivable and inventory, however, normally must be converted into cash before payment is made. An excessive amount of receivables and inventory weakens a company's ability to pay current liabilities. The acid-test ratio (see below) can help with this assessment.

Turnover rate of assets.   Asset turnover measures a company's efficiency in using its assets. One relevant measure of asset efficiency is the revenue generated. A measure of total asset turnover is revenues divided by total assets, but evaluation of turnover for individual assets is also useful. We discuss both receivables turnover and inventory turnover on the next page.

 Decision Maker   Answer — p. 581

Banker   A company requests a one-year, $200,000 loan for expansion. This company's current ratio is 4:1, with current assets of $160,000. Key competitors carry a current ratio of about 1.9:1. Using this information, do you approve the loan application? Does your decision change if the application is for a 10-year loan? ■

Acid-Test Ratio   Quick assets are cash, short-term investments, and current receivables. These are the most liquid types of current assets. The *acid-test ratio,* also called *quick ratio,* and introduced in Chapter 4, reflects on a company's short-term liquidity.

$$\text{Acid-test ratio} = \frac{\text{Cash + Short-term investments + Current receivables}}{\text{Current liabilities}}$$

RIM's acid-test ratio is computed in Exhibit 13.15. RIM's 2010 acid-test ratio (1.94) is between that for Apple (2.33) and Palm (0.94), and greater than the 1:1 common guideline for an

EXHIBIT 13.15

Acid-Test Ratio

($ thousands)	2010	2009
Cash and equivalents	$1,550,861	$ 835,546
Short-term investments	360,614	682,666
Current receivables	2,800,115	2,269,845
Total quick assets	$4,711,590	$3,788,057
Current liabilities	$2,431,777	$2,115,351
Acid-test ratio		
$4,711,590/$2,431,777	1.94 to 1	
$3,788,057/$2,115,351		1.79 to 1

Acid-test ratio
Apple = 2.33
Palm = 0.94
Industry = 1.5

acceptable acid-test ratio. The ratios for both RIM and Apple exceed the 1.5 industry norm. As with analysis of the current ratio, we need to consider other factors. For instance, the frequency with which a company converts its current assets into cash affects its working capital requirements. This implies that analysis of short-term liquidity should also include an analysis of receivables and inventories, which we consider next.

Accounts Receivable Turnover   We can measure how frequently a company converts its receivables into cash by computing the *accounts receivable turnover*. This ratio is defined as follows (see Chapter 7 for additional explanation):

$$\text{Accounts receivable turnover} = \frac{\text{Net sales}}{\text{Average accounts receivable, net}}$$

Short-term receivables from customers are often included in the denominator along with accounts receivable. Also, accounts receivable turnover is more precise if credit sales are used for the numerator, but external users generally use net sales (or net revenues) because information about credit sales is typically not reported. RIM's 2010 accounts receivable turnover is computed as follows ($ millions).

$$\frac{14,953,224}{(\$2,593,742 + \$2,112,117)/2} = 6.4 \text{ times}$$

RIM's value of 6.4 is between that of Apple's 14.8 and Palm's 8.0. Accounts receivable turnover is high when accounts receivable are quickly collected. A high turnover is favorable because it means the company need not commit large amounts of funds to accounts receivable. However, an accounts receivable turnover can be too high; this can occur when credit terms are so restrictive that they negatively affect sales volume.

Inventory Turnover   How long a company holds inventory before selling it will affect working capital requirements. One measure of this effect is *inventory turnover,* also called *merchandise turnover* or *merchandise inventory turnover,* which is defined as follows (see Chapter 5 for additional explanation):

$$\text{Inventory turnover} = \frac{\text{Cost of goods sold}}{\text{Average inventory}}$$

Using RIM's cost of goods sold and inventories information, we compute its inventory turnover for 2010 as follows (if the beginning and ending inventories for the year do not represent the usual inventory amount, an average of quarterly or monthly inventories can be used).

$$\frac{\$8,368,958}{(\$621,611 + \$682,400)/2} = 12.84 \text{ times}$$

RIM's inventory turnover of 12.84 is less than Apple's 53.28, but similar to Palm's 13.22, and the industry's 10.1. A company with a high turnover requires a smaller investment in inventory than one producing the same sales with a lower turnover. Inventory turnover can be too high, however, if the inventory a company keeps is so small that it restricts sales volume.

Days' Sales Uncollected   Accounts receivable turnover provides insight into how frequently a company collects its accounts. Days' sales uncollected is one measure of this activity, which is defined as follows (Chapter 6 provides additional explanation):

$$\text{Days' sales uncollected} = \frac{\text{Accounts receivable, net}}{\text{Net sales}} \times 365$$

Any short-term notes receivable from customers are normally included in the numerator.

RIM's 2010 days' sales uncollected follows.

Day's sales uncollected
Apple = 28.59
Palm = 32.96

$$\frac{\$2,593,742}{\$14,953,224} \times 365 = 63.31 \text{ days}$$

Both Apple's days' sales uncollected of 28.59 days and Palm's 32.96 days are less than the 63.31 days for RIM. Days' sales uncollected is more meaningful if we know company credit terms. A rough guideline states that days' sales uncollected should not exceed $1\frac{1}{3}$ times the days in its (1) credit period, *if* discounts are not offered or (2) discount period, *if* favorable discounts are offered.

Days' Sales in Inventory   *Days' sales in inventory* is a useful measure in evaluating inventory liquidity. Days' sales in inventory is linked to inventory in a way that days' sales uncollected is linked to receivables. We compute days' sales in inventory as follows (Chapter 5 provides additional explanation).

$$\text{Days' sales in inventory} = \frac{\text{Ending inventory}}{\text{Cost of goods sold}} \times 365$$

RIM's days' sales in inventory for 2010 follows.

Days' sales in inventory
Apple = 6.5
Palm = 12.5
Industry = 25

$$\frac{\$621,611}{\$8,368,958} \times 365 = 27.1 \text{ days}$$

Point: *Average collection period* is estimated by dividing 365 by the accounts receivable turnover ratio. For example, 365 divided by an accounts receivable turnover of 6.1 indicates a 60-day average collection period.

If the products in RIM's inventory are in demand by customers, this formula estimates that its inventory will be converted into receivables (or cash) in 27.1 days. If all of RIM's sales were credit sales, the conversion of inventory to receivables in 27.1 days *plus* the conversion of receivables to cash in 63.31 days implies that inventory will be converted to cash in about 90.41 days (27.1 + 63.31).

Total Asset Turnover   *Total asset turnover* reflects a company's ability to use its assets to generate sales and is an important indication of operating efficiency. The definition of this ratio follows (Chapter 8 offers additional explanation).

$$\text{Total asset turnover} = \frac{\text{Net sales}}{\text{Average total assets}}$$

RIM's total asset turnover for 2010 follows and is greater than that for both Apple (1.03) and Palm (0.81).

Total asset turnover
Apple = 1.03
Palm = 0.81
Industry = 1.0

$$\frac{\$14,953,224}{(\$10,204,409 + \$8,101,372)/2} = 1.63 \text{ times}$$

Quick Check   Answers – p. 581

8. Information from Paff Co. at Dec. 31, 2010, follows: cash, $820,000; accounts receivable, $240,000; inventories, $470,000; plant assets, $910,000; accounts payable, $350,000; and income taxes payable, $180,000. Compute its (*a*) current ratio and (*b*) acid-test ratio.

9. On Dec. 31, 2011, Paff Company (see question 8) had accounts receivable of $290,000 and inventories of $530,000. During 2011, net sales amounted to $2,500,000 and cost of goods sold was $750,000. Compute (*a*) accounts receivable turnover, (*b*) days' sales uncollected, (*c*) inventory turnover, and (*d*) days' sales in inventory.

Solvency

Solvency refers to a company's long-run financial viability and its ability to cover long-term obligations. All of a company's business activities—financing, investing, and operating—affect its solvency. Analysis of solvency is long term and uses less precise but more encompassing measures than liquidity. One of the most important components of solvency analysis is the composition of a company's capital structure. *Capital structure* refers to a company's financing sources. It ranges from relatively permanent equity financing to riskier or more temporary short-term financing. Assets represent security for financiers, ranging from loans secured by specific assets to the assets available as general security to unsecured creditors. This section describes the tools of solvency analysis. Our analysis focuses on a company's ability to both meet its obligations and provide security to its creditors *over the long run.* Indicators of this ability include *debt* and *equity* ratios, the relation between *pledged assets and secured liabilities,* and the company's capacity to earn sufficient income to *pay fixed interest charges.*

Debt and Equity Ratios   One element of solvency analysis is to assess the portion of a company's assets contributed by its owners and the portion contributed by creditors. This relation is reflected in the debt ratio (also described in Chapter 2). The *debt ratio* expresses total liabilities as a percent of total assets. The **equity ratio** provides complementary information by expressing total equity as a percent of total assets. **RIM**'s debt and equity ratios follow.

Point: For analysis purposes, Minority Interest is usually included in equity.

($ thousands)	2010	Ratios	
Total liabilities	$ 2,601,746	25.5%	[Debt ratio]
Total equity	7,602,663	74.5	[Equity ratio]
Total liabilities and equity	$10,204,409	100.0%	

Debt ratio :: Equity ratio
Apple = 33.4% :: 66.6%
Industry = 40% :: 60%

RIM's financial statements reveal more equity than debt. A company is considered less risky if its capital structure (equity and long-term debt) contains more equity. One risk factor is the required payment for interest and principal when debt is outstanding. Another factor is the greater the stockholder financing, the more losses a company can absorb through equity before the assets become inadequate to satisfy creditors' claims. From the stockholders' point of view, if a company earns a return on borrowed capital that is higher than the cost of borrowing, the difference represents increased income to stockholders. The inclusion of debt is described as *financial leverage* because debt can have the effect of increasing the return to stockholders. Companies are said to be highly leveraged if a large portion of their assets is financed by debt.

Point: Bank examiners from the FDIC and other regulatory agencies use debt and equity ratios to monitor compliance with regulatory capital requirements imposed on banks and S&Ls.

Debt-to-Equity Ratio   The ratio of total liabilities to equity is another measure of solvency. We compute the ratio as follows (Chapter 10 offers additional explanation).

$$\text{Debt-to-equity ratio} = \frac{\text{Total liabilities}}{\text{Total equity}}$$

RIM's debt-to-equity ratio for 2010 is

$$\$2,601,746/\$7,602,663 = 0.34$$

Debt-to-equity
Apple = 0.50
Industry = 0.7

RIM's 0.34 debt-to-equity ratio is less than the 0.50 ratio for Apple, and less than the industry ratio of 0.7. Consistent with our inferences from the debt ratio, RIM's capital structure has more equity than debt, which decreases risk. Recall that debt must be repaid with interest, while equity does not. These debt requirements can be burdensome when the industry and/or the economy experience a downturn. A larger debt-to-equity ratio also implies less opportunity to expand through use of debt financing.

Times Interest Earned   The amount of income before deductions for interest expense and income taxes is the amount available to pay interest expense. The following

Point: The times interest earned ratio and the debt and equity ratios are of special interest to bank lending officers.

times interest earned ratio reflects the creditors' risk of loan repayments with interest (see Chapter 9 for additional explanation).

$$\text{Times interest earned} = \frac{\text{Income before interest expense and income taxes}}{\text{Interest expense}}$$

The larger this ratio, the less risky is the company for creditors. One guideline says that creditors are reasonably safe if the company earns its fixed interest expense two or more times each year. RIM's times interest earned ratio follows; its value suggests that its creditors have little risk of nonrepayment.

Times interest earned
Apple = n.a.

$$\frac{\$2,457,144 + \sim\$0 \text{ (see RIM note \#16)} + \$809,366}{\sim\$0} = \text{"infinite" (not applicable)}$$

Decision **Insight**

Bears and Bulls   A *bear market* is a declining market. The phrase comes from bear-skin jobbers who often sold the skins before the bears were caught. The term *bear* was then used to describe investors who sold shares they did not own in anticipation of a price decline. A *bull market* is a rising market. This phrase comes from the once popular sport of bear and bull baiting. The term *bull* came to mean the opposite of *bear*. ∎

Profitability

We are especially interested in a company's ability to use its assets efficiently to produce profits (and positive cash flows). *Profitability* refers to a company's ability to generate an adequate return on invested capital. Return is judged by assessing earnings relative to the level and sources of financing. Profitability is also relevant to solvency. This section describes key profitability measures and their importance to financial statement analysis.

Profit Margin   A company's operating efficiency and profitability can be expressed by two components. The first is *profit margin,* which reflects a company's ability to earn net income from sales (Chapter 3 offers additional explanation). It is measured by expressing net income as a percent of sales (*sales* and *revenues* are similar terms). **RIM**'s profit margin follows.

Profit margin
Apple = 19.2%
Industry = 3%

$$\text{Profit margin} = \frac{\text{Net income}}{\text{Net sales}} = \frac{\$2,457,144}{\$14,953,224} = 16.4\%$$

To evaluate profit margin, we must consider the industry. For instance, an appliance company might require a profit margin between 10% and 15%; whereas a retail supermarket might require a profit margin of 1% or 2%. Both profit margin and *total asset turnover* make up the two basic components of operating efficiency. These ratios reflect on management because managers are ultimately responsible for operating efficiency. The next section explains how we use both measures to analyze return on total assets.

Return on Total Assets   *Return on total assets* is defined as follows.

$$\text{Return on total assets} = \frac{\text{Net income}}{\text{Average total assets}}$$

RIM's 2010 return on total assets is

Return on total assets
Apple = 19.7%
Industry = 4%

$$\frac{\$2,457,144}{(\$10,204,409 + \$8,101,372)/2} = 26.8\%$$

RIM's 26.8% return on total assets is higher than that for many businesses and is higher than Apple's return of 19.7% and the industry's 4% return. We also should evaluate any trend in the rate of return.

The following equation shows the important relation between profit margin, total asset turnover, and return on total assets.

Point: Many analysts add back *Interest expense* × *(1 − Tax rate)* to net income in computing return on total assets.

$$\textbf{Profit margin} \times \textbf{Total asset turnover} = \textbf{Return on total assets}$$

or

$$\frac{\textbf{Net income}}{\textbf{Net sales}} \times \frac{\textbf{Net sales}}{\textbf{Average total assets}} = \frac{\textbf{Net income}}{\textbf{Average total assets}}$$

Both profit margin and total asset turnover contribute to overall operating efficiency, as measured by return on total assets. If we apply this formula to RIM, we get

$$16.4\% \times 1.63 = 26.8\% \text{ (with rounding error)}$$

Apple: 19.2% × 1.03 = 19.7%
(with rounding)

This analysis shows that RIM's superior return on assets versus that of Apple is driven mainly by its higher total asset turnover.

Return on Common Stockholders' Equity   Perhaps the most important goal in operating a company is to earn net income for its owner(s). *Return on common stockholders' equity* measures a company's success in reaching this goal and is defined as follows.

$$\textbf{Return on common stockholders' equity} = \frac{\textbf{Net income} - \textbf{Preferred dividends}}{\textbf{Average common stockholders' equity}}$$

RIM's 2010 return on common stockholders' equity is computed as follows:

$$\frac{\$2,457,144 - \$0}{(\$5,874,128 + \$7,602,663)/2} = 36.5\%$$

Return on common equity
Apple = 30.5%
Industry = 6%

The denominator in this computation is the book value of common equity (minority interest is often included in common equity for this ratio). In the numerator, the dividends on cumulative preferred stock are subtracted whether they are declared or are in arrears. If preferred stock is noncumulative, its dividends are subtracted only if declared.

Decision Insight

Wall Street   *Wall Street* is synonymous with financial markets, but its name comes from the street location of the original New York Stock Exchange. The street's name derives from stockades built by early settlers to protect New York from pirate attacks. ■

Market Prospects

Market measures are useful for analyzing corporations with publicly traded stock. These market measures use stock price, which reflects the market's (public's) expectations for the company. This includes expectations of both company return and risk—as the market perceives it.

Price-Earnings Ratio   Computation of the *price-earnings ratio* follows (Chapter 11 provides additional explanation).

$$\textbf{Price-earnings ratio} = \frac{\textbf{Market price per common share}}{\textbf{Earnings per share}}$$

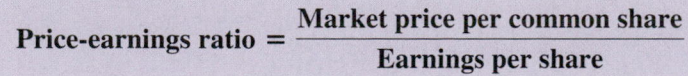

Predicted earnings per share for the next period is often used in the denominator of this computation. Reported earnings per share for the most recent period is also commonly used. In both cases, the ratio is used as an indicator of the future growth and risk of a company's earnings as perceived by the stock's buyers and sellers.

The market price of RIM's common stock at the start of fiscal year 2010 was $50.84. Using RIM's $4.35 basic earnings per share, we compute its price-earnings ratio as follows (some analysts compute this ratio using the median of the low and high stock price).

$$\frac{\$50.84}{\$4.35} = 11.7$$

PE (year-end)
Apple = 13.9

RIM's price-earnings ratio is less than that for Apple, but is slightly higher than the norm for the recessionary period 2009–2010. (Palm's ratio is negative due to its abnormally low earnings.) RIM's middle-of-the-pack ratio likely reflects investors' expectations of stagnant growth but normal earnings.

Dividend Yield *Dividend yield* is used to compare the dividend-paying performance of different investment alternatives. We compute dividend yield as follows (Chapter 11 offers additional explanation).

$$\text{Dividend yield} = \frac{\textbf{Annual cash dividends per share}}{\textbf{Market price per share}}$$

RIM's dividend yield, based on its fiscal year-end market price per share of $50.84 and its policy of $0.00 cash dividends per share, is computed as follows.

$$\frac{\$0.00}{\$50.84} = 0.0\%$$

Dividend yield
Apple = 0.0%
Palm = 0.0%

Some companies do not declare and pay dividends because they wish to reinvest the cash.

Summary of Ratios

Exhibit 13.16 summarizes the major financial statement analysis ratios illustrated in this chapter and throughout the book. This summary includes each ratio's title, its formula, and the purpose for which it is commonly used.

■ Decision Insight

Ticker Prices *Ticker prices* refer to a band of moving data on a monitor carrying up-to-the-minute stock prices. The phrase comes from *ticker tape,* a 1-inch-wide strip of paper spewing stock prices from a printer that ticked as it ran. Most of today's investors have never seen actual ticker tape, but the phrase survives. ■

Quick Check   Answers — p. 581

10. Which ratio best reflects a company's ability to meet immediate interest payments? (*a*) Debt ratio. (*b*) Equity ratio. (*c*) Times interest earned.

11. Which ratio best measures a company's success in earning net income for its owner(s)? (*a*) Profit margin. (*b*) Return on common stockholders' equity. (*c*) Price-earnings ratio. (*d*) Dividend yield.

12. If a company has net sales of $8,500,000, net income of $945,000, and total asset turnover of 1.8 times, what is its return on total assets?

EXHIBIT 13.16

Financial Statement Analysis Ratios*

Ratio	Formula	Measure of
Liquidity and Efficiency		
Current ratio	$= \dfrac{\text{Current assets}}{\text{Current liabilities}}$	Short-term debt-paying ability
Acid-test ratio	$= \dfrac{\text{Cash} + \text{Short-term investments} + \text{Current receivables}}{\text{Current liabilities}}$	Immediate short-term debt-paying ability
Accounts receivable turnover	$= \dfrac{\text{Net sales}}{\text{Average accounts receivable, net}}$	Efficiency of collection
Inventory turnover	$= \dfrac{\text{Cost of goods sold}}{\text{Average inventory}}$	Efficiency of inventory management
Days' sales uncollected	$= \dfrac{\text{Accounts receivable, net}}{\text{Net sales}} \times 365$	Liquidity of receivables
Days' sales in inventory	$= \dfrac{\text{Ending inventory}}{\text{Cost of goods sold}} \times 365$	Liquidity of inventory
Total asset turnover	$= \dfrac{\text{Net sales}}{\text{Average total assets}}$	Efficiency of assets in producing sales
Solvency		
Debt ratio	$= \dfrac{\text{Total liabilities}}{\text{Total assets}}$	Creditor financing and leverage
Equity ratio	$= \dfrac{\text{Total equity}}{\text{Total assets}}$	Owner financing
Debt-to-equity ratio	$= \dfrac{\text{Total liabilities}}{\text{Total equity}}$	Debt versus equity financing
Times interest earned	$= \dfrac{\text{Income before interest expense and income taxes}}{\text{Interest expense}}$	Protection in meeting interest payments
Profitability		
Profit margin ratio	$= \dfrac{\text{Net income}}{\text{Net sales}}$	Net income in each sales dollar
Gross margin ratio	$= \dfrac{\text{Net sales} - \text{Cost of goods sold}}{\text{Net sales}}$	Gross margin in each sales dollar
Return on total assets	$= \dfrac{\text{Net income}}{\text{Average total assets}}$	Overall profitability of assets
Return on common stockholders' equity	$= \dfrac{\text{Net income} - \text{Preferred dividends}}{\text{Average common stockholders' equity}}$	Profitability of owner investment
Book value per common share	$= \dfrac{\text{Shareholders' equity applicable to common shares}}{\text{Number of common shares outstanding}}$	Liquidation at reported amounts
Basic earnings per share	$= \dfrac{\text{Net income} - \text{Preferred dividends}}{\text{Weighted-average common shares outstanding}}$	Net income per common share
Market Prospects		
Price-earnings ratio	$= \dfrac{\text{Market price per common share}}{\text{Earnings per share}}$	Market value relative to earnings
Dividend yield	$= \dfrac{\text{Annual cash dividends per share}}{\text{Market price per share}}$	Cash return per common share

* Additional ratios also examined in previous chapters included credit risk ratio; plant asset useful life; plant asset age; days' cash expense coverage; cash coverage of growth; cash coverage of debt; free cash flow; cash flow on total assets; and payout ratio.

GLOBAL VIEW

The analysis and interpretation of financial statements is, of course, impacted by the accounting system in effect. This section discusses similarities and differences for analysis of financial statements when prepared under U.S. GAAP vis-à-vis IFRS.

Horizontal and Vertical Analyses Horizontal and vertical analyses help eliminate many differences between U.S. GAAP and IFRS when analyzing and interpreting financial statements. Financial numbers are converted to percentages that are, in the best case scenario, consistently applied across and within periods. This enables users to effectively compare companies across reporting regimes. However, when fundamental differences in reporting regimes impact financial statements, such as with certain recognition rule differences, the user must exercise caution when drawing conclusions. Some users will reformulate one set of numbers to be more consistent with the other system to enable comparative analysis. This reformulation process is covered in advanced courses. The important point is that horizontal and vertical analyses help strip away differences between the reporting regimes, but several key differences sometimes remain and require adjustment of the numbers. **Nokia** reports the following partial vertical analysis to its shareholders as part of its MD&A report.

NOKIA

As a Percentage of Revenue	2010
Research and development	6.5%
Selling, marketing and administration	12.8
Amortization	2.1
Litigation	1.1
Total operating expenses	22.5%

Ratio Analysis Ratio analysis of financial statement numbers has many of the advantages and disadvantages of horizontal and vertical analyses discussed above. Importantly, ratio analysis is useful for business decisions, with some possible changes in interpretation depending on what is and what is not included in accounting measures across U.S. GAAP and IFRS. Still, we must take care in drawing inferences from a comparison of ratios across reporting regimes because what a number measures can differ across regimes. **Nokia** offers the following example of its own ratio analysis applied to gross margin: "Consolidated gross margin increased by $1.48 billion, or 29.2%, to $6.58 billion, or 44.0% of revenue, in fiscal 2010, compared to $5.10 billion, or 46.1% of revenue, in fiscal 2009. The decrease of 2.1% in consolidated gross margin percentage was primarily due to a decrease in the blended device margins."

Decision Insight

Not Created Equal Financial regulation has several goals. Two of them are to ensure adequate accounting disclosure and to strengthen corporate governance. For disclosure purposes, companies must now provide details of related-party transactions and material off-balance-sheet agreements. This is motivated by several major frauds. For corporate governance, the CEO and CFO must now certify the fairness of financial statements and the effectiveness of internal controls. Yet, concerns remain. A study reports that 23% of management and administrative employees observed activities that posed a conflict of interest in the past year (KPMG 2009). Another 12% witnessed the falsifying or manipulating of accounting information. The bottom line: All financial statements are not of equal quality. ■

 Decision Analysis    Analysis Reporting

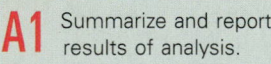

Understanding the purpose of financial statement analysis is crucial to the usefulness of any analysis. This understanding leads to efficiency of effort, effectiveness in application, and relevance in focus. The purpose of most financial statement analyses is to reduce uncertainty in business decisions through a rigorous and sound evaluation. A *financial statement analysis report* helps by directly addressing the building blocks of analysis and by identifying weaknesses in inference by requiring explanation: It forces us to organize our reasoning and to verify its flow and logic. A report also serves as a communication link with readers, and the writing process reinforces our judgments and vice versa. Finally, the report helps us (re)evaluate evidence and refine conclusions on key building blocks. A good analysis report usually consists of six sections:

1. **Executive summary**—brief focus on important analysis results and conclusions.
2. **Analysis overview**—background on the company, its industry, and its economic setting.
3. **Evidential matter**—financial statements and information used in the analysis, including ratios, trends, comparisons, statistics, and all analytical measures assembled; often organized under the building blocks of analysis.
4. **Assumptions**—identification of important assumptions regarding a company's industry and economic environment, and other important assumptions for estimates.
5. **Key factors**—list of important favorable and unfavorable factors, both quantitative and qualitative, for company performance; usually organized by areas of analysis.
6. **Inferences**—forecasts, estimates, interpretations, and conclusions drawing on all sections of the report.

We must remember that the user dictates relevance, meaning that the analysis report should include a brief table of contents to help readers focus on those areas most relevant to their decisions. All irrelevant matter must be eliminated. For example, decades-old details of obscure transactions and detailed miscues of the analysis are irrelevant. Ambiguities and qualifications to avoid responsibility or hedging inferences must be eliminated. Finally, writing is important. Mistakes in grammar and errors of fact compromise the report's credibility.

Decision **Insight**

Short Selling *Short selling* refers to selling stock before you buy it. Here's an example: You borrow 100 shares of Nike stock, sell them at $40 each, and receive money from their sale. You then wait. You hope that Nike's stock price falls to, say, $35 each and you can replace the borrowed stock for less than you sold it for, reaping a profit of $5 each less any transaction costs. ■

DEMONSTRATION PROBLEM

Use the following financial statements of Precision Co. to complete these requirements.

1. Prepare comparative income statements showing the percent increase or decrease for year 2011 in comparison to year 2010.
2. Prepare common-size comparative balance sheets for years 2011 and 2010.
3. Compute the following ratios as of December 31, 2011, or for the year ended December 31, 2011, and identify its building block category for financial statement analysis.
   a. Current ratio
   b. Acid-test ratio
   c. Accounts receivable turnover
   d. Days' sales uncollected
   e. Inventory turnover
   f. Debt ratio
   g. Debt-to-equity ratio
   h. Times interest earned
   i. Profit margin ratio
   j. Total asset turnover
   k. Return on total assets
   l. Return on common stockholders' equity

PRECISION COMPANY
Comparative Income Statements
For Years Ended December 31, 2011 and 2010

	2011	2010
Sales	$2,486,000	$2,075,000
Cost of goods sold	1,523,000	1,222,000
Gross profit	963,000	853,000
Operating expenses		
Advertising expense	145,000	100,000
Sales salaries expense	240,000	280,000
Office salaries expense	165,000	200,000
Insurance expense	100,000	45,000
Supplies expense	26,000	35,000
Depreciation expense	85,000	75,000
Miscellaneous expenses	17,000	15,000
Total operating expenses	778,000	750,000
Operating income	185,000	103,000
Interest expense	44,000	46,000
Income before taxes	141,000	57,000
Income taxes	47,000	19,000
Net income	$ 94,000	$ 38,000
Earnings per share	$ 0.99	$ 0.40

PRECISION COMPANY
Comparative Balance Sheets
December 31, 2011 and 2010

	2011	2010
Assets		
Current assets		
Cash	$ 79,000	$ 42,000
Short-term investments	65,000	96,000
Accounts receivable, net	120,000	100,000
Merchandise inventory	250,000	265,000
Total current assets	514,000	503,000
Plant assets		
Store equipment, net	400,000	350,000
Office equipment, net	45,000	50,000
Buildings, net	625,000	675,000
Land	100,000	100,000
Total plant assets	1,170,000	1,175,000
Total assets	$1,684,000	$1,678,000
Liabilities		
Current liabilities		
Accounts payable	$ 164,000	$ 190,000
Short-term notes payable	75,000	90,000
Taxes payable	26,000	12,000
Total current liabilities	265,000	292,000
Long-term liabilities		
Notes payable (secured by		
mortgage on buildings)	400,000	420,000
Total liabilities	665,000	712,000
Stockholders' Equity		
Common stock, $5 par value	475,000	475,000
Retained earnings	544,000	491,000
Total stockholders' equity	1,019,000	966,000
Total liabilities and equity	$1,684,000	$1,678,000

PLANNING THE SOLUTION

- Set up a four-column income statement; enter the 2011 and 2010 amounts in the first two columns and then enter the dollar change in the third column and the percent change from 2010 in the fourth column.
- Set up a four-column balance sheet; enter the 2011 and 2010 year-end amounts in the first two columns and then compute and enter the amount of each item as a percent of total assets.
- Compute the required ratios using the data provided. Use the average of beginning and ending amounts when appropriate (see Exhibit 13.16 for definitions).

SOLUTION TO DEMONSTRATION PROBLEM

1.

PRECISION COMPANY
Comparative Income Statements
For Years Ended December 31, 2011 and 2010

	2011	2010	Increase (Decrease) in 2011 Amount	Increase (Decrease) in 2011 Percent
Sales	$2,486,000	$2,075,000	$411,000	19.8%
Cost of goods sold	1,523,000	1,222,000	301,000	24.6
Gross profit	963,000	853,000	110,000	12.9

[continued on next page]

[continued from previous page]

Operating expenses				
Advertising expense	145,000	100,000	45,000	45.0
Sales salaries expense	240,000	280,000	(40,000)	(14.3)
Office salaries expense	165,000	200,000	(35,000)	(17.5)
Insurance expense	100,000	45,000	55,000	122.2
Supplies expense	26,000	35,000	(9,000)	(25.7)
Depreciation expense	85,000	75,000	10,000	13.3
Miscellaneous expenses	17,000	15,000	2,000	13.3
Total operating expenses	778,000	750,000	28,000	3.7
Operating income	185,000	103,000	82,000	79.6
Interest expense	44,000	46,000	(2,000)	(4.3)
Income before taxes	141,000	57,000	84,000	147.4
Income taxes	47,000	19,000	28,000	147.4
Net income	$ 94,000	$ 38,000	$ 56,000	147.4
Earnings per share	$ 0.99	$ 0.40	$ 0.59	147.5

2.

PRECISION COMPANY
Common-Size Comparative Balance Sheets
December 31, 2011 and 2010

	December 31		Common-Size Percents	
	2011	2010	2011*	2010*
Assets				
Current assets				
Cash	$ 79,000	$ 42,000	4.7%	2.5%
Short-term investments	65,000	96,000	3.9	5.7
Accounts receivable, net	120,000	100,000	7.1	6.0
Merchandise inventory	250,000	265,000	14.8	15.8
Total current assets	514,000	503,000	30.5	30.0
Plant assets				
Store equipment, net	400,000	350,000	23.8	20.9
Office equipment, net	45,000	50,000	2.7	3.0
Buildings, net	625,000	675,000	37.1	40.2
Land	100,000	100,000	5.9	6.0
Total plant assets	1,170,000	1,175,000	69.5	70.0
Total assets	$1,684,000	$1,678,000	100.0	100.0
Liabilities				
Current liabilities				
Accounts payable	$ 164,000	$ 190,000	9.7%	11.3%
Short-term notes payable	75,000	90,000	4.5	5.4
Taxes payable	26,000	12,000	1.5	0.7
Total current liabilities	265,000	292,000	15.7	17.4
Long-term liabilities				
Notes payable (secured by mortgage on buildings)	400,000	420,000	23.8	25.0
Total liabilities	665,000	712,000	39.5	42.4
Stockholders' equity				
Common stock, $5 par value	475,000	475,000	28.2	28.3
Retained earnings	544,000	491,000	32.3	29.3
Total stockholders' equity	1,019,000	966,000	60.5	57.6
Total liabilities and equity	$1,684,000	$1,678,000	100.0	100.0

* Columns do not always exactly add to 100 due to rounding.

3. **Ratios for 2011:**

   a. Current ratio: $514,000/$265,000 = 1.9:1 (liquidity and efficiency)

   b. Acid-test ratio: ($79,000 + $65,000 + $120,000)/$265,000 = 1.0:1 (liquidity and efficiency)

   c. Average receivables: ($120,000 + $100,000)/2 = $110,000
   Accounts receivable turnover: $2,486,000/$110,000 = 22.6 times (liquidity and efficiency)

   d. Days' sales uncollected: ($120,000/$2,486,000) × 365 = 17.6 days (liquidity and efficiency)

   e. Average inventory: ($250,000 + $265,000)/2 = $257,500
   Inventory turnover: $1,523,000/$257,500 = 5.9 times (liquidity and efficiency)

   f. Debt ratio: $665,000/$1,684,000 = 39.5% (solvency)

   g. Debt-to-equity ratio: $665,000/$1,019,000 = 0.65 (solvency)

   h. Times interest earned: $185,000/$44,000 = 4.2 times (solvency)

   i. Profit margin ratio: $94,000/$2,486,000 = 3.8% (profitability)

   j. Average total assets: ($1,684,000 + $1,678,000)/2 = $1,681,000
   Total asset turnover: $2,486,000/$1,681,000 = 1.48 times (liquidity and efficiency)

   k. Return on total assets: $94,000/$1,681,000 = 5.6% or 3.8% × 1.48 = 5.6% (profitability)

   l. Average total common equity: ($1,019,000 + $966,000)/2 = $992,500
   Return on common stockholders' equity: $94,000/$992,500 = 9.5% (profitability)

APPENDIX

13A

Sustainable Income

A2 Explain the form and assess the content of a complete income statement.

When a company's revenue and expense transactions are from normal, continuing operations, a simple income statement is usually adequate. When a company's activities include income-related events not part of its normal, continuing operations, it must disclose information to help users understand these events and predict future performance. To meet these objectives, companies separate the income statement into continuing operations, discontinued segments, extraordinary items, comprehensive income, and earnings per share. For illustration, Exhibit 13A.1 shows such an income statement for ComUS. These separate distinctions help us measure *sustainable income,* which is the income level most likely to continue into the future. Sustainable income is commonly used in PE ratios and other market-based measures of performance.

Continuing Operations   The first major section (①) shows the revenues, expenses, and income from continuing operations. Users especially rely on this information to predict future operations. Many users view this section as the most important. Earlier chapters explained the items comprising income from continuing operations.

Discontinued Segments   A **business segment** is a part of a company's operations that serves a particular line of business or class of customers. A segment has assets, liabilities, and financial results of operations that can be distinguished from those of other parts of the company. A company's gain or loss from selling or closing down a segment is separately reported. Section ② of Exhibit 13A.1 reports both (1) income from operating the discontinued segment for the current period prior to its disposal and (2) the loss from disposing of the segment's net assets. The income tax effects of each are reported separately from the income taxes expense in section ①.

Extraordinary Items   Section ③ reports **extraordinary gains and losses,** which are those that are *both unusual* and *infrequent.* An **unusual gain or loss** is abnormal or otherwise unrelated to the company's regular activities and environment. An **infrequent gain or loss** is not expected to recur given the company's operating environment. Reporting extraordinary items in a separate category helps users predict future performance, absent the effects of extraordinary items. Items usually considered extraordinary include (1) expropriation (taking away) of property by a foreign government, (2) condemning of property by a domestic government body, (3) prohibition against using an asset by a newly enacted law, and (4) losses and gains from an unusual and infrequent calamity ("act of God"). Items *not* considered extraordinary include (1) write-downs of inventories and write-offs of receivables, (2) gains and losses from disposing of segments, and (3) financial effects of labor strikes.

EXHIBIT 13A.1

Income Statement (all-inclusive) for a Corporation

ComUS Income Statement For Year Ended December 31, 2011		
Net sales		$8,478,000
Operating expenses		
Cost of goods sold	$5,950,000	
Depreciation expense	35,000	
Other selling, general, and administrative expenses	515,000	
Interest expense	20,000	
① Total operating expenses		(6,520,000)
Other gains (losses)		
Loss on plant relocation		(45,000)
Gain on sale of surplus land		72,000
Income from continuing operations before taxes		1,985,000
Income taxes expense		(595,500)
Income from continuing operations		1,389,500
Discontinued segment		
② Income from operating Division A (net of $180,000 taxes)	420,000	
Loss on disposal of Division A (net of $66,000 tax benefit)	(154,000)	266,000
Income before extraordinary items		1,655,500
Extraordinary items		
③ Gain on land expropriated by state (net of $85,200 taxes)	198,800	
Loss from earthquake damage (net of $270,000 tax benefit)	(630,000)	(431,200)
Net income		$1,224,300
Earnings per common share (200,000 outstanding shares)		
Income from continuing operations		$ 6.95
Discontinued operations		1.33
④ Income before extraordinary items		8.28
Extraordinary items		(2.16)
Net income (basic earnings per share)		$ 6.12

Gains and losses that are neither unusual nor infrequent are reported as part of continuing operations. Gains and losses that are *either* unusual *or* infrequent, but *not* both, are reported as part of continuing operations *but* after the normal revenues and expenses.

Decision Maker   Answer — p. 581

Small Business Owner   You own an orange grove near Jacksonville, Florida. A bad frost destroys about one-half of your oranges. You are currently preparing an income statement for a bank loan. Can you claim the loss of oranges as extraordinary? ∎

Earnings per Share   The final section ④ of the income statement in Exhibit 13A.1 reports earnings per share for each of the three subcategories of income (continuing operations, discontinued segments, and extraordinary items) when they exist. Earnings per share is discussed in Chapter 11.

Changes in Accounting Principles   The *consistency concept* directs a company to apply the same accounting principles across periods. Yet a company can change from one acceptable accounting principle (such as FIFO, LIFO, or weighted-average) to another as long as the change improves the usefulness of information in its financial statements. A footnote would describe the accounting change and why it is an improvement.

Changes in accounting principles require retrospective application to prior periods' financial statements. *Retrospective application* involves applying a different accounting principle to prior periods as if that principle had always been used. Retrospective application enhances the consistency of financial information between periods, which improves the usefulness of information, especially with comparative

Point: Changes in principles are sometimes required when new accounting standards are issued.

analyses. (Prior to 2005, the cumulative effect of changes in accounting principles was recognized in net income in the period of the change.) Accounting standards also require that *a change in depreciation, amortization, or depletion method for long-term operating assets is accounted for as a change in accounting estimate*—that is, prospectively over current and future periods. This reflects the notion that an entity should change its depreciation, amortization, or depletion method only with changes in estimated asset benefits, the pattern of benefit usage, or information about those benefits.

Quick Check   Answers — p. 581

13. Which of the following is an extraordinary item? (*a*) a settlement paid to a customer injured while using the company's product, (*b*) a loss to a plant from damages caused by a meteorite, or (*c*) a loss from selling old equipment.

14. Identify the four major sections of an income statement that are potentially reportable.

15. A company using FIFO for the past 15 years decides to switch to LIFO. The effect of this event on prior years' net income is (*a*) reported as if the new method had always been used; (*b*) ignored because it is a change in an accounting estimate; or (*c*) reported on the current year income statement.

Summary

C1 **Explain the purpose and identify the building blocks of analysis.** The purpose of financial statement analysis is to help users make better business decisions. Internal users want information to improve company efficiency and effectiveness in providing products and services. External users want information to make better and more informed decisions in pursuing their goals. The common goals of all users are to evaluate a company's (1) past and current performance, (2) current financial position, and (3) future performance and risk. Financial statement analysis focuses on four "building blocks" of analysis: (1) liquidity and efficiency—ability to meet short-term obligations and efficiently generate revenues; (2) solvency—ability to generate future revenues and meet long-term obligations; (3) profitability—ability to provide financial rewards sufficient to attract and retain financing; and (4) market prospects—ability to generate positive market expectations.

C2 **Describe standards for comparisons in analysis.** Standards for comparisons include (1) intracompany—prior performance and relations between financial items for the company under analysis; (2) competitor—one or more direct competitors of the company; (3) industry—industry statistics; and (4) guidelines (rules of thumb)—general standards developed from past experiences and personal judgments.

A1 **Summarize and report results of analysis.** A financial statement analysis report is often organized around the building blocks of analysis. A good report separates interpretations and conclusions of analysis from the information underlying them. An analysis report often consists of six sections: (1) executive summary, (2) analysis overview, (3) evidential matter, (4) assumptions, (5) key factors, and (6) inferences.

A2ᴬ **Explain the form and assess the content of a complete income statement.** An income statement has four *potential* sections: (1) continuing operations, (2) discontinued segments, (3) extraordinary items, and (4) earnings per share.

P1 **Explain and apply methods of horizontal analysis.** Horizontal analysis is a tool to evaluate changes in data across time. Two important tools of horizontal analysis are comparative statements and trend analysis. Comparative statements show amounts for two or more successive periods, often with changes disclosed in both absolute and percent terms. Trend analysis is used to reveal important changes occurring from one period to the next.

P2 **Describe and apply methods of vertical analysis.** Vertical analysis is a tool to evaluate each financial statement item or group of items in terms of a base amount. Two tools of vertical analysis are common-size statements and graphical analyses. Each item in common-size statements is expressed as a percent of a base amount. For the balance sheet, the base amount is usually total assets, and for the income statement, it is usually sales.

P3 **Define and apply ratio analysis.** Ratio analysis provides clues to and symptoms of underlying conditions. Ratios, properly interpreted, identify areas requiring further investigation. A ratio expresses a mathematical relation between two quantities such as a percent, rate, or proportion. Ratios can be organized into the building blocks of analysis: (1) liquidity and efficiency, (2) solvency, (3) profitability, and (4) market prospects.

Guidance Answers to Decision Maker

Auditor The *joint relation* referred to is the combined increase in sales and the decrease in expenses yielding more than a 5% increase in income. Both *individual* accounts (sales and expenses) yield percent changes within the ±5% acceptable range. However, a joint analysis suggests a different picture. For example, consider a joint analysis using the profit margin ratio. The client's profit margin is 11.46% ($206,000 − $182,400/$206,000) for the current year compared with 5.0% ($200,000 − $190,000/$200,000) for the prior year—yielding a 129% increase in profit margin! This is what concerns the partner, and it suggests expanding audit tests to verify or refute the client's figures.

Banker   Your decision on the loan application is positive for at least two reasons. First, the current ratio suggests a strong ability to meet short-term obligations. Second, current assets of $160,000 and a current ratio of 4:1 imply current liabilities of $40,000 (one-fourth of current assets) and a working capital excess of $120,000. This working capital excess is 60% of the loan amount. However, if the application is for a 10-year loan, our decision is less optimistic. The

current ratio and working capital suggest a good safety margin, but indications of inefficiency in operations exist. In particular, a 4:1 current ratio is more than double its key competitors' ratio. This is characteristic of inefficient asset use.

Small Business Owner   The frost loss is probably not extraordinary. Jacksonville experiences enough recurring frost damage to make it difficult to argue this event is both unusual and infrequent. Still, you want to highlight the frost loss and hope the bank views this uncommon event separately from continuing operations.

Guidance Answers to Quick Checks

1. General-purpose financial statements are intended for a variety of users interested in a company's financial condition and performance—users without the power to require specialized financial reports to meet their specific needs.

2. General-purpose financial statements include the income statement, balance sheet, statement of stockholders' (owners') equity, and statement of cash flows plus the notes related to these statements.

3. *a*

4. Data from one or more direct competitors are usually preferred for comparative purposes.

5. *d*

6. Percents on comparative income statements show the increase or decrease in each item from one period to the next. On common-size comparative income statements, each item is shown as a percent of net sales for that period.

7. *c*

8. (a) ($820,000 + $240,000 + $470,000)/
    ($350,000 + $180,000) = 2.9 to 1.

   (b) ($820,000 + $240,000)/($350,000 + $180,000) = 2:1.

9. (a) $2,500,000/[($290,000 + $240,000)/2] = 9.43 times.

   (b) ($290,000/$2,500,000) × 365 = 42 days.

   (c) $750,000/[($530,000 + $470,000)/2] = 1.5 times.

   (d) ($530,000/$750,000) × 365 = 258 days.

10. *c*

11. *b*

12. $\text{Profit margin} \times \dfrac{\text{Total asset}}{\text{turnover}} = \dfrac{\text{Return on}}{\text{total assets}}$

    $\dfrac{\$945,000}{\$8,500,000} \times 1.8 = 20\%$

13. (b)

14. The four (potentially reportable) major sections are income from continuing operations, discontinued segments, extraordinary items, and earnings per share.

15. (a); known as retrospective application.

Key Terms

mhhe.com/wildFINMAN4e

Business segment (p. 578)
Common-size financial statement (p. 561)
Comparative financial statements (p. 556)
Efficiency (p. 555)
Equity ratio (p. 569)
Extraordinary gains and losses (p. 578)
Financial reporting (p. 555)

Financial statement analysis (p. 554)
General-purpose financial statements (p. 555)
Horizontal analysis (p. 556)
Infrequent gain or loss (p. 578)
Liquidity (p. 555)
Market prospects (p. 555)

Profitability (p. 555)
Ratio analysis (p. 556)
Solvency (p. 555)
Unusual gain or loss (p. 578)
Vertical analysis (p. 556)
Working capital (p. 565)

Multiple Choice Quiz

Answers on p. 597   mhhe.com/wildFINMAN4e

Additional Quiz Questions are available at the book's Website.

1. A company's sales in 2010 were $300,000 and in 2011 were $351,000. Using 2010 as the base year, the sales trend percent for 2011 is:

   a. 17%
   b. 85%
   c. 100%
   d. 117%
   e. 48%

Use the following information for questions 2 through 5.

GALLOWAY COMPANY
Balance Sheet
December 31, 2011

Assets

Cash	$ 86,000
Accounts receivable	76,000
Merchandise inventory	122,000
Prepaid insurance	12,000
Long-term investments	98,000
Plant assets, net	436,000
Total assets	$830,000

Liabilities and Equity

Current liabilities	$124,000
Long-term liabilities	90,000
Common stock	300,000
Retained earnings	316,000
Total liabilities and equity	$830,000

2. What is Galloway Company's current ratio?
   a. 0.69
   b. 1.31

   c. 3.88
   d. 6.69
   e. 2.39

3. What is Galloway Company's acid-test ratio?
   a. 2.39
   b. 0.69
   c. 1.31
   d. 6.69
   e. 3.88

4. What is Galloway Company's debt ratio?
   a. 25.78%
   b. 100.00%
   c. 74.22%
   d. 137.78%
   e. 34.74%

5. What is Galloway Company's equity ratio?
   a. 25.78%
   b. 100.00%
   c. 34.74%
   d. 74.22%
   e. 137.78%

^A Superscript letter A denotes assignments based on Appendix 13A.

  Icon denotes assignments that involve decision making.

Discussion Questions

1. What is the difference between comparative financial statements and common-size comparative statements?

2. Which items are usually assigned a 100% value on (*a*) a common-size balance sheet and (*b*) a common-size income statement?

3. Explain the difference between financial reporting and financial statements.

4. What three factors would influence your evaluation as to whether a company's current ratio is good or bad?

5. Suggest several reasons why a 2:1 current ratio might not be adequate for a particular company.

6. Why is working capital given special attention in the process of analyzing balance sheets?

7. What does the number of days' sales uncollected indicate?

8. What does a relatively high accounts receivable turnover indicate about a company's short-term liquidity?

9. Why is a company's capital structure, as measured by debt and equity ratios, important to financial statement analysts?

10. How does inventory turnover provide information about a company's short-term liquidity?

11. What ratios would you compute to evaluate management performance?

12. Why would a company's return on total assets be different from its return on common stockholders' equity?

13. Where on the income statement does a company report an unusual gain not expected to occur more often than once every two years or so?

14. Use **Research In Motion**'s financial statements in Appendix A to compute its return on total assets for fiscal years ended February 27, 2010, and February 28, 2009. Total assets at March 1, 2008, were $5,511,187 (in thousands).   RIM

15. Refer to **Palm**'s financial statements in Appendix A to compute its equity ratio as of May 31, 2009 and May 31, 2008.   Palm

16. Refer to **Nokia**'s financial statements in Appendix A. Compute its debt ratio as of December 31, 2009, and December 31, 2008.   NOKIA

17. Refer to **Apple**'s financial statements in Appendix A. Compute its profit margin for the fiscal year ended September 26, 2009.   Apple

Mc Graw Hill connect

Which of the following items (1) through (9) are part of financial reporting but are *not* included as part of general-purpose financial statements? (1) stock price information and analysis, (2) statement of cash flows, (3) management discussion and analysis of financial performance, (4) income statement, (5) company news releases, (6) balance sheet, (7) financial statement notes, (8) statement of shareholders' equity, (9) prospectus.

QUICK STUDY

QS 13-1
Financial reporting   C1

What are four possible standards of comparison used to analyze financial statement ratios? Which of these is generally considered to be the most useful? Which one is least likely to provide a good basis for comparison?

QS 13-2
Standard of comparison   C2

Use the following information for Tipster Corporation to determine the 2010 and 2011 trend percents for net sales using 2010 as the base year.

QS 13-3
Trend percents

P1

($ thousands)	2011	2010
Net sales	$201,600	$114,800
Cost of goods sold	109,200	60,200

Refer to the information in QS 13-3. Use that information for Tipster Corporation to determine the 2010 and 2011 common-size percents for cost of goods sold using net sales as the base.

QS 13-4
Common-size analysis   P2

Compute the annual dollar changes and percent changes for each of the following accounts.

QS 13-5
Horizontal analysis

P1

	2011	2010
Short-term investments	$217,800	$165,000
Accounts receivable	42,120	48,000
Notes payable	57,000	0

For each ratio listed, identify whether the change in ratio value from 2010 to 2011 is usually regarded as favorable or unfavorable.

QS 13-6
Ratio interpretation

P3

Ratio	2011	2010	Ratio	2011	2010
1. Profit margin	8%	6%	5. Accounts receivable turnover	5.4	6.6
2. Debt ratio	45%	40%	6. Basic earnings per share	$1.24	$1.20
3. Gross margin	33%	45%	7. Inventory turnover	3.5	3.3
4. Acid-test ratio	0.99	1.10	8. Dividend yield	1%	0.8%

The following information is available for Silverado Company and Titan Company, similar firms operating in the same industry. Write a half-page report comparing Silverado and Titan using the available information. Your discussion should include their ability to meet current obligations and to use current assets efficiently.

QS 13-7
Analysis of short-term financial condition

A1

Microsoft Excel - Book1

File Edit View Insert Format Tools Data Accounting Window Help

100% Arial 10 B I U $ %

	Silverado			Titan		
	2012	2011	2010	2012	2011	2010
Current ratio	1.6	1.7	2.0	3.1	2.6	1.8
Acid-test ratio	0.9	1.0	1.1	2.7	2.4	1.5
Accounts receivable turnover	29.5	24.2	28.2	15.4	14.2	15.0
Merchandise inventory turnover	23.2	20.9	16.1	13.5	12.0	11.6
Working capital	$60,000	$48,000	$42,000	$121,000	$93,000	$68,000

Sheet1 Sheet2 Sheet3

Team Project: Assume that the two companies apply for a one-year loan from the team. Identify additional information the companies must provide before the team can make a loan decision.

QS 13-8ᴬ
Error adjustments
A2

A review of the notes payable files discovers that three years ago the company reported the entire amount of a payment (principal and interest) on an installment note payable as interest expense. This mistake had a material effect on the amount of income in that year. How should the correction be reported in the current year financial statements?

QS 13-9
International ratio analysis
C2

Answer each of the following related to international accounting and analysis.
a. Identify an advantage to using horizontal and vertical analyses when examining companies reporting under different currencies.
b. Identify a limitation to using ratio analysis when examining companies reporting under different accounting systems such as IFRS versus U.S. GAAP.

EXERCISES

Exercise 13-1
Building blocks of analysis
C1

Match the ratio to the building block of financial statement analysis to which it best relates.
A. Liquidity and efficiency   **C.** Profitability
B. Solvency   **D.** Market prospects

1. _____ Book value per common share   6. _____ Gross margin ratio
2. _____ Days' sales in inventory   7. _____ Acid-test ratio
3. _____ Accounts receivable turnover   8. _____ Equity ratio
4. _____ Debt-to-equity   9. _____ Return on total assets
5. _____ Times interest earned   10. _____ Dividend yield

Exercise 13-2
Identifying financial ratios
C2

1. Which two short-term liquidity ratios measure how frequently a company collects its accounts?
2. What measure reflects the difference between current assets and current liabilities?
3. Which two ratios are key components in measuring a company's operating efficiency? Which ratio summarizes these two components?

Exercise 13-3
Computation and analysis of trend percents
P1

Compute trend percents for the following accounts, using 2009 as the base year. State whether the situation as revealed by the trends appears to be favorable or unfavorable for each account.

	2013	2012	2011	2010	2009
Sales	$283,880	$271,800	$253,680	$235,560	$151,000
Cost of goods sold	129,200	123,080	116,280	107,440	68,000
Accounts receivable	19,100	18,300	17,400	16,200	10,000

Exercise 13-4
Determination of income effects from common-size and trend percents
P1 P2

Common-size and trend percents for Aziz Company's sales, cost of goods sold, and expenses follow. Determine whether net income increased, decreased, or remained unchanged in this three-year period.

	Common-Size Percents			Trend Percents		
	2012	2011	2010	2012	2011	2010
Sales	100.0%	100.0%	100.0%	104.4%	103.2%	100.0%
Cost of goods sold	62.4	60.9	58.1	102.0	108.1	100.0
Total expenses	14.3	13.8	14.1	105.9	101.0	100.0

Express the following comparative income statements in common-size percents and assess whether or not this company's situation has improved in the most recent year.

Exercise 13-5
Common-size percent
computation and interpretation

P2

GERALDO CORPORATION Comparative Income Statements For Years Ended December 31, 2011 and 2010		
	2011	**2010**
Sales	$720,000	$535,000
Cost of goods sold	475,200	280,340
Gross profit	244,800	254,660
Operating expenses	151,200	103,790
Net income	$ 93,600	$150,870

Rolf Company and Kent Company are similar firms that operate in the same industry. Kent began operations in 2011 and Rolf in 2008. In 2013, both companies pay 7% interest on their debt to creditors. The following additional information is available.

Exercise 13-6
Analysis of efficiency and
financial leverage

A1

	Rolf Company			Kent Company		
	2013	2012	2011	2013	2012	2011
Total asset turnover	3.0	2.7	2.9	1.6	1.4	1.1
Return on total assets	8.9%	9.5%	8.7%	5.8%	5.5%	5.2%
Profit margin ratio	2.3%	2.4%	2.2%	2.7%	2.9%	2.8%
Sales	$400,000	$370,000	$386,000	$200,000	$160,000	$100,000

Write a half-page report comparing Rolf and Kent using the available information. Your analysis should include their ability to use assets efficiently to produce profits. Also comment on their success in employing financial leverage in 2013.

Sanderson Company's year-end balance sheets follow. Express the balance sheets in common-size percents. Round amounts to the nearest one-tenth of a percent. Analyze and comment on the results.

Exercise 13-7
Common-size percents

P2

At December 31	2012	2011	2010
Assets			
Cash	$ 30,800	$ 35,625	$ 36,800
Accounts receivable, net	88,500	62,500	49,200
Merchandise inventory	111,500	82,500	53,000
Prepaid expenses	9,700	9,375	4,000
Plant assets, net	277,500	255,000	229,500
Total assets	$518,000	$445,000	$372,500
Liabilities and Equity			
Accounts payable	$128,900	$ 75,250	$ 49,250
Long-term notes payable secured by mortgages on plant assets	97,500	102,500	82,500
Common stock, $10 par value	162,500	162,500	162,500
Retained earnings	129,100	104,750	78,250
Total liabilities and equity	$518,000	$445,000	$372,500

Refer to Sanderson Company's balance sheets in Exercise 13-7. Analyze its year-end short-term liquidity position at the end of 2012, 2011, and 2010 by computing (1) the current ratio and (2) the acid-test ratio. Comment on the ratio results. (Round ratio amounts to two decimals.)

Exercise 13-8
Liquidity analysis

P3

Exercise 13-9
Liquidity analysis and
interpretation
P3

Refer to the Sanderson Company information in Exercise 13-7. The company's income statements for the
years ended December 31, 2012 and 2011, follow. Assume that all sales are on credit and then compute:
(1) days' sales uncollected, (2) accounts receivable turnover, (3) inventory turnover, and (4) days' sales in
inventory. Comment on the changes in the ratios from 2011 to 2012. (Round amounts to one decimal.)

For Year Ended December 31	2012		2011	
Sales		$672,500		$530,000
Cost of goods sold	$410,225		$344,500	
Other operating expenses	208,550		133,980	
Interest expense	11,100		12,300	
Income taxes	8,525		7,845	
Total costs and expenses		638,400		498,625
Net income		$ 34,100		$ 31,375
Earnings per share		$ 2.10		$ 1.93

Exercise 13-10
Risk and capital structure
analysis P3

Refer to the Sanderson Company information in Exercises 13-7 and 13-9. Compare the company's long-
term risk and capital structure positions at the end of 2012 and 2011 by computing these ratios: (1) debt
and equity ratios, (2) debt-to-equity ratio, and (3) times interest earned. Comment on these ratio results.

Exercise 13-11
Efficiency and
profitability analysis P3

Refer to Sanderson Company's financial information in Exercises 13-7 and 13-9. Evaluate the company's
efficiency and profitability by computing the following for 2012 and 2011: (1) profit margin ratio, (2) total
asset turnover, and (3) return on total assets. Comment on these ratio results.

Exercise 13-12
Profitability analysis
P3

Refer to Sanderson Company's financial information in Exercises 13-7 and 13-9. Additional information
about the company follows. To help evaluate the company's profitability, compute and interpret the following ratios for 2012 and 2011: (1) return on common stockholders' equity, (2) price-earnings ratio on
December 31, and (3) dividend yield.

Common stock market price, December 31, 2012	$15.00
Common stock market price, December 31, 2011	14.00
Annual cash dividends per share in 2012	0.30
Annual cash dividends per share in 2011	0.15

Exercise 13-13ᴬ
Income statement categories
A2

In 2011, Jin Merchandising, Inc., sold its interest in a chain of retail outlets, taking the company completely
out of the retailing business. The company still operates its wholesale outlets. A listing of the major sections
of an income statement follows:

A. Income (loss) from continuing operations
B. Income (loss) from operating, or gain (loss) from disposing, a discontinued segment
C. Extraordinary gain (loss)

Indicate where each of the following income-related items for this company appears on its 2011 income
statement by writing the letter of the appropriate section in the blank beside each item.

Section	Item	Debit	Credit
_____	1. Net sales		$3,000,000
_____	2. Gain on state's condemnation of company property (net of tax)		330,000
_____	3. Salaries expense	$ 640,000	
_____	4. Income taxes expense	117,000	
_____	5. Depreciation expense	432,500	
_____	6. Gain on sale of retail business segment (net of tax)		875,000
_____	7. Loss from operating retail business segment (net of tax)	544,000	
_____	8. Cost of goods sold	1,580,000	

Use the financial data for Jin Merchandising, Inc., in Exercise 13-13 to prepare its income statement for calendar year 2011. (Ignore the earnings per share section.)

Exercise 13-14[A]
Income statement presentation
A2

Nintendo Company, Ltd., reports the following financial information as of, or for the year ended, March 31, 2008. Nintendo reports its financial statements in both Japanese yen and U.S. dollars as shown (amounts in millions).

Exercise 13-15
Ratio analysis under different currencies

P3

Current assets	¥1,646,834	$16,468.348
Total assets	1,802,490	18,024.903
Current liabilities	567,222	5,672.229
Net sales	1,672,423	16,724.230
Net income	257,342	2,573.426

1. Compute Nintendo's current ratio, net profit margin, and sales-to-total-assets using the financial information reported in (a) yen and (b) dollars.
2. What can we conclude from a review of the results for part 1?

 connect

Selected comparative financial statements of Bennington Company follow.

PROBLEM SET A

Problem 13-1A
Ratios, common-size statements, and trend percents

P1 P2 P3

mhhe.com/wildFINMAN4e

BENNINGTON COMPANY
Comparative Income Statements
For Years Ended December 31, 2012, 2011, and 2010

	2012	2011	2010
Sales	$444,000	$340,000	$236,000
Cost of goods sold	267,288	212,500	151,040
Gross profit	176,712	127,500	84,960
Selling expenses	62,694	46,920	31,152
Administrative expenses	40,137	29,920	19,470
Total expenses	102,831	76,840	50,622
Income before taxes	73,881	50,660	34,338
Income taxes	13,764	10,370	6,962
Net income	$ 60,117	$ 40,290	$ 27,376

BENNINGTON COMPANY
Comparative Balance Sheets
December 31, 2012, 2011, and 2010

	2012	2011	2010
Assets			
Current assets	$ 48,480	$ 37,924	$ 50,648
Long-term investments	0	500	3,720
Plant assets, net	90,000	96,000	57,000
Total assets	$138,480	$134,424	$111,368
Liabilities and Equity			
Current liabilities	$ 20,200	$ 19,960	$ 19,480
Common stock	72,000	72,000	54,000
Other paid-in capital	9,000	9,000	6,000
Retained earnings	37,280	33,464	31,888
Total liabilities and equity	$138,480	$134,424	$111,368

Required

1. Compute each year's current ratio. (Round ratio amounts to one decimal.)
2. Express the income statement data in common-size percents. (Round percents to two decimals.)

Check   (3) 2012, Total assets trend,
124.34%

3. Express the balance sheet data in trend percents with 2010 as the base year. (Round percents to two decimals.)

Analysis Component

4. Comment on any significant relations revealed by the ratios and percents computed.

Problem 13-2A
Calculation and analysis of trend percents

A1 P1

Selected comparative financial statements of Sugo Company follow.

SUGO COMPANY							
Comparative Income Statements							
For Years Ended December 31, 2012–2006							
($ thousands)	2012	2011	2010	2009	2008	2007	2006
Sales	$1,594	$1,396	$1,270	$1,164	$1,086	$1,010	$828
Cost of goods sold	1,146	932	802	702	652	610	486
Gross profit	448	464	468	462	434	400	342
Operating expenses	340	266	244	180	156	154	128
Net income	$ 108	$ 198	$ 224	$ 282	$ 278	$ 246	$214

SUGO COMPANY							
Comparative Balance Sheets							
December 31, 2012–2006							
($ thousands)	2012	2011	2010	2009	2008	2007	2006
Assets							
Cash	$ 68	$ 88	$ 92	$ 94	$ 98	$ 96	$ 99
Accounts receivable, net	480	504	456	350	308	292	206
Merchandise inventory	1,738	1,264	1,104	932	836	710	515
Other current assets	46	42	24	44	38	38	19
Long-term investments	0	0	0	136	136	136	136
Plant assets, net	2,120	2,114	1,852	1,044	1,078	960	825
Total assets	$4,452	$4,012	$3,528	$2,600	$2,494	$2,232	$1,800
Liabilities and Equity							
Current liabilities	$1,120	$ 942	$ 618	$ 514	$ 446	$ 422	$ 272
Long-term liabilities	1,194	1,040	1,012	470	480	520	390
Common stock	1,000	1,000	1,000	840	840	640	640
Other paid-in capital	250	250	250	180	180	160	160
Retained earnings	888	780	648	596	548	490	338
Total liabilities and equity	$4,452	$4,012	$3,528	$2,600	$2,494	$2,232	$1,800

Required

Check   (1) 2012, Total assets trend,
247.3%

1. Compute trend percents for all components of both statements using 2006 as the base year. (Round percents to one decimal.)

Analysis Component

2. Analyze and comment on the financial statements and trend percents from part 1.

Problem 13-3A
Transactions, working capital, and liquidity ratios

P3

mhhe.com/wildFINMAN4e

Park Corporation began the month of May with $650,000 of current assets, a current ratio of 2.50:1, and an acid-test ratio of 1.10:1. During the month, it completed the following transactions (the company uses a perpetual inventory system).

May   2   Purchased $75,000 of merchandise inventory on credit.
       8   Sold merchandise inventory that cost $58,000 for $103,000 cash.
      10   Collected $19,000 cash on an account receivable.
      15   Paid $21,000 cash to settle an account payable.

17 Wrote off a $3,000 bad debt against the Allowance for Doubtful Accounts account.
22 Declared a $1 per share cash dividend on its 40,000 shares of outstanding common stock.
26 Paid the dividend declared on May 22.
27 Borrowed $75,000 cash by giving the bank a 30-day, 10% note.
28 Borrowed $90,000 cash by signing a long-term secured note.
29 Used the $165,000 cash proceeds from the notes to buy new machinery.

Check May 22: Current ratio, 2.12; Acid-test ratio, 1.04

May 29: Current ratio, 1.82; Working capital, $320,000

Required

Prepare a table showing Park's (1) current ratio, (2) acid-test ratio, and (3) working capital, after each transaction. Round ratios to two decimals.

Selected year-end financial statements of McCord Corporation follow. (All sales were on credit; selected balance sheet amounts at December 31, 2010, were inventory, $32,400; total assets, $182,400; common stock, $90,000; and retained earnings, $31,300.)

Problem 13-4A
Calculation of financial statement ratios

P3

mhhe.com/wildFINMAN4e

McCORD CORPORATION
Income Statement
For Year Ended December 31, 2011

Sales	$348,600
Cost of goods sold	229,150
Gross profit	119,450
Operating expenses	52,500
Interest expense	3,100
Income before taxes	63,850
Income taxes	15,800
Net income	$ 48,050

McCORD CORPORATION
Balance Sheet
December 31, 2011

Assets		Liabilities and Equity	
Cash	$ 9,000	Accounts payable	$ 16,500
Short-term investments	7,400	Accrued wages payable	2,200
Accounts receivable, net	28,200	Income taxes payable	2,300
Notes receivable (trade)*	3,500	Long-term note payable, secured	
Merchandise inventory	31,150	by mortgage on plant assets	62,400
Prepaid expenses	1,650	Common stock	90,000
Plant assets, net	152,300	Retained earnings	59,800
Total assets	$233,200	Total liabilities and equity	$233,200

* These are short-term notes receivable arising from customer (trade) sales.

Required

Compute the following: (1) current ratio, (2) acid-test ratio, (3) days' sales uncollected, (4) inventory turnover, (5) days' sales in inventory, (6) debt-to-equity ratio, (7) times interest earned, (8) profit margin ratio, (9) total asset turnover, (10) return on total assets, and (11) return on common stockholders' equity.

Check Acid-test ratio, 2.3 to 1; Inventory turnover, 7.2

Summary information from the financial statements of two companies competing in the same industry follows.

Problem 13-5A
Comparative ratio analysis

A1 P3

	Ryan Company	Priest Company		Ryan Company	Priest Company
Data from the current year-end balance sheets			**Data from the current year's income statement**		
Assets			Sales	$660,000	$780,200
Cash	$ 18,500	$ 33,000	Cost of goods sold	485,100	532,500
Accounts receivable, net	36,400	56,400	Interest expense	6,900	11,000
Current notes receivable (trade)	8,100	6,200	Income tax expense	12,800	19,300
Merchandise inventory	83,440	131,500	Net income	67,770	105,000
Prepaid expenses	4,000	5,950	Basic earnings per share	1.94	2.56
Plant assets, net	284,000	303,400			
Total assets	$434,440	$536,450			
			Beginning-of-year balance sheet data		
Liabilities and Equity			Accounts receivable, net	$ 28,800	$ 53,200
Current liabilities	$ 60,340	$ 92,300	Current notes receivable (trade)	0	0
Long-term notes payable	79,800	100,000	Merchandise inventory	54,600	106,400
Common stock, $5 par value	175,000	205,000	Total assets	388,000	372,500
Retained earnings	119,300	139,150	Common stock, $5 par value	175,000	205,000
Total liabilities and equity	$434,440	$536,450	Retained earnings	94,300	90,600

Required

Check (1) Priest: Accounts receivable turnover, 13.5; Inventory turnover, 4.5

(2) Ryan: Profit margin, 10.3%; PE, 12.9

1. For both companies compute the (*a*) current ratio, (*b*) acid-test ratio, (*c*) accounts (including notes) receivable turnover, (*d*) inventory turnover, (*e*) days' sales in inventory, and (*f*) days' sales uncollected. Identify the company you consider to be the better short-term credit risk and explain why.

2. For both companies compute the (*a*) profit margin ratio, (*b*) total asset turnover, (*c*) return on total assets, and (*d*) return on common stockholders' equity. Assuming that each company paid cash dividends of $1.50 per share and each company's stock can be purchased at $25 per share, compute their (*e*) price-earnings ratios and (*f*) dividend yields. Identify which company's stock you would recommend as the better investment and explain why.

Problem 13-6A[A]
Income statement computations and format

A2

Selected account balances from the adjusted trial balance for Zen Corporation as of its calendar year-end December 31, 2011, follow.

	Debit	Credit
a. Income taxes expense	$?	
b. Correction of overstatement of prior year's sales (pretax)	17,000	
c. Loss on sale of machinery	26,850	
d. Loss from settlement of lawsuit	24,750	
e. Other operating expenses	107,400	
f. Accumulated depreciation—Machinery		$ 72,600
g. Gain from settlement of lawsuit		45,000
h. Accumulated depreciation—Buildings		175,500
i. Loss from operating a discontinued segment (pretax)	19,250	
j. Gain on insurance recovery of tornado damage (pretax and extraordinary)		30,120
k. Net sales		999,500
l. Depreciation expense—Buildings	53,000	
m. Depreciation expense—Machinery	35,000	
n. Gain on sale of discontinued segment's assets (pretax)		35,000
o. Accounts payable		45,000
p. Interest revenue		15,000
q. Cost of goods sold	483,500	

Required

Answer each of the following questions by providing supporting computations.

1. Assume that the company's income tax rate is 30% for all items. Identify the tax effects and after-tax amounts of the four items labeled pretax.
2. What is the amount of income from continuing operations before income taxes? What is the amount of the income taxes expense? What is the amount of income from continuing operations?
3. What is the total amount of after-tax income (loss) associated with the discontinued segment?
4. What is the amount of income (loss) before the extraordinary items?
5. What is the amount of net income for the year?

Check   (3) $11,025

(4) $241,325

(5) $262,409

Selected comparative financial statement information of Sawgrass Corporation follows.

PROBLEM SET B

Problem 13-1B
Ratios, common-size statements, and trend percents

P1 P2 P3

SAWGRASS CORPORATION Comparative Income Statements For Years Ended December 31, 2012, 2011, and 2010			
	2012	**2011**	**2010**
Sales	$199,800	$167,000	$144,800
Cost of goods sold	109,890	87,175	67,200
Gross profit	89,910	79,825	77,600
Selling expenses	23,680	20,790	19,000
Administrative expenses	17,760	15,610	16,700
Total expenses	41,440	36,400	35,700
Income before taxes	48,470	43,425	41,900
Income taxes	5,050	4,910	4,300
Net income	$ 43,420	$ 38,515	$ 37,600

SAWGRASS CORPORATION Comparative Balance Sheets December 31, 2012, 2011, and 2010			
	2012	**2011**	**2010**
Assets			
Current assets	$ 55,860	$ 33,660	$ 37,300
Long-term investments	0	2,700	11,600
Plant assets, net	113,810	114,660	80,000
Total assets	$169,670	$151,020	$128,900
Liabilities and Equity			
Current liabilities	$ 23,370	$ 20,180	$ 17,500
Common stock	47,500	47,500	38,000
Other paid-in capital	14,850	14,850	12,300
Retained earnings	83,950	68,490	61,100
Total liabilities and equity	$169,670	$151,020	$128,900

Required

1. Compute each year's current ratio. (Round ratio amounts to one decimal.)
2. Express the income statement data in common-size percents. (Round percents to two decimals.)
3. Express the balance sheet data in trend percents with 2010 as the base year. (Round percents to two decimals.)

Check   (3) 2012, Total assets trend, 131.63%

Analysis Component

4. Comment on any significant relations revealed by the ratios and percents computed.

Problem 13-2B
Calculation and analysis of
trend percents

A1 P1

Selected comparative financial statements of Deuce Company follow.

DEUCE COMPANY Comparative Income Statements For Years Ended December 31, 2012–2006							
($ thousands)	2012	2011	2010	2009	2008	2007	2006
Sales	$660	$710	$730	$780	$840	$870	$960
Cost of goods sold	376	390	394	414	440	450	480
Gross profit	284	320	336	366	400	420	480
Operating expenses	184	204	212	226	240	244	250
Net income	$100	$116	$124	$140	$160	$176	$230

DEUCE COMPANY Comparative Balance Sheets December 31, 2012–2006							
($ thousands)	2012	2011	2010	2009	2008	2007	2006
Assets							
Cash	$ 34	$ 36	$ 42	$ 44	$ 50	$ 52	$ 58
Accounts receivable, net	120	126	130	134	140	144	150
Merchandise inventory	156	162	168	170	176	180	198
Other current assets	24	24	26	28	28	30	30
Long-term investments	26	20	16	100	100	100	100
Plant assets, net	410	414	420	312	320	328	354
Total assets	$770	$782	$802	$788	$814	$834	$890
Liabilities and Equity							
Current liabilities	$138	$146	$176	$180	$200	$250	$270
Long-term liabilities	82	110	132	138	184	204	250
Common stock	150	150	150	150	150	150	150
Other paid-in capital	60	60	60	60	60	60	60
Retained earnings	340	316	284	260	220	170	160
Total liabilities and equity	$770	$782	$802	$788	$814	$834	$890

Required

Check (1) 2012, Total assets trend, 86.5%

1. Compute trend percents for all components of both statements using 2006 as the base year. (Round percents to one decimal.)

Analysis Component

2. Analyze and comment on the financial statements and trend percents from part 1.

Problem 13-3B
Transactions, working capital,
and liquidity ratios P3

Ready Corporation began the month of June with $280,000 of current assets, a current ratio of 2.8:1, and an acid-test ratio of 1.2:1. During the month, it completed the following transactions (the company uses a perpetual inventory system).

Check June 1: Current ratio, 3.19; Acid-test ratio, 2.21

June 1 Sold merchandise inventory that cost $62,000 for $101,000 cash.
    3 Collected $78,000 cash on an account receivable.
    5 Purchased $130,000 of merchandise inventory on credit.
    7 Borrowed $90,000 cash by giving the bank a 60-day, 10% note.
    10 Borrowed $180,000 cash by signing a long-term secured note.
    12 Purchased machinery for $280,000 cash.
    15 Declared a $1 per share cash dividend on its 60,000 shares of outstanding common stock.
    19 Wrote off a $7,000 bad debt against the Allowance for Doubtful Accounts account.
    22 Paid $11,000 cash to settle an account payable.
    30 Paid the dividend declared on June 15.

June 30: Working capital, $59,000; Current ratio, 1.19

Required

Prepare a table showing the company's (1) current ratio, (2) acid-test ratio, and (3) working capital after each transaction. Round ratios to two decimals.

Selected year-end financial statements of Overland Corporation follow. (All sales were on credit; selected balance sheet amounts at December 31, 2010, were inventory, $16,400; total assets, $95,900; common stock, $41,500; and retained earnings, $19,800.)

Problem 13-4B
Calculation of financial statement ratios
P3

OVERLAND CORPORATION Income Statement For Year Ended December 31, 2011	
Sales	$215,500
Cost of goods sold	136,100
Gross profit	79,400
Operating expenses	50,200
Interest expense	1,200
Income before taxes	28,000
Income taxes	2,200
Net income	$ 25,800

OVERLAND CORPORATION
Balance Sheet
December 31, 2011

Assets		Liabilities and Equity	
Cash	$ 5,100	Accounts payable	$ 10,500
Short-term investments	5,900	Accrued wages payable	2,300
Accounts receivable, net	11,100	Income taxes payable	1,600
Notes receivable (trade)*	2,000	Long-term note payable, secured	
Merchandise inventory	12,500	by mortgage on plant assets	25,000
Prepaid expenses	1,000	Common stock, $5 par value	41,000
Plant assets, net	72,900	Retained earnings	30,100
Total assets	$110,500	Total liabilities and equity	$110,500

* These are short-term notes receivable arising from customer (trade) sales.

Required

Compute the following: (1) current ratio, (2) acid-test ratio, (3) days' sales uncollected, (4) inventory turnover, (5) days' sales in inventory, (6) debt-to-equity ratio, (7) times interest earned, (8) profit margin ratio, (9) total asset turnover, (10) return on total assets, and (11) return on common stockholders' equity.

Check   Acid-test ratio, 1.7 to 1; Inventory turnover, 9.4

Summary information from the financial statements of two companies competing in the same industry follows.

Problem 13-5B
Comparative ratio analysis
A1 P3

	Loud Company	Clear Company		Loud Company	Clear Company
Data from the current year-end balance sheets			**Data from the current year's income statement**		
Assets			Sales	$395,600	$669,500
Cash	$ 22,000	$ 38,500	Cost of goods sold	292,600	482,000
Accounts receivable, net	79,100	72,500	Interest expense	7,900	12,400
Current notes receivable (trade)	13,600	11,000	Income tax expense	7,700	14,300
Merchandise inventory	88,800	84,000	Net income	35,850	63,700
Prepaid expenses	11,700	12,100	Basic earnings per share	1.33	2.23
Plant assets, net	178,900	254,300			
Total assets	$394,100	$472,400			
			Beginning-of-year balance sheet data		
Liabilities and Equity			Accounts receivable, net	$ 74,200	$ 75,300
Current liabilities	$ 92,500	$ 99,000	Current notes receivable (trade)	0	0
Long-term notes payable	95,000	95,300	Merchandise inventory	107,100	82,500
Common stock, $5 par value	135,000	143,000	Total assets	385,400	445,000
Retained earnings	71,600	135,100	Common stock, $5 par value	135,000	143,000
Total liabilities and equity	$394,100	$472,400	Retained earnings	51,100	111,700

Required

1. For both companies compute the (*a*) current ratio, (*b*) acid-test ratio, (*c*) accounts (including notes) receivable turnover, (*d*) inventory turnover, (*e*) days' sales in inventory, and (*f*) days' sales uncollected. Identify the company you consider to be the better short-term credit risk and explain why.

2. For both companies compute the (*a*) profit margin ratio, (*b*) total asset turnover, (*c*) return on total assets, and (*d*) return on common stockholders' equity. Assuming that each company paid cash dividends of $3.00 per share and each company's stock can be purchased at $25 per share, compute their (*e*) price-earnings ratios and (*f*) dividend yields. Identify which company's stock you would recommend as the better investment and explain why.

Problem 13-6B[A]

Income statement computations and format

A2

Selected account balances from the adjusted trial balance for Halogen Corp. as of its calendar year-end December 31, 2011, follow.

	Debit	Credit
a. Other operating expenses	$ 338,000	
b. Depreciation expense—Buildings	110,000	
c. Loss from settlement of lawsuit	46,000	
d. Income taxes expense	?	
e. Loss on hurricane damage (pretax and extraordinary)	74,000	
f. Accumulated depreciation—Buildings		$ 230,000
g. Accumulated depreciation—Equipment		410,000
h. Interest revenue		30,000
i. Net sales		2,650,000
j. Gain from settlement of lawsuit		78,000
k. Loss on sale of building	34,000	
l. Loss from operating a discontinued segment (pretax)	130,000	
m. Accounts payable		142,000
n. Correction of overstatement of prior year's expense (pretax)		58,000
o. Cost of goods sold	1,050,000	
p. Loss on sale of discontinued segment's assets (pretax)	190,000	
q. Depreciation expense—Equipment	166,000	

Required

Answer each of the following questions by providing supporting computations.

1. Assume that the company's income tax rate is 25% for all items. Identify the tax effects and after-tax amounts of the four items labeled pretax.

2. What is the amount of income from continuing operations before income taxes? What is the amount of income taxes expense? What is the amount of income from continuing operations?

3. What is the total amount of after-tax income (loss) associated with the discontinued segment?

4. What is the amount of income (loss) before the extraordinary items?

5. What is the amount of net income for the year?

SERIAL PROBLEM

Business Solutions

P3

(This serial problem began in Chapter 1 and continues through most of the book. If previous chapter segments were not completed, the serial problem can begin at this point. It is helpful, but not necessary, to use the Working Papers that accompany the book.)

SP 13   Use the following selected data from Business Solutions' income statement for the three months ended March 31, 2012, and from its March 31, 2012, balance sheet to complete the requirements below: computer services revenue, $25,307; net sales (of goods), $18,693; total sales and revenue, $44,000; cost of goods sold, $14,052; net income, $18,833; quick assets, $90,924; current assets, $95,568; total assets, $120,268; current liabilities, $875; total liabilities, $875; and total equity, $119,393.

Required

1. Compute the gross margin ratio (both with and without services revenue) and net profit margin ratio.

2. Compute the current ratio and acid-test ratio.

3. Compute the debt ratio and equity ratio.

4. What percent of its assets are current? What percent are long term?

Beyond the Numbers

BTN 13-1   Refer to **Research In Motion** financial statements in Appendix A to answer the following.

1. Using fiscal 2008 as the base year, compute trend percents for fiscal years 2008, 2009, and 2010 for revenues, cost of sales, operating expenses, income taxes, and net income. (Round percents to one decimal.)

2. Compute common-size percents for fiscal years 2009 and 2010 for the following categories of assets: (*a*) total current assets, (*b*) property and equipment, net, and (*c*) intangible assets. (Round to the nearest tenth of a percent.)

3. Comment on any notable changes across the years for the income statement trends computed in part 1 and the balance sheet percents computed in part 2.

REPORTING IN ACTION

A1 P1 P2

RIM

Fast Forward

4. Access Research In Motion's financial statements for fiscal years ending after February 27, 2010, from its Website (**RIM.com**) or the SEC database (**www.sec.gov**). Update your work for parts 1, 2, and 3 using the new information accessed.

BTN 13-2   Key figures for **Research In Motion** and **Apple** follow.

COMPARATIVE ANALYSIS

C2 P2

RIM

Apple

($ millions)	Research In Motion	Apple
Cash and equivalents	$ 1,551	$ 5,263
Accounts receivable, net	2,594	3,361
Inventories	622	455
Retained earnings	5,274	23,353
Cost of sales	8,369	25,683
Revenues	14,953	42,905
Total assets	10,204	47,501

Required

1. Compute common-size percents for each of the companies using the data provided. (Round percents to one decimal.)

2. Which company retains a higher portion of cumulative net income in the company?

3. Which company has a higher gross margin ratio on sales?

4. Which company holds a higher percent of its total assets as inventory?

BTN 13-3   As Baldwin Company controller, you are responsible for informing the board of directors about its financial activities. At the board meeting, you present the following information.

ETHICS CHALLENGE

A1

	2011	2010	2009
Sales trend percent	147.0%	135.0%	100.0%
Selling expenses to sales	10.1%	14.0%	15.6%
Sales to plant assets ratio	3.8 to 1	3.6 to 1	3.3 to 1
Current ratio	2.9 to 1	2.7 to 1	2.4 to 1
Acid-test ratio	1.1 to 1	1.4 to 1	1.5 to 1
Inventory turnover	7.8 times	9.0 times	10.2 times
Accounts receivable turnover	7.0 times	7.7 times	8.5 times
Total asset turnover	2.9 times	2.9 times	3.3 times
Return on total assets	10.4%	11.0%	13.2%
Return on stockholders' equity.........	10.7%	11.5%	14.1%
Profit margin ratio	3.6%	3.8%	4.0%

After the meeting, the company's CEO holds a press conference with analysts in which she mentions the following ratios.

	2011	2010	2009
Sales trend percent	147.0%	135.0%	100.0%
Selling expenses to sales	10.1%	14.0%	15.6%
Sales to plant assets ratio	3.8 to 1	3.6 to 1	3.3 to 1
Current ratio	2.9 to 1	2.7 to 1	2.4 to 1

Required

1. Why do you think the CEO decided to report 4 ratios instead of the 11 prepared?
2. Comment on the possible consequences of the CEO's reporting of the ratios selected.

COMMUNICATING IN PRACTICE

A1 P3

BTN 13-4   Each team is to select a different industry, and each team member is to select a different company in that industry and acquire its financial statements. Use those statements to analyze the company, including at least one ratio from each of the four building blocks of analysis. When necessary, use the financial press to determine the market price of its stock. Communicate with teammates via a meeting, e-mail, or telephone to discuss how different companies compare to each other and to industry norms. The team is to prepare a single one-page memorandum reporting on its analysis and the conclusions reached.

TAKING IT TO THE NET

P3

BTN 13-5   Access the February 19, 2010, filing of the December 31, 2009, 10-K report of **The Hershey Company** (ticker HSY) at **www.SEC.gov** and complete the following requirements.

Required

Compute or identify the following profitability ratios of Hershey for its years ending December 31, 2009, *and* December 31, 2008. Interpret its profitability using the results obtained for these two years.

1. Profit margin ratio.
2. Gross profit ratio.
3. Return on total assets. (Total assets at year-end 2007 were $4,247,113,000.)
4. Return on common stockholders' equity. (Total shareholders' equity at year-end 2007 was $592,922,000.)
5. Basic net income per common share.

TEAMWORK IN ACTION

P1 P2 P3

BTN 13-6   A team approach to learning financial statement analysis is often useful.

Required

1. Each team should write a description of horizontal and vertical analysis that all team members agree with and understand. Illustrate each description with an example.
2. *Each* member of the team is to select *one* of the following categories of ratio analysis. Explain what the ratios in that category measure. Choose one ratio from the category selected, present its formula, and explain what it measures.

    a. Liquidity and efficiency   **c.** Profitability
    b. Solvency   **d.** Market prospects

3. Each team member is to present his or her notes from part 2 to teammates. Team members are to confirm or correct other teammates' presentation.

Hint: Pairing within teams may be necessary for part 2. Use as an in-class activity or as an assignment. Consider presentations to the entire class using team rotation with transparencies.

ENTREPRENEURIAL DECISION

A1 P1 P2 P3

BTN 13-7   Assume that David and Tom Gardner of **The Motley Fool** (**Fool.com**) have impressed you since you first heard of their rather improbable rise to prominence in financial circles. You learn of a staff opening at The Motley Fool and decide to apply for it. Your resume is successfully screened from the thousands received and you advance to the interview process. You learn that the interview consists of analyzing the following financial facts and answering analysis questions. (*Note:* The data are taken from a small merchandiser in outdoor recreational equipment.)

	2010	2009	2008
Sales trend percents	137.0%	125.0%	100.0%
Selling expenses to sales	9.8%	13.7%	15.3%
Sales to plant assets ratio	3.5 to 1	3.3 to 1	3.0 to 1
Current ratio	2.6 to 1	2.4 to 1	2.1 to 1
Acid-test ratio	0.8 to 1	1.1 to 1	1.2 to 1
Merchandise inventory turnover	7.5 times	8.7 times	9.9 times
Accounts receivable turnover	6.7 times	7.4 times	8.2 times
Total asset turnover	2.6 times	2.6 times	3.0 times
Return on total assets	8.8%	9.4%	11.1%
Return on equity	9.75%	11.50%	12.25%
Profit margin ratio	3.3%	3.5%	3.7%

Required

Use these data to answer each of the following questions with explanations.

1. Is it becoming easier for the company to meet its current liabilities on time and to take advantage of any available cash discounts? Explain.

2. Is the company collecting its accounts receivable more rapidly? Explain.

3. Is the company's investment in accounts receivable decreasing? Explain.

4. Is the company's investment in plant assets increasing? Explain.

5. Is the owner's investment becoming more profitable? Explain.

6. Did the dollar amount of selling expenses decrease during the three-year period? Explain.

BTN 13-8   You are to devise an investment strategy to enable you to accumulate $1,000,000 by age 65. Start by making some assumptions about your salary. Next compute the percent of your salary that you will be able to save each year. If you will receive any lump-sum monies, include those amounts in your calculations. Historically, stocks have delivered average annual returns of 10–11%. Given this history, you should probably not assume that you will earn above 10% on the money you invest. It is not necessary to specify exactly what types of assets you will buy for your investments; just assume a rate you expect to earn. Use the future value tables in Appendix B to calculate how your savings will grow. Experiment a bit with your figures to see how much less you have to save if you start at, for example, age 25 versus age 35 or 40. (For this assignment, do not include inflation in your calculations.)

HITTING THE ROAD

C1   P3

BTN 13-9   Nokia (www.Nokia.com), which is a leading manufacturer of mobile devices and services, along with **Research In Motion** and **Apple** are competitors in the global marketplace. Key figures for Nokia follow (in euro millions).

GLOBAL DECISION

A1

NOKIA

RIM

Apple

Cash and equivalents	1,142
Accounts receivable, net	7,981
Inventories	1,865
Retained earnings	10,132
Cost of sales	27,720
Revenues	40,984
Total assets	35,738

Required

1. Compute common-size percents for Nokia using the data provided. (Round percents to one decimal.)

2. Compare the results with Research In Motion and Apple from BTN 13-2.

ANSWERS TO MULTIPLE CHOICE QUIZ

1. d; ($351,000/$300,000) × 100 = 117%

2. e; ($86,000 + $76,000 + $122,000 + $12,000)/$124,000 = 2.39

3. c; ($86,000 + $76,000)/$124,000 = 1.31

4. a; ($124,000 + $90,000)/$830,000 = 25.78%

5. d; ($300,000 + $316,000)/$830,000 = 74.22%

14

Managerial Accounting Concepts and Principles

A Look Back

Chapter 13 described the analysis and interpretation of financial statement information. We applied horizontal, vertical, and ratio analyses to better understand company performance and financial condition.

A Look at This Chapter

We begin our study of managerial accounting by explaining its purpose and describing its major characteristics. We also discuss cost concepts and describe how they help managers gather and organize information for making decisions. The reporting of manufacturing activities is also discussed.

A Look Ahead

The remaining chapters discuss the types of decisions managers must make and how managerial accounting helps with those decisions. The first of these chapters, Chapter 15, considers how we measure costs assigned to certain types of projects.

Learning Objectives

CAP

CONCEPTUAL

C1 Explain the purpose and nature of, and the role of ethics in, managerial accounting. (p. 600)

C2 Describe accounting concepts useful in classifying costs. (p. 604)

C3 Define product and period costs and explain how they impact financial statements. (p. 606)

C4 Explain how balance sheets and income statements for manufacturing and merchandising companies differ. (p. 608)

C5 Explain manufacturing activities and the flow of manufacturing costs. (p. 612)

C6 Describe trends in managerial accounting. (p. 615)

ANALYTICAL

A1 Compute cycle time and cycle efficiency, and explain their importance to production management (p. 617)

LP14

PROCEDURAL

P1 Compute cost of goods sold for a manufacturer. (p. 609)

P2 Prepare a manufacturing statement and explain its purpose and links to financial statements. (p. 613)

Hot Late Nights

"I didn't know I was a baker . . ."

—COREY RIMMEL

COLUMBIA, MO—Hanging out in a friend's basement one night, college students Corey Rimmel, Adam Hendin, and David Melnick thought a late-night bakery would be the perfect recipe for their hunger. But, the enterprising trio's thoughts weren't just on eating cookies but also on starting a business. "At first we were just joking, kicking the idea around," Corey says. "Before long, we were in the library every night doing research. One day we said, 'Well, let's just see if we can do it.'" After weeks of research, talking to entrepreneurs, writing a business plan, and setting up a managerial accounting system, the friends started **Hot Box Cookies (HotBoxCookies.com).**

Hot Box Cookies focuses on meeting individual customer's tastes. Starting with homemade dough in four flavors, the company's bakers mix in whatever the customer wants—chocolate chips, Reese's pieces, candy bars. After placing their orders, customers can play board games or surf the Internet in the Hot Box store or have their fresh cookies delivered. The owners say their biggest surprise is how incredibly busy they were from the very beginning of their business. "We haven't had time to work our way through our marketing plan . . . we've just been too busy," explains Corey.

The owners insist college is a great time to start a new business. Risk is low, and "if the owners are passionate and have a good plan, banks will lend money to get the business going," says Corey. "It's nice having something to call our own," Adam says. "A lot of people want to own a business, but they don't." But the trio, two of whom are accounting majors, emphasize that understanding basic managerial principles, product and period costs, manufacturing statements, and cost flow is crucial. The owners use managerial accounting information from the baking process to monitor and control costs and to assess what cookies are most popular and profitable. Success has enabled the business to expand and grow into other product lines such as catering, coffee, and "Dough on the Go" sold in local markets.

Corey, Adam, and David believe that entrepreneurs fill a void by creating a niche. "I've always had it in my mind that I would work for myself," says Corey. However, financial success depends on monitoring and controlling operations to best meet customer needs. By staying focused and applying sound managerial accounting principles and concepts to their business, the owners hope to expand to other college campuses across the country. Ah, the sweet smell of success.

[Sources: *Hot Box Cookies* Website, January 2011; *Columbia Missourian,* October 2008; *The MOVE Magazine,* October 2008; *Columbia Business Times,* August 2008; *Columbia Tribune,* November 2008.]

Managerial accounting, like financial accounting, provides information to help users make better decisions. However, managerial accounting and financial accounting differ in important ways, which this chapter explains. This chapter also compares the accounting and reporting practices used by manufacturing and merchandising companies. A merchandising company sells products without changing their condition. A manufacturing company buys raw materials and turns them into finished products for sale to customers. A third type of company earns revenues by providing services rather than products. The skills, tools, and techniques developed for measuring a manufacturing company's activities apply to service companies as well. The chapter concludes by explaining the flow of manufacturing activities and preparing the manufacturing statement.

Managerial Accounting Concepts and Principles

Managerial Accounting Basics

- Purpose of managerial accounting
- Nature of managerial accounting
- Managerial decisions
- Fraud and ethics in managerial accounting

Managerial Cost Concepts

- Types of cost classifications
- Identification of cost classifications
- Cost concepts for service companies

Reporting Manufacturing Activities

- Balance sheet
- Income statement
- Flow of activities
- Manufacturing statement
- Trends in managerial accounting

MANAGERIAL ACCOUNTING BASICS

Managerial accounting is an activity that provides financial and nonfinancial information to an organization's managers and other internal decision makers. This section explains the purpose of managerial accounting (also called *management accounting*) and compares it with financial accounting. The main purpose of the financial accounting system is to prepare general-purpose financial statements. That information is incomplete for internal decision makers who manage organizations.

Purpose of Managerial Accounting

C1 Explain the purpose and nature of, and the role of ethics in, managerial accounting.

The purpose of both managerial accounting and financial accounting is providing useful information to decision makers. They do this by collecting, managing, and reporting information in demand by their users. Both areas of accounting also share the common practice of reporting monetary information, although managerial accounting includes the reporting of nonmonetary information. They even report some of the same information. For instance, a company's financial statements contain information useful for both its managers (insiders) and other persons interested in the company (outsiders).

The remainder of this book looks carefully at managerial accounting information, how to gather it, and how managers use it. We consider the concepts and procedures used to determine the costs of products and services as well as topics such as budgeting, break-even analysis, product costing, profit planning, and cost analysis. Information about the costs of products and services is important for many decisions that managers make. These decisions include predicting the future costs of a product or service. Predicted costs are used in product pricing, profitability analysis, and in deciding whether to make or buy a product or component. More generally, much of managerial accounting involves gathering information about costs for planning and control decisions.

Planning is the process of setting goals and making plans to achieve them. Companies formulate long-term strategic plans that usually span a 5- to 10-year horizon and then refine them with medium-term and short-term plans. Strategic plans usually set a firm's long-term direction by developing a road map based on opportunities such as new products, new markets, and capital investments. A strategic plan's goals and objectives are broadly defined given its long-term

Point: Nonfinancial information, also called nonmonetary information, includes customer and employee satisfaction data, the percentage of on-time deliveries, and product defect rates.

Point: Costs are important to managers because they impact both the financial position and profitability of a business. Managerial accounting assists in analysis, planning, and control of costs.

orientation. Medium- and short-term plans are more operational in nature. They translate the strategic plan into actions. These plans are more concrete and consist of better defined objectives and goals. A short-term plan often covers a one-year period that, when translated in monetary terms, is known as a budget.

Control is the process of monitoring planning decisions and evaluating an organization's activities and employees. It includes the measurement and evaluation of actions, processes, and outcomes. Feedback provided by the control function allows managers to revise their plans. Measurement of actions and processes also allows managers to take corrective actions to avoid undesirable outcomes. For example, managers periodically compare actual results with planned results. Exhibit 14.1 portrays the important management functions of planning and control.

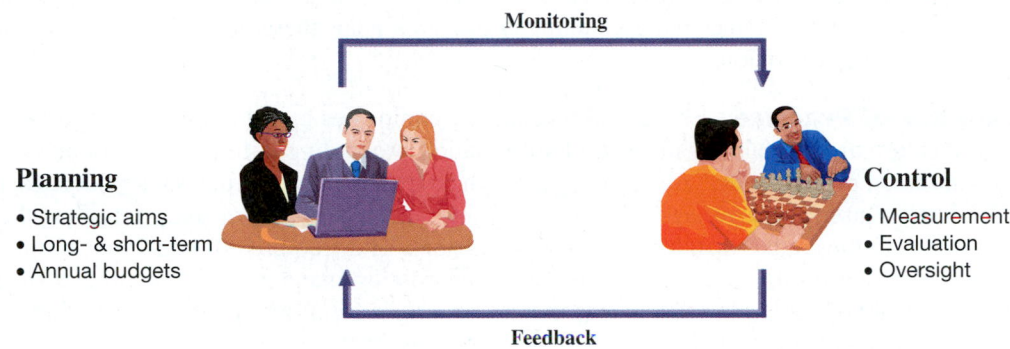

EXHIBIT 14.1

Planning and Control (including monitoring and feedback)

Managers use information to plan and control business activities. In later chapters, we explain how managers also use this information to direct and improve business operations.

Nature of Managerial Accounting

Managerial accounting has its own special characteristics. To understand these characteristics, we compare managerial accounting to financial accounting; they differ in at least seven important ways. These differences are summarized in Exhibit 14.2. This section discusses each of these characteristics.

EXHIBIT 14.2

Key Differences between Managerial Accounting and Financial Accounting

	Financial Accounting	Managerial Accounting
1. Users and decision makers	Investors, creditors, and other users external to the organization	Managers, employees, and decision makers internal to the organization
2. Purpose of information	Assist external users in making investment, credit, and other decisions	Assist managers in making planning and control decisions
3. Flexibility of practice	Structured and often controlled by GAAP	Relatively flexible (no GAAP constraints)
4. Timeliness of information	Often available only after an audit is complete	Available quickly without the need to wait for an audit
5. Time dimension	Focus on historical information with some predictions	Many projections and estimates; historical information also presented
6. Focus of information	Emphasis on whole organization	Emphasis on an organization's projects, processes, and subdivisions
7. Nature of information	Monetary information	Mostly monetary; but also nonmonetary information

Point: It is desirable to accumulate certain information for management reports in a database separate from financial accounting records.

Users and Decision Makers   Companies accumulate, process, and report financial accounting and managerial accounting information for different groups of decision makers. Financial accounting information is provided primarily to external users including investors, creditors, analysts, and regulators. External users rarely have a major role in managing a company's daily activities. Managerial accounting information is provided primarily to internal users who are responsible for making and implementing decisions about a company's business activities.

Purpose of Information   Investors, creditors, and other external users of financial accounting information must often decide whether to invest in or lend to a company. If they have already done so, they must decide whether to continue owning the company or carrying the loan. Internal decision makers must plan a company's future. They seek to take advantage of opportunities or to overcome obstacles. They also try to control activities and ensure their effective and efficient implementation. Managerial accounting information helps these internal users make both planning and control decisions.

Point: The *Institute of Management Accountants* issues statements that govern the practice of managerial accounting. Accountants who pass a qualifying exam are awarded the CMA.

Flexibility of Practice   External users compare companies by using financial reports and need protection against false or misleading information. Accordingly, financial accounting relies on accepted principles that are enforced through an extensive set of rules and guidelines, or GAAP. Internal users need managerial accounting information for planning and controlling their company's activities rather than for external comparisons. They require different types of information depending on the activity. This makes standardizing managerial accounting systems across companies difficult. Instead, managerial accounting systems are flexible. The design of a company's managerial accounting system depends largely on the nature of the business and the arrangement of its internal operations. Managers can decide for themselves what information they want and how they want it reported. Even within a single company, different managers often design their own systems to meet their special needs. The important question a manager must ask is whether the information being collected and reported is useful for planning, decision making, and control purposes.

Point: Financial statements are usually issued several weeks after the period-end. GAAP requires the reporting of important events that occur while the statements are being prepared. These events are called *subsequent events.*

Point: Independent auditors test the integrity of managerial accounting records when they are used in preparing financial statements.

Timeliness of Information   Formal financial statements reporting past transactions and events are not immediately available to outside parties. Independent certified public accountants often must *audit* a company's financial statements before it provides them to external users. Thus, because audits often take several weeks to complete, financial reports to outsiders usually are not available until well after the period-end. However, managers can quickly obtain managerial accounting information. External auditors need not review it. Estimates and projections are acceptable. To get information quickly, managers often accept less precision in reports. As an example, an early internal report to management prepared right after the year-end could report net income for the year between $4.2 and $4.8 million. An audited income statement could later show net income for the year at $4.6 million. The internal report is not precise, but its information can be more useful because it is available earlier.

   Internal auditing plays an important role in managerial accounting. Internal auditors evaluate the flow of information not only inside but also outside the company. Managers are responsible for preventing and detecting fraudulent activities in their companies.

Time Dimension   To protect external users from false expectations, financial reports deal primarily with results of both past activities and current conditions. While some predictions such as service lives and salvage values of plant assets are necessary, financial accounting avoids predictions whenever possible. Managerial accounting regularly includes predictions of conditions and events. As an example, one important managerial accounting report is a budget, which predicts revenues, expenses, and other items. If managerial accounting reports were restricted to the past and present, managers would be less able to plan activities and less effective in managing and evaluating current activities.

EXHIBIT 14.3

Focus of External Reports

Focus of Information   Companies often organize into divisions and departments, but investors rarely can buy shares in one division or department. Nor do creditors lend money to a company's single division or department. Instead, they own shares in or make loans to the entire company. Financial accounting focuses primarily on a company as a whole as depicted in Exhibit 14.3. The

focus of managerial accounting is different. While top-level managers are responsible for managing the whole company, most other managers are responsible for much smaller sets of activities. These middle-level and lower-level managers need managerial accounting reports dealing with specific activities, projects, and subdivisions for which they are responsible. For instance, division sales managers are directly responsible only for the results achieved in their divisions. Accordingly, division sales managers need information about results achieved in their own divisions to improve their performance. This information includes the level of success achieved by each individual, product, or department in each division as depicted in Exhibit 14.4.

EXHIBIT 14.4

Focus of Internal Reports

Nature of Information Both financial and managerial accounting systems report monetary information. Managerial accounting systems also report considerable nonmonetary information. Monetary information is an important part of managerial decisions, and nonmonetary information plays a crucial role, especially when monetary effects are difficult to measure. Common examples of nonmonetary information are the quality and delivery criteria of purchasing decisions.

Decision Ethics   Answer — p. 623

Production Manager You invite three friends to a restaurant. When the dinner check arrives, David, a self-employed entrepreneur, picks it up saying, "Here, let me pay. I'll deduct it as a business expense on my tax return." Denise, a salesperson, takes the check from David's hand and says, "I'll put this on my company's credit card. It won't cost us anything." Derek, a factory manager for a company, laughs and says, "Neither of you understands. I'll put this on my company's credit card and call it overhead on a cost-plus contract my company has with a client." (*A cost-plus contract means the company receives its costs plus a percent of those costs.*) Adds Derek, "That way, my company pays for dinner *and* makes a profit." Who should pay the bill? Why? ∎

Managerial Decision Making

The previous section emphasized differences between financial and managerial accounting, but they are not entirely separate. Similar information is useful to both external and internal users. For instance, information about costs of manufacturing products is useful to all users in making decisions. Also, both financial and managerial accounting affect peoples' actions. For example, **Trek**'s design of a sales compensation plan affects the behavior of its salesforce when selling its manufactured bikes. It also must estimate the dual effects of promotion and sales compensation plans on buying patterns of customers. These estimates impact the equipment purchase decisions for manufacturing and can affect the supplier selection criteria established by purchasing. Thus, financial and managerial accounting systems do more than measure; they also affect people's decisions and actions.

Fraud and Ethics in Managerial Accounting

Fraud, and the role of ethics in reducing fraud, are important factors in running business operations. Fraud involves the use of one's job for personal gain through the deliberate misuse of the employer's assets. Examples include theft of the employer's cash or other assets, overstating reimbursable expenses, payroll schemes, and financial statement fraud. Fraud affects all business and it is costly: A 2008 *Report to the Nation* from the Association of Certified Fraud Examiners estimates the average U.S. business loses 7% of its annual revenues to fraud.

The most common type of fraud, where employees steal or misuse the employer's resources, results in an average loss of $175,000 per occurrence. For example, in a billing fraud, an employee sets up a bogus supplier. The employee then prepares bills from the supplier and pays these bills from the employer's checking account. The employee cashes the checks sent to the bogus supplier and uses them for his or her own personal benefit.

More generally, although there are many types of fraud schemes, all fraud:

- Is done to provide direct or indirect benefit to the employee.
- Violates the employee's obligations to the employer.
- Costs the employer money or loss of other assets.
- Is hidden from the employer.

Implications for Managerial Accounting   Fraud increases a business's costs. Left undetected, these inflated costs can result in poor pricing decisions, an improper product mix, and faulty performance evaluations. Management can develop accounting systems to closely track costs and identify deviations from expected amounts. In addition, managers rely on an **internal control system** to monitor and control business activities. An internal control system is the policies and procedures managers use to:

- Urge adherence to company policies.
- Promote efficient operations.
- Ensure reliable accounting.
- Protect assets.

Combating fraud and other dilemmas requires ethics in accounting. **Ethics** are beliefs that distinguish right from wrong. They are accepted standards of good and bad behavior. Identifying the ethical path can be difficult. The preferred path is a course of action that avoids casting doubt on one's decisions.

The **Institute of Management Accountants** (IMA), the professional association for management accountants, has issued a code of ethics to help accountants involved in solving ethical dilemmas. The IMA's Statement of Ethical Professional Practice requires that management accountants be competent, maintain confidentiality, act with integrity, and communicate information in a fair and credible manner.

The IMA provides a "road map" for resolving ethical conflicts. It suggests that an employee follow the company's policies on how to resolve such conflicts. If the conflict remains unresolved, an employee should contact the next level of management (such as the immediate supervisor) who is not involved in the ethical conflict.

Point: The IMA also issues the Certified Management Accountant (CMA) and the Certified Financial Manager (CFM) certifications. Employees with the CMA or CFM certifications typically earn higher salaries than those without.

Point: The **Sarbanes-Oxley Act** requires each issuer of securities to disclose whether it has adopted a code of ethics for its senior officers and the content of that code.

Quick Check	Answers — p. 624

1. Managerial accounting produces information (*a*) to meet internal users' needs, (*b*) to meet a user's specific needs, (*c*) often focusing on the future, or (*d*) all of these.
2. What is the difference between the intended users of financial and managerial accounting?
3. Do generally accepted accounting principles (GAAP) control and dictate managerial accounting?

MANAGERIAL COST CONCEPTS

C2 Describe accounting concepts useful in classifying costs.

An organization incurs many different types of costs that are classified differently, depending on management needs (different costs for different purposes). We can classify costs on the basis of their (1) behavior, (2) traceability, (3) controllability, (4) relevance, and (5) function. This section explains each concept for assigning costs to products and services.

Types of Cost Classifications

Classification by Behavior   At a basic level, a cost can be classified as fixed or variable. A **fixed cost** does not change with changes in the volume of activity (within a range of activity known as an activity's *relevant range*). For example, straight-line depreciation on equipment is a fixed cost. A **variable cost** changes in proportion to changes in the volume of activity. Sales commissions computed as a percent of sales revenue are variable costs. Additional examples of fixed and variable costs for a bike manufacturer are provided in Exhibit 14.5. When cost items are combined, total cost can be fixed, variable, or mixed. *Mixed* refers to a combination of fixed and variable costs. Equipment rental often includes a fixed cost for some minimum amount and a variable cost based on amount of usage. Classification of costs by behavior is helpful in cost-volume-profit analyses and short-term decision making. We discuss these in Chapters 18 and 23.

EXHIBIT 14.5

Fixed and Variable Costs

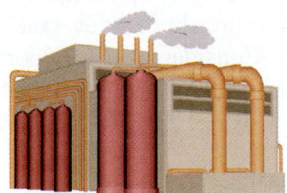

Fixed Cost: Rent for Rocky Mountain Bikes' building is $22,000, and it doesn't change with the number of bikes produced.

Variable Cost: Cost of bicycle tires is variable with the number of bikes produced—this cost is $15 per pair.

Classification by Traceability   A cost is often traced to a **cost object,** which is a product, process, department, or customer to which costs are assigned. **Direct costs** are those traceable to a single cost object. For example, if a product is a cost object, its material and labor costs are usually directly traceable. **Indirect costs** are those that cannot be easily and cost–beneficially traced to a single cost object. An example of an indirect cost is a maintenance plan that benefits two or more departments. Exhibit 14.6 identifies examples of both direct and indirect costs for the maintenance department in a manufacturing plant. Thus, salaries of Rocky Mountain Bikes' maintenance department employees are considered indirect if the cost object is bicycles and direct if the cost object is the maintenance department. Classification of costs by traceability is useful for cost allocation. This is discussed in Chapter 22.

EXHIBIT 14.6

Direct and Indirect Costs of a Maintenance Department

Direct Costs		Indirect Costs	
• Salaries of maintenance department employees	• Materials purchased by maintenance department	• Factory accounting	• Factory light and heat
• Equipment purchased by maintenance department	• Maintenance department equipment depreciation	• Factory administration	• Factory internal audit
		• Factory rent	• Factory intranet
		• Factory manager's salary	• Insurance on factory

Decision Maker   Answer — p. 623

Entrepreneur   You wish to trace as many of your assembly department's direct costs as possible. You can trace 90% of them in an economical manner. To trace the other 10%, you need sophisticated and costly accounting software. Do you purchase this software? ■

Classification by Controllability   A cost can be defined as **controllable** or **not controllable.** Whether a cost is controllable or not depends on the employee's responsibilities, as shown in Exhibit 14.7. This is referred to as *hierarchical levels* in management, or *pecking order.* For example, investments in machinery are controllable by upper-level managers but not lower-level managers. Many daily operating expenses such as overtime often are controllable by lower-level managers. Classification of costs by controllability is especially useful for assigning responsibility to and evaluating managers.

EXHIBIT 14.7

Controllability of Costs

Senior Manager Controls costs of investments in land, buildings, and equipment.

Supervisor Controls daily expenses such as supplies, maintenance, and overtime.

Point: Opportunity costs are not recorded by the accounting system.

Classification by Relevance   A cost can be classified by relevance by identifying it as either a sunk cost or an out-of-pocket cost. A **sunk cost** has already been incurred and cannot be avoided or changed. It is irrelevant to future decisions. One example is the cost of a company's office equipment previously purchased. An **out-of-pocket cost** requires a future outlay of cash and is relevant for decision making. Future purchases of equipment involve out-of-pocket costs. A discussion of relevant costs must also consider opportunity costs. An **opportunity cost** is the potential benefit lost by choosing a specific action from two or more alternatives. One example is a student giving up wages from a job to attend evening classes. Consideration of opportunity cost is important when, for example, an insurance company must decide whether to outsource its payroll function or maintain it internally. This is discussed in Chapter 23.

C3 Define product and period costs and explain how they impact financial statements.

Classification by Function   Another cost classification (for manufacturers) is capitalization as inventory or to expense as incurred. Costs capitalized as inventory are called **product costs,** which refer to expenditures necessary and integral to finished products. They include direct materials, direct labor, and indirect manufacturing costs called *overhead costs*. Product costs pertain to activities carried out to manufacture the product. Costs expensed are called **period costs,** which refer to expenditures identified more with a time period than with finished products. They include selling and general administrative expenses. Period costs pertain to activities that are not part of the manufacturing process. A distinction between product and period costs is important because period costs are expensed in the income statement and product costs are assigned to inventory on the balance sheet until that inventory is sold. An ability to understand and identify product costs and period costs is crucial to using and interpreting a *manufacturing statement* described later in this chapter.

Point: Only costs of production and purchases are classed as product costs.

Exhibit 14.8 shows the different effects of product and period costs. Period costs flow directly to the current income statement as expenses. They are not reported as assets. Product costs are first assigned to inventory. Their final treatment depends on when inventory is sold or disposed of. Product costs assigned to finished goods that are sold in year 2011 are reported on the 2011 income statement as part of cost of goods sold. Product costs assigned to unsold inventory are carried forward on the balance sheet at the end of year 2011. If this inventory is sold in year 2012 product costs assigned to it are reported as part of cost of goods sold in that year's income statement.

Point: Product costs are either in the income statement as part of cost of goods sold or in the balance sheet as inventory. Period costs appear only on the income statement under operating expenses. See Exhibit 14.8.

The difference between period and product costs explains why the year 2011 income statement does not report operating expenses related to either factory workers' wages or depreciation on factory buildings and equipment. Instead, both costs are combined with the cost of raw materials to compute the product cost of finished goods. A portion of these manufacturing costs

EXHIBIT 14.8

Period and Product Costs in Financial Statements

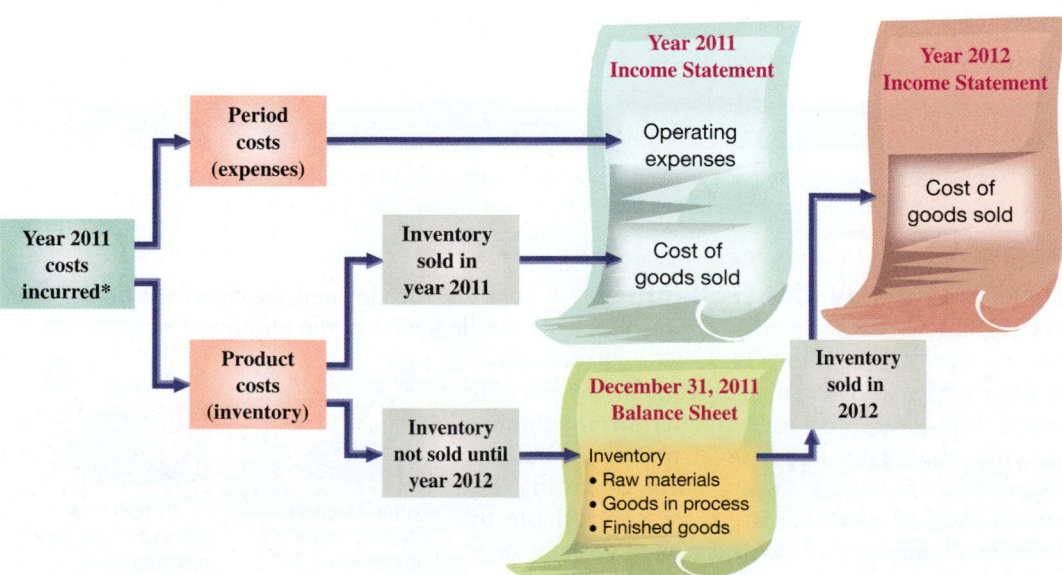

* This diagram excludes costs to acquire assets other than inventory.

Point: For a team approach to identifying period and product costs, see *Teamwork in Action* in the *Beyond the Numbers* section.

(related to the goods sold) is reported in the year 2011 income statement as part of Cost of Goods Sold. The other portion is reported on the balance sheet at the end of that year as part of Inventory. The portion assigned to inventory could be included in any or all of raw materials, goods in process, or finished goods inventories.

Decision Maker   Answer — p. 624

Purchase Manager   You are evaluating two potential suppliers of seats for the manufacturing of motor-cycles. One supplier (A) quotes a $145 price per seat and ensures 100% quality standards and on-time delivery. The second supplier (B) quotes a $115 price per seat but does not give any written assurances on quality or delivery. You decide to contract with the second supplier (B), saving $30 per seat. Does this decision have opportunity costs? ■

Identification of Cost Classifications

It is important to understand that a cost can be classified using any one (or combination) of the five different means described here. To do this we must understand costs and operations. Specifically, for the five classifications, we must be able to identify the *activity* for behavior, *cost object* for traceability, *management hierarchical level* for controllability, *opportunity cost* for relevance, and *benefit period* for function. Factory rent, for instance, can be classified as a product cost; it is fixed with respect to number of units produced, it is indirect with respect to the product, and it is not controllable by a production supervisor. Potential multiple classifications are shown in Exhibit 14.9 using different cost items incurred in manufacturing mountain bikes. The finished bike is the cost object. Proper allocation of these costs and the managerial decisions based on cost data depend on a correct cost classification.

Cost Item	By Behavior	By Traceability	By Function
Bicycle tires	Variable	Direct	Product
Wages of assembly worker*	Variable	Direct	Product
Advertising	Fixed	Indirect	Period
Production manager's salary	Fixed	Indirect	Product
Office depreciation	Fixed	Indirect	Period

EXHIBIT 14.9

Examples of Multiple Cost Classifications

* Although an assembly worker's wages are classified as variable costs, their actual behavior depends on how workers are paid and whether their wages are based on a union contract (such as piece rate or monthly wages).

Cost Concepts for Service Companies

The cost concepts described are generally applicable to service organizations. For example, consider **Southwest Airlines**. Its cost of beverages for passengers is a variable cost based on number of passengers. The cost of leasing an aircraft is fixed with respect to number of passengers. We can also trace a flight crew's salary to a specific flight whereas we likely cannot trace wages for the ground crew to a specific flight. Classification by function (such as product versus period costs) is not relevant to service companies because services are not inventoried. Instead, costs incurred by a service firm are expensed in the reporting period when incurred.

Managers in service companies must understand and apply cost concepts. They seek and rely on accurate cost estimates for many decisions. For example, an airline manager must often decide between canceling or rerouting flights. The manager must also be able to estimate costs saved by canceling a flight versus rerouting. Knowledge of fixed costs is equally important. We explain more about the cost requirements for these and other managerial decisions in Chapter 23.

Point: All expenses of service companies are period costs because these companies do not have inventory.

Service Costs
- Beverages and snacks
- Cleaning fees
- Pilot and copilot salaries
- Attendant salaries
- Fuel and oil costs
- Travel agent fees
- Ground crew salaries

Quick Check   Answers — p. 624

4. Which type of cost behavior increases total costs when volume of activity increases?

5. How could traceability of costs improve managerial decisions?

REPORTING MANUFACTURING ACTIVITIES

Companies with manufacturing activities differ from both merchandising and service companies. The main difference between merchandising and manufacturing companies is that merchandisers buy goods ready for sale while manufacturers produce goods from materials and labor. **Payless** is an example of a merchandising company. It buys and sells shoes without physically changing them. **Adidas** is primarily a manufacturer of shoes, apparel, and accessories. It purchases materials such as leather, cloth, dye, plastic, rubber, glue, and laces and then uses employees' labor to convert these materials to products. **Southwest Airlines** is a service company that transports people and items.

Manufacturing activities differ from both selling merchandise and providing services. Also, the financial statements for manufacturing companies differ slightly. This section considers some of these differences and compares them to accounting for a merchandising company.

Manufacturer's Balance Sheet

> **C4** Explain how balance sheets and income statements for manufacturing and merchandising companies differ.

Manufacturers carry several unique assets and usually have three inventories instead of the single inventory that merchandisers carry. Exhibit 14.10 shows three different inventories in the current asset section of the balance sheet for Rocky Mountain Bikes, a manufacturer. The three inventories are raw materials, goods in process, and finished goods.

Raw Materials Inventory **Raw materials inventory** refers to the goods a company acquires to use in making products. It uses raw materials in two ways: directly and indirectly. Most raw materials physically become part of a product and are identified with specific units or batches of a product. Raw materials used directly in a product are called *direct materials*. Other materials used to support production processes are sometimes not as clearly identified with specific units or batches of product. These materials are called **indirect materials** because they are not clearly identified with specific product units or batches. Items used as indirect materials often appear on a balance sheet as factory supplies or are included in raw materials. Some direct materials are classified as indirect materials when their costs are low (insignificant). Examples include screws and nuts used in assembling mountain bikes and staples and glue used in manufacturing shoes. Using

> **Point:** Reducing the size of inventories saves storage costs and frees money for other uses.

EXHIBIT 14.10

Balance Sheet for a Manufacturer

ROCKY MOUNTAIN BIKES Balance Sheet December 31, 2011			
Assets		**Liabilities and Equity**	
Current assets		Current liabilities	
Cash	$ 11,000	Accounts payable	$ 14,000
Accounts receivable, net	30,150	Wages payable	540
Raw materials inventory	**9,000**	Interest payable	2,000
Goods in process inventory	**7,500**	Income taxes payable	32,600
Finished goods inventory	**10,300**	Total current liabilities	49,140
Factory supplies	350		
Prepaid insurance	300	Long-term liabilities	
Total current assets	68,600	Long-term notes payable	50,000
Plant assets		Total liabilities	99,140
Small tools, net	1,100		
Delivery equipment, net	5,000	Stockholders' equity	
Office equipment, net	1,300	Common stock, $1.2 par	24,000
Factory machinery, net	65,500	Paid-in capital	76,000
Factory building, net	86,700	Retained earnings	49,760
Land	9,500	Total stockholders' equity	149,760
Total plant assets, net	169,100		
Intangible assets (patents), net	11,200	Total liabilities and equity	$248,900
Total assets	$248,900		

the *materiality principle,* individually tracing the costs of each of these materials and classifying them separately as direct materials does not make much economic sense. For instance, keeping detailed records of the amount of glue used to manufacture one shoe is not cost beneficial.

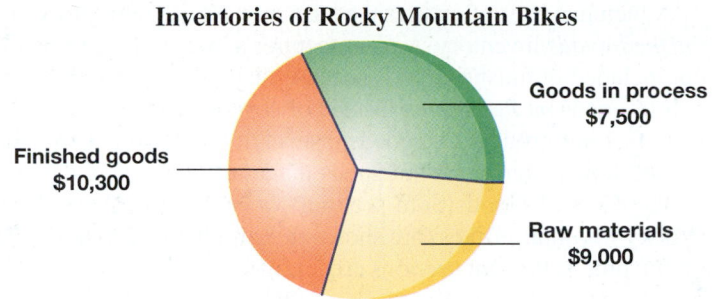

Inventories of Rocky Mountain Bikes

Finished goods $10,300

Goods in process $7,500

Raw materials $9,000

Goods in Process Inventory   Another inventory held by manufacturers is **goods in process inventory,** also called *work in process inventory.* It consists of products in the process of being manufactured but not yet complete. The amount of goods in process inventory depends on the type of production process. If the time required to produce a unit of product is short, the goods in process inventory is likely small; but if weeks or months are needed to produce a unit, the goods in process inventory is usually larger.

Finished Goods Inventory   A third inventory owned by a manufacturer is **finished goods inventory,** which consists of completed products ready for sale. This inventory is similar to merchandise inventory owned by a merchandising company. Manufacturers also often own unique plant assets such as small tools, factory buildings, factory equipment, and patents to manufacture products. The balance sheet in Exhibit 14.10 shows that Rocky Mountain Bikes owns all of these assets. Some manufacturers invest millions or even billions of dollars in production facilities and patents. **Briggs & Stratton**'s recent balance sheet shows about $1 billion net investment in land, buildings, machinery and equipment, much of which involves production facilities. It manufactures more racing engines than any other company in the world.

Manufacturer's Income Statement

The main difference between the income statement of a manufacturer and that of a merchandiser involves the items making up cost of goods sold. Exhibit 14.11 compares the components of cost of goods sold for a manufacturer and a merchandiser. A merchandiser adds cost of goods purchased to beginning merchandise inventory and then subtracts ending merchandise inventory to get cost of goods sold. A manufacturer adds cost of goods manufactured to beginning finished goods inventory and then subtracts ending finished goods inventory to get cost of goods sold.

P1 Compute cost of goods sold for a manufacturer.

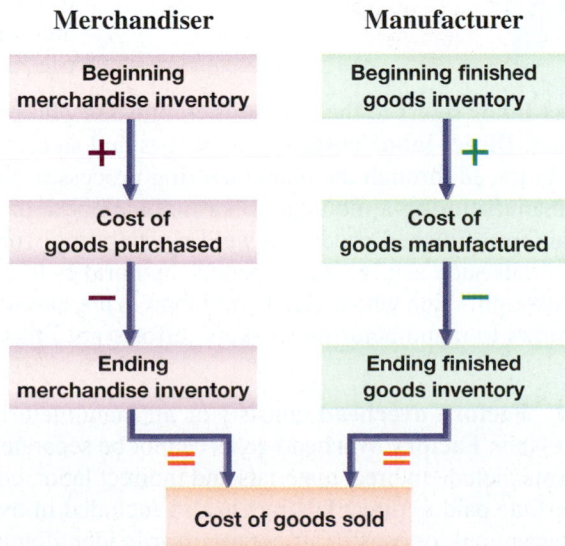

Merchandiser

Beginning merchandise inventory

+

Cost of goods purchased

−

Ending merchandise inventory

=

Manufacturer

Beginning finished goods inventory

+

Cost of goods manufactured

−

Ending finished goods inventory

=

Cost of goods sold

EXHIBIT 14.11

Cost of Goods Sold Computation

A merchandiser often uses the term *merchandise* inventory; a manufacturer often uses the term *finished goods* inventory. A manufacturer's inventories of raw materials and goods in process are not included in finished goods because they are not available for sale. A manufacturer also shows cost of goods *manufactured* instead of cost of goods *purchased*. This difference occurs because a manufacturer produces its goods instead of purchasing them ready for sale. We show later in this chapter how to derive cost of goods manufactured from the manufacturing statement.

EXHIBIT 14.12

Cost of Goods Sold for a Merchandiser and Manufacturer

The Cost of Goods Sold sections for both a merchandiser (Tele-Mart) and a manufacturer (Rocky Mountain Bikes) are shown in Exhibit 14.12 to highlight these differences. The remaining income statement sections are similar.

Merchandising (Tele-Mart) Company		Manufacturing (Rocky Mtn. Bikes) Company	
Cost of goods sold		Cost of goods sold	
Beginning *merchandise* inventory	$ 14,200	**Beginning *finished goods* inventory**	$ 11,200
Cost of merchandise *purchased*	234,150	**Cost of goods *manufactured***	170,500
Goods available for sale	248,350	Goods available for sale	181,700
Less ending *merchandise* inventory	12,100	**Less ending *finished goods* inventory**	10,300
Cost of goods sold	$236,250	Cost of goods sold	$171,400

* Cost of goods manufactured is reported in the income statement of Exhibit 14.14.

Although the cost of goods sold computations are similar, the numbers in these computations reflect different activities. A merchandiser's cost of goods purchased is the cost of buying products to be sold. A manufacturer's cost of goods manufactured is the sum of direct materials, direct labor, and factory overhead costs incurred in producing products. The remainder of this section further explains these three manufacturing costs and describes prime and conversion costs.

Direct Materials   **Direct materials** are tangible components of a finished product. **Direct material costs** are the expenditures for direct materials that are separately and readily traced through the manufacturing process to finished goods. Examples of direct materials in manufacturing a mountain bike include its tires, seat, frame, pedals, brakes, cables, gears, and handlebars. The chart in the margin shows that direct materials generally make up about 45% of manufacturing costs in today's products, but this amount varies across industries and companies.

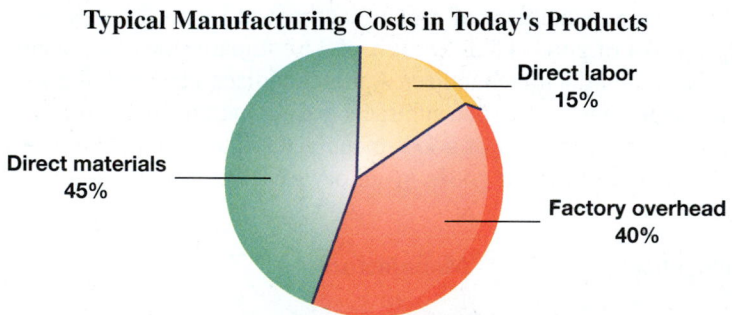

Typical Manufacturing Costs in Today's Products

Direct labor 15%

Direct materials 45%

Factory overhead 40%

Direct Labor   **Direct labor** refers to the efforts of employees who physically convert materials to finished product. **Direct labor costs** are the wages and salaries for direct labor that are separately and readily traced through the manufacturing process to finished goods. Examples of direct labor in manufacturing a mountain bike include operators directly involved in converting raw materials into finished products (welding, painting, forming) and assembly workers who attach materials such as tires, seats, pedals, and brakes to the bike frames. Costs of other workers on the assembly line who assist direct laborers are classified as **indirect labor costs**. **Indirect labor** refers to manufacturing workers' efforts not linked to specific units or batches of the product.

Point: Indirect labor costs are part of factory overhead.

Factory Overhead   **Factory overhead** consists of all manufacturing costs that are not direct materials or direct labor. **Factory overhead costs** cannot be separately or readily traced to finished goods. These costs include indirect materials and indirect labor, costs not directly traceable to the product. Overtime paid to direct laborers is also included in overhead because overtime is due to delays, interruptions, or constraints not necessarily identifiable to a specific product or batches of product. Factory overhead costs also include maintenance of the mountain bike

Point: Factory overhead is also called *manufacturing overhead.*

factory, supervision of its employees, repairing manufacturing equipment, factory utilities (water, gas, electricity), production manager's salary, factory rent, depreciation on factory buildings and equipment, factory insurance, property taxes on factory buildings and equipment, and factory accounting and legal services. Factory overhead does *not* include selling and administrative expenses because they are not incurred in manufacturing products. These expenses are called *period costs* and are recorded as expenses on the income statement when incurred.

Prime and Conversion Costs   Direct material costs and direct labor costs are also called **prime costs**—expenditures directly associated with the manufacture of finished goods. Direct labor costs and overhead costs are called **conversion costs**—expenditures incurred in the process of converting raw materials to finished goods. Direct labor costs are considered both prime costs and conversion costs. Exhibit 14.13 conveys the relation between prime and conversion costs and their components of direct material, direct labor, and factory overhead.

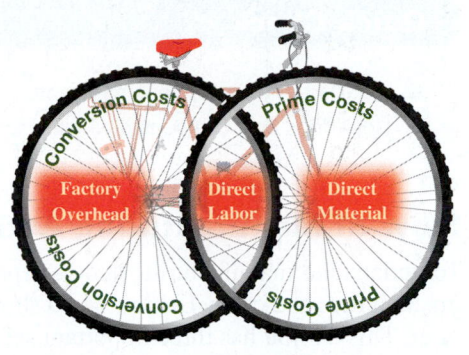

EXHIBIT 14.13

Prime and Conversion Costs and Their Makeup

Prime costs =
Direct materials + Direct labor.
Conversion costs =
Direct labor + Factory overhead.

Reporting Performance   Exhibit 14.14 shows the income statement for Rocky Mountain Bikes. Its operating expenses include sales salaries, office salaries, and depreciation of delivery and office equipment. Operating expenses do not include manufacturing costs such as

EXHIBIT 14.14

Income Statement for a Manufacturer

ROCKY MOUNTAIN BIKES Income Statement For Year Ended December 31, 2011		
Sales...		$310,000
Cost of goods sold		
Finished goods inventory, Dec. 31, 2010	$ 11,200	
Cost of goods manufactured	170,500	
Goods available for sale	181,700	
Less finished goods inventory, Dec. 31, 2011	10,300	
Cost of goods sold		171,400
Gross profit......................................		138,600
Operating expenses		
Selling expenses		
Sales salaries expense	18,000	
Advertising expense	5,500	
Delivery wages expense	12,000	
Shipping supplies expense.......................	250	
Insurance expense—Delivery equipment	300	
Depreciation expense—Delivery equipment	2,100	
Total selling expenses		38,150
General and administrative expenses		
Office salaries expense	15,700	
Miscellaneous expense	200	
Bad debts expense	1,550	
Office supplies expense	100	
Depreciation expense—Office equipment	200	
Interest expense	4,000	
Total general and administrative expenses		21,750
Total operating expenses		59,900
Income before income taxes		78,700
Income taxes expense		32,600
Net income		$ 46,100

Point: Manufacturers treat costs such as depreciation and rent as product costs if they are related to manufacturing.

factory workers' wages and depreciation of production equipment and the factory buildings. These manufacturing costs are reported as part of cost of goods manufactured and included in cost of goods sold. We explained why and how this is done in the section "Classification by Function."

Quick Check   Answers — p. 624

6. What are the three types of inventory on a manufacturing company's balance sheet?
7. How does cost of goods sold differ for merchandising versus manufacturing companies?

Flow of Manufacturing Activities

C5 Explain manufacturing activities and the flow of manufacturing costs.

To understand manufacturing and its reports, we must first understand the flow of manufacturing activities and costs. Exhibit 14.15 shows the flow of manufacturing activities for a manufacturer. This exhibit has three important sections: *materials activity, production activity,* and *sales activity.* We explain each activity in this section.

EXHIBIT 14.15

Activities and Cost Flows in Manufacturing

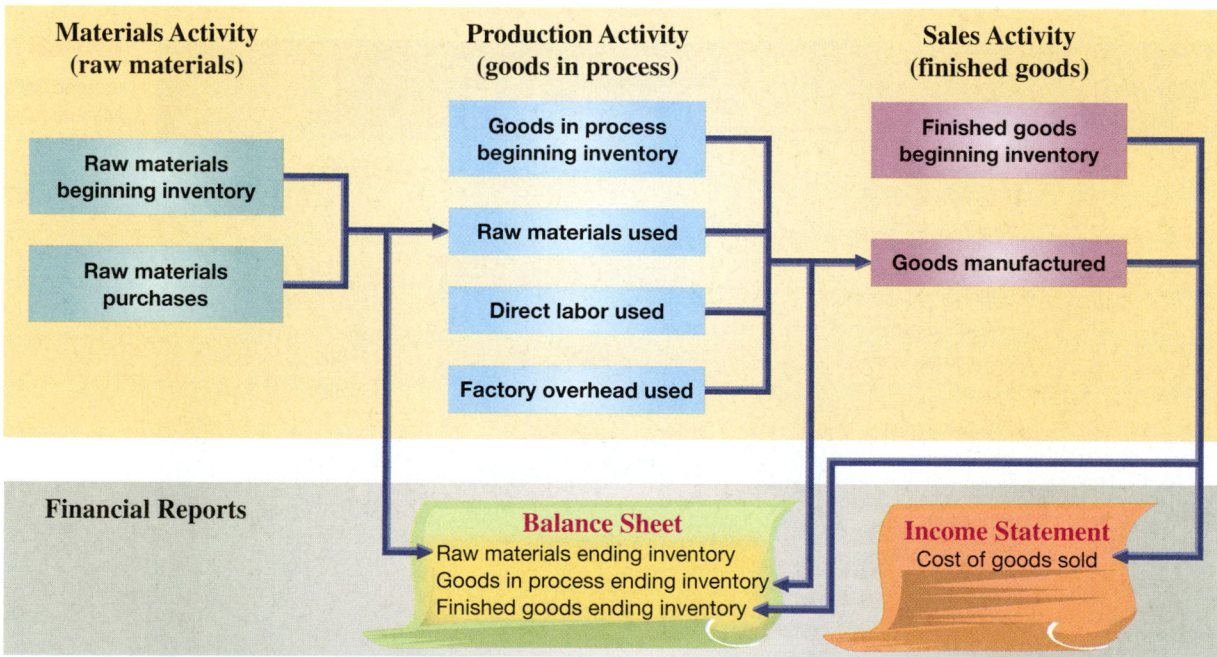

Point: Knowledge of managerial accounting provides us a means of measuring manufacturing costs and is a sound foundation for studying advanced business topics.

Materials Activity   The far left side of Exhibit 14.15 shows the flow of raw materials. Manufacturers usually start a period with some beginning raw materials inventory carried over from the previous period. The company then acquires additional raw materials in the current period. Adding these purchases to beginning inventory gives total raw materials available for use in production. These raw materials are then either used in production in the current period or remain in inventory at the end of the period for use in future periods.

Production Activity   The middle section of Exhibit 14.15 describes production activity. Four factors come together in production: beginning goods in process inventory, direct materials, direct labor, and overhead. Beginning goods in process inventory consists of partly assembled products from the previous period. Production activity results in products that are either finished or remain unfinished. The cost of finished products makes up the cost of goods manufactured for the current period. Unfinished products are identified as ending goods in process inventory. The cost of unfinished products consists of direct materials, direct labor, and factory overhead, and is reported on the current period's balance sheet. The costs of both finished goods manufactured and goods in process are *product costs.*

Sales Activity   The company's sales activity is portrayed in the far right side of Exhibit 14.15. Newly completed units are combined with beginning finished goods inventory to make up total finished goods available for sale in the current period. The cost of finished products sold is reported on the income statement as cost of goods sold. The cost of products not sold is reported on the current period's balance sheet as ending finished goods inventory.

Manufacturing Statement

A company's manufacturing activities are described in a **manufacturing statement,** also called the *schedule of manufacturing activities* or the *schedule of cost of goods manufactured.* The manufacturing statement summarizes the types and amounts of costs incurred in a company's manufacturing process. Exhibit 14.16 shows the manufacturing statement for Rocky Mountain Bikes. The statement is divided into four parts: *direct materials, direct labor, overhead,* and *computation of cost of goods manufactured.* We describe each of these parts in this section.

P2 Prepare a manufacturing statement and explain its purpose and links to financial statements.

① The manufacturing statement begins by computing direct materials used. We start by adding beginning raw materials inventory of $8,000 to the current period's purchases of $86,500. This yields $94,500 of total raw materials available for use. A physical count of inventory shows $9,000 of ending raw materials inventory. This implies a total cost of raw materials used during the period of $85,500 ($94,500 total raw materials available for use − $9,000 ending inventory). (*Note:* All raw materials are direct materials for Rocky Mountain Bikes.)

EXHIBIT 14.16

Manufacturing Statement

ROCKY MOUNTAIN BIKES Manufacturing Statement For Year Ended December 31, 2011		
Direct materials		
Raw materials inventory, Dec. 31, 2010	$ 8,000	
Raw materials purchases	86,500	
Raw materials available for use	94,500	
Less raw materials inventory, Dec. 31, 2011	9,000	
Direct materials used		$ 85,500
Direct labor		60,000
Factory overhead		
Indirect labor	9,000	
Factory supervision	6,000	
Factory utilities	2,600	
Repairs—Factory equipment	2,500	
Property taxes—Factory building	1,900	
Factory supplies used	600	
Factory insurance expired	1,100	
Depreciation expense—Small tools	200	
Depreciation expense—Factory equipment	3,500	
Depreciation expense—Factory building	1,800	
Amortization expense—Patents	800	
Total factory overhead		30,000
Total manufacturing costs		175,500
Add goods in process inventory, Dec. 31, 2010		2,500
Total cost of goods in process		178,000
Less goods in process inventory, Dec. 31, 2011		7,500
Cost of goods manufactured		$170,500

Point: Direct material and direct labor costs increase with increases in production volume and are called *variable costs*. Overhead can be both variable and fixed. When overhead costs vary with production, they are called *variable overhead*. When overhead costs don't vary with production, they are called *fixed overhead*.

Point: Manufacturers sometimes report variable and fixed overhead separately in the manufacturing statement to provide more information to managers about cost behavior.

② The second part of the manufacturing statement reports direct labor costs. Rocky Mountain Bikes had total direct labor costs of $60,000 for the period. This amount includes payroll taxes and fringe benefits.

③ The third part of the manufacturing statement reports overhead costs. The statement lists each important factory overhead item and its cost. Total factory overhead cost for the period is $30,000. Some companies report only *total* factory overhead on the manufacturing statement and attach a separate schedule listing individual overhead costs.

④ The final section of the manufacturing statement computes and reports the *cost of goods manufactured*. (Total manufacturing costs for the period are $175,500 [$85,500 + $60,000 + $30,000], the sum of direct materials used and direct labor and overhead costs incurred.) This amount is first added to beginning goods in process inventory. This gives the total goods in process inventory of $178,000 ($175,500 + $2,500). We then compute the current period's cost of goods manufactured of $170,500 by taking the $178,000 total goods in process and subtracting the $7,500 cost of ending goods in process inventory that consists of direct materials, direct labor, and factory overhead. The cost of goods manufactured amount is also called *net cost of goods manufactured* or *cost of goods completed*. Exhibit 14.14 shows that this item and amount are listed in the Cost of Goods Sold section of Rocky Mountain Bikes' income statement and the balance sheet.

A managerial accounting system records costs and reports them in various reports that eventually determine financial statements. Exhibit 14.17 shows how overhead costs flow through the system: from an initial listing of specific costs, to a section of the manufacturing statement, to the reporting on the income statement and the balance sheet.

Management uses information in the manufacturing statement to plan and control the company's manufacturing activities. To provide timely information for decision making, the

EXHIBIT 14.17

Overhead Cost Flows across Accounting Reports

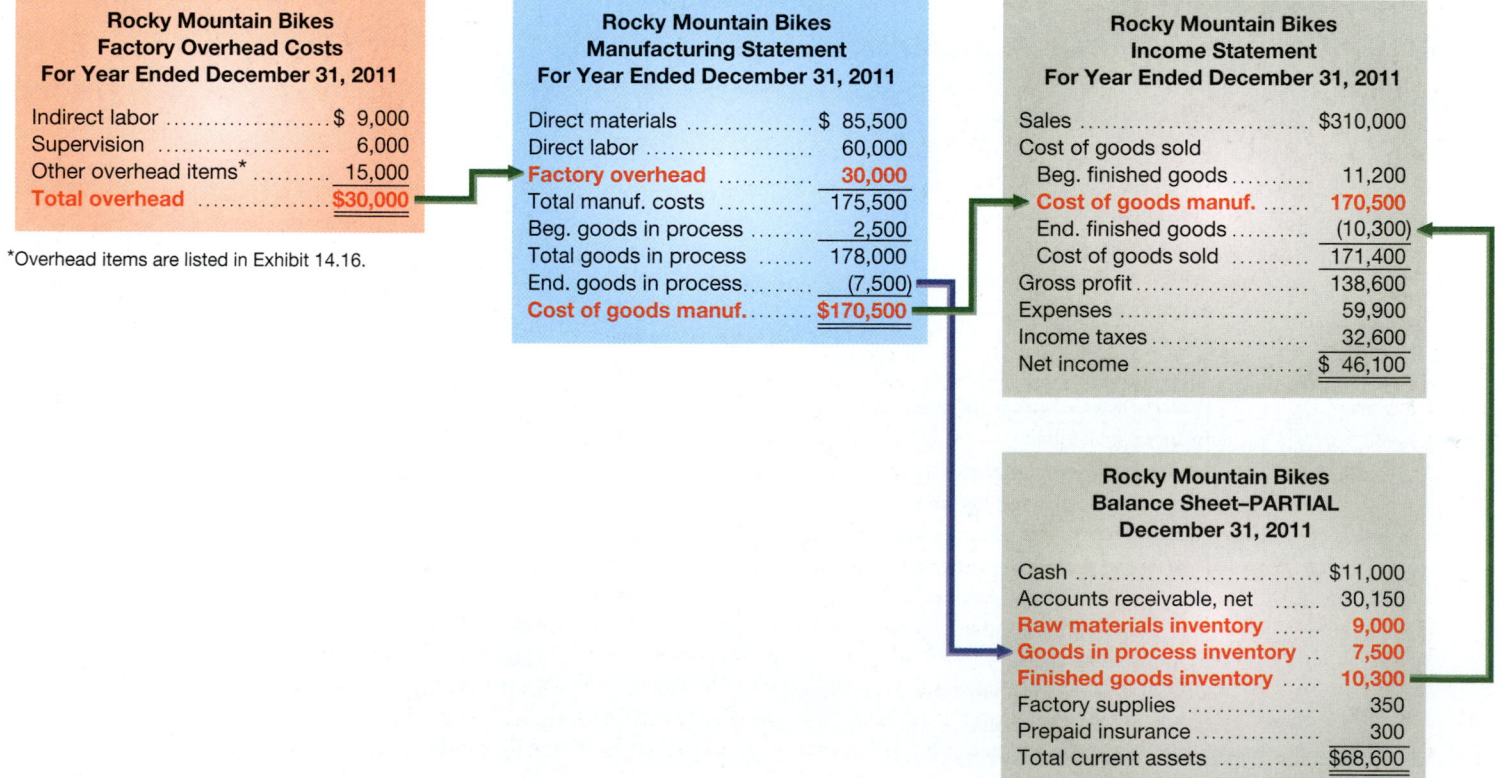

*Overhead items are listed in Exhibit 14.16.

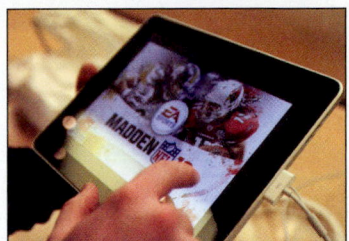

statement is often prepared monthly, weekly, or even daily. In anticipation of release of its much-hyped iPad, **Apple** grew its inventory of critical components, and its finished goods inventory. The manufacturing statement contains information useful to external users but is not a general-purpose financial statement. Companies rarely publish the manufacturing statement because managers view this information as proprietary and potentially harmful to them if released to competitors.

Quick Check   Answers — p. 624

8. A manufacturing statement (*a*) computes cost of goods manufactured for the period, (*b*) computes cost of goods sold for the period, or (*c*) reports operating expenses incurred for the period.

9. Are companies required to report a manufacturing statement?

10. How are both beginning and ending goods in process inventories reported on a manufacturing statement?

Trends in Managerial Accounting

The analytical tools and techniques of managerial accounting have always been useful, and their relevance and importance continue to increase. This is so because of changes in the business environment. This section describes some of these changes and their impact on managerial accounting.

C6 Describe trends in managerial accounting.

Customer Orientation   There is an increased emphasis on *customers* as the most important constituent of a business. Customers expect to derive a certain value for the money they spend to buy products and services. Specifically, they expect that their suppliers will offer them the right service (or product) at the right time and the right price. This implies that companies accept the notion of **customer orientation,** which means that employees understand the changing needs and wants of their customers and align their management and operating practices accordingly.

Global Economy   Our *global economy* expands competitive boundaries and provides customers more choices. The global economy also produces changes in business activities. One notable case that reflects these changes in customer demand and global competition is auto manufacturing. The top three Japanese auto manufacturers (**Honda**, **Nissan**, and **Toyota**) once controlled more than 40% of the U.S. auto market. Customers perceived that Japanese auto manufacturers provided value not available from other manufacturers. Many European and North American auto manufacturers responded to this challenge and regained much of the lost market share.

E-Commerce   People have become increasingly interconnected via smartphones, text messaging, and other electronic applications. Consumers thus expect and demand to be able to buy items electronically, whenever and wherever they want. Many businesses have enhanced their Websites to allow for online transactions. Online sales now make up over 7% of total retail sales.

Service Economy   Businesses that provide services, such as telecommunications and health care, constitute an ever-growing part of our economy. In developed economies like the United States, service businesses typically account for over 60% to 70% of total economic activity.

Companies must be alert to these and other factors. Many companies have responded by adopting the **lean business model,** whose goal is to *eliminate waste* while "satisfying the customer" and "providing a positive return" to the company.

Lean Practices   **Continuous improvement** rejects the notions of "good enough" or "acceptable" and challenges employees and managers to continuously experiment with new and improved business practices. This has led companies to adopt practices such as total quality management (TQM) and just-in-time (JIT) manufacturing. The philosophy underlying both practices is continuous improvement; the difference is in the focus.

Point: Goals of a TQM process include reduced waste, better inventory control, fewer defects, and continuous improvement. Just-in-time concepts have similar goals.

    Total quality management focuses on quality improvement and applies this standard to all aspects of business activities. In doing so, managers and employees seek to uncover waste in business activities including accounting activities such as payroll and disbursements. To encourage an emphasis on quality, the U.S. Congress established the Malcolm Baldrige National Quality Award (MBNQA). Entrants must conduct a thorough analysis and evaluation of their business using guidelines from the Baldrige committee. **Ritz Carlton Hotel** is a recipient of the Baldrige award in the service category. The company applies a core set of values, collectively called *The Gold Standards,* to improve customer service.

Point: The time between buying raw materials and selling finished goods is called *throughput time.*

    Just-in-time manufacturing is a system that acquires inventory and produces only when needed. An important aspect of JIT is that companies manufacture products only after they receive an order (a *demand-pull* system) and then deliver the customer's requirements on time. This means that processes must be aligned to eliminate any delays and inefficiencies including inferior inputs and outputs. Companies must also establish good relations and communications with their suppliers. On the downside, JIT is more susceptible to disruption than traditional systems. As one example, several **General Motors** plants were temporarily shut down due to a strike at an assembly division; the plants supplied components *just in time* to the assembly division.

Value Chain   The **value chain** refers to the series of activities that add value to a company's products or services. Exhibit 14.18 illustrates a possible value chain for a retail cookie company. Companies can use lean practices to increase efficiency and profits.

EXHIBIT 14.18

Typical Value Chain (Cookie Retailer)

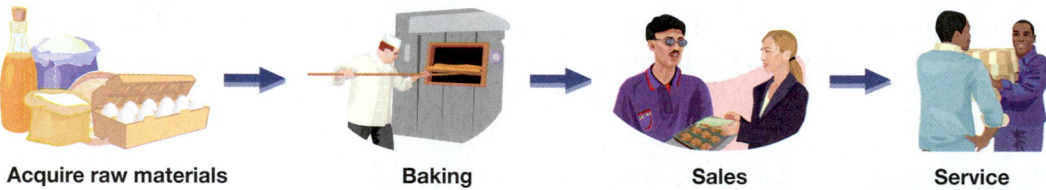

Acquire raw materials   Baking   Sales   Service

Decision Insight

Global Lean   **Toyota Motor Corporation** pioneered lean manufacturing, and it has since spread to other manufacturers throughout the world. The goals include improvements in quality, reliability, inventory turnover, productivity, exports, and—above all—sales and income. ■

"My boss wants us to appeal to a younger and hipper crowd. So, I'd like to get a tattoo that says-- 'Accounting rules!'"

Implications for Managerial Accounting   Adopting the lean business model can be challenging because to foster its implementation, all systems and procedures that a company follows must be realigned. Managerial accounting has an important role to play by providing accurate cost and performance information. Companies must understand the nature and sources of cost and must develop systems that capture costs accurately. Developing such a system is important to measuring the "value" provided to customers. The price that customers pay for acquiring goods and services is an important determinant of value. In turn, the costs a company incurs are key determinants of price. All else being equal, the better a company is at controlling its costs, the better its performance.

Decision Insight

Balanced Scorecard The *balanced scorecard* aids continuous improvement by augmenting financial measures with information on the "drivers" (indicators) of future financial performance along four dimensions: (1) *financial*—profitability and risk, (2) *customer*—value creation and product and service differentiation, (3) *internal business processes*—business activities that create customer and owner satisfaction, and (4) *learning and growth*—organizational change, innovation, and growth. ■

 ## GLOBAL VIEW

Managerial accounting is more flexible than financial accounting and does not follow a set of strict rules. However, many international businesses use the managerial accounting concepts and principles described in this chapter.

Customer Focus **Nestlé**, one of the world's leading nutrition and wellness companies, adopts a customer focus and strives to understand its customers' tastes. For example, Nestlé employees spent three days living with people in Lima, Peru, to understand their motivations, routines, buying habits, and everyday lives. This allowed Nestlé to adjust its products to suit local tastes.

Reporting Manufacturing Activities Nestlé must classify and report costs. In reporting inventory, Nestlé includes direct production costs, production overhead, and factory depreciation. A recent Nestlé annual report shows the following:

(in millions of Swiss francs)	Ending Inventory	Beginning Inventory
Raw materials, work in progress, and sundry supplies	3,708	3,590
Finished goods	5,901	3,590

Nestlé managers use this information, along with the more detailed information found in a manufacturing statement, to plan and control manufacturing activities.

Cycle Time and Cycle Efficiency      **Decision Analysis**

As lean manufacturing practices help companies move toward just-in-time manufacturing, it is important for these companies to reduce the time to manufacture their products and to improve manufacturing efficiency. One metric that measures that time element is **cycle time (CT).** A definition of cycle time is in Exhibit 14.19.

A1 Compute cycle time and cycle efficiency, and explain their importance to production management.

> **Cycle time = Process time + Inspection time + Move time + Wait time**

EXHIBIT 14.19

Cycle Time

Process time is the time spent producing the product. *Inspection time* is the time spent inspecting (1) raw materials when received, (2) goods in process while in production, and (3) finished goods prior to shipment. *Move time* is the time spent moving (1) raw materials from storage to production and (2) goods in process from one factory location to another factory location. *Wait time* is the time that an order or job sits with no production applied to it; this can be due to order delays, bottlenecks in production, and poor scheduling.

Process time is considered **value-added time** because it is the only activity in cycle time that adds value to the product from the customer's perspective. The other three time activities are considered **non-value-added time** because they add no value to the customer.

Companies strive to reduce non-value-added time to improve **cycle efficiency (CE).** Cycle efficiency is the ratio of value-added time to total cycle time—see Exhibit 14.20.

EXHIBIT 14.20

Cycle Efficiency

$$\text{Cycle efficiency} = \frac{\text{Value-added time}}{\text{Cycle time}}$$

To illustrate, assume that Rocky Mountain Bikes receives and produces an order for 500 Tracker® mountain bikes. Assume that the following times were measured during production of this order.

Process time... 1.8 days   **Inspection time... 0.5 days**   **Move time... 0.7 days**   **Wait time... 3.0 days**

In this case, cycle time is 6.0 days, computed as 1.8 days + 0.5 days + 0.7 days + 3.0 days. Also, cycle efficiency is 0.3, or 30%, computed as 1.8 days divided by 6.0 days. This means that Rocky Mountain Bikes spends 30% of its time working on the product (value-added time). The other 70% is spent on non-value-added activities.

If a company has a CE of 1, it means that its time is spent entirely on value-added activities. If the CE is low, the company should evaluate its production process to see if it can identify ways to reduce non-value-added activities. The 30% CE for Rocky Mountain Bikes is low and its management should look for ways to reduce non-value-added activities.

DEMONSTRATION PROBLEM 1: COST BEHAVIOR AND CLASSIFICATION

Understanding the classification and assignment of costs is important. Consider a company that manufactures computer chips. It incurs the following costs in manufacturing chips and in operating the company.

1. Plastic board used to mount the chip, $3.50 each.
2. Assembly worker pay of $15 per hour to attach chips to plastic board.
3. Salary for factory maintenance workers who maintain factory equipment.
4. Factory supervisor pay of $55,000 per year to supervise employees.
5. Real estate taxes paid on the factory, $14,500.
6. Real estate taxes paid on the company office, $6,000.
7. Depreciation costs on machinery used by workers, $30,000.
8. Salary paid to the chief financial officer, $95,000.
9. Advertising costs of $7,800 paid to promote products.
10. Salespersons' commissions of $0.50 for each assembled chip sold.
11. Management has the option to rent the manufacturing plant to six local hospitals to store medical records instead of producing and assembling chips.

Classify each cost in the following table according to the categories listed in the table header. A cost can be classified under more than one category. For example, the plastic board used to mount chips is classified as a direct material product cost and as a direct unit cost.

Cost	Period Costs Selling and Administrative	Product Costs Direct Material (Prime Cost)	Direct Labor (Prime and Conversion)	Factory Overhead (Conversion Cost)	Unit Cost Classification Direct	Indirect	Sunk Cost	Opportunity Cost
1. Plastic board used to mount the chip, $3.50 each		✔			✔			

SOLUTION TO DEMONSTRATION PROBLEM 1

Cost*	Period Costs Selling and Administrative	Product Costs Direct Material (Prime Cost)	Direct Labor (Prime and Conversion)	Factory Overhead (Conversion Cost)	Unit Cost Classification Direct	Indirect	Sunk Cost	Opportunity Cost
1.		✔			✔			
2.			✔		✔			
3.				✔		✔		
4.				✔		✔		
5.				✔		✔		
6.	✔							
7.				✔		✔	✔	
8.	✔							
9.	✔							
10.	✔							
11.								✔

* Costs 1 through 11 refer to the 11 cost items described at the beginning of the problem.

DEMONSTRATION PROBLEM 2: REPORTING FOR MANUFACTURERS

A manufacturing company's balance sheet and income statement differ from those for a merchandising or service company.

Required

1. Fill in the [BLANK] descriptors on the partial balance sheets for both the manufacturing company and the merchandising company. Explain why a different presentation is required.

Manufacturing Company

ADIDAS GROUP Partial Balance Sheet December 31, 2011	
Current assets	
Cash	$10,000
[BLANK]	8,000
[BLANK]	5,000
[BLANK]	7,000
Supplies	500
Prepaid insurance	500
Total current assets	$31,000

Merchandising Company

PAYLESS SHOE OUTLET Partial Balance Sheet December 31, 2011	
Current assets	
Cash	$ 5,000
[BLANK]	12,000
Supplies	500
Prepaid insurance	500
Total current assets	$18,000

2. Fill in the [**BLANK**] descriptors on the income statements for the manufacturing company and the merchandising company. Explain why a different presentation is required.

Manufacturing Company

ADIDAS GROUP Partial Income Statement For Year Ended December 31, 2011	
Sales	$200,000
Cost of goods sold	
Finished goods inventory, Dec. 31, 2010	10,000
[BLANK]	120,000
Goods available for sale	130,000
Finished goods inventory, Dec. 31, 2011	(7,000)
Cost of goods sold	123,000
Gross profit	$ 77,000

Merchandising Company

PAYLESS SHOE OUTLET Partial Income Statement For Year Ended December 31, 2011	
Sales	$190,000
Cost of goods sold	
Merchandise inventory, Dec. 31, 2010	8,000
[BLANK]	108,000
Goods available for sale	116,000
Merchandise inventory, Dec. 31, 2011	(12,000)
Cost of goods sold	104,000
Gross profit	$ 86,000

3. A manufacturer's cost of goods manufactured is the sum of (a) _____, (b) _____, and (c) _____ costs incurred in producing the product.

SOLUTION TO DEMONSTRATION PROBLEM 2

1. Inventories for a manufacturer and for a merchandiser.

Manufacturing Company

ADIDAS GROUP Partial Balance Sheet December 31, 2011	
Current assets	
Cash	$10,000
Raw materials inventory	8,000
Goods in process inventory	5,000
Finished goods inventory	7,000
Supplies	500
Prepaid insurance	500
Total current assets	$31,000

Merchandising Company

PAYLESS SHOE OUTLET Partial Balance Sheet December 31, 2011	
Current assets	
Cash	$ 5,000
Merchandise inventory	12,000
Supplies	500
Prepaid insurance	500
Total current assets	$18,000

Explanation: A manufacturing company must control and measure three types of inventories: raw materials, goods in process, and finished goods. In the sequence of making a product, the raw materials move into production—called *goods in process inventory*—and then to finished goods. All raw materials and goods in process inventory at the end of each accounting period are considered current assets. All unsold finished inventory is considered a current asset at the end of each accounting period. The merchandising company must control and measure only one type of inventory, purchased goods.

2. Cost of goods sold for a manufacturer and for a merchandiser.

Manufacturing Company

ADIDAS GROUP Partial Income Statement For Year Ended December 31, 2011		
Sales		$ 200,000
Cost of goods sold		
Finished goods inventory, Dec. 31, 2010	10,000	
Cost of goods manufactured	120,000	
Goods available for sale	130,000	
Finished goods inventory, Dec. 31, 2011	(7,000)	
Cost of goods sold	123,000	
Gross profit		$ 77,000

Merchandising Company

PAYLESS SHOE OUTLET Partial Income Statement For Year Ended December 31, 2011		
Sales		$ 190,000
Cost of goods sold		
Merchandise inventory, Dec. 31, 2010	8,000	
Cost of purchases	108,000	
Goods available for sale	116,000	
Merchandise inventory, Dec. 31, 2011	(12,000)	
Cost of goods sold	104,000	
Gross profit		$ 86,000

Explanation: Manufacturing and merchandising companies use different reporting terms. In particular, the terms *finished goods* and *cost of goods manufactured* are used to reflect the production of goods, yet the concepts and techniques of reporting cost of goods sold for a manufacturing company and merchandising company are similar.

3. A manufacturer's cost of goods manufactured is the sum of (a) *direct material,* (b) *direct labor,* and (c) *factory overhead* costs incurred in producing the product.

DEMONSTRATION PROBLEM 3: MANUFACTURING STATEMENT

The following account balances and other information are from SUNN Corporation's accounting records for year-end December 31, 2011. Use this information to prepare (1) a table listing factory overhead costs, (2) a manufacturing statement (show only the total factory overhead cost), and (3) an income statement.

Advertising expense	$ 85,000	Goods in process inventory, Dec. 31, 2010	$ 8,000
Amortization expense—Factory Patents	16,000	Goods in process inventory, Dec. 31, 2011	9,000
Bad debts expense	28,000	Income taxes	53,400
Depreciation expense—Office equipment	37,000	Indirect labor	26,000
Depreciation expense—Factory building	133,000	Interest expense	25,000
Depreciation expense—Factory equipment	78,000	Miscellaneous expense	55,000
Direct labor	250,000	Property taxes on factory equipment	14,000
Factory insurance expired	62,000	Raw materials inventory, Dec. 31, 2010	60,000
Factory supervision	74,000	Raw materials inventory, Dec. 31, 2011	78,000
Factory supplies used	21,000	Raw materials purchases	313,000
Factory utilities	115,000	Repairs expense—Factory equipment	31,000
Finished goods inventory, Dec. 31, 2010	15,000	Salaries expense	150,000
Finished goods inventory, Dec. 31, 2011	12,500	Sales	1,630,000

PLANNING THE SOLUTION

● Analyze the account balances and select those that are part of factory overhead costs.

● Arrange these costs in a table that lists factory overhead costs for the year.

● Analyze the remaining costs and select those related to production activity for the year; selected costs should include the materials and goods in process inventories and direct labor.

● Prepare a manufacturing statement for the year showing the calculation of the cost of materials used in production, the cost of direct labor, and the total factory overhead cost. When presenting overhead cost on this statement, report only total overhead cost from the table of overhead costs for the year. Show the costs of beginning and ending goods in process inventory to determine cost of goods manufactured.

● Organize the remaining revenue and expense items into the income statement for the year. Combine cost of goods manufactured from the manufacturing statement with the finished goods inventory amounts to compute cost of goods sold for the year.

SOLUTION TO DEMONSTRATION PROBLEM 3

SUNN CORPORATION
Factory Overhead Costs
For Year Ended December 31, 2011

Amortization expense—Factory patents	$ 16,000
Depreciation expense—Factory building	133,000
Depreciation expense—Factory equipment	78,000
Factory insurance expired	62,000
Factory supervision	74,000
Factory supplies used	21,000
Factory utilities	115,000
Indirect labor	26,000
Property taxes on factory equipment	14,000
Repairs expense—Factory equipment	31,000
Total factory overhead	$570,000

SUNN CORPORATION
Manufacturing Statement
For Year Ended December 31, 2011

Direct materials		
Raw materials inventory, Dec. 31, 2010	$ 60,000	
Raw materials purchase	313,000	
Raw materials available for use	373,000	
Less raw materials inventory, Dec. 31, 2011	78,000	
Direct materials used		295,000
Direct labor		250,000
Factory overhead		570,000
Total manufacturing costs		1,115,000
Goods in process inventory, Dec. 31, 2010		8,000
Total cost of goods in process		1,123,000
Less goods in process inventory, Dec. 31, 2011		9,000
Cost of goods manufactured		$1,114,000

SUNN CORPORATION
Income Statement
For Year Ended December 31, 2011

Sales			$1,630,000
Cost of goods sold			
Finished goods inventory, Dec. 31, 2010	$ 15,000		
Cost of goods manufactured	1,114,000		
Goods available for sale	1,129,000		
Less finished goods inventory, Dec. 31, 2011	12,500		
Cost of goods sold		1,116,500	
Gross profit		513,500	
Operating expenses			
Advertising expense	85,000		
Bad debts expense	28,000		
Depreciation expense—Office equipment	37,000		
Interest expense	25,000		
Miscellaneous expense	55,000		
Salaries expense	150,000		
Total operating expenses		380,000	
Income before income taxes		133,500	
Income taxes		53,400	
Net income		$ 80,100	

Summary

C1 **Explain the purpose and nature of, and the role of ethics in, managerial accounting.** The purpose of managerial accounting is to provide useful information to management and other internal decision makers. It does this by collecting, managing, and reporting both monetary and nonmonetary information in a manner useful to internal users. Major characteristics of managerial accounting include (1) focus on internal decision makers, (2) emphasis on planning and control, (3) flexibility, (4) timeliness, (5) reliance on forecasts and estimates, (6) focus on segments and projects, and (7) reporting both monetary and nonmonetary information. Ethics are beliefs that distinguish right from wrong. Ethics can be important in reducing fraud in business operations.

C2 **Describe accounting concepts useful in classifying costs.** We can classify costs on the basis of their (1) behavior—fixed vs. variable, (2) traceability—direct vs. indirect, (3) controllability—controllable vs. uncontrollable, (4) relevance—sunk vs. out of pocket, and (5) function—product vs. period. A cost can be classified in more than one way, depending on the purpose for which the cost is being determined. These classifications help us understand cost patterns, analyze performance, and plan operations.

C3 **Define product and period costs and explain how they impact financial statements.** Costs that are capitalized because they are expected to have future value are called *product costs;* costs that are expensed are called *period costs*. This classification is important because it affects the amount of costs expensed in the income statement and the amount of costs assigned to inventory on the balance sheet. Product costs are commonly made up of direct materials, direct labor, and overhead. Period costs include selling and administrative expenses.

C4 **Explain how balance sheets and income statements for manufacturing and merchandising companies differ.** The main difference is that manufacturers usually carry three inventories on their balance sheets—raw materials, goods in process, and finished goods—instead of one inventory that merchandisers carry. The main difference between income statements of manufacturers and merchandisers is the items making up cost of goods sold. A merchandiser adds beginning merchandise inventory to cost of goods purchased and then subtracts ending merchandise inventory to get cost of goods sold. A manufacturer adds beginning finished goods inventory to cost of goods

manufactured and then subtracts ending finished goods inventory to get cost of goods sold.

C5 **Explain manufacturing activities and the flow of manufacturing costs.** Manufacturing activities consist of materials, production, and sales activities. The materials activity consists of the purchase and issuance of materials to production. The production activity consists of converting materials into finished goods. At this stage in the process, the materials, labor, and overhead costs have been incurred and the manufacturing statement is prepared. The sales activity consists of selling some or all of finished goods available for sale. At this stage, the cost of goods sold is determined.

C6 **Describe trends in managerial accounting.** Important trends in managerial accounting include an increased focus on satisfying customers, the impact of a global economy, and the growing presence of e-commerce and service-based businesses. The lean business model, designed to eliminate waste and satisfy customers, can be useful in responding to recent trends. Concepts such as total quality management, just-in-time production, and the value chain often aid in application of the lean business model.

A1 **Compute cycle time and cycle efficiency, and explain their importance to production management.** It is important for companies to reduce the time to produce their products and to improve manufacturing efficiency. One measure of that time is cycle time (CT), defined as Process time + Inspection time + Move time + Wait time. Process time is value-added time; the others are non-value-added time. Cycle efficiency (CE) is the ratio of value-added time to total cycle time. If CE is low, management should evaluate its production process to see if it can reduce non-value-added activities.

P1 **Compute cost of goods sold for a manufacturer.** A manufacturer adds beginning finished goods inventory to cost of goods manufactured and then subtracts ending finished goods inventory to get cost of goods sold.

P2 **Prepare a manufacturing statement and explain its purpose and links to financial statements.** The manufacturing statement reports computation of cost of goods manufactured for the period. It begins by showing the period's costs for direct materials, direct labor, and overhead and then adjusts these numbers for the beginning and ending inventories of the goods in process to yield cost of goods manufactured.

Guidance Answers to Decision Maker and Decision Ethics

Production Manager   It appears that all three friends want to pay the bill with someone else's money. David is using money belonging to the tax authorities, Denise is taking money from her company, and Derek is defrauding the client. To prevent such practices, companies have internal audit mechanisms. Many companies also adopt ethical codes of conduct to help guide employees. We must recognize that some entertainment expenses are justifiable and even encouraged. For example, the tax law allows certain deductions for entertainment that have a business purpose. Corporate policies also sometimes allow and encourage reimbursable spending for social activities, and contracts can include entertainment as allowable costs.

Nevertheless, without further details, payment for this bill should be made from personal accounts.

Entrepreneur   Tracing all costs directly to cost objects is always desirable, but you need to be able to do so in an economically feasible manner. In this case, you are able to trace 90% of the assembly department's direct costs. It may not be economical to spend more money on a new software to trace the final 10% of costs. You need to make a cost–benefit trade-off. If the software offers benefits beyond tracing the remaining 10% of the assembly department's costs, your decision should consider this.

Purchase Manager   Opportunity costs relate to the potential quality and delivery benefits given up by not choosing supplier (A). Selecting supplier (B) might involve future costs of poor-quality seats (inspection, repairs, and returns). Also, potential delivery delays could interrupt work and increase manufacturing costs. Your company could also incur sales losses if the product quality of supplier (B) is low. As purchase manager, you are responsible for these costs and must consider them in making your decision.

Guidance Answers to Quick Checks

1. *d*
2. Financial accounting information is intended for users external to an organization such as investors, creditors, and government authorities. Managerial accounting focuses on providing information to managers, officers, and other decision makers within the organization.
3. No, GAAP do not control the practice of managerial accounting. Unlike external users, the internal users need managerial accounting information for planning and controlling business activities rather than for external comparison. Different types of information are required, depending on the activity. Therefore it is difficult to standardize managerial accounting.
4. Variable costs increase when volume of activity increases.
5. By being able to trace costs to cost objects (say, to products and departments), managers better understand the total costs associated with a cost object. This is useful when managers consider making changes to the cost object (such as when dropping the product or expanding the department).
6. Raw materials inventory, goods in process inventory, and finished goods inventory.
7. The cost of goods sold for merchandising companies includes all costs of acquiring the merchandise; the cost of goods sold for manufacturing companies includes the three costs of manufacturing: direct materials, direct labor, and overhead.
8. *a*
9. No; companies rarely report a manufacturing statement.
10. Beginning goods in process inventory is added to total manufacturing costs to yield total goods in process. Ending goods in process inventory is subtracted from total goods in process to yield cost of goods manufactured for the period.

Continuous improvement (p. 616)
Control (p. 601)
Controllable or not controllable cost (p. 605)
Conversion costs (p. 611)
Cost object (p. 605)
Customer orientation (p. 615)
Cycle efficiency (CE) (p. 618)
Cycle time (CT) (p. 617)
Direct costs (p. 605)
Direct labor (p. 610)
Direct labor costs (p. 610)
Direct material (p. 610)
Direct material costs (p. 610)
Ethics (p. 604)

Factory overhead (p. 610)
Factory overhead costs (p. 610)
Finished goods inventory (p. 609)
Fixed cost (p. 604)
Goods in process inventory (p. 609)
Indirect costs (p. 605)
Indirect labor (p. 610)
Indirect labor costs (p. 610)
Indirect material (p. 608)
Institute of Management Accountants (IMA) (p. 604)
Internal control system (p. 604)
Just-in-time (JIT) manufacturing (p. 616)
Lean business model (p. 615)
Managerial accounting (p. 600)

Manufacturing statement (p. 613)
Non-value-added time (p. 618)
Opportunity cost (p. 606)
Out-of-pocket cost (p. 606)
Period costs (p. 606)
Planning (p. 600)
Prime costs (p. 611)
Product costs (p. 606)
Raw materials inventory (p. 608)
Sunk cost (p. 606)
Total quality management (TQM) (p. 616)
Value-added time (p. 618)
Value chain (p. 616)
Variable cost (p. 604)

Additional Quiz Questions are available at the book's Website.

1. Continuous improvement
   a. Is used to reduce inventory levels.
   b. Is applicable only in service businesses.
   c. Rejects the notion of "good enough."
   d. Is used to reduce ordering costs.
   e. Is applicable only in manufacturing businesses.

2. A direct cost is one that is
   a. Variable with respect to the cost object.
   b. Traceable to the cost object.
   c. Fixed with respect to the cost object.
   d. Allocated to the cost object.
   e. A period cost.

3. Costs that are incurred as part of the manufacturing process, but are not clearly traceable to the specific unit of product or batches of product, are called
   a. Period costs.
   b. Factory overhead.
   c. Sunk costs.
   d. Opportunity costs.
   e. Fixed costs.

4. The three major cost components of manufacturing a product are
   a. Direct materials, direct labor, and factory overhead.
   b. Period costs, product costs, and sunk costs.

   c. Indirect labor, indirect materials, and fixed expenses.
   d. Variable costs, fixed costs, and period costs.
   e. Opportunity costs, sunk costs, and direct costs.

5. A company reports the following for the current year.

Finished goods inventory, beginning year	$6,000
Finished goods inventory, ending year	3,200
Cost of goods sold	7,500

Its cost of goods manufactured for the current year is
   a. $1,500.
   b. $1,700.
   c. $7,500.
   d. $2,800.
   e. $4,700.

Ⅰ Icon denotes assignments that involve decision making.

Discussion Questions

1. Describe the managerial accountant's role in business planning, control, and decision making.

2. Distinguish between managerial and financial accounting on
   a. Users and decision makers. **b.** Purpose of information.
   c. Flexibility of practice. **d.** Time dimension.
   e. Focus of information. **f.** Nature of information.

3. Ⅰ Identify the usual changes that a company must make when it adopts a customer orientation.

4. Distinguish between direct material and indirect material.

5. Distinguish between direct labor and indirect labor.

6. Distinguish between (*a*) factory overhead and (*b*) selling and administrative overhead.

7. What product cost is listed as both a prime cost and a conversion cost?

8. Ⅰ Assume that you tour **Apple**'s factory where it makes its products. List three direct costs and three indirect costs that you are likely to see. *Apple*

9. Ⅰ Should we evaluate a manager's performance on the basis of controllable or noncontrollable costs? Why?

10. Ⅰ Explain why knowledge of cost behavior is useful in product performance evaluation.

11. Explain why product costs are capitalized but period costs are expensed in the current accounting period.

12. Ⅰ Explain how business activities and inventories for a manufacturing company, a merchandising company, and a service company differ.

13. Ⅰ Why does managerial accounting often involve working with numerous predictions and estimates?

14. How do an income statement and a balance sheet for a manufacturing company and a merchandising company differ?

15. Besides inventories, what other assets often appear on manufacturers' balance sheets but not on merchandisers' balance sheets?

16. Why does a manufacturing company require three different inventory categories?

17. Manufacturing activities of a company are described in the _____. This statement summarizes the types and amounts of costs incurred in its manufacturing _____.

18. What are the three categories of manufacturing costs?

19. List several examples of factory overhead.

20. Ⅰ List the four components of a manufacturing statement and provide specific examples of each for **Apple**. *Apple*

21. Ⅰ Prepare a proper title for the annual "manufacturing statement" of **Palm**. Does the date match the balance sheet or income statement? Why? *Palm*

22. Ⅰ Describe the relations among the income statement, the manufacturing statement, and a detailed listing of factory overhead costs.

23. Ⅰ Define and describe *cycle time* and identify the components of cycle time.

24. Ⅰ Explain the difference between value-added time and non-value-added time.

25. Define and describe *cycle efficiency*.

26. Ⅰ Can management of a company such as **Research In Motion** use cycle time and cycle efficiency as useful measures of performance? Explain. *RIM*

27. Access **Dell**'s annual report (10-K) for the fiscal year ended January 29, 2010, at the SEC's EDGAR database (**SEC.gov**) or its Website (**Dell.com**). From its financial statement notes, identify the titles and amounts of its inventory components.

QUICK STUDY

QS 14-1

Managerial accounting versus financial accounting

C1

Identify whether each description most likely applies to managerial or financial accounting.

1. _____ Its primary focus is on the organization as a whole.
2. _____ Its principles and practices are very flexible.
3. _____ It is directed at external users in making investment, credit, and other decisions.
4. _____ Its primary users are company managers.
5. _____ Its information is often available only after an audit is complete.

QS 14-2

Managerial accounting defined

C1

Managerial accounting (choose one)

1. Must follow generally accepted accounting principles.
2. Provides information to aid management in planning and controlling business activities.
3. Is directed at reporting aggregate data on the company as a whole.
4. Provides information that is widely available to all interested parties.

QS 14-3

Fixed and variable costs

C2

Which of these statements is true regarding fixed and variable costs?

1. Fixed costs increase and variable costs decrease in total as activity volume decreases.
2. Fixed costs stay the same and variable costs increase in total as activity volume increases.
3. Both fixed and variable costs increase as activity volume increases.
4. Both fixed and variable costs stay the same in total as activity volume increases.

QS 14-4

Direct and indirect costs

C2

Kasey Anthony Company produces sporting equipment, including basketballs. Identify each of the following costs as direct or indirect if the cost object is a basketball produced by Kasey Anthony.

1. Materials used to produce basketballs.
2. Electricity used in the production plant.
3. Labor used on the basketball production line.
4. Salary of manager who supervises the entire plant.
5. Depreciation on equipment used to produce basketballs.

QS 14-5

Product and period costs

C3

Which of these statements is true regarding product and period costs?

1. Sales commission is a product cost and factory rent is a period cost.
2. Factory wages are a product cost and direct material is a period cost.
3. Factory maintenance is a product cost and sales commission is a period cost.
4. Sales commission is a product cost and depreciation on factory equipment is a product cost.

QS 14-6

Inventory reporting for manufacturers   C4

Three inventory categories are reported on a manufacturing company's balance sheet: (i) raw materials, (ii) goods in process, and (iii) finished goods. Identify the usual order in which these inventory items are reported on the balance sheet.

1. (i)(ii)(iii)   **2.** (ii)(i)(iii)   **3.** (ii)(iii)(i)   **4.** (iii)(ii)(i)

QS 14-7

Cost of goods sold   P1

A company has year-end cost of goods manufactured of $5,000, beginning finished goods inventory of $700, and ending finished goods inventory of $850. Its cost of goods sold is

1. $4,250   **2.** $4,000   **3.** $4,850   **4.** $6,550

QS 14-8

Manufacturing flows identified

C5

Identify the usual sequence of manufacturing activities by filling in the blank (with i, ii or iii) corresponding to its order: _____ Production activities; _____ sales activities; _____ materials activities.

Match each lean business concept with its best description by entering its letter in the blank.

1. _____ Customer orientation

2. _____ Total quality management

3. _____ Just-in-time manufacturing

4. _____ Continuous improvements

A. Inventory is acquired or produced only as needed.

B. Flexible product designs can be modified to accommodate customer choices.

C. Every manager and employee constantly looks for ways to improve company operations.

D. Focuses on quality throughout the production process.

QS 14-9
Lean business concepts
C6

Compute cost of goods sold for year 2011 using the following information.

Finished goods inventory, Dec. 31, 2010	$321,500
Goods in process inventory, Dec. 31, 2010	74,550
Goods in process inventory, Dec. 31, 2011	81,200
Cost of goods manufactured, year 2011	972,345
Finished goods inventory, Dec. 31, 2011	297,200

QS 14-10
Cost of goods sold
P1

Prepare the 2011 manufacturing statement for Carmichael Company using the following information.

Direct materials	$192,500
Direct labor	65,150
Factory overhead costs	26,000
Goods in process, Dec. 31, 2010	159,600
Goods in process, Dec. 31, 2011	144,750

QS 14-11
Cost of goods manufactured
P2

Compute and interpret (_a_) manufacturing cycle time and (_b_) manufacturing cycle efficiency using the following information from a manufacturing company.

Process time	15 minutes
Inspection time	2 minutes
Move time	6.4 minutes
Wait time	36.6 minutes

QS 14-12
Manufacturing cycle time and efficiency
A1

Nestlé reports beginning raw materials inventory of 3,590 and ending raw materials inventory of 3,708 (both numbers in millions of Swiss francs). If Nestlé purchased 12,000 (in millions of Swiss francs) of raw materials during the year, what is the amount of raw materials it used during the year?

QS 14-13
Direct materials used
C5

Both managerial accounting and financial accounting provide useful information to decision makers. Indicate in the following chart the most likely source of information for each business decision (a decision can require major input from both sources, in which case both can be marked).

EXERCISES

Exercise 14-1
Sources of accounting information
C1

	Primary Information Source	
Business Decision	**Managerial**	**Financial**
1. Plan the budget for next quarter	____	____
2. Measure profitability of all individual stores	____	____
3. Prepare financial reports according to GAAP	____	____
4. Determine location and size for a new plant	____	____
5. Determine amount of dividends to pay stockholders	____	____
6. Evaluate a purchasing department's performance	____	____
7. Report financial performance to board of directors	____	____
8. Estimate product cost for a new line of shoes	____	____

Exercise 14-2

Characteristics of financial accounting and managerial accounting

C1

In the following chart, compare financial accounting and managerial accounting by describing how each differs for the items listed. Be specific in your responses.

	Financial Accounting	Managerial Accounting
1. Nature of information	_____	_____
2. Flexibility of practice	_____	_____
3. Focus of information	_____	_____
4. Time dimension	_____	_____
5. Users and decision makers	_____	_____
6. Timeliness of information	_____	_____
7. Purpose of information	_____	_____

Exercise 14-3

Planning and control descriptions

C1

Complete the following statements by filling in the blanks.

1. _____ is the process of setting goals and making plans to achieve them.
2. _____ _____ usually covers a period of 5 to 10 years.
3. _____ _____ usually covers a period of one year.
4. _____ is the process of monitoring planning decisions and evaluating an organization's activities and employees.

Exercise 14-4

Cost analysis and identification

C3

Georgia Pacific, a manufacturer, incurs the following costs. (1) Classify each cost as either a product or a period cost. If a product cost, identify it as a prime and/or conversion cost. (2) Classify each product cost as either a direct cost or an indirect cost using the product as the cost object.

Cost	Product Cost Prime	Product Cost Conversion	Period Cost	Direct Cost	Indirect Cost
1. Office supplies used	____	____	____	____	____
2. Bad debts expense	____	____	____	____	____
3. Small tools used	____	____	____	____	____
4. Factory utilities	____	____	____	____	____
5. Advertising.............................	____	____	____	____	____
6. Amortization of patents on factory machine...	____	____	____	____	____
7. Payroll taxes for production supervisor	____	____	____	____	____
8. Accident insurance on factory workers	____	____	____	____	____
9. Depreciation—Factory building	____	____	____	____	____
10. State and federal income taxes	____	____	____	____	____
11. Wages to assembly workers	____	____	____	____	____
12. Direct materials used	____	____	____	____	____

Exercise 14-5

Cost classifications   C2

(1) Identify each of the five cost classifications discussed in the chapter. (2) List two purposes of identifying these separate cost classifications.

Exercise 14-6

Cost analysis and classification

C2

Listed here are product costs for the production of soccer balls. (1) Classify each cost (a) as either fixed or variable and (b) as either direct or indirect. (2) What pattern do you see regarding the relation between costs classified by behavior and costs classified by traceability?

Product Cost	Cost by Behavior Variable	Cost by Behavior Fixed	Cost by Traceability Direct	Cost by Traceability Indirect
1. Taxes on factory	____	____	____	____
2. Machinery depreciation	____	____	____	____
3. Coolants for machinery	____	____	____	____
4. Wages of assembly workers	____	____	____	____
5. Lace to hold leather together	____	____	____	____
6. Leather covers for soccer balls	____	____	____	____
7. Annual flat fee paid for office security	____	____	____	____

Current assets for two different companies at calendar year-end 2011 are listed here. One is a manufacturer, Roller Blades Mfg., and the other, Sunny Foods, is a grocery distribution company. (1) Identify which set of numbers relates to the manufacturer and which to the merchandiser. (2) Prepare the current asset section for each company from this information. Discuss why the current asset section for these two companies is different.

Exercise 14-7
Balance sheet identification and preparation
C4

Account	Company 1	Company 2
Cash	$ 9,000	$ 7,000
Raw materials inventory	—	44,000
Merchandise inventory	47,000	—
Goods in process inventory	—	32,000
Finished goods inventory	—	52,000
Accounts receivable, net	64,000	77,000
Prepaid expenses	3,500	700

Compute cost of goods sold for each of these two companies for the year ended December 31, 2011.

Exercise 14-8
Cost of goods sold computation
P1

	Century Merchandising	New Homes Manufacturing
Beginning inventory		
Merchandise	$250,000	
Finished goods		$500,000
Cost of purchases	460,000	
Cost of goods manufactured		886,000
Ending inventory		
Merchandise	150,000	
Finished goods		144,000

Check   Century Merchandising COGS, $560,000

Using the following data, compute (1) the cost of goods manufactured and (2) the cost of goods sold for both Canyon Company and Rossings Company.

Exercise 14-9
Cost of goods manufactured and cost of goods sold computation
P1 P2

	Canyon Company	Rossings Company
Beginning finished goods inventory	$14,000	$18,450
Beginning goods in process inventory	16,500	21,950
Beginning raw materials inventory	9,250	11,000
Rental cost on factory equipment	29,000	24,750
Direct labor	21,000	37,000
Ending finished goods inventory	19,650	15,300
Ending goods in process inventory	24,000	18,000
Ending raw materials inventory	7,300	9,200
Factory utilities	11,000	14,000
Factory supplies used	10,200	5,200
General and administrative expenses	23,000	45,000
Indirect labor	3,250	9,660
Repairs—Factory equipment	6,780	3,500
Raw materials purchases	35,000	54,000
Sales salaries	52,000	48,000

Check   Canyon COGS, $105,030

Exercise 14-10

Components of accounting reports

P2

For each of the following accounts for a manufacturing company, place a ✔ in the appropriate column indicating that it appears on the balance sheet, the income statement, the manufacturing statement, and/or a detailed listing of factory overhead costs. Assume that the income statement shows the calculation of cost of goods sold and the manufacturing statement shows only the total amount of factory overhead. (An account can appear on more than one report.)

	File Edit View Insert Format Tools Data Window Help				
	Account	Balance Sheet	Income Statement	Manufacturing Statement	Overhead Report
3	Accounts receivable				
4	Computer supplies used in office				
5	Beginning finished goods inventory				
6	Beginning goods in process inventory				
7	Beginning raw materials inventory				
8	Cash				
9	Depreciation expense—Factory building				
10	Depreciation expense—Factory equipment				
11	Depreciation expense—Office building				
12	Depreciation expense—Office equipment				
13	Direct labor				
14	Ending finished goods inventory				
15	Ending goods in process inventory				
16	Ending raw materials inventory				
17	Factory maintenance wages				
18	Computer supplies used in factory				
19	Income taxes				
20	Insurance on factory building				
21	Rent cost on office building				
22	Office supplies used				
23	Property taxes on factory building				
24	Raw materials purchases				
25	Sales				

Exercise 14-11

Manufacturing statement preparation

P2

Given the following selected account balances of Randa Company, prepare its manufacturing statement for the year ended on December 31, 2011. Include a listing of the individual overhead account balances in this statement.

Sales	$1,252,000
Raw materials inventory, Dec. 31, 2010	39,000
Goods in process inventory, Dec. 31, 2010	55,900
Finished goods inventory, Dec. 31, 2010	64,750
Raw materials purchases	177,600
Direct labor	227,000
Factory computer supplies used	19,840
Indirect labor	49,000
Repairs—Factory equipment	7,250
Rent cost of factory building	59,000
Advertising expense	96,000
General and administrative expenses	131,300
Raw materials inventory, Dec. 31, 2011	44,700
Goods in process inventory, Dec. 31, 2011	43,500
Finished goods inventory, Dec. 31, 2011	69,300

Check Cost of goods manufactured, $546,390

Exercise 14-12

Income statement preparation

P2

Use the information in Exercise 14-11 to prepare an income statement for Randa Company (a manufacturer). Assume that its cost of goods manufactured is $546,390.

The following chart shows how costs flow through a business as a product is manufactured. Some boxes in the flowchart show cost amounts. Compute the cost amounts for the boxes that contain question marks.

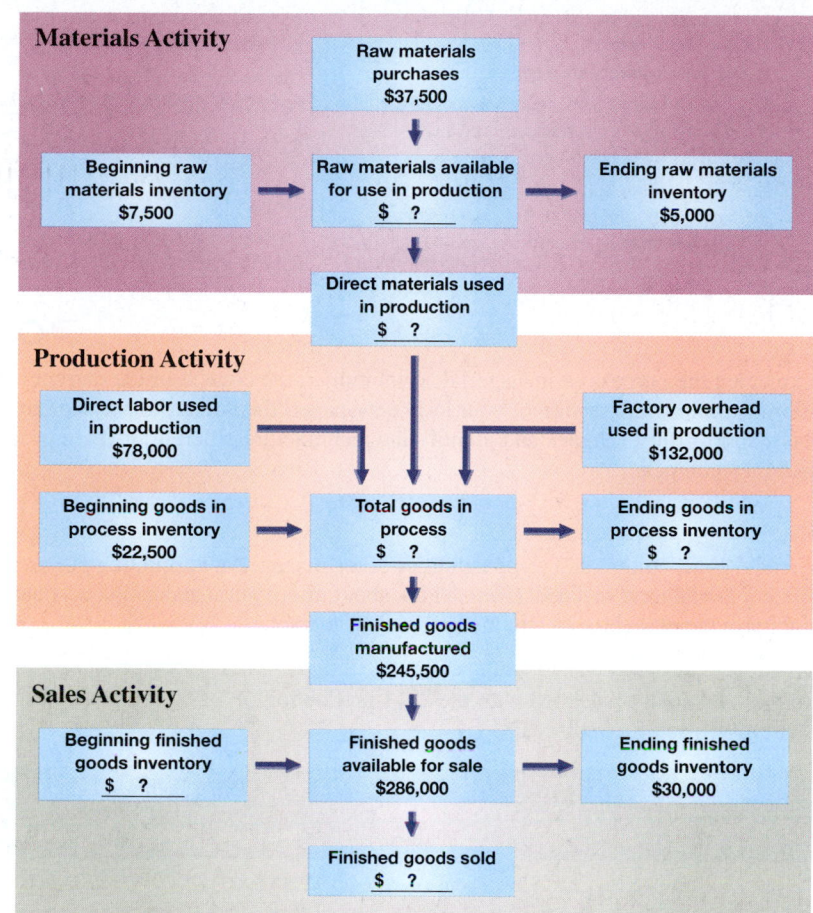

Customer orientation means that a company's managers and employees respond to customers' changing wants and needs. A manufacturer of metal parts has created a customer satisfaction survey that it asks each of its customers to complete. The survey asks about the following factors: (A) product performance; (B) price; (C) lead time; (D) delivery. Each factor is to be rated as unsatisfactory, marginal, average, satisfactory, or very satisfied.

a. Match the competitive forces 1 through 4 to the factors on the survey. A factor can be matched to more than one competitive force.

Survey Factor	Competitive Force
A. Product performance	_____ **1.** Cost
B. Price	_____ **2.** Time
C. Lead time	_____ **3.** Quality
D. Delivery	_____ **4.** Flexibility of service

b. How can managers of this company use the information from this customer satisfaction survey to better meet competitive forces and satisfy their customers?

Following are three separate events affecting the managerial accounting systems for different companies. Match the management concept(s) that the company is likely to adopt for the event identified. There is some overlap in the meaning of customer orientation and total quality management and, therefore, some responses can include more than one concept.

Event	Management Concept
_____ 1. The company starts measuring inventory turnover and discontinues elaborate inventory records. Its new focus is to pull inventory through the system.	a. Total quality management (TQM)
	b. Just-in-time (JIT) system
_____ 2. The company starts reporting measures on customer complaints and product returns from customers.	c. Continuous improvement (CI)
	d. Customer orientation (CO)
_____ 3. The company starts reporting measures such as the percent of defective products and the number of units scrapped.	

PROBLEM SET A

Problem 14-1A
Managerial accounting role

C1

This chapter explained the purpose of managerial accounting in the context of the current business environment. Review the *automobile* section of your local newspaper; the Sunday paper is often best. Review advertisements of sport-utility vehicles and identify the manufacturers that offer these products and the factors on which they compete.

Required

Discuss the potential contributions and responsibilities of the managerial accounting professional in helping an automobile manufacturer succeed. (*Hint:* Think about information and estimates that a managerial accountant might provide new entrants into the sport-utility market.)

Problem 14-2A
Cost computation, classification, and analysis

C2 C3

Listed here are the total costs associated with the 2011 production of 1,000 drum sets manufactured by NeatBeat. The drum sets sell for $300 each.

	Cost by Behavior		Cost by Function	
Costs	**Variable**	**Fixed**	**Product**	**Period**
1. Plastic for casing—$12,000.	$12,000		$12,000	
2. Wages of assembly workers—$60,000.				
3. Property taxes on factory—$6,000				
4. Accounting staff salaries—$45,000				
5. Drum stands (1,000 stands outsourced)—$25,000				
6. Rent cost of equipment for sales staff—$7,000				
7. Upper management salaries—$100,000				
8. Annual flat fee for maintenance service—$9,000				
9. Sales commissions—$10 per unit				
10. Machinery depreciation—$10,000				

Required

Check (1) Total variable
manufacturing cost, $97,000

1. Classify each cost and its amount as (*a*) either fixed or variable and (*b*) either product or period. (The first cost is completed as an example.)
2. Compute the manufacturing cost per drum set.

Analysis Component

3. Assume that 1,200 drum sets are produced in the next year. What do you predict will be the total cost of plastic for the casings and the per unit cost of the plastic for the casings? Explain.
4. Assume that 1,200 drum sets are produced in the next year. What do you predict will be the total cost of property taxes and the per unit cost of the property taxes? Explain.

Problem 14-3A
Cost classification
and explanation

C2 C3

Assume that you must make a presentation to the marketing staff explaining the difference between product and period costs. Your supervisor tells you the marketing staff would also like clarification regarding prime and conversion costs and an explanation of how these terms fit with product and period cost. You are told that many on the staff are unable to classify costs in their merchandising activities.

Required

Prepare a one-page memorandum to your supervisor outlining your presentation to the marketing staff.

Refer to *Decision Maker,* **Purchase Manager,** in this chapter. Assume that you are the motorcycle manufacturer's managerial accountant. The purchasing manager asks you about preparing an estimate of the related costs for buying motorcycle seats from supplier (B). She tells you this estimate is needed because unless dollar estimates are attached to nonfinancial factors, such as lost production time, her supervisor will not give it full attention. The manager also shows you the following information.

- Production output is 3,000 motorcycles per year based on 250 production days a year.
- Production time per day is 8 hours at a cost of $2,000 per hour to run the production line.
- Lost production time due to poor quality is 1%.
- Satisfied customers purchase, on average, three motorcycles during a lifetime.
- Satisfied customers recommend the product, on average, to 10 other people.
- Marketing predicts that using seat (B) will result in 10 lost customers per year from repeat business and referrals.
- Average gross profit per motorcycle is $3,000.

Required

Estimate the costs (including opportunity costs) of buying motorcycle seats from supplier (B). This problem requires that you think creatively and make reasonable estimates; thus there could be more than one correct answer. (*Hint:* Reread the answer to *Decision Maker* and compare the cost savings for buying from supplier [B] to the sum of lost customer revenue from repeat business and referrals and the cost of lost production time.)

Problem 14-4A
Opportunity cost estimation and application
C1 C2

Check Estimated cost of lost production time, $40,000

Shepler Boot Company makes specialty boots for the rodeo circuit. On December 31, 2010, the company had (*a*) 500 pairs of boots in finished goods inventory and (*b*) 1,500 heels at a cost of $5 each in raw materials inventory. During 2011, the company purchased 50,000 additional heels at $5 each and manufactured 20,000 pairs of boots.

Required

1. Determine the unit and dollar amounts of raw materials inventory in heels at December 31, 2011.

Analysis Component

2. Write a one-half page memorandum to the production manager explaining why a just-in-time inventory system for heels should be considered. Include the amount of working capital that can be reduced at December 31, 2011, if the ending heel raw material inventory is cut by half.

Problem 14-5A
Ending inventory computation and evaluation
C4

Check (1) Ending (heel) inventory, 11,500 units; $57,500

Shown here are annual financial data at December 31, 2011, taken from two different companies.

	Pinnacle Retail	Slope Board Manufacturing
Beginning inventory		
Merchandise	$150,000	
Finished goods		$300,000
Cost of purchases	250,000	
Cost of goods manufactured		586,000
Ending inventory		
Merchandise	100,000	
Finished goods		200,000

Problem 14-6A
Inventory computation and reporting
C4 P1

mhhe.com/wildFINMAN4e

Required

1. Compute the cost of goods sold section of the income statement at December 31, 2011, for each company. Include the proper title and format in the solution.

2. Write a half-page memorandum to your instructor (*a*) identifying the inventory accounts and (*b*) describing where each is reported on the income statement and balance sheet for both companies.

Check (1) Slope Board's cost of goods sold, $686,000

Problem 14-7A
Lean business concepts

C6

Many fast-food restaurants compete on lean business concepts. Match each of the following activities at a fast-food restaurant with the lean business concept it strives to achieve. Some activities might relate to more than one lean business concept.

_____ **1.** Clean tables and floors
_____ **2.** Orders filled within three minutes
_____ **3.** Standardized food making processes
_____ **4.** Courteous employees
_____ **5.** Food produced to order
_____ **6.** New product development
_____ **7.** Customer satisfaction surveys
_____ **8.** Continually changing menus
_____ **9.** Drive-through windows
_____ **10.** Standardized menus from location to location

a. Just-in-time (JIT)
b. Continuous improvement (CI)
c. Total quality management (TQM)

Problem 14-8A
Manufacturing and income
statements; inventory analysis   P2

The following calendar year-end information is taken from the December 31, 2011, adjusted trial balance and other records of Plaza Company.

Advertising expense	$ 30,750	Direct labor	$ 677,480
Depreciation expense—Office equipment	9,250	Income taxes expense	235,725
Depreciation expense—Selling equipment	10,600	Indirect labor	58,875
Depreciation expense—Factory equipment	35,550	Miscellaneous production costs	10,425
Factory supervision	104,600	Office salaries expense	65,000
Factory supplies used	9,350	Raw materials purchases	927,000
Factory utilities	35,000	Rent expense—Office space	24,000
Inventories		Rent expense—Selling space	28,100
Raw materials, December 31, 2010	168,850	Rent expense—Factory building	78,800
Raw materials, December 31, 2011	184,000	Maintenance expense—Factory equipment	37,400
Goods in process, December 31, 2010	17,700	Sales	4,527,000
Goods in process, December 31, 2011	21,380	Sales discounts	64,500
Finished goods, December 31, 2010	169,350	Sales salaries expense	394,560
Finished goods, December 31, 2011	138,490		

Check (1) Cost of goods
manufactured, $1,955,650

Required

1. Prepare the company's 2011 manufacturing statement.

2. Prepare the company's 2011 income statement that reports separate categories for (*a*) selling expenses and (*b*) general and administrative expenses.

Analysis Component

3. Compute the (*a*) inventory turnover, defined as cost of goods sold divided by average inventory, and (*b*) days' sales in inventory, defined as 365 times ending inventory divided by cost of goods sold, for both its raw materials inventory and its finished goods inventory. (To compute turnover and days' sales in inventory for raw materials, use raw materials used rather than cost of goods sold.) Discuss some possible reasons for differences between these ratios for the two types of inventories. Round answers to one decimal place.

Problem 14-9A
Manufacturing cycle time and
efficiency

A1

White Maple Company produces maple bookcases to customer order. It received an order from a customer to produce 15,000 bookcases. The following information is available for the production of the bookcases.

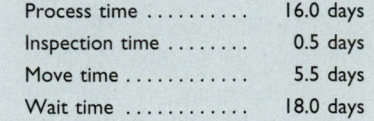

Process time	16.0 days
Inspection time	0.5 days
Move time	5.5 days
Wait time	18.0 days

Required

1. Compute the company's manufacturing cycle time.
2. Compute the company's manufacturing cycle efficiency. Interpret your answer.

Check (2) Manufacturing cycle efficiency, 0.40

Analysis Component

3. Assume that White Maple wishes to increase its manufacturing cycle efficiency to 0.75. What are some ways that it can accomplish this?

This chapter described the purpose of managerial accounting in the context of the current business environment. Review the *home electronics* section of your local newspaper; the Sunday paper is often best. Review advertisements of home electronics and identify the manufacturers that offer these products and the factors on which they compete.

Required

Discuss the potential contributions and responsibilities of the managerial accounting professional in helping a home electronics manufacturer succeed. (*Hint:* Think about information and estimates that a managerial accountant might provide new entrants into the home electronics market.)

PROBLEM SET B

Problem 14-1B
Managerial accounting role

C1

Listed here are the total costs associated with the 2011 production of 10,000 Blu-ray Discs (BDs) manufactured by Hip-Hop. The BDs sell for $15 each.

Problem 14-2B
Cost computation, classification, and analysis

C2 C3

Costs	Cost by Behavior		Cost by Function	
	Variable	Fixed	Product	Period
1. Plastic for BDs—$1,000	$1,000		$1,000	
2. Wages of assembly workers—$20,000				
3. Cost of factory rent—$4,500				
4. Systems staff salaries—$10,000				
5. Labeling (outsourced)—$2,500				
6. Cost of office equipment rent—$700				
7. Upper management salaries—$100,000				
8. Annual fixed fee for cleaning service—$3,000				
9. Sales commissions—$0.50 per BD				
10. Machinery depreciation—$15,000				

Required

1. Classify each cost and its amount as (*a*) either fixed or variable and (*b*) either product or period. (The first cost is completed as an example.)
2. Compute the manufacturing cost per BD.

Check (2) Total variable manufacturing cost, $23,500

Analysis Component

3. Assume that 15,000 BDs are produced in the next year. What do you predict will be the total cost of plastic for the BDs and the per unit cost of the plastic for the BDs? Explain.
4. Assume that 15,000 BDs are produced in the next year. What do you predict will be the total cost of factory rent and the per unit cost of the factory rent? Explain.

Assume that you must make a presentation to a client explaining the difference between prime and conversion costs. The client makes and sells 50,000 cookies per week. The client tells you that her sales staff also would like a clarification regarding product and period costs. She tells you that most of the staff lack training in managerial accounting.

Problem 14-3B
Cost classification and explanation

C2 C3

Required

Prepare a one-page memorandum to your client outlining your planned presentation to her sales staff.

Problem 14-4B

Opportunity cost estimation and application

C1 C2

Refer to *Decision Maker,* **Purchase Manager,** in this chapter. Assume that you are the motorcycle manufacturer's managerial accountant. The purchasing manager asks you about preparing an estimate of the related costs for buying motorcycle seats from supplier (B). She tells you this estimate is needed because unless dollar estimates are attached to nonfinancial factors such as lost production time, her supervisor will not give it full attention. The manager also shows you the following information.

- Production output is 2,000 motorcycles per year based on 250 production days a year.
- Production time per day is 8 hours at a cost of $500 per hour to run the production line.
- Lost production time due to poor quality is 1%.
- Satisfied customers purchase, on average, three motorcycles during a lifetime.
- Satisfied customers recommend the product, on average, to 10 other people.
- Marketing predicts that using seat (B) will result in 8 lost customers per year from repeat business and referrals.
- Average gross profit per motorcycle is $4,000.

Required

Check Cost of lost gross profit, $32,000

Estimate the costs (including opportunity costs) of buying motorcycle seats from supplier (B). This problem requires that you think creatively and make reasonable estimates; thus there could be more than one correct answer. (*Hint:* Reread the answer to *Decision Maker,* and compare the cost savings for buying from supplier [B] to the sum of lost customer revenue from repeat business and referrals and the cost of lost production time.)

Problem 14-5B

Ending inventory computation and evaluation

C4

The Edge Company makes specialty skates for the ice skating circuit. On December 31, 2010, the company had (*a*) 500 skates in finished goods inventory and (*b*) 2,000 blades at a cost of $15 each in raw materials inventory. During 2011, Edge Company purchased 45,000 additional blades at $15 each and manufactured 20,000 pairs of skates.

Required

Check (1) Ending (blade) inventory, 7,000 units; $105,000

1. Determine the unit and dollar amounts of raw materials inventory in blades at December 31, 2011.

Analysis Component

2. Write a one-half page memorandum to the production manager explaining why a just-in-time inventory system for blades should be considered. Include the amount of working capital that can be reduced at December 31, 2011, if the ending blade raw material inventory is cut in half.

Problem 14-6B

Inventory computation and reporting

C4 P1

Shown here are annual financial data at December 31, 2011, taken from two different companies.

	Cardinal Drug (Retail)	Nandina (Manufacturing)
Beginning inventory		
Merchandise	$ 50,000	
Finished goods		$200,000
Cost of purchases	350,000	
Cost of goods manufactured		686,000
Ending inventory		
Merchandise	25,000	
Finished goods		300,000

Required

Check (1) Cardinal Drug cost of goods sold, $375,000

1. Compute the cost of goods sold section of the income statement at December 31, 2011, for each company. Include the proper title and format in the solution.

2. Write a half-page memorandum to your instructor (*a*) identifying the inventory accounts and (*b*) identifying where each is reported on the income statement and balance sheet for both companies.

Eastman-Kodak manufactures digital cameras and must compete on lean manufacturing concepts. Match each of the following activities that it engages in with the lean manufacturing concept it strives to achieve. (Some activities might relate to more than one lean manufacturing concept.)

Problem 14-7B
Lean business concepts

C6

_____ **1.** Kodak monitors the market to determine what features its competitors are offering on digital cameras.

_____ **2.** Kodak asks production workers for ideas to improve production.

_____ **3.** Lenses are received daily based on customer orders.

_____ **4.** Customers receive a satisfaction survey with each camera purchased.

_____ **5.** The manufacturing process is standardized and documented.

_____ **6.** Cameras are produced in small lots, and only to customer order.

_____ **7.** Manufacturing facilities are arranged to reduce move time and wait time.

_____ **8.** Kodak conducts focus groups to determine new features that customers want in digital cameras.

_____ **9.** Orders received are filled within two business days.

_____ **10.** Kodak works with suppliers to reduce inspection time of incoming materials.

a. Just-in-time (JIT)

b. Continuous improvement (CI)

c. Total quality management (TQM)

The following calendar year-end information is taken from the December 31, 2011, adjusted trial balance and other records of Firethorn Furniture.

Problem 14-8B
Manufacturing and income statements; analysis of inventories P2

Advertising expense	$ 22,250	Direct labor	$ 564,500	
Depreciation expense—Office equipment	10,440	Income taxes expense	138,700	
Depreciation expense—Selling equipment	12,125	Indirect labor	61,000	
Depreciation expense—Factory equipment	37,400	Miscellaneous production costs	10,440	
Factory supervision	123,500	Office salaries expense	72,875	
Factory supplies used	8,060	Raw materials purchases	896,375	
Factory utilities	39,500	Rent expense—Office space	25,625	
Inventories		Rent expense—Selling space	29,000	
Raw materials, December 31, 2010	42,375	Rent expense—Factory building	95,500	
Raw materials, December 31, 2011	72,430	Maintenance expense—Factory equipment	32,375	
Goods in process, December 31, 2010	14,500	Sales	5,002,000	
Goods in process, December 31, 2011	16,100	Sales discounts	59,375	
Finished goods, December 31, 2010	179,200	Sales salaries expense	297,300	
Finished goods, December 31, 2011	143,750			

Required

1. Prepare the company's 2011 manufacturing statement.

2. Prepare the company's 2011 income statement that reports separate categories for (a) selling expenses and (b) general and administrative expenses.

Check (1) Cost of goods manufactured, $1,836,995

Analysis Component

3. Compute the (a) inventory turnover, defined as cost of goods sold divided by average inventory, and (b) days' sales in inventory, defined as 365 times ending inventory divided by cost of goods sold, for both its raw materials inventory and its finished goods inventory. (To compute turnover and days' sales in inventory for raw materials, use raw materials used rather than cost of goods sold.) Discuss some possible reasons for differences between these ratios for the two types of inventories. Round answers to one decimal place.

Problem 14-9B
Manufacturing cycle time and efficiency

A1

Quick Dry Ink produces ink-jet printers for personal computers. It received an order for 600 printers from a customer. The following information is available for this order.

Process time	16.0 hours
Inspection time	3.4 hours
Move time	9.0 hours
Wait time	21.6 hours

Required

1. Compute the company's manufacturing cycle time.

2. Compute the company's manufacturing cycle efficiency. Interpret your answer.

Analysis Component

3. Assume that Quick Dry Ink wishes to increase its manufacturing cycle efficiency to 0.80. What are some ways that it can accomplish this?

SERIAL PROBLEM
Business Solutions

C2 C4 P2

(This serial problem begins in Chapter 1 and continues through most of the book. If previous chapter segments were not completed, the serial problem can begin at this point. It is helpful, but not necessary, to use the Working Papers that accompany the book.)

SP 14   Santana Rey, owner of Business Solutions, decides to diversify her business by also manufacturing computer workstation furniture.

Required

1. Classify the following manufacturing costs of Business Solutions by behavior and traceability.

Product Costs	Cost by Behavior		Cost by Traceability	
	Variable	Fixed	Direct	Indirect
1. Monthly flat fee to clean workshop	____	____	____	____
2. Laminate coverings for desktops	____	____	____	____
3. Taxes on assembly workshop	____	____	____	____
4. Glue to assemble workstation component parts	____	____	____	____
5. Wages of desk assembler	____	____	____	____
6. Electricity for workshop	____	____	____	____
7. Depreciation on tools	____	____	____	____

2. Prepare a manufacturing statement for Business Solutions for the month ended January 31, 2012. Assume the following manufacturing costs:

Direct materials: $2,200

Factory overhead: $490

Direct labor: $900

Beginning goods in process: none (December 31, 2011)

Ending goods in process: $540 (January 31, 2012)

Beginning finished goods inventory: none (December 31, 2011)

Ending finished goods inventory: $350 (January 31, 2012)

Check   (3) COGS, $2,700

3. Prepare the cost of goods sold section of a partial income statement for Business Solutions for the month ended January 31, 2012.

Beyond the Numbers

BTN 14-1   Managerial accounting is more than recording, maintaining, and reporting financial results. Managerial accountants must provide managers with both financial and nonfinancial information including estimates, projections, and forecasts. There are many accounting estimates that management accountants must make, and **Research In Motion** must notify shareholders of these estimates.

REPORTING IN ACTION

C1

RIM

Required

1. Access and read Research In Motion's "Use of Estimates" section of the "Summary of Significant Accounting Policies" footnote to its financial statements, from Appendix A. What are some of the accounting estimates that Research In Motion made in preparing its financial statements? What are some of the effects if the company's actual results differ from its estimates?

2. What is the management accountant's role in determining those estimates?

Fast Forward

3. Access **Research In Motion**'s annual report for a fiscal year ending after February 27, 2010, from either its Website [**RIM.com**] or the SEC's EDGAR database [**www.SEC.gov**]. Answer the questions in parts (1) and (2) after reading the current "Summary of Significant Accounting Policies". Identify any major changes.

BTN 14-2   Manufacturing companies must decide whether to operate their own manufacturing facilities or instead outsource the manufacturing function to a third-party (outside) company. This decision impacts both company managers and also financial statement items. Access the annual report or 10-K for both **Research In Motion** (RIM) and **Apple**. The RIM report is for the year ended February 27, 2010 and the Apple report is for the year ended September 26, 2009.

COMPARATIVE ANALYSIS

C1

RIM

Apple

Required

1. Determine whether RIM operates its own manufacturing facilities or outsources the manufacturing function. (*Hint:* Search for "Manufacturing Capacity.")

2. Determine whether Apple operates its own manufacturing facilities or outsources the manufacturing function. (*Hint:* Search for "product manufacturing.")

3. For both companies, determine the amounts they report for (a) raw materials inventory, (b) work-in-process inventory, and (c) finished goods inventory. Explain how the decision on outsourcing (or not) of manufacturing operations is related to the components of inventory.

BTN 14-3   Assume that you are the managerial accountant at Infostore, a manufacturer of hard drives, CDs, and DVDs. Its reporting year-end is December 31. The chief financial officer is concerned about having enough cash to pay the expected income tax bill because of poor cash flow management. On November 15, the purchasing department purchased excess inventory of CD raw materials in anticipation of rapid growth of this product beginning in January. To decrease the company's tax liability, the chief financial officer tells you to record the purchase of this inventory as part of supplies and expense it in the current year; this would decrease the company's tax liability by increasing expenses.

ETHICS CHALLENGE

C1 C3

Required

1. In which account should the purchase of CD raw materials be recorded?

2. How should you respond to this request by the chief financial officer?

BTN 14-4   Write a one-page memorandum to a prospective college student about salary expectations for graduates in business. Compare and contrast the expected salaries for accounting (including different subfields such as public, corporate, tax, audit, and so forth), marketing, management, and finance majors. Prepare a graph showing average starting salaries (and those for experienced professionals in those fields if available). To get this information, stop by your school's career services office; libraries also have this information. The Website **JobStar.org** (click on *Salary Info*) also can get you started.

COMMUNICATING IN PRACTICE

C6

**TAKING IT TO
THE NET**

C1

BTN 14-5 Managerial accounting professionals follow a code of ethics. As a member of the Institute of Management Accountants, the managerial accountant must comply with Standards of Ethical Conduct.

Required

1. Identify, print, and read the *Statement of Ethical Professional Practice* posted at **www.IMAnet.org**. (Search using "ethical professional practice.")
2. What four overarching ethical principles underlie the IMA's statement?
3. Describe the courses of action the IMA recommends in resolving ethical conflicts.

**TEAMWORK IN
ACTION**

C5 P2

BTN 14-6 The following calendar-year information is taken from the December 31, 2011, adjusted trial balance and other records of Azalea Company.

Advertising expense	$ 19,125	Direct labor	$ 650,750
Depreciation expense—Office equipment	8,750	Indirect labor	60,000
Depreciation expense—Selling equipment	10,000	Miscellaneous production costs	8,500
Depreciation expense—Factory equipment	32,500	Office salaries expense	100,875
Factory supervision	122,500	Raw materials purchases	872,500
Factory supplies used	15,750	Rent expense—Office space	21,125
Factory utilities	36,250	Rent expense—Selling space	25,750
Inventories		Rent expense—Factory building	79,750
Raw materials, December 31, 2010	177,500	Maintenance expense—Factory equipment	27,875
Raw materials, December 31, 2011	168,125	Sales	3,275,000
Goods in process, December 31, 2010	15,875	Sales discounts	57,500
Goods in process, December 31, 2011	14,000	Sales salaries expense	286,250
Finished goods, December 31, 2010	164,375		
Finished goods, December 31, 2011	129,000		

Required

1. *Each* team member is to be responsible for computing **one** of the following amounts. You are not to duplicate your teammates' work. Get any necessary amounts from teammates. Each member is to explain the computation to the team in preparation for reporting to class.

   a. Materials used.   **d.** Total cost of goods in process.
   b. Factory overhead.   **e.** Cost of goods manufactured.
   c. Total manufacturing costs.

2. Check your cost of goods manufactured with the instructor. If it is correct, proceed to part (3).

3. *Each* team member is to be responsible for computing **one** of the following amounts. You are not to duplicate your teammates' work. Get any necessary amounts from teammates. Each member is to explain the computation to the team in preparation for reporting to class.

   a. Net sales.   **d.** Total operating expenses.
   b. Cost of goods sold.   **e.** Net income or loss before taxes.
   c. Gross profit.

Point: Provide teams with transparencies and markers for presentation purposes.

**ENTREPRENEURIAL
DECISION**

C1 C2 C6

BTN 14-7 Corey Rimmel, Adam Hendin, and David Melnick of **Hot Box Cookies** must understand manufacturing costs to effectively operate and succeed as a profitable and efficient business.

Required

1. What are the three main categories of manufacturing costs the owners must monitor and control? Provide examples of each.

2. How can the owners make Hot Box Cookies' manufacturing process more cost-effective? Provide examples of two useful managerial measures of time and efficiency.

3. What are four goals of a total quality management process? How can Hot Box Cookies use TQM to improve its business activities?

BTN 14-8   Visit your favorite fast-food restaurant. Observe its business operations.

HITTING THE ROAD

C1 C2

Required

1. Describe all business activities from the time a customer arrives to the time that customer departs.

2. List all costs you can identify with the separate activities described in part 1.

3. Classify each cost from part 2 as fixed or variable, and explain your classification.

BTN 14-9   Access Nokia's Website (www.nokia.com/about-nokia) and select "Corporate Governance" and then select "Overview." Read the section dealing with the responsibilities of its board of directors.

GLOBAL DECISION

C1

NOKIA

Required

1. Identify the responsibilities of Nokia's board of directors.

2. How would management accountants be involved in assisting the board of directors in carrying out their responsibilities? Explain.

ANSWERS TO MULTIPLE CHOICE QUIZ

1. c
2. b
3. b
4. a

5. Beginning finished goods + Cost of goods manufactured (COGM) −
Ending finished goods = Cost of goods sold
$6,000 + COGM − $3,200 = $7,500
COGM = $4,700

15

Job Order Costing and Analysis

A Look Back

Chapter 14 introduced managerial accounting and explained basic cost concepts. We also described the lean business model and the reporting of manufacturing activities, including the manufacturing statement.

A Look at This Chapter

We begin this chapter by describing a cost accounting system. We then explain the procedures used to determine costs using a job order costing system. We conclude with a discussion of over- and underapplied overhead.

A Look Ahead

Chapter 16 focuses on measuring costs in process production companies. We explain process production, describe how to assign costs to processes, and compute and analyze cost per equivalent unit.

Learning Objectives

CAP

CONCEPTUAL

C1 Describe important features of job order production. (p. 644)

C2 Explain job cost sheets and how they are used in job order cost accounting. (p. 646)

ANALYTICAL

A1 Apply job order costing in pricing services. (p. 657)

LP15

PROCEDURAL

P1 Describe and record the flow of materials costs in job order cost accounting. (p. 648)

P2 Describe and record the flow of labor costs in job order cost accounting. (p. 650)

P3 Describe and record the flow of overhead costs in job order cost accounting. (p. 651)

P4 Determine adjustments for overapplied and underapplied factory overhead. (p. 656)

Decision Insight

Riding the Wavers

"Results are what count . . . it's not how you start, but how you finish"

—**JOHN T. HEWITT** (CEO and founder)

VIRGINIA BEACH, VA—Don't be surprised if we find Uncle Sam and Lady Liberty waving to us around tax time. Use of these characters to market tax services is the brainchild of John Hewitt, founder of **Liberty Tax Service (LibertyTax.com),** a tax return preparation service. On street corners across America, Uncle Sam and Lady Liberty wave, dance, do cartwheels, and play air guitar, all to draw customers into Liberty's stores. This unconventional marketing scheme has helped Liberty become the fastest growing retail tax business ever.

The company started humbly, finalizing its business plan in a spare bedroom and renting a tiny office for a business address. John explains that one of his key tasks was developing a cost accounting system. Manufacturers of custom products, and providers of custom services like Liberty Tax Services, use state-of-the-art job order cost accounting to track costs. This includes tracking the cost of materials, labor, and overhead and managing those expenses. With job order costing, a company tracks costs separately for each job. If a job's cost is too high,

the company must reduce any future costs and perhaps also increase its selling price. Job order costing systems allow entrepreneurs such as John to better isolate costs and avoid the run-away costs often experienced by start-ups that fail to use costing techniques.

John's mission is simple: Set the standard, improve each day, and have some fun. While Uncle Sam and Lady Liberty get customers in the door, the company's fanatical focus on customer satisfaction and retention drive its growth. John continually works to improve services and adapt to market trends and competitors. With every successful customer contact his company approaches its ultimate goal: To be the largest tax preparation company in the universe. With Uncle Sam on air guitar, Liberty expects to ride the wave of growth.

[Sources: *Liberty Tax Service Website,* January 2011; *The Wall Street Journal,* April 17, 2006; *Hampton Roads Website,* February 2007]

This chapter introduces a system for assigning costs to the flow of goods through a production process. We then describe the details of a *job order cost accounting system*. Job order costing is frequently used by manufacturers of custom products or providers of custom services. Manufacturers that use job order costing typically base it on a perpetual inventory system, which provides a continuous record of materials, goods in process, and finished goods inventories.

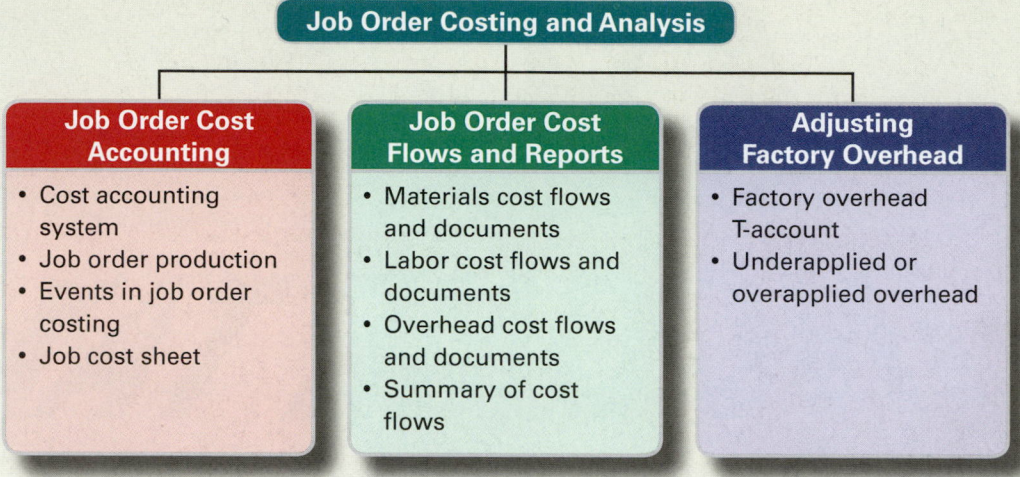

JOB ORDER COST ACCOUNTING

This section describes a cost accounting system and job order production and costing.

Cost Accounting System

An ever-increasing number of companies use a cost accounting system to generate timely and accurate inventory information. A **cost accounting system** records manufacturing activities using a *perpetual* inventory system, which continuously updates records for costs of materials, goods in process, and finished goods inventories. A cost accounting system also provides timely information about inventories and manufacturing costs per unit of product. This is especially helpful for managers' efforts to control costs and determine selling prices. (A **general accounting system** records manufacturing activities using a *periodic* inventory system. Some companies still use a general accounting system, but its use is declining as competitive forces and customer demands have increased pressures on companies to better manage inventories.)

The two basic types of cost accounting systems are *job order cost accounting* and *process cost accounting*. We describe job order cost accounting in this chapter. Process cost accounting is explained in the next chapter.

Job Order Production

C1 Describe important features of job order production.

Many companies produce products individually designed to meet the needs of a specific customer. Each customized product is manufactured separately and its production is called **job order production,** or *job order manufacturing* (also called *customized production,* which is the production of products in response to special orders). Examples of such products include synthetic football fields, special-order machines, a factory building, custom jewelry, wedding invitations, and artwork.

The production activities for a customized product represent a **job.** The principle of customization is equally applicable to both manufacturing *and* service companies. Most service companies meet customers' needs by performing a custom service for a specific customer. Examples of such services include an accountant auditing a client's financial statements, an interior designer remodeling an office, a wedding consultant planning and supervising a reception, and a lawyer defending a client. Whether the setting is manufacturing or services, job order operations involve meeting the needs of customers by producing or performing custom jobs.

Boeing's aerospace division is one example of a job order production system. Its primary business is twofold: (1) design, develop, and integrate space carriers and (2) provide systems engineering and integration of Department of Defense (DoD) systems. Many of its orders are customized and produced through job order operations.

When a job involves producing more than one unit of a custom product, it is often called a **job lot.** Products produced as job lots could include benches for a church, imprinted T-shirts for a 10K race or company picnic, or advertising signs for a chain of stores. Although these orders involve more than one unit, the volume of production is typically low, such as 50 benches, 200 T-shirts, or 100 signs. Another feature of job order production is the diversity, often called *heterogeneity,* of the products produced. Namely, each customer order is likely to differ from another in some important respect. These variations can be minor or major.

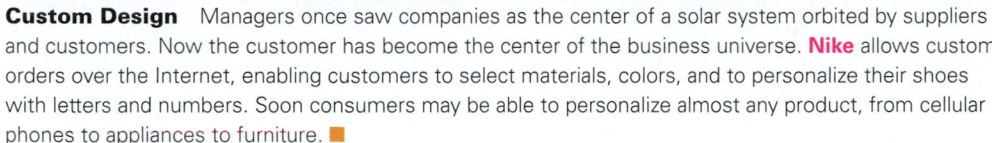

Custom Design Managers once saw companies as the center of a solar system orbited by suppliers and customers. Now the customer has become the center of the business universe. **Nike** allows custom orders over the Internet, enabling customers to select materials, colors, and to personalize their shoes with letters and numbers. Soon consumers may be able to personalize almost any product, from cellular phones to appliances to furniture. ■

Events in Job Order Costing

The initial event in a normal job order operation is the receipt of a customer order for a custom product. This causes the company to begin work on a job. A less common case occurs when management decides to begin work on a job before it has a signed contract. This is referred to as *jobs produced on speculation.*

Step 1: **Predict the cost to complete the job.** This cost depends on the product design prepared by either the customer or the producer.

Step 2: **Negotiate price and decide whether to pursue the job.** Other than for government or other cost-plus contracts, the selling price is determined by market factors. Producers evaluate the market price, compare it to cost, and determine whether the profit on the job is reasonable. If the profit is not reasonable, the producer would determine a desired **target cost.**

Point: Some jobs are priced on a *cost-plus basis:* The customer pays the manufacturer for costs incurred on the job plus a negotiated amount or rate of profit.

Step 3: **Schedule production of the job.** This must meet the customer's needs and fit within the company's own production constraints. Preparation of this work schedule should consider work-place facilities including equipment, personnel, and supplies. Once this schedule is complete, the producer can place orders for raw materials. Production occurs as materials and labor are applied to the job.

An overview of job order production activity is shown in Exhibit 15.1. This exhibit shows the March production activity of Road Warriors, which installs security devices into cars and trucks. The company converts any vehicle by adding alarms, reinforced exterior, bulletproof glass, and bomb detectors. The company began by catering to high-profile celebrities, but it now caters to anyone who desires added security in a vehicle.

Job order production for Road Warriors requires materials, labor, and overhead costs. Recall that direct materials are goods used in manufacturing that are clearly identified with a particular job. Similarly, direct labor is effort devoted to a particular job. Overhead costs support production of more than one job. Common overhead items are depreciation on factory buildings and equipment, factory supplies, supervision, maintenance, cleaning, and utilities.

Exhibit 15.1 shows that materials, labor, and overhead are added to Jobs B15, B16, B17, B18, and B19, which were started during March. Special tires and bulletproof glass are added to Jobs B15 and B16, while Job B17 receives a reinforced exterior and bulletproof glass. Road Warriors completed Jobs B15, B16, and B17 in March and delivered Jobs B15 and B16 to customers. At the end of March, Jobs B18 and B19 remain in goods in process inventory and Job B17 is in finished goods inventory. Both labor and materials costs are also separated into their direct and indirect components. Their indirect amounts are added to overhead. Total overhead cost is then allocated to the various jobs.

Point: Many professional examinations including the CPA and CMA exams require knowledge of job order and process cost accounting.

EXHIBIT 15.1

Job Order Production Activities

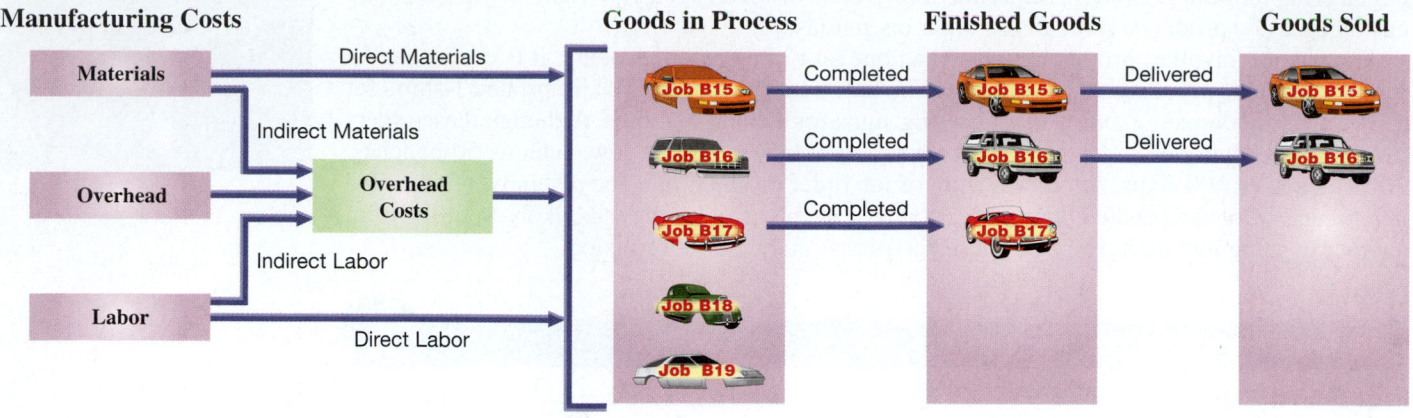

Decision Insight

Target Costing   Many producers determine a target cost for their jobs. Target cost is determined as follows: Expected selling price − Desired profit = Target cost. If the projected target cost of the job as determined by job costing is too high, the producer can apply *value engineering*, which is a method of determining ways to reduce job cost until the target cost is met. ■

Job Cost Sheet

C2 Explain job cost sheets and how they are used in job order cost accounting.

General ledger accounts usually do not provide the accounting information that managers of job order cost operations need to plan and control production activities. This is so because the needed information often requires more detailed data. Such detailed data are usually stored in subsidiary records controlled by general ledger accounts. Subsidiary records store information about raw materials, overhead costs, jobs in process, finished goods, and other items. This section describes the use of these records.

A major aim of a **job order cost accounting system** is to determine the cost of producing each job or job lot. In the case of a job lot, the system also aims to compute the cost per unit. The accounting system must include separate records for each job to accomplish this, and it must capture information about costs incurred and charge these costs to each job.

A **job cost sheet** is a separate record maintained for each job. Exhibit 15.2 shows a job cost sheet for an alarm system that Road Warriors produced for a customer. This job cost sheet identifies the customer, the job number assigned, the product, and key dates. Costs incurred on the job are immediately recorded on this sheet. When each job is complete, the supervisor enters the date of completion, records any remarks, and signs the sheet. The job cost sheet in Exhibit 15.2 classifies costs as direct materials, direct labor, or overhead. It shows that a total of $600 in direct materials is added to Job B15 on four different dates. It also shows seven entries for direct labor costs that total $1,000. Road Warriors *allocates* (also termed *applies, assigns,* or *charges*) factory overhead costs of $1,600 to this job using an allocation rate of 160% of direct labor cost (160% × $1,000)—we discuss overhead allocation later in this chapter.

Point: Factory overhead consists of costs (other than direct materials and direct labor) that ensure the production activities are carried out.

Cost Flows: During Production   While a job is being produced, its accumulated costs are kept in **Goods in Process Inventory.** The collection of job cost sheets for all jobs in process makes up a subsidiary ledger controlled by the Goods in Process Inventory account in the general ledger. Managers use job cost sheets to monitor costs incurred to date and to predict and control costs for each job.

EXHIBIT 15.2

Job Cost Sheet

Accounting System: Exhibit 15-2

File   Edit   Maintain   Tasks   Analysis   Options   Reports   Window   Help

Road Warriors, Los Angeles, California   **JOB COST SHEET**

Customer's Name	Carroll Connor		Job No.	B15
Address	1542 High Point Dr.		City & State	Malibu, California
Job Description	Level 1 Alarm System on Ford Expedition			
Date promised	March 15	Date started	March 3	Date completed	March 11

Direct Materials			Direct Labor			Overhead		
Date	Requisition	Cost	Date	Time Ticket	Cost	Date	Rate	Cost
3/3/2011	R-4698	100.00	3/3/2011	L-3393	120.00	3/11/2011	160% of Direct Labor Cost	1,600.00
3/7/2011	R-4705	225.00	3/4/2011	L-3422	150.00			
3/9/2011	R-4725	180.00	3/5/2011	L-3456	180.00			
3/10/2011	R-4777	95.00	3/8/2011	L-3479	60.00			
			3/9/2011	L-3501	90.00			
			3/10/2011	L-3535	240.00			
			3/11/2011	L-3559	160.00			
	Total	600.00		Total	1,000.00		Total	1,600.00

REMARKS: Completed job on March 11, and shipped to customer on March 15. Met all specifications and requirements.

SUMMARY:

Materials	600.00
Labor	1,000.00
Overhead	1,600.00

Signed: *C. Luther, Supervisor*

Total cost	3,200.00

Cost Flows: Job Completion   When a job is finished, its job cost sheet is completed and moved from the jobs in process file to the finished jobs file. This latter file acts as a subsidiary ledger controlled by the **Finished Goods Inventory** account.

Cost Flows: Job Delivery   When a finished job is delivered to a customer, the job cost sheet is moved to a permanent file supporting the total cost of goods sold. This permanent file contains records from both current and prior periods. When the job is finished, the company also prepares a journal entry that credits Sales and debits Cash (or Accounts Receivable).

Point: Documents (electronic and paper) are crucial in a job order system, and the job cost sheet is a cornerstone. Understanding it aids in grasping concepts of capitalizing product costs and product cost flow.

Decision Maker   Answer — p. 661

Management Consultant   One of your tasks is to control and manage costs for a consulting company. At the end of a recent month, you find that three consulting jobs were completed and two are 60% complete. Each unfinished job is estimated to cost $10,000 and to earn a revenue of $12,000. You are unsure how to recognize goods in process inventory and record costs and revenues. Do you recognize any inventory? If so, how much? How much revenue is recorded for unfinished jobs this month? ■

Quick Check   Answers — p. 661

1. Which of these products is likely to involve job order production? (*a*) inexpensive watches, (*b*) racing bikes, (*c*) bottled soft drinks, or (*d*) athletic socks.

2. What is the difference between a job and a job lot?

3. Which of these statements is correct? (*a*) The collection of job cost sheets for unfinished jobs makes up a subsidiary ledger controlled by the Goods in Process Inventory account, (*b*) Job cost sheets are financial statements provided to investors, or (*c*) A separate job cost sheet is maintained in the general ledger for each job in process.

4. What three costs are normally accumulated on job cost sheets?

JOB ORDER COST FLOWS AND REPORTS

Materials

P1	Describe and record the flow of materials costs in job order cost accounting.

Point: Some companies certify certain suppliers based on the quality of their materials. Goods received from these suppliers are not always inspected by the purchaser to save costs.

Materials Cost Flows and Documents

This section focuses on the flow of materials costs and the related documents in a job order cost accounting system. We begin analysis of the flow of materials costs by examining Exhibit 15.3. When materials are first received from suppliers, the employees count and inspect them and record the items' quantity and cost on a receiving report. The receiving report serves as the *source document* for recording materials received in both a materials ledger card and in the general ledger. In nearly all job order cost systems, **materials ledger cards** (or files) are perpetual records that are updated each time units are purchased and each time units are issued for use in production.

To illustrate the purchase of materials, Road Warriors acquired $450 of wiring and related materials on March 4, 2011. This purchase is recorded as follows.

Assets = Liabilities + Equity
+450   +450

Mar. 4	Raw Materials Inventory—M-347	450	
	Accounts Payable		450
	To record purchase of materials for production.		

EXHIBIT 15.3

Materials Cost Flows through Subsidiary Records

Job B15

Materials	Labor	Overhead
600.00		

Requisitions

Job Cost Sheets

Direct Cost

Alarm System Wiring

Received	Issued	Balance
450.00		675.00
	225.00	450.00

Receiving Reports

Materials Ledger Cards

Indirect Cost

Indirect Materials

550.00

Factory Overhead Ledger

Requisitions

Exhibit 15.3 shows that materials can be requisitioned for use either on a specific job (direct materials) or as overhead (indirect materials). Cost of direct materials flows from the materials ledger card to the job cost sheet. The cost of indirect materials flows from the materials ledger card to the Indirect Materials account in the factory overhead ledger, which is a subsidiary ledger controlled by the Factory Overhead account in the general ledger.

Exhibit 15.4 shows a materials ledger card for material received and issued by Road Warriors. The card identifies the item as alarm system wiring and shows the item's stock number, its location in the storeroom, information about the maximum and minimum quantities that should be available, and the reorder quantity. For example, alarm system wiring is issued

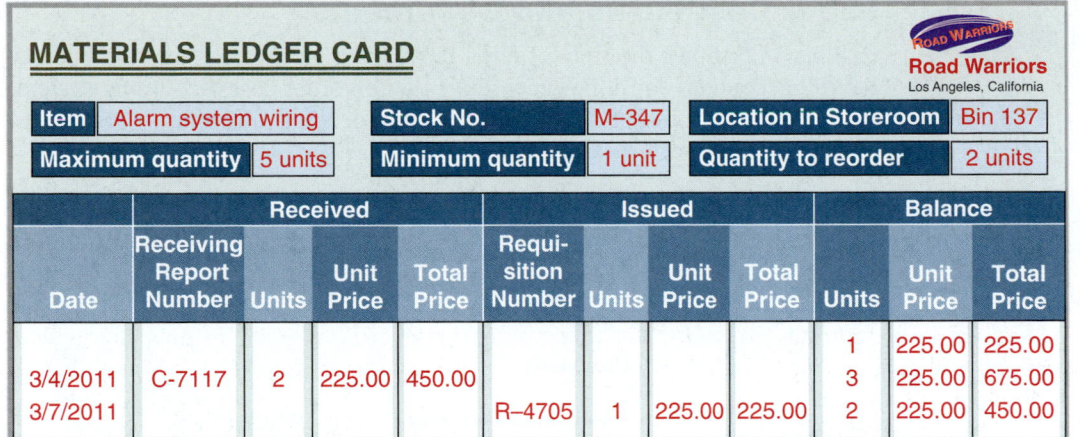

EXHIBIT 15.4

Materials Ledger Card

and recorded on March 7, 2011. The job cost sheet in Exhibit 15.2 showed that Job B15 used this wiring.

When materials are needed in production, a production manager prepares a **materials requisition** and sends it to the materials manager. The requisition shows the job number, the type of material, the quantity needed, and the signature of the manager authorized to make the requisition. Exhibit 15.5 shows the materials requisition for alarm system wiring for Job B15. To see how this requisition ties to the flow of costs, compare the information on the requisition with the March 7, 2011, data in Exhibits 15.2 and 15.4.

Point: Requisitions are often accumulated and recorded in one entry. The frequency of entries depends on the job, the industry, and management procedures.

MATERIALS REQUISITION   No. R–4705

Road Warriors
Los Angeles, California

Job No.	B15	Date	3/7/2011
Material Stock No.	M–347	Material Description	Alarm system wiring
Quantity Requested	1	Requested By	C. Luther
Quantity Provided	1	Date Provided	3/7/2011
Filled By	M. Bateman	Material Received By	C. Luther
Remarks			

EXHIBIT 15.5

Materials Requisition

The use of alarm system wiring on Job B15 yields the following entry (locate this cost item in the job cost sheet shown in Exhibit 15.2).

Mar. 7	Goods in Process Inventory—Job B15	225	
	Raw Materials Inventory—M-347		225
	To record use of material on Job B15.		

Assets = Liabilities + Equity
+225
−225

This entry is posted both to its general ledger accounts and to subsidiary records. Posting to subsidiary records includes a debit to a job cost sheet and a credit to a materials ledger card. (*Note:* An entry to record use of indirect materials is the same as that for direct materials *except* the debit is to Factory Overhead. In the subsidiary factory overhead ledger, this entry is posted to Indirect Materials.)

P2	Describe and record the flow of labor costs in job order cost accounting.

Labor

Labor Cost Flows and Documents

Exhibit 15.6 shows the flow of labor costs from clock cards and the Factory Payroll account to subsidiary records of the job order cost accounting system. Recall that costs in subsidiary records give detailed information needed to manage and control operations.

EXHIBIT 15.6

Labor Cost Flows through Subsidiary Records

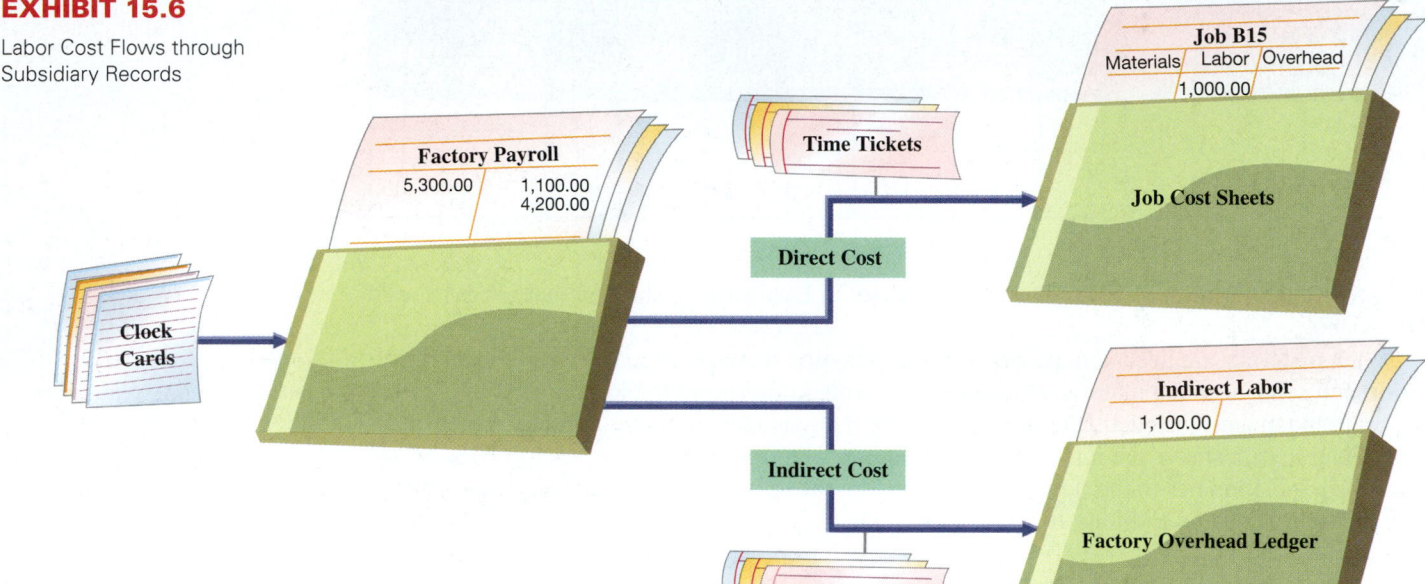

Point: Many employee fraud schemes involve payroll, including overstated hours on clock cards.

Point: In the accounting equation, we treat accounts such as Factory Payroll and Factory Overhead as temporary accounts, which hold various expenses until they are allocated to balance sheet or income statement accounts.

The flow of costs in Exhibit 15.6 begins with **clock cards.** Employees commonly use these cards to record the number of hours worked, and they serve as source documents for entries to record labor costs. Clock card data on the number of hours worked is used at the end of each pay period to determine total labor cost. This amount is then debited to the Factory Payroll account, a temporary account containing the total payroll cost (both direct and indirect). Payroll cost is later allocated to both specific jobs and overhead.

According to clock card data, workers earned $1,500 for the week ended March 5. Illustrating the flow of labor costs, the accrual and payment of these wages are recorded as follows.

Assets = Liabilities + Equity
−1,500   −1,500

Mar. 6	Factory Payroll	1,500	
	Cash		1,500
	To record the weekly payroll.		

"It's on Corporate Standard Time...
It loses an hour of your pay every day."

To assign labor costs to specific jobs and to overhead, we must know how each employee's time is used and its costs. Source documents called **time tickets** usually capture these data. Employees regularly fill out time tickets to report how much time they spent on each job. An employee who works on several jobs during a day completes a separate time ticket for each job. Tickets are also prepared for time charged to overhead as indirect labor. A supervisor signs an employee's time ticket to confirm its accuracy.

Exhibit 15.7 shows a time ticket reporting the time a Road Warrior employee spent working on Job B15. The employee's supervisor signed the ticket to confirm its accuracy. The hourly rate and total labor cost are computed after the time ticket is turned in. To see the effect of this time ticket on the job cost sheet, look at the entry dated March 8, 2011, in Exhibit 15.2.

EXHIBIT 15.7

Time Ticket

TIME TICKET			No. L–3479

Road Warriors
Los Angeles, California

Date ......March 8...... 20 ...11...

Employee Name	Employee Number	Job No.
T. Zeller	3969	B15

TIME AND RATE INFORMATION:

Start Time	Finish Time	Elapsed Time	Hourly Rate
9:00	12:00	3.0	$20.00

Remarks

....
....
....

Approved By ....*C. Luther*............. | Total Cost | $60.00 |

When time tickets report labor used on a specific job, this cost is recorded as direct labor. The following entry records the data from the time ticket in Exhibit 15.7.

Mar. 8	Goods in Process Inventory—Job B15	60	
	Factory Payroll		60
	To record direct labor used on Job B15.		

Assets = Liabilities + Equity
+60   +60

The debit in this entry is posted both to the general ledger account and to the appropriate job cost sheet. (*Note:* An entry to record indirect labor is the same as for direct labor *except* that it debits Factory Overhead and credits Factory Payroll. In the subsidiary factory overhead ledger, the debit in this entry is posted to the Indirect Labor account.)

Overhead Cost Flows and Documents

Factory overhead (or simply overhead) cost flows are shown in Exhibit 15.8. Factory overhead includes all production costs other than direct materials and direct labor. Two sources of overhead costs are indirect materials and indirect labor. These costs are recorded from requisitions for indirect materials and time tickets for indirect labor. Two other sources of overhead are (1) vouchers authorizing payments for items such as supplies or utilities and (2) adjusting entries for costs such as depreciation on factory assets.

Overhead

P3 Describe and record the flow of overhead costs in job order cost accounting.

Factory overhead usually includes many different costs and, thus, a separate account for each is often maintained in a subsidiary factory overhead ledger. This ledger is controlled by the Factory Overhead account in the general ledger. Factory Overhead is a temporary account that accumulates costs until they are allocated to jobs.

Recording Overhead   Recall that overhead costs are recorded with debits to the Factory Overhead account and with credits to other accounts such as Cash, Accounts Payable, and

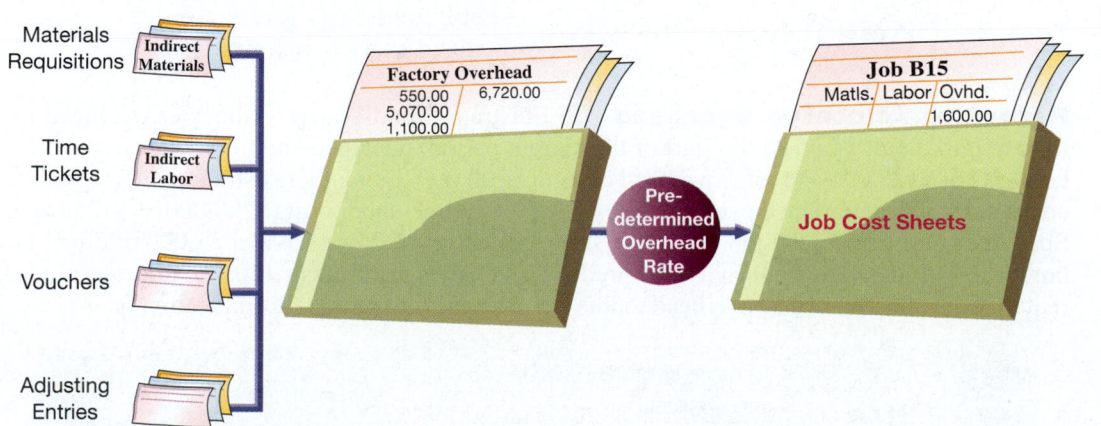

EXHIBIT 15.8

Overhead Cost Flows through Subsidiary Records

Accumulated Depreciation—Equipment. In the subsidiary factory overhead ledger, the debits are posted to their respective accounts such as Depreciation Expense—Equipment, Insurance Expense—Warehouse, or Amortization Expense—Patents.

To illustrate the recording of overhead, the following two entries reflect the depreciation of factory equipment and the accrual of utilities, respectively, for the week ended March 6.

Assets = Liabilities + Equity
−600   −600

Assets = Liabilities + Equity
            +250   −250

Mar. 6	Factory Overhead	600	
	Accumulated Depreciation—Equipment		600
	To record depreciation on factory equipment.		
Mar. 6	Factory Overhead	250	
	Utilities Payable		250
	To record the accrual of factory utilities.		

Exhibit 15.8 shows that overhead costs flow from the Factory Overhead account to job cost sheets. Because overhead is made up of costs not directly associated with specific jobs or job lots, we cannot determine the dollar amount incurred on a specific job. We know, however, that overhead costs represent a necessary part of business activities. If a job cost is to include all costs needed to complete the job, some amount of overhead must be included. Given the difficulty in determining the overhead amount for a specific job, however, we allocate overhead to individual jobs in some reasonable manner.

Overhead Allocation Bases We generally allocate overhead by linking it to another factor used in production, such as direct labor or machine hours. The factor to which overhead costs are linked is known as the *allocation base.* A manager must think carefully about how many and which allocation bases to use. This managerial decision influences the accuracy with which overhead costs are allocated to individual jobs. In turn, the cost of individual jobs might impact a manager's decisions for pricing or performance evaluation. In Exhibit 15.2, overhead is expressed as 160% of direct labor. We then allocate overhead by multiplying 160% by the estimated amount of direct labor on the jobs.

Point: The predetermined overhead rate is computed at the start of the period and is used throughout the period to allocate overhead to jobs.

Point: Predetermined overhead rates can be estimated using mathematical equations, statistical analysis, or professional experience.

Overhead Allocation Rates We cannot wait until the end of a period to allocate overhead to jobs because perpetual inventory records are part of the job order costing system (demanding up-to-date costs). Instead, we must predict overhead in advance and assign it to jobs so that a job's total costs can be estimated prior to its completion. This estimated cost is useful for managers in many decisions including setting prices and identifying costs that are out of control. Being able to estimate overhead in advance requires a **predetermined overhead rate,** also called *predetermined overhead allocation* (or *application*) *rate.* This rate requires an estimate of total overhead cost and an allocation factor such as total direct labor cost before the start of the period. Exhibit 15.9 shows the usual formula for computing a predetermined overhead rate (estimates are commonly based on annual amounts). This rate is used during the period to allocate overhead to jobs. It is common for companies to use multiple activity (allocation) bases and multiple predetermined overhead rates for different types of products and services.

EXHIBIT 15.9

Predetermined Overhead
Allocation Rate Formula

$$\text{Predetermined overhead rate} = \frac{\text{Estimated}}{\text{overhead costs}} \div \frac{\text{Estimated}}{\text{activity base}}$$

Recording Allocated Overhead To illustrate, Road Warriors allocates overhead by linking it to direct labor. At the start of the current period, management predicts total direct labor costs of $125,000 and total overhead costs of $200,000. Using these estimates, management computes its predetermined overhead rate as 160% of direct labor cost ($200,000 ÷ $125,000). Specifically, reviewing the job order cost sheet in Exhibit 15.2, we see that $1,000 of direct labor went into Job B15. We then use the predetermined overhead rate of 160% to allocate $1,600 (equal to $1,000 × 1.60) of overhead to this job. The entry to record this allocation is

Example: If management predicts total direct labor costs of $100,000 and total overhead costs of $200,000, what is its predetermined overhead rate? *Answer:* 200% of direct labor cost.

Assets = Liabilities + Equity
+1,600   +1,600

Mar. 11	Goods in Process Inventory—Job B15	1,600	
	Factory Overhead		1,600
	To assign overhead to Job B15.		

Since the allocation rate for overhead is estimated at the start of a period, the total amount assigned to jobs during a period rarely equals the amount actually incurred. We explain how this difference is treated later in this chapter.

Decision Ethics   Answer — p. 661

Web Consultant You are working on seven client engagements. Two clients reimburse your firm for actual costs plus a 10% markup. The other five pay a fixed fee for services. Your firm's costs include overhead allocated at $47 per labor hour. The managing partner of your firm instructs you to record as many labor hours as possible to the two markup engagements by transferring labor hours from the other five. What do you do? ■

Summary of Cost Flows

We showed journal entries for charging Goods in Process Inventory (Job B15) with the cost of (1) direct materials requisitions, (2) direct labor time tickets, and (3) factory overhead. We made separate entries for each of these costs, but they are usually recorded in one entry. Specifically, materials requisitions are often collected for a day or a week and recorded with a single entry summarizing them. The same is done with labor time tickets. When summary entries are made, supporting schedules of the jobs charged and the types of materials used provide the basis for postings to subsidiary records.

To show all production cost flows for a period and their related entries, we again look at Road Warriors' activities. Exhibit 15.10 shows costs linked to all of Road Warriors' production activities for March. Road Warriors did not have any jobs in process at the beginning of March, but it did apply materials, labor, and overhead costs to five new jobs in March. Jobs B15 and B16 are completed and delivered to customers in March, Job B17 is completed but not delivered, and Jobs B18 and B19 are still in process. Exhibit 15.10 also shows purchases of raw materials for $2,750, labor costs incurred for $5,300, and overhead costs of $6,720.

Point: Study the flow of manufacturing costs through general ledger accounts and job cost sheets. Use Exhibit 15.11 as reinforcement.

EXHIBIT 15.10

Job Order Costs of All Production Activities

			Overhead		Goods in	Finished	Cost of Goods
ROAD WARRIORS							
Job Order Manufacturing Costs							
For Month Ended March 31, 2011							
Explanation	Materials	Labor	Incurred	Allocated	Process	Goods	Sold
Job B15	$ 600	$1,000		$1,600			$3,200
Job B16	300	800		1,280			2,380
Job B17	500	1,100		1,760		$3,360	
Job B18	150	700		1,120	$1,970		
Job B19	250	600		960	1,810		
Total job costs	1,800	4,200		$6,720	$3,780	$3,360	$5,580
Indirect materials	550		$ 550				
Indirect labor		1,100	1,100				
Other overhead			5,070				
Total costs used in production	2,350	$5,300	$6,720				
Ending materials inventory	1,400						
Materials available	3,750						
Less beginning materials inventory	(1,000)						
Materials purchased	$2,750						

The upper part of Exhibit 15.11 shows the flow of these costs through general ledger accounts and the end-of-month balances in key subsidiary records. Arrow lines are numbered to show the flows of costs for March. Each numbered cost flow reflects several entries made in March. The lower part of Exhibit 15.11 shows summarized job cost sheets and their status at the end of March. The sum of costs assigned to the jobs in process ($1,970 + $1,810) equals the

EXHIBIT 15.11

Job Order Cost Flows and Ending Job Cost Sheets

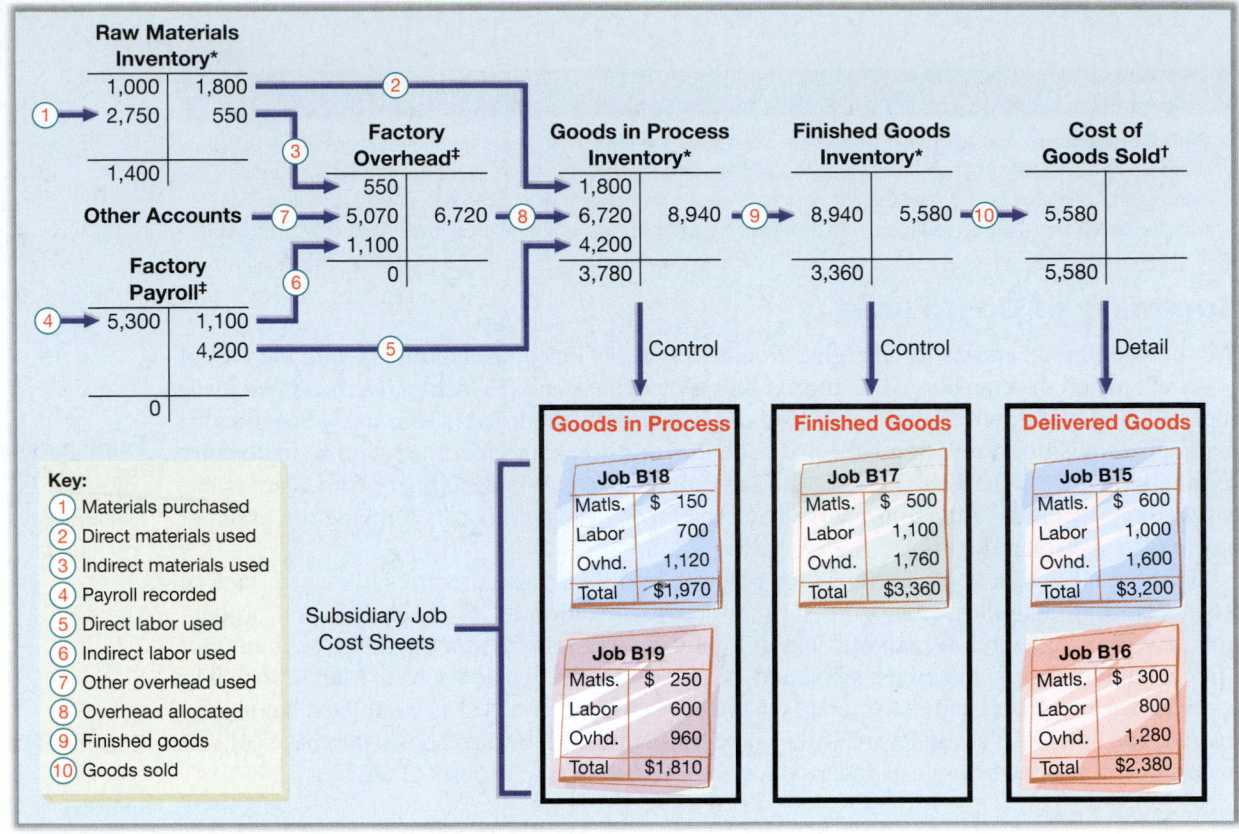

* The ending balances in the inventory accounts are carried to the balance sheet.
† The Cost of Goods Sold balance is carried to the income statement.
‡ Factory Payroll and Factory Overhead are considered temporary accounts; when these costs are allocated to jobs, the balances in these accounts are reduced.

$3,780 balance in Goods in Process Inventory shown in Exhibit 15.10. Also, costs assigned to Job B17 equal the $3,360 balance in Finished Goods Inventory. The sum of costs assigned to Jobs B15 and B16 ($3,200 + $2,380) equals the $5,580 balance in Cost of Goods Sold.

Exhibit 15.12 shows each cost flow with a single entry summarizing the actual individual entries made in March. Each entry is numbered to link with the arrow lines in Exhibit 15.11.

Decision Maker   Answer — p. 661

Entrepreneur   Competitors' prices on one of your product segments are lower than yours. Of the total product cost used in setting your prices, 53% is overhead allocated using direct labor hours. You believe that product costs are distorted and wonder whether there is a better way to allocate overhead and to set product price. What do you suggest? ■

Quick Check   Answers — p. 661

5. In job order cost accounting, which account is debited in recording a raw materials requisition? (*a*) Raw Materials Inventory, (*b*) Raw Materials Purchases, (*c*) Goods in Process Inventory if for a job, or (*d*) Goods in Process Inventory if they are indirect materials.

6. What are four sources of information for recording costs in the Factory Overhead account?

7. Why does job order cost accounting require a predetermined overhead rate?

8. What events result in a debit to Factory Payroll? What events result in a credit?

EXHIBIT 15.12

Entries for Job Order Production Costs*

①	Raw Materials Inventory	2,750	
	Accounts Payable		2,750
	Acquired materials on credit for factory use.		
②	Goods in Process Inventory	1,800	
	Raw Materials Inventory		1,800
	To assign costs of direct materials used.		
③	Factory Overhead	550	
	Raw Materials Inventory		550
	To record use of indirect materials.		
④	Factory Payroll	5,300	
	Cash (and other accounts)		5,300
	To record salaries and wages of factory workers (including various payroll liabilities).		
⑤	Goods in Process Inventory	4,200	
	Factory Payroll		4,200
	To assign costs of direct labor used.		

⑥	Factory Overhead	1,100	
	Factory Payroll		1,100
	To record indirect labor costs as overhead.		
⑦	Factory Overhead	5,070	
	Cash (and other accounts)		5,070
	To record factory overhead costs such as insurance, utilities, rent, and depreciation.		
⑧	Goods in Process Inventory	6,720	
	Factory Overhead		6,720
	To apply overhead at 160% of direct labor.		
⑨	Finished Goods Inventory	8,940	
	Goods in Process Inventory		8,940
	To record completion of Jobs B15, B16, and B17.		
⑩	Cost of Goods Sold	5,580	
	Finished Goods Inventory		5,580
	To record sale of Jobs B15 and B16.		

* Exhibit 15.12 provides summary journal entries. Remember, applied overhead is recorded *during* the period, while actual overhead is recorded at the end of the period. *Actual* overhead is debited to Factory Overhead. *Allocated* overhead is credited to Factory Overhead.

ADJUSTING FACTORY OVERHEAD

Refer to the debits in the Factory Overhead account in Exhibit 15.11 (or Exhibit 15.12). The total cost of factory overhead incurred during March is $6,720 ($550 + $5,070 + $1,100). The $6,720 exactly equals the amount assigned to goods in process inventory (see ⑧). Therefore, the overhead incurred equals the overhead applied in March. The amount of overhead incurred rarely equals the amount of overhead applied, however, because estimates rarely equal the exact amounts actually incurred. This section explains what we do when too much or too little overhead is applied to jobs.

Factory Overhead T-Account

Exhibit 15.13 shows a Factory Overhead T-account. The company applies overhead using a predetermined rate estimated at the beginning of the period. At the end of the period, the company receives bills for its actual overhead costs.

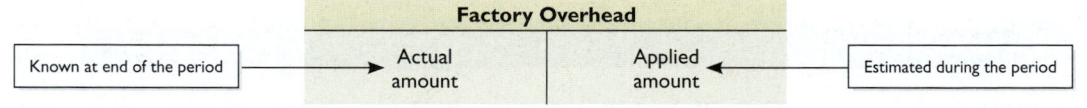

EXHIBIT 15.13

Factory Overhead T-account

Exhibit 15.14 shows what to do when actual overhead does not equal applied overhead. When less overhead is applied than is actually incurred, the remaining debit balance in the Factory Overhead account is called **underapplied overhead.** When the overhead applied in a period exceeds the overhead incurred, the resulting credit balance in the Factory Overhead account is called **overapplied overhead.** In either case, a journal entry is needed to adjust Factory Overhead and Cost of Goods Sold. Exhibit 15.14 summarizes this entry.

EXHIBIT 15.14

Adjusting Factory Overhead

Overhead Costs	Factory Overhead Balance Is	Overhead Is	Journal Entry Needed Is	
Actual > Applied	Debit	Underapplied	Cost of Goods Sold ...... #	
			Factory Overhead	#
Actual < Applied	Credit	Overapplied	Factory Overhead .... #	
			Cost of Goods Sold	#

P4 Determine adjustments for overapplied and underapplied factory overhead.

Underapplied or Overapplied Overhead

To illustrate, assume that Road Warriors actually incurred *other overhead costs* of $5,550 instead of the $5,070 shown in Exhibit 15.11. This yields an actual total overhead cost of $7,200 in March. Since the amount of overhead applied was only $6,720, the Factory Overhead account is left with a $480 debit balance as shown in the ledger account in Exhibit 15.15.

EXHIBIT 15.15

Underapplied Overhead in the Factory Overhead Ledger Account

Factory Overhead				Acct. No. 540
Date	Explanation	Debit	Credit	Balance
Mar. 31	Indirect materials cost	550		550 Dr.
31	Indirect labor cost	1,100		1,650 Dr.
31	Other overhead cost	5,550		7,200 Dr.
31	Overhead costs applied to jobs		6,720	480 Dr.

The $480 debit balance reflects manufacturing costs not assigned to jobs. This means that the balances in Goods in Process Inventory, Finished Goods Inventory, and Cost of Goods Sold do not include all production costs incurred. When the underapplied overhead amount is immaterial, it is allocated (closed) to the Cost of Goods Sold account with the following adjusting entry.

Example: If we do not adjust for underapplied overhead, will net income be overstated or understated? *Answer:* Overstated.

Assets = Liabilities + Equity
−480
+480

Mar. 31	Cost of Goods Sold	480	
	Factory Overhead		480
	To adjust for underapplied overhead costs.		

The $480 debit (increase) to Cost of Goods Sold reduces income by $480. (When the underapplied (or overapplied) overhead is material, the amount is normally allocated to the Cost of Goods Sold, Finished Goods Inventory, and Goods in Process Inventory accounts. This process is covered in advanced courses.)

We treat overapplied overhead at the end of the period in the same way we treat underapplied overhead, except that we debit Factory Overhead and credit Cost of Good Sold for the amount.

Decision Insight

Job Order Education   Many companies invest in their employees, and the demand for executive education is strong. Annual spending on training and education exceeds $20 billion. Annual revenues for providers of executive education continue to rise, with about 40% of revenues coming from custom programs designed for one or a select group of companies. ∎

Quick Check

Answers — p. 662

9. In a job order cost accounting system, why does the Factory Overhead account usually have an overapplied or underapplied balance at period-end?

10. When the Factory Overhead account has a debit balance at period-end, does this reflect overapplied or underapplied overhead?

GLOBAL VIEW

Porsche AG manufactures high-performance cars. Each car is built according to individual customer specifications. Customers can use the Internet to place orders for their dream cars. Porsche employs just-in-time inventory techniques to ensure a flexible production process that can respond rapidly to customer orders. For fiscal 2009, Porsche reported €33,781 million in costs of materials and €9,038 million in personnel costs, which helped generate €57,081 million in revenue.

The chapter described job order costing mainly using a manufacturing setting. However, these concepts and procedures are applicable to a service setting. Consider AdWorld, an advertising agency that develops Web-based ads for small firms. Each of its customers has unique requirements, so costs for each individual job must be tracked separately.

> **A1** Apply job order costing in pricing services.

AdWorld uses two types of labor: Web designers ($65 per hour) and computer staff ($50 per hour). It also incurs overhead costs that it assigns using two different predetermined overhead allocation rates: $125 per designer hour and $96 per staff hour. For each job, AdWorld must estimate the number of designer and staff hours needed. Then total costs pertaining to each job are determined using the procedures in the chapter. (*Note:* Most service firms have neither the category of materials cost nor inventory.)

To illustrate, a manufacturer of golf balls requested a quote from AdWorld for an advertising engagement. AdWorld estimates that the job will require 43 designer hours and 61 staff hours, with the following total estimated cost for this job.

Direct Labor		
Designers (43 hours × $65)	$ 2,795	
Staff (61 hours × $50)	3,050	
Total direct labor		$ 5,845
Overhead		
Designer related (43 hours × $125)	5,375	
Staff related (61 hours × $96)	5,856	
Total overhead		11,231
Total estimated job cost		$17,076

AdWorld can use this cost information to help determine the price quote for the job (see *Decision Maker, Sales Manager,* scenario below).

Another source of information that AdWorld must consider is the market, that is, how much competitors will quote for this job. Competitor information is often unavailable; therefore, AdWorld's managers must use estimates based on their assessment of the competitive environment.

◼ Decision Maker   Answer — p. 661

Sales Manager As AdWorld's sales manager, assume that you estimate costs pertaining to a proposed job as $17,076. Your normal pricing policy is to apply a markup of 18% from total costs. However, you learn that three other agencies are likely to bid for the same job, and that their quotes will range from $16,500 to $22,000. What price should you quote? What factors other than cost must you consider? ◼

DEMONSTRATION PROBLEM—JOB ORDER COSTING

The following information reflects Walczak Company's job order production activities for May.

Raw materials purchases	$16,000
Factory payroll cost	15,400
Overhead costs incurred	
Indirect materials	5,000
Indirect labor	3,500
Other factory overhead	9,500

Walczak's predetermined overhead rate is 150% of direct labor cost. Costs are allocated to the three jobs worked on during May as follows.

	Job 401	Job 402	Job 403
In-process balances on April 30			
Direct materials	$3,600		
Direct labor	1,700		
Applied overhead	2,550		
Costs during May			
Direct materials	3,550	$3,500	$1,400
Direct labor	5,100	6,000	800
Applied overhead	?	?	?
Status on May 31	**Finished (sold)**	**Finished (unsold)**	**In process**

Required

1. Determine the total cost of:
   a. The April 30 inventory of jobs in process.
   b. Materials used during May.
   c. Labor used during May.
   d. Factory overhead incurred and applied during May and the amount of any over- or underapplied overhead on May 31.
   e. Each job as of May 31, the May 31 inventories of both goods in process and finished goods, and the goods sold during May.
2. Prepare summarized journal entries for the month to record:
   a. Materials purchases (on credit), the factory payroll (paid with cash), indirect materials, indirect labor, and the other factory overhead (paid with cash).
   b. Assignment of direct materials, direct labor, and overhead costs to the Goods in Process Inventory account. (Use separate debit entries for each job.)
   c. Transfer of each completed job to the Finished Goods Inventory account.
   d. Cost of goods sold.
   e. Removal of any underapplied or overapplied overhead from the Factory Overhead account. (Assume the amount is not material.)
3. Prepare a manufacturing statement for May.

PLANNING THE SOLUTION

- Determine the cost of the April 30 goods in process inventory by totaling the materials, labor, and applied overhead costs for Job 401.
- Compute the cost of materials used and labor by totaling the amounts assigned to jobs and to overhead.
- Compute the total overhead incurred by summing the amounts for the three components. Compute the amount of applied overhead by multiplying the total direct labor cost by the predetermined overhead rate. Compute the underapplied or overapplied amount as the difference between the actual cost and the applied cost.
- Determine the total cost charged to each job by adding the costs incurred in April (if any) to the cost of materials, labor, and overhead applied during May.
- Group the costs of the jobs according to their completion status.
- Record the direct materials costs assigned to the three jobs, using a separate Goods in Process Inventory account for each job; do the same for the direct labor and the applied overhead.
- Transfer costs of Jobs 401 and 402 from Goods in Process Inventory to Finished Goods.
- Record the costs of Job 401 as cost of goods sold.
- Record the transfer of underapplied overhead from the Factory Overhead account to the Cost of Goods Sold account.
- On the manufacturing statement, remember to include the beginning and ending goods in process inventories and to deduct the underapplied overhead.

SOLUTION TO DEMONSTRATION PROBLEM

1. Total cost of

   a. April 30 inventory of jobs in process (Job 401).

Direct materials..........	$3,600
Direct labor	1,700
Applied overhead	2,550
Total cost	$7,850

   b. Materials used during May.

Direct materials		
Job 401..................		$ 3,550
Job 402..................		3,500
Job 403..................		1,400
Total direct materials		8,450
Indirect materials		5,000
Total materials used		$13,450

   c. Labor used during May.

Direct labor		
Job 401...............		$ 5,100
Job 402...............		6,000
Job 403...............		800
Total direct labor		11,900
Indirect labor		3,500
Total labor used..........		$15,400

   d. Factory overhead incurred in May.

Actual overhead		
Indirect materials......................		$ 5,000
Indirect labor........................		3,500
Other factory overhead		9,500
Total actual overhead		18,000
Overhead applied (150% × $11,900)		17,850
Underapplied overhead....................		$ 150

   e. Total cost of each job.

	401	402	403
In-process costs from April			
Direct materials.................	$ 3,600		
Direct labor	1,700		
Applied overhead*	2,550		
Cost incurred in May			
Direct materials.................	3,550	$ 3,500	$1,400
Direct labor	5,100	6,000	800
Applied overhead*	7,650	9,000	1,200
Total costs	$24,150	$18,500	$3,400

   * Equals 150% of the direct labor cost.

   Total cost of the May 31 inventory of goods in process (Job 403) = $3,400

   Total cost of the May 31 inventory of finished goods (Job 402) = $18,500

   Total cost of goods sold during May (Job 401) = $24,150

2. Journal entries.

   a.

Raw Materials Inventory	16,000	
Accounts Payable		16,000
To record materials purchases.		
Factory Payroll..................................	15,400	
Cash.......................................		15,400
To record factory payroll.		
Factory Overhead	5,000	
Raw Materials Inventory		5,000
To record indirect materials.		
Factory Overhead	3,500	
Factory Payroll		3,500
To record indirect labor.		
Factory Overhead	9,500	
Cash.......................................		9,500
To record other factory overhead.		

b. Assignment of costs to Goods in Process Inventory.

Goods in Process Inventory (Job 401)	3,550	
Goods in Process Inventory (Job 402)	3,500	
Goods in Process Inventory (Job 403)	1,400	
Raw Materials Inventory		8,450
To assign direct materials to jobs.		
Goods in Process Inventory (Job 401)	5,100	
Goods in Process Inventory (Job 402)	6,000	
Goods in Process Inventory (Job 403)	800	
Factory Payroll		11,900
To assign direct labor to jobs.		
Goods in Process Inventory (Job 401)	7,650	
Goods in Process Inventory (Job 402)	9,000	
Goods in Process Inventory (Job 403)	1,200	
Factory Overhead		17,850
To apply overhead to jobs.		

c. Transfer of completed jobs to Finished Goods Inventory.

Finished Goods Inventory	42,650	
Goods in Process Inventory (Job 401)		24,150
Goods in Process Inventory (Job 402)		18,500
To record completion of jobs.		

d.

Cost of Goods Sold	24,150	
Finished Goods Inventory		24,150
To record sale of Job 401.		

e.

Cost of Goods Sold	150	
Factory Overhead		150
To assign underapplied overhead.		

3.

WALCZAK COMPANY
Manufacturing Statement
For Month Ended May 31

Direct materials.....................		$ 8,450
Direct labor		11,900
Factory overhead		
Indirect materials	$5,000	
Indirect labor	3,500	
Other factory overhead	9,500	18,000
Total production costs		38,350
Add goods in process, April 30.........		7,850
Total cost of goods in process		46,200
Less goods in process, May 31		3,400
Less underapplied overhead		150
Cost of goods manufactured		$42,650

Note how underapplied overhead is reported. Overapplied overhead is similarly reported, but is added.

Summary

C1 **Describe important features of job order production.** Certain companies called *job order manufacturers* produce custom-made products for customers. These customized products are produced in response to a customer's orders. A job order manufacturer produces products that usually are different and, typically, produced in low volumes. The production systems of job order companies are flexible and are not highly standardized.

C2 **Explain job cost sheets and how they are used in job order cost accounting.** In a job order cost accounting system, the costs of producing each job are accumulated on a separate job cost sheet. Costs of direct materials, direct labor, and overhead are accumulated separately on the job cost sheet and then added to determine the total cost of a job. Job cost sheets for jobs in process, finished jobs, and jobs sold make up subsidiary records controlled by general ledger accounts.

A1 **Apply job order costing in pricing services.** Job order costing can usefully be applied to a service setting. The resulting job cost estimate can then be used to help determine a price for services.

P1 **Describe and record the flow of materials costs in job order cost accounting.** Costs of materials flow from receiving reports to materials ledger cards and then to either job cost sheets or the Indirect Materials account in the factory overhead ledger.

P2 **Describe and record the flow of labor costs in job order cost accounting.** Costs of labor flow from clock cards to the Factory Payroll account and then to either job cost sheets or the Indirect Labor account in the factory overhead ledger.

P3 **Describe and record the flow of overhead costs in job order cost accounting.** Overhead costs are accumulated in the Factory Overhead account that controls the subsidiary factory overhead ledger. Then, using a predetermined overhead rate, overhead costs are charged to jobs.

P4 **Determine adjustments for overapplied and underapplied factory overhead.** At the end of each period, the Factory Overhead account usually has a residual debit (underapplied overhead) or credit (overapplied overhead) balance. If the balance is not material, it is transferred to Cost of Goods Sold, but if it is material, it is allocated to Goods in Process Inventory, Finished Goods Inventory, and Cost of Goods Sold.

Guidance Answers to Decision Maker and Decision Ethics

Management Consultant   Service companies (such as this consulting firm) do not recognize goods in process inventory or finished goods inventory—an important difference between service and manufacturing companies. For the two jobs that are 60% complete, you could recognize revenues and costs at 60% of the total expected amounts. This means you could recognize revenue of $7,200 (0.60 × $12,000) and costs of $6,000 (0.60 × $10,000), yielding net income of $1,200 from each job.

Web Consultant   The partner has a monetary incentive to *manage* the numbers and assign more costs to the two cost-plus engagements. This also would reduce costs on the fixed-price engagements. To act in such a manner is unethical. As a professional and an honest person, it is your responsibility to engage in ethical behavior. You must not comply with the partner's instructions. If the partner insists you act in an unethical manner, you should report the matter to a higher authority in the organization.

Entrepreneur   An inadequate cost system can distort product costs. You should review overhead costs in detail. Once you know the different cost elements in overhead, you can classify them into groups such as material related, labor related, or machine related. Other groups can also be formed (we discuss this in Chapter 22). Once you have classified overhead items into groups, you can better establish overhead allocation bases and use them to compute predetermined overhead rates. These multiple rates and bases can then be used to assign overhead costs to products. This will likely improve product pricing.

Sales Manager   The price based on AdWorld's normal pricing policy is $20,150 ($17,076 × 1.18), which is within the price range offered by competitors. One option is to apply normal pricing policy and quote a price of $20,150. On the other hand, assessing the competition, particularly in terms of their service quality and other benefits they might offer, would be useful. Although price is an input customers use to select suppliers, factors such as quality and timeliness (responsiveness) of suppliers are important. Accordingly, your price can reflect such factors.

Guidance Answers to Quick Checks

1. *b*

2. A job is a special order for a custom product. A job lot consists of a quantity of identical, special-order items.

3. *a*

4. Three costs normally accumulated on a job cost sheet are direct materials, direct labor, and factory overhead.

5. *c*

6. Four sources of factory overhead are materials requisitions, time tickets, vouchers, and adjusting entries.

7. Since a job order cost accounting system uses perpetual inventory records, overhead costs must be assigned to jobs before the end of a period. This requires the use of a predetermined overhead rate.

8. Debits are recorded when wages and salaries of factory employees are paid or accrued. Credits are recorded when direct labor costs are assigned to jobs and when indirect labor costs are transferred to the Factory Overhead account.

9. Overapplied or underapplied overhead usually exists at the end of a period because application of overhead is based on estimates

of overhead and another variable such as direct labor. Estimates rarely equal actual amounts incurred.

10. A debit balance reflects underapplied factory overhead.

Key Terms   mhhe.com/wildFINMAN4e

Clock card (p. 650)
Cost accounting system (p. 644)
Finished Goods Inventory (p. 647)
General accounting system (p. 644)
Goods in Process Inventory (p. 646)
Job (p. 644)

Job cost sheet (p. 646)
Job lot (p. 645)
Job order cost accounting system (p. 646)
Job order production (p. 644)
Materials ledger card (p. 648)

Materials requisition (p. 649)
Overapplied overhead (p. 655)
Predetermined overhead rate (p. 652)
Target cost (p. 645)
Time ticket (p. 650)
Underapplied overhead (p. 655)

Multiple Choice Quiz   Answers on p. 679   mhhe.com/wildFINMAN4e

Additional Quiz Questions are available at the book's Website.

1. A company's predetermined overhead allocation rate is 150% of its direct labor costs. How much overhead is applied to a job that requires total direct labor costs of $30,000?
   a. $15,000
   b. $30,000
   c. $45,000
   d. $60,000
   e. $75,000

2. A company's cost accounting system uses direct labor costs to apply overhead to goods in process and finished goods inventories. Its production costs for the period are: direct materials, $45,000; direct labor, $35,000; and overhead applied, $38,500. What is its predetermined overhead allocation rate?
   a. 10%
   b. 110%
   c. 86%
   d. 91%
   e. 117%

3. A company's ending inventory of finished goods has a total cost of $10,000 and consists of 500 units. If the overhead applied to these goods is $4,000, and the predetermined overhead rate is 80% of direct labor costs, how much direct materials cost was incurred in producing these 500 units?
   a. $10,000
   b. $ 6,000
   c. $ 4,000
   d. $ 5,000
   e. $ 1,000

4. A company's Goods in Process Inventory T-account follows.

Goods in Process Inventory			
Beginning balance	9,000		
Direct materials	94,200		
Direct labor	59,200	?	Finished goods
Overhead applied	31,600		
Ending balance	17,800		

The cost of units transferred to Finished Goods inventory is
   a. $193,000
   b. $211,800
   c. $185,000
   d. $144,600
   e. $176,200

5. At the end of its current year, a company learned that its overhead was underapplied by $1,500 and that this amount is not considered material. Based on this information, the company should
   a. Close the $1,500 to Finished Goods Inventory.
   b. Close the $1,500 to Cost of Goods Sold.
   c. Carry the $1,500 to the next period.
   d. Do nothing about the $1,500 because it is not material and it is likely that overhead will be overapplied by the same amount next year.
   e. Carry the $1,500 to the Income Statement as "Other Expense."

I Icon denotes assignments that involve decision making.

Discussion Questions

1. Why must a company estimate the amount of factory overhead assigned to individual jobs or job lots?

2. **I** The chapter used a percent of labor cost to assign factory overhead to jobs. Identify another factor (or base) a company might reasonably use to assign overhead costs.

3. 🏺 What information is recorded on a job cost sheet? How do management and employees use job cost sheets?

4. In a job order cost accounting system, what records serve as a subsidiary ledger for Goods in Process Inventory? For Finished Goods Inventory?

5. What journal entry is recorded when a materials manager receives a materials requisition and then issues materials (both direct and indirect) for use in the factory?

6. 🏺 How does the materials requisition help safeguard a company's assets?

7. **Palm** uses a "time ticket" for some employees. What is the difference between a clock card and a time ticket? **Palm**

8. What events cause debits to be recorded in the Factory Overhead account? What events cause credits to be recorded in the Factory Overhead account?

9. **Nokia** applies overhead to product costs. What account(s) is(are) used to eliminate overapplied **NOKIA**

or underapplied overhead from the Factory Overhead account, assuming the amount is not material?

10. 🏺 Assume that **Apple** produces a batch of 1,000 iPods. Does it account for this as 1,000 individual jobs or as a job lot? Explain (consider costs and benefits). **Apple**

11. Why must a company prepare a predetermined overhead rate when using job order cost accounting?

12. 🏺 How would a hospital apply job order costing? Explain.

13. 🏺 **Harley-Davidson** manufactures 30 custom-made, luxury-model motorcycles. Does it account for these motorcycles as 30 individual jobs or as a job lot? Explain. **Harley-Davidson**

14. Assume **Research In Motion** will install and service a server to link all of a customer's employees' smartphones to a centralized company server, for an upfront flat price. How can RIM use a job order costing system? **RIM**

🔴 connect

Determine which products are most likely to be manufactured as a job and which as a job lot.

1. A hand-crafted table.
2. A 90-foot motor yacht.
3. Wedding dresses for a chain of stores.
4. A custom-designed home.
5. Hats imprinted with company logo.
6. Little League trophies.

QUICK STUDY

QS 15-1
Jobs and job lots C1

List the three types of costs that are typically recorded on a job cost sheet. How can managers use job cost sheets?

QS 15-2
Job cost sheets C2

During the current month, a company that uses a job order cost accounting system purchases $70,000 in raw materials for cash. It then uses $22,000 of raw materials indirectly as factory supplies and uses $42,000 of raw materials as direct materials. Prepare entries to record these three transactions.

QS 15-3
Direct materials journal entries
P1

During the current month, a company that uses a job order cost accounting system incurred a monthly factory payroll of $120,000, paid in cash. Of this amount, $30,000 is classified as indirect labor and the remainder as direct. Prepare entries to record these transactions.

QS 15-4
Direct labor journal entries P2

A company incurred the following manufacturing costs this period: direct labor, $605,000; direct materials, $672,000; and factory overhead, $129,500. Compute its overhead cost as a percent of (1) direct labor and (2) direct materials. Express your answers as percents, rounded to one decimal place.

QS 15-5
Factory overhead rates P3

During the current month, a company that uses a job order cost accounting system incurred a monthly factory payroll of $120,000, paid in cash. Of this amount, $30,000 is classified as indirect labor and the remainder as direct for the production of Job 65A. Factory overhead is applied at 150% of direct labor. Prepare the entry to apply factory overhead to this job lot.

QS 15-6
Factory overhead journal entries
P3

A company allocates overhead at a rate of 140% of direct labor cost. Actual overhead cost for the current period is $745,000, and direct labor cost is $500,000. Prepare the entry to close over- or underapplied overhead to cost of goods sold.

QS 15-7
Entry for over- or underapplied overhead P4

A company's Factory Overhead T-account shows total debits of $325,000 and total credits of $331,000 at the end of a period. Prepare the journal entry to close the balance in the Factory Overhead account to Cost of Goods Sold.

QS 15-8
Entry for over- or underapplied overhead P4

QS 15-9
Pricing services   **A1**

An advertising agency is estimating costs for advertising a music festival. The job will require 50 direct labor hours at a cost of $60 per hour. Overhead costs are applied at a rate of $95 per direct labor hour. What is the total estimated cost for this job?

QS 15-10
Predetermined overhead rate

P3

At the beginning of a period a company predicts total direct materials costs of $175,000 and total overhead costs of $218,750. If the company uses direct materials costs as its activity base to allocate overhead, what is the predetermined overhead rate it should use during the period?

QS 15-11
Job cost sheets   **C2**

Road Warriors' job cost sheet for job A75 shows that the cost to add security features to a car was $13,500. The car was delivered to the customer, who paid $18,900 in cash for the added features. What journal entries should Road Warriors record for the completion and delivery of job A75?

QS 15-12
Job order production   **C1**

Refer to this chapter's Global View. **Porsche AG** is the manufacturer of the Porsche automobile line. Does Porsche produce in jobs or in job lots? Explain.

EXERCISES

Exercise 15-1
Job order production

C1

Match the terms below with their definitions.

1. Job
2. Job order production
3. Job lot
4. Cost accounting system
5. Target cost
6. General accounting system

    a. The expected selling price of a job minus its desired profit.
    b. Production activities for a customized product.
    c. A system that records manufacturing costs using a perpetual inventory system.
    d. Production of products in response to customer orders.
    e. Production of more than one unit of a custom product.
    f. A system that records manufacturing costs using a periodic inventory system.

Exercise 15-2
Documents in job order cost accounting

P1 P2 P3

The left column lists the titles of documents and accounts used in job order cost accounting. The right column presents short descriptions of the purposes of the documents. Match each document in the left column to its numbered description in the right column.

A. Factory Payroll account
B. Materials ledger card
C. Time ticket
D. Voucher
E. Materials requisition
F. Factory Overhead account
G. Clock card

    _____ **1.** Communicates the need for materials to complete a job.
    _____ **2.** Shows only total time an employee works each day.
    _____ **3.** Shows amount approved for payment of an overhead or other cost.
    _____ **4.** Shows amount of time an employee works on a job.
    _____ **5.** Temporarily accumulates the cost of incurred overhead until the cost is assigned to specific jobs.
    _____ **6.** Temporarily accumulates incurred labor costs until they are assigned to specific jobs or to overhead.
    _____ **7.** Perpetual inventory record of raw materials received, used, and available for use.

Exercise 15-3
Job cost computation

C2

The following information is from the materials requisitions and time tickets for Job 9-1005 completed by Wright Boats. The requisitions are identified by code numbers starting with the letter Q and the time tickets start with W. At the start of the year, management estimated that overhead cost would equal 140% of direct labor cost for each job. Determine the total cost on the job cost sheet for Job 9-1005.

Date	Document	Amount
7/1/2011	Q-4698	$1,350
7/1/2011	W-3393	700
7/5/2011	Q-4725	1,100
7/5/2011	W-3479	550
7/10/2011	W-3559	400

As of the end of June, the job cost sheets at Racing Wheels, Inc., show the following total costs accumulated on three custom jobs.

Exercise 15-4
Analysis of cost flows
C2 P1 P2 P3

	Job 102	Job 103	Job 104
Direct materials.........	$30,000	$66,000	$54,000
Direct labor	16,000	28,400	42,000
Overhead..............	8,000	14,200	21,000

Job 102 was started in production in May and the following costs were assigned to it in May: direct materials, $12,000; direct labor, $3,600; and overhead, $1,800. Jobs 103 and 104 are started in June. Overhead cost is applied with a predetermined rate based on direct labor cost. Jobs 102 and 103 are finished in June, and Job 104 is expected to be finished in July. No raw materials are used indirectly in June. Using this information, answer the following questions. (Assume this company's predetermined overhead rate did not change across these months).

1. What is the cost of the raw materials requisitioned in June for each of the three jobs?
2. How much direct labor cost is incurred during June for each of the three jobs?
3. What predetermined overhead rate is used during June?
4. How much total cost is transferred to finished goods during June?

Check   (4) $162,600

In December 2010, Kent Computer's management establishes the year 2011 predetermined overhead rate based on direct labor cost. The information used in setting this rate includes estimates that the company will incur $756,000 of overhead costs and $540,000 of direct labor cost in year 2011. During March 2011, Kent began and completed Job No. 13-56.

1. What is the predetermined overhead rate for year 2011?
2. Use the information on the following job cost sheet to determine the total cost of the job.

Exercise 15-5
Overhead rate; costs assigned to jobs
P3

Check   (2) $23,280

JOB COST SHEET

| **Customer's Name** | Keiser Co. | | | **Job No.** | 13-56 | |

Job Description   5 color monitors—21 inch

	Direct Materials			**Direct Labor**		**Overhead Costs Applied**	
Date	**Requisition No.**	**Amount**		**Time-Ticket No.**	**Amount**	**Rate**	**Amount**
Mar. 8	4-129	$5,000		T-306	$ 640		
Mar. 11	4-142	7,050		T-432	1,280		
Mar. 18	4-167	3,550		T-456	1,280		
Totals							

Lopez Company uses a job order cost accounting system that charges overhead to jobs on the basis of direct material cost. At year-end, the Goods in Process Inventory account shows the following.

Exercise 15-6
Analysis of costs assigned to goods in process
P3

Accounting System

File Edit Maintain Tasks Analysis Options Reports Window Help

Goods in Process Inventory   Acct. No. 121

Date	Explanation	Debit	Credit	Balance
2011				
Dec. 31	Direct materials cost	1,500,000		1,500,000
31	Direct labor cost	240,000		1,740,000
31	Overhead costs	450,000		2,190,000
31	To finished goods		2,100,000	90,000

Sales Purchases General Ledger Payroll Inventory Company Analysis

1. Determine the overhead rate used (based on direct material cost).
2. Only one job remained in the goods in process inventory at December 31, 2011. Its direct materials cost is $30,000. How much direct labor cost and overhead cost are assigned to it?

Check   (2) Direct labor cost, $51,000

Exercise 15-7
Cost flows in a job order cost system

P1 P2 P3 P4

The following information is available for Lock-Down Company, which produces special-order security products and uses a job order cost accounting system.

	April 30	May 31
Inventories		
Raw materials	$40,000	$ 50,000
Goods in process	9,600	19,500
Finished goods	60,000	33,200
Activities and information for May		
Raw materials purchases (paid with cash)		189,000
Factory payroll (paid with cash)		400,000
Factory overhead		
Indirect materials..		12,000
Indirect labor		75,000
Other overhead costs.....................................		100,500
Sales (received in cash)		1,200,000
Predetermined overhead rate based on direct labor cost		65%

Compute the following amounts for the month of May.

1. Cost of direct materials used.   **4.** Cost of goods sold.*

2. Cost of direct labor used.   **5.** Gross profit.

Check (3) $693,350

3. Cost of goods manufactured.   **6.** Overapplied or underapplied overhead.

*Do not consider any underapplied or overapplied overhead.

Exercise 15-8
Journal entries for materials

P1

Use information in Exercise 15-7 to prepare journal entries for the following events for the month of May.

1. Raw materials purchases for cash.

2. Direct materials usage.

3. Indirect materials usage.

Exercise 15-9
Journal entries for labor

P2

Use information in Exercise 15-7 to prepare journal entries for the following events for the month of May.

1. Factory payroll costs in cash.

2. Direct labor usage.

3. Indirect labor usage.

Exercise 15-10
Journal entries for overhead

P3

Use information in Exercise 15-7 to prepare journal entries for the following events for the month of May.

1. Factory overhead excluding indirect materials and indirect labor (record credit to Other Accounts).

2. Application of overhead to goods in process.

Exercise 15-11
Adjusting factory overhead   P4

Refer to information in Exercise 15-7. Prepare the journal entry to allocate (close) overapplied or underapplied overhead to Cost of Goods Sold.

Exercise 15-12
Adjusting factory overhead

P4

Record the journal entry to close over- or underapplied factory overhead to Cost of Goods Sold for each of the independent cases below.

	JK Concert Promotions	EL Home Builders
Actual indirect materials costs	$12,000	$ 6,500
Actual indirect labor costs	56,000	46,500
Other overhead costs	17,000	49,000
Overhead applied	96,200	106,800

In December 2010, Ultravision established its predetermined overhead rate for movies produced during year 2011 by using the following cost predictions: overhead costs, $1,800,000, and direct labor costs, $450,000. At year end 2011, the company's records show that actual overhead costs for the year are $1,770,000. Actual direct labor cost had been assigned to jobs as follows.

Exercise 15-13
Factory overhead computed, applied, and adjusted

P3 P4

Movies completed and released	$400,000
Movies still in production	45,000
Total actual direct labor cost	$445,000

1. Determine the predetermined overhead rate for year 2011.
2. Set up a T-account for overhead and enter the overhead costs incurred and the amounts applied to movies during the year using the predetermined overhead rate.
3. Determine whether overhead is overapplied or underapplied (and the amount) during the year.
4. Prepare the adjusting entry to allocate any over- or underapplied overhead to Cost of Goods Sold.

Check   (3) $10,000 overapplied

In December 2010, Perez Company established its predetermined overhead rate for jobs produced during year 2011 by using the following cost predictions: overhead costs, $600,000, and direct labor costs, $500,000. At year end 2011, the company's records show that actual overhead costs for the year are $680,000. Actual direct labor cost had been assigned to jobs as follows.

Exercise 15-14
Factory overhead computed, applied, and adjusted

P3 P4

Jobs completed and sold	$420,000
Jobs in finished goods inventory	84,000
Jobs in goods in process inventory	56,000
Total actual direct labor cost	$560,000

1. Determine the predetermined overhead rate for year 2011.
2. Set up a T-account for Factory Overhead and enter the overhead costs incurred and the amounts applied to jobs during the year using the predetermined overhead rate.
3. Determine whether overhead is overapplied or underapplied (and the amount) during the year.
4. Prepare the adjusting entry to allocate any over- or underapplied overhead to Cost of Goods Sold.

Check   (3) $8,000 underapplied

Red Wing Company applies factory overhead based on direct labor costs. The company incurred the following costs during 2011: direct materials costs, $637,500; direct labor costs, $2,500,000; and factory overhead costs applied, $1,000,000.

Exercise 15-15
Overhead rate calculation, allocation, and analysis

P3

1. Determine the company's predetermined overhead rate for year 2011.
2. Assuming that the company's $57,000 ending Goods in Process Inventory account for year 2011 had $18,000 of direct labor costs, determine the inventory's direct materials costs.
3. Assuming that the company's $337,485 ending Finished Goods Inventory account for year 2011 had $137,485 of direct materials costs, determine the inventory's direct labor costs and its overhead costs.

Check   (3) $57,143 overhead costs

Vegas Company's ending Goods in Process Inventory account consists of 4,500 units of partially completed product, and its Finished Goods Inventory account consists of 11,700 units of product. The factory manager determines that Goods in Process Inventory includes direct materials cost of $10 per unit and direct labor cost of $7 per unit. Finished goods are estimated to have $12 of direct materials cost per unit and $9 of direct labor cost per unit. The company established the predetermined overhead rate using the following predictions: estimated direct labor cost, $300,000, and estimated factory overhead, $360,000. The company allocates factory overhead to its goods in process and finished goods inventories based on direct labor cost. During the period, the company incurred these costs: direct materials, $460,000; direct labor, $277,000; and factory overhead applied, $332,400.

Exercise 15-16
Costs allocated to ending inventories

P1 P2 P3

1. Determine the predetermined overhead rate.
2. Compute the total cost of the two ending inventories.
3. Compute cost of goods sold for the year (assume no beginning inventories and no underapplied or overapplied overhead).

Check   (3) Cost of goods sold, $583,040

Exercise 15-17
Cost-based pricing

A1

Multiplex Corporation has requested bids from several architects to design its new corporate headquarters. Friesen Architects is one of the firms bidding on the job. Friesen estimates that the job will require the following direct labor.

	Labor	Estimated Hours	Hourly Rate
1			
2	Architects	200	$300
3	Staff	400	75
4	Clerical	700	20

Friesen applies overhead to jobs at 160% of direct labor cost. Friesen would like to earn at least $80,000 profit on the architectural job. Based on past experience and market research, it estimates that the competition will bid between $325,000 and $400,000 for the job.

Check (1) $270,400

1. What is Friesen's estimated cost of the architectural job?
2. What bid would you suggest that Friesen submit?

Exercise 15-18
Direct materials journal entries

P1

A recent balance sheet for **Porsche AG** shows beginning raw materials inventory of €83 million and ending raw materials inventory of €85 million. Assume the company purchased raw materials (on account) for €3,108 million during the year. (1) Prepare journal entries to record (a) the purchase of raw materials and (b) the use of raw materials in production. (2) What do you notice about the € amounts in your journal entries?

PROBLEM SET A

Problem 15-1A
Production costs computed and recorded; reports prepared

C2 P1 P2 P3 P4

Winfrey Co.'s March 31 inventory of raw materials is $150,000. Raw materials purchases in April are $400,000, and factory payroll cost in April is $220,000. Overhead costs incurred in April are: indirect materials, $30,000; indirect labor, $14,000; factory rent, $20,000; factory utilities, $12,000; and factory equipment depreciation, $30,000. The predetermined overhead rate is 50% of direct labor cost. Job 306 is sold for $380,000 cash in April. Costs of the three jobs worked on in April follow.

	Job 306	Job 307	Job 308
Balances on March 31			
Direct materials.............	$ 14,000	$ 18,000	
Direct labor...............	18,000	16,000	
Applied overhead...........	9,000	8,000	
Costs during April			
Direct materials.............	100,000	170,000	$ 80,000
Direct labor...............	30,000	56,000	120,000
Applied overhead...........	?	?	?
Status on April 30.............	Finished (sold)	Finished (unsold)	In process

Required

1. Determine the total of each production cost incurred for April (direct labor, direct materials, and applied overhead), and the total cost assigned to each job (including the balances from March 31).
2. Prepare journal entries for the month of April to record the following.
   a. Materials purchases (on credit), factory payroll (paid in cash), and actual overhead costs including indirect materials and indirect labor. (Factory rent and utilities are paid in cash.)
   b. Assignment of direct materials, direct labor, and applied overhead costs to the Goods in Process Inventory.
   c. Transfer of Jobs 306 and 307 to the Finished Goods Inventory.
   d. Cost of goods sold for Job 306.
   e. Revenue from the sale of Job 306.
   f. Assignment of any underapplied or overapplied overhead to the Cost of Goods Sold account. (The amount is not material.)

Check (2f) $3,000 underapplied

(3) Cost of goods manufactured, $482,000

3. Prepare a manufacturing statement for April (use a single line presentation for direct materials and show the details of overhead cost).
4. Compute gross profit for April. Show how to present the inventories on the April 30 balance sheet.

Analysis Component

5. The over- or underapplied overhead is closed to Cost of Goods Sold. Discuss how this adjustment impacts business decision making regarding individual jobs or batches of jobs.

Thai Bay's computer system generated the following trial balance on December 31, 2011. The company's manager knows something is wrong with the trial balance because it does not show any balance for Goods in Process Inventory but does show balances for the Factory Payroll and Factory Overhead accounts.

Problem 15-2A
Source documents, journal entries, overhead, and financial reports

P1 P2 P3 P4

	Debit	Credit
Cash	$ 48,000	
Accounts receivable	42,000	
Raw materials inventory	26,000	
Goods in process inventory	0	
Finished goods inventory	9,000	
Prepaid rent	3,000	
Accounts payable		$ 10,500
Notes payable		13,500
Common stock		30,000
Retained earnings		87,000
Sales		180,000
Cost of goods sold	105,000	
Factory payroll	16,000	
Factory overhead	27,000	
Operating expenses	45,000	
Totals	$321,000	$321,000

After examining various files, the manager identifies the following six source documents that need to be processed to bring the accounting records up to date.

Materials requisition 21-3010:	$4,600 direct materials to Job 402
Materials requisition 21-3011:	$7,600 direct materials to Job 404
Materials requisition 21-3012:	$2,100 indirect materials
Labor time ticket 6052:	$5,000 direct labor to Job 402
Labor time ticket 6053:	$8,000 direct labor to Job 404
Labor time ticket 6054:	$3,000 indirect labor

Jobs 402 and 404 are the only units in process at year-end. The predetermined overhead rate is 200% of direct labor cost.

Required

1. Use information on the six source documents to prepare journal entries to assign the following costs.
   a. Direct materials costs to Goods in Process Inventory.
   b. Direct labor costs to Goods in Process Inventory.
   c. Overhead costs to Goods in Process Inventory.
   d. Indirect materials costs to the Factory Overhead account.
   e. Indirect labor costs to the Factory Overhead account.
2. Determine the revised balance of the Factory Overhead account after making the entries in part 1. Determine whether there is any under- or overapplied overhead for the year. Prepare the adjusting entry to allocate any over- or underapplied overhead to Cost of Goods Sold, assuming the amount is not material.
3. Prepare a revised trial balance.
4. Prepare an income statement for year 2011 and a balance sheet as of December 31, 2011.

Check (2) $6,100 underapplied overhead

(3) T. B. totals, $321,000
(4) Net income, $23,900

Analysis Component

5. Assume that the $2,100 on materials requisition 21-3012 should have been direct materials charged to Job 404. Without providing specific calculations, describe the impact of this error on the income statement for 2011 and the balance sheet at December 31, 2011.

Problem 15-3A
Source documents, journal
entries, and accounts in job
order cost accounting

P1 P2 P3

Westin Watercraft's predetermined overhead rate for year 2011 is 200% of direct labor. Information on the company's production activities during May 2011 follows.

a. Purchased raw materials on credit, $125,000.

b. Paid $84,000 cash for factory wages.

c. Paid $11,000 cash to a computer consultant to reprogram factory equipment.

d. Materials requisitions record use of the following materials for the month.

Job 136....................	$30,000
Job 137....................	20,000
Job 138....................	12,000
Job 139....................	14,000
Job 140....................	4,000
Total direct materials.........	80,000
Indirect materials............	12,000
Total materials used..........	$92,000

e. Time tickets record use of the following labor for the month.

Job 136	$ 8,000
Job 137	7,000
Job 138	25,000
Job 139	26,000
Job 140	2,000
Total direct labor	68,000
Indirect labor	16,000
Total	$84,000

f. Applied overhead to Jobs 136, 138, and 139.

g. Transferred Jobs 136, 138, and 139 to Finished Goods.

h. Sold Jobs 136 and 138 on credit at a total price of $340,000.

i. The company incurred the following overhead costs during the month (credit Prepaid Insurance for expired factory insurance).

Depreciation of factory building	$37,000
Depreciation of factory equipment	21,000
Expired factory insurance	7,000
Accrued property taxes payable	31,000

j. Applied overhead at month-end to the Goods in Process (Jobs 137 and 140) using the predetermined overhead rate of 200% of direct labor cost.

Required

1. Prepare a job cost sheet for each job worked on during the month. Use the following simplified form.

Job No. _____	
Materials	$ _____
Labor............	_____
Overhead	_____
Total cost	$ _____

Check (2f) Cr. Factory Overhead,
$118,000

2. Prepare journal entries to record the events and transactions *a* through *j*.

3. Set up T-accounts for each of the following general ledger accounts, each of which started the month with a zero balance: Raw Materials Inventory; Goods in Process Inventory; Finished Goods Inventory;

Factory Payroll; Factory Overhead; Cost of Goods Sold. Then post the journal entries to these T-accounts and determine the balance of each account.

4. Prepare a report showing the total cost of each job in process and prove that the sum of their costs equals the Goods in Process Inventory account balance. Prepare similar reports for Finished Goods Inventory and Cost of Goods Sold.

Check (4) Finished Goods Inventory, $92,000

In December 2010, Gomez Company's manager estimated next year's total direct labor cost assuming 50 persons working an average of 2,000 hours each at an average wage rate of $15 per hour. The manager also estimated the following manufacturing overhead costs for year 2011.

Problem 15-4A

Overhead allocation and adjustment using a predetermined overhead rate

P3 P4

mhhe.com/wildFINMAN4e

Indirect labor	$159,600
Factory supervision	120,000
Rent on factory building	70,000
Factory utilities	44,000
Factory insurance expired	34,000
Depreciation—Factory equipment	240,000
Repairs expense—Factory equipment	30,000
Factory supplies used	34,400
Miscellaneous production costs	18,000
Total estimated overhead costs	$750,000

At the end of 2011, records show the company incurred $725,000 of actual overhead costs. It completed and sold five jobs with the following direct labor costs: Job 201, $354,000; Job 202, $330,000; Job 203, $175,000; Job 204, $420,000; and Job 205, $184,000. In addition, Job 206 is in process at the end of 2011 and had been charged $10,000 for direct labor. No jobs were in process at the end of 2010. The company's predetermined overhead rate is based on direct labor cost.

Required

1. Determine the following.

 a. Predetermined overhead rate for year 2011.

 b. Total overhead cost applied to each of the six jobs during year 2011.

 c. Over- or underapplied overhead at year-end 2011.

2. Assuming that any over- or underapplied overhead is not material, prepare the adjusting entry to allocate any over- or underapplied overhead to Cost of Goods Sold at the end of year 2011.

Check (1c) $11,500 overapplied

(2) Dr. Factory Overhead $11,500

If the working papers that accompany this book are unavailable, do not attempt to solve this problem.
Sagrillo Company manufactures variations of its product, a technopress, in response to custom orders from its customers. On May 1, the company had no inventories of goods in process or finished goods but held the following raw materials.

Problem 15-5A

Production transactions, subsidiary records, and source documents

P1 P2 P3 P4

Material M	120 units @ $200 =	$24,000
Material R	80 units @ 160 =	12,800
Paint	44 units @ 72 =	3,168
Total cost		$39,968

On May 4, the company began working on two technopresses: Job 102 for Global Company and Job 103 for Rolf Company.

Required

Follow the instructions in this list of activities and complete the sheets provided in the working papers.

a. Purchased raw materials on credit and recorded the following information from receiving reports and invoices.

Receiving Report No. 426, Material M, 150 units at $200 each.
Receiving Report No. 427, Material R, 70 units at $160 each.

Instructions: Record these purchases with a single journal entry and post it to general ledger T-accounts, using the transaction letter *a* to identify the entry. Enter the receiving report information on the materials ledger cards.

b. Requisitioned the following raw materials for production.

> Requisition No. 35, for Job 102, 80 units of Material M.
> Requisition No. 36, for Job 102, 60 units of Material R.
> Requisition No. 37, for Job 103, 40 units of Material M.
> Requisition No. 38, for Job 103, 30 units of Material R.
> Requisition No. 39, for 12 units of paint.

Instructions: Enter amounts for direct materials requisitions on the materials ledger cards and the job cost sheets. Enter the indirect material amount on the materials ledger card and record a debit to the Indirect Materials account in the subsidiary factory overhead ledger. Do not record a journal entry at this time.

c. Received the following employee time tickets for work in May.

> Time tickets Nos. 1 to 10 for direct labor on Job 102, $40,000.
> Time tickets Nos. 11 to 30 for direct labor on Job 103, $32,000.
> Time tickets Nos. 31 to 36 for equipment repairs, $12,000.

Instructions: Record direct labor from the time tickets on the job cost sheets and then debit indirect labor to the Indirect Labor account in the subsidiary factory overhead ledger. Do not record a journal entry at this time.

d. Paid cash for the following items during the month: factory payroll, $84,000, and miscellaneous overhead items, $36,000.

Instructions: Record these payments with journal entries and then post them to the general ledger accounts. Also record a debit in the Miscellaneous Overhead account in the subsidiary factory overhead ledger.

e. Finished Job 102 and transferred it to the warehouse. The company assigns overhead to each job with a predetermined overhead rate equal to 70% of direct labor cost.

Instructions: Enter the allocated overhead on the cost sheet for Job 102, fill in the cost summary section of the cost sheet, and then mark the cost sheet "Finished." Prepare a journal entry to record the job's completion and its transfer to Finished Goods and then post it to the general ledger accounts.

f. Delivered Job 102 and accepted the customer's promise to pay $290,000 within 30 days.

Instructions: Prepare journal entries to record the sale of Job 102 and the cost of goods sold. Post them to the general ledger accounts.

g. Applied overhead to Job 103 based on the job's direct labor to date.

Instructions: Enter overhead on the job cost sheet but do not make a journal entry at this time.

h. Recorded the total direct and indirect materials costs as reported on all the requisitions for the month.

Instructions: Prepare a journal entry to record these costs and post it to general ledger accounts.

i. Recorded the total direct and indirect labor costs as reported on all time tickets for the month.

Instructions: Prepare a journal entry to record these costs and post it to general ledger accounts.

j. Recorded the total overhead costs applied to jobs.

Instructions: Prepare a journal entry to record the allocation of these overhead costs and post it to general ledger accounts.

PROBLEM SET B

Problem 15-1B
Production costs computed and recorded; reports prepared

C2 P1 P2 P3 P4

Pak Co.'s August 31 inventory of raw materials is $16,000. Raw materials purchases in September are $60,000, and factory payroll cost in September is $68,000. Overhead costs incurred in September are: indirect materials, $6,000; indirect labor, $4,000; factory rent, $24,000; factory utilities, $22,000; and factory equipment depreciation, $25,000. The predetermined overhead rate is 130% of direct labor cost. Job 114 is sold for $100,000 cash in September. Costs for the three jobs worked on in September follow.

	Job 114	Job 115	Job 116
Balances on August 31			
Direct materials..............	$ 4,000	$ 6,000	
Direct labor	2,000	2,200	
Applied overhead	2,600	2,860	
Costs during September			
Direct materials..............	10,000	30,000	$16,000
Direct labor	16,000	28,000	20,000
Applied overhead	?	?	?
Status on September 30	Finished (sold)	Finished (unsold)	In process

Required

1. Determine the total of each production cost incurred for September (direct labor, direct materials, and applied overhead), and the total cost assigned to each job (including the balances from August 31).

2. Prepare journal entries for the month of September to record the following.

   a. Materials purchases (on credit), factory payroll (paid in cash), and actual overhead costs including indirect materials and indirect labor. (Factory rent and utilities are paid in cash.)

   b. Assignment of direct materials, direct labor, and applied overhead costs to Goods in Process Inventory.

   c. Transfer of Jobs 114 and 115 to the Finished Goods Inventory.

   d. Cost of Job 114 in the Cost of Goods Sold account.

   e. Revenue from the sale of Job 114.

   f. Assignment of any underapplied or overapplied overhead to the Cost of Goods Sold account. (The amount is not material.)

3. Prepare a manufacturing statement for September (use a single line presentation for direct materials and show the details of overhead cost).

4. Compute gross profit for September. Show how to present the inventories on the September 30 balance sheet.

Check (2f) $2,200 overapplied

(3) Cost of goods manufactured, $160,860

Analysis Component

5. The over- or underapplied overhead adjustment is closed to Cost of Goods Sold. Discuss how this adjustment impacts business decision making regarding individual jobs or batches of jobs.

Metro's computer system generated the following trial balance on December 31, 2011. The company's manager knows that the trial balance is wrong because it does not show any balance for Goods in Process Inventory but does show balances for the Factory Payroll and Factory Overhead accounts.

Problem 15-2B
Source documents, journal entries, overhead, and financial reports
P1 P2 P3 P4

	Debit	Credit
Cash	$ 40,000	
Accounts receivable	80,000	
Raw materials inventory	24,000	
Goods in process inventory	0	
Finished goods inventory	50,000	
Prepaid rent	4,000	
Accounts payable		$ 16,000
Notes payable		30,000
Common stock		60,000
Retained earnings		33,800
Sales		250,000
Cost of goods sold	140,000	
Factory payroll	20,000	
Factory overhead	9,800	
Operating expenses	22,000	
Totals	$389,800	$389,800

After examining various files, the manager identifies the following six source documents that need to be processed to bring the accounting records up to date.

Materials requisition 94-231:	$ 5,000 direct materials to Job 603
Materials requisition 94-232:	$ 8,000 direct materials to Job 604
Materials requisition 94-233:	$ 1,500 indirect materials
Labor time ticket 765:	$ 6,000 direct labor to Job 603
Labor time ticket 766:	$12,000 direct labor to Job 604
Labor time ticket 777:	$ 2,000 indirect labor

Jobs 603 and 604 are the only units in process at year-end. The predetermined overhead rate is 80% of direct labor cost.

Required

1. Use information on the six source documents to prepare journal entries to assign the following costs.
   a. Direct materials costs to Goods in Process Inventory.
   b. Direct labor costs to Goods in Process Inventory.
   c. Overhead costs to Goods in Process Inventory.
   d. Indirect materials costs to the Factory Overhead account.
   e. Indirect labor costs to the Factory Overhead account.

Check   (2) $1,100 overapplied
          overhead

2. Determine the revised balance of the Factory Overhead account after making the entries in part 1. Determine whether there is under- or overapplied overhead for the year. Prepare the adjusting entry to allocate any over- or underapplied overhead to Cost of Goods Sold, assuming the amount is not material.

(3) T. B. totals, $389,800

3. Prepare a revised trial balance.

(4) Net income, $89,100

4. Prepare an income statement for year 2011 and a balance sheet as of December 31, 2011.

Analysis Component

5. Assume that the $1,500 indirect materials on materials requisition 94-233 should have been direct materials charged to Job 604. Without providing specific calculations, describe the impact of this error on the income statement for 2011 and the balance sheet at December 31, 2011.

Problem 15-3B
Source documents, journal entries, and accounts in job order cost accounting
P1 P2 P3

Troupe Company's predetermined overhead rate is 90% of direct labor. Information on the company's production activities during September 2011 follows.
a. Purchased raw materials on credit, $57,000.
b. Paid $99,750 cash for factory wages.
c. Paid $11,250 cash for miscellaneous factory overhead costs.
d. Materials requisitions record use of the following materials for the month.

Job 487	$13,500
Job 488	9,000
Job 489	12,000
Job 490	10,500
Job 491	1,500
Total direct materials	46,500
Indirect materials	3,750
Total materials used	$50,250

e. Time tickets record use of the following labor for the month.

Job 487	$16,500
Job 488	19,500
Job 489	25,500
Job 490	18,000
Job 491	7,500
Total direct labor	87,000
Indirect labor	12,750
Total	$99,750

f. Allocated overhead to Jobs 487, 489, and 490.

g. Transferred Jobs 487, 489, and 490 to Finished Goods.

h. Sold Jobs 487 and 489 on credit for a total price of $225,000.

i. The company incurred the following overhead costs during the month (credit Prepaid Insurance for expired factory insurance).

Depreciation of factory building	$24,750
Depreciation of factory equipment	18,750
Expired factory insurance	2,250
Accrued property taxes payable	5,250

j. Applied overhead at month-end to the Goods in Process (Jobs 488 and 491) using the predetermined overhead rate of 90% of direct labor cost.

Required

1. Prepare a job cost sheet for each job worked on in the month. Use the following simplified form.

Job No. _____	
Materials	$ _____
Labor	_____
Overhead	_____
Total cost	$ _____

2. Prepare journal entries to record the events and transactions *a* through *j*.

3. Set up T-accounts for each of the following general ledger accounts, each of which started the month with a zero balance: Raw Materials Inventory, Goods in Process Inventory, Finished Goods Inventory, Factory Payroll, Factory Overhead, Cost of Goods Sold. Then post the journal entries to these T-accounts and determine the balance of each account.

4. Prepare a report showing the total cost of each job in process and prove that the sum of their costs equals the Goods in Process Inventory account balance. Prepare similar reports for Finished Goods Inventory and Cost of Goods Sold.

Check (2f) Cr. Factory Overhead, $54,000

(3) Finished goods inventory, $44,700

In December 2010, Monk Company's manager estimated next year's total direct labor cost assuming 40 persons working an average of 1,500 hours each at an average wage rate of $50 per hour. The manager also estimated the following manufacturing overhead costs for year 2011.

Problem 15-4B
Overhead allocation and adjustment using a predetermined overhead rate

P3 P4

Indirect labor	$ 540,000
Factory supervision	450,000
Rent on factory building	360,000
Factory utilities	200,000
Factory insurance expired	60,000
Depreciation—Factory equipment	300,000
Repairs expense—Factory equipment	180,000
Factory supplies used	110,000
Miscellaneous production costs	200,000
Total estimated overhead costs	$2,400,000

At the end of 2011, records show the company incurred $2,200,000 of actual overhead costs. It completed and sold five jobs with the following direct labor costs: Job 625, $300,000; Job 626, $225,000; Job 627, $975,000; Job 628, $240,000; and Job 629, $375,000. In addition, Job 630 is in process at the end of 2011 and had been charged $75,000 for direct labor. No jobs were in process at the end of 2010. The company's predetermined overhead rate is based on direct labor cost.

Required

1. Determine the following.
   a. Predetermined overhead rate for year 2011.
   b. Total overhead cost applied to each of the six jobs during year 2011.
   c. Over- or underapplied overhead at year-end 2011.

2. Assuming that any over- or underapplied overhead is not material, prepare the adjusting entry to allocate any over- or underapplied overhead to Cost of Goods Sold at the end of year 2011.

Check   (1c) $448,000 underapplied

(2) Cr. Factory Overhead, $448,000

Problem 15-5B
Production transactions, subsidiary records, and source documents

P1 P2 P3 P4

If the working papers that accompany this book are unavailable, do not attempt to solve this problem.
Sim Company produces variations of its product, a megatron, in response to custom orders from its customers. On June 1, the company had no inventories of goods in process or finished goods but held the following raw materials.

Material M	150 units @ $ 40 =	$ 6,000
Material R	50 units @ 160 =	8,000
Paint	20 units @ 20 =	400
Total cost		$14,400

On June 3, the company began working on two megatrons: Job 450 for Olivas Company and Job 451 for Ireland, Inc.

Required

Follow instructions in this list of activities and complete the sheets provided in the working papers.

a. Purchased raw materials on credit and recorded the following information from receiving reports and invoices.

> Receiving Report No. 20, Material M, 150 units at $40 each.
> Receiving Report No. 21, Material R, 200 units at $160 each.

Instructions: Record these purchases with a single journal entry and post it to general ledger T-accounts, using the transaction letter *a* to identify the entry. Enter the receiving report information on the materials ledger cards.

b. Requisitioned the following raw materials for production.

> Requisition No. 223, for Job 450, 60 units of Material M.
> Requisition No. 224, for Job 450, 100 units of Material R.
> Requisition No. 225, for Job 451, 30 units of Material M.
> Requisition No. 226, for Job 451, 75 units of Material R.
> Requisition No. 227, for 10 units of paint.

Instructions: Enter amounts for direct materials requisitions on the materials ledger cards and the job cost sheets. Enter the indirect material amount on the materials ledger card and record a debit to the Indirect Materials account in the subsidiary factory overhead ledger. Do not record a journal entry at this time.

c. Received the following employee time tickets for work in June.

> Time tickets Nos. 1 to 10 for direct labor on Job 450, $24,000.
> Time tickets Nos. 11 to 20 for direct labor on Job 451, $20,000.
> Time tickets Nos. 21 to 24 for equipment repairs, $4,000.

Instructions: Record direct labor from the time tickets on the job cost sheets and then debit indirect labor to the Indirect Labor account in the subsidiary factory overhead ledger. Do not record a journal entry at this time.

d. Paid cash for the following items during the month: factory payroll, $48,000, and miscellaneous overhead items, $47,000.

Instructions: Record these payments with journal entries and post them to the general ledger accounts. Also record a debit in the Miscellaneous Overhead account in the subsidiary factory overhead ledger.

e. Finished Job 450 and transferred it to the warehouse. The company assigns overhead to each job with a predetermined overhead rate equal to 120% of direct labor cost.

Instructions: Enter the allocated overhead on the cost sheet for Job 450, fill in the cost summary section of the cost sheet, and then mark the cost sheet "Finished." Prepare a journal entry to record the job's completion and its transfer to Finished Goods and then post it to the general ledger accounts.

f. Delivered Job 450 and accepted the customer's promise to pay $130,000 within 30 days.

Instructions: Prepare journal entries to record the sale of Job 450 and the cost of goods sold. Post them to the general ledger accounts.

g. Applied overhead cost to Job 451 based on the job's direct labor used to date.

Instructions: Enter overhead on the job cost sheet but do not make a journal entry at this time.

h. Recorded the total direct and indirect materials costs as reported on all the requisitions for the month.

Instructions: Prepare a journal entry to record these costs and post it to general ledger accounts.

> **Check** (h) Dr. Goods in Process Inventory, $31,600

i. Recorded the total direct and indirect labor costs as reported on all time tickets for the month.

Instructions: Prepare a journal entry to record these costs and post it to general ledger accounts.

j. Recorded the total overhead costs applied to jobs.

Instructions: Prepare a journal entry to record the allocation of these overhead costs and post it to general ledger accounts.

> **Check** Balance in Factory Overhead, $1,600 Cr., overapplied

---

(This serial problem began in Chapter 1 and continues through most of the book. If previous chapter segments were not completed, the serial problem can begin at this point. It is helpful, but not necessary, to use the Working Papers that accompany the book.)

SERIAL PROBLEM
Business Solutions
P1 P2 P3

SP 15 The computer workstation furniture manufacturing that Santana Rey started in January is progressing well. As of the end of June, Business Solutions' job cost sheets show the following total costs accumulated on three furniture jobs.

	Job 6.02	Job 6.03	Job 6.04
Direct materials	$1,500	$3,300	$2,700
Direct labor	800	1,420	2,100
Overhead	400	710	1,050

Job 6.02 was started in production in May, and these costs were assigned to it in May: direct materials, $600; direct labor, $180; and overhead, $90. Jobs 6.03 and 6.04 were started in June. Overhead cost is applied with a predetermined rate based on direct labor costs. Jobs 6.02 and 6.03 are finished in June, and Job 6.04 is expected to be finished in July. No raw materials are used indirectly in June. (Assume this company's predetermined overhead rate did not change over these months).

Required

1. What is the cost of the raw materials used in June for each of the three jobs and in total?

> **Check** (1) Total materials, $6,900

2. How much total direct labor cost is incurred in June?

3. What predetermined overhead rate is used in June?

> (3) 50%

4. How much cost is transferred to finished goods inventory in June?

Beyond the Numbers

BTN 15-1 **Research In Motion**'s financial statements and notes in Appendix A provide evidence of growth potential in its sales.

REPORTING IN ACTION

C1

RIM

Required

1. Identify at least two types of costs that will predictably increase as a percent of sales with growth in sales.

2. Explain why you believe the types of costs identified for part 1 will increase, and describe how you might assess RIM's success with these costs. (*Hint:* You might consider the gross margin ratio.)

Fast Forward

3. Access RIM's annual report for a fiscal year ending after February 27, 2010, from its Website [**RIM.com**] or the SEC's EDGAR database [**www.SEC.gov**]. Review and report its growth in sales along with its cost and income levels (including its gross margin ratio).

COMPARATIVE ANALYSIS

C1

RIM

Apple

BTN 15-2   Retailers as well as manufacturers can apply just-in-time (JIT) to their inventory management. Both **Research In Motion** and **Apple** want to know the impact of a JIT inventory system for their operating cash flows. Review each company's statement of cash flows in Appendix A to answer the following. (For RIM, also review Note 16.)

Required

1. Identify the impact on operating cash flows (increase or decrease) for changes in inventory levels (increase or decrease) for both companies for each of the three most recent years.

2. What impact would a JIT inventory system have on both RIM's and Apple's operating income? Link the answer to your response for part 1.

3. Would the move to a JIT system have a one-time or recurring impact on operating cash flow?

ETHICS CHALLENGE

P3

BTN 15-3   An accounting professional requires at least two skill sets. The first is to be technically competent. Knowing how to capture, manage, and report information is a necessary skill. Second, the ability to assess manager and employee actions and biases for accounting analysis is another skill. For instance, knowing how a person is compensated helps anticipate information biases. Draw on these skills and write a one-half page memo to the financial officer on the following practice of allocating overhead.

Background: Assume that your company sells portable housing to both general contractors and the government. It sells jobs to contractors on a bid basis. A contractor asks for three bids from different manufacturers. The combination of low bid and high quality wins the job. However, jobs sold to the government are bid on a cost-plus basis. This means price is determined by adding all costs plus a profit based on cost at a specified percent, such as 10%. You observe that the amount of overhead allocated to government jobs is higher than that allocated to contract jobs. These allocations concern you and motivate your memo.

Point: Students could compare responses and discuss differences in concerns with allocating overhead.

COMMUNICATING IN PRACTICE

C1 C2

BTN 15-4   Assume that you are preparing for a second interview with a manufacturing company. The company is impressed with your credentials but has indicated that it has several qualified applicants. You anticipate that in this second interview, you must show what you offer over other candidates. You learn the company currently uses a periodic inventory system and is not satisfied with the timeliness of its information and its inventory management. The company manufactures custom-order holiday decorations and display items. To show your abilities, you plan to recommend that it use a cost accounting system.

Required

In preparation for the interview, prepare notes outlining the following:

1. Your cost accounting system recommendation and why it is suitable for this company.

2. A general description of the documents that the proposed cost accounting system requires.

3. How the documents in part 2 facilitate the operation of the cost accounting system.

Point: Have students present a mock interview, one assuming the role of the president of the company and the other the applicant.

TAKING IT TO THE NET

C1

BTN 15-5   Many contractors work on custom jobs that require a job order costing system.

Required

Access the Website **AMSI.com** and click on *Construction Management Software,* and then on STARBUILDER. Prepare a one-page memorandum for the CEO of a construction company providing information about the job order costing software this company offers. Would you recommend that the company purchase this software?

BTN 15-6   Consider the activities undertaken by a medical clinic in your area.

Required

1. Do you consider a job order cost accounting system appropriate for the clinic?
2. Identify as many factors as possible to lead you to conclude that it uses a job order system.

TEAMWORK IN ACTION

C1

BTN 15-7   Refer to the chapter opener regarding John Hewitt and his company, **Liberty Tax Service**. All successful businesses track their costs, and it is especially important for start-up businesses to monitor and control costs.

Required

1. Assume that Liberty Tax Service uses a job order costing system. For the basic cost category of direct materials, explain how a job cost sheet for Liberty Tax Service would differ from a job cost sheet for a manufacturing company.
2. For the basic cost categories of direct labor and overhead, provide examples of the types of costs that would fall into each category for Liberty Tax Service.

ENTREPRENEURIAL DECISION

C1

BTN 15-8   Job order cost accounting is frequently used by home builders.

Required

1. You (or your team) are to prepare a job cost sheet for a single-family home under construction. List four items of both direct materials and direct labor. Explain how you think overhead should be applied.
2. Contact a builder and compare your job cost sheet to this builder's job cost sheet. If possible, speak to that company's accountant. Write your findings in a short report.

HITTING THE ROAD

C2 P1 P2 P3

BTN 15-9   **Nokia** and **Palm** are competitors in the global marketplace. Access Nokia's annual report (www.Nokia.com) for the year ended December 31, 2009. The following information is available for Nokia.

(Euro millions)	Current Year	One Year Prior	Two Years Prior
Inventories	€1,865	€2,533	€2,876

Required

1. Determine the change in Nokia's inventories for the last two years. Then identify the impact on net resources generated by operating activities (increase or decrease) for changes in inventory levels (increase or decrease) for Nokia for the last two years.
2. Would a move to a JIT system likely impact Nokia more than it would Palm? Explain.

GLOBAL DECISION

C1

NOKIA

Palm

ANSWERS TO MULTIPLE CHOICE QUIZ

1. c; $30,000 × 150% = $45,000
2. b; $38,500/$35,000 = 110%
3. e; Direct materials + Direct labor + Overhead = Total cost;
   Direct materials + ($4,000/.80) + $4,000 = $10,000
   Direct materials = $1,000

4. e; $9,000 + $94,200 + $59,200 + $31,600 − Finished goods = $17,800
   Thus, finished goods = $176,200
5. b

16

Process Costing and Analysis

A Look Back

Chapter 14 introduced managerial accounting and described cost concepts and the reporting of manufacturing activities. Chapter 15 explained job order costing—an important cost accounting system for customized products and services.

A Look at This Chapter

This chapter focuses on how to measure and account for costs in process operations. We explain process production, describe how to assign costs to processes, and compute cost per equivalent unit for a process.

A Look Ahead

Chapter 17 introduces the activity-based costing (ABC) system, which provides managers with strategic cost information that is not readily available from other costing methods.

Learning Objectives

CONCEPTUAL

C1 Explain process operations and the way they differ from job order operations. (p. 682)

C2 Define and compute equivalent units and explain their use in process cost accounting. (p. 689)

C3 Define and prepare a process cost summary and describe its purposes. (p. 694)

C4 *Appendix 16A*—Explain and illustrate the accounting for production activity using FIFO. (p. 701)

ANALYTICAL

A1 Compare process cost accounting and job order cost accounting. (p. 685)

A2 Explain and illustrate a hybrid costing system. (p. 697)

LP16

PROCEDURAL

P1 Record the flow of direct materials costs in process cost accounting. (p. 686)

P2 Record the flow of direct labor costs in process cost accounting. (p. 687)

P3 Record the flow of factory overhead costs in process cost accounting. (p. 687)

P4 Record the transfer of completed goods to Finished Goods Inventory and Cost of Goods Sold. (p. 695)

Writing on Walls

"We're selling a dynamic environment. . . . it energizes you"
—JEFF AVALLON

CAMBRIDGE, MA—Brainstorming for a class, John Goscha and friends became frustrated with having to constantly erase a tiny whiteboard or hang paper all over their walls. Then, Goscha said, "Wouldn't it be great if we could have a dry erase board that just took up the entire wall?" John pursued the idea and started a company, **IdeaPaint (IdeaPaint.com),** bringing his friends Jeff Avallon and Morgen Newman on-board to help build the business. Their product is a paint that turns any wall into a dry-erase surface, at a lower cost than actually installing whiteboards.

Though the idea is simple, the process for turning their vision to reality was hard. The business partners spent time in their school's chemistry lab with all kinds of paint to develop a crude prototype. Two labs the group contacted gave up, concluding the idea was impossible. Finally, a third lab stumbled upon the proper chemistry and developed a paint from which markers can be wiped off.

IdeaPaint's production process offers clear advantages over those of companies that produce dry-erase whiteboards. Competitors use a host of raw materials, including wood, steel, and aluminum, and then use high-intensity ovens to make whiteboards. IdeaPaint is made in a process that combines paint pigment, additives, and water. IdeaPaint holds few materials in inventory, and as Jeff notes, IdeaPaint is "simply mixed and stirred." Still, entrepreneurs like Jeff, John, and Morgen rely on process cost summaries to help them monitor and control the costs of material, labor, and overhead applied to their production processes. Morgen admits that "every company has overhead to deal with," but IdeaPaint is able to beat competitors by saving on shipping and energy costs. Managerial accounting information provides insights into those production costs and aids in company decisions.

Having perfected their production process, the trio is now focused on the process of running their operation. "We assigned tasks based on who had slept more than four hours the past few days," says Morgen. Now, the partners each focus on different aspects of the business. As John explains, "We are learning how to take this from just an idea and paint in a can to a real business with distribution and sales." A focus on cost management minimizes their risk of bad decisions as the company pursues further expansion. With sales growing rapidly, the company recently raised over $3 million in venture-capital to finance entry into hospitals, schools, and retail stores. And, in addition to "working at their dream jobs" as Jeff puts it, they get to write on walls.

Sources: *IdeaPaint Company Website,* January 2011; *Inc.com; Businessweek.com,* September 2009; *CNNMoney.com,* March 2010.

The type of product or service a company offers determines its cost accounting system. Job order costing is used to account for custom products and services that meet the demands of a particular customer. Not all products are manufactured in this way; many carry standard designs so that one unit is no different than any other unit. Such a system often produces large numbers of units on a continuous basis, all of which pass through similar processes.

This chapter describes how to use a process cost accounting system to account for these types of products. It also explains how costs are accumulated for each process and then assigned to units passing through those processes. This information helps us understand and estimate the cost of each process as well as find ways to reduce costs and improve processes.

Process Costing and Analysis

Process Operations
- Comparing job order and process operations
- Organization of process operations
- GenX Company—an illustration

Process Cost Accounting
- Direct and indirect costs
- Accounting for materials costs
- Accounting for labor costs
- Accounting for factory overhead

Equivalent Units of Production (EUP)
- Accounting for goods in process
- Differences between EUP for materials, labor, and overhead

Process Costing Illustration
- Physical flow of units
- EUP
- Cost per EUP
- Cost reconciliation
- Process cost summary
- Transfers to finished goods and to cost of goods sold

PROCESS OPERATIONS

C1 Explain process operations and the way they differ from job order operations.

Process operations, also called *process manufacturing* or *process production,* is the mass production of products in a continuous flow of steps. This means that products pass through a series of sequential processes. Petroleum refining is a common example of process operations. Crude oil passes through a series of steps before it is processed into different grades of petroleum. **Exxon Mobil**'s oil activities reflect a process operation. An important characteristic of process operations is the high level of standardization necessary if the system is to produce large volumes of products. Process operations also extend to services. Examples include mail sorting in large post offices and order processing in large mail-order firms such as **L.L. Bean**. The common feature in these service organizations is that operations are performed in a sequential manner using a series of standardized processes. Other companies using process operations include:

Company	Product or Service	Company	Product or Service
Kellogg	Cereals	Heinz	Ketchup
Pfizer	Pharmaceuticals	Penn	Tennis balls
Procter & Gamble	Household products	Hershey	Chocolate
Coca-Cola	Soft drinks	Jiffy Lube	Oil changes

For virtual tours of process operations visit **PennRacquet.com/factory.html** (tennis balls) and **Hersheys.com/discover/tour_video.asp** (chocolate).

Each of these examples of products and services involves operations having a series of *processes,* or steps. Each process involves a different set of activities. A production operation that processes chemicals, for instance, might include the four steps shown in Exhibit 16.1. Understanding such processes for companies with process operations is crucial for measuring their costs. Increasingly, process operations use machines and automation to control product quality and reduce manufacturing costs.

EXHIBIT 16.1

Process Operations: Chemicals

Comparing Job Order and Process Operations

Job order and process operations can be considered as two ends of a continuum. Important features of both systems are shown in Exhibit 16.2. We often describe job order and process operations with manufacturing examples, but both also apply to service companies. In a job order costing system, the measurement focus is on the individual job or batch. In a process costing system, the measurement focus is on the process itself and the standardized units produced.

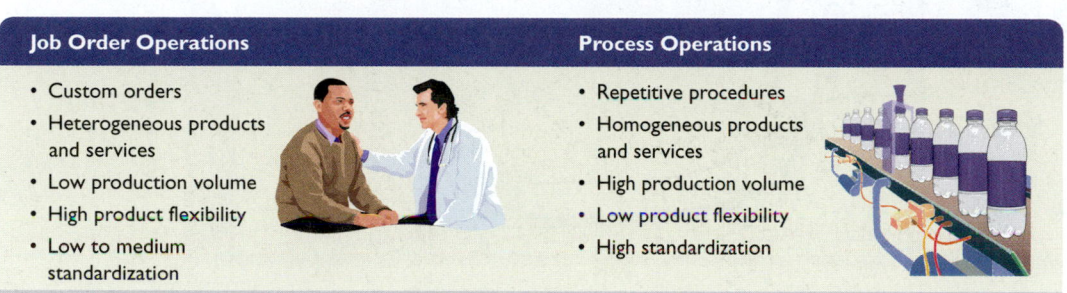

EXHIBIT 16.2

Comparing Job Order and Process Operations

Organization of Process Operations

In a process operation, each process is identified as a separate *production department, workstation,* or *work center.* With the exception of the first process or department, each receives the output from the prior department as a partially processed product. Depending on the nature of the process, a company applies direct labor, overhead, and, perhaps, additional direct materials to move the product toward completion. Only the final process or department in the series produces finished goods ready for sale to customers.

Tracking costs for several related departments can seem complex. Yet because process costing procedures are applied to the activity of each department or process separately, we need to consider only one process at a time. This simplifies the procedures.

When the output of one department becomes an input to another department, as is the case in sequential processing, we simply transfer the costs associated with those units from the first department into the next. We repeat these steps from department to department until the final process is complete. At that point the accumulated costs are transferred with the product from Goods in Process Inventory to Finished Goods Inventory. The next section illustrates a company with a single process, but the methods illustrated apply to a multiprocess scenario as each department's costs are handled separately for each department.

Decision Insight

Accounting for Health Many service companies use process departments to perform specific tasks for consumers. Hospitals, for instance, have radiology and physical therapy facilities with special equipment and trained employees. When patients need services, they are processed through departments to receive prescribed care. Service companies need process cost accounting information as much as manufacturers to estimate costs of services, to plan future operations, to control costs, and to determine customer charges. ■

GenX Company—An Illustration

The GenX Company illustrates process operations. It produces Profen®, an over-the-counter pain reliever for athletes. GenX sells Profen to wholesale distributors, who in turn sell it to

EXHIBIT 16.3

Floor Plan of GenX's Factory

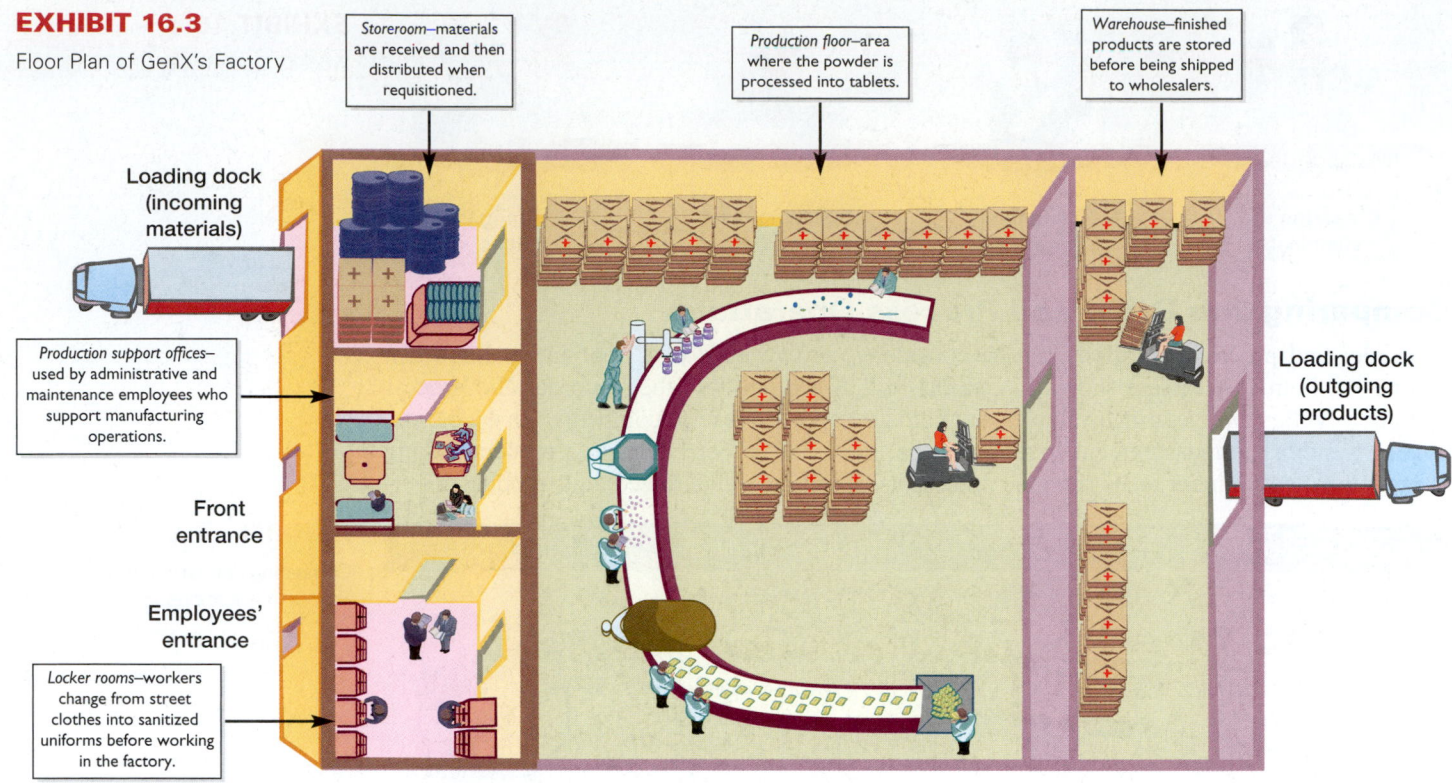

Storeroom—materials are received and then distributed when requisitioned.

Production floor—area where the powder is processed into tablets.

Warehouse—finished products are stored before being shipped to wholesalers.

Loading dock (incoming materials)

Production support offices— used by administrative and maintenance employees who support manufacturing operations.

Front entrance

Employees' entrance

Locker rooms—workers change from street clothes into sanitized uniforms before working in the factory.

Loading dock (outgoing products)

Point: Electronic monitoring of operations is common in factories.

retailers. Profen is produced by mixing its active ingredient, Profelene, with flavorings and preservatives, molding it into Profen tablets, and packaging the tablets. Exhibit 16.3 shows a summary floor plan of the GenX factory, which has five areas.

The first step in process manufacturing is to decide when to produce a product. Management determines the types and quantities of materials and labor needed and then schedules the work. Unlike a job order process, where production often begins only after receipt of a custom order, managers of companies with process operations often forecast the demand expected for their products. Based on these plans, production begins. The flowchart in Exhibit 16.4 shows the production steps for GenX. The following sections explain how GenX uses a process cost accounting system to compute these costs. Many of the explanations refer to this exhibit and its numbered cost flows ① through ⑩. (*Hint:* The amounts for the numbered cost flows in Exhibit 16.4 are summarized in Exhibit 16.21. Those amounts are explained in the following pages, but it can help to refer to Exhibit 16.21 as we proceed through the explanations.)

EXHIBIT 16.4

Process Operations and Costs: GenX

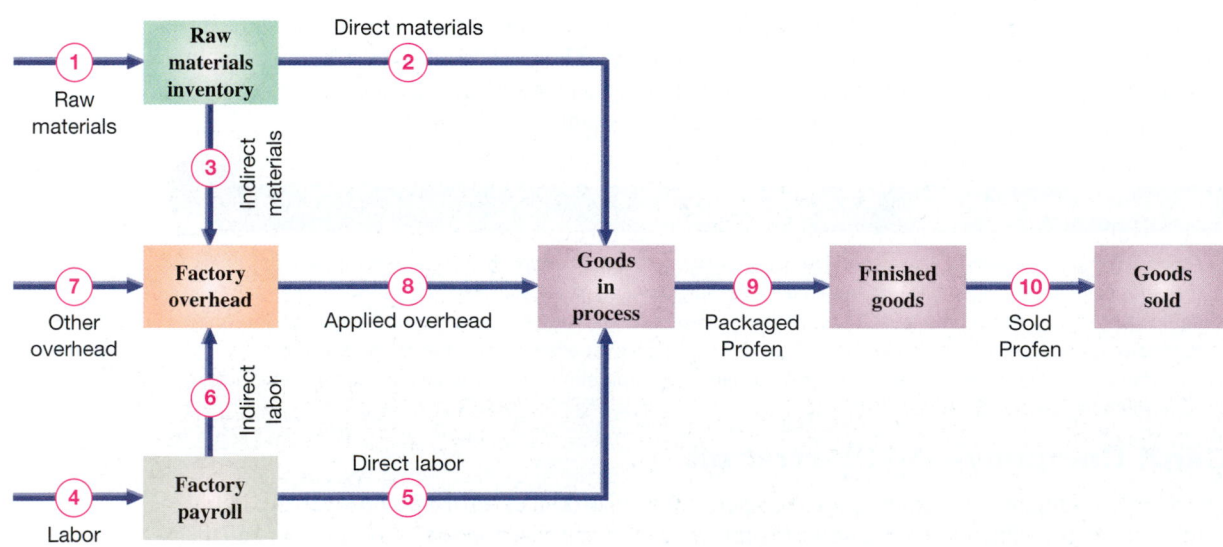

PROCESS COST ACCOUNTING

Comparing Job Order and Process Cost Accounting Systems

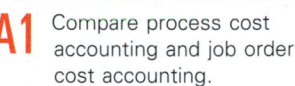

Process and job order operations are similar in that both combine materials, labor, and overhead in the process of producing products. They differ in how they are organized and managed. The measurement focus in a job order costing system is on the individual job or batch, whereas in a process costing system, it is on the individual process. Regardless of the measurement focus, we are ultimately interested in determining the cost per unit of product (or service) resulting from either system.

Specifically, the **job order cost accounting system** assigns direct materials, direct labor, and overhead to jobs. The total job cost is then divided by the number of units to compute a cost per unit for that job. The **process cost accounting system** assigns direct materials, direct labor, and overhead to specific processes (or departments). The total costs associated with each process are then divided by the number of units passing through that process to determine the cost per equivalent unit (defined later in the chapter) for that process. Differences in the way these two systems apply materials, labor, and overhead costs are highlighted in Exhibit 16.5.

Point: The cost object in a job order system is the specific job; the cost object in a process costing system is the process.

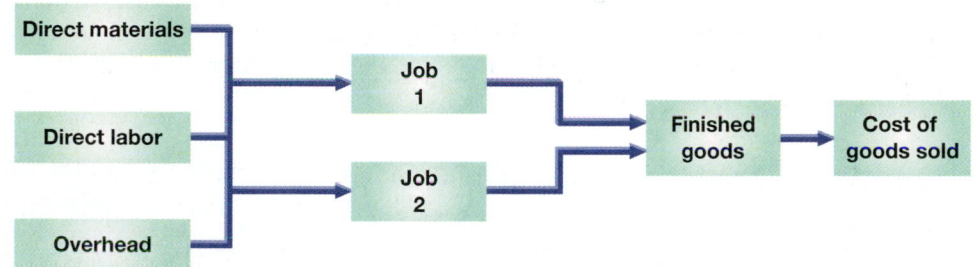

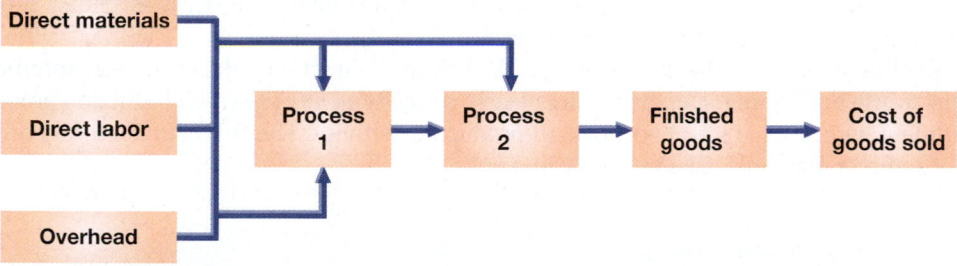

EXHIBIT 16.5

Comparing Job Order and Process Cost Accounting Systems

Direct and Indirect Costs

Like job order operations, process cost accounting systems use the concepts of direct and indirect costs. If a cost can be traced to the cost object, it is direct; if it cannot, it is indirect. Materials and labor that can be traced to specific processes are assigned to those processes as direct costs. Materials and labor that cannot be traced to a specific process are indirect costs and are assigned to overhead. Some costs classified as overhead in a job order system may be classified as direct costs in process cost accounting. For example, depreciation of a machine used entirely by one process is a direct cost of that process.

Decision Insight

JIT Boon to Process Operations   Companies that adopt JIT manufacturing often organize their production system as a series of sequential processes. One survey found 60% of companies that converted to JIT used process operations; this compares to only 20% before converting to JIT. ■

P1 Record the flow of direct materials costs in process cost accounting.

Accounting for Materials Costs

In Exhibit 16.4, arrow line ① reflects the arrival of materials at GenX's factory. These materials include Profelene, flavorings, preservatives, and packaging. They also include supplies for the production support office. GenX uses a perpetual inventory system and makes all purchases on credit. The summary entry for receipts of raw materials in April follows (dates in journal entries numbered ① through ⑩ are omitted because they are summary entries, often reflecting two or more transactions or events).

Assets = Liabilities + Equity
+11,095   +11,095

①	Raw Materials Inventory	11,095	
	Accounts Payable		11,095
	Acquired materials on credit for factory use.		

Arrow line ② in Exhibit 16.4 reflects the flow of direct materials to production, where they are used to produce Profen. Most direct materials are physically combined into the finished product; the remaining direct materials include those used and clearly linked with a specific process. The manager of a process usually obtains materials by submitting a *materials requisition* to the materials storeroom manager. In some situations, materials move continuously from raw materials inventory through the manufacturing process. **Pepsi Bottling**, for instance, uses a process in which inventory moves continuously through the system. In these cases, a **materials consumption report** summarizes the materials used by a department during a reporting period and replaces materials requisitions. The entry to record the use of direct materials by GenX's production department in April follows.

Assets = Liabilities + Equity
+9,900
−9,900

②	Goods in Process Inventory	9,900	
	Raw Materials Inventory		9,900
	To assign costs of direct materials used in production.		

This entry transfers costs from one asset account to another asset account. (When two or more production departments exist, a company uses two or more Goods in Process Inventory accounts to separately accumulate costs incurred by each.)

Example: What types of materials might the flow of arrow line ③ in Exhibit 16.4 reflect? *Answer:* Goggles, gloves, protective clothing, recordkeeping supplies, and cleaning supplies.

In Exhibit 16.4, the arrow line ③ reflects the flow of indirect materials from the storeroom to factory overhead. These materials are not clearly linked with any specific production process or department but are used to support overall production activity. The following entry records the cost of indirect materials used by GenX in April.

Assets = Liabilities + Equity
−1,195   −1,195

③	Factory Overhead	1,195	
	Raw Materials Inventory		1,195
	To record indirect materials used in April.		

After the entries for both direct and indirect materials are posted, the Raw Materials Inventory account appears as shown in Exhibit 16.6. The April 30 balance sheet reports the $4,000 Raw Materials Inventory account as a current asset.

EXHIBIT 16.6

Raw Materials Inventory

Raw Materials Inventory				Acct. No. 132		
Date		Explanation	Debit	Credit	Balance
Mar.	31	Balance			4,000
Apr.	30	Materials purchases	11,095		15,095
	30	Direct materials usage		9,900	5,195
	30	Indirect materials usage		1,195	4,000

Accounting for Labor Costs

Exhibit 16.4 shows GenX factory payroll costs as reflected in arrow line ④. Total labor costs of $8,920 are paid in cash and are recorded in the Factory Payroll account.

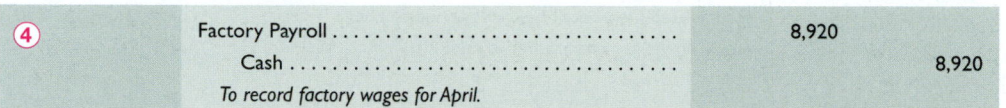

④	Factory Payroll	8,920	
	Cash		8,920
	To record factory wages for April.		

Assets = Liabilities + Equity
−8,920   −8,920

Time reports from the production department and the production support office triggered this entry. (For simplicity, we do not separately identify withholdings and additional payroll taxes for employees.) In a process operation, the direct labor of a production department includes all labor used exclusively by that department. This is the case even if the labor is not applied to the product itself. If a production department in a process operation, for instance, has a full-time manager and a full-time maintenance worker, their salaries are direct labor costs of that process and are not factory overhead.

Arrow line ⑤ in Exhibit 16.4 shows GenX's use of direct labor in the production department. The following entry transfers April's direct labor costs from the Factory Payroll account to the Goods in Process Inventory account.

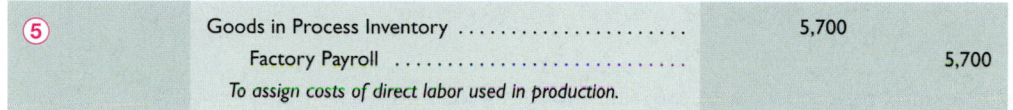

⑤	Goods in Process Inventory	5,700	
	Factory Payroll		5,700
	To assign costs of direct labor used in production.		

Assets = Liabilities + Equity
+5,700   +5,700

Arrow line ⑥ in Exhibit 16.4 reflects GenX's indirect labor costs. These employees provide clerical, maintenance, and other services that help produce Profen efficiently. For example, they order materials, deliver them to the factory floor, repair equipment, operate and program computers used in production, keep payroll and other production records, clean up, and move the finished goods to the warehouse. The following entry charges these indirect labor costs to factory overhead.

Point: A department's indirect labor cost might include an allocated portion of the salary of a manager who supervises two or more departments. Allocation of costs between departments is discussed in a later chapter.

⑥	Factory Overhead	3,220	
	Factory Payroll		3,220
	To record indirect labor as overhead.		

Assets = Liabilities + Equity
                       −3,220
                       +3,220

After these entries for both direct and indirect labor are posted, the Factory Payroll account appears as shown in Exhibit 16.7. The temporary Factory Payroll account is now closed to another temporary account, Factory Overhead, and is ready to receive entries for May. Next we show how to apply overhead to production and close the temporary Factory Overhead account.

Factory Payroll					Acct. No. 530
Date		**Explanation**	**Debit**	**Credit**	**Balance**
Mar.	31	Balance			0
Apr.	30	Total payroll for April	8,920		8,920
	30	Direct labor costs		5,700	3,220
	30	Indirect labor costs		3,220	0

EXHIBIT 16.7

Factory Payroll

Accounting for Factory Overhead

Overhead costs other than indirect materials and indirect labor are reflected by arrow line ⑦ in Exhibit 16.4. These overhead items include the costs of insuring production assets, renting the factory building, using factory utilities, and depreciating equipment not directly related to a specific process. The following entry records overhead costs for April.

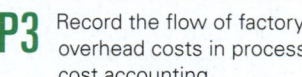

P2 Record the flow of direct labor costs in process cost accounting.

P3 Record the flow of factory overhead costs in process cost accounting.

Assets = Liabilities + Equity
−180   +645   −2,425
−750
−850

⑦	Factory Overhead	2,425	
	Prepaid Insurance		180
	Utilities Payable		645
	Cash		750
	Accumulated Depreciation—Factory Equipment ...		850
	To record overhead items incurred in April.		

After this entry is posted, the Factory Overhead account balance is $6,840, comprising indirect materials of $1,195, indirect labor of $3,220, and $2,425 of other overhead.

Arrow line ⑧ in Exhibit 16.4 reflects the application of factory overhead to production. Factory overhead is applied to processes by relating overhead cost to another variable such as direct labor hours or machine hours used. With increasing automation, companies with process operations are more likely to use machine hours to allocate overhead. In some situations, a single allocation basis such as direct labor hours (or a single rate for the entire plant) fails to provide useful allocations. As a result, management can use different rates for different production departments. Based on an analysis of its operations, GenX applies its April overhead at a rate of 120% of direct labor cost, as shown in Exhibit 16.8.

Point: The time it takes to process (cycle) products through a process is sometimes used to allocate costs.

EXHIBIT 16.8

Applying Factory Overhead
(Production Department)

$$\textbf{Overhead applied = Direct labor cost} \times \textbf{Predetermined rate}$$
$$\$6,840 \quad = \quad \$5,700 \quad \times \quad 120\%$$

GenX records its applied overhead with the following entry.

Assets = Liabilities + Equity
+6,840   +6,840

⑧	Goods in Process Inventory	6,840	
	Factory Overhead		6,840
	Allocated overhead costs to production at 120% of direct labor cost.		

After posting this entry, the Factory Overhead account appears as shown in Exhibit 16.9. For GenX, the amount of overhead applied equals the actual overhead incurred during April. In most cases, using a predetermined overhead rate leaves an overapplied or underapplied balance in the Factory Overhead account. At the end of the period, this overapplied or underapplied balance should be closed to the Cost of Goods Sold account, as described in the job order costing chapter.

EXHIBIT 16.9

Factory Overhead

Example: If applied overhead results in a $6,940 credit to the factory overhead account, does it yield an over- or underapplied overhead amount? *Answer:* $100 overapplied overhead

		Factory Overhead			Acct. No. 540
Date		**Explanation**	**Debit**	**Credit**	**Balance**
Mar.	31	Balance			0
Apr.	30	Indirect materials usage	1,195		1,195
	30	Indirect labor costs	3,220		4,415
	30	Other overhead costs	2,425		6,840
	30	Applied to production departments		6,840	0

Decision Ethics   Answer — p. 706

Budget Officer   You are working to identify the direct and indirect costs of a new processing department that has several machines. This department's manager instructs you to classify a majority of the costs as indirect to take advantage of the direct labor-based overhead allocation method so it will be charged a lower amount of overhead (because of its small direct labor cost). This would penalize other departments with higher allocations. It also will cause the performance ratings of managers in these other departments to suffer. What action do you take? ■

Quick Check

Answers — p. 706

1. A process operation (*a*) is another name for a job order operation, (*b*) does not use the concepts of direct materials or direct labor, or (*c*) typically produces large quantities of homogeneous products or services.
2. Under what conditions is a process cost accounting system more suitable for measuring production costs than a job order cost accounting system?
3. When direct materials are assigned and used in production, the entry to record their use includes (*a*) a credit to Goods in Process Inventory, (*b*) a debit to Goods in Process Inventory, or (*c*) a debit to Raw Materials Inventory.
4. What are the three cost categories incurred by both job order and process operations?
5. How many Goods in Process Inventory accounts are needed in a process cost system?

EQUIVALENT UNITS OF PRODUCTION

We explained how materials, labor, and overhead costs for a period are accumulated in the Goods in Process Inventory account, but we have not explained the arrow lines labeled ⑨ and ⑩ in Exhibit 16.4. These lines reflect the transfer of products from the production department to finished goods inventory, and from finished goods inventory to cost of goods sold. To determine the costs recorded for these flows, we must first determine the cost per unit of product and then apply this result to the number of units transferred.

 C2 Define and compute equivalent units and explain their use in process cost accounting.

Accounting for Goods in Process

If a process has *no beginning and no ending goods in process inventory,* the unit cost of goods transferred out of a process is computed as follows.

> **Total cost assigned to the process (direct materials, direct labor, and overhead)**
> **Total number of units started and finished in the period**

If a process has a beginning or ending inventory of partially processed units (or both), then the total cost assigned to the process must be allocated to all completed and incomplete units worked on during the period. Therefore, the denominator must measure the entire production activity of the process for the period, called **equivalent units of production** (or **EUP**), a phrase that refers to the number of units that could have been started *and* completed given the cost incurred during a period. This measure is then used to compute the cost per equivalent unit and to assign costs to finished goods and goods in process inventory.

To illustrate, assume that GenX adds (or introduces) 100 units into its process during a period. Suppose at the end of that period, the production supervisor determines that those 100 units are 60% of the way through the process. Therefore, equivalent units of production for that period total 60 EUP (100 units × 60%). This means that with the resources used to put 100 units 60% of the way through the process, GenX could have started and completed 60 whole units.

Point: For GenX, "units" might refer to individual Profen tablets. For a juice maker, units might refer to gallons.

Differences in Equivalent Units for Materials, Labor, and Overhead

In many processes, the equivalent units of production for direct materials are not the same with respect to direct labor and overhead. To illustrate, consider a five-step process operation shown in Exhibit 16.10.

EXHIBIT 16.10

An Illustrative Five-Step Process Operation

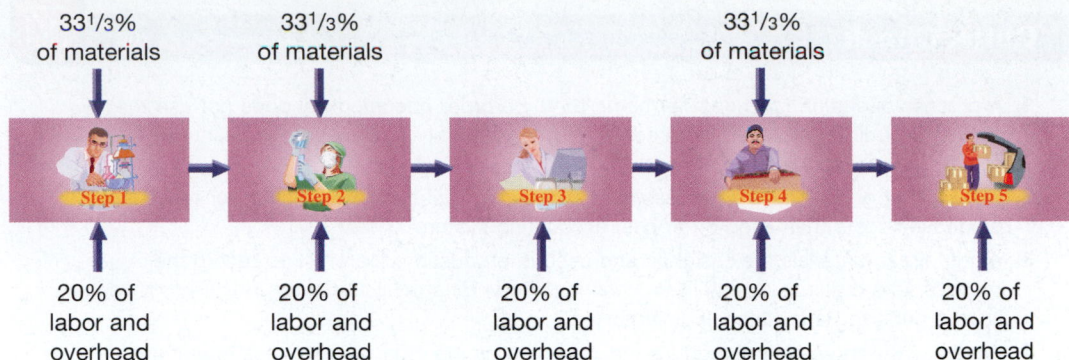

This exhibit shows that one-third of the direct material cost is added at each of three steps: 1, 2, and 4. One-fifth of the direct labor cost is added at each of the five steps. One-fifth of the overhead also is added at each step because overhead is applied as a percent of direct labor for this company.

When units finish step 1, they are one-third complete with respect to direct materials but only one-fifth complete with respect to direct labor and overhead. When they finish step 2, they are two-thirds complete with respect to direct materials but only two-fifths complete with respect to direct labor and overhead. When they finish step 3, they remain two-thirds complete with respect to materials but are now three-fifths complete with respect to labor and overhead. When they finish step 4, they are 100% complete with respect to materials (all direct materials have been added) but only four-fifths complete with respect to labor and overhead.

For example, if 300 units of product are started and processed through step 1 of Exhibit 16.10, they are said to be one-third complete *with respect to materials*. Expressed in terms of equivalent finished units, the processing of these 300 units is equal to finishing 100 EUP with respect to materials (300 units × 33⅓%). However, only one-fifth of direct labor and overhead has been applied to the 300 units at the end of step 1. This means that the equivalent units of production *with respect to labor and overhead* total 60 EUP (300 units × 20%).

Decision Insight

Process Services   Customer interaction software is a hot item in customer service processes. Whether in insurance, delivery, or technology services, companies are finding that this software can turn their customer service process into an asset. How does it work? For starters, it cuts time spent on service calls because a customer describes a problem only once. It also yields a database of customer questions and complaints that gives insights into needed improvements. It recognizes incoming phone numbers and accesses previous dealings. ■

PROCESS COSTING ILLUSTRATION

This section applies process costing concepts and procedures to GenX. **This illustration uses the weighted-average method for inventory costs. The FIFO method is illustrated in Appendix 16A.** (Assume a weighted-average cost flow for all computations and assignments in this chapter unless explicitly stated differently. When using a just-in-time inventory system, different inventory methods yield similar results because inventories are immaterial.)

Exhibit 16.11 shows selected information from the production department for the month of April. Accounting for a department's activity for a period includes four steps involving analysis of (1) physical flow, (2) equivalent units, (3) cost per equivalent unit, and (4) cost assignment and reconciliation. The next sections describe each step.

Beginning goods in process inventory (March 31)	
Units of product	30,000 units
Percentage of completion—Direct materials	100%
Percentage of completion—Direct labor	65%
Direct materials costs	$ 3,300
Direct labor costs	$ 600
Factory overhead costs applied (120% of direct labor)	$ 720
Activities during the current period (April)	
Units started this period	90,000 units
Units transferred out (completed)	100,000 units
Direct materials costs	$ 9,900
Direct labor costs	$ 5,700
Factory overhead costs applied (120% of direct labor)	$ 6,840
Ending goods in process inventory (April 30)	
Units of product	20,000 units
Percentage of completion—Direct materials	100%
Percentage of completion—Direct labor	25%

EXHIBIT 16.11

Production Data

Step 1: Determine the Physical Flow of Units

A *physical flow reconciliation* is a report that reconciles (1) the physical units started in a period with (2) the physical units completed in that period. A physical flow reconciliation for GenX is shown in Exhibit 16.12 for April.

Units to Account For		Units Accounted For	
Beginning goods in process inventory	30,000 units	Units completed and transferred out	100,000 units
Units started this period	90,000 units	Ending goods in process inventory	20,000 units
Total units to account for	**120,000 units**	Total units accounted for	**120,000 units**

reconciled

EXHIBIT 16.12

Physical Flow Reconciliation

The weighted-average method does not require us to separately track the units in beginning work in process from those units started this period. Instead, the units are treated as part of a large pool with an average cost per unit.

Step 2: Compute Equivalent Units of Production

The second step is to compute *equivalent units of production* for direct materials, direct labor, and factory overhead for April. Overhead is applied using direct labor as the allocation base for GenX. This also implies that equivalent units are the same for both labor and overhead.

GenX used its direct materials, direct labor, and overhead to make finished units of Profen and to begin processing some units that are not yet complete. We must convert the physical units measure to equivalent units based on how each input has been used. Equivalent units are computed by multiplying the number of physical units by the percentage of completion for each input—see Exhibit 16.13.

Equivalent Units of Production	Direct Materials	Direct Labor	Factory Overhead
Equivalent units completed and transferred out (100,000 × 100%)	100,000 EUP	100,000 EUP	100,000 EUP
Equivalent units for ending goods in process			
Direct materials (20,000 × 100%)	20,000		
Direct labor (20,000 × 25%)		5,000	
Factory overhead (20,000 × 25%)			5,000
Equivalent units of production	120,000 EUP	105,000 EUP	105,000 EUP

EXHIBIT 16.13

Equivalent Units of Production—Weighted Average

The first row of Exhibit 16.13 reflects units transferred out in April. The production department entirely completed its work on the 100,000 units transferred out. These units have 100% of the materials, labor, and overhead required, or 100,000 equivalent units of each input (100,000 × 100%).

The second row references the ending goods in process, and rows three, four, and five break it down by materials, labor, and overhead. For direct materials, the units in ending goods in process inventory (20,000 physical units) include all materials required, so there are 20,000 equivalent units (20,000 × 100%) of materials in the unfinished physical units. Regarding labor, the units in ending goods in process inventory include 25% of the labor required, which implies 5,000 equivalent units of labor (20,000 × 25%). These units are only 25% complete and labor is used uniformly through the process. Overhead is applied on the basis of direct labor for GenX, so equivalent units for overhead are computed identically to labor (20,000 × 25%).

The final row reflects the whole units of product that could have been manufactured with the amount of inputs used to create some complete and some incomplete units. For GenX, the amount of inputs used to produce 100,000 complete units and to start 20,000 additional units is equivalent to the amount of direct materials in 120,000 whole units, the amount of direct labor in 105,000 whole units, and the amount of overhead in 105,000 whole units.

Step 3: Compute the Cost per Equivalent Unit

Equivalent units of production for each product (from step 2) is used to compute the average cost per equivalent unit. Under the **weighted-average method,** the computation of EUP does not separate the units in beginning inventory from those started this period; similarly, this method combines the costs of beginning goods in process inventory with the costs incurred in the current period. This process is illustrated in Exhibit 16.14.

EXHIBIT 16.14

Cost per Equivalent Unit of Production—Weighted Average

Cost per Equivalent Unit of Production	Direct Materials	Direct Labor	Factory Overhead
Costs of beginning goods in process inventory	$ 3,300	$ 600	$ 720
Costs incurred this period	9,900	5,700	6,840
Total costs	$13,200	$6,300	$7,560
÷ Equivalent units of production (from Step 2)	120,000 EUP	105,000 EUP	105,000 EUP
= Cost per equivalent unit of production	$0.11 per EUP*	$0.06 per EUP†	$0.072 per EUP‡

*$13,200 ÷ 120,000 EUP   †$6,300 ÷ 105,000 EUP   ‡$7,560 ÷ 105,000 EUP

For direct materials, the cost averages $0.11 per EUP, computed as the sum of direct materials cost from beginning goods in process inventory ($3,300) and the direct materials cost incurred in April ($9,900), and this sum ($13,200) is then divided by the 120,000 EUP for materials (from step 2). The costs per equivalent unit for labor and overhead are similarly computed. Specifically, direct labor cost averages $0.06 per EUP, computed as the sum of labor cost in beginning goods in process inventory ($600) and the labor costs incurred in April ($5,700), and this sum ($6,300) divided by 105,000 EUP for labor. Overhead costs averages $0.072 per EUP, computed as the sum of overhead cost in the beginning goods in process inventory ($720) and the overhead costs applied in April ($6,840), and this sum ($7,560) divided by 105,000 EUP for overhead.

Step 4: Assign and Reconcile Costs

The EUP from step 2 and the cost per EUP from step 3 are used in step 4 to assign costs to (a) units that production completed and transferred to finished goods and (b) units that remain in process. This is illustrated in Exhibit 16.15.

EXHIBIT 16.15

Report of Costs Accounted For—Weighted Average

Cost of units completed and transferred out		
Direct materials (100,000 EUP × $0.11 per EUP)	$11,000	
Direct labor (100,000 EUP × $0.06 per EUP)	6,000	
Factory overhead (100,000 EUP × $0.072 per EUP)	7,200	
Cost of units completed this period......................		$ 24,200
Cost of ending goods in process inventory		
Direct materials (20,000 EUP × $0.11 per EUP)	2,200	
Direct labor (5,000 EUP × $0.06 per EUP).................	300	
Factory overhead (5,000 EUP × $0.072 per EUP)	360	
Cost of ending goods in process inventory		2,860
Total costs accounted for		**$27,060**

Cost of Units Completed and Transferred The 100,000 units completed and transferred to finished goods inventory required 100,000 EUP of direct materials. Thus, we assign $11,000 (100,000 EUP × $0.11 per EUP) of direct materials cost to those units. Similarly, those units had received 100,000 EUP of direct labor and 100,000 EUP of factory overhead (recall Exhibit 16.13). Thus, we assign $6,000 (100,000 EUP × $0.06 per EUP) of direct labor and $7,200 (100,000 EUP × $0.072 per EUP) of overhead to those units. The total cost of the 100,000 completed and transferred units is $24,200 ($11,000 + $6,000 + $7,200) and their average cost per unit is $0.242 ($24,200 ÷ 100,000 units).

Cost of Units for Ending Goods in Process There are 20,000 incomplete units in goods in process inventory at period-end. For direct materials, those units have 20,000 EUP of material (from step 2) at a cost of $0.11 per EUP (from step 3), which yields the materials cost of goods in process inventory of $2,200 (20,000 EUP × $0.11 per EUP). For direct labor, the in-process units have 25% of the required labor, or 5,000 EUP (from step 2). Using the $0.06 labor cost per EUP (from step 3) we obtain the labor cost of goods in process inventory of $300 (5,000 EUP × $0.06 per EUP). For overhead, the in-process units reflect 5,000 EUP (from step 2). Using the $0.072 overhead cost per EUP (from step 3) we obtain overhead costs with in-process inventory of $360 (5,000 EUP × $0.072 per EUP). Total cost of goods in process inventory at period-end is $2,860 ($2,200 + $300 + $360).

As a check, management verifies that total costs assigned to those units completed and transferred plus the costs of those in process (from Exhibit 16.15) equal the costs incurred by production. Exhibit 16.16 shows the costs incurred by production this period. We then reconcile the *costs accounted for* in Exhibit 16.15 with the *costs to account for* in Exhibit 16.16.

EXHIBIT 16.16

Report of Costs to Account For—Weighted Average

Cost of beginning goods in process inventory		
Direct materials......................................	$3,300	
Direct labor..	600	
Factory overhead	720	$ 4,620
Cost incurred this period		
Direct materials......................................	9,900	
Direct labor..	5,700	
Factory overhead	6,840	22,440
Total costs to account for		**$27,060**

At GenX, the production department manager is responsible for $27,060 in costs: $4,620 that is assigned to the goods in process at the start of the period plus $22,440 of materials, labor, and overhead incurred in the period. At period-end, that manager must show where these costs are assigned. The manager for GenX reports that $2,860 are assigned to units in process and $24,200 are assigned to units completed (per Exhibit 16.15). The sum of these amounts equals $27,060. Thus, the total *costs to account for* equal the total *costs accounted for* (minor differences can sometimes occur from rounding).

C3 Define and prepare a process cost summary and describe its purposes.

Point: Managers can examine changes in monthly costs per equivalent unit to help control the production process. When prices are set in a competitive market, managers can use process cost summary information to determine which costs should be cut to achieve a profit.

Process Cost Summary   An important managerial accounting report for a process cost accounting system is the **process cost summary** (also called *production report*), which is prepared separately for each process or production department. Three reasons for the summary are to (1) help department managers control and monitor their departments, (2) help factory managers evaluate department managers' performances, and (3) provide cost information for financial statements. A process cost summary achieves these purposes by describing the costs charged to each department, reporting the equivalent units of production achieved by each department, and determining the costs assigned to each department's output. For our purposes, it is prepared using a combination of Exhibits 16.13, 16.14, 16.15, and 16.16.

The process cost summary for GenX is shown in Exhibit 16.17. The report is divided into three sections. Section ① lists the total costs charged to the department, including direct materials, direct labor, and overhead costs incurred, as well as the cost of the beginning goods in process inventory. Section ② describes the equivalent units of production for the department. Equivalent units for materials, labor, and overhead are in separate columns. It also reports direct

EXHIBIT 16.17

Process Cost Summary

GenX COMPANY
Process Cost Summary
For Month Ended April 30, 2011

① Costs Charged to Production

Costs of beginning goods in process

Direct materials	$3,300	
Direct labor	600	
Factory overhead	720	$ 4,620

Costs incurred this period

Direct materials	9,900	
Direct labor	5,700	
Factory overhead	6,840	22,440
Total costs to account for		**$27,060**

Unit Cost Information

Units to account for:		Units accounted for:	
Beginning goods in process	30,000	Completed and transferred out	100,000
Units started this period	90,000	Ending goods in process	20,000
Total units to account for	120,000	Total units accounted for	120,000

② Equivalent Units of Production (EUP)

	Direct Materials	Direct Labor	Factory Overhead
Units completed and transferred out	100,000 EUP	100,000 EUP	100,000 EUP
Units of ending goods in process			
Direct materials (20,000 × 100%)	20,000		
Direct labor (20,000 × 25%)		5,000	
Factory overhead (20,000 × 25%)			5,000
Equivalent units of production	120,000 EUP	105,000 EUP	105,000 EUP

Cost per EUP

	Direct Materials	Direct Labor	Factory Overhead
Costs of beginning goods in process	$ 3,300	$ 600	$ 720
Costs incurred this period	9,900	5,700	6,840
Total costs	$13,200	$6,300	$7,560
÷ EUP	120,000 EUP	105,000 EUP	105,000 EUP
Cost per EUP	$0.11 per EUP	$0.06 per EUP	$0.072 per EUP

③ Cost Assignment and Reconciliation

Costs transferred out (cost of goods manufactured)

Direct materials (100,000 EUP × $0.11 per EUP)	$11,000	
Direct labor (100,000 EUP × $0.06 per EUP)	6,000	
Factory overhead (100,000 EUP × $0.072 per EUP)	7,200	$ 24,200

Costs of ending goods in process

Direct materials (20,000 EUP × $0.11 per EUP)	2,200	
Direct labor (5,000 EUP × $0.06 per EUP)	300	
Factory overhead (5,000 EUP × $0.072 per EUP)	360	2,860
Total costs accounted for		**$27,060**

reconciled

materials, direct labor, and overhead costs per equivalent unit. Section ③ allocates total costs among units worked on in the period. The $24,200 is the total cost of goods transferred out of the department, and the $2,860 is the cost of partially processed ending inventory units. The assigned costs are then added to show that the total $27,060 cost charged to the department in section ① is now assigned to the units in section ③.

Quick Check

Answers — p. 706

6. Equivalent units are (*a*) a measure of a production department's productivity in using direct materials, direct labor, or overhead; (*b*) units of a product produced by a foreign competitor that are similar to units produced by a domestic company; or (*c*) generic units of a product similar to brand name units of a product.

7. Interpret the meaning of a department's equivalent units with respect to direct labor.

8. A department began the period with 8,000 units that were one-fourth complete with respect to direct labor. It completed 58,000 units, and ended with 6,000 units that were one-third complete with respect to direct labor. What were its direct labor equivalent units for the period using the weighted-average method?

9. A process cost summary for a department has three sections. What information is presented in each of them?

Transfers to Finished Goods Inventory and Cost of Goods Sold

P4 Record the transfer of completed goods to Finished Goods Inventory and Cost of Goods Sold.

Arrow line ⑨ in Exhibit 16.4 reflects the transfer of completed products from production to finished goods inventory. The process cost summary shows that the 100,000 units of finished Profen are assigned a cost of $24,200. The entry to record this transfer follows.

⑨	Finished Goods Inventory	24,200	
	Goods in Process Inventory		24,200
	To record transfer of completed units.		

Assets = Liabilities + Equity
+24,200
−24,200

The credit to Goods in Process Inventory reduces that asset balance to reflect that 100,000 units are no longer in production. The cost of these units has been transferred to Finished Goods Inventory, which is recognized as a $24,200 increase in this asset. After this entry is posted, there remains a balance of $2,860 in the Goods in Process Inventory account, which is the amount computed in Step 4 previously. The cost of units transferred from Goods in Process Inventory to Finished Goods Inventory is called the **cost of goods manufactured.** Exhibit 16.18 reveals the activities in the Goods in Process Inventory account for this period. The ending balance of this account equals the cost assigned to the partially completed units in section ③ of Exhibit 16.17.

Goods in Process Inventory			Acct. No. 134			
Date		Explanation	Debit	Credit	Balance	
Mar.	31	Balance			4,620	
Apr.	30	Direct materials usage	9,900		14,520	
	30	Direct labor costs incurred	5,700		20,220	
	30	Factory overhead applied	6,840		27,060	
	30	Transfer completed product to warehouse		24,200	2,860	

EXHIBIT 16.18

Goods in Process Inventory

Arrow line ⑩ in Exhibit 16.4 reflects the sale of finished goods. Assume that GenX sold 106,000 units of Profen this period, and that its beginning inventory of finished goods consisted of 26,000 units with a cost of $6,292. Also assume that its ending finished goods inventory consists of 20,000 units at a cost of $4,840. Using this information, we can compute its cost of goods sold for April as shown in Exhibit 16.19.

Point: We omit the journal entry for sales, but it totals the number of units sold times price per unit.

EXHIBIT 16.19

Cost of Goods Sold

Beginning finished goods inventory...............	$ 6,292
+ Cost of goods manufactured this period	24,200
= Cost of goods available for sale	$30,492
– Ending finished goods inventory...............	4,840
= Cost of goods sold	$25,652

The summary entry to record cost of goods sold for this period follows.

Assets = Liabilities + Equity
–25,652   –25,652

⑩
Cost of Goods Sold.............................	25,652	
Finished Goods Inventory		25,652
To record cost of goods sold for April.		

The Finished Goods Inventory account now appears as shown in Exhibit 16.20.

EXHIBIT 16.20

Finished Goods Inventory

Finished Goods Inventory				Acct. No. 135		
Date		Explanation		Debit	Credit	Balance
Mar.	31	Balance				6,292
Apr.	30	Transfer in cost of goods manufactured		24,200		30,492
	30	Cost of goods sold			25,652	4,840

Summary of Cost Flows   Exhibit 16.21 shows GenX's manufacturing cost flows for April. Each of these cost flows and the entries to record them have been explained. The flow of costs through the accounts reflects the flow of production activities and products.

EXHIBIT 16.21*

Cost Flows through GenX

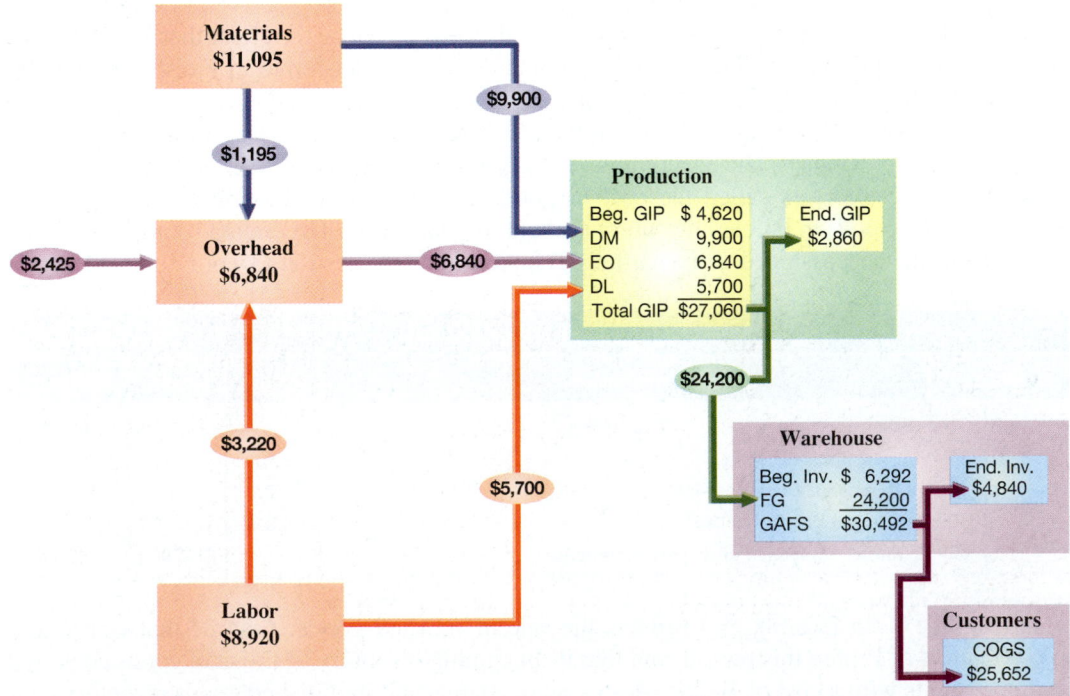

*Abbreviations: GIP (goods in process); DM (direct materials); DL (direct labor); FO (factory overhead);
FG (finished goods); GAFS (goods available for sale); COGS (cost of goods sold).

Trends in Process Operations

Some of the recent trends in process operations are discussed in the following paragraphs.

Process Design Management concerns with production efficiency can lead companies to entirely reorganize production processes. For example, instead of producing different types of computers in a series of departments, a separate work center for each computer can be established in one department. The process cost system is then changed to account for each work center's costs.

Just-in-Time Production Companies are increasingly adopting just-in-time techniques. With a just-in-time inventory system, inventory levels can be minimal. If raw materials are not ordered or received until needed, a Raw Materials Inventory account might be unnecessary. Instead, materials cost is immediately debited to the Goods in Process Inventory account. Similarly, a Finished Goods Inventory account may not be needed. Instead, cost of finished goods may be immediately debited to the Cost of Goods Sold account.

Automation Advances in technology increasingly enable companies to automate their production processes. This allows them to reduce direct labor costs. Reflecting this, some companies focus on **conversion costs per equivalent unit,** which is the combined costs of direct labor and factory overhead per equivalent unit.

Services Service-based businesses are increasingly prevalent. For routine, standardized services like oil changes and simple tax returns, computing costs based on the process is simpler and more useful than a cost per individual job.

Customer Orientation Focus on customer orientation also leads to improved processes. A manufacturer of control devices improved quality and reduced production time by forming teams to study processes and suggest improvements. An ice cream maker studied customer tastes to develop a more pleasing ice cream texture.

 **GLOBAL VIEW**

As part of a series of global environmental goals, the international giant **Anheuser-Busch InBev** set targets to reduce its water usage. The company uses massive amounts of water in beer production and in its cleaning and cooling processes. To meet these goals, the company followed recent trends in process operations. These included extensive redesign of production processes and the use of advanced technology to increase efficiency at wastewater treatment plants. As a result water usage decreased by almost 37 percent in its global operations.

Hybrid Costing System  **Decision Analysis**

This chapter explained the process costing system and contrasted it with the job order costing system. Many organizations use a *hybrid system* that contains features of both process and job order operations. A recent survey of manufacturers revealed that a majority use hybrid systems.

A2 Explain and illustrate a hybrid costing system.

To illustrate, consider a car manufacturer's assembly line. On one hand, the line resembles a process operation in that the assembly steps for each car are nearly identical. On the other hand, the specifications of most cars have several important differences. At the **Ford** Mustang plant, each car assembled on a given day can be different from the previous car and the next car. This means that the costs of materials (subassemblies or components) for each car can differ. Accordingly, while the conversion costs (direct labor and overhead) can be accounted for using a process costing system, the component costs (direct materials) are accounted for using a job order system (separately for each car or type of car).

A hybrid system of processes requires a *hybrid costing system* to properly cost products or services. In the Ford plant, the assembly costs per car are readily determined using process costing. The costs of additional components can then be added to the assembly costs to determine each car's total cost (as in job order costing). To illustrate, consider the following information for a daily assembly process at Ford.

Assembly process costs	
Direct materials	$10,600,000
Direct labor	$5,800,000
Factory overhead	$6,200,000
Number of cars assembled	1,000
Costs of three different types of steering wheels	$240, $330, $480
Costs of three different types of seats	$620, $840, $1,360

The assembly process costs $22,600 per car. Depending on the type of steering wheel and seats the customer requests, the cost of a car can range from $23,460 to $24,440 (a $980 difference).

Today companies are increasingly trying to standardize processes while attempting to meet individual customer needs. To the extent that differences among individual customers' requests are large, understanding the costs to satisfy those requests is important. Thus, monitoring and controlling both process and job order costs are important.

Decision Ethics   Answer – p. 706

Entrepreneur   You operate a process production company making similar products for three different customers. One customer demands 100% quality inspection of products at your location before shipping. The added costs of that inspection are spread across all customers, not just the one demanding it. If you charge the added costs to that customer, you could lose that customer and experience a loss. Moreover, your other two customers have agreed to pay 110% of full costs. What actions (if any) do you take? ■

DEMONSTRATION PROBLEM

Pennsylvania Company produces a product that passes through a single production process. Then completed products are transferred to finished goods in its warehouse. Information related to its manufacturing activities for July follows.

Raw Materials	
Beginning inventory	$100,000
Raw materials purchased on credit	211,400
Direct materials used	(190,000)
Indirect materials used	(51,400)
Ending inventory	$ 70,000

Factory Payroll	
Direct labor incurred	$ 55,500
Indirect labor incurred	50,625
Total payroll (paid in cash)	$106,125

Factory Overhead	
Indirect materials used	$ 51,400
Indirect labor used	50,625
Other overhead costs	71,725
Total factory overhead incurred	$173,750

Factory Overhead Applied	
Overhead applied (200% of direct labor)	$111,000

Production Department	
Beginning goods in process inventory (units)	5,000
Percentage completed—Materials	100%
Percentage completed—Labor and overhead	60%
Beginning goods in process inventory (costs)	
Direct materials used	$ 20,000
Direct labor incurred	9,600
Overhead applied (200% of direct labor)	19,200
Total costs of beginning goods in process	$ 48,800
Units started this period	20,000
Units completed this period	17,000
Ending goods in process inventory (units)	8,000
Percentage completed—Materials	100%
Percentage completed—Labor and overhead	20%

Finished Goods Inventory	
Beginning finished goods inventory	$ 96,400
Cost transferred in from production	321,300
Cost of goods sold	(345,050)
Ending finished goods inventory	$ 72,650

Required

1. Prepare a physical flow reconciliation for July as illustrated in Exhibit 16.12.
2. Compute the equivalent units of production in July for direct materials, direct labor, and factory overhead.
3. Compute the costs per equivalent units of production in July for direct materials, direct labor, and factory overhead.
4. Prepare a report of costs accounted for and a report of costs to account for.
5. Prepare summary journal entries to record the transactions and events of July for (a) raw materials purchases, (b) direct materials usage, (c) indirect materials usage, (d) factory payroll costs, (e) direct labor usage, (f) indirect labor usage, (g) other overhead costs (credit Other Accounts), (h) application of overhead to production, (i) transfer of finished goods from production, and (j) the cost of goods sold.

PLANNING THE SOLUTION

- Track the physical flow to determine the number of units completed in July.
- Compute the equivalent unit of production for direct materials, direct labor, and factory overhead.
- Compute the costs per equivalent unit of production with respect to direct materials, direct labor, and overhead; and determine the cost per unit for each.
- Compute the total cost of the goods transferred to production by using the equivalent units and unit costs. Determine (a) the cost of the beginning in-process inventory, (b) the materials, labor, and overhead costs added to the beginning in-process inventory, and (c) the materials, labor, and overhead costs added to the units started and completed in the month.
- Determine the cost of goods sold using balances in finished goods and cost of units completed this period.
- Use the information to record the summary journal entries for July.

SOLUTION TO DEMONSTRATION PROBLEM

1. Physical flow reconciliation.

Units to Account For		Units Accounted For	
Beginning goods in process inventory	5,000 units	Units completed and transferred out	17,000 units
Units started this period	20,000 units	Ending goods in process inventory.	8,000 units
Total units to account for	**25,000 units**	Total units accounted for	**25,000 units**

reconciled

2. Equivalent units of production.

Equivalent Units of Production	Direct Materials	Direct Labor	Factory Overhead
Equivalent units completed and transferred out	17,000 EUP	17,000 EUP	17,000 EUP
Equivalent units in ending goods in process			
Direct materials (8,000 × 100%)	8,000		
Direct labor (8,000 × 20%)		1,600	
Factory overhead (8,000 × 20%)			1,600
Equivalent units of production	25,000 EUP	18,600 EUP	18,600 EUP

3. Costs per equivalent unit of production.

Costs per Equivalent Unit of Production	Direct Materials	Direct Labor	Factory Overhead
Costs of beginning goods in process	$ 20,000	$ 9,600	$ 19,200
Costs incurred this period	190,000	55,500	111,000*
Total costs	$210,000	$65,100	$130,200
÷ Equivalent units of production (from part 2) . .	25,000 EUP	18,600 EUP	18,600 EUP
= Costs per equivalent unit of production	$8.40 per EUP	$3.50 per EUP	$7.00 per EUP

*Factory overhead applied

4. Reports of costs accounted for and of costs to account for

Report of Costs Accounted For

Cost of units transferred out (cost of goods manufactured)

Direct materials ($8.40 per EUP × 17,000 EUP)	$142,800	
Direct labor ($3.50 per EUP × 17,000 EUP)	59,500	
Factory overhead ($7.00 per EUP × 17,000 EUP)	119,000	
Cost of units completed this period		$ 321,300

Cost of ending goods in process inventory

Direct materials ($8.40 per EUP × 8,000 EUP)	67,200	
Direct labor ($3.50 per EUP × 1,600 EUP)	5,600	
Factory overhead ($7.00 per EUP × 1,600 EUP)	11,200	
Cost of ending goods in process inventory		84,000
Total costs accounted for		**$405,300** ◄

Report of Costs to Account For

Cost of beginning goods in process inventory

Direct materials	$ 20,000	
Direct labor	9,600	
Factory overhead	19,200	$ 48,800

Cost incurred this period

Direct materials	190,000	
Direct labor	55,500	
Factory overhead	111,000	356,500
Total costs to account for		**$405,300** ◄

reconciled

5. Summary journal entries for the transactions and events in July.

a.	Raw Materials Inventory	211,400		**g.**	Factory Overhead	71,725	
	Accounts Payable		211,400		Other Accounts		71,725
	To record raw materials purchases.				*To record other overhead costs.*		
b.	Goods in Process Inventory	190,000		**h.**	Goods in Process Inventory	111,000	
	Raw Materials Inventory		190,000		Factory Overhead		111,000
	To record direct materials usage.				*To record application of overhead.*		
c.	Factory Overhead	51,400		**i.**	Finished Goods Inventory	321,300	
	Raw Materials Inventory		51,400		Goods in Process Inventory		321,300
	To record indirect materials usage.				*To record transfer of finished goods*		
d.	Factory Payroll	106,125			*from production.*		
	Cash		106,125	**j.**	Cost of Goods Sold	345,050	
	To record factory payroll costs.				Finished Goods Inventory		345,050
e.	Goods in Process Inventory	55,500			*To record cost of goods sold.*		
	Factory Payroll		55,500				
	To record direct labor usage.						
f.	Factory Overhead	50,625					
	Factory Payroll		50,625				
	To record indirect labor usage.						

FIFO Method of Process Costing

16A

The **FIFO method** of process costing assigns costs to units assuming a first-in, first-out flow of product. The objectives, concepts, and journal entries (not amounts) are the same as for the weighted-average method, but computation of equivalent units of production and cost assignment are slightly different.

> **C4** Explain and illustrate the accounting for production activity using FIFO.

Exhibit 16A.1 shows selected information from GenX's production department for the month of April. Accounting for a department's activity for a period includes four steps: (1) determine physical flow, (2) compute equivalent units, (3) compute cost per equivalent unit, and (4) determine cost assignment and reconciliation. This appendix describes each of these steps using the FIFO method for process costing.

Beginning goods in process inventory (March 31)	
Units of product	30,000 units
Percentage of completion—Direct materials	100%
Percentage of completion—Direct labor	65%
Direct materials costs	$ 3,300
Direct labor costs	$ 600
Factory overhead costs applied (120% of direct labor)	$ 720
Activities during the current period (April)	
Units started this period	90,000 units
Units transferred out (completed)	100,000 units
Direct materials costs.................................	$ 9,900
Direct labor costs....................................	$ 5,700
Factory overhead costs applied (120% of direct labor)..........	$ 6,840
Ending goods in process inventory (April 30)	
Units of product	20,000 units
Percentage of completion—Direct materials	100%
Percentage of completion—Direct labor	25%

EXHIBIT 16A.1

Production Data

Step 1: Determine Physical Flow of Units   A *physical flow reconciliation* is a report that reconciles (1) the physical units started in a period with (2) the physical units completed in that period. The physical flow reconciliation for GenX is shown in Exhibit 16A.2 for April.

Units to Account For		Units Accounted For	
Beginning goods in process inventory	30,000 units	Units completed and transferred out	100,000 units
Units started this period	90,000 units	Ending goods in process inventory	20,000 units
Total units to account for	**120,000 units**	Total units accounted for	**120,000 units**

reconciled

EXHIBIT 16A.2

Physical Flow Reconciliation

FIFO assumes that the 100,000 units transferred to finished goods during April include the 30,000 units from the beginning goods in process inventory. The remaining 70,000 units transferred out are from units started in April. Of the total 90,000 units started in April, 70,000 were completed, leaving 20,000 units unfinished at period-end.

Step 2: Compute Equivalent Units of Production—FIFO   GenX used its direct materials, direct labor, and overhead both to make complete units of Profen and to start some units that are not yet complete. We need to convert the physical measure of units to equivalent units based on how much of each input has been used. We do this by multiplying the number of physical units by the percentage of processing applied to those units in the current period; this is done for each input (materials, labor, and overhead). The FIFO method accounts for cost flow in a sequential manner—earliest costs are the first to flow out. (This is different from the weighted-average method, which combines prior period costs—those in beginning Goods in Process Inventory—with costs incurred in the current period.)

Three distinct groups of units must be considered in determining the equivalent units of production under the FIFO method: (a) units in beginning Goods in Process Inventory that were completed this period, (b) units started *and* completed this period, and (c) units in ending Goods in Process Inventory. We must determine how much material, labor, and overhead are used for each of these unit groups. These computations are shown in Exhibit 16A.3. The remainder of this section explains these computations.

EXHIBIT 16A.3

Equivalent Units of Production—FIFO

Equivalent Units of Production	Direct Materials	Direct Labor	Factory Overhead
(a) Equivalent units to complete beginning goods in process			
Direct materials (30,000 × 0%)	0 EUP		
Direct labor (30,000 × 35%)		10,500 EUP	
Factory overhead (30,000 × 35%)			10,500 EUP
(b) Equivalent units started and completed*	70,000	70,000	70,000
(c) Equivalent units in ending goods in process			
Direct materials (20,000 × 100%)	20,000		
Direct labor (20,000 × 25%)		5,000	
Factory overhead (20,000 × 25%)			5,000
Equivalent units of production	90,000 EUP	85,500 EUP	85,500 EUP

*Units completed this period . . . .   100,000 units
Less units in beginning goods in process   30,000
Units started and completed this period . . . .   70,000 units

(a) Beginning Goods in Process   Under FIFO, we assume that production first completes any units started in the prior period. There were 30,000 physical units in beginning goods in process inventory. Those units were 100% complete with respect to direct materials as of the end of the prior period. This means that no materials (0%) are needed in April to complete those 30,000 units. So the equivalent units of *materials* to complete beginning goods in process are zero (30,000 × 0%)—see first row under row "(a)" in Exhibit 16A.3. The units in process as of April 1 had already been through 65% of production prior to this period and need only go through the remaining 35% of production. The equivalent units of *labor* to complete the beginning goods in process are 10,500 (30,000 × 35%)—see the second row under row "(a)." This implies that the amount of labor required this period to complete the 30,000 units started in the prior period is the amount of labor needed to make 10,500 units, start-to-finish. Finally, overhead is applied based on direct labor costs, so GenX computes equivalent units for overhead as it would for direct labor.

(b) Units Started and Completed This Period   After completing any beginning goods in process, FIFO assumes that production begins on newly started units. GenX began work on 90,000 new units this period. Of those units, 20,000 remain incomplete at period-end. This means that 70,000 of the units started in April were completed in April. These complete units have received 100% of materials, labor, and overhead. Exhibit 16A.3 reflects this by including 70,000 equivalent units (70,000 × 100%) of materials, labor, and overhead in its equivalent units of production—see row "(b)."

(c) Ending Goods in Process   The 20,000 units started in April that GenX was not able to complete by period-end consumed materials, labor, and overhead. Specifically, those 20,000 units received 100% of materials and, therefore, the equivalent units of materials in ending goods in process inventory are 20,000 (20,000 × 100%)—see the first row under row "(c)." For labor and overhead, the units in ending goods in process were 25% complete in production. This means the equivalent units of labor and overhead for those units are 5,000 (20,000 × 25%) as GenX incurs labor and overhead costs uniformly throughout its production process. Finally, for each input (direct materials, direct labor, and factory overhead), the equivalent units for each of the unit groups (a), (b), and (c) are added to determine the total equivalent units of production with respect to each—see the final row in Exhibit 16A.3.

Step 3: Compute Cost per Equivalent Unit—FIFO   To compute cost per equivalent unit, we take the product costs (for each of direct materials, direct labor, and factory overhead from Exhibit 16A.1) added in April and divide by the equivalent units of production from step 2. Exhibit 16A.4 illustrates these computations.

EXHIBIT 16A.4

Cost per Equivalent Unit of Production—FIFO

Cost per Equivalent Unit of Production	Direct Materials	Direct Labor	Factory Overhead
Costs incurred this period	$9,900	$5,700	$6,840
÷ Equivalent units of production (from Step 2)	90,000 EUP	85,500 EUP	85,500 EUP
Cost per equivalent unit of production	$0.11 per EUP	$0.067 per EUP	$0.08 per EUP

It is essential to compute costs per equivalent unit for *each* input because production inputs are added at different times in the process. The FIFO method computes the cost per equivalent unit based solely on this period's EUP and costs (unlike the weighted-average method, which adds in the costs of the beginning goods in process inventory).

Step 4: Assign and Reconcile Costs   The equivalent units determined in step 2 and the cost per equivalent unit computed in step 3 are both used to assign costs (1) to units that the production department completed and transferred to finished goods and (2) to units that remain in process at period-end.

In Exhibit 16A.5, under the section for cost of units transferred out, we see that the cost of units completed in April includes the $4,620 cost carried over from March for work already applied to the 30,000 units that make up beginning Goods in Process Inventory, plus the $1,544 incurred in April to complete those units. This section also includes the $17,990 of cost assigned to the 70,000 units started and completed this period. Thus, the total cost of goods manufactured in April is $24,154 ($4,620 + $1,544 + $17,990). The average cost per unit for goods completed in April is $0.242 ($24,154 ÷ 100,000 completed units).

Cost of units transferred out (cost of goods manufactured)		
Cost of beginning goods in process inventory		$ 4,620
Cost to complete beginning goods in process		
Direct materials ($0.11 per EUP × 0 EUP)	$ 0	
Direct labor ($0.067 per EUP × 10,500 EUP)	704	
Factory overhead ($0.08 per EUP × 10,500 EUP)	840	1,544
Cost of units started and completed this period		
Direct materials ($0.11 per EUP × 70,000 EUP)	7,700	
Direct labor ($0.067 per EUP × 70,000 EUP)	4,690	
Factory overhead ($0.08 per EUP × 70,000 EUP)	5,600	17,990
Total cost of units finished this period		24,154
Cost of ending goods in process inventory		
Direct materials ($0.11 per EUP × 20,000 EUP)	2,200	
Direct labor ($0.067 per EUP × 5,000 EUP)	335	
Factory overhead ($0.08 per EUP × 5,000 EUP)	400	
Total cost of ending goods in process inventory		2,935
Total costs accounted for		**$27,089**

EXHIBIT 16A.5

Report of Costs Accounted For—FIFO

The computation for cost of ending goods in process inventory is in the lower part of Exhibit 16A.5. The cost of units in process includes materials, labor, and overhead costs corresponding to the percentage of these resources applied to those incomplete units in April. That cost of $2,935 ($2,200 + $335 + $400) also is the ending balance for the Goods in Process Inventory account.

Management verifies that the total costs assigned to units transferred out and units still in process equal the total costs incurred by production. We reconcile the costs accounted for (in Exhibit 16A.5) to the costs that production was charged for as shown in Exhibit 16A.6.

Cost of beginning goods in process inventory		
Direct materials	$3,300	
Direct labor	600	
Factory overhead	720	$ 4,620
Costs incurred this period		
Direct materials	9,900	
Direct labor	5,700	
Factory overhead	6,840	22,440
Total costs to account for		**$27,060**

EXHIBIT 16A.6

Report of Costs to Account For—FIFO

The production manager is responsible for $27,060 in costs: $4,620 that had been assigned to the department's Goods in Process Inventory as of April 1 plus $22,440 of materials, labor, and overhead costs the department incurred in April. At period-end, the manager must identify where those costs were assigned. The production manager can report that $24,154 of cost was assigned to units completed in April and $2,935 was assigned to units still in process at period-end. The sum of these amounts is $29 different from the $27,060 total costs incurred by production due to rounding in step 3—rounding errors are common and not a concern.

The final report is the process cost summary, which summarizes key information from Exhibits 16A.3, 16A.4, 16A.5, and 16A.6. Reasons for the summary are to (1) help managers control and monitor costs, (2) help upper management assess department manager performance, and (3) provide cost information for financial reporting. The process cost summary, using FIFO, for GenX is in Exhibit 16A.7. Section ◇ lists

EXHIBIT 16A.7

Process Cost Summary

GenX COMPANY
Process Cost Summary
For Month Ended April 30, 2011

Costs charged to production

Costs of beginning goods in process inventory

Direct materials..	$3,300	
Direct labor	600	
Factory overhead	720	$ 4,620

① Costs incurred this period

Direct materials	9,900	
Direct labor	5,700	
Factory overhead	6,840	22,440
Total costs to account for		$27,060 ◄

Unit cost information

Units to account for		Units accounted for	
Beginning goods in process.........	30,000	Transferred out..................	100,000
Units started this period...........	90,000	Ending goods in process	20,000
Total units to account for	120,000	Total units accounted for	120,000

Equivalent units of production	Direct Materials	Direct Labor	Factory Overhead
Equivalent units to complete beginning goods in process			
Direct materials (30,000 × 0%)	0 EUP		
Direct labor (30,000 × 35%)		10,500 EUP	
② Factory overhead (30,000 × 35%)			10,500 EUP
Equivalent units started and completed	70,000	70,000	70,000
Equivalent units in ending goods in process			
Direct materials (20,000 × 100%)	20,000		
Direct labor (20,000 × 25%)		5,000	
Factory overhead (20,000 × 25%)			5000
Equivalent units of production	90,000 EUP	85,500 EUP	85,500 EUP

Cost per equivalent unit of production	Direct Materials	Direct Labor	Factory Overhead
Costs incurred this period	$9,900	$5,700	$6,840
÷ Equivalent units of production	90,000 EUP	85,500 EUP	85,500 EUP
Cost per equivalent unit of production	$0.11 per EUP	$0.067 per EUP	$0.08 per EUP

Cost assignment and reconciliation

(cost of units completed and transferred out)

Cost of beginning goods in process		$ 4,620
Cost to complete beginning goods in process		
Direct materials ($0.11 per EUP × 0 EUP)	$ 0	
Direct labor ($0.067 per EUP × 10,500 EUP).............................	704	
Factory overhead ($0.08 per EUP × 10,500 EUP)	840	1,544
Cost of units started and completed this period		
③ Direct materials ($0.11 per EUP × 70,000 EUP)	7,700	
Direct labor ($0.067 per EUP × 70,000 EUP).............................	4,690	
Factory overhead ($0.08 per EUP × 70,000 EUP)	5,600	17,990
Total cost of units finished this period		24,154

Cost of ending goods in process

Direct materials ($0.11 per EUP × 20,000 EUP)	2,200	
Direct labor ($0.067 per EUP × 5,000 EUP)................................	335	
Factory overhead ($0.08 per EUP × 5,000 EUP)	400	
Total cost of ending goods in process......................................		2,935
Total costs accounted for		$27,089* ◄

reconciled

*$29 difference due to rounding

the total costs charged to the department, including direct materials, direct labor, and overhead costs incurred, as well as the cost of the beginning goods in process inventory. Section ② describes the equivalent units of production for the department. Equivalent units for materials, labor, and overhead are in separate columns. It also reports direct materials, direct labor, and overhead costs per equivalent unit. Section ③ allocates total costs among units worked on in the period.

Decision Maker   Answer — p. 706

Cost Manager   As cost manager for an electronics manufacturer, you apply a process costing system using FIFO. Your company plans to adopt a just-in-time system and eliminate inventories. What is the impact of the use of FIFO (versus the weighted-average method) given these plans? ■

Summary

C1 Explain process operations and the way they differ from job order operations. Process operations produce large quantities of similar products or services by passing them through a series of processes, or steps, in production. Like job order operations, they combine direct materials, direct labor, and overhead in the operations. Unlike job order operations that assign the responsibility for each job to a manager, process operations assign the responsibility for each *process* to a manager.

C2 Define and compute equivalent units and explain their use in process cost accounting. Equivalent units of production measure the activity of a process as the number of units that would be completed in a period if all effort had been applied to units that were started and finished. This measure of production activity is used to compute the cost per equivalent unit and to assign costs to finished goods and goods in process inventory. To compute equivalent units, determine the number of units that would have been finished if all materials (or labor or overhead) had been used to produce units that were started and completed during the period. The costs incurred by a process are divided by its equivalent units to yield cost per unit.

C3 Define and prepare a process cost summary and describe its purposes. A process cost summary reports on the activities of a production process or department for a period. It describes the costs charged to the department, the equivalent units of production for the department, and the costs assigned to the output. The report aims to (1) help managers control their departments, (2) help factory managers evaluate department managers' performances, and (3) provide cost information for financial statements. A process cost summary includes the physical flow of units, equivalent units of production, costs per equivalent unit, and a cost reconciliation. It reports the units and costs to account for during the period and how they were accounted for during the period. In terms of units, the summary includes the beginning goods in process inventory and the units started during the month. These units are accounted for in terms of the goods completed and transferred out, and the ending goods in process inventory. With respect to costs, the summary includes materials, labor, and overhead costs assigned to the process during the period. It shows how these costs are assigned to goods completed and transferred out, and to ending goods in process inventory.

C4ᴬ Explain and illustrate the accounting for production activity using FIFO. The FIFO method for process costing is applied and illustrated to (1) report the physical flow of units, (2) compute the equivalent units of production, (3) compute the cost per equivalent unit of production, and (4) assign and reconcile costs.

A1 Compare process cost accounting and job order cost accounting. Process and job order manufacturing operations are similar in that both combine materials, labor, and factory overhead to produce products or services. They differ in the way they are organized and managed. In job order operations, the job order cost accounting system assigns materials, labor, and overhead to specific jobs. In process operations, the process cost accounting system assigns materials, labor, and overhead to specific processes. The total costs associated with each process are then divided by the number of units passing through that process to get cost per equivalent unit. The costs per equivalent unit for all processes are added to determine the total cost per unit of a product or service.

A2 Explain and illustrate a hybrid costing system. A hybrid costing system contains features of both job order and process costing systems. Generally, certain direct materials are accounted for by individual products as in job order costing, but direct labor and overhead costs are accounted for similar to process costing.

P1 Record the flow of direct materials costs in process cost accounting. Materials purchased are debited to a Raw Materials Inventory account. As direct materials are issued to processes, they are separately accumulated in a Goods in Process Inventory account for that process.

P2 Record the flow of direct labor costs in process cost accounting. Direct labor costs are initially debited to the Factory Payroll account. The total amount in it is then assigned to the Goods in Process Inventory account pertaining to each process.

P3 Record the flow of factory overhead costs in process cost accounting. The different factory overhead items are first accumulated in the Factory Overhead account and are then allocated, using a predetermined overhead rate, to the different processes. The allocated amount is debited to the Goods in Process Inventory account pertaining to each process.

P4 Record the transfer of completed goods to Finished Goods Inventory and Cost of Goods Sold. As units complete the final process and are eventually sold, their accumulated cost is transferred to Finished Goods Inventory and finally to Cost of Goods Sold.

Guidance Answers to Decision Maker and Decision Ethics

Budget Officer   By instructing you to classify a majority of costs as indirect, the manager is passing some of his department's costs to a common overhead pool that other departments will partially absorb. Since overhead costs are allocated on the basis of direct labor for this company and the new department has a relatively low direct labor cost, the new department will be assigned less overhead. Such action suggests unethical behavior by this manager. You must object to such reclassification. If this manager refuses to comply, you must inform someone in a more senior position.

Entrepreneur   By spreading the added quality-related costs across three customers, the entrepreneur is probably trying to remain competitive with respect to the customer that demands the 100%

quality inspection. Moreover, the entrepreneur is partly covering the added costs by recovering two-thirds of them from the other two customers who are paying 110% of total costs. This act likely breaches the trust placed by the two customers in this entrepreneur's application of its costing system. The costing system should be changed, and the entrepreneur should consider renegotiating the pricing and/or quality test agreement with this one customer (at the risk of losing this currently loss-producing customer).

Cost Manager   Differences between the FIFO and weighted-average methods are greatest when large work in process inventories exist and when costs fluctuate. The method used if inventories are eliminated does not matter; both produce identical costs.

Guidance Answers to Quick Checks

1. *c*

2. When a company produces large quantities of similar products/ services, a process cost system is often more suitable.

3. *b*

4. The costs are direct materials, direct labor, and overhead.

5. A goods in process inventory account is needed for *each* production department.

6. *a*

7. Equivalent units with respect to direct labor are the number of units that would have been produced if all labor had been used on units that were started and finished during the period.

8.

Units completed and transferred out	58,000 EUP
Units of ending goods in process	
Direct labor (6,000 × 1/3)	2,000 EUP
Units of production	60,000 EUP

9. The first section shows the costs charged to the department. The second section describes the equivalent units produced by the department. The third section shows the assignment of total costs to units worked on during the period.

Key Terms   mhhe.com/wildFINMAN4e

Conversion costs per equivalent unit (p. 697)

Cost of goods manufactured (p. 695)

Equivalent units of production (EUP) (p. 689)

FIFO method (p. 701)

Job order cost accounting system (p. 685)

Materials consumption report (p. 686)

Process cost accounting system (p. 685)

Process cost summary (p. 694)

Process operations (p. 682)

Weighted-average method (p. 692)

Multiple Choice Quiz   Answers on p. 723   mhhe.com/wildFINMAN4e

Additional Quiz Questions are available at the book's Website.

1. Equivalent units of production are equal to
- **a.** Physical units that were completed this period from all effort being applied to them.
- **b.** The number of units introduced into the process this period.
- **c.** The number of finished units actually completed this period.
- **d.** The number of units that could have been started and completed given the cost incurred.
- **e.** The number of units in the process at the end of the period.

2. Recording the cost of raw materials purchased for use in a process costing system includes a
- **a.** Credit to Raw Materials Inventory.
- **b.** Debit to Goods in Process Inventory.
- **c.** Debit to Factory Overhead.
- **d.** Credit to Factory Overhead.
- **e.** Debit to Raw Materials Inventory.

3. The production department started the month with a beginning goods in process inventory of $20,000. During the month, it was assigned the following costs: direct materials, $152,000; direct labor, $45,000; overhead applied at the rate of 40% of direct labor cost. Inventory with a cost of $218,000 was transferred to finished goods. The ending balance of goods in process inventory is
   a. $330,000.
   b. $ 17,000.
   c. $220,000.
   d. $112,000.
   e. $118,000.

4. A company's beginning work in process inventory consists of 10,000 units that are 20% complete with respect to direct labor costs. A total of 40,000 units are completed this period. There are 15,000 units in goods in process, one-third complete for direct labor, at period-end. The equivalent units of production (EUP) with respect to direct labor at period-end, assuming the weighted-average method, are
   a. 45,000 EUP.
   b. 40,000 EUP.
   c. 5,000 EUP.
   d. 37,000 EUP.
   e. 43,000 EUP.

5. Assume the same information as in question 4. Also assume that beginning work in process had $6,000 in direct labor cost and that $84,000 in direct labor is added during this period. What is the cost per EUP for labor?
   a. $0.50 per EUP
   b. $1.87 per EUP
   c. $2.00 per EUP
   d. $2.10 per EUP
   e. $2.25 per EUP

> *Assume the weighted-average inventory method is used for all assignments unless stated differently.*

^{A} *Superscript letter A denotes assignments based on Appendix 16A.*

🔲 Icon denotes assignments that involve decision making.

Discussion Questions

1. 🔲 Can services be delivered by means of process operations? Support your answer with an example.

2. 🔲 What is the main factor for a company in choosing between the job order costing and process costing accounting systems? Give two likely applications of each system.

3. Identify the control document for materials flow when a materials requisition slip is not used.

4. The focus in a job order costing system is the job or batch. Identify the main focus in process costing.

5. Are the journal entries that match cost flows to product flows in process costing primarily the same or much different than those in job order costing? Explain.

6. 🔲 Explain in simple terms the notion of equivalent units of production (EUP). Why is it necessary to use EUP in process costing?

7. 🔲 What are the two main inventory methods used in process costing? What are the differences between these methods?

8. 🔲 Why is it possible for direct labor in process operations to include the labor of employees who do not work directly on products or services?

9. Assume that a company produces a single product by processing it first through a single production department. Direct labor costs flow through what accounts in this company's process cost system?

10. After all labor costs for a period are allocated, what balance should remain in the Factory Payroll account?

11. 🔲 Is it possible to have under- or overapplied overhead costs in a process cost accounting system? Explain.

12. Explain why equivalent units of production for both direct labor and overhead can be the same as, and why they can be different from, equivalent units for direct materials.

13. Companies such as **Palm** apply process operations. List the four steps in accounting for production activity in a reporting period (for process operations). **Palm**

14. Companies such as **Nokia** commonly prepare a process cost summary. What purposes does a process cost summary serve? **NOKIA**

15. 🔲 Are there situations where **Research In Motion** can use process costing? Identify at least one and explain it. *RIM*

16. 🔲 **Apple** produces iMacs with a multiple production line. Identify and list some of its production processing steps and departments. **Apple**

📕 **connect**™ ───────────────────────────────────

For each of the following products and services, indicate whether it is most likely produced in a process operation or in a job order operation.

1. Luxury cars
2. Vanilla ice cream
3. Apple juice
4. Tennis courts

QUICK STUDY

QS 16-1
Process vs. job order operations

C1

QS 16-2
Recording costs of direct materials   P1

Sturdy Packaging makes cardboard shipping cartons in a single operation. This period, Sturdy purchased $125,000 in raw materials. Its production department requisitioned $90,000 of those materials for use in producing cartons. Prepare journal entries to record its (1) purchase of raw materials and (2) requisition of direct materials.

QS 16-3
Recording costs of direct labor
P2

Refer to the information in QS 16-2. Sturdy Packaging incurred $165,000 in factory payroll costs, of which $110,000 was direct labor. Prepare journal entries to record its (1) total factory payroll incurred and (2) direct labor used in production.

QS 16-4
Recording costs of factory overhead
P3

Refer to the information in QS 16-2 and QS 16-3. Sturdy Packaging requisitioned $62,000 of indirect materials from its raw materials and used $55,000 of indirect labor in its production of boxes. Also, it incurred $220,000 of other factory overhead costs. It applies factory overhead at the rate of 130% of direct labor costs. Prepare journal entries to record its (1) indirect materials requisitioned, (2) indirect labor used in production, (3) other factory overhead costs incurred, and (4) application of overhead to production.

QS 16-5
Recording transfer of costs to finished goods   P4

Refer to the information in QS 16-2, QS 16-3, and QS 16-4. Sturdy Packaging completed 175,000 boxes costing $335,000 and transferred them to finished goods. Prepare its journal entry to record the transfer of the boxes from production to finished goods inventory.

QS 16-6
Computing equivalent units of production
C2

The following refers to units processed in Heath Printing's binding department in June. Compute the total equivalent units of production with respect to labor for June using the weighted-average inventory method.

	Units of Product	Percent of Labor Added
Beginning goods in process	150,000	85%
Goods started	310,000	100
Goods completed	340,000	100
Ending goods in process	120,000	25

QS 16-7
Computing EUP cost   C2

The cost of beginning inventory plus the costs added during the period should equal the cost of units _____ plus the cost of _____ .

QS 16-8
Hybrid costing   A2

Explain how a car maintenance and repair garage might use a hybrid costing system.

QS 16-9^A
Computing equivalent units—FIFO   C4

Refer to QS 16-6 and compute the total equivalent units of production with respect to labor for June using the FIFO inventory method.

QS 16-10
Steps in process costing
C3

Put the four steps in accounting for production activities in the order in which they would occur.
  a. Assign and reconcile costs
  b. Compute the cost per equivalent unit
  c. Compute equivalent units of production
  d. Determine physical flow of units

List the headings of the three major sections of a process cost summary. Refer to Exhibit 16.17.

QS 16-11
Process cost summary   **C3**

Anheuser-Busch InBev is attempting to reduce its water usage. How could a company manager use a process cost summary to determine if the program to reduce water usage is successful?

QS 16-12
Process cost summary   **C3**

Label each statement below as either true ("T") or false ("F").

1. Job order and process operations both combine materials, labor, and overhead in producing products or services.
2. Costs per job are computed in both job order and process costing systems.
3. Service companies are not able to use process costing.
4. The cost per equivalent unit is computed as the total costs of a process divided by the number of equivalent units passing through that process.

QS 16-13
Process vs. job order costing
A1

Mc Graw Hill connect

Match each of the following items A through G with the best numbered description of its purpose.

A. Process cost summary
B. Equivalent units of production
C. Goods in Process Inventory account
D. Raw Materials Inventory account

E. Materials requisition
F. Finished Goods Inventory account
G. Factory Overhead account

_____ **1.** Holds costs of materials until they are used in production or as factory overhead.
_____ **2.** Holds costs of indirect materials, indirect labor, and similar costs until assigned to production.
_____ **3.** Holds costs of direct materials, direct labor, and applied overhead until products are transferred from production to finished goods (or another department).
_____ **4.** Standardizes partially completed units into equivalent completed units.
_____ **5.** Holds costs of finished products until sold to customers.
_____ **6.** Describes the activity and output of a production department for a period.
_____ **7.** Notifies the materials manager to send materials to a production department.

EXERCISES

Exercise 16-1
Terminology in process cost accounting

C1   A1   P1   P2   P3

Prepare journal entries to record its following production activities.

1. Purchased $80,000 of raw materials on credit.
2. Used $34,000 of direct materials in production.
3. Used $41,000 of indirect materials.

Exercise 16-2
Recording costs of materials
P1

Prepare journal entries to record the following production activities.

1. Incurred total labor cost of $77,000, which is paid in cash.
2. Used $58,000 of direct labor in production.
3. Used $19,000 of indirect labor.

Exercise 16-3
Recording costs of labor
P2

Refer to information in Exercise 16-3. Prepare journal entries to record the following production activities.

1. Paid overhead costs (other than indirect materials and indirect labor) of $22,000.
2. Applied overhead at 90% of direct labor costs.

Exercise 16-4
Recording overhead costs
P3

Prepare journal entries to record the following production activities.

1. Transferred completed products with a cost of $137,000 to finished goods inventory.
2. Sold $450,000 of products on credit. Their cost is $150,000.

Exercise 16-5
Recording cost of completed goods
P4

Exercise 16-6

Recording cost flows in a process cost system

P1 P2 P3 P4

Lowes Lumber produces bagged bark for use in landscaping. Production involves packaging bark chips in plastic bags in a bagging department. The following information describes production operations for October.

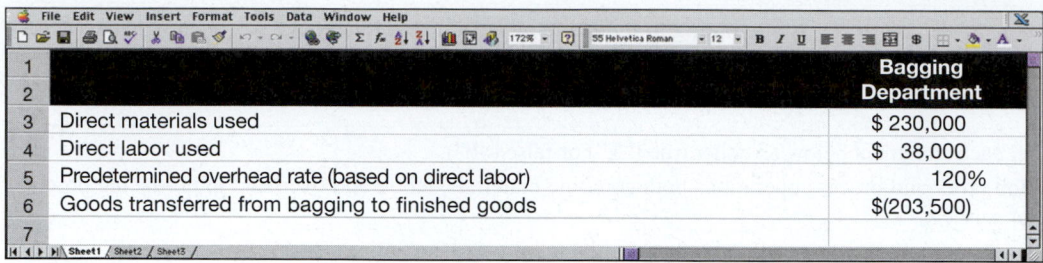

		Bagging Department
3	Direct materials used	$ 230,000
4	Direct labor used	$ 38,000
5	Predetermined overhead rate (based on direct labor)	120%
6	Goods transferred from bagging to finished goods	$(203,500)

The company's revenue for the month totaled $450,000 from credit sales, and its cost of goods sold for the month is $250,000. Prepare summary journal entries dated October 31 to record its October production activities for (1) direct material usage, (2) direct labor usage, (3) overhead allocation, (4) goods transfer from production to finished goods, and (5) sales.

Check   (3) Cr. Factory Overhead, $45,600

Exercise 16-7

Interpretation of journal entries in process cost accounting

P1 P2 P3 P4

The following journal entries are recorded in Kiera Co.'s process cost accounting system. Kiera produces handbags and scarves. Overhead is applied to production based on direct labor cost for the period. Prepare a brief explanation (including any overhead rates applied) for each journal entry *a* through *j*.

a.	Raw Materials Inventory	54,000	
	Accounts Payable		54,000
b.	Goods in Process Inventory	44,000	
	Raw Materials Inventory		44,000
c.	Factory Payroll	36,000	
	Cash		36,000
d.	Goods in Process Inventory	28,000	
	Factory Payroll		28,000
e.	Factory Overhead	10,500	
	Cash		10,500
f.	Factory Overhead	3,000	
	Raw Materials Inventory		3,000

g.	Factory Overhead	8,000	
	Factory Payroll		8,000
h.	Goods in Process Inventory	35,000	
	Factory Overhead		35,000
i.	Finished Goods Inventory	98,000	
	Goods in Process Inventory		98,000
j.	Accounts Receivable	256,000	
	Sales		256,000
	Cost of Goods Sold	104,000	
	Finished Goods Inventory		104,000

Exercise 16-8

Computing equivalent units of production—weighted average

C2

During April, the production department of a process manufacturing system completed a number of units of a product and transferred them to finished goods. Of these transferred units, 37,500 were in process in the production department at the beginning of April and 150,000 were started and completed in April. April's beginning inventory units were 60% complete with respect to materials and 40% complete with respect to labor. At the end of April, 51,250 additional units were in process in the production department and were 80% complete with respect to materials and 30% complete with respect to labor.

1. Compute the number of units transferred to finished goods.

Check   (2) EUP for materials, 228,500

2. Compute the number of equivalent units with respect to both materials used and labor used in the production department for April using the weighted-average method.

Exercise 16-9

Costs assigned to output and inventories—weighted average

C2 P4

The production department described in Exercise 16-8 had $531,480 of direct materials and $407,689 of direct labor cost charged to it during April. Also, its beginning inventory included $74,075 of direct materials cost and $28,493 of direct labor.

1. Compute the direct materials cost and the direct labor cost per equivalent unit for the department.

Check   (1) $2.65 per EUP of direct materials

2. Using the weighted-average method, assign April's costs to the department's output—specifically, its units transferred to finished goods and its ending goods in process inventory.

Refer to the information in Exercise 16-8 to compute the number of equivalent units with respect to both materials used and labor used in the production department for April using the FIFO method.

Exercise 16-10^A
Computing equivalent units of
production—FIFO **C4**

Refer to the information in Exercise 16-8 and complete its parts (1) and (2) using the FIFO method.

Exercise 16-11^A
Costs assigned to output—FIFO

C4 P4

The production department in a process manufacturing system completed 191,500 units of product and transferred them to finished goods during a recent period. Of these units, 31,500 were in process at the beginning of the period. The other 160,000 units were started and completed during the period. At period-end, 29,500 units were in process. Compute the department's equivalent units of production with respect to direct materials under each of three separate assumptions:

Exercise 16-12
Equivalent units computed—
weighted average

C2

1. All direct materials are added to products when processing begins.
2. Direct materials are added to products evenly throughout the process. Beginning goods in process inventory was 40% complete, and ending goods in process inventory was 75% complete.
3. One-half of direct materials is added to products when the process begins and the other half is added when the process is 75% complete as to direct labor. Beginning goods in process inventory is 40% complete as to direct labor, and ending goods in process inventory is 60% complete as to direct labor.

Check (3) EUP for materials, 206,250

Refer to the information in Exercise 16-12 and complete it for each of the three separate assumptions using the FIFO method for process costing.

Exercise 16-13^A
Equivalent units computed—
FIFO **C4**

Check (3) EUP for materials, 190,500

The following flowchart shows the August production activity of the The Spade Company. Use the amounts shown on the flowchart to compute the missing four numbers identified by blanks.

Exercise 16-14
Flowchart of costs for a process
operation **P1 P2 P3 P4**

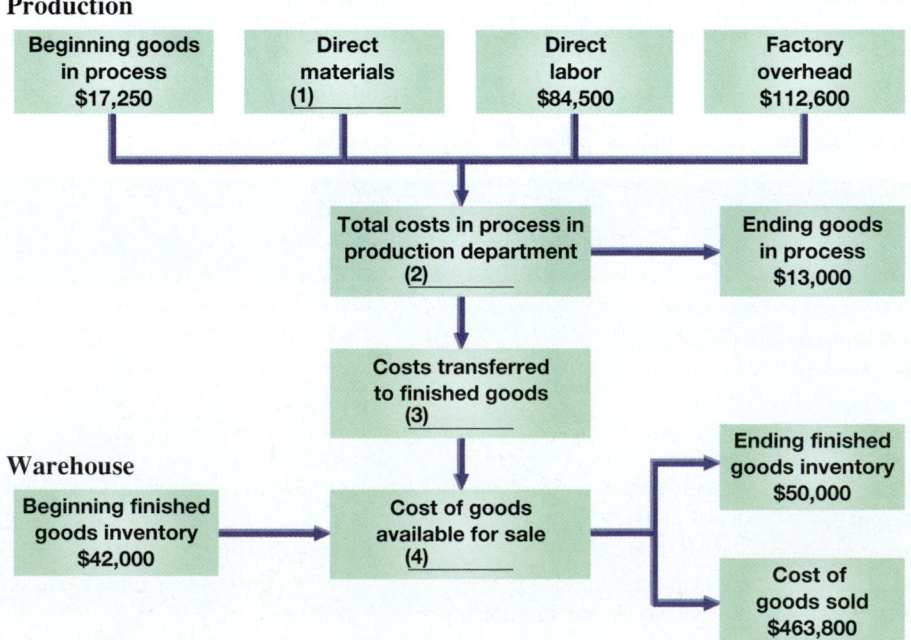

Exercise 16-15
Completing a process cost summary

C3

The following partially completed process cost summary describes the May production activities of Raman Company. Its production output is sent to its warehouse for shipping. Prepare its process cost summary using the weighted-average method.

Equivalent Units of Production	Direct Materials	Direct Labor	Factory Overhead
Units transferred out	128,000	128,000	128,000
Units of ending goods in process	10,000	6,000	6,000
Equivalent units of production	138,000	134,000	134,000

Costs per EUP	Direct Materials	Direct Labor	Factory Overhead
Costs of beginning goods in process	$ 37,100	$ 1,520	$ 3,040
Costs incurred this period	715,000	125,780	251,560
Total costs	$752,100	$127,300	$254,600

Units in beginning goods in process	8,000
Units started this period	130,000
Units completed and transferred out	128,000
Units in ending goods in process	10,000

Exercise 16-16
Process costing—weighted average C3

Ebony Company uses the weighted-average method of process costing to assign production costs to its products. Information for April follows. Assume that all materials are added at the beginning of its production process, and that direct labor and factory overhead are added uniformly throughout the process.

Goods in process inventory, April 1 (4,000 units, 100% complete with respect to direct materials, 80% complete with respect to direct labor and overhead; includes $90,000 of direct material cost, $51,200 in direct labor cost, $61,440 overhead cost)	$202,640
Units started in April	56,000
Units completed and transferred to finished goods inventory	46,000
Goods in process inventory, April 30 (? units, 100% complete with respect to direct materials, 40% complete with respect to direct labor and overhead)	?
Costs incurred in April	
Direct materials	$750,000
Direct labor	$310,000
Overhead applied at 120% of direct labor cost	?

Required

Fill in the blanks labeled *a* through *uu* in the following process cost summary.

EBONY COMPANY Process Cost Summary For Month Ended April 30		
Costs Charged to Production		
Costs of beginning goods in process		
Direct materials	$ 90,000	
Direct labor	51,200	
Factory overhead	61,440	$202,640
Costs incurred this period		
Direct materials	$750,000	
Direct labor	310,000	
Factory overhead	(a)_____	(b)_____
Total costs to account for		(c)_____

Check (c) $1,634,640

[continued on next page]

[continued from previous page]

Unit Cost Information

Units to account for		Units accounted for	
Beginning goods in process	4,000	Completed and transferred out	46,000
Units started this period	56,000	Ending goods in process	(d)_____
Total units to account for	(e)_____	Total units accounted for	(f)_____

Equivalent Units of Production (EUP)			**Direct Materials**	**Direct Labor**	**Factory Overhead**
Units completed and transferred out			(g)_____EUP	(h)_____EUP	(i)_____EUP
Units of ending goods in process					
Materials	(j)_____	× 100%	(k)_____EUP		
Direct labor	(l)_____	× 40%		(m)_____EUP	
Factory overhead	(n)_____	× 40%			(o)_____EUP
Equivalent units of production (EUP)			(p)_____EUP	(q)_____EUP	(r)_____EUP

Cost per EUP	**Direct Materials**	**Direct Labor**	**Factory Overhead**
Costs of beginning goods in process	$ 90,000	$ 51,200	$61,440
Costs incurred this period	750,000	310,000	(s)_____
Total costs	$840,000	$361,200	(t)_____
÷ EUP	(u)_____	(v)_____	(w)_____
Cost per EUP	(x)_____	(y)_____	(z)_____

Check (z) $8.40 per EUP

Cost Assignment and Reconciliation

Costs transferred out		Cost/EUP	×	EUP	
Direct materials		(aa)_____	×	(bb)_____	(cc)_____
Direct labor		(dd)_____	×	(ee)_____	(ff)_____
Factory overhead		(gg)_____	×	(hh)_____	(ii)_____
Costs of goods completed and transferred out					(jj)_____
Costs of ending goods in process					
Direct materials		(kk)_____	×	(ll)_____	(mm)_____
Direct labor		(nn)_____	×	(oo)_____	(pp)_____
Factory overhead		(qq)_____	×	(rr)_____	(ss)_____
Costs of ending goods in process					(tt)_____
Total costs accounted for					(uu)_____

For each of the following products and services, indicate whether it is most likely produced in a process operation or in a job order operation.

1. Door hardware
2. Cut flower arrangements
3. House paints
4. Concrete swimming pools
5. Custom tailored dresses
6. Grand pianos
7. Table lamps
8. Beach towels
9. Bolts and nuts
10. Lawn chairs
11. Headphones
12. Designed patio

Exercise 16-17
Matching of product to cost accounting system

C1

Label each item *a* through *h* below as a feature of either a job order or process operation.

a. Routine, repetitive procedures
b. Custom orders
c. Low production volume
d. Heterogeneous products and services
e. Low product flexibility
f. Low product standardization
g. Focus on individual batch
h. Focus on standardized units

Exercise 16-18
Compare process and job order operations

C1

Explain a hybrid costing system. Identify a product or service operation that might well fit a hybrid costing system.

Exercise 16-19
Hybrid costing system

A2

PROBLEM SET A

Problem 16-1A
Production cost flow and measurement; journal entries

P1 P2 P3 P4

Edison Company manufactures wool blankets and accounts for product costs using process costing. The following information is available regarding its May inventories.

	Beginning Inventory	Ending Inventory
Raw materials inventory	$ 28,000	$ 25,500
Goods in process inventory	220,750	252,000
Finished goods inventory	319,000	277,000

The following additional information describes the company's production activities for May.

Raw materials purchases (on credit)	$ 135,000
Factory payroll cost (paid in cash)	791,500
Other overhead cost (Other Accounts credited)	43,000
Materials used	
Direct	$ 93,500
Indirect	31,000
Labor used	
Direct	$ 352,000
Indirect	439,500
Overhead rate as a percent of direct labor	110%
Sales (on credit)	$1,500,000

Check (1b) Cost of goods sold $843,450

Required

1. Compute the cost of (a) products transferred from production to finished goods, and (b) goods sold.
2. Prepare summary journal entries dated May 31 to record the following production activities during May: (a) raw materials purchases, (b) direct materials usage, (c) indirect materials usage, (d) payroll costs, (e) direct labor costs, (f) indirect labor costs, (g) other overhead costs, (h) overhead applied, (i) goods transferred from production to finished goods, and (j) sale of finished goods.

Problem 16-2A
Cost per equivalent unit; costs assigned to products

C2 C3

mhhe.com/wildFINMAN4e

Fairfax Company uses weighted-average process costing to account for its production costs. Direct labor is added evenly throughout the process. Direct materials are added at the beginning of the process. During September, the company transferred 735,000 units of product to finished goods. At the end of September, the goods in process inventory consists of 207,000 units that are 90% complete with respect to labor. Beginning inventory had $244,920 of direct materials and $69,098 of direct labor cost. The direct labor cost added in September is $1,312,852, and the direct materials cost added is $1,639,080.

Required

1. Determine the equivalent units of production with respect to (a) direct labor and (b) direct materials.
2. Compute both the direct labor cost and the direct materials cost per equivalent unit.
3. Compute both direct labor cost and direct materials cost assigned to (a) units completed and transferred out, and (b) ending goods in process inventory.

Check (2) Direct labor cost per equivalent unit, $1.50

(3b) $693,450

Analysis Component

4. The company sells and ships all units to customers as soon as they are completed. Assume that an error is made in determining the percentage of completion for units in ending inventory. Instead of being 90% complete with respect to labor, they are actually 65% complete. Write a one-page memo to the plant manager describing how this error affects its September financial statements.

Li Company produces large quantities of a standardized product. The following information is available for its production activities for January.

Problem 16-3A
Journalizing in process costing; equivalent units and costs

C2 P1 P2 P3

Raw materials		Factory overhead incurred	
Beginning inventory	$ 26,000	Indirect materials used	$ 81,500
Raw materials purchased (on credit)	255,000	Indirect labor used	50,000
Direct materials used	(172,000)	Other overhead costs	159,308
Indirect materials used	(81,500)	Total factory overhead incurred	$290,808
Ending inventory	$ 27,500		
		Factory overhead applied	
Factory payroll		**(140% of direct labor cost)**	
Direct labor used	$207,720	Total factory overhead applied	$290,808
Indirect labor used	50,000		
Total payroll cost (paid in cash)	$257,720		

Additional information about units and costs of production activities follows.

Units		Costs		
Beginning goods in process inventory	2,200	Beginning goods in process inventory		
Started	30,000	Direct materials	$3,500	
Ending goods in process inventory	5,900	Direct labor	3,225	
		Factory overhead	4,515	$ 11,240
Status of ending goods in process inventory		Direct materials added		172,000
Materials—Percent complete	50%	Direct labor added		207,720
Labor and overhead—Percent complete	65%	Overhead applied (140% of direct labor)		290,808
		Total costs		$681,768
		Ending goods in process inventory		$ 82,128

During January, 55,000 units of finished goods are sold for $50 cash each. Cost information regarding finished goods follows.

Beginning finished goods inventory	$155,000
Cost transferred in	599,640
Cost of goods sold	(612,500)
Ending finished goods inventory	$142,140

Required

1. Prepare journal entries dated January 31 to record the following January activities: (a) purchase of raw materials, (b) direct materials usage, (c) indirect materials usage, (d) factory payroll costs, (e) direct labor costs used in production, (f) indirect labor costs, (g) other overhead costs—credit Other Accounts, (h) overhead applied, (i) goods transferred to finished goods, and (j) sale of finished goods.

2. Prepare a process cost summary report for this company, showing costs charged to production, units cost information, equivalent units of production, cost per EUP, and its cost assignment and reconciliation.

Check   (2) Cost per equivalent unit: materials, $6.00; labor, $7.00; overhead, $9.80

Analysis Component

3. The company provides incentives to its department managers by paying monthly bonuses based on their success in controlling costs per equivalent unit of production. Assume that the production department underestimates the percentage of completion for units in ending inventory with the result that its equivalent units of production in ending inventory for January are understated. What impact does this error have on the January bonuses paid to the production managers? What impact, if any, does this error have on February bonuses?

Problem 16-4A

Process cost summary; equivalent units

C2 C3 P4

mhhe.com/wildFINMAN4e

Easton Co. produces its product through a single processing department. Direct materials are added at the start of production, and direct labor and overhead are added evenly throughout the process. The company uses monthly reporting periods for its weighted-average process cost accounting system. Its Goods in Process Inventory account follows after entries for direct materials, direct labor, and overhead costs for October.

		Goods in Process Inventory			Acct. No. 133
Date		Explanation	Debit	Credit	Balance
Oct.	1	Balance			348,638
	31	Direct materials	104,090		452,728
	31	Direct labor	416,360		869,088
	31	Applied overhead	244,920		1,114,008

Its beginning goods in process consisted of $60,830 of direct materials, $176,820 of direct labor, and $110,988 of factory overhead. During October, the company started 280,000 units and transferred 306,000 units to finished goods. At the end of the month, the goods in process inventory consisted of 41,200 units that were 80% complete with respect to direct labor and factory overhead.

Required

Check (1) Costs transferred to finished goods, $1,002,150

1. Prepare the company's process cost summary for October using the weighted-average method.
2. Prepare the journal entry dated October 31 to transfer the cost of the completed units to finished goods inventory.

Problem 16-5A

Process cost summary, equivalent units, cost estimates

C2 C3 P4

Ogden Co. manufactures a single product in one department. All direct materials are added at the beginning of the manufacturing process. Direct labor and overhead are added evenly throughout the process. The company uses monthly reporting periods for its weighted-average process cost accounting. During October, the company completed and transferred 22,200 units of product to finished goods inventory. Its 3,000 units of beginning goods in process consisted of $9,900 of direct materials, $61,650 of direct labor, and $49,320 of factory overhead. It has 2,400 units (100% complete with respect to direct materials and 80% complete with respect to direct labor and overhead) in process at month-end. After entries to record direct materials, direct labor, and overhead for October, the company's Goods in Process Inventory account follows.

		Goods in Process Inventory			Acct. No. 133
Date		Explanation	Debit	Credit	Balance
Oct.	1	Balance			120,870
	31	Direct materials	248,400		369,270
	31	Direct labor	601,650		970,920
	31	Applied overhead	481,320		1,452,240

Required

Check (1) EUP for labor and overhead, 24,120 EUP

(2) Cost transferred to finished goods, $1,332,000

1. Prepare the company's process cost summary for October using the weighted-average method.
2. Prepare the journal entry dated October 31 to transfer the cost of completed units to finished goods inventory.

Analysis Components

3. The cost accounting process depends on numerous estimates.

  a. Identify two major estimates that determine the cost per equivalent unit.

  b. In what direction might you anticipate a bias from management for each estimate in part 3a (assume that management compensation is based on maintaining low inventory amounts)? Explain your answer.

Refer to the data in Problem 16-5A. Assume that Ogden uses the FIFO method to account for its process costing system. The following additional information is available:

- Beginning goods in process consisted of 3,000 units that were 100% complete with respect to direct materials and 40% complete with respect to direct labor and overhead.
- Of the 22,200 units completed, 3,000 were from beginning goods in process. The remaining 19,200 were units started and completed during October.

Required

1. Prepare the company's process cost summary for October using FIFO.

2. Prepare the journal entry dated October 31 to transfer the cost of completed units to finished goods inventory.

Problem 16-6A
Process cost summary; equivalent units; cost estimates—FIFO

C3 C4 P4

Check (1) EUP for labor and overhead, 22,920 EUP

(2) Cost transferred to finished goods, $1,333,920

Tarick Toys Company manufactures video game consoles and accounts for product costs using process costing. The following information is available regarding its June inventories.

PROBLEM SET B

Problem 16-1B
Production cost flow and measurement; journal entries

P1 P2 P3 P4

	Beginning Inventory	Ending Inventory
Raw materials inventory	$ 54,000	$ 82,500
Goods in process inventory	117,000	187,500
Finished goods inventory	120,000	148,500

The following additional information describes the company's production activities for June.

Raw materials purchases (on credit)	$150,000
Factory payroll cost (paid in cash)	300,000
Other overhead cost (Other Accounts credited)	127,875
Materials used	
Direct	$ 90,000
Indirect	31,500
Labor used	
Direct	$262,500
Indirect	37,500
Overhead rate as a percent of direct labor	75%
Sales (on credit)	$750,000

Required

1. Compute the cost of (a) products transferred from production to finished goods, and (b) goods sold.

2. Prepare journal entries dated June 30 to record the following production activities during June: (a) raw materials purchases, (b) direct materials usage, (c) indirect materials usage, (d) payroll costs, (e) direct labor costs, (f) indirect labor costs, (g) other overhead costs, (h) overhead applied, (i) goods transferred from production to finished goods, and (j) sale of finished goods.

Check (1b) Cost of goods sold, $450,375

Eden Company uses process costing to account for its production costs. Direct labor is added evenly throughout the process. Direct materials are added at the beginning of the process. During April, the production department transferred 40,000 units of product to finished goods. Beginning goods in process had $116,000 of direct materials and $172,800 of direct labor cost. At the end of April, the goods in process inventory consists of 4,000 units that are 25% complete with respect to labor. The direct materials cost added in April is $1,424,000, and direct labor cost added is $3,960,000.

Problem 16-2B
Cost per equivalent unit; costs assigned to products

C2 C3

Required

1. Determine the equivalent units of production with respect to (a) direct labor and (b) direct materials.

2. Compute both the direct labor cost and the direct materials cost per equivalent unit.

3. Compute both direct labor cost and direct materials cost assigned to (a) units completed and transferred out, and (b) ending goods in process inventory.

Analysis Component

4. The company sells and ships all units to customers as soon as they are completed. Assume that an error is made in determining the percentage of completion for units in ending inventory. Instead of being 30% complete with respect to labor, they are actually 75% complete. Write a one-page memo to the plant manager describing how this error affects its April financial statements.

Problem 16-3B
Journalizing in process costing; equivalent units and costs

C2 P1 P2 P3 P4

Ying Company produces large quantities of a standardized product. The following information is available for its production activities for March.

Raw materials		Factory overhead incurred	
Beginning inventory	$ 16,000	Indirect materials used	$20,280
Raw materials purchased (on credit)	110,560	Indirect labor used	18,160
Direct materials used	(98,560)	Other overhead costs	17,216
Indirect materials used	(20,280)	Total factory overhead incurred	$55,656
Ending inventory	$ 7,720		
		Factory overhead applied	
Factory payroll		**(90% of direct labor cost)**	
Direct labor used	$ 61,840	Total factory overhead applied	$55,656
Indirect labor used	18,160		
Total payroll cost (paid in cash)	$ 80,000		

Additional information about units and costs of production activities follows.

Units		Costs		
Beginning goods in process inventory	8,000	Beginning goods in process inventory		
Started	24,000	Direct materials	$2,240	
Ending goods in process inventory	6,000	Direct labor	1,410	
		Factory overhead	1,269	$ 4,919
Status of ending goods in process inventory		Direct materials added		98,560
Materials—Percent complete	100%	Direct labor added		61,840
Labor and overhead—Percent complete	25%	Overhead applied (90% of direct labor) . . .		55,656
		Total costs		$220,975
		Ending goods in process inventory		$ 25,455

During March, 45,000 units of finished goods are sold for $25 cash each. Cost information regarding finished goods follows.

Beginning finished goods inventory	$ 74,200
Cost transferred in from production	195,520
Cost of goods sold	(225,000)
Ending finished goods inventory	$ 44,720

Required

1. Prepare journal entries dated March 31 to record the following March activities: (a) purchase of raw materials, (b) direct materials usage, (c) indirect materials usage, (d) factory payroll costs, (e) direct labor costs used in production, (f) indirect labor costs, (g) other overhead costs—credit Other Accounts, (h) overhead applied, (i) goods transferred to finished goods, and (j) sale of finished goods.

2. Prepare a process cost summary report for this company, showing costs charged to production, unit cost information, equivalent units of production, cost per EUP, and its cost assignment and reconciliation.

Analysis Component

3. This company provides incentives to its department managers by paying monthly bonuses based on their success in controlling costs per equivalent unit of production. Assume that production overestimates the percentage of completion for units in ending inventory with the result that its equivalent units of production in ending inventory for March are overstated. What impact does this error have on bonuses paid to the managers of the production department? What impact, if any, does this error have on these managers' April bonuses?

Basilex Company produces its product through a single processing department. Direct materials are added at the beginning of the process. Direct labor and overhead are added to the product evenly throughout the process. The company uses monthly reporting periods for its weighted-average process cost accounting. Its Goods in Process Inventory account follows after entries for direct materials, direct labor, and overhead costs for November.

Problem 16-4B

Process cost summary; equivalent units

C2 C3 P4

Goods in Process Inventory				Acct. No. 133
Date	**Explanation**	**Debit**	**Credit**	**Balance**
Nov. 1	Balance			10,650
30	Direct materials	58,200		68,850
30	Direct labor	213,400		282,250
30	Applied overhead	320,100		602,350

The 7,500 units of beginning goods in process consisted of $3,400 of direct materials, $2,900 of direct labor, and $4,350 of factory overhead. During November, the company finished and transferred 100,000 units of its product to finished goods. At the end of the month, the goods in process inventory consisted of 12,000 units that were 100% complete with respect to direct materials and 25% complete with respect to direct labor and factory overhead.

Required

1. Prepare the company's process cost summary for November using the weighted-average method.

2. Prepare the journal entry dated November 30 to transfer the cost of the completed units to finished goods inventory.

Check (1) Cost transferred to finished goods, $580,000

Oakley International Co. manufactures a single product in one department. Direct labor and overhead are added evenly throughout the process. Direct materials are added as needed. The company uses monthly reporting periods for its weighted-average process cost accounting. During March, Oakley completed and transferred 220,000 units of product to finished goods inventory. Its 10,000 units of beginning goods in process consisted of $16,800 of direct materials, $27,920 of direct labor, and $69,800 of factory overhead. 40,000 units (50% complete with respect to direct materials and 30% complete with respect to direct labor and overhead) are in process at month-end. After entries for direct materials, direct labor, and overhead for March, the company's Goods in Process Inventory account follows.

Problem 16-5B

Process cost summary; equivalent units; cost estimates

C2 C3 P4

Goods in Process Inventory				Acct. No. 133
Date	**Explanation**	**Debit**	**Credit**	**Balance**
Mar. 1	Balance			114,520
31	Direct materials	223,200		337,720
31	Direct labor	352,560		690,280
31	Applied overhead	881,400		1,571,680

Required

1. Prepare the company's process cost summary for March using the weighted-average method.

2. Prepare the journal entry dated March 31 to transfer the cost of completed units to finished goods inventory.

Check (1) EUP for labor and overhead, 232,000

(2) Cost transferred to finished goods, $1,482,800

Analysis Components

3. The cost accounting process depends on several estimates.

    a. Identify two major estimates that affect the cost per equivalent unit.

    b. In what direction might you anticipate a bias from management for each estimate in part 3a (assume that management compensation is based on maintaining low inventory amounts)? Explain your answer.

Problem 16-6B[A]

Process cost summary;
equivalent units; cost
estimates—FIFO

C3   C4   P4

Refer to the information in Problem 16-5B. Assume that Oakley International uses the FIFO method to account for its process costing system. The following additional information is available.

● Beginning goods in process consists of 10,000 units that were 75% complete with respect to direct materials and 60% complete with respect to direct labor and overhead.

● Of the 220,000 units completed, 10,000 were from beginning goods in process; the remaining 210,000 were units started and completed during March.

Required

Check (1) Labor and overhead EUP, 226,000

     (2) Cost transferred, $1,486,960

1. Prepare the company's process cost summary for March using FIFO. Round cost per EUP to one-tenth of a cent.

2. Prepare the journal entry dated March 31 to transfer the cost of completed units to finished goods inventory.

SERIAL PROBLEM

Business Solutions

C1   A1

(This serial problem began in Chapter 1 and continues through most of the book. If previous chapter segments were not completed, the serial problem can begin at this point.)

SP 16   The computer workstation furniture manufacturing that Santana Rey started is progressing well. At this point, Santana is using a job order costing system to account for the production costs of this product line. Santana has heard about process costing and is wondering whether process costing might be a better method for her to keep track of and monitor her production costs.

Required

1. What are the features that distinguish job order costing from process costing?

2. Do you believe that Santana should continue to use job order costing or switch to process costing for her workstation furniture manufacturing? Explain.

**COMPREHENSIVE
PROBLEM**

**Major League Bat
Company**

(Review of Chapters 2, 4, 14, 16)

CP 16   Major League Bat Company manufactures baseball bats. In addition to its goods in process inventories, the company maintains inventories of raw materials and finished goods. It uses raw materials as direct materials in production and as indirect materials. Its factory payroll costs include direct labor for production and indirect labor. All materials are added at the beginning of the process, and direct labor and factory overhead are applied uniformly throughout the production process.

Required

You are to maintain records and produce measures of inventories to reflect the July events of this company. Set up the following general ledger accounts and enter the June 30 balances: Raw Materials Inventory, $25,000; Goods in Process Inventory, $8,135 ($2,660 of direct materials, $3,650 of direct labor, and $1,825 of overhead); Finished Goods Inventory, $110,000; Sales, $0; Cost of Goods Sold, $0; Factory Payroll, $0; and Factory Overhead, $0.

1. Prepare journal entries to record the following July transactions and events.

    a. Purchased raw materials for $125,000 cash (the company uses a perpetual inventory system).

    b. Used raw materials as follows: direct materials, $52,440; and indirect materials, $10,000.

    c. Incurred factory payroll cost of $227,250 paid in cash (ignore taxes).

    d. Assigned factory payroll costs as follows: direct labor, $202,250; and indirect labor, $25,000.

    e. Incurred additional factory overhead costs of $80,000 paid in cash.

Check (1f) Cr. Factory Overhead, $101,125

    f. Allocated factory overhead to production at 50% of direct labor costs.

2. Information about the July inventories follows. Use this information with that from part 1 to prepare a process cost summary, assuming the weighted-average method is used.

Check   (2) EUP for overhead, 14,200

Units	
Beginning inventory	5,000 units
Started	14,000 units
Ending inventory	8,000 units
Beginning inventory	
Materials—Percent complete	100%
Labor and overhead—Percent complete	75%
Ending inventory	
Materials—Percent complete	100%
Labor and overhead—Percent complete	40%

3. Using the results from part 2 and the available information, make computations and prepare journal entries to record the following:

   a. Total costs transferred to finished goods for July (label this entry g).

   b. Sale of finished goods costing $265,700 for $625,000 in cash (label this entry h).

(3a) $271,150

4. Post entries from parts 1 and 3 to the ledger accounts set up at the beginning of the problem.

5. Compute the amount of gross profit from the sales in July. (*Note:* Add any underapplied overhead to, or deduct any overapplied overhead from, the cost of goods sold. Ignore the corresponding journal entry.)

Beyond the Numbers

BTN 16-1   **Research In Motion** reports in notes to its financial statements that, in addition to its merchandise sold, it includes the following costs (among others) in cost of goods sold: customer shipping and handling expenses, warranty expenses, and depreciation expense on assets used in manufacturing.

REPORTING IN ACTION

C2

RIM

Required

1. Why do you believe Research In Motion includes these costs in its cost of goods sold?

2. What effect does this cost accounting policy for its cost of goods sold have on Research In Motion's financial statements and any analysis of these statements? Explain.

Fast Forward

3. Access Research In Motion's financial statements for the fiscal years after February 27, 2010, from its Website (**RIM.com**) or the SEC's EDGAR Website (**sec.gov**). Review its footnote relating to Critical Accounting Policies and Estimates. Has Research In Motion changed its policy with respect to what costs are included in the cost of goods sold? Explain.

BTN 16-2   Manufacturers such as **Research In Motion**, **Apple**, and **Palm** usually work to maintain a high-quality and low-cost operation. One ratio routinely computed for this assessment is the cost of goods sold divided by total expenses. A decline in this ratio can mean that the company is spending too much on selling and administrative activities. An increase in this ratio beyond a reasonable level can mean that the company is not spending enough on selling activities. (Assume for this analysis that total expenses equal the cost of goods sold plus selling, general, and administrative expenses.)

COMPARATIVE ANALYSIS

C1

RIM

Apple

Palm

Required

1. For Research In Motion, Apple, and Palm refer to Appendix A and compute the ratios of cost of goods sold to total expenses for their two most recent fiscal years. (Record answers as percents, rounded to one decimal.)

2. Comment on the similarities or differences in the ratio results across both years among the companies.

ETHICS CHALLENGE

C1

BTN 16-3 Many accounting and accounting-related professionals are skilled in financial analysis, but most are not skilled in manufacturing. This is especially the case for process manufacturing environments (for example, a bottling plant or chemical factory). To provide professional accounting and financial services, one must understand the industry, product, and processes. We have an ethical responsibility to develop this understanding before offering services to clients in these areas.

Required

Write a one-page action plan, in memorandum format, discussing how you would obtain an understanding of key business processes of a company that hires you to provide financial services. The memorandum should specify an industry, a product, and one selected process and should draw on at least one reference, such as a professional journal or industry magazine.

COMMUNICATING IN PRACTICE

A1 C1 P1 P2

BTN 16-4 You hire a new assistant production manager whose prior experience is with a company that produced goods to order. Your company engages in continuous production of homogeneous products that go through various production processes. Your new assistant e-mails you questioning some cost classifications on an internal report—specifically why the costs of some materials that do not actually become part of the finished product, including some labor costs not directly associated with producing the product, are classified as direct costs. Respond to this concern via memorandum.

TAKING IT TO THE NET

C1

BTN 16-5 Many companies acquire software to help them monitor and control their costs and as an aid to their accounting systems. One company that supplies such software is **proDacapo** (**prodacapo.com**). There are many other such vendors. Access proDacapo's Website, click on "Prodacapo Process Management," and review the information displayed.

Required

How is process management software helpful to businesses? Explain with reference to costs, efficiency, and examples, if possible.

TEAMWORK IN ACTION

C1 P1 P2 P3 P4

BTN 16-6 The purpose of this team activity is to ensure that each team member understands process operations and the related accounting entries. Find the activities and flows identified in Exhibit 16.4 with numbers ①–⑩. Pick a member of the team to start by describing activity number ① in this exhibit, then verbalizing the related journal entry, and describing how the amounts in the entry are computed. The other members of the team are to agree or disagree; discussion is to continue until all members express understanding. Rotate to the next numbered activity and next team member until all activities and entries have been discussed. If at any point a team member is uncertain about an answer, the team member may pass and get back in the rotation when he or she can contribute to the team's discussion.

ENTREPRENEURIAL DECISION

C3 A2

BTN 16-7 This chapter's opener featured Jeff Avallon, John Goscha and Morgen Newman and their company **IdeaPaint**.

Required

1. How would a process cost summary differ between IdeaPaint and a competitor making dry-erase whiteboards?

2. How does not holding raw materials inventories reduce costs? If the items are not used in production, how can they impact profits? Explain.

3. Suppose IdeaPaint decides to allow customers to make their own unique paint colors. Why might the company then use a process costing system?

BTN 16-8 In process costing, the process is analyzed first and then a unit measure is computed in the form of equivalent units for direct materials, direct labor, overhead, and all three combined. The same analysis applies to both manufacturing and service processes.

HITTING THE ROAD

C2

Required

Visit your local **U.S. Mail** center. Look into the back room, and you will see several ongoing processes. Select one process, such as sorting, and list the costs associated with this process. Your list should include materials, labor, and overhead; be specific. Classify each cost as fixed or variable. At the bottom of your list, outline how overhead should be assigned to your identified process. The following format (with an example) is suggested.

Point: The class can compare and discuss the different processes studied and the answers provided.

Cost Description	Direct Material	Direct Labor	Overhead	Variable Cost	Fixed Cost
Manual sorting		X		X	
⋮					

Overhead allocation suggestions:

BTN 16-9   **Nokia**, **Research In Motion**, **Apple**, and **Palm** are competitors in the global marketplace. Selected data for Nokia follow.

GLOBAL DECISION

C1

NOKIA

RIM

Apple

Palm

(millions of euros)	Current Year	Prior Year
Cost of goods sold	€27,720	€33,337
General, selling, and administrative expenses	5,078	5,664
Total expenses	€32,798	€39,001

Required

1. Review the discussion of the importance of the cost of goods sold divided by total expenses ratio in BTN 16-2. Compute the cost of goods sold to total expenses ratio for Nokia for the two years of data provided. (Record answers as percents, rounded to one decimal.)

2. Comment on the similarities or differences in the ratio results calculated in part 1 and in BTN 16-2 across years and companies. (Record answers as percents, rounded to one decimal.)

ANSWERS TO MULTIPLE CHOICE QUIZ

1. d

2. e

3. b; $20,000 + $152,000 + $45,000 + $18,000 − $218,000 = $17,000

4. a; 40,000 + (15,000 × 1/3) = 45,000 EUP

5. c; ($6,000 + $84,000) ÷ 45,000 EUP = $2 per EUP

17

Activity-Based Costing and Analysis

A Look Back

Chapters 15 and 16 described costing systems used by companies to accumulate product costing information for the reporting of inventories and cost of goods sold.

A Look at This Chapter

This chapter introduces the activity-based costing (ABC) system with the potential for greater accuracy of cost allocations. ABC provides managers with cost information for strategic decisions that is not readily available with other costing methods.

A Look Ahead

Chapter 18 discusses the importance of information on both costs and sales behavior for managers in performing cost-volume-profit (CVP) analysis, which is a valuable managerial tool.

Learning Objectives

CONCEPTUAL

C1 Distinguish between the plantwide overhead rate method, the departmental overhead rate method, and the activity-based costing method. (p. 726)

C2 Explain cost flows for activity-based costing. (p. 731)

C3 Describe the four types of activities that cause overhead costs. (p. 738)

ANALYTICAL

A1 Identify and assess advantages and disadvantages of the plantwide overhead and departmental overhead rate methods. (p. 731)

A2 Identify and assess advantages and disadvantages of activity-based costing. (p. 737)

LP17

PROCEDURAL

P1 Allocate overhead costs to products using the plantwide overhead rate method. (p. 727)

P2 Allocate overhead costs to products using the departmental overhead rate method. (p. 728)

P3 Allocate overhead costs to products using activity-based costing. (p. 732)

Sweet Success

"Anyone can do it . . ."

—NEAL GOTTLIEB

SAN FRANCISCO—After returning from a stint in the Peace Corps, Neal Gottlieb wanted to start the "most Earth-friendly business I could think of." Using the $70,000 he saved from delivering newspapers and other boyhood jobs, Neal started **Three Twins Ice Cream**, a manufacturer and seller of organic ice cream. Business started slowly, with Neal as the lone employee in a single ice cream shop. "I made ice cream in the morning, ran the shop all day, then cleaned up and did paperwork at night," recalls Neal.

Working 166 straight days without a day off and recording gross sales of $49 on one cold, rainy Monday, Neal decided he had to expand into the wholesale ice cream business or abandon his dreams. Neal's gamble paid off—today Three Twins Ice Cream is certified organic in more ice cream flavors than any ice cream company in the world, and as Neal says, "I'm happy to say I don't mop floors anymore."

In addition to using only organic ingredients, Neal strives to make his entire operation Earth-friendly. "Everything we give the customer can be composted," explains Neal. Cups and spoons are made from pressed sugar cane, potatoes, and corn starch. His production strategy adds overhead costs; for example, spoons cost 4 cents each instead of 1 cent each for plastic spoons. Neal explains that "using organic ingredients isn't the cheapest option, but it's the best." With costly raw materials and overhead costs, Neal must be adept at interpreting product cost reports. Without good cost and production process controls, his income would quickly evaporate.

In smaller businesses, a single plantwide overhead allocation rate is often sufficient. But as businesses grow and offer more diverse product lines, more sophisticated costing techniques are often needed. Activity-based costing (ABC) procedures help managers monitor and control costs and ensure product quality. ABC is especially useful in companies like Neal's, where different products require different processes and varying levels of overhead. Traditional flavors like vanilla, chocolate, and strawberry can be made in large quantities in long production runs, while treats like Peanut Butter Confetti Crunch, Mocha Difference, and The Chocolate Project are made in small batches. ABC helps in allocating overhead costs, such as product development, plant maintenance, and clean-up costs, to different products.

Neal's recipe is working. Three Twins recently built a 4,200 square foot manufacturing facility to expand its business and reduce costs. Neal's factory allows him to produce larger quantities of ice cream at lower cost, because he now makes his own mix. "We used to pay $15 per gallon for our mix; we can now make mix for less than $7 per gallon," explains Neal. Neal responded to these cost savings by lowering his selling prices and saw demand for his products grow.

From humble beginnings, Three Twins' sales are growing at almost 100 percent per year. "We want to be a national brand," says Neal. "We believe we have the potential to find a huge market." Still, Neal advises would-be entrepreneurs to "enjoy what they do, work hard, and give back."

[Sources: *Three Twins Ice Cream Company* Website, January 2011; *Marin Independent Journal*, July 2010; sf.eater.com, April 2010; *North Bay Business* Journal, April 2010; *Napa Valley Register*, April 2007]

Prior chapters described costing systems used to assign costs to product units. This discussion emphasized the valuation of inventory and the cost of goods sold. Although the information from these prior costing systems conforms to generally accepted accounting principles (GAAP) for external reporting, it has limitations. This chapter introduces the activity-based costing (ABC) system, which is used by managers who desire more accurate product cost information.

Activity-Based Costing and Analysis

Assigning Overhead Costs	Applying Activity-Based Costing	Assessing Activity-Based Costing
• Single plantwide overhead rate method • Multiple departmental overhead rate method • Activity-based costing rates and method	• Step 1 Identify activities and their costs • Step 2 Trace overhead costs to cost pools • Step 3 Determine activity rates • Step 4 Assign overhead costs to cost objects	• Advantages of activity-based costing • Disadvantages of activity-based costing • Types of activities

ASSIGNING OVERHEAD COSTS

C1 Distinguish between the plantwide overhead rate method, the departmental overhead rate method, and the activity-based costing method.

Managerial activities such as product pricing, product mix decisions, and cost control depend on accurate product cost information. Distorted product cost information can result in poor decisions. Knowing accurate costs for producing, delivering, and servicing products helps managers set a price to cover product costs and yield a profit.

In competitive markets, price is established through the forces of supply and demand. In these situations, managers must understand product costs to assess whether the market price is high enough to justify the cost of entering the market. Disparities between market prices and producer costs give managers insight into their efficiency relative to competitors.

Product costs consist of direct materials, direct labor, and overhead (indirect costs). Since the physical components of a product (direct materials) and the work of making a product (direct labor) can be traced to units of output, the assignment of costs of these factors is usually straightforward. Overhead costs, however, are not directly related to production volume, and therefore cannot be traced to units of product in the same way that direct materials and direct labor can.

Point: Evidence suggests overhead costs have steadily increased while direct labor costs have steadily decreased as a percentage of total manufacturing costs over recent decades. This puts greater importance on accurate cost allocations.

For example, we can trace the cost of putting tires on a car because we know there is a logical relation between the number of cars produced and the number of tires needed for each car. The cost to heat an automobile manufacturing factory, however, is not readily linked with the number of cars made. Consequently, we must use an allocation system to assign overhead costs such as utilities and factory maintenance. This chapter introduces three methods of overhead allocation: (1) the single plantwide overhead rate method, (2) the departmental overhead rate method, and (3) the activity-based costing method.

Exhibit 17.1 summarizes some key features of these three alternative methods. Both the *plantwide overhead rate method* and the *departmental overhead rate method* use volume-based measures such as direct labor hours, direct labor dollars, or machine hours to allocate overhead costs to products. These methods differ in that the plantwide method uses a single rate for allocating overhead costs, and the departmental rate method uses at least two rates. The departmental method arguably provides more accurate cost allocations than the single rate allocations of the plantwide method. In contrast, *activity-based costing* focuses on activities and the costs of carrying out activities. Rates based on these activities are then used to assign overhead to products in proportion to the amount of activity required to produce them. Activity-based costing typically uses more overhead allocation rates than the plantwide and departmental methods.

EXHIBIT 17.1

Overhead Cost Allocation Methods

Method	Overhead Allocations Based on	Overhead Allocation Rates Based on
Plantwide rate	One rate	Volume-based measures such as direct labor hours or machine hours
Departmental rate	Two or more rates	Volume-based measures such as direct labor hours or machine hours
Activity-based costing	At least two (but often many) rates	Activities that drive costs, such as number of batches of product produced

Plantwide Overhead Rate Method

Cost Flows under Plantwide Overhead Rate Method   The first method is known as the *single plantwide overhead rate method,* or simply the *plantwide overhead rate method,* for allocating overhead costs to products. For this method, the target of the cost assignment, or **cost object,** is the unit of product—see Exhibit 17.2. The rate is determined using volume-related measures such as direct labor hours, direct labor cost dollars, or machine hours, which are readily available in most manufacturing settings. In some industries, overhead costs are closely related to these volume-related measures. In such cases it is logical to use this method as a basis for assigning indirect manufacturing costs to products.

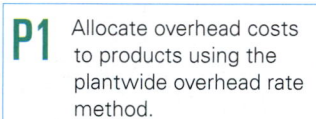

P1 Allocate overhead costs to products using the plantwide overhead rate method.

EXHIBIT 17.2

Plantwide Overhead Rate Method

```
Indirect          ┌──────────────────────────────────────┐
Costs    ──────►  │           Overhead Cost              │
                  └──────────────────────────────────────┘
                                    │
                                    ▼
Cost              ┌──────────────────────────────────────┐
Allocation ─────► │     Single Plantwide Overhead Rate   │
Base              └──────────────────────────────────────┘
                                    │
                    ┌───────────────┼───────────────┐
                    ▼               ▼               ▼
Cost           ┌─────────┐    ┌─────────┐    ┌─────────┐
Objects ─────► │Product 1│    │Product 2│    │Product 3│
               └─────────┘    └─────────┘    └─────────┘
```

Applying the Plantwide Overhead Rate Method   Under the single plantwide overhead rate method, total budgeted overhead costs are combined into one overhead cost pool. This cost pool is then divided by the chosen allocation base, such as total direct labor hours, to arrive at a single plantwide overhead rate. This rate then is applied to assign costs to all products based on the allocation base such as direct labor hours required to manufacture each product.

To illustrate, consider data from KartCo, a go-kart manufacturer that produces both standard and custom go-karts for amusement parks. The standard go-kart is a basic model sold primarily to amusement parks that service county and state fairs. Custom go-karts are produced for theme parks who want unique go-karts that coordinate with their respective themes.

Assume that KartCo applies the plantwide overhead rate method and uses direct labor hours (DLH) as its overhead allocation base. KartCo's budgeted DLH information is in Exhibit 17.3.

EXHIBIT 17.3

KartCo's Budgeted Direct Labor Hours

	Number of Units	Direct Labor Hours per Unit	Total Direct Labor Hours
Standard go-kart . . .	5,000	15	75,000
Custom go-kart	1,000	25	25,000
Total			100,000

KartCo's budgeted overhead cost information is in Exhibit 17.4. Its overhead cost consists of indirect labor and factory utilities.

EXHIBIT 17.4

KartCo's Budgeted Overhead Cost

Indirect labor cost	$4,000,000
Factory utilities	800,000
Total overhead cost	$4,800,000

The single plantwide overhead rate for KartCo is computed as follows.

$$\begin{array}{c}\text{Plantwide} \\ \text{overhead rate}\end{array} = \frac{\text{Total budgeted}}{\text{overhead cost}} \div \frac{\text{Total budgeted direct}}{\text{labor hours}}$$
$$= \$4,800,000 \div 100,000 \text{ DLH}$$
$$= \$48 \text{ per DLH}$$

This plantwide overhead rate is then used to allocate overhead cost to products based on the number of direct labor hours required to produce each unit as follows.

Overhead allocated to each product unit = Plantwide overhead rate × DLH per unit

For KartCo, overhead cost is allocated to its two products as follows (on a per unit basis).

Standard go-kart:	$48 per DLH × 15 DLH = $ 720
Custom go-kart:	$48 per DLH × 25 DLH = $1,200

KartCo uses these per unit overhead costs to compute the total unit cost of each product as follows.

	Direct Materials	Direct Labor	Overhead	Total Cost per Unit
Standard go-kart	$400	$350	$ 720	$1,470
Custom go-kart	600	500	1,200	2,300

During the most recent period, KartCo sold its standard model go-karts for $2,000 and its custom go-karts for $3,500. A recent report from its marketing staff indicates that competitors are selling go-karts similar to KartCo's standard model for as low as $1,200. KartCo management believes it must be competitive, but management is concerned that meeting this lower price would result in a loss of $270 ($1,200 − $1,470) on each standard go-kart sold.

In the case of its custom go-kart, KartCo has been swamped with orders and is unable to meet demand. Accordingly, management is considering a change in strategy. Some discussion has ensued about dropping its standard model and concentrating on its custom model. Yet management recognizes that its pricing and cost decisions are influenced by its cost allocations. Thus, before making any strategic decisions, management has directed its cost analysts to further review production costs for both the standard and custom go-kart models. To pursue this analysis, the cost analysts first turned to the departmental rate method.

Departmental Overhead Rate Method

Cost Flows under Departmental Overhead Rate Method　　Many companies have several departments that produce various products and consume overhead resources in substantially different ways. Under such circumstances, use of a single plantwide overhead rate can produce cost assignments that fail to accurately reflect the cost to manufacture a specific product. In these cases, use of multiple overhead rates can result in better overhead cost allocations and improve management decisions.

P2 Allocate overhead costs to products using the departmental overhead rate method.

The *departmental overhead rate method* uses a different overhead rate for each production department. This is usually done through a two-stage assignment process, each with its different cost objects (target of cost assignment). In the first stage the departments are the cost objects and in the second stage the products are the cost objects (see Exhibit 17.5).

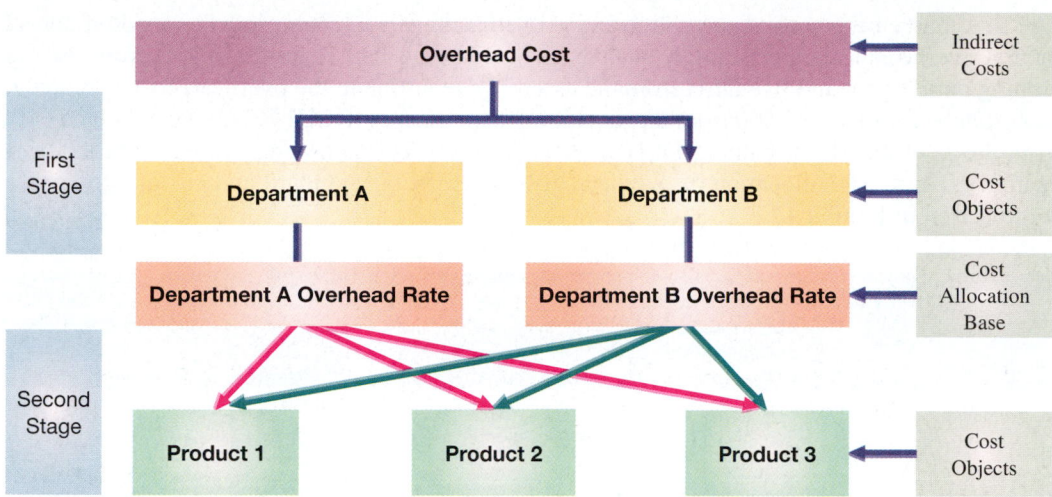

EXHIBIT 17.5

Departmental Overhead
Rate Method

Exhibit 17.5 shows that under the departmental overhead rate method, overhead costs are first determined separately for each production department. Next, an overhead rate is computed for each production department to allocate the overhead costs of each department to products passing through that department. The departmental overhead rate method allows each department to have its own overhead rate and its own allocation base. For example, an assembly department can use direct labor hours to allocate its overhead cost while the machining department can use machine hours as its base.

Applying the Departmental Overhead Rate Method To illustrate the departmental overhead rate method, let's return to KartCo. KartCo has two production departments, the machining department and the assembly department. The first stage requires that KartCo assign its $4,800,000 overhead cost to its two production departments. KartCo determines from an analysis of its indirect labor and factory utilities that $4,200,000 of overhead costs are traceable to its machining department and the remaining $600,000 are traceable to its assembly department.

The second stage demands that after overhead costs are assigned to departments, each department determines an allocation base for its operations. For KartCo, the machining department uses machine hours (MH) as a base for allocating its overhead and the assembly department uses direct labor hours (DLH) as the base for allocating its overhead. For this stage, the relevant information for the machining and assembly departments is in Exhibit 17.6.

Point: In some cases it is difficult for companies to trace overhead costs to distinct departments as some overhead costs can be common to several departments. In these cases, companies must allocate overhead to departments applying reasonable allocation bases.

EXHIBIT 17.6

Allocation Information for
Machining and Assembly
Departments

	Number of Units	Machining Department		Assembly Department	
		Hours per Unit	Total Hours	Hours per Unit	Total Hours
Standard go-kart	5,000	10 MH per unit	50,000 MH	5 DLH per unit	25,000 DLH
Custom go-kart	1,000	20 MH per unit	20,000 MH	5 DLH per unit	5,000 DLH
Totals			70,000 MH		30,000 DLH

Each department computes its own overhead rate using the following formula.

$$\text{Departmental overhead rate} = \frac{\text{Total departmental overhead cost}}{\text{Total units in departmental allocation base}}$$

For KartCo, its departmental overhead rates are computed as follows.

$$\text{Machining department overhead rate} = \frac{\$4,200,000}{70,000 \text{ MH}} = \$60 \text{ per MH}$$

$$\text{Assembly department overhead rate} = \frac{\$600,000}{30,000 \text{ DLH}} = \$20 \text{ per DLH}$$

The final part of the second stage is to apply overhead costs to each product based on depart-mental overhead rates. For KartCo, since each standard go-kart requires 10 MH from the machining department and five DLH from the assembly department, the overhead cost allocated to each standard go-kart is $600 from the machining department (10 MH × $60 per MH) and $100 from the assembly department (5 DLH × $20 per DLH). The same procedure is applied for its custom go-kart. The allocation of overhead costs to KartCo's standard and custom go-karts is summarized in Exhibit 17.7.

EXHIBIT 17.7

Overhead Allocation Using Departmental Overhead Rates

	Departmental Overhead Rate	Standard Go-Kart		Custom Go-Kart	
		Hours per Unit	Overhead Allocated	Hours per Unit	Overhead Allocated
Machining department	$60 per MH	10 MH per unit	$600	20 MH per unit	$1,200
Assembly department	$20 per DLH	5 DLH per unit	100	5 DLH per unit	100
Totals			$700		$1,300

Allocated overhead costs vary depending upon the allocation methods used. Exhibit 17.8 summarizes and compares the allocated overhead costs for standard and custom go-karts under the single plantwide overhead rate and the departmental overhead rate methods. The overhead cost allocated to each standard go-kart decreased from $720 under the plantwide overhead rate method to $700 under the departmental overhead rate method, whereas overhead cost allocated to each custom go-kart increased from $1,200 to $1,300. These differences occur because the custom go-kart requires more hours in the machining department (20 MH) than the standard go-kart requires (10 MH).

EXHIBIT 17.8

Comparison of Plantwide Overhead Rate and Departmental Overhead Rate Methods

	Standard Go-Kart	Custom Go-Kart
Overhead under plantwide overhead rate method	$720	$1,200
Overhead under departmental overhead rate method	$700	$1,300

Compared to the plantwide overhead rate method, the departmental overhead rate method usually results in more accurate overhead allocations. When cost analysts are able to logically trace costs to cost objects, costing accuracy is improved. For KartCo, costs are traced to depart-ments and then assigned to units based on how long they spend in each department. The single plantwide overhead rate of $48 per hour is a combination of the $60 per hour machining depart-ment rate and the $20 per hour assembly department rate.

For KartCo, using the multiple departmental overhead rate method yields the following total costs for its products.

	Direct Materials	Direct Labor	Overhead Total	Cost per Unit
Standard go-kart	$400	$350	$ 700	$1,450
Custom go-kart	600	500	1,300	2,400

These costs per unit under the departmental overhead rate method are different from those under the plantwide overhead rate method. Further, this information suggests that KartCo management seri-ously review future production for its standard go-kart product. Specifically, these cost data imply that KartCo cannot make a profit on its standard go-kart if it meets competitors' $1,200 price.

Assessing the Plantwide and Departmental Overhead Rate Methods   The plantwide and departmental overhead rate methods have three key advantages: (1) They are based on readily available information, like direct labor hours. (2) They are easy to implement.

(3) They are consistent with GAAP and can be used for external reporting needs. Both suffer from an important disadvantage, in that overhead costs are frequently too complex to be explained by one factor like direct labor hours or machine hours. Further, technological advances often lower direct labor costs as a percentage of total manufacturing costs. (In some companies, direct labor cost is such a small part of total cost that it is treated as overhead.)

The usefulness of overhead allocations based on the single plantwide overhead rate for managerial decisions depends on two critical assumptions: (1) overhead costs change with the allocation base (such as direct labor hours); and (2) all products use overhead costs in the same proportions.

The reasonableness of these assumptions varies. For companies that manufacture few products or whose operations are labor-intensive, the single plantwide method can yield reasonably useful information for managerial decisions. However, for companies with many different products or those with products that use overhead costs in very different ways, the assumptions of the single plantwide rate are not reasonable. When overhead costs, like machinery depreciation, bear little if any relation to direct labor hours used, allocating overhead cost using a single plantwide overhead rate based on direct labor hours can distort product cost and lead to poor managerial decisions. Despite such shortcomings, some companies continue to use the plantwide method for its simplicity.

The departmental overhead rate method is more refined than the plantwide overhead rate method, but it too has limitations that can distort product costs. The departmental overhead rate method assumes that different products are similar in volume, complexity, and batch size, and that departmental overhead costs are directly proportional to the department allocation base (such as direct labor hours and machine hours for KartCo). When products differ in batch size and complexity, they usually consume different amounts of overhead costs. This is likely the case for KartCo with its high-volume standard model and its low-volume custom model built to customer specifications. In addition, since the departmental overhead rate method still allocates overhead costs based on measures closely related to production volume, it also fails to accurately assign many overhead costs, like machine depreciation or utility costs, that are not driven by production volume.

The next section describes the activity-based costing method, which is designed to overcome some of the limitations of the plantwide and departmental overhead rate methods.

A1 Identify and assess advantages and disadvantages of the plantwide overhead and departmental overhead rate methods.

🟥 **Decision Ethics**   Answer — p. 744   ♟

Department Manager   Three department managers jointly decide to hire a consulting firm for advice on increasing departmental effectiveness and efficiency. The consulting firm spends 50% of its efforts on department "A" and 25% on each of the other two departments. The manager for department "A" suggests that the three departments equally share the consulting fee. As a manager of one of the other two departments, do you believe equal sharing is fair? 🟥

Activity-Based Costing Rates and Method

Cost Flows under Activity-Based Costing Method   Activity-based costing **(ABC)** attempts to more accurately assign overhead costs to the users of overhead by focusing on *activities*. The basic principle underlying activity-based costing is that an **activity**, which is a task, operation, or procedure, is what causes costs to be incurred. For example, cutting raw materials consumes labor and machine hours. Likewise, warehousing products consumes resources (costs) such as employee time for driving a forklift, the electricity to power the forklift, and the wear and tear on a forklift. Also, training employees drives costs such as fees or salaries paid to trainers and the training supplies required. Generally, all activities of an organization can be linked to use of resources. An **activity cost pool** is a collection of costs that are related to the same or similar activity. Pooling costs to determine an **activity overhead (pool) rate** for all costs incurred by the same activity reduces the number of cost assignments required.

There are two basic stages to ABC as shown in Exhibit 17.9. The first stage of ABC cost assignment is to identify the activities (cost objects) involved in manufacturing products and match those activities with the costs they cause (drive). To reduce the total number of activities

C2 Explain cost flows for activity-based costing.

EXHIBIT 17.9

Activity-Based
Costing Method

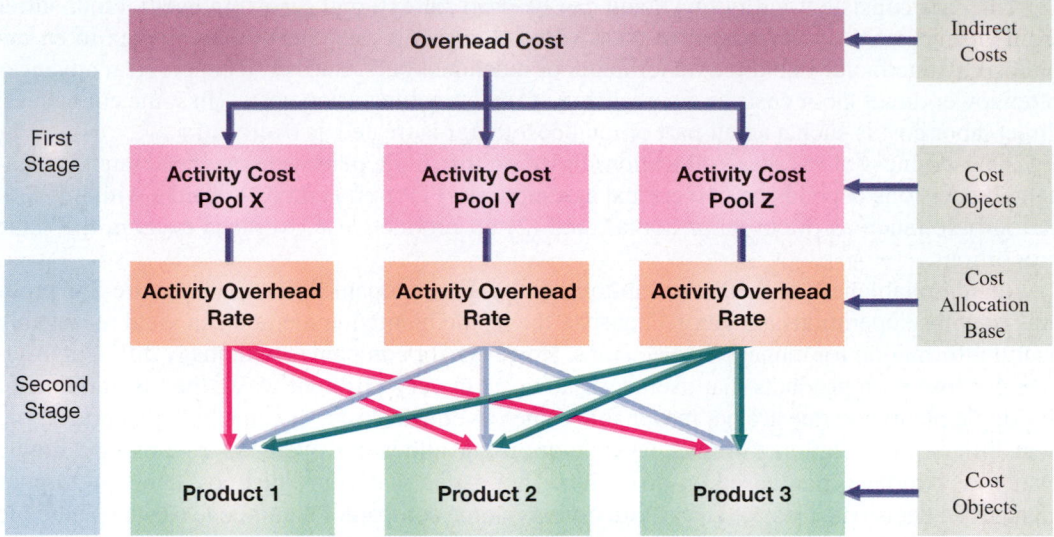

that must be assigned costs, the homogeneous activities (those caused by the same factor such as cutting metal) are grouped into activity cost *pools*. The second stage of ABC is to compute an activity rate for each cost pool and then use this rate to allocate overhead costs to products, which are the cost objects of this second stage.

Quick Check   Answers — p. 744

1. Which method of cost assignment requires more than one overhead rate? (a) Plantwide overhead rate method (b) Departmental overhead rate method (c) ABC (d) Both *b* and *c*.
2. Which method of overhead costing is the most accurate when products differ in level of complexity? (a) ABC (b) Plantwide overhead rate method (c) Departmental overhead rate method.
3. ABC assumes that costs are incurred because of what? (a) Management decisions (b) Activities (c) Financial transactions.

APPLYING ACTIVITY-BASED COSTING

P3 Allocate overhead costs to products using activity-based costing.

Activity-based costing accumulates overhead costs into activity cost pools and then uses activity rates to allocate those costs to products. This involves four steps: (1) identify activities and the costs they cause; (2) group similar activities into activity cost pools; (3) determine an activity rate for each activity cost pool; and (4) allocate overhead costs to products using those activity rates. To illustrate, let's return to KartCo and apply steps 1 through 4.

Step 1: Identify Activities and the Costs They Cause

Step 1 in applying ABC is to identify activities. This is commonly done through discussions with employees in production departments and through reviews of production activities. The more activities that ABC tracks, the more accurately overhead costs are assigned. However, tracking too many activities makes the system cumbersome and costly to maintain. Consequently, we try to reach a balance where it is often necessary to reduce the number of activities tracked by combining similar activities. An activity can also involve several related tasks. The aim of this first step is to understand actions performed in the organization that drive costs.

KartCo has total overhead cost of $4,800,000 consisting of $4,000,000 indirect labor costs and $800,000 factory utilities costs. Details gathered by KartCo about its overhead costs are shown in Exhibit 17.10. Column totals for indirect labor and factory utilities correspond to amounts in Exhibit 17.4. Activity-based costing provides more detail about the activities and the costs they cause than is provided from traditional costing methods.

Activity	Indirect Labor	Factory Utilities	Total Overhead
Machine setup	$ 700,000	—	$ 700,000
Machine repair	1,300,000	—	1,300,000
Factory maintenance	800,000	—	800,000
Engineer salaries	1,200,000	—	1,200,000
Assembly line power	—	$600,000	600,000
Heating and lighting	—	200,000	200,000
Totals	$4,000,000	$800,000	$4,800,000

EXHIBIT 17.10

KartCo Overhead Cost Details

Decision Maker

Answer — p. 744

Cost Analyst Your employer is exploring the possibility of implementing an activity-based costing system in the plant where you are newly assigned as a cost analyst. Your responsibilities are to identify manufacturing activities and link them to the costs they drive. You have never worked in this type of manufacturing operation and you are unsure about what activities are performed and their costs. What steps should you pursue to yield a quality report? ■

Step 2: Trace Overhead Costs to Cost Pools

Step 2 in applying ABC is to assign activities and their overhead costs to cost pools. Overhead costs are commonly accumulated by each department in a traditional accounting system. Some of these overhead costs are traced directly to a specific activity cost pool. At KartCo, for example, the assembly department supervisor's salary is assigned to its design modification cost pool and its machine repair costs are traced to its setup cost pool. Companies try to trace as many overhead costs to specific activity cost pools as possible to improve costing accuracy.

Recall that a premise of ABC is that operations are a series of activities that cause costs to be incurred. Instead of combining costs from different activities into one plantwide pool or multiple departmental pools, ABC focuses on activities as the cost object in the first step of cost assignment. We are then able to *trace* costs to a cost object and then combine activities that are used by products in similar ways to reduce the number of cost allocations.

After a review and analysis of its activities, KartCo management assigns its overhead costs into its four activity cost pools as shown in Exhibit 17.11. To assign costs to pools, management looks for costs that are caused by the activities of that pool and activity level. It is crucial that activities in each cost pool be similar and reflect a similar activity level.

Activity Pools	Activity Cost	Pool Cost
Craftsmanship		
Assembly line power	$ 600,000	$ 600,000
Setup		
Machine setup	700,000	
Machine repair	1,300,000	2,000,000
Design modification		
Engineer salaries	1,200,000	1,200,000
Plant services		
Factory maintenance	800,000	
Heating and lighting	200,000	1,000,000
Total overhead cost		$4,800,000

EXHIBIT 17.11

Assigning Overhead to Activity Cost Pools

Exhibit 17.11 shows that $600,000 of overhead costs are assigned to the craftsmanship cost pool; $2,000,000 to the setup cost pool; $1,200,000 to the design-modification cost pool; and $1,000,000 to the plant services cost pool. This reduces the potential number of overhead rates from six (one for each of its six activities) to four (one for each pool).

⬛ Decision Insight

Measuring Health   Activity-based costing is used in many settings. Its only requirements are existence of costs and demand for reliable cost information. A study found that activity-based costing improves health care costing accuracy, enabling improved profitability analysis and decision making. Identifying cost drivers in a health care setting is challenging and fraught with ethical concerns. ■

Step 3: Determine Activity Rates

Step 3 is to compute activity rates used to assign overhead costs to final cost objects such as products. Proper determination of activity rates depends on (1) proper identification of the factor that drives the cost in each activity cost pool and (2) proper measures of activities.

Identifying the factor that drives cost, the **activity cost driver,** is that activity causing costs in the pool to be incurred. For KartCo's overhead, craftsmanship costs are mainly driven (caused) by assembling products, setup costs are driven by system repairs and retooling, design-modification costs are driven by new features, and plant service costs are driven by building occupancy. The activity cost driver, a measure of activity level, serves as the allocation base. KartCo uses the following activity drivers for its activity pools.

Activity Pool	Activity Driver (# of)
Craftsmanship	Direct labor hours
Setup	Batches
Design modification.	Designs
Plant services.	Square feet

KartCo expects the following activity levels: 30,000 direct labor hours, 200 batches of go-karts produced, 10 design modifications, and use of 20,000 square feet of floor space.

In general, cost pool activity rates are computed as:

Cost pool activity rate = Overhead costs assigned to pool ÷ Number of activities

For KartCo, the activity rate for the craftsmanship cost pool is computed as:

Craftsmanship cost pool activity rate = $600,000 ÷ 30,000 DLH = $20 per DLH

The activity rate computations for KartCo are summarized in Exhibit 17.12.

EXHIBIT 17.12

Activity Rates for KartCo

Activity Cost Pools	Activity Measure Chosen	Overhead Costs Assigned to Pool	× Number of Activities =	Activity Rate
Craftsmanship	DLH	$ 600,000	30,000 DLH	$20 per DLH
Setup	Batches	2,000,000	200 batches	$10,000 per batch
Design modification	Number of designs	1,200,000	10 designs	$120,000 per design
Plant services	Square feet	1,000,000	20,000 sq. ft.	$50 per sq. ft.

Step 4: Assign Overhead Costs to Cost Objects

Step 4 is to assign overhead costs in each activity cost pool to final cost objects using activity rates. (This is referred to as the *second-stage assignment;* where steps 1 through 3 make up the *first-stage assignment.*) To accomplish this, overhead costs in each activity cost pool are allocated to product lines based on the level of activity for each product line. After costs in all cost pools are allocated, the costs for each product line are totaled and then divided by the number of units of that product line to arrive at overhead cost per product unit.

For KartCo, overhead costs in each pool are allocated to the standard go-karts and the custom go-karts using the activity rates from Exhibit 17.12. The activities used by each product line and the overhead costs allocated to standard and custom go-karts under ABC for KartCo are summarized in Exhibit 17.13. To illustrate, the $500,000 of overhead costs in the craftsmanship cost pool is allocated to standard go-karts as follows.

> **Overhead from craftsmanship pool allocated to standard go-kart** = Activities consumed × Activity rate
> = 25,000 DLH × $20 per DLH = $500,000

We know that standard go-karts require 25,000 direct labor hours and the activity rate for craftsmanship is $20 per direct labor hour. Multiplying the number of direct labor hours by the activity rate yields the craftsmanship costs assigned to standard go-karts. Custom go-karts consumed 5,000 direct labor hours, so we assign $100,000 (5,000 DLH × $20 per DLH) to that product line. We similarly allocate overhead to setup, design modification, and plant services pools for each type of go-kart.

	Standard Go-Karts			**Custom Go-Karts**		
	Activities Consumed	Activity Rate	Activity Cost Allocated	Activities Consumed	Activity Rate	Activity Cost Allocated
Craftsmanship	25,000 DLH	$20 per DLH	$ 500,000	5,000 DLH	$20 per DLH	$ 100,000
Setup	40 batches	$10,000 per batch	400,000	160 batches	$10,000 per batch	1,600,000
Design modification	0 designs	$120,000 per design	0	10 designs	$120,000 per design	1,200,000
Plant services	12,000 sq. ft.	$50 per sq. ft.	600,000	8,000 sq. ft.	$50 per sq. ft.	400,000
Total cost			$1,500,000			$3,300,000

EXHIBIT 17.13

Overhead Allocated to Go-Karts for KartCo

In assigning overhead costs to products, KartCo assigned no design modification costs to standard go-karts because standard go-karts are sold as "off-the-shelf" items.

Overhead cost per unit is computed by dividing total overhead cost allocated to each product line by the number of product units. KartCo's overhead cost per unit for its standard and custom go-karts is computed and shown in Exhibit 17.14.

	(A) Total Overhead Cost Allocated	(B) Budgeted Units of Production	(A ÷ B) Overhead Cost per Unit
Standard go-kart	$1,500,000	5,000 units	$ 300 per unit
Custom go-kart	3,300,000	1,000 units	$3,300 per unit

EXHIBIT 17.14

Overhead Cost per Unit for Go-Karts Using ABC

Total cost per unit for KartCo using ABC for its two products follows.

	Direct Materials	Direct Labor	Overhead	Total Cost per Unit
Standard go-kart . . .	$400	$350	$ 300	$1,050
Custom go-kart	600	500	3,300	4,400

Assuming that ABC more accurately assigns costs, we now are able to help KartCo's management understand how its competitors can sell their standard models at $1,200 and why KartCo is flooded with orders for custom go-karts. Specifically, if the cost to produce a standard go-kart is $1,050, as shown above (and not $1,470 as computed using the plantwide rate or $1,450 computed using departmental rates), a profit of $150 ($1,200 − $1,050) occurs on each standard unit sold at the competitive $1,200 market price. Further, selling its custom go-kart at $3,500 is a mistake by KartCo management because it is losing $900 ($3,500 − $4,400) on each custom go-kart sold. That is, KartCo has underpriced its custom go-kart relative to its production costs and competitors' prices, which explains why the company has more custom orders than it can supply.

Overhead allocation per go-kart under the single plantwide rate method, multiple departmental rate method, and ABC is summarized in Exhibit 17.15. Overhead cost allocated to standard go-karts is much less under ABC than under either of the volume-based costing methods. One reason for this difference is the large design modification costs that were spread over all go-karts under both the plantwide rate and the departmental rate methods even though standard go-karts require no engineering modification. When ABC is used, overhead costs commonly shift from standardized, large-volume products to low-volume, customized specialty products that consume disproportionate resources.

EXHIBIT 17.15

Comparison of Overhead Allocations by Method

Overhead Cost Allocation Method	Overhead Cost per Go-Kart	
	Standard Go-Kart	Custom Go-Kart
Plantwide method	$720	$1,200
Departmental method	700	1,300
Activity-based costing	300	3,300

Differences between ABC and Multiple Departmental Rates   Using ABC differs from using multiple departmental rates in how overhead cost pools are identified and in how overhead cost in each pool is allocated. When using multiple departmental rates, each department is a cost pool, and overhead cost allocated to each department is assigned to products using a volume-based factor (such as direct labor hours or machine hours). This assumes that overhead costs in each department are directly proportional to the volume-based factor. ABC, on the other hand, recognizes that overhead costs are more complex. For example, purchasing costs might make up one activity cost pool (spanning more than one department) that would include activities such as the number of invoices. ABC emphasizes activities and costs of carrying out these activities. Under ABC, only costs related to the same activity are grouped into a cost pool. Therefore, ABC arguably better reflects the complex nature of overhead costs and how these costs are used in making products.

Decision Insight

ABCs of Banking   **First Tennessee National Corporation**, a bank, applied ABC to reveal that 30% of its CD customers provided nearly 90% of its profits from CDs. Further, another 30% of its CD customers were actually losing money for the bank. Management used ABC to correct this problem. ■

Quick Check   Answers — p. 744

4. What is a cost driver? Provide an example of a typical cost driver.

5. What is an activity driver? Provide an example of a typical activity driver.

6. Traditional volume-based costing methods tend to: (a) overstate the cost of low-volume products, (b) overstate the cost of high-volume products, or (c) both a and b.

ASSESSING ACTIVITY-BASED COSTING

While activity-based costing improves the accuracy of overhead cost allocations to products, it too has limitations. This section describes the major advantages and disadvantages of activity-based costing.

A2 Identify and assess advantages and disadvantages of activity-based costing.

Advantages of Activity-Based Costing

More Accurate Overhead Cost Allocation Companies have typically used either a plantwide overhead rate or multiple departmental overhead rates because these methods are more straightforward than ABC and are acceptable under GAAP for external reporting. Under these traditional systems, overhead costs are pooled in a few large pools and are spread uniformly across high- and low-volume products. With ABC, overhead costs are grouped into activity pools. There are usually more activity pools under ABC than cost pools under traditional costing, which usually increases costing accuracy. More important is that overhead costs in each ABC pool are caused by a single activity. This means that overhead costs in each activity pool are allocated to products based on the cost of resources consumed by a product (input) rather than on how many units are produced (output). In sum, overhead cost allocation under ABC is more accurate because (1) there are more cost pools, (2) costs in each pool are more similar, and (3) allocation is based on activities that cause overhead costs.

Point: ABC can allocate the selling and administrative costs expensed by GAAP to activities; such costs can include marketing costs, costs to process orders, and costs to process customer returns.

More Effective Overhead Cost Control In traditional costing, overhead costs are usually allocated to products based on either direct labor hours or machine hours. Such allocation typically leads management to focus attention on direct labor cost or machine hours. Yet, direct labor or machine hours are often not the cause of overhead costs and often not even linked with these volume-related measures. As we saw with KartCo, design modifications markedly affect its overhead costs. Consequently, a plantwide overhead rate or departmental overhead rate based on direct labor or machine hours can mislead managers, preventing effective control of overhead costs and leading to product mispricing. ABC, on the other hand, can be used to identify activities that can benefit from process improvement. ABC can also help managers effectively control overhead cost by focusing on processes or activities such as batching setups, order processing, and design modifications instead of focusing only on direct labor or machine hours. For KartCo, identification of large design-modification costs would allow managers to work on initiatives to improve this process. Besides controlling overhead costs, KartCo's better assignment of overhead costs (particularly design-modification costs) for its go-karts helps its managers make better production and pricing decisions.

Focus on Relevant Factors Basing cost assignment on activities is not limited to determining product costs, as illustrated by KartCo. ABC can be used to assign costs to any cost object that is of management interest. For instance, a marketing manager often wants to determine the profitability of various market segments. Activity-based costing can be used to accurately assign costs of shipping, advertising, order-taking, and customer service that are unrelated to sales and costs of products sold. Such an activity-based analysis can reveal to the marketing department some customers that are better left to the competition if they consume a larger amount of marketing resources than the gross profit generated by sales to those customers. Generally, ABC provides better customer profitability information by including all resources consumed to serve a customer. This allows managers to make better pricing decisions on custom orders and to better manage customers by focusing on those that are most profitable.

Point: The *Demonstration Problem* illustrates how ABC is applied for a services company.

Better Management of Activities Being competitive requires that managers be able to use resources efficiently. Understanding how costs are incurred is a first step toward controlling costs. One important contribution of ABC is helping managers identify the causes of costs, that is, the activities driving them. **Activity-based management (ABM)** is an outgrowth of ABC that draws on the link between activities and cost incurrence for better management. Activity-based management can be useful in distinguishing **value-added activities,** which add value to a product, from *non-value-added activities,* which do not. For KartCo, its value-added activities include machining, assembly, and the costs of engineering design changes. Its non-value-added activity is machine repair. The way to control a cost requires changing how much of an activity is performed.

Decision Maker
Answer — p. 744

Entrepreneur   You are the entrepreneur of a start-up pharmaceutical company. You are assigning overhead to product units based on machine hours in the packaging area. Profits are slim due to increased competition. One of your larger overhead costs is $10,000 for cleaning and sterilization that occurs each time the packaging system is converted from one product to another. These overhead costs average $0.10 per product unit. Can you reduce cleaning and sterilizing costs by reducing the number of units produced? If not, what should you do to control these overhead costs? ■

Disadvantages of Activity-Based Costing

Costs to Implement and Maintain ABC   Designing and implementing an activity-based costing system requires management commitment and financial resources. For ABC to be effective, a thorough analysis of cost activities must be performed and appropriate cost pools must be determined. Collecting and analyzing cost data are expensive and so is maintaining an ABC system. While technology, such as bar coding, has made it possible for many companies to use ABC, it is still too costly for some. Managers must weigh the cost of implementing and maintaining an ABC system against the potential benefits of ABC in light of company circumstances.

Uncertainty with Decisions Remains   As with all cost information, managers must interpret ABC data with caution in making managerial decisions. In the KartCo case, given the huge design-modification costs for custom go-karts determined under the ABC system, a manager might be tempted to decline some custom go-kart orders to save overhead costs. However, in the short run, some or all of the design-modification costs cannot be saved even if some custom go-kart orders are rejected. Managers must examine carefully the controllability of costs before making decisions.

Types of Activities

C3   Describe the four types of activities that cause overhead costs.

Activities causing overhead cost can be separated into four levels of types of activities: (1) **unit level activities,** (2) **batch level activities,** (3) **product level activities,** and (4) **facility level activities.** These four activities are described as follows.

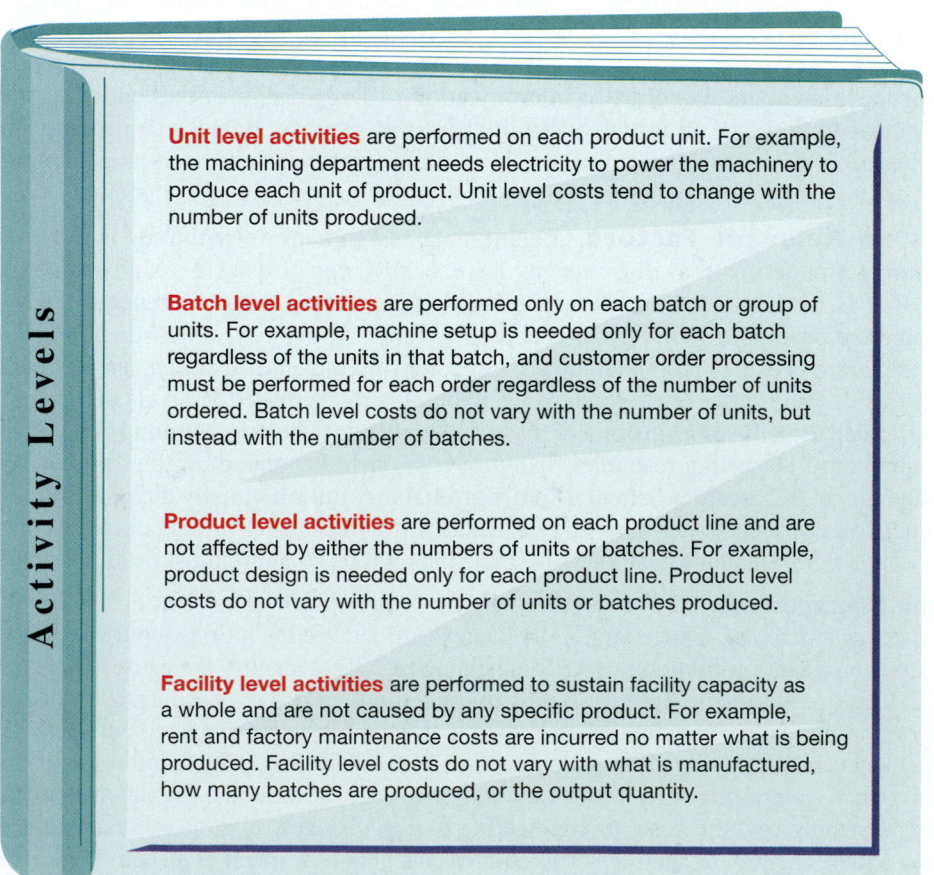

Activity Levels

Unit level activities are performed on each product unit. For example, the machining department needs electricity to power the machinery to produce each unit of product. Unit level costs tend to change with the number of units produced.

Batch level activities are performed only on each batch or group of units. For example, machine setup is needed only for each batch regardless of the units in that batch, and customer order processing must be performed for each order regardless of the number of units ordered. Batch level costs do not vary with the number of units, but instead with the number of batches.

Product level activities are performed on each product line and are not affected by either the numbers of units or batches. For example, product design is needed only for each product line. Product level costs do not vary with the number of units or batches produced.

Facility level activities are performed to sustain facility capacity as a whole and are not caused by any specific product. For example, rent and factory maintenance costs are incurred no matter what is being produced. Facility level costs do not vary with what is manufactured, how many batches are produced, or the output quantity.

In the KartCo example, the craftsmanship pool reflects unit level costs, the setup pool reflects batch level costs, the design-modification pool reflects product level costs, and plant services reflect facility level costs.

Additional examples of activities commonly found within each of the four activity levels are shown in the following table. This is not a complete list, but reviewing it can help in understanding this hierarchy of production activities. This list also includes common measures used to reflect the specific activity identified. Knowing this hierarchy can help us simplify and understand activity-based costing.

Activity Level	Examples of Activity	Activity Driver (Measure)
Unit level	Cutting parts	Machine hours
	Assembling components	Direct labor hours
	Printing checks	Number of checks
Batch level	Calibrating machines	Number of batches
	Receiving shipments	Number of orders
	Sampling product quality	Number of lots produced
Product level	Designing modifications	Change requests
	Organizing production	Engineering hours
	Controlling inventory	Parts per product
Facility level	Cleaning workplace	Square feet of floors*
	Providing electricity	Kilowatt hours*
	Providing personnel support	Number of employees*

* Facility level costs are not traceable to individual product lines, batches, or units. They are normally assigned to units using a unit level driver such as direct labor hours or machine hours even though they are caused by another activity.

Quick Check   Answers — p. 744

7. What are three advantages of ABC over traditional volume-based allocation methods?
8. What is the main advantage of traditional volume-based allocation methods compared to activity-based costing? How should a manager decide which method to use?

 ## GLOBAL VIEW

Toyota Motor Corporation pioneered *lean manufacturing,* which focuses on eliminating waste while satisfying customers. Many lean manufacturers embrace **lean accounting,** which has two key components. First, the company applies lean thinking to eliminate waste in its accounting process. Second, instead of focusing on cost allocation methods such as activity-based costing, the company develops alternative performance measures that better reflect the benefits of manufacturing process changes. Examples include the percentage of products produced without defects, the percentage of ontime deliveries, and the level of sales per employee.

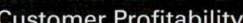 Customer Profitability      **Decision Analysis**

Are all customers equal? To help answer this, let's return to the KartCo case and assume that costs of providing customer support (such as delivery, installation, and warranty work) are related to the distance a technician must travel to provide services. Also assume that, as a result of applying activity-based costing, KartCo plans to sell its standard go-kart for $1,200 per unit. If the annual cost of customer services is expected to be $250,000 and the distance traveled by technicians is 100,000 miles annually, KartCo would want to link the cost of customer services with individual customers to make efficient marketing decisions.

Using these data, an activity rate of $2.50 per mile ($250,000/100,000 miles) is computed for assigning customer service costs to individual customers. For KartCo, it would compute a typical customer profitability report for one of its customers, Six Flags, as follows.

Customer Profitability Report—Six Flags			
Sales (10 standard go-karts × $1,200)			$12,000
Less: Product costs			
Direct materials (10 go-karts × $400 per go-kart)		$4,000	
Direct labor (10 go-karts × $350 per go-kart)...................		3,500	
Overhead (10 go-karts × $300 per go-kart, Exhibit 17.14)		3,000	10,500
Product profit margin			1,500
Less: Customer service costs (200 miles × $2.50 per mile)			500
Customer profit margin			$ 1,000

Analysis indicates that a total profit margin of $1,000 is generated from this customer. The management of KartCo can see that if this customer requires service technicians to travel more than 600 miles ($1,500 ÷ $2.50 per mile), the sale of 10 standard go-karts to this customer would be unprofitable. ABC encourages management to consider all resources consumed to serve a customer, not just manufacturing costs that are the focus of traditional costing methods.

DEMONSTRATION PROBLEM

Silver Law Firm provides litigation and mediation services to a variety of clients. Attorneys keep track of the time they spend on each case, which is used to charge fees to clients at a rate of $300 per hour. A management advisor commented that activity-based costing might prove useful in evaluating the costs of its legal services, and the firm has decided to evaluate its fee structure by comparing ABC to its alternative cost allocations. The following data relate to a typical month at the firm. During a typical month the firm handles seven mediation cases and three litigation cases.

	Activity Driver	Total Amount	Consumption by Service Type		Activity Cost
			Litigation	Mediation	
Providing legal advice.................	Billable hours	200	75	125	$30,000
Overhead costs					
Internal support departments					
Preparing documents	Documents	30	16	14	$ 4,000
Occupying office space	Billable hours	200	75	125	1,200
Heating and lighting of office	Billable hours	200	75	125	350
External support departments					
Registering court documents	Documents	30	16	14	1,250
Retaining consultants					
(investigators, psychiatrists)	Court dates	6	5	1	10,000
Using contract services					
(couriers, security guards)	Court dates	6	5	1	5,000
Total overhead costs					$21,800

Required

1. Determine the cost of providing legal services to each type of case using activity-based costing (ABC).
2. Determine the cost of each type of case using a single plantwide rate for nonattorney costs based on billable hours.

3. Determine the cost of each type of case using multiple departmental overhead rates for the internal support department (based on number of documents) and external support department (based on billable hours).

4. Compare and discuss the costs assigned under each method for management decisions.

PLANNING THE SOLUTION

- Compute pool rates and assign costs to cases using ABC.
- Compute costs for the cases using the volume-based methods and discuss differences between these costs and the costs computed using ABC.

SOLUTION TO DEMONSTRATION PROBLEM

1. We need to set up activity pools and compute pool rates for ABC. All activities except "occupying office space" and "heating and lighting" are unit level (meaning they are traceable to the individual cases handled by the law firm). "Preparing documents" and "registering documents" are both driven by the number of documents associated with each case. We can therefore combine these activities and their costs into a single pool, which we call "clerical support." Similarly, "retaining consultants" and "using services" are related to the number of times the attorneys must go to court (court dates). We combine these activities and their costs into another activity cost pool labeled "litigation support." The costs associated with occupying office space and the heating and lighting are facility level activities and are not traceable to individual cases. Yet they are costs that must be covered by fees charged to clients. We assign these costs using a convenient base—in this example we use the number of billable hours, which attorneys record for each client. Providing legal advice is the direct labor for a law firm.

Activity Pool	Activity Cost	Pool Cost	Activity Driver	Pool Rate (Pool Cost ÷ Activity Driver)
Providing legal advice	$30,000	$30,000	200 billable hours	$150 per billable hour
Clerical support				
Preparing documents	4,000			
Registering documents	1,250	5,250	30 documents	$175 per document
Litigation support				
Retaining consultants	10,000			
Using services	5,000	15,000	6 court dates	$2,500 per court date
Facility costs				
Occupying office space	1,200			
Heating and lighting	350	1,550	200 billable hours	$7.75 per billable hour

We next determine the cost of providing each type of legal service as shown in the following table. Specifically, the pool rates from above are used to assign costs to each type of service provided by the law firm. Since litigation consumed 75 billable hours of attorney time, we assign $11,250 (75 billable hours × $150 per billable hour) of the cost of providing legal advice to this type of case. Mediation required 125 hours of attorney time, so $18,750 (125 billable hours × $150 per billable hour) of the cost to provide legal advice is assigned to mediation cases. Clerical support cost $175 per document, so the costs associated with activities in this cost pool are assigned to litigation cases (16 documents × $175 per document = $2,800) and mediation cases (14 documents × $175 per document = $2,450). The costs of activities in the litigation support and the facility cost pools are similarly assigned to the two case types.

    We compute the total cost of litigation ($27,131.25) and mediation ($24,668.75) and divide these totals by the number of cases of each type to determine the average cost of each case type: $9,044 for litigation and $3,524 for mediation. This analysis shows that charging clients $300 per billable hour without regard to the type of case results in litigation clients being charged less than the cost to provide that service ($7,500 versus $9,044).

	Pool Rate	Litigation		Mediation	
Providing legal advice......	$150 per billable hour	75 hours	$11,250.00	125 hours	$18,750.00
Clerical support..........	$175 per document	16 docs	2,800.00	14 docs	2,450.00
Litigation support	$2,500 per court date	5 court dates	12,500.00	1 court date	2,500.00
Facility costs	$7.75 per billable hour	75 hours	581.25	125 hours	968.75
Total cost...............			$27,131.25		$24,668.75
÷ Number of cases.......			3 cases		7 cases
Average cost per case			**$9,044**		**$3,524**
Average fee per case			**$7,500***		**$5,357**†

* (75 billable hours × $300 per hour) ÷ 3 cases

† (125 billable hours × $300 per hour) ÷ 7 cases

2. The cost of each type of case using a single plantwide rate for nonattorney costs (that is, all costs except for those related to providing legal advice) based on billable hours is as follows.

> Total overhead cost/ Total billable hours = $21,800/200 billable hours = **$109 per hour**

We then determine the cost of providing each type of legal service as follows.

		Litigation		Mediation	
Providing legal advice...........	$150 per billable hour	75 hours	$11,250	125 hours	$18,750
Overhead (from part 2).........	$109 per billable hour	75 hours	8,175	125 hours	13,625
Total cost....................			$19,425		$32,375
÷ Number of cases............			3 cases		7 cases
Average cost per case			**$6,475**		**$4,625**
Average fee per case .... (from part 1)			**$7,500**		**$5,357**

3. The cost of each type of case using multiple departmental overhead rates for the internal support department (based on number of documents) and external support department (based on billable hours) is determined as follows.

	Departmental Cost	Base	Departmental Rate (Departmental Cost ÷ Base)
Internal support departments			
Preparing documents.........	$ 4,000		
Occupying office space	1,200		
Heating and lighting of office	350	$ 5,550	30 documents	$185 per document
External support departments			
Registering documents	1,250		
Retaining consultants	10,000		
Using contract services	5,000	16,250	200 billable hours	$81.25 per hour

The departmental overhead rates computed above are used to assign overhead costs to the two types of legal services. For the internal support department we use the overhead rate of $185 per document to assign $2,960 ($185 × 16 documents) to litigation and $2,590 ($185 × 14 documents) to mediation. For the external support department we use the overhead rate of $81.25 per hour to assign $6,093.75 ($81.25 × 75 hours) to litigation and $10,156.25 ($81.25 × 125 hours) to mediation. As shown below, the resulting average costs of litigation cases and mediation cases are $6,768 and $4,499, respectively.

Using this method of cost assignment, it *appears* that the fee of $300 per billable hour is adequate to cover costs associated with each case.

		Litigation		Mediation	
Attorney fees.............	$150 per billable hour	75 hours	$11,250.00	125 hours	$18,750.00
Internal support...........	$185 per document	16 documents	2,960.00	14 documents	2,590.00
External support	$81.25 per hour	75 hours	6,093.75	125 hours	10,156.25
Total cost................			$20,303.75		$31,496.25
÷ Number of cases........			3 cases		7 cases
Average cost per case			**$6,768**		**$4,499**
Average fee per case .... (from part 1)			**$7,500**		**$5,357**

4. A comparison and discussion of the costs assigned under each method follows.

	Method of Assigning Overhead Costs		
Average Cost per Case	Activity-Based Costing	Plantwide Overhead Rate	Departmental Overhead Rates
Litigation cases...................	$9,044	$6,475	$6,768
Mediation cases	3,524	4,625	4,499

The departmental and plantwide overhead rate methods assign overhead on the basis of volume-related measures (billable hours and document filings). Litigation costs *appear* profitable under these methods, because the average costs are below the average revenue of $7,500. ABC, however, focuses attention on activities that drive costs. A large part of overhead costs was for consultants and contract services, which were unrelated to the number of cases, but related to the type of cases consuming those resources. Using ABC, the costs shift from the high-volume cases (mediation) to the low-volume cases (litigation). When the firm considers the consumption of resources for these cases using ABC, it finds that the fees charged to litigate cases is insufficient (average revenue of $7,500 versus average cost of $9,044). The law firm is charging too little for the complex cases that require litigation.

Summary

C1 Distinguish between the plantwide overhead rate method, the departmental overhead rate method, and the activity-based costing method. Overhead costs can be assigned to cost objects using a plantwide rate that combines all overhead costs into a single rate, usually based on direct labor hours, machine hours, or direct labor cost. Multiple departmental overhead rates that include overhead costs traceable to departments are used to allocate overhead based on departmental functions. ABC links overhead costs to activities and assigns overhead based on how much of each activity is required for a product.

C2 Explain cost flows for activity-based costing. With ABC, overhead costs are first traced to the activities that cause them, and then cost pools are formed combining costs caused by the same activity. Overhead rates based on these activities are then used to assign overhead to products in proportion to the amount of activity required to produce them.

C3 Describe the four types of activities that cause overhead costs. The four types of activities that cause overhead costs are: (1) unit level activities, (2) batch level activities, (3) product level activities, and (4) facility level activities. Unit level activities

are performed on each unit, batch level activities are performed only on each group of units, and product level activities are performed only on each product line. Facility level activities are performed to sustain facility capacity and are not caused by any specific product. Understanding these types of activities can help in applying activity-based costing.

A1 Identify and assess advantages and disadvantages of the plantwide overhead and departmental overhead rate methods. A single plantwide overhead rate is a simple way to assign overhead cost. A disadvantage is that it can inaccurately assign costs when costs are caused by multiple factors and when different products consume different amounts of inputs. Overhead costing accuracy is improved by use of multiple departmental rates because differences across departmental functions can be linked to costs incurred in departments. Yet, accuracy of cost assignment with departmental rates suffers from the same problems associated with plantwide rates because activities required for each product are not identified with costs of providing those activities.

A2 Identify and assess advantages and disadvantages of activity-based costing. ABC improves product costing accuracy and draws management attention to relevant factors to control. The cost of constructing and maintaining an ABC system can sometimes outweigh its value.

P1 **Allocate overhead costs to products using the plantwide overhead rate method.** The plantwide overhead rate equals total budgeted overhead divided by budgeted plant volume, the latter often measured in direct labor hours or machine hours. This rate multiplied by the number of direct labor hours (or machine hours) required for each product provides the overhead assigned to each product.

P2 **Allocate overhead costs to products using the departmental overhead rate method.** When using multiple departmental rates, overhead cost must first be traced to each department and then divided by the measure of output for that department to yield the departmental overhead rate. Overhead is applied to products using this rate as products pass through each department.

P3 **Allocate overhead costs to products using activity-based costing.** With ABC, overhead costs are matched to activities that cause them. If there is more than one cost with the same activity, these costs are combined into pools. An overhead rate for each pool is determined by dividing total cost for that pool by its activity measure. Overhead costs are assigned to products by multiplying the ABC pool rate by the amount of the activity required for each product.

Guidance Answers to Decision Maker and Decision Ethics

Department Manager   When dividing a bill, common sense suggests fairness. That is, if one department consumes more services than another, we attempt to share the bill in proportion to consumption. Equally dividing the bill among the number of departments is fair if each consumed equal services. This same notion applies in assigning costs to products and services. For example, dividing overhead costs by the number of units is fair if all products consumed overhead in equal proportion.

Cost Analyst   Before the accounting system can report information, relevant and accurate data must be collected. One step is to ask questions—it is a good way to leverage others' experience and knowledge to quickly learn operations. A cost analyst must also understand the manufacturing operation to itemize activities for ABC. Thus, step two might be to tour the manufacturing facility, observing manufacturing operations, asking probing questions, and requesting recommendations from the people who work in those operations. We must remember that these employees are the experts who can provide the data we need to implement an activity-based costing system.

Entrepreneur   Cleaning and sterilizing costs are not directly related to the volume of product manufactured. Thus, changing the number of units produced does not necessarily reduce these costs. Further, expressing costs of cleaning and sterilizing on a per unit basis is often misleading for the person responsible for controlling costs. Costs of cleaning and sterilizing are related to changing from one product line to another. Consequently, the way to control those costs is to control the number of times the packing system has to be changed for a different product line. Thus, efficient product scheduling would help reduce those overhead costs and improve profitability.

Guidance Answers to Quick Checks

1. d

2. a

3. b

4. A cost driver is an activity that causes costs to be incurred. Setup costs, design modifications, and plant services such as maintenance and utilities are examples of typical cost drivers.

5. An activity driver is the measurement used for cost drivers. An example is machine hours.

6. b

7. Three advantages of ABC over traditional methods are: (a) more accurate product costing; (b) more effective cost control; and (c) focus on relevant factors for decision making.

8. Traditional volume-based methods are easier and less costly to implement and maintain. The choice of accounting method should be made by comparing the costs of alternatives with their benefits.

Key Terms   mhhe.com/wildFINMAN4e

Activity (p. 731)

Activity-based costing (ABC) (p. 731)

Activity-based management (p. 737)

Activity cost driver (p. 734)

Activity cost pool (p. 731)

Activity overhead (pool) rate (p. 731)

Batch level activities (p. 738)

Cost object (p. 727)

Facility level activities (p. 738)

Lean accounting (p. 739)

Product level activities (p. 738)

Unit level activities (p. 738)

Value-added activities (p. 737)

Additional Quiz Questions are available at the book's Website.

1. In comparison to a traditional cost system, and when there are batch level or product level costs, an activity-based costing system usually:
   a. Shifts costs from low-volume to high-volume products.
   b. Shifts costs from high-volume to low-volume products.
   c. Shifts costs from standardized to specialized products.
   d. Shifts costs from specialized to standardized products.

2. Which of the following statements is (are) true?
   a. An activity-based costing system is generally easier to implement and maintain than a traditional costing system.
   b. One of the goals of activity-based management is the elimination of waste by allocating costs to products that waste resources.
   c. Activity-based costing uses a number of activity cost pools, each of which is allocated to products on the basis of direct labor hours.
   d. Activity rates in activity-based costing are computed by dividing costs from the first-stage allocations by the activity measure for each activity cost pool.

3. All of the following are examples of batch level activities except:
   a. Purchase order processing.
   b. Setting up equipment.
   c. Clerical activity associated with processing purchase orders to produce an order for a standard product.
   d. Employee recreational facilities.

4. A company has two products: A and B. It uses activity-based costing and prepares the following analysis showing budgeted cost and activity for each of its three activity cost pools.

Activity Cost Pool	Budgeted Overhead Cost	Budgeted Activity		
		Product A	Product B	Total
Activity 1	$ 80,000	200	800	1,000
Activity 2	58,400	1,000	500	1,500
Activity 3	360,000	600	5,400	6,000

Annual production and sales level of Product A is 18,188 units, and the annual production and sales level of Product B is 31,652 units. The approximate overhead cost per unit of Product B under activity-based costing is:
   a. $2.02
   b. $5.00
   c. $12.87
   d. $22.40

5. A company uses activity-based costing to determine the costs of its two products: A and B. The budgeted cost and activity for each of the company's three activity cost pools follow.

Activity Cost Pool	Budgeted Cost	Budgeted Activity		
		Product A	Product B	Total
Activity 1	$19,800	800	300	1,100
Activity 2	16,000	2,200	1,800	4,000
Activity 3	14,000	400	300	700

The activity rate under the activity-based costing method for Activity 3 is approximately:
   a. $4.00
   b. $8.59
   c. $18.00
   d. $20.00

 Icon denotes assignments that involve decision making.

Discussion Questions

1. Why are overhead costs allocated to products and not traced to products as direct materials and direct labor are?

2. What are three common methods of assigning overhead costs to a product?

3. What is a cost object?

4. Why are direct labor hours and machine hours commonly used as the bases for overhead allocation?

5. What are the advantages of using a single plantwide overhead rate?

6. The usefulness of a single plantwide overhead rate is based on two assumptions. What are those assumptions?

7. Explain why a single plantwide overhead rate can distort the cost of a particular product.

8. **Nokia** reports costs in financial statements. If plantwide overhead rates are allowed for reporting costs to external users, why might a company choose to use a more complicated and more expensive method for assigning overhead costs to products?   **NOKIA**

9. Why are multiple departmental overhead rates more accurate for product costing than a single plantwide overhead rate?

10. In what way are departmental overhead rates similar to a single plantwide overhead rate? How are they different?

11. What is the first step in applying activity-based costing?

12. **Apple**'s production requires activities. What are value-added activities? Apple

13. What is an activity cost driver?

14. What are the four activity levels associated with activity-based costing? Define each.

15. ⓘ **Research In Motion** must assign overhead costs to its products. Activity-based costing is generally RIM

considered more accurate than other methods of assigning overhead. If this is so, why do all manufacturing companies not use it?

16. ⓘ **Palm** is a manufacturer. "Activity-based costing is only useful for manufacturing companies." Is this a true statement? Explain. Palm

---

connect

QUICK STUDY

QS 17-1
Overhead cost allocation methods
C1

In the blank next to each of the following terms, place the letter *A* through *D* that corresponds to the description of that term. Some letters are used more than once.

1. _____ Activity-based costing

2. _____ Plantwide overhead rate method

3. _____ Departmental overhead rate method

A. Uses only volume-based measures such as direct labor hours to allocate overhead costs to products.

B. Focuses on the costs of carrying out activities.

C. Uses more than one rate to allocate overhead costs to products.

D. Typically uses the most overhead allocation rates.

QS 17-2
Costing terminology
C2

In the blank next to the following terms, place the letter *A* through *D* corresponding to the best description of that term.

1. _____ Activity

2. _____ Activity driver

3. _____ Cost pool

4. _____ Cost object

A. Measurement associated with an activity.

B. A group of costs that have the same activity drivers.

C. Anything to which costs will be assigned.

D. A task that causes a cost to be incurred.

QS 17-3
Identify activity levels
C3

Identify each of the following activities as unit level (U), batch level (B), product level (P), or facility level (F) to indicate the way each is incurred with respect to production.

1. _____ Sampling cookies to determine quality.

2. _____ Paying real estate taxes on the factory building.

3. _____ Attaching labels to collars of shirts.

4. _____ Mixing of bread dough in a commercial bakery.

5. _____ Polishing of gold wedding rings.

6. _____ Cleaning the assembly department.

7. _____ Redesigning a bicycle seat in response to customer feedback.

QS 17-4
Advantages of plantwide and departmental rate methods **A1**

List the three main advantages of the plantwide and departmental overhead rate methods.

QS 17-5
Compute plantwide overhead rates
P1

Renfro Manufacturing identified the following data in its two production departments.

	Assembly	Finishing
Manufacturing overhead costs.........	$600,000	$1,200,000
Direct labor hours worked	12,000 DLH	20,000 DLH
Machine hours used................	6,000 MH	16,000 MH

Required

1. What is the company's single plantwide overhead rate based on direct labor hours?

2. What is the company's single plantwide overhead rate based on machine hours?

Refer to the information in QS 17-5. What are the company's departmental overhead rates if the assembly department assigns overhead based on direct labor hours and the finishing department assigns overhead based on machine hours?

QS 17-6
Compute departmental
overhead rates   **P2**

Chan Company identified the following activities, costs, and activity drivers. The company manufactures two types of go-karts: Fast and Standard. Production volume is 10,000 units of the Fast model and 30,000 units of the Standard model.

QS 17-7
Compute plantwide
overhead rates

P1

Activity	Expected Costs	Expected Activity
Handling materials	$625,000	100,000 parts in stock
Inspecting product	900,000	1,500 batches
Processing purchase orders.	105,000	700 orders
Paying suppliers	175,000	500 invoices
Insuring the factory	300,000	40,000 square feet
Designing packaging	375,000	10 models

Required

1. Compute a single plantwide overhead rate assuming that the company assigns overhead based on 100,000 budgeted direct labor hours.

2. Assign overhead costs to each model assuming the Fast model requires 25,000 direct labor hours and the Standard model requires 60,000 direct labor hours. What is the overhead cost per unit for each model?

Refer to the information in QS 17-7. Compute the activity rate for each activity, assuming the company uses activity-based costing.

QS 17-8
Compute overhead rates
under ABC   **P3**

Refer to the data in QS17-7. Assume that the following information is available for the company's two products.

QS 17-9
Assigning costs using ABC

P3

	Fast Model	Standard Model
Production volume.	10,000 units	30,000 units
Parts required	20,000 parts	30,000 parts
Batches made.	250 batches	100 batches
Purchase orders	50 orders	20 orders
Invoices	50 invoices	10 invoices
Space occupied	10,000 sq. ft.	7,000 sq. ft.
Models	1 model	1 model

Required

Assign overhead costs to each product model using activity-based costing (ABC). What is the overhead cost per unit of each model?

Qinto Company sells two types of products, Basic and Deluxe. The company provides technical support for users of its products, at an expected cost of $250,000 per year. The company expects to process 10,000 customer service calls per year.

QS 17-10
Assigning costs using ABC

P3

Required

1. Determine the company's cost of technical support per customer service call.

2. During the month of January, Qinto received 650 calls for customer service on its Deluxe model, and 150 calls for customer service on its Basic model. Assign technical support costs to each model using activity-based costing (ABC).

QS 17-11

Multiple choice overhead questions

A2

1. Which costing method tends to overstate the cost of high-volume products?
   a. Traditional volume-based costing
   b. Activity-based costing
   c. Job order costing
   d. Differential costing

2. If management wants the most accurate product cost, which of the following costing methods should be used?
   a. Volume-based costing using departmental overhead rates
   b. Volume-based costing using a plantwide overhead rate
   c. Normal costing using a plantwide overhead rate
   d. Activity-based costing

3. Disadvantages of activity-based costing include
   a. It is not acceptable under GAAP for external reporting.
   b. It can be costly to implement.
   c. It can be used in an activity-based management.
   d. Both a. and b.

QS 17-12

Activity-based costing and overhead cost allocation

P3

The following is taken from Mortan Co.'s internal records of its factory with two operating departments. The cost driver for indirect labor and supplies is direct labor costs, and the cost driver for the remaining overhead items is number of hours of machine use. Compute the total amount of overhead cost allocated to Operating Department 1 using activity-based costing.

	Direct Labor	Machine Use Hours
Operating department 1	$18,800	2,000
Operating department 2	13,200	1,200
Totals	$32,000	3,200
Factory overhead costs		
Rent and utilities		$12,200
Indirect labor		5,400
General office expense		4,000
Depreciation—Equipment		3,000
Supplies		2,600
Total factory overhead.............		$27,200

Check   Dept. 1 allocation, $16,700

QS 17-13

Computing activity rates

P3

A company uses activity-based costing to determine the costs of its three products: A, B, and C. The budgeted cost and cost driver activity for each of the company's three activity cost pools follow.

Activity Cost Pool	Budgeted Cost	Budgeted Activity of Cost Driver		
		Product A	Product B	Product C
Activity 1	$70,000	6,000	9,000	20,000
Activity 2	$45,000	7,000	15,000	8,000
Activity 3	$82,000	2,500	1,000	1,625

Compute the activity rates for each of the company's three activities.

QS 17-14

Activity-based costing rates and allocations

P3

A company has two products: standard and deluxe. The company expects to produce 34,300 standard units and 69,550 deluxe units. It uses activity-based costing and has prepared the following analysis showing budgeted cost and cost driver activity for each of its three activity cost pools.

Activity Cost Pool	Budgeted Cost	Budgeted Activity of Cost Driver	
		Standard	Deluxe
Activity 1	$87,000	3,000	2,800
Activity 2	$62,000	4,500	5,500
Activity 3	$93,000	2,500	5,250

[continued on next page]

Required

1. What is the overhead cost per unit for the standard units?

2. What is the overhead cost per unit for the deluxe units?

Toyota embraces lean techniques, including lean accounting. What are the two key components of lean accounting?

QS 17-15
Lean accounting and ABC

A2

---

connect
_____

1. With ABC, overhead costs should be traced to which cost object first?
  a. Units of product   **c.** Activities
  b. Departments   **d.** Product batches

2. When using departmental overhead rates, which of the following cost objects is the first in the cost allocation process?
  a. Activities   **c.** Product lines
  b. Units of product   **d.** Departments

3. Which costing method assumes all products use overhead costs in the same proportions?
  a. Activity-based costing   **c.** Departmental overhead rate method
  b. Plantwide overhead rate method   **d.** All cost allocation methods

4. Which of the following would usually *not* be used in computing plantwide overhead rates?
  a. Direct labor hours   **c.** Direct labor dollars
  b. Number of quality inspections   **d.** Machine hours

EXERCISES

Exercise 17-1
Cost allocation methods
C1

Why is overhead allocation under ABC usually more accurate than either the plantwide overhead allocation method or the departmental overhead allocation method?

Exercise 17-2
Comparing overhead allocation methods   A2

Explain the two basic stages of cost flows for activity-based costing.

Exercise 17-3
Cost flows under activity-based costing   C2

Following are activities in providing medical services at Healthcare Clinic.

A. Ordering medical equipment   **E.** Registering patients
B. Heating the clinic   **F.** Cleaning beds
C. Filling prescriptions   **G.** Washing linens
D. Providing security services   **H.** Stocking examination rooms

Required

1. Classify each activity as unit level (U), batch level (B), product level (P), or facility level (F).

2. Identify an activity driver that might be used to measure these activities at the clinic.

Exercise 17-4
Activity classification
C3

Teradyne Crystal makes fine tableware in its Ireland factory. The following data are taken from its production plans for 2011.

Direct labor costs	€5,870,000
Setup costs.	630,000

	Wine Glasses	Commemorative Vases
Expected production	211,000 units	17,000 units
Direct labor hours required	254,000 DLH	16,400 DLH
Machine setups required	200 setups	800 setups

Exercise 17-5
Comparing costs under ABC to traditional plantwide overhead rate
P1 P3 A1 A2

Required

1. Determine the setup cost per unit for the wine glasses and for the commemorative vases if setup costs are assigned using a single plantwide overhead rate based on direct labor hours.

2. Determine setup costs per unit for the wine glasses and for the commemorative vases if the setup costs are assigned based on the number of setups.

3. Which method is better for assigning costs to each product? Explain.

Exercise 17-6
Plantwide overhead rate
P1

Textra Polymers produces parts for a variety of small machine manufacturers. Most products go through two operations, molding and trimming, before they are ready for packaging. Expected costs and activities for the molding department and for the trimming department for 2011 follow.

	Molding	Trimming
Direct labor hours.........	52,000 DLH	48,000 DLH
Machine hours	30,500 MH	3,600 MH
Overhead costs	$730,000	$590,000

Data for two special order parts to be manufactured by the company in 2011 follow:

	Part A27C	Part X82B
Number of units	9,800 units	54,500 units
Machine hours		
Molding	5,100 MH	1,020 MH
Trimming	2,600 MH	650 MH
Direct labor hours		
Molding	5,500 DLH	2,150 DLH
Trimming	700 DLH	3,500 DLH

Required

1. Compute the plantwide overhead rate using direct labor hours as the base.

2. Determine the overhead cost assigned to each product line using the plantwide rate computed in requirement 1.

Exercise 17-7
Departmental overhead rates
P2

Refer to the information in Exercise 17-6.

Required

1. Compute a departmental overhead rate for the molding department based on machine hours and a department overhead rate for the trimming department based on direct labor hours.

2. Determine the total overhead cost assigned to each product line using the departmental overhead rates from requirement 2.

3. Determine the overhead cost per unit for each product line using the departmental rate.

Exercise 17-8
Assigning overhead costs using the plantwide rate and departmental rate methods
P1 P2

Lavor produces lamps and home lighting fixtures. Its most popular product is a brushed aluminum desk lamp. This lamp is made from components shaped in the fabricating department and assembled in its implementation department. Information related to the 35,000 desk lamps produced annually follow.

Direct materials...	$280,000
Direct labor	
Fabricating department (7,000 DLH × $20 per DLH)	$140,000
Implementation department (16,000 DLH × $29 per DLH)	$464,000
Machine hours	
Fabricating department	15,040 MH
Implementation department	21,000 MH

Expected overhead cost and related data for the two production departments follow.

	Fabricating	Implementation
Direct labor hours.........	75,000 DLH	125,000 DLH
Machine hours............	80,000 MH	62,500 MH
Overhead cost............	$300,000	$200,000

Required

1. Determine the plantwide overhead rate for Lavor using direct labor hours as a base.
2. Determine the total manufacturing cost per unit for the aluminum desk lamp using the plantwide overhead rate.
3. Compute departmental overhead rates based on machine hours in the fabricating department and direct labor hours in the implementation department.
4. Use departmental overhead rates from requirement 3 to determine the total manufacturing cost per unit for the aluminum desk lamps.

Check (2) $26.90 per unit

Check (4) $27.60 per unit

Real Cool produces two different models of air conditioners. The company produces the mechanical systems in their components department. The mechanical systems are combined with the housing assembly in its finishing department. The activities, costs, and drivers associated with these two manufacturing processes and the production support process follow.

Exercise 17-9
Using the plantwide overhead rate to assess prices
P1

Process	Activity	Overhead Cost	Driver	Quantity
Components	Changeover	$ 500,000	Number of batches	800
	Machining	279,000	Machine hours	6,000
	Setups	225,000	Number of setups	120
		$1,004,000		
Finishing	Welding	$ 180,300	Welding hours	3,000
	Inspecting	210,000	Number of inspections	700
	Rework	75,000	Rework orders	300
		$ 465,300		
Support	Purchasing	$ 135,000	Purchase orders	450
	Providing space	32,000	Number of units	5,000
	Providing utilities	65,000	Number of units	5,000
		$ 232,000		

Additional production information concerning its two product lines follows.

	Model 145	Model 212
Units produced	1,500	3,500
Welding hours	800	2,200
Batches	400	400
Number of inspections	400	300
Machine hours	1,800	4,200
Setups	60	60
Rework orders	160	140
Purchase orders	300	150

Required

1. Using a plantwide overhead rate based on machine hours, compute the overhead cost per unit for each product line.
2. Determine the total cost per unit for each product line if the direct labor and direct materials costs per unit are $250 for Model 145 and $180 for Model 212.
3. If the market price for Model 145 is $800 and the market price for Model 212 is $470, determine the profit or loss per unit for each model. Comment on the results.

Check (3) Model 212, $(50.26) per unit loss

Exercise 17-10
Using departmental overhead rates to assess prices
P2

Refer to the information in Exercise 17-9 to answer the following requirements.

Required

1. Determine departmental overhead rates and compute the overhead cost per unit for each product line. Base your overhead assignment for the components department on machine hours. Use welding hours to assign overhead costs to the finishing department. Assign costs to the support department based on number of purchase orders.

2. Determine the total cost per unit for each product line if the direct labor and direct materials costs per unit are $250 for Model 145 and $180 for Model 212.

Check (3) Model 212, $(30.38) per unit loss

3. If the market price for Model 145 is $800 and the market price for Model 212 is $470, determine the profit or loss per unit for each model. Comment on the results.

Exercise 17-11
Using ABC to assess prices
P3

Refer to the information in Exercise 17-9 to answer the following requirements.

Required

1. Using ABC, compute the overhead cost per unit for each product line.

2. Determine the total cost per unit for each product line if the direct labor and direct materials costs per unit are $200 for Model 145 and $180 for Model 212.

Check (3) Model 212, $24.88 per unit profit

3. If the market price for Model 145 is $800 and the market price for Model 212 is $470, determine the profit or loss per unit for each model. Comment on the results.

Exercise 17-12
Using ABC in a service company
P3

Singh and Smythe is an architectural firm that provides services for residential construction projects. The following data pertain to a recent reporting period.

	Activities	Costs
Design department		
Client consultation	1,500 contact hours	$270,000
Drawings	2,000 design hours	115,000
Modeling	40,000 square feet	30,000
Project management department		
Supervision	600 days	$120,000
Billings	8 jobs	10,000
Collections	8 jobs	12,000

Required

1. Using ABC, compute the firm's activity overhead rates. Form activity cost pools where appropriate.

Check (2) $150,200

2. Assign costs to a 9,200 square foot job that requires 450 contact hours, 340 design hours, and 200 days to complete.

Exercise 17-13
Using ABC for strategic decisions
P1 P3

Consider the following data for two products of Vigano Manufacturing.

	Overhead Cost	Product A	Product B
Number of units produced		10,000 units	2,000 units
Direct labor cost (@$24 per DLH)		0.20 DLH per unit	0.25 DLH per unit
Direct materials cost....................		$2 per unit	$3 per unit
Activity			
Machine setup	$121,000		
Materials handling	48,000		
Quality control	80,000		
	$249,000		

Required

1. Using direct labor hours as the basis for assigning overhead costs, determine the total production cost per unit for each product line.

2. If the market price for Product A is $20 and the market price for Product B is $60, determine the profit or loss per unit for each product. Comment on the results.

3. Consider the following additional information about these two product lines. If ABC is used for assigning overhead costs to products, what is the cost per unit for Product A and for Product B?

Check   (2) Product B, $26.10 per unit profit

	Product A	Product B
Number of setups required for production	10 setups	12 setups
Number of parts required......................	1 part/unit	3 parts/unit
Inspection hours required	40 hours	210 hours

4. Determine the profit or loss per unit for each product. Should this information influence company strategy? Explain.

(4) Product B, ($24.60) per unit loss

Northwest Company produces two types of glass shelving, rounded edge and squared edge, on the same production line. For the current period, the company reports the following data.

Exercise 17-14
Activity-based costing

P3 A2

	Rounded Edge	Squared Edge	Total
Direct materials	$19,000	$ 43,200	$ 62,200
Direct labor	12,200	23,800	36,000
Overhead (300% of direct labor cost)	36,600	71,400	108,000
Total cost	$67,800	$138,400	$206,200
Quantity produced	10,500 ft.	14,100 ft.	
Average cost per ft.	$ 6.46	$ 9.82	

Northwest's controller wishes to apply activity-based costing (ABC) to allocate the $108,000 of overhead costs incurred by the two product lines to see whether cost per foot would change markedly from that reported above. She has collected the following information.

Overhead Cost Category (Activity Cost Pool)	Cost
Supervision	$ 5,400
Depreciation of machinery	56,600
Assembly line preparation.............................	46,000
Total overhead.......................................	$108,000

She has also collected the following information about the cost drivers for each category (cost pool) and the amount of each driver used by the two product lines.

Overhead Cost Category (Activity Cost Pool)	Driver	Usage		
		Rounded Edge	Squared Edge	Total
Supervision	Direct labor cost($)	$12,200	$23,800	$36,000
Depreciation of machinery	Machine hours	500 hours	1,500 hours	2,000 hours
Assembly line preparation	Setups (number)	40 times	210 times	250 times

Required

1. Assign these three overhead cost pools to each of the two products using ABC.

2. Determine average cost per foot for each of the two products using ABC.

3. Compare the average cost per foot under ABC with the average cost per foot under the current method for each product. Explain why a difference between the two cost allocation methods exists.

Check   (2) Rounded edge, $5.19; Squared edge, $10.76

Exercise 17-15

Activity-based costing

P3

Health Co-op is an outpatient surgical clinic that was profitable for many years, but Medicare has cut its reimbursements by as much as 40%. As a result, the clinic wants to better understand its costs. It decides to prepare an activity-based cost analysis, including an estimate of the average cost of both general surgery and orthopedic surgery. The clinic's three cost centers and their cost drivers follow.

Cost Center	Cost	Cost Driver	Driver Quantity
Professional salaries...............	$1,600,000	Professional hours	10,000
Patient services and supplies	27,000	Number of patients	600
Building cost	150,000	Square feet	1,500

The two main surgical units and their related data follow.

Service	Hours	Square Feet*	Patients
General surgery............	2,500	600	400
Orthopedic surgery.........	7,500	900	200

* Orthopedic surgery requires more space for patients, supplies, and equipment.

Required

Check (2) Average cost of general (orthopedic) surgery, $1,195 ($6,495) per patient

1. Compute the cost per cost driver for each of the three cost centers.
2. Use the results from part 1 to allocate costs from each of the three cost centers to both the general surgery and the orthopedic surgery units. Compute total cost and average cost per patient for both the general surgery and the orthopedic surgery units.

Mc Graw Hill **connect**

PROBLEM SET A

Problem 17-1A

Evaluating product line costs and prices using ABC

P3

Healthy Day Company produces two beverages, PowerPunch and SlimLife. Data about these products follow.

	PowerPunch	SlimLife
Production volume	12,500 bottles	180,000 bottles
Liquid materials	1,400 gallons	37,000 gallons
Dry materials	620 pounds	12,000 pounds
Bottles	12,500 bottles	180,000 bottles
Labels	3 labels per bottle	1 label per bottle
Machine setups	500 setups	300 setups
Machine hours	200 MH	3,750 MH

Additional data from its two production departments follow.

Department	Driver	Cost
Mixing department		
Liquid materials	Gallons	$ 2,304
Dry materials............	Pounds	6,941
Utilities................	Machine hours	1,422
Bottling department		
Bottles	Units	$77,000
Labeling	Labels per bottle	6,525
Machine setup	Setups	20,000

Required

Check (3) $2.22 profit per bottle

1. Determine the cost of each product line using ABC.
2. What is the cost per bottle for PowerPunch? What is the cost per bottle of SlimLife? (*Hint:* Your answer should draw on the total cost for each product line computed in requirement 1.)
3. If PowerPunch sells for $3.75 per bottle, how much profit does the company earn per bottle of PowerPunch that it sells?
4. What is the minimum price that the company should set per bottle of SlimLife? Explain.

Craftmore Machining produces machine tools for the construction industry. The following details about overhead costs were taken from its company records.

Problem 17-2A
Applying activity-based costing
P1 P3 A1 A2 C3

Production Activity	Indirect Labor	Indirect Materials	Other Overhead
Grinding.....................	$320,000		
Polishing		$135,000	
Product modification	600,000		
Providing power..............			$255,000
System calibration	500,000		

Additional information on the drivers for its production activities follows.

Grinding...................	13,000 machine hours
Polishing...................	13,000 machine hours
Product modification.........	1,500 engineering hours
Providing power.............	17,000 direct labor hours
System calibration	400 batches

Required

1. Classify each activity as unit level, batch level, product level, or facility level.
2. Compute the activity overhead rates using ABC. Form cost pools as appropriate.
3. Determine overhead costs to assign to the following jobs using ABC.

	Job 3175	Job 4286
Number of units	200 units	2,500 units
Machine hours	550 MH	5,500 MH
Engineering hours	26 eng. hours	32 eng. hours
Batches	30 batches	90 batches
Direct labor hours	500 DLH	4,375 DLH

4. What is the overhead cost per unit for Job 3175? What is the overhead cost per unit for Job 4286?
5. If the company used a plantwide overhead rate based on direct labor hours, what is the overhead cost for each unit of Job 3175? Of Job 4286?
6. Compare the overhead costs per unit computed in requirements 4 and 5 for each job. Which method more accurately assigns overhead costs?

Check (4) Job 3175, $373.25 per unit

Maxlon Company manufactures custom-made furniture for its local market and produces a line of home furnishings sold in retail stores across the country. The company uses traditional volume-based methods of assigning direct materials and direct labor to its product lines. Overhead has always been assigned by using a plantwide overhead rate based on direct labor hours. In the past few years, management has seen its line of retail products continue to sell at high volumes, but competition has forced it to lower prices on these items. The prices are declining to a level close to its cost of production.

Problem 17-3A
Assessing impacts of using a plantwide overhead rate versus ABC
A1 A2

Meanwhile, its custom-made furniture is in high demand and customers have commented on its favorable (lower) prices compared to its competitors. Management is considering dropping its line of retail products and devoting all of its resources to custom-made furniture.

Required

1. What reasons could explain why competitors are forcing the company to lower prices on its high-volume retail products?
2. Why do you believe the company charges less for custom-order products than its competitors?
3. Does a company's costing method have any effect on its pricing decisions? Explain.
4. Aside from the differences in volume of output, what production differences do you believe exist between making custom-order furniture and mass-market furnishings?
5. What information might the company obtain from using ABC that it might not obtain using volume-based costing methods?

Problem 17-4A

Comparing costs using ABC with the plantwide overhead rate

P1   P3   A1   A2

The following data are for the two products produced by Shakti Company.

	Product A	Product B
Direct materials	$15 per unit	$24 per unit
Direct labor hours	0.3 DLH per unit	1.6 DLH per unit
Machine hours	0.1 MH per unit	1.2 MH per unit
Batches	125 batches	225 batches
Volume	10,000 units	2,000 units
Engineering modifications	12 modifications	58 modifications
Number of customers	500 customers	400 customers
Market price	$30 per unit	$120 per unit

The company's direct labor rate is $20 per direct labor hour (DLH). Additional information follows.

	Costs	Driver
Indirect manufacturing		
Engineering support	$24,500	Engineering modifications
Electricity	34,000	Machine hours
Setup costs	52,500	Batches
Nonmanufacturing		
Customer service	81,000	Number of customers

Required

Check   (1) Product A, $26.37 per unit cost

1. Compute the manufacturing cost per unit using the plantwide overhead rate based on direct labor hours. What is the gross profit per unit?

2. How much gross profit is generated by each customer of Product A using the plantwide overhead rate? How much gross profit is generated by each customer of Product B using the plantwide overhead rate? What is the cost of providing customer service to each customer? What information is provided by this comparison?

(3) Product A, $24.30 per unit cost

3. Determine the manufacturing cost per unit of each product line using ABC. What is the gross profit per unit?

4. How much gross profit is generated by each customer of Product A using ABC? How much gross profit is generated by each customer of Product B using ABC? Is the gross profit per customer adequate?

5. Which method of product costing gives better information to managers of this company? Explain why.

Problem 17-5A

Pricing analysis with ABC and a plantwide overhead rate

A1   A2   P1   P3

Tent Master produces two lines of tents sold to outdoor enthusiasts. The tents are cut to specifications in department A. In department B the tents are sewn and folded. The activities, costs, and drivers associated with these two manufacturing processes and its production support activities follow.

Process	Activity	Overhead Cost	Driver	Quantity
Department A	Pattern alignment	$ 64,400	Batches	560
	Cutting	50,430	Machine hours	12,300
	Moving product	100,800	Moves	2,400
		$215,630		
Department B	Sewing	$327,600	Direct labor hours	4,200
	Inspecting	24,000	Inspections	600
	Folding	47,880	Units	22,800
		$399,480		
Support	Design	$280,000	Modification orders	280
	Providing space	51,600	Square feet	8,600
	Materials handling	184,000	Square yards	920,000
		$515,600		

Additional production information on the two lines of tents follows.

	Pup Tent	Pop-Up Tent
Units produced	15,200 units	7,600 units
Moves......................	800 moves	1,600 moves
Batches.....................	140 batches	420 batches
Number of inspections	240 inspections	360 inspections
Machine hours	7,000 MH	5,300 MH
Direct labor hours............	2,600 DLH	1,600 DLH
Modification orders	70 modification orders	210 modification orders
Space occupied	4,300 square feet	4,300 square feet
Material required.............	450,000 square yards	470,000 square yards

Required

1. Using a plantwide overhead rate based on direct labor hours, compute the overhead cost that is assigned to each pup tent and each pop-up tent.

2. Using the plantwide overhead rate, determine the total cost per unit for the two products if the direct materials and direct labor cost is $25 per pup tent and $32 per pop-up tent.

3. If the market price of the pup tent is $65 and the market price of the pop-up tent is $200, determine the gross profit per unit for each tent. What might management conclude about the pup tent?

4. Using ABC, compute the total cost per unit for each tent if the direct labor and direct materials cost is $25 per pup tent and $32 per pop-up tent.

5. If the market price is $65 per pup tent and $200 per pop-up tent, determine the gross profit per unit for each tent. Comment on the results.

6. Would your pricing analysis be improved if the company used, instead of ABC, departmental rates determined using machine hours in Department A and direct labor hours in Department B? Explain.

Check (4) Pup tent, $58.46 per unit cost

MathGames produces two electronic, handheld educational games: *Fun with Fractions* and *Count Calculus*. Data on these products follow.

	Fun with Fractions	Count Calculus
Production volume	150,000 units	10,000 units
Components	450,000 parts	100,000 parts
Direct labor hours	15,000 DLH	2,000 DLH
Packaging materials	150,000 boxes	10,000 boxes
Shipping cartons	100 units per carton	25 units per carton
Machine setups	52 setups	52 setups
Machine hours	5,000 MH	2,000 MH

PROBLEM SET B

Problem 17-1B
Evaluating product line costs and prices using ABC

P3

Additional data from its two production departments follow.

Department	Driver	Cost
Assembly department		
Component cost	Parts	$495,000
Assembly labor.............	Direct labor hours	244,800
Maintenance	Machine hours	100,800
Wrapping department		
Packaging materials	Boxes	$460,800
Shipping	Cartons	27,360
Machine setup	Setups	187,200

Required

1. Using ABC, determine the cost of each product line.

2. What is the cost per unit for Fun with Fractions? What is the cost per unit of Count Calculus?

Check (3) $32.37 profit per unit

3. If Count Calculus sells for $59.95 per unit, how much profit does the company earn per unit of Count Calculus sold?

4. What is the minimum price that the company should set per unit of Fun with Fractions? Explain.

Problem 17-2B
Applying activity-based costing
P1 P3 A1 A2 C3

Fancy Foods produces gourmet gift baskets that it distributes online as well as from its small retail store. The following details about overhead costs are taken from its records.

Production Activity	Indirect Labor	Indirect Materials	Other Overhead
Wrapping	$300,000	$200,000	
Assembling	400,000		
Product design	180,000		
Obtaining business licenses			$100,000
Cooking	150,000	120,000	

Additional information on the drivers for its production activities follows.

Wrapping	100,000 units
Assembling	20,000 direct labor hours
Product design	3,000 design hours
Obtaining business licenses	20,000 direct labor hours
Cooking	1,000 batches

Required

1. Classify each activity as unit level, batch level, product level, or facility level.

2. Compute the activity overhead rates using ABC. Form cost pools as appropriate.

3. Determine the overhead cost to assign to the following jobs using ABC.

	Holiday Basket	Executive Basket
Number of units	8,000 units	1,000 units
Direct labor hours	2,000 DLH	500 DLH
Design hours	40 design hours	40 design hours
Batches	80 batches	200 batches

Check (4) Holiday Basket, $14.25 per unit

(5) Holiday Basket, $18.13 per unit

4. What is the cost per unit for the Holiday Basket? What is the cost per unit for the Executive Basket?

5. If the company used a plantwide overhead rate based on direct labor hours, what is the overhead cost for each Holiday Basket unit? What would be the overhead cost for each Executive Basket unit if a single plantwide overhead rate is used?

6. Compare the costs per unit computed in requirements 4 and 5 for each job. Which cost assignment method provides the most accurate cost? Explain.

Problem 17-3B
Assessing impacts of using a plantwide overhead rate versus ABC

A1 A2

Lakeside Paper produces cardboard boxes. The boxes require designing, cutting, and printing. (The boxes are shipped flat and customers fold them as necessary.) Lakeside has a reputation for providing high-quality products and excellent service to customers, who are major U.S. manufacturers. Costs are assigned to products based on the number of machine hours required to produce them.

Three years ago, a new marketing executive was hired. She suggested the company offer custom design and manufacturing services to small specialty manufacturers. These customers required boxes for their products and were eager to have Lakeside as a supplier. Within one year Lakeside found that it was so busy with orders from small customers, that it had trouble supplying boxes to all its customers on a timely basis. Large, long-time customers began to complain about slow service and several took their business elsewhere. Within another 18 months, Lakeside was in financial distress with a backlog of orders to be filled.

Required

1. What do you believe are the major costs of making its boxes? How are those costs related to the volume of boxes produced?
2. How did Lakeside's new customers differ from its previous customers?
3. Would the unit cost to produce a box for new customers be different from the unit cost to produce a box for its previous customers? Explain.
4. Could Lakeside's fate have been different if it had used ABC for determining the cost of its boxes?
5. What information would have been available with ABC that might have been overlooked using a traditional volume-based costing method?

Vargo Company makes two distinct products with the following information available for each.

Problem 17-4B
Comparing costs using ABC with the plantwide overhead rate

A1 A2 P1 P3

	Standard	Deluxe
Direct materials	$4 per unit	$8 per unit
Direct labor hours	4 DLH per unit	5 DLH per unit
Machine hours	3 MH per unit	3 MH per unit
Batches	175 batches	75 batches
Volume	40,000 units	10,000 units
Engineering modifications	50 modifications	25 modifications
Number of customers	1,000 customers	1,000 customers
Market price	$92 per unit	$125 per unit

The company's direct labor rate is $20 per direct labor hour (DLH). Additional information follows.

	Costs	Driver
Indirect manufacturing		
Engineering support	$ 56,250	Engineering modifications
Electricity	112,500	Machine hours
Setup costs	41,250	Batches
Nonmanufacturing		
Customer service	250,000	Number of customers

Required

1. Compute the manufacturing cost per unit using the plantwide overhead rate based on machine hours. What is the gross profit per unit?
2. How much gross profit is generated by each customer of the standard product using the plantwide overhead rate? How much gross profit is generated by each customer of the deluxe product using the plantwide overhead rate? What is the cost of providing customer service to each customer? What information is provided by this comparison?
3. Determine the manufacturing cost per unit of each product line using ABC. What is the gross profit per unit?
4. How much gross profit is generated by each customer of the standard product using ABC? How much gross profit is generated by each customer of the deluxe product using ABC? Is the gross profit per customer adequate?
5. Which method of product costing gives better information to managers of this company? Explain.

Check (1) Gross profit per unit:
Standard, $3.80; Deluxe, $12.80

(3) Gross profit per unit:
Standard, $4.09; Deluxe, $11.64

Spicy Salsa Company produces its condiments in two types: Extra Fine for restaurant customers and Family Style for home use. Salsa is prepared in department 1 and packaged in department 2. The activities, overhead costs, and drivers associated with these two manufacturing processes and its production support activities follow.

Problem 17-5B
Pricing analysis with ABC and a plantwide overhead rate

A1 A2 P1 P3

Process	Activity	Overhead Cost	Driver	Quantity
Department 1	Mixing	$ 4,500	Machine hours	1,500
	Cooking	11,250	Machine hours	1,500
	Product testing	112,500	Batches	600
		$128,250		
Department 2	Machine calibration	$250,000	Production runs	400
	Labeling	12,000	Cases of output	120,000
	Defects	6,000	Cases of output	120,000
		$268,000		
Support	Recipe formulation	$ 90,000	Focus groups	45
	Heat, lights, and water	27,000	Machine hours	1,500
	Materials handling	65,000	Container types	8
		$182,000		

Additional production information about its two product lines follows.

	Extra Fine	Family Style
Units produced	20,000 cases	100,000 cases
Batches................	200 batches	400 batches
Machine hours	500 MH	1,000 MH
Focus groups	30 groups	15 groups
Container types.........	5 containers	3 containers
Production runs.........	200 runs	200 runs

Required

1. Using a plantwide overhead rate based on cases, compute the overhead cost that is assigned to each case of Extra Fine Salsa and each case of Family Style Salsa.

Check (2) Cost per case: Extra Fine, $10.82; Family Style, $9.82

2. Using the plantwide overhead rate, determine the total cost per unit for the two products if the direct materials and direct labor cost is $6 per case of Extra Fine and $5 per case of Family Style.

3. If the market price of Extra Fine Salsa is $18 per case and the market price of Family Style Salsa is $9 per case, determine the gross profit per case for each product. What might management conclude about each product line?

(4) Cost per case: Extra Fine, $20.02; Family Style, $7.98

4. Using ABC, compute the total cost per case for each product type if the direct labor and direct materials cost is $6 per case of Extra Fine and $5 per case of Family Style.

5. If the market price is $18 per case of Extra Fine and $9 per case of Family Style, determine the gross profit per case for each product. How should management interpret the market prices given your computations?

6. Would your pricing analysis be improved if the company used departmental rates based on machine hours in department 1 and number of cases in department 2, instead of ABC? Explain.

SERIAL PROBLEM
Business Solutions

P3

(This serial problem began in Chapter 1 and continues through most of the book. If previous chapter segments were not completed, the serial problem can begin at this point. It is helpful, but not necessary, to use the Working Papers that accompany the book.)

SP 17 After reading an article about activity-based costing in a trade journal for the furniture industry, Santana Rey wondered if it was time to critically analyze overhead costs at Business Solutions. In a recent month, Rey found that setup costs, inspection costs, and utility costs made up most of its overhead. Additional information about overhead follows.

Activity	Cost	Driver
Setting up machines...........	$20,000	25 batches
Inspecting components	$ 7,500	5,000 parts
Providing utilities	$10,000	5,000 machine hours

Overhead has been applied to output at a rate of 50% of direct labor costs. The following data pertain to Job 6.15.

Direct materials	$2,500
Direct labor	$3,500
Batches	2 batches
Number of parts	400 parts
Machine hours	600 machine hours

Required

1. Classify each of its three overhead activities as unit level, batch level, product level, or facility level.
2. What is the total cost of Job 6.15 if Business Solutions applies overhead at 50% of direct labor cost?
3. What is the total cost of Job 6.15 if Business Solutions uses activity-based costing?
4. Which approach to assigning overhead gives a better representation of the costs incurred to produce Job 6.15? Explain.

Beyond the Numbers

BTN 17-1 Refer to financial statements of **Research In Motion** (**RIM.com**) and **Apple** (**Apple.com**) to answer the following.

REPORTING IN ACTION

C3 A2

RIM

Apple

Required

1. Identify at least two activities at Research In Motion and at Apple that cause costs to be incurred. Do you believe these companies should be concerned about controlling costs of the activities you identified? Explain.
2. Would you classify Research In Motion and Apple as service, merchandising, or manufacturing companies? Explain.
3. Is activity-based costing useful for companies such as Research In Motion and Apple? Explain.

BTN 17-2 **Research In Motion** and **Apple** are competitors in the sales of handheld devices such as wireless phones. Compare these companies' income statements and answer the following.

COMPARATIVE ANALYSIS

C2 A2

RIM

Apple

Required

1. Which company has a higher ratio of costs, defined as cost of goods sold plus total operating expenses, to revenues? Use the two most recent years' income statements from Appendix A. Show your analysis.
2. How might the use of activity-based costing help the less competitive company become *more* competitive?
3. Apple sells some of its products through its own retail stores while Research In Motion sells most of its products through wireless carriers. Assume Research In Motion is considering opening its own retail stores. What are the activities associated with opening a new retail store?

BTN 17-3 In conducting interviews and observing factory operations to implement an activity-based costing system, you determine that several activities are unnecessary or redundant. For example, warehouse personnel were inspecting purchased components as they were received at the loading dock. Later that day, the components were inspected again on the shop floor before being installed in the final product. Both of these activities caused costs to be incurred but were not adding value to the product. If you include this observation in your report, one or more employees who perform inspections will likely lose their jobs.

ETHICS CHALLENGE

A2 C3

Required

1. As a plant employee, what is your responsibility to report your findings to superiors?
2. Should you attempt to determine if the redundancy is justified? Explain.
3. What is your responsibility to the employees whose jobs will likely be lost by your report?
4. What facts should you consider before making your decision to report or not?

COMMUNICATING IN PRACTICE
A2

BTN 17-4   The chief executive officer (CEO) of your company recently returned from a luncheon meeting where activity-based costing was presented and discussed. Though her background is not in accounting, she has worked for the company for 15 years and is thoroughly familiar with its operations. Her impression of the presentation about ABC was that it was just another way of dividing up total overhead cost and that the total would still be the same "no matter how you sliced it."

Required

Write a memorandum to the CEO, no more than one page, explaining how ABC is different from traditional volume-based costing methods. Also, identify its advantages and disadvantages vis-à-vis traditional methods. Be sure it is written to be understandable to someone who is not an accountant.

TAKING IT TO THE NET
A2

BTN 17-5   Accounting professionals that work for private companies often obtain the Certified Management Accountant (CMA) designation to indicate their proficiency in several business areas in addition to managerial accounting. The CMA examination is administered by the Institute of Management Accountants (IMA).

Required

Go to the IMA Website (**IMAnet.org**) and determine which parts of the CMA exam likely cover activity-based costing. A person planning to become a CMA should take what college course work?

TEAMWORK IN ACTION
C2 C3

BTN 17-6   Observe the operations at your favorite fast-food restaurant.

Required

1. How many people does it take to fill a typical order of sandwich, beverage, and one side-order?
2. Describe the activities involved in its food service process.
3. What costs are related to each activity identified in requirement 2?

ENTREPRENEURIAL DECISION
C3

BTN 17-7   **Three Twins Ice Cream** has expanded its product offerings from basic chocolate and vanilla type flavors to include many varieties of certified organic ice cream flavors. Neal Gottlieb, founder of Three Twins Ice Cream, realizes that financial success depends on cost control as well as revenue generation.

Required

1. If Three Twins Ice Cream wanted to expand its product line to include yogurt smoothies, what activities would it need to perform that are not required for its current product lines?
2. Related to part 1, should the additional overhead costs related to new product lines be shared by existing product lines? Explain your reasoning.

HITTING THE ROAD
C2 C3

BTN 17-8   Visit and observe the processes of three different fast-food restaurants—these visits can be done as individuals or as teams. The objective of activity-based costing is to accurately assign costs to products and to improve operational efficiency.

Required

1. Individuals (or teams) can be assigned to each of three different fast-food establishments. Make a list of the activities required to process an order of a sandwich, beverage, and one side-order at each restaurant. Record the time required for each process, from placing the order to receiving the completed order.
2. What activities do the three establishments have in common? What activities are different across the establishments?
3. Is the number of activities related to the time required to process an order? Is the number of activities related to the price charged to customers? Explain both.
4. Make recommendations for improving the processes you observe. Would your recommendations increase or decrease the cost of operations?

BTN 17-9   Visit the Websites and review the financial statements for **Nokia** (**Nokia.com**) and **Apple** (**Apple.com**). Each of these companies sells handheld phones and devices in global markets.

GLOBAL DECISION

C3

NOKIA

Apple

Required

1. For Nokia in 2009, what are the largest three geographic markets in which it sells products? What is the amount (in millions of euros) of sales in each market?

2. For Apple in 2009, what are the largest three geographic markets (countries) in which it sells products? What is the amount (in millions of U.S. dollars) of sales in each market?

3. How would customer service activities differ across different geographic markets?

ANSWERS TO MULTIPLE CHOICE QUIZ

1. b; Under traditional costing methods, overhead costs are allocated to products on the basis of some measure of volume such as direct labor hours or machine hours. This results in much of the overhead cost being allocated to high-volume products. In contrast, under activity-based costing, some overhead costs are allocated on the basis of batch level or product level activities. This change in allocation bases results in shifting overhead costs from high-volume products to low-volume products.

2. d; Generally, an activity-based costing system is more difficult to implement and maintain than a traditional costing system (thus answer **a** is false). Instead of eliminating waste by allocating costs to products that waste resources, activity-based management is a management approach that focuses on managing activities as a means of eliminating waste and reducing delays and defects (thus answer **b** is false). Instead of using a single allocation base (such as direct labor hours), activity-based costing uses a number of allocation bases for assigning costs to products (thus answer **c** is false). Answer **d** is true.

3. d; Batch level activities are activities that are performed each time a batch of goods is handled or processed, regardless of how many units are in a batch. Further, the amount of resources consumed depends on the number of batches rather than on the number of units in the batch. Worker recreational facilities relate to the organization as a whole rather than to specific batches and, as such, are not considered to be batch level. On the other hand, purchase order processing, setting up equipment, and the clerical activities described are activities that are performed each time a batch of goods is handled or processed, and, as such, are batch level activities.

4. c;

	(A) Activity Rate (Budgeted overhead cost ÷ Budgeted activity)	(B) Actual Activity	(A × B) Overhead Cost Applied to Production
Activity 1....	($80,000 ÷ 1,000) = $80.00	800	$ 64,000
Activity 2....	($58,400 ÷ 1,500) = $38.93*	500	19,465
Activity 3....	($360,000 ÷ 6,000) = $60.00	5,400	324,000
Total overhead cost per unit for Product B			$407,465
Divided by number of units produced			÷ 31,652
Overhead cost per unit of Product B			$ 12.87

* rounded

5. d; The activity rate for Activity 3 is determined as follows:

Budgeted cost ÷ Budgeted activity = Activity rate

$14,000 ÷ 700 = $20

18

Cost Behavior and Cost-Volume-Profit Analysis

A Look Back

Chapter 17 introduced the activity-based costing (ABC) system, which has the potential for greater accuracy of cost allocations and for providing managers with better cost information for strategic decisions.

A Look at This Chapter

This chapter shows how information on both costs and sales behavior is useful to managers in performing cost-volume-profit analysis. This analysis is an important part of successful management and sound business decisions.

A Look Ahead

Chapter 19 compares reports prepared under variable costing with those under absorption costing, and it explains how variable costing can improve managerial decisions.

Learning Objectives

CAP

CONCEPTUAL

C1 Describe different types of cost behavior in relation to production and sales volume. (p. 766)

C2 Describe several applications of cost-volume-profit analysis. (p. 777)

ANALYTICAL

A1 Compute the contribution margin and describe what it reveals about a company's cost structure. (p. 772)

A2 Analyze changes in sales using the degree of operating leverage. (p. 782)

LP18

PROCEDURAL

P1 Determine cost estimates using the scatter diagram, high-low, and regression methods of estimating costs. (p. 769)

P2 Compute the break-even point for a single product company. (p. 773)

P3 Graph costs and sales for a single product company. (p. 774)

P4 Compute the break-even point for a multiproduct company. (p. 779)

Heeeere's Johnny!

"People ask for my autograph . . . it's unbelievable"
—JOHN EARLE

BOSTON, MS—Working at a music store, John Earle's co-workers coined new nicknames for him on an almost daily basis: Johnny Appleseed, Johnny Pancakes, Johnny Cupcakes. As a joke, John printed up a few t-shirts with the Johnny Cupcakes nickname for the heavy-metal band he played in. The shirts, based on a skull and crossbones design with a cupcake replacing the skull, drew attention, and John dropped his heavy-metal dreams to start his company, **Johnny Cupcakes, Inc. (JohnnyCupcakes.com).**

John was always a small-scale serial entrepreneur, operating lemonade stands, peddling glow sticks on the beach near his home, and selling packs of pranks and magic tricks. Like his itching powder prank that went awry at his school, "the Johnny Cupcakes brand started as a complete joke," admits John. One day John's mother Lorraine interrupted his band's tour to tell him he had a real business on his hands. Now, the company's designs—like a Statue of Liberty holding a cupcake, Marilyn Monroe with a tiny cupcake-shaped mole, and the cupcakes and crossbones motif—attract a cult following. By the time John opened his first store, over 500 people had lined up to get in (see photo above).

Though still a prankster, John knows that successful entrepreneurs must understand cost behavior to succeed. Identifying fixed and variable costs is key to understanding break-even points and maintaining the right mix of t-shirt choices. With t-shirts selling at prices between $40–$70 each, John focuses on making limited editions to keep demand high. In performing cost-volume-profit analyses, John's mother Lorraine, the company's chief financial officer, typically estimates sales at about half the amount John does. "A large gap between our estimates is pretty typical, but John is happy when we beat our break-even points and produce profits," says Lorraine. Johnny Cupcakes recently expanded into other product lines, including button-down shirts, jackets, sweaters, and baseball caps. With a diverse product line, an understanding of contribution margins and how costs relate to volume and profits become even more important.

From a handful of gag t-shirts made as a joke, Johnny Cupcakes now boasts sales of $3.4 million per year. "I never expected it to get this big," John says, encouraging potential entrepreneurs to get out and make it happen. "I work very hard," he says, "and I enjoy every minute of it."

[Sources: *Johnny Cupcakes Website,* January 2011; *Boston Globe,* October 2007; *Businessweek.com,* August 2008; *Inc magazine,* May 2010; *NPR.org,* August 2006]

This chapter describes different types of costs and shows how changes in a company's operating volume affect these costs. The chapter also analyzes a company's costs and sales to explain how different operating strategies affect profit or loss. Managers use this type of analysis to forecast what will happen if changes are made to costs, sales volume, selling prices, or product mix. They then use these forecasts to select the best business strategy for the company.

Cost Behavior and Cost-Volume-Profit Analysis

Identifying Cost Behavior	Measuring Cost Behavior	Using Break-Even Analysis	Applying Cost-Volume-Profit Analysis
• Fixed costs • Variable costs • Mixed costs • Step-wise costs • Curvilinear costs	• Scatter diagrams • High-low method • Least-squares regression • Comparison of cost estimation methods	• Computing contribution margin • Computing break-even • Preparing a cost-volume-profit chart • Making assumptions in cost-volume-profit analysis	• Computing income from sales and costs • Computing sales for target income • Computing margin of safety • Using sensitivity analysis • Computing multiproduct break-even

IDENTIFYING COST BEHAVIOR

Point: *Profit* is another term for *income.*

Planning a company's future activities and events is a crucial phase in successful management. One of the first steps in planning is to predict the volume of activity, the costs to be incurred, sales to be made, and profit to be received. An important tool to help managers carry out this step is **cost-volume-profit (CVP) analysis,** which helps them predict how changes in costs and sales levels affect income. In its basic form, CVP analysis involves computing the sales level at which a company neither earns an income nor incurs a loss, called the *break-even point.* For this reason, this basic form of cost-volume-profit analysis is often called *break-even analysis.* Managers use variations of CVP analysis to answer questions such as these:

- What sales volume is needed to earn a target income?
- What is the change in income if selling prices decline and sales volume increases?
- How much does income increase if we install a new machine to reduce labor costs?
- What is the income effect if we change the sales mix of our products or services?

Consequently, cost-volume-profit analysis is useful in a wide range of business decisions.

Conventional cost-volume-profit analysis requires management to classify all costs as either *fixed* or *variable* with respect to production or sales volume. The remainder of this section discusses the concepts of fixed and variable cost behavior as they relate to CVP analysis.

Decision Insight

No Free Lunch   Hardly a week goes by without a company advertising a free product with the purchase of another. Examples are a free printer with a digital camera purchase or a free monitor with a computer purchase. Can these companies break even, let alone earn profits? We are reminded of the *no-free-lunch* adage, meaning that companies expect profits from the companion or add-on purchase to make up for the free product. ∎

C1 Describe different types of cost behavior in relation to production and sales volume.

Fixed Costs

A *fixed cost* remains unchanged in amount when the volume of activity varies from period to period within a relevant range. For example, $5,000 in monthly rent paid for a factory building remains the same whether the factory operates with a single eight-hour shift or around the clock with three shifts. This means that rent cost is the same each month at any level of output from zero to the plant's full productive capacity. Notice that while *total* fixed cost does not change as the level of production changes, the fixed cost *per unit* of output decreases as volume increases. For instance, if 20 units are produced when monthly rent is $5,000, the average rent cost per unit is $250 (computed as $5,000/20 units). When production increases to 100 units per month, the average cost per unit decreases to $50 (computed as $5,000/100 units). The average cost decreases to $10 per unit if production increases to 500 units per month. Common examples of fixed costs include depreciation, property taxes, office salaries, and many service department costs.

When production volume and costs are graphed, units of product are usually plotted on the *horizontal axis* and dollars of cost are plotted on the *vertical axis.* Fixed costs then are represented as a horizontal line because they remain constant at all levels of production. To illustrate, the graph in Exhibit 18.1 shows that fixed costs remain at $32,000 at all production levels up to the company's monthly capacity of 2,000 units of output. The *relevant range* for fixed costs in Exhibit 18.1 is 0 to 2,000 units. If the relevant range changes (that is, production capacity extends beyond this range), the amount of fixed costs will likely change.

Example: If the fixed cost line in Exhibit 18.1 is shifted upward, does the total cost line shift up, down, or remain in the same place? *Answer:* It shifts up by the same amount.

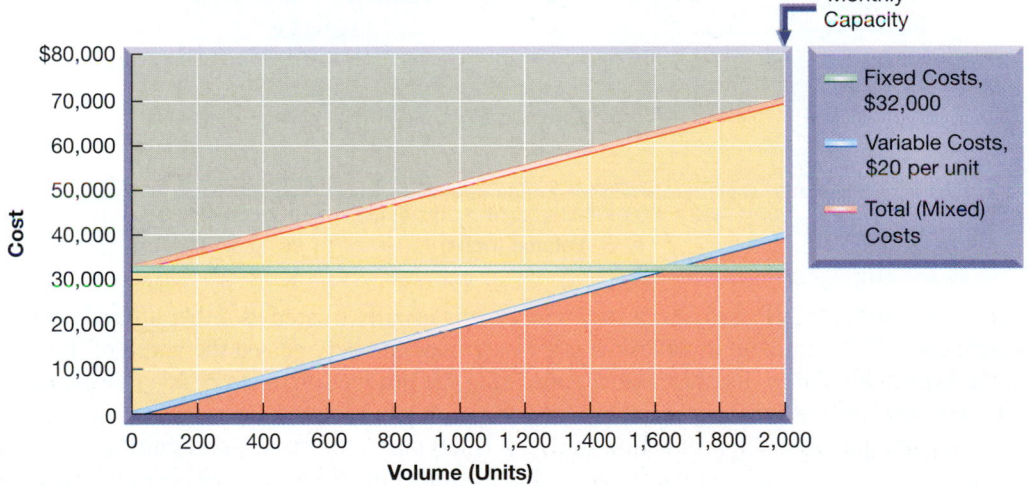

EXHIBIT 18.1

Relations of Fixed and Variable Costs to Volume

Example: If the level of fixed costs in Exhibit 18.1 changes, does the slope of the total cost line change? *Answer:* No, the slope doesn't change. The total cost line is simply shifted upward or downward.

Variable Costs

A *variable cost* changes in proportion to changes in volume of activity. The direct materials cost of a product is one example of a variable cost. If one unit of product requires materials costing $20, total materials costs are $200 when 10 units of product are manufactured, $400 for 20 units, $600 for 30 units, and so on. Notice that variable cost *per unit* remains constant but the *total* amount of variable cost changes with the level of production. In addition to direct materials, common variable costs include direct labor (if employees are paid per unit), sales commissions, shipping costs, and some overhead costs.

Point: Fixed costs are constant in total but vary (decline) per unit as more units are produced. Variable costs vary in total but are fixed per unit.

When variable costs are plotted on a graph of cost and volume, they appear as a straight line starting at the zero cost level. This straight line is upward (positive) sloping. The line rises as volume of activity increases. A variable cost line using a $20 per unit cost is graphed in Exhibit 18.1.

Mixed Costs

A **mixed cost** includes both fixed and variable cost components. For example, compensation for sales representatives often includes a fixed monthly salary and a variable commission based on sales. The total cost line in Exhibit 18.1 is a mixed cost. Like a fixed cost, it is greater than zero when volume is zero; but unlike a fixed cost, it increases steadily in proportion to increases in volume. The mixed cost line in Exhibit 18.1 starts on the vertical axis at the $32,000 fixed cost point. Thus, at the zero volume level, total cost equals the fixed costs. As the activity level increases, the mixed cost line increases at an amount equal to the variable cost per unit. This line is highest when volume of activity is at 2,000 units (the end point of the relevant range). In CVP analysis, mixed costs are often separated into fixed and variable components. The fixed component is added to other fixed costs, and the variable component is added to other variable costs.

Step-Wise Costs

A **step-wise cost** reflects a step pattern in costs. Salaries of production supervisors often behave in a step-wise manner in that their salaries are fixed within a *relevant range* of the current production volume. However, if production volume expands significantly (for example, with the addition of another shift), additional supervisors must be hired. This means that the total cost for supervisory salaries goes up by a lump-sum amount. Similarly, if volume takes another significant step up, supervisory salaries will increase by another lump sum. This behavior reflects a step-wise cost, also known as a *stair-step cost,* which is graphed in Exhibit 18.2. See how the step-wise cost line is flat within ranges (steps). Then, when volume significantly changes, it shifts to another level for that range (step).

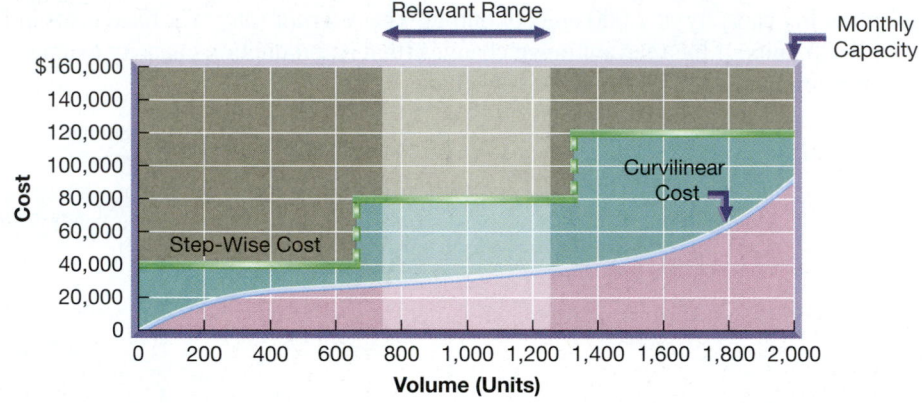

In a conventional CVP analysis, a step-wise cost is usually treated as either a fixed cost or a variable cost. This treatment involves manager judgment and depends on the width of the range and the expected volume. To illustrate, suppose after the production of every 25 snowboards, an operator lubricates the finishing machine. The cost of this lubricant reflects a step-wise pattern. Also, suppose that after the production of every 1,000 units, the snowboard cutting tool is replaced. Again, this is a step-wise cost. Note that the range of 25 snowboards is much narrower than the range of 1,000 snowboards. Some managers might treat the lubricant cost as a variable cost and the cutting tool cost as a fixed cost.

Point: Computer spreadsheets are important and effective tools for CVP analysis and for analyzing alternative "what-if" strategies.

Curvilinear Costs

A variable cost, as explained, is a *linear* cost; that is, it increases at a constant rate as volume of activity increases. A **curvilinear cost,** also called a *nonlinear cost,* increases at a nonconstant rate as volume increases. When graphed, curvilinear costs appear as a curved line. Exhibit 18.2 shows a curvilinear cost beginning at zero when production is zero and then increasing at different rates.

An example of a curvilinear cost is total direct labor cost when workers are paid by the hour. At low to medium levels of production, adding more employees allows each of them to specialize by doing certain tasks repeatedly instead of doing several different tasks. This often yields additional units of output at lower costs. A point is eventually reached at which adding more employees creates inefficiencies. For instance, a large crew demands more time and effort in communicating and coordinating their efforts. While adding employees in this case increases output, the labor cost per unit increases, and the total labor cost goes up at a steeper slope. This pattern is seen in Exhibit 18.2 where the curvilinear cost curve starts at zero, rises, flattens out, and then increases at a faster rate as output nears the maximum.

Point: Cost-volume-profit analysis helped Rod Canion, Jim Harris, and Bill Murto raise start-up capital of $20 million to launch **Compaq Computer.** They showed that break-even volumes were attainable within the first year.

1. Which of the following statements is typically true? (*a*) Variable cost per unit increases as volume increases, (*b*) fixed cost per unit decreases as volume increases, or (*c*) a curvilinear cost includes both fixed and variable elements.
2. Describe the behavior of a fixed cost.
3. If cost per unit of activity remains constant (fixed), why is it called a variable cost?

MEASURING COST BEHAVIOR

Identifying and measuring cost behavior requires careful analysis and judgment. An important part of this process is to identify costs that can be classified as either fixed or variable, which often requires analysis of past cost behavior. Three methods are commonly used to analyze past costs: scatter diagrams, high-low method, and least-squares regression. Each method is discussed in this section using the unit and cost data shown in Exhibit 18.3, which are taken from a start-up company that uses units produced as the activity base in estimating cost behavior.

P1 Determine cost estimates using the scatter diagram, high-low, and regression methods of estimating costs.

Month	Units Produced	Total Cost
January	17,500	$20,500
February.......	27,500	21,500
March.........	25,000	25,000
April..........	35,000	21,500
May...........	47,500	25,500
June	22,500	18,500
July	30,000	23,500
August	52,500	28,500
September	37,500	26,000
October	57,500	26,000
November	62,500	31,000
December	67,500	29,000

EXHIBIT 18.3

Data for Estimating Cost Behavior

Scatter Diagrams

Scatter diagrams display past cost and unit data in graphical form. In preparing a scatter diagram, units are plotted on the horizontal axis and cost is plotted on the vertical axis. Each individual point on a scatter diagram reflects the cost and number of units for a prior period. In Exhibit 18.4, the prior 12 months' costs and numbers of units are graphed. Each point reflects total costs incurred and units produced for one of those months. For instance, the point labeled March had units produced of 25,000 and costs of $25,000.

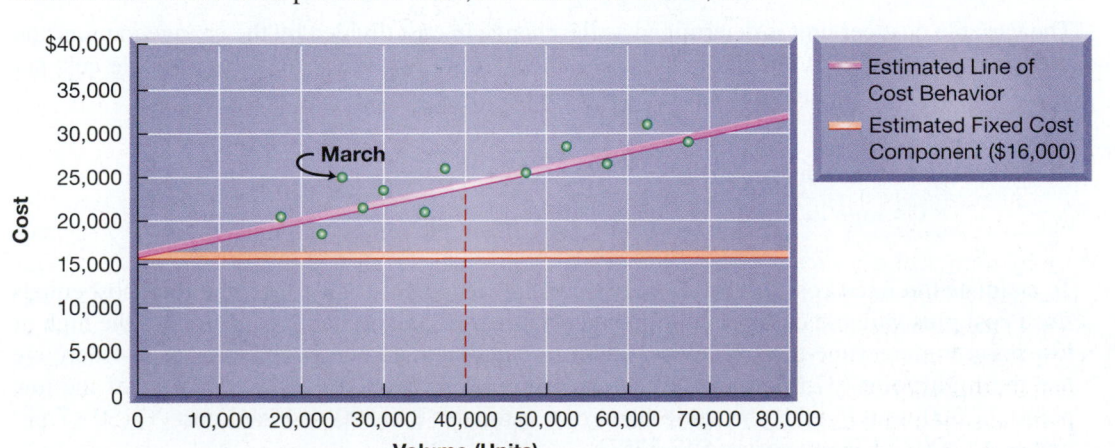

EXHIBIT 18.4

Scatter Diagram

The **estimated line of cost behavior** is drawn on a scatter diagram to reflect the relation between cost and unit volume. This line best visually "fits" the points in a scatter diagram. Fitting this line demands judgment. The line drawn in Exhibit 18.4 intersects the vertical axis at approximately $16,000, which reflects fixed cost. To compute variable cost per unit, or the slope, we perform three steps. First, we select any two points on the horizontal axis (units), say 0 and 40,000. Second, we draw a vertical line from each of these points to intersect the estimated line of cost behavior. The point on the vertical axis (cost) corresponding to the 40,000 units point that intersects the estimated line is roughly $24,000. Similarly, the cost corresponding to zero units is $16,000 (the fixed cost point). Third, we compute the slope of the line, or variable cost, as the change in cost divided by the change in units. Exhibit 18.5 shows this computation.

EXHIBIT 18.5

Variable Cost per Unit
(Scatter Diagram)

$$\frac{\text{Change in cost}}{\text{Change in units}} = \frac{\$24,000 - \$16,000}{40,000 - 0} = \frac{\$8,000}{40,000} = \$0.20 \text{ per unit}$$

Example: In Exhibits 18.4 and 18.5, if units are projected at 30,000, what is the predicted cost? *Answer:* Approximately $22,000.

Variable cost is $0.20 per unit. Thus, the cost equation that management will use to estimate costs for different unit levels is **$16,000 plus $0.20 per unit**.

High-Low Method

The **high-low method** is a way to estimate the cost equation by graphically connecting the two cost amounts at the highest and lowest unit volumes. In our case, the lowest number of units is 17,500, and the highest is 67,500. The costs corresponding to these unit volumes are $20,500 and $29,000, respectively (see the data in Exhibit 18.3). The estimated line of cost behavior for the high-low method is then drawn by connecting these two points on the scatter diagram corresponding to the lowest and highest unit volumes as follows.

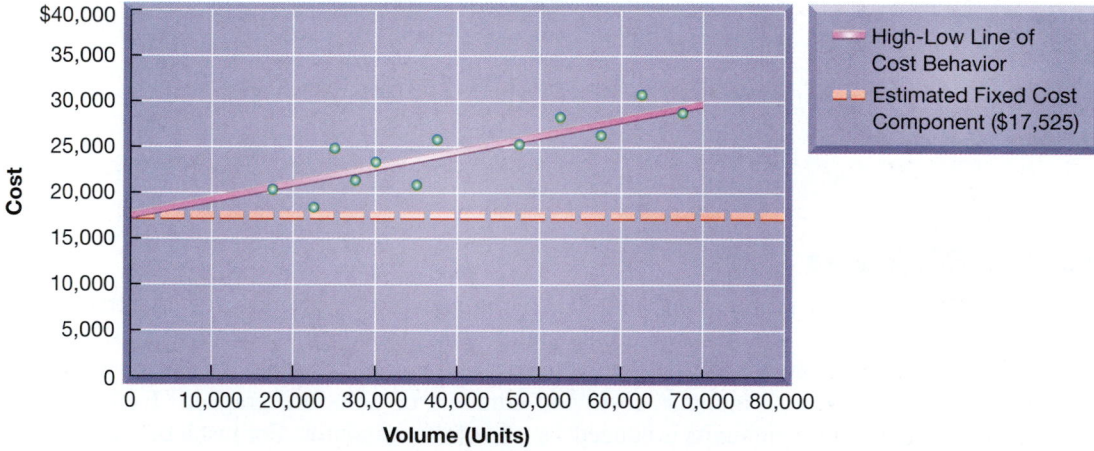

Point: Note that the high-low method identifies the high and low points of the volume (activity) base, and the costs linked with those extremes—which may not be the highest and lowest costs.

The variable cost per unit is determined as the change in cost divided by the change in units and uses the data from the high and low unit volumes. This results in a slope, or variable cost per unit, of $0.17 as computed in Exhibit 18.6.

EXHIBIT 18.6

Variable Cost per Unit
(High-Low Method)

$$\frac{\text{Change in cost}}{\text{Change in units}} = \frac{\$29,000 - \$20,500}{67,500 - 17,500} = \frac{\$8,500}{50,000} = \$0.17 \text{ per unit}$$

To estimate the fixed cost for the high-low method, we use the knowledge that total cost equals fixed cost plus variable cost per unit times the number of units. Then we pick either the high or low point to determine the fixed cost. This computation is shown in Exhibit 18.7—where we use the high point (67,500 units) in determining the fixed cost of $17,525. Use of the low point (17,500 units) yields the same fixed cost estimate: $20,500 = Fixed cost + ($0.17 per unit × 17,500), or Fixed cost = $17,525.

> **Total cost = Fixed cost + (Variable cost × Units)**
>
> $29,000 = Fixed cost + ($0.17 per unit × 67,500 units)
>
> Then,   Fixed cost = $17,525

EXHIBIT 18.7

Fixed Cost (High-Low Method)

Thus, the cost equation used to estimate costs at different units is **$17,525 plus $0.17 per unit**. This cost equation differs slightly from that determined from the scatter diagram method. A deficiency of the high-low method is that it ignores all cost points except the highest and lowest. The result is less precision because the high-low method uses the most extreme points rather than the more usual conditions likely to recur.

Least-Squares Regression

Least-squares regression is a statistical method for identifying cost behavior. For our purposes, we use the cost equation estimated from this method but leave the computational details for more advanced courses. Such computations for least-squares regression are readily done using most spreadsheet programs or calculators. We illustrate this using Excel® in Appendix 18A.

The regression cost equation for the data presented in Exhibit 18.3 is **$16,947 plus $0.19 per unit**; that is, the fixed cost is estimated as $16,947 and the variable cost at $0.19 per unit. Both costs are reflected in the following graph.

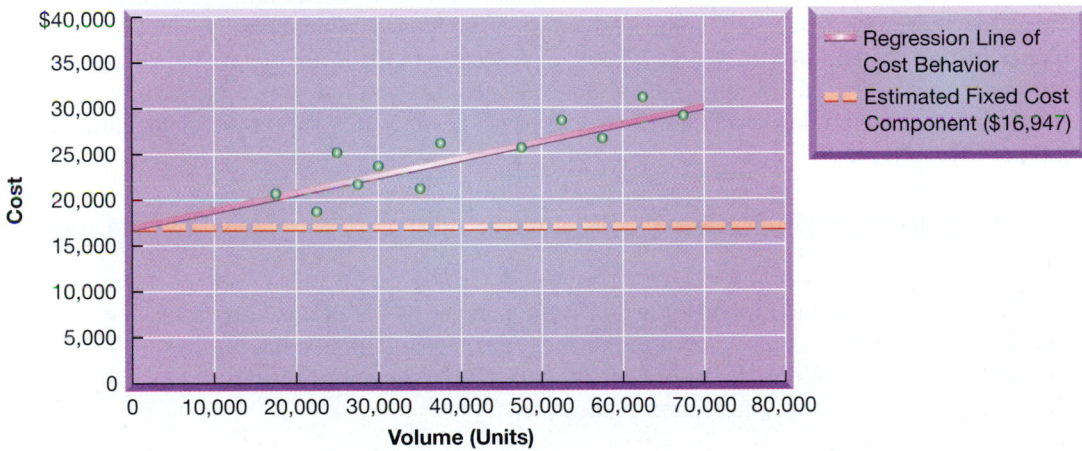

Comparison of Cost Estimation Methods

The three cost estimation methods result in slightly different estimates of fixed and variable costs as summarized in Exhibit 18.8. Estimates from the scatter diagram are based on a visual fit of the cost line and are subject to interpretation. Estimates from the high-low method use only two sets of values corresponding to the lowest and highest unit volumes. Estimates from least-squares regression use a statistical technique and all available data points.

Estimation Method	Fixed Cost	Variable Cost
Scatter diagram	$16,000	$0.20 per unit
High-low method	17,525	0.17 per unit
Least-squares regression	16,947	0.19 per unit

EXHIBIT 18.8

Comparison of Cost Estimation Methods

We must remember that all three methods use *past data*. Thus, cost estimates resulting from these methods are only as good as the data used for estimation. Managers must establish that the data are reliable in deriving cost estimates for the future.

4. Which of the following methods is likely to yield the most precise estimated line of cost behavior? (*a*) High-low, (*b*) least-squares regression, or (*c*) scatter diagram.
5. What is the primary weakness of the high-low method?
6. Using conventional CVP analysis, a mixed cost should be (*a*) disregarded, (*b*) treated as a fixed cost, or (*c*) separated into fixed and variable components.

USING BREAK-EVEN ANALYSIS

Break-even analysis is a special case of cost-volume-profit analysis. This section describes break-even analysis by computing the break-even point and preparing a CVP (or break-even) chart.

Contribution Margin and Its Measures

A1 Compute the contribution margin and describe what it reveals about a company's cost structure.

We explained how managers classify costs by behavior. This often refers to classifying costs as being fixed or variable with respect to volume of activity. In manufacturing companies, volume of activity usually refers to the number of units produced. We then classify a cost as either fixed or variable, depending on whether total cost changes as the number of units produced changes. Once we separate costs by behavior, we can then compute a product's contribution margin. **Contribution margin per unit,** or *unit contribution margin,* is the amount by which a product's unit selling price exceeds its total unit variable cost. This excess amount contributes to covering fixed costs and generating profits on a per unit basis. Exhibit 18.9 shows the contribution margin per unit formula.

EXHIBIT 18.9

Contribution Margin per Unit

$$\text{Contribution margin per unit} = \text{Sales price per unit} - \text{Total variable cost per unit}$$

The **contribution margin ratio,** which is the percent of a unit's selling price that exceeds total unit variable cost, is also useful for business decisions. It can be interpreted as the percent of each sales dollar that remains after deducting the total unit variable cost. Exhibit 18.10 shows the formula for the contribution margin ratio.

EXHIBIT 18.10

Contribution Margin Ratio

$$\text{Contribution margin ratio} = \frac{\text{Contribution margin per unit}}{\text{Sales price per unit}}$$

To illustrate the use of contribution margin, let's consider **Rydell,** which sells footballs for $100 per unit and incurs variable costs of $70 per unit sold. Its fixed costs are $24,000 per month with monthly capacity of 1,800 units (footballs). Rydell's contribution margin per unit is $30, which is computed as follows.

Selling price per unit	$100
Variable cost per unit	70
Contribution margin per unit	$ 30

Its contribution margin ratio is 30%, computed as $30/$100. This reveals that for each unit sold, Rydell has $30 that contributes to covering fixed cost and profit. If we consider sales in dollars, a contribution margin of 30% implies that for each $1 in sales, Rydell has $0.30 that contributes to fixed cost and profit.

Decision Maker   Answer — p. 785

Sales Manager   You are evaluating orders from two customers but can accept only one of the orders because of your company's limited capacity. The first order is for 100 units of a product with a contribution margin ratio of 60% and a selling price of $1,000. The second order is for 500 units of a product with a contribution margin ratio of 20% and a selling price of $800. The incremental fixed costs are the same for both orders. Which order do you accept? ■

Computing the Break-Even Point

The **break-even point** is the sales level at which a company neither earns a profit nor incurs a loss. The concept of break-even is applicable to nearly all organizations, activities, and events. One of the most important items of information when launching a project is whether it will break even—that is, whether sales will at least cover total costs. The break-even point can be expressed in either units or dollars of sales.

To illustrate the computation of break-even analysis, let's again look at Rydell, which sells footballs for $100 per unit and incurs $70 of variable costs per unit sold. Its fixed costs are $24,000 per month. Rydell breaks even for the month when it sells 800 footballs (sales volume of $80,000). We compute this break-even point using the formula in Exhibit 18.11. This formula uses the contribution margin per unit, which for Rydell is $30 ($100 − $70). From this we can compute the break-even sales volume as $24,000/$30, or 800 units per month.

P2 Compute the break-even point for a single product company.

$$\text{Break-even point in units} = \frac{\text{Fixed costs}}{\text{Contribution margin per unit}}$$

EXHIBIT 18.11

Formula for Computing Break-Even Sales (in Units)

At a price of $100 per unit, monthly sales of 800 units yield sales dollars of $80,000 (called *break-even sales dollars*). This $80,000 break-even sales can be computed directly using the formula in Exhibit 18.12.

$$\text{Break-even point in dollars} = \frac{\text{Fixed costs}}{\text{Contribution margin ratio}}$$

EXHIBIT 18.12

Formula for Computing Break-Even Sales (in Dollars)

Rydell's break-even point in dollars is computed as $24,000/0.30, or $80,000 of monthly sales. To verify that Rydell's break-even point equals $80,000 (or 800 units), we prepare a simplified income statement in Exhibit 18.13. It shows that the $80,000 revenue from sales of 800 units exactly equals the sum of variable and fixed costs.

Point: Even if a company operates at a level in excess of its break-even point, management may decide to stop operating because it is not earning a reasonable return on investment.

RYDELL COMPANY Contribution Margin Income Statement (at Break-Even) For Month Ended January 31, 2011	
Sales (800 units at $100 each)	$80,000
Variable costs (800 units at $70 each)	56,000
Contribution margin	24,000
Fixed costs	24,000
Net income	$ 0

EXHIBIT 18.13

Contribution Margin Income Statement for Break-Even Sales

The statement in Exhibit 18.13 is called a *contribution margin income statement*. It differs in format from a conventional income statement in two ways. First, it separately classifies costs and expenses as variable or fixed. Second, it reports contribution margin (Sales − Variable costs). The contribution margin income statement format is used in this chapter's assignment materials because of its usefulness in CVP analysis.

Point: A contribution margin income statement is also referred to as a *variable costing income statement*. This differs from the traditional *absorption costing* approach where all product costs are assigned to units sold and to units in ending inventory. Recall that variable costing expenses all fixed product costs. Thus, income for the two approaches differs depending on the level of finished goods inventory; the lower inventory is, the more similar the two approaches are.

Preparing a Cost-Volume-Profit Chart

Exhibit 18.14 is a graph of Rydell's cost-volume-profit relations. This graph is called a **cost-volume-profit (CVP) chart,** or a *break-even chart* or *break-even graph.* The horizontal axis is the number of units produced and sold and the vertical axis is dollars of sales and costs. The lines in the chart depict both sales and costs at different output levels.

EXHIBIT 18.14

Cost-Volume-Profit Chart

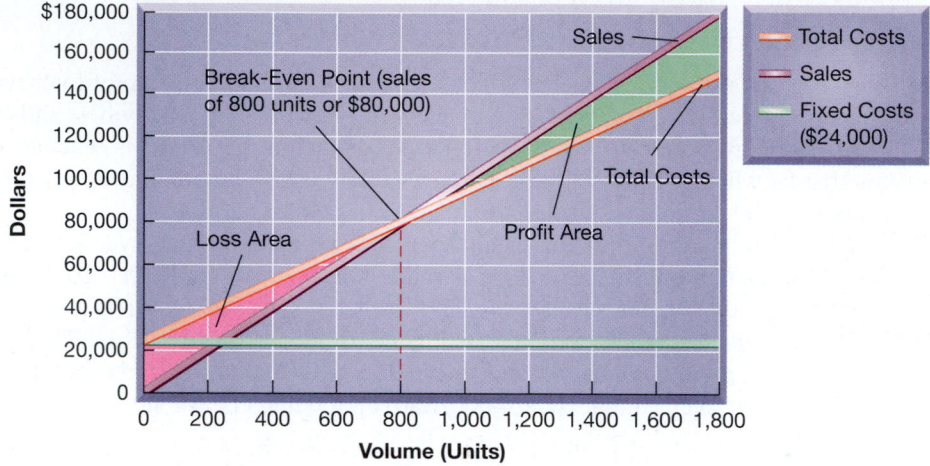

We follow three steps to prepare a CVP chart, which can also be drawn with computer programs that convert numeric data to graphs:

1. Plot fixed costs on the vertical axis ($24,000 for Rydell). Draw a horizontal line at this level to show that fixed costs remain unchanged regardless of output volume (drawing this fixed cost line is not essential to the chart).

2. Draw the total (variable plus fixed) costs line for a relevant range of volume levels. This line starts at the fixed costs level on the vertical axis because total costs equal fixed costs at zero volume. The slope of the total cost line equals the variable cost per unit ($70). To draw the line, compute the total costs for any volume level, and connect this point with the vertical axis intercept ($24,000). Do not draw this line beyond the productive capacity for the planning period (1,800 units for Rydell).

3. Draw the sales line. Start at the origin (zero units and zero dollars of sales) and make the slope of this line equal to the selling price per unit ($100). To sketch the line, compute dollar sales for any volume level and connect this point with the origin. Do not extend this line beyond the productive capacity. Total sales will be at the highest level at maximum capacity.

Example: In Exhibit 18.14, the sales line intersects the total cost line at 800 units. At what point would the two lines intersect if selling price is increased by 20% to $120 per unit? *Answer:* $24,000/($120 − $70) = 480 units

The total costs line and the sales line intersect at 800 units in Exhibit 18.14, which is the break-even point—the point where total dollar sales of $80,000 equals the sum of both fixed and variable costs ($80,000).

On either side of the break-even point, the vertical distance between the sales line and the total costs line at any specific volume reflects the profit or loss expected at that point. At volume levels to the left of the break-even point, this vertical distance is the amount of the expected loss because the total costs line is above the total sales line. At volume levels to the right of the break-even point, the vertical distance represents the expected profit because the total sales line is above the total costs line.

■ **Decision Maker**   Answer — p. 785

Operations Manager   As a start-up manufacturer, you wish to identify the behavior of manufacturing costs to develop a production cost budget. You know three methods can be used to identify cost behavior from past data, but past data are unavailable because this is a start-up. What do you do? ■

Making Assumptions in Cost-Volume-Profit Analysis

Cost-volume-profit analysis assumes that relations can normally be expressed as simple lines similar to those in Exhibits 18.4 and 18.14. Such assumptions allow users to answer several important questions, but the usefulness of the answers depends on the validity of three assumptions: (1) constant selling price per unit, (2) constant variable costs per unit, and (3) constant total fixed costs. These assumptions are not always realistic, but CVP analysis can be very useful for business decision making even when its assumptions are not strictly met. This section discusses these assumptions and other issues for CVP analysis.

Working with Assumptions   The behavior of individual costs and sales often is not perfectly consistent with CVP assumptions. If the expected costs and sales behavior differ from the assumptions, the results of CVP analysis can be limited. Still, we can perform useful analyses in spite of limitations with these assumptions for several reasons.

Summing costs can offset individual deviations.   Deviations from assumptions with individual costs are often minor when these costs are summed. That is, individual variable cost items may not be perfectly variable, but when we sum these variable costs, their individual deviations can offset each other. This means the assumption of variable cost behavior can be proper for total variable costs. Similarly, an assumption that total fixed costs are constant can be proper even when individual fixed cost items are not exactly constant.

CVP is applied to a relevant range of operations.   Sales, variable costs, and fixed costs often are reasonably reflected in straight lines on a graph when the assumptions are applied over a relevant range. The **relevant range of operations** is the normal operating range for a business. Except for unusually difficult or prosperous times, management typically plans for operations within a range of volume neither close to zero nor at maximum capacity. The relevant range excludes extremely high and low operating levels that are unlikely to occur. The validity of assuming that a specific cost is fixed or variable is more acceptable when operations are within the relevant range. As shown in Exhibit 18.2, a curvilinear cost can be treated as variable and linear if the relevant range covers volumes where it has a nearly constant slope. If the normal range of activity changes, some costs might need reclassification.

CVP analysis yields estimates.   CVP analysis yields approximate answers to questions about costs, volumes, and profits. These answers do not have to be precise because the analysis makes rough estimates about the future. As long as managers understand that CVP analysis gives estimates, it can be a useful tool for starting the planning process. Other qualitative factors also must be considered.

Working with Output Measures   CVP analysis usually describes the level of activity in terms of *sales volume,* which can be expressed in terms of either units sold or dollar sales. However, other measures of output exist. For instance, a manufacturer can use the number of units produced as a measure of output. Also, to simplify analysis, we sometimes assume that the production level is the same as the sales level. That is, inventory levels do not change. This often is justified by arguing that CVP analysis provides only approximations.

Example: If the selling price declines, what happens to the break-even point? *Answer:* It increases.

Quick Check

Answers — p. 786

7. Fixed cost divided by the contribution margin ratio yields the (*a*) break-even point in dollars, (*b*) contribution margin per unit, or (*c*) break-even point in units.

8. A company sells a product for $90 per unit with variable costs of $54 per unit. What is the contribution margin ratio?

9. Refer to Quick Check (8). If fixed costs for the period are $90,000, what is the break-even point in dollars?

10. What three basic assumptions are used in CVP analysis?

Working with Changes in Estimates   Because CVP analysis uses estimates, knowing how changes in those estimates impact break-even is useful. For example, a manager might form three estimates for each of the components of break-even: optimistic, most likely, and pessimistic. Then ranges of break-even points in units can be computed using the formula in Exhibit 18.11.

To illustrate, assume Rydell's managers provide the set of estimates in Exhibit 18.15.

EXHIBIT 18.15

Alternative Estimates for Break-Even Analysis

	Selling Price per Unit	Variable Cost per Unit	Total Fixed Costs
Optimistic	$105	$68	$21,000
Most likely	100	70	24,000
Pessimistic	95	72	27,000

If, for example, Rydell's managers believe they can raise the selling price of a football to $105, without any change in variable or fixed costs, then the revised contribution margin per football is $35, and the revised break-even in units follows in Exhibit 18.16.

EXHIBIT 18.16

Revised Break-Even in Units

$$\text{Revised break-even} \atop \text{point in units} = \frac{\$24,000}{\$35} = 686 \text{ units}$$

EXHIBIT 18.17

Scatter Diagrams—Break-Even Points for Alternative Estimates

Repeating this calculation using each of the other eight separate estimates above, and graphing the results, yields the three scatter diagrams in Exhibit 18.17.

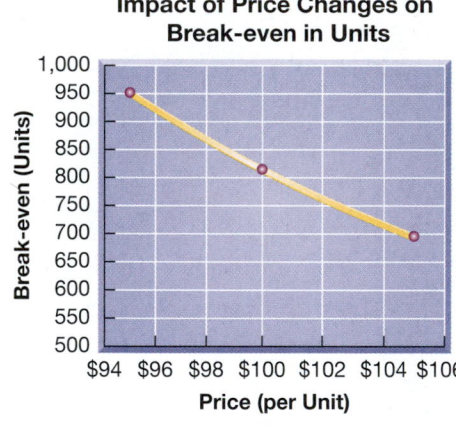

Impact of Price Changes on Break-even in Units

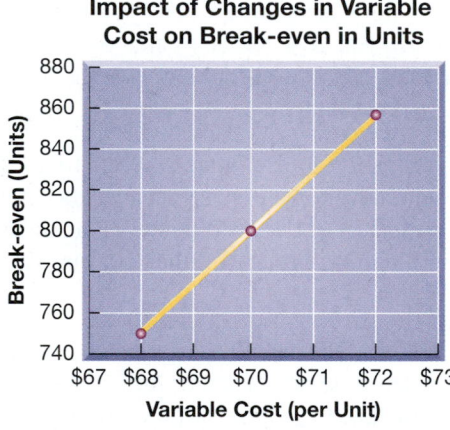

Impact of Changes in Variable Cost on Break-even in Units

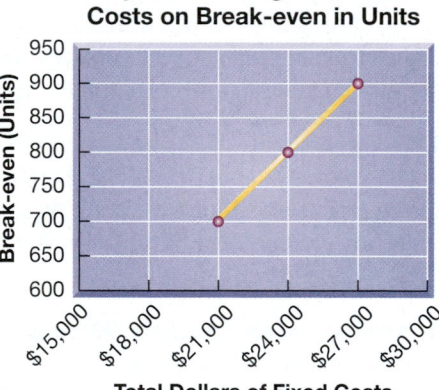

Impact of Changes in Fixed Costs on Break-even in Units

These scatter diagrams show how changes in selling prices, variable costs, and fixed costs impact break-even. When selling prices can be increased without impacting costs, break-even decreases. When competition drives selling prices down, and the company cannot reduce costs, break-even increases. Increases in either variable or fixed costs, if they cannot be passed on to customers via higher selling prices, will increase break-even. If costs can be reduced and selling prices held constant, the break-even decreases.

Point: This analysis changed only one estimate at a time; managers can examine how combinations of changes in estimates will impact break-even.

APPLYING COST-VOLUME-PROFIT ANALYSIS

Managers consider a variety of strategies in planning business operations. Cost-volume-profit analysis is useful in helping managers evaluate the likely effects of these strategies, which is the focus of this section.

Computing Income from Sales and Costs

An important question managers often need an answer to is "What is the predicted income from a predicted level of sales?" To answer this, we look at four variables in CVP analysis. These variables and their relations to income (pretax) are shown in Exhibit 18.18. We use these relations to compute expected income from predicted sales and cost levels.

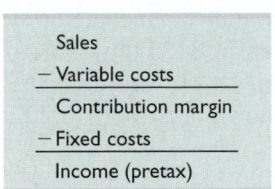

| C2 | Describe several applications of cost-volume-profit analysis. |

EXHIBIT 18.18

Income Relations in CVP Analysis

To illustrate, let's assume that Rydell's management expects to sell 1,500 units in January 2011. What is the amount of income if this sales level is achieved? Following Exhibit 18.18, we compute Rydell's expected income in Exhibit 18.19.

RYDELL COMPANY
Contribution Margin Income Statement
For Month Ended January 31, 2011

Sales (1,500 units at $100 each)	$150,000
Variable costs (1,500 units at $70 each)	105,000
Contribution margin	45,000
Fixed costs	24,000
Income (pretax)	$ 21,000

EXHIBIT 18.19

Computing Expected Pretax Income from Expected Sales

The $21,000 income is pretax. To find the amount of *after-tax* income from selling 1,500 units, management must apply the proper tax rate. Assume that the tax rate is 25%. Then we can prepare the after-tax income statement shown in Exhibit 18.20. We can also compute pretax income as after-tax income divided by (1 − tax rate); for Rydell, this is $15,750/(1 − 0.25), or $21,000.

RYDELL COMPANY
Contribution Margin Income Statement
For Month Ended January 31, 2011

Sales (1,500 units at $100 each)	$150,000
Variable costs (1,500 units at $70 each)	105,000
Contribution margin	45,000
Fixed costs	24,000
Pretax income	21,000
Income taxes (25%)	5,250
Net income (after tax)	$ 15,750

EXHIBIT 18.20

Computing Expected After-Tax Income from Expected Sales

Management then assesses whether this income is an adequate return on assets invested. Management should also consider whether sales and income can be increased by raising or lowering prices. CVP analysis is a good tool for addressing these kinds of "what-if" questions.

Computing Sales for a Target Income

Many companies' annual plans are based on certain income targets (sometimes called *budgets*). Rydell's income target for this year is to increase income by 10% over the prior year. When prior year income is known, Rydell easily computes its target income. CVP analysis helps to determine the sales level needed to achieve the target income. Computing this sales level is important because planning for the year is then based on this level. We use the formula shown in Exhibit 18.21 to compute sales for a target *after-tax* income.

"How many units must I sell to earn $50,000?"

EXHIBIT 18.21

Computing Sales (Dollars) for
a Target After-Tax Income

$$\text{Dollar sales at target after-tax income} = \frac{\text{Fixed costs} + \text{Target pretax income}}{\text{Contribution margin ratio}}$$

To illustrate, Rydell has monthly fixed costs of $24,000 and a 30% contribution margin ratio. Assume that it sets a target monthly after-tax income of $9,000 when the tax rate is 25%. This means the pretax income is targeted at $12,000 [$9,000/(1 − 0.25)] with a tax expense of $3,000. Using the formula in Exhibit 18.21, we find that $120,000 of sales are needed to produce a $9,000 after-tax income as shown in Exhibit 18.22.

EXHIBIT 18.22

Rydell's Dollar Sales for a
Target Income

$$\text{Dollar sales at target after-tax income} = \frac{\$24,000 + \$12,000}{30\%} = \$120,000$$

Point: Break-even is a special case of the formulas in Exhibits 18.21 and 18.23; simply set target pretax income to $0 and the formulas reduce to those in Exhibits 18.11 and 18.12.

We can alternatively compute *unit sales* instead of dollar sales. To do this, we substitute *contribution margin per unit* for the contribution margin ratio in the denominator. This gives the number of units to sell to reach the target after-tax income. Exhibit 18.23 illustrates this for Rydell. The two computations in Exhibits 18.22 and 18.23 are equivalent because sales of 1,200 units at $100 per unit equal $120,000 of sales.

EXHIBIT 18.23

Computing Sales (Units)
for a Target After-Tax
Income

$$\text{Unit sales at target after-tax income} = \frac{\text{Fixed costs} + \text{Target pretax income}}{\text{Contribution margin per unit}}$$

$$= \frac{\$24,000 + \$12,000}{\$30} = 1,200 \text{ units}$$

Computing the Margin of Safety

All companies wish to sell more than the break-even number of units. The excess of expected sales over the break-even sales level is called a company's **margin of safety,** the amount that sales can drop before the company incurs a loss. It can be expressed in units, dollars, or even as a percent of the predicted level of sales. To illustrate, if Rydell's expected sales are $100,000, the margin of safety is $20,000 above break-even sales of $80,000. As a percent, the margin of safety is 20% of expected sales as shown in Exhibit 18.24.

EXHIBIT 18.24

Computing Margin of Safety
(in Percent)

$$\text{Margin of safety (in percent)} = \frac{\text{Expected sales} - \text{Break-even sales}}{\text{Expected sales}}$$

$$= \frac{\$100,000 - \$80,000}{\$100,000} = 20\%$$

Management must assess whether the margin of safety is adequate in light of factors such as sales variability, competition, consumer tastes, and economic conditions.

| Decision **Ethics** | Answer — p. 785 |

Supervisor Your team is conducting a cost-volume-profit analysis for a new product. Different sales projections have different incomes. One member suggests picking numbers yielding favorable income because any estimate is "as good as any other." Another member points to a scatter diagram of 20 months' production on a comparable product and suggests dropping unfavorable data points for cost estimation. What do you do? ∎

Using Sensitivity Analysis

Earlier we showed how changing one of the estimates in a CVP analysis impacts break-even. We can also examine strategies that impact several estimates in the CVP analysis. For instance, we might want to know what happens to income if we automate a currently manual process. We can use CVP analysis to predict income if we can describe how these changes affect a company's fixed costs, variable costs, selling price, and volume.

To illustrate, assume that Rydell Company is looking into buying a new machine that would increase monthly fixed costs from $24,000 to $30,000 but decrease variable costs from $70 per unit to $60 per unit. The machine is used to produce output whose selling price will remain unchanged at $100. This results in increases in both the unit contribution margin and the contribution margin ratio. The revised contribution margin per unit is $40 ($100 − $60), and the revised contribution margin ratio is 40% of selling price ($40/$100). Using CVP analysis, Rydell's revised break-even point in dollars would be $75,000 as computed in Exhibit 18.25.

Example: If fixed costs decline, what happens to the break-even point? *Answer:* It decreases.

$$\text{Revised break-even point in dollars} = \frac{\text{Revised fixed costs}}{\text{Revised contribution margin ratio}} = \frac{\$30,000}{40\%} = \$75,000$$

EXHIBIT 18.25

Revising Break-even When Changes Occur

The revised fixed costs and the revised contribution margin ratio can be used to address other issues including computation of (1) expected income for a given sales level and (2) the sales level needed to earn a target income. Once again, we can use sensitivity analysis to generate different sets of revenue and cost estimates that are *optimistic, pessimistic,* and *most likely.* Different CVP analyses based on these estimates provide different scenarios that management can analyze and use in planning business strategy.

Decision Insight

Eco-CVP Auto makers are increasingly offering hybrid cars, including the **Ford** Fusion, **Toyota** Prius, and **Nissan** Altima Hybrid. Hybrids yield better gas mileage and generate fewer greenhouse gases, but they are priced higher. Are hybrid models economically feasible for buyers? A study by **Edmunds.com** shows it take several years for consumers to break even (save enough money on gas to offset the higher purchase price) on most hybrid models. ■

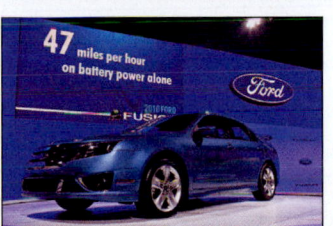

Quick Check

Answers — p. 786

11. A company has fixed costs of $50,000 and a 25% contribution margin ratio. What dollar sales are necessary to achieve an after-tax net income of $120,000 if the tax rate is 20%? (*a*) $800,000, (*b*) $680,000, or (*c*) $600,000.

12. If a company's contribution margin ratio decreases from 50% to 25%, what can be said about the unit sales needed to achieve the same target income level?

13. What is a company's margin of safety?

Computing a Multiproduct Break-Even Point

To this point, we have looked only at cases where the company sells a single product or service. This was to keep the basic CVP analysis simple. However, many companies sell multiple products or services, and we can modify the CVP analysis for use in these cases. An important assumption in a multiproduct setting is that the sales mix of different products is known and remains constant during the planning period. **Sales mix** is the ratio (proportion) of the sales volumes for the various products. For instance, if a company normally sells 10,000 footballs, 5,000 softballs, and 4,000 basketballs per month, its sales mix can be expressed as 10:5:4 for footballs, softballs, and basketballs.

P4 Compute the break-even point for a multiproduct company.

To apply multiproduct CVP analysis, we can estimate the break-even point by using a **composite unit,** which consists of a specific number of units of each product in proportion to their expected sales mix. Multiproduct CVP analysis treats this composite unit as a single product. To illustrate, let's look at **Hair-Today,** a styling salon that offers three cuts: basic, ultra, and budget in the ratio of 4 basic units to 2 ultra units to 1 budget unit (expressed as 4:2:1). Management wants to estimate its break-even point for next year. Unit selling prices for these three cuts are basic, $20; ultra, $32; and budget, $16. Using the 4:2:1 sales mix, the selling price of a composite unit of the three products is computed as follows.

4 units of basic @ $20 per unit	$ 80
2 units of ultra @ $32 per unit	64
1 unit of budget @ $16 per unit	16
Selling price of a composite unit	**$160**

Point: Selling prices and variable costs are usually expressed in per unit amounts. Fixed costs are usually expressed in total amounts.

Hair-Today's fixed costs are $192,000 per year, and its variable costs of the three products are basic, $13; ultra, $18.00; and budget, $8.00. Variable costs for a composite unit of these products follow.

4 units of basic @ $13 per unit	$52
2 units of ultra @ $18 per unit	36
1 unit of budget @ $8 per unit	8
Variable costs of a composite unit	**$96**

Hair-Today's $64 contribution margin for a composite unit is computed by subtracting the variable costs of a composite unit ($96) from its selling price ($160). We then use the contribution margin to determine Hair-Today's break-even point in composite units in Exhibit 18.26.

EXHIBIT 18.26

Break-Even Point in Composite Units

$$\text{Break-even point in composite units} = \frac{\text{Fixed costs}}{\text{Contribution margin per composite unit}}$$

$$= \frac{\$192,000}{\$64} = 3{,}000 \text{ composite units}$$

Point: The break-even point in dollars for Exhibit 18.26 is $192,000/($64/$160) = $480,000.

This computation implies that Hair-Today breaks even when it sells 3,000 composite units. To determine how many units of each product it must sell to break even, we multiply the number of units of each product in the composite by 3,000 as follows.

Basic:	4 × 3,000	. . . .	12,000 units
Ultra:	2 × 3,000	. . . .	6,000 units
Budget:	1 × 3,000	. . . .	3,000 units

Instead of computing contribution margin per composite unit, a company can compute a **weighted-average contribution margin.** Given the 4:2:1 product mix, basic cuts comprise 57.14% (computed as 4/7) of the company's haircuts, ultra makes up 28.57% of its business, and budget cuts comprise 14.29%. The weighted-average contribution margin follows in Exhibit 18.27.

EXHIBIT 18.27

Weighted-Average Contribution Margin

	Unit contribution margin	×	Percentage of sales mix	=	Weighted unit contribution margin
Basic.	$ 7		57.14%		$4.000
Ultra	14		28.57		4.000
Budget	8		14.29		1.143
Weighted-average contribution margin					**$9.143**

The company's break-even point in units is computed in Exhibit 18.28 as follows:

$$\text{Break-even point in units} = \frac{\text{Fixed costs}}{\text{Weighted-average contribution margin}}$$

$$= \frac{\$192,000}{\$9.143} = 21,000 \text{ units}$$

EXHIBIT 18.28

Break-Even in Units Using Weighted-Average Contribution Margin

We see that the weighted-average contribution margin method yields 21,000 whole units as the break-even amount, the same total as the composite unit approach.

Exhibit 18.29 verifies the results for composite units by showing Hair-Today's sales and costs at this break-even point using a contribution margin income statement.

EXHIBIT 18.29

Multiproduct Break-Even Income Statement

HAIR-TODAY
Forecasted Contribution Margin Income Statement (at Break-even)

	Basic	Ultra	Budget	Totals
Sales				
Basic (12,000 @ $20)	$240,000			
Ultra (6,000 @ $32)		$192,000		
Budget (3,000 @ $16)			$48,000	
Total sales				$480,000
Variable costs				
Basic (12,000 @ $13)	156,000			
Ultra (6,000 @ $18)		108,000		
Budget (3,000 @ $8)			24,000	
Total variable costs				288,000
Contribution margin	$ 84,000	$ 84,000	$24,000	192,000
Fixed costs				192,000
Net income				$ 0

A CVP analysis using composite units can be used to answer a variety of planning questions. Once a product mix is set, all answers are based on the assumption that the mix remains constant at all relevant sales levels as other factors in the analysis do. We also can vary the sales mix to see what happens under alternative strategies.

Decision Maker   Answer — p. 786

Entrepreneur   A CVP analysis indicates that your start-up, which markets electronic products, will break even with the current sales mix and price levels. You have a target income in mind. What analysis might you perform to assess the likelihood of achieving this income? ■

Quick Check   Answers — p. 786

14. The sales mix of a company's two products, X and Y, is 2:1. Unit variable costs for both products are $2, and unit sales prices are $5 for X and $4 for Y. What is the contribution margin per composite unit? (a) $5, (b) $10, or (c) $8.

15. What additional assumption about sales mix must be made in doing a conventional CVP analysis for a company that produces and sells more than one product?

GLOBAL VIEW

Decision Analysis    Degree of Operating Leverage

A2 Analyze changes in sales using the degree of operating leverage.

CVP analysis is especially useful when management begins the planning process and wishes to predict outcomes of alternative strategies. These strategies can involve changes in selling prices, fixed costs, variable costs, sales volume, and product mix. Managers are interested in seeing the effects of changes in some or all of these factors.

One goal of all managers is to get maximum benefits from their fixed costs. Managers would like to use 100% of their output capacity so that fixed costs are spread over the largest number of units. This would decrease fixed cost per unit and increase income. The extent, or relative size, of fixed costs in the total cost structure is known as **operating leverage.** Companies having a higher proportion of fixed costs in their total cost structure are said to have higher operating leverage. An example of this is a company that chooses to automate its processes instead of using direct labor, increasing its fixed costs and lowering its variable costs. A useful managerial measure to help assess the effect of changes in the level of sales on income is the **degree of operating leverage (DOL)** defined in Exhibit 18.30.

EXHIBIT 18.30

Degree of Operating Leverage

DOL = Total contribution margin (in dollars)/Pretax income

To illustrate, let's return to Rydell Company. At a sales level of 1,200 units, Rydell's total contribution margin is $36,000 (1,200 units × $30 contribution margin per unit). Its pretax income, after subtracting fixed costs of $24,000, is $12,000 ($36,000 − $24,000). Rydell's degree of operating leverage at this sales level is 3.0, computed as contribution margin divided by pretax income ($36,000/$12,000). We then use DOL to measure the effect of changes in the level of sales on pretax income. For instance, suppose Rydell expects sales to increase by 10%. If this increase is within the relevant range of operations, we can expect this 10% increase in sales to result in a 30% increase in pretax income computed as DOL multiplied by the increase in sales (3.0 × 10%). Similar analyses can be done for expected decreases in sales.

DEMONSTRATION PROBLEM

Sport Caps Co. manufactures and sells caps for different sporting events. The fixed costs of operating the company are $150,000 per month, and the variable costs for caps are $5 per unit. The caps are sold for $8 per unit. The fixed costs provide a production capacity of up to 100,000 caps per month.

Required

1. Use the formulas in the chapter to compute the following:
   a. Contribution margin per cap.
   b. Break-even point in terms of the number of caps produced and sold.
   c. Amount of net income at 30,000 caps sold per month (ignore taxes).
   d. Amount of net income at 85,000 caps sold per month (ignore taxes).

e. Number of caps to be produced and sold to provide $45,000 of after-tax income, assuming an income tax rate of 25%.

2. Draw a CVP chart for the company, showing cap output on the horizontal axis. Identify (*a*) the break-even point and (*b*) the amount of pretax income when the level of cap production is 70,000. (Omit the fixed cost line.)

3. Use the formulas in the chapter to compute the

  a. Contribution margin ratio.

  b. Break-even point in terms of sales dollars.

  c. Amount of net income at $250,000 of sales per month (ignore taxes).

  d. Amount of net income at $600,000 of sales per month (ignore taxes).

  e. Dollars of sales needed to provide $45,000 of after-tax income, assuming an income tax rate of 25%.

PLANNING THE SOLUTION

- Identify the formulas in the chapter for the required items expressed in units and solve them using the data given in the problem.

- Draw a CVP chart that reflects the facts in the problem. The horizontal axis should plot the volume in units up to 100,000, and the vertical axis should plot the total dollars up to $800,000. Plot the total cost line as upward sloping, starting at the fixed cost level ($150,000) on the vertical axis and increasing until it reaches $650,000 at the maximum volume of 100,000 units. Verify that the break-even point (where the two lines cross) equals the amount you computed in part 1.

- Identify the formulas in the chapter for the required items expressed in dollars and solve them using the data given in the problem.

SOLUTION TO DEMONSTRATION PROBLEM

1. a. Contribution margin per cap = Selling price per unit − Variable cost per unit
= $8 − $5 = $3

b. Break-even point in caps $= \dfrac{\text{Fixed costs}}{\text{Contribution margin per cap}} = \dfrac{\$150,000}{\$3} = 50,000 \text{ caps}$

c. Net income at 30,000 caps sold = (Units × Contribution margin per unit) − Fixed costs
= (30,000 × $3) − $150,000 = $(60,000) loss

d. Net income at 85,000 caps sold = (Units × Contribution margin per unit) − Fixed costs
= (85,000 × $3) − $150,000 = $105,000 profit

e. Pretax income = $45,000/(1 − 0.25) = $60,000
Income taxes = $60,000 × 25% = $15,000

Units needed for $45,000 income $= \dfrac{\text{Fixed costs} + \text{Target pretax income}}{\text{Contribution margin per cap}}$

$= \dfrac{\$150,000 + \$60,000}{\$3} = 70,000 \text{ caps}$

2. CVP chart.

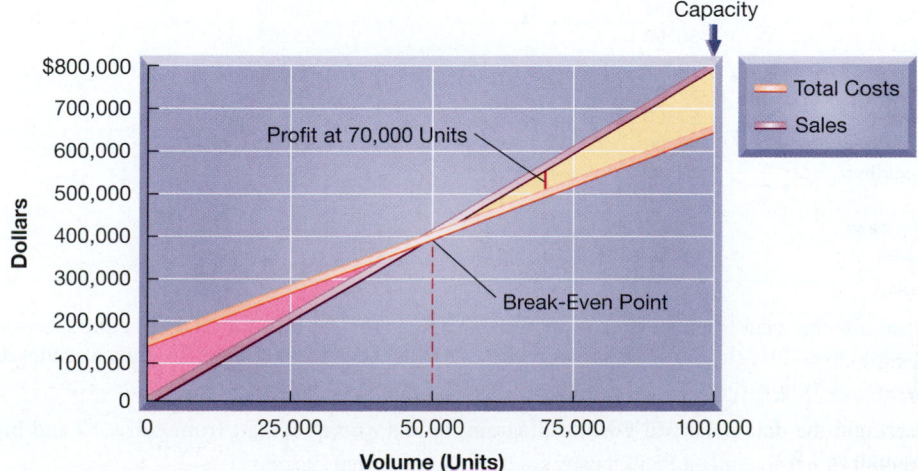

3. a. Contribution margin ratio $= \dfrac{\text{Contribution margin per unit}}{\text{Selling price per unit}} = \dfrac{\$3}{\$8} = 0.375, \text{ or } 37.5\%$

b. Break-even point in dollars $= \dfrac{\text{Fixed costs}}{\text{Contribution margin ratio}} = \dfrac{\$150,000}{37.5\%} = \$400,000$

c. Net income at sales of $250,000 $= (\text{Sales} \times \text{Contribution margin ratio}) - \text{Fixed costs}$
$= (\$250,000 \times 37.5\%) - \$150,000 = \$(56,250) \text{ loss}$

d. Net income at sales of $600,000 $= (\text{Sales} \times \text{Contribution margin ratio}) - \text{Fixed costs}$
$= (\$600,000 \times 37.5\%) - \$150,000 = \$75,000 \text{ income}$

e. Dollars of sales to yield
$45,000 after-tax income $= \dfrac{\text{Fixed costs} + \text{Target pretax income}}{\text{Contribution margin ratio}}$
$= \dfrac{\$150,000 + \$60,000}{37.5\%} = \$560,000$

18A   Using Excel to Estimate Least-Squares Regression

Microsoft Excel® 2007 and other spreadsheet software can be used to perform least-squares regressions to identify cost behavior. In Excel®, the INTERCEPT and SLOPE functions are used. The following screen shot reports the data from Exhibit 18.3 in cells A1 through C13 and shows the cell contents to find the intercept (cell B16) and slope (cell B17). Cell B16 uses Excel® to find the intercept from a least-squares regression of total cost (shown as C2:C13 in cell B16) on units produced (shown as B2:B13 in cell B16). Spreadsheet software is useful in understanding cost behavior when many data points (such as monthly total costs and units produced) are available.

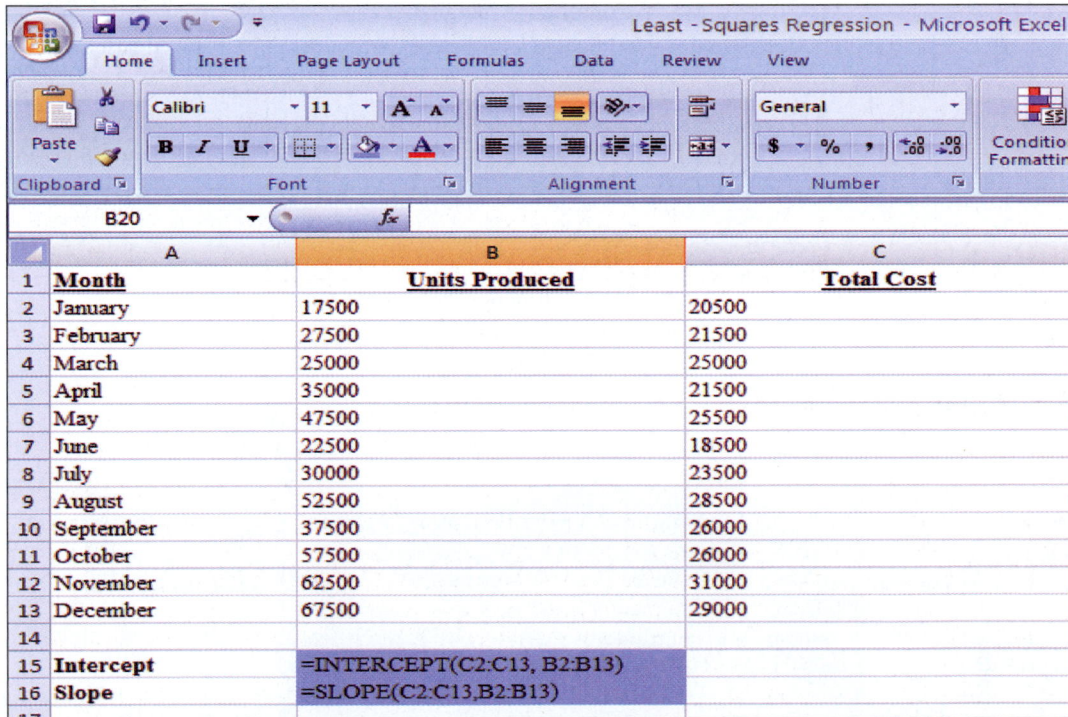

Excel® can also be used to create scatter diagrams such as that in Exhibit 18.4. In contrast to visually drawing a line that "fits" the data, Excel® more precisely fits the regression line. To draw a scatter diagram with a line of fit, follow these steps:

1. Highlight the data cells you wish to diagram; in this example, start from cell C13 and highlight through cell B2.

2. Then select "Insert" and "Scatter" from the drop-down menus. Selecting the chart type in the upper left corner of the choices under Scatter will produce a diagram that looks like that in Exhibit 18.4, without a line of fit.

3. To add a line of fit (also called trend line), select "Layout" and "Trendline" from the drop-down menus. Selecting "Linear Trendline" will produce a diagram that looks like that in Exhibit 18.4, including the line of fit.

Summary

C1 **Describe different types of cost behavior in relation to production and sales volume.** Cost behavior is described in terms of how its amount changes in relation to changes in volume of activity within a relevant range. Fixed costs remain constant to changes in volume. Total variable costs change in direct proportion to volume changes. Mixed costs display the effects of both fixed and variable components. Step-wise costs remain constant over a small volume range, then change by a lump sum and remain constant over another volume range, and so on. Curvilinear costs change in a non-linear relation to volume changes.

C2 **Describe several applications of cost-volume-profit analysis.** Cost-volume-profit analysis can be used to predict what can happen under alternative strategies concerning sales volume, selling prices, variable costs, or fixed costs. Applications include "what-if" analysis, computing sales for a target income, and break-even analysis.

A1 **Compute the contribution margin and describe what it reveals about a company's cost structure.** Contribution margin per unit is a product's sales price less its total variable costs. Contribution margin ratio is a product's contribution margin per unit divided by its sales price. Unit contribution margin is the amount received from each sale that contributes to fixed costs and income. The contribution margin ratio reveals what portion of each sales dollar is available as contribution to fixed costs and income.

A2 **Analyze changes in sales using the degree of operating leverage.** The extent, or relative size, of fixed costs in a company's total cost structure is known as *operating leverage.* One tool useful in assessing the effect of changes in sales on income is the degree of operating leverage, or DOL. DOL is the ratio of the contribution margin divided by pretax income. This ratio can be used to determine the expected percent change in income given a percent change in sales.

P1 **Determine cost estimates using the scatter diagram, high-low, and regression methods of estimating costs.** Three different methods used to estimate costs are the scatter diagram, the high-low method, and least-squares regression. All three methods use past data to estimate costs. Cost estimates from a scatter diagram are based on a visual fit of the cost line. Estimates from the high-low method are based only on costs corresponding to the lowest and highest sales. The least-squares regression method is a statistical technique and uses all data points.

P2 **Compute the break-even point for a single product company.** A company's break-even point for a period is the sales volume at which total revenues equal total costs. To compute a break-even point in terms of sales units, we divide total fixed costs by the contribution margin per unit. To compute a break-even point in terms of sales dollars, divide total fixed costs by the contribution margin ratio.

P3 **Graph costs and sales for a single product company.** The costs and sales for a company can be graphically illustrated using a CVP chart. In this chart, the horizontal axis represents the number of units sold and the vertical axis represents dollars of sales or costs. Straight lines are used to depict both costs and sales on the CVP chart.

P4 **Compute the break-even point for a multiproduct company.** CVP analysis can be applied to a multiproduct company by expressing sales volume in terms of composite units. A composite unit consists of a specific number of units of each product in proportion to their expected sales mix. Multiproduct CVP analysis treats this composite unit as a single product.

Guidance Answers to Decision Maker and Decision Ethics

Sales Manager The contribution margin per unit for the first order is $600 (60% of $1,000); the contribution margin per unit for the second order is $160 (20% of $800). You are likely tempted to accept the first order based on its high contribution margin per unit, but you must compute the total contribution margin based on the number of units sold for each order. Total contribution margin is $60,000 ($600 per unit × 100 units) and $80,000 ($160 per unit × 500 units) for the two orders, respectively. The second order provides the largest return in absolute dollars and is the order you would accept. Another factor to consider in your selection is the potential for a long-term relationship with these customers including repeat sales and growth.

Operations Manager Without the availability of past data, none of the three methods described in the chapter can be used to measure cost behavior. Instead, the manager must investigate whether

data from similar manufacturers can be accessed. This is likely difficult due to the sensitive nature of such data. In the absence of data, the manager should develop a list of the different production inputs and identify input-output relations. This provides guidance to the manager in measuring cost behavior. After several months, actual cost data will be available for analysis.

Supervisor Your dilemma is whether to go along with the suggestions to "manage" the numbers to make the project look like it will achieve sufficient profits. You should not succumb to these suggestions. Many people will likely be affected negatively if you manage the predicted numbers and the project eventually is unprofitable. Moreover, if it does fail, an investigation would likely reveal that data in the proposal were "fixed" to make it look good. Probably the only benefit from managing the numbers is the short-term payoff of pleasing those who proposed the product. One way to deal with this dilemma is to prepare several analyses showing results under different assumptions and then let senior management make the decision.

Entrepreneur   You must first compute the level of sales required to achieve the desired net income. Then you must conduct sensitivity analysis by varying the price, sales mix, and cost estimates. Results from the sensitivity analysis provide information you can use to assess the possibility of reaching the target sales level. For instance, you might have to pursue aggressive marketing strategies to push the high-margin products, or you might have to cut prices to increase sales and profits, or another strategy might emerge.

Guidance Answers to Quick Checks

1. *b*

2. A fixed cost remains unchanged in total amount regardless of output levels. However, fixed *cost per unit* declines with increased output.

3. Such a cost is considered variable because the *total* cost changes in proportion to volume changes.

4. *b*

5. The high-low method ignores all costs and sales (activity base) volume data points except the costs corresponding to the highest and lowest (most extreme) sales (activity base) volume.

6. *c*

7. *a*

8. ($90 − $54)/$90 = 40%

9. $90,000/40% = $225,000

10. Three basic CVP assumptions are that (1) selling price per unit is constant, (2) variable costs per unit are constant, and (3) total fixed costs are constant.

11. *a*; Two steps are required for explanation:
    (1) Pretax income = $120,000/(1 − 0.20) = $150,000
    (2) $\dfrac{\$50,000 + \$150,000}{25\%} = \$800,000$

12. If the contribution margin ratio decreases from 50% to 25%, unit sales would have to double.

13. A company's margin of safety is the excess of the predicted sales level over its break-even sales level.

14. *c*; Selling price of a composite unit:

2 units of X @ $5 per unit	$10
1 unit of Y @ $4 per unit	4
Selling price of a composite unit	$14

Variable costs of a composite unit:

2 units of X @ $2 per unit	$4
1 unit of Y @ $2 per unit	2
Variable costs of a composite unit	$6

Therefore, the contribution margin per composite unit is $8.

15. It must be assumed that the sales mix remains unchanged at all sales levels in the relevant range.

Key Terms   mhhe.com/wildFINMAN4e

Absorption costing (p. 773)
Break-even point (p. 773)
Composite unit (p. 780)
Contribution margin per unit (p. 772)
Contribution margin ratio (p. 772)
Cost-volume-profit (CVP) analysis (p. 766)
Cost-volume-profit (CVP) chart (p. 774)
Curvilinear cost (p. 768)

Degree of operating leverage (DOL) (p. 782)
Estimated line of cost behavior (p. 770)
High-low method (p. 770)
Least-squares regression (p. 771)
Margin of safety (p. 778)
Mixed cost (p. 767)
Operating leverage (p. 782)

Relevant range of operations (p. 775)
Sales mix (p. 779)
Scatter diagram (p. 769)
Step-wise cost (p. 768)
Variable costing income statement (p. 773)
Weighted-average contribution margin (p. 780)

Multiple Choice Quiz   Answers on p. 801   mhhe.com/wildFINMAN4e

Additional Quiz Questions are available at the book's Website.

1. A company's only product sells for $150 per unit. Its variable costs per unit are $100, and its fixed costs total $75,000. What is its contribution margin per unit?
    a. $50
    b. $250
    c. $100
    d. $150
    e. $25

2. Using information from question 1, what is the company's contribution margin ratio?
    a. 66⅔%
    b. 100%
    c. 50%
    d. 0%
    e. 33⅓%

3. Using information from question 1, what is the company's break-even point in units?
  a. 500 units
  b. 750 units
  c. 1,500 units
  d. 3,000 units
  e. 1,000 units

4. A company's forecasted sales are $300,000 and its sales at break-even are $180,000. Its margin of safety in dollars is
  a. $180,000.
  b. $120,000.
  c. $480,000.
  d. $60,000.
  e. $300,000.

5. A product sells for $400 per unit and its variable costs per unit are $260. The company's fixed costs are $840,000. If the company desires $70,000 pretax income, what is the required dollar sales?
  a. $2,400,000
  b. $200,000
  c. $2,600,000
  d. $2,275,000
  e. $1,400,000

---

^{A} *Superscript letter A denotes assignments based on Appendix 18A*

🔲 Icon denotes assignments that involve decision making.

Discussion Questions

1. 🔲 How is cost-volume-profit analysis useful?

2. What is a variable cost? Identify two variable costs.

3. 🔲 When output volume increases, do variable costs per unit increase, decrease, or stay the same within the relevant range of activity? Explain.

4. 🔲 When output volume increases, do fixed costs per unit increase, decrease, or stay the same within the relevant range of activity? Explain.

5. How do step-wise costs and curvilinear costs differ?

6. Define and describe *contribution margin* per unit.

7. Define and explain the *contribution margin ratio*.

8. Describe the contribution margin ratio in layperson's terms.

9. In performing CVP analysis for a manufacturing company, what simplifying assumption is usually made about the volume of production and the volume of sales?

10. What two arguments tend to justify classifying all costs as either fixed or variable even though individual costs might not behave exactly as classified?

11. 🔲 How does assuming that operating activity occurs within a relevant range affect cost-volume-profit analysis?

12. List three methods to measure cost behavior.

13. How is a scatter diagram used to identify and measure the behavior of a company's costs?

14. In cost-volume-profit analysis, what is the estimated profit at the break-even point?

15. 🔲 Assume that a straight line on a CVP chart intersects the vertical axis at the level of fixed costs and has a positive slope that rises with each additional unit of volume by the amount of the variable costs per unit. What does this line represent?

16. **Palm** has both fixed and variable costs. Why are fixed costs depicted as a horizontal line on a CVP chart? **Palm**

17. 🔲 Each of two similar companies has sales of $20,000 and total costs of $15,000 for a month. Company A's total costs include $10,000 of variable costs and $5,000 of fixed costs. If Company B's total costs include $4,000 of variable costs and $11,000 of fixed costs, which company will enjoy more profit if sales double?

18. _____ of _____ reflects expected sales in excess of the level of break-even sales.

19. 🔲 **Apple** produces iPods for sale. Identify some of the variable and fixed product costs associated with that production. [*Hint:* Limit costs to product costs.] **Apple**

20. 🔲 Should **Research In Motion** use single product or multiproduct break-even analysis? Explain. **RIM**

21. 🔲 **Nokia** is thinking of expanding sales of its most popular cell-phone model by 65%. Do you expect its variable and fixed costs for this model to stay within the relevant range? Explain. **NOKIA**

Connect

Determine whether each of the following is best described as a fixed, variable, or mixed cost with respect to product units.

1. Maintenance of factory machinery.
2. Depreciation expense of warehouse.
3. Taxes on factory building.
4. Factory supervisor's salary.
5. Wages of an assembly-line worker paid on the basis of acceptable units produced.
6. Packaging expense.
7. Rubber used to manufacture athletic shoes.

QUICK STUDY

QS 18-1
Cost behavior identification

C1

QS 18-2
Cost behavior identification
C1

Listed here are four series of separate costs measured at various volume levels. Examine each series and identify whether it is best described as a fixed, variable, step-wise, or curvilinear cost. (It can help to graph the cost series.)

Volume (Units)	Series 1	Series 2	Series 3	Series 4
0	$ 0	$900	$ 400	$200
100	400	900	400	210
200	800	900	400	240
300	1,200	900	800	290
400	1,600	900	800	380
500	2,000	900	1,200	500
600	2,400	900	1,200	640

QS 18-3
Cost behavior estimation—
scatter diagram
P1

This scatter diagram reflects past maintenance hours and their corresponding maintenance costs.

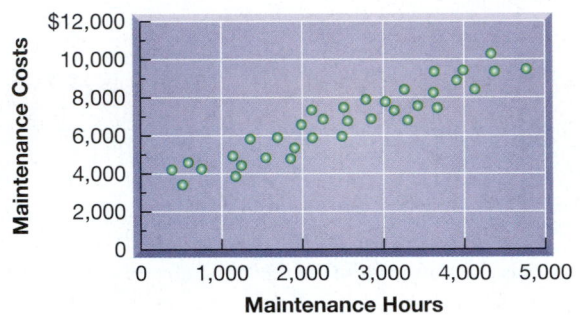

1. Draw an estimated line of cost behavior.
2. Estimate the fixed and variable components of maintenance costs.

QS 18-4
Cost behavior estimation—
high-low method
P1

The following information is available for a company's maintenance cost over the last seven months. Using the high-low method, estimate both the fixed and variable components of its maintenance cost.

Month	Maintenance Hours	Maintenance Cost
June..............	20	$6,020
July	48	8,100
August	24	5,100
September	38	7,000
October..........	42	6,900
November	36	6,900
December	12	3,600

QS 18-5
Contribution margin ratio
A1

Compute and interpret the contribution margin ratio using the following data: sales, $150,000; total variable cost, $90,000.

QS 18-6
Contribution margin per unit
and break-even units
P2

MCU Phone Company sells its cordless phone for $300 per unit. Fixed costs total $540,000, and variable costs are $120 per unit. Determine the (1) contribution margin per unit and (2) break-even point in units.

QS 18-7
Assumptions in CVP analysis
C2

Refer to the information from QS 18-6. How will the break-even point in units change in response to each of the following independent changes in selling price per unit, variable cost per unit, or total fixed costs? Use I for increase and D for decrease. (It is not necessary to compute new break-even points.)

Change	Break-even in Units Will
1. Total fixed cost to $520,000	_____
2. Variable cost to $134 per unit	_____
3. Selling price per unit to $290	_____
4. Variable cost to $100 per unit	_____
5. Total fixed cost to $544,000	_____
6. Selling price per unit to $320	_____

Refer to QS 18-6. Determine the (1) contribution margin ratio and (2) break-even point in dollars.

QS 18-8
Contribution margin ratio
and break-even dollars   **P2**

Refer to QS 18-6. Assume that MCU Phone Co. is subject to a 30% income tax rate. Compute the units of product that must be sold to earn after-tax income of $504,000.

QS 18-9
CVP analysis and target income

P2

Which one of the following is an assumption that underlies cost-volume-profit analysis?

1. All costs have approximately the same relevant range.

2. The selling price per unit must change in proportion to the number of units sold.

3. For costs classified as variable, the costs per unit of output must change constantly.

4. For costs classified as fixed, the costs per unit of output must remain constant.

QS 18-10
CVP assumptions

C2

A high proportion of Company X's total costs are variable with respect to units sold; a high proportion of Company Y's total costs are fixed with respect to units sold. Which company is likely to have a higher degree of operating leverage (DOL)? Explain.

QS 18-11
Operating leverage analysis   **A2**

M-Mobile Company manufactures and sells two products, black phones and white phones, in the ratio of 5:3. Fixed costs are $85,000, and the contribution margin per composite unit is $170. What number of both black and white phones is sold at the break-even point?

QS 18-12
Multiproduct break-even   **P4**

Corme Company expects sales of $34 million (400,000 units). The company's total fixed costs are $17.5 million and its variable costs are $35 per unit. Prepare a CVP chart from this information.

QS 18-13
CVP graph   **P3**

A recent income statement for **Volkswagen** reports the following (in € millions). Assume 70 percent of the cost of sales and 70 percent of the selling and administrative costs are variable costs, and the remaining 30 percent of each is fixed. Compute the contribution margin (in € millions). (Round computations using percentages to the nearest whole euro.)

QS 18-14
Contribution margin   **A1**

Sales	€105,187
Cost of sales	91,608
Selling and administrative expenses	13,276

---

connect

A company reports the following information about its sales and its cost of sales. Each unit of its product sells for $500. Use these data to prepare a scatter diagram. Draw an estimated line of cost behavior and determine whether the cost appears to be variable, fixed, or mixed.

EXERCISES

Exercise 18-1
Measurement of cost behavior using a scatter diagram

P1

Period	Sales	Cost of Sales	Period	Sales	Cost of Sales
1	$15,000	$10,100	4	7,500	5,500
2	11,500	7,500	5	9,000	6,000
3	10,500	7,000	6	12,500	9,500

Exercise 18-2

Cost behavior in graphs

C1

Following are five graphs representing various cost behaviors. (1) Identify whether the cost behavior in each graph is mixed, step-wise, fixed, variable, or curvilinear. (2) Identify the graph (by number) that best illustrates each cost behavior: (a) Factory policy requires one supervisor for every 30 factory workers; (b) real estate taxes on factory; (c) electricity charge that includes the standard monthly charge plus a charge for each kilowatt hour; (d) commissions to salespersons; and (e) costs of hourly paid workers that provide substantial gains in efficiency when a few workers are added but gradually smaller gains in efficiency when more workers are added.

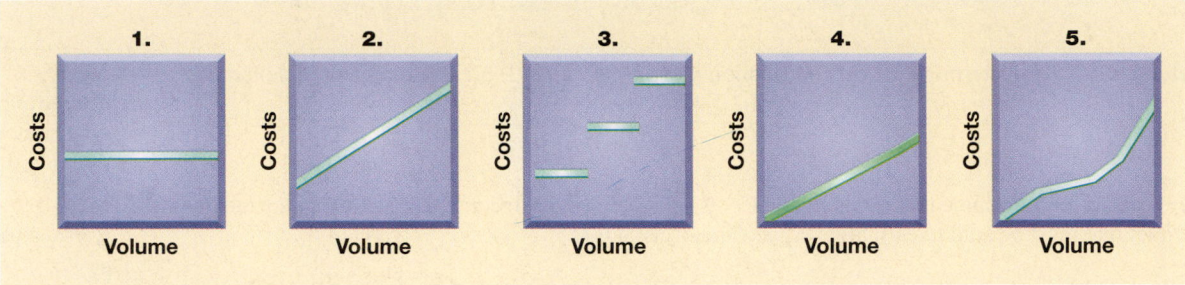

Exercise 18-3

Cost behavior defined

C1

The left column lists several cost classifications. The right column presents short definitions of those costs. In the blank space beside each of the numbers in the right column, write the letter of the cost best described by the definition.

A. Curvilinear cost

B. Step-wise cost

C. Fixed cost

D. Mixed cost

E. Variable cost

F. Total cost

_____ **1.** This cost increases in direct proportion to increases in volume; its amount is constant for each unit produced.

_____ **2.** This cost remains constant over a limited range of volume; when it reaches the end of its limited range, it changes by a lump sum and remains at that level until it exceeds another limited range.

_____ **3.** This cost has a component that remains the same over all volume levels and another component that increases in direct proportion to increases in volume.

_____ **4.** This cost increases when volume increases, but the increase is not constant for each unit produced.

_____ **5.** This cost remains constant over all volume levels within the productive capacity for the planning period.

_____ **6.** This cost is the combined amount of all the other costs.

Exercise 18-4

Cost behavior identification

C1

Following are five series of costs *A* through *E* measured at various volume levels. Examine each series and identify which is fixed, variable, mixed, step-wise, or curvilinear.

	Volume (Units)	Series A	Series B	Series C	Series D	Series E
1	0	$ 0	$2,500	$ 0	$2,000	$4,000
2	200	3,600	3,100	6,000	2,000	4,000
3	400	7,200	3,700	6,600	4,000	4,000
4	600	10,800	4,300	7,200	4,000	4,000
5	800	14,400	4,900	8,200	6,000	4,000
6	1,000	18,000	5,500	9,600	6,000	4,000
7	1,200	21,600	6,100	13,500	8,000	4,000

Exercise 18-5

Predicting sales and variable costs using contribution margin

C2

Orlando Company management predicts that it will incur fixed costs of $250,000 and earn pretax income of $350,000 in the next period. Its expected contribution margin ratio is 60%. Use this information to compute the amounts of (1) total dollar sales and (2) total variable costs.

Use the following information about sales and costs to prepare a scatter diagram. Draw a cost line that reflects the behavior displayed by this cost. Determine whether the cost is variable, step-wise, fixed, mixed, or curvilinear.

Period	Sales	Costs	Period	Sales	Costs
1	$760	$590	9	$580	$390
2	800	560	10	320	240
3	200	230	11	240	230
4	400	400	12	720	550
5	480	390	13	280	260
6	620	550	14	440	410
7	680	590	15	380	260
8	540	430			

Exercise 18-6
Scatter diagram and measurement of cost behavior
P1

Felix & Co. reports the following information about its sales and cost of sales. Draw an estimated line of cost behavior using a scatter diagram, and compute fixed costs and variable costs per unit sold. Then use the high-low method to estimate the fixed and variable components of the cost of sales.

Period	Units Sold	Cost of Sales	Period	Units Sold	Cost of Sales
1	0	$2,500	6	2,000	5,500
2	400	3,100	7	2,400	6,100
3	800	3,700	8	2,800	6,700
4	1,200	4,300	9	3,200	7,300
5	1,600	4,900	10	3,600	7,900

Exercise 18-7
Cost behavior estimation—scatter diagram and high-low
P1

Refer to the information from Exercise 18-7. Use spreadsheet software to use ordinary least-squares regression to estimate the cost equation, including fixed and variable cost amounts.

Exercise 18-8[A]
Measurement of cost behavior using regression   P1

A pants maker is designing a new line of pants called the Redbird. The pants will sell for $325 per pair and cost $260 per pair in variable costs to make. (1) Compute the contribution margin per pair. (2) Compute the contribution margin ratio. (3) Describe what the contribution margin ratio reveals about this new pants line.

Exercise 18-9
Contribution margin
A2

Apollo Company manufactures a single product that sells for $168 per unit and whose total variable costs are $126 per unit. The company's annual fixed costs are $630,000. (1) Use this information to compute the company's (a) contribution margin, (b) contribution margin ratio, (c) break-even point in units, and (d) break-even point in dollars of sales.

Exercise 18-10
Contribution margin, break-even, and CVP chart   P2

Refer to the information in Exercise 18-10. Prepare a CVP chart for the company.

Exercise 18-11
CVP chart   P3

Refer to Exercise 18-10. (1) Prepare a contribution margin income statement for Apollo Company showing sales, variable costs, and fixed costs at the break-even point. (2) If the company's fixed costs increase by $135,000, what amount of sales (in dollars) is needed to break even? Explain.

Exercise 18-12
Income reporting and break-even analysis   C2

Apollo Company management (in Exercise 18-10) targets an annual after-tax income of $840,000. The company is subject to a 20% income tax rate. Assume that fixed costs remain at $630,000. Compute the (1) unit sales to earn the target after-tax net income and (2) dollar sales to earn the target after-tax net income.

Exercise 18-13
Computing sales to achieve target income   C2

Exercise 18-14
Forecasted income statement
C2

Check   Forecasted income,
$1,416,000

Apollo Company's sales manager (in Exercise 18-10) predicts that annual sales of the company's product will soon reach 40,000 units and its price will increase to $200 per unit. According to the production manager, the variable costs are expected to increase to $140 per unit but fixed costs will remain at $630,000. The income tax rate is 20%. What amounts of pretax and after-tax income can the company expect to earn from these predicted changes? (*Hint:* Prepare a forecasted contribution margin income statement as in Exhibit 18.20.)

Exercise 18-15
Predicting unit and dollar sales
C2

Greenspan Company management predicts $500,000 of variable costs, $800,000 of fixed costs, and a pretax income of $100,000 in the next period. Management also predicts that the contribution margin per unit will be $60. Use this information to compute the (1) total expected dollar sales for next period and (2) number of units expected to be sold next period.

Exercise 18-16
Computation of variable and fixed costs
C2

Cinquante Company expects to sell 100,000 units of its product next year, which would generate total sales of $12 million. Management predicts that pretax net income for next year will be $3,000,000 and that the contribution margin per unit will be $40. Use this information to compute next year's total expected (a) variable costs and (b) fixed costs.

Exercise 18-17
CVP analysis using composite units   P4

Check   (3) 1,000 composite units

Home Builders sells windows and doors in the ratio of 8:2 (windows:doors). The selling price of each window is $100 and of each door is $250. The variable cost of a window is $62.50 and of a door is $175. Fixed costs are $450,000. Use this information to determine the (1) selling price per composite unit, (2) variable costs per composite unit, (3) break-even point in composite units, and (4) number of units of each product that will be sold at the break-even point.

Exercise 18-18
CVP analysis using weighted-average contribution margin
P4

Refer to the information from Exercise 18-17. Use the information to determine the (1) weighted-average contribution margin, (2) break-even point in units, and (3) number of units of each product that will be sold at the break-even point.

Exercise 18-19
CVP analysis using composite units
P4

Hubert Tax Service offers tax and consulting services to individuals and small businesses. Data for fees and costs of three types of tax returns follow. Hubert provides services in the ratio of 4:4:2 (easy, moderate, business). Fixed costs total $20,000 for the tax season. Use this information to determine the (1) selling price per composite unit, (2) variable costs per composite unit, (3) break-even point in composite units, and (4) number of units of each product that will be sold at the break-even point. Round answer for part (3) to two decimals.

Type of Return	Fee Charged	Variable Cost per Return
Easy (form 1040EZ)	$ 50	$ 30
Moderate (form 1040)	125	75
Business	275	100

Exercise 18-20
CVP analysis using weighted-average contribution margin
P4

Refer to the information from Exercise 18-19. Use the information to determine the (1) weighted-average contribution margin, (2) break-even point in units, and (3) number of units of each product that will be sold at the break-even point. Round answer for part (2) to one decimal.

Exercise 18-21
Operating leverage computed and applied
A2

Company A is a manufacturer with current sales of $3,000,000 and a 60% contribution margin. Its fixed costs equal $1,300,000. Company B is a consulting firm with current service revenues of $3,000,000 and a 25% contribution margin. Its fixed costs equal $250,000. Compute the degree of operating leverage (DOL) for each company. Identify which company benefits more from a 20% increase in sales and explain why.

The following costs result from the production and sale of 4,000 drum sets manufactured by Vince Drum Company for the year ended December 31, 2011. The drum sets sell for $250 each. The company has a 25% income tax rate.

Variable production costs	
Plastic for casing	$ 68,000
Wages of assembly workers	328,000
Drum stands	104,000
Variable selling costs	
Sales commissions	60,000
Fixed manufacturing costs	
Taxes on factory	10,000
Factory maintenance	20,000
Factory machinery depreciation	80,000
Fixed selling and administrative costs	
Lease of equipment for sales staff	20,000
Accounting staff salaries	70,000
Administrative management salaries	150,000

PROBLEM SET A

Problem 18-1A
Contribution margin income statement and contribution margin ratio

A1

Check (1) Net income, $67,500

Required

1. Prepare a contribution margin income statement for the company.

2. Compute its contribution margin per unit and its contribution margin ratio.

Analysis Component

3. Interpret the contribution margin and contribution margin ratio from part 2.

Edge Equipment Co. manufactures and markets a number of rope products. Management is considering the future of Product XT, a special rope for hang gliding, that has not been as profitable as planned. Since Product XT is manufactured and marketed independently of the other products, its total costs can be precisely measured. Next year's plans call for a $150 selling price per 100 yards of XT rope. Its fixed costs for the year are expected to be $200,000, up to a maximum capacity of 550,000 yards of rope. Forecasted variable costs are $100 per 100 yards of XT rope.

Problem 18-2A
CVP analysis and charting

P2 P3

mhhe.com/wildFINMAN4e

Required

1. Estimate Product XT's break-even point in terms of (a) sales units and (b) sales dollars.

2. Prepare a CVP chart for Product XT like that in Exhibit 18.14. Use 5,500 units (550,000 yards/100 yards) as the maximum number of sales units on the horizontal axis of the graph, and $900,000 as the maximum dollar amount on the vertical axis.

3. Prepare a contribution margin income statement showing sales, variable costs, and fixed costs for Product XT at the break-even point.

Check (1) Break-even sales, 4,000 units

Alden Co.'s monthly sales and cost data for its operating activities of the past year follow. Management wants to use these data to predict future fixed and variable costs.

Problem 18-3A
Scatter diagram and cost behavior estimation

P1

Month	Sales	Total Cost	Month	Sales	Total Cost
1	$325,000	$162,500	7	$355,000	$242,000
2	170,000	106,250	8	275,000	156,750
3	270,000	210,600	9	75,000	60,000
4	210,000	105,000	10	155,000	135,625
5	295,000	206,500	11	99,000	99,000
6	195,000	117,000	12	105,000	76,650

Required

1. Prepare a scatter diagram for these data with sales volume (in $) plotted on the horizontal axis and total cost plotted on the vertical axis.

2. Estimate both the variable costs per sales dollar and the total monthly fixed costs using the high-low method. Draw the total costs line on the scatter diagram in part 1.

3. Use the estimated line of cost behavior and results from part 2 to predict future total costs when sales volume is (a) $380,000 and (b) $420,000.

Problem 18-4A

Break-even analysis; income targeting and forecasting

C2 P2 A1

Jetson Co. sold 20,000 units of its only product and incurred a $50,000 loss (ignoring taxes) for the current year as shown here. During a planning session for year 2012's activities, the production manager notes that variable costs can be reduced 50% by installing a machine that automates several operations. To obtain these savings, the company must increase its annual fixed costs by $150,000. The maximum output capacity of the company is 40,000 units per year.

JETSON COMPANY	
Contribution Margin Income Statement	
For Year Ended December 31, 2011	
Sales	$750,000
Variable costs	600,000
Contribution margin	150,000
Fixed costs	200,000
Net loss	$ (50,000)

Required

1. Compute the break-even point in dollar sales for year 2011.

2. Compute the predicted break-even point in dollar sales for year 2012 assuming the machine is installed and there is no change in the unit sales price.

3. Prepare a forecasted contribution margin income statement for 2012 that shows the expected results with the machine installed. Assume that the unit sales price and the number of units sold will not change, and no income taxes will be due.

4. Compute the sales level required in both dollars and units to earn $140,000 of after-tax income in 2012 with the machine installed and no change in the unit sales price. Assume that the income tax rate is 30%. (*Hint:* Use the procedures in Exhibits 18.21 and 18.23.)

5. Prepare a forecasted contribution margin income statement that shows the results at the sales level computed in part 4. Assume an income tax rate of 30%.

Problem 18-5A

Break-even analysis, different cost structures, and income calculations

C2 A1 P4

Letter Co. produces and sells two products, T and O. It manufactures these products in separate factories and markets them through different channels. They have no shared costs. This year, the company sold 50,000 units of each product. Sales and costs for each product follow.

	Product T	Product O
Sales	$800,000	$800,000
Variable costs..................	560,000	100,000
Contribution margin	240,000	700,000
Fixed costs	100,000	560,000
Income before taxes	140,000	140,000
Income taxes (32% rate)	44,800	44,800
Net income	$ 95,200	$ 95,200

Required

1. Compute the break-even point in dollar sales for each product.

2. Assume that the company expects sales of each product to decline to 33,000 units next year with no change in unit sales price. Prepare forecasted financial results for next year following the format of the contribution margin income statement as just shown with columns for each of the two products (assume a 32% tax rate). Also, assume that any loss before taxes yields a 32% tax savings.

3. Assume that the company expects sales of each product to increase to 64,000 units next year with no change in unit sales price. Prepare forecasted financial results for next year following the format of the contribution margin income statement shown with columns for each of the two products (assume a 32% tax rate).

Analysis Component

4. If sales greatly decrease, which product would experience a greater loss? Explain.

5. Describe some factors that might have created the different cost structures for these two products.

Check (2) After-tax income:
T, $39,712; O, $(66,640)

(3) After-tax income:
T, $140,896; O, $228,480

This year Cairo Company sold 35,000 units of its only product for $16 per unit. Manufacturing and selling the product required $120,000 of fixed manufacturing costs and $180,000 of fixed selling and administrative costs. Its per unit variable costs follow.

Material	$4.00
Direct labor (paid on the basis of completed units)..........	3.00
Variable overhead costs	0.40
Variable selling and administrative costs	0.20

Problem 18-6A

Analysis of price, cost, and volume changes for contribution margin and net income

P2 A1

eXcel

mhhe.com/wildFINMAN4e

Next year the company will use new material, which will reduce material costs by 60% and direct labor costs by 40% and will not affect product quality or marketability. Management is considering an increase in the unit sales price to reduce the number of units sold because the factory's output is nearing its annual output capacity of 40,000 units. Two plans are being considered. Under plan 1, the company will keep the price at the current level and sell the same volume as last year. This plan will increase income because of the reduced costs from using the new material. Under plan 2, the company will increase price by 25%. This plan will decrease unit sales volume by 10%. Under both plans 1 and 2, the total fixed costs and the variable costs per unit for overhead and for selling and administrative costs will remain the same.

Required

1. Compute the break-even point in dollar sales for both (a) plan 1 and (b) plan 2.

2. Prepare a forecasted contribution margin income statement with two columns showing the expected results of plan 1 and plan 2. The statements should report sales, total variable costs, contribution margin, total fixed costs, income before taxes, income taxes (30% rate), and net income.

Check (1) Break-even: Plan 1,
$400,000; Plan 2, $375,000

(2) Net income: Plan 1,
$84,000; Plan 2, $142,800

National Co. manufactures and sells three products: red, white, and blue. Their unit sales prices are red, $55; white, $85; and blue, $110. The per unit variable costs to manufacture and sell these products are red, $40; white, $60; and blue, $80. Their sales mix is reflected in a ratio of 5:4:2 (red:white:blue). Annual fixed costs shared by all three products are $150,000. One type of raw material has been used to manufacture all three products. The company has developed a new material of equal quality for less cost. The new material would reduce variable costs per unit as follows: red, by $10; white, by $20; and blue, by $10. However, the new material requires new equipment, which will increase annual fixed costs by $20,000. (Round answers to whole composite units.)

Problem 18-7A

Break-even analysis with composite units

P4

Required

1. If the company continues to use the old material, determine its break-even point in both sales units and sales dollars of each individual product.

2. If the company uses the new material, determine its new break-even point in both sales units and sales dollars of each individual product.

Check (1) Old plan break-even,
639 composite units (rounded)

(2) New plan break-even,
442 composite units (rounded)

Analysis Component

3. What insight does this analysis offer management for long-term planning?

PROBLEM SET B

Problem 18-1B
Contribution margin income statement and contribution margin ratio

A1

The following costs result from the production and sale of 480,000 CD sets manufactured by Trace Company for the year ended December 31, 2011. The CD sets sell for $4.50 each. The company has a 25% income tax rate.

Variable manufacturing costs	
Plastic for CD sets	$ 43,200
Wages of assembly workers	600,000
Labeling	86,400
Variable selling costs	
Sales commissions	48,000
Fixed manufacturing costs	
Rent on factory	100,000
Factory cleaning service	75,000
Factory machinery depreciation	125,000
Fixed selling and administrative costs	
Lease of office equipment	120,000
Systems staff salaries	600,000
Administrative management salaries	300,000

Required

Check (1) Net income, $46,800

1. Prepare a contribution margin income statement for the company.
2. Compute its contribution margin per unit and its contribution margin ratio.

Analysis Component

3. Interpret the contribution margin and contribution margin ratio from part 2.

Problem 18-2B
CVP analysis and charting

P2 P3

Jammin Co. manufactures and markets several products. Management is considering the future of one product, electronic keyboards, that has not been as profitable as planned. Since this product is manufactured and marketed independently of the other products, its total costs can be precisely measured. Next year's plans call for a $225 selling price per unit. The fixed costs for the year are expected to be $30,000, up to a maximum capacity of 700 units. Forecasted variable costs are $150 per unit.

Required

Check (1) Break-even sales, 400 units

1. Estimate the keyboards' break-even point in terms of (a) sales units and (b) sales dollars.
2. Prepare a CVP chart for keyboards like that in Exhibit 18.14. Use 700 keyboards as the maximum number of sales units on the horizontal axis of the graph, and $180,000 as the maximum dollar amount on the vertical axis.
3. Prepare a contribution margin income statement showing sales, variable costs, and fixed costs for keyboards at the break-even point.

Problem 18-3B
Scatter diagram and cost behavior estimation

P1

Koto Co.'s monthly sales and costs data for its operating activities of the past year follow. Management wants to use these data to predict future fixed and variable costs.

Month	Sales	Total Cost	Month	Sales	Total Cost
1	$390	$194	7	$290	$186
2	250	174	8	370	210
3	210	146	9	270	170
4	310	178	10	170	116
5	190	162	11	350	190
6	430	220	12	230	158

Required

1. Prepare a scatter diagram for these data with sales volume (in $) plotted on the horizontal axis and total costs plotted on the vertical axis.

2. Estimate both the variable costs per sales dollar and the total monthly fixed costs using the high-low method. Draw the total costs line on the scatter diagram in part 1.

3. Use the estimated line of cost behavior and results from part 2 to predict future total costs when sales volume is (a) $150 and (b) $250.

Check   (2) Variable costs, $0.40 per sales dollar; fixed costs, $48

Caruso Co. sold 40,000 units of its only product and incurred a $100,000 loss (ignoring taxes) for the current year as shown here. During a planning session for year 2012's activities, the production manager notes that variable costs can be reduced 50% by installing a machine that automates several operations. To obtain these savings, the company must increase its annual fixed costs by $300,000. The maximum output capacity of the company is 80,000 units per year.

Problem 18-4B
Break-even analysis; income targeting and forecasting

C2   P2   A1

CARUSO COMPANY	
Contribution Margin Income Statement	
For Year Ended December 31, 2011	
Sales	$1,500,000
Variable costs..............	1,200,000
Contribution margin	300,000
Fixed costs................	400,000
Net loss	$ (100,000)

Required

1. Compute the break-even point in dollar sales for year 2011.

2. Compute the predicted break-even point in dollar sales for year 2012 assuming the machine is installed and no change occurs in the unit sales price. (Round the change in variable costs to a whole number.)

3. Prepare a forecasted contribution margin income statement for 2012 that shows the expected results with the machine installed. Assume that the unit sales price and the number of units sold will not change, and no income taxes will be due.

4. Compute the sales level required in both dollars and units to earn $280,000 of after-tax income in 2012 with the machine installed and no change in the unit sales price. Assume that the income tax rate is 30%. (*Hint:* Use the procedures in Exhibits 18.21 and 18.23.)

5. Prepare a forecasted contribution margin income statement that shows the results at the sales level computed in part 4. Assume an income tax rate of 30%.

Check   (3) Net income, $200,000

(4) Required sales, $1,833,333 or 48,889 units

Dominico Co. produces and sells two products, BB and TT. It manufactures these products in separate factories and markets them through different channels. They have no shared costs. This year, the company sold 120,000 units of each product. Sales and costs for each product follow.

Problem 18-5B
Break-even analysis, different cost structures, and income calculations

C2   P4   A1

	Product BB	Product TT
Sales	$3,000,000	$3,000,000
Variable costs.................	1,800,000	600,000
Contribution margin	1,200,000	2,400,000
Fixed costs...................	600,000	1,800,000
Income before taxes	600,000	600,000
Income taxes (35% rate)	210,000	210,000
Net income	$ 390,000	$ 390,000

Required

1. Compute the break-even point in dollar sales for each product.

2. Assume that the company expects sales of each product to decline to 104,000 units next year with no change in the unit sales price. Prepare forecasted financial results for next year following the format of the contribution margin income statement as shown here with columns for each of the two products (assume a 35% tax rate, and that any loss before taxes yields a 35% tax savings).

3. Assume that the company expects sales of each product to increase to 190,000 units next year with no change in the unit sales prices. Prepare forecasted financial results for next year following the format of the contribution margin income statement as shown here with columns for each of the two products (assume a 35% tax rate).

Check   (2) After-tax income: BB, $286,000; TT, $182,000

(3) After-tax income: BB, $845,000; TT, $1,300,000

Analysis Component

4. If sales greatly increase, which product would experience a greater increase in profit? Explain.

5. Describe some factors that might have created the different cost structures for these two products.

Problem 18-6B
Analysis of price, cost, and volume changes for contribution margin and net income

A1   P2

This year Jostens Company earned a disappointing 4.2% after-tax return on sales (Net income/Sales) from marketing 100,000 units of its only product. The company buys its product in bulk and repackages it for resale at the price of $25 per unit. Jostens incurred the following costs this year.

Total variable unit costs.............	$1,000,000
Total variable packaging costs.........	$ 100,000
Fixed costs.......................	$1,250,000
Income tax rate...................	30%

The marketing manager claims that next year's results will be the same as this year's unless some changes are made. The manager predicts the company can increase the number of units sold by 80% if it reduces the selling price by 20% and upgrades the packaging. This change would increase variable packaging costs by 25%. Increased sales would allow the company to take advantage of a 20% quantity purchase discount on the cost of the bulk product. Neither the packaging change nor the volume discount would affect fixed costs, which provide an annual output capacity of 200,000 units.

Required

Check (1) Break-even sales for new strategy, $2,325,581

(2) Net income: Existing strategy, $105,000; new strategy, $479,500

1. Compute the break-even point in dollar sales under the (a) existing business strategy and (b) new strategy that alters both unit sales price and variable costs.

2. Prepare a forecasted contribution margin income statement with two columns showing the expected results of (a) the existing strategy and (b) changing to the new strategy. The statements should report sales, total variable costs (unit and packaging), contribution margin, fixed costs, income before taxes, income taxes, and net income. Also determine the after-tax return on sales for these two strategies.

Problem 18-7B
Break-even analysis with composite units

P4

Texon Co. manufactures and sells three products: product 1, product 2, and product 3. Their unit sales prices are product 1, $40; product 2, $30; and product 3, $14. The per unit variable costs to manufacture and sell these products are product 1, $30; product 2, $20; and product 3, $8. Their sales mix is reflected in a ratio of 6:3:5. Annual fixed costs shared by all three products are $200,000. One type of raw material has been used to manufacture products 1 and 2. The company has developed a new material of equal quality for less cost. The new material would reduce variable costs per unit as follows: product 1 by $10, and product 2, by $5. However, the new material requires new equipment, which will increase annual fixed costs by $50,000.

Required

Check (1) Old plan break-even, 1,667 composite units (rounded)

(2) New plan break-even, 1,282 composite units (rounded)

1. If the company continues to use the old material, determine its break-even point in both sales units and sales dollars of each individual product.

2. If the company uses the new material, determine its new break-even point in both sales units and sales dollars of each individual product.

Analysis Component

3. What insight does this analysis offer management for long-term planning?

SERIAL PROBLEM
Business Solutions

P4

(This serial problem began in Chapter 1 and continues through most of the book. If previous chapter segments were not completed, the serial problem can begin at this point. It is helpful, but not necessary, to use the working papers that accompany the book.)

SP 18 Business Solutions sells upscale modular desk units and office chairs in the ratio of 3:2 (desk unit:chair). The selling prices are $1,250 per desk unit and $500 per chair. The variable costs are $750 per desk unit and $250 per chair. Fixed costs are $120,000.

Required

1. Compute the selling price per composite unit.

2. Compute the variable costs per composite unit.

3. Compute the break-even point in composite units.

Check   (3) 60 composite units

4. Compute the number of units of each product that would be sold at the break-even point.

Beyond the Numbers

BTN 18-1   **Research In Motion** offers services to Blackberry customers that allows them subscription access for wireless connectivity via a mobile carrier. As you complete the following requirements, assume that the Blackberry services department uses many of Research In Motion's existing resources such as its software, phone systems, account databases and buildings.

REPORTING IN ACTION

C1

RIM

Required

1. Identify several of the variable, mixed, and fixed costs that the Blackberry services department is likely to incur in carrying out its services.

2. Assume that Blackberry services revenues are expected to grow by 25% in the next year. How do you expect the costs identified in part 1 to change, if at all?

3. Based on your answer to part 2, can Research In Motion use the contribution margin ratio to predict how income will change in response to increases in Blackberry services revenues?

BTN 18-2   Both **Research In Motion** and **Apple** sell numerous hand-held consumer products, and each of these companies has a different product mix.

COMPARATIVE ANALYSIS

P2 A2

RIM

Apple

Required

1. Assume the following data are available for both companies. Compute each company's break-even point in unit sales. (Each company sells many hand-held consumer products at many different selling prices, and each has its own variable costs. This assignment assumes an *average* selling price per unit and an *average* cost per item.)

	Research In Motion	Apple
Average selling price per item sold	$350	$280
Average variable cost per item sold	$140	$110
Total fixed costs.	$14,980 million	$12,580 million

2. If unit sales were to decline, which company would experience the larger decline in operating profit? Explain.

BTN 18-3   Labor costs of an auto repair mechanic are seldom based on actual hours worked. Instead, the amount paid a mechanic is based on an industry average of time estimated to complete a repair job. The repair shop bills the customer for the industry average amount of time at the repair center's billable cost per hour. This means a customer can pay, for example, $120 for two hours of work on a car when the actual time worked was only one hour. Many experienced mechanics can complete repair jobs faster than the industry average. The average data are compiled by engineering studies and surveys conducted in the auto repair business. Assume that you are asked to complete such a survey for a repair center. The survey calls for objective input, and many questions require detailed cost data and analysis. The mechanics and owners know you have the survey and encourage you to complete it in a way that increases the average billable hours for repair work.

ETHICS CHALLENGE

C1

Required

Write a one-page memorandum to the mechanics and owners that describes the direct labor analysis you will undertake in completing this survey.

COMMUNICATING IN PRACTICE

C2

BTN 18-4   Several important assumptions underlie CVP analysis. Assumptions often help simplify and focus our analysis of sales and costs. A common application of CVP analysis is as a tool to forecast sales, costs, and income.

Required

Assume that you are actively searching for a job. Prepare a one-half page report identifying (1) three assumptions relating to your expected revenue (salary) and (2) three assumptions relating to your expected costs for the first year of your new job. Be prepared to discuss your assumptions in class.

TAKING IT TO THE NET

C1

BTN 18-5   Access and review the entrepreneurial information at **Business Owner's Toolkit** [**Toolkit. cch.com**]. Access and review its *New Business Cash Needs Estimate* under the Business Tools/Business Finance menu bar or similar work sheets related to controls of cash and costs.

Required

Write a one-half page report that describes the information and resources available at the Business Owner's Toolkit to help the owner of a start-up business to control and monitor its costs.

TEAMWORK IN ACTION

C2

BTN 18-6   A local movie theater owner explains to you that ticket sales on weekends and evenings are strong, but attendance during the weekdays, Monday through Thursday, is poor. The owner proposes to offer a contract to the local grade school to show educational materials at the theater for a set charge per student during school hours. The owner asks your help to prepare a CVP analysis listing the cost and sales projections for the proposal. The owner must propose to the school's administration a charge per child. At a minimum, the charge per child needs to be sufficient for the theater to break even.

Required

Your team is to prepare two separate lists of questions that enable you to complete a reliable CVP analysis of this situation. One list is to be answered by the school's administration, the other by the owner of the movie theater.

ENTREPRENEURIAL DECISION

C1 A1

BTN 18-7   Johnny Cupcakes, launched by entrepreneur John Earle, produces t-shirts in unique styles and limited quantities. Selling prices typically range from $40 per shirt to $70 per shirt.

Required

1. Identify at least two fixed costs that will not change regardless of how many t-shirts Johnny Cupcakes produces.
2. How could overly optimistic sales estimates potentially hurt John Earle's business?
3. Explain how cost-volume-profit analysis can help John Earle manage Johnny Cupcakes.

HITTING THE ROAD

P4

BTN 18-8   Multiproduct break-even analysis is often viewed differently when actually applied in practice. You are to visit a local fast-food restaurant and count the number of items on the menu. To apply multiproduct break-even analysis to the restaurant, similar menu items must often be fit into groups. A reasonable approach is to classify menu items into approximately five groups. We then estimate average selling price and average variable cost to compute average contribution margin. (*Hint:* For fast-food restaurants, the highest contribution margin is with its beverages, at about 90%.)

Required

1. Prepare a one-year multiproduct break-even analysis for the restaurant you visit. Begin by establishing groups. Next, estimate each group's volume and contribution margin. These estimates are necessary to compute each group's contribution margin. Assume that annual fixed costs in total are $500,000 per year. (*Hint:* You must develop your own estimates on volume and contribution margin for each group to obtain the break-even point and sales.)

2. Prepare a one-page report on the results of your analysis. Comment on the volume of sales necessary to break even at a fast-food restaurant.

BTN 18-9   Access and review Nokia's Website (www.Nokia.com) to answer the following questions.

GLOBAL DECISION

P4

NOKIA

Required

1. Do you believe that Nokia's managers use single product CVP analysis or multiproduct break-even point analysis? Explain.

2. How does the addition of a new product line affect Nokia's CVP analysis?

ANSWERS TO MULTIPLE CHOICE QUIZ

1. a; $150 − $100 = $50
2. e; ($150 − $100)/$150 = 33⅓%
3. c; $75,000/$50 CM per unit = 1,500 units
4. b; $300,000 − $180,000 = $120,000
5. c; Contribution margin ratio = ($400 − $260)/$400 = 0.35
   Targeted sales = ($840,000 + $70,000)/0.35 = $2,600,000

19

Variable Costing and Performance Reporting

A Look Back

Chapter 18 looked at cost behavior and its use by managers in performing cost-volume-profit analysis. It also illustrated the application of cost-volume-profit analysis.

A Look at This Chapter

This chapter describes managerial accounting reports that reflect variable costing. It also compares reports prepared under variable costing with those under absorption costing, and it explains how variable costing can improve business decisions.

A Look Ahead

Chapter 20 introduces and describes the budgeting process and its importance to management. It also explains the master budget and its usefulness to the planning of future company activities.

Learning Objectives

CONCEPTUAL

C1 Describe how absorption costing can result in over-production. (p. 811)

C2 Explain the role of variable costing in pricing special orders. (p. 813)

ANALYTICAL

A1 Compute and interpret break-even volume in units. (p. 815)

LP19

PROCEDURAL

P1 Compute unit cost under both absorption and variable costing. (p. 805)

P2 Prepare and analyze an income statement using absorption costing and using variable costing. (p. 806)

P3 Prepare a contribution margin report. (p. 807)

P4 Convert income under variable costing to the absorption cost basis. (p. 811)

A Fitting Pair

"Be your best, make a difference, and live with passion"
—SAMANTA AND KELVIN JOSEPH

NEW YORK—Business recipe: Take one information systems graduate, mix a bit of international flair, add an accountant, and stir. The result is **Samanta Shoes (SamantaShoes.com),** a start-up shoe manufacturer. Founded by Samanta and Kelvin Joseph, their company is aimed at providing "stylish, comfortable, and affordable" shoes, explains Samanta. "I design every shoe, and nothing less than the best material is used."

Kelvin's focus is on the accounting and financial side of Samanta Shoes. "The knowledge gained from my years at Ernst & Young LLP [a major accounting firm]," explains Kelvin, "has enabled me to be more helpful." Kelvin's knowledge of cost accounting and the importance of controlling costs is crucial to Samanta's success. Both partners stress the importance of attending to variable manufacturing costs, overhead, and product contribution margins to stay afloat.

Success is causing their company to evolve, but the partners adhere to a quality-first mentality. "It's all in the design," insists Samanta. "[A quality design] allows for more comfort and support." But quality also extends to style and uniqueness. "Women don't like other women having their shoe," explains Samanta. "We don't want to dilute our brand by being too mass market." Kelvin explains that the smallest manufacturing run they can have is 18 pairs of a special line. With small production runs, variable production costs drive decisions regarding product lines and product pricing. Accordingly, a variable costing system, with reports on variable costs, contribution margins, and break-even points, is key.

The partners also continue to apply managerial accounting fundamentals. "Our business cannot survive," says Kelvin, "unless it is profitable." They regularly review the accounting results and assess contribution margins, although Kelvin adds, "money does not equal happiness." Samanta explains, "Live your dreams . . . make a difference . . . give back to your community"—advice that we can all live by. "If you're not enjoying it," continues Samanta, "there's no point to doing it."

[Sources: *Samanta Shoes Website,* January 2011; *New York Resident,* August 2004; *Caribbean Vibe,* August 2004; *Black Enterprise,* June 2006; *Regine Magazine,* Spring 2004; *Inc.com,* July 2007]

Product-costing information is crucial for most business decisions. This chapter explains and illustrates the concept of variable costing. We then compare variable costing to that of absorption costing commonly used for financial reporting. We show that income is different when computed under variable or absorption costing whenever the number of units produced is different from units sold. We also show how absorption costing can be misleading (though not wrong) and how variable costing can result in better production and pricing decisions.

Variable Costing and Performance Reporting

Variable Costing and Absorption Costing	Performance Reporting (Income) Implications	Comparing Variable Costing and Absorption Costing
• Absorption costing • Variable costing • Computing unit costs	• When production equals sales • When production exceeds sales • When production is less than sales • Income reporting • Converting variable cost income to absorption cost	• Planning production • Setting prices • Controlling costs • Limitations of variable costing • Variable costing for service firms

INTRODUCING VARIABLE COSTING AND ABSORPTION COSTING

Product costs consist of direct materials, direct labor, and overhead. Direct materials and direct labor costs are those that can be identified and traced to the product(s). Overhead, which consists of costs such as electricity, equipment depreciation, and supervisor salaries, is not traceable to the product. Overhead costs must be allocated to products.

There are a variety of costing methods for identifying and allocating overhead costs to products. A prior chapter focused on *how* to allocate overhead costs to products. This chapter focuses on *what* overhead costs are included in product costs.

Under the traditional costing approach, *all* manufacturing costs are assigned to products. Those costs consist of direct materials, direct labor, variable overhead, and fixed overhead. This traditional approach is referred to as **absorption costing** (also called *full costing*), which assumes that products *absorb* all costs incurred to produce them. While widely used for external financial reporting (GAAP), this costing method can result in misleading product cost information for managers' business decisions.

Under **variable costing,** only costs that change in total with changes in production level are included in product costs. Those consist of direct materials, direct labor, and variable overhead. Fixed overhead does not change with changes in production and, thus, it is excluded from product costs. Instead, fixed overhead is treated as a period cost; meaning it is expensed in the period when it is incurred.

The following diagram compares the absorption and variable costing methods. Under both methods, direct materials, direct labor, and variable overhead are included in product costs. The key difference between the methods lies in their treatment of *fixed* overhead costs—such costs are included in product costs under absorption costing but included in period expenses under variable costing. Recall that product costs are included in inventory until the goods are sold, at which time they are included in cost of goods sold. Period expenses are reported as expenses immediately in the period in which they are incurred.

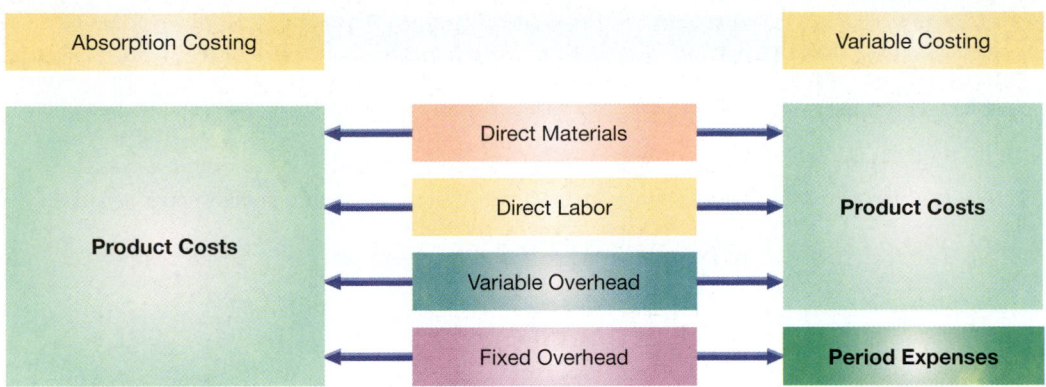

The diagram above helps us understand when the absorption and variable costing methods will yield different income amounts. In particular, differences in income resulting from the alternative methods will be *small* when:

- Fixed overhead is small as a percentage of total manufacturing costs.
- Inventory levels are low. As more companies adopt lean techniques, including just-in-time manufacturing, inventory levels fall. Lower inventory levels reduce differences between absorption and variable costing.
- Inventory turnover is rapid. The more quickly inventory turns over, the more product costs are included in cost of goods sold, relative to the product costs that remain in inventory.

Computing Unit Cost

To illustrate the difference between absorption costing and variable costing, let's consider the product cost data in Exhibit 19.1 from IceAge, a skate manufacturer.

P1 Compute unit cost under both absorption and variable costing.

Direct materials cost	$4 per unit
Direct labor cost	8 per unit
Overhead cost	
Variable overhead cost	$ 180,000
Fixed overhead cost	600,000
Total overhead cost	$ 780,000
Expected units produced	60,000 units

EXHIBIT 19.1

Summary Product Cost Data

Drawing on the product cost data, Exhibit 19.2 shows the product unit cost computations for both absorption and variable costing. For absorption costing, the product unit cost is $25, which consists of $4 in direct materials, $8 in direct labor, $3 in variable overhead ($180,000/60,000 units), and $10 in fixed overhead ($600,000/60,000 units).

For variable costing, the product unit cost is $15, which consists of $4 in direct materials, $8 in direct labor, and $3 in variable overhead. Fixed overhead costs of $600,000 are treated as a period cost and are recorded as expense in the period incurred. The difference between the two costing methods is the exclusion of fixed overhead from product costs for variable costing.

	Absorption Costing	Variable Costing
Direct materials cost per unit	$ 4	$ 4
Direct labor cost per unit	8	8
Overhead cost		
Variable overhead cost per unit	3	3
Fixed overhead cost per unit	10	—
Total product cost per unit	$25	$15

EXHIBIT 19.2

Unit Cost Computation

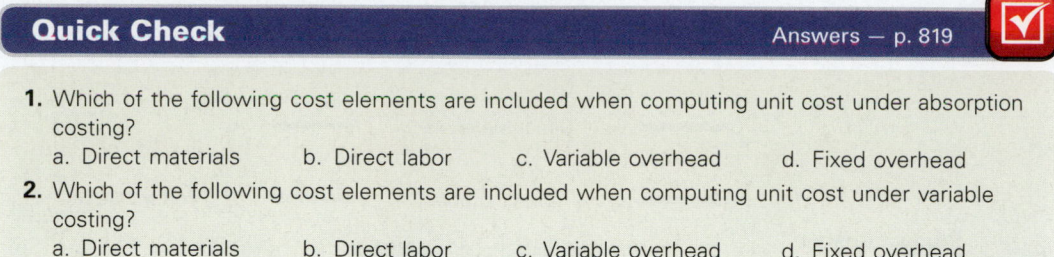

1. Which of the following cost elements are included when computing unit cost under absorption costing?
   a. Direct materials   b. Direct labor   c. Variable overhead   d. Fixed overhead
2. Which of the following cost elements are included when computing unit cost under variable costing?
   a. Direct materials   b. Direct labor   c. Variable overhead   d. Fixed overhead

PERFORMANCE REPORTING (INCOME) IMPLICATIONS

The prior section illustrated the differences between absorption costing and variable costing in computing unit cost. This section shows the implications of those differences for performance (income) reporting.

To illustrate the reporting implications, we return to IceAge Company. Exhibit 19.3 summarizes the production cost data for IceAge as well as additional data on nonproduction costs. Assume that IceAge's variable costs per unit are constant and that its annual fixed costs remain unchanged during the three-year period 2009 through 2011.

EXHIBIT 19.3

Summary Cost Information for 2009–2011

Production Costs		Nonproduction Costs	
Direct materials cost . .	$4 per unit	Variable selling and administrative expenses . .	$2 per unit
Direct labor cost	$8 per unit	Fixed selling and administrative expenses	$200,000 per year
Variable overhead cost .	$3 per unit		
Fixed overhead cost . . .	$600,000 per year		

The reported sales and production information for IceAge follows. Its sales price was a constant $40 per unit over this time period. We see that the units produced equal those sold for 2009, but exceed those sold for 2010, and are less than those sold for 2011.

	Units Produced	Units Sold	Units in Ending Inventory
2009	60,000	60,000	0
2010	60,000	40,000	20,000
2011	60,000	80,000	0

Drawing on the information above, we next prepare the income statement for IceAge both under absorption costing and under variable costing. Our purpose is to highlight differences between these two costing methods under three different cases: when units produced are equal to, exceed, or are less than units sold.

Units Produced Equal Units Sold

P2 Prepare and analyze an income statement using absorption costing and using variable costing.

Exhibit 19.4 presents the 2009 income statement for both costing methods (2010 and 2011 statements will follow). The income statement under variable costing (on the right) is referred to as the **contribution margin income statement.** Contribution margin is the excess of sales over variable costs. This amount contributes to covering all fixed costs and earning income. Under variable costing, the expenses are grouped according to cost behavior—variable or fixed, and production or nonproduction. Under the traditional format of absorption costing, expenses are grouped according to function.

EXHIBIT 19.4

Income for 2009—Quantity Produced Equals Quantity Sold*

ICEAGE COMPANY Income Statement (Absorption Costing) For Year Ended December 31, 2009		
Sales† (60,000 × $40)		$2,400,000
Cost of goods sold (60,000 × $25*)		1,500,000
Gross margin		900,000
Selling and administrative expenses [$200,000 + (60,000 × $2)]		320,000
Net income		$ 580,000

* See Exhibit 19.2 for unit cost computation under absorption and under variable costing.

† Units produced equal 60,000; units sold equal 60,000.

ICEAGE COMPANY Income Statement (Variable Costing) For Year Ended December 31, 2009		
Sales† (60,000 × $40)		$2,400,000
Variable expenses		
Variable production costs (60,000 × $15*)	$900,000	
Variable selling and administrative expenses (60,000 × $2)	120,000	1,020,000
Contribution margin		1,380,000
Fixed expenses		
Fixed overhead	600,000	
Fixed selling and administrative expense	200,000	800,000
Net income		$ 580,000

A performance report that excludes fixed expenses and net income is a contribution margin report.

Point: Contribution margin income statements prepared under variable costing are useful in performing cost-volume-profit analyses.

Exhibit 19.4 reveals that *reported income is identical under absorption costing and variable costing when the units produced equal the units sold.*

Contribution Margin Report A performance report that excludes fixed expenses and net income is known as a **contribution margin report.** Looking at the variable costing income statement in Exhibit 19.4, a contribution margin report would end with the contribution margin of $1,380,000. However, a *contribution margin income statement* includes fixed expenses and net income as shown in Exhibit 19.4.

Exhibit 19.5 reorganizes the information from Exhibit 19.4 to show the assignment of costs to different expenses and assets under both absorption costing and variable costing. When quantity produced equals quantity sold there is no difference in total costs assigned. Yet, there is a difference in what categories receive those costs. Absorption costing assigns $1,500,000 to cost of goods sold compared to $900,000 for variable costing. The $600,000 difference is a period cost for variable costing.

P3 Prepare a contribution margin report.

Point: Contribution margin (Sales − Variable expenses) is different from gross margin (Sales − Cost of sales).

EXHIBIT 19.5

Production Cost Assignment for 2009

	Cost of Goods Sold (Expense)		Ending Inventory (Asset)		Period Cost (Expense)	2009 Expense
Absorption Costing						
Direct materials	60,000 × $4	$ 240,000	0 × $4	$ 0		$ 240,000
Direct labor	60,000 × $8	480,000	0 × $8	0		480,000
Variable overhead	60,000 × $3	180,000	0 × $3	0		180,000
Fixed overhead	60,000 × $10	600,000	0 × $10	0		600,000
Total costs		$1,500,000		$ 0		$1,500,000
Variable Costing						
Direct materials	60,000 × $4	$ 240,000	0 × $4	$ 0		$ 240,000
Direct labor	60,000 × $8	480,000	0 × $8	0		480,000
Variable overhead	60,000 × $3	180,000	0 × $3	0		180,000
Fixed overhead					$600,000	600,000
Total costs		$ 900,000		$ 0	$600,000	$1,500,000
Cost difference						$ 0

Decision Insight

Manufacturing Margin   Some managers compute *manufacturing margin* (also called *production margin*), which is sales less variable production costs. Some managers also require that internal income statements show this amount to highlight variable product costs on income. The contribution margin section of IceAge's variable costing income statement would appear as follows (compare this to Exhibit 19.4).

Sales............................	$2,400,000
Variable production costs	900,000
Manufacturing margin	1,500,000
Variable selling & admin. exp.........	120,000
Contribution margin	$1,380,000

Units Produced Exceed Units Sold

Exhibit 19.6 shows absorption costing and variable costing income statements for 2010. In 2010, 60,000 units were produced, which is the same as in 2009. However, only 40,000 units were sold.

The income statements reveal that for 2010, income is $320,000 under absorption costing. Under variable costing, income is $120,000, which is $200,000 less than under absorption costing. The cause of this $200,000 difference rests with the different treatment of fixed overhead under the two costing methods.

EXHIBIT 19.6

Income for 2010—Quantity Produced Exceeds Quantity Sold*

ICEAGE COMPANY Income Statement (Absorption Costing) For Year Ended December 31, 2010		
Sales† (40,000 × $40)...............		$1,600,000
Cost of goods sold (40,000 × $25*) ...		1,000,000
Gross margin		600,000
Selling and administrative expenses [$200,000 + (40,000 × $2)]		280,000
Net income......................		$ 320,000

* See Exhibit 19.2 for unit cost computation under absorption and under variable costing.

† Units produced equal 60,000; units sold equal 40,000.

ICEAGE COMPANY Income Statement (Variable Costing) For Year Ended December 31, 2010		
Sales† (40,000 × $40).......		$1,600,000
Variable expenses		
Variable production costs (40,000 × $15*)	$600,000	
Variable selling and administrative expenses (40,000 × $2)..	80,000	680,000
Contribution margin........		920,000
Fixed expenses		
Fixed overhead	600,000	
Fixed selling and administrative expense ...	200,000	800,000
Net income..............		$ 120,000

Under variable costing, the entire $600,000 fixed overhead cost is treated as an expense in computing 2010 income. Under absorption costing, the fixed overhead cost is allocated to each unit of product at the rate of $10 per unit (from Exhibit 19.2). When production exceeds sales by 20,000 units (60,000 versus 40,000), the $200,000 ($10 × 20,000 units) of fixed overhead cost allocated to these 20,000 units is carried as part of the cost of ending inventory (see Exhibit 19.7). This means that $200,000 of fixed overhead cost incurred in 2010 is not expensed until future periods when it is reported in cost of goods sold as those products are sold. Consequently, income for 2010 under absorption costing is $200,000 higher than income under variable costing.

Exhibit 19.7 reorganizes the information from Exhibit 19.6 to show the assignment of costs to different expenses and assets under both absorption costing and variable costing. When quantity produced exceeds quantity sold there is a difference in total costs assigned. As a result, income under absorption costing is greater than under variable costing because of the greater fixed overhead cost allocated to ending inventory (asset) under absorption costing. Those cost differences extend to cost of goods sold, ending inventory, and period costs.

EXHIBIT 19.7

Production Cost Assignment for 2010

		Cost of Goods Sold (Expense)		Ending Inventory (Asset)		Period Cost (Expense)	2010 Expense
Absorption Costing							
Direct materials....	40,000 × $4	$ 160,000	20,000 × $4	$ 80,000			$ 160,000
Direct labor.......	40,000 × $8	320,000	20,000 × $8	160,000			320,000
Variable overhead ..	40,000 × $3	120,000	20,000 × $3	60,000			120,000
Fixed overhead.....	40,000 × $10	400,000	20,000 × $10	200,000			400,000
Total costs		$1,000,000		$500,000			$1,000,000
Variable Costing							
Direct materials....	40,000 × $4	$ 160,000	20,000 × $4	$ 80,000			$ 160,000
Direct labor.......	40,000 × $8	320,000	20,000 × $8	160,000			320,000
Variable overhead ..	40,000 × $3	120,000	20,000 × $3	60,000			120,000
Fixed overhead.....						$600,000	600,000
Total costs		$ 600,000		$300,000		$600,000	$1,200,000
Cost difference ...							$ (200,000)

Units Produced Are Less Than Units Sold

Exhibit 19.8 shows absorption costing and variable costing income statements for 2011. In 2011, IceAge produced 20,000 fewer units than it sold. Production equaled 60,000 units, but units sold were 80,000. IceAge's income statements reveal that income is $840,000 under absorption costing, but it is $1,040,000 under variable costing.

The cause of this $200,000 difference lies with the treatment of fixed overhead. Beginning inventory in 2011 under absorption costing included $200,000 of fixed overhead cost incurred in 2010, which is assigned to cost of goods sold in 2011 under absorption costing.

Point: IceAge can sell more units than it produced in 2011 because of inventory carried over from 2010.

EXHIBIT 19.8

Income for 2011—Quantity Produced Is Less Than Quantity Sold*

ICEAGE COMPANY Income Statement (Absorption Costing) For Year Ended December 31, 2011	
Sales† (80,000 × $40)...............	$3,200,000
Cost of goods sold (80,000 × $25*)...	2,000,000
Gross margin	1,200,000
Selling and administrative expenses [$200,000 + (80,000 × $2)]	360,000
Net income.......................	$ 840,000

* See Exhibit 19.2 for unit cost computation under absorption and under variable costing.

† Units produced equal 60,000; units sold equal 80,000.

ICEAGE COMPANY Income Statement (Variable Costing) For Year Ended December 31, 2011		
Sales† (80,000 × $40).....		$3,200,000
Variable expenses		
Variable production costs (80,000 × $15*)	$1,200,000	
Variable selling and administrative expenses (80,000 × $2)	160,000	1,360,000
Contribution margin......		1,840,000
Fixed expenses		
Fixed overhead	600,000	
Fixed selling and administrative expense.....	200,000	800,000
Net income.............		$1,040,000

Exhibit 19.9 reorganizes the information from Exhibit 19.8 to show the assignment of costs to different expenses and assets under both absorption costing and variable costing. When quantity produced is less than quantity sold there is a difference in total costs assigned.

Specifically, ending inventory in 2010 under absorption costing was $500,000 (20,000 units × $25) whereas it was only $300,000 (20,000 units × $15) under variable costing—see Exhibit 19.7. Consequently, when that inventory is sold in 2011, the 2011 income under absorption costing is $200,000 less than the income under variable costing. That inventory cost difference flows through cost of goods sold and then to income.

EXHIBIT 19.9

Production Cost Assignment for 2011

	Cost of Goods Sold (Expense)		Ending Inventory (Asset)		Period Cost (Expense)	2011 Expense
Absorption Costing						
Direct materials.....	80,000 × $4	$ 320,000	0 × $4	$ 0		$ 320,000
Direct labor........	80,000 × $8	640,000	0 × $8	0		640,000
Variable overhead ...	80,000 × $3	240,000	0 × $3	0		240,000
Fixed overhead	80,000 × $10	800,000	0 × $10	0		800,000
Total costs		$2,000,000		$ 0		$2,000,000
Variable Costing						
Direct materials.....	80,000 × $4	$ 320,000	0 × $4	$ 0		$ 320,000
Direct labor........	80,000 × $8	640,000	0 × $8	0		640,000
Variable overhead ...	80,000 × $3	240,000	0 × $3	0		240,000
Fixed overhead					$600,000	600,000
Total costs		$1,200,000		$ 0	$600,000	$1,800,000
Cost difference ...						$ 200,000

Summarizing Income Reporting

Income reported under both variable costing and absorption costing for the years 2009 through 2011 for IceAge is summarized in Exhibit 19.10. We see that the differences in income are due to timing, as total income is $1,740,000 for this time period for *both* methods. Further, income under absorption costing and that under variable costing will be different whenever the quantity produced and the quantity sold are different. Specifically, *income under absorption costing is higher when more units are produced relative to units sold and is lower when fewer units are produced than are sold.*

EXHIBIT 19.10

Summary of Income Reporting

	Units Produced	Units Sold	Income under Absorption Costing	Income under Variable Costing	Differences
2009	60,000	60,000	$ 580,000	$ 580,000	$ 0
2010	60,000	40,000	320,000	120,000	200,000
2011	60,000	80,000	840,000	1,040,000	(200,000)
Totals	180,000	180,000	$1,740,000	$1,740,000	$ 0

Our illustration using IceAge had the total number of units produced over 2009–2011 exactly equal to the number of units sold over that period. This meant that the difference between absorption costing income and variable costing income for the *total* three-year period is zero. In reality, it is unusual for production and sales quantities to exactly equal each other over such a short period of time. This means that we normally continue to see differences in income for these two methods extending over several years.

Quick Check   Answers — p. 819

3. Which of the following statements is true when units produced exceed units sold?
   a. Variable costing income exceeds absorption costing income.
   b. Variable costing income equals absorption costing income.
   c. Variable costing income is less than absorption costing income.

4. Which of the following statements is true when units produced are less than units sold?
   a. Variable costing income exceeds absorption costing income.
   b. Variable costing income equals absorption costing income.
   c. Variable costing income is less than absorption costing income.

Converting Income under Variable Costing to Absorption Costing

Companies commonly use variable costing for internal reporting and business decisions, and use absorption costing for external reporting and tax reporting. For companies concerned about the cost of maintaining two costing systems, it is comforting to know that we can readily convert reports under variable costing to that using absorption costing.

Income under variable costing is restated to that under absorption costing by adding the fixed production cost in ending inventory and subtracting the fixed production cost in beginning inventory, as follows.

P4 Convert income under variable costing to the absorption cost basis.

Income under absorption costing	=	Income under variable costing	+	Fixed production cost in ending inventory	−	Fixed production cost in beginning inventory

Using IceAge's data, in 2010, absorption costing income was $200,000 higher than variable costing income. The $200,000 difference was because the fixed overhead cost incurred in 2010 was allocated to the 20,000 units of ending inventory under absorption costing (and not expensed in 2010 under absorption costing). On the other hand, the $200,000 fixed overhead costs (along with all other fixed costs) were expensed in 2010 under variable costing.

Exhibit 19.11 shows the computations for restating income under the two costing methods. To restate variable costing income to absorption costing income for 2010, we must add back the **fixed overhead cost deferred in** (ending) **inventory.** Similarly, to restate variable costing income to absorption costing income for 2011, we must deduct the **fixed overhead cost recognized from** (beginning) **inventory,** which was incurred in 2010, but expensed in the 2011 cost of goods sold when the inventory was sold.

	2009	2010	2011
Variable costing income	$580,000	$120,000	$1,040,000
Add: Fixed overhead cost deferred in ending inventory			
(20,000 × $10)	0	200,000	0
Less: Fixed overhead cost recognized from beginning inventory			
(20,000 × $10)	0	0	(200,000)
Absorption costing income	$580,000	$320,000	$ 840,000

EXHIBIT 19.11

Converting Variable Costing Income to Absorption Costing Income

COMPARING VARIABLE COSTING AND ABSORPTION COSTING

This section discusses how absorption costing can lead to undesirable production and pricing decisions and how variable costing can result in better business decisions.

Planning Production

Production planning is an important managerial function. Producing too much leads to excess inventory, which in turn leads to higher storage and financing costs, and to greater risk of product obsolescence. On the other hand, producing too little can lead to lost sales and customer dissatisfaction.

C1 Describe how absorption costing can result in over-production.

Production levels should be based on reliable sales forecasts. However over-production and inventory buildup can occur because of how managers are evaluated and rewarded. For instance, many companies link manager bonuses to income computed under absorption costing because this is how income is reported to shareholders (per GAAP).

To illustrate how a reward system can lead to over-production under absorption costing, let's use IceAge's 2009 data with one change: assume that its manager decides to produce 100,000 units instead of 60,000. Since only 60,000 units are sold, the 40,000 units of excess production will be stored in inventory.

The left side of Exhibit 19.12 shows the unit cost when 60,000 units are produced (same as Exhibit 19.2). The right side shows unit cost when 100,000 units are produced. The exhibit is prepared under absorption costing for 2009.

EXHIBIT 19.12

Unit Cost under Absorption
Costing for Different
Production Levels

Absorption Costing When 60,000 Units Are Produced		Absorption Costing When 100,000 Units Are Produced	
Direct materials cost	$ 4 per unit	Direct materials cost	$ 4 per unit
Direct labor cost	8 per unit	Direct labor cost	8 per unit
Variable overhead cost	3 per unit	Variable overhead cost.............	3 per unit
Total variable cost	15 per unit	Total variable cost	15 per unit
Fixed overhead ($600,000/60,000 units)	10 per unit	Fixed overhead ($600,000/100,000 units)	6 per unit
Total product cost	$25 per unit	Total product cost	$21 per unit

Total production cost *per unit* is $4 less when 100,000 units are produced. Specifically, cost per unit is $21 when 100,000 units are produced versus $25 per unit at 60,000 units. The reason for this difference is because the company is spreading the $600,000 fixed overhead cost over more units when 100,000 units are produced than when 60,000 are produced.

The difference in cost per unit impacts performance reporting. Exhibit 19.13 presents the 2009 income statement under absorption costing for the two alternative production levels.

EXHIBIT 19.13

Income under Absorption Costing
for Different Production Levels

ICEAGE COMPANY Income Statement (Absorption Costing) For Year Ended December 31, 2009 [60,000 Units Produced; 60,000 Units Sold]			ICEAGE COMPANY Income Statement (Absorption Costing) For Year Ended December 31, 2009 [100,000 Units Produced; 60,000 Units Sold]		
Sales (60,000 × $40)		$2,400,000	Sales (60,000 × $40)		$2,400,000
Cost of goods sold (60,000 × $25)		1,500,000	Cost of goods sold (60,000 × $21).....		1,260,000
Gross margin		900,000	Gross margin		1,140,000
Selling and administrative expenses			Selling and administrative expenses		
Variable (60,000 × $2)	$120,000		Variable (60,000 × $2)...	$120,000	
Fixed	200,000	320,000	Fixed	200,000	320,000
Net income		$ 580,000	Net income		$ 820,000

Point: The 41% income increase is computed as:

$$\frac{\$820,000 - \$580,000}{\$580,000} = 0.41$$

Common sense suggests that because the company's variable cost per unit, total fixed costs, and sales are identical in both cases, merely producing more units and creating excess ending inventory should not increase income. Yet, as we see in Exhibit 19.13, income under absorption costing is 41% greater if management produces 40,000 more units than necessary and builds up ending inventory. The reason is that $240,000 of fixed overhead (40,000 units × $6) is assigned to ending inventory instead of being expensed as cost of goods sold in 2009. This shows that a manager can report increased income merely by producing more and disregarding whether the excess units can be sold or not.

Manager bonuses are tied to income computed under absorption costing for many companies. Accordingly, these managers may be enticed to increase production that increases income and their bonuses. This incentive problem encourages inventory buildup, which leads to increased costs in storage, financing, and obsolescence. If the excess inventory is never sold, it will be disposed of at a loss.

The manager incentive problem can be avoided when income is measured using variable costing. To illustrate, Exhibit 19.14 reports income under variable costing for the same production levels used in Exhibit 19.13. This demonstrates that managers cannot increase income under variable costing by merely increasing production without increasing sales.

Why is income under absorption costing affected by the production level when that for variable costing is not? The answer lies in the different treatment of fixed overhead costs for the two methods. Under absorption costing, fixed overhead *per unit* is lower when 100,000 units are produced than when 60,000 units are produced, and then fixed overhead cost is allocated to more units—recall Exhibit 19.12. If those excess units produced are not sold, the fixed overhead cost allocated to those units is not expensed until a future period when those units are sold.

EXHIBIT 19.14

Income under Variable Costing for Different Production Levels

ICEAGE COMPANY Income Statement (Variable Costing) For Year Ended December 31, 2009 [60,000 Units Produced; 60,000 Units Sold]		
Sales (60,000 × $40)		$2,400,000
Variable expenses		
Variable production costs (60,000 × $15)	$900,000	
Variable selling and administrative expenses (60,000 × $2)	120,000	1,020,000
Contribution margin		1,380,000
Fixed expenses		
Fixed overhead	600,000	
Fixed selling and administrative expense.	200,000	800,000
Net income		$ 580,000

ICEAGE COMPANY Income Statement (Variable Costing) For Year Ended December 31, 2009 [100,000 Units Produced; 60,000 Units Sold]		
Sales (60,000 × $40) . .		$2,400,000
Variable expenses		
Variable production costs (60,000 × $15) . . .	$900,000	
Variable selling and administrative expenses (60,000 × $2)	120,000	1,020,000
Contribution margin . . .		1,380,000
Fixed expenses		
Fixed overhead	600,000	
Fixed selling and administrative expense.	200,000	800,000
Net income		$ 580,000

Reported income under variable costing, on the other hand, is not affected by production level changes because *all* fixed production costs are expensed in the year when incurred. Under variable costing, companies increase reported income by selling more units—it is not possible to increase income just by producing more units and creating excess inventory.

Point: A per unit cost that is constant at all production levels is a *variable cost per unit*.

Decision Ethics   Answer — p. 819

Production Manager   Your company produces and sells MP3 players. Due to competition, your company projects sales to be 35% less than last year. In a recent meeting, the CEO expressed concern that top executives may not receive bonuses because of the expected sales decrease. The controller suggests that if the company continues to produce as many units as last year, reported income might achieve the level for bonuses to be paid. Should your company produce excess inventory to maintain income? What ethical issues arise? ■

Setting Prices

Setting prices for products and services is one of the more complex and important managerial decisions. Although many factors impact pricing, cost is a crucial factor. Cost information from both absorption costing and variable costing can aid managers in pricing.

C2 Explain the role of variable costing in pricing special orders.

Over the long run, price must be high enough to cover all costs, including variable costs and fixed costs, and still provide an acceptable return to owners. For this purpose, absorption cost information is useful because it reflects the full costs that sales must exceed for the company to be profitable.

Over the short run, however, fixed production costs such as the cost to maintain plant capacity does not change with changes in production levels. With excess capacity, increases in production level would increase variable production costs, but not fixed costs. This implies that while managers try to maintain the long-run price on existing orders, which covers all production costs, managers should accept special orders *provided the special order price exceeds variable cost.*

To illustrate, let's return to the data of IceAge Company. Recall that its variable production cost per unit is $15 and its total production cost per unit is $25 (at production level of 60,000 units). Assume that it receives a special order for 1,000 pairs of skates at an offer price of $22 per pair from a foreign skating school. This special order will not affect IceAge's regular sales and its plant has excess capacity to fill the order.

Drawing on absorption costing information, we observe that cost is $25 per unit and that the special order price is $22 per unit. These data would suggest that management reject the order as it would lose $3,000, computed as 1,000 units at $3 loss per pair ($22 − $25).

Point: Use of relevant costs in special order and other managerial decisions is covered more extensively in a later chapter.

However, closer analysis suggests that this order should be accepted. This is because the $22 order price exceeds the $15 variable cost of the product. Specifically, Exhibit 19.15 reveals that the incremental revenue from accepting the order is $22,000 (1,000 units at $22 per unit), whereas the incremental production cost of the order is $15,000 (1,000 units at $15 per unit) and the incremental variable selling and administrative cost is $2,000 (1,000 units at $2 per unit). Thus, both its contribution margin and net income would increase by $5,000 from accepting the order. Variable costing reveals this opportunity while absorption costing hides it.

EXHIBIT 19.15

Computing Incremental Income for a Special Order

Rejecting Special Order		Accepting Special Order	
Incremental sales	$ 0	Incremental sales (1,000 × $22)	$22,000
Incremental costs	0	Incremental costs	
		Variable production cost (1,000 × $15)	15,000
		Variable selling and admin. expense (1,000 × $2)	2,000
Incremental income	$ 0	Incremental income.	$ 5,000

The reason for increased income from accepting the special order lies in the different behavior of variable and fixed production costs. We see that if the order is rejected, only variable costs are saved. Fixed costs, on the other hand, do not change in the short run regardless of rejecting or accepting this order. Since incremental revenue from the order exceeds incremental costs (only variable cost in this case), accepting the special order increases company income.

Point: Fixed overhead costs won't increase when these additional units are sold because the company already has the capacity.

Controlling Costs

Every company strives to control costs to be competitive. An effective cost control practice is to hold managers responsible only for their **controllable costs.** A cost is controllable if a manager has the power to determine or at least markedly affect the amount incurred. **Uncontrollable costs** are not within the manager's control or influence. For example, direct materials cost is controllable by a production supervisor. On the other hand, costs related to production capacity are not controllable by that supervisor as that supervisor does not have authority to change factory size or add new machinery. Generally, variable production costs and fixed production costs are controlled at different levels of management. Similarly, variable selling and administrative costs are usually controlled at a level of management different from that which controls fixed selling and administrative costs.

Under absorption costing, both variable production costs and fixed production costs are included in product cost. This makes it difficult to evaluate the effectiveness of cost control by different levels of managers. Variable costing separates the variable costs from fixed costs and, therefore, makes it easier to identify and assign control over costs.

Decisions to change a company's fixed costs are usually assigned to higher-level managers. This is different from most variable costs that are assigned to lower-level managers and supervisors. When we separately report variable and fixed cost elements, as is done with an income statement in the **contribution format,** it highlights the impact of each cost element for income. This makes it easier for us to identify problem areas and to take cost control measures by appropriate levels of management. This approach is also useful in evaluating the performance of managers of different segments within a company.

Decision Maker   Answer — p. 819

Internal Auditor   Your company uses absorption costing for preparing its GAAP-based income statement and balance sheet. Management is disappointed because its external auditors are requiring it to write off an inventory amount because it exceeds what the company could reasonably sell in the foreseeable future. Why would management produce more than it sells? Why would management be disappointed about the write-off? ∎

Limitations of Reports Using Variable Costing

An important generally accepted accounting principle is that of matching. Most managers interpret the matching principle as expensing all manufacturing costs, both variable and fixed, in the period when the related product is sold rather than when incurred. Consequently, absorption costing is almost exclusively used for external reporting. For income tax purposes, absorption costing is the only acceptable basis for filings with the Internal Revenue Service (IRS) under the Tax Reform Act of 1986.

Thus, and despite the many useful applications and insights provided by variable cost reports, *absorption costing is the only acceptable basis for both external reporting and tax reporting*. Also, as we discussed, top executives are often awarded bonuses based on income computed using absorption costing. These realities contribute to the widespread use of absorption costing by companies.

Variable Costing for Service Firms

Although most of this chapter's examples used data for a manufacturer, variable costing also applies to service companies. Since service companies do not produce inventory, the differences in income from absorption and variable costing shown for a manufacturer do not apply. Still, a focus on variable costs can be useful in managerial decisions for service firms. One example is "special order" pricing for airlines when they sell tickets a day or so before a flight at deeply discounted prices. Provided the discounted price exceeds variable costs, such sales increase contribution margin and net income.

Quick Check

Answers — p. 819

5. Why is information under variable costing useful in making short-run pricing decisions when idle capacity exits?
6. Discuss the usefulness of absorption costing versus variable costing in controlling costs.
7. What are the limitations of variable costing?

 **GLOBAL VIEW**

Survey evidence shows that many German companies have elaborate and detailed cost accounting systems. Over 90 percent of companies surveyed report their systems focus on *contribution margin*. This focus helps German companies like **Volkswagen** control costs and plan their production levels.

Break-Even Analysis  **Decision Analysis**

The previous chapter discussed cost-volume-profit (CVP) analysis for making managerial decisions. However, if the income statement is prepared under absorption costing, the data needed for CVP analysis are not readily available. Accordingly, substantial effort is required to go back to the accounting records and reclassify the cost data to obtain information necessary for conducting CVP analysis.

On the other hand, if the income statement is prepared using the contribution format, the data needed for CVP analysis are readily available. To illustrate, we can draw on IceAge's contribution margin income statement from Exhibit 19.4 (reproduced below) to readily compute its contribution margin per unit and its break-even volume in units.

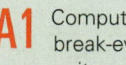 **A1** Compute and interpret break-even volume in units.

ICEAGE COMPANY Income Statement (Variable Costing) For Year Ended December 31, 2009			
		Dollars	Per Unit
Sales (60,000 × $40)		$2,400,000	$40
Variable expenses			
Variable production costs (60,000 × $15)	$900,000		$15
Variable selling and administrative expenses (60,000 × $2)	120,000	1,020,000	2 17
Contribution margin		1,380,000	$23
Fixed expenses			
Fixed overhead	600,000		
Fixed selling and administrative expense	200,000	800,000	
Net income		$ 580,000	

We compute and report the company's contribution margin per unit and its components in the far right columns of the exhibit above. Recall that contribution margin per unit is defined as follows.

$$\text{Contribution margin per unit} = \text{Sales price per unit} - \text{Variable cost per unit}$$
$$= \$40 - \$17 = \$23$$

The above report shows that its variable cost per unit consists of $15 in variable production costs and $2 in variable selling and administrative costs.

We also see that the company's total fixed costs of $800,000 is the sum of $600,000 in fixed overhead cost and $200,000 in fixed selling and administrative cost. From this information we can compute the company's break-even volume in units as follows.

$$\text{Break-even volume in units} = \frac{\text{Total fixed costs}}{\text{Contribution margin per unit}} = \frac{\$800,000}{\$23} = 34{,}783 \text{ units (rounded)}$$

This finding implies that the company must produce and sell 34,783 units to break even (zero income). Sales less than that amount would yield a net loss and sales above that amount would yield net income.

DEMONSTRATION PROBLEM

Navaroli Company began operations on January 5, 2010. Cost and sales information for its first two calendar years of operations are summarized below.

Manufacturing costs	
Direct materials	$80 per unit
Direct labor	$120 per unit
Factory overhead costs for the year	
Variable overhead	$30 per unit
Fixed overhead	$14,000,000
Nonmanufacturing costs	
Variable selling and administrative	$10 per unit
Fixed selling and administrative	$ 8,000,000
Production and sales data	
Units produced, 2010	200,000 units
Units sold, 2010	140,000 units
Units in ending inventory, 2010	60,000 units
Units produced, 2011	80,000 units
Units sold, 2011	140,000 units
Units in ending inventory, 2011	0 units
Sales price per unit	$600 per unit

Required

1. Prepare an income statement for the company for 2010 under absorption costing.
2. Prepare an income statement for the company for 2010 under variable costing.
3. Explain the source(s) of the difference in reported income for 2010 under the two costing methods.
4. Prepare an income statement for the company for 2011 under absorption costing.
5. Prepare an income statement for the company for 2011 under variable costing.
6. Prepare a schedule to convert variable costing income to absorption costing income for the years 2010 and 2011. Use the format in Exhibit 19.11.

PLANNING THE SOLUTION

- Set up a table to compute the unit cost under the two costing methods (refer to Exhibit 19.2).
- Prepare an income statement under both of the two costing methods (refer to Exhibit 19.6).
- Consider differences in the treatment of fixed production costs for the income statement to answer requirements 3 and 6.

SOLUTION TO DEMONSTRATION PROBLEM

Before the income statement for 2010 is prepared, unit costs for 2010 are computed under the two costing methods as follows.

	Absorption Costing	Variable Costing
Direct materials per unit..............	$ 80	$ 80
Direct labor per unit.................	120	120
Overhead per unit		
Variable overhead per unit	30	30
Fixed overhead per unit*	70	—
Total production cost per unit	$300	$230

* Fixed overhead per unit = $14,000,000 ÷ 200,000 units = $70 per unit.

1. Absorption costing income statement for 2010.

NAVAROLI COMPANY
Income Statement
For Year Ended December 31, 2010

Sales (140,000 × $600)	$84,000,000
Cost of goods sold (140,000 × $300)	42,000,000
Gross margin	42,000,000
Selling and administrative expenses ($1,400,000 + $8,000,000)	9,400,000
Net income	$32,600,000

2. Variable costing income statement for 2010.

NAVAROLI COMPANY
Income Statement (Contribution Format)
For Year Ended December 31, 2010

Sales (140,000 × $600)		$84,000,000
Variable expenses		
Variable production costs (140,000 × $230)	$32,200,000	
Variable selling and administrative costs.............	1,400,000	33,600,000
Contribution margin...............................		50,400,000
Fixed expenses		
Fixed overhead	14,000,000	
Fixed selling and administrative	8,000,000	22,000,000
Net income......................................		$28,400,000

3. Income under absorption costing is $4,200,000 more than that under variable costing even though sales are identical for each. This difference is due to the different treatment of fixed overhead cost. Under variable costing, the entire $14,000,000 of fixed overhead is expensed on the 2010 income statement. However, under absorption costing, $70 of fixed overhead cost is allocated to each of the 200,000 units produced. Since there were 60,000 units unsold at year-end, $4,200,000 (60,000 units × $70 per unit) of fixed overhead cost allocated to these units will be carried on its balance sheet in ending inventory. Consequently, reported income under absorption costing is $4,200,000 higher than variable costing income for the current period.

Before the income statement for 2011 is prepared, unit costs are computed under the two costing methods as follows.

	Absorption Costing	Variable Costing
Direct materials per unit	$ 80	$ 80
Direct labor per unit	120	120
Overhead per unit		
Variable overhead per unit	30	30
Fixed overhead per unit*	175	
Total production cost per unit	$405	$230

* Fixed overhead per unit = $14,000,000/80,000 units = $175 per unit.

4. Absorption costing income statement for 2011.

NAVAROLI COMPANY
Income Statement
For Year Ended December 31, 2011

Sales (140,000 × $600)		$84,000,000
Cost of goods sold		
From beginning inventory (60,000 × $300)	$18,000,000	
Produced during the year (80,000 × $405)	32,400,000	50,400,000
Gross margin		33,600,000
Selling and administrative expenses ($1,400,000 + $8,000,000)		9,400,000
Net income		$24,200,000

5. Variable costing income statement for 2011.

NAVAROLI COMPANY
Income Statement (Contribution Format)
For Year Ended December 31, 2011

Sales (140,000 × $600)		$84,000,000
Variable expenses		
Variable production costs (140,000 × $230)	$32,200,000	
Variable selling and administrative costs	1,400,000	33,600,000
Contribution margin		50,400,000
Fixed expenses		
Fixed overhead	14,000,000	
Fixed selling and administrative	8,000,000	22,000,000
Net income		$28,400,000

6. Conversion of variable costing income to absorption costing income.

	2010	2011
Variable costing income	$28,400,000	$28,400,000
Add: Fixed overhead cost deferred in ending inventory (60,000 × $70)	4,200,000	0
Less: Fixed overhead cost recognized from beginning inventory (60,000 × $70)	0	(4,200,000)
Absorption costing income	$32,600,000	$24,200,000

Summary

C1 **Describe how absorption costing can result in over-production.** Under absorption costing, fixed overhead costs are allocated to all units including both units sold and units in ending inventory. Consequently, expenses associated with the fixed overhead allocated to ending inventory are deferred to a future period. As a result, the larger ending inventory is, the more overhead cost is deferred to the future, and the greater current period income is.

C2 **Explain the role of variable costing in pricing special orders.** Over the short run, fixed production costs such as cost of maintaining plant capacity do not change with changes in production levels. When there is excess capacity, increases in production levels would only increase variable costs. Thus, managers should accept special orders as long as the order price is greater than the variable cost. This is because accepting the special order would increase only variable costs.

A1 **Compute and interpret break-even volume in units.** Break-even volume in units is defined as total fixed costs divided by contribution margin per unit. The result gives managers a unit goal to achieve breakeven; if the goal is surpassed, the company earns income.

P1 **Compute unit cost under both absorption and variable costing.** Absorption cost per unit includes direct materials, direct labor, and *all* overhead, whereas variable cost per unit includes direct materials, direct labor, and only *variable* overhead.

P2 **Prepare and analyze an income statement using absorption costing and using variable costing.** The variable costing income statement differs from the absorption costing income statement in that it classifies expenses based on cost behavior rather than function. Instead of gross margin, the variable costing income statement shows contribution margin. This contribution margin format focuses attention on the relation between costs and sales that is not evident from the absorption costing format. Under absorption costing, some fixed overhead cost is allocated to ending inventory and is carried on the balance sheet to the next period. However, all fixed costs are expensed in the period incurred under variable costing. Consequently, absorption costing income is generally greater than variable costing income if units produced exceed units sold, and conversely.

P3 **Prepare a contribution margin report.** Under variable costing, the total variable costs are first deducted from sales to arrive at contribution margin. Variable costs and contribution margin are also shown as ratios (after dividing by dollar sales).

P4 **Convert income under variable costing to the absorption cost basis.** Variable costing income can be adjusted to absorption costing income by adding the fixed cost allocated to ending inventory and subtracting the fixed cost previously allocated to beginning inventory.

Guidance Answers to Decision Ethics and Decision Maker

Production Manager Under absorption costing, fixed production costs are spread over all units produced. Thus, fixed cost for each unit would be lower if more units are produced because the fixed cost is spread over more units. This means the company can increase income by producing excess units even if sales remain constant. With sales lagging, producing excess inventory leads to increased financing cost and inventory obsolescence. Also, producing excess inventory to meet income levels for bonuses harms company owners and is unethical. You must discuss this with the appropriate managers.

Internal Auditor If manager bonuses are tied to income, they would have incentives to increase income for personal gain. If absorption costing is used to determine income, management can reduce current period expenses (and raise income) with over-production, which shifts fixed production costs to future periods. This decision fails to consider whether there is a viable market for all units that are produced. If there is not, an auditor can conclude that the inventory does not have "future economic value" and pressure management to write it off. Such a write-off reduces income by the cost of the excess inventory.

Guidance Answers to Quick Checks

1. a, b, c, and d; Direct materials, direct labor, variable overhead, and fixed overhead.
2. a, b, and c; Direct materials, direct labor, and variable overhead.
3. c; see Exhibit 19.6
4. a; see Exhibit 19.8
5. This is because only the variable cost will be avoided if a special order is rejected, as fixed cost does not change with changes to short-run sales. This means a company is better off taking an order provided the order price exceeds variable cost.

6. Variable costs and fixed costs are typically influenced by decisions at different managerial levels. Since reports under variable costing separate variable costs from fixed costs, variable costing makes it easier to identify and control these cost elements.
7. Variable costing is not accepted for external reporting and income tax purposes—only absorption costing is acceptable for those purposes.

Key Terms   mhhe.com/wildFINMAN4e

Absorption costing (also called full costing) (p. 804)

Contribution format (p. 814)

Contribution margin income statement (p. 806)

Contribution margin report (p. 807)

Controllable costs (p. 814)

Fixed overhead cost deferred in inventory (p. 811)

Fixed overhead cost recognized from inventory (p. 811)

Uncontrollable costs (p. 814)

Variable costing (also called direct or marginal costing) (p. 804)

Multiple Choice Quiz   Answers on p. 833   mhhe.com/wildFINMAN4e

Additional Quiz Questions are available at the book's Website.

Answer questions 1 and 2 using the following company data.

Units produced..........................	1,000
Variable costs	
Direct materials	$3 per unit
Direct labor	$5 per unit
Variable overhead	$3 per unit
Variable selling and administrative	$1 per unit
Fixed overhead........................	$3,000
Fixed selling and administrative	$1,000

1. Product cost per unit under absorption costing is:
   a. $11
   b. $12
   c. $14
   d. $15
   e. $16

2. Product cost per unit under variable costing is:
   a. $11
   b. $12
   c. $14
   d. $15
   e. $16

3. Under variable costing, which costs are included in product cost?
   a. All variable product costs, including direct materials, direct labor, and variable overhead.
   b. All variable and fixed allocations of product costs, including direct materials, direct labor, and both variable and fixed overhead.
   c. All variable product costs except for variable overhead.
   d. All variable and fixed allocations of product costs, except for both variable and fixed overhead.

4. The difference between unit product cost under absorption costing as compared to that under variable costing is:
   a. Direct materials and direct labor.
   b. Fixed and variable portions of overhead.
   c. Fixed overhead only.
   d. Variable overhead only.

5. When production exceeds sales, which of the following is true?
   a. No change occurs to inventories for either absorption costing or variable costing methods.
   b. Use of absorption costing produces a higher net income than the use of variable costing.
   c. Use of absorption costing produces a lower net income than the use of variable costing.
   d. Use of absorption costing causes inventory value to decrease more than it would through the use of variable costing.

[i] Icon denotes assignments that involve decision making.

Discussion Questions

1. What costs are normally included as part of product costs under the method of absorption costing?

2. What costs are normally included as part of product costs under the method of variable costing?

3. Describe how the following items are computed: *a.* Gross margin, and *b.* Contribution margin

4. [i] When units produced exceed units sold for a reporting period, would income under variable costing be greater than, equal to, or less than income under absorption costing? Explain.

5. [i] Describe how use of absorption costing in determining income can lead to over-production and a buildup of inventory. Explain how variable costing can avoid this same problem.

6. [i] How can absorption costing lead to incorrect short-run pricing decisions?

7. What conditions must exist to achieve accurate short-run pricing decisions using variable costing?

8. [i] Describe the usefulness of variable costing for controlling company costs.

9. [i] Explain how contribution margin analysis is useful for managerial decisions and performance evaluations.

10. What are the major limitations of variable costing?

11. How can variable costing income statements be converted to absorption costing?

12. [i] Nokia's managers rely on reports of variable costs. How can variable costing reports prepared using the contribution margin format help managers in computing break-even volume in units?   **NOKIA**

13. 🔒 How can **Palm** use variable costing to help better understand its operations and to make better pricing decisions?   **Palm**   is a one-time order, which will not require any additional capacity or fixed costs. What should Apple consider when determining a selling price for these iPads?

14. 🔒 Assume that **Apple** has received a special order from a retailer for 1,000 specially outfitted iPads. This   **Apple**

Under absorption costing a company had the following per unit costs when 10,000 units were produced.

Direct labor	$ 2
Direct material	3
Variable overhead	4
Total variable cost	9
Fixed overhead ($50,000/10,000 units)	5
Total production cost per unit	$14

QUICK STUDY

QS 19-1
Absorption costing and over-production

C1

Required

1. Compute the company's total production cost per unit if 25,000 units had been produced.
2. Why might a manager of a company using absorption costing produce more units than can currently be sold?

Rajeev Company reports the following information regarding its production costs. Compute its production cost per unit under absorption costing.

Direct materials.	$10 per unit
Direct labor.	$20 per unit
Overhead costs for the year	
Variable overhead	$10 per unit
Fixed overhead	$160,000
Units produced	20,000 units

QS 19-2
Computing unit cost under absorption costing

P1

Refer to Rajeev Company's data in QS 19-2. Compute its production cost per unit under variable costing.

QS 19-3
Computing unit cost under variable costing   P1

AirTel Company sold 10,000 units of its product at a price of $80 per unit. Total variable cost is $50 per unit, consisting of $40 in variable production cost and $10 in variable selling and administrative cost. Compute the manufacturing (production) margin for the company under variable costing.

QS 19-4
Computing manufacturing margin   P3

Refer to the information for AirTel Company in QS 19-4. Compute the contribution margin.

QS 19-5
Computing contribution margin

P3

Slams Inc., a manufacturer of tennis rackets, began operations this year. The company produced 6,000 rackets and sold 4,900. Each racket was sold at a price of $90. Fixed overhead costs are $78,000 and fixed selling and administrative costs are $65,200. The company also reports the following per unit costs for the year:

Variable production costs	$25.00
Variable selling and administrative expenses.	2.00

Prepare an income statement under absorption costing.

QS 19-6
Absorption costing income statement

P2

Refer to information in QS 19-6. Prepare an income statement under variable costing.

QS 19-7
Variable costing income statement   P2

QS 19-8

Production level, absorption costing, and gross margin

P3

Tramor Company reports the following cost data for its single product. The company regularly sells 20,000 units of its product at a price of $80 per unit. If Tramor doubles its production to 40,000 units while sales remain at the current 20,000 unit level, by how much would the company's gross margin increase or decrease under absorption costing?

Direct materials	$10 per unit
Direct labor	$12 per unit
Overhead costs for the year	
Variable overhead	$3 per unit
Fixed overhead per year	$40,000
Normal production level (in units)	20,000 units

QS 19-9

Production level, variable costing, gross margin   **P2 P3**

Refer to the information about Tramor Company in QS 19-8. Would the answer to the question in QS 19-8 change if the company uses variable costing? Explain.

QS 19-10

Break-even volume in units   **A1**

Assume a company sells a given product for $85 per unit. How many units must be sold to break even if variable selling costs are $27 per unit, variable production costs are $23 per unit, and total fixed costs are $700,000?

QS 19-11

Special order pricing

C2

Xu Company produces a product that sells for $84 per unit. A customer contacts Xu and offers to purchase 2,000 units of its product at a price of $68 per unit. Variable production costs with this order would be $30 per unit, and variable selling expenses would be $18 per unit. Assuming that this special order would not require any additional fixed costs, and that Xu has sufficient capacity to produce the product without affecting regular sales, explain to Xu's management why it might be a good decision to accept this special order.

QS 19-12

Converting variable costing income to absorption costing

P4

Aivars Company reports the following variable costing income statement for its single product. This company's sales totaled 50,000 units, but its production was 80,000 units. It had no beginning finished goods inventory for the current period.

AIVARS COMPANY	
Income Statement (Variable Costing)	
Sales (50,000 units × $60 per unit)	$3,000,000
Variable expenses	
Variable manufacturing expense (50,000 units × $28 per unit)	1,400,000
Variable selling and admin. expense (50,000 units × $5 per unit)	250,000
Total variable expenses	1,650,000
Contribution margin	1,350,000
Fixed expenses	
Fixed overhead	320,000
Fixed selling and administrative expense	160,000
Total fixed expenses	480,000
Net income	$ 870,000

1. Convert this company's variable costing income statement to an absorption costing income statement.

2. Explain the difference in income between the variable costing and absorption costing income statement.

QS 19-13

Converting variable costing income to absorption costing income   **P4**

Techmore had net income of $250,000 based on variable costing. Beginning and ending inventories were 50,000 units and 48,000 units, respectively. Assume the fixed overhead per unit was $0.75 for both the beginning and ending inventory. What is net income under absorption costing?

QS 19-14

Converting variable costing income to absorption costing income   **P4**

Singh Company had net income of $772,200 based on variable costing. Beginning and ending inventories were 7,800 units and 5,200 units, respectively. Assume the fixed overhead per unit was $3.00 for both the beginning and ending inventory. What is net income under absorption costing?

 connect

Adams Company, a manufacturer of in-home decorative fountains, began operations on September 1 of the current year. Its cost and sales information for this year follows.

EXERCISES

Exercise 19-1
Income reporting under absorption costing and variable costing

P2

Production costs	
Direct materials...................	$40 per unit
Direct labor	$60 per unit
Overhead costs for the year	
Variable overhead................	$3,000,000
Fixed overhead	$7,000,000
Nonproduction costs for the year	
Variable selling and administrative.........	$ 770,000
Fixed selling and administrative..........	$4,250,000
Production and sales for the year	
Units produced	100,000 units
Units sold.....................	70,000 units
Sales price per unit	$350 per unit

1. Prepare an income statement for the company using absorption costing.
2. Prepare an income statement for the company using variable costing.
3. Under what circumstance(s) is reported income identical under both absorption costing and variable costing?

Check   (1) Absorption costing income, $5,480,000; (2) Variable costing income, $3,380,000

Duo Company reports the following information for the current year, which is its first year of operations.

Exercise 19-2
Computing unit and inventory costs under absorption costing and variable costing

P1

Direct materials............................	$15 per unit
Direct labor	$16 per unit
Overhead costs for the year	
Variable overhead.........................	$ 80,000 per year
Fixed overhead	$160,000 per year
Units produced this year.....................	20,000 units
Units sold this year.........................	14,000 units
Ending finished goods inventory in units.........	6,000 units

1. Compute the cost per unit of finished goods using absorption costing.
2. Compute the cost per unit of finished goods using variable costing.
3. Determine the cost of ending finished goods inventory using absorption costing.
4. Determine the cost of ending finished goods inventory using variable costing.

Check   (1) Absorption cost per unit, $43; (2) Variable cost per unit, $35

Kenai Kayaking, a manufacturer of kayaks, began operations this year. During this first year, the company produced 1,050 kayaks and sold 800. At the current year-end, the company reported the following income statement information using absorption costing.

Exercise 19-3
Converting absorption costing income to variable costing income

P2 P4

Sales (800 × $1,050).....................	$840,000
Cost of goods sold (800 × $500)	400,000
Gross margin	440,000
Selling and administrative expenses	230,000
Net income	$210,000

Additional Information

a. Production cost per kayak totals $500, which consists of $400 in variable production cost and $100 in fixed production cost—the latter amount is based on $105,000 of fixed production costs allocated to the 1,050 kayaks produced.
b. The $230,000 in selling and administrative expense consists of $75,000 that is variable and $155,000 that is fixed.

Required

1. Prepare an income statement for the current year under variable costing.
2. Explain the difference in income between the variable costing and absorption costing income statement.

Exercise 19-4
Income reporting under absorption costing and variable costing

P2 P4

Woodson Company, a producer of solid oak tables, reports the following data from its current year operations, which is its second year of business.

Sales price per unit	$320 per unit
Units produced this year	115,000 units
Units sold this year	118,000 units
Units in beginning-year inventory	3,000 units
Beginning inventory costs	
Variable (3,000 units × $135)	$405,000
Fixed (3,000 units × $80)	240,000
Total	$645,000
Production costs this year	
Direct materials.......................	$40 per unit
Direct labor	$62 per unit
Overhead costs this year	
Variable overhead.....................	$3,220,000
Fixed overhead	$7,400,000
Nonproduction costs this year	
Variable selling and administrative	$1,416,000
Fixed selling and administrative	4,600,000

1. Prepare the current year income statement for the company using absorption costing.
2. Prepare the current year income statement for the company using variable costing.
3. Explain any difference between the two income numbers under the two costing methods in parts 1 and 2.

Exercise 19-5
Break-even volume in units

A1

Lor Company's single product sells at a price of $108 per unit. Cost data for its single product follows. Compute this company's break-even volume in units.

Direct materials........................	$20 per unit
Direct labor	$28 per unit
Overhead costs	
Variable overhead	$ 6 per unit
Fixed overhead per year	$160,000 per year
Selling and administrative expenses	
Variable.............................	$ 18 per unit
Fixed................................	$200,000 per year

Exercise 19-6
Converting variable costing income to absorption costing income P2 P4

Lyon Furnaces prepares the income statement under variable costing for its managerial reports, and it prepares the income statement under absorption costing for external reporting. For its first month of operations, 375 furnaces were produced and 225 were sold; this left 150 furnaces in ending inventory. The income statement information under variable costing follows.

Sales (225 × $1,600)..	$360,000
Variable production cost (225 × $625)	140,625
Variable selling and administrative expenses (225 × $65)	14,625
Contribution margin	204,750
Fixed overhead cost	56,250
Fixed selling and administrative expense	75,000
Net income	$ 73,500

1. Prepare this company's income statement for its first month of operations under absorption costing.
2. Explain the difference in income between the variable costing and absorption costing income statement.

Blue Sky Company reports the following costing data on its product for its first year of operations. During this first year, the company produced 44,000 units and sold 36,000 units at a price of $140 per unit.

Production costs	
Direct materials per unit	$60
Direct labor per unit	$22
Variable overhead per unit	$8
Fixed overhead for the year	$528,000
Selling and administrative cost	
Variable selling and administrative cost per unit	$11
Fixed selling and administrative cost per year	$105,000

Exercise 19-7
Unit costs and income statement under absorption costing and variable costing
P1 P2

1. Assume that this company uses absorption costing.

    a. Determine its unit product cost.

    b. Prepare its income statement for the year under absorption costing.

2. Assume that this company uses variable costing.

    a. Determine its unit product cost.

    b. Prepare its income statement for the year under variable costing.

Check   (1a) Absorption cost per unit, $102

(2a) Variable cost per unit, $90

Mountain Airlines provides charter airplane services. In October this year, the company was operating at 60% of its capacity when it received a bid from the local community college. The college was organizing a Washington, D.C., trip for its international student group. The college only budgeted $30,000 for round-trip airfare. Mountain Airlines normally charges between $50,000 and $60,000 for such service given the number of travelers. Mountain determined its cost for the roundtrip flight to Washington to be $44,000, which consists of the following:

Exercise 19-8
Variable costing for services
C2

Variable cost	$15,000
Fixed cost	29,000
Total cost	$44,000

Although the manager at Mountain supports the college's educational efforts, she could not justify accepting the $30,000 bid for the trip given the projected $14,000 loss. Still, she decides to consult with you, an independent financial consultant. Do you believe the airline should accept the bid from the college? Prepare a memorandum, with supporting computations, explaining why or why not.

Polarix is a retailer of ATVs (all terrain vehicles) and accessories. An income statement for its Consumer ATV Department for the current year follows. ATVs sell, on average, for $3,800. Variable selling expenses are $270 each. The remaining selling expenses are fixed. Administrative expenses are 40% variable and 60% fixed. The company does not manufacture its own ATVs; it purchases them from a supplier for $1,830 each.

Exercise 19-9
Contribution margin format income statement   **P3**

POLARIX		
Income Statement—Consumer ATV Department		
For Year Ended December 21, 2011		
Sales		$646,000
Cost of goods sold		311,100
Gross margin		334,900
Operating expenses		
Selling expenses	$135,000	
Administrative expenses	59,500	194,500
Net income		$140,400

Required

1. Prepare an income statement for this current year using the contribution margin format.

2. For each ATV sold during this year, what is the contribution toward covering fixed expenses and earning income?

Check   (2) $1,560

Exercise 19-10
Variable costing and contribution margin statement
P3

Down Jackets has three types of costs: jacket cost, factory rent cost, and utilities cost. This company sells its jackets for $16.50 each. Management has prepared the following estimated cost information for next month under two different sales levels.

	At 10,000 Jackets	At 12,000 Jackets
Jacket cost	$80,000	$96,000
Rent cost	6,000	6,000
Utilities cost	8,400	9,900

Required

Check   (2) Contribution margin, $93,000

1. Compute what the company should expect for total variable cost if 11,000 jackets are sold next month. (*Hint:* Use the high-low method to separate jacket and utilities costs into their variable and fixed components.)

2. Prepare its contribution margin statement for a monthly sales volume of 12,000 jackets.

Exercise 19-11
Absorption costing and over-production
C1

Rourke Inc. reports the following annual cost data for its single product.

Normal production and sales level	60,000 units
Sales price	$56.00 per unit
Direct materials.......................	$9.00 per unit
Direct labor	$6.50 per unit
Variable overhead	$11.00 per unit
Fixed overhead	$720,000 in total

If Rourke increases its production to 80,000 units, while sales remain at the current 60,000 unit level, by how much would the company's gross margin increase or decrease under absorption costing? Assume the company has idle capacity to double current production.

Exercise 19-12
Contribution margin
P3

A recent income statement for **Volkswagen** reports the following (in € millions).

Sales	€105,187
Cost of sales	91,608
Selling and administrative expenses	13,276

Assume 70 percent of the cost of sales and 70 percent of the selling and administrative costs are variable costs, and the remaining 30 percent of each is fixed. Round all calculations involving percentages to the nearest whole euro (€).

Required

Compute the (1) gross margin, (2) contribution margin, and (3) manufacturing margin. Express your answers in € millions.

PROBLEM SET A

Torres Company began operations this year. During this first year, the company produced 100,000 units and sold 80,000 units. The absorption costing income statement for its first year of operations follows.

Problem 19-1A
Variable costing income statement and conversion to absorption costing income
P2   P4

Sales (80,000 units × $50 per unit)		$4,000,000
Cost of goods sold		
Beginning inventory	$ 0	
Cost of goods manufactured (100,000 units × $30 per unit)	3,000,000	
Cost of goods available for sale..................................	3,000,000	
Ending inventory (20,000 × $30)	600,000	
Cost of goods sold..		2,400,000
Gross margin		1,600,000
Selling and administrative expenses		530,000
Net income		$1,070,000

Additional Information

a. Selling and administrative expenses consist of $350,000 in annual fixed expenses and $2.25 per unit in variable selling and administrative expenses.

b. The company's product cost of $30 per unit is computed as follows.

Direct materials................................	$5 per unit
Direct labor......................................	$14 per unit
Variable overhead	$2 per unit
Fixed overhead ($900,000/100,000 units)	$9 per unit

Required

1. Prepare an income statement for the company under variable costing.

2. Explain any difference between the income under variable costing (from part 1) and the income reported above.

Check (1) Variable costing income, $890,000

Powell Company produces a single product. Its income statement under absorption costing for its first two years of operation follow.

Problem 19-2A
Variable costing income statement and conversion to absorption costing income (two consecutive years)

P2 P4

	2010	2011
Sales ($46 per unit)	$920,000	$1,840,000
Cost of goods sold ($31 per unit)	620,000	1,240,000
Gross margin..........................	300,000	600,000
Selling and administrative expenses	290,000	340,000
Net income...........................	$ 10,000	$ 260,000

Additional Information

a. Sales and production data for these first two years follow.

	2010	2011
Units produced	30,000	30,000
Units sold	20,000	40,000

b. Variable cost per unit and total fixed costs are unchanged during 2010 and 2011. The company's $31 per unit product cost consists of the following.

Direct materials............................	$ 5
Direct labor...............................	9
Variable overhead	7
Fixed overhead ($300,000/30,000 units)	10
Total product cost per unit..................	$31

c. Selling and administrative expenses consist of the following.

	2010	2011
Variable selling and administrative ($2.5 per unit)	$ 50,000	$100,000
Fixed selling and administrative.......................	240,000	240,000
Total selling and administrative	$290,000	$340,000

Required

1. Prepare income statements for the company for each of its first two years under variable costing.

2. Explain any difference between the absorption costing income and the variable costing income for these two years.

Check (1) 2010 net loss, $(90,000)

Problem 19-3A

CVP analysis, absorption costing, and variable costing

A1

Refer to information about Powell Company in Problem 19-2A. In the company's planning documents, Kyra Powell, the company's president, reports that the break-even volume (in units) for the company is 24,000 units. This break-even point is computed as follows.

$$\text{Break-even volume} = \frac{\text{Total fixed cost}}{\text{Contribution margin per unit}} = \frac{\$540,000}{\$22.50} = 24,000 \text{ units}$$

Total fixed cost consists of $300,000 in fixed production cost and $240,000 in fixed selling and administrative expenses. The contribution margin per unit of $22.50 is computed by deducting the $23.50 variable cost per unit (which consists of $21 in variable production cost and $2.50 in variable selling and administrative cost) from the $46 sales price per unit. In 2010, the company sold 20,000 units, which was below break-even, and Kyra was concerned that the company's income statement would show a net loss. To her surprise, the company's 2010 income statement revealed a net income of $10,000 as shown in Problem 19-2A.

Required

Prepare a one-half-page memorandum to the president explaining how the company could report net income when it sold less than its break-even volume in units.

Problem 19-4A

Variable cost analysis for a services company

C2

Winter Garden is a luxury hotel with 150 suites. Its regular suite rate is $250 per night per suite. The hotel's cost per night is $140 per suite and consists of the following.

Variable direct labor and materials cost	$ 30
Fixed cost [($6,022,500/150 suites) ÷ 365 days]..........	110
Total cost per night per suite	$140

The hotel manager received an offer to hold the local Bikers' Club annual meeting at the hotel in March, which is the hotel's low season with an occupancy rate of under 50%. The Bikers' Club would reserve 50 suites for three nights if the hotel could offer a 50% discount, or a rate of $125 per night. The hotel manager is inclined to reject the offer because the cost per suite per night is $140. The manager believes that if 50 suites are offered at the rate of $125 per night for three nights, the hotel would lose $2,250, computed as ($125 − $140) × 50 suites × 3 nights.

Required

Check $14,250 contribution margin

Prepare an analysis of this offer for the hotel manager. Explain (with supporting computations) whether the offer from the Bikers' Club should be accepted or rejected.

Problem 19-5A

Income reporting, absorption costing, and managerial ethics

C1 P2

Safety Chemical produces and sells an ice-melting granular used on roadways and sidewalks in winter. It annually produces and sells about 100 tons of its granular. In its nine-year history, the company has never reported a net loss. However, because of this year's unusually mild winter, projected demand for its product is only 60 tons. Based on its predicted production and sales of 60 tons, the company projects the following income statement (under absorption costing).

Sales (60 tons at $21,000 per ton)	$1,260,000
Cost of goods sold (60 tons at $16,000 per ton)	960,000
Gross margin	300,000
Selling and administrative expenses	318,600
Net loss	$ (18,600)

Its product cost information follows and consists mainly of fixed cost because of its automated production process requiring expensive equipment.

Variable direct labor and material costs per ton	$ 3,500
Fixed cost per ton ($750,000 ÷ 60 tons)	12,500
Total product cost per ton	$16,000

Selling and administrative expenses consist of variable selling and administrative expenses of $310 per ton and fixed selling and administrative expenses of $300,000 per year. The company's president is concerned about the adverse reaction from its creditors and shareholders if the projected net loss is reported. The operations manager mentions that since the company has large storage capacity, it can report a net income by keeping its production at the usual 100-ton level even though it expects to sell only 60 tons. The president was puzzled by the suggestion that the company can report income by producing more without increasing sales.

Required

1. Can the company report a net income by increasing production to 100 tons and storing the excess production in inventory? Your explanation should include an income statement (using absorption costing) based on production of 100 tons and sales of 60 tons.

2. Should the company produce 100 tons given that projected demand is 60 tons? Explain, and also refer to any ethical implications of such a managerial decision.

Check (1) $281,400 absorption costing income

Mitchell Company began operations this year. During this first year, the company produced 300,000 units and sold 250,000 units. Its income statement under absorption costing for its first year of operations follows.

PROBLEM SET B

Problem 19-1B
Variable costing income statement and conversion to absorption costing income

P2 P4

Sales (250,000 units × $18 per unit)		$4,500,000
Cost of goods sold		
Beginning inventory	$ 0	
Cost of goods manufactured (300,000 units × $7.50 per unit)	2,250,000	
Cost of goods available for sale	2,250,000	
Ending inventory (50,000 × $7.50)	375,000	
Cost of goods sold		1,875,000
Gross margin		2,625,000
Selling and administrative expenses		2,200,000
Net income		$ 425,000

Additional Information

a. Selling and administrative expenses consist of $1,200,000 in annual fixed expenses and $4 per unit in variable selling and administrative expenses.

b. The company's product cost of $7.50 per unit is computed as follows.

Direct materials	$2.00 per unit
Direct labor	$2.40 per unit
Variable overhead	$1.60 per unit
Fixed overhead ($450,000/300,000 units)	$1.50 per unit

Required

1. Prepare the company's income statement under variable costing.

2. Explain any difference between the company's income under variable costing (from part 1) and the income reported above.

Check (1) Variable costing income, $350,000

Flores Company produces a single product. Its income statement under absorption costing for its first two years of operation follow.

Problem 19-2B
Variable costing income statement and conversion to absorption costing income (two consecutive years)

P2 P4

	2010	2011
Sales ($35 per unit)	$1,925,000	$2,275,000
Cost of goods sold ($26 per unit)	1,430,000	1,690,000
Gross margin	495,000	585,000
Selling and administrative expenses	465,000	495,000
Net income	$ 30,000	$ 90,000

Additional Information

a. Sales and production data for these first two years follow.

	2010	2011
Units produced	60,000	60,000
Units sold.............	55,000	65,000

b. Its variable cost per unit and total fixed costs are unchanged during 2010 and 2011. Its $26 per unit product cost consists of the following.

Direct materials............................	$ 4
Direct labor	6
Variable overhead	8
Fixed overhead ($480,000/60,000 units)........	8
Total product cost per unit	$26

c. Its selling and administrative expenses consist of the following.

	2010	2011
Variable selling and administrative ($3 per unit)..........	$165,000	$195,000
Fixed selling and administrative.......................	300,000	300,000
Total selling and administrative	$465,000	$495,000

Required

Check (1) 2010 net loss, $(10,000)

1. Prepare this company's income statements under variable costing for each of its first two years.

2. Explain any difference between the absorption costing income and the variable costing income for these two years.

Problem 19-3B
CVP analysis, absorption costing, and variable costing

A1

Refer to information about Flores Company in Problem 19-2B. In the company's planning documents, Roberto Flores, the company president, reports that the company's break-even volume in unit sales is 55,715 units. This break-even point is computed as follows.

$$\text{Break-even volume} = \frac{\text{Total fixed cost}}{\text{Contribution margin per unit}} = \frac{\$780,000}{\$14} = 55,715 \text{ units (rounded)}$$

Total fixed cost consists of $480,000 in fixed production cost and $300,000 in fixed selling and administrative expenses. The contribution margin per unit of $14 is computed by deducting the $21 variable cost per unit (which consists of $18 in variable production cost and $3 in variable selling and administrative cost) from the $35 sales price per unit. In 2010, it sold 55,000 units, which was below break-even, and Roberto Flores was concerned that the company's income statement would show a net loss. To his surprise, the company's 2010 income statement revealed a net income of $30,000 as shown in Problem 19-2B.

Required

Prepare a one-half-page memorandum to the president explaining how the company could report net income when it sold less than its break-even volume in units.

Problem 19-4B
Variable cost analysis for a services company

C2

Elegant Plaza Hotel is a luxury hotel with 400 rooms. Its regular room rate is $300 per night per room. The hotel's cost is $165 per night per room and consists of the following.

Variable direct labor and materials cost	$ 40
Fixed cost [($18,250,000/400 rooms) ÷ 365 days].........	125
Total cost per night per room........................	$165

The hotel manager received an offer to hold the Junior States of America (JSA) convention at the hotel in February, which is the hotel's low season with an occupancy rate of under 45%. JSA would reserve 100 rooms for four nights if the hotel could offer a 50% discount, or a rate of $150 per night. The hotel manager is inclined to reject the offer because the cost per room per night is $165. The manager believes that if 100 rooms are offered at the rate of $150 per night for four nights, the hotel would lose $6,000, computed as ($150 − $165) × 100 rooms × 4 nights.

Required

Prepare an analysis of this offer for the hotel manager. Explain (with supporting computations) whether the offer from JSA should be accepted or rejected.

Check   Contribution margin, $44,000

Proto Chemical produces and sells an ice-melting granular used on roadways and sidewalks in winter. The company annually produces and sells about 300,000 lbs of its granular. In its ten-year history, the company has never reported a net loss. Because of this year's unusually mild winter, projected demand for its product is only 250,000 lbs. Based on its predicted production and sales of 250,000 lbs, the company projects the following income statement under absorption costing.

Problem 19-5B
Income reporting, absorption costing, and managerial ethics

C1 P2

Sales (250,000 lbs at $8 per lb.)	$ 2,000,000
Cost of goods sold (250,000 lbs at $6.80 per lb.)	1,700,000
Gross margin	300,000
Selling and administrative expenses	450,000
Net loss	$ (150,000)

Its product cost information follows and consists mainly of fixed production cost because of its automated production process requiring expensive equipment.

Variable direct labor and materials costs per lb.	$2.00
Fixed production cost per lb ($1,200,000/250,000 lbs.)	4.80
Total product cost per lb.	$6.80

The company's selling and administrative expenses are all fixed. The president is concerned about the adverse reaction from its creditors and shareholders if the projected net loss is reported. The controller suggests that since the company has large storage capacity, it can report a net income by keeping its production at the usual 300,000 lbs level even though it expects to sell only 250,000 lbs. The president was puzzled by the suggestion that the company can report a profit by producing more without increasing sales.

Required

1. Can the company report a net income by increasing production to 300,000 lbs and storing the excess production in inventory? Your explanation should include an income statement (using absorption costing) based on production of 300,000 lbs and sales of 250,000 lbs.

2. Should the company produce 300,000 lbs given that projected demand is 250,000 lbs? Explain, and also refer to any ethical implications of such a managerial decision.

Check   (1) $50,000 absorption income

(This serial problem began in Chapter 1 and continues through most of the book. If previous chapter segments were not completed, the serial problem can begin at this point. It is helpful, but not necessary, to use the Working Papers that accompany the book.)

SERIAL PROBLEM
Business Solutions
P2 P4

SP 19   Santana Rey expected sales of her line of computer workstation furniture to equal 300 workstations (at a sales price of $3,000) for 2012. The workstations' manufacturing costs include the following.

Direct materials	$800 per unit
Direct labor	$400 per unit
Variable overhead	$100 per unit
Fixed overhead	$24,000 per year

The selling expenses related to these workstations follow.

Variable selling expenses	$50 per unit
Fixed selling expenses	$4,000 per year

Santana is considering how many workstations to produce in 2012. She is confident that she will be able to sell any workstations in her 2012 ending inventory during 2013. However, Santana does not want to overproduce as she does not have sufficient storage space for many more workstations.

Required

1. Compute Business Solutions' absorption costing income assuming
   a. 300 workstations are produced.
   b. 320 workstations are produced.
2. Compute Business Solutions' variable costing income assuming
   a. 300 workstations are produced.
   b. 320 workstations are produced.
3. Explain to Santana any differences in the income figures determined in parts 1 and 2. How should Santana use the information from parts 1 and 2 to help make production decisions?

Beyond the Numbers

REPORTING IN ACTION

P2

RIM

BTN 19-1   Innovative technologies like **Research In Motion**'s Blackberry often require considerable customer service after the sale. Assume Research In Motion is considering starting a group called the Tech Team, designed to address customers' technology problems. The Tech Team would offer a wide variety of services, including repairing defective Blackberrys, containing virus outbreaks, removing spyware, and helping protect and back up important data.

Required

For Research In Motion to determine what services and products to offer through its Tech Team, would variable or absorption costing be a better approach to analyze those new services or products? Explain.

COMPARATIVE ANALYSIS

P2

RIM

Apple

BTN 19-2   To compete with **Apple**'s iTunes (**itunes.com**) music download store, assume **Research In Motion** is considering starting a similar download store.

Required

1. What are some of the costs that Research In Motion should consider when deciding whether to offer the music download service? Are those costs different from what Apple must consider when offering additional new iTunes or services? Explain.
2. Would variable or absorption costing be more useful to Research In Motion in analyzing whether its new service is profitable? Explain.

ETHICS CHALLENGE

P2

BTN 19-3   FDP Company produces a variety of home security products. Gary Price, the company's president, is concerned with the fourth quarter market demand for the company's products. Unless something is done in the last two months of the year, the company is likely to miss its earnings expectation of Wall Street analysts. Price still remembers when FDP's earnings were below analysts' expectation by two cents a share three years ago, and the company's share price fell 19% the day earnings were announced. In a recent meeting, Price told his top management that something must be done quickly. One proposal by the marketing vice president was to give a deep discount to the company's major customers to increase the company's sales in the fourth quarter. The company controller pointed out that while the discount could increase sales, it may not help the bottom line; to the contrary, it could lower income. The controller said, "Since we have enough storage capacity, we might simply increase our production in the fourth quarter to increase our reported profit."

Required

1. Gary Price is not sure how the increase in production without a corresponding increase in sales could help boost the company's income. Explain to Price how reported income varies with respect to production level.
2. Is there an ethical concern in this situation? If so, which parties are affected? Explain.

COMMUNICATING IN PRACTICE

A1

BTN 19-4   Mertz Chemical has three divisions. Its consumer product division faces strong competition from companies overseas. During its recent teleconference, Ryan Peterson, the consumer product division manager, reported that his division's sales for the current year were below its break-even point. However, when the division's annual reports were received, Billie Mertz, the company president, was surprised that the consumer product division actually reported a profit of $264,000. How could this be possible?

Required

Assume that you work in the corporate controller's office. Write a one-half-page memorandum to the president explaining how the division can report income even if its sales are below the break-even point.

BTN 19-5   This chapter discussed the variable costing method and how to use variable costing information to make various business decisions. We also can find several Websites on variable costing and its business applications.

Required

1. Review the Website of **Value Based Management** at **ValueBasedManagement.net**. Identify and print the site page on the topic of variable costing (**ValueBasedManagement.net/Methods_Variable_Costing.html**).
2. What other phrases are used in practice for *variable costing?*
3. According to this Website, what are the consequences of variable costing for profit calculation?

TAKING IT TO THE NET
P2

BTN 19-6   This chapter identified many decision contexts in which variable costing information is more relevant than absorption costing. However, absorption costing is still used by many companies and remains the only acceptable basis for external (and tax) reporting.

Required

Break into teams and identify at least one specific decision context in which absorption costing information is more relevant than variable costing. Be prepared to discuss your answers in class.

TEAMWORK IN ACTION
P4

BTN 19-7   **Samanta Shoes**, which was launched by entrepreneurs Samanta and Kelvin Joseph produces high-quality shoes in unique styles and limited quantities. Selling prices for a pair of Samanta shoes can range from $100 per pair to $350 per pair.

Required

1. Based on information in this chapter's opener, identify at least four examples of the types of costs that likely explain the wide range of shoe selling prices.
2. The founders of Samanta Shoes use variable costing in their business decisions. If Samanta Shoes used absorption costing, would you expect the company's income to be more, less than, or about the same as its income measured under variable costing? Explain.

ENTREPRENEURIAL DECISION
P4

BTN 19-8   Visit a local hotel and observe its daily operating activities. The costs associated with some of its activities are variable while others are fixed with respect to occupancy levels.

Required

1. List cost items that are likely variable for the hotel.
2. List cost items that are likely fixed for the hotel.
3. Compare the fixed cost items with variable cost items. Rank costs within each category based on your perception of which ones you believe are the larger.
4. Based on your observations and the answers to parts 1 through 3, explain why many hotels offer discounts as high as 50% or more during their low occupancy season.

HITTING THE ROAD
C2

BTN 19-9   Assume that **Nokia** (**Nokia.com**) is considering offering a service similar to **Apple**'s iTunes music download store. However, instead of developing the group internally, Nokia is considering buying a company that already offers such services.

Required

Would absorption or variable costing be most useful to Nokia in evaluating whether to acquire an existing business that provides services similar to the iTunes? Explain.

GLOBAL DECISION
P2

NOKIA

Apple

ANSWERS TO MULTIPLE CHOICE QUIZ

1. c; $14, computed as $3 + $5 + $3 + ($3,000/1,000 units).
2. a; $11, computed as $3 + $5 + $3 (consisting of all variable product costs).

3. a
4. c
5. b

20

Master Budgets and Performance Planning

A Look Back

Chapter 19 compared reports prepared under variable costing with those under absorption costing, and it explained how variable costing can improve managerial decisions.

A Look at This Chapter

This chapter explains the importance of budgeting and describes the master budget and its preparation. It also discusses the value of the master budget to the planning of future business activities.

A Look Ahead

Chapter 21 focuses on flexible budgets, standard costs, and variance reporting. It explains the usefulness of these procedures and reports for business decisions.

Learning Objectives

CONCEPTUAL

C1 Describe the importance and benefits of budgeting and the process of budget administration. (p. 836)

C2 Describe a master budget and the process of preparing it. (p. 840)

ANALYTICAL

A1 Analyze expense planning using activity-based budgeting. (p. 850)

LP20

PROCEDURAL

P1 Prepare each component of a master budget and link each to the budgeting process. (p. 842)

P2 Link both operating and capital expenditures budgets to budgeted financial statements. (p. 846)

P3 *Appendix 20A*—Prepare production and manufacturing budgets. (p. 856)

Not Grandma's Needlepoint

"This is incredible . . . people thought it was a foolish idea"
—AUSTIN BRANSON

Bethesda, MD—Peter Smathers Carter and Austin Branson's entrepreneurial adventure began with needlepoint belts they each received as gifts. Noting the interest the belts received, the duo began planning a company to manufacture cool hand-stitched belts. The result is **Smathers and Branson (SmathersAndBranson.com),** with annual sales now exceeding $2.5 million.

The company's products are best summed up as "not your grandmother's needlepoint." Belt designs include a string of banded beer cans, a "jolly roger" with skull and crossbones, and a martini-sipping pink elephant. As Austin explains, "we keep having random brainstorming sessions and adding good patterns." Yet their belts are more than just funky designs. Peter and Austin's belts are hand-stitched and use some of the best materials —the finest threads from Europe, full-grain leather tanned in Asia, and belt buckles from the United States.

Using top-quality materials and hand-stitching each belt rather than mass producing is not cheap, something the pair quickly realized in their budget planning process. Noting it takes about 40 to 50 hours to hand-stitch a single belt, Peter explains that "we calculated the materials and labor it cost our girlfriends to make the belts at around $300 per belt—more than the market would bear." The use of direct materials, direct labor, and factory overhead budgets led them to focus on reducing direct labor costs as essential. Now, the company employs almost 2,000 stitchers in Vietnam, enabling the duo to sell their handcrafted belts at prices the market will pay. Sales, production, and manufacturing budgets help Peter and Austin continue to plan their use of materials, labor, and overhead.

As Austin puts it, "our original plan was to be finance majors. But the belts seemed more fun and unique and different." Keeping it fun and profitable however requires attention to plans. As the company continues to expand into additional product lines—dog collars, key fobs, wallets, headbands, and flasks—master budgets and the budgeting process become even more important. Budgets help formalize business plans and goals, and help direct and monitor employees. Peter and Austin also use budgeted income statements to determine how changes in the costs of material, labor, or overhead, impact the bottom line.

While linking budgeted data to budgeted financial statements and using that information to control costs is important, both Peter and Austin stress the importance of having fun and a passion for what they do as keys to their success. Austin explains "we're having a great time and growing rapidly."

[Sources: *Smathers and Branson Website*, January 2011; *Inc.com*, 2009; *Golfbusinesswire.com*; *Thrillist.com*]

Management seeks to turn its strategies into action plans. These action plans include financial details that are compiled in a master budget. The budgeting process serves several purposes, including motivating employees and communicating with them. The budget process also helps coordinate a company's activities toward common goals and is useful in evaluating results and management performance. This chapter explains how to prepare a master budget and use it as a formal plan of a company's future activities. The ability to prepare this type of plan is of enormous help in starting and operating a company. Such planning gives managers a glimpse into the future, and it can help translate ideas into actions.

Master Budgets and Performance Planning

Budget Process
- Strategic budgeting
- Benchmarking budgets
- Budgeting and human behavior
- Budgeting as a management tool
- Budgeting communication

Budget Administration
- Budget committee
- Budget reporting
- Budget timing

Master Budget
- Master budget components
- Operating budgets
- Capital expenditures budget
- Financial budgets

BUDGET PROCESS

Strategic Budgeting

C1 Describe the importance and benefits of budgeting and the process of budget administration.

Most companies prepare long-term strategic plans spanning 5 to 10 years. They then fine-tune them in preparing medium-term and short-term plans. Strategic plans usually set a company's long-term direction. They provide a road map for the future about potential opportunities such as new products, markets, and investments. The strategic plan can be inexact, given its long-term focus. Medium- and short-term plans are more operational and translate strategic plans into actions. These action plans are fairly concrete and consist of defined objectives and goals.

Short-term financial plans are called *budgets* and typically cover a one-year period. A **budget** is a formal statement of a company's future plans. It is usually expressed in monetary terms because the economic or financial aspects of the business are the primary factors driving management's decisions. All managers should be involved in **budgeting,** the process of planning future business actions and expressing them as formal plans. Managers who plan carefully and formalize plans in a budgeting process increase the likelihood of both personal and company success. (Although most firms prepare annual budgets, it is not unusual for organizations to prepare three-year and five-year budgets that are revised at least annually.)

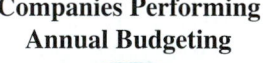

Companies Performing Annual Budgeting

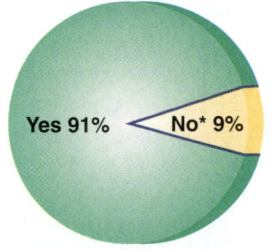

Yes 91% No* 9%

*Most of the 9% have eliminated annual budgeting in favor of rolling or continual budgeting.

The relevant focus of a budgetary analysis is the future. Management must focus on future transactions and events and the opportunities available. A focus on the future is important because the pressures of daily operating problems often divert management's attention and take precedence over planning. A good budgeting system counteracts this tendency by formalizing the planning process and demanding relevant input. Budgeting makes planning an explicit management responsibility.

Benchmarking Budgets

The control function requires management to evaluate (benchmark) business operations against some norm. Evaluation involves comparing actual results against one of two usual alternatives: (1) past performance or (2) expected performance.

An evaluation assists management in identifying problems and taking corrective actions if necessary. Evaluation using expected, or budgeted, performance is potentially superior to using past performance to decide whether actual results trigger a need for corrective actions. This is so because past performance fails to consider several changes that can affect current and future activities. Changes in economic conditions, shifts in competitive advantages within the industry, new product developments, increased or decreased advertising, and other factors reduce the usefulness of comparisons with past results. In hi-tech industries, for instance, increasing competition, technological advances, and other innovations often reduce the usefulness of performance comparisons across years.

Budgeted performance is computed after careful analysis and research that attempts to anticipate and adjust for changes in important company, industry, and economic factors. Therefore, budgets usually provide management an effective control and monitoring system.

Budgeting and Human Behavior

Budgeting provides standards for evaluating performance and can affect the attitudes of employees evaluated by them. It can be used to create a positive effect on employees' attitudes, but it can also create negative effects if not properly applied. Budgeted levels of performance, for instance, must be realistic to avoid discouraging employees. Personnel who will be evaluated should be consulted and involved in preparing the budget to increase their commitment to meeting it. Performance evaluations must allow the affected employees to explain the reasons for apparent performance deficiencies.

The budgeting process has three important guidelines: (1) Employees affected by a budget should be consulted when it is prepared (*participatory budgeting*), (2) goals reflected in a budget should be attainable, and (3) evaluations should be made carefully with opportunities to explain any failures. Budgeting can be a positive motivating force when these guidelines are followed. Budgeted performance levels can provide goals for employees to attain or even exceed as they carry out their responsibilities. This is especially important in organizations that consider the annual budget a "sacred" document.

Managers must also be aware of potential negative outcomes of budgeting. Under participatory budgeting, some employees might understate sales budgets and overstate expense budgets to allow them a cushion, or *budgetary slack,* to aid in meeting targets. For some businesses, pressure to meet budgeted results might lead employees to engage in unethical behavior or commit fraud. Finally, some employees might always spend their budgeted amounts, even on unnecessary items, to ensure their budgets aren't reduced for the next period.

Point: The practice of involving employees in the budgeting process is known as *participatory budgeting.*

Example: Assume a company's sales force receives a bonus when sales exceed the budgeted amount. How would this arrangement affect the participatory sales forecasts? *Answer:* Sales reps may understate their budgeted sales.

 **Decision Ethics**   Answer — p. 858

Budget Staffer   Your company's earnings for the current period will be far below the budgeted amount reported in the press. One of your superiors, who is aware of the upcoming earnings shortfall, has accepted a management position with a competitor. This superior is selling her shares of the company. What are your ethical concerns, if any? ∎

Budgeting as a Management Tool

An important management objective in large companies is to ensure that activities of all departments contribute to meeting the company's overall goals. This requires coordination. Budgeting helps to achieve this coordination.

We describe later in this chapter that a company's budget, or operating plan, is based on its objectives. This operating plan starts with the sales budget, which drives all other budgets including production, materials, labor, and overhead. The budgeting process coordinates the activities of these various departments to meet the company's overall goals.

Budgeting Communication

Managers of small companies can adequately explain business plans directly to employees through conversations and other informal communications. However, conversations can create uncertainty and confusion if not supported by clear documentation of the plans. A written budget is preferred and can inform employees in all types of organizations about management's plans. The budget can also communicate management's specific action plans for the employees in the budget period.

Decision Insight

Budgets Exposed   When companies go public and their securities trade on an organized stock exchange, management usually develops specific future plans and budgets. For this purpose, companies often develop detailed six- to twelve-month budgets and less-detailed budgets spanning two to five years. ■

BUDGET ADMINISTRATION

Budget Committee

The task of preparing a budget should not be the sole responsibility of any one department. Similarly, the budget should not be simply handed down as top management's final word. Instead, budget figures and budget estimates developed through a *bottom-up* process

usually are more useful. This includes, for instance, involving the sales department in preparing sales estimates. Likewise, the production department should have initial responsibility for preparing its own expense budget. Without active employee involvement in preparing budget figures, there is a risk these employees will feel that the numbers fail to reflect their special problems and needs.

Most budgets should be developed by a bottom-up process, but the budgeting system requires central guidance. This guidance is supplied by a budget committee of department heads and other executives responsible for seeing that budgeted amounts are realistic and coordinated. If a de-

Point: In a large company, developing a budget through a bottom-up process can involve hundreds of employees and take several weeks to finalize.

partment submits initial budget figures not reflecting efficient performance, the budget committee should return them with explanatory comments on how to improve them. Then the originating department must either adjust its proposals or explain why they are acceptable. Communication between the originating department and the budget committee should continue as needed to ensure that both parties accept the budget as reasonable, attainable, and desirable.

The concept of continuous improvement applies to budgeting as well as production. For example, one of the world's largest energy companies streamlined its monthly budget report from a one-inch-thick stack of monthly control reports to a tidy, two-page flash report on monthly earnings and key production statistics. The key to this efficiency gain was the integration of new budgeting and cost allocation processes with its strategic planning process. Its controller explained the new role of the finance department with respect to the budgetary control process as follows: "there's less of an attitude that finance's job is to control. People really have come to see that our job is to help attain business objectives."

Budget Reporting

The budget period usually coincides with the accounting period. Most companies prepare at least an annual budget, which reflects the objectives for the next year. To provide specific guidance, the annual budget usually is separated into quarterly or monthly budgets. These short-term budgets allow management to periodically evaluate performance and take needed corrective action.

Managers can compare actual results to budgeted amounts in a report such as that shown in Exhibit 20.1. This report shows actual amounts, budgeted amounts, and their differences. A difference is called a *variance*. Management examines variances, particularly large ones, to identify areas for improvement and corrective action.

EXHIBIT 20.1

Comparing Actual Performance with Budgeted Performance

ECCENTRIC MUSIC — Income Statement with Variances from Budget — For Month Ended April 30, 2011	Actual	Budget	Variance
Net sales	$60,500	$57,150	$+3,350
Cost of goods sold	41,350	39,100	+2,250
Gross profit	19,150	18,050	+1,100
Operating expenses			
Selling expenses			
Sales salaries	6,250	6,000	+250
Advertising	900	800	+100
Store supplies	550	500	+50
Depreciation—Store equipment	1,600	1,600	
Total selling expenses	9,300	8,900	+400
General and administrative expenses			
Office salaries	2,000	2,000	
Office supplies used	165	150	+15
Rent	1,100	1,100	
Insurance	200	200	
Depreciation—Office equipment	100	100	
Total general and administrative expenses	3,565	3,550	+15
Total operating expenses	12,865	12,450	+415
Net income	$ 6,285	$ 5,600	$ +685

Example: Assume that you must explain variances to top management. Which variances in Exhibit 20.1 would you research and why? *Answer:* Sales and cost of goods sold—due to their large variances.

Budget Timing

The time period required for the annual budgeting process can vary considerably. For example, budgeting for 2012 can begin as early as January 2011 or as late as December 2011. Large, complex organizations usually require a longer time to prepare their budgets than do smaller organizations. This is so because considerable effort is required to coordinate the different units (departments) within large organizations.

Many companies apply **continuous budgeting** by preparing **rolling budgets.** As each monthly or quarterly budget period goes by, these companies revise their entire set of budgets for the months or quarters remaining and add new monthly or quarterly budgets to replace the ones that have lapsed. At any point in time, monthly or quarterly budgets are available for the next 12 months or four quarters. Exhibit 20.2 shows rolling budgets prepared at the end of five consecutive

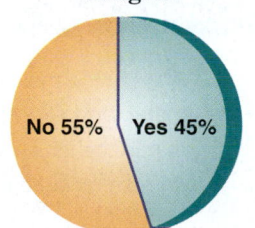

Companies Using Rolling Budgets

No 55%   Yes 45%

EXHIBIT 20.2

Rolling Budgets

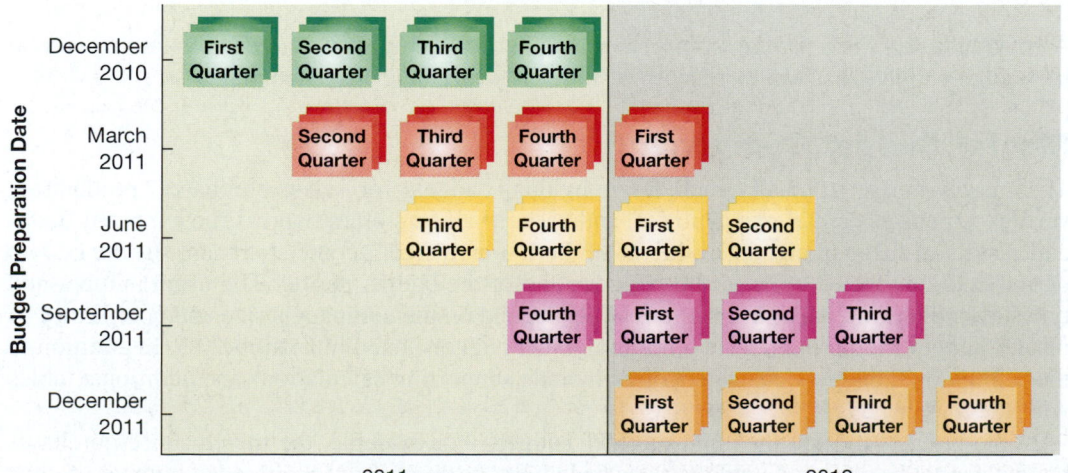

periods. The first set (at top) is prepared in December 2010 and covers the four calendar quarters of 2011. In March 2011, the company prepares another rolling budget for the next four quarters through March 2012. This same process is repeated every three months. As a result, management is continuously planning ahead.

Exhibit 20.2 reflects an annual budget composed of four quarters prepared four times per year using the most recent information available. For example, the budget for the fourth quarter of 2011 is prepared in December 2010 and revised in March, June, and September of 2011. When continuous budgeting is not used, the fourth-quarter budget is nine months old and perhaps out of date when applied.

Decision Insight

Budget Calendar   Many companies use long-range operating budgets. For large companies, three groups usually determine or influence the budgets: creditors, directors, and management. All three are interested in the companies' future cash flows and earnings. The annual budget process often begins six months or more before the budget is due to the board of directors. A typical budget calendar, shown here, provides insight into the budget process during a typical calendar year. ∎

Quick Check

Answers — p. 858

1. What are the major benefits of budgeting?
2. What is the main responsibility of the budget committee?
3. What is the usual time period covered by a budget?
4. What are rolling budgets?

MASTER BUDGET

C2   Describe a master budget and the process of preparing it.

A **master budget** is a formal, comprehensive plan for a company's future. It contains several individual budgets that are linked with each other to form a coordinated plan.

Master Budget Components

The master budget typically includes individual budgets for sales, purchases, production, various expenses, capital expenditures, and cash. Managers often express the expected financial results of these planned activities with both a budgeted income statement for the budget period and a budgeted balance sheet for the end of the budget period. The usual number and types of budgets included in a master budget depend on the company's size and complexity. A master budget should include, at a minimum, the budgets listed in Exhibit 20.3. In addition to these individual budgets, managers often include supporting calculations and additional tables with the master budget.

Some budgets require the input of other budgets. For example, the merchandise purchases budget cannot be prepared until the sales budget has been prepared because the number of units

EXHIBIT 20.3

Basic Components of a
Master Budget

Operating budgets
- *Sales budget*
- For merchandisers add: *Merchandise purchases budget* (units to be purchased)
- For manufacturers add: *Production budget* (units to be produced)
  Manufacturing budget (manufacturing costs)
- *Selling expense budget*
- *General and administrative expense budget*

Capital expenditures budget (expenditures for plant assets)

Financial budgets
- *Cash budget* (cash receipts and disbursements)
- *Budgeted income statement*
- *Budgeted balance sheet*

to be purchased depends on how many units are expected to be sold. As a result, we often must sequentially prepare budgets within the master budget.

A typical sequence for a master budget consists of the five steps in Exhibit 20.4. Any stage in this budgeting process might reveal undesirable outcomes, so changes often must be made to prior budgets by repeating the previous steps. For instance, an early version of the cash budget could show an insufficient amount of cash unless cash outlays are reduced. This could yield a reduction in planned equipment purchases. A preliminary budgeted balance sheet could also reveal too much debt from an ambitious capital expenditures budget. Findings such as these often result in revised plans and budgets.

EXHIBIT 20.4

Master Budget Sequence

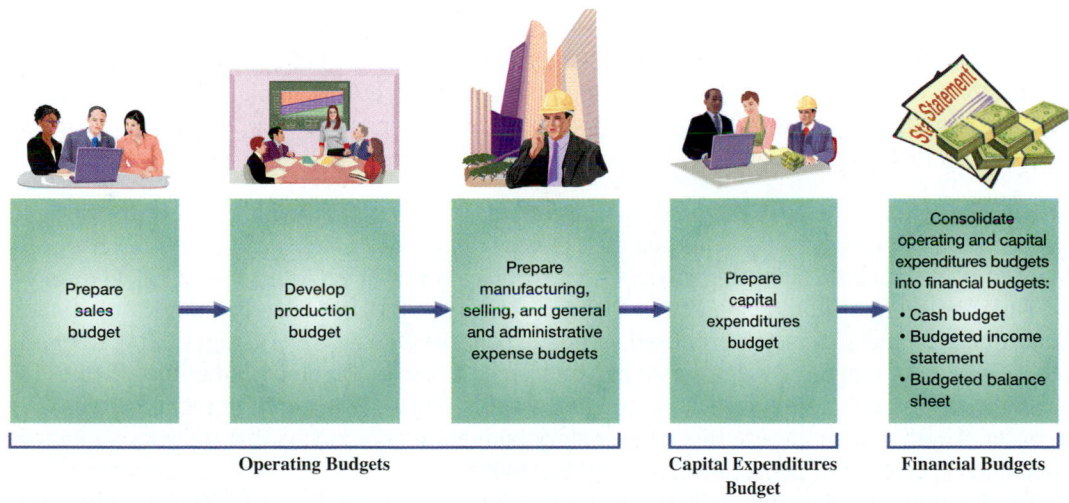

| Prepare sales budget | Develop production budget | Prepare manufacturing, selling, and general and administrative expense budgets | Prepare capital expenditures budget | Consolidate operating and capital expenditures budgets into financial budgets:
• Cash budget
• Budgeted income statement
• Budgeted balance sheet |

Operating Budgets   **Capital Expenditures Budget**   **Financial Budgets**

The remainder of this section explains how Hockey Den (HD), a retailer of youth hockey sticks, prepares its master budget. Its master budget includes operating, capital expenditures, and cash budgets for each month in each quarter. It also includes a budgeted income statement for each quarter and a budgeted balance sheet as of the last day of each quarter. We show how HD prepares budgets for October, November, and December 2011. Exhibit 20.5 presents HD's balance sheet at the start of this budgeting period, which we often refer to as we prepare the component budgets.

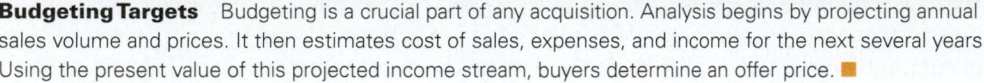

Decision Insight

Budgeting Targets   Budgeting is a crucial part of any acquisition. Analysis begins by projecting annual sales volume and prices. It then estimates cost of sales, expenses, and income for the next several years. Using the present value of this projected income stream, buyers determine an offer price. ■

EXHIBIT 20.5

Balance Sheet Prior to the
Budgeting Periods

HOCKEY DEN
Balance Sheet
September 30, 2011

Assets

Cash		$ 20,000
Accounts receivable		42,000
Inventory (900 units @ $60)		54,000
Equipment*	$200,000	
Less accumulated depreciation	36,000	164,000
Total assets		$280,000

Liabilities and Equity

Liabilities		
Accounts payable	$ 58,200	
Income taxes payable (due 10/31/2011)	20,000	
Note payable to bank	10,000	$ 88,200
Stockholders' equity		
Common stock	150,000	
Retained earnings	41,800	191,800
Total liabilities and equity		$280,000

* Equipment is depreciated on a straight-line basis over 10 years (salvage value is $20,000).

Operating Budgets

This section explains HD's preparation of operating budgets. Its operating budgets consist of the sales budget, merchandise purchases budget, selling expense budget, and general and administrative expense budget. HD does not prepare production and manufacturing budgets because it is a merchandiser. (The preparation of production budgets and manufacturing budgets is described in Appendix 20A.)

Sales Budget The first step in preparing the master budget is planning the **sales budget**, which shows the planned sales units and the expected dollars from these sales. The sales budget is the starting point in the budgeting process because plans for most departments are linked to sales.

The sales budget should emerge from a careful analysis of forecasted economic and market conditions, business capacity, proposed selling expenses (such as advertising), and predictions of unit sales. A company's sales personnel are usually asked to develop predictions of sales for each territory and department because people normally feel a greater commitment to goals they help set. Another advantage to this participatory budgeting approach is that it draws on knowledge and experience of people involved in the activity.

To illustrate, in September 2011, HD sold 700 hockey sticks at $100 per unit. After considering sales predictions and market conditions, HD prepares its sales budget for the next quarter (three months) plus one extra month (see Exhibit 20.6). The sales budget includes

P1 Prepare each component of a master budget and link each to the budgeting process.

EXHIBIT 20.6

Sales Budget for Planned Unit and Dollar Sales

HOCKEY DEN
Monthly Sales Budget
October 2011–January 2012

	Budgeted Unit Sales	Budgeted Unit Price	Budgeted Total Sales
September 2011 (actual)	700	$100	$ 70,000
October 2011	1,000	$100	$100,000
November 2011	800	100	80,000
December 2011	1,400	100	140,000
Totals for the quarter	3,200	100	$320,000
January 2012	900	100	$ 90,000

January 2012 because the purchasing department relies on estimated January sales to decide on December 2011 inventory purchases. The sales budget in Exhibit 20.6 includes forecasts of both unit sales and unit prices. Some sales budgets are expressed only in total sales dollars, but most are more detailed. Management finds it useful to know budgeted units and unit prices for many different products, regions, departments, and sales representatives.

Decision Maker   Answer — p. 858

Entrepreneur You run a start-up that manufactures designer clothes. Business is seasonal, and fashions and designs quickly change. How do you prepare reliable annual sales budgets? ■

Merchandise Purchases Budget Companies use various methods to help managers make inventory purchasing decisions. These methods recognize that the number of units added to inventory depends on budgeted sales volume. Whether a company manufactures or purchases the product it sells, budgeted future sales volume is the primary factor in most inventory management decisions. A company must also consider its inventory system and other factors that we discuss next.

Just-in-time inventory systems. Managers of *just-in-time* (JIT) inventory systems use sales budgets for short periods (often as few as one or two days) to order just enough merchandise or materials to satisfy the immediate sales demand. This keeps the amount of inventory to a minimum (or zero in an ideal situation). A JIT system minimizes the costs of maintaining inventory, but it is practical only if customers are content to order in advance or if managers can accurately determine short-term sales demand. Suppliers also must be able and willing to ship small quantities regularly and promptly.

> **Point:** Accurate estimates of future sales are crucial in a JIT system.

Safety stock inventory systems. Market conditions and manufacturing processes for some products do not allow use of a just-in-time system. Companies in these cases maintain sufficient inventory to reduce the risk and cost of running short. This practice requires enough purchases to satisfy the budgeted sales amounts and to maintain a **safety stock,** a quantity of inventory that provides protection against lost sales caused by unfulfilled demands from customers or delays in shipments from suppliers.

Merchandise purchases budget preparation. A merchandiser usually expresses a **merchandise purchases budget** in both units and dollars. Exhibit 20.7 shows the general layout for this budget in equation form. If this formula is expressed in units and only one product is involved, we can compute the number of dollars of inventory to be purchased for the budget by multiplying the units to be purchased by the cost per unit.

Inventory to be purchased	=	Budgeted ending inventory	+	Budgeted cost of sales for the period	−	Budgeted beginning inventory

EXHIBIT 20.7

General Formula for a Merchandise Purchases Budget

To illustrate, after assessing the cost of keeping inventory along with the risk and cost of inventory shortages, HD decided that the number of units in its inventory at each month-end should equal 90% of next month's predicted sales. For example, inventory at the end of October should equal 90% of budgeted November sales, and the November ending inventory should equal 90% of budgeted December sales, and so on. Also, HD's suppliers expect the September 2011 per unit cost of $60 to remain unchanged through January 2012. This information along with knowledge of 900 units in inventory at September 30 (see Exhibit 20.5) allows the company to prepare the merchandise purchases budget shown in Exhibit 20.8.

The first three lines of HD's merchandise purchases budget determine the required ending inventories (in units). Budgeted unit sales are then added to the desired ending inventory to give the required units of available merchandise. We then subtract beginning inventory to

> **Example:** Assume Hockey Den adopts a JIT system in purchasing merchandise. How will its sales budget differ from its merchandise purchases budget? *Answer:* The two budgets will be similar because future inventory should be near zero.

EXHIBIT 20.8

Merchandise Purchases Budget

HOCKEY DEN Merchandise Purchases Budget October 2011–December 2011	October	November	December
Next month's budgeted sales (units)	800	1,400	900
Ratio of inventory to future sales	× 90%	× 90%	× 90%
Budgeted ending inventory (units)	720	1,260	810
Add budgeted sales (units)	1,000	800	1,400
Required units of available merchandise	1,720	2,060	2,210
Deduct beginning inventory (units)	900	720	1,260
Units to be purchased	820	1,340	950
Budgeted cost per unit	$ 60	$ 60	$ 60
Budgeted cost of merchandise purchases	$49,200	$80,400	$57,000

Example: If ending inventory in Exhibit 20.8 is required to equal 80% of next month's predicted sales, how many units must be purchased each month? *Answer:* Budgeted ending inventory: Oct. = 640 units; Nov. = 1,120 units; Dec. = 720 units. Required purchases: Oct. = 740 units; Nov. = 1,280 units; Dec. = 1,000 units.

determine the budgeted number of units to be purchased. The last line is the budgeted cost of the purchases, computed by multiplying the number of units to be purchased by the predicted cost per unit.

We already indicated that some budgeting systems describe only the total dollars of budgeted sales. Likewise, a system can express a merchandise purchases budget only in terms of the total cost of merchandise to be purchased, omitting the number of units to be purchased. This method assumes a constant relation between sales and cost of goods sold. HD, for instance, might assume the expected cost of goods sold to be 60% of sales, computed from the budgeted unit cost of $60 and the budgeted sales price of $100. However, it still must consider the effects of changes in beginning and ending inventories in determining the amounts to be purchased.

Selling Expense Budget   The **selling expense budget** is a plan listing the types and amounts of selling expenses expected during the budget period. Its initial responsibility usually rests with the vice president of marketing or an equivalent sales manager. The selling expense budget is normally created to provide sufficient selling expenses to meet sales goals reflected in the sales budget. Predicted selling expenses are based on both the sales budget and the experience of previous periods. After some or all of the master budget is prepared, management might decide that projected sales volume is inadequate. If so, subsequent adjustments in the sales budget can require corresponding adjustments in the selling expense budget.

To illustrate, HD's selling expense budget is in Exhibit 20.9. The firm's selling expenses consist of commissions paid to sales personnel and a $2,000 monthly salary paid to the sales manager. Sales commissions equal 10% of total sales and are paid in the month sales occur. Sales commissions are variable with respect to sales volume, but the sales manager's salary is fixed. No advertising expenses are budgeted for this particular quarter.

EXHIBIT 20.9

Selling Expense Budget

HOCKEY DEN Selling Expense Budget October 2011–December 2011	October	November	December	Totals
Budgeted sales	$100,000	$80,000	$140,000	$320,000
Sales commission percent	× 10%	× 10%	× 10%	× 10%
Sales commissions	10,000	8,000	14,000	32,000
Salary for sales manager	2,000	2,000	2,000	6,000
Total selling expenses	$ 12,000	$10,000	$ 16,000	$ 38,000

Example: If sales commissions in Exhibit 20.9 are increased, which budgets are affected? *Answer:* Selling expenses budget, cash budget, and budgeted income statement.

General and Administrative Expense Budget The **general and administrative expense budget** plans the predicted operating expenses not included in the selling expenses budget. General and administrative expenses can be either variable or fixed with respect to sales volume. The office manager responsible for general administration often is responsible for preparing the initial general and administrative expense budget.

Exhibit 20.10 shows HD's general and administrative expense budget. It includes salaries of $54,000 per year, or $4,500 per month (paid each month when they are earned). Using information in Exhibit 20.5, the depreciation on equipment is computed as $18,000 per year [($200,000 − $20,000)/10 years], or $1,500 per month ($18,000/12 months).

HOCKEY DEN General and Administrative Expense Budget October 2011–December 2011				
	October	November	December	Totals
Administrative salaries	$4,500	$4,500	$4,500	$13,500
Depreciation of equipment	1,500	1,500	1,500	4,500
Total general and administrative expenses	$6,000	$6,000	$6,000	$18,000

EXHIBIT 20.10

General and Administrative Expense Budget

Interest expense and income tax expense are often classified as general and administrative expenses in published income statements but normally cannot be planned at this stage of the budgeting process. The prediction of interest expense follows the preparation of the cash budget and the decisions regarding debt. The predicted income tax expense depends on the budgeted amount of pretax income. Both interest and income taxes are usually beyond the control of the office manager. As a result, they are not used in comparison to the budget to evaluate that person's performance.

Example: In Exhibit 20.10, how would a rental agreement of $5,000 per month plus 1% of sales affect the general and administrative expense budget? (Budgeted sales are in Exhibit 20.6.) *Answer: Rent expense:* Oct. = $6,000; Nov. = $5,800; Dec. = $6,400; Total = $18,200; *Revised total general and administrative expenses:* Oct. = $12,000; Nov. = $11,800; Dec. = $12,400; Total = $36,200.

Decision Insight

No Biz Like Snow Biz Ski resorts' costs of making snow are in the millions of dollars for equipment alone. Snowmaking involves spraying droplets of water into the air, causing them to freeze and come down as snow. Making snow can cost more than $2,000 an hour. Snowmaking accounts for 40 to 50 percent of the operating budgets for many ski resorts. ■

Quick Check   Answers — p. 858

5. What is a master budget?

6. A master budget (a) always includes a manufacturing budget specifying the units to be produced; (b) is prepared with a process starting with the operating budgets and continues with the capital expenditures budget and then financial budgets; or (c) is prepared with a process ending with the sales budget.

7. What are the three primary categories of budgets in the master budget?

8. In preparing monthly budgets for the third quarter, a company budgeted sales of 120 units for July and 140 units for August. Management wants each month's ending inventory to be 60% of next month's sales. The June 30 inventory consists of 50 units. How many units of product for July acquisition should the merchandise purchases budget specify for the third quarter? (a) 84, (b) 120, (c) 154, or (d) 204.

9. How do the operating budgets for merchandisers and manufacturers differ?

10. How does a just-in-time inventory system differ from a safety stock system?

Capital Expenditures Budget

The **capital expenditures budget** lists dollar amounts to be both received from plant asset disposals and spent to purchase additional plant assets to carry out the budgeted business activities. It is usually prepared after the operating budgets. Since a company's plant assets determine its productive capacity, this budget is usually affected by long-range plans for the business. Yet the process of preparing a sales or purchases budget can reveal that the company requires more (or less) capacity, which implies more (or less) plant assets.

Capital budgeting is the process of evaluating and planning for capital (plant asset) expenditures. This is an important management task because these expenditures often involve long-run commitments of large amounts, affect predicted cash flows, and impact future debt and equity financing. This means that the capital expenditures budget is often linked with management's evaluation of the company's ability to take on more debt. We describe capital budgeting in Chapter 24.

Hockey Den does not anticipate disposal of any plant assets through December 2011, but it does plan to acquire additional equipment for $25,000 cash near the end of December 2011. This is the only budgeted capital expenditure from October 2011 through January 2012. Thus, no separate budget is shown. Hockey Den's cash budget will reflect this $25,000 planned expenditure.

Financial Budgets

After preparing its operating and capital expenditures budgets, a company uses information from these budgets to prepare at least three financial budgets: the cash budget, budgeted income statement, and budgeted balance sheet.

P2 Link both operating and capital expenditures budgets to budgeted financial statements.

Cash Budget After developing budgets for sales, merchandise purchases, expenses, and capital expenditures, the next step is to prepare the **cash budget,** which shows expected cash inflows and outflows during the budget period. It is especially important to maintain a cash balance necessary to meet ongoing obligations. By preparing a cash budget, management can prearrange loans to cover anticipated cash shortages before they are needed. A cash budget also helps management avoid a cash balance that is too large. Too much cash is undesirable because it earns a relatively low (if any) return. Exhibit 20.11 shows the general formula for the cash budget.

EXHIBIT 20.11

General Formula for Cash Budget

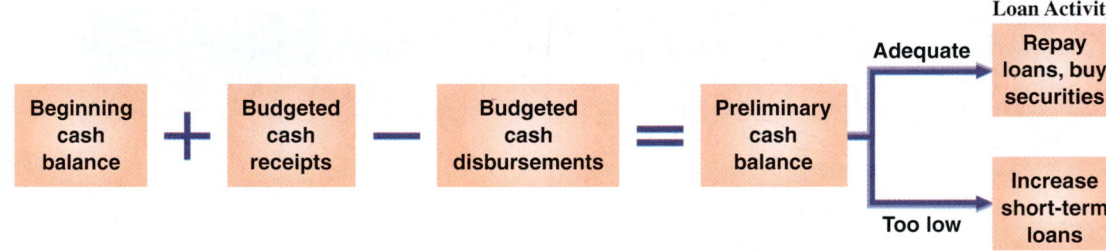

When preparing a cash budget, we add expected cash receipts to the beginning cash balance and deduct expected cash disbursements. If the expected (preliminary) ending cash balance is too low, additional cash requirements appear in the budget as planned increases from short-term loans. If the expected ending cash balance exceeds the desired balance, the excess is used to repay loans or to acquire short-term investments. Information for preparing the cash budget is mainly taken from the operating and capital expenditures budgets.

Cash Receipts from Sales To illustrate, Exhibit 20.12 presents HD's budgeted cash receipts.

EXHIBIT 20.12

Computing Budgeted Cash Receipts

	September	October	November	December
Sales	$70,000	$100,000	$80,000	$140,000
Less ending accounts receivable (60%)	42,000	60,000	48,000	84,000
Cash receipts from				
Cash sales (40% of sales)		40,000	32,000	56,000
Collections of prior month's receivables		42,000	60,000	48,000
Total cash receipts		$ 82,000	$92,000	$104,000

We begin with reference to HD's budgeted sales (Exhibit 20.6). Analysis of past sales indicates that 40% of the firm's sales are for cash. The remaining 60% are credit sales; these customers are expected to pay in full in the month following the sales. We now can compute the budgeted cash receipts from customers as shown in Exhibit 20.12. October's budgeted cash receipts consist of $40,000 from expected cash sales ($100,000 × 40%) plus the anticipated collection of $42,000 of accounts receivable from the end of September.

Cash Disbursements for Merchandise   Next, we see that HD's merchandise purchases are entirely on account. It makes full payment during the month following its purchases. Therefore, cash disbursements for purchases can be computed from the September 30, 2011, balance sheet (Exhibit 20.5), for October disbursements, and the merchandise purchases budget (Exhibit 20.8), for November and December disbursements. This is shown in Exhibit 20.13.

	October	November	December
Purchases (from Exhibit 20.8)	$49,200	$80,400	$57,000
Cash disbursements for			
Current month purchases (0%)	0	0	0
Prior month purchases (100%)	58,200*	49,200	80,400
Total cash disbursements for purchases	$58,200	$49,200	$80,400

*From September 30 balance sheet (Exhibit 20.5)

EXHIBIT 20.13

Computing Cash Disbursements for Purchases

The schedule above can be modified for alternative payment timing. For example, if Hockey Den paid for 20% of its purchases in the month of purchase, and paid the remaining 80% of a month's purchases in the following month, its cash disbursements in December would equal $75,720, computed as (20% × $57,000) plus (80% × $80,400).

Exhibit 20.14 shows the full cash budget for Hockey Den, beginning with information on budgeted cash receipts from Exhibit 20.13 and budgeted cash purchases for merchandise from Exhibit 20.13. Next we discuss HD's other cash disbursements and loan activity on its cash budget.

EXHIBIT 20.14

Cash Budget

HOCKEY DEN Cash Budget October 2011–December 2011			
	October	November	December
Beginning cash balance	$ 20,000	$ 20,000	$ 22,272
Cash receipts from customers (Exhibit 20.12)	82,000	92,000	104,000
Total cash available	102,000	112,000	126,272
Cash disbursements			
Payments for merchandise (Exhibit 20.13)	58,200	49,200	80,400
Sales commissions (Exhibit 20.9)	10,000	8,000	14,000
Salaries			
Sales (Exhibit 20.9)	2,000	2,000	2,000
Administrative (Exhibit 20.10)	4,500	4,500	4,500
Income taxes payable (Exhibit 20.5)	20,000		
Dividends ($150,000 × 2%)		3,000	
Interest on bank loan			
October ($10,000 × 1%)*	100		
November ($22,800 × 1%)		228	
Purchase of equipment			25,000
Total cash disbursements	94,800	66,928	125,900
Preliminary cash balance	$ 7,200	$ 45,072	$ 372
Loan activity			
Additional loan from bank	12,800		19,628
Repayment of loan to bank		22,800	
Ending cash balance	$ 20,000	$ 22,272	$ 20,000
Loan balance, end of month	$ 22,800	$ 0	$ 19,628

* Beginning loan balance from Exhibit 20.5

Example: If the minimum ending cash balance in Exhibit 20.14 is changed to $25,000 for each month, what is the projected loan balance at Dec. 31, 2011?
Answer:

Loan balance, Oct. 31.......	$27,800
November interest	278
November payment........	25,022
Loan balance, Nov. 30	2,778
December interest	28
Additional loan in Dec.	21,928
Loan balance, Dec. 31.......	$24,706

The monthly budgeted cash disbursements for sales commissions and salaries are taken from the selling expense budget (Exhibit 20.9) and the general and administrative expense budget (Exhibit 20.10). The cash budget is unaffected by depreciation as reported in the general and administrative expenses budget.

Cash Disbursements for Other Items   Income taxes are due and payable in October as shown in the September 30, 2011, balance sheet (Exhibit 20.5). The cash budget in Exhibit 20.14 shows this $20,000 expected payment in October. Predicted income tax expense for the quarter ending December 31 is 40% of net income and is due in January 2012. It is therefore not reported in the October–December 2011 cash budget but in the budgeted income statement as income tax expense and on the budgeted balance sheet as income tax liability.

Hockey Den also pays a cash dividend equal to 2% of the par value of common stock in the second month of each quarter. The cash budget in Exhibit 20.14 shows a November payment of $3,000 for this purpose (2% of $150,000; see Exhibit 20.5).

Loan Activity   Analyzing Hockey Den's loan activity is necessary in computing its budgeted cash disbursements for interest. Hockey Den has an agreement with its bank that promises additional loans at each month-end, if necessary, to keep a minimum cash balance of $20,000. If the cash balance exceeds $20,000 at a month-end, HD uses the excess to repay loans. Interest is paid at each month-end at the rate of 1% of the beginning balance of these loans. For October, this payment is 1% of the $10,000 amount reported in the balance sheet of Exhibit 20.5. For November, HD expects to pay interest of $228, computed as 1% of the $22,800 expected loan balance at October 31. No interest is budgeted for December because the company expects to repay the loans in full at the end of November. Exhibit 20.14 shows that the October 31 cash balance declines to $7,200 (before any loan-related activity). This amount is less than the $20,000 minimum. Hockey Den will bring this balance up to the minimum by borrowing $12,800 with a short-term note. At the end of November, the budget shows an expected cash balance of $45,072 before any loan activity. This means that HD expects to repay $22,800 of debt. The equipment purchase budgeted for December reduces the expected cash balance to $372, far below the $20,000 minimum. The company expects to borrow $19,628 in that month to reach the minimum desired ending balance.

Decision Insight

Cash Cushion   Why do some companies maintain a minimum cash balance when the budget shows extra cash is not needed? For example, iPhone sales have pushed Apple's cash and investments balance to over $40 billion. Per CEO Steve Jobs the cushion provides "flexibility and security," important in navigating uncertain economic times. ■

Budgeted Income Statement   One of the final steps in preparing the master budget is to summarize the income effects. The **budgeted income statement** is a managerial accounting report showing predicted amounts of sales and expenses for the budget period. Information needed for preparing a budgeted income statement is primarily taken from already prepared budgets. The volume of information summarized in the budgeted income statement is so large for some companies that they often use spreadsheets to accumulate the budgeted transactions and classify them by their effects on income. We condense HD's budgeted income statement and show it in Exhibit 20.15. All information in this exhibit is taken from earlier budgets. Also, we now can predict the amount of income tax expense for the quarter, computed as 40% of the budgeted pretax income. This amount is included in the cash budget and/or the budgeted balance sheet as necessary.

Point: Lenders often require potential borrowers to provide cash budgets, budgeted income statements, and budgeted balance sheets, as well as data on past performance.

Budgeted Balance Sheet   The final step in preparing the master budget is summarizing the company's financial position. The **budgeted balance sheet** shows predicted amounts for the

EXHIBIT 20.15

Budgeted Income Statement

HOCKEY DEN
Budgeted Income Statement
For Three Months Ended December 31, 2011

Sales (Exhibit 20.6, 3,200 units @ $100)		$320,000
Cost of goods sold (3,200 units @ $60)		192,000
Gross profit		128,000
Operating expenses		
Sales commissions (Exhibit 20.9)	$32,000	
Sales salaries (Exhibit 20.9)	6,000	
Administrative salaries (Exhibit 20.10)	13,500	
Depreciation on equipment (Exhibit 20.10)	4,500	
Interest expense (Exhibit 20.14)	328	56,328
Income before income taxes		71,672
Income tax expense ($71,672 × 40%)		28,669
Net income		$ 43,003

company's assets, liabilities, and equity as of the end of the budget period. HD's budgeted balance sheet in Exhibit 20.16 is prepared using information from the other budgets. The sources of amounts are reported in the notes to the budgeted balance sheet.[1]

EXHIBIT 20.16

Budgeted Balance Sheet

HOCKEY DEN
Budgeted Balance Sheet
December 31, 2011

Assets		
Cash[a]		$ 20,000
Accounts receivable[b]		84,000
Inventory[c]		48,600
Equipment[d]	$225,000	
Less accumulated depreciation[e]	40,500	184,500
Total assets		$337,100
Liabilities and Equity		
Liabilities		
Accounts payable[f]	$ 57,000	
Income taxes payable[g]	28,669	
Bank loan payable[h]	19,628	$105,297
Stockholders' equity		
Common stock[i]	150,000	
Retained earnings[j]	81,803	231,803
Total liabilities and equity		$337,100

[a] Ending balance for December from the cash budget in Exhibit 20.14.

[b] 60% of $140,000 sales budgeted for December from the sales budget in Exhibit 20.6.

[c] 810 units in budgeted December ending inventory at the budgeted cost of $60 per unit (from the purchases budget in Exhibit 20.8).

[d] September 30 balance of $200,000 from the beginning balance sheet in Exhibit 20.5 plus $25,000 cost of new equipment from the cash budget in Exhibit 20.14.

[e] September 30 balance of $36,000 from the beginning balance sheet in Exhibit 20.5 plus $4,500 expense from the general and administrative expense budget in Exhibit 20.10.

[f] Budgeted cost of purchases for December from the purchases budget in Exhibit 20.8.

[g] Income tax expense from the budgeted income statement for the fourth quarter in Exhibit 20.15.

[h] Budgeted December 31 balance from the cash budget in Exhibit 20.14.

[i] Unchanged from the beginning balance sheet in Exhibit 20.5.

[j] September 30 balance of $41,800 from the beginning balance sheet in Exhibit 20.5 plus budgeted net income of $43,003 from the budgeted income statement in Exhibit 20.15 minus budgeted cash dividends of $3,000 from the cash budget in Exhibit 20.14.

---

[1] An eight-column spreadsheet, or work sheet, can be used to prepare a budgeted balance sheet (and income statement). The first two columns show the ending balance sheet amounts from the period prior to the budget period. The budgeted transactions and adjustments are entered in the third and fourth columns in the same manner as adjustments are entered on an ordinary work sheet. After all budgeted transactions and adjustments have been entered, the amounts in the first two columns are combined with the budget amounts in the third and fourth columns and sorted to the proper Income Statement (fifth and sixth columns) and Balance Sheet columns (seventh and eighth columns). Amounts in these columns are used to prepare the budgeted income statement and balance sheet.

Decision Insight

Plan Ahead Most companies allocate dollars based on budgets submitted by department managers. These managers verify the numbers and monitor the budget. Managers must remember, however, that a budget is judged by its success in helping achieve the company's mission. One analogy is that a hiker must know the route to properly plan a hike and monitor hiking progress. ■

Quick Check

Answers — p. 858

11. In preparing a budgeted balance sheet, (a) plant assets are determined by analyzing the capital expenditures budget and the balance sheet from the beginning of the budget period, (b) liabilities are determined by analyzing the general and administrative expense budget, or (c) retained earnings are determined from information contained in the cash budget and the balance sheet from the beginning of the budget period.

12. What sequence is followed in preparing the budgets that constitute the master budget?

GLOBAL VIEW

Royal Phillips Electronics of the Netherlands is a diversified company. Preparing budgets and evaluating progress helps the company achieve its goals. In a recent annual report the company reports that it expects sales to grow at a faster pace than overall economic growth. Based on this sales target, company managers prepare detailed operating, capital expenditure, and financial budgets.

Decision Analysis

Activity-Based Budgeting

 A1 Analyze expense planning using activity-based budgeting.

Activity-based budgeting (ABB) is a budget system based on expected activities. Knowledge of expected activities and their levels for the budget period enables management to plan for resources required to perform the activities. To illustrate, we consider the budget of a company's accounting department. Traditional budgeting systems list items such as salaries, supplies, equipment, and utilities. Such an itemized budget informs management of the use of the funds budgeted (for example, salaries), but management cannot assess the basis for increases or decreases in budgeted amounts as compared to prior periods. Accordingly, management often makes across-the-board cuts or increases. In contrast, ABB requires management to list activities performed by, say, the accounting department such as auditing, tax reporting, financial reporting, and cost accounting. Exhibit 20.17 contrasts a traditional budget with an activity-based budget for a company's accounting department. An understanding of the resources required to perform the activities, the costs associated with these resources, and the way resource use changes with

EXHIBIT 20.17

Activity-Based Budgeting versus Traditional Budgeting (for an accounting department)

Activity-Based Budget		Traditional Budget	
Auditing	$ 58,000	Salaries.	$152,000
Tax reporting	71,000	Supplies	22,000
Financial reporting	63,000	Depreciation	36,000
Cost accounting	32,000	Utilities	14,000
Total	$224,000	Total	$224,000

changes in activity levels allows management to better assess how expenses will change to accommodate changes in activity levels. Moreover, by knowing the relation between activities and costs, management can attempt to reduce costs by eliminating nonvalue-added activities.

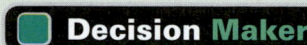 **Decision** Maker

Answer – p. 858

Environmental Manager You hold the new position of environmental control manager for a chemical company. You are asked to develop a budget for your job and identify job responsibilities. How do you proceed? ■

DEMONSTRATION PROBLEM

Wild Wood Company's management asks you to prepare its master budget using the following information. The budget is to cover the months of April, May, and June of 2011.

WILD WOOD COMPANY Balance Sheet March 31, 2011			
Assets		**Liabilities and Equity**	
Cash	$ 50,000	Accounts payable	$156,000
Accounts receivable	175,000	Short-term notes payable	12,000
Inventory	126,000	Total current liabilities	168,000
Total current assets	351,000	Long-term note payable	200,000
Equipment, gross	480,000	Total liabilities	368,000
Accumulated depreciation	(90,000)	Common stock	235,000
Equipment, net	390,000	Retained earnings	138,000
		Total stockholders' equity	373,000
Total assets	$741,000	Total liabilities and equity	$741,000

Additional Information

a. Sales for March total 10,000 units. Each month's sales are expected to exceed the prior month's results by 5%. The product's selling price is $25 per unit.

b. Company policy calls for a given month's ending inventory to equal 80% of the next month's expected unit sales. The March 31 inventory is 8,400 units, which complies with the policy. The purchase price is $15 per unit.

c. Sales representatives' commissions are 12.5% of sales and are paid in the month of the sales. The sales manager's monthly salary will be $3,500 in April and $4,000 per month thereafter.

d. Monthly general and administrative expenses include $8,000 administrative salaries, $5,000 depreciation, and 0.9% monthly interest on the long-term note payable.

e. The company expects 30% of sales to be for cash and the remaining 70% on credit. Receivables are collected in full in the month following the sale (none is collected in the month of the sale).

f. All merchandise purchases are on credit, and no payables arise from any other transactions. One month's purchases are fully paid in the next month.

g. The minimum ending cash balance for all months is $50,000. If necessary, the company borrows enough cash using a short-term note to reach the minimum. Short-term notes require an interest payment of 1% at each month-end (before any repayment). If the ending cash balance exceeds the minimum, the excess will be applied to repaying the short-term notes payable balance.

h. Dividends of $100,000 are to be declared and paid in May.

i. No cash payments for income taxes are to be made during the second calendar quarter. Income taxes will be assessed at 35% in the quarter.

j. Equipment purchases of $55,000 are scheduled for June.

Required

Prepare the following budgets and other financial information as required:

1. Sales budget, including budgeted sales for July.
2. Purchases budget, the budgeted cost of goods sold for each month and quarter, and the cost of the June 30 budgeted inventory.
3. Selling expense budget.
4. General and administrative expense budget.
5. Expected cash receipts from customers and the expected June 30 balance of accounts receivable.
6. Expected cash payments for purchases and the expected June 30 balance of accounts payable.
7. Cash budget.
8. Budgeted income statement.
9. Budgeted statement of retained earnings.
10. Budgeted balance sheet.

PLANNING THE SOLUTION

- The sales budget shows expected sales for each month in the quarter. Start by multiplying March sales by 105% and then do the same for the remaining months. July's sales are needed for the purchases budget. To complete the budget, multiply the expected unit sales by the selling price of $25 per unit.

- Use these results and the 80% inventory policy to budget the size of ending inventory for April, May, and June. Add the budgeted sales to these numbers and subtract the actual or expected beginning inventory for each month. The result is the number of units to be purchased each month. Multiply these numbers by the per unit cost of $15. Find the budgeted cost of goods sold by multiplying the unit sales in each month by the $15 cost per unit. Compute the cost of the June 30 ending inventory by multiplying the expected units available at that date by the $15 cost per unit.

- The selling expense budget has only two items. Find the amount of the sales representatives' commissions by multiplying the expected dollar sales in each month by the 12.5% commission rate. Then include the sales manager's salary of $3,500 in April and $4,000 in May and June.

- The general and administrative expense budget should show three items. Administrative salaries are fixed at $8,000 per month, and depreciation is $5,000 per month. Budget the monthly interest expense on the long-term note by multiplying its $200,000 balance by the 0.9% monthly interest rate.

- Determine the amounts of cash sales in each month by multiplying the budgeted sales by 30%. Add to this amount the credit sales of the prior month (computed as 70% of prior month's sales). April's cash receipts from collecting receivables equals the March 31 balance of $175,000. The expected June 30 accounts receivable balance equals 70% of June's total budgeted sales.

- Determine expected cash payments on accounts payable for each month by making them equal to the merchandise purchases in the prior month. The payments for April equal the March 31 balance of accounts payable shown on the beginning balance sheet. The June 30 balance of accounts payable equals merchandise purchases for June.

- Prepare the cash budget by combining the given information and the amounts of cash receipts and cash payments on account that you computed. Complete the cash budget for each month by either borrowing enough to raise the preliminary balance to the minimum or paying off short-term debt as much as the balance allows without falling below the minimum. Show the ending balance of the short-term note in the budget.

- Prepare the budgeted income statement by combining the budgeted items for all three months. Determine the income before income taxes and multiply it by the 35% rate to find the quarter's income tax expense.

- The budgeted statement of retained earnings should show the March 31 balance plus the quarter's net income minus the quarter's dividends.

- The budgeted balance sheet includes updated balances for all items that appear in the beginning balance sheet and an additional liability for unpaid income taxes. Amounts for all asset, liability, and equity accounts can be found either in the budgets, other calculations, or by adding amounts found there to the beginning balances.

SOLUTION TO DEMONSTRATION PROBLEM

1. Sales budget

	April	May	June	July
Prior period's unit sales	10,000	10,500	11,025	11,576
Plus 5% growth	500	525	551	579
Projected unit sales	10,500	11,025	11,576	12,155

	April	May	June	Quarter
Projected unit sales	10,500	11,025	11,576	
Selling price per unit	× $25	× $25	× $25	
Projected sales	$262,500	$275,625	$289,400	$827,525

2. Purchases budget

	April	May	June	Quarter
Next period's unit sales (part 1)	11,025	11,576	12,155	
Ending inventory percent	× 80%	× 80%	× 80%	
Desired ending inventory	8,820	9,261	9,724	
Current period's unit sales (part 1)	10,500	11,025	11,576	
Units to be available	19,320	20,286	21,300	
Less beginning inventory	8,400	8,820	9,261	
Units to be purchased	10,920	11,466	12,039	
Budgeted cost per unit	× $15	× $15	× $15	
Projected purchases	$163,800	$171,990	$180,585	$516,375

Budgeted cost of goods sold

	April	May	June	Quarter
This period's unit sales (part 1)	10,500	11,025	11,576	
Budgeted cost per unit	× $15	× $15	× $15	
Projected cost of goods sold	$157,500	$165,375	$173,640	$496,515

Budgeted inventory for June 30

Units (part 2)	9,724
Cost per unit	× $15
Total	$145,860

3. Selling expense budget

	April	May	June	Quarter
Budgeted sales (part 1)	$262,500	$275,625	$289,400	$827,525
Commission percent	× 12.5%	× 12.5%	× 12.5%	× 12.5%
Sales commissions	32,813	34,453	36,175	103,441
Manager's salary	3,500	4,000	4,000	11,500
Projected selling expenses	$ 36,313	$ 38,453	$ 40,175	$114,941

4. General and administrative expense budget

	April	May	June	Quarter
Administrative salaries	$ 8,000	$ 8,000	$ 8,000	$24,000
Depreciation	5,000	5,000	5,000	15,000
Interest on long-term note payable (0.9% × $200,000)	1,800	1,800	1,800	5,400
Projected expenses	$14,800	$14,800	$14,800	$44,400

5. Expected cash receipts from customers

	April	May	June	Quarter
Budgeted sales (part 1)	$262,500	$275,625	$289,400	
Ending accounts receivable (70%)	$183,750	$192,938	$202,580	
Cash receipts				
Cash sales (30% of budgeted sales)	$ 78,750	$ 82,687	$ 86,820	$248,257
Collections of prior month's receivables	175,000	183,750	192,938	551,688
Total cash to be collected	$253,750	$266,437	$279,758	$799,945

6. Expected cash payments to suppliers

	April	May	June	Quarter
Cash payments (equal to prior month's purchases)	$156,000	$163,800	$171,990	$491,790
Expected June 30 balance of accounts payable (June purchases)			$180,585	

7. Cash budget

	April	May	June
Beginning cash balance	$ 50,000	$ 89,517	$ 50,000
Cash receipts (part 5)	253,750	266,437	279,758
Total cash available	303,750	355,954	329,758
Cash payments			
Payments for merchandise (part 6)	156,000	163,800	171,990
Sales commissions (part 3)	32,813	34,453	36,175
Salaries			
Sales (part 3)	3,500	4,000	4,000
Administrative (part 4)	8,000	8,000	8,000
Interest on long-term note (part 4)	1,800	1,800	1,800
Dividends		100,000	
Equipment purchase			55,000
Interest on short-term notes			
April ($12,000 × 1.0%)	120		
June ($6,099 × 1.0%)			61
Total cash payments	202,233	312,053	277,026
Preliminary balance	101,517	43,901	52,732
Loan activity			
Additional loan		6,099	
Loan repayment	(12,000)		(2,732)
Ending cash balance	$ 89,517	$ 50,000	$ 50,000
Ending short-term notes	$ 0	$ 6,099	$ 3,367

8.

WILD WOOD COMPANY
Budgeted Income Statement
For Quarter Ended June 30, 2011

Sales (part 1)		$827,525
Cost of goods sold (part 2)		496,515
Gross profit		331,010
Operating expenses		
Sales commissions (part 3)	$103,441	
Sales salaries (part 3)	11,500	
Administrative salaries (part 4)	24,000	
Depreciation (part 4)	15,000	
Interest on long-term note (part 4)	5,400	
Interest on short-term notes (part 7)	181	
Total operating expenses		159,522
Income before income taxes		171,488
Income taxes (35%)		60,021
Net income		$111,467

9.

WILD WOOD COMPANY
Budgeted Statement of Retained Earnings
For Quarter Ended June 30, 2011

Beginning retained earnings (given)	$138,000
Net income (part 8)	111,467
	249,467
Less cash dividends (given)	100,000
Ending retained earnings	$149,467

10.

WILD WOOD COMPANY
Budgeted Balance Sheet
June 30, 2011

Assets

Cash (part 7)		$ 50,000
Accounts receivable (part 5)		202,580
Inventory (part 2)		145,860
Total current assets		398,440
Equipment (given plus purchase)	$535,000	
Less accumulated depreciation (given plus expense)	105,000	430,000
Total assets		$828,440

Liabilities and Equity

Accounts payable (part 6)	$180,585
Short-term notes payable (part 7)	3,367
Income taxes payable (part 8)	60,021
Total current liabilities	243,973
Long-term note payable (given)	200,000
Total liabilities	443,973
Common stock (given)	235,000
Retained earnings (part 9)	149,467
Total stockholders' equity	384,467
Total liabilities and equity	$828,440

20A

Production and Manufacturing Budgets

P3 Prepare production and manufacturing budgets.

Unlike a merchandising company, a manufacturer must prepare a **production budget** instead of a merchandise purchases budget. A production budget, which shows the number of units to be produced each month, is similar to merchandise purchases budgets except that the number of units to be purchased each month (as shown in Exhibit 20.8) is replaced by the number of units to be manufactured each month. A production budget does not show costs; it is *always expressed in units of product*. Exhibit 20A.1 shows the production budget for **Toronto Sticks Company (TSC),** a manufacturer of hockey sticks. TSC is an exclusive supplier of hockey sticks to Hockey Den, meaning that TSC uses HD's budgeted sales figures (Exhibit 20.6) to determine its production and manufacturing budgets.

EXHIBIT 20A.1

Production Budget

TSC Production Budget October 2011–December 2011			
	October	November	December
Next period's budgeted sales (units)	800	1,400	900
Ratio of inventory to future sales	× 90%	× 90%	× 90%
Budgeted ending inventory (units)	720	1,260	810
Add budgeted sales for the period (units)	1,000	800	1,400
Required units of available production	1,720	2,060	2,210
Deduct beginning inventory (units)	(900)	(720)	(1,260)
Units to be produced	820	1,340	950

A **manufacturing budget** shows the budgeted costs for direct materials, direct labor, and overhead. It is based on the budgeted production volume from the production budget. The manufacturing budget for most companies consists of three individual budgets: direct materials budget, direct labor budget, and overhead budget. Exhibits 20A.2–20A.4 show these three manufacturing budgets for TSC. These budgets yield the total expected cost of goods to be manufactured in the budget period.

The *direct materials budget* is driven by the budgeted materials needed to satisfy each month's production requirement. To this we must add the desired ending inventory requirements. The desired ending inventory of direct materials as shown in Exhibit 20A.2 is 50% of next month's budgeted materials requirements of wood. For instance, in October 2011, an ending inventory of 335 units of material is desired (50% of November's 670 units). The desired ending inventory for December 2011 is 225 units, computed from the direct material requirement of 450 units for a production level of 900 units in January 2012. The total materials requirements are computed by adding the desired ending inventory figures to that month's budgeted production material requirements. For October 2011, the total materials requirement is 745 units (335 + 410). From the total materials requirement, we then subtract the units of

EXHIBIT 20A.2

Direct Materials Budget

TSC Direct Materials Budget October 2011–December 2011			
	October	November	December
Budget production (units)	820	1,340	950
Materials requirements per unit	× 0.5	× 0.5	× 0.5
Materials needed for production (units)	410	670	475
Add budgeted ending inventory (units)	335	237.5	225
Total materials requirements (units)	745	907.5	700
Deduct beginning inventory (units)	(205)	(335)	(237.5)
Materials to be purchased (units)	540	572.5	462.5
Material price per unit	$ 20	$ 20	$ 20
Total cost of direct materials purchases	$10,800	$11,450	$9,250

materials available in beginning inventory. For October 2011, the materials available from September 2011 are computed as 50% of October's materials requirements to satisfy production, or 205 units (50% of 410). Therefore, direct materials purchases in October 2011 are budgeted at 540 units (745 − 205). See Exhibit 20A.2.

TSC's *direct labor budget* is shown in Exhibit 20A.3. About 15 minutes of labor time is required to produce one unit. Labor is paid at the rate of $12 per hour. Budgeted labor hours are computed by multiplying the budgeted production level for each month by one-quarter (0.25) of an hour. Direct labor cost is then computed by multiplying budgeted labor hours by the labor rate of $12 per hour.

EXHIBIT 20A.3
Direct Labor Budget

TSC Direct Labor Budget October 2011–December 2011	October	November	December
Budgeted production (units)	820	1,340	950
Labor requirements per unit (hours)	× 0.25	× 0.25	× 0.25
Total labor hours needed	205	335	237.5
Labor rate (per hour)	$ 12	$ 12	$ 12
Labor dollars	$2,460	$4,020	$2,850

TSC's *factory overhead budget* is shown in Exhibit 20A.4. The variable portion of overhead is assigned at the rate of $2.50 per unit of production. The fixed portion stays constant at $1,500 per month. The budget in Exhibit 20A.4 is in condensed form; most overhead budgets are more detailed, listing each overhead cost item.

EXHIBIT 20A.4
Factory Overhead Budget

TSC Factory Overhead Budget October 2011–December 2011	October	November	December
Budgeted production (units)	820	1,340	950
Variable factory overhead rate	× $2.50	× $2.50	× $2.50
Budgeted variable overhead	2,050	3,350	2,375
Budgeted fixed overhead	1,500	1,500	1,500
Budgeted total overhead	$3,550	$4,850	$3,875

Summary

C1 Describe the importance and benefits of budgeting and the process of budget administration. Planning is a management responsibility of critical importance to business success. Budgeting is the process management uses to formalize its plans. Budgeting promotes management analysis and focuses its attention on the future. Budgeting also provides a basis for evaluating performance, serves as a source of motivation, is a means of coordinating activities, and communicates management's plans and instructions to employees. Budgeting is a detailed activity that requires administration. At least three aspects are important: budget committee, budget reporting, and budget timing. A budget committee oversees the budget preparation. The budget period pertains to the time period for which the budget is prepared such as a year or month.

C2 Describe a master budget and the process of preparing it. A master budget is a formal overall plan for a company. It consists of plans for business operations and capital expenditures, plus the financial results of those activities. The budgeting process begins with a

sales budget. Based on expected sales volume, companies can budget purchases, selling expenses, and administrative expenses. Next, the capital expenditures budget is prepared, followed by the cash budget and budgeted financial statements. Manufacturers also must budget production quantities, materials purchases, labor costs, and overhead.

A1 Analyze expense planning using activity-based budgeting. Activity-based budgeting requires management to identify activities performed by departments, plan necessary activity levels, identify resources required to perform these activities, and budget the resources.

P1 Prepare each component of a master budget and link each to the budgeting process. The term *master budget* refers to a collection of individual component budgets. Each component budget is designed to guide persons responsible for activities covered by that component. A master budget must reflect the components of a company and their interaction in pursuit of company goals.

P2 **Link both operating and capital expenditures budgets to budgeted financial statements.** The operating budgets, capital expenditures budget, and cash budget contain much of the information to prepare a budgeted income statement for the budget period and a budgeted balance sheet at the end of the budget period. Budgeted financial statements show the expected financial consequences of the planned activities described in the budgets.

P3ᴬ **Prepare production and manufacturing budgets.** A manufacturer must prepare a *production budget* instead of a purchases budget. A *manufacturing budget* shows the budgeted production costs for direct materials, direct labor, and overhead.

Guidance Answers to Decision Maker and Decision Ethics

Budget Staffer   Your superior's actions appear unethical because she is using private information for personal gain. As a budget staffer, you are low in the company's hierarchical structure and probably unable to confront this superior directly. You should inform an individual with a position of authority within the organization about your concerns.

Entrepreneur   You must deal with two issues. First, because fashions and designs frequently change, you cannot heavily rely on previous budgets. As a result, you must carefully analyze the market to understand what designs are in vogue. This will help you plan the product mix and estimate demand. The second issue is the budgeting

period. An annual sales budget may be unreliable because tastes can quickly change. Your best bet might be to prepare monthly and quarterly sales budgets that you continuously monitor and revise.

Environmental Manager   You are unlikely to have data on this new position to use in preparing your budget. In this situation, you can use activity-based budgeting. This requires developing a list of activities to conduct, the resources required to perform these activities, and the expenses associated with these resources. You should challenge yourself to be absolutely certain that the listed activities are necessary and that the listed resources are required.

Guidance Answers to Quick Checks

1. Major benefits include promoting a focus on the future; providing a basis for evaluating performance; providing a source of motivation; coordinating the departments of a business; and communicating plans and instructions.

2. The budget committee's responsibility is to provide guidance to ensure that budget figures are realistic and coordinated.

3. Budget periods usually coincide with accounting periods and therefore cover a month, quarter, or a year. Budgets can also be prepared for longer time periods, such as five years.

4. Rolling budgets are budgets that are periodically revised in the ongoing process of continuous budgeting.

5. A master budget is a comprehensive or overall plan for the company that is generally expressed in monetary terms.

6. *b*

7. The master budget includes operating budgets, the capital expenditures budget, and financial budgets.

8. *c*; Computed as $(60\% \times 140) + 120 - 50 = 154$.

9. Merchandisers prepare merchandise purchases budgets; manufacturers prepare production and manufacturing budgets.

10. A just-in-time system keeps the level of inventory to a minimum and orders merchandise or materials to meet immediate sales demand. A safety stock system maintains an inventory that is large enough to meet sales demands plus an amount to satisfy unexpected sales demands and an amount to cover delayed shipments from suppliers.

11. *a*

12. (a) Operating budgets (such as sales, selling expense, and administrative budgets), (b) capital expenditures budget, (c) financial budgets: cash budget, budgeted income statement, and budgeted balance sheet.

Key Terms   mhhe.com/wildFINMAN4e

Activity-based budgeting (ABB) (p. 850)
Budget (p. 836)
Budgeted balance sheet (p. 848)
Budgeted income statement (p. 848)
Budgeting (p. 836)
Capital expenditures budget (p. 846)

Cash budget (p. 846)
Continuous budgeting (p. 839)
General and administrative expense budget (p. 845)
Manufacturing budget (p. 856)
Master budget (p. 840)

Merchandise purchases budget (p. 843)
Production budget (p. 856)
Rolling budgets (p. 839)
Safety stock (p. 843)
Sales budget (p. 842)
Selling expense budget (p. 844)

Additional Quiz Questions are available at the book's Website.

1. A plan that reports the units or costs of merchandise to be purchased by a merchandising company during the budget period is called a
   a. Capital expenditures budget.
   b. Cash budget.
   c. Merchandise purchases budget.
   d. Selling expenses budget.
   e. Sales budget.

2. A hardware store has budgeted sales of $36,000 for its power tool department in July. Management wants to have $7,000 in power tool inventory at the end of July. Its beginning inventory of power tools is expected to be $6,000. What is the budgeted dollar amount of merchandise purchases?
   a. $36,000
   b. $43,000
   c. $42,000
   d. $35,000
   e. $37,000

3. A store has the following budgeted sales for the next five months.

May	$210,000
June	186,000
July	180,000
August	220,000
September	240,000

   Cash sales are 25% of total sales and all credit sales are expected to be collected in the month following the sale. The total amount of cash expected to be received from customers in September is

   a. $240,000
   b. $225,000
   c. $ 60,000
   d. $165,000
   e. $220,000

4. A plan that shows the expected cash inflows and cash outflows during the budget period, including receipts from loans needed to maintain a minimum cash balance and repayments of such loans, is called
   a. A rolling budget.
   b. An income statement.
   c. A balance sheet.
   d. A cash budget.
   e. An operating budget.

5.^A The following sales are predicted for a company's next four months.

	September	October	November	December
Unit sales . .	480	560	600	480

   Each month's ending inventory of finished goods should be 30% of the next month's sales. At September 1, the finished goods inventory is 140 units. The budgeted production of units for October is
   a. 572 units.
   b. 560 units.
   c. 548 units.
   d. 600 units.
   e. 180 units.

^A Superscript letter A denotes assignments based on Appendix 20A.

[I] Icon denotes assignments that involve decision making.

Discussion Questions

1. [I] Identify at least three roles that budgeting plays in helping managers control and monitor a business.

2. What two common benchmarks can be used to evaluate actual performance? Which of the two is generally more useful?

3. [I] What is the benefit of continuous budgeting?

4. Identify three usual time horizons for short-term planning and budgets.

5. [I] Why should each department participate in preparing its own budget?

6. [I] How does budgeting help management coordinate and plan business activities?

7. [I] Why is the sales budget so important to the budgeting process?

8. What is a selling expense budget? What is a capital expenditures budget?

9. Budgeting promotes good decision making by requiring managers to conduct _____ and by focusing their attention on the _____.

10. **Nokia** prepares a cash budget. What is a cash budget? Why must operating budgets and the capital expenditures budget be prepared before the cash budget?   **NOKIA**

11.^A What is the difference between a production budget and a manufacturing budget?

12. [I] Would a manager of an **Apple** retail store participate more in budgeting than a manager at the corporate offices? Explain.   **Apple**

13. [I] Does the manager of a **Research In Motion** distribution center participate in long-term budgeting? Explain.   **RIM**

14. [I] Assume that **Palm**'s smartphone division is charged with preparing a master budget. Identify the participants—for example, the sales manager for the sales budget—and describe the information each person provides in preparing the master budget.   **Palm**

QUICK STUDY

QS 20-1
Budget motivation   C1

The motivation of employees is one goal of budgeting. Identify three guidelines that organizations should follow if budgeting is to serve effectively as a source of motivation for employees.

QS 20-2
Budgeting process   C1

Good management includes good budgeting. (1) Explain why the bottom-up approach to budgeting is considered a more successful management technique than a top-down approach. (2) Provide an example of implementation of the bottom-up approach to budgeting.

QS 20-3
Components of a master budget
C2

Which one of the following sets of items are all necessary components of the master budget?

1. Operating budgets, historical income statement, and budgeted balance sheet.
2. Sales budget, operating budgets, and historical financial budgets.
3. Operating budgets, financial budgets, and capital expenditures budget.
4. Prior sales reports, capital expenditures budget, and financial budgets.

QS 20-4
Purchases budget   P1

Rockgate Company's July sales budget calls for sales of $400,000. The store expects to begin July with $40,000 of inventory and to end the month with $50,000 of inventory. Gross margin is typically 30% of sales. Determine the budgeted cost of merchandise purchases for July.

QS 20-5
Computing budgeted accounts receivable
P2

Treehouse Company anticipates total sales for June and July of $420,000 and $398,000, respectively. Cash sales are normally 60% of total sales. Of the credit sales, 10% are collected in the same month as the sale, 70% are collected during the first month after the sale, and the remaining 20% are collected in the second month. Determine the amount of accounts receivable reported on the company's budgeted balance sheet as of July 31.

QS 20-6
Cash budget
P1

Use the following information to prepare a cash budget for the month ended on March 31 for Sosa Company. The budget should show expected cash receipts and cash disbursements for the month of March and the balance expected on March 31.

a. Beginning cash balance on March 1, $82,000.
b. Cash receipts from sales, $300,000.
c. Budgeted cash disbursements for purchases, $120,000.
d. Budgeted cash disbursements for salaries, $80,000.
e. Other budgeted cash expenses, $55,000.
f. Cash repayment of bank loan, $30,000.

QS 20-7
Activity-based budgeting
A1

Activity-based budgeting is a budget system based on *expected activities*. (1) Describe activity-based budgeting, and explain its preparation of budgets. (2) How does activity-based budgeting differ from traditional budgeting?

QS 20-8

QS 20-8[A]
Production budget
P3

Goldenlock Company manufactures watches and has a JIT policy that ending inventory must equal 20% of the next month's sales. It estimates that October's actual ending inventory will consist of 95,000 watches. November and December sales are estimated to be 350,000 and 400,000 watches, respectively. Compute the number of watches to be produced that would appear on the company's production budget for the month of November.

QS 20-9[A]
Factory overhead budget   P3

Refer to information from QS 20-8[A]. Goldenlock Company assigns variable overhead at the rate of $1.75 per unit of production. Fixed overhead equals $5,000,000 per month. Prepare a factory overhead budget for November.

QS 20-10
Sales budget   P1

Turks sells miniature digital cameras for $400 each. 900 units were sold in May, and it forecasts 5% growth in unit sales each month. Determine (a) the number of camera sales and (b) the dollar amount of camera sales for the month of June.

Refer to information from QS 20-10. Turks pays a sales manager a monthly salary of $4,000 and a commission of 10% of camera sales (in dollars). Prepare a selling expense budget for the month of June.

QS 20-11
Selling expense budget P1

Refer to information from QS 20-10. Assume 20% of Turks's sales are for cash. The remaining 80% are credit sales; these customers pay in the month following the sale. Compute the budgeted cash receipts for June.

QS 20-12
Cash budget P1

Following are selected accounts for a company. For each account, indicate whether it will appear on a budgeted income statement (BIS) or a budgeted balance sheet (BBS). If an item will not appear on either budgeted financial statement, label it NA.

QS 20-13
Budgeted financial statements
P2

Sales	_____	Interest paid on bank loan	_____
Administrative salaries paid	_____	Cash dividends paid	_____
Accumulated depreciation	_____	Bank loan owed	_____
Depreciation expense	_____	Cost of goods sold	_____

The Candy Shoppe reports the following sales forecast: August, $110,000; September, $120,000. Cash sales are normally 25% of total sales and all credit sales are expected to be collected in the month following the date of sale. Prepare a schedule of cash receipts for September.

QS 20-14
Cash receipts P1

Zen Den reports the following sales forecast: September, $25,000; October, $36,000; and November, $30,000. All sales are on account. Collections of credit sales are received as follows: 15% in the month of sale, 60% in the first month after sale, 20% in the second month after sale, and 5% is uncollectible. Prepare a schedule of cash receipts for November.

QS 20-15
Cash receipts P1

T-Mart purchased $100,000 of merchandise in August and expects to purchase $120,000 in September. Merchandise purchases are paid as follows: 25% in the month of purchase and 75% in the following month. Compute cash disbursements for merchandise for September.

QS 20-16
Cash disbursements for merchandise P1

Jam Co. forecasts merchandise purchases of $11,600 in January, $11,800 in February, and $15,400 in March; 40% of purchases are paid in the month of purchase and 60% are paid in the following month. At December 31 of the prior year, the balance of Accounts Payable (for December purchases) is $8,000. Prepare a schedule of cash disbursements for merchandise for each of the months of January, February, and March.

QS 20-17
Cash disbursements for merchandise
P1

Splinter Company forecasts sales of 6,000 units for April. Beginning inventory is 1,000 units. The desired ending inventory is 30% higher than the beginning inventory. How many units should Splinter purchase in April?

QS 20-18
Computing purchases
P1

Li Company forecasts unit sales of 640,000 in April, 720,000 in May, 780,000 in June, and 620,000 in July. Beginning inventory on April 1 is 192,000 units, and the company wants to have 30% of next month's sales in inventory at the end of each month. Prepare a merchandise purchases budget for the months of April, May, and June.

QS 20-19
Computing purchases
P1

Kyoto, Inc. predicts the following sales in units for the coming three months:

QS 20-20[A]
Production budget
P3

	May	June	July
Sales in units	280	300	240

Each month's ending inventory of finished units should be 60% of the next month's sales. The April 30 finished goods inventory is 168 units. Compute Kyoto's budgeted production (in units) for May.

Zyton Corp. budgets production of 292 units in January and 264 units in February. Each finished unit requires five pounds of raw material Z, which costs $6 per pound. Each month's ending inventory of raw materials should be 30% of the following month's budgeted production. The January 1 raw materials inventory has 438 pounds of Z. Prepare a direct materials budget for January.

QS 20-21[A]
Direct materials budget
P3

QS 20-22^A
Direct labor budget   P3

Tek Co. plans to produce 620 units in July. Each unit requires two hours of direct labor. The direct labor rate is $16 per hour. Prepare a direct labor budget for July.

QS 20-23
Sales budget   P1

Shay, Inc., is preparing its master budget for the quarter ending March 31. It sells a single product for $25 per unit. Budgeted sales for the next four months follow. Prepare a sales budget for the months of January, February, and March.

	January	February	March	April
Sales in units	1,200	1,000	1,600	1,400

QS 20-24
Cash receipts budget   P1

Refer to information in QS 20-23. In addition, sales are 40% cash and 60% on credit. All credit sales are collected in the month following the sale. The January 1 balance in accounts receivable is $10,000. Prepare a schedule of budgeted cash receipts for January, February, and March.

QS 20-25
Selling expense budget   P1

Refer to information in QS 20-23. In addition, sales commissions are 10% of sales and the company pays a sales manager a salary of $5,000 per month. Sales commissions and salaries are paid in the month incurred. Prepare a selling expense budget for January, February, and March.

QS 20-26
Budgeted loan activity
P1

Mink Company is preparing a cash budget for February. The company has $30,000 cash at the beginning of February and anticipates $75,000 in cash receipts and $96,250 in cash disbursements during February. What amount, if any, must the company borrow during February to maintain a $10,000 cash balance? The company has no loans outstanding on February 1.

QS 20-27
Operating budgets
P1

Royal Phillips Electronics of the Netherlands reports sales of €23,200 million for a recent year. Assume that the company expects sales growth of 3 percent for the next year. Also assume that selling expenses are typically 20 percent of sales, while general and administrative expenses are 4 percent of sales.

Required

1. Compute budgeted sales for the next year.
2. Assume budgeted sales for next year is €24,000 million, and then compute budgeted selling expenses and budgeted general and administrative expenses for the next year. Round amounts to one decimal.

McGraw Hill **connect**

EXERCISES

Exercise 20-1
Preparation of merchandise purchases budgets (for three periods)
P1

Formworks Company prepares monthly budgets. The current budget plans for a September ending inventory of 15,000 units. Company policy is to end each month with merchandise inventory equal to a specified percent of budgeted sales for the following month. Budgeted sales and merchandise purchases for the three most recent months follow. (1) Prepare the merchandise purchases budget for the months of July, August, and September. (2) Compute the ratio of ending inventory to the next month's sales for each budget prepared in part 1. (3) How many units are budgeted for sale in October?

	Sales (Units)	Purchases (Units)
July	120,000	138,000
August	210,000	204,000
September	180,000	159,000

Exercise 20-2
Preparation of cash budgets (for three periods)
P1

Kasik Co. budgeted the following cash receipts and cash disbursements for the first three months of next year.

	Cash Receipts	Cash Disbursements
January	$500,000	$450,000
February.........	300,000	250,000
March	400,000	500,000

According to a credit agreement with the company's bank, Kasik promises to have a minimum cash balance of $30,000 at each month-end. In return, the bank has agreed that the company can borrow up to $150,000 at an annual interest rate of 12%, paid on the last day of each month. The interest is computed based on the beginning balance of the loan for the month. The company has a cash balance of $30,000 and a loan balance of $60,000 at January 1. Prepare monthly cash budgets for each of the first three months of next year.

Check January ending cash balance, $30,000

Use the following information to prepare the July cash budget for Sanchez Co. It should show expected cash receipts and cash disbursements for the month and the cash balance expected on July 31.

a. Beginning cash balance on July 1: $50,000.

b. Cash receipts from sales: 30% is collected in the month of sale, 50% in the next month, and 20% in the second month after sale (uncollectible accounts are negligible and can be ignored). Sales amounts are: May (actual), $1,720,000; June (actual), $1,200,000; and July (budgeted), $1,400,000.

c. Payments on merchandise purchases: 60% in the month of purchase and 40% in the month following purchase. Purchases amounts are: June (actual), $430,000; and July (budgeted), $600,000.

d. Budgeted cash disbursements for salaries in July: $211,000.

e. Budgeted depreciation expense for July: $12,000.

f. Other cash expenses budgeted for July: $150,000.

g. Accrued income taxes due in July: $80,000.

h. Bank loan interest due in July: $6,600.

Exercise 20-3
Preparation of a cash budget
P1

Check Ending cash balance, $434,400

Use the information in Exercise 20-3 and the following additional information to prepare a budgeted income statement for the month of July and a budgeted balance sheet for July 31.

a. Cost of goods sold is 44% of sales.

b. Inventory at the end of June is $80,000 and at the end of July is $64,000.

c. Salaries payable on June 30 are $50,000 and are expected to be $40,000 on July 31.

d. The equipment account balance is $1,600,000 on July 31. On June 30, the accumulated depreciation on equipment is $280,000.

e. The $6,600 cash payment of interest represents the 1% monthly expense on a bank loan of $660,000.

f. Income taxes payable on July 31 are $124,320, and the income tax rate applicable to the company is 30%.

g. The only other balance sheet accounts are: Common Stock, with a balance of $600,000 on June 30; and Retained Earnings, with a balance of $1,072,000 on June 30.

Exercise 20-4
Preparing a budgeted income statement and balance sheet
P2

Check Net income, $290,080; Total assets, $3,026,400

Powerdyne Company's cost of goods sold is consistently 60% of sales. The company plans to carry ending merchandise inventory for each month equal to 40% of the next month's budgeted cost of good sold. All merchandise is purchased on credit, and 50% of the purchases made during a month is paid for in that month. Another 35% is paid for during the first month after purchase, and the remaining 15% is paid for during the second month after purchase. Expected unit sales are: August (actual), 150,000; September (actual), 350,000; October (estimated), 200,000; November (estimated), 300,000. Use this information to determine October's expected cash payments for purchases. (*Hint:* Use the layout of Exhibit 20.8, but revised for the facts given here.)

Exercise 20-5
Computing budgeted cash payments for purchases
P1

Check Budgeted purchases: August, $138,000; October, $144,000

Sand Dollar Company purchases all merchandise on credit. It recently budgeted the following month-end accounts payable balances and merchandise inventory balances. Cash payments on accounts payable during each month are expected to be: May, $1,300,000; June, $1,450,000; July, $1,350,000; and August, $1,400,000. Use the available information to compute the budgeted amounts of (1) merchandise purchases for June, July, and August and (2) cost of goods sold for June, July, and August.

Exercise 20-6
Computing budgeted purchases and costs of goods sold
P1

	Accounts Payable	Merchandise Inventory
May 31	$120,000	$250,000
June 30	170,000	400,000
July 31	200,000	300,000
August 31	160,000	330,000

Check June purchases, $1,500,000; June cost of goods sold, $1,350,000

Exercise 20-7
Computing budgeted accounts payable and purchases—sales forecast in dollars

P1   P2

Sound Check, a merchandising company specializing in home computer speakers, budgets its monthly cost of goods sold to equal 70% of sales. Its inventory policy calls for ending inventory in each month to equal 25% of the next month's budgeted cost of goods sold. All purchases are on credit, and 20% of the purchases in a month is paid for in the same month. Another 50% is paid for during the first month after purchase, and the remaining 30% is paid for in the second month after purchase. The following sales budgets are set: July, $300,000; August, $240,000; September, $270,000; October, $240,000; and November, $210,000. Compute the following: (1) budgeted merchandise purchases for July, August, September, and October; (2) budgeted payments on accounts payable for September and October; and (3) budgeted ending balances of accounts payable for September and October. (*Hint:* For part 1, refer to Exhibits 20.7 and 20.8 for guidance, but note that budgeted sales are in dollars for this assignment.)

Exercise 20-8ᴬ
Preparing production budgets (for two periods)   P3

Nascar Company manufactures an innovative automobile transmission for electric cars. Management predicts that ending inventory for the first quarter will be 37,500 units. The following unit sales of the transmissions are expected during the rest of the year: second quarter, 225,000 units; third quarter, 262,500 units; and fourth quarter, 237,500 units. Company policy calls for the ending inventory of a quarter to equal 20% of the next quarter's budgeted sales. Prepare a production budget for both the second and third quarters that shows the number of transmissions to manufacture.

Exercise 20-9ᴬ
Direct materials budget

P3

Refer to information from Exercise 20-8ᴬ. Each transmission requires 0.60 pounds of a key raw material. Nascar Company aims to end each quarter with an ending inventory of direct materials equal to 50% of next quarter's budgeted materials requirements. Direct materials cost $175 per unit. Prepare a direct materials budget for the second quarter.

Exercise 20-10ᴬ
Direct labor budget   P3

Refer to information from Exercise 20-8ᴬ. Each transmission requires 4 direct labor hours, at a cost of $9 per hour. Prepare a direct labor budget for the second quarter.

Exercise 20-11
Budgeted cash disbursements

P1

Jake Company reports the following:

	July	August	September
Sales	$24,000	$32,000	$36,000
Purchases	14,400	19,200	21,600

Payments for purchases are made in the month after purchase. Selling expenses are 15% of sales, administrative expenses are 10% of sales, and both are paid in the month of sale. Rent expense of $2,400 is paid monthly. Depreciation expense is $1,300 per month. Prepare a schedule of budgeted cash disbursements for August and September.

Exercise 20-12
Budgeted cash receipts

P1

Emily Company has sales on account and sales for cash. Specifically, 60% of its sales are on account and 40% are for cash. Credit sales are collected in full in the month following the sale. The company forecasts sales of $525,000 for April, $535,000 for May, and $560,000 for June. The beginning balance of Accounts Receivable is $300,000 on April 1. Prepare a schedule of budgeted cash receipts for April, May, and June.

Exercise 20-13
Cash budget

P1

Kaizen Corp. requires a minimum $8,000 cash balance. If necessary, loans are taken to meet this requirement at a cost of 1% interest per month (paid monthly). Any excess cash is used to repay loans at month-end. The cash balance on July 1 is $8,400 and the company has no outstanding loans. Forecasted cash receipts (other than for loans received) and forecasted cash payments (other than for loan or interest payments) are:

	July	August	September
Cash receipts	$24,000	$32,000	$40,000
Cash disbursements	28,000	30,000	32,000

Prepare a cash budget for July, August, and September. Round interest payments to the nearest whole dollar.

Fabrice Corp. requires a minimum $6,000 cash balance. If necessary, loans are taken to meet this requirement at a cost of 1% interest per month (paid monthly). Any excess cash is used to repay loans at month-end. The cash balance on October 1 is $6,000 and the company has an outstanding loan of $2,000. Forecasted cash receipts (other than for loans received) and forecasted cash payments (other than for loan or interest payments) follow. Prepare a cash budget for October, November, and December. Round interest payments to the nearest whole dollar.

Exercise 20-14
Cash budget
P1

	October	November	December
Cash receipts	$22,000	$16,000	$20,000
Cash disbursements	24,000	15,000	16,000

Cambridge, Inc. is preparing its master budget for the quarter ended June 30. Budgeted sales and cash payments for merchandise for the next three months follow:

Exercise 20-15
Cash budget
P1

	April	May	June
Budgeted sales	$32,000	$40,000	$24,000
Budgeted cash payments for merchandise.................	20,200	16,800	17,200

Sales are 60% cash and 40% on credit. All credit sales are collected in the month following the sale. The March 30 balance sheet includes balances of $12,000 in cash, $12,000 in accounts receivable, $11,000 in accounts payable, and a $2,000 balance in loans payable. A minimum cash balance of $12,000 is required. Loans are obtained at the end of any month when a cash shortage occurs. Interest is 1% per month based on the beginning of the month loan balance and is paid at each month-end. If an excess balance of cash exists, loans are repaid at the end of the month. Operating expenses are paid in the month incurred and consist of sales commissions (10% of sales), shipping (3% of sales), office salaries ($3,000 per month) and rent ($5,000 per month). Prepare a cash budget for each of the months of April, May, and June (round all dollar amounts to the nearest whole dollar).

Kool-Ray is preparing its master budget for the quarter ended September 30. Budgeted sales and cash payments for merchandise for the next three months follow:

Exercise 20-16
Cash budget
P1

	July	August	September
Budgeted sales	$64,000	$80,000	$48,000
Budgeted cash payments for merchandise.................	40,400	33,600	34,400

Sales are 20% cash and 80% on credit. All credit sales are collected in the month following the sale. The June 30 balance sheet includes balances of $12,000 in cash; $45,000 in accounts receivable; $4,500 in accounts payable; and a $2,000 balance in loans payable. A minimum cash balance of $12,000 is required. Loans are obtained at the end of any month when a cash shortage occurs. Interest is 1% per month based on the beginning of the month loan balance and is paid at each month-end. If an excess balance of cash exists, loans are repaid at the end of the month. Operating expenses are paid in the month incurred and consist of sales commissions (10% of sales), office salaries ($4,000 per month), and rent ($6,500 per month). (1) Prepare a cash receipts budget for July, August, and September. (2) Prepare a cash budget for each of the months of July, August, and September. (Round all dollar amounts to the nearest whole dollar.)

Exercise 20-17
Budgeted balance sheet
P2

The following information is available for Zhao Company:

a. The cash budget for March shows an ending bank loan of $10,000 and an ending cash balance of $48,000.

b. The sales budget for March indicates sales of $120,000. Accounts receivable are expected to be 70% of the current-month sales.

c. The merchandise purchases budget indicates that $89,000 in merchandise will be purchased on account in March. Purchases on account are paid 100% in the month following the purchase. Ending inventory for March is predicted to be 600 units at a cost of $35 each.

d. The budgeted income statement for March shows net income of $48,000. Depreciation expense of $1,000 and $26,000 in income tax expense were used in computing net income for March. Accrued taxes will be paid in April.

e. The balance sheet for February shows equipment of $84,000 with accumulated depreciation of $30,000, common stock of $25,000, and ending retained earnings of $8,000. There are no changes budgeted in the equipment or common stock accounts.

Prepare a budgeted balance sheet for March.

Exercise 20-18
Budgeted income statement
P2

Zulu, Inc., is preparing its master budget for the first quarter. The company sells a single product at a price of $25 per unit. Sales (in units) are forecasted at 40,000 for January, 60,000 for February, and 50,000 for March. Cost of goods sold is $14 per unit. Other expense information for the first quarter follows. Prepare a budgeted income statement for this first quarter.

Commissions	10% of sales
Rent	$20,000 per month
Advertising	15% of sales
Office salaries	$75,000 per month
Depreciation	$50,000 per month
Interest	15% annually on a $250,000 note payable
Tax rate.	40%

Exercise 20-19^A
Direct labor budget
P3

The production budget for Zink Company shows units to be produced as follows: July, 620; August, 680; September, 540. Each unit produced requires two hours of direct labor. The direct labor rate is currently $16 per hour but is predicted to be $16.75 per hour in September. Prepare a direct labor budget for the months July, August, and September.

Exercise 20-20^A
Production budget
P3

Rad Co. provides the following sales forecast for the next four months:

	April	May	June	July
Sales (units)	500	580	530	600

The company wants to end each month with ending finished goods inventory equal to 20% of next month's sales. Finished goods inventory on April 1 is 174 units. Assume July's budgeted production is 540 units. Prepare a production budget for the months of April, May, and June.

Exercise 20-21^A
Direct materials budget
P3

Refer to the information in Exercise 20-20^A. In addition, assume each finished unit requires five pounds of raw materials and the company wants to end each month with raw materials inventory equal to 30% of next month's production needs. Beginning raw materials inventory for April was 663 pounds.

Prepare a direct materials budget for April, May, and June.

Match the definitions 1 through 9 with the term or phrase a through i.

A. Master budget
B. General and administrative expense budget
C. Budget
D. Safety stock
E. Budgeted income statement
F. Budgeted balance sheet
G. Sales budget
H. Cash budget
I. Merchandise purchases budget

_____ 1. A plan that shows the units or costs of merchandise to be purchased by a merchandising company during the budget period.

_____ 2. An accounting report that presents predicted amounts of the company's assets, liabilities, and equity balances at the end of the budget period.

_____ 3. A plan showing the units of goods to be sold and the sales to be derived; the usual starting point in the budgeting process.

_____ 4. An accounting report that presents predicted amounts of the company's revenues and expenses for the budgeting period.

_____ 5. A quantity of inventory or materials over the minimum to reduce the risk of running short.

_____ 6. A comprehensive business plan that includes specific plans for expected sales, the units of product to be produced, the merchandise or materials to be purchased, the expenses to be incurred, the long-term assets to be purchased, and the amounts of cash to be borrowed or loans to be repaid, as well as a budgeted income statement and balance sheet.

_____ 7. A formal statement of a company's future plans, usually expressed in monetary terms.

_____ 8. A plan that shows predicted operating expenses not included in the selling expenses budget.

_____ 9. A plan that shows the expected cash inflows and cash outflows during the budget period, including receipts from any loans needed to maintain a minimum cash balance and repayments of such loans.

Exercise 20-22
Master budget definitions
C2

Participatory budgeting can sometimes lead to negative consequences. Identify three potential negative outcomes that can arise from participatory budgeting.

Exercise 20-23
Budget consequences   C1

Kirk Co. CPA is preparing activity-based budgets for 2011. The partners expect the firm to generate billable hours for the year as follows:

Data entry	1,100 hours
Auditing	2,400 hours
Tax	2,150 hours
Consulting	375 hours

The company pays $8 per hour to data-entry clerks, $40 per hour to audit personnel, $50 per hour to tax personnel, and $50 per hour to consulting personnel. Prepare a schedule of budgeted labor costs for 2011 using activity-based budgeting.

Exercise 20-24
Activity-based budgeting
A1

---

 connect

Pinsetter's Supply is a merchandiser of three different products. The company's February 28 inventories are footwear, 15,500 units; sports equipment, 70,000 units; and apparel, 40,000 units. Management believes that excessive inventories have accumulated for all three products. As a result, a new policy dictates that ending inventory in any month should equal 40% of the expected unit sales for the following month. Expected sales in units for March, April, May, and June follow.

	Budgeted Sales in Units			
	March	April	May	June
Footwear	10,000	20,000	30,000	33,000
Sports equipment	66,000	85,000	90,000	80,000
Apparel	36,000	30,000	30,000	18,000

PROBLEM SET A

Problem 20-1A
Preparation and analysis of merchandise purchases budgets

C2 P1

eXcel
mhhe.com/wildFINMAN4e

Required

1. Prepare a merchandise purchases budget (in units) for each product for each of the months of March, April, and May.

Analysis Component

2. The purchases budgets in part 1 should reflect fewer purchases of all three products in March compared to those in April and May. What factor caused fewer purchases to be planned? Suggest business conditions that would cause this factor to both occur and impact the company in this way.

Problem 20-2A

Preparation of cash budgets
(for three periods)

C2   P2

mhhe.com/wildFINMAN4e

During the last week of August, Apache Arts Company's owner approaches the bank for an $80,000 loan to be made on September 2 and repaid on November 30 with annual interest of 12%, for an interest cost of $2,400. The owner plans to increase the store's inventory by $60,000 during September and needs the loan to pay for inventory acquisitions. The bank's loan officer needs more information about Apache Arts' ability to repay the loan and asks the owner to forecast the store's November 30 cash position. On September 1, Apache Arts is expected to have a $3,000 cash balance, $135,000 of accounts receivable, and $100,000 of accounts payable. Its budgeted sales, merchandise purchases, and various cash disbursements for the next three months follow.

Budgeted Figures*	September	October	November
Sales	$220,000	$300,000	$380,000
Merchandise purchases	210,000	180,000	220,000
Cash disbursements			
Payroll	16,000	17,000	18,000
Rent	6,000	6,000	6,000
Other cash expenses	64,000	8,000	7,000
Repayment of bank loan			80,000
Interest on the bank loan			2,400

* Operations began in August; August sales were $180,000 and purchases were $100,000.

The budgeted September merchandise purchases include the inventory increase. All sales are on account. The company predicts that 25% of credit sales is collected in the month of the sale, 45% in the month following the sale, 20% in the second month, 9% in the third, and the remainder is uncollectible. Applying these percents to the August credit sales, for example, shows that $81,000 of the $180,000 will be collected in September, $36,000 in October, and $16,200 in November. All merchandise is purchased on credit; 80% of the balance is paid in the month following a purchase, and the remaining 20% is paid in the second month. For example, of the $100,000 August purchases, $80,000 will be paid in September and $20,000 in October.

Required

Prepare a cash budget for September, October, and November for Apache Arts Company. Show supporting calculations as needed.

Problem 20-3A

Preparation and analysis of
cash budgets with supporting
inventory and purchases
budgets

C2   P2

Abacus Company sells its product for $125 per unit. Its actual and projected sales follow.

	Units	Dollars
April (actual)	8,000	$1,000,000
May (actual)	4,000	500,000
June (budgeted)	12,000	1,500,000
July (budgeted)............	6,000	750,000
August (budgeted)	7,600	950,000

All sales are on credit. Recent experience shows that 20% of credit sales is collected in the month of the sale, 30% in the month after the sale, 48% in the second month after the sale, and 2% proves to be uncollectible. The product's purchase price is $100 per unit. All purchases are payable within 12 days. Thus, 60% of purchases made in a month is paid in that month and the other 40% is paid in the next month. The company has a policy to maintain an ending monthly inventory of 25% of the next month's unit sales plus a safety stock of 100 units. The April 30 and May 31 actual inventory levels are consistent with this policy. Selling and administrative expenses for the year are $1,200,000 and are paid evenly throughout the year in cash. The company's minimum cash balance at month-end is $60,000. This minimum is maintained, if necessary, by borrowing cash from the bank. If the balance exceeds $60,000, the company repays as much of the loan as it can without going below the minimum. This type of loan carries an annual 9% interest rate. On May 31, the loan balance is $32,000, and the company's cash balance is $60,000.

Required

1. Prepare a table that shows the computation of cash collections of its credit sales (accounts receivable) in each of the months of June and July.

2. Prepare a table that shows the computation of budgeted ending inventories (in units) for April, May, June, and July.

3. Prepare the merchandise purchases budget for May, June, and July. Report calculations in units and then show the dollar amount of purchases for each month.

4. Prepare a table showing the computation of cash payments on product purchases for June and July.

5. Prepare a cash budget for June and July, including any loan activity and interest expense. Compute the loan balance at the end of each month.

Analysis Component

6. Refer to your answer to part 5. Abacus's cash budget indicates the company will need to borrow more than $40,000 in June and will need to borrow $60,000 in July. Suggest some reasons that knowing this information in May would be helpful to management.

Check (1) Cash collections: June, $930,000; July, $840,000

(3) Budgeted purchases: May, $600,000; June, $1,050,000

(5) Budgeted ending loan balance: June, $72,240; July, $136,782

Lilliput, a one-product mail-order firm, buys its product for $60 per unit and sells it for $130 per unit. The sales staff receives a 10% commission on the sale of each unit. Its December income statement follows.

Problem 20-4A
Preparation and analysis of budgeted income statements

C2 P2

LILLIPUT COMPANY	
Income Statement	
For Month Ended December 31, 2011	
Sales	$1,300,000
Cost of goods sold	600,000
Gross profit	700,000
Expenses	
Sales commissions (10%)	130,000
Advertising	200,000
Store rent	24,000
Administrative salaries	40,000
Depreciation	50,000
Other expenses	12,000
Total expenses	456,000
Net income	$ 244,000

Management expects December's results to be repeated in January, February, and March of 2012 without any changes in strategy. Management, however, has an alternative plan. It believes that unit sales will increase at a rate of 10% *each* month for the next three months (beginning with January) if the item's selling price is reduced to $115 per unit and advertising expenses are increased by 25% and remain at that level for all three months. The cost of its product will remain at $60 per unit, the sales staff will continue to earn a 10% commission, and the remaining expenses will stay the same.

Required

1. Prepare budgeted income statements for each of the months of January, February, and March that show the expected results from implementing the proposed changes. Use a three-column format, with one column for each month.

Check (1) Budgeted net income: January, $102,500; February, $150,350; March, $202,985

Analysis Component

2. Use the budgeted income statements from part 1 to recommend whether management should implement the proposed changes. Explain.

Problem 20-5A
Preparation of a complete
master budget

C2 P1 P2

Near the end of 2011, the management of Simid Sports Co., a merchandising company, prepared the following estimated balance sheet for December 31, 2011.

SIMID SPORTS COMPANY
Estimated Balance Sheet
December 31, 2011

Assets

Cash		$ 18,000
Accounts receivable		262,500
Inventory		75,000
Total current assets		355,500
Equipment	$270,000	
Less accumulated depreciation	33,750	236,250
Total assets		$591,750

Liabilities and Equity

Accounts payable	$180,000	
Bank loan payable	7,500	
Taxes payable (due 3/15/2012)	45,000	
Total liabilities		$232,500
Common stock	236,250	
Retained earnings	123,000	
Total stockholders' equity		359,250
Total liabilities and equity		$591,750

To prepare a master budget for January, February, and March of 2012, management gathers the following information.

a. Simid Sports' single product is purchased for $30 per unit and resold for $55 per unit. The expected inventory level of 2,500 units on December 31, 2011, is more than management's desired level for 2012, which is 20% of the next month's expected sales (in units). Expected sales are: January, 3,500 units; February, 4,500 units; March, 5,500 units; and April, 5,000 units.

b. Cash sales and credit sales represent 25% and 75%, respectively, of total sales. Of the credit sales, 60% is collected in the first month after the month of sale and 40% in the second month after the month of sale. For the December 31, 2011, accounts receivable balance, $62,500 is collected in January and the remaining $200,000 is collected in February.

c. Merchandise purchases are paid for as follows: 20% in the first month after the month of purchase and 80% in the second month after the month of purchase. For the December 31, 2011, accounts payable balance, $40,000 is paid in January and the remaining $140,000 is paid in February.

d. Sales commissions equal to 20% of sales are paid each month. Sales salaries (excluding commissions) are $30,000 per year.

e. General and administrative salaries are $72,000 per year. Maintenance expense equals $1,000 per month and is paid in cash.

f. Equipment reported in the December 31, 2011, balance sheet was purchased in January 2011. It is being depreciated over eight years under the straight-line method with no salvage value. The following amounts for new equipment purchases are planned in the coming quarter: January, $18,000; February, $48,000; and March, $14,400. This equipment will be depreciated under the straight-line method over eight years with no salvage value. A full month's depreciation is taken for the month in which equipment is purchased.

g. The company plans to acquire land at the end of March at a cost of $75,000, which will be paid with cash on the last day of the month.

h. Simid Sports has a working arrangement with its bank to obtain additional loans as needed. The interest rate is 12% per year, and interest is paid at each month-end based on the beginning balance. Partial or full payments on these loans can be made on the last day of the month. The company has agreed to maintain a minimum ending cash balance of $12,500 in each month.

i. The income tax rate for the company is 40%. Income taxes on the first quarter's income will not be paid until April 15.

Required

Prepare a master budget for each of the first three months of 2012; include the following component budgets (show supporting calculations as needed, and round amounts to the nearest dollar):

1. Monthly sales budgets (showing both budgeted unit sales and dollar sales).

2. Monthly merchandise purchases budgets.

3. Monthly selling expense budgets.

4. Monthly general and administrative expense budgets.

5. Monthly capital expenditures budgets.

6. Monthly cash budgets.

7. Budgeted income statement for the entire first quarter (not for each month).

8. Budgeted balance sheet as of March 31, 2012.

Check   (2) Budgeted purchases: January, $57,000; February, $141,000

(3) Budgeted selling expenses: January, $41,000; February, $52,000

(6) Ending cash bal.: January, $15,050; February, $105,150

(8) Budgeted total assets at March 31, $784,325

Diamond Slope Company produces snow skis. Each ski requires 2 pounds of carbon fiber. The company's management predicts that 7,000 skis and 10,000 pounds of carbon fiber will be in inventory on June 30 of the current year and that 120,000 skis will be sold during the next (third) quarter. Management wants to end the third quarter with 4,000 skis and 5,000 pounds of carbon fiber in inventory. Carbon fiber can be purchased for $12 per pound.

Problem 20-6A[A]
Preparing production and direct materials budgets

C2   P3

Required

1. Prepare the third-quarter production budget for skis.

2. Prepare the third-quarter direct materials (carbon fiber) budget; include the dollar cost of purchases.

Check   (1) Units manuf., 117,000;

(2) Cost of carbon fiber purchases, $2,748,000

H20 Company is a merchandiser of three different products. The company's March 31 inventories are water skis, 40,000 units; tow ropes, 90,000 units; and life jackets, 250,000 units. Management believes that excessive inventories have accumulated for all three products. As a result, a new policy dictates that ending inventory in any month should equal 10% of the expected unit sales for the following month. Expected sales in units for April, May, June, and July follow.

PROBLEM SET B

Problem 20-1B
Preparation and analysis of merchandise purchases budgets

C2   P1

	Budgeted Sales in Units			
	April	May	June	July
Water skis	70,000	90,000	130,000	140,000
Tow ropes	100,000	90,000	110,000	100,000
Life jackets	300,000	260,000	310,000	260,000

Required

1. Prepare a merchandise purchases budget (in units) for each product for each of the months of April, May, and June.

Check   (1) April budgeted purchases: Water skis, 39,000; Tow ropes, 19,000; Life jackets, 76,000

Analysis Component

2. The purchases budgets in part 1 should reflect fewer purchases of all three products in April compared to those in May and June. What factor caused fewer purchases to be planned? Suggest business conditions that would cause this factor to both occur and affect the company as it has.

During the last week of March, Siro Stereo's owner approaches the bank for a $125,000 loan to be made on April 1 and repaid on June 30 with annual interest of 10%, for an interest cost of $3,125. The owner plans to increase the store's inventory by $100,000 in April and needs the loan to pay for inventory acquisitions. The bank's loan officer needs more information about Siro Stereo's ability to repay the loan and asks the owner to forecast the store's June 30 cash position. On April 1, Siro Stereo is expected to have a $12,000 cash balance, $121,500 of accounts receivable, and $90,000 of accounts

Problem 20-2B
Preparation of cash budgets (for three periods)

C2   P2

payable. Its budgeted sales, merchandise purchases, and various cash disbursements for the next three months follow.

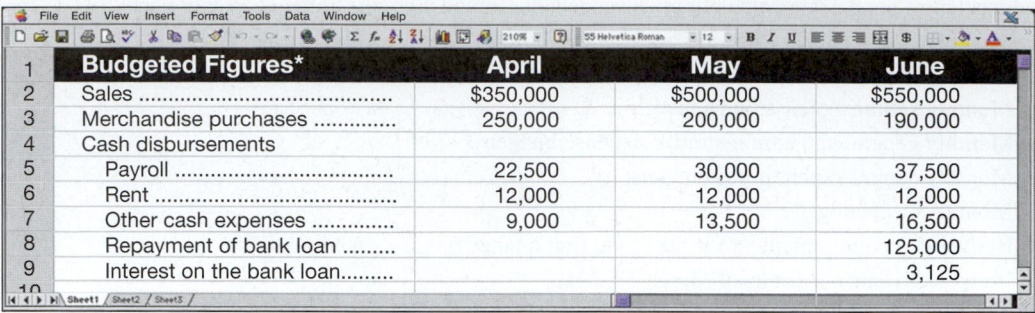

Budgeted Figures*	April	May	June
1			
2 Sales	$350,000	$500,000	$550,000
3 Merchandise purchases	250,000	200,000	190,000
4 Cash disbursements			
5 Payroll	22,500	30,000	37,500
6 Rent	12,000	12,000	12,000
7 Other cash expenses	9,000	13,500	16,500
8 Repayment of bank loan			125,000
9 Interest on the bank loan.........			3,125

*Operations began in March; March sales were $135,000 and purchases were $90,000.

The budgeted April merchandise purchases include the inventory increase. All sales are on account. The company predicts that 10% of credit sales is collected in the month of the sale, 60% in the month following the sale, 25% in the second month, 3% in the third, and the remainder is uncollectible. Applying these percents to the March credit sales, for example, shows that $81,000 of the $135,000 will be collected in April, $33,750 in May, and $4,050 in June. All merchandise is purchased on credit; 80% of the balance is paid in the month following a purchase and the remaining 20% is paid in the second month. For example, of the $90,000 March purchases, $72,000 will be paid in April and $18,000 in May.

Check Budgeted cash balance:
April, $137,500; May, $157,750;
June, $200,175

Required

Prepare a cash budget for April, May, and June for Siro Stereo. Show supporting calculations as needed.

Problem 20-3B

Preparation and analysis of cash budgets with supporting inventory and purchases budgets

C2 P2

LaRocca Company sells its product for $20 per unit. Its actual and projected sales follow.

	Units	Dollars
January (actual)	18,000	$360,000
February (actual)	27,000	540,000
March (budgeted)	15,000	300,000
April (budgeted)	27,000	540,000
May (budgeted)	33,000	660,000

All sales are on credit. Recent experience shows that 40% of credit sales is collected in the month of the sale, 30% in the month after the sale, 25% in the second month after the sale, and 5% proves to be uncollectible. The product's purchase price is $12 per unit. All purchases are payable within 21 days. Thus, 30% of purchases made in a month is paid in that month and the other 70% is paid in the next month. The company has a policy to maintain an ending monthly inventory of 30% of the next month's unit sales plus a safety stock of 300 units. The January 31 and February 28 actual inventory levels are consistent with this policy. Selling and administrative expenses for the year are $1,440,000 and are paid evenly throughout the year in cash. The company's minimum cash balance for month-end is $45,000. This minimum is maintained, if necessary, by borrowing cash from the bank. If the balance exceeds $45,000, the company repays as much of the loan as it can without going below the minimum. This type of loan carries an annual 12% interest rate. At February 28, the loan balance is $12,000, and the company's cash balance is $45,000.

Required

Check (1) Cash collections: March, $372,000; April, $441,000

1. Prepare a table that shows the computation of cash collections of its credit sales (accounts receivable) in each of the months of March and April.

2. Prepare a table showing the computations of budgeted ending inventories (units) for January, February, March, and April.

Check (3) Budgeted purchases: February, $280,800; March, $223,200

3. Prepare the merchandise purchases budget for February, March, and April. Report calculations in units and then show the dollar amount of purchases for each month.

4. Prepare a table showing the computation of cash payments on product purchases for March and April.

Check (5) Ending cash balance: March, $45,000, April, $82,204

5. Prepare a cash budget for March and April, including any loan activity and interest expense. Compute the loan balance at the end of each month.

Analysis Component

6. Refer to your answer to part 5. LaRocca's cash budget indicates whether the company must borrow additional funds at the end of March. Suggest some reasons that knowing the loan needs in advance would be helpful to management.

Computa-Cations buys its product for $20 and sells it for $50 per unit. The sales staff receives a 10% commission on the sale of each unit. Its June income statement follows.

Problem 20-4B

Preparation and analysis of budgeted income statements

C2 P2

COMPUTA-CATIONS COMPANY Income Statement For Month Ended June 30, 2011	
Sales	$1,000,000
Cost of goods sold	400,000
Gross profit	600,000
Expenses	
Sales commissions (10%)	100,000
Advertising	100,000
Store rent	10,000
Administrative salaries	20,000
Depreciation	12,000
Other expenses	24,000
Total expenses	266,000
Net income	$ 334,000

Management expects June's results to be repeated in July, August, and September without any changes in strategy. Management, however, has another plan. It believes that unit sales will increase at a rate of 10% *each* month for the next three months (beginning with July) if the item's selling price is reduced to $45 per unit and advertising expenses are increased by 20% and remain at that level for all three months. The cost of its product will remain at $20 per unit, the sales staff will continue to earn a 10% commission, and the remaining expenses will stay the same.

Required

1. Prepare budgeted income statements for each of the months of July, August, and September that show the expected results from implementing the proposed changes. Use a three-column format, with one column for each month.

Check Budgeted net income: July, $265,000; August, $310,100; September, $359,710

Analysis Component

2. Use the budgeted income statements from part 1 to recommend whether management should implement the proposed plan. Explain.

Near the end of 2011, the management of Oasis Corp., a merchandising company, prepared the following estimated balance sheet for December 31, 2011.

Problem 20-5B

Preparation of a complete master budget

C2 P1 P2

OASIS CORPORATION Estimated Balance Sheet December 31, 2011		
Assets		
Cash		$ 160,000
Accounts receivable		400,000
Inventory		180,000
Total current assets		740,000
Equipment	$1,200,000	
Less accumulated depreciation	120,000	1,080,000
Total assets		$1,820,000

[continued on next page]

[continued from previous page]

Liabilities and Equity		
Accounts payable	$ 300,000	
Bank loan payable	20,000	
Taxes payable (due 3/15/2012)	200,000	
Total liabilities		$ 520,000
Common stock	1,500,000	
Retained earnings	(200,000)	
Total stockholders' equity		1,300,000
Total liabilities and equity		$1,820,000

To prepare a master budget for January, February, and March of 2012, management gathers the following information.

a. Oasis Corp.'s single product is purchased for $10 per unit and resold for $24 per unit. The expected inventory level of 18,000 units on December 31, 2011, is more than management's desired level for 2012, which is 40% of the next month's expected sales (in units). Expected sales are: January, 30,000 units; February, 24,000 units; March, 40,000 units; and April, 50,000 units.

b. Cash sales and credit sales represent 40% and 60%, respectively, of total sales. Of the credit sales, 70% is collected in the first month after the month of sale and 30% in the second month after the month of sale. For the $400,000 accounts receivable balance at December 31, 2011, $280,000 is collected in January 2012 and the remaining $120,000 is collected in February 2012.

c. Merchandise purchases are paid for as follows: 80% in the first month after the month of purchase and 20% in the second month after the month of purchase. For the $300,000 accounts payable balance at December 31, 2011, $240,000 is paid in January 2012 and the remaining $60,000 is paid in February 2012.

d. Sales commissions equal to 10% of sales are paid each month. Sales salaries (excluding commissions) are $288,000 per year.

e. General and administrative salaries are $336,000 per year. Maintenance expense equals $6,000 per month and is paid in cash.

f. Equipment reported in the December 31, 2011, balance sheet was purchased in January 2011. It is being depreciated over 10 years under the straight-line method with no salvage value. The following amounts for new equipment purchases are planned in the coming quarter: January, $240,000; February, $120,000; and March, $96,000. This equipment will be depreciated using the straight-line method over 10 years with no salvage value. A full month's depreciation is taken for the month in which equipment is purchased.

g. The company plans to acquire land at the end of March at a cost of $232,000, which will be paid with cash on the last day of the month.

h. Oasis Corp. has a working arrangement with its bank to obtain additional loans as needed. The interest rate is 12% per year, and interest is paid at each month-end based on the beginning balance. Partial or full payments on these loans can be made on the last day of the month. Oasis has agreed to maintain a minimum ending cash balance of $160,000 in each month.

i. The income tax rate for the company is 30%. Income taxes on the first quarter's income will not be paid until April 15.

Required

Prepare a master budget for each of the first three months of 2012; include the following component budgets (show supporting calculations as needed, and round amounts to the nearest dollar):

1. Monthly sales budgets (showing both budgeted unit sales and dollar sales).

2. Monthly merchandise purchases budgets.

3. Monthly selling expense budgets.

4. Monthly general and administrative expense budgets.

5. Monthly capital expenditures budgets.

6. Monthly cash budgets.

Check (2) Budgeted purchases: January, $216,000; February, $304,000;

(3) Budgeted selling expenses: January, $96,000; February, $81,600

(6) Ending cash bal.: January, $160,000; February, $281,578

7. Budgeted income statement for the entire first quarter (not for each month).

8. Budgeted balance sheet as of March 31, 2012.

RBI Company produces baseball bats. Each bat requires 4 pounds of aluminum alloy. Management predicts that 10,000 bats and 28,000 pounds of aluminum alloy will be in inventory on March 31 of the current year and that 100,000 bats will be sold during this year's second quarter. Management wants to end the second quarter with 3,000 finished bats and 2,000 pounds of aluminum alloy in inventory. Aluminum alloy can be purchased for $3 per pound.

Problem 20-6B^A
Preparing production and direct materials budgets

C2 P3

Required

1. Prepare the second-quarter production budget for bats.

2. Prepare the second-quarter direct materials (aluminum alloy) budget; include the dollar cost of purchases.

Check (1) Units manuf., 93,000;
(2) Cost of aluminum purchases, $1,038,000

(This serial problem began in Chapter 1 and continues through most of the book. If previous chapter segments were not completed, the serial problem can begin at this point. It is helpful, but not necessary, to use the Working Papers that accompany the book.)

SERIAL PROBLEM
Business Solutions

P2

SP 20 Santana Rey expects second quarter 2012 sales of her new line of computer furniture to be the same as the first quarter's sales (reported below) without any changes in strategy. Monthly sales averaged 40 desk units (sales price of $1,250) and 20 chairs (sales price of $500).

BUSINESS SOLUTIONS
Segment Income Statement*
For Quarter Ended March 31, 2012

Sales†	$180,000
Cost of goods sold‡	115,000
Gross profit	65,000
Expenses	
Sales commissions (10%)	18,000
Advertising expenses	9,000
Other fixed expenses	18,000
Total expenses	45,000
Net income	$ 20,000

* Reflects revenue and expense activity only related to the computer furniture segment.
† Revenue: (120 desks × $1,250) + (60 chairs × $500) = $150,000 + $30,000 = $180,000
‡ Cost of goods sold: (120 desks × $750) + (60 chairs × $250) + $10,000 = $115,000

Santana Rey believes that sales will increase each month for the next three months (April, 48 desks, 32 chairs; May, 52 desks, 35 chairs; June, 56 desks, 38 chairs) *if* selling prices are reduced to $1,150 for desks and $450 for chairs, and advertising expenses are increased by 10% and remain at that level for all three months. The products' variable cost will remain at $750 for desks and $250 for chairs. The sales staff will continue to earn a 10% commission, the fixed manufacturing costs per month will remain at $10,000 and other fixed expenses will remain at $6,000 per month.

Required

1. Prepare budgeted income statements for each of the months of April, May, and June that show the expected results from implementing the proposed changes. Use a three-column format, with one column for each month.

2. Use the budgeted income statements from part 1 to recommend whether Santana Rey should implement the proposed changes. Explain.

Check (1) Budgeted income (loss):
April, $(660); May, $945

Beyond the Numbers

REPORTING IN ACTION

P2

RIM

BTN 20-1   Financial statements often serve as a starting point in formulating budgets. Review **Research In Motion**'s financial statements to determine its cash paid for acquisitions of property, plant and equipment in the current year and the budgeted cash needed for such acquisitions in the next year.

Required

1. Which financial statement reports the amount of cash paid for acquisitions of property, plant, and equipment? Explain where on the statement this information is reported.
2. Indicate the amount of cash (a) paid for acquisitions of property, plant, and equipment in the year ended February 27, 2010, and (b) to be paid (budgeted for) next year under the assumption that annual acquisitions of property, plant and equipment equal 60% of the prior year's net income.

Fast Forward

3. Access Research In Motion's financial statements for a year ending after February 27, 2010, from either its Website [**RIM.com**] or the SEC's EDGAR database [**www.sec.gov**]. Compare your answer for part 2 with actual cash paid for acquisitions of property, plant and equipment for that fiscal year. Compute the error, if any, in your estimate. Speculate as to why cash paid for acquisitions of property, plant and equipment was higher or lower than your estimate.

COMPARATIVE ANALYSIS

P2

RIM
Apple

BTN 20-2   One source of cash savings for a company is improved management of inventory. To illustrate, assume that **Research In Motion** and **Apple** both have $200,000 per month in sales of one model of handheld devices in Canada, and both forecast this level of sales per month for the next 24 months. Also assume that both Research In Motion and Apple have a 20% contribution margin and equal fixed costs, and that cost of goods sold is the only variable cost. Assume that the main difference between Research In Motion and Apple is the distribution system. Research In Motion uses a just-in-time system and requires ending inventory of only 10% of next month's sales in inventory at each month-end. However, Apple is building an improved distribution system and currently requires 40% of next month's sales in inventory at each month-end.

Required

1. Compute the amount by which Apple can reduce its inventory level if it can match Research In Motion's system of maintaining an inventory equal to 10% of next month's sales. (*Hint:* Focus on the facts given and only on the Canada area.)
2. Explain how the analysis in part 1 that shows ending inventory levels for both the 40% and 10% required inventory policies can help justify a just-in-time inventory system. You can assume a 15% interest cost for resources that are tied up in ending inventory.

ETHICS CHALLENGE

C1

BTN 20-3   Both the budget process and budgets themselves can impact management actions, both positively and negatively. For instance, a common practice among not-for-profit organizations and government agencies is for management to spend any amounts remaining in a budget at the end of the budget period, a practice often called "use it or lose it." The view is that if a department manager does not spend the budgeted amount, top management will reduce next year's budget by the amount not spent. To avoid losing budget dollars, department managers often spend all budgeted amounts regardless of the value added to products or services. All of us pay for the costs associated with this budget system.

Required

Write a one-half page report to a local not-for-profit organization or government agency offering a solution to the "use it or lose it" budgeting problem.

COMMUNICATING IN PRACTICE

C2

BTN 20-4   The sales budget is usually the first and most crucial of the component budgets in a master budget because all other budgets usually rely on it for planning purposes.

Required

Assume that your company's sales staff provides information on expected sales and selling prices for items making up the sales budget. Prepare a one-page memorandum to your supervisor outlining concerns with the sales staff's input in the sales budget when its compensation is at least partly tied to these budgets. More generally, explain the importance of assessing any potential bias in information provided to the budget process.

BTN 20-5   Access information on e-budgets through The Manage Mentor:
http://www.themanagementor.com/kuniverse/kmailers_universe/finance_kmailers/cfa/budgeting2.htm
Read the information provided.

Required

1. Assume the role of a senior manager in a large, multidivision company. What are the benefits of using e-budgets?

2. As a senior manager, what concerns do you have with the concept and application of e-budgets?

TAKING IT TO THE NET

C1

BTN 20-6   Your team is to prepare a budget report outlining the costs of attending college (full-time) for the next two semesters (30 hours) or three quarters (45 hours). This budget's focus is solely on attending college; do not include personal items in the team's budget. Your budget must include tuition, books, supplies, club fees, food, housing, and all costs associated with travel to and from college. This budgeting exercise is similar to the initial phase in activity-based budgeting. Include a list of any assumptions you use in completing the budget. Be prepared to present your budget in class.

TEAMWORK IN ACTION

A1

BTN 20-7   **Smathers and Branson** handcrafts needlepoint belts and other products. Company founders, Peter Smathers Carter and Austin Branson stress the importance of planning and budgeting.

Required

1. How can budgeting help the owners efficiently develop and operate their business?

2. Why would direct materials budgets and direct labor budgets be particularly important for a business like Smathers and Branson?

ENTREPRENEURIAL DECISION

C1

BTN 20-8   To help understand the factors impacting a sales budget, you are to visit three businesses with the same ownership or franchise membership. Record the selling prices of two identical products at each location, such as regular and premium gas sold at **Chevron** stations. You are likely to find a difference in prices for at least one of the three locations you visit.

Required

1. Identify at least three external factors that must be considered when setting the sales budget. (*Note:* There is a difference between internal and external factors that impact the sales budget.)

2. What factors might explain any differences identified in the prices of the businesses you visited?

HITTING THE ROAD

C2 P1

BTN 20-9   Access **Nokia**'s income statement (www.Nokia.com) for the year ended December 31, 2009.

Required

1. Is Nokia's administrative and general expense budget likely to be an important budget in its master budgeting process? Explain.

2. Identify three types of expenses that would be reported as administrative and general expenses on Nokia's income statement.

3. Who likely has the initial responsibility for Nokia's administrative and general expense budget? Explain.

GLOBAL DECISION

P1

NOKIA

ANSWERS TO MULTIPLE CHOICE QUIZ

1. c

2. e; Budgeted purchases = $36,000 + $7,000 − $6,000 = $37,000

3. b; Cash collected = 25% of September sales + 75% of August sales =
(0.25 × $240,000) + (0.75 × $220,000) = $225,000

4. d

5. a; 560 units + (0.30 × 600 units) − (0.30 × 560 units) = 572 units

21

Flexible Budgets and Standard Costs

A Look Back

Chapter 20 explained the master budget and its component budgets as well as their usefulness for planning and monitoring company activities.

A Look at This Chapter

This chapter describes flexible budgets, variance analysis, and standard costs. It explains how each is used for purposes of better controlling and monitoring of business activities.

A Look Ahead

Chapter 22 introduces responsibility accounting and managerial control. It also describes useful measures of departmental performance.

Learning Objectives

CAP

CONCEPTUAL

C1 Define *standard costs* and explain how standard cost information is useful for management by exception. (p. 885)

C2 Describe variances and what they reveal about performance. (p. 887)

ANALYTICAL

A1 Analyze changes in sales from expected amounts. (p. 895)

LP21

PROCEDURAL

P1 Prepare a flexible budget and interpret a flexible budget performance report. (p. 882)

P2 Compute materials and labor variances. (p. 888)

P3 Compute overhead variances. (p. 892)

P4 *Appendix 21A*—Prepare journal entries for standard costs and account for price and quantity variances. (p. 902)

Behind the Curtains

"Don't back down . . . find ways to overcome problems"
—MEGAN DUCKETT

RANCHO DOMINGUEZ, CA—What do Kenny Chesney and Alice in Chains have in common? Both have played shows with custom backdrops and drapes sewed by Megan Duckett's company, **SewWhat? Inc. (SewWhatInc.com).** Megan's company has quickly become a top provider of customized stage curtains, drapes, and backdrops for the entertainment and special events industries, providing the "soft goods" for hard-edged clients like Green Day and Sonic Youth.

Founder Megan Duckett immigrated to the United States from Australia at age 19. Working as a technician for a concert production company, she started sewing in her spare time. Her first gig? Sewing fabric coffin linings for a Halloween show. "I rented a sewing machine and lined 10 coffins. I discovered I had an ability to sew, and I really enjoyed it," says Megan. The business stayed on the sidelines until Megan's husband Adam noticed she made more money "sewing on the kitchen table than at her 40-hour-per-week commuter job." Megan boldly invested $2,000 in a small office and sewing machine and pursued her passion.

SewWhat? Inc. adheres to tight standards. As with many manufacturers, production problems can arise from materials, processes, or employees. Main drapes are made from cotton or synthetic material, and factors like light blockage, sound absorption, and budget are important in determining materials re-

quirements. Megan stresses the importance of "having exact specifications and controls to detect problems; we don't use any material that doesn't satisfy our requirements." As for process, the company monitors its sewing machines to ensure excessive wear does not impair production efficiency and product quality. Megan uses innovative software to guide production. "Our application calculates yardage and purchasing requirements and prints out sewing instructions both in Spanish and English. It allows us to standardize pricing," explains Megan. Employees have work quotas, and the company knows how much labor costs and how long projects should take.

Achieving high standards is the goal at SewWhat? Inc. "We've made a commitment to push ourselves in order to grow," says Megan. From modest beginnings at Megan's kitchen table, the company's sales have grown to over $4.6 million per year. Megan encourages entrepreneurs to "build a business around something you are good at and feel passionate about." After phenomenal successes with massive installations for recent Carrie Underwood and Rod Stewart tours, the company's future looks bright. Proclaims Megan, "Bring on the next one!"

[Sources: *SewWhat? Inc. Website,* January 2011; *Dell Website, Trailblazer Stories,* May 2010; *Inc.com,* May 2009; *Entreprenuer.com,* October 2007]

Budgeting helps organize and formalize management's planning activities. This chapter extends the study of budgeting to look more closely at the use of budgets to evaluate performance. Evaluations are important for controlling and monitoring business activities. This chapter also describes and illustrates the use of standard costs and variance analyses. These managerial tools are useful for both evaluating and controlling organizations and for the planning of future activities.

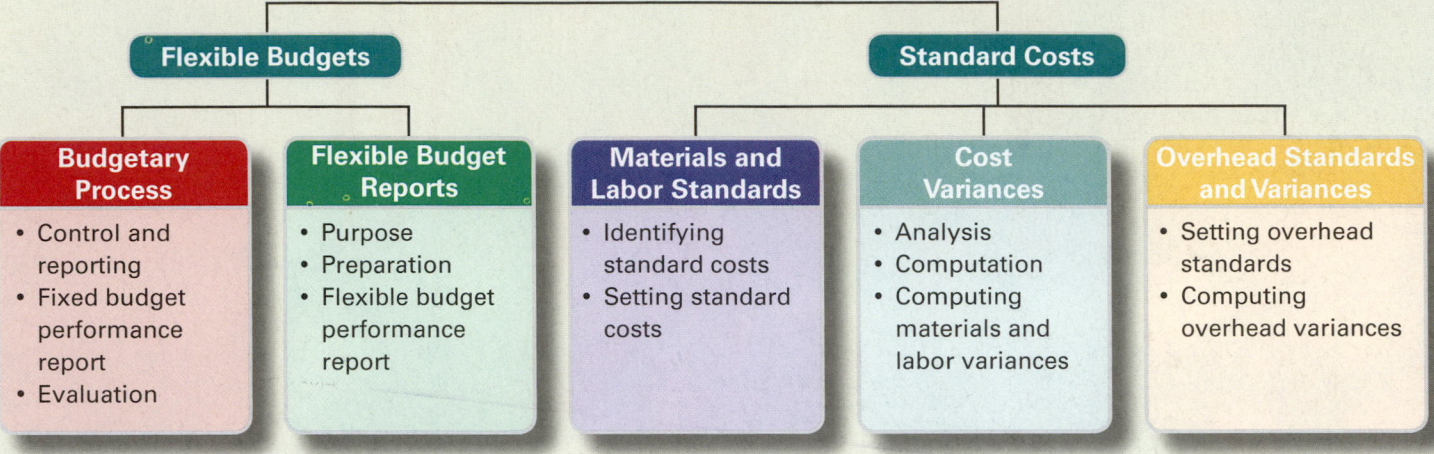

Flexible Budgets

Budgetary Process
- Control and reporting
- Fixed budget performance report
- Evaluation

Flexible Budget Reports
- Purpose
- Preparation
- Flexible budget performance report

Standard Costs

Materials and Labor Standards
- Identifying standard costs
- Setting standard costs

Cost Variances
- Analysis
- Computation
- Computing materials and labor variances

Overhead Standards and Variances
- Setting overhead standards
- Computing overhead variances

Section 1—Flexible Budgets

This section introduces fixed budgets and fixed budget performance reports. It then introduces flexible budgets and flexible budget performance reports and illustrates their advantages.

BUDGETARY PROCESS

A master budget reflects management's planned objectives for a future period. The preparation of a master budget is based on a predicted level of activity such as sales volume for the budget period. This section discusses the effects on the usefulness of budget reports when the actual level of activity differs from the predicted level.

Budgetary Control and Reporting

Budgetary control refers to management's use of budgets to monitor and control a company's operations. This includes using budgets to see that planned objectives are met. **Budget reports** contain relevant information that compares actual results to planned activities. This comparison is motivated by a need to both monitor performance and control activities. Budget reports are sometimes viewed as progress reports, or *report cards,* on management's performance in achieving planned objectives. These reports can be prepared at any time and for any period. Three common periods for a budget report are a month, quarter, and year.

Point: Budget reports are often used to determine bonuses of managers.

The budgetary control process involves at least four steps: (1) develop the budget from planned objectives, (2) compare actual results to budgeted amounts and analyze any differences, (3) take corrective and strategic actions, and (4) establish new planned objectives and prepare a new budget. Exhibit 21.1 shows this continual process of budgetary control. Budget reports and

EXHIBIT 21.1

Process of Budgetary Control

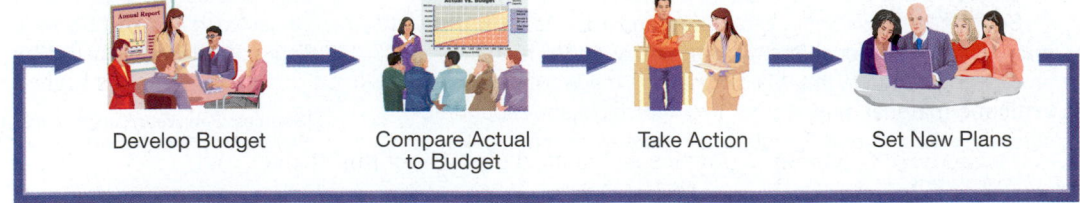

Develop Budget → Compare Actual to Budget → Take Action → Set New Plans

related documents are effective tools for managers to obtain the greatest benefits from this budgetary process.

Fixed Budget Performance Report

In a fixed budgetary control system, the master budget is based on a single prediction for sales volume or other activity level. The budgeted amount for each cost essentially assumes that a specific (or *fixed*) amount of sales will occur. A **fixed budget,** also called a *static budget,* is based on a single predicted amount of sales or other measure of activity.

One benefit of a budget is its usefulness in comparing actual results with planned activities. Information useful for analysis is often presented for comparison in a performance report. As shown in Exhibit 21.2, a **fixed budget performance report** for **Optel** compares actual results for January 2011 with the results expected under its fixed budget that predicted 10,000 (composite) units of sales. Optel manufactures inexpensive eyeglasses, frames, contact lens, and related supplies. For this report, its production volume equals sales volume (its inventory level did not change).

EXHIBIT 21.2

Fixed Budget Performance Report

OPTEL Fixed Budget Performance Report For Month Ended January 31, 2011	Fixed Budget	Actual Results	Variances*
Sales (in units)	10,000	12,000	
Sales (in dollars)	$100,000	$125,000	$25,000 F
Cost of goods sold			
Direct materials	10,000	13,000	3,000 U
Direct labor	15,000	20,000	5,000 U
Overhead			
Factory supplies	2,000	2,100	100 U
Utilities	3,000	4,000	1,000 U
Depreciation—machinery	8,000	8,000	0
Supervisory salaries	11,000	11,000	0
Selling expenses			
Sales commissions	9,000	10,800	1,800 U
Shipping expenses	4,000	4,300	300 U
General and administrative expenses			
Office supplies	5,000	5,200	200 U
Insurance expenses	1,000	1,200	200 U
Depreciation—office equipment	7,000	7,000	0
Administrative salaries	13,000	13,000	0
Total expenses	88,000	99,600	11,600 U
Income from operations	$ 12,000	$ 25,400	$13,400 F

* F = Favorable variance; U = Unfavorable variance.

This type of performance report designates differences between budgeted and actual results as variances. We see the letters *F* and *U* located beside the numbers in the third number column of this report. Their meanings are as follows:

F = **Favorable variance**   When compared to budget, the actual cost or revenue contributes to a *higher* income. That is, actual revenue is higher than budgeted revenue, or actual cost is lower than budgeted cost.

U = **Unfavorable variance**   When compared to budget, the actual cost or revenue contributes to a *lower* income; actual revenue is lower than budgeted revenue, or actual cost is higher than budgeted cost.

This convention is common in practice and is used throughout this chapter.

Example: How is it that the favorable sales variance in Exhibit 21.2 is linked with so many unfavorable cost and expense variances? *Answer:* Costs have increased with the increase in sales.

Budget Reports for Evaluation

A primary use of budget reports is as a tool for management to monitor and control operations. Evaluation by Optel management is likely to focus on a variety of questions that might include these:

- Why is actual income from operations $13,400 higher than budgeted?
- Are amounts paid for each expense item too high?
- Is manufacturing using too much direct material?
- Is manufacturing using too much direct labor?

The performance report in Exhibit 21.2 provides little help in answering these questions because actual sales volume is 2,000 units higher than budgeted. A manager does not know if this higher level of sales activity is the cause of variations in total dollar sales and expenses or if other factors have influenced these amounts. This inability of fixed budget reports to adjust for changes in activity levels is a major limitation of a fixed budget performance report. That is, it fails to show whether actual costs are out of line due to a change in actual sales volume or some other factor.

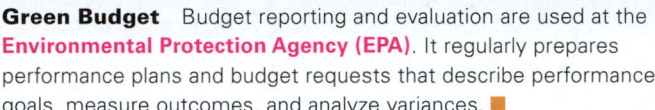

Green Budget   Budget reporting and evaluation are used at the **Environmental Protection Agency (EPA)**. It regularly prepares performance plans and budget requests that describe performance goals, measure outcomes, and analyze variances. ■

FLEXIBLE BUDGET REPORTS

Purpose of Flexible Budgets

To help address limitations with the fixed budget performance report, particularly from the effects of changes in sales volume, management can use a flexible budget. A **flexible budget,** also called a *variable budget,* is a report based on predicted amounts of revenues and expenses corresponding to the actual level of output. Flexible budgets are useful both before and after the period's activities are complete.

A flexible budget prepared before the period is often based on several levels of activity. Budgets for those different levels can provide a "what-if" look at operations. The different levels often include both a best case and worst case scenario. This allows management to make adjustments to avoid or lessen the effects of the worst case scenario.

A flexible budget prepared after the period helps management evaluate past performance. It is especially useful for such an evaluation because it reflects budgeted revenues and costs based on the actual level of activity. Thus, comparisons of actual results with budgeted performance are more likely to identify the causes of any differences. This can help managers focus attention on real problem areas and implement corrective actions. This is in contrast to a fixed budget, whose primary purpose is to assist managers in planning future activities and whose numbers are based on a single predicted amount of budgeted sales or production.

Point: A flexible budget yields an "apples to apples" comparison because budgeted activity levels are the same as the actual.

Preparation of Flexible Budgets

P1 Prepare a flexible budget and interpret a flexible budget performance report.

A flexible budget is designed to reveal the effects of volume of activity on revenues and costs. To prepare a flexible budget, management relies on the distinctions between fixed and variable costs. Recall that the cost per unit of activity remains constant for variable costs so that the total amount of a variable cost changes in direct proportion to a change in activity level. The total amount of fixed cost remains unchanged regardless of changes in the level of activity within a relevant (normal) operating range. (Assume that costs can be reasonably classified as variable or fixed within a relevant range.)

When we create the numbers constituting a flexible budget, we express each variable cost as either a constant amount per unit of sales or as a percent of a sales dollar. In the case of a fixed cost, we express its budgeted amount as the total amount expected to occur at any sales volume within the relevant range.

Exhibit 21.3 shows a set of flexible budgets for Optel for January 2011. Seven of its expenses are classified as variable costs. Its remaining five expenses are fixed costs. These classifications result from management's investigation of each expense. Variable and fixed expense categories are *not* the same for every company, and we must avoid drawing conclusions from specific cases. For example, depending on the nature of a company's operations, office supplies expense can be either fixed or variable with respect to sales.

Point: The usefulness of a flexible budget depends on valid classification of variable and fixed costs. Some costs are mixed and must be analyzed to determine their variable and fixed portions.

EXHIBIT 21.3

Flexible Budgets

OPTEL
Flexible Budgets
For Month Ended January 31, 2011

	Flexible Budget — Variable Amount per Unit	Total Fixed Cost	Flexible Budget for Unit Sales of 10,000	Flexible Budget for Unit Sales of 12,000	Flexible Budget for Unit Sales of 14,000
Sales	$10.00		$100,000	$120,000	$140,000
Variable costs					
Direct materials	1.00		10,000	12,000	14,000
Direct labor	1.50		15,000	18,000	21,000
Factory supplies	0.20		2,000	2,400	2,800
Utilities	0.30		3,000	3,600	4,200
Sales commissions	0.90		9,000	10,800	12,600
Shipping expenses	0.40		4,000	4,800	5,600
Office supplies	0.50		5,000	6,000	7,000
Total variable costs	4.80		48,000	57,600	67,200
Contribution margin	$ 5.20		$ 52,000	$ 62,400	$ 72,800
Fixed costs					
Depreciation—machinery		$ 8,000	8,000	8,000	8,000
Supervisory salaries		11,000	11,000	11,000	11,000
Insurance expense		1,000	1,000	1,000	1,000
Depreciation—office equipment		7,000	7,000	7,000	7,000
Administrative salaries		13,000	13,000	13,000	13,000
Total fixed costs		$40,000	40,000	40,000	40,000
Income from operations			$ 12,000	$ 22,400	$ 32,800

The layout for the flexible budgets in Exhibit 21.3 follows a *contribution margin format*—beginning with sales followed by variable costs and then fixed costs. Both the expected individual and total variable costs are reported and then subtracted from sales. The difference between sales and variable costs equals contribution margin. The expected amounts of fixed costs are listed next, followed by the expected income from operations before taxes.

The first and second number columns of Exhibit 21.3 show the flexible budget amounts for variable costs per unit and each fixed cost for any volume of sales in the relevant range. The third, fourth, and fifth columns show the flexible budget amounts computed for three different sales volumes. For instance, the third column's flexible budget is based on 10,000 units. These numbers are the same as those in the fixed budget of Exhibit 21.2 because the expected volumes are the same for these two budgets.

Recall that Optel's actual sales volume for January is 12,000 units. This sales volume is 2,000 units more than the 10,000 units originally predicted in the master budget. When differences between actual and predicted volume arise, the usefulness of a flexible budget is apparent. For instance, compare the flexible budget for 10,000 units in the third column (which is the same as the fixed budget in Exhibit 21.2) with the flexible budget for 12,000 units in the fourth

Example: Using Exhibit 21.3, what is the budgeted income from operations for unit sales of (a) 11,000 and (b) 13,000? *Answers:* $17,200 for unit sales of 11,000; $27,600 for unit sales of 13,000.

Point: Flexible budgeting allows a budget to be prepared at the *actual* output level. Performance reports are then prepared comparing the flexible budget to actual revenues and costs.

column. The higher levels for both sales and variable costs reflect nothing more than the increase in sales activity. Any budget analysis comparing actual with planned results that ignores this information is less useful to management.

To illustrate, when we evaluate Optel's performance, we need to prepare a flexible budget showing actual and budgeted values at 12,000 units. As part of a complete profitability analysis, managers could compare the actual income of $25,400 (from Exhibit 21.2) with the $22,400 income expected at the actual sales volume of 12,000 units (from Exhibit 21.3). This results in a total favorable income variance of $3,000 to be explained and interpreted. This variance is markedly lower from the $13,400 favorable variance identified in Exhibit 21.2 using a fixed budget, but still suggests good performance. After receiving the flexible budget based on January's actual volume, management must determine what caused this $3,000 difference. The next section describes a flexible budget performance report that provides guidance in this analysis.

Decision Maker   Answer — p. 904

Entrepreneur   The heads of both the strategic consulting and tax consulting divisions of your financial services firm complain to you about the unfavorable variances on their performance reports. "We worked on more consulting assignments than planned. It's not surprising our costs are higher than expected. To top it off, this report characterizes our work as *poor!*" How do you respond? ■

Flexible Budget Performance Report

A **flexible budget performance report** lists differences between actual performance and budgeted performance based on actual sales volume or other activity level. This report helps direct management's attention to those costs or revenues that differ substantially from budgeted amounts. Exhibit 21.4 shows Optel's flexible budget performance report for January. We prepare this report after the actual volume is known to be 12,000 units. This report shows a $5,000 favorable variance in total dollar sales. Because actual and budgeted volumes are both 12,000 units, the $5,000 sales variance must have resulted from a higher than expected selling price.

EXHIBIT 21.4

Flexible Budget
Performance Report

OPTEL Flexible Budget Performance Report For Month Ended January 31, 2011	Flexible Budget	Actual Results	Variances*
Sales (12,000 units)	$120,000	$125,000	$5,000 F
Variable costs			
Direct materials	12,000	13,000	1,000 U
Direct labor	18,000	20,000	2,000 U
Factory supplies	2,400	2,100	300 F
Utilities	3,600	4,000	400 U
Sales commissions	10,800	10,800	0
Shipping expenses	4,800	4,300	500 F
Office supplies	6,000	5,200	800 F
Total variable costs	57,600	59,400	1,800 U
Contribution margin	62,400	65,600	3,200 F
Fixed costs			
Depreciation—machinery	8,000	8,000	0
Supervisory salaries	11,000	11,000	0
Insurance expense	1,000	1,200	200 U
Depreciation—office equipment	7,000	7,000	0
Administrative salaries	13,000	13,000	0
Total fixed costs	40,000	40,200	200 U
Income from operations	$ 22,400	$ 25,400	$3,000 F

* F = Favorable variance; U = Unfavorable variance.

Further analysis of the facts surrounding this $5,000 sales variance reveals a favorable sales variance per unit of nearly $0.42 as shown here:

Actual average price per unit (rounded to cents)	$125,000/12,000 = $10.42
Budgeted price per unit	$120,000/12,000 = 10.00
Favorable sales variance per unit	$5,000/12,000 = $ 0.42

The other variances in Exhibit 21.4 also direct management's attention to areas where corrective actions can help control Optel's operations. Each expense variance is analyzed as the sales variance was. We can think of each expense as the joint result of using a given number of units of input and paying a specific price per unit of input. Optel's expense variances total $2,000 unfavorable, suggesting poor control of some costs, particularly direct materials and direct labor.

Each variance in Exhibit 21.4 is due in part to a difference between *actual price* per unit of input and *budgeted price* per unit of input. This is a **price variance.** Each variance also can be due in part to a difference between *actual quantity* of input used and *budgeted quantity* of input. This is a **quantity variance.** We explain more about this breakdown, known as **variance analysis,** later in the standard costs section.

Quick Check

Answers — p. 905

1. A flexible budget (a) shows fixed costs as constant amounts of cost per unit of activity, (b) shows variable costs as constant amounts of cost per unit of activity, or (c) is prepared based on one expected amount of budgeted sales or production.
2. What is the initial step in preparing a flexible budget?
3. What is the main difference between a fixed and a flexible budget?
4. What is the contribution margin?

Section 2—Standard Costs

Standard costs are preset costs for delivering a product or service under normal conditions. These costs are established by personnel, engineering, and accounting studies using past experiences and data. Management uses these costs to assess the reasonableness of actual costs incurred for producing the product or service. When actual costs vary from standard costs, management follows up to identify potential problems and take corrective actions. **Management by exception** means that managers focus attention on the most significant differences between actual costs and standard costs and give less attention to areas where performance is reasonably close to standard. Management by exception is especially useful when directed at controllable items, enabling top management to affect the actions of lower-level managers responsible for the company's revenues and costs.

Standard costs are often used in preparing budgets because they are the anticipated costs incurred under normal conditions. Terms such as *standard materials cost, standard labor cost,* and *standard overhead cost* are often used to refer to amounts budgeted for direct materials, direct labor, and overhead.

While many managers use standard costs to investigate manufacturing costs, standard costs can also help control *nonmanufacturing* costs. Companies providing services instead of products can also benefit from the use of standard costs. For example, while quality medical service is paramount, efficiency in providing that service is also important to medical professionals. The use of budgeting and standard costing is touted as an effective means to control and monitor medical costs, especially overhead.

 C1 Define *standard costs* and explain how standard cost information is useful for management by exception.

Point: Since standard costs are often budgeted costs, they can be used to prepare both fixed budgets and flexible budgets.

Decision Ethics   Answer — p. 904

Internal Auditor   You discover a manager who always spends exactly what is budgeted. About 30% of her budget is spent just before the period-end. She admits to spending what is budgeted, whether or not it is needed. She offers three reasons: (1) she doesn't want her budget cut, (2) "management by exception" focuses on budget deviations; and (3) she believes the money is budgeted to be spent. What action do you take? ■

MATERIALS AND LABOR STANDARDS

This section explains how to set materials and labor standards and how to prepare a standard cost card.

Identifying Standard Costs

Point: Business practice often uses the word *budget* when speaking of total amounts and *standard* when discussing per unit amounts.

Managerial accountants, engineers, personnel administrators, and other managers combine their efforts to set standard costs. To identify standards for direct labor costs, we can conduct time and motion studies for each labor operation in the process of providing a product or service. From these studies, management can learn the best way to perform the operation and then set the standard labor time required for the operation under normal conditions. Similarly, standards for materials are set by studying the quantity, grade, and cost of each material used. Standards for overhead costs are explained later in the chapter.

Example: What factors might be considered when deciding whether to revise standard costs? *Answer:* Changes in the processes and/or resources needed to carry out the processes.

Regardless of the care used in setting standard costs and in revising them as conditions change, actual costs frequently differ from standard costs, often as a result of one or more factors. For instance, the actual quantity of material used can differ from the standard, or the price paid per unit of material can differ from the standard. Quantity and price differences from standard amounts can also occur for labor. That is, the actual labor time and actual labor rate can vary from what was expected. The same analysis applies to overhead costs.

Decision Insight

Cruis'n Standards   The **Corvette** consists of hundreds of parts for which engineers set standards. Various types of labor are also involved in its production, including machining, assembly, painting, and welding, and standards are set for each. Actual results are periodically compared with standards to assess performance. ■

Setting Standard Costs

To illustrate the setting of a standard cost, we consider a professional league baseball bat manufactured by **ProBat.** Its engineers have determined that manufacturing one bat requires 0.90 kg. of high-grade wood. They also expect some loss of material as part of the process because of inefficiencies and waste. This results in adding an *allowance* of 0.10 kg., making the standard requirement 1.0 kg. of wood for each bat.

Point: Companies promoting continuous improvement strive to achieve ideal standards by eliminating inefficiencies and waste.

The 0.90 kg. portion is called an *ideal standard;* it is the quantity of material required if the process is 100% efficient without any loss or waste. Reality suggests that some loss of material usually occurs with any process. The standard of 1.0 kg. is known as the *practical standard,* the quantity of material required under normal application of the process.

High-grade wood can be purchased at a standard price of $25 per kg. The purchasing department sets this price as the expected price for the budget period. To determine this price, the purchasing department considers factors such as the quality of materials, future economic conditions, supply factors (shortages and excesses), and any available discounts. The engineers also decide that two hours of labor time (after including allowances) are required to manufacture a bat. The wage rate is $20 per hour (better than average skilled labor is required). ProBat assigns all overhead at the rate of $10 per labor hour. The standard costs of direct materials, direct labor, and overhead for one bat are shown in Exhibit 21.5 in what is called a *standard cost card.* These cost amounts are then used to prepare manufacturing budgets for a budgeted level of production.

EXHIBIT 21.5

Standard Cost Card

STANDARD COST CARD		▪ □ ✕
Production factor	**Cost factor**	**Total**
Direct materials (wood)	**1 kg. @ $25 per kg.**	**$25**
Direct labor	**2 hours @ $20 per hour**	**40**
Overhead	**2 labor hours @ $10 per hour**	**20**
	Total	**$85**

REMARKS:

Based on standard costs of direct materials, direct labor, and overhead for a single ProBat

SUMMARY:

Materials	$25
Labor	40
Overhead	20
Total cost	$85

COST VARIANCES

A **cost variance,** also simply called a *variance,* is the difference between actual and standard costs. A cost variance can be favorable or unfavorable. A variance from standard cost is considered favorable if actual cost is less than standard cost. It is considered unfavorable if actual cost is more than standard cost.[1] This section discusses variance analysis.

C2 Describe variances and what they reveal about performance.

Cost Variance Analysis

Variances are usually identified in performance reports. When a variance occurs, management wants to determine the factors causing it. This often involves analysis, evaluation, and explanation. The results of these efforts should enable management to assign responsibility for the variance and then to take actions to correct the situation.

To illustrate, ProBat's standard materials cost for producing 500 bats is $12,500. Assume that its actual materials cost for those 500 bats is $13,000. The $500 unfavorable variance raises questions that call for answers that, in turn, can lead to changes to correct the situation and eliminate this variance in the next period. A performance report often identifies the existence of a problem, but we must follow up with further investigation to see what can be done to improve future performance.

Exhibit 21.6 shows the flow of events in the effective management of variance analysis. It shows four steps: (1) preparing a standard cost performance report, (2) computing and analyzing variances, (3) identifying questions and their explanations, and (4) taking corrective and strategic actions. These variance analysis steps are interrelated and are frequently applied in good organizations.

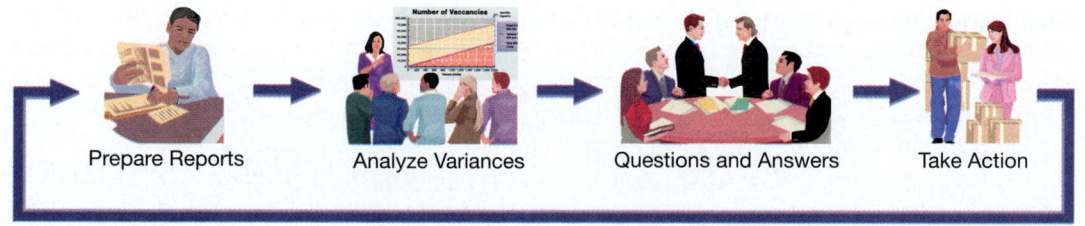

Prepare Reports   Analyze Variances   Questions and Answers   Take Action

EXHIBIT 21.6

Variance Analysis

Cost Variance Computation

Management needs information about the factors causing a cost variance, but first it must properly compute the variance. In its most simple form, a cost variance (CV) is computed as the difference between actual cost (AC) and standard cost (SC) as shown in Exhibit 21.7.

---

[1] Short-term favorable variances can sometimes lead to long-term unfavorable variances. For instance, if management spends less than the budgeted amount on maintenance or insurance, the performance report would show a favorable variance. Cutting these expenses can lead to major losses in the long run if machinery wears out prematurely or insurance coverage proves inadequate.

EXHIBIT 21.7

Cost Variance Formulas

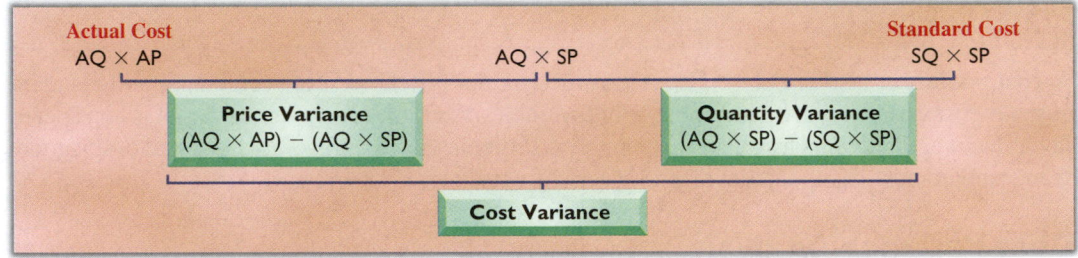

> **Cost Variance (CV) = Actual Cost (AC) − Standard Cost (SC)**
>
> where:
>
> **Actual Cost (AC) = Actual Quantity (AQ) × Actual Price (AP)**
> **Standard Cost (SC) = Standard Quantity (SQ) × Standard Price (SP)**

A cost variance is further defined by its components. Actual quantity (AQ) is the input (material or labor) used to manufacture the quantity of output. Standard quantity (SQ) is the expected input for the quantity of output. Actual price (AP) is the amount paid to acquire the input (material or labor), and standard price (SP) is the expected price.

Point: Price and quantity variances for direct labor are nearly always referred to as *rate* and *efficiency variances,* respectively.

   Two main factors cause a cost variance: (1) the difference between actual price and standard price results in a *price* (or rate) *variance* and (2) the difference between actual quantity and standard quantity results in a *quantity* (or usage or efficiency) *variance*. To assess the impacts of these two factors in a cost variance, we use the formulas in Exhibit 21.8.

EXHIBIT 21.8

Price Variance and Quantity Variance Formulas

Actual Cost		**Standard Cost**
AQ × AP	AQ × SP	SQ × SP

Price Variance
(AQ × AP) − (AQ × SP)

Quantity Variance
(AQ × SP) − (SQ × SP)

Cost Variance

In computing a price variance, the quantity (actual) is held constant. In computing a quantity variance, the price (standard) is held constant. The cost variance, or total variance, is the sum of the price and quantity variances. These formulas identify the sources of the cost variance. Managers sometimes find it useful to apply an alternative (but equivalent) computation for the price and quantity variances as shown in Exhibit 21.9.

EXHIBIT 21.9

Alternative Price Variance and Quantity Variance Formulas

> **Price Variance (PV) = [Actual Price (AP) − Standard Price (SP)] × Actual Quantity (AQ)**
> **Quantity Variance (QV) = [Actual Quantity (AQ) − Standard Quantity (SQ)] × Standard Price (SP)**

The results from applying the formulas in Exhibits 21.8 and 21.9 are identical.

Computing Materials and Labor Variances

P2 Compute materials and labor variances.

We illustrate the computation of the materials and labor cost variances using data from **G-Max,** a company that makes specialty golf equipment and accessories for individual customers. This company has set the following standard quantities and costs for materials and labor per unit for one of its hand-crafted golf clubheads:

Direct materials (0.5 lb. per unit at $20 per lb.)	$10.00
Direct labor (1 hr. per unit at $8 per hr.)	8.00
Total standard direct cost per unit	$18.00

Materials Cost Variances   During May 2011, G-Max budgeted to produce 4,000 clubheads (units). It actually produced only 3,500 units. It used 1,800 pounds of direct materials (titanium) costing $21.00 per pound, meaning its total materials cost was $37,800. This information allows us to compute both actual and standard direct materials costs for G-Max's 3,500 units and its direct materials cost variance as follows:

Actual cost	1,800 lbs. @ $21.00 per lb.	= $37,800
Standard cost	1,750 lbs. @ $20.00 per lb.	= 35,000
Direct materials cost variance (unfavorable)		= **$ 2,800**

To better isolate the causes of this $2,800 unfavorable total direct materials cost variance, the materials price and quantity variances for these G-Max clubheads are computed and shown in Exhibit 21.10.

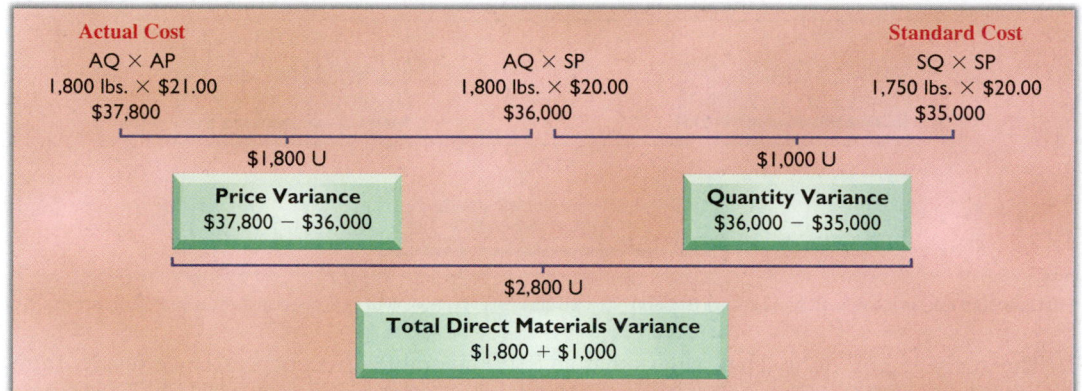

EXHIBIT 21.10

Materials Price and Quantity Variances*

*AQ is actual quantity; AP is actual price; SP is standard price; SQ is standard quantity allowed for actual output.

The $1,800 unfavorable price variance results from paying $1 more per unit than the standard price, computed as 1,800 lbs. × $1. The $1,000 unfavorable quantity variance is due to using 50 lbs. more materials than the standard quantity, computed as 50 lbs. × $20. The total direct materials variance is $2,800 and it is unfavorable. This information allows management to ask the responsible individuals for explanations and corrective actions.

The purchasing department is usually responsible for the price paid for materials. Responsibility for explaining the price variance in this case rests with the purchasing manager if a price higher than standard caused the variance. The production department is usually responsible for the amount of material used and in this case is responsible for explaining why the process used more than the standard amount of materials.

Variance analysis presents challenges. For instance, the production department could have used more than the standard amount of material because its quality did not meet specifications and led to excessive waste. In this case, the purchasing manager is responsible for explaining why inferior materials were acquired. However, the production manager is responsible for explaining what happened if analysis shows that waste was due to inefficiencies, not poor quality material.

In evaluating price variances, managers must recognize that a favorable price variance can indicate a problem with poor product quality. **Redhook Ale**, a micro brewery in the Pacific Northwest, can probably save 10% to 15% in material prices by buying six-row barley malt instead of the better two-row from Washington's Yakima valley. Attention to quality, however, has helped Redhook Ale become the first craft brewer to be kosher certified. Redhook's purchasing activities are judged on both the quality of the materials and the purchase price variance.

Example: Identify at least two factors that might have caused the unfavorable quantity variance and the unfavorable price variance in Exhibit 21.10. *Answer:* Poor quality materials or untrained workers for the former; poor price negotiation or higher-quality materials for the latter.

Labor Cost Variances Labor cost for a specific product or service depends on the number of hours worked (quantity) and the wage rate paid to employees (price). When actual amounts for a task differ from standard, the labor cost variance can be divided into a rate (price) variance and an efficiency (quantity) variance.

To illustrate, G-Max's direct labor standard for 3,500 units of its hand-crafted clubheads is one hour per unit, or 3,500 hours at $8 per hour. Since only 3,400 hours at $8.30 per hour were actually used to complete the units, the actual and standard labor costs are

Actual cost	3,400 hrs. @ $8.30 per hr.	= $28,220
Standard cost	3,500 hrs. @ $8.00 per hr.	= 28,000
Direct labor cost variance (unfavorable)		= $ 220

This analysis shows that actual cost is merely $220 over the standard and suggests no immediate concern. Computing both the labor rate and efficiency variances reveals a different picture, however, as shown in Exhibit 21.11.

EXHIBIT 21.11

Labor Rate and
Efficiency Variances*

Actual Cost	AH × SR	Standard Cost
AH × AR	3,400 hrs. × $8.00	SH × SR
3,400 hrs. × $8.30	$27,200	3,500 hrs. × $8.00
$28,220		$28,000

$1,020 U

Rate Variance
$28,220 − $27,200

$800 F

Efficiency Variance
$27,200 − $28,000

$220 U

Total Direct Labor Variance
$1,020 − $800

* AH is actual direct labor hours; AR is actual wage rate; SH is standard direct labor hours allowed for actual output; SR is standard wage rate.

Example: Compute the rate variance and the efficiency variance for Exhibit 21.11 if 3,700 actual hours are used at an actual price of $7.50 per hour. *Answer:* $1,850 favorable labor rate variance and $1,600 unfavorable labor efficiency variance.

The analysis in Exhibit 21.11 shows that an $800 favorable efficiency variance results from using 100 fewer direct labor hours than standard for the units produced, but this favorable variance is more than offset by a wage rate that is $0.30 per hour higher than standard. The personnel administrator or the production manager needs to explain why the wage rate is higher than expected. The production manager should also explain how the labor hours were reduced. If this experience can be repeated and transferred to other departments, more savings are possible.

One possible explanation of these labor rate and efficiency variances is the use of workers with different skill levels. If this is the reason, senior management must discuss the implications with the production manager who has the responsibility to assign workers to tasks with the appropriate skill level. In this case, an investigation might show that higher-skilled workers were used to produce 3,500 units of hand-crafted clubheads. As a result, fewer labor hours might be required for the work, but the wage rate paid these workers is higher than standard because of their greater skills. The effect of this strategy is a higher than standard total cost, which would require actions to remedy the situation or adjust the standard.

Decision Maker   Answer — p. 904

Human Resource Manager   You receive the manufacturing variance report for June and discover a large unfavorable labor efficiency (quantity) variance. What factors do you investigate to identify its possible causes? ■

Quick Check   Answers — p. 905

5. A standard cost (*a*) changes in direct proportion to changes in the level of activity, (*b*) is an amount incurred at the actual level of production for the period, or (*c*) is an amount incurred under normal conditions to provide a product or service.

6. What is a cost variance?

7. The following information is available for York Company.

Actual direct labor hours per unit	2.5 hours
Standard direct labor hours per unit	2.0 hours
Actual production (units)	2,500 units
Budgeted production (units)	3,000 units
Actual rate per hour	$3.10
Standard rate per hour	$3.00

The labor efficiency variance is (*a*) $3,750 U, (*b*) $3,750 F, or (*c*) $3,875 U.

8. Refer to Quick Check 7; the labor rate variance is (*a*) $625 F or (*b*) $625 U.

9. If a materials quantity variance is favorable and a materials price variance is unfavorable, can the total materials cost variance be favorable?

OVERHEAD STANDARDS AND VARIANCES

When standard costs are used, a predetermined overhead rate is used to assign standard overhead costs to products or services produced. This predetermined rate is often based on some overhead allocation base (such as standard labor cost, standard labor hours, or standard machine hours).

Setting Overhead Standards

Standard overhead costs are the amounts expected to occur at a certain activity level. Unlike direct materials and direct labor, overhead includes fixed costs and variable costs. This results in the average overhead cost per unit changing as the predicted volume changes. Since standard costs are also budgeted costs, they must be established before the reporting period begins. Standard overhead costs are therefore average per unit costs based on the predicted activity level.

To establish the standard overhead cost rate, management uses the same cost structure it used to construct a flexible budget at the end of a period. This cost structure identifies the different overhead cost components and classifies them as variable or fixed. To get the standard overhead rate, management selects a level of activity (volume) and predicts total overhead cost. It then divides this total by the allocation base to get the standard rate. Standard direct labor hours expected to be used to produce the predicted volume is a common allocation base and is used in this section.

Point: With increased automation, machine hours are frequently used in applying overhead instead of labor hours.

To illustrate, Exhibit 21.12 shows the overhead cost structure used to develop G-Max's flexible overhead budgets for May 2011. The predetermined standard overhead rate for May is set before the month begins. The first two number columns list the per unit amounts of variable costs and the monthly amounts of fixed costs. The four right-most columns show the costs expected to occur at four different levels of production activity. The predetermined overhead rate per labor hour is smaller as volume of activity increases because total fixed costs remain constant.

EXHIBIT 21.12

Flexible Overhead Budgets

G-MAX Flexible Overhead Budgets For Month Ended May 31, 2011	Variable Amount per Unit	Total Fixed Cost	Flexible Budget at 70% Capacity	Flexible Budget at 80% Capacity	Flexible Budget at 90% Capacity	Flexible Budget at 100% Capacity
Production (in units)	1 unit		3,500	4,000	4,500	5,000
Factory overhead						
Variable costs						
Indirect labor	$0.40/unit		$1,400	$1,600	$1,800	$2,000
Indirect materials	0.30/unit		1,050	1,200	1,350	1,500
Power and lights	0.20/unit		700	800	900	1,000
Maintenance	0.10/unit		350	400	450	500
Total variable overhead costs	$1.00/unit		3,500	4,000	4,500	5,000
Fixed costs (per month)						
Building rent		$1,000	1,000	1,000	1,000	1,000
Depreciation—machinery		1,200	1,200	1,200	1,200	1,200
Supervisory salaries		1,800	1,800	1,800	1,800	1,800
Total fixed overhead costs		$4,000	4,000	4,000	4,000	4,000
Total factory overhead			$7,500	$8,000	$8,500	$9,000
Standard direct labor hours 1 hr./unit . .			3,500 hrs.	4,000 hrs.	4,500 hrs.	5,000 hrs.
Predetermined overhead rate per standard direct labor hour			$ 2.14	$ 2.00	$ 1.89	$ 1.80

G-Max managers predicted an 80% activity level for May, or a production volume of 4,000 clubheads. At this volume, they budget $8,000 as the May total overhead. This choice implies a $2 per unit (labor hour) average overhead cost ($8,000/4,000 units). Since G-Max has a standard of one direct labor hour per unit, the predetermined standard overhead rate for May is $2 per standard direct labor hour. The variable overhead rate remains constant at $1 per direct labor hour regardless of the budgeted production level. The fixed overhead rate changes according to the budgeted production volume. For instance, for the predicted level of 4,000 units of production, the fixed rate is $1 per hour ($4,000 fixed costs/4,000 units). For a production level of 5,000 units, however, the fixed rate is $0.80 per hour ($4,000 fixed costs/5,000 units).

Point: Variable costs per unit remain constant, but fixed costs per unit decline with increases in volume. This means the average total overhead cost per unit declines with increases in volume.

When choosing the predicted activity level, management considers many factors. The level can be set as high as 100% of capacity, but this is rare. Factors causing the activity level to be less than full capacity include difficulties in scheduling work, equipment under repair or maintenance, and insufficient product demand. Good long-run management practices often call for some plant capacity in excess of current operating needs to allow for special opportunities and demand changes.

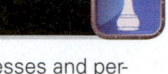

Decision Insight

Measuring Up   In the spirit of continuous improvement, competitors compare their processes and performance standards against benchmarks established by industry leaders. Those that use **benchmarking** include Precision Lube, Jiffy Lube, All Tune and Lube, and Speedee Oil Change and Tune-Up. ∎

Total Overhead Cost Variance

P3 Compute overhead variances.

EXHIBIT 21.13

Overhead Cost Variance

When standard costs are used, the cost accounting system applies overhead to the good units produced using the predetermined standard overhead rate. At period-end, the difference between the total overhead cost applied to products and the total overhead cost actually incurred is called an **overhead cost variance** (total overhead variance), which is defined in Exhibit 21.13.

> **Overhead cost variance (OCV) = Actual overhead incurred (AOI) − Standard overhead applied (SOA)**

The standard overhead applied is based on the predetermined overhead rate and the standard number of hours that should have been used, based on the actual production. To illustrate, G-Max produced 3,500 units during the month, which should have used 3,500 direct labor hours. From Exhibit 21.12, G-Max's predetermined overhead rate at the predicted capacity level of 4,000 units was $2.00 per direct labor hour, so the standard overhead applied is $7,000 (computed as 3,500 × $2.00). Additional data from cost reports show that the actual overhead cost incurred in the month is $7,650. G-Max's total overhead variance is thus $650, computed as $7,650 − $7,000. This variance is unfavorable, as G-Max's actual overhead was higher than it should have been based on budgeted amounts.

Controllable and Volume Variances   To help identify factors causing the overhead cost variance, managers analyze this variance separately for controllable and volume variances, as illustrated in Exhibit 21.14. The results provide information useful for taking strategic actions to improve company performance.

EXHIBIT 21.14

Framework for Understanding Total Overhead Variance

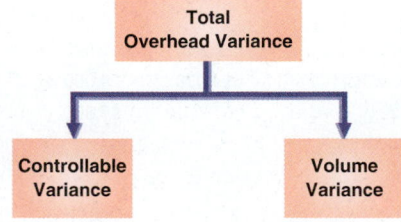

The **controllable variance** is the difference between actual overhead costs incurred and the budgeted overhead costs based on a flexible budget. The controllable variance is so named because it refers to activities usually under management control. A **volume variance** occurs when there is a difference between the actual volume of production and the standard volume of production. The budgeted fixed overhead amount is the same regardless of the volume of production (within the relevant range). This budgeted amount is computed based on the standard direct labor hours that the budgeted production volume allows. The applied fixed overhead is based, however, on the standard direct labor hours allowed for the actual volume of production, using the flexible budget. When a company operates at a capacity different from what it expected, the volume variance will differ from zero.

Returning to the G-Max data, the flexible budget in Exhibit 21.12 shows budgeted factory overhead of $7,500 at the production volume of 3,500 units during the month. The controllable variance is then computed as:

Actual total overhead (given)	$7,650
Applied total overhead (from flexible budget)	7,500
Controllable variance (unfavorable)	$ 150

We then compute the volume variance. It is important to note that the volume variance is based solely on *fixed* overhead. G-Max's budgeted fixed overhead at the predicted capacity level for the month was $4,000. Recall from Exhibit 21.12 that G-Max's predetermined fixed overhead at the predicted capacity level of 4,000 units was $1 per hour. Thus, G-Max's applied fixed overhead was $3,500, computed as 3,500 units $\times$ $1.00 per unit. G-Max's volume variance is then computed as:

Budgeted fixed overhead (at predicted capacity)	$4,000
Applied fixed overhead (3,500 $\times$ $1.00)	3,500
Volume variance (unfavorable)	$ 500

Analyzing Controllable and Volume Variances How should the top management of G-Max interpret the unfavorable controllable and volume variances? An unfavorable volume variance implies that the company did not reach its predicted operating level. In this case, 80% of manufacturing capacity was budgeted but only 70% was used. Management needs to know why the actual level of production differs from the expected level. The main purpose of the volume variance is to identify what portion of the total overhead variance is caused by failing to meet the expected production level. Often the reasons for failing to meet this expected production level are due to factors, for example customer demand, that are beyond employees' control. This information permits management to focus on explanations for the controllable variance, as we discuss next.

Overhead Variance Reports To help management isolate the reasons for the $150 unfavorable controllable variance, an *overhead variance report* can be prepared. A complete overhead variance report provides managers information about specific overhead costs and how they differ from budgeted amounts. Exhibit 21.15 shows G-Max's overhead variance report for May. It reveals that (1) fixed costs and maintenance costs were incurred as expected, (2) costs for indirect labor and power and lights were higher than expected, and (3) indirect materials cost was less than expected.

"Well, according to the books, you've got too much overhead."

EXHIBIT 21.15

Overhead Variance Report

G-MAX
Overhead Variance Report
For Month Ended May 31, 2011

Volume Variance

Expected production level	80% of capacity
Production level achieved.	70% of capacity
Volume variance	**$500 (unfavorable)**

Controllable Variance	Flexible Budget	Actual Results	Variances*
Variable overhead costs			
Indirect labor	$1,400	$1,525	**$125 U**
Indirect materials	1,050	1,025	25 F
Power and lights	700	750	50 U
Maintenance	350	350	0
Total variable overhead costs	3,500	3,650	150 U
Fixed overhead costs			
Building rent	1,000	1,000	0
Depreciation—machinery	1,200	1,200	0
Supervisory salaries	1,800	1,800	0
Total fixed overhead costs	4,000	4,000	0
Total overhead costs	$7,500	$7,650	$150 U

* F = Favorable variance; U = Unfavorable variance.

The total controllable variance amount is also readily available from Exhibit 21.15. The overhead variance report shows the total volume variance as $500 unfavorable (shown at the top) and the $150 unfavorable controllable variance (reported at the bottom right). The sum of the controllable variance and the volume variance equals the total overhead variance of $650 unfavorable.

Appendix 21A describes an expanded analysis of overhead variances.

Quick Check

Answers — p. 905

10. Under what conditions is an overhead volume variance considered favorable?
11. To use management by exception, a company (*a*) need not study fixed overhead variances, (*b*) should compute variances from flexible budget amounts to allow management to focus its attention on significant differences between actual and budgeted results, or (*c*) should analyze only variances for direct materials and direct labor.

GLOBAL VIEW

BMW, a German automobile manufacturer, uses concepts of standard costing and variance analysis. Production begins with huge rolls of steel and aluminum, which are then cut and pressed by large machines. Material must meet high quality standards, and the company sets standards for each of its machine operations. In the Assembly department, highly-trained employees complete the assembly of the painted car chassis, often to customer specifications. Again, BMW sets standards for how much labor should be used and monitors its employee performance.

This chapter explained the computation and analysis of cost variances. A similar variance analysis can be applied to sales. To illustrate, consider the following sales data from G-Max for two of its golf products, Excel golf balls and Big Bert® drivers.

A1 Analyze changes in sales from expected amounts.

	Budgeted	Actual
Sales of Excel golf balls (units)	1,000 units	1,100 units
Sales price per Excel golf ball	$10	$10.50
Sales of Big Bert® drivers (units)	150 units	140 units
Sales price per Big Bert® driver	$200	$190

Using this information, we compute both the *sales price variance* and the *sales volume variance* as shown in Exhibit 21.16. The total sales price variance is $850 unfavorable, and the total sales volume variance is $1,000 unfavorable. Neither total variance implies anything positive about these two products. However, further analysis of these total sales variances reveals that both the sales price and sales volume variances for Excel golf balls are favorable, meaning that both the unfavorable total sales price variance and the unfavorable total sales volume variance are due to the Big Bert driver.

EXHIBIT 21.16

Computing Sales Variances*

Excel Golf Balls	Actual Results AS × AP	Flexible Budget AS × BP	Fixed Budget BS × BP
Sales dollars (balls)	(1,100 × $10.50) **$11,550**	(1,100 × $10) **$11,000**	(1,000 × $10) **$10,000**
	$550 F	$1,000 F	
	Sales Price Variance	**Sales Volume Variance**	
Big Bert® Drivers			
Sales dollars (drivers)	(140 × $190) **$26,600**	(140 × $200) **$28,000**	(150 × $200) **$30,000**
	$1,400 U	$2,000 U	
	Sales Price Variance	**Sales Volume Variance**	
Total	**$850 U**	**$1,000 U**	

* AS = actual sales units; AP = actual sales price; BP = budgeted sales price; BS = budgeted sales units (fixed budget).

Managers use sales variances for planning and control purposes. The sales variance information is used to plan future actions to avoid unfavorable variances. G-Max sold 90 total combined units (both balls and drivers) more than planned, but these 90 units were not sold in the proportion budgeted. G-Max sold fewer than the budgeted quantity of the higher-priced driver, which contributed to the unfavorable total sales variances. Managers use such detail to question what caused the company to sell more golf balls and fewer drivers. Managers also use this information to evaluate and even reward their salespeople. Extra compensation is paid to salespeople who contribute to a higher profit margin. Finally, with multiple products, the sales volume variance can be separated into a *sales mix variance* and a *sales quantity variance*. The sales mix variance is the difference between the actual and budgeted sales mix of the products. The sales quantity variance is the difference between the total actual and total budgeted quantity of units sold.

 **Decision Maker**   Answer — p. 904

Sales Manager   The current performance report reveals a large favorable sales volume variance but an unfavorable sales price variance. You did not expect to see a large increase in sales volume. What steps do you take to analyze this situation? ■

DEMONSTRATION PROBLEM

Pacific Company provides the following information about its budgeted and actual results for June 2011. Although the expected June volume was 25,000 units produced and sold, the company actually produced and sold 27,000 units as detailed here:

	Budget (25,000 units)	Actual (27,000 units)
Selling price	$5.00 per unit	$5.23 per unit
Variable costs (per unit)		
Direct materials	1.24 per unit	1.12 per unit
Direct labor	1.50 per unit	1.40 per unit
Factory supplies*	0.25 per unit	0.37 per unit
Utilities*	0.50 per unit	0.60 per unit
Selling costs	0.40 per unit	0.34 per unit
Fixed costs (per month)		
Depreciation—machinery*	$3,750	$3,710
Depreciation—building*	2,500	2,500
General liability insurance	1,200	1,250
Property taxes on office equipment	500	485
Other administrative expense	750	900

* Indicates factory overhead item; $0.75 per unit or $3 per direct labor hour for variable overhead, and $0.25 per unit or $1 per direct labor hour for fixed overhead.

Standard costs based on expected output of 25,000 units

	Per Unit of Output	Quantity to Be Used	Total Cost
Direct materials, 4 oz. @ $0.31/oz.	$1.24/unit	100,000 oz.	$31,000
Direct labor, 0.25 hrs. @ $6.00/hr.	1.50/unit	6,250 hrs.	37,500
Overhead	1.00/unit		25,000

Actual costs incurred to produce 27,000 units

	Per Unit of Output	Quantity Used	Total Cost
Direct materials, 4 oz. @ $0.28/oz.	$1.12/unit	108,000 oz.	$30,240
Direct labor, 0.20 hrs. @ $7.00/hr.	1.40/unit	5,400 hrs.	37,800
Overhead	1.20/unit		32,400

Standard costs based on expected output of 27,000 units

	Per Unit of Output	Quantity to Be Used	Total Cost
Direct materials, 4 oz. @ $0.31/oz.	$1.24/unit	108,000 oz.	$33,480
Direct labor, 0.25 hrs. @ $6.00/hr.	1.50/unit	6,750 hrs.	40,500
Overhead			26,500

Required

1. Prepare June flexible budgets showing expected sales, costs, and net income assuming 20,000, 25,000, and 30,000 units of output produced and sold.
2. Prepare a flexible budget performance report that compares actual results with the amounts budgeted if the actual volume had been expected.
3. Apply variance analysis for direct materials and direct labor.
4. Compute the total overhead variance, and the controllable and volume variances.
5. Compute spending and efficiency variances for overhead. (Refer to Appendix 21A.)
6. Prepare journal entries to record standard costs, and price and quantity variances, for direct materials, direct labor, and factory overhead. (Refer to Appendix 21A.)

PLANNING THE SOLUTION

- Prepare a table showing the expected results at the three specified levels of output. Compute the variable costs by multiplying the per unit variable costs by the expected volumes. Include fixed costs at the given amounts. Combine the amounts in the table to show total variable costs, contribution margin, total fixed costs, and income from operations.
- Prepare a table showing the actual results and the amounts that should be incurred at 27,000 units. Show any differences in the third column and label them with an *F* for favorable if they increase income or a *U* for unfavorable if they decrease income.
- Using the chapter's format, compute these total variances and the individual variances requested:
  - Total materials variance (including the direct materials quantity variance and the direct materials price variance).
  - Total direct labor variance (including the direct labor efficiency variance and rate variance).
  - Total overhead variance (including both controllable and volume overhead variances and their component variances).

SOLUTION TO DEMONSTRATION PROBLEM

1.

PACIFIC COMPANY
Flexible Budgets
For Month Ended June 30, 2011

	Flexible Budget — Variable Amount per Unit	Flexible Budget — Total Fixed Cost	Flexible Budget for Unit Sales of 20,000	Flexible Budget for Unit Sales of 25,000	Flexible Budget for Unit Sales of 30,000
Sales	$5.00		$100,000	$125,000	$150,000
Variable costs					
Direct materials	1.24		24,800	31,000	37,200
Direct labor	1.50		30,000	37,500	45,000
Factory supplies	0.25		5,000	6,250	7,500
Utilities	0.50		10,000	12,500	15,000
Selling costs	0.40		8,000	10,000	12,000
Total variable costs	3.89		77,800	97,250	116,700
Contribution margin	$1.11		22,200	27,750	33,300
Fixed costs					
Depreciation—machinery		$3,750	3,750	3,750	3,750
Depreciation—building		2,500	2,500	2,500	2,500
General liability insurance		1,200	1,200	1,200	1,200
Property taxes on office equipment		500	500	500	500
Other administrative expense		750	750	750	750
Total fixed costs		$8,700	8,700	8,700	8,700
Income from operations			$ 13,500	$ 19,050	$ 24,600

2.

PACIFIC COMPANY Flexible Budget Performance Report For Month Ended June 30, 2011	Flexible Budget	Actual Results	Variance*
Sales (27,000 units)	$135,000	$141,210	$6,210 F
Variable costs			
Direct materials	33,480	30,240	3,240 F
Direct labor	40,500	37,800	2,700 F
Factory supplies	6,750	9,990	3,240 U
Utilities.................................	13,500	16,200	2,700 U
Selling costs	10,800	9,180	1,620 F
Total variable costs	105,030	103,410	1,620 F
Contribution margin	29,970	37,800	7,830 F
Fixed costs			
Depreciation—machinery...................	3,750	3,710	40 F
Depreciation—building	2,500	2,500	0
General liability insurance	1,200	1,250	50 U
Property taxes on office equipment	500	485	15 F
Other administrative expense	750	900	150 U
Total fixed costs	8,700	8,845	145 U
Income from operations	$ 21,270	$ 28,955	$7,685 F

* F = Favorable variance; U = Unfavorable variance.

3. Variance analysis of materials and labor costs.

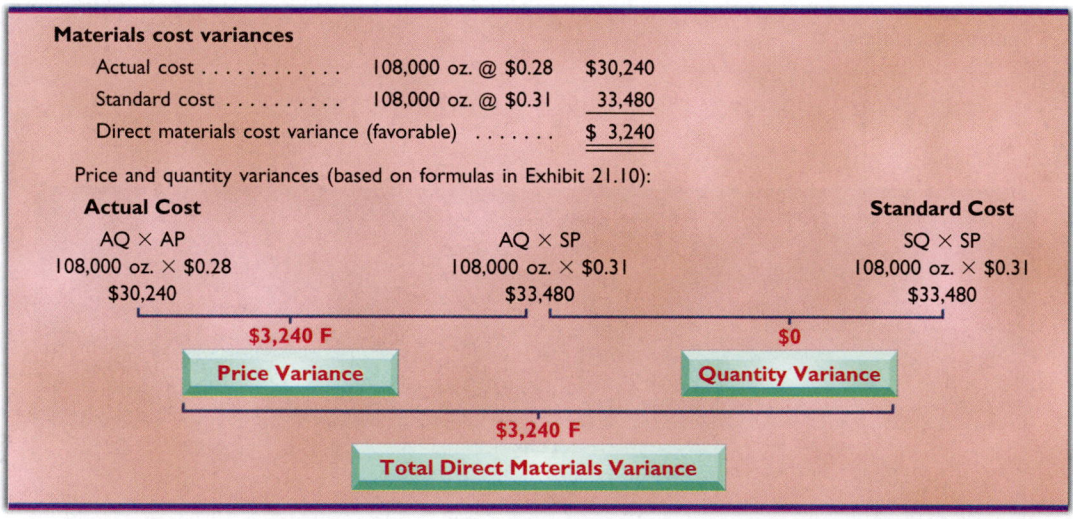

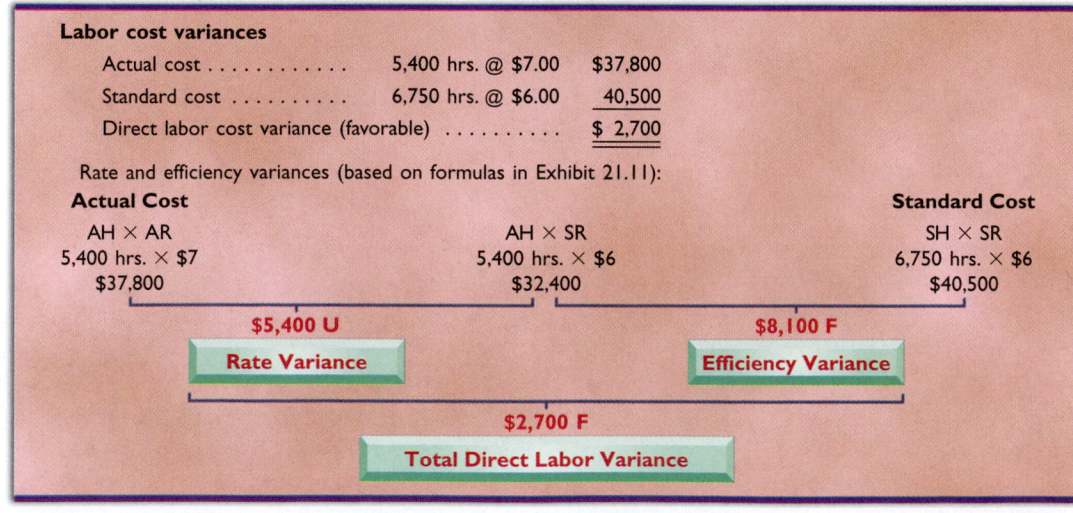

4. Total, controllable, and volume variances for overhead.

Overhead cost variances

Total overhead cost incurred	27,000 units @ $1.20	$32,400
Total overhead applied	27,000 units @ $1.00	27,000
Overhead cost variance (unfavorable)		$ 5,400

Controllable variance

Actual overhead (given)	$32,400
Applied overhead (from flexible budget for 27,000 units)	26,500
Controllable variance (unfavorable)	$ 5,900

Volume variance

Budgeted fixed overhead (at predicted capacity)	$ 6,250
Applied fixed overhead (6,750 × $1.00)	6,750
Volume variance (favorable).........................	$ 500

5. Variable and fixed overhead spending and efficiency variances.

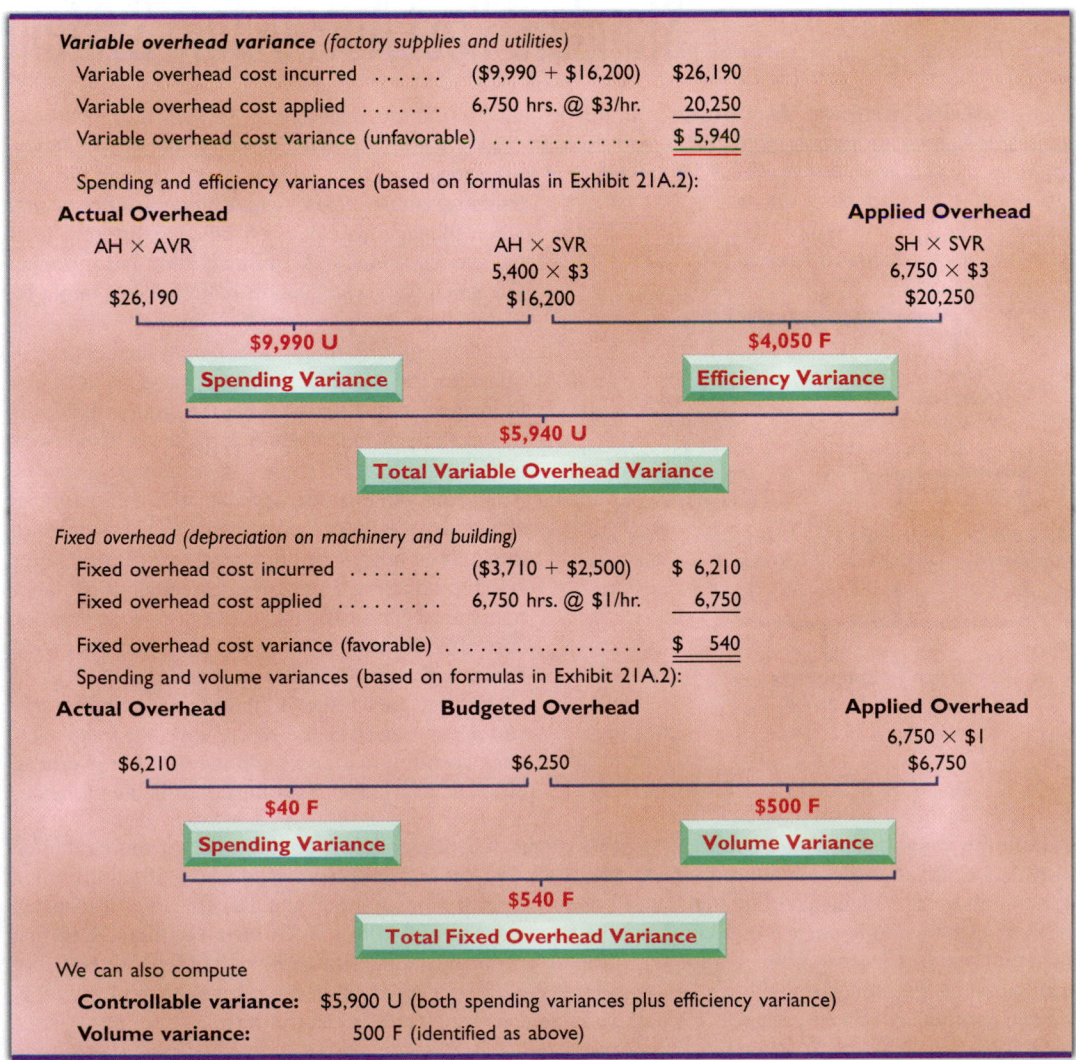

Variable overhead variance _(factory supplies and utilities)_

Variable overhead cost incurred	($9,990 + $16,200)	$26,190
Variable overhead cost applied	6,750 hrs. @ $3/hr.	20,250
Variable overhead cost variance (unfavorable)		$ 5,940

Spending and efficiency variances (based on formulas in Exhibit 21A.2):

Actual Overhead		**Applied Overhead**
AH × AVR	AH × SVR	SH × SVR
	5,400 × $3	6,750 × $3
$26,190	$16,200	$20,250

$9,990 U — **Spending Variance** $4,050 F — **Efficiency Variance**

$5,940 U — **Total Variable Overhead Variance**

Fixed overhead (depreciation on machinery and building)

Fixed overhead cost incurred	($3,710 + $2,500)	$ 6,210
Fixed overhead cost applied	6,750 hrs. @ $1/hr.	6,750
Fixed overhead cost variance (favorable)		$ 540

Spending and volume variances (based on formulas in Exhibit 21A.2):

Actual Overhead	**Budgeted Overhead**	**Applied Overhead**
		6,750 × $1
$6,210	$6,250	$6,750

$40 F — **Spending Variance** $500 F — **Volume Variance**

$540 F — **Total Fixed Overhead Variance**

We can also compute

Controllable variance:	$5,900 U (both spending variances plus efficiency variance)
Volume variance:	500 F (identified as above)

6.

Goods in Process Inventory	33,480	
Direct Materials Price Variance		3,240
Raw Materials Inventory		30,240
Goods in Process Inventory	40,500	
Direct Labor Rate Variance	5,400	
Direct Labor Efficiency Variance		8,100
Factory Payroll		37,800
Goods in Process Inventory*	27,000	
Variable Overhead Spending Variance	9,990	
Variable Overhead Efficiency Variance		4,050
Fixed Overhead Spending Variance		40
Fixed Overhead Volume Variance		500
Factory Overhead†		32,400

* $20,250 + $6,750   † $26,190 + $6,210

21A

Expanded Overhead Variances and Standard Cost Accounting System

Expanded Overhead Variances   Similar to analysis of direct materials and direct labor, overhead variances can be more completely analyzed. Exhibit 21A.1 shows an expanded framework for understanding these component overhead variances. This framework uses classifications of overhead costs as either variable or fixed. A **spending variance** occurs when management pays an amount different than the standard price to acquire an item. For instance, the actual wage rate paid to indirect labor might be higher than the standard rate. Similarly, actual supervisory salaries might be different than expected. Spending variances such as these cause management to investigate the reasons that the amount paid differs from the standard. Both variable and fixed overhead costs can yield their own spending variances. Analyzing variable overhead includes computing an **efficiency variance,** which occurs when standard direct labor hours (the allocation base) expected for actual production differ from the actual direct labor hours used. This efficiency variance reflects on the cost-effectiveness in using the overhead allocation base (such as direct labor).

EXHIBIT 21A.1

Expanded Framework for Total Overhead Variance

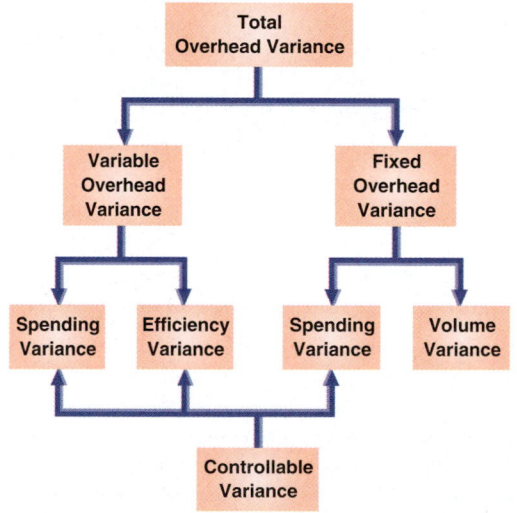

Exhibit 21A.1 shows that we can combine the variable overhead spending variance, the fixed overhead spending variance, and the variable overhead efficiency variance to get the controllable variance.

Computing Variable and Fixed Overhead Cost Variances   To illustrate the computation of more detailed overhead cost variances, we return to the G-Max data. We know that G-Max produced 3,500 units when 4,000 units were budgeted. Additional data from cost reports show that the actual overhead cost incurred is $7,650 (the variable portion of $3,650 and the fixed portion of $4,000). Recall from Exhibit 21.12 that each unit requires 1 hour of direct labor, that variable overhead is applied at a rate of $1.00 per direct labor hour, and that the predetermined fixed overhead rate is $1.00 per direct labor hour. Using this information, we can compute overhead variances for both variable and fixed overhead as follows:

Actual variable overhead (given)	$3,650
Applied variable overhead (3,500 × $1.00)	3,500
Variable overhead variance (unfavorable)	$ 150

Actual fixed overhead (given)	$4,000
Applied fixed overhead (3,500 × $1.00)	3,500
Fixed overhead variance (unfavorable)	$ 500

Management should seek to determine the causes of these unfavorable variances and take corrective action. To help better isolate the causes of these variances, more detailed overhead variances can be used, as shown in the next section.

Expanded Overhead Variance Formulas   Exhibit 21A.2 shows formulas to use in computing detailed overhead variances that can better identify reasons for variable and fixed overhead variances.

EXHIBIT 21A.2

Variable and Fixed Overhead Variances

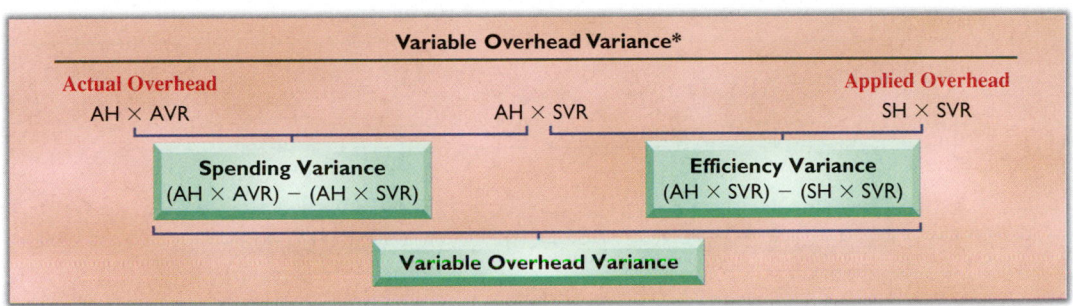

* AH = actual direct labor hours; AVR = actual variable overhead rate; SH = standard direct labor hours; SVR = standard variable overhead rate.

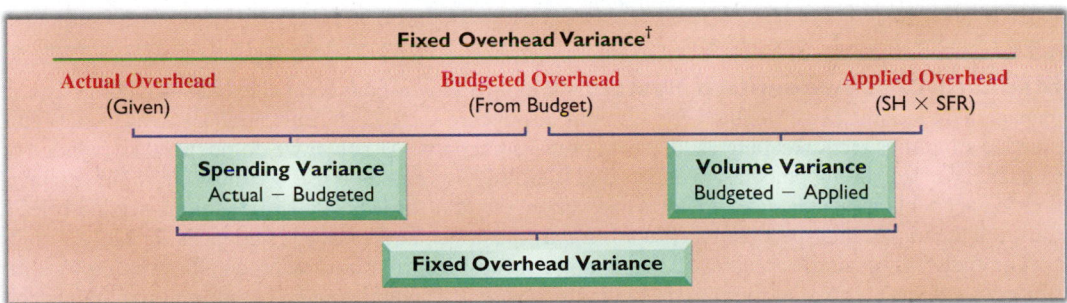

†SH = standard direct labor hours; SFR = standard fixed overhead rate.

Variable Overhead Cost Variances   Using these formulas, Exhibit 21A.3 offers insight into the causes of G-Max's $150 unfavorable variable overhead cost variance. Recall that G-Max applies overhead based on direct labor hours as the allocation base. We know that it used 3,400 direct labor hours to produce 3,500 units. This compares favorably to the standard requirement of 3,500 direct labor hours at one labor hour per unit. At a standard variable overhead rate of $1.00 per direct labor hour, this should have resulted in variable overhead costs of $3,400 (middle column of Exhibit 21A.3).

EXHIBIT 21A.3

Computing Variable Overhead Cost Variances

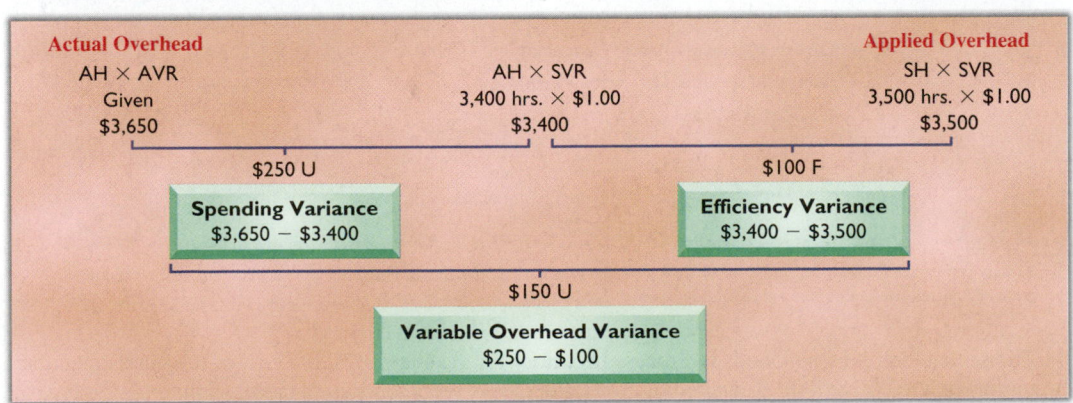

G-Max's cost records, however, report actual variable overhead of $3,650, or $250 higher than expected. This means G-Max has an unfavorable variable overhead spending variance of $250 ($3,650 − $3,400). On the other hand, G-Max used 100 fewer labor hours than expected to make 3,500 units, and its actual variable overhead is lower than its applied variable overhead. Thus, G-Max has a favorable variable overhead efficiency variance of $100 ($3,400 − $3,500).

Fixed Overhead Cost Variances   Exhibit 21A.4 provides insight into the causes of G-Max's $500 unfavorable fixed overhead variance. G-Max reports that it incurred $4,000 in actual fixed overhead; this amount equals the budgeted fixed overhead for May at the expected production level of 4,000 units (see Exhibit 21.12). Thus, the fixed overhead spending variance is zero, suggesting good control of fixed overhead costs. G-Max's budgeted fixed overhead application rate is $1 per hour ($4,000/4,000 direct labor hours), but the actual production level is only 3,500 units. Using this information, we can compute the fixed overhead volume variance shown in Exhibit 21A.4. The applied fixed overhead is computed by multiplying 3,500 standard hours allowed for the actual production by the $1 fixed overhead allocation rate. The volume variance of $500 occurs because 500 fewer units are produced than budgeted; namely, 80% of the manufacturing capacity is budgeted but only 70% is used.

EXHIBIT 21A.4

Computing Fixed Overhead Cost Variances

Standard Cost Accounting System   We have shown how companies use standard costs in management reports. Most standard cost systems also record these costs and variances in accounts. This practice simplifies recordkeeping and helps in preparing reports. Although we do not need knowledge of standard cost accounting practices to understand standard costs and their use, we must know how to interpret the accounts in which standard costs and variances are recorded. The entries in this section briefly illustrate the important aspects of this process for G-Max's standard costs and variances for May.

P4 Prepare journal entries for standard costs and account for price and quantity variances.

The first of these entries records standard materials cost incurred in May in the Goods in Process Inventory account. This part of the entry is similar to the usual accounting entry, but the amount of the debit equals the standard cost ($35,000) instead of the actual cost ($37,800). This entry credits Raw Materials Inventory for actual cost. The difference between standard and actual direct materials costs is recorded with debits to two separate materials variance accounts (recall Exhibit 21.10). Both the materials price and quantity variances are recorded as debits because they reflect additional costs higher than the standard cost (if actual costs were less than the standard, they are recorded as credits). This treatment (debit) reflects their unfavorable effect because they represent higher costs and lower income.

Assets = Liabilities + Equity
+35,000   −1,000
−37,800   −1,800

May 31	Goods in Process Inventory	35,000	
	Direct Materials Price Variance*	1,800	
	Direct Materials Quantity Variance	1,000	
	Raw Materials Inventory		37,800
	To charge production for standard quantity of materials used (1,750 lbs.) at the standard price ($20 per lb.), and to record material price and material quantity variances.		

* Many companies record the materials price variance when materials are purchased. For simplicity, we record both the materials price and quantity variances when materials are issued to production.

The second entry debits Goods in Process Inventory for the standard labor cost of the goods manufactured during May ($28,000). Actual labor cost ($28,220) is recorded with a credit to the Factory Payroll account. The difference between standard and actual labor costs is explained by two variances (see Exhibit 21.11). The direct labor rate variance is unfavorable and is debited to that account. The direct labor efficiency variance is favorable and that account is credited. The direct labor efficiency variance is favorable because it represents a lower cost and a higher net income.

May 31	Goods in Process Inventory	28,000	
	Direct Labor Rate Variance	1,020	
	Direct Labor Efficiency Variance		800
	Factory Payroll		28,220
	To charge production with 3,500 standard hours of direct labor at the standard $8 per hour rate, and to record the labor rate and efficiency variances.		

Assets = Liabilities + Equity
+28,000   +28,220
                       − 1,020
                       + 800

The entry to assign standard predetermined overhead to the cost of goods manufactured must debit the $7,000 predetermined amount to the Goods in Process Inventory account. Actual overhead costs of $7,650 were debited to Factory Overhead during the period (entries not shown here). Thus, when Factory Overhead is applied to Goods in Process Inventory, the actual amount is credited to the Factory Overhead account. To account for the difference between actual and standard overhead costs, the entry includes a $250 debit to the Variable Overhead Spending Variance, a $100 credit to the Variable Overhead Efficiency Variance, and a $500 debit to the Volume Variance (recall Exhibits 21A.3 and 21A.4). An alternative (simpler) approach is to record the difference with a $150 debit to the Controllable Variance account and a $500 debit to the Volume Variance account (recall from Exhibit 21A.1 that controllable variance is the sum of both variable overhead variances and the fixed overhead spending variance).

May 31	Goods in Process Inventory	7,000	
	Volume Variance	500	
	Variable Overhead Spending Variance	250	
	Variable Overhead Efficiency Variance		100
	Factory Overhead		7,650
	To apply overhead at the standard rate of $2 per standard direct labor hour (3,500 hours), and to record overhead variances.		

Assets = Liabilities + Equity
+7,000   +7,650
                     − 250
                     − 500
                     + 100

The balances of these different variance accounts accumulate until the end of the accounting period. As a result, the unfavorable variances of some months can offset the favorable variances of other months.

These ending variance account balances, which reflect results of the period's various transactions and events, are closed at period-end. If the amounts are *immaterial,* they are added to or subtracted from the balance of the Cost of Goods Sold account. This process is similar to that shown in the job order costing chapter for eliminating an underapplied or overapplied balance in the Factory Overhead account. (*Note:* These variance balances, which represent differences between actual and standard costs, must be added to or subtracted from the materials, labor, and overhead costs recorded. In this way, the recorded costs equal the actual costs incurred in the period; a company must use actual costs in external financial statements prepared in accordance with generally accepted accounting principles.)

Point: If variances are material they can be allocated between Goods in Process Inventory, Finished Goods Inventory, and Cost of Goods Sold. This closing process is explained in advanced courses.

Quick Check

Answers — p. 905

12. A company uses a standard cost accounting system. Prepare the journal entry to record these direct materials variances:

Direct materials cost actually incurred..................	$73,200
Direct materials quantity variance (favorable)...........	3,800
Direct materials price variance (unfavorable)	1,300

13. If standard costs are recorded in the manufacturing accounts, how are recorded variances treated at the end of an accounting period?

Summary

C1 Define *standard costs* and explain how standard cost information is useful for management by exception. Standard costs are the normal costs that should be incurred to produce a product or perform a service. They should be based on a careful examination of the processes used to produce a product or perform a service as well as the quantities and prices that should be incurred in carrying out those processes. On a performance report, standard costs (which are flexible budget amounts) are compared to actual costs, and the differences are presented as variances. Standard cost accounting provides management information about costs that differ from budgeted (expected) amounts. Performance reports disclose the costs or areas of operations that have significant variances from budgeted amounts. This allows managers to focus attention on the exceptions and less attention on areas proceeding normally.

C2 Describe variances and what they reveal about performance. Management can use variances to monitor and control activities. Total cost variances can be broken into price and quantity variances to direct management's attention to those responsible for quantities used and prices paid.

A1 Analyze changes in sales from expected amounts. Actual sales can differ from budgeted sales, and managers can investigate this difference by computing both the sales price and sales volume variances. The *sales price variance* refers to that portion of total variance resulting from a difference between actual and budgeted selling prices. The *sales volume variance* refers to that portion of total variance resulting from a difference between actual and budgeted sales quantities.

P1 Prepare a flexible budget and interpret a flexible budget performance report. A flexible budget expresses variable costs in per unit terms so that it can be used to develop budgeted amounts for any volume level within the relevant range. Thus, managers compute budgeted amounts for evaluation after a period for the volume that actually occurred. To prepare a flexible budget, we express each variable cost as a constant amount per unit of sales (or as a percent of sales dollars). In contrast, the budgeted amount

of each fixed cost is expressed as a total amount expected to occur at any sales volume within the relevant range. The flexible budget is then determined using these computations and amounts for fixed and variable costs at the expected sales volume.

P2 Compute materials and labor variances. Materials and labor variances are due to differences between the actual costs incurred and the budgeted costs. The price (or rate) variance is computed by comparing the actual cost with the flexible budget amount that should have been incurred to acquire the actual quantity of resources. The quantity (or efficiency) variance is computed by comparing the flexible budget amount that should have been incurred to acquire the actual quantity of resources with the flexible budget amount that should have been incurred to acquire the standard quantity of resources.

P3 Compute overhead variances. Overhead variances are due to differences between the actual overhead costs incurred and the overhead applied to production. An overhead spending variance arises when the actual amount incurred differs from the budgeted amount of overhead. An overhead efficiency (or volume) variance arises when the flexible overhead budget amount differs from the overhead applied to production. It is important to realize that overhead is assigned using an overhead allocation base, meaning that an efficiency variance (in the case of variable overhead) is a result of the overhead application base being used more or less efficiently than planned.

P4ᴬ Prepare journal entries for standard costs and account for price and quantity variances. When a company records standard costs in its accounts, the standard costs of materials, labor, and overhead are debited to the Goods in Process Inventory account. Based on an analysis of the material, labor, and overhead costs, each quantity variance, price variance, volume variance, and controllable variance is recorded in a separate account. At period-end, if the variances are material, they are allocated among the balances of the Goods in Process Inventory, Finished Goods Inventory, and Cost of Goods Sold accounts. If they are not material, they are simply debited or credited to the Cost of Goods Sold account.

Guidance Answers to Decision Maker and Decision Ethics

Entrepreneur   From the complaints, this performance report appears to compare actual results with a fixed budget. This comparison is useful in determining whether the amount of work actually performed was more or less than planned, but it is not useful in determining whether the divisions were more or less efficient than planned. If the two consulting divisions worked on more assignments than expected, some costs will certainly increase. Therefore, you should prepare a flexible budget using the actual number of consulting assignments and then compare actual performance to the flexible budget.

Internal Auditor   Although the manager's actions might not be unethical, this action is undesirable. The internal auditor should report this behavior, possibly recommending that for the purchase of such discretionary items, the manager must provide budgetary requests using an activity-based budgeting process. The internal auditor would then be given full authority to verify this budget request.

Human Resource Manager   As HR manager, you should investigate the causes for any labor-related variances although you may not be responsible for them. An unfavorable labor efficiency variance occurs because more labor hours than standard were used during the period. There are at least three possible reasons for this: (1) materials quality could be poor, resulting in more labor consumption due to rework; (2) unplanned interruptions (strike, breakdowns, accidents) could have occurred during the period; and (3) the production manager could have used a different labor mix to expedite orders. This new labor mix could have consisted of a larger proportion of untrained labor, which resulted in more labor hours.

Sales Manager   The unfavorable sales price variance suggests that actual prices were lower than budgeted prices. As the sales manager, you want to know the reasons for a lower than expected price. Perhaps your salespeople lowered the price of certain products by offering quantity discounts. You then might want to know what prompted them to offer the quantity discounts (perhaps competitors were offering discounts). You want to break the sales volume variance into both the sales mix and sales quantity variances. You could find that although the sales quantity variance is favorable, the sales mix variance is not. Then you need to investigate why the actual sales mix differs from the budgeted sales mix.

Guidance Answers to Quick Checks

1. *b*

2. The first step is classifying each cost as variable or fixed.

3. A fixed budget is prepared using an expected volume of sales or production. A flexible budget is prepared using the actual volume of activity.

4. The contribution margin equals sales less variable costs.

5. *c*

6. It is the difference between actual cost and standard cost.

7. *a*; Total actual hours: 2,500 × 2.5 = 6,250
  Total standard hours: 2,500 × 2.0 = 5,000
  Efficiency variance = (6,250 − 5,000) × $3.00
          = $3,750 U

8. *b*; Rate variance = ($3.10 − $3.00) × 6,250 = $625 U

9. Yes, this will occur when the materials quantity variance is more than the materials price variance.

10. The overhead volume variance is favorable when the actual operating level is higher than the expected level.

11. *b*

12.

Goods in Process Inventory	75,700	
Direct Materials Price Variance	1,300	
Direct Materials Quantity Variance		3,800
Raw Materials Inventory		73,200

13. If the variances are material, they should be prorated among the Goods in Process Inventory, Finished Goods Inventory, and Cost of Goods Sold accounts. If they are not material, they can be closed to Cost of Goods Sold.

Key Terms   mhhe.com/wildFINMAN4e

Benchmarking (p. 892)	**Fixed budget** (p. 881)	**Quantity variance** (p. 885)
Budget report (p. 880)	**Fixed budget performance report** (p. 881)	**Spending variance** (p. 900)
Budgetary control (p. 880)	**Flexible budget** (p. 882)	**Standard costs** (p. 885)
Controllable variance (p. 893)	**Flexible budget performance report** (p. 884)	**Unfavorable variance** (p. 881)
Cost variance (p. 887)	**Management by exception** (p. 885)	**Variance analysis** (p. 885)
Efficiency variance (p. 900)	**Overhead cost variance** (p. 892)	**Volume variance** (p. 893)
Favorable variance (p. 881)	**Price variance** (p. 885)	

Multiple Choice Quiz   Answers on p. 923   mhhe.com/wildFINMAN4e

Additional Quiz Questions are available at the book's Website.

1. A company predicts its production and sales will be 24,000 units. At that level of activity, its fixed costs are budgeted at $300,000, and its variable costs are budgeted at $246,000. If its activity level declines to 20,000 units, what will be its fixed costs and its variable costs?
  a. Fixed, $300,000; variable, $246,000
  b. Fixed, $250,000; variable, $205,000
  c. Fixed, $300,000; variable, $205,000
  d. Fixed, $250,000; variable, $246,000
  e. Fixed, $300,000; variable, $300,000

2. Using the following information about a single product company, compute its total actual cost of direct materials used.
  • Direct materials standard cost: 5 lbs. × $2 per lb. = $10.
  • Total direct materials cost variance: $15,000 unfavorable.
  • Actual direct materials used: 300,000 lbs.
  • Actual units produced: 60,000 units.

  a. $585,000
  b. $600,000
  c. $300,000
  d. $315,000
  e. $615,000

3. A company uses four hours of direct labor to produce a product unit. The standard direct labor cost is $20 per hour. This period the company produced 20,000 units and used 84,160 hours of direct labor at a total cost of $1,599,040. What is its labor rate variance for the period?
  a. $83,200 F
  b. $84,160 U
  c. $84,160 F
  d. $83,200 U
  e. $ 960 F

4. A company's standard for a unit of its single product is $6 per unit in variable overhead (4 hours × $1.50 per hour). Actual data for the period show variable overhead costs of $150,000 and production of 24,000 units. Its total variable overhead cost variance is
   a. $ 6,000 F.
   b. $ 6,000 U.
   c. $114,000 U.
   d. $114,000 F.
   e. $ 0.

5. A company's standard for a unit of its single product is $4 per unit in fixed overhead ($24,000 total/6,000 units budgeted). Actual data for the period show total actual fixed overhead of $24,100 and production of 4,800 units. Its volume variance is
   a. $4,800 U.
   b. $4,800 F.
   c. $ 100 U.
   d. $ 100 F.
   e. $4,900 U.

A *Superscript letter A denotes assignments based on Appendix 21A.*
🛈 Icon denotes assignments that involve decision making.

Discussion Questions

1. 🛈 What limits the usefulness to managers of fixed budget performance reports?
2. 🛈 Identify the main purpose of a flexible budget for managers.
3. Prepare a flexible budget performance report title (in proper form) for Spalding Company for the calendar year 2011. Why is a proper title important for this or any report?
4. 🛈 What type of analysis does a flexible budget performance report help management perform?
5. In what sense can a variable cost be considered constant?
6. 🛈 What department is usually responsible for a direct labor rate variance? What department is usually responsible for a direct labor efficiency variance? Explain.
7. What is a price variance? What is a quantity variance?
8. 🛈 What is the purpose of using standard costs?
9. **Nokia** monitors its fixed overhead. In an analysis of fixed overhead cost variances, what is the volume variance? **NOKIA**
10. What is the predetermined standard overhead rate? How is it computed?

11. In general, variance analysis is said to provide information about _____ and _____ variances.
12. 🛈 **Research In Motion** monitors its overhead. In an analysis of overhead cost variances, what is the controllable variance and what causes it? **RIM**
13. What are the relations among standard costs, flexible budgets, variance analysis, and management by exception?
14. 🛈 How can the manager of handheld devices at an **Apple** retail store use flexible budgets to enhance performance? **Apple**
15. 🛈 Is it possible for a retail store such as **Apple** to use variances in analyzing its operating performance? Explain. **Apple**
16. 🛈 Assume that **Palm** is budgeted to operate at 80% of capacity but actually operates at 75% of capacity. What effect will the 5% deviation have on its controllable variance? Its volume variance? **Palm**

🅜 **connect**

QUICK STUDY

QS 21-1
Flexible budget performance report
P1

Santana Company sold 100,000 units of its product in May. For the level of production achieved in May, the budgeted amounts were: sales, $850,000; variable costs, $675,000; and fixed costs, $150,000. The following actual financial results are available for May. Prepare a flexible budget performance report for May.

Sales (100,000 units)	$837,500
Variable costs..............	656,250
Fixed costs	150,000

QS 21-2
Management by exception
C1 🛈

Managers use *management by exception* for control purposes. (1) Describe the concept of management by exception. (2) Explain how standard costs help managers apply this concept to monitor and control costs.

QS 21-3
Standard cost card **C1**

BatPro makes metal baseball bats. Each bat requires 1 kg. of aluminum at $20 per kg. and 0.50 direct labor hours at $16 per hour. Overhead is assigned at the rate of $40 per labor hour. What amounts would appear on a standard cost card for BatPro?

QS 21-4
Cost variances **C2**

Refer to information in QS 21-3. Assume the actual cost to manufacture one metal bat was $54. Compute the cost variance and classify it as favorable or unfavorable.

Jacomo Company's output for the current period was assigned a $300,000 standard direct materials cost. The direct materials variances included a $44,000 favorable price variance and a $6,000 favorable quantity variance. What is the actual total direct materials cost for the current period?

QS 21-5
Materials cost variances   P2

Reflection Company's output for the current period results in a $40,000 unfavorable direct labor rate variance and a $20,000 unfavorable direct labor efficiency variance. Production for the current period was assigned an $800,000 standard direct labor cost. What is the actual total direct labor cost for the current period?

QS 21-6
Labor cost variances   P2

For the current period, Kawaga Company's manufacturing operations yield a $4,000 favorable price variance on its direct materials usage. The actual price per pound of material is $77; the standard price is $77.50. How many pounds of material are used in the current period?

QS 21-7
Materials cost variances   P2

Hewitt Company's output for the current period yields a $30,000 favorable overhead volume variance and a $50,400 unfavorable overhead controllable variance. Standard overhead charged to production for the period is $225,000. What is the actual total overhead cost incurred for the period?

QS 21-8
Overhead cost variances   P3

Refer to the information in QS 21-8. Hewitt records standard costs in its accounts. Prepare the journal entry to charge overhead costs to the Goods in Process Inventory account and to record any variances.

QS 21-9[A]
Preparing overhead entries   P4

Masters Company applies overhead using machine hours and reports the following information. Compute the total variable overhead cost variance.

Actual machine hours used	4,950 hours
Standard machine hours	5,000 hours
Actual variable overhead rate per hour	$4.10
Standard variable overhead rate per hour	$4.00

QS 21-10[A]
Overhead cost variances
P3

Refer to the information from QS 21-10. Compute the variable overhead spending variance and the variable overhead efficiency variance.

QS 21-11[A]
Overhead spending and efficiency variances   P3

VanWay, Inc. specializes in selling used SUVs. During the first six months of 2011, the dealership sold 100 trucks at an average price of $10,000 each. The budget for the first six months of 2011 was to sell 90 trucks at an average price of $10,500 each. Compute the dealership's sales price variance and sales volume variance for the first six months of 2011.

QS 21-12
Computing sales price and volume variances   A1

Based on predicted production of 12,000 units, a company anticipates $150,000 of fixed costs and $123,000 of variable costs. If the company actually produces 10,000 units, what are the flexible budget amounts of fixed and variable costs?

QS 21-13
Flexible budget   P1

Beck Company expects to produce 10,000 units for the year ending December 31. A flexible budget for 10,000 units of production reflects sales of $200,000; variable costs of $40,000; and fixed costs of $75,000. If the company instead produces and sells 13,000 units for the year, calculate the expected level of income from operations.

QS 21-14
Flexible budget
P1

Refer to information in QS 21-14. Assume that actual sales are $265,000, actual variable costs for the year are $59,000, and actual fixed costs for the year are $73,400. Prepare a flexible budget performance report for the year.

QS 21-15
Flexible budget performance report   P1

TenPro reports the following on one of its products. Compute the direct materials price and quantity variances.

QS 21-16
Materials variances
P2

Direct materials standard (4 lbs. @ $2/lb.)	$8 per finished unit
Actual direct materials used	150,000 lbs.
Actual finished units produced	30,000 units
Actual cost of direct materials used	$267,500

QS 21-17
Direct labor variances
P2

The following information describes a company's usage of direct labor in a recent period. Compute the direct labor rate and efficiency variances for the period.

Actual direct labor hours used	45,000
Actual direct labor rate per hour	$15
Standard direct labor rate per hour	$14
Standard direct labor hours for units produced	47,000

QS 21-18
Controllable overhead variance
P3

Funk Co. expects to produce 48,000 units for the year. The company's flexible budget for 48,000 units of production shows variable overhead costs of $72,000 and fixed overhead costs of $64,000. For the year, the company incurred actual overhead costs of $122,800 while producing 40,000 units. Compute the controllable overhead variance.

QS 21-19
Controllable overhead variance
P3

Aigne Corp. reports the following for November. Compute the controllable overhead variance for November.

Actual total factory overhead incurred	$28,175
Standard factory overhead:	
Variable overhead	$3.10 per unit produced
Fixed overhead	
($12,000/6,000 predicted units to be produced)	$2 per unit
Predicted units produced	6,000 units
Actual units produced	4,800 units

QS 21-20
Volume variance **P3**

Refer to information in QS 21-19. Compute the volume variance for November.

QS 21-21
Sales variances **A1**

In a recent year, **BMW** sold 216,944 of its 1 Series cars. Assume the company expected to sell 225,944 of these cars during the year. Also assume the budgeted sales price for each car was $30,000, and the actual sales price for each car was $30,200. Compute the sales price variance and the sales volume variance.

---

connect

EXERCISES

Exercise 21-1
Preparation of flexible budgets
P1

Mesa Company's fixed budget for the first quarter of calendar year 2011 reveals the following. Prepare flexible budgets following the format of Exhibit 21.3 that show variable costs per unit, fixed costs, and three different flexible budgets for sales volumes of 7,500, 10,000, and 12,500 units.

Sales (10,000 units)		$3,000,000
Cost of goods sold		
Direct materials	$320,000	
Direct labor	680,000	
Production supplies	264,000	
Plant manager salary	60,000	1,324,000
Gross profit		1,676,000
Selling expenses		
Sales commissions	120,000	
Packaging	210,000	
Advertising	100,000	430,000
Administrative expenses		
Administrative salaries	80,000	
Depreciation—office equip.	30,000	
Insurance	18,000	
Office rent	24,000	152,000
Income from operations		$1,094,000

Check Income (at 7,500 units), $742,500

KMAR Company manufactures and sells mountain bikes. It normally operates eight hours a day, six days a week. Using this information, classify each of the following costs as fixed or variable. If additional information would affect your decision, describe the information.

a. Incoming shipping expenses
b. Office supplies
c. Depreciation on tools
d. Taxes on property

e. Bike tires
f. Gas used for heating
g. Bike frames
h. Direct labor

i. Screws for assembly
j. Repair expense for tools
k. Management salaries

Exercise 21-2
Classification of costs as fixed or variable
P1

Cimarron Company's fixed budget performance report for July follows. The $630,000 budgeted expenses include $588,000 variable expenses and $42,000 fixed expenses. Actual expenses include $54,000 fixed expenses. Prepare a flexible budget performance report that shows any variances between budgeted results and actual results. List fixed and variable expenses separately.

Exercise 21-3
Preparation of a flexible budget performance report
P1

	Fixed Budget	Actual Results	Variances
Sales (in units)	8,400	10,800	
Sales (in dollars)	$840,000	$1,080,000	$240,000 F
Total expenses	630,000	756,000	126,000 U
Income from operations	$210,000	$ 324,000	$114,000 F

Check Income variance, $42,000 F

Daytec Company's fixed budget performance report for June follows. The $440,000 budgeted expenses include $300,000 variable expenses and $140,000 fixed expenses. Actual expenses include $130,000 fixed expenses. Prepare a flexible budget performance report showing any variances between budgeted and actual results. List fixed and variable expenses separately.

Exercise 21-4
Preparation of a flexible budget performance report
P1

	Fixed Budget	Actual Results	Variances
Sales (in units)	6,000	4,800	
Sales (in dollars)	$480,000	$422,400	$57,600 U
Total expenses	440,000	394,000	46,000 F
Income from operations	$ 40,000	$ 28,400	$11,600 U

Check Income variance, $24,400 F

After evaluating Zero Company's manufacturing process, management decides to establish standards of 1.5 hours of direct labor per unit of product and $11 per hour for the labor rate. During October, the company uses 3,780 hours of direct labor at a $45,360 total cost to produce 2,700 units of product. In November, the company uses 4,480 hours of direct labor at a $47,040 total cost to produce 2,800 units of product. (1) Compute the rate variance, the efficiency variance, and the total direct labor cost variance for each of these two months. (2) Interpret the October direct labor variances.

Exercise 21-5
Computation and interpretation of labor variances P2

Check (1) October rate variance, $3,780 U

Sonic Company set the following standard costs for one unit of its product for 2011.

Exercise 21-6[A]
Computation of total variable and fixed overhead variances
P3

Direct material (20 lbs. @ $2.50 per lb.)	$ 50.00
Direct labor (15 hrs. @ $8.00 per hr.)	120.00
Factory variable overhead (15 hrs. @ $2.50 per hr.)	37.50
Factory fixed overhead (15 hrs. @ $0.50 per hr.)	7.50
Standard cost	$215.00

The $3.00 ($2.50 + $0.50) total overhead rate per direct labor hour is based on an expected operating level equal to 75% of the factory's capacity of 50,000 units per month. The following monthly flexible budget information is also available.

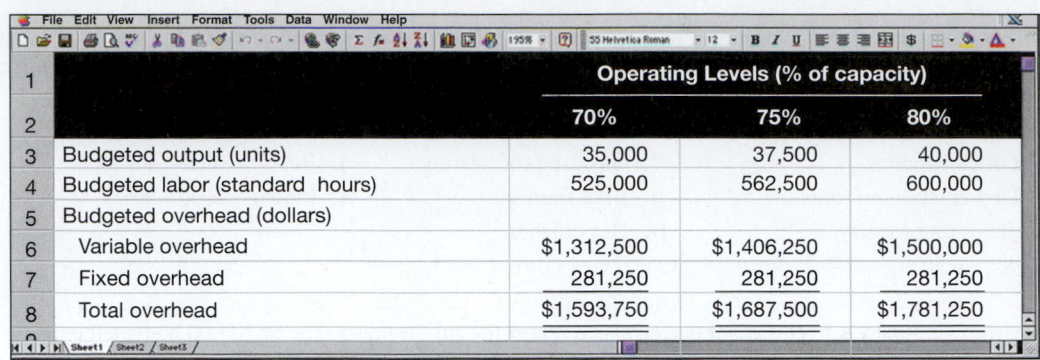

	Operating Levels (% of capacity)		
	70%	**75%**	**80%**
3 Budgeted output (units)	35,000	37,500	40,000
4 Budgeted labor (standard hours)	525,000	562,500	600,000
5 Budgeted overhead (dollars)			
6 Variable overhead	$1,312,500	$1,406,250	$1,500,000
7 Fixed overhead	281,250	281,250	281,250
8 Total overhead	$1,593,750	$1,687,500	$1,781,250

During the current month, the company operated at 70% of capacity, employees worked 500,000 hours, and the following actual overhead costs were incurred.

Variable overhead costs	$1,267,500
Fixed overhead costs	285,000
Total overhead costs	$1,552,500

Check (2) Variable overhead cost variance, $45,000 F

(1) Show how the company computed its predetermined overhead application rate per hour for total overhead, variable overhead, and fixed overhead. (2) Compute the variable and fixed overhead variances.

Exercise 21-7^A

Exercise 21-7[A]

Computation and interpretation of overhead spending, efficiency, and volume variances **P3**

Check (1) Variable overhead: Spending, $17,500 U; Efficiency, $62,500 F

Refer to the information from Exercise 21-6. Compute and interpret the following.

1. Variable overhead spending and efficiency variances.

2. Fixed overhead spending and volume variances.

3. Controllable variance.

Exercise 21-8

Computation and interpretation of materials variances **P2**

Check Price variance, $8,800 F

BTS Company made 6,000 bookshelves using 88,000 board feet of wood costing $607,200. The company's direct materials standards for one bookshelf are 16 board feet of wood at $7 per board foot. (1) Compute the direct materials variances incurred in manufacturing these bookshelves. (2) Interpret the direct materials variances.

Exercise 21-9^A

Materials variances recorded and closed

P4

Check (2) Cr. to Cost of Goods Sold, $64,800

Refer to Exercise 21-8. BTS Company records standard costs in its accounts and its material variances in separate accounts when it assigns materials costs to the Goods in Process Inventory account. (1) Show the journal entry that both charges the direct materials costs to the Goods in Process Inventory account and records the materials variances in their proper accounts. (2) Assume that BTS's material variances are the only variances accumulated in the accounting period and that they are immaterial. Prepare the adjusting journal entry to close the variance accounts at period-end. (3) Identify the variance that should be investigated according to the management by exception concept. Explain.

Exercise 21-10

Computation of total overhead rate and total overhead variance

P3

Check (1) Variable overhead rate, $7.00 per hour

Earth Company expects to operate at 80% of its productive capacity of 25,000 units per month. At this planned level, the company expects to use 40,000 standard hours of direct labor. Overhead is allocated to products using a predetermined standard rate based on direct labor hours. At the 80% capacity level, the total budgeted cost includes $40,000 fixed overhead cost and $280,000 variable overhead cost. In the current month, the company incurred $340,000 actual overhead and 39,000 actual labor hours while producing 19,500 units. (1) Compute its overhead application rate for total overhead. (2) Compute its total overhead variance.

Exercise 21-11

Computation of volume and controllable overhead variances

P3

Check (2) $27,000 U

Refer to the information from Exercise 21-10. Compute the (1) overhead volume variance and (2) overhead controllable variance.

Comp Wiz sells computers. During May 2011, it sold 500 computers at a $900 average price each. The May 2011 fixed budget included sales of 550 computers at an average price of $850 each. (1) Compute the sales price variance and the sales volume variance for May 2011. (2) Interpret the findings.

Exercise 21-12
Computing and interpreting sales variances

A1

Match the terms a through e with their correct definition 1 through 5.

a. Standard cost
b. Practical standard
c. Standard cost card
d. Ideal standard
e. Management by exception

1. Record that accumulates standard cost information.
2. Quantity of input required if a production process is 100% efficient.
3. Managing by focusing on large differences from standard costs.
4. Quantity of input required under normal conditions.
5. Preset cost for delivering a product or service under normal conditions.

Exercise 21-13
Standard costs

C1

Presented below are terms preceded by letters a through j and a list of definitions 1 through 10. Enter the letter of the term with the definition, using the space preceding the definition.

a. Cost variance
b. Volume variance
c. Price variance
d. Quantity variance
e. Standard costs
f. Controllable variance
g. Fixed budget
h. Flexible budget
i. Variance analysis
j. Management by exception

Exercise 21-14
Cost variances

C2

_____ **1.** The difference between the total budgeted overhead cost and the overhead cost that was allocated to products using the predetermined fixed overhead rate.

_____ **2.** A planning budget based on a single predicted amount of sales or production volume; unsuitable for evaluations if the actual volume differs from the predicted volume.

_____ **3.** Preset costs for delivering a product, component, or service under normal conditions.

_____ **4.** A process of examining the differences between actual and budgeted sales or costs and describing them in terms of the amounts that resulted from price and quantity differences.

_____ **5.** The difference between actual and budgeted sales or cost caused by the difference between the actual price per unit and the budgeted price per unit.

_____ **6.** A budget prepared based on predicted amounts of revenues and expenses corresponding to the actual level of output.

_____ **7.** The difference between actual and budgeted cost caused by the difference between the actual quantity and the budgeted quantity.

_____ **8.** The combination of both overhead spending variances (variable and fixed) and the variable overhead efficiency variance.

_____ **9.** A management process to focus on significant variances and give less attention to areas where performance is close to the standard.

_____ **10.** The difference between actual cost and standard cost, made up of a price variance and a quantity variance.

Dee-Daw Co. provides the following results of April's operations: F indicates favorable and U indicates unfavorable. Applying the management by exception approach, which of the variances are of greatest concern? Why?

Exercise 21-15
Analyzing variances

C1

Direct materials price variance	$ 400 F
Direct materials quantity variance	2,000 U
Direct labor rate variance	100 U
Direct labor efficiency variance	1,200 F
Controllable overhead variance	400 U
Fixed overhead volume variance	600 F

Exercise 21-16
Direct materials and direct labor variances
P2

The following information describes production activities of Truzor Manufacturing for the year:

Actual raw materials used	16,000 lbs. at $4.05 per lb.
Actual factory payroll	5,545 hours for a total of $72,085
Actual units produced	30,000

Budgeted standards for each unit produced are 0.50 pounds of raw material at $4.15 per pound and 10 minutes of direct labor at $12.50 per hour. (1) Compute the direct materials price and quantity variances. Round to the nearest whole dollar. (2) Compute the direct labor rate and efficiency variances. Indicate whether each variance is favorable or unfavorable.

PROBLEM SET A

Problem 21-1A
Computation of materials, labor, and overhead variances
P2　P3

mhhe.com/wildFINMAN4e

Tuna Company set the following standard unit costs for its single product.

Direct materials (25 lbs. @ $4 per lb.)	$100.00
Direct labor (6 hrs. @ $8 per hr.)	48.00
Factory overhead—variable (6 hrs. @ $5 per hr.)	30.00
Factory overhead—fixed (6 hrs. @ $7 per hr.)	42.00
Total standard cost	$220.00

The predetermined overhead rate is based on a planned operating volume of 80% of the productive capacity of 60,000 units per quarter. The following flexible budget information is available.

	Operating Levels		
	70%	80%	90%
Production in units	42,000	48,000	54,000
Standard direct labor hours	252,000	288,000	324,000
Budgeted overhead			
Fixed factory overhead	$2,016,000	$2,016,000	$2,016,000
Variable factory overhead	$1,260,000	$1,440,000	$1,620,000

During the current quarter, the company operated at 70% of capacity and produced 42,000 units of product; actual direct labor totaled 250,000 hours. Units produced were assigned the following standard costs:

Direct materials (1,050,000 lbs. @ $4 per lb.)	$4,200,000
Direct labor (252,000 hrs. @ $8 per hr.)	2,016,000
Factory overhead (252,000 hrs. @ $12 per hr.)	3,024,000
Total standard cost.	$9,240,000

Actual costs incurred during the current quarter follow:

Direct materials (1,000,000 lbs. @ $4.25)	$4,250,000
Direct labor (250,000 hrs. @ $7.75)	1,937,500
Fixed factory overhead costs	1,960,000
Variable factory overhead costs	1,200,000
Total actual costs	$9,347,500

Required

Check　(1) Materials variances: Price, $250,000 U; Quantity, $200,000 F.
　　　　(2) Labor variances: Rate, $62,500 F; Efficiency, $16,000 F

1. Compute the direct materials cost variance, including its price and quantity variances.
2. Compute the direct labor variance, including its rate and efficiency variances.
3. Compute the overhead controllable and volume variances.

Problem 21-2A^A
Expanded overhead variances
P3

Refer to information in Problem 21-1A.

Required

Compute these variances: (a) variable overhead spending and efficiency, (b) fixed overhead spending and volume, and (c) total overhead controllable.

Pebco Company's 2011 master budget included the following fixed budget report. It is based on an expected production and sales volume of 20,000 units.

Problem 21-3A
Preparation and analysis of a flexible budget   **P1**

PEBCO COMPANY
Fixed Budget Report
For Year Ended December 31, 2011

Sales		$3,000,000
Cost of goods sold		
Direct materials.........................	$1,200,000	
Direct labor	260,000	
Machinery repairs (variable cost)	57,000	
Depreciation—plant equipment	250,000	
Utilities ($50,000 is variable)	200,000	
Plant management salaries	140,000	2,107,000
Gross profit		893,000
Selling expenses		
Packaging	80,000	
Shipping	116,000	
Sales salary (fixed annual amount)	160,000	356,000
General and administrative expenses		
Advertising expense	81,000	
Salaries...............................	241,000	
Entertainment expense	90,000	412,000
Income from operations		$ 125,000

Required

1. Classify all items listed in the fixed budget as variable or fixed. Also determine their amounts per unit or their amounts for the year, as appropriate.

2. Prepare flexible budgets (see Exhibit 21.3) for the company at sales volumes of 18,000 and 24,000 units.

Check   (2) Budgeted income at 24,000 units, $372,400

3. The company's business conditions are improving. One possible result is a sales volume of approximately 28,000 units. The company president is confident that this volume is within the relevant range of existing capacity. How much would operating income increase over the 2011 budgeted amount of $125,000 if this level is reached without increasing capacity?

4. An unfavorable change in business is remotely possible; in this case, production and sales volume for 2011 could fall to 14,000 units. How much income (or loss) from operations would occur if sales volume falls to this level?

(4) Potential operating loss, $(240,100)

Refer to the information in Problem 21-3A. Pebco Company's actual income statement for 2011 follows.

Problem 21-4A
Preparation and analysis of a flexible budget performance report

P1 P2 A1

mhhe.com/wildFINMAN4e

PEBCO COMPANY
Statement of Income from Operations
For Year Ended December 31, 2011

Sales (24,000 units)		$3,648,000
Cost of goods sold		
Direct materials.........................	$1,400,000	
Direct labor	360,000	
Machinery repairs (variable cost)	60,000	
Depreciation—plant equipment	250,000	
Utilities (fixed cost is $154,000)	218,000	
Plant management salaries................	155,000	2,443,000
Gross profit		1,205,000
Selling expenses		
Packaging	90,000	
Shipping	124,000	
Sales salary (annual).....................	162,000	376,000
General and administrative expenses		
Advertising expense	104,000	
Salaries...............................	232,000	
Entertainment expense	100,000	436,000
Income from operations		$ 393,000

Required

1. Prepare a flexible budget performance report for 2011.

Analysis Component

2. Analyze and interpret both the (a) sales variance and (b) direct materials variance.

Problem 21-5A
Flexible budget preparation;
computation of materials, labor,
and overhead variances; and
overhead variance report

P1   P2   P3   C2

Kwikeze Company set the following standard costs for one unit of its product.

Direct materials (4.5 lbs. @ $6 per lb.)	$27.00
Direct labor (1.5 hrs. @ $12 per hr.)	18.00
Overhead (1.5 hrs. @ $16 per hr.)	24.00
Total standard cost......................	$69.00

The predetermined overhead rate ($16 per direct labor hour) is based on an expected volume of 75% of the factory's capacity of 20,000 units per month. Following are the company's budgeted overhead costs per month at the 75% level.

Overhead Budget (75% Capacity)

Variable overhead costs		
Indirect materials	$22,500	
Indirect labor	90,000	
Power	22,500	
Repairs and maintenance	45,000	
Total variable overhead costs		$180,000
Fixed overhead costs		
Depreciation—building	24,000	
Depreciation—machinery	72,000	
Taxes and insurance	18,000	
Supervision	66,000	
Total fixed overhead costs		180,000
Total overhead costs		$360,000

The company incurred the following actual costs when it operated at 75% of capacity in October.

Direct materials (69,000 lbs. @ $6.10 per lb.)		$ 420,900
Direct labor (22,800 hrs. @ $12.30 per hr.)		280,440
Overhead costs		
Indirect materials	$21,600	
Indirect labor	82,260	
Power	23,100	
Repairs and maintenance	46,800	
Depreciation—building	24,000	
Depreciation—machinery	75,000	
Taxes and insurance	16,500	
Supervision	66,000	355,260
Total costs		$1,056,600

Required

1. Examine the monthly overhead budget to (a) determine the costs per unit for each variable overhead item and its total per unit costs, and (b) identify the total fixed costs per month.

2. Prepare flexible overhead budgets (as in Exhibit 21.12) for October showing the amounts of each variable and fixed cost at the 65%, 75%, and 85% capacity levels.

3. Compute the direct materials cost variance, including its price and quantity variances.

4. Compute the direct labor cost variance, including its rate and efficiency variances.
5. Prepare a detailed overhead variance report (as in Exhibit 21.15) that shows the variances for individual items of overhead.

(4) Labor variances: Rate, $6,840 U; Efficiency, $3,600 U

Kudos Company has set the following standard costs per unit for the product it manufactures.

Direct materials (10 lbs. @ $3 per lb.)............	$30.00
Direct labor (4 hrs. @ $6 per hr.)	24.00
Overhead (4 hrs. @ $2.50 per hr.)	10.00
Total standard cost	$64.00

Problem 21-6A[A]

Materials, labor, and overhead variances; and overhead variance report

C2 P2 P3

The predetermined overhead rate is based on a planned operating volume of 80% of the productive capacity of 10,000 units per month. The following flexible budget information is available.

	Operating Levels		
	70%	80%	90%
Production in units	7,000	8,000	9,000
Standard direct labor hours	28,000	32,000	36,000
Budgeted overhead			
Variable overhead costs			
Indirect materials................	$ 8,750	$10,000	$11,250
Indirect labor	14,000	16,000	18,000
Power........................	3,500	4,000	4,500
Maintenance....................	1,750	2,000	2,250
Total variable costs	28,000	32,000	36,000
Fixed overhead costs			
Rent of factory building	12,000	12,000	12,000
Depreciation—machinery	20,000	20,000	20,000
Supervisory salaries	16,000	16,000	16,000
Total fixed costs	48,000	48,000	48,000
Total overhead costs	$76,000	$80,000	$84,000

During May, the company operated at 90% of capacity and produced 9,000 units, incurring the following actual costs.

Direct materials (92,000 lbs. @ $2.95 per lb.).........		$271,400
Direct labor (37,600 hrs. @ $6.05 per hr.)		227,480
Overhead costs		
Indirect materials	$10,000	
Indirect labor	16,000	
Power	4,500	
Maintenance	3,000	
Rent of factory building	12,000	
Depreciation—machinery	19,200	
Supervisory salaries	17,000	81,700
Total costs		$580,580

Required

1. Compute the direct materials variance, including its price and quantity variances.
2. Compute the direct labor variance, including its rate and efficiency variances.

Check (1) Materials variances: Price, $4,600 F; Quantity, $6,000 U
(2) Labor variances: Rate, $1,880 U; Efficiency, $9,600 U

3. Compute these variances: (a) variable overhead spending and efficiency, (b) fixed overhead spending and volume, and (c) total overhead controllable.

4. Prepare a detailed overhead variance report (as in Exhibit 21.15) that shows the variances for individual items of overhead.

Problem 21-7A^A

Materials, labor, and overhead variances recorded and analyzed

C1   P4

Loretto Company's standard cost accounting system recorded this information from its December operations.

Standard direct materials cost	$130,000
Direct materials quantity variance (unfavorable)	5,000
Direct materials price variance (favorable)	1,500
Actual direct labor cost	65,000
Direct labor efficiency variance (favorable)	7,000
Direct labor rate variance (unfavorable)	500
Actual overhead cost	250,000
Volume variance (unfavorable)	12,000
Controllable variance (unfavorable)	8,000

Required

Check (1) Dr. Goods in Process Inventory (for overhead), $230,000

1. Prepare December 31 journal entries to record the company's costs and variances for the month. (Do not prepare the journal entry to close the variances.)

Analysis Component

2. Identify the areas that would attract the attention of a manager who uses management by exception. Explain what action(s) the manager should consider.

PROBLEM SET B

Problem 21-1B

Computation of materials, labor, and overhead variances

P2   P3

Sabates Company set the following standard unit costs for its single product.

Direct materials (5 lbs. @ $10 per lb.)	$ 50.00
Direct labor (3 hrs. @ $15 per hr.)	45.00
Factory overhead—variable (3 hrs. @ $5 per hr.)	15.00
Factory overhead—fixed (3 hrs. @ $3 per hr.)	9.00
Total standard cost	$119.00

The predetermined overhead rate is based on a planned operating volume of 90% of the productive capacity of 100,000 units per quarter. The following flexible budget information is available.

	Operating Levels		
	80%	**90%**	**100%**
Production in units	32,000	36,000	40,000
Standard direct labor hours	96,000	108,000	120,000
Budgeted overhead			
Fixed factory overhead	$324,000	$324,000	$324,000
Variable factory overhead	480,000	540,000	600,000

During the current quarter, the company operated at 80% of capacity and produced 32,000 units of product; direct labor hours worked were 100,000. Units produced were assigned the following standard costs:

Direct materials (160,000 lbs. @ $10 per lb.)	$1,600,000
Direct labor (96,000 hrs. @ $15 per hr.)	1,440,000
Factory overhead (96,000 hrs. @ $8 per hr.)	768,000
Total standard cost	$3,808,000

Actual costs incurred during the current quarter follow:

Direct materials (155,000 lbs. @ $10.20)	$1,581,000
Direct labor (100,000 hrs. @ $14)	1,400,000
Fixed factory overhead costs	370,000
Variable factory overhead costs	480,000
Total actual costs	$3,831,000

Required

1. Compute the direct materials cost variance, including its price and quantity variances.
2. Compute the direct labor variance, including its rate and efficiency variances.
3. Compute the total overhead controllable and volume variances.

Check (1) Materials variances: Price, $31,000 U; Quantity, $50,000 F
(2) Labor variances: Rate, $100,000 F; Efficiency, $60,000 U

Refer to information in Problem 21-1B.

Required

Compute these variances: (a) variable overhead spending and efficiency, (b) fixed overhead spending and volume, and (c) total overhead controllable.

Problem 21-2B^A
Expanded overhead variances
P3

Razorback Company's 2011 master budget included the following fixed budget report. It is based on an expected production and sales volume of 10,000 units.

Problem 21-3B
Preparation and analysis of a flexible budget **P1 A1**

RAZORBACK COMPANY
Fixed Budget Report
For Year Ended December 31, 2011

Sales		$250,000
Cost of goods sold		
Direct materials	$100,000	
Direct labor	20,000	
Machinery repairs (variable cost)	3,000	
Depreciation—machinery	11,920	
Utilities (80% is variable cost)	8,000	
Plant manager salaries	6,000	148,920
Gross profit		101,080
Selling expenses		
Packaging	9,000	
Shipping	30,000	
Sales salary (fixed annual amount)	18,000	57,000
General and administrative expenses		
Advertising	4,000	
Salaries	9,360	
Entertainment expense	10,000	23,360
Income from operations		$ 20,720

Required

1. Classify all items listed in the fixed budget as variable or fixed. Also determine their amounts per unit or their amounts for the year, as appropriate.
2. Prepare flexible budgets (see Exhibit 21.3) for the company at sales volumes of 8,000 and 12,000 units.
3. The company's business conditions are improving. One possible result is a sales volume of approximately 14,400 units. The company president is confident that this volume is within the relevant range of existing capacity. How much would operating income increase over the 2011 budgeted amount of $20,720 if this level is reached without increasing capacity?
4. An unfavorable change in business is remotely possible; in this case, production and sales volume for 2011 could fall to 5,000 units. How much income (or loss) from operations would occur if sales volume falls to this level?

Check (2) Budgeted income at 12,000 units, $37,040

(4) Potential operating loss, $(20,080)

Problem 21-4B
Preparation and analysis
of a flexible budget
performance report
P1 A1

Refer to the information in Problem 21-3B. Razorback Company's actual income statement for 2011 follows.

RAZORBACK COMPANY Statement of Income from Operations For Year Ended December 31, 2011		
Sales (12,000 units)		$288,000
Cost of goods sold		
Direct materials	$95,000	
Direct labor	16,000	
Machinery repairs (variable cost)	3,300	
Depreciation—machinery	11,920	
Utilities (variable cost, $7,160)	8,520	
Plant manager salaries	6,720	141,460
Gross profit		146,540
Selling expenses		
Packaging	10,800	
Shipping	37,200	
Sales salary (annual)	19,200	67,200
General and administrative expenses		
Advertising expense	4,200	
Salaries	9,360	
Entertainment expense	10,000	23,560
Income from operations		$ 55,780

Required

Check   (1) Variances: Fixed costs,
$1,880 U; Income, $18,740 F

1. Prepare a flexible budget performance report for 2011.

Analysis Component

2. Analyze and interpret both the (a) sales variance and (b) direct materials variance.

Problem 21-5B
Flexible budget preparation;
computation of materials, labor,
and overhead variances; and
overhead variance report
P1 P2 P3 C2

Sunburst Company set the following standard costs for one unit of its product.

Direct materials (48 kgs. @ $4 per kg.)	$192.00
Direct labor (12 hrs. @ $9 per hr.)	108.00
Overhead (12 hrs. @ $4.50 per hr.)	54.00
Total standard cost	$354.00

The predetermined overhead rate ($4.50 per direct labor hour) is based on an expected volume of 50% of the factory's capacity of 10,000 units per month. Following are the company's budgeted overhead costs per month at the 50% level.

Overhead Budget (50% Capacity)	
Variable overhead costs	
Indirect materials	$40,000
Indirect labor	80,000
Power	20,000
Repairs and maintenance	30,000
Total variable overhead costs	$170,000
Fixed overhead costs	
Depreciation—building	20,000
Depreciation—machinery	30,000
Taxes and insurance	10,000
Supervision	40,000
Total fixed overhead costs	100,000
Total overhead costs	$270,000

The company incurred the following actual costs when it operated at 40% of capacity in December.

Direct materials (196,000 kgs. @ $4.00)		$ 784,000
Direct labor (46,000 hrs. @ $9.15)		420,900
Overhead costs		
Indirect materials	$30,000	
Indirect labor	66,000	
Power	15,600	
Repairs and maintenance	21,000	
Depreciation—building	20,000	
Depreciation—machinery	30,000	
Taxes and insurance	9,600	
Supervision	39,600	231,800
Total costs		$1,436,700

Required

1. Examine the monthly overhead budget to (a) determine the costs per unit for each variable overhead item and its total per unit costs, and (b) identify the total fixed costs per month.
2. Prepare flexible overhead budgets (as in Exhibit 21.12) for December showing the amounts of each variable and fixed cost at the 40%, 50%, and 60% capacity levels.
3. Compute the direct materials cost variance, including its price and quantity variances.
4. Compute the direct labor cost variance, including its rate and efficiency variances.
5. Prepare a detailed overhead variance report (as in Exhibit 21.15) that shows the variances for individual items of overhead.

Check (2) Budgeted total overhead at 6,000 units, $304,000

(3) Materials variances: Price, $0 U; Quantity, $16,000 U

(4) Labor variances: Rate, $6,900 U; Efficiency, $18,000 F

Carlsbad Company has set the following standard costs per unit for the product it manufactures.

Direct materials (40 oz. @ $0.75 per oz.)		$ 30.00
Direct labor (2 hr. @ $20 per hr.)		40.00
Overhead (2 hr. @ $53.50 per hr.)		107.00
Total standard cost		$177.00

Problem 21-6B[A]
Materials, labor, and overhead variances; and overhead variance report

C2 P2 P3

The predetermined overhead rate is based on a planned operating volume of 60% of the productive capacity of 3,000 units per month. The following flexible budget information is available.

	Operating Levels		
	50%	**60%**	**70%**
Production in units	1,500	1,800	2,100
Standard direct labor hours	3,000	3,600	4,200
Budgeted overhead			
Variable overhead costs			
Indirect materials	$ 18,000	$21,600	$25,200
Indirect labor	10,500	12,600	14,700
Power	7,500	9,000	10,500
Maintenance	4,500	5,400	6,300
Total variable costs	40,500	48,600	56,700
Fixed overhead costs			
Rent of factory building	48,000	48,000	48,000
Depreciation—machinery	44,000	44,000	44,000
Taxes and insurance	20,000	20,000	20,000
Supervisory salaries	32,000	32,000	32,000
Total fixed costs	144,000	144,000	144,000
Total overhead costs	$184,500	$192,600	$200,700

During March, the company operated at 70% of capacity and produced 2,100 units, incurring the following actual costs.

Direct materials (88,000 oz. @ $0.70 per oz.)		$ 61,600
Direct labor (4,000 hrs. @ $19.50 per hr.)		78,000
Overhead costs		
Indirect materials.	$23,600	
Indirect labor	14,800	
Power.	10,000	
Maintenance.	3,200	
Rent of factory building	48,000	
Depreciation—machinery	44,000	
Taxes and insurance	24,000	
Supervisory salaries.	31,600	199,200
Total costs		$338,800

Required

1. Compute the direct materials cost variance, including its price and quantity variances.
2. Compute the direct labor variance, including its rate and efficiency variances.
3. Compute these variances: (a) variable overhead spending and efficiency, (b) fixed overhead spending and volume, and (c) total overhead controllable.
4. Prepare a detailed overhead variance report (as in Exhibit 21.15) that shows the variances for individual items of overhead.

Problem 21-7B[A]

Materials, labor, and overhead variances recorded and analyzed

C1 P4

Kincaid Company's standard cost accounting system recorded this information from its June operations.

Standard direct materials cost	$220,500
Direct materials quantity variance (favorable)	20,250
Direct materials price variance (favorable)	14,500
Actual direct labor cost	335,000
Direct labor efficiency variance (favorable)	26,700
Direct labor rate variance (unfavorable)	3,500
Actual overhead cost	359,000
Volume variance (unfavorable)	1,650
Controllable variance (unfavorable)	32,500

Required

1. Prepare journal entries dated June 30 to record the company's costs and variances for the month. (Do not prepare the journal entry to close the variances.)

Analysis Component

2. Identify the areas that would attract the attention of a manager who uses management by exception. Describe what action(s) the manager should consider.

SERIAL PROBLEM

Business Solutions

P1

(This serial problem began in Chapter 1 and continues through most of the book. If previous chapter segments were not completed, the serial problem can begin at this point. It is helpful, but not necessary, to use the working papers that accompany the book.)

SP 21 Business Solutions' second quarter 2012 fixed budget performance report for its computer furniture operations follows. The $156,000 budgeted expenses include $108,000 in variable expenses for desks and $18,000 in variable expenses for chairs, as well as $30,000 fixed expenses. The actual expenses include $31,000 fixed expenses. Prepare a flexible budget performance report that shows any variances between budgeted results and actual results. List fixed and variable expenses separately.

	Fixed Budget	Actual Results	Variances
Desk sales (in units).............	144	150	
Chair sales (in units)	72	80	
Desk sales (in dollars)	$180,000	$186,000	$6,000 F
Chair sales (in dollars)...........	$ 36,000	$ 41,200	$5,200 F
Total expenses	$156,000	$163,880	$7,880 U
Income from operations	$ 60,000	$ 63,320	$3,320 F

Check Variances: Fixed expenses, $1,000 U

Beyond the Numbers

BTN 21-1 Analysis of flexible budgets and standard costs emphasizes the importance of a similar unit of measure for meaningful comparisons and evaluations. When **Research In Motion** compiles its financial reports in compliance with GAAP, it applies the same unit of measurement, U.S. dollars, for most measures of business operations. One issue for Research In Motion is how best to adjust account values for its subsidiaries that compile financial reports in currencies other than the U.S. dollar.

REPORTING IN ACTION

C1

RIM

Required

1. Read Research In Motion's Note 1 in Appendix A and identify the financial statement where it reports the annual adjustment (remeasurement) for foreign currency translation.
2. Translating financial statements requires the use of a currency exchange rate. For each of the following three financial statement items, explain the exchange rate the company would apply to translate into U.S. dollars.
   a. Cash
   b. Sales revenue
   c. Property, plant and equipment

BTN 21-2 The usefulness of budgets, variances, and related analyses often depends on the accuracy of management's estimates of future sales activity.

COMPARATIVE ANALYSIS

A1

RIM

Apple

Palm

Required

1. Identify and record the prior three years' sales (in dollars) for **Research In Motion**, **Apple**, and **Palm** using their financial statements in Appendix A.
2. Using the data in part 1, predict all three companies' sales activity for the next two to three years. (If possible, compare your predictions to actual sales figures for these years.)

BTN 21-3 Setting materials, labor, and overhead standards is challenging. If standards are set too low, companies might purchase inferior products and employees might not work to their full potential. If standards are set too high, companies could be unable to offer a quality product at a profitable rate and employees could be overworked. The ethical challenge is to set a high but reasonable standard. Assume that as a manager, you are asked to set the standard materials price and quantity for the new 1,000 CKB Mega-Max chip, a technically advanced product. To properly set the price and quantity standards, you assemble a team of specialists to provide input.

ETHICS CHALLENGE

C1

Required

Identify four types of specialists that you would assemble to provide information to help set the materials price and quantity standards. Briefly explain why you chose each individual.

COMMUNICATING IN PRACTICE

P4 C2

BTN 21-4 The reason we use the words *favorable* and *unfavorable* when evaluating variances is made clear when we look at the closing of accounts. To see this, consider that (1) all variance accounts are closed at the end of each period (temporary accounts), (2) a favorable variance is always a credit balance, and (3) an unfavorable variance is always a debit balance. Write a one-half page memorandum to your instructor with three parts that answer the three following requirements. (Assume that variance accounts are closed to Cost of Goods Sold.)

Required

1. Does Cost of Goods Sold increase or decrease when closing a favorable variance? Does gross margin increase or decrease when a favorable variance is closed to Cost of Goods Sold? Explain.
2. Does Cost of Goods Sold increase or decrease when closing an unfavorable variance? Does gross margin increase or decrease when an unfavorable variance is closed to Cost of Goods Sold? Explain.
3. Explain the meaning of a favorable variance and an unfavorable variance.

TAKING IT TO THE NET

C1

BTN 21-5 Access **iSixSigma**'s Website (**iSixSigma.com**) to search for and read information about *benchmarking* to complete the following requirements.

Required

1. Write a one-paragraph explanation (in layperson's terms) of benchmarking.
2. How does standard costing relate to benchmarking?

TEAMWORK IN ACTION

C2

BTN 21-6 Many service industries link labor rate and time (quantity) standards with their processes. One example is the standard time to board an aircraft. The reason time plays such an important role in the service industry is that it is viewed as a competitive advantage: best service in the shortest amount of time. Although the labor rate component is difficult to observe, the time component of a service delivery standard is often readily apparent—for example, "Lunch will be served in less than five minutes, or it is free."

Required

Break into teams and select two service industries for your analysis. Identify and describe all the time elements each industry uses to create a competitive advantage.

ENTREPRENEURIAL DECISION

C1 C2

BTN 21-7 **SewWhat? Inc.**, as discussed in the chapter opener, uses a costing system with standard costs for direct materials, direct labor, and overhead costs. Two comments frequently are mentioned in relation to standard costing and variance analysis: "Variances are not explanations" and "Management's goal is not to minimize variances."

Required

Write a short memo to Megan Duckett, SewWhat? Inc.'s CEO, (no more than 1 page) interpreting these two comments.

HITTING THE ROAD

C1

BTN 21-8 Training employees to use standard amounts of materials in production is common. Typically large companies invest in this training but small organizations do not. One can observe these different practices in a trip to two different pizza businesses. Visit both a local pizza business and a national pizza chain business and then complete the following.

Required

1. Observe and record the number of raw material items used to make a typical cheese pizza. Also observe how the person making the pizza applies each item when preparing the pizza.
2. Record any differences in how items are applied between the two businesses.
3. Estimate which business is more profitable from your observations. Explain.

BTN 21-9   Access the annual report of Nokia (at www.Nokia.com) for the year ended December 31, 2009. The usefulness of its budgets, variances, and related analyses depends on the accuracy of management's estimates of future sales activity.

GLOBAL DECISION

A1

NOKIA

Required

1. Identify and record the prior two years' sales (in € millions) for Nokia from its income statement.
2. Using the data in part 1, predict sales activity for Nokia for the next two years. Explain your prediction process.

ANSWERS TO MULTIPLE CHOICE QUIZ

1. c; Fixed costs remain at $300,000; Variable costs = ($246,000/24,000 units) × 20,000 units = $205,000.

2. e; Budgeted direct materials + Unfavorable variance = Actual cost of direct materials used; or, 60,000 units × $10 per unit = $600,000 + $15,000 U = $615,000.

3. c; (AH × AR) − (AH × SR) = $1,599,040 – (84,160 hours × $20 per hour) = $84,160 F.

4. b; Actual variable overhead − Variable overhead applied to production = Variable overhead cost variance; or $150,000 − (96,000 hours × $1.50 per hour) = $6,000 U.

5. a; Budgeted fixed overhead − Fixed overhead applied to production = Volume variance; or $24,000 − (4,800 units × $4 per unit) = $4,800 U.

22

Decentralization and Performance Evaluation

A Look Back

Chapter 21 discussed flexible budgets, variance analysis, and standard costs. It explained how management uses each to control and monitor business activities.

A Look at This Chapter

This chapter describes responsibility accounting, measuring departmental performance, transfer pricing, and allocating common costs across departments. It also identifies managerial reports useful in directing a company's activities.

A Look Ahead

Chapter 23 explains several tools and procedures used in making and evaluating short-term managerial decisions.

Learning Objectives

CONCEPTUAL

C1 Distinguish between direct and indirect expenses and identify bases for allocating indirect expenses to departments. (p. 927)

C2 Explain controllable costs and responsibility accounting. (p. 937)

C3 *Appendix 22A*—Explain transfer pricing and methods to set transfer prices. (p. 944)

C4 *Appendix 22B*—Describe allocation of joint costs across products. (p. 945)

ANALYTICAL

A1 Analyze investment centers using return on assets, residual income, and balanced scorecard. (p. 935)

A2 Analyze investment centers using profit margin and investment turnover. (p. 940)

LP22

PROCEDURAL

P1 Prepare departmental income statements and contribution reports. (p. 929)

© MATTHEW TURLEY

This Buds for You

"No good ideas come from sitting in an office"
—RICK ALDEN

PARK CITY, UT—Inspiration hit Rick Alden on a ski lift in Utah. While he was listening to music, his cell phone rang, and Rick fumbled around for the right device. Then a thought struck Rick: Why not make headphones that work together with cellphones and other mobile accessories? Why not target the 12 to 25 year-olds he saw snowboarding? Immediately getting to work, Rick designed headphones and earbuds in bright colors and skater patterns and came up with a cool name for his company.

Today, Rick's company **Skullcandy** (**SkullCandy.com**) is a fast-growing business that designs headphones, audio accessories, apparel, and audio-enabled lifestyle products like backpacks with built-in speakers and iPod controls. Skullcandy's product designs, drawn from hip-hop culture, let wearers show the world they are into the cool lifestyle of skiers, surfers, and skaters. The company also partners with brands like Burton Snowboards and users like Metallica and Snoop Dogg to stay cool. Skullcandy headquarters is a fun place to work, with surf retreats to reward good work, skateboards for traveling between offices, and a half-pipe behind the office. "The vibe is creative," says art director Kevin Horsburgh.

The company offers a diverse product line of edgy headphones, speaker-equipped backpacks and helmets, and MP3-equipped watches. This diversity of product offerings requires attention to cost management. Explaining that production factories were not willing to take a risk on his ideas, Rick laughs that "the first year we had to pay 100 percent of our costs upfront." Now, company managers monitor direct, indirect, and controllable costs and allocate them to departments and products. Understanding how its product lines are performing and their contribution margins helps Skullcandy plan for expansion. "We measure return on investment (ROI)," explains Rick. "We will expand as long as there are customers to win." Currently number two in its industry, the company hopes customer loyalty will propel it to number one.

As Skullcandy continues to grow, Rick critically focuses on contribution margins, investment turnover, and other performance indicators such as customer approval ratings and on-time delivery rates. But, to seek inspiration, Rick and his team "head to the mountain." "No good ideas ever come from sitting in an office," says Rick. "Not around here at least."

Sources: *Skullcandy Website,* January 2011; *Salt Lake Tribune,* April 20, 2009; *Entrepreneur,* January 2010; *Fortune,* December 30, 2008.

This chapter describes how to allocate costs shared by more than one product across those different products and how to allocate indirect costs of shared items such as utilities, advertising, and rent. This knowledge helps managers better understand how to assign costs and assess company performance. The chapter also introduces additional managerial accounting reports useful in managing a company's activities and explains how and why management divides companies into departments.

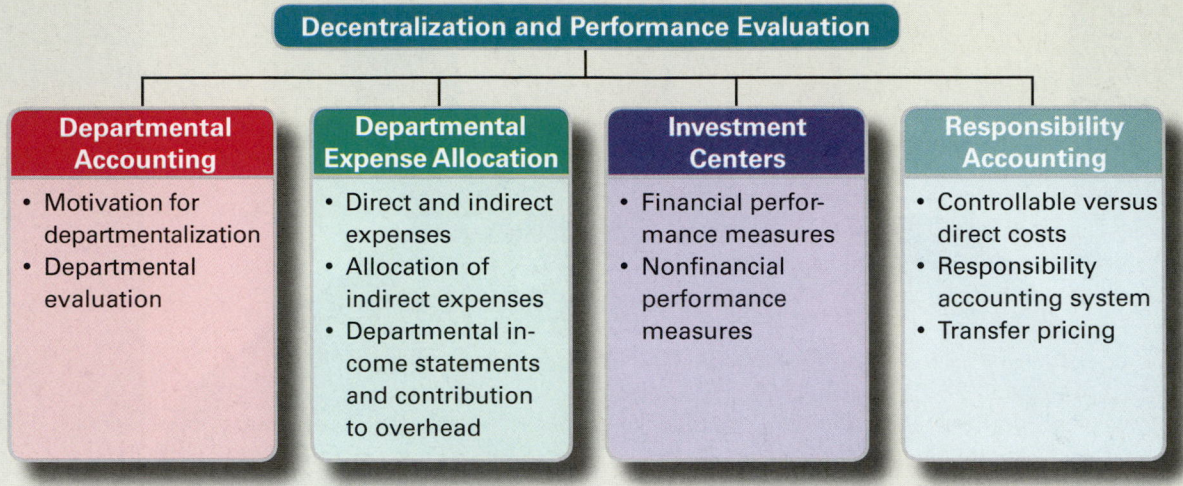

Decentralization and Performance Evaluation

Departmental Accounting	Departmental Expense Allocation	Investment Centers	Responsibility Accounting
• Motivation for departmentalization • Departmental evaluation	• Direct and indirect expenses • Allocation of indirect expenses • Departmental income statements and contribution to overhead	• Financial performance measures • Nonfinancial performance measures	• Controllable versus direct costs • Responsibility accounting system • Transfer pricing

This chapter describes and illustrates allocation of costs for performance evaluation. We begin with departmental accounting and expense allocations and conclude with responsibility accounting.

DEPARTMENTAL ACCOUNTING

Companies are divided into *departments,* also called *subunits,* when they are too large to be managed effectively as a single unit. Managerial accounting for departments has two main goals. The first is to set up a **departmental accounting system** to provide information for managers to evaluate the profitability or cost effectiveness of each department's activities. The second goal is to set up a **responsibility accounting system** to control costs and expenses and evaluate managers' performances by assigning costs and expenses to the managers responsible for controlling them. Departmental and responsibility accounting systems are related and share much information.

Motivation for Departmentalization

Many companies are so large and complex that they are broken into separate divisions for efficiency and/or effectiveness purposes. Divisions then are usually organized into separate departments. When a company is departmentalized, each department is often placed under the direction of a manager. As a company grows, management often divides departments into new departments so that responsibilities for a department's activities do not overwhelm the manager's ability to oversee and control them. A company also creates departments to take advantage of the skills of individual managers. Departments are broadly classified as either operating or service departments.

Departmental Evaluation

Point: To improve profitability, **Sears, Roebuck & Co.** eliminated several departments, including its catalog division.

When a company is divided into departments, managers need to know how each department is performing. The accounting system must supply information about resources used and outputs achieved by each department. This requires a system to measure and accumulate revenue and expense information for each department whenever possible.

Departmental information is rarely distributed publicly because of its potential usefulness to competitors. Information about departments is prepared for internal managers to help control operations, appraise performance, allocate resources, and plan strategy. If a department is highly profitable, management may decide to expand its operations, or if a department is performing poorly, information about revenues or expenses can suggest useful changes.

More companies are emphasizing customer satisfaction as a main responsibility of many departments. This has led to changes in the measures reported. Increasingly, financial measurements are being supplemented with quality and customer satisfaction indexes. **Motorola**, for instance, uses two key measures: the number of defective parts per million parts produced and the percent of orders delivered on time to customers. (Note that some departments have only "internal customers.")

Financial information used to evaluate a department depends on whether it is evaluated as a profit center, cost center, or investment center. A **profit center** incurs costs and generates revenues; selling departments are often evaluated as profit centers. A **cost center** incurs costs without directly generating revenues. An **investment center** incurs costs and generates revenues, and is responsible for effectively using center assets. The manufacturing departments of a manufacturer and its service departments such as accounting, advertising, and purchasing, are all cost centers.

Evaluating managers' performance depends on whether they are responsible for profit centers, cost centers, or investment centers. Profit center managers are judged on their abilities to generate revenues in excess of the department's costs. They are assumed to influence both revenue generation and cost incurrence. Cost center managers are judged on their abilities to control costs by keeping them within a satisfactory range under an assumption that only they influence costs. Investment center managers are evaluated on their use of center assets to generate income.

Point: Selling departments are often treated as *revenue centers*; their managers are responsible for maximizing sales revenues.

Quick Check

Answers — p. 948

1. What is the difference between a departmental accounting system and a responsibility accounting system?
2. Service departments (*a*) manufacture products, (*b*) make sales directly to customers, (*c*) produce revenues, (*d*) assist operating departments.
3. Explain the difference between a cost center and a profit center. Cite an example of each.

DEPARTMENTAL EXPENSE ALLOCATION

When a company computes departmental profits, it confronts some accounting challenges that involve allocating its expenses across its operating departments.

C1 Distinguish between direct and indirect expenses and identify bases for allocating indirect expenses to departments.

Direct and Indirect Expenses

Direct expenses are costs readily traced to a department because they are incurred for that department's sole benefit. They require no allocation across departments. For example, the salary of an employee who works in only one department is a direct expense of that one department.

Indirect expenses are costs that are incurred for the joint benefit of more than one department and cannot be readily traced to only one department. For example, if two or more departments share a single building, all enjoy the benefits of the expenses for rent, heat, and light. Indirect expenses are allocated across departments benefiting from them when we need information about departmental profits. Ideally, we allocate indirect expenses by using a cause-effect relation. When we cannot identify cause-effect relations, we allocate each indirect expense on a basis approximating the relative benefit each department receives. Measuring the benefit for each department from an indirect expense can be difficult.

Point: Utility expense has elements of both direct and indirect expenses.

Illustration of Indirect Expense Allocation To illustrate how to allocate an indirect expense, we consider a retail store that purchases janitorial services from an outside company. Management allocates this cost across the store's three departments according to the floor space each occupies. Costs of janitorial services for a recent month are $300. Exhibit 22.1 shows the square feet of floor space each department occupies. The store computes the percent of total square feet allotted to each department and uses it to allocate the $300 cost.

EXHIBIT 22.1

Indirect Expense Allocation

Department	Square Feet	Percent of Total	Allocated Cost
Jewelry	2,400	60%	$180
Watch repair	600	15	45
China and silver	1,000	25	75
Totals	4,000	100%	$300

Specifically, because the jewelry department occupies 60% of the floor space, 60% of the total $300 cost is assigned to it. The same procedure is applied to the other departments. When the allocation process is complete, these and other allocated costs are deducted from the gross profit for each department to determine net income for each. One consideration in allocating costs is to motivate managers and employees to behave as desired. As a result, a cost incurred in one department might be best allocated to other departments when one of the other departments caused the cost.

Allocation of Indirect Expenses

This section describes how to identify the bases used to allocate indirect expenses across departments. No standard rule identifies the best basis because expense allocation involves several factors, and the relative importance of these factors varies across departments and organizations. Judgment is required, and people do not always agree. Employee morale suffers when allocations are perceived as unfair. Thus, it is important to carefully design and explain the allocation of service department costs. In our discussion, note the parallels between activity-based costing and the departmental expense allocation procedures described here.

Wages and Salaries Employee wages and salaries can be either direct or indirect expenses. If their time is spent entirely in one department, their wages are direct expenses of that department. However, if employees work for the benefit of more than one department, their wages are indirect expenses and must be allocated across the departments benefited. An employee's contribution to a department usually depends on the number of hours worked in contributing to that department. Thus, a reasonable basis for allocating employee wages and salaries is the *relative amount of time spent in each department*. In the case of a supervisor who manages more than one department, recording the time spent in each department may not always be practical. Instead, a company can allocate the supervisor's salary to departments on the basis of the number of employees in each department—a reasonable basis if a supervisor's main task is managing people. Another basis of allocation is on sales across departments, also a reasonable basis if a supervisor's job reflects on departmental sales.

Point: Some companies ask supervisors to estimate time spent supervising specific departments for purposes of expense allocation.

Rent and Related Expenses Rent expense for a building is reasonably allocated to a department on the basis of floor space it occupies. Location can often make some floor space more valuable than other space. Thus, the allocation method can charge departments that occupy more valuable space a higher expense per square foot. Ground floor retail space, for instance, is often more valuable than basement or upper-floor space because all customers pass departments near the entrance but fewer go beyond the first floor. When no precise measures of floor space values exist, basing allocations on data such as customer traffic and real estate assessments is helpful. When a company owns its building, its expenses for depreciation, taxes, insurance, and other related building expenses are allocated like rent expense.

Advertising Expenses Effective advertising of a department's products increases its sales and customer traffic. Moreover, advertising products for some departments usually helps other departments' sales because customers also often buy unadvertised products. Thus, many stores treat advertising as an indirect expense allocated on the basis of each department's proportion of total sales. For example, a department with 10% of a store's total sales is assigned 10% of advertising expense. Another method is to analyze each advertisement to compute the Web/newspaper space or TV/radio time devoted to the products of a department and charge that department for the proportional costs of advertisements. Management must consider whether this more detailed and costly method is justified.

Equipment and Machinery Depreciation Depreciation on equipment and machinery used only in one department is a direct expense of that department. Depreciation on equipment and machinery used by more than one department is an indirect expense to be allocated across departments. Accounting for each department's depreciation expense requires a company to keep records showing which departments use specific assets. The number of hours that a department uses equipment and machinery is a reasonable basis for allocating depreciation.

Utilities Expenses Utilities expenses such as heating and lighting are usually allocated on the basis of floor space occupied by departments. This practice assumes their use is uniform across departments. When this is not so, a more involved allocation can be necessary, although there is often a trade-off between the usefulness of more precise allocations and the effort to compute them. Manufacturers often allocate electricity cost to departments on the basis of the horsepower of equipment located in each department.

Service Department Expenses To generate revenues, operating departments require support services provided by departments such as personnel, payroll, advertising, and purchasing. Such service departments are typically evaluated as cost centers because they do not produce revenues. (Evaluating them as profit centers requires the use of a system that "charges" user departments a price that then serves as the "revenue" generated by service departments.) A departmental accounting system can accumulate and report costs incurred directly by each service department for this purpose. The system then allocates a service department's expenses to operating departments benefiting from them. This is often done, for example, using traditional two-stage cost allocation (see Chapter 17). Exhibit 22.2 shows some commonly used bases for allocating service department expenses to operating departments.

Point: When a service department "charges" its user departments within a company, a *transfer pricing system* must be set up to determine the "revenue" from its services provided.

Service Department	Common Allocation Bases
Office expenses	Number of employees or sales in each department
Personnel expenses	Number of employees in each department
Payroll expenses	Number of employees in each department
Advertising expenses	Sales or amount of advertising charged directly to each department
Purchasing costs	Dollar amounts of purchases or number of purchase orders processed
Cleaning expenses	Square feet of floor space occupied
Maintenance expenses	Square feet of floor space occupied

EXHIBIT 22.2

Bases for Allocating Service Department Expenses

Departmental Income Statements

An income statement can be prepared for each operating department once expenses have been assigned to it. Its expenses include both direct expenses and its share of indirect expenses. For this purpose, compiling all expenses incurred in service departments before assigning them to operating departments is useful. We illustrate the steps to prepare departmental income statements using **A-1 Hardware** and its five departments. Two of them (office and purchasing) are service departments and the other three (hardware, housewares, and appliances) are operating (selling) departments. Allocating costs to operating departments and preparing departmental income statements involves four steps.

P1 Prepare departmental income statements and contribution reports.

1. Accumulating direct expenses by department.
2. Allocating indirect expenses across departments.
3. Allocating service department expenses to operating department.
4. Preparing departmental income statements.

Step 1   Step 1 accumulates direct expenses for each service and operating department as shown in Exhibit 22.3. Direct expenses include salaries, wages, and other expenses that each department incurs but does not share with any other department. This information is accumulated in departmental expense accounts.

EXHIBIT 22.3

Step 1: Direct Expense Accumulation

Accumulate Direct Expenses in Departmental Expense Accounts

Point: We sometimes allocate service department costs across other service departments before allocating them to operating departments. This "step-wise" process is in advanced courses.

Step 2   Step 2 allocates indirect expenses across all departments as shown in Exhibit 22.4. Indirect expenses can include items such as depreciation, rent, advertising, and any other expenses that cannot be directly assigned to a department. Indirect expenses are recorded in company expense accounts, an allocation base is identified for each expense, and costs are allocated using a *departmental expense allocation spreadsheet* described in step 3.

EXHIBIT 22.4

Step 2: Indirect Expense Allocation

Accumulate Indirect Expenses in Company Accounts and Allocate

Step 3   Step 3 allocates expenses of the service departments (office and purchasing) to the operating departments. Service department costs are not allocated to other service departments. Exhibit 22.5 reflects the allocation of service department expenses using the allocation base(s). All of the direct and indirect expenses of service departments are allocated to operating departments.[1]

EXHIBIT 22.5

Step 3: Service Department Expense Allocation to Operating Departments

General Office Department Expense Allocation

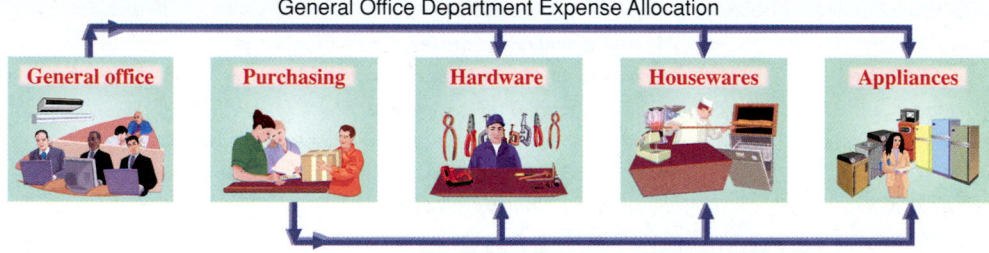

Purchasing Department Expense Allocation

Computations for both steps 2 and 3 are commonly made using a departmental expense allocation spreadsheet as shown in Exhibit 22.6. The first two sections of this spreadsheet list direct expenses and indirect expenses by department. The third section lists the service department expenses and their allocations to operating departments. The allocation bases are identified in the second column, and total expense amounts are reported in the third column.

Illustration of Steps 1, 2, and 3   The departmental expense allocation spreadsheet is useful in implementing the first three steps. To illustrate, first (step 1) the three direct expenses of salaries, depreciation, and supplies are accumulated in each of the five departments.

---

[1] In some cases we allocate a service department's expenses to other service departments when they use its services. For example, expenses of a payroll office benefit all service and operating departments and can be assigned to all departments. Nearly all examples and assignment materials in this book allocate service expenses only to operating departments for simplicity.

EXHIBIT 22.6

Departmental Expense Allocation Spreadsheet

| | File Edit View Insert Format Tools Data Window Help | | | | | | | | |

A-1 HARDWARE
Departmental Expense Allocations
For Year Ended December 31, 2011

	Allocation Base	Expense Account Balance	General Office Dept.	Purchas- ing Dept.	Hard- ware Dept.	House- wares Dept.	Appli- ances Dept.
Direct expenses							
Salaries expense....................	Payroll records.........................	$51,900	$13,300	$8,200	$15,600	$ 7,000	$ 7,800
Depreciation—Equipment......	Depreciation records.............	1,500	500	300	400	100	200
Supplies expense....................	Requisitions............................	900	200	100	300	200	100
Indirect expenses							
Rent expense	Amount and value of space..	12,000	600	600	4,860	3,240	2,700
Utilities expense.....................	Floor space............................	2,400	300	300	810	540	450
Advertising expense	Sales......................................	1,000			500	300	200
Insurance expense..................	Value of insured assets	2,500	400	200	900	600	400
Total department expenses		72,200	15,300	9,700	23,370	11,980	11,850
Service department expenses							
General office department.....	Sales......................................		(15,300)		7,650	4,590	3,060
Purchasing department	Purchase orders....................			(9,700)	3,880	2,630	3,190
Total expenses allocated to operating departments..		$72,200	$ 0	$ 0	$34,900	$19,200	$18,100

Sheet1 / Sheet2 / Sheet3 /

Second (step 2), the four indirect expenses of rent, utilities, advertising, and insurance are allocated to all departments using the allocation bases identified. For example, consider rent allocation. Exhibit 22.7 lists the five departments' square footage of space occupied.

Department	Floor Space (Square Feet)	Value of Insured Assets ($)	Sales ($)	Number of Purchase Orders
General office	1,500	$ 38,000		—
Purchasing	1,500	19,000		—*
Hardware	4,050	85,500	$119,500	394
Housewares	2,700	57,000	71,700	267
Appliances	2,250	38,000	47,800	324
Total	12,000	$237,500	$239,000	985

EXHIBIT 22.7

Departments' Allocation Bases

* Purchasing department tracks purchase orders by department.

The two service departments (office and purchasing) occupy 25% of the total space (3,000 sq. feet/ 12,000 sq. feet). However, they are located near the back of the building, which is of lower value than space near the front that is occupied by operating departments. Management esti- mates that space near the back accounts for $1,200 of the total rent expense of $12,000. Exhibit 22.8 shows how we allocate the $1,200 rent expense between these two service departments in proportion to their square footage. Exhibit 22.8 shows a simple rule for cost

Department	Square Feet	Percent of Total	Allocated Cost
General office	1,500	50.0%	$ 600
Purchasing	1,500	50.0	600
Totals	3,000	100.0%	$1,200

EXHIBIT 22.8

Allocating Indirect (Rent) Expense to Service Departments

allocations: Allocated cost = Percentage of allocation base × Total cost. We then allocate the remaining $10,800 of rent expense to the three operating departments as shown in Exhibit 22.9.

EXHIBIT 22.9

Allocating Indirect (Rent)
Expense to Operating Departments

Department	Square Feet	Percent of Total	Allocated Cost
Hardware	4,050	45.0%	$ 4,860
Housewares	2,700	30.0	3,240
Appliances	2,250	25.0	2,700
Totals	9,000	100.0%	$10,800

We continue step 2 by allocating the $2,400 of utilities expense to all departments based on the square footage occupied as shown in Exhibit 22.10.

EXHIBIT 22.10

Allocating Indirect (Utilities)
Expense to All Departments

Department	Square Feet	Percent of Total	Allocated Cost
General office	1,500	12.50%	$ 300
Purchasing	1,500	12.50	300
Hardware	4,050	33.75	810
Housewares	2,700	22.50	540
Appliances	2,250	18.75	450
Totals	12,000	100.00%	$2,400

Exhibit 22.11 shows the allocation of $1,000 of advertising expense to the three operating departments on the basis of sales dollars. We exclude service departments from this allocation because they do not generate sales.

Department	Sales	Percent of Total	Allocated Cost
Hardware	$119,500	50.0%	$ 500
Housewares	71,700	30.0	300
Appliances	47,800	20.0	200
Totals	$239,000	100.0%	$1,000

To complete step 2 we allocate insurance expense to each service and operating department as shown in Exhibit 22.12.

EXHIBIT 22.12

Allocating Indirect (Insurance)
Expense to All Departments

Department	Value of Insured Assets	Percent of Total	Allocated Cost
General office	$ 38,000	16.0%	$ 400
Purchasing	19,000	8.0	200
Hardware	85,500	36.0	900
Housewares	57,000	24.0	600
Appliances	38,000	16.0	400
Total	$237,500	100.0%	$2,500

Third (step 3), total expenses of the two service departments are allocated to the three operating departments as shown in Exhibits 22.13 and 22.14.

Department	Sales	Percent of Total	Allocated Cost
Hardware	$119,500	50.0%	$ 7,650
Housewares	71,700	30.0	4,590
Appliances	47,800	20.0	3,060
Total	$239,000	100.0%	$15,300

Department	Number of Purchase Orders	Percent of Total	Allocated Cost
Hardware	394	40.00%	$3,880
Housewares	267	27.11	2,630
Appliances	324	32.89	3,190
Total	985	100.00%	$9,700

EXHIBIT 22.14

Allocating Service Department (Purchasing) Expenses to Operating Departments

Step 4 The departmental expense allocation spreadsheet can now be used to prepare performance reports for the company's service and operating departments. The general office and purchasing departments are cost centers, and their managers will be evaluated on their control of costs. Actual amounts of service department expenses can be compared to budgeted amounts to help assess cost center manager performance.

Amounts in the operating department columns are used to prepare departmental income statements as shown in Exhibit 22.15. This exhibit uses the spreadsheet for its operating expenses; information on sales and cost of goods sold comes from departmental records.

Example: If the $15,300 general office expenses in Exhibit 22.6 are allocated equally across departments, what is net income for the hardware department and for the combined company? *Answer:* Hardware income, $13,350; combined income, $19,000.

A-1 HARDWARE
Departmental Income Statements
For Year Ended December 31, 2011

	Hardware Department	Housewares Department	Appliances Department	Combined
Sales	$119,500	$71,700	$47,800	$239,000
Cost of goods sold	73,800	43,800	30,200	147,800
Gross profit	45,700	27,900	17,600	91,200
Operating expenses				
Salaries expense	15,600	7,000	7,800	30,400
Depreciation expense—Equipment	400	100	200	700
Supplies expense	300	200	100	600
Rent expense.........................	4,860	3,240	2,700	10,800
Utilities expense	810	540	450	1,800
Advertising expense	500	300	200	1,000
Insurance expense....................	900	600	400	1,900
Share of general office expenses	7,650	4,590	3,060	15,300
Share of purchasing expenses	3,880	2,630	3,190	9,700
Total operating expenses	34,900	19,200	18,100	72,200
Net income (loss)	**$10,800**	**$ 8,700**	**$ (500)**	**$19,000**

EXHIBIT 22.15

Departmental Income Statements

Departmental Contribution to Overhead

Data from departmental income statements are not always best for evaluating each profit center's performance, especially when indirect expenses are a large portion of total expenses and when weaknesses in assumptions and decisions in allocating indirect expenses can markedly affect net income. In these and other cases, we might better evaluate profit center performance using the **departmental contribution to overhead,** which is a report of the amount of sales less *direct* expenses.[2] We can also examine cost center performance by focusing on control of direct expenses.

---

[2] A department's contribution is said to be "to overhead" because of the practice of considering all indirect expenses as overhead. Thus, the excess of a department's sales over direct expenses is a contribution toward at least a portion of its total overhead.

EXHIBIT 22.16

Departmental Contribution
to Overhead

A-1 HARDWARE Income Statement Showing Departmental Contribution to Overhead For Year Ended December 31, 2011				
	Hardware Department	Housewares Department	Appliances Department	Combined
Sales	$119,500	$ 71,700	$47,800	$239,000
Cost of goods sold	73,800	43,800	30,200	147,800
Gross profit	45,700	27,900	17,600	91,200
Direct expenses				
Salaries expense	15,600	7,000	7,800	30,400
Depreciation expense—Equipment	400	100	200	700
Supplies expense	300	200	100	600
Total direct expenses	16,300	7,300	8,100	31,700
Departmental contributions to overhead........................	**$29,400**	**$20,600**	**$ 9,500**	**$59,500**
Indirect expenses				
Rent expense........................				10,800
Utilities expense				1,800
Advertising expense..................				1,000
Insurance expense				1,900
General office department expense				15,300
Purchasing department expense				9,700
Total indirect expenses				40,500
Net income				**$19,000**
Contribution as percent of sales	24.6%	28.7%	19.9%	24.9%

Point: Net income is the same in Exhibits 22.15 and 22.16. The method of reporting indirect expenses in Exhibit 22.16 does not change total net income but does identify each department's contribution to overhead and net income.

The upper half of Exhibit 22.16 shows a departmental (profit center) contribution to overhead as part of an expanded income statement. This format is common when reporting departmental contributions to overhead. Using the information in Exhibits 22.15 and 22.16, we can evaluate the profitability of the three profit centers. For instance, let's compare the performance of the appliances department as described in these two exhibits. Exhibit 22.15 shows a $500 net loss resulting from this department's operations, but Exhibit 22.16 shows a $9,500 positive contribution to overhead, which is 19.9% of the appliance department's sales. The contribution of the appliances department is not as large as that of the other selling departments, but a $9,500 contribution to overhead is better than a $500 loss. This tells us that the appliances department is not a money loser. On the contrary, it is contributing $9,500 toward defraying total indirect expenses of $40,500.

Quick Check

Answers — p. 948

4. If a company has two operating (selling) departments (shoes and hats) and two service departments (payroll and advertising), which of the following statements is correct? (a) Wages incurred in the payroll department are direct expenses of the shoe department, (b) Wages incurred in the payroll department are indirect expenses of the operating departments, or (c) Advertising department expenses are allocated to the other three departments.

5. Which of the following bases can be used to allocate supervisors' salaries across operating departments? (a) Hours spent in each department, (b) number of employees in each department, (c) sales achieved in each department, or (d) any of the above, depending on which information is most relevant and accessible.

6. What three steps are used to allocate expenses to operating departments?

7. An income statement showing departmental contribution to overhead, (a) subtracts indirect expenses from each department's revenues, (b) subtracts only direct expenses from each department's revenues, or (c) shows net income for each department.

INVESTMENT CENTERS

This section introduces both financial and nonfinancial measures of investment center performance.

Financial Performance Evaluation Measures

Investment center managers are typically evaluated using performance measures that combine income and assets. Consider the following data for ZTel, a company which operates two divisions: LCD and S-Phone. The LCD division manufactures liquid crystal display (LCD) touch-screen monitors and sells them for use in computers, cellular phones, and other products. The S-Phone division sells smartphones, mobile phones that also function as personal computers, MP3 players, cameras, and global positioning satellite (GPS) systems. Exhibit 22.17 shows current year income and assets for those divisions.

A1 Analyze investment centers using return on assets, residual income, and balanced scorecard.

	LCD	S-Phone
Net income	$ 526,500	$ 417,600
Average invested assets	2,500,000	1,850,000

EXHIBIT 22.17

Investment Center Income and Assets

Investment Center Return on Total Assets   One measure to evaluate division performance is the **investment center return on total assets,** also called *return on investment* (ROI). This measure is computed as follows

$$\text{Return on investment} = \frac{\text{Investment center net income}}{\text{Investment center average invested assets}}$$

The return on investment for the LCD division is 21% (rounded), computed as $526,500/ $2,500,000. The S-Phone division's return on investment is 23% (rounded), computed as $417,600/$1,850,000. Though the LCD division earned more dollars of net income, it was less efficient in using its assets to generate income compared to the S-Phone division.

Investment Center Residual Income   Another way to evaluate division performance is to compute **investment center residual income,** which is computed as follows

$$\text{Residual income} = \frac{\text{Investment center}}{\text{net income}} - \frac{\text{Target investment center}}{\text{net income}}$$

Assume ZTel's top management sets target net income at 8% of divisional assets. For an investment center, this **hurdle rate** is typically the cost of obtaining financing. Applying this hurdle rate using the data from Exhibit 22.17 yields the residual income for ZTel's divisions in Exhibit 22.18.

	LCD	S-Phone
Net income	$526,500	$417,600
Less: Target net income		
$2,500,000 × 8%	200,000	
$1,850,000 × 8%		148,000
Investment center residual income	$326,500	$269,600

EXHIBIT 22.18

Investment Center Residual Income

Unlike return on assets, residual income is expressed in dollars. The LCD division outperformed the S-Phone division on the basis of residual income. However, this result is due in part to the LCD division having a larger asset base than the S-Phone division.

Using residual income to evaluate division performance encourages division managers to accept all opportunities that return more than the target net income, thus increasing company value. For example, the S-Phone division might not want to accept a new customer that will provide a 15% return on investment, since that will reduce the S-Phone division's overall return on investment (23% as shown above). However, the S-Phone division should accept this opportunity because the new customer would increase residual income by providing net income above the target net income.

Nonfinancial Performance Evaluation Measures

Evaluating performance solely on financial measures such as return on investment or residual income has limitations. For example, some investment center managers might forgo profitable opportunities to keep their return on investment high. Also, residual income is less useful when comparing investment centers of different size. And, both return on investment and residual income can encourage managers to focus too heavily on short-term financial goals.

In response to these limitations, companies consider nonfinancial measures. For example, a delivery company such as **FedEx** might track the percentage of on-time deliveries. The percentage of defective tennis balls manufactured can be used to assess performance of **Penn**'s production managers. **Walmart**'s credit card screens commonly ask customers at check-out whether the cashier was friendly or the store was clean. This kind of information can help division managers run their divisions and help top management evaluate division manager performance.

Balanced Scorecard

The **balanced scorecard** is a system of performance measures, including nonfinancial measures, used to assess company and division manager performance. The balanced scorecard requires managers to think of their company from four perspectives:

1. **Customer:** What do customers think of us?
2. **Internal processes:** Which of our operations are critical to meeting customer needs?
3. **Innovation and learning:** How can we improve?
4. **Financial:** What do our owners think of us?

Point: One survey indicates that nearly 60% of global companies use some form of a balanced scorecard.

The balanced scorecard collects information on several key performance indicators within each of the four perspectives. These key indicators vary across companies. Exhibit 22.19 lists common performance measures.

EXHIBIT 22.19

Balanced Scorecard Performance Indicators

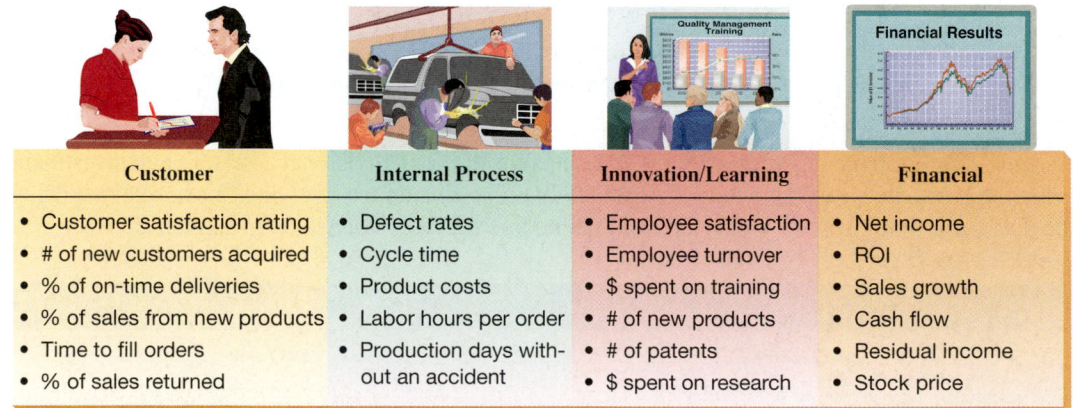

Customer	Internal Process	Innovation/Learning	Financial
• Customer satisfaction rating	• Defect rates	• Employee satisfaction	• Net income
• # of new customers acquired	• Cycle time	• Employee turnover	• ROI
• % of on-time deliveries	• Product costs	• $ spent on training	• Sales growth
• % of sales from new products	• Labor hours per order	• # of new products	• Cash flow
• Time to fill orders	• Production days without an accident	• # of patents	• Residual income
• % of sales returned		• $ spent on research	• Stock price

After selecting key performance indicators, companies collect data on each indicator and compare actual amounts to expected amounts to assess performance. For example, a company might have a goal of filling 98% of customer orders within two hours. Balanced scorecard reports are often presented in graphs or tables that can be updated frequently. Such timely information aids division managers in their decisions, and can be used by top management to evaluate division manager performance.

Customer Perspective	Actual	Goal
Checkout success	62%	⬆
Orders returned	2.2%	↔
Customer satisfaction rating	9.5	⬆
Number of customer complaints	142	⬇

EXHIBIT 22.20

Balanced Scorecard Reporting:
Internet Retailer

Exhibit 22.20 is an example of balanced scorecard reporting on the customer perspective for an Internet retailer. This scorecard reports for example that the retailer is getting 62% of its potential customers successfully through the checkout process, and that 2.2% of all orders are returned. The *color* of the arrows in the right-most column reveals whether the company is exceeding its goal (green), barely meeting the goal (yellow), or not meeting the goal (red). The *direction* of the arrows reveals any trend in performance: an upward arrow indicates improvement, a downward arrow indicates declining performance, and an arrow pointing sideways indicates no change. A review of these arrows' color and direction suggests the retailer is meeting or exceeding its goals on checkout success, orders returned, and customer satisfaction. Further, checkout success and customer satisfaction are improving. The red arrow shows the company has received more customer complaints than was hoped for; however, the number of customer complaints is declining. A manager would combine this information with similar information on the internal process, innovation and learning, and financial perspectives to get an overall view of division performance.

 **Decision Maker**   Answer — p. 947

Center Manager   Your center's usual return on total assets is 19%. You are considering two new investments for your center. The first requires a $250,000 average investment and is expected to yield annual net income of $50,000. The second requires a $1 million average investment with an expected annual net income of $175,000. Do you pursue either? ■

RESPONSIBILITY ACCOUNTING

Departmental accounting reports often provide data used to evaluate a department's performance, but are they useful in assessing how well a department *manager* performs? Neither departmental income nor its contribution to overhead may be useful because many expenses can be outside a manager's control. Instead, we often evaluate a manager's performance using responsibility accounting reports that describe a department's activities in terms of **controllable costs**.[3] A cost is controllable if a manager has the power to determine or at least significantly affect the amount incurred. **Uncontrollable costs** are not within the manager's control or influence.

C2 Explain controllable costs and responsibility accounting.

Controllable versus Direct Costs

Controllable costs are not always the same as direct costs. Direct costs are readily traced to a department, but the department manager might or might not control their amounts. For example, department managers often have little or no control over depreciation expense because

---

[3] The terms *cost* and *expense* are often used interchangeably in managerial accounting, but they are not necessarily the same. *Cost* often refers to the monetary outlay to acquire some resource that can have present and future benefit. *Expense* usually refers to an expired cost. That is, as the benefit of a resource expires, a portion of its cost is written off as an expense.

they cannot affect the amount of equipment assigned to their departments. Also, department managers rarely control their own salaries. However, they can control or influence items such as the cost of supplies used in their department. When evaluating managers' performances, we should use data reflecting their departments' outputs along with their controllable costs and expenses.

Distinguishing between controllable and uncontrollable costs depends on the particular manager and time period under analysis. For example, the cost of property insurance is usually not controllable at the department manager's level but by the executive responsible for obtaining the company's insurance coverage. Likewise, this executive might not control costs resulting from insurance policies already in force. However, when a policy expires, this executive can renegotiate a replacement policy and then controls these costs. Therefore, all costs are controllable at some management level if the time period is sufficiently long. We must use good judgment in identifying controllable costs.

Responsibility Accounting System

A *responsibility accounting system* uses the concept of controllable costs to assign managers the responsibility for costs and expenses under their control. Prior to each reporting period, a company prepares plans that identify costs and expenses under each manager's control. These plans are called **responsibility accounting budgets.** To ensure the cooperation of managers and the reasonableness of budgets, managers should be involved in preparing their budgets.

A responsibility accounting system also involves performance reports. A **responsibility accounting performance report** accumulates and reports costs and expenses that a manager is responsible for and their budgeted amounts. Management's analysis of differences between budgeted amounts and actual costs and expenses often results in corrective or strategic managerial actions. Upper-level management uses performance reports to evaluate the effectiveness of lower-level managers in controlling costs and expenses and keeping them within budgeted amounts.

A responsibility accounting system recognizes that control over costs and expenses belongs to several levels of management. We illustrate this by considering the organization chart in Exhibit 22.21. The lines in this chart connecting the managerial positions reflect channels of authority. For example, the four department managers of this consulting firm (benchmarking, cost management, outsourcing, and service) are responsible for controllable costs and expenses incurred in their departments, but these same costs are subject to the overall control of the vice president (VP) for operational consulting. Similarly, this VP's costs are subject to the control of the executive vice president (EVP) for operations, the president, and, ultimately, the board of directors.

At lower levels, managers have limited responsibility and relatively little control over costs and expenses. Performance reports for low-level management typically cover few controllable costs. Responsibility and control broaden for higher-level managers; therefore, their reports span a wider range of costs. However, reports to higher-level managers seldom contain the details reported to their subordinates but are summarized for two reasons: (1) lower-level managers are often responsible for these detailed costs and (2) detailed reports can obscure broader, more important issues facing a company.

Exhibit 22.22 shows summarized performance reports for the three management levels identified in Exhibit 22.21. Exhibit 22.22 shows that costs under the control of the benchmarking

EXHIBIT 22.21

Organizational Responsibility Chart

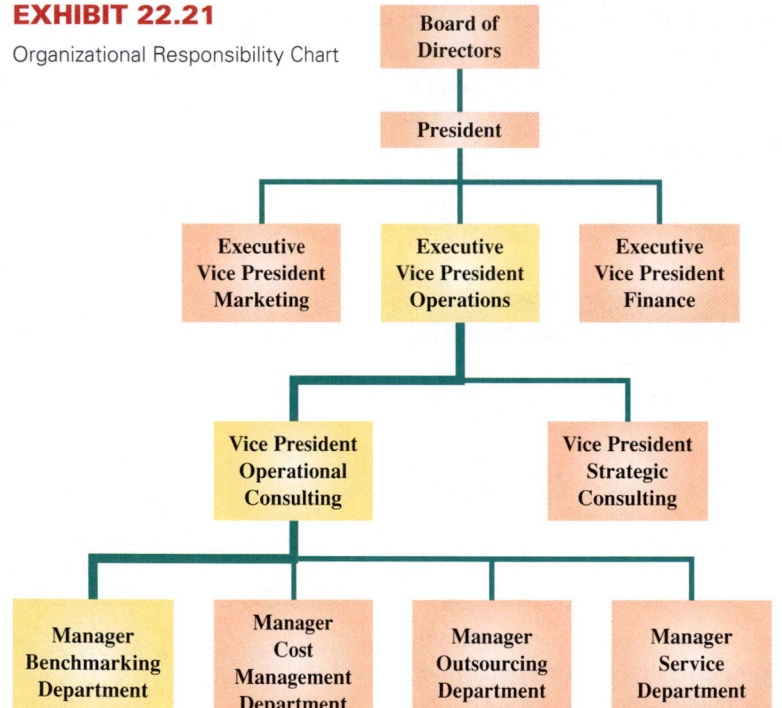

Point: Responsibility accounting does not place blame. Instead, responsibility accounting is used to identify opportunities for improving performance.

EXHIBIT 22.22

Responsibility Accounting
Performance Reports

Executive Vice President, Operations

Controllable Costs	Budgeted Amount	Actual Amount	Over (Under) Budget
		For July	
Salaries, VPs	$ 80,000	$ 80,000	$ 0
Quality control costs	21,000	22,400	1,400
Office costs	29,500	28,800	(700)
Operational consulting	276,700	279,500	2,800
Strategic consulting	390,000	380,600	(9,400)
Totals	$ 797,200	$ 791,300	$ (5,900)

Vice President, Operational Consulting

Controllable Costs	Budgeted Amount	Actual Amount	Over (Under) Budget
		For July	
Salaries, department managers	$ 75,000	$ 78,000	$ 3,000
Depreciation	10,600	10,600	0
Insurance	6,800	6,300	(500)
Benchmarking department	79,600	79,900	300
Cost management department	61,500	60,200	(1,300)
Outsourcing department	24,300	24,700	400
Service department	18,900	19,800	900
Totals	$276,700	$279,500	$2,800

Manager, Benchmarking Department

Controllable Costs	Budgeted Amount	Actual Amount	Over (Under) Budget
		For July	
Salaries	$ 51,600	$ 52,500	$ 900
Supplies	8,000	7,800	(200)
Other controllable costs	20,000	19,600	(400)
Totals	$ 79,600	$ 79,900	$ 300

department manager are totaled and included among controllable costs of the VP for operational consulting. Also, costs under the control of the VP are totaled and included among controllable costs of the EVP for operations. In this way, a responsibility accounting system provides relevant information for each management level.

Technological advances increase our ability to produce vast amounts of information that often exceed our ability to use it. Good managers select relevant data for planning and controlling the areas under their responsibility. A good responsibility accounting system makes every effort to provide relevant information to the right person (the one who controls the cost) at the right time (before a cost is out of control).

Point: Responsibility accounting usually divides a company into subunits, or *responsibility centers*. A center manager is evaluated on how well the center performs, as reported in responsibility accounting reports.

Summary of Cost Allocation

Exhibit 22.23 summarizes the cost allocation techniques shown in this chapter. These methods focus on different types of costs, as managers need different information for different decisions.

EXHIBIT 22.23

Cost Allocation Methods

Cost Definition	Accounting Task	Managerial Decision
Indirect expenses	Assign indirect expenses to departments	Evaluate department performance
Uncontrollable costs	Remove uncontrollable costs from responsibility accounting reports	Evaluate department manager performance

Quick Check

Answers — p. 948

8. Are the reports of departmental net income and the departmental contribution to overhead useful in assessing a department manager's performance? Explain.

9. Performance reports to evaluate managers should (*a*) include data about controllable expenses, (*b*) compare actual results with budgeted levels, or (*c*) both (*a*) and (*b*).

GLOBAL VIEW

L'Oreal is an international cosmetics company incorporated in France. With multiple brands and operations in over 100 countries, the company uses concepts of departmental accounting and controllable costs to evaluate performance. For example, a recent annual report shows the following for the major divisions in its Cosmetics branch:

Division	Operating Profit (€ millions)	
Consumer products	€1,578	
Professional products	519	
Luxury products	766	
Active cosmetics	259	
Other cosmetics	(12)	€3,110
Nonallocated costs		(502)
Cosmetics branch total		€2,608

For L'Oreal, nonallocated costs include costs that are not controllable by division managers, including fundamental research and development and costs of service operations like insurance and banking. Excluding noncontrollable costs enables L'Oreal to prepare more meaningful division performance evaluations.

Decision Analysis    Investment Center Profit Margin and Investment Turnover

A2 Analyze investment centers using profit margin and investment turnover.

We can further examine investment center (division) performance by splitting return on investment into **profit margin** and **investment turnover** as follows

Return on investment	=	Profit margin	×	Investment turnover

$$\frac{\text{Investment center net income}}{\text{Investment center average assets}} = \frac{\text{Investment center net income}}{\text{Investment center sales}} \times \frac{\text{Investment center sales}}{\text{Investment center average assets}}$$

Profit margin measures the income earned per dollar of sales. **Investment turnover** measures how efficiently an investment center generates sales from its invested assets. Higher profit margin and higher investment turnover indicate better performance. To illustrate, consider **Best Buy** which reports in Exhibit 22.24 results for two divisions (segments): Domestic and International.

EXHIBIT 22.24

Best Buy Division Sales, Income, and Assets

($ millions)	Domestic	International
Sales........................	$37,314	$12,380
Net income	2,071	164
Average invested assets	9,745	7,319

Profit margin and investment turnover for its Domestic and International divisions are computed and shown in Exhibit 22.25:

($ millions)	Domestic	International
Profit Margin		
$2,071/$37,314	5.55%	
$164/$12,380		1.32%
Investment Turnover		
$37,314/9,745	3.83	
$12,380/$7,319		1.69

EXHIBIT 22.25

Best Buy Division Profit Margin and Investment Turnover

Best Buy's Domestic division generates 5.55 cents of profit per $1 of sales, while its International division generates only 1.32 cents of profit per dollar of sales. Its Domestic division also uses its assets more efficiently; its investment turnover of 3.83 is over twice that of its International division's 1.69. Top management can use profit margin and investment turnover to evaluate the performance of division managers. The measures can also aid management when considering further investment in its divisions.

Decision Maker   Answer — p. 948

Division Manager   You manage a division in a highly competitive industry. You will receive a cash bonus if your division achieves an ROI above 12%. Your division's profit margin is 7%, equal to the industry average, and your division's investment turnover is 1.5. What actions can you take to increase your chance of receiving the bonus? ■

DEMONSTRATION PROBLEM

Management requests departmental income statements for Hacker's Haven, a computer store that has five departments. Three are operating departments (hardware, software, and repairs) and two are service departments (general office and purchasing).

	General Office	Purchasing	Hardware	Software	Repairs
Sales	—	—	$960,000	$600,000	$840,000
Cost of goods sold	—	—	500,000	300,000	200,000
Direct expenses					
Payroll	$60,000	$45,000	80,000	25,000	325,000
Depreciation	6,000	7,200	33,000	4,200	9,600
Supplies	15,000	10,000	10,000	2,000	25,000

The departments incur several indirect expenses. To prepare departmental income statements, the indirect expenses must be allocated across the five departments. Then the expenses of the two service departments must be allocated to the three operating departments. Total cost amounts and the allocation bases for each indirect expense follow.

Indirect Expense	Total Cost	Allocation Basis
Rent	$150,000	Square footage occupied
Utilities	50,000	Square footage occupied
Advertising	125,000	Dollars of sales
Insurance	30,000	Value of assets insured
Service departments		
General office	?	Number of employees
Purchasing	?	Dollars of cost of goods sold

The following additional information is needed for indirect expense allocations.

Department	Square Feet	Sales	Insured Assets	Employees	Cost of Goods Sold
General office	500		$ 60,000		
Purchasing	500		72,000		
Hardware............	4,000	$ 960,000	330,000	5	$ 500,000
Software............	3,000	600,000	42,000	5	300,000
Repairs.............	2,000	840,000	96,000	10	200,000
Totals	10,000	$2,400,000	$600,000	20	$1,000,000

Required

1. Prepare a departmental expense allocation spreadsheet for Hacker's Haven.
2. Prepare a departmental income statement reporting net income for each operating department and for all operating departments combined.

PLANNING THE SOLUTION

- Set up and complete four tables to allocate the indirect expenses—one each for rent, utilities, advertising, and insurance.
- Allocate the departments' indirect expenses using a spreadsheet like the one in Exhibit 22.6. Enter the given amounts of the direct expenses for each department. Then enter the allocated amounts of the indirect expenses that you computed.
- Complete two tables for allocating the general office and purchasing department costs to the three operating departments. Enter these amounts on the spreadsheet and determine the total expenses allocated to the three operating departments.
- Prepare departmental income statements like the one in Exhibit 22.15. Show sales, cost of goods sold, gross profit, individual expenses, and net income for each of the three operating departments and for the combined company.

SOLUTION TO DEMONSTRATION PROBLEM

Allocations of the four indirect expenses across the five departments.

Rent	Square Feet	Percent of Total	Allocated Cost
General office	500	5.0%	$ 7,500
Purchasing	500	5.0	7,500
Hardware............	4,000	40.0	60,000
Software	3,000	30.0	45,000
Repairs.............	2,000	20.0	30,000
Totals	10,000	100.0%	$150,000

Utilities	Square Feet	Percent of Total	Allocated Cost
General office	500	5.0%	$ 2,500
Purchasing	500	5.0	2,500
Hardware............	4,000	40.0	20,000
Software	3,000	30.0	15,000
Repairs.............	2,000	20.0	10,000
Totals	10,000	100.0%	$50,000

Advertising	Sales Dollars	Percent of Total	Allocated Cost
Hardware...........	$ 960,000	40.0%	$ 50,000
Software............	600,000	25.0	31,250
Repairs.............	840,000	35.0	43,750
Totals	$2,400,000	100.0%	$125,000

Insurance	Assets Insured	Percent of Total	Allocated Cost
General office	$ 60,000	10.0%	$ 3,000
Purchasing	72,000	12.0	3,600
Hardware	330,000	55.0	16,500
Software	42,000	7.0	2,100
Repairs.............	96,000	16.0	4,800
Totals	$600,000	100.0%	$30,000

1. Allocations of service department expenses to the three operating departments.

General Office Allocations to	Employees	Percent of Total	Allocated Cost
Hardware..............	5	25.0%	$23,500
Software..............	5	25.0	23,500
Repairs...............	10	50.0	47,000
Totals	20	100.0%	$94,000

Purchasing Allocations to	Cost of Goods Sold	Percent of Total	Allocated Cost
Hardware..............	$ 500,000	50.0%	$37,900
Software..............	300,000	30.0	22,740
Repairs...............	200,000	20.0	15,160
Totals	$1,000,000	100.0%	$75,800

HACKER'S HAVEN
Departmental Expense Allocations
For Year Ended December 31, 2011

	Allocation Base	Expense Account Balance	General Office Dept.	Purchasing Dept.	Hardware Dept.	Software Dept.	Repairs Dept.
Direct Expenses							
Payroll............		$ 535,000	$ 60,000	$ 45,000	$ 80,000	$ 25,000	$ 325,000
Depreciation		60,000	6,000	7,200	33,000	4,200	9,600
Supplies		62,000	15,000	10,000	10,000	2,000	25,000
Indirect Expenses							
Rent	Square ft.	150,000	7,500	7,500	60,000	45,000	30,000
Utilities............	Square ft.	50,000	2,500	2,500	20,000	15,000	10,000
Advertising	Sales	125,000	—	—	50,000	31,250	43,750
Insurance	Assets	30,000	3,000	3,600	16,500	2,100	4,800
Total expenses		1,012,000	94,000	75,800	269,500	124,550	448,150
Service Department Expenses							
General office	Employees		(94,000)		23,500	23,500	47,000
Purchasing	Goods sold			(75,800)	37,900	22,740	15,160
Total expenses allocated to operating departments		$1,012,000	$ 0	$ 0	$330,900	$170,790	$510,310

2. Departmental income statements for Hacker's Haven.

HACKER'S HAVEN
Departmental Income Statements
For Year Ended December 31, 2011

	Hardware	Software	Repairs	Combined
Sales	$ 960,000	$ 600,000	$ 840,000	$2,400,000
Cost of goods sold	500,000	300,000	200,000	1,000,000
Gross profit	460,000	300,000	640,000	1,400,000
Expenses				
Payroll	80,000	25,000	325,000	430,000
Depreciation	33,000	4,200	9,600	46,800
Supplies	10,000	2,000	25,000	37,000
Rent	60,000	45,000	30,000	135,000
Utilities	20,000	15,000	10,000	45,000
Advertising	50,000	31,250	43,750	125,000
Insurance	16,500	2,100	4,800	23,400
Share of general office	23,500	23,500	47,000	94,000
Share of purchasing	37,900	22,740	15,160	75,800
Total expenses	330,900	170,790	510,310	1,012,000
Net income	**$129,100**	**$129,210**	**$129,690**	**$ 388,000**

22A

Transfer Pricing

C3 Explain transfer pricing and methods to set transfer prices.

Divisions in decentralized companies sometimes do business with one another. For example, a separate division of **Harley-Davidson** manufactures its plastic and fiberglass parts used in the company's motorcycles. **Anheuser-Busch**'s metal container division makes cans and lids used in its brewing operations, and also sells cans and lids to soft-drink companies. A division of **Prince** produces strings used in tennis rackets made by Prince and other manufacturers.

Determining the price that should be used to record transfers between divisions in the same company is the focus of this appendix. Because these transactions are transfers within the same company, the price to record them is called the **transfer price.** In decentralized organizations, division managers have input on or decide those prices. Transfer prices can be used in cost, profit, and investment centers. Since these transfers are not with customers outside the company, the transfer price has no direct impact on the company's overall profits. However, transfer prices can impact performance evaluations and, if set incorrectly, lead to bad decisions.

Point: Transfer pricing can impact company profits when divisions are located in countries with different tax rates; this is covered in advanced courses.

Alternative Transfer Prices   Exhibit 22A.1 reports data on the LCD division of ZTel. LCD manufactures liquid crystal display (LCD) touch-screen monitors for use in ZTel's S-Phone division's smartphones, which sell for $400 each. The monitors can also be used in other products. So, LCD can sell its monitors to buyers other than S-Phone. Likewise, the S-Phone division can purchase monitors from suppliers other than LCD.

EXHIBIT 22A.1

LCD Division Manufacturing Information—Monitors

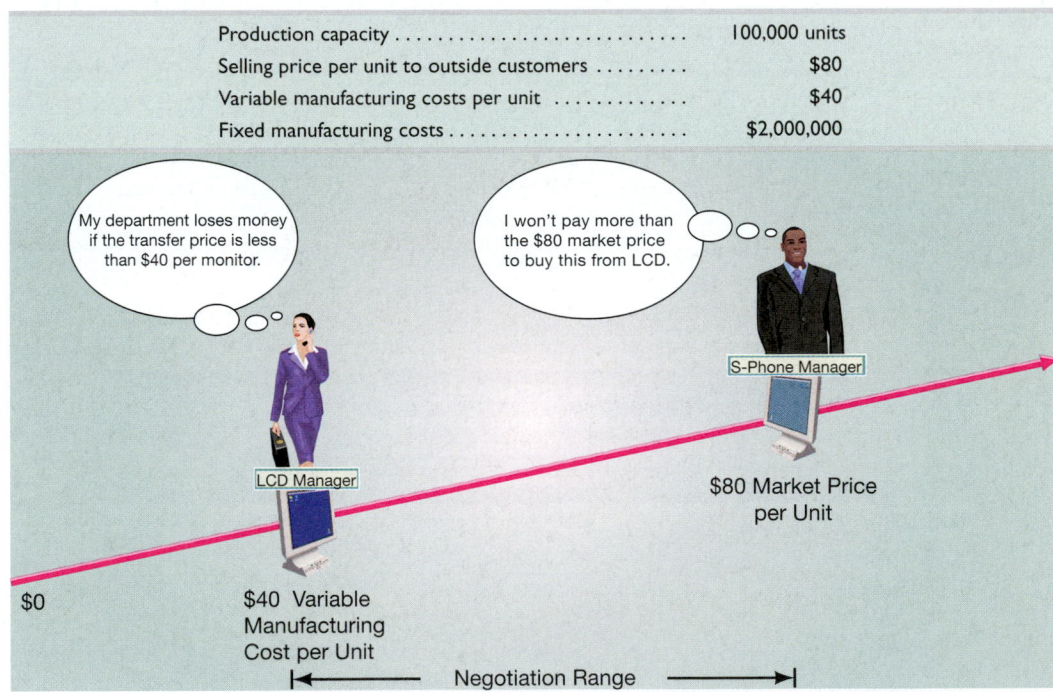

Production capacity	100,000 units
Selling price per unit to outside customers	$80
Variable manufacturing costs per unit	$40
Fixed manufacturing costs	$2,000,000

Exhibit 22A.1 reveals the range of transfer prices for transfers of monitors from LCD to S-Phone. The manager of LCD wants to report a division profit; thus, this manager will not accept a transfer price less than $40 (variable manufacturing cost per unit) because doing so would cause the division to lose money on each monitor transferred. The LCD manager will only consider transfer prices of $40 or more. On the other hand, the S-Phone division manager also wants to report a division profit. Thus, this manager will not pay more than $80 per monitor because similar monitors can be bought from outside suppliers at that price. The S-Phone manager will only consider transfer prices of $80 or less. As any transfer price between $40 and $80 per monitor is possible, how does ZTel determine the transfer price? The answer depends in part on whether the LCD division has excess capacity to manufacture monitors.

No Excess Capacity Assume the LCD division can sell every monitor it produces, and thus is producing 100,000 units. In that case, a **market-based transfer price** of $80 per monitor is preferred. At that price, the LCD division manager is willing to either transfer monitors to S-Phone or sell to outside customers. The S-Phone manager cannot buy monitors for less than $80 from outside suppliers, so the $80 price is acceptable. Further, with a transfer price of $80 per monitor, top management of ZTel is indifferent to S-Phone buying from LCD or buying similar-quality monitors from outside suppliers.

With no excess capacity, the LCD manager will not accept a transfer price less than $80 per monitor. For example, suppose the S-Phone manager suggests a transfer price of $70 per monitor. At that price the LCD manager incurs an unnecessary *opportunity cost* of $10 per monitor (computed as $80 market price minus $70 transfer price). This would lower the LCD division's income and hurt its performance evaluation.

Excess Capacity Assume that the LCD division has excess capacity. For example, the LCD division might currently be producing only 80,000 units. Because LCD has $2,000,000 of fixed manufacturing costs, both LCD and the top management of ZTel prefer that S-Phone purchases its monitors from LCD. For example, if S-Phone purchases its monitors from an outside supplier at the market price of $80 each, LCD manufactures no units. Then, LCD reports a division loss equal to its fixed costs, and ZTel overall reports a lower net income as its costs are higher. Consequently, with excess capacity, LCD should accept any transfer price of $40 per unit or greater and S-Phone should purchase monitors from LCD. This will allow LCD to recover some (or all) of its fixed costs and increase ZTel's overall profits. For example, if a transfer price of $50 per monitor is used, the S-Phone manager is pleased to buy from LCD, since that price is below the market price of $80. For each monitor transferred from LCD to S-Phone at $50, the LCD division receives a *contribution margin* of $10 (computed as $50 transfer price less $40 variable cost) to contribute towards recovering its fixed costs. This form of transfer pricing is called **cost-based transfer pricing.** Under this approach the transfer price might be based on variable costs, total costs, or variable costs plus a markup. Determining the transfer price under excess capacity is complex and is covered in advanced courses.

Additional Issues in Transfer Pricing Several additional issues arise in determining transfer prices which include the following:

- **No market price exists.** Sometimes there is no market price for the product being transferred. The product might be a key component that requires additional conversion costs at the next stage and is not easily replicated by an outside company. For example, there is no market for a console for a **Nissan Maxima** and there is no substitute console **Nissan** can use in assembling a Maxima. In this case a market-based transfer price cannot be used.
- **Cost control.** To provide incentives for cost control, transfer prices might be based on standard, rather than actual costs. For example, if a transfer price of actual variable costs plus a markup of $20 per unit is used in the case above, LCD has no incentive to control its costs.
- **Division managers' negotiation.** With excess capacity, division managers will often negotiate a transfer price that lies between the variable cost per unit and the market price per unit. In this case, the **negotiated transfer price** and resulting departmental performance reports reflect, in part, the negotiating skills of the respective division managers. This might not be best for overall company performance.
- **Nonfinancial factors.** Factors such as quality control, reduced lead times, and impact on employee morale can be important factors in determining transfer prices.

Transfer Pricing Approaches Used by Companies

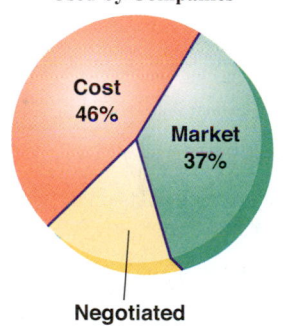

Cost 46%

Market 37%

Negotiated 17%

Joint Costs and Their Allocation

22B

C4 Describe allocation of joint costs across products.

Most manufacturing processes involve **joint costs,** which refer to costs incurred to produce or purchase two or more products at the same time. A joint cost is like an indirect expense in the sense that more than one cost object share it. For example, a sawmill company incurs a joint cost when it buys logs that it cuts into lumber as shown in Exhibit 22B.1. The joint cost includes the logs (raw material) and its cutting (conversion) into boards classified as Clear, Select, No. 1 Common, No. 2 Common, No. 3 Common, and other types of lumber and by-products.

When a joint cost is incurred, a question arises as to whether to allocate it to different products resulting from it. The answer is that when management wishes to estimate the costs of individual products, joint

EXHIBIT 22B.1

Joint Products from Logs

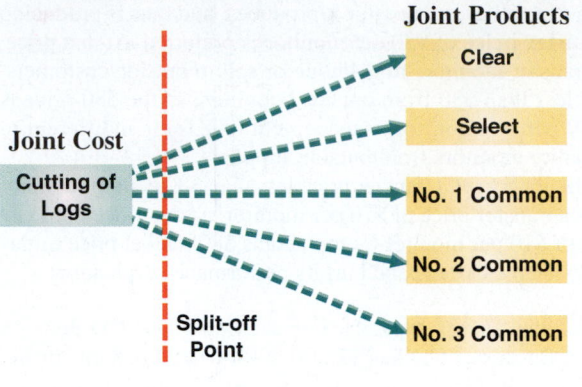

costs are included and must be allocated to these joint products. However, when management needs information to help decide whether to sell a product at a certain point in the production process or to process it further, the joint costs are ignored.

Financial statements prepared according to GAAP must assign joint costs to products. To do this, management must decide how to allocate joint costs across products benefiting from these costs. If some products are sold and others remain in inventory, allocating joint costs involves assigning costs to both cost of goods sold and ending inventory.

The two usual methods to allocate joint costs are the (1) *physical basis* and (2) the *value basis*. The physical basis typically involves allocating joint cost using physical characteristics such as the ratio of pounds, cubic feet, or gallons of each joint product to the total pounds, cubic feet, or gallons of all joint products flowing from the cost. This method is not preferred because the resulting cost allocations do not reflect the relative market values the joint cost generates. The preferred approach is the value basis, which allocates joint cost in proportion to the sales value of the output produced by the process at the "split-off point"; see Exhibit 22B.1.

Physical Basis Allocation of Joint Cost   To illustrate the physical basis of allocating a joint cost, we consider a sawmill that bought logs for $30,000. When cut, these logs produce 100,000 board feet of lumber in the grades and amounts shown in Exhibit 22B.2. The logs produce 20,000 board feet of No. 3 Common lumber, which is 20% of the total. With physical allocation, the No. 3 Common lumber is assigned 20% of the $30,000 cost of the logs, or $6,000 ($30,000 × 20%). Because this low-grade lumber sells for $4,000, this allocation gives a $2,000 loss from its production and sale. The physical basis for allocating joint costs does not reflect the extra value flowing into some products or the inferior value flowing into others. That is, the portion of a log that produces Clear and Select grade lumber is worth more than the portion used to produce the three grades of common lumber, but the physical basis fails to reflect this.

EXHIBIT 22B.2

Allocating Joint Costs on a Physical Basis

Grade of Lumber	Board Feet Produced	Percent of Total	Allocated Cost	Sales Value	Gross Profit
Clear and Select............	10,000	10.0%	$ 3,000	$12,000	$ 9,000
No. 1 Common	30,000	30.0	9,000	18,000	9,000
No. 2 Common	40,000	40.0	12,000	16,000	4,000
No. 3 Common	20,000	20.0	6,000	4,000	(2,000)
Totals	100,000	100.0%	$30,000	$50,000	$20,000

Value Basis Allocation of Joint Cost   Exhibit 22B.3 illustrates the value basis method of allocation. It determines the percents of the total costs allocated to each grade by the ratio of each grade's sales value to the total sales value of $50,000 (sales value is the unit selling price multiplied by the number of units produced). The Clear and Select lumber grades receive 24% of the total cost ($12,000/$50,000) instead of the 10% portion using a physical basis. The No. 3 Common lumber receives only 8% of the total cost, or $2,400, which is much less than the $6,000 assigned to it using the physical basis.

EXHIBIT 22B.3

Allocating Joint Costs on a Value Basis

Grade of Lumber	Sales Value	Percent of Total	Allocated Cost	Gross Profit
Clear and Select	$12,000	24.0%	$ 7,200	$ 4,800
No. 1 Common	18,000	36.0	10,800	7,200
No. 2 Common	16,000	32.0	9,600	6,400
No. 3 Common	4,000	8.0	2,400	1,600
Totals	$50,000	100.0%	$30,000	$20,000

An outcome of value basis allocation is that *each* grade produces exactly the same 40% gross profit at the split-off point. This 40% rate equals the gross profit rate from selling all the lumber made from the $30,000 logs for a combined price of $50,000.

Example: Refer to Exhibit 22B.3. If the sales value of Clear and Select lumber is changed to $10,000, what is the revised ratio of the market value of No. 1 Common to the total? *Answer:* $18,000/$48,000 = 37.5%

Quick Check   Answers — p. 948

10. A company produces three products, B1, B2, and B3. The joint cost incurred for the current month for these products is $180,000. The following data relate to this month's production:

Product	Units Produced	Unit Sales Value
B1	96,000	$3.00
B2	64,000	6.00
B3	32,000	9.00

The amount of joint cost allocated to product B3 using the value basis allocation is (*a*) $30,000, (*b*) $54,000, or (*c*) $90,000.

Summary

C1 **Distinguish between direct and indirect expenses and identify bases for allocating indirect expenses to departments.** Direct expenses are traced to a specific department and are incurred for the sole benefit of that department. Indirect expenses benefit more than one department. Indirect expenses are allocated to departments when computing departmental net income. Ideally, we allocate indirect expenses by using a cause-effect relation for the allocation base. When a cause-effect relation is not identifiable, each indirect expense is allocated on a basis reflecting the relative benefit received by each department.

C2 **Explain controllable costs and responsibility accounting.** A controllable cost is one that is influenced by a specific management level. The total expenses of operating a department often include some items a department manager does not control. Responsibility accounting systems provide information for evaluating the performance of department managers. A responsibility accounting system's performance reports for evaluating department managers should include only the expenses (and revenues) that each manager controls.

C3^A **Explain transfer pricing and methods to set transfer prices.** Transfer prices are used to record transfers of items between divisions of the same company. Transfer prices can be based on costs or market prices, or can be negotiated by division managers.

C4^B **Describe allocation of joint costs across products.** A joint cost refers to costs incurred to produce or purchase two or more products at the same time. When income statements are prepared, joint costs are usually allocated to the resulting joint products using either a physical or value basis.

A1 **Analyze investment centers using return on assets, residual income, and balanced scorecard.** A financial measure often

used to evaluate an investment center manager is the *investment center return on total assets,* also called *return on investment.* This measure is computed as the center's net income divided by the center's average total assets. Residual income, computed as investment center net income minus a target net income is an alternative financial measure of investment center performance. A balanced scorecard uses a combination of financial and non-financial measures to evaluate performance.

A2 **Analyze investment centers using profit margin and investment turnover.** Return on investment can also be computed as profit margin times investment turnover. Profit margin (equal to net income/sales) measures the income earned per dollar of sales and investment turnover (equal to sales/assets) measures how efficiently a division uses its assets.

P1 **Prepare departmental income statements and contribution reports.** Each profit center (department) is assigned its expenses to yield its own income statement. These costs include its direct expenses and its share of indirect expenses. The departmental income statement lists its revenues and costs of goods sold to determine gross profit. Its operating expenses (direct expenses and its indirect expenses allocated to the department) are deducted from gross profit to yield departmental net income. The departmental contribution report is similar to the departmental income statement in terms of computing the gross profit for each department. Then the direct operating expenses for each department are deducted from gross profit to determine the contribution generated by each department. Indirect operating expenses are deducted *in total* from the company's combined contribution.

Guidance Answers to Decision Maker and Decision Ethics

Center Manager We must first realize that the two investment opportunities are not comparable on the basis of absolute dollars of income or on assets. For instance, the second investment provides a

higher income in absolute dollars but requires a higher investment. Accordingly, we need to compute return on total assets for each alternative: (1) $50,000 ÷ $250,000 = 20%, and (2) $175,000 ÷

$1 million = 17.5%. Alternative 1 has the higher return and is preferred over alternative 2. Do you pursue one, both, or neither? Because alternative 1's return is higher than the center's usual return of 19%, it should be pursued, assuming its risks are acceptable. Also, since alternative 1 requires a small investment, top management is likely to be more agreeable to pursuing it. Alternative 2's return is lower than the usual 19% and is not likely to be acceptable.

Division Manager Your division's ROI without further action is 10.5% (equal to 7% × 1.5). In a highly competitive industry, it is difficult to increase profit margins by raising prices. Your division might be better able to control its costs to increase its profit margin. In addition, you might engage in a marketing program to increase sales without increasing your division's invested assets. Investment turnover and thus ROI will increase if the marketing campaign attracts customers.

Guidance Answers to Quick Checks

1. A departmental accounting system provides information used to evaluate the performance of *departments*. A responsibility accounting system provides information used to evaluate the performance of *department managers*.

2. *d*

3. A cost center, such as a service department, incurs costs without directly generating revenues. A profit center, such as a product division, incurs costs but also generates revenues.

4. *b*

5. *d*

6. (1) Assign the direct expenses to each department. (2) Allocate indirect expenses to all departments. (3) Allocate the service department expenses to the operating departments.

7. *b*

8. No, because many expenses that enter into these calculations are beyond the manager's control, and managers should not be evaluated using costs they do not control.

9. *c*

10. *b*; $180,000 × ([32,000 × $9]/[96,000 × $3 + 64,000 × $6 + 32,000 × $9]) = $54,000.

Key Terms   mhhe.com/wildFINMAN4e

Balanced scorecard (p. 936)
Controllable costs (p. 937)
Cost-based transfer pricing (p. 945)
Cost center (p. 927)
Departmental accounting system (p. 926)
Departmental contribution to overhead (p. 933)
Direct expenses (p. 927)
Hurdle rate (p. 935)

Indirect expenses (p. 927)
Investment center (p. 927)
Investment center residual income (p. 935)
Investment center return on total assets (p. 935)
Investment turnover (p. 940)
Joint cost (p. 945)
Market-based transfer price (p. 945)

Negotiated transfer price (p. 945)
Profit center (p. 927)
Profit margin (p. 940)
Responsibility accounting budget (p. 938)
Responsibility accounting performance report (p. 938)
Responsibility accounting system (p. 926)
Transfer price (p. 944)
Uncontrollable costs (p. 937)

Multiple Choice Quiz   Answers on p. 965   mhhe.com/wildFINMAN4e

Additional Quiz Questions are available at the book's Website.

1. A retailer has three departments—housewares, appliances, and clothing—and buys advertising that benefits all departments. Advertising expense is $150,000 for the year, and departmental sales for the year follow: housewares, $356,250; appliances, $641,250; clothing, $427,500. How much advertising expense is allocated to appliances if allocation is based on departmental sales?
   a. $37,500
   b. $67,500
   c. $45,000
   d. $150,000
   e. $641,250

2. Expenses that are easily traced and assigned to a specific department because they are incurred for the sole benefit of that department are called

   a. Uncontrollable expenses
   b. Fixed expenses
   c. Direct expenses
   d. Controllable expenses
   e. Indirect expenses

3. A difficult challenge in computing the total expenses of a department is
   a. Determining the direct expenses of the department.
   b. Determining the amount of sales of the department.
   c. Determining the gross profit ratio.
   d. Assigning indirect expenses to the department.
   e. Assigning direct expenses to the department.

4. A company operates three retail departments as profit centers, and the following information is available for each. Which department has the largest dollar amount of departmental contribution to overhead and what is the dollar amount contributed?

Department	Sales	Cost of Goods Sold	Direct Expenses	Allocated Indirect Expenses
X	$500,000	$350,000	$50,000	$40,000
Y	200,000	75,000	20,000	50,000
Z	350,000	150,000	75,000	10,000

  a. Department Y, $ 55,000
  b. Department Z, $125,000
  c. Department X, $500,000
  d. Department Z, $200,000
  e. Department X, $ 60,000

5. Using the data in question 4, Department X's contribution to overhead as a percentage of sales is
  a. 20%
  b. 30%
  c. 12%
  d. 48%
  e. 32%

$^{A(B)}$ *Superscript letter A (B) denotes assignments based on Appendix 22A (22B).*

🏛 Icon denotes assignments that involve decision making.

Discussion Questions

1. Why are many companies divided into departments?

2. What is the difference between operating departments and service departments?

3. 🏛 What are two main goals in managerial accounting for reporting on and analyzing departments?

4. 🏛 Is it possible to evaluate a cost center's profitability? Explain.

5. What is the difference between direct and indirect expenses?

6. 🏛 Suggest a reasonable basis for allocating each of the following indirect expenses to departments: (a) salary of a supervisor who manages several departments, (b) rent, (c) heat, (d) electricity for lighting, (e) janitorial services, (f) advertising, (g) expired insurance on equipment, and (h) property taxes on equipment.

7. **Research In Motion** has many departments. How is a department's contribution to overhead measured? *RIM*

8. 🏛 What are controllable costs?

9. Controllable and uncontrollable costs must be identified with a particular _____ and a definite _____ period.

10. 🏛 Why should managers be closely involved in preparing their responsibility accounting budgets?

11. 🏛 **Nokia** aims to give its managers timely cost reports. In responsibility accounting, who receives timely cost reports and specific cost information? Explain. **NOKIA**

12.^{A} What is a transfer price? Under what conditions is a market-based transfer price most likely to be used?

13.^{B} What is a joint cost? How are joint costs usually allocated among the products produced from them?

14.^{B} 🏛 Give two examples of products with joint costs.

15. 🏛 Each retail store of **Apple** has several departments. Why is it useful for its management to (a) collect accounting information about each department and (b) treat each department as a profit center? *Apple*

16. 🏛 **Palm** delivers its products to locations around the world. List three controllable and three uncontrollable costs for its delivery department. **Palm**

_{Mc Graw Hill} **connect**

In each blank next to the following terms, place the identifying letter of its best description.

1. _____ Operating department
2. _____ Profit center
3. _____ Responsibility accounting system
4. _____ Cost center
5. _____ Investment center
6. _____ Departmental accounting system
7. _____ Service department

  A. Holds manager responsible for revenues, costs, and investments.
  B. Does not directly manufacture products but contributes to profitability of the entire company.
  C. Incurs costs and also generates revenues.
  D. Provides information used to evaluate the performance of a department.
  E. Incurs costs without directly yielding revenues.
  F. Provides information used to evaluate the performance of a department manager.
  G. Engages directly in manufacturing or in making sales directly to customers.

QUICK STUDY

QS 22-1
Allocation and measurement terms

C1

QS 22-2

Basis for cost allocation

C1

For each of the following types of indirect expenses and service department expenses, identify one allocation basis that could be used to distribute it to the departments indicated.

1. Electric utility expenses of all departments.
2. General office department expenses of the operating departments.
3. Maintenance department expenses of the operating departments.
4. Computer service expenses of production scheduling for operating departments.

QS 22-3

Allocating costs to departments

P1

Macee Department Store has three departments, and it conducts advertising campaigns that benefit all departments. Advertising costs are $100,000 this year, and departmental sales for this year follows. How much advertising cost is allocated to each department if the allocation is based on departmental sales?

Department	Sales
Department I	$220,000
Department 2	400,000
Department 3	180,000

QS 22-4

Allocating costs to departments

P1

Mervon Company has two operating departments: Mixing and Bottling. Mixing has 300 employees and occupies 22,000 square feet. Bottling has 200 employees and occupies 18,000 square feet. Indirect factory costs for the current period follow: Administrative, $160,000; and Maintenance, $200,000. Administrative costs are allocated to operating departments based on the number of workers. Determine the administrative cost allocated to each operating department.

QS 22-5

Allocating costs to departments

P1

Refer to the information in QS 22-4. If the maintenance costs are allocated to operating departments based on square footage, determine the amount of maintenance costs allocated to each operating department.

QS 22-6

Departmental contribution to overhead

P1

Use the information in the following table to compute each department's contribution to overhead (both in dollars and as a percent). Which department contributes the largest dollar amount to total overhead? Which contributes the highest percent (as a percent of sales)? Round percents to one decimal.

	Dept. A	Dept. B	Dept. C
Sales	$53,000	$170,000	$84,000
Cost of goods sold	34,185	103,700	49,560
Gross profit	18,815	66,300	34,440
Total direct expenses	6,360	37,060	8,736
Contribution to overhead	$	$	$
Contribution percent	%	%	%

QS 22-7

Investment center analysis

A1

Compute return on assets for each of these **Best Buy** divisions (each is an investment center). Comment on the relative performance of each investment center. Round percents to one decimal.

Investment Center	Net Income	Average Assets	Return on Assets
Cameras and camcorders	$4,500,000	$20,000,000	_____
Phones and communications.........	1,500,000	12,500,000	_____
Computers and accessories	800,000	10,000,000	_____

QS 22-8

Computing residual income

A1

Refer to information in QS 22-7. Assume a target income of 12% of average invested assets. Compute residual income for each of Best Buy's divisions.

A company's shipping division (an investment center) has sales of $4,700,000, net income of $916,000, and average invested assets of $3,000,000. Compute the division's profit margin and investment turnover.

QS 22-9
Computing performance measures A2

Fill in the blanks in the schedule below for two separate investment centers A and B.

QS 22-10
Performance measures

A1 A2

	Investment Center	
	A	B
Sales...................	$_____	$6,400,000
Net income	$ 252,000	$_____
Average invested assets	$1,400,000	_____
Profit margin	6%	_____%
Investment turnover	_____	1.6
Return on assets	_____%	10%

Classify each of the performance measures below into the most likely balanced scorecard perspective it relates to. Label your answers using C (customer), P (internal process), I (innovation and growth), or F (financial).

1. Number of new products introduced   _____
2. Length of time raw materials are in inventory   _____
3. Profit margin   _____
4. Customer wait time   _____
5. Change in market share   _____
6. Employee training sessions attended   _____
7. Number of days of employee absences   _____
8. Customer satisfaction index   _____

QS 22-11
Performance measures—balanced scorecard

A1

Walt Disney reports the following information for its two Parks and Resorts divisions.

QS 22-12
Performance measures—balanced scorecard

A1

	East Coast		West Coast	
	Current year	Prior year	Current year	Prior year
Hotel occupancy rates	89%	86%	92%	93%

Assume Walt Disney uses a balanced scorecard and sets a target of 90% occupancy in its resorts. Using Exhibit 22.20 as a guide, show how the company's performance on hotel occupancy would appear on a balanced scorecard report.

The Windshield division of Cargo Co. makes windshields for use in Cargo's Assembly division. The Windshield division incurs variable costs of $350 per windshield and has capacity to make 100,000 windshields per year. The market price is $600 per windshield. The Windshield division incurs total fixed costs of $3,000,000 per year. If the Windshield division is operating at full capacity, what transfer price should be used on transfers between the Windshield and Assembly divisions? Explain.

QS 22-13ᴬ
Determining transfer prices without excess capacity

C3

Refer to information in QS 22-13. If the Windshield division has excess capacity, what is the range of possible transfer prices that could be used on transfers between the Windshield and Assembly divisions? Explain.

QS 22-14ᴬ
Determining transfer prices with excess capacity C3

A company purchases a 10,000 square foot commercial building for $400,000 and spends an additional $65,000 to divide the space into two separate rental units and prepare it for rent. Unit A, which has the desirable location on the corner and contains 2,500 square feet, will be rented for $2.00 per square foot. Unit B contains 7,500 square feet and will be rented for $1.50 per square foot. How much of the joint cost should be assigned to Unit B using the value basis of allocation?

QS 22-15ᴮ
Joint cost allocation

C4

QS 22-16
Rent expense allocated
to departments

C1

Auto Market pays $128,000 rent each year for its two-story building. The space in this building is occupied by five departments as specified here.

Paint department	1,200 square feet of first-floor space
Engine department	3,600 square feet of first-floor space
Window department	1,920 square feet of second-floor space
Electrical department	1,056 square feet of second-floor space
Accessory department	1,824 square feet of second-floor space

The company allocates 65% of total rent expense to the first floor and 35% to the second floor, and then allocates rent expense for each floor to the departments occupying that floor on the basis of space occupied. Determine the rent expense to be allocated to each department. (Round percents to the nearest one-tenth and dollar amounts to the nearest whole dollar.)

Check Allocated to Paint Dept.,
$20,800

QS 22-17
Return on investment

A1

For a recent year **L'Oreal** reported operating profit of €3,110 (in millions) for its Cosmetics division. Total assets were €11,314 at the beginning of the year and €12,988 (in millions) at the end of the year. Compute return on investment for the year. State your answer as a percent, rounded to one decimal.

EXERCISES

Exercise 22-1
Departmental expense
allocations

C1

Won Han Co. has four departments: materials, personnel, manufacturing, and packaging. In a recent month, the four departments incurred three shared indirect expenses. The amounts of these indirect expenses and the bases used to allocate them follow.

Indirect Expense	Cost	Allocation Base
Supervision	$ 75,000	Number of employees
Utilities	60,000	Square feet occupied
Insurance	16,500	Value of assets in use
Total	$151,500	

Departmental data for the company's recent reporting period follow.

Department	Employees	Square Feet	Asset Values
Materials	18	27,000	$ 6,000
Personnel	6	4,500	1,200
Manufacturing	66	45,000	37,800
Packaging	30	13,500	15,000
Total	120	90,000	$60,000

Check (2) Total of $30,900 assigned
to Materials Dept.

(1) Use this information to allocate each of the three indirect expenses across the four departments. (2) Prepare a summary table that reports the indirect expenses assigned to each of the four departments.

Exercise 22-2
Departmental contribution report

P1

Below are departmental income statements for a guitar manufacturer. The manufacturer is considering dropping its electric guitar department since it has a net loss. The company classifies advertising, rent, and utilities expenses as indirect. (1) Prepare a departmental contribution report that shows each department's contribution to overhead. (2) Based on contribution to overhead, should the electric guitar department be eliminated?

BEST GUITAR
Departmental Income Statements
For Year Ended December 31, 2011

	Acoustic	Electric
Sales	$101,500	$85,000
Cost of goods sold	45,675	46,750
Gross profit	55,825	38,250
Operating expenses		
Advertising expense	5,075	4,250
Depreciation expense-equipment	10,150	8,500
Salaries expense	20,300	17,000
Supplies expense	2,030	1,700
Rent expense	7,105	5,950
Utilities expense....................	3,045	2,550
Total operating expenses	47,705	39,950
Net income (loss)	**$ 8,120**	**($1,700)**

Overroad Cycle Shop has two service departments (advertising and administration) and two operating departments (cycles and clothing). During 2011, the departments had the following direct expenses and occupied the following amount of floor space.

Department	Direct Expenses	Square Feet
Advertising	$ 16,000	1,088
Administrative	18,500	1,152
Cycles	101,600	6,336
Clothing	11,900	4,224

The advertising department developed and distributed 100 advertisements during the year. Of these, 76 promoted cycles and 24 promoted clothing. The store sold $300,000 of merchandise during the year. Of this amount, $225,000 is from the cycles department, and $75,000 is from the clothing department. The utilities expense of $64,000 is an indirect expense to all departments. Prepare a departmental expense allocation spreadsheet for Overroad Cycle Shop. The spreadsheet should assign (1) direct expenses to each of the four departments, (2) the $64,000 of utilities expense to the four departments on the basis of floor space occupied, (3) the advertising department's expenses to the two operating departments on the basis of the number of ads placed that promoted a department's products, and (4) the administrative department's expenses to the two operating departments based on the amount of sales. Provide supporting computations for the expense allocations.

Exercise 22-3
Departmental expense allocation spreadsheet

C1

Check Total expenses allocated to Cycles Dept., $167,769

The following is a partially completed lower section of a departmental expense allocation spreadsheet for Bookworm Bookstore. It reports the total amounts of direct and indirect expenses allocated to its five departments. Complete the spreadsheet by allocating the expenses of the two service departments (advertising and purchasing) to the three operating departments.

Exercise 22-4
Service department expenses allocated to operating departments P1

File Edit View Insert Format Tools Data Window Help

	Allocation Base	Expense Account Balance	Advertising Dept.	Purchasing Dept.	Books Dept.	Magazines Dept.	Newspapers Dept.
1			Allocation of Expenses to Departments				
5 Total department expenses..........		$654,000	$22,000	$30,000	$425,000	$86,000	$91,000
6 **Service department expenses**							
7 Advertising department.............Sales			?		?	?	?
8 Purchasing department............Purch. orders				?	?	?	?
9 Total expenses allocated to							
10 operating departments.............		?	$ 0	$ 0	?	?	?

Sheet1 / Sheet2 / Sheet3

Advertising and purchasing department expenses are allocated to operating departments on the basis of dollar sales and purchase orders, respectively. Information about the allocation bases for the three operating departments follows.

Department	Sales	Purchase Orders
Books	$448,000	424
Magazines	144,000	312
Newspapers	208,000	264
Total	$800,000	1,000

Check Total expenses allocated to Books Dept., $450,040

Exercise 22-5

Indirect payroll expense allocated to departments

C1

Monica Gellar works in both the jewelry department and the hosiery department of a retail store. Gellar assists customers in both departments and arranges and stocks merchandise in both departments. The store allocates Gellar's $30,000 annual wages between the two departments based on a sample of the time worked in the two departments. The sample is obtained from a diary of hours worked that Gellar kept in a randomly chosen two-week period. The diary showed the following hours and activities spent in the two departments. Allocate Gellar's annual wages between the two departments. (Round percents to one decimal.)

Selling in jewelry department	64 hours
Arranging and stocking merchandise in jewelry department	6 hours
Selling in hosiery department	14 hours
Arranging and stocking merchandise in hosiery department	12 hours
Idle time spent waiting for a customer to enter one of the selling departments	4 hours

Check Assign $8,130 to Hosiery

Exercise 22-6

Managerial performance evaluation

C2

Bob Daniels manages an auto dealership's service department. The recent month's income statement for his department follows. (1) Analyze the items on the income statement and identify those that definitely should be included on a performance report used to evaluate Daniels's performance. List them and explain why you chose them. (2) List and explain the items that should definitely be excluded. (3) List the items that are not definitely included or excluded and explain why they fall into that category.

Revenues		
Sales of parts	$144,000	
Sales of services	210,000	$354,000
Costs and expenses		
Cost of parts sold	60,000	
Building depreciation	18,600	
Income taxes allocated to department	17,400	
Interest on long-term debt	15,000	
Manager's salary	24,000	
Payroll taxes	16,200	
Supplies	31,800	
Utilities	8,800	
Wages (hourly)	32,000	
Total costs and expenses		223,800
Departmental net income		$130,200

Exercise 22-7

Investment center analysis

A1

You must prepare a return on investment analysis for the regional manager of Out-and-In Burgers. This growing chain is trying to decide which outlet of two alternatives to open. The first location (A) requires a $500,000 investment and is expected to yield annual net income of $80,000. The second location (B) requires a $200,000 investment and is expected to yield annual net income of $38,000. Compute the return on investment for each Out-and-In Burgers alternative and then make your recommendation in a one-half page memorandum to the regional manager. (The chain currently generates an 18% return on total assets.)

Comart, a retailer of consumer goods, provides the following information on two of its departments (each considered an investment center).

Exercise 22-8
Computing performance measures
A1

Investment Center	Sales	Net Income	Average Invested Assets
Electronics	$20,000,000	$1,500,000	$ 7,500,000
Sporting goods..............	16,000,000	1,600,000	10,000,000

(1) Compute return on investment for each department. Using return on investment, which department is most efficient at using assets to generate returns for the company? (2) Assume a target income level of 12% of average invested assets. Compute residual income for each department. Which department generated the most residual income for the company? (3) Assume the Electronics department is presented with a new investment opportunity that will yield a 15% return on assets. Should the new investment opportunity be accepted? Explain.

Refer to information in Exercise 22-8. Compute profit margin and investment turnover for each department. Which department generates the most net income per dollar of sales? Which department is most efficient at generating sales from average invested assets?

Exercise 22-9
Computing performance measures   A2

MidCoast Airlines uses the following performance measures. Classify each of the performance measures below into the most likely balanced scorecard perspective it relates to. Label your answers using C (customer), P (internal process), I (innovation and growth), or F (financial).

Exercise 22-10
Performance measures—balanced scorecard
A1

 1. Flight attendant training sessions attended   ———
 2. Customer complaints   ———
 3. Percentage of on-time departures   ———
 4. Market value   ———
 5. Percentage of ground crew trained   ———
 6. Return on investment   ———
 7. On-time flight percentage   ———
 8. Accidents or safety incidents per mile flown   ———
 9. Number of reports of mishandled or lost baggage   ———
 10. Cash flow from operations   ———
 11. Time airplane is on ground between flights   ———
 12. Airplane miles per gallon of fuel   ———
 13. Revenue per seat   ———
 14. Cost of leasing airplanes   ———

The Trailer department of Soni Bicycles makes bike trailers that attach to bicycles and can carry children or cargo. The trailers have a retail price of $100 each. Each trailer incurs $40 of variable manufacturing costs. The Trailer department has capacity for 40,000 trailers per year, and incurs fixed costs of $800,000 per year.

Exercise 22-11[A]
Determining transfer prices
C3

Required

 1. Assume the Assembly division of Soni Bicycles wants to buy 10,000 trailers per year from the Trailer division. If the Trailer division can sell all of the trailers it manufactures to outside customers, what price should be used on transfers between Soni Bicycle's divisions? Explain.

 2. Assume the Trailer division currently only sells 20,000 trailers to outside customers, and the Assembly division wants to buy 10,000 trailers per year from the Trailer division. What is the range of acceptable prices that could be used on transfers between Soni Bicycle's divisions? Explain.

 3. Assume transfer prices of either $40 per trailer or $70 per trailer are being considered. Comment on the preferred transfer prices from the perspectives of the Trailer division manager, the Assembly division manager, and the top management of Soni Bicycles.

Tidy Home Properties is developing a subdivision that includes 300 home lots. The 225 lots in the Garden section are below a ridge and do not have views of the neighboring gardens and hills; the 75 lots in the Premier section offer unobstructed views. The expected selling price for each Garden lot is $50,000 and for each Premier lot is $100,000. The developer acquired the land for $2,500,000 and spent another $2,000,000 on street and utilities improvements. Assign the joint land and improvement costs to the lots using the value basis of allocation and determine the average cost per lot.

Exercise 22-12[B]
Joint real estate costs assigned
C4

Check   Total Garden cost, $2,700,000

Exercise 22-13ᴮ
Joint product costs assigned
C4

Check (2) Inventory cost, $1,826

Pike Seafood Company purchases lobsters and processes them into tails and flakes. It sells the lobster tails for $20 per pound and the flakes for $15 per pound. On average, 100 pounds of lobster are processed into 57 pounds of tails and 24 pounds of flakes, with 19 pounds of waste. Assume that the company purchased 3,000 pounds of lobster for $6.00 per pound and processed the lobsters with an additional labor cost of $1,800. No materials or labor costs are assigned to the waste. If 1,510 pounds of tails and 710 pounds of flakes are sold, what is (1) the allocated cost of the sold items and (2) the allocated cost of the ending inventory? The company allocates joint costs on a value basis. (Round the dollar cost per pound to the nearest thousandth.)

Exercise 22-14
Profit margin and investment turnover
A2

L'Oreal reports the following for a recent year for the major divisions in its Cosmetics branch.

(€ millions)	Sales	Income	Total Assets End of Year	Total Assets Beginning of Year
Professional products	€ 2,472	€ 519	€ 2,516	€ 2,440
Consumer products	8,355	1,578	5,496	5,361
Luxury products	4,170	766	4,059	2,695
Active cosmetics	1,289	259	817	818
Total	€16,286	€3,122	€12,888	€11,314

1. Compute profit margin for each division. State your answers as percents, rounded to two decimal places. Which L'Oreal division has the highest profit margin?
2. Compute investment turnover for each division. Round your answers to two decimal places. Which L'Oreal division has the best investment turnover?

PROBLEM SET A

Problem 22-1A
Allocation of building occupancy costs to departments
P1

mhhe.com/wildFINMAN4e

City Bank has several departments that occupy both floors of a two-story building. The departmental accounting system has a single account, Building Occupancy Cost, in its ledger. The types and amounts of occupancy costs recorded in this account for the current period follow.

Depreciation—Building	$18,000
Interest—Building mortgage	27,000
Taxes—Building and land	8,000
Gas (heating) expense	2,500
Lighting expense	3,000
Maintenance expense	5,500
Total occupancy cost	$64,000

The building has 4,000 square feet on each floor. In prior periods, the accounting manager merely divided the $64,000 occupancy cost by 8,000 square feet to find an average cost of $8 per square foot and then charged each department a building occupancy cost equal to this rate times the number of square feet that it occupied.

Laura Diaz manages a first-floor department that occupies 1,000 square feet, and Lauren Wright manages a second-floor department that occupies 1,800 square feet of floor space. In discussing the departmental reports, the second-floor manager questions whether using the same rate per square foot for all departments makes sense because the first-floor space is more valuable. This manager also references a recent real estate study of average local rental costs for similar space that shows first-floor space worth $30 per square foot and second-floor space worth $20 per square foot (excluding costs for heating, lighting, and maintenance).

Check (1) Total allocated to Diaz and Wright, $22,400 (2) Total occupancy cost to Diaz, $9,330

Required

1. Allocate occupancy costs to the Diaz and Wright departments using the current allocation method.
2. Allocate the depreciation, interest, and taxes occupancy costs to the Diaz and Wright departments in proportion to the relative market values of the floor space. Allocate the heating, lighting, and maintenance costs to the Diaz and Wright departments in proportion to the square feet occupied (ignoring floor space market values).

Analysis Component

3. Which allocation method would you prefer if you were a manager of a second-floor department? Explain.

Vortex Company operates a retail store with two departments. Information about those departments follows.

	Department A	Department B
Sales	$800,000	$450,000
Cost of goods sold	497,000	291,000
Direct expenses		
Salaries	125,000	88,000
Insurance	20,000	10,000
Utilities	24,000	14,000
Depreciation	21,000	12,000
Maintenance	7,000	5,000

The company also incurred the following indirect costs.

Salaries	$36,000
Insurance	6,000
Depreciation	15,000
Office expenses	50,000

Indirect costs are allocated as follows: salaries on the basis of sales; insurance and depreciation on the basis of square footage; and office expenses on the basis of number of employees. Additional information about the departments follows.

Department	Square footage	Number of employees
A	28,000	75
B	12,000	50

Required

1. For each department, determine the departmental contribution to overhead and the departmental net income.

2. Should Department B be eliminated? Explain.

Problem 22-2A
Departmental contribution to income

P1

Check   (1) Dept. A net income, $38,260

Time-To-See Company began operations in January 2011 with two operating (selling) departments and one service (office) department. Its departmental income statements follow.

TIME-TO-SEE COMPANY Departmental Income Statements For Year Ended December 31, 2011			
	Clock	Mirror	Combined
Sales	$122,500	$52,500	$175,000
Cost of goods sold	60,000	32,000	92,000
Gross profit	62,500	20,500	83,000
Direct expenses			
Sales salaries	20,000	7,000	27,000
Advertising	1,200	500	1,700
Store supplies used	900	400	1,300
Depreciation—Equipment	1,500	300	1,800
Total direct expenses	23,600	8,200	31,800
Allocated expenses			
Rent expense	7,020	3,780	10,800
Utilities expense	2,600	1,400	4,000
Share of office department expenses	10,500	4,500	15,000
Total allocated expenses	20,120	9,680	29,800
Total expenses	43,720	17,880	61,600
Net income	$ 18,780	$ 2,620	$ 21,400

Problem 22-3A
Departmental income statements; forecasts

P1

mhhe.com/wildFINMAN4e

Time-To-See plans to open a third department in January 2012 that will sell paintings. Management predicts that the new department will generate $35,000 in sales with a 55% gross profit margin and will require the following direct expenses: sales salaries, $8,000; advertising, $800; store supplies, $500; and equipment depreciation, $200. It will fit the new department into the current rented space by taking some square footage from the other two departments. When opened the new painting department will fill one-fifth of the space presently used by the clock department and one-sixth used by the mirror department. Management does not predict any increase in utilities costs, which are allocated to the departments in proportion to occupied space (or rent expense). The company allocates office department expenses to the operating departments in proportion to their sales. It expects the painting department to increase total office department expenses by $7,000. Since the painting department will bring new customers into the store, management expects sales in both the clock and mirror departments to increase by 7%. No changes for those departments' gross profit percents or their direct expenses are expected except for store supplies used, which will increase in proportion to sales.

Required

Check   2012 forecasted combined
net income (sales), $29,869
($222,250)

Prepare departmental income statements that show the company's predicted results of operations for calendar year 2012 for the three operating (selling) departments and their combined totals. (Round percents to the nearest one-tenth and dollar amounts to the nearest whole dollar.)

Problem 22-4A

Responsibility accounting
performance reports;
controllable and budgeted costs

C2

Becky Hoefer, the plant manager of Travel Far's Indiana plant, is responsible for all of that plant's costs other than her own salary. The plant has two operating departments and one service department. The camper and trailer operating departments manufacture different products and have their own managers. The office department, which Hoefer also manages, provides services equally to the two operating departments. A budget is prepared for each operating department and the office department. The company's responsibility accounting system must assemble information to present budgeted and actual costs in performance reports for each operating department manager and the plant manager. Each performance report includes only those costs that a particular operating department manager can control: raw materials, wages, supplies used, and equipment depreciation. The plant manager is responsible for the department managers' salaries, utilities, building rent, office salaries other than her own, and other office costs plus all costs controlled by the two operating department managers. The annual departmental budgets and actual costs for the two operating departments follow.

	Budget			Actual		
	Campers	Trailers	Combined	Campers	Trailers	Combined
Raw materials	$160,000	$250,000	$ 410,000	$159,400	$246,500	$ 405,900
Employee wages	99,000	191,000	290,000	102,300	193,700	296,000
Dept. manager salary	40,000	44,000	84,000	41,000	47,000	88,000
Supplies used	34,000	83,000	117,000	31,900	84,600	116,500
Depreciation—Equip.	58,000	110,000	168,000	58,000	110,000	168,000
Utilities..................	2,800	4,200	7,000	2,700	3,800	6,500
Building rent	5,000	8,000	13,000	4,800	7,200	12,000
Office department costs	56,000	56,000	112,000	54,450	54,450	108,900
Totals	$454,800	$746,200	$1,201,000	$454,550	$747,250	$1,201,800

The office department's annual budget and its actual costs follow.

	Budget	Actual
Plant manager salary	$ 60,000	$ 62,000
Other office salaries	30,000	27,700
Other office costs	22,000	19,200
Totals	$112,000	$108,900

Required

1. Prepare responsibility accounting performance reports like those in Exhibit 22.22 that list costs controlled by the following:

Check   (1a) $600 total over budget

   a. Manager of the camper department.

   b. Manager of the trailer department.

(1c) Indiana plant controllable
costs, $1,200 total under budget

   c. Manager of the Indiana plant.

   In each report, include the budgeted and actual costs and show the amount that each actual cost is over or under the budgeted amount.

   [continued on next page]

Analysis Component

2. Did the plant manager or the operating department managers better manage costs? Explain.

Bloom Orchards produced a good crop of peaches this year. After preparing the following income statement, the company believes it should have given its No. 3 peaches to charity and saved its efforts.

Problem 22-5A^B
Allocation of joint costs

C4

BLOOM ORCHARDS				
Income Statement				
For Year Ended December 31, 2011				
	No. 1	No. 2	No. 3	Combined
Sales (by grade)				
No. 1: 300,000 lbs. @ $1.50/lb	$450,000			
No. 2: 300,000 lbs. @ $1.00/lb		$300,000		
No. 3: 750,000 lbs. @ $0.20/lb			$ 150,000	
Total sales				$900,000
Costs				
Tree pruning and care @ $0.20/lb	60,000	60,000	150,000	270,000
Picking, sorting, and grading @ $0.12/lb	36,000	36,000	90,000	162,000
Delivery costs $0.03/lb	9,000	9,000	22,500	40,500
Total costs	105,000	105,000	262,500	472,500
Net income (loss)	$345,000	$195,000	$(112,500)	$427,500

In preparing this statement, the company allocated joint costs among the grades on a physical basis as an equal amount per pound. The company's delivery cost records show that $30,000 of the $40,500 relates to crating the No. 1 and No. 2 peaches and hauling them to the buyer. The remaining $10,500 of delivery costs is for crating the No. 3 peaches and hauling them to the cannery.

Required

1. Prepare reports showing cost allocations on a sales value basis to the three grades of peaches. Separate the delivery costs into the amounts directly identifiable with each grade. Then allocate any shared delivery costs on the basis of the relative sales value of each grade.

2. Using your answers to part 1, prepare an income statement using the joint costs allocated on a sales value basis.

Check (1) $89,910 tree pruning and care costs allocated to No. 2

(2) Net income from No. 1 & No. 2 peaches, $216,000 & $144,144

Analysis Component

3. Do you think delivery costs fit the definition of a joint cost? Explain.

Dixon's has several departments that occupy all floors of a two-story building that includes a basement floor. Dixon rented this building under a long-term lease negotiated when rental rates were low. The departmental accounting system has a single account, Building Occupancy Cost, in its ledger. The types and amounts of occupancy costs recorded in this account for the current period follow.

PROBLEM SET B

Problem 22-1B
Allocation of building occupancy costs to departments

P1

Building rent	$300,000
Lighting expense	24,000
Cleaning expense	16,000
Total occupancy cost	$340,000

The building has 7,500 square feet on each of the upper two floors but only 5,000 square feet in the basement. In prior periods, the accounting manager merely divided the $340,000 occupancy cost by 20,000 square feet to find an average cost of $17 per square foot and then charged each department a building occupancy cost equal to this rate times the number of square feet that it occupies.

Alex Ferrero manages a department that occupies 2,000 square feet of basement floor space. In discussing the departmental reports with other managers, she questions whether using the same rate per square foot for all departments makes sense because different floor space has different values. Ferrero checked a recent real estate report of average local rental costs for similar space that shows first-floor space worth $40 per square foot, second-floor space worth $20 per square foot, and basement space worth $10 per square foot (excluding costs for lighting and cleaning).

Required

1. Allocate occupancy costs to Ferrero's department using the current allocation method.

2. Allocate the building rent cost to Ferrero's department in proportion to the relative market value of the floor space. Allocate to Ferrero's department the lighting and heating costs in proportion to the square feet occupied (ignoring floor space market values). Then, compute the total occupancy cost allocated to Ferrero's department.

Analysis Component

3. Which allocation method would you prefer if you were a manager of a basement department?

Problem 22-2B
Departmental contribution to income

P1

Sadar Company operates a store with two departments: videos and music. Information about those departments follows.

	Videos Department	Music Department
Sales	$370,500	$279,500
Cost of goods sold	320,000	175,000
Direct expenses		
Salaries	35,000	25,000
Maintenance	12,000	10,000
Utilities	5,000	4,500
Insurance	4,200	3,700

The company also incurred the following indirect costs.

Advertising	$15,000
Salaries	27,000
Office expenses	3,200

Indirect costs are allocated as follows: advertising on the basis of sales; salaries on the basis of number of employees; and office expenses on the basis of square footage. Additional information about the departments follows.

Department	Square footage	Number of employees
Videos	5,000	3
Music	3,000	2

Required

1. For each department, determine the departmental contribution to overhead and the departmental net income.

2. Should the video department be eliminated? Explain.

Problem 22-3B
Departmental income
statements; forecasts P1

Hollywood Entertainment began operations in January 2011 with two operating (selling) departments and one service (office) department. Its departmental income statements follow.

HOLLYWOOD ENTERTAINMENT
Departmental Income Statements
For Year Ended December 31, 2011

	Movies	Video Games	Combined
Sales	$540,000	$180,000	$720,000
Cost of goods sold	378,000	138,600	516,600
Gross profit	162,000	41,400	203,400
Direct expenses			
Sales salaries	35,000	14,000	49,000
Advertising	10,500	5,500	16,000
Store supplies used	3,300	700	4,000
Depreciation—Equipment	4,200	2,800	7,000
Total direct expenses	53,000	23,000	76,000
Allocated expenses			
Rent expense	29,520	6,480	36,000
Utilities expense	4,100	900	5,000
Share of office department expenses	39,000	14,000	53,000
Total allocated expenses	72,620	21,380	94,000
Total expenses	125,620	44,380	170,000
Net income (loss)	$ 36,380	$ (2,980)	$ 33,400

The company plans to open a third department in January 2012 that will sell compact discs. Management predicts that the new department will generate $250,000 in sales with a 35% gross profit margin and will require the following direct expenses: sales salaries, $18,000; advertising, $10,000; store supplies, $1,500; and equipment depreciation, $1,000. The company will fit the new department into the current rented space by taking some square footage from the other two departments. When opened, the new compact disc department will fill one-fourth of the space presently used by the movie department and one-third of the space used by the video game department. Management does not predict any increase in utilities costs, which are allocated to the departments in proportion to occupied space (or rent expense). The company allocates office department expenses to the operating departments in proportion to their sales. It expects the compact disc department to increase total office department expenses by $8,000. Since the compact disc department will bring new customers into the store, management expects sales in both the movie and video game departments to increase by 10%. No changes for those departments' gross profit percents or for their direct expenses are expected, except for store supplies used, which will increase in proportion to sales.

Required

Prepare departmental income statements that show the company's predicted results of operations for calendar year 2012 for the three operating (selling) departments and their combined totals. (Round percents to the nearest one-tenth and dollar amounts to the nearest whole dollar.)

Check   2012 forecasted movies net income (sales), $64,885 ($594,000)

Aaron Braun, the plant manager of SOS Co.'s Chicago plant, is responsible for all of that plant's costs other than his own salary. The plant has two operating departments and one service department. The refrigerator and dishwasher operating departments manufacture different products and have their own managers. The office department, which Braun also manages, provides services equally to the two operating departments. A monthly budget is prepared for each operating department and the office department. The company's responsibility accounting system must assemble information to present budgeted and actual costs in performance reports for each operating department manager and the plant manager. Each performance report includes only those costs that a particular operating department manager can control: raw materials, wages, supplies used, and equipment depreciation. The plant manager is responsible for the department managers' salaries, utilities, building rent, office salaries other than his own, and other office costs plus all costs controlled by the two operating department managers. The April departmental budgets and actual costs for the two operating departments follow.

Problem 22-4B
Responsibility accounting performance reports; controllable and budgeted costs

C2

	Budget			Actual		
	Refrigerators	Dishwashers	Combined	Refrigerators	Dishwashers	Combined
Raw materials	$400,000	$200,000	$ 600,000	$375,000	$200,000	$ 575,000
Employee wages	172,000	80,000	252,000	174,700	76,800	251,500
Dept. manager salary	55,000	49,000	104,000	55,000	46,500	101,500
Supplies used	15,000	9,000	24,000	14,000	10,000	24,000
Depreciation—Equip.	53,000	37,000	90,000	53,000	37,000	90,000
Utilities.......................	30,000	18,000	48,000	34,500	20,700	55,200
Building rent	63,000	17,000	80,000	61,000	15,000	76,000
Office department costs	70,500	70,500	141,000	75,000	75,000	150,000
Totals	$858,500	$480,500	$1,339,000	$842,200	$481,000	$1,323,200

The office department's budget and its actual costs for April follow.

	Budget	Actual
Plant manager salary	$ 80,000	$ 85,000
Other office salaries	40,000	35,200
Other office costs	21,000	29,800
Totals	$141,000	$150,000

Required

1. Prepare responsibility accounting performance reports like those in Exhibit 22.22 that list costs controlled by the following:

   Check (1a) $23,300 total under budget

   a. Manager of the refrigerator department.

   b. Manager of the dishwasher department.

   (1c) Chicago plant controllable costs, $20,800 total under budget

   c. Manager of the Chicago plant.

   In each report, include the budgeted and actual costs for the month and show the amount by which each actual cost is over or under the budgeted amount.

Analysis Component

2. Did the plant manager or the operating department managers better manage costs? Explain.

Problem 22-5B^B
Allocation of joint costs

C4

Sarah and Stew Salsa own and operate a tomato grove. After preparing the following income statement, Sarah believes they should have offered the No. 3 tomatoes to the public for free and saved themselves time and money.

SARAH AND STEW SALSA Income Statement For Year Ended December 31, 2011				
	No. 1	No. 2	No. 3	Combined
Sales (by grade)				
No. 1: 400,000 lbs. @ $1.50/lb	$600,000			
No. 2: 300,000 lbs. @ $1.00/lb		$300,000		
No. 3: 100,000 lbs. @ $0.30/lb			$ 30,000	
Total sales				$930,000
Costs				
Land preparation, seeding, and cultivating @ $0.50/lb	200,000	150,000	50,000	400,000
Harvesting, sorting, and grading @ $0.02/lb....................	8,000	6,000	2,000	16,000
Delivery costs @ $0.01/lb	4,000	3,000	1,000	8,000
Total costs	212,000	159,000	53,000	424,000
Net income (loss)	$388,000	$141,000	$(23,000)	$506,000

In preparing this statement, Sarah and Stew allocated joint costs among the grades on a physical basis as an equal amount per pound. Also, their delivery cost records show that $7,000 of the $8,000 relates to crating the No. 1 and No. 2 tomatoes and hauling them to the buyer. The remaining $1,000 of delivery costs is for crating the No. 3 tomatoes and hauling them to the cannery.

Required

1. Prepare reports showing cost allocations on a sales value basis to the three grades of tomatoes. Separate the delivery costs into the amounts directly identifiable with each grade. Then allocate any shared delivery costs on the basis of the relative sales value of each grade. (Round percents to the nearest one-tenth and dollar amounts to the nearest whole dollar.)

2. Using your answers to part 1, prepare an income statement using the joint costs allocated on a sales value basis.

Check (1) $512 harvesting, sorting and grading costs allocated to No. 3

(2) Net income from No. 1 & No. 2 tomatoes, $327,011 & $163,301

Analysis Component

3. Do you think delivery costs fit the definition of a joint cost? Explain.

Beyond the Numbers

BTN 22-1 Review **Research In Motion**'s income statement in Appendix A and identify its revenues for the years ended February 27, 2010, February 28, 2009, and March 1, 2008. For the year ended February 27, 2010, Research In Motion reports the following product revenue mix. (Assume that its product revenue mix is the same for each of the three years reported when answering the requirements.)

REPORTING IN ACTION

C1

RIM

Devices	Service	Software	Other
81%	14%	2%	3%

Required

1. Compute the amount of revenue from each of its product lines for the years ended February 27, 2010, February 28, 2009, and March 1, 2008.

2. If Research In Motion wishes to evaluate each of its product lines, how can it allocate its operating expenses to each of them to determine each product line's profitability?

Fast Forward

3. Access Research In Motion's annual report for a fiscal year ending after February 27, 2010, from its Website (**RIM.com**) or the SEC's EDGAR database (**sec.gov**). Compute its revenues for its product lines for the most recent year(s). Compare those results to those from part 1. How has its product mix changed?

BTN 22-2 **Research In Motion**, **Apple**, and **Palm** compete across the world in several markets.

COMPARATIVE ANALYSIS

C2

RIM

Apple

Palm

Required

1. Design a three-tier responsibility accounting organizational chart assuming that you have available internal information for all three companies. Use Exhibit 22.21 as an example. The goal of this assignment is to design a reporting framework for the companies; numbers are not required. Limit your reporting framework to sales activity only.

2. Explain why it is important to have similar performance reports when comparing performance within a company (and across different companies). Be specific in your response.

BTN 22-3 Senior Security Co. offers a range of security services for senior citizens. Each type of service is considered within a separate department. Mary Pincus, the overall manager, is compensated partly on the basis of departmental performance by staying within the quarterly cost budget. She often revises operations to make sure departments stay within budget. Says Pincus, "I will not go over budget even if it means slightly compromising the level and quality of service. These are minor compromises that don't significantly affect my clients, at least in the short term."

ETHICS CHALLENGE

P1

Required

1. Is there an ethical concern in this situation? If so, which parties are affected? Explain.

2. Can Mary Pincus take action to eliminate or reduce any ethical concerns? Explain.

3. What is Senior Security's ethical responsibility in offering professional services?

COMMUNICATING IN PRACTICE

P1

BTN 22-4   Home Station is a national home improvement chain with more than 100 stores throughout the country. The manager of each store receives a salary plus a bonus equal to a percent of the store's net income for the reporting period. The following net income calculation is on the Denver store manager's performance report for the recent monthly period.

Sales	$2,500,000
Cost of goods sold	800,000
Wages expense	500,000
Utilities expense	200,000
Home office expense	75,000
Net income	$ 925,000
Manager's bonus (0.5%)	$ 4,625

In previous periods, the bonus had also been 0.5% of net income, but the performance report had not included any charges for the home office expense, which is now assigned to each store as a percent of its sales.

Required

Assume that you are the national office manager. Write a one-half page memorandum to your store managers explaining why home office expense is in the new performance report.

TAKING IT TO THE NET

P1

BTN 22-5   This chapter described and used spreadsheets to prepare various managerial reports (see Exhibit 22-6). You can download from Websites various tutorials showing how spreadsheets are used in managerial accounting and other business applications.

Required

1. Link to the Website Lacher.com. Select "Excel Examples." Identify and list three tutorials for review.
2. Describe in a one-half page memorandum to your instructor how the applications described in each tutorial are helpful in business and managerial decision making.

TEAMWORK IN ACTION

P1 C2

BTN 22-6   Refer to Problem 22-1A involving the allocation of building occupancy costs to departments to answer the following requirements.

Required

1. Separate the class into 3-person teams. Each member of the 3-person team is assigned to complete one of the following tasks individually: (i) Allocate occupancy costs to the Diaz and Wright departments using the current allocation method. (ii) Allocate the depreciation, interest, and taxes occupancy costs to the Diaz and Wright departments in proportion to the relative market values of floor space. (iii) Allocate the heating, lighting, and maintenance costs to the Diaz and Wright departments in proportion to the square feet occupied (ignoring floor space market values). Confirm your answers with the instructor.
2. The two people assigned to task *ii* and task *iii* from part 1 are to meet and determine the total occupancy costs allocated to the Diaz and Wright departments. The person assigned to task *i* is to help with this determination.
3. Using answers for parts 1 and 2, the 3-person team is to discuss and explain which allocation method a manager of a second-floor department would prefer. Each team should be prepared to present their solutions to the class.

ENTREPRENEURIAL DECISION

P1

BTN 22-7   Skullcandy sells headphones and other audio-mobile accessories and apparel. The company's plans call for continued expansion into other types of products.

Required

1. How can Skullcandy use departmental income statements to assist in understanding and controlling operations?
2. Are departmental income statements always the best measure of a department's performance? Explain.
3. Provide examples of nonfinancial performace indicators Skullcandy might use as part of a balanced scorecard system of performance evaluation.

BTN 22-8   Visit a local movie theater and check out both its concession area and its showing areas. The manager of a theater must confront questions such as:

HITTING THE ROAD

C1 C2

- How much return do we earn on concessions?
- What types of movies generate the greatest sales?
- What types of movies generate the greatest net income?

Required

Assume that you are the new accounting manager for a 16-screen movie theater. You are to set up a responsibility accounting reporting framework for the theater.

1. Recommend how to segment the different departments of a movie theater for responsibility reporting.

2. Propose an expense allocation system for heat, rent, insurance, and maintenance costs of the theater.

BTN 22-9   Selected product data from Nokia (www.Nokia.com) follow.

GLOBAL DECISION

P1

NOKIA

Product Segment for Year Ended (EURm)	Net Sales		Operating Income	
	December 31, 2009	December 31, 2008	December 31, 2009	December 31, 2008
Devices & Services	€27,841	€35,084	€3,314	€5,816
NAVTEQ	579	318	(344)	(153)
Nokia Siemens Networks	12,564	15,308	(1,639)	(301)

Required

1. Compute the percentage growth in net sales for each product line from fiscal year 2008 to 2009. Round percents to one decimal.

2. Which product line's net sales grew the fastest?

3. Which segment was the most profitable?

4. How can Nokia's managers use this information?

ANSWERS TO MULTIPLE CHOICE QUIZ

1. b; [$641,250/($356,250 + $641,250 + $427,500)] × $150,000 = $67,500
2. c
3. d
4. b;

	Department X	Department Y	Department Z
Sales	$500,000	$200,000	$350,000
Cost of goods sold	350,000	75,000	150,000
Gross profit	150,000	125,000	200,000
Direct expenses............	50,000	20,000	75,000
Departmental contribution	$100,000	$105,000	$125,000

5. a; $100,000/$500,000 = 20%

23

Relevant Costing for Managerial Decisions

A Look Back

Chapter 22 focused on cost allocation and performance measurement. We identified several reports useful in measuring and analyzing the activities of a company, its departments, and its managers.

A Look at This Chapter

This chapter explains several tools and procedures useful for making and evaluating short-term managerial decisions. It also describes how to assess the consequences of such decisions.

A Look Ahead

Chapter 24 focuses on capital budgeting decisions. It explains and illustrates several methods that help identify projects with the higher return on investment.

Learning Objectives

CAP

CONCEPTUAL

C1 Describe the importance of relevant costs for short-term decisions. (p. 969)

ANALYTICAL

A1 Evaluate short-term managerial decisions using relevant costs. (p. 969)

A2 Determine product selling price based on total costs. (p. 977)

LP23

PROCEDURAL

P1 Identify relevant costs and apply them to managerial decisions. (p. 970)

Decision Insight

Top Dog!

SAN FRANCISCO, CA—Bothered by dealing with his dog's painful health problems, Marco Giannini started **Dogswell LLC (Dogswell.com),** a company devoted to developing foods to fight disease in dogs. The company combines natural ingredients with nutritional supplements like flaxseed, glucosamine, and taurine to make Happy Hips™, Mellow Mut™, and Biscuits with Benefits™.

Marco started with $30,000 of his own money and insight into the benefits of nutritional supplements after the failure of his venture into nutritional beverages. His first product was cage-free chicken jerky sold from plastic bags hanging from grocery store hooks. "The treat was very cost-effective, and it was easy to get shelf space for a small product that provided good contribution margins for retailers," explains Marco. Focusing on contribution margins also helps Marco and his Dogswell team make decisions on sales mix and whether to eliminate certain products. "Not all of our products have been successful, but we quickly push the successful ones and we take the bottom ones out of the market," admits Marco. Focusing on relevant costs and incremental revenues guides these important business decisions.

Marco applies high standards to his production process. Unlike some companies that might be able to rework substandard materials into a viable product, Marco says "raw materials that do not meet our specifications never enter our processing facilitities." Assessing payback periods, rates of return, and break-even points helps Marco make decisions on what, and when, to buy. While relevant costs are important, Marco stresses the importance of employees—"We didn't bring on human capital fast enough," he admits. And, says Marco, don't ignore factors such as employee morale and the company's image in making decisions.

Marco advises would-be entrepreneurs to develop the best product they can. He stresses "simplicity" as one key to success. "Make everything easy for the customer," says Marco. "We have a simple product line with easy-to-read ingredients. People appreciate that." With projected sales of over $21 million, that recipe is working.

[Sources: *Dogswell Company Website*, January 2011; *Los Angeles Business Journal,* November 2008; *Entrepeneur.com*, August 2008; *Pet Business,* September 2008]

Making business decisions involves choosing between alternative courses of action. Many factors affect business decisions, yet analysis typically focuses on finding the alternative that offers the highest return on investment or the greatest reduction in costs. In all situations, managers can reach a sounder decision if they identify the consequences of alternative choices in financial terms. This chapter explains several methods of analysis that can help managers make short-term business decisions.

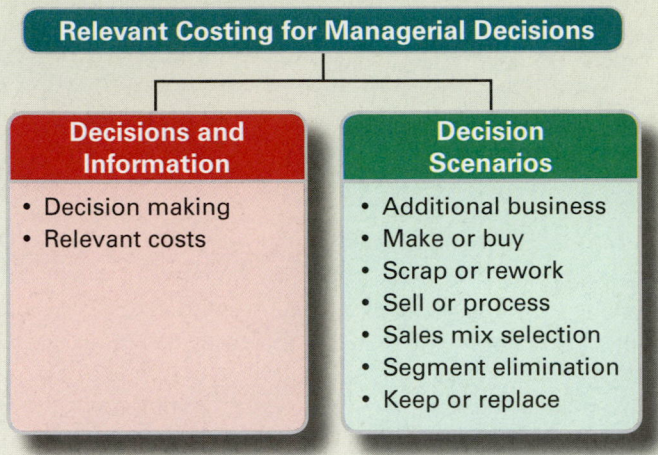

Relevant Costing for Managerial Decisions

Decisions and Information
- Decision making
- Relevant costs

Decision Scenarios
- Additional business
- Make or buy
- Scrap or rework
- Sell or process
- Sales mix selection
- Segment elimination
- Keep or replace

This chapter focuses on methods that use accounting information to make important managerial decisions. Most of these cases involve short-term decisions. This differs from methods used for longer-term managerial decisions that are described in the next chapter.

DECISIONS AND INFORMATION

This section explains how managers make decisions and the information relevant to those decisions.

Decision Making

Managerial decision making involves five steps: (1) define the decision task, (2) identify alternative courses of action, (3) collect relevant information and evaluate each alternative, (4) select the preferred course of action, and (5) analyze and assess decisions made. These five steps are illustrated in Exhibit 23.1.

EXHIBIT 23.1

Managerial Decision Making

Define Task and Goal → Identify Alternative Actions → Collect Relevant Information → Select Course of Action → Analyze and Assess Decision

Both managerial and financial accounting information play an important role in most management decisions. The accounting system is expected to provide primarily *financial* information such as performance reports and budget analyses for decision making. *Nonfinancial* information is also relevant, however; it includes information on environmental effects, political sensitivities, and social responsibility.

Relevant Costs

Most financial measures of revenues and costs from accounting systems are based on historical costs. Although historical costs are important and useful for many tasks such as product pricing and the control and monitoring of business activities, we sometimes find that an analysis of *relevant costs,* or *avoidable costs,* is especially useful. Three types of costs are pertinent to our discussion of relevant costs: sunk costs, out-of-pocket costs, and opportunity costs.

A *sunk cost* arises from a past decision and cannot be avoided or changed; it is irrelevant to future decisions. An example is the cost of computer equipment previously purchased by a company. Most of a company's allocated costs, including fixed overhead items such as depreciation and administrative expenses, are sunk costs.

An *out-of-pocket cost* requires a future outlay of cash and is relevant for current and future decision making. These costs are usually the direct result of management's decisions. For instance, future purchases of computer equipment involve out-of-pocket costs.

An *opportunity cost* is the potential benefit lost by taking a specific action when two or more alternative choices are available. An example is a student giving up wages from a job to attend summer school. Companies continually must choose from alternative courses of action. For instance, a company making standardized products might be approached by a customer to supply a special (nonstandard) product. A decision to accept or reject the special order must consider not only the profit to be made from the special order but also the profit given up by devoting time and resources to this order instead of pursuing an alternative project. The profit given up is an opportunity cost. Consideration of opportunity costs is important. The implications extend to internal resource allocation decisions. For instance, a computer manufacturer must decide between internally manufacturing a chip versus buying it externally. In another case, management of a multidivisional company must decide whether to continue operating or close a particular division.

Besides relevant costs, management must also consider the relevant benefits associated with a decision. **Relevant benefits** refer to the additional or *incremental* revenue generated by selecting a particular course of action over another. For instance, a student must decide the relevant benefits of taking one course over another. In sum, both relevant costs and relevant benefits are crucial to managerial decision making.

 Describe the importance of relevant costs for short-term decisions.

Example: Depreciation and amortization are allocations of the original cost of plant and intangible assets. Are they out-of-pocket costs? *Answer:* No; they are sunk costs.

Point: Opportunity costs are not entered in accounting records. This does not reduce their relevance for managerial decisions.

MANAGERIAL DECISION SCENARIOS

Managers experience many different scenarios that require analyzing alternative actions and making a decision. We describe several different types of decision scenarios in this section. We set these tasks in the context of FasTrac, an exercise supplies and equipment manufacturer introduced earlier. *We treat each of these decision tasks as separate from each other.*

 Evaluate short-term managerial decisions using relevant costs.

Additional Business

FasTrac is operating at its normal level of 80% of full capacity. At this level, it produces and sells approximately 100,000 units of product annually. Its per unit and annual total costs are shown in Exhibit 23.2.

	Per Unit	Annual Total
Sales (100,000 units)	$10.00	$1,000,000
Direct materials	(3.50)	(350,000)
Direct labor	(2.20)	(220,000)
Overhead	(1.10)	(110,000)
Selling expenses	(1.40)	(140,000)
Administrative expenses	(0.80)	(80,000)
Total costs and expenses	(9.00)	(900,000)
Operating income	$ 1.00	$ 100,000

EXHIBIT 23.2

Selected Operating Income Data

A current buyer of FasTrac's products wants to purchase additional units of its product and export them to another country. This buyer offers to buy 10,000 units of the product at $8.50 per unit, or $1.50 less than the current price. The offer price is low, but FasTrac is considering the proposal because this sale would be several times larger than any single previous sale and it would use idle capacity. Also, the units will be exported, so this new business will not affect current sales.

To determine whether to accept or reject this order, management needs to know whether accepting the offer will increase net income. The analysis in Exhibit 23.3 shows that if management relies on per unit historical costs, it would reject the sale because it yields a loss. However, historical costs are *not* relevant to this decision. Instead, the relevant costs are the additional costs, called **incremental costs.** These costs, also called *differential costs,* are the additional costs incurred if a company pursues a certain course of action. FasTrac's incremental costs are those related to the added volume that this new order would bring.

EXHIBIT 23.3

Analysis of Additional Business Using Historical Costs

	Per Unit	Total
Sales (10,000 additional units)	$ 8.50	$ 85,000
Direct materials	(3.50)	(35,000)
Direct labor	(2.20)	(22,000)
Overhead	(1.10)	(11,000)
Selling expenses	(1.40)	(14,000)
Administrative expenses	(0.80)	(8,000)
Total costs and expenses	(9.00)	(90,000)
Operating loss	$(0.50)	$(5,000)

P1 Identify relevant costs and apply them to managerial decisions.

To make its decision, FasTrac must analyze the costs of this new business in a different manner. The following information regarding the order is available:

- Manufacturing 10,000 additional units requires direct materials of $3.50 per unit and direct labor of $2.20 per unit (same as for all other units).
- Manufacturing 10,000 additional units adds $5,000 of incremental overhead costs for power, packaging, and indirect labor (all variable costs).
- Incremental commissions and selling expenses from this sale of 10,000 additional units would be $2,000 (all variable costs).
- Incremental administrative expenses of $1,000 for clerical efforts are needed (all fixed costs) with the sale of 10,000 additional units.

We use this information, as shown in Exhibit 23.4, to assess how accepting this new business will affect FasTrac's income.

EXHIBIT 23.4

Analysis of Additional Business Using Relevant Costs

	Current Business	Additional Business	Combined
Sales	$1,000,000	$ 85,000	$1,085,000
Direct materials	(350,000)	(35,000)	(385,000)
Direct labor	(220,000)	(22,000)	(242,000)
Overhead	(110,000)	(5,000)	(115,000)
Selling expenses	(140,000)	(2,000)	(142,000)
Administrative expense	(80,000)	(1,000)	(81,000)
Total costs and expenses	(900,000)	(65,000)	(965,000)
Operating income	$ 100,000	$ 20,000	$ 120,000

The analysis of relevant costs in Exhibit 23.4 suggests that the additional business be accepted. It would provide $85,000 of added revenue while incurring only $65,000 of added costs. This would yield $20,000 of additional pretax income, or a pretax profit margin of 23.5%. More generally, FasTrac would increase its income with any price that exceeded $6.50 per unit ($65,000 incremental cost/10,000 additional units).

An analysis of the incremental costs pertaining to the additional volume is always relevant for this type of decision. We must proceed cautiously, however, when the additional volume approaches or exceeds the factory's existing available capacity. If the additional volume requires the company to expand its capacity by obtaining more equipment, more space, or more personnel, the incremental costs could quickly exceed the incremental revenue. Another cautionary note is the effect on existing sales. All new units of the extra business will be sold outside FasTrac's normal domestic sales channels. If accepting additional business would cause existing sales to decline, this information must be included in our analysis. The contribution margin lost from a decline in sales is an opportunity cost.

The key point is that *management must not blindly use historical costs, especially allocated overhead costs.* Instead, the accounting system needs to provide information about the incremental costs to be incurred if the additional business is accepted.

Example: Exhibit 23.4 uses quantitative information. Suggest some qualitative factors to be considered when deciding whether to accept this project. *Answer:* (1) Impact on relationships with other customers and (2) Improved relationship with customer buying additional units.

■ Decision Maker   Answer — p. 980

Partner You are a partner in a small accounting firm that specializes in keeping the books and preparing taxes for clients. A local restaurant is interested in obtaining these services from your firm. Identify factors that are relevant in deciding whether to accept the engagement. ■

Make or Buy

The managerial decision to make or buy a component for one of its current products is commonplace and depends on incremental costs. To illustrate, FasTrac has excess productive capacity it can use to manufacture Part 417, a component of the main product it sells. The part is currently purchased and delivered to the plant at a cost of $1.20 per unit. FasTrac estimates that making Part 417 would cost $0.45 for direct materials, $0.50 for direct labor, and an undetermined amount for overhead. The task is to determine how much overhead to add to these costs so we can decide whether to make or buy Part 417. If FasTrac's normal predetermined overhead application rate is 100% of direct labor cost, we might be tempted to conclude that overhead cost is $0.50 per unit, computed as 100% of the $0.50 direct labor cost. We would then mistakenly conclude that total cost is $1.45 ($0.45 of materials + $0.50 of labor + $0.50 of overhead). A wrong decision in this case would be to conclude that the company is better off buying the part at $1.20 each than making it for $1.45 each.

Instead, as we explained earlier, only incremental overhead costs are relevant in this situation. Thus, we must compute an *incremental overhead rate.* Incremental overhead costs might include, for example, additional power for operating machines, extra supplies, added cleanup costs, materials handling, and quality control. We can prepare a per unit analysis in this case as shown in Exhibit 23.5.

	Make	Buy
Direct materials	$0.45	—
Direct labor	0.50	—
Overhead costs	[?]	—
Purchase price	—	$1.20
Total incremental costs	$0.95 + [?]	$1.20

EXHIBIT 23.5

Make or Buy Analysis

We can see that if incremental overhead costs are less than $0.25 per unit, the total cost of making the component is less than the purchase price of $1.20 and FasTrac should make the part. FasTrac's decision rule in this case is that any amount of overhead less than $0.25 per unit yields a total cost for Part 417 that is less than the $1.20 purchase price. FasTrac must consider several nonfinancial factors in the make or buy decision, including product quality, timeliness of delivery (especially in a just-in-time setting), reactions of customers and suppliers, and other intangibles such as employee morale and workload. It must also consider whether making the part requires incremental fixed costs to expand plant capacity. When these added factors are considered, small cost differences may not matter.

Point: Managers must consider nonfinancial factors when making decisions.

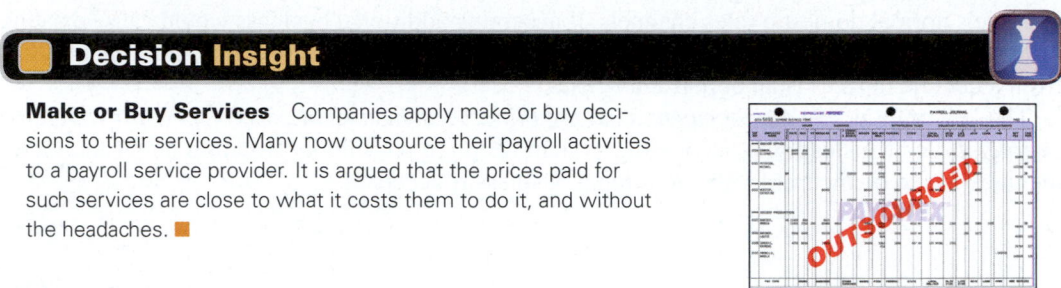

Decision Insight

Make or Buy Services   Companies apply make or buy decisions to their services. Many now outsource their payroll activities to a payroll service provider. It is argued that the prices paid for such services are close to what it costs them to do it, and without the headaches. ∎

Scrap or Rework

Managers often must make a decision on whether to scrap or rework products in process. Remember that costs already incurred in manufacturing the units of a product that do not meet quality standards are sunk costs that have been incurred and cannot be changed. Sunk costs are irrelevant in any decision on whether to sell the substandard units as scrap or to rework them to meet quality standards.

To illustrate, assume that FasTrac has 10,000 defective units of a product that have already cost $1 per unit to manufacture. These units can be sold as is (as scrap) for $0.40 each, or they can be reworked for $0.80 per unit and then sold for their full price of $1.50 each. Should FasTrac sell the units as scrap or rework them?

To make this decision, management must recognize that the already incurred manufacturing costs of $1 per unit are sunk (unavoidable). These costs are *entirely irrelevant* to the decision. In addition, we must be certain that all costs of reworking defects, including interfering with normal operations, are accounted for in our analysis. For instance, reworking the defects means that FasTrac is unable to manufacture 10,000 *new* units with an incremental cost of $1 per unit and a selling price of $1.50 per unit, meaning it incurs an opportunity cost equal to the lost $5,000 net return from making and selling 10,000 new units. This opportunity cost is the difference between the $15,000 revenue (10,000 units × $1.50) from selling these new units and their $10,000 manufacturing costs (10,000 units × $1). Our analysis is reflected in Exhibit 23.6.

EXHIBIT 23.6

Scrap or Rework Analysis

	Scrap	Rework
Sale of scrapped/reworked units	$ 4,000	$15,000
Less costs to rework defects		(8,000)
Less opportunity cost of not making new units		**(5,000)**
Incremental net income	**$4,000**	**$ 2,000**

The analysis yields a $2,000 difference in favor of scrapping the defects, yielding a total incremental net income of $4,000. If we had failed to include the opportunity costs of $5,000, the rework option would have shown an income of $7,000 instead of $2,000, mistakenly making the reworking appear more favorable than scrapping.

Quick Check

Answers — p. 981

1. A company receives a special order for 200 units that requires stamping the buyer's name on each unit, yielding an additional fixed cost of $400 to its normal costs. Without the order, the company is operating at 75% of capacity and produces 7,500 units of product at the following costs:

Direct materials	$37,500
Direct labor	60,000
Overhead (30% variable)	20,000
Selling expenses (60% variable)	25,000

The special order will not affect normal unit sales and will not increase fixed overhead and selling expenses. Variable selling expenses on the special order are reduced to one-half the normal amount. The price per unit necessary to earn $1,000 on this order is (*a*) $14.80, (*b*) $15.80, (*c*) $19.80, (*d*) $20.80, or (*e*) $21.80.

2. What are the incremental costs of accepting additional business?

Sell or Process

The managerial decision to sell partially completed products as is or to process them further for sale depends significantly on relevant costs. To illustrate, suppose that FasTrac has 40,000 units of partially finished Product Q. It has already spent $0.75 per unit to manufacture these 40,000 units at a $30,000 total cost. FasTrac can sell the 40,000 units to another manufacturer as raw material for $50,000. Alternatively, it can process them further and produce finished products X, Y, and Z at an incremental cost of $2 per unit. The added processing yields the products and revenues shown in Exhibit 23.7. FasTrac must decide whether the added revenues from selling finished products X, Y, and Z exceed the costs of finishing them.

Product	Price	Units	Revenues
Product X	$4.00	10,000	$ 40,000
Product Y	6.00	22,000	132,000
Product Z	8.00	6,000	48,000
Spoilage	—	2,000	0
Totals		40,000	**$220,000**

EXHIBIT 23.7

Revenues from Processing Further

Exhibit 23.8 shows the two-step analysis for this decision. First, FasTrac computes its incremental revenue from further processing Q into products X, Y, and Z. This amount is the difference between the $220,000 revenue from the further processed products and the $50,000 FasTrac will give up by not selling Q as is (a $50,000 opportunity cost). Second, FasTrac computes its incremental costs from further processing Q into X, Y, and Z. This amount is $80,000 (40,000 units × $2 incremental cost). The analysis shows that FasTrac can earn incremental net income of $90,000 from a decision to further process Q. (Notice that the earlier incurred $30,000 manufacturing cost for the 40,000 units of Product Q does not appear in Exhibit 23.8 because it is a sunk cost and as such is irrelevant to the decision.)

Example: Does the decision change if incremental costs in Exhibit 23.8 increase to $4 per unit and the opportunity cost increases to $95,000? *Answer:* Yes. There is now an incremental net loss of $35,000.

Revenue if processed	$220,000
Revenue if sold as is	(50,000)
Incremental revenue	170,000
Cost to process	(80,000)
Incremental net income	**$ 90,000**

EXHIBIT 23.8

Sell or Process Analysis

Quick Check
Answers — p. 981

3. A company has already incurred a $1,000 cost in partially producing its four products. Their selling prices when partially and fully processed follow with additional costs necessary to finish these partially processed units:

Product	Unfinished Selling Price	Finished Selling Price	Further Processing Costs
Alpha	$300	$600	$150
Beta.	450	900	300
Gamma.	275	425	125
Delta.	150	210	75

Which product(s) should *not* be processed further, (a) Alpha, (b) Beta, (c) Gamma, or (d) Delta?

4. Under what conditions is a sunk cost relevant to decision making?

Sales Mix Selection

Point: A method called *linear programming* is useful for finding the optimal sales mix for several products subject to many market and production constraints. This method is described in advanced courses.

When a company sells a mix of products, some are likely to be more profitable than others. Management is often wise to concentrate sales efforts on more profitable products. If production facilities or other factors are limited, an increase in the production and sale of one product usually requires reducing the production and sale of others. In this case, management must identify the most profitable combination, or *sales mix* of products. To identify the best sales mix, management must know the contribution margin of each product, the facilities required to produce each product, any constraints on these facilities, and its markets.

To illustrate, assume that FasTrac makes and sells two products, A and B. The same machines are used to produce both products. A and B have the following selling prices and variable costs per unit:

	Product A	Product B
Selling price per unit.................	$5.00	$7.50
Variable costs per unit	3.50	5.50
Contribution margin per unit.........	$1.50	$2.00

The variable costs are included in the analysis because they are the incremental costs of producing these products within the existing capacity of 100,000 machine hours per month. We consider three separate cases.

Demand Is Unlimited and Products Use Same Inputs   Assume that (1) each product requires 1 machine hour per unit for production and (2) the markets for these products are unlimited. Under these conditions, FasTrac should produce as much of Product B as it can because of its larger contribution margin of $2 per unit. At full capacity, FasTrac would produce $200,000 of total contribution margin per month, computed as $2 per unit times 100,000 machine hours.

Demand Is Unlimited and Products Use Different Inputs   Assume that (1) Product A requires 1 machine hour per unit, (2) Product B requires 2 machine hours per unit, and (3) the markets for these products are unlimited. Under these conditions, FasTrac should produce as much of Product A as it can because it has a contribution margin of $1.50 per machine hour compared with only $1 per machine hour for Product B. Exhibit 23.9 shows the relevant analysis.

EXHIBIT 23.9

Sales Mix Analysis

	Product A	Product B
Selling price per unit	$5.00	$7.50
Variable costs per unit	3.50	5.50
Contribution margin per unit	$1.50	$2.00
Machine hours per unit...........................	1.0	2.0
Contribution margin per machine hour.........	**$1.50**	**$1.00**

At its full capacity of 100,000 machine hours, FasTrac would produce 100,000 units of Product A, yielding $150,000 of total contribution margin per month. In contrast, if it uses all 100,000 hours to produce Product B, only 50,000 units would be produced yielding a contribution margin of $100,000. These results suggest that when a company faces excess demand and limited capacity, only the most profitable product per input should be manufactured.

Demand Is Limited   The need for a mix of different products arises when market demand is not sufficient to allow a company to sell all that it produces. For instance, assume that (1) Product A requires 1 machine hour per unit, (2) Product B requires 2 machine hours per unit, and (3) the market for Product A is limited to 80,000 units. Under these conditions, FasTrac should produce no more than 80,000 units of Product A. This would leave another 20,000 machine hours of capacity for making Product B. FasTrac should use this spare capacity to produce 10,000 units of Product B. This sales mix would maximize FasTrac's total contribution margin per month at an amount of $140,000.

Example: If Product B's variable costs per unit increase to $6, Product A's variable costs per unit decrease to $3, and the same machine hours per unit are used, which product should FasTrac produce? *Answer:* Product A. Its contribution margin of $2 per machine hour is higher than B's $.75 per machine hour.

Decision Insight

Companies such as **Gap**, **Abercrombie & Fitch**, and **American Eagle** must continuously monitor and manage the sales mix of their product lists. Selling their products in hundreds of countries and territories further complicates their decision process. The contribution margin of each product is crucial to their product mix strategies. ■

Segment Elimination

When a segment such as a department or division is performing poorly, management must consider eliminating it. Segment information on either net income (loss) or its contribution to overhead is not sufficient for this decision. Instead, we must look at the segment's avoidable expenses and unavoidable expenses. **Avoidable expenses,** also called *escapable expenses,* are amounts the company would not incur if it eliminated the segment. **Unavoidable expenses,** also called *inescapable expenses,* are amounts that would continue even if the segment is eliminated.

To illustrate, FasTrac considers eliminating its treadmill division because its $48,300 total expenses are higher than its $47,800 sales. Classification of this division's operating expenses into avoidable or unavoidable expenses is shown in Exhibit 23.10.

Point: FasTrac might consider buying another machine to reduce the constraint on production. A strategy designed to reduce the impact of constraints or bottlenecks, on production, is called the *theory of constraints.*

	Total	Avoidable Expenses	Unavoidable Expenses
Cost of goods sold	$ 30,000	$ 30,000	—
Direct expenses			
Salaries expense	7,900	7,900	—
Depreciation expense—Equipment	200	—	$ 200
Indirect expenses			
Rent and utilities expense	3,150	—	3,150
Advertising expense	400	400	—
Insurance expense	400	300	100
Service department costs			
Share of office department expenses	3,060	2,200	860
Share of purchasing expenses	3,190	1,000	2,190
Total	**$48,300**	**$41,800**	**$6,500**

EXHIBIT 23.10

Classification of Segment Operating Expenses for Analysis

FasTrac's analysis shows that it can avoid $41,800 expenses if it eliminates the treadmill division. Because this division's sales are $47,800, eliminating it will cause FasTrac to lose $6,000 of income. *Our decision rule is that a segment is a candidate for elimination if its revenues are less than its avoidable expenses.* Avoidable expenses can be viewed as the costs to generate this segment's revenues.

When considering elimination of a segment, we must assess its impact on other segments. A segment could be unprofitable on its own, but it might still contribute to other segments' revenues and profits. It is possible then to continue a segment even when its revenues are less than its avoidable expenses. Similarly, a profitable segment might be discontinued if its space, assets, or staff can be more profitably used by expanding existing segments or by creating new ones. Our decision to keep or eliminate a segment requires a more complex analysis than simply looking at a segment's performance report. Such reports provide useful information, but they do not provide all the information necessary for this decision.

Keep or Replace Equipment

Businesses periodically must decide whether to keep using equipment or replace it. Advances in technology typically mean newer equipment can operate more efficiently and at lower cost than older equipment. In making the decision to keep or replace equipment, managers must decide whether the reduction in *variable* manufacturing costs with the new equipment over its useful life is greater than the net purchase price of the equipment. In this setting, the net purchase price of the equipment is its total cost minus any trade-in allowance or cash receipt for the old equipment.

For example, FasTrac has a piece of manufacturing equipment with a book value (cost minus accumulated depreciation) of $20,000 and a remaining useful life of four years. At the end of four years the equipment will have a salvage value of zero. The market value of the equipment is currently $25,000.

FasTrac can purchase a new machine for $100,000 and receive $25,000 in return for trading in its old machine. The new machine will reduce FasTrac's variable manufacturing costs by $18,000 per year over the four-year life of the new machine. FasTrac's incremental analysis is shown in Exhibit 23.11.

EXHIBIT 23.11

Keep or Replace Analysis

	Increase or (Decrease) in Net Income
Cost to buy new machine	$(100,000)
Cash received to trade in old machine	25,000
Reduction in variable manufacturing costs*	72,000
Total increase (decrease) in net income	$ (3,000)

*18,000 × 4 years

The analysis in Exhibit 23.11 shows that FasTrac should not replace the old equipment with this newer version as it will decrease income by $3,000. Note, the book value of the old equipment ($20,000) is not relevant to this analysis. Book value is a sunk cost, and it cannot be changed regardless of whether FasTrac keeps or replaces this equipment.

Qualitative Decision Factors

Managers must consider qualitative factors in making managerial decisions. Consider a decision on whether to buy a component from an outside supplier or continue to make it. Several qualitative decision factors must be considered. For example, the quality, delivery, and reputation of the proposed supplier are important. The effects from deciding not to make the component can include potential layoffs and impaired worker morale. Consider another situation in which a company is considering a one-time sale to a new customer at a special low price. Qualitative factors to consider in this situation include the effects of a low price on the company's image and the threat that regular customers might demand a similar price. The company must also consider whether this customer is really a one-time customer. If not, can it continue to offer this low price in the long run? Clearly, management cannot rely solely on financial data to make such decisions.

Quick Check

Answers — p. 981

5. What is the difference between avoidable and unavoidable expenses?

6. A segment is a candidate for elimination if (*a*) its revenues are less than its avoidable expenses, (*b*) it has a net loss, (*c*) its unavoidable expenses are higher than its revenues.

Setting Product Price      **Decision Analysis**

Relevant costs are useful to management in determining prices for special short-term decisions. But longer run pricing decisions of management need to cover both variable and fixed costs, and yield a profit.

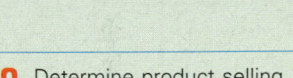
A2   Determine product selling price based on total costs.

There are several methods to help management in setting prices. The *cost-plus* methods are probably the most common, where management adds a **markup** to cost to reach a target price. We will describe the **total cost method,** where management sets price equal to the product's total costs plus a desired profit on the product. This is a four-step process:

1. Determine total costs.

$$\text{Total costs} = \frac{\text{Production (direct materials,}}{\text{direct labor, and overhead)}} + \frac{\text{Nonproduction (selling and}}{\text{administrative) costs}}$$

2. Determine total cost per unit.

$$\text{Total cost per unit} = \text{Total costs} \div \text{Total units expected to be produced and sold}$$

3. Determine the dollar markup per unit.

$$\text{Markup per unit} = \text{Total cost per unit} \times \text{Markup percentage}$$

where Markup percentage = Desired profit/Total costs

4. Determine selling price per unit.

$$\text{Selling price per unit} = \text{Total cost per unit} + \text{Markup per unit}$$

To illustrate, consider a company that produces MP3 players. The company desires a 20% return on its assets of $1,000,000, and it expects to produce and sell 10,000 players. The following additional company information is available:

Variable costs (per unit)	
Production costs	$44
Nonproduction costs	6
Fixed costs (in dollars)	
Overhead.	$140,000
Nonproduction	60,000

We apply our four-step process to determine price.

1. Total costs = Production costs + Nonproduction costs
   = [($44 × 10,000 units) + $140,000] + [($6 × 10,000 units) + $60,000]
   = $700,000

2. Total cost per unit = Total costs/Total units expected to be produced and sold
   = $700,000/10,000
   = $70

3. Markup per unit = Total cost per unit × (Desired profit/Total costs)
   = $70 × [(20% × $1,000,000)/$700,000]
   = $20

4. Selling price per unit = Total cost per unit + Markup per unit
   = $70 + $20
   = $90

To verify that our price yields the $200,000 desired profit (20% × $1,000,000), we compute the following simplified income statement using the information above.

Sales ($90 × 10,000)	$900,000
Expenses	
Variable ($50 × 10,000)	500,000
Fixed ($140,000 + $60,000)	200,000
Income	$200,000

Companies use cost-plus pricing as a starting point for determining selling prices. Many factors determine price, including consumer preferences and competition.

DEMONSTRATION PROBLEM

Determine the appropriate action in each of the following managerial decision situations.

1. Packer Company is operating at 80% of its manufacturing capacity of 100,000 product units per year. A chain store has offered to buy an additional 10,000 units at $22 each and sell them to customers so as not to compete with Packer Company. The following data are available.

Costs at 80% Capacity	Per Unit	Total
Direct materials	$ 8.00	$ 640,000
Direct labor	7.00	560,000
Overhead (fixed and variable)	12.50	1,000,000
Totals	$27.50	$2,200,000

In producing 10,000 additional units, fixed overhead costs would remain at their current level but incremental variable overhead costs of $3 per unit would be incurred. Should the company accept or reject this order?

2. Green Company uses Part JR3 in manufacturing its products. It has always purchased this part from a supplier for $40 each. It recently upgraded its own manufacturing capabilities and has enough excess capacity (including trained workers) to begin manufacturing Part JR3 instead of buying it. The company prepares the following cost projections of making the part, assuming that overhead is allocated to the part at the normal predetermined rate of 200% of direct labor cost.

Direct materials	$11
Direct labor	15
Overhead (fixed and variable) (200% of direct labor)	30
Total	$56

The required volume of output to produce the part will not require any incremental fixed overhead. Incremental variable overhead cost will be $17 per unit. Should the company make or buy this part?

3. Gold Company's manufacturing process causes a relatively large number of defective parts to be produced. The defective parts can be (a) sold for scrap, (b) melted to recover the recycled metal for reuse, or (c) reworked to be good units. Reworking defective parts reduces the output of other good units because no excess capacity exists. Each unit reworked means that one new unit cannot be produced. The following information reflects 500 defective parts currently available.

Proceeds of selling as scrap	$2,500
Additional cost of melting down defective parts	400
Cost of purchases avoided by using recycled metal from defects	4,800
Cost to rework 500 defective parts	
Direct materials	0
Direct labor	1,500
Incremental overhead	1,750
Cost to produce 500 new parts	
Direct materials	6,000
Direct labor	5,000
Incremental overhead	3,200
Selling price per good unit	40

Should the company melt the parts, sell them as scrap, or rework them?

PLANNING THE SOLUTION

- Determine whether Packer Company should accept the additional business by finding the incremental costs of materials, labor, and overhead that will be incurred if the order is accepted. Omit fixed costs that the order will not increase. If the incremental revenue exceeds the incremental cost, accept the order.

- Determine whether Green Company should make or buy the component by finding the incremental cost of making each unit. If the incremental cost exceeds the purchase price, the component should be purchased. If the incremental cost is less than the purchase price, make the component.

- Determine whether Gold Company should sell the defective parts, melt them down and recycle the metal, or rework them. To compare the three choices, examine all costs incurred and benefits received from the alternatives in working with the 500 defective units versus the production of 500 new units. For the scrapping alternative, include the costs of producing 500 new units and subtract the $2,500 proceeds from selling the old ones. For the melting alternative, include the costs of melting the defective units, add the net cost of new materials in excess over those obtained from recycling, and add the direct labor and overhead costs. For the reworking alternative, add the costs of direct labor and incremental overhead. Select the alternative that has the lowest cost. The cost assigned to the 500 defective units is sunk and not relevant in choosing among the three alternatives.

SOLUTION TO DEMONSTRATION PROBLEM

1. This decision involves accepting additional business. Since current unit costs are $27.50, it appears initially as if the offer to sell for $22 should be rejected, but the $27.50 cost includes fixed costs. When the analysis includes only *incremental* costs, the per unit cost is as shown in the following table. The offer should be accepted because it will produce $4 of additional profit per unit (computed as $22 price less $18 incremental cost), which yields a total profit of $40,000 for the 10,000 additional units.

Direct materials	$ 8.00
Direct labor	7.00
Variable overhead (given)	3.00
Total incremental cost	$18.00

2. For this make or buy decision, the analysis must not include the $13 nonincremental overhead per unit ($30 − $17). When only the $17 incremental overhead is included, the relevant unit cost of manufacturing the part is shown in the following table. It would be better to continue buying the part for $40 instead of making it for $43.

Direct materials	$11.00
Direct labor	15.00
Variable overhead	17.00
Total incremental cost	$43.00

3. The goal of this scrap or rework decision is to identify the alternative that produces the greatest net benefit to the company. To compare the alternatives, we determine the net cost of obtaining 500 marketable units as follows:

Incremental Cost to Produce 500 Marketable Units	Sell as Is	Melt and Recycle	Rework Units
Direct materials			
New materials	$ 6,000	$6,000	
Recycled metal materials		(4,800)	
Net materials cost		1,200	
Melting costs		400	
Total direct materials cost	6,000	1,600	
Direct labor	5,000	5,000	$1,500
Incremental overhead	3,200	3,200	1,750
Cost to produce 500 marketable units	14,200	9,800	3,250
Less proceeds of selling defects as scrap	(2,500)		
Opportunity costs*			5,800
Net cost	$11,700	$9,800	$9,050

* The $5,800 opportunity cost is the lost contribution margin from not being able to produce and sell 500 units because of reworking, computed as ($40 − [$14,200/500 units]) × 500 units.

The incremental cost of 500 marketable parts is smallest if the defects are reworked.

Summary

C1 Describe the importance of relevant costs for short-term decisions. A company must rely on relevant costs pertaining to alternative courses of action rather than historical costs. Out-of-pocket expenses and opportunity costs are relevant because these are avoidable; sunk costs are irrelevant because they result from past decisions and are therefore unavoidable. Managers must also consider the relevant benefits associated with alternative decisions.

A1 Evaluate short-term managerial decisions using relevant costs. Relevant costs are useful in making decisions such as to accept additional business, make or buy, and sell as is or process further. For example, the relevant factors in deciding whether to produce and sell additional units of product are incremental costs and incremental revenues from the additional volume.

A2 Determine product selling price based on total costs. Product selling price is estimated using total production and nonproduction costs plus a markup. Price is set to yield management's desired profit for the company.

P1 Identify relevant costs and apply them to managerial decisions. Several illustrations apply relevant costs to managerial decisions, such as whether to accept additional business; make or buy; scrap or rework products; sell products or process them further; or eliminate a segment and how to select the best sales mix.

Guidance Answers to Decision Maker and Decision Ethics

Partner You should identify the differences between existing clients and this potential client. A key difference is that the restaurant business has additional inventory components (groceries, vegetables, meats, etc.) and is likely to have a higher proportion of depreciable assets. These differences imply that the partner must spend more hours auditing the records and understanding the business, regulations, and standards that pertain to the restaurant business. Such differences suggest that the partner must use a different "formula" for quoting a price to this potential client vis-à-vis current clients.

Guidance Answers to Quick Checks

1. *e*; Variable costs per unit for this order of 200 units follow:

Direct materials ($37,500/7,500)	$ 5.00
Direct labor ($60,000/7,500)	8.00
Variable overhead [(0.30 × $20,000)/7,500]	0.80
Variable selling expenses [(0.60 × $25,000 × 0.5)/7,500]	1.00
Total variable costs per unit	$14.80

Cost to produce special order: (200 × $14.80) + $400
= $3,360.
Price per unit to earn $1,000: ($3,360 + $1,000)/200 = $21.80.

2. They are the additional (new) costs of accepting new business.

3. *d*;

	Incremental benefits		Incremental costs
Alpha	$300 ($600 − $300)	>	$150 (given)
Beta	$450 ($900 − $450)	>	$300 (given)
Gamma	$150 ($425 − $275)	>	$125 (given)
Delta	$ 60 ($210 − $150)	<	$ 75 (given)

4. A sunk cost is *never* relevant because it results from a past decision and is already incurred.

5. Avoidable expenses are ones a company will not incur by eliminating a segment; unavoidable expenses will continue even after a segment is eliminated.

6. *a*

Key Terms
mhhe.com/wildFINMAN4e

Avoidable expense (p. 975)   **Markup** (p. 977)   **Total cost method** (p. 977)

Incremental cost (p. 970)   **Relevant benefits** (p. 969)   **Unavoidable expense** (p. 975)

Multiple Choice Quiz   Answers on p. 995   mhhe.com/wildFINMAN4e

Additional Quiz Questions are available at the book's Website.

1. A company inadvertently produced 3,000 defective MP3 players. The players cost $12 each to produce. A recycler offers to purchase the defective players as they are for $8 each. The production manager reports that the defects can be corrected for $10 each, enabling them to be sold at their regular market price of $19 each. The company should:
  a. Correct the defect and sell them at the regular price.
  b. Sell the players to the recycler for $8 each.
  c. Sell 2,000 to the recycler and repair the rest.
  d. Sell 1,000 to the recycler and repair the rest.
  e. Throw the players away.

2. A company's productive capacity is limited to 480,000 machine hours. Product X requires 10 machine hours to produce; and Product Y requires 2 machine hours to produce. Product X sells for $32 per unit and has variable costs of $12 per unit; Product Y sells for $24 per unit and has variable costs of $10 per unit. Assuming that the company can sell as many of either product as it produces, it should:
  a. Produce X and Y in the ratio of 57% and 43%.
  b. Produce X and Y in the ratio of 83% X and 17% Y.
  c. Produce equal amounts of Product X and Product Y.
  d. Produce only Product X.
  e. Produce only Product Y.

3. A company receives a special one-time order for 3,000 units of its product at $15 per unit. The company has excess capacity and it currently produces and sells the units at $20 each to its regular customers. Production costs are $13.50 per unit, which includes $9 of variable costs. To produce the special order, the company must incur additional fixed costs of $5,000. Should the company accept the special order?
  a. Yes, because incremental revenue exceeds incremental costs.
  b. No, because incremental costs exceed incremental revenue.
  c. No, because the units are being sold for $5 less than the regular price.
  d. Yes, because incremental costs exceed incremental revenue.
  e. No, because incremental cost exceeds $15 per unit when total costs are considered.

4. A cost that cannot be changed because it arises from a past decision and is irrelevant to future decisions is
  a. An uncontrollable cost.
  b. An out-of-pocket cost.
  c. A sunk cost.
  d. An opportunity cost.
  e. An incremental cost.

5. The potential benefit of one alternative that is lost by choosing another is known as
  a. An alternative cost.
  b. A sunk cost.
  c. A differential cost.
  d. An opportunity cost.
  e. An out-of-pocket cost.

▮ Icon denotes assignments that involve decision making.

Discussion Questions

1. **▮** Identify the five steps involved in the managerial decision-making process.

2. Is nonfinancial information ever useful in managerial decision making?

3. What is a relevant cost? Identify the two types of relevant costs.

4. **▮** Why are sunk costs irrelevant in deciding whether to sell a product in its present condition or to make it into a new product through additional processing?

5. **Palm** has many types of costs. What is an out-of-pocket cost? Are out-of-pocket costs recorded in the accounting records?   **Palm**

6. **Nokia** confronts opportunity costs. What is an opportunity cost? Are opportunity costs recorded in the accounting records?   **NOKIA**

7. **▮** Identify some qualitative factors that should be considered when making managerial decisions.

8. **▮** Identify the incremental costs incurred by **Apple** for shipping one additional iPod from a warehouse to a retail store along with the store's normal order of 75 iPods.   **Apple**

9. **Apple** is considering eliminating one of its stores in a large U.S. city. What are some factors that it should consider in making this decision?   **Apple**

10. **▮** Assume that **Research In Motion** manufactures and sells 500,000 units of a product at $30 per unit in domestic markets. It costs $20 per unit to manufacture ($13 variable cost per unit, $7 fixed cost per unit). Can you describe a situation under which the company is willing to sell an additional 25,000 units of the product in an international market at $15 per unit?   **RIM**

▮▮ connect

QUICK STUDY

QS 23-1

Identification of relevant costs

P1

Lopez Company has been approached by a new customer to provide 2,000 units of its regular product at a special price of $6 per unit. The regular selling price of the product is $8 per unit. Lopez is operating at 75% of its capacity of 10,000 units. Identify whether the following costs are relevant to Lopez's decision as to whether to accept the order at the special selling price. No additional fixed manufacturing overhead will be incurred because of this order. The only additional selling expense on this order will be a $0.50 per unit shipping cost. There will be no additional administrative expenses because of this order. Place an X in the appropriate column to identify whether the cost is relevant or irrelevant to accepting this order.

Item	Relevant	Not relevant
a. Selling price of $6.00 per unit	_____	_____
b. Direct materials cost of $1.00 per unit	_____	_____
c. Direct labor of $2.00 per unit	_____	_____
d. Variable manufacturing overhead of $1.50 per unit	_____	_____
e. Fixed manufacturing overhead of $0.75 per unit	_____	_____
f. Regular selling expenses of $1.25 per unit	_____	_____
g. Additional selling expenses of $0.50 per unit	_____	_____
h. Administrative expenses of $0.60 per unit	_____	_____

QS 23-2

Analysis of relevant costs

A1

Refer to the data in QS 23-1. Based on financial considerations alone, should Lopez accept this order at the special price? Explain.

QS 23-3

Identification of relevant nonfinancial factors

P1

Refer to QS 23-1 and QS 23-2. What nonfinancial factors should Lopez consider before accepting this order? Explain.

QS 23-4

Sell or process

P1 A1

Garcia Company has 10,000 units of its product that were produced last year at a total cost of $150,000. The units were damaged in a rain storm because the warehouse where they were stored developed a leak in the roof. Garcia can sell the units as is for $2 each or it can repair the units at a total cost of $18,000 and then sell them for $5 each. Should Garcia sell the units as is or repair them and then sell them? Explain.

Label each of the following statements as either true ("T") or false ("F").

1. An opportunity cost is the potential benefit that is lost by taking a specific action when two or more alternative choices are available.

2. A sunk cost will change with a future course of action.

3. An out-of-pocket cost requires a current and/or future outlay of cash.

4. Relevant costs are also known as unavoidable costs.

5. Incremental costs are also known as differential costs.

QS 23-5
Relevant costs
C1

Mo-Kan Company incurs a $6 per unit cost for Product A, which it currently manufactures and sells for $9 per unit. Instead of manufacturing and selling this product, the company can purchase Product B for $5 per unit and sell it for $8 per unit. If it does so, unit sales would remain unchanged and $5 of the $6 per unit costs assigned to Product A would be eliminated. Should the company continue to manufacture Product A or purchase Product B for resale?

QS 23-6
Analysis of incremental costs
A1 P1

Memory Lane Company can sell all units of computer memory X and Y that it can produce, but it has limited production capacity. It can produce four units of X per hour *or* three units of Y per hour, and it has 8,000 production hours available. Contribution margin is $10 for product X and $8 for product Y. What is the most profitable sales mix for this company?

QS 23-7
Selection of sales mix
A1

Kirk Company sells bikes for $600 each. The company currently sells 7,500 bikes per year and could make as many as 10,000 bikes per year. The bikes cost $450 each to make; $300 in variable costs per bike and $150 of fixed costs per bike. Kirk received an offer from a potential customer who wants to buy 1,500 bikes for $500 each. Incremental fixed costs to make this order are $100,000. No other costs will change if this order is accepted. Compute Kirk's additional income (ignore taxes) if it accepts this order.

QS 23-8
Decision to accept additional business
A1 P1

Z-Tech mistakenly produced 10,000 defective cell phones. The phones cost $60 each to produce. A salvage company will buy the defective phones as they are for $30 each. It would cost Z-Tech $80 per phone to rework the phones. If the phones are reworked, Z-Tech could sell them for $125 each. Compute the incremental net income from reworking the phones.

QS 23-9
Scrap or rework
A1 P1

Bartel Company produces a product that can either be sold as is or processed further. Bartel has already spent $10,000 to produce 250 units that can be sold now for $13,500 to another manufacturer. Alternatively, Bartel can process the units further at an incremental cost of $36 per unit. If Bartel processes further, the units can be sold for $100 each. Compute the incremental income if Bartel processes further.

QS 23-10
Sell or process decision
A1 P1

A guitar manufacturer is considering eliminating its electric guitar division because its $76,000 expenses are higher than its $72,000 sales. The company reports the following expenses for this division. Should the division be eliminated?

QS 23-11
Segment elimination
A1 P1

	Avoidable Expenses	Unavoidable Expenses
Cost of goods sold	$55,000	
Direct expenses	6,250	$2,250
Indirect expenses	470	3,600
Service department costs	7,000	1,430

Tak Company has a machine with a book value of $50,000 and a remaining five-year useful life. A new machine is available at a cost of $75,000, and Tak can also receive $40,000 for trading in its old machine. The new machine will reduce variable manufacturing costs by $12,000 per year over its five-year useful life. Should the machine be replaced?

QS 23-12
Keep or replace decision
A1 P1

EXERCISES

Exercise 23-1
Relevant costs
C1

Fill in each of the blanks below with the correct term.

1. Relevant costs are also known as _____.
2. An _____ requires a future outlay of cash and is relevant for current and future decision making.
3. An _____ is the potential benefit lost by taking a specific action when two or more alternative choices are available.
4. A _____ arises from a past decision and cannot be avoided or changed; it is irrelevant to future decisions.
5. _____ refer to the incremental revenue generated from taking one particular action over another.

Exercise 23-2
Scrap or rework
A1 P1

A company must decide between scrapping or reworking units that do not pass inspection. The company has 15,000 defective units that cost $6 per unit to manufacture. The units can be sold as is for $2.50 each, or they can be reworked for $4.50 each and then sold for the full price of $9 each. If the units are sold as is, the company will have to build 15,000 replacement units at a cost of $6 each, and sell them at the full price of $9 each. (1) What is the incremental income from selling the units as scrap? (2) What is the incremental income from reworking and selling the units? (3) Should the company sell the units as scrap or rework them?

Exercise 23-3
Keep or replace
A1 P1

Xu Company is considering replacing one of its manufacturing machines. The machine has a book value of $45,000 and a remaining useful life of 4 years, at which time its salvage value will be zero. It has a current market value of $55,000. Variable manufacturing costs are $34,000 per year for this machine. Information on two alternative replacement machines follows. Should Xu keep or replace its manufacturing machine? If the machine should be replaced, which alternative new machine should Xu purchase?

	Alternative A	Alternative B
Cost.....................................	$115,000	$125,000
Variable manufacturing costs per year.........	22,000	12,000

Exercise 23-4
Decision to accept additional business or not
A1 P1

Feist Co. expects to sell 200,000 units of its product in the next period with the following results.

Sales (200,000 units)	$3,000,000
Costs and expenses	
Direct materials................	400,000
Direct labor	800,000
Overhead.....................	200,000
Selling expenses................	300,000
Administrative expenses	514,000
Total costs and expenses...........	2,214,000
Net income	$ 786,000

The company has an opportunity to sell 20,000 additional units at $12 per unit. The additional sales would not affect its current expected sales. Direct materials and labor costs per unit would be the same for the additional units as they are for the regular units. However, the additional volume would create the following incremental costs: (1) total overhead would increase by 15% and (2) administrative expenses would increase by $86,000. Prepare an analysis to determine whether the company should accept or reject the offer to sell additional units at the reduced price of $12 per unit.

Check   Income increase, $4,000

Exercise 23-5
Decision to accept new business or not
P1 A1

Goshford Company produces a single product and has capacity to produce 100,000 units per month. Costs to produce its current sales of 80,000 units follow. The regular selling price of the product is $100 per unit. Management is approached by a new customer who wants to purchase 20,000 units of the product for $75 per unit. If the order is accepted, there will be no additional fixed manufacturing overhead, and no additional fixed selling and administrative expenses. The customer is not in the company's regular selling territory, so there will be a $5 per unit shipping expense in addition to the regular variable selling and administrative expenses.

	Per Unit	Costs at 80,000 Units
Direct materials..............................	$12.50	$1,000,000
Direct labor......................................	15.00	1,200,000
Variable manufacturing overhead	10.00	800,000
Fixed manufacturing overhead	17.50	1,400,000
Variable selling and administrative expenses	14.00	1,120,000
Fixed selling and administrative expenses	13.00	1,040,000
Totals	$82.00	$6,560,000

Required

1. Determine whether management should accept or reject the new business.
2. What nonfinancial factors should management consider when deciding whether to take this order?

Check (1) Additional volume effect on net income, $370,000

Santos Company currently manufactures one of its crucial parts at a cost of $3.40 per unit. This cost is based on a normal production rate of 50,000 units per year. Variable costs are $1.50 per unit, fixed costs related to making this part are $50,000 per year, and allocated fixed costs are $45,000 per year. Allocated fixed costs are unavoidable whether the company makes or buys the part. Santos is considering buying the part from a supplier for a quoted price of $2.70 per unit guaranteed for a three-year period. Should the company continue to manufacture the part, or should it buy the part from the outside supplier? Support your answer with analyses.

Exercise 23-6
Make or buy decision

A1 P1

Check $10,000 increased costs to buy

Gelb Company currently manufactures 40,000 units of a key component for its manufacturing process at a cost of $4.45 per unit. Variable costs are $1.95 per unit, fixed costs related to making this component are $65,000 per year, and allocated fixed costs are $58,500 per year. The allocated fixed costs are unavoidable whether the company makes or buys this component. The company is considering buying this component from a supplier for $3.50 per unit. Should it continue to manufacture the component, or should it buy this component from the outside supplier? Support your decision with analysis of the data provided.

Exercise 23-7
Make or buy decision   P1 A1

Check Increased cost to make, $3,000

Cantrell Company has already manufactured 20,000 units of Product A at a cost of $20 per unit. The 20,000 units can be sold at this stage for $500,000. Alternatively, the units can be further processed at a $300,000 total additional cost and be converted into 4,000 units of Product B and 8,000 units of Product C. Per unit selling price for Product B is $75 and for Product C is $50. Prepare an analysis that shows whether the 20,000 units of Product A should be processed further or not.

Exercise 23-8
Sell or process decision

A1 P1

Varto Company has 7,000 units of its sole product in inventory that it produced last year at a cost of $22 each. This year's model is superior to last year's and the 7,000 units cannot be sold at last year's regular selling price of $35 each. Varto has two alternatives for these items: (1) they can be sold to a wholesaler for $8 each, or (2) they can be reworked at a cost of $125,000 and then sold for $25 each. Prepare an analysis to determine whether Varto should sell the products as is or rework them and then sell them.

Exercise 23-9
Sell or rework decision
P1 A1

Check Incremental net income of reworking, $(6,000)

Suresh Co. expects its five departments to yield the following income for next year.

Exercise 23-10
Analysis of income effects from eliminating departments

A1

File Edit View Insert Format Tools Data Window Help

		Dept. M	Dept. N	Dept. O	Dept. P	Dept. T
2	Sales	$31,500	$17,500	$28,000	$21,000	$14,000
3	Expenses					
4	Avoidable	4,900	18,200	11,200	7,000	18,900
5	Unavoidable	25,900	6,300	2,100	14,700	4,900
6	Total expenses	30,800	24,500	13,300	21,700	23,800
7	Net income (loss)	$ 700	$ (7,000)	$14,700	$ (700)	$ (9,800)

Sheet1 Sheet2 Sheet3

Recompute and prepare the departmental income statements (including a combined total column) for the company under each of the following separate scenarios: Management (1) does not eliminate any department, (2) eliminates departments with expected net losses, and (3) eliminates departments with sales dollars that are less than avoidable expenses. Explain your answers to parts 2 and 3.

Check Total income (loss)
(2) $(10,500), (3) $3,500

Exercise 23-11
Income analysis of eliminating departments
A1

Marinette Company makes several products, including canoes. The company has been experiencing losses from its canoe segment and is considering dropping that product line. The following information is available regarding its canoe segment. Should management discontinue the manufacturing of canoes? Support your decision.

MARINETTE COMPANY Income Statement—Canoe Segment		
Sales		$2,000,000
Variable costs		
Direct materials	$450,000	
Direct labor	500,000	
Variable overhead	300,000	
Variable selling and administrative	200,000	
Total variable costs		1,450,000
Contribution margin		550,000
Fixed costs		
Direct	375,000	
Indirect	300,000	
Total fixed costs		675,000
Net income		$ (125,000)

Check Income impact if canoe segment dropped, $(175,000)

Exercise 23-12
Sales mix determination and analysis
A1

Bethel Company owns a machine that can produce two specialized products. Production time for Product TLX is two units per hour and for Product MTV is five units per hour. The machine's capacity is 2,200 hours per year. Both products are sold to a single customer who has agreed to buy all of the company's output up to a maximum of 3,750 units of Product TLX and 2,000 units of Product MTV. Selling prices and variable costs per unit to produce the products follow. Determine (1) the company's most profitable sales mix and (2) the contribution margin that results from that sales mix.

	Product TLX	Product MTV
Selling price per unit	$12.50	$7.50
Variable costs per unit	3.75	4.50

Check (2) $37,688

Exercise 23-13
Sales mix
A1

Childress Company produces three products, K1, S5, and G9. Each product uses the same type of direct material. K1 uses 4 pounds of the material, S5 uses 3 pounds of the material, and G9 uses 6 pounds of the material. Demand for all products is strong, but only 50,000 pounds of material are available. Information about the selling price per unit and variable cost per unit of each product follows. Orders for which product should be produced and filled first, then second, and then third? Support your answer.

	K1	S5	G9
Selling price	$160	$112	$210
Variable costs	96	85	144

Check K1 contribution margin per pound, $16

 connect

Cayman Products manufactures and sells to wholesalers approximately 300,000 packages per year of underwater markers at $4 per package. Annual costs for the production and sale of this quantity are shown in the table.

Direct materials................	$384,000
Direct labor	96,000
Overhead.....................	288,000
Selling expenses...............	120,000
Administrative expenses	80,000
Total costs and expenses.........	$968,000

A new wholesaler has offered to buy 50,000 packages for $3.44 each. These markers would be marketed under the wholesaler's name and would not affect Cayman Products' sales through its normal channels. A study of the costs of this additional business reveals the following:

● Direct materials costs are 100% variable.

● Per unit direct labor costs for the additional units would be 50% higher than normal because their production would require overtime pay at one-and-one-half times the usual labor rate.

● 25% of the normal annual overhead costs are fixed at any production level from 250,000 to 400,000 units. The remaining 75% of the annual overhead cost is variable with volume.

● Accepting the new business would involve no additional selling expenses.

● Accepting the new business would increase administrative expenses by a $4,000 fixed amount.

Required

Prepare a three-column comparative income statement that shows the following:

1. Annual operating income without the special order (column 1).

2. Annual operating income received from the new business only (column 2).

3. Combined annual operating income from normal business and the new business (column 3).

Calla Company produces skateboards that sell for $50 per unit. The company currently has the capacity to produce 90,000 skateboards per year, but is selling 80,000 skateboards per year. Annual costs for 80,000 skateboards follow.

Direct materials................	$ 800,000
Direct labor	640,000
Overhead.....................	960,000
Selling expenses...............	560,000
Administrative expenses	480,000
Total costs and expenses.........	$3,440,000

A new retail store has offered to buy 10,000 of its skateboards for $45 per unit. The store is in a different market from Calla's regular customers and it would not affect regular sales. A study of its costs in anticipation of this additional business reveals the following:

● Direct materials and direct labor are 100% variable.

● Thirty percent of overhead is fixed at any production level from 80,000 units to 90,000 units; the remaining 70% of annual overhead costs are variable with respect to volume.

● Selling expenses are 60% variable with respect to number of units sold, and the other 40% of selling expenses are fixed.

● There will be an additional $2 per unit selling expense for this order.

● Administrative expenses would increase by a $1,000 fixed amount.

PROBLEM SET A

Problem 23-1A
Analysis of income effects of additional business

A1 P1

 eXcel

mhhe.com/wildFINMAN4e

Check   Operating income:
(1) $232,000, (2) $44,000

Problem 23-2A
Analysis of income effects of additional business

P1 A1

Required

1. Prepare a three-column comparative income statement that reports the following:

    a. Annual income without the special order.

Check (1b) Added income from
order, $123,000

    b. Annual income from the special order.

    c. Combined annual income from normal business and the new business.

2. Should Calla accept this order? What nonfinancial factors should Calla consider? Explain.

Analysis Component

3. Assume that the new customer wants to buy 15,000 units instead of 10,000 units—it will only buy 15,000 units or none and will not take a partial order. Without any computations, how does this change your answer for part 2?

Problem 23-3A

Make or buy

P1 A1

Haver Company currently produces component RX5 for its sole product. The current cost per unit to manufacture the required 50,000 units of RX5 follows.

Direct materials	$ 5.00
Direct labor	8.00
Overhead	9.00
Total cost per unit	$22.00

Direct materials and direct labor are 100% variable. Overhead is 80% fixed. An outside supplier has offered to supply the 50,000 units of RX5 for $18.00 per unit.

Required

Check (1) Incremental cost to
make RX5, $740,000

1. Determine whether the company should make or buy the RX5.

2. What factors beside cost must management consider when deciding whether to make or buy RX5?

Problem 23-4A

Sell or process

P1 A1

Harold Manufacturing produces denim clothing. This year, it produced 5,000 denim jackets at a manufacturing cost of $45 each. These jackets were damaged in the warehouse during storage. Management investigated the matter and identified three alternatives for these jackets.

1. Jackets can be sold to a second-hand clothing shop for $6 each.

2. Jackets can be disassembled at a cost of $32,000 and sold to a recycler for $12 each.

3. Jackets can be reworked and turned into good jackets. However, with the damage, management estimates it will be able to assemble the good parts of the 5,000 jackets into only 3,000 jackets. The remaining pieces of fabric will be discarded. The cost of reworking the jackets will be $102,000, but the jackets can then be sold for their regular price of $45 each.

Required

Check Incremental income for
alternative 2, $28,000

Which alternative should Harold choose? Show analysis for each alternative.

Problem 23-5A

Analysis of sales mix strategies

A1

Ortiz Company is able to produce two products, G and B, with the same machine in its factory. The following information is available.

	Product G	Product B
Selling price per unit	$120	$160
Variable costs per unit.	40	90
Contribution margin per unit	$ 80	$ 70
Machine hours to produce 1 unit	0.8 hours	2.0 hours
Maximum unit sales per month.	400 units	350 units

The company presently operates the machine for a single eight-hour shift for 22 working days each month. Management is thinking about operating the machine for two shifts, which will increase its productivity by another eight hours per day for 22 days per month. This change would require $6,500 additional fixed costs per month.

Required

1. Determine the contribution margin per machine hour that each product generates.

2. How many units of Product G and Product B should the company produce if it continues to operate with only one shift? How much total contribution margin does this mix produce each month?

3. If the company adds another shift, how many units of Product G and Product B should it produce? How much total contribution margin would this mix produce each month? Should the company add the new shift? Explain.

4. Suppose that the company determines that it can increase Product G's maximum sales to 440 units per month by spending $2,000 per month in marketing efforts. Should the company pursue this strategy and the double shift? Explain.

Check   Units of Product G: (2) 220, (3) 400, (4) 440

Home Decor Company's management is trying to decide whether to eliminate Department 200, which has produced losses or low profits for several years. The company's 2011 departmental income statement shows the following.

Problem 23-6A
Analysis of possible elimination of a department

A1

HOME DECOR COMPANY Departmental Income Statements For Year Ended December 31, 2011			
	Dept. 100	Dept. 200	Combined
Sales	$872,000	$580,000	$1,452,000
Cost of goods sold	524,000	414,000	938,000
Gross profit	348,000	166,000	514,000
Operating expenses			
Direct expenses			
Advertising	34,000	24,000	58,000
Store supplies used	8,000	7,600	15,600
Depreciation—Store equipment.........	10,000	6,600	16,600
Total direct expenses	52,000	38,200	90,200
Allocated expenses			
Sales salaries	130,000	78,000	208,000
Rent expense.........................	18,880	9,440	28,320
Bad debts expense	19,800	16,200	36,000
Office salary	37,440	24,960	62,400
Insurance expense	4,000	2,200	6,200
Miscellaneous office expenses	4,800	3,200	8,000
Total allocated expenses	214,920	134,000	348,920
Total expenses	266,920	172,200	439,120
Net income (loss)	$ 81,080	$ (6,200)	$ 74,880

In analyzing whether to eliminate Department 200, management considers the following:

a. The company has one office worker who earns $1,200 per week, or $62,400 per year, and four salesclerks who each earn $1,000 per week, or $52,000 per year.

b. The full salaries of two salesclerks are charged to Department 100. The full salary of one salesclerk is charged to Department 200. The salary of the fourth clerk, who works half-time in both departments, is divided evenly between the two departments.

c. Eliminating Department 200 would avoid the sales salaries and the office salary currently allocated to it. However, management prefers another plan. Two salesclerks have indicated that they will be quitting soon. Management believes that their work can be done by the other two clerks if the one office worker works in sales half-time. Eliminating Department 200 will allow this shift of duties. If this change is implemented, half the office worker's salary would be reported as sales salaries and half would be reported as office salary.

d. The store building is rented under a long-term lease that cannot be changed. Therefore, Department 100 will use the space and equipment currently used by Department 200.

e. Closing Department 200 will eliminate its expenses for advertising, bad debts, and store supplies; 70% of the insurance expense allocated to it to cover its merchandise inventory; and 25% of the miscellaneous office expenses presently allocated to it.

Required

Check (1) Total expenses:
(a) $1,377,120, (b) $568,140

(2) Forecasted net income
without Department 200, $63,020

1. Prepare a three-column report that lists items and amounts for (a) the company's total expenses (including cost of goods sold)—in column 1, (b) the expenses that would be eliminated by closing Department 200—in column 2, and (c) the expenses that will continue—in column 3.

2. Prepare a forecasted annual income statement for the company reflecting the elimination of Department 200 assuming that it will not affect Department 100's sales and gross profit. The statement should reflect the reassignment of the office worker to one-half time as a salesclerk.

Analysis Component

3. Reconcile the company's combined net income with the forecasted net income assuming that Department 200 is eliminated (list both items and amounts). Analyze the reconciliation and explain why you think the department should or should not be eliminated.

PROBLEM SET B

Problem 23-1B
Analysis of income effects of additional business

A1 P1

Windtrax Company manufactures and sells to local wholesalers approximately 200,000 units per month at a sales price of $1 per unit. Monthly costs for the production and sale of this quantity follow.

Direct materials..............	$ 30,000
Direct labor.................	12,000
Overhead....................	50,000
Selling expenses..............	7,500
Administrative expenses........	31,500
Total costs and expenses.......	$131,000

A new out-of-state distributor has offered to buy 20,000 units next month for $0.80 each. These units would be marketed in other states and would not affect Windtrax's sales through its normal channels. A study of the costs of this new business reveals the following:

● Direct materials costs are 100% variable.

● Per unit direct labor costs for the additional units would be 100% higher than normal because their production would require double overtime pay to meet the distributor's deadline.

● Eighty percent of the normal annual overhead costs are fixed at any production level from 120,000 to 300,000 units. The remaining 20% is variable with volume.

● Accepting the new business would involve no additional selling expenses.

● Accepting the new business would increase administrative expenses by a $750 fixed amount.

Required

Prepare a three-column comparative income statement that shows the following:

1. Monthly operating income without the special order (column 1).

Check Operating income:
(1) $69,000, (2) $8,850

2. Monthly operating income received from the new business only (column 2).

3. Combined monthly operating income from normal business and the new business (column 3).

Problem 23-2B
Analysis of income effects of additional business

P1 A1

Mervin Company produces circuit boards that sell for $8 per unit. It currently has capacity to produce 600,000 circuit boards per year, but is selling 550,000 boards per year. Annual costs for the 550,000 circuit boards follow.

Direct materials..............	$ 825,000
Direct labor.................	1,100,000
Overhead....................	1,375,000
Selling expenses..............	275,000
Administrative expenses........	550,000
Total costs and expenses.......	$4,125,000

An overseas customer has offered to buy 50,000 circuit boards for $6 per unit. The customer is in a different market from its regular customers and would not affect regular sales. A study of its costs in anticipation of this additional business reveals the following:

- Direct materials and direct labor are 100% variable.
- Twenty percent of overhead is fixed at any production level from 550,000 units to 600,000 units; the remaining 80% of annual overhead costs are variable with respect to volume.
- Selling expenses are 40% variable with respect to number of units sold, and the other 60% of selling expenses are fixed.
- There will be an additional $0.20 per unit selling expense for this order.
- Administrative expenses would increase by a $700 fixed amount.

Required

1. Prepare a three-column comparative income statement that reports the following:
   a. Annual income without the special order.
   b. Annual income from the special order.
   c. Combined annual income from normal business and the new business.
2. Should management accept the order? What nonfinancial factors should Mervin consider? Explain.

Check   (1b) Additional income from order, $4,300

Analysis Component

3. Assume that the new customer wants to buy 100,000 units instead of 50,000 units—it will only buy 100,000 units or none and will not take a partial order. Without any computations, how does this change your answer in part 2?

Alto Company currently produces component TH1 for its sole product. The current cost per unit to manufacture its required 400,000 units of TH1 follows.

Problem 23-3B
Make or buy

P1 A1

Direct materials	$1.20
Direct labor	1.50
Overhead	6.00
Total cost per unit	$8.70

Direct materials and direct labor are 100% variable. Overhead is 75% fixed. An outside supplier has offered to supply the 400,000 units of TH1 for $4 per unit.

Required

1. Determine whether management should make or buy the TH1.
2. What factors besides cost must management consider when deciding whether to make or buy TH1?

Check   (1) Incremental cost to make TH1, $1,680,000

Micron Manufacturing produces electronic equipment. This year, it produced 7,500 oscilloscopes at a manufacturing cost of $300 each. These oscilloscopes were damaged in the warehouse during storage and, while usable, cannot be sold at their regular selling price of $500 each. Management has investigated the matter and has identified three alternatives for these oscilloscopes.

Problem 23-4B
Sell or process

P1   A1

1. They can be sold to a wholesaler for $75 each.
2. They can be disassembled at a cost of $400,000 and the parts sold to a recycler for $130 each.
3. They can be reworked and turned into good units. The cost of reworking the units will be $3,200,000, after which the units can be sold at their regular price of $500 each.

Required

Which alternative should management pursue? Show analysis for each alternative.

Check   Incremental income for alternative 2, $575,000

Problem 23-5B
Analysis of sales mix strategies

A1

Digits Company is able to produce two products, 22 and 44, with the same machine in its factory. The following information is available.

	Product 22	Product 44
Selling price per unit	$175	$200
Variable costs per unit..................	100	150
Contribution margin per unit	$ 75	$ 50
Machine hours to produce 1 unit	0.8 hours	0.5 hours
Maximum unit sales per month...........	525 units	450 units

The company presently operates the machine for a single eight-hour shift for 23 working days each month. Management is thinking about operating the machine for two shifts, which will increase its productivity by another eight hours per day for 23 days per month. This change would require $5,000 additional fixed costs per month.

Required

1. Determine the contribution margin per machine hour that each product generates.

2. How many units of Product 22 and Product 44 should the company produce if it continues to operate with only one shift? How much total contribution margin does this mix produce each month?

Check Units of Product 44: (2) 368, (3) 450, (4) 500

3. If the company adds another shift, how many units of Product 22 and Product 44 should it produce? How much total contribution margin would this mix produce each month? Should the company add the new shift? Explain.

4. Suppose that the company determines that it can increase Product 44's maximum sales to 500 units per month by spending $500 per month in marketing efforts. Should the company pursue this strategy and the double shift? Explain.

Problem 23-6B
Analysis of possible elimination of a department

A1

Turftime Company's management is trying to decide whether to eliminate Department Z, which has produced low profits or losses for several years. The company's 2011 departmental income statement shows the following.

TURFTIME COMPANY Departmental Income Statements For Year Ended December 31, 2011			
	Dept. A	Dept. Z	Combined
Sales	$350,000	$87,500	$437,500
Cost of goods sold	230,650	62,550	293,200
Gross profit	119,350	24,950	144,300
Operating expenses			
Direct expenses			
Advertising	13,500	1,500	15,000
Store supplies used	2,800	700	3,500
Depreciation—Store equipment	7,000	3,500	10,500
Total direct expenses.................	23,300	5,700	29,000
Allocated expenses			
Sales salaries	35,100	11,700	46,800
Rent expense........................	11,040	2,760	13,800
Bad debts expense	10,500	2,000	12,500
Office salary	10,400	2,600	13,000
Insurance expense...................	2,100	700	2,800
Miscellaneous office expenses	850	1,250	2,100
Total allocated expenses	69,990	21,010	91,000
Total expenses.........................	93,290	26,710	120,000
Net income (loss)	$ 26,060	$(1,760)	$ 24,300

In analyzing whether to eliminate Department Z, management considers the following items:

a. The company has one office worker who earns $250 per week or $13,000 per year and four sales-clerks who each earn $225 per week or $11,700 per year.

b. The full salaries of three salesclerks are charged to Department A. The full salary of one salesclerk is charged to Department Z.

c. Eliminating Department Z would avoid the sales salaries and the office salary currently allocated to it. However, management prefers another plan. Two salesclerks have indicated that they will be quitting soon. Management believes that their work can be done by the two remaining clerks if the one office worker works in sales half-time. Eliminating Department Z will allow this shift of duties. If this change is implemented, half the office worker's salary would be reported as sales salaries and half would be reported as office salary.

d. The store building is rented under a long-term lease that cannot be changed. Therefore, Department A will use the space and equipment currently used by Department Z.

e. Closing Department Z will eliminate its expenses for advertising, bad debts, and store supplies; 65% of the insurance expense allocated to it to cover its merchandise inventory; and 30% of the miscellaneous office expenses presently allocated to it.

Required

1. Prepare a three-column report that lists items and amounts for (a) the company's total expenses (including cost of goods sold)—in column 1, (b) the expenses that would be eliminated by closing Department Z—in column 2, and (c) the expenses that will continue—in column 3.

2. Prepare a forecasted annual income statement for the company reflecting the elimination of Department Z assuming that it will not affect Department A's sales and gross profit. The statement should reflect the reassignment of the office worker to one-half time as a salesclerk.

Check   (1) Total expenses:
(a) $413,200, (b) $90,980

(2) Forecasted net income
without Department Z, $27,780

Analysis Component

3. Reconcile the company's combined net income with the forecasted net income assuming that Department Z is eliminated (list both items and amounts). Analyze the reconciliation and explain why you think the department should or should not be eliminated.

(This serial problem began in Chapter 1 and continues through most of the book. If previous chapter segments were not completed, the serial problem can begin at this point. It is helpful, but not necessary, to use the Working Papers that accompany the book.)

SERIAL PROBLEM
Business Solutions

A1

SP 23   Santana Rey has found that her line of computer desks and chairs has become very popular and she is finding it hard to keep up with demand. She knows that she cannot fill all of her orders for both items, so she decides she must determine the optimal sales mix given the resources she has available. Information about the desks and chairs follows.

	Desks	Chairs
Selling price per unit	$1,125	$375
Variable costs per unit	500	200
Contribution margin per unit	$ 625	$175
Direct labor hours per unit	5 hours	4 hours
Expected demand for next quarter	175 desks	50 chairs

Santana has determined that she only has 1,015 direct labor hours available for the next quarter and wants to optimize her contribution margin given the limited number of direct labor hours available.

Required

Determine the optimal sales mix and the contribution margin the business will earn at that sales mix.

Beyond the Numbers

REPORTING IN ACTION

A1

RIM

BTN 23-1   Assume that next year **Research In Motion** sells off its interest in TIP Communications (one of its subsidiaries). Forecasted information about the operations for RIM and TIP for that future fiscal year immediately prior to the proposed sale follows.

$ millions	RIM*	TIP	Total
Revenues	$20,943	$1,727	$22,670
Operating expenses†	20,321	1,971	22,292

* Does not include TIP results. † Includes cost of goods sold.

Required

1. Compute operating income for RIM and TIP, separately, and the total operating income for both.
2. If the results in part 1 for TIP are typical, why do you believe RIM decided to sell off its interest in TIP?

COMPARATIVE ANALYSIS

A1

RIM

Apple

Palm

BTN 23-2   **Research In Motion**, **Apple**, and **Palm** sell several different products; most are profitable but some are not. Teams of employees in each company make advertising, investment, and product mix decisions. A certain portion of advertising for both companies is on a local basis to a target audience.

Required

1. Find one major advertisement of a product or group of products for each company in your local newspaper. Contact the newspaper and ask the approximate cost of this ad space (for example, cost of one page or one-half page of advertising).
2. Estimate how many products this advertisement must sell to justify its cost. Begin by taking the product's sales price advertised for each company and assume a 20% contribution margin.
3. Prepare a one-half page memorandum explaining the importance of effective advertising when making a product mix decision. Be prepared to present your ideas in class.

ETHICS CHALLENGE

P1 A1

BTN 23-3   Bert Asiago, a salesperson for Convertco, received an order from a potential new customer for 50,000 units of Convertco's single product at a price $25 below its regular selling price of $65. Asiago knows that Convertco has the capacity to produce this order without affecting regular sales. He has spoken to Convertco's controller, Bia Morgan, who has informed Asiago that at the $40 selling price, Convertco will not be covering its variable costs of $42 for the product, and she recommends the order not be accepted. Asiago knows that variable costs include his sales commission of $4 per unit. If he accepts a $2 per unit commission, the sale will produce a contribution margin of zero. Asiago is eager to get the new customer because he believes that this could lead to the new customer becoming a regular customer.

Required

1. Determine the contribution margin per unit on the order as determined by the controller.
2. Determine the contribution margin per unit on the order as determined by Asiago if he takes the lower commission.
3. Do you recommend Convertco accept the special order? What factors must management consider?

COMMUNICATING IN PRACTICE

P1

BTN 23-4   Assume that you work for Greeble's Department Store, and your manager requests that you outline the pros and cons of discontinuing its hardware department. That department appears to be generating losses, and your manager believes that discontinuing it will increase overall store profits.

Required

Prepare a memorandum to your manager outlining what Greeble's management should consider when trying to decide whether to discontinue its hardware department.

TAKING IT TO THE NET

P1

BTN 23-5   Many companies must determine whether to internally produce their component parts or to outsource them. Further, some companies now outsource key components or business processes to international providers. Access the Website **BizBrim.com** and review the available information on outsourcing—especially as it relates to both the advantages and the negative effects of outsourcing.

Required

1. What does Bizbrim identify as the major advantages and the major disadvantages of outsourcing?
2. Does it seem that Bizbrim is generally in favor of or opposed to outsourcing? Explain.

BTN 23-6   Break into teams and identify costs that an airline such as **Delta Airlines** would incur on a flight from Green Bay to Minneapolis. (1) Identify the individual costs as variable or fixed. (2) Assume that Delta is trying to decide whether to drop this flight because it seems to be unprofitable. Determine which costs are likely to be saved if the flight is dropped. Set up your answer in the following format.

TEAMWORK IN ACTION

P1

Cost	Variable or Fixed	Cost Saved if Flight Is Dropped	Rationale

---

BTN 23-7   Marco Giannini of **Dogswell** makes food for dogs. Marco must decide on the best sales mix for his products. Assume that his company has a capacity of 80 hours of processing time available each month and it makes two types of dog food, Deluxe and Premium. Information on these foods follows.

ENTREPRENEURIAL DECISION

A1

	Deluxe	Premium
Selling price per carton	$70	$90
Variable costs per carton	$40	$50
Processing minutes per carton	6 minutes	12 minutes

Required

1. Assume the markets for both cartons of dog food are unlimited. How many Deluxe cartons and how many Premium cartons should the company make each month? Explain. How much total contribution margin does this mix produce each month?
2. Assume the market for the Deluxe carton is limited to 600 cartons per month, with no market limit for the Premium cartons. How many Deluxe cartons and how many Premium cartons should the company make each month? Explain. How much total contribution margin does this mix produce each month?

BTN 23-8   Restaurants are often adding and removing menu items. Visit a restaurant and identify a new food item. Make a list of costs that the restaurant must consider when deciding whether to add that new item. Also, make a list of nonfinancial factors that the restaurant must consider when adding that item.

HITTING THE ROAD

P1

BTN 23-9   Access **Nokia**'s 2009 annual report dated December 31, 2009, from its Website **www.Nokia.com**. Identify and read the section on *Environment—Corporate Responsibility*.

GLOBAL DECISION

C1

Required

Nokia reports that up to 80 percent of a Nokia mobile device can be recycled and the remainder can be recovered as energy or materials so that nothing goes to a landfill. These recycling efforts are costly. Why would a company like Nokia pursue these costly efforts?

NOKIA

ANSWERS TO MULTIPLE CHOICE QUIZ

1. a; Reworking provides incremental revenue of $11 per unit ($19 − $8); and, it costs $10 to rework them. The company is better off by $1 per unit when it reworks these products and sells them at the regular price.
2. e; Product X has a $2 contribution margin per machine hour [($32 − $12)/10 MH]; Product Y has a $7 contribution margin per machine hour [($24 − $10)/2 MH]. It should produce as much of Product Y as possible.
3. a; Total revenue from the special order = 3,000 units × $15 per unit = $45,000; and, Total costs for the special order = (3,000 units × $9 per unit) + $5,000 = $32,000. Net income from the special order = $45,000 − $32,000 = $13,000. Thus, yes, it should accept the order.
4. c
5. d

24

Capital Budgeting and Investment Analysis

A Look Back

Chapter 23 described several procedures useful for making and evaluating short-term managerial decisions. It also assessed the consequences of such decisions.

A Look at This Chapter

This chapter focuses on evaluating capital budgeting decisions. Several methods are described and illustrated that help managers identify projects with the greater return on investment.

CONCEPTUAL

C1 Describe the selection of a hurdle rate for an investment. (p. 1003)

ANALYTICAL

A1 Analyze a capital investment project using break-even time. (p. 1008)

LP24

PROCEDURAL

P1 Compute payback period and describe its use. (p. 999)

P2 Compute accounting rate of return and explain its use. (p. 1001)

P3 Compute net present value and describe its use. (p. 1003)

P4 Compute internal rate of return and explain its use. (p. 1005)

Decision Insight

Gamer Grub!

"Be in front of your customer . . . [and] have a little bit of an edge"
—**KEITH MULLIN** (far left)

SAN DIEGO—"I have been battling greasy fingers and keyboard crumbs," complained gamer Keith Mullin. "I thought '*there has to be a better way!*'" So, Keith-the-gamer morphed into Keith-the-entrepreneur. In 2008, Keith set up what he calls his "garage startup" and introduced **Gamer Grub**® (**GamerGrub.com**), which is performance snack food for gamers. "I got tired of wiping my hands on my jeans," laughs Keith. "And, I like to multi-task."

Success, however, requires Keith to monitor and minimize costs. "I made the first Gamer Grub prototypes in my mom's kitchen," explains Keith. He eventually set up an accounting system to track costs and match them with revenues. But, Keith says, it is a constant struggle as his business has been tripling in revenues each month. He explains that properly applying capital budgeting methods and acting on that information has helped in his success. However, admits Keith, "it is more of a collaborative effort."

To date, Keith has successfully controlled his costs while monitoring both revenues and customer needs. "You need to be in front of your customer, watch them taste it, watch them understand what you're doing," says Keith. "You have to be out there . . . we have given out at least 16,000 samples!" Keith adds that he applies capital budgeting methods such as net present value and internal rate of return. These methods enable Keith to expand his capacity and enter new markets that deliver high returns. He also relies on analyses from these methods to assess which snacks have positive returns and which investments in production operations to make. But, what keeps him going, admits Keith, is knowing that he offers "different ways to snack while you're computer gaming or multi-tasking."

Keith is on a mission. What motivates him, explains Keith, is the "Wow! If you get that 'Wow' reaction, that's a really good thing." To make that happen, he tracks the accounting numbers to be sure his "Wow food" is a money-making venture. "Gamer Grub allows gamers to consume healthy, game-enhancing snacks," insists Keith. "Without greasy fingers or keyboard crumbs!"

[Sources: *GamerGrub* Website, January 2011; *Entrepreneur,* October 2009; *Business Wire,* September 2008; *MGC* Website, January 2010]

Management must assess alternative long-term strategies and investments, and then decide which assets to acquire or sell to achieve company objectives. This analysis process is called capital budgeting, which is one of the more challenging, risky, and important tasks that management undertakes. This task requires predictions and estimates, and management's capital budgeting decisions impact the company for years. This chapter explains and illustrates several methods to aid management in the capital budgeting decisions.

Capital Budgeting and Investment Analysis

Non-present Value Methods
- Payback period
- Accounting rate of return

Present Value Methods
- Net present value
- Internal rate of return
- Comparison of methods

INTRODUCTION TO CAPITAL BUDGETING

The capital expenditures budget is management's plan for acquiring and selling plant assets. **Capital budgeting** is the process of analyzing alternative long-term investments and deciding which assets to acquire or sell. These decisions can involve developing a new product or process, buying a new machine or a new building, or acquiring an entire company. An objective for these decisions is to earn a satisfactory return on investment.

Capital budgeting decisions require careful analysis because they are usually the most difficult and risky decisions that managers make. These decisions are difficult because they require predicting events that will not occur until well into the future. Many of these predictions are tentative and potentially unreliable. Specifically, a capital budgeting decision is risky because (1) the outcome is uncertain, (2) large amounts of money are usually involved, (3) the investment involves a long-term commitment, and (4) the decision could be difficult or impossible to reverse, no matter how poor it turns out to be. Risk is especially high for investments in technology due to innovations and uncertainty.

Managers use several methods to evaluate capital budgeting decisions. Nearly all of these methods involve predicting cash inflows and cash outflows of proposed investments, assessing the risk of and returns on those flows, and then choosing the investments to make. Management often restates future cash flows in terms of their present value. This approach applies the time value of money: A dollar today is worth more than a dollar tomorrow. Similarly, a dollar tomorrow is worth less than a dollar today. The process of restating future cash flows in terms of their present value is called *discounting*. The time value of money is important when evaluating capital investments, but managers sometimes apply evaluation methods that ignore present value. This section describes four methods for comparing alternative investments.

Point: The nature of capital spending has changed with the business environment. Budgets for information technology have increased from about 25% of corporate capital spending 20 years ago to an estimated 35% today.

METHODS NOT USING TIME VALUE OF MONEY

All investments, whether they involve the purchase of a machine or another long-term asset, are expected to produce net cash flows. *Net cash flow* is cash inflows minus cash outflows. Sometimes managers perform simple analyses of the financial feasibility of an investment's net cash flow without using the time value of money. This section explains two of the most common methods in this category: (1) payback period and (2) accounting rate of return.

Payback Period

An investment's **payback period (PBP)** is the expected time period to recover the initial investment amount. Managers prefer investing in assets with shorter payback periods to reduce the risk of an unprofitable investment over the long run. Acquiring assets with short payback periods reduces a company's risk from potentially inaccurate long-term predictions of future cash flows.

P1 Compute payback period and describe its use.

Computing Payback Period with Even Cash Flows   To illustrate use of the payback period for an investment with even cash flows, we look at data from FasTrac, a manufacturer of exercise equipment and supplies. (*Even cash flows* are cash flows that are the same each and every year; *uneven cash flows* are cash flows that are not all equal in amount.) FasTrac is considering several different capital investments, one of which is to purchase a machine to use in manufacturing a new product. This machine costs $16,000 and is expected to have an eight-year life with no salvage value. Management predicts this machine will produce 1,000 units of product each year and that the new product will be sold for $30 per unit. Exhibit 24.1 shows the expected annual net cash flows for this asset over its life as well as the expected annual revenues and expenses (including depreciation and income taxes) from investing in the machine.

EXHIBIT 24.1

Cash Flow Analysis

FASTRAC Cash Flow Analysis—Machinery Investment January 15, 2011	Expected Accrual Figures	Expected Net Cash Flows
Annual sales of new product	$30,000	$30,000
Deduct annual expenses		
Cost of materials, labor, and overhead (except depreciation)	15,500	15,500
Depreciation—Machinery	2,000	
Additional selling and administrative expenses	9,500	9,500
Annual pretax accrual income	3,000	
Income taxes (30%)	900	900
Annual net income	$ 2,100	
Annual net cash flow		$ 4,100

The amount of net cash flow from the machinery is computed by subtracting expected cash outflows from expected cash inflows. The cash flows column of Exhibit 24.1 excludes all noncash revenues and expenses. Depreciation is FasTrac's only noncash item. Alternatively, managers can adjust the projected net income for revenue and expense items that do not affect cash flows. For FasTrac, this means taking the $2,100 net income and adding back the $2,000 depreciation.

The formula for computing the payback period of an investment that yields even net cash flows is in Exhibit 24.2.

Point: Annual net cash flow in Exhibit 24.1 equals net income plus depreciation (a noncash expense).

$$\text{Payback period} = \frac{\text{Cost of investment}}{\text{Annual net cash flow}}$$

EXHIBIT 24.2

Payback Period Formula with Even Cash Flows

The payback period reflects the amount of time for the investment to generate enough net cash flow to return (or pay back) the cash initially invested to purchase it. FasTrac's payback period for this machine is just under four years:

$$\text{Payback period} = \frac{\$16,000}{\$4,100} = 3.9 \text{ years}$$

Example: If an alternative machine (with different technology) yields a payback period of 3.5 years, which one does a manager choose? Answer: The alternative (3.5 is less than 3.9).

The initial investment is fully recovered in 3.9 years, or just before reaching the halfway point of this machine's useful life of eight years.

Decision Insight

Payback Phones   Profits of telecoms have declined as too much capital investment chased too little revenue. Telecom success depends on new technology, and communications gear is evolving at a dizzying rate. Consequently, managers of telecoms often demand short payback periods and large expected net cash flows to compensate for the investment risk. ∎

Computing Payback Period with Uneven Cash Flows   Computing the payback period in the prior section assumed even net cash flows. What happens if the net cash flows are uneven? In this case, the payback period is computed using the *cumulative total of net cash flows*. The word *cumulative* refers to the addition of each period's net cash flows as we progress through time. To illustrate, consider data for another investment that FasTrac is considering. This machine is predicted to generate uneven net cash flows over the next eight years. The relevant data and payback period computation are shown in Exhibit 24.3.

EXHIBIT 24.3

Payback Period Calculation with Uneven Cash Flows

Period*	Expected Net Cash Flows	Cumulative Net Cash Flows
Year 0	$(16,000)	$(16,000)
Year 1	3,000	(13,000)
Year 2	4,000	(9,000)
Year 3...........	4,000	(5,000)
Year 4	4,000	(1,000)
Year 5	5,000	4,000
Year 6	3,000	7,000
Year 7	2,000	9,000
Year 8	2,000	11,000
		Payback period = 4.2 years

* All cash inflows and outflows occur uniformly during the year.

Example: Find the payback period in Exhibit 24.3 if net cash flows for the first 4 years are:
Year 1 = $6,000; Year 2 = $5,000;
Year 3 = $4,000; Year 4 = $3,000.
Answer: 3.33 years

Year 0 refers to the period of initial investment in which the $16,000 cash outflow occurs at the end of year 0 to acquire the machinery. By the end of year 1, the cumulative net cash flow is reduced to $(13,000), computed as the $(16,000) initial cash outflow plus year 1's $3,000 cash inflow. This process continues throughout the asset's life. The cumulative net cash flow amount changes from negative to positive in year 5. Specifically, at the end of year 4, the cumulative net cash flow is $(1,000). As soon as FasTrac receives net cash inflow of $1,000 during the fifth year, it has fully recovered the investment. If we assume that cash flows are received uniformly *within* each year, receipt of the $1,000 occurs about one-fifth of the way through the year. This is computed as $1,000 divided by year 5's total net cash flow of $5,000, or 0.20. This yields a payback period of 4.2 years, computed as 4 years plus 0.20 of year 5.

Using the Payback Period   Companies desire a short payback period to increase return and reduce risk. The more quickly a company receives cash, the sooner it is available for other uses and the less time it is at risk of loss. A shorter payback period also improves the company's ability to respond to unanticipated changes and lowers its risk of having to keep an unprofitable investment.

Payback period should never be the only consideration in evaluating investments. This is so because it ignores at least two important factors. First, it fails to reflect differences in the timing of net cash flows within the payback period. In Exhibit 24.3, FasTrac's net cash flows in the first five years were $3,000, $4,000, $4,000, $4,000, and $5,000. If another investment had predicted cash flows of $9,000, $3,000, $2,000, $1,800, and $1,000 in these five years, its payback period would also be 4.2 years, but this second alternative could be more desirable because it provides cash more quickly. The second important factor is that the payback period ignores *all* cash flows after the point where its costs are fully recovered. For example, one investment might pay back its cost in 3 years but stop producing cash after 4 years. A second investment might require 5 years to pay back its cost yet continue to produce net cash flows for another 15 years. A focus on only the payback period would mistakenly lead management to choose the first investment over the second.

"So what if I underestimated costs and overestimated revenues? It all averages out in the end."

Quick Check

Answers — p. 1013

1. Capital budgeting is (*a*) concerned with analyzing alternative sources of capital, including debt and equity, (*b*) an important activity for companies when considering what assets to acquire or sell, or (*c*) best done by intuitive assessments of the value of assets and their usefulness.
2. Why are capital budgeting decisions often difficult?
3. A company is considering purchasing equipment costing $75,000. Future annual net cash flows from this equipment are $30,000, $25,000, $15,000, $10,000, and $5,000. The payback period is (*a*) 4 years, (*b*) 3.5 years, or (*c*) 3 years.
4. If depreciation is an expense, why is it added back to an investment's net income to compute the net cash flow from that investment?
5. If two investments have the same payback period, are they equally desirable? Explain.

Accounting Rate of Return

The **accounting rate of return,** also called *return on average investment,* is computed by dividing a project's after-tax net income by the average amount invested in it. To illustrate, we return to FasTrac's $16,000 machinery investment described in Exhibit 24.1. We first compute (1) the after-tax net income and (2) the average amount invested. The $2,100 after-tax net income is already available from Exhibit 24.1. To compute the average amount invested, we assume that net cash flows are received evenly throughout each year. Thus, the average investment for each year is computed as the average of its beginning and ending book values. If FasTrac's $16,000 machine is depreciated $2,000 each year, the average amount invested in the machine for each year is computed as shown in Exhibit 24.4. The average for any year is the average of the beginning and ending book values.

P2 Compute accounting rate of return and explain its use.

	Beginning Book Value	Annual Depreciation	Ending Book Value	Average Book Value
Year 1	$16,000	$2,000	$14,000	$15,000
Year 2	14,000	2,000	12,000	13,000
Year 3	12,000	2,000	10,000	11,000
Year 4	10,000	2,000	8,000	9,000
Year 5	8,000	2,000	6,000	7,000
Year 6	6,000	2,000	4,000	5,000
Year 7	4,000	2,000	2,000	3,000
Year 8	2,000	2,000	0	1,000
All years				**$ 8,000**

EXHIBIT 24.4

Computing Average Amount Invested (Book Value)

Next we need the average book value for the asset's entire life. This amount is computed by taking the average of the individual yearly averages. This average equals $8,000, computed as $64,000 (the sum of the individual years' averages) divided by eight years (see last column of Exhibit 24.4).

If a company uses straight-line depreciation, we can find the average amount invested by using the formula in Exhibit 24.5. Because FasTrac uses straight-line depreciation, its average

Point: General formula for *annual average investment* is the sum of individual years' average book values divided by the number of years of the planned investment.

amount invested for the eight years equals the sum of the book value at the beginning of the asset's investment period and the book value at the end of its investment period, divided by 2, as shown in Exhibit 24.5.

EXHIBIT 24.5

Computing Average Amount Invested under Straight-Line Depreciation

$$\text{Annual average investment} = \frac{\textbf{Beginning book value} + \textbf{Ending book value}}{\textbf{2}}$$

$$\text{(straight-line case only)}$$

$$= \frac{\$16{,}000 + \$0}{2} = \$8{,}000$$

If an investment has a salvage value, the average amount invested when using straight-line depreciation is computed as (Beginning book value + Salvage value)/2.

Once we determine the after-tax net income and the average amount invested, the accounting rate of return on the investment can be computed from the annual after-tax net income divided by the average amount invested, as shown in Exhibit 24.6.

EXHIBIT 24.6

Accounting Rate of Return Formula

$$\text{Accounting rate of return} = \frac{\textbf{Annual after-tax net income}}{\textbf{Annual average investment}}$$

This yields an accounting rate of return of 26.25% ($2,100/$8,000). FasTrac management must decide whether a 26.25% accounting rate of return is satisfactory. To make this decision, we must factor in the investment's risk. For instance, we cannot say an investment with a 26.25% return is preferred over one with a lower return unless we recognize any differences in risk. Thus, an investment's return is satisfactory or unsatisfactory only when it is related to returns from other investments with similar lives and risk.

When accounting rate of return is used to choose among capital investments, the one with the least risk, the shortest payback period, and the highest return for the longest time period is often identified as the best. However, use of accounting rate of return to evaluate investment opportunities is limited because it bases the amount invested on book values (not predicted market values) in future periods. Accounting rate of return is also limited when an asset's net incomes are expected to vary from year to year. This requires computing the rate using *average* annual net incomes, yet this accounting rate of return fails to distinguish between two investments with the same average annual net income but different amounts of income in early years versus later years or different levels of income variability.

Quick Check   Answers — p. 1013

6. The following data relate to a company's decision on whether to purchase a machine:

Cost	$180,000
Salvage value	15,000
Annual after-tax net income	40,000

The machine's accounting rate of return, assuming the even receipt of its net cash flows during the year and use of straight-line depreciation, is (a) 22%, (b) 41%, or (c) 21%.

7. Is a 15% accounting rate of return for a machine a good rate?

METHODS USING TIME VALUE OF MONEY

This section describes two methods that help managers with capital budgeting decisions and that use the time value of money: (1) net present value and (2) internal rate of return. *(To apply these methods, you need a basic understanding of the concept of present value. An expanded explanation of present value concepts is in Appendix B near the end of the book. You can use the present value tables at the end of Appendix B to solve many of this chapter's assignments that use the time value of money.)*

Net Present Value

Net present value analysis applies the time value of money to future cash inflows and cash out-flows so management can evaluate a project's benefits and costs at one point in time. Specifically, **net present value (NPV)** is computed by discounting the future net cash flows from the investment at the project's required rate of return and then subtracting the initial amount invested. A company's required return, often called its hurdle rate, is typically its **cost of capital,** which is the rate the company must pay to its long-term creditors and shareholders.

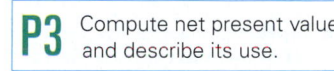

P3 Compute net present value and describe its use.

To illustrate, let's return to FasTrac's proposed machinery purchase described in Exhibit 24.1. Does this machine provide a satisfactory return while recovering the amount invested? Recall that the machine requires a $16,000 investment and is expected to provide $4,100 annual net cash inflows for the next eight years. If we assume that net cash flows from this machine are received at each year-end and that FasTrac requires a 12% annual return, net present value can be computed as in Exhibit 24.7.

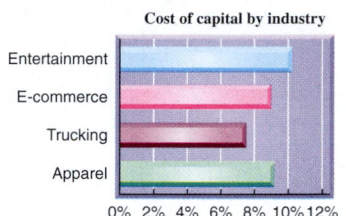

	Net Cash Flows*	Present Value of 1 at 12%†	Present Value of Net Cash Flows
Year 1	$ 4,100	0.8929	$ 3,661
Year 2	4,100	0.7972	3,269
Year 3	4,100	0.7118	2,918
Year 4	4,100	0.6355	2,606
Year 5	4,100	0.5674	2,326
Year 6	4,100	0.5066	2,077
Year 7	4,100	0.4523	1,854
Year 8	4,100	0.4039	1,656
Totals	$32,800		20,367
Amount invested			(16,000)
Net present value			$ 4,367

EXHIBIT 24.7

Net Present Value Calculation with Equal Cash Flows

* Cash flows occur at the end of each year.

† Present value of 1 factors are taken from Table B.1 in Appendix B.

The first number column of Exhibit 24.7 shows the annual net cash flows. Present value of 1 factors, also called *discount factors,* are shown in the second column. Taken from Table B.1 in Appendix B, they assume that net cash flows are received at each year-end. *(To simplify present value computations and for assignment material at the end of this chapter, we assume that net cash flows are received at each year-end.)* Annual net cash flows from the first column of Exhibit 24.7 are multiplied by the discount factors in the second column to give present values shown in the third column. The last three lines of this exhibit show the final NPV computations. The asset's $16,000 initial cost is deducted from the $20,367 total present value of all future net cash flows to give this asset's NPV of $4,367. The machine is thus expected to (1) recover its cost, (2) provide a 12% compounded return, and (3) generate $4,367 above cost. We summarize this analysis by saying the present value of this machine's future net cash flows to FasTrac exceeds the $16,000 investment by $4,367.

Point: The assumption of end-of-year cash flows simplifies computations and is common in practice.

Point: The amount invested includes all costs that must be incurred to get the asset in its proper location and ready for use.

Example: What is the net present value in Exhibit 24.7 if a 10% return is required? *Answer:* $5,873

Net Present Value Decision Rule The decision rule in applying NPV is as follows: When an asset's expected cash flows are discounted at the required rate and yield a *positive* net present value, the asset should be acquired. This decision rule is reflected in the graphic below. When comparing several investment opportunities of about the same cost and same risk, we prefer the one with the highest positive net present value.

C1 Describe the selection of a hurdle rate for an investment.

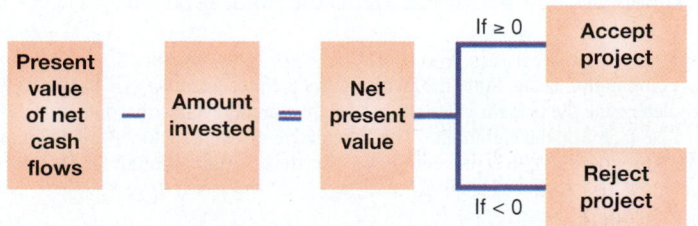

Example: Why does the net present value of an investment increase when a lower discount rate is used? *Answer:* The present value of net cash flows increases.

Simplifying Computations   The computations in Exhibit 24.7 use separate present value of 1 factors for each of the eight years. Each year's net cash flow is multiplied by its present value of 1 factor to determine its present value. The individual present values for each of the eight net cash flows are added to give the asset's total present value. This computation can be simplified in two ways if annual net cash flows are equal in amount. One way is to add the eight annual present value of 1 factors for a total of 4.9676 and multiply this amount by the annual $4,100 net cash flow to get the $20,367 total present value of net cash flows.[1] A second simplification is to use a calculator with compound interest functions or a spreadsheet program. We show how to use Excel functions to compute net present value in this chapter's Appendix. Whatever procedure you use, it is important to understand the concepts behind these computations.

■ **Decision Ethics**   Answer — p. 1012

Systems Manager   Top management adopts a policy requiring purchases in excess of $5,000 to be submitted with cash flow projections to the cost analyst for capital budget approval. As systems manager, you want to upgrade your computers at a $25,000 cost. You consider submitting several orders all under $5,000 to avoid the approval process. You believe the computers will increase profits and wish to avoid a delay. What do you do? ■

Uneven Cash Flows   Net present value analysis can also be applied when net cash flows are uneven (unequal). To illustrate, assume that FasTrac can choose only one capital investment from among projects A, B, and C. Each project requires the same $12,000 initial investment. Future net cash flows for each project are shown in the first three number columns of Exhibit 24.8.

EXHIBIT 24.8

Net Present Value Calculation with Uneven Cash Flows

	Net Cash Flows			Present Value of 1 at 10%	Present Value of Net Cash Flows		
	A	**B**	**C**		**A**	**B**	**C**
Year 1	$ 5,000	$ 8,000	$ 1,000	0.9091	$ 4,546	$ 7,273	$ 909
Year 2	5,000	5,000	5,000	0.8264	4,132	4,132	4,132
Year 3	5,000	2,000	9,000	0.7513	3,757	1,503	6,762
Totals	$15,000	$15,000	$15,000		12,435	12,908	11,803
Amount invested					(12,000)	(12,000)	(12,000)
Net present value					**$ 435**	**$ 908**	**$ (197)**

Example: If 12% is the required return in Exhibit 24.8, which project is preferred? *Answer:* Project B. Net present values are: A = $10; B = $553; C = $(715).

Example: Will the rankings of Projects A, B, and C change with the use of different discount rates, assuming the same rate is used for all projects? *Answer:* No; only the NPV amounts will change.

The three projects in Exhibit 24.8 have the same expected total net cash flows of $15,000. Project A is expected to produce equal amounts of $5,000 each year. Project B is expected to produce a larger amount in the first year. Project C is expected to produce a larger amount in the third year. The fourth column of Exhibit 24.8 shows the present value of 1 factors from Table B.1 assuming 10% required return.

Computations in the right-most columns show that Project A has a $435 positive NPV. Project B has the largest NPV of $908 because it brings in cash more quickly. Project C has a $(197) *negative* NPV because its larger cash inflows are delayed. If FasTrac requires a 10% return, it should reject Project C because its NPV implies a return *under* 10%. If only one project can be accepted, project B appears best because it yields the highest NPV.

---

[1] We can simplify this computation using Table B.3, which gives the present value of 1 to be received periodically for a number of periods. To determine the present value of these eight annual receipts discounted at 12%, go down the 12% column of Table B.3 to the factor on the eighth line. This cumulative discount factor, also known as an *annuity* factor, is 4.9676. We then compute the $20,367 present value for these eight annual $4,100 receipts, computed as 4.9676 × $4,100.

Salvage Value and Accelerated Depreciation   FasTrac predicted the $16,000 machine to have zero salvage value at the end of its useful life (recall Exhibit 24.1). In many cases, assets are expected to have salvage values. If so, this amount is an additional net cash inflow received at the end of the final year of the asset's life. All other computations remain the same.

Depreciation computations also affect net present value analysis. FasTrac computes depreciation using the straight-line method. Accelerated depreciation is also commonly used, especially for income tax reports. Accelerated depreciation produces larger depreciation deductions in the early years of an asset's life and smaller deductions in later years. This pattern results in smaller income tax payments in early years and larger payments in later years. Accelerated depreciation does not change the basics of a present value analysis, but it can change the result. Using accelerated depreciation for tax reporting affects the NPV of an asset's cash flows because it produces larger net cash inflows in the early years of the asset's life and smaller ones in later years. Being able to use accelerated depreciation for tax reporting always makes an investment more desirable because early cash flows are more valuable than later ones.

Use of Net Present Value   In deciding whether to proceed with a capital investment project, we approve the proposal if the NPV is positive but reject it if the NPV is negative. When considering several projects of similar investment amounts and risk levels, we can compare the different projects' NPVs and rank them on the basis of their NPVs. However, if the amount invested differs substantially across projects, the NPV is of limited value for comparison purposes. One means to compare projects, especially when a company cannot fund all positive net present value projects, is to use the **profitability index,** which is computed as:

$$\text{Profitability index} = \frac{\textbf{Net present value of cash flows}}{\textbf{Investment}}$$

A higher profitability index suggests a more desirable project. To illustrate, suppose that Project X requires a $1 million investment and provides a $100,000 NPV. Project Y requires an investment of only $100,000 and returns a $75,000 NPV. Ranking on the basis of NPV puts Project X ahead of Y, yet X's profitability index is only 0.10 ($100,000/$1,000,000) whereas Y's profitability index is 0.75. We must also remember that when reviewing projects with different risks, we computed the NPV of individual projects using different discount rates. The higher the risk, the higher the discount rate.

Inflation   Large price-level increases should be considered in NPV analyses. Hurdle rates already include investor's inflation forecasts. Net cash flows can be adjusted for inflation by using *future value* computations. For example, if the expected net cash inflow in year 1 is $4,100 and 5% inflation is expected, then the expected net cash inflow in year 2 is $4,305, computed as $4,100 × 1.05 (1.05 is the future value of $1 (Table B.2) for 1 period with a 5% rate).

Internal Rate of Return

Another means to evaluate capital investments is to use the **internal rate of return (IRR),** which equals the rate that yields an NPV of zero for an investment. This means that if we compute the total present value of a project's net cash flows using the IRR as the discount rate and then subtract the initial investment from this total present value, we get a zero NPV.

To illustrate, we use the data for FasTrac's Project A from Exhibit 24.8 to compute its IRR. Exhibit 24.9 shows the two-step process in computing IRR.

EXHIBIT 24.9

Computing Internal Rate of Return
(with even cash flows)

Step 1: Compute the present value factor for the investment project.

$$\text{Present value factor} = \frac{\text{Amount invested}}{\text{Net cash flows}} = \frac{\$12,000}{\$5,000} = 2.4000$$

Step 2: Identify the discount rate (IRR) yielding the present value factor

Search Table B.3 for a present value factor of 2.4000 in the three-year row (equaling the 3-year project duration). The 12% discount rate yields a present value factor of 2.4018. This implies that the IRR is approximately 12%.*

* Since the present value factor of 2.4000 is not exactly equal to the 12% factor of 2.4018, we can more precisely estimate the IRR as follows:

Discount rate	Present Value Factor from Table B.3
12%	2.4018
15%	2.2832
	0.1186 = difference

Then, $\text{IRR} = 12\% + \left[(15\% - 12\%) \times \dfrac{2.4018 - 2.4000}{0.1186} \right] = \underline{\underline{12.05\%}}$

When cash flows are equal, as with Project A, we compute the present value factor (as shown in Exhibit 24.9) by dividing the initial investment by its annual net cash flows. We then use an annuity table to determine the discount rate equal to this present value factor. For FasTrac's Project A, we look across the three-period row of Table B.3 and find that the discount rate corresponding to the present value factor of 2.4000 roughly equals the 2.4018 value for the 12% rate. This row is reproduced here:

Present Value of an Annuity of 1 for Three Periods

	Discount Rate				
Periods	1%	5%	10%	12%	15%
3	2.9410	2.7232	2.4869	2.4018	2.2832

The 12% rate is the Project's IRR. A more precise IRR estimate can be computed following the procedure shown in the note to Exhibit 24.9. Spreadsheet software and calculators can also compute this IRR. We show how to use an Excel function to compute IRR in this chapter's appendix.

Uneven Cash Flows   If net cash flows are uneven, we must use trial and error to compute the IRR. We do this by selecting any reasonable discount rate and computing the NPV. If the amount is positive (negative), we recompute the NPV using a higher (lower) discount rate. We continue these steps until we reach a point where two consecutive computations result in NPVs having different signs (positive and negative). Because the NPV is zero using IRR, we know that the IRR lies between these two discount rates. We can then estimate its value. Spreadsheet programs and calculators can do these computations for us.

▮ Decision Insight

Fun-IRR   Many theme parks use both financial and nonfinancial criteria to evaluate their investments in new rides and activities. The use of IRR is a major part of this evaluation. This requires good estimates of future cash inflows and outflows. It also requires risk assessments of the uncertainty of the future cash flows. ▮

Use of Internal Rate of Return When we use the IRR to evaluate a project, we compare it to a predetermined **hurdle rate,** which is a minimum acceptable rate of return and is applied as follows.

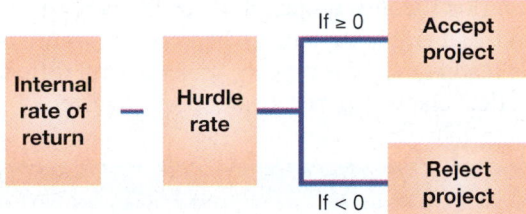

Top management selects the hurdle rate to use in evaluating capital investments. Financial formulas aid in this selection, but the choice of a minimum rate is subjective and left to management. For projects financed from borrowed funds, the hurdle rate must exceed the interest rate paid on these funds. The return on an investment must cover its interest and provide an additional profit to reward the company for its risk. For instance, if money is borrowed at 10%, an average risk investment often requires an after-tax return of 15% (or 5% above the borrowing rate). Remember that lower-risk investments require a lower rate of return compared with higher-risk investments.

If the project is internally financed, the hurdle rate is often based on actual returns from comparable projects. If the IRR is higher than the hurdle rate, the project is accepted. Multiple projects are often ranked by the extent to which their IRR exceeds the hurdle rate. The hurdle rate for individual projects is often different, depending on the risk involved. IRR is not subject to the limitations of NPV when comparing projects with different amounts invested because the IRR is expressed as a percent rather than as an absolute dollar value in NPV.

Decision Maker   Answer — p. 1012

Entrepreneur You are developing a new product and you use a 12% discount rate to compute its NPV. Your banker, from whom you hope to obtain a loan, expresses concern that your discount rate is too low. How do you respond? ■

Comparison of Capital Budgeting Methods

We explained four methods that managers use to evaluate capital investment projects. How do these methods compare with each other? Exhibit 24.10 addresses that question. Neither the payback period nor the accounting rate of return considers the time value of money. On the other hand, both the net present value and the internal rate of return do.

Example: How does management evaluate the risk of an investment? *Answer:* It must assess the uncertainty of future cash flows.

Point: A survey reports that 41% of top managers would reject a project with an internal rate of return *above* the cost of capital, *if* the project would cause the firm to miss its earnings forecast. The roles of benchmarks and manager compensation plans must be considered in capital budgeting decisions.

EXHIBIT 24.10

Comparing Capital Budgeting Methods

	Payback Period	Accounting Rate of Return	Net Present Value	Internal Rate of Return
Measurement basis	• Cash flows	• Accrual income	• Cash flows • Profitability	• Cash flows • Profitability
Measurement unit	• Years	• Percent	• Dollars	• Percent
Strengths	• Easy to understand	• Easy to understand	• Reflects time value of money	• Reflects time value of money
	• Allows comparison of projects	• Allows comparison of projects	• Reflects varying risks over project's life	• Allows comparisons of dissimilar projects
Limitations	• Ignores time value of money	• Ignores time value of money	• Difficult to compare dissimilar projects	• Ignores varying risks over life of project
	• Ignores cash flows after payback period	• Ignores annual rates over life of project		

The payback period is probably the simplest method. It gives managers an estimate of how soon they will recover their initial investment. Managers sometimes use this method when they have limited cash to invest and a number of projects to choose from. The accounting rate of return yields a percent measure computed using accrual income instead of cash flows. The accounting rate of return is an average rate for the entire investment period. Net present value considers all estimated net cash flows for the project's expected life. It can be applied to even and uneven cash flows and can reflect changes in the level of risk over a project's life. Since it yields a dollar measure, comparing projects of unequal sizes is more difficult. The internal rate of return considers all cash flows from a project. It is readily computed when the cash flows are even but requires some trial and error estimation when cash flows are uneven. Because the IRR is a percent measure, it is readily used to compare projects with different investment amounts. However, IRR does not reflect changes in risk over a project's life.

Decision Insight

And the Winner Is . . . How do we choose among the methods for evaluating capital investments? Management surveys consistently show the internal rate of return (IRR) as the most popular method followed by the payback period and net present value (NPV). Few companies use the accounting rate of return (ARR), but nearly all use more than one method. ■

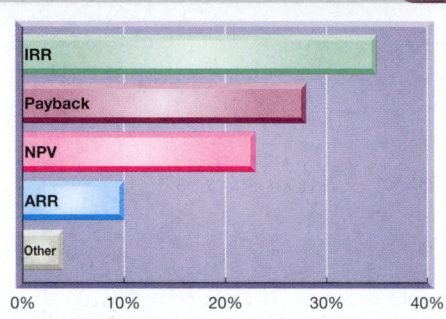

Company Usage of Capital Budgeting Methods

Quick Check

Answers — p. 1013

8. A company can invest in only one of two projects, A or B. Each project requires a $20,000 investment and is expected to generate end-of-period, annual cash flows as follows:

	Year 1	Year 2	Year 3	Total
Project A	$12,000	$8,500	$4,000	$24,500
Project B	4,500	8,500	13,000	26,000

Assuming a discount rate of 10%, which project has the higher net present value?

9. Two investment alternatives are expected to generate annual cash flows with the same net present value (assuming the same discount rate applied to each). Using this information, can you conclude that the two alternatives are equally desirable?

10. When two investment alternatives have the same total expected cash flows but differ in the timing of those flows, which method of evaluating those investments is superior, (a) accounting rate of return or (b) net present value?

GLOBAL VIEW

Siemens AG is a global electrical engineering and electronics company headquartered in Germany. Recently, the company announced plans to invest £80 million to build a wind turbine plant in the United Kingdom. Net present value analyses support such decisions. In this case, Siemens foresees strong future cash flows based on increased demand for clean sources of energy, like wind power.

Decision Analysis    Break-Even Time

A1   Analyze a capital investment project using break-even time.

The first section of this chapter explained several methods to evaluate capital investments. Break-even time of an investment project is a variation of the payback period method that overcomes the limitation of not using the time value of money. **Break-even time (BET)** is a time-based measure used to evaluate a capital investment's acceptability. Its computation yields a measure of expected time, reflecting the time period until the *present value* of the net cash flows from an investment equals the initial cost of the investment. In basic terms, break-even time is computed by restating future cash flows in terms of present values and then determining the payback period using these present values.

To illustrate, we return to the FasTrac case described in Exhibit 24.1 involving a $16,000 investment in machinery. The annual net cash flows from this investment are projected at $4,100 for eight years. Exhibit 24.11 shows the computation of break-even time for this investment decision.

Year	Cash Flows	Present Value of 1 at 10%	Present Value of Cash Flows	Cumulative Present Value of Cash Flows
0	$(16,000)	1.0000	$(16,000)	$(16,000)
1	4,100	0.9091	3,727	(12,273)
2	4,100	0.8264	3,388	(8,885)
3	4,100	0.7513	3,080	(5,805)
4	4,100	0.6830	2,800	(3,005)
5	4,100	0.6209	2,546	(459)
6	4,100	0.5645	2,314	1,855
7	4,100	0.5132	2,104	3,959
8	4,100	0.4665	1,913	5,872

EXHIBIT 24.11

Break-Even Time Analysis*

* The time of analysis is the start of year 1 (same as end of year 0). All cash flows occur at the end of each year.

The right-most column of this exhibit shows that break-even time is between 5 and 6 years, or about 5.2 years—also see margin graph (where the line crosses the zero point). This is the time the project takes to break even after considering the time value of money (recall that the payback period computed without considering the time value of money was 3.9 years). We interpret this as cash flows earned after 5.2 years contribute to a positive net present value that, in this case, eventually amounts to $5,872.

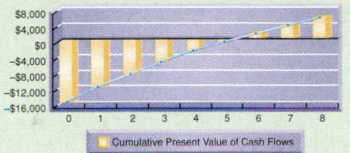

Cumulative Present Value of Cash Flows

Break-even time is a useful measure for managers because it identifies the point in time when they can expect the cash flows to begin to yield net positive returns. Managers expect a positive net present value from an investment if break-even time is less than the investment's estimated life. The method allows managers to compare and rank alternative investments, giving the project with the shortest break-even time the highest rank.

Decision Maker   Answer — p. 1012

Investment Manager Management asks you, the investment manager, to evaluate three alternative investments. Investment recovery time is crucial because cash is scarce. The time value of money is also important. Which capital budgeting method(s) do you use to assess the investments? ■

DEMONSTRATION PROBLEM

White Company can invest in one of two projects, TD1 or TD2. Each project requires an initial investment of $101,250 and produces the year-end cash inflows shown in the following table.

	Net Cash Flows	
	TD1	TD2
Year 1	$ 20,000	$ 40,000
Year 2	30,000	40,000
Year 3	70,000	40,000
Totals	$120,000	$120,000

Required

1. Compute the payback period for both projects. Which project has the shortest payback period?
2. Assume that the company requires a 10% return from its investments. Compute the net present value of each project.
3. Drawing on your answers to parts 1 and 2, determine which project, if any, should be chosen.
4. Compute the internal rate of return for project TD2. Based on its internal rate of return, should project TD2 be chosen?

PLANNING THE SOLUTION

- Compute the payback period for the series of unequal cash flows (Project TD1) and for the series of equal cash flows (Project TD2).
- Compute White Company's net present value of each investment using a 10% discount rate.
- Use the payback and net present value rules to determine which project, if any, should be selected.
- Compute the internal rate of return for the series of equal cash flows (Project TD2) and determine whether that internal rate of return is greater than the company's 10% discount rate.

SOLUTION TO DEMONSTRATION PROBLEM

1. The payback period for a project with a series of equal cash flows is computed as follows:

$$\text{Payback period} = \frac{\text{Cost of investment}}{\text{Annual net cash flow}}$$

For project TD2, the payback period equals 2.53 (rounded), computed as $101,250/$40,000. This means that the company expects to recover its investment in Project TD2 after approximately two and one-half years of its three-year life.

Next, determining the payback period for a series of unequal cash flows (as in Project TD1) requires us to compute the cumulative net cash flows from the project at the end of each year. Assuming the cash outflow for Project TD1 occurs at the end of year 0, and cash inflows occur continuously over years 1, 2, and 3, the payback period calculation follows.

TD1:

Period	Expected Net Cash Flows	Cumulative Net Cash Flows
0	$(101,250)	$(101,250)
1	20,000	(81,250)
2	30,000	(51,250)
3	70,000	18,750

The cumulative net cash flow for Project TD1 changes from negative to positive in year 3. As cash flows are received continuously, the point at which the company has recovered its investment into year 3 is 0.27 (rounded), computed as $18,750/$70,000. This means that the payback period for TD1 is 2.27 years, computed as 2 years plus 0.27 of year 3.

2. TD1:

	Net Cash Flows	Present Value of 1 at 10%	Present Value of Net Cash Flows
Year 1	$ 20,000	0.9091	$ 18,182
Year 2	30,000	0.8264	24,792
Year 3	70,000	0.7513	52,591
Totals	$120,000		95,565
Amount invested			(101,250)
Net present value			**$ (5,685)**

TD2:

	Net Cash Flows	Present Value of 1 at 10%	Present Value of Net Cash Flows
Year 1	$ 40,000	0.9091	$ 36,364
Year 2	40,000	0.8264	33,056
Year 3	40,000	0.7513	30,052
Totals	$120,000		99,472
Amount invested			(101,250)
Net present value			**$ (1,778)**

3. White Company should not invest in either project. Both are expected to yield a negative net present value, and it should invest only in positive net present value projects. Although the company expects to recover its investment from both projects before the end of these projects' useful lives, the projects are not acceptable after considering the time value of money.

4. To compute Project TD2's internal rate of return, we first compute a present value factor as follows:

$$\text{Present value factor} = \frac{\text{Amount invested}}{\text{Net cash flow}} = \$101{,}250/\$40{,}000 = 2.5313 \text{ (rounded)}$$

Then, we search Table B.3 for the discount rate that corresponds to the present value factor of 2.5313 for three periods. From Table B.3, this discount rate is 9%. Project TD2's internal rate of return of 9% is below this company's hurdle rate of 10%. Thus, Project TD2 should *not* be chosen.

APPENDIX

Using Excel to Compute Net Present Value and Internal Rate of Return

24A

Computing present values and internal rates of return for projects with uneven cash flows is tedious and error prone. These calculations can be performed simply and accurately by using functions built into Excel. Many calculators and other types of spreadsheet software can perform them too. To illustrate, consider FasTrac, a company that is considering investing in a new machine with the expected cash flows shown in the following spreadsheet. Cash outflows are entered as negative numbers, and cash inflows are entered as positive numbers. Assume FasTrac requires a 12% annual return, entered as 0.12 in cell C1.

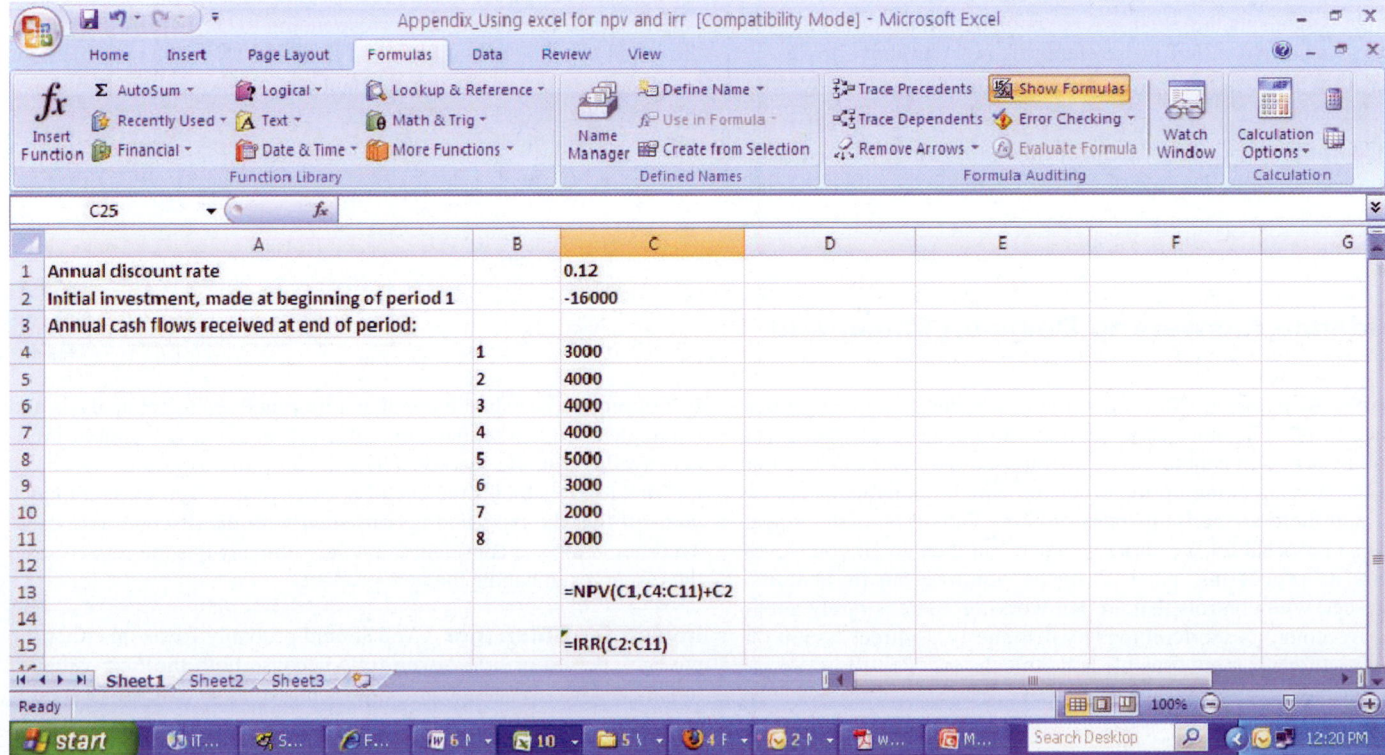

To compute the net present value of this project, the following is entered into cell C13:

$$=\text{NPV}(C1,C4:C11)+C2.$$

This instructs Excel to use its NPV function to compute the present value of the cash flows in cells C4 through C11, using the discount rate in cell C1, and then add the amount of the (negative) initial investment. For this stream of cash flows and a discount rate of 12%, the net present value is $1,326.03.

To compute the internal rate of return for this project, the following is entered into cell C15:

$$=\text{IRR}(C2:C11).$$

This instructs Excel to use its IRR function to compute the internal rate of return of the cash flows in cells C2 through C11. By default, Excel starts with a guess of 10%, and then uses trial and error to find the IRR. The IRR equals 14% for this project.

Summary

C1 **Describe the selection of a hurdle rate for an investment.** Top management should select the hurdle (discount) rate to use in evaluating capital investments. The required hurdle rate should be at least higher than the interest rate on money borrowed because the return on an investment must cover the interest and provide an additional profit to reward the company for risk.

A1 **Analyze a capital investment project using break-even time.** Break-even time (BET) is a method for evaluating capital investments by restating future cash flows in terms of their present values (discounting the cash flows) and then calculating the payback period using these present values of cash flows.

P1 **Compute payback period and describe its use.** One way to compare potential investments is to compute and compare their payback periods. The payback period is an estimate of the expected time before the cumulative net cash inflow from the investment equals its initial cost. A payback period analysis fails to reflect risk of the cash flows, differences in the timing of cash flows within the payback period, and cash flows that occur after the payback period.

P2 **Compute accounting rate of return and explain its use.** A project's accounting rate of return is computed by dividing the expected annual after-tax net income by the average amount of investment in the project. When the net cash flows are received evenly throughout each period and straight-line depreciation is used, the average investment is computed as the average of the investment's initial book value and its salvage value.

P3 **Compute net present value and describe its use.** An investment's net present value is determined by predicting the future cash flows it is expected to generate, discounting them at a rate that represents an acceptable return, and then by subtracting the investment's initial cost from the sum of the present values. This technique can deal with any pattern of expected cash flows and applies a superior concept of return on investment.

P4 **Compute internal rate of return and explain its use.** The internal rate of return (IRR) is the discount rate that results in a zero net present value. When the cash flows are equal, we can compute the present value factor corresponding to the IRR by dividing the initial investment by the annual cash flows. We then use the annuity tables to determine the discount rate corresponding to this present value factor.

Guidance Answers to Decision Maker and Decision Ethics

Systems Manager   Your dilemma is whether to abide by rules designed to prevent abuse or to bend them to acquire an investment that you believe will benefit the firm. You should not pursue the latter action because breaking up the order into small components is dishonest and there are consequences of being caught at a later stage. Develop a proposal for the entire package and then do all you can to expedite its processing, particularly by pointing out its benefits. When faced with controls that are not working, there is rarely a reason to overcome its shortcomings by dishonesty. A direct assault on those limitations is more sensible and ethical.

Entrepreneur   The banker is probably concerned because new products are risky and should therefore be evaluated using a higher rate of return. You should conduct a thorough technical analysis and obtain detailed market data and information about any similar products available in the market. These factors might provide sufficient information to support the use of a lower return. You must convince yourself that the risk level is consistent with the discount rate used. You should also be confident that your company has the capacity and the resources to handle the new product.

Investment Manager   You should probably focus on either the payback period or break-even time because both the time value of money and recovery time are important. Break-even time method is superior because it accounts for the time value of money, which is an important consideration in this decision.

Guidance Answers to Quick Checks

1. *b*

2. A capital budgeting decision is difficult because (1) the outcome is uncertain, (2) large amounts of money are usually involved, (3) a long-term commitment is required, and (4) the decision could be difficult or impossible to reverse.

3. *b*

4. Depreciation expense is subtracted from revenues in computing net income but does not use cash and should be added back to net income to compute net cash flows.

5. Not necessarily. One investment can continue to generate cash flows beyond the payback period for a longer time period than the other. The timing of their cash flows within the payback period also can differ.

6. *b*; Annual average investment = ($180,000 + $15,000)/2
                          = $97,500

  Accounting rate of return = $40,000/$97,500 = 41%

7. For this determination, we need to compare it to the returns expected from alternative investments with similar risk.

8. Project A has the higher net present value as follows:

		Project A		Project B	
Year	Present Value of 1 at 10%	Net Cash Flows	Present Value of Net Cash Flows	Net Cash Flows	Present Value of Net Cash Flows
1	0.9091	$12,000	$10,909	$ 4,500	$ 4,091
2	0.8264	8,500	7,024	8,500	7,024
3	0.7513	4,000	3,005	13,000	9,767
Totals		$24,500	$20,938	$26,000	$20,882
Amount invested			(20,000)		(20,000)
Net present value			**$ 938**		**$ 882**

9. No, the information is too limited to draw that conclusion. For example, one investment could be riskier than the other, or one could require a substantially larger initial investment.

10. *b*

Key Terms
mhhe.com/wildFINMAN4e

Accounting rate of return (p. 1001)
Break-even time (BET) (p. 1008)
Capital budgeting (p. 998)

Cost of capital (p. 1003)
Hurdle rate (p. 1007)
Internal rate of return (IRR) (p. 1005)

Net present value (NPV) (p. 1003)
Payback period (PBP) (p. 999)
Profitability index (p. 1005)

Multiple Choice Quiz
Answers on p. 1024
mhhe.com/wildFINMAN4e

Additional Quiz Questions are available at the book's Website.

1. The minimum acceptable rate of return for an investment decision is called the
  a. Hurdle rate of return.
  b. Payback rate of return.
  c. Internal rate of return.
  d. Average rate of return.
  e. Maximum rate of return.

2. A corporation is considering the purchase of new equipment costing $90,000. The projected after-tax annual net income from the equipment is $3,600, after deducting $30,000 depreciation. Assume that revenue is to be received at each year-end, and the machine has a useful life of three years with zero salvage value. Management requires a 12% return on its investments. What is the net present value of this machine?
  a. $ 60,444
  b. $ 80,700
  c. $(88,560)
  d. $ 90,000
  e. $ (9,300)

3. A disadvantage of using the payback period to compare investment alternatives is that it
  a. Ignores cash flows beyond the payback period.
  b. Cannot be used to compare alternatives with different initial investments.

  c. Cannot be used when cash flows are not uniform.
  d. Involves the time value of money.
  e. Cannot be used if a company records depreciation.

4. A company is considering the purchase of equipment for $270,000. Projected annual cash inflow from this equipment is $61,200 per year. The payback period is:
  a. 0.2 years
  b. 5.0 years
  c. 4.4 years
  d. 2.3 years
  e. 3.9 years

5. A company buys a machine for $180,000 that has an expected life of nine years and no salvage value. The company expects an annual net income (after taxes of 30%) of $8,550. What is the accounting rate of return?
  a. 4.75%
  b. 42.75%
  c. 2.85%
  d. 9.50%
  e. 6.65%

🛇 Icon denotes assignments that involve decision making.

Discussion Questions

1. What is capital budgeting?

2. 🛇 Identify four reasons that capital budgeting decisions by managers are risky.

3. Capital budgeting decisions require careful analysis because they are generally the _____ _____ and _____ decisions that management faces.

4. Identify two disadvantages of using the payback period for comparing investments.

5. 🛇 Why is an investment more attractive to management if it has a shorter payback period?

6. What is the average amount invested in a machine during its predicted five-year life if it costs $200,000 and has a $20,000 salvage value? Assume that net income is received evenly throughout each year and straight-line depreciation is used.

7. If the present value of the expected net cash flows from a machine, discounted at 10%, exceeds the amount to be invested, what can you say about the investment's expected rate of return? What can you say about the expected rate of return if the present value of the net cash flows, discounted at 10%, is less than the investment amount?

8. Why is the present value of $100 that you expect to receive one year from today worth less than $100 received today? What is the present value of $100 that you expect to receive one year from today, discounted at 12%?

9. 🛇 **Nokia** deals with capital budgeting decisions. Why should managers set the required rate of return higher than the rate at which money can be borrowed when making a typical capital budgeting decision?   **NOKIA**

10. 🛇 **Palm** managers must select depreciation methods. Why does the use of the accelerated depreciation method (instead of straight line) for income tax reporting increase an investment's value?   **Palm**

11. 🛇 The management of **Research In Motion** is planning to invest in a new companywide computerized inventory tracking system. What makes this potential investment risky?   **RIM**

12. 🛇 **Apple** is considering expanding a store. Identify three methods management can use to evaluate whether to expand.   **Apple**

13. 🛇 The management of **Apple** is planning to acquire new equipment to manufacture some of its computer peripherals, and it intends to evaluate that investment decision using net present value. What are some of the costs and benefits that would be included in Apple's analysis?   **Apple**

Mc Graw Hill connect

QUICK STUDY

QS 24-1

Analyzing payback periods   P1

Ting Company is considering two alternative investments. The payback period is 3.5 years for investment A and 5 years for investment B. (1) If management relies on the payback period, which investment is preferred? (2) Why might Ting's analysis of these two alternatives lead to the selection of B over A?

QS 24-2

Payback period   P1

Fabiano Brothers Co. is considering an investment that requires immediate payment of $550,000 and provides expected cash inflows of $100,000 annually for eight years. What is the investment's payback period?

QS 24-3

Computation of net present value   P3

If Kelsey K. Company invests $250,000 today, it can expect to receive $50,000 at the end of each year for the next seven years, plus an extra $32,000 at the end of the seventh year. What is the net present value of this investment assuming a required 8% return on investments?

QS 24-4

Computation of accounting rate of return   P2

Cardinal Company is considering an investment expected to generate an average net income after taxes of $1,300 for three years. The investment costs $30,000 and has an estimated $4,000 salvage value. Compute the accounting rate of return for this investment; assume the company uses straight-line depreciation. Hint: Use the formula in Exhibit 24.5 when computing the average annual investment.

QS 24-5

Net present value analysis

P3

Tinto Company is planning to invest in a project at a cost of $135,000. This project has the following expected cash flows over its three-year life: Year 1, $45,000; Year 2, $52,000; and Year 3, $78,000. Management requires a 10% rate of return on its investments. Compute the net present value of this investment.

QS 24-6

Internal rate of return   P4

A company is considering investing in a new machine that requires a cash payment of $15,982 today. The machine will generate annual cash flows of $7,000 for the next three years. What is the internal rate of return if the company buys this machine?

Soles, a shoe manufacturer, is evaluating the costs and benefits of new equipment that would custom fit each pair of athletic shoes. The customer would have his or her foot scanned by digital computer equipment; this information would be used to cut the raw materials to provide the customer a perfect fit. The new equipment costs $100,000 and is expected to generate an additional $35,000 in cash flows for five years. A bank will make a $100,000 loan to the company at a 10% interest rate for this equipment's purchase. Use the following table to determine the break-even time for this equipment. (Round the present value of cash flows to the nearest dollar.)

QS 24-7
Computation of break-even time
A1

Year	Cash Flows*	Present Value of 1 at 10%	Present Value of Cash Flows	Cumulative Present Value of Cash Flows
0	$(100,000)	1.0000		
1	35,000	0.9091		
2	35,000	0.8264		
3	35,000	0.7513		
4	35,000	0.6830		
5	35,000	0.6209		

* All cash flows occur at year-end.

Jester Company is considering two alternative projects. Project 1 requires an initial investment of $500,000 and has a net present value of cash flows of $1,200,000. Project 2 requires an initial investment of $3,500,000 and has a net present value of cash flows of $1,900,000. Compute the profitability index for each project. Based on the profitability index, which project should the company prefer? Explain.

QS 24-8
Profitability index
P3

Siemens AG invests €80 million to build a manufacturing plant to build wind turbines. The company predicts net cash flows of €16 million per year for the next 8 years. Assume the company requires an 8% rate of return from its investments. (1) What is the payback period of this investment? (2) What is the net present value of this investment?

QS 24-9
Capital budgeting methods
P1 P3

connect

Compute the payback period for each of these two separate investments (round the payback period to two decimals):

a. A new operating system for an existing machine is expected to cost $260,000 and have a useful life of five years. The system yields an incremental after-tax income of $75,000 each year after deducting its straight-line depreciation. The predicted salvage value of the system is $10,000.

b. A machine costs $190,000, has a $10,000 salvage value, is expected to last nine years, and will generate an after-tax income of $30,000 per year after straight-line depreciation.

EXERCISES

Exercise 24-1
Payback period computation; even cash flows
P1

Wenro Company is considering the purchase of an asset for $90,000. It is expected to produce the following net cash flows. The cash flows occur evenly throughout each year. Compute the payback period for this investment.

Exercise 24-2
Payback period computation; uneven cash flows
P1

	Year 1	Year 2	Year 3	Year 4	Year 5	Total
Net cash flows	$30,000	$20,000	$30,000	$60,000	$19,000	$159,000

Check   3.167 years

A machine can be purchased for $300,000 and used for 5 years, yielding the following net incomes. In projecting net incomes, double-declining balance depreciation is applied, using a 5-year life and a $50,000 salvage value. Compute the machine's payback period (ignore taxes). (Round the payback period to two decimals.)

Exercise 24-3
Payback period computation; declining-balance depreciation
P1

	Year 1	Year 2	Year 3	Year 4	Year 5
Net incomes	$20,000	$50,000	$100,000	$75,000	$200,000

Check   2.265 years

Exercise 24-4
Accounting rate of return   P2

A machine costs $500,000 and is expected to yield an after-tax net income of $15,000 each year. Management predicts this machine has a 10-year service life and a $100,000 salvage value, and it uses straight-line depreciation. Compute this machine's accounting rate of return.

Exercise 24-5
Payback period and accounting rate of return on investment
P1   P2

K2B Co. is considering the purchase of equipment that would allow the company to add a new product to its line. The equipment is expected to cost $240,000 with a 12-year life and no salvage value. It will be depreciated on a straight-line basis. The company expects to sell 96,000 units of the equipment's product each year. The expected annual income related to this equipment follows. Compute the (1) payback period and (2) accounting rate of return for this equipment.

Sales	$150,000
Costs	
Materials, labor, and overhead (except depreciation)	80,000
Depreciation on new equipment	20,000
Selling and administrative expenses	15,000
Total costs and expenses	115,000
Pretax income	35,000
Income taxes (30%)	10,500
Net income	$ 24,500

Check (1) 5.39 years (2) 20.42%

Exercise 24-6
Computing net present value   P3

After evaluating the risk of the investment described in Exercise 24-5, K2B Co. concludes that it must earn at least an 8% return on this investment. Compute the net present value of this investment. (Round the net present value to the nearest dollar.)

Exercise 24-7
Computation and interpretation of net present value and internal rate of return

P3   P4

Kase Company can invest in each of three cheese-making projects: C1, C2, and C3. Each project requires an initial investment of $190,000 and would yield the following annual cash flows.

	C1	C2	C3
Year 1	$ 10,000	$ 80,000	$150,000
Year 2	90,000	80,000	50,000
Year 3	140,000	80,000	40,000
Totals	$240,000	$240,000	$240,000

Check (1) C2 net present value, $2,152

(1) Assuming that the company requires a 12% return from its investments, use net present value to determine which projects, if any, should be acquired. (2) Using the answer from part 1, explain whether the internal rate of return is higher or lower than 12% for project C2. (3) Compute the internal rate of return for project C2.

Exercise 24-8
NPV and profitability index   P3

Following is information on two alternative investments being considered by Jin Company. The company requires a 10% return from its investments.

	Project A	Project B
Initial investment	$(175,000)	$(145,000)
Expected net cash flows in year:		
1	40,000	32,000
2	56,000	50,000
3	80,295	66,000
4	90,400	72,000
5	55,000	29,000

For each alternative project compute the (a) net present value, and (b) profitability index. If the company can only select one project, which should it choose? Explain.

Exercise 24-9^A
Using Excel to compute IRR   P4

Refer to the information in Exercise 24-8. Create an Excel spreadsheet to compute the internal rate of return for each of the projects. Round the percentage return to two decimals.

This chapter explained two methods to evaluate investments using recovery time, the payback period and break-even time (BET). Refer to QS 24-7 and (1) compute the recovery time for both the payback period and break-even time, (2) discuss the advantage(s) of break-even time over the payback period, and (3) list two conditions under which payback period and break-even time are similar.

Exercise 24-10
Comparison of payback and BET

P1   A1

connect

Elite Company is planning to add a new product to its line. To manufacture this product, the company needs to buy a new machine at a $300,000 cost with an expected four-year life and a $20,000 salvage value. All sales are for cash, and all costs are out of pocket except for depreciation on the new machine. Additional information includes the following.

PROBLEM SET A

Problem 24-1A
Computation of payback period, accounting rate of return, and net present value

P1   P2   P3

mhhe.com/wildFINMAN4e

Expected annual sales of new product	$1,150,000
Expected annual costs of new product	
Direct materials	300,000
Direct labor	420,000
Overhead excluding straight-line depreciation on new machine	210,000
Selling and administrative expenses	100,000
Income taxes	30%

Required

1. Compute straight-line depreciation for each year of this new machine's life. (Round depreciation amounts to the nearest dollar.)
2. Determine expected net income and net cash flow for each year of this machine's life. (Round answers to the nearest dollar.)
3. Compute this machine's payback period, assuming that cash flows occur evenly throughout each year. (Round the payback period to two decimals.)
4. Compute this machine's accounting rate of return, assuming that income is earned evenly throughout each year. (Round the percentage return to two decimals.)
5. Compute the net present value for this machine using a discount rate of 7% and assuming that cash flows occur at each year-end. (*Hint:* Salvage value is a cash inflow at the end of the asset's life. Round the net present value to the nearest dollar.)

Check   (4) 21.88%

(5) $70,915

Pleasant Company has an opportunity to invest in one of two new projects. Project Y requires a $700,000 investment for new machinery with a four-year life and no salvage value. Project Z requires a $700,000 investment for new machinery with a three-year life and no salvage value. The two projects yield the following predicted annual results. The company uses straight-line depreciation, and cash flows occur evenly throughout each year.

Problem 24-2A
Analysis and computation of payback period, accounting rate of return, and net present value

P1   P2   P3

	Project Y	Project Z
Sales	$700,000	$560,000
Expenses		
Direct materials	98,000	70,000
Direct labor	140,000	84,000
Overhead including depreciation	252,000	252,000
Selling and administrative expenses	50,000	50,000
Total expenses	540,000	456,000
Pretax income	160,000	104,000
Income taxes (30%)	48,000	31,200
Net income	$112,000	$ 72,800

Required

1. Compute each project's annual expected net cash flows. (Round the net cash flows to the nearest dollar.)
2. Determine each project's payback period. (Round the payback period to two decimals.)
3. Compute each project's accounting rate of return. (Round the percentage return to one decimal.)

Check   For Project Y: (2) 2.44 years, (3) 32%, (4) $250,573

4. Determine each project's net present value using 8% as the discount rate. For part 4 only, assume that cash flows occur at each year-end. (Round the net present value to the nearest dollar.)

Analysis Component

5. Identify the project you would recommend to management and explain your choice.

Problem 24-3A

Computation of cash flows and net present values with alternative depreciation methods

P3

Angiletta Corporation is considering a new project requiring a $30,000 investment in test equipment with no salvage value. The project would produce $12,000 of pretax income before depreciation at the end of each of the next six years. The company's income tax rate is 40%. In compiling its tax return and computing its income tax payments, the company can choose between the two alternative depreciation schedules shown in the table.

	Straight-Line Depreciation	MACRS Depreciation*
Year 1	$ 3,000	$ 6,000
Year 2	6,000	9,600
Year 3	6,000	5,760
Year 4	6,000	3,456
Year 5	6,000	3,456
Year 6	3,000	1,728
Totals	$30,000	$30,000

* The modified accelerated cost recovery system (MACRS) for depreciation is discussed in Chapter 8.

Required

1. Prepare a five-column table that reports amounts (assuming use of straight-line depreciation) for each of the following for each of the six years: (a) pretax income before depreciation, (b) straight-line depreciation expense, (c) taxable income, (d) income taxes, and (e) net cash flow. Net cash flow equals the amount of income before depreciation minus the income taxes. (Round answers to the nearest dollar.)

2. Prepare a five-column table that reports amounts (assuming use of MACRS depreciation) for each of the following for each of the six years: (a) pretax income before depreciation, (b) MACRS depreciation expense, (c) taxable income, (d) income taxes, and (e) net cash flow. Net cash flow equals the income amount before depreciation minus the income taxes. (Round answers to the nearest dollar.)

Check   Net present value:
(3) $10,041, (4) $10,635

3. Compute the net present value of the investment if straight-line depreciation is used. Use 10% as the discount rate. (Round the net present value to the nearest dollar.)

4. Compute the net present value of the investment if MACRS depreciation is used. Use 10% as the discount rate. (Round the net present value to the nearest dollar.)

Analysis Component

5. Explain why the MACRS depreciation method increases this project's net present value.

Problem 24-4A

Computing net present value of alternate investments

P3

Interstate Manufacturing is considering either replacing one of its old machines with a new machine or having the old machine overhauled. Information about the two alternatives follows. Management requires a 10% rate of return on its investments.

Alternative 1: Keep the old machine and have it overhauled. If the old machine is overhauled, it will be kept for another five years and then sold for its salvage value.

Cost of old machine	$112,000
Cost of overhaul	150,000
Annual expected revenues generated	95,000
Annual cash operating costs after overhaul	42,000
Salvage value of old machine in 5 years	15,000

Alternative 2: Sell the old machine and buy a new one. The new machine is more efficient and will yield substantial operating cost savings with more product being produced and sold.

Cost of new machine	$300,000
Salvage value of old machine now	29,000
Annual expected revenues generated	100,000
Annual cash operating costs.	32,000
Salvage value of new machine in 5 years	20,000

Required

1. Determine the net present value of alternative 1.

2. Determine the net present value of alternative 2.

3. Which alternative do you recommend that management select? Explain.

Check   (1) Net present value of Alternative 1, $60,226

Sentinel Company is considering an investment in technology to improve its operations. The investment will require an initial outlay of $250,000 and will yield the following expected cash flows. Management requires investments to have a payback period of three years, and it requires a 10% return on investments.

Problem 24-5A
Payback period, break-even time, and net present value

P1 A1

Period	Cash Flow
1	$ 47,000
2	52,000
3	75,000
4	94,000
5	125,000

Required

1. Determine the payback period for this investment. (Round the answer to one decimal.)

2. Determine the break-even time for this investment. (Round the answer to one decimal.)

3. Determine the net present value for this investment.

Check   (1) Payback period, 3.8 years

Analysis Component

4. Should management invest in this project? Explain.

Lenitnes Company is considering an investment in technology to improve its operations. The investment will require an initial outlay of $250,000 and will yield the following expected cash flows. Management requires investments to have a payback period of three years, and it requires a 10% return on its investments.

Problem 24-6A
Payback period, break-even time, and net present value

P1 A1

Period	Cash Flow
1	$125,000
2	94,000
3	75,000
4	52,000
5	47,000

Required

1. Determine the payback period for this investment. (Round the answer to one decimal.)

2. Determine the break-even time for this investment. (Round the answer to one decimal.)

3. Determine the net present value for this investment.

Check   (1) Payback period, 2.4 years

Analysis component

4. Should management invest in this project? Explain.

5. Compare your answers for parts 1 through 4 with those for Problem 24-5A. What are the causes of the differences in results and your conclusions?

PROBLEM SET B

Problem 24-1B
Computation of payback period, accounting rate of return, and net present value

P1 P2 P3

Concorde Company is planning to add a new product to its line. To manufacture this product, the company needs to buy a new machine at a $100,000 cost with an expected five-year life and a $25,000 salvage value. All sales are for cash and all costs are out of pocket, except for depreciation on the new machine. Additional information includes the following.

Expected annual sales of new product	$350,000
Expected annual costs of new product	
Direct materials	150,000
Direct labor	50,000
Overhead excluding straight-line depreciation on new machine	100,000
Selling and administrative expenses	23,000
Income taxes	20%

Required

1. Compute straight-line depreciation for each year of this new machine's life. (Round depreciation amounts to the nearest dollar.)

2. Determine expected net income and net cash flow for each year of this machine's life. (Round answers to the nearest dollar.)

3. Compute this machine's payback period, assuming that cash flows occur evenly throughout each year. (Round the payback period to two decimals.)

Check (4) 15.36%

4. Compute this machine's accounting rate of return, assuming that income is earned evenly throughout each year. (Round the percentage return to two decimals.)

(5) $2,862

5. Compute the net present value for this machine using a discount rate of 12% and assuming that cash flows occur at each year-end. (*Hint:* Salvage value is a cash inflow at the end of the asset's life.)

Problem 24-2B
Analysis and computation of payback period, accounting rate of return, and net present value

P1 P2 P3

Micelli Company has an opportunity to invest in one of two projects. Project A requires a $480,000 investment for new machinery with a three-year life and no salvage value. Project B also requires a $480,000 investment for new machinery with a four-year life and no salvage value. The two projects yield the following predicted annual results. The company uses straight-line depreciation, and cash flows occur evenly throughout each year.

	Project A	Project B
Sales	$750,000	$800,000
Expenses		
Direct materials	125,000	250,000
Direct labor	130,000	80,000
Overhead including depreciation	330,000	276,000
Selling and administrative expenses	120,000	120,000
Total expenses	705,000	726,000
Pretax income	45,000	74,000
Income taxes (30%)	13,500	22,200
Net income	$ 31,500	$ 51,800

Required

1. Compute each project's annual expected net cash flows. (Round net cash flows to the nearest dollar.)
2. Determine each project's payback period. (Round the payback period to two decimals.)
3. Compute each project's accounting rate of return. (Round the percentage return to one decimal.)

Check For Project A: (2) 2.5 years, (3) 13.1%, (4) $(3,759)

4. Determine each project's net present value using 10% as the discount rate. For part 4 only, assume that cash flows occur at each year-end. (Round net present values to the nearest dollar.)

Analysis Component

5. Identify the project you would recommend to management and explain your choice.

Cologne Corporation is considering a new project requiring a $25,000 investment in an asset having no salvage value. The project would produce $15,000 of pretax income before depreciation at the end of each of the next six years. The company's income tax rate is 30%. In compiling its tax return and computing its income tax payments, the company can choose between two alternative depreciation schedules as shown in the table.

Problem 24-3B
Computation of cash flows and net present values with alternative depreciation methods

P3

	Straight-Line Depreciation	MACRS Depreciation*
Year 1	$ 2,500	$ 5,000
Year 2	5,000	8,000
Year 3	5,000	4,800
Year 4	5,000	2,880
Year 5	5,000	2,880
Year 6	2,500	1,440
Totals	$25,000	$25,000

* The modified accelerated cost recovery system (MACRS) for depreciation is discussed in Chapter 8.

Required

1. Prepare a five-column table that reports amounts (assuming use of straight-line depreciation) for each of the following items for each of the six years: (a) pretax income before depreciation, (b) straight-line depreciation expense, (c) taxable income, (d) income taxes, and (e) net cash flow. Net cash flow equals the amount of income before depreciation minus the income taxes. (Round answers to the nearest dollar.)

2. Prepare a five-column table that reports amounts (assuming use of MACRS depreciation) for each of the following items for each of the six years: (a) income before depreciation, (b) MACRS depreciation expense, (c) taxable income, (d) income taxes, and (e) net cash flow. Net cash flow equals the amount of income before depreciation minus the income taxes. (Round answers to the nearest dollar.)

3. Compute the net present value of the investment if straight-line depreciation is used. Use 15% as the discount rate. (Round the net present value to the nearest dollar.)

Check   Net present value:
(3) $19,437, (4) $19,914

4. Compute the net present value of the investment if MACRS depreciation is used. Use 15% as the discount rate. (Round the net present value to the nearest dollar.)

Analysis Component

5. Explain why the MACRS depreciation method increases the net present value of this project.

Archer Foods has a freezer that is in need of repair and is considering whether to replace the old freezer with a new freezer or have the old freezer extensively repaired. Information about the two alternatives follows. Management requires a 10% rate of return on its investments.

Problem 24-4B
Computing net present value of alternate investments

P3

Alternative 1: Keep the old freezer and have it repaired. If the old freezer is repaired, it will be kept for another 8 years and then sold for its salvage value.

Cost of old freezer	$75,000
Cost of repair	50,000
Annual expected revenues generated	63,000
Annual cash operating costs after repair	55,000
Salvage value of old freezer in 8 years	3,000

Alternative 2: Sell the old freezer and buy a new one. The new freezer is larger than the old one and will allow the company to expand its product offerings, thereby generating more revenues. Also, it is more energy efficient and will yield substantial operating cost savings.

Cost of new freezer	$150,000
Salvage value of old freezer now	5,000
Annual expected revenues generated	68,000
Annual cash operating costs..................	30,000
Salvage value of new freezer in 8 years	8,000

Required

1. Determine the net present value of alternative 1.

2. Determine the net present value of alternative 2.

3. Which alternative do you recommend that management select? Explain.

Check   (1) Net present value of Alternative 1, $(5,921)

Problem 24-5B
Payback period, break-even
time, and net present value

P1 A1

Aster Company is considering an investment in technology to improve its operations. The investment will
require an initial outlay of $800,000 and yield the following expected cash flows. Management requires
investments to have a payback period of two years, and it requires a 10% return on its investments.

Period	Cash Flow
1	$300,000
2	350,000
3	400,000
4	450,000

Required

Check (1) Payback period,
2.4 years

1. Determine the payback period for this investment.
2. Determine the break-even time for this investment.
3. Determine the net present value for this investment.

Analysis Component

4. Should management invest in this project? Explain.

Problem 24-6B
Payback period, break-even
time, and net present value

P1 A1

Retsa Company is considering an investment in technology to improve its operations. The investment will
require an initial outlay of $800,000 and will yield the following expected cash flows. Management re-
quires investments to have a payback period of two years, and it requires a 10% return on its investments.

Period	Cash Flow
1	$450,000
2	400,000
3	350,000
4	300,000

Required

Check (1) Payback period, 1.9 years

1. Determine the payback period for this investment. (Round the answer to one decimal.)
2. Determine the break-even time for this investment. (Round the answer to one decimal.)
3. Determine the net present value for this investment.

Analysis Component

4. Should management invest in this project? Explain.
5. Compare your answers for parts 1 through 4 with those for Problem 24-5B. What are the causes of the
differences in results and your conclusions?

SERIAL PROBLEM
Business Solutions

P1 P2

*(This serial problem began in Chapter 1 and continues through most of the book. If previous chapter seg-
ments were not completed, the serial problem can begin at this point. It is helpful, but not necessary, to use
the Working Papers that accompany the book.)*

SP 24   Santana Rey is considering the purchase of equipment for Business Solutions that would allow
the company to add a new product to its computer furniture line. The equipment is expected to cost
$300,000 and to have a six-year life and no salvage value. It will be depreciated on a straight-line basis.
Business Solutions expects to sell 100 units of the equipment's product each year. The expected annual
income related to this equipment follows.

Sales	$375,000
Costs	
Materials, labor, and overhead (except depreciation)	200,000
Depreciation on new equipment	50,000
Selling and administrative expenses	37,500
Total costs and expenses	287,500
Pretax income	87,500
Income taxes (30%)	26,250
Net income	$ 61,250

Required

Compute the (1) payback period and (2) accounting rate of return for this equipment. (Record answers as
percents, rounded to one decimal.)

Beyond the Numbers

BTN 24-1   Assume **Research In Motion** invested $834 million to expand its manufacturing capacity. Assume that these assets have a seven-year life, and that Research In Motion requires a 12% internal rate of return on these assets.

Required

1. What is the amount of annual cash flows that Research In Motion must earn from these projects to have a 12% internal rate of return? (*Hint:* Identify the seven-period, 12% factor from the present value of an annuity table, and then divide $834 million by this factor to get the annual cash flows necessary.)

Fast Forward

2. Access RIM's financial statements for fiscal years ended after February 27, 2010, from its Website (**RIM.com**) or the SEC's Website (**SEC.gov**).
    a. Determine the amount that RIM invested in capital assets for the most recent year. (*Hint:* Refer to the statement of cash flows.)
    b. Assume a seven-year life and a 12% internal rate of return. What is the amount of cash flows that RIM must earn on these new projects?

REPORTING IN ACTION

P3

RIM

BTN 24-2   Assume that **Apple** invests $242 million in capital expenditures, including $108 million related to store relocations, remodeling, and new store construction. Assume that these projects have a seven-year life and that management requires a 15% internal rate of return on those projects.

Required

1. What is the amount of annual cash flows that Apple must earn from those store-related projects to achieve a 15% internal rate of return? (*Hint:* Identify the 7-period, 15% factor from the present value of an annuity table and then divide $108 million by the factor to get the annual cash flows required.)
2. BTN 24-1 must be completed to answer part 2. How does your answer to part 1 compare to **RIM**'s required cash flows determined in BTN 24-1? What does this imply about each company's cash flow requirements for these types of projects?

COMPARATIVE ANALYSIS

P3 P4

RIM

Apple

BTN 24-3   A consultant commented that "too often the numbers look good but feel bad." This comment often stems from estimation error common to capital budgeting proposals that relate to future cash flows. Three reasons for this error often exist. First, reliably predicting cash flows several years into the future is very difficult. Second, the present value of cash flows many years into the future (say, beyond 10 years) is often very small. Third, it is difficult for personal biases and expectations not to unduly influence present value computations.

Required

1. Compute the present value of $100 to be received in 10 years assuming a 12% discount rate.
2. Why is understanding the three reasons mentioned for estimation errors important when evaluating investment projects? Link this response to your answer for part 1.

ETHICS CHALLENGE

P3

BTN 24-4   Payback period, accounting rate of return, net present value, and internal rate of return are common methods to evaluate capital investment opportunities. Assume that your manager asks you to identify the type of measurement basis and unit that each method offers and to list the advantages and disadvantages of each. Present your response in memorandum format of less than one page.

COMMUNICATING IN PRACTICE

P1 P2 P3 P4

BTN 24-5   Capital budgeting is an important topic and there are Websites designed to help people understand the methods available. Access **TeachMeFinance.com**'s capital budgeting Webpage (**teachmefinance.com/capitalbudgeting.html**). This Webpage contains an example of a capital budgeting case involving a $15,000 initial cash outflow.

Required

Compute the payback period and the net present value (assuming a 10% required rate of return) of the following investment—assume that its cash flows occur at year-end. Compared to the example case at the

TAKING IT TO THE NET

P1 P3

Website, the larger cash inflows in the example below occur in the later years of the project's life. Is this investment acceptable based on the application of these two capital budgeting methods? Explain.

Year	Cash Flow
0	$(15,000)
1	1,000
2	2,000
3	3,000
4	6,000
5	7,000

TEAMWORK IN ACTION

P1 P3

BTN 24-6   Break into teams and identify four reasons that an international airline such as Southwest, Delta, or American would invest in a project when its direct analysis using both payback period and net present value indicate it to be a poor investment. (*Hint:* Think about qualitative factors.) Provide an example of an investment project supporting your answer.

ENTREPRENEURIAL DECISION

P1 P2 P3 P4

BTN 24-7   Read the chapter opener about Keith Mullin and his company, Gamer Grub. Keith is considering building a new, larger warehousing center to make his business more efficient and reduce costs. He expects that an efficient warehouse could reduce his costs by 20%.

Required

1. What are some of the management tools that he can use to evaluate whether the new warehousing center will be a good investment?
2. What information does he need to use the tools that are identified in your answer to part 1?
3. What are some of the advantages and disadvantages of each tool identified in your answer to part 1?

HITTING THE ROAD

P3

BTN 24-8   Visit or call a local auto dealership and inquire about leasing a car. Ask about the down payment and the required monthly payments. You will likely find the salesperson does not discuss the cost to purchase this car but focuses on the affordability of the monthly payments. This chapter gives you the tools to compute the cost of this car using the lease payment schedule in present dollars and to estimate the profit from leasing for an auto dealership.

Required

1. Compare the cost of leasing the car to buying it in present dollars using the information from the dealership you contact. (Assume you will make a final payment at the end of the lease and then own the car.)
2. Is it more costly to lease or buy the car? Support your answer with computations.

GLOBAL DECISION

C1

BTN 24-9   Nokia's annual report includes information about its debt and interest rates. One statement in its annual report reveals that Nokia recently issued 10-year bonds with a market return of about 6.8%.

Required

Explain how Nokia would use that 6.8% rate to evaluate its investments in capital projects.

ANSWERS TO MULTIPLE CHOICE QUIZ

1. a

2. e;

	Net Cash Flow	Present Value of an Annuity of 1 at 12%	Present Value of Cash Flows
Years 1–3	$3,600 + $30,000	2.4018	$ 80,700
Amount invested			(90,000)
Net present value			$ (9,300)

3. a

4. c; Payback = $270,000/$61,200 per year = 4.4 years.

5. d; Accounting rate of return = $8,550/[($180,000 + $0)/2] = 9.5%.

Appendix

Financial Statement Information

This appendix includes financial information for (1) **Research In Motion**, (2) **Apple**, (3) **Palm**, and (4) **Nokia**. This information is taken from their annual 10-K reports (20-F for Nokia) filed with the SEC. An **annual report** is a summary of a company's financial results for the year along with its current financial condition and future plans. This report is directed to external users of financial information, but it also affects the actions and decisions of internal users.

A company often uses an annual report to showcase itself and its products. Many annual reports include photos, diagrams, and illustrations related to the company. The primary objective of annual reports, however, is the *financial section,* which communicates much information about a company, with most data drawn from the accounting information system. The layout of an annual report's financial section is fairly established and typically includes the following:

- Letter to Shareholders
- Financial History and Highlights
- Management Discussion and Analysis
- Management's Report on Financial Statements and on Internal Controls
- Report of Independent Accountants (Auditor's Report) and on Internal Controls
- Financial Statements
- Notes to Financial Statements
- List of Directors and Officers

This appendix provides the financial statements for Research In Motion (plus selected notes), Apple, Palm, and Nokia. The appendix is organized as follows:

- **Research In Motion** **A-2** through **A-18**
- **Apple** **A-19** through **A-23**
- **Palm** **A-24** through **A-28**
- **Nokia** **A-29** through **A-33**

Many assignments at the end of each chapter refer to information in this appendix. We encourage readers to spend time with these assignments; they are especially useful in showing the relevance and diversity of financial accounting and reporting.

Special note: The SEC maintains the EDGAR (**E**lectronic **D**ata **G**athering, **A**nalysis, and **R**etrieval) database at **www.SEC.gov**. (Over the next few years, the SEC will be moving to IDEA, short for Interactive Data Electronic Applications, which will eventually replace the EDGAR system.) The **Form 10-K** is the annual report form for most companies. It provides electronically accessible information. The **Form 10-KSB** is the annual report form filed by small businesses. It requires slightly less information than the Form 10-K. One of these forms must be filed within 90 days after the company's fiscal year-end. (Forms 10-K405, 10-KT, 10-KT405, and 10-KSB405 are slight variations of the usual form due to certain regulations or rules.)

Research In Motion Financial Report

Research In Motion Limited
Summary Data—Management's Discussion and Analysis of Financial Condition and Results of Operations

As at and for the Fiscal Year Ended	February 27, 2010	February 28, 2009	March 1, 2008	March 3, 2007	March 4, 2006
	(in thousands, except for per share amounts)				
Revenue	$ 14,953,224	$ 11,065,186	$ 6,009,395	$ 3,037,103	$ 2,065,845
Cost of sales	8,368,958	5,967,888	2,928,814	1,379,301	925,598
Gross margin	6,584,266	5,097,298	3,080,581	1,657,802	1,140,247
Operating expenses					
Research and development	964,841	684,702	359,828	236,173	158,887
Selling, marketing and administration	1,907,398	1,495,697	881,482	537,922	314,317
Amortization	310,357	194,803	108,112	76,879	49,951
Litigation	163,800	—	—	—	201,791
Total operating expenses	3,346,396	2,375,202	1,349,422	850,974	724,946
Income from operations	3,237,870	2,722,096	1,731,159	806,828	415,301
Investment income	28,640	78,267	79,361	52,117	66,218
Income before income taxes	3,266,510	2,800,363	1,810,520	858,945	481,519
Provision for income taxes	809,366	907,747	516,653	227,373	106,863
Net income	$ 2,457,144	$ 1,892,616	$ 1,293,867	$ 631,572	$ 374,656
Earnings per share					
Basic	$ 4.35	$ 3.35	$ 2.31	$ 1.14	$ 0.66
Diluted	$ 4.31	$ 3.30	$ 2.26	$ 1.10	$ 0.64
Weighted-average number of shares outstanding (000's)					
Basic	564,492	565,059	559,778	556,059	566,742
Diluted	569,759	574,156	572,830	571,809	588,468
Total asset	$ 10,204,409	$ 8,101,372	$ 5,511,187	$ 3,088,949	$ 2,314,349
Total liabilities	$ 2,601,746	$ 2,227,244	$ 1,577,621	$ 605,449	$ 318,934
Total long-term liabilities	$ 169,969	$ 111,893	$ 103,190	$ 58,874	$ 34,709
Shareholders' equity	$ 7,602,663	$ 5,874,128	$ 3,933,566	$ 2,483,500	$ 1,995,415

REPORT OF
INDEPENDENT REGISTERED PUBLIC ACCOUNTING FIRM

To the Shareholders of **Research In Motion Limited**

We have audited the accompanying consolidated balance sheets of **Research In Motion Limited** [the "Company"] as at February 27, 2010 and February 28, 2009, and the related consolidated statements of operations, shareholders' equity and cash flows for the years ended February 27, 2010, February 28, 2009 and March 1, 2008. These financial statements are the responsibility of the Company's management. Our responsibility is to express an opinion on these financial statements based on our audits.

We conducted our audits in accordance with Canadian generally accepted auditing standards and the standards of the Public Company Accounting Oversight Board (United States). Those standards require that we plan and perform the audit to obtain reasonable assurance about whether the financial statements are free of material misstatement. An audit includes examining, on a test basis, evidence supporting the amounts and disclosures in the financial statements. An audit also includes assessing the accounting principles used and significant estimates made by management, as well as evaluating the overall financial statement presentation. We believe that our audits provide a reasonable basis for our opinion.

In our opinion, the consolidated financial statements referred to above present fairly, in all material respects, the financial position of the Company as at February 27, 2010 and February 28, 2009, and the results of its operations and its cash flows for the years ended February 27, 2010, February 28, 2009 and March 1, 2008, in conformity with United States generally accepted accounting principles.

We also have audited, in accordance with the standards of the Public Company Accounting Oversight Board (United States), the Company's internal control over financial reporting as of February 27, 2010, based on criteria established in Internal Control-Integrated Framework issued by the Committee of Sponsoring Organizations of the Treadway Commission and our report dated April 1, 2010 expressed an unqualified opinion thereon.

Ernst & Young LLP

Kitchener, Canada,
April 1, 2010.

Chartered Accountants
Licensed Public Accountants

RESEARCH IN MOTION

RESEARCH IN MOTION

**REPORT OF
INDEPENDENT REGISTERED PUBLIC ACCOUNTING FIRM
ON INTERNAL CONTROL OVER FINANCIAL REPORTING**

To the Shareholders of **Research In Motion Limited**

We have audited **Research In Motion Limited's** [the "Company"] internal control over financial reporting as of February 27, 2010, based on criteria established in Internal Control — Integrated Framework issued by the Committee of Sponsoring Organizations of the Treadway Commission ["the COSO criteria"]. The Company's management is responsible for maintaining effective internal control over financial reporting, and for its assessment of the effectiveness of internal control over financial reporting. Our responsibility is to express an opinion on the Company's internal control over financial reporting based on our audit.

We conducted our audit in accordance with the standards of the Public Company Accounting Oversight Board (United States). Those standards require that we plan and perform the audit to obtain reasonable assurance about whether effective internal control over financial reporting was maintained in all material respects. Our audit included obtaining an understanding of internal control over financial reporting, assessing the risk that a material weakness exists, testing and evaluating the design and operating effectiveness of internal control based on the assessed risk, and performing such other procedures as we considered necessary in the circumstances. We believe that our audit provides a reasonable basis for our opinion.

A company's internal control over financial reporting is a process designed to provide reasonable assurance regarding the reliability of financial reporting and the preparation of financial statements for external purposes in accordance with generally accepted accounting principles. A company's internal control over financial reporting includes those policies and procedures that [1] pertain to the maintenance of records that, in reasonable detail, accurately and fairly reflect the transactions and dispositions of the assets of the company; [2] provide reasonable assurance that transactions are recorded as necessary to permit preparation of financial statements in accordance with generally accepted accounting principles, and that receipts and expenditures of the company are being made only in accordance with authorizations of management and directors of the company; and [3] provide reasonable assurance regarding prevention or timely detection of unauthorized acquisition, use or disposition of the company's assets that could have a material effect on the financial statements.

Because of its inherent limitations, internal control over financial reporting may not prevent or detect misstatements. Also, projections of any evaluation of effectiveness to future periods are subject to the risk that controls may become inadequate because of changes in conditions, or that the degree of compliance with the policies or procedures may deteriorate.

In our opinion, the Company maintained, in all material respects, effective internal control over financial reporting as of February 27, 2010, based on the COSO criteria**.**

We also have audited, in accordance with the standards of the Public Company Accounting Oversight Board (United States), the consolidated balance sheets of the Company as at February 27, 2010 and February 28, 2009, and the consolidated statements of operations, shareholders' equity and cash flows for the years ended February 27, 2010, February 28, 2009 and March 1, 2008 of the Company and our report dated April 1, 2010 expressed an unqualified opinion thereon.

Ernst & Young LLP

Kitchener, Canada,
April 1, 2010.

Chartered Accountants
Licensed Public Accountants

Research In Motion Limited
Consolidated Balance Sheets

($US, in thousands)	February 27, 2010	February 28, 2009
Assets		
Current		
Cash and cash equivalents	$ 1,550,861	$ 835,546
Short-term investments	360,614	682,666
Accounts receivable, net	2,593,742	2,112,117
Other receivables	206,373	157,728
Inventories	621,611	682,400
Other current assets	285,539	187,257
Deferred income tax asset	193,916	183,872
Total current assets	5,812,656	4,841,586
Long-term investments	958,248	720,635
Property, plant and equipment, net	1,956,581	1,334,648
Intangible assets, net	1,326,363	1,066,527
Goodwill	150,561	137,572
Deferred income tax asset	—	404
Total assets	$10,204,409	$8,101,372
Liabilities		
Current		
Accounts payable	$ 615,620	$ 448,339
Accrued liabilities	1,638,260	1,238,602
Income taxes payable	95,650	361,460
Deferred revenue	67,573	53,834
Deferred income tax liability	14,674	13,116
Total current liabilities	2,431,777	2,115,351
Deferred income tax liability	141,382	87,917
Income taxes payable	28,587	23,976
Total liabilities	2,601,746	2,227,244
Shareholders' Equity		
Capital stock		
Preferred shares, authorized unlimited number of non-voting, cumulative, redeemable and retractable	—	—
Common shares, authorized unlimited number of non-voting, redeemable, retractable Class A common shares and unlimited number of voting common shares. Issued — 557,328,394 voting common shares (February 28, 2009 — 566,218,819)	2,207,609	2,208,235
Treasury stock		
February 27, 2010 — 1,458,950 (February 28, 2009 — nil)	(94,463)	—
Retained earnings	5,274,365	3,545,710
Additional paid-in capital	164,060	119,726
Accumulated other comprehensive income	51,092	457
Total shareholders equity	7,602,663	5,874,128
Total liabilities and shareholders' equity	$10,204,409	$8,101,372

RESEARCH IN MOTION

Research In Motion Limited
Consolidated Statements of Operations

($US, in thousands, except per share data)

For the Year Ended	February 27, 2010	February 28, 2009	March 1, 2008
Revenue			
Devices and other	$12,535,998	$ 9,410,755	$4,914,366
Service and software	2,417,226	1,654,431	1,095,029
Total revenue	$14,953,224	11,065,186	6,009,395
Cost of sales			
Devices and other	7,979,163	5,718,041	2,758,250
Service and software	389,795	249,847	170,564
Total cost of sales	8,368,958	5,967,888	2,928,814
Gross margin	6,584,266	5,097,298	3,080,581
Operating expenses			
Research and development	964,841	684,702	359,828
Selling, marketing and administration	1,907,398	1,495,697	881,482
Amortization	310,357	194,803	108,112
Litigation	163,800	—	—
Total operating expenses	3,346,396	2,375,202	1,349,422
Income from operations	3,237,870	2,722,096	1,731,159
Investment income	28,640	78,267	79,361
Income before income taxes	3,266,510	2,800,363	1,810,520
Provision for income taxes	809,366	907,747	516,653
Net income	$ 2,457,144	$ 1,892,616	$1,293,867
Earnings per share			
Basic	$ 4.35	$ 3.35	$ 2.31
Diluted	$ 4.31	$ 3.30	$ 2.26

Research In Motion Limited

Consolidated Statements of Shareholders' Equity

($US, in thousands)	Capital Stock	Additional Paid-In Capital	Treasury Stock	Retained Earnings	Accumulated Other Comprehensive Income (Loss)	Total
Balance as at March 3, 2007	$2,099,696	$ 36,093	$ —	$ 359,227	$(11,516)	$2,483,500
Comprehensive income (loss):						
Net income	—	—	—	1,293,867	—	1,293,867
Net change in unrealized gains on available-for-sale investments	—	—	—	—	13,467	13,467
Net change in fair value of derivatives designated as cash flow hedges during the year	—	—	—	—	37,564	37,564
Amounts reclassified to earnings during the year	—	—	—	—	(9,232)	(9,232)
Other paid-in capital	—	9,626	—	—	—	9,626
Shares issued:						
Exercise of stock options	62,889	—	—	—	—	62,889
Transfers to capital stock from stock option exercises	7,271	(7,271)	—	—	—	—
Stock-based compensation	—	33,700	—	—	—	33,700
Excess tax benefits from stock-based compensation	—	8,185	—	—	—	8,185
Balance as at March 1, 2008	$2,169,856	$ 80,333	$ —	$1,653,094	$ 30,283	$3,933,566
Comprehensive income (loss):						
Net income	—	—	—	1,892,616	—	1,892,616
Net change in unrealized gains on available-for-sale investments	—	—	—	—	(7,161)	(7,161)
Net change in fair value of derivatives designated as cash flow hedges during the year	—	—	—	—	(6,168)	(6,168)
Amounts reclassified to earnings during the year	—	—	—	—	(16,497)	(16,497)
Shares issued:						
Exercise of stock options	27,024	—	—	—	—	27,024
Transfers to capital stock from stock option exercises	11,355	(11,355)	—	—	—	—
Stock-based compensation	—	38,100	—	—	—	38,100
Excess tax benefits from stock-based compensation	—	12,648	—	—	—	12,648
Balance as at February 28, 2009	$2,208,235	$119,726	$ —	$3,545,710	$ 457	$5,874,128
Comprehensive income:						
Net income	—	—	—	2,457,144	—	2,457,144
Net change in unrealized gains on available-for-sale investments	—	—	—	—	6,803	6,803
Net change in fair value of derivatives designated as cash flow hedges during the year	—	—	—	—	28,324	28,324
Amounts reclassified to earnings during the year	—	—	—	—	15,508	15,508
Shares issued:						
Exercise of stock options	30,246	—	—	—	—	30,246
Transfers to capital stock from stock option exercises	15,647	(15,647)	—	—	—	—
Stock-based compensation	—	58,038	—	—	—	58,038
Excess tax benefits from stock-based compensation	—	1,943	—	—	—	1,943
Purchase of treasury stock	—	—	(94,463)	—	—	(94,463)
Common shares repurchased	(46,519)	—	—	(728,489)	—	(775,008)
Balance as at February 27, 2010	$2,207,609	$164,060	$(94,463)	$5,274,365	$ 51,092	$7,602,663

RESEARCH IN MOTION

Research In Motion Limited
Consolidated Statements of Cash Flows

For the Year Ended ($US, in thousands)	February 27, 2010	February 28, 2009	March 1, 2008
Cash flows from operating activities			
Net income	$ 2,457,144	$ 1,892,616	$ 1,293,867
Adjustments to reconcile net income to net cash provided by operating activities:			
Amortization	615,621	327,896	177,366
Deferred income taxes	51,363	(36,623)	(67,244)
Income taxes payable	4,611	(6,897)	4,973
Stock-based compensation	58,038	38,100	33,700
Other	8,806	5,867	3,303
Net changes in working capital items	(160,709)	(769,114)	130,794
Net cash provided by operating activities	3,034,874	1,451,845	1,576,759
Cash flows from investing activities			
Acquisition of long-term investments	(862,977)	(507,082)	(757,656)
Proceeds on sale or maturity of long-term investments	473,476	431,713	260,393
Acquisition of property, plant and equipment	(1,009,416)	(833,521)	(351,914)
Acquisition of intangible assets	(421,400)	(687,913)	(374,128)
Business acquisitions, net of cash acquired	(143,375)	(48,425)	(6,200)
Acquisition of short-term investments	(476,956)	(917,316)	(1,249,919)
Proceeds on sale or maturity of short-term investments	970,521	739,021	1,325,487
Net cash used in investing activities	(1,470,127)	(1,823,523)	(1,153,937)
Cash flows from financing activities			
Issuance of common shares	30,246	27,024	62,889
Additional paid-in capital	—	—	9,626
Excess tax benefits from stock-based compensation	1,943	12,648	8,185
Purchase of treasury stock	(94,463)	—	—
Common shares repurchased	(775,008)	—	—
Repayment of debt	(6,099)	(14,305)	(302)
Net cash provided by (used in) financing activities	(843,381)	25,367	80,398
Effect of foreign exchange gain (loss) on cash and cash equivalents	(6,051)	(2,541)	4,034
Net increase (decrease) in cash and cash equivalents for the year	715,315	(348,852)	507,254
Cash and cash equivalents, beginning of year	835,546	1,184,398	677,144
Cash and cash equivalents, end of year	$ 1,550,861	$ 835,546	$ 1,184,398

RIM—SELECTED Notes to the Consolidated Financial Statements

$US in thousands, except share and per share data, and where otherwise indicated

1. RESEARCH IN MOTION LIMITED AND SUMMARY OF SIGNIFICANT ACCOUNTING POLICIES

Research In Motion Limited ("RIM" or the "Company") is a leading designer, manufacturer and marketer of innovative wireless solutions for the worldwide mobile communications market. Through the development of integrated hardware, software and services that support multiple wireless network standards, RIM provides platforms and solutions for seamless access to time-sensitive information including email, phone, short messaging service (SMS), Internet and intranet-based applications. RIM technology also enables a broad array of third party developers and manufacturers to enhance their products and services with wireless connectivity to data. RIM's portfolio of award-winning products, services and embedded technologies are used by thousands of organizations and millions of consumers around the world and include the BlackBerry wireless solution, and other software and hardware. The Company's sales and marketing efforts include collaboration with strategic partners and distribution channels, as well as its own supporting sales and marketing teams, to promote the sale of its products and services.

Basis of presentation and preparation

The consolidated financial statements include the accounts of all subsidiaries of the Company with intercompany transactions and balances eliminated on consolidation. All of the Company's subsidiaries are wholly-owned. These consolidated financial statements have been prepared by management in accordance with United States generally accepted accounting principles ("U.S. GAAP") on a basis consistent for all periods presented except as described in note 2. Certain of the comparative figures have been reclassified to conform to the current year presentation. The Company's fiscal year end date is the 52 or 53 weeks ending on the last Saturday of February, or the first Saturday of March. The fiscal years ended February 27, 2010, February 28, 2009, and March 1, 2008 comprise 52 weeks.

The significant accounting policies used in these U.S. GAAP consolidated financial statements are as follows:

Use of estimates

The preparation of the consolidated financial statements requires management to make estimates and assumptions with respect to the reported amounts of assets, liabilities, revenues and expenses and the disclosure of contingent assets and liabilities. Significant areas requiring the use of management estimates relate to the determination of reserves for various litigation claims, provisions for excess and obsolete inventories and liabilities for purchase commitments with contract manufacturers and suppliers, fair values of assets acquired and liabilities assumed in business combinations, royalties, amortization expense, implied fair value of goodwill, provision for income taxes, realization of deferred income tax assets and the related components of the valuation allowance, provisions for warranty and the fair values of financial instruments. Actual results could differ from these estimates.

Foreign currency translation

The U.S. dollar is the functional and reporting currency of the Company. Foreign currency denominated assets and liabilities of the Company and all of its subsidiaries are translated into U.S. dollars. Accordingly, monetary assets and liabilities are translated using the exchange rates in effect at the consolidated balance sheet date and revenues and expenses at the rates of exchange prevailing when the transactions occurred. Remeasurement adjustments are included in income. Non-monetary assets and liabilities are translated at historical exchange rates.

Cash and cash equivalents

Cash and cash equivalents consist of balances with banks and liquid investments with maturities of three months or less at the date of acquisition.

Accounts receivable, net

The accounts receivable balance which reflects invoiced and accrued revenue is presented net of an allowance for doubtful accounts. The allowance for doubtful accounts reflects estimates of probable losses in accounts receivables. The Company is dependent on a number of significant customers and on large complex contracts with respect to sales of the majority of its products, software and services. The Company expects the majority of its accounts receivable balances to continue to come from large customers as it sells the majority of its devices and software products and service relay access through network carriers and resellers rather than directly.

The Company evaluates the collectability of its accounts receivables based upon a combination of factors on a periodic basis such as specific credit risk of its customers, historical trends and economic circumstances. The Company, in the normal course of business, monitors the financial condition of its customers and reviews the credit history of each new

RESEARCH IN MOTION

$US in thousands, except share and per share data, and where otherwise indicated

customer. When the Company becomes aware of a specific customer's inability to meet its financial obligations to the Company (such as in the case of bankruptcy filings or material deterioration in the customer's operating results or financial position, and payment experiences), RIM records a specific bad debt provision to reduce the customer's related accounts receivable to its estimated net realizable value. If circumstances related to specific customers change, the Company's estimates of the recoverability of accounts receivables balances could be further adjusted. The allowance for doubtful accounts as at February 27, 2010 is $2.0 million (February 28, 2009- $2.1 million).

Investments

The Company's investments, other than cost method investments of $2.5 million and equity method investments of $4.1 million, consist of money market and other debt securities, and are classified as available-for-sale for accounting purposes. The Company does not exercise significant influence with respect to any of these investments.

Investments with maturities one year or less, as well as any investments that management intends to hold for less than one year, are classified as short-term investments. Investments with maturities in excess of one year are classified as long-term investments.

The Company determines the appropriate classification of investments at the time of purchase and subsequently reassesses the classification of such investments at each balance sheet date. Investments classified as available-for-sale are carried at fair value with unrealized gains and losses recorded in accumulated other comprehensive income (loss) until such investments mature or are sold. The Company uses the specific identification method of determining the cost basis in computing realized gains or losses on available-for-sale investments which are recorded in investment income.

The Company assesses individual investments in an unrealized loss position to determine whether the unrealized loss is other-than-temporary. The Company makes this assessment by considering available evidence, including changes in general market conditions, specific industry and individual company data, the length of time and the extent to which the fair value has been less than cost, the financial condition, the near-term prospects of the individual investment and the Company's intent and ability to hold the investments. In the event that a decline in the fair value of an investment occurs and the decline in value is considered to be other-than-temporary, an impairment charge is recorded in investment income equal to the difference between the cost basis and the fair value of the individual investment at the balance sheet date of the reporting period for which the assessment was made. The fair value of the investment then becomes the new cost basis of the investment.

Effective in the second quarter of fiscal 2010, if a debt security's market value is below its amortized cost and the Company either intends to sell the security or it is more likely than not that the Company will be required to sell the security before its anticipated recovery, the Company records an other-than-temporary impairment charge to investment income for the entire amount of the impairment. For other-than-temporary impairments on debt securities that the Company does not intend to sell and it is not more likely than not that the entity will be required to sell the security before its anticipated recovery, the Company would separate the other-than-temporary impairment into the amount representing the credit loss and the amount related to all other factors. The Company would record the other-than-temporary impairment related to the credit loss as a charge to investment income and the remaining other-than-temporary impairment would be recorded as a component of accumulated other comprehensive income.

Derivative financial instruments

The Company uses derivative financial instruments, including forward contracts and options, to hedge certain foreign currency exposures. The Company does not use derivative financial instruments for speculative purposes.

Inventories

Raw materials are stated at the lower of cost and replacement cost. Work in process and finished goods inventories are stated at the lower of cost and net realizable value. Cost includes the cost of materials plus direct labour applied to the product and the applicable share of manufacturing overhead. Cost is determined on a first-in-first-out basis.

Property, plant and equipment, net

Property, plant and equipment is stated at cost less accumulated amortization. No amortization is provided for construction in progress until the assets are ready for use. Amortization is provided using the following rates and methods:

Buildings, leaseholds and other	Straight-line over terms between 5 and 40 years
BlackBerry operations and other information technology . . .	Straight-line over terms between 3 and 5 years
Manufacturing equipment, R&D equipment and tooling . . .	Straight-line over terms between 2 and 8 years
Furniture and fixtures	Declining balance at 20% per annum

$US in thousands, except share and per share data, and where otherwise indicated

Intangible assets, net

Intangible assets are stated at cost less accumulated amortization and are comprised of acquired technology, licenses, and patents. Acquired technology consists of purchased developed technology arising from the Company's business acquisitions. Licenses include licenses or agreements that the Company has negotiated with third parties upon use of third parties' technology. Patents comprise trademarks, internally developed patents, as well as individual patents or portfolios of patents acquired from third parties. Costs capitalized and subsequently amortized include all costs necessary to acquire intellectual property, such as patents and trademarks, as well as legal defense costs arising out of the assertion of any Company-owned patents.

Intangible assets are amortized as follows:

Acquired technology	Straight-line over 2 to 5 years
Licenses	Straight-line over terms of the license agreements or on a per unit basis based upon the anticipated number of units sold during the terms, subject to a maximum of 5 years
Patents	Straight-line over 17 years or over estimated useful life

Goodwill

Goodwill represents the excess of the purchase price of business acquisitions over the fair value of identifiable net assets acquired. Goodwill is allocated as at the date of the business combination. Goodwill is not amortized, but is tested for impairment annually, or more frequently if events or changes in circumstances indicate the asset may be impaired.

Impairment of long-lived assets

The Company reviews long-lived assets such as property, plant and equipment and intangible assets with finite useful lives for impairment whenever events or changes in circumstances indicate that the carrying amount may not be recoverable. If the total of the expected undiscounted future cash flows is less than the carrying amount of the asset, a loss is recognized for the excess of the carrying amount over the fair value of the asset.

Income taxes

The Company uses the liability method of tax allocation to account for income taxes. Deferred income tax assets and liabilities are recognized based upon temporary differences between the financial reporting and tax bases of assets and liabilities, and measured using enacted tax rates and laws that will be in effect when the differences are expected to reverse. The Company records a valuation allowance to reduce deferred income tax assets to the amount that is more likely than not to be realized. The Company considers both positive evidence and negative evidence, to determine whether, based upon the weight of that evidence, a valuation allowance is required. Judgment is required in considering the relative impact of negative and positive evidence.

Revenue recognition

The Company recognizes revenue when it is realized or realizable and earned. The Company considers revenue realized or realizable and earned when it has persuasive evidence of an arrangement, the product has been delivered or the services have been provided to the customer, the sales price is fixed or determinable and collectability is reasonably assured. In addition to this general policy, the following paragraphs describe the specific revenue recognition policies for each major category of revenue.

Devices

Revenue from the sales of BlackBerry devices is recognized when title is transferred to the customer and all significant contractual obligations that affect the customer's final acceptance have been fulfilled. For hardware products for which software is deemed not to be incidental, the Company recognizes revenue in accordance with industry specific software revenue recognition guidance. The Company records reductions to revenue for estimated commitments related to price protection and for customer incentive programs, including reseller and end-user rebates. The estimated cost of the incentive programs are accrued based on historical experience, as a reduction to revenue in the period the Company has sold the product and committed to a plan. Price protection is accrued as a reduction to revenue based on estimates of future price reductions and certain agreed customer inventories at the date of the price adjustment. In addition, provisions are made at the time of sale for warranties and royalties.

Service

Revenue from service is recognized rateably on a monthly basis when the service is provided. In instances where the Company bills the customer prior to performing the service, the prebilling is recorded as deferred revenue.

Software

Revenue from licensed software is recognized at the inception of the license term and in accordance with industry

$US in thousands, except share and per share data, and where otherwise indicated

specific software revenue recognition guidance. When the fair value of a delivered element has not been established, the Company uses the residual method to recognize revenue if the fair value of undelivered elements is determinable. Revenue from software maintenance, unspecified upgrades and technical support contracts is recognized over the period that such items are delivered or that services are provided.

Other

Revenue from the sale of accessories is recognized when title is transferred to the customer and all significant contractual obligations that affect the customer's final acceptance have been fulfilled. Technical support ("T-Support") contracts extending beyond the current period are recorded as deferred revenue. Revenue from repair and maintenance programs is recognized when the service is delivered which is when the title is transferred to the customer and all significant contractual obligations that affect the customer's final acceptance have been fulfilled. Revenue for non-recurring engineering contracts is recognized as specific contract milestones are met. The attainment of milestones approximates actual performance.

Shipping and handling costs

Shipping and handling costs charged to income are included in cost of sales where they can be reasonably attributed to certain revenue; otherwise they are included in selling, marketing and administration.

Multiple-element arrangements

The Company enters into transactions that represent multiple-element arrangements which may include any combination of hardware and/or service or software and T-Support. These multiple-element arrangements are assessed to determine whether they can be separated into more than one unit of accounting or element for the purpose of revenue recognition. When the appropriate criteria for separating revenue into more than one unit of accounting is met and there is vendor specific objective evidence of fair value for all units of accounting or elements in an arrangement, the arrangement consideration is allocated to the separate units of accounting or elements based on each unit's relative fair value. When the fair value of a delivered element has not been established, the Company uses the residual method to recognize revenue if the fair value of undelivered elements is determinable. This vendor specific objective evidence of fair value is established through prices charged for each revenue element when that element is sold separately. The revenue recognition policies described above are then applied to each unit of accounting.

Research and development

Research costs are expensed as incurred. Development costs for BlackBerry devices and licensed software to be sold, leased or otherwise marketed are subject to capitalization beginning when a product's technological feasibility has been established and ending when a product is available for general release to customers. The Company's products are generally released soon after technological feasibility has been established and therefore costs incurred subsequent to achievement of technological feasibility are not significant and have been expensed as incurred.

Comprehensive income (loss)

Comprehensive income (loss) is defined as the change in net assets of a business enterprise during a period from transactions and other events and circumstances from non-owner sources and includes all changes in equity during a period except those resulting from investments by owners and distributions to owners. The Company's reportable items of comprehensive income are cash flow hedges and changes in the fair value of available-for-sale investments. Realized gains or losses on available-for-sale investments are reclassified into investment income using the specific identification basis.

Earnings per share

Earnings per share is calculated based on the weighted-average number of shares outstanding during the year. The treasury stock method is used for the calculation of the dilutive effect of stock options.

Stock-based compensation plans

The Company has stock-based compensation plans.

Warranty

The Company provides for the estimated costs of product warranties at the time revenue is recognized. BlackBerry devices are generally covered by a time-limited warranty for varying periods of time. The Company's warranty obligation is affected by product failure rates, differences in warranty periods, regulatory developments with respect to warranty obligations in the countries in which the Company carries on business, freight expense, and material usage and other related repair costs. The Company's estimates of costs are based upon historical experience and expectations of future return rates and unit warranty repair cost. If the Company experiences increased or decreased warranty activity, or increased or decreased costs associated with servicing those obligations, revisions to the estimated warranty liability would be recognized in the reporting period when such revisions are made.

Advertising costs

The Company expenses all advertising costs as incurred. These costs are included in selling, marketing and administration.

$US in thousands, except share and per share data, and where otherwise indicated

4.   CASH, CASH EQUIVALENTS AND INVESTMENTS

The components of cash, cash equivalents and investments were as follows:

	Cost Basis	Unrealized Gains	Unrealized Losses	Recorded Basis	Cash and Cash Equivalents	Short-term Investments	Long-term Investments
As at February 27, 2010							
Bank balances	$ 535,445	$ —	$ —	$ 535,445	$ 535,445	$ —	$ —
Money market fund	3,278	—	—	3,278	3,278	—	—
Bankers acceptances and term deposits/certificates	377,596	—	—	377,596	377,596	—	—
Commercial paper and corporate notes/bonds	855,145	6,528	(49)	861,624	472,312	187,369	201,943
Treasury bills/notes	203,514	129	(12)	203,631	92,272	50,786	60,573
Government sponsored enterprise notes	447,131	2,590	(13)	449,708	69,958	111,977	267,773
Asset-backed securities	393,751	5,280	(50)	398,981	—	10,482	388,499
Auction-rate securities	40,527	—	(7,688)	32,839	—	—	32,839
Other investments	6,621	—	—	6,621	—	—	6,621
	$2,863,008	$14,527	$ (7,812)	$2,869,723	$1,550,861	$360,614	$958,248

Realized gains and losses on available-for-sale securities comprise the following:

For the year ended	February 27, 2010	February 28, 2009	March 1, 2008
Realized gains	$439	$ 158	$ 10
Realized losses	(17)	(1,801)	(410)
Net realized gains (losses)	$422	$(1,643)	$(400)

The contractual maturities of available-for-sale investments at February 27, 2010 were as follows:

	Cost Basis	Fair Value
Due in one year or less	$1,371,047	$1,372,752
Due in one to five years	773,471	783,451
Due after five years	173,146	168,176
No fixed maturity date	3,278	3,278
	$2,320,942	$2,327,657

5.   FAIR VALUE MEASUREMENTS

The Company defines fair value as the price that would be received to sell an asset or paid to transfer a liability in an orderly transaction between market participants at the measurement date. When determining the fair value measurements for assets and liabilities required to be recorded at fair value, the Company considers the principal or most advantageous market in which it would transact and considers assumptions that market participants would use in pricing the asset or liability such as inherent risk, non-performance risk and credit risk. The Company applies the following fair value hierarchy, which prioritizes the inputs used in the valuation methodologies in measuring fair value into three levels:

- Level 1 — Unadjusted quoted prices at the measurement date for identical assets or liabilities in active markets.

- Level 2 — Observable inputs other than quoted prices included in Level 1, such as quoted prices for similar assets and liabilities in active markets; quoted prices for identical or similar assets and liabilities in markets that are not active; or other inputs that are observable or can be corroborated by observable market data.

- Level 3 — Significant unobservable inputs which are supported by little or no market activity.

The fair value hierarchy also requires the Company to maximize the use of observable inputs and minimize the use of unobservable inputs when measuring fair value. The carrying amounts of the Company's cash and cash equivalents, accounts receivable, other receivables, accounts payable and accrued liabilities, approximate fair value due to their short maturities. When determining the fair value of its investments held, the Company primarily relies on an independent third party valuator for the fair valuation of securities.

$US in thousands, except share and per share data, and where otherwise indicated

6.　INVENTORIES

Inventories were comprised as follows:

	February 27, 2010	February 28, 2009
Raw materials	$ 490,063	$464,497
Work in process	231,939	250,728
Finished goods	17,068	35,264
Provision for excess and obsolete inventories	(117,459)	(68,089)
	$ 621,611	$682,400

7.　PROPERTY, PLANT AND EQUIPMENT, NET

Property, plant and equipment were comprised of the following:

February 27, 2010	Cost	Accumulated amortization	Net book value
Land	$ 104,254	$ —	$ 104,254
Buildings, leaseholds and other	926,747	115,216	811,531
BlackBerry operations and other information technology	1,152,637	484,180	668,457
Manufacturing equipment, research and development equipment, and tooling	347,692	182,228	165,464
Furniture and fixtures	346,641	139,766	206,875
	$2,877,971	$921,390	$1,956,581

As at February 27, 2010, the carrying amount of assets under construction was $254.3 million (February 28, 2009 — $88.9 million). Of this amount, $110.9 million (February 28, 2009 — $50.0 million) was included in buildings, leaseholds and other; $102.5 million (February 28, 2009 - $35.8 million) was included in BlackBerry operations and other information technology; and $40.9 million (February 28, 2009 — $3.2 million) was included in manufacturing equipment, research and development equipment, and tooling. As at February 27, 2010, $31.7 million has been classified as an asset held for sale and accordingly has been reclassified from property, plant and equipment to other current assets. For the year ended February 27, 2010, amortization expense related to property, plant and equipment was $344.5 million (February 28, 2009 — $203.4 million; March 1, 2008 — $133.1 million).

8.　INTANGIBLE ASSETS, NET

Intangible assets were comprised of the following:

February 27, 2010	Cost	Accumulated amortization	Net book value
Acquired technology	$ 165,791	$ 70,777	$ 95,014
Licenses	711,969	196,618	515,351
Patents	889,467	173,469	715,998
	$1,767,227	$440,864	$1,326,363

For the year ended February 27, 2010, amortization expense related to intangible assets was $271.1 million (February 28, 2009 — $124.5 million; March 1, 2008 — $44.3 million). Total additions to intangible assets in fiscal 2010 were $531.0 million (2009 — $721.1 million). Based on the carrying value of the identified intangible assets as at February 27, 2010 and assuming no subsequent impairment of the underlying assets, the annual amortization expense for the next five fiscal years is expected to be as follows: 2011 — $324 million; 2012 — $275 million; 2013 — $227 million; 2014 — $139 million; and 2015 — $61 million. The weighted-average remaining useful life of the acquired technology is 3.4 years (2009 – 3.7 years).

$US in thousands, except share and per share data, and where otherwise indicated

10.   INCOME TAXES

The difference between the amount of the provision for income taxes and the amount computed by multiplying income before income taxes by the statutory Canadian tax rate is reconciled as follows:

For the year ended	February 27, 2010	February 28, 2009
Statutory Canadian tax rate	32.8%	33.4%
Expected income tax provision	$1,072,395	$935,881
Differences in income taxes resulting from:		
Impact of Canadian U.S. dollar functional currency election	(145,000)	—
Investment tax credits	(101,214)	(81,173)
Manufacturing and processing activities	(52,053)	(49,808)
Foreign exchange	2,837	99,575
Foreign tax rate differences	5,291	(16,273)
Non-deductible stock compensation	9,600	10,500
Adjustments to deferred tax balances for enacted changes in tax laws and rates	7,927	1,260
Other differences	9,583	7,785
	$ 809,366	$907,747

11.   CAPITAL STOCK

(a) Capital stock

The Company is authorized to issue an unlimited number of non-voting, redeemable, retractable Class A common shares, an unlimited number of voting common shares and an unlimited number of non-voting, cumulative, redeemable, retractable preferred shares. At February 27, 2010 and February 28, 2009, there were no Class A common shares or preferred shares outstanding. The Company declared a 3-for-1 stock split of the Company's outstanding common shares on June 28, 2007. The stock split was implemented by way of a stock dividend. Shareholders received an additional two common shares of the Company for each common share held. The stock dividend was paid on August 20, 2007 to common shareholders of record at the close of business on August 17, 2007. All share, earnings per share and stock option data have been adjusted to reflect this stock dividend.

The following details the changes in issued and outstanding common shares for the year ended February 27, 2010:

	Capital Stock		Treasury Stock	
	Stock Outstanding (000's)	Amount	Stock Outstanding (000's)	Amount
Common shares outstanding as at February 28, 2009	566,219	2,208,235	—	—
Exercise of stock options	3,408	30,246	—	—
Conversion of restricted share units	2	—	—	—
Transfers to capital stock resulting from stock option exercises	—	15,647	—	—
Restricted share unit plan purchase of shares	—	—	1,459	(94,463)
Common shares repurchased	(12,300)	(46,519)	—	—
Common shares outstanding as at February 27, 2010	557,329	$2,207,609	1,459	$(94,463)

On November 4, 2009, the Company's Board of Directors authorized a Common Share Repurchase Program for the repurchase and cancellation, through the facilities of the NASDAQ Stock Market, common shares having an aggregate purchase price of up to $1.2 billion, or approximately 21 million common shares based on trading prices at the time of the authorization. This represents approximately 3.6% of the outstanding common shares of the Company at the time of the authorization. All common shares repurchased by the Company pursuant to the Common Share Repurchase Program have been cancelled. The Common Share Repurchase Program will remain in place for up to 12 months from November 4, 2009 or until the purchases are completed or the program is terminated by the Company.

(b) Stock-based compensation

Stock Option Plan

The Company recorded a charge to income and a credit to paid-in-capital of $37.0 million in fiscal 2010 (fiscal 2009 — $38.1 million; fiscal 2008 — $33.7 million) in relation to stock-based compensation expense.

The Company has not paid a dividend in the previous twelve fiscal years and has no current expectation of paying cash dividends on its common shares.

Restricted Share Unit Plan

During fiscal 2010, the trustee purchased 1,458,950 common shares for total consideration of approximately $94.5 million

$US in thousands, except share and per share data, and where otherwise indicated

to comply with its obligations to deliver shares upon vesting. These purchased shares are classified as treasury stock for accounting purposes and included in the shareholders' equity section of the Company's consolidated balance sheet. The Company recorded compensation expense with respect to RSUs of $21.0 million in the year ended February 27, 2010 (February 28, 2009 — $196; March 1, 2008 — $33).

Deferred Share Unit Plan

The Company issued 14,593 DSUs in the year ended February 27, 2010. There are 34,801 DSUs outstanding as at February 27, 2010 (February 28, 2009 — 20,208). The Company had a liability of $2.5 million in relation to the DSU plan as at February 27, 2010 (February 28, 2009 — $834).

12.   COMMITMENTS AND CONTINGENCIES

(a) Credit Facility

The Company has $150.0 million in unsecured demand credit facilities (the "Facilities") to support and secure operating and financing requirements. As at February 27, 2010, the Company has utilized $6.9 million of the Facilities for outstanding letters of credit, and $143.1 million of the Facilities are unused.

(b) Lease commitments

The Company is committed to future minimum annual lease payments under operating leases as follows:

	Real Estate	Equipment and other	Total
For the years ending			
2011	$ 35,088	$1,917	$ 37,005
2012	30,611	1,202	31,813
2013	27,841	163	28,004
2014	26,178	—	26,178
2015	21,755	—	21,755
Thereafter	63,631	—	63,631
	$205,104	$3,282	$208,386

For the year ended February 27, 2010, the Company incurred rental expense of $39.6 million (February 28, 2009 — $22.7 million; March 1, 2008 — $15.5 million).

(c) Litigation

The Company is involved in litigation in the normal course of its business, both as a defendant and as a plaintiff. The Company may be subject to claims (including claims related to patent infringement, purported class actions and derivative actions) either directly or through indemnities against these claims that it provides to certain of it partners.

13.   PRODUCT WARRANTY

The Company estimates its warranty costs at the time of revenue recognition based on historical warranty claims experience and records the expense in cost of sales. The warranty accrual balance is reviewed quarterly to establish that it materially reflects the remaining obligation based on the anticipated future expenditures over the balance of the obligation period. Adjustments are made when the actual warranty claim experience differs from estimates. The change in the Company's warranty expense and actual warranty experience from March 3, 2007 to February 27, 2010 as well as the accrued warranty obligations as at February 27, 2010 are set forth in the following table:

Accrued warranty obligations as at March 3, 2007	$ 36,669
Actual warranty experience during fiscal 2008	(68,166)
Fiscal 2008 warranty provision	116,045
Accrued warranty obligations as at March 1, 2008	84,548
Actual warranty experience during fiscal 2009	(146,434)
Fiscal 2009 warranty provision	258,757
Adjustments for changes in estimate	(12,536)
Accrued warranty obligations as at February 28, 2009	184,335
Actual warranty experience during fiscal 2010	(416,393)
Fiscal 2010 warranty provision	462,834
Adjustments for changes in estimate	21,541
Accrued warranty obligations as at February 27, 2010	$ 252,317

$US in thousands, except share and per share data, and where otherwise indicated

14. EARNINGS PER SHARE

The following table sets forth the computation of basic and diluted earnings per share:

For the year ended	February 27, 2010	February 28, 2009	March 1, 2008
Net income for basic and diluted earnings per share available to common shareholders	$2,457,144	$1,892,616	$1,293,867
Weighted-average number of shares outstanding (000's) — basic	564,492	565,059	559,778
Effect of dilutive securities (000's) — stock-based compensation	5,267	9,097	13,052
Weighted-average number of shares and assumed conversions (000's) — diluted	569,759	574,156	572,830
Earnings per share — reported			
Basic	$ 4.35	$ 3.35	$ 2.31
Diluted	$ 4.31	$ 3.30	$ 2.26

15. COMPREHENSIVE INCOME (LOSS)

The components of comprehensive income (loss) are shown in the following table:

For the year ended	February 27, 2010	February 28, 2009	March 1, 2008
Net income	$2,457,144	$1,892,616	$1,293,867
Net change in unrealized gains (losses) on available-for-sale investments	6,803	(7,161)	13,467
Net change in fair value of derivatives designated as cash flow hedges during the year, net of income taxes of $13,190 (February 28, 2009 - tax recovery of $8,641; March 1, 2008 - income taxes of $19,238)	28,324	(6,168)	37,564
Amounts reclassified to earnings during the year, net of income tax recovery of $6,079 (February 28, 2009 - income taxes of $4,644; March 1, 2008 - income taxes of $5,142)	15,508	(16,497)	(9,232)
Comprehensive income	$2,507,779	$1,862,790	$1,335,666

The components of accumulated other comprehensive income (loss) are as follows:

	February 27, 2010	February 28, 2009	March 1, 2008
Accumulated net unrealized gains (losses) on available- for-sale investments	$ 6,715	$ (88)	$ 7,073
Accumulated net unrealized gains on derivative instruments designated as cash flow hedges	44,377	545	23,210
Total accumulated other comprehensive income	$51,092	$457	$30,283

16. SUPPLEMENTAL INFORMATION

(a) Cash flows resulting from net changes in working capital items are as follows:

For the year ended	February 27, 2010	February 28, 2009	March 1, 2008
Accounts receivable	$(480,610)	$(936,514)	$(602,055)
Other receivables	(44,719)	(83,039)	(34,515)
Inventories	60,789	(286,133)	(140,360)
Other current assets	(52,737)	(50,280)	(26,161)
Accounts payable	167,281	177,263	140,806
Accrued liabilities	442,065	506,859	383,020
Income taxes payable	(266,517)	(113,868)	401,270
Deferred revenue	13,739	16,598	8,789
	$(160,709)	$(769,114)	$ 130,794

(b) Certain statement of cash flow information related to interest and income taxes paid is summarized as follows:

For the year ended	February 27, 2010	February 28, 2009	March 1, 2008
Interest paid during the year	$ —	$ 502	$ 518
Income taxes paid during the year	$1,081,720	$946,237	$216,095

$US in thousands, except share and per share data, and where otherwise indicated

(c) The following items are included in the accrued liabilities balance:

	February 27, 2010	February 28, 2009
Marketing costs	$ 91,554	$ 91,160
Vendor inventory liabilities	125,761	18,000
Warranty	252,316	184,335
Royalties	383,939	279,476
Rebates	146,304	134,788
Other	638,386	530,843
	$1,638,260	$1,238,602

Other accrued liabilities as noted in the above chart, include, among other things, salaries, payroll withholding taxes and incentive accruals, none of which are greater than 5% of the current liability balance.

(d) Additional information

Advertising expense, which includes media, agency and promotional expenses totalling $790.8 million (February 28, 2009 — $718.9 million; March 1, 2008 — $336.0 million) is included in selling, marketing and administration expense.

Selling, marketing and administration expense for the fiscal year includes $58.4 million with respect to foreign exchange losses (February 28, 2009 – loss of $6.1 million; March 1, 2008 – loss of $5.3 million). For the year ended February 27, 2010, the Company recorded a $54.3 million charge primarily relating to the reversal of foreign exchange gains previously recorded in fiscal 2009 on the revaluation of Canadian dollar denominated tax liability balances.

17.   DERIVATIVE FINANCIAL INSTRUMENTS

The Company uses derivative instruments to manage exposures to foreign exchange risk resulting from transactions in currencies other than its functional currency, the U.S. dollar. The Company's risk management objective in holding derivative instruments is to reduce the volatility of current and future income as a result of changes in foreign currency. To limit its exposure to adverse movements in foreign currency exchange rates, the Company enters into foreign currency forward and option contracts.

18.   SEGMENT DISCLOSURES

The Company is organized and managed as a single reportable business segment. The Company's operations are substantially all related to the research, design, manufacture and sales of wireless communications products, services and software. Selected financial information is as follows:

Revenue, classified by major geographic segments in which our customers are located, was as follows:

For the year ended	February 27, 2010	February 28, 2009	March 1, 2008
Revenue			
Canada	$ 843,762	$ 887,005	$ 438,302
United States	8,619,762	6,967,598	3,528,858
United Kingdom	1,447,417	711,536	461,592
Other	4,042,283	2,499,047	1,580,643
	$14,953,224	$11,065,186	$6,009,395

	February 27, 2010	February 28, 2009
Total assets		
Canada	$ 4,502,522	$3,218,640
United States	4,059,174	2,646,783
United Kingdom	1,195,534	1,931,387
Other	447,179	304,562
	$10,204,409	$8,101,372

Apple Financial Report

APPLE

APPLE INC.
CONSOLIDATED BALANCE SHEETS
(in millions, except share amounts)

	September 26, 2009	September 27, 2008
ASSETS		
Current assets		
Cash and cash equivalents	$ 5,263	$11,875
Short-term marketable securities	18,201	10,236
Accounts receivable, less allowances of $52 and $47, respectively	3,361	2,422
Inventories	455	509
Deferred tax assets	1,135	1,044
Other current assets	3,140	3,920
Total current assets	31,555	30,006
Long-term marketable securities	10,528	2,379
Property, plant and equipment, net	2,954	2,455
Goodwill	206	207
Acquired intangible assets, net	247	285
Other assets	2,011	839
Total assets	$47,501	$36,171
LIABILITIES AND SHAREHOLDERS' EQUITY		
Current liabilities		
Accounts payable	$ 5,601	$ 5,520
Accrued expenses	3,852	4,224
Deferred revenue	2,053	1,617
Total current liabilities	11,506	11,361
Deferred revenue – non-current	853	768
Other non-current liabilities	3,502	1,745
Total liabilities	15,861	13,874
Shareholders' equity		
Common stock, no par value; 1,800,000,000 shares authorized; 899,805,500 and 888,325,973 shares issued and outstanding, respectively	8,210	7,177
Retained earnings	23,353	15,129
Accumulated other comprehensive income/(loss)	77	(9)
Total shareholders' equity	31,640	22,297
Total liabilities and shareholders' equity	$47,501	$36,171

APPLE

APPLE INC.
CONSOLIDATED STATEMENTS OF OPERATIONS
(in millions, except share amounts which are reflected in thousands and per share amounts)

For fiscal year ended	September 26, 2009	September 27, 2008	September 29, 2007
Net sales.	$ 42,905	$ 37,491	$ 24,578
Cost of sales	25,683	24,294	16,426
Gross margin	17,222	13,197	8,152
Operating expenses			
Research and development	1,333	1,109	782
Selling, general and administrative	4,149	3,761	2,963
Total operating expenses	5,482	4,870	3,745
Operating income.	11,740	8,327	4,407
Other income and expense.	326	620	599
Income before provision for income taxes.	12,066	8,947	5,006
Provision for income taxes	3,831	2,828	1,511
Net income.	$ 8,235	$ 6,119	$ 3,495
Earnings per common share:			
Basic	$ 9.22	$ 6.94	$ 4.04
Diluted	$ 9.08	$ 6.78	$ 3.93
Shares used in computing earnings per share:			
Basic.	893,016	881,592	864,595
Diluted	907,005	902,139	889,292

APPLE

APPLE

APPLE INC.
CONSOLIDATED STATEMENTS OF SHAREHOLDERS' EQUITY
(in millions, except share amounts which are reflected in thousands)

	Common Stock		Retained Earnings	Accumulated Other Comprehensive Income	Total Shareholders' Equity
	Shares	Amount			
Balances as of September 30, 2006	855,263	$ 4,355	$ 5,607	$ 22	$ 9,984
Components of comprehensive income:					
Net income	—	—	3,495	—	3,495
Change in foreign currency translation	—	—	—	51	51
Change in unrealized loss on available-for-sale securities, net of tax	—	—	—	(7)	(7)
Change in unrealized gain on derivative instruments, net of tax	—	—	—	(3)	(3)
Total comprehensive income					3,536
Stock-based compensation	—	251	—	—	251
Common stock issued under stock plans, net of shares withheld for employee taxes	17,066	364	(2)	—	362
Tax benefit from employee stock plan awards	—	398	—	—	398
Balances as of September 29, 2007	872,329	5,368	9,100	63	14,531
Cumulative effect of change in accounting principle	—	45	11	—	56
Components of comprehensive income:					
Net income	—	—	6,119	—	6,119
Change in foreign currency translation	—	—	—	(28)	(28)
Change in unrealized loss on available-for-sale securities, net of tax	—	—	—	(63)	(63)
Change in unrealized gain on derivative instruments, net of tax	—	—	—	19	19
Total comprehensive income					6,047
Stock-based compensation	—	513	—	—	513
Common stock issued under stock plans, net of shares withheld for employee taxes	15,888	460	(101)	—	359
Issuance of common stock in connection with an asset acquisition	109	21	—	—	21
Tax benefit from employee stock plan awards	—	770	—	—	770
Balances as of September 27, 2008	888,326	7,177	15,129	(9)	22,297
Components of comprehensive income:					
Net income	—	—	8,235	—	8,235
Change in foreign currency translation	—	—	—	(14)	(14)
Change in unrealized loss on available-for-sale securities, net of tax	—	—	—	118	118
Change in unrealized gain on derivative instruments, net of tax	—	—	—	(18)	(18)
Total comprehensive income					8,321
Stock-based compensation	—	707	—	—	707
Common stock issued under stock plans, net of shares withheld for employee taxes	11,480	404	(11)	—	393
Tax benefit from employee stock plan awards, including transfer pricing adjustments	—	(78)	—	—	(78)
Balances as of September 26, 2009	899,806	$ 8,210	$23,353	$ 77	$31,640

APPLE INC.
CONSOLIDATED STATEMENTS OF CASH FLOWS
(in millions)

For fiscal year ended	September 26, 2009	September 27, 2008	September 29, 2007
Cash and cash equivalents, beginning of the year	$ 11,875	$ 9,352	$ 6,392
Operating Activities			
Net income.	8,235	6,119	3,495
Adjustments to reconcile net income to cash			
generated by operating activities			
Depreciation, amortization and accretion	734	496	327
Stock-based compensation expense.	710	516	242
Deferred income tax expense.	1,040	398	73
Loss on disposition of property, plant and equipment	26	22	12
Changes in operating assets and liabilities			
Accounts receivable, net	(939)	(785)	(385)
Inventories	54	(163)	(76)
Other current assets	749	(274)	(1,279)
Other assets	(902)	289	285
Accounts payable.	92	596	1,494
Deferred revenue	521	718	566
Other liabilities.	(161)	1,664	716
Cash generated by operating activities	10,159	9,596	5,470
Investing Activities			
Purchases of marketable securities	(46,724)	(22,965)	(11,719)
Proceeds from maturities of marketable securities	19,790	11,804	6,483
Proceeds from sales of marketable securities	10,888	4,439	2,941
Purchases of other long-term investments	(101)	(38)	(17)
Payments made in connection with business acquisitions,			
net of cash acquired	—	(220)	—
Payment for acquisition of property, plant and equipment	(1,144)	(1,091)	(735)
Payment for acquisition of intangible assets	(69)	(108)	(251)
Other	(74)	(10)	49
Cash used in investing activities	(17,434)	(8,189)	(3,249)
Financing Activities			
Proceeds from issuance of common stock.	475	483	365
Excess tax benefits from stock-based compensation	270	757	377
Cash used to net share settle equity awards.	(82)	(124)	(3)
Cash generated by financing activities.	663	1,116	739
(Decrease)/increase in cash and cash equivalents	(6,612)	2,523	2,960
Cash and cash equivalents, end of the year	$ 5,263	$11,875	$ 9,352
Supplemental cash flow disclosures:			
Cash paid for income taxes, net.	$ 2,997	$ 1,267	$ 863

Palm Financial Report

Palm, Inc.

Consolidated Balance Sheets

(In thousands, except par value amounts)

	May 31, 2009	May 31, 2008
ASSETS		
Current assets		
Cash and cash equivalents	$ 152,400	$ 176,918
Short-term investments	102,733	81,830
Accounts receivable, net of allowance for doubtful accounts of $350 and $1,169, respectively	66,452	116,430
Inventories	19,716	67,461
Deferred income taxes	174	82,011
Prepaids and other	12,104	15,436
Total current assets	353,579	540,086
Restricted investments	9,496	8,620
Non-current auction rate securities	6,105	29,944
Deferred costs	14,896	—
Property and equipment, net	31,167	39,636
Goodwill	166,320	166,332
Intangible assets, net	48,914	61,048
Deferred income taxes	331	318,850
Other assets	12,428	15,746
Total assets	$ 643,236	$1,180,262
LIABILITIES AND STOCKHOLDERS' EQUITY (DEFICIT)		
Current liabilities		
Accounts payable	$ 105,628	$ 161,642
Income taxes payable	475	1,088
Deferred revenues	18,429	4,080
Accrued restructuring	6,090	8,058
Current portion of long-term debt	4,000	4,000
Other accrued liabilities	207,820	232,478
Total current liabilities	342,442	411,346
Non-current liabilities		
Long-term debt	390,000	394,000
Non-current deferred revenues	13,077	—
Non-current tax liabilities	5,783	6,127
Other non-current liabilities	—	2,098
Series B redeemable convertible preferred stock, $0.001 par value, 325 shares authorized and outstanding; aggregate liquidation value: $325,000	265,412	255,671
Series C redeemable convertible preferred stock, $0.001 par value, 100 shares authorized; outstanding: 51 shares and 0 shares, respectively; aggregate liquidation value: $51,000 and $0, respectively	40,387	—
Stockholders' equity (deficit)		
Preferred stock, $0.001 par value, 125,000 shares authorized:		
Series A: 2,000 shares authorized, none outstanding	—	—
Common stock, $0.001 par value, 2,000,000 shares authorized; outstanding: 139,687 shares and 108,369 shares, respectively	140	108
Additional paid-in capital	854,649	659,141
Accumulated deficit	(1,269,672)	(537,484)
Accumulated other comprehensive income (loss)	1,018	(10,745)
Total stockholders' equity (deficit)	(413,865)	111,020
Total liabilities and stockholders' equity (deficit)	$ 643,236	$1,180,262

Palm, Inc.

Consolidated Statements of Operations

(In thousands, except per share amounts)

Years Ended May 31	2009	2008	2007
Revenues	$ 735,872	$1,318,691	$1,560,507
Cost of revenues	576,113	916,810	985,369
Gross profit	159,759	401,881	575,138
Operating expenses			
Sales and marketing	174,052	229,702	248,685
Research and development	177,210	202,764	190,952
General and administrative	55,923	60,778	59,762
Amortization of intangible assets	3,054	3,775	1,981
Restructuring charges	16,134	30,353	—
Casualty recovery	(268)	—	—
Patent acquisition cost (refund)	(1,537)	5,000	—
Gain on sale of land	—	(4,446)	—
In-process research and development	—	—	3,700
Total operating expenses	424,568	527,926	505,080
Operating income (loss)	(264,809)	(126,045)	70,058
Impairment of non-current auction rate securities	(35,885)	(32,175)	—
Interest (expense)	(25,299)	(20,397)	(1,970)
Interest income	5,840	21,860	25,958
Loss on series C derivative	(2,515)	—	—
Other income (expense), net	(5,255)	(1,471)	(1,619)
Income (loss) before income taxes	(327,923)	(158,228)	92,427
Income tax provision (benefit)	404,265	(52,809)	36,044
Net income (loss)	(732,188)	(105,419)	56,383
Accretion of series B and series C redeemable convertible preferred stock	21,285	5,516	—
Net income (loss) applicable to common shareholders	$(753,473)	$ (110,935)	$ 56,383
Net income (loss) per common share:			
Basic	$ (6.51)	$ (1.05)	$ 0.55
Diluted	$ (6.51)	$ (1.05)	$ 0.54
Shares used to compute net income (loss) per common share:			
Basic	115,725	105,891	102,757
Diluted	115,725	105,891	104,442

PALM

Palm, Inc.
Consolidated Statements of Stockholders' Equity (Deficit) and Comprehensive Income (Loss)
(In thousands)

	Common Stock	Additional Paid-In Capital	Unamortized Deferred Stock-Based Compensation	Accumulated Deficit	Accumulated Other Comprehensive Income (Loss)	Total
Balances, May 31, 2006	$ 103	$1,475,319	$ (2,752)	$ (488,081)	$ (684)	$ 983,905
Components of comprehensive income:						
Net income	—	—	—	56,383	—	56,383
Net unrealized gains on available-for-sale investments	—	—	—	—	1,522	1,522
Recognized gains included in results of operations	—	—	—	—	(110)	(110)
Accumulated translation adjustments	—	—	—	—	915	915
Total comprehensive income	—	—	—	—	—	58,710
Common stock issued under stock plans, net	3	21,923		—	—	21,926
Stock-based compensation expense	—	21,503	2,752	—	—	24,255
Tax benefit from employee stock options	—	4,578	—	—	—	4,578
Shares repurchased and retired	(2)	(30,961)				(30,963)
Balances, May 31, 2007	104	1,492,362	—	(431,698)	1,643	1,062,411
Components of comprehensive loss:						
Net loss	—	—	—	(105,419)	—	(105,419)
Net unrealized losses on available-for-sale investments	—	—	—	—	(1,261)	(1,261)
Net unrealized losses in value of non-current auction rate securities	—	—	—	—	(44,706)	(44,706)
Net recognized losses on non-current auction rate securities included in results of operations	—	—	—	—	32,175	32,175
Net recognized gains on available-for-sale investments included in results of operations	—	—	—	—	(68)	(68)
Accumulated translation adjustments	—	—	—	—	1,472	1,472
Total comprehensive loss	—	—	—	—	—	(117,807)
Common stock issued under stock plans, net	4	28,433	—	—	—	28,437
Stock-based compensation expense	—	32,181	—	—	—	32,181
Tax deficiency from employee stock options	—	(3,663)	—	—	—	(3,663)
Cash distribution to stockholders	—	(949,691)	—	—	—	(949,691)
Discount recognized on issuance of series B redeemable convertible preferred stock	—	65,035	—	—	—	65,035
Accretion of series B redeemable convertible preferred stock	—	(5,516)	—	—	—	(5,516)
Adjustment to accumulated deficit due to adoption of FIN No. 48 (see Note 16)	—	—	—	(367)	—	(367)
Balances, May 31, 2008	108	659,141	—	(537,484)	(10,745)	111,020
Components of comprehensive loss:						
Net loss	—	—	—	(732,188)	—	(732,188)
Net unrealized losses on available-for-sale investments	—	—	—	—	(1,649)	(1,649)
Net unrealized losses in value of non-current auction rate securities	—	—	—	—	(23,354)	(23,354)
Net recognized losses on non-current auction rate securities included in results of operations	—	—	—	—	35,885	35,885
Net recognized losses on available-for-sale investments included in results of operations	—	—	—	—	3,594	3,594
Accumulated translation adjustments	—	—	—	—	(2,713)	(2,713)
Total comprehensive loss	—	—	—	—	—	(720,425)
Common stock issued under stock plans, net	5	15,531	—	—	—	15,536
Stock-based compensation expense	—	23,853	—	—	—	23,853
Tax benefit from employee stock options	—	1,924	—	—	—	1,924
Distribution liability related to canceled shares of restricted stock	—	34	—	—	—	34
Accretion of series B and series C redeemable convertible preferred stock	—	(21,285)	—	—	—	(21,285)
Warrants recorded in connection with issuance of series C units	—	21,966	—	—	—	21,966
Conversion of series C units and issuance of additional common stock, net	27	101,544	—	—	—	101,571
Discount recognized on issuance of series C redeemable convertible preferred stock	—	51,941	—	—	—	51,941
Balances, May 31, 2009	$ 140	$ 854,649	$ —	$ (1,269,672)	$ 1,018	$ (413,865)

Palm, Inc.
Consolidated Statements of Cash Flows
(In thousands)

Years Ended May 31	2009	2008	2007
Cash flows from operating activities			
Net income (loss)	$(732,188)	$(105,419)	$ 56,383
Adjustments to reconcile net income (loss) to net cash flows from operating activities			
Depreciation	19,677	19,699	13,316
Stock-based compensation	23,853	32,181	24,255
Amortization of intangible assets	12,134	16,510	8,315
Amortization of debt issuance costs	3,139	1,834	—
In-process research and development	—	—	3,700
Deferred income taxes	401,670	(58,227)	11,313
Realized (gain) loss on short-term investments	3,594	(68)	(110)
Excess tax benefit related to stock-based compensation	(142)	(40)	(5,241)
Realized loss (gain) on disposition of property and equipment and sale of land	619	(4,446)	—
Impairment of non-current auction rate securities	35,885	32,175	—
Loss on series C derivative	2,515	—	—
Changes in assets and liabilities			
Accounts receivable	48,425	89,312	2
Inventories	47,571	(28,147)	18,842
Prepaids and other	4,542	736	1,790
Accounts payable	(54,883)	(35,840)	11,654
Income taxes payable	(346)	3,033	16,421
Accrued restructuring	(361)	6,303	(1,803)
Deferred revenues/costs, net	12,530	—	—
Other accrued liabilities	(16,746)	12,866	9,354
Net cash provided by (used in) operating activities	(188,512)	(17,538)	168,191
Cash flows from investing activities			
Purchase of brand name intangible asset	—	(1,500)	(44,000)
Purchase of property and equipment	(13,452)	(22,999)	(24,651)
Proceeds from sale of land	—	64,446	—
Cash paid for business acquisitions	—	(495)	(19,000)
Purchase of short-term investments	(112,385)	(517,104)	(682,882)
Sales/maturities of short-term investments	88,109	777,917	671,623
Purchase of restricted investments	(2,000)	(8,951)	—
Sale of restricted investments	1,124	331	—
Proceeds related to investments in non-current auction rate securities	485	250	—
Net cash provided by (used in) investing activities	(38,119)	291,895	(98,910)
Cash flows from financing activities			
Proceeds from issuance of common stock, net	104,049	—	—
Proceeds from issuance of common stock, employee stock plans	15,536	28,437	21,926
Purchase and subsequent retirement of common stock	—	—	(30,963)
Excess tax benefit related to stock-based compensation	142	40	5,241
Proceeds from issuance of redeemable convertible preferred stock and series C units, net	99,173	315,190	—
Proceeds from issuance of debt, net	—	381,107	—
Repayment of debt	(14,446)	(3,089)	(50,816)
Cash distribution to stockholders	(439)	(948,949)	—
Net cash provided by (used in) financing activities	204,015	(227,264)	(54,612)
Effects of exchange rate changes on cash and cash equivalents	(1,902)	1,695	—
Change in cash and cash equivalents	(24,518)	48,788	14,669
Cash and cash equivalents, beginning of period	176,918	128,130	113,461
Cash and cash equivalents, end of period	$ 152,400	$ 176,918	$ 128,130
Supplemental cash flow information:			
Cash paid for income taxes	$ 3,402	$ 3,391	$ 8,900
Cash paid for interest	$ 21,828	$ 18,042	$ 1,741
Non-cash investing and financing activities:			
Liability for property and equipment acquired	$ —	$ 3,334	$ 2,309

Nokia Financial Report

Nokia Corporation and Subsidiaries
Consolidated Statements of Financial Position

December 31	2009 EURm	2008 EURm
ASSETS		
Non-current assets		
Capitalized development costs	143	244
Goodwill	5 171	6 257
Other intangible assets	2 762	3 913
Property, plant and equipment	1 867	2 090
Investments in associated companies	69	96
Available-for-sale investments	554	512
Deferred tax assets	1 507	1 963
Long-term loans receivable	46	27
Other non-current assets	6	10
	12 125	15 112
Current assets		
Inventories	1 865	2 533
Accounts receivable, net of allowances for doubtful accounts (2009: EUR 391 million, 2008: EUR 415 million)	7 981	9 444
Prepaid expenses and accrued income	4 551	4 538
Current portion of long-term loans receivable	14	101
Other financial assets	329	1 034
Investments at fair value through profit and loss, liquid assets	580	—
Available-for-sale investments, liquid assets	2 367	1 272
Available-for-sale investments, cash equivalents	4 784	3 842
Bank and cash	1 142	1 706
	23 613	24 470
Total assets	35 738	39 582
SHAREHOLDERS' EQUITY AND LIABILITIES		
Capital and reserves attributable to equity holders of the parent		
Share capital	246	246
Share issue premium	279	442
Treasury shares, at cost	(681)	(1 881)
Translation differences	(127)	341
Fair value and other reserves	69	62
Reserve for invested non-restricted equity	3 170	3 306
Retained earnings	10 132	11 692
	13 088	14 208
Minority interests	1 661	2 302
Total equity	14 749	16 510
Non-current liabilities		
Long-term interest-bearing liabilities	4 432	861
Deferred tax liabilities	1 303	1 787
Other long-term liabilities	66	69
	5 801	2 717
Current liabilities		
Current portion of long-term loans	44	13
Short-term borrowings	727	3 578
Other financial liabilities	245	924
Accounts payable	4 950	5 225
Accrued expenses	6 504	7 023
Provisions	2 718	3 592
	15 188	20 355
Total shareholders' equity and liabilities	35 738	39 582

Nokia Corporation and Subsidiaries
Consolidated Income Statements

Financial Year Ended December 31	2009 EURm	2008 EURm	2007 EURm
Net sales	**40 984**	50 710	51 058
Cost of sales	**(27 720)**	(33 337)	(33 781)
Gross profit	**13 264**	17 373	17 277
Research and development expenses	**(5 909)**	(5 968)	(5 636)
Selling and marketing expenses	**(3 933)**	(4 380)	(4 379)
Administrative and general expenses	**(1 145)**	(1 284)	(1 165)
Impairment of goodwill	**(908)**	–	–
Other income	**338**	420	2 312
Other expenses	**(510)**	(1 195)	(424)
Operating profit	**1 197**	4 966	7 985
Share of results of associated companies	**30**	6	44
Financial income and expenses	**(265)**	(2)	239
Profit before tax	**962**	4 970	8 268
Tax	**(702)**	(1 081)	(1 522)
Profit	**260**	3 889	6 746
Profit attributable to equity holders of the parent	**891**	3 988	7 205
Loss attributable to minority interests	**(631)**	(99)	(459)
	260	3 889	6 746

Earnings per share	2009 EUR	2008 EUR	2007 EUR
(for profit attributable to the equity holders of the parent)			
Basic	**0.24**	1.07	1.85
Diluted	**0.24**	1.05	1.83

	2009	2008	2007
Average number of shares (000's shares)			
Basic	**3 705 116**	3 743 622	3 885 408
Diluted	**3 721 072**	3 780 363	3 932 008

Nokia Corporation and Subsidiaries
Consolidated Statements of Comprehensive Income

Financial Year Ended December 31	2009 EURm	2008 EURm	2007 EURm
Profit	**260**	3 889	6 746
Other comprehensive income			
Translation differences	**(563)**	595	(151)
Net investment hedge gains (losses)	**114**	(123)	51
Cash flow hedges	**25**	(40)	(7)
Available-for-sale investments	**48**	(15)	49
Other increase (decrease), net	**(7)**	28	(46)
Income tax related to components of other comprehensive income	**(44)**	58	(12)
Other comprehensive income (expense), net of tax	**(427)**	503	(116)
Total comprehensive income (expense)	**(167)**	4 392	6 630
Total comprehensive income (expense) attributable to:			
Equity holders of the parent	**429**	4 577	7 073
Minority interests	**(596)**	(185)	(443)
	(167)	4 392	6 630

NOKIA

Nokia Corporation and Subsidiaries

Consolidated Statements of Changes in Shareholders' Equity

	Number of shares (000's)	Share capital	Share issue premium	Treasury shares	Translation differences	Fair value and other reserves	Reserve for invested non-restrict. equity	Retained earnings	Before minority interests	Minority interests	Total
Balance at December 31, 2007	**3 845 950**	**246**	**644**	**(3 146)**	**(163)**	**23**	**3 299**	**13 870**	**14 773**	**2 565**	**17 338**
Translation differences					595				595		595
Net investment hedge gains, net of tax					(91)				(91)		(91)
Cash flow hedges, net of tax						42			42	(67)	(25)
Available-for-sale investments, net of tax						(3)			(3)	(2)	(5)
Other increase, net								46	46	(17)	29
Profit								3 988	3 988	(99)	3 889
Total comprehensive income		**—**	**—**	**—**	**504**	**39**	**—**	**4 034**	**4 577**	**(185)**	**4 392**
Stock options exercised	3 547						51		51		51
Stock options exercised related to acquisitions			1						1		1
Share-based compensation			74						74		74
Excess tax benefit on share-based compensation			(117)						(117)	(6)	(124)
Settlement of performance and restricted shares	5 622		(179)	154			(44)		(69)		(69)
Acquisition of treasury shares	(157 390)			(3 123)					(3 123)		(3 123)
Reissuance of treasury shares	143			2					2		2
Cancellation of treasury shares			0	4 232				(4 232)	—		—
Dividend								(1 992)	(1 992)	(35)	(2 027)
Acquisitions and other change in minority interests										(37)	(37)
Vested portion of share-based payment awards related to acquisitions			19						19		19
Acquisition of Symbian								12	12		12
Total of other equity movements		**—**	**(202)**	**1 265**	**—**	**—**	**7**	**(6 212)**	**(5 142)**	**(78)**	**(5 220)**
Balance at December 31, 2008	**3 697 872**	**246**	**442**	**(1 881)**	**341**	**62**	**3 306**	**11 692**	**14 208**	**2 302**	**16 510**
Translation differences					(552)				(552)	(9)	(561)
Net investment hedge gains, net of tax					84				84		84
Cash flow hedges, net of tax						(35)			(35)	49	14
Available-for-sale investments, net of tax						42			42	2	44
Other decrease, net								(1)	(1)	(7)	(8)
Profit								891	891	(631)	260
Total comprehensive income		**—**	**—**	**—**	**(468)**	**7**	**—**	**890**	**429**	**(596)**	**(167)**
Stock options exercised	7						—				—
Stock options exercised related to acquisitions			(1)						(1)		(1)
Share-based compensation			16						16		16
Excess tax benefit on share-based compensation			(12)						(12)	(1)	(13)
Settlement of performance and restricted shares	10 352		(166)	230			(136)		(72)		(72)
Acquisition of treasury shares									—		—
Reissuance of treasury shares	31			1					1		1
Cancellation of treasury shares				969				(969)	—		—
Dividend								(1 481)	(1 481)	(44)	(1 525)
Total of other equity movements		**—**	**(163)**	**1 200**	**—**	**—**	**(136)**	**(2 450)**	**(1 549)**	**(45)**	**(1 594)**
Balance at December 31, 2009	**3 708 262**	**246**	**279**	**(681)**	**(127)**	**69**	**3 170**	**10 132**	**13 088**	**1 661**	**14 749**

Dividends declared per share were EUR 0.40 for 2009 (EUR 0.40 for 2008 and EUR 0.53 for 2007), subject to shareholders' approval.

Nokia Corporation and Subsidiaries
Consolidated Statements of Cash Flows

Financial Year Ended December 31	2009 EURm	2008 EURm	2007 EURm
Cash flow from operating activities			
Profit attributable to equity holders of the parent	**891**	3 988	7 205
Adjustments, total	**3 390**	3 024	1 159
Change in net working capital	**140**	(2 546)	605
Cash generated from operations	**4 421**	4 466	8 969
Interest received	**125**	416	362
Interest paid	**(256)**	(155)	(59)
Other financial income and expenses, net received	**(128)**	250	67
Income taxes paid, net received	**(915)**	(1 780)	(1 457)
Net cash from operating activities	**3 247**	3 197	7 882
Cash flow from investing activities			
Acquisition of Group companies, net of acquired cash	**(29)**	(5 962)	253
Purchase of current available-for-sale investments, liquid assets	**(2 800)**	(669)	(4 798)
Purchase of investments at fair value through profit and loss, liquid assets	**(695)**	—	—
Purchase of non-current available-for-sale investments	**(95)**	(121)	(126)
Purchase of shares in associated companies	**(30)**	(24)	(25)
Additions to capitalized development costs	**(27)**	(131)	(157)
Long-term loans made to customers	**—**	—	(261)
Proceeds from repayment and sale of long-term loans receivable	**—**	129	163
Proceeds from (+) / payment of (-) other long-term receivables	**2**	(1)	5
Proceeds from (+) / payment of (-) short-term loans receivable	**2**	(15)	(119)
Capital expenditures	**(531)**	(889)	(715)
Proceeds from disposal of shares in associated companies	**40**	3	6
Proceeds from disposal of businesses	**61**	41	—
Proceeds from maturities and sale of current available-for-sale investments, liquid assets	**1 730**	4 664	4 930
Proceeds from maturities and sale of investments at fair value through profit and loss, liquid assets	**108**	—	—
Proceeds from sale of non-current available-for-sale investments	**14**	10	50
Proceeds from sale of fixed assets	**100**	54	72
Dividends received	**2**	6	12
Net cash used in investing activities	**(2 148)**	(2 905)	(710)
Cash flow from financing activities			
Proceeds from stock option exercises	**—**	53	987
Purchase of treasury shares	**—**	(3 121)	(3 819)
Proceeds from long-term borrowings	**3 901**	714	115
Repayment of long-term borrowings	**(209)**	(34)	(16)
Proceeds from (+) / repayment of (-) short-term borrowings	**(2 842)**	2 891	661
Dividends paid	**(1 546)**	(2 048)	(1 760)
Net cash used in financing activities	**(696)**	(1 545)	(3 832)
Foreign exchange adjustment	**(25)**	(49)	(15)
Net increase (+) / decrease (-) in cash and cash equivalents	**378**	(1 302)	3 325
Cash and cash equivalents at beginning of period	**5 548**	6 850	3 525
Cash and cash equivalents at end of period	**5 926**	5 548	6 850
Cash and cash equivalents comprise of:			
Bank and cash	**1 142**	1 706	2 125
Current available-for-sale investments, cash equivalents	**4 784**	3 842	4 725
	5 926	5 548	6 850

NOKIA

B

Time Value of Money

Learning Objectives

CAP

CONCEPTUAL

C1 Describe the earning of interest and the concepts of present and future values. (p. B-1)

PROCEDURAL

P1 Apply present value concepts to a single amount by using interest tables. (p. B-3)

P2 Apply future value concepts to a single amount by using interest tables. (p. B-4)

P3 Apply present value concepts to an annuity by using interest tables. (p. B-5)

P4 Apply future value concepts to an annuity by using interest tables. (p. B-6)

The concepts of present and future values are important to modern business, including the preparation and analysis of financial statements. The purpose of this appendix is to explain, illustrate, and compute present and future values. This appendix applies these concepts with reference to both business and everyday activities.

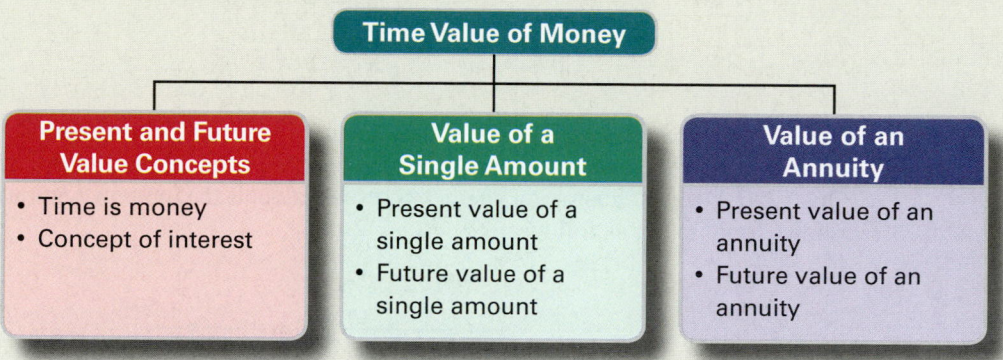

PRESENT AND FUTURE VALUE CONCEPTS

The old saying "Time is money" reflects the notion that as time passes, the values of our assets and liabilities change. This change is due to *interest*, which is a borrower's payment to the owner of an asset for its use. The most common example of interest is a savings account asset. As we keep a balance of cash in the account, it earns interest that the financial institution pays us. An example of a liability is a car loan. As we carry the balance of the loan, we accumulate interest costs on it. We must ultimately repay this loan with interest.

Present and future value computations enable us to measure or estimate the interest component of holding assets or liabilities over time. The present value computation is important when we want to know the value of future-day assets *today*. The future value computation is important when we want to know the value of present-day assets *at a future date*. The first section focuses on the present value of a single amount. The second section focuses on the future value of a single amount. Then both the present and future values of a series of amounts (called an *annuity*) are defined and explained.

C1 Describe the earning of interest and the concepts of present and future values.

Decision Insight

Keep That Job Lottery winners often never work again. Kenny Dukes, a recent Georgia lottery winner, doesn't have that option. He is serving parole for burglary charges, and Georgia requires its parolees to be employed (or in school). For his lottery winnings, Dukes had to choose between $31 million in 30 annual payments or $16 million in one lump sum ($10.6 million after-tax); he chose the latter. ■

PRESENT VALUE OF A SINGLE AMOUNT

We graphically express the present value, called *p*, of a single future amount, called *f*, that is received or paid at a future date in Exhibit B.1.

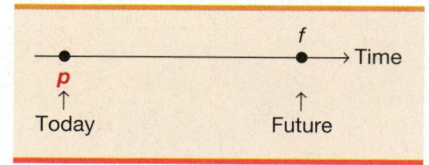

EXHIBIT B.1

Present Value of a Single Amount Diagram

The formula to compute the present value of a single amount is shown in Exhibit B.2, where p = present value; f = future value; i = rate of interest per period; and n = number of periods. (Interest is also called the *discount,* and an interest rate is also called the *discount rate.*)

EXHIBIT B.2

Present Value of a Single Amount Formula

$$p = \frac{f}{(1 + i)^n}$$

To illustrate present value concepts, assume that we need $220 one period from today. We want to know how much we must invest now, for one period, at an interest rate of 10% to provide for this $220. For this illustration, the p, or present value, is the unknown amount—the specifics are shown graphically as follows:

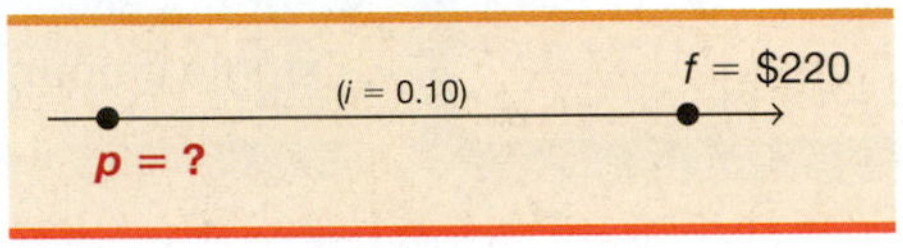

Conceptually, we know p must be less than $220. This is obvious from the answer to this question: Would we rather have $220 today or $220 at some future date? If we had $220 today, we could invest it and see it grow to something more than $220 in the future. Therefore, we would prefer the $220 today. This means that if we were promised $220 in the future, we would take less than $220 today. But how much less? To answer that question, we compute an estimate of the present value of the $220 to be received one period from now using the formula in Exhibit B.2 as follows:

$$p = \frac{f}{(1 + i)^n} = \frac{\$220}{(1 + 0.10)^1} = \$200$$

We interpret this result to say that given an interest rate of 10%, we are indifferent between $200 today or $220 at the end of one period.

We can also use this formula to compute the present value for *any number of periods.* To illustrate, consider a payment of $242 at the end of two periods at 10% interest. The present value of this $242 to be received two periods from now is computed as follows:

$$p = \frac{f}{(1 + i)^n} = \frac{\$242}{(1 + 0.10)^2} = \$200$$

Together, these results tell us we are indifferent between $200 today, or $220 one period from today, or $242 two periods from today given a 10% interest rate per period.

The number of periods (n) in the present value formula does not have to be expressed in years. Any period of time such as a day, a month, a quarter, or a year can be used. Whatever period is used, the interest rate (i) must be compounded for the same period. This means that if a situation expresses n in months and i equals 12% per year, then i is transformed into interest earned per month (or 1%). In this case, interest is said to be *compounded monthly.*

A present value table helps us with present value computations. It gives us present values (factors) for a variety of both interest rates (i) and periods (n). Each present value in a present value table assumes that the future value (f) equals 1. When the future value (f) is different from 1, we simply multiply the present value (p) from the table by that future value to give us the estimate. The formula used to construct a table of present values for a single future amount of 1 is shown in Exhibit B.3.

EXHIBIT B.3

Present Value of 1 Formula

$$p = \frac{1}{(1 + i)^n}$$

This formula is identical to that in Exhibit B.2 except that *f* equals 1. Table B.1 at the end of this appendix is such a present value table. It is often called a **present value of 1 table**. A present value table involves three factors: *p*, *i*, and *n*. Knowing two of these three factors allows us to compute the third. (A fourth is *f*, but as already explained, we need only multiply the 1 used in the formula by *f*.) To illustrate the use of a present value table, consider three cases.

> **P1** Apply present value concepts to a single amount by using interest tables.

Case 1   (solve for *p* when knowing *i* and *n*). To show how we use a present value table, let's look again at how we estimate the present value of $220 (the *f* value) at the end of one period (*n* = 1) where the interest rate (*i*) is 10%. To solve this case, we go to the present value table (Table B.1) and look in the row for 1 period and in the column for 10% interest. Here we find a present value (*p*) of 0.9091 based on a future value of 1. This means, for instance, that $1 to be received one period from today at 10% interest is worth $0.9091 today. Since the future value in this case is not $1 but $220, we multiply the 0.9091 by $220 to get an answer of $200.

Case 2   (solve for *n* when knowing *p* and *i*). To illustrate, assume a $100,000 future value (*f*) that is worth $13,000 today (*p*) using an interest rate of 12% (*i*) but where *n* is unknown. In particular, we want to know how many periods (*n*) there are between the present value and the future value. To put this in context, it would fit a situation in which we want to retire with $100,000 but currently have only $13,000 that is earning a 12% return and we will be unable to save any additional money. How long will it be before we can retire? To answer this, we go to Table B.1 and look in the 12% interest column. Here we find a column of present values (*p*) based on a future value of 1. To use the present value table for this solution, we must divide $13,000 (*p*) by $100,000 (*f*), which equals 0.1300. This is necessary because *a present value table defines* f *equal to 1, and* p *as a fraction of 1.* We look for a value nearest to 0.1300 (*p*), which we find in the row for 18 periods (*n*). This means that the present value of $100,000 at the end of 18 periods at 12% interest is $13,000; alternatively stated, we must work 18 more years.

Case 3   (solve for *i* when knowing *p* and *n*). In this case, we have, say, a $120,000 future value (*f*) worth $60,000 today (*p*) when there are nine periods (*n*) between the present and future values, but the interest rate is unknown. As an example, suppose we want to retire with $120,000, but we have only $60,000 and we will be unable to save any additional money, yet we hope to retire in nine years. What interest rate must we earn to retire with $120,000 in nine years? To answer this, we go to the present value table (Table B.1) and look in the row for nine periods. To use the present value table, we must divide $60,000 (*p*) by $120,000 (*f*), which equals 0.5000. Recall that this step is necessary because a present value table defines *f* equal to 1 and *p* as a fraction of 1. We look for a value in the row for nine periods that is nearest to 0.5000 (*p*), which we find in the column for 8% interest (*i*). This means that the present value of $120,000 at the end of nine periods at 8% interest is $60,000 or, in our example, we must earn 8% annual interest to retire in nine years.

| **Quick Check** | Answer — p. B-7 | |

1. A company is considering an investment expected to yield $70,000 after six years. If this company demands an 8% return, how much is it willing to pay for this investment?

FUTURE VALUE OF A SINGLE AMOUNT

We must modify the formula for the present value of a single amount to obtain the formula for the future value of a single amount. In particular, we multiply both sides of the equation in Exhibit B.2 by $(1 + i)^n$ to get the result shown in Exhibit B.4.

$$f = p \times (1 + i)^n$$

EXHIBIT B.4

Future Value of a Single Amount Formula

The future value (f) is defined in terms of p, i, and n. We can use this formula to determine that \$200 (p) invested for 1 (n) period at an interest rate of 10% (i) yields a future value of \$220 as follows:

$$f = p \times (1 + i)^n$$
$$= \$200 \times (1 + 0.10)^1$$
$$= \$220$$

P2 Apply future value concepts to a single amount by using interest tables.

This formula can also be used to compute the future value of an amount for *any number of periods* into the future. To illustrate, assume that \$200 is invested for three periods at 10%. The future value of this \$200 is \$266.20, computed as follows:

$$f = p \times (1 + i)^n$$
$$= \$200 \times (1 + 0.10)^3$$
$$= \$266.20$$

A future value table makes it easier for us to compute future values (f) for many different combinations of interest rates (i) and time periods (n). Each future value in a future value table assumes the present value (p) is 1. As with a present value table, if the future amount is something other than 1, we simply multiply our answer by that amount. The formula used to construct a table of future values (factors) for a single amount of 1 is in Exhibit B.5.

EXHIBIT B.5

Future Value of 1 Formula

$$f = (1 + i)^n$$

Table B.2 at the end of this appendix shows a table of future values for a current amount of 1. This type of table is called a **future value of 1 table**.

There are some important relations between Tables B.1 and B.2. In Table B.2, for the row where $n = 0$, the future value is 1 for each interest rate. This is so because no interest is earned when time does not pass. We also see that Tables B.1 and B.2 report the same information but in a different manner. In particular, one table is simply the *inverse* of the other. To illustrate this inverse relation, let's say we invest \$100 for a period of five years at 12% per year. How much do we expect to have after five years? We can answer this question using Table B.2 by finding the future value (f) of 1, for five periods from now, compounded at 12%. From that table we find $f = 1.7623$. If we start with \$100, the amount it accumulates to after five years is \$176.23 (\$100 $\times$ 1.7623). We can alternatively use Table B.1. Here we find that the present value (p) of 1, discounted five periods at 12%, is 0.5674. Recall the inverse relation between present value and future value. This means that $p = 1/f$ (or equivalently, $f = 1/p$). We can compute the future value of \$100 invested for five periods at 12% as follows: $f = \$100 \times (1/0.5674) = \$176.24$ (which equals the \$176.23 just computed, except for a 1 cent rounding difference).

A future value table involves three factors: f, i, and n. Knowing two of these three factors allows us to compute the third. To illustrate, consider these three possible cases.

Case 1   (solve for f when knowing i and n). Our preceding example fits this case. We found that \$100 invested for five periods at 12% interest accumulates to \$176.24.

Case 2   (solve for n when knowing f and i). In this case, we have, say, \$2,000 (p) and we want to know how many periods (n) it will take to accumulate to \$3,000 (f) at 7% (i) interest. To answer this, we go to the future value table (Table B.2) and look in the 7% interest column. Here we find a column of future values (f) based on a present value of 1. To use a future value table, we must divide \$3,000 (f) by \$2,000 (p), which equals 1.500. This is necessary because *a future value table defines* p *equal to 1, and* f *as a multiple of 1*. We look for a value nearest to 1.50 (f), which we find in the row for six periods (n). This means that \$2,000 invested for six periods at 7% interest accumulates to \$3,000.

Case 3   (solve for i when knowing f and n). In this case, we have, say, \$2,001 (p), and in nine years (n) we want to have \$4,000 (f). What rate of interest must we earn to accomplish this? To answer that, we go to Table B.2 and search in the row for nine periods. To use a future value table, we must divide \$4,000 (f) by \$2,001 (p), which equals 1.9990. Recall that this is necessary because a future value table defines *p* equal to 1 and *f* as a multiple of 1. We look for a value nearest to 1.9990 (*f*), which we find in the column for 8% interest (*i*). This means that $2,001 invested for nine periods at 8% interest accumulates to $4,000.

| **Quick Check** | Answer — p. B-7 | |

2. Assume that you win a $150,000 cash sweepstakes. You decide to deposit this cash in an account earning 8% annual interest, and you plan to quit your job when the account equals $555,000. How many years will it be before you can quit working?

PRESENT VALUE OF AN ANNUITY

An *annuity* is a series of equal payments occurring at equal intervals. One example is a series of three annual payments of $100 each. An *ordinary annuity* is defined as equal end-of-period payments at equal intervals. An ordinary annuity of $100 for three periods and its present value (*p*) are illustrated in Exhibit B.6.

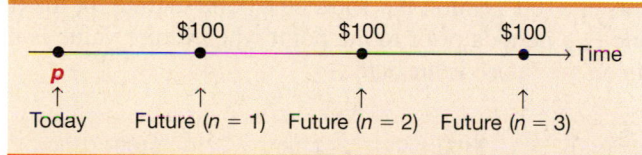

EXHIBIT B.6

Present Value of an Ordinary Annuity Diagram

One way to compute the present value of an ordinary annuity is to find the present value of each payment using our present value formula from Exhibit B.3. We then add each of the three present values. To illustrate, let's look at three $100 payments at the end of each of the next three periods with an interest rate of 15%. Our present value computations are

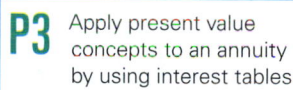

P3 Apply present value concepts to an annuity by using interest tables.

$$p = \frac{\$100}{(1 + 0.15)^1} + \frac{\$100}{(1 + 0.15)^2} + \frac{\$100}{(1 + 0.15)^3} = \$228.32$$

This computation is identical to computing the present value of each payment (from Table B.1) and taking their sum or, alternatively, adding the values from Table B.1 for each of the three payments and multiplying their sum by the $100 annuity payment.

A more direct way is to use a present value of annuity table. Table B.3 at the end of this appendix is one such table. This table is called a **present value of an annuity of 1 table**. If we look at Table B.3 where *n* = 3 and *i* = 15%, we see the present value is 2.2832. This means that the present value of an annuity of 1 for three periods, with a 15% interest rate, equals 2.2832.

A present value of an annuity formula is used to construct Table B.3. It can also be constructed by adding the amounts in a present value of 1 table. To illustrate, we use Tables B.1 and B.3 to confirm this relation for the prior example:

From Table B.1		From Table B.3	
i = 15%, *n* = 1	0.8696		
i = 15%, *n* = 2	0.7561		
i = 15%, *n* = 3	0.6575		
Total	2.2832	*i* = 15%, *n* = 3	2.2832

We can also use business calculators or spreadsheet programs to find the present value of an annuity.

Decision Insight

Better Lucky Than Good   "I don't have good luck—I'm blessed," proclaimed Andrew "Jack" Whittaker, 55, a sewage treatment contractor, after winning the largest ever undivided jackpot in a U.S. lottery. Whittaker had to choose between $315 million in 30 annual installments or $170 million in one lump sum ($112 million after-tax). ■

Quick Check   Answer — p. B-7

3. A company is considering an investment paying $10,000 every six months for three years. The first payment would be received in six months. If this company requires an 8% annual return, what is the maximum amount it is willing to pay for this investment?

FUTURE VALUE OF AN ANNUITY

The future value of an *ordinary annuity* is the accumulated value of each annuity payment with interest as of the date of the final payment. To illustrate, let's consider the earlier annuity of three annual payments of $100. Exhibit B.7 shows the point in time for the future value (f). The first payment is made two periods prior to the point when future value is determined, and the final payment occurs on the future value date.

EXHIBIT B.7

Future Value of an Ordinary Annuity Diagram

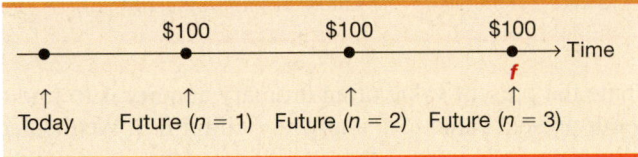

One way to compute the future value of an annuity is to use the formula to find the future value of *each* payment and add them. If we assume an interest rate of 15%, our calculation is

$$f = \$100 \times (1 + 0.15)^2 + \$100 \times (1 + 0.15)^1 + \$100 \times (1 + 0.15)^0 = \$347.25$$

This is identical to using Table B.2 and summing the future values of each payment, or adding the future values of the three payments of 1 and multiplying the sum by $100.

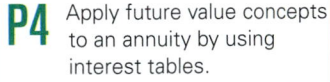

P4 Apply future value concepts to an annuity by using interest tables.

A more direct way is to use a table showing future values of annuities. Such a table is called a **future value of an annuity of 1 table**. Table B.4 at the end of this appendix is one such table. Note that in Table B.4 when $n = 1$, the future values equal 1 ($f = 1$) for all rates of interest. This is so because such an annuity consists of only one payment and the future value is determined on the date of that payment—no time passes between the payment and its future value. The future value of an annuity formula is used to construct Table B.4. We can also construct it by adding the amounts from a future value of 1 table. To illustrate, we use Tables B.2 and B.4 to confirm this relation for the prior example:

From Table B.2		From Table B.4	
$i = 15\%, n = 0$	1.0000		
$i = 15\%, n = 1$	1.1500		
$i = 15\%, n = 2$	1.3225		
Total	3.4725	$i = 15\%, n = 3$	3.4725

Note that the future value in Table B.2 is 1.0000 when $n = 0$, but the future value in Table B.4 is 1.0000 when $n = 1$. Is this a contradiction? No. When $n = 0$ in Table B.2, the future value is determined on the date when a single payment occurs. This means that no interest is earned because no time has passed, and the future value equals the payment. Table B.4 describes annuities with equal payments occurring at the end of each period. When $n = 1$, the annuity has one payment, and its future value equals 1 on the date of its final and only payment. Again, no time passes between the payment and its future value date.

Quick Check   Answer — p. B-7

> **4.** A company invests $45,000 per year for five years at 12% annual interest. Compute the value of this annuity investment at the end of five years.

Summary

C1 **Describe the earning of interest and the concepts of present and future values.** Interest is payment by a borrower to the owner of an asset for its use. Present and future value computations are a way for us to estimate the interest component of holding assets or liabilities over a period of time.

P1 **Apply present value concepts to a single amount by using interest tables.** The present value of a single amount received at a future date is the amount that can be invested now at the specified interest rate to yield that future value.

P2 **Apply future value concepts to a single amount by using interest tables.** The future value of a single amount invested

at a specified rate of interest is the amount that would accumulate by the future date.

P3 **Apply present value concepts to an annuity by using interest tables.** The present value of an annuity is the amount that can be invested now at the specified interest rate to yield that series of equal periodic payments.

P4 **Apply future value concepts to an annuity by using interest tables.** The future value of an annuity invested at a specific rate of interest is the amount that would accumulate by the date of the final payment.

Guidance Answers to Quick Checks

1. $70,000 \times 0.6302 = \$44,114$ (use Table B.1, $i = 8\%$, $n = 6$).

2. $555,000/\$150,000 = 3.7000$; Table B.2 shows this value is not achieved until after 17 years at 8% interest.

3. $10,000 \times 5.2421 = \$52,421$ (use Table B.3, $i = 4\%$, $n = 6$).

4. $45,000 \times 6.3528 = \$285,876$ (use Table B.4, $i = 12\%$, $n = 5$).

---

connect

Assume that you must make future value estimates using the *future value of 1 table* (Table B.2). Which interest rate column do you use when working with the following rates?

1. 8% compounded quarterly

2. 12% compounded annually

3. 6% compounded semiannually

4. 12% compounded monthly

QUICK STUDY

QS B-1
Identifying interest
rates in tables

C1

Ken Francis is offered the possibility of investing $2,745 today and in return to receive $10,000 after 15 years. What is the annual rate of interest for this investment? (Use Table B.1.)

QS B-2
Interest rate
on an investment   **P1**

Megan Brink is offered the possibility of investing $6,651 today at 6% interest per year in a desire to accumulate $10,000. How many years must Brink wait to accumulate $10,000? (Use Table B.1.)

QS B-3
Number of periods
of an investment   **P1**

Flaherty is considering an investment that, if paid for immediately, is expected to return $140,000 five years from now. If Flaherty demands a 9% return, how much is she willing to pay for this investment?

QS B-4
Present value of an amount   **P1**

CII, Inc., invests $630,000 in a project expected to earn a 12% annual rate of return. The earnings will be reinvested in the project each year until the entire investment is liquidated 10 years later. What will the cash proceeds be when the project is liquidated?

QS B-5
Future value of an amount   **P2**

QS B-6
Present value
of an annuity   P3

Beene Distributing is considering a project that will return $150,000 annually at the end of each year for six years. If Beene demands an annual return of 7% and pays for the project immediately, how much is it willing to pay for the project?

QS B-7
Future value
of an annuity   P4

Claire Fitch is planning to begin an individual retirement program in which she will invest $1,500 at the end of each year. Fitch plans to retire after making 30 annual investments in the program earning a return of 10%. What is the value of the program on the date of the last payment?

EXERCISES

Exercise B-1
Number of periods
of an investment   P2

Bill Thompson expects to invest $10,000 at 12% and, at the end of a certain period, receive $96,463. How many years will it be before Thompson receives the payment? (Use Table B.2.)

Exercise B-2
Interest rate on
an investment   P2

Ed Summers expects to invest $10,000 for 25 years, after which he wants to receive $108,347. What rate of interest must Summers earn? (Use Table B.2.)

Exercise B-3
Interest rate on
an investment   P3

Jones expects an immediate investment of $57,466 to return $10,000 annually for eight years, with the first payment to be received one year from now. What rate of interest must Jones earn? (Use Table B.3.)

Exercise B-4
Number of periods
of an investment   P3

Keith Riggins expects an investment of $82,014 to return $10,000 annually for several years. If Riggins earns a return of 10%, how many annual payments will he receive? (Use Table B.3.)

Exercise B-5
Interest rate on
an investment   P4

Algoe expects to invest $1,000 annually for 40 years to yield an accumulated value of $154,762 on the date of the last investment. For this to occur, what rate of interest must Algoe earn? (Use Table B.4.)

Exercise B-6
Number of periods
of an investment   P4

Kate Beckwith expects to invest $10,000 annually that will earn 8%. How many annual investments must Beckwith make to accumulate $303,243 on the date of the last investment? (Use Table B.4.)

Exercise B-7
Present value
of an annuity   P3

Sam Weber finances a new automobile by paying $6,500 cash and agreeing to make 40 monthly payments of $500 each, the first payment to be made one month after the purchase. The loan bears interest at an annual rate of 12%. What is the cost of the automobile?

Exercise B-8
Present value of bonds

P1 P3

Spiller Corp. plans to issue 10%, 15-year, $500,000 par value bonds payable that pay interest semiannually on June 30 and December 31. The bonds are dated December 31, 2011, and are issued on that date. If the market rate of interest for the bonds is 8% on the date of issue, what will be the total cash proceeds from the bond issue?

Exercise B-9
Present value
of an amount   P1

McAdams Company expects to earn 10% per year on an investment that will pay $606,773 six years from now. Use Table B.1 to compute the present value of this investment. (Round the amount to the nearest dollar.)

Exercise B-10
Present value of
an amount and
of an annuity   P1 P3

Compute the amount that can be borrowed under each of the following circumstances:
1. A promise to repay $90,000 seven years from now at an interest rate of 6%.
2. An agreement made on February 1, 2011, to make three separate payments of $20,000 on February 1 of 2012, 2013, and 2014. The annual interest rate is 10%.

Exercise B-11
Present value
of an amount   P1

On January 1, 2011, a company agrees to pay $20,000 in three years. If the annual interest rate is 10%, determine how much cash the company can borrow with this agreement.

Find the amount of money that can be borrowed today with each of the following separate debt agreements *a* through *f.* (Round amounts to the nearest dollar.)

Exercise B-12
Present value
of an amount **P1**

Case	Single Future Payment	Number of Periods	Interest Rate
a.	$40,000	3	4%
b.	75,000	7	8
c.	52,000	9	10
d.	18,000	2	4
e.	63,000	8	6
f.	89,000	5	2

C&H Ski Club recently borrowed money and agrees to pay it back with a series of six annual payments of $5,000 each. C&H subsequently borrows more money and agrees to pay it back with a series of four annual payments of $7,500 each. The annual interest rate for both loans is 6%.

1. Use Table B.1 to find the present value of these two separate annuities. (Round amounts to the nearest dollar.)

2. Use Table B.3 to find the present value of these two separate annuities. (Round amounts to the nearest dollar.)

Exercise B-13
Present values of annuities

P3

Otto Co. borrows money on April 30, 2011, by promising to make four payments of $13,000 each on November 1, 2011; May 1, 2012; November 1, 2012; and May 1, 2013.

1. How much money is Otto able to borrow if the interest rate is 8%, compounded semiannually?

2. How much money is Otto able to borrow if the interest rate is 12%, compounded semiannually?

3. How much money is Otto able to borrow if the interest rate is 16%, compounded semiannually?

Exercise B-14
Present value with semiannual compounding

C1 P3

Mark Welsch deposits $7,200 in an account that earns interest at an annual rate of 8%, compounded quarterly. The $7,200 plus earned interest must remain in the account 10 years before it can be withdrawn. How much money will be in the account at the end of 10 years?

Exercise B-15
Future value
of an amount **P2**

Kelly Malone plans to have $50 withheld from her monthly paycheck and deposited in a savings account that earns 12% annually, compounded monthly. If Malone continues with her plan for two and one-half years, how much will be accumulated in the account on the date of the last deposit?

Exercise B-16
Future value
of an annuity **P4**

Starr Company decides to establish a fund that it will use 10 years from now to replace an aging production facility. The company will make a $100,000 initial contribution to the fund and plans to make quarterly contributions of $50,000 beginning in three months. The fund earns 12%, compounded quarterly. What will be the value of the fund 10 years from now?

Exercise B-17
Future value of
an amount plus
an annuity **P2 P4**

Catten, Inc., invests $163,170 today earning 7% per year for nine years. Use Table B.2 to compute the future value of the investment nine years from now. (Round the amount to the nearest dollar.)

Exercise B-18
Future value of
an amount **P2**

For each of the following situations, identify (1) the case as either (*a*) a present or a future value and (*b*) a single amount or an annuity, (2) the table you would use in your computations (but do not solve the problem), and (3) the interest rate and time periods you would use.

a. You need to accumulate $10,000 for a trip you wish to take in four years. You are able to earn 8% compounded semiannually on your savings. You plan to make only one deposit and let the money accumulate for four years. How would you determine the amount of the one-time deposit?

b. Assume the same facts as in part (*a*) except that you will make semiannual deposits to your savings account.

c. You want to retire after working 40 years with savings in excess of $1,000,000. You expect to save $4,000 a year for 40 years and earn an annual rate of interest of 8%. Will you be able to retire with more than $1,000,000 in 40 years? Explain.

d. A sweepstakes agency names you a grand prize winner. You can take $225,000 immediately or elect to receive annual installments of $30,000 for 20 years. You can earn 10% annually on any investments you make. Which prize do you choose to receive?

Exercise B-19
Using present and future value tables

C1 P1 P2 P3 P4

TABLE B.1
Present Value of 1

$$p = 1/(1 + i)^n$$

Periods	rate

Periods	1%	2%	3%	4%	5%	6%	7%	8%	9%	10%	12%	15%
1	0.9901	0.9804	0.9709	0.9615	0.9524	0.9434	0.9346	0.9259	0.9174	0.9091	0.8929	0.8696
2	0.9803	0.9612	0.9426	0.9246	0.9070	0.8900	0.8734	0.8573	0.8417	0.8264	0.7972	0.7561
3	0.9706	0.9423	0.9151	0.8890	0.8638	0.8396	0.8163	0.7938	0.7722	0.7513	0.7118	0.6575
4	0.9610	0.9238	0.8885	0.8548	0.8227	0.7921	0.7629	0.7350	0.7084	0.6830	0.6355	0.5718
5	0.9515	0.9057	0.8626	0.8219	0.7835	0.7473	0.7130	0.6806	0.6499	0.6209	0.5674	0.4972
6	0.9420	0.8880	0.8375	0.7903	0.7462	0.7050	0.6663	0.6302	0.5963	0.5645	0.5066	0.4323
7	0.9327	0.8706	0.8131	0.7599	0.7107	0.6651	0.6227	0.5835	0.5470	0.5132	0.4523	0.3759
8	0.9235	0.8535	0.7894	0.7307	0.6768	0.6274	0.5820	0.5403	0.5019	0.4665	0.4039	0.3269
9	0.9143	0.8368	0.7664	0.7026	0.6446	0.5919	0.5439	0.5002	0.4604	0.4241	0.3606	0.2843
10	0.9053	0.8203	0.7441	0.6756	0.6139	0.5584	0.5083	0.4632	0.4224	0.3855	0.3220	0.2472
11	0.8963	0.8043	0.7224	0.6496	0.5847	0.5268	0.4751	0.4289	0.3875	0.3505	0.2875	0.2149
12	0.8874	0.7885	0.7014	0.6246	0.5568	0.4970	0.4440	0.3971	0.3555	0.3186	0.2567	0.1869
13	0.8787	0.7730	0.6810	0.6006	0.5303	0.4688	0.4150	0.3677	0.3262	0.2897	0.2292	0.1625
14	0.8700	0.7579	0.6611	0.5775	0.5051	0.4423	0.3878	0.3405	0.2992	0.2633	0.2046	0.1413
15	0.8613	0.7430	0.6419	0.5553	0.4810	0.4173	0.3624	0.3152	0.2745	0.2394	0.1827	0.1229
16	0.8528	0.7284	0.6232	0.5339	0.4581	0.3936	0.3387	0.2919	0.2519	0.2176	0.1631	0.1069
17	0.8444	0.7142	0.6050	0.5134	0.4363	0.3714	0.3166	0.2703	0.2311	0.1978	0.1456	0.0929
18	0.8360	0.7002	0.5874	0.4936	0.4155	0.3503	0.2959	0.2502	0.2120	0.1799	0.1300	0.0808
19	0.8277	0.6864	0.5703	0.4746	0.3957	0.3305	0.2765	0.2317	0.1945	0.1635	0.1161	0.0703
20	0.8195	0.6730	0.5537	0.4564	0.3769	0.3118	0.2584	0.2145	0.1784	0.1486	0.1037	0.0611
25	0.7798	0.6095	0.4776	0.3751	0.2953	0.2330	0.1842	0.1460	0.1160	0.0923	0.0588	0.0304
30	0.7419	0.5521	0.4120	0.3083	0.2314	0.1741	0.1314	0.0994	0.0754	0.0573	0.0334	0.0151
35	0.7059	0.5000	0.3554	0.2534	0.1813	0.1301	0.0937	0.0676	0.0490	0.0356	0.0189	0.0075
40	0.6717	0.4529	0.3066	0.2083	0.1420	0.0972	0.0668	0.0460	0.0318	0.0221	0.0107	0.0037

TABLE B.2
Future Value of 1

$$f = (1 + i)^n$$

Periods	1%	2%	3%	4%	5%	6%	7%	8%	9%	10%	12%	15%
0	1.0000	1.0000	1.0000	1.0000	1.0000	1.0000	1.0000	1.0000	1.0000	1.0000	1.0000	1.0000
1	1.0100	1.0200	1.0300	1.0400	1.0500	1.0600	1.0700	1.0800	1.0900	1.1000	1.1200	1.1500
2	1.0201	1.0404	1.0609	1.0816	1.1025	1.1236	1.1449	1.1664	1.1881	1.2100	1.2544	1.3225
3	1.0303	1.0612	1.0927	1.1249	1.1576	1.1910	1.2250	1.2597	1.2950	1.3310	1.4049	1.5209
4	1.0406	1.0824	1.1255	1.1699	1.2155	1.2625	1.3108	1.3605	1.4116	1.4641	1.5735	1.7490
5	1.0510	1.1041	1.1593	1.2167	1.2763	1.3382	1.4026	1.4693	1.5386	1.6105	1.7623	2.0114
6	1.0615	1.1262	1.1941	1.2653	1.3401	1.4185	1.5007	1.5869	1.6771	1.7716	1.9738	2.3131
7	1.0721	1.1487	1.2299	1.3159	1.4071	1.5036	1.6058	1.7138	1.8280	1.9487	2.2107	2.6600
8	1.0829	1.1717	1.2668	1.3686	1.4775	1.5938	1.7182	1.8509	1.9926	2.1436	2.4760	3.0590
9	1.0937	1.1951	1.3048	1.4233	1.5513	1.6895	1.8385	1.9990	2.1719	2.3579	2.7731	3.5179
10	1.1046	1.2190	1.3439	1.4802	1.6289	1.7908	1.9672	2.1589	2.3674	2.5937	3.1058	4.0456
11	1.1157	1.2434	1.3842	1.5395	1.7103	1.8983	2.1049	2.3316	2.5804	2.8531	3.4785	4.6524
12	1.1268	1.2682	1.4258	1.6010	1.7959	2.0122	2.2522	2.5182	2.8127	3.1384	3.8960	5.3503
13	1.1381	1.2936	1.4685	1.6651	1.8856	2.1329	2.4098	2.7196	3.0658	3.4523	4.3635	6.1528
14	1.1495	1.3195	1.5126	1.7317	1.9799	2.2609	2.5785	2.9372	3.3417	3.7975	4.8871	7.0757
15	1.1610	1.3459	1.5580	1.8009	2.0789	2.3966	2.7590	3.1722	3.6425	4.1772	5.4736	8.1371
16	1.1726	1.3728	1.6047	1.8730	2.1829	2.5404	2.9522	3.4259	3.9703	4.5950	6.1304	9.3576
17	1.1843	1.4002	1.6528	1.9479	2.2920	2.6928	3.1588	3.7000	4.3276	5.0545	6.8660	10.7613
18	1.1961	1.4282	1.7024	2.0258	2.4066	2.8543	3.3799	3.9960	4.7171	5.5599	7.6900	12.3755
19	1.2081	1.4568	1.7535	2.1068	2.5270	3.0256	3.6165	4.3157	5.1417	6.1159	8.6128	14.2318
20	1.2202	1.4859	1.8061	2.1911	2.6533	3.2071	3.8697	4.6610	5.6044	6.7275	9.6463	16.3665
25	1.2824	1.6406	2.0938	2.6658	3.3864	4.2919	5.4274	6.8485	8.6231	10.8347	17.0001	32.9190
30	1.3478	1.8114	2.4273	3.2434	4.3219	5.7435	7.6123	10.0627	13.2677	17.4494	29.9599	66.2118
35	1.4166	1.9999	2.8139	3.9461	5.5160	7.6861	10.6766	14.7853	20.4140	28.1024	52.7996	133.1755
40	1.4889	2.2080	3.2620	4.8010	7.0400	10.2857	14.9745	21.7245	31.4094	45.2593	93.0510	267.8635

$$p = \left[1 - \frac{1}{(1+i)^n}\right]/i$$

TABLE B.3

Present Value of an Annuity of 1

Periods	1%	2%	3%	4%	5%	6%	7%	8%	9%	10%	12%	15%
1	0.9901	0.9804	0.9709	0.9615	0.9524	0.9434	0.9346	0.9259	0.9174	0.9091	0.8929	0.8696
2	1.9704	1.9416	1.9135	1.8861	1.8594	1.8334	1.8080	1.7833	1.7591	1.7355	1.6901	1.6257
3	2.9410	2.8839	2.8286	2.7751	2.7232	2.6730	2.6243	2.5771	2.5313	2.4869	2.4018	2.2832
4	3.9020	3.8077	3.7171	3.6299	3.5460	3.4651	3.3872	3.3121	3.2397	3.1699	3.0373	2.8550
5	4.8534	4.7135	4.5797	4.4518	4.3295	4.2124	4.1002	3.9927	3.8897	3.7908	3.6048	3.3522
6	5.7955	5.6014	5.4172	5.2421	5.0757	4.9173	4.7665	4.6229	4.4859	4.3553	4.1114	3.7845
7	6.7282	6.4720	6.2303	6.0021	5.7864	5.5824	5.3893	5.2064	5.0330	4.8684	4.5638	4.1604
8	7.6517	7.3255	7.0197	6.7327	6.4632	6.2098	5.9713	5.7466	5.5348	5.3349	4.9676	4.4873
9	8.5660	8.1622	7.7861	7.4353	7.1078	6.8017	6.5152	6.2469	5.9952	5.7590	5.3282	4.7716
10	9.4713	8.9826	8.5302	8.1109	7.7217	7.3601	7.0236	6.7101	6.4177	6.1446	5.6502	5.0188
11	10.3676	9.7868	9.2526	8.7605	8.3064	7.8869	7.4987	7.1390	6.8052	6.4951	5.9377	5.2337
12	11.2551	10.5753	9.9540	9.3851	8.8633	8.3838	7.9427	7.5361	7.1607	6.8137	6.1944	5.4206
13	12.1337	11.3484	10.6350	9.9856	9.3936	8.8527	8.3577	7.9038	7.4869	7.1034	6.4235	5.5831
14	13.0037	12.1062	11.2961	10.5631	9.8986	9.2950	8.7455	8.2442	7.7862	7.3667	6.6282	5.7245
15	13.8651	12.8493	11.9379	11.1184	10.3797	9.7122	9.1079	8.5595	8.0607	7.6061	6.8109	5.8474
16	14.7179	13.5777	12.5611	11.6523	10.8378	10.1059	9.4466	8.8514	8.3126	7.8237	6.9740	5.9542
17	15.5623	14.2919	13.1661	12.1657	11.2741	10.4773	9.7632	9.1216	8.5436	8.0216	7.1196	6.0472
18	16.3983	14.9920	13.7535	12.6593	11.6896	10.8276	10.0591	9.3719	8.7556	8.2014	7.2497	6.1280
19	17.2260	15.6785	14.3238	13.1339	12.0853	11.1581	10.3356	9.6036	8.9501	8.3649	7.3658	6.1982
20	18.0456	16.3514	14.8775	13.5903	12.4622	11.4699	10.5940	9.8181	9.1285	8.5136	7.4694	6.2593
25	22.0232	19.5235	17.4131	15.6221	14.0939	12.7834	11.6536	10.6748	9.8226	9.0770	7.8431	6.4641
30	25.8077	22.3965	19.6004	17.2920	15.3725	13.7648	12.4090	11.2578	10.2737	9.4269	8.0552	6.5660
35	29.4086	24.9986	21.4872	18.6646	16.3742	14.4982	12.9477	11.6546	10.5668	9.6442	8.1755	6.6166
40	32.8347	27.3555	23.1148	19.7928	17.1591	15.0463	13.3317	11.9246	10.7574	9.7791	8.2438	6.6418

$$f = [(1+i)^n - 1]/i$$

TABLE B.4

Future Value of an Annuity of 1

Periods	1%	2%	3%	4%	5%	6%	7%	8%	9%	10%	12%	15%
1	1.0000	1.0000	1.0000	1.0000	1.0000	1.0000	1.0000	1.0000	1.0000	1.0000	1.0000	1.0000
2	2.0100	2.0200	2.0300	2.0400	2.0500	2.0600	2.0700	2.0800	2.0900	2.1000	2.1200	2.1500
3	3.0301	3.0604	3.0909	3.1216	3.1525	3.1836	3.2149	3.2464	3.2781	3.3100	3.3744	3.4725
4	4.0604	4.1216	4.1836	4.2465	4.3101	4.3746	4.4399	4.5061	4.5731	4.6410	4.7793	4.9934
5	5.1010	5.2040	5.3091	5.4163	5.5256	5.6371	5.7507	5.8666	5.9847	6.1051	6.3528	6.7424
6	6.1520	6.3081	6.4684	6.6330	6.8019	6.9753	7.1533	7.3359	7.5233	7.7156	8.1152	8.7537
7	7.2135	7.4343	7.6625	7.8983	8.1420	8.3938	8.6540	8.9228	9.2004	9.4872	10.0890	11.0668
8	8.2857	8.5830	8.8923	9.2142	9.5491	9.8975	10.2598	10.6366	11.0285	11.4359	12.2997	13.7268
9	9.3685	9.7546	10.1591	10.5828	11.0266	11.4913	11.9780	12.4876	13.0210	13.5795	14.7757	16.7858
10	10.4622	10.9497	11.4639	12.0061	12.5779	13.1808	13.8164	14.4866	15.1929	15.9374	17.5487	20.3037
11	11.5668	12.1687	12.8078	13.4864	14.2068	14.9716	15.7836	16.6455	17.5603	18.5312	20.6546	24.3493
12	12.6825	13.4121	14.1920	15.0258	15.9171	16.8699	17.8885	18.9771	20.1407	21.3843	24.1331	29.0017
13	13.8093	14.6803	15.6178	16.6268	17.7130	18.8821	20.1406	21.4953	22.9534	24.5227	28.0291	34.3519
14	14.9474	15.9739	17.0863	18.2919	19.5986	21.0151	22.5505	24.2149	26.0192	27.9750	32.3926	40.5047
15	16.0969	17.2934	18.5989	20.0236	21.5786	23.2760	25.1290	27.1521	29.3609	31.7725	37.2797	47.5804
16	17.2579	18.6393	20.1569	21.8245	23.6575	25.6725	27.8881	30.3243	33.0034	35.9497	42.7533	55.7175
17	18.4304	20.0121	21.7616	23.6975	25.8404	28.2129	30.8402	33.7502	36.9737	40.5447	48.8837	65.0751
18	19.6147	21.4123	23.4144	25.6454	28.1324	30.9057	33.9990	37.4502	41.3013	45.5992	55.7497	75.8364
19	20.8109	22.8406	25.1169	27.6712	30.5390	33.7600	37.3790	41.4463	46.0185	51.1591	63.4397	88.2118
20	22.0190	24.2974	26.8704	29.7781	33.0660	36.7856	40.9955	45.7620	51.1601	57.2750	72.0524	102.4436
25	28.2432	32.0303	36.4593	41.6459	47.7271	54.8645	63.2490	73.1059	84.7009	98.3471	133.3339	212.7930
30	34.7849	40.5681	47.5754	56.0849	66.4388	79.0582	94.4608	113.2832	136.3075	164.4940	241.3327	434.7451
35	41.6603	49.9945	60.4621	73.6522	90.3203	111.4348	138.2369	172.3168	215.7108	271.0244	431.6635	881.1702
40	48.8864	60.4020	75.4013	95.0255	120.7998	154.7620	199.6351	259.0565	337.8824	442.5926	767.0914	1,779.0903

Appendix

C

Investments and International Operations

A Look at This Appendix

This appendix focuses on investments in securities. We explain how to identify, account for, and report investments in both debt and equity securities. We also explain accounting for transactions listed in a foreign currency.

Learning Objectives

CAP

CONCEPTUAL

C1 Distinguish between debt and equity securities and between short-term and long-term investments. (p. C-2)

C2 Describe how to report equity securities with controlling influence. (p. C-9)

C3 *Appendix C-A*—Explain foreign exchange rates and record transactions listed in a foreign currency. (p. C-16)

ANALYTICAL

A1 Compute and analyze the components of return on total assets. (p. C-11)

LP-C

PROCEDURAL

P1 Account for trading securities. (p. C-5)

P2 Account for held-to-maturity securities. (p. C-6)

P3 Account for available-for-sale securities. (p. C-6)

P4 Account for equity securities with significant influence. (p. C-8)

Schooling the Market

"There's this whole new emerging category of academic technology"

—**MICHAEL CHASEN**

WASHINGTON, DC—Michael Chasen and Matthew Pittinsky had just finished college—Michael earning a degree in accounting and Matthew Pittinsky in education. Both took jobs at KPMG. "Matthew and I had decided to leave KPMG and start an e-learning business, which we called **Blackboard (Blackboard.com),**" explains Michael. "Campuses nationwide were beginning to connect to the Internet but had no way to put courses online."

What Michael and Matthew did was leverage online technology to enhance education and learning for both students and instructors. "[Students and instructors] want improved ease of use," insists Michael. "They want the teaching and learning kept not just inside the class, but outside the classroom." Michael and Matthew have been so successful that their company's operations now extend over many countries. "We not only continue to expand within higher education but we are expanding internationally," says Michael. "I travel all over the world for Blackboard."

This broad reach has led to business challenges involving both investments and international operations. "I am asked a lot of questions about . . . education on the Internet," explains Michael. "[Investments are] often one of the better ways to deploy capital."

Blackboard's annual report states: "[We] pursue strategic relationships with, acquisitions of, and investments in, companies that would enhance the technological features of our products, offer complementary products, services and technologies, or broaden the scope of our product offerings." Also, investments in international operations require them to translate their performance into U.S. dollars for financial reporting. Those tasks require knowledge of accounting and reporting requirements for investments, including investments in securities of other companies.

Blackboard's annual report reveals that it has "a variety of marketable investments." It reports that "for those investments in entities where the Company has significant influence over operations . . . [it] follows the equity method of accounting." It also explains that Blackboard "consolidates investments where it has a controlling financial interest." Still, Michael insists that their investment in the future of learning is the key. "We are very much focused on innovation," says Michael. "[The market's] ripe for a technology explosion in e-learning."

[Sources: *Blackboard Website,* January 2011; *Entrepreneur,* March 2009; *The New York Times,* November 2009; *The Washington Post,* August 2007; *Washington Business Journal,* October 2008]

This appendix's main focus is investments in securities. Many companies have investments, and many of these are in the form of debt and equity securities issued by other companies. We describe investments in these securities and how to account for them. An increasing number of companies also invest in international operations. We explain how to account for and report international transactions listed in foreign currencies.

Investments and International Operations

Basics of Investments	Noninfluential Investments	Influential Investments
• Motivation for investments • Short-term versus long-term • Classification and reporting • Accounting basics	• Trading securities • Held-to-maturity securities • Available-for-sale securities	• Securities with significant influence • Securities with controlling influence • Accounting summary

BASICS OF INVESTMENTS

C1 Distinguish between debt and equity securities and between short-term and long-term investments.

This section describes the motivation for investments, the distinction between short- and long-term investments, and the different classes of investments.

Motivation for Investments

Companies make investments for at least three reasons. First, companies transfer *excess cash* into investments to produce higher income. Second, some entities, such as mutual funds and pension funds, are set up to produce income from investments. Third, companies make investments for strategic reasons. Examples are investments in competitors, suppliers, and even customers. Exhibit C.1 shows short-term (S-T) and long-term (L-T) investments as a percent of total assets for several companies.

EXHIBIT C.1

Investments of Selected Companies

Pfizer — S-T 19% — L-T 4%
Gap — S-T 2% — L-T 1%
Starbucks — S-T 3% — L-T 5%
Coca-Cola — S-T 1% — L-T 18%

0% — 25%

Percent of total assets

Short-Term Investments Cash equivalents are investments that are both readily converted to known amounts of cash and mature within three months. Many investments, however, mature between 3 and 12 months. These investments are **short-term investments,** also called *temporary investments* and *marketable securities*. Specifically, short-term investments are securities that (1) management intends to convert to cash within one year or the operating cycle, whichever is longer, and (2) are readily convertible to cash. Short-term investments are reported under current assets and serve a purpose similar to cash equivalents.

Long-Term Investments **Long-term investments** in securities are defined as those securities that are not readily convertible to cash or are not intended to be converted into cash in the short term. Long-term investments can also include funds earmarked for a special purpose, such as bond sinking funds and investments in land or other assets not used in the company's operations. Long-term investments are reported in the noncurrent section of the balance sheet, often in its own separate line titled *Long-Term Investments*.

Debt Securities versus Equity Securities Investments in securities can include both debt and equity securities. *Debt securities* reflect a creditor relationship such as investments in notes, bonds, and certificates of deposit; they are issued by governments, companies, and individuals. *Equity securities* reflect an owner relationship such as shares of stock issued by companies.

Classification and Reporting

Accounting for investments in securities depends on three factors: (1) security type, either debt or equity, (2) the company's intent to hold the security either short term or long term, and (3) the company's (investor's) percent ownership in the other company's (investee's) equity securities. Exhibit C.2 identifies five classes of securities using these three factors. It describes each of these five classes of securities and the standard reporting required under each class.

EXHIBIT C.2

Investments in Securities

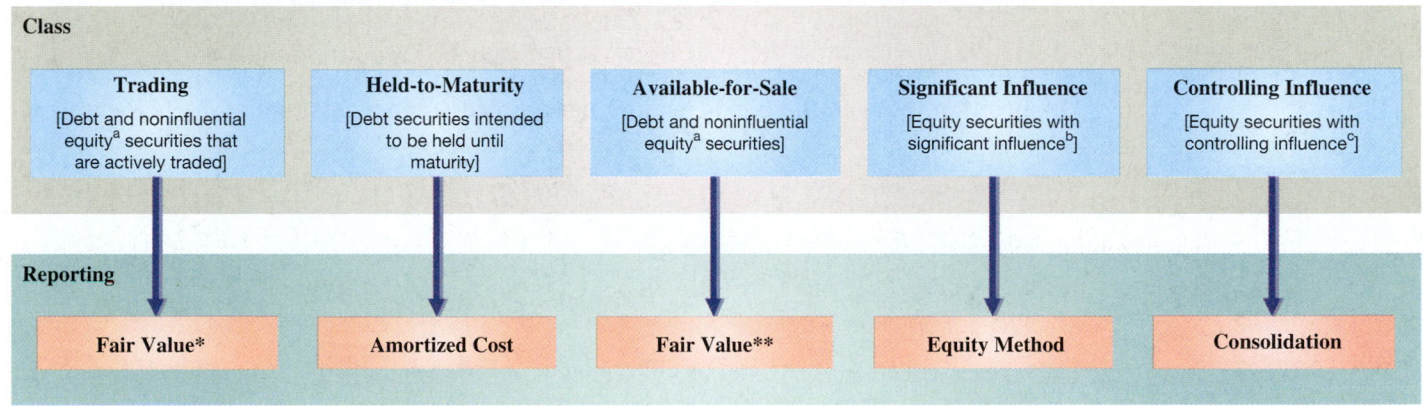

Class				
Trading [Debt and noninfluential equity[a] securities that are actively traded]	**Held-to-Maturity** [Debt securities intended to be held until maturity]	**Available-for-Sale** [Debt and noninfluential equity[a] securities]	**Significant Influence** [Equity securities with significant influence[b]]	**Controlling Influence** [Equity securities with controlling influence[c]]
Reporting				
Fair Value*	Amortized Cost	Fair Value**	Equity Method	Consolidation

[a] Holding less than 20% of voting stock (equity securities only). [b] Holding 20% or more, but not more than 50%, of voting stock.
[c] Holding more than 50% of voting stock.
* Unrealized gains and losses reported on the income statement.
** Unrealized gains and losses reported in the equity section of the balance sheet and in comprehensive income.

Debt Securities: Accounting Basics

This section explains the accounting basics for *debt securities,* including that for acquisition, disposition, and any interest.

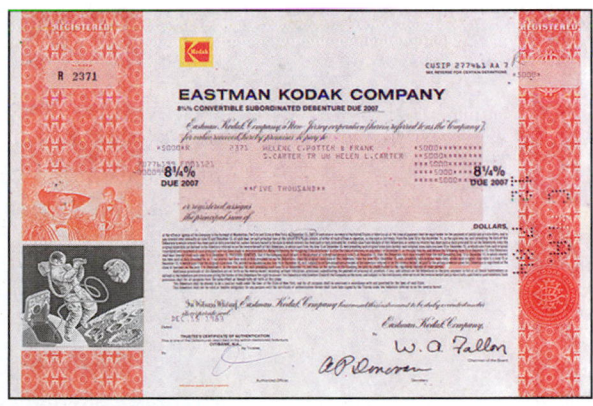

Acquisition.   Debt securities are recorded at cost when purchased. To illustrate, assume that Music City paid $29,500 plus a $500 brokerage fee on September 1, 2010, to buy Dell's 7%, two-year bonds payable with a $30,000 par value. The bonds pay interest semiannually on August 31 and February 28. Music City intends to hold the bonds until they mature on August 31, 2012; consequently, they are classified as held-to-maturity (HTM) securities. The entry to record this purchase follows. (If the maturity of the securities was short term, and management's intent was to hold them until they mature, then they would be classified as Short-Term Investments—HTM.)

2010			
Sept. I	Long-Term Investments—HTM (Dell)	30,000	
	Cash		30,000
	Purchased bonds to be held to maturity.		

Assets = Liabilities + Equity
+30,000
−30,000

Interest earned.   Interest revenue for investments in debt securities is recorded when earned. To illustrate, on December 31, 2010, at the end of its accounting period, Music City accrues interest receivable as follows.

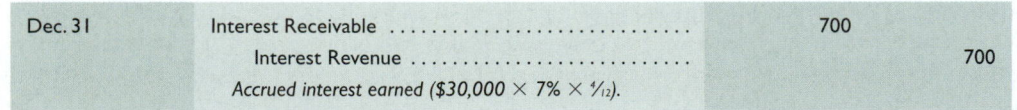

Dec. 31	Interest Receivable	700	
	Interest Revenue		700
	Accrued interest earned ($30,000 × 7% × ⅟₁₂).		

Assets = Liabilities + Equity
+700   +700

The $700 reflects 4/6 of the semiannual cash receipt of interest—the portion Music City earned as of December 31. Relevant sections of Music City's financial statements at December 31, 2010, are shown in Exhibit C.3.

EXHIBIT C.3

Financial Statement Presentation
of Debt Securities

On the income statement for year 2010:	
Interest revenue	**$ 700**
On the December 31, 2010, balance sheet:	
Long-term investments—Held-to-maturity securities (at amortized cost)	**$30,000**

On February 28, 2011, Music City records receipt of semiannual interest.

Assets = Liabilities + Equity
+1,050   +350
−700

Feb. 28	Cash	1,050	
	Interest Receivable		700
	Interest Revenue		350
	Received six months' interest on Dell bonds.		

Disposition.   When the bonds mature, the proceeds (not including the interest entry) are recorded as:

Assets = Liabilities + Equity
+30,000
−30,000

2012			
Aug. 31	Cash	30,000	
	Long-Term Investments—HTM (Dell)...........		30,000
	Received cash from matured bonds.		

Example: What is cost per share?
Answer: Cost per share is the total cost of acquisition, including broker fees, divided by number of shares acquired.

The cost of a debt security can be either higher or lower than its maturity value. When the investment is long term, the difference between cost and maturity value is amortized over the remaining life of the security. We assume for ease of computations that the cost of a long-term debt security equals its maturity value.

Equity Securities: Accounting Basics

This section explains the accounting basics for *equity securities,* including that for acquisition, dividends, and disposition.

Acquisition.   Equity securities are recorded at cost when acquired, including commissions or brokerage fees paid. To illustrate, assume that Music City purchases 1,000 shares of Intex common stock at par value for $86,000 on October 10, 2010. It records this purchase of available-for-sale (AFS) securities as follows.

Assets = Liabilities + Equity
+86,000
−86,000

Oct. 10	Long-Term Investments—AFS (Intex)	86,000	
	Cash		86,000
	Purchased 1,000 shares of Intex.		

Dividend earned.   Any cash dividends received are credited to Dividend Revenue and reported in the income statement. To illustrate, on November 2, Music City receives a $1,720 quarterly cash dividend on the Intex shares, which it records as:

Assets = Liabilities + Equity
+1,720   +1,720

Nov. 2	Cash	1,720	
	Dividend Revenue		1,720
	Received dividend of $1.72 per share.		

Disposition.   When the securities are sold, sale proceeds are compared with the cost, and any gain or loss is recorded. To illustrate, on December 20, Music City sells 500 of the Intex shares for $45,000 cash and records this sale as:

Assets = Liabilities + Equity
+45,000   +2,000
−43,000

Dec. 20	Cash	45,000	
	Long-Term Investments—AFS (Intex)		43,000
	Gain on Sale of Long-Term Investments		2,000
	Sold 500 Intex shares ($86,000 × 500/1,000).		

REPORTING OF NONINFLUENTIAL INVESTMENTS

Companies must value and report most noninfluential investments at *fair value.* The exact reporting requirements depend on whether the investments are classified as (1) trading, (2) held-to-maturity, or (3) available-for-sale.

Trading Securities

Trading securities are *debt and equity securities* that the company intends to actively manage and trade for profit. Frequent purchases and sales are expected and are made to earn profits on short-term price changes. Trading securities are *always* reported as current assets.

 **P1** Account for trading securities.

Valuing and reporting trading securities.   The entire portfolio of trading securities is reported at its fair value; this requires a "fair value adjustment" from the cost of the portfolio. The term *portfolio* refers to a group of securities. Any unrealized gain (or loss) from a change in the fair value of the portfolio of trading securities is reported on the income statement. Most users believe accounting reports are more useful when changes in fair value for trading securities are reported in income.

To illustrate, TechCom's portfolio of trading securities had a total cost of $11,500 and a fair value of $13,000 on December 31, 2010, the first year it held trading securities. The difference between the $11,500 cost and the $13,000 fair value reflects a $1,500 gain. It is an unrealized gain because it is not yet confirmed by actual sales. The fair value adjustment for trading securities is recorded with an adjusting entry at the end of each period to equal the difference between the portfolio's cost and its fair value. TechCom records this gain as follows.

Point: '*Unrealized gain (or loss)*' refers to a change in fair value that is not yet realized through actual sale.

Point: 'Fair Value Adjustment—Trading' is a *permanent account,* shown as a deduction or addition to 'Short-Term Investments—Trading.'

Dec. 31	Fair Value Adjustment—Trading	1,500	
	Unrealized Gain—Income		1,500
	To reflect an unrealized gain in fair values of trading securities.		

Assets = Liabilities + Equity
+1,500   +1,500

The **Unrealized Gain (or Loss)** is reported in the Other Revenues and Gains (or Expenses and Losses) section on the income statement. Unrealized Gain (or Loss)—Income is a *temporary* account that is closed to Income Summary at the end of each period. Fair Value Adjustment—Trading is a *permanent* account, which adjusts the reported value of the trading securities portfolio from its prior period fair value to the current period fair value. The total cost of the trading securities portfolio is maintained in one account, and the fair value adjustment is recorded in a separate account. For example, TechCom's investment in trading securities is reported in the current assets section of its balance sheet as follows.

Example: If TechCom's trading securities have a cost of $14,800 and a fair value of $16,100 at Dec. 31, 2011, its adjusting entry is
Unrealized Loss—Income 200
  Fair Value Adj.—Trading   200
This is computed as: $1,500 Beg. Dr. bal. + $200 Cr. = $1,300 End. Dr. bal.

Current Assets		
Short-term investments—Trading (at cost)	$11,500	
Fair Value adjustment—Trading	1,500	
Short-term investments—Trading (at fair value)		$13,000
or simply		
Short-term investments—Trading (at fair value; cost is $11,500)		$13,000

Selling trading securities.   When individual trading securities are sold, the difference between the net proceeds (sale price less fees) and the cost of the individual trading securities that are sold is recognized as a gain or a loss. Any prior period fair value adjustment to the portfolio is *not* used to compute the gain or loss from sale of individual trading securities. For example, if TechCom sold some of its trading securities that had cost $1,000 for $1,200 cash on January 9, 2011, it would record the following.

Point: Reporting securities at fair value is referred to as *mark-to-market* accounting.

Assets = Liabilities + Equity
+1,200   +200
−1,000

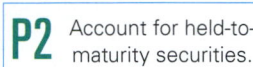

Jan. 9	Cash	1,200	
	Short-Term Investments—Trading		1,000
	Gain on Sale of Short-Term Investments		200
	Sold trading securities costing $1,000 for $1,200 cash.		

A gain is reported in the Other Revenues and Gains section on the income statement, whereas a loss is shown in Other Expenses and Losses. When the period-end fair value adjustment for the portfolio of trading securities is computed, it excludes the cost and fair value of any securities sold.

Held-to-Maturity Securities

P2 Account for held-to-maturity securities.

Held-to-maturity (HTM) securities are *debt* securities a company intends and is able to hold until maturity. They are reported in current assets if their maturity dates are within one year or the operating cycle, whichever is longer. HTM securities are reported in long-term assets when the maturity dates extend beyond one year or the operating cycle, whichever is longer. All HTM securities are recorded at cost when purchased, and interest revenue is recorded when earned.

Point: Only debt securities can be classified as *held-to-maturity;* equity securities have no maturity date.

The portfolio of HTM securities is usually reported at (amortized) cost, which is explained in advanced courses. There is no fair value adjustment to the portfolio of HTM securities—neither to the short-term nor long-term portfolios. The basics of accounting for HTM securities were described earlier in this appendix.

Decision Maker   Answer — p. C-19

Money Manager   You expect interest rates to sharply fall within a few weeks and remain at this lower rate. What is your strategy for holding investments in fixed-rate bonds and notes? ■

Available-for-Sale Securities

P3 Account for available-for-sale securities.

Available-for-sale (AFS) securities are *debt and equity securities* not classified as trading or held-to-maturity securities. AFS securities are purchased to yield interest, dividends, or increases in fair value. They are not actively managed like trading securities. If the intent is to sell AFS securities within the longer of one year or operating cycle, they are classified as short-term investments. Otherwise, they are classified as long-term.

Valuing and reporting available-for-sale securities.   As with trading securities, companies adjust the cost of the portfolio of AFS securities to reflect changes in fair value. This is done with a fair value adjustment to its total portfolio cost. However, any unrealized gain or loss for the portfolio of AFS securities is *not* reported on the income statement. Instead, it is reported in the equity section of the balance sheet (and is part of *comprehensive income,* explained later). To illustrate, assume that Music City had no prior period investments in available-for-sale securities other than those purchased in the current period. Exhibit C.4 shows both the cost and fair value of those investments on December 31, 2010, the end of its reporting period.

Example: If fair value in Exhibit C.4 is $70,000 (instead of $74,550), what entry is made? *Answer:*
Unreal. Loss—Equity 3,000
    Fair Value Adj.—AFS. . .   3,000

EXHIBIT C.4

Cost and Fair Value of Available-for-Sale Securities

	Cost	Fair Value	Unrealized Gain (Loss)
Improv bonds	$30,000	$29,050	$ (950)
Intex common stock, 500 shares	43,000	45,500	2,500
Total	$73,000	$74,550	$1,550

The year-end adjusting entry to record the fair value of these investments follows.

Assets = Liabilities + Equity
+1,550   +1,550

Dec. 31	Fair Value Adjustment—Available-for-Sale (LT)	1,550	
	Unrealized Gain—Equity		1,550
	To record adjustment to fair value of		
	available-for-sale securities.		

Exhibit C.5 shows the December 31, 2010, balance sheet presentation—it assumes these investments are long term, but they can also be short term. It is also common to combine the cost of investments with the balance in the Fair Value Adjustment account and report the net as a single amount.

Point: 'Unrealized Loss—Equity' and 'Unrealized Gain—Equity' are *permanent* (balance sheet) equity *accounts*.

EXHIBIT C.5

Balance Sheet Presentation of Available-for-Sale Securities

Assets	
Long-term investments—Available-for-sale (at cost)	$73,000
Fair value adjustment—Available-for-sale	1,550
Long-term investments—Available-for-sale (at fair value)	$74,550
or simply	
Long-term investments—Available-for-sale (at fair value; cost is $73,000)	$74,550
Equity	
. . . consists of usual equity accounts . . .	
Add unrealized gain on available-for-sale securities*	$ 1,550

Reconciled

* Often included under the caption Accumulated Other Comprehensive Income.

Let's extend this illustration and assume that at the end of its next calendar year (December 31, 2011), Music City's portfolio of long-term AFS securities has an $81,000 cost and an $82,000 fair value. It records the adjustment to fair value as follows.

Point: Income can be window-dressed upward by selling AFS securities with unrealized gains; income is reduced by selling those with unrealized losses.

Dec. 31	Unrealized Gain—Equity	550
	Fair Value Adjustment—Available-for-Sale (LT)	550
	To record adjustment to fair value of	
	available-for-sale securities.	

Assets = Liabilities + Equity
−550   −550

The effects of the 2010 and 2011 securities transactions are reflected in the following T-accounts.

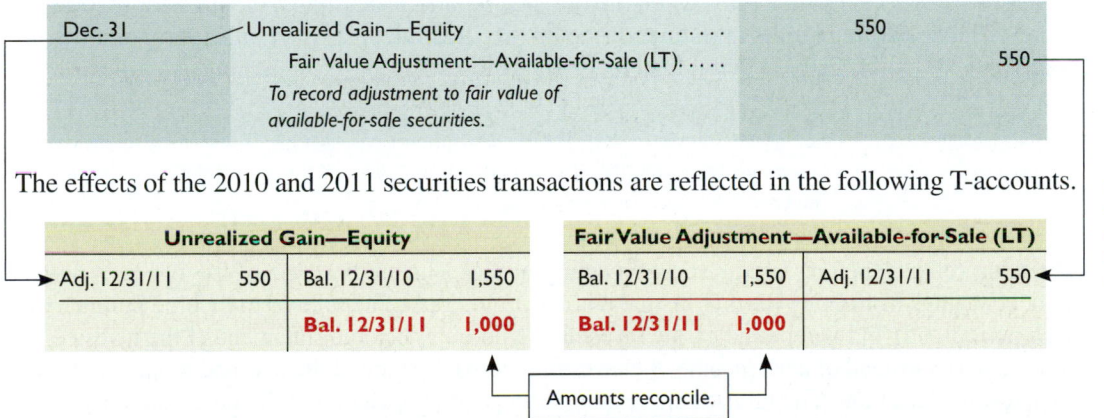

Unrealized Gain—Equity		
Adj. 12/31/11	550	Bal. 12/31/10	1,550
		Bal. 12/31/11	**1,000**

Fair Value Adjustment—Available-for-Sale (LT)		
Bal. 12/31/10	1,550	Adj. 12/31/11	550
Bal. 12/31/11	**1,000**		

Amounts reconcile.

Example: If cost is $83,000 and fair value is $82,000 at Dec. 31, 2011, it records the following adjustment:
Unreal. Gain—Equity 1,550
Unreal. Loss—Equity 1,000
    Fair Value Adj.—AFS . .   2,550

Selling available-for-sale securities.   Accounting for the sale of individual AFS securities is identical to that described for the sale of trading securities. When individual AFS securities are sold, the difference between the cost of the individual securities sold and the net proceeds (sale price less fees) is recognized as a gain or loss.

Point: 'Fair Value Adjustment—Available-for-Sale' is a permanent account, shown as a deduction or addition to the Investment account.

Quick Check

Answers — p. C-19

1. How are short-term held-to-maturity securities reported (valued) on the balance sheet?
2. How are trading securities reported (valued) on the balance sheet?
3. Where are unrealized gains and losses on available-for-sale securities reported?
4. Where are unrealized gains and losses on trading securities reported?

Alert   *Both U.S. GAAP (and IFRS) permit companies to use fair value in reporting financial assets (referred to as the fair value option). This option allows companies to report any financial asset at fair value and recognize value changes in income. This method was previously reserved only for trading securities, but is now an option for available-for-sale and held-to-maturity securities (and other 'financial assets and liabilities' such as accounts and notes receivable, accounts and notes payable, and bonds). U.S. standards also set a 3-level system to determine fair value:*
—Level 1: Use quoted market values
—Level 2: Use observable values from related assets or liabilities
—Level 3: Use unobservable values from estimates or assumptions
To date, a fairly small set of companies has chosen to broadly apply the fair value option—but, we continue to monitor its use . . .

REPORTING OF INFLUENTIAL INVESTMENTS

Investment in Securities with Significant Influence

P4 Account for equity securities with significant influence.

A long-term investment classified as **equity securities with significant influence** implies that the investor can exert significant influence over the investee. An investor that owns 20% or more (but not more than 50%) of a company's voting stock is usually presumed to have a significant influence over the investee. In some cases, however, the 20% test of significant influence is over-ruled by other, more persuasive, evidence. This evidence can either lower the 20% requirement or increase it. The **equity method** of accounting and reporting is used for long-term investments in equity securities with significant influence, which is explained in this section.

Long-term investments in equity securities with significant influence are recorded at cost when acquired. To illustrate, Micron Co. records the purchase of 3,000 shares (30%) of Star Co. common stock at a total cost of $70,650 on January 1, 2010, as follows.

Assets = Liabilities + Equity
+70,650
−70,650

Jan. 1	Long-Term Investments—Star	70,650	
	Cash		70,650
	To record purchase of 3,000 Star shares.		

The investee's (Star) earnings increase both its net assets and the claim of the investor (Micron) on the investee's net assets. Thus, when the investee reports its earnings, the investor records its share of those earnings in its investment account. To illustrate, assume that Star reports net income of $20,000 for 2010. Micron then records its 30% share of those earnings as follows.

Assets = Liabilities + Equity
+6,000   +6,000

Dec. 31	Long-Term Investments—Star	6,000	
	Earnings from Long-Term Investment		6,000
	To record 30% equity in investee earnings.		

The debit reflects the increase in Micron's equity in Star. The credit reflects 30% of Star's net income. Earnings from Long-Term Investment is a *temporary* account (closed to Income Summary at each period-end) and is reported on the investor's (Micron's) income statement. If the investee incurs a net loss instead of a net income, the investor records its share of the loss and reduces (credits) its investment account. The investor closes this earnings or loss account to Income Summary.

The receipt of cash dividends is not revenue under the equity method because the investor has already recorded its share of the investee's earnings. Instead, cash dividends received by an investor from an investee are viewed as a conversion of one asset to another; that is, dividends reduce the balance of the investment account. To illustrate, Star declares and pays $10,000 in cash dividends on its common stock. Micron records its 30% share of these dividends received on January 9, 2011, as:

Assets = Liabilities + Equity
+3,000
−3,000

Jan. 9	Cash	3,000	
	Long-Term Investments—Star		3,000
	To record share of dividend paid by Star.		

The book value of an investment under the equity method equals the cost of the investment plus (minus) the investor's equity in the *undistributed* (*distributed*) earnings of the investee. Once Micron records these transactions, its Long-Term Investments account appears as in Exhibit C.6.

EXHIBIT C.6

Investment in Star Common Stock (Ledger Account)

Long-Term Investment—Star				
1/ 1/2010 Investment acquisition	70,650			
12/31/2010 Share of earnings	6,000			
12/31/2010 Balance	76,650			
		1/ 9/2011 Share of dividend	3,000	
1/ 9/2011 Balance	73,650			

Micron's account balance on January 9, 2011, for its investment in Star is $73,650. This is the investment's cost *plus* Micron's equity in Star's earnings since its purchase *less* Micron's equity in Star's cash dividends since its purchase. When an investment in equity securities is sold, the gain or loss is computed by comparing proceeds from the sale with the book value of the investment on the date of sale. If Micron sells its Star stock for $80,000 on January 10, 2011, it records the sale as:

Point: Security prices are sometimes listed in fractions. For example, a debt security with a price of $22\frac{1}{4}$ is the same as $22.25.

Jan. 10	Cash	80,000	
	Long-Term Investments—Star		73,650
	Gain on Sale of Investment		6,350
	Sold 3,000 shares of stock for $80,000.		

Assets = Liabilities + Equity
+80,000   +6,350
−73,650

Investment in Securities with Controlling Influence

A long-term investment classified as **equity securities with controlling influence** implies that the investor can exert a controlling influence over the investee. An investor who owns more than 50% of a company's voting stock has control over the investee. This investor can dominate all other shareholders in electing the corporation's board of directors and has control over the investee's management. In some cases, controlling influence can extend to situations of less than 50% ownership. Exhibit C.7 summarizes the accounting for investments in equity securities based on an investor's ownership in the stock.

C2 Describe how to report equity securities with controlling influence.

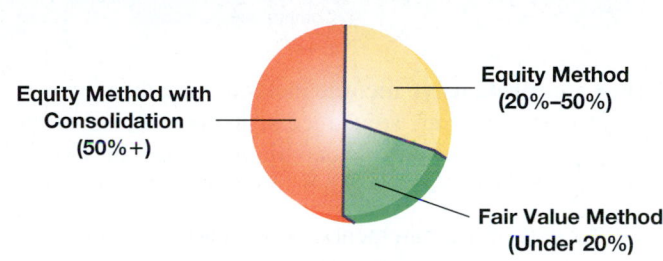

Equity Method with Consolidation (50%+)

Equity Method (20%–50%)

Fair Value Method (Under 20%)

EXHIBIT C.7

Accounting for Equity Investments by Percent of Ownership

The *equity method with consolidation* is used to account for long-term investments in equity securities with controlling influence. The investor reports *consolidated financial statements* when owning such securities. The controlling investor is called the **parent,** and the investee is called the **subsidiary.** Many companies are parents with subsidiaries. Examples are (1) **McGraw-Hill**, the parent of J.D. Power and Associates, Standard & Poor's, and Platt's; (2) **Gap, Inc.,** the parent of Gap, Old Navy, and Banana Republic; and (3) **Brunswick**, the parent of Mercury Marine, Sea Ray, and U.S. Marine. A company owning all the outstanding stock of a subsidiary can, if it desires, take over the subsidiary's assets, retire the subsidiary's stock, and merge the subsidiary into the parent. However, there often are financial, legal, and tax advantages if a business operates as a parent controlling one or more subsidiaries. When a company operates as a parent with subsidiaries, each entity maintains separate accounting records. From a legal viewpoint, the parent and each subsidiary are separate entities with all rights, duties, and responsibilities of individual companies.

Consolidated financial statements show the financial position, results of operations, and cash flows of all entities under the parent's control, including all subsidiaries. These statements are prepared as if the business were organized as one entity. The parent uses the equity method in its accounts, but the investment account is *not* reported on the parent's financial statements. Instead, the individual assets and liabilities of the parent and its subsidiaries are combined on one balance sheet. Their revenues and expenses also are combined on one income statement, and their cash flows are combined on one statement of cash flows. The procedures for preparing consolidated financial statements are in advanced courses.

 **IFRS**

Unlike U.S. GAAP, IFRS requires uniform accounting policies be used throughout the group of consolidated subsidiaries. Also, unlike U.S. GAAP, IFRS offers no detailed guidance on valuation procedures. ■

Accounting Summary for Investments in Securities

Exhibit C.8 summarizes the standard accounting for investments in securities. Recall that many investment securities are classified as either short term or long term depending on management's intent and ability to convert them in the future. Understanding the accounting for these investments enables us to draw better conclusions from financial statements in making business decisions.

EXHIBIT C.8

Accounting for Investments
in Securities

Classification	Accounting
Short-Term Investment in Securities	
Held-to-maturity (debt) securities	**Cost** (without any discount or premium amortization)
Trading (debt and equity) securities	**Fair value** (with fair value adjustment to income)
Available-for-sale (debt and equity) securities	**Fair value** (with fair value adjustment to equity)
Long-Term Investment in Securities	
Held-to-maturity (debt) securities	**Cost** (with any discount or premium amortization)
Available-for-sale (debt and equity) securities	**Fair value** (with fair value adjustment to equity)
Equity securities with significant influence	Equity method
Equity securities with controlling influence	Equity method (with consolidation)

Comprehensive Income   **Comprehensive income** is defined as all changes in equity during a period except those from owners' investments and dividends. Specifically, comprehensive income is computed by adding or subtracting *other comprehensive income* to net income:

Net income	$ #
Other comprehensive income	#
Comprehensive income	$ #

Other comprehensive income includes unrealized gains and losses on available-for-sale securities, foreign currency adjustments, and pension adjustments. (*Accumulated other comprehensive income* is defined as the cumulative impact of *other comprehensive income.*)
   Comprehensive income can be reported in financial statements:

1. As part of the statement of stockholders' equity
2. On the income statement
3. In a statement of comprehensive income

Apple   Option 1 is the most common. **Apple**, for example, reports comprehensive income as part of its statement of shareholders' equity in Appendix A near the end of the book as follows ($ millions):

Net income	$8,235	
Change in foreign currency translation	(14)	
Change in unrealized loss on AFS securities	118	Other comprehensive income
Change in unrealized gain on derivatives	(18)	
Comprehensive income	$8,321	

The 2009 *cumulative* total of Apple's *other comprehensive income* from all prior periods is $77, which is reported in its statement of shareholders' equity and is its *accumulated other comprehensive income*. That total is carried over to the equity section of its balance sheet as follows:

Common stock	$ 8,210
Retained earnings	23,353
Accumulated other comprehensive income	77
Total shareholders' equity	$31,640

Point: Some users believe that since AFS securities are not actively traded, reporting fair value changes in income would unnecessarily increase income variability and decrease usefulness.

Quick Check   Answers – p. C-19

5. Give at least two examples of assets classified as long-term investments.
6. What are the requirements for an equity security to be listed as a long-term investment?
7. Identify similarities and differences in accounting for long-term investments in debt securities that are held-to-maturity versus those available-for-sale.
8. What are the three possible classifications of long-term equity investments? Describe the criteria for each class and the method used to account for each.

GLOBAL VIEW

This section discusses similarities and differences for the accounting and reporting of investments when financial statements are prepared under U.S. GAAP vis-à-vis IFRS.

Accounting for Noninfluential Securities   The accounting for noninfluential securities is broadly similar between U.S. GAAP and IFRS. *Trading securities* are accounted for using fair values with unrealized gains and losses reported in net income as fair values change. *Available-for-sale securities* are accounted for using fair values with unrealized gains and losses reported in other comprehensive income as fair values change (and later in net income when realized). *Held-to-maturity securities* are accounted for using amortized cost. Similarly, companies have the option under both systems to apply the fair value option for available-for-sale and held-to-maturity securities. Also, both systems review held-to-maturity securities for impairment. There are some differences in terminology under IFRS: (1) trading securities are commonly referred to as *financial assets at fair value through profit and loss,* and (2) available-for-sale securities are commonly referred to as *available-for-sale financial assets.* NOKIA reports the following categories for noninfluential securities: (1) *Financial assets at fair value through profit or loss,* consisting of financial assets held for trading and financial assets designated upon initial recognition as at fair value through profit or loss, (2) *Available-for-sale financial assets,* which are measured at fair value.

NOKIA

Accounting for Influential Securities   The accounting for influential securities is broadly similar across U.S. GAAP and IFRS. Specifically, under the *equity method,* the share of investee's net income is reported in the investor's income in the same period the investee earns that income; also, the investment account equals the acquisition cost plus the share of investee income less the share of investee dividends (minus amortization of excess on purchase price above fair value of identifiable, limited-life assets). Under the *consolidation method,* investee and investor revenues and expenses are combined, absent intercompany transactions, and subtracting noncontrolling interests. Also, nonintercompany assets and liabilities are similarly combined (eliminating the need for an investment account), and noncontrolling interests are subtracted from equity. There are some differences in terminology: (1) U.S. GAAP companies commonly refer to earnings from long-term investments as *equity in earnings of affiliates* whereas IFRS companies commonly use *equity in earnings of associated (or associate) companies,* (2) U.S. GAAP companies commonly refer to noncontrolling interests in consolidated subsidiaries as *minority interests* whereas IFRS companies commonly use *noncontrolling interests.*

Components of Return on Total Assets      **Decision Analysis**

A company's **return on total assets** (or simply *return on assets*) is important in assessing financial performance. The return on total assets can be separated into two components, profit margin and total asset turnover, for additional analyses. Exhibit C.9 shows how these two components determine return on total assets.

A1 Compute and analyze the components of return on total assets.

Return on total assets = Profit margin × Total asset turnover

$$\frac{\text{Net income}}{\text{Average total assets}} = \frac{\text{Net income}}{\text{Net sales}} \times \frac{\text{Net sales}}{\text{Average total assets}}$$

EXHIBIT C.9

Components of Return on Total Assets

Profit margin reflects the percent of net income in each dollar of net sales. Total asset turnover reflects a company's ability to produce net sales from total assets. All companies desire a high return on total assets. By considering these two components, we can often discover strengths and weaknesses not revealed by return on total assets alone. This improves our ability to assess future performance and company strategy.

To illustrate, consider return on total assets and its components for **Gap Inc.** in Exhibit C.10.

EXHIBIT C.10

Gap's Components of Return on Total Assets

Fiscal Year	Return on Total Assets	=	Profit Margin	×	Total Asset Turnover
2009	12.6%	=	6.66%	×	1.89
2008	10.2*	=	5.28	×	1.92
2007	9.0	=	4.9	×	1.84
2006	11.8*	=	6.9	×	1.70
2005	11.1	=	7.1	×	1.57

* Differences due to rounding.

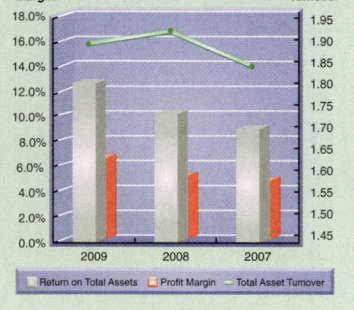

At least three findings emerge. First, Gap's return on total assets improved from 9.0% in 2007 to 12.6% in 2009. Second, total asset turnover has slightly improved over this period, from 1.84 to 1.89. Third, Gap's profit margin steadily increased over this period, from 4.9% in 2007 to 6.66% in 2009. These components reveal the dual role of profit margin and total asset turnover in determining return on total assets. They also reveal that the driver of Gap's recent improvement in return on total assets is not total asset turnover but profit margin.

Generally, if a company is to maintain or improve its return on total assets, it must meet any decline in either profit margin or total asset turnover with an increase in the other. If not, return on assets will decline. Companies consider these components in planning strategies. A component analysis can also reveal where a company is weak and where changes are needed, especially in a competitor analysis. If asset turnover is lower than the industry norm, for instance, a company should focus on raising asset turnover at least to the norm. The same applies to profit margin.

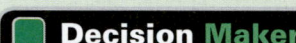 **Decision Maker**   Answer — p. C-19

Retailer You are an entrepreneur and owner of a retail sporting goods store. The store's recent annual performance reveals (industry norms in parentheses): return on total assets = 11% (11.2%); profit margin = 4.4% (3.5%); and total asset turnover = 2.5 (3.2). What does your analysis of these figures reveal? ■

DEMONSTRATION PROBLEM—1

Garden Company completes the following selected transactions related to its short-term investments during 2011.

May 8   Purchased 300 shares of FedEx stock as a short-term investment in available-for-sale securities at $40 per share plus $975 in broker fees.

Sept. 2   Sold 100 shares of its investment in FedEx stock at $47 per share and held the remaining 200 shares; broker's commission was $225.

Oct. 2   Purchased 400 shares of Ajay stock for $60 per share plus $1,600 in commissions. The stock is held as a short-term investment in available-for-sale securities.

Required

1. Prepare journal entries for the above transactions of Garden Company for 2011.
2. Prepare an adjusting journal entry as of December 31, 2011, if the fair values of the equity securities held by Garden Company are $48 per share for FedEx and $55 per share for Ajay. (Year 2011 is the first year Garden Company acquired short-term investments.)

SOLUTION TO DEMONSTRATION PROBLEM—1

1.

May 8	Short-Term Investments—AFS (FedEx)	12,975	
	Cash		12,975
	Purchased 300 shares of FedEx stock		
	(300 × $40) + $975.		

[continued on next page]

[continued from previous page]

Sept. 2	Cash	4,475	
	Gain on Sale of Short-Term Investment		150
	Short-Term Investments—AFS (FedEx)		4,325
	Sold 100 shares of FedEx for $47 per share less a $225 commission. The original cost is ($12,975 × 100/300).		
Oct. 2	Short-Term Investments—AFS (Ajay)	25,600	
	Cash		25,600
	Purchased 400 shares of Ajay for $60 per share plus $1,600 in commissions.		

2. Computation of unrealized gain or loss follows.

Short-Term Investments in Available-for-Sale Securities	Shares	Cost per Share	Total Cost	Fair Value per Share	Total Fair Value	Unrealized Gain (Loss)
FedEx	200	$43.25	$ 8,650	$48.00	$ 9,600	
Ajay	400	64.00	25,600	55.00	22,000	
Totals			$34,250		$31,600	$(2,650)

The adjusting entry follows.

Dec. 31	Unrealized Loss—Equity	2,650	
	Fair Value Adjustment—Available-for-Sale (ST)		2,650
	To reflect an unrealized loss in fair values of available-for-sale securities.		

DEMONSTRATION PROBLEM—2

The following transactions relate to Brown Company's long-term investments during 2010 and 2011. Brown did not own any long-term investments prior to 2010. Show (1) the appropriate journal entries and (2) the relevant portions of each year's balance sheet and income statement that reflect these transactions for both 2010 and 2011.

2010

Sept. 9 Purchased 1,000 shares of Packard, Inc., common stock for $80,000 cash. These shares represent 30% of Packard's outstanding shares.

Oct.   2 Purchased 2,000 shares of AT&T common stock for $60,000 cash as a long-term investment. These shares represent less than a 1% ownership in AT&T.

  17 Purchased as a long-term investment 1,000 shares of Apple Computer common stock for $40,000 cash. These shares are less than 1% of Apple's outstanding shares.

Nov. 1 Received $5,000 cash dividend from Packard.

  30 Received $3,000 cash dividend from AT&T.

Dec. 15 Received $1,400 cash dividend from Apple.

  31 Packard's net income for this year is $70,000.

  31 Fair values for the investments in equity securities are Packard, $84,000; AT&T, $48,000; and Apple Computer, $45,000.

  31 For preparing financial statements, note the following post-closing account balances: Common Stock, $500,000, and Retained Earnings, $350,000.

2011

Jan.   1 Sold Packard, Inc., shares for $108,000 cash.

May 30 Received $3,100 cash dividend from AT&T.

June 15 Received $1,600 cash dividend from Apple.

Aug. 17   Sold the AT&T stock for $52,000 cash.
      19   Purchased 2,000 shares of Coca-Cola common stock for $50,000 cash as a long-term invest-
           ment. The stock represents less than a 5% ownership in Coca-Cola.
Dec. 15   Received $1,800 cash dividend from Apple.
      31   Fair values of the investments in equity securities are Apple, $39,000, and Coca-Cola,
           $48,000.
      31   For preparing financial statements, note the following post-closing account balances: Common
           Stock, $500,000, and Retained Earnings, $410,000.

PLANNING THE SOLUTION

● Account for the investment in Packard under the equity method.
● Account for the investments in AT&T, Apple, and Coca-Cola as long-term investments in available-for-
  sale securities.
● Prepare the information for the two years' balance sheets by including the relevant asset and equity
  accounts, and the two years' income statements by identifying the relevant revenues, earnings, gains,
  and losses.

SOLUTION TO DEMONSTRATION PROBLEM—2

1. Journal entries for 2010.

Sept. 9	Long-Term Investments—Packard	80,000	
	Cash		80,000
	Acquired 1,000 shares, representing a 30% equity in Packard.		
Oct. 2	Long-Term Investments—AFS (AT&T)	60,000	
	Cash		60,000
	Acquired 2,000 shares as a long-term investment in available-for-sale securities.		
Oct. 17	Long-Term Investments—AFS (Apple)	40,000	
	Cash		40,000
	Acquired 1,000 shares as a long-term investment in available-for-sale securities.		
Nov. 1	Cash	5,000	
	Long-Term Investments—Packard		5,000
	Received dividend from Packard.		
Nov. 30	Cash	3,000	
	Dividend Revenue		3,000
	Received dividend from AT&T.		
Dec. 15	Cash	1,400	
	Dividend Revenue		1,400
	Received dividend from Apple.		
Dec. 31	Long-Term Investments—Packard	21,000	
	Earnings from Investment (Packard)		21,000
	To record 30% share of Packard's annual earnings of $70,000.		
Dec. 31	Unrealized Loss—Equity	7,000	
	Fair Value Adjustment—Available-for-Sale (LT)* ...		7,000
	To record change in fair value of long-term available-for-sale securities.		

* Fair value adjustment computations:

	Cost	Fair Value	Unrealized Gain (Loss)
AT&T	$ 60,000	$48,000	$(12,000)
Apple	40,000	45,000	5,000
Total	$100,000	$93,000	$ (7,000)

Required balance of the Fair Value Adjustment—Available-for-Sale (LT) account (credit)	$(7,000)
Existing balance	0
Necessary adjustment (credit)	$(7,000)

2. The December 31, 2010, selected balance sheet items appear as follows.

Assets	
Long-term investments	
Available-for-sale securities (at fair value; cost is $100,000)	$ 93,000
Investment in equity securities	96,000
Total long-term investments	189,000
Stockholders' Equity	
Common stock	500,000
Retained earnings	350,000
Unrealized loss—Equity	(7,000)

The relevant income statement items for the year ended December 31, 2010, follow.

Dividend revenue	$ 4,400
Earnings from investment	21,000

1. Journal entries for 2011.

Jan. 1	Cash	108,000	
	Long-Term Investments—Packard		96,000
	Gain on Sale of Long-Term Investments		12,000
	Sold 1,000 shares for cash.		
May 30	Cash	3,100	
	Dividend Revenue		3,100
	Received dividend from AT&T.		
June 15	Cash	1,600	
	Dividend Revenue		1,600
	Received dividend from Apple.		
Aug. 17	Cash	52,000	
	Loss on Sale of Long-Term Investments	8,000	
	Long-Term Investments—AFS (AT&T)		60,000
	Sold 2,000 shares for cash.		
Aug. 19	Long-Term Investments—AFS (Coca-Cola)	50,000	
	Cash		50,000
	Acquired 2,000 shares as a long-term investment in available-for-sale securities.		
Dec. 15	Cash	1,800	
	Dividend Revenue		1,800
	Received dividend from Apple.		
Dec. 31	Fair Value Adjustment—Available-for-Sale (LT)*	4,000	
	Unrealized Loss—Equity		4,000
	To record change in fair value of long-term available-for-sale securities.		

* Fair value adjustment computations:

	Cost	Fair Value	Unrealized Gain (Loss)
Apple	$40,000	$39,000	$(1,000)
Coca-Cola	50,000	48,000	(2,000)
Total	$90,000	$87,000	$(3,000)

Required balance of the Fair Value Adjustment—Available-for-Sale (LT) account (credit) .... $(3,000)
Existing balance (credit) .... (7,000)
Necessary adjustment (debit) .... $ 4,000

2. The December 31, 2011, balance sheet items appear as follows.

Assets	
Long-term investments	
Available-for-sale securities (at fair value; cost is $90,000)	$ 87,000
Stockholders' Equity	
Common stock	500,000
Retained earnings	410,000
Unrealized loss—Equity	(3,000)

The relevant income statement items for the year ended December 31, 2011, follow.

Dividend revenue	$ 6,500
Gain on sale of long-term investments..........	12,000
Loss on sale of long-term investments..........	(8,000)

APPENDIX

C-A

Investments in International Operations

Many entities from small entrepreneurs to large corporations conduct business internationally. Some entities' operations occur in so many different countries that the companies are called **multinationals.** Many of us think of **Coca-Cola** and **McDonald's**, for example, as primarily U.S. companies, but most of their sales occur outside the United States. Exhibit C-A.1 shows the percent of international sales and income for selected U.S. companies. Managing and accounting for multinationals present challenges. This section describes some of these challenges and how to account for and report these activities.

Two major accounting challenges that arise when companies have international operations relate to transactions that involve more than one currency. The first is to account for sales and purchases listed in a foreign currency. The second is to prepare consolidated financial statements with international subsidiaries. For ease in this discussion, we use companies with a U.S. base of operations and assume the need to prepare financial statements in U.S. dollars. This means the *reporting currency* of these companies is the U.S. dollar.

EXHIBIT C-A.1

International Sales and Income as a Percent of Their Totals

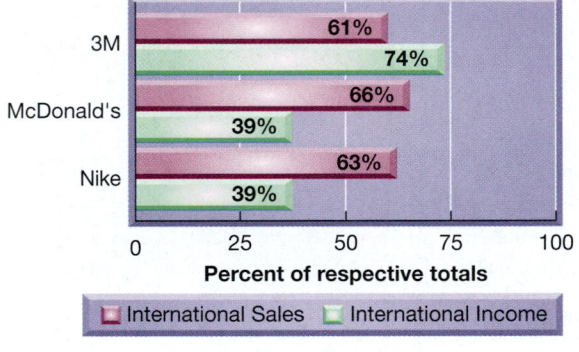

Point: Transactions *listed* or *stated* in a foreign currency are said to be *denominated* in that currency.

C3 Explain foreign exchange rates and record transactions listed in a foreign currency.

Point: To convert currency, see XE.com

Exchange Rates between Currencies   Markets for the purchase and sale of foreign currencies exist all over the world. In these markets, U.S. dollars can be exchanged for Canadian dollars, British pounds, Japanese yen, Euros, or any other legal currencies. The price of one currency stated in terms of another currency is called a **foreign exchange rate.** Exhibit C-A.2 lists recent exchange rates for selected currencies. The exchange rate for British pounds and U.S. dollars is $1.8980, meaning 1 British pound could be purchased for $1.8980. On that same day, the exchange rate between Mexican pesos and U.S. dollars is $0.0925, or 1 Mexican peso can be purchased for $0.0925. Exchange rates fluctuate due to changing economic and political conditions, including the supply and demand for currencies and expectations about future events.

Decision Insight

Rush to Russia   Investors are still eager to buy Russian equities even in the face of rampant crime, corruption, and slow economic growth. Why? Many argue Russia remains a bargain-priced, if risky, bet on future growth. Some analysts argue that natural-resource-rich Russia is one of the least expensive emerging markets. ■

Source (unit)	Price in $U.S.	Source (unit)	Price in $U.S.
Britain (pound)	$1.8980	Canada (dollar)	$0.9793
Mexico (peso)	0.0925	Japan (yen)	0.0090
Taiwan (dollar)	0.0305	Europe (Euro)	1.2920

EXHIBIT C-A.2

Foreign Exchange Rates for Selected Currencies*

* Rates will vary over time based on economic, political, and other changes.

Sales and Purchases Listed in a Foreign Currency   When a U.S. company makes a credit sale to an international customer, accounting for the sale and the account receivable is straightforward if sales terms require the international customer's payment in U.S. dollars. If sale terms require (or allow) payment in a foreign currency, however, the U.S. company must account for the sale and the account receivable in a different manner.

Sales in a Foreign Currency   To illustrate, consider the case of the U.S.-based manufacturer Boston Company, which makes credit sales to London Outfitters, a British retail company. A sale occurs on December 12, 2010, for a price of £10,000 with payment due on February 10, 2011. Boston Company keeps its accounting records in U.S. dollars. To record the sale, Boston Company must translate the sales price from pounds to dollars. This is done using the exchange rate on the date of the sale. Assuming the exchange rate on December 12, 2010, is $1.80, Boston records this sale as follows.

Dec. 12	Accounts Receivable—London Outfitters	18,000	
	Sales*		18,000
	*To record a sale at £10,000, when the exchange rate equals $1.80. * (£10,000 × $1.80/£)*		

Assets = Liabilities + Equity
+18,000   +18,000

When Boston Company prepares its annual financial statements on December 31, 2010, the current exchange rate is $1.84. Thus, the current dollar value of Boston Company's receivable is $18,400 (£10,000 × $1.84/£). This amount is $400 higher than the amount recorded on December 12. Accounting principles require a receivable to be reported in the balance sheet at its current dollar value. Thus, Boston Company must make the following entry to record the increase in the dollar value of this receivable at year-end.

Dec. 31	Accounts Receivable—London Outfitters	400	
	Foreign Exchange Gain		400
	To record the increased value of the British pound for the receivable.		

Assets = Liabilities + Equity
+400   +400

On February 10, 2011, Boston Company receives London Outfitters' payment of £10,000. It immediately exchanges the pounds for U.S. dollars. On this date, the exchange rate for pounds is $1.78. Thus, Boston Company receives only $17,800 (£10,000 × $1.78/£). It records the cash receipt and the loss associated with the decline in the exchange rate as follows.

Point: Foreign exchange gains are credits, and foreign exchange losses are debits.

Feb. 10	Cash	17,800	
	Foreign Exchange Loss	600	
	Accounts Receivable—London Outfitters		18,400
	Received foreign currency payment of an account and converted it into dollars.		

Assets = Liabilities + Equity
+17,800   −600
−18,400

Gains and losses from foreign exchange transactions are accumulated in the Foreign Exchange Gain (or Loss) account. After year-end adjustments, the balance in the Foreign Exchange Gain (or Loss) account is reported on the income statement and closed to the Income Summary account.

Purchases in a Foreign Currency   Accounting for credit purchases from an international seller is similar to the case of a credit sale to an international customer. In particular, if the U.S. company is required to make payment in a foreign currency, the account payable must be translated into dollars before the U.S. company can record it. If the exchange rate is different when preparing financial statements and when paying for the purchase, the U.S. company must recognize a foreign exchange gain or loss at those dates. To illustrate, assume NC Imports, a U.S. company, purchases products costing €20,000 (euros) from

Example: Assume that a U.S. company makes a credit purchase from a British company for £10,000 when the exchange rate is $1.62. At the balance sheet date, this rate is $1.72. Does this imply a gain or loss for the U.S. company? *Answer:* A loss.

Hamburg Brewing on January 15, when the exchange rate is $1.20 per euro. NC records this transaction as follows.

Assets = Liabilities + Equity
+24,000   +24,000

Jan. 15	Inventory	24,000	
	Accounts Payable—Hamburg Brewing		24,000
	To record a €20,000 purchase when exchange rate is $1.20 (€20,000 × $1.20/€)		

NC Imports makes payment in full on February 14 when the exchange rate is $1.25 per euro, which is recorded as follows.

Assets = Liabilities + Equity
−25,000   −24,000   −1,000

Feb. 14	Accounts Payable—Hamburg Brewing	24,000	
	Foreign Exchange Loss	1,000	
	Cash		25,000
	To record cash payment towards €20,000 account when exchange rate is $1.25 (€20,000 × $1.25/€).		

Decision Insight

Global Greenback   What do changes in foreign exchange rates mean? A decline in the price of the U.S. dollar against other currencies usually yields increased international sales for U.S. companies, without hiking prices or cutting costs, and puts them on a stronger competitive footing abroad. At home, they can raise prices without fear that foreign rivals will undercut them. ■

Consolidated Statements with International Subsidiaries   A second challenge in accounting for international operations involves preparing consolidated financial statements when the parent company has one or more international subsidiaries. Consider a U.S.-based company that owns a controlling interest in a French subsidiary. The reporting currency of the U.S. parent is the dollar. The French subsidiary maintains its financial records in euros. Before preparing consolidated statements, the parent must translate financial statements of the French company into U.S. dollars. After this translation is complete (including that for accounting differences), it prepares consolidated statements the same as for domestic subsidiaries. Procedures for translating an international subsidiary's account balances depend on the nature of the subsidiary's operations. The process requires the parent company to select appropriate foreign exchange rates and to apply those rates to the foreign subsidiary's account balances. This is described in advanced courses.

Global: A weaker U.S. dollar often increases global sales for U.S. companies.

Decision Maker   Answer — p. C-19

Entrepreneur   You are a U.S. home builder that purchases lumber from mills in both the U.S. and Canada. The price of the Canadian dollar in terms of the U.S. dollar jumps from US$0.70 to US$0.80. Are you now more or less likely to buy lumber from Canadian or U.S. mills? ■

Summary

C1   **Distinguish between debt and equity securities and between short-term and long-term investments.** *Debt securities* reflect a creditor relationship and include investments in notes, bonds, and certificates of deposit. *Equity securities* reflect an owner relationship and include shares of stock issued by other companies. Short-term investments in securities are current assets that meet two criteria: (1) They are expected to be converted into cash within one year or the current operating cycle of the business, whichever is longer and (2) they are readily convertible to cash, or *marketable*. All other investments in securities are long-term. Long-term investments also include assets not used in operations and those held for special purposes, such as land for expansion.

Investments in securities are classified into one of five groups: (1) trading securities, which are always short-term, (2) debt securities held-to-maturity, (3) debt and equity securities available-for-sale, (4) equity securities in which an investor has a significant influence over the investee, and (5) equity securities in which an investor has a controlling influence over the investee.

C2   **Describe how to report equity securities with controlling influence.** If an investor owns more than 50% of another company's voting stock and controls the investee, the investor's financial reports are prepared on a consolidated basis. These reports are prepared as if the company were organized as one entity.

C3^A **Explain foreign exchange rates and record transactions listed in a foreign currency.** A foreign exchange rate is the price of one currency stated in terms of another. An entity with transactions in a foreign currency when the exchange rate changes between the transaction dates and their settlement will experience exchange gains or losses. When a company makes a credit sale to a foreign customer and sales terms call for payment in a foreign currency, the company must translate the foreign currency into dollars to record the receivable. If the exchange rate changes before payment is received, exchange gains or losses are recognized in the year they occur. The same treatment is used when a company makes a credit purchase from a foreign supplier and is required to make payment in a foreign currency.

A1 **Compute and analyze the components of return on total assets.** Return on total assets has two components: profit margin and total asset turnover. A decline in one component must be met with an increase in another if return on assets is to be maintained. Component analysis is helpful in assessing company performance compared to that of competitors and its own past.

P1 **Account for trading securities.** Investments are initially recorded at cost, and any dividend or interest from these investments is recorded in the income statement. Investments classified as trading securities are reported at fair value. Unrealized gains and losses on trading securities are reported in income. When investments are sold, the difference between the net proceeds from the sale and the cost of the securities is recognized as a gain or loss.

P2 **Account for held-to-maturity securities.** Debt securities held-to-maturity are reported at cost when purchased. Interest revenue is recorded as it accrues. The cost of long-term held-to-maturity securities is adjusted for the amortization of any difference between cost and maturity value.

P3 **Account for available-for-sale securities.** Debt and equity securities available-for-sale are recorded at cost when purchased. Available-for-sale securities are reported at their fair values on the balance sheet with unrealized gains or losses shown in the equity section. Gains and losses realized on the sale of these investments are reported in the income statement.

P4 **Account for equity securities with significant influence.** The equity method is used when an investor has a significant influence over an investee. This usually exists when an investor owns 20% or more of the investee's voting stock but not more than 50%. The equity method means an investor records its share of investee earnings with a debit to the investment account and a credit to a revenue account. Dividends received reduce the investment account balance.

Guidance Answers to Decision Maker

Money Manager   If you have investments in fixed-rate bonds and notes when interest rates fall, the value of your investments increases. This is so because the bonds and notes you hold continue to pay the same (high) rate while the market is demanding a new lower interest rate. Your strategy is to continue holding your investments in bonds and notes, and, potentially, to increase these holdings through additional purchases.

Retailer   Your store's return on assets is 11%, which is similar to the industry norm of 11.2%. However, disaggregation of return on assets reveals that your store's profit margin of 4.4% is much higher than the norm of 3.5%, but your total asset turnover of 2.5 is much lower than the norm of 3.2. These results suggest that, as compared with competitors, you are less efficient in using assets. You need to focus on increasing sales or reducing assets. You might consider reducing prices to increase sales, provided such a strategy does not reduce your return on assets. For instance, you could reduce your profit margin to 4% to increase sales. If total asset turnover increases to more than 2.75 when profit margin is lowered to 4%, your overall return on assets is improved.

Entrepreneur   You are now less likely to buy Canadian lumber because it takes more U.S. money to buy a Canadian dollar (and lumber). For instance, the purchase of lumber from a Canadian mill with a $1,000 (Canadian dollars) price would have cost the U.S. builder $700 (U.S. dollars, computed as C$1,000 × US$0.70) before the rate change, and $800 (US dollars, computed as C$1,000 × US$0.80) after the rate change.

Guidance Answers to Quick Checks

1. Short-term held-to-maturity securities are reported at cost.
2. Trading securities are reported at fair value.
3. The equity section of the balance sheet (and in comprehensive income).
4. The income statement.
5. Long-term investments include (1) long-term funds earmarked for a special purpose, (2) debt and equity securities that do not meet current asset requirements, and (3) long-term assets not used in the regular operations of the business.
6. An equity investment is classified as long term if it is not marketable or, if marketable, it is not held as an available source of cash to meet the needs of current operations.

7. Debt securities held-to-maturity and debt securities available-for-sale are both recorded at cost. Also, interest on both is accrued as earned. However, only long-term securities held-to-maturity require amortization of the difference between cost and maturity value. In addition, only securities available-for-sale require a period-end adjustment to fair value.
8. Long-term equity investments are placed in one of three categories and accounted for as follows: (a) **available-for-sale** (noninfluential, less than 20% of outstanding stock)—fair value; (b) **significant influence** (20% to 50% of outstanding stock)—equity method; and (c) **controlling influence** (holding more than 50% of outstanding stock)—equity method with consolidation.

Available-for-sale (AFS) securities (p. C-6)
Comprehensive income (p. C-10)
Consolidated financial statements (p. C-9)
Equity method (p. C-8)
Equity securities with controlling influence (p. C-9)

Equity securities with significant influence (p. C-8)
Foreign exchange rate (p. C-16)
Held-to-maturity (HTM) securities (p. C-6)
Long-term investments (p. C-2)
Multinational (p. C-16)

Other comprehensive income (p. C-10)
Parent (p. C-9)
Return on total assets (p. C-11)
Short-term investments (p. C-2)
Subsidiary (p. C-9)
Trading securities (p. C-5)
Unrealized gain (loss) (p. C-5)

Multiple Choice Quiz   Answers on p. C-35   mhhe.com/wildFINMAN4e

Additional Quiz Questions are available at the book's Website.

1. A company purchased $30,000 of 5% bonds for investment purposes on May 1. The bonds pay interest on February 1 and August 1. The amount of interest revenue accrued at December 31 (the company's year-end) is:
   a. $1,500
   b. $1,375
   c. $1,000
   d. $625
   e. $300

2. Earlier this period, Amadeus Co. purchased its only available-for-sale investment in the stock of Bach Co. for $83,000. The period-end fair value of this stock is $84,500. Amadeus records a:
   a. Credit to Unrealized Gain—Equity for $1,500.
   b. Debit to Unrealized Loss—Equity for $1,500.
   c. Debit to Investment Revenue for $1,500.
   d. Credit to Fair Value Adjustment—Available-for-Sale for $3,500.
   e. Credit to Cash for $1,500.

3. Mozart Co. owns 35% of Melody Inc. Melody pays $50,000 in cash dividends to its shareholders for the period. Mozart's entry to record the Melody dividend includes a:
   a. Credit to Investment Revenue for $50,000.
   b. Credit to Long-Term Investments for $17,500.

   c. Credit to Cash for $17,500.
   d. Debit to Long-Term Investments for $17,500.
   e. Debit to Cash for $50,000.

4. A company has net income of $300,000, net sales of $2,500,000, and total assets of $2,000,000. Its return on total assets equals:
   a. 6.7%
   b. 12.0%
   c. 8.3%
   d. 80.0%
   e. 15.0%

5. A company had net income of $80,000, net sales of $600,000, and total assets of $400,000. Its profit margin and total asset turnover are:

	Profit Margin	Total Asset Turnover
a.	1.5%	13.3
b.	13.3%	1.5
c.	13.3%	0.7
d.	7.0%	13.3
e.	10.0%	26.7

A Superscript A denotes assignments based on Appendix C-A.
[I] Icon denotes assignments that involve decision making.

Discussion Questions

1. Under what two conditions should investments be classified as current assets?
2. [I] On a balance sheet, what valuation must be reported for short-term investments in trading securities?
3. If a short-term investment in available-for-sale securities costs $6,780 and is sold for $7,500, how should the difference between these two amounts be recorded?
4. Identify the three classes of noninfluential and two classes of influential investments in securities.

5. Under what conditions should investments be classified as current assets? As long-term assets?
6. If a company purchases its only long-term investments in available-for-sale debt securities this period and their fair value is below cost at the balance sheet date, what entry is required to recognize this unrealized loss?
7. On a balance sheet, what valuation must be reported for debt securities classified as available-for-sale?

8. Under what circumstances are long-term investments in debt securities reported at cost and adjusted for amortization of any difference between cost and maturity value?

9. For investments in available-for-sale securities, how are unrealized (holding) gains and losses reported?

10. In accounting for investments in equity securities, when should the equity method be used?

11. Under what circumstances does a company prepare consolidated financial statements?

12.ᴬ What are two major challenges in accounting for international operations?

13.ᴬ Assume a U.S. company makes a credit sale to a foreign customer that is required to make payment in its foreign currency. In the current period, the exchange rate is $1.40 on the date of the sale and is $1.30 on the date the customer pays the receivable. Will the U.S. company record an exchange gain or loss?

14.ᴬ If a U.S. company makes a credit sale to a foreign customer required to make payment in U.S. dollars, can the U.S. company have an exchange gain or loss on this sale?

15. Refer to **Apple**'s statement of changes in shareholders' equity in Appendix A. What is the amount of foreign currency translation adjustment for the year ended September 26, 2009? Is this adjustment an unrealized gain or an unrealized loss? **Apple**

16. Refer to **Palm**'s statement of stockholders' equity. What was the amount of its fiscal 2009 unrealized gain or loss on securities? **Palm**

17. Refer to the balance sheet of **Nokia** in Appendix A. How can you tell that Nokia uses the consolidated method of accounting? **NOKIA**

18. Refer to the financial statements of **Research In Motion** in Appendix A. Compute its return on total assets for the year ended February 27, 2010. **RIM**

---

connect

Complete the following descriptions by filling in the blanks.

1. Accrual of interest on bonds held as long-term investments requires a credit to _____ _____.

2. The controlling investor (more than 50% ownership) is called the _____, and the investee company is called the _____.

3. Trading securities are classified as _____ assets.

4. Equity securities giving an investor significant influence are accounted for using the _____ _____.

5. Available-for-sale debt securities are reported on the balance sheet at _____ _____.

QUICK STUDY

QS C-1
Describing investments in securities
C1 C2

Which of the following statements are true of long-term investments?

a. They can include investments in trading securities.

b. They are always easily sold and therefore qualify as being marketable.

c. They can include debt and equity securities available-for-sale.

d. They are held as an investment of cash available for current operations.

e. They can include debt securities held-to-maturity.

f. They can include bonds and stocks not intended to serve as a ready source of cash.

g. They can include funds earmarked for a special purpose, such as bond sinking funds.

QS C-2
Identifying long-term investments
C1

On April 18, Dice Co. made a short-term investment in 500 common shares of XLT Co. The purchase price is $45 per share and the broker's fee is $150. The intent is to actively manage these shares for profit. On May 30, Dice Co. receives $1 per share from XLT in dividends. Prepare the April 18 and May 30 journal entries to record these transactions.

QS C-3
Short-term equity investments P1

Fender Co. purchased short-term investments in available-for-sale securities at a cost of $100,000 on November 25, 2011. At December 31, 2011, these securities had a fair value of $94,000. This is the first and only time the company has purchased such securities.

1. Prepare the December 31, 2011, year-end adjusting entry for the securities' portfolio.

2. For each account in the entry for part 1, explain how it is reported in financial statements.

3. Prepare the April 6, 2012, entry when Fender sells one-half of these securities for $52,000.

QS C-4
Available-for-sale securities
P3

Prepare Hoffman Company's journal entries to reflect the following transactions for the current year.

May 7 Purchases 100 shares of Lov stock as a short-term investment in available-for-sale securities at a cost of $25 per share plus $200 in broker fees.

June 6 Sells 100 shares of its investment in Lov stock at $28 per share. The broker's commission on this sale is $75.

QS C-5
Available-for-sale securities
P3

QS C-6
Available-for-sale securities
P3

Galaxy Company completes the following transactions during the current year.

May 9   Purchases 400 shares of X&O stock as a short-term investment in available-for-sale securities at a cost of $50 per share plus $400 in broker fees.

June 2   Sells 200 shares of its investment in X&O stock at $56 per share. The broker's commission on this sale is $180.

Dec. 31   The closing market price (fair value) of the X&O stock is $46 per share.

Prepare the May 9 and June 2 journal entries and the December 31 adjusting entry. This is the first and only time the company purchased such securities.

QS C-7
Recording equity securities
P3

On May 20, 2011, Alexis Co. paid $750,000 to acquire 25,000 common shares (10%) of TKR Corp. as a long-term investment. On August 5, 2012, Alexis sold one-half of these shares for $475,000. What valuation method should be used to account for this stock investment? Prepare entries to record both the acquisition and the sale of these shares.

QS C-8
Equity method transactions
P4

Assume the same facts as in QS C-7 except that the stock acquired represents 40% of TKR Corp.'s outstanding stock. Also assume that TKR Corp. paid a $125,000 dividend on November 1, 2011, and reported a net income of $550,000 for 2011. Prepare the entries to record (a) the receipt of the dividend and (b) the December 31, 2011, year-end adjustment required for the investment account.

QS C-9
Debt securities transactions
P2

On February 1, 2011, Charo Mendez purchased 6% bonds issued by CR Utilities at a cost of $30,000, which is their par value. The bonds pay interest semiannually on July 31 and January 31. For 2011, prepare entries to record Mendez's July 31 receipt of interest and its December 31 year-end interest accrual.

QS C-10
Recording fair value adjustment
for securities
P3

During the current year, Patton Consulting Group acquired long-term available-for-sale securities at a $35,000 cost. At its December 31 year-end, these securities had a fair value of $29,000. This is the first and only time the company purchased such securities.

1. Prepare the necessary year-end adjusting entry related to these securities.
2. Explain how each account used in part 1 is reported in the financial statements.

QS C-11
Return on total
assets A1

The return on total assets is the focus of analysts, creditors, and other users of financial statements.

1. How is the return on total assets computed?
2. What does this important ratio reflect?

QS C-12
Component return on total
assets A1

Return on total assets can be separated into two important components.

1. Write the formula to separate the return on total assets into its two basic components.
2. Explain how these components of the return on total assets are helpful to financial statement users for business decisions.

QS C-13ᴬ
Foreign currency transactions
C3

A U.S. company sells a product to a British company with the transaction listed in British pounds. On the date of the sale, the transaction total of $16,000 is billed as £10,000, reflecting an exchange rate of 1.60 (that is, $1.60 per pound). Prepare the entry to record (1) the sale and (2) the receipt of payment in pounds when the exchange rate is 1.50.

QS C-14ᴬ
Foreign currency transactions
C3

On March 1, 2011, a U.S. company made a credit sale requiring payment in 30 days from a Malaysian company, Hamac Sdn. Bhd., in 20,000 Malaysian ringgits. Assuming the exchange rate between Malaysian ringgits and U.S. dollars is $0.6811 on March 1 and $0.6985 on March 31, prepare the entries to record the sale on March 1 and the cash receipt on March 31.

QS C-15
Equity securities with
controlling influence
C2

Complete the following descriptions by filling in the blanks.

1. A long-term investment classified as equity securities with controlling influence implies that the investor can exert a _____ influence over the investee.
2. The controlling investor is called the _____, and the investee is called the _____.

The **Carrefour Group** reports the following description of its trading securities (titled "financial assets reported at fair value in the income statement").

> These are financial assets held by the Group in order to make a short-term profit on the sale. These assets are valued at their fair value with variations in value recognized in the income statement.

Note 10 to Carrefour's 2008 financial statements reports €117 million in unrealized gains for 2008 and €63 million in unrealized losses for 2008, both included in the fair value of those financial assets held for trading. What amount of these unrealized gains and unrealized losses, if any, are reported in its 2008 income statement? Explain.

QS C-16
International accounting for investments
P1

connect

Prepare journal entries to record the following transactions involving the short-term securities investments of Maxwell Co., all of which occurred during year 2011.

a. On February 15, paid $100,000 cash to purchase FTR's 90-day short-term debt securities ($100,000 principal), dated February 15, that pay 8% interest (categorized as held-to-maturity securities).

b. On May 16, received a check from FTR in payment of the principal and 90 days' interest on the debt securities purchased in transaction *a*.

EXERCISES

Exercise C-1
Accounting for short-term held-to-maturity securities **P2**

Prepare journal entries to record the following transactions involving the short-term securities investments of Smart Co., all of which occurred during year 2011.

a. On March 22, purchased 700 shares of FIX Company stock at $30 per share plus a $150 brokerage fee. These shares are categorized as trading securities.

b. On September 1, received a $1.00 per share cash dividend on the FIX Company stock purchased in transaction *a*.

c. On October 8, sold 350 shares of FIX Co. stock for $40 per share, less a $140 brokerage fee.

Exercise C-2
Accounting for short-term trading securities
P1

(*c*) Dr. Cash $13,860

Prepare journal entries to record the following transactions involving the short-term securities investments of Prairie Co., all of which occurred during year 2011.

a. On August 1, paid $60,000 cash to purchase Better Buy's 10% debt securities ($60,000 principal), dated July 30, 2011, and maturing January 30, 2012 (categorized as available-for-sale securities).

b. On October 30, received a check from Better Buy for 90 days' interest on the debt securities purchased in transaction *a*.

Exercise C-3
Accounting for short-term available-for-sale securities
P3

Complete the following descriptions by filling in the blanks.

1. Short-term investments are securities that (1) management intends to convert to cash within ___ ___ or the ___ ___ whichever is longer, and (2) are readily convertible to ___.

2. Long-term investments in securities are defined as those securities that are ___ ___ convertible to cash or are ___ ___ to be converted into cash in the short term.

3. Debt securities reflect a ___ relationship such as investments in notes, bonds, and certificates of deposit.

4. Equity securities reflect an ___ relationship such as shares of stock issued by companies.

Exercise C-4
Debt and equity securities and short- and long-term investments
C1

Complete the following descriptions by filling in the blanks.

1. The equity method with ___ is used to account for long-term investments in equity securities with controlling influence.

2. Consolidated ___ ___ show the financial position, results of operations, and cash flows of all entities under the parent's control, including all subsidiaries.

Exercise C-5
Equity securities with controlling influence
C2

Forex Co. purchases various investments in trading securities at a cost of $56,000 on December 27, 2011. (This is its first and only purchase of such securities.) At December 31, 2011, these securities had a fair value of $66,000.

1. Prepare the December 31, 2011, year-end adjusting entry for the trading securities' portfolio.

2. Explain how each account in the entry of part 1 is reported in financial statements.

3. Prepare the January 3, 2012, entry when Forex sells a portion of its trading securities (that had originally cost $28,000) for $30,000.

Exercise C-6
Accounting for trading securities
P1

Check (3) Gain, $2,000

Exercise C-7
Adjusting available-for-sale
securities to fair value

P3

On December 31, 2011, Rollo Company held the following short-term investments in its portfolio of available-for-sale securities. Rollo had no short-term investments in its prior accounting periods. Prepare the December 31, 2011, adjusting entry to report these investments at fair value.

	Cost	Fair Value
Vicks Corporation bonds payable	$79,600	$90,600
Pace Corporation notes payable	60,600	52,900
Lake Lugano Company common stock	85,500	82,100

Check   Unrealized loss, $100

Exercise C-8
Transactions in short-term and
long-term investments

P1 P2 P3

Prepare journal entries to record the following transactions involving both the short-term and long-term investments of Sophia Corp., all of which occurred during calendar year 2011. Use the account Short-Term Investments for any transactions that you determine are short term.

a. On February 15, paid $150,000 cash to purchase American General's 120-day short-term notes at par, which are dated February 15 and pay 10% interest (classified as held-to-maturity).

b. On March 22, bought 700 shares of Frain Industries common stock at $25 cash per share plus a $250 brokerage fee (classified as long-term available-for-sale securities).

c. On June 15, received a check from American General in payment of the principal and 120 days' interest on the notes purchased in transaction *a*.

d. On July 30, paid $50,000 cash to purchase MP3 Electronics' 8% notes at par, dated July 30, 2011, and maturing on January 30, 2012 (classified as trading securities).

e. On September 1, received a $0.50 per share cash dividend on the Frain Industries common stock purchased in transaction *b*.

f. On October 8, sold 350 shares of Frain Industries common stock for $32 cash per share, less a $175 brokerage fee.

g. On October 30, received a check from MP3 Electronics for three months' interest on the notes purchased in transaction *d*.

Exercise C-9
Fair value adjustment to
available-for-sale securities

P3

On December 31, 2011, Manhattan Co. held the following short-term available-for-sale securities.

	Cost	Fair Value
Nintendo Co. common stock	$68,900	$75,300
Atlantic bonds payable	24,500	22,800
Kellogg Co. notes payable	50,000	47,200
McDonald's Corp. common stock	91,400	86,600

Manhattan had no short-term investments prior to the current period. Prepare the December 31, 2011, year-end adjusting entry to record the fair value adjustment for these securities.

Exercise C-10
Fair value adjustment to
available-for-sale securities

P3

Berroa Co. began operations in 2010. The cost and fair values for its long-term investments portfolio in available-for-sale securities are shown below. Prepare Berroa's December 31, 2011, adjusting entry to reflect any necessary fair value adjustment for these investments.

	Cost	Fair Value
December 31, 2010	$79,483	$72,556
December 31, 2011	85,120	90,271

Exercise C-11
Multiyear fair value adjustments
to available-for-sale securities

P3

Ticker Services began operations in 2009 and maintains long-term investments in available-for-sale securities. The year-end cost and fair values for its portfolio of these investments follow. Prepare journal entries to record each year-end fair value adjustment for these securities.

	Cost	Fair Value
December 31, 2009	$374,000	$362,560
December 31, 2010	426,900	453,200
December 31, 2011	580,700	686,450
December 31, 2012	875,500	778,800

Information regarding Central Company's individual investments in securities during its calendar-year 2011, along with the December 31, 2011, fair values, follows.

a. Investment in Beeman Company bonds: $418,500 cost, $455,000 fair value. Central intends to hold these bonds until they mature in 2016.

b. Investment in Baybridge common stock: 29,500 shares; $332,450 cost; $361,375 fair value. Central owns 32% of Baybridge's voting stock and has a significant influence over Baybridge.

c. Investment in Carroll common stock: 12,000 shares; $169,750 cost; $183,000 fair value. This investment amounts to 3% of Carroll's outstanding shares, and Central's goal with this investment is to earn dividends over the next few years.

d. Investment in Newtech common stock: 3,500 shares; $95,300 cost; $93,625 fair value. Central's goal with this investment is to reap an increase in fair value of the stock over the next three to five years. Newtech has 30,000 common shares outstanding.

e. Investment in Flock common stock: 16,300 shares; $102,860 cost; $109,210 fair value. This stock is marketable and is held as an investment of cash available for operations.

Required

1. Identify whether each investment should be classified as a short-term or long-term investment. For each long-term investment, indicate in which of the long-term investment classifications it should be placed.

2. Prepare a journal entry dated December 31, 2011, to record the fair value adjustment of the long-term investments in available-for-sale securities. Central had no long-term investments prior to year 2011.

Exercise C-12
Classifying investments in securities; recording fair values

C1 P2 P3 P4

Check (2) Unrealized gain, $11,575

Prepare journal entries to record the following transactions and events of Kash Company.

2011

Jan. 2 Purchased 30,000 shares of Bushtex Co. common stock for $204,000 cash plus a broker's fee of $3,480 cash. Bushtex has 90,000 shares of common stock outstanding and its policies will be significantly influenced by Kash.

Sept. 1 Bushtex declared and paid a cash dividend of $3.10 per share.
Dec. 31 Bushtex announced that net income for the year is $624,900.

2012

June 1 Bushtex declared and paid a cash dividend of $3.60 per share.
Dec. 31 Bushtex announced that net income for the year is $699,750.
Dec. 31 Kash sold 10,000 shares of Bushtex for $162,500 cash.

Exercise C-13
Securities transactions; equity method

P4

The following information is available from the financial statements of Wright Industries. Compute Wright's return on total assets for 2011 and 2012. (Round returns to one-tenth of a percent.) Comment on the company's efficiency in using its assets in 2011 and 2012.

Exercise C-14
Return on total assets

A1

	2010	2011	2012
Total assets, December 31	$190,000	$320,000	$750,000
Net income	28,200	36,400	58,300

Desi of New York sells its products to customers in the United States and the United Kingdom. On December 16, 2011, Desi sold merchandise on credit to Bronson Ltd. of London at a price of 17,000 pounds. The exchange rate on that day for £1 was $1.5238. On December 31, 2011, when Desi prepared its financial statements, the rate was £1 for $1.4990. Bronson paid its bill in full on January 15, 2012, at which time the exchange rate was £1 for $1.5156. Desi immediately exchanged the 17,000 pounds for U.S. dollars. Prepare Desi's journal entries on December 16, December 31, and January 15 (round to the nearest dollar).

Exercise C-15ᴬ
Foreign currency transactions

C3

Exercise C-16[A]
Computing foreign exchange
gains and losses on receivables

C3

On May 8, 2011, Jett Company (a U.S. company) made a credit sale to Lopez (a Mexican company). The terms of the sale required Lopez to pay 800,000 pesos on February 10, 2012. Jett prepares quarterly financial statements on March 31, June 30, September 30, and December 31. The exchange rates for pesos during the time the receivable is outstanding follow.

May 8, 2011	$0.1984
June 30, 2011	0.2013
September 30, 2011	0.2029
December 31, 2011.	0.1996
February 10, 2012	0.2047

Compute the foreign exchange gain or loss that Jett should report on each of its quarterly income statements for the last three quarters of 2011 and the first quarter of 2012. Also compute the amount reported on Jett's balance sheets at the end of each of its last three quarters of 2011.

Exercise C-17
International accounting
for investments

P3

The **Carrefour Group** reports the following description of its financial assets available-for-sale.

> Assets available for sale are . . . valued at fair value. Unrealized . . . gains or losses are recorded as shareholders' equity until they are sold.

Note 10 to Carrefour's 2008 financial statements reports €6 million in *net* unrealized losses (net of unrealized gains) for 2008, which is included in the fair value of its available-for-sale securities reported on the balance sheet.

1. What amount of the €6 million net unrealized losses, if any, is reported in its 2008 income statement? Explain.
2. If the €6 million net unrealized losses are not reported in the income statement, in which statement are they reported, if any? Explain.

PROBLEM SET A

Ryder Company, which began operations in 2011, invests its idle cash in trading securities. The following transactions are from its short-term investments in its trading securities.

Problem C-1A
Recording transactions and
fair value adjustments for
trading securities

P1

2011

Jan. 20   Purchased 900 shares of Ford Motor Co. at $36 per share plus a $125 commission.
Feb. 9   Purchased 4,400 shares of Lucent at $10 per share plus a $200 commission.
Oct. 12   Purchased 500 shares of Z-Seven at $8 per share plus a $100 commission.

2012

Apr. 15   Sold 900 shares of Ford Motor Co. at $39 per share less a $185 commission.
July   5   Sold 500 shares of Z-Seven at $10.25 per share less a $100 commission.
July 22   Purchased 800 shares of Hunt Corp. at $30 per share plus a $225 commission.
Aug. 19   Purchased 1,000 shares of Donna Karan at $12 per share plus a $100 commission.

2013

Feb. 27   Purchased 3,400 shares of HCA at $22 per share plus a $220 commission.
Mar. 3   Sold 800 shares of Hunt at $25 per share less a $125 commission.
June 21   Sold 4,400 shares of Lucent at $8 per share less a $180 commission.
June 30   Purchased 1,000 shares of Black & Decker at $47.50 per share plus a $195 commission.
Nov. 1   Sold 1,000 shares of Donna Karan at $22 per share less a $208 commission.

Required

1. Prepare journal entries to record these short-term investment activities for the years shown. (Ignore any year-end adjusting entries.)

Check (2) Dr. Fair Value
Adjustment—Trading $2,385

2. On December 31, 2013, prepare the adjusting entry to record any necessary fair value adjustment for the portfolio of trading securities when HCA's share price is $24 and Black & Decker's share price is $43.50. (Assume the Fair Value Adjustment—Trading account had an unadjusted balance of zero.)

Perry Company had no short-term investments prior to year 2011. It had the following transactions involving short-term investments in available-for-sale securities during 2011.

Apr. 16 Purchased 8,000 shares of Gem Co. stock at $24.25 per share plus a $360 brokerage fee.
May   1 Paid $200,000 to buy 90-day U.S. Treasury bills (debt securities): $200,000 principal amount, 6% interest, securities dated May 1.
July   7 Purchased 4,000 shares of PepsiCo stock at $49.25 per share plus a $350 brokerage fee.
       20 Purchased 2,000 shares of Xerox stock at $16.75 per share plus a $410 brokerage fee.
Aug.   3 Received a check for principal and accrued interest on the U.S. Treasury bills that matured on July 29.
       15 Received an $0.85 per share cash dividend on the Gem Co. stock.
       28 Sold 4,000 shares of Gem Co. stock at $30 per share less a $450 brokerage fee.
Oct.   1 Received a $1.90 per share cash dividend on the PepsiCo shares.
Dec. 15 Received a $1.05 per share cash dividend on the remaining Gem Co. shares.
       31 Received a $1.30 per share cash dividend on the PepsiCo shares.

Required

1. Prepare journal entries to record the preceding transactions and events.
2. Prepare a table to compare the year-end cost and fair values of Perry's short-term investments in available-for-sale securities. The year-end fair values per share are: Gem Co., $26.50; PepsiCo, $46.50; and Xerox, $13.75.
3. Prepare an adjusting entry, if necessary, to record the year-end fair value adjustment for the portfolio of short-term investments in available-for-sale securities.

Analysis Component

4. Explain the balance sheet presentation of the fair value adjustment for Perry's short-term investments.
5. How do these short-term investments affect Perry's (a) income statement for year 2011 and (b) the equity section of its balance sheet at year-end 2011?

Problem C-2A

Recording, adjusting, and reporting short-term available-for-sale securities

P3

Check (2) Cost = $328,440

(3) Dr. Unrealized Loss—Equity $8,940

Shaq Security, which began operations in 2011, invests in long-term available-for-sale securities. Following is a series of transactions and events determining its long-term investment activity.

Problem C-3A

Recording, adjusting, and reporting long-term available-for-sale securities

P3

2011

Jan. 20 Purchased 900 shares of Johnson & Johnson at $18.75 per share plus a $590 commission.
Feb. 9 Purchased 2,200 shares of Sony at $46.88 per share plus a $2,578 commission.
June 12 Purchased 500 shares of Mattel at $55.50 per share plus an $832 commission.
Dec. 31 Per share fair values for stocks in the portfolio are Johnson & Johnson, $20.38; Mattel, $57.25; Sony, $39.

2012

Apr. 15 Sold 900 shares of Johnson & Johnson at $21.75 per share less a $685 commission.
July 5 Sold 500 shares of Mattel at $49.13 per share less a $491 commission.
July 22 Purchased 1,600 shares of Sara Lee at $36.25 per share plus a $1,740 commission.
Aug. 19 Purchased 1,800 shares of Eastman Kodak at $28 per share plus a $1,260 commission.
Dec. 31 Per share fair values for stocks in the portfolio are: Kodak, $31.75; Sara Lee, $30.00; Sony, $36.50.

2013

Feb. 27 Purchased 3,400 shares of Microsoft at $23.63 per share plus a $1,606 commission.
June 21 Sold 2,200 shares of Sony at $40.00 per share less a $2,640 commission.
June 30 Purchased 1,200 shares of Black & Decker at $47.50 per share plus a $1,995 commission.
Aug. 3 Sold 1,600 shares of Sara Lee at $31.25 per share less a $1,750 commission.
Nov. 1 Sold 1,800 shares of Eastman Kodak at $42.75 per share less a $2,309 commission.
Dec. 31 Per share fair values for stocks in the portfolio are: Black & Decker, $56.50; Microsoft, $28.

Required

1. Prepare journal entries to record these transactions and events and any year-end fair value adjustments to the portfolio of long-term available-for-sale securities.

Check (2b) Fair Value Adjustment bal.: 12/31/11, $(18,994); 12/31/12; $(31,664)

(3b) Unrealized Gain at 12/31/2013, $22,057

2. Prepare a table that summarizes the (a) total cost, (b) total fair value adjustment, and (c) total fair value of the portfolio of long-term available-for-sale securities at each year-end.

3. Prepare a table that summarizes (a) the realized gains and losses and (b) the unrealized gains or losses for the portfolio of long-term available-for-sale securities at each year-end.

Problem C-4A
Long-term investment transactions; unrealized and realized gains and losses

C2 P3 P4

Park Co.'s long-term available-for-sale portfolio at December 31, 2010, consists of the following.

Available-for-Sale Securities	Cost	Fair Value
80,000 shares of Company A common stock	$1,070,600	$ 980,000
14,000 shares of Company B common stock	318,750	308,000
35,000 shares of Company C common stock	1,325,500	1,281,875

Park enters into the following long-term investment transactions during year 2011.

Jan. 29 Sold 7,000 shares of Company B common stock for $158,375 less a brokerage fee of $3,100.
Apr. 17 Purchased 20,000 shares of Company W common stock for $395,000 plus a brokerage fee of $3,500. The shares represent a 30% ownership in Company W.
July 6 Purchased 9,000 shares of Company X common stock for $253,125 plus a brokerage fee of $3,500. The shares represent a 10% ownership in Company X.
Aug. 22 Purchased 100,000 shares of Company Y common stock for $750,000 plus a brokerage fee of $8,200. The shares represent a 51% ownership in Company Y.
Nov. 13 Purchased 17,000 shares of Company Z common stock for $533,800 plus a brokerage fee of $6,900. The shares represent a 5% ownership in Company Z.
Dec. 9 Sold 80,000 shares of Company A common stock for $1,030,000 less a brokerage fee of $4,100.

The fair values of its investments at December 31, 2011, are: B, $162,750; C, $1,220,625; W, $382,500; X, $236,250; Y, $1,062,500; and Z, $557,600.

Required

1. Determine the amount Park should report on its December 31, 2011, balance sheet for its long-term investments in available-for-sale securities.

Check (2) Cr. Unrealized Loss— Equity, $40,000

2. Prepare any necessary December 31, 2011, adjusting entry to record the fair value adjustment for the long-term investments in available-for-sale securities.

3. What amount of gains or losses on transactions relating to long-term investments in available-for-sale securities should Park report on its December 31, 2011, income statement?

Problem C-5A
Accounting for long-term investments in securities; with and without significant influence

P3 P4

Pillar Steel Co., which began operations on January 4, 2011, had the following subsequent transactions and events in its long-term investments.

2011

Jan. 5 Pillar purchased 30,000 shares (20% of total) of Kildaire's common stock for $780,000.
Oct. 23 Kildaire declared and paid a cash dividend of $1.60 per share.
Dec. 31 Kildaire's net income for 2011 is $582,000, and the fair value of its stock at December 31 is $27.75 per share.

2012

Oct. 15 Kildaire declared and paid a cash dividend of $1.30 per share.
Dec. 31 Kildaire's net income for 2012 is $738,000, and the fair value of its stock at December 31 is $30.45 per share.

2013

Jan. 2 Pillar sold all of its investment in Kildaire for $947,000 cash.

Part 1
Assume that Pillar has a significant influence over Kildaire with its 20% share of stock.

Required

1. Prepare journal entries to record these transactions and events for Pillar.

Check (2) Carrying value per share, $31.90

2. Compute the carrying (book) value per share of Pillar's investment in Kildaire common stock as reflected in the investment account on January 1, 2013.

3. Compute the net increase or decrease in Pillar's equity from January 5, 2011, through January 2, 2013, resulting from its investment in Kildaire.

Part 2

Assume that although Pillar owns 20% of Kildaire's outstanding stock, circumstances indicate that it does not have a significant influence over the investee and that it is classified as an available-for-sale security investment.

Required

1. Prepare journal entries to record the preceding transactions and events for Pillar. Also prepare an entry dated January 2, 2013, to remove any balance related to the fair value adjustment.

2. Compute the cost per share of Pillar's investment in Kildaire common stock as reflected in the investment account on January 1, 2013.

3. Compute the net increase or decrease in Pillar's equity from January 5, 2011, through January 2, 2013, resulting from its investment in Kildaire.

(1) 1/2/2013 Dr. Unrealized Gain—Equity $133,500

(3) Net increase, $254,000

Roundtree Company, a U.S. corporation with customers in several foreign countries, had the following selected transactions for 2011 and 2012.

Problem C-6A[A]
Foreign currency transactions

C3

2011

Apr. 8   Sold merchandise to Salinas & Sons of Mexico for $7,938 cash. The exchange rate for pesos is $0.1323 on this day.

July 21   Sold merchandise on credit to Sumito Corp. in Japan. The price of 1.5 million yen is to be paid 120 days from the date of sale. The exchange rate for yen is $0.0096 on this day.

Oct. 14   Sold merchandise for 19,000 pounds to Smithers Ltd. of Great Britain, payment in full to be received in 90 days. The exchange rate for pounds is $1.5181 on this day.

Nov. 18   Received Sumito's payment in yen for its July 21 purchase and immediately exchanged the yen for dollars. The exchange rate for yen is $0.0091 on this day.

Dec. 20   Sold merchandise for 17,000 ringgits to Hamid Albar of Malaysia, payment in full to be received in 30 days. On this day, the exchange rate for ringgits is $0.6852.

Dec. 31   Recorded adjusting entries to recognize exchange gains or losses on Roundtree's annual financial statements. Rates for exchanging foreign currencies on this day follow.

Pesos (Mexico)	$0.1335
Yen (Japan)	0.0095
Pounds (Britain)	1.5235
Ringgits (Malaysia)	0.6807

2012

Jan. 12   Received full payment in pounds from Smithers for the October 14 sale and immediately exchanged the pounds for dollars. The exchange rate for pounds is $1.5314 on this day.

Jan. 19   Received Hamid Albar's full payment in ringgits for the December 20 sale and immediately exchanged the ringgits for dollars. The exchange rate for ringgits is $0.6771 on this day.

Required

1. Prepare journal entries for the Roundtree transactions and adjusting entries (round amounts to the nearest dollar).

2. Compute the foreign exchange gain or loss to be reported on Roundtree's 2011 income statement.

Check (2) 2011 total foreign exchange loss, $723

Analysis Component

3. What actions might Roundtree consider to reduce its risk of foreign exchange gains or losses?

Deal Company, which began operations in 2011, invests its idle cash in trading securities. The following transactions relate to its short-term investments in its trading securities.

PROBLEM SET B

Problem C-1B
Recording transactions and fair value adjustments for trading securities **P1**

2011

Mar. 10   Purchased 1,200 shares of AOL at $59.15 per share plus a $773 commission.
May 7   Purchased 2,500 shares of MTV at $36.25 per share plus a $1,428 commission.
Sept. 1   Purchased 600 shares of UPS at $57.25 per share plus a $625 commission.

2012

Apr. 26   Sold 2,500 shares of MTV at $34.50 per share less a $1,025 commission.
Apr. 27   Sold 600 shares of UPS at $60.50 per share less an $894 commission.

June   2   Purchased 1,800 shares of SPW at $172 per share plus a $1,625 commission.
June 14   Purchased 450 shares of Walmart at $50.25 per share plus a $541.50 commission.

2013

Jan. 28   Purchased 1,000 shares of PepsiCo at $43 per share plus a $1,445 commission.
Jan. 31   Sold 1,800 shares of SPW at $168 per share less a $1,020 commission.
Aug. 22   Sold 1,200 shares of AOL at $56.75 per share less a $1,240 commission.
Sept. 3   Purchased 750 shares of Vodaphone at $40.50 per share plus an $840 commission.
Oct.   9   Sold 450 shares of Walmart at $53.75 per share less a $610.50 commission.

Required

1. Prepare journal entries to record these short-term investment activities for the years shown. (Ignore any year-end adjusting entries.)

Check (2) Cr. Fair Value Adjustment—Trading $6,910

2. On December 31, 2013, prepare the adjusting entry to record any necessary fair value adjustment for the portfolio of trading securities when PepsiCo's share price is $41 and Vodaphone's share price is $37. (Assume the Fair Value Adjustment—Trading account had an unadjusted balance of zero.)

Problem C-2B
Recording, adjusting, and reporting short-term available-for-sale securities

P3

Day Systems had no short-term investments prior to 2011. It had the following transactions involving short-term investments in available-for-sale securities during 2011.

Feb.   6   Purchased 1,700 shares of Nokia stock at $41.25 per share plus a $1,500 brokerage fee.
      15   Paid $10,000 to buy six-month U.S. Treasury bills (debt securities): $10,000 principal amount, 6% interest, securities dated February 15.
Apr.   7   Purchased 600 shares of Dell Co. stock at $39.50 per share plus a $627 brokerage fee.
June   2   Purchased 1,250 shares of Merck stock at $72.50 per share plus a $1,945 brokerage fee.
      30   Received a $0.19 per share cash dividend on the Nokia shares.
Aug. 11   Sold 425 shares of Nokia stock at $46 per share less a $525 brokerage fee.
      16   Received a check for principal and accrued interest on the U.S. Treasury bills purchased February 15.
      24   Received a $0.10 per share cash dividend on the Dell shares.
Nov.   9   Received a $0.20 per share cash dividend on the remaining Nokia shares.
Dec. 18   Received a $0.15 per share cash dividend on the Dell shares.

Required

1. Prepare journal entries to record the preceding transactions and events.

Check (2) Cost = $170,616

2. Prepare a table to compare the year-end cost and fair values of the short-term investments in available-for-sale securities. The year-end fair values per share are: Nokia, $40.25; Dell, $41; and Merck, $59.

(3) Dr. Unrealized Loss—Equity, $20,947

3. Prepare an adjusting entry, if necessary, to record the year-end fair value adjustment for the portfolio of short-term investments in available-for-sale securities.

Analysis Component

4. Explain the balance sheet presentation of the fair value adjustment to Day's short-term investments.

5. How do these short-term investments affect (*a*) its income statement for year 2011 and (*b*) the equity section of its balance sheet at the 2011 year-end?

Problem C-3B
Recording, adjusting, and reporting long-term available-for-sale securities

P3

Venice Enterprises, which began operations in 2011, invests in long-term available-for-sale securities. Following is a series of transactions and events involving its long-term investment activity.

2011

Mar. 10   Purchased 2,400 shares of Apple at $33.25 per share plus $1,995 commission.
Apr.   7   Purchased 5,000 shares of Ford at $17.50 per share plus $2,625 commission.
Sept. 1   Purchased 1,200 shares of Polaroid at $49.00 per share plus $1,176 commission.
Dec. 31   Per share fair values for stocks in the portfolio are: Apple, $35.50; Ford, $17.00; Polaroid, $51.75.

2012

Apr. 26   Sold 5,000 shares of Ford at $16.38 per share less a $2,237 commission.
June   2   Purchased 3,600 shares of Duracell at $18.88 per share plus a $2,312 commission.
June 14   Purchased 900 shares of Sears at $24.50 per share plus a $541 commission.
Nov. 27   Sold 1,200 shares of Polaroid at $52 per share less a $1,672 commission.
Dec. 31   Per share fair values for stocks in the portfolio are: Apple, $35.50; Duracell, $18.00; Sears, $26.00.

2013

Jan. 28   Purchased 2,000 shares of Coca-Cola Co. at $41 per share plus a $3,280 commission.
Aug. 22   Sold 2,400 shares of Apple at $29.75 per share less a $2,339 commission.
Sept. 3   Purchased 1,500 shares of Motorola at $29 per share plus a $870 commission.
Oct.   9   Sold 900 shares of Sears at $27.50 per share less a $619 commission.
Oct. 31   Sold 3,600 shares of Duracell at $16.00 per share less a $1,496 commission.
Dec. 31   Per share fair values for stocks in the portfolio are: Coca-Cola, $46.00; Motorola, $22.00.

Required

1. Prepare journal entries to record these transactions and events and any year-end fair value adjustments to the portfolio of long-term available-for-sale securities.

2. Prepare a table that summarizes the (*a*) total cost, (*b*) total fair value adjustment, and (*c*) total fair value for the portfolio of long-term available-for-sale securities at each year-end.

3. Prepare a table that summarizes (*a*) the realized gains and losses and (*b*) the unrealized gains or losses for the portfolio of long-term available-for-sale securities at each year-end.

Check   (2b) Fair Value Adjustment bal.: 12/31/11, $404; 12/31/12, $(1,266)

(3b) Unrealized Loss at 12/31/2013, $4,650

Capollo's long-term available-for-sale portfolio at December 31, 2010, consists of the following.

Available-for-Sale Securities	Cost	Fair Value
45,000 shares of Company R common stock	$1,118,250	$1,198,125
17,000 shares of Company S common stock	616,760	586,500
22,000 shares of Company T common stock	294,470	303,600

Problem C-4B
Long-term investment transactions; unrealized and realized gains and losses

C2 P3 P4

Capollo enters into the following long-term investment transactions during year 2011.

Jan. 13   Sold 4,250 shares of Company S stock for $144,500 less a brokerage fee of $2,390.
Mar. 24   Purchased 31,000 shares of Company U common stock for $565,750 plus a brokerage fee of $9,900. The shares represent a 62% ownership interest in Company U.
Apr.   5   Purchased 85,000 shares of Company V common stock for $267,750 plus a brokerage fee of $4,500. The shares represent a 10% ownership in Company V.
Sept. 2   Sold 22,000 shares of Company T common stock for $313,500 less a brokerage fee of $5,400.
Sept. 27   Purchased 5,000 shares of Company W common stock for $101,000 plus a brokerage fee of $2,100. The shares represent a 25% ownership interest in Company W.
Oct. 30   Purchased 10,000 shares of Company X common stock for $97,500 plus a brokerage fee of $2,340. The shares represent a 13% ownership interest in Company X.

The fair values of its investments at December 31, 2011, are: R, $1,136,250; S, $420,750; U, $545,600; V, $269,875; W, $109,375; and X, $91,250.

Required

1. Determine the amount Capollo should report on its December 31, 2011, balance sheet for its long-term investments in available-for-sale securities.

2. Prepare any necessary December 31, 2011, adjusting entry to record the fair value adjustment of the long-term investments in available-for-sale securities.

3. What amount of gains or losses on transactions relating to long-term investments in available-for-sale securities should Capollo report on its December 31, 2011, income statement?

Check   (2) Dr. Unrealized Loss— Equity, $34,785; Cr. Fair Value Adjustment—AFS (LT), $93,530

Bengal Company, which began operations on January 3, 2011, had the following subsequent transactions and events in its long-term investments.

2011

Jan.   5   Bengal purchased 15,000 shares (25% of total) of Bloch's common stock for $187,500.
Aug.   1   Bloch declared and paid a cash dividend of $0.95 per share.
Dec. 31   Bloch's net income for 2011 is $92,000, and the fair value of its stock is $12.90 per share.

2012

Aug.   1   Bloch declared and paid a cash dividend of $1.25 per share.
Dec. 31   Bloch's net income for 2012 is $76,000, and the fair value of its stock is $13.55 per share.

Problem C-5B
Accounting for long-term investments in securities; with and without significant influence

P3 P4

2013

Jan.   8   Bengal sold all of its investment in Bloch for $204,750 cash.

Part 1

Assume that Bengal has a significant influence over Bloch with its 25% share.

Required

1. Prepare journal entries to record these transactions and events for Bengal.
2. Compute the carrying (book) value per share of Bengal's investment in Bloch common stock as reflected in the investment account on January 7, 2013.
3. Compute the net increase or decrease in Bengal's equity from January 5, 2011, through January 8, 2013, resulting from its investment in Bloch.

Part 2

Assume that although Bengal owns 25% of Bloch's outstanding stock, circumstances indicate that it does not have a significant influence over the investee and that it is classified as an available-for-sale security investment.

Required

1. Prepare journal entries to record these transactions and events for Bengal. Also prepare an entry dated January 8, 2013, to remove any balance related to the fair value adjustment.
2. Compute the cost per share of Bengal's investment in Bloch common stock as reflected in the investment account on January 7, 2013.
3. Compute the net increase or decrease in Bengal's equity from January 5, 2011, through January 8, 2013, resulting from its investment in Bloch.

Check (2) Carrying value per share, $13.10

(1) 1/8/2013 Dr. Unrealized Gain—Equity $15,750

(3) Net increase, $50,250

Problem C-6B[A]

Foreign currency transactions

C3

Datamix, a U.S. corporation with customers in several foreign countries, had the following selected transactions for 2011 and 2012.

2011

May 26   Sold merchandise for 6.5 million yen to Fuji Company of Japan, payment in full to be received in 60 days. On this day, the exchange rate for yen is $0.0094.

June   1   Sold merchandise to Fordham Ltd. of Great Britain for $72,613 cash. The exchange rate for pounds is $1.5277 on this day.

July 25   Received Fuji's payment in yen for its May 26 purchase and immediately exchanged the yen for dollars. The exchange rate for yen is $0.0090 on this day.

Oct. 15   Sold merchandise on credit to Martinez Brothers of Mexico. The price of 373,000 pesos is to be paid 90 days from the date of sale. On this day, the exchange rate for pesos is $0.1340.

Dec.   6   Sold merchandise for 242,000 yuans to Chi-Ying Company of China, payment in full to be received in 30 days. The exchange rate for yuans is $0.1975 on this day.

Dec. 31   Recorded adjusting entries to recognize exchange gains or losses on Datamix's annual financial statements. Rates of exchanging foreign currencies on this day follow.

Yen (Japan)	$0.0094
Pounds (Britain)	1.5318
Pesos (Mexico)	0.1560
Yuans (China)	0.2000

2012

Jan.   5   Received Chi-Ying's full payment in yuans for the December 6 sale and immediately exchanged the yuans for dollars. The exchange rate for yuans is $0.2060 on this day.

Jan. 13   Received full payment in pesos from Martinez for the October 15 sale and immediately exchanged the pesos for dollars. The exchange rate for pesos is $0.1420 on this day.

Required

1. Prepare journal entries for the Datamix transactions and adjusting entries.
2. Compute the foreign exchange gain or loss to be reported on Datamix's 2011 income statement.

Analysis Component

3. What actions might Datamix consider to reduce its risk of foreign exchange gains or losses?

Check (2) 2011 total foreign exchange gain, $6,211

(This serial problem began in Chapter 1 and continues through most of the book. If previous chapter segments were not completed, the serial problem can begin at this point. It is helpful, but not necessary, to use the Working Papers that accompany the book.)

SP C   While reviewing the March 31, 2012, balance sheet of Business Solutions, Santana Rey notes that the business has built a large cash balance of $68,057. Its most recent bank money market statement shows that the funds are earning an annualized return of 0.75%. S. Rey decides to make several investments with the desire to earn a higher return on the idle cash balance. Accordingly, in April 2012, Business Solutions makes the following investments in trading securities:

April 16   Purchases 400 shares of Johnson & Johnson stock at $50 per share plus $300 commission.
April 30   Purchases 200 shares of Starbucks Corporation at $22 per share plus $250 commission.

On June 30, 2012, the per share market price (fair value) of the Johnson & Johnson shares is $55 and the Starbucks shares is $19.

Required

1. Prepare journal entries to record the April purchases of trading securities by Business Solutions.
2. On June 30, 2012, prepare the adjusting entry to record any necessary fair value adjustment to its port-folio of trading securities.

Beyond the Numbers

BTN C-1   Refer to **Research In Motion**'s financial statements in Appendix A to answer the following.
1. Are Research In Motion's financial statements consolidated? How can you tell?
2. What is Research In Motion's *comprehensive income* for the year ended February 27, 2010?
3. Does Research In Motion have any foreign operations? How can you tell?
4. Compute Research In Motion's return on total assets for the year ended February 27, 2010.

Fast Forward

5. Access Research In Motion's annual report for a fiscal year ending after February 27, 2010, from either its Website (**RIM.com**) or the SEC's database (**www.SEC.gov**). Recompute Research In Motion's return on total assets for the years subsequent to February 27, 2010.

BTN C-2   Key figures for **Research In Motion** and **Apple** follow.

($ millions)	Research In Motion			Apple		
	Current Year	1 Year Prior	2 Years Prior	Current Year	1 Year Prior	2 Years Prior
Net income	$ 2,457	$1,893	$1,294	$ 8,235	$ 6,119	$ 3,495
Net sales	12,536	9,411	4,914	42,905	37,491	24,578
Total assets	10,204	8,101	5,511	47,501	36,171	25,347

Required

1. Compute return on total assets for Research In Motion and Apple for the two most recent years.
2. Separate the return on total assets computed in part 1 into its components for both companies and both years according to the formula in Exhibit C.9.
3. Which company has the highest total return on assets? The highest profit margin? The highest total asset turnover? What does this comparative analysis reveal? (Assume an industry average of 10.0% for return on assets.)

BTN C-3   Kendra Wecker is the controller for Wildcat Company, which has numerous long-term investments in debt securities. Wildcat's investments are mainly in 10-year bonds. Wecker is preparing its year-end financial statements. In accounting for long-term debt securities, she knows that each long-term investment must be designated as a held-to-maturity or an available-for-sale security. Interest rates rose sharply this past year causing the portfolio's fair value to substantially decline. The company does not intend to hold the bonds for the entire 10 years. Wecker also earns a bonus each year, which is computed as a percent of net income.

Required

1. Will Wecker's bonus depend in any way on the classification of the debt securities? Explain.
2. What criteria must Wecker use to classify the securities as held-to-maturity or available-for-sale?
3. Is there likely any company oversight of Wecker's classification of the securities? Explain.

COMMUNICATING IN PRACTICE
P4

BTN C-4 Assume that you are Jackson Company's accountant. Company owner Abel Terrio has reviewed the 2011 financial statements you prepared and questions the $6,000 loss reported on the sale of its investment in Blackhawk Co. common stock. Jackson acquired 50,000 shares of Blackhawk's common stock on December 31, 2009, at a cost of $500,000. This stock purchase represented a 40% interest in Blackhawk. The 2010 income statement reported that earnings from all investments were $126,000. On January 3, 2011, Jackson Company sold the Blackhawk stock for $575,000. Blackhawk did not pay any dividends during 2010 but reported a net income of $202,500 for that year. Terrio believes that because the Blackhawk stock purchase price was $500,000 and was sold for $575,000, the 2011 income statement should report a $75,000 gain on the sale.

Required

Draft a one-half page memorandum to Terrio explaining why the $6,000 loss on sale of Blackhawk stock is correctly reported.

TAKING IT TO THE NET
C1

BTN C-5 Access the July 30, 2009, 10-K filing (for year-end June 30, 2009) of **Microsoft** (MSFT) at **www.SEC.gov**. Review its note 4, "Investments."

Required

1. How does the "cost-basis" total amount for its investments as of June 30, 2009, compare to the prior year-end amount?
2. Identify at least eight types of short-term investments held by Microsoft as of June 30, 2009.
3. What were Microsoft's unrealized gains and its unrealized losses from its investments for 2009?
4. Was the cost or fair value ("recorded basis") of the investments higher as of June 30, 2009?

TEAMWORK IN ACTION
C1 C2 P1 P2 P3 P4

BTN C-6 Each team member is to become an expert on a specific classification of long-term investments. This expertise will be used to facilitate other teammates' understanding of the concepts and procedures relevent to the classification chosen.

1. Each team member must select an area for expertise by choosing one of the following classifications of long-term investments.
    a. Held-to-maturity debt securities
    b. Available-for-sale debt and equity securities
    c. Equity securities with significant influence
    d. Equity securities with controlling influence
2. Learning teams are to disburse and expert teams are to be formed. Expert teams are made up of those who select the same area of expertise. The instructor will identify the location where each expert team will meet.
3. Expert teams will collaborate to develop a presentation based on the following requirements. Students must write the presentation in a format they can show to their learning teams in part (4).

Requirements for Expert Presentation

    a. Write a transaction for the acquisition of this type of investment security. The transaction description is to include all necessary data to reflect the chosen classification.
    b. Prepare the journal entry to record the acquisition.
    [*Note:* The expert team on equity securities with controlling influence will substitute requirements (*d*) and (*e*) with a discussion of the reporting of these investments.]

    c. Identify information necessary to complete the end-of-period adjustment for this investment.

    d. Assuming that this is the only investment owned, prepare any necessary year-end entries.

    e. Present the relevant balance sheet section(s).

4. Re-form learning teams. In rotation, experts are to present to their teams the presentations they developed in part 3. Experts are to encourage and respond to questions.

BTN C-7ᴬ   Assume that you are planning a spring break trip to Europe. Identify three locations where you can find exchange rates for the dollar relative to the Euro or other currencies.

HITTING THE ROAD

C3

BTN C-8   **Nokia**, **Research In Motion**, and **Apple** are competitors in the global marketplace. Following are selected data from each company.

GLOBAL DECISION

A1

NOKIA

RIM

Apple

Key Figure	Nokia (Euro millions)			Research In Motion		Apple	
	Current Year	One Year Prior	Two Years Prior	Current Year	Prior Year	Current Year	Prior Year
Net income	€ 260	€ 3,889	€ 6,746	—	—	—	—
Net sales	40,984	50,710	51,058	—	—	—	—
Total assets	35,738	39,582	37,599	—	—	—	—
Profit margin	?	?	—	19.6%	20.1%	19.2%	16.3%
Total asset turnover	?	?	—	1.37	1.38	1.03	1.22

Required

1. Compute Nokia's return on total assets, and its components of profit margin and total asset turnover, for the most recent two years using the data provided.

2. Which of these three companies has the highest return on total assets? Highest profit margin? Highest total asset turnover? Interpret these results.

ANSWERS TO MULTIPLE CHOICE QUIZ

1. d; $30,000 × 5% × 5/12 = $625

2. a; Unrealized gain = $84,500 − $83,000 = $1,500

3. b; $50,000 × 35% = $17,500

4. e; $300,000/$2,000,000 = 15%

5. b; Profit margin = $80,000/$600,000 = 13.3%
       Total asset turnover = $600,000/$400,000 = 1.5

Glossary

Absorption costing A costing method that includes all manufacturing costs—direct materials, direct labor, and both variable and fixed manufacturing overhead—in unit product costs. Absorption costing is also referred to as the full cost method; also called *full costing*. (p. 794)

Accelerated depreciation method Method that produces larger depreciation charges in the early years of an asset's life and smaller charges in its later years. (p. 332)

Account Record within an accounting system in which increases and decreases are entered and stored in a specific asset, liability, equity, revenue, or expense. (p. 51)

Account balance Difference between total debits and total credits (including the beginning balance) for an account. (p. 55)

Account form balance sheet Balance sheet that lists assets on the left side and liabilities and equity on the right. (p. 18)

Account payable Liability created by buying goods or services on credit; backed by the buyer's general credit standing. (p. 50)

Accounting Information and measurement system that identifies, records, and communicates relevant information about a company's business activities. (p. 4)

Accounting cycle Recurring steps performed each accounting period, starting with analyzing transactions and continuing through the post-closing trial balance (or reversing entries). (p. 112)

Accounting equation Equality involving a company's assets, liabilities, and equity; Assets = Liabilities + Equity; also called *balance sheet equation*. (p. 14)

Accounting information system People, records, and methods that collect and process data from transactions and events, organize them in useful forms, and communicate results to decision makers. (p. E-2)

Accounting period Length of time covered by financial statements; also called *reporting period*. (p. 94)

Accounting rate of return Rate used to evaluate the acceptability of an investment; equals the after-tax periodic income from a project divided by the average investment in the asset; also called *rate of return on average investment*. (p. 1001)

Accounts payable ledger Subsidiary ledger listing individual creditor (supplier) accounts. (p. E-7)

Accounts receivable Amounts due from customers for credit sales; backed by the customer's general credit standing. (p. 292)

Accounts receivable ledger Subsidiary ledger listing individual customer accounts. (p. E-7)

Accounts receivable turnover Measure of both the quality and liquidity of accounts receivable; indicates how often receivables are received and collected during the period; computed by dividing net sales by average accounts receivable. (p. 307)

Accrual basis accounting Accounting system that recognizes revenues when earned and expenses when incurred; the basis for GAAP. (p. 95)

Accrued expenses Costs incurred in a period that are both unpaid and unrecorded; adjusting entries for recording accrued expenses involve increasing expenses and increasing liabilities. (p. 101)

Accrued revenues Revenues earned in a period that are both unrecorded and not yet received in cash (or other assets); adjusting entries for recording accrued revenues involve increasing assets and increasing revenues. (pp. 103 & 960)

Accumulated depreciation Cumulative sum of all depreciation expense recorded for an asset. (p. 97)

Acid-test ratio Ratio used to assess a company's ability to settle its current debts with its most liquid assets; defined as quick assets (cash, short-term investments, and current receivables) divided by current liabilities. (p. 172)

Activity An event that causes the consumption of overhead resources in an entity. (p. 723)

Activity-based budgeting (ABB) Budget system based on expected activities. (p. 850)

Activity-based costing (ABC) Cost allocation method that focuses on activities performed; traces costs to activities and then assigns them to cost objects. (p. 731)

Activity-based management A management approach that focuses on managing activities as a way of eliminating waste and reducing delays and defects. (p. 730)

Activity cost driver Variable that causes an activity's cost to go up or down; a causal factor. (p. 861)

Activity cost pool Temporary account that accumulates costs a company incurs to support an activity. (p. 861)

Activity overhead (pool) rate A predetermined overhead rate in activity-based costing; each activity cost pool has its own activity rate that is used to apply overhead to products and services. (p. 731)

Adjusted trial balance List of accounts and balances prepared after period-end adjustments are recorded and posted. (p. 106)

Adjusting entry Journal entry at the end of an accounting period to bring an asset or liability account to its proper amount and update the related expense or revenue account. (p. 96)

Aging of accounts receivable Process of classifying accounts receivable by how long they are past due for purposes of estimating uncollectible accounts. (p. 300)

Allowance for Doubtful Accounts Contra asset account with a balance approximating uncollectible accounts receivable; also called *Allowance for Uncollectible Accounts*. *(p. 297)*

Allowance method Procedure that (a) estimates and matches bad debts expense with its sales for the period and/or (b) reports accounts receivable at estimated realizable value. *(p. 296)*

Amortization Process of allocating the cost of an intangible asset to expense over its estimated useful life. *(p. 341)*

Annual financial statements Financial statements covering a one-year period; often based on a calendar year, but any consecutive 12-month (or 52-week) period is acceptable. *(p. 94)*

Annual report Summary of a company's financial results for the year with its current financial condition and future plans; directed to external users of financial information. *(p. A-1)*

Annuity Series of equal payments at equal intervals. *(p. 431)*

Appropriated retained earnings Retained earnings separately reported to inform stockholders of funding needs. *(p. 473)*

Asset book value (See *book value.*)

Assets Resources a business owns or controls that are expected to provide current and future benefits to the business. *(p. 14)*

Audit Analysis and report of an organization's accounting system, its records, and its reports using various tests. *(p. 12)*

Auditors Individuals hired to review financial reports and information systems. *Internal auditors* of a company are employed to assess and evaluate its system of internal controls, including the resulting reports. *External auditors* are independent of a company and are hired to assess and evaluate the "fairness" of financial statements (or to perform other contracted financial services) *(p. 13)*.

Authorized stock Total amount of stock that a corporation's charter authorizes it to issue. *(p. 459)*

Available-for-sale (AFS) securities Investments in debt and equity securities that are not classified as trading securities or held-to-maturity securities. *(p. C-6)*

Average cost See *weighted average.* *(pp. 210 & 225)*

Avoidable expense Expense (or cost) that is relevant for decision making; expense that is not incurred if a department, product, or service is eliminated. *(p. 975)*

Bad debts Accounts of customers who do not pay what they have promised to pay; an expense of selling on credit; also called *uncollectible accounts.* *(p. 295)*

Balance column account Account with debit and credit columns for recording entries and another column for showing the balance of the account after each entry. *(p. 58)*

Balance sheet Financial statement that lists types and dollar amounts of assets, liabilities, and equity at a specific date. *(p. 19)*

Balance sheet equation (See *accounting equation.*)

Balanced scorecard A system of performance measurement that collects information on several key performance indicators within each of four perspectives: customer, internal processes, innovation and learning, and financial. *(p. 936)*

Bank reconciliation Report that explains the difference between the book (company) balance of cash and the cash balance reported on the bank statement. *(p. 263)*

Bank statement Bank report on the depositor's beginning and ending cash balances, and a listing of its changes, for a period. *(p. 262)*

Basic earnings per share Net income less any preferred dividends and then divided by weighted-average common shares outstanding. *(p. 475)*

Batch level activities Activities that are performed each time a batch of goods is handled or processed, regardless of how many units are in a batch; the amount of resources used depends on the number of batches run rather than on the number of units in the batch. *(p. 738)*

Batch processing Accumulating source documents for a period of time and then processing them all at once such as once a day, week, or month. *(p. E-16)*

Bearer bonds Bonds made payable to whoever holds them (the *bearer*); also called *unregistered bonds.* *(p. 426)*

Benchmarking Practice of comparing and analyzing company financial performance or position with other companies or standards. *(p. 1002)*

Betterments Expenditures to make a plant asset more efficient or productive; also called *improvements.* *(p. 337)*

Bond Written promise to pay the bond's par (or face) value and interest at a stated contract rate; often issued in denominations of $1,000. *(p. 412)*

Bond certificate Document containing bond specifics such as issuer's name, bond par value, contract interest rate, and maturity date. *(p. 414)*

Bond indenture Contract between the bond issuer and the bondholders; identifies the parties' rights and obligations. *(p. 414)*

Book value Asset's acquisition costs less its accumulated depreciation (or depletion, or amortization); also sometimes used synonymously as the *carrying value* of an account. *(p. 100)*

Book value per common share Recorded amount of equity applicable to common shares divided by the number of common shares outstanding. *(p. 476)*

Book value per preferred share Equity applicable to preferred shares (equals its call price [or par value if it is not callable] plus any cumulative dividends in arrears) divided by the number of preferred shares outstanding. *(p. 476)*

Bookkeeping (See *recordkeeping.*) *(p. 4)*

Break-even point Output level at which sales equals fixed plus variable costs; where income equals zero. *(p. 773)*

Break-even time (BET) Time-based measurement used to evaluate the acceptability of an investment; equals the time expected to pass before the present value of the net cash flows from an investment equals its initial cost. *(p. 1008)*

Budget Formal statement of future plans, usually expressed in monetary terms. *(p. 836)*

Budget report Report comparing actual results to planned objectives; sometimes used as a progress report. *(p. 880)*

Budgetary control Management use of budgets to monitor and control company operations. *(p. 880)*

Budgeted balance sheet Accounting report that presents predicted amounts of the company's assets, liabilities, and equity balances as of the end of the budget period. *(p. 848)*

Budgeted income statement Accounting report that presents predicted amounts of the company's revenues and expenses for the budget period. *(p. 848)*

Budgeting Process of planning future business actions and expressing them as formal plans. *(p. 836)*

Business An organization of one or more individuals selling products and/or services for profit. *(p. 10)*

Business entity assumption Principle that requires a business to be accounted for separately from its owner(s) and from any other entity. *(p. 11)*

Business segment Part of a company that can be separately identified by the products or services that it provides or by the geographic markets that it serves; also called *segment*. *(p. 578)*

C corporation Corporation that does not qualify for nor elect to be treated as a proprietorship or partnership for income tax purposes and therefore is subject to income taxes; also called *C corp*. *(p. D-4)*

Call price Amount that must be paid to call and retire a callable preferred stock or a callable bond. *(p. 469)*

Callable bonds Bonds that give the issuer the option to retire them at a stated amount prior to maturity. *(p. 426)*

Callable preferred stock Preferred stock that the issuing corporation, at its option, may retire by paying the call price plus any dividends in arrears. *(p. 469)*

Canceled checks Checks that the bank has paid and deducted from the depositor's account. *(p. 263)*

Capital budgeting Process of analyzing alternative investments and deciding which assets to acquire or sell. *(p. 998)*

Capital expenditures Additional costs of plant assets that provide material benefits extending beyond the current period; also called *balance sheet expenditures*. *(p. 336)*

Capital expenditures budget Plan that lists dollar amounts to be both received from disposal of plant assets and spent to purchase plant assets. *(p. 846)*

Capital leases Long-term leases in which the lessor transfers substantially all risk and rewards of ownership to the lessee. *(p. 437)*

Capital stock General term referring to a corporation's stock used in obtaining capital (owner financing). *(p. 459)*

Capitalize Record the cost as part of a permanent account and allocate it over later periods.

Carrying (book) value of bonds Net amount at which bonds are reported on the balance sheet; equals the par value of the bonds less any unamortized discount or plus any unamortized premium; also called *carrying amount or book value*. *(p. 416)*

Cash Includes currency, coins, and amounts on deposit in bank checking or savings accounts. *(p. 253)*

Cash basis accounting Accounting system that recognizes revenues when cash is received and records expenses when cash is paid. *(p. 95)*

Cash budget Plan that shows expected cash inflows and outflows during the budget period, including receipts from loans needed to maintain a minimum cash balance and repayments of such loans. *(p. 846)*

Cash disbursements journal Special journal normally used to record all payments of cash; also called *cash payments journal*. *(p. E-14)*

Cash discount Reduction in the price of merchandise granted by a seller to a buyer when payment is made within the discount period. *(p. 159)*

Cash equivalents Short-term, investment assets that are readily convertible to a known cash amount or sufficiently close to their maturity date (usually within 90 days) so that market value is not sensitive to interest rate changes. *(p. 253)*

Cash flow on total assets Ratio of operating cash flows to average total assets; not sensitive to income recognition and measurement; partly reflects earnings quality. *(p. 518)*

Cash Over and Short Income statement account used to record cash overages and cash shortages arising from errors in cash receipts or payments. *(p. 255)*

Cash receipts journal Special journal normally used to record all receipts of cash. *(p. E-11)*

Change in an accounting estimate Change in an accounting estimate that results from new information, subsequent developments, or improved judgment that impacts current and future periods. *(pp. 335 & 473)*

Chart of accounts List of accounts used by a company; includes an identification number for each account. *(p. 54)*

Check Document signed by a depositor instructing the bank to pay a specified amount to a designated recipient. *(p. 260)*

Check register Another name for a cash disbursements journal when the journal has a column for check numbers. *(pp. 272 & E-14)*

Classified balance sheet Balance sheet that presents assets and liabilities in relevant subgroups, including current and noncurrent classifications. *(p. 113)*

Clock card Source document used to record the number of hours an employee works and to determine the total labor cost for each pay period. *(p. 782)*

Closing entries Entries recorded at the end of each accounting period to transfer end-of-period balances in revenue, gain, expense, loss, and withdrawal (dividend for a corporation) accounts to the capital account (to retained earnings for a corporation). *(p. 108)*

Closing process Necessary end-of-period steps to prepare the accounts for recording the transactions of the next period. *(p. 108)*

Columnar journal Journal with more than one column. *(p. E-8)*

Committee on Sponsoring Organizations (COSO) Committee devoted to improving the quality of financial reporting through effective internal controls, consisting of five interrelated components, along with other mechanisms (www.COSO.org). *(p. 249)*

Common stock Corporation's basic ownership share; also generically called *capital stock*. *(pp. 12 & 458)*

Common-size financial statement Statement that expresses each amount as a percent of a base amount. In the balance sheet, total assets is usually the base and is expressed as 100%. In the income statement, net sales is usually the base. *(p. 561)*

Comparative financial statement Statement with data for two or more successive periods placed in side-by-side columns, often with changes shown in dollar amounts and percents. *(p. 556)*

Compatibility principle Information system principle that prescribes an accounting system to conform with a company's activities, personnel, and structure. *(p. E-3)*

Complex capital structure Capital structure that includes outstanding rights or options to purchase common stock, or securities that are convertible into common stock. *(p. 475)*

Components of accounting systems Five basic components of accounting systems are source documents, input devices, information processors, information storage, and output devices. *(p. E-3)*

Composite unit Generic unit consisting of a specific number of units of each product; unit comprised in proportion to the expected sales mix of its products. *(p. 780)*

Compound journal entry Journal entry that affects at least three accounts. *(p. 61)*

Comprehensive income Net change in equity for a period, excluding owner investments and distributions. *(p. C-10)*

Computer hardware Physical equipment in a computerized accounting information system.

Computer network Linkage giving different users and different computers access to common databases and programs. *(p. E-16)*

Computer software Programs that direct operations of computer hardware.

Conceptual framework A written framework to guide the development, preparation, and interpretation of financial accounting information. *(p. 9)*

Conservatism constraint Principle that prescribes the less optimistic estimate when two estimates are about equally likely. *(p. 214)*

Consignee Receiver of goods owned by another who holds them for purposes of selling them for the owner. *(p. 204)*

Consignor Owner of goods who ships them to another party who will sell them for the owner. *(p. 204)*

Consistency concept Principle that prescribes use of the same accounting method(s) over time so that financial statements are comparable across periods. *(p. 213)*

Consolidated financial statements Financial statements that show all (combined) activities under the parent's control, including those of any subsidiaries. *(p. C-9)*

Contingent liability Obligation to make a future payment if, and only if, an uncertain future event occurs. *(p. 380)*

Continuous budgeting Practice of preparing budgets for a selected number of future periods and revising those budgets as each period is completed. *(p. 839)*

Continuous improvement Concept requiring every manager and employee continually to look to improve operations. *(p. 616)*

Contra account Account linked with another account and having an opposite normal balance; reported as a subtraction from the other account's balance. *(p. 99)*

Contract rate Interest rate specified in a bond indenture (or note); multiplied by the par value to determine the interest paid each period; also called *coupon rate, stated rate,* or *nominal rate. (p. 415)*

Contributed capital Total amount of cash and other assets received from stockholders in exchange for stock; also called *paid-in capital. (p. 14)*

Contributed capital in excess of par value Difference between the par value of stock and its issue price when issued at a price above par.

Contribution format An income statement format that is geared to cost behavior in that costs are separated into variable and fixed categories rather than being separated according to the functions of production, sales, and administration. *(p. 804)*

Contribution margin Sales revenue less total variable costs.

Contribution margin income statement Income statement that separates variable and fixed costs; highlights the contribution margin, which is sales less variable expenses. *(p. 806)*

Contribution margin per unit Amount that the sale of one unit contributes toward recovering fixed costs and earning profit; defined as sales price per unit minus variable expense per unit. *(p. 772)*

Contribution margin ratio Product's contribution margin divided by its sale price. *(p. 772)*

Contribution margin report A performance report that lists sales less the variable costs, ending with the contribution margin; fixed costs are excluded. *(p. 807)*

Control Process of monitoring planning decisions and evaluating the organization's activities and employees. *(p. 601)*

Control principle Information system principle that prescribes an accounting system to aid managers in controlling and monitoring business activities. *(p. E-2)*

Controllable costs Costs that a manager has the power to control or at least strongly influence. *(pp. 605, 814 & 937)*

Controllable variance Combination of both overhead spending variances (variable and fixed) and the variable overhead efficiency variance. *(p. 893)*

Controlling account General ledger account, the balance of which (after posting) equals the sum of the balances in its related subsidiary ledger. *(p. E-7)*

Conversion costs Expenditures incurred in converting raw materials to finished goods; includes direct labor costs and overhead costs. *(p. 611)*

Conversion costs per equivalent unit The combined costs of direct labor and factory overhead per equivalent unit. *(p. 697)*

Convertible bonds Bonds that bondholders can exchange for a set number of the issuer's shares. *(p. 426)*

Convertible preferred stock Preferred stock with an option to exchange it for common stock at a specified rate. *(p. 468)*

Copyright Right giving the owner the exclusive privilege to publish and sell musical, literary, or artistic work during the creator's life plus 70 years. *(p. 342)*

Corporation Business that is a separate legal entity under state or federal laws with owners called *shareholders* or *stockholders. (pp. 12 & 456)*

Cost All normal and reasonable expenditures necessary to get an asset in place and ready for its intended use. *(p. 327 & 329)*

Cost accounting system Accounting system for manufacturing activities based on the perpetual inventory system. *(p. 776)*

Cost-based transfer pricing A form of pricing transfers between divisions of the same company based on costs to the transferring division; typically used when the transferring division has excess capacity. *(p. 945)*

Cost-benefit constraint Notion that only information with benefits of disclosure greater than the costs of disclosure need be disclosed. *(p. 12)*

Cost-benefit principle Information system principle that prescribes the benefits from an activity in an accounting system to outweigh the costs of that activity. *(p. E-3)*

Cost center Department that incurs costs but generates no revenues; common example is the accounting or legal department. *(p. 927)*

Cost object Product, process, department, or customer to which costs are assigned. *(p. 605)*

Cost of capital Rate the company must pay to its long-term creditors and shareholders; also called *hurdle rate*. *(p. 1003)*

Cost of goods available for sale Consists of beginning inventory plus net purchases of a period.

Cost of goods manufactured Total manufacturing costs (direct materials, direct labor, and factory overhead) for the period plus beginning goods in process less ending goods in process; also called *net cost of goods manufactured* and *cost of goods completed*. *(p. 695)*

Cost of goods sold Cost of inventory sold to customers during a period; also called *cost of sales*. *(p. 156)*

Cost principle Accounting principle that prescribes financial statement information to be based on actual costs incurred in business transactions. *(p. 10)*

Cost variance Difference between the actual incurred cost and the standard cost. *(p. 887)*

Cost-volume-profit (CVP) analysis Planning method that includes predicting the volume of activity, the costs incurred, sales earned, and profits received. *(p. 766)*

Cost-volume-profit (CVP) chart Graphic representation of cost-volume-profit relations. *(p. 774)*

Coupon bonds Bonds with interest coupons attached to their certificates; bondholders detach coupons when they mature and present them to a bank or broker for collection. *(p. 426)*

Credit Recorded on the right side; an entry that decreases asset and expense accounts, and increases liability, revenue, and most equity accounts; abbreviated Cr. *(p. 55)*

Credit memorandum Notification that the sender has credited the recipient's account in the sender's records. *(p. 165)*

Credit period Time period that can pass before a customer's payment is due. *(p. 159)*

Credit terms Description of the amounts and timing of payments that a buyer (debtor) agrees to make in the future. *(p. 159)*

Creditors Individuals or organizations entitled to receive payments. *(p. 52)*

Cumulative preferred stock Preferred stock on which undeclared dividends accumulate until paid; common stockholders cannot receive dividends until cumulative dividends are paid. *(p. 467)*

Current assets Cash and other assets expected to be sold, collected, or used within one year or the company's operating cycle, whichever is longer. *(p. 114)*

Current liabilities Obligations due to be paid or settled within one year or the company's operating cycle, whichever is longer. *(p. 115 & 369)*

Current portion of long-term debt Portion of long-term debt due within one year or the operating cycle, whichever is longer; reported under current liabilities. *(p. 377)*

Current ratio Ratio used to evaluate a company's ability to pay its short-term obligations, calculated by dividing current assets by current liabilities. *(p. 117)*

Curvilinear cost Cost that changes with volume but not at a constant rate. *(p. 768)*

Customer orientation Company position that its managers and employees be in tune with the changing wants and needs of consumers. *(p. 615)*

Cycle efficiency (CE) A measure of production efficiency, which is defined as value-added (process) time divided by total cycle time. *(p. 618)*

Cycle time (CT) A measure of the time to produce a product or service, which is the sum of process time, inspection time, move time, and wait time; also called *throughput time*. *(p. 617)*

Date of declaration Date the directors vote to pay a dividend. *(p. 463)*

Date of payment Date the corporation makes the dividend payment. *(p. 463)*

Date of record Date directors specify for identifying stockholders to receive dividends. *(p. 463)*

Days' sales in inventory Estimate of number of days needed to convert inventory into receivables or cash; equals ending inventory divided by cost of goods sold and then multiplied by 365; also called days' *stock on hand*. *(p. 217)*

Days' sales uncollected Measure of the liquidity of receivables computed by dividing the current balance of receivables by the annual credit (or net) sales and then multiplying by 365; also called *days' sales in receivables*. *(p. 267)*

Debit Recorded on the left side; an entry that increases asset and expense accounts, and decreases liability, revenue, and most equity accounts; abbreviated Dr. *(p. 55)*

Debit memorandum Notification that the sender has debited the recipient's account in the sender's records. *(p. 160)*

Debtors Individuals or organizations that owe money. *(p. 51)*

Debt ratio Ratio of total liabilities to total assets; used to reflect risk associated with a company's debts. *(p. 69)*

Debt-to-equity ratio Defined as total liabilities divided by total equity; shows the proportion of a company financed by non-owners (creditors) in comparison with that financed by owners. *(p. 427)*

Declining-balance method Method that determines depreciation charge for the period by multiplying a depreciation rate (often twice the straight-line rate) by the asset's beginning-period book value. *(p. 332)*

Deferred income tax liability Corporation income taxes that are deferred until future years because of temporary differences between GAAP and tax rules. *(p. 392)*

Degree of operating leverage (DOL) Ratio of contribution margin divided by pretax income; used to assess the effect on income of changes in sales. *(p. 782)*

Departmental accounting system Accounting system that provides information useful in evaluating the profitability or cost effectiveness of a department. *(p. 926)*

Departmental contribution to overhead Amount by which a department's revenues exceed its direct expenses. *(p. 933)*

Depletion Process of allocating the cost of natural resources to periods when they are consumed and sold. *(p. 340)*

Deposit ticket Lists items such as currency, coins, and checks deposited and their corresponding dollar amounts. *(p. 260)*

Deposits in transit Deposits recorded by the company but not yet recorded by its bank. *(p. 263)*

Depreciable cost Cost of a plant asset less its salvage value.

Depreciation Expense created by allocating the cost of plant and equipment to periods in which they are used; represents the expense of using the asset. *(pp. 99 & 329)*

Diluted earnings per share Earnings per share calculation that requires dilutive securities be added to the denominator of the basic EPS calculation. *(p. 475)*

Dilutive securities Securities having the potential to increase common shares outstanding; examples are options, rights, convertible bonds, and convertible preferred stock. *(p. 475)*

Direct costs Costs incurred for the benefit of one specific cost object. *(p. 605)*

Direct expenses Expenses traced to a specific department (object) that are incurred for the sole benefit of that department. *(p. 927)*

Direct labor Efforts of employees who physically convert materials to finished product. *(p. 610)*

Direct labor costs Wages and salaries for direct labor that are separately and readily traced through the production process to finished goods. *(p. 610)*

Direct material Raw material that physically becomes part of the product and is clearly identified with specific products or batches of product. *(p. 610)*

Direct material costs Expenditures for direct material that are separately and readily traced through the production process to finished goods. *(p. 610)*

Direct method Presentation of net cash from operating activities for the statement of cash flows that lists major operating cash receipts less major operating cash payments. *(p. 506)*

Direct write-off method Method that records the loss from an uncollectible account receivable at the time it is determined to be uncollectible; no attempt is made to estimate bad debts. *(p. 295)*

Discount on bonds payable Difference between a bond's par value and its lower issue price or carrying value; occurs when the contract rate is less than the market rate. *(p. 415)*

Discount on note payable Difference between the face value of a note payable and the (lesser) amount borrowed; reflects the added interest to be paid on the note over its life.

Discount on stock Difference between the par value of stock and its issue price when issued at a price below par value. *(p. 461)*

Discount period Time period in which a cash discount is available and the buyer can make a reduced payment. *(p. 159)*

Discount rate Expected rate of return on investments; also called *cost of capital, hurdle rate,* or *required rate of return.* *(p. B-2)*

Discounts lost Expenses resulting from not taking advantage of cash discounts on purchases. *(p. 273)*

Dividend in arrears Unpaid dividend on cumulative preferred stock; must be paid before any regular dividends on preferred stock and before any dividends on common stock. *(p. 467)*

Dividends Corporation's distributions of assets to its owners. *(p. 14)*

Dividend yield Ratio of the annual amount of cash dividends distributed to common shareholders relative to the common stock's market value (price). *(p. 476)*

Double-declining-balance (DDB) depreciation Depreciation equals beginning book value multiplied by 2 times the straight-line rate.

Double taxation Corporate income is taxed and then its later distribution through dividends is normally taxed again for shareholders.

Double-entry accounting Accounting system in which each transaction affects at least two accounts and has at least one debit and one credit. *(p. 55)*

Earnings (See *net income.*)

Earnings per share (EPS) Amount of income earned by each share of a company's outstanding common stock; also called *net income per share.* *(p. 475)*

Effective interest method Allocates interest expense over the bond life to yield a constant rate of interest; interest expense for a period is found by multiplying the balance of the liability at the beginning of the period by the bond market rate at issuance; also called *interest method.* *(p. 433)*

Efficiency Company's productivity in using its assets; usually measured relative to how much revenue a certain level of assets generates. *(p. 555)*

Efficiency variance Difference between the actual quantity of an input and the standard quantity of that input. *(p. 900)*

Electronic funds transfer (EFT) Use of electronic communication to transfer cash from one party to another. *(p. 361)*

Employee benefits Additional compensation paid to or on behalf of employees, such as premiums for medical, dental, life, and disability insurance, and contributions to pension plans. *(p. 377)*

Employee earnings report Record of an employee's net pay, gross pay, deductions, and year-to-date payroll information. *(p. 388)*

Enterprise resource planning (ERP) software Programs that manage a company's vital operations, which range from order taking to production to accounting. *(p. E-17)*

Entity Organization that, for accounting purposes, is separate from other organizations and individuals.

EOM Abbreviation for *end of month;* used to describe credit terms for credit transactions. *(p. 159)*

Equity Owner's claim on the assets of a business; equals the residual interest in an entity's assets after deducting liabilities; also called *net assets.* *(p. 14)*

Equity method Accounting method used for long-term investments when the investor has "significant influence" over the investee. *(p. C-8)*

Equity ratio Portion of total assets provided by equity, computed as total equity divided by total assets. *(p. 569)*

Equity securities with controlling influence Long-term investment when the investor is able to exert controlling influence over the investee; investors owning 50% or more of voting stock are presumed to exert controlling influence. *(p. C-9)*

Equity securities with significant influence Long-term investment when the investor is able to exert significant influence over the investee;

investors owning 20 percent or more (but less than 50 percent) of voting stock are presumed to exert significant influence. *(p. C-8)*

Equivalent units of production (EUP) Number of units that would be completed if all effort during a period had been applied to units that were started and finished. *(p. 689)*

Estimated liability Obligation of an uncertain amount that can be reasonably estimated. *(p. 377)*

Estimated line of cost behavior Line drawn on a graph to visually fit the relation between cost and sales. *(p. 770)*

Ethics Codes of conduct by which actions are judged as right or wrong, fair or unfair, honest or dishonest. *(pp. 8 & 604)*

Events Happenings that both affect an organization's financial position and can be reliably measured. *(p. 15)*

Expanded accounting equation Assets = Liabilities + Equity; Equity equals [Owner capital − Owner withdrawals + Revenues − Expenses] for a noncorporation; Equity equals [Contributed capital + Retained earnings + Revenues − Expenses] for a corporation where dividends are subtracted from retained earnings. *(p. 14)*

Expense recognition (or **matching**) **principle** (See *matching principle*.) *(pp. 11 & 96)*

Expenses Outflows or using up of assets as part of operations of a business to generate sales. *(p. 14)*

External transactions Exchanges of economic value between one entity and another entity. *(p. 15)*

External users Persons using accounting information who are not directly involved in running the organization. *(p. 5)*

Extraordinary gains and losses Gains or losses reported separately from continuing operations because they are both unusual and infrequent. *(p. 578)*

Extraordinary repairs Major repairs that extend the useful life of a plant asset beyond prior expectations; treated as a capital expenditure. *(p. 337)*

Facility level activities Activities that relate to overall production and cannot be traced to specific products; costs associated with these activities pertain to a plant's general manufacturing process. *(p. 725)*

Factory overhead Factory activities supporting the production process that are not direct material or direct labor; also called *overhead and manufacturing overhead*. *(p. 610)*

Factory overhead costs Expenditures for factory overhead that cannot be separately or readily traced to finished goods; also called *overhead costs*. *(p. 610)*

Fair value option Reporting option that permits a company to use fair value in reporting certain assets and liabilities, which is presently based on a 3-level system to determine fair value. *(p. 425)*

Favorable variance Difference in actual revenues or expenses from the budgeted amount that contributes to a higher income. *(p. 881)*

Federal depository bank Bank authorized to accept deposits of amounts payable to the federal government. *(p. 385)*

Federal Insurance Contributions Act (FICA) taxes Taxes assessed on both employers and employees; for Social Security and Medicare programs. *(p. 374)*

Federal Unemployment Taxes (FUTA) Payroll taxes on employers assessed by the federal government to support its unemployment insurance program. *(p. 376)*

FIFO method (See *first-in, first-out*.) *(pp. 209 & 701)*

Financial accounting Area of accounting aimed mainly at serving external users. *(p. 5)*

Financial Accounting Standards Board (FASB) Independent group of full-time members responsible for setting accounting rules. *(p. 9)*

Financial leverage Earning a higher return on equity by paying dividends on preferred stock or interest on debt at a rate lower than the return earned with the assets from issuing preferred stock or debt; also called *trading on the equity*. *(p. 469)*

Financial reporting Process of communicating information relevant to investors, creditors, and others in making investment, credit, and business decisions. *(p. 555)*

Financial statement analysis Application of analytical tools to general-purpose financial statements and related data for making business decisions. *(p. 554)*

Financial statements Includes the balance sheet, income statement, statement of owner's (or stockholders') equity, and statement of cash flows.

Financing activities Transactions with owners and creditors that include obtaining cash from issuing debt, repaying amounts borrowed, and obtaining cash from or distributing cash to owners. *(p. 502)*

Finished goods inventory Account that controls the finished goods files, which acts as a subsidiary ledger (of the Inventory account) in which the costs of finished goods that are ready for sale are recorded. *(pp. 609 & 779)*

First-in, first-out (FIFO) Method to assign cost to inventory that assumes items are sold in the order acquired; earliest items purchased are the first sold. *(p. 209)*

Fiscal year Consecutive 12-month (or 52-week) period chosen as the organization's annual accounting period. *(p. 95)*

Fixed budget Planning budget based on a single predicted amount of volume; unsuitable for evaluations if the actual volume differs from predicted volume. *(p. 881)*

Fixed budget performance report Report that compares actual revenues and costs with fixed budgeted amounts and identifies the differences as favorable or unfavorable variances. *(p. 881)*

Fixed cost Cost that does not change with changes in the volume of activity. *(p. 604)*

Fixed overhead cost deferred in inventory The portion of the fixed manufacturing overhead cost of a period that goes into inventory under the absorption costing method as a result of production exceeding sales. *(p. 801)*

Fixed overhead cost recognized from inventory The portion of the fixed manufacturing overhead cost of a prior period that becomes an expense of the current period under the absorption costing method as a result of sales exceeding production. *(p. 801)*

Flexibility principle Information system principle that prescribes an accounting system be able to adapt to changes in the company, its operations, and needs of decision makers. *(p. E-3)*

Flexible budget Budget prepared (using actual volume) once a period is complete that helps managers evaluate past performance; uses fixed and variable costs in determining total costs. *(p. 882)*

Flexible budget performance report Report that compares actual revenues and costs with their variable budgeted amounts based on actual sales volume (or other level of activity) and identifies the differences as variances. *(p. 884)*

FOB Abbreviation for *free on board;* the point when ownership of goods passes to the buyer; *FOB shipping point* (or *factory*) means the buyer pays shipping costs and accepts ownership of goods when the seller transfers goods to carrier; *FOB destination* means the seller pays shipping costs and buyer accepts ownership of goods at the buyer's place of business. *(p. 161)*

Foreign exchange rate Price of one currency stated in terms of another currency. *(p. C-16)*

Form 940 IRS form used to report an employer's federal unemployment taxes (FUTA) on an annual filing basis. *(p. 385)*

Form 941 IRS form filed to report FICA taxes owed and remitted. *(p. 385)*

Form 10-K (or 10-KSB) Annual report form filed with SEC by businesses (small businesses) with publicly traded securities. *(p. A-1)*

Form W-2 Annual report by an employer to each employee showing the employee's wages subject to FICA and federal income taxes along with amounts withheld. *(p. 387)*

Form W-4 Withholding allowance certificate, filed with the employer, identifying the number of withholding allowances claimed. *(p. 390)*

Franchises Privileges granted by a company or government to sell a product or service under specified conditions. *(p. 342)*

Full disclosure principle Principle that prescribes financial statements (including notes) to report all relevant information about an entity's operations and financial condition. *(p. 11)*

GAAP (See *generally accepted accounting principles.*)

General accounting system Accounting system for manufacturing activities based on the *periodic* inventory system. *(p. 776)*

General and administrative expenses Expenses that support the operating activities of a business. *(p. 169)*

General and administrative expense budget Plan that shows predicted operating expenses not included in the selling expenses budget. *(p. 845)*

General journal All-purpose journal for recording the debits and credits of transactions and events. *(pp. E-6)*

General ledger (See *ledger.*) *(p. 51)*

General partner Partner who assumes unlimited liability for the debts of the partnership; responsible for partnership management. *(p. D-3)*

General partnership Partnership in which all partners have mutual agency and unlimited liability for partnership debts. *(p. D-3)*

Generally accepted accounting principles (GAAP) Rules that specify acceptable accounting practices. *(p. 8)*

Generally accepted auditing standards (GAAS) Rules that specify auditing practices.

General-purpose financial statements Statements published periodically for use by a variety of interested parties; includes the income statement, balance sheet, statement of owner's equity (or statement of retained earnings for a corporation), statement of cash flows, and notes to these statements. *(p. 555)*

Going-concern assumption Principle that prescribes financial statements to reflect the assumption that the business will continue operating. *(p. 11)*

Goods in process inventory Account in which costs are accumulated for products that are in the process of being produced but are not yet complete; also called *work in process inventory.* *(pp. 609 & 778)*

Goodwill Amount by which a company's (or a segment's) value exceeds the value of its individual assets less its liabilities. *(p. 343)*

Gross margin (See *gross profit.*) *(p. 157)*

Gross margin ratio Gross margin (net sales minus cost of goods sold) divided by net sales; also called *gross profit ratio.* *(p. 172)*

Gross method Method of recording purchases at the full invoice price without deducting any cash discounts. *(p. 273)*

Gross pay Total compensation earned by an employee. *(p. 374)*

Gross profit Net sales minus cost of goods sold; also called *gross margin.* *(p. 156)*

Gross profit method Procedure to estimate inventory when the past gross profit rate is used to estimate cost of goods sold, which is then subtracted from the cost of goods available for sale. *(p. 228)*

Held-to-maturity (HTM) securities Debt securities that a company has the intent and ability to hold until they mature. *(p. C-6)*

High-low method Procedure that yields an estimated line of cost behavior by graphically connecting costs associated with the highest and lowest sales volume. *(p. 770)*

Horizontal analysis Comparison of a company's financial condition and performance across time. *(p. 556)*

Hurdle rate Minimum acceptable rate of return (set by management) for an investment. *(pp. 935 & 1007)*

Impairment Diminishment of an asset value. *(pp. 336 & 342)*

Imprest system Method to account for petty cash; maintains a constant balance in the fund, which equals cash plus petty cash receipts.

Inadequacy Condition in which the capacity of plant assets is too small to meet the company's production demands. *(p. 329)*

Income (See *net income.*)

Income statement Financial statement that subtracts expenses from revenues to yield a net income or loss over a specified period of time; also includes any gains or losses. *(p. 19)*

Income Summary Temporary account used only in the closing process to which the balances of revenue and expense accounts (including any gains or losses) are transferred; its balance is transferred to the capital account (or retained earnings for a corporation). *(p. 809)*

Incremental cost Additional cost incurred only if a company pursues a specific course of action. *(p. 970)*

Indefinite life Asset life that is not limited by legal, regulatory, contractual, competitive, economic, or other factors. *(p. 341)*

Indirect costs Costs incurred for the benefit of more than one cost object. *(p. 605)*

Indirect expenses Expenses incurred for the joint benefit of more than one department (or cost object). *(p. 927)*

Indirect labor Efforts of production employees who do not work specifically on converting direct materials into finished products and who are not clearly identified with specific units or batches of product. *(p. 610)*

Indirect labor costs Labor costs that cannot be physically traced to production of a product or service; included as part of overhead. *(p. 610)*

Indirect material Material used to support the production process but not clearly identified with products or batches of product. *(p. 608)*

Indirect method Presentation that reports net income and then adjusts it by adding and subtracting items to yield net cash from operating activities on the statement of cash flows. *(p. 506)*

Information processor Component of an accounting system that interprets, transforms, and summarizes information for use in analysis and reporting. *(p. E-4)*

Information storage Component of an accounting system that keeps data in a form accessible to information processors. *(p. E-4)*

Infrequent gain or loss Gain or loss not expected to recur given the operating environment of the business. *(p. 578)*

Input device Means of capturing information from source documents that enables its transfer to information processors. *(p. E-4)*

Installment note Liability requiring a series of periodic payments to the lender. *(p. 422)*

Institute of Management Accountants (IMA) A professional association of management accountants. *(p. 604)*

Intangible assets Long-term assets (resources) used to produce or sell products or services; usually lack physical form and have uncertain benefits. *(pp. 115 & 341)*

Interest Charge for using money (or other assets) loaned from one entity to another. *(p. 302)*

Interim financial statements Financial statements covering periods of less than one year; usually based on one-, three-, or six-month periods. *(pp. 94 & 227)*

Internal controls or **Internal control system** All policies and procedures used to protect assets, ensure reliable accounting, promote efficient operations, and urge adherence to company policies. *(pp. 248, 604 & E-2)*

Internal rate of return (IRR) Rate used to evaluate the acceptability of an investment; equals the rate that yields a net present value of zero for an investment. *(p. 1005)*

Internal transactions Activities within an organization that can affect the accounting equation. *(p. 15)*

Internal users Persons using accounting information who are directly involved in managing the organization. *(p. 6)*

International Accounting Standards Board (IASB) Group that identifies preferred accounting practices and encourages global acceptance; issues International Financial Reporting Standards (IFRS). *(p. 9)*

International Financial Reporting Standards (IFRS) International Financial Reporting Standards (IFRS) are required or allowed by over 100 countries; IFRS is set by the International Accounting Standards Board (IASB), which aims to develop a single set of global standards, to promote those standards, and to converge national and international standards globally. *(p. 9)*

Inventory Goods a company owns and expects to sell in its normal operations. *(p. 157)*

Inventory turnover Number of times a company's average inventory is sold during a period; computed by dividing cost of goods sold by average inventory; also called *merchandise turnover*. *(p. 217)*

Investing activities Transactions that involve purchasing and selling of long-term assets, includes making and collecting notes receivable and investments in other than cash equivalents. *(p. 502)*

Investment center Center of which a manager is responsible for revenues, costs, and asset investments. *(p. 927)*

Investment center residual income The net income an investment center earns above a target return on average invested assets. *(p. 935)*

Investment center return on total assets Center net income divided by average total assets for the center. *(p. 935)*

Investment turnover The efficiency with which a company generates sales from its available assets; computed as sales divided by average invested assets. *(p. 940)*

Invoice Itemized record of goods prepared by the vendor that lists the customer's name, items sold, sales prices, and terms of sale. *(p. 271)*

Invoice approval Document containing a checklist of steps necessary for approving the recording and payment of an invoice; also called *check authorization*. *(p. 271)*

Job Production of a customized product or service. *(p. 776)*

Job cost sheet Separate record maintained for each job. *(p. 778)*

Job lot Production of more than one unit of a customized product or service. *(p. 777)*

Job order cost accounting system Cost accounting system to determine the cost of producing each job or job lot. *(pp. 685 & 817)*

Job order production Production of special-order products; also called *customized production*. *(p. 776)*

Joint cost Cost incurred to produce or purchase two or more products at the same time. *(p. 945)*

Journal Record in which transactions are entered before they are posted to ledger accounts; also called *book of original entry*. *(p. 56)*

Journalizing Process of recording transactions in a journal. *(p. 56)*

Just-in-time (JIT) manufacturing Process of acquiring or producing inventory only when needed. *(p. 616)*

Known liabilities Obligations of a company with little uncertainty; set by agreements, contracts, or laws; also called *definitely determinable liabilities*. *(p. 370)*

Land improvements Assets that increase the benefits of land, have a limited useful life, and are depreciated. *(p. 328)*

Large stock dividend Stock dividend that is more than 25% of the previously outstanding shares. *(p. 464)*

Last-in, first-out (LIFO) Method to assign cost to inventory that assumes costs for the most recent items purchased are sold first and charged to cost of goods sold. *(p. 209)*

Lean accounting System designed to eliminate waste in the accounting process and better reflect the benefits of lean manufacturing techniques.

Lean business model Practice of eliminating waste while meeting customer needs and yielding positive company returns. *(p. 615)*

Lease Contract specifying the rental of property. *(pp. 343 & 436)*

Leasehold Rights the lessor grants to the lessee under the terms of a lease. *(p. 343)*

Leasehold improvements Alterations or improvements to leased property such as partitions and storefronts. *(p. 343)*

Least-squares regression Statistical method for deriving an estimated line of cost behavior that is more precise than the high-low method and the scatter diagram. *(p. 776)*

Ledger Record containing all accounts (with amounts) for a business; also called *general ledger*. *(p. 51)*

Lessee Party to a lease who secures the right to possess and use the property from another party (the lessor). *(p. 343)*

Lessor Party to a lease who grants another party (the lessee) the right to possess and use its property. *(p. 343)*

Liabilities Creditors' claims on an organization's assets; involves a probable future payment of assets, products, or services that a company is obligated to make due to past transactions or events. *(p. 14)*

Licenses (See *franchises.*) *(p. 342)*

Limited liability Owner can lose no more than the amount invested. *(p. 11)*

Limited liability company Organization form that combines select features of a corporation and a limited partnership; provides limited liability to its members (owners), is free of business tax, and allows members to actively participate in management. *(p. D-4)*

Limited liability partnership Partnership in which a partner is not personally liable for malpractice or negligence unless that partner is responsible for providing the service that resulted in the claim. *(p. D-3)*

Limited life (See *useful life.*)

Limited partners Partners who have no personal liability for partnership debts beyond the amounts they invested in the partnership. *(p. D-3)*

Limited partnership Partnership that has two classes of partners, limited partners and general partners. *(p. D-3)*

Liquid assets Resources such as cash that are easily converted into other assets or used to pay for goods, services, or liabilities. *(p. 253)*

Liquidating cash dividend Distribution of assets that returns part of the original investment to stockholders; deducted from contributed capital accounts. *(p. 464)*

Liquidation Process of going out of business; involves selling assets, paying liabilities, and distributing remainder to owners.

Liquidity Availability of resources to meet short-term cash requirements. *(pp. 253 & 555)*

List price Catalog (full) price of an item before any trade discount is deducted. *(p. 158)*

Long-term investments Long-term assets not used in operating activities such as notes receivable and investments in stocks and bonds. *(pp. 115 & C-2)*

Long-term liabilities Obligations not due to be paid within one year or the operating cycle, whichever is longer. *(pp. 115 & 369)*

Lower of cost or market (LCM) Required method to report inventory at market replacement cost when that market cost is lower than recorded cost. *(p. 213)*

Maker of the note Entity who signs a note and promises to pay it at maturity. *(p. 302)*

Management by exception Management process to focus on significant variances and give less attention to areas where performance is close to the standard. *(p. 885)*

Managerial accounting Area of accounting aimed mainly at serving the decision-making needs of internal users; also called *management accounting*. *(pp. 6 & 600)*

Manufacturer Company that uses labor and operating assets to convert raw materials to finished goods.

Manufacturing budget Plan that shows the predicted costs for direct materials, direct labor, and overhead to be incurred in manufacturing units in the production budget. *(p. 856)*

Manufacturing statement Report that summarizes the types and amounts of costs incurred in a company's production process for a period; also called *cost of goods manufacturing statement*. *(p. 613)*

Margin of safety Excess of expected sales over the level of break-even sales. *(p. 778)*

Market-based transfer price The market price of a good or service being transferred between divisions within a company; typically used when the transferring division does not have excess capacity. *(p. 945)*

Market prospects Expectations (both good and bad) about a company's future performance as assessed by users and other interested parties. *(p. 555)*

Market rate Interest rate that borrowers are willing to pay and lenders are willing to accept for a specific lending agreement given the borrowers' risk level. *(p. 415)*

Market value per share Price at which stock is bought or sold. *(p. 459)*

Master budget Comprehensive business plan that includes specific plans for expected sales, product units to be produced, merchandise (or materials) to be purchased, expenses to be incurred, plant assets to be purchased, and amounts of cash to be borrowed or loans to be repaid, as well as a budgeted income statement and balance sheet. *(p. 840)*

Matching (or expense recognition) principle Prescribes expenses to be reported in the same period as the revenues that were earned as a result of the expenses. *(pp. 11 & 296)*

Materiality constraint Prescribes that accounting for items that significantly impact financial statement and any inferences from them adhere strictly to GAAP. *(pp. 12 & 296)*

Materials consumption report Document that summarizes the materials a department uses during a reporting period; replaces materials requisitions. *(p. 686)*

Materials ledger card Perpetual record updated each time units are purchased or issued for production use. *(p. 780)*

Materials requisition Source document production managers use to request materials for production; used to assign materials costs to specific jobs or overhead. *(p. 781)*

Maturity date of a note Date when a note's principal and interest are due. *(p. 302)*

Measurement principle Accounting information is based on cost with potential subsequent adjustments to fair value; see also *cost principle*. *(p. 10)*

Merchandise (See *merchandise inventory.*) *(p. 156)*

Merchandise inventory Goods that a company owns and expects to sell to customers; also called *merchandise* or *inventory*. *(p. 157)*

Merchandise purchases budget Plan that shows the units or costs of merchandise to be purchased by a merchandising company during the budget period. *(p. 843)*

Merchandiser Entity that earns net income by buying and selling merchandise. *(p. 156)*

Merit rating Rating assigned to an employer by a state based on the employer's record of employment. *(p. 376)*

Minimum legal capital Amount of assets defined by law that stockholders must (potentially) invest in a corporation; usually defined as par value of the stock; intended to protect creditors. *(p. 459)*

Mixed cost Cost that behaves like a combination of fixed and variable costs. *(p. 767)*

Modified Accelerated Cost Recovery System (MACRS) Depreciation system required by federal income tax law. *(p. 334)*

Monetary unit assumption Principle that assumes transactions and events can be expressed in money units. *(p. 11)*

Mortgage Legal loan agreement that protects a lender by giving the lender the right to be paid from the cash proceeds from the sale of a borrower's assets identified in the mortgage. *(p. 424)*

Multinational Company that operates in several countries. *(p. C-16)*

Multiple-step income statement Income statement format that shows subtotals between sales and net income, categorizes expenses, and often reports the details of net sales and expenses. *(p. 169)*

Mutual agency Legal relationship among partners whereby each partner is an agent of the partnership and is able to bind the partnership to contracts within the scope of the partnership's business. *(p. D-2)*

Natural business year Twelve-month period that ends when a company's sales activities are at their lowest point. *(p. 95)*

Natural resources Assets physically consumed when used; examples are timber, mineral deposits, and oil and gas fields; also called *wasting assets*. *(p. 340)*

Negotiated transfer price A price, determined by negotiation between division managers, to record transfers between divisions; typically lies between the variable cost and the market price of the item transferred. *(p. 945)*

Net assets (See *equity*.)

Net income Amount earned after subtracting all expenses necessary for and matched with sales for a period; also called *income, profit,* or *earnings*. *(p. 14)*

Net loss Excess of expenses over revenues for a period. *(p. 14)*

Net method Method of recording purchases at the full invoice price less any cash discounts. *(p. 273)*

Net pay Gross pay less all deductions; also called *take-home pay*. *(p. 374)*

Net present value (NPV) Dollar estimate of an asset's value that is used to evaluate the acceptability of an investment; computed by discounting future cash flows from the investment at a satisfactory rate and then subtracting the initial cost of the investment. *(p. 1003)*

Net realizable value Expected selling price (value) of an item minus the cost of making the sale. *(p. 204)*

Noncumulative preferred stock Preferred stock on which the right to receive dividends is lost for any period when dividends are not declared. *(p. 467)*

Noninterest-bearing note Note with no stated (contract) rate of interest; interest is implicitly included in the note's face value.

Nonparticipating preferred stock Preferred stock on which dividends are limited to a maximum amount each year. *(p. 468)*

Nonsufficient funds (NSF) check Maker's bank account has insufficient money to pay the check; also called *hot check*.

Non-value-added time The portion of cycle time that is not directed at producing a product or service; equals the sum of inspection time, move time, and wait time. *(p. 618)*

No-par value stock Stock class that has not been assigned a par (or stated) value by the corporate charter. *(p. 459)*

Not controllable costs Costs that a manager does not have the power to control or strongly influence. *(p. 605)*

Note (See *promissory note*.)

Note payable Liability expressed by a written promise to pay a definite sum of money on demand or on a specific future date(s).

Note receivable Asset consisting of a written promise to receive a definite sum of money on demand or on a specific future date(s).

Objectivity principle Principle that prescribes independent, unbiased evidence to support financial statement information. *(p. 9)*

Obsolescence Condition in which, because of new inventions and improvements, a plant asset can no longer be used to produce goods or services with a competitive advantage. *(p. 329)*

Off-balance-sheet financing Acquisition of assets by agreeing to liabilities not reported on the balance sheet. *(p. 437)*

Online processing Approach to inputting data from source documents as soon as the information is available. *(p. E-16)*

Operating activities Activities that involve the production or purchase of merchandise and the sale of goods or services to customers, including expenditures related to administering the business. *(p. 501)*

Operating cycle Normal time between paying cash for merchandise or employee services and receiving cash from customers. *(p. 113)*

Operating leases Short-term (or cancelable) leases in which the lessor retains risks and rewards of ownership. *(p. 436)*

Operating leverage Extent, or relative size, of fixed costs in the total cost structure. *(p. 782)*

Opportunity cost Potential benefit lost by choosing a specific action from two or more alternatives. *(p. 606)*

Ordinary repairs Repairs to keep a plant asset in normal, good operating condition; treated as a revenue expenditure and immediately expensed. *(p. 336)*

Organization expenses (costs) Costs such as legal fees and promoter fees to bring an entity into existence. *(pp. 457 & 462)*

Other comprehensive income Equals net income less comprehensive income; includes unrealized gains and losses on available-for-sale securities, foreign currency adjustments, and pension adjustments. *(p. C-10)*

Out-of-pocket cost Cost incurred or avoided as a result of management's decisions. *(p. 606)*

Output devices Means by which information is taken out of the accounting system and made available for use. *(p. E-5)*

Outsourcing Manager decision to buy a product or service from another part of a *make-or-buy* decision; also called *make or buy.*

Outstanding checks Checks written and recorded by the depositor but not yet paid by the bank at the bank statement date. *(p. 263)*

Outstanding stock Corporation's stock held by its shareholders.

Overapplied overhead Amount by which the overhead applied to production in a period using the predetermined overhead rate exceeds the actual overhead incurred in a period. *(p. 787)*

Overhead cost variance Difference between the total overhead cost applied to products and the total overhead cost actually incurred. *(p. 892)*

Owner, Capital Account showing the owner's claim on company assets; equals owner investments plus net income (or less net losses) minus owner withdrawals since the company's inception; also referred to as *equity. (p. 14)*

Owner investment Assets put into the business by the owner. *(p. 14)*

Owner's equity (See *equity.*)

Owner, withdrawals Account used to record asset distributions to the owner. (See also *withdrawals.*) *(p. 14)*

Paid-in capital (See *contributed capital.*) *(p. 460)*

Paid-in capital in excess of par value Amount received from issuance of stock that is in excess of the stock's par value. *(p. 461)*

Par value Value assigned a share of stock by the corporate charter when the stock is authorized. *(p. 459)*

Par value of a bond Amount the bond issuer agrees to pay at maturity and the amount on which cash interest payments are based; also called *face amount* or *face value* of a bond. *(p. 412)*

Par value stock Class of stock assigned a par value by the corporate charter. *(p. 459)*

Parent Company that owns a controlling interest in a corporation (requires more than 50% of voting stock). *(p. C-9)*

Participating preferred stock Preferred stock that shares with common stockholders any dividends paid in excess of the percent stated on preferred stock. *(p. 468)*

Partner return on equity Partner net income divided by average partner equity for the period. *(p. D-14)*

Partnership Unincorporated association of two or more persons to pursue a business for profit as co-owners. *(pp. 11 & D-2)*

Partnership contract Agreement among partners that sets terms under which the affairs of the partnership are conducted; also called *articles of partnership. (p. D-2)*

Partnership liquidation Dissolution of a partnership by (1) selling noncash assets and allocating any gain or loss according to partners' income-and-loss ratio, (2) paying liabilities, and (3) distributing any remaining cash according to partners' capital balances. *(p. D-11)*

Patent Exclusive right granted to its owner to produce and sell an item or to use a process for 20 years. *(p. 342)*

Payback period (PBP) Time-based measurement used to evaluate the acceptability of an investment; equals the time expected to pass before an investment's net cash flows equal its initial cost. *(p. 999)*

Payee of the note Entity to whom a note is made payable. *(p. 302)*

Payroll bank account Bank account used solely for paying employees; each pay period an amount equal to the total employees' net pay is deposited in it and the payroll checks are drawn on it. *(p. 390)*

Payroll deductions Amounts withheld from an employee's gross pay; also called *withholdings. (p. 374)*

Payroll register Record for a pay period that shows the pay period dates, regular and overtime hours worked, gross pay, net pay, and deductions. *(p. 387)*

Pension plan Contractual agreement between an employer and its employees for the employer to provide benefits to employees after they retire; expensed when incurred. *(p. 438)*

Period costs Expenditures identified more with a time period than with finished products costs; includes selling and general administrative expenses. *(p. 606)*

Periodic inventory system Method that records the cost of inventory purchased but does not continuously track the quantity available or sold to customers; records are updated at the end of each period to reflect the physical count and costs of goods available. *(p. 158)*

Permanent accounts Accounts that reflect activities related to one or more future periods; balance sheet accounts whose balances are not closed; also called *real accounts. (p. 108)*

Perpetual inventory system Method that maintains continuous records of the cost of inventory available and the cost of goods sold. *(p. 158)*

Petty cash Small amount of cash in a fund to pay minor expenses; accounted for using an imprest system. *(p. 258)*

Planning Process of setting goals and preparing to achieve them. *(p. 600)*

Plant asset age Estimate of the age of a company's plant assets, computed by dividing accumulated depreciation by depreciation expense. *(p. 345)*

Plant assets Tangible long-lived assets used to produce or sell products and services; also called *property, plant and equipment (PP&E)* or *fixed assets. (pp. 99 & 326)*

Pledged assets to secured liabilities Ratio of the book value of a company's pledged assets to the book value of its secured liabilities.

Post-closing trial balance List of permanent accounts and their balances from the ledger after all closing entries are journalized and posted. *(p. 110)*

Posting Process of transferring journal entry information to the ledger; computerized systems automate this process. *(p. 56)*

Posting reference (PR) column A column in journals in which individual ledger account numbers are entered when entries are posted to those ledger accounts. *(p. 58)*

Predetermined overhead rate Rate established prior to the beginning of a period that relates estimated overhead to another variable, such as estimated direct labor, and is used to assign overhead cost to production. *(p. 784)*

Preemptive right Stockholders' right to maintain their proportionate interest in a corporation with any additional shares issued. *(p. 458)*

Preferred stock Stock with a priority status over common stockholders in one or more ways, such as paying dividends or distributing assets. *(p. 466)*

Premium on bonds Difference between a bond's par value and its higher carrying value; occurs when the contract rate is higher than the market rate; also called *bond premium*. (p. 418)

Premium on stock (See *contributed capital in excess of par value*.) (p. 461)

Prepaid expenses Items paid for in advance of receiving their benefits; classified as assets. (p. 97)

Price-earnings (PE) ratio Ratio of a company's current market value per share to its earnings per share; also called *price-to-earnings*. (p. 475)

Price variance Difference between actual and budgeted revenue or cost caused by the difference between the actual price per unit and the budgeted price per unit. (p. 885)

Prime costs Expenditures directly identified with the production of finished goods; include direct materials costs and direct labor costs. (p. 611)

Principal of a note Amount that the signer of a note agrees to pay back when it matures, not including interest. (p. 302)

Principles of internal control Principles prescribing management to establish responsibility, maintain records, insure assets, separate record-keeping from custody of assets, divide responsibility for related transactions, apply technological controls, and perform reviews. (p. 249)

Prior period adjustment Correction of an error in a prior year that is reported in the statement of retained earnings (or statement of stockholders' equity) net of any income tax effects. (p. 473)

Pro forma financial statements Statements that show the effects of proposed transactions and events as if they had occurred. (p. 124)

Process cost accounting system System of assigning direct materials, direct labor, and overhead to specific processes; total costs associated with each process are then divided by the number of units passing through that process to determine the cost per equivalent unit. (p. 685)

Process cost summary Report of costs charged to a department, its equivalent units of production achieved, and the costs assigned to its output. (p. 694)

Process operations Processing of products in a continuous (sequential) flow of steps; also called *process manufacturing* or *process production*. (p. 682)

Product costs Costs that are capitalized as inventory because they produce benefits expected to have future value; include direct materials, direct labor, and overhead. (p. 606)

Product level activities Activities that relate to specific products that must be carried out regardless of how many units are produced and sold or batches run. (p. 725)

Production budget Plan that shows the units to be produced each period. (p. 856)

Profit (See *net income*.)

Profit center Business unit that incurs costs and generates revenues. (p. 927)

Profit margin Ratio of a company's net income to its net sales; the percent of income in each dollar of revenue; also called *net profit margin*. (pp. 117 & 940)

Profitability Company's ability to generate an adequate return on invested capital. (p. 555)

Profitability index A measure of the relation between the expected benefits of a project and its investment, computed as the present value of expected future cash flows from the investment divided by the cost of the investment; a higher value indicates a more desirable investment, and a value below 1 indicates an unacceptable project. (p. 1005)

Promissory note (or **note**) Written promise to pay a specified amount either on demand or at a definite future date; is a *note receivable* for the lender but a *note payable* for the lendee. (p. 302)

Proprietorship (See *sole proprietorship*.) (p. 11)

Proxy Legal document giving a stockholder's agent the power to exercise the stockholder's voting rights. (p. 457)

Purchase discount Term used by a purchaser to describe a cash discount granted to the purchaser for paying within the discount period. (p. 159)

Purchase order Document used by the purchasing department to place an order with a seller (vendor). (p. 270)

Purchase requisition Document listing merchandise needed by a department and requesting it be purchased. (p. 270)

Purchases journal Journal normally used to record all purchases on credit. (p. E-13)

Quantity variance Difference between actual and budgeted revenue or cost caused by the difference between the actual number of units and the budgeted number of units. (p. 885)

Ratio analysis Determination of key relations between financial statement items as reflected in numerical measures. (p. 556)

Raw materials inventory Goods a company acquires to use in making products. (p. 608)

Realizable value Expected proceeds from converting an asset into cash. (p. 297)

Receiving report Form used to report that ordered goods are received and to describe their quantity and condition. (p. 271)

Recordkeeping Part of accounting that involves recording transactions and events, either manually or electronically; also called *bookkeeping*. (p. 4)

Registered bonds Bonds owned by investors whose names and addresses are recorded by the issuer; interest payments are made to the registered owners. (p. 426)

Relevance principle Information system principle prescribing that its reports be useful, understandable, timely, and pertinent for decision making. (p. E-2)

Relevant benefits Additional or incremental revenue generated by selecting a particular course of action over another. (p. 969)

Relevant range of operations Company's normal operating range; excludes extremely high and low volumes not likely to occur. (p. 775)

Report form balance sheet Balance sheet that lists accounts vertically in the order of assets, liabilities, and equity.

Responsibility accounting budget Report of expected costs and expenses under a manager's control. (p. 938)

Responsibility accounting performance report Responsibility report that compares actual costs and expenses for a department with budgeted amounts. (p. 938)

Responsibility accounting system System that provides information that management can use to evaluate the performance of a department's manager. *(p. 926)*

Restricted retained earnings Retained earnings not available for dividends because of legal or contractual limitations. *(p. 472)*

Retail inventory method Method to estimate ending inventory based on the ratio of the amount of goods for sale at cost to the amount of goods for sale at retail. *(p. 227)*

Retailer Intermediary that buys products from manufacturers or wholesalers and sells them to consumers. *(p. 156)*

Retained earnings Cumulative income less cumulative losses and dividends. *(pp. 14 & 460)*

Retained earnings deficit Debit (abnormal) balance in Retained Earnings; occurs when cumulative losses and dividends exceed cumulative income; also called *accumulated deficit*. *(p. 463)*

Return Monies received from an investment; often in percent form. *(p. 26)*

Return on assets (See *return on total assets*) *(p. 22)*

Return on equity Ratio of net income to average equity for the period.

Return on total assets Ratio reflecting operating efficiency; defined as net income divided by average total assets for the period; also called *return on assets* or *return on investment*. *(p. C-11)*

Revenue expenditures Expenditures reported on the current income statement as an expense because they do not provide benefits in future periods. *(p. 336)*

Revenue recognition principle The principle prescribing that revenue is recognized when earned. *(p. 10)*

Revenues Gross increase in equity from a company's business activities that earn income; also called *sales*. *(p. 14)*

Reverse stock split Occurs when a corporation calls in its stock and replaces each share with less than one new share; increases both market value per share and any par or stated value per share. *(p. 466)*

Reversing entries Optional entries recorded at the beginning of a period that prepare the accounts for the usual journal entries as if adjusting entries had not occurred in the prior period. *(p. 125)*

Risk Uncertainty about an expected return. *(p. 26)*

Rolling budget New set of budgets a firm adds for the next period (with revisions) to replace the ones that have lapsed. *(p. 839)*

S corporation Corporation that meets special tax qualifications so as to be treated like a partnership for income tax purposes. *(p. D-4)*

Safety stock Quantity of inventory or materials over the minimum needed to satisfy budgeted demand. *(p. 843)*

Sales (See *revenues*.)

Sales budget Plan showing the units of goods to be sold or services to be provided; the starting point in the budgeting process for most departments. *(p. 842)*

Sales discount Term used by a seller to describe a cash discount granted to buyers who pay within the discount period. *(p. 159)*

Sales journal Journal normally used to record sales of goods on credit. *(p. E-8)*

Sales mix Ratio of sales volumes for the various products sold by a company. *(p. 779)*

Salvage value Estimate of amount to be recovered at the end of an asset's useful life; also called *residual value* or *scrap value*. *(p. 329)*

Sarbanes-Oxley Act (SOX) Created the *Public Company Accounting Oversight Board,* regulates analyst conflicts, imposes corporate governance requirements, enhances accounting and control disclosures, impacts insider transactions and executive loans, establishes new types of criminal conduct, and expands penalties for violations of federal securities laws. *(pp. 12 & 248)*

Scatter diagram Graph used to display data about past cost behavior and sales as points on a diagram. *(p. 769)*

Schedule of accounts payable List of the balances of all accounts in the accounts payable ledger and their totals. *(p. E-14)*

Schedule of accounts receivable List of the balances of all accounts in the accounts receivable ledger and their totals. *(p. E-9)*

Section 404 (of SOX) Section 404 of SOX requires that company management document and assess the effectiveness of all internal control processes that can affect financial reporting; company auditors express an opinion on whether management's assessment of the effectiveness of internal controls is fairly stated. *(p. 249)*

Secured bonds Bonds that have specific assets of the issuer pledged as collateral. *(p. 426)*

Securities and Exchange Commission (SEC) Federal agency Congress has charged to set reporting rules for organizations that sell ownership shares to the public. *(p. 9)*

Segment return on assets Segment operating income divided by segment average (identifiable) assets for the period. *(p. E-18)*

Selling expense budget Plan that lists the types and amounts of selling expenses expected in the budget period. *(p. 844)*

Selling expenses Expenses of promoting sales, such as displaying and advertising merchandise, making sales, and delivering goods to customers. *(p. 169)*

Serial bonds Bonds consisting of separate amounts that mature at different dates. *(p. 426)*

Service company Organization that provides services instead of tangible products.

Shareholders Owners of a corporation; also called *stockholders*. *(p. 12)*

Shares Equity of a corporation divided into ownership units; also called *stock*. *(p. 12)*

Short-term investments Debt and equity securities that management expects to convert to cash within the next 3 to 12 months (or the operating cycle if longer); also called *temporary investments* or *marketable securities*. *(p. C-2)*

Short-term note payable Current obligation in the form of a written promissory note. *(p. 371)*

Shrinkage Inventory losses that occur as a result of theft or deterioration. *(p. 166)*

Signature card Includes the signatures of each person authorized to sign checks on the bank account. *(p. 260)*

Simple capital structure Capital structure that consists of only common stock and nonconvertible preferred stock; consists of no dilutive securities. *(p. 475)*

Single-step income statement Income statement format that includes cost of goods sold as an expense and shows only one subtotal for total expenses. *(p. 170)*

Sinking fund bonds Bonds that require the issuer to make deposits to a separate account; bondholders are repaid at maturity from that account. *(p. 426)*

Small stock dividend Stock dividend that is 25% or less of a corporation's previously outstanding shares. *(p. 464)*

Social responsibility Being accountable for the impact that one's actions might have on society. *(p. 8)*

Sole proprietorship Business owned by one person that is not organized as a corporation; also called *proprietorship*. *(p. 11)*

Solvency Company's long-run financial viability and its ability to cover long-term obligations. *(p. 555)*

Source documents Source of information for accounting entries that can be in either paper or electronic form; also called *business papers*. *(p. 50)*

Special journal Any journal used for recording and posting transactions of a similar type. *(p. E-6)*

Specific identification Method to assign cost to inventory when the purchase cost of each item in inventory is identified and used to compute cost of inventory. *(p. 207)*

Spending variance Difference between the actual price of an item and its standard price. *(p. 900)*

Spreadsheet Computer program that organizes data by means of formulas and format; also called *electronic work sheet*.

Standard costs Costs that should be incurred under normal conditions to produce a product or component or to perform a service. *(p. 885)*

State Unemployment Taxes (SUTA) State payroll taxes on employers to support its unemployment programs. *(p. 376)*

Stated value stock No-par stock assigned a stated value per share; this amount is recorded in the stock account when the stock is issued. *(p. 460)*

Statement of cash flows A financial statement that lists cash inflows (receipts) and cash outflows (payments) during a period; arranged by operating, investing, and financing. *(pp. 19 & 500)*

Statement of owner's equity Report of changes in equity over a period; adjusted for increases (owner investment and net income) and for decreases (withdrawals and net loss). *(p. 19)*

Statement of partners' equity Financial statement that shows total capital balances at the beginning of the period, any additional investment by partners, the income or loss of the period, the partners' withdrawals, and the partners' ending capital balances; also called *statement of partners' capital*. *(p. D-7)*

Statement of retained earnings Report of changes in retained earnings over a period; adjusted for increases (net income), for decreases (dividends and net loss), and for any prior period adjustment. *(p. 19)*

Statement of stockholders' equity Financial statement that lists the beginning and ending balances of each major equity account and describes all changes in those accounts. *(p. 473)*

Statements of Financial Accounting Standards (SFAS) FASB publications that establish U.S. GAAP.

Step-wise cost Cost that remains fixed over limited ranges of volumes but changes by a lump sum when volume changes occur outside these limited ranges. *(p. 768)*.

Stock (See *shares*.) *(p. 12)*

Stock dividend Corporation's distribution of its own stock to its stockholders without the receipt of any payment. *(p. 464)*

Stock options Rights to purchase common stock at a fixed price over a specified period of time. *(p. 473)*

Stock split Occurs when a corporation calls in its stock and replaces each share with more than one new share; decreases both the market value per share and any par or stated value per share. *(p. 466)*

Stock subscription Investor's contractual commitment to purchase unissued shares at future dates and prices.

Stockholders (See *shareholders*.) *(p. 12)*

Stockholders' equity A corporation's equity; also called *shareholders' equity* or *corporate capital*. *(p. 460)*

Straight-line depreciation Method that allocates an equal portion of the depreciable cost of plant asset (cost minus salvage) to each accounting period in its useful life. *(pp. 99 & 330)*

Straight-line bond amortization Method allocating an equal amount of bond interest expense to each period of the bond life. *(p. 416)*

Subsidiary Entity controlled by another entity (parent) in which the parent owns more than 50% of the subsidiary's voting stock. *(p. C-9)*

Subsidiary ledger List of individual subaccounts and amounts with a common characteristic; linked to a controlling account in the general ledger. *(p. E-6)*

Sunk cost Cost already incurred and cannot be avoided or changed. *(p. 606)*

Supplementary records Information outside the usual accounting records; also called *supplemental records*. *(p. 162)*

Supply chain Linkages of services or goods extending from suppliers, to the company itself, and on to customers.

T-account Tool used to show the effects of transactions and events on individual accounts. *(p. 55)*

Target cost Maximum allowable cost for a product or service; defined as expected selling price less the desired profit. *(p. 777)*

Temporary accounts Accounts used to record revenues, expenses, and withdrawals (dividends for a corporation); they are closed at the end of each period; also called *nominal accounts*. *(p. 108)*

Term bonds Bonds scheduled for payment (maturity) at a single specified date. *(p. 426)*

Throughput time (See *cycle time*.)

Time period assumption Assumption that an organization's activities can be divided into specific time periods such as months, quarters, or years. *(pp. 11 & 94)*

Time ticket Source document used to report the time an employee spent working on a job or on overhead activities and then to determine the amount of direct labor to charge to the job or the amount of indirect labor to charge to overhead. *(p. 782)*

Times interest earned Ratio of income before interest expense (and any income taxes) divided by interest expense; reflects risk of covering interest commitments when income varies. *(p. 382)*

Total asset turnover Measure of a company's ability to use its assets to generate sales; computed by dividing net sales by average total assets. *(p. 345)*

Total quality management (TQM) Concept calling for all managers and employees at all stages of operations to strive toward higher standards and reduce number of defects. *(p. 616)*

Trade discount Reduction from a list or catalog price that can vary for wholesalers, retailers, and consumers. *(p. 158)*

Trademark or **trade (brand) name** Symbol, name, phrase, or jingle identified with a company, product, or service. *(p. 343)*

Trading on the equity (See *financial leverage.*)

Trading securities Investments in debt and equity securities that the company intends to actively trade for profit. *(p. C-5)*

Transfer price The price used to record transfers of goods or services between divisions in the same company. *(p. 444)*

Transaction Exchange of economic consideration affecting an entity's financial position that can be reliably measured.

Treasury stock Corporation's own stock that it reacquired and still holds. *(p. 470)*

Trial balance List of accounts and their balances at a point in time; total debit balances equal total credit balances. *(p. 65)*

Unadjusted trial balance List of accounts and balances prepared before accounting adjustments are recorded and posted. *(p. 106)*

Unavoidable expense Expense (or cost) that is not relevant for business decisions; an expense that would continue even if a department, product, or service is eliminated. *(p. 975)*

Unclassified balance sheet Balance sheet that broadly groups assets, liabilities, and equity accounts. *(p. 113)*

Uncontrollable costs Costs that a manager does not have the power to determine or strongly influence. *(pp. 814 & 937)*

Underapplied overhead Amount by which overhead incurred in a period exceeds the overhead applied to that period's production using the predetermined overhead rate. *(p. 787)*

Unearned revenue Liability created when customers pay in advance for products or services; earned when the products or services are later delivered. *(pp. 52 & 100)*

Unfavorable variance Difference in revenues or costs, when the actual amount is compared to the budgeted amount, that contributes to a lower income. *(881)*

Unit contribution margin Amount a product's unit selling price exceeds its total unit variable cost.

Unit level activities Activities that arise as a result of the total volume of goods and services that are produced, and that are performed each time a unit is produced. *(p. 738)*

Units-of-production depreciation Method that charges a varying amount to depreciation expense for each period of an asset's useful life depending on its usage. *(p. 331)*

Unlimited liability Legal relationship among general partners that makes each of them responsible for partnership debts if the other partners are unable to pay their shares. *(p. D-3)*

Unrealized gain (loss) Gain (loss) not yet realized by an actual transaction or event such as a sale. *(p. C-5)*

Unsecured bonds Bonds backed only by the issuer's credit standing; almost always riskier than secured bonds; also called *debentures*. *(p. 426)*

Unusual gain or loss Gain or loss that is abnormal or unrelated to the company's ordinary activities and environment. *(p. 578)*

Useful life Length of time an asset will be productively used in the operations of a business; also called *service life* or *limited life*. *(p. 329)*

Value-added activities Activities that add to the value of a product or service.

Value-added time The portion of cycle time that is directed at producing a product or service; equals process time. *(p. 618)*

Value chain Sequential activities that add value to an entity's products or services; includes design, production, marketing, distribution, and service. *(p. 616)*

Variable cost Cost that changes in proportion to changes in the activity output volume. *(p. 604)*

Variable costing A costing method that includes only variable manufacturing costs—direct materials, direct labor, and variable manufacturing overhead—in unit product costs; also called *direct or marginal costing*. *(p. 794)*

Variable costing income statement An income statement which reports variable costs and fixed costs separately; also called a *contribution margin income statement*. *(p. 773)*

Variance analysis Process of examining differences between actual and budgeted revenues or costs and describing them in terms of price and quantity differences. *(p. 885)*

Vendee Buyer of goods or services. *(p. 271)*

Vendor Seller of goods or services. *(p. 270)*

Vertical analysis Evaluation of each financial statement item or group of items in terms of a specific base amount. *(p. 556)*

Volume variance Difference between two dollar amounts of fixed overhead cost; one amount is the total budgeted overhead cost, and the other is the overhead cost allocated to products using the predetermined fixed overhead rate. *(p. 893)*

Voucher Internal file used to store documents and information to control cash disbursements and to ensure that a transaction is properly authorized and recorded. *(p. 257)*

Voucher register Journal (referred to as *book of original entry*) in which all vouchers are recorded after they have been approved. *(p. 272)*

Voucher system Procedures and approvals designed to control cash disbursements and acceptance of obligations. *(p. 256)*

Wage bracket withholding table Table of the amounts of income tax withheld from employees' wages. *(p. 390)*

Warranty Agreement that obligates the seller to correct or replace a product or service when it fails to perform properly within a specified period. *(p. 378)*

Weighted average Method to assign inventory cost to sales; the cost of available-for-sale units is divided by the number of units available to determine per unit cost prior to each sale that is then multiplied by the units sold to yield the cost of that sale. *(pp. 210–225 & 692)*

Weighted-average contribution margin Contribution margin for a multiproduct company; computed based on each products' percentage of the company's sales mix. *(p. 780)*

Weighted-average method (See *weighted average.*)

Wholesaler Intermediary that buys products from manufacturers or other wholesalers and sells them to retailers or other wholesalers. *(p. 156)*

Withdrawals Payment of cash or other assets from a proprietorship or partnership to its owner or owners. *(p. 14)*

Work sheet Spreadsheet used to draft an unadjusted trial balance, adjusting entries, adjusted trial balance, and financial statements. *(p. 123)*

Working capital Current assets minus current liabilities at a point in time. *(p. 565)*

Working papers Analyses and other informal reports prepared by accountants and managers when organizing information for formal reports and financial statements. *(p. 123)*

Credits

Index

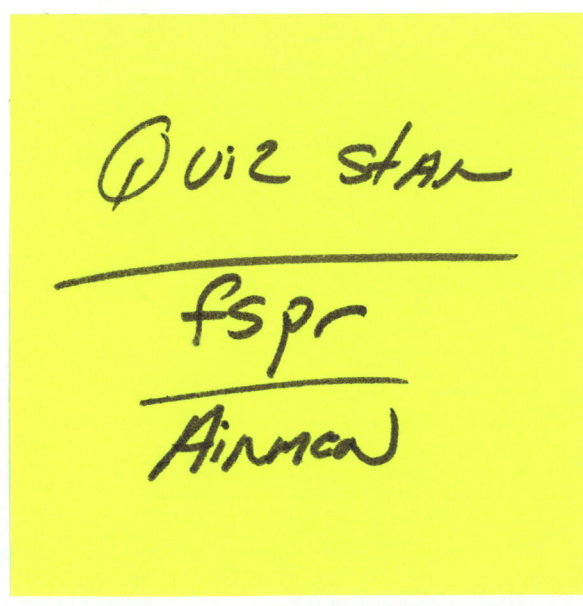

A Rose by Any Other Name

The same financial statement sometimes receives different titles. Following are some of the more common aliases.*

Balance Sheet	Statement of Financial Position Statement of Financial Condition
Income Statement	Statement of Income Operating Statement Statement of Operations Statement of Operating Activity Earnings Statement Statement of Earnings Profit and Loss (P&L) Statement
Statement of Cash Flows	Statement of Cash Flow Cash Flows Statement Statement of Changes in Cash Position Statement of Changes in Financial Position
Statement of Stockholders' Equity	Statement of Shareholders' Equity Statement of Changes in Shareholders' Equity Statement of Stockholders' Equity and Comprehensive Income Statement of Changes in Owner's Equity Statement of Changes in Owner's Capital Statement of Changes in Capital Accounts

* The term **Consolidated** often precedes or follows these statement titles to reflect the combination of different entities, such as a parent company and its subsidiaries.

We thank Dr. Louella Moore from Arkansas State University for suggesting this listing.

Chart of Accounts

Following is a typical chart of accounts, which is used in several assignments. Every company has its own unique accounts and numbering system.

Assets

Current Assets

101 Cash
102 Petty cash
103 Cash equivalents
104 Short-term investments
105 Fair value adjustment, _____ securities (S-T)
106 Accounts receivable
107 Allowance for doubtful accounts
108 Legal fees receivable
109 Interest receivable
110 Rent receivable
111 Notes receivable
119 Merchandise inventory
120 _____ inventory
121 _____ inventory
124 Office supplies
125 Store supplies
126 _____ supplies
128 Prepaid insurance
129 Prepaid interest
131 Prepaid rent
132 Raw materials inventory
133 Goods in process inventory, _____
134 Goods in process inventory, _____
135 Finished goods inventory

Long-Term Investments

141 Long-term investments
142 Fair value adjustment, _____ securities (L-T)
144 Investment in _____
145 Bond sinking fund

Plant Assets

151 Automobiles
152 Accumulated depreciation—Automobiles
153 Trucks
154 Accumulated depreciation—Trucks
155 Boats
156 Accumulated depreciation—Boats
157 Professional library
158 Accumulated depreciation—Professional library
159 Law library
160 Accumulated depreciation—Law library
161 Furniture
162 Accumulated depreciation—Furniture
163 Office equipment
164 Accumulated depreciation—Office equipment
165 Store equipment

166 Accumulated depreciation—Store equipment
167 _____ equipment
168 Accumulated depreciation—_____ equipment
169 Machinery
170 Accumulated depreciation—Machinery
173 Building _____
174 Accumulated depreciation—Building _____
175 Building _____
176 Accumulated depreciation—Building _____
179 Land improvements _____
180 Accumulated depreciation—Land improvements _____
181 Land improvements _____
182 Accumulated depreciation—Land improvements _____
183 Land

Natural Resources

185 Mineral deposit
186 Accumulated depletion—Mineral deposit

Intangible Assets

191 Patents
192 Leasehold
193 Franchise
194 Copyrights
195 Leasehold improvements
196 Licenses
197 Accumulated amortization—_____

Liabilities

Current Liabilities

201 Accounts payable
202 Insurance payable
203 Interest payable
204 Legal fees payable
207 Office salaries payable
208 Rent payable
209 Salaries payable
210 Wages payable
211 Accrued payroll payable
214 Estimated warranty liability
215 Income taxes payable
216 Common dividend payable
217 Preferred dividend payable
218 State unemployment taxes payable
219 Employee federal income taxes payable
221 Employee medical insurance payable

222 Employee retirement program payable
223 Employee union dues payable
224 Federal unemployment taxes payable
225 FICA taxes payable
226 Estimated vacation pay liability

Unearned Revenues

230 Unearned consulting fees
231 Unearned legal fees
232 Unearned property management fees
233 Unearned _____ fees
234 Unearned _____ fees
235 Unearned janitorial revenue
236 Unearned _____ revenue
238 Unearned rent

Notes Payable

240 Short-term notes payable
241 Discount on short-term notes payable
245 Notes payable
251 Long-term notes payable
252 Discount on long-term notes payable

Long-Term Liabilities

253 Long-term lease liability
255 Bonds payable
256 Discount on bonds payable
257 Premium on bonds payable
258 Deferred income tax liability

Equity

Owner's Equity

301 _____, Capital
302 _____, Withdrawals
303 _____, Capital
304 _____, Withdrawals
305 _____, Capital
306 _____, Withdrawals

Paid-In Capital

307 Common stock, $_____ par value
308 Common stock, no-par value
309 Common stock, $_____ stated value
310 Common stock dividend distributable
311 Paid-in capital in excess of par value, Common stock

312 Paid-in capital in excess of stated value, No-par common stock
313 Paid-in capital from retirement of common stock
314 Paid-in capital, Treasury stock
315 Preferred stock
316 Paid-in capital in excess of par value, Preferred stock

Retained Earnings

318 Retained earnings
319 Cash dividends (or Dividends)
320 Stock dividends

Other Equity Accounts

321 Treasury stock, Common
322 Unrealized gain—Equity
323 Unrealized loss—Equity

Revenues

401 _____ fees earned
402 _____ fees earned
403 _____ services revenue
404 _____ services revenue
405 Commissions earned
406 Rent revenue (or Rent earned)
407 Dividends revenue (or Dividend earned)
408 Earnings from investment in _____
409 Interest revenue (or Interest earned)
410 Sinking fund earnings
413 Sales
414 Sales returns and allowances
415 Sales discounts

Cost of Sales

Cost of Goods Sold

502 Cost of goods sold
505 Purchases
506 Purchases returns and allowances
507 Purchases discounts
508 Transportation-in

Manufacturing

520 Raw materials purchases
521 Freight-in on raw materials
530 Factory payroll
531 Direct labor
540 Factory overhead
541 Indirect materials
542 Indirect labor
543 Factory insurance expired
544 Factory supervision
545 Factory supplies used
546 Factory utilities
547 Miscellaneous production costs
548 Property taxes on factory building
549 Property taxes on factory equipment
550 Rent on factory building
551 Repairs, factory equipment
552 Small tools written off
560 Depreciation of factory equipment
561 Depreciation of factory building

Standard Cost Variance

580 Direct material quantity variance
581 Direct material price variance
582 Direct labor quantity variance
583 Direct labor price variance
584 Factory overhead volume variance
585 Factory overhead controllable variance

Expenses

Amortization, Depletion, and Depreciation

601 Amortization expense—_____
602 Amortization expense—_____
603 Depletion expense—_____
604 Depreciation expense—Boats
605 Depreciation expense—Automobiles
606 Depreciation expense—Building _____
607 Depreciation expense—Building _____
608 Depreciation expense—Land improvements _____
609 Depreciation expense—Land improvements _____
610 Depreciation expense—Law library
611 Depreciation expense—Trucks
612 Depreciation expense—_____ equipment
613 Depreciation expense—_____ equipment
614 Depreciation expense—_____
615 Depreciation expense—_____

Employee-Related Expenses

620 Office salaries expense
621 Sales salaries expense
622 Salaries expense
623 _____ wages expense
624 Employees' benefits expense
625 Payroll taxes expense

Financial Expenses

630 Cash over and short
631 Discounts lost
632 Factoring fee expense
633 Interest expense

Insurance Expenses

635 Insurance expense—Delivery equipment
636 Insurance expense—Office equipment
637 Insurance expense—_____

Rental Expenses

640 Rent expense
641 Rent expense—Office space
642 Rent expense—Selling space
643 Press rental expense
644 Truck rental expense
645 _____ rental expense

Supplies Expenses

650 Office supplies expense
651 Store supplies expense
652 _____ supplies expense
653 _____ supplies expense

Miscellaneous Expenses

655 Advertising expense
656 Bad debts expense
657 Blueprinting expense
658 Boat expense
659 Collection expense
661 Concessions expense
662 Credit card expense
663 Delivery expense
664 Dumping expense
667 Equipment expense
668 Food and drinks expense
671 Gas and oil expense
672 General and administrative expense
673 Janitorial expense
674 Legal fees expense
676 Mileage expense
677 Miscellaneous expenses
678 Mower and tools expense
679 Operating expense
680 Organization expense
681 Permits expense
682 Postage expense
683 Property taxes expense
684 Repairs expense—_____
685 Repairs expense—_____
687 Selling expense
688 Telephone expense
689 Travel and entertainment expense
690 Utilities expense
691 Warranty expense
695 Income taxes expense

Gains and Losses

701 Gain on retirement of bonds
702 Gain on sale of machinery
703 Gain on sale of investments
704 Gain on sale of trucks
705 Gain on _____
706 Foreign exchange gain or loss
801 Loss on disposal of machinery
802 Loss on exchange of equipment
803 Loss on exchange of _____
804 Loss on sale of notes
805 Loss on retirement of bonds
806 Loss on sale of investments
807 Loss on sale of machinery
808 Loss on _____
809 Unrealized gain—Income
810 Unrealized loss—Income
811 Impairment gain
812 Impairment loss

Clearing Accounts

901 Income summary
902 Manufacturing summary

SELECTED TRANSACTIONS AND RELATIONS

① Merchandising Transactions Summary

Merchandising Transactions		Merchandising Entries	Dr.	Cr.
Purchases	Purchasing merchandise for resale.	• Merchandise Inventory	#	
		Cash or Accounts Payable		#
	Paying freight costs on purchases; FOB shipping point.	• Merchandise Inventory	#	
		Cash		#
	Paying within discount period.	• Accounts Payable	#	
		Merchandise Inventory		#
		Cash		#
	Recording purchase returns or allowances.	• Cash or Accounts Payable	#	
		Merchandise Inventory		#
Sales	Selling merchandise.	• Cash or Accounts Receivable	#	
		Sales		#
		• Cost of Goods Sold...................	#	
		Merchandise Inventory		#
	Receiving payment within discount period.	• Cash	#	
		Sales Discounts	#	
		Accounts Receivable................		#
	Granting sales returns or allowances.	• Sales Returns and Allowances..........	#	
		Cash or Accounts Receivable		#
		• Merchandise Inventory	#	
		Cost of Goods Sold		#
	Paying freight costs on sales; FOB destination.	• Delivery Expense	#	
		Cash		#

Merchandising Events		Adjusting and Closing Entries		
Adjusting	Adjusting due to shrinkage (occurs when recorded amount larger than physical inventory).	Cost of Goods Sold	#	
		Merchandise Inventory		#
Closing	Closing temporary accounts with credit balances.	Sales	#	
		Income Summary		#
	Closing temporary accounts with debit balances.	Income Summary	#	
		Sales Returns and Allowances		#
		Sales Discounts		#
		Cost of Goods Sold		#
		Delivery Expense		#
		"Other Expenses"		#

② Merchandising Cash Flows

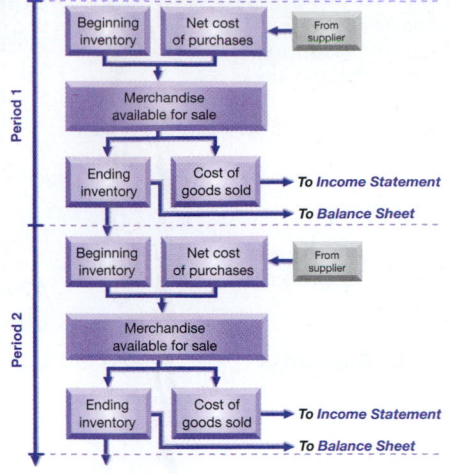

③ Credit Terms and Amounts

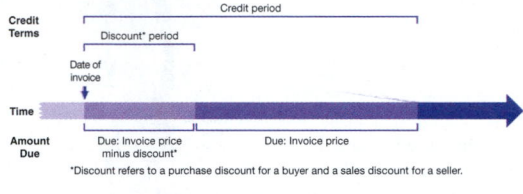

*Discount refers to a purchase discount for a buyer and a sales discount for a seller.

④ Bad Debts Estimation

Bad Debts Estimation
or

Income Statement Focus

Balance Sheet Focus
or

Percent of Sales [Emphasis on Matching]

Sales × Rate = Bad Debts Expense

Percent of Receivables [Emphasis on Realizable Value]

Accounts Receivable × Rate = Allowance for Doubtful Accounts

Aging of Receivables [Emphasis on Realizable Value]

Accounts Receivable (by Age) × Rates (by Age) = Allowance for Doubtful Accounts

⑤ Bond Valuation

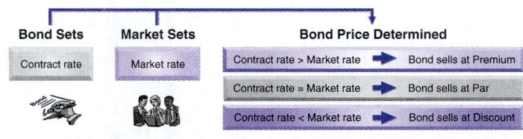

Bond Sets	Market Sets	Bond Price Determined	
Contract rate	Market rate	Contract rate > Market rate	Bond sells at Premium
		Contract rate = Market rate	Bond sells at Par
		Contract rate < Market rate	Bond sells at Discount

⑦ Dividend Transactions

Account Affected	Type of Dividend		
	Cash Dividend	Stock Dividend	Stock Split
Cash	Decrease	—	—
Common Stock	—	Increase	—
Retained Earnings ..	Decrease	Decrease	—

⑥ Stock Transactions Summary

Stock Transactions		Stock Entries	Dr.	Cr.
Issue Common Stock	Issue par value common stock at par (par stock recorded at par).	Cash	#	
		Common Stock		#
	Issue par value common stock at premium (par stock recorded at par).	Cash	#	
		Common Stock		#
		Paid-In Capital in Excess of Par Value, Common Stock		#
	Issue no-par value common stock (no-par stock recorded at amount received).	Cash	#	
		Common Stock		#
	Issue stated value common stock at stated value (stated stock recorded at stated value).	Cash	#	
		Common stock		#
	Issue stated value common stock at premium (stated stock recorded at stated value).	Cash	#	
		Common stock		#
		Paid-In Capital in Excess of Stated Value, Common Stock		#
Issue Preferred Stock	Issue par value preferred stock at par (par stock recorded at par).	Cash	#	
		Preferred Stock		#
	Issue par value preferred stock at premium (par stock recorded at par).	Cash	#	
		Preferred Stock		#
		Paid-In Capital in Excess of Par Value, Preferred Stock		#
Reacquire Common Stock	Reacquire its own common stock (treasury stock recorded at cost).	Treasury Stock, Common	#	
		Cash		#
Reissue Common Stock	Reissue its treasury stock at cost (treasury stock removed at cost).	Cash	#	
		Treasury Stock, Common		#
	Reissue its treasury stock above cost (treasury stock removed at cost).	Cash	#	
		Treasury Stock, Common		#
		Paid-In Capital, Treasury		#
	Reissue its treasury stock below cost (treasury stock removed at cost; if paid-in capital is insufficient to cover amount below cost, retained earnings is debited for remainder).	Cash	#	
		Paid-In Capital, Treasury		#
		Treasury Stock, Common		#
		Retained Earnings (if necessary) ...		#

⑧ A Rose by Any Other Name

The same financial statement sometimes receives different titles. Following are some of the more common aliases.*

Balance Sheet	Statement of Financial Position Statement of Financial Condition
Income Statement	Statement of Income Operating Statement Statement of Operations Statement of Operating Activity Earnings Statement Statement of Earnings Profit and Loss (P&L) Statement
Statement of Cash Flows	Statement of Cash Flow Cash Flows Statement Statement of Changes in Cash Position Statement of Changes in Financial Position
Statement of Stockholders' Equity	Statement of Shareholders' Equity Statement of Changes in Shareholders' Equity Statement of Stockholders' Equity and Comprehensive Income Statement of Changes in Owner's Equity Statement of Changes in Owner's Capital Statement of Changes in Capital Accounts

*The term **Consolidated** often precedes or follows these statement titles to reflect the combination of different entities, such as a parent company and its subsidiaries.

MANAGERIAL ANALYSES AND REPORTS

① Cost Types

Variable costs:	Total cost changes in proportion to volume of activity
Fixed costs:	Total cost does not change in proportion to volume of activity
Mixed costs:	Cost consists of both a variable and a fixed element

② Cost Sources

Direct materials:	Raw materials costs directly linked to finished product
Direct labor:	Employee costs directly linked to finished product
Overhead:	Costs indirectly linked to finished product

③ Costing Systems

Job order costing:	Costs assigned to each unique unit or batch of units
Process costing:	Costs assigned to similar products that are mass-produced in a continuous manner

④ Costing Ratios

Contribution margin ratio = (Net sales − Variable costs)/Net sales
Predetermined overhead rate = Estimated overhead costs/Estimated activity base
Break-even point in units = Total fixed costs/Contribution margin per unit

⑤ Planning and Control Metrics

Cost variance = Actual cost − Standard (budgeted) cost
Sales (revenue) variance = Actual sales − Standard (budgeted) sales

⑥ Capital Budgeting

Payback period = Time expected to recover investment cost
Accounting rate of return = Expected annual net income/Average annual investment
Net present value (NPV) = Present value of future cash flows − Investment cost

NPV rule: 1. Compute net present value (NPV in $)
2. If NPV ≥ 0, then accept project; If NPV < 0, then reject project

Internal rate   1. Compute internal rate of return (IRR in %)
of return rule: 2. If IRR ≥ hurdle rate, accept project; If IRR < hurdle rate, reject project

⑦ Costing Terminology

Relevant range:	Organization's normal range of operating activity.
Direct cost:	Cost incurred for the benefit of one cost object.
Indirect cost:	Cost incurred for the benefit of more than one cost object.
Product cost:	Cost that is necessary and integral to finished products.
Period cost:	Cost identified more with a time period than with finished products.
Overhead cost:	Cost not separately or directly traceable to a cost object.
Relevant cost:	Cost that is pertinent to a decision.
Opportunity cost:	Benefit lost by choosing an action from two or more alternatives.
Sunk cost:	Cost already incurred that cannot be avoided or changed.
Standard cost:	Cost computed using standard price and standard quantity.
Budget:	Formal statement of an organization's future plans.
Break-even point:	Sales level at which an organization earns zero profit.
Incremental cost:	Cost incurred only if the organization undertakes a certain action.
Transfer price:	Price on transactions between divisions within a company.

⑧ Standard Cost Variances

Total materials variance =	Materials price variance	+	Materials quantity variance

Total labor variance =	Labor (rate) variance	+	Labor efficiency (quantity) variance

Total overhead variance =	Overhead controllable variance	+	Fixed overhead volume variance

Overhead controllable variance = Actual total overhead − Applied total overhead from flexible budget

Fixed overhead volume variance = Budgeted fixed overhead − Applied fixed overhead

Variable overhead variance = Variable overhead spending variance + Variable overhead efficiency variance ⎫
Fixed overhead variance = Fixed overhead spending variance + Fixed overhead volume variance ⎬ = Total overhead variance
⎭

Materials price variance	= [AQ × AP] − [AQ × SP]
Materials quantity variance	= [AQ × SP] − [SQ × SP]
Labor (rate) variance	= [AH × AR] − [AH × SR]
Labor efficiency (quantity) variance	= [AH × SR] − [SH × SR]

Variable overhead spending variance = [AH × AVR] − [AH × SVR]
Variable overhead efficiency variance = [AH × SVR] − [SH × SVR]
Fixed overhead spending variance = Actual fixed overhead − Budgeted fixed overhead

where AQ is actual quantity of materials; AP is actual price of materials; AH is actual hours of labor; AR is actual rate of wages; AVR is actual variable rate of overhead; SQ is standard quantity of materials; SP is standard price of materials; SH is standard hours of labor; SR is standard rate of wages; SVR is standard variable rate of overhead.

⑨ Sales Variances

Sales price variance	= [AS × AP] − [AS × BP]
Sales volume variance	= [AS × BP] − [BS × BP]

where AS = actual sales units; AP = actual sales price; BP = budgeted sales price; BS = budgeted sales units (fixed budget)

Manufacturing Statement
For _period_ Ended _date_

Direct materials		
Raw materials inventory, Beginning	$	#
Raw materials purchases		#
Raw materials available for use		#
Raw materials inventory, Ending		(#)
Direct materials used		#
Direct labor		#
Overhead costs		
Total overhead costs		#
Total manufacturing costs		#
Add goods in process inventory, Beginning		#
Total cost of goods in process		#
Deduct goods in process inventory, Ending		(#)
Cost of goods manufactured	$	#

Contribution Margin Income Statement
For _period_ Ended _date_

Net sales (revenues)	$	#
Total variable costs		#
Contribution margin		#
Total fixed costs		#
Net income	$	#

Flexible Budget
For _period_ Ended _date_

	Flexible Budget — Variable Amount per Unit	Flexible Budget — Fixed Cost	Flexible Budget for Unit Sales of #
Sales (revenues)	$ #		$ #
Variable costs			
Examples: Direct materials, Direct labor, ...			
Other variable costs	#		#
Total variable costs	#		#
Contribution margin	$ #		#
Fixed costs			
Examples: Depreciation, Manager salaries, Administrative salaries		$ # #	# #
Total fixed costs		$ #	#
Income from operations			$ #

Fixed Budget Performance Report
For _period_ Ended _date_

	Fixed Budget	Actual Performance	Variances[†]
Sales: In units	#	#	
In dollars	$ #	$ #	$ # F or U
Cost of sales			
Direct costs	#	#	# F or U
Indirect costs	#	#	# F or U
Selling expenses			
Examples: Commissions,	#	#	# F or U
Shipping expenses	#	#	# F or U
General and administrative expenses			
Examples: Administrative salaries	#	#	# F or U
Total expenses	$ #	$ #	$ # F or U
Income from operations	$ #	$ #	$ # F or U

[†]F = Favorable variance; U = Unfavorable variance.

Master Budget Sequence

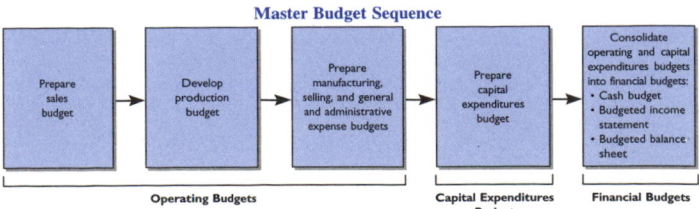

Prepare sales budget → Develop production budget → Prepare manufacturing, selling, and general and administrative expense budgets → Prepare capital expenditures budget → Consolidate operating and capital expenditures budgets into financial budgets: • Cash budget • Budgeted income statement • Budgeted balance sheet

Operating Budgets   Capital Expenditures Budget   Financial Budgets

FUNDAMENTALS

① Accounting Equation

Assets	=	Liabilities	+	Equity

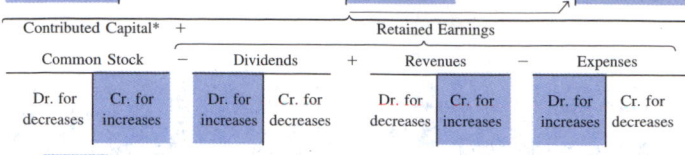

Debit for increases ↑	Credit for decreases ↓	Debit for decreases ↓	Credit for increases ↑	Debit for decreases ↓	Credit for increases ↑

Contributed Capital* + Retained Earnings

Common Stock	− Dividends +	Revenues −	Expenses

Dr. for decreases	Cr. for increases	Dr. for increases	Cr. for decreases	Dr. for decreases	Cr. for increases	Dr. for increases	Cr. for decreases

▓ Indicates normal balance.

*Includes common stock and any preferred stock.

② Accounting Cycle

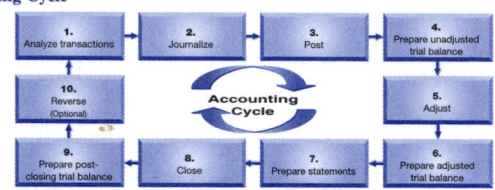

1. Analyze transactions
2. Journalize
3. Post
4. Prepare unadjusted trial balance
5. Adjust
6. Prepare adjusted trial balance
7. Prepare statements
8. Close
9. Prepare post-closing trial balance
10. Reverse (Optional)

Accounting Cycle

③ Adjustments and Entries

Type	Adjusting Entry	
Prepaid Expenses	Dr. Expense	Cr. Asset*
Unearned Revenues	Dr. Liability	Cr. Revenue
Accrued Expenses	Dr. Expense	Cr. Liability
Accrued Revenues	Dr. Asset	Cr. Revenue

*For depreciation, credit Accumulated Depreciation (contra asset).

④ 4-Step Closing Process

1. Transfer revenue and gain account balances to Income Summary.
2. Transfer expense and loss account balances to Income Summary.
3. Transfer Income Summary balance to Retained Earnings.
4. Transfer Dividends balance to Retained Earnings.

⑤ Accounting Concepts

Characteristics	Assumptions	Principles	Constraints
Relevance	Business entity	Historical cost	Cost-benefit
Reliability	Going concern	Revenue recognition	Materiality
Comparability	Monetary unit	Expense recognition	Industry practice
Consistency	Periodicity	Full disclosure	Conservatism

⑥ Ownership of Inventory

	Ownership Transfers When Goods Passed To	Transportation Costs Paid By
FOB Shipping Point	Carrier	Buyer
FOB Destination	Buyer	Seller

⑦ Inventory Costing Methods

- Specific Identification
- First-In, First-Out (FIFO)
- Weighted-Average
- Last-In, First-Out (LIFO)

⑧ Depreciation and Depletion

Straight-Line: $\dfrac{\text{Cost} - \text{Salvage value}}{\text{Useful life in periods}} \times \text{Periods expired}$

Units-of-Production: $\dfrac{\text{Cost} - \text{Salvage value}}{\text{Useful life in units}} \times \text{Units produced}$

Declining-Balance: Rate* × Beginning-of-period book value
*Rate is often double the straight-line rate, or 2 × (1/Useful life)

Depletion: $\dfrac{\text{Cost} - \text{Salvage value}}{\text{Total capacity in units}} \times \text{Units extracted}$

⑨ Interest Computation

Interest = Principal (face) × Rate × Time

⑩ Accounting for Investment Securities

Classification*	Accounting
Short-Term Investment in Securities	
Held-to-maturity (debt) securities	**Cost** (without any discount or premium amortization)
Trading (debt and equity) securities	**Fair value** (with fair value adjustment to income)
Available-for-sale (debt and equity) securities	**Fair value** (with fair value adjustment to equity)
Long-Term Investment in Securities	
Held-to-maturity (debt) securities	**Cost** (with any discount or premium amortization)
Available-for-sale (debt and equity) securities	**Fair value** (with fair value adjustment to equity)
Equity securities with significant influence	Equity method
Equity securities with controlling influence	Equity method (with consolidation)

*A *fair value option* allows companies to report HTM and AFS securities much like trading securities.

ANALYSES

① Liquidity and Efficiency

Current ratio $= \dfrac{\text{Current assets}}{\text{Current liabilities}}$ — p. 117

Working capital = Current assets − Current liabilities — p. 565

Acid-test ratio $= \dfrac{\text{Cash} + \text{Short-term investments} + \text{Current receivables}}{\text{Current liabilities}}$ — p. 172

Accounts receivable turnover $= \dfrac{\text{Net sales}}{\text{Average accounts receivable, net}}$ — p. 307

Credit risk ratio $= \dfrac{\text{Allowance for doubtful accounts}}{\text{Accounts receivable, net}}$ — p. 307

Inventory turnover $= \dfrac{\text{Cost of goods sold}}{\text{Average inventory}}$ — p. 217

Days' sales uncollected $= \dfrac{\text{Accounts receivable, net}}{\text{Net sales}} \times 365$* — p. 267

Days' sales in inventory $= \dfrac{\text{Ending inventory}}{\text{Cost of goods sold}} \times 365$* — p. 217

Total asset turnover $= \dfrac{\text{Net sales}}{\text{Average total assets}}$ — p. 345

Plant asset useful life $= \dfrac{\text{Plant asset cost}}{\text{Depreciation expense}}$ — p. 345

Plant asset age $= \dfrac{\text{Accumulated depreciation}}{\text{Depreciation expense}}$ — p. 345

Days' cash expense coverage $= \dfrac{\text{Cash and cash equivalents}}{\text{Average daily cash expenses}}$ — p. 254

*360 days is also commonly used.

② Solvency

Debt ratio $= \dfrac{\text{Total liabilities}}{\text{Total assets}}$ Equity ratio $= \dfrac{\text{Total equity}}{\text{Total assets}}$ — pp. 69 & 573

Debt-to-equity $= \dfrac{\text{Total liabilities}}{\text{Total equity}}$ — p. 427

Times interest earned $= \dfrac{\text{Income before interest expense and income taxes}}{\text{Interest expense}}$ — p. 382

Cash coverage of growth $= \dfrac{\text{Cash flow from operations}}{\text{Cash outflow for plant assets}}$ — p. 519

Cash coverage of debt $= \dfrac{\text{Cash flow from operations}}{\text{Total noncurrent liabilities}}$ — p. 519

③ Profitability

Profit margin ratio $= \dfrac{\text{Net income}}{\text{Net sales}}$ — p. 117

Gross margin ratio $= \dfrac{\text{Net sales} - \text{Cost of goods sold}}{\text{Net sales}}$ — p. 172

Return on total assets $= \dfrac{\text{Net income}}{\text{Average total assets}}$ — p. 22

$= $ Profit margin ratio × Total asset turnover — p. 571

Return on common stockholders' equity $= \dfrac{\text{Net income} - \text{Preferred dividends}}{\text{Average common stockholders' equity}}$ — p. 571

Book value per common share $= \dfrac{\text{Stockholders' equity applicable to common shares}}{\text{Number of common shares outstanding}}$ — p. 476

Basic earnings per share $= \dfrac{\text{Net income} - \text{Preferred dividends}}{\text{Weighted-average common shares outstanding}}$ — p. 475

Cash flow on total assets $= \dfrac{\text{Cash flow from operations}}{\text{Average total assets}}$ — p. 518

Payout ratio $= \dfrac{\text{Cash dividends declared on common stock}}{\text{Net income}}$ — p. 476

④ Market

Price-earnings ratio $= \dfrac{\text{Market value (price) per share}}{\text{Earnings per share}}$ — p. 475

Dividend yield $= \dfrac{\text{Annual cash dividends per share}}{\text{Market price per share}}$ — p. 476

Residual income = Net income − Target net income